International Directory of
COMPANY
HISTORIES

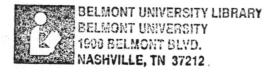

International Directory of
COMPANY
HISTORIES

VOLUME 67

Editor

Jay P. Pederson

ST. JAMES PRESS

An imprint of Thomson Gale, a part of The Thomson Corporation

Detroit • New York • San Francisco • San Diego • New Haven, Conn. • Waterville, Maine • London • Munich

International Directory of Company Histories, Volume 67

Jay P. Pederson, Editor

Project Editor
Miranda H. Ferrara

Editorial
Virgil Burton, Donna Craft, Louise Gagné,
Peggy Geeseman, Julie Gough, Linda Hall,
Sonya Hill, Keith Jones, Lynn Pearce,
Maureen Puhl, Holly Selden,
Justine Ventimiglia

Imaging and Multimedia
Randy Bassett, Lezlie Light

Manufacturing
Rhonda Williams

Product Manager
Gerald L. Sawchuk

LIBRARY OF CONGRESS CATALOG NUMBER 89-190943

ISBN: 1-55862-512-7

BRITISH LIBRARY CATALOGUING IN PUBLICATION DATA

International directory of company histories. Vol. 67
I. Jay P. Pederson
33.87409

Printed in the United States of America
10 9 8 7 6 5 4 3 2 1

CONTENTS _____

Preface . . . . page vii
List of Abbreviations ix

Company Histories

Advanced Circuits Inc. 3
AGCO Corporation 6
AMERCO 11
American Axle & Manufacturing
    Holdings, Inc. 15
American Power Conversion Corporation . 18
American Technical Ceramics Corp. 21
Ameron International Corporation 24
Ampacet Corporation 27
Amylin Pharmaceuticals, Inc. 30
AnnTaylor Stores Corporation 33
AU Optronics Corporation 38
AVX Corporation 41
B.J. Alan Co., Inc. 44
Benetton Group S.p.A. 47
BenQ Corporation 52
Berjaya Group Bhd. 55
BHP Billiton 58
The Black & Decker Corporation 65
Brascan Corporation 71
Brioni Roman Style S.p.A. 74
Brush Engineered Materials Inc. 77
BSH Bosch und Siemens
    Hausgeräte GmbH 80
California Steel Industries, Inc. 85
Cantine Giorgio Lungarotti S.R.L. 88
Car Toys, Inc. 91
Carbo PLC 94
Celgene Corporation 97
CHC Helicopter Corporation 101
Chelsfield PLC 104
Chipotle Mexican Grill, Inc. 107
The Coca-Cola Company 111
Cold Spring Granite Company Inc. 118

Cone Mills LLC 123
Conn's, Inc. 128
Cox Enterprises, Inc. 131
Cristalerias de Chile S.A. 136
Denbury Resources, Inc. 139
Doctor's Associates Inc. 142
Dynaction S.A. 146
EastGroup Properties, Inc. 149
Eaton Corporation 152
eBay Inc. 157
The Economist Group Ltd. 162
Edge Petroleum Corporation 166
Electrabel N.V. 169
Eon Labs, Inc. 172
Exxon Mobil Corporation 175
Geodis S.A. 187
Graco Inc. 191
Groupe Bolloré 196
Grupo Clarín S.A. 200
GSI Commerce, Inc. 204
Hollander Home Fashions Corp. 207
Industrie Zignago Santa Margherita S.p.A. . . 210
International Shipbreaking Ltd. L.L.C. 213
Ipiranga S.A. 216
Knight Ridder, Inc. 219
Lancair International, Inc. 224
Laserscope 227
Le Cordon Bleu S.A. 230
Level 3 Communications, Inc. 233
Linde AG 236
Mag Instrument, Inc. 240
Manhattan Associates, Inc. 243
Marzotto S.p.A. 246
Medtronic, Inc. 250

National Journal Group Inc. 256
NeighborCare, Inc. 259
NGK Insulators Ltd. 264
Niman Ranch, Inc. 267
Nintendo Company, Ltd. 270
Nordstrom, Inc. 277
Oracle Corporation 282
Outdoor Research, Incorporated 288
Outrigger Enterprises, Inc. 291
Pacific Coast Feather Company 294
PepsiAmericas, Inc. 297
Pilot Air Freight Corp. 301
The Procter & Gamble Company 304
PVC Container Corporation 312
Quilmes Industrial (QUINSA) S.A. 315
Radio One, Inc. 318
Reed & Barton Corporation 322
Renault Argentina S.A. 325
Robert W. Baird & Co. Incorporated 328

Rolls-Royce Group PLC 331
Schott Brothers, Inc. 337
SDL PLC 340
Seddon Group Ltd. 343
Sideco Americana S.A. 346
Skalli Group 349
Société Norbert Dentressangle S.A. 352
Spectrum Control, Inc. 355
SRC Holdings Corporation 358
Stratasys, Inc. 361
Tilley Endurables, Inc. 364
Viacom Inc. 367
Viasystems Group, Inc. 372
Vidrala S.A. 375
AB Volvo 378
Warners' Stellian Inc. 384
WellChoice, Inc. 388
Westcon Group, Inc. 392
Zones, Inc. 395

Index to Companies 399
Index to Industries 577
Geographic Index 621
Notes on Contributors 661

PREFACE

The St. James Press series *The International Directory of Company Histories (IDCH)* is intended for reference use by students, business people, librarians, historians, economists, investors, job candidates, and others who seek to learn more about the historical development of the world's most important companies. To date, *IDCH* has covered over 6,900 companies in 67 volumes.

Inclusion Criteria

Most companies chosen for inclusion in *IDCH* have achieved a minimum of US$25 million in annual sales and are leading influences in their industries or geographical locations. Companies may be publicly held, private, or nonprofit. State-owned companies that are important in their industries and that may operate much like public or private companies also are included. Wholly owned subsidiaries and divisions are profiled if they meet the requirements for inclusion. Entries on companies that have had major changes since they were last profiled may be selected for updating.

The *IDCH* series highlights 10% private and nonprofit companies, and features updated entries on approximately 50 companies per volume.

Entry Format

Each entry begins with the company's legal name, the address of its headquarters, its telephone, toll-free, and fax numbers, and its web site. A statement of public, private, state, or parent ownership follows. A company with a legal name in both English and the language of its headquarters country is listed by the English name, with the native-language name in parentheses.

The company's founding or earliest incorporation date, the number of employees, and the most recent available sales figures follow. Sales figures are given in local currencies with equivalents in U.S. dollars. For some private companies, sales figures are estimates and indicated by the abbreviation *est.* The entry lists the exchanges on which a company's stock is traded and its ticker symbol, as well as the company's NAIC codes.

Entries generally contain a *Company Perspectives* box which provides a short summary of the company's mission, goals, and ideals, a *Key Dates* box highlighting milestones in the company's history, lists of *Principal Subsidiaries, Principal Divisions, Principal Operating Units, Principal Competitors,* and articles for *Further Reading.*

American spelling is used throughout *IDCH*, and the word ''billion'' is used in its U.S. sense of one thousand million.

Sources

Entries have been compiled from publicly accessible sources both in print and on the Internet such as general and academic periodicals, books, annual reports, and material supplied by the companies themselves.

Cumulative Indexes

IDCH contains three indexes: the **Index to Companies**, which provides an alphabetical index to companies discussed in the text as well as to companies profiled, the **Index to Industries**, which allows researchers to locate companies by their principal industry, and the **Geographic Index**, which lists companies alphabetically by the country of their headquarters. The indexes are cumulative and specific instructions for using them are found immediately preceding each index.

Suggestions Welcome

Comments and suggestions from users of *IDCH* on any aspect of the product as well as suggestions for companies to be included or updated are cordially invited. Please write:

The Editor
International Directory of Company Histories
St. James Press
27500 Drake Rd.
Farmington Hills, Michigan 48331-3535

AB	Aktiebolag (Finland, Sweden)
AB Oy	Aktiebolag Osakeyhtiot (Finland)
A.E.	Anonimos Eteria (Greece)
AG	Aktiengesellschaft (Austria, Germany, Switzerland, Liechtenstein)
A.O.	Anonim Ortaklari/Ortakligi (Turkey)
ApS	Amparteselskab (Denmark)
A.Š.	Anonim Širketi (Turkey)
A/S	Aksjeselskap (Norway); Aktieselskab (Denmark, Sweden)
Ay	Avoinyhtio (Finland)
B.A.	Buttengewone Aansprakeiijkheid (The Netherlands)
Bhd.	Berhad (Malaysia, Brunei)
B.V.	Besloten Vennootschap (Belgium, The Netherlands)
C.A.	Compania Anonima (Ecuador, Venezuela)
C. de R.L.	Compania de Responsabilidad Limitada (Spain)
Co.	Company
Corp.	Corporation
CRL	Companhia a Responsabilidao Limitida (Portugal, Spain)
C.V.	Commanditaire Vennootschap (The Netherlands, Belgium)
G.I.E.	Groupement d'Interet Economique (France)
GmbH	Gesellschaft mit beschraenkter Haftung (Austria, Germany, Switzerland)
Inc.	Incorporated (United States, Canada)
I/S	Interessentselskab (Denmark); Interesentselskap (Norway)
KG/KGaA	Kommanditgesellschaft/Kommanditgesellschaft auf Aktien (Austria, Germany, Switzerland)
KK	Kabushiki Kaisha (Japan)
K/S	Kommanditselskab (Denmark); Kommandittselskap (Norway)
Lda.	Limitada (Spain)
L.L.C.	Limited Liability Company (United States)
Ltd.	Limited (Various)
Ltda.	Limitada (Brazil, Portugal)
Ltee.	Limitee (Canada, France)
mbH	mit beschraenkter Haftung (Austria, Germany)
N.V.	Naamloze Vennootschap (Belgium, The Netherlands)
OAO	Otkrytoe Aktsionernoe Obshchestve (Russia)
OOO	Obschestvo s Ogranichennoi Otvetstvennostiu (Russia)
Oy	Osakeyhtiö (Finland)
PLC	Public Limited Co. (United Kingdom, Ireland)
Pty.	Proprietary (Australia, South Africa, United Kingdom)
S.A.	Société Anonyme (Belgium, France, Greece, Luxembourg, Switzerland, Arab speaking countries); Sociedad Anónima (Latin America [except Brazil], Spain, Mexico); Sociedades Anônimas (Brazil, Portugal)
SAA	Societe Anonyme Arabienne
S.A.R.L.	Sociedade Anonima de Responsabilidade Limitada (Brazil, Portugal); Société à Responsabilité Limitée (France, Belgium, Luxembourg)
S.A.S.	Societá in Accomandita Semplice (Italy); Societe Anonyme Syrienne (Arab speaking countries)
Sdn. Bhd.	Sendirian Berhad (Malaysia)
S.p.A.	Società per Azioni (Italy)
Sp. z.o.o.	Spólka z ograniczona odpowiedzialnoscia (Poland)
S.R.L.	Società a Responsabilità Limitata (Italy); Sociedad de Responsabilidad Limitada (Spain, Mexico, Latin America [except Brazil])
S.R.O.	Spolecnost s Rucenim Omezenym (Czechoslovakia
Ste.	Societe (France, Belgium, Luxembourg, Switzerland)
VAG	Verein der Arbeitgeber (Austria, Germany)
YK	Yugen Kaisha (Japan)
ZAO	Zakrytoe Aktsionernoe Obshchestve (Russia)

ABBREVIATIONS FOR CURRENCY

$	United States dollar	ISK	Icelandic krona
£	United Kingdom pound	ITL	Italian lira
¥	Japanese yen	JMD	Jamaican dollar
AED	Emirati dirham	KPW	North Korean won
ARS	Argentine peso	KRW	South Korean won
ATS	Austrian shilling	KWD	Kuwaiti dinar
AUD	Australian dollar	LUF	Luxembourg franc
BEF	Belgian franc	MUR	Mauritian rupee
BHD	Bahraini dinar	MXN	Mexican peso
BRL	Brazilian real	MYR	Malaysian ringgit
CAD	Canadian dollar	NGN	Nigerian naira
CHF	Swiss franc	NLG	Netherlands guilder
CNY	Chinese yuan	NOK	Norwegian krone
COP	Colombian peso	NZD	New Zealand dollar
CLP	Chilean peso	OMR	Omani rial
CZK	Czech koruna	PHP	Philippine peso
DEM	German deutsche mark	PKR	Pakistani rupee
DKK	Danish krone	PLN	Polish zloty
DZD	Algerian dinar	PTE	Portuguese escudo
EEK	Estonian Kroon	RMB	Chinese renminbi
EGP	Egyptian pound	RUB	Russian ruble
ESP	Spanish peseta	SAR	Saudi riyal
EUR	euro	SEK	Swedish krona
FIM	Finnish markka	SGD	Singapore dollar
FRF	French franc	THB	Thai baht
GRD	Greek drachma	TND	Tunisian dinar
HKD	Hong Kong dollar	TRL	Turkish lira
HUF	Hungarian forint	TWD	new Taiwan dollar
IDR	Indonesian rupiah	VEB	Venezuelan bolivar
IEP	Irish pound	VND	Vietnamese dong
ILS	new Israeli shekel	ZAR	South African rand
INR	Indian rupee	ZMK	Zambian kwacha

International Directory of

COMPANY HISTORIES

Advanced Circuits Inc.

21101 E. 32nd Parkway
Aurora, Colorado 80011
U.S.A.
Telephone: (303) 576-6610
Toll Free: (800) 289-1724
Fax: (303) 418-2334
Web site: http://www.4pcb.com

Private Company
Founded: 1979 as Seiko Circuits
Employees: 250
Sales: $36 million (2004 est.)
NAIC: 334412 Printed Circuit Board Manufacturing

A private company based in the Denver suburb of Aurora, Colorado, Advanced Circuits Inc. is one of the nation's few thriving printed circuit board (PCB) manufacturers. While most PCB manufacturing is now done overseas, Advanced Circuits has found a niche by specializing in the quick turnaround of engineering prototypes and limited production runs, the kind of jobs that the larger offshore PCB manufacturers are not suited to service. A PCB is a thin plate containing chips and other electronic components. A typical computer includes a main PCB, the motherboard, as well as smaller expansion cards, adapters, controllers, interfaces. To ensure that a PCB works as intended, designers turn to Advanced Circuits to produce prototypes for testing purposes. The company has a solid reputation as a reliable vendor in its field, boasting an on-time or early delivery rate in excess of 99 percent. As a result, Advanced Circuits has many loyal customers, including major companies such as IBM, Apple Computer, Lucent, and Texas Instruments. The company is more technically advanced than the competition, and has for several years provided quotes over the Internet. More recently it launched FreeDFM.com, a free Internet-based program that allows engineers to check designs for flaws that could lead to unnecessary delays in manufacturing. In addition, the program provides a quote to help drum up new business. Advanced Circuits also has succeeded in developing an attractive company culture and enjoys a 98 percent employee reten-

tion rate, one of the highest in its industry. It has a solid reputation for complying with state and federal environmental regulations, a problem for PCB manufacturers, which work with a number of toxic chemicals.

A Failed Company in the 1980s

Advanced Circuits was established in 1979 as Seiko Circuits but ten years later was going out of business. A pair of brothers-in-law, Ron Huston and Paul Bustabade, entered the picture to bail out the business. Huston, 25 years old in 1989, had earned a degree in electrical engineering from Wichita State University and moved to Los Angeles to work as a design engineer with McDonnell-Douglas Corp. After he was on the job four years, Bustabade called him from Colorado to tell him about an area "board shop" that they might be able to pick up on the cheap. Huston flew out to find a two-layer fabrication operation located in a 5,000-square-foot garage. The business lacked a computer or even a fax machine, but it had enough serviceable equipment that Huston and Bustabade decided to make a lowball offer, which to their surprise was accepted. They turned to family and friends to raise the purchase price, renamed the business Advanced Circuits, and with just one other employee went to work for themselves.

The early years were difficult. The partners' only goal was mere survival. Huston wore any number of hats, sometimes on the phone as salesman and often in the back building boards with Bustabade. In addition, he acted as head bookkeeper, chief operations manager, and collections manager. The company offered customers a 1 to 2 percent discount if payments were made within ten days, but they had to allow a person to pick up a check to make sure the money was received quickly. In the first few years Huston personally retrieved local checks. A courier service was employed for out-of-state clients.

Changing Conditions for PCB Industry in the Early 1990s

PCB manufacturers located in the United States were starting to be squeezed out of the market by offshore companies, particularly in Taiwan, that could take advantage of cheap labor.

The situation was exacerbated by a downturn in the economy that crippled the PCB industry in 1991 and 1992, just as Advanced Circuits was beginning to establish itself. During this period the number of domestic board makers fell from 2,500 to just 700. It was in 1992 that Advanced Circuits reached a major turning point. The company either had to learn to adapt to business conditions or perish. Huston recognized that the company could take advantage of its location to offer faster service to U.S. customers. Overnight delivery of PCBs made in Asia took at least two days, and at the time at least one week was needed to complete a project on a quick turnaround basis. Unable to compete on larger contracts with long lead times, Huston concluded at the beginning of 1992 that he could drum up business if he could offer three-day turnaround, something that was impossible for larger board makers due to their high set-up costs. Moreover, because there was no language barrier, Advanced Circuits would be able to offer personalized service.

Over the course of the next year, Advanced Circuits reorganized its production routines to minimize the amount of time a board lay idle. While a project might only require 20 hours of manufacturing, it could sit unfinished for several days. The first step the company took was to institute batching, so that a number of jobs were combined in the same production run. Not only was time saved, but the use of materials was optimized, leading to lower costs that could be passed on to customers in the form of savings. Next, as he recounted in an article he wrote for *Logistics Today,* Huston "spent the entire month of July spreadsheeting. My living room was covered with spreadsheets experimenting with every possible combination of lead-time, order size and engineering assumptions (based on three jobs per batch). My objective was to discover the optimum combination of lead-time and order-size variables that could be priced attractively and be of no interest to big offshore providers." His conclusion was that Advanced Circuits should concentrate on prototypes, which were needed quickly in limited quantities and often required clarification on design specifications, a factor that played to the company's advantage in language compatibility. In the words of Huston, "We stopped fishing for whales and started fishing for minnows."

In November 1992 Huston mailed out some 5,000 brochures to potential customers, pitching Advanced Circuits' quick turnaround, promising that boards would be delivered on time or they were free. To make the offer even more attractive, the company accepted credit cards for the work. The response was immediate and strong: the telephone began ringing with new orders, making it necessary for Huston to hire his first sales associate. To achieve success with its new strategy, Advanced Circuits eventually broke down the manufacturing of PCBs to 20 processes. Although automated, they were complex and required oversight. The status of each order, where it was on the shop floor and how it stood against the deadline, was closely monitored. At the start of each day product managers and senior managers took stock on where they stood with orders.

Advanced Circuits began a string of profitable years, as it continued to exploit gaps in the offshore PCB manufacturing business model. The making of prototype PCBs accounted for 10 percent of the company's business by the end of 1993, an amount that would reach 50 percent a decade later. The rest of the company's business was in limited production runs. The sweet spot for the company's success lay with orders of ten units or less needed within a week.

As Advanced Circuits grew, it hired an increasing number of people, and Huston displayed an innovative way to manage people that resulted in company loyalty and an extremely low level of employee turnover. He was good at establishing goals that, if met, rewarded employees, sometimes with money and sometimes in less tangible ways. In 1998, in order to increase daily sales from $28,000 to $30,000, he promised each of his eight sales people $50 cash each week that they achieved a daily average above $30,000. The goal was met in the first week. A year later, he devised a more flamboyant way to improve production. He had a $200 car hauled into the parking lot along with a sledgehammer. Every day the employees could bludgeon the car if they had no redo jobs. The goal was to flatten the car in three months. It was a fun diversion, but seeing the car as employees drove into work was a visual reminder about the company's emphasis on quality control. When the company hit a sales ceiling, unable to crack the $1 million mark in monthly sales, Huston promised to take employees and their families out to lunch once the ceiling was pierced. The very next month sales totaled $1.1 million and Huston picked up a $7,000 lunch tab. A more traditional incentive was the company's profit-sharing plan instituted in 2002, that was more than generous for a business its size. By meeting sales and productivity goals, employees received a 5 percent monthly bonus, plus performance bonuses awarded three times a year. As a result, employees received an additional 20 percent of their salary over the course of a year. Having a highly motivated workforce paid off in other ways as well. When employees were surveyed in 2004, many complained that management was too slow to fire nonperformers. Thus the drive to create an even more productive workforce was being generated from the bottom up and allowed management to weed out poor performers with the blessing of the group.

Business grew so steadily in the 1990s that Advanced Circuits became overwhelmed by the number of requests for quotes by phone or fax. The company turned to the Internet, becoming the first in the industry to bring online instant price quoting, ordering, and order status capabilities to the Web. The demand for its services became so strong in 1999 and 2000 that one of the greatest challenges facing the company was capacity management. Rather than raise prices to ease the pressure, Advanced Circuits decided instead to reexamine its operations. It identified bottlenecks in both the design and manufacturing areas and took steps to manage capacity issues by simply building boards faster.

Avoiding Industry Fate Early in the New Century

The early years of the new century, troubled by a recession, were another difficult time for U.S. PCB manufacturers. From 2001 to 2003 the number of PCB makers was reduced by

Key Dates:

1979:   The company is founded as Seiko Circuits.
1989:   Ron Huston and Paul Bustabade buy the company, renaming it Advanced Circuits.
1992:   The company focuses on building prototypes.
1998:   Internet ordering begins.
2003:   FreeDFM is launched.

another 40 percent. Despite conditions that devastated the tech sector across the board, Advanced Circuits found a way to continue its pattern of growth. In fact, from 1998 to 2002, the company grew sales by 237 percent, and in 2003 it built a new 62,000-square-foot office and manufacturing facility. Several months into the recession, when Huston concluded that the downturn was so steep that the company could not afford to simply ride it out, he called together his senior managers to plot a strategy. What they quickly came to realize was that the company needed to continue using the tools that had made it successful in the first place: speed, quality, innovation, and culture. As long as it could turn out boards faster than airplanes could travel from Asia to the United States, the company would have ready customers no matter what the economic conditions. In addition, the workforce was already highly motivated, leaving quality and innovation as the areas that required some focus.

The management team came to realize that what hindered quality and cost time were problems that occurred at the start of a project, caused by fundamental design flaws that had to be addressed either before work began or later, when unnecessary delays resulted. Advanced Circuits devoted two years to developing a Web-based design-for-manufacturability (DFM) review service, providing design rule checks. The idea had been kicking around for some time, but only now did Huston free up IT and engineering people to concentrate on the task of developing the program, taking advantage of the Web capabilities the company already possessed. The way it worked, designers could send files for each layer of a board. Potential manufacturing problems that resulted in unnecessary production delays and frustrated designers were discovered. In this way, Advanced Circuits made designers look good with their customers while lining up new business for itself. Each evaluation came with a quote for building the submitted design. The program was dubbed FreeDFM and came online in October 2003. It was well received by customers, and because of its use less than 2 percent of orders were held up because of a design flaw.

Advanced Circuits grew revenues from an estimated $28 million in 2003 to $36 million in 2004. Given its advanced capabilities and reputation for speed and reliability, there was every reason to believe that the company would continue to enjoy long-term success.

Principal Competitors

Custom PCB Manufacturing Inc.; PCB Fab Express.

Further Reading

''Change Is Good,'' *Manufacturer,* June 1, 2004.
DiBattista, Laurie, ''Huston Expanding Advanced Circuits,'' *Denver Business Journal,* June 9, 2000, p. 4B.
Freeman, Diane, ''Aurora Firm Running on Circuits,'' *Rocky Mountain News,* May 17, 2004, p. 6B.
Huston, Ron, ''Fishing for Minnows,'' *Logistics Today,* May 1, 2004.
Sloane, Julie, ''The Best Bosses: The Number Cruncher,'' *Fortune Small Business,* October 1, 2004.

—Ed Dinger

AGCO Corporation

4205 River Green Parkway
Duluth, Georgia 30096-2568
U.S.A.
Telephone: (770) 813-9200
Fax: (770) 813-6118
Web site: http://www.agcocorp.com

Public Company
Incorporated: 1985 as Deutz-Allis Corp.
Employees: 11,300
Sales: $3.5 billion (2003)
Stock Exchanges: New York
Ticker Symbol: AG
NAIC: 333111 Farm Machinery and Equipment
  Manufacturing

AGCO Corporation is the world's third largest manufacturer and distributor of tractors and other farm equipment (behind Deere & Company and CNH Global N.V.). Through its extensive network of more than 9,200 dealers serving more than 140 countries, AGCO builds and distributes products under brands that include AGCO, Ag-Chem, Challenger, Fendt, Gleaner, Hesston, Massey Ferguson, Valtra, and White, among others. AGCO has achieved explosive growth since 1990 through savvy business management and by acquiring competitors.

Although AGCO itself was not created until 1990, the company boasts a rich history of success and innovation in the farm machinery industry. In fact, AGCO is the successor to Deutz-Allis Corp., which was formed in 1985 when Klöckner-Humboldt-Deutz AG purchased the agricultural unit of Allis-Chalmers Corp. In 1990 Klöckner spun off Deutz-Allis to a group of executives who formed AGCO. Thus, AGCO is effectively the offspring of the renowned Allis-Chalmers Corp.

Earliest Roots

The Allis-Chalmers Corp. was the progeny of an American named Edward P. Allis. Allis was born in New York in 1824 and graduated from Geneva College in 1845. After college, Allis and a friend, William Allen, moved to Milwaukee, Wis-

consin, where they opened the Empire Leather Store. This venture was a natural progression for Allis because his family was already involved in the leather business in that area. Through either sheer luck or great foresight, Allis sold his interest in Empire Leather shortly before the financial panic of 1857. A number of businesses, including Empire Leather, failed during the economic downturn. For the cash-rich Allis, the disaster was an opportunity. In 1861 he used his savings to purchase the financially troubled Reliance Works at a sheriff's auction. Reliance Works was a leading manufacturer of sawmills, flour milling equipment, and castings. Before 1857, Reliance had been one of Milwaukee's largest employers with a workforce of about 75.

During the 1860s, Reliance Works of Edward P. Allis & Co., as the company was called, employed about 40 people working 55 hours per week. Allis constructed a new plant in 1868, and one year later he purchased his biggest rival, Bay State Iron Manufacturing Co. The company enjoyed strong profits until the financial panic of 1873, during which Allis went bankrupt. Chiefly because of the goodwill and faith of his creditors, Allis successfully renegotiated his debt and eventually recovered from the depression. The company remained intact, and even enjoyed a period of strong growth during much of the 1880s. By 1889, Allis employed 1,500 workers and shipped about $3 million worth of equipment annually. Allis died on April 1 of that year. He is still recognized as a pioneer in several machinery industry segments.

A number of gifted inventors and managers contributed to Allis's business efforts during the late 1800s. George M. Hinkley, for example, was a talented engineer and salesman who joined Allis in 1873. Among his most notable inventions was the bandsaw, which replaced the circular saw in many milling applications. The innovation was credited with revolutionizing the logging industry at the time, and the great demand for the saw helped the Edward P. Allis Company achieve a global presence in the machinery industry. Throughout his career, Hinkley accrued 35 patents on a wide range of sawmill machinery and accessories. Other notable Allis Company inventors included William Dixon Gray, who invented important new milling devices, and Edwin Reynolds, a pioneer in steam engine technology.

Company Perspectives:

AGCO is a publicly held corporation focused on the global distribution of farm equipment through independent dealers and distributors to farmers engaged in agricultural production to meet the demand to feed an ever expanding population and provide crops for new industrial applications.

The Company should be recognized throughout the world for the superior reliability of its products as measured by its market share leadership and the full service capability of its dealers in every market.

Formation of Allis-Chalmers: 1901

After Allis's death, his company continued to introduce breakthrough machines to the industry, particularly steam and pumping equipment. By the turn of the 20th century, the Edward P. Allis Company was the largest supplier of steam engines in the world. In 1901 Allis merged with another prominent machinery manufacturer, Fraser & Chalmers, to form Allis-Chalmers Company. Chalmers brought several new lines of machinery, particularly mining equipment, to the newly formed group, giving Allis-Chalmers a comprehensive product line. Further acquisitions during the next few years significantly broadened the company's product offerings, and Allis-Chalmers (the name was changed to Allis-Chalmers Manufacturing Company in 1913) continued to enter new machinery industries throughout the coming decades. Of greatest import to the history of AGCO was Allis-Chalmers's foray into the farm tractors market. Allis-Chalmers made many significant contributions to the farm machinery industry during the 1920s and 1930s, though its participation in that burgeoning market was dwarfed by competitors such as International Harvester and John Deere.

While it trailed a few industry leaders, Allis-Chalmers was recognized as a major U.S. manufacturer of farm equipment following its acquisition of Advance-Rumely Thresher Co. in 1931. The company parlayed its legacy of innovation into substantial gains with the division, introducing the first rubber-tired tractor in 1932 and, a few years later, a machine called the "All-Crop" harvester, which eventually eliminated the grain binder and threshing machine. One of the company's most profitable early innovations was the color it chose for its tractors—orange, in contrast to the industry-standard green. That move, devised by Allis-Chalmers's clever tractor division manager, Harry Merritt, proved to be a savvy publicity gimmick. The company's distinctive bright orange tractors eventually dotted the American landscape and became an excellent advertising tool.

During the 1940s and 1950s, Allis-Chalmers's farm machinery division assumed an increasingly prominent position within the company's many product groups. Ongoing innovation, such as the landmark multiple V-belt drive (Texrope drive), which the company introduced in the 1940s, spurred steady growth of the agricultural unit. To compete more effectively within its various markets, the company reorganized into separate tractor and general machinery divisions in the 1950s and several non–farm equipment lines were gradually phased out. Simultaneously, the company moved to expand its presence in foreign markets with the creation of Allis-Chalmers International. By the early 1960s, Allis-Chalmers operated factories in Mexico, Australia, England, France, and several other countries.

Corporate Mismanagement Leading to 1985 Sale of Farm Equipment Division

During the 1960s and early 1970s, Allis-Chalmers Corp., as it was named in 1971, experienced turbulence in several of its key markets. Fortunately, demand for agricultural equipment boomed during this period, and the company was able to offset losses in other areas with sales of tractors and other farm machinery. Despite the success of the agricultural division, general mismanagement and faulty strategy resulted in huge overall losses for the company. To make matters worse, the demand for farm equipment dropped significantly in the late 1970s. Battered by years of poor planning and a sagging economy, Allis-Chalmers's executives began searching in the early 1980s for a way to bring capital into the cash-starved organization.

During this period, Allis-Chalmers's farm equipment division became so unprofitable that the company was forced to close down its tractor and combine production plants for three months in 1984. This move stunned longtime Allis-Chalmers employees, many of whom were laid off. Desperate for cash and impatient with agricultural markets, Allis-Chalmers executives reached an agreement within six months of the shutdown to sell the farm machinery division. In 1985, the Allis-Chalmers Agricultural Equipment Co., along with a related credit subsidiary, was sold to Klöckner-Humboldt-Deutz AG (KHD) for approximately $132 million and other consideration. At the time, the division was producing about $260 million in annual sales. KHD combined the new purchase with its established Deutz Farm Equipment subsidiary to create a new company called Deutz-Allis Corp.

Between 1985 and 1989, KHD labored to cut costs and restore profitability to the ailing Deutz-Allis Corp. It closed down U.S. tractor production facilities and began relying solely on its imported German-built tractors. However, KHD continued to operate the Allis-Chalmers combine manufacturing facility in Independence, Missouri, and even invested about $8 million in capital improvements at the plant. Importantly, KHD drastically reduced the number of equipment dealers from about 1,800 to just 800 and slashed its U.S. workforce from more than 1,800 to just 900. The company also eliminated some unprofitable product lines and worked to reduce unnecessary operational costs. The effort succeeded in reducing Deutz-Allis's losses from about $82 million in 1987 to just $1.9 million in 1989.

Creation of AGCO Through 1990 Management Buyout

Despite these noteworthy gains with its new Deutz-Allis unit, KHD was disappointed with the performance of its U.S. farm equipment operations. Importantly, the company had underestimated the loyalty of American farmers, many of whom were World War II veterans, to U.S.-built machinery. One of the Deutz-Allis gleaners, for example, was nicknamed the "Kraut Can" by import-wary farmers, despite the fact that the machine was built in Missouri. By 1989, KHD had tired of its Deutz-Allis experiment and was ready to sell the division. Robert Ratliff, the head of Deutz-Allis in the United States, recognized the company's potential; along with a group of fellow executives, Ratliff arranged to purchase the division by selling off Deutz-Allis

Key Dates:

1901: Edward P. Allis Company merges with Fraser & Chalmers to form Allis-Chalmers Company, based in Milwaukee.

1913: Company name is changed to Allis-Chalmers Manufacturing Company.

1920s: Company enters the farm tractors market.

1971: Company changes its name to Allis-Chalmers Corp.

1984: Industry downturn leads to three-month shutdown of tractor and combine production plants.

1985: Farm equipment division is sold to Klöckner-Humboldt-Deutz AG (KHD); the German firm combines the division with its Deutz Farm Equipment subsidiary to form Deutz-Allis Corp.

1990: Robert Ratliff leads a management buyout of Deutz-Allis, which is soon operating as AGCO Corporation; headquarters are shifted to near Atlanta, Georgia.

1991: Acquisition spree begins with purchases of Hesston Corporation and White Tractor.

1992: One-half of AGCO's stock is sold via an initial public offering.

1993: AGCO purchases Massey Ferguson's North American operations.

1994: Company's stock listing shifts from the NASDAQ to the New York Stock Exchange; company buys the international operations of Massey Ferguson.

1997: Xaver Fendt GmbH & Co. KG, the leading German tractor maker, is acquired.

2004: The Valtra tractor and diesel engine operations of the Finnish firm Kone Corporation are acquired for $756 million.

receivables and using the money to finance a management buyout. Ratliff's management group completed the acquisition of Deutz-Allis in 1990 and renamed the company Allis-Gleaner Corporation, or AGCO Corporation.

Ratliff was well acquainted with both AGCO's operations and the machinery industry when he took control of the company. He had worked at Uniroyal and at International Harvester, where he headed the truck group, before KHD hired him in 1988 to turn around the ailing Deutz-Allis. Upon purchasing the company, he and four other executives, with the help of investment firm Hamilton, Robinson & Co., moved quickly to assume control of the $200-million-per-year equipment manufacturer. "We never looked back," Ratliff recalled in the October 30, 1994, *Topeka (Kans.) Capital-Journal*. Ratliff and his partners moved AGCO's headquarters to near Atlanta, Georgia, where the company could get a clean start by taking advantage of strong transportation and labor markets. Among other changes, they brought back the distinguished bright orange color to the farm equipment, which KHD had previously jettisoned in favor of dark green.

In the early 1990s, AGCO executives launched an aggressive plan to cut costs and increase efficiency. More importantly, they devised an ambitious strategy for growth. In 1991, Ratliff went to his home state of Kansas to negotiate the purchase of

Hesston Corporation, a small hay handling equipment company with an excellent reputation for quality but a long history of financial problems. Founded by a group of Mennonite farmers, the company prospered for a short time before giant round-balers were introduced to the industry. Hesston was then purchased by Fiat, of Italy, which achieved uneven success in attempting to turn the company around. Ratliff believed that his team stood a better chance of reviving the company. A few months after the Hesston purchase, AGCO bought the White Tractor division of Allied Products. The acquisition of both Hesston and White Tractor not only rounded out AGCO's product line, but it also added 1,100 dealerships for the distribution of AGCO's existing machinery.

The Hesston and White Tractor acquisitions provided an insight into Ratliff's long-term profit strategy for AGCO. He realized that AGCO would be fighting an uphill battle if it was going to try to compete with manufacturing giants such as John Deere and J.I. Case. "You've got 70 percent of the industry in North America controlled by two companies . . . neither of which has made money for a number of years," explained Allen Ritchie, head of AGCO's acquisition team, in the May 1994 issue of *Georgia Trend*. "[Those] businesses were really being driven by the manufacturing side of the business—low cost production . . . and nobody won." Thus, instead of profiting by building more farm equipment, AGCO hoped to succeed by beating Deere and Case in the marketing and distribution arenas. To that end, AGCO executives planned to concentrate on building a comprehensive, efficient network of dealers that could supply an expansive, reputable product line.

Mid-1990s Acquisition of Massey Ferguson

AGCO paid $36 million for both Hesston and White Tractor, financing each deal by selling more receivables. To help stabilize the ballooning organization, Ratliff hired John Shumejda to serve as chief operating officer. Shumejda was an engineer and an expert at farm machinery technology. While Shumejda worked to streamline AGCO's manufacturing and distribution operations, Ratliff and Ritchie continued to make acquisitions. In January 1993 AGCO paid $94.8 million to Varity Corp. for the assets of farm-tractor giant Massey Ferguson's North American operations. This move represented a major coup for AGCO in that Massey added 1,100 new dealers to AGCO's network and $200 million in sales. In addition, AGCO bought a related credit company for about $45 million which became a primary profit center for the corporation. Later that year, AGCO acquired White-New Idea for $53 million. This baling equipment manufacturer added $83 million to AGCO's revenue and tagged 300 new dealers onto its burgeoning network. In the meantime, AGCO's acquisition spree was aided by an initial public offering of one-half of the company's stock. Initially traded on the NASDAQ, AGCO gained a listing on the New York Stock Exchange in 1994.

By mid-1994, AGCO had established itself as the top North American distributor of tractors and a leading distributor of a wide range of farm machinery. Its giant distribution network had swelled to include 2,600 dealers, compared to John Deere's 1,400. AGCO was selling 20 different tractor models under the AGCO Allis name, four different Gleaner combines, 11 White tractors, and a range of equipment marketed under the names of Massey Ferguson and other brands. Although AGCO's debt burden had increased significantly, sales rocketed from about $220 million in 1990 to $314 million in 1992 and then $596 million in 1993. More importantly, AGCO's net income bounded to a healthy $34 million in 1993 (including a $14 million charge related to the Massey Ferguson buyout).

In 1994 AGCO transformed itself from a midsized North American farm equipment company to an international industry leader when it paid the equivalent of about $330 million for the international operations of Massey Ferguson. Prior to the buyout, only about 2 percent of AGCO's revenue came from outside North America. That figure shot up past 50 percent after the sale, giving AGCO immediate access to 140 different countries where Massey Ferguson was active. Furthermore, the giant division more than doubled AGCO's revenues, which surged in 1994 to an impressive $1.32 billion, about $76 million of which was net income. AGCO also continued to cut costs, particularly in its foreign operations, and to enhance its distribution network.

In 1995 AGCO bought the AgEquipment Group, manufacturer and marketer of agricultural implements and tillage equipment under the Glencoe, Tye, and Farmhand brands. The recent acquisitions helped revenues surge past the $2 billion mark, hitting $2.13 billion. Profits jumped to $129.1 million.

Late 1990s: International Acquisitions, Industry Downturn

International growth was at the forefront during 1996 and 1997. In June 1996 AGCO paid about $260 million for Iochpe-Mexion, the company's Massey Ferguson licensee in Brazil. Iochpe-Mexion held about a 45 percent share of Brazil's farm tractor market, along with significant portions of the combine harvester and loader-backhoe markets as well. That November, Jean-Paul Richard was named AGCO president and CEO, with Ratliff remaining chairman. Richard, a one-time president and CEO of Massey Ferguson, had served on the AGCO board since the acquisition of that firm. Further South American expansion came in December 1996 when AGCO completed a $61 million purchase of Deutz Argentina S.A. to gain the leading producer of farm tractors in the continent's second largest market. In early 1997 the company acquired the German firm Xaver Fendt GmbH & Co. KG for $320 million. Fendt was known as a producer of some of the world's most technologically advanced tractors and heavy farm equipment. With annual revenues of $580 million, Fendt was the market leader in Germany, where it held a market share of 25 percent, and had significant market shares in several other Western European nations: 23 percent in the Netherlands, 20 percent in the United Kingdom, 18 percent in Scandinavia, and 17 percent in France. On the strength of these deals, AGCO's revenues leaped 39 percent during 1997, reaching $3.22 billion. Net income reached a new high as well, amounting to $168.7 million. Richard, however, was not around when these stellar results were announced. He had resigned in August 1997, apparently after clashing with Ratliff, who seemed reluctant to give up too much day-to-day control over the company whose formation he had spearheaded. Ratliff reassumed the CEO spot following Richard's departure.

The 1990s ended on a down note for AGCO, as economic difficulties in Asia and Russia, which reduced the grain exports of U.S. farmers, coupled with three straight years of record crops, drastically reduced crop prices—to 20-year lows—and in turn sharply depressed demand for farm equipment. Agricultural equipment makers, including AGCO, began laying off workers, cutting production, and in some cases closing plants. In October 1998 AGCO announced that it was cutting 1,400 jobs, or about 12 percent of its workforce. Tractor and combine production was cut by 13 percent below 1997 levels, and the company saw its revenues and profits both drop for the year, to $2.94 billion and $60.6 million, respectively. AGCO also announced that it would sell its manufacturing plant in Argentina, consolidating the production there at its plant in Brazil. Late in 1999 AGCO revealed plans to close plants in Coldwater, Ohio; and Lockney, Texas. For 1999, the company suffered a net loss of $11.5 million on sales of just $2.41 billion. In February 1999, meantime, Shumejda was named president and CEO; Ratliff continued to serve as chairman.

Early 2000s and Beyond

As the downturn in the agricultural equipment market continued, AGCO cut its workforce by a further 5 percent in 2000 and closed its factory in Independence, Missouri. The company also reentered the acquisition arena. In mid-2000 AGCO bought out CNH Global N.V.'s stake in a hay-farming equipment joint venture called Hay and Forage Industries, based in Hesston, Kansas. (CNH Global had been formed in November 1999 through the merger of New Holland N.V. and Case Corporation.) Later in 2000 AGCO entered into a joint venture with Italian agriculture equipment maker Same DeutzFahr S.p.A. to distribute Same, Deutz-Fahr, Lamborghini, and Huerlimann brands in North America. AGCO next purchased the Minnesota firm Ag-Chem Equipment Co., Inc. in early 2001 for $247.2 million. The addition of Ag-Chem gave AGCO the leading position in self-propelled sprayers that spread fertilizer and chemicals on fields. In January 2002 AGCO bought Caterpillar Inc.'s agricultural tractor business. It featured the Challenger line of tractors, launched in the late 1980s, which had rubber-belted bulldozer-like tracks.

Just a week before the Caterpillar deal was completed, tragedy hit the company. A corporate jet carrying Shumejda and Edward Swingle, AGCO's senior vice-president of sales and marketing worldwide, crashed on takeoff in Birmingham, England, killing all aboard. An investigation later revealed that the failure of the flight crew to de-ice the plane was the likely cause of the crash. Within hours of the crash, Ratliff reassumed the position of president and CEO. Ratliff went on to complete one more deal that year, the $48 million purchase of Sunflower Manufacturing Co., Inc., finalized in November. Based in Beloit, Kansas, Sunflower was a leading producer of tillage, seeding, and specialty harvesting equipment. Also in 2002 AGCO announced plans to close its tractor plant in Coventry, England, shifting production to facilities in France and Brazil. During 2003 the Challenger tractor factory in DeKalb, Illinois, was also shut down, and production of the Challenger line was relocated to a plant in Jackson, Minnesota. Overall, 2003 was AGCO's best year since 1997. Whereas the company suffered a net loss of $84.4 million on sales of $2.92 billion in 2002, results for 2003 showed profits of $74.4 million on record revenues of $3.5 billion.

In early January 2004 AGCO completed its largest acquisition yet, acquiring the Valtra tractor and diesel engine operations of the Finnish firm Kone Corporation for about $756 million. Valtra held a market-leading position in the Nordic region of Europe and had a significant presence in Latin America as well. It also provided AGCO with an in-house engine maker. In the fiscal year ending in June 2003, Valtra had an operating profit of about $65 million on $900 million in revenue.

A lengthy executive search also came to fruition in 2004. In July, Martin Richenhagen came onboard as president and CEO, as Ratliff continued as chairman of the board. Richenhagen had most recently served as a group vice-president of Forbo International S.A., a flooring materials concern based in Zurich, Switzerland, and prior to that had been group president from 1998 through 2003 of Claas KgaA mbH, a German farm equipment manufacturer and distributor. The selection of Richenhagen showed how important Europe was to AGCO. Even prior to the Valtra deal, Europe was AGCO's largest market, accounting for 46 percent of 2003 sales. Under Richenhagen's leadership, further major acquisitions did not seem in the offing. In May 2004, prior to officially assuming his position, he told the *Atlanta Business Chronicle* that "AGCO has put together a fine selection of businesses. My challenge is to create a corporate identity and to grow the business, to harvest what is already in place." Among his specific areas of focus were digesting Valtra, continuing to bolster the distribution of the Challenger line, improving the manufacturing operations, and strengthening the company's worldwide network of dealers.

Principal Subsidiaries

AGCO Equipment Company; Fendt GmbH (Germany); Massey Ferguson Corp.; Valtra Holding Oy (Finland).

Principal Competitors

Deere & Company; CNH Global N.V.

Further Reading

"Action at AGCO," *Diesel Progress North American Edition*, July 2002, p. 34.

"AGCO: Challenging Times, Rewarding Performance," *Implement and Tractor*, July/August 2002, pp. 12–13.

Baldo, Anthony, "Tricks with Tractors," *Financial World*, January 4, 1994, p. 68.

Barry, Tom, "The Wizard of Ag," *Georgia Trend*, September 1997, pp. 23–28.

Connola, Jon, and John Fauber, "Allis-Chalmers Files State Plant Closing Notice," *Business Journal-Milwaukee*, July 27, 1987, p. 1.

Fogarty, Bill, and Scott Nesbitt, "Deutz and Allis Get Hitched," *Implement and Tractor*, July 1985, p. 8.

Freiberg, Bill, "AGCO Corporation: 'A Living Example of the American Dream,'" *Implement and Tractor*, May/June 1995, pp. 4–6.

Hitchcock, Doug, "Analysts Say Deutz-Allis Slowdown at Combine Factory to Be Temporary," *Kansas City Business Journal*, February 8, 1988, p. 11.

Jordan, Meredith, "Acquisitions Sow Seeds for Growth," *Atlanta Business Chronicle*, May 7, 2004.

Kotlowitz, Alex, and Jeffrey Zaslow, "Allis-Chalmers Completes Sale of Units, Agrees with Lenders on Restructuring," *Wall Street Journal*, May 28, 1985.

Kotlowitz, Alex, and William Power, "Allis-Chalmers Seeks Shelter of Chapter 11," *Wall Street Journal*, June 30, 1987.

Levine, Joshua, "Plant Pals," *Forbes*, May 8, 1995, pp. 130+.

Lovel, Jim, "After Tragedy: AGCO, CEO Move On," *Atlanta Business Chronicle*, February 1, 2002, pp. A1+.

Luke, Robert, and Hank Ezell, "Global Experience Scored Points for New AGCO CEO," *Atlanta Journal and Constitution*, November 20, 1996, p. D3.

Mallory, Maria, "AGCO Tractors Roar Down the Fast Track," *Business Week*, February 7, 1994.

——, "Sharp Jump in Earnings Drives Up AGCO Stock, Analysts' Projections," *Atlanta Constitution*, October 28, 1994, p. D1.

Nesbitt, Scott, "Deutz-Allis Execs Buy U.S. Operation," *Implement and Tractor*, May 1990, p. 2.

Osenga, Mike, "AGCO: The Unknown OEM Goes Global," *Diesel Progress: Engines and Drives*, April 1995, pp. 12, 14, 18.

Paul, Peralte C., "AGCO Takes Step on Succession Plan: Company Names President/CEO," *Atlanta Journal-Constitution*, March 17, 2004, p. C1.

Peterson, Walter, and C. Edward Weber, *An Industrial Heritage: Allis-Chalmers Corporation*, Milwaukee: Milwaukee County Historical Society, 1976, 407 p.

Quinn, Matthew C., "Duluth's AGCO to Cut 1,400 Jobs," *Atlanta Constitution*, October 30, 1998, p. E1.

Quintanilla, Carl, "Plowing Ahead: A Remarkable Gamble in an Industry Slump Pays Off Fast for AGCO," *Wall Street Journal*, August 19, 1997, p. A1.

Richards, Bill, "Allis-Chalmers Plans to Spin Off Its Overseas Units," *Wall Street Journal*, February 11, 1987.

——, "The Rust Bowl: Allis-Chalmers Corp.'s Survival Strategy Involves Risky Reliance on Synthetic Fuel," *Wall Street Journal*, June 26, 1984.

Rubinger, David, "Biggest Deal in Southeast This Year Brings Allis Home to U.S.," *Atlanta Business Chronicle*, July 23, 1990, p. A1.

Sparks, Debra, "Betting the Farm; Can the New Massey Ferguson Reap Rewards in the Depressed European Market?," *Financial World*, October 25, 1994, p. 74.

Suber, Jim, "A Farm Equipment Company Led by a Native Kansan Has Quietly Pulled Off a Machinery Miracle," *Topeka (Kans.) Capital-Journal*, October 30, 1994, p. C1.

Swinford, Norm, *The Proud Heritage of AGCO Tractors*, St. Joseph, Mich.: American Society of Agricultural Engineers, 1999, 279 p.

Van Dusen, Christine, "Rising from Tragedy," *Atlanta Journal-Constitution*, January 5, 2003, p. Q1.

Verespej, Michael A., "Bob Ratliff Sticks to Basics," *Industry Week*, May 1, 1995, p. 67.

Wendel, Charles H., *The Allis-Chalmers Story*, Sarasota, Fla.: Crestline Publishing, 1988, 372 p.

Wilkinson, Bruce, "Well-Run Companies Always Make Money," *Georgia Trend*, May 1994, p. 43.

—Dave Mote
—update: David E. Salamie

AMERCO

1325 Airmotive Way, Suite 100
Reno, Nevada 89502-3239
U.S.A.
Telephone: (775) 688-6300
Fax: (775) 688-6338
Web site: http://www.amerco.com

Public Company
Incorporated: 1969
Employees: 17,230
Sales: $2.17 billion (2004)
Stock Exchanges: NASDAQ New York
Ticker Symbol: UHAL (NASDAQ); AOPRA (New York)
NAIC: 532120 Truck, Utility Trailer, and RV
(Recreational Vehicle) Rental and Leasing; 531130
Lessors of Miniwarehouses and Self-Storage Units

AMERCO is a holding company whose primary subsidiary is Phoenix-based U-Haul International, Inc., North America's leading provider of move-it-yourself rental equipment, one of the largest operators of self-storage facilities, and the world's largest installer of permanent trailer hitches. The U-Haul rental system, which includes a fleet of nearly 200,000 vehicles (including moving vans, trucks, and trailers) and automobile towing devices, operates through more than 1,350 company-owned U-Haul retail centers in the United States and Canada and nearly 14,000 independent U-Haul dealers. U-Haul was founded in the 1940s by Leonard Samuel (L.S.) Shoen as what he hoped would be the cornerstone of a family business empire. From the 1970s into the 1990s, control of the company was the subject of one of the bitterest family feuds in the history of American business. In the early 2000s the Shoen family continued to own about 40 percent of AMERCO, which was now led by Edward J. (Joe) Shoen, son of the founder.

Do-It-Yourself Moving Pioneer

L.S. Shoen was the son of an Oregon farmer who lost his land during the Great Depression. The younger Shoen worked picking fruit, butchering cattle, and cutting hair to pay for a three-year stint at college, which ended when he was expelled for providing answers for a classmate. He then entered the U.S. Navy just in time for World War II. During the war he moved his family from military base to military base in borrowed trailers, an experience that led him to envision a nationwide company that would provide mobile Americans with reliable, rented trailers that they could use to move their belongings without worrying about how they would return the vehicles.

With the help of his wife, Anna Mary, Shoen launched U-Haul Trailer Rental Company in Ridgefield, Washington, a city just outside Portland, Oregon, in 1945. With a $5,000 investment, the Shoens began to buy and build trailers, painting and stenciling the company's name on each of the trailers themselves. They were originally rented for $2 a day. The couple had six children by the time Anna Mary Shoen died in 1957, and L.S. Shoen eventually had a total of 12 children with three wives.

Throughout the 1940s and 1950s, L.S. Shoen built a business empire of trailer dealerships that had automobile service stations as their main outlets. Traveling by car for weeks at a time, he recruited new dealers for his U-Haul trailers and used the tool box he carried to patch and repair his company's rolling stock, often by the light of street lamps late at night. He also rented trailers to people who would travel to cities he could not visit, provided that they return those trailers to service stations he thought were potential U-Haul dealers. By the mid-1950s his dealer network stretched from Portland, Oregon, to Miami, Florida, and from Los Angeles, California, to New York City.

In *You and Me,* a 1980 book in which he chronicled his family's history and outlined his corporate philosophy, Shoen illustrated his entrepreneurial spirit and homespun management style. "The first day we rented a trailer, I set my sights on 1,000 trailers, and when we got 1,000 trailers on the road, I wanted 10,000," he wrote. He made surprise visits to his dealers, sometimes at night, and as an example to his employees of wasteful spending, he once threw $1,000 in cash from the 11th floor of his headquarters building. Shoen stressed economy in all areas, mandating that his executives eat at fast-food restaurants and stay at cheap hotels on company business trips. Because he planned to hand over his business empire to his children, they were fully instructed in running the company, including painting and repairing the U-Haul fleet. As they grew up, his first four sons joked that they had orange U-Haul paint in their veins rather than blood.

Reorganizing the Company, New Competitive Threat: Late 1960s and Early 1970s

In the 1960s U-Haul was the preeminent do-it-yourself trailer rental company in the United States and Canada. In 1967, at the height of the company's success, Shoen moved his corporate headquarters to Phoenix, Arizona. Two years later, in 1969, Shoen incorporated American Family Corporation (AMERCO) in Reno, Nevada, as the holding company for what he hoped would become a diversified corporation. AMERCO later started the Ponderosa Group, a captive insurance company established to cover corporate risks. Through its real estate subsidiary, AMERCO also acquired a property portfolio with an estimated value of $1 billion.

Events of the 1970s significantly altered AMERCO's future. The first critical change arose from the founding in 1970 of Ryder System, Inc. in Miami. Eventually becoming a formidable competitor, Ryder copied the idea and style established for the trailer and truck rental business that Shoen had founded. In 1989 U-Haul and Ryder each controlled nearly 45 percent of the United States market for do-it-yourself rentals of trailers and trucks.

While the long-term effects of Ryder's presence in the market was largely indeterminable in the early 1970s, the second threat to AMERCO's business was more immediate and forced the company to consider new businesses and directions. The 1973 oil crisis, which struck at the heart of the company's basic business by curtailing the mobility of Americans, also caused fundamental changes in the way gasoline was distributed and resulted in the closing of many of the independently owned service stations that comprised U-Haul's dealership network. In response, U-Haul expanded its operations starting in 1974 by establishing U-Haul Centers—company-owned stores that offered a variety of rental services, from jet skis and party goods to sexually explicit videocassettes. A huge investment expense for AMERCO at a time when its sales and profits were declining and competition was increasing, the stores were ultimately unsuccessful and brought the company additional losses.

Beginning of Family Feud, Mid- to Late 1970s

As these changes were occurring, strife arose between Shoen and his eldest children, who were not getting along with his second wife, Suzanne Gilbert. Disputes between Gilbert and the Shoen children while L.S. Shoen was out of town on business sometimes had to be settled by the Phoenix police. In 1977 the couple divorced.

Over the years Shoen gave his children progressively greater shares of the company in preparation for eventually handing it over to their control, so that by the early 1980s, his seven sons and five daughters owned 95 percent of the outstanding shares of the company, while he controlled only 2 percent. Relations between Shoen and his four eldest sons, Sam, Mike, Edward J. (Joe), and Mark, began to deteriorate in the mid-1970s, when the four siblings had moved into the upper management of the company. The sons believed that the investment in the 1,100 U-Haul Center stores, which offered a wide variety of rental items, was not benefitting U-Haul. They argued that the stores detracted from the servicing and maintenance of U-Haul's aging fleet of trucks and trailers, which were put in greater jeopardy with the growth of rival Ryder Systems.

By 1979 Joe and Mark Shoen had resigned from U-Haul because of this dispute over the direction of the company, and a year later Mark's relationship with his father and brother Sam deteriorated still further when they refused to help him out of a financial predicament by buying some of his AMERCO stock. Mark Shoen, who later became president of U-Haul International, noted in an interview with the *Los Angeles Times*, "[We] were millionaires in name only. We were told we were wealthy, but we didn't have enough money to buy a car."

1986: Ousting of Founder by Sons

Mark and Joe Shoen set out to wrest control of the company from their father and brother Sam. By 1986 Joe and Mark Shoen had drummed up enough support among their brothers and sisters to oust L.S. Shoen as chairman of the corporation. The brothers moved quickly after assuming control of the company to return it to its basic businesses. They kept U-Haul's rental storage facilities but eliminated many of the company's extraneous rental offerings, focusing on trucks and trailers, boxes, moving pads, and packing materials as featured items at the company's U-Haul Centers. In addition, they cut back on the company's workforce, purging executives who supported L.S. and Sam Shoen.

At the 1987 annual meeting, Sam and L.S. Shoen appeared to have convinced enough family members to return to their side; by early 1988 Sam and L.S. Shoen hoped to control 52 percent of the corporation. Joe Shoen, a lawyer with an M.B.A. degree from Harvard University, foiled that plan by wooing 53 percent of those voting to his side.

To retain his control of the corporation, Joe Shoen issued 8,099 shares of the corporation's treasury stock to friendly executives. In March 1989 the company's annual meeting allegedly turned into a brawl when L.S. Shoen and his son Mike attempted to set up a tape recorder to record the proceedings. After the meeting Mike Shoen posed shirtless for a photographer and alleged that his brother Mark had hit him, while Joe Shoen said in an interview with the *Arizona Republic* that no one was "beaten up."

On August 6, 1990, Eva Shoen, the 44-year-old wife of Sam Shoen, was murdered. The homicide, which news reports claimed had signs of a professional hit, was under investigation for months with no official police suspects. The murder became the source of a libel suit filed by Joe Shoen against his father,

Key Dates:

1945: L.S. Shoen launches U-Haul Trailer Rental Company in Ridgefield, Washington.
1967: Corporate headquarters is moved to Phoenix, Arizona.
1969: Shoen incorporates American Family Corporation (AMERCO) as a Reno, Nevada-based holding company, with U-Haul the main operating company.
1974: First company-owned U-Haul Centers are established.
1986: Control of the company is wrested from L.S. Shoen by his sons Joe and Mark.
1988: The new leaders fend off an attempt by the founder and his allies to regain control.
1994: In a lawsuit stemming from the 1988 battle, a jury returns a $1.47 billion judgment against Joe Shoen and five other AMERCO directors.
1995: A judge reduces the judgment to $461.8 million; AMERCO is forced to shoulder the payments based on an indemnification agreement.
2002: Company restates its financial results for the previous seven years because of accounting irregularities.
2003: AMERCO files for Chapter 11 bankruptcy protection.
2004: Having refinanced its debt, the company emerges from bankruptcy.

L.S. Shoen, who said publicly that he believed Joe was involved in it. In November 1994, however, a New Mexico man was sentenced to 24 years in prison for shooting Eva Shoen in a botched robbery. The libel suit, meanwhile, was one of several court proceedings involving the Shoen family and the company that carried on well into the 1990s; all of the cases argued that one or another of the family factions was the rightful manager of the company.

During the 1980s AMERCO's annual income rose from a $2 million loss in 1981 to gains of more than $41 million in 1984, but the corporation's earnings were never steady. Though in the late 1980s and early 1990s revenues increased in part because of AMERCO's improvements of U-Haul's core rental business, income generally remained on a downward trend. Net income for 1990, for example, dropped 39 percent from the previous year to $28.3 million; revenues, however, rose significantly to $737.6 million in 1990 and to $986 million in 1991. During 1991 a corporate restructuring that eliminated and consolidated second-tier subsidiaries and cut the workforce from 18,000 to 10,900 led to income for the year of just $416,000. Analysts blamed inconsistencies and roller coaster-like changes in the company's profit on the instability brought on by feuding among Shoen family members.

Culmination of Family Feud in the 1990s

During fiscal 1993 net income nearly doubled to $40.1 million, while revenues surpassed the $1 billion mark for the first time, reaching $1.04 billion. In October 1993 stock in

AMERCO began trading on the New York Stock Exchange through an offering of 6.1 million shares of preferred stock. Then the following year AMERCO common stock began trading on the NASDAQ.

The lawsuits stemming from the late 1980s family feud came to a head in the mid-1990s. In October 1994 a jury sided with the L.S. Shoen/Sam Shoen side, agreeing that the 1988 sale of shares was improper and had prevented the plaintiffs from gaining control of the company board. They stipulated that Joe Shoen and five other AMERCO directors had to pay the plaintiffs $1.47 billion in compensation and that Joe Shoen had to pay an additional $70 million in punitive damages. The following February, however, an Arizona state court judge slashed the two awards to $461.8 million and $7 million, respectively, finding them "excessive." The directors, claiming they could not shoulder the judgment, then filed for bankruptcy court protection, leading AMERCO to indemnify them for the award, as part of a preexisting indemnification agreement. AMERCO was forced to sell or lease back millions of dollars worth of assets, including vehicles and trailers, to fulfill the judgment. Meantime, the company founder and his allies had to agree to give up their shares in the company. Joe Shoen carried on the battle, appealing the $7 million personal judgment against him for acting with malice in his 1988 dealings with family members. He lost his appeal in 1998 and was ordered to pay the punitive damages. In a sad postscript to the family feud, L.S. Shoen died in October 1999 at the age of 83, apparently having committed suicide by driving his car into a power pole.

Over the course of the 1990s AMERCO's revenues grew fairly steadily, culminating in $1.68 billion in sales for the fiscal year ending in March 2000. Net income was stagnant, ending at $65.5 million, not much above the $60 million or $60.4 million figures for 1995 and 1996, respectively.

Early 2000s: Accounting Irregularities, Bankruptcy, More Lawsuits

The soap opera-like history of AMERCO continued in the early 2000s. In 2002 AMERCO became the latest company facing allegations of accounting irregularities. In 1994 so-called special purpose entities (made infamous by Enron Corporation) collectively known as SAC Holdings had been set up by U-Haul President Mark Shoen to own land where U-Haul storage facilities were based. In February 2002, in the wake of the Enron scandal, AMERCO's auditor, PricewaterhouseCoopers (PwC), told AMERCO that it had to consolidate the results of SAC Holdings with AMERCO and restate the latter's financial results for the previous seven years. During fiscal 2003 the company did so, and the consolidation of SAC Holdings' debt sharply reduced AMERCO's net earnings and net worth. For example, the net income figure for fiscal 2000 was cut to $21.8 million, and the company now posted a net loss for fiscal 2001 of $42.1 million. AMERCO, however, soon fired PwC and then later sued the accounting firm for $2.5 billion, accusing it of providing flawed financial advice that brought the company to the brink of bankruptcy.

Indeed, in October 2002, AMERCO missed a $100 million bond payment and later missed a second payment. Unable to secure new financing, the company filed for Chapter 11 bankruptcy protection in June 2003 to expedite the restructuring of its debt. The filing was unusual in that the company aimed to pay all of its creditors in full and to leave its preferred and common stock intact. In this it was successful. In March 2004 the company emerged from bankruptcy on the back of a $550 million credit facility through a banking syndicate.

Clouding the company's future was still more litigation. Paul Shoen, another brother of Joe and Mark, sued AMERCO in connection with the SAC accounting irregularities in a reprise of the family feud. His case was consolidated with four others before being dismissed in May 2003, but the plaintiffs planned to appeal. AMERCO additionally faced four class-action lawsuits, again connected with SAC, on behalf of company shareholders. In May 2003 the Securities and Exchange Commission (SEC) opened an investigation into AMERCO's accounting practices, and twice had to go to court seeking orders to compel the company to comply with SEC document requests.

Principal Subsidiaries

AMERCO Real Estate Company; Oxford Life Insurance Company; Republic Western Insurance Company; U-Haul International, Inc.

Principal Competitors

Budget Rent A Car System, Inc.; Penske Truck Leasing; Public Storage, Inc.; Shurgard Storage Centers, Inc.; Storage USA, Inc.

Further Reading

Adelson, Andrea, "Gains at U-Haul Dampened by Feud in Owning Family," *New York Times,* January 31, 1989.

Atlas, Riva D., "U-Haul's Parent Finds Equity Gains in Bankruptcy," *New York Times,* August 20, 2003, p. C1.

Berke, Jonathan, "Amerco Wrestles with Credibility Gap," *Daily Deal,* August 11, 2003.

——, "Mission Impossible," *Daily Deal,* November 20, 2003.

Blumenthal, Karen, "Award in Dispute over Amerco Is Cut to $461.8 Million," *Wall Street Journal,* February 6, 1995, p. B9.

Boorstein, Michelle, "U-Haul Making a Turnaround Move," *Las Vegas Review-Journal,* December 7, 1995, p. 11D.

Buckler, Arthur, "Jury Sets Damages in Amerco Lawsuit at $1.47 Billion," *Wall Street Journal,* October 11, 1994, p. B9.

Fiscus, Chris, "Don't Judge U-Haul by Feud, Leader Says," *Arizona Business Gazette,* April 26, 1991, pp. 1+.

Fix, Janet, "No More Mr. Nice Guy," *Forbes,* February 11, 1985, pp. 64+.

Freudmann, Aviva, "IRS May Appeal Tax Court Rulings on Captive Insurers," *Journal of Commerce,* April 9, 1991.

Friedland, Jonathan, and Jonathan Weil, "U-Haul Parent Amerco Inc. Sues Pricewaterhouse over Accounting," *Wall Street Journal,* April 21, 2003, p. A2.

Gately, Edward, "U-Haul Parent Alters Accounting Practices amid Greater Scrutiny," *East Valley Tribune* (Mesa, Ariz.), August 27, 2002.

——, "U-Haul Parent Files Suit Against Auditor over Loss of Shareholder Confidence," *East Valley Tribune* (Mesa, Ariz.), April 22, 2003.

Groves, Martha, "Family Feud Weighs Down U-Haul," *Los Angeles Times,* September 4, 1990.

Kang, Stephanie, "Parent of U-Haul, Amerco Inc., Files for Chapter 11," *Wall Street Journal,* June 23, 2003, p. B8.

Luebke, Cathy, "Net Income at U-Haul up Dramatically," *Phoenix Business Journal,* July 23, 1993, pp. 1+.

Michaels, Adrian, "A Moving Tale As Financial Woes Deluge Rental Group," *Financial Times,* October 19, 2002, p. 19.

Tomsho, Robert, "Supporters of Joe Shoen Take New Steps to Strengthen Grip on U-Haul Empire," *Wall Street Journal,* September 28, 1990.

——, "U-Haul's Patriarch Now Battles Offspring in Bitterest of Feuds," *Wall Street Journal,* July 16, 1990.

Toy, Stewart, "A New Generation Takes the Wheel at U-Haul," *Business Week,* March 28, 1988, p. 57.

Toy, Stewart, and Judith H. Dobrzynski, "The Family That Hauls Together Brawls Together," *Business Week,* August 29, 1988, pp. 64+.

Watkins, Ronald J., *Birthright: Murder, Greed, and Power in the U-Haul Family Dynasty,* New York: Morrow, 1993, 425 p.

—Bruce Vernyi
—update: David E. Salamie

American Axle & Manufacturing Holdings, Inc.

1840 Holbrook Avenue
Detroit, Michigan 48212
U.S.A.
Telephone: (313) 974-2000
Toll Free: (800) 299-2953
Fax: (313) 974-3090
Web site: http://www.aam.com

Public Company
Incorporated: 1994 as American Axle & Manufacturing
    of Michigan, Inc.
Employees: 11,800
Sales: $3.68 billion (2003)
Stock Exchanges: New York
Ticker Symbol: AXL
NAIC: 336399 All Other Motor Vehicle Parts and
    Accessories; 551112 Offices of Other Holding
    Companies

American Axle & Manufacturing Holdings, Inc. (AAM) designs and manufactures driveline systems, chassis systems, and forged products for trucks, sport utility vehicles, buses, and passenger cars. AAM relies heavily on General Motors Corporation (GM) for its business, deriving more than 80 percent of its sales from the car maker. AAM also supplies driveline components (the parts that transfer power from the transmission and deliver it to the drive wheels) to DaimlerChrysler AG, Ford Motor Company, Nissan, Renault, Visteon Automotive, and others. AAM operates 17 manufacturing facilities in the United States, Mexico, Brazil, and the United Kingdom. Company-owned sales and business offices are located in Tokyo, Japan, and Ulm, Germany.

Origins

The dominant figure behind AAM's impressive success was the architect of its development, Richard Dauch. Dauch was a 30-year veteran of the automotive industry when he decided to resurrect a handful of manufacturing plants neglected by GM.

A hard-nosed, pragmatic executive, Dauch began his illustrious career at GM, joining the car manufacturer in 1964 after earning a Bachelor of Science degree in industrial management and science at Purdue University. Dauch spent a dozen years at GM, rising from an entry level position to become the youngest plant manager in Chevrolet's history. From there, Dauch moved on to Volkswagen of America, serving for four years as the company's group vice-president of manufacturing operations. Dauch was becoming an expert in his field, something of a manufacturing evangelist whose views were regarded as visionary. His reputation as a forward-thinking executive drew the admiration of Lee Iacocca, Chrysler's influential chairman.

In 1980, Iacocca recruited Dauch from Volkswagen, tapping the rising executive to apply his salubrious touch to Chrysler's troubled manufacturing operations. At Chrysler, Dauch confirmed his reputation as a manufacturing guru, becoming the driving force behind the car maker's well-publicized resurgence during the 1980s. Chrysler's comeback made Iacocca a household name, but those in the industry were quick to bestow the company's executive vice-president of worldwide manufacturing with a large portion of the credit for the company's revival. Dauch's success at Chrysler prompted him to write a book about his favorite subject, the title of which neatly described its author. *Passion for Manufacturing*, published in 1993, contained 280 pages of wisdom from the renowned automotive authority that eventually would be sold in 80 countries and used as a textbook in numerous colleges and universities. One year after finishing his book, Dauch directed his manufacturing zeal toward the dilapidated factory where he once worked as a GM employee.

During the early 1990s, Dauch turned his attention to a business unit of his former employer. The Final Drive and Forge Business Unit of GM's Saginaw Division was a collection of neglected manufacturing facilities that represented the car maker's axle, forge, and driveshaft driveline assets. GM executives thought little of the business. They viewed the business of making axles and driveshafts as a low technology, low profit-margin business and their attention to the factories reflected their ambivalence. Dauch, on the other hand, saw a perfect opportunity to demonstrate his manufacturing acumen and apply new technology to the business. With the help of two

---

Company Perspectives:

American Axle & Manufacturing and its associates are committed to meeting customer requirements through measurable quality improvement, cost reduction, and on-time delivery of products and services, while achieving profitable growth and increasing shareholder value.

---

investors, Raymond Park and Morten Harris, Dauch acquired five plants from GM for an undisclosed sum, though industry observers speculated that the trio paid approximately $300 million for assets located "in a horrible part of town . . . surrounded by abandoned houses, crack houses, prostitution, and plenty of bars," as described by *Crain's Detroit Business* in a July 26, 2004 article.

Dauch incorporated his company, initially called American Axle & Manufacturing of Michigan, Inc. in March 1994. (American Axle & Manufacturing Holdings, Inc. was adopted as the company's corporate title in January 1999.) From its inception under Dauch's control, AAM was a more than $1 billion business with more than a half-century of existence behind it, but its assets were in dire need of a visionary's touch. Dauch began with core manufacturing operations based in Michigan and New York and a commitment from GM to be the car maker's sole-source supplier of the components it previously had made for itself. To turn this base into a flourishing enterprise, which AAM did become, Dauch applied his three decades of experience to the company's improvement. He focused on improving product quality, manufacturing efficiency, and, perhaps most importantly, he demonstrated an unwavering commitment to research and development.

Cash Infusion in 1997

The rehabilitation of AAM's assets turned the company into one of North America's largest and most profitable suppliers to the automotive industry. The development toward such status was consistent but slow during the company's first years in business, as Dauch faced the daunting challenge of breathing new life into the massive and neglected facilities that supported GM. The establishment of a new research and development center in 1995—a facility treated with several expansion and improvement programs before the end of the decade—was one of the first significant successes achieved by Dauch. His investments and changes in manufacturing techniques drove the company's sales up to $2.2 billion in 1996, by which point his efforts had produced sufficient tangible results to attract a large cash infusion. A New York investment firm, Blackstone Capital Partners II Merchant Banking Fund L.P., looked at Dauch's work and decided to invest substantially in the company's future. In October 1997, Blackstone acquired a controlling stake in the company, giving Dauch as much as $700 million to funnel toward AAM's expansion and improvement.

In the wake of Blackstone's leveraged recapitalization of AAM, Dauch assumed a more aggressive posture as the company's chairman and chief executive officer. In 1998, the company acquired Scotland-based Albion Automotive (Holdings)

Limited, a supplier of front steerable and rear axles, driving heads, crankshafts, chassis components, and transmission parts. Albion's parts were used in medium-duty trucks and buses for customers in the United Kingdom and continental Europe. In 1999, when AAM completed its initial public offering of stock, Dauch completed two acquisitions on the domestic front, paying roughly $223 million for two forging companies, Colfer Manufacturing Inc. and MSP Industries Corp. He also built an axle plant in Mexico and acquired a majority interest in a joint venture in Brazil that machined forging and driveline components. The acquisitions represented Dauch's efforts to vertically integrate AAM, aping what GM had done roughly 70 years earlier. Dauch's purchases were intended to allow AAM to forge more parts for the company's axles and drivelines, part of his plan to nearly quintuple sales within five years to $10 billion. "We are a consolidator," Dauch announced in the May 17, 1999 issue of *Crain's Detroit Business*, "the goal is to be a strategic supplier." Dauch fell well short of reaching his financial goal, but his accomplishments hardly could be dismissed as AAM entered the 21st century.

In 2000, after six years of working to improve AAM's manufacturing capabilities, Dauch could point to convincing evidence that his expertise had worked wonders. Between 1994 and 2000, roughly $1.5 billion was spent on capital expenditures. During that period, the average number of axles produced per day increased from 10,000 to 16,000. The number of defect parts for every million parts shipped to GM plummeted from 13,441 to 89. The dramatic improvements drove the growth of the company, enabling it to edge past the $3-billion-in-sales mark in 2000, 84.5 percent of which was derived from sales to GM.

As Dauch focused on improving manufacturing methods, he also concentrated on developing another area of AAM's business. The company's relationship with GM was a strength, with the car maker's success translating into commensurate success for AAM, but the company's dependence on GM was also a potential weakness. Dauch, wishing to reduce the company's reliance on a single customer, worked to develop relationships with other car makers and other automotive suppliers. By the end of 2000, the company's sales to customers other than GM had more than tripled in comparison to 1998. In 2001, progress in the company's customer diversification was highlighted by two contracts. In September, the company was awarded a contract to supply gears for automatic transmissions in selected Ford Motor Company vehicles. The following month, AAM announced it had been selected to supply front and rear driveshafts for DaimlerChrysler AG's heavy-duty Dodge Ram pickup truck program. Dauch's continued attention to customer diversification enabled the company to reduce its dependence on GM in subsequent years. GM accounted for 87 percent of the company's business in 2001. In 2003, when sales to non-GM customers were up nearly 50 percent, the company derived 82 percent of its sales from GM.

AAM in the 21st Century

Investments in new technology underpinned the company's progress during the first years of the new decade. By 2002, three-quarters of the products AAM was supplying had been developed within the previous three years, putting Dauch's offerings on the technological vanguard. At this point, the company was supplying the driveline systems for the long-wheelbase versions of the Chevrolet TrailBlazer and GMC Envoy sport utility vehicles, the Hummer H2, and the heavy-duty version of the 2003 Dodge Ram pickup truck. The company received a new contract to supply GM with a new driveline system in 2006, a deal of tremendous importance to its future business. The contract, which potentially was worth more than $1.5 billion annually, was hailed by Dauch. "This is the largest driveline-system award program by any vehicle manufacturer in the world," he explained in a May 20, 2002 interview with *Crain's Detroit Business.* "It will secure our revenue (from 2006) through 2015 with this one program," he added. Revenues at the end of the year reached a record high of $3.5 billion, and the company's net income, after increasing 53 percent, reached a record high of $176 million.

As AAM entered the mid-2000s, it continued to register significant improvements in its manufacturing methods. The number of defects per million parts shipped to GM, which stood at 13,441 in 1994 before being whittled down to 89 in 2000, was only 15 by the end of 2003. The company was producing 19,300 axles per day by this point, nearly twice the daily production average in 1994. New-technology-related sales represented only 3 percent of the company's business when Dauch took control of its factories. By the end of 2003, AAM derived 80 percent of its revenue from products featuring new technology. The influence of Dauch on the company's operations was immense, representing more than a restoration of the facilities formerly owned by GM. Dauch reinvented the business, creating an automotive supplier that ranked as the most profitable enterprise in its industry. As the company plotted its course, its future success rested almost as heavily on the presence of Dauch as it did on the business supplied by GM.

AAM dedicated its new headquarters facility in mid-2004, a seven-story, 250,000-square-foot, $40-million building that promised to be the focal point of the company's future success. The dedication occurred during the company's 10th anniversary, an occasion marked by Dauch in a July 23, 2004 AAM press release. "When this company was formed in 1994," he wrote, "it was a priority for us that we locate our headquarters in the city of Detroit, the motor capital of the world. The new AAM world headquarters tops off more than 10 years of improvements and contributions that we have made in the community. It is a true capstone for our corporation. Now, we have all our functional capabilities under one roof, for the first time in AAM's history."

Principal Subsidiaries

American Axle & Manufacturing, Inc.; AAM Receivables Corp.; American Axle International Sales, Ltd.; Colfer Manufacturing Inc.; MASP Industries Corporation; MSP Team, LLC (99%); American Axle & Manufacturing de Mexico Holdings S. de R.L. de C.V. (99.99%); Guanajuato Gear & Axle de Mexico S. de R.L. de C.V. (99.99%); American Axle & Manufacturing de Mexico S.A. de C.V. (99.99%); AAM International Holdings, Inc.; Albion Automotive (Holdings) Limited (Scotland); Albion Automotive Limited (Scotland); Farington Components Limited (U.K.); AAM Comercio e Participacoes Ltda. (99.99%); AAM do Brasil Ltda. (Brazil).

Principal Competitors

ArvinMeritor, Inc.; Dana Corporation; Metaldyne Corporation.

Further Reading

"American Axle's Dauch Rewarded Handsomely for Company Success," *Crain's Detroit Business,* April 21, 2003, p. 4.
Crain, Keith, "A Success Story," *Crain's Detroit Business,* July 26, 2004, p. 8.
Fahey, Jonathan, "Consumer Durables," *Forbes,* January 12, 2004, p. 162.
Kosdrosky, Terry, "American Axle Continues Forging Biz Consolidation," *Crain's Detroit Business,* May 17, 1999, p. 16.
——, "American Axle Dedicates HQ," *Crain's Detroit Business,* August 2, 2004, p. 15.
——, "American Axle Hopes New 4WD Unit Can Shift into High Gear," *Crain's Detroit Business,* December 23, 2002, p. 17.
——, "2 Suppliers Compete for Sport-Utility Steering Business," *Automotive News,* July 15, 2002, p. 20J.
McCracken, Jeffrey, "Parts Makers to Cut Suppliers," *Crain's Detroit Business,* February 21, 2000, p. 1.
Morath, Eric, "American Axle Still Covets GM Work but Pursues Others," *Crain's Detroit Business,* May 20, 2002, p. 6.
Sherefkin, Robert, "American Axle Gets GM Boost," *Automotive News,* May 20, 2002, p. 8.
Strong, Michael, "Some Manufacturers Defy Slow Economy, Increase Revenue," *Crain's Detroit Business,* July 7, 2003, p. 12.
Williams, Fred O., "Investment Group Purchases American Axle," *Buffalo News,* September 26, 1997, p. A11.
Zoia, David E., "New Vision," *Ward's Auto World,* January 1, 2004, p. 45.

—Jeffrey L. Covell

American Power Conversion Corporation

132 Fairgrounds Road
West Kingston, Rhode Island 02892
U.S.A.
Telephone: (401) 789-5735
Toll Free: (800) 788-2208
Fax: (401) 789-3710
Web site: http://www.apcc.com

Public Company
Incorporated: 1981
Employees: 6,365
Sales: $1.46 billion (2003)
Stock Exchanges: NASDAQ
Ticker Symbol: APCC
NAIC: 335999 All Other Miscellaneous Electrical
     Equipment and Component Manufacturing; 333319
     Other Commercial and Service Industry Machinery
     Manufacturing

American Power Conversion Corporation (APC) designs and manufactures power protection and management solutions for computer, communications, and electronic applications. APC helps customers overcome problems with erratic electricity, making a wide range of products that serve as backup power supplies and analyze energy consumption and quality. The company's core product is an uninterruptible power supply device that regulates the flow of utility power. APC's uninterruptible power supply products range in price from $29.99 to $210,000. The company manufactures its products in the United States, Brazil, China, India, Ireland, the Philippines, and Switzerland.

Origins

APC began as a failure. The company was founded by three electronic power engineers from the Massachusetts Institute of Technology (MIT), two of whom—Neil E. Rasmussen and Emanuel E. Landsman—remained with the company during its formative decades. Landsman spent 15 years at MIT's Lincoln Library before cofounding APC, working in the Space Communications Group from 1966 to 1977 before joining the Energy

Systems Engineering Group. Rasmussen joined Landsman at the Energy Systems Engineering Group in 1979, spending two years there before starting APC. APC was founded to make solar power products, but the business idea began to show its fallibility not long after APC was incorporated in March 1981.

The company floundered during its first months of existence, unable to find a product to sustain its operation and precariously reliant on government funding. In 1982, APC, in a desperate attempt to stay alive, began making lead batteries, designing its batteries to serve as backup power supplies to personal computers. The batteries were designed to provide temporary power in the event of a momentary power blackout or surge, thereby giving the computer user time to save data before it was otherwise lost. The foray into lead battery manufacture was a sideline venture, but soon making backup power supplies became the central focus of the company. In 1984, government funding and incentive programs for solar research began to disappear, portending the worst for APC. The company's management responded by introducing its first uninterruptible power supply (UPS) product the same year. The 750, using a lead-acid battery, provided power surge protection and backup power for personal computers, local area networks (LANs), and engineering workstations. The decision to shelve its solar power business and enter the power protection business not only saved the company from bankruptcy but also moved it into a market capable of creating a billion-in-sales company. APC became that company, the first company to generate $1 billion in revenue by manufacturing and marketing UPS products.

When APC entered the UPS market, no one either outside or inside the company had any idea how large the market for UPS products would become. The decision to enter the field was a decision to be relished in hindsight. Personal computer usage was in its infancy at the time of the 750's introduction. Computer networking, the Internet, and other factors that fueled the growth of the UPS market trailed considerably further behind the maturation of the personal computer market. The nascence of the markets that would come to depend on UPS technology helped APC considerably during its early years, allowing the company to secure a foothold without fear of competition from large computer companies. Further, the technology inside the

Company Perspectives:

APC's mission: To create delighted customers by improving the manageability, availability and performance of information and communication systems through the rapid delivery of innovative solutions to real customer problems.

750 and its successors discouraged competition from another direction. The power supply of a UPS consisted of a lead-acid battery, circuitry designed to even out surges and lulls in the power, and a switch to detect a lapse in incoming power and automatically turn to the battery for backup. The electronic circuitry in the power supply discouraged conventional battery makers from entering the business. APC was shielded from larger, more established competition by the nature of its business, allowed to operate freely in a market perceived to be too small to entice computer companies and too sophisticated to seduce battery manufacturers into entering the fray.

Dowdell's Arrival in 1985

APC's advantageous position perhaps would have been worth nothing were it not for Rodger Dowdell, Jr. Though not a founder of the company, Dowdell was a particularly important figure in APC's history. Dowdell joined APC as its president in August 1985, beginning an enduring length of service that would see him preside over the company for more than two decades. For nine months before his appointment as president, Dowdell worked as a consultant for APC, developing a marketing and production strategy for UPS products. Before that, he served a six-year term as president of Independent Energy, Inc., a maker of electronic temperature controls.

Dowdell's strength was in manufacturing. He knew how to achieve optimal efficiency in manufacturing a product, a skill that would serve APC well as it established itself in its fledgling market and later as it contended with the pressures of a burgeoning market. Within months of becoming president, Dowdell directed the company's manufacturing operations to be moved from alongside Massachusetts Route 128 to Peacedale, Rhode Island. By moving to Rhode Island, Dowdell gave the young APC several advantages. Tax incentives were part of the benefits of a Rhode Island manufacturing base, where real estate was inexpensive and skilled labor was available. Dowdell was an executive, not an engineer, and his emphasis on reducing operating costs to increase profit margins helped APC gain its footing in a soon-to-be lucrative market. The company also was aided by a quality product. In 1986, the year APC relocated to Rhode Island, the 750 was awarded the "Editor's Choice" award by the influential trade publication *PC Magazine*. APC ended its fifth year of business with its product on the map and its manufacturing facility situated in an ideal geographic location.

During the latter half of the 1980s, the use of personal computers in corporate settings and the networking of personal computers proliferated. Data was flying from desktop to desktop in increasing volume, its vulnerability to erratic electricity threatening a major crisis to any business reliant on computers. Power protection was a necessity, and APC began to reap the rewards of

its leading position in a once miniscule market. To keep pace with the growth of its market and to exploit it to its fullest potential, APC needed capital. Dowdell, realizing the need for an infusion of cash, decided to take APC public in 1988. In July, he completed the company's initial public offering, when the company's stock debuted on the NASDAQ for $7.50 per share.

The energetic growth of the markets APC served ignited APC's own growth. The company's sales increased impressively during the latter half of the decade, rising from $400,000 in 1984 to more than $35 million in 1989. Industry observers took notice of APC's advances and gave new merit to the market for power protection. In 1989, *Business Week* ranked APC number four on its list of the 100 "hottest" companies in the country, the same year *Fortune* listed the company as one of the ten "stock superstars of the 1990s" and *Inc.* ranked the company as number 40 on its list of the 100 fastest-growing public companies in the country. APC had arrived, holding sway with a 30 percent share of the backup power-supply market. Its products, ranging from a $2,000 power supply for minicomputers to a $169 backup for desktops, were respected and coveted, putting the company in an ideal position to grab the lion's share of the power protection business in the 1990s, a decade that would bring phenomenal growth to personal computers and related markets.

Becoming a Giant in the 1990s

The 1990s began with another move of the company's headquarters and an award to APC's influential leader. In 1990, *Inc.* recognized Dowdell as the magazine's New England "Entrepreneur of the Year," the same year the company moved its headquarters to West Kingston, Rhode Island. A look inside the company's new offices reflected Dowdell's focus on the manufacturing side of APC's operations. The offices, with papers stacked on the floor and only the bare minimum of furniture, belied the success the company was enjoying. All the trappings of a company fast on the rise were found in its production plant, a facility outfitted with an automated assembly line that placed and soldered components onto circuit boards. APC's strength was in its products, and as the 1990s began it possessed the products that would capture the bulk of the decade's business. The company introduced its Smart-UPS brand in 1990, a line of products that grew to become the industry's leading network power protection solution.

APC grew with ferocity during the 1990s, expanding its presence across the globe as sales skyrocketed. The company entered the surge protection market in 1991 and the UPS market for mainframe computers the following year. In 1994, APC made its first move overseas, where most of the company's products would be produced in the future. The first plant was established in Galway, Ireland, and was followed by a plant in the Philippines in 1996. At the end of 1996, Dowdell announced he was planning to build seven new plants in 1997 at a cost of between $10 million and $15 million each. His ambition was justifiable. The $35 million company that exited the 1980s generated $515 million in sales in 1995. A giant in the making, APC was seizing the opportunities produced by the terrific growth of the computer industry.

Exponential growth prompted Dowdell to push forward and expand APC's business scope. As the company built new manu-

Key Dates:

1981: APC is founded by three engineers from the Massachusetts Institute of Technology.
1982: To stay afloat, APC begins manufacturing lead batteries.
1984: APC abandons the solar power business and introduces its first uninterruptible power supply product, the 750.
1988: APC completes its initial public offering of stock.
1994: APC establishes its first overseas facility in Galway, Ireland.
1998: APC acquires Silicon A/S; sales eclipse $1 billion.
2003: Sales approach $1.5 billion.

facturing plants in Brazil, China, India, and elsewhere, its long-term leader sized up other avenues of growth for the company. In 1998, APC spent nearly $70 million for Silicon A/S, a Denmark-based company that ranked as the third largest supplier of UPS products in Europe. The acquisition gave the company products designed for systems that used large amounts of electricity, such as those found at large data-storage centers and mainframe computer facilities. In 2000, Dowdell acquired EnergyOn.com, an Internet company that allowed customers in deregulated energy markets to shop for the most inexpensive electricity and natural gas prices. The acquisition pointed APC in two new directions, toward e-commerce and toward the energy marketing business. In the years to come, the company was expected to continue to diversify its interests.

As APC made its way in the early years of the 21st century, it exuded enormous strength. The pace of sales growth recorded during the first half of the 1990s continued during the late 1990s. In 1998, APC became the first company focused on UPS products to generate $1 billion in sales, posting $1.1 billion in revenue for the year. The company ended the decade with $1.3 billion in sales and began to demonstrate less vigorous growth at the dawn of the 21st century, as recessive economic conditions and a downturn in the technology sector delivered stinging blows. Despite the absence of frenetic sales growth—difficult to achieve for a company of APC's size—the company stood strong in the early years of the century's first decade, fueling optimism for a successful future.

As APC neared its 25th anniversary, the company stood atop its industry. Revenues reached nearly $1.5 billion in 2003, a year that offered evidence of the company's prowess. In a survey conducted by *Computer Reseller News,* solution providers selected APC as the winner in the UPS category. The company trounced its competition, emerging the favorite in 10 out of 11 criteria used to judge performance and customer satisfaction. The company's dominance must have provided satisfaction to Dowdell, whose tenure at APC had seen the march of UPS products from the periphery of the computer

industry to its center. On the company's web site in 2004, Dowdell reflected on the growth of the UPS market and APC's fortune to have abandoned designing solar power products. "In 1984, when we built our first UPS," Dowdell wrote, "I don't think anyone at APC could have imagined a better scenario for the company than what we are seeing today. Data has become money, and it is flying around the globe, without bounds, at an incredible rate of speed. As a company we could not have hoped for a better business opportunity than one in which network downtime correlates to a loss of revenue."

Principal Subsidiaries

APC America, Inc.; APC Sales & Service Corporation; Systems Enhancement Corporation; APC DC Network Solutions Inc.: American Power Conversion Europe S.A.R.L. (France); American Power Conversion Corporation (A.P.C.) B.V.; APC Distribution Limited (Ireland); APC Deutschland GmbH (Germany); American Power Conversion UK Ltd.; American Power Conversion Sweden AB; APC Australia Pty. Limited; American Power Conversion Portugal, Ltda.; American Power Conversion Spain S.L.; American Power Conversion Italia S.R.L. (Italy); APC Korea Corporation; American Power Conversion Hong Kong Limited; American Power Conversion (Phils.) Inc. (Philippines); APC Japan, Inc.; American Power Conversion Brasil Ltda. (Brazil).

Principal Competitors

Liebert Corporation; Powerware Corporation; MGE UPS Systems; Trippe Manufacturing Company; Phoenixtee Power Company Ltd.; Belkin Components; Chloride Power.

Further Reading

"American Power Conversion," *Communications News,* March 2002, p. 6.
"APC Acquiring Colorado Web Firm," *Providence Business News,* February 14, 2000, p. 17.
"APC Buying Product Lines from Georgia Firm," *Providence Business News,* December 3, 2001, p. 21.
Autry, Ret, "American Power Conversion," *Fortune,* May 6, 1991, p. 100.
Barmann, Timothy C., "Rhode Island's American Power Conversion to Build Two More Plants Overseas," *Knight Ridder/Tribune Business News,* February 4, 1997.
Caywood, Thomas, "APC's Latest Venture to Include E-Commerce," *Providence Business News,* February 21, 2000, p. 4.
Churbuck, David, "When the Lights Go Out," *Forbes,* February 17, 1992, p. 135.
"Overall Winner: APC—American Power Conversion Pulls the Plug on Rivals with Near Sweep in UPS Category," *Computer Reseller News,* March 10, 2003, p. 87.
Tooher, Nora Lockwood, "Rhode Island Surge Protector Maker Buys a Danish Firm for $68.6 Million," *Knight Ridder/Tribune Business News,* April 27, 1998.

—Jeffrey L. Covell

American Technical Ceramics Corp.

17 Stepar Place
Huntington Station, New York 11746
U.S.A.
Telephone: (631) 622-4700
Fax: (631) 622-4748
Web site: http:///www.atceramics.com

Public Company
Incorporated: 1966 as Phase Industries Inc.
Employees: 537
Sales: $61.2 million (2004)
Stock Exchanges: American
Ticker Symbol: AMK
NAIC: 334414 Electronic Capacitor Manufacturing

American Technical Ceramics Corp. (ATC) produces multilayer capacitors, single-layer capacitors, resistor products, inductors, low temperature co-fired ceramics, and custom thin film products for use in a wide range of industries, including cell phones, broadcast satellites, fiber optics, radar and navigation systems, medical electronics, aerospace, defense, and semiconductors. Capacitors store electrical energy for temporary use and because they filter and condition electronic signals they are an important component in the architecture of electrical or electronic circuits. The company is based in Huntington Station, New York, where most of the manufacturing is done, but majority owner and CEO Victor Insetta works out of ATC's facility in Jacksonville, Florida. In addition, the company owns a subsidiary in Sweden to handle European sales, as well as offices in England and Germany. For the Asian market, ATC operates a technical support subsidiary located in China. Sales are conducted by ATC's own staff as well as independent representatives. The company is publicly traded on the American Stock Exchange.

Founding the Company in the 1960s

ATC was cofounded in 1964 by Victor Insetta in Brooklyn, New York, as Phase Industries Inc. (Phase). Insetta graduated from Brooklyn Technical High School, and followed with a degree at Brooklyn College. At the time, the use of transistors was in the early stages, as the electronics industry was still dependent on electron tubes. Insetta recognized the direction the industry was taking and Phase developed a capacitor for the solid-state radio-frequency power product markets. It was such a new field that Phase engineers often had to invent the tools needed to manufacture the capacitors. In 1966 Phase Industries was incorporated in New York and moved its operations to the Long Island community of Huntington Station. In that same year the company introduced its 100 Series high Q porcelain multilayer capacitors for microwave, RF/IF Applications. The next major product debuted in 1970—the 700 Series high self-resonance, porcelain and ceramic multilayer capacitors. A year later Phase opened a nearby facility for administration, production, sales, and engineering. Also in 1971 the company introduced its 200 Series BX ceramic multilayer capacitors.

Phase was successful enough that by the late 1970s Insetta was ready to open a research and development facility. He looked first in south Florida, but was eventually attracted to Jacksonville, which boasted a younger population and could offer a more consistent pool of employees. The Jacksonville Technology Center opened in 1982 and Insetta would ultimately move to the area and run the company from Jacksonville while continuing to maintain the official headquarters in New York.

Phase introduced another new product in 1980: millimeter wavelength single-layer capacitors for high-frequency applications. In June 1984 Phase changed its name to American Technical Ceramics Corp. The company, producing multiple-layer ceramic and porcelain capacitors, was reincorporated in Delaware in April 1985 in preparation of taking ATC public. The offering, underwritten by D.H. Blair Co., was completed in July of that year, and the stock began trading on an over-the-counter basis. In May 1986 ATC gained its listing on the American Stock Exchange. The year 1985 was also noteworthy for several other reasons. A 20,000-square-foot addition was made to its New York manufacturing facility; the company introduced its 900 Series multilayer capacitors; and in September of that year ATC enjoyed the first million dollar quarter in its history.

In August 1988, ATC agreed to be acquired by a rival, South Carolina-based AVX Corporation. During the 1970s AVX had conducted in-depth market research that indicated the potential

---

---

demand for multilayer ceramic capacitors (MLCs) in the fast-growing semiconductor market and focused all of its attention on this product. ATC, like other capacitor makers, recognized that MLCs were gaining more usage, but failed to anticipate the enormous growth of the market. As a result, AVX had a head start, was able to ramp up production, allowing it to cut prices, and staked out a dominant position in the marketplace. ATC and the rest of the industry were forced to play catch-up. Becoming part of AVX appeared to be a good deal for ATC shareholders, who were originally offered $5.50 per share by AVX, but the price was then lowered to $5.25 per share, or $22 million total. By the end of August 1988 AVX decided to scuttle the deal when the two sides failed to reach a final agreement. An AVX spokesperson maintained, "It wasn't a price consideration. Some things came up."

Whatever the actual reasons for the breakdown in negotiations with AVX, ATC continued on in the capacitor business as a much smaller player. By the end of the 1980s sales totaled $24.5 million, with net income of $791,000. Much of the company's business was defense related, and with the end of the Cold War that sector would soon be hard hit. As ATC entered a new decade it also faced another serious problem: a slowdown in the worldwide electronics market, which led to increased competition over prices. ATC lost ground in fiscal 1990 (which ended June 30, 1990), posting $21.5 million in sales, a 12 percent drop over the previous year. Net income totaled just $62,000, but it took a concerted effort on the part of management to cut overhead costs in order to retain profitability. Insetta and his management team remained optimistic about the future, as evidenced by the decision to institute a stock repurchase program to take advantage of a stock price that they felt was not a proper reflection of the company's underlying strength.

Early 1990s Bringing Difficult Times

With the economy in recession, continued cutbacks in defense and sluggish sales overseas, business was not about to improve for some time. Revenues dropped another 13 percent to $18.8 million in fiscal 1991, leading to a net loss of $841,000. To counterbalance the drop in sales, the company took steps to mechanize and improve the manufacturing process to reduce costs, and also made further overhead cuts, including the trimming of the workforce by nearly one-fifth. Management's hope was that with a leaner operation, ATC would be in a better competitive position when the economy eventually recovered, and indeed business began to pick up in fiscal 1992. Revenues improved to $19.4 million and the company returned to profitability, recording net income of nearly $400,000.

Business grew at a steady pace in the first half of the 1990s, as many industries began to spend money to modernize equipment after years of retrenchment. There was also a greater demand for ATC products from customers in the telecommuni-

cations and wireless communications industries, as well as an increasing demand for the company's high-reliability products, which commanded a higher profit margin. MLCs were either classified as commercial or "hi-rel." "Hi-rel" capacitors were subjected to more rigorous performance and environmental tests and were used primarily in applications such as satellites, high-performance military aircraft, spacecraft, and missiles, as well as radar and other electronic countermeasures. Commercial MLCs also were tested to make sure they met performance specifications but were not subjected to the kind of environmental tests required by "hi-rel" capacitors. In addition to an increase in domestic sales during this period, ATC benefited from rising demand for electronic products around the world. Revenues reached $20.6 million in 1993, $23.1 million in 1994, and more than $28.6 million in 1995. Net income during this period grew from $991,000 in 1993 to nearly $1.9 million in 1995. Sales also were helped by the 1993 launch of a new division in the Jacksonville facility to produce thin film products, which were used in circuit fabrication.

The second half of the 1990s started out strong. Not only was demand up, but ATC also benefited from the opening of a new chip element facility that increased the number of capacitors the company could produce, resulting in the ability to lower prices and gain a competitive advantage. Sales for the year reached $33.9 million, an 18 percent increase over the previous year, and net income topped the $2 million mark. Lower manufacturing overhead costs and improved processes that led to greater production yields helped ATC to maintain its growth in fiscal 1997, when revenues increased to $36.5 million and net income held steady at $2.1 million. The year was also noteworthy for producing the company's first $10 million quarter.

During fiscal 1998 ATC introduced power capacitor assemblies and a new broadband microwave surface-mount ceramic capacitor series, aimed at the wireless and satellite communications systems markets. For the year, revenues increased 11 percent to $40.4 million, and net income doubled, totaling $4.2 million, but sales began to slow down in the fourth quarter due to weakening foreign business. A sluggish global economy caused many customers to delay projects until conditions improved, resulting in a significant drop in demand for ATC projects. The company responded by eliminating some jobs and by moving some manufacturing from Jacksonville to the New York facility, allowing Jacksonville, the center of ATC research and development efforts, to concentrate on new products. In fiscal 1999 ATC experienced a 7 percent drop in sales to $37.6 million, all in the company's core capacitor products. Thin film products continued to enjoy strong growth, with sales increasing 88 percent, from $2.4 million in fiscal 1998 to more than $4.5 million. Net income for the year fell to $2.1 million. During the second half of the year, however, business began to improve, leading to a record year for ATC.

Record Results in the New Century

The main driver for ATC's business in fiscal 2000 was the rapidly growing wireless communications industry, but demand was strong across the board for the company's products. As a result of posting record quarterly profits, ATC, despite being little known, saw its stock price rise rapidly. It would peak at $52.75 per share in May 2000. To take advantage of its momentum, ATC established a Swedish subsidiary in fiscal 2000 to grow European sales, which also were aided by expanding the company's direct sales operation in Germany. In addition, ATC beefed up its e-commerce capabilities by offering design kits for sale, thus permitting engineers to work ATC products into their original designs. Unable to make as many products as the market would buy, ATC also began taking steps to build a new facility in Jacksonville to house its thin film manufacturing. When the year came to a close, ATC smashed all records for sales and profits. Revenues for fiscal 2000 increased by 77 percent to $66.5 million and net income soared to more than $9 million. The good times continued into fiscal 2001, resulting in another record year. The company recorded a 27 percent increase in sales to $84.6 million and net income improved to $10.3 million. However, the boom times quickly came to an end.

In the early months of 2001, during ATC's fourth quarter, the electronics and telecommunications industries suffered a sudden collapse in business at a time when the worldwide economy was beginning to struggle, leading to canceled projects and orders for ATC products. As the fiscal year came to a close, ATC cut costs to protect profits, but there was little that could be done to offset steadily declining orders other than to retrench and wait for better times. The company was strong enough, however, that it could take advantage of the slowdown to concentrate on new product development to put ATC in a better position when conditions improved. For instance, the company took steps to introduce a new category of product, low-

temperature co-fired ceramics (LTCC), suitable for aerospace and military applications. The company also tested new high-power resistive products during this period. During fiscal 2002 ATC added thin film resistor manufacturing capability to this product line.

Revenues fell to $49.6 million in fiscal 2002, a 41 percent decrease over the previous year, leading to a net loss of $4.2 million. Sales continued to slip slightly in fiscal 2003, totaling $49 million, but the company cut its loss on the year to $501,000. It was not until fiscal 2004 that ATC was able to rebound, as sales improved to $61.2 million, and the company returned to profitability posting net income of nearly $2.2 million. ATC had weathered the storm and was now ready to resume the steady pattern of growth it had exhibited over 40 years.

Principal Subsidiaries

American Technical Ceramics, Inc.; Phase Components, Ltd.; American Technical Ceramics Europe Aktiebolag (Sweden); American Technical Ceramics (China) Ltd.; American Technical Ceramics Costa Rica, S.A.

Principal Competitors

AVX Corporation; KEMET Corporation; Vishay Intertechnology, Inc.

Further Reading

Alexander, Kobi, "Entrepreneur of the Year Finalists," *Long Island Business News,* June 15, 2001, p. 6C.

Basch, Mark, "A Closer Look; Demand Growing for Tiny High-Tech Capacitors, Film Products," *Florida Times Union,* May 3, 2000, p. F1.

——, "Huntington Station, N.Y.-Based High-Tech Manufacturer Cuts Jobs," *Florida Times Union,* May 4, 2001.

——, "Slow Sales Force Plant to Cut Jobs," *Florida Union Times,* September 23, 1998, p. D1.

—Ed Dinger

Ameron International Corporation

245 South Los Robles Avenue
Pasadena, California 91101
U.S.A.
Telephone: (626) 683-4000
Fax: (626) 683-4060
Web site: http://www.ameron.com

Public Company
Incorporated: 1929 as American Concrete Pipe Co.
Employees: 2,700
Sales: $600.49 million (2003)
Stock Exchanges: New York
Ticker Symbol: AMN
NAIC: 327999 All Other Miscellaneous Nonmetallic
   Mineral Product Manufacturing; 327320 Ready-Mix
   Concrete Manufacturing; 327390 Other Concrete
   Product Manufacturing; 331210 Iron and Steel Pipes
   and Tubes Manufacturing from Purchased Steel;
   332312 Fabricated Structural Metal Manufacturing;
   332812 Metal Coating, Engraving, and Allied
   Services (Except Jewelry and Silverware) to
   Manufacturers; 332999 All Other Miscellaneous
   Fabricated Metal Product Manufacturing

Ameron International Corporation is a manufacturer of highly engineered products that are sold to customers in the chemical, industrial, energy, transportation, and infrastructure industries. Ameron's business is divided into four operating groups: Performance Coatings and Finishes, Fiberglass-Composite Pipe, Water Transmission, and Infrastructure Products. Through its Performance Coatings & Finishes group, the company makes coatings and surfacer systems that protect metallic and concrete facilities and equipment. The Fiberglass-Composite Pipe group makes fiberglass pipe and fittings used by industrial, petroleum, chemical processing, and petrochemical industries, offering an alternative to metallic piping systems, which inevitably are destroyed under corrosive operating conditions. The company's Water Transmission group manufactures concrete and steel pipe used in the construction of water pipe-lines. Ameron's Infrastructure Products group includes operations that manufacture concrete and steel poles for highway, street, and outdoor area lighting and for traffic signals. The Infrastructure Products Group also supplies ready-mix concrete, crushed and sized basaltic aggregates, dune sand, and concrete pipe to the construction industry in Hawaii. Ameron operates in North America, South America, Europe, Australasia, and Asia. Through joint-venture companies, Ameron operates in the Middle East, maintaining a presence in Saudi Arabia and Kuwait.

Origins

The earliest precursor to Ameron was established in 1907, but company historians point to 1929 as the true beginning of their enterprise. Early in the year, two companies merged to form American Concrete Pipe Co., the company recognized as Ameron's oldest, direct antecedent. The company's name changed several times during the Great Depression, finally finding some permanence in 1942, when the American Pipe and Construction Co. name first appeared. The company operated under that corporate banner for roughly the next 30 years, as it gradually began to develop interests in the businesses that would support it late in the century.

Ameron Develops Its Modern Structure After the 1970s

During Ameron's formative decades, there were several defining events. The most significant of those milestone moments occurred after the late 1960s. Ameron, at that point, operated nearly exclusively as a manufacturer. Its product line had expanded beyond concrete and steel pipe to include high-performance protective coatings, ready-mix concrete, construction aggregates, and reinforced thermosetting resin pipe and fittings—product categories that became the pillars supporting Ameron. The other principal components of the company's business were added after the beginning of the 1970s, when the name Ameron, Inc. was adopted as the company's official corporate title.

In the years leading up to the company's 50th anniversary, an important addition was made to Ameron's portfolio of products. During the 1970s, the company began to manufacture

Ameron has consistently achieved quality earnings by developing and executing specific strategies that are unique for each business and by relying on a common set of strategic fundamentals. These can be summarized as: selective investments, value-added growth, and operational efficiency. By selective investments, we mean making capital investment decisions after rigorous risk examination to ensure that the investment returns are commensurate with the risk.

concrete and steel poles used for lighting streets and other areas. Ameron also began to manufacture tapered steel vertical and cantilevered poles for traffic signals.

During the 1980s, Ameron's moves on the acquisition front added a new business line and greatly increased its involvement in another business line. In 1984, the company acquired a major domestic fiberglass pipe business, marking its entry into the manufacture of fiberglass pipe. The acquisition gave the company a manufacturing plant in Burkburnett, Texas. Ameron gained another important facility four years later, when the company purchased a major steel pipe fabricating facility in Fontana, California. The addition of the plant substantially increased the company's ability to serve the water transmission and distribution market, making its production of water transmission lines one of its primary businesses.

By the end of the 1980s, 60 years of expansion had produced a company with more than $400 million in annual revenue. The company's financial growth during the ensuing two decades occurred at a measured pace—nothing to dazzle Wall Street—but Ameron was not a company operating in markets capable of fueling electric financial growth. The company was a reliable profit generator that achieved revenue growth incrementally, steadily improving its position in markets fundamental to industry.

James Marlen Taking Control: 1993

During the early 1990s, Ameron fell under the control of the leader who would guide it into the 21st century. James Marlen was appointed president and chief executive officer of the company in mid-1993. Marlen joined Ameron after spending nearly 30 years at GenCorp, Inc., a suburban Sacramento, California-based company that underwent significant change during Marlen's lengthy service. When Marlen joined GenCorp, the company ranked as one of the largest tire manufacturers in the world, but by the time he left the company it was beginning to concentrate on manufacturing rocket propulsion systems. Marlen was named vice-president of the company in 1988, the same year he was named president of the company's primary consumer and industrial products segment, GenCorp Polymer Products.

When Marlen joined Ameron, the company was generating approximately $450 million in annual revenue. The company derived the total from four business groups: Protective Coatings Systems, Fiberglass Pipe Systems, Concrete and Steel Pipe Systems, and Construction and Allied Products. The company's Protective Coatings Systems group made high-performance coatings that prevented corrosion, abrasion, and other forms of chemical and physical attack. The coatings, which were used by a broad range of industries, were manufactured at the company's plants in California, Arkansas, and overseas in the Netherlands. Ameron's Fiberglass Pipe Systems group manufactured fiberglass pipe and fittings used by a variety of customers, including operators of offshore oil platforms and marine vessels, who avoided metallic piping systems because of their vulnerability to corrosion. Through its Concrete and Steel Pipe Systems group, Ameron made pipe used by utility companies to transport water and for industrial wastewater and sewage collection. The company conducted such activity at eight manufacturing plants located in the western United States. The Construction and Allied Products group comprised two divisions, the HC&D division, which supplied ready-mix concrete, basaltic aggregates, and dune sand to the construction industry in Hawaii, and the Pole Products and Systems division, which manufactured poles for highway, street, and outdoor area lighting and for traffic signals.

Under Marlen's leadership, Ameron expanded its operations along the company's four business lines, increasing its interests both domestically and abroad. The company's involvement in international markets, which preceded Marlen's appointment as president and chief executive officer, increased under his rule. In 1996, one year after Marlen was named chairman, the company changed its name to Ameron International Corporation to reflect the multinational composition of its business. The year also included two acquisitions that strengthened the company's Protective Coatings Systems group and Fiberglass Pipe Systems group. The former was enriched by the acquisition of the Devoe marine coatings business belonging to Imperial Chemical Industries, Plc, while the latter was bolstered by the purchase of Centron, a leading manufacturer of fiberglass pipe for the oilfield market.

During Marlen's first five years of leadership, Ameron increased its revenue volume by roughly $100 million. The company generated $552 million in sales in 1998, a year that saw it acquire the industrial paints business belonging to a British company, Croda International. The acquisition, which supplied paints for heavy duty and general industrial applications, comprised operations in the United Kingdom, Australia, and New Zealand. Ameron also acquired Hope Composites 2000, Inc. in 1998. Hope, a privately owned company based in Georgia, manufactured fiberglass pipe and fittings.

Ameron in the 21st Century

As Ameron entered the 21st century, it altered the names of its four business groups. The Protective Coatings Systems group was renamed the Performance Coatings and Finishes group. The Fiberglass Pipe Systems group was renamed the Fiberglass-Composite Pipe group. The Concrete and Steel Pipe Systems group was renamed the Water Transmission group. The Construction and Allied Products group was renamed the Infrastructure Products group. Ameron's reliance on its four business groups was fairly balanced, with the company's largest segment, its Performance Coatings and Finishes group, generating $186 million in sales in 2000 and its smallest segment, the Fiberglass-Composite Pipe group, generating $103 million in sales for the year. Of the $550 million collected in revenue in

Key Dates:

1929: American Concrete Pipe Co. is formed.
1942: American Concrete Pipe Co. changes its name to American Pipe and Construction Co.
1970: American Pipe and Construction Co. changes its name to Ameron, Inc.
1984: Ameron enters the fiberglass pipe business.
1988: Ameron acquires its Fontana, California, manufacturing plant.
1993: James Marlen is appointed president and chief executive officer.
1996: Ameron, Inc. changes its name to Ameron International Corporation.
1998: Ameron acquires the industrial paints business of Croda International.
2003: Ameron registers its eighth consecutive year of record earnings.

2000, nearly $390 million was derived from sales to customers in the United States.

Although Ameron achieved only modest sales growth during the early years of the 21st century, the company's ability to squeeze increasing profits from its operations was impressive. At the end of the company's fiscal year in 2001, it posted record earnings of $27.7 million, the sixth consecutive year it increased its net income. Ameron recorded the gain despite flagging sales. An economic recession negatively affected its business, particularly the company's Fiberglass-Composite Pipe group, but the company was able to offset the adverse conditions through the performance of its Water Transmission group. The demand in the western United States for water piping to meet the needs of population growth and infrastructure modernization held the company in good stead.

Ameron continued its remarkable record of earnings growth after 2001, making Marlen's 10th anniversary at the company an event to celebrate. Earnings increased in 2002 and 2003, marking eight consecutive years of earnings growth. During Marlen's first decade in command, earnings increased at a compounded annual growth rate of 15 percent. His 10th anniversary also marked a return to more favorable market conditions, as the company recorded a substantial increase in revenues in 2003, collecting $600 million for the first time in its history. The gain in revenues—a more than $60 million increase from 2002's total, was driven by each segment of the company's business, as each facet of Ameron's business demonstrated growth.

As Ameron prepared for the future, the company looked to each of its business segments to carry it toward continued financial growth. The company's Fiberglass-Composite Pipe group was expected to benefit from what the company hailed as a revolutionary new product, steel-strip laminate (SSL) pipe, which was undergoing final specification and product qualification tests with major oil companies. Ameron perceived SSL as having the potential to deliver substantial, long-term growth.

The company's Water Transmission group, after being inundated with orders at the dawn of the new millennium, was experiencing a lull in activity as the company entered the mid-2000s. There was encouraging news, however, in the group's collaboration with the Fiberglass-Composite Pipe group to develop a new composite-pipe product to serve the growing domestic sewer rehabilitation market. The Performance Coatings & Finishes group was also working on developing new products to introduce to its markets. The group was preparing to introduce an epoxy-based coatings line for the industrial flooring market. It also was developing a coating for the fire protection of steel in high-rise buildings. Ameron's Infrastructure Products Group introduced a new lightweight concrete—Isle Cell Crete—in Hawaii, which was expected to strengthen the company's leading market position. Management also wanted to extend the geographic reach of the group's pole products operations.

Principal Subsidiaries

Amercoat Japan Company, Limited; American Pipe & Construction International; Ameron (Australia) Pty. Limited; Ameron B.V. (Netherlands); Ameron Composites Inc.; Ameron (Hong Kong) Ltd.; Ameron Malaysia Sdn. Bhd.; Ameron (New Zealand) Limited; Ameron (Pte) Ltd. (Singapore); Ameron (UK) Limited; Centron International, Inc.; Island Ready-Mix Concrete, Inc.; TAMCO (50%); Bondstrand, Ltd. (Saudi Arabia; 40%); Oasis-Ameron, Ltd. (Saudi Arabia; 40%); Ameron Saudi Arabia, Ltd. (30%).

Principal Operating Units

Performance Coatings & Finishes; Fiberglass-Composite Pipe; Water Transmission; Infrastructure Products.

Principal Competitors

NS Group, Inc.; PPG Industries, Inc.; RPM International, Inc.

Further Reading

"Ameron Forms Venture in Kuwait," *Oil Daily,* December 6, 1999, p. 13.
"Ameron International Corporation Announces Major New Orders," *Business Wire,* February 18, 1997.
"Ameron Reports Sixth Consecutive Year of Record Earnings," *Advanced Materials & Composite News,* February 4, 2002, p. 32.
Blazier, Andrew, "Pasadena, Calif., Manufacturer Ameron Settles Another Strike with Union," *Knight Ridder/Tribune Business News,* April 6, 2004.
——, "War May Be Bonanza for Pasadena, Calif.-Based Maker of Oil-Bearing Equipment," *Knight Ridder/Tribune Business News,* March 27, 2003.
"Company Disposes of Its Industrial Paint Business," *Polymers Paint Colour Journal,* May 1998, p. 3.
Moyle, Andrew, "Pasadena, Calif.-Based Pipe Manufacturer Reports $2.75 Million Loss," *Inland Valley Daily Bulletin,* March 25, 2004, p. 7.
Peterson, Anne M., "Union Strikes Ameron Plant in Fontana, Calif.," *Knight Ridder/Tribune Business News,* February 13, 1998.

—Jeffrey L. Covell

Ampacet Corporation

660 White Plains Road
Tarrytown, New York 10591-5130
U.S.A.
Telephone: (914) 631-6600
Toll Free: (800) 267-2238
Fax: (914) 631-7197
Web site: http://www.ampacet.com

Private Company
Founded: 1937 as American Molding Powder &
    Chemical Corp.
Sales: $550 million (2003 est.)
NAIC: 325131 Inorganic Dye and Pigment
    Manufacturing

In terms of volume, Ampacet Corporation is the world's largest provider of color compounds and concentrates used by plastic manufacturers to produce consistent colors and chemical characteristics. Each year the Tarrytown, New York-based company produces about 900 million pounds of utility and specialty white, black, and additive masterbatches, and custom and stock colorants. The products, sold to more than 80 countries, can be used by almost all plastic processing methods, including extrusion coating, blown and cast films, blownware, injection molding, wire and cable, pipe and conduit, and fiber spinning. Industries served include agricultural, consumer, fiber, industrial, packaging, pipe and conduit, and wire and cable. In North America, Ampacet operates manufacturing facilities in Terre Haute, Indiana; Cartersville, Georgia; DeRidder, Louisiana; Crockett, Texas; Heath, Ohio; and two plants in Canada. The company also maintains a research and development center in Terre Haute. In South America, Ampacet operates plants in Argentina, Brazil, and Chile. In Europe, facilities are found in the United Kingdom, Italy, and Belgium. The company also maintains a strong sales presence in Asia, with offices located in India, Malaysia, Australia, and China. Ampacet is owned by Norman E. Alexander, chairman and CEO of Sequa Corporation. Alexander, who turned 90 in 2004, has never considered taking Ampacet public and has taken steps to allow the company to continue on as a private concern after his death.

The Company's Founding in the 1930s

Ampacet was founded in Brooklyn, New York, in 1937 as American Molding Powder & Chemical Corp. It was acquired by Anton Bamberger, well known in the plastics field at the time, and a group of investors in 1941. During the war years the company recycled acetate from nylon stockings, which was then used to make parachutes for the military. For the next 25 years the company acted as a recycler, using scrap to produce products such as injection-molded combs, brushes, toys, and houseware items. In 1954 Norman Alexander bought the business.

Alexander was born in New York City in 1914 and grew up in the South Bronx. His father ran a business making spats, and when they went out of style he switched to children's leggings. Alexander attended Columbia University, where he earned an undergraduate degree in 1934 and a law degree two years later. Because of the Great Depression, finding work as a lawyer was difficult, and he joined the family business instead of practicing law. Rather than focusing entirely on the garment trade, he began investing in New York and Florida real estate. In 1947 he became involved in the entertainment field, acquiring the rights to old films produced by Universal Studios, and three years later he and his partners began making their own movies.

During this period he bought a more mundane business, Ansbacher-Siegel Corp., a Staten Island manufacturer of organic pigments, which were used to make inks, paints, plastics, cosmetics, and textiles. One of its customers was American Molding Powder & Chemical Corp., which Alexander added to his portfolio in 1954. He would then take control of Sun Chemical Corp. in 1957 and merge it with Ansbacher-Siegel. Sun eventually changed its name to Sequa Corporation and exited the ink and pigment business in the 1980s in favor of aerospace. The running of it consumed much of Alexander's time, as did his real estate speculation and other business interests. Because he was always striving to become the market leader in whatever industry he was involved, Alexander supported American Molding Powder & Chemical, investing profits to grow the business. But he essentially took a hands-off approach, allowing the executives he hired to run the show.

In 1958 the man who would lead the company for close to two decades, David Weil, joined American Molding Powder & Chemical. After a three-year stint in the military he earned a degree from the City College of New York, then became an export manager at Raven Mills Corp. in New York City. At first he was also an export manager at American Molding Powder & Chemical, then from 1960 to 1970 he served as executive vice-president and general manager. In 1970 he became president and chief executive officer. When Weil went to work for the company it was doing around $450,000 in annual sales, but with Alexander's backing the company began to produce steady growth.

In 1964 the company opened a plant in Mount Vernon, New York, which also housed its headquarters. A year later the name changed to Ampacet, an acronym drawn from American Molding Powder & Chemical Corp. At this stage its primary business was in plastic compounding and scrap and regrind recycling. Yearly sales had reached the $1 million level, but in the mid-1960s Ampacet's management realized there was little future in scrap recycling and decided to shift the company's focus to color compounds and concentrates. It was a move that took advantage of new developments by pigment makers, such as sister company Sun, which produced pigments that were more forgiving when made in concentrates. Moreover, resin manufacturers increasingly turned to outside compounders like Ampacet that devoted their resources to color rather than maintain an in-house unit with less capability. The most important customer for Ampacet as it completed its transformation was Mobil Chemical Co., a large producer of polyethylene film, used to make trash can liners and other products. The film market was the most important reason that Ampacet prospered.

New Capabilities in the 1970s

Ampacet added other capabilities as well. In 1969 it developed color concentrates for extrusion coating, and a year later began to produce fire retardant concentrates. In 1976 it introduced multifunction concentrates and in 1979 began offering single pigment concentrates for engineering products. To serve its expanding business, the company opened its Terre Haute plant in 1972, and another manufacturing facility in DeRidder, Louisiana, in 1977. By 1980, 15 years after switching its focus from a $1 million a year plastic scrap business to the production of concentrate pigments, Ampacet had grown annual sales to $40 million.

The 1980s was a decade of international expansion for Ampacet and reorganization for its domestic manufacturing operations. In 1987 the company opened a manufacturing facility with 30 million pounds of capacity in Messancy, Belgium, to begin production for the increasingly important European market. The technology employed in this plant served as a starting point for a major $20 million expansion at Terre Haute, work that was completed in 1988 and 1989. The result was a pair of fully automated production lines and an additional 120 million pounds of capacity. Terre Haute now relied more heavily on statistical process controls, the need for which had increased as customers demanded more exact specifications in concentrate formulations. The plant's automated production lines could now store a customer's formulation to replicate exact batches of concentrate. As the Terre Haute lines became operational, the Mt. Vernon plant, Ampacet's oldest, was gradually decommissioned, and work was sent to Indiana as well as to a newer Louisiana facility. In addition, in 1987 the company headquarters was moved from Mt. Vernon to Tarrytown, New York. Ampacet closed the decade well entrenched in North America, gaining market share in Europe, and beginning to turn its attention to the Far East as an avenue for future growth. Malaysia and Indonesia looked especially promising because of their emerging plastics industries.

A key to the future would also be the ability to offer new and innovative solutions to customers, whose needs had grown more complicated because of more stringent environmental regulations. To beef up its research and development capabilities, Ampacet in 1990 opened the Corporate Technical Center in Terre Haute. By the early 1990s these efforts were a factor in the company's ability to maintain a 10 percent annual growth rate and top $300 million in revenues. In addition, in many industries, like automotive, metal parts were increasingly being replaced with plastic, which would require the services of colorant and pigment companies. Other growth markets for colorants included wire and cable, vinyl building products, and synthetic fiber. To improve profitability, Ampacet also began to offer high-performance specialty additives and high-gloss colors that commanded a much higher price than could commodity items. In 1995 Ampacet opened its $17.5 million Cartersville, Georgia, plant north of Atlanta, adding to its ability to enter new areas. It began offering pigment concentrates to color nylon, polyester, and other synthetic fibers. Cartersville also allowed Ampacet to become more involved in the engineering plastics market, in which previously the company had only been able to serve polypropylene.

Going Global in the 1990s

In addition to new products, Ampacet in the 1990s was eager to become more of a global company, in essence to follow the market for its products. By the middle of the decade North America accounted for 35 percent of the world masterbatch market, followed by Europe with 33 percent, Asia with 27 percent, and other markets with 5 percent. Ampacet claimed a 13 percent market share on world masterbatch sales and established a target of 20 percent within five years. A sales target of $700 million to be reached by 2002 also was set. In 1993 Ampacet established a sales office in Kuala Lumpur. Ampacet then bolstered its position in the European market with the 1996 acquisition of Tisco S.R.L. in Telgate, Italy, maker of engineering grade thermoplastic compounds. In addition, Ampacet forged alliances with Pomini S.R.L., an Italian maker of continuous extrusion and compounding equipment, and with the Israeli firm of Kafrit Industries to develop and sell value-added agricultural film masterbatches. Ampacet was especially active

Key Dates:

1937: The company is founded as American Molding Powder & Chemical Corp.
1954: Norman Alexander acquires the company.
1965: The name is changed to Ampacet Corporation.
1972: The Terre Haute, Indiana, plant opens.
1987: A Belgian plant opens.
1990: The Corporate Technical Center opens.
1999: Equistar Chemicals' Color & Compound division is acquired.
2000: A Thailand plant opens.

in 1998 when it created a joint venture in Argentina with Biblos Color to serve the fast-growing South American market. Ampacet also acquired a Canadian company in 1998, Baron Colour Concentrates Ltd., a masterbatch supplier that mostly served the flexible packaging sector. In addition, Ampacet added 33 million pounds of capacity to its Belgian plant. Also of note in 1998 was David Weil stepping down as Ampacet's president, turning over the position to David DeFalco, who had spent eight years heading the European operation from Luxembourg. At this stage the company had reached $400 million in yearly revenues. Three years later Weil retired, making DeFalco CEO of the company as well.

Ampacet completed a major acquisition in 1999, buying Equistar Chemicals' Color & Compound division. Ampacet picked up manufacturing plants in Crockett, Texas, and Heath, Ohio, and added 160 million pounds of capacity. The acquisition also brought Ampacet into the compounding business, which primarily served the wire and cable industry. Also of great importance was the addition of Equistar's Cincinnati research and development center, a smaller affair than Terre Haute but one that was well equipped and employed five researchers experienced in developing concentrates for the wire and cable, foam, and rotational molding markets.

Ampacet opened a plant with 30 million pounds of capacity in Thailand in 2000 to produce biaxially oriented polypropylene (BOPP) films similar to cellophane used in food and snack packaging, which was a strong product area in the region despite problems in the Asian economy. The company also expanded capacity in its Italian plant and in 2003 opened a blow molding facility in its Heath plant. A poor economy that emerged in 2001 hurt business somewhat, leading to a minor reduction in Ampacet's worldwide workforce, but cutbacks were essentially accomplished through attrition rather than layoffs. The company also underwent a minor restructuring of reporting responsibilities, so that regional managers more directly reported to DeFalco. The company's business was strong enough that it was able soon to complete three acquisitions and begin work on expansion projects at six other plants. In position to take advantage of a poor global economy, Ampacet bought Polimaster S.R.L. of Italy and PolyColour Ltd. of England, both of which produced specialty color concentrates for the blow molding and injection molding markets, and Corland of Brazil, maker of commodity-grade white concentrates. Ampacet also built a replacement plant in British Columbia, expanded its facility in Thailand, and broke ground on a new plant in China, scheduled to open in late 2005 or early 2006. On the research side, Ampacet continued to focus its efforts on increasing the number of higher-margin, value-added products the company offered.

For half a century the company had prospered under the private ownership of Norman Alexander, free from the pressures that accompany a public company. Although Alexander turned 90 in 2004 there was little concern about the fate of Ampacet after his death. His estate was set up to allow Ampacet to continue conducting business in the way that had proved so successful for so many years.

Principal Divisions

North America; South America; Europe; Asia.

Principal Competitors

A. Schulman, Inc.; Ciba Specialty Chemicals Holding Inc.; Spartech Corporation.

Further Reading

Bernstein, Peter W., "Norman Alexander Just Won't Go Away," *Fortune,* January 28, 1980, p. 82.

Esposito, Frank, "Alexander Shapes Ampacet Present, Future," *Plastic News,* July 15, 2002, p. 13.

Schmitt, Bill, "Ampacet Weathers a Slowdown," *Chemical Week,* October 2, 2002, p. 37.

Tullo, Alex, "Ampacet Pushes for Aggressive Growth," *Chemical Market Reporter,* June 28, 1999, p. 4.

—Ed Dinger

Amylin Pharmaceuticals, Inc.

9360 Towne Centre Drive, Suite 110
San Diego, California 92121
U.S.A.
Telephone: (858) 552-2200
Fax: (858) 552-2212
Web site: http://www.amylin.com

Public Company
Incorporated: 1987
Employees: 535
Sales: $85.65 million (2003)
Stock Exchanges: NASDAQ
Ticker Symbol: AMLN
NAIC: 541710 Research and Development in the
    Physical Sciences and Engineering Sciences; 325412
    Pharmaceutical Preparation Manufacturing; 621511
    Medical Laboratories

Amylin Pharmaceuticals, Inc. develops medicines to treat diabetes, obesity, and cardiovascular disease. The company's two lead drugs are SYMLIN and exenatide, both developed to treat diabetes. SYMLIN and exenatide are in late-stage development, nearing full approval for commercialization. Amylin also has several other drugs in earlier stages of the development and approval process, including pharmaceuticals known as AC2592, AC137, and AC162352. Most of Amylin's financial support comes from a collaboration agreement with Eli Lilly & Co. to develop and market exenatide.

Beginning a Hard Corporate Life in the Late 1980s

Biopharmaceutical companies, particularly those that are publicly held, suffer a somewhat tortuous existence. The costs incurred in developing a drug are immense. The process of guiding a drug through the various stages of regulatory approval is excruciatingly lengthy. While waiting to get the green light to begin marketing a drug, companies invest hundreds of millions of dollars without the ability to recoup their investment. All the while, investors critically assess every move of the company, trying to anticipate failure and share in success, holding the market value of the company hostage while its potential is subjected to the vagaries of a drug's development. Amylin experienced the pains and the pleasures of a publicly held biopharmaceutical company. More than 15 years after its formation, the company, racking up substantial debt through the years, did not have a marketable product. Along the way, the company experienced the roller-coaster ride of an investor-backed venture in the pharmaceutical industry. At times, the company's potential excited industry observers, fueling optimism that Amylin was destined for great success. At other times, the company appeared headed toward collapse, its troubles portending bankruptcy and the nullification of research that promised to help millions of patients. Amylin, during its formative years, typified the struggle of a biopharmaceutical company trying to establish itself.

Amylin's work in helping diabetes patients centered on a namesake peptide named amylin, discovered by researchers at Oxford University in 1987, the year of Amylin's formation. Researchers at Oxford discover that amylin was made in and secreted from the same cells—beta cells—that make and secrete insulin. In someone not afflicted with diabetes, amylin complements the actions of insulin, with the two hormones working together with another pancreatic hormone, glucagon, to maintain normal glucose concentrations. In normal physiology, insulin and amylin concentrations increase after food is ingested. Glucagon levels, in contrast, decrease after food is ingested. In diabetic patients, the complementary functions of the three pancreatic hormones are thrown out of balance. The disease is manifested in two forms: Type I (juvenile-onset) consists of patients whose insulin-producing pancreatic beta cells have been destroyed; Type II (maturity-onset) includes diabetics whose insulin-producing cells do not produce enough insulin. Insulin deficiency in both forms results in abnormally high blood-glucose concentration, or hyperglycemia, which causes degenerative complications such as blindness, kidney failure, nerve damage, and, according to many authorities, heart disease.

Amylin was formed in September 1987 to develop further the amylin research of the Oxford scientists. A founder of the company, Howard E. Greene, Jr., wanted to continue the work begun in England to develop a drug to treat both Type I and

Type II diabetics, a drug that would be a synthetic analog of amylin. In the late 1980s, Greene was an executive of note, having participated in either the founding or management of 11 medical technology companies during the previous two decades. An alumnus of Harvard University, where he earned an M.B.A., Greene served as the chief executive officer of Hybritech for most of the 1980s. He joined the company in 1979 and co-invented the company's patented monoclonal antibody assay technology. He left the company in March 1986, when Hybritech was acquired by the giant pharmaceutical company Eli Lilly & Co. Greene's next venture, Amylin, put him in a position to help millions of people and make millions of dollars. An estimated 16 million people suffered from diabetes in the United States, with the incidence of diagnoses as a percentage of the country's population tripling between the late 1950s and late 1980s. Diabetes ranked as the fourth or fifth leading cause of death in most developed countries. The cost of treating diabetics in the United States was estimated to be more than $100 billion annually, accounting for one in seven healthcare dollars spent during the early 1990s. Starting out in 1987, Green and Amylin's team of scientists were intent on making a drug to improve the treatment of diabetes and, by consequence, to garner a sizable share of the money spent on treating diabetes.

1995 Collaboration Agreement with Johnson & Johnson

Amylin focused on the synthetic equivalent of amylin, pramlintide—a drug developed to improve glucose control in Type I and Type II diabetics. The company, whose progress became public knowledge after it completed its initial public offering of stock in 1992, began the methodical, slow journey through development and federal approval at great cost. Amylin was sustained by investments in the potential of pramlintide, racking up heavy annual losses as it engaged exclusively in research and development activities. Amylin's first major breakthrough as a drug developer and the first surge in investor confidence in the company occurred in June 1995, when Johnson & Johnson, through its subsidiary LifeScan Inc., signed a worldwide collaboration agreement with Amylin. Johnson & Johnson agreed to support financially the development and commercialization of pramlintide, giving Amylin its first meaningful stream of revenue. Between 1992 and 1994, the company registered a total of $1.8 million in research fees associated with an agreement with Glaxo-Wellcome. In 1995, Amylin recorded $17 million in revenue, a total derived from Johnson & Johnson's one-half share of development expenses and a license fee paid at the signing of the collaboration agreement.

With the backing of Johnson & Johnson, Amylin's fortunes improved significantly. The massive healthcare products company agreed to invest more money once certain points were reached in pramlintide's development, known as "milestone payments" in the drug development industry. Amylin received its first milestone payment in August 1996, when, after reviewing data of pramlintide's development, Johnson & Johnson agreed to give Amylin $22 million and to continue with the collaboration. Revenues for the year reached $35.8 million, by which point Amylin had accumulated a $155 million deficit.

Reaching the first milestone in the collaboration agreement with Johnson & Johnson fueled confidence at Amylin. "We remain on track to achieve our goal of filing regulatory applications in North America and Europe during 1998," Greene remarked in an August 19, 1996 interview with *San Diego Business Journal.* Pramlintide, which became known as SYMLIN, was in Phase III clinical trails, the last of three progressive testing stages required by the Food and Drug Administration (FDA) before a drug is considered for final approval. After years of research and development, the company was nearing commercialization of its first product, but much remained to be accomplished. The closer a drug came to gaining approval for introduction to the public, the more stringent the testing became, often making the late-stage development process a slow crawl to the finish line.

Amylin suffered a severe setback in SYMLIN's passage through the product pipeline exactly two years after the company achieved its first milestone. In August 1998, after investing more than $170 million in SYMLIN's development, Johnson & Johnson terminated its collaboration agreement with Amylin. Greene's company was rocked by Johnson & Johnson's departure. Revenue, which totaled $42.6 million in 1997, fell to $16.2 million in 1998 before disappearing altogether the following year. The financial community took a giant step back from Amylin, causing its stock value to plummet to $.68 per share by October 1998.

Amylin kept its faith in SYMLIN after Johnson & Johnson terminated the collaboration agreement and pressed ahead with bringing the drug to market. Joseph C. Cook, Jr., a 28-year veteran at Eli Lilly & Co. and an Amylin board member since 1994, came out of retirement in 1998 to help the company recover its footing, taking the title of chief executive officer. Under Cook's stewardship, Amylin dealt with the blow incurred by the loss of its drug development partner and began to effect a turnaround. Cook reduced the company's workforce by 75 percent to conserve cash and raised capital from investors to keep SYMLIN moving through the regulatory pipeline. He also had to be mindful of Wall Street's perception of the company, a critical item on his checklist. In this area, Cooke achieved success not long after he took control of the company. In 1999, intrigued by the announcement of positive results on clinical trials of SYMLIN, the financial community renewed its interest in Amylin. The company's stock was trading at $7 per share at the end of the year, increasing 1,568 percent in value in 1999. By the beginning of 2000, shares in Amylin hovered in the $14 range. The return of investors' faith was an important achievement for Cook, but his greatest test arrived in 2001, when the fate of SYMLIN, and with it most probably the fate of Amylin, hung in the balance.

SYMLIN Going Before an FDA Panel in 2001

In 2001, SYMLIN was scheduled for review by the FDA's Endocrinologic and Metabolic Drugs and Advisory Committee

Key Dates:

1987: Amylin is formed.
1992: The company completes its initial public offering of stock.
1995: Amylin and Johnson & Johnson sign a collaboration agreement.
1998: Johnson & Johnson terminates its collaboration agreement.
2001: The Food and Drug Administration issues an "approvable letter" for SYMLIN.
2002: Amylin signs a collaboration agreement with Eli Lilly & Co.
2003: Ginger Graham is appointed president and chief executive officer.

(EMDAC). The drug's existence was at stake. SYMLIN, slated to be the first drug to work with insulin to lower levels of blood glucose without having the side effect of weight gain, needed to gain EMDAC's approval if it had any chance of passing through final regulatory review and entering the market. The FDA not only typically heeded the rulings of EMDAC, but also was more conservative than its panel, often ruling against a drug EMDAC had approved. As the July 2001 review with EMDAC neared, Cook and other executives went to great lengths to ensure SYMLIN earned EMDAC's approval. The company rehearsed its presentation of SYMLIN, creating a simulated setting that followed the exact configuration of the tables and chairs in EMDAC's presentation room in Washington, D.C. The company invited diabetes specialists from throughout the country to ask Amylin's staff the same type of questions the panel's specialists were expected to ask. "We trained our people to use slides and how to present," Cook said in an April 7, 2003 interview with *San Diego Business Journal.* "We wanted them to be totally comfortable with the physical surroundings of the event so that when they went in front of the panel they wouldn't have stage fright." Amylin staged a final rehearsal in Washington, D.C., before appearing before EMDAC.

Amylin's team of SYMLIN presenters made their case before EMDAC in July and waited for the nine-member panel's findings. EMDAC voted 8–1 that SYMLIN's trials proved efficacy, but the panel ruled 8–1 against using the drug for Type I diabetes and 6–3 against using it for Type II diabetes. EMDAC also voted 8–1 that SYMLIN appeared not to be safe. The panel's findings portended disaster, suggesting that nearly 15 years of work had been in vain. "The jury is still out," Cook told reporters after the panel's votes were revealed, as quoted in the April 7, 2003 issue of *San Diego Business Journal,* but few observers shared his muted optimism.

Amylin appeared on the verge of collapse. The deathblow of a drug developer had been delivered, but in October 2001, three months after EMDAC's ruling, a stunning announcement offered a lifeline. In a decision the April 7, 2003 issue of *San Diego Business Journal* described as "baffling," the FDA voted against the recommendations of EMDAC and issued an "approvable

letter" for SYMLIN. Although the FDA said it wanted to see more data before approving SYMLIN for market, the unusual reversal renewed hope that the drug, which one analyst claimed could generate $260 million in worldwide revenue annually, would give Amylin its first marketable product.

Amylin and Eli Lilly & Co. in 2002

Amylin received additional good news not long after the FDA's reversal breathed new life into the company. By September 2002, the company had about one year left of funding when Cook secured another collaboration agreement. Eli Lilly & Co., where Cook had spent nearly three decades, agreed to a $300 million collaboration agreement with Amylin to develop another diabetes drug, exenatide, which was designed to treat Type II diabetics. Eli Lilly & Co. agreed to an initial $80 million payment and to split the development costs and U.S. profits with Amylin, with Cook's company getting up to $300 million in milestone payments. The deal sparked new excitement in the financial community. "The fact that Joe (Cook) got a profit-sharing deal out of Eli Lilly as opposed to a royalty-based deal makes the terms much more generous for Amylin," an analyst remarked in an April 7, 2003 interview with *San Diego Business Journal.*

With SYMLIN under regulatory review and exenatide undergoing Phase III clinical trials, Amylin was edging closer to having two drugs on the market. Cook, after engineering a remarkable turnaround at the company, decided to step down in 2003 and hand the opportunity of guiding Amylin toward a future of potential prosperity to another board member. Ginger Graham, an Amylin board member since 1994, was named president and chief executive officer in September 2003. Formerly an executive at Guidant Corp. and Eli Lilly & Co., Graham took charge of the company at yet another critical point in its development. In the not too distant future, Amylin would discover the commercial and medical worth of more than 15 years of research and development. The existence of the company depended on a successful denouement.

Further Reading

"Amylin Completes $175 Million Secondary," *Corporate Financing Week,* February 10, 2003, p. 4.
"Eli Lilly and Amylin Enter Pact," *Chemical Market Reporter,* September 30, 2002, p. 14.
"Ginger L. Graham," *Chemical Market Reporter,* June 16, 2003, p. 30.
Webb, Marion, "Amylin Gets Nod from FDA for Drug Condidate," *San Diego Business Journal,* October 22, 2001, p. 9.
——, "Amylin's Success a Survival Lesson," *San Diago Business Journal,* April 7, 2003, p. 1.
——, "Amylin Watches Its R&D Costs Continue to Rise," *San Diego Business Journal,* November 4, 2002, p. 13.
——, "CEO's Challenge: Building on Foundation; Amylin's Joseph Cook Is Stepping Down for Board Member Ginger Graham," *San Diego Business Journal,* June 16, 2003, p. 9.
——, "Diabetes Drug Results Drive Amylin Stock," *San Diego Business Journal,* August 11, 2003, p. 12.
——, "Lilly Deal Buoys Biotech Amylin," *San Diego Business Journal,* September 30, 2002, p. 1.

—Jeffrey L. Covell

AnnTaylor Stores Corporation

142 West 57th Street
New York, New York 10019
U.S.A.
Telephone: (212) 541-3300
Toll Free: (800) 342-5266
Fax: (212) 541-3379
Web site: http://www.anntaylor.com

Public Company
Incorporated: 1988
Employees: 13,000
Sales: $1.58 billion (2004)
Stock Exchanges: New York
Ticker Symbol: ANN
NAIC: 448120 Women's Clothing Stores

Through its wholly owned subsidiary, AnnTaylor Inc., Ann-Taylor Stores Corporation is a retailer of women's apparel, with stores in major downtown city locations and shopping malls across the United States. Noted for its classic, tailored designs for career women, AnnTaylor strives to provide what is referred to as "a head to toe concept of dressing with an edited assortment of tasteful, fashion-updated classic apparel and accessories in a one-stop shopping environment." After a shaky sales spell in the 1990s brought on by a departure from the company's signature style, the company rebounded in large part due to the success and expansion of its AnnTaylor Loft stores in the early 2000s.

The 1950s–70s: From College Town Boutique to Manhattan

The original AnnTaylor store was founded in New Haven, Connecticut, in 1954, by Robert Liebskind. Interestingly, there was never an actual Ann Taylor; the name was simply selected to characterize the target customer. The company's line of classic clothing became popular and eventually new shops were opened primarily in such eastern college towns as New Haven, Providence, Boston, Cambridge, and Georgetown. In 1977, Liebskind sold his stores to Garfinckel, Brooks Brothers, Miller

Rhodes Corporation (known as Garfinckels). Under new management, AnnTaylor stores began to spread rapidly during the late 1970s.

During this time, AnnTaylor began showcasing the work of Perry Ellis, who designed clothing for the AnnTaylor label. AnnTaylor also had exclusive contracts with Marimeko and other cutting-edge, upscale designers. The stores eventually began to offer European fashions, as management found that loyal AnnTaylor customers were generally willing to spend a little more for unique, less conservative styles but still less likely to pay the prices or risk the fashion statements available in designer boutiques. Moreover, by refraining from carrying a wide variety of designer labels and brands offered by department stores, AnnTaylor had less competition and thus more pricing flexibility; the company could also produce fast reactions to fashion trends and regional needs.

The value of AnnTaylor's name as a brand increased steadily, and the stores became increasingly popular. The flagship store for the company, on 57th Street in Manhattan, featured a chic restaurant on the third floor. The AnnTaylor customer during this time was characterized as a new breed of well-dressed career woman who favored classic fabrics in fashionable designs. Describing a 1978 AnnTaylor catalogue, one writer for *Working Woman* magazine noted that the catalogue showed "a duo of well-dressed working women ganging up on a would-be mugger, hitting him with their AnnTaylor purses. The message: The AnnTaylor woman might wear silk and cashmere, but watch out—she's taken karate."

The 1980s: A Series of New Owners and Management

In 1981, AnnTaylor, as part of Garfinckels, was acquired by Allied Stores Corporation and quickly became the most profitable among the group of Allied retailers, outperforming even Brooks Brothers and Bonwit Teller. Allied subsequently unloaded unprofitable subsidiaries and further polished its core stores' image of upscale, high-profile specialty and department stores. In 1983, Sally Frame Kasaks, who had started in the fashion industry as a salesperson, was named president of the company, and she served in that capacity until 1985, when she left to join Talbots and, eventually, Abercrombie & Fitch.

A new president and CEO, Mark Shulman, faced new challenges. A Canadian financier, Robert Campeau, was attracted by Allied's cache of healthy, upscale stores with recognizable names. In 1986, his Campeau Corporation made an overture to acquire Allied but was rebuffed. Campeau was tiny compared with Allied; it had 1985 revenues of $153 million, while Allied reported $4.1 billion for the same year. Nevertheless, in the leveraged buyout-crazed 1980s, it was not hard for Campeau to get financial backing. After securing $3 billion in credit, Campeau launched a hostile takeover of Allied. The final price for the deal was more than $5 billion by some estimates, and Campeau had to sell off many of Allied's units to pay for the purchase, retaining only the best performers, such as Brooks Brothers and AnnTaylor. By the end of 1987, more than $1 billion of Allied's holdings had been sold off, and Campeau was able to pay down some of its debts.

Although it was ahead of schedule on debt payments, Campeau was still feeling the effects of the transaction, earning only $44 million in the first three quarters of 1987. Moreover, its interest payments for that same time period were $244 million. Thus some analysts were surprised when Campeau quickly set its sights on Federated Department Stores, Inc., a giant holding company of department stores then three times the size of Allied. With more than $4 billion in fresh loans, Campeau initiated a similar takeover, again increasing the initial per-share offer, until the final cost for Federated reached $6.6 billion. Campeau sold off Brooks Brothers to a British department store to get cash for its debts and for Federated stock. Although Campeau vowed he would not sell AnnTaylor, the retailer was put on the block by June 1988, when Campeau claimed that AnnTaylor's spot in specialty retailing no longer complemented Campeau's department store holdings. At the time, AnnTaylor had 100 stores nationwide and accounted for 8 percent of Allied's $3.96 billion in sales in 1988. AnnTaylor was the last of Allied's specialty stores. Proceeds from the sale would go toward Allied's bank debt, as well as for Federated stock.

It was not hard to find a buyer for AnnTaylor. Joseph E. Brooks, formerly the chief executive officer of Lord & Taylor, led a group of investors that included Merrill Lynch Capital Partners, Inc. and some of AnnTaylor's management. The price paid was $430 million, which, to some observers, seemed a tad high for a company that, like many companies in the women's apparel industry, had recently reported flat earnings. In fact, although AnnTaylor had more than 36 percent annual growth in both earnings and sales between 1983 and 1987, its earnings seemed to have peaked in 1986. Expectations soared, however, now that Brooks was in charge.

Brooks was noted for making Lord & Taylor over into an upscale store offering classic merchandise. Under his leadership, Lord & Taylor had expanded from 19 to 46 units and sales had quadrupled. Brooks moved quickly at AnnTaylor, bringing in a new management team, some of whom had been with him at Lord & Taylor, including his son, Thomas H.K. Brooks, who was named AnnTaylor's president. Faced with staggering interest payments and a tricky debt-to-equity load, the company focused on rapid expansion and cost-cutting tactics.

1990s: Hard Times in the Industry; Instability at Home

By 1991, AnnTaylor had spread as far from its East Coast roots as Jackson, Mississippi, and now boasted 58 new outlets and a total of 176 stores. With new stores helping to boost sales, Brooks felt confident enough to make bids for Saks Fifth Avenue and Bloomingdale's. He was outbid for Saks, however, and the $1 billion he offered for Bloomingdale's failed to tempt its owner, Federated Stores. With the debt load still pressuring AnnTaylor to perform, the company's buyout bosses proposed a public offering of AnnTaylor stock. The industry was limping and a stock offering seemed a good way to raise equity enough to tide AnnTaylor over the rough spots. Despite the fact that AnnTaylor was not faring well in same-store sales, the offering went well. Seven million shares were sold at $26 per share, providing the cash flow necessary to continue planned expansions.

The offering also increased AnnTaylor's burden to perform well in sales and earnings growth, however, and it was in the face of such pressures that some decisions were made that would eventually prove detrimental to the company. The new management decided that the typical AnnTaylor customer of 1990 was not as affluent as its earlier clientele had been, and, in an effort to broaden its appeal and cut expenses, the company began using fabrics of lesser quality for the first time.

Management also opted to end AnnTaylor's long and profitable relationship with Joan & David shoes, a product that had accounted for roughly 14 percent of AnnTaylor's sales for 30 years and had a fine reputation of its own, pulling many customers into AnnTaylor stores. AnnTaylor began offering its own line of shoes instead, at about half the price. Early reviews of these shoes bordered on snide, and earnings and revenues became weak. The stock collapsed and some stockholders sued, alleging misrepresentation of the facts by the prospectus that accompanied the public offering.

Then, in December 1991, Joseph E. Brooks abruptly announced his retirement from his position as chairman. His son, Thomas Brooks, had quit the presidency just as suddenly a few weeks earlier, as had Gerald H. Blum, the company's vice-chairman. With their company suddenly being run by a commit-

Key Dates:

1954: Robert Liebskind opens the first AnnTaylor store in New Haven, Connecticut.

1977: Liebskind sells his stores to Garfinckel, Brooks Brothers, Miller Rhodes Corporation.

1981: AnnTaylor, as part of Garfinckels, is acquired by Allied Stores Corporation.

1983: Sally Frame Kasaks becomes president of the company.

1985: Mark Shulman replaces Kasaks as chief executive officer.

1987: The Campeau Corporation implements a hostile takeover of Allied Stores.

1988: The Campeau Corporation sells AnnTaylor to Merrill Lynch Capital Partners, Inc. and some of AnnTaylor's management.

1991: AnnTaylor goes public.

1992: Sally Frame Kasaks returns to head AnnTaylor.

1996: AnnTaylor buys Cygne Designs' stock in its joint ventures; J. Patrick Spainhour and Patricia DeRosa replace Kasaks.

1998: AnnTaylor expands its AnnTaylor Loft Stores.

2001: Katherine Lawther Krill is appointed president of Loft Division.

2002: Loft stores rapidly expand; company posts most profitable third quarter in its history.

2003: Kim Roy resigns as president of AnnTaylor Division.

2004: Company moves back office work to Milford, Connecticut; celebrates 50th "ANNiversary."

tee, stockholders and investors became anxious. The company had lost about two-thirds of its market value since going public in 1991 and was losing its most loyal customers daily. That year, AnnTaylor lost $15.8 million on sales of $438 million.

In February 1992, AnnTaylor wooed former President Sally Frame Kasaks back. Her first action, like Brooks's, was to install a solid management team. Kasaks chose a primarily female management staff, composed of seasoned veterans of the specialty retail trade. Kasaks then worked to reestablish AnnTaylor's reputation for high-quality clothing, getting rid of the cheap synthetic fabrics and overseeing a new autumn line of clothes that borrowed heavily from popular and costly designs of Donna Karan and Ralph Lauren. Four months after Kasaks rejoined AnnTaylor, the company's same-store sales were up 10 percent.

After reassuring the customer of the quality of AnnTaylor merchandise, Kasaks sought a strategy for keeping prices reasonable. Toward that end, she explored several manufacturing options, finally reaching an agreement with Cygne Designs for the manufacture of apparel through a joint venture called CAT. A private-label company with factory contracts mainly overseas, Cygne worked with AnnTaylor to produce items made to specification more cheaply and quickly. As a result, what few designer labels the AnnTaylor stores stocked nearly disappeared, and lines of casual and weekend clothes were added, as were lines of petite sizes and whole new lines meant to attract younger women.

By her own admission, Kasaks worked hard to stay in touch with suppliers and customers. "This is very much a business of relationships," she was quoted as saying in a 1995 *Chain Store Executive* article, adding "and as a symbol of this business, I need to stay out there." Thus she visited an average of 100 stores a year, refused to fly first class on business trips "because it is something that most AnnTaylor customers do not do on a regular basis," and tried to see that overseas factories maintained responsible manufacturing and production practices.

Sales at new stores opened in 1993 grew an impressive 13.6 percent by March 1994, and Merrill Lynch Capital Partners and other affiliates—still holding 52 percent of AnnTaylor's stock—prepared to make another public offering. During the first six months of 1994, same-store sales grew 10.6 percent, while other popular specialty stores, such as The Gap and Nordstrom's, were reporting gains of less than half that amount. By year's end, the company's sales had increased considerably to $659 million with earnings of $32 million, as formerly loyal customers began to return to AnnTaylor, and analysts were hailing AnnTaylor as being "back on track." A new fragrance line was introduced, five freestanding shoe and accessory stores were opened, and a mail-order catalogue was launched in 1994. Kasaks also expanded AnnTaylor's traditional career offerings to include casual clothes, denims, and petites. The company updated its systems and controls for supplying stores with merchandise. It opened a new business, AnnTaylor Loft, intended to have greater appeal to younger customers with its more fashionable, less basics-oriented approach.

The Loft was also an attempt to compete with discount apparel stores, the most potent threat to apparel specialty stores at that time because of the price deflation they caused in the moderate and lower priced lines. By early 1995, AnnTaylor was feeling this threat as it was forced to cut prices by 10 to 15 percent. The board, in an attempt to maintain the company's growth, tripled its capital spending budget as plans were undertaken for further aggressive expansion. By the end of the year, however, AnnTaylor's spectacular comeback was being labeled a flop. The spring line, which included cropped T-shirts and leather jackets in an attempt to woo the younger customer, had not sold well.

Kasaks attributed the company's sales problems to the difficult retail environment, but others attributed them to Kasaks herself. Known for her mercurial disposition, she had ostensibly shaken up more than one staff meeting. More than a dozen executives, including the company's senior vice-president and general merchandising manager, had resigned as AnnTaylor's stock dipped from its December 1994 high of almost $45 to a low of $10 in October 1995. The company became unable to meet the conditions of its loans.

In April 1996, two shareholders filed a class-action suit accusing the company of concealing its financial problems and hiding inventory. In September 1996, in an effort to salvage its ailing principal supplier, AnnTaylor bought Cygne's 60 percent stake in CAT and Cygne's AnnTaylor Woven Division. After 14 straight months of declining sales and losses or lower profits in five of six quarters, Kasaks resigned under pressure from the board in August 1996, replaced by J. Patrick Spainhour, former chief financial officer of Donna Karan International, as chief executive, and Patricia DeRosa, former president of Gap Kids, as president and chief operating officer.

In 1997, AnnTaylor invested heavily in advertising for its fall line of clothes, the more conservatively stylish, businesslike attire with which it had made its name. Sales remained sluggish through most of 1997, when sales for the entire company fell 2.1 percent. By 1998, however, the company seemed to have solidified its comeback. For this, AnnTaylor had its loyal customer base to thank, who, according to at least one analyst in the *Milwaukee Journal Sentinel,* kept coming back to browse the racks even after styles disappointed them. Sales for the year increased to $912 million, yielding profits of $39.3 million.

Sales at AnnTaylor continued to improve, albeit slowly, throughout 1999 and into 2000, when there was talk of a company buyout by May Department Stores. The company's share price continued to be volatile throughout this period, reaching an April 1999 high of about $53, but dropping as low as about $15 in early 2000. By mid-2000, when AnnTaylor offered a new Internet shopping service to customers, the future of the company was still far from certain.

The end of the1990s was spent expanding AnnTaylor's Loft spinoff which proved both popular and profitable for the company. As industry analysts predicted, some market share of the company's more expensive retail AnnTaylor stores was lost when AnnTaylor shoppers defected, becoming loyal Loft shoppers instead. AnnTaylor was not alone in "losing" customers; The Gap experienced the same effect when it opened its lower priced and trendier Old Navy stores. The company took note of the Loft stores' burgeoning success and by May 2000 Ann-Taylor had 70 loft stores throughout the United States, with plans for further expansion.

In the early 2000s AnnTaylor was shoring up its internet business by partnering with a variety of internet service providers including ProfitLogic, Interworld, Convergys Corporation and Delano Technology. Internet retailing made the shopping experience easier for the average woman career professional and AnnTaylor capitalized on its appeal to working women, drawing them in with aggressive marketing and giving them the excellent customer service they demanded.

The company reached agreements with J.C. Penney's subsidiary JCP Logistics in June 2000 to provide distribution for its web-based retailing at www.anntaylor.com. In November 2000 AnnTaylor chose Interworld Commerce Suite to help power the company's growing e-tail business. AnnTaylor's reputation as a top-notch customer service provider at its retail stores was transferred to its web-based business as through its association with Interworld. Even more emphasis was placed on its internet shop when in January 2001 AnnTaylor chose Delano Velocity Marketing to assist with its e-marketing and client relations.

Sales had declined in the 1990s and by 2000 the company looked to recapture its lost market share. A campaign began with an emphasis on a return to its signature look and style—a classic style with solid wardrobe pieces for the career minded woman. The company was known for its classic mix and match outfits but had strayed toward trendier styles in the 1990s. Cathy Rano was hired at the AnnTaylor division as vice-president of design and charged to bring back the basics while updating

color scheme trends and modernizing inventory along traditional fashion variations such as hemline length, lapel width, and jacket style.

The company decided to consolidate some of its operations in 2004. AnnTaylor's data center and some of its back-office work would move to Milford, Connecticut. The new building provided 42,000 square feet with a six-year lease. That same year marked the 50th anniversary of AnnTaylor and the company celebrated its milestone with a new advertising campaign shot by world renowned photographer Annie Leibovitz. The slogan chosen for the campaign was "I AM ANN TAYLOR" with ads featuring fashion icons from the past, as well as beautiful women who were beginning to grace the pages of fashionable women's magazines. The ads captured the return of the classic AnnTaylor look with a focus on its timeless yet modern design. AnnTaylor was refashioning itself and, despite inconsistent sales, attempting to solidify its market share by the mid-2000s.

Principal Subsidiaries

AnnTaylor Inc.

Principal Divisions

AnnTaylor Loft; Anntaylor.com; AnnTaylor Factory Stores.

Principal Competitors

The Gap Inc.; Liz Claiborne Inc.; Donna Karan International Inc.; The Talbots Inc.; Chicos FAS, Inc.

Further Reading

"AnnTaylor Sells Card Portfolio to Alliance Data," *Cardline,* February 1, 2002, p. 1.

"Brooks Group Gets AnnTaylor for $430 Million," *Women's Wear Daily,* November 30, 1988, pp. 1, 26.

Caminiti, Susan, "How to Win Back Customers," *Fortune,* June 14, 1993, p. 118.

Coleman, Lisa, "Welcome Back," *Forbes,* August 17, 1992, p. 124.

Colodny, Mark, "Mr. Ann Taylor," *Fortune,* March 11, 1991, p. 105.

Contavski, Vicki, "Who'll Mind the Store?," *Forbes,* December 9, 1991, p. 16.

Croghan, Iore, "AnnTaylor Arrives Near Grand Central," *Crain's New York Business,* January 28, 2002, p. 12.

Curan, Catherine, "New AnnTaylor Lead Must Fashion Turnaround," *Crain's New York Business*, May 26, 2003, p. 4.

Dawkins, Pam, "AnnTaylor to Consolidate Data," *Connecticut Post*, March 30, 2004.

Daykin, Tom, "Wauwatosa, Wisconsin, J.C. Penney Distribution Center Lands Deal with AnnTaylor," *Milwaukee Journal Sentinel,* June 16, 2000.

Donahue, Christine, "AnnTaylor Turns Barbara Bush into a Fashion Plate," *Adweek's Marketing Index,* September 4, 1989, p. 31.

Furman, Phyllis, "Fashionable AnnTaylor to Sell Stock," *Crain's New York Business,* March 25, 1991, pp. 3, 34.

Gross, Esther, "Specialty Retailers Boom; Profits Climbing at Limited, AnnTaylor," *New York Daily News,* November 18, 1998 p. 41.

Jeresky, Laura, "Rags to Riches," *Forbes,* April 15, 1991, p. 42.

Mahar, Maggie, "Mission Impossible?," *Working Woman,* December 1993, pp. 60–68.

McNally, Pamela, "The AnnTaylor Footwear Formula," *Footwear News,* August 1, 1994, p. S6.

McNish, Jacquie, "Campeau Plans to Sell Allied's AnnTaylor Unit," *Wall Street Journal,* June 16, 1988, p. 10.

Moore, Janet, "A Harsh Classic Education," *Star Tribune*, June 28, 2001, p. 1D.

Pate, Kelly, "AnnTaylor Offshoot Eyes 16th St. Mall," *Denver Post*, May 12, 2000, p. C2.

Power, William, "Soaring AnnTaylor May Need Some Caution As Accessory," *Wall Street Journal,* April 15, 1994.

Schoolman, Judith, "AnnTaylor Widens Scope; Clothier Expands Its Lower-Priced Loft Stores," *New York Daily News*, September 20, 1999, p. 27.

Souccar, Miriam Kreinin, "AnnTaylor Rolls Up Sleeves to Find Suitable President," *Crain's New York Business*, February 10, 2003, p. 12.

Steinhauer, Jennifer, "Can AnnTaylor Dust Itself Off?," *New York Times,* December 2, 1995, p. 35.

——, "In a Surprise, AnnTaylor's Chief Resigns," *New York Times,* August 24, 1996, p. 35.

Trachtenberg, Jeffrey, "AnnTaylor Plans Expansion to Pay $37 Million in Interest from Buy-Out," *Wall Street Journal,* May 11, 1989, p. A4.

Wachs Book, Esther, "The Treachery of Success," *Forbes,* September 12, 1994, pp. 88–90.

Wilson, Marianne, "Reinventing AnnTaylor," *Chain Store Age Executive,* January 1995, pp. 26–45.

Zinn, Laura, "Trouble Stalks the Aisles at AnnTaylor," *Business Week,* December 9, 1991, p. 38.

—Carol I. Keeley
—updates: Carrie Rothburd, Susan B. Culligan

AU Optronics Corporation

1 Li-Hsin Rd. 2, Science-Based I
Hsinchu
Taiwan
Telephone: +886 3 563 2899
Fax: 886 3 564 3370
Web site: http://www.auo.com

Public Company
Incorporated: 2001
Employees: 9,780
Sales: TWD 104.86 billion ($3.1 billion) (2003)
Stock Exchanges: Taiwan
Ticker Symbol: AUO
NAIC: 334419 Other Electronic Component
    Manufacturing

AU Optronics Corporation is Taiwan's largest producer of flat panel displays—that is, thin film transistor liquid crystal display panels, or TFT-LCDs—and is also the world's number three manufacturer, trailing only South Korea's Samsung and LG-Philips. As the first Taiwanese company to begin producing active matrix LCDs in the early 1990s, AU Optronics has played a leading role in Taiwan's transformation as one of the world's high-technology centers. The company has expanded its production from small-sized panels to the latest-generation large-scale panels, such as Taiwan's first high-definition 46-inch television panel, debuted in late 2003. AU Optronics also has developed a strong in-house research and development component, which has enabled it to become the first in the world to produce an amorphous silicon-based TFT OLED (organic light-emitting display). The company expects to put this technology into practice producing panels for new generation mobile telephones—including those produced by sister company BenQ, Taiwan's leading mobile phone producer. AU Optronics operates subsidiaries in Taiwan, Japan, China, the United States, and The Netherlands, with production based in Taiwan and in Suzhou, China. In 2003, AU Optronics posted revenues of more than TWD 104 billion ($3.1 billion), multiplying its sales by more than 18 times since 1999. The company is led by Chairman K.Y. Lee, who is also chairman of BenQ Corporation.

Technology Drive in the 1990s

Taiwan began an effort to shift its economy from a reliance on low-margin mass production items to the higher-margin and higher-prestige markets such as the technology sector in the early 1980s. As part of that effort, the government established the Industrial Technology Research Institute (ITRI), attached to the Ministry of Economic Affairs. By the late 1970s, the ITRI had targeted the integrated circuit market for growth, and established a new division, the Electronic Research Service Organization (ERSO), which began acquiring the technology—through technology transfers with Western partners such as RCA—for the creation of Taiwan's own integrated circuit (IC) production industry.

With RCA's assistance, ERSO successfully launched Taiwan's first IC production facility. In 1980, the government body spun off the IC line into a new company, United Microelectronics Corporation (UMC). UMC at first turned out small chips for the consumer market, such as for use in digital wristwatches. Through the decade, however, UMC continued to develop its technology—and the sophistication of its production capacity. Commodity production remained, however, a major part of the company's business.

In 1985, UMC became the first of Taiwan's IC producers to go public, listing on the Taiwan Stock Exchange. The listing enabled the company to begin pursuing a diversification into other emerging technologies. One of these was the small but potentially vast market for liquid crystal display (LCD) panels. UMC's interest turned toward the development of thin-film transistor (TFT) technology, and in 1990 the company backed the founding of a new company dedicated to the development of TFT-LCD technology, called Unipac Optoelectronics. UMC was to remain a major Unipac shareholder throughout the decade.

Turning once again to foreign partners in a series of technology transfer agreements, Unipac set out to build its own first-generation production plant, known as Fab L1 within the company, at the newly built HsinChu Science-based Industrial Park.

Company Perspectives:

Mission: Be A Global Leader in Flat Panel Displays.
Vision: Enrich Digital Lifestyle with Optronic Innovations.

That facility began testing in the early 1990s, and by 1994 had launched full-scale production.

Unipac's initial production was limited to a range of sizes between 1.8 inches and 4-inch screen formats, but by 1995 the company had ramped up to production on the 5.6-inch format as well. By then, the company was able to produce some 30,000 four-inch screens per month. The smaller formats were geared, in large part, to such end uses as navigation displays and television monitors, and also found a market later in the decade as passenger airline seatback displays.

Portable computers, however, represented the most buoyant market for TFT-LCD technology. At the middle of the decade, the 10.5-inch form factor became the industry standard. Yet, Unipac, like other emerging Taiwanese LCD manufacturers, continued to lag behind its larger competitors in Japan and Korea, while depending on technology brought in from these countries and elsewhere. At the same time, Unipac faced impending pressure from a number of new competitors, which were ramping up to production of their own large-size panels in the latter half of the 1990s.

One of the new companies was Acer Display Technologies (ADT), which was founded as a subsidiary of the fast-growing computer group in 1996. ADT's ambitions took a big step forward in 1998, when the company signed a technology transfer agreement with IBM. Not to be outdone, Unipac reached its own technology transfer agreement that year with Japan's Matsushita. Both agreements promised to boost Taiwan's capacity for producing large-sized TFT-LCD panels.

Challenging Global Leadership in the New Century

The agreement with Matsushita enabled Unipac to complete its second-generation fab, which began mass production in 1999. The company's entry into the large-sized panels market launched its transformation. From sales of just $20 million in 1998, Unipac entered a period of explosive growth. By the end of 1999, the company's revenues topped $70 million.

By March 2000, Unipac launched its first 17-inch TFT-LCD, becoming the first in Taiwan to produce in the larger than 15-inch category. The company followed that triumph with a listing on the Taiwan Stock Exchange, ultimately reducing UMC's stake in Unipac to just 40 percent. Soon after Unipac's public offering, it was joined on the stock exchange by ADT, also making its stock market debut. By the end of 2000, Unipac had launched mass production in its newest Generation 3.5 facility, FAB L3m, capable of producing 60,000 sheets per month. In the meantime, Unipac continued producing its original small-sized screens, capturing the world's number two position in that market, behind leader Sharp of Japan.

UMC had in the meantime been structuring its operations, shedding its commodity ICs business to refocus itself as a

Key Dates:

1990: Unipac Optoelectronics is launched as a TFT-LCD affiliate of Taiwanese semiconductor manufacturer United Microelectronics Corporation.
1994: Production begins at Unipac's first TFT-LCD fab.
1996: Acer forms the TFT-LCD subsidiary, Acer Display Technologies (ADT).
1998: Unipac forms a technology transfer partnership with Matsushita; ADT forms a technology transfer agreement with IBM.
2000: Both ADT and Unipac go public on the Taiwan Stock Exchange.
2001: ADT and Unipac merge as AU Optronics.
2002: The company's first production facility opens in mainland China.
2003: AU Optronics claims the number three spot in the worldwide TFT-LCD market.
2004: The company launches construction of a sixth-generation production plant, slated to open in 2005; the company considers suspending construction of a seventh-generation plant due to poor market conditions.

pure-play semiconductor foundry. As part of that effort, UMC sought a means to spin off its LCD business. In 2001, Unipac found a new partner when Acer agreed to spin off its own display panels subsidiary ADT into a new, merged company together with Unipac, called AU Optronics. The chairman's seat at the new company was taken by K.Y. Lee, who also served as chairman at another Acer offshoot, BenQ Corporation.

AU Optronics' combined production capacity—which included two LCD facilities from ADT—placed it among the global industry's leaders, and also gave it the top position in the domestic market. The company's combined clout encouraged it to launch an effort to gain greater control of its technology requirement. In 2000, AU Optronics opened its research and development facility in Hsinchu. As the company's executive vice-president, Lu Po-Yen told *EBN:* "The research and development of various types of new products has become the key for us to surpass our current high position and quicken the pace of our ascension to the world's no. 1 flat-panel-display company."

As part of that effort, the company pledged to spend some $300 million leading up to 2005, doubling its previous research spending. The effort began to pay off toward the end of 2002, when the company displayed its first fifth-generation LCD panel. By then, the company also had finished development on the world's first amorphous silicon-based organic light-emitted display (OLED). The company formally debuted the completed product, a four-inch screen, in 2003.

By the end of 2002, AU Optronics' research and development push began paying off for the company—in that year, AU Optronics led the market in filing for new patents, with 265 patent rights applications. AU Optronics also had been stepping up its production, including the June 2002 launch of a new fab in Suzhou, on the Chinese mainland, with a production capacity of 50,000 LCD modules per month.

By 2003, AU Optronics was able to claim the number three position worldwide in shipments of large-sized TFT-LCD panels, as the market for computer peripherals and especially for new LCD-based televisions began to take off worldwide. In August of that year, the company launched production of the world's first 30-inch wide LCD television panel. This was followed soon after by the debut of the first Taiwan-built 46-inch HDTV LCD panel. At the other end of the scale, AU Optronics began targeting the mobile phone market, launching production of its own low-power screens. The company also sought to gain a foothold in the palm-sized market, debuting Taiwan's first two-inch transreflective LCD screen in October 2003. By the end of that year, the company's annual sales had soared past TWD 104 billion ($3.1 billion).

As it entered 2004, AU Optronics had launched construction of a new sixth-generation LCD fab, slated for completion in 2005. The company also began plans for a new seventh-generation fab, originally scheduled to enter mass production in 2007. However, poor market conditions—a drop-off in demand in late 2004 combined with the rapidly falling prices of LCD-based televisions and computer monitors—forced AU Optronics to consider placing the opening of the new facility on hold. Nonetheless, AU Optronics seemed on course to achieve its goal of becoming the world's leading maker of TFT-LCD screens by the middle of the decade.

Principal Subsidiaries

AU Optronics (Suzhou) Corporation (China); AU Optronics Corporation America; AU Optronics Corporation Japan; AU Optronics Europe B.V. (Netherlands); AU Optronics Korea.

Principal Competitors

Samsung Corporation; LG-Philips; Sharp Corporation.

Further Reading

"Acer Display Tech and Unipac to Merge," *Futures World News,* May 17, 2001.

"AU Optronics," *Euroweek,* June 4, 2004, p. 21.

"AU Optronics Readies for 2003 Rollout of LTPS Cell Phone Displays," *Taiwan Economic News,* October 25, 2002.

"AU Optronics' 6th Generation TFT-LCD," *Taiwan Economic News,* September 17, 2003.

"AUO Ties Up with Changhong for TFT-LCD Market," *SinoCast China IT Watch,* October 14, 2003.

Hung, Faith, "Au Optronics Establishes Display Technology Center," *EBN,* November 11, 2002, p. 4.

"TFT-LCD Panel Makers to Invest in New Generation Plants," *Taiwan Economic News,* April 23, 2003.

Wang, Lisa, "Poor Demand Prompts AU Optronics to Delay Plans to Set Up a New Facility," *Tapei Times,* September 15, 2004, p. 10.

—M.L. Cohen

AVX Corporation

801 17th Avenue South
Myrtle Beach, South Carolina 29577
U.S.A.
Telephone: (843) 448-9411
Toll Free: (843) 448-7139
Fax: (843) 448-7139
Web site: http://www.avxcorp.com

Public Company
Incorporated: 1972
Employees: 13,150
Sales: $1.14 billion (2004)
Stock Exchanges: New York
Ticker Symbol: AVX
NAIC: 334417 Electronic Connector Manufacturing

AVX Corporation is a global manufacturer of passive electronic components. The Myrtle Beach, South Carolina-based company is publicly traded on the New York Stock Exchange but is majority-owned by Japanese electronics giant Kyocera Corporation. AVX products include ceramic and tantalum capacitors, film capacitors, varistors, and nonlinear resistors. (Capacitors temporarily store electrical energy and are a vital component in the architecture of electrical or electronic circuits, filtering and conditioning electronic signals.) Markets served include automotive, consumer, data processing, medical, and telecommunications. AVX operates 20 manufacturing facilities located in 11 countries and maintains five research and development centers. In addition, AVX sells and distributes some of the electronic connectors manufactured by its corporate parent.

Lineage Dating to the 1920s

The history of AVX can be traced to 1922 and the founding of the Radiola Wireless Corp., an early maker of radios. The company changed its name to Aerovox Wireless Corp. and then shortened it to Aerovox Corp. AVX was formed as a subsidiary in 1972 to manufacture ceramic capacitors and in June 1973 took over the parent corporation after the other assets of

Aerovox were sold. Also in 1973 Marshall D. Butler, the man most responsible for the growth of the company, was hired as chief executive officer and chairman. Butler had experience in the semiconductor industry: in 1957 he cofounded Alloys Unlimited Inc., which sold components and other materials to semiconductor makers. After the business was sold to a British company, Plessey Co., in 1970, Butler stayed on as president of the Plessey subsidiary, but after three years he had a falling out with the corporate parent over strategy and quit. He was soon recruited by AVX to jumpstart the company, which had enjoyed only modest success with electrical capacitors.

Butler quickly decided to focus on multilayer ceramic capacitors (MLCs), the kind used in the integrated circuits of semiconductors, a fast-growing area. Butler sold off two other operations to concentrate on the MLC market, with goals of ramping up production, cutting prices, and gaining a dominant market share. He launched a $20 million, five-year program that increased the company's production capacity by 20 times. Everyone in the capacitor industry realized that MLCs were gaining momentum but only AVX conducted in-depth market studies, which gave Butler the confidence to spend $20 million to win market share. By the time the rest of the industry understood what was happening, AVX had achieved a stranglehold on the market. In 1979 sales reached $95 million, well more than the $83 million target based on a projected growth rate of 30 percent a year. During this period AVX established a European operation, and in its efforts to sell products in Japan began a fruitful relationship with Kyocera. When Butler took over AVX he was saddled with a licensing agreement that did not allow the company to sell in Japan, while at the same time Kyocera could use AVX technology to sell into the United States. Butler complained to Kyocera, whose CEO, Kazuo Inamori, agreed that the arrangement was not fair and had the contract voided. In April 1979 AVX formed a subsidiary with Japanese partners to enter the Japanese market.

Steady Growth in the 1980s

AVX enjoyed steady growth through the early 1980s. In 1983 the company recorded sales of $160.9 million and net income of $8.7 million. Business remained strong through most of 1984,

---

Company Perspectives:

The goal of AVX is Total Customer Satisfaction through continuous improvement.

---

when AVX produced $235 million in revenues and net income topped $15 million, but by the end of the year semiconductor sales began to slump. In retrospect, it appeared that computer makers had bought more capacitors than they really needed during the early 1980s, a situation that led to a glut in the marketplace and an inevitable consolidation in the capacitor industry. AVX was well positioned to weather the storm and was able to grow larger by way of acquisitions. It also invested heavily in research and development during the late 1980s to develop the next generation of MLCs and noncapacitor products to help AVX in its efforts to diversify. By the end of the decade AVX was achieving some $450 million in annual revenues.

In the late 1980s Butler approached Inamori about forging a joint venture, with AVX manufacturing some Kyocera parts in Europe where the Japanese company lacked manufacturing capacity. By this stage, AVX had built up its European operations, which accounted for about one-quarter of the company's sales. Kyocera, on the other hand, generated less than 2 percent of its $2.5 billion of annual sales in Europe and was eager to expand its presence in the market before 1992, when internal trade barriers in the European Community would be curtailed. Rather than create a joint venture with AVX, however, Inamori offered to buy AVX. Because AVX would gain access to Kyocera parts to sell in Europe and have the financial backing of the Japanese company to fuel further growth, not to mention the cordial relationship that had existed between the two companies over the course of 15 years, Butler was agreeable to the idea. Kyocera had some regulatory hurdles in Japan to overcome, but in January 1990 Kyocera completed the $267 million stock purchase of AVX.

Butler continued to act as CEO until he retired in 1993, although he stayed on as a member of the board. He was replaced as CEO by Benedict P. Rosen, who had been with AVX since 1972, holding a number of executive positions. Unlike many purchases made by Japanese companies during this time, Kyocera's acquisition of AVX was a success for both parties. Sales reached $795.6 million in fiscal 1994 and approached $1 billion ($988.9 million) a year later. Net income for fiscal 1995 totaled $74.9 million. In large measure, this period of robust growth for AVX was due to expansion in the electronics industry and the growing popularity of personal computers and cellular telephones. There was an increased use of electronic components in the automotive, home appliance, and medical markets, as well as the need for capacitors in advanced electronic systems. AVX also prospered by distributing Kyocera products around the world. Moreover, AVX benefited from its relationship with Kyocera in less visible ways. Rosen told *Forbes* in 1995, "We never imagined we could make the kind of money we're making. Kyocera showed us how." The Japanese were especially helpful in improving manufacturing efficiency and controlling costs in general. Kyocera also helped AVX to enter the connector field, an area of electronics closely

associated with capacitors. For its part, AVX used experience gained in Indonesia and Mexico to aid Kyocera in its efforts to set up manufacturing operations in those countries.

Kyocera turned to the public markets in 1995 to cash in on the success of its subsidiary in addition to the $62 million it had already received in dividends since buying the company. Kyocera sold about 25 percent of AVX, netting more than $557 million. Thus after five years Kyocera had all but earned back the money it spent on AVX and still owned the lion's share of the company. AVX received approximately $50 million from the offering, the money earmarked to fund the expansion of its ceramic and tantalum capacitor business as well as its entry into the connector field.

The second half of the 1990s was marked by cyclical reversals. For most of 1995 capacitor manufacturers could not keep up with demand, but as had been the case 20 years earlier, appearances proved deceptive. The real demand for capacitors fell far short of the perceived demand, a situation that resulted in swollen inventories that would take time to work through. Most companies, like AVX, ramped up production just in time to see the bottom fall out of the market in late 1995. For fiscal 1996, which ended on March 31, AVX posted sales of $1.2 billion and a net profit of $137.8 million, but because of oversupply problems and the resulting drop in prices, the company saw its revenues fall to $1.13 billion in fiscal 1997 and net income drop to $121.3 million. AVX resumed its growth in 1998 as the need for passive electronic components once again grew in response to the demand for personal computers and cell phones and the increased use of electronics by automakers. Revenues in fiscal 1998 reached $1.27 billion and net income improved to $137.8 million. But once again the company's momentum was checked by poor market conditions including an Asian currency crisis, the high cost of precious metals, and low prices caused by inventory reductions by major customers. To meet the challenge AVX attempted to control costs by cutting its workforce. In the end, sales held up, decreasing modestly to $1.24 billion, but net income was severely impacted, dropping to $41.5 million.

Demand for AVX products surged once again in 2000 across all markets, leading to favorable pricing. To keep up with demand, AVX added a plant in the Czech Republic and boosted production in its El Salvador facility. Although the price of palladium, a key raw material, was high, AVX was able to post strong results for fiscal 2000. Sales grew by a third to $1.63 billion and net sales rebounded, totaling close to $157 million. The company enjoyed an unprecedented boom period for the rest of calendar 2000 and into 2001. To meet the need AVX operated its 26 plants in 12 countries around the clock, but it was still unable to keep up with demand, most of which was driven by the telecommunications sector and the ubiquitous nature of cell phones. When fiscal 2001 ended on March 31, 2001, AVX recorded staggering numbers. Sales grew by 60 percent over the previous year to $2.6 billion, while net income soared to $567.6 million.

Early 21st-Century Recession Forcing Retrenchment

The expectation was that demand would return to normal over the next year and a half, but even as AVX was finishing up the final quarter of a highly successful year, demand began to

<table>
<tr><td colspan="2">Key Dates:</td></tr>
<tr><td>1972:</td><td>The company is formed as a subsidiary of Aerovox Corp.</td></tr>
<tr><td>1973:</td><td>Marshall Butler is named CEO and chairman.</td></tr>
<tr><td>1990:</td><td>Kyocera Corp. acquires AVX.</td></tr>
<tr><td>1993:</td><td>Butler retires.</td></tr>
<tr><td>1995:</td><td>Kyocera sells a 25 percent stake in a public offering.</td></tr>
<tr><td>2001:</td><td>Sales total $2.6 billion, and net income amounts to $567.5 million.</td></tr>
</table>

slow down dramatically in early 2001. The economy worldwide lapsed into recession, with the telecom sector particularly hard hit. Just as rapidly as AVX had taken steps to ramp up production, it now began to retrench, launching a cost-cutting initiative. The company tried putting employees on week-long hiatuses and cutting hours to avoid slashing the workforce, but as it became clear that business would not be rebounding in the near term, AVX finally began implementing long-term layoffs. The workforce that numbered 21,000 in December 2000 dropped to 12,500 a year later. When fiscal 2002 was completed, the balance sheet revealed a drop in revenues of more than 50 percent over the previous year to $1.25 billion. AVX also recorded some $60 million in restructuring and special charges, which led to a net loss of $7.2 million in fiscal 2002.

Poor business conditions lasted much longer than expected, leading AVX to make further job cuts and to begin shifting some production from the United States to such countries as the Czech Republic and China, where labor costs were significantly lower. In fiscal 2003 sales continued to slip, to $1.13 billion, as the company lost an additional $12.4 million. Although sales began to pick up during the close of fiscal 2003, it proved to be just a marginal improvement. Revenues improved slightly to $1.14 billion in fiscal 2004, but because of a number of restruc-

turing charges the company took during the year, AVX posted a loss of $109.4 million for the year.

In 2004 there were strong indications that the cost of raw materials and pricing were stabilizing. If so, AVX could expect to enjoy a significant rebound. The company had no debt and had $718 million in cash investments at its disposal. With that money AVX was interested in making acquisitions, likely in the $50 million range, involving connectors or specialty connectors. Despite going on a roller coaster ride with much of the tech sector for the past decade, AVX appeared well positioned to enjoy a prosperous future when the demand for electronic products resumed its upward trend.

Principal Subsidiaries

AVX Tantalum Corporation; Elco USA, Inc.

Principal Competitors

KEMET Corporation; Murata Manufacturing Co., Ltd.; Vishay Intertechnology, Inc.

Further Reading

Carroll, Paul B., "Kyocera Corp. of Japan Agrees to Buy AVX," *Wall Street Journal,* September 29, 1989, p. 1.

Easton, Thomas, "A Smart Japanese Buy," *Forbes,* November 20, 1995, p. 80.

Hussey, Allan F., "AVX, Ceramics Capacitor Maker, Cashes in on Fast-Growing Market," *Barron's National Business and Financial Weekly,* November 15, 1976, p. 40.

"How AVX Became No. 1 in Ceramic Capacitors," *Business Week,* October 29, 1979, p. 54J.

Lappen, Alyssa A., "Living Dangerously," *Forbes,* June 26, 1989, p. 100.

Silverman, Edward R., "Surging Computer Sales Charge Up AVX," *Crain's New York Business,* May 8, 1989, p. 15.

—Ed Dinger

B.J. Alan Co., Inc.

555 Martin Luther King, Jr. Boulevard
Youngstown, Ohio 44502-1102
U.S.A.
Telephone: (330) 746-1064
Fax: (330) 746-4410
Web site: http://www.fireworks.com

Private Company
Incorporated: 1977
Employees: 400
Sales: $100 million (2004 est.)
NAIC: 421920 Toy and Hobby Goods and Supplies
    Wholesalers; 325998 All Other Miscellaneous
    Chemical Product and Preparation Manufacturing

B.J. Alan Co., Inc. is the second largest importer and wholesaler of consumer fireworks in the country, operating 41 permanent retail outlets in 12 states and more than 1,000 temporary sales venues under the Phantom Fireworks banner. The company also owns Diamond Sparkler Manufacturing Co. Inc., which is the last sparkler manufacturing plant in the United States and produces up to 800,000 sparklers a day. The two companies, which are located on a 17-acre complex in the Mahoning Valley of Ohio, sell their goods under the tradenames Phantom, Wolfpack, Grucci Collection, and Silver Salute. In addition to its own private label products, B.J. Alan also sells Black Cat, Longhorn, Brothers, Zenith, and other fireworks.

1977–90: Developing a Business in Pyrotechnics

Beginning in the late 1980s, the pyrotechnics industry began to grow steadily. In 1985, B.J. Alan acquired the assets of Chicago-based Acme, the last sparkler manufacturing company in the United States, which had been started in 1922 by the Callen family. B.J. Alan moved Acme to Youngstown, Ohio, and renamed it Diamond Sparkler Manufacturing Co., Inc. In its heyday, Acme had employed 150 workers and produced as many as 1.5 million sparklers a day. However, by the time B.J. Alan purchased the company, it struggled each

year to make a profit. This was due at least in part to the import of sparklers from China and the illegal dumping of foreign-made sparklers in the United States. Zoldan's rationale for buying the sparkler manufacturer, according to company literature, was that he couldn't "envision something as American as sparklers, with its association with the [Fourth] of July, not being made in this country."

The 1990s: Growth Parallels Increased Popularity of Fireworks

In 1990, a surge in fireworks' popularity coincided with an increased interest in special pyrotechnic effects and "close proximity" fireworks. Phantom Fireworks entered the California market in 1991 under the banner of Big Bear Fireworks, Inc. By 1996, B.J. Alan sold its products to distributors in 15 states, at 30 stores, and from more than 500 roadside stands. According to Zoldan, "The fireworks industry has witnessed a great increase in sales over the years. This increase is expressed through the many family celebrations that take place over the [Fourth of July] holiday and the additional fireworks displays that take place throughout the country. There is enthusiasm for celebrating all sorts of occasions with fireworks. . . ."

The fireworks consumption rate in the United States climbed steadily throughout the 1990s, increasing from about 68 million pounds of fireworks purchased in 1990 to 153 million pounds in 2000. Consumption continued to grow into the early years of the next century, with 161 million pounds of fireworks purchased in 2001, and more than 190 million pounds in 2002.

Diamond Sparkler did not fare as well as its sister company throughout the 1990s. It lost money—$1.4 million between the years 1995 and 2001—largely as a result of keeping its prices low enough to match illegal Chinese imports. But after the United States International Trade Commission found that the pyrotechnics industry was being harmed by "dumping," Congress passed a law in 2001 requiring that the government turn over the tariffs it imposed on Chinese sparklers. This resulted in a $1.6 million award for Diamond. By 2002–03, sales and production at Diamond's Youngstown facilities were up more than 30 percent, fueled by the renewed spirit of patriotism in evidence across the United States.

As the purchase of fireworks increased, so, too, did concern over the legality of their sale and the safety of their use. In 1991, the attorney general of Pennsylvania ordered B.J. Alan to issue a warning notifying potential purchasers of the illegality of fireworks in that state when it advertised its wares for sale. "Fireworks aren't toys," Attorney General Preate announced in a statement. "They are explosive devices that injure an estimated 10,000 Americans each year. . . ." In Nevada, Assemblywoman Chowning pushed for legislation that would ban the sale of all but "Safe and Sane" fireworks statewide. Three years later, the New York state attorney general sued B.J. Alan for marketing fireworks illegally in that state by selling them to people who did not have a permit. In New York State, only localities, fair associations, and organizations authorized to put on a display were allowed to purchase fireworks.

In 1997, ten states still outlawed fireworks of any kind and 39 severely restricted their use. Only Hawaii had no state law regarding fireworks, although it did have local fireworks restrictions. Purchasers in B.J. Alan's home state of Ohio had to fill out a Fireworks Purchaser's Form from the State Fire Marshal, which granted them permission to buy fireworks, but required that they remove them from the state within 48 hours.

New Millennium: Increased Emphasis on Safety Accompanying Rise in Pyrotechnics Use

Debate continued to surround the sale and use of fireworks into the new millennium. Proponents of consumers' right to purchase pyrotechnics cited favorable safety statistics. According to the Consumer Products Safety Commission in Maryland in 2003, in 1993 there were a reported 12,500 fireworks-related injuries, while by 2003, that number had decreased to 9,300. During the same period of time, fireworks sales had increased from 87 million pounds of imported pyrotechnics in 1993 to 220 million pounds in 2003.

Legislators in Connecticut, reasoning that it was better to set safety standards than to outlaw the explosives that consumers would buy even if illegal, legalized the sale of non-aerial, non-exploding sparklers containing up to 3.5 ounces of pyrotechnic mixture to people 16 and older in 2000. In 2002, The National Council on Fireworks Safety, an industry-sponsored organization, set standards for the amount of explosive material in fireworks and mandated that fuses burn for at least three and no more than nine seconds.

B.J. Alan responded by emphasizing the safe use of fireworks. In 2001, it launched a company web site, Fireworks .com, which included an extensive safety section with a series of general "dos and don'ts" along with a step-by-step guide to safe fireworks use. The award-winning site also featured the company's merchandise catalog and a full virtual fireworks show that could be set for viewing over major cities throughout the United States.

The pyrotechnics industry experienced a continued upward trend in sales in 2002, boosted by the increase in number of states that allowed the purchase of consumer grade fireworks. B.J. Alan had its best year ever in 2002, with double-digit sales growth in stores open a year or longer. The company added five new showrooms and 100 seasonal locations to reach a total of around 40 showrooms in 11 states and 1,200 seasonal sales centers in 17 states. It employed 300 workers year round. In 2002, it landed its first national contract with consumer goods supplier Fleming Companies and began selling in Kmart and Rite Aid stores.

In 2003, B.J. Alan opened a new 75,000-square-foot fireworks warehouse in Wheatland, Pennsylvania, which was double the size of its Youngstown warehouse. Sales for 2003 reached 221 million pounds of fireworks. During the peak six weeks leading up to the 4th of July, B.J. Alan did 93 to 95 percent of its approximately $100 million in annual revenue, selling 25 million pounds of fireworks at its 41 stores in 12 states and 1,200 temporary sales locations in 17 states.

Yet turmoil surrounding the sale of fireworks continued. B.J. Alan, like other fireworks distributors, had a history of entering into fundraising alliances with nonprofit organizations that would sell their wares for a share of the profits. In California, in 2003, two stands operated by nonprofits were closed for not having proper permits and for selling B.J. Alan's fireworks to minors. In Pinellas County, Florida, a new county ordinance effectively put fireworks dealers out of business. The new rules required sellers to get a county permit before opening shop and to demand paperwork from buyers assuring use of the explosives for legal purposes, which in Florida meant only agricultural or industrial use.

Seven states banned fireworks by 2004, and federal law banned the retail sale of large reloadable mortar shells, cherry bombs, aerial bombs, M-80 salutes, and firecrackers with more than two grains of powder. Yet the popularity of fireworks throughout the United States showed no signs of abating—43 states permitted some level of fireworks sales—and B.J. Alan remained optimistic about its future and the future of its industry. With an office and representatives in Hunan, China, B.J. Alan was well prepared to meet increased sales with ever increasing firepower.

Principal Competitors

American Promotional Events; Fireworks Over America; TNT Fireworks.

Further Reading

Bonfatti, John F., ''The Fireworks Next Door; Just Over the State Line, a Pennsylvania Store Is Marketing All Kinds of Fireworks to New Yorkers,'' *Buffalo News*, June 16, 2002, p. C1.

Bounds, Gwendolyn, ''Fireworks Sales Takes Off with a Bang; Manufacturers Spend Entire Year Preparing for Fourth of July,'' *Chicago Sun Times*, July 1, 2004, p. 18.

——, ''Preparing for the Big Bang; For a Fireworks Company, Gearing Up for July 4th Takes 11 Months of Effort,'' *Wall Street Journal*, June 29, 2004, p. B 1.

Collier, Gene, ''Oh, Say, Can You See the Fireworks Loophole: Buy 'Em in Ohio and Ignite Rockets' Red Glare in Another State Where They're Illegal,'' *Pittsburgh Post Gazette*, July 4, 1997, p. A1.

Eksten, Bonnie, ''Exploding Profits; Fireworks Business Is Like Any Other, Except Product Should Go Up in Smoke,'' *Star News*, July 4, 2004, p. 1 E.

Holtz, Jeff, ''Red, White, Blue (and Profitable),'' *New York Times*, June 29, 2003, p. 14.

Shilling, Don, ''Youngstown, Ohio, Fireworks Distributor to Open Warehouse in Wheatland, Pennsylvania,'' *Knight Ridder Tribune Business News*, March 10, 2003, p. 1.

——, ''Youngstown, Ohio, Sparkler Manufacturer Wins $1.6 Million from Tariffs,'' *Vindicator*, December 14, 2001, p. B1.

—Carrie Rothburd

Benetton Group S.p.A.

Villa Minelli
Ponzano Veneto
I-31050 TV
Italy
Telephone: +39 0422 519111
Fax: +39 0422 519930
Web site: http://www.benetton.it

Public Company
Incorporated: 1965 as Maglificio di Ponzano Veneto dei
    Fratelli Benetton
Employees: 6,949
Sales: $2.33 billion (2003)
Stock Exchanges: Borsa Italiana New York Frankfurt
    Bolsa de Madrid Toronto London
Ticker Symbol: BNG
NAIC: 315999 Other Apparel Accessories and Other
    Apparel Manufacturing; 315191 Outerwear Knitting
    Mills; 315228 Men's and Boys' Cut and Sew Other
    Outerwear Manufacturing; 339920 Sporting and
    Athletic Good Manufacturing; 423910 Sporting and
    Recreational Goods and Supplies Merchant
    Wholesalers; 424320 Men's and Boys' Clothing and
    Furnishings Merchant Wholesalers; 448140 Family
    Clothing Stores

Benetton Group S.p.A. has toned down its controversial advertising campaigns as it seeks to restore its momentum in the 2000s. Formerly one of the world's fastest-growing fashion chains, Benetton is now playing catch-up to H&M, Zara, The Gap, and others that emerged as challengers during the late 1990s. Nonetheless, Benetton remains one of the world's largest and most well-known clothing empires, operating more than 5,000 stores in 120 countries. Benetton markets its clothing under several brand names, including flagship brand United Colors of Benetton. The company has struck back at its edgier competitors with the launch of the fashion-oriented Sisley brand, and has entered the sportswear sector with Playlife, launched in 1998. In 2003, Benetton completed its exit from an ill-fated diversification into the sporting goods sector. The Benetton family also has stepped back from active management of the company, turning over its operations to CEO Silvano Cassano, appointed in 2003.

Family Partnership in the 1960s

Luciano and Giuliana Benetton, the founders of the Benetton Group, came from humble origins. The Benetton family grew up poor; their father, who owned a car and bicycle rental business, died while they were children. But Giuliana Benetton developed a skill that would make her family rich. At age five, she fell in love with knitting. In her early teens, Giuliana worked during the day in a tiny knitting business, producing scratchy, somber-colored woolen sweaters. At night, she used a borrowed knitting machine to make her own brightly colored designs. Her brother Luciano, who was then 20 and had worked as a men's clothing salesman in Treviso, realized his 17-year-old sister's talent. The two siblings sold their bicycle and accordion and scraped together enough cash to buy their first secondhand knitting machine in 1955. Then Luciano sold a small collection of Giuliana's knitted creations to local Veneto area stores. The enthusiastic reception of her designs gave the company a solid start.

In the early 1960s, the "Brothers of the Rainbow" invested about $2,000 to buy another secondhand hosiery knitting machine, which Luciano converted to make sweaters and jersey materials, and to build a small factory in Ponzano, a few miles from Treviso. Then in 1965, the Benetton company was formed as a partnership, called Maglificio di Ponzano Veneto dei Fratelli Benetton, with Luciano as chairman, his brother Gilberto in charge of administration, their younger brother Carlo running production, and Giuliana as chief designer.

To compete in the casual clothing market, which is marked by its competitive and volatile nature, the small company's designs needed to be creative but so did its management. The company flourished by making "industrial fashion," fashionable apparel made and sold through flexible, cost-effective retailing and production systems.

To attract attention to their sweaters, Luciano decided to sell directly to the consumer through specialized knitwear shops

---

Company Perspectives:

Today the Benetton Group is present in 120 countries around the world. Its core business is clothing: a group with a strong Italian character whose style, design expertise and passion are clearly seen in the United Colors of Benetton and the more fashion-oriented Sisley brands, and in sportswear brands Playlife and Killer Loop. The Group produces over 110 million garments every year, over 90% in Europe.

rather than to retail outlets that sold competing products. This decision formed the basis for the Benetton retail outlets, which sell the Benetton line exclusively; the first such store was opened in 1968 in Belluno in the Italian Alps. The following year, the company opened its first shop in Paris. Luciano thought that it would be a challenge to bring Italian fashion to the sophisticated Paris market, but if Benetton was successful there, Benetton could make it anywhere.

Production at the company was also unique. In 1972 Luciano introduced a time- and money-saving production technique. By dyeing assembled garments made of unbleached wool rather than batches of yarn before knitting, manufacturing time was trimmed and Benetton could produce garments upon demand, which minimized the need to maintain an extensive inventory.

To produce many sweaters at reduced cost and financial risk, Benetton took advantage of an old Italian cottage industry. Benetton farmed out labor-intensive production—knitting and sewing—to small, family-owned companies (many owned in whole, or part, by Benetton management) throughout northeast Italy. Employing advanced technology, these companies allowed Benetton to manufacture in response to increased market demand both domestically and abroad with reduced financial risk. About 80 percent of production was farmed out to 450 subcontractors who employed about 20,000 workers in the Veneto region. The remaining 20 percent of value-added, capital-intensive production—quality control and cutting and dyeing—was performed in house. By 1983 Benetton payments for contract work equaled nearly six times the labor expense for work performed in its factories, according to the Harvard School of Business.

Benetton's early success is attributable as much to Luciano's genius, as to the Italian and local business climate, however. According to journalist Dante Ferrari of the Italian business daily *Il Sole-24 Ore,* Benetton's management style evolved from the heritage of the Veneto region, which offered a strong artisan tradition, an abundance of labor created from shrinking agricultural production, and hydraulic energy provided by many rivers and springs. During the years 1971 to 1981, despite weak governments and rampant inflation, highly productive, technologically advanced small-to-medium businesses in Italy outpaced those of the other European Community (EC) partners. By 1977 Italy had become the largest producer of knitted overwear in Europe, producing 60 percent of all EC output.

Foreign Expansion in the 1970s

In 1978 Benetton became a limited liability company. Sales, which included T-shirts and denim jeans, reached $78 million,

98 percent of which came from the domestic market. With 1,000 stores in Italy alone, Benetton realized that the home market was saturated, and launched a major export campaign. Benetton targeted the rest of Europe and made plans to enter U.S. and Japanese markets. In 1979 the first store was opened in North America. By 1981, Benetton, operating under the name Invep S.p.A., had become the world leader in the field of knitwear, generating three times the sales volume of the next largest manufacturer. By 1982, with 1,900 shops in Europe (1,165 of which were in Italy), Benetton was opening stores at the rate of one each working day. To handle its expansion, Benetton invested in distribution and marketing operations, building a $30 million computerized state-of-the-art warehouse, which made it possible for a staff of seven to handle more than 30,000 incoming and outgoing boxes in a 16-hour work day in 1983.

Having grown to a mature multinational company, Benetton needed expert managerial direction. Aldo Palmieri, from the Bank of Italy, became Benetton's first managing director in 1982, and brought the company into an era of wide expansion, globalizing its capital base. Although Luciano Benetton was not initially receptive, leading Palmieri to leave in 1990, the company eventually adopted Palmieri's vision after he had been rehired in 1992.

In 1984, 55 percent of Benetton's $303 million in sales was generated from foreign turnover, outperforming domestic sales for the first time. The United States became Benetton's fastest growing market by early 1985, boosting sales by 35 percent. Retail operations also were opened in Eastern Europe—Budapest in March and Prague in September—marking the opening of the first shop by a Western manufacturer since 1948. Following a corporate reorganization in December 1985, the company was renamed Benetton Group S.p.A. It was now one of the world's largest garment producers, with four factories in Italy and one each in France, Spain, Scotland, and North Carolina, and an annual production growth rate of about 30 percent.

In July 1986, Benetton made its first public offering on the Milan and Venice Stock Exchanges, and the listing was subsequently extended to the Rome and Turin Stock Exchanges. Through an innovative corporate finance deal, Benetton sold 20 percent of its equity on the London and Frankfurt capital markets, raising about $500 million, of which some $100 million was earmarked for research and development over the next three years.

In early 1987, Palmieri approached the international capital market, focusing on the United States, and also began to finance acquisitions and joint ventures. In March, he raised an international syndicated loan with Citibank and authorized Morgan Guaranty Trust to place in behalf of Benetton Group S.p.A. eight to nine million American Depository Receipts—worth about $150 million—on the New York Stock Exchange. This was the first time that an Italian company had attempted to float stock directly on Wall Street. In addition, Benetton formed Benetton U.S.A. Corporation, listed on the Toronto, Madrid, Tokyo, and Frankfurt exchanges, and made private placements in Europe and Japan. These moves were aimed not only at eliminating short-term debt but also at broadening the shareholder base between Italian and international investors, as Benetton attempted to expand in North America and the Far East,

Key Dates:

1955: Giuliana and Luciano Benetton buy their first knitting machine and begin selling Giuliana's woolen sweaters.

1965: The Benetton family forms a partnership, Maglificio di Ponzano Veneto dei Fratelli Benetton.

1972: The company introduces a new dyeing technique that enables on-demand production.

1978: The company incorporates as a limited liability company, Invep S.p.A.

1979: The company begins international expansion with its first stores in North America and Europe.

1983: The company builds a state-of-the-art warehouse.

1985: The company is renamed as Benetton S.p.A.

1986: Benetton is listed on the Borsa Italiana.

1989: The Benetton family acquires Nordica as the first part of its entry into the sporting goods sector under Benetton Sportsystem; the company's first controversial United Colors of Benetton advertising campaign is launched.

1993: The company opens a state-of-the-art production facility in Castrette, Italy.

1997: Benetton buys the money-losing Benetton Sportsystem.

2001: The company begins selling off its sporting goods holdings; the Sisley youth-oriented brand is launched.

2003: The company completes the sell-off of sporting goods divisions; the company announces a $526 million spending effort to produce higher-quality goods and adds accessories, cosmetics, and home furnishings under the Benetton brand.

and instilling the discipline required by the U.S. Securities and Stock Exchange into its corporate culture.

Diversification in the 1980s

Because financial services were poor in Italy, Benetton began lending to its suppliers. By 1986 this informal business grew to $400 million in leasing and factoring. Bencom S.p.A. was incorporated as a subsidiary in 1987 to undertake leasing activities, and a financial services company was formed. Like the retail line, financial services were structured with the Benetton management philosophy—independent entrepreneurs selling and receiving commissions. The financial services evolved to include insurance products and personal and corporate financial services. Other nonretail interests included stakes in Italy's largest department store chains, banks, hotels, and real estate. Unfortunately, these ventures required heavy capital investments and took away concentration of management time from the retail sector. Nevertheless, Benetton's retail line was expanded.

Palmieri pushed Benetton to extend the retail product line and introduce a nonretail line, to shift to global manufacturing, and to find local partners able to penetrate difficult or emerging markets in the developing world. The company introduced a new watch and cosmetic line, incorporated Benetton Japan K.K. to penetrate the Japanese and potential Far East market, and

signed licensing agreements to produce clothing in the Middle East and Far East through Benetton International N.V. Benetton Group sales rose to $2.5 billion in 1987, an increase of about 15 percent over 1986 figures. At that time, there were about 5,000 shops in 70 countries; the EC accounted for 68 percent of sales, North America for 20 percent, and the Far East for 2 percent.

In 1988, after years of double-digit profit growth, Benetton's attempts to diversify faltered with consolidated net income flat at about $99.5 million and stock at about half its initial offering price. Sales stalled in Italy. In the United States, which accounted for about 15 percent of total sales, revenue fell 20 percent. The slowdown was due to a weak dollar, rising apparel prices, saturated markets, the rising cost of Italian labor, and shifting tastes, especially in the United States.

Moreover, in late 1988, several Benetton store owners filed suit in the United States against Benetton's agents, alleging unfair trade practices and also complaining about the disorganization of U.S. operations and the Benetton Group's practice of clustering stores, which was intended to promote competition among store owners. Benetton countersued two former store owners for alleged defamation. Conceding that these problems were brought about by rapid expansion (250 shops in 1983 to 758 shops in 1988) in North America, Benetton brought in former McKinsey & Co. consultant Federico Minoli to head Benetton U.S.A. Corporation as an autonomous entity and to improve relations with store owners.

Although Benetton spent three years expanding into financial services, reaching the $300 million mark, in 1988 it sold its merchant banking interests and refocused on its retail line. Benetton acquired interests in four apparel-related manufacturing companies: Calzaturificio di Varese S.p.A., a shoe manufacturer and distributor; Galli Filati S.p.A., a producer of woolen yarn; and Columbia S.p.A. and Altana Uno S.p.A., both licensed to produce and market under the Benetton trademark. To integrate group logistics, Benetton also acquired Azimut S.p.A., Benair S.p.A., and Benlog S.p.A. To enhance global production and marketing, Benetton built a factory in Argentina to add to facilities built the year before in Brazil; acquired, incorporated, or sold marketing companies in various countries; opened stores in Warsaw, Moscow, and Cairo; listed on the New York and Toronto Stock Exchanges; planned to expand Benetton Cosmetics, which had operated in North America and Europe for the last three years, into the Japanese and South American markets; and entered into a joint venture with the Japanese trading company Marubeni, creating Benetton Shoes Corporation, to sell shoes in the United States and Canada. Negotiations also were made with Toyobo on joint plans to enter both the Japanese and Brazilian markets, and with Seibu-Saison to convert its license to a production and marketing joint venture.

These developments were representative of Benetton's strategy to first use licensees to gain wide exposure in new markets and then to convert the license into production and marketing joint ventures. Accordingly, growth also was accelerated by granting licenses to producers in noncompeting industries. The Home Colors trademark was developed by acquiring an interest in Eliolona S.p.A., which was to produce linens under license agreements in Brazil and Israel and to sell them in European markets. A new joint venture called United Optical was formed between H.J.

Heinz and the Italian manufacturer Anser to produce spectacles. Furthermore, W.I.D.E. Corporation was incorporated in the United States as a joint venture with Avendero S.p.A. to manage international forwarding and customs clearance operations.

By 1989 exports rose to 65.5 percent of total annual sales. To finance this expansion, Benetton aimed to attract investors in the United States, Canada, Japan, and Europe by making a capital issue of 24 million shares. In that year, Benetton's holding company, Edizione Holding, reinvested its funds from the sale of financial services by buying Nordica, a ski equipment firm, for $150 million and soon acquired several other retail sports lines. Moreover, the trademark United Colors of Benetton was adopted. In the meantime, the Federal Trade Commission conducted a preliminary investigation to determine whether Benetton had violated federal statutes by failing to file as a franchiser but dropped the inquiry after Benetton asserted that contracts are negotiated by independent sales agents and that store owners pay no fees or royalties, even though they are required to follow stringent merchandising rules.

In the late 1980s, Benetton gained additional competitive advantage by implementing global networking to connect sales and production. A point-of-sale computerized program, which linked the shops to headquarters, was designed to handle order management, cost accounting, production control, and distribution support. Thus agents began booking 80 percent of each seasonal order six months in advance; the remaining orders were placed midseason and relayed to headquarters by computer. The point-of-sale program was replaced by late 1989, and Benetton's decentralized operations were linked by a global electronic data interchange network, which also included freight forwarding and customs applications.

Although sales grew by 24 percent in 1990, Benetton lost $6.6 million in the United States that year, and another $10 million in 1991, a loss of 28 percent since 1987. Thus in 1991 Benetton started to consolidate its stores in the United States as well as Europe, replacing the clusters of smaller stores with the megastore concept, which carried the full Benetton line. In addition, Benetton turned its marketing and sales efforts once again to developing markets in the Near and Far East and to Eastern Europe, and halved its dividend to have more funds for expansion and acquisition. In December, Benetton signed a joint manufacturing agreement with Alexanian in Egypt in light of plans to open 30 stores in that country, and in 1992, 12 stores were opened in Poland. A joint venture agreement was signed for manufacturing facilities in Armenia, which was to produce apparel for the Soviet market under the United Colors of Benetton trademark; future expansion plans came to a halt, however, owing to lagging productivity at this plant.

To beat the worldwide recession and increase market share, in 1992 Benetton developed strategies to achieve the following goals: to improve operating margins, reducing prices by about 15 percent, increasing production volume, improving product mix, and taking advantage of the devaluation of the lira; to improve operating efficiency, reducing number of styles of its collection from 4,000 to 2,600, and acquiring and integrating the operations of four key former subcontractors; and to improve cash flows, refinancing short- and medium-term debt. The mix of items was improved by introducing sophisticated classic professional apparel through shops dedicated to these higher-margin product lines—*And* for dress shirts, Di Varese for shoes, and Benetton Uomo and Benetton Donna for mature men and women—and by continuing to expand into the sporting goods market. By mid-1992, Benetton bought the remaining interest in Galli Filati and consolidated interests in four suppliers of woolen and cotton materials; now about 68 percent of the cost of production was represented by charges from subcontractors, compared with 87 percent in 1991. As a result, 1992 group sales rose 10 percent.

Notoriety in the 1990s

By early 1993, Benetton had continued to close stores in the United States and, for production and marketing reasons, ceased operations at the Rocky Mountain plant in North Carolina. A technologically advanced factory opened at Castrette, Italy, which was designed to expand manufacturing capacity to 20 million pieces per year with about 15 people, using sophisticated robotic technology. Goods were now exported in greater numbers from Italy, where Benetton benefited from the abolition of the wage indexation system and the devaluation of the lira following its withdrawal from the exchange rate mechanism of the European Monetary System. At this point, Benetton had 32 factories, of which 27 were in Italy, and license agreements in 13 countries. In addition, Benetton decided to expand in developing countries, forming a joint venture with a major Indian manufacturer to produce linens and stationery, opening its 7,047th store, in Cuba, and transforming Benetton Mexico from a sales subsidiary to a manufacturing operation for the North American market. These developments, particularly the continued effort to rationalize production, resulted in Benetton's stock reaching a five-year high. Consolidated revenues increased in 1993 by about 10 percent compared with the previous year, and net income rose 39 percent since 1990.

Benetton's global advertising campaign succeeded in generating a mix of praise and criticism and, ultimately, a fair amount of free publicity since about 1989. The ads, which were initially product-oriented campaigns on themes of multinational and multiracial harmony, eventually focused on institutional-oriented campaigns that featured documentaries on AIDS, sexuality, the environment, interracial relationships, and the war in Bosnia-Herzegovina. Although many of the ads became the subject of controversy and were withdrawn or banned throughout the world, the United Colors of Benetton ad campaign, which hinged on racial diversity, won Benetton's art director Oliviero Toscani the UNESCO Grand Prix award.

Despite the ad controversy, Benetton managed to maintain a sterling corporate image during Italian government kickback investigations conducted in 1993 that involved more than 5,000 of the country's political and business elite. In fact, Luciano had gotten involved in national politics as part of a movement to overthrow the old system, and in 1992 was elected to the Italian Senate as a member of the Republican party. In 1994, however, Luciano retreated from politics, believing that the Italian government had met its objective, to devote himself to the family business.

In early 1994, Palmieri diversified Benetton by planning substantial acquisitions of either well-known brands or companies in the developing world. One such expansion was a joint venture agreement signed with Timex and Junghans Uhren to produce watches and alarm clocks. In addition, Palmieri planned to double turnover by 1996. To fund these ambitious plans, he placed 11 million shares in foreign markets. This issue was expected to raise the float from 20 to 30 percent, with the remaining stock controlled by the Benetton family.

New Start for the 2000s

In the mid-1990s, Benetton's efforts to crack the U.S. market appeared to run out of steam. While the company's clothing continued to attract European consumers, American shoppers turned away from the brand and its all too controversial advertising campaigns. The company's attempts to enter the Asian and Eastern European markets met with similar indifference on the part of consumers. In the meantime, the 1990s saw the rise of a new breed of trendy designer-retailers who soon were beating Benetton at its own game. Such names as H&M, Zara, The Gap, Diesel, and many others began drawing consumers from Benetton stores.

With its apparel sales in a slump, Benetton also faced a crunch from its effort to crack the sporting goods market. Since the late 1980s, the Benetton family's Edizione holding had been building up a portfolio of sporting goods companies, starting with its purchase of Nordica in 1989. By the late 1990s, the company had tennis manufacturer Prince, racquetball equipment maker Ektelon, the United States' Rollerblade, and others, including golf equipment from Langert, skis from Kastlë, and mountaineering boots from Asolo. These holdings were placed under a new unit, Benetton Sportsystem, which was then sold to Benetton S.p.A. between 1997 and 1998, for $300 million. Yet the sporting goods division never jelled with the company, and after years of posting losses, Benetton began selling off the sporting goods division. This process was completed in large part by 2003, with the sale of Nordica.

In the meantime, Benetton's problems with its clothing division deepened. The late 1990s saw the company attempt a massive licensing scheme, placing its brand name on items ranging from condoms to mineral water to wallpaper. As one consultant told *Forbes:* "That is not a good sign. It's usually an indication that a brand is over the hill."

Benetton's desperation to recapture its former glory was highlighted by a distribution agreement reached with staid U.S. department store group Sears, Roebuck and Co. in 1998. The hoped-for sales never materialized. Worse, Benetton's advertising campaign inspired only revulsion in the United States, when it launched its "We, On Death Row" campaign featuring prison inmates. The resulting controversy convinced Sears, Roebuck to pull out of its distribution agreement.

Benetton continued to struggle into the 2000s, with a lack of focus and little enthusiasm for its clothing designs. The company appointed a new CEO, Luigi de Puppi, who was replaced in 2003 by Silvano Cassano, a former Fiat executive. At the same time, the Benetton family announced that it planned to draw back from the day-to-day operation of the clothing company.

Cassano installed new management and led a revamp of the company's clothing designs and a redesign of its retail stores, with a focus on the group's 166 megastores. The company also launched a new brand, Sisley, featuring trendier, edgier youth fashions. By the end of 2003, as the company's sales continued to slip—back to $2.3 billion, Cassano announced plans to spend nearly $530 million on an effort to revitalize the company's retail offer. As part of that strategy, the company intended to introduce a new range of higher-quality goods, and diversification into cosmetics, accessories, and home furnishings. Benetton hoped to recapture the flair that had made it one of Italy's major fashion success stories.

Principal Subsidiaries

Benfin S.p.A.; Bencom S.p.A.; Galli Filati S.p.A.; Fabrica S.p.A.; Benetton Fashion S.p.A.; Benlong S.p.A.; Benetton Services Ltd. (U.K.); Benetton U.S.A. Corporation; Benetton Capital Investments N.V. (Netherlands); Benetton Holdings N.V. (Netherlands); Benetton International N.V. (Netherlands).

Principal Competitors

Industria de Diseno Textil S.A.; The Gap Inc.; Hennes & Mauritz AB; Vivarte; Gruppo Coin S.p.A.; Kiabi S.A.; La Redoute; Charles Vogele Holding AG; Peek und Cloppenburg KG; Somfy International S.A.; Cortefiel S.A.; Mango S.A.

Further Reading

Benetton, Luciano, with Andrea Lee, *Io e i miei fratelli: La storia del nostro successo,* Milan: Sperling and Kupfer Editori, 1990.

"Benetton to Sell Rollerblade," *WWD,* January 7, 2003, p. 16.

Camuffo, Arnaldo, and Giovanni Costa, "Strategic Human Resource Management—Italian Style," *Sloan Management Review,* Winter 1993, pp. 59–67.

Carlson, Scott, "Benetton Write-Offs Add Up to Loss," *Financial Post,* April 1, 2003.

Cento Bull, Anna, and Paul Corner, *From Peasant to Entrepreneur: The Survival of the Family Economy in Italy,* Oxford: Berg Publishers Limited, 1993.

Dapiran, Peter, "Benetton- -Global Logistics in Action," *International Journal of Physical Distribution and Logistics Management,* volume 22, number 6, 1992, pp. 7–11.

Edmondson, Gail, "Has Benetton Stopped Unraveling?," *Business Week,* June 30, 2003, p. 76.

Gallagher, Leigh, "About Face," *Forbes,* March 19, 2001, p. 178.

Harvard Business School, "Benetton S.p.A.: Industrial Fashion" (case study), Boston: HBS Services, 1987.

"How Benetton Has Streamlined and Branched Out Worldwide in Casual Clothing Market: Case Studies from Academia," *International Management,* May 1985, pp. 79–82.

Kaiser, Amanda, "Benetton Invests $526m to Expand Range of Product," *WWD,* December 10, 2003, p. 2.

Ketelhohn, Werner, "An Interview with Aldo Palmieri of Benetton: The Early Growth Years," *European Management Journal,* September 1993, pp. 321–31.

——, "An Interview with Aldo Palmieri of Benetton: The Return As CEO," *European Management Journal,* December 1993, pp. 481–84.

Lee, Andrea, "Profiles," *New Yorker,* November 1986, pp. 53–74.

Pepper, Curtis Bill, "Fast Forward," *Business Month,* February 1989, pp. 25–30.

Stillit, Daniel, "Benetton: Italy's Smart Operator," *Corporate Finance,* June 1993, pp. 30–39.

Vergani, Guido, "A Family Affair," *Harper's Bazaar,* December 2002, p. S16.

—Marina L. Rota
—update: M.L. Cohen

Enjoyment Matters

BenQ Corporation

157 San Ying Road, Kweisan Hsiang
Taoyuan 333
Taiwan
Telephone: +886 3 359 5000
Fax: +886 3 359 9000
Web site: http://www.benq.com

Public Company
Incorporated: 1984 as Continental Systems
Employees: 13,000
Sales: $3.75 billion (2003)
Stock Exchanges: Taiwan
Ticker Symbol: BenQ
NAIC: 334119 Other Computer Peripheral Equipment
   Manufacturing (pt)

Once the contract manufacturing arm of Taiwan's Acer Computer Corporation, BenQ Corporation has come into its own as a world-leading manufacturer of computer peripherals, digital media equipment, and mobile telephone and other networking and communications devices. BenQ produces LCD and CRT monitors, LCD televisions, digital projectors, and other display systems; CD-ROM, CD-RW, DVD-ROM, and DVD+RW drives, color laser printers, digital cameras, and scanners; and mobile telephones and wireless networking and communications equipment. Contract manufacturing continues to make up more than two-thirds of BenQ's revenues. Since splitting off from Acer in 2001, however, BenQ has begun a push to establish its own name—which comes from the slogan, ''Bringing Enjoyment and Quality to Life''—as a world-leading peripheral products brand. The effort seems to be paying off. In just four years, the company's sales have more than doubled, topping $3.75 billion in 2003. BenQ operates manufacturing facilities in Taiwan, China, Malaysia, and Mexico. The company's operations also include a network of affiliated companies, including AU Optronics; Daxon Technology; Darfon Electronics; Airoha Technology; Copax Photonics; Darly Venture; and BenQ Guru Software Co. BenQ is led by Kuen-Yao (K.Y.) Lee and is listed on the Taiwan Stock

Exchange. Acer remains a major shareholder, with 14 percent of the company's stock.

Acer Offshoot in the 1980s

Stan Shih and a group of university friends founded Multitech in 1976, becoming one of the pioneers of Taiwan's computer industry. Among the new company's earliest employees was Kuen-Yao Lee, a graduate from Taiwan's prestigious National Chiao Tung University who also held an M.B.A. from Lausanne University in Switzerland. Lee quickly became an important member of the fast-rising Multitech group. In 1984, when the company—which adopted the Acer brand name in 1986—formed a dedicated contract manufacturing subsidiary, Lee became head of the new subsidiary, originally known as Continental Systems.

Continental Systems at first began producing components such as power supplies and monitors for integrated engineering workstations and other computer systems, supplying both Multitech and the fast-growing OEM market. As such the company was part of a strong trend through the 1980s, which saw Taiwan become one of the world's most important centers for contract computer component manufacturing. After Multitech adopted the Acer trade name in 1986, the subsidiary became known as Acer Continental.

In the late 1980s, Acer Continental began to focus more strongly on the computer peripherals market—leaving the development of completed systems to its parent company. The subsidiary then changed its name to Acer Peripherals to underscore its commitment to the components market. The production of monitors then became one of the company's main markets, and by the early 1990s, Acer Peripherals emerged as a significant supplier to the global OEM computer market, supplying computer manufacturers such as IBM and others.

The early part of this phase, however, occurred without Lee. After being passed over for the CEO position at the Acer parent in 1989, Lee left the company to take a position in Lausanne instead. Meanwhile, Acer Peripherals continued to expand in the early 1990s, opening a manufacturing subsidiary in Malaysia, and a series of global sales offices, such as the Acer Periph-

Company Perspectives:

Corporate Vision: Combining Culture and Core Values.

While we have been refining the traditional technology sector to generate exceptional speed, flexibility, efficiency and enhancing our quality and channel connections, we have also been successfully building a BenQ culture that supports our vision.

Through our four core values we motivate our people, get closer to our customers, and build our future.

We Care: We want to have lifelong relationships with our customers, we seek to understand and meet their needs, care about our employees, and are concerned about our environment.

We Innovate: We create, build and market innovative solutions; constantly looking for new and innovative ways to work and new ways to spark new innovation.

We Uphold: Quality: We produce reliable products, but quality for us also encompasses the quality of the experience of using the product as part of a total solution that delivers lifestyle benefits.

We Celebrate: Enjoyment: We aim to bring enjoyment and pleasure to our customers as we celebrate the beauty we see in life.

What we have learned over the years is that the true strength of these core values is how they work together to help us bring enjoyment and quality to life. And we believe that our future success will increasingly depend on our ability to integrate not just at cultural and business-model levels but also with our customers as well.

erals Labs in the United States in 1992. In this way, Acer Peripherals was able to supply support for Acer's own global expansion effort, which saw the Taiwan company emerge as one of the world's top PC makers by mid-decade.

Acer Peripherals turned to mainland China in 1993, establishing a manufacturing facility in Suzhou in order to meet the rapidly rising demand for computer peripheral products. Among these were the first CD-ROM drives, which began appearing in the early part of the decade. By 1994, Acer Peripherals had succeeded in producing its first 2X CD-ROM drive. The development of this new technology, permitting the extension of the computer's multimedia capabilities, became one of the primary drivers behind the mid-decade personal computing boom worldwide.

Acer Peripherals further extended its product range in 1995, when it debuted the AcerScan 300C flatbed scanner, one of the first scanners made affordable as a consumer-level product. This launch coincided with Acer's own emergence as one of the world's top consumer PC brands. It also coincided with K.Y. Lee's return to Acer in 1995. Arriving back at the firm, Lee was placed in charge of the Acer Peripherals subsidiary.

As a mark of independence, and of Acer Peripherals' own importance not only as a supplier to Acer, but as a leading supplier to the OEM and contract manufacturing markets, Lee moved Acer Peripherals out of the parent company's headquar-

ters, and into its own—in Taoyuan, more than an hour's drive from its parent's headquarters.

Diversification in the 1990s

Lee now led Acer Peripherals on an ambitious drive to diversify its range of products and deepen its international penetration. One of the company's first moves was to set up Acer Display Technologies in 1996 in order to produce TFT-LCD panels for the rapidly growing LCD monitor market. Acer Peripherals also took a step toward independence that year, when it launched its stock on the Taiwan Stock Exchange.

By 1997, Acer Peripherals had succeeded in developing its first LCD-based computer monitor. The company also extended its scanner technologies with the launch of its first sheet-fed scanner that year. Meanwhile, Acer Peripherals had spotted the potential of the market for mobile telephone handsets, and in 1997 the company debuted its first GSM 900-compatible cellular phone.

The company backed up its diversification effort with the 1998 opening of a new production plant in Suzhou, called the Acer Suzhou Technology Park. In that year, as well, Acer Peripherals debuted a number of important new products, such as its first CD-RW drive, its first digital projector, and its first dye-sub photo printer. The following year, the company added a new factory in Taoyuan, and a research and development center in Taipei. The company also expanded through acquisition, buying Bri-Link Technology Co. in 2000.

Acer's rise as a world-leading computer brand had by then brought the company into increasing conflict with the customers of its contract manufacturing business—most of which were direct competitors on the computer market. In response, Acer moved to refocus itself around its core computer business and transfer its contract manufacturing and peripherals businesses to independent companies. As such, Acer Peripherals was itself spun off as a separate company, Acer Communications & Multimedia, in 2000. Acer maintained a share of just 14 percent of its former subsidiary, and also remained one of its most important customers.

The new company, led by K.Y. Lee, now grouped many of Acer's former contract manufacturing specialists, including the Acer Display Technologies (ADT) unit and others. With his new freedom to guide the company, Lee set out to turn Acer Communications & Multimedia into a global computing giant in its own right. The company took a step in the right direction in 2001 when it engineered the merger of ADT with Unipac Optoelectronics, creating AU Optronics, the world's third largest maker of TFT-LDC panels.

Global Brand Leader in the 2000s

Lee's ambitions ran still higher, however. In 2002, the company decided to adopt a new corporate and brand name, BenQ, an acronym suggested by the company's new slogan: "Bringing Enjoyment and Quality to Life." The success of the BenQ brand was swift: the company's sales began to soar, climbing from $1.7 billion in 2000, to more than $3 billion by the end of 2002—and nearly $4 billion by the end of 2003.

Key Dates:

1976: Acer Computers is founded as Multitech.

1984: Computer OEM components and systems subsidiary, Continental Systems, is established.

1986: The company becomes Acer Continental.

1989: The company becomes Acer Peripherals and refocuses as a dedicated peripherals product business, producing computer monitors and the like.

1992: The company opens a production subsidiary in Malaysia; a sales and marketing subsidiary is opened in the United States.

1993: A manufacturing subsidiary is established in Suzhou, China.

1996: The company goes public as Acer Peripherals; the Acer Display Technologies unit is formed to produce TFT-LCD panels.

1997: The company debuts its first LCD monitor; the company enters the mobile telephone market.

1998: The company opens a new manufacturing facility, Acer Suzhou Techno Park.

2000: The company is spun off as a separate company, Acer Communications & Multimedia, grouping most of Acer's contract manufacturing businesses; Bri-Link Technology Co. is acquired.

2002: The company changes its name to BenQ, derived from the company slogan, "Bringing Enjoyment and Quality to Life," and begins a drive to establish itself as a global brand name in computer and electronic peripherals.

2003: A joint venture optical drives company is formed with Philips.

By then BenQ was one of the world's leading computer peripherals brands in certain segments, such as LCD monitors and optical drives and other products. The group's production and technology capacity was further enhanced by the formation of a joint venture with Dutch appliances giant Philips to produce digital store products, including CD-ROM, CD-RW, DVD-ROM, and DVD + RW drives, which were then marketed under the Philips, BenQ, or as OEM products for other brands.

Sales of BenQ's LCD monitors and televisions also took off in the early 2000s, and by 2004 the company had emerged as the world's number two-selling LCD monitor brand, trailing only Samsung of South Korea. The company also was quick to spot openings in new trends, such as the emergence of the so-called convergence of computing and home entertainment systems. In 2002, the company launched its first product to meet this fast-growing new category, the Joybook 8000 "multimedia hub." This product also marked the group's entry into the highly competitive notebook computing market.

By 2004, BenQ had become Taiwan's top-selling consumer electronics brand. BenQ also had become a prominent brand in markets such as Japan (where it was the leading seller of 17-inch monitors), China, and India. The company also was making strong headway in its drive to enter the North American and European markets. Europe was seen as holding special potential for the company, given the relatively small numbers of locally based brands there. Under K.Y. Lee's guidance, BenQ promised to fulfill its ambition to become a global brand leader in the new century.

Principal Subsidiaries

Airoha Technology Corporation; AU Optronics Corporation; BenQ Guru Software Company, Ltd.; Copax Photonics Corporation; Darfon Electronics Corporation; Darly Venture Incorporated; Daxon Technology, Inc.

Principal Competitors

Sony Corporation; IBM Corporation; Fujitsu Corporation; Toshiba Corporation; Samsung Corporation.

Further Reading

Del Nibletto, Paolo, "Who Is BenQ and Why Isn't It Acer?," *Computer Dealer News,* January 10, 2003, p. 1.

Einhorn, Bruce, "The Apple of the Island?," *Business Week,* August 9, 2004, p. 26.

Flannery, Russell, "Breakout of a Brand," *Forbes Global,* February 3, 2003, p. 18.

"No Joybook in Canada, Not Yet: Peripheral Vendor BenQ Trying Hard to Release First Notebook Ever in Canada," *Computer Dealer News,* May 7, 2004, p. 12.

Taylor, Paul, "Spin-Off Establishes Its Very Own Identity," *Financial Times,* March 17, 2004, p. 2.

"Watch Out Sony, Toshiba, Panasonic, Fujitsu! Here Comes BenQ," *Online Reporter,* March 15, 2003.

—M.L. Cohen

BERJAYA

Strength In Diversity

Berjaya Group Bhd.

11th Fl. Menara Berjaya, KL Plz.
Kuala Lumpur
50250
Malaysia
Telephone: +60 3 2935 8888
Fax: +60 3 2935 8043
Web site: http://www.berjaya.com.my

Public Company
Incorporated: 1990
Employees: 24,000
Sales: MYR 7.7 billion ($1.9 billion) (2003)
Stock Exchanges: Kuala Lumpur
NAIC: 551112 Offices of Other Holding Companies;
517212 Cellular and Other Wireless
Telecommunications; 622110 General Medical and
Surgical Hospitals; 713990 All Other Amusement and
Recreation Industries; 721110 Hotels (Except Casino
Hotels) and Motels

Berjaya Group Bhd. is a major Malaysian conglomerate with holdings ranging from lottery and casino operations; hotel, resort development, and time-share development and management; mobile telephone services, through its holding in DiGi, the country's third largest; food and beverages, notably through its McDonald's, Starbucks, Roasters, 7-Eleven, and other franchises; motor vehicle sales through its Hyundai-Berjaya joint venture; the distribution of consumer goods and brands, including Cosway, Singer, and others; and the manufacturing and distribution of air conditioning, refrigeration, and related systems through subsidiary Dunham-Bush Malaysia, among others. The company is also a major real estate developer in Malaysia—the company's most recently completed project is the massive Berjaya Times Square complex, which, at more than 675,000 square meters of retail, entertainment, and leisure space, is the largest in the Asia Pacific region. Like many Asian conglomerates, Berjaya reflects the work of a single person—in Berjaya's case, the company's fortunes have been developed by Tan Sri Dato' Seri Vincent Tan Chee, who transformed the

company from a tiny insurance agency to one of Malaysia's most powerful financial groups. In addition to his own dealings within the Berjaya Group, Tan also has a range of personal investments, such as his backing of Malaysia's second pay-TV service, MiTV, launched in October 2004. Berjaya Group is listed on the Kuala Lumpur Stock Exchange. In 2003, the company posted revenues of MYR 7.7 billion ($1.9 billion).

Deserving a Break in the 1980s

Vincent Tan left school at the age of 16 and began his career as a bank clerk. Yet Tan quickly displayed an ambitious nature, and by the end of the 1960s had launched a second career selling insurance in the evenings. Tan's ability as a salesman soon won him a job as an agency supervisor for American International Insurance when he was just 21 years old.

Toward the end of the 1970s, Tan decided to go into business on his own, founding what was to become one of Malaysia's—and the Asian Pacific region's—wealthiest business empires. Tan's initial business foray kept him close to the insurance industry. In the late 1970s, Tan set up a joint venture with Tokyo Marine & Fire Insurance.

Insurance proved only a means to an end, however. In 1981, Tan scored another noteworthy business victory when he won the franchise to bring McDonald's fast food restaurants into Malaysia. By mid-decade, Tan had emerged as one of the country's fastest-rising entrepreneurs. Part of Tan's success came through building a strong relationship with the government, particularly with longtime leader Mahathir Maohamad. Although this relationship raised questions at times, Tan acknowledged the importance of his link with Mahathir. As he told *Fortune:* "It's only prudent for a businessman to be friendly with the government of the day, but I'm not into politics and our companies are well run."

The next phase in the development of the future Berjaya business empire came in 1985, when Tan convinced the Malaysian government to privatize the state-run Sports Toto lottery and turn over its operation to Berjaya. The government agreed, and Berjaya bought up 70 percent of the lottery, which had been founded in 1969 in order to raise funds for sports programs and other cultural activities. Sports Toto was listed on the Kuala Lumpur Stock Exchange in 1987. In 1990, however, a restructuring of the lottery and gaming business gave Tan full control of that operation. Sports Toto was then placed into one of many Berjaya holding companies, Berjaya Land Berhad. At the same time, Tan and Berjaya were able to acquire a number of other Malaysian real estate and leisure activities. By the mid-1990s, Berjaya had emerged as a strong player in the country's hotel and resort vacation industry, with holdings including the Bukit Tinggi Resort complex.

During this time, Tan made use of the strong cash flow from Sports Toto to begin building a diversified, and ever changing, conglomerate. The company entered a wide variety of industries, with holdings ranging from manufacturing to advertising to distribution and restaurants. An example of this effort was the company acquisition of a 48 percent stake in the Singer Sewing Machine Company's (SSMC) Malaysian subsidiary, acquired in 1985. Berjaya, which did not wish to limit itself to the Asian Pacific region, next targeted SSMC itself, launching a takeover bid for the well-known U.S. company. Although that bid failed, Berjaya was able to gain majority control of the Singer Malaysia operations. That stake was later placed under the holding company Cosway, established in 1998 as Berjaya's manufacturing and distribution arm.

Malaysian Tycoon in the 1990s

Cosway became one of Berjaya's main operating subsidiaries. In addition to the Singer business, Cosway developed its own "network-marketing" sales model, based on a multilevel sales model similar to that of Tupperware, Avon, and others. The company became a major Malaysian distributor of cosmetics, toiletries, and fashion jewelry, among other products. Cosway also distributed durable consumer goods, and by the beginning of the 2000s had expanded to include the distribution of audiovisual products, both in the retail and rental markets, including films and children's educational products.

The Cosway holding was further expanded in 1992 with the purchase of the Unza Malaysia and Manufacturing Services Sendirian Berhard (MSSB), both manufacturers of personal care and household products, with a combined presence in more than 20 countries, including subsidiaries in Singapore, Indonesia, Vietnam, Hong Kong, and China, and manufacturing operations in China and Vietnam. These operations, expanded with the purchase of Unza International Limited in 2000, were then placed on the Kuala Lumpur Main Board in 2000. The following year, Unza acquired two more companies, Gervas Corporation Sdn. Bhd. and Formapac Sdn. Bhd., the latter a contract manufacturer for the former's line of personal care products.

Cosway also branched out its manufacturing side, acquiring Dunham-Bush Malaysia. Originally set up in 1984, Dunham-Bush specialized in the production of refrigeration and air conditioning equipment, marketed under brand names including Dunham-Bush, Anemostat, Polacel, Topaire, and DataAire. Dunham-Bush was taken public in 1994, although majority control rested firmly with Berjaya Group.

Meanwhile, Tan returned to the restaurant sector in the early 1990s. In 1993, Tan bought up the Roadhouse Grill restaurant concept, promoted by country singer Kenny Rogers, and began opening restaurants in the United States. That operation quickly spread, with company-owned restaurants in 11 states and franchise stores added in Brazil, Italy, and Malaysia. The company had similar success with the acquisition of the 7-Eleven convenience store franchise for the Malaysian market. By the 2000s, the company had opened nearly 220 7-Eleven stores in Malaysia.

By the mid-1990s, Tan had emerged as one of the most ambitious and most successful of Malaysia's growing class of business tycoons. In 1995, Tan launched a new project in order to highlight his and Berjaya's success in building a wide range of successful businesses. That project called for the construction of a massive shopping, entertainment, and leisure center, named Berjaya Times Square, in Kuala Lumpur.

Work began on the structure that year. The complex at completion was to include more than 900 stores, as well as an amusement park, hotel rooms, and other leisure and entertainment amenities. Covering more than 675,000 square meters, the complex became the largest in the Asian region, and one of the largest such sites in the world.

Progress on the complex was slowed by the Asian economic crisis of the late 1990s, and the corresponding property slump, which was then exacerbated by uncertainty following the September 11, 2001 terrorist attacks on the U.S. Nonetheless, Tan pushed through with the project—which originally remained a personal project and not included within the Berjaya Group's financial structure—and the doors opened at the Times Square Complex in October 2003.

Restructured for the New Century

Yet the difficult economic climate at the beginning of the 2000s, coupled with Berjaya's soaring debt levels, forced Tan to lead the company through an extensive restructuring effort. The restructuring essentially created a "new" Berjaya Group, transferring most of the former company's assets into the new vehicle. Investors in the "old" Berjaya were then given one share in the new company for every four shares they had previously held. Tan sweetened the deal by adding a number of his personal assets, such as part of the Times Square development.

Another key asset added to the Berjaya group was 24 percent of Tan's 33 percent of mobile telephone service operator DiGi. That company had originally been established as Mutiara Swisscom in 1995, and was the first in the country to offer a fully digital phone service. Joining Tan in setting up the company was partner Telenor, of Norway, which also took 33 percent of the company. Mutiara placed its stock on the Kuala Lumpur Stock Exchange in 1997, then changed its name to

Key Dates:

1981: Vincent Tan gains a franchise to open McDonald's restaurants in Malaysia.
1985: The Malaysian government privatizes Sports Toto, the state lottery, and sells 70 percent to Tan.
1990: Tan acquires full control of Sports Toto, and launches a new holding company, Berjaya Group.
1992: The company acquires Unza Malaysia and Manufacturing Services Sendirian Berhad (MSSB), establishing personal care products and other consumer products sales.
1993: The company acquires Roasters Grill Inc. in the United States.
1994: The company acquires Dunham-Bush, manufacturer of refrigeration and air conditioning systems.
1995: Tan launches construction of the Berjaya Times Square complex; the company joins in the launch of the Mutiara Swisscom mobile telephone service (later DiGi).
1998: The company acquires the Malaysian franchise for the Starbucks coffee shop operations.
2001: Berjaya restructures, and takes over 24 percent of DiGi
2003: Berjaya acquires the Hyundai concession in Malaysia.
2004: Berjaya acquires 70 percent of organic food stores Country Farms; Tan joins in the launch of MiTV pay-television service.

DiGi in 2000. By the dawn of the 21st century it had developed into Malaysia's third largest mobile phone operator, and number one in pre-paid services sales.

Tan and Berjaya continued to look for new expansion opportunities into the next decade. In 1998, the company expanded its restaurant offerings with the acquisition of the Malaysian license for the Starbucks coffee shop franchise. Through subsidiary Berjaya Coffee Company, Berjaya opened its first Starbucks in 1998 and had ten stores in operation by 2002. In October 2001, the company, through another of its holding companies, Matrix International, acquired Nature Avenue Sdn. Bhd., which operated the Special Cash Sweep Number Forecast Lotteries in Sarawak.

Berjaya entered the automotive market in 2003, buying up Hyundai-Berjaya Sdn. Bhd. That business provided oversight for a network of some 80 dealers selling Hyundai-branded cars and other vehicles in Malaysia. By 2004, however, Berjaya had begun reducing its stake in the Hyundai franchise. The company also sold off a number of other holdings, including the Unza Holdings group and another subsidiary, Taiga Forest Products Bhd.

Instead, Berjaya and Tan were looking in new directions. One of these came in September 2004, when the company bought a 70 percent stake in Country Farms Sdn. Bhd. That company operated two organic food stores in Malaysia. At the same time Tan continued to build on his personal holdings. In July 2004, Tan moved to acquire more than 28 percent of Informatics Holdings, in an effort to gain control of the educational products provider. That effort brought Tan head to head with another Malaysian business tycoon, Oie Hong Leong. Meanwhile, Tan had joined a group of investors preparing the launch of a pay-TV service, MiTV, in October 2004. Tan, and Berjaya, had become firm fixtures at the top of Malaysia's business community in the new century.

Principal Subsidiaries

Berjaya Land Berhad; Berjaya Capital Berhad; Berjaya Sports Toto Berhad; Cosway Corporation Berhad; Dunham-Bush (Malaysia) Bhd.; Matrix International Berhad; Hyundai-Berjaya Corporation.

Principal Competitors

CCL Industries Inc.; New World Development Company Limited; Sime Darby Berhad.

Further Reading

Ahmad, Baidura, "Another Feather in Berjaya's Cap," *New Straits Time,* October 2, 2003.
"Berjaya Incurs RM27.5m Q1 Loss," *Business Times (Malaysia),* October 1, 2004.
"Berjaya's Vincent Tan in Battle Royale for Informatics," *Bernama,* July 5, 2004.
"Berjaya Ventures into Food Distribution," *Business Times,* September 8, 2004.
Kraar, Louis, "Dedicated to Their Work," *Fortune,* Fall 1990, p. 81.
Ranawana, Arjuna, "Restructuring or Reshuffling?," *Asiaweek,* June 22, 2001.
"Tycoon to Launch Malaysia's Second Pay-TV Service in October," *Catcha News,* June 17, 2004.

—M.L. Cohen

BHP Billiton

180 Lonsdale Street
Melbourne 3000
Australia
Telephone: +61 396093333
Fax: +61 396093015
Web site: http://www.bhpbilliton.com

Public Company
Incorporated: 1885 as Broken Hill Proprietary
Employees: 38,000
Sales: $24.94 billion (2004)
Stock Exchanges: Australian London New York
Ticker Symbol: BHP
NAIC: 213112 Support Activities for Oil and Gas Field
    Exploration; 211111 Crude Petroleum and Natural
    Gas Extraction; 212111 Bituminous Coal and Lignite
    Surface Mining; 212210 Iron Ore Mining; 212299
    Other Metal Ore Mining; 212319 Other Crushed and
    Broken Stone Mining and Quarrying; 324110
    Petroleum Refineries; 331111 Iron and Steel Mills

BHP Billiton was formed through the 2001 merger of Australia's mining and oil giant BHP and U.K.-based mining group Billiton. The merger created the world's largest diversified resources company, with operations in 20 countries spanning the aluminum, coal, copper, ferro-alloys, iron ore, titanium, nickel, diamond, and silver mining sectors, as well as the oil, gas, and liquefied natural gas markets. BHP Billiton is leader or near-leader in nearly every market it covers. In 2004, BHP Billiton posted revenues of nearly $25 billion. The company's operations are segmented into seven major divisions: Petroleum, Aluminum, Base Metals, Carbon Steel Materials, Diamonds and Specialty Products, Energy Coal, and Stainless Steel Materials. Despite the merger, BHP and Billiton continue to operate as separate entities—in Australia as BHP Billiton Ltd., and in the United Kingdom as BHP Billiton PLC. The company is listed on the New York, Australian, and London Stock Exchanges.

Late 19th-Century Foundation

BHP owes its foundation to Charles Rasp, a boundary rider working in the early 1880s on the Mt. Gipps station near Silverton in New South Wales. As a boundary rider, Rasp patrolled the property, repairing fences and generally checking the property. The station was managed by George McCulloch. Rasp believed that a low broken-backed ridge on the property—the Broken Hill—contained argentiferous ores. He persuaded McCulloch and five others to form a syndicate for the purpose of testing the ridge. The first shaft sunk proved disappointing and some of the original syndicate members sold their shares, but the core members decided to raise the capital necessary for further investigation by floating a public company; they issued a prospectus in 1885 in the name of the Broken Hill Proprietary Company. Almost simultaneously, news arrived of a significant silver strike. BHP shares rose sharply in value once it was announced that the company's first consignment of 48 tons of ore had realized 35,605 ounces of silver, worth nearly £7,500.

None of the directors of the new company had been trained as mining engineers. BHP, therefore, imported the talents of two U.S. engineers, William Patton and Hermann Schlapp, whose technical work rescued the company's collapsing Big Mine at Broken Hill.

Easily accessible high-grade ores, low labor and equipment costs, and high silver and lead prices made the 15-year period to the end of the 19th century extremely profitable for BHP. The establishment of a head office in Melbourne and a lead refinery at Port Pirie were evidence of the company's increasing contribution to and investment in the states of Victoria and South Australia, but in New South Wales (NSW), around Broken Hill itself, the laissez-faire attitude of both BHP and the state government led to the growth of a primitive shanty town. The dangerous conditions in which the miners themselves had to work and the squalid circumstances in which their families had to live brought the Amalgamated Miners' Association (AMA) and other unions into conflict with BHP in 1889 and 1890. As a result of the 1892 slump in world silver and lead prices, BHP decided to scrap a work-practice agreement with the AMA and to prompt a showdown with a union movement it openly regarded with contempt. BHP led the other mining companies established at Broken Hill in the bitter and violent strike that ensued, declaring its intention of breaking free from union-imposed wage agreements by offering freedom of contract instead as the basis for future employment. After four months, with their leaders imprisoned, the unions capitulated and the workforce returned to the mines, with the exception of known strike leaders whom BHP refused to re-employ. A legacy of bitterness had been created between labor and management, which was to surface repeatedly to poison BHP's relations both with its own employees and with the Australian labor movement in general. The ambivalent attitude many Australians still retain toward their country's largest company arose from the 1892 strike and the many others that followed.

Early 20th-Century Expansion into Steel

In the first decade of the 20th century, BHP faced a decline in silver prices coupled with the mining-out of the accessible top-side ores that had been cheap to mine. Henceforth it had to work the deeper-lying sulfide ores, a more costly operation compounded by the greater difficulty of extracting silver from this type of ore.

Guillaume Delprat, a Dutch engineer and chemist whom BHP had brought to Australia from Europe, provided the solution to the problem of treating sulfide ores with his invention in 1902 of the flotation process. This method and later variants enabled BHP and other Broken Hill companies to extract silver, lead, and especially zinc from sulfide tailings, which had until then been deemed almost worthless. Delprat had become BHP's general manager in 1899 and under his careful but imaginative stewardship BHP's productivity rose steadily.

Delprat and BHP's directors insisted that an important factor in the company's success was the flexibility that the free contract system of employment allowed amid fluctuating and uncertain world metals markets. They were staunch believers in loyalty to the company, hard work, and self-help, and held that these virtues rather than socialism or unionism were the real allies of the Australian worker. The union movement disagreed with this analysis and in 1905 militants urged the NSW government not to renew BHP's leases at the Big Mine. Two years later BHP announced that it could no longer honor the remainder of its existing wage agreements on the grounds that plunging metals prices made these unworkable.

Early in 1909 the AMA launched a new strike. This time BHP stood alone, its intransigence and stubborn refusal to deal

with the union having alienated it from the other Broken Hill companies. The strike was marked throughout by exceptional violence and intimidation of scab labor brought in by BHP to work the mine. When Australia's Arbitration Court ruled against the company, the latter appealed to the High Court, unsuccessfully. BHP's response was to delay the opening of the mine and then reduce the number of workers employed.

Delprat and his fellow directors had already perceived that the Big Mine's days of economic productivity were numbered. Rather than buying new leases and opening new mines they decided that BHP's future lay in steel manufacture. At that time Australia possessed no steel industry and there was considerable skepticism both in Australia and abroad as to whether such an industry could be established successfully in a country far removed from the world's traditional steel markets and with no appreciable industrial base.

Delprat, however, was certain that a local steel producer could quickly capture a growing local market still dependent on costly imports from the United Kingdom and pointed to the advantages that Australia and BHP possessed—cheap energy in the form of large and accessible coal fields in NSW, and the company's own sizable and high-quality iron ore deposits at Iron Knob in South Australia. On the advice of a U.S. steel expert, David Baker, BHP chose Newcastle on the NSW coast as the site of its first steelworks due to the proximity of the coalfields and the presence of both labor and manufacturing industry in the area. Newcastle was also connected by rail to Sydney, Australia's largest city and manufacturing center.

BHP acted swiftly to forestall the setting up of a proposed state-owned steelworks. Baker designed the new plant along the latest U.S. lines, the whole project being financed out of an increase in share capital, two debenture issues, and the sale in 1915 of BHP's Port Pirie lead smelter to the Broken Hill Associated Smelters Company for £300,000. Steel production commenced in April 1915.

World War I Bringing Increased Demand, Labor Unrest

Wartime demand for armaments and sheet steel ensured production at full capacity and guaranteed the steel mill's early years. At Broken Hill, however, inflation during World War I worsened conditions, producing strikes in 1915, 1917, and 1919, the last of which was settled in the unions' favor, resulting in a new 35-hour work week and a rise in wage rates. By this time, however, BHP's energies were focused on its expanding steel business and the Big Mine played a progressively smaller role in the company's calculations, closing altogether in 1939 and thereby ending BHP's association with Broken Hill.

In 1921 Delprat was succeeded by Essington Lewis, a mining engineer who had joined BHP in the first decade of the century and risen swiftly in the corporate hierarchy. Lewis continued the policy of supporting the establishment of secondary manufacturers who would use BHP steel in their products, thus creating new customers for the company and new industries for Australia.

The short-lived postwar steel boom was followed by a scramble for shrinking world markets. BHP suffered several

Key Dates:

1885: Charles Rasp and George McCulloch form Broken Hill Proprietary Company (BHP).
1902: BHP begins extracting silver, lead, and zinc.
1915: BHP enters steel production.
1935: The company acquires Australian Iron & Steel Company.
1960: The company relaunches iron ore prospecting and mining operations.
1964: The company commissions the first oil well off the coast of Victoria.
1979: The company opens the Gregory coal mine.
1985: The company acquires 80 percent of Thiess Dampier Mitsui, operator of Moura and Kianga.
1984: The U.S. mining and construction group Utah Mines Ltd. is acquired from General Electric.
1986: Monsanto Oil is acquired.
1987: Hamilton Oil is acquired.
1988: Gulf Energy Development is acquired.
1995: Magma Copper Company is acquired.
1996: The White Pine refinery is acquired from Inmet Mining Corporation.
1999: New CEO Paul Anderson begins a companywide restructuring, cutting 20,000 jobs.
2001: BHP merges with the United Kingdom's Billiton, creating BHP-Billiton, the world's largest diversified resources group.
2003: The company begins a $5 billion investment program to boost oil operations.
2004: The company launches a $412 million expansion of the Hillside aluminum smelter in South Africa; the company announces interest in acquiring one of Australia's smaller oil producers.

handicaps in the race. The most serious of these was its having to serve a small home market with a diverse range of products, thereby failing to obtain the economies of scale achieved by its foreign competitors. In addition, freight costs for export had soared due to the postwar shortage of shipping, and rises in the price of coal were reducing BHP's margins.

Lewis campaigned for protection, and the William M. Hughes government eventually imposed import duties on imported steel. The 1920 seamen's strike convinced BHP that it had to control its own shipping. This belief led to the foundation of BHP's fleet of dedicated ore carriers.

Despite import duties, foreign steel was still managing to undersell the local product. BHP announced that it would have to shut down capacity unless the steel unions—chiefly the Federated Ironworkers Association (FIA)—were willing to accept wage reductions. This acceptance was not forthcoming and in May 1922 temporary closure of the Newcastle mill for a month was followed by a total shutdown lasting nine months until a ruling of the Arbitration Court compelled BHP to reopen it. Terrible hardship had been caused in the Newcastle area, and union leaders and elements in the Labour Party began to call for BHP's nationalization.

After this difficult start Lewis launched a program concentrating on improving the efficiency, safety, and cleanliness of the steel plant, all concepts closely linked in Lewis's mind and to which he attached the greatest importance. He placed particular emphasis on the replacement of old machinery, with the result that by the end of the 1920s BHP was operating one of the cleanest, safest, and most cost-effective steel plants in the world. Thus the Depression, which began in 1929 and devastated other Australian industries, left the steel industry comparatively unscathed.

Just as control of shipping was essential to reduce freight costs, so Lewis reasoned that ownership of coal would make BHP independent of the demands of the mine owners. BHP, therefore, began to buy up coal mines, a foretaste of the great expansion of its coal interests in the 1970s and 1980s.

Challenges and Opportunities During the Great Depression

Although BHP entered the Depression with an unusually small debt burden—Lewis disliked paying for new machinery with borrowed money—and an efficient steel operation, it was not immune from the effects. A collapse of world prices in steel, silver, and lead forced BHP to reduce production levels and lay off large numbers of mill workers. The Big Mine was shut down until a rise in metals prices made reopening worthwhile, and from 1930 until 1932 BHP did not pay dividends to its shareholders. The company viewed with distrust the economic policies of Scullin's Labour government, which it regarded as populist and shortsighted. This attitude was mollified when the government sought to stimulate local industry by imposing a new round of duties on imports, and devalued the Australian currency to encourage Australian exporters. These measures, in tandem with BHP's underlying financial strength and Lewis's policy of low-cost selling, ensured the company's survival.

In 1935 BHP's only competitor in Australia, the struggling Australian Iron & Steel Company (AIS), sought a merger with its larger rival. BHP was quick to agree and at a stroke acquired AIS's valuable steelworks at Port Kembla, NSW, and its iron ore deposits at Yampi Sound in Western Australia. BHP's opponents attacked the merger as monopolistic and called for an official enquiry. The issue became intensely political with two future Australian prime ministers, John Curtin and Robert Menzies, respectively, attacking and defending the merger.

Two years later the South Australian government asked BHP to construct a steel plant in the state. BHP, anxious to see its leases at Iron Knob extended, agreed to build a furnace and port at Whyalla on the Spencer Gulf. This and other investments in the years immediately prior to World War II were paid for by four major restructurings in the company's capital base.

In 1938 BHP became embroiled in another political battle when union labor refused to handle cargos of iron ore destined for Japan, at that time engaged in a brutal and aggressive war in China. BHP's insistence on carrying through its contractual obligations aroused strong emotions in Australia and Attorney General Robert Menzies's defense of BHP's action earned him the unflattering sobriquet of "pig-iron Bob."

In 1940 Menzies appointed Lewis Director General of Munitions with the responsibility of harnessing the nations' entire manufacturing industry to the war effort. Lewis applied to this demanding job all the energy and concentration that enabled BHP to achieve the new targets set by his wartime planning. New blast and open-hearth furnaces were built at Port Kembla and a shipyard was established at Whyalla. Comparatively far removed from the area of battle, BHP's mills suffered no physical damage during the war, but were subjected to brief and ineffectual shelling of Newcastle by a Japanese submarine. The company lost two of its ore carriers, however, to enemy torpedoes. Japan's frighteningly rapid advance into Southeast Asia up to Australia's not-so-distant neighbor, New Guinea, in 1942, served to quell union antagonism toward BHP. As this threat receded, the unions renewed their attacks, culminating in a protracted strike in late 1945, which began at Port Kembla and then drew in coal miners and seamen, rapidly assuming the proportions of a national crisis. Although the militant far Left in the unions failed to achieve its objective of BHP's nationalization and lost its influence during the strike, this episode had the effect of dampening BHP's plans for renewed investment in its steel business. Not until the end of the 1940s did this situation change, when a rising demand for steel encouraged increased production and investment.

In 1950 Lewis became chairman of BHP. Two years later he relinquished his position to Colin Syme, a lawyer who had joined BHP's board in 1937.

Return to Mining in Post-World War II Era

During the early 1950s Japan's resuscitated steel industry began to demonstrate its capacity for large-scale, low-cost production, which in the 1960s helped underwrite Japan's extraordinary economic growth. Once again the Japanese renewed their search abroad for low-cost iron ore reserves. The Australian government's lifting in 1960 of its prewar restrictions on the export of iron ore encouraged BHP to enter the field once again as a prospector. This entry led to the identification of large iron ore deposits, notably at Koolanyobbing, Western Australia, and Koolan Island, Western Australia. Quarries were commissioned at these two sites, but the centerpiece of BHP's iron ore business became the Mt. Newman ore body in the Pilbara region of Western Australia. In association with AMAX (American Metal Climax, Inc.) and CSR, the company established a joint venture operation to develop and operate the world's largest open-pit iron ore mine. BHP initially held a 30 percent interest but in 1985 bought out the remaining AMAX and CSR shareholdings.

During the early 1960s BHP transformed the nature of its business by deciding to enter the oil exploration and production industry. Australia's geology had tended to discourage oil prospecting but in 1960, true to its tradition of seeking expertise outside Australia, BHP asked the U.S. petroleum expert L.G. Weekes to examine some of its leases. Weekes advised BHP to drill offshore in the Bass Strait area. Despite the considerable technical difficulties involved, but encouraged by the subsidies of an Australian government keen to see the country's costly dependence on imported oil reduced, BHP went into a 50/50 partnership with Standard Oil's Australian subsidiary, Esso Standard. In 1964 the first well was commissioned in the Gippsland Basin area off the coast of Victoria. The extensive gas fields found as a corollary were developed for domestic use and export to Japan.

At about the same time, BHP began the development of a manganese mine at Groote Eylandte in the Gulf of Carpentaria.

As at Mt. Newman, this enterprise involved not only the commissioning of the mine itself but also the building of a whole township, transport links, and a port area.

A booming minerals and steel market enabled BHP to double its net profit between 1960 and 1970. Such rapid growth began to outdistance a management structure that had remained essentially unaltered since Essington Lewis's day. On the advice of a firm of U.S. management consultants, BHP adopted the concept of independent profit centers, each responsible for its own performance.

Loss of Many Government Protections in the 1970s

Such moves did not prevent BHP's critics from claiming that the company was still too large, too secretive, and above all too unaccountable to the Australian public for its decisions. Antimonopolists held that BHP's stranglehold on sales outlets prevented any rival steelmaker from setting up operations in Australia, while environmentalists questioned the company's record on industrial pollution. The unions attacked it for its strict adherence to the "minimum wage policy" laid down by the Arbitration Court, justified by BHP as a necessary measure in the light of competition from producers with lower labor costs, such as Japan and Taiwan.

The Labour Government elected in 1972 took several actions against BHP. Rex Connor, Minister for Minerals and Energy, attacked BHP for profiteering and proceeded to remove the subsidies BHP had been given for its oil exploration work. Tax concessions were canceled. Particularly irritating for the company were the decisions and comments of the Government's Prices Justification Tribunal before which BHP was required to defend its pricing policies.

In the middle of the decade BHP announced its decision to enter into a partnership with Shell to exploit the natural gas deposits found off the northern coast of Western Australia. Known as the North West Shelf Natural Gas Project, the justification for the huge investment needed lay in the interest shown by foreign energy consumers, especially the Japanese. Construction work began in 1981 and by 1984 the domestic gas phase of the project had been commissioned, followed by the launch of the export phase in 1989. Further offshore oil discoveries in the Timor Sea at Jabiru in the early 1980s launched another production program.

Aside from Australia's vast iron ore deposits, foreign industries looked toward the country's coal fields as a source of energy not subject to the vagaries of Middle Eastern power politics and price instability. The sharp rises in oil prices in 1973 and 1979 began to renew BHP's interest in coal and coal mining for export purposes. In 1976–77, BHP acquired Peabody Coal's Australian assets, thereby gaining a 60 percent interest in the Moura and Kianga coal mines in Queensland. In 1979 the huge Gregory mine was opened, followed a year later by the Saxonvale mine in NSW. In 1985 BHP increased its holding in Thiess Dampier Mitsui, operator of the Moura and Kianga mines, to more than 80 percent.

External Events Fostering Internal Change in the 1980s

The early 1980s brought two separate threats that effected widescale change at BHP. In 1982, the conglomerate was subjected to an unwelcome takeover raid by Robert Holmes a Court, who would plague BHP throughout most of the decade. Having accumulated 30 percent of the corporation's stock, Holmes a Court proposed a drastic restructuring. At the same time, BHP's steel business was struggling with rising production costs and falling world steel prices as overcapacity in world production undercut world steel prices. In the wake of the 1987 stock market crash, Holmes a Court sold his stake back to BHP. The deal also gave BHP a one-third stake in International Brewing Investments (IBI), including a one-third share of Foster's Brewing. Holmes a Court was successful in one regard, however, for his raid and the crisis of the global steel industry had forced BHP into a major rationalization. Under the direction of CEO Brian Loton and John Prescott, the head of the steel business, BHP invested AUD 22 billion in a decade-long restructuring.

The company reorganized into three main divisions: steel, minerals, and oil. In 1983 alone, nearly a third of the Steel Division's employees were made redundant. In an effort to safeguard the steel industry's future, the Labour Government of the day announced a five-year Steel Industry Plan under which the steel unions promised to refrain from industrial action in return for guarantees from BHP relating to security of employment for their members. Under the new dispensation BHP managed to transform itself from one of the world's most inefficient steelmakers into one of the few to achieve profitability in 1992. Productivity increased from only 150 tons per worker per annum in 1982 to some 250 tons in 1984. The five-year plan was widely regarded as a milestone in Australian industrial relations. By the end of the decade, BHP had three integrated steelworks in Australia with total steelmaking capacity of almost seven million tons per year. It also operated a range of downstream processing facilities in Australia, and steel forming and building products facilities in Asia and the West Coast of the United States.

In 1984 BHP bought the U.S. mining and construction company Utah Mines Ltd. from General Electric. This move extended BHP's interests abroad into the United States, Canada, and South America; greatly enlarged BHP's interests in coal and iron ore; and helped make it one of the world's top copper miners. The acquisition also gave it a controlling interest in Chile's Escondida copper mine, the third largest in the world. This mine's low production costs and large reserves base meant it was also competitively positioned. Another significant acquisition for BHP was a 30 percent interest in the OK Tedi gold and copper mine in Papua New Guinea, which began producing in 1984. In Australia during the 1980s BHP commissioned gold mines at Ora Banda and Boddington and a new lead and zinc mine at Cadjebut. BHP added to its iron ore interests in the Pilbara region of Australia through the purchase in 1990 of the remaining 70 percent of Mt. Goldsworthy Mining Associates it did not already own. It since sold a minority interest in Mt. Goldsworthy and a new iron ore mine named Yandi to its Japanese partners in the Mt. Newman joint venture. BHP Gold Mines Ltd. merged with Newmont Australia Ltd. in 1990. The merger created a major Australian gold company renamed Newcrest Mining Ltd. in which BHP had the largest single shareholding, 23 percent.

BHP invested AUD 5 billion in its oil division from 1987 to 1992. The major acquisitions of Monsanto Oil in 1986, Hamilton Oil in 1987, Gulf Energy Development in 1988, and of Pacific Resources Inc. in 1989 further increased BHP's strength in the fields of oil exploration and refining in the North Sea and Pacific Ocean. By 1992, it ranked tenth among the world's oil companies, and petroleum had become a significant contributor to overall profits, which totaled $900 million on revenues of $12 billion in 1992.

Merging Resources Giants in the 20th Century

Loton advanced to chairman in 1991, at which time John Prescott succeeded him as CEO. While remaining focused on BHP's core businesses, Prescott aimed to broaden the conglomerate's global reach. Acquisitions increased foreign properties from 28 percent of assets to more than 40 percent from 1991 to 1996. By the latter year, international operations generated 70 percent of annual revenues. But not all of these purchases actually improved BHP's bottom line. In 1995, for example, BHP acquired Magma Copper Company, the United States' largest copper smelter, for AUD 3.2 billion ($1.8 billion). At the time, copper prices were high and the deal was hailed as a major coup. But in 1996, an international trading scandal slashed copper prices by 30 percent. Other investments that lost money during this period included a Vietnamese oil field, the Foster's Brewing stake, and the Pacific Resources refinery in Hawaii. In fiscal 1997 (ended May 31), BHP was forced to write off AUD 1 billion on these and other investments, thereby reducing its net operating profits to AUD 410 million, down from a record AUD 1.6 billion in fiscal 1995. The company's stock dropped by more than 20 percent in the middle of 1996.

Observers inside as well as outside the conglomerate began to suggest that BHP's parts were worth more than the whole. In August 1997, the heads of BHP's minerals and petroleum divisions resigned. An article in that month's *Economist* magazine noted that the petroleum executive John J. O'Connor had favored a spinoff of his division—BHP's most profitable operation at the time—and quit when a deal was not forthcoming. The *Economist* seemed to concur with O'Connor when it surmised that "the big Australian might be better off smaller."

BHP's diversity remained one of its strong points, however. In his 1997 message to shareholders, CEO and Managing Director Prescott reasserted the company's dedication to diversity, noting, "We have six groups of businesses that we are confident will continue to perform strongly against our criteria. These include the oil and gas activities in Bass Strait and the North West Shelf (Australia), Escondida (Chile) copper mine, our various iron ore businesses and most of our coal and flat products steel activities. These are the businesses we know best, where we see our major comparative advantages and where we achieve great results." At the same time, BHP appeared poised to become a major player in the global markets for precious metals and gems. In 1997, it received permission from the Canadian government to begin mining a major trove of diamonds in that country's Northwest Territories. BHP expected to begin production at the site in 1998, and forecast annual output at four million carats by 1999. Also in Canada, the company acquired the White Pine refinery from Inmet Mining Corporation in 1996. The company also owned one of the world's most valuable gold mines, and was gleaning platinum from a site in Zimbabwe.

As it approached the dawn of the 21st century, however, BHP was described as "a dysfunctional family" by new CEO

Paul Anderson, an American appointed to restructure the group in 1999. Anderson launched BHP on a huge restructuring effort, trimming its number of divisions from eight to just four, and selling off some $2.2 billion in noncore and underperforming assets. The company also shed more than 20,000 employees. In 2000, the company continued its restructuring, launching a AUD 3 billion sell-off of noncore steel assets in the United States and Australia. The program included the sale of BHP Coated Steel Corp. and BHP Steel Building Products USA in 2000 to Mexico's IMSA Acero.

Yet Anderson's most significant change to BHP came in 2001—in that year, Anderson engineered the merger of BHP with U.K.-owned, South Africa-based Billiton. The resulting business became the world's largest "diversified resources" company, as it called itself, creating a new company, BHP Billiton. The former Billiton and BHP companies nonetheless continued to operate as separate companies, renamed BHP Billiton PLC, in the United Kingdom, and BHP Billiton Ltd. in Australia. For a time, the company also operated under two CEOs, Anderson and Billiton's Brian Gilbertson. Anderson stepped down in 2002, at which time Gilbertson became sole CEO of the entire operation. Gilbertson did not last long, however, resigning just six months later.

In the meantime, BHP Billiton continued seeking out growth areas. At the beginning of 2004, the company launched a new $412 million expansion of its Hillside aluminum smelter in South Africa, and announced its intention to continue its expansion in that sector in the near future. At the same time, BHP Billiton sought to enhance its standing in the international oil market—the company lingered at the bottom of the top 20 companies—earmarking some $5 billion between 2003 and 2006 for new developments in that sector. As part of that effort, the company paid $1.1 billion to acquire Atlantis, based in the Gulf of Mexico. In Australia, meanwhile, the company indicated its interest in acquiring one of the country's two smaller oil producers, Woodside and Santos, in an effort to boost its international status. As the world's largest resources company, BHP Billiton appeared to have struck a rich vein for the new century.

Principal Subsidiaries

Aquila Steel Company Pty. Ltd.; Associated Airlines Pty. Ltd. (55%); Australian Iron and Steel Pty. Ltd.; Australian Manganese Co. Ltd.; Australian Wire Industries Pty. Ltd.; AWI Holdings Pty. Ltd.; BHP Aerospace & Electronics Pty. Ltd.; BHP Capital No. 20 Pty. Ltd.; BHP Development Finance Pty. Ltd.; BHP Engineering International Pte. Ltd. (Singapore); BHP Engineering Malaysia Sdn. Bdn.; BHP Engineering Pty. Ltd.; BHP Finance Ltd.; BHP Finance (U.S.A.) Ltd.; BHP Finance Services Pty. Ltd.; BHP Financial Services (U.K.) Ltd.; BHP Holdings (U.S.A.) Inc.; BHP Information Technology Sdn. Bhd. (Malaysia); BHP International Holdings Ltd. (Hong Kong); BHP Investment Holdings Ltd. (U.K.); BHP Iron Ore Ltd.; BHP Japan Pty. Ltd.; BHP Marine & General Insurances Pty. Ltd.; BHP Minerals Holdings Pty. Ltd.; BHP Minerals Norway Pty. Ltd.; BHP Minerals Zimbabwe Pty. Ltd.; BHP Nominees Pty. Ltd.; BHP Papua New Guinea Pty. Ltd.; BHP Petroleum International Pty. Ltd.; BHP Rail Products (Canada) Ltd.; BHP Rail Products Pty. Ltd.; BHP Refractories Ltd.; BHP Steel (AIS) Pty. Ltd.; BHP Steel Building Products (Guangzhou) Ltd.

(China); BHP Steel Building Products (Shanghai) Ltd. (China); BHP Steel Building Products Vietnam Co. Ltd.; BHP Steel Canada Inc.; BHP Steel (JLA) Pty. Ltd.; BHP Stevedoring Pty. Ltd.; BHP Superannuation Investment Co. Pty. Ltd.; BHP Trading New Zealand Ltd.; BHP Transport Pty. Ltd.; Groote Eylandt Mining Company Pty. Ltd.; John Lysaght (Australia) Pty. Ltd.; Keithen Ltd.; NSW BHP Steel Ltd.; PT BHP Steel Indonesia (65%); Resources Insurances Pte. Ltd. (Singapore); Tasmanian Electro Metallurgical Company Pty. Ltd.; Tavela Ltd.; The World Marine & General Insurance PLC (U.K.); Bekaert-BHP Steel Cord Pty. Ltd. (50%); Elkem Mangan KS (Norway; 49%); Foster's Brewing Group Ltd. (36.6%); Koppers Australia Pty. Ltd. (50%); Orbital Engine Corporation Ltd. (25.1%); Samarco Mineracao S.A. (Brazil; 49%); Tubemakers of Australia Ltd. (49.4%).

Principal Divisions

BHP Copper; BHP Minerals; BHP Steel; BHP Petroleum; BHP Service Companies.

Principal Competitors

Dagang Petroleum Administration Bureau; Perusahaan Pertambangan Minyak and Gas Bumi Negara; Sinopec Shengli Oilfield Dynamic Group Company Ltd.; Komineft Joint Stock Co.; Da Qing Petroleum Administrative Bureau; Exxon Mobil Corporation; Eastern Oil Joint Stock Co.; Yamburggazdobycha Ltd.; Shell Transport and Trading Company PLC; Uzbekneftegaz State Holding Co; Petrom S.A; Fushun Coal Mine Bureau; Sonat Offshore S.A.

Further Reading

Aarons, Eric, *The Steel Octopus: The Story of BHP*, Sydney: Current Book Distributors, 1961.

Berman, Phyllis, "Magma-nificent Deal," *Forbes*, January 22, 1996, pp. 14–15.

"BHP Billiton Eyes Domestic Rivals," *International Petroleum Finance*, April 2003, p. 11.

BHP: 100 Years of Growing with Australia, Dubbo, N.S.W: Macquarie Publications, 1985.

"The Big Australian and the Tigers: Broken Hill Proprietary," *Economist*, July 8, 1995, pp. 60–61.

"The Big Australian Stumbles," *Economist*, September 28, 1996, p. 72.

Blainey, Geoffrey, *The Steel Master: A Life of Essington Lewis*, Carlton South, Victoria, Australia: Melbourne University Press, 1995.

Caney, Derek J., "BHP Deal with Magma Applauded by Industry," *American Metal Market*, December 4, 1995, p. 1.

"Corporate Carpentry: BHP," *Economist*, May 16, 1992, p. 88.

Dale, George, *The Industrial History of Broken Hill*, Melbourne: Fraser & Jenkinson, 1918.

The Fabulous Hill, Melbourne: Broken Hill Proprietary Company, 1961.

Fulford, Benjamin, "The Big Dig," *Forbes*, September 2, 2002, p. 88.

Haign, Gideon, *The Battle for BHP*, Melbourne: Information Australia with Allen & Unwin Australia, 1987.

Hoskins, Donald G., *The Ironmaster: The Life of Charles Hoskins, 1851–1926*, North Wollongong, N.S.W.: University of Wollongong Press, 1995.

How It All Began: BHP in Its 100th Year, Melbourne: BHP, 1985.

"Is There Life After Steel: Australia," *Economist*, June 21, 1997, p. 46.

Jacques, Bruce, "Minnows Swallowing Up the Whales," *Euromoney*, August 1986, pp. 132–36.

Jokiel, Lucy, "Striking It Big," *Hawaii Business,* April 1989, pp. 18–23.

Kriegler, Roy J., *Working for the Company,* Melbourne: Oxford University Press, 1980.

LaRue, Gloria T., "BHP Chief Executive Committed to Change," *American Metal Market,* October 14, 1996, p. 3.

Norman, James R., "Wake Up, Mate," *Forbes,* October 25, 1993, pp. 216–17.

Quinlan, Michael, *Monopoly Employer, The State and Industrial Conflict: Managerial Strategy in the Australian Steel Industry, 1945–1983,* Nathan, Qld.: Griffith University, School of Social and Industrial Administration, 1984.

Raggatt, H.G., *Mountains of Ore,* Melbourne: Lansdowne Press, 1968.

Sawer, Derek, *Australians in Company: BHP in Its 100th Year,* Melbourne: Broken Hill Proprietary Company Ltd., 1985.

"Sparkling: Diamond-Mining in Canada," *Economist,* January 25, 1997, pp. 59–60.

"Still Digging: BHP," *Economist,* August 16, 1997, p. 50.

Swindells, Steve, "BHPB Gears Up for Further Growth at S. Africa, Mozambique Smelters," *American Metal Market,* February 11, 2004, p. 5.

Trengrove, A., *"What's Good for Australia . . . !": A History of BHP,* Stanmore, N.S.W.: Cassell Australia, 1975.

"The Yank Who Pulled BHP Out of the Shaft," *Business Week,* January 8, 2001, p. 25.

—D.H. O'Leary
—updates: April Dougal Gasbarre, M.L. Cohen

The Black & Decker Corporation

701 East Joppa Road
Towson, Maryland 21286-5559
U.S.A.
Telephone: (410) 716-3900
Fax: (410) 716-2933
Web site: http://www.bdk.com

Public Company
Incorporated: 1910 as The Black & Decker
    Manufacturing Company
Employees: 22,100
Sales: $4.48 billion (2003)
Stock Exchanges: New York Pacific
Ticker Symbol: BDK
NAIC: 326191 Plastics Plumbing Fixture Manufacturing;
    332212 Hand and Edge Tool Manufacturing; 332213
    Saw Blade and Handsaw Manufacturing; 332510
    Hardware Manufacturing; 332913 Plumbing Fixture
    Fitting and Trim Manufacturing; 333112 Lawn and
    Garden Tractor and Home Lawn and Garden Equipment
    Manufacturing; 333319 Other Commercial and Service
    Industry Machinery Manufacturing; 333515 Cutting
    Tool and Machine Tool Accessory Manufacturing;
    333912 Air and Gas Compressor Manufacturing;
    333991 Power-Driven Handtool Manufacturing; 335129
    Other Lighting Equipment Manufacturing; 335212
    Household Vacuum Cleaner Manufacturing

The Black & Decker Corporation is the leading maker of
power tools and accessories in the United States—and is the
firm most responsible for the creation of the post-World War II
consumer market for power tools. The firm's key power tool
brands are Black & Decker and DeWalt. Black & Decker
(B&D) is also a leading producer of electric lawn and garden
tools, security hardware (locks and locksets under the Kwikset,
Baldwin, and Weiser brands), general and decorative hardware
products (Baldwin), plumbing products (Price Pfister), and specialty fastening and assembly systems (Emhart). B&D products

are sold in more than 100 countries and are manufactured at 36
plants, 18 in the United States and 18 abroad, located in Brazil,
China, the Czech Republic, Germany, Italy, Japan, Mexico, and
the United Kingdom.

Early History

Alonzo G. Decker and S. Duncan Black, two industrial tool
designers and engineers, formed The Black & Decker Manufacturing Company in September 1910. With $600 from the sale of
Black's second-hand car and a loan of $1,200, they set up a
machine shop in a rented warehouse in Baltimore, Maryland.
Black was the president of the company. In their first years the
partners contracted to manufacture industrial products invented
and sold by others, such as a milk bottle cap machine, a cotton
picker, candy dippers, and machinery for the U.S. Mint.

In 1916 Black and Decker began to design and manufacture
their own electric-powered tools. The German-made electric
tools then available were heavy and difficult to operate, and, as
a result, had not been commercially successful. Black and
Decker designed a universal motor—the first for electric-tool
use—which employed either alternating or direct current, and a
trigger switch modeled after the mechanism in the Colt re-
volver. The first tool incorporating these innovative elements
was a ½-inch portable drill with the innovative "pistol grip and
trigger switch" that have remained standard for electric drills
ever since. The drill was comparatively light at 21½ pounds,
and it was considered inexpensive at $230.

B&D grew consistently during the 1920s, as businesses
bought labor-saving devices to deal with rising labor costs. In
1917 the company was awarded patents for its pistol grip and
trigger switch and constructed a factory on the outskirts of
Towson, Maryland. By 1918 sales surpassed $1 million. Imme-
diately after World War I, more portable electric tools were
introduced, including a ⅜-inch drill, a grinder, and a screwdriver. To accommodate demand the Towson plant was expanded three times by 1927. A Towson headquarters building
was also constructed in 1924.

Black & Decker used aggressive salesmanship and product
services to build its client base. The company's first service

65

centers were opened in Boston and New York in 1918. B&D also organized clinics to teach distributors how to use and sell the tools; demonstrators toured the country in two buses. At the end of the 1920s the company even outfitted a monoplane to showcase its tools. In addition, the firm began its first mass-media campaign in the *Saturday Evening Post* in 1921.

With its initial success The Black & Decker Manufacturing Company expanded outside the United States, marking the beginning of its development into a global business. During the last year of World War I, burgeoning overseas sales led the company to establish representatives in Canada, Great Britain, the Soviet Union, Australia, and Japan. Canada was the site of B&D's first foreign subsidiary, started in 1922. Three years later a London sales and service subsidiary was formed. In 1928 the British company began manufacturing operations at a leased facility in Slough, outside London. The British company eventually built its own plant at Harmondsworth, Middlesex, in 1939. In 1929 an Australian subsidiary was established in Sydney. Until the 1950s the British subsidiary remained Black & Decker's only foreign manufacturing operation. It was the most important of B&D's many foreign operations after World War II.

In the latter half of the 1920s Black & Decker expanded its U.S. operations through several acquisitions. In 1926 the Marschke Manufacturing Company of Indianapolis, Indiana, a maker of grinders, was purchased. Two years later the Van Dorn Electric Tool Company of Cleveland, Ohio, was acquired. In 1929 B&D purchased the Fleming Machine Company of Worcester, Massachusetts, and the Domestic Electric Company of Cleveland. Fleming Machine made wire brushes, saws, and grinding stones, and Domestic Electric was a major producer of electric motors. In addition Black & Decker acquired the Loadometer Company, from which it previously had bought the rights to a portable truckweighing scale. Meantime, in 1927, the company's shares traded publicly for the first time in 1927; Black & Decker gained a listing on the New York Stock Exchange in 1936.

Like other businesses, The Black & Decker Manufacturing Company experienced great difficulties during the Great Depression. Despite huge layoffs, including Alonzo Decker's son, the company nearly went bankrupt. Employee loyalty—some workers continued to work although the company could not pay them—and a large influx of capital from outside investors kept Black & Decker afloat. The Marschke Manufacturing Company acquisition did not prove successful, and that company was sold in 1932. Black & Decker continued to develop new products. In 1930 and 1931 the firm marketed a portable circular saw, an adjustable-clutch electric screwdriver, and a new, streamlined housing for its drills. A line of power tools using the new

induction motors, the High Cycle line, was introduced in 1935. As the decade ended there was a cascade of new B&D products, including an electric hammer, an industrial vacuum cleaner, a portable metal cutter, a portable trim saw, and the Shorty series of drills.

Successful Marketing to Postwar Consumers

When the United States entered World War II Black & Decker switched to the production of fuses, shells, and other products to contribute to the war effort. Alonzo Decker and S. Duncan Black were determined to avoid the problems that had followed World War I. They believed that the key would be postwar consumers. Although the company had developed an inexpensive ½-inch drill in 1923, and introduced the Cinderella washing machine in 1930, its forays into the consumer market had not been successful. In 1942 the Black & Decker Post-War Planning Committee was established. This group developed plans for Black & Decker to manufacture power tools for do-it-yourselfers and homeowners. The committee believed B&D could provide cheaper tools using new, less-expensive plastic housings to tap this unexplored market.

In 1946 The Black & Decker Manufacturing Company introduced the world's first power tools for the consumer market, the inexpensive Home Utility line of ¼-inch and ½-inch drills and accessories. In the first five years, one million ¼-inch drills were produced. This success led to the addition of other products to the Home Utility line. A set of circular saws was introduced in 1949, and a finishing sander and jigsaw in 1953. Black & Decker also continued to market new tools for professional users, including an impact socket wrench introduced in 1949 and two heavy-duty routers introduced in 1957. As a result of great demand, the company began construction of a large new plant in Hampstead, Maryland, in 1951; by 1955 this facility had been expanded to more than four times its original size. The old Towson plant ceased production in 1965, although the site remained Black & Decker's headquarters.

In the 1950s and 1960s B&D resumed the overseas expansion begun in the 1920s. Manufacturing operations were organized in Australia and South Africa in 1956. During the 1960s production facilities were built or acquired in West Germany, France, Italy, Spain, Canada, and Mexico. In addition, sales and service subsidiaries were established in many other countries. The U.K. subsidiary successfully expanded into other European markets, and, as a result, a new plant was built at Maidenhead in 1962. Three years later this factory was expanded, and another plant was opened in Spennymoor, Durham. By 1969, 43 percent of B&D's sales and earnings came from its foreign operations.

Despite personnel changes, The Black & Decker Manufacturing Company remained under the leadership of the Black and Decker families during the 1950s and 1960s. In 1951 president and cofounder S. Duncan Black died at age 67. Black was succeeded as president by his partner, Alonzo G. Decker, who also took on the new post of chairman in 1954. Two years later, however, Decker died at age 72. Robert D. Black, S. Duncan Black's brother, succeeded Decker. In 1960 Decker's son, Alonzo G. Decker, Jr., was named president. The 54-year-old Alonzo Decker, Jr., had started at B&D as a floor sweeper in the early 1920s. In 1964 he replaced Black as chief executive officer.

Key Dates:

1910: Alonzo G. Decker and S. Duncan Black form The Black & Decker Manufacturing Company, based in Baltimore, Maryland, and begin making industrial products invented and sold by others.

1916: Company begins designing and manufacturing their own electric-powered tools, including a ½-inch portable drill.

1917: First manufacturing plant is built in Towson, Maryland.

1922: First foreign subsidiary is established in Canada.

1924: Headquarters are shifted to Towson.

1927: Black & Decker's shares begin trading publicly.

1936: Company shares are listed on the New York Stock Exchange.

1946: Company introduces the world's first power tools for the consumer market.

1960: DeWalt of Lancaster, Pennsylvania, is acquired.

1975: Francis P. Lucier is named CEO, ending the founding families' executive control of the company.

1978: Dustbuster cordless vacuum cleaner is introduced.

1984: General Electric Company's small appliance business is acquired.

1985: Company changes its name to The Black & Decker Corporation.

1986: Nolan D. Archibald is named CEO.

1989: Emhart Corporation, a conglomerate whose holdings include Price Pfister faucets and Kwikset locks, is acquired for $2.7 billion.

1992: Black & Decker relaunches the DeWalt line of high-end power tools.

1994: Company introduces the VersaPak interchangeable battery system and the SnakeLight flexible flashlight.

1998: As part of a "strategic repositioning," Black & Decker divests its household appliance operations.

2003: Baldwin Hardware Corporation and Weiser Lock Corporation are acquired from Masco Corporation.

2004: Black & Decker buys Pentair, Inc.'s Tools Group for $775 million.

Diversified Product Line in 1960s and 1970s

Although Black & Decker enjoyed healthy profits, by the late 1950s the company was not increasing beyond its 20 percent share of the U.S. market. To generate growth the company branched out into other types of labor-saving machinery. The Master Pneumatic Tool Company of Bedford, Ohio, maker of portable pneumatic tools, was acquired in 1959. Production of portable air tools was begun at a new facility in Solon, Ohio, in 1960. The Value line was introduced in 1967 to offer standardized, less-expensive models. The pneumatic tools business remained a minor part of B&D's operations, until that sector was sold in 1986.

In 1960 Black & Decker purchased DeWalt of Lancaster, Pennsylvania, makers of radial arm saws and other woodworking equipment. An improved line of radial arm saws was introduced in 1966. To expand the woodworking operations Black & Decker bought the Carbide Router Company of Moonachie, New Jersey, in 1970 and the Wisconsin Knife Works of Beloit, Wisconsin, the following year.

Black & Decker also entered the garden- and lawn-care field in the late 1950s. It introduced electric lawn edgers and hedge trimmers in 1957. The first electric lawnmowers were unveiled in 1966, and a cordless model went into production three years later. In 1973 the business was expanded by the purchase of McCulloch Corporation, a manufacturer of gasoline engines and chainsaws. During the mid-1970s production of certain outdoor-tool models was scaled back because of the unpredictable nature of their sales. Sales of outdoor tools depended upon weather conditions and seasonal buying patterns. McCulloch performed very well during the energy crisis of the early 1970s, which spurred the use of woodburning stoves, thus popularizing chainsaws, but in the early 1980s the subsidiary began losing money. In 1983 the chainsaw business was sold.

Black & Decker power tools continued to enjoy success during the 1960s and early 1970s, as prices were cut and products improved. The cost of B&D's ¼-inch drill was reduced in increments from $15.98 in 1963 to $7.99 in 1970. A research-and-development task force brought out dozens of new tools each year, maintaining Black & Decker's status as an industry innovator. The Workmate portable worktable and accessories were first marketed in England in 1973, and soon proved very successful around the world. Beginning in 1964 Black & Decker also made extensive use of television advertising. Sales surpassed $100 million in 1964, $200 million in 1969, and $500 million in 1974. To accommodate the new demand the company built two plants in North Carolina, at Fayetteville and Tarboro, in 1966 and 1970, respectively. In 1974 a plant also was constructed in Easton, Maryland.

In 1975 Decker retired as CEO, to be replaced by Francis P. Lucier who had been named president in 1970. Although Decker remained chairman, this marked the end of the founding families' executive control of the company. In 1975 B&D also experienced its first break in postwar growth, and many employees were laid off. The firm's future looked dim in the face of growing competition from Japanese and German toolmakers. Offering lower-priced, high-quality tools, the Japanese firm Makita Electric Works steadily gained on Black & Decker. By the early 1980s Makita had nearly equaled Black & Decker's 20 percent share of the world market in professional tools. High turnover among the top executives also contributed to Black & Decker's woes.

Restructurings and Major Acquisitions in the 1980s

Promoting a program of globalization, 48-year-old Laurence Farley was promoted to president and CEO in 1983. The new head of B&D was determined to develop a world market for standardized consumer goods, including housewares. He implemented a sweeping reorganization scheme, closing five plants in England, Ireland, and the United States. Two years later more plants were closed in the United States, Brazil, Mexico, and Canada. Farley also integrated the global operations of Black & Decker, in the process firing 25 European managers and closing the European headquarters in Brussels. In 1985, to help bring home the reorganization, The Black & Decker Manufacturing

Company revamped its hexagonal trademark and changed its name to The Black & Decker Corporation. The name change was meant to give greater emphasis to the marketing and sales side of the company.

Black & Decker's new path under Farley grew out of the firm's earlier development of cordless technology. In 1961 Black & Decker had introduced the world's first self-contained cordless electric drill. This tool and others that soon followed were powered by nickel-cadmium batteries, which failed to deliver the necessary performance. Nevertheless, the firm developed a cordless minimum-torque-recreation tool and a lunar surface drill, both of which were used by NASA on several space missions.

Using this earlier experience, Black & Decker introduced the Dustbuster cordless vacuum cleaner in 1978. This product was an immediate success, establishing B&D as the leader in the hitherto untapped small-appliance niche market. The Dustbuster was followed by the Spotliter rechargeable light and other cordless appliances. To put Black & Decker squarely in this new business, Farley paid $300 million in 1984 for the small-appliance operations of General Electric Company (GE). By purchasing the largest U.S. producer of irons, toaster ovens, portable mixers, coffee makers, and hairdryers, Black & Decker was able to gain a large chunk of the market immediately, without risking the loss of Black & Decker hardware shelf space to its housewares. Farley also believed production costs would be lowered by integrating the research and production of power tools and housewares.

During the two years following the 1984 purchase, Black & Decker undertook a $100 million brand-transition program. Meanwhile, the company also developed its own upscale light appliances, such as the Spacemaker series, a line of under-the-cabinet kitchen appliances. Black & Decker also introduced more cordless appliances, including a mixer and an electric knife. Farley began marketing the company's small-appliance line overseas. In Britain, where B&D had long enjoyed considerable name recognition, the first Black & Decker appliances were introduced in 1985. Other markets soon followed. In addition, GE's expertise in manufacturing electric motors enabled Black & Decker to design more efficient power tools using a smaller and more powerful 47-millimeter motor.

Yet Black & Decker's sales performance remained unspectacular, and fears that Laurence Farley was not sufficiently committed to product development contributed to his replacement as president by Nolan D. Archibald. A year later Archibald also was named CEO and chairman of the board of Black & Decker. Archibald came to The Black & Decker Corporation from Beatrice Company, where he headed the consumer durables group. Bringing in his own management team, the new B&D chief cut 3,000 jobs by 1987 and spurred product development. The company's worldwide operations were restructured into product groups. In 1986 the household-products group introduced a number of successful products, including the Cup-at-A-Time coffee maker. Greater efficiency at Black & Decker led to record sales of $1.9 billion and improved profits in 1987.

Once he had returned Black & Decker to efficiency and profitability, Archibald set out to expand the company's operations through acquisition. In January 1988 he attempted to purchase American Standard to obtain its line of plumbing fixtures, but American Standard escaped through a leveraged buyout. Archibald then acquired Emhart Corporation, a conglomerate, in early 1989 for $2.7 billion. With its True Temper lawn and garden tools, Kwikset locks, GardenAmerica sprinkler systems, Price Pfister faucets, and various fastening systems, Emhart's product line—at least parts of it—complemented Black & Decker's own products. Archibald combined the two companies' distribution and sales networks.

Plagued by Debt Burden in Early 1990s

Unfortunately, Emhart, whose $2.7 billion in revenue exceeded B&D's own $2.3 billion, turned into a bit of a nightmare after the economy moved into recession in the early 1990s and the market for asset sales dried up. B&D's debt had increased to more than $4 billion as a result of the highly leveraged acquisition and Archibald had planned to sell Emhart's numerous noncomplementary operations—about $1.8 billion worth—to reduce this debt burden. With the go-go years of the 1980s over, however, Archibald ran into difficulty finding buyers and in getting the kinds of prices he needed to quickly pay down the debt. By 1991 several Emhart businesses had been sold, including Bostik chemical adhesives and Arotronics nondomestic capacitors, but only for a total of $762 million. Debt still stood at $3.2 billion and annual net interest expense was about $300 million.

Meanwhile the recession hit the housing market particularly hard, reducing demand for power tools among both professional builders and do-it-yourselfers. As a result company sales declined sharply in 1991 and increased only marginally in 1992. B&D's net margin was less than one-half percent in 1991, then B&D posted a loss in 1992 thanks to a $135 million restructuring charge primarily associated with its Dynapert operations. Dynapert, which made equipment used in the assembly of printed circuit boards, had been acquired with Emhart and slated for sale but a buyer had yet to be found. Clearly, Emhart was dragging Black & Decker down.

Mid-1990s Turnaround Based on Savvy Marketing and Innovative New Products

A company turnaround had its start during 1992 with the launch of the DeWalt line of high-end power tools. This was actually a relaunch since B&D took the existing line of Black & Decker brand professional power tools, improved their quality, guaranteed 48-hour service center repair, *increased* their price (to be slightly *higher* than the competing Makita brand), and resurrected the 1960-acquired DeWalt brand, which was still highly respected by contractors. The company was now able to offer the low-end Black & Decker line of power tools aimed at do-it-yourselfers and the high-end DeWalt line aimed at professional contractors. This brilliant strategy—in part the brainchild of marketing whiz Joseph Galli, who soon headed B&D's entire worldwide power tool group—was immensely successful. The company's share of the domestic professional power tool market increased from 8 percent in 1991 to more than 40 percent in 1995. Sales of the DeWalt line increased from less than $30 million during the launch year to more than $600 million by 1997. In 1993 a similar high-end/low-end strategy began to be employed in B&D's security hardware group, when the Titan line of locksets were added to complement the Kwikset line.

Increased cash flow from these introductions helped Black & Decker decrease its debt load. During the record revenue year of 1994, when sales hit $4.37 billion, total debt was reduced to $2.39 billion. Reinvigorated new product development resulted in several successful 1994 introductions, most notably the VersaPak interchangeable battery system used in a new line of consumer cordless power tools and SnakeLight, a flashlight with a flexible base which became the fastest-selling product in company history.

Meanwhile Archibald was also able to further reduce debt by belatedly selling off additional Emhart businesses. In 1993 B&D sold the Corwin Russwin Architectural Hardware unit to Williams Holdings for $80 million, and Dynapert's through-hole circuit business for $28 million. In 1995 Archibald was finally able to sell the PRC information technology and services businesses in three separate deals totaling $520.5 million.

To further strengthen its financial health, Black & Decker also closed several plants in Europe in 1994 and restructured its consumer businesses in 1996, eliminating about 1,400 jobs and incurring an after-tax charge of $74.8 million. In 1995 efforts also began to further expand Black & Decker internationally, through joint ventures in India and China and the debut of the DeWalt line in Europe and Latin America. By 1996, when sales neared the $5 billion mark and total debt was down to $1.71 billion, Black & Decker seemed back on track. Although earnings were reduced because of the restructuring charge, the net margin of 3.2 percent was a significant improvement over that of the dark days of the early 1990s.

Restructuring Again in the Late 1990s

Results were similar in 1997, a year marked by the recall of 224,000 Black & Decker under-the-cabinet Spacemaker toasters, which were found to pose a fire danger. (B&D later had to pay a $575,000 civil penalty to the Consumer Product Safety Commission for failing to report defects in the toaster quickly enough.) Early the following year, the company announced plans for another restructuring, termed a "strategic repositioning," intended to heighten the firm's focus on its core operations and improve its financial performance. Black & Decker said it would sell three of its least profitable businesses: its household appliance operations in North America, Latin America, and Australia; Emhart Glass, maker of equipment for manufacturing glass containers; and True Temper Sports, producer of steel and graphite golf-club shafts—the latter two making up the last of the unwanted Emhart businesses. After selling the Australian household appliance business, Black & Decker sold its household appliance operations in North America and Latin America (excluding Brazil) in June 1998 to Windmere-Durable Holdings, Inc. (later renamed Applica Incorporated) for $315 million. B&D retained, however, its profitable Dustbuster and SnakeLight lines. In September the company sold Emhart Glass to Bucher Holding AG of Switzerland for $178.7 million and True Temper Sports to Cornerstone Equity Investors LLC for $177.7 million.

These divestments enabled Black & Decker to refocus on its core power tools and hardware lines, particularly the DeWalt line, which was now generating nearly $1 billion in annual revenues, or fully 20 percent of the company total. The repositioning also involved the repurchase of 10 percent of the company's stock by the end of 1999 and a restructuring of the remaining operations in order to reduce fixed costs. About 5,000 employees were laid off and several facilities were closed, including four overseas production plants. Restructuring charges of $164.7 million and a $900 million writeoff of goodwill led to a net loss for 1998 of $754.8 million. B&D returned to the black in 1999, posting profits of $300.3 million on revenues of $4.52 billion. Also that year, Galli, considered Archibald's heir apparent, left the company, when it became clear that Archibald, then 55, was not ready to retire any time soon. (Galli later became CEO of Newell Rubbermaid Inc.)

Early 2000s: Further Restructuring and a Return to the Acquisitions Arena

Black & Decker continued to churn out new products in the early 2000s, but sales and earnings growth stagnated in the sluggish economic environment. A number of cost-saving measures were enacted, including a three-year restructuring plan launched in early 2002. The key objective of this plan was to reduce manufacturing costs by shifting production from the United States and England to lower-cost facilities in Mexico, China, and the Czech Republic; and by sourcing more products from third party manufacturers. Several U.S. plants were closed that year and the following one, including the facility in Easton, Maryland, the last of B&D's home-state plants. Restructuring charges for 2001, 2002, and 2003 totaled $99.7 million, $46.6 million, and $31.6 million, respectively. The company estimated that over the three-year period it eliminated 5,200 positions in high-cost manufacturing locations and added 4,500 replacement positions in low-cost locales. By 2003 the restructuring had already yielded $50 million in annual cost savings, and B&D expected to achieve $130 million in yearly savings by 2005.

Also during 2002 Black & Decker was forced to recall 140,000 cordless electric lawnmowers because of potential problems with overheating. During the following year the company returned to the acquisition arena, but with an eye toward smaller, product-line purchases that would complement existing operations. In September 2003 B&D acquired Baldwin Hardware Corporation and Weiser Lock Corporation from Masco Corporation for $277.6 million. Based in Reading, Pennsylvania, Baldwin was a manufacturer of high-end architectural and decorative hardware for the home. Weiser, headquartered in Tucson, Arizona, produced locksets and decorative exterior hardware. This acquisition, coupled with the existing Kwikset line, made Black & Decker the clear leader in the North American residential lockset market, with several brands at various price points sold through a variety of retail channels. Black & Decker followed up this deal by selling its European security unit to the Swedish firm Assa Abloy for $108 million in early 2004.

Black & Decker enjoyed a solid year in 2003 as revenues increased 4 percent, to $4.48 billion, while net earnings of $293 million were 27 percent higher than the previous year's total. In March 2004 the company announced that it was reorganizing its power tools and accessories business into two separate groups: Black & Decker Consumer and DeWalt Professional. In July of that year B&D reached an agreement to buy Pentair, Inc.'s Tools Group, a unit that had 2003 operating profits of $82 million on $1.08 billion in sales. The Tools Group included

Porter-Cable portable power tools, Delta woodworking machinery, DeVillbiss Air Power air compressors and pressure washers, Oldham Saw saw blades and router bits, and the German-based Flex business, specializing in grinders and masonry and metalworking tools. The brands were mainly aimed at professionals, so they were a good fit with B&D's DeWalt line. Black & Decker closed the $775 million deal in October 2004.

Principal Subsidiaries

Baldwin Hardware Corporation; Black & Decker (Ireland) Inc.; Black & Decker Abrasives Inc.; Black & Decker India Inc.; Kwikset Corporation; Momentum Laser, Inc.; Price Pfister, Inc.; Weiser Lock Corporation; Black & Decker Argentina S.A.; Black & Decker Werkzeuge Vertriebs-Gesellschaft M.B.H. (Austria); Black & Decker (Belgium) N.V.; Black & Decker Do Brasil Ltda. (Brazil); Refal Industria e Comercio de Rebites e Rebitadeiras Ltda. (Brazil); Black & Decker Canada Inc.; Maquinas y Herramientas Black & Decker de Chile S.A.; Black & Decker (Suzhou) Co. Ltd. (China); Black & Decker (Suzhou) Power Tools Co., Ltd. (China); Shanghai Emhart Fastening Systems Ltd. (China); Black & Decker de Colombia S.A.; Black & Decker (Czech) S.R.O. (Czech Republic); Emhart Harttung A/S (Denmark); Black & Decker de El Salvador, S.A. de C.V.; Black & Decker Oy (Finland); Black & Decker (France) S.A.S.; Emhart S.A.R.L. (France); Black & Decker G.m.b.H. (Germany); Black & Decker (Hellas) S.A. (Greece); Black & Decker Hong Kong Limited; Black & Decker (Ireland); Chesapeake Factoring Company (Ireland); Black & Decker Italia S.P.A. (Italy); Fasteners & Tools, Ltd. (Japan); Nippon Pop Rivets & Fasteners Ltd. (Japan); Black & Decker (Overseas) A.G. (Liechtenstein); Black & Decker Luxembourg S.A.; Black & Decker Macao; Black & Decker (Malaysia) Sdn. Bhd.; Black & Decker Asia Pacific (Malaysia) Sdn. Bhd.; BD Power Tools Mexicana, S. de R.L. de C.V. (Mexico); Black & Decker de Reynosa S. de R.L. de C.V. (Mexico); Black & Decker, S.A. de C.V. (Mexico); DeWalt Industrial Tools, S.A. de C.V. (Mexico); Price-Pfister de Mexico, S. de R.L. de C.V.; Technolock, S. de R.L. de C.V. (Mexico); Weiser Lock Mexico, S.A. De C.V.; Black & Decker (Nederland) B.V. (Netherlands); Black & Decker (New Zealand) Limited; Black & Decker (Norge) A/S (Norway); Black & Decker de Panama, S.A.; Black & Decker Del Peru S.A.; Black & Decker Asia Pacific Pte. Ltd. (Singapore); Black & Decker (South Africa) Pty. Ltd.; Emhart Fastening Teknologies Korea, Inc. (South Korea); Black & Decker Iberica S.Com por A. (Spain); Black & Decker Aktiebolag (Sweden); Black & Decker (Switzerland) S.A.; Black & Decker (Thailand) Limited; Aven Tools Limited (U.K.); Bandhart (U.K.); Black & Decker (U.K.); Black & Decker Europe (U.K.); Black & Decker International (U.K.); Emhart International Limited (U.K.); Tucker Fasteners Limited (U.K.); Weiser Lock Limited (U.K.); Black & Decker de Venezuela, C.A.

Principal Operating Units

Black & Decker Consumer Group; DeWalt Professional Group; Hardware and Home Improvement Group; Fastening and Assembly Systems Group.

Principal Competitors

Makita Corporation; The Stanley Works; Danaher Corporation; American Standard Companies Inc.; Kohler Co.; Snap-on Incorporated.

Further Reading

"A.G. Decker of Black & Decker," *Nation's Business,* December 1969.

Anderson, Lauren Bayne, "Black & Decker Buying Pentair's Tool Division," *Washington Post,* July 20, 2004, p. E2.

Barrett, Amy, and Gail DeGeorge, "Home Improvement at Black & Decker," *Business Week,* May 11, 1998, pp. 54, 56.

Berselli, Beth, "Retooling at Black & Decker: In a Return to Core Products, the Home Appliance Line Will Go," *Washington Post,* February 9, 1998, p. F10.

Brown, Warren, and Sandra Sugawara, "Wall Street Worries over Black & Decker: Buying Emhart Corp. Caused Debt Difficulties," *Washington Post,* February 5, 1990, p. WB5.

Defotis, Dimitra, "Cool Tools: Renovations to Power Black & Decker," *Barron's,* January 29, 2001, p. 43.

Flack, Stuart, "All Leverage Is Not Created Equal," *Forbes,* March 19, 1990, p. 39.

Highlights of Progress, Towson, Md.: The Black & Decker Corporation, 1987.

Hamilton, Martha McNeil, "Black & Decker to Shut Plants: Local Jobs Are Among 2,400 Moving to Lower-Wage Countries," *Washington Post,* January 30, 2002, p. E1.

Huey, John, "The New Power in Black & Decker," *Fortune,* January 2, 1989, p. 89.

Mirabella, Lorraine, "Black & Decker Buys Minnesota-Based Tool Business for $775 Million," *Baltimore Sun,* July 20, 2004.

Schifrin, Matthew, "Cut-and-Build Archibald," *Forbes,* September 23, 1996, pp. 44–48.

Sellers, Patricia, "New Selling Tool: The Acura Concept," *Fortune,* February 24, 1992, pp. 88–89.

Sentementes, Gus G., "Black & Decker to Purchase Hardware, Lock Divisions from Michigan Manufacturer," *Baltimore Sun,* July 2, 2003.

Weber, Joseph, and Brian Bremner, "The Screws Are Tightening at Black & Decker," *Business Week,* September 23, 1991, pp. 61, 64.

Welsh, Jonathan, "Black & Decker to Shed Some Lines and Focus on Tools," *Wall Street Journal,* January 28, 1998, p. A6.

—Neal R. McCrillis
—update: David E. Salamie

⫶BRASCAN

Brascan Corporation

BCE Place, Suite 300
181 Bay Street
Toronto, Ontario M5J 2T3
Canada
Telephone: (416) 363-9491
Fax: (416) 363-2856
Web site: http://www.brascancorp.com

Public Company
Incorporated: 1912 as Brazilian Traction, Light and
    Power Company Limited
Employees: 6,000
Operating Revenues: $3.37 billion (2003)
Stock Exchanges: New York Toronto
Ticker Symbols: BNN; BNNa
NAIC: 531210 Office of Real Estate Agents and Brokers;
    213114 Support Activities for Metal Mining; 322121
    Paper Mills (Except Newsprint, Uncoated
    Groundwood Paper Mills)

Brascan Corporation is working on an image change, from being known as one of Canada's largest conglomerates to a tightly focused company more appealing to investors. The company's core businesses are real estate and power generation. In addition to billions in direct investments, Brascan is growing its portfolio of assets under management. Hard assets include over 70 office properties in North America and the United Kingdom and more than 100 power generation plants, mainly in the Northeast.

From South to North: 1899–1979

Brascan Corporation can be traced back to the dawn of the 20th century and South America, where Canadians played a role in the early development of hydroelectric power generation, street car lines, and gas and telephone systems. The power business came first, beginning in 1899. The Brazilian Traction, Light and Power Company Limited, formed in 1912, amalgamated infrastructure operations in Sao Paulo and Rio de Janeiro.

The company's northern hemisphere roots were established as the second half of the century was getting underway. Edper Investments Limited, incorporated in Montreal in 1954, was owned by Peter, Edward, and Mildred Mona Bronfman trusts. From 1954 to 1968, Edper involved itself in real estate, financial, and industrial ventures.

Edward and Peter Bronfman, nephews of Samuel Bronfman, the builder of Seagram Co. Ltd., became known for the dizzying array of companies they amassed under one or another holding company. "It really was a very, very complex organization," Desjardins Securities analyst Michael Goldberg told the *Financial Post* in 2003.

Brazilian Traction, Light and Power Company, meanwhile, sold off its telephone operations to the Brazilian government. The company was renamed Brascan. A decade later, in 1979, the power business, too, was sold to the government, and Edper acquired controlling interest in Brascan. North America became the central focus for investment in the power industry. In 1973, Brascan had acquired Great Lakes Power Company and its hydroelectric facilities. The independent company had been incorporated in the early 1920s to provide power in northern Ontario.

A Complicated Design: 1980s–90s

Merchant bank Hees International Bankcorp served "as the nerve centre for Brascan in its glory days in the late 1980s," wrote Deirdre McMurdy for *Canadian Business* in 2002. For two decades, South African-born Jack Cockwell had led the charge, investing Bronfman money in dozens of publicly traded firms, gaining significant or controlling interest.

Distiller John Labatt Ltd., forest products giant MacMillan Bloedel, financial concern Royal Trustco, mining company Noranda, and real estate broker Royal LePage represented the diverse interests held by the Bronfmans. According to *Maclean's,* in 1989 the Bronfman empire consisted of more than 150 companies, with assets worth about $120 billion and 100,000 employees. That year the company announced a restructuring to decrease family ownership, offer shares to the public, and open the door for greater management control.

Company Perspectives:

Brascan has a proud history spanning over 100 years that includes the successful operation of world-class real estate, power generation, financial management and resource assets as well as ownership interests in some of Canada's best known corporations, which in the past included Labatts, London Life and Seagram. While the core of our business in the past decade has narrowed to three areas—real estate, power generation and asset management—we remain singularly focused on enhancing value for our shareholders.

The fortunes of Hees, Brascan, and Cockwell soured with the economy in the early 1990s. The North American recession particularly hurt core business segments real estate and natural resources. Hees International Bancorp Inc. and Brascan Ltd., both publicly traded holding companies, felt the strain.

In February 1993, the Edper group sold off a pair of assets with a combined value of $1.96 billion. McMurdy wrote for *Maclean's*, "Indeed, the sale of MacMillan Bloedel and Labatt by the Toronto-based Hees-Edper corporate empire clearly marks the end of an era. After more than a decade as the most dominant and acquisitive force in the Canadian economy, the Edper group is literally losing control. The Bronfman family and its senior managers have come under mounting pressure and scrutiny from bankers, regulators and disgruntled minority shareholders to address the financial leverage of their complex structure. By selling assets, the group has made a clear attempt to raise capital, reducing both debt and uncertainty."

The rise of another company helped turn the tide for Brascan. Canadian Arena Company (Carena) was incorporated in 1923 to own and manage the Montreal Forum and the Canadiens hockey team. During the mid-1970s, Carena bought a 50.1 percent stake in Toronto developer Trizec, gaining control of BCE Developments and billions in property. Those considerable assets eventually found their way into Brookfield Properties Inc., the BCED subsidiary that built BEC Place in Toronto, according to *Canadian Business*. At that time, Edper became the major shareholder.

Brookfield gained a foothold in New York City, through a stake in the World Financial Center owned by the unraveling Olympia & York. Bruce Flatt, the son of the cofounder of a giant Canadian-based mutual fund, built an impressive portfolio of properties.

In 1997 the Edper Group Limited and Brascan Limited amalgamated to form EdperBrascan Corporation.

A Change in the Wind: 2000–04

As the new century began EdperBrascan took a new name, Brascan Corporation, but its future was uncertain. Conglomerates were on their way to extinction and investors were cheering on their demise. "In general, the market does not like the idea of conglomerates. It consistently values them at a substantial discount to asset values, a penalty imposed because of the extra corporate layer between the investor and operating compa-

nies," explained Dan Westell in *Canadian Business*. The massive companies countered by maintaining that their complexity gave them the advantage during tough times.

The planned breakup of Canadian Pacific Ltd. drove up Brascan's share price in 2001, as investors anticipated split-offs by three remaining Canadian conglomerates. Internal moves, including improvements in operations and capital investments and continued simplification of the corporate structure, were expected to fare well with investors even if no restructuring was in the immediate future. In addition, a New York Stock Exchange listing beginning in late 2000 brought the company to the attention of American investors.

Bruce Flatt, president and CEO of Brookfield Properties Corp., took over the post of president and CEO of Brascan Corporation in 2002, succeeding Jack Cockwell, who had tapped him as his successor. Flatt's operating results at Brookfield led him to his advancement to the head of Brascan. But it was his performance post-9/11 that solidified the choice of the young man.

When the World Trade Center fell, the nearby Brookfield properties became the subject of speculation as to their safety, driving down share price. Flatt went to New York to check out the property and brought in materials from its forest product concern to help board up blown-out windows in theirs and other buildings near ground zero.

While his quick action helped stabilize the company's stock during a trying time, it remained to be seen if he could produce the same magic at the conglomerate as he did with Brookfield, especially given the status of holding companies, the senior executives' lock hold on the company's board, and Jay Cockwell's ongoing influence in the position of co-chair. Cockwell's strategy lay in the cross ownership; Flatt would have to abandon that to make significant change.

Brascan found itself looking to its other foreign investments with some concern as the political and economic situation in Brazil destabilized. The Brascan Brazil Ltd. subsidiary held interest in the real estate, mining, agriculture, power generation, and financial services sectors. When Brazil's currency went on a slide in 2002, the company's financial operations were exposed to possible losses and highlighted again the many and varied dangers inherent to international business.

In an effort to beef up its already impressive real estate business, in 2003, Brascan got involved in a bidding war for the control of the United Kingdom's Canary Wharf Group. It also entered into one of the largest financing deals ever constructed in the commercial real estate market.

In 2004, Brascan acknowledged that Noranda Inc. was involved in merger talks with global mining companies. The natural resource company gained the majority of its sales from copper and nickel mining and smelting. Forest product subsidiaries Norbord Inc. and Fraser Papers Inc. were expected to be next on the trading block.

Although losing the bid for control of London's Canary Wharf in 2004, Brascan gained 72 New York State hydroelectric generating plants. The two deals represented the wave of

Key Dates:

1899: Power business is established in Sao Paulo, Brazil.
1912: Brazilian Traction, Light and Power Company is incorporated in Toronto.
1923: Canadian Arena Company (Carena) is incorporated.
1954: Edper Investments Limited is incorporated in Montreal.
1969: Brazilian telephone operations are sold and the name is changed to Brascan.
1973: Brascan acquires Great Lakes Power.
1976: Edper Investments becomes the major shareholder of Trizec.
1979: Edper acquires a controlling interest in Brascan.
1989: Edper Investments Ltd. is renamed Edper Enterprises and makes its public offering.
1997: The Edper Group and Brascan Limited combine to form EdperBrascan Corporation.
2000: The company is renamed Brascan Corporation.

the future. "For Canada's Brascan Corp., it's goodbye, rocks and trees, and hello, buildings and dams," wrote Elena Cherney for the *Wall Street Journal*. By focusing on power generation and real estate, Brascan felt it would draw in more institutional investors growing portfolios for the wave of retirees on the horizon.

Principal Subsidiaries

Brascan Financial Corporation; Great Lakes Power Inc.

Principal Competitors

Domtar Inc.; Inco Limited; Trizec Properties.

Further Reading

Best, Patricia, and Ann Shortell, *The Brass Ring: Power, Influence, and the Brascan Empire,* Toronto, Ontario: Random House, 1988.

"Brascan Increases Canary Wharf Holding to 9%," *Property Week,* May 16, 2003, p. 17.

"Brascan Issues Bond to Beat Uncertainty," *Corporate Financing Week,* March 10, 2003, p. 5.

"Canary Wharf Group PLC: Morgan Stanley, Brascan Place Final Bids for British Company," *Wall Street Journal,* April 19, 2004, p. 1.

Cherney, Elena, "Canada's Brascan Aims to Change Focus," *Wall Street Journal,* August 17, 2004, p. B6.

Clemence, Sara, "Toronto Company to Buy Upstate Power Plants," *Times Union* (Albany, N.Y.), May 22, 2004, p. B8.

"The Countdown Continues: 52 Brookfield Properties," *Canadian Business,* May 12, 2003.

"EuroHypo, Brascan Join Wachovia for GM Financing," *Real Estate Finance and Investment,* September 22, 2003, p. 1.

Haliechuk, Rick, "Peter Bronfman Giving Up Control of Hees/Edper," *Toronto Star,* February 24, 1995, p. B5.

"Hees, Edper Group to Amalgamate," *Toronto Star,* October 18, 1996, p. E8.

Jenish, D'Arcy, "Reshaping an Empire," *Maclean's,* May 29, 1989, p. 43.

McDowall, Duncan, *The Light: Brazilian Traction, Light and Power Company Limited, 1899–1945,* Toronto, Ontario: University of Toronto Press, 1988.

McMurdy, Deirdre, "At the Top of His Game," *Canadian Business,* March 4, 2002.

——, "Bay Street Bonanza," *Maclean's,* February 22, 1993, p. 18.

Raghavan, Anita, and Sarah Turner, "Deals & Deal Makers: Canary Wharf Battle Heats Up As Morgan Stanley Boosts Bid," *Wall Street Journal,* February 6, 2004, p. C4.

"Real Estate Brief—Canary Wharf Group PLC: Offer from Canadian Group Doesn't Get Panel's Support," *Wall Street Journal,* March 8, 2004, p. 1.

Robin, Raizel, "A Real Downer," *Canadian Business,* September 2, 2002.

Theobald, Steven, "Shareholders Approve Birth of EdperBrascan," *Toronto Star,* July 11, 1997, p. E3.

Thompson, Peter, "Brascan Plans Debt Financing for N.Y. Acquisitions," *Power, Finance and Risk,* May 24, 2004, p. 1.

Westell, Dan, "And Then There Were Three," *Canadian Business,* April 2, 2001.

—Kathleen Peippo

Brioni Roman Style S.p.A.

1, Piazza Duomo
65017 Penne, Abruzzo
Italy
Telephone: (39) (08) 582-171
Fax: (39) (0858) 279-200
Web site: http://www.brioni.com

Private Company
Incorporated: 1945
Employees: 5,800
Sales: $200 million (2003 est.)
NAIC: 424320 Men's and Boys' Clothing and
Furnishings Merchant Wholesalers; 424330 Women's,
Children's, and Infants' Clothing and Accessories
Merchant Wholesalers; 448110 Men's Clothing
Stores; 448120 Women's Clothing Stores; 315222
Men's and Boys' Cut and Sew Suit, Coat, and
Overcoat Manufacturing; 315234 Women's and Girls'
Cut and Sew Suit, Coat, Tailored Jacket, and Skirt
Manufacturing

Brioni Roman Style S.p.A. is an apparel maker of the highest order, selling the most expensive off-the-rack suits in the world. Brioni's garments are stitched by hand, retailing for as much $5,500. The company's custom-made suits sell for $15,000. Brioni makes roughly 80 percent of its money as a wholesaler, distributing its men's and women's apparel to exclusive retailers through the world. The company also operates its own network of stores, maintaining a presence in Europe, the United States, and Asia through 19 shops. The United States ranks as the company's largest market. Brioni operates one of Italy's most respected tailoring schools, offering a four-year program that creates recruits for its factories.

Origins

Brioni, the name of luxury and elegance in the fashion world, began its business life surrounded by the devastation of World War II. Rubble-strewn streets and mortar-pocked build-ings provided the backdrop for Rome's new sartorial master, a surreal setting for a business based on fine design and geared toward wealthy clientele. The business started with the opening of an exclusive tailor shop in Rome in 1945, a venture pairing a well-connected Roman socialite, Gaetano Savini, who would serve as the business's fashion coordinator, and a talented tailor from the central Italian city of Penne, Nazareno Fonticoli.

The founders selected a name that harkened to more prosperous, carefree times, taking the name of an island off the coast of Croatia that was once owned by Italy. In the decades before the war, Brioni was the exclusive destination of aristocrats and the wealthy, a popular playground for the elite who enjoyed polo matches, golf, and the comforts of high society. The memory of Brioni rather than the reality of 1945 Rome fit the image Savini and Fonticoli strove to cultivate, but the adoption of the Brioni name also served another purpose. According to Ettore Perrone, Savini's son-in-law, the selection of the name was a marketing ploy. "You see," he informed the *Daily News Record* in a June 23, 1983 interview, "the partners needed a short Italian name the Americans would remember. When they opened the store after World War II that's who they wanted to sell to. After all, Americans had the money."

Brioni quickly established itself as one of Rome's finest tailors. Fonticoli's work distinguished the shop, enabling it to evolve into a fashion house. Savini, well known by the wealthy and famous—Brioni's target customer—kept the business busy with new clients, cultivating a customer base that grew exclusively through word of mouth (the company did not advertise for nearly a half-century). After only six years in business, the Brioni name achieved the prestigious status that later defined it. In 1951, the company became one of the first men's fashion houses to stage a fashion show in Rome's Sala Bianca.

Brioni's rise in Rome provided a springboard for the company's international expansion. The exportation of Italian fashion into the international marketplace, particularly into U.S. markets, was, in large part, the work of Brioni, a migration that was aided immeasurably by the cast of luminaries who wore Brioni suits. Film stars such as Gary Cooper, Cary Grant, Henry Fonda, and John Wayne were Brioni customers, with their celebrity status serving as an effective means of giving recognition to the Brioni name outside of Rome. Although the company became a genuinely global business, serving customers in Europe, Asia, and the Middle East, its largest market was the United States. Brioni began distributing its apparel in the United States in 1961, selling its hand-sewn suits to a select few upscale retail outlets on the East Coast.

As Brioni grew, it did so primarily as a wholesaler. Although the company developed a greater retail presence as it expanded, the basis of its business was as a wholesaler. Brioni focused its efforts not toward developing a chain of stores but toward making the finest suits, a painstaking process whose reliance on hand-stitching belied the technology-driven production processes of the 20th century. Brioni's factories, located in Penne and the surrounding region, bore little resemblance to the production facilities prevalent in other industries. The company's machinery consisted of a few rows of old sewing machines used only to stitch inner linings or other areas of the garment that benefited little from hand stitching. Instead of cutting-edge machinery, Brioni relied on tailors, 750 of whom sewed each suit by hand, stitch by stitch. The company, like the cadre of other exclusive fashion houses, was an anachronism of sorts, facing far different impediments to survival and growth than the legions of high-volume apparel manufacturers. One of the most pressing and enduring problems confronting the company was finding qualified tailors to make Brioni garments. Finding highly skilled tailors was a daunting challenge for other prestigious apparel firms, but Brioni was one of only a few companies that tried to take the matter in its own hands. In 1978, the company opened what would become one of Italy's most highly respected tailoring schools. The school, located in the central Italian region of Abruzzo, offered a four-year program, producing a pool of tailors that helped Brioni avoid, for the most part, skilled labor shortages.

Retail Network Beginning to Grow in the 1980s

By the beginning of the 1980s, Brioni epitomized Italian high fashion, holding sway as a nearly 40-year-old brand conducting business on a global scale. The company maintained an extremely exclusive retail operation, managing three stores, two in Rome and a third in Sardinia. Its suits, however, traveled far beyond Italy's borders, underpinning a wholesale business that drove the company's sales. Brioni's suits were on stock at a small number of retail outlets in Europe, Asia, and the Middle East, retailing for roughly $1,300. Brioni shirts sold for approximately $145. The importance of the U.S. market to the company's financial growth increased considerably during the decade. A store in New York opened in 1982, with its success convincing officials in Italy to establish a division in the United States shortly after the store's debut. The store was located a mile from Madison Avenue's "Gold Coast," the heart of the city's upscale, European retail district, but Brioni management expressed little concern that the store was removed from the Gold Coast. They chose the location,

in the Fisher Building off Park Avenue and 52nd Street, because of its association with the building's owner, a real estate tycoon and Brioni customer. "Fisher wanted us," Ettore Perrone told *Daily New Record* in a June 23, 1983 interview. "Besides," he added, "we don't have to see our customers walk by the store. It's all very personal here."

As Brioni entered the 1990s, the company gained the leadership of the individual who would orchestrate the greatest growth period in its history. Umberto Angeloni was named chief executive officer of Brioni in 1990, beginning a highly effective reign of command that extended into the 21st century. Angeloni presided over a fivefold increase in Brioni's size during his first decade in control, engineering the diversification of the company's product line and the expansion of its retail network. When the company celebrated its 50th anniversary in 1995, an occasion marked by a ten-day exhibition of Brioni apparel in Florence, sales stood at $53 million, a total collected from the 60,000 garments produced during the year. Brioni, by this point, operated three factories near Pescara, Italy, using its tailors to hand-sew a product line consisting of suits, sportswear, and ties. The company also produced a small women's collection distributed under the Lady Brioni label that represented roughly 5 percent of the company's total production. Most of these garments were distributed to select retail locations throughout the world, while the rest were sold at five company-owned shops in Rome, New York, Florence, and at a store in Malaysia that Brioni operated through a joint venture agreement.

The growth achieved by Brioni during the 1990s belied the projections of industry pundits. In the company's biggest market, the United States, the trend toward more casual business wear was expected to hurt apparel makers of Brioni's ilk, but instead the trend worked in the company's favor. Fewer suits were purchased during the decade, but the suits that were purchased tended to be more expensive. Volume manufacturers of relatively inexpensive suits felt the sting of the trend toward casual wear, but Brioni and its $3,500 to $5,500 suits thrived during the decade, particularly during the latter half of the 1990s. The growth achieved during the period was most evident in the expansion of the company's retail operations, although Angeloni did not intend to alter the focus of the company. "We don't want to become a chain of stores," he asserted in an October 23, 2002 interview with trade publication *WWD*. Between 1996 and 2001, the number of Brioni retail shops increased substantially, jumping from 5 to 13 stores. The expansion included the opening of a new flagship store in Milan in 1999, a 64,800-square-foot shop that was part of an 18th-century villa. The store, staffed with a full-time tailor, generated sales of more than $4 million during its first year of operation.

Although the trend toward more casual attire worked in Brioni's favor, the 1990s presented other challenges that forced the company to make some changes. One of the most difficult issues the company had to deal with stemmed from the unusual place it occupied in the modern world of high technology and industrialization. As a company competing in the global economy, Brioni was subject to the ever increasing costs of distribution and other expenses that any company faced, but expanding production to keep ahead of escalating costs threatened to mutate Brioni's essence. Expansion beyond a certain point

Key Dates:

1945: Brioni opens a tailor shop in Rome.
1961: Brioni begins distribution to the United States.
1978: Brioni opens its own tailoring school.
1982: A retail shop is opened in New York.
1990: Umberto Angeloni is named chief executive officer.
1995: Pierce Brosnan, in the James Bond film *Goldeneye*, wears a Brioni suit.
2002: Brioni opens its first two women's apparel stores in Milan and New York.

meant incorporating machinery and other aspects of modern, industrialized manufacturing, an evolutionary step that would be anathema to Brioni's identity as a maker of hand-made apparel. The question centered on how to make Brioni's 19th-century manufacturing practices fuel a growing enterprise at the turn of the 21st century.

One way to increase sales was to expand the company's product line by adding accessories and developing a women's line of clothing. Another way was developing a marketing program, something the company did for the first time in its history in the early 1990s when it began to advertise in print media. The company's biggest marketing move occurred in 1995 when Brioni was selected as the suit to be worn by Pierce Brosnan in the James Bond film *Goldeneye*. Designers Hugo Boss, Ermenegildo Zegna, and Giorgio Armani jockeyed for selection, but the film's costume designer picked Brioni after reading an article about the company in a London newspaper. The exposure given by a Brioni-draped James Bond did much to promote the brand name, providing a marketing boon whose worth increased when in subsequent installments of the James Bond series, Brosnan wore Brioni suits.

Brioni at the Beginning of the 21st Century

Brioni recorded electric financial growth during the late 1990s, making the start of the company's second half-century of business one of the most remarkable periods in its existence. By 2000, the $53 million in sales generated five years earlier had trebled to $150 million. By this point the company operated eight hand-production factories in Abruzzo, Bologna, and near Milan. The company's product line was diverse, including the shirts, ties, belts, and women's wear that were vital to the company's expansion. The growth was encouraging, but An-

geloni was not intoxicated by the results. "We are not interested in generating billion-dollar sales at the expense of brand equity," he remarked in a March 8, 2001 interview with *WWD*.

As Brioni prepared for the future, the esteem accorded to its brand name was as strong as ever. Although Angeloni consistently tempered any growth of the company's retail network by insisting the development of a retail chain was not in the company's future, the number of Brioni shops increased, nonetheless. In 2002, the company opened its first freestanding women's store in Milan followed by a second women's store in New York later that year. In 2004, in what was expected to be an annual event, Angeloni hosted a polo tournament on the company's namesake island, flying in players from South America to revive the glamorous days that had defined Brioni 80 years earlier. Angeloni planned to construct guest villas to accommodate the event's well-heeled attendants. Participants at the first event typified the exclusivity of a Brioni customer, a guest list that included Count Alvaro de Marichalar, a brother-in-law to Princess Elena of Spain, Winston Churchill III, and property tycoon Oliver Rothschild.

Principal Subsidiaries

Brioni Roman Style U.S.A. Corporation.

Principal Competitors

Georgio Armani S.p.A.; Gianni Versace S.p.A.; I Pellettieri d'Italia S.p.A.

Further Reading

Forden, Sara Gay, "Brioni Turns 50 with a Bang," *Daily News Record,* June 19, 1995, p. 22.

Geller, Stan, "Brioni Goes Beyond Its Sartorial Suits," *Daily News Record,* May 21, 1997, p. 5.

——, "Ettore Perrone Transforming Brioni to a Gentler Image," *Daily News Record,* June 23, 1983, p. 10.

Heller, Richard, "Making Money in Style," *Forbes,* September 18, 2000, p. 138.

Muir, Lucie, "Brioni Does Brisk Business at New Milan Flagship," *Daily News Record,* January 4, 1999, p. 10.

"A Stitch in Time," *Forbes,* July 31, 1995, p. 96.

"Why a $3,000 Suit?," *Business Week,* September 8, 2003, p. 114.

Wilson, Anamaria, "Brioni Women's Line Has a New Home," *WWD,* October 23, 2002, p. 6.

Zargani, Luisa, "Horse Play," *WWD,* July 15, 2004, p. 4.

—Jeffrey L. Covell

Brush Engineered Materials Inc.

17876 St. Clair Avenue
Cleveland, Ohio 44110
U.S.A.
Telephone: (216) 486-4200
Fax: (216) 383-4091
Web site: http://www.beminc.com

Public Company
Incorporated: 1931 as Brush Beryllium Co.
Employees: 1,833
Sales: $401.04 million (2003)
Stock Exchanges: New York
Ticker Symbol: BW
NAIC: 331419 Primary Smelting and Refining of
   Nonferrous Metal (Except Copper and Aluminum)

Through its wholly owned subsidiaries, Brush Engineered Materials Inc. is a leading maker of high-performance engineered materials, operating through two major business groups. A part of the Metal Systems Group, the Brush Wellman Inc. subsidiary is the world's only fully integrated producer of beryllium—a stiff metal lighter than aluminum but closer to the strength of steel, possessing thermal properties—beryllium-containing alloys, and beryllium ceramic. Beryllium is used in a number of high-performance applications, mostly in the defense and aerospace industries. Because in addition to strength and hardness copper beryllium offers high electrical and thermal conductivity, it makes an ideal material for many demanding applications in automotive electronics, aerospace, computers, oil exploration, plastic mold tooling, and undersea fiber-optic cables. Another subsidiary, Engineered Materials Systems, combines precious and nonprecious metals into continuous strips for use in automobiles, computers, and telecommunications systems. Brush's Microelectronics Group uses pure metal and specialty metal alloys to produce materials needed for high reliability applications in the aerospace, crystal, electron tube, hybrid microelectronics, magnetic head, optical media, and performance film industries. Brush also combines ceramics, powder metallurgy, thick film metallization, and electronic pack-

ages for use in highly demanding electronic applications in the aerospace, automotive, medical, and wireless communication fields. In addition to its headquarters, research center, and manufacturing facility in Cleveland, Ohio, Brush maintains two other plants in Ohio, and manufacturing operations in Arizona, California, Massachusetts, New York, Ohio, Pennsylvania, Rhode Island, Utah, and the Philippines. Brush is a public company, trading on the New York Stock Exchange.

Heritage Linked to 19th-Century Inventor

Brush's history is linked to one of the great American inventors of the 1800s, Charles Francis Brush. The son of a woolen manufacturer and farmer, he was born in 1849 in Ohio near Cleveland. Because he was the youngest of nine children he had more free time than his siblings while growing up on the family farm, providing him ample opportunity to indulge an early passion for science and electricity. He became obsessed with building his own arc light after reading how Sir Humphrey Davy in the early 1800s showed that light could be produced by passing electricity between the gap of two carbon electrodes. To help further his education, Brush's parents sent him to Cleveland's Central High School, where he would succeed in building an arc light and graduate in 1867 with honors. Another young man who stayed at the same boarding house where Brush resided also was destined to make his mark on the world: John D. Rockefeller. With a loan from an uncle, Brush was able to enroll at the University of Michigan. He chose a practical major, mining engineering. and graduated in just two years, eager to find work to repay his uncle.

After a less than stellar attempt to work as an analytical and consulting chemist, he went to work with a boyhood friend marketing Lake Superior pig iron. In his spare time he conducted experiments on arc lighting systems and came to the conclusion that a dynamo would be a necessary part of generating the needed electricity. He related his efforts to another childhood friend, George Stockly, general manager of the Telegraph Supply Company, who agreed to fund Brush's efforts to build a small dynamo. In 1876 Brush succeeded and a year later received a patent for his dynamo. He then developed the first electric arc light that featured a regulating system good enough to make it economically viable. Soon after he lit Cleveland's Public Square in 1879, a number of cities installed his arc lamps to illuminate their streets. In 1880 Telegraph Supply Company of Cleveland was reorganized to form Brush Electric Company, which in 1891 was merged with Edison General Electric Company to form today's General Electric Company.

Brush Laboratories Beginning Beryllium Research in the 1920s

With the creation of General Electric, Brush walked away a rich man, but he continued to conduct experiments in his laboratory leading to other patents, such as the storage battery, and he became involved in other business ventures. He was also a devoted family man with two daughters and a son, Charles Francis Brush, Jr., born in 1893. When the boy was only eight years old, however, Brush's wife, Mary, died. He now spent a great deal of time raising his son, whom he taught chemistry and electricity in his basement laboratory. Charles Brush, Jr., would then study chemistry and physics at Harvard University and go on to postgraduate work at the Massachusetts Institute of Technology. In 1921 the young Brush, with the financial backing of his father and facilities on the family property, founded Brush Laboratories with a college friend, Charles Baldwin Sawyer. One of the areas that Charles Brush, Jr., pursued starting in 1926 was finding industrial uses for beryllium.

Tragedy again struck the Brush family in 1927, when Charles, Jr., agreed to give a blood transfusion to his gravely ill daughter. Not only did she not survive, but he also died from complications caused by the transfusion. Two years later the elder Brush, now 80, contracted bronchitis. His condition worsened until June 15, 1929, when he succumbed to pneumonia. Twenty years later, in April 1949, Charles F. Brush III joined the board of the company his father cofounded. His service as a director would be interrupted, but starting in December 1958 he served on the board continuously until his retirement at the age of 80 in December 2003.

After the death of his partner, Sawyer continued to run Brush Laboratories. In 1931 he and Bengyt Kjellgreen developed a process to extract beryllium from ore, prompting a name change for the company: Brush Beryllium Company. Two years later the first electrically heated Beryl furnace was built, and the company gradually increased the amount of beryllium metal it produced, from 60 grams in 1936 to more than 1,000 grams in 1942. An early use for beryllium was the U.S. military's effort to build the first atom bomb. After the war beryllium continued to be used in the development of nuclear weapons as well as peaceful uses for atomic energy. Business improved steadily, topping the $1 million mark in annual revenues in 1943. In addition to beryllium metal, Brush also sold alloys, oxides, and

ceramics. In the second half of the 1950s, the United States ramped up a space program in response to the successes enjoyed by the Soviet Union, beginning with the 1957 launch of the world's first satellite, Sputnik. Brush quadrupled its sales by 1960. The company moved all operations to Elmore, Ohio, where in 1953 Brush had established its alloy division.

Because of its unique properties, beryllium was especially useful in making heat shields for missiles, satellites, and other aerospace applications, but it was with beryllium-copper alloys that Brush enjoyed the most profits in the early 1960s. This material was used in such common applications as automobile parts, welding electrodes, circuit breakers, switches, bearings, gears, valves, casting molds for plastic, dies, and tools that do not spark. From 1964 to 1968 Brush's revenues grew by 58 percent, to $35.3 million. About 90 percent of sales came from beryllium-related products. Also during this period beryl ore was discovered in Utah's Topaz Mountains, leading Brush to form subsidiary Beryllium Resources which then acquired the rights to explore this region and later stake a claim. In 1969 the company took the next step in becoming a more integrated company by building a $10 million mining and milling facility in Utah, located close to a one-pit mine Brush owned and operated. The mill would process ore into beryllium oxide, the raw material for the company's three product lines: beryllium metal, alloys, and ceramics. As a result, Brush became the first beryllium producer in the world to control its own source of ore, thus setting the stage for ongoing growth. The company's mine was also the only beryl mine located in the non-Communist world.

In August 1971 Brush acquired assets of the S.K. Wellman Division of Abex Corp. Wellman manufactured metallic friction material to make robust clutches and brakes required by heavy duty off-road equipment. Brush changed its name to Brush Wellman Inc. When the United States began to withdraw from Vietnam in the early 1970s, Brush's business fell off as military spending declined and government contracts for beryllium metal expired. The company now looked to diversify and develop new markets. It completed several acquisitions in the 1970s, including the 1973 $5.45 million purchase of Sawyer Research Products Inc., the $6.1 million addition of Bucyrus Blades, Inc. a year later, and the 1979 purchase of Crystal Systems, Inc. for $1.14 million. The most important new market to emerge during this time was Silicon Valley, which needed heat-resistant beryllium-copper alloy to make microelectronic chips, which generated more heat as they grew in capability, thus requiring an increase in the need for beryllium-copper. Brush also found more demand for beryllia ceramics, a material with strong insulating properties and an excellent dissipater of heat. Long a money-losing product line, by 1980 it accounted for about 10 percent of the company's pretax profit margin.

Brush Well Positioned for the 1980s

Brush entered the 1980s in a strong position. With the election of Ronald Reagan as President of the United States, military spending grew dramatically, increasing the demand for metallic beryllium. Moreover, Brush's only competitor in this line discontinued production, allowing Brush to raise the price for pure beryllium by 30 percent, a change that did not dissuade the U.S. government from awarding the company a major contract to upgrade the U.S. beryllium metals stockpile. Never-

Key Dates:

1921: Brush Laboratories is launched.
1926: Brush Laboratories begins researching uses for beryllium.
1931: Brush Beryllium grows out of Brush Laboratories.
1971: S.K. Wellman is acquired, leading to the name change to Brush Wellman.
1982: Technical Materials, Inc. is acquired.
1991: Gordon D. Harnett is named CEO.
2000: Brush Wellman becomes Brush Engineered Materials Inc.

theless, Brush endured some struggles in the early 1980s because of a recession. To become involved in the specialty clad metals field—providing materials to be used in power-shift, clutch and brake systems, and cutting edges—Brush paid nearly $46.7 million to acquire Technical Materials, Inc. in late 1982. As a consequence, revenues increased to $245 million and profits to $25.7 million in 1983. With renewed momentum, Brush launched a $57 million capital improvement program in 1984. Of that amount $30 million was earmarked for new casting furnaces, rolling equipment, and other facilities in the Elmore plant; $15 million to build the company's first finishing mill in Europe; $10 million to upgrade a Pennsylvania finishing mill; and $2 million to improve warehouses.

Brush's growth trajectory reversed course in 1988, leading to four straight years of declining revenues caused by a drop in military sales with the end of the Cold War and the rise in popularity of the personal computer, which eclipsed mainframe computers, a major customer for Brush's beryllium materials. The company was forced to cut employment, and in January 1990 it terminated its chairman, president, and CEO, Raymond A. Foos, and began looking for a new chief executive who would be more aggressive in seeking out new applications and markets for Brush's products. Taking over on an interim basis was Foos's predecessor, Henry G. Piper. He held the post for a full year before Gordon D. Harnett, a former senior vice-president at B.F. Goodrich Co., was hired. Harnett was responsible for building up Goodrich's specialty chemicals segment.

Instrumental in Brush's comeback in the early 1990s was the discovery of new applications for beryllium alloys, such as automobile relays, connectors, surge protectors, fuse terminals, and switches. By 1994 sales grew to about $330 million. Later in the 1990s Brush was hurt by the dumping of beryllium at extremely low prices by a refining operation in the former Soviet republic of Kazakhstan. Another area of concern was the rise of lawsuits from former employees claiming they had been exposed to dangerous levels of beryllium particles, which lead to a lung condition called chronic beryllium disease, or CBD. The health hazards of beryllium were first recognized in the 1940s when workers and their wives, who inhaled particles from their husbands' work clothes while doing the laundry, and even people who simply lived close to plant, developed a deadly lung disease that, if it ran its course, resulted in suffocation. Stringent standards were imposed by the U.S. Environmental Protection Agency and the Occupational Safety and Health Administration, by which Brush abided, but workers continued to claim they were victims of CBD. Years of litigation ensued, but Brush was consistently cleared of wrongdoing. Despite these problems, the company launched a $110 million expansion in 1996 to add new equipment for melting, casting, and finishing copper beryllium strip. By the end of the decade, sales grew to a record $456 million.

In 2000 Brush Wellman reorganized its business under a new holding company named Brush Engineered Materials, Inc. The Wellman operations had been sold off in the 1980s and the new company name also better reflected the current breadth of Brush's product offerings. In the early part of the 21st century, Brush experienced a significant drop in business, exacerbated by poor economic conditions in Asia and the United States. Revenues dipped to $372.8 million in 2002 but rebounded to $401 million in 2003 and continued to improve in 2004. The future also looked promising, as end-use markets showed strong growth trends, and automobiles continued to add electronics that would rely on beryllium-based products.

Principal Subsidiaries

BEM Services, Inc.; Brush Wellman Inc.; Brush International, Inc.; Brush Resources Inc.; Technical Materials, Inc.; Williams Advanced Materials Inc.; Zentrix Technologies Inc.

Principal Competitors

NGK Insulators, Ltd.; Olin Corporation; Sumitomo Metal Industries, Ltd.

Further Reading

Gerdel, Thomas W., "Brush Wellman Is Proposing New Structure, Name Change," *Plain Dealer,* February 3, 2000, p. 2C.

Meier, Barry, "The Dark Side of a Magical Metal," *New York Times,* August 25, 1996, p. 3.

Nolan, Kevin, "Beryllium Products: Demand Has Faltered But Hopes Are High," *Metal Center News,* March 1994, p. 54.

Prizinsky, David, "Brush Wellman Sweeps Aside Poor Sales Years," *Crain's Cleveland Business,* October 3, 1994, p. 2.

Quirt, John, "Fat Years at Brush Wellman," *Fortune,* June 15, 1981, p. 148.

Sherman, Joseph V., "Competitive Mettle," *Barron's National Business and Financial Weekly,* January 12, 1970, p. 50.

——, "Space-Age Metal," *Barron's National Business and Financial Weekly,* February 25, 1963, p. 43.

Troxell, Thomas N., Jr., "Brush Wellman: After a Momentous Year, It's Making Bigger Profits," *Barron's National Business and Financial Weekly,* July 25, 1983, p. 63.

—Ed Dinger

B/S/H/

BSH Bosch und Siemens Hausgeräte GmbH

Carl-Wery-Straße 34
D-81739 Munich
Germany
Telephone: (089) 45 90-01
Fax: (089) 45 90-23 47
Web site: http://www.bsh-group.com

Joint Venture of Robert Bosch GmbH and Siemens AG
Incorporated: 1967 as Bosch-Siemens Hausgeräte GmbH
Employees: 34,400
Sales: DEM 6.30 billion ($7.93 billion) (2003)
NAIC: 333415 Air-Conditioning and Warm Air Heating
   Equipment and Commercial and Industrial
   Refrigeration Equipment Manufacturing; 335211
   Electric Housewares and Household Fan
   Manufacturing; 335212 Household Vacuum Cleaner
   Manufacturing; 335221 Household Cooking Appliance
   Manufacturing; 335222 Household Refrigerator and
   Home Freezer Manufacturing; 335224 Household
   Laundry Equipment Manufacturing; 335228 Other
   Major Household Appliance Manufacturing

BSH Bosch und Siemens Hausgeräte GmbH, a joint venture between German industrial giants Robert Bosch GmbH and Siemens AG, is the largest maker of household appliances in both Germany and Western Europe, and ranks third worldwide, trailing only the Swedish firm AB Electrolux of Sweden and the U.S.-based Whirlpool Corporation. In addition to its flagship Bosch and Siemens brands, BSH also sells products under a number of specialized brands (Gaggenau, Neff, Thermador, Constructa, and Ufesa) and regional brands: Balay (Spain), Lynx (Spain), Profilo (Turkey), Pitsos (Greece), Continental (South America), and Coldex (Peru). At its 43 factories located in 15 countries (Germany, France, Greece, Poland, Russia, Slovakia, Slovenia, Spain, Turkey, the United States, Mexico, Brazil, Peru, China, and Thailand), BSH produces a full range of major household appliances, including cooking equipment, dishwashers, refrigerators, freezers, washing machines, and dryers, as well as vacuum cleaners and small appliances such as coffeemakers, food processors, deep fryers, and irons. Its worldwide sales and customer service network is composed of about 70 subsidiary operations in 30 countries. Nearly three-quarters of BSH's sales are generated outside of Germany: 54 percent in Western Europe excluding Germany, 6 percent in Eastern Europe, 5 percent each in North America and Asia, and 3 percent in Latin America. A hallmark of BSH is its consistent aim to establish itself, wherever it operates, as a leader of the premium sector of the market by producing high-quality, innovative products significantly more expensive than the average for that market.

Foundation of BSH: 1967

Bosch and Siemens merged their household appliance operations in 1967, creating a 50–50 joint venture originally called Bosch-Siemens Hausgeräte GmbH (BSH). The rationale behind this joining of forces was to provide a stronger platform for competing in an increasingly global marketplace. Bosch had developed a reputation in Germany for its advanced refrigerators and freezers, based at least in part on its introduction of the first electric domestic refrigerator in 1933. The company extended its range of appliances in the 1950s as part of a diversification drive. In 1952 Bosch introduced the "New Era" electric kitchen appliance, a combination mixer/food processor that could mix, knead, chop, slice, make purees, grind, grate, and more. Next came washing machines, in 1958, and then dishwashers, in 1964. Siemens, which had emerged only in 1966 as an amalgamation of several predecessor firms, had a long history of innovation in household appliances—the first vacuum cleaner in 1906, the first baking oven in 1925, and the first automatic dishwasher in 1964. Key developments in appliances occurred in the immediate aftermath of World War II. In 1949 one of the Siemens predecessors opened a factory in Giengen, West Germany, for the production of refrigerators and freezers and another in Traunreut, West Germany, for cooking appliances and water heaters. These two plants, along with a factory in Berlin where washers and dryers were produced, were contributed to the BSH joint venture in 1967. BSH thus began with three plants, all in West Germany, and about 14,000 employees. First-year revenues of DEM 1 billion were generated in the home country and a few of its neighbors. Western Europe remained the venture's sole focus for nearly the first ten years of its existence.

Company Perspectives:

A consistent innovation and quality policy governs everything we do and how the company evolves. One of the most important principles embraced by BSH is to offer consumers genuine added value in terms of performance, comfort and ease of use by developing new and improved products. This approach is based on the firm conviction that pushing forward with new technologies not only creates competitive advantages and added convenience for the customer—but also ensures that the environment constantly benefits. Know-how transfer within the BSH group ensures that environmental protection standards are also adopted worldwide. BSH is wholeheartedly committed to the principle of sustainability and to the responsible utilization of resources.

Whereas major household appliances were BSH's main focus from the start, the company also started out as a manufacturer of consumer electronics products, such as televisions and radios. Fierce competition from Asian importers, however, overwhelmed many Western manufacturers, and BSH soon abandoned the manufacturing of such goods. The company continued to market consumer electronics products made by third parties, before leaving this sector for good in 1996.

BSH produced products under both the Bosch and Siemens names. The venture was able to get off to a strong start because the two brands had similar positions in the market. They were both premium brands known for their high quality and innovation. These characteristics were in clear evidence in the founding year: It was then that BSH introduced the first dishwasher with a stainless steel interior.

First Moves Abroad: Mid-1970s Through Late 1980s

After achieving steady growth in its home market for several years, BSH made its first move abroad in the mid-1970s. The company acquired a stake in Pitsos A.E. of Athens, Greece, in 1976. BSH later gained full control of this company, which was eventually renamed BSH Ikiakes Syskeves A.B.E. Despite the name change, this subsidiary continued to produce refrigerators and cooking appliances under the Pitsos name. Also in 1976, BSH was given control of a factory in Dillingen, West Germany, that had been opened by Bosch in 1960. Under BSH, the plant, located on the Danube in northwestern Bavaria, began producing dishwashers. Innovation also remained on the agenda in the late 1970s: BSH introduced a refrigerator in 1978 that could store food in multiple temperature zones and that featured pull-out drawers for more convenient removal of stored items.

In the early 1980s intense competition within the European domestic appliance sector coupled with a recession led to industry overcapacity and the collapse of two market leaders in West Germany, AEG Telefunken and Bauknecht. A European-wide shakeout ensued with numerous mergers and bankruptcies throughout the 1980s. In 1980, 150 companies controlled 80 percent of the European market, but by 1990, that number had fallen to just 15. The consolidation wave was engendered in part in anticipation of the creation of a single European market in 1992.

By 1990, BSH had gained the number one position in the newly reunified German market and was number two in Europe, trailing only Electrolux, with a market share of approximately 17 percent. BSH was not the most active consolidator of the 1980s but did manage to add an additional factory in Germany and several in Spain. In 1982 BSH acquired the high-end Neff brand from AEG for about DEM 80 million. Neff had been founded in 1877 in Bretten (Baden-Württemberg) by Carl Andreas Neff, originally producing coal-fired stoves. The company later moved into production of gas- and electric-powered appliances, introduced Europe's first microwave oven in 1957, and invented induction cooking one year later. At the time of its acquisition by BSH, Neff was best known as a producer of premium built-in cooking appliances. Under BSH it would operate as a subsidiary called Neff GmbH.

BSH entered the Spanish market in 1988 and 1989 when it gained majority control of Zaragoza-based Balay, S.A. and acquired Pamplona-based Safel, S.A. Safel's product line included refrigerators, freezers, and ovens, while Balay's included washers and dryers. Among the product development advancements in the 1980s, meantime, was the introduction in 1981 of a universal built-in cooking appliance featuring an integrated microwave oven. In 1985 BSH introduced the Aqua-Stop system into its dishwashers and washing machines. With this feature, in the event of a leak the supply of water would be cut off to prevent flooding. By 1985, BSH had seen its revenue grow to DEM 3.57 billion and its workforce to 15,400. By decade's end, revenues were just short of DEM 6 billion, half of which was generated abroad, and the workforce had reached nearly 23,000.

Continuous Global Expansion in the 1990s

As BSH began to take advantage of the additional domestic opportunities afforded by German reunification, the firm also continued to grow abroad. In 1991 a toehold was established in the United States when it began exporting dishwashers there, shipping models that were nearly identical to those sold in Germany. Dishwashers were selected for this initial assault of the highly competitive U.S. market because that appliance was the most "international" in design; cooking, refrigeration, and laundry appliances needed to be much more tailored to individual markets because of local differences in cooking traditions, cleaning preferences, and climates. Also in 1991, BSH began selling a compact/tabletop dishwasher. Two years later the company moved into Eastern Europe for the first time, acquiring a factory in Nararje, Slovenia, where small domestic appliances—such as hand mixers, blenders, and food processors—and vacuum cleaners were made. This factory became the center of BSH's worldwide small appliance operations. Reacting to concerns that the refrigerants chlorofluorocarbon (CFC) and hydrochlorofluorocarbon (HCFC) were depleting the protective ozone layer in the upper atmosphere, BSH in 1993 began phasing out the use of CFCs and HCFCs in its refrigerators and freezers. In another move that burnished the firm's image as environmentally responsible, BSH launched a program for recycling old appliances.

Under the continued leadership of Herbert Wörner, who had served as chief executive since 1987, BSH's acquisitions pace rapidly increased in the mid-1990s. Late in 1994 Gaggenau,

Key Dates:

1967: German industrial giants Robert Bosch GmbH and Siemens AG create Bosch-Siemens Hausgeräte GmbH (BSH), a joint venture specializing in household appliances.

1976: In its first move outside its home country, BSH acquires a stake in Pitsos A.E. of Athens, Greece.

1982: The company acquires the high-end German cooking appliance brand Neff.

1988–89: BSH enters the Spanish market with the acquisitions of Balay, S.A. and Safel, S.A.

1991: A toehold is established in the United States through the export of dishwashers there.

1994: Gaggenau, German producer of high-end cooking appliances, is acquired.

1995: Production of washers begins in China—the first move into that market.

1997: BSH's first U.S. production plant begins operating in New Bern, North Carolina.

1998: Thermador Corporation, U.S.-based maker of high-end cooking appliances, is acquired; the company changes its name to BSH Bosch und Siemens Hausgeräte GmbH.

2004: Via a $200 million expansion, two new plants are added in New Bern.

maker of high-end built-in cooking appliances, was acquired. A long established German manufacturer, Gaggenau traced its history back to 1683 and began producing stoves in the late 19th century. Among Gaggenau's assets was a factory in Lipsheim, France, which eventually became the center of development for BSH's high-end gas cooking appliances. The factory in Gaggenau itself was closed in 1997.

There were several other developments in late 1994. BSH acquired majority control of Continental 2001 S.A., the third largest producer of domestic appliances in Brazil with annual sales of DEM 420 million ($294 million). This deal gave BSH five manufacturing plants in Brazil and one in Mexico and provided a platform for introducing a full line of Bosch and Siemens brand cooking, refrigeration, laundry, and dishwasher products. Continental brand products continued to be manufactured as well. BSH also entered into a joint venture with Wuxi Little Swan Co., a leading maker of laundry appliances in China, for the manufacture of European-style, front-loading washing machines. Production began the following year at the plant in Wuxi, located in Jiangsu province. BSH revenues for 1994 totaled DEM 6.88 billion ($4.8 billion), up 3 percent from the previous year. Of the total, 42 percent was generated outside Germany.

During 1995 BSH completed a continent-wide restructuring of its distribution system, reducing its European warehouses from 36 to 10 and thereby achieving yearly cost savings of DEM 30 million. Also that year BSH acquired a majority stake in PEG Profilo Elektrikli Gereçler Sanayii A.S., based in Çerkezköy, Turkey. BSH now controlled a production site in Turkey that produced Profilo brand cooking appliances, refrig-

erators, washing machines, and dishwashers. Similar to the Continental deal, BSH planned to use the acquired company as a base for expanding its flagship Bosch and Siemens brands. In the spring of 1995 BSH opened a new factory in Nauen, located in the eastern German state of Brandenburg, capable of producing 400,000 tumble dryers annually. A second plant opened on the same site in the summer of 1996 and had the capacity to make 350,000 top-loading washing machines each year.

BSH in early 1996 entered into a joint venture with China's Yangzi Group to manufacture and supply refrigerators and freezers in China from a factory in Chuzhou, Anhui province. To facilitate marketing throughout Asia, two sales companies were set up in Hong Kong and Singapore. Expansion in Latin America was achieved through a purchase of a majority interest in Lima-based Coldex, S.A. Coldex, the largest appliance maker in Peru, specialized in freestanding cooking appliances, refrigerators, and freezers. Back home, BSH took over control of a factory in Bad Neustadt, in northern Bavaria, that was the largest vacuum cleaner plant in the country. On the innovation front, BSH introduced the Aqua-Sensor system for dishwashers in 1996. This feature enabled the machine to automatically adjust the cleaning process depending on how soiled the water, thus saving time, water, and energy. Washing machine models began offering this feature in 1997.

The most significant developments during the late 1990s centered around a major expansion into the lucrative U.S. market. In March 1997 BSH began producing dishwashers at a plant in New Bern, North Carolina, where Robert Bosch had been making power tools. Production of cooking equipment was added to this plant two years later. These products, positioned in the premium sector of the market, were initially sold under the Bosch brand. BSH next added another high-end brand through the acquisition of Thermador Corporation of Huntington Beach, California, for about $83 million. Well established and prestigious, Thermador produced a variety of high-end cooking appliances—freestanding ranges, built-in cooktops, and range hoods—as well as semiprofessional ranges. The company had plants in Vernon, California, and La Follette, Tennessee. Revenues for fiscal 1997 totaled $115 million.

In 1997 the company's BSH Continental subsidiary in Brazil opened a new refrigerator/freezer production site in the Campinas region. The next year saw further ventures into Eastern European territory: Production of washing machines began at a new plant in Lódz, Poland, and a new plant opened in Chernogolovka, Russia, for the manufacture of a full range of freestanding gas cooking appliances. There were several more acquisitions in 1998. BSH bought Eval, a maker of small appliances in Turkey, and Ufesa, the leading producer of small appliances in Spain. Based in northern Spain, Ufesa was particularly strong in irons, and its plant in Vitoria became BSH's worldwide center for iron manufacturing. Other products produced by Ufesa included coffeemakers, deep fryers, and oil radiators. BSH endeavored to add component development and production to its core competencies, leading Siemens to give the joint venture control of two factories: a controls and sensors facility in Regensburg, Germany, and a motors and pump plant in Michalovce, Slovakia. BSH also joined with Fedders Corporation of the United States in the creation of a joint venture to manufacture room air conditioners in Estella, Spain. In April

1998, meantime, the company changed its name to BSH Bosch und Siemens Hausgeräte GmbH as part of an effort to provide a more consistent global face for a firm whose operations were increasingly far-flung. ''BSH'' began to be incorporated into the firm's growing roster of subsidiaries around the world.

After the hectic activity of 1998, BSH paused to consolidate its newly won operations the following year. Although there were no further acquisitions, a couple of new products for 1999 were particularly noteworthy. BSH debuted a fully automatic dishwasher, one that included sensors to gauge the size of the load and the degree of soiling and then automatically start the appropriate washing program. Also introduced was the world's first food processor designed to be built right into a kitchen counter.

BSH ended the 1990s with its best sales year ever, totaling DEM 10.73 billion ($5.53 billion), despite a difficult economic environment in most of Europe. Net income for 1999, however, amounted to only DEM 111 million ($57.1 million), a significant drop from the peak figure of DEM 198.2 million recorded two years earlier. Thanks to its aggressive global expansion, BSH now had 30 production sites located on four continents, and 68 percent of revenues were coming from outside Germany.

Early 2000s and Beyond

A rebounding economy in Europe and an expanding product portfolio augmented by many new products helped push revenues up 14.5 percent in 2000, to DEM 12.28 billion ($5.97 billion), while net income soared to DEM 384.4 million ($187.4 million). The resulting net profit margin of 3.1 percent was a huge improvement over the previous year's 1 percent. In October 2000 BSH entered into a joint venture with Japan's Hitachi, Ltd. to make front-loading washing machines at a Hitachi plant in Kabinburi, Thailand. The venture, 60 percent owned by BSH, began production in January 2002, marketing the washers under the Bosch, Siemens, and Hitachi brands for the southeast Asian and Pacific region. At the end of 2000, Wörner left the company after 13 years of globalizing and having shepherded the firm into position as the world's third largest maker of white goods. Taking over as president and CEO was Kurt-Ludwig Gutberlet, who had worked his way up to executive vice-president after joining the company in 1983 as a strategic planning associate.

In mid-2001 BSH launched a restructuring of its European refrigerator/freezer operations, which were under severe competitive pressure. To cut costs and improve efficiency, the workforce in Germany was to be gradually reduced by 600 over a two-to three-year period. Despite the high labor costs at home—and the addition of numerous factories abroad—more than half of BSH's production continued to come from German plants.

During 2002 a modern dishwasher production plant was added to the Lódź site and ground was broken in New Bern, North Carolina, for a $200 million expansion of BSH's main U.S. facility that was to add more than 1,400 new jobs. The latter was the company's largest ever plant expansion outside of Germany. Two new plants opened at the site in March 2004 producing washing machines, dryers, and freestanding cooking ranges, designed specifically for the U.S. market. The New Bern factories, already also producing Bosch dishwashers and

Thermidor built-in ovens, soon began churning out Siemens dishwashers, which were initially available only at consumer electronics retailer Best Buy Co., Inc. outlets. Siemens washers, dryers, and countertop small appliances soon followed. BSH now sold three brands in the United States, aiming Siemens at tech-savvy urbanites, Bosch at upwardly mobile families, and Thermador at the trophy kitchen set. U.S. advertising in 2004 doubled to $6 million as North America was targeted as BSH's number one growth market. BSH aimed to more than double its North American sales, hoping to reach $1 billion by about 2006. With the expansion in New Bern, the Thermador plant in Vernon, California, was closed down in mid-2004 in order to cut costs and better exploit the potential of the new facilities.

Meanwhile, in September 2003, BSH moved into a new headquarters in the Neuperlach-Süd district of Munich. The new building enabled the company to concentrate under one roof 1,500 people from various corporate areas who had previously been scattered among several locations. Reflecting the company's cutting-edge, innovative, and high-quality product lines, the new headquarters was said to be the first European office complex to be constructed according to the principles of feng shui. Ecologically friendly materials were featured throughout, and all the furniture met state-of-the-art standards for ergonomics.

As part of a drive to concentrate on core products, BSH completed its exit from the commercial refrigeration sector by selling Metalfrio Solutions, a Brazilian subsidiary of BSH Continental, in early 2004. Around the same time, BSH bought out its partner, Fedders, in the Spain-based air conditioning venture. Despite intense competition that placed downward pressure on prices, BSH remained consistently profitable, enabling it to embark on further global growth initiatives. During 2004 the company began construction on a new dryer factory at the Lódź site and also launched a three-year expansion in China slated to cost between $80 million and $100 million. In China new factories were to be built, the product range was to be extended to include cooking appliances and small appliances, and the Bosch brand would be introduced into the market to be used alongside the Siemens brand, which had been BSH's only brand in China. BSH also was studying the possibility of introducing Bosch refrigerators into the U.S. market, which would enable the company to offer a full line of major appliances in that country for the first time.

Principal Subsidiaries

Robert Bosch Hausgeräte GmbH; Siemens-Electrogeräte GmbH; Constructa-Neff Vertriebs-GmbH; Gaggenau Hausgeräte GmbH; Neff GmbH; BSH Hausgeräte Service GmbH; BSH Hausgeräte Service Nauen GmbH; BSH Hausgerätewerk Nauen GmbH; BSH Electrodomesticos S.A. (Argentina); BSH Hausgeräte Gesellschaft m.b.H. (Austria); BSH Home Appliances S.A. (Belgium); BSH Continental Eletrodomésticos Ltda. (Brazil); Anhui BSH Cooling Appliances Co. Ltd. (China); BSW Household Appliances Co. Ltd. (China; 60%); Jiangsu BS Home Appliances Sales Co., Ltd.; BSH domácí spotřebiče s.r.o. (Czech Republic); BSH Hvidevarer A/S (Denmark); BSH Kodinkoneet Oy (Finland); BSH Electroménager S.A.S. (France); Gaggenau Industrie S.A. (France); BSH Ikiakes Syskeves A.B.E. (Greece); Euroservice A.B.E.-Service Ikiakon

Syskevon (Greece); BSH Home Appliances Ltd. (Hong Kong); BSH Háztartási Készülék Kereskedelmi Kft. (Hungary); BSH Home Appliances Ltd. (Israel); BSH Elettrodomestici S.p.A. (Italy); BSH Electrodomésticos, S.A. de C.V. (Mexico); BSH Huishoud-elektro B.V. (Netherlands); BSH Husholdningsapparater A/S (Norway); BSH Electrodomésticos S.A.C. (Peru); BSH Sprzet Gospodarstwa Domowego Sp. z.o.o. (Poland); BSHP Electrodomésticos, S.U., Lda. (Portugal); BSH Electrocasnice S.R.L. (Romania); OOO BSH Bytowaja Technika (Russia); BSH Home Appliances Pte. Ltd. (Singapore); BSH Drives and Pumps s.r.o. (Slovakia); BSH Hišni Aparati d.o.o. (Slovenia); BSH Home Appliances (Pty.) Ltd. (South Africa); BSH Electrodomésticos España, S.A. (Spain); BSH Balay, S.A. (Spain); BSH Fabricación, S.A. (Spain); BSH Interservice, S.A. (Spain); BSH PAE, S.L. (Spain); BSH Ufesa Industrial, S.A. (Spain); BSH Krainel, S.A. (Spain); BSH and FEDDERS International Air Conditioning, S.A. (Spain); BSH Hushållsapparater AB (Sweden); BSH Hausgeräte AG (Switzerland); BSH Home Appliances Ltd. (Thailand); BHST Washing Appliances Ltd. (Thailand; 60%); BSH Home Appliances Sarl (Tunisia); BSH Profilo Elektrikli Gereçler Sanayii A.Ş. (Turkey); BSH PEG Beyaz Esya Servis A.Ş. (Turkey); BSH Küçük Ev Aletleri Sanayii A.Ş. (Turkey); BSH Home Appliances FZE (United Arab Emirates); BSH Home Appliances Ltd. (U.K.); BSH Home Appliances Corporation (U.S.A.).

Principal Competitors

AB Electrolux; Whirlpool Corporation; GE Consumer & Industrial; Merloni Elettrodomestici S.p.A.; Candy S.p.A.; Haier Group Company; Maytag Corporation.

Further Reading

Baxter, Andrew, "Bosch-Siemens Casts Eye Over New Ground," *Financial Times,* May 25, 1994, p. 29.
Beatty, Gerry, "Bosch-Thermador Deal Sets Upscale Course," *HFN—The Weekly Newspaper for the Home Furnishing Network,* June 22, 1998, p. 50.
——, "BSH Plant Expansion to Fuel Growth Plans," *HFN—The Weekly Newspaper for the Home Furnishing Network,* February 18, 2002, p. 37.
Birkner, Claus, "Bosch-Siemens' Globalization Strategy," *Appliance,* August 1997, p. 20.
——, "BSHG Consolidates Operations in Eastern Europe," *Appliance,* April 1998, p. 22.
Bonnema, Lisa, "Expanding Its Reach," *Appliance,* April 2004, p. B2.
Fallon, James, "Bosch-Siemens Looks for Clout Through Acquisitions," *HFD—The Weekly Home Furnishings Newspaper,* June 13, 1994, p. 78.
Jancsurak, Joe, "Big Plans for Europe's Big Three," *Appliance Manufacturer,* April 1995, p. 26.
Le Blanc, Jenny, "Expansion in the U.S.," *Appliance,* February 1997, p. B11.
Marsh, Peter, "German Venture to Make Dishwashers in the U.S.," *Financial Times,* December 23, 1996, p. 22.
Roggema, Paul, "Bosch/Siemens Hausgeräte: Saturated? Innovate!," *Appliance,* August 2001, p. 24.
Simpson, David, "A Simple Answer," *Appliance,* April 2004, p. B10.
Stevens, Scot, "Welcome to America," *Appliance,* September 1997, p. 67.
——, "Worldwide Encounters," *Appliance,* February 1997, p. B4.
Wolf, Alan, "Best Buy Adds BSH's Siemens Brand to Assortment," *Twice,* January 8, 2004, p. 152.

—David E. Salamie

California Steel Industries, Inc.

14000 San Bernadino Avenue
Fontana, California 92335
U.S.A.
Telephone: (909) 350-6200
Fax: (909) 350-6223
Web site: http://www.californiasteel.com

Private Company
Incorporated: 1984
Employees: 923
Sales: $763.55 million (2003)
NAIC: 331221 Rolled Steel Shape Manufacturing;
331210 Iron and Steel Pipe and Tube Manufacturing
from Purchased Steel

California Steel Industries, Inc. (CSI) ranks as the largest producer of flat-rolled steel in the western United States. CSI does not manufacture steel. The company buys steel slab from third-party vendors and processes the slab into finished steel products, producing hot-rolled, cold-rolled, and galvanized coil and sheet. CSI also produces electric resistance welded pipe. The company's steel products are used in a variety of goods, including appliances, home furnaces, automobile wheels and rims, plumbing fixtures, water heaters, lighting fixtures, decking, and tanks. CSI serves customers in the 11 states west of the Rocky Mountains from its 450-acre manufacturing facility in Fontana, California, 50 miles east of Los Angeles. The company is owned by JFE Steel Corporation (formerly Kawasaki Steel Corp.), a major steel producer in Japan, and Companhia Vale do Rio Doce Ltd., a state-owned Brazilian natural resources company that ranks as the world's largest iron ore producer and exporter.

Origins

CSI began its business life by occupying what had once been home to the largest steelworks in the western United States. The integrated mill in Fontana, California, was built in the 1940s, becoming the jewel of the steelmaking empire controlled by Kaiser Steel Corp. The 350-acre facility bustled with activity in its prime, employing more than 2,500 workers and holding sway as the largest of its kind west of the Mississippi. By the beginning of the 1980s, however, the luster was gone from the Fontana steelworks. The success of foreign competitors, high interest rates in the United States, and adverse conditions in the domestic steel industry drained the factory of its vitality. Financial losses mounted, forcing Kaiser's management to admit defeat and declare bankruptcy. Employees at the Fontana plant were laid off and the mill was closed down, its machinery, presses, and equipment left to lay idle in late 1983.

One individual who was acutely aware of the Fontana closure was Michael Wilkinson, a British-born entrepreneur and steel executive who relied heavily on Kaiser's output. At the time of the Fontana closure, Wilkinson had spent the previous quarter-century owning and managing various steel-related enterprises, building a career that eventually tied his success to the success of Kaiser—the nexus that motivated the formation of CSI. Wilkinson worked at Steel Company of Canada in Hamilton, Ontario, between 1957 and 1962. For the next five years he managed several divisions of steel distributing companies in Toronto and Vancouver. His career in the United States began in 1975 when he formed a partnership with an Italian trading company to acquire Lafayette Metals, a steel producing and distributing company based in Long Beach, California. In 1978, he formed Tecrim, an automobile wheel rim manufacturer, and he acquired 50 percent of Cal Metal Corp., operator of a mill in Irwindale, California. It was through Tecrim and Cal Metal that Wilkinson felt the sting of the Fontana closure; both companies obtained nearly all their steel from Kaiser, ranking among the steelmaker's largest customers.

The closure of the Fontana plant struck the region's steel community hard, particularly Wilkinson. Steel prices rose after Kaiser's steelworks closed. Wilkinson labored to find other suppliers to feed his companies with sufficient amounts of steel product. The idea of acquiring the deserted Fontana plant occurred to Wilkinson soon after Kaiser declared bankruptcy, its genesis springing from his own need for steel and by impending legislation. Wilkinson believed the International Trade Commission (ITC) was preparing to take a stand against subsidized steel imports. "It was very apparent," he said in a May 17, 1985 interview with *Iron Age*, "that the government was going to do something about unfairly traded steel coming into this market. That was an attraction." The threat of foreign-made steel becoming harder to secure and more expensive to buy exacerbated the effect of Kaiser's collapse, prompting Wilkinson to move ahead with acquiring the Fontana plant. Shortly after the ITC ruled in July 1984 to impose sanctions against subsidized imports, Wilkinson made his offer to acquire the Fontana plant. He sold 49 percent of his Tecrim assets to a Japanese trading company, Itoman & Co., and enlisted the support of two well-financed, well-known corporate partners, Japan-based Kawasaki Steel Corp. and Rio Doce Ltd., the U.S. subsidiary of the state-owned Brazilian natural resources company, Companhia Vale do Rio Doce Ltd. (CVRD). The three partners paid $110 million for the former Kaiser plant, concluding the deal in August 1984. The company formed to manage the plant was CSI, a steel company 50 percent owned by Wilkinson, 25 percent owned by Kawasaki Steel, and 25 percent owned by CVRD.

In the hands of Wilkinson and his two partners, the Kaiser complex was geared to be a quite different type of steel factory. Kaiser had produced steel in Fontana; CSI would not make steel. Instead, Wilkinson intended to purchase steel slab from suppliers—primarily from offshore sources in Mexico, Europe, and South America—and to create finished steel products from the slab, the cold-rolled, hot-rolled, flat-rolled sheet, strip, and coils that would compose CSI's product line. Wilkinson, who initially employed only a fraction of the workforce Kaiser had employed, also changed the way the factory operated. "We chucked out the time clocks and put all our people on salary," he explained in his interview with *Iron Age,* eschewing the unionized workforce of Kaiser's day. "We got away from the old job descriptions limiting what an employee can do," he added. Wilkinson hoped the combination of reduced labor costs, greater efficiency, and the proximity of CSI's customers (Wilkinson's nearby companies were expected to consume roughly a third of the plant's output) would enable him to compete against the foreign competition that had brought down the once-mighty Kaiser.

CSI's attempt to succeed where Kaiser failed officially began in late November 1984. Using slabs shipped from Brazilian steelmaker Companhia Siderurgica de Tubarao (24.5 percent owned by Kawasaki Steel), CSI delivered its first order to a tubing manufacturer. During its first full year of operation, profits eluded the company as it struggled to eclipse the breakeven output of 600,000 tons targeted by Wilkinson. The company achieved profitability in 1986, but by the time CSI moved into the black more dramatic news took center stage. What ensued in 1986 became a struggle for CSI itself.

Ownership Battle in 1986

At the start of 1986, talks of restructuring CSI touched off a bitter battle among the company's three owners. The episode began without acrimony, first made public in January 1986 when

discussions of a realignment were revealed by *American Metal Market.* The company was on the verge of profitability, but the losses incurred since CSI's inception required an injection of cash, $25 million according to reports. Because Wilkinson lacked the financial resources of his two massive corporate partners, his contribution to CSI's capital infusion presumably meant his stake in the company would be reduced. In a January 10, 1986 *American Metal Market* article, Wilkinson said the proposed changes "are not significant one way or another," but within months the tenor of the discussions changed. Negotiations broke down among the partners, leading Wilkinson to assert, "I'm not selling any of my stock and I'm not going down to a minority position," according to the June 20, 1986 issue of *American Metal Market.* Kawasaki and CVRD responded by taking Wilkinson to court. Wilkinson filed a countersuit in July 1986. The contentious struggle was resolved several months later, ending with the sale of Wilkinson's 50 percent stake and his complete disassociation with CSI.

In the aftermath of the ownership battle, CSI settled on its course, developing into a profitable, growing steel enterprise. The first profits registered in 1986 set a precedent that was followed for the remainder of the 1980s and throughout the 1990s. The success of the company coupled with the financial resources of CVRD and Kawasaki Steel allowed for a major capital improvement program, giving the company modern and efficient machinery to expand its production output. In 1993, the company embarked on a six-year modernization program aimed at reducing operating costs, broadening its product line, and increasing production capacity. CSI spent roughly $250 million on the program, increasing the amount of tons billed during the period by nearly 90 percent.

An indication of the prosperity and optimism pervading the Fontana headquarters was demonstrated during the late 1990s. In 1997, with still two years to go on its modernization program, company officials began discussing the possibility of another major expansion program. Their confidence drew its strength from the company's admirable performance during the mid-1990s. Annual sales topped $700 million as production increased 70 percent to 1.7 million tons. The increase was achieved by only increasing payroll from 850 to 945 workers, which meant the gains were realized, in large part, by operating more efficiently. In response, management began considering another $250 million improvement project, one that flirted with the idea of CSI making steel for the first time in its history. The plan to produce steel for the company's sheet metal rolling operation was abandoned in 1998, but the exploration into the idea pointed to the vitality of CSI.

By the end of the 1990s, CSI was a well-established, profit-making enterprise, firmly footed as a fixture of the steel community in the western United States. In 1999, a year in which the company posted a record high $47 million in net income, it ranked as the largest producer of the flat-rolled steel in the West. CSI served customers in the 11 states located west of the Rocky Mountains, devoting much of its manufacturing operations to the production of hot-rolled sheet and coil, which accounted for 47 percent of total tons billed at the end of the decade.

CSI in the 21st Century

CSI's impressive record of profitability came to an end as the company entered the 21st century. In the first three months of 2001, the company posted a quarterly loss of $1.9 million, the first loss recorded in 15 years. The company's president and chief executive officer, Lourenco Goncalves, listed a combination of weak demand, low prices, and out-of-state competition as causes for the loss, but most of his frustration was directed at escalating energy prices in California. In the first quarter of 2001, CSI's electricity bill increased 25 percent, a price hike far outstripped by the $5 million the company had to pay for natural gas, a 725 percent increase. The company recovered in the second quarter, but the $3.4 million posted in net income for the period was wiped away by a $3.4 million loss in the third quarter. For the year, CSI ended with a deficit, registering a $3.7 million loss.

When the severity of California's energy crisis ebbed, CSI regained its financial health. In 2002, the company billed more than two million tons of steel products for the first time in its history. More important, the losses recorded the previous year were thoroughly swept away with the $35 million in profit recorded in 2002.

As CSI prepared for its 20th anniversary, the company could claim to have achieved what Kaiser did not: make the Fontana steelworks a profitable, thriving enterprise. The leadership of the company changed as its anniversary approached, giving it the management team to guide its future course. In 2003, Goncalves resigned to head Houston-based Metals USA, leading to the appointment of Vincente Wright as president and chief executive officer. Wright, who joined CVRD in 1975, put together the slab supply contract in 1984 that helped CSI begin

operations when he was the 29-year-old marketing manager at Siderurgica de Tubarao. In mid-2004, Wright was appointed chairman of the company, paving the way for the promotion of Masakazu Kurushima to the posts of president and chief executive officer. Kurushima began his career at Kawasaki Steel in 1972, rising to head the company's U.S. subsidiary before being tapped to lead CSI. To these two individuals fell the responsibility of ensuring that CSI's future was as successful as its past.

Principal Subsidiaries

CSI Rolling Mills, Inc.

Principal Competitors

Oregon Steel Mills, Inc.; USS-POSCO Industries; Steelscape, Inc.

Further Reading

Haflich, Frank, "California Steel Brings Fontana into Production After 10-Month Shutdown," *American Metal Market,* November 16, 1984, p. 2.

——, "California Steel Eyes 'Little Guys' Accounts," *American Metal Market,* August 3, 1984, p. 1.

——, "California Steel Posts 1st Loss in 15 Years," *American Metal Market,* April 25, 2001, p. 3.

——, "Calif. Steel Chairman to Keep 50% Interest," *American Metal Market,* June 20, 1986, p. 1.

——, "Calif. Steel Makes a Commitment; Assures Fontana Unit Will Be Producing in 2 Months," *American Metal Market,* September 13, 1984, p. 1.

——, "Calif. Steel Partners in Legal Battle," *American Metal Market,* July 2, 1986, p. 1.

——, "Despite Lure of Good Times, CSI Resists Call to Expand," *American Metal Market,* February 24, 2004, p. 1.

——, "Legal Battle Between CSI's Wilkinson and Two Foreign Partners Escalates," *American Metal Market,* July 15, 1986, p. 1.

——, "Wilkinson's California Steel Interest Might Be Reduced," *American Metal Market,* January 10, 1986, p. 1.

——, "Wright at the Helm at CSI, Braces for Challenges," *American Metal Market,* April 9, 2003, p. 1.

Katzanek, Jack, "Fontana, Calif., Steel Company Posts $1.9 Million Loss," *Knight Ridder/Tribune Business News,* April 25, 2001.

"Owners Install New Chairman, President/CEO at California," *Metal Producing & Processing,* July-August 2004, p. 14.

Scott, Gray, "California Steel Eyes $250 Million Expansion for Steel Making," *Knight Ridder/Tribune Business News,* December 1, 1997.

Senia, Al, "How Michael Wilkinson Will Make California Steel Go," *Iron Age,* May 17, 1985, p. 24.

—Jeffrey L. Covell

Cantine Giorgio Lungarotti S.R.L.

Via Mario Angeloni, 16
06089 Torgiano
Perugia
Italy
Telephone: +39-075-988-0348
Fax: +39-075-988-0294
Web site: http://www.lungarotti.it

Private Company
Incorporated: 1962
NAIC: 312130 Wineries

Cantine Giorgio Lungarotti S.R.L. has literally put Italy's Umbria region on the winemaker's map of the world. The Torgiano-based company is behind the region's renaissance as one of Italy's most well-known winemaking regions. Lungarotti is also the area's dominant winemaker, with more than 300 acres of vineyard owned or directly controlled by the company. In this way, Lungarotti ensures a near-autonomous supply of grapes for its production of fine wines. The company limits its wine production to just a few labels, including the company's strongest seller, Rubesco DOC. Other labels in the Lungarotti stable include Aurente, Cabernet Sauvignon, Chardonnay, Giubilante, Grappa di Rubesco, Pinot Grigio, Rubesco Riserva Vigna Monticchio DOCG, San Giorgio, Torre di Giano, and Vino Santo. Many of Lungarotti's wines are aged for some ten years before they are bottled. Lungarotti targets the higher-priced bracket of the wine market, with prices ranging from $12 to $60 per bottle. The company also produces a fortified wine, Grappa di Rubesco. In addition to its core winemaking operations, Lungarotti produces olive oil and balsamic vinegar. The company also has developed a number of tourism initiatives, including the four-star Le Tre Vasalle; the Lungarotti Wine Museum, considered by many as one of the best in the world; the Olive and Olive Oil Museum; and La Spolla, a gift shop featuring traditional handcrafts. Cantine Giorgio Lungarotti is led by the founder's daughter, Chiara Lungarotti, who serves as company CEO. Stepdaughter Teresa Severini, who became the first female Italian oenologist in 1978, serves as the company's winemaker.

Restoring the Umbrian Wine Legacy in the 1960s

The Umbria region, south of Italy's more well-known Tuscany wine region, had developed its own winemaking culture stretching back at least 3,000 years, during the Etruscan period. The region's caves, formed naturally in the volcanic rock, served as ideal wine cellars. During the Roman era, the region's winemaking practices—such as a tradition of mixed agricultural use of the land—were codified, and remained in place, for the most part, into the late 20th century. The mixed agriculture also gave rise to the region's prominence as a major Italian olive oil producer.

In the late 19th century, an outbreak of the phylloxera virus decimated Europe's vineyards, including those in the Umbrian region. Winemakers replanted, but with inferior quality and nontraditional grape varieties. While Umbrian olive oil retained its prestige into the 20th century, the region's wine reputation suffered. Overshadowed by the more popular and respected wines from the Tuscany region, Umbria's wines earned a reputation as "perennially mediocre," as *Town & Country* put it.

If Umbrian wines nonetheless achieved a worldwide reputation by the dawn of the 21st century, it was through the efforts, in large part, of Dr. Giorgio Lungarotti, who held doctorate degrees in oenology and agronomy. The Lungarotti family had long been a prominent agricultural family in the region, and Lungarotti himself had made a fortune as an olive oil producer in the years following World War II.

In the 1950s, Lungarotti became convinced that his lands could also produce high-quality wines as well. Lungarotti recognized that such a transformation required abandoning the region's traditional agricultural methods, in particular the mixed-used farming method, where vines were spaced widely apart and surrounded by other plants and crops. Lungarotti began experimenting with new planting techniques, as well as new vine varieties. Lungarotti also brought a scientific approach to developing his vineyards, performing soil analysis and other testing procedures in order to match vine and soil types.

Lungarotti began buying up additional lands in the area, a move that enabled the company to develop a near-autonomy in

Company Perspectives:

Created by Giorgio Lungarotti, an entrepreneur with exceptional capabilities, the Company has become identified with its founder and his family, which is completely involved in the management. Today with the determination and communicative skills of sisters Chiara Lungarotti and Teresa Severini and the culture expressed by the Lungarotti Foundation embodied by their mother Maria Grazia, the Company is advancing in a logic of entrepreneurial connections that has always made this family known as a veritable "volcano" of ideas.

Key Dates:

1962: Giorgio Lungarotti establishes a winery and begins experimenting with grape varieties and growing techniques.

1968: Cantine Giorgio Lungarotti's Rubesco becomes one of the first Italian wines to receive the DOC appellation.

1974: The company opens the Lungarotti Wine Museum.

1983: The company begins aging a "single-hill" wine, Rubesco Riserva Vigna Monticchio.

1990: Rubesco Riserva Vigna Monticchio receives the new DOCG appellation; the company opens the Olive and Olive Oil Museum.

1999: Giorgio Lungarotti dies at age 88 and daughters Chiara Lungarotti and Teresa Severini become the first women to operate a major winery in Italy.

2001: The company releases a new label, Giubilante.

its grape production. This also allowed the company close control of planting, growing, and harvesting techniques. In the early 1960s, Lungarotti became one of the first in Italy to begin importing grape varieties, such as the Cabernet Sauvignon and Chardonnay grapes. Yet Lungarotti also was inspired by the Umbrian region's long winemaking history, and began planting vineyards based on varieties used before the phylloxera outbreak in the 19th century. The success of these early initiatives convinced Lungarotti to set up his company, Cantine Giorgio Lungarotti, in 1962.

Then 52 years old, Lungarotti built a modern winery and began bottling his wines by the mid-1960s, launching the flagship wine label, Rubesco, from the Latin "rubescere," meaning "to blush." The quality of the company's wines was instantly recognized, and by 1968, Lungarotti became one of the first in Italy to achieve the newly instituted Demoninazione di Origine Controllata (DOC) established by the Italian government.

Lungarotti married Maria Grazia in 1970. Grazia's own background was as an art historian, and her association with the company led Lungarotti to establish its own wine museum in 1974. Under Grazia's curatorship, the Lungarotti Wine Museum soon became world famous, and was considered one of the finest museums devoted to wine and winemaking in the world.

New Generation for a New Century

Grazia's daughter, Teresa Severini, also became an important part of the company. In 1978, Severini, who studied agronomy at the University of Perugia and winemaking at the University of Bordeaux, became the first woman in Italy to receive a degree as an oenologist. Severini's acceptance in the company's operations was by no means guaranteed. As Lungarotti's daughter explained to *Decanter:* "Initially both my sister and I had to prove ourselves as winemakers. My father was a conservative and rather prejudiced. It took him time to accept that both his daughters were worthy winemakers."

Yet both recognized Lungarotti's importance in developing Umbria's new reputation as a quality wine region. As Severini told the *Sarah Jane English Newsletter:* "I like quoting our friend author Hugh Johnson who said my father put Umbria on the world wine map. Father realized our region's potential at a time many Italian wines had a mediocre image, especially abroad. His transformation of the family holdings to specialized interests differentiated the product line to reach higher stan-

dards. He believed that wine and culture were inherent to each other and planned our company to include the development of cultural and hospitality activities. Giorgio was a great, great entrepreneur, an enlightened man who 40 years ago understood the necessity of change, maintaining at the same time an intelligent respect for roots and tradition. He considered his family his precious collaborators. We carry on."

Daughter Chiara, born in the early 1970s, also became an important part of the family business. As she explained to *Decanter:* "The winery was my world. This is where I grew up. Some of my most precious memories are of being hoisted onto my father's knees as he drove the tractor through the vineyards." Chiara, who also went on to study agronomy at the University of Perugia, joined the company in 1992, gaining experience in all aspects of the winery's operation.

Lungarotti continued developing new wines through the 1980s and into the 1990s. The company's willingness to age its wines for ten years or more before bottling them became something of a company hallmark, and helped enhance its reputation for high quality wines. The company released its Cabernet Sauvignon di Torgiano, initially planted in 1970, which received its own DOC designation. The company also continued to experiment with its growing and planting techniques. This led to the creation of a new wine, Rubesco Riserva Vigna Monticchio, in 1983. While featuring a similar blend to the company's earlier Rubesco, the new variety featured grapes from a single hillside, called Monticchio, with particularly fertile soil. The new label, aged for a minimum of ten years, received the new DOCG (Demoninazione di Origine Controllata e Garantita) designation when it was created in 1990. The DOCG designation was made retroactive to the first Monticchio vintage in 1983.

Lungarotti continued to contribute to the region in other ways, especially its tourism infrastructure. In 1990, the company opened its second museum, dedicated to olives and olive oil. Lungarotti also developed its own four-star hotel and restaurant, La Tre Vassale. After Lungarotti died in 1999, his daughters took over as operators of the winery—marking the first time in Italian history that a major winery was run by women. Severini became the company's top winemaker, and Chiara Lungarotti became company CEO.

Into the 2000s, Lungarotti continued to attract recognition from the world of wine. The new generation of family leadership also emerged as capable winemakers in their own right, releasing a number of new wine types. These included the Giubilante, a blend of five grape varieties, released in 2001, and the "supervinodatavola" Rosso dell' Umbria IGT, created from a blend of Sangiovese, Canaiolo, and Cabernet Sauvignon grapes. In the meantime, the Lungarotti tradition appeared set to spread beyond Umbria—in 2003, Chiara Lungarotti married Matteo Lupi Grassi, owner of a wine estate in Tuscany.

Principal Subsidiaries

La Spola; Le Tre Vaselle; Lungarotti Wine Museum; Olive and Olive Oil Museum; Poggio alle Vigne.

Principal Competitors

Antinori S.p.A.; Diageo PLC; Gruppo Italiano Vini Soc. Coop. S.R.L.

Further Reading

Bergonzini, Renato, "Giorgio Lungarotti: 'Tutti assieme appassionatamente,'" *Premiata Salumeria Italiana,* March-April 2002.

Collins, Glenn, "A Wine Lover's Dream," *Town & Country,* May 2004, p. 105.

Ejbich, Konrad, "The Good Doctor of Lunarotto," *eye,* September 24, 1992.

English, Sarah Jane, "Lungarotti—A Travel and Wine Destination in Umbria, Italy," *Sarah Jane English Newsletter,* April 28, 2001.

Gismondi, Anthony, "Turning Away from Tradition Paid Off for Producers," *Vancouver Sun,* May 2004.

Passmore, Nick, "Stunning Umbrian," *Forbes,* March 12, 2003.

—M.L. Cohen

CAR·TOYS
A better way to go.

Car Toys, Inc.

20 West Galer Street
Seattle, Washington 98119
U.S.A.
Telephone: (206) 443-0980
Fax: (206) 443-2525
Web site: http://www.cartoys.com

Private Company
Incorporated: 1987
Employees: 1,200
Sales: $150 million (2003 est.)
NAIC: 443112 Radio, Television, and Other Electronics
  Stores

Car Toys, Inc. ranks as the fifth largest mobile electronics retailer in the United States. The company operates more than 50 stores in Washington, Oregon, Colorado, and Texas, selling cellular phones and service, car audio systems, car alarm systems, radar detectors, and a variety of car accessories. A substantial portion of the company's business is derived from the installation of the products sold at its stores. Car Toys places an emphasis on training its salespeople in customer service and product knowledge, presenting itself as an expert in the field of mobile electronics. The company is led by its founder, chairman, chief executive officer, and president, Daniel Brettler.

Origins

Daniel Brettler's drive to found Car Toys was motivated by a belief common among entrepreneurs. He believed he could do a better job than his employer could. Brettler began developing his conviction, and the experience that would help him manage Car Toys, during his first job. In 1981, after earning a college degree, Brettler started working for an electronics retailer, Pacific Stereo, based in Tacoma, Washington. Brettler was hired as a salesman, earning $4.25 an hour selling car stereos, home stereos, and video equipment. His disillusionment with working within the hierarchy of a corporate retailer started building almost immediately. "I was a young kid who had nothing to lose and everything to prove," he reflected in a

September 15, 2002 interview with the *Seattle Times*. "I quickly became one of the top salesman on the floor, but I was on an hourly wage and not on commission like the rest of the guys. They had a limit on the number of salespeople they could put on commission, so I left."

Brettler, a proven, albeit young, salesperson, had little trouble finding another job. He spent a year at Pacific Stereo before leaving to join Northwest Auto Sound in 1982. Brettler distinguished himself at Northwest Auto, rising to the post of vice-president of sales and marketing within a few years, but his dissatisfaction persisted. At Pacific Stereo, he experienced an organization that was unwilling to reward his efforts. At Northwest Auto, his success was acknowledged by a series of promotions, but he grew frustrated at the way the business was run. "I just felt I could do it better," he remarked in a July 16, 1993 interview with *Puget Sound Business Journal*. "I wanted to put my own identity on a project and see if I could deliver a better product," he added. His decision to leave Northwest Auto was well timed. The retailer expanded too quickly, jumping into other product categories such as home audio and cellular installation. The company went out of business in 1987, the same year the 28-year-old Brettler opened his own store.

Brettler had left Northwest Auto the previous year and had begun planning for the start of his entrepreneurial career. He, like his employers, planned to sell car audio equipment, radar detectors, car alarms, and other electronic accessories designed for cars. He planned to name his store "Mobile Electronics World," but his wife suggested an alternative, "Car Toys." "It (the name of the store) was very instrumental to his success," one of Brettler's business associates explained in a July 16, 1993 interview with *Puget Sound Business Journal*. "Everybody wants that trick name that describes exactly what the business does." Brettler opened his first store east of Seattle, in Bellevue, Washington, in 1987. The store, which focused on installing the products it sold, performed remarkably well during its first year, collecting $1.5 million in sales.

Brettler's confidence in his abilities to succeed in the car electronics field was demonstrated in the expansion of the Car Toys concept. Within four years of its inception, the company opened two more stores, one in Seattle and another in Lynnwood, a suburb of Seattle. Together, these stores generated $9 million in sales in 1991, the year Brettler redoubled his efforts to make Car Toys a leader in customer service. Nearly every company espoused a great emphasis on customer service, but not every company succeeded in turning words into reality. Brettler succeeded, shaping Car Toys into a retailer renowned for a high level of customer service. Brettler's increased commitment to customer service was well timed, occurring before the expected wave of mass merchandisers flooded the Pacific Northwest and, as industry pundits projected, forever changed the way regional chains operated. Aware that some other retailer could always offer merchandise at a lower price, Brettler focused on employee training, "the biggest thing we do," he said in an August 3, 1992 interview with *HFD-The Weekly Home Furnishings Newspaper.* "We decided about a year ago to make a huge, huge investment in training our people, so as our growth continued there would still be a high quality of expertise," he explained. Attention to customer service, Brettler believed, would help the company compete against the approaching major retailers. "We've been lucky," he said in his August 3, 1992 interview, "because we haven't had a real strong mass merchandiser like Circuit City or Good Guys come into town yet, but we will. It's only a matter of time," he added.

Expansion of the Concept in the 1990s

Brettler succeeded in establishing an identity for Car Toys, creating a retail brand that could be expanded. Brettler's winning formula was a combination of aggressive marketing, attractive pricing, and attention to customer service. Salespeople were given four to five weeks of training, including two days at Cellular One, the leading provider of cellular communication services in the Pacific Northwest. (Car Toys was a Cellular One authorized agent, signing customers up for service when they purchased a cellular phone.) Installation staff, whose work was responsible for a fifth of the company's sales, were tested and certified on a three-level scale based on a national certification program. The company's well-trained staff sold and installed just four categories of merchandise—cellular phones, car audio systems, car alarms, and radar detectors—giving Car Toys a limited yet distinct product line. "He's carved out a niche as a specialist," one of Brettler's vendors noted in a July 16, 1993 interview with *Puget Sound Business Journal.* "But he also advertises the best deals. He's been the best at combining the two—great value to the customer and a lot of training and testing of salespeople."

Brettler steadily expanded his concept during the 1990s, building Car Toys into a regional chain. The company's 5,500-square-foot format, featuring neon décor and large windows overlooking the installation area, proved to be a successful blueprint for other stores. Between 1991 and 1993, Brettler

doubled the size of his company, giving him six stores, including two in Portland, Oregon, the first units established outside Washington. Brettler opened new stores at a pace of nearly three stores a year during the mid-1990s, making Car Toys a 20-store, $65 million regional chain by 1998. At this point, after a decade of guiding the company, Brettler was contemplating a major move on the financial side of the company's operation. "I felt it was a good time to diversify my own assets and find another way to finance Car Toys' growth," he explained in an April 2, 1999 interview with *Puget Sound Business Journal.*

Taking on an Investment Partner: 1999

The decision Brettler made in the late 1990s fueled Car Toys' expansion, making the period one of fast-paced growth for the company. Brettler wanted to obtain capital to accelerate Car Toys' expansion, while, at the same time, take some of his own cash out of the company. He also wanted to give nine principal managers an equity position in the company. Initially, Brettler thought about taking Car Toys public to achieve his three objectives, but he was advised to eclipse the $100-million-sales mark and to prove to Wall Street that the concept worked outside the Pacific Northwest before completing an initial public offering (IPO) of stock. Brettler heeded the advice and took another approach, hiring a Seattle-based investment banking firm, Windswept LLC, to locate an investment partner. Ideally, Brettler wanted an investor to acquire a stake in the company, but not interfere in the company's operation. Windswept found a perfect match to Brettler's criteria, a Boston, Massachusetts-based investment firm, TA Associates.

Car Toys' recapitalization program was announced in early 1999. The deal involved selling 45 percent of the company, with most of the equity stake taken on by TA Associates. New York-based First Dominion Capital, which offered a revolving credit line, and the group of Car Toys managers secured smaller equity positions. The infusion of capital—an undisclosed amount—gave Brettler the financial resources to expand the chain aggressively, something that already was underway when the recapitalization package was made public. Car Toys made its first move outside the Pacific Northwest in 1999, opening a store in Denver, Colorado, in March. Brettler's ambitions had grown, and a new approach to the company's expansion emerged. The company had determined that the Denver area was capable of supporting nine Car Toys stores, enabling it to expand in a burst, with a cluster of stores targeted for the area. By the time the first Denver store opened, seven additional stores were in the process of receiving building permits or already under construction.

Brettler did not wait long before expanding Car Toys into its fourth major market, leading industry pundits to wonder whether the company's chairman, chief executive officer, and president was trying to prove to the financial community that Car Toys was worthy of an IPO. In September 2000, the 30-store chain entered the Dallas market, an area chosen because of its substantial population and the absence of a major competitor. The company's expansion came in a burst, following the pattern established by its foray into the Denver area. Three stores were opened in the Dallas suburbs of Hurst, Irving, and McKinney at the end of September, followed by the establishment of stores in Lewisville and Duncanville by the end of

Key Dates:

1987:	The first Car Toys store opens in Bellevue, Washington.
1991:	Car Toys invests heavily in an employee-training program.
1999:	TA Associates takes a minority equity position in Car Toys.
2000:	One year after entering the Denver market, Car Toys expands into Dallas.
2004:	Car Toys ranks as the fifth largest mobile electronics retailer in the country.

landscape between Washington and Texas midway through the decade, the company already had outgrown the definition of a regional chain. In the years ahead, the company's conversion to public ownership seemed likely, as Brettler set his sights on making Car Toys a retail brand with national appeal.

Principal Competitors

Circuit City Stores, Inc.; Magnolia Hi-Fi Inc.; Good Guys, Inc.

Further Reading

Parkhurst, Terry, "The Toys Car Buffs Crave," *Puget Sound Business Journal,* October 28, 1991, p. 18.

Sather, Jeanne, "Car Toys' Boss Pumps Up the Volume," *Puget Sound Business Journal,* July 16, 1993, p. 1.

Spector, Robert, "Car Toys: Hottest Technology; Mobile Electronics Chain Readies for Mass Merchants with Customer Service, Newest Goods," *HFD-The Weekly Home Furnishings Newspaper,* August 3, 1992, p. 76.

Tice, Carol, "Car Toys Revving Up Dallas Market," *Puget Sound Business Journal,* September 15, 2000, p. 12.

——, "Seattle-Based Car Toys Finds Its Dream Partner," *Business Journal-Portland,* April 2, 1999, p. 5.

——, "Sound Move," *Puget Sound Business Journal,* April 2, 1999, p. 1.

—Jeffrey L. Covell

the year. "Our advertising plan is built around radio and television ads," Brettler explained in a September 15, 2000 interview with *Puget Sound Business Journal.* "So we like markets where we can put a cluster or set of stores, with 10 to 20 in a single ad umbrella. We want to get our brand going extremely strong, and to do that we've got to spend some ad dollars."

Car Toys stretched the parameters defining a regional chain during the early years of the century's first decade. With a model of expansion established, the company likely could export its concept to additional major markets, eventually becoming a national chain. With more than 50 stores dotting the

Carbo PLC

Trafford Park Road, Trafford Park
Manchester
M17 1HP
United Kingdom
Telephone: +44 161 872 8291
Fax: +44 161 872 1471
Web sites: http://www.angloabrasives.com
http://www.carbogb.co.uk

Public Company
Founded: 1891 as Carborundum Company
Employees: 838
Sales: £53 million ($96.9 million) (2003)
Stock Exchanges: London
Ticker Symbol: CAB.L
NAIC: 327910 Abrasive Product Manufacturing; 335314
Relay and Industrial Control Manufacturing

Carbo PLC, through subsidiary Carborundum Abrasives GB Ltd., is one of the world's leading manufacturers of abrasives products. The company focuses on high-specification abrasives for the professional sector, leaving the consumer do-it-yourself (DIY) market to competitors such as Saint-Gobain's Norton. Carbo produces a full range of bonded, and coated, abrasives, as well as high-performance superabrasives. The company's production takes place in Manchester, England, as well as in company-owned sites in Germany. Carbo is also one of the leading distributors of its own and others' abrasives products in the United Kingdom through subsidiaries Anglo-Abrasives and Abrafract. The company operates a countrywide network of distribution centers, ranging from Glasgow to Newton Abbot in far south England, and including sites in Sheffield, Manchester, Nuneaton, Strensham, Worcester, Kingston, Surry, New Milton, and Newton Aycliffe. Carbo has been hit hard by the economic slowdown at the beginning of the 21st century and has been battling losses in the early 2000s. By 2004, however, with sales at £53 million ($96 million), the company started to see signs of a turnaround, as orders began to rise. Carbo PLC is listed on the London Stock Exchange, and is led by Managing Director Lars Nyquist.

Abrasives Import in the 20th Century

Carbo's origins traced back to the foundation of the Carborundum Company in the United States at the end of the 19th century. Edward Acheson had been performing experiments using electricity in order to create artificial diamonds. Instead of diamonds, Acheson discovered a new type of crystal created as a byproduct of his experiments.

Acheson quickly determined that the crystals were able to cut not only glass, but diamonds as well. The crystals also possessed excellent refractory properties. Acheson decided to commercialize the new product, adopting the name Carborundum because he mistakenly believed that the crystals were a combination of carbon and aluminum oxide, also known as corundum. The crystals were later revealed to be silicon carbide, and recognized as the world's first man-made mineral. Acheson set up his company in 1891 and began producing grinding wheels using the new substance.

Carborundum's first market came from the New York diamond trade, replacing traditional materials used for polishing gemstones. The company's first big contract, however, came from George Westinghouse, who placed an order for 60,000 grinding wheels in 1893. The company initially produced only bonded abrasives; by 1898, however, Carborundum had developed a range of coated adhesives as well.

For many, the invention of Carborundum represented a milestone in the history of industrial growth. The crystals' abrasives capability, coupled with their high level of heat tolerance, played an important role in the development of mass production techniques. Demand for the crystals rose quickly throughout the world. The company also continued to research new abrasives materials, and in 1905 introduced a fused aluminum oxide called Aloxite. The new substance proved even more resistant than Acheson's original silicon carbide.

To supply strong demand from Europe, Carborundum began investing in overseas production. In 1906, the company built a

Company Perspectives:

Carborundum has a proud history, but we are not content to rest on past glories. The Company's commitment to product quality, technological excellence and exemplary customer service confirm our continued leadership in an industry founded by Edward Goodrich Acheson over a century ago.

factory near Düsseldorf, Deutsche Carborundum Werke. Germany quickly emerged as a major world center for abrasives production. Meanwhile, Carborundum continued to seek new production sites, launching a French subsidiary in 1910. England came next, with the establishment of a British subsidiary, The Carborundum Company Ltd., in Manchester, England. The Trafford Park site remained the British operation's main site into the next century.

The U.S. Carborundum Company expanded rapidly in the United States, then focused on continuing its international expansion. In the years following World War II, the parent company entered a number of new markets, including Switzerland, Belgium, Brazil, Australia and New Zealand, and India. Carborundum also began an ambitious diversification effort, adding production of metals, ceramics, other minerals, and various manufacturing operations as well.

New Owners in the 1980s and 1990s

The U.K. Carborundum meanwhile remained focused on its core abrasives products. The company made a series of investments in order to increase its manufacturing capacity. At the same time, it expanded its abrasives line, building a dedicated Resin Plant in 1960. This allowed Carborundum UK to begin producing a line of resin bonded abrasive wheels, as well as coated papers and cloths.

By the mid-1970s, the U.S. parent company had begun to attract a series of takeover offers, starting with a hostile offer from Eaton Corporation. After successfully fighting off that attempt, Carborundum accepted a $571 million cash offer from Kennecott Copper Corporation in 1978. Within just three years, however, Kennecott was scooped up by Standard Oil of Ohio, also known as Sohio.

Soon after, Sohio began stripping its abrasives operations, especially Carborundum's international operations. Like much of Carborundum's international businesses, the British unit had slumped into losses with the 1970s economic recession. Sohio had named a new management team to try to turn the British subsidiary around. Then, after Sohio announced its intention to shed its foreign abrasives holdings, Carbo's management, led by Ken Jackson, engineered a buyout of the British subsidiary. The purchase price amounted to just £2.6 million. The company, primarily composed of Carborundum's British and German operations, then adopted the name Carborundum Abrasives GB Ltd. (Carbo). Carbo listed its shares on the London Stock Exchange's OTC market that year, before moving to a full listing in 1988.

The abrasives market during the 1980s remained a highly fragmented, and highly cyclical, market, in which profits proved difficult to realize. As Carbo was unable to gain a significant market share in its core markets, Jackson led the company on a diversification drive, expanding into a number of areas including drainage products and plastics. The company's largest single market during this period was West Germany. Yet the deep economic difficulties in that country during the recession at the beginning of the 1990s were slated to be exacerbated by the German reunification.

In response, Jackson sought a buyer for the company. In 1991, Carborundum agreed to be acquired by the United Kingdom's Hopkinsons Group for £33 million. Hopkinsons was itself in the process of restructuring, having sold off its main Hopkinsons Limited business in 1987, and its large valve business to the Weir Group in 1990. The ''new'' Hopkinsons now operated through two primary divisions, Carborundum, and Bryan Donkin, for gas distribution equipment and systems.

Focusing on Abrasives for the New Century

In 1993, Ken Jackson took over as Hopkinsons' chief executive, backed up by another Carborundum alumnus, Martin Sanderson, as finance director. The pair now began to refocus Hopkinsons around its abrasives operations. The company also plotted a strategy to build market share in bonded abrasives in its core U.K. and German markets, in order to position itself as a major player in the global abrasives market.

Acquisitions formed an important part of this strategy. In 1996, Hopkinsons launched its acquisition drive in earnest. The purchase of Abrafract Abrasives that year boosted the group's U.K. operations by some 25 percent, and gave it a leading 20 percent share of the British market. The company also bought Hodges Jacques, which enabled the company to target the French market. The company boosted its capacity in Germany by acquiring Acton & Borman.

By 1997, abrasives accounted for 70 percent of the company's turnover, prompting Hopkinsons to change its name to Carbo PLC that year. The company continued building up its abrasives operations, while phasing out its noncore operations. The Bryan Donkin business was sold off in 1998.

As it approached the end of the decade, Carbo restructured its German operations, shifting its exports business to the United Kingdom. In 1998, Carbo announced its plans to spend £10 million on new acquisitions, starting with abrasives distributor Noble & Macauley. In Germany, Carbo bought family-owned Dilumit that year as well. In 1999, the company attempted to enter Italy, acquiring the country's BMA Group for £4 million. The purchase added some 21 percent to the company's coated abrasives revenues and a 10 percent boost to the company's overall sales.

Yet Carbo's hopes for gaining a significant stake in the wider European market were thwarted by the rise of the Saint-Gobain group's abrasives subsidiary, which had acquired world leader Norton in 1990 and also controlled another major abrasives maker, Unicorn/Universal. As Saint-Gobain continued to buy abrasives companies—including the remains of the original Carborundum group in 1995—Carbo was forced to draw back to its core German and U.K. markets.

Key Dates:

1891: Carborundum Company is founded in the United States.

1908: Carborundum establishes a manufacturing plant in Düsseldorf, Germany.

1913: The company launches a U.K. subsidiary, with a plant in Trafford Park, Manchester.

1960: Carborundum UK establishes the Resin Plant.

1978: Carborundum is acquired by Standard Oil (Sohio).

1981: Kennecott Copper acquires Sohio; Carborundum UK gets new management under CEO Ken Jackson.

1984: Kennecott begins the sell-off of Carborundum operations; Jackson leads the management buyout of Carborundum UK, including the German assets; the company goes public on the London Stock Exchange OTC board as Carborundum Abrasives GB.

1988: The company shifts its stock to the London Stock Exchange's main board.

1991: Hopkinsons acquires Carborundum for £33 million.

1993: Ken Jackson becomes CEO of Hopkinsons and begins refocusing the company as an abrasives group.

1996: As part of a drive to gain market share, the company acquires Abrafract Abrasives, Hodges Jacques, and Acton & Borman in Germany.

1997: The company changes its name to Carbo PLC.

1998: The company acquires abrasives distributor Noble & Macauley in the United Kingdom and Dilumit in Germany.

1999: The company acquires the BMA Group in Italy.

2002: The company shifts distribution operations, including export business, to the United Kingdom, and refocuses manufacturing operations on Germany; Ekamunt, an abrasives conversion and distribution company in the United Kingdom, is acquired.

2004: After posting £25 million in losses since the beginning of the decade, the company shuts down its original Trafford Park site, shifting production to Germany.

The economic slump at the start of the 2000s also began to grind down on Carbo. The company's revenues began to slip, and its profits disappeared. As its losses began to mount, Carbo worked at consolidating its manufacturing operations. By 2002, the company's difficulties caused it to place its Trafford Park plant under bankruptcy protection; the company later bought the facility back for £150,000. Payroll at the site, the company's home for nearly 100 years, was slashed to a minimum. Not all of Carbo's efforts were negative, however. In 2002 the company bought Ekamant UK Ltd., extending its business into the conversion and distribution of abrasives for the woodworking sector.

Nonetheless, Carbo's losses continued to sap the company's health. By 2004, its net assets had dwindled from £26.5 million at the end of the 1990s, to just £200,000. In dire straits, the company found temporary relief from GMAC, which pledged £9.5 million ($15 million) in working capital facilities. The company's major shareholders then brought in a new management team, led by Lars Nyquist, who had been active in the abrasives market in Sweden, as company CEO.

Under Nyquist, Carbo moved to complete the restructuring of the group's operations, announcing in September 2004 its decision to shut down the Trafford Park plant and shift production to the company's Düsseldorf factories. In this way, the company expected to cut some £700,000 per year in operating costs. Carbo nonetheless remained committed to maintaining its position in the U.K. abrasives sector, now focused on its Anglo-Abrasives distribution network.

Principal Subsidiaries

Abrafract Abrasives; Anglo-Abrasives Ltd.; Carborundum Abrasives GB Ltd.

Principal Competitors

GE Superabrasives; Universal Superabrasives Inc; Saint-Gobain Abrasives Inc.; Ilyich Abrasive Co.; Sia Abrasives Holding AG; 3M Nederland B.V.; Flugger A/S.

Further Reading

"Carbo Move," *Birmingham Evening Mail,* September 6, 2004, p. 40.

"GMAC Steps in to Rescue Carbo," *Financial Times,* February 20, 2004, p. 20.

Gould, Anthony, "Carbo Plans a GBP10m Spree," *Engineer,* May 15, 1998, p. 8.

"Production Up," *TTJ-The Timber Industry Magazine,* April 17, 2004, p. 10.

"Refinancings (Carbo)," *European Venture Capital Journal,* March 2004, p. 29.

Roberts, Patricia, "Carbo Wields Axe on Jobs," *Manchester Evening News,* August 2, 2003.

—M.L. Cohen

Celgene Corporation

7 Powder Horn Drive
Warren, New Jersey 07059
U.S.A.
Telephone: (732) 271-1001
Fax: (732) 271-4184
Web site: http://www.celgene.com

Public Company
Incorporated: 1986
Employees: 679
Sales: $271.47 million (2003)
Stock Exchanges: NASDAQ
Ticker Symbol: CELG
NAIC: 541710 Research and Development in the
   Physical Sciences and Engineering; 325412
   Pharmaceutical Preparation Manufacturing; 325998
   All Other Miscellaneous Chemical Product
   Manufacturing

Celgene Corporation is a biopharmaceutical company focused on developing and marketing therapies to treat leprosy, cancer, and immunological diseases. The company's technology centers on using small molecules to prevent tumors from forming blood vessels and regulating the pathways of cellular, genomic, and proteomic targets. Celgene markets a brand of thalidomide called Thalomid, a product first introduced by the company to treat complications of leprosy.

Origins

Celgene underwent several permutations during its development, subsisting on one type of business and then delving into another line of work before ultimately gaining prominence as a biotechnology company that relied on one of the most notorious pharmaceutical products in history. Celgene began as a unit of Celanese Corp., a major chemical company that specialized in man-made fibers. The business unit took the definition of its business scope from its parent company, instructed by Celanese to apply biotechnology to the production of fine and specialty chemicals. Celgene's progenitor pursued such work until a dramatic development in Celanese's history directly influenced its biotechnology unit. In 1986, Celanese merged with another large chemical company, American Hoechst Corp., a transaction that ushered in an era of freedom for the business that would become Celgene. As part of the merger process, Celanese's biotechnology unit was spun off into a separate enterprise, Celgene Corporation.

Celgene's first leader as an independent company was Louis Fernandez, an executive of consequence that gave the young company legitimacy in the industry. Fernandez joined Celgene as its chief executive officer in 1986, four months after retiring as chairman of Monsanto Company, one of the largest chemical companies in the world. Joining Fernandez were a number of high-profile executives who served as Celgene's board of directors, a list of corporate luminaries that included Frank Cary, a former chief executive officer of IBM, John Horan, a former chief executive officer of Merck, and the chief executive officer of Chase Manhattan, Willard Butcher. Guided by this list of distinguished executives, Celgene's scientists and engineers focused their efforts on a field close to Fernandez's heart, bioremediation. Celgene concentrated on the research and development of chemical and biotreatment processes for the chemical and pharmaceutical industries. Fernandez, in one of his last moves as Monsanto's chairman, helped form Clean Sites Inc., a nonprofit organization dedicated to accelerating the cleanup of toxic waste dumps. The mandate of Clean Sites dovetailed with Celgene's purpose, presenting Fernandez with an opportunity that prompted him to forsake retirement.

Celgene worked on finding bacteria capable of eliminating toxic waste. One of the company's most significant discoveries was a microorganism that digested toluene—a highly toxic gasoline additive—and broke it down into water and carbon dioxide, rendering it harmless. "Microorganisms are little bugs," Fernandez explained in a January 30, 1989 interview with *Fortune*, "and like all bugs, they have to eat. So when you find organisms that love hazardous wastes, why, you let them at it." The bioremediation field showed promise, but it did not catapult Celgene anywhere close to the multi-billion-dollar stature of Monsanto. Celgene posted $2.3 million in sales in

1988, almost the same amount the company collected a decade later in an entirely different line of business.

Celgene Changes Its Strategic Course in the Early 1990s

As Celgene entered the 1990s, it continued to look for biological solutions to the problems of hazardous waste, but— almost accidentally—the company began moving toward entering a new line of business. The circumstance that eventually led to Celgene's destiny occurred in 1991, when the company's vice-president, Sol Barer, and its chief scientist went to meet Gilla Kaplan at New York's Rockefeller University. The Celgene pair went to discuss a project about developing a drug to treat tuberculosis, but Kaplan interjected. "You know," Kaplan said, according to a March 28, 2004 interview with *The Star-Ledger*, "this is all very interesting. But I think I have a better project for you." Kaplan's suggestion involved a drug named thalidomide, a name that rekindled dreadful memories for those within and without the pharmaceutical industry.

Thalidomide first appeared in Germany in October 1957, when the drug was marketed as a sedative. Soon, the drug gained favor as a treatment for morning sickness, finding a receptive audience among pregnant women. Tragedy soon followed, as the use of thalidomide led to a surge of birth defects and the infamous appellation, "Thalidomide Babies." Thalidomide, it was discovered, stopped the growth of blood cells necessary for fetal development and for the growth of arms and legs. Children were born with horrible deformities, the most common of which, *Pharcomelia*, described the flipper-like limbs of Thalidomide Babies. At its peak, thalidomide was prescribed to pregnant women in 46 countries, resulting in roughly 20,000 infants born during the 1960s with deformities caused by the drug. Thalidomide became the scourge of the pharmaceutical industry. The drug was taken off the market in the early 1960s, as affected children and their parents dealt with the horrific consequences of its use.

Kaplan's mention of thalidomide as a drug for a small company like Celgene to base its existence on was a proposal rife with complexities. The process of taking any drug through regulatory and approval processes was exceptionally lengthy and risky. For a drug like thalidomide, the path to market promised to be strewn with even more formidable obstacles. There were thalidomide victims' groups who likely would oppose the drug's re-introduction with the same zeal of a mother opposing the parole of her child's killer. Further, the Food and Drug Administration (FDA), the federal agency whose consent meant everything to any pharmaceutical company, had suffi-

cient cause never to entertain the possibility of thalidomide entering the U.S. market. In some ways, the very essence of the FDA was tied to keeping thalidomide out of the U.S. market.

By the beginning of the 1960s, when doctors in countries such as Germany, Canada, England, and Australia were prescribing the drug for morning sickness treatment, the application for U.S. approval landed at the desk of the FDA's Frances Kelsey. At the time, approving a drug for public use was a perfunctory process, with scant attention paid to the possible damages of a drug. Thalidomide was Kelsey's first case as an FDA researcher, which further diminished the odds that thalidomide would be denied approval. Kelsey, however, noticed the disturbing occurrence of birth defects and denied approval. Fewer than 20 cases of thalidomide-caused birth defects occurred in the United States because of Kelsey's scrutiny. The FDA, largely because of the thalidomide case, gained a higher state of legitimacy and began to transform into the watchdog organization it later became. When Kaplan suggested thalidomide to Barer, the FDA had every reason to distance itself from the drug that had helped it establish its reputation, a crucible not forgotten by Kelsey, who was an FDA official when Kaplan met Barer in 1991.

There was a litany of reasons for Barer to dismiss the idea of delving into the development of thalidomide, but he listened to Kaplan. Kaplan explained that new research showed thalidomide could treat the painful skin lesions caused by leprosy. There were also indications that the drug could treat AIDS and cancer. Rockefeller University, Kaplan explained, needed a business partner to explore the potential of thalidomide further. Celgene, Barer responded, needed to find a drug to develop. The pair agreed to answer each other's needs, leading to Celgene's 1992 acquisition of exclusive worldwide rights for thalidomide. "It was greeted with a lot of skepticism by the Wall Street community and internally, too," Barer reflected in a March 28, 2004 interview with the *Star-Ledger*. "People said, 'You're going to take the most vilified drug in history, and you're going to build a pharmaceutical company around it?' "

Celgene's bold undertaking soon diverted its attention away from bioremediation. The company discontinued its biotreatment operations in 1994 to devote itself exclusively to the commercialization of thalidomide. Celgene racked up huge annual losses as it conducted experiments and clinical trials, endeavoring to gain approval from the FDA. The company was financially strapped, barely able to keep afloat as it labored in the lab and outside the lab, building the necessary political relationships to bring thalidomide to market. Much of the company's ability to survive during these difficult years was credited to its management, a team led by Barer, who was promoted to president in 1993, and John Jackson, who became Celgene's chief executive officer and chairman in January 1996. A veteran of American Cyanamid and Merck & Co., Jackson was running his own consultancy business, Gemini Medical, when he joined Celgene. "The company was on death's door," a friend remarked in a March 28, 2004 interview with the *Star-Ledger*, remembering his surprise when he learned of Jackson's decision to head Celgene. "I thought, 'Boy, is this guy nuts or what?' " Jackson, in an October 18, 1999 interview with *Bioworld Financial Watch*, explained why he took the job: "I thought that the potential of thalidomide coming back to the market to treat

Key Dates:

1980: Celgene's precursor is formed as a unit of Celanese Corp.
1986: Celgene is spun off as a separate company.
1987: Celgene completes its initial public offering of stock.
1992: Celgene acquires the rights to thalidomide.
1996: John Jackson is appointed Celgene's chief executive officer and chairman.
1998: Celgene begins shipping Thalomid.
2000: Signal Pharmaceuticals Inc. is acquired
2003: Celgene records its first annual profit.

serious, debilitating, life-threatening diseases would be a very worthwhile project. At the same time, it was a tremendous challenge working with the FDA and other interested parties.''

Jackson's marketing and business experience complemented Barer's scientific expertise. Celgene would need both skill sets from its leadership as it continued along its controversial path. In 1997, the company desperately needed the talents of Jackson, as it teetered on the brink of insolvency. At one point during the year, the company only had two week's worth of cash left, but Jackson, with the help of some of the Marines he served with in Vietnam, was able to secure $18 million in capital to keep the company alive. His intervention was timely; within a year Celgene succeeded in gaining approval from the FDA to market thalidomide.

Thalidomide Entering the Market in 1998

In July 1998, the FDA approved the use of thalidomide, marketed by Celgene under the brand Thalomid, for treating leprosy. Barer commented on the event, saying in a July 16, 1998 interview with *Knight Ridder/Tribune Business News:* "It's an historic event for us. It's our first product and there can be nothing more important for a pharmaceutical company, especially a small one like ours." Randolph Warren, head of the Thalidomide Victims Association of Canada, offered his reaction in the same article. "We knew it was coming, but this is a very somber day for us. There ought to be a skull and crossbones on the package." The concern was justifiable, and both the FDA and Celgene acknowledged the hazards inherent in introducing thalidomide into the market. Thalomid became the most restricted drug ever sold in the United States, subject to an elaborate distribution system designed by the FDA in conjunction with patient advocacy groups and Celgene. The FDA stipulated that Thalomid could be prescribed only by doctors who registered with a special FDA program. Weekly pregnancy tests were to be given to female patients during the first month of Thalomid therapy, and once monthly for the duration of its use. Female patients were required to use two forms of contraception simultaneously, while male patients were given written and oral warnings of the risk of contraception failure and the need to use condoms. Photographs of children afflicted with thalidomide-caused birth defects were inserted in the drug's packaging to ensure that patients were aware of the risks involved.

Celgene began shipping Thalomid in September 1998. Despite the excitement at Celgene's New Jersey headquarters, the

financial gains from the release of Thalomid were expected to be only modest in size. Fewer than 100 new cases of leprosy were reported each year in the United States and roughly 4,000 people were afflicted with the disease in North America, presenting the company with a very small potential customer base. Celgene hoped to broaden Thalomid's scope, however, and seek approval from the FDA to sell the drug as a treatment for cancer and AIDs patients.

Celgene in the 21st Century

Celgene's history of recording annual losses continued as the company exited the 1990s and entered the 21st century. The company hoped to gain financial success by using thalidomide as a springboard to build a pipeline of drugs whose chemical structures were derived from thalidomide. These offshoots, or thalidomide analogs, were called IMiDS, immunomodulatory drugs that were small-molecule, orally-administered compounds that modulated the immune system. Celgene achieved promising success in using one such IMiD to treat multiple myeloma, a cancer of the plasma cells. The company also began advancing the development of a drug it called Revlimid, which, Celgene-sponsored studies showed, was a stronger, safer version of Thalomid.

Celgene completed two important acquisitions at the turn of the millennium, purchases that opened up new avenues of opportunities while it pursued business opportunities related to thalidomide and its analogs. In 2000, the company acquired Signal Pharmaceutical Inc., a privately held, California-based biopharmaceutical company, in a stock-for-stock-merger worth an estimated $200 million. Signal focused on discovering and developing new classes of drugs that regulated genes associated with disease. In 2003, Celgene acquired New Jersey-based Anthrogenesis Corp. in a $45 million deal. Anthrogenesis was a biotherapeutics company involved in the recovery of stem cells from human placental tissue following the completion of a full-term, successful pregnancy.

As Celgene plotted its future course, the potential for long-term financial success was present, but the true measure of any biopharmaceutical company rested on turning potential into reality. Celgene was just beginning to reap the rewards of its research and development efforts as it entered the mid-2000s. In 2003, for the first time in its history, the company posted an annual profit, recording $13.5 million in net income. The company also had accumulated a sizeable deficit by the end of its 17th year as an independent concern, registering $308 million of debt. The future success of Celgene rested on the effectiveness of Thalomid and its derivatives in treating various forms of cancer and AIDs, the outcome of which would determine whether Barer's gamble in 1991 would have a long-term payoff.

Principal Subsidiaries

Signal Pharmaceuticals, Inc.; Anthrogenesis Corp.; Celgene International, Inc.; Celgene Cellular Therapeutics; Celgene International SARL (Switzerland).

Principal Competitors

Bristol Myers Squibb Co.; Amgen Inc.; Genentech Inc.; Aventis Inc.; Novartis AG; AstraZeneca p.l.c.; Millennium Pharmaceuticals Inc.; Genta Co.; Cell Therapeutics Inc.; Vertex Pharmaceuticals Inc.; Biogen IDEC Inc.; Ilex Oncology Inc.

Further Reading

Bellucci, Neal M., "Lack of Efficacy Stops Melanoma Drug Trial," *R&D Directions,* July-August 2004, p. 62.

"Celgene Acquires Signal," *Chemical Market Reporter,* July 10, 2000, p. 19.

"Celgene Gains Rights to Thalidomide," *The Record,* December 11, 1998, p. B3.

"Celgene Seeking to Recast Drug for New FDA Approval," *PR Week,* July 26, 2004, p. 7.

Colchamiro, Russ, "Thalidomide Approved for Leprosy," *American Druggist,* August 1998, p. 25.

Gerena-Morales, Rafael, "FDA Approves Use of Thalidomide for Treatment of Leprosy," *Knight Ridder/Tribune Business News,* July 16, 1998.

Henderson, Charles W., "Rights to Thalidomide under Rockefeller Patent Attained," *TB Weekly,* February 13, 1995, p. 32.

Klempin, Raymond, "ENSR Forms Joint Venture with British Conglomerate," *Houston Business Journal,* March 13, 1989, p. 12.

Madden, Stephen, "All They Can Eat," *Fortune,* January 30, 1989, p. 191.

Mather, Joan, "Access-Designed Celgene Exhibit Is Visual Metaphor for Company's Products," *Tradeshow Week,* June 24, 2002, p. 10.

Osborne, Randall, "Celgene's Revlimid Looks Strong in Bid to Grab MDS Market," *Bioworld Financial Watch,* September 20, 2004, p. 1.

Shook, David, " 'We Had the Wind at Our Backs,' " *The Record,* February 25, 2000, p. B1.

Silverman, Edward R., "FDA Approves Highly Restricted Use of Birth-Defect-Causing Thalidomide," *Knight Ridder/Tribune Business News,* July 16, 1998.

Steenhuysen, Julie, "Celgene Sets Stock Split; Will Seek Cancer Drug," *Star-Ledger,* September 10, 2004, p. 46.

Strickland, Debbie, "Resurrection of Thalidomide Portends New Celgene Pipeline," *Bioworld Financial Watch,* October 18, 1999, p. 1.

Todd, Susan, "Drug Program Could Pay Off for Celgene," *Star-Ledger,* June 25, 2004, p. 62.

——, "A Drug's Reincarnation," *Star-Ledger,* March 28, 2004, p. 1.

——, "In Crowded Biotech Field, Street Is Noticing Celgene," *Star Ledger,* July 30, 2003, p. 58.

"Trial Finds Celgene Medicine Effective Vs. Myeloma," *Star-Ledger,* June 8, 2004, p. 57.

Webb, Marion, "Celgene Moves into Larger Quarters," *San Diego Business Journal,* October 21, 2002, p. 10.

—Jeffrey L. Covell

CHC

CHC Helicopter Corporation

4740 Agar Drive
Richmond, British Columbia
V7B 1A3
Canada
Telephone: (604) 276-7500
Web site: http://www.chc.ca

Public Company
Incorporated: 1975 as Sealand Helicopters Ltd.
Employees: 3,400
Sales: CAD 733.65 million ($535.2 million) (2004)
Stock Exchanges: Toronto New York
Ticker Symbols: FLY.A FLY.B; FLI
NAIC: 481211 Nonscheduled Chartered Passenger Air
    Transportation; 481212 Nonscheduled Chartered
    Freight Air Transportation; 621910 Ambulance
    Services

CHC Helicopter Corporation is the largest provider of helicopter support to the world's offshore oil industry. It operates in more than 30 countries and has a fleet of 160 helicopters. Its chief business is flying workers and supplies to offshore oilrigs. CHC also conducts air ambulance services and performs maintenance and overhaul work and flight training.

Origins

CHC Helicopter Corporation was created in 1987 when three Canadian helicopter firms combined their operations. Craig Dobbin, owner of Sealand Helicopters Ltd., became the new firm's chief executive officer.

A Newfoundland real estate developer, Dobbin had acquired a helicopter to take him to his remote fishing lodge (a place where Dobbin would entertain dignitaries such as U.S. President George H.W. Bush and Canadian Prime Minister Brian Mulroney). He later told the *Financial Post* it cost CAD 85,000 to buy the helicopter and the same amount each year to operate it. Dobbin decided to hire the aircraft out, forming Sealand Helicopters Ltd. in December 1975.

Sealand soon won a five-year contract to supply Newfoundland's air ambulance service. Mobil Oil Canada Ltd.'s exploration of the Hibernia oilfield provided another impetus for early growth. The fleet was expanded by a third to 38 aircraft. (Dobbin also formed an engineering firm to support the energy industry.)

Dobbin began gathering helicopter companies to help Sealand survive through an industry downturn. In the early 1980s, Toronto Helicopters Ltd., which provided air ambulance and forestry-related services, was acquired in a leveraged buyout.

Laden with debt, Dobbin then went after the industry leader. Vancouver's Okanagan Helicopters Ltd. had been founded in 1947 in the pioneering days of rotary wing flight. Once publicly traded, in 1982 the company was acquired by Calgary's Resource Service Group Ltd. Revenues were CAD 70.9 million in 1986, when operations stretched across Canada and as far abroad as Turkey and New Zealand. Okanagan had 561 employees and 125 helicopters before the merger.

The combined operation had revenues of about $118 million a year. It had 162 aircraft, 230 pilots, and 750 employees altogether. Principal owners of the company included Dobbin and the United Kingdom's Bristow Helicopter Group Ltd., the world's largest commercial helicopter operator. Bristow had acquired a 49 percent holding in Okanagan a couple years earlier.

Public in 1987

CHC acquired two more firms in 1987, fuel distributor Aero Flight Holdings Ltd. and Offshore Helicopter Technologies Ltd., which was developing a flight simulator facility in St. John's. CHC's shares began trading on the Toronto Stock Exchange in August of that year, raising CAD 44 million in the initial public offering (IPO). (This financed the Okanagan acquisition.) It was, noted the *Financial Post,* the market's last IPO before the crash of October 1987. CHC was Canada's largest helicopter firm and the third largest in the world, reported Toronto's *Financial Post.*

CHC acquired Ranger Helicopters Canada, a geology specialist, in April 1988 for CAD 9.7 million. Ranger had briefly

Company Perspectives:

Our customers want one consistent standard of safety and service around the globe. Our shareholders expect CHC to continue to create exceptional value. We will do both.

Key Dates:

1975: Craig Dobbin forms Sealand Helicopters with one aircraft.
1987: Sealand is combined with Okanagan and Toronto Helicopters to form CHC; the company makes its initial public offering.
1994: CHC acquires control of British International Helicopters.
1999: Norway's Helikopter Services Group (HSG) is acquired.
2004: CHC lists shares on the New York Stock Exchange; the company moves its headquarters to Vancouver.

operated an airport shuttle in Toronto. Close rival Viking Helicopters Ltd. was taken over in April 1989. Viking operated a fleet of five dozen helicopters centered in Quebec. Annual revenues were about $20 million.

European Expansion in the 1990s

By 1990 CHC had a fleet of 256 aircraft operating in 16 countries. In June of that year it announced a joint venture with Irish aircraft leasing giant GPA Group PLC.

CHC won a contract for United Nations peacekeeping flights in Kuwait, Cambodia, and Thailand in 1991, reported the *Financial Post*. This was, however, an unprofitable and difficult line of work.

CHC acquired 40 percent of the voting shares of British International Helicopters Ltd. (BIH) in 1993. BIH, also called Brintel, was based in Aberdeen, Scotland, and dated back to 1947. It operated 20 large twin-engine helicopters and had revenues of about CAD 100 million a year. CHC's shareholding was raised to 90 percent within a year.

The Brintel acquisition made CHC second only to Norway's Helikopter Services Group AS among helicopter operators. The company had 1,600 employees and a fleet of 250 rotary wing aircraft. In December 1994 CHC had promoted a new president and CEO from within, Rudy Palladina, while Dobbin remained chairman and the largest shareholder. (Dobbin, diagnosed with idiopathic pulmonary fibrosis, moved to the United States for a few years to seek a lung transplant.)

Norway's Helikopter Services Group (HSG) unsuccessfully challenged CHC's right to acquire a European Community company. Dobbin had earlier become a national of Ireland on the strength of his historic ties to the country (and an endowment to the University of Dublin). HSG took a significant swipe at CHC in 1995 when it wrested away a contract to service the Hibernia oil platform.

CHC entered the Gulf of Mexico market in the late 1990s through an alliance with American Helicopters. CHC had previously lacked a license to do this flying in the United States.

Repair and Overhaul Focus in the Late 1990s

Repair and overhaul contributed more than a third of revenues in 1997. This work was performed at two subsidiaries, Atlantic Turbines Inc. on Prince Edward Island and Acro Aerospace in British Columbia.

CHC aimed to expand the repair side of the business since it was less cyclical than helicopter operations. In 1998 the company bought Hunting Airmotive in southern England for CAD 60 million.

The engine overhaul business was spun off in June 1998 as Vector Aerospace Corp. in a CAD 300 million IPO. CHC sold off its remaining 20 percent stake in September 1999.

CHC's revenues were CAD 354 million in 1998. The company had 200 aircraft operating from 69 bases across the globe. A new CAD 22.5 million, 60,000-square-foot aerospace composites fabrication plant opened in August 1999 in Gander, Newfoundland.

Number One in 1999

Years of cutthroat competition between the big three of CHC, HSG, and Offshore Logistics Inc. of the United States made the field ripe for consolidation. CHC was able to acquire HSG itself for CAD 206 million in 1999. The HSG buy, conducted through CHC's Vinland Helicopters AS subsidiary, left CHC with a debt of CAD 600 million, noted *Canadian Business*, and this was a significant priority. The purchase made CHC the world's largest helicopter firm, with a combined fleet of 370 aircraft and 3,000 employees. More than three quarters of revenues (CAD 554 million in fiscal 2000) came from outside Canada; the U.S. market was relatively untapped.

Dobbin's favorite part of entrepreneurship was building companies, noted a March 2000 profile in the *National Post*. He started a Newfoundland-Nova Scotia executive charter service called Touch Down Aviation. He established the Newfoundland commuter airline Air Atlantic Ltd. 15 years earlier.

Demand for energy resulted in more offshore oil and gas exploration, generating more business for CHC. CHC was active across the globe as it picked up new oilfield contracts in Malaysia and India. CHC also was providing search and rescue helicopters for the Royal Australian Air Force.

On the Big Board in 2004

In February 2004, CHC acquired Schreiner Aviation Group of The Netherlands in a deal worth EUR 87 million (CAD 144 million). Schreiner provided support for the offshore oil industry in Europe, Africa, and Asia with a fleet of about 50 rotary and fixed wing aircraft.

CHC agreed to acquire a majority holding in Aero Turbine Support Ltd. in September 2004, expanding CHC's repair and overhaul business. Aero Turbine was based in Langley, British Columbia, and specialized in maintaining General Electric CT58/T58 and Pratt & Whitney PT6T engines.

CHC's shares began trading on the New York Stock Exchange on October 11, 2004. The company was already listed in Toronto. CHC moved its main offices cross country from St. John's, Newfoundland, to Vancouver, British Columbia, in 2004. Dobbin had earlier told the *Financial Post* he expected CHC to have annual revenues of CAD 1 billion around 2007.

Principal Subsidiaries

CHC Helicopters International Inc.; CHC Helicopters (Barbados) Limited; CHC Leasing (Barbados) Limited; CHC Capital (Barbados) Limited; Canadian Helicopters (UK) Limited (Scotland); CHC Scotia Limited (England and Wales); Vinland Denmark A.S.; Vinland Helicopters A.S. (Norway); Helikopter Services Group A.S. (Norway); CHC Helikopter Service A.S. (Norway); Astec Helicopter Services A.S. (Norway); Heliwest A.S. (Norway); Lloyd Helicopter Services Pty. Ltd. (Australia); CHC Helicopters (Africa) Pty. Ltd.; Court Helicopters Limited (Mauritius); CHC Composites Inc.; CHC Denmark ApS (Denmark); CHC Ireland Limited; Brintel Holdings Limited (Scotland); 4083423 Canada Inc.; CHC Netherlands B.V.; CHC Sweden AB; Schreiner Luchtvaart Groep B.V. (Netherlands); Schreiner North Sea Helicopters B.V. (Netherlands); Schreiner Airways, B.V. (Netherlands); Schreiner Aircraft Maintenance Company B.V. (Netherlands); Schreiner & Co., B.V. (Netherlands); Schreiner Chad; Whirly Bird Services Limited (U.K.).

Principal Divisions

Helicopter Operations; Repair and Overhaul; Composites; Flight Training.

Principal Operating Units

CHC Global Support; CHC Global Operations; CHC Europe.

Principal Competitors

Offshore Logistics, Inc.

Further Reading

"Aberdeen's Offshore Oil and Gas Workers Take the High Road to Work," *Business a.m.* (Scotland), September 3, 2001.
Blackwell, Richard, "No. 1 Domestic Helicopter Firm Buys Rival, Raises Market Share," *Financial Post* (Toronto), April 7, 1989, p. 21.
——, "Oil Action Could Lift CHC Helicopter," *Financial Post* (Toronto), May 16, 1988, p. 27.
"CHC Helicopter Sells Remaining Stake in Vector Aerospace," *National Post,* September 24, 1999, p. C2.
"CHC Helicopter's Norwegian Deal to Go Through," *National Post,* August 3, 1999, p. C7.
Daw, James, "Three Big Helicopter Operators to Join Forces Under New Name," *Toronto Star,* July 8, 1987, p. F3.
Fitzpatrick, Peter, "CHC Buys Air Service Unit of Britain's Hunting," *Financial Post,* March 17, 1998, p. 6.
——, "CHC Chief Quits Over Moves to Boost Stock," *Financial Post,* April 2, 1998, p. 5.
——, "CHC Gets Access to Gulf of Mexico," *Financial Post* (Toronto), October 9, 1997, p. 6.
——, "CHC Reaches Deal with Regulator," *Financial Post* (Toronto), October 15, 1997, p. 13.
Flanagan, Chris, "Birdman of Newfoundland," *Canadian Business,* August 27, 1999, p. 55.
Francis, Diane, "The Tiny Helicopter Firm That Took Off: Dobbin's CHC Joins the Wall Street Elite," *Financial Post* (Canada), October 12, 2002, p. 1.
"Gander Gets Aerospace Plant; CHC Helicopters Creating 250 Jobs at New Facility," *Toronto Star,* July 24, 1998, p. E5.
Hunter, Dough, "Helicopter Firm Harkens Back," *Financial Post* (Toronto), May 4, 1987.
Jones, Deborah, "CHC Helicopters on Aggressive Course," *Financial Post* (Toronto), February 20, 1993, p. S31.
MacDonald, Michael, "CHC Helicopter OKs Controversial Stock Options Plan," *National Post's Financial Post & FP Investing* (Canada), September 27, 2002, p. FP9.
MacNamara, Kate, "The Builder: Craig Dobbin Tells Kate MacNamara How He Became the Copter King," *National Post Business,* July 2001, p. 27.
McQueen, Rod, "Will Debt-Laden CHC Helicopter Take Off?," *Financial Post* (Toronto), June 21, 1995, p. 27.
Moulton, Donalee, "He's Not Flying by the Seat of His Pants," *National Post,* March 15, 2000, p. E1.
Newman, Peter C., "Two Dramatic Tales of Personal Survival," *Maclean's,* February 15, 1999, p. 48.
Roche, Pat, "Flying High on Newfoundland's Promise," *Maclean's,* February 17, 1986, p. 28.
Rojo, Oscar, "CHC Flies High with Irish Giant," *Toronto Star,* June 15, 1990, p. F7.
——, "CHC Flies on Board U.K. Firm," *Toronto Star,* January 28, 1993, p. C8.
——, "CHC Helicopter Takes U.K. Firm Under Its Wing," *Toronto Star,* January 8, 1994, p. E7.
——, "Helicopter Firm Is Taking Time to Get Airborne," *Toronto Star,* February 8, 1988, p. E7.
Shinkle, Kirk, "The High Seas Produce High Returns Here," *Investor's Business Daily,* October 31, 2002, p. A14.
Stone, Cynthia, "Sky-High Aspirations," *Canadian Business,* April 1989, pp. 25 +.
Warwick, Graham, "CHC Helicopter Reorganises," *Flight International,* September 21, 2004, p. 26.
Westell, Dan, "CHC Helicopter Faces Court Challenge," *Financial Post* (Toronto), December 12, 1996, p. 7.

—Frederick C. Ingram

Chelsfield PLC

67 Brook Street
London
W1Y 2NJ
United Kingdom
Telephone: +44 20 7493 3977
Fax: +44 20 7491 9369
Web site: http://www.chelsfield.com

Private Company
Incorporated: 1986
Employees: 553
Sales: $285.60 million (2003)
NAIC: 531190 Lessors of Other Real Estate Property;
236210 Industrial Building Construction; 236220
Commercial and Institutional Building Construction;
237210 Land Subdivision; 531120 Lessors of
Nonresidential Buildings (Except Miniwarehouses);
551112 Offices of Other Holding Companies

Chelsfield PLC is one of the United Kingdom's major property development groups. Chelsfield has been the motivating force behind a number of prominent U.K. developments, including Merry Hill, in the West Midlands, one of the United Kingdom's largest shopping centers, and the huge White City project, which at the time of its completion in 2007 will be the largest retail site in the Greater London area. Chelsfield also holds a 50 percent stake in the Paddington Basin commercial, office, and retail project, which, like White City, will include an extension of the London rail and subway network. The company also has been chosen to assist London & Continental Railways in developing its proposed £3 billion Stratford city project, in East London. Other Chelsfield holdings include the Wentworth Golf Club and a 75 percent stake in money-losing Global Switch. Chelsfield was founded by Elliott Bernerd, who remains the company's hands-on chairman. After Bernerd took the company private in 2004, however, he faced a challenge for control, and by October 2004 the company had received buyout offers from Australia's shopping mall giant Westfield. That bid was countered by a rival offer from another Australian property group, Multiplex, which holds a 7 percent stake in Chelsfield.

Investment Success in the 1980s

The son of a wealthy British film executive, Elliott Bernerd was just 15 when he left school. In 1962, at the age of 16, Bernerd began working with a property agent in London, and by the time he was 21, Bernerd had become a partner in that firm. Yet Bernerd never received formal certification as an estate agent—a move that would have barred him from becoming an investor in the property deals themselves.

In the late 1960s, Bernerd teamed up with London property heavyweight Stuart Laurie, who served as Bernerd's mentor as the pair began acquiring a portfolio of West End properties in the 1970s. Bernerd quickly earned a reputation as a shrewd investor, locating inexpensive properties that quickly rose in value. Nonetheless, Bernerd nearly lost his first business during the collapse of the British real estate sector in the mid-1970s. Bernerd managed to save the business through an alliance with Lord Sterling, of the P&O group. Soon after, Bernerd found a buyer for the business in Morgan Grenfell, then in the process of an ambitious acquisition drive.

One of Bernerd's most successful projects came in the early 1980s, when Bernerd led an investor team including Jacob Rothschild and Stuart Lipton in the purchase of a plot of land near Heathrow Airport. Paying just £8 million for the site, a former landfill, Bernerd became the first in the United Kingdom to develop an American-style business park. For this project, Bernerd set up a new company, Stockley Group. The site's proximity to the country's major international airport quickly attracted interest from the rising number of multinational companies that were then just beginning to transform the global economic scene. In 1988, the investment group sold off most of Stockley Park for £365 million. Bernerd himself earned some £20 million on that deal.

By then, Bernerd had set up a new property investment vehicle, Chelsfield PLC, founded in 1986. Chelsfield quickly began amassing a property portfolio. Among the company's most noteworthy deals in the late 1980s was its purchase of the exclusive Wentworth Golf Club in 1988. Bernerd paid just £17.7 million for the club—just ahead of a sudden boom in the golf market. By 1989, Bernerd had sold off 40 percent of the club to a group of Japanese investors, raising a total of £32 million.

Chelsfield's property interests were not limited to the United Kingdom. In 1990, the company formed a 50/50 partnership with P&O in order to acquire Laing Inc. and its portfolio of 6,700 rental apartments and 2.7 million square feet of commercial property in Atlanta, Georgia. While initially the deal seemed to be a dud, given the crash in the global housing market in the early 1990s, the portfolio regained its value toward the middle of the decade and the Atlanta Olympic Games of 1996.

Property Developer in the 1990s

By then Chelsfield had already disposed of the major part of its Laing holdings as the company re-focused itself from a property investment group to one of Britain's major property developers. Launching that process was the company's listing on the London Stock Exchange in 1993.

The listing coincided with the company's acquisition of the then-bankrupt Merry Hill Shopping Centre project. At the time, the original preferred buyer of the project had put off acquiring the site, claiming that it was contaminated. Bernerd convinced the receivers of the site to allow him to conduct environmental tests and when these proved that the contamination of the site was minimal, Chelsfield won the right to purchase the site. Bernerd brought in a group of Saudi Arabian investors to put up some £120 million in debt and equity, and Chelsfield itself gained control of some £90 million of the site for just £35 million. At the same time, Bernerd himself pocketed a £6 million finder's fee paid to him by the Saudi investors.

Chelsfield later bought out the Saudi investors, gaining full control of the Merry Hill site. Under the company's management, the shopping center became one of the largest in all of the United Kingdom and by 2004 was worth some £2 billion. Chelsfield continued building up its portfolio, with investments including hotel conversions in New York City and business parks in New Jersey, although the majority of the group's property portfolio remained focused on the London area.

Not all of the company's investments provided it with success, at least in the short term. The company was forced to sell off the New Jersey properties in 2004 amid a soft market there. More troubling for the company was its investment in Global Switch International Ltd. Founded in 1998, Global Switch appeared to have created a new niche—that of technical real estate. Global Switch promised to develop properties providing purpose built data center facilities for the growing ranks of IT and telecommunications companies during the high-tech boom at the beginning of the new millennium.

Chelsfield initially bought a 33.3 percent stake in Global Switch in 1999, as that company readied the opening of its first site in London's Docklands in September of that year. Global Switch then began rolling out its concept to other markets, including Amsterdam, Frankfurt, Paris, Singapore, and Sydney, as well as a second site in London. Chelsfield continued to increase its stake in Global Switch, taking majority control, at 75 percent, by 2002.

Yet by then, the crash of the global IT market left Global Switch vulnerable—as its tenant companies collapsed in the early 2000s, Global Switch suddenly found its vacancy rates rising. By 2001, Global Switch's difficulties had dragged Chelsfield into losses as well. At the end of that year, Chelsfield posted a loss of £25 million. Losses due to the Global Switch holding continued into the next year. Chelsfield attempted to unload Global Switch as early as 2001; that deal fell through, however. By the end of 2003, Global Switch's poor performance had again dragged Chelsfield into the red, with losses of more than £20 million.

Up for Grabs in the Mid-2000s?

Chelsfield's problems were exacerbated by Bernerd's health problems, as he battled jaw cancer in the early 2000s. At the same time, Bernerd and Chelsfield were in the process of putting together a new shopping center for London, White City, slated to become the city's largest upon its scheduled completion in 2007. Chelsfield took charge of developing the project, while the construction work was being carried out by Australia's Multiplex. The company also was developing another ambitious project, Paddington Basin.

By 2003, facing increasing shareholder pressure, Bernerd launched a drive to take Chelsfield private. Bernerd's initial offers were rejected by the company's shareholders. Finally, at the beginning of 2004, the shareholders agreed to a new offer of 320p per share, valuing the company at £895 million.

To finance the buyout, Bernerd began gathering a range of investors, including Multiplex, which bought more than 7 percent of the company; Israeli diamond magnate Beny Steinmetz, who bought 2 percent; and the Bank of East Asia, led by Bernerd's friend (and best man) David Li, which acquired 3.5 percent. A still larger stake went to the Reuben brothers, David and Simon, who had parlayed businesses in scrap metals and carpets into a fortune worth more than £2 billion.

Although longtime acquaintances, Bernerd had never done business with the Reuben brothers before. The Reubens agreed to acquire 35 percent of Chelsfield, which cost them £135 million, compared with Bernerd's 17 percent. Yet Bernerd also had a series of agreements with other investors that gave him effective control of the company.

Chelsfield began selling a number of assets in order to help pay off the company's debt, which reached £1.6 billion after the buyout. In August 2004, the company sold the White City development to Germany's CGI, which paid £1.4 billion for the prestigious project. Chelsfield, however, retained an option to buy back 50 percent of White City upon its 2007 completion.

Key Dates:

1983: Elliott Bernerd founds Stockley Group to develop Stockley Park near Heathrow Airport in London.

1986: Bernerd founds a new property investment portfolio, Chelsfield.

1988: Chelsfield buys Wentworth Golf Club for £17.7 million; Stockley Park is sold for £365 million.

1989: Chelsfield sells 40 percent of Wentworth Golf Club for £32 million.

1990: Chelsfield acquires 50 percent of Atlanta, Georgia-based Liang Inc.

1993: Chelsfield is listed on the London Stock Exchange; Merry Hill Shopping Centre is acquired.

1996: Chelsfield refocuses from a property investment group to a property development group.

1999: Chelsfield acquires an initial stake in Global Switch International.

2000: Chelsfield launches development of the White City project, to become London's largest shopping center in 2007.

2002: Chelsfield acquires 75 percent of Global Switch.

2003: Bernerd makes a bid to acquire Chelsfield and take it private.

2004: Bernerd succeeds in taking Chelsfield private; White City is sold off to Germany's CGI in August, and Wentworth is put up for sale as well.

By September 2004, Chelsfield also had begun looking for buyers for its 60 percent stake in the Wentworth Golf Club.

By then, however, Bernerd's relationship with the Reubens had soured. The Reubens were said to have misunderstood the nature of their investment in Chelsfield, hoping to achieve a rapid and short-term gain by selling off the company's holdings. Yet Bernerd remained focused on the long term, and proved reluctant to strip the company of the assets.

When word of the conflict emerged, Chelsfield suddenly found itself the target of a takeover bid from Australian shopping center giant Westfield, which made an offer of £585 million ($1.3 billion) for Chelsfield in October 2004. Multiplex, with its 7 percent stake in the company giving it the preemptive rights, immediately announced that it too was preparing an offer for Chelsfield.

Despite the effort to take over the company he had founded and nurtured since the mid-1980s, Bernerd remained pragmatic. In September 2004, Bernerd suggested to the *Times* that should he indeed lose control of Chelsfield, he would simply move on to start up a new business. As he told the *Times:* "When Frank Lloyd Wright was asked what his favorite project had been he would say 'the next one.'" With or without control of Chelsfield, Bernerd was certain to remain one of the United Kingdom's most influential property developers.

Principal Competitors

GUS PLC; Taylor Woodrow PLC; Singer and Friedlander Group PLC; Arriva PLC; BAA PLC; M.J. Gleeson Group PLC; Enterprise Inns PLC; Birse Group PLC; Heron International.

Further Reading

Barrie, Giles, "Chelsfield Hit by New Global Switch Losses: Analysts Urge Developer to Offload Internet Hotels That Wiped Out £25m Profits," *Property Week,* September 13, 2002, p. 17.

Cattell, Brian, "Chelsfield Bidder Looks Triumphant," *Daily Deal,* December 16, 2003.

"CGI Seizes White City for £1.4bn," *Estates Gazette,* August 21, 2004, p. 9.

"Chelsfield's £20m Loss," *Property Week,* March 5, 2004, p. 19.

Chong, Florence, and Emily Pettafor, "Multiplex Yet to Make Move for Chelsfield," *Australasian Business Intelligence,* October 6, 2004.

"Great Survivor Faces Threat of Demolition," *Observer,* September 19, 2004.

Marriot, Robin, "Bernerd's Other World," *Property Week,* January 23, 2004, p. 12.

Riechmann, Deb, "Mall Giant Westfield Bids $1.3b for UK's Chelsfield," *Financial Post,* October 1, 2004.

Rossiter, James, "Quiet Man Who's a Big Noise in London Property," *Evening Standard,* September 9, 2003.

Waples, John, "Tycoons at War," *Times,* September 12, 2004.

—M.L. Cohen

Chipotle Mexican Grill, Inc.

1543 Wazee Street, Suite 200
Denver, Colorado 80202-1442
U.S.A.
Telephone: (303) 595-4000
Fax: (303) 595-4014
Web site: http://www.chipotle.com

*90-Percent-Owned Subsidiary of McDonald's
Corporation*
Incorporated: 1993
Employees: 6,600
Sales: $321 million (2003 est.)
NAIC: 722211 Limited-Service Restaurants

Chipotle Mexican Grill, Inc. is one of the leading fast-casual Mexican restaurant chains, with approximately 400 outlets in about 20 states, mainly in the West and Midwest. Known for its fresh, gourmet, and increasingly organic ingredients, Chipotle (pronounced chi-POAT-lay) offers a fairly simple menu of burritos, fajitas, and tacos featuring pork, shredded beef, chicken, steak, and vegetarian fillings. Customer checks average about $8.50. From a single location in Denver, Colorado, in 1993, the chain is now growing at the rate of 100 new restaurants per year thanks to the deep pockets of its parent, fast-food giant McDonald's Corporation. McDonald's first invested in the company in 1998, before taking majority control the following year, and it now holds a 90 percent stake. The vast majority of Chipotle restaurants are company-owned; fewer than ten are franchised. Annual revenues per unit are an estimated $1.2 million.

Early 1990s Brainchild of Steve Ells

Born on September 12, 1965, in Indianapolis, Steve Ells, the founder and CEO of Chipotle, developed a deep interest in cuisine, cooking, and restaurant eating at an early age. He told *Nation's Restaurant News* in January 1999 that in family travels across the United States and Europe he had an opportunity to taste many different foods and to develop an appreciation for fine cuisine at an unusually young age. Instead of cartoons, he was interested in watching Julia Child cooking shows. ''When I was in fourth grade, I used to make eggs Benedict before I had to catch the school bus.''

Ells attended the University of Colorado at Boulder, where he received an art history degree in 1988. He then decided to pursue his lifelong interest in fine food by attending the Culinary Institute of America in Hyde Park, New York. After graduating in 1990, he worked for two years at the high-end Stars restaurant in San Francisco under famed chef Jeremiah Tower. His inspiration for creating Chipotle, however, came from his frequent off-hour visits to little *taquerias* in San Francisco's Mission District. There he was struck by the fat burritos prepared to order, everything bundled in a giant flour tortilla wrapped in foil. Ells's idea was to put a twist on this traditional Mexican peasant food by stuffing the tortillas with gourmet ingredients, leveraging his culinary knowledge.

After a year of planning during which he arranged an $80,000 loan and persuaded his father, a former president of the pharmaceuticals firm Syntex Corporation, to invest an additional $85,000, the then 27-year-old Ells returned to the Denver area, where he had lived during his junior/senior high years, to open the first Chipotle Mexican Grill. It was named after a smoked and dried jalapeño pepper that figured prominently among the ingredients, particularly the marinades used to flavor the meats. Located on Evans Avenue in Denver near the campus of the University of Denver, the restaurant opened in July 1993. The configuration of the restaurant made for a somewhat rough beginning. The kitchen was in the back, and customers and employees had to yell back and forth during ordering. Ells soon developed an open-kitchen design in which the food prep was brought out front, and the customers could interact directly with the staff and have more control over the food they were ordering.

The simple menu enabled customers to choose among burrito, taco, and fajita items; select a filling of steak, chicken, pork carnitas, or vegetarian; and then add various other fillings or toppings—all as they moved along a serving line. The huge burritos, weighing a pound and a quarter and wrapped in enormous 14-inch flour tortillas, held rice and beans in addition to the aforementioned fillings. All the ingredients were of high quality and fresh, and Ells put special gourmet touches on nearly everything: cilantro and lime juice in the rice; chopped serranos, more

Company Perspectives:

"When I created Chipotle in 1993, I had a very simple idea: Offer a simple menu of great food prepared fresh each day, using many of the same cooking techniques as gourmet restaurants. Then serve the food quickly, in a cool atmosphere. It was food that I wanted, and thought others would like too. We've never strayed from that original idea. The critics raved and customers began lining up at my tiny burrito joint. Since then, we've opened a few more."

—Steve Ells, founder and CEO

cilantro, and marinated red onions in the guacamole; romaine lettuce rather than the typical iceberg in the tacos. In an early rave review, Bill St. John, writing in the *Rocky Mountain News* enthused: "Nothing is plain here; everything has depth, character, nuance, layers of flavor." The main items on the menu were quite reasonably priced, initially ranging from $3.95 to $4.55. Among the drink offerings were margaritas and beer.

After working out the initial kinks, the first Chipotle became a huge hit. Ells's father got his investment back within a month or so. Over the next few years, more outlets were opened in the Denver metro area, funded by an additional $1.5 million investment by Ells's father and a $1.5 million private stock offering. The second store opened in February 1995, and then six more debuted during 1996. Ells concentrated first on siting restaurants in Denver's trendier neighborhoods before moving into the suburbs. Backing this growth initiative and adding efficiency to the overall operations was the addition of a central commissary where some of the ingredients were prepared. By this time, Chipotle was considered a pioneer in two national restaurant trends: so-called wraps and the fast-casual sector. The latter category encompassed chains that were a bit fancier than typical fast-food restaurants such as Taco Bell and a bit faster than casual-dining chains such as Chevys. Each Chipotle was estimated to be generating just over $1 million in annual sales at this time. Sales were divided about 50–50 between eat-in and carry-out customers. Chipotle's clientele was mainly composed of adults between the ages of 18 and 49, a contrast to most fast-food restaurants, which catered to teenagers and families.

Whereas the first Chipotle was a cramped 800 square feet in size, the subsequent units covered 1,600 to 2,800 square feet, and they employed about 17 workers each. Although the design differed from unit to unit, the architecture aimed for a hip, urban feel. The decor was spare and industrial: halogen lighting, metal tabletops, wooden benches and seats, concrete floors, and arched metal ceilings. At this time, design and construction costs totaled about $249,000 per unit. Also noteworthy during this initial period of growth was that Chipotle did little in the way of advertising or promotion, relying instead on word-of-mouth testimonials.

Rapid Expansion Funded by Late 1990s McDonald's Buyout

As six more Chipotle Mexican Grills opened in the Denver area during 1997, bringing the total to 14, Ells and other company leaders were seeking more funding to accelerate the growth rate. Venture capital firms were more interested in the high-flying tech world at the time, so a member of the Chipotle board of directors sent an unsolicited business plan to fast-food leader McDonald's Corporation. The timing was perfect. Domestic sales were flattening at the burger giant, and executives were seeking a way to jump-start growth. In February 1998, after a year of negotiations and due diligence, McDonald's made its first-ever investment in a restaurant chain it did not itself develop, buying a minority stake in Chipotle. (Later, it bought the Boston Market chain and owned the Donatos Pizza chain for a few years.) Chipotle continued to be run independently, headed by Ells as CEO, and neither its management structure nor its menu changed. Growth would continue to be generated through company-owned outlets—now with the backing of much deeper pockets—but there was the clear potential for franchising, eventually, through McDonald's system of franchisees.

Following the McDonald's infusion, Chipotle began expanding outside of Colorado, sometimes aided by McDonald's expertise in site selection. Two units were opened in Kansas City (one in Kansas and one in Missouri) in 1998, and several new markets were entered in 1999: Chicago; Cleveland, Columbus, and Dayton, Ohio; Minneapolis-St. Paul; Phoenix; Dallas; and Washington, D.C. The restaurant count more than doubled in 1999, ending at 37. Revenues for the year totaled approximately $31 million, compared to $13 million for 1997. McDonald's increased its stake in Chipotle to more than 50 percent in 1999 and would later bump its ownership interest to 90 percent.

Another early benefit of the McDonald's relationship was that Chipotle could leverage McDonald's industry clout in, for example, getting a better supplier of avocados. Chipotle was also able to have supplies such as avocados shipped immediately through McDonald's massive distribution system. Such access was indispensable as Chipotle's operations spread out geographically.

Early 2000s: Accelerating Growth, Shifting to Organic Ingredients

Expansion accelerated in the early 2000s, with the store count reaching 100 by the end of 2000 and then 175 at year-end 2001. Among the new markets were Baltimore, Houston, Los Angeles, and San Francisco. A McDonald's franchisee began operating two Chipotle units in Dayton, Ohio, but there was not yet a major move into franchising the concept. During 2001 Chipotle dropped the phrase "Mexican Grill" from the name of its restaurants (though the company name itself did not change). Officials at the chain reasoned that "Mexican Grill" had become too commonly used throughout the industry and might prove limiting, given that the menu already went well beyond typical Mexican fare. Around this same time, the company made the first significant changes to the menu since the first store opened. In addition to fine-tuning the recipe for its homemade guacamole, Chipotle switched to free-range pork for its carnitas. The supplier, Oakland, California-based Niman Ranch, raised its pigs "naturally"; Niman allowed them to roam free and did not feed them antibiotics. The result, according to Ells, was better-tasting pork. To use the higher-end and higher-priced product, Chipotle had to raise the price of its pork

Key Dates:

1993: Steve Ells opens the first Chipotle Mexican Grill in Denver, Colorado.
1995: Second Chipotle restaurant opens.
1997: Six more Chipotle Mexican Grills open, bringing the total to 14.
1998: McDonald's Corporation purchases a minority stake in Chipotle; first units outside Colorado open in Kansas City.
1999: McDonald's purchases majority control of Chipotle; several new markets are entered as store count reaches 37.
2001: Menu begins featuring Niman Ranch free-range pork.
2003: Store count reaches 300.

burritos by more than $1, to $5.50, but sales hardly suffered. Ells told *Nation's Restaurant News* in July 2001 that "our customers can't get enough of the new recipe. . . . In fact, we are selling two-and-a-half times more carnitas than before, and sales continue to rise." Food industry research and consulting firm Technomic estimated that overall revenues at Chipotle more than doubled in 2001, reaching $145 million.

About 55 more Chipotles opened in 2002 and another 70 the following year, bringing the total to 300. As it celebrated its tenth anniversary, Chipotle ranked as one of the fastest-growing restaurant chains in the country. The chain entered the Las Vegas, Atlanta, and New York markets, among others, in 2003, by which time Technomic estimated revenues at $321 million. Same-unit sales (that is, sales at units open more than one year) were growing at an impressive rate of 20 percent per year. Late in 2003 McDonald's announced, contrary to earlier rumors, that it would sell neither Chipotle nor Boston Market, both of which were operating in the black (it soon sold Donatos Pizza, however). Chipotle remained a major growth avenue for McDonald's.

Continuing to upgrade his food ingredients, Ells switched from yellow corn, which could contain genetically modified stock, to organic white corn, which did not have any genetically modified stock. He also began switching to organic beans, but a shortage of suppliers meant that Chipotle could get only 10 percent of the beans it needed from organic sources. In addition, he was running into similar problems finding suppliers of organic chicken. By mid-2004 Chipotle was offering naturally raised, antibiotic-free chicken from Bell & Evans in 50 restaurants in Washington, D.C., New York, and Ohio. Eight restaurants in Chicago and New York were using naturally raised beef.

Starting with 2004, Chipotle increased its growth rate to 100 new units per year, aiming to hit the 500 restaurant mark by the end of 2005. The chain expanded into the Pacific Northwest by entering the Seattle and Portland, Oregon, markets and also moved into Florida, specifically Orlando and Tampa. Chipotle also beefed up its marketing efforts by hiring its first outside advertising agency, the New York office of an irreverent British agency, Mother. Chipotle had been producing its own humorous radio, print, and billboard ads featuring a photo of a burrito

wrapped in foil accompanied by brief, witty copy, such as "A complete, four-course meal in a handy tortilla carrying pouch" or "Burrito? Or body pillow?" Chipotle's marketing budget was estimated to be $10 million per year. Another development was an addition to the menu in response to the low-carb diet craze: Chipotle began offering its burritos and fajitas in a bowl, sans tortilla, and with romaine lettuce standing in for rice.

By late 2004, with the store count nearing 400, nothing appeared to be slowing Chipotle's remarkable growth. Ells had made only small changes to the still-simple menu in the 11-plus years he had been in business, and he continued to seek out new sources for organic ingredients. "It's not just about fresh anymore; fresh is sort of the minimum that you have to do in this category now," Ells told *Nation's Restaurant News* in October 2004. "You have to be concerned where your food comes from and how the animals were raised. I call it 'Food with Integrity.'" Backed by the cash-rich McDonald's, Ells was positioned to maintain the rapid growth of Chipotle: "I think there's a huge demand in the U.S. for the brand. And so the challenge is to improve the experience and deliver it to more and more people."

Principal Competitors

Fresh Enterprises, Inc.; Rubio's Restaurants, Inc.; Moe's Southwest Grill, LLC; Qdoba Restaurant Corporation; El Pollo Loco, Inc.

Further Reading

Alsever, Jennifer, "Quest for a New Burrito: CEO Brings Natural Foods to Fold," *Denver Post,* May 9, 2004, p. K1.

Bernstein, Charles, "The Right Combination: Chipotle Grows with Steve Ells' Youth and Food Fanaticism Plus McDonald's Experience and Deep Pockets," *Chain Leader,* May 2001, pp. 54–56, 58, 60.

Bunn, Dina, "McDonald's Takes Bite of Chipotle," *Rocky Mountain News,* February 10, 1998, p. 1B.

Cavanaugh, Bonnie Brewer, "Steve Ells," *Nation's Restaurant News,* October 4, 2004, pp. 114+.

Cebrzynski, Gregg, "Chipotle Seeks 'Fresh Thinking,' Hires First Formal Agency," *Nation's Restaurant News,* February 23, 2004, p. 14.

Chandler, Susan, "Burrito Chain Spices McDonald's," *Chicago Tribune,* August 2, 1998, p. 1.

Cohen, Deborah L., "McD's Takes Control of Mexican-Food Restaurant Chain," *Crain's Chicago Business,* October 11, 1999, p. 3.

Dunn, Julie, "Free-Range Burritos: Is This McDonald's?," *New York Times,* September 29, 2002, sec. 3, p. 6.

Elliott, Stuart, "Restaurant Chain Known for Irreverent Advertising," *New York Times,* January 8, 2004, p. C7.

Forgrieve, Janet, "Chipotle Serves Up a Winner," *Rocky Mountain News,* July 11, 2003, p. 7B.

Guy, Sandra, "McDonald's Plans Big Chipotle Boost," *Chicago Sun-Times,* May 24, 2002, p. 51.

Hamstra, Mark, "McD's Buys Stake in Chipotle Mexican Grill," *Nation's Restaurant News,* February 23, 1998, pp. 1, 6.

Hochwarth, Patricia, "The Gospel According to Chipotle," *Restaurant Hospitality,* April 2004, p. 58.

Landwehr, Rebecca, "Big Macs and Burritos," *Denver Business Journal,* February 18, 2000, p. 1A.

Parker, Penny, "Married Life Suits Chipotle: McDonald's Stake Carries Clout," *Denver Post,* May 23, 1999, p. K1.

——, "McDonald's Acquires Taste for Burritos: Fast-Food Giant Invests in Local Chipotle Chain," *Denver Post,* February 10, 1998, p. A1.

Raffio, Ralph, ''Steve's Big McBreak,'' *Restaurant Business,* April 1, 1998, pp. 38–41, 44, 46.

Ruggless, Ron, ''Southwestern Cuisine Keeps Palates Sizzling,'' *Nation's Restaurant News,* June 30, 1997, pp. 35–36.

——, ''Steve Ells: Taking Quick Service to New Levels of Sophistication at Chipotle Mexican Grill,'' *Nation's Restaurant News,* January 1999, pp. 68, 77.

St. John, Bill, ''Chipotle Mexican Grill: Just Like the Pepper, It's All Jazzed Up,'' *Rocky Mountain News,* October 22, 1993, p. 20D.

Thorn, Bret, ''Steve Ells,'' *Nation's Restaurant News,* January 27, 2003, pp. 36, 40.

Yee, Laura, ''Did Someone Say, Chipotle Mexican Grill?,'' *Restaurants and Institutions,* July 1, 1999, pp. 51–52.

Zuber, Amy, ''Chipotle's Challenge: Create a Unique Design for Each Site,'' *Nation's Restaurant News,* November 9, 1998, p. 24.

——, ''Chipotle Upgrades Menu Items, Will Drop 'Mexican Grill' Name,'' *Nation's Restaurant News,* July 30, 2001, pp. 4, 69.

——, ''Donatos Shuts Units, Cuts Staff As Chipotle Heats Up,'' *Nation's Restaurant News,* December 2, 2002, pp. 1 + .

——, ''Regional Powerhouse Chains: Chipotle,'' *Nation's Restaurant News,* January 28, 2002, pp. 58–59.

—David E. Salamie

The Coca-Cola Company

The Coca-Cola Company

The Coca-Cola Company

One Coca-Cola Plaza
Atlanta, Georgia 30313-2420
U.S.A.
Telephone: (404) 676-2121
Toll Free: (800) 468-7856
Fax: (404) 676-6792
Web site: http://www.cocacola.com

Public Company
Incorporated: 1892
Employees: 49,000
Sales: $21.04 billion (2003)
Stock Exchanges: New York Boston Chicago National
   (NSX) Pacific Philadelphia
Ticker Symbol: KO
NAIC: 312111 Soft Drink Manufacturing; 311930
   Flavoring Syrup and Concentrate Manufacturing;
   311411 Frozen Fruit, Juice, and Vegetable
   Manufacturing; 311920 Coffee and Tea
   Manufacturing; 312112 Bottled Water Manufacturing

The Coca-Cola Company is the world's number one maker of soft drinks, selling 1.3 billion beverage servings every day. Coca-Cola's red and white trademark is probably the best-known brand symbol in the world. Headquartered since its founding in Atlanta, Coca-Cola makes four of the top five soft drinks in the world, Coca-Cola at number one and Diet Coke, Fanta, and Sprite at numbers three through five. The company also operates one of the world's most pervasive distribution systems, offering its nearly 400 beverage products in more than 200 countries worldwide. Nearly 70 percent of sales are generated outside North America, with revenues breaking down as follows: North America, 30 percent; Europe, Eurasia, and the Middle East, 31 percent; Asia, 24 percent; Latin America (including Mexico), 10 percent; and Africa, 4 percent. Among the company's products are a variety of carbonated beverages (including the aforementioned brands and many others, such as Fresca, Barq's, and Cherry and Vanilla Coke); sports drinks (POWERade and Aquarius); juices and juice drinks (Minute

Maid, Fruitopia, Hi-C, Five Alive, Qoo, Maaza, and Bibo); teas (Sokenbicha and Marocha); coffees (Georgia); and bottled waters (Ciel, Dasani, and Bonaqua). Moreover, the company holds the rights to the Schweppes, Canada Dry, Dr Pepper, and Crush brands outside of North America, Europe, and Australia. Coca-Cola's development into one of the most powerful and admired firms in the world has been credited to proficiency in four basic areas: consumer marketing, infrastructure (production and distribution), product packaging, and customer (or vendor) marketing.

Creation of a Brand Legend

The inventor of Coca-Cola, Dr. John Styth Pemberton, came to Atlanta from Columbus, Georgia, in 1869. In 1885 he set up a chemical laboratory in Atlanta and went into the patent medicine business. Pemberton invented such products as Indian Queen hair dye, Gingerine, and Triplex liver pills. In 1886 he concocted a mixture of sugar, water, and extracts of the coca leaf and the kola nut. He added caffeine to the resulting syrup so that it could be marketed as a headache remedy. Through his research Pemberton arrived at the conclusion that this medication was capable of relieving indigestion and exhaustion in addition to being refreshing and exhilarating.

The pharmacist and his business partners could not decide whether to market the mixture as a medicine or to extol its flavor for its own sake, so they did both. In *Coca-Cola: An Illustrated History,* Pat Watters cited a Coca-Cola label from 1887 which stated that the drink, ''makes not only a delicious . . . and invigorating beverage . . . but a valuable Brain Tonic and a cure for all nervous affections.'' The label also claimed that ''the peculiar flavor of Coca-Cola delights every palate; it is dispensed from the soda fountain in the same manner as any fruit syrup.'' The first newspaper advertisement for Coca-Cola appeared exactly three weeks after the first batch of syrup was produced, and the famous trademark, white Spenserian script on a red background, made its debut at about the same time.

Coca-Cola was not, however, immediately successful. During the product's first year in existence, Pemberton and his partners spent around $74 in advertising their unique beverage and made only $50 in sales. The combined pressures of poor

111

Company Perspectives:

The Coca-Cola Company exists to benefit and refresh everyone it touches.

The basic proposition of our business is simple, solid and timeless. When we bring refreshment, value, joy and fun to our stakeholders, then we successfully nurture and protect our brands, particularly Coca-Cola. That is the key to fulfilling our ultimate obligation to provide consistently attractive returns to the owners of our business.

business and ill health led Pemberton to sell two-thirds of his business in early 1888. By 1891, a successful druggist named Asa G. Candler owned the entire enterprise. It had cost him $2,300. Dr. Pemberton, who died three years earlier, was never to know the enormous success his invention would have in the coming century.

Candler, a religious man with excellent business sense, infused the enterprise with his personality. Candler became a notable philanthropist, associating the name of Coca-Cola with social awareness in the process. He was also an integral part of Atlanta both as a citizen and as a leader. Candler endowed Emory University and its Wesley Memorial Hospital with more than $8 million. Indeed, the university could not have come into existence without his aid. In 1907 he prevented a real estate panic in Atlanta by purchasing $1 million worth of homes and reselling them to people of moderate income at affordable prices. During World War I, Candler helped to avert a cotton crisis by using his growing wealth to stabilize the market. After he stepped down as the president of Coca-Cola, he became the mayor of Atlanta and introduced such reforms as motorizing the fire department and augmenting the water system with his private funds.

1891–1919: Rapid Growth Under the Candlers

Under Candler's leadership, which spanned a 26-year period, the Coca-Cola Company grew quickly. Between 1888 and 1907, the factory and offices of the business were moved to eight different buildings in order to keep up with the company's growth and expansion. As head of the company, Candler was most concerned with the quality and promotion of his product. He was particularly concerned with production of the syrup, which was boiled in kettles over a furnace and stirred by hand with large wooden paddles. He improved Pemberton's formula with the help of a chemist, a pharmacist, and a prescriptionist. In 1901, responding to complaints about the presence of minute amounts of cocaine in the Coca-Cola syrup, Candler devised the means to remove all traces of the substance. By 1905, the syrup was completely free of cocaine.

In 1892, the newly incorporated Coca-Cola Company allocated $11,401 for advertising its drink. Advertising materials included signs, free sample tickets, and premiums such as ornate soda fountain urns, clocks, and stained-glass lampshades, all with the words "Coca-Cola" engraved upon them. These early advertising strategies initiated the most extensive promotional campaign for one product in history. Salesmen traveled the entire country selling the company's syrup,

and by 1895 Coca-Cola was being sold and consumed in every state in the nation. Soon it was available in some Canadian cities and in Honolulu, and plans were underway for its introduction into Mexico. By the time Asa Candler left the company in 1916, Coke had also been sold in Cuba, Jamaica, Germany, Bermuda, Puerto Rico, the Philippines, France, and England.

An event that had an enormous impact on the future and very nature of the company was the 1899 agreement made between Candler and two young lawyers that allowed them to bottle and sell Coca-Cola throughout the United States: the first bottling franchise had been established. Five years later, in 1904, the one-millionth gallon of Coca-Cola syrup had been sold. In 1916 the now universally recognized, uniquely contour-shaped Coke bottle was invented. The management of all company advertising was assigned to the D'Arcy Advertising Agency, and the advertising budget had ballooned to $1 million by 1911. During this time, all claims for the medicinal properties of Coca-Cola were quietly dropped from its advertisements.

World War I and the ensuing sugar rationing measures slowed the growth of the company, but the pressure of coal rations led Candler's son, Charles Howard, to invent a process whereby the sugar and water could be mixed without using heat. This process saved the cost of fuel, relieved the company of the need for a boiler, and saved a great amount of time since there was no need for the syrup to go through a cooling period. The company continued to use this method of mixing into the 1990s.

Although Candler was fond of his company, he became disillusioned with it in 1916 and retired. One of the reasons for this decision was the new tax laws which, in Candler's words, did not allow for "the accumulation of surplus in excess of the amount necessary for profitable and safe conduct of our particular business." (It has also been suggested that Candler refused to implement the modernization of company facilities.)

1919–55: The Woodruff Era

Robert Winship Woodruff became president of the company in 1923 at the age of 33. His father, Ernest Woodruff, along with an investor group, had purchased it from the Candler family in 1919 for $25 million, and the company went public in the same year at $40 a share. After leaving college before graduation, Woodruff held various jobs, eventually becoming the Atlanta branch manager and then the vice-president of an Atlanta motor company, before becoming the president of Coca-Cola.

Having entered the company at a time when its affairs were quite tumultuous, Woodruff worked rapidly to improve Coca-Cola's financial condition. In addition to low sales figures in 1922, he had to face the problem of animosity toward the company on the part of the bottlers as a result of an imprudent sugar purchase that management had made. This raised the price of the syrup and angered the bottlers. Woodruff was aided in particular by two men, Harrison Jones and Harold Hirsch, who were adept at maintaining good relations between the company and its bottling franchises.

Woodruff set to work improving the sales department; he emphasized quality control, and began advertising and promotional campaigns that were far more sophisticated than those of the past. He established a research department that became a

<table>
<tr><td colspan="2">Key Dates:</td></tr>
</table>

Key Dates:

1886: Pharmacist Dr. John Styth Pemberton concocts Coca-Cola, a mixture of sugar, water, caffeine, and extracts of the coca leaf and the kola nut.

1891: Asa G. Candler, a druggist, gains complete control of Pemberton's enterprise.

1892: Candler incorporates The Coca-Cola Company.

1899: The first bottling franchise is established.

1905: Coca-Cola syrup is completely free of cocaine.

1916: The unique, contour-shaped Coke bottle is introduced.

1919: Ernest Woodruff and an investor group buy the company for $25 million; the company goes public at $40 per share.

1923: Robert Winship Woodruff becomes president of the firm.

1943: Coca-Cola plants are set up near fighting fronts in North Africa and Europe, helping boost American GI spirits and introduce Coke to the world market.

1960: The Minute Maid Corporation is acquired.

1961: Sprite makes its debut.

1981: Roberto Goizueta becomes chairman.

1982: Columbia Pictures is acquired for $750 million; Diet Coke is introduced to the market.

1985: Coca-Cola is reformulated; New Coke is rejected by consumers, and the company brings back the original formula, calling it Coca-Cola Classic.

1987: Company sells its entertainment business to Tri-Star Pictures.

1990: Sales surpass the $10 billion mark for the first time.

1997: Douglas Ivester succeeds Goizueta as chairman and CEO.

1999: Company acquires the rights to sell Schweppes, Canada Dry, Dr Pepper, and Crush brands in 157 countries, not including the United States, Canada, Mexico, and most of Europe.

2000: New CEO Douglas N. Daft launches major restructuring involving job cuts of 5,200.

2002: Company launches Vanilla Coke.

2004: E. Neville Isdell is named chairman and CEO.

Emory University for a cancer diagnosis and treatment center, and over the years gave more than $100 million to the clinic. He donated $8 million for the construction of the Atlanta Memorial Arts Center. Under his leadership the Coca-Cola Company pioneered such company benefits as group life insurance and group accident and health policies, and in 1948 introduced a retirement program.

Woodruff was to see the Coca-Cola Company through an era marked by important and varied events. Even during the Great Depression the company did not suffer thanks to Woodruff's cost-cutting measures. When Prohibition was repealed, Coca-Cola continued to experience rising sales. It was World War II, however, that catapulted Coca-Cola into the world market and made it one of the country's first multinational companies.

Woodruff and Archie Lee of the D'Arcy Advertising Agency worked to equate Coca-Cola with the American way of life. Advertisements had, in Candler's era, been targeted at the wealthy population. In Woodruff's time the advertising was aimed at all Americans. By early 1950, African Americans were featured in advertisements, and by the mid-1950s there was an increase in advertising targeted at other minority groups. Advertising never reflected the problems of the world, only the good and happy life. Radio advertising began in 1927, and through the years Coca-Cola sponsored many musical programs. During World War II, Woodruff announced that every man in uniform would be able to get a bottle of Coke for five cents no matter what the cost to the company. This was an extremely successful marketing maneuver and provided Coke with good publicity. In 1943, at the request of General Eisenhower, Coca-Cola plants were set up near the fighting fronts in North Africa and eventually throughout Europe in order to help increase the morale of U.S. soldiers. Thus, Coca-Cola was introduced to the world.

Coke was available in Germany prior to the war, but its survival there during the war years was due to a man named Max Keith who kept the company going even when there was little Coca-Cola syrup available. Keith developed his own soft drink, using ingredients available to him, and called his beverage Fanta. By selling this beverage he kept the enterprise intact until after the war. When the war was over the company continued to market Fanta. By 1944, the Coca-Cola company had sold one billion gallons of syrup, by 1953 two billion gallons had been sold, and by 1969 the company had sold six billion gallons.

1955–81: Diversification, New Products, and Foreign Expansion

The years from the end of World War II to the early 1980s were years of extensive and rapid change. Although Woodruff stepped down officially in 1955, he still exerted a great amount of influence on the company over the coming years. There were a series of chairmen and presidents to follow before the next major figure, J. Paul Austin, took the helm in 1970; he was followed by Roberto Goizueta in 1981. In 1956, after 50 years with the D'Arcy Advertising Agency, the Coca-Cola Company turned its accounts over to McCann-Erickson and began enormous promotional campaigns. The decade of the 1950s was a time of the greatest European expansion for the company. During this decade Coca-Cola opened approximately 15 to 20 plants a year throughout the world.

pioneering market research agency. He also worked hard to provide his customers with the latest in technological developments that would facilitate their selling Coca-Cola to the public, and he labored to increase efficiency at every step of the production process so as to raise the percentage of profit from every sale of Coca-Cola syrup.

Through the 1920s and 1930s such developments as the six-pack carton of Coke, which encouraged shoppers to purchase the drink for home consumption, coin-operated vending machines in the workplace, and the cooler designed by John Stanton expanded the domestic market considerably. Also, by the end of 1930, as a result of the company's quality control efforts, Coca-Cola tasted exactly the same everywhere.

Considered slightly eccentric, Woodruff was a fair employer and an admired philanthropist. In 1937, he donated $50,000 to

The company also began to diversify extensively, beginning in 1960, when the Minute Maid Corporation, maker of fruit juices and Hi-C fruit drinks, was acquired by Coca-Cola. Four years later the Duncan Foods Corporation also merged with the company. In 1969 Coca-Cola acquired the Belmont Springs Water Company, Inc., which produced natural spring water and processed water for commercial and home use. The following year the company purchased Aqua-Chem, Inc., producers of desalting machines and other such equipment, and in 1977 Coca-Cola acquired the Taylor Wines Company and other wineries. These last two companies were sold later under Goizueta's leadership.

In addition to its diversification program, the Coca-Cola Company also expanded its product line. Fanta became available in the United States during 1960 and was followed by the introduction of Sprite (1961), TAB (1963), and Fresca (1966), along with diet versions of these drinks. One reason that Coca-Cola began to introduce new beverages during the 1960s was competition from Pepsi Cola, sold by PepsiCo, Inc. Pepsi's success also motivated the Coca-Cola Company to promote its beverage with the slogan ''It's the Real Thing,'' a subtle, comparative form of advertising that the company had never before employed.

Things did not always run smoothly for Coca-Cola. When Coke was first introduced to France, the Communist party, as well as conservative vineyard owners, did what they could to get the product removed from the country. They were unsuccessful. Swiss breweries also felt threatened, and spread rumors about the caffeine content of the drink. More consequential was the Arab boycott in 1967 which significantly hindered the company's relations with Israel. In 1970 the company was involved in a scandal in the United States when an NBC documentary reported on the bad housing and working conditions of Minute Maid farm laborers in Florida. In response, the company established a program that improved the workers' situation. In 1977 it was discovered that Coca-Cola, for various reasons, had made $1.3 million in illegal payments over a period of six years, mostly to executives and government officials in foreign countries.

During the 1970s, under the direction of Chairman J. Paul Austin and President J. Lucian Smith, Coca-Cola was introduced in Russia as well as in China. To enter the Chinese market, the company sponsored five scholarships for Chinese students at the Harvard Business School, and supported China's soccer and table-tennis teams. The beverage also became available in Egypt in 1979, after an absence there of 12 years. Austin strongly believed in free trade and opposed boycotts. He felt that business, in terms of international relations, should be used to improve national economies, and could be a strong deterrent to war. Under Austin, Coca-Cola also started technological and educational programs in the Third World countries in which it conducted business, introducing clean water technology and sponsoring sports programs in countries too poor to provide these benefits for themselves.

Austin's emphasis was on foreign expansion. Furthermore, under Austin's management the company became more specialized. Where Woodruff was aware of all facets of the company, Austin would delegate authority to various departments. For instance, he would give general approval to an advertising scheme, but would not review it personally. Smith was responsible for the everyday operations of the company, and Austin would, among other things, set policies, negotiate with foreign countries, and direct the company's relations with the U.S. government.

1981–97: The Goizueta Era

Roberto Goizueta became chairman in 1981, replacing Austin. The Cuban immigrant immediately shook up what had become a risk-averse, tradition-obsessed, barely profitable company. Less than a year after becoming chairman, he made two controversial decisions. First, he acquired Columbia Pictures for about $750 million in 1982. Goizueta thought that the entertainment field had good growth prospects, and that it would benefit from Coca-Cola's expertise in market research. Secondly, without much consumer research, Goizueta introduced Diet Coke to the public, risking the well-guarded trademark that until then had stood only for the original formula. Something had to be done about the sluggish domestic sales of Coca-Cola and the intense competition presented by Pepsi. In 1950, Coke had outsold Pepsi by more than five to one, but by 1984 Pepsi had a 22.8 percent share of the market while Coke had a 21.6 percent share. Goizueta's second 1982 gamble paid off handsomely when Diet Coke went on to become the most successful consumer product launch of the 1980s, and eventually the number three soft drink in the entire world.

In 1985 Goizueta took another chance. Based on information gathered from blind taste tests, Goizueta decided to reformulate the 99-year-old drink in the hope of combating Pepsi's growing popularity. The change to New Coke was not enthusiastically greeted by the U.S. public. Apparently Goizueta did not take into account the public's emotional attachment to the name ''Coca-Cola'' and all that it stood for: stability, memories, and the idea of a ''golden America.'' Within less than a year the company brought back the ''old'' Coke, calling it Coca-Cola Classic. New Coke was universally considered the biggest consumer product blunder of the 1980s, but it was also viewed in a longer term perspective as a positive thing, because of the massive amount of free publicity that the Coke brand received from the debacle.

In September 1987, Coca-Cola agreed to sell its entertainment business to TriStar Pictures, 30 percent of which was owned by Coca-Cola. In return, Coca-Cola's interest in TriStar was increased to 80 percent. Coca-Cola's holding in TriStar was gradually distributed as a special dividend to Coca-Cola shareholders until the company's interest was reduced to a minority, when TriStar changed its name to Columbia Pictures Entertainment and sought its own listing on the New York Stock Exchange. Although the company's flirtation with entertainment appeared to be ill-advised, Coca-Cola ended up with $1 billion in profits from its short-term venture.

In a 1984 article in the *New York Times,* Goizueta stated that he saw Coca-Cola's challenge as ''continuing the growth in profits of highly successful main businesses, and [those] it may choose to enter, at a rate substantially in excess of inflation, in order to give shareholders an above average total return on their investment.'' Goizueta projected that by 1990 his new strategy would nearly double the company's net income to $1 billion.

His prediction came true in 1988. Two years later revenues surpassed the $10 billion mark.

In the mid-1980s, Coca-Cola reentered the bottling business, which had long been dominated by family-operated independents. Coca-Cola began repurchasing interests in bottlers worldwide with a view toward providing those bottlers with financial and managerial strength, improving operating efficiencies, and promoting expansion into emerging international markets. The trend started domestically, when the parent company formed Coca-Cola Enterprises Inc. through the acquisition and consolidation of two large bottlers in the South and West in 1986. The parent company acquired more than 30 bottlers worldwide from 1983 to 1993. By then, the market value of the company's publicly traded bottlers exceeded the company's book value by $1.5 billion.

Called "one of the world's most sophisticated and powerful marketing organizations," the company's schemes for the 1990s included the 1993 global launch of the "Always Coca-Cola" advertising theme. The new campaign was formulated by Creative Artists Agency, which took over much of the brand's business in 1992 from longtime agency McCann-Erickson Worldwide. In addition to the new campaign, a 32-page catalog of about 400 licensed garments, toys, and gift items featuring Coke slogans or advertising themes was released. The 1994 introduction of a PET plastic bottle in the brand's distinctive, contour shape resulted from corporate marketing research indicating that an overwhelming 84 percent of consumers would choose the trademarked bottle over a generic straight-walled bottle. But the company's primary challenge for the last decade of the 20th century came in the diet segment, where top-ranking Diet Coke was losing share to ready-to-drink teas, bottled waters, and other "New Age" beverages, which were perceived as healthier and more natural than traditional soft drinks. Coca-Cola fought back by introducing its own new alternative drinks, including POWERade (1990), the company's first sports drink, and the Fruitopia line (1994). In 1992 the company and Nestlé S.A. of Switzerland formed a 50–50 joint venture, Coca-Cola Nestlé, Refreshment Company, to produce ready-to-drink tea and coffee beverages under the Nestea and Nescafé, brand names. Also during this time, Coca-Cola purchased Barq's, a maker of root beer and other soft drinks.

Goizueta died of lung cancer in October 1997, having revitalized and awakened what had been a sleeping giant. Goizueta had turned the company into one of the most admired companies in the world, racking up an impressive list of accomplishments during his 16-year tenure. Coca-Cola's share of the global soft drink market was approaching 50 percent, while in the United States Coke had increased its share to 42 percent, overtaking and far surpassing Pepsi's 31 percent. Revenues increased from $4.8 billion in 1981 to $18.55 billion in 1996; net income grew from $500 million to $3.49 billion over the same period. Perhaps Goizueta's most important—and influential—contribution to the storied history of Coca-Cola was his relentless focus on the company's shareholders. The numbers clearly showed that he delivered for his company's owners: return on equity increased from 20 percent to 60 percent, while the market value of the Coca-Cola Company made a tremendous increase, from $4.3 billion to $147 billion. Perhaps most telling, a $1,000 investment in Coca-Cola in 1981 was worth,

assuming that dividends were reinvested, $62,000 by the time of Goizueta's death.

Challenging and Stormy Times in the Late 1990s

Goizueta's right-hand man, Douglas Ivester, was given the unenviable task of succeeding perhaps the most admired chief executive in the United States; Ivester's reign turned out to be both brief and stormy. Although Coca-Cola remained steadily profitable, it was beset by one problem after another in the late 1990s. Having restructured its worldwide bottling operations under Goizueta, the firm moved into a new phase of growth based on the acquisition of other companies' brands. Its already dominant market share and a sometimes arrogant and aggressive approach to acquisition led some countries, particularly in Europe, to take a hard line toward the company. In late 1997, for example, Coca-Cola announced it would acquire the Orangina brand in France from Paris-based Pernod Ricard for about $890 million. French authorities, who had fined Coca-Cola for anticompetitive practices earlier that year, blocked the purchase. In December 1998 Coca-Cola announced that it would purchase several soft drink brands—including Schweppes, Dr Pepper, Canada Dry, and Crush—outside the United States, France, and South Africa from Cadbury Schweppes plc for $1.85 billion. After encountering regulatory resistance in Europe, Australia, Mexico, and Canada, the two companies in July 1999 received regulatory approval for a new scaled-down deal valued at about $700 million, which included 155 countries but not the United States, Norway, Switzerland, and the member states of the European Union with the exception of the United Kingdom, Ireland, and Greece. Later in 1999 separate agreements were reached that gave Coca-Cola the Schweppes brands in South Africa and New Zealand.

With nearly two-thirds of sales originating outside North America, Coca-Cola was hit particularly hard by the global economic crisis of the late 1990s, which moved from Asia to Russia to Latin America. In Russia, where the company had invested $750 million from 1991 through the end of the decade, sales fell about 60 percent from August 1998, when the value of the ruble crashed, to September 1999. Rather than retreating from the world stage, however, Ivester viewed the downturn as an opportunity to make additional foreign investments at bargain prices, essentially sacrificing the short term for potentially huge long-term gains. While the economic crisis was still wreaking havoc, Coca-Cola was faced with another crisis in June 1998 when several dozen Belgian schoolchildren became ill after drinking Coke that had been made with contaminated carbon dioxide. Soon, 14 million cases of Coca-Cola products were recalled in five European countries in the largest recall in company history, and France and Belgium placed a temporary ban on the company's products. The crisis, though short-lived, was a public relations disaster because company officials appeared to wait too long to take the situation seriously, admit that there had been a manufacturing error, and apologize to its customers. Meanwhile, around this same time, four current and former employees had filed a racial discrimination suit against the firm in the United States, a suit that was later granted class-action status.

Despite the seemingly endless string of challenges the company faced in the late 1990s, Coca-Cola was also moving forward with new initiatives. In February 1999 the company announced plans to launch its first bottled water brand in North America. Dasani was described as a "purified, non-carbonated water enhanced with minerals." In October 1999 the company announced that it would redesign the look of its Coca-Cola Classic brand in 2000 in an attempt to revitalize the flagship's stagnant sales. Labels would continue to feature the iconic contour bottle but with a cap popped off and soda fizzing out. In addition, the Coke Classic slogan "Always," which had been used since 1993, would be replaced with the tag line "Enjoy," which had been used on Coke bottles periodically for decades. The company also planned to increase the appearances of the eight-ounce contour bottle, in a particularly nostalgic move.

The renewed emphasis on this classic brand icon and the resurrection of the "Enjoy" slogan seemed to be a fitting way for a U.S.—if not global—institution to launch itself into the new millennium. But the company ended 1999 with the surprising news that the beleaguered Ivester would retire in early 2000 after just two and a half years at the helm—a tenure marked perhaps most tellingly by seven straight quarters of earnings declines. Taking over was Douglas N. Daft, a native Australian and 30-year Coke veteran who had headed the company's operating group covering the Middle and Far East and Africa; he was named president and chief operating officer in December 1999 before becoming chairman and CEO the following February.

Continuing Struggles in the Early 2000s

Daft's first year was a hectic one. In January 2000 the company announced a drastic restructuring based on a plan drafted by a Daft-led team. Coca-Cola said it would lay off about 6,000 employees, representing a slashing of the workforce by 20 percent—the largest cutbacks in Coke history. The cuts were later scaled back to about 5,200, but the company still took about $1.6 billion in one-time charges for a plan that aimed to save $300 million in operating costs per year. The restructuring, which centered on marketing, sales, and customer support jobs, was envisioned as a slashing of bureaucracy in an attempt to create a more decentralized company, one in which ideas could more readily bubble up from managers in the field rather than those at the Atlanta headquarters. In November 2000 Daft engineered a tentative deal to take over the Quaker Oats Company for $15.75 billion. This would have added to the Coke portfolio the Gatorade brand, which dominated the sports drink sector, a perennial Coke weakness, and would also have complemented the company's strategy of strengthening its lineup of noncarbonated beverages. But at the last minute, Coca-Cola's board pulled the plug on the deal, mainly concerned that the price was too high. The company's arch-rival PepsiCo quickly swooped in to complete a $13.4 billion acquisition of Quaker Oats. Also in November, Coca-Cola reached an agreement to settle the race-discrimination class-action lawsuit that had been brought against it. The company agreed to a $192.5 million settlement and also to have certain of its employment practices overseen by an outside task force. About 2,000 current and former African American employees were eligible for settlement awards.

Another of Daft's main objectives was pumping up an arid new product pipeline, but he garnered only mixed results. The company found moderate success with the 2001-debuting Diet Coke with Lemon, before making a much bigger splash with Vanilla Coke one year later. The latter received the firm's largest new product launch since the New Coke debacle. To supplement these meager advances—and particularly to try to capture a greater share of the noncarbonated beverage sector, which was growing at a much faster clip than the stagnant carbonated sector—Daft turned to partnerships as a potential source of renewed growth. In January 2001 an agreement was reached with Nestlé S.A. to form a joint venture called Beverage Partners Worldwide. Within a couple of years, this venture was marketing ready-to-drink tea (Nestea, Belté, Yang Guang, and several other brands) and coffee (Nescafé, Taster's Choice, and Georgia Club) products in the United States and about 45 other countries. Coca-Cola and the Procter & Gamble Company (P&G) agreed in March 2001 to create a $4 billion joint venture that would have joined Coke's Minute Maid brand and distribution network with P&G's snack and juice brands. However, Coca-Cola pulled out of the deal just a few months later, having decided to try to build the Minute Maid brand on its own. Then in July 2002 Coca-Cola and Groupe Danone formed a joint venture to produce, market, and distribute Danone's Dannon and Sparkletts bottled-water brands in the United States. In a separate deal, Coke took over the U.S. marketing, sales, and distribution of Danone's Evian water brand, the French firm's biggest seller.

In March 2003 the company slashed another 1,000 jobs from the payroll, half of them at headquarters. Also that year, Coca-Cola was the recipient of more negative publicity when it was revealed that several midlevel employees had rigged a marketing test for Frozen Coke done three years earlier at Burger King restaurants in the Richmond, Virginia, area. The scandal led to the departure of the head of Coke's fountain division, and the company issued an apology to Burger King and its franchisees and offered to pay them $21 million. An early 2004 launch of the Dasani brand into the European market was aborted when bottles in Britain were found to contain elevated levels of bromate, a substance that can cause cancer after long-term exposure.

This latest product recall came as Coca-Cola was in the midst of yet another change at the top. In February 2004 Daft announced his intention to retire following a search for a new chief executive. After considering a number of outside candidates, the company hired a semi-outsider, E. Neville Isdell, in June 2004. An Irish citizen who had grown up in Africa, Isdell was a former senior executive at Coke who had led the company's push into a number of new markets around the globe in the 1980s and 1990s. He left the company in 1998 to become chairman of Coca-Cola Beverages, a major Coke bottler, and then retired in 2001. The new leader was faced with many of the same challenges that his predecessor struggled with little success to overcome: improving marketing, forging better relations with the company's bottlers, and satisfying consumer demand for more healthful beverage products, particularly of the non-carbonated variety.

Principal Subsidiaries

The Minute Maid Company.

Principal Divisions

Foodservice and Hospitality; North & West Africa; Southern & East Africa; East & South Asia; China; India; Southeast & West Asia; Philippines; Japan; South Pacific & Korea; Central Europe, Eurasia & Middle East; Central Europe & Russia; Italy & Alpine; Southeast Europe & Gulf; Germany & Nordic; Northwest Europe; Iberian; Brazil; Latin Center; Mexico; South Latin.

Principal Competitors

PepsiCo, Inc.; Nestlé S.A.; Cadbury Schweppes plc; Groupe Danone; Kraft Foods Inc.

Further Reading

Allen, Frederick, *Secret Formula: How Brilliant Marketing and Relentless Salesmanship Made Coca-Cola the Best-Known Product in the World,* New York: HarperBusiness, 1994, 500 p.

Applegate, Howard L., *Coca-Cola: A History in Photographs, 1930 Through 1969,* Osceola, Wis.: Iconografix, 1996, 126 p.

Beatty, Sally, and Nikhil Deogun, "Coke Revisits Its Emotional Ads of the '70s," *Wall Street Journal,* July 8, 1998, p. B8.

Bernstein, Peter W., "Coke Strikes Back," *Fortune,* June 1, 1981, pp. 30 + .

Candler, Charles Howard, *Asa Griggs Candler,* Atlanta: Emory University, 1950, 502 p.

The Chronicle of Coca-Cola, Since 1886, Atlanta: Coca-Cola Company, [n.d.].

The Coca-Cola Company: An Illustrated Profile of a Worldwide Company, Atlanta: Coca-Cola Company, 1974.

"Coke's Big Marketing Blitz," *Business Week,* May 30, 1983, pp. 58 + .

Cowell, Alan, "The Coke Stomach Ache Heard Round the World," *New York Times,* June 25, 1999, p. C1.

Deogun, Nikhil, "Aggressive Push Abroad Dilutes Coke's Strength As Big Markets Stumble," *Wall Street Journal,* February 8, 1999, pp. A1 + .

——, "Can Coke Rise to the Global Challenge?," *Wall Street Journal,* September 24, 1998, p. C1.

Deogun, Nikhil, et al., "Anatomy of a Recall: How Coke's Controls Fizzled Out in Europe," *Wall Street Journal,* June 29, 1999, pp. A1 + .

Echikson, William, "Have a Coke and a Smile—Please," *Business Week,* August 30, 1999, p. 214A.

Enrico, Roger, and Jesse Kornbluth, *The Other Guy Blinked: And Other Dispatches from the Cola Wars,* New York: Bantam, 1988, 280 p.

Foust, Dean, "Things Go Better with . . . Juice," *Business Week,* May 17, 2004, pp. 81–82.

Foust, Dean, and Deborah Rubin, "Now, Coke Is No Longer 'It,' " *Business Week,* February 28, 2000, pp. 148, 150–51.

Foust, Dean, David Rocks, and Mark L. Clifford, "Is Douglas Daft the Real Thing?," *Business Week,* December 20, 1999, pp. 44, 46.

Foust, Dean, and Gerry Khermouch, "Repairing the Coke Machine," *Business Week,* March 19, 2001, pp. 86–88.

Graham, Elizabeth C., and Ralph Roberts, *The Real Ones: Four Generations of the First Family of Coca-Cola,* New York: Barricade Books, 1992, 344 p.

Greisling, David, *I'd Like the World to Buy a Coke: The Life and Leadership of Roberto Goizueta,* New York: Wiley, 1998, 334 p.

Hagerty, James R., and Amy Barrett, "Can Douglas Ivester End Coke's Crisis?," *Wall Street Journal,* June 18, 1999, p. B1.

Harrison, DeSales, *"Footprints on the Sands of Time": A History of Two Men and the Fulfillment of a Dream,* New York: Newcomen Society in North America, 1969, 24 p.

Hays, Constance L., *The Real Thing: Truth and Power at the Coca-Cola Company,* New York: Random House, 2004, 398 p.

——, "A Sputter in the Coke Machine: When Its Customers Fell Ill, a Master Marketer Faltered," *New York Times,* June 30, 1999, p. C1.

Huey, John, "In Search of Roberto's Secret Formula," *Fortune,* December 29, 1997, pp. 230–32, 234.

Kahn, Ely Jacques, *The Big Drink: The Story of Coca-Cola,* New York: Random House, 1960, 174 p.

Kemp, Kathryn W., *God's Capitalist: Asa Candler of Coca-Cola,* Macon, Ga.: Mercer, 2002, 312 p.

Laing, Jonathan R., "Is Coke Still It?," *Barron's,* May 9, 1994, pp. 29–33.

Louis, J.C., and Harvey Z. Yazijian, *The Cola Wars,* New York: Everest House, 1980, 386 p.

McKay, Betsy, "Coca-Cola Agrees to Settle Bias Suit for $192.5 Million," *Wall Street Journal,* November 17, 2000, p. A3.

——, "Coke Faces the Return of Recycling Issue," *Wall Street Journal,* September 13, 1999, p. B8.

——, "Cola on the Rocks, Coke Plans a 'Classic' Redesign," *Wall Street Journal,* October 13, 1999, pp. B1, B4.

McKay, Betsy, and Joann S. Lublin, "Coke Names Isdell Chairman, CEO," *Wall Street Journal,* May 5, 2004, p. A3.

McKay, Betsy, and Nikhil Deogun, "After Short, Stormy Tenure, Coke's Ivester to Retire," *Wall Street Journal,* December 7, 1999, p. B1.

Moore, Thomas, and Susan Caminiti, "He Put the Kick Back into Coke," *Fortune,* October 26, 1987, pp. 46 + .

Morris, Betsy, "Doug Is It," *Fortune,* May 25, 1998, pp. 70–74, 78, 80, 82, 84.

Neff, Jack, "Trouble Bubbles for Coke," *Food Processing,* November 2003, pp. 24–26.

Oliver, Thomas, *The Real Coke: The Real Story,* New York: Viking Penguin, 1987, 195 p.

Pendergrast, Mark, *For God, Country and Coca-Cola: The Definitive History of the Great American Soft Drink and the Company That Makes It,* 2nd edition, New York: Basic, 2000, 621 p.

Santoli, Michael, "Coke Is No Longer It," *Barron's,* April 5, 1999, p. 15.

——, "How Coke Is Kicking Pepsi's Can," *Fortune,* October 28, 1996, pp. 70–73 + .

Scredon, Scott, and Marc Frons, "Coke's Man on the Spot: The Changes Goizueta Is Making Outweigh One Spectacular Blunder," *Business Week,* July 29, 1985, pp. 56 + .

Sellers, Patricia, "Coke's CEO Doug Daft Has to Clean Up the Big Spill," *Fortune,* March 6, 2000, pp. 58–59.

——, "Who's in Charge Here?," *Fortune,* December 24, 2001, pp. 76–80, 83, 86.

Terhune, Chad, "CEO Says Things Aren't Going Better with Coke," *Wall Street Journal,* September 16, 2004, pp. A1, A10.

——, "Coke's CEO Is to Retire at Year End," *Wall Street Journal,* February 20, 2004, p. A3.

Terhune, Chad, and Betsy McKay, "Bottled Up—Behind Coke's CEO Travails: A Long Struggle over Strategy," *Wall Street Journal,* May 4, 2004, p. A1.

Watters, Pat, *Coca-Cola,* New York: Doubleday, 1978, 288 p.

Yazijian, Harvey Z., and J.C. Louis, *The Cola Wars,* New York: Everest House, 1980, 386 p.

—updates: April Dougal Gasbarre, David E. Salamie

Cold Spring Granite Company Inc.

202 S. Third Avenue
Cold Spring, Minnesota 56320
U.S.A.
Telephone: (320) 685-3621
Toll Free: (800) 328-5040
Fax: (320) 685-8490
Web site: http://www.coldspringgranite.com

Private Company
Incorporated: 1920 as Rockville Granite Company
Employees: 1,250
Sales: $128 million (2003 est.)
NAIC: 327991 Cut Stone and Stone Products
     Manufacturing

Cold Spring Granite Company Inc. is one of the largest granite quarrying and fabrication operations in the world. The small-town business over the years earned the respect of architects and gained an international reputation on its ability to provide a complete array of services from mining and finishing to installation. The company offers products for commercial and memorialization applications, ranging from building facing and countertop slabs to flat markers and family mausoleums. The privately held company has been led by three generations of the Alexander family.

The Early Years in Rockville: 1880s–1910s

Henry Nair Alexander worked in the granite and slate quarries of his native Scotland alongside his father and brothers. In 1880, he and two of his brothers immigrated to the United States and cut stone in Portland, Maine. He returned to Scotland two years later in order to finish a contract for granite barns. While back home he met and married Maggie Milne.

The American granite industry started to develop west of Chicago just as the second half of the 19th century began. Alexander decided to follow other Scotsmen to the massive granite fields in central Minnesota. In 1889 he and seven other men working for the Breen and Young quarry struck out on

their own to form the Rockville Granite Company. Their first big contract—eight large columns—was for the Minnesota State Capitol in St. Paul.

Alexander bought out his partners on September 29, 1898, and became sole owner of Rockville Granite Company. He then moved the business to a quarry location closer to the Great Northern Railroad right-of-way and began modernizing his equipment. He also purchased a farm in the Rockville area to help support his growing family. Carrying on the family tradition, Henry's sons started working in the quarry at a young age. A daughter received business training and took over the bookkeeping. In general, Alexander believed a family was a stabilizing influence on his workers, and that belief would come to influence the philosophy of the business, then and in the future.

Rockville Granite Company faced stiff competition when a larger concern, the Clark and McCormick Granite Company, set up shop in 1907 and began quarrying the gray granite which was so plentiful in the area. Alexander kept the business going with projects such as Chicago's Iroquois Theatre and the Minneapolis disposal system. When Henry became ill from pneumonia in 1912, 22-year-old Patrick Alexander, who had left home to work in quarries around the country and in Canada, came home and took over management of the company. Fourteen-year-old John Alexander also helped out at the plant, but their brother William Alexander continued to farm.

When Henry died in 1913, Maggie Alexander decided to try to sell the business to the Clark and McCormick quarry. Unable to get what she felt was a fair price she kept the business, and Patrick became the youngest granite company manager in the country. John, a high school student, helped on weekends, and William assisted with blacksmith work when needed. Maggie died in 1916, and Patrick and John became the owners of Rockville Granite Company, which was valued at about $6,000, including plant, equipment, and property.

John was intent on getting a college education, but that changed when Patrick was called to serve in World War I. John had to return home to help run the plant. By the end of the war the amount of work coming into the plant was on the rise, but business was good for the company's competitor, too. The

Company Perspectives:

Henry Alexander brought to Minnesota the stone skills, heritage and work ethic that has become the company culture for Cold Spring Granite Company. These skills and attitudes have been passed down from generation to generation within the company as many employees represent second, third and fourth generations of loyal and dedicated granite craftsmen.

Clark and McCormick Quarry had acquired practically all the gray granite outcroppings in the area to supply granite for the cathedral being built in St. Paul. Rockville Granite Company had to find a new site in order to keep running. John gave up his plans to return to college and helped Patrick look for a new location for the company.

The Move to Cold Spring: 1920s

The site of a burned down flour mill, just west of Rockville in Cold Spring, looked like a promising location. It was on a river with a dam for supplying power, and the town needed new businesses. The loss of the mill had cost jobs, and the other big employer, Cold Spring Brewing Company, was suffering because of Prohibition. Cold Spring banker Fred Stein and Cold Spring Brewing Company owner Ferdinand Peters recruited several other businessmen to help bring the quarry company to town.

On October 5, 1920, Rockville Granite Company was incorporated with Peters as president, Patrick Alexander as vice-president, John Alexander as secretary, and Fred Stein as treasurer. The mill purchase price was $30,000. The company made a $200,000 stock offering and quickly sold over 40 percent of that and then borrowed additional cash to finance the startup costs. The new plant began operation in the spring of 1921. The Alexander brothers, as managers of the newly incorporated company, searched for new granite outcroppings to supply material for the plant. The stone they found had a pink tinge and was used to supply their first major job, the Stearns County Court House in St. Cloud.

The Rockville Granite Company was now on solid financial ground, and the company could begin growing. A full-time draftsman and later drafting assistants were hired and concentrated on architectural projects. A sales force was formed and opened offices near large building construction sites in Minneapolis, Chicago, St. Louis, and Philadelphia. New equipment was purchased and quarry and plant operations were revamped to cut down waste and increase efficiency. By 1923 the company could retire its debts and pay interest on its stock. Well-established in its new location, with an expanded physical plant and about 75 full-time employees, the company was ready for a name change. In 1924 Rockville Granite Company became Cold Spring Granite Company.

Growth created its share of problems for Cold Spring Granite. The company, which had operated a union, or closed, shop for many years, was struck when a contract was made to deliver granite to an open shop on the West Coast. The labor movement

was in its formative years and working to gain strength and momentum; a compromise which would have allowed Cold Spring to fill its contract could not be negotiated. The closed shop policy was ended, and about one-quarter of the men left the company. However, due to relatively high wages the vacancies were quickly filled. Many of the men hired then later moved to supervisory positions. Others who joined on at the time were to be the first in a line of family members stretching for several generations that worked for the company.

According to John Dominik, author of *Cold Spring Granite: A History,* the company found early success due to the experience of the employees and their ability to innovate. Men with expertise in the industry were drawn on board, and Patrick Alexander strove to introduce production techniques that enhanced their competitiveness. Together they adapted equipment from other heavy industries for use with granite and became leaders in the field.

The Depression and War Years: 1930s–40s

The economic depression of the 1930s dried up the architectural work Cold Spring Granite had depended on in its early years, and the company had to temporarily shut down. After resuming operations, the company responded by shifting to monument work and by becoming increasingly self-sufficient. Employees painstakingly built their own surfacing wheels, which were needed to finish the stone, and when the cost of the steel shot used in the cutting process rose dramatically, they made that, too.

During the Depression, John Alexander took over the management of monument sales. In order to keep the plant running in the winter months he offered incentives to monument dealers who placed off-season orders. Promotional materials with drawings and photographs of the monuments and mausoleums were also generated. After the economy improved and architectural work increased, monument sales continued to hold an important position in the company.

Transportation was a large part of the expense of granite production. Cold Spring Granite had persistent difficulties connected to delivery of its unwieldy product. Most shipments were made by rail: breakage and long delays were common. In the mid-1930s, a trucker who hauled the company's granite from the plant to the railroad proposed that finished granite could be shipped directly to work sites on semi-trailer trucks. Consequently, Cold Spring shifted away from rail to truck transportation, ending its dependence on railroad schedules and routes, cutting shipping costs, and lessening the risk of damage which occurred during the transfer of stone from truck to train to truck.

The company suffered an important loss in 1938 with the death of its president. Ferdinand Peters had guided the company through its incorporation and managed the financial aspects of Cold Spring Granite while the Alexanders concentrated on production. With Peters's death, Patrick Alexander once again headed the company his father had founded. He soon faced another crisis.

When the United States entered World War II architectural steel manufacturers diverted their efforts to military production: construction jobs became scarce. But Cold Spring Granite

Key Dates:

1889: Rockville Granite Company is formed.
1898: Henry N. Alexander becomes sole owner.
1912: Son Patrick takes over management of company.
1920: Company incorporates.
1921: New plant in Cold Spring begins operations.
1924: Company is renamed after its new location.
1929: Beginning of economic depression marks transition from building projects to monument work.
1939: Company is hit hard by loss of men called off to war.
1945: John Alexander becomes president following the death of his brother Patrick.
1957: Company is chosen as granite supplier for Air Force Academy located in Colorado Springs.
1968: Third generation Alexander, Thomas, is named president.
1989: Company controls 30 percent of domestic market for granite.
1998: Cold Spring Granite celebrates its 100th anniversary.
2004: Company begins test marketing high-end product directly to public.

had the experience and equipment for handling large, heavy material. John Alexander pursued war contracts and then managed production. The plants were converted to handle steel instead of stone and manufactured—among other things—ships bottoms and hull sections. Men who had been quarriers learned to be welders.

With the end of the war came a flood of structural granite orders. But the quarries had been nearly idle for four years, and experienced men had been lost to the war. Cold Spring fell behind in production. To ease the burden the Royal Granite Company in St. Cloud was purchased. The monument end of the business also needed some attention, for consumer preferences had changed. Flat markers—which allowed for easier care of cemetery land and created a park-like look—had cut into the market. Ferdinand "Frosty" Peters, son of the late Cold Spring president, promoted a line of bronze markers anchored in granite, and a wholly owned subsidiary, Granit-Bronz, Inc., was established. During this time of change the company again lost its president when Patrick Alexander died in 1945 and was succeeded by his brother.

Time of Expansion: 1950s–70s

"John Alexander's tenure as president of Cold Spring Granite Company was marked by unprecedented expansion," wrote John Dominik. It was through those acquisitions that the company "became the largest granite concern in the world." Prior to World War II Cold Spring Granite had already obtained quarries that allowed it to supply a rich variety of colors to its market: "black" Canadian granite; South Dakota Ruby Red granite; and Minnesota Rainbow granite. During the war the company purchased the quarries situated in the original Rockville location. The postwar expansion began with Royal Granite and was fol-

lowed by the purchase of the Texas Granite Company of Marble Falls; a Purple Crystal granite quarry near Rockville; a quarry and a small plant in Raymond, California; the Lake Placid Granite Company in New York; and still more quarries in Minnesota, South Dakota, California, and Canada. The quarries and plants purchased during the 1950s and 1960s benefited the company in terms of proximity to desirable market areas or job sites and with the added expertise of the new employees.

As the company expanded Cold Spring Granite won larger architectural contracts. In 1957, the company was chosen as granite supplier for the new Air Force Academy in Colorado Springs, Colorado. Rockville granite was used for fortress walls, building facing, walkway steps, and the plaza. The million-dollar project was the beginning of a push to convince architectural firms to use company granite in large construction projects.

Just as the combined talent of the Cold Spring crew had solved production problems in the past, they came together to meet the architectural challenges of the 1960s. New techniques were developed in order to apply granite to modern office towers such as the 54-story Bank of America building in San Francisco. After completing several skyscraper projects, the company shifted its focus to large plazas including those at the Atlanta International Headquarters of Coca-Cola Company, the Chicago Civic Center, and the Twenty State Street Mall in Boston.

Even though the architecture of the 1960s and 1970s was dominated by modernism—more large commercial buildings were faced with glass, metal, and precast concrete than with stone—Cold Spring grew. Between 1975 and 1980 sales increased by $5 million per year, topping $50 million in 1980. By the early 1980s builders had begun to move away from modernism and emphasized the color and tradition found in stone. Cold Spring Granite Company rode with that resurgence.

Third Generation of Alexander Family Leadership: 1980s to Mid-1990s

The leadership of Cold Spring Granite had passed on to a third generation by this time. Thomas Alexander, Patrick's middle son, had been named president in 1968. Like his father and uncle before him, his involvement in the company started at an early age, first with small jobs around the office and then work in the plant. An experienced pilot, Thomas nearly left the granite business, but his uncle, John Alexander, brought him on as his assistant. Through doing the company's production cost accounting Thomas became familiar with every aspect of the company, which enabled him to guide the development of new products and production methods.

In 1983 Patrick Alexander, the namesake of his uncle, became the fifth Alexander to lead the company. He had followed in their footsteps and learned the business from the ground up. He worked in the quarries and the pre-casting plant while still in high school. After graduating from St. Edward's College in Austin, Texas, he went on to the Marble Falls plant. Eventually Patrick took over supervision of operations at Raymond, Lake Placid, Texas, and Cold Spring Granite of Canada, Ltd.

The first five years of Patrick Alexander's term as president were marked by rapid growth. The number of employees increased from 700 to 1,700, annual revenues rose to more than

$110 million, and the company spent $40 million for quarry and plant improvements. But it also was a time marked by uncertainty. In the mid-1980s the granite industry was hit by high building vacancy rates and apprehension about federal tax law revision: the result was a slowdown of office and apartment construction. Foreign competitors were also a concern for the American granite industry. Italy held 70 percent of the total structural granite market, compared with Cold Spring's 15 percent.

In 1987 Cold Spring along with two other American granite companies filed a suit with the International Trade Commission (ITC) against Italian and Spanish granite firms. They claimed that government subsidies were allowing the foreign companies to sell granite below cost. Patrick Alexander was quoted in the *Star Tribune* as saying that the Italian and Spanish firms "are slowly but surely driving otherwise competitive U.S. companies out of business." The companies were seeking penalty duties on foreign granite. Even though the commission initially found that there was a "reasonable indication" that U.S. granite firms were being hurt, ultimately it ruled against them.

Although the purchase of new granite and plant sites had slowed in the 1970s and 1980s, it had not ceased entirely. Cold Spring acquired Capitol Marble and Granite Company, Inc., in Granite Falls, Texas, in 1988. With Capitol's annual revenues of $20 million, the investment was expected to boost Cold Spring's sales to $130 million.

In 1989, *Corporate Report Minnesota* reported that Cold Spring Granite controlled 30 percent of the $500 million domestic market for granite, employed 1,900 workers, and operated 31 quarries. Structural granite still provided its greatest source of revenue, but one-third of its business came from tombstones and mausoleums, and another 10 percent from a new commercial line of highly polished granite tiles and countertops.

Cold Spring Granite laid off over 400 employees in 1991 in response to a severe downturn in the construction business. To help boost sales it introduced a line of unfinished granite slabs targeted for sale to international granite fabricators. Continued diversification resulted in a drop of architectural sales to about 28 percent of business by 1995. With a long history of successful adaptation to rapidly changing circumstances, a powerful legacy in itself, Cold Spring Granite appeared solidly positioned in the industry as it prepared to enter its second century in business.

Second Hundred Years: Late 1990s to 2004

The MonuWest facility, designed for memorial fabrications, opened in January 1997. The first phase of a new foundry was completed in 1998. International sales, a business begun in the late 1980s, continued its yearly rise. Cold Spring Granite was 100 years old and growing.

As 1999 wound down, Cold Spring Granite was set to begin delivery of stone for the national World War II Memorial. More than one million pounds of granite quarried from sites in Minnesota, South Dakota, North Carolina, and Canada would be fabricated and shipped to Washington, D.C., for the monument honoring soldiers involved in the Normandy invasion.

According to an April 2000 *PR Newswire* article, "no single company has contributed more raw and finished granite building material to the development of national memorials in the last century." Among the memorials Cold Spring Granite had worked to build were ones dedicated to Franklin Delano Roosevelt, the Vietnam and Korean wars, and the U.S.S. Indianapolis.

Despite the high visibility of such projects, it was the personal memorial which continued to help drive the company. Over time, too, the products had taken on color. In a departure from traditional neutral toned stone, in the 1970s colored granites began gaining greater acceptance and availability. "Cold Spring was one of the first companies to successfully market granite colors for use in memorials and grave markers," according to a November 2000 *PR Newswire* article. The colored granites were marketed under equally colorful names such as "Mountain Red" or "Lake Superior Green." The company also offered limited supply colors such as "Autumn Blaze," found in a Wisconsin quarry, and supplemented its own color line by materials brought in from other continents.

Historically innovative, Cold Spring Granite had set its sites on another goal, achieving heightened manufacturing standards. In 1996 the company earned ISO certification and began pumping millions into updating plants and equipment. In 1999 the company was re-certified for the ISO 9001standard for quality management and began bolstering continuous improvement efforts with lean manufacturing and time-based management techniques. Cold Spring Granite strove to not only increase productivity and flexibility but improve customer satisfaction.

The company's results in terms of its on-time performance challenged the industry. Chief Financial Officer Greg Flint told *IIE Solutions:* "A colleague of mine was flabbergasted that we were doing something so cutting edge and unique in a mature company and industry. I told him the same people that expect meals, pictures and oil changes in minutes order from us and that if we did not reduce our lead times we would be left by the wayside." The company's dedicated workforce contributed to the firm's success. In 2002, Cold Spring Granite employed around 1,230; more than 190 of them had 25 or more years of service to the company.

Private mausoleums, the stone tombs which largely fell out of fashion in the United States in the 1920s, were experiencing resurgence as the number of wealthy Americans grew. In 1985, only about 65 private mausoleums were constructed in North America. In 2002, the number had climbed to 1,300 and the next year 1,400, even while death rates remained relatively stable. Cold Spring Granite, the largest mausoleum builder in the country, began test marketing direct sales to the public in 2004. Traditionally these sales had been made through monument retailers and cemeteries. The price tag ranged from $180,000 to more than $1 million. Once more Cold Spring Granite made a move in line with the times.

Principal Competitors

Georgia Marble Company; Pete Lien and Sons.

Further Reading

Adams, Jennifer, "Changing with the Times," *Stone World*," January 2002, pp. 34+.

Bjorhus, Jennifer, "Mausoleums Begin to Make a Comeback in U.S.," *Knight Ridder/Tribune Business News,* May 14, 2004.

"Cold Spring Granite Acquires Texas Firm," *Star Tribune* (Minneapolis), November 22, 1988, p. 8D.

"The Company Behind the Memorials," *PR Newswire,* April 27, 2000.

"Completion of D-Day Memorial in Sight," *PR Newswire,* December 1, 1999.

Dominik, John, *Cold Spring Granite: A History,* Cold Spring, Minn.: Cold Spring Granite Company, 1982.

Kahn, Aron, "Granite Firm Stonewalled by Economy," *St. Paul Pioneer Press,* September 13, 1991.

Klobuchar, Jim, "Firm Will Help You Say It with Granite," *Star Tribune* (Minneapolis), November 1, 1988, p. 1B.

McDonnell, Lynda, "Trade Deficit Keeps Rising; Hits at Home," *St. Paul Pioneer Press and Dispatch,* September 15, 1986, p. 1.

"Minnesota Shares in Stone Revival," *St. Paul Pioneer Press and Dispatch,* October 19, 1986, p. 1D.

"1995 CEOs of Minnesota," *Corporate Report Minnesota,* July 1995, p. 35.

"A Not-So-Rocky Road to Lean Manufacturing," *IIE Solutions,* October 2001, p. 11.

"Once Rare in American Cemeteries, Colorful Granite Brings New Life to Memorials," *PR Newswire, January* 18, 2001.

"Perfect Record," *Stone World,* September 2001, p. 22.

"Pet Memorials Help Owners Cope with Loss," *PR Newswire,* January 18, 2001.

Phelps, David, "Business Visas to Japan Called Hard to Get," *Star Tribune* (Minneapolis) February 29, 1988, p. 5D.

——, "Granite Firms Charge Unfair Competition by Europeans," *Star Tribune* (Minneapolis), July 29, 1987, p. 1M.

Rosengren, John, "Ground-Breaking Growth," *Corporate Report Minnesota,* July 1989, pp. 60+.

Sundstrom, Ingrid, "Business Is Solid at Cold Spring Granite," Star Tribune (Minneapolis), October 9, 1988, p. 1D.

Thomma, Steven, "Panel Acts to Bolster Granite Firm," *St. Paul Pioneer Press and Dispatch,* September 10, 1987.

Weinberger, Betsy, "Cold Spring Granite Wants Out of Carlson Center Lease," *Minneapolis/St. Paul City Business,* August 14, 1992.

Wickland, John A., "Saws Scream Night and Day at Big Granite Works," *Minneapolis Tribune,* September 5, 1954.

—Kathleen Peippo

Cone Mills LLC

804 Green Valley Road, Ste. 300
Greensboro, North Carolina 27408
U.S.A.
Telephone: (336) 379-6220
Fax: (336) 379-6287
Web site: http://www.cone.com

Private Company
Incorporated: 1891 as the Cone Export & Commission
    Company
Employees: 2,300
Sales: $445.6 million (2002)
NAIC: 313210 Broad Woven Fabric Mills

Cone Mills LLC has more than a century of experience in the textile industry. While operating as Cone Mills Corporation, it was known as the world's largest manufacturer of denim fabric and the United States' largest printer of home-furnishings fabrics. Started by two brothers with a background in wholesale groceries, Cone grew steadily throughout its early years, concentrating on the manufacture of denim for work clothes. The competitive world textile industry caused the company to begin making cutbacks in the late 1970s, and it moved to diversify its product mix in order to maintain profitability. Despite resurgence in the popularity of denim with the baby boomers, Cone Mills found itself unable to thrive in the wake of rising raw material costs, narrowing profit margins, and the changing global marketplace. The company filed for Chapter 11 bankruptcy protection in the fall of 2003 and was acquired by WL Ross & Co. the next spring. Cone Mills now operates as part of International Textile Group which also includes former competitor Burlington Industries.

Roots in Family Grocery Business: 1840s–90s

Cone Mills was founded by Moses and Caesar Cone. They were the two eldest sons of a Baltimore wholesale grocery merchant, Herman Cone, who had immigrated to the United States from Bavaria in the 1840s, changing his name from Kahn to what he considered a more American spelling. In their teens,

Cone's sons worked with him in his store. By 1876, the business had expanded to include tobacco and leather goods, and Moses and Caesar had begun to travel the Southeast, taking orders from merchants for their father's goods.

In their travels, the brothers had an opportunity to observe the textile industry of the South. Beginning in the late 1880s, the Cones made investments in three Southern cotton mills: the C.E. Graham Manufacturing Company of Asheville, North Carolina, the Salisbury Cotton Mills, and the Minneola Manufacturing Company. All three of these factories used outmoded equipment to produce coarse, low quality plaids and sheeting. The fabrics enjoyed a vogue as a result of their low cost, yet in competition with the products of more modern Northern mills, they sold slowly.

Convinced that there was a glut of coarse plaids on the market, the Cone brothers persuaded their own business partners, as well as other Southern mill owners, to diversify their offerings. The Cones assigned brand names to key products, and published guarantees of quality. With these steps, sales began to rise. By 1890, the Cones had convinced 38 of the roughly 50 southern mill owners that they could benefit from hiring a selling agency to market their products. Faced with declining profits in their grocery business, Moses and Caesar, along with their father and another brother, Julius, liquidated H. Cone & Sons, in order to form the Cone Export & Commission Company in 1891. The enterprise was known facetiously by its competitors as the "plaid trust." The brothers signed five-year contracts with the mill owners to market their goods, at a 5 percent commission.

With fundraising for the new business complete, Moses Cone went to New York in 1891 to set up an office. Although as a Southerner he met with some hostility, he soon established his place in the business community, and the company was able to move to Worth Street, in the heart of the textile industry. In short order, the Cones were selling more fabric than they could provide, as mill owners left their selling syndicate.

The Cone brothers vowed to go into the fabric production business themselves. Their plans to build two mills, one for denim and one for flannel, were delayed by a financial panic in

1893, but within two years, the Cones had moved ahead, constructing a denim mill on land they owned in Greensboro, North Carolina. Since the plant was near its supply of raw materials, the cotton fields of the South, the Cones named their new factory the Proximity Cotton Mill, and set up a holding company for this plant and the others in which they held an interest called the Proximity Manufacturing Company. In 1896, the first lengths of fabric rolled off the big looms at Proximity. Caesar Cone felt that denim, a sturdy fabric for use in work clothes, would be in constant demand as the United States expanded and industrialized.

More Mills: 1900s–20s

Just three years later, the Cones opened Revolution Mills, a modern facility to weave soft cotton flannel. In 1902, a second denim plant was under construction. Called White Oak, it was named for the enormous tree that grew on its site. With ten different warehouses for cotton and its own power plant, the mill began turning out indigo blue denim by 1905. Moses Cone died at age 51 in 1908, and his brother carried on the company, opening a fourth mill, the Proximity Print Works, in 1912. This facility was designed to "finish" or print cotton with multiple colors, creating a type of cotton product new to the South.

More than just a workplace, the Cone mills became an entire world for their employees, who were cared for in a paternalistic, and some would say totalitarian, system by the mill owners. The Cones built housing near their mills, both boarding houses and single family homes, which made up segregated Cone villages. Stores sold dairy products and meat produced on company farms. For each village, the company built a school and donated land for churches. Two mill YMCAs were built to provide outlets for recreation, and the company also instituted a Welfare Office, with social workers and nurses to look after its employees.

By 1913, the Proximity Manufacturing Company owned all or half interests in seven cotton production facilities. During the following year, the company paid both its first dividend, and its first income taxes. In 1915, the company began to produce denim fabric for Levi's jeans, opening up an important new market. With the coming of World War I in 1914, Cone products continued to be in demand, both by the Allies overseas, and then, after 1917, by the American armed forces. In March of that year, Caesar Cone, the company's only living founder, died after a brief illness, and leadership of the company was turned over to his younger brothers, Julius and Bernard.

During the 1920s, as the American economy boomed in the Jazz Age, the Cones undertook cautious expansion, as they converted from wartime practices back to civilian production.

In 1920, the company bought the Salisbury Cotton Mills, which produced chambrays, coverts, ticking, and upholstery cloth. Further diversification came in 1925, when the company's New York distribution arm began marketing cotton blankets and felts produced by the Houston Textile Company of Texas. Over the next six years, the company gradually took over the Eno Cotton Mills of Hillsborough, North Carolina, which manufactured fine combed broadcloth for shirts.

In the late 1920s, the company also bought two gingham mills, the Cliffside Mill and Haynes Mill, which also had their own railroad to bring their products to the nearest main rail line. The Cones scrapped the mills' old box looms and installed terrycloth manufacturing equipment, enabling the Cones to enter the towel market. In addition, the company bought a mill built on solid granite called the Granite Cotton Factory from a Greensboro bank. On the same property, Cone also established the Tabardrey Manufacturing Company.

Economic Depression and Warfare: 1930s–40s

With the stock market crash of 1929 and the ensuing Great Depression, the Cones refrained from any further expansion throughout most of the 1930s. The company did introduce two new cotton fabrics, a light-weight flannel called "flannelette," and a crepe called "Proximity Plisse." Despite the popularity these products enjoyed, the company was forced to curtail production at its plants as the Depression wore on. In a move that would bode well for the future, however, Cone introduced "deeptone" denim in 1936, a smoother, darker indigo fabric that was designed to appeal to wearers more than the earlier, rougher fabrics.

By 1941, Cone was on more secure financial footing, and the company acquired the Florence Mills and its subsidiary, the American Spinning Company. Further expansion was halted with the American entry into World War II, when wartime production goals were implemented. In addition to an accelerated output of denim, Cone found itself producing such unfamiliar items as camouflage cloth, tent cloth, and osnaburg, for use in sandbags.

Seventy percent of the output of the fabric mills of North Carolina was diverted to the defense effort during the war, and at its end, it was clear that the Cones' operations needed to undergo a reorganization to thrive in the newly competitive civilian market. Accordingly, in 1945, the company merged all its separate mill properties into the Proximity Manufacturing Company, and also dissolved the old Cone Export and Commission Company, replacing it with a similar entity under the control of Proximity.

This move was followed in 1946 by the purchase of two more cotton mills, bringing to 16 the number of textile manufacturing facilities owned by Cone. In the next year, Cone branched out for the first time into synthetic fibers, purchasing a rayon plant next to one of its old cotton mills, and later adding a rayon spinning plant to bolster its production.

On the first day of 1948, Proximity's president announced that the company would change its name to Cone Mills Corporation. Further expansion followed this switch. In 1950, Cone merged with the Dwight Manufacturing Company, a producer

Key Dates:

1891: Cone Export & Commission Company is formed from liquidated grocery business H. Cone & Sons to market textile goods.

1896: The company's first denim manufacturing plant, Proximity Cotton Mill, begins production.

1899: Company begins weaving soft cotton flannel.

1905: Second denim plant begins turning out indigo blue denim.

1912: Fourth mill is opened to print cotton with multiple colors.

1929: Stock market crash puts an end to decade of expansion.

1945: Separate mills merge under Proximity Manufacturing Company.

1948: Name is changed to Cone Mills Corporation.

1951: Company goes public, begins trading on New York Stock Exchange.

1957: Decline in demand for denim prompts formation of Spinco fabrics for blended and synthetic goods.

1961: Company expands geographically with interest in South American company.

1962: Cone Mills steps outside textile industry for first time.

1969: Flooded warehouse results in fashion trend.

1975: Begins plant modernization drive to cut costs, combat cheap imports.

1983: Company goes private to circumvent takeover.

1992: Cone goes public again.

1995: Company enters into joint denim manufacturing effort in Mexico.

2003: Company files for Chapter 11 bankruptcy protection.

2004: Assets are acquired by WL Ross & Co.

of twills and drills located in Alabama, and in the following year, the company was purchased outright. Also in that year, Cone formed the Guilford Products Company, manufacturing cloth diapers to serve the growing market produced by the postwar baby boom.

In the Public Eye: 1950s–60s

In November 1951, Cone made its largest organizational shift to date, selling stock to the public for the first time. In trading on the New York Stock Exchange, the company's shares were valued at $28.58. In the wake of the company's debut as a publicly traded enterprise, Cone moved to further consolidate its similar operations, and to diversify its activities to protect itself against weakness in demand for any one product. In 1952, the company purchased the Union Bleachery in Greenville, South Carolina. In doing so, Cone gained the first license for the ''Sanforizing'' process granted in the United States.

Despite the fact that denim pants were beginning to be worn by teenagers as fashion statements, as opposed to being worn exclusively by manual laborers, the demand for denim began to drop in the mid-1950s, causing Cone to look to development in

its other areas of business for growth. The company began to emphasize its dyeing, printing, and finishing operations. Its flagship Proximity Cotton Mills was converted from the manufacture of denim, which was no longer in high demand, to the production of poplins, twills, and corduroy.

In 1957, Cone purchased three converting companies, and also moved further into the synthetics field, forming Spinco fabrics for blended and synthetic goods. Increasingly, the company found its market share threatened by products from other nations, where labor costs were lower. In response to this threat, in the following year, Cone stepped up its marketing efforts, and streamlined its manufacturing operations further, forming a finishing division to coordinate its various activities in that field. In addition, Cone inaugurated a Research and Development Department, to facilitate innovation in textile production. Overall, despite these efforts, the company's financial results throughout the 1950s were somewhat uneven.

In the 1960s, Cone began to diversify its operations further. In the first year of the decade, the company branched out into the decorative fabrics field, purchasing a controlling interest in John Wolf Textiles, which marketed fabrics for use in home furnishings. In the following year, Cone strengthened its presence in the furniture industry by organizing Olympic Products, which made polyurethane foam cushions and other foam products. This marked the company's first step outside the textile industry. In addition to this expansion in its activities, Cone broadened its geographical scope in 1961, buying an 11 percent interest in Fabrica Argentina de Alpargatas, which manufactured fabric, shoes, and other consumer goods in Brazil, Argentina, and Uruguay.

As a result of cotton pricing structures imposed by the federal government, Cone found itself losing its competitive edge in pricing for all-cotton fabrics to foreign producers. To combat this trend, the company began to increase the amount of synthetic fibers that it used in the fabrics it wove. These synthetic blends resulted in the introduction of stretch fabrics in 1962, and permanent press fabrics in 1964. In the following year, the company made a major shift in emphasis from all-cotton products to those made from a mix of cotton and synthetic fibers. These fabrics, which were used for newly fashionable casual and leisure-wear clothes, brought a higher price than simple cotton. Cone eventually offered more than 170 different blended cotton and synthetic products.

Denim Back in Demand: 1970s–80s

By the end of the decade, however, Cone had also seen a resurgence in the demand for its first product, denim, as jeans became a staple among the baby boom generation, evolving from functional work clothes to a fashion item. The extent of denim's domination of the youth fashion market was demonstrated in 1969, when Cone's denim warehouse at its White Oak plant was flooded after a torrential downpour fell on Greensboro. Faced with the task of washing and dying vast amounts of fabric, the company decided, at the suggestion of one of its marketing employees, to run the damaged fabric through a bleach solution while restoring it, to randomly remove its indigo dye. The resulting product, dubbed ''pinto wash'' denim, touched off a fashion fad. As further evidence of denim's popularity, Cone's Proximity Cotton Mills were converted back to their original function, the manufacture of denim, in 1970, to meet the rising demand. In addition, the company was producing a growing quantity of corduroy, as this fabric became a popular fashion item.

Cone continued to purchase companies that fit into its existing operations, adding a cushion manufacturer, the Prelude Company, in 1970. By the following year, however, it had become clear that some divisions of the company were not profitable, and Cone shut down two weak operations, a blanket plant in Houston, and the John Wolf Apparel Fabrics Division.

In 1972, Cone expanded its program to sell off unused real estate that the company had acquired over the years, buying the Cornwallis Development Company, a real estate developer, which became a separate Cone division. This company would eventually profitably develop over 1,000 acres of land in the Greensboro area.

Throughout the 1970s, Cone struggled against an industry-wide tide of cheap imported fabrics, which worked to keep profits down. The company relied heavily on its two main products, denim and corduroy, which enjoyed continuing fashion popularity. In 1974, Cone opened a new denim factory at its Cliffside plant. In 1975, the company embarked upon a nine-year program of plant modernization that was designed to make operations as efficient as possible, so that costs could be kept low.

Early in the 1980s, Cone entered another new market when it purchased the Chemical Chair House company, which manufactured molded urethane foam for use in the furniture and transportation industries. After changing its acquisition's name to Conitron, Cone built a new urethane plant for this company in Trinity, North Carolina. In the following year, Cone added to its polyurethane plant holdings when it purchased Ragan Hardware to add to its Olympic Division.

In 1983, Cone became a victim of the rage for corporate stock speculation when it was targeted for hostile takeover by Western Pacific Industries. In response, the company engineered a leveraged buyout of all of its outstanding stock, going private once again.

In further efforts to combat the impact of imported fabrics on its market, Cone joined with other American textile manufacturers to promote increased consumption of domestic products. "Crafted with Pride in the U.S.A." became the rallying cry for a public relations campaign designed to offset the impact of lower prices for imported products. Nevertheless, this factor, in combination with a loss in popularity for corduroy, caused Cone to close, convert, or sell ten of its mills in the years between 1977 and 1990. Such founding pillars of the company as the Proximity Cotton Mills and Print Works, the Revolution Mill, and the Minneola Mill shut their doors forever during this time.

Shrinking Fabric: 1990s

In addition to these measures, Cone streamlined its operations, and turned its attention to quality improvement programs and customer service. In 1990, the company also decided to move its marketing division to Greensboro. In the following year, Cone returned to the stock market, offering shares in the company in

June 1992. At the same time that it strengthened its financial standing through this move, Cone—continuing a strategy begun in late 1991—moved to shrink its operations, withdrawing from the corduroy manufacturing business, as well as other areas.

Cone Mills had returned to the public market on a high note, but earnings began to slip in subsequent years and dropped into the red in 1995. Although 1995 sales reached a record high of about $910 million, the company posted a $3.3 million net loss.

According to the *Daily News Record*, Cone Mills attributed the shortfall to "high raw cotton prices, the weak apparel retail market, continued deterioration of decorative print markets and a troubled Mexican economy." During the year, Cone Mills had opened a denim facility, Parras Cone de Mexico, in a joint venture with Compania Industrial de Parras, SA de CV, Mexico's largest denim producer.

In 1996, 85 percent of Cone Mills' revenue came from apparel fabric—primarily denim—with the remaining 15 percent from home furnishings and other businesses. A loss again was posted on the year. The company was selling off noncore businesses in an effort to turn things around, but the bleak news continued.

In 1998, Cone Mills launched a major restructuring effort to cut costs. The following year, investment group Summit Capital Corp., which had gradually acquired a 12.6 percent stake in Cone Mills, offered to take the company private through a buyout. The offer was rejected and Cone Mills adopted a poison pill defense to prevent a hostile takeover of the company down the road.

Under restructuring the company's workforce was reduced, plants closed, and lines of business ended. To be sure, Cone wasn't the only U.S. fabric manufacturer struggling. The North American Free Trade Agreement, enacted in 1994, while increasing trade, had not helped the slumping industry, according to the *Atlanta Journal-Constitution* in December 2000. "In fact, the elimination of quotas and duties between the United States and Mexico has encouraged Mexican firms to set up fabric mills, contributing to the surplus of fabrics that makes it harder for U.S. manufacturers to compete," Fernando Silva, managing partner for Atlanta-based Kurt Salmon Associates' soft goods practice, told Chris Burritt. The global oversupply of denim had driven the wholesale price down nearly 27 percent in four years.

Still, Cone Mills remained the world's largest producer of denim fabrics and North America's largest commission printer of home furnishing fabrics as the 21st century began and planned to continue to invest in manufacturing plants south of the border.

A New Life for Century-Old Fabric Maker: 2000–04

In 2002, Cone Mills reported its first profitable year since 1994. The company earned $7.2 million versus a $40.6 million loss in 2001. While pleased with the turnaround, CEO John Bakane was critical of the U.S. trade policy and tied it to the ongoing downturn in the economy, Scott Malone reported for *WWD*. Bakane "noted that China's manufacturing plants are attracting 20 million new workers a year at a time when the entire U.S. manufacturing sector employs 17 million." He also noted that "Cone and other U.S.

manufacturers need to modernize their plants and migrate to lower-cost nations to prepare for the onslaught of competition in 2005, when the 145 nations of the World Trade Organization are to drop quotas on apparel and textiles.''

Cone Mills' Parras Cone de Mexico joint venture contributed $8.3 million to 2002 operation income. In addition, a Turkish joint venture, established in 2002, had begun serving the European division of Levi Strauss & Co.

But in September 2003, Cone Mills failed to make a scheduled bond interest payment of $4.1 million. As part of a deal to be purchased by WL Ross & Co., Cone Mills planned to file for Chapter 11 bankruptcy protection. Likewise, competitor Burlington Industries had filed for bankruptcy in 2001 and was set to be purchased by financier Wilbur Ross.

WL Ross & Co. paid $46 million in cash for Cone Mills and assumed certain liabilities in the deal that was completed in March 2004. WL Ross & Co. formed International Textile Group (ITG) from Cone Mills and Burlington Industries. Ross had completed a similar deal when he formed International Steel Group out of three bankrupt steel companies.

Both textile companies had made large cuts in the work force in the year before the bankruptcies and together employed about 7,300. The new company's total revenue was $900 million. To exceed the $1 billion mark, ITG was planning to develop new fabric technologies, boost brand name identities, and lower operating costs.

Ross, chairman of the combined companies, said in the *Daily News Record*, ''Consumers know apparel brands but they're ignorant of fabric brands. If you can make a banana into Chiquita, we can do this with our fabrics.''

In May 2004, the company announced plans for a denim plant to begin operation in Guatemala City in 2005 and was looking toward additional manufacturing opportunities in Asia. Already under the Cone Mills division of the IT were the Mexican plant and joint ventures in India and Turkey.

In operation for over a century and providing denim and casual sportswear fabrics internationally for about a half century, perhaps as part of ITG, Cone Mills would finally become a household word.

Principal Competitors

Milliken & Co.; Springs Industries, Inc.; W.L. Gore & Associates, Inc.

Further Reading

Burritt, Chris, ''Seven Years into NAFTA, U.S. Textile Makers Seek Payoff in Mexico,'' *Atlanta Journal-Constitution,* December 17, 2000.

A Century of Excellence: The History of Cone Mills, 1891 to 1991, Greensboro, N.C.: Cone Mills Corporation, 1991.

Clune, Ray, Spirited Denim Sales Are Helping Cone Mills Weather Troubled Times,'' *Daily News Record,* May 16, 1996, pp. 9+.

''Cone Mills Announces 1999 Results,'' *PR Newswire,* February 10, 2000.

''Cone Mills Down 15% on Continued Denim Glut,'' *Dow Jones Newswire,* July 2, 1997.

''Cone Mills Drops $2.5M in 'Worst Quarter' Ever,'' *WWD,* February 13, 2002, p. 23.

''Cone Mills Quarter Best Since 1996,'' *WWD,* July 24, 2002, p. 17.

''Cone Mills Sets Poison Pill,'' *WWD,* October 15, 1999, p. 2.

''Cone Mills to Discontinue Khaki Fabric,'' *WWD,* October 31, 2001, p. 3.

''Cone Mills, WL Ross Complete Sale,'' *PR Newswire,* March 12, 2004.

Elliott, Frank, ''Cone Goes Hungry on a High-Fiber Diet,'' *Business North Carolina,* April 1997, pp. 20+.

''ITG Finalizes Burlington, Cone Mills Additions,'' *HFN The Weekly Newspaper for the Home Furnishing Network,* August 9, 2004, p. 18.

Lloyd, Brenda, ''Rose's Strategy: A Branding Blitz for Textile Firms,'' *Daily News Record,* March 22, 2004, p. 1.

Malone, Scott, ''Cone Reverses Loss with $3M in Income,'' *WWD,* February 7, 2003, p. 1.

——, ''Mills Break Losing Streak,'' *WWD,* June 6, 2000, p. 10.

——, ''Ross Combines Burlington, Cone Mills into $900M ITG,'' *HFN The Weekly Newspaper for the Home Furnishing Network,* March 29, 2004, p. 4.

——, ''Wilbur Ross Plans Guatemalan Plant,'' *WWD,* May 14, 2004, p.3.

''Ross to Buy Cone Mills,'' *Business Journal Serving the Greater Triad Area,'' September 16, 2003.

''Ross's Strategy: Branding Blitz for Textile Firms,'' *Daily News Record,* March 22, 2004, p.1.

—Elizabeth Rourke
—update: Kathleen Peippo

Conn's, Inc.

3295 College Street
Beaumont, Texas 77701
U.S.A.
Telephone: (409) 832-1696
Fax: (409) 832-4344
Web site: http://www.conns.com

Public Company
Founded: 1890 as Eastham Plumbing and Heat Co.
Employees: 2,050
Sales: $499.3 million (2003)
Stock Exchanges: NASDAQ
Ticker Symbol: CONN
NAIC: 443111 Household Appliance Stores

Conn's, Inc., a publicly traded company based in Beaumont, Texas, operates a chain of some 50 appliance stores in Texas and Louisiana, including 18 units in Houston; 13 in the San Antonio and Austin market; five in the "Golden Triangle" of Texas and Louisiana; five in the Baton Rouge and Lafayette, Louisiana, area; and one in Corpus Christi, Texas. About 40 percent of all stores are stand-alone buildings, with the rest found in shopping strip centers and larger enclosed malls. Units generally include 19,000 square feet of selling space and offer more than 1,100 product items. Merchandise includes such major home appliances as ranges, washers, dryers, refrigerators, and freezers; consumer electronics products such as televisions, DVD players, home theater systems, digital cameras, and video cameras; computers and handhelds for home office use; bedding by Serta; air conditioners and combination heaters and air conditioners; lawn and garden items such as lawnmowers, tractors, and grills; small appliances, including vacuum cleaners, air purifiers, water coolers, and wine coolers; kitchen products including cookware, cutlery sets, coffee makers, toasters, toaster ovens, slow cookers, griddles, mixers, ice makers, rotisseries, and deep fryers; and miscellaneous appliances such as sewing machines, electric shavers, and hair trimmers. Because it often competes with much larger retailing chains—Wal-Mart, Target, Circuit City, and Best Buy—that can use their size to offer lower prices, Conn's places a great deal of emphasis on customer service and timeliness. Complaints are generally resolved within 48 hours and stores offer same-day or next-day delivery. Conn's has been publicly traded on the NASDAQ since 2003, and hopes to take advantage of its new status to accelerate the chain's growth in existing and new markets.

Lineage Dating to 19th Century

Conn's traces its history to 1890 when Edward Eastham founded Eastham Plumbing and Heat Company in Beaumont, Texas. After the Republic of Texas was formed, years before it became part of the United States, Beaumont in 1838 was designated a county seat, which ensured local prominence. At the start of the 20th century, the city, located between Houston and the Louisiana border, boasted four railroads and a population approaching 10,000. Then, in 1901, oil was discovered in the vicinity, leading to a rapid increase in Beaumont's population, which doubled within ten years and increased to 58,000 by 1930. Eastham Plumbing and Heating grew with the town, but in 1931, in the midst of the Depression, the business failed. It was taken over by the First National Bank of Beaumont and renamed Plumbing and Heating Inc. The company soon came into the hands of an area oil baron who essentially bought the business to make sure he had an available plumber, after a recent cold snap had burst his pipes and he had been unable to get someone to do the repair work. In 1933 C.W. Conn, Sr., who had been selling appliances for an area gas company, was hired to run Plumbing and Heating with an option to buy it. A year later he exercised the option, bought the company, and renamed it Conn Plumbing and Heating Company. In 1937 he began the transition away from plumbing and heating when he started selling refrigerators, soon adding gas ranges. By the end of the decade he was selling his wares out of a downtown Beaumont storefront.

C.W. Conn would be joined by his son, C.W. Conn, Jr., who as early as the age of three earned a dollar for cleaning out a bathtub at the store. After he grew up, in 1953, he went to work at the store on a full-time basis. It was during this period that Conn's present-day chief executive and chairman, Thomas J. Frank, Sr., and his family began their association with the

Company Perspectives:

We are known for providing excellent customer service, and we believe that our customer-focused business strategies make us an attractive alternative to appliance and electronics superstores, department stores and other national, regional and local retailers.

company. His father, John J. Frank, Jr., first went to work for Conn's in 1956, taking a job as a salesman on the floor. He was in his late 30s at the time, and some 50 years later, when he was well into his 80s, would still be employed by the company selling trade-in appliances and doing some customer relations work. His son started out working at Conn's in 1957 when he was a high school junior, serving as a delivery truck helper. He would go on to college at Sam Houston State University, earning a degree in industrial arts and later taking graduate courses at Texas A&M University and Harvard University. Tom Frank began his full-time career at Conn's in the early 1960s and alongside C.W. Conn, Jr., would play an instrumental role in growing the Beaumont appliance store into a major regional chain. During his ascent to the top, Frank held key positions in all areas of the organization, involved in distribution, service, credit, information technology, accounting, and general operations. He became a member of the board of directors in 1980.

C.W. Conn, Jr., succeeded his father as the head of the business, and took it to an entirely new level. A second store, also in Beaumont, was not added until 1959. During the Baby Boom years of the 1950s the town was growing at a fast clip and able to support a second location. The population increased from 94,000 in 1950 to nearly 120,000 ten years later. The site for the second Conn Appliance store was considered remote at the time, located in the rural outskirts of Beaumont. In fact, the store was set up in an old dairy barn that was converted by laying down a cement floor. The younger Conn also was responsible for launching a credit operation; offering financing to customers was a key element in the retailer's growth.

Chain Beginning to Form in the 1960s

Conn's added two more stores in Beaumont by 1966 and at this stage was generating annual sales of $4 million. The next step for the small chain was to expand into the so-called Golden Triangle region that extended from southeastern Texas into the southwestern part of Louisiana. In 1969 Conn's opened its first two Louisiana stores. Additional stores were added in 1975, in Port Arthur, Orange, and Baytown, Texas, and Lafayette, Louisiana. In short order, a second Lafayette location was opened, as well as stores in Opelousas, Louisiana. Also in 1975, C.W. Conn, Sr., died and was replaced as chairman by his namesake.

In 1983 the emerging appliance chain would expand westward to the Houston market. It was not the best of times to do business in a city very much dependent on the oil business. Plummeting commodity prices crippled the industry, bankrupting a large number of companies and resulting in the loss of many jobs and a reduction in the number of people looking to

buy new televisions and washing machines. But the retailer persevered until conditions improved, so that Houston with 18 units would eventually enjoy the greatest concentration of Conn Appliance stores in the chain's area of operations.

Conn's expanded into San Antonio in 1993, the same year that the company cracked the $100 million mark in revenues. But Conn's had now reached a key moment: Management concluded that it had to reposition the chain if it were to realize even greater growth. Tom Frank succeeded C.W. Conn, Jr., as CEO and chairman and new talent was added to the management team, including David R. Atnip, who took over as chief financial officer. Williams C. Nylin, Jr., would become president and chief operating officer in 1995, and Frank's brother, C. William Frank, also would join the company, taking over as CFO while Atnip became secretary/treasurer of the company. In addition, Conn's made the investments necessary to upgrade its infrastructure and took steps to refine its operating strategy. Also in 1994 Conn's moved into another Texas market, opening its first store in the San Antonio/Austin area. All told, by the end of fiscal 1994 the chain totaled 21 stores.

Despite the changes made, between fiscal 1994 and fiscal 1999, Conn's added only another five stores, but operating margins improved from 5.3 percent to 8.7 percent. The chain reached $200 million in annual sales volume in 1999. The chain would now begin an accelerated rate of expansion, due in large part to new ownership, which possessed the financial resources to grow the business. In 1998 the Arkansas-based Stephens family and its business interests bought a controlling interest in the chain from the Conn family. The Stephens family ran a major regional investment banking firm, which had fallen out of step with the way investment banking was being conducted in the 1990s. It was now actively looking for opportunities with small and midsized companies such as Conn's.

Stephens Inc. was founded by Wilton R. Stephens in 1933 to broker cheap Arkansas highway bonds hurt by the Depression, which his father, a state legislator, convinced him the state would eventually honor. When the economy recovered during the early 1940s, spurred by the military spending of World War II, the bonds were paid off at par and Stephens was well positioned to grow into an important regional banking firm, one that followed in the tradition of merchant banks, in which relationships between gentlemen were as important in landing business as the strength of a firm's balance sheet. Witt Stephens's brother, Jackson, joined the firm in 1946 and ten years later became an equal partner and took over as CEO. He headed the firm for the next 30 years, growing it into what many regarded as the premier regional investment banking firm in the country, and 15th largest in the industry. Jack Stephens took full advantage of his connections with Arkansas's business elite, including Don Tyson of Tyson Foods Inc. and Sam Walton of Wal-Mart fame. After he retired in 1986 and was succeeded by his son Warren, the firm continued to play an influential role in Arkansas business and politics, but it began to lose its edge in the wider arena. Such major Wall Street firms as Merrill Lynch and Morgan Stanley Dean Witter began invading Stephens's traditional turf and the Arkansas firm was slow to take up the challenge and adapt to changing conditions. The result was that business dried up, the firm was afforded few opportunities to underwrite stock offerings, and Stephens slipped to the 80th

Key Dates:

1890: The company is founded as Eastham Plumbing and Heat Co.
1934: C.W. Conn takes over the company.
1937: The company begins selling ranges and refrigerators.
1959: The second store opens.
1983: The first Houston store opens.
1994: Tom Frank succeeds C.W. Conn as CEO.
1998: The Stephens family acquires a controlling interest.
2003: The company is taken public.

spot in terms of size. Finally, in the late 1990s, Stephens hired a roster of new investment bankers, analysts, and sales people to drum up opportunities, one of which was the purchase of a regional appliance store chain.

Preparing to Go Public in the Late 1990s

Over the next five years, Conn's management team and Stephens grew the retailer in preparation of taking the company public and realizing a profit for the investment banker. The chain moved into the Baton Rouge, Louisiana, market in 1999. It added more warehouse space and in 2000 thought about moving its headquarters to Houston, where it operated its largest number of stores and maintained a distribution center. Beaumont city officials as well as the Chamber of Commerce convinced the company to stay. Conn's acquired a former supermarket and converted it into a new corporate center, remodeling some 66,000 square feet for credit, customer service, and administrative offices. Subsequently, the company remodeled another 18,000 square feet to create a new parts distribution center. In addition, Conn's opened a new store close by to replace the chain's second location. It would also be used to help in some aspects of employee training, all the operations of which would now be moved to Beaumont. The chain then opened its first stores in Austin and Corpus Christi in 2002.

In fiscal 1999, which ended July 31 of that year, Conn's recorded sales of $236.7 million and net income of nearly $9 million. With the addition of new stores, the chain improved revenues to $279.7 million in fiscal 2000 and $330.3 million a year later. Net income during this period improved from $12.6 million to more than $15 million. The company then changed its fiscal year to end on January 31 of the ensuing year. Thus in fiscal 2002, ending January 2003, Conn's saw its revenues increase to $382.1 million and net income approach $20 million. Also in January 2003 Conn's, Inc. was incorporated in Delaware in preparation of taking the appliance chain public. An initial offering of stock, priced at $14 per share, was completed in

December 2003, underwritten in part by Stephens Inc. The proceeds were earmarked to pay down debt by nearly $35 million as well as for future growth. At the time of the offering, Conn's was operating 42 stores. Markets the chain hoped to penetrate over the next several years included the Dallas-Fort Worth area and the Texas-Mexican border region of the Rio Grande Valley in southwest Texas. In Louisiana, Conn's targeted New Orleans as well as Shreveport, Monroe, and Alexandria in central Louisiana. In addition, Conn's intended to expand its market presence in areas where it already operated stores.

Preparing for the public offering had diverted some of management's focus away from meeting a goal of reaching $500 million in sales for fiscal 2003. The situation was exacerbated by dropping prices in electronics, which required the chain to move more merchandise to make up the difference. For the first time, the chain had to contend with a dip in same-store sales, minus 3 percentage points, prompting management to institute a recovery plan. New merchandise was added, such as bedding, lawn and garden products, and small electronic components. By the end of the year same-store sales improved to plus 3.57 percentage points and the company fell just $700,000 short of the $500 million mark. The company planned to open three to five stores in fiscal 2004 and another four to six in fiscal 2005. Conn's also was taking steps to adopt a new, larger prototype store, offering as much as 24,000 square feet of retail space, some 15 percent larger that the previous one. Moreover, management established a new and ambitious goal, reaching the $1 billion mark in annual sales.

Principal Subsidiaries

CAIAIR Inc.; Conn Appliances Inc.; Conn Credit Corporation, Inc.; Conn Funding, LLC.

Principal Competitors

Best Buy Co., Inc.; Circuit City Stores, Inc.; Wal-Mart Stores, Inc.

Further Reading

Clausen, Christopher, ''Appliance Retailer Conn's Inc. Targets Growth Along Texas-Mexico Border,'' *Beaumont Enterprise,* June 4, 2004.
Elstein, Aaron, ''Stephens Remaking Itself for More Aggressive Era,'' *American Banker,* July 17, 1998, p. 24.
Moritz, Gwen, ''Stephens Owns Majority of Texas IPO,'' *Arkansas Business,* December 1, 2003, p. 10.
Wallach, Dan, ''Beaumont, Texas, Appliance Retailer Applies to Make Public Stock Offering,'' *Beaumont Enterprise,* September 25, 2003.
——, ''Beaumont, Texas-Based Appliance Store Chain Continues to Grow,'' *Beaumont Enterprise,* July 23, 2001.

—Ed Dinger

Cox Enterprises, Inc.

6205 Peachtree Dunwoody Road
Atlanta, Georgia 30328
U.S.A.
Telephone: (678) 645-0000
Fax: (678) 645-1079
Web site: http://www.coxenterprises.com

Private Company
Incorporated: 1968
Employees: 77,000
Sales: $10.7 billion (2003)
NAIC: 511110 Newspaper Publishers; 515112 Radio
Stations; 515210 Cable and Other Subscription
Programming; 517212 Cellular and Other Wireless
Telecommunications; 517910 Other Telecommunications

Cox Enterprises, Inc. is a media conglomerate composed of four core companies: Cox Communications, Inc.; Cox Newspapers, Inc.; Cox Broadcasting, Inc.; and Manheim Auctions, Inc. Cox Communications, one of the largest cable systems in the country with 6.3 million subscribers in 20 states, is a publicly traded firm majority-owned by Cox Enterprises. Cox Newspapers publishes 17 daily and 25 weekly newspapers in Colorado, Florida, Georgia, Ohio, North Carolina, and Texas. Cox Broadcasting operates 15 television stations. Cox Radio, 62 percent owned by Cox Enterprises, owns more than 80 radio stations. Manheim Auctions is the largest wholesale automobile auction company in the world with 115 auction facilities worldwide. Until incorporated as a single entity in 1968, Cox Enterprises operated as an assortment of media businesses owned by the Cox family. A dizzying series of acquisitions, mergers, divestments, public offerings, rearrangements of operations, and new ventures in the 1980s and 1990s led Cox Enterprises to its position as a leading media conglomerate in the 21st century.

Cox Family Empire Beginning with Ohio Newspapers in the Late 19th Century

In 1898, James M. Cox bought the *Dayton Evening News*—now the *Dayton Daily News*—in Dayton, Ohio, for $26,000 that he had raised from several friends. Cox, a native of rural Ohio, had been a schoolteacher; a reporter for the *Middletown Signal* in Middletown, Ohio, and for the *Cincinnati Enquirer,* in Cincinnati, Ohio; and a Washington, D.C.-based secretary to Ohio Congressman Paul J. Sorg. Cox quickly became an influential newspaper publisher; in 1905 he bought the *Springfield Press-Republic,* also in Ohio, changed its name to the *Springfield Daily News,* and established a newspaper chain, which he called the News League of Ohio. He also entered politics; he represented Ohio's third district in Congress from 1909 to 1913 and was elected governor of Ohio in 1913. Cox was defeated when he ran for reelection in 1915, but won in 1917 and 1919, making him the state's first three-term governor. In 1920 he was the Democratic Party's presidential candidate, with future-president Franklin D. Roosevelt as his running mate. He lost the election to Warren G. Harding.

After the defeat and his completion of his gubernatorial term in 1921, Cox returned to public life only once, when Roosevelt, by then president, appointed him a delegate to the 1933 World Monetary and Economic Conference in London. Instead, Cox focused on his media business. In 1923 he acquired the *Miami Metropolis,* in Florida, changing its name to the *Miami Daily News,* and the *Canton News,* in Canton, Ohio. In 1930 he sold the Canton paper and bought the *Springfield Sun,* in Ohio. He entered broadcasting in 1934, establishing Dayton's first radio station, WHIO.

In 1939 Cox acquired the *Atlanta Journal,* in Georgia, and its AM radio station, WSB. The newspaper had been founded in 1883 and had gone through several owners; the radio station, which began broadcasting in 1922, was the South's first. As with other newspapers he had acquired, Cox wanted the Atlanta paper to maintain its own style and personality.

In 1948 Cox entered the new medium of television with WSB-TV in Atlanta; the company also set up WSB-FM as a companion to the original AM radio station. In 1949 the company acquired a second Dayton, Ohio, newspaper, the *Journal Herald,* and put WHIO-TV and WHIO-FM radio on the air in that city. In 1950 Cox acquired the *Atlanta Constitution.* The *Atlanta Journal* and the *Atlanta Constitution* began a combined Sunday edition while publishing separately during the week.

Company Perspectives:

At the Cox companies, we encourage employee creativity, inclusion and calculated risk taking. We're dedicated to customers' and audiences' needs. We seize new business opportunities when the time is right. And, we do what's right for our communities, through sponsorships, donations, and volunteer activities. For some corporations, these concepts make good PR "sound bites." But at the Cox companies, they're the values that guide us in every decision we make.

James Cox died in 1957 at age 87. His son, James M. Cox, Jr., succeeded him as the leader of the family businesses and oversaw continued expansion. The family acquired AM and FM radio stations and a television station, all operating under the call letters WSOC, in Charlotte, North Carolina, in 1959.

Entry into Cable TV in the Early 1960s

The Coxes were among the first major broadcasters to enter cable television, acquiring a cable system in Lewistown, Pennsylvania, in 1962. In 1963 they acquired KTVU-TV in the San Francisco-Oakland, California, area and radio stations WIOD-AM and WAIA-FM in Miami. In 1964 the Cox family established Cox Broadcasting Corporation to run the radio and television operations. The broadcasting concern had its shares publicly traded on the New York Stock Exchange, but the family retained substantial ownership. The same year, broadcasting and cable operations expanded with the purchase of WPXI-TV in Pittsburgh, Pennsylvania, and cable systems in Washington, Oregon, and California.

In 1966 Cox Broadcasting added a business- and technical-publishing division; in 1967 it went into motion picture production. Its Bing Crosby Productions unit eventually made movies such as *Ben, Walking Tall,* and *The Reincarnation of Peter Proud.* In 1968 all the various Cox-owned newspapers were organized into Cox Enterprises, Inc., which remained a private company. The same year, Cox Broadcasting set up Cox Cable Communications, Inc. as a publicly traded, partially owned subsidiary.

Another 1968 event was the company's entry into the automobile auction business, with the broadcasting group's purchase of auction facilities in Manheim, Pennsylvania; Bordentown, New Jersey; and Fredericksburg, Virginia. New and used car dealers traditionally have used auto auctions to buy and sell from each other. During the 1980s, banks with repossessed cars, car rental agencies, and fleet operators began to use auction facilities for sales.

In 1969 the newspaper group added three Florida daily papers: the *Palm Beach Daily News,* the *Palm Beach Evening Times,* and the *Palm Beach Post.* The broadcasting group's operations expanded that year with the purchase of Tele-Systems, a California cable operation, and of auto auctions in Kansas City, Missouri, and Lakeland, Florida. An auction facility in High Point, North Carolina, was added in 1970; a cable system in Santa Barbara, California, and an auto auction in Pittsburgh came on in 1971.

Acquiring TeleRep in 1972

The following year brought the acquisition of TeleRep, a national television-advertising-sales representation firm, which sells time on client stations to national advertisers. The firm eventually added a programming arm, Television Program Enterprises, to produce and sell syndicated programming, including *Entertainment Tonight, Star Search,* and *Lifestyles of the Rich and Famous.* An auto auction facility in Milwaukee, Wisconsin, also came into the company lineup in 1972.

The presidential election of 1972 brought a break in James Cox, Jr.'s, association with the Democratic Party. Cox, who had attended the 1912 Democratic convention with his father, decided in 1972 to endorse President Richard M. Nixon for reelection over Senator George McGovern, and ordered all Cox Enterprises newspapers to do the same—the only time Cox ever became involved in the newspapers' editorial policies. Two editors resigned as a result. Eventually, the family allied itself with the Democrats again; Anne Cox Chambers, one of James Cox, Jr.'s, two sisters, was an early supporter of Georgia Governor Jimmy Carter and served as ambassador to Belgium when Carter became president. In the mid-1970s the Coxes' Atlanta newspapers switched from an anti-Carter to a pro-Carter stance, but management said the switch was not related to Chambers's support of Carter.

Also in 1972, Cox Cable announced plans to merge with American Television and Communications Corporation, but the Justice Department sued to block the deal. The suit led the companies to call off the transaction early in 1973; both contended the merger would not violate federal antitrust law, but noted the litigation could delay the deal by several months. Later in 1973, Cox Cable set a merger with LVO Cable Inc., but subsequently called it off because of market conditions. Another major event of 1973 was Cox Broadcasting's purchase of KFI-AM, Los Angeles.

James Cox, Jr., died in 1974 at the age of 71. His sister Barbara Cox Anthony's husband, Garner Anthony, took over the primary direction of the family companies, and the expansion continued.

Cox Broadcasting added an auto auction in Orlando, Florida, in 1974, and one in Fresno, California, in 1975. Also in 1975, it bought a cable television system in Myrtle Beach, South Carolina. Cox Enterprises acquired four Texas newspapers in 1976—the *Austin American-Statesman,* the *Waco Tribune-Herald,* the *Port Arthur News,* and the *Lufkin Daily News.* The same year, Cox Broadcasting added KOST-FM, Los Angeles, and acquired a cable system in Pensacola, Florida. It also acquired an auto-auction facility in Anaheim, California, and built one in Atlanta.

In 1977 the Cox Cable subsidiary was merged back into Cox Broadcasting; over the next three years, the broadcasting group added 26 cable television franchises, including one in Omaha, Nebraska, and another in New Orleans, Louisiana. Also in 1977, the broadcasting operation acquired WLIF-FM, Baltimore, Maryland, and Cox Enterprises bought the *Mesa Tribune* in Arizona.

The broadcasting company acquired WZGO-FM in Philadelphia, Pennsylvania, in 1979; the newspaper group acquired

Key Dates:

1898: James M. Cox pays $26,000 for the *Dayton Evening News.*

1934: The formation of WHIO in Dayton marks the company's entry into broadcasting.

1948: The company establishes the first television station and the first FM radio station in the southern United States.

1964: Cox Broadcasting Corporation, consisting of radio and television properties, debuts as a publicly traded company.

1968: Cox Enterprises, Inc. is formed to control all of the Cox family's newspapers.

1982: Cox Broadcasting becomes Cox Communications, Inc.

1985: Cox Communications is merged into Cox Enterprises.

1988: James C. Kennedy is named chairman and chief executive officer of Cox Enterprises.

1996: Cox Radio, Inc. becomes a publicly traded company, the same year Cox Interactive media is formed.

1999: Autotrader.com is launched.

2004: Kennedy announces a plan to buy $8 billion worth of Cox Communications' stock to take the company private.

Texas's *Longview Morning Journal* and the *Longview Daily News* in 1978 and the *Daily Sentinel,* of Grand Junction, Colorado, in 1979. Also in 1979, Cox Broadcasting discontinued motion picture production, but continued to market its inventory, in favor of concentrating on its broadcasting and cable television businesses.

The major event of 1979, however, was the Cox family's negotiation of a sale of Cox Broadcasting to General Electric Company (GE), in what would have been the biggest broadcasting merger in history. The Coxes wanted to sell the broadcast concern apparently because they feared the Federal Communications Commission (FCC) eventually would force a breakup of their newspaper and broadcast operations in the cities where they had both—Atlanta, Dayton, and Miami. GE's extensive broadcast holdings, however, resulted in a barrage of complaints to the FCC about concentration of ownership; the delays resulting from these complaints postponed the sale and paved the way for price renegotiations, which led to the deal's collapse early in 1980. The Coxes were asking $637 million; GE's final offer was $570 million.

Both Cox companies went through more changes and expansion in the early 1980s. WSB-TV changed its network affiliation to ABC in 1980, after having been an NBC affiliate for more than 30 years. Cox Enterprises bought the *Tempe Daily News* in Arizona in 1980; Cox Broadcasting bought a Boston auto auction in 1981, and KDNL-TV, St. Louis, Missouri, in 1982.

The broadcasting concern sold its business- and technical-publishing arm to Hearst Corporation in 1980; the aim, as with the end of film production, was to concentrate on the broadcasting and cable businesses. The auto auctions, although unrelated to these businesses, were retained because of their growth and profitability.

In 1982 Cox Broadcasting changed its name to Cox Communications, Inc. to better reflect its positions in both broadcasting and cable. The year 1983 was an acquisitive one. Cox Communications acquired auto auctions in Phoenix, Arizona, and in Toronto, Ontario, and a cable franchise in Staten Island, New York. The company also agreed to swap WLIF-FM in Baltimore for a Chicago FM station, WXFM, whose call letters subsequently were changed to WCKG; to buy a Detroit television station, WKBD, after divesting itself of a cable system in St. Clair Shores, Michigan; and to buy 90 percent of CyberTel, a radio common carrier system in St. Louis. These transactions were completed the following year. Also in 1983, Cox Enterprises bought the *Chandler Arizonan,* followed by the acquisition of another Arizona newspaper, the *Yuma Daily Sun,* in 1984. Cox Communications bought another auto auction, in Houston, Texas, in 1984.

1985 Merger of Cox Enterprises and Cox Communications

In 1985 Cox Enterprises purchased Cox Communications for $75 a share. Cox Enterprises had owned or controlled 40.2 percent of the communications company's 28.2 million outstanding shares. The combined corporation became the nation's 13th largest media company; before the merger, Cox Communications ranked 19th and Cox Enterprises 21st.

Other 1985 events were the acquisition of a Texas newspaper, the *Orange Leader,* and an Orlando, Florida, TV station, WFTV; and a swap of a cable television system in Avon Park, Florida, for one owned by Storer Communications in Fortuna, California. In 1987 Cox Enterprises sold its Philadelphia radio station to Malrite Communications Group and sold its Datext unit to Lotus Development Corporation. It had established Datext, which packaged financial information on compact discs, in 1984. It also sold CyberTel to a St. Louis investor.

At the end of 1987 the company had another change in top leadership, as Garner Anthony stepped down from the post of chairman and chief executive officer of Cox Enterprises and was succeeded by his stepson, James C. Kennedy. Into the late 1990s, sisters Barbara Cox Anthony and Anne Cox Chambers remained active in the company, chairing the Dayton and Atlanta newspapers, respectively.

By 1988 Cox Enterprises' *Miami News,* like many afternoon newspapers, was suffering declining readership and advertising. Cox sought a buyer for the paper; there were discussions with a group of Chicago investors. A sale, however, could not be worked out, and Cox closed the paper at year-end. In 1989 Cox sold its St. Louis television station to Better Communications, but expanded in other areas. It acquired an equity stake in Blockbuster Entertainment Corporation and became a franchisee of Blockbuster Video stores. Other acquisitions included Trader Publications, a publisher of advertising-only magazines; The Clipper, Inc., a publisher of coupon magazines; The Stuffit Company, a direct mailer of coupons and custom mailings; Main Street Advertising USA, a direct mail advertising company; Cox In-Store Advertising, formerly Buckler Broadcast Group, a point-of-purchase advertising business; and an interest in IP Services, Inc., a software company. It also entered into a joint venture with Picture Classified Network (PCN) to expand coverage and distribution of PCN's Gold Book automobile price guide. Also in 1989, Cox's cable group topped the 1.5 million customer mark.

By the early 1990s, Cox Enterprises consisted of four main operating companies: Cox Newspapers, Cox Cable Communications, Cox Broadcasting (television and radio stations, TeleRep, and Television Program Enterprises), and Manheim Auctions (the auto auctions business). In 1990 Cox sold two of its Texas newspapers, the *Port Arthur News* and *Orange Leader,* to American Publishing Company; Cox officials said they wanted to concentrate on the company's other Texas papers. The same year, Cox acquired two radio stations, WSUN-AM of Tampa, Florida, and KKWM-FM, later KLRX-FM of Dallas. Revenues for Cox Enterprises topped the $2 billion mark for the first time that year.

In March 1991 the Justice Department sued Cox Enterprises for $3.67 million for failing, in 1986, to seek federal approval before buying a $101 million stake in Knight-Ridder, another communications company. The Justice Department asserted that Cox violated a law requiring individuals and groups to seek federal approval before buying large amounts of stock in another company. A lawyer for Cox Enterprises stated that Cox believed its purchase was not subject to the law because the shares were bought for investment purposes. Also in March, Manheim Auctions acquired GE auto auctions, adding 20 auctions to Manheim's 26, and making Manheim the world's largest auto auction company.

In April 1991 Trader Publications was merged with Landmark Target Media of Norfolk, Virginia, and Cox held 50 percent of the resulting company. In May the company announced it would sell its Blockbuster stores. In September, Cox added to its direct marketing operations—which were collectively known as Cox Target Media, Inc., part of Cox Newspapers—with the acquisition of Val-Pak Direct Marketing Systems, Inc. of Largo, Florida. Val-Pak was the leading U.S. cooperative direct mailer and specialized in sending several business ads in one envelope to targeted households.

PCS, Rysher, and Times Mirror: Highlights of the Mid-1990s

In 1991 Cox began testing cable-based personal communications services (PCS), leading to the first PCS call over cable lines in 1992. As a leader in the development of PCS—which functioned as a phone, pager, answering machine, and voice mail system, while also delivering crisper sound and more security than analog cellular phone technology—Cox was one of three companies awarded a pioneer's preference license from the FCC. Initially, this designation was to lead to free PCS licenses for Cox. But the federal government revised the rules surrounding PCS in 1994, and by early 1995 Cox had purchased two licenses, at only a 15 percent pioneer's discount, one covering southern California and the other for Omaha, Nebraska. In 1996 Cox launched PCS phone service in San Diego.

In 1994 Cox entered into an alliance that formed the Sprint Telecommunications Venture, renamed Sprint Spectrum LP in 1995. The alliance partners were Sprint Corp., with 40 percent of the venture; Tele-Communications Inc., 30 percent; and Cox and Comcast Corp., 15 percent each. In the early 1995 FCC auction of PCS licenses, Sprint Spectrum was the biggest winner, gaining the rights to wireless licenses in 31 major U.S. markets, covering a population of 156 million.

Cox Broadcasting, meanwhile, acquired Rysher Entertainment, a distributor of syndicated television shows, in March 1993, and later that year merged Television Program Enterprises into it. Rysher subsequently evolved into a network television and film production company, developing *Nash Bridges* for CBS, the television movie *Rasputin* for HBO, and the motion pictures *Primal Fear, Evening Star,* and *Big Night,* all in 1996 alone.

The heightened merger activity in the media industries in the 1990s led Cox to conclude that it had to grow to survive. Kennedy, in fact, set an ambitious goal for Cox Enterprises: to double its 1993 revenues of $2.68 billion within the next five years. The cable operations of Cox Cable Communications were the first major area targeted for expansion. In December 1993 Southwestern Bell Corp., one of the Baby Bells, announced that it would invest $1.6 billion for a 40 percent stake in a joint venture with Cox that would own Cox Cable. Through this cash infusion, Cox Cable planned to quickly increase its base from 1.7 million subscribers, which made it the nation's sixth largest cable system, to at least 4 million, which would vault it into the number three slot. The deal collapsed, however, when the FCC announced new cable regulations in early 1994 calling for a rollback in cable rates. The rollback altered the value that Southwestern Bell put on its investment in Cox Cable, and led to its backing out of the merger in April 1994.

A successful deal was consummated just months later, however, when Cox purchased the cable operations of Times Mirror Company for $2.3 billion in cash and stock. The deal closed in February 1995, increasing Cox Cable's base from 1.9 to 3.2 million customers and moving it into fifth place among cable operators. With the completion of the acquisition, Cox Cable became a publicly traded company under the name Cox Communications, Inc., with Cox Enterprises holding a 75 percent stake. Cox Communications then began selling and trading cable systems that were not strategically clustered in order to take advantage of economies of scale and achieve operational efficiencies.

By 1996, revenues for Cox Enterprises had reached an astonishing $4.59 billion, a 21 percent increase over 1995 and up 70 percent since 1993, when Kennedy set the goal of doubling revenue in five years. Various activities during 1996 set the stage for the company to meet this ambitious goal ahead of schedule. TeleRep, by this time the nation's leading television sales rep firm, jumped into the Internet field with the formation of Cox Interactive Sales to sell online advertising. Cox Communications launched the Cox@Home Network in Orange County, California, which provided high-speed Internet service via a cable modem. Cox Enterprises formed Cox Interactive Media, Inc. to produce and manage interactive Web products, targeting the local markets where the company already operated newspapers, television and radio stations, and cable systems. Manheim

Auctions added an additional 11 auction locations, including nine gained through the acquisition of Gateway Auto Auction of Granite City, Illinois. Manheim also entered the U.K. auto auction market through a joint venture called Independent Car Auctions Holdings Limited.

Perhaps the most significant event of 1996 came on the heels of the 1996 Telecommunications Act, which loosened federal regulations regarding ownership of radio and television stations. This act led to additional media mergers, and Cox Broadcasting positioned itself for growth by completing an initial public offering of its radio station group, which became known as Cox Radio Inc. Cox Broadcasting retained a 70 percent stake in the new company. With the $120 million generated through the offering, Cox Radio was able to more than double the number of stations it owned in a short span. By mid-1997, Cox Radio owned 49 stations, making it the ninth largest radio group in the country.

Striding into the 21st Century

As Cox Enterprises celebrated its centennial in 1998 and prepared for its next 100 years of business, the company held sway as one of the most powerful media conglomerates in the world. Kennedy's salubrious touch garnered much of the credit for the company's vitality at the end of the decade. During the company's anniversary year, he met his five-year goal of doubling the size of the company, and ended the 1990s presiding over a $6.1 billion empire.

The end of the 1990s marked the end of robust economic times and the beginning of a recession. Kennedy showed his leadership skill by anticipating the downturn and the resulting decline in advertising spending by taking action before the damaging economic conditions could take their toll on Cox Enterprises. Kennedy consolidated the company's flagship newspapers, merging the *Atlanta Constitution,* a morning paper, with the *Atlanta Journal,* an evening paper, in November 2001. The combination emerged 35 percent more profitable than during the previous recession a decade earlier. Kennedy also cut overhead, but he did not retreat from opportunities for growth. The company launched AutoTrader.com, destined to become the largest online marketplace for used cars, in 1999 and continued to fund the business's development as economic conditions worsened. His commitment paid off when AutoTrader.com became a profitable venture in 2002, a year that also saw the Web property record a 75 percent increase in revenue to roughly $100 million.

Cox Enterprises emerged from the recession essentially unscathed. Revenues swelled to more than $10 billion in 2003, representing a massive increase from the $1.8 billion generated when Kennedy took over in 1988. In 2004, Kennedy made a startling announcement, declaring his intention to purchase the 38 percent of Cox Communications that Cox Enterprises did not already own and return the company to private ownership. Kennedy felt the financial community was not recognizing the strides the company had made. In his mind, the success of the company's advances in cable television distribution, telephone service, high-speed Internet service, and other broadband service were undervalued. In August 2004, he announced a $7.9 billion plan to purchase Cox Communications stock. As Kennedy worked to complete the transaction, Cox Enterprises prepared for the future, its position as a mighty media force unlikely to weaken in the years ahead.

Principal Subsidiaries

Cox Communications, Inc. (62%); Cox Newspapers, Inc.; Cox Target Media, Inc.; Longstreet Press; Trader Publishing Co. (50%); Cox Broadcasting, Inc.; Cox Radio, Inc. (62%); Manheim Auctions, Inc.; Independent Car Auctions Holdings Limited (U.K.); AutoTrader.com L.L.C.; Cox Interactive Media.

Principal Competitors

Gannett Co., Inc.; Knight-Ridder, Inc.; Tribune Company.

Further Reading

Cohen, Jodi B., "Cox Goes Digital," *Editor & Publisher,* August 3, 1996, p. 28.

Cook, Lynn J., "Survival Instincts," *Forbes,* November 25, 2002, p. 182.

"Cox Announces $7.9 Billion Acquisition Plan," *eWeek,* August 2, 2004, p. 31.

Cox, James M., *Journey Through My Years,* New York: Simon & Schuster, 1946.

"Cox to Buy Back Public CCI Shares for $7.9 Billion," *InternetWeek,* August 2, 2004, p. 35.

Criner, Kathleen, and Jane Wilson, "Watch Out for Cable, Easterly Says," *Editor & Publisher,* April 27, 1996, pp. 38, 105.

Greising, David, and Mark Landler, "This Time, Cox Reels in a Big Fish," *Business Week,* June 20, 1994, p. 39.

Gubernick, Lisa, "Big Decisions," *Forbes,* November 2, 1987, p. 222.

Harrigan, Susan, "Powerful Clan: The Coxes of Atlanta Rule a Media Empire with Quiet Authority," *Wall Street Journal,* September 26, 1980.

Jessell, Harry, "Cox's Jim Kennedy: Big Is Better," *Broadcasting & Cable,* June 20, 1994, pp. 23–27.

Keller, John J., "Sprint, Partners Map $4 Billion Phone Invasion," *Wall Street Journal,* March 29, 1995, p. B9.

Landler, Mark, and Bart Ziegler, "Southwestern Bell and Cox: A Deal with a Difference," *Business Week,* December 20, 1993, p. 39.

Learmonth, Michael, "Cable on the Table: Sibs Seek to Take Cox Private in $7.9 Bil. Bid," *Daily Variety,* August 3, 2004, p. 4.

O'Shea, Dan, "Cable Deal Could Keep Cox Ticking," *Telephony,* June 13, 1994, p. 6.

Romano, Allison, "Take That, Wall Street: Seeking Freedom from Investor Whims, Undervalued Cable Company Cox to Move to Go Private," *Broadcasting & Cable,* August 9, 2004, p. 8.

Rose, Frederick, "Times Mirror Says Litigation Settlement Leaves Basic Agreement with Cox Intact," *Wall Street Journal,* October 13, 1994, p. B10.

——, "Times Mirror's Plan to Sell Cable TV Sparks Several Shareholder Lawsuits," *Wall Street Journal,* June 9, 1994, p. B6.

Rose, Frederick, and Anita Sharpe, "Cox Agrees to Buy Cable-TV Operations from Times Mirror in $2.3 Billion Deal," *Wall Street Journal,* June 6, 1994, pp. A3, A6.

Sharpe, Anita, and Mark Robichaux, "Cox Sees Times Mirror Cable System As Key to Survival," *Wall Street Journal,* July 7, 1994, p. B4.

——, "Southwestern Bell and Cox Cancel Venture," *Wall Street Journal,* April 6, 1994, pp. A3, A4.

—Trudy Ring
—updates: David E. Salamie, Jeffrey L. Covell

Cristalerias de Chile S.A.

Hendaya 60 - Of 201, Las Condes
Santiago
Chile
Telephone: +56 2 246 8888
Fax: 56 2 246 8800
Web site: http://www.cristalchile.cl

Public Company
Incorporated: 1904 as Fábrica Nacional de Vidrios
Employees: 711
Sales: CLP 169.7 billion ($283 million) (2003)
Stock Exchanges: Bolsa de Comercio de Santiago New
    York
Ticker Symbol: Cristales; CGW
NAIC: 327213 Glass Container Manufacturing; 326160
    Plastics Bottle Manufacturing; 326199 All Other
    Plastics Product Manufacturing (pt); 511120
    Periodical Publishers; 513120 Television Broadcasting

Cristalerias de Chile S.A., or Cristalchile, is that country's leading producer of glass and plastic containers and related packaging. The Santiago-based company produces bottles for the domestic wine sector and also bottles for the country's fast-growing export wine market. The company also develops bottles for the domestic liquor industry, which is focused especially on the local Pisco fortified wine. For Chile's breweries, Cristalchile manufactures refundable and refillable bottles, which is the dominant beer packaging type in the country. The company holds a virtual monopoly in this sector, with the capacity to supply 100 percent of the Chile beer industry's bottle requirement. Cristalchile also has developed a range of bottles for the nonalcoholic beverage segment, including mineral water, fruit juice, and soft drinks, supplying nearly all of the bottles for this area as well. The company develops and produces glass-based packaging for the processed food industry, including jars for baby food, sauces, preserves, oil, and the like, and for the pharmaceutical industry. Cristalchile also has diversified its packaging operations to include plastics, through its 50 percent share of the PET joint venture CMF Envases formed in

partnership with Embotelladora Andina S.A. Beyond packaging, Christalchile has built up a diversified portfolio of businesses. The company holds controlling stakes in winemaker Sociedad Anónima Viña Santa Rita and nearly all of Red Televisiva Megavision S.A. through subsidiary CIESCSA, representing the group's Communications, Information, Entertainment and Culture division. Total group sales amounted to nearly CLP 170 billion ($283 million) in 2003. Glass packaging accounts for 42 percent of the group's sales, matched by its wine operations, while Cristalchile's media holdings add 16 percent to its total sales. Listed on the Bolsa de Comercio de Santiago, Cristalchile's shares are also traded on the New York Stock Exchange as ADRs. Compania Electro Metallurgica, through the Elecmetal Group, is Cristalchile's primary shareholder.

Bottling Origins in the Early 1900s

Cristalerias de Chile was established in 1904 as Fábrica Nacional de Vidrios and started producing glass and glass bottles for the domestic market. By the 1930s, the company had outgrown its original facility. Cristalerias de Chile, or Cristalchile, as it came to be called, then opened a new facility on Santiago's Avenue Vicuna Mackenna. That plant's capacity, backed by 15 smelting furnaces, enabled Cristalchile to become the dominant glass packaging producer in the country.

Cristalchile supported its growth by developing an extensive mining and sand washing capacity. The company eventually built up a real estate portfolio based on two primary properties. The first was located in San Sebastian, in the Cartagena region, with an area of some 500,000 square meters providing both mining operations and sand washing capacity. The second focused on mining over a holding of 400 hectares in the El Turco zone of Cartagena.

In the 1970s, Cristalchile also found support through a new majority shareholder. In 1975, Chilean conglomerate Compania Electro Metallurgica bought a controlling stake in Cristalchile, which was placed under the parent's Elecmetal group.

Under Elecmetal, Cristalchile launched a companywide modernization effort. The company not only revamped its marketing and distribution operations, it also began construction of a new, more modern glass production facility. That effort was boosted in 1977 when Cristalchile signed a Technical Assistance Agreement with the United States' Owens-Illinois, then the world's leading glass packaging group. The technology transfer agreement enabled Cristalchile to launch production at a new state-of-the-art facility in Padre Hurtado in 1978.

Built on a property extending more than 325,000 square meters, the Padre Hurtado plant gave Cristalchile an administrative and production headquarters spanning 50,000 square meters. The plant featured four smelting furnaces and 12 IS package forming lines. With its increased capacity, Cristalchile was able to provide 100 percent of the country's beer and soft-drink industry bottling needs.

Until 1980, Cristalchile had focused wholly on its glass bottle production. In that year, however, the company began a diversification effort. Part of the group's expansion strategy kept it close to its historic packaging core, as the company moved into the market for plastic packaging. After establishing a dedicated plastic packaging subsidiary, Crowpla, the company acquired a 50 percent stake in Reicolite. These moves enabled the company to begin production of an extensive line of PET-based plastic bottles, buckets, caps, containers, and buckets.

Diversified Holdings in the 1990s

Yet Cristalchile also sought expansion beyond the packaging sector. For its first effort, the company did not stray too far, however. In 1980, the company made its first move in this direction, with the purchase of a majority stake in Sociedad Anónima Viña Santa Rita.

Santa Rita played an important part in establishing the worldwide reputation for Chilean wines. Chile had long been a fixture on the global winemaking map; the first vines were planted in the country in the mid-16th century, making Chile the first American state to develop its own wine industry. The area was later planted with French vine stock, including the Cabernet Sauvignon variety, considered to be superior to Chile's local grapes.

In the second half of the 19th century, while French and Californian vineyards were devastated by the phylloxera plague, Chile remained free of the virus. The country, and the Santa Rita region in particular, emerged as a principal supplier of Cabernet Sauvignon vine stock to the rest of the world. The region's wines also began winning international recognition, with exports starting as early as 1877. By 1880, the Santa Rita winery was officially founded by Don Domingo Fernandez. Under Fernandez, the vineyard brought in French wine experts to help it develop its technological expertise.

By 1980, Santa Rita had emerged as Chile's leading domestic producer of wine. The company also held the number three spot among the ranks of Chile's fast-growing wine exporters. Cristalchile joined a group of investors, including Don Ricardo Claro Valdes, which acquired a 50 percent stake in the company. In 1988, the group acquired the remaining 50 percent. Cristalchile stepped up its own stake in the wine company. At the end of 2003, Cristalchile's holding in Santa Rita topped 54 percent.

With the close of the 1980s, Cristalchile sought new growth opportunities. In 1989, its attention turned toward the communications industry. In that year, Cristalchile acquired the license to operate 21 television stations across Chile. Shortly after, the company created a new subsidiary, Red Televisiva Megavision S.A., in a partnership with Mexico's Televisa S.A. de C.V. Red Televisiva was placed under a new subsidiary, CIECSA, the acronym for the company's Communications, Information, Entertainment, and Culture division. CIECSA was soon expanded to include other media as well, such as Ediciones Financerias S.A., publisher of the Diario Financiero, and Editorial Zig-Zag S.A.

In the early 1990s, Cristalchile sought to step up its media interests and in 1994 the company listed its stock as ADRs on the New York Stock Exchange. The share offering fueled the group's expansion into cable television, which Cristalchile entered in 1994, through an association with TCI-Bresnan (later Liberty Media Corporation). The new company was called Cordillera Comunicaciones Ltd., and took Metropolis as its brand name. The following year, however, Cristalchile reached an agreement with rival Intercom—owned by Telefonica CTC Chile—to merge Metropolis into a new company, Metropolis Intercom. That company then began to explore expansion into other communications areas, notably Internet access services.

Triple Focus for the New Century

Cristalchile stepped up its holding in its Crowpla and Reicolite plastics operations in 1996. With 99.99 percent control of each, Cristalchile engineered their merger in 1996. The combined Crowpla-Reicolite's production operations were then transferred to a new central production plant, in Santiago's Pudahuel district.

Meanwhile, the company moved to boost its core glassmaking business. In 1999, the company bought a 40 percent stake in Rayen Cura SAIC, based in Argentina and held by Saint-Gobain-owned Vicasa. This acquisition marked Cristalchile's first international acquisition.

As it entered the new century, Cristalchile moved to reduce its focus to just three core operations—Glass Packaging, Wine, and Media. As part of this strategy, the company agreed to merge Crowpla-Reicolite with Evases Multipack, the PET

Key Dates:

1904: The company is established as Fábrica Nacional de Vidrios to produce glass and glass bottles for the Chilean domestic market.

1975: Chilean conglomerate Compania Electro Metallurgica buys a controlling stake in the company, now known as Cristalchile.

1977: Cristalchile signs a Technical Assistance Agreement with Owens-Illinois, the world's leading glass packaging group.

1980: The company purchases a majority stake in Sociedad Anónima Viña Santa Rita.

1989: Cristalchile acquires a license to operate 21 television stations across Chile.

1994: The company lists its stock as ADRs on the New York Stock Exchange, enabling it to expand into cable television.

1999: The company buys a 40 percent stake in Argentina-based Rayen Cura SAIC.

2000: The company joins with partner Liberty Media to buy out Metropolis Intercom, gaining a 50 percent stake.

2003: Cristalchile gains full control of Red Televisiva Megavision, after buying the stake previously held by Televisa.

packaging operation of Embotelladora Andina S.A., creating the new CMF Envases. Cristalchile's stake in that business, created in 2001, stood at 50 percent.

Cristalchile also moved to consolidate its media interests. In 2000, the company firmed up its control of Metropolis Intercom, joining with partner Liberty Media to buy out the company from Telefonica CTC Chile. Cristalchile then took a 50 percent stake in the new Metropolis Intercom. In 2003, Cristalchile also took full control of Red Televisiva Megavision, buying out the stake previously held by Televisa. At the end of that year, Cristalchile's Media holdings represented 16 percent of its consolidated group sales of nearly CLP 170 billion. Balancing out that business were the group's Glass and Wine divisions, both of which represented 42 percent of the company's consolidated sales. Cristalchile then looked forward to celebrating its 100th anniversary, marking the occasion with the launch of plans to build a new production plant for the new century.

Principal Subsidiaries

Cristalchile Inversiones S.A.; Ciecsa S.A.; Constructora Apoger S.A.; Cordillera Comunicaciones Holding Limitada; Cristalchile Comunicaciones S.A.; Sociedad Anónima Viña Santa Rita; Red Televisiva Megavision S.A.

Principal Competitors

Ball Plastic Container Div.; Schott Glas; Owens-Illinois Inc.; OSRAM GmbH; Saint-Gobain Container Inc.; Rexam Beverage Packaging AB; Arc International; Nipro Corporation; BSN GLASSPACK S.A.; Nueva Fabrica Nacional de Vidrio S.A.; Belopal AD; Turkiye Sise ve Cam Fabrikalari A.S.; Villeroy und Boch AG; Vitrocrisa S.A. de C.V.

Further Reading

"Cristalerias de Chile Approves US$210 Investment Plan," *South American Business Information,* June 24, 2004.

"Cristalerias de Chile Filed Environmental Impact Study for New Plant," *South American Business Information,* September 22, 2004.

"Cristalerias de Chile to Buy Control of Megavision," *South American Business Information,* September 2, 2002.

"Cristalerias de Chile Took Out US$100mil Loan," *South American Business Information,* September 6, 2000.

"Sales of Cristalerias de Chile Rise by 10.2%," *South American Business Information,* March 24, 2003.

—M.L. Cohen

Denbury Resources, Inc.

5100 Tennyson Parkway, Suite 3000
Plano, Texas 75024
U.S.A.
Telephone: (972) 673-2000
Fax: (972) 673-2150
Web site: http://www.denbury.com

Public Company
Incorporated: 1951 as Key Lake Mines Limited (N.P.L.)
Employees: 374
Sales: $393.70 million (2003)
Stock Exchanges: New York
Ticker Symbol: DNR
NAIC: 211111 Crude Petroleum and Natural Gas
  Exploration

Denbury Resources, Inc. is an independent oil and gas company that ranks as the largest operator in Mississippi. Denbury also owns producing fields in Louisiana, but its signature properties are in Mississippi, where the company owns the largest reserves of carbon dioxide. Carbon dioxide, when injected into an oilfield, acts as a type of solvent for the oil, causing it to expand and become mobile, easing its recovery. Denbury began using carbon dioxide to extract oil from proven oilfields in the late 1990s, a move that led to the transformation of the company into what is known as a tertiary exploitation producer, as opposed to an exploration and production company reliant on traditional acquire-drill-exploit tactics. Denbury's carbon dioxide properties are located in western Mississippi. In eastern Mississippi, the company owns interests in 504 wells, deriving the majority of its business from the largest field in the region, the Heidelberg field. Denbury owns interests in 87 wells in Louisiana, maintaining a presence in the southern part of the state.

Origins

Denbury underwent significant changes during its first half-century of business, changing its name, its corporate structure, its nationality, and its business strategy. The outward inconstancy of the company developed from one common characteristic, however its involvement in oil and gas exploration and development. Denbury began its business life as "Key Lake Mines Limited (N.P.L.)," a company incorporated under the laws of Manitoba, Canada, in March 1951. During this era of the company's existence, it was focused on developing oil and natural gas properties in Manitoba, although it did maintain a small presence in Saskatchewan. For the next three decades, the company's geographic scope of operations remained essentially the same, with the bulk of its business being conducted in Manitoba and, to a lesser extent, in Saskatchewan.

The company changed its name to "Newscope Resources Limited" in September 1984, a somewhat superficial event, to be sure, but one that symbolized the sweeping changes about to take place. After adopting Newport Resources as its corporate title, the company changed its name three more times during the ensuing nine years, eventually settling on Denbury Resources, Inc. in December 1995. During this period, the profile of the company changed dramatically, as Denbury's predecessor sold its assets, abandoned its home country, and chose a new geographic base.

The company spent more than 35 years earning its living in Manitoba and Saskatchewan. After 1987, however, the unvarying quality of its existence began to change. Between 1988 and 1990, the majority of the company's exploration and development activities shifted west, to Alberta. The change in geographic stance marked the beginning of a far more dramatic alteration in the company's geographic focus.

Divesting Canadian Operations: Early 1990s

During the early 1990s, Newscope's management decided to divest its Canadian operations and focus on operating in the United States instead. In March 1992, the company sold its Manitoba oil and gas properties—the historical roots of the organization. In a transaction completed four months later, the company acquired all the outstanding shares of Denbury Management, a Mississippi-based company formed in 1990, and appointed its leader, Gareth Roberts, president and chief executive officer of Newscope. The acquisition pointed the company in a new direction, giving it oil and gas properties in Texas, Louisiana, and Mississippi. In September 1993, the geographic transformation was completed when Newscope sold all its remaining Canadian oil and gas properties, operations that consisted primarily of producing oil and gas properties in Saskatchewan and Alberta, as well as undeveloped lands in British Columbia, Alberta, and Saskatchewan.

Following a new business strategy, Newscope, in the years immediately following its last Canadian divestiture, focused primarily on onshore properties in Louisiana and Mississippi. It was two years before Newscope changed its name to Denbury to reflect the name of its U.S. subsidiary, and another six years before the company moved its headquarters to the United States (Denbury moved to Texas in April 1999). As these events occurred in the background, Gareth Roberts and his executives worked to build the company's presence in the southern United States. They bolstered Denbury's position largely through the acquisition of oil and gas properties. As a rule, roughly three-quarters of the company's oil and gas reserves during the 1990s were obtained from acquisitions. During the second half of the decade, Denbury completed four acquisitions that provided the base for its rapid expansion as it entered the new century.

The first of Denbury's signal purchases occurred in May 1996. The company paid $37 million for properties owned by Amerada Hess Corp. that averaged nearly 3,000 barrels of oil equivalent per day, or BOE/D, a measurement that quantified both oil and gas production into one figure. Next, the company completed the largest acquisition in its history. In December 1997, Denbury paid $202 million to Chevron U.S.A., Inc. for the Heidelberg field in Jasper County, Mississippi. The purchase, which gave the company the vast majority of holdings in the Mississippi Salt Flats Basin, more than doubled the company's total reserves. Before the acquisition, the company's reserves totaled 27.4 million barrels of oil equivalent (BOE), a volume that exponentially increased after the addition of Heidelberg's 30.2 million BOE.

Additional acquisitions were completed during the late 1990s, but before the deals were concluded, Denbury's management needed to resolve a difficult situation. The company's cash flow declined sharply in 1998, when depressed oil prices delivered a stinging blow to its operations. Low oil prices continued into 1999, further draining the company's cash flow and increasing debt levels. To resolve the problem, Denbury sought an infusion of capital from its largest shareholder, Texas Pacific Group. In April 1999, the deal was concluded, when Texas Pacific gave Denbury $100 million in return for increasing its ownership in the company from 32 percent to 60 percent.

Denbury Acquiring First Carbon Dioxide Asset in 1999

By the end of the 1990s, the properties acquired from Amerada Hess and Chevron ranked as two of the five largest fields

supporting Denbury. Of the other three largest fields, two were acquired in 1999, including one that gave the company a new strategic focus for the 21st century. Denbury paid nearly $5 million for the King Bee oilfield in Mississippi and $12.3 million for the Little Creek tertiary recovery oilfield, also located in Mississippi. Although the Little Creek purchase paled in stature to the Heidelberg acquisition, its addition to Denbury's property portfolio had a tremendous influence on the company. With Little Creek, a project originally developed by Shell Oil Company, Denbury acquired its first carbon dioxide assets, leading the company to begin approaching its production efforts in a new way.

The use of carbon dioxide in oil extraction gave Denbury a new way of conducting its business and new potential to old oil wells. When injected, or "flooded," into an oil well, carbon dioxide acted as a solvent, causing oil to expand and become mobile, which eased the recovery of both the oil and the carbon dioxide. Once recovered, the carbon dioxide was extracted from the oil, compressed back into a liquid state, and reinjected into the oil reservoir. After repeating this cycle several times, nearly as much oil could be recovered as in the primary production phase of an oil reservoir.

Pilot studies sponsored by major oil companies during the 1970s and 1980s demonstrated carbon dioxide-induced oil extraction could work. However, its financial feasibility was contingent on there being a sufficient supply of carbon dioxide available at a reasonable cost. There were few regions that possessed abundant supplies of carbon dioxide, but Mississippi was one of them, rich in reserves produced from a volcano near Jackson, Mississippi. The carbon dioxide reserves were discovered during the 1960s, when exploration efforts to find oil and gas revealed large volumes of carbon dioxide. Denbury, situated ideally to take advantage of a bountiful supply of inexpensive carbon dioxide, seized an opportunity available to few other oil producers. After the August 1999 acquisition of Little Creek—a momentous event in the company's history—Denbury moved to acquire additional carbon dioxide assets and to breathe new life into its business and into established oilfields.

By 2000, Denbury dominated ownership of carbon dioxide properties in Mississippi. In February 2001, the company paid $42 million for properties that assured its supply of carbon dioxide, confirming the company as the leader in its niche. The acquisition, purchased from a business unit of Airgas, Inc., gave Denbury 800 billion cubic feet of carbon dioxide—most of the carbon dioxide supply in Mississippi—and ownership of a 183-mile carbon dioxide pipeline. With the ability to control the price and availability of carbon dioxide, the company acquired oil wells within its carbon-dioxide service area, typically purchasing old oil properties for a low price relative to their tertiary recovery value. In two such cases, Denbury paid $4 million for the West Mallalieu and Olive fields in southwestern Mississippi in 2001. In 2002, the company acquired the McComb field for $2.3 million.

Denbury also expanded its business in other areas at this time. In mid-2001, the company acquired Matrix Oil & Gas, Inc., a Louisiana-based company with most of its properties located offshore in the Gulf of Mexico. The acquisition, completed for $158 million, increased Denbury's reserves by ap-

Key Dates:

1951: Denbury's predecessor organization, Key Lake Mines Limited (N.P.L.), is incorporated in Manitoba, Canada.

1984: Key Lake changes its name to Newscope Resources Limited.

1992: Newscope decides to divest its Canadian holdings and turn its focus to the southern United States.

1995: Newscope changes its name to Denbury Resources, Inc.

1997: Denbury acquires the Heidelberg field from Chevron.

1999: The acquisition of the Little Creek field moves Denbury into the carbon dioxide business.

2001: The acquisition of carbon dioxide properties from Airgas, Inc. confirms Denbury as the region's dominant carbon dioxide owner.

2004: Denbury sells its properties in the Gulf Coast, divesting Denbury Offshore, Inc.

proximately 12 percent and its production by approximately 22 percent. In August 2002, the company added to its offshore portfolio, acquiring COHO Energy Inc.'s Gulf Coast properties for $48 million. Denbury eventually divested its interests in the Gulf of Mexico, selling its offshore subsidiary, Denbury Offshore, Inc., for $200 million in July 2004.

Denbury recorded explosive growth in the years following its decision to extract oil with carbon dioxide. The company exited the 1990s with less than $90 million in annual revenue. By 2003, the company was generating nearly $400 million in revenue. The effectiveness of carbon dioxide extraction contributed greatly to the company's growth. Its original carbon dioxide property, Little Creek, served as a prime example of the gains to be achieved by employing carbon dioxide. When Denbury acquired the property, it was producing 1,350 barrels of oil per day. By 2003, after carbon dioxide flooding of the property, Little Creek was averaging 3,201 barrels of oil per day. The company by this point owned every carbon dioxide producing well in western Mississippi, vanquishing any competitor's hope of following Denbury's lead. Further, in the area stretching from eastern Texas to Florida, the company owned all the natural sources of carbon dioxide.

As Denbury prepared for the future, the company's stranglehold on carbon dioxide assets boded well for growth in the coming years. The company was preparing to expand the geo-graphic scope of its operations by building new carbon dioxide pipelines to service other oilfields. In February 2004, the company initiated feasibility studies concerning extending carbon dioxide recovery operations into eastern Mississippi. In August 2004, after arriving at positive conclusions, Denbury announced it had begun to acquire leases for the construction of an 84-mile pipeline to transport carbon dioxide eastward from its source near Jackson. The pipeline, which was expected to be completed by 2006, was designed to carry carbon dioxide into the company's Eucutta field, the primary producing property acquired in the 1996 Amerada Hess purchase. In the years ahead, Denbury was expected to increase the coverage of its pipeline system and to acquire oil properties in proximity to its supply of carbon dioxide, as the company endeavored to leverage its power and record robust growth.

Principal Subsidiaries

Denbury Gathering & Marketing, Inc.; Genesis Energy, Inc.; Denbury Operating Company; Denbury Onshore, L.L.C.; Denbury Marine, L.L.C.; Tuscaloosa Royalty Fund L.L.C.

Principal Competitors

The Meridian Resource Corporation; Newfield Exploration Company; Swift Energy Company.

Further Reading

Cleveland, Crystal, "Denbury Resources Inc., Dallas, Has Acquired Coho Energy Inc.'s Gulf Coast Properties from Bankruptcy Court for $50.3 Million," *Oil and Gas Investor,* September 2002, p. 105.

"Denbury Closes $42 Million Acquisition of CO2 Assets," *Canadian Corporate News,* February 6, 2001.

"Denbury Resources Announces Internal Holding Company Reorganization," *Canadian Corporate News,* December 23, 2003, p. 32.

"Denbury Resources Announces Plans to De-List from the Toronto Stock Exchange," *Canadian Corporate News,* March 21, 2002.

"Denbury Resources Announces Record Quarterly and Annual Earnings," *Canadian Corporate News,* February 23, 2001.

"Denbury Resources Completes Matrix Oil & Gas Acquisition," *Canadian Corporate News,* July 13, 2001.

"Denbury Resources Inc.," *Market News Publishing,* May 1, 2001.

"Denbury Resources Inc. Announces New CO2 Pipeline," *Canadian Corporate News,* August 31, 2004, p. 45.

"Denbury Sells Offshore Assets," *Mississippi Business Journal,* August 2, 2004, p. 10.

"Denbury to Acquire Matrix," *Oil Daily,* June 6, 2001.

Fletcher, Sam, "HS Resources, Denbury Snap Up Properties from Majors in Multi-Million-Dollar Deals," *Oil Daily,* November 26, 1997, p. 1.

—Jeffrey L. Covell

Doctor's Associates Inc.

325 Bic Drive
Milford, Connecticut 06460
U.S.A.
Telephone: (203) 877-4281
Toll Free: (800) 888-4848
Fax: (203) 876-6695
Web site: http://www.subway.com

Private Company
Incorporated: 1965 as Pete's Super Submarines
Employees: 730
Sales: $468.4 billion (2004 est.)
NAIC: 722211 Restaurants, Fast Food

With more than 22,000 worldwide locations, Subway—owned and operated by privately held Doctor's Associates Inc.—is almost as ubiquitous as McDonald's, which it overtook in 2001 as the United States' largest fast-food chain. Subway shops are increasingly visible worldwide with shops in 77 countries including the Bahamas, Bolivia, Chile, Cyprus, Germany, Hungary, Iceland, Iraq, Paraguay, Russia, and Venezuela. Fred Deluca and Peter Buck, the partners who control this $7 billion (in systemwide sales) private empire, have no immediate plans to take their goldmine public. Their collaboration has become the largest and most successful sandwich franchise in the world. Subway's claim to fame continues to be its freshly made-to-order sandwiches, several of which have seven grams of fat or less—made famous by Jared Fogle, the college student turned Subway poster boy who claimed to have lost 245 pounds eating Subway subs.

Evolution of a Sub Sandwich: 1960s–70s

Fred DeLuca was born in Brooklyn in the late 1940s, a time when Harry S. Truman was president, Arthur Miller's *Death of a Salesman* had won a Pulitzer Prize for drama, and Rodgers and Hammerstein's *South Pacific* was a hit on Broadway. Although there were not many ways a kid his age could earn money in the 1950s, DeLuca did—returning two-cent bottles found around the Bronx housing project where he lived. When his family moved

upstate to Schenectady, young Fred delivered newspapers, gradually increasing his clientele until his route covered some 400 patrons on Sundays. Originally planning to study pre-med in college, DeLuca was faced with the daunting challenge of raising tuition money. It was 1965 and DeLuca was 17.

Concentrating on his immediate future, he worked in a hardware store earning little cash ($1.25 per hour) but possessing plenty of ambition. He was looking for another job, something paying more than minimum wage, when he struck up a conversation with family friend Dr. Peter Buck at a barbecue. Buck was a nuclear physicist, and he talked about a popular sandwich shop near his hometown. Buck wondered aloud if DeLuca should open a shop serving submarine sandwiches, a food item gaining considerable popularity. Over the next four hours, the two drew up a business plan; with a $1,000 start-up loan from Buck, the two became partners.

DeLuca moved quickly, looking for a location the very next day. On August 25, 1965, Pete's Super Submarines opened in Bridgeport, Connecticut, serving fresh made-to-order sandwiches with a choice of toppings and condiments, though oddly, without lettuce (it appeared on the menu later). The shop location was not ideal, but was only a short distance from the hardware store where DeLuca had worked. There was little fanfare and few customers, but Buck and DeLuca met regularly in the latter's family home, discussing strategy over homemade pasta. The new enterprise, however, did not stop DeLuca from beginning his freshman year at the University of Bridgeport in September (he graduated in 1971 with a B.S. in psychology). Juggling his studies and the sandwich shop, weeks turned into months for DeLuca and the business never soared as planned. Yet rather than give up and abandon the partnership, Buck and DeLuca decided on another gambit—to open a second location in 1966. They hoped that increased visibility and name recognition would steer more customers to Pete's Super Submarines. They then decided to take their gamble even further, by opening a third location.

The third time was the charm. The old adage proved right on the money as the third store—in a highly accessible and visible location—began to take off. Not particularly superstitious, DeLuca and Buck did consider "three" their lucky number and later emphasized positive numerology in their corporate marketing campaigns. As the business progressed, the partners found the name cumbersome and thought it sounded like "pizza marine." Consequently, Pete's Super Submarines was renamed Subway, taken from New York City's underground railways built in the early 20th century. The shop's name was emblazoned in yellow, and the inside decor consisted of faux newspaper articles heralding the new mode of transportation.

In 1974, as the partners approached the tenth year of their alliance, they were supposed to have had 32 submarine shops according to their initial business plan. Instead, they had half this number and decided to explore another option: franchising. DeLuca believed franchising was the wave of the future and had soon convinced a friend to become the first franchisee. The new store opened in upstate Wallingford. The move, though a sound business decision, was a profound risk. The world was experiencing inflation, the dollar had been devalued twice in two years, an energy crisis had forced Americans to cut back on power and fuel usage, and unemployment was on the rise.

DeLuca and Buck, however, seemed to have the golden touch. The franchised Subway did well, as did its successors (another 14 or so within the year). Although franchising was an excellent way to expand a business, DeLuca and Buck tinkered with the system for years before finding a formula with which they were completely happy. Yet both had discovered the incontrovertible truth that new business owners needed to invent a product and entice an ever-growing number of customers. Doing both was demanding, but with franchising, the idea and product were already established so the new business owner simply had to bring in a clientele and keep them happy.

From Nowhere to Everywhere: 1980–94

By 1983 there were 200 Subway shops and DeLuca and Buck discovered one of the largest hurdles was keeping their brand consistent in all locations. This was when the partners decided to have each location bake its own bread on the premises. As the first fast-food chain to bake bread at each location, Subway's sales steadily increased. The bread became a signature product with its ingredients and oven time trade secrets. Just two years later, in 1985, after 20 years of partnership, DeLuca and Buck had 596 Subway stores in the United States and abroad; by 1987, the number had more than tripled to 1,810 shops.

Subway's phenomenal growth continued unabated throughout the remainder of the 1980s and into the 1990s. In 1988

Subway earned the top spot on *Entrepreneur* magazine's Franchise 500 as the number one sandwich franchiser in the United States (a title it would hold for four years in a row). By 1989 there were 4,071 stores and by 1992 there were 7,327. As more and more Subway franchises popped up across the nation as well as outside the United States, the partners had created the "University of Subway," an intensive two-week course at headquarters. Prospective franchisees learned the ins and outs of the Subway business, from the standard decor to bookkeeping, from baking the signature bread to the varied ingredients that made up the chain's popular sandwiches.

Another key to Subway's ongoing expansion was innovation and taking convenience a step further than its competitors. Subway stores began appearing in unusual locations, catering to consumers where they might not expect a sandwich shop—at convenience stores and truck stops. These "nontraditional" locations were a hit with traveling consumers and by 1993 some 50 such shops dotted the nation, with more on the way. Although these uniquely placed shops were a fraction of Subway's 8,450 locations worldwide, they thrived and came to make up a fifth of the company's global sales in coming years.

In 1994 Subway was nearing the 10,000 mark and DeLuca was determined to take on the world's largest fast-food chain, McDonald's Corporation. Although Subway was aggressively targeting the leader, the burger giant, founded in 1948, had nearly 20 years on the upstart. No slough to ingenuity, McDonald's had stores in such nontraditional locations as Wal-Mart stores and gas stations. A key to the success of both chains had been consistency. Customers counted on McDonald's decor and menu to be virtually the same from town to town; the same was true of Subway. Each chain, of course, made menu concessions in some countries—for Subway it was no pork products in areas with large Muslim populations; lots of salmon at the Norway shop; chicken salad with curry in British Subways; and chicken satay with peanut sauce in Australian locations.

A Global Leader: 1995–99

By 1995 Subway had sales of nearly $2.6 billion and 11,420 locations. DeLuca and Buck became increasingly active in charitable causes, giving to a variety of groups including the Girl Scouts of America, Habitat for Humanity, Junior Achievement, the Muscular Dystrophy Association, the Yale-New Haven Children's Hospital, and many others. The company also held several business association memberships (Better Business Bureau of Western Connecticut, the Connecticut Restaurant Association, the International Franchise Association, the Milford Chamber of Commerce) and even turned to environmental issues. In this vein, Subway introduced the Chocolate Brazil Nut cookie in 1995, full of Brazilian nuts harvested from the Peruvian rainforests, which in turn employed some 250 people and helped keep the rainforest alive.

In Subway's history 1996 turned out to be a stellar year—the company continued to dominate *Entrepreneur* magazine's Franchise 500 (regaining the title in 1993 and holding on to it into the early 2000s), and revenues increased nearly 25 percent to $3.2 billion, an incredible financial spurt by any standard. Part of the leap had come from further expansion to 12,516 locations, much of it in nontraditional settings. This was backed

---

Key Dates:

1965: Partners Fred DeLuca and Dr. Peter Buck open Pete's Super Submarines.

1974: The first Subway franchise opens in Wallingford, Connecticut.

1979: Subway stores surpass 130 locations.

1984: The first international Subway opens in Bahrain, Saudi Arabia; U.S. locations total 360.

1989: Subway stores number more than 3,500 worldwide.

1995: The company celebrates its 30th anniversary by opening the 11,000th Subway.

1999: Subway's 14,000th store opens; wraps become part of the permanent menu.

2000: Jared Fogle makes his first commercial; gourmet breads and sauces are added to Subway's menu.

2001: Subway surpasses McDonald's as the United States' largest fast-food chain; the 15,000th Subway opens.

2002: Systemwide Subway sales have reportedly reached $5 billion worldwide.

2004: Subway surpassed 22,000 stores worldwide; Atkins-themed wraps are added to the menu.

2005: Subway celebrates its 40th year in business.

---

up by the numbers in 1997, when nontraditional shops reached 2,700, or about 20 percent of the chain's locations. The company had explored a myriad of unusual possibilities, including railway and bus stations, airports, casinos, amusement parks, arenas, hospitals, museums, and department stores. Subway shops in high schools, colleges, and universities were especially successful for both the company and the schools, as students stopped leaving campuses for lunch, bringing profits and jobs back into these establishments. Yet another major coup had been an exclusive agreement with NEXCOM (Naval Exchange Commission) to put Subway shops on naval bases worldwide.

With Subway's ongoing success and rapid expansion, Wall Street and franchisees alike wondered if DeLuca and Buck would ever take their privately owned company public. The response was usually vague—not an unequivocal denial, but a carefully evasive statement. "We think that going public could take the focus off developing the business for our franchisees," DeLuca told the Winston-Salem (N.C.) *Journal* in 1997, leaving the possibility open.

By the fall of 1998 Subway had more than 13,229 shops worldwide and made changes to both its marketing strategy and its menu. A family-oriented advertising campaign was launched to bring kids into the stores, while three "wraps" (using tortillas instead of bread) were added to the menu for health-conscious adults. The wraps, which had gained popularity in restaurants as a healthy alternative to bread, had been tried on a limited basis and proved successful enough to be added to the menu permanently. Although sales for 1998 did not climb significantly ($3.4 billion, up from $3.3 billion the year before), Subway was still in solid financial shape.

Having overtaken Burger King as the second largest international restaurant chain (it had less than 11,000 stores, though it

remained the number two burger chain), Subway continued to target McDonald's, which still owned the lion's share (more than one-third) of the sandwich market. In 1999 McDonald's had more than 25,000 locations worldwide and 40 percent of the U.S. fast-food market. Subway planned to topple McDonald's by opening 950 shops annually until 2005, including new locations in India, Germany, and Scotland, and eventually to have Subway shops in every country in the world.

In the submarine sandwich marketplace, however, both Blimpie (ranked second to Subway) and Quizno's (ranked third) were gaining ground. Although the New York-based Blimpie International had 2,000 shops by the end of 1999 and the Denver-based Quizno's Corporation had only 600 in the United States, Canada, and Japan, each chain had ambitious plans mirroring those of Subway—to expand and conquer in 2000 and beyond. In addition, there was the entry into the market of another specialty sandwich chain, Schlotzsky's Inc., an Austin-based company. Schlotzsky's was nearing 800 deli stores in 1999 and, though it did not consider its "sub" sandwiches the primary success of the company (which had experienced 40 percent growth from 1998 to 1999), the competitors were certainly eating into Subway's bottom line.

The Jared Phenomenon: Early 2000s

An Indiana University college student named Jared Fogle revolutionized Subway's marketing when he claimed to have lost 245 pounds eating Subway sandwiches with six grams of fat or less, low-fat chips, and diet pop. Fogle's remarkable transformation made the college newspaper, the *Indiana Daily Student,* in April 1999, and both his and Subway's fortunes changed forever. Living in an apartment next to a Subway shop, Fogle was amazed when the store's sales picked up and he became a local celebrity. *Men's Health* magazine covered the weight loss story and Subway executives heard about it from Jared's mother, who wrote to thank them. Fogle was brought on board as a spokesman in January 2000, the year of Subway's 35th anniversary.

In addition to the Jared Fogle ads touting its low-fat sandwiches, Subway upgraded its menu with better meats, new items (Subway Selects with flavored breads and gourmet sauces), and additional advertising to broaden its customer base. For years Subway ads had targeted adults who wanted a quick yet healthy meal, and children who enjoyed the Nickelodeon-themed toys available in kids' meals. In the 2000s, Subway added teenagers to their lineup, attracting the highly fickle and yet lucrative market of 13- to 17-year-olds, who were generally more concerned with good taste than fat content. The gambit worked, and Subway pulled in an increasing number of teens and adults who favored delicious, made-the-way-you-want-them subs.

By 2001 Subway had 15,000 stores, with sales reaching $4 billion and an estimated customer base expanding to more than 725 million. The company credited menu additions and upbeat advertising campaigns featuring the increasingly popular Jared Fogle. Other sandwich franchisees, however, were gaining ground. Quizno's had grown to 870 stores and had gained significant market distinction by touting its toasted subs, while Blimpie had opened few shops (only about 100 in two years), concentrating instead on raising individual store sales rather than rapid expansion. Two other franchises were earning reputations as well, the East Coast-based Jersey Mike's Subs and Cousins Subs, based in the Midwest, though each chain was considerably smaller than its competitors.

Subway sold a record 2,000 franchises in 2001, besting previous years by a large margin. The chain had stores in 76 countries including new stores in France, Finland, and Poland, despite slower sales for the fast-food industry as a whole due to the terrorist attacks of September 11 and a weakened economy. These factors, however, did not prevent Subway from overtaking McDonald's as for having the most fast-food stores in the United States. Subway had 13,247 outlets by December 31, 2001, compared to McDonald's 13,099 according to *Nation's Restaurant News* (February 11, 2002). As McDonald's struggled with market saturation, some questioned whether Subway's growth could continue without facing the same perils, despite its burgeoning sales of nearly $5 billion for 2001 (compared with McDonald's sales of $40 billion for the same period).

In 2002 Subway wore its new title—as the nation's largest fast-food chain—proudly and decided to revamp its shops and image. Stores were redone in muted colors and a more sophisticated "Tuscan" design, leaning toward a casual and not strictly fast-food dining experience. The upscale image was implemented, as well, to help new franchisees locate in better locations, such as trendy shopping or business areas. By mid-2002 a new bilingual (English and Spanish) advertising campaign featuring Subway poster boy Jared was launched, touting new gourmet sandwiches such as Red Wine Vinaigrette and Chicken Teriyaki.

As Subway expanded internationally to further compete with rival McDonald's, the question of going public continued to plague everyone but its owners. Commenting to *Business Week Online* (August 19, 2002), DeLuca said he and Buck considered the idea briefly, finding the benefits did not outweigh the risks in their case. "Do we want a bunch of additional people—shareholders—to distract us from our mission? We did the calculations and decided we didn't have to go public."

Onward and Upward: 2003 and Beyond

In 2003 and 2004 Subway continued its growth both domestically and abroad. New international locations included India, Chile, and Iraq (through the Army-Air Force Exchange Service to provide service men and women fighting in Iraq "comfort food"), with additional stores opening in Germany and the United Kingdom (which reached 200 outlets). Sales for international locations, including Canada, topped $1.1 billion for 2003, while domestic sales reached an astonishing $5.7 billion for the same period. In addition, Jared continued to pop up in commercials, and his story inspired others to try the "Subway diet." The company frequently received letters from successful dieters, crediting their weight loss to Subway's fresh, low-fat sandwiches.

Subway continued to tweak its menu by adding salads and Aktins-friendly wraps (following the Atkins diet, which blamed carbohydrates for weight gain). Subway also entered into a long-term deal with the Coca-Cola Company by signing a ten-year contract to serve Coke products in its stores. The contract was a major coup for Coca-Cola, considering Coke products had been available in only a fraction of Subway's 22,000 stores,

with the vast majority selling Pepsi offerings. The new contract covered *all* Subway stores, both domestically and worldwide.

As Subway approached its 40th year, there were few signs middle age would slow the sandwich chain down. In a January 2004 interview with *Entrepreneur* magazine (after topping the magazine's Franchise 500 for the 12th time), DeLuca discussed the importance of franchisees in the decision-making process and the future: "The important thing for me and for anybody in this business is to appreciate the abilities of the franchisees and what they can do to improve a company and help a company grow." DeLuca believed most franchise chains had only "scratched the surface" of their potential. "Twenty-five years from now, the most successful franchise companies will have 50,000 outlets worldwide. There's a big opportunity for the future—especially for those companies able to develop not only the domestic market, but also an international brand."

Principal Competitors

McDonald's Corporation; Tricon Global Restaurants, Inc.; Blimpie International Inc.; Schlotzsky's Inc.; Quizno's Corporation.

Further Reading

"The Army-Air Force Exchange Service Opened Iraq's First Subway," *Nation's Restaurant News Daily NewsFax,* September 20, 2004, p. 1.

Ball, Brian R., "Master Minds," *Business First-Columbus* (Ohio), March 9, 2001, p. C3.

Biddle, RiShawn, "Split Personality," *Forbes,* September 3, 2001, p. 85.

Brady, Diane, "Subway Is on a Roll," *Business Week Online,* August 19, 2002.

Doss, Lorrie, "Sub Standard No Longer," *Nation's Restaurant News,* March 11, 2002, pp. 8+.

"Franchise Success Secrets," *Successful Franchising,* June 1998.

Hill, Suzette, "Subway's Fresh Approach," *Points of Purchase,* February 2001, p. 10.

Kaplan, David, "Jared's Back Plugging for Subway," *Adweek Eastern Edition,* May 13, 2002, p. 8.

Kuhn, Susan, "#13 Lucky for Subway Restaurants and Its Customer 7/6 Campaign Proves to Be a Winner," *Total Food Service,* February 1998.

Marshall, Charlee, "Six Grams of Fat Still Adds Up to a Good Tasting Sub," *Index-Journal* (Greenwood, S.C.), January 28, 1999.

McQuilkin, Steve, "Subway Founder Shares Recipe for Success," *Journal* (Winston-Salem, N.C.), November 12, 1997.

Morse, Dan, "School Cafeterias Are Enrolling As Fast-Food Franchisees," *Wall Street Journal,* July 28, 1998.

Prather, Michelle, "No. 1 with Everything," *Entrepreneur,* January 2002, p. 134.

Sperber, Bob, "In Search of Fresh Ideas," *Brandweek,* October 15, 2001, p. M54.

Strong, Michael, "Piling It On: Local Sandwich Chains Face Onslaught of Competition from National Companies," *Crain's Detroit Business,* November 10, 2003, p. 3.

"Subway Eclipses McD in Domestic Unit Tally," *Nation's Restaurant News,* February 11, 2002, pp. 3+.

Torres, Nichole, "From Zero to Hero," *Entrepreneur,* January 2004, pp. 148+.

——, "Sub-Liminable (Company Profile)," *Entrepreneur,* January 2001, p. 162.

—Nelson Rhodes

Dynaction S.A.

39 rue des Peupliers
Boulogne Billancourt
F-92773 Cedex
France
Telephone: +33 1 46 20 02 32
Fax: +33 1 46 08 14 09
Web site: http://www.dynaction.fr

Public Company
Incorporated: 1982 as Cryo Diffusion
Employees: 1,895
Sales: EUR 190.6 million ($220 million) (2003)
Stock Exchanges: Euronext Paris
Ticker Symbol: DYNP.PA
NAIC: 325412 Pharmaceutical Preparation
    Manufacturing; 325998 All Other Miscellaneous
    Chemical Product and Preparation Manufacturing

Once a model ''mini-conglomerate,'' Dynaction S.A. is shedding its holding company status and focusing itself as a pure-play Fine and Specialty Chemicals group. As such, Dynaction is in the process of divesting most of its holdings in order to regroup around a core represented by subsidiary PCAS. The company expects to complete a full merger with PCAS by the end of 2004. PCAS is active in five specialty chemicals areas: pharmaceutical synthesis and pharmaceutical formulation (41.6 percent and 15.1 percent, respectively, of sales); aroma chemical and cosmetics (11.8 percent); fine mineral chemicals (7.0 percent); specialty industrial chemicals (9.7 percent); and photochemicals and new technologies (10.7 percent). The company produces chemicals and chemical components for major pharmaceuticals companies. Among these is Adventis, with which the company is engaged in a partnership for the production of active ingredients, as well as the synthesis of Adventis-developed molecules. PCAS operates ten production plants, including a plant in Finland and one in Quebec, Canada. Three of the company's plants also meet the U.S. Food and Drug Administration requirements, giving the company access to that market. PCAS generated EUR 190 million, or approximately three-fourths of Dynaction's total revenues. (The remainder was generated by industrial group CMD Engrenages et Réducteurs, slated to be sold by the end of 2004.) France accounts for 38.6 percent of the company's sales, while the rest of Europe adds 42 percent of the group's sales, followed by North America, at 11.5 percent of sales. PCAS itself serves as a holding company for a number of subsidiaries, including Expansia, PCAS, PCAS Finland, PCF, Saint Jean Photochimie, in Canada, and Société Béarnaise de Synthèse. Dynaction is quoted on the Euronext Paris Stock Exchange and is led by cofounder and Chairman Christian Moretti.

Founding a Mini-Conglomerate in the 1980s

Dynaction specialized in acquiring and developing new and growing businesses long before ''start-up'' became an investors circle buzzword. The company was founded by Christian Moretti and Henri Blanchet. Both men had backgrounds in the banking and finance industries. Moretti, a native of Nice and a graduate of Columbia Business School, also had taught finance in Paris in the 1970s. In 1982, Moretti and Blanchet joined together to form an investment partnership and that year acquired Cryo Diffusion, paying a symbolic amount for the money-losing cryogenics company.

Moretti and Blanchet launched Cryo Diffusion on a restructuring that quickly brought it back in the black. In the meantime the partners had been scouting for new acquisition candidates for their young holding company. Their next purchases came in 1983, with the acquisition of two small industrial manufacturers, CEE, one of the world's top producers of electronic security systems, and CCS, a maker of remote control devices. CEE was then listed on the Paris Stock Exchange's Secondary Market in 1984 in order to fund more acquisitions. By the end of that year, Moretti and Blanchet had acquired Matlabo. Then in 1985, the partners added Risoud S.A.

In that year, Moretti and Blanchet restructured their cryogenics operations as a new subsidiary and adopted the name Dynaction for the holding company. Dynaction's strategy was by then mostly in place. Moretti and Blanchet targeted purchases of small-scale industrial companies, choosing such solid if ''unglamorous'' sectors as mechanical engineering, packaging, re-

Company Perspectives:

Dynaction is an industrial company focused on a single growth sector: Fine and Speciality Chemicals. This is the sole business of PCAS, Dynaction's subsidiary, where its majority stake is close to 70%.

Dynaction's single-sector strategy is the result of a refocusing dynamic under way since 1995. Its last phase, the sale of CMD Engrenages et Réducteurs, is scheduled for 2004.

Dynaction's objective is to allocate all its resources to Fine and Speciality Chemicals, a growing, value-creating sector that is generally sheltered from international business cycles. At the end of 2003, this sector represented 74% of Dynaction's turnover. PCAS has earned a leadership position in this market thanks to constant and sustained growth, averaging 17% per annum over the last eight years. Dynaction is an industrial company with optimised and streamlined structures, a well-targeted strategy and very low operating costs. Dynaction has embarked on a move to combine with its subsidiary PCAS, which will lead to a merger during the second half of 2004.

frigeration, and the like. These companies, however, were chosen among the leaders in their markets, and especially those with strong operations on the export market. At the same time, Dynaction never embarked on hostile takeovers, bucking the prevailing trend in a decade dominated by corporate raiders. Instead, the company preferred the less expensive friendly takeover.

Once brought into Dynaction, the new subsidiaries retained a high degree of independence. Managers of the group's companies were given a free rein in their decision-making, and only required to seek Dynaction's approval for matters such as acquisitions and financing. Moretti and Blanchet also sought to transform a company's management into entrepreneurs, rather than employees. In order to encourage this, managers of Dynaction subsidiaries were given stakes as high as 25 percent. This enabled Moretti and Blanchet to attract a pool of highly competent managers. In this way, also, Dynaction itself remained quite small, with just two other employees in addition to Moretti and Blanchet.

Another feature of Dynaction's investment process was its willingness to open the capital of its subsidiaries to outside investors. Selling stakes in the companies, whether through stock exchange listings as with CEE or through placements with institutional investors, permitted Dynaction to raise capital necessary to continue its acquisition strategy.

Dynaction itself went public, listing on the Paris Stock Exchange's Secondary Market in 1986. That year, the company acquired Jeulin and Jeulin, which was then merged into the Matlabo subsidiary. Dynaction also created a new subsidiary, Mecadyne, by spinning off the industrial operations of Risoud and by acquiring two other small businesses. Mecadyne itself grew into a sort of "mini-Dynaction," overseeing its own range of subsidiaries. Other Dynaction vehicles followed this pattern, giving rise to subsidiaries Dynelec, Dynalog, Dynaspring, and Cellier, the world leader in coated paper.

This last group represented an example of what could go wrong under Dynaction's management style. Acquired through Dynaction's acquisition of Frankel in 1987, Cellier was hit hard by the economic recession of the early 1990s. By 1992, the company was forced into bankruptcy proceedings. Nonetheless, on the whole Dynaction proved highly successful in developing its diversified holdings. These included Dynelec, which had been acquired as Metanic, and Fontaine Electronique in 1987; and Eurodyne, Grantil, Regma, a maker of office equipment acquired from Rhone Poulenc, and RMA in 1988. The latter two were combined with Fontaine Electronique to form Dynaspring in 1989.

Scaling Back in the 1990s

By the beginning of the 1990s, Dynaction represented a diversified, if small-scale, conglomerate of more than 70 companies, including 32 subsidiaries directly controlled by Dynaction. Total sales among the conglomerate's holdings neared FRF 5.5 billion (approximately $900 million) by 1991. In that year, Dynaction transferred its stock listing to the Paris main board. The company also acquired a new subsidiary that year, CMD Engrenages et Réducteurs, bought from PSA, the makers of Peugeot and Citroën automobiles.

The year 1992 marked the first change in strategy for the group. The failure of Cellier, and difficulties among the group's other operations during the drawn-out economic recession in Europe, led Dynaction to take tighter control of its operations. The company began a process of streamlining and refocusing its holdings. By 1995, Dynaction had reduced its holdings to just 28 companies, most of which were grouped under ten primary subsidiaries. The disposal program played a major part in helping to reduce the company's exposure to the hard-hit industrial manufacturing sector.

At the same time, Dynaction sought to diversify into less cyclical business sectors. In the early 1990s, Dynaction targeted two sectors for this effort. With the acquisition of Mediascience, Dynaction entered the educational materials, systems, and publishing market. Through Mediascience, Dynaction moved into the distribution market, offering some 4,500 products for the secondary and university markets. Still more significant for the company was its 1992 acquisition of PCAS, a fine and specialty chemicals operation of The Netherlands' Akzo. PCAS, which stood for Produits Chimiques Auxiliaires de Synthèse, gave Dynaction a variety of operations, including the production of aroma molecules and products, and active ingredients and other specialty chemicals for the pharmaceuticals market.

As it pared away at its industrial holdings, Dynaction began building up its two newest areas of operations. In 1993, for example, the company acquired Canada's Saint-Jean Photochimie, extending PCAS into the production of photosensitive resins. The company also formed a new Spanish division for its Mediascience operation, called Euroscience, that year.

Both Mediascience and PCAS were then listed on the Paris Stock Exchange. Mediascience's listing came in 1994, reducing Dynaction's stake in the company to just 54 percent. PCAS's turn came the following year, as a result of which the stake dropped to slightly less than 71 percent.

Key Dates:

1982: Christian Moretti and Henri Blanchet acquire Cryo Diffusion and create a holding company structure to acquire other businesses.

1985: The holding company's name is changed to Dynaction.

1986: Dynaction lists on the Paris Stock Exchange's Secondary Market.

1991: The company transfers its listing to the Paris main board.

1992: The company acquires PCAS from Akzo and begins streamlining its holdings.

1995: Henri Blanchet dies; Dynaction continues restructuring around three core divisions; PCAS lists on the Paris Stock Exchange's Secondary Market.

1996: PCAS forms the Béarnaise de Synthèse partnership with Elf-Atochem.

1998: PCAS acquires Seloc.

1999: PCAS acquires Vernolab and Pharmacie Centrale.

2000: PCAS acquires active principals business from Sanofi-Synthelabo.

2001: PCAS acquires Expansia, Leira Fine Chemicals (Finland), and E-Pharma.

2002: PCAS acquires, through the Créapharm subsidiary, Euclidis and Sci Maude.

2003: Dynaction announces a plan to sell off its remaining noncore holdings and merge with PCAS.

2004: The merger with PCAS is slated for completion by the end of the year.

Focused Specialty Chemicals Group for the New Century

The year 1995 marked the true turning point for Dynaction. In large part, the company's change in focus appeared to come as a result of the sudden death of Henri Blanchet that year. Now led by Moretti alone, Dynaction continued its policy of streamlining its operations through the late 1990s. By 1995, the company sales had been scaled back to just FRF 3.1 billion (approximately $530 million), and by 2000, Dynaction's total revenues amounted to just EUR 327 million ($300 million). As part of its restructuring, Dynaction regrouped its continuing operations under three primary divisions: Industrial Manufacturing; Components and Services; and Technical Distribution.

By the early 2000s, however, Dynaction's focus had narrowed still further. The investors' climate had changed dramatically from the boom years of the late 1990s, brought on by the collapse of the high-technology sector, and by increasing investor preference for ''pure-play'' stocks. Dynaction continued to shed operations and by the end of 2003, the company's holdings consisted of just two main groups: PCAS and CMD Engrenages et Réducteurs.

With the latter scheduled for disposal by the end of 2004, Dynaction had transformed itself from a diversified conglomerate to a specialist company in the fine and specialty chemicals industry. PCAS had grown strongly since its acquisition in the early 1990s. In 1996, PCAS formed a partnership with Elf-Atochem, forming Bèarnaise de Synthèse to produce molecules for the Elf subsidiary. This was followed by the acquisition of Seloc in 1998, and Vernolab, a leading provider of oils analysis and services, and Pharmacie Centrale in 1999.

In 2000, PCAS acquired the active principal ingredients operation of Sanofi-Synthelabo. The following year, PCAS acquired three more companies, Expansia, E-pharma, and Finland-based Leiras Fine Chemicals Oy. The company also acquired the Bessay industrial site that year, located near Vichy in France. Through its Créapharm subsidiary, PCAS made several more acquisitions into the 2000s, including Euclidis and Sci Maude in 2002. The following year, the decision was made to refocus PCAS on a core of Fine and Specialty Chemicals. As part of that decision, the company sold off Vernolab in 2004.

By then, Dynaction was ready to complete the final process of its transformation, and in 2003 the company announced its intention to merge with PCAS, creating a single entity. Poor market conditions forced the company to postpone the merger. Nonetheless, in 2004, Moretti reaffirmed the company's commitment to the merger, intending to complete the move by the end of the year. The form of the merger—whether to merge Dynaction into PCAS, or vice versa—had yet to be decided. Dynaction looked forward, however, to its new beginning as a specialty chemicals group in the new century.

Principal Subsidiaries

CMD Engrenages et Réducteurs; Créapharm; Expansia; PCAS; PCAS Finland; PCF; Saint Jean Photochimie (Canada); Société Béarnaise de Synthèse.

Principal Divisions

Industrial Manufacturing; Components and Services; Technical Distribution.

Principal Competitors

Bayer AG; Ciba Specialty Chemicals Corporation; Clariant Ltd.; Imperial Chemical Industries PLC; SKW Trostberg AG; Rhodia S.A.

Further Reading

''Conglomerateurs Par Excellence,'' *Economist,* June 16, 1990, p. 82.

''Merger Planned Between PCAS and Dynaction,'' *Chemical Business NewsBase,* January 27, 2003.

—M.L. Cohen

EastGroup Properties, Inc.

300 One Jackson Place, 188 East Capitol Street
Jackson, Mississippi 39201
U.S.A.
Telephone: (601) 354-3555
Fax: (601) 352-1441
Web site: http://www.eastgroup.net

Public Company
Incorporated: 1969 as Third ICM Realty
Employees: 57
Sales: $108.44 million (2003)
Stock Exchanges: New York
Ticker Symbol: EGP
NAIC: 525930 Real Estate Investment Trusts

EastGroup Properties, Inc. acquires, operates, and develops industrial real estate properties in the southern and southwestern United States, focusing primarily on markets in Florida, Texas, Arizona, and California. EastGroup concentrates on acquiring distribution centers near transportation centers. The company's properties range in size from 20,000 square feet to more than one million square feet. EastGroup's portfolio of properties contains nearly 20 million square feet.

Origins

Mississippi-based EastGroup began its business life under a different name in a different part of the country. The one thread connecting the company from its past to its existence in the 21st century was its classification as a real estate investment trust, or REIT. The birth of EastGroup followed not long after REITs were encouraged to be formed by the Real Estate Investment Trust Act of 1960. The law sought to stimulate investment in real estate by granting special tax concessions to companies, trusts, or associations that qualified as REITs. The qualification standards were numerous, but as a general rule REITs were exempt from federal income taxation provided they distributed nearly all of their taxable income as dividends to shareholders and held at least 75 percent of their assets in real property. The special tax status provided by the law was intended to be limited to passive investors in real estate, not to entities that actively operated a real estate business.

The exemption from taxation opened the doors to investors who otherwise would have been barred from engaging in real estate ownership and professional real estate management. For the first time, small investors, encouraged by the provisions of the Real Estate Investment Trust Act, could pool their investments and participate in business activities that historically had been restricted to institutions or to the wealthy. With a pooling of investments, the risk of loss was spread out, lessened by the greater number of investors involved in a purchase. A greater number of investors also allowed involvement in projects that the individual investor did not have the resources to undertake. The benefits were substantial, spawning a wave of REIT formations during the 1960s, particularly later in the decade when technical changes in the tax code invigorated interest in REITs. It was at this point that EastGroup's predecessor was formed. In July 1969, Third ICM Realty was incorporated, commencing operations several months later in December 1969.

Initially, ICM Realty invested in real estate projects in the northeastern United States, developing its portfolio in markets far removed from the company's geographic focus in later years. Many of the REITs in existence during the late 1960s and early 1970s grew rapidly, funding their expansion through offerings of stock to the public, which provided substantially more capital than traditional sources of real estate financing. ICM Realty followed suit, completing its initial public offering (IPO) of stock in 1971, the same year the company dropped "Third" from its corporate title.

After an initial burst of growth, the REIT industry experienced one of the more difficult periods in its history. Capital, obtained through public offerings, was relatively easy to come by, creating a glut of cash in the industry. Few industries could complain of having access to too much money, but for REITs the supply of funds exceeded the number of quality real estate investments available, which, in turn, drove property prices skyward. The industry, particularly those REITs involved in development projects, suffered as it entered the mid-1970s, experiencing a general downturn that was exacerbated by recessive economic conditions between 1974 and 1975. Numerous real estate projects failed during the period, prompting a series of amendments to the provisions governing REITs. ICM Realty withstood the downturn, enduring the grim conditions that beset the industry early in the company's development. ICM Realty survived, giving it a chance to some day make its mark on the national scene—a day, as it happened, that was years away.

New Management in 1983

For more than two decades, ICM Realty operated in near obscurity. The company's path towards prominence did not begin until it gained the management team that would lead it into the 21st century. In 1983, the year the company adopted the name EastGroup Properties, the two most influential individuals in the company's history arrived. Leland R. Speed, who earned a B.S. in industrial management from Georgia Institute of Technology and an M.B.A. from Harvard Business School, became EastGroup's chief strategist. Before joining the company, Speed was involved in the general securities and real estate development business. In 1983, Speed was joined by David H. Hoster II, who received a B.A. in history from Princeton University and an M.B.A. from Stanford University. Before joining EastGroup, Hoster spent eight years in Washington, D.C., serving as president of Riviere Realty Trust, a position he was given after spending three years as a project manager with K.S. Sweet Associates.

With Speed in the lead and Hoster at his side, EastGroup Properties gradually developed into a REIT of note. It took more than a decade after the pair's arrival before the company began its rise, however. EastGroup, despite the implication in its name and its region of origin, created its identity in the southern and southwestern United States, in the region commonly referred to as the Sunbelt. The company made its mark not as a Maryland-based company but as a Jackson, Mississippi-based company, one that started to exhibit impressive growth during the 1990s. EastGroup entered the decade having never generated more than $10 million in annual revenue. The company exited the decade flirting with the $100 million-in-sales mark.

EastGroup, as led by Speed and Hoster, focused on acquiring and developing industrial properties, particularly distribution centers located near transportation hubs. REITs commonly pursued specific segments of the real estate market, describing themselves as healthcare REITs, residential REITs, retail REITs, hotel and motel REITS, and numerous other classifica-

tions. EastGroup positioned itself as an industrial REIT with a particular focus on distribution centers near transportation hubs, although the company occasionally acquired office space that did not meet its principal strategic criteria.

Speed applied EastGroup's strategy to the Sunbelt, concentrating much of his efforts in Florida, Texas, Arizona, and California. The company's revenue volume edged passed $13 million in 1992, beginning a measured march upwards. Growth came as Speed expanded the company's portfolio of property holdings, with sharp increases realized by acquiring other industrial REITs. Speed assumed an acquisitive posture as his company exited the mid-1990s, when EastGroup was generating roughly $30 million in revenue. Between 1996 and 1998, the company acquired three publicly held REITs, beginning with the May 1996 purchase of LNH REIT, Inc. LNH, with approximately $2.5 million in 1995 revenues, had $6.2 million worth of real estate properties in its portfolio, including a 122,000-square-foot commercial facility in Kansas City, Missouri, a 135,000-square-foot shopping center in Warwick, Rhode Island, and a 100,000-square-foot industrial building in Fort Lauderdale, Florida. A much larger acquisition followed the next month, when EastGroup purchased Copley Properties, Inc. in a $166 million transaction. Formed in 1985, Copley owned and operated 15 properties with more than 2.5 million square feet of leasable space, possessing more than $80 million in assets. Copley's properties, primarily located in Arizona and California, bolstered EastGroup's presence in the Sunbelt. In June 1998, the company completed another acquisition on the scale of the Copley purchase, acquiring Meridian Trust VIII Co. in a $103 million deal. Meridian owned 18 industrial properties in major Sunbelt markets, giving EastGroup more than 2.6 million square feet of leasable space.

The acquisition of REITs and the expansion of the company's own portfolio through internal means greatly accelerated EastGroup's growth during the late 1990s. By the end of 1999, the company was a $74-million-in-revenues REIT, having increased its revenue volume nearly fivefold in five years. The company maintained the intensified pace in 1999, completing 13 acquisitions in five states that added more than 1.6 million square feet of leasable space. By this point, Hoster had assumed day-to-day control over the company, becoming EastGroup's chief executive officer in September 1997. Speed presided as chairman. Under Hoster's leadership, EastGroup entered the 21st century with roughly 16 million square feet of leasable space. He focused his efforts on expanding the company's base, guiding EastGroup past the $100 million-in-revenue mark.

EastGroup in the New Millennium

EastGroup's pattern of robust financial growth, which described the company for much of the 1990s, continued at the start of the new century. Revenues reached nearly $98 million in 2000 before eclipsing a financial milestone the following year, when the company's sales volume totaled $105 million. From there, EastGroup's financial growth stagnated, as a national recession delivered a discernible blow to the real estate market. Vacancy rates increased during the economic downturn, causing the company's financial progress to stall. In 2002, EastGroup's revenues only increased by roughly $650,000. Further, market conditions did not justify aggressive expansion, making the early years of

Key Dates:
1969: Incorporated as Third ICM Realty, EastGroup Properties is formed.
1971: The company completes its initial public offering of stock.
1983: Concurrent with a name change to EastGroup Properties, the company hires the two senior executives who will lead it into the 21st century.
1996: EastGroup Properties acquires LNH REIT, Inc. and Copley Properties, Inc.
1998: Meridian Trust VIII Co. is acquired.
2003: Nearly $20 million is spent on acquiring real estate properties.

the decade a period of little significant progress. When the economic climate improved, however, Hoster quickly seized the opportunities available to him, ushering EastGroup into a period of expansion first demonstrated in 2003.

As EastGroup neared its 35th anniversary, Hoster directed the company's growth in California, Arizona, Texas, and Florida, where more than 80 percent of its properties were located. Hoster purchased five properties in 2003, adding 442,000 square feet of leasable space and 82 acres of land for future development. The properties acquired included the 62,000-square-foot Altamonte Commerce Center II in Orlando, Florida, and the 63,000-square-foot Airport Commons Distribution Center in Phoenix, Arizona, both acquired in May for a total of just under $6 million. In September, the company paid $4.2 million for the Shady Trail Distribution Center in Dallas, Texas. In October, the 72,000-square-foot Expressway Commerce Center II in Tampa, Florida, was acquired, followed by the purchase of another Tampa-based property the following month, the 127,000-square-foot Oak Creek Distribution Center. Each Tampa property was acquired for $4.2 million. The company ended the year with a modest gain in revenues to $108 million, a total generated from the 19.4 million square feet of leasable space that constituted its portfolio.

EastGroup remained in the acquisitive mode as it celebrated its 35th year in business. Among the purchases made during 2004 was the acquisition in April of the Kirby Business Center in Houston. Located near the city's sports complex, Reliant Stadium, the Kirby property was a 125,000-square-foot distribution center. "This acquisition," Hoster said in an April 5, 2004 interview with *Mississippi Business Journal*, "increases EastGroup's ownership in Houston to three million square feet including our properties under development." A significant acquisition followed in August, when EastGroup entered the San Antonio market for the first time. The company purchased the Alamo Downs Distribution Center for $8.4 million, gaining a two-building, distribution complex with more than 250,000 square feet of leasable space. In an August 23, 2004 interview with the *Mississippi Business Journal*, Hoster marked the occasion by explaining, "San Antonio is a new market for EastGroup, and we see the potential for growing ownership there to over one million square feet. We believe that a portfolio of quality properties in San Antonio will complement our operations in Houston, Dallas, and El Paso." As Hoster guided the company forward, he sought to increase the 20.2 million square feet owned by the company in late 2004 and create a bigger presence for EastGroup in the Sunbelt.

Principal Subsidiaries

EastGroup Properties General Partners, Inc.; EastGroup Properties Holdings, Inc.; Nash IND Corporation; EastGroup TRS, Inc.

Principal Competitors

Duke Realty Corp.; Kilroy Realty Corporation; Prentiss Properties Trust.

Further Reading

Bivans, Ralph, "Mississippi-Based REIT Plans to Build Warehouses Near Houston Airport," *Knight Ridder/Tribune Business News,* January 17, 2001.

"EastGroup Acquires Tampa Property," *Mississippi Business Journal,* November 3, 2003, p. 30.

"EastGroup Buys Houston Facility," *Mississippi Business Journal,* July 29, 2002, p. 13.

"EastGroup Completes Ariz, Buy," *Mississippi Business Journal,* June 24, 2002, p. 10.

"EastGroup Enters San Antonio," *Mississippi Business Journal,* August 23, 2004, p. 10.

"EastGroup Makes Houston Purchase," *Mississippi Business Journal,* April 5, 2004, p. 8.

"EastGroup Properties," *Real Estate Finance and Investment,* December 9, 2002, p. 4.

Hollahan, Terry, "EastGroup Expands Industrial Real Estate Presence with Acquisition," *Memphis Business Journal,* February 18, 2000, p. 2.

Northway, Wally, "EastGroup Closes Public Offering," *Mississippi Business Journal,* July 14, 2003, p. 11.

Perez, Christine, "EastGroup Pays $2.5M for Distribution Center," *Dallas Business Journal,* June 2, 2000, p. 18.

Simanoff, Dave, "EastGroup Buys Five Properties," *Business Journal,* August 20, 1999, p. 1.

—Jeffrey L. Covell

Eaton Corporation

Eaton Center
1111 Superior Avenue
Cleveland, Ohio 44114-2584
U.S.A.
Telephone: (216) 523-5000
Toll Free: (800) 386-1911
Fax: (216) 523-4787
Web site: http://www.eaton.com

Public Company
Incorporated: 1911 as the Torbensen Gear and Axle
    Company
Employees: 55,000
Sales: $8.06 billion (2003)
Stock Exchanges: New York Chicago Pacific
Ticker Symbol: ETN
NAIC: 332912 Fluid Power Valve and Hose Fitting
    Manufacturing; 333995 Fluid Power Cylinder and
    Actuator Manufacturing; 333996 Fluid Power Pump
    and Motor Manufacturing; 334513 Instruments for
    Measuring and Displaying Industrial Process
    Variables; 335311 Power, Distribution, and Specialty
    Transformer Manufacturing; 335313 Switchgear and
    Switchboard Apparatus Manufacturing; 335314 Relay
    and Industrial Control Manufacturing; 335999 All
    Other Miscellaneous Electrical Equipment and
    Component Manufacturing; 336322 Other Motor
    Vehicle Electrical and Electronic Equipment
    Manufacturing; 336350 Motor Vehicle Transmission
    and Power Train Parts Manufacturing; 336399 All
    Other Motor Vehicle Parts Manufacturing

Eaton Corporation is a diversified industrial manufacturer whose operations are divided into four main groups: fluid power, electrical, automotive, and trucks. The company is a global leader in fluid power systems and services for industrial, mobile, and aircraft equipment; electrical systems and components for power quality, distribution, and control; automotive engine air management systems and power-train controls for fuel economy; and intelligent drive-train systems for fuel economy and safety in trucks. Among the brands that Eaton uses to market its products and services are Aeroquip, Airflex, Bill, Boston, Char-Lynn, Challenger, Durant, Eaton Electrical, Elek, Fuller, Golf Pride, Heinemann, Holec, Home Automation, Hydro-Line, MEM, Sterer, Tabula, Tedeco, Vickers, VORAD, and Weatherhead. Eaton generates business in more than 100 countries worldwide, with about one-third of revenues originating outside the United States—19 percent in Europe and about 6 percent each in Latin America and the Asia-Pacific region. The company's roots are in low-tech commodity parts for trucks and automobiles, but—particularly since the mid-1990s—Eaton has shifted focus to the manufacture of a variety of electronics-based products.

Pioneering Auto Supplier

In 1911 Joseph Oriel Eaton established a small machine shop in Bloomfield, New Jersey, manufacturing heavy-duty truck axles for the expanding automotive industry. With the help of brother-in-law Henning O. Taube and Viggo V. Torbensen, who had patented an internal-gear rear truck axle in 1902, the Torbensen Gear and Axle Company built seven axles by hand in its first year. Three years later, the company's operations were moved to Cleveland, in order to be closer to the auto manufacturers there and in Detroit. Then in 1917, by which time production had soared to 33,000, the company was sold to Republic Motor Truck Co., the largest truck maker in the country.

In 1922 Eaton reentered the picture, buying back his original company from Republic Motor Truck Co. and renaming it one year later the Eaton Axle and Spring Co. Over the next several years, the company acquired several smaller auto parts manufacturers, including makers of chassis leaf springs, bumpers, engine valves and tappets, and coil springs. Diversification of its product line also included a new line of parts for aircraft engines.

The company weathered the Great Depression, acquiring several companies that were nearing bankruptcy. By the late 1930s industrial growth was stimulated by President Roose-

Company Perspectives:

From our earliest days, when Eaton invented, hand-manufactured and then sold some of the first truck axles in the industry, it has been a primary tenet of business that the company carries a responsibility to deliver breakthrough solutions to its customers. Innovative entrepreneurship continues to drive Eaton in the 21st century.

velt's New Deal program, and demand for products from the Eaton Manufacturing Company—a name change registered in May 1932—increased slowly and steadily. When the United States became involved in World War II, Eaton, as a primary manufacturer of vehicle parts, produced a variety of items for the war effort.

In 1946 Eaton purchased the Dynamatic Corporation and one year later established a joint sales and engineering company with two British firms, Rubry Owen and E.N.V. Engineering. These companies soon became suppliers of axles and gears to Ford Motor Company and General Motors Corporation in England. In 1953 Livia, a small Italian manufacturer of engine valves, acquired technological assistance and a production license from Eaton. As a result, Livia become the exclusive supplier of engine valves for Simca of France as well as for all trucks built by Fiat. Livia was purchased by Eaton in 1961.

Diversification Through Acquisition: 1958–73

John C. Virden was named president of Eaton in 1958 and followed the company's diversification policy. A strong believer in "divisional autonomy," Virden ensured that Eaton's subsidiaries and divisions maintained a large degree of managerial independence. Under Virden, Eaton made 23 major acquisitions between 1958 and 1973, including Fuller Manufacturing Co., which produced automotive transmissions (1958); Dole Valve Co. (1963), the deal through which Eaton entered the appliance and automotive controls sectors; and, perhaps more importantly, the Yale & Towne Manufacturing Company. Yale & Towne was founded in the 1870s by the inventor Linus Yale, Jr., who developed a revolutionary pin-tumbler cylinder lock, or padlock, which proved popular and has remained essentially unchanged since its invention. When Yale died in 1913 at the age of 47, Henry Towne took over the company and served as its leader for the next 50 years. Yale & Towne was acquired by Eaton on October 31, 1963, and a full merger occurred on January 1, 1966, under the name of Eaton Yale & Towne Inc.

During this time, Eaton's auto parts division suffered a temporary setback when General Motors, one of Eaton's primary customers, reduced its orders after model changes and higher wages forced the auto manufacturer to scale down production. Nevertheless, Eaton Yale & Towne remained profitable, as its other divisions supported the company until demand for auto parts recovered. In 1966 Eaton Yale & Towne experienced record growth in sales and profits, largely as a result of an expansion in industrial growth.

Following the merger with Yale & Towne, the company executed a careful integration of managerial personnel; officials at Yale & Towne were given important permanent positions in the new company. Gordon Patterson, formerly president of Yale & Towne, was named vice-chairperson, and John Virden became chairperson, as Elliot Ludvigsen, a former president of Fuller Manufacturing, was named president. When Virden retired in 1969, E. Mandell de Windt, who had joined the company as a production clerk, was elected chairperson. The company's name was changed once again on April 21, 1971, to Eaton Corporation.

Expansion into Factory Automation in the Late 1970s

In the 1970s, decreased demand for American cars severely affected the three largest manufacturers of automobile components: Bendix Corporation, Rockwell International, and Eaton. As a result, all three companies attempted further diversification of their operations. Whereas Bendix acquired new product lines, and Rockwell added electronics products to its line, Eaton began to focus on the less volatile truck components market, as well as on expansion into foreign markets. Eaton also initiated a $470 million diversification program to develop a new line of factory automation products.

In 1978, with the automotive market still sluggish, Eaton made three acquisitions: Samuel Moore & Company, a manufacturer of hydraulic motors and transmissions; Kenway, a company specializing in robotic warehouse storage systems; and, most importantly, the electronics company Cutler-Hammer Inc., whose AIL electronics division had developed the ALQ-161 advanced radar counter-measures system for Rockwell's B-1 bomber and had also been chosen by NASA to build the landing system for the space shuttles. Eaton intended to combine the resources of these three companies in order to develop a new line of factory automation products. During the development stage, however, high capital investments and low profit margins ensued, and Eaton began to struggle financially. Moreover, the Yale & Towne division's ventures in forest equipment and lift-truck manufacturing proved barely profitable (in February 1978 Eaton had sold the Yale lock and security business to Thomas Telling Ltd.); 1980 was a particularly bad year for Eaton.

Restructuring in the 1980s

The following year, Eaton sold or closed down 18 subsidiaries whose profits were marginal or nonexistent. The forestry equipment and lift-truck businesses were written off and sold in 1982 for $200 million. That year, Eaton registered its first loss in 50 years, $189.6 million on sales of $2.4 billion. Determined to reduce the company's exposure to the vagaries of the automotive components business, de Windt declared that Eaton had now dedicated itself to becoming a "high technology company servicing the growth markets of the 1980s."

Ironically, the automotive division generated most of the company's profit the following year. Eaton's major automotive customers, International Harvester (later renamed Navistar International Corp.), Ford, General Motors, and Paccar Inc., had fully recovered from the recession of the mid-1970s and were once again selling a wide range of trucks. Even so, automotive components, which had accounted for 79 percent of Eaton's sales in 1977, were down to 46 percent by 1983. In 1984, 12 of

Key Dates:

1911: Joseph Oriel Eaton, Henning O. Taube, and Viggo V. Torbensen establish the Torbensen Gear and Axle Company, a small machine shop in Bloomfield, New Jersey, manufacturing heavy-duty truck axles.

1914: Company moves its operations to Cleveland.

1917: Company is sold to Republic Motor Truck Co.

1922: Eaton reacquires the firm.

1923: Company is renamed Eaton Axle and Spring Co.

1932: Company's name is changed to Eaton Manufacturing Company.

1958: Fuller Manufacturing Co., maker of automotive transmissions, is acquired.

1963: Eaton acquires lockmaker Yale & Towne Manufacturing Company and Dole Valve Co., maker of appliance and automotive controls.

1966: Eaton is renamed Eaton Yale & Towne Inc.

1971: Company's name is changed to Eaton Corporation.

1978: Electronics company Cutler-Hammer Inc. is acquired; the Yale lock and security business is divested.

1982: Eaton reports its first loss in 50 years.

1994: Eaton acquires Westinghouse Electric Corporation's distribution and control unit for $1.1 billion.

1998: The company's truck axle and brake business—its founding business—is sold to Dana Corporation.

1999: Aeroquip-Vickers, Inc., producer of industrial hydraulic equipment, is acquired for $1.7 billion.

2000: Semiconductor equipment business is spun off as Axcelis Technologies, Inc.

2004: Powerware Corporation is acquired.

the company's automotive components plants were closed, and the workforce was reduced to 41,000, down from 63,000 in 1979. During this time, sales from the electronic components division rose dramatically from 21 percent of turnover in 1977 to 54 percent in 1983.

Jim Stover, president and chief operating officer of Eaton since 1979, was named chairperson and CEO when de Windt retired on April 23, 1986. Stover maintained de Windt's commitment to the company's substantial foreign markets, remarking that Eaton had learned from the recession that "you compete on a global basis or you don't compete at all." Stover took over after Eaton had reported a 1985 profit of $231 million on sales of $3.7 billion.

At the beginning of 1986, Eaton had $1 billion available for financing acquisitions, and, by July of that year, it had purchased three more companies: Consolidated Controls (precision instruments), Singer Controls (switches and valves), and Pacific-Sierra Research (defense and computer systems). At the end of the year, Stover unexpectedly placed the company's defense electronics business, AIL Systems, Inc., up for sale, noting quality control problems and reduced orders for the division's B-1B bomber systems. This segment of Eaton's business had suffered several other setbacks during this period as well. It was suspended from bidding on new Air Force

contracts, and, in March 1988, AIL paid the Department of Defense $9.5 million to settle improper billing charges. Unable to sell the subsidiary, Eaton sustained it as a discontinued operation until mid-1993, when it was "reconsolidated," according to that year's annual report.

Two Huge Acquisitions in the 1990s

From 1984 to 1993, Eaton invested almost $1.7 billion in capital improvements and $2.3 billion in research and development, which enabled it to introduce several new products in the early 1990s. One noteworthy innovation was the AutoSelect automatic transmission, the result of $10 million and six years of planning. Introduced in 1993, AutoSelect promised the trucking industry increased fuel efficiency, safer and easier driving, and drastically lowered training costs. An article in the June 1993 issue of *Forbes* magazine suggested that AutoSelect might also be intended to attract more female drivers to the short-handed trucking industry, an allegation that Eaton strongly denied. It was also during this period that William E. Butler took over as CEO, starting in 1991.

Eaton's global expansion resulted in annual sales increases from 13.4 percent in 1985 to nearly 30 percent by 1993. Domestic sales from its automotive division continued, however, to provide the largest share, over 50 percent, of Eaton's revenues. Still susceptible to market fluctuations, the company recorded rather meager profits from 1989 to 1991, and reported a loss in 1992. Nevertheless, profits rebounded the following year, fueled by surging sales in the North American market for sport utility vehicles.

That year, Eaton announced a plan to lessen its dependence on automotive components through the $1.1 billion acquisition of Westinghouse Electric Corporation's distribution and controls business unit—a bold move for a traditionally conservative company. The purchase, completed in February 1994 and at that point the largest in the company's history, advanced Eaton to a top position in industrial control and power distribution markets, providing such products as circuit breakers. The company aimed to pay off the $930 million debt it incurred for the acquisition by 1998. Shortly after completion of the deal, Eaton merged the Westinghouse business into its Cutler-Hammer unit, in the process closing eight plants and warehouses and laying off 1,200 employees. The Westinghouse deal was a significant force behind a 37 percent increase in revenues in 1994, to $6.05 billion.

During 1995 Butler retired after 38 years with the company. Stephen R. Hardis, vice-chairman and CFO since 1986, was named CEO and chairman. Alexander M. Cutler, a strong operations executive who had run the controls group since 1989 and who had joined the company when Cutler-Hammer was acquired in 1978, was named president and chief operating officer. Also that year, Eaton bought the IKU Group, a Dutch maker of automotive mirror controls, and Emwest Products, a manufacturer of electrical switch gear and controls based in Australia. In an example of the company's increasing shift to high-tech business lines—and as a reflection of a 50 percent increase in R&D spending that Hardis enacted—Eaton introduced the VORAD Safety System, a radar unit designed to provide visual and audible warnings to truck drivers if they are too close to a vehicle ahead.

Continuing to seek strategic acquisitions and grow overseas, Eaton spent $135 million in March 1996 for CAPCO Automotive Products, a Brazilian producer of manual transmissions for medium trucks. Brazil was one of five countries the company was targeting for foreign growth, the others being China, India, Mexico, and South Korea. Building its semiconductor business, through which Eaton had a dominant position in the market for ion implanters, used to produce memory chips, the company in July 1997 acquired Fusion Systems Corp., a maker of semiconductor equipment based in Rockville, Maryland, for about $293 million. Eaton also continued to divest operations in which it did not hold clear leadership positions. Late in 1997, for example, its appliance controls business was sold to Siebe plc for $310 million. Eaton also finally unloaded the noncore AIL defense electronics business, selling a majority of its stock to AIL's management and an AIL employee stock ownership plan. Then, in a historic move, Eaton engineered a swap of businesses with Dana Corporation in January 1998 that involved Eaton's founding business. Eaton sold its truck axle and brake business to Dana for $287 million, while simultaneously buying Dana's clutch business for $180 million, gaining a business that meshed well with Eaton's truck transmission product line.

In April 1999, in its biggest acquisition yet, Eaton paid $1.7 billion in cash for Aeroquip-Vickers, Inc., a producer of industrial hydraulic equipment based in Maumee, Ohio. Aeroquip-Vickers produced hydraulic pumps, cylinders, motors, and drives as well as fittings and hoses for industrial, aerospace, and automotive markets. Its revenues for 1998 were $2.15 billion. The deal made Eaton the number two player in the hydraulic equipment market, trailing only Parker Hannifin Corporation. To finance the acquisition, Eaton subsequently sold off several operations, some of which had come to the company through Aeroquip-Vickers: Eaton's engineered fasteners business, to TransTechnology Corp.; its fluid power division, producer of engine cooling systems for cars and trucks, to Borg-Warner Automotive, Inc.; its Vickers electronic systems division, to Siemens Energy and Automation, Inc.; and its mobile hydraulic cylinder business, to Hyco International, Inc. Eaton also reorganized its operations into five segments: automotive components, fluid power and other components, industrial and commercial controls, semiconductor equipment, and truck components. Eaton enjoyed its best year ever in 1999, posting net income of $617 million on revenues of $8.4 billion.

Continuing to Evolve in the Early 21st Century

Having thoroughly overhauled both the operations and the management ranks—59 of the top 73 positions at the company were filled by new people, half outsiders, since 1995—Hardis retired in July 2000. Taking over as chairman, president, and CEO was Cutler. The new leader oversaw the separation of the semiconductor equipment business. This unit was taken public as Axcelis Technologies, Inc. in July 2000 through an initial public offering of 18 percent of its stock. Eaton then spun off its remaining 82 percent interest to shareholders in December of that year. Proceeds from the IPO were used to pay down debt, which stood at approximately $3 billion early in 2000.

Over the next few years, with the economic downturn providing a particularly difficult environment for industrial manufacturers, Eaton managed to consistently beat the expectations of Wall Street and remain profitable, culminating in 2003 in net income of $386 million on sales of $8.06 billion. The balance sheet improved significantly as total debt was reduced to less than $2 billion. In addition, the company completed several smaller, "fill-in" acquisitions as well as the divestment of a number of nonproductive businesses.

In March 2001 Eaton purchased Sumitomo Heavy Industries, Ltd.'s 50 percent interest in the two companies' fluid-power joint venture in Japan, which was subsequently renamed Eaton Fluid Power Limited. One month later, Eaton sold its vehicle-switch and electronics division to Delphi Automotive Systems Corp. for $300 million. Eaton next sold its Navy Controls unit, maker of shipboard integrated electrical power distribution and control systems for the Navy, to DRS Technologies, Inc. in July 2002 for $92.2 million. In November 2002 the company bought the Boston Weatherhead division of Dana Corp. for $130 million. This division produced hose, tubing, and fluid connectors for fluid power systems mainly for the industrial distribution, mobile off-highway, and heavy-duty truck markets. In January 2003 Eaton acquired the electrical division of Delta plc for $215 million. Headquartered in the United Kingdom with operations in Europe and the Asia-Pacific region, the acquired division specialized in electrical products, systems, and services used for the control and distribution of medium- and low-voltage electricity to protect life, equipment, and buildings. The division's brands included MEM, Holec, Bill, Home Automation, Elek, and Tabula. Also in 2003 the industrial and commercial control business along with the Cutler-Hammer unit were renamed Eaton Electrical Inc. In June 2004 Eaton acquired Powerware Corporation, the power systems business of Invensys plc, for $560 million. Based in Raleigh, North Carolina, Powerware was a global leader in uninterruptible power systems (UPS) and other devices and services for protecting factories and offices from power surges and power interruptions. With ten plants and more than 100 locations worldwide, Powerware had revenues of $775 million for the fiscal year ending in March 2004. Eaton also bolstered its fluid power business by acquiring Walterscheid Rohrverbindungstechnik GmbH, a German manufacturer of hydraulic tube connectors and fittings, from GKN plc in September 2004 for $48 million.

Principal Subsidiaries

Eaton MDH Co. Inc.; Aeroquip International Inc.; Eaton Electrical Inc.; Eaton Hydraulics Inc.; Eaton International Corporation; Integrated Partial Discharge Diagnostics, Inc.; Modern Molded Products, Inc.; Vickers International Inc.; CAPCO Automotive Products Corporation; Eaton Aeroquip Inc.; Eaton Inoac Company; G.T. Products, Inc.; Powerware Corporation; Aeroquip-Vickers, Inc.; Eaton Electrical IDT Inc.; Eaton Leasing Corporation; U.S. Engine Valve; Eaton Pty. Ltd. (Australia); Eaton Holding G.m.b.H. (Austria); Eaton Holec Componenten N.V. (Belgium); Eaton Ltda. (Brazil); Aeroquip-Vickers Canada Inc.; Eaton Yale Ltd. (Canada); Eaton China Investments Co., Ltd. (China); Eaton Truck & Bus Components Company (Shanghai) Co. Ltd. (China); Eaton Fluid Power (Jining) Co. Ltd. (China); Eaton Fluid Power (Shanghai) Co. Ltd. (China); Shanghai Eaton Engine Components Company, Ltd. (China); Zhenjiang Holec Electrical Systems Company Limited (China); Eaton Industries s.r.o. (Czech Republic);

Eaton Holec, AS (Denmark); Eaton Holec, OY (Finland); Eaton S.A. (France); Eaton Technologies S.A. (France); Eaton Automotive G.m.b.H. (Germany); Eaton G.m.b.H. & Co. K.G. (Germany); Eaton Fluid Power G.m.b.H. (Germany); Eaton Holding G.m.b.H. (Germany); Walterscheid Rohrverbindungstechnik GmbH (Germany); Eaton Electric & Engineering Services, Limited (Hong Kong); Eaton Limited (Hong Kong); Eaton Industries Private Ltd. (India); Eaton Automotive Ltd. (Ireland); Eaton Automotive Srl (Italy); Eaton Srl (Italy); Eaton Fluid Power Srl (Italy); Eaton Fluid Power Limited (Japan); Eaton Japan Co., Ltd.; Eaton Holding S.a r.l. (Luxembourg); Eaton Electric Switchgear Sdn. Bhd. (Malaysia); Eaton Electrical Mexicana, S.A. (Mexico); Eaton Controls, S. de R.L. de C.V. (Mexico); Eaton Finance, S. de R.L. de C.V. (Mexico); Eaton Industries S. de R.L. de C.V. (Mexico); Eaton Molded Products S. de R.L. de C.V. (Mexico); Eaton Truck Components, S. de R.L. de C.V. (Mexico); Eaton Automotive B.V. (Netherlands); Eaton B.V. (Netherlands); Eaton International B.V. (Netherlands); Vickers Systems Limited (New Zealand); Eaton Automotive Spolka z o.o. (Poland); Eaton Truck Components S.A. (Poland); Eaton Electric Switchgear (Asia Pacific) Pte. Ltd. (Singapore); Eaton Truck Components (Pty.) Limited (South Africa); Eaton Automotive Controls Limited (South Korea); Eaton Limited (South Korea); Eaton S.L. (Spain); Eaton Holec, AB (Sweden); Eaton Industries G.m.b.H. (Switzerland); Eaton SA (Switzerland); Rubberon Technology Corporation Limited (Thailand); Eaton Electric Limited (U.K.); Eaton Limited (U.K.); Cutler-Hammer de Venezuela S.A.

Principal Operating Units

Fluid Power Group; Electrical Group; Automotive Group; Truck Group.

Principal Competitors

Johnson Controls, Inc.; Parker Hannifin Corporation; Emerson Electric Co.; ITT Industries, Inc.; Siemens AG; Rockwell Automation, Inc.; General Electric Company.

Further Reading

Aeppel, Timothy, "Eaton to Pay $1.7 Billion for Aeroquip," *Wall Street Journal,* February 2, 1999, p. A3.

Bergstrom, Robin Yale, "Eaton: The Next Level," *Automotive Production,* May 1996, pp. 70–71.

Cochran, Thomas N., "Rusty No More: Eaton Corp. Shifts into New Businesses and New Products," *Barron's,* July 8, 1996, pp. 23–24.

"Eaton: Poised for Profits from Its Shift to High Technology," *Business Week,* June 8, 1981, pp. 133+.

"Eaton: Spinning Its Wheels on the Road to High-Tech Profits," *Business Week,* March 28, 1983, p. 132.

Gerdel, Thomas W., "Controlling Its Destiny: Eaton Takes Big Bite with Westinghouse Deal," *Cleveland Plain Dealer,* November 14, 1993, p. 1E.

——, "Cultivating Success: Eaton Corp. Enjoys Bounty of Seeds Planted Years Ago," *Cleveland Plain Dealer,* June 23, 1995, p. 2E.

——, "Eaton Buys Powerware for $560 Million," *Cleveland Plain Dealer,* April 28, 2004, p. C1.

——, "Eaton Plans $1.1 Billion Acquisition," *Cleveland Plain Dealer,* August 12, 1993, p. 1A.

——, "Eaton's New CEO Values Team Play: Cutler Will Continue to Streamline Efforts, Seek Diversification," *Cleveland Plain Dealer,* April 28, 2000, p. 1C.

——, "Eaton to Buy Manufacturer for $1.7 Billion," *Cleveland Plain Dealer,* February 2, 1999, p. 1C.

——, "Taking a High-Tech Turn: Eaton Corp. Is Pursuing New Business in New Ways," *Cleveland Plain Dealer,* October 19, 1997, p. 1H.

Gold, Howard, "Eaton Redux," *Forbes,* June 3, 1985, pp. 166+.

History of Eaton Corporation, 1911–1985, Cleveland: Eaton, [1985 or 1986], 94 p.

Hussey, Allan F., "Profitable Overhaul: A Slimmer Eaton Moves into High-Growth Fields," *Barron's,* September 3, 1984, pp. 39+.

Illingworth, Montieth M., "Road to Recovery: Eaton's Drive to Cut Costs Begins to Pay Off," *Barron's,* August 15, 1983, pp. 11+.

Lewis, Morgan, Jr., "Change Maker: At Only 53, Eaton Corp. CEO Alexander 'Sandy' Cutler Has Distinguished Himself As One of the Region's Foremost Business and Civic Leaders—and He's Just Getting Started," *Inside Business,* October 2004, pp. 86+.

Ludvigsen, E.L., *Eaton Yale & Towne: A Corporate Portrait,* New York: Newcomen Society in North America, 1968, 20 p.

Machan, Dyan, "Don't Clutch," *Forbes,* June 21, 1993, p. 46.

——, "Down and Dirty," *Forbes,* May 11, 1992, p. 66.

Norton, Erle, "Westinghouse Plans to Sell Unit to Eaton Corp.," *Wall Street Journal,* August 12, 1993, p. A3.

Phillips, Stephen, "Eaton Sees Its Future—and It's on the Ground," *Business Week,* November 16, 1987, pp. 113+.

Sherefkin, Robert, "Hardis Handing over Top Spot," *Crain's Cleveland Business,* June 26, 2000, p. 35.

Stern, Andrew, "Eaton: Keep on Truckin'?," *Financial World,* September 14, 1993, p. 16.

Stevens, Tim, "Growth by Innovation," *Industry Week,* December 16, 1996, pp. 73–74+.

Upbin, Bruce, "Power Trains Made Sexy," *Forbes,* August 9, 1999, pp. 62, 64–65.

Verespej, Michael A., "Eaton Corp.," *Industry Week,* June 7, 1999, p. 34.

——, "Unfazed by the Challenge: Eaton Corp.," *Industry Week,* July 21, 1986, pp. 47–48.

Whitney, Allison A., "Eaton AIL Settles DOD Probe: Agrees to Pay $9.5 Million," *Manufacturing Week,* March 7, 1988, pp. 12–13.

—updates: April Dougal Gasbarre, David E. Salamie

eBay Inc.

2005 Hamilton Ave., Suite 204
San Jose, California 95125
U.S.A.
Telephone: (408) 558-7400
Fax: (408) 558-7401
Web site: http://www.ebay.com

Public Company
Incorporated: 1996
Employees: 6,200
Sales: $2.17 billion (2003)
Stock Exchanges: NASDAQ
Ticker Symbol: EBAY
NAIC: 453998 Other Miscellaneous Store Retailers

Millions of buyers and sellers have made eBay Inc. the world's largest and most popular Internet site for individuals and businesses to exchange goods. By 1999 eBay had 5.6 million registered users and listed over 3.1 million items for sale; by 2004 there were an estimated 65 million registered users from 150 countries, 971 million items for sale, and gross merchandise sales hit $15 billion. eBay owns local sites in 19 countries, has stakes in another eight foreign nations, and provides users with its own online pay service, PayPal Inc. As eBay's revenues continue to grow, the sky seems the limit despite competition from Yahoo!, Amazon.com, and an ever increasing number of imitators.

Looking for Pez Dispensers: 1995–96

Paris-born Pierre Omidyar, who immigrated with his family to the United States when he was six, graduated from Tufts University in 1988 with a degree in computer science. While at Tufts, Omidyar met his future wife, Pam, who had an unusual hobby: she collected and traded Pez candy dispensers. When Pam complained it was hard to find people with similar interests, Omidyar decided to create a small online auction service. AuctionWeb was launched Labor Day weekend in 1995. Set up as a sole proprietorship in San Jose, California, the online bazaar was considered a ''grand experiment'' by its creator.

Little did he know the impact his brainchild would have on the Internet, auctions, and corporate history.

At the time he launched AuctionWeb, Omidyar was working at the General Magic Corporation as a software developer. His background included cofounding Ink Development Corp., which became eShop, a pioneer of online shopping before it was bought by Microsoft. Omidyar also developed consumer applications for Claris, a subsidiary of Apple Computer, and had even written a software program for his high school library at the age of 14.

For the first five months of AuctionWeb's existence, Omidyar offered the new service for free, building a base of buyers and sellers through word of mouth. In May 1996 he incorporated eBay (which stood for ''electronic Bay Area''), becoming its chief executive and quit his day job. By the end of 1996 the company had six employees, including Jerry Skoll, eBay's original president.

The Concept

Prior to AuctionWeb, online auctions were either business-to-business or business-to-consumer. There was nothing comparable to Omidyar's concept either online or offline; flea markets and yard sales were the most similar kind of person-to-person interaction offered by the precursor of eBay. Unlike traditional auctions, there was no auctioneer. At AuctionWeb sellers posted information about their items, and buyers were able to browse the site and submit bids by electronic mail (e-mail). The actual auction for an item was held over three to four days, with bidders receiving e-mail notices when someone made a higher bid. They could then counter the bid or drop out. The winning bidder made arrangements with the seller for payment and shipping.

eBay served the role of a broker; the firm did not own any of the items being sold and was not responsible for distribution. Bidding was free, but it did cost between 25 cents and $2 to list an item for sale, plus a commission of between 2.5 and 5 percent of the sale price. The site was profitable almost from the beginning, unlike the vast majority of e-commerce sites. Much of the site's success appeared due to Omidyar's sense of what people

Company Perspectives:

eBay is The World's Online Marketplace. Founded in 1995, eBay created a powerful platform for the sale of goods and services by a passionate community of individuals and businesses. On any given day, there are millions of items across thousands of categories for sale on eBay. eBay enables trade on a local, national and international basis with customized sites in markets around the world. Through an array of services, such as its payment solution provider PayPal, eBay is enabling global e-commerce for an ever-growing online community.

wanted: a simple, central location to buy and sell items, and the ability to talk with (and perhaps eventually meet) people with similar interests. From the beginning, eBay's auction service sought to create the sense of an old-fashioned marketplace and encouraged communication between hobbyists and collectors.

During 1996 the site hosted more than 250,000 auctions in some 60 categories including Beanie Babies, stamps, coins, and computers. By the end of the year it was overseeing about 15,000 simultaneous auctions daily, with 2,000 of them new each day. The site received over two million hits a week, and the amount of money exchanged for goods sold exceeded $6 million for the year.

Fighting Fraud: 1997

The site's popularity continued to increase and in the first quarter of 1997 AuctionWeb saw over 330,000 completed auctions, with the total transaction value of goods sold worth more than $10.25 million. Among these items was an original 1959 "Suburban Shopper" Barbie doll, which sold for $7,999. In a May 1997 press release, eBay President Jerry Skoll stated that the growth "clearly demonstrates the receptivity and the eagerness of the general public to participate in online commerce. Our goal is to provide a fun, efficient, and reliable forum for both buyers and sellers."

Omidyar and Skoll decided the company needed venture capital and a more experienced management team. In mid-1997 Benchmark Capital, a venture capital firm in Menlo Park, California, put $5 million into the company to acquire a 22 percent stake. With their advice, the company began targeted advertising, renamed itself eBay in September, and launched a second-generation service with a redesigned site. By the end of the year the company had about 340,000 registered users and was hosting approximately 200,000 auctions at any given time. eBay had also established a relationship with America Online Inc. (AOL), and eBay became featured in AOL's Hobby and Classifieds prompts. A year later, in 1998, eBay became the exclusive auctioneer in the Classifieds area, paying AOL a guaranteed $12 million over three years.

Internet fraud soon became a growing concern, with buyers paying for goods that were never delivered. In November 1997 the U.S. Senate's Permanent Subcommittee on Investigations conducted hearings into Internet commerce. The National Consumers League found fraud reports had tripled after it created its

Internet Fraud Watch project in March 1996. In addition to false promises for discounted services and charges for Internet services that were supposed to be free, people were experiencing problems at auction sites such as eBay as well. Between January and October 1997, Internet Fraud Watch received 141 complaints about auction sites. As Susan Grant of the National Consumers League told *Internet World*, "The problem basically is that auction sites really don't take responsibility for the sales if they go bad. They merely put the buyer together with the seller."

In the same article, eBay reported it had only 27 disputes from over one million transactions between May and August 1997. To keep such disputes to a minimum, eBay instituted a feedback system for buyers to post reviews of their transactions. Sellers were then given a rating based on the number of their successful auctions: positive comments received one point, neutral responses a zero, and negative comments a minus one. Potential buyers were able to read the comments as well as view the rating. A rating of minus four (−4) resulted in a seller being denied use of the service.

Major Growth and Change: 1998

eBay grew phenomenally, recording gross merchandise sales of $100 million and revenues of $6 million in the first quarter of 1998. The first quarter had become the company's best, as eBay promoted the auctioning off of unwanted Christmas gifts.

Some competition, however, was beginning to develop. Late 1997 saw the business-to-business auction service OnSale Inc. add person-to-person auctions and the launch of Auction Universe Inc., a web auction firm owned by *Los Angeles Times* parent Times Mirror Company. During 1998 Auction Universe began providing city-oriented auction sites through a group of affiliated newspapers, each offering its own local auction site (but run by Auction Universe). Such web sites, aimed primarily at the newspapers' local areas, made it easier to auction large items, since it was expensive to ship a used car or a large piece of furniture across the country. It also offered newspapers a way to regain revenues lost when classified ads became too expensive for low cost items.

eBay bought Jump, Inc., the developer and operator of Up4Sale, an advertising-supported trading/auction site, launched in 1997. Planning to use Up4Sale to introduce complementary future services, eBay operated the site as a separate service. In May, Meg Whitman was appointed president and CEO of eBay, with Pierre Omidyar becoming chairman. Whitman came from Hasbro Inc.'s preschool division, where she had been general manager. She had previously headed FTD Inc., where she launched its web site and oversaw the transition of the organization from a network of individual florists to a private company. Known for her experience in managing and marketing consumer brands, including Teletubbies and Playskool, Whitman concentrated on raising eBay's profile through increased advertising aimed at hobbyists and groups of collectors.

At the time Whitman came on board, eBay claimed more than 950,000 registered users, hosted more than two million auctions a month in 846 categories, and had a success rate of more than 70 percent (offered items actually being sold). Whit-

Key Dates:

1995: Pierre Omidyar launches AuctionWeb.
1996: Omidyar incorporates the company as eBay Inc. in San Jose, California.
1998: eBay gets a new chief executive, reincorporates in Delaware, and goes public.
1999: The "Great Collections" auction site is launched for high ticket items.
2000: Firm buys into AutoTrader.com and brings Japan, Canada, and Austria into the fold.
2001: Registered users reach nearly 43 million.
2002: eBay revenues top the $1 billion mark.
2003: Revenues climb to a remarkable $2.17 billion.
2004: eBay buys three international dot.coms and a stake in classified ads provider craigslist.
2005: eBay auctions are available in 46,000 merchandise categories worldwide.

man and Omidyar reincorporated eBay in Delaware in September 1998 and took the company public, watching the price of their stock triple within a few days. Among those selling shares in the $63 million initial public offering was the eBay Foundation, established by eBay several months before the initial public offering (IPO) with a grant of 100,000 shares.

According to the Community Foundation Silicon Valley, which administered the foundation, this was the first time a company had launched a charitable fund with pre-IPO stock. "It is fairly unusual, [and] it's a fairly effective way to do it because it doesn't cost them much," a Community Foundation official told the *Business Journal-San Jose*. The eBay Foundation sold just over 10,000 shares at the IPO, generating cash to make grants.

At the end of 1998 eBay was hosting nearly 1.8 million auctions and reported a profit of $2.4 million on revenues of $47.4 million, making it one of the few Internet retailers to return solid profits. At the same time, its growth and popularity were putting the spotlight on the company and user expectations became more sophisticated.

Ups and Downs: 1999

The first quarter of 1999 was again record-setting, with gross merchandise sales of $541 million and net revenues of $34 million. During the quarter eBay stopped selling guns and ammunition on its site, announced a second public offering, a four-year $75 million marketing alliance with AOL, and a 3-for-1 stock split. The day before the secondary offering, Amazon.com, the Web's leading "e-tailer," began hosting its own daily auctions.

In May the company made three acquisitions. Both Butterfield, a 135-year-old San Francisco auction house, and Kruse International, an automobile auctioneer in Indiana known for collector cars, helped eBay move into a higher-priced market. The third purchase, Billpoint Inc., was a California company specializing in credit card payments over the Internet. Sellers on eBay could now use Billpoint to instantly accept credit cards and buyers would be able to receive reference reports listing all

their transactions. The company issued $275 million in common stock to finance the purchases.

Moving overseas, eBay next entered a joint venture with Australia-based PBL Online. In addition, to provide its members with more news and information about their collectibles, eBay signed an agreement with the Collecting Channel to provide "content" on the site. The first offering was information about Star Wars memorabilia.

In June 1999, however, eBay was shaken as its web site experienced numerous crashes. The company was a few days away from completing installation of a backup system when outages began, including one lasting 22 hours. eBay refunded from $3 to $5 million in waived listing fees, conducted free auctions, and moved to hire more computer network experts and senior technology managers. As other big Internet companies such as AOL and E*Trade had learned, site reliability was a critical factor in retaining customer loyalty. Competitors such as Amazon.com and Auction Universe reported increased traffic at their sites as a result of eBay's problems.

Within days of the outages, however, eBay gave journalists something else to write about: global expansion. It moved into Europe with the acquisition of Alando de AG, Germany's largest online trading site, and considered adding a Japanese-language corner to provide support for its 6,500 members in Japan. Yahoo, however, beat eBay to the punch and launched its own site in September 1999, a full five months before eBay officially added its Japanese site. This delay would prove a pivotal mistake in eBay's plans for global expansion.

Competition also moved to the high end of the auction market as 1999 drew to a close. Amazon.com, which had acquired a minority stake in Sotheby's Holding Inc., paired up with its new partner to launch a joint auction site. Christie's International indicated it would soon be adding an interactive section to its web site, and smaller companies handling decorative and fine art or antiques were also going online. Behind all the action was the tremendous potential for sales. Experts predicted the online auction field would grow to 17.5 million registered buyers and sales of $15.5 billion by 2001, up from 1.5 millions users and $1.5 billion in sales in 1998.

eBay had already recognized the opportunity to use online auctions for high-priced items, but noted such offerings needed to be presented in a different manner. After acquiring Butterfield and Butterfield, the world's third largest auction house for over $250 million, the company began structuring such a site. Great Collections (later renamed eBay Premier) was launched in October 1999, with partnering auction houses, galleries, and dealers having their own branded areas and offering the same authentication services they did in their brick-and-mortar locations.

A New Century, a New Frontier: 2000–01

By the new millennium eBay had become the Internet's top auction site with ten million registered users, selling around $10 million of merchandise a day. In the week of January 9, eBay set a new record for attracting just under 1.8 million users that week, prompting CEO Whitman to tell *DSN Retailing Today* (May 8, 2000): "Our unique community of passionate buyers and sellers continue to take eBay to new heights."

Some of the firm's more creative users, however, had learned how to rig bids and outcomes; buyers teamed up with bidding partners, while sellers had buddies submitting fake high bids. eBay, however, was not terribly concerned since by 2000 fraud occurred only once in every 25,000 transactions according to company spokesperson Kevin Pursglove. This was due in part to measures taken two years before when the subject of fraud was addressed by CEO Whitman and eBay's board. Though founder and Chairman Omidyar feared tighter controls might alienate some of eBay's diehard users, several measures had been implemented including the ban on weapons, placing adult-themed items in a secure area, offering buyers insurance from the esteemed Lloyds of London, and allowing sellers a discounted rate at Equifax to run credit checks.

The biggest news of early 2000 was not security but the possible merger between eBay and mega-portal Yahoo. Both firms owned pay-online businesses (Yahoo bought Arthas.com and eBay had acquired Billpoint.com) and each brought clout to the bargaining table: Yahoo had a customer base of 120 million users, while eBay had already established itself as the premier online auction house. Talks, however, fell apart.

In mid-2000 eBay bought the Philadelphia-based Half.com, an auction site specializing in used goods, for $312 million. Half.com, which sold used goods for half their original retail price, already had four million registered users and earned 15 percent on every sale. While eBay finalized its acquisition of Half.com, its chairman founded the Omidyar Foundation to donate $20 million annually to worthy causes.

While eBay Chairman Omidyar spent time in Paris working on eBay's international expansion, Whitman continued to expand the company's domestic operations. At the end of 2000 a new service called BusinessExchange, a business-to-business marketplace for small companies to buy office products and equipment, was launched by eBay to maintain its lead as the world's top online auctioneer. According to Forrester Research, an Internet market research firm, eBay controlled 85 percent of the online auction action, which Forrester estimated would top $3.3 billion for the year (*Fortune*, June 26, 2000).

In January 2001 eBay suffered another outage, this time a crash lasting for 11 hours. While the company blamed the crash on a series of "glitches," IT analysts believed eBay's Sun Microsystems hardware and Oracle software were no longer up to the task of handling millions of transactions a day. The company denied such reports, claiming confidence in its systems. With eBay's difficulties, minor as they were, competitors were still unable to topple its reign. Yahoo, which had gained considerable ground and was the Web's third most visited firm, lost the majority of its online auction clients after starting to charge fees in the first quarter of 2001.

Not waiting for Yahoo to regain its footing, eBay inked a deal with Microsoft, the Internet's second most visited firm behind AOL, to be featured on a myriad of its web sites and to serve as its default auction provider. With online auctions growing at an exponential rate, eBay was determined to hang on to the lion's share of what Forrester Research claimed would rise to $6.4 billion in sales by 2003.

As 2001 ended, eBay earned the top slot on the Deloitte & Touche Technology Fast 500 as the fastest-growing technology company in North America, based on an average of its revenue growth over a five-year period. For the years in question, eBay had gone from $372,000 in 1996 to an astounding $431 million in revenues for 2000, with nearly 30 million registered users. Better yet were eBay's figures for the year 2001: revenues topped $748 million and registered users had climbed to more than 40 million.

Staving Off Competition: 2002 and Beyond

In early 2002 eBay signed an agreement with Priceline.com to dabble in the travel and leisure market, for which the company's 42 million registered users had already shown a keen interest. Next came a partnership with Sotheby's to market high-end collectibles. The new Sotheby's site would supersede both eBay's Premier site and Sotheby's own online auction site. Both the Priceline.com and Sotheby's deals spearheaded new frontiers, as eBay struggled with overseas competition. Rival Yahoo had gained control of Japan's lucrative online auctions, the globe's second largest online auction marketplace.

Yahoo's dominance was a stinging reminder of entering the Asian market with too little too late. Yahoo controlled 95 percent of the market by 2002 and eBay's dismal performance affected its hopes for worldwide dominion. Despite its problems in Japan, however, eBay remained the leading online auctioneer in Australia, Canada, Germany, and the United Kingdom and its year-end figures reflected its status as revenues topped the billion-dollar mark for the first time, reaching $1.1 billion on total auction sales of some $15 billion for 2002.

eBay's CEO Meg Whitman made news in early 2003 by following in the footsteps of Pierre and Pam Omidyar. Whitman donated $30 million to her alma mater, Princeton University, where she had graduated with a degree in economics in 1977. Whitman's contribution was earmarked for the New Jersey school's campus expansion and to increase student enrollment over the next ten years. On the corporate front, eBay paid a reported $1.5 billion for the Internet's premier online-pay service, PayPal, to replace its own Billpoint service. Both Billpoint and PayPal's online gambling service were phased out after the purchase.

As 2003 wound down, eBay still dominated the world's online auctions with close to 63 million registered users, revenues hitting $2.17 billion, and net income reaching $442 million. In 2004 the firm went on an acquisitions spree, buying Germany's mobile.de, India's Baazee.com, Korea's Internet Auction Company, Ltd., and a stake in online classifieds forum craigslist. Though eBay retained its status as the planet's favorite online auction host, the company had learned from its mistakes: Kruse International and Butterfields were sold; it withdrew from the Japanese market; Half.com was phased out; and Billpoint was shuttered in favor of PayPal. Despite or because of these missteps, eBay refocused on what it did best: providing a comfortable and competitive environment for online buyers and sellers in an ever increasing range of auctions.

Principal Subsidiaries

Baazee.com; Eachnet. Inc.; Internet Auction Company, Ltd.; MercadoLibre.com; mobile.de; PayPal Inc.

Principal Competitors

Amazon.com; Auction Universe; First Auction; OnSale Inc.; uBid.com; Yahoo.com.

Further Reading

Alexander, Steve, "Digital Auction," *Star Tribune* (Minneapolis), March 1, 1998, p. 1D.

Anders, George, "Customers' Loyalty Tested As eBay Repairs System," *South Bend Tribune,* June 21, 1999, p. C7.

——, "Nation's Latest Cybermogul Got the Bidding Started Online," *Orange County Register,* September 27, 1998, p. 22.

Avery, Simon, "AOL, eBay in $75M Marketing Alliance," *National Post,* March 26, 1999, p. C8.

Barmann, Timothy, "eBay Manages to Thrive As Other Internet Startups Drop Like Flies," *Knight-Ridder/Tribune Business News,* November 11, 2002.

Buel, Stephen, "Amazon.com to Challenge eBay for Online Auction Market," *San Jose Mercury News,* March 30, 1999.

Bedell, Doug, "eBay Is a Social Phenomenon As Well As a Trailblazing Auction Site," *Knight-Ridder/Tribune Business News,* December 5, 2000.

——, "Online Trader eBay Feeling Growing Pains," *San Jose Mercury News,* December 29, 1998.

Carrell, Paul, "eBay Buys German Online Trader," *National Post,* June 23, 1999, p. C11.

"The eBay Economy," *Business Week,* August 25, 2003, p. 124.

"eBay's AuctionWeb Completes Record $10 Million in Auctions," *Business Wire,* May 1, 1997.

"eBay's AuctionWeb Tops One Million Bids," *Business Wire,* December 12, 1996.

"eBay Leads Top 500 Tech List," *United Press International,* November 16, 2001.

"eBay's CEO Meg Whitman," *Investor's Business Daily,* March 24, 2000, p. A04.

"eBay to Buy Out PayPal," *Electronic Payments International,* July 2002, p. 1.

Evangelista, Benny, "New eBay Site Auctions High-Ticket Items," *San Francisco Chronicle,* October 20, 1999, p. C2.

Gaw, Jonathan, "Nearly Daylong Outage Plagues Online Auction House eBay," *Los Angeles Times,* June 12, 1999, p. C1.

"Going, Going, Gone—Sucker!," *Business Week Online,* March 20, 2000, p. 124.

Green, Heather, "Online Merchants—Cyberspace Winners: How They Did It," *Business Week,* June 22, 1998, p. 154.

Hardy, Quentin, "The Radical Philanthropist," *Forbes,* May 1, 2000, p. 114.

Heim, Kristi, and Joelle Tessler, "Rumors Abound Over Possible Merger of Yahoo, eBay," *Knight-Ridder/Tribune Business News,* March 24, 2000.

Hof, Robert D., "eBay Vs. Amazon.com," *Business Week,* May 31, 1999, p. 128.

——, and Peter Burrows, "Meet eBay's Auctioneer-in-Chief," *Business Week Online,* May 29, 2003.

"How Yahoo! Japan Beat eBay at Its Own Game," *Business Week,* June 4, 2001, p. 58.

Lashinsky, Adam, "Meg and The Machine: Unstoppable eBay . . . ," *Fortune,* September 1, 2003, p. 68

"Meg Whitman: eBay," *Business Week,* May 31, 1999, p. 134.

Murphy, Kathleen, "Fraud Follows Buyers onto Web," *Internet World,* October 20, 1997.

"Net Auctioneer eBay Names Hasbro GM As President and CEO," *Network Briefing,* May 8, 1998.

O'Brien, Chris, "eBay Buys Half.com," *Knight-Ridder/Tribune Business News,* June 14, 2000.

"Online Buying Could Top $51 Billion This Year," *Investor's Business Daily,* January 3, 2003, p. A04.

Razzi, Elizabeth, "Auction Fever," *Kiplinger's Personal Finance,* May 2000, p. 114.

Roth, Daniel, "Meet eBay's Worst Nightmare," *Fortune,* June 26, 2000, p. 1299

Scally, Robert, "The Auction Network Making a Bid for Online Dominance," *DSN Retailing Today,* May 8, 2000, p. 64

Smith, Rebecca, "eBay, Butterfield Make a Bid for the Bourgeoisie," *San Francisco Chronicle,* June 28, 1999, p. E1.

"U.S. Online Auctioneer Wooing Japanese Trade," *Nikkei Weekly,* June 28, 1999, p. 11.

Vierira, Paul, "Going, Going, Gone . . . Online," *National Post,* November 27, 1999, p. C7.

Wagner, Mitch, and Ted Kemp, "What's Wrong with eBay?," *InternetWeek,* January 1, 2001, p. 1.

—Ellen D. Wernick
—update: Nelson Rhodes

The Economist Group Ltd.

25 St. James's Street
London
SW1A 1HG
United Kingdom
Telephone: +44-20-7830-7000
Fax: +44-20-7839-2968
Web site: http://www.economist.com

Private Company (50% owned by The Financial Times Group/Pearson)
Incorporated: 1843
Employees: 942
Sales: £191 million ($342.7 million) (2004)
NAIC: 511110 Newspaper Publishers; 511120 Periodical Publishers; 519110 New Syndicates; 531190 Lessors of Other Real Estate Property; 541810 Advertising Agencies

The Economist Group Ltd. is the owner of the prestigious Economist brand. The group's flagship is the *Economist* weekly "newspaper." Published for more than 160 years, the *Economist* is one of the world's leading economic, news, and political opinion magazines, with a circulation of more than 900,000 in the early 2000s. Approximately one-third of the British-based group's sales come from the United States. Other members of the Economist brand family include the Economist Intelligence Unit (EIU), a provider of business information and analysis, covering more than 200 international markets; Economist Conferences, which hosts roundtable meetings, conferences, and similar events for government and corporate groups in 50 countries; as well as a range of ancillary products sold through the company's Economist Shop in London and online. The Economist brand family accounted for more than 83 percent of the company's total revenues of £191 million ($342 million) in 2004. Other brands within The Economist Group include CFO, with its 500,000-plus circulation *CFO* magazine, and its *CFO Asia* and *CFO Europe* editions, as well as the CFO.com web site and CFO Enterprises product group. The Economist Group also controls the Capitol Hill-oriented *Roll Call,* said to be the second most widely read newspaper in Washington, D.C., behind the *Washington Post.* Approximately 82 percent of *Roll Call's* circulation of more than 17,000 is distributed free to Congressional and Senate members and their staffs. The Economist Group also has launched a similar publication, *European Voice,* targeting the European Parliament. The Economist Group has been 50 percent-owned by the Pearson publishing group, through its Financial Times Group, since 1928. The other 50 percent is controlled by a trust, in turned owned by a range of shareholders, allowing the *Economist* to continue its long tradition of objective editorial independence.

Liberal Opinion Setter in the 19th Century

The *Economist* stemmed from the economic and political upheaval of the rapidly industrializing United Kingdom in the mid-19th century. As the country's population shifted from a predominantly rural agricultural base to the growing number of large industrial cities, the country's political base also began to shift. Long dominated by the country's wealthy landowners, who used the government to pass laws to protect their interests, the British Parliament came under pressure to adopt its economic policies to reflect the country's new industrial reality.

Among the most-hated of British legislation favoring the landholders were the Corn Laws. Initially drafted in 1804, the Corn Laws significantly raised the duties on corn imports, favoring the growth of the country's wheat crop. Related legislation was drafted in 1815, following the end of the Napoleonic Wars, restricting wheat imports as well. The legislation proved highly controversial and the government was forced to deploy troops to protect Parliament members.

The high wheat prices led to high bread prices, particularly in the country's growing urban sectors. The inflated prices also placed pressure on the country's manufacturers to increase wages for workers hit hard by the high bread prices. Into the late 1830s, a series of poor harvests further put pressure on the population, as bread prices soared.

The situation inspired the creation of the Anti-Corn Law League in 1837. The league was joined by Richard Cobden, who entered Parliament in 1841. As a member of Parliament, Cobden was able to lobby his fellow members for a repeal of the Corn Laws. In 1843, the Anti-Corn Law League found a new ally in James Wilson, a hat maker from Hawick, in Scotland. A dedicated believer in the principles of the free market system, Wilson decided to publish a newspaper directed at the country's business class. Wilson called his newspaper the *Economist,* to underscore the newspaper's commitment to publishing only verifiable fact.

Although a staunch backer of the Anti-Corn Law League, Wilson's aims went beyond that single cause. As he wrote in the newspaper's prospectus: "We seriously believe that free trade, free intercourse, will do more than any other visible agent to extend civilisation and morality throughout the world."

By then, the Anti-Corn Law League had grown into one of England's largest and wealthiest political organizations, and Wilson himself was a close ally of the movement. In return, the Anti-Corn Law League became the newspaper's earliest backer, guaranteeing a large percentage of the *Economist*'s initial circulation. Yet Wilson was careful to maintain the newspaper's independence.

The failure of the potato crop in 1845 and resulting widespread famine at last brought a repeal of the Corn Laws in 1846. If the Anti-Corn Law League no longer had a reason for existence, the independent editorial and financial policies of the *Economist* allowed it not only to continue publishing, but to become a prominent economic and political voice in the second half of the century.

Wilson himself remained editor of the newspaper until 1857. Ownership of the weekly nonetheless remained within the Wilson family, at first directly by the family, later through a trust, into the 1920s. The appointment of Walter Bagehot in 1861 marked a major milestone in the *Economist*'s history. Under Bagehot, the newspaper firmly established its reputation for editorial integrity and independence. The newspaper also developed many of its most long-lasting features, not the least of which was its principle of anonymity. Instead of attributing bylines, the *Economist* sought a collective voice, one in which the focus was placed on the words, and not on who wrote them. Nonetheless, many of the *Economist*'s writers enjoyed distinguished careers in government, journalism, and business.

Although specifically targeted at the British market, the *Economist* quickly became internationally recognized. Sales abroad, to Europe and to the United States, began as early as the late 1840s. The Economist Group's holdings also extended beyond its own title, with the addition of the *Bankers' Gazette* in 1845 and of *Railway Monitor*. The company continued to produce these titles through to the early 1930s. Another step

forward for the company was its decision to accept advertising in 1888. Yet for this, the newspaper limited itself to the smaller market for business notices such as company meetings.

New Ownership Structure in the 1920s

Walter Layton was appointed editor of the *Economist* in 1922, launching a new era of prestige for the newspaper. At that time, the *Economist* remained under the control of the trust established by the Wilson family. Layton led a policy of buying up shares in the company. Yet in that he was soon challenged by Brendan Backen, a later ally of, and minister of information under, Winston Churchill, who had acquired the rival *Financial News,* the precursor to the *Financial Times.*

After a lengthy battle for ownership of the newspaper, the two sides reached an agreement in 1928. Under the terms of that agreement, Backen gained control of 50 percent of the *Economist.* The other half was controlled by the *Economist*'s trust, which in turn was owned by a larger group of shareholders, including members of the *Economist* itself, as well as other prominent British financial figures. An important feature of the agreement was the guarantee that the *Economist* would remain editorially and financially independent.

The battle for control of the *Economist* drove up the group's value to all of £100,000 (the equivalent of just £4 million in the 2000s). This reflects the newspaper's rather restricted circulation: under Bagehot, the *Economist*'s circulation stood at less than 4,000. By 1920, the company's print run had only reached 6,000. Despite these small numbers, the *Economist* remained a highly influential voice. It was also consistently profitable, for the most part.

Financial News Leader in the Mid-to-Late 1900s

Layton was succeeded by Geoffrey Crowther, who became one of the most influential editors in the *Economist*'s history. Under Crowther, the *Economist* opened its pages more and more to foreign development, especially to the United States. By the late 1930s, half of the newspaper's circulation was being sent abroad. The company's international focus culminated in the launch of a new section, American Survey, dedicated to developments in the United States, in 1941.

Crowther also led a redesign of the newspaper into a more or less magazine format featuring a distinctive blue cover with the title in red. Yet the *Economist* continued to refer to itself as a newspaper—distinguishing itself from the rising number of news weeklies in the postwar era.

From 18,000 at the end of the war, the newspaper's circulation rose to more than 50,000 by the end of the 1950s. The year 1959 marked the introduction of a new and distinctive red logo. The following year, the *Economist* added full-color advertisements for the first time. The use of color remained limited, however, and the newspaper's first full-color cover appeared only in 1969. By then, the company also had built up a strong intelligence services component, called Economist Intelligence Unit (EIU), stemming from 1946.

Despite its somewhat stodgy appearance, the *Economist* steadily built up an international reputation—and readership.

Key Dates:

1843: James Wilson launches the *Economist,* in part to provide backing to the Anti-Corn Law League.

1888: The *Economist* begins accepting advertisements.

1928: An agreement to a 50–50 ownership structure between Economist Trust and *Financial News* (later *Financial Times*) is formed.

1941: A dedicated "American" section is launched as U.S. sales grow.

1946: The company launches its first intelligence activities, giving rise to the creation of the Economist Intelligence Unit.

1960: The first full-color advertisements are introduced.

1974: Circulation tops 100,000.

1987: A new "Asia" section is introduced.

1989: The company acquires *CFO* magazine in the United States.

1995: The company acquires *Journal of Commerce.*

2001: The company sells *Journal of Commerce*; a redesign of the magazine features full-color editorial content.

2004: The *Intelligent Life* glossy annual is launched.

Circulation topped 100,000 for the first time in 1974. Driving much of the newspaper's growth was its ability to impose itself in the United States as one of the most important sources of news and information on the world's business, financial, and political sectors. By the early 1990s, the *Economist* had extended its readership into Asia as well, leading to the launch of a specially dedicated Asia section in 1987.

By then, the *Economist* had developed a second brand family, buying up U.S.-based *CFO* magazine in 1989. That title, geared specifically to the interests of chief financial officers, became a strong seller for the company, rising to more than 500,000 by the end of the century.

In 1991, the company attempted a new expansion effort. In that year, The Economist Group launched the first new company-developed title in its history, *Treasury* magazine. Targeting the U.S. market's company treasurers, the new magazine launched with a circulation of 40,000. These were provided free of charge, with revenues generated by advertising. Yet *Treasury* proved a short-lived effort.

The *Economist* had long been solidly if unspectacularly profitable. The appointment of Marjorie Scardino as company CEO in 1992 introduced more momentum into the company's balance sheet. By the mid-1990s, the Economist's profit had jumped ahead some 130 percent—propelling Scardino herself into the CEO spot of Pearson, then, as owner of the *Financial Times,* holder of 50 percent of the *Economist.* Before she left, Scardino had engineered the company's biggest acquisition to date, that of U.S.-based *Journal of Commerce* (JoC). Paying $115 million, The Economist Group added the 168-year-old JoC and other titles, including *Florida Shipper, Gulf Shipper,* and *Traffic World,* as well as industry directories and other products.

Scardino was replaced by Helen Alexander as chief executive. The Economist Group now began a new drive to extend its range of titles, as well as its international scope. The company by then published *Roll Call,* a magazine produced specifically—and, in large part, provided free of charge—for the Washington political market. The Economist Group then launched a sister publication, *European Voice,* targeting the European Parliament. The company attempted to expand beyond print media, launching the short-lived Economist TV.

Changes in the 21st Century

A slump in the U.S. shipping market forced the company to reduce the JoC's printing schedule, converting it into a weekly. By the early 2000s, however, with its own profits sinking quickly, The Economist Group decided that the JoC no longer fit its strategic objectives. In 2001, the company sold off the JoC to Commonwealth Business Media, a company set up specifically for the acquisition.

That year marked a major redesign of the *Economist,* including, among other features, the addition of four-color editorial content. The company also began developing a new range of products and services under the *Economist* banner, including a web site offering access to its Economist Intelligence Unit content. In 2002, the company added to its portfolio again, launching *CFO Asia,* targeting the fast-growing Asian markets.

The early 2000s represented a difficult period for the company, as sales and profits dipped. In 2002, the company initiated a difficult restructuring effort, letting go some one-third of its employees in a bid to restore profit growth. This effort paid off, as profits once again began to climb, despite continued drops in sales. By 2004, sales were down to £191 million, from £272 million in 2001. Nonetheless, circulation continued to build, nearing the 900,000 mark.

The Economist Group continued to add to its range of titles and services. In June 2004, the company launched a new title, a glossy, consumer-oriented annual magazine called *Intelligent Life.* The magazine, although published just once per year, was meant to help broaden the group's appeal beyond its core readership, in particular by attracting more consumer and female readers. After more than 160 years, the *Economist* itself remained one of the few globally respected news titles.

Principal Subsidiaries

(Brands and Titles) CFO; CFO Asia; CFO Europe; European Voice; Roll Call; The Economist; The Economist Intelligence Unit; The Economist Enterprises; The Economist Conferences; The Economist Diaries.

Principal Competitors

Berkshire Hathaway Inc.; Bertelsmann AG; News Corporation Ltd.; Cox Enterprises Inc.; Quebecor Inc.; Pearson PLC; Gannett Company Inc.; ABC Inc.; Tribune Co.; VNU NV; Reed Elsevier PLC; Hearst Corporation; New York Times Co.

Further Reading

Aitken, Lucy, "The *Economist* Gets a Lifestyle with Annual Launch," *Campaign,* June 18, 2004, p. 21.

Burt, Tim, "Tough Cutbacks Lift *Economist,*" *Financial Times,* June 16, 2003, p. 25.

"The *Economist* Announces Global Redesign," *AsiaPulse News,* May 10, 2001.

"The Economist Group Launches New Magazine for China," *Business Publisher,* August 16, 2002, p. 2.

"Economist Intelligence Unit Sold to Executive Insight," *Business Publisher,* October 31, 2001, p. 6.

Edwards, Ruth, *The Pursuit of Reason: The Economist, 1843–1993,* London: Hamish Hamilton, 1993.

Gapper, John, "Restructuring at U.S. Unit Slows Economist," *Financial Times,* August 7, 1998, p. 21.

Mills, Dominic, "The *Economist:* An Expert's View," *Campaign,* May 18, 2001, p. 16.

O'Connor, Ashling, "Economist Sells JoC to US Group," *Financial Times,* August 29, 2001, p. 18.

Reece, Damian, "Economist Profits Plunge," *Sunday Telegraph,* August 4, 2002.

Trefgame, George, "International Growth Planned for Economist," *Daily Telegraph,* July 23, 2001.

—M.L. Cohen

EDGE PETROLEUM CORPORATION

Edge Petroleum Corporation

1301 Travis Suite 2000
Houston, Texas 77002
U.S.A.
Telephone: (713) 654-8960
Fax: (713) 654-7722
Web site: http://www.edgepet.com

Public Company
Founded: 1983
Employees: 35
Sales: $33.9 million (2003)
Stock Exchanges: NASDAQ
Ticker Symbol: EPEX
NAIC: 211111 Crude Petroleum and Natural Gas
    Extraction

Edge Petroleum Corporation is a Houston, Texas-based, publicly traded, independent energy company. Using 3-D seismic information and visualization software, it is engaged in the exploration, development, and production of oil and natural gas, concentrating its activities onshore in the Gulf of Mexico in south Texas and Louisiana, where the company has either options or leases on nearly 100,000 acres. Edge also works acreage in the northern Rocky Mountains in the states of Wyoming and Montana, and a 2003 acquisition has brought new properties in Michigan to evaluate. All told, Edge has proved reserves of some 64 million cubic feet of natural gas equivalent.

Early 1980s Foundation

Edge was founded by John E. Calaway in 1983. As a son of a successful independent Houston oilman, James C. Calaway, he grew up in the energy business. His parents also were interested in other areas, including the arts, and expected John and his twin brother, James D. Calaway, to earn college degrees. But after just a single semester, John quit school, eager to begin a career in oil exploration. After initially opposing the idea, the elder Calaway eventually relented and helped his son get a start in the industry. When John Calaway was still in his early 20s he was

able to line up investors to form an energy company that would act as a prospect generator using cutting-edge technology. Hence, Calaway chose the name Edge Petroleum when he founded his new company in 1983. In 1986 he became chief executive officer and chairman of the board.

Because the most readily available sources of oil and gas had long since been tapped out, energy companies operating in the United States had to drill much deeper wells. These "deep plays" were more expensive to develop and required the use of seismic surveys to locate prospects. The use of seismic instruments dates to the mid-1800s when they were used to measure ground movements during earthquakes. Early in the 20th century sound waves were used to detect icebergs and determine water depths, and during World War I became an effective way for the German army to determine the location of opposing artillery. In Oklahoma in the early 1920s John C. Karchner and colleagues developed reflection seismology, which used underground sound waves to map geological structures beneath the earth to locate likely oil and gas deposits. They formed a company known as Geophysical Service. Because such technology required computing power, the company became involved in calculators and computers and is better known as Texas Instruments.

During its first decade of operation Edge relied on 2-D seismic technology. Although more sophisticated 3-D seismic technology had been developed, it required the use of expensive computers that put it out of reach of all but the largest energy companies. Nevertheless, Edge was able to use the tools at hand to enjoy considerable drilling success, hitting on one out of every three attempts. As a result, Edge was able to remain viable during the mid-1980s when the industry was suffering through one of the worst periods in its history and many companies failed. Unlike most energy executives, John Calaway found a unique way to cope with the stress of these difficult times: art. Although not formally trained, Calaway grew into an accomplished painter and sculptor, whose work was bought by the likes of playwright Edward Albee and financier Feyez Sarofim. According to a 1990 *Business Month* profile, "His sculptures range from classic nude torsos to abstract bronze arcs. . . . His paintings are dark canvases overlaid with rich but often somber

Key Dates:

1983: The company is founded by John Calaway.
1992: The company switches to 3-D seismic technology.
1997: Edge goes public.
1998: John Elias succeeds John Calaway as CEO and chairman.
2003: Miller Exploration Company is acquired.

colors augmented by a pale, matte-textured substance—marble dust.'' Until he got married, Calaway found time to work in his studio seven days a week. During the workweek he spent his evenings there, from 5:30 to 11:00, and on Saturday and Sunday he spent his days in the studio. He told *Business Month,* ''During 1986, at the bottom of the bust, a lot of good people in this business were terribly depressed because we'd all run up against a brick wall, and there was nothing we could do about it. But I'd go down to my studio and get onto a big piece of stone with my chisel, and all my worries would fall away. The next morning, I'd walk into my office, and people would say, 'How can you be so up?' I was up because I had made progress on my rock.''

Better Times Emerging in the 1990s

Edge survived the crash of the 1980s and with the emergence of better times in the 1990s changed its strategy. In 1992 the company began to make the transition from 2-D seismic technology to 3-D, due to the advent of robust but affordable computers as well as the availability of economic 3-D seismic surveys. Over the next few years, Edge cut back on its reliance on 2-D data in favor of building up a library of 3-D seismic data for use in developing drilling prospects. Moreover, Edge began to do some drilling on its own account, primarily in south Texas and Louisiana. By 1995 Edge was almost totally reliant on 3-D seismic data. The company's success rate jumped from 33 percent to about 67 percent, making it an attractive drilling partner for the likes of Chevron Corp., KCS Energy Inc., and Pennzoil Co. In 1995 and 1996 Edge used its 3-D data to drill 69 wells in south Texas and to a lesser extent in Mississippi and Alabama. By focusing on specific geologic areas, Edge was able to gain insights that allowed it to locate overlooked deposits.

John Calaway was joined by his twin brother James, who became a director of Edge in 1991. He had displayed an entrepreneurial spirit as well. In 1982 he cofounded Space Industries International, Inc. to produce spaceflight equipment and later became involved in the funding and organization of a number of high-tech start-ups. In December 1996 he became president of Edge as part of a reorganization of the company in preparation for going public. An initial public offering (IPO) of common stock was successfully completed in March 1997, underwritten by Raymond James & Associates Inc., which acted as lead manager. Co-managing were Jefferies and Co. Inc. and Principal Financial Securities Inc. The parties had hoped to sell two million shares priced from $15 million to $17 million, but interest was strong enough that Edge was able to command a price in the upper range of the asking price, $16.5 million, and sell 760,000 additional shares. Edge netted some $40 million, earmarked to pay down debt and finance a capital expenditure

program to collect more 3-D seismic data on onshore Gulf Coast properties and pursue an aggressive exploration strategy in 1997 and 1998.

The proceeds of the IPO also came in handy in August 1997 when Edge paid $3.6 million to acquire a 10 percent stake in Houston-based Frontera Resources Corp. and forge a mutually beneficial alliance. Frontera was involved in producing fields in Russia and Latin America, a situation that allowed Edge to apply its 3-D seismic technology to international plays and gain valuable knowledge in doing business outside of the United States. Investment in Edge's domestic drilling program paid off more immediately in 1997. The company drilled 75 new wells, and despite a drop in oil prices, revenues grew from $7.7 million to $13.5 million in 1998.

New Leadership in the Late 1990s

Oil prices continued to slump in 1998 and presented some challenges for Edge, which tried to market its drilling prospects to industry partners as a way to spread the risk inherent in deep plays. In general, however, the company was involved in too many of these risky projects and took steps during the year to develop an inventory of prospects that offered a better balance between risk and reward. Leading this effort at Edge would be a new CEO and chairman, as John Calaway decided in November 1998 that the time had arrived to step away from the company he founded and devote more time to his artistic career and other business interests. His replacement was John W. Elias, who had 35 years of experience in the oil and gas industry. After graduating from the University of Oklahoma with a degree in geology and attending the Advanced Management Program at Harvard University, he spent 30 years with Amoco Corporation and another five years with Seagull Energy Corporation. Calaway expressed his faith in his successor, noting that Elias had the kind of international experience that would help Edge reach the next level in its development. James Calaway would stay on as president and help with the transition for the next year before he too resigned as an officer and director in order to pursue other opportunities in the vein of his early work with start-up companies. In addition to bringing strong organizational skills to the company, Elias was also instrumental in changing the compensation structure of the company, making it performance-based, and using stock to reward all employees rather than rely on a royalty compensation system. In this way, Edge became more competitive with its peers in attracting and retaining key talent.

Edge made other fundamental changes to the way it traditionally did business. Throughout its history, the company generated all of its prospects but it relied on the selling of individual prospects to raise necessary capital. But selling these prospects placed demands on the staff and there was too much uncertainty about when a prospect would be drilled. The goal now was to build a program that was more predictable. In addition to producing its own prospects, Edge was open to acquisitions, farm-ins, and alliances. The company's stake in Frontera, however, was no longer considered a strategic asset and management decided to sell its position. The company also took steps in 1999 to better control overhead costs, which were not in keeping with the company's size. Headcount was cut by some 30 percent and a salary freeze went into effect. In the field in 1999, Edge enjoyed continued success in south Texas but was disappointed with two dry holes drilled in southern Louisiana. All told in 1999, Edge participated in the drilling of 13 exploratory wells, of which nine were successful, and six development wells, of which five were successful.

Edge prospered on a number of fronts in 2000. It participated in the drilling of 26 wells, of which 24 were successful. As a result, the company replaced 190 percent of its total production and a 19 percent increase in proved reserves. Edge benefited from higher than expected gas prices, but could have realized even greater growth were it not for a hedging program that failed to correctly anticipate the market. Also during the year, Edge and its partners acquired new 3-D seismic data on acreage in south central Louisiana, and after some analysis identified a number of prospects. However, while they held a great deal of potential, these leads were highly risky.

The energy sector faced a number of challenges in 2001, including a glut of natural gas and a sluggish worldwide economy. Entering the year with a strong balance sheet, Edge again enjoyed solid success with the drill bit, succeeding with 17 out of 22 wells it completed. It also spent $6.7 million to add 5.6 billion cubic feet of proven reserves during the year. Edge planned to drill slightly more wells in 2002, but because of delays in acquiring and processing some new 3-D data, it managed to drill only 13. Again the company enjoyed a high success rate, around 85 percent, but the dry holes, all located in Louisiana, were expensive ventures, leading to an unacceptable development cost of $1.74 per thousand cubic feet of gas equivalent (Mfce).

Edge performed much better in 2003, more in keeping with its strategic plan. It drilled 36 new wells and proved reserves grew by 30 percent. As a result, the price of Edge stock improved by more than 200 percent, rising from $3.75 per share to a high of $11.40. Edge also completed a significant acquisition in 2003, using $13 million in stock to buy Miller Exploration Company, a Traverse City, Michigan-based company with operations in the Mississippi Salt basin of central Mississippi as well as options on some 100,000 undeveloped acres in northern Montana. The deal provided some diversity and added about 10 percent to Edge's proved reserves.

Edge came under pressure from its largest shareholder, Chicago-based Capital Corp., which expressed displeasure with the company's pursuit of high-risk wells. Marlin wanted to declassify the company's board and made no secret that it would prefer Edge to be open to acquisition overtures as a way to maximize shareholder value. Edge's management disagreed and continued to pursue its strategy of improving shareholder value through the drill bit. During the first half of 2004 Edge enjoyed record success, due to increased production and higher commodity prices, putting to rest, at least temporarily, talk of selling the company.

Principal Subsidiaries

Edge Petroleum Exploration Company; Edge Petroleum Operating Company, Inc.; Miller Oil Corporation; Miller Exploration Company.

Principal Competitors

The Meridian Resource Company; Remington Oil and Gas Corporation; TransTexas Gas Corporation.

Further Reading

Beago, Brad L., "Edge Petroleum Corp.," *Oil & Gas Investor,* June 1998, p. 72.
"Edge Petroleum Corp.," *Oil & Gas Investor,* March 1998, p. 14.
Pybus, Kenneth R., "Calaway Brothers to Offer Shares of Edge Petroleum," *Houston Business Journal,* December 13, 1996, p. 1.
Sheehy, Sandy, "Mixing Oil and Sculpture," *Business Month,* July 1990, p. 74.
Shinkle, Kirk, "Driller Opens Wallet to Fuel Opportunities," *Investor's Business Daily,* February 13, 2004, p. A05.

—Ed Dinger

Electrabel N.V.

Blvd. du Regent 8
Bruxelles
B-1000
Belgium
Telephone: + 32 2 518 61 11
Fax: +32 2 518 64 00
Web site: http://www.electrabel.com

Public Company
Incorporated: 1892 as Compagnie Hydro-Electrique
    Anversoise
Employees: 14,642
Sales: EUR 10.85 billion ($13.39 billion) (2003)
Stock Exchanges: Euronext Brussels
Ticker Symbol: ELEB
NAIC: 221122 Electric Power Distribution; 221210
    Natural Gas Distribution; 221310 Water Supply and
    Irrigation Systems; 221330 Steam and Air-
    Conditioning Supply; 515210 Cable and Other
    Subscription Programming

Electrabel N.V. is Belgium's dominant electric power producer, controlling more than 95 percent of all domestic power generation and distribution. In Belgium alone, Electrabel produces nearly 13,000 MW from a diverse park of nuclear, hydroelectric, coal, and gas-fired and wind-powered generation plants, serving nearly four million customers. Electrabel also has powered itself into the ranks of Europe's top five power companies, with an additional 16,000 MW of generation capacity outside of Belgium. Electrabel's international operations include The Netherlands, Luxembourg, France, Spain, Portugal, Germany, Poland, Hungary, and Italy. The company's total output amounted to more than 137,000 GWh in 2003, with Belgium accounting for about 60 percent of that total. Together, the company's operations produced revenues of EUR 10.85 billion ($13.39 billion) in 2003. Listed on the Euronext Brussels Stock Exchange, Electrabel is majority controlled by France's Suez, and operates within that company's Tractebel subsidiary. In the early 2000s, Electrabel and Suez have been negotiating a transfer of Tractebel's European power generation operations to Electrabel so that Tractebel can concentrate on its international holdings beyond Europe. As of 2004, Tractebel's holding of Electrabel topped 55 percent.

Emerging Belgian Power Leaders in the 1900s

Electrabel in the 2000s represented more than 100 years of consolidation in the Belgian power sector, creating the country's dominant electrical power supplier and one of Europe's top energy companies. The earliest member of the future Electrabel family was founded in 1892 as the Compagnie Hydro-Electrique Anversoise. Backed by a starting capital of BEF 2.75 million, that company focused on generating electrical power for the Antwerp market.

In 1905, the Antwerp-based group formed a joint venture with the city's tram operator, Compagnie Generale des Tramways, to build and operate an electrical power generating plant in the town of Merksem, outside of Antwerp. The new company was named Electricteitsmaatschappij der Schelde (EMS). By 1908, EMS had completed the new plant and had begun providing power to Antwerp.

EMS ultimately became the dominant power producer in Antwerp, supplanting Compagnie Hydro-Electrique Anversoise in the Flemish-speaking city. In 1956, EMS orchestrated a merger with three other power generating companies in the Flanders region, including Société d'Electricité de l'Escaut, founded in 1905. The merger created a new publicly listed group, Sociétés Reunis d'Energie du Bassin de l'Escaut, or EBES SA. The following year, EBES made its first acquisition, buying Société d'Electricité du Littoral.

By then, many of the other members of the later Electrabel had also been formed. One of the largest of these was founded in 1901 as Société Intercommunale Belge d'Electricité, or INTERCOM. Starting with a capital of just BEF 300,000, INTERCOM was a major motor for the development of Belgium's electrical power market. INTERCOM itself launched a number of regionally operating power generating and distribution companies. For the most part, INTERCOM's earliest power generation capacity was distributed to customers through INTERCOM's subsidiaries.

Company Perspectives:

Strategy

Electrabel is determined to pursue its development in Europe whilst remaining the leader in Benelux. It is constantly improving its performance in all of its business segments and at all levels. Whatever the country or the customer segment concerned, its objective is to provide its customers with quality local products and services.

To achieve this, it forms alliances with local partners and draws on its strength as a major European company. In the production field, Electrabel intends to reinforce its profile as a "low cost producer," in particular by using its trading assets. Its objective is to increase sales without increasing production resources to the same degree.

Finally, the company is guided by four constant values: customer-orientation, performance, caring for staff and a sense of responsibility.

In 1921, however, after building a new generator at Monceau-sur-Sabre, INTERCOM began direct distribution operations for the first time. However, INTERCOM restricted this activity, at least initially, to its institutional customers.

In the years following World War II, INTERCOM began a long series of acquisitions, culminating in the 1961 merger with Gazelec. Other INTERCOM purchases included Henelgaz, Société d'Electricité du Nord de la Belgique, and Compagnie Belge pour l'Exploitation du Gaz et de l'Electricité. These acquisitions helped propel INTERCOM into the top tier of Belgium's still fragmented power generation industry.

Another major Belgian power group also emerged during this period. In 1933, two Meuse region power generators, Centrale Electrique de l'Entre Sambre et Meuse and Société d'Electricité de la Region de Malmedy, merged to form Centrales Electriques de l'Entre Sambre et Meuse et de la Region de Malmedy. That company became more familiarly known as Esma.

Esma too began a growth drive in the 1950s, as Belgian power consumption soared during the long period of economic prosperity. In 1956, Esma bought Compagnie d'Electricité des Ardennes, as well as the Centrale d'Electricité, Eau et Gaz de Malmedy. By 1960, Esma had added several more companies, including Compagnie des Distributions Electriques and the Compagnie d'Electricité de Walcourt et Extensions. Featured among Esma's acquisitions were two Luxembourg-based companies, Société d'Electricité de la Province du Luxembourg and Compagnie Luxembourgeoise d'Electricité. Following these purchases Esma adopted the new name of Société d'Electricité de Sambre et Meuse, des Ardennes et du Luxembourg—or Esmalux, for short.

Esmalux consolidated its position as an emerging power generation and distribution leader with three new acquisitions in 1962, Electricité du Val de Poix, Electricité de Bastogne, and the J. Lambert company. In 1971, Esmalux grew again, acquiring Electricité de la Vierre. Then, in 1976, Esmalux joined a three-way merger with UCE LinaluxHainaut and Compagnie Nationale d'Eclairage—founded in Brussels in 1906—forming UNERG.

Unified Power Leader in the 1990s

The Belgian power market moved steadily closer to consolidation through the 1970s and 1980s. UNERG, INTERCOM, and EBES emerged as the country's three major privately held power generation groups. INTERCOM had grown during this period through the 1976 acquisition of Union Intercommunale des Centrales Electriques du Brabant, and the purchase of Intersambre in 1982. UNERG in the meantime added the Société de Production d'Electricité d'Amercoeur that same year. The company also began developing electricity generation and gas distribution operations outside of Belgium.

In the mid-1980s, INTERCOM and UNERG launched an effort to restructure the country's power generation grid. In 1985 the two companies agreed to an exchange of customers in an effort to coordinate their territories of operation. Under terms of that agreement, INTERCOM picked up UNERG's industrial customers in the Hainaut area, while INTERCOM transferred its own industrial customers in Liege to UNERG. Following that agreement, INTERCOM picked up a new subsidiary, Electricité de Herve, in 1986.

The Belgian power sector, however, remained fragmented. The approach of European economic unification, however, placed new pressure on the sector to consolidate. Under terms of the unification process, trade barriers were slated to be lowered in the early 1990s. Barriers to cross-border utility ownership were also lowered, leading up to the opening of national power markets—typically operated as government-owned monopolies—to competition.

Talks began among Belgium's three power generation leaders, and by 1990, EBES, INTERCOM, and UNERG had reached an agreement to merge their operations into a single company, renamed as Electrabel. Also joining the merger were a number of smaller companies, including Société d'Electricité d'Eupen et Extensions, Sautrac, and Interescaut. Two other companies joined Electrabel by the end of 1991, Electronucleaire and Antwerpse Gasmaatschappij. While INTERCOM and EBES were absorbed completely in the new company, UNERG contributed its electricity production and transmission business, then changed its name to Powerfin in order to continue building up its gas and electricity operations outside of Belgium.

Emerging European Leader in the New Century

By 1992, Electrabel had consolidated its near monopoly status in Belgium. The company then accounted for nearly 95 percent of all of Belgium's electricity supply. The company, which had a market capitalization worth some BEF 304 billion, was also profitable, with net profits topping BEF 22.5 billion that year.

The European power generation market braced itself for the coming competition. While many of the European Union members dragged their feet on liberalizing their domestic energy markets, the Benelux countries moved forward, signaling the start of a new era of European energy consolidation. Electrabel quickly joined in that process, buying 80 percent of the largest electrical power generator in The Netherlands, EPON, in 1999.

Key Dates:

1892: The founding of Compagnie Hydro-Electrique Anversoise leads to the formation of EMS in 1905.

1901: INTERCOM is founded.

1933: The merger of two electricity companies forms Esma (Centrales Electriques de l'Entre Sambre et Meuse et de la region de Malmedy).

1956: EMS leads a merger with three other companies to form EBES (Sociétés Réunies d'Energie du Bassin de l'Escaut).

1960: Esma acquires four companies, including two Luxembourg companies, and becomes Esmalux.

1961: INTERCOM acquires Gazelec and becomes one of the top power companies in Belgium.

1976: UNERG is created through the merger of Esmalux with Electrogaz, and others.

1990: INTERCOM, UNERG, and EBES merge to form Electrabel.

1999: Electrabel acquires 80 percent of The Netherlands' EPON.

2001: Electrabel acquires Spark Energy in The Netherlands.

2003: The stake in Compagnie Nationale du Rhône in France is increased to 48 percent.

2004: Electrabel plans to enter the Polish power market.

Electrabel next turned to Spain, entering a takeover battle with U.S.-based TXU to acquire Hidroelectrica del Cantabrico S.A., that country's fourth largest utility. Although Electrabel gained a 10 percent stake in Cantabrico in 2000, the two sides agreed to end the takeover effort. Electrabel profitably sold its stake in Cantabrico the following year. Instead, Electrabel acquired Dutch power distribution group Spark Energy in 2001.

Electrabel itself had gained new owners. In the mid-1990s, Tractebel, formed from Belgium government-owned Société Générale, had acquired a 40 percent stake in Electrabel. When Tractebel faced a hostile takeover attempt led by Italy's Silvio Berlusconi, the company was "rescued" by French white knight Suez, which took over both Tractebel and its stake in Electrabel. Suez quickly moved to increase its holding in Electrabel, boosting its position to 45 percent by the end of the century. By 2004, Suez had succeeded in gaining a clear majority, boosting its shareholding to 50.1 percent. Electrabel in the meantime operated as a subsidiary of Tractebel.

Electrabel's European expansion plans were given a strong boost from its new owners. In the early 2000s, Tractebel transferred a number of its European power generation facilities to Electrabel. In this way, Electrabel was able to extend its range of operations to Germany, Italy, Hungary, Spain, Portugal, and elsewhere. At the same time, Electrabel, Tractebel, and Suez began discussions over the transfer of all of Tractebel's European energy operations to Electrabel, so that Tractebel would be able to concentrate on its overseas operations. By 2002, the parties had hammered out a basic agreement.

In 2002, Electrabel increased its profile in Italy with a cooperation agreement with that country's Acea, which included Electrabel buying a minority stake in the Italian power producer. Electrabel also began investing in new clean energy capacity, buying a 250 MW wind farm portfolio in Portugal and a 175 MW wind farm portfolio in Italy from Gamesa.

Electrabel also expanded into France, acquiring a stake in Compagnie Nationale du Rhône (CNR). In 2003, Electrabel stepped up its position in that company, the second largest power generator in the country, buying the 22 percent held by government-owned Electricité de France. As a result, Electrabel's stake in CNR neared 48 percent.

Electrabel next turned to Poland as that country, which joined the European Union in 2004, prepared to liberalize its own energy sector. Electrabel appeared a strong candidate to acquire a number of the country's soon-to-be privatized electricity distribution companies. In the meantime, the transfer of Tractebel's European assets to Electrabel was put on hold in early 2004, after the parties were unable to reach an agreement on the price of the transfer. Nonetheless, by then Electrabel had established itself as Europe's fifth largest power generation and distribution group, with annual sales of nearly EUR 11 billion, covering most of the key European markets.

Principal Subsidiaries

Aquinter S.A.; Cocetrel S.C.; Electrabel Customer Solutions S.A.; Electrabel Finance S.A. (Luxembourg); Electrabel Netten Vlaanderen S.A.; Twinerg S.A. (Germany); Electrabel Deutschland AG; Energie SaarLorLux AG (Germany); Castelnou Energia S.L. (Spain); Electrabel España S.A.; Hidrobages S.A. (Spain); Electrabel France S.A.

Principal Competitors

Royal Dutch Petroleum Co.; Enel Distribuzione S.p.A.; Stockholms Stad; Termoelectrica S.A; ENEL S.p.A.; TRACTEBEL S.A.; Alcatel; E.ON Energie AG.

Further Reading

Arnold, Martin, Joshua Levitt, and Raphael Minder, "Suez Denies 'Spying' on Electrabel," *Financial Times*, May 12, 2004, p. 28.

Betts, Paul, "Suez Takes Control of Electrabel," *Financial Times*, December 16, 2003, p. 29.

Dombey, Daniel, "Electrabel Aims for Belgian Power Cut," *Financial Times*, April 24, 2001, p. 27.

"Electrabel Nears Rhone Acquisitions," *Utility Week*, July 18, 2003, p. 13.

Electrabel: Ses Origines, Brussels: Electrabel, 1992.

"European Drivers Lift Electrabel," *Power Economics*, September 14, 2004, p. 9.

Jones, Simon, "Tractebel Takes the Reins at Electrabel," *Utility Week*, May 30, 2003, p. 12.

Russell, Eric, "At the Very Heart of the Action," *European Power News*, September 1998, p. 7.

—M.L. Cohen

Eon Labs, Inc.

227-15 North Conduit Avenue
Laurelton, New York 11413
U.S.A.
Telephone: (718) 276-8600
Toll Free: (800) 526-0225
Fax: (718) 949-3120
Web site: http://www.eonlabs.com

Public Company
Incorporated: 1992 as Eon Labs Manufacturing, Inc.
Employees: 531
Sales: $329.53 million (2003)
Stock Exchanges: NASDAQ
Ticker Symbol: ELAB
NAIC: 325412 Pharmaceutical Preparation Manufacturing

Eon Labs, Inc. is a generic drug manufacturer that develops, manufactures, and markets a broad range of prescription pharmaceutical products. The company focuses on drugs that are difficult to make and it strives to introduce the generic equivalent of brand name drugs on the first day patent protection expires. Eon's pharmaceutical product line comprises more than 200 products representing various dosage strengths for 60 drugs. Nearly two-thirds of Eon's drugs rank either first or second in market share. The company operates two manufacturing plants, one at its headquarters in Laurelton, New York, and another in Wilson, North Carolina. The company is majority-owned by Hexal AG, the second largest generic drug manufacturer in Germany.

Origins

Eon sprang from disgrace and failure. Its predecessor company, Vitarine Pharmaceuticals, Inc. became engulfed in a generic drug scandal that made Eon's first years in business a trying time. Vitarine and a handful of other generic drug companies were accused of fixing prices, falsifying test results, and providing erroneous information on applications filed with the U.S. Food and Drug Administration (FDA). In 1991, Vitarine's director of research and development, Steven Colton, was sen-

tenced to 27 months without parole. The company also was punished. Vitarine was fined $500,000 and barred from applying to make new drugs by being listed on the "application integrity policy list," the FDA's blacklist. The FDA also removed from the market about a dozen drugs sold by Vitarine, stripping the company of some of its best-selling drugs. With no way to make money on its past achievements and no way to develop new drugs, Vitarine wilted quickly from the intensity of the government's indignation. The company filed for bankruptcy and sold its assets to an investor group that included J.H. Whitney & Co., Citicorp Ventures, and Canaan Partners. The transaction was completed in 1992.

The investor group recruited Edward C. Shinal to the lead the new company, an enterprise named Eon Labs Manufacturing, Inc. Shinal, a former director of American Cyanamid Co.'s Lederle Laboratories, was given the task of rebuilding the company's reputation, a challenge the chief executive officer completed within several years of his appointment. Shinal tightened control over manufacturing, separating oversight of quality control from regulatory affairs, and implemented 250 new procedures to comply with FDA standards. Shinal also spent $4 million improving the equipment in the company's plant in Laurelton, New York, priming the company for its return from disrepute.

Eon overcame Vitarine's legacy of errancy in September 1994, when the company was removed from the FDA's blacklist. By the beginning of 1995, the company was well positioned to reap the rewards of Shinal's restorative measures. The company's relationship with the FDA had improved dramatically, a relationship of vital importance to any generic manufacturer and of particular importance to Eon, whose strategy hinged on moving quickly through the approval process. In February 1995, the FDA approved Eon's application to manufacture the drug Sulfadiazine, which was used to combat toxoplasmosis, a disease associated with AIDS. Sulfadiazine was just one of Eon's stable of drugs. By the beginning of 1995, the company had 30 drugs in production, with applications filed for the introduction of 14 additional drugs. With this portfolio of drugs—and more to follow in the coming years—Eon prepared to enter a period of great promise for generic drug companies. During the previous decade, the size of the industry had in-

Company Perspectives:

The employees of Eon Labs are dedicated to develop, manufacture and be first to market with a broad range of affordable multi-source pharmaceutical products to the U.S. healthcare community. Eon's professional team will progressively utilize modern technology and innovative thinking to apply the highest standards throughout our operation and processes.

creased significantly: In the mid-1980s, generic drugs accounted for 2 percent of the prescription drug market; by the mid-1990s, generic manufacturers generated $10 billion in revenue annually, accounting for 40 percent of the prescriptions dispensed in the United States. The generic portion of the market was expected to increase to 50 percent by the end of the decade. Between 1993 and 2000, the patents of 140 brand name drugs were scheduled to expire, releasing $25 billion worth of business to generic producers.

Hexal and Eon Joining Together in 1995

As Eon prepared for the potentially lucrative years ahead, it gained the support of a valuable partner. Small, independent drug companies such as Eon often forged partnerships and agreements with larger pharmaceutical concerns as a way to survive, alliances that helped small companies avoid being crushed in the highly competitive pharmaceutical industry. Eon formed more than a partnership in September 1995, when Hexal AG agreed to purchase one-half of the company. Hexal ranked as the second largest generic drug manufacturer in Germany, providing Eon with a massive parent company to foster its growth. Under the terms of the arrangement with Hexal, Eon had first rights to all the drugs made by its parent company and exclusive rights to market Hexal drugs in the United States.

When Hexal assumed half-ownership of Eon (J.H. Whitney owned the other half), the German company appointed one of its own executives to lead Eon. Bernhard Hampl, who received a Ph.D. in pharmaceutical chemistry from Ludwig Maximillian University in Munich, spent 15 years working for Cyanamid GmbH, where he served as the company's director of research and development and technical director. In 1995, he was hired by Hexal to explore the possibility of establishing a Hexal subsidiary in the United States, a job that led to his appointment as Eon's chief executive officer in October 1995. Under Bernhard Hampl's stewardship, which would continue into the 21st century, Eon developed a particular identity for itself in the generic drug industry. The company focused on developing generic drugs that were particularly difficult to make, either because of technological challenges, hard-to-find raw materials, or legal problems. Eon pursued the development of drugs few other companies chose to pursue, selecting drugs that positioned the company in less competitive niches of the generic drug market. The strategy placed a premium on execution, on the company's ability to overcome the particular problems a drug's development posed. In this area, Eon excelled, with Hampl recording encouraging success during the latter half of the 1990s.

Hampl's success convinced his German superiors to increase their commitment to the company. Between 1992 and 1999, the company's revenues increased from $10 million to $77 million. Profits were growing steadily, eclipsing $5 million in 1999. The financial results and Hampl's success in executing the company's strategy convinced Hexal to purchase the entire company in 2000. Hexal acquired J.H. Whitney's half of Eon and became the sole owner of the company. In the next few years, Hexal's investment proved to be shrewd, as Eon enjoyed the most successful years in its history.

Robust Growth in the 21st Century

Eon's success in the early 2000s rested on the execution of its operating strategy. The company selected drugs with what it called "high barriers to entry," leaving it less vulnerable to the competitive pressures of the drug industry. "They're not going after your typical commodity generics," an analyst explained in a February 14, 2004 interview with *Investor's Business Daily*. "A lot of the products may have two, three, or four competitors instead of 10, 11, or 12, so that certainly helps them on the margin side." Eon also endeavored, and in most cases succeeded, in being the first to market a generic alternative, introducing its version on the first day the patent protection on a branded pharmaceutical expired. By being the first generic on the market, Eon typically enjoyed a 180-day period granted by the FDA to market the drug without any competition, one of the rewards of moving expeditiously through the drug approval process. The exclusive marketing period gave the first generic entrant a jump on securing market share and higher profit margins because the price of the first generic alternative started high before the introduction of other generic alternatives drove prices downward.

Eon strove to be first to market with every drug it produced, a strategy that depended upon winning quick approval from the FDA. The company's compliance record with the federal agency, in sharp contrast with Vitarine's woeful transgressions, was exemplary, enabling Eon to move quickly and expand its portfolio of generic drugs. By the end of 2001, the company was marketing more than 80 generic drugs in various dosage strengths, ranking as one of the top five companies in the country in terms of gaining FDA approvals. At this point, the company was recording explosive growth. The addition of a second manufacturing plant in Wilson, North Carolina, in December 2000—a facility that was more than twice the size of the Laurelton plant—had provided a substantial increase in Eon's production capacity. Sales leaped upwards as a result, reaching $165 million in 2001, or more than twice the total generated two years earlier.

By the end of 2001, the stage was set for Eon's debut as a publicly traded company. Substantial debt had been incurred by Hexal's buyout of J.H. Whitney's interest in 2000, prompting management to file for an initial public offering (IPO) of stock to take advantage of Eon's vibrant growth. Eon's IPO was completed in June 2002, when it debuted on the NASDAQ at $15 per share. The offering raised $139 million in net proceeds. Hexal remained the majority owner of Eon, controlling nearly three-quarters of the company's stock.

Gains in Eon's stock value remained negligible for several months after the IPO, but once the financial community took

Key Dates:

1992: Eon is formed to acquire the assets of Vitarine Pharmaceuticals, Inc.
1995: Hexal AG acquires 50 percent of Eon.
2000: Hexal acquires all of Eon.
2002: Eon completes its initial public offering of stock, with Hexal remaining a majority owner.
2004: Eon begins shipping a generic version of Wellbutrin.

note of the company its stock value began to increase sharply. By May 2003, Eon's stock was trading at more than $31 per share, having doubled in price since September 2002. Investors were watching a company astutely execute a strategy that delivered consistent financial growth. In 2002, sales increased to $244 million and net income soared to $43.2 million, nearly three times the total posted a year earlier. Attention from investors intensified in late 2003 when Eon broke with tradition and gave onlookers a glimpse at what the future held for the company.

In late November 2003, Eon received approval for Bupropion, the generic version of GlaxoSmithKline's 100-milligram antidepressant Wellbutrin. The drug, which generated between $250 million and $350 million in annual revenue, marked a significant departure from the company's practice of targeting drugs that drew the interest of only a few competitors. Wellbutrin was a blockbuster drug, one that attracted the attention of the biggest generic producers. Once it gained approval for Bupropion, Eon next demonstrated perhaps its greatest skill in rapidly bringing the drug to market. Analysts predicted Bupropion would be introduced by the end of 2004, but Hampl and his team began shipping their generic alternative in early February 2004.

As Eon plotted its future course, the company's foray into high profile, blockbuster drug manufacture suggested the adoption of a broader operating strategy. If Hampl chose to pursue making generic versions of branded bestsellers, there were numerous opportunities ahead for Eon to exploit. More than 30 of the top-selling 57 pharmaceutical products were expected to lose patent protection by 2008. Although nearly all of the company's achievements had been made by manufacturing drugs that many other companies avoided, its record of success offered ample evidence to support a wider strategic scope. By 2004, three of every four drugs produced by the company entered the market on the first day, or shortly thereafter, the patents for the branded drug expired. In the years ahead, Eon was expected to demonstrate its first-to-market capabilities with an ever increasing product line.

Principal Subsidiaries

Eon Pharma, LLC; Forte Pharma, Inc.

Principal Competitors

Alpharma, Inc.; Geneva Pharmaceuticals, Inc.; IVAX Corporation; Mylan Laboratories Inc.; Teva Pharmaceuticals Industries Limited; Watson Pharmaceuticals, Inc.

Further Reading

Buckley, Bruce, "Wholesalers Look to Programs, Services to Sharpen Relationships at Retail," *Drug Store News,* February 17, 2003, p. 52.
"Eon Labs," *Drug Store News,* June 17, 2002, p. 53.
Fugazy, Danielle, "No Longer a Secret, Eon Going Public," *IPO Reporter,* March 11, 2002.
Gondo, Nancy, "Fast FDA Approvals Give Eon Labs an Edge in Fierce Generic Market," *Investor's Business Daily,* February 17, 2004, p. B2.
Maiello, Michael, "Life Among the Ruins," *Forbes,* November 1, 2004, p. 178.
Reeves, Amy, "Eon Labs Inc.," *Investor's Business Daily,* September 9, 2002, p. A11.
Sisson, Mary, "Stock Watch: Eon Lab's Growth Formula Overheats Its Share Price," *Crain's New York Business,* May 19, 2003, p. 4.

—Jeffrey L. Covell

Exxon Mobil Corporation

5959 Las Colinas Boulevard
Irving, Texas 75039
U.S.A.
Telephone: (972) 444-1000
Fax: (972) 444-1350
Web site: http://www.exxon.mobil.com

Public Company
Incorporated: 1882 as Standard Oil Company of New
Jersey
Employees: 88,300
Sales: $213.19 billion (2003)
Stock Exchanges: New York
Ticker Symbol: XOM
NAIC: 324110 Petroleum Refineries; 211111 Crude
Petroleum and Natural Gas Extraction; 213112
Support Activities for Oil and Gas Field Exploration;
447110 Gasoline Stations with Convenience Stores

Exxon Mobil Corporation is the second largest integrated oil company in the world, trailing only BP p.l.c. The company is involved in oil and gas exploration, production, transportation, and marketing in more than 200 countries and territories. Exxon Mobil is a major manufacturer of basic petrochemicals, such as olefins, aromatics, and polyethylene and polypropylene plastics. The company supplies refined products to more than 40,000 service stations operating under the brand names Exxon, Mobil, and Esso. Created from the 1999 merger of Mobil Corporation and Exxon Corporation, Exxon Mobil's history is the story of two companies, each an influential constituent of modern business history.

The Development of Mobil's Predecessor Companies

The 1931 merger of Standard Oil Company of New York (Socony) and Vacuum Oil Company created Mobil. Of Mobil's two progenitors, Socony was the larger and more generalized oil company, while Vacuum's expertise lay in the production of high-quality machine lubricants. Vacuum got its start in 1866

when Matthew Ewing, a carpenter and part-time inventor in Rochester, New York, devised a new method of distilling kerosene from oil using a vacuum. The process itself proved to be no great discovery, but Ewing's partner, Hiram Bond Everest, who had invested $20 in seed capital in the project, noticed that its gummy residue was suitable for lubrication, and the two men took out a patent on behalf of the Vacuum Oil Company in 1866. Ewing sold his interest in Vacuum to Everest shortly thereafter. The heavy Vacuum oil was soon much in demand by manufacturers of steam engines and the new internal-combustion engines. In 1869 Everest patented Gargoyle 600-W Steam Cylinder Oil, which was still in use into the 1990s, and the firm continued to prosper.

Within a decade Vacuum had expanded sufficiently to catch the eye of John D. Rockefeller's Standard Oil Company. Beginning in 1872, Standard had bought up scores of refineries and marketing companies around the country, and in 1879 it added Vacuum Oil to its list of conquests, paying $200,000 for 75 percent of Vacuum's stock. By that date Standard Oil had achieved an effective monopoly on the oil business in the United States. Despite its small size, Vacuum was given latitude by the Standard management, who respected its excellent products and the acumen of Hiram Everest and his son, C.M. Everest.

The Everests pursued an independent course in foreign sales. As early as 1885 Vacuum had opened affiliates in Montreal and in Liverpool, where its staff included 19 salespeople, and within the next decade the company added branches in Toronto, Milan, and Bombay. Vacuum became the leader among Standard's companies in the use of efficient marketing and sales techniques, packaging its lubricants in attractive tins, pursuing customers with a well-organized, efficient sales team, and, when necessary, bringing in a lubricants specialist to help customers choose the oil best suited to their needs. Company oils were made according to a secret formula, and by 1911 the Vacuum marketers had made the name Mobil oil known on five continents. In the United States, Vacuum products were sold nationwide by the Standard chain of distributors and in the Northeast by Vacuum's own agents.

In 1906 Vacuum added a second refinery to its original Rochester plant, and in 1910 Standard Oil Company of New

Jersey (Jersey Standard), the holding company for the Standard interests, invested $500,000 to enable its big Bayonne, New Jersey, refinery to manufacture some of Vacuum's lubricants for export. In 1911 the Standard companies were ordered to break up by the U.S. Supreme Court, and among the 34 splinters were Vacuum Oil and Standard Oil Company of New York (Socony). Socony, the second largest of the newly independent companies, had been created along with Jersey Standard in 1882, both as a legal domicile for Standard's New York assets and to serve as the administrative and banking center for the entire Standard Oil Trust. William Rockefeller, John D. Rockefeller's younger brother and longtime business partner, remained the president of Socony from its inception until 1911.

From the first it was planned that in addition to serving as Standard's headquarters, Socony would handle the great bulk of the trust's growing foreign sales. It took over from Standard Oil Company of Ohio ownership of the merchant firm of Meissner, Ackermann & Company, with offices in New York and Hamburg and agents around Europe. At first Standard relied exclusively on such brokers for its foreign business, but as the years went on the company set up its own foreign subsidiaries around the world. By 1910 the Standard subsidiaries had usurped almost all of the foreign sales, with Socony's affiliates handling about 30 percent, while Vacuum Oil, which also had built a small but widespread sales group, contributed 6 percent to the total. In addition to the sales it made itself, Socony also bought and then resold all Standard products leaving New York, and even for a time those shipped out of California to Asia. Bolstered by its double role, Socony's sales were among the largest of any Standard company, and as Standard's official overseas representative, it became a familiar name in many countries.

Another of Socony's important functions, especially prior to 1899, when Jersey Standard began assuming such duties, was to administer most of the Standard group's internal affairs. In the New York City office building at 26 Broadway were housed not only Socony's own corporate leaders, but also the small group of men who ran Standard Oil. Some individuals, such as William Rockefeller, served on both boards, and the interplay between Socony and the Standard group was intimate and complex. Socony also assumed banking functions for the group. After 1899 Jersey Standard became the sole holding company for all of the Standard interests, but Socony continued much as before in its various key roles.

Regrouping Following Supreme Court Ruling in 1911

By the time of the dissolution of Standard in 1911, Socony had established its position in Europe and Africa and built a thriving business in Asia as well. China became an important market for Socony. Socony eventually built a network of subsidiaries from Japan to Turkey that by 1910 was handling nearly 50 percent of the kerosene sold in Asia. In the United States, Socony's five refineries turned out kerosene, gasoline, and naphtha for sale in New York and New England, through jobbers and a growing number of the new roadside stores known as "gas stations."

In 1911 the Supreme Court upheld a lower court's conviction of Jersey Standard for violation of the Sherman Antitrust Act and ordered the organization dissolved. Each of the 34 new companies created by the order was allotted varying proportions of the three basic oil assets—crude production, refining, and marketing—but neither Socony nor Vacuum Oil ended up with any sources of crude. Both companies were strong marketers and refiners, and both became occupied by the search for enough crude oil to keep their plants and salesmen busy. Socony's need for its own crude supplies was greater since it produced a large volume of oil-based fuels and lubricants, whereas Vacuum's business was more limited in both volume and variety. Socony set out to secure ownership of its own wells.

At that point in the history of U.S. oil production, the natural area in which to explore was Texas, Louisiana, and Oklahoma. In 1918 Socony bought 45 percent of Magnolia Petroleum Company, which owned wells, pipelines, and a refinery in Beaumont, Texas, and did most of its marketing in Texas and the Southwest. After buying the rest of Magnolia in 1925, Socony purchased General Petroleum Corporation of California to help supply its large market in Asia. Then it entered the Midwest for the first time with a 1930 purchase of White Eagle Oil & Refining Company, with gas stations in 11 states. Socony now needed even more crude oil to supply these additional market outlets, and like most of the other big international oil concerns, Socony looked to the Middle East.

World War I had demonstrated the crucial role of oil in modern warfare and prompted the U.S. government to encourage U.S. participation in the newly formed Turkish Petroleum Company, operating in present-day Iraq. A consortium of U.S. oil companies was sold 25 percent of Turkish Petroleum. By the early 1930s only Jersey Standard and Socony were left in the partnership, with each eventually holding 12 percent. Oil was first struck by the company, renamed Iraq Petroleum, in 1928, and by 1934 the partners had built a pipeline across the Levant to Haifa, Palestine. From Haifa, Socony could ship oil to its many European subsidiaries.

In the meantime, Vacuum Oil had made a number of important domestic acquisitions and had strengthened its already far-flung network of foreign subsidiaries, but continued to share Socony's chronic shortage of crude. The two companies, similar in profile and complementary in product mix, joined forces

Key Dates:

1870: John D. Rockefeller and Henry Flagler incorporate the Standard Oil Company.

1878: Standard controls $33 million of the country's $35 million annual refining capacity.

1882: Rockefeller reorganizes Standard Oil into a trust, creating Standard Oil Company of New Jersey as one of many regional corporations controlled by the trust.

1888: Standard founds its first foreign affiliate, Anglo-American Oil Company, Limited.

1890: The Sherman Antitrust Act is passed, in large part, in response to Standard's oil monopoly.

1891: The trust has secured a quarter of the total oilfield production in the United States.

1892: A lawsuit leads to dissolution of the trust; the renamed Standard Oil Company (New Jersey) becomes the main vessel of the Standard holdings.

1899: Jersey becomes the sole holding company for all of the Standard interests.

1906: The federal government files a suit against Jersey under the Sherman Antitrust Act, charging it with running a monopoly.

1911: The U.S. Supreme Court upholds a lower court conviction of the company and orders that it be separated into 34 unrelated companies, one of which continues to be called Standard Oil Company (New Jersey).

1926: The Esso brand is used for the first time on the company's refined products.

1931: The merger of Standard Oil Company of New York and Vacuum Oil Company creates Socony-Vacuum Corp., Mobil's immediate predecessor company.

1946: A 30 percent interest in Arabian American Oil Company, and its vast Saudi Arabian oil concessions, is acquired.

1954: The company gains a 7 percent stake in an Iranian oil production consortium.

1960: Mobil Chemical Company is formed.

1966: Mobil Oil Corporation becomes the official corporate title of Socony-Vacuum.

1972: Standard Oil Company (New Jersey) changes its name to Exxon Corporation.

1973: OPEC cuts off oil supplies to the United States.

1976: Mobil Oil Corporation changes its name to Mobil Corporation.

1980: Exxon's revenues exceed $100 billion because of the rapid increase in oil prices.

1984: Mobil acquires Superior Oil Company for $5.7 billion, obtaining extensive reserves of oil and natural gas.

1989: The crash of the *Exxon Valdez* in Prince William Sound off the port of Valdez, Alaska, releases about 260,000 barrels of crude oil.

1990: Exxon's headquarters are moved from Rockefeller Center in New York City to Irving, Texas.

1994: Federal jury finds company guilty of "recklessness" and orders it to pay $286.8 million in compensatory damages and $5 billion in punitive damages.

1997: Exxon appeals the $5 billion punitive damages award; it reports profits of $8.46 billion on revenues of $120.28 billion for the year.

1998: Exxon agrees to buy Mobil in one of the largest mergers in U.S. history.

1999: Exxon and Mobil complete their $83 billion merger, forming Exxon Mobil Corporation.

2001: Cost savings from the merger are tallied at $4.6 billion.

2004: Rex Tillerson is appointed president of Exxon Mobil, leading observers to predict his appointment as chief executive officer upon Lee Raymond's retirement.

in 1931 when Socony purchased the assets of Vacuum and changed its name to Socony-Vacuum Corporation. The union was the first alliance between members of the former Jersey Standard conglomerate and created a company with formidable refining and marketing strengths both at home and abroad. To supply its joint Far East markets more efficiently, in 1933 Socony-Vacuum (SV) and Jersey Standard created another venture called Standard-Vacuum Oil Company (Stan-Vac). Stan-Vac would ship oil from Jersey Standard's large Indonesian holdings to SV's extensive marketing outlets from Japan to East Africa. By 1941 it was contributing 35 percent of SV's corporate earnings.

In 1934 Socony-Vacuum Corporation changed its name to Socony-Vacuum Oil Company, Inc. (SVO). The company's growth made SVO the second largest U.S. oil concern by the mid-1930s, with nearly $500 million in sales, exclusive of Stan-Vac. From warehouses and gas stations in 43 states and virtually every country in the world, SVO sold a full line of petroleum products, many of them sporting some variety of Vacuum's famous Mobil brand name or its equally familiar flying red horse logo. With 14 refineries in Europe alone and a fleet of 54 oceangoing tankers, by 1941 SVO's holdings were truly international in scope and balance—a situation that caused growing anxiety as World War II approached. When the Nazis stormed across Western Europe they found working SVO refineries that they promptly put into the service of the Third Reich. The largest prize, a huge refinery at Gravenchon, France, was destroyed by the retreating French in a blaze that lasted for seven days. Similarly, the $30 million Stan-Vac refinery at Palembang, Indonesia, was kept out of Japanese hands by burning it to the ground. The war also cost SVO some 32 ships and the lives of 432 crew members, lost to German submarines. Throughout this period, increased military sales generally made up for SVO's wartime capital losses and declining civilian revenue.

Socony-Vacuum Oil Company's search for crude oil continued. In the immediate postwar years SVO completed a transaction that would provide the company with oil for many years to come. In the 1930s, Standard Oil Company (California) and the Texas Company—later known as Chevron and Texaco, respectively—had bought drilling rights to a huge chunk of Saudi Arabia, and when they realized the extent of the fields there the two companies sought partners with investment capital and overseas markets. SVO and Jersey Standard had ample amounts of both, and they agreed to split the offered 40 percent interest in the newly formed Arabian American Oil Company (Aramco). SVO had second thoughts about so large an investment and settled for 10 percent instead. This miscalculation was rendered less painful by the truly enormous scale of the Arabian oil reserves. In the coming decade of economic growth and skyrocketing consumption of oil, SVO would develop and depend upon its Arabian connection even more strongly than the other major oil concerns.

Postwar Rise in Demand

In the United States a new culture based on the automobile and abundant supplies of cheap gasoline spread the boundaries of cities and built a nationwide system of interstate highways. SV's long use of its Mobil trade names and flying red horse logo had made these symbols known around the country, and in 1955 the company capitalized on this by changing its name to Socony Mobil Oil Company, Inc. (SM). In 1958 sales reached $2.8 billion and continued upward with the steadily growing U.S. economy, hitting $4.3 billion five years later and $6.5 billion in 1967. In 1960 a subsidiary, Mobil Chemical Company, was formed to take advantage of the many discoveries in the field of petrochemicals. Mobil Chemical manufactured a wide range of plastic packaging, petrochemicals, and chemical additives. In 1989 it contributed 32 percent of Mobil's net operating income—generated on sales representing less than 7 percent of the corporate total.

Egypt's nationalization of the Suez Canal in 1956 was one of many indications that SM's Middle Eastern dependence could one day prove to be problematic, but there was little the company could do to reduce this dependence. Even significant new finds in Texas and the Gulf of Mexico were not able to keep pace with the nation's oil consumption, and by 1966 the Middle East, principally Saudi Arabia, supplied 43 percent of SM's crude production. Also in 1966 Socony Mobil Oil Company changed its name to Mobil Oil Corporation, using ''Mobil'' as its sole corporate and trade name and de-emphasizing the use of the Pegasus logo in favor of a streamlined ''Mobil'' with a bright red ''o.'' Still constantly searching for alternative sources of crude, Mobil got a piece of both the North Sea fields and the Prudhoe Bay region of Alaska in the late 1960s, although neither would be of much help for a number of years. In the meantime, world oil consumption had slowly overtaken production and shifted the market balance in favor of the Organization of Petroleum Exporting Countries (OPEC), which would soon take advantage of the relative scarcity to enforce its world cartel.

The Oil Crisis of the 1970s

During the 1960s Mobil Oil's 9 percent annual increase in net income was the best of all major oil companies, and it continued as a major supplier of natural gas and oil to the world's two fastest-growing economies, West Germany and Japan. In 1973, however, OPEC placed an embargo on oil shipments to the United States for six months and began gradual annexation of U.S.-owned oil properties. The price of oil quadrupled overnight, and a new era of energy awareness began, as the international oil companies lost the comfortable positions they had held in the Middle East since the 1920s. On the other hand, the immediate result of OPEC's move was to boost sales and profits at all the oil majors. Mobil Oil's sales nearly tripled

between 1973 and 1977 to $32 billion, and 1974 profits hit record highs, prompting a barrage of congressional and media criticism that was answered by Mobil Oil's own public relations department. Mobil Oil quickly became famous as the most outspoken defender of the oil industry's right to conduct its business as it saw fit.

Despite its apparent ability to make money in any oil environment, Mobil Oil was concerned about the imminent loss of its legal control over the Middle Eastern oil on which it depended. Under the special guidance of President and Chief Operating Officer William Tavoulareas, Mobil Oil chose to strengthen its ties with Saudi Arabia, spending large amounts of time and money courting the Saudi leaders, investing in industrial projects, and in 1974 acquiring an additional 5 percent of the stock in Aramco from its partners. In 1976 Mobil Oil Corporation again changed its name, to Mobil Corporation. In the early 1990s, it enjoyed one of the closest relationships with the Saudis of any oil firm, a bond whose value increased sharply when oil was scarce but was a liability when plentiful supplies made Mobil's purchases of the expensive Saudi crude less than a bargain. In addition, Mobil considerably increased its budget for oil exploration, concentrating mainly on the North Sea and Gulf of Mexico regions. Although these efforts succeeded, in large part, in replacing Mobil's reserves as fast as they were used up, the company bought Superior Oil Company in 1984. Mobil paid $5.7 billion for Superior, mainly for its extensive reserves of natural gas and oil.

By that time the oil market had once again changed course. Conservation measures and a generally sluggish world economy reversed the price of oil in 1981, and it continued to drop throughout the decade. Mobil thus found itself locked into contracts for expensive Saudi crude and burdened with the debts incurred in the Superior purchase at a time of falling revenues. To make ends meet, Chairman Rawleigh Warner, Jr., and his 1986 successor, Allen E. Murray, made substantial cuts in refineries and service stations, upgrading Mobil's holdings of both to a smaller number of more modern, efficient units. By 1988 Mobil had pulled out of the retail gasoline business in 20 states and derived 88 percent of its retail revenue from just 14 states, mostly in the Northeast. It also had cut its oil-related employment by 20 percent as well as jettisoned its Montgomery Ward and Container Corporation of America subsidiaries, holdovers from a move toward diversification in the mid-1970s.

The $6 billion sale of assets was used to reduce debt, and Mobil's financial performance improved accordingly as the decade drew to a close, although not enough to please Wall Street analysts. The 1980s were generally not a good period for Mobil, which continued, on paper at least, to show a worrisome decline in proven oil reserves.

Challenges in the 1990s

World events in the early 1990s had contradictory repercussions for Mobil and the petroleum industry as a whole. The Persian Gulf War in particular, and instability in the Middle East in general, heightened the importance of Mobil's carefully cultivated friendship with Saudi Arabia. But a recession in the United States and the worldwide economic slowdown lowered the demand for energy and chemicals, thereby weakening prices.

The corporation marked its 125th anniversary in 1991, but there was little cause for celebration. As earnings across the gas and oil industry dropped, Mobil's profits fell by only ½ percent, but the corporation braced for a deepening recession with restructuring and internal investment. Asset sales of $570 million in 1991 included a Wyoming coal mine and hundreds of wells in western Texas. Capital and exploration spending crested that year at more than $5 billion, up almost 16 percent from the previous year.

The recession deepened in 1992, and Mobil Chairman and CEO Allen E. Murray continued restructuring as earnings plunged precipitously across the industry. By the end of the year, Mobil had divested itself of a polyethylene bread bag manufacturing business, a polystyrene resin business, and its interests in nine oilfields in west Texas and southeast New Mexico. Mobil also cut its domestic workforce by more than 2,000 in 1992 and slashed $800 million from that year's capital and exploration budget. It may have seemed that even nature moved against the oil industry: August's Hurricane Andrew forced the evacuation of oil and gas rigs and platforms on the Gulf of Mexico, in Alabama, on Mobile Bay, and even as far inland as Beaumont, Texas. Gulf operations began the return to normal within a week of the devastating storm.

Environmental and philanthropic efforts were a hallmark of Mobil's operations. In 1991 Mobil started the industry's first nationwide used oil collection program, and it continued to contribute to such cultural and educational projects as "Teach for America," a nonprofit teacher corps. But Mobil's environmental record was marred in 1992 when, after three years of litigation, an environmental manager at Mobil Chemical proved that his superiors attempted to force him to falsify the findings of environmental audits. A jury awarded the former employee $1.75 million in damages and interest in his wrongful discharge suit against Mobil.

Mobil's worldwide influence, with strong positions in Saudi Arabia, Nigeria, and Asia's Pacific Rim, included a commanding presence in Indonesia. In the early 1990s, Mobil was the largest U.S. firm extracting natural gas in Indonesia, which was one of the world's largest producers of that resource. Natural gas constituted 50 percent of Mobil's worldwide resources at that time, making the Indonesian activities doubly important.

By 1994, Mobil's position had stabilized, as rising natural gas prices pushed up the company's profits, one-third of which were from natural gas. The following year the company undertook a restructuring of worldwide staff support services, including a 28 percent reduction in staffing. Overall, the company had shaved nearly $2 billion from operating expenses since 1992. In 1995 profits jumped to an estimated $1.9 billion (in large part driven by Mobil's 30 percent stake in the rich Indonesian Arun field, which contributed one-quarter of that figure); as a result, Mobil ranked number one in the industry in terms of profitability.

Analysts predicted that the company's profits would increase by another 50 percent in 1996. At the same time, Arun's reserves had peaked, and Mobil was pressed to find additional supplies. Chairman Lucio Noto, who had succeeded Murray in 1994, set his sights on Ras Laffan, a natural gas field in the Persian Gulf, off the coast of Qatar. With deliveries scheduled to begin in 1999,

Mobil's 30 percent stake in the field was expected to add $300 million in annual operating earnings in its first decade, and as much as $700 million after Mobil's initial investment was paid down. According to a Mobil executive, when Qatar was first proposed, Noto's response was ". . . this is something that could get carved on my tombstone, if we do it right."

Other projects proceeded apace. In May, Mobil announced that the company and a partner would launch a second petrochemical operation at Yanbu, Saudi Arabia, at a cost of $2 billion. The company also was investigating the construction of an ethylene plant in Singapore, and formed a joint venture with a Venezuelan firm to develop a $1.5 billion olefins complex in Jose, Venezuela. Other investments included a 25 percent stake in the Tengiz oilfield in Kazakhstan and the acquisition of Ampolex, an Australian oil and gas company. Total resources rose 28 percent. Disinvestments, on the other hand, included the sale of $1.8 billion in assets in land development, chemicals, mining, and gas processing.

In June Mobil announced a new management structure, in which 11 new business groups would take the place of the existing three worldwide divisions. Noto explained, "In this new competitive climate, these changes better focus on our entrepreneurial talent of seizing new business opportunities, while maintaining our commitment to technology and functional excellence in our upstream and downstream activities."

On the retail side, Mobil operated 7,711 highly successful gas stations, concentrated in 18 states, only 600 of which were company-owned. Expanding into full-scale convenience stores, the company introduced about 150 "On the Run" outlets, which it described as "brighter, bigger, bolder convenience stores." On the Run was part of a plan to eventually offer franchises of car care, convenience stores, car washes, and gasoline.

Ending 1996 with $81.5 billion in revenues, the company announced that it had essentially met its target for two years hence, 1998, of more than $3 billion in earnings. The restructuring initiatives that were initiated were expected to reduce annual costs by $1.3 billion annually, and dividends to shareholders increased for the ninth consecutive year. Said Noto: "We began working several years ago toward becoming a great, global company. Today, as a result, Mobil is more efficient, more responsive, and better positioned for growth. In that respect, 1996 was a pivotal year for our company. We can now see the Mobil of tomorrow taking shape—more profitable, a recognized leader in all our businesses, with unprecedented opportunities for long-term growth for our shareholders, better products and services for our customers, and a challenging and inclusive environment for our employees."

Mid-19th-Century Developments Leading to Exxon's Beginnings As Standard Oil

The individual most responsible for the creation of Standard Oil, John D. Rockefeller, was born in 1839 to a family of modest means living in the Finger Lakes region of New York State. His father, William A. Rockefeller, was a sporadically successful merchant and part-time hawker of medicinal remedies. William Rockefeller moved his family to Cleveland, Ohio, when John D. Rockefeller was in his early teens, and it was there that the young man finished his schooling and began work as a bookkeeper in 1855. From a very young age John D. Rockefeller developed an interest in business. Before getting his first job with the merchant firm of Hewitt Tuttle, Rockefeller had already demonstrated an innate affinity for business, later honed by a few months at business school.

Rockefeller worked at Hewitt Tuttle for four years, studying large-scale trading in the United States. In 1859 the 19-year-old Rockefeller set himself up in a similar venture—Clark Rockefeller, merchants handling the purchase and resale of grain, meat, farm implements, salt, and other basic commodities. Although still very young, Rockefeller had impressed Maurice Clark and his other business associates as an unusually capable, cautious, and meticulous businessman. He was a reserved, undemonstrative individual, never allowing emotion to cloud his thinking. Bankers found that they could trust John D. Rockefeller, and his associates in the merchant business began looking to him for judgment and leadership.

Clark Rockefeller's already healthy business was given a boost by the Civil War economy, and by 1863 the firm's two partners had put away a substantial amount of capital and were looking for new ventures. The most obvious and exciting candidate was oil. A few years before, the nation's first oil well had been drilled at Titusville, in western Pennsylvania, and by 1863 Cleveland had become the refining and shipping center for a trail of newly opened oilfields in the so-called Oil Region. Activity in the oilfields, however, was extremely chaotic, a scene of unpredictable wildcatting, and John D. Rockefeller was a man who prized above all else the maintenance of order. He and Clark, therefore, decided to avoid drilling and instead go into the refining of oil, and in 1863 they formed Andrews, Clark Company with an oil specialist named Samuel Andrews. Rockefeller, never given to publicity, was the "Company."

With excellent railroad connections as well as the Great Lakes to draw upon for transportation, the city of Cleveland and the firm of Andrews, Clark Company both did well. The discovery of oil wrought a revolution in U.S. methods of illumination. Kerosene soon replaced animal fat as the source of light across the country, and by 1865 Rockefeller was fully convinced that oil refining would be his life's work. Unhappy with his Clark family partners, Rockefeller bought them out for $72,000 in 1865 and created the new firm of Rockefeller Andrews, already Cleveland's largest oil refiner. It was a typically bold move by Rockefeller, who although innately conservative and methodical was never afraid to make difficult decisions. He thus found himself, at the age of 25, co-owner of one of the world's leading oil concerns.

Talent, capital, and good timing combined to bless Rockefeller Andrews. Cleveland handled the lion's share of Pennsylvania crude and, as the demand for oil continued to explode, Rockefeller Andrews soon dominated the Cleveland scene. By 1867, when a young man of exceptional talent named Henry Flagler became a third partner, the firm was already operating the world's number one oil refinery; there was as yet little oil produced outside the United States. The year before, John Rockefeller's brother, William Rockefeller, had opened a New York office to encourage the rapidly growing export of kerosene and oil byproducts, and it was not long before foreign sales

became an important part of Rockefeller's strength. In 1869 the young firm allocated $60,000 for plant improvements—an enormous sum of money for that day.

The Standard Oil Monopoly: 1870–92

The early years of the oil business were marked by tremendous swings in the production and price of both crude and refined oil. With a flood of newcomers entering the field every day, size and efficiency already had become critically important for survival. As the biggest refiner, Rockefeller was in a better position than anyone to weather the price storms. Rockefeller and Henry Flagler, with whom Rockefeller enjoyed a long and harmonious business relationship, decided to incorporate their firm to raise the capital needed to enlarge the company further. On January 10, 1870, the Standard Oil Company was formed, with the two Rockefellers, Flagler, and Andrews owning the great majority of stock, valued at $1 million. The new company was not only capable of refining approximately 10 percent of the entire country's oil, it also owned a barrel-making plant, dock facilities, a fleet of railroad tank cars, New York warehouses, and forest land for the cutting of lumber used to produce barrel staves. At a time when the term was yet unknown, Standard Oil had become a vertically integrated company.

One of the great advantages of Standard Oil's size was the leverage it gave the company in railroad negotiations. Most of the oil refined at Standard made its way to New York and the Eastern Seaboard. Because of Standard's great volume—60 carloads a day by 1869—it was able to win lucrative rebates from the warring railroads. In 1871 the various railroads concocted a plan whereby the nation's oil refiners and railroads would agree to set and maintain prohibitively high freight rates while awarding large rebates and other special benefits to those refiners who were part of the scheme. The railroads would avoid disastrous price wars while the large refiners forced out of business those smaller companies who refused to join the cartel, known as the South Improvement Company.

The plan was denounced immediately by Oil Region producers and many independent refiners, with near-riots breaking out in the oilfields. After a bitter war of words and a flood of press coverage, the oil refiners and the railroads abandoned their plan and announced the adoption of public, inflexible transport rates. In the meantime, however, Rockefeller and Flagler were already far advanced on a plan to combat the problems of excess capacity and dropping prices in the oil industry. To Rockefeller the remedy was obvious, though unprecedented: the eventual unification of all oil refiners in the United States into a single company. Rockefeller approached the Cleveland refiners and a number of important firms in New York and elsewhere with an offer of Standard Oil stock or cash in exchange for their often-ailing plants. By the end of 1872, all 34 refiners in the area had agreed to sell—some freely and for profit, and some, competitors alleged, under coercion. Because of Standard's great size and the industry's overbuilt capacity, Rockefeller and Flagler were in a position to make their competitors irresistible offers. All indications are that Standard regularly paid top dollar for viable companies.

By 1873 Standard Oil was refining more oil—10,000 barrels per day—than any other region of the country, employing 1,600 workers, and netting around $500,000 per year. With great confidence, Rockefeller proceeded to duplicate his Cleveland success throughout the rest of the country. By the end of 1874 he had absorbed the next three largest refiners in the nation, located in New York, Philadelphia, and Pittsburgh. Rockefeller also began moving into the field of distribution with the purchase of several of the new pipelines then being laid across the country. With each new acquisition it became more difficult for Rockefeller's next target to refuse his cash. Standard interests rapidly grew so large that the threat of monopoly was clear. The years 1875 to 1879 saw Rockefeller push through his plan to its logical conclusion. In 1878, a mere six years after beginning its annexation campaign, Standard Oil controlled $33 million of the country's $35 million annual refining capacity, as well as a significant proportion of the nation's pipelines and oil tankers. At the age of 39, Rockefeller was one of the five wealthiest men in the country.

Standard's involvement in the aborted South Improvement Company, however, had earned it lasting criticism. The company's subsequent absorption of the refining industry did not mend its image among the few remaining independents and the mass of oil producers who found in Standard a natural target for their wrath when the price of crude dropped precipitously in the late 1870s. Although the causes of producers' failing fortunes are unclear, it is evident that given Standard's extraordinary position in the oil industry it was fated to become the target of dissatisfaction. In 1879 nine Standard Oil officials were indicted by a Pennsylvania grand jury for violating state antimonopoly laws. Although the case was not pursued, it indicated the depth of feeling against Standard Oil, and was only the first in a long line of legal battles waged to curb the company's power.

In 1882 Rockefeller and his associates reorganized their dominions, creating the first "trust" in U.S. business history. This move overcame state laws restricting the activity of a corporation to its home state. Henceforth the Standard Oil Trust, domiciled in New York City, held "in trust" all assets of the various Standard Oil companies. Of the Standard Oil Trust's nine trustees, John D. Rockefeller held the largest number of shares. Together the trust's 30 companies controlled 80 percent of the refineries and 90 percent of the oil pipelines in the United States, constituting the leading industrial organization in the world. The trust's first year's combined net earnings were $11.2 million, of which some $7 million was immediately plowed back into the companies for expansion. Almost lost in the flurry of big numbers was the 1882 creation of Standard Oil Company of New Jersey, one of the many regional corporations created to handle the trust's activities in surrounding states. Barely worth mentioning at the time, Standard Oil Company of New Jersey, or "Jersey" as it came to be called, would soon become the dominant Standard company and, much later, rename itself Exxon.

The 1880s were a period of exponential growth for Standard. The trust not only maintained its lock on refining and distribution but also seriously entered the field of production. By 1891 the trust had secured a quarter of the country's total output, most of it in the new regions of Indiana and Illinois. Standard's overseas business also was expanding rapidly, and in 1888 it founded its first foreign affiliate, London-based Anglo-American Oil Company, Limited (later known as Esso Petroleum Company, Limited). The overseas trade in kerosene was

especially important to Jersey, which derived as much as three-fourths of its sales from the export trade. Jersey's Bayonne, New Jersey refinery was soon the third largest in the Standard family, putting out 10,000 to 12,000 barrels per day by 1886. In addition to producing and refining capacity, Standard also was extending gradually its distribution system from pipelines and bulk wholesalers toward the retailer and eventual end user of kerosene, the private consumer.

Jersey at Head of Standard Oil Empire: 1892–1911

The 1890 Sherman Antitrust Act, passed in large part in response to Standard's oil monopoly, laid the groundwork for a second major legal assault against the company, an 1892 Ohio Supreme Court order forbidding the trust to operate Standard of Ohio. As a result, the trust was promptly dissolved, but taking advantage of newly liberalized state law in New Jersey, the Standard directors made Jersey the main vessel of their holdings. Standard Oil Company of New Jersey became Standard Oil Company (New Jersey) at this time. The new Standard Oil structure now consisted of only 20 much-enlarged companies, but effective control of the interests remained in the same few hands as before. Jersey added a number of important manufacturing plants to its already impressive refining capacity and was the leading Standard unit. It was not until 1899, however, that Jersey became the sole holding company for all of the Standard interests. At that time the entire organization's assets were valued at about $300 million and it employed 35,000 people. John D. Rockefeller continued as nominal president, but the most powerful active member of Jersey's board was probably John D. Archbold.

Rockefeller had retired from daily participation in Standard Oil in 1896 at the age of 56. Once Standard's consolidation was complete Rockefeller spent his time reversing the process of accumulation, seeing to it that his immense fortune—estimated at $900 million in 1913—was redistributed as efficiently as it had been made.

The general public was only dimly aware of Rockefeller's philanthropy, however. More obvious were the frankly monopolistic policies of the company he had built. With its immense size and complete vertical integration, Standard Oil piled up huge profits ($830 million in the 12 years from 1899 to 1911). In relative terms, however, its domination of the U.S. industry was steadily decreasing. By 1911 its percentage of total refining was down to 66 percent from the 90 percent of a generation before, but in absolute terms Standard Oil had grown to monstrous proportions. Therefore, it was not surprising that in 1905 a U.S. congressman from Kansas launched an investigation of Standard Oil's role in the falling price of crude in his state. The commissioner of the Bureau of Corporations, James R. Garfield, decided to widen the investigation into a study of the national oil industry—in effect, Standard Oil.

Garfield's critical report prompted a barrage of state lawsuits against Standard Oil (New Jersey) and, in November 1906, a federal suit was filed charging the company, John D. Rockefeller, and others with running a monopoly. In 1911, after years of litigation, the U.S. Supreme Court upheld a lower court's conviction of Standard Oil for monopoly and restraint of trade under the Sherman Antitrust Act. The Court ordered the separation from Standard Oil Company (New Jersey) of 33 of the major Standard Oil subsidiaries, including those that subsequently kept the Standard name.

Independent Growth into a "Major": 1911–72

Standard Oil Company (New Jersey) retained an equal number of smaller companies spread around the United States and overseas, representing $285 million of the former Jersey's net value of $600 million. Notable among the remaining holdings were a group of large refineries, four medium-sized producing companies, and extensive foreign marketing affiliates. Absent were the pipelines needed to move oil from well to refinery, much of the former tanker fleet, and access to a number of important foreign markets, including Great Britain and the Far East.

John D. Archbold, a longtime intimate of the elder Rockefeller and whose Standard service had begun in 1879, remained president of Standard Oil (New Jersey). Archbold's first problem was to secure sufficient supplies of crude oil for Jersey's extensive refining and marketing capacity. Jersey's former subsidiaries were more than happy to continue selling crude to Jersey; the dissolution decree had little immediate effect on the coordinated workings of the former Standard Oil group, but Jersey set about finding its own sources of crude. The company's first halting steps toward foreign production met with little success; ventures in Romania, Peru, Mexico, and Canada suffered political or geological setbacks and were of no help. In 1919, however, Jersey made a domestic purchase that would prove to be of great long-term value. For $17 million Jersey acquired 50 percent of the Humble Oil Refining Company of Houston, Texas, a young but rapidly growing network of Texas producers that immediately assumed first place among Jersey's domestic suppliers. Although only the fifth leading producer in Texas at the time of its purchase, Humble would soon become the dominant drilling company in the United States and eventually was wholly purchased by Jersey. Humble, later known as Exxon Company U.S.A., remained one of the leading U.S. producers of crude oil and natural gas through the end of the century.

Despite initial disappointments in overseas production, Jersey remained a company oriented to foreign markets and supply sources. On the supply side, Jersey secured a number of valuable Latin American producing companies in the 1920s, especially several Venezuelan interests consolidated in 1943 into Creole Petroleum Corporation. By that time Creole was the largest and most profitable crude producer in the Jersey group. In 1946 Creole produced an average of 451,000 barrels per day, far more than the 309,000 by Humble and almost equal to all other Jersey drilling companies combined. Four years later, Creole generated $157 million of the Jersey group's total net income of $408 million and did so on sales of only $517 million. Also in 1950, Jersey's British affiliates showed sales of $283 million but a bottom line of about $2 million. In contrast to the industry's early days, oil profits now lay in the production of crude, and the bulk of Jersey's crude came from Latin America. The company's growing Middle Eastern affiliates did not become significant resources until the early 1950s. Jersey's Far East holdings, from 1933 to 1961 owned jointly with Socony-Vacuum Oil Company—formerly Standard Oil Company of New York and now Mobil Corporation—never provided sizable amounts of crude oil.

In marketing, Jersey's income showed a similar preponderance of foreign sales. Jersey's domestic market had been limited by the dissolution decree to a handful of mid-Atlantic states, whereas the company's overseas affiliates were well entrenched and highly profitable. Jersey's Canadian affiliate, Imperial Oil Limited, had a monopolistic hold on that country's market, while in Latin America and the Caribbean the West India Oil Company performed superbly during the second and third decades of the 20th century. Jersey also had incorporated eight major marketing companies in Europe by 1927, and these, too, sold a significant amount of refined products—most of them under the Esso brand name introduced the previous year (the name was derived from the initials for Standard Oil). Esso became Jersey's best known and most widely used retail name both at home and abroad.

Jersey's mix of refined products changed considerably over the years. As the use of kerosene for illumination gave way to electricity and the automobile continued to grow in popularity, Jersey's sales reflected a shift away from kerosene and toward gasoline. Even as late as 1950, however, gasoline had not yet become the leading seller among Jersey products. That honor went to the group of residual fuel oils used as a substitute for coal to power ships and industrial plants. Distillates used for home heating and diesel engines were also strong performers. Even in 1991, when Exxon distributed its gasoline through a network of 12,000 U.S. and 26,000 international service stations, the earnings of all marketing and refining activities were barely one-third of those derived from the production of crude. In 1950 that proportion was about the same, indicating that regardless of the end products into which oil was refined, it was the production of crude that yielded the big profits.

Indeed, by mid-century the international oil business had become, in large part, a question of controlling crude oil at its source. With Standard Oil Company (New Jersey) and its multinational competitors having built fully vertically integrated organizations, the only leverage remaining was control of the oil as it came out of the ground. Although it was not yet widely known in the United States, production of crude was shifting rapidly from the United States and Latin America to the Middle East. As early as 1908 oil had been verified in present-day Iran, but it was not until 1928 that Jersey and Socony-Vacuum, prodded by chronic shortages of crude, joined three European companies in forming Iraq Petroleum Company. Also in 1928, Jersey, Shell, and Anglo-Persian secretly agreed to limit each company's share of world production to their present relative amounts, attempting, by means of this "As Is" agreement, to limit competition and keep prices at comfortably high levels. As with Rockefeller's similar tactics 50 years before, it was not clear in 1928 that the agreement was illegal, because its participants were located in a number of different countries each with its own set of trade laws. Already in 1928, Jersey and the other oil giants were stretching the very concept of nationality beyond any simple application.

Following World War II, Jersey was again in need of crude to supply the resurgent economies of Europe. Already the world's largest producer, the company became interested in the vast oil concessions in Saudi Arabia recently won by Texaco and Socal. The latter companies, in need of both capital for expansion and world markets for exploitation, sold 30 percent of the newly formed Arabian American Oil Company (Aramco) to Jersey and 10 percent to Socony-Vacuum in 1946. Eight years later, after Iran's nationalization of Anglo-Persian's holdings was squelched by a combination of CIA assistance and an effective worldwide boycott of Iranian oil by competitors, Jersey was able to take 7 percent of the consortium formed to drill in that oil-rich country. With a number of significant tax advantages attached to foreign crude production, Jersey drew an increasing percentage of its oil from its holdings in all three of the major Middle Eastern fields—Iraq, Iran, and Saudi Arabia—and helped propel the 20-year postwar economic boom in the West. With oil prices exceptionally low, the United States and Europe busily shifted their economies to complete dependence on the automobile and on oil as the primary industrial fuel.

Exxon, Oil Shocks, and Diversification: 1972–89

Despite the growing strength of newcomers to the international market, such as Getty and Conoco, the big companies continued to exercise decisive control over the world oil supply and thus over the destinies of the Middle East producing countries. Growing nationalism and an increased awareness of the extraordinary power of the large oil companies led to the 1960 formation of the Organization of Petroleum Exporting Countries (OPEC). Later, a series of increasingly bitter confrontations erupted between countries and companies concerned about control over the oil upon which the world had come to depend. The growing power of OPEC and the concomitant nationalization of oil assets by various producing countries prompted Jersey to seek alternative sources of crude. Exploration resulted in discoveries in Alaska's Prudhoe Bay and the North Sea in the late 1960s. The Middle Eastern sources remained paramount, however, and when OPEC cut off oil supplies to the United States in 1973—in response to U.S. sponsorship of Israel—the resulting 400 percent price increase induced a prolonged recession and permanently changed the industrial world's attitude to oil. Control of oil was, in large part, taken out of the hands of the oil companies, who began exploring new sources of energy and business opportunities in other fields.

For Standard Oil Company (New Jersey), which had changed its name to Exxon in 1972, the oil embargo had several major effects. Most obviously it increased corporate sales; the expensive oil allowed Exxon to double its 1972 revenue of $20 billion in only two years and then pushed that figure over the $100 billion mark by 1980. After a year of windfall profits made possible by the sale of inventoried oil bought at much lower prices, Exxon was able to make use of its extensive North Sea and Alaskan holdings to keep profits at a steady level. The company had suffered a strong blow to its confidence, however, and soon was investigating a number of diversification measures that eventually included office equipment, a purchase of Reliance Electric Company (the fifth largest holdings of coal in the United States), and an early 1980s venture into shale oil. With the partial exception of coal, all of these were expensive failures, costing Exxon approximately $6 billion to $7 billion.

By the early 1980s the world oil picture had eased considerably and Exxon felt less urgency about diversification. With the price of oil peaking around 1981 and then tumbling for most of the decade, Exxon's sales dropped sharply. The company's confidence rose, however, as OPEC's grip on the marketplace

proved to be weaker than advertised. Having abandoned its forays into other areas, Exxon refocused on the oil and gas business, cutting its assets and workforce substantially to accommodate the drop in revenue without losing profitability. In 1986 the company consolidated its oil and gas operations outside North America, which had been handled by several separate subsidiaries, into a new division called Exxon Company, International, with headquarters in New Jersey. Exxon Company, U.S.A. and Imperial Oil Limited continued to handle the company's oil and gas operations in the United States and Canada, respectively.

Exxon also bought back a sizable number of its own shares to bolster per-share earnings, which reached excellent levels and won the approval of Wall Street. The stock buyback was partially in response to Exxon's embarrassing failure to invest its excess billions profitably—the company was somewhat at a loss as to what to do with its money. It could not expand further into the oil business without running into antitrust difficulties at home, and investments outside of oil would have had to be mammoth to warrant the time and energy required.

The **Exxon Valdez***: 1989–98*

In 1989 Exxon was no longer the world's largest company, and soon it would not even be the largest oil group (Royal Dutch/Shell would take over that position in 1990), but with the help of the March 24, 1989 *Exxon Valdez* disaster the company heightened its notoriety. The crash of the *Exxon Valdez* in Prince William Sound off the port of Valdez, Alaska, released about 260,000 barrels, or 11.2 million gallons, of crude oil. The disaster cost Exxon $1.7 billion in 1989 alone, and the company and its subsidiaries were faced with more than 170 civil and criminal lawsuits brought by state and federal governments and individuals.

By late 1991 Exxon had paid $2.2 billion to clean up Prince William Sound and had reached a tentative settlement of civil and criminal charges that levied a $125 million criminal fine against the oil conglomerate. Fully $100 million of the fine was forgiven and the remaining amount was split between the North American Wetlands Conservation Fund (which received $12 million) and the U.S. Treasury (which received $13 million). Exxon and a subsidiary, Exxon Shipping Co., also were required to pay an additional $1 billion to restore the spill area.

Although the *Valdez* disaster was a costly public relations nightmare—a nightmare made worse by the company's slow response to the disaster and by CEO Lawrence G. Rawl's failure to visit the site in person—Exxon's financial performance actually improved in the opening years of the last decade in the 20th century. The company enjoyed record profits in 1991, netting $5.6 billion and earning a special place in the *Fortune* 500. Of the annual list's top ten companies, Exxon was the only one to post a profit increase over 1990. *Business Week*'s ranking of companies according to market value also found Exxon at the top of the list.

The company's performance was especially dramatic when compared with the rest of the fuel industry: As a group the 44 fuel companies covered by *Business Week*'s survey lost $35 billion in value, or 11 percent, in 1991. That year, Exxon also scrambled to the top of the profits heap, according to *Forbes* magazine. With a profit increase of 12 percent over 1990, Exxon's $5.6 billion in net income enabled the company to unseat IBM as the United States' most profitable company. At 16.5 percent, Exxon's return on equity was also higher than any other oil company. The company also significantly boosted the value of its stock through its long-term and massive stock buyback program, through which it spent about $15.5 billion to repurchase 518 million shares—or 30 percent of its outstanding shares—between 1983 and 1991.

Like many of its competitors, Exxon was forced to trim expenses to maintain such outstanding profitability. One of the favorite methods was to cut jobs. Citing the globally depressed economy and the need to streamline operations, Exxon eliminated 5,000 employees from its payrolls between 1990 and 1992. With oil prices in a decade-long slide, Exxon also cut spending on exploration from $1.7 billion in 1985 to $900 million in 1992. The company's exploration budget constituted less than 1 percent of revenues and played a large part in Exxon's good financial performance. Meantime, Exxon in 1990 abandoned its fancy headquarters at Rockefeller Center in New York City to reestablish its base in the heart of oil territory, in the Dallas suburb of Irving, Texas. In 1991 the company established a new Houston-based division, Exxon Exploration Company, to handle the company's exploration operations everywhere in the world except for Canada.

At the end of 1993 Lee R. Raymond took over as CEO from the retiring Rawl. Raymond continued Exxon's focus on cost-cutting, with the workforce falling to 79,000 employees by 1996, the lowest level since the breakup of Standard Oil in 1911. Other savings were wrung out by reengineering production, transportation, and marketing processes. Over a five-year period ending in 1996, Exxon had managed to reduce its operating costs by $1.3 billion annually. The result was increasing levels of profits. In 1996 the company reported net income of $7.51 billion, more than any other company on the *Fortune* 500. The following year it made $8.46 billion on revenues of $120.28 billion, a 7 percent profit margin. The huge profits enabled Exxon in the middle to late 1990s to take some gambles, and it risked tens of billion of dollars on massive new oil and gas fields in Russia, Indonesia, and Africa. In addition, Exxon and Royal Dutch/Shell joined forces in a worldwide petroleum additives joint venture in 1996.

Yet Exxon was unable—some said unwilling—to shake itself free of its *Exxon Valdez* legacy. Having already spent some $1.1 billion to settle state and federal criminal charges related to the spill, Exxon faced a civil trial in which the plaintiffs sought compensatory and punitive damages amounting to $16.5 billion. The 14,000 plaintiffs in the civil suit included fishermen, Alaskan natives, and others claiming harm from the spill. In June 1994 a federal jury found that the huge oil spill had been caused by "recklessness" on the part of Exxon. Two months later the same jury ruled that the company should pay $286.8 million in compensatory damages; then in August the panel ordered Exxon to pay $5 billion in punitive damages. Although Wall Street reacted positively to what could have been much larger damage amounts and Exxon's huge profits placed it in a position to reach a final settlement and perhaps put the *Exxon Valdez* nightmare in its past, the company chose to

continue to take a hard line. It vowed to exhaust all its legal avenues to overturn the verdict—including seeking a mistrial and a new trial and filing appeals. In June 1997, in fact, Exxon formally appealed the $5 billion verdict. Exxon seemed to make another PR gaffe in the late 1990s when it attempted to reverse a federal ban on the return to Alaskan waters of the *Exxon Valdez,* which had by then been renamed the *Sea-River Mediterranean.* Environmentalists continued to berate the company for its refusal to operate double-hulled tankers, a ship design that may have prevented the oil spill in the first place. In addition, in an unrelated but equally embarrassing development, Exxon in 1997 reached a settlement with the Federal Trade Commission in which it agreed to run advertisements that refuted earlier ads claiming that its high-octane gasoline reduced automobile maintenance costs.

Nearing the Dawn of the 21st Century: The Merger of Exxon and Mobil

In December 1998 Exxon agreed to buy Mobil for about $75 billion in what promised to be one of the largest takeovers ever. The megamerger was one of a spate of petroleum industry deals brought about by an oil glut that forced down the price of a barrel of crude by late 1998 to about $11, the cheapest price in history with inflation factored in. Just one year earlier, the price had been about $23. The oil glut was caused by a number of factors, principally the Asian economic crisis and the sharp decline in oil consumption engendered by it, and the virtual collapse of OPEC, which was unable to curb production by its own members. In such an environment, pressure to cut costs was again exerted, and Exxon and Mobil cited projected savings of $2.8 billion per year as a prime factor behind the merger.

Based on 1998 results, the proposed Exxon Mobil Corporation would have combined revenues of $168.8 billion, making it the largest oil company in the world, and $8.1 billion in profits. Raymond would serve as chairman, CEO, and president of the Irving, Texas-based goliath, with the head of Mobil, Lucio A. Noto, acting as vice-chairman. Shareholders of both Exxon and Mobil approved the merger in May 1999. In September of that year the European Commission granted antitrust approval to the deal with the only major stipulation being that Mobil divest its share of a joint venture with BP Amoco p.l.c. in European refining and marketing. In November 1999, the historic and massive merger was completed in an $83 billion stock transaction. Mobil Corporation became a wholly owned subsidiary of Exxon Corporation concurrent with Exxon changing its name to Exxon Mobil Corporation.

Exxon Mobil in the 21st Century

The integration of Mobil into Exxon promised to deliver cost savings and to interweave two contrasting corporate cultures. Historically, Exxon's strengths had been in finance and engineering, while Mobil's strengths had been in marketing and deal-making. Exxon was as rigid as its leader, Lee Raymond, while Noto, "renowned from Riyadh to Jakarta for his high-octane energy and charm," as *Business Week* noted in its April 9, 2001 issue, personified the more relaxed culture of Mobil. As these two dissimilar, but potentially complementary, heritages combined, the corporate personality of Exxon dominated Exxon Mobil. Throughout the merged company's senior management ranks, Mobil executives generally served under Exxon executives. Noto, whose responsibilities and influence were diminished as vice-chairman, announced his retirement in January 2001, the same year the Exxon Mobil board of directors made an exception to the company's mandatory retirement age and asked Raymond to continue leading the company.

Under Raymond's tight control, Exxon Mobil demonstrated its skill as an efficient, financially prudent behemoth. By 2001, cost savings from the merger reached $4.6 billion. These savings were used to fund the company's growth by internal means, as the company prepared to expand its output of oil and gas—something it had not done since the 1970s. The company planned to invest $10 billion in exploration and production in 2001, an amount Exxon Mobil planned to spend annually through the end of the decade.

Five years after the merger, its success was confirmed. Between 1999 and 2004, Exxon Mobil earned $75 billion in net profits and generated $123 billion in cash. By 2004, the company was enjoying what Raymond, in a March 11, 2004 interview with the *Oil Daily,* referred to as "unprecedented developments" in Angola, Equatorial Guinea, Chad, and the Caspian Sea. The profile of the company's production portfolio was expected to be altered substantially by these developments. Africa, the Mideast, and Russia accounted for less than 20 percent of Exxon Mobil's oil and gas production in 2004. By 2010, the regions were expected to account for 40 percent of the company's oil and gas production.

As Exxon Mobil prepared for the future, perhaps the most significant event on the horizon was a change in leadership. Industry observers were expecting Raymond to retire at some point midway through the decade, and the consensus on his replacement was Rex Tillerson, who joined Exxon in 1975. Following the 1999 merger, Tillerson was appointed executive vice-president of Exxon Mobil Development Co., the entity responsible for guiding oil and gas development and drilling activities for Exxon Mobil. In February 2004, in a move that appeared to confirm his imminent promotion to chief executive officer, Tillerson was elected president of Exxon Mobil. "Tillerson has a reputation as a good 'hands on' guy, and a solid exploration and production manager," an analyst said in a March 1, 2004 interview with the *Oil Daily.* "He's a Texas engineer type in a company with a history of being run by engineers." If Tillerson did in fact succeed Raymond, his challenge was to keep Exxon Mobil moving forward, as the largest oil company in the United States endeavored to maintain its reputation on the global scene.

Principal Subsidiaries

Exxon Luxembourg Holdings L.L.C.; Exxon Mobile Bay Limited Partnership; Exxon Neftegas Limited; Exxon Overseas Corporation; Exxon Yemen Inc.; ExxonMobil Alaska Production Inc.; ExxonMobil Asia Pacific Pte. Ltd. (Singapore); ExxonMobil Aviation International Limited (U.K.); ExxonMobil Canada Ltd.; ExxonMobil Capital N.V. (Netherlands); ExxonMobil Central Europe Holding GmbH (Germany); ExxonMobil Chemical Central Europe GmbH (Germany); ExxonMobil Chemical Films Europe, Inc.; ExxonMobil Chemical France S.A.R.L. (France; 99.77%); ExxonMobil Chemical Holland B.V.; ExxonMobil Chemical Holland L.L.C.; ExxonMobil Chemical Limited (U.K.); ExxonMobil Chemical Operations Private Limited (Singapore); ExxonMobil Chemical Polymeres SNC (France; 99.77%); ExxonMobil de Colombia S.A.; ExxonMobil Egypt (S.A.E.); ExxonMobil Energy Limited (Hong Kong); ExxonMobil Exploration and Production Malaysia Inc.; ExxonMobil Far East Holdings Ltd. (Bahamas); ExxonMobil Gas Marketing Europe Limited (U.K.); ExxonMobil Global Services Company; ExxonMobil Holding Company Holland L.L.C.; ExxonMobil Hong Kong Limited; ExxonMobil International Holdings Inc.; ExxonMobil International Services, S.A.R.L. (Luxembourg); ExxonMobil Kazakhstan Inc. (Malaysia); ExxonMobil Kazakhstan Ventures Inc.; ExxonMobil Luxembourg UK, S.A.R.L.; ExxonMobil Malaysia Sdn. Bhd.; ExxonMobil Marine Limited (U.K.); ExxonMobil Mediterranea S.R.L. (Italy); ExxonMobil Middle East Gas Marketing Limited (Bahamas); ExxonMobil Oil Corporation; ExxonMobil Oil Indonesia Inc.; ExxonMobil Oil Singapore Pte. Ltd.; ExxonMobil Petroleum & Chemical (Belgium); ExxonMobil Pipeline Company; ExxonMobil Production Deutschland GmbH (Germany); ExxonMobil Qatargas Inc.; ExxonMobil Rasgas Inc.; ExxonMobil Sales and Supply Corporation; ExxonMobil Yugen Kaisha (Japan); Fina Antwerp Olefins N.V. (Belgium; 35%); Imperial Oil Limited (Canada; 69.6%); Infineum Holdings B.V. (Belgium; 49.6%); Kyokuto Sekiyu Kogyo Kabushiki Kaisha (Japan; 50%); Mineraloelraffinerie Oberrhein GmbH & Co. KG (Germany; 25%); Mobil Argentina S.A.; Mobil Australia Resources Company Pty. Limited; Mobil California Exploration & Producing Asset Company; Mobil Caspian Pipeline Company; Mobil Cerro Negro, Ltd. (Bahamas); Mobil Corporation; Mobil Equatorial Guinea Inc.; Mobil Erdgas-Erdoel GmbH (Germany; 99.99%); Mobil Exploration and Development Argentina Inc.; Mobil Exploration Indonesia Inc.; Mobil Exploration Norway Inc.; Mobil Fairfax Inc.; Mobil North Sea Limited; Mobil Oil Australia Pty. Ltd.; Mobil Oil Exploration & Producing Southeast Inc.; Mobil Oil New Zealand Limited; Mobil Oil Nigeria Public Limited Company (59.99%); Mobil Producing Nigeria Unlimited; Mobil Producing Texas & New Mexico Inc.; Mobil Refining Australia Pty. Ltd.; Mobil Yanbu Petrochemical Company Inc.; Mobil Yanbu Refining Company Inc.; Nansei Sekiyu Kabushiki Kaisha (Japan; 43.77%); Nederlandse Aardolie Maatschappij B.V. (Netherlands; 50%); Paxon Polymer Company, L.P. II (92.84%); QM Tanker Co., L.L.C. (Cayman Islands; 50%); Ras Laffan Liquefied Natural Gas Company Limited (Qatar; 26.5%); Ras Laffan Liquefied Natural Gas Company Limited (Qatar; 29.99%); Samoco L.L.C. (Cayman Islands; 50%); Saudi Aramco Mobil Refinery Company Ltd. (Saudi Arabia; 50%); Saudi Yanbu Petrochemical Co. (Saudi Arabia; 50%); Schubert Beteiligungs-GmbH (Germany; 72.99%); SeaRiver Maritime Financial Holdings, Inc.; SeaRiver Maritime, Inc.; Societa per Azioni Raffineria Padana Olii Minerali-SARPOM (Italy; 74.14%); Superior Oil (U.K.) Limited; Tengizchevroil, LLP (Kazakhstan; 25%); TonenGeneral Sekiyu K.K. (Japan; 50.02%); Tonen Kagaku K.K. (Japan; 50.02%).

Principal Competitors

BP p.l.c.; ChevronTexaco Corporation; Royal Dutch/Shell Group of Companies.

Further Reading

Abcede, Angel, "Mobil Opts for Caution with Transition from 'G' to 'C' Stores," *National Petroleum News,* January 1997.

Akin, Edward N., *Flagler: Rockefeller Partner and Florida Baron,* Kent, Ohio: Kent State University Press, 1988.

"Alabama Judge Reduces Exxon Mobil Ruling 70 Percent to $3.6 Billion," *Dallas Morning News,* March 30, 2004, p. B1.

Beatty, Sally, "Exxon-Mobil Is Marketing Dilemma," *Wall Street Journal,* December 3, 1998, p. B11.

A Brief History of Mobil, New York: Mobil Corporation, 1991.

Byrne, Harlan S., "Well-Oiled: Exxon Has Shaped Itself into a Nimble and Even More Formidable Giant," *Barron's,* May 20, 1996, pp. 17–18.

Caney, Derek, "Ethylene Snaps Back After Andrew," *Chemical Marketing Reporter,* September 7, 1992.

Caragata, Warren, "Union of Giants: Exxon and Mobil Create a Colossus," *Maclean's,* December 14, 1998, pp. 44–46.

Chernow, Ron, *Titan: The Life of John D. Rockefeller, Sr.,* New York: Random House, 1998.

Cooper, Christopher, "Fears Linger on 10th Anniversary of *Exxon Valdez* Spill," *Wall Street Journal,* March 23, 1999, p. B4.

Cooper, Christopher, and Steve Liesman, "Exxon Agrees to Buy Mobil for $75.3 Billion," *Wall Street Journal,* December 2, 1998, p. A3.

Cropper, Carol M., et al., "The *Forbes* 500's Annual Directory," *Forbes,* April 27, 1992.

"Environmental Manager's Ethical Stand Vindicated," *Environmental Manager,* September 1992.

"ExxonMobil Opens Its 1,000th On the Run Site," *National Petroleum News,* April 2004, p. 61.

"Exxon-Mobil, Total-Petrofina Mergers Slated," *Oil Gas Journal,* December 7, 1998, pp. 37–38, 40–41.

"Exxon Unleashed," *Business Week,* April 9, 2001, p. 58.

Fan, Eliza, "Mobil Restructures Its Organization to Shift Power to Regional Managers," *Oil Daily,* June 4, 1996.

"Federal Appeals Court Overturns $4 Billion Ruling Against Exxon," *Dallas Morning News,* August 23, 2003, p. B2.

Finch, Peter, "The *Business Week* 1000," *Business Week,* special issue, 1992.

"Gas Dominates Exxon's Development Portfolio," *Oil Daily,* September 10, 2004.

Gibb, George Sweet, and Evelyn H. Knowlton, *History of Standard Oil Company (New Jersey): The Resurgent Years, 1911–1927,* New York: Harper Brothers, 1956.

Grabarek, Brooke H., "Exxon: Forget the *Valdez,*" *Financial World,* September 27, 1994, p. 14.

Hedges, Stephen J., "The Cost of Cleaning Up," *U.S. News World Report,* August 30/September 6, 1993, pp. 26–28, 30.

Hidy, Ralph W., and Murrel E. Hidy, *History of Standard Oil Company (New Jersey): Pioneering in Big Business, 1882–1911,* New York: Harper Brothers, 1955.

"Hurricane Slams Gulf Operations," *Oil & Gas Journal,* September 7, 1992.

"Indonesia—Looking for Oil and Gas: As Explorations Step Up So Do Equipment Imports," *East Asian Executive Reports,* June 15, 1992.

"Industry Earnings Plunge from 1990 Level," *Oil & Gas Journal,* December 2, 1991.

"Inside the Empire of Exxon the Unloved," *Economist,* March 5, 1994, p. 69.

"Irani: Oxy Winds Up Restructuring Program; Murray, Mobil Discussing More Moves," *Oil & Gas Journal,* March 23, 1992.

Koen, A.D., "Hurricane Shuts Down Gulf Activity," *Oil & Gas Journal,* August 31, 1992.

Kopp, Wendy, "The ABCs of Raising Millions," *Working Woman,* June 1992.

Larson, Henrietta M., Evelyn H. Knowlton, and Charles S. Popple, *History of Standard Oil Company (New Jersey): New Horizons, 1927–1950,* New York: Harper Row, 1971.

Liesman, Steve, "Exxon Suspends Exploration in Russia," *Wall Street Journal,* August 19, 1999, p. A2.

Liesman, Steve, and John R. Wilke, "Exxon and Mobil Get Antitrust Approval in Europe for Their Planned Merger," *Wall Street Journal,* September 30, 1999, p. A4.

Longman, Phillip J., and Jack Egan, "Why Big Oil Is Getting a Lot Bigger," *U.S. News World Report,* December 14, 1998, pp. 26–28.

Mack, Toni, "Mobil's Great Challenge," *Forbes,* January 22, 1996.

——, "The Tiger Is on the Prowl," *Forbes,* April 21, 1997, p. 42.

McCoy, Charles, "Exxon's Secret *Valdez* Deals Anger Judge," *Wall Street Journal,* June 13, 1996, p. A3.

Merolli, Paul, "Raymond Sees No Reason to Change Exxon," *Oil Daily,* March 11, 2004.

Michels, Antony, "Sailing Straight with Growth Stocks," *Fortune,* August 8, 1994.

"More U.S. Production Changes Hands," *Oil & Gas Journal,* July 20, 1992.

Nevins, Allan, *Study in Power: John D. Rockefeller—Industrialist and Philanthropist,* 2 vols., New York: Charles Scribner's Sons, 1953.

Norman, James R., "A Tale of Two Strategies," *Forbes,* August 17, 1992, p. 48.

"Oil Companies Report Sharply Lower Earnings," *Chemical Marketing Reporter,* April 27, 1992.

"Oil Majors Make Tough Decisions on Jobs, Assets," *Chemical Marketing Reporter,* July 13, 1992.

Pillar, Dan, "Exxon Mobil Leader Talks to Analysts About Annual Report," *Forth Worth Star-Telegram,* March 11, 2004, p. B4.

Raeburn, Paul, "It's Time to Put the *Valdez* Behind Us," *Business Week,* March 29, 1999, p. 90.

"Restructuring Still Rampant in U.S.," *Oil & Gas Journal,* July 13, 1992.

Richards, Bill, "Exxon Is Battling a Ban on an Infamous Tanker," *Wall Street Journal,* July 29, 1998, p. B1.

Rogers, Alison, "The *Fortune* 500: It Was the Worst of Years," *Fortune,* April 20, 1992.

Sampson, Anthony, *The Seven Sisters: The Great Oil Companies and the World They Made,* New York: Viking, 1975; New York: Bantam, 1991.

Solomon, Caleb, "Exxon Is Told to Pay $5 Billion for *Valdez* Spill," *Wall Street Journal,* September 19, 1994, p. A3.

——, "Exxon Verdict Comes Amid Problems of Old Oil Fields, Few New Prospects," *Wall Street Journal,* September 19, 1994, p. A3.

——, "Jury Decides Exxon Must Pay $286.8 Million," *Wall Street Journal,* August 12, 1994, p. A3.

——, "Jury Finds Exxon Reckless in Oil Spill," *Wall Street Journal,* June 14, 1994, p. A3.

Sullivan, Allanna, "Exxon and Mobil Are Already Devising Their New Brand," *Wall Street Journal,* April 6, 1999, p. B4.

Tarbell, Ida M., *The History of the Standard Oil Company,* New York: Harper Row, 1966.

Teitelbaum, Richard, "Exxon: Pumping Up Profits," *Fortune,* April 28, 1997, pp. 134–36, 140–42.

"Tillerson Seen As Next CEO at Exxon Mobil," *Oil Daily,* March 1, 2004.

Wall, Bennett H., *Growth in a Changing Environment: A History of Standard Oil Company (New Jersey),* New York: McGraw-Hill, 1988.

Wilke, John R., and Steve Liesman, "Exxon, Mobil May Be Forced into Divestitures," *Wall Street Journal,* January 20, 1999, p. A3.

—Jonathan Martin
—updates: April Dougal, Paula Kepos,
David E. Salamie, Jeffrey L. Covell

Geodis S.A.

183 avenue de Clichy
75017 Paris
France
Telephone: +33 1 53 06 12 00
Fax: +33 1 53 06 12 01
Web site: http://www.geodis.fr

Public Company
Incorporated: 1925 as Société des Transports Rapides
    Calberson
Employees: 22,519
Sales: EUR 22.5 billion (2003)
Stock Exchanges: Euronext Paris
Ticker Symbol: GEO
NAIC: 541614 Process, Physical Distribution, and
    Logistics Consulting Services; 484121 General Freight
    Trucking, Long-Distance, Truckload

Geodis S.A. is one of Europe's leading logistics groups, providing a full range of logistics services and supply side management to corporations around the world. Founded in 1995 as a spinoff of French national railway SNCF's nonrail goods transport operations, Geodis has extended its reach to include some 120 countries, with services through nearly 700 agencies. France remains the company's dominant market, however, at 69 percent of its sales of EUR 22.5 billion in 2003. Geodis operates through a number of primary brands, including Geodis BM, focused on the French and European transport market; Geodis Calberson, the group's largest component, which provides groupage and express delivery services; Geodis Logistics, a provider of global logistics solutions; Geodis Vitesse, based in The Netherlands, providing logistics, supply chain management, overseas, and related services in the Benelux market; Geodis Züst Ambrosetti, one of Italy's leading logistics companies; Geodis Teisa, which provides transport and logistics services to the Iberian Peninsula; and Geodis Overseas, a France-based multimodal freight-forwarding and intercontinental logistics services provider. The company also operates under a number of regional brands in France, including Geodis Walbaum, Geodis Dusolier Calberson, Geodis Mes-

sageries Parisiennes de Livre, Geodis Valena, and Geodis MG Transports. Geodis is listed on the Euronext Paris Stock Exchange. The SNCF controls approximately 45 percent of Geodis's shares. La Poste, the French postal service, is also a major Geodis shareholder.

Early 20th-Century Origins

In 1995, the Société National de Chemins de Fer Français, or SNCF, restructured its nonrail transport holdings into a new company, Geodis, which was then spun off in a public offering. The new company quickly became a leading player in France's transport and logistics sectors. Geodis, however, had its origins at the beginning of the 20th century, providing services to rail customers in Le Havre, one of France's major industrial ports.

The development of France's national rail system had by the beginning of the 20th century given the country one of the Western world's densest railway grids. Part of the reason for this is the fact that France's railroads, although encouraged and financially supported by the French government, had been almost entirely built by private interests. This situation also led to the development of a number of ancillary service professions, such as the "commissionnaire bagagiste," or baggage delivery service, responsible for picking up and delivering passengers' luggage and other goods from their homes to the trains, and accompanying the baggage en route in order to see the luggage through to its final destination.

Among these delivery men was Emile Calberson, who started his own business in 1904 in the port town of Le Havre. Calberson began providing delivery services along the Le Havre-Rouen-Paris line, at the time one of the most important and busiest in France. By 1907, Calberson had set up his first branch office in Rouen, followed by an office in Paris in 1910, allowing him to provide delivery services along the entire line.

Deliveries were made by horse-drawn carriage until just before World War I, when Calberson's company—led by son Leon and wife Philomene since Calberson's death in 1913—introduced motorized coaches for the first time. Although these were soon after requisitioned by the French army for the war effort, Calberson had recognized the potential offered by motor

Company Perspectives:

New Ambitions for the Group: Pursuit of improvement in our profitability.

2003 was a watershed year for Geodis. Having reached and even surpassed its objectives, the Group improved its financial situation. It has realised profits, controlled its costs, reduced its indebtedness and generated a positive free cash flow. When combined with the quality of its offer, the strength of its fundamentals provides it with the means to achieve its ambition: accelerate its development in order to strengthen its positions in Europe and widen its worldwide coverage while improving its profitability.

vehicle transport, and in 1919 the company relaunched its operation as a full-fledged goods transporter along the Paris-Rouen-Le Havre line. Joining the company at this time was René Marquand, at first as head of the Le Havre office, then as partner in the company alongside Leon Calberson.

Calberson's destiny changed in 1921 when, after the company was denied its request for authorization to transport large-sized bulk goods on the line's trains, it decided to put into place a road-based delivery service. As an early entrant in France's road transport industry, Calberson grew quickly. By 1925, the company had incorporated as Société des Transports Rapides Calberson, and, taking advantage of the flexibility of the road system, the company expanded its territory, with routes covering much of France's north region. This led the company to open a new series of branch offices, and by the end of the decade, Calberson had offices in Lille, Roubais, Tourcoing, Nantes, Caen, Laval, Rennes, and Flers, in addition to its offices in Le Havre, Rouen, and Paris.

Calberson's growing fleet enabled it to become a strong partner for the region's railroads, themselves soon to be nationalized under a single government-run entity, the Société National de Chemins de Fer Français, or SNCF. In the early 1930s, the French government began encouraging the closer cooperation among the different transport modes in the country—in addition to the rail and road network, the country also boasted a well-developed canal network. Marquand favored cooperation with the railroads. This led Calberson, who preferred to remain in competition with the railroads, to leave the company in 1931. The following year, Société des Transports Rapides Calberson sold the majority of its shares to France Transport Domicile. The company moved its headquarters to Paris, where Marquand became president.

During the early 1930s, the French government laid the groundwork for the creation of the SNCF, passing new legislation including a decree in 1934 establishing a system of cooperation among the railroad and other transporters in the country. Calberson was now well placed to become a major partner for the railroads in connecting the country's rail and road grid, and, backed by contracts with the developing national railroad, the company began extending its operations into the southwest region in the middle of the decade. The establishment of the SNCF in 1938 led Calberson to adopt a new corporate status, as a limited liability company that same year.

During World War II, Calberson restricted its operations to the Brittany and western regions. In 1942, however, the company acquired Marseilles-based Transports Carré, giving it access to the south of the country and to the French presence in North Africa. By the end of the war, Calberson emerged as one of the country's primary road transporters specialized in the delivery sector.

The Logistics of Restructuring in the 1990s

Calberson's position in the French transport market was cemented in 1955 when the shares in the company formerly held by France Transport Domicile were acquired by Sceta, the road transport subsidiary of the SNCF. Calberson now became a government-owned company, but nonetheless continued as an independently operating entity. Backed by Sceta and the SNCF, Calberson began a series of acquisitions enabling it to expand its operations to provide national coverage by the mid-1960s.

Next, Calberson turned toward developing its international operations, starting with the 1966 purchase of Schenker France. The company then established a dedicated international subsidiary, Société Nouvelle des Transports Internationaux Calberson (SNTI), later known as Calberson Overseas.

Calberson also began expanding its range of services. In 1969, the company inaugurated a new warehouse in Paris. At 130,000 square meters, the facility boasted being the world's largest distribution center. In 1971, Calberson added another new service, that of express delivery. The group's national network enabled it to launch its own 24-hour and 48-hour delivery services. That offering was extended soon after with the launch of Calexpress, which promised 12-hour delivery to more than 36,000 locations throughout the country. By 1974, the growth of the group's delivery operations led it to open a new dedicated express delivery facility in Paris.

The acquisition of Transports Legat in 1976 allowed the company to extend its international operations. That year, as well, Calberson reached a cooperation agreement with another leading delivery group, France Express, providing for a merging of the two groups' national networks.

Calberson restructured in the early 1980s, creating the holding company Compagnie Générale Calberson (CGC), which went public on the Paris stock exchange in 1984. The SNCF, through Sceta, nonetheless remained the group's majority shareholder. By mid-decade, Calberson had emerged as the country's second largest land-based transport group, following only the SNCF itself.

Calberson restructured in 1992, splitting its operations into 12 regions. At the same time, the SNCF was also under pressure to carry out its own restructuring, in large part in order to meet European Union directives meant to develop a competitive market among the union's railroads. As part of that process, the SNCF moved to spin off much of Sceta's operations into a new, independent company, Geodis. The SNCF nonetheless remained Geodis's major shareholder, with more than 45 percent of its stock.

Calberson, including Calberson Overseas, formed the major part of the new company, complemented by the addition of

Key Dates:

1904: Emile Calberson begins offering services as "commissionnaire bagagiste" for Le Havre railroad.
1907: Calberson opens a branch office in Rouen.
1910: A branch office is opened in Paris, completing service along the entire Le Havre-Rouen-Paris line.
1919: The company begins operating as a general goods transporter.
1921: The company focuses on developing road transport operations.
1925: The company incorporates as Société des Transports Rapides Calberson.
1931: Bourgey-Montreuil, which grows into a major road transport group in France, is founded.
1932: FTD acquires a majority share of the company, renamed Société Nouvelle des Transportes Rapides Calberson (SNTR).
1942: The company acquires Transports Carré in Marseilles.
1955: SNCF subsidiary Sceta acquires SNTR.
1966: The company acquires Schenker France, establishing international operations.
1969: The company opens a 130,000-square-meter warehouse in Paris.
1970: Express delivery service is launched.
1984: The company restructures under holding Compagnie Générale Calberson and lists on the Paris Stock Exchange.
1995: SNCF spins off its road transport and logistics division, including Calberson, Calberson Overseas, and Bourgey-Montreuil, as Geodis.
1997: Geodis acquires Tailleur Industrie as part of a strategic focus on logistics operations.
1999: Vitesse, in The Netherlands, is acquired.
2001: Züst Ambrosetti, in Italy, is acquired.
2003: Geodis opens a 30,000-square-meter logistics platform in Ireland.

Bourgey-Montreuil, founded in 1931 and one of France's leading road transporters, as well as a number of Sceta's logistics holdings. Yet a number of the company's operations were losing money—part of its heritage as a member of the perennially unprofitable SNCF—leading to the company posting a loss of FRF 240 million in 1996. In response the group named Alain Poinssot as company CEO in 1997. Poinssot then led the company on a new restructuring design to refocus it as a logistics specialist.

The European logistics market was then in the process of a strong development. The arrival of a single currency at the end of the decade offered new perspectives for internationally operating companies, not least of which was the creation of unified logistics networks. As distribution, warehousing, supply chain management, and other functions extended beyond a local scale, the complexity of these operations had become too difficult and too expensive for corporations seeking at the same time to reduce their lead times, speed up their order-to-delivery rates, and minimize their raw materials and other inventories.

Corporations increasingly sought all-in-one and internationally based solutions for their logistics needs. Geodis responded by boosting its own logistics capacity through a series of strategic acquisitions, starting with France's Tailleur Industrie in 1997. The company then moved to extend its reach deeper into Europe, and in 1999, Geodis acquired The Netherlands' Vitesse B.V. That purchase, which created Geodis Vitesse, gave the company access to the Benelux markets as well as other parts of northern Europe.

For the Spanish and Portuguese markets, the company acquired Teisa, forming Geodis Teisa. With a fleet of nearly 500 vehicles and warehousing space of more than 100,000 square meters, Geodis Teisa emerged as one of the leading logistics players for the Iberian Peninsula market. Geodis also moved into the United Kingdom, acquiring United Carriers Group in 1999; that purchase proved short-lived, however, as the company shut down its struggling U.K. operation at the beginning of 2002. At the same time, Geodis stepped up its focus on its logistics operations when it sold off its express parcel delivery service, regrouped under a new subsidiary, Extand, to the British Post Office for EUR 122 million.

Instead, Geodis turned to Italy, where it had purchased that country's Züst Ambrosetti at the beginning of 2001. That company brought Geodis a major logistics operation featuring nearly 60 distribution centers, and more than one million square meters of warehousing space across 11 facilities. Geodis's Italian holdings were expanded further with the purchase of a 50 percent stake in Trate Sud. In 2004, Geodis moved to acquire complete control of that business.

Back at home, Geodis acquired a new shareholder in 2001 when the SNCF and La Poste reached an agreement to exchange between Geodis's Extand and La Poste's logistics subsidiary Sernam. As part of the agreement, La Poste agreed to acquire as much as 25 percent of Geodis shares. Ultimately, La Poste decided not to acquire Extand. The two sides agreed, however, to the transfer of Sernam to Geodis. That move, however, remained blocked by the French government.

As it moved toward mid-decade, Geodis focused on establishing partnerships to enhance its range of logistics services. In 2002, the company reached a partnership agreement with Rohde & Liesenfeld, gaining access to that company's expertise in air and maritime-based transport and logistics. That year, as well, the company partnered with groupage specialist Elix. The two companies expanded their partnership the following year, when Geodis Züst Ambrosetti became Elix's exclusive partner in its Italy-Germany network. As part of the partnership agreement, Geodis acquired 34 percent of Elix's shares. Also that year, Geodis opened a new 30,000-square-meter logistics platform in Ireland as part of its outsourcing services for IBM. With sales of more than EUR 22 billion, Geodis counted among the leaders of Europe's logistics sector in the new century.

Principal Subsidiaries

Geodis Bm; Geodis Calberson; Geodis Dusolier Calberson: Geodis Logistics; Geodis Messageries Parisiennes du Livre: Geodis mg transports; Geodis Overseas; Geodis Teisa (Spain); Geodis Valenda; Geodis Vitesse (Netherlands); Geodis Walbaum: Geodis Züst Ambrosetti (Italy).

Principal Competitors

Deutsche Post; Exel PLC; Kuhne und Nagel International AG; Schenker AG; Inchcape PLC; J Lauritzen A/S; Danzas Group; IDS Logistik GmbH; Société Norbert Dentressangle S.A.

Further Reading

Coia, Anthony, "Logistics Alliances Cross European Borders," *Logistics Management & Distribution Report,* September 2000, p. S3.

Collomp, Florentin, "Comment IBM a vendu ses camions, ses entrepots et ses salariés," *L'Expansion,* January 21, 1999, p. 106.

"La filiale italienne du logisticien français Geodis vient de monter à 100 pc dans le capital de Trate Sud," *Les Echos,* June 9, 2004.

Parker, John G., "Geodis Acquires Vitesse," *Traffic World,* August 9, 1999, p. 17.

"Sernam: le colis piégé de la SNCF," *Nouvel Observateur,* August 30, 2001.

—M.L. Cohen

Graco Inc.

88 11th Avenue Northeast
Minneapolis, Minnesota 55413-1829
U.S.A.
Telephone: (612) 623-6000
Fax: (612) 623-6777
Web site: http://www.graco.com

Public Company
Incorporated: 1926 as Gray Company, Inc.
Employees: 1,750
Sales: $535.1 million (2003)
Stock Exchanges: New York
Ticket Symbol: GGG
NAIC: 333911 Pump and Pumping Equipment
    Manufacturing; 333912 Air and Gas Compressor
    Manufacturing; 333913 Measuring and Dispensing
    Pump Manufacturing; 333996 Fluid Power Pump and
    Motor Manufacturing

Graco Inc. is a world leader in fluid-handling systems and components. The company designs and manufactures products that move, measure, mix, proportion, control, dispense, and apply a wide range of fluids and viscous materials for a variety of industries, ranging from shipbuilding and aerospace to construction contracting and fast-lube outlets. According to Harlan S. Byrne in a February 1997 *Barron's* article, "Graco is one of those companies, nearly invisible to investors, that makes a steady living by supplying humdrum products—in its case, application systems for paint, sealants, adhesives and lubricants." Low-profile Graco serves such industry giants as Andersen Windows and Caterpillar Inc. while quietly holding a number one position in a majority of its markets.

First Products: 1920s–30s

Graco traces its history to Gray Company, Inc., which was founded in 1926 by Leil and Russell Gray to manufacture and sell the air-powered grease gun the brothers had developed for use in automobile maintenance. The men, who worked in a downtown Minneapolis garage, found hand-operated grease guns cumbersome to use, especially in the winter months when lubricants were more difficult to move. After field tests showed their invention was easier to handle and more effective than the hand-operated devices, the brothers hired three employees and began manufacturing "Graco" air-powered grease guns. First year sales were about $35,000.

Within two years, the men added other products to the Graco line, such as an air-powered pumping unit that moved automotive fluids directly from shipping containers through a flexible hose to the service area. The company also began a nationwide marketing program directed primarily to car dealers and service station owners.

Sales had reached $65,000 by 1931. The company continued to grow even during the Great Depression years, and in 1938 the business moved into a new plant, where Russell Gray further expanded the product line. Leil Gray, as company president, accelerated marketing and sales efforts; a branch office opened in New York, and salesmen carried Graco products in trailers bearing the company insignia. Sales topped $1 million in 1941.

Postwar Change of Focus and Rapid Growth

During World War II, Gray Company designed mobile lubrication equipment for use on the battlefield, while a tire retreading system helped extend limited resources at home. After the war the company turned its attention to industrial uses of the pumping technology it had been developing over the years. Spraying units, finishing equipment, and dispensing systems were designed for uses ranging from spreading adhesives to handling food.

By the mid-1950s, the 400-employee company had revenues in excess of $5 million. Driven by the needs of its customers, Gray Company continued to play the role of innovator. The company was the first to use hydraulics for cleaning, and the first to develop cold airless atomization (a process that used pressure to separate liquid into fine particles) for spray painting and coating. The company also began to design automated systems for manufacturing plants and implement plans for international operations.

Company Perspectives:

Graco's mission is to generate sustained profitable growth to benefit its customers, employees, shareholders and communities. We will be the world's leading supplier of fluid management products and packages in the markets we target.

In 1958 Leil Gray died, and Harry A. Murphy, Sr., was named president and CEO. That same year, Gray Company introduced Hydra-Spray, the first airless paint spray unit, and airless-spray technology propelled the company's growth in the 1960s. In 1965 Gray Company developed an electrically powered airless-spray system that freed painting contractors from bulky compressors. The company also introduced equipment that permitted hot airless pumping, proportionate mixing, and automatically controlled dispensing of fluids.

In 1962 Leil Gray's son-in-law David A. Koch was named president, succeeding Murphy. In the early years of his tenure, Koch guided the company through a plant modernization program and an important period of growth. In 1969, Gray Company, Inc. was taken public and changed its name to Graco Inc. Sales for the year were $33 million up from about $12 million when Koch assumed company leadership.

International expansion moved forward with the purchase of a majority interest in French automobile servicing equipment and products manufacturer Fogautolube S.A. and also with the establishment of a Canadian sales subsidiary. Domestically, Graco purchased Chicago-based H.G. Fischer & Co., a finishing and electrostatics business, in 1970. Sales topped $50 million in 1971. The company experienced an annual growth rate of 17 percent in sales and about 20 percent in net earnings over the ten-year period from 1963 to 1973.

A Decade of Change: 1970s

Graco's rapid growth faltered in 1974. Financial analyst Ken Johnson, in a 1975 *Corporate Report* article, suggested that Graco was surprised by a weakening market that had been disguised by customer purchases made in response to rapidly rising raw material prices. Net sales for 1974 rose only 6.3 percent, and net earnings fell 50 percent. The slide continued in 1975 with a significant drop in revenues.

Nevertheless, Graco rebounded in 1976. Pumps and spray-painting equipment for the construction and decorating trades led the recovery. Graco sales more than doubled over four years, and earnings reached a high of $10 million or $4.45 per share in 1979. Concern regarding future growth prompted the company to develop technology acquired earlier in the decade.

Electrostatic painting, which required less paint and reduced emissions, had become a preferred finishing method in increasingly cost-conscious, competitive, and environmentally concerned times. A heavy investment in the technology paid off: Graco developed a successful new line of sophisticated products and positioned itself as an electrostatic equipment supplier for automobile makers.

Robotics Venture

In 1981 the company established a joint venture, Graco Robotics, Inc. (GRI), with Edon Finishing Systems of Troy, Michigan, in order to develop a robotics paint-finishing system. According to Eben Shapiro, in a June 1987 *Minneapolis/St. Paul CityBusiness* article, Graco saw robotics as "a logical and necessary extension of its finishing business."

In 1982 Graco sales and earnings were hit by a combination of poor market and economic conditions, but the company continued to pump research and development dollars into the slowly progressing robotics venture and even increased its ownership from 51 to 80 percent. GRI sold its first robots in 1983 and became profitable in 1984. With 1985 sales around $20 million, GRI contributed about 10 percent of total Graco sales.

Koch stepped down as president of Graco in 1985, remaining chairman and CEO. Walter Weyler, a vice-president with General Electric Company, succeeded him. Quoted in an April 1985 *Minneapolis Star Tribune* article, Koch remarked that he intended to focus on the strategic direction of the company as it made the transition from an emphasis on components to high-tech systems.

Activity continued in other business segments. In 1984 Graco discontinued a consumer painting business started in the late 1970s. The purchase of Lockwood Technology, Inc. (LTI), a supplier of chemical bonding and sealing equipment, broadened the fluid handling group that same year. The company acquired 100 percent ownership of a former Japanese joint venture in 1985, thus expanding its international operations in the Far East. The following year Graco's common stock was listed on the New York Stock Exchange.

By 1986, GRI had become a major supplier of paint-spraying robots, and its customers included Chrysler, Ford, Fiat, Ferrari, Volvo, and Rolls-Royce. Moreover, Japanese automakers purchased robotics paint sprayers for plants located in the United States. GRI was one of only a few U.S. robot makers that had been able to maintain profitability.

A Changing Marketplace: The 1990s

Demand for finishing equipment fell off, however, as U.S. automakers completed installation of the new generation of paint sprayers in the late 1980s; and profits on foreign sales of large automated systems were low because of customizing costs. Graco's 1988 domestic sales were flat, while a 31.7 percent increase in international sales was attributable to its traditional products, such as portable airless-spray painters.

International sales slowed in 1990, but increased U.S. sales in architectural coating and cleaning equipment helped Graco achieve both record sales and earnings for the year; net revenues were $321.3 million, and net earnings were $17.7 million. Continuing recession in the United States and poor economic conditions in several European countries resulted in decreased earnings in 1991, which fell by nearly 50 percent. The company also reported losses associated with the divestment of its robotics division; pressure from larger competitors had prompted the sale.

The company initiated a year-long strategic review in 1992, while it refined various aspects of its businesses. As a result,

---

Key Dates:

1926: Leil and Russell Gray found Gray Company, Inc. in Minneapolis to make and sell "Graco" air-powered grease guns.

1941: Sales reach $1 million; as part of the war effort, Gray Company designs mobile lubrication equipment for use on the battlefield.

1958: Company introduces Hydra-Spray, the first airless paint spray unit.

1962: David A. Koch, son-in-law of Leil Gray, takes over leadership as president.

1969: Company goes public as Graco Inc.

1970: Chicago-based H.G. Fischer & Co., a finishing and electrostatics business, is acquired.

1986: Company stock begins trading on the New York Stock Exchange.

1993: New spray gun manufacturing plant is opened in Sioux Falls, South Dakota.

1996: A distribution and manufacturing center is opened in Rogers, Minnesota.

1999: The German firm Böllhoff Verfahrenstechnik is acquired.

2001: Graco acquires ASM Company, Inc.

2003: Sharpe Manufacturing Company is acquired.

Graco exited the packaging and converting aspect of the adhesive equipment market with the sale of LTI and a related joint venture, two Detroit-area operations were consolidated in the building that was constructed for Graco Robotics, and a new spray-gun manufacturing plant was planned.

Weyler resigned his positions as president and chief operating officer in January 1993. Koch—who was the major company shareholder as well as CEO and chairman—commented at the time that he and Weyler had important differences regarding the future direction of the company. "The sudden resignation of a president is enough to throw most public companies into a tailspin," wrote Scott Carlson, in the *St. Paul Pioneer Press Dispatch* in March 1993. But with Koch once again at the helm, Wall Street was not fazed; Graco had a solid reputation as a well-run company, with little long-term debt, no across-the-board competition, and the ability to meet the challenges of changing internal and external conditions.

George Aristides, a 20-year Graco veteran, was promoted to president and chief operating officer in June 1993. Aristides had served as vice-president of manufacturing operations since 1985 and led the $20 million, five-year conversion of Graco's two sprawling Minneapolis plants to a cellular operation with work groups producing components or products from start to finish. Also in 1993 Graco opened up a new factory for manufacturing spray guns in Sioux Falls, South Dakota.

Graco in 1993 became the first company in its industry to become ISO 9000—registered at all its major sites. ISO 9000, which set business practice standards, was adopted by the International Organization for Standardization in 1987. Forty percent of Graco's 1992 sales had been in the international market-

place where certification was increasingly expected. More American companies, such as the Sherwin-Williams Company, one of Graco's largest customers for pumps and paint spraying equipment, were also asking their vendors to be certified.

Ongoing recessions in Europe and Japan, both important overseas markets, had forced Graco to downsize operations in those regions. In 1994, Graco restructured its operations in the Pacific and in Europe. In order to boost product development, the company pumped in $23.1 million in capital expenditures into engineering and manufacturing capabilities in 1994 and added another $19.8 million in 1995. Late in 1995 plans for a $70 million distribution and manufacturing center were announced, and the David A. Koch Center opened in Rogers, Minnesota, the following year. This last move enabled the company to transfer its fast-growing contractor equipment manufacturing operation out of its crowded main plant in Minneapolis.

After 33 years as CEO, Koch stepped down from the post in January 1996. Koch was succeeded by Aristides, while maintaining his position as chairman. Net earnings grew by 31 percent to $36.2 million in 1996 on little change in revenue, which was up just 1 percent to $391.8 million. But profits were slim on foreign sales which contributed nearly one-third of total volume.

Harlan S. Byrne, in a February 1997 *Barron's* article, credited Aristides with shaking up "the once sleepy organization." Product development spending was increased by nearly 50 percent from 1992 to 1996. Graco introduced 130 new items in 1996 and expected to increase that number to 160 in 1997. Products introduced in the previous three years generated 21 percent of 1996 worldwide sales. Selling, general, and administrative expenses were cut from 40 to 31 percent of revenues from 1992 to 1996. Byrne regarded Graco's gains in earnings under Aristides as dramatic. Net earnings, before special items, had more than tripled since 1992. Nevertheless, he noted that "Aristides won't be happy until annual revenues rise, on average, at a double-digit clip."

Revenues increased 6 percent in 1997, reaching a record $423.9 million, but net earnings surged 24 percent, to $44.7 million, thanks to Aristides's efforts to permanently reduce expenses. The following year the company spent about $191 million to buy back 22 percent of its outstanding common stock that had been held by a trust for heirs of the company founders.

In February 1999 James Earnshaw was named president and CEO of Graco, with Aristides becoming vice-chairman. Earnshaw was brought in from the outside, having spent 26 years at Cleveland diversified manufacturer Eaton Corporation, where he most recently served as head of the Eden Prairie, Minnesota–based hydraulics division. In June 1999 Graco acquired Böllhoff Verfahrenstechnik (BV), based in Bielefeld, Germany, a producer of piston pumps, diaphragm pumps, two-component proportioning equipment, and applicators used in the automotive and industrial markets, primarily in Europe. BV had 1998 sales of about $20 million.

Quietly Reaching New Heights: Early 2000s

At the end of 1999 Earnshaw resigned "to pursue other opportunities," and Aristides returned as CEO. Dale Johnson, a

23-year Graco veteran, was named president and COO. During 2000 the company moved its corporate headquarters from Golden Valley, Minnesota, back to the site of its largest manufacturing plant in Minneapolis, and also began a 130,000-square-foot expansion of that same plant. Behind the corporate move was a desire by management to get closer to the production operations. In early 2000 Graco introduced the Magnum line of spray-painting products for smaller paint contractors. The new line was sold through home center and paint store channels, with the Home Depot, Inc. big-box chain being the main distribution outlet.

More management changes were on tap for 2001. In March, Johnson, the heir apparent to Aristides, stepped down as president and COO to become vice-president of Graco's contractor equipment division. After an outside search for a new leader, the company hired David A. Roberts as president and CEO in June 2001. Roberts had been a group vice-president of the Marmon Group, a privately held group of diverse companies based in the Chicago area, overseeing several manufacturing firms. Meantime, in April 2001 Aristides was named company chairman, succeeding longtime Chairman Koch.

Also in 2001 Graco acquired ASM Company, Inc., maker and marketer of spray tips, guns, poles, and other accessories for the professional painter. Headquartered in Orange, California, ASM had sales of approximately $11 million in 2000. ASM distributed its products through the paint store, home center, and rental channels. Following the acquisition, the ASM operation was transferred to Graco's Sioux Falls plant. Overall, Graco struggled during 2001 because of the global economic recession. Revenues of $472.8 million were down about 4 percent from the previous year, and net earnings of $65.3 million represented a drop of approximately 9 percent.

By 2002 Graco's financial position was so strong that it had retired all of its long-term debt. Cash-rich, the firm was on the lookout for significant acquisitions while continuing to pour money into new product development. In mid-2002 Graco closed the manufacturing plant in Bielefeld, Germany, it had gained in the BV deal. Some product lines that had been manufactured there were discontinued and the rest were transferred to the Minneapolis facilities. Aristides resigned as chairman during 2002 and was succeeded by Lee R. Mitau, who had served as a Graco director since 1990.

In early 2003 Graco used some of its cash hoard to buy back 2.2 million shares of its stock from the founding family, spending $54.8 million to do so. Later in the year the company began construction of a new 42,000-square-foot building on its corporate campus where some of the company's manufacturing and administrative employees would be housed. This building was completed in February 2004. Graco also continued to seek growth in emerging markets by developing distributors in such countries and regions as China, Korea, India, the Middle East, and Eastern Europe. By 2003 the company had distributors in more than 100 countries and was generating 37 percent of its sales outside the United States. Growth was further aided by the April 2003 acquisition of Sharpe Manufacturing Company of Santa Fe Springs, California, for $13.5 million. Sharpe, which had 2002 revenues of $11 million, produced spray guns and related parts and accessories for the automotive refinishing

market, a new sector for Graco. Early in 2004 the manufacturing operations of Sharpe were relocated to the Sioux Falls plant.

Graco's low-profile, methodical approach yielded its best results yet in 2003, when revenues reached a record $535.1 million, a 10 percent jump from 2002, and net income totaled a best-ever $86.7 million, a 15 percent increase. Looking to the future, Graco aimed to continue to grow by developing new products, expanding into new market segments, adding to its global distribution system, and pursuing strategic acquisitions. On the manufacturing side, the company also announced in mid-2004 that it would spend about $4 million to open a 50,000-square-foot manufacturing plant in the Shanghai region of China. A leased facility, the plant was expected to become operational during the second half of 2005.

Principal Subsidiaries

Equipos Graco Argentina S.A.; Graco Barbados FSC Limited; Graco Canada Inc.; Graco do Brasil Limitada (Brazil); Graco Europe N.V. (Belgium); Graco Fluid Equipment (Shanghai) Co., Ltd. (China); Graco GmbH (Germany); Graco Hong Kong Limited; Graco K.K. (Japan); Graco Korea Inc.; Graco Limited (U.K.); Graco Minnesota Inc.; Graco N.V. (Belgium); Graco S.A.S. (France); Graco South Dakota Inc.

Principal Divisions

Contractor Equipment; Industrial/Automotive Equipment; Lubrication Equipment.

Principal Competitors

Illinois Tool Works Inc.; Nordson Corporation; Exel Industries SA; Raven Industries, Inc.

Further Reading

Black, Sam, "Cash-Rich, Debtless, Graco Wants to Buy," *Minneapolis/St. Paul Business Journal*, February 1, 2002.
——, "Toro, Graco Chasing Big-Box Retail Market," *Minneapolis/St. Paul CityBusiness*, January 26, 2001, p. 5.
Byrne, Harlan S., "Revitalized," *Barron's*, February 3, 1997, p. 22.
Carlson, Scott, "Restructuring Graco," *St. Paul Pioneer Press Dispatch*, March 1, 1993.
"Corporate Capsule: Graco Inc.," *Minneapolis/St. Paul CityBusiness*, July 15, 1991 and April 23, 1993.
"David Koch Ending His 33-Year Tenure As CEO at Graco," *Minneapolis Star Tribune*, December 16, 1995, p. 2D.
Ewen, Beth, "Graco Reports Earnings Downturn Due to Lower Profit Margins," *Minneapolis/St. Paul CityBusiness*, August 7-20, 1989, p. 16.
"Fast-Forward on the Paint-Spray Line," *Financial World*, October 31–November 13, 1984, pp. 70–71.
Feyder, Susan, " 'Stick-To-Itiveness' Pays Off for Graco," *Minneapolis Star Tribune*, May 5, 1986, p. 1M.
Fredrickson, Tom, "Aristides Primes the Pump at Graco," *Minneapolis/St. Paul CityBusiness*, November 12–19, 1993, p. 1.
——, "Woes Across the Water," *Minneapolis/St. Paul CityBusiness*, May 27–June 2, 1994, p. 1.
"Graco Hires GE Official As President," *Minneapolis Star Tribune*, April 12, 1985.
Johnson, Ken, "Graco at the Gap," *Corporate Report Minnesota*, June 1975, pp. 35–36.

——, "Graco at the Ready," *Corporate Report Minnesota,* September 1981.

Kearney, Robert P., "A Pumped Up Graco," *Corporate Report Minnesota,* April 1986, pp. 45+.

The Graco Story, Minneapolis: Graco Inc., 2001.

Maturi, Richard J., "The Age of Robots," *Barron's,* August 18, 1986, p. 36.

Peterson, Susan E., "Aggressive Graco Pumps Up the Volume," *Minneapolis Star Tribune,* May 17, 1993, p. 1D.

——, "Global Competition Spurs ISO 9000," *Minneapolis Star Tribune,* November 22, 1993, p. 1D.

——, "Graco Names Aristides President, COO," *Minneapolis Star Tribune,* June 25, 1993, p. 3D.

——, "Graco Reports Record Sales and Earnings for Last Year," *Minneapolis Star Tribune,* February 15, 1991, p. 2D.

——, "Long-Term Changes Paying Off at Graco," *Minneapolis Star Tribune,* November 12, 1997, p. 1D.

——, "Osborne Resigns As Graco President After One Year," *Minneapolis Star Tribune,* May 27, 1998, p. 1D.

——, "Walter Weyler Resigns from Graco Because of 'Differences' with CEO," *Minneapolis Star Tribune,* January 16, 1993, p. 1D.

Randle, Wilma, "Dollar's Strength Hit Graco in '84," *St. Paul Pioneer Press Dispatch,* May 8, 1985.

St. Anthony, Neal, "Graco Is Returning to Its Northeast Minneapolis Roots," *Minneapolis Star Tribune,* May 5, 2000, p. 1D.

——, "With Little Notice, Graco Keeps Growing," *Minneapolis Star Tribune,* February 15, 2002, p. 1D.

Shapiro, Eben, "Graco Robots Wow Even the Japanese," *Minneapolis/ St. Paul CityBusiness,* June 3, 1987, p. 1.

—Kathleen Peippo
—update: David E. Salamie

Groupe Bolloré

Tour Bolloré, 31-32 quai de Dion
Puteaux
F-92811
France
Telephone: +33 1 46 96 44 33
Fax: +33 1 46 96 40 83
Web site: http://www.bollore.com

Public Company
Incorporated: 1822
Employees: 33,411
Sales: EUR 5.39 billion ($6 billion) (2003)
Stock Exchanges: Euronext Paris
Ticker Symbol: BOL
NAIC: 325211 Plastics Material and Resin
   Manufacturing; 326113 Unsupported Plastics Film and
   Sheet (Except Packaging) Manufacturing; 424720
   Petroleum and Petroleum Products Merchant
   Wholesalers (Except Bulk Stations and Terminals);
   481111 Scheduled Passenger Air Transportation;
   483113 Coastal and Great Lakes Freight
   Transportation; 488320 Marine Cargo Handling

Groupe Bolloré is a diversified industrial conglomerate with leadership status in most of its operating areas. Led by Vincent Bolloré, who gained fame as one of France's most successful corporate raiders, Bolloré represents the continuation of a family-owned business with roots in the early 19th century. The company continues to operate in that historical sector, producing specialty thin papers for the publishing, advertising, pharmaceutical, beauty care, and other industries. Bolloré's thin paper production comes from two plants, Papeteries du Léman and a new facility in the Vosges opened in 2003, with combined production of 95,000 tons per year. Bolloré is the world leader in the thin paper segment, with some 20 percent of the global market. Since the early 1980s, Bolloré also has built a leading presence in the global plastic films market. The company produces polypropylene film for capacitors, shrink-wrap packaging films, and related products. The company also has deployed the

technological expertise gained from this division into development of a lithium-based automotive battery. A pet project of Vincent Bolloré himself, the battery, through the company's batScap division, was launched in 2004. Other parts of the Bolloré Group include international shipping and logistics, primarily through subsidiary SDV, with a particularly strong presence in Africa. The company is also the second largest independent fuel distributor in Europe, through the Bolloré Energie and Calpam names, with a focus on the French, Swiss, Dutch, and German markets. Bolloré Energie also controls 90 percent of SFDM, which operates the Donges-Melun-Metz oil pipeline and other fuel logistics facilities in France and Switzerland. Bolloré is perhaps best known for its financial dealings, which have included the purchase of significant stakes of many of France's best-known firms, such as Bouyges, Pathé, Lazard Frères, and others. In 2004, the company's portfolio included positions with Italy's Mediobanca and industrial group Vallourec, among others. Bolloré also has begun a drive to build its own media operations, taking stakes in film distributor Gaumont, advertising group Havas, the Mac-Mahon movie theater in Paris, French video streaming leader Steampower, production studio SFP, Radio New Talents, and a digital television station, Direct 8. Bolloré Group is listed on the Euronext Paris Stock Exchange. Nonetheless, Vincent Bolloré and other members of the Bolloré family control close to 90 percent of the group's shares. In 2003, Bolloré Group posted sales of EUR 5.39 billion ($6 billion).

Paper-Based Fortune in the 1800s

The Bolloré Group stemmed from a small, family-owned business founded near Quimper, on the coast of France's Brittany region, in the early 19th century. René Bolloré had traveled to China, where he had been introduced to the country's rice paper-making techniques. Back in France, Bolloré invented a means of machine-producing a similar thin paper, and launched his company in 1822. Bolloré's thin papers proved suitable for such uses as the pages for Bibles, tracing paper, and rolling papers for handmade cigarettes.

The Bolloré company grew into one of the leading paper producers in Brittany and in France, and the Bolloré family

Company Perspectives:

The commitments of the Bolloré Group: Ethics, human resources, the environment, and humanitarian work.

The Bolloré Group develops its strategy with a view to sustainable growth. Its objective is to anchor its development, along with its social, ethical and environmental concerns, in the long-term.

As a creator of innovative high-tech products, it strives to become a major player as well as to fuel economic growth and maintain a clean, healthy environment.

Thanks to its ongoing policy of research and innovation, its international development strategy and the sizeable investments it has made in recent years, the Bolloré Group boasts a leadership position in each of its industrial and service activities.

itself became a powerful financial force in the region. The development of the tobacco industry in the latter half of the 19th century, and especially the gradual shift in tobacco use from pipe and cigar smoking to cigarettes, offered new opportunities for the family-owned company's growth.

Bolloré's son, also named René and grandfather of Vincent Bolloré, recognized the potential of the rising new market and in 1893 the company built a new factory, in Cascadet on the Odet River. The new paper mill specialized in thin papers using flax and textile fibers.

True success for the family-owned company came after World War I. In 1918, with the market for cigarette tobacco and roll-your-owns growing rapidly, René Bolloré launched a new cigarette paper on the market—OCB, for Odet Cascadet Bolloré.

Over the next decades, OCB grew into France's leading cigarette paper brand. The brand enjoyed international success as well, and by the early 1950s the company claimed to have captured some 10 percent of the worldwide cigarette market, including pre-rolled cigarettes. The company continued to exploit new markets for its thin paper technologies as well, launching production of papers for use in capacitors in 1948. Teabags were also a strongly growing market for the company.

Saving the Family Firm in the 1970s

Bolloré also grew through external expansion. In the 1950s, Bolloré bought control of another well-known French cigarette paper manufacturer, Zig-Zag. That company had been founded by Maurice and Jacques Braunstein in 1879. Based in Paris, the company built a dedicated cigarette paper production plant, the Papeterie de Gassicourt, near the town of Mantes in 1882. The Braunsteins began developing new cigarette paper production technologies, and in 1894 launched the product that was to make the company famous the world over: the Zig-Zag brand of cigarette papers. The product owed its name to the company's patent overlap packaging technique.

Zig-Zag, OCB, and a third brand, JOB, enabled France to claim the vast majority of the world market for cigarette rolling papers by the late 1930s. The Braunstein company grew strongly, opening a new mill in Thonon in 1936. Following World War II, which destroyed the company's original facility, production was transferred to the Thonon site.

By the 1950s, however, Zig-Zag's heavy investments had brought it into financial difficulties. By 1959, the company had been acquired by Bolloré, with main rival JOB acquiring a significant stake as well. Under Bolloré, the Thonon facility became dedicated to the production of carbon paper, a fast-growing paper segment, while the Zig-Zag brand was transferred to a new facility. Through the 1960s and into the 1970s the rolling paper market, despite losing sales to the rising popularity of packaged cigarettes, discovered a new market rooted in the era's counterculture.

Bolloré continued to seek out new markets through the 1960s. In 1969, the company made its first move into the production of polypropylene-based films, launching test production for a range of capacitor films. By 1972, the company was ready to launch full production. At the same time, Bolloré began production of aluminum-coated film. The company had high hopes for its new division, and sought entry for its products, and its other paper products, into the North American market through the creation of two U.S. subsidiaries, Bolloré Inc. and Bolmet, in 1978.

Yet declining cigarette paper sales, rising fuel costs, the long economic recession, and the high investment costs needed to launch polypropylene film production took its toll on Bolloré. The company also suffered somewhat from a lack of strong direction, as Michel Bolloré, the second René Bolloré's son, had left Brittany to live in Paris, and attempted to run the company from there. By the end of the 1970s, Bolloré faced bankruptcy. In order to save the company, Vincent Bolloré asked friend and mentor Edmond de Rothschild to buy the family-owned business in 1975.

Vincent Bolloré, born in 1952 and raised in Paris, began his career at Compagnie Financiere Rothschild, where he first served as deputy director in 1976. During this time, Bolloré also earned a law degree, attending night classes. By the early 1980s, as the Bolloré company appeared to be heading toward bankruptcy, Bolloré, joined by older brother Michel-Yves, convinced Rothschild to sell them back the family business. Rothschild did so, demanding a symbolic one franc.

Rise of a Financial Power Player in the 1980s

The Bollorés quickly found backing from Sébastien Piccioto, who agreed to invest FRF 10 million, in exchange for 50 percent of the company. The Bollorés then began restructuring the operation, selling off Zig-Zag to JOB in 1981. That year also marked the start of Vincent Bolloré's legendary deal-making: As part of the paper company's restructuring, Bolloré traveled to the factory near Quimper, where he climbed up on a crate and asked workers to accept a 15 percent cut in pay. The workers agreed.

Bolloré now stepped up its focus on polypropylene film and capacitor production. In 1983, the company entered a new and fast-growing market, that for polypropylene-based shrink-wrap films. The following year, Bolloré established a subsidiary in

Key Dates:

1822: Rene Bolloré invents a process for manufacturing thin papers and founds a paper plant near Quimper, France.

1893: The company establishes a second plant in Cascadet, on the Odet River, to produce cigarette papers.

1918: The OCB rolling paper brand is launched.

1948: The company begins producing paper for capacitors.

1972: The production of polypropylene film is launched.

1975: The company is sold to Edmond de Rothschild.

1978: Two subsidiaries, Bolloré Inc. and Bolmet, are established in the United States.

1981: Vincent Bolloré buys back the company.

1983: The company launches shrink-wrap production.

1985: The company goes public as Bolloré Technologies.

1988: The company acquires SCAC.

1991: The company acquires Delmas-Vieljeux, which is merged with SCAC to form SDV.

1992: The Rivaud Group is acquired.

1997: The company acquires Saga.

1999: The company acquires the OT Africa Line.

2001: The tobacco and cigarette holdings are sold off.

2004: The company acquires a stake in Havas advertising as part of an extension into the media sector.

Japan, Bolloré KK. In 1985, the company restructured itself, becoming Bolloré Technologies, and listing its shares on the Paris Stock Exchange's Secondary Market.

The public offering marked the start of Bolloré's rise as a diversified industrial group. In 1986, Bolloré bought out JOB, taking control of the world's three leading cigarette rolling paper brands, JOB, Zig-Zag, and OCB. In that year, also, Bolloré went a step further and bought up tobacco company Sofical, primarily active in Africa. That purchase transformed Bolloré into one of the African continent's major cigarette producers. Through Sofical, Bolloré next went after Société Commercial d'Affrètements et de Combustibles, or SCAC, which was France's leading freight-forward firm. Founded in 1885, SCAC primarily focused on freight routes to Africa. Yet in order to gain control of SCAC, Bolloré was forced into a takeover battle with venerable French shipping giant Delmas-Vieljeux.

Bolloré won that battle, earning a reputation as one of France's brightest deal-makers. In 1988, Bolloré put into place a new holding structure, a multi-level investment vehicle that received financial backing from a number of France's leading financiers, including Claude Bébéar, head of French insurance giant AXA. Other backers included Antoine Bernheim of Lazard, Crédit National, Clinvest, Italy's Agnelli family, and South Africa's Rupert. The company listed on the Paris Exchange's main monthly settlement board the following year.

The holding structure enabled Vincent Bolloré to eye a new wave of investments that earned him the nickname the "Prince

of Cash Flow." One of Bolloré's first purchases under the new structure was that of Rhin Rhône, a fuel distribution subsidiary of Elf-Aquitaine. This purchase, in which Bolloré was forced to stand down resistance from the company, the governments, and its employees, helped create Bolloré's reputation as a fiercely determined deal-maker. The acquisition formed the basis of the later Bolloré Energie.

A flurry of deals followed, including taking control of car leasing group Mattei in 1989; acquiring fuel companies Calpam and Satramin in 1990; buying up Copigraph, a maker of carbonless paper, which enabled the company to exit carbon paper production; a joint venture with France's Seita tobacco monopoly, reinforcing the company's tobacco interests in Africa; and purchasing controlling stakes in Matlavuoto, which specialized in producing plastic films for capacitors. Vincent Bolloré's penchant for risk-taking proved too much for brother Michel-Yves, who left the company in 1991. Longtime partner Piccioto also left the company after a dispute over its direction.

Rebuilding the Empire for the New Century

Bolloré's deal-making nearly sank the company in the early 1990s. The bitter rivalry between Bolloré and Delmas-Vieljeux had continued into the new decade and culminated in Bolloré acquiring a significant stake in the venerable, but ailing, shipping company. Bolloré meant only to buy up a minority stake in the company—enough to enable him to demand a seat on the board of directors and a say in the company's direction. Yet Bolloré's enemy Tristan Vieljeux ultimately outmaneuvered Bolloré, orchestrating a ruling from the French SEC equivalent forcing Bolloré to buy up all of Delmas-Vieljeux. The ruling forced Bolloré to pay far more than Delmas-Vieljeux's worth. Bolloré soon discovered the extent of the company's problems, including a debt of some FRF 3 billion.

The deal appeared to have put an end to Bolloré's winning streak. Yet, with backing from some of France's most important financiers, Bolloré stayed afloat, restructuring the company's shipping holdings by merging SCAC and Delmas-Vieljeux into a new company, SDV. Another factor in Bolloré's successful resurrection was its acquisition of diversified conglomerate Rivaud, which gave Bolloré a strong source of cash flow from the group's banking, forests, plantations, and other holdings, as well as a strong treasury. In addition, Bolloré was able to sell off much of Rivaud to pay down debt.

Into the new century, Bolloré continued to build up its core operations, even as Vincent Bolloré continued to make headlines for his hobby as a corporate raider. In 1997, Bolloré stepped up its international freight and logistics operations with the purchase of Saga, a leading French cargo handler. Two years later, the company acquired OT Africa Line, or OTAL, a British-registered roll-on roll-off specialist founded in Nigeria in 1975. Bolloré then expanded its Bolloré Energie subsidiary through the acquisition of the Donges-Melun-Metz oil pipeline in 2000. By then, Bolloré had merged SDV and Bolloré Technologies into a single structure, Bolloré Group. The company also began narrowing its focus around a core of plastic films, specialty thin papers, and shipping and logistics. As such, the company sold off its rolling paper operations in 2000, and 75 percent of its cigarette and tobacco business, Tobaccor, in 2001.

The company also sold its African logging operations in 2002, amid criticism from the World Bank.

In the meantime, Vincent Bolloré continued to make headlines, acquiring stakes in such giant French operations as Bouygues, Pathé, Lazard Frères, and others. In each case, Bolloré was able to cash out on the acquired shares at a handsome profit. Bolloré did not cash out on all of its investment, however. As the company approached mid-decade, its intention to establish itself as a major media group had become clear. In the early 2000s, Bolloré had made a number of media purchases, including a stake in the Gaumont film distribution company, as well as interests in production, through SFP, Internet video services through Streampower, and the launch of Radio New Talents and the digital terrestrial television station Direct 8.

Bolloré's media ambitions gained scale in 2004 when Bolloré revealed that it had begun building a stake in the Havas advertising agency, one of France's largest. By the end of the year, Bolloré had amassed some 13 percent of Havas's shares. Although questions remained over Bolloré's intentions in the acquisition, few doubted that Vincent Bolloré would achieve his aims. After 25 years at the helm of the Bolloré Group, Bolloré had transformed the company from failing family firm to one of Europe's top industrial conglomerates.

Principal Subsidiaries

batScap; Bolloré Energie; Bolloré Investissement; Bolloré, Division Films Plastiques; Delmas-Vieljeux; IER; OT Africa Line; Papeteries du Léman; Saga; SDV.

Principal Competitors

A.P. Møller - Maersk A/S; CP Ships Limited; Neptune Orient Lines Limited.

Further Reading

Arnold, Martin, ''The Uninvited Guest Who Has Feasted on Some of France's Leading Companies,'' *Financial Times,* September 18, 2004, p. 21.

Basini, Bruna, ''Vincent Bolloré ou la tentation patrimonale,'' *L'Expansion,* February 18, 1999, p. 68.

Groom, Brian, ''Bolloré's Pitch,'' *Financial Times,* September 29, 2004.

Le Bourdonnec, Yannick, ''Bolloré essuie son premier coup de tabac,'' *L'Expansion,* October 7, 1993, p. 88.

Raulin, Nathalie, and Renaud Lecadre, *Bolloré. Enquête sur un capitaliste au- dessus de tout soupçon,* Paris: Denoël.

Tagliabue, John, ''Raiding French Banking's Citadel,'' *New York Times,* January 7, 2001, p. 2(L).

—M.L. Cohen

Grupo Clarín S.A.

Piedras 1473
Buenos Aires, C.F. C1140ABK
Argentina
Telephone: (54) (11) 4309-7500
Fax: (54) (11) 4309-7200
Web site: http://www.grupoClarín.com.ar

Private Company
Incorporated: 1999
Employees: 7,000
Sales: ARS 1.84 billion ($623.73 million) (2003)
NAIC: 322122 Newsprint Mills; 323110 Commercial
Lithographic Printing; 323111 Commercial Gravure
Printing; 511110 Newspaper Publishers; 511120
Periodical Publishers; 512110 Motion Picture and
Video Production; 515112 Radio Stations; 515120
Television Production Broadcasting; 515210 Cable
and Other Subscription Programming; 517212 Cellular
and Other Wireless Telecommunications; 517410
Satellite Telecommunications; 518111 Internet Service
Providers; 519110 News Syndicates

Grupo Clarín S.A., a privately owned Argentine holding company, is the leading media group in the Spanish-speaking world. Its principal holdings are *Clarín,* the Buenos Aires-based daily newspaper whose circulation is the largest in the Hispanic world, and Multicanal S.A., one of the two companies that dominates cable television in Argentina. Grupo Clarín also owns, or has a share in, other newspapers and magazines and a news service; a printing plant and a newsprint manufacturer; television channels and radio stations; cellular mobile telephone service; film and sports-TV production; and an Internet service provider and search engine. By these means the group enters each day the homes of at least three out of every four Argentines.

Rising to Highest Circulation in the Hispanic World: 1945–85

Roberto Jose Noble was a lawyer who served in Argentina's Congress and as a provincial-government minister before leaving politics in 1939 to become a rancher. Six years later, with an initial investment of $1.6 million, he founded a Buenos Aires tabloid newspaper, which he named *Clarín* (Bugle). Noble sold his ranch to buy the rolls of newsprint that at this time were as valuable as precious metals. The paper sold 60,000 copies on its first day. Populist in tone, it emphasized local news, sports, and entertainment.

Clarín first appeared as Juan Perón was rising to power to become Argentina's authoritarian leader. Although the paper declared itself free from ties to any traditional political group, and Noble's official biographer later wrote that Noble was anti-Perónist, *Clarín* and other papers are said to have engaged in self-censorship to avoid Perón's anger. The paper backed the Perónist nationalist position of government support for Argentine industry. The Perón regime intimidated the press through its control of labor unions and by the curbs it imposed on newsprint in 1948. After it shut down *La Prensa* in 1951, it turned this opposition daily over to the nation's labor federation. *La Prensa*'s middle-class readers then deserted the paper in droves, many of them gravitating to *Clarín,* which also picked up much of *La Prensa*'s lucrative classified advertisements.

Clarín continued to advance after Perón's fall in 1955. In 1960 its own building on its own downtown Buenos Aires lot was erected for *Clarín.* It rose to become the paper of highest circulation in Buenos Aires in 1965 and, two years later, added a color press and a Sunday magazine, which it also supplied to provincial newspapers. Noble died in 1969 at the age of 66. His widow, Ernestina Herrera de Noble, succeeded him as publisher.

Despite its large circulation, *Clarín* is said to have been on the verge of bankruptcy when, in 1971, Herrera de Noble turned to Rogelio Frigerio, the head of the political group Movement for Integration and Development. According to one account, Frigerio's allies rescued *Clarín* with $10 million in contributions, and for the next decade it hewed to the party's line, which centered on government aid for national infrastructure and industrial development. On Frigerio's advice, Herrera de Noble brought in Héctor Magnetto, who took charge of the newspaper's finances, and two of Magnetto's associates, José Antonio Aranda and Lucio Rafael Pagliaro. These four still controlled the paper, and the additional media properties of Grupo Clarín, in 2004.

Company Perspectives:

Every day Grupo Clarín faces up to its commitment to offer honest and independent communications, exercised with professional integrity, to give its audiences a comprehensive and up to date vision of reality. . . . The objectives of the Group are to employ leading edge technology in order to widen the range of information, cultural and entertainment options available and to promote Argentine talent in the context of globalization.

Throughout a period of military rule (1966–73), followed by a second Perónist period (1973–76) and another military dictatorship (1976–83), *Clarín* again tread softly. Since military censorship made it virtually impossible to write candidly about politics, *Clarín* filled its paper with more and more soccer news, lurid crime stories, and entertainment. It even generated its own news by sponsoring events such as movie festivals, chess competitions, and marathon races. In 1977, however, the paper and two other Buenos Aires dailies succeeded in securing their own newsprint supply, and they opened their own paper plant the following year. By 1979 *Clarín* was selling an average of 500,000 copies a day and about 770,000 for the Sunday edition, with distribution in all parts of Argentina. It also had a large lead over its rivals in classified advertisements. In 1980 the enterprise had sales of about $300 million and was the 26th largest in Argentina. The same three newspapers founded the news agency Diarios y Noticias (DyN) in 1982. By 1985 *Clarín* had the highest circulation of any newspaper in the Spanish-speaking world—a lead it maintained in subsequent years.

Multimedia Colossus in the 1990s

The next decade saw the enterprise convert itself into a multimedia corporation. Under the presidency of Carlos Menem, Argentina began selling numerous state-owned enterprises, including two Buenos Aires television stations. After a law that prohibited newspapers from control of other mass media was repealed, *Clarín,* in 1990, purchased a Buenos Aires television station, Channel 13, which was losing $20 million a year but ranked second in viewers. In the same year the company bought its first radio station, Mitre (soon adding an FM station as well), and established a subsidiary named Arte Radiotelevision Argentino (Artear) for its radio and television properties. By 1997 Radio Mitre was Argentina's largest station.

In 1991 *Clarín* began broadcasting and distributing the broadcasting of sports events for television. The following year it purchased a fledgling cable television venture, Multicanal S.A., and in 1993 it established two cable channels: one for news 24 hours a day, the other to show old movies and television shows. *Clarín,* in a joint venture with the French publisher Hachette Filipacchi, launched a women's magazine, *Elle Argentina,* in 1994. (*Clarín* bought Hachette's share in 2001.) It took a stake in the same year in Compania de Telefonos del Interior S.A. (CTI), which was starting a cellular mobile-telephone service.

With so many new ventures on its plate, the enterprise was reorganized under the name Grupo Clarín in 1995. In that year its revenues passed $1 billion, with print media now accounting for less than half of the total. The company garnered another $276 million in cash when, in 1995–96, it sold 55 percent of Multicanal (which now had 550,000 subscribers and was proving highly profitable), to Telefonica International S.A. and CEI Citicorp Holdings S.A. These partners provided not only capital but also financial expertise. Magnetto and his collaborators were uncomfortable with sharing power in Multicanal, however, and the partnership broke up in 1997–98 by means of a complex web of purchases and sales. CEI and Telefonica became proprietors of a rival venture, Cablevision S.A. Clarín also was bracing for competition from direct-satellite television by partnering with others to offer direct-to-home digital television in Argentina.

Grupo Clarín was also busy in its traditional area of print journalism. In 1996 it introduced *Ole,* Argentina's first sports daily newspaper, and the following year it joined Cimeco S.A., a consortium, to acquire regional newspapers. *Clarín* and rival *La Nación* were partners in Cimeco, which purchased 85 percent of two large provincial newspapers, *Los Andes* of Mendoza and *La Voz del Interior* of Córdoba, for $170 million. In 1998 Clarín introduced a children's magazine called *Genios.*

Grupo Clarín became a power in sports telecasting by its majority stake in a firm that owned Argentina's main sports cable channel, TyC Sports (established in 1994), the premium channel TyC Max, and rights to telecast basketball, volleyball, auto racing, boxing, handball, ice hockey, and all weekend matches of Argentina's professional soccer league. The contract for the latter was good through 2006, with an option through 2014. Clarín also had half-ownership of another company holding the rights to telecast championship tournaments of Argentina's professional soccer league and the most important South American competitions. Through Patagonik Film Group S.A., the group was participating in producing films to be distributed throughout Latin America.

By 1998 Grupo Clarín was reaching three out of every four Argentine homes. Its eponymous newspaper had the highest circulation in the Hispanic world, and Multicanal was the largest cable system in Latin America, with a network covering Buenos Aires and the principal cities of eight provinces. The AM and FM radio stations each rated as the most listened-to ones in Buenos Aires. Channel 13 still ranked second among over-the-air television stations; its highest-rating program was a Sunday evening soccer review produced by TyC. Through Prima S.A., a subsidiary founded in 1997, Ciudad Internet was Argentina's second largest Internet service provider. Prima's holdings also included a broadband-access data network. Grupo Clarín also held half of Audiotel, a search engine.

Harder Times in the New Millennium

These gains came at a price—namely a debt that had reached $1.4 billion. Despite its growth, Multicanal had fallen into the red because of the interest it had to pay on its debt of $780 million. The various media—newspapers, magazines, radio, television, cellular phones, and the Internet—did not add up to an integrated whole, even though the group was formally incorporated in 1999 as Grupo Clarín S.A., a holding company encompassing its 18 business units. Each unit continued to operate independently under separate management, although a corporate management

Key Dates:

1945: Roberto José Noble founds *Clarín* in Buenos Aires.
1965: *Clarín* becomes the newspaper of highest circulation in Buenos Aires.
1969: Noble's widow, Ernestina Herrera de Noble, succeeds him as publisher.
1985: *Clarín* now has the largest circulation of any newspaper in the Hispanic world.
1990: The company buys the second largest television channel in Buenos Aires, as well as a Buenos Aires radio station, which grows to become Argentina's largest.
1992: *Clarín* takes a stake in a cable television network, Multicanal.
1995: Now Grupo Clarín, the media giant has annual revenue surpassing $1 billion.
1997: Grupo Clarín founds Ciudad Internet, an Internet service provider.
1999: Grupo Clarín incorporates and sells an 18 percent share to Goldman, Sachs Group, Inc.
2002: Struggling Multicanal, the cable-TV subsidiary, "defers" payments on its sizable debts.
2003: Grupo Clarín returns to profitability.

group was established to oversee the group's finances, human resources, and new businesses. Near the end of the year Clarín sold an 18 percent interest in the group to Goldman, Sachs Group, Inc. for $500 million. In addition to the capital gained, Clarín was planning to use Goldman, Sachs as a way to take the company public and tap the U.S. equity market. In *LatinFinance,* Lisa Wing quoted a Goldman, Sachs executive as saying, "Clarín is a long-term investment for us. Even after the company goes public, we will hold the shares."

Multicanal, now with 1.4 million subscribers and a 43 percent share of Argentine homes wired for cable, was considered worth nearly as much as Grupo Clarín itself. Few countries anywhere had taken to cable television as had Argentina, where people considered it an essential utility, like water and electricity. Cable television, in more than 60 percent of all homes, was among the highest in the world in market share for TV viewing. Clarín's cable unit had ambitious plans to develop its digital broadband capacity in order to offer voice data services to its Internet subscribers and the content of its newspapers, television channels, and film productions for premium channels and pay-per-view events. Digital broadband also carried with it the possibility of interactive television, video on demand, and telephonic services in a now deregulated marketplace.

The reality proved quite different. Argentina's economy failed to break out of recession, and as a consequence many of Multicanal's subscribers found themselves not only unable to take on added services but to pay the average $32-a-month cost for basic service itself. In order to reduce its own operating costs by $330 million a year, the cable company cut 15 percent of its staff and dropped some channels from its offerings. By mid-2001 one bank analyst forecast a 60 percent chance that Multicanal would default on its debt before the end of the year,

and Standard & Poor's dropped its credit rating to five levels below investment grade. The company survived the crisis by floating $144 million in two-year bonds and selling its 4 percent interest in DirecTV Latin America LLC for $150 million.

The inability of the Argentine government, in January 2002, to make payments on its debts resulted in the devaluation of the peso and pushed many companies into default on their own debts. Multicanal missed payments in February and announced that it was "deferring" $138 million in coupon and principal payments. Its $680 million in dollar-denominated debt—about 65 percent of parent Grupo Clarín's total—now had been effectively more than tripled because of the decline of the peso to about 30 cents on the dollar. To add insult to injury, by March 2003 Multicanal had lost 18 percent of its subscribers (982,000 at the end of 2003) compared with only 9 percent for rival Cablevisión, indicating that the latter's subscribers were more affluent and creditworthy than the former's. In December 2003, however, Multicanal won support from some creditors for an offer to buy back its bonds at 30 percent of their face value or to trade them for new securities. In the same year Agea Diario Clarín restructured its $408 million in debts.

Grupo Clarín's revenues came to ARS 1.84 billion ($623.73 million) in 2003, a 24 percent increase over the previous year but a far cry from its peak of ARS 1.74 billion in 1998, when the peso was at parity with the dollar. Agea Diario Clarín (the two wholly owned newspapers plus *Genios*) accounted for 30 percent and Multicanal for 28 percent. Artear, the radio and television business, accounted for 12 percent; the newsprint business for 9 percent; Artes Gráfica Rioplatense (Agr), the printing subsidiary, for 5 percent; Cimeco, the regional newspaper alliance, for 4 percent; Ciudad Internet for 3 percent; and other properties for 9 percent. The group earned ARS 695 million (about $235 million) in 2003 after a loss of ARS 1.1 billion (about $375 million) in 2002. Multicanal returned to profitability after losing ARS 938 million (about $318 million) in 2002. By one ranking, Agea Diario Clarín was second in the nation in profit margin in 2003, and Agr was fourth.

Agr was printing newspaper supplements, magazines, telephone books, and circulars for supermarkets and commercial chains. It also offered prepostal services, distribution, and finishing of documents. The group's other graphic holdings, as of 2002, included *Elle Argentina,* 75 percent of *La Razón,* 37 percent of Papel Prensa, one-third of Cimeco, and 25.6 percent of the news agency DyN. The audiovisual holdings, in addition to Multicanal, Artear, Radio Mitre, and its sports events units, included all of channel 7 in Bahia Blanca, Buenos Aires, 85 percent of channel 12 in Córdoba, 82 percent of Prima Argentina and Prima do Brasil, half of Audiotel, and 30 percent of Patagonik Film Group.

Principal Subsidiaries

Arte Gráfico Editorial Argentino S.A.; Artear S.A. (98%); Artes Grafica Rioplatense S.A.; Multicanal S.A. (94%); Prima S.A. (82%).

Principal Competitors

Cablevisión S.A.; La Nación S.A.; Telecom Internet S.A.

Further Reading

Bachelet, Pablo, ''Ciudad Clarín,'' *América economia,* December 1998, p. 57.

Benechi, Mario, ''La próxima batalla,'' *Mercado,* August 1998, pp. 136–46.

Llonto, Pablo, *La Noble Ernestina,* Buenos Aires: Astralib, 2003.

''La misión de Multicanal,'' *Multichannel News International,* October 2001, pp. 28+.

Paxman, Andrew, ''Quiet Clarín Making Moves,'' *Variety,* March 25–31, 1996, pp. 40, 60.

Ramos, Julio A., *Los Cerrojos a la Prensa,* Buenos Aires: Editorial Amfin, 1993.

Ryst, Sonja, ''Argentine Companies Make Serious Headway in Digging Out of Debt,'' *Wall Street Journal,* January 5, 2004, p. 13.

Sciutto, Luis A., *Robert Noble: Un gran argentino,* Buenos Aires: Fundación Roberto Noble, 1979.

Sencio, Gustavo, ''La verdad sobre Clarín,'' *Apertura,* August 2002, pp. 22–28.

Ulanovsky, Carlos, *Paren las rotativas,* Buenos Aires: Espasa, 1997.

Wing, Lisa, ''Opening Capital Campaign,'' *LatinFinance,* March 2000, pp. 63–64.

—Robert Halasz

GSI Commerce, Inc.

1075 1st Avenue
King of Prussia, Pennsylvania 19406
U.S.A.
Telephone: (610) 265-3229
Fax: (610) 491-7366
Web site: http://www.gsicommerce.com

Public Company
Incorporated: 1997 as Global Sports, Inc.
Employees: 1,074
Sales: $241.91 million (2003)
Stock Exchanges: NASDAQ
Ticker Symbol: GSIC
NAIC: 541512 Computer Systems Design Services

GSI Commerce, Inc. helps other companies conduct business on the Internet, providing a comprehensive set of e-commerce services to retailers, branded manufacturers, media companies, and professional sports organizations. GSI assumes responsibility for web site design and maintenance, merchandise procurement and fulfillment, and customer service matters. The company operates a 450,000-square-foot warehouse in Louisville, Kentucky, and a customer service center in Melbourne, Florida. GSI's clients include The Athlete's Foot, Kmart, Ace Hardware, the Web store for cable television channel Comedy Central, the National Football League's Denver Broncos, and The Sports Authority, among others. The company serves nearly 50 customers who pay GSI a percentage of each sale made online.

Origins

GSI lived two distinctly different corporate lives in its business history. The thread connecting the disparate periods of the company's existence was Michael G. Rubin, a Villanova University dropout whose creation of a successful e-commerce business model turned a teenage entrepreneur into the leader of a potentially $1 billion-in-sales company. Rubin's withdrawal from Villanova was not because of a lack of drive on his part—the last characteristic anyone could impugn on the enterprising teenager. While in high school, Rubin owned and operated a chain of five retail stores selling skiing and sporting goods in

Pennsylvania and New York. It was his early business success that precluded Rubin from finishing his studies at Villanova. The Lafayette, Pennsylvania native started a discount sporting goods distribution business named KPR Sports International, Inc. at age 19, founding the company in 1991. The success of KPR enabled Rubin to introduce his own line of footwear in 1994, a line branded under the name Yukon.

While Rubin raced forward in the business world, another member of the sporting goods industry floundered. Its failure gave Rubin the opportunity to advance his remarkable career. In Portland, Oregon, a company that designed, marketed, and distributed a line of footwear design for women was in trouble. The company and the line of branded footwear shared the name RYKA. RYKA, Inc. was organized in 1986, introducing its first two styles of high-performance athletic footwear in 1987. The company shipped its first products in 1988. The company lost money perennially, but in the mid-1990s salvation appeared imminent. In January 1995, RYKA and L.A. Gear, Inc., a sports apparel company, announced a merger, a union that promised to alleviate RYKA's financial burdens considerably. At the end of April 1995, however, the company was notified that L.A. Gear was terminating the merger agreement. Less than three weeks later, RYKA's position became precarious when it received notice of another terminated agreement. Pro-Specs America Corporation, which provided the principal source of financing for RYKA's production activities, announced that it was ending its support in May 1995. RYKA reeled from the effect of the two termination notices. Employees were fired, employees quit, and sales efforts were cut back drastically after the company was unable to obtain products from overseas production sources.

RYKA's situation was desperate by mid-1995. The company had posted annual losses every year since its inception, racking up a deficit of nearly $18 million. Sales, which had steadily increased from $7.9 million in 1991 to $16.2 million in 1994, plummeted to $7.6 million in 1995, a year in which the company posted a $3.6 million loss. The company teetered on the edge of bankruptcy, but its collapse was staved off when MR Acquisitions, L.L.C. intervened in July 1995. The "MR" in MR Acquisitions stood for Michael Rubin. The company, indirectly owned by Rubin, gave RYKA its financial salvation, providing the company with an $8 million financing agreement.

Company Perspectives:

We offer a quality and cost effective solution for our partners to capitalize on e-commerce and direct response opportunities while remaining focused on their core businesses. By outsourcing with us, our partners benefit from our scalable infrastructure, which is designed to operate multiple e-commerce businesses. As a result, our partners are able to avoid the significant capital investments and operating expenses that would be required to operate their online retailing and direct response marketing businesses on their own. GSI Commerce benefits from aggregating the demand of our partners' businesses to achieve operational efficiencies. Depending on the needs of the partner, we can offer either a complete outsourcing of their online retailing and direct response activities or a more customized solution that uses portions of our platform.

"Without this financing arrangement," RYKA's filing with the Securities and Exchange Commission explained, "management believed there was substantial doubt that the company would be able to remain in business." Rubin, as a result of the deal, gained a 40 percent stake in RYKA and, because RYKA was listed on the NASDAQ, he became chairman and chief executive officer of a publicly traded company at age 23.

Contemplating E-Commerce in 1998

Although RYKA was in dire shape when he took control, Rubin eventually was able to effect a turnaround. In 1997, he combined RYKA with KPR, forming Global Sports, Inc. as the entity with control over the RYKA and Yukon brand names. Global Sports led a profitable existence as a distributor of discount footwear, apparel, and sporting goods, but both Rubin and the company were destined for success in a different line of business. Rubin made the decision to forsake his involvement in the sporting goods business only a year after forming Global Sports, initiating a thorough transformation of the company that would take nearly two years to complete. Rubin decided to enter the e-commerce sector, a young, emerging industry with growth projections capable of seducing any ambitious businessperson. E-commerce sales in 1998 were $13 billion. Within five years, according to industry pundits, e-commerce sales were expected to reach $3.2 trillion.

The first evidence of the new Global Sports Rubin envisioned emerged in the first half of 1999. A new e-commerce division was formed called Global Sports Interactive whose mission was to build, maintain, and update web sites for sporting goods retailers. Rubin set up the division to perform nearly every task associated with a retailer's online business. Global Sports Interactive purchased merchandise directly from vendors, shipped the products, and handled all sales and customer service details. Rubin offered a complete outsourcing of Internet business for retailers, many of whom lacked the personnel, finances, and expertise to develop their own in-house departments.

Global Sports Interactive rose to the forefront of Rubin's business focus as the sporting goods footwear and apparel business receded. The web sites of the company's first four clients launched in November 1999, when Global Sports took control of the online business of Grand Rapids, Michigan-based MC Sports, La Canada, California-based Sport Chalet, Ft. Lauderdale, Florida-based The

Sports Authority, and Kennesaw, Georgia-based The Athlete's Foot. By the end of the year, Rubin had divested the company's historical business, selling the Yukon and RYKA brands to a California-based company named American Sporting Goods.

Global Sports' first four clients represented the beginning of a wave of customers. As new clients signed on for the company's comprehensive services, Rubin realized he had erred in outsourcing the fulfillment services he offered. It was one of the few mistakes he made in launching his e-commerce business. Rubin could not offer adequate service by relying on third-party companies to warehouse merchandise, so, within nine months of starting the venture, he opened Global Sports' own 300,000-square-foot warehouse in Louisville, Kentucky. The addition of the warehouse left virtually everything Internet-related in Global Sports' hands, an acceptance of responsibility that appealed to retailers. The company's agreement with The Athlete's Foot typified what the relationship between Rubin's company and its customers entailed. Global Sports designed the retailer's web site, bought the inventory, stored the merchandise, shipped the products to customers, and fielded customer service phone calls. The Athlete's Foot limited its involvement to marketing the web site, establishing online prices, and advising on design to ensure the web site reflected its image. For his services, Rubin charged a percentage of sales instead of a flat fee. With each product sold online, Global Sports received 92.5 percent of the sale and The Athlete's Foot received 7.5 percent.

Moving Beyond Sporting Goods in 2001

Rubin's business model showed potential for retailers outside the sporting goods industry not long after it was introduced. In March 2000, the company's newest client was the $40 billion-in-sales retailer Kmart, a company with sporting goods sales that eclipsed $2 billion. The agreement signed in March gave Global Sports control over the merchandise procurement and fulfillment for BlueLightSports.com, Kmart's online sporting goods department that served as prelude for BlueLight.com, Kmart's full-fledged online offering. In September 2001, Global Sports moved beyond its niche in sporting goods and sports-related e-commerce by taking control over BlueLight.com.

When Global Sports was awarded control of Kmart's Internet business, Rubin, by then 29 years old, was perceived by many onlookers as a perceptive visionary. Kmart was one of roughly 20 customers, a client list that included WebMD, Fox Sports, the National Football League's Denver Broncos, and the Ladies Professional Golf Association. The remarkable part of Global Sports' success was not its growing client list, but that the company was succeeding while the rest of its dot-com brethren were suffering from a combination of illusion and delusion. The collapse of the dot-com sector had arrived, its fall the subject of daily headlines, but the business press still rallied behind Rubin and his e-commerce business model.

Rubin, as *Business Week* noted in a November 20, 2000 article, did not represent one of the "let's-spend-everything-we-have-on-TV-advertising dot-coms." Global Sports was invisible to any consumer whom it counted as its ultimate customer, a behind-the-scenes company that never tried to create its own brand. Instead, the company relied on the proven strength of existing brands. "What [Global Sports is] trying to do is not develop their own brand name, but utilize and leverage the brand names of their

Key Dates:

1991: Michael Rubin starts a sporting goods distribution business named KPR Sport International, Inc.
1994: KPR introduces Yukon, its own brand of footwear.
1995: Rubin acquires 40 percent of a troubled footwear company, RYKA, Inc.
1997: Rubin combines the Yukon and RYKA brands to form Global Sports, Inc.
1998: Rubin decides to sell his two sporting goods brands and create an e-commerce company.
1999: Global Sports begins operating the online business of its first four retail clients.
2001: Global Sports takes control of BlueLight.com, Kmart's web site, a move that marks Rubin's diversification outside the sporting goods sector.
2002: Global Sports changes its name to GSI Commerce, Inc.
2004: A second warehouse is constructed in Shepherdsville, Kentucky, as GSI records robust growth.

partners, which makes a lot more sense,'' an analyst commented in a November 11, 2001 *Knight Ridder/Tribune Business News* article. Another analyst, in the same article, echoed praise for Rubin's approach. ''They're one of the real success stories in e-commerce,'' the analyst explained. ''They took a decidedly different approach by partnering with existing brick-and-mortar brands. Back in the dot-com heyday, it was all about building a new brand, and the existing brick-and-mortar brands were going to be replaced by these new-economy brands. Michael Rubin believed that wasn't going to be the case.''

Rubin enjoyed robust sales growth after his conversion to e-commerce. Revenue leaped from $5.5 million in 1999 to $42 million in 2000 before recording explosive gains to $103 million in 2001 and $172 million in 2002. Profits were harder to come by, however, a trait shared by the legions of the dot-com companies that failed at the turn of the 21st century. GSI did not record its first profitable quarter until the last three months of 2001, when it registered $258,000 in net income. Although the lack of consistent profitability was a concern, the company's financial state was strong thanks to sizable investments gained through several partnerships. When Rubin began developing an e-commerce business in 1999, Softbank Corp. acquired 30 percent of Global Sports, giving Rubin $80 million to fund business development. In September 2000, the company received $40.8 million by selling a 19.8 percent interest to Interactive Technology Holdings L.L.C., jointly owned by QVC Inc. and Comcast Inc. The investments, coupled with a business model that drew its strength from established and proven brands, mitigated concerns about profitability.

As Global Sports concluded its first five years as an e-commerce enterprise, the company was applying its expertise outside of the sporting goods sector. QVC's investment in the company led to the formation of a Global Sports subsidiary in 2002 whose focus was selling e-commerce services to television and cable networks looking to sell merchandise online. Through this venture, Global Sports signed agreements with

Comedy Central, Pax TV, The Golf Channel, and TV Land. The growth of the company's media-related business, combined with its involvement with companies such as Kmart and Ace Hardware, created a need for a new name. Global Sports no longer restricted its operating scope to sporting goods retailers. Accordingly, in May 2002 the company changed its name to GSI Commerce, Inc. to better reflect its diversified interests.

As Rubin planned for the future, his thoughts centered on expansion. ''We feel it's very important to be profitable,'' he said in an August 25, 2004 interview with the *Philadelphia Inquirer*, ''but not maximize profits. That would take away from growing the business.'' GSI was expected to post its first annual profit in 2004, but the addition of new e-commerce partners such as Kate Spade, Liz Claiborne, Timberland, and Wilson Leathers in 2004 encouraged Rubin to invest in the infrastructure to support its growing roster of clients. The company moved into a new 104,000-square-foot headquarters facility in 2004 and was expected to open another warehouse in Shepherdsville, Kentucky, by the end of the year. Although few industry pundits questioned the financial viability of Rubin's approach to e-commerce, the future progress of GSI ultimately would determine the soundness of its business model.

Principal Subsidiaries

Global-QVC Solutions.

Principal Competitors

Amazon.com, Inc.; Digital River, Inc.; Electronic Data Systems Corporation.

Further Reading

Geiger, Mia, ''CEO Profile: Michael G. Rubin,'' *Philadelphia Business Journal,* September 14, 2001, p. 16.

''Global Sports Forms a Pact with BlueLight.Com,'' *Daily News Record,* March 13, 2000, p. 1A.

''It Ain't Over 'Til It's Over,'' *Business Week,* November 20, 2000, p. EB108.

Kanaley, Reid, ''King of Prussia, Pa.-Based Sports E-Tailer Thrives in Spite of Downturn,'' *Knight Ridder/Tribune Business News,* November 11, 2001.

McKinney, Melonee, ''Global Sports Forms New E-Commerce Division; Off-Pricer Links Up with Five Athletic Specialty Store Chains,'' *Daily News Record,* May 12, 1999, p. 1A.

''Pennsylvania-Based Web Retailer Global Sports Posts Its First Profit,'' *Knight Ridder/Tribune Business News,* February 7, 2002.

''Softbank Buys 30-Percent Stake in Global Sports,'' *Footwear News,* August 2, 1999, p. 126.

Solnik, Claude, ''American Sports Taking Yukon, RYKA into Apparel,'' *Footwear News,* January 31, 2000, p. 17.

——, ''Global Quits Wholesaling; Yukon and RYKA Brands Will Be Put on the Block,'' *Footwear News,* June 14, 1999, p. 4.

——, ''QVC and Comcast Purchasing $40.8 Million Stake in Global Sports,'' *Footwear News,* September 18, 2000, p. 35.

Tanaka, Wendy, ''King of Prussia, Pa.-Based E-Commerce Firm Grows by Expanding Beyond Original Niche,'' *Philadelphia Inquirer,* August 25, 2004, p. 39.

Tedeschi, Mark, ''Global Sports Emerging from Closeout Roots,'' *Sporting Goods Business,* March 25, 1998, p. 22.

—Jeffrey L. Covell

Hollander Home Fashions Corp.

6560 W. Rogers Circle, Suite 19
Boca Raton, Florida 33487
U.S.A.
Telephone: (561) 997-6900
Fax: (561) 997-8738
Web site: http://www.hollander.com

Private Company
Founded: 1953
Employees: 1,200
Sales: $211 million (2002 est.)
NAIC: 314129 Other Household Textile and Product Mills

Hollander Home Fashions Corp. is a privately owned major bedding manufacturer based in Boca Raton, Florida. Products are organized under three business groups: basic, fashion, and designer. Pillows are the most important product line in the basic bedding group, which specializes in white goods. Hollander sells more pillows, some 30 million across all groups, than any other company in the world. In addition, the basic bedding group offers mattress pads, down comforters, featherbeds, fiberbeds, throws, and blankets. The company also produces much of the group's raw materials by processing its own down, feathers, and polyester fiber fill. The fashion bedding group offers complete ensembles aimed at the juvenile, teen, and adult markets. Products include decorative pillows, pillow shams, comforters, duvet covers, sheets, bed skirts, and layered window treatments. Some of the juvenile lines are licensed with such designers as Hank Player USA, Todd Parr, and Libby & Friends. Hollander has stepped back from an earlier push to license well-known properties, due to mixed results. The designer bedding group offers basic bedding products through licensing agreements: Laura Ashley and Karen Neuburger for a more upscale market; and Countess York, JG Hook, and Beauty Rest for mid-market retailers. Traditionally involved in private-label manufacturing, Hollander also has taken steps in recent years to build its own brand: "Hollander Home Fashions: Live Comfortably." In addition to its corporate offices in Boca Raton, Hollander maintains a New York City showroom and nine manufacturing plants in the United States and Canada,

factories in Germany to serve the European market, and five factories in China.

Founder's Emigration Following World War II

The company's founder, Bernard Hollander, emigrated from Uruguay to the United States in the late 1940s. Settling in New Jersey, he made his living peddling such everyday items as glasses and combs to retailers on a wholesale basis. He also began acting as a bed pillow jobber. One of his clients was Two Guys, the first discount store chain in the United States. The pillow maker that he represented decided to sell directly to the chain and cut him out. He vowed on a Friday that he would have a factory by Monday to start making bed pillows himself. He kept his word by converting his Irvington, New Jersey garage into a makeshift plant, relying on a single sewing machine and a homemade measuring board. Thus in 1953 he launched Hollander Home Fashions. It was a shoestring operation in the beginning: He sold his pillows by going door-to-door to home furnishings retailers, keeping track of orders on sheets of wrapping paper. A major turning point was a decision by the U.S. government, because of the Korean War, to commandeer all large supplies of feathers in order to make sleeping bags for the military. Because Hollander's operation was small and unnoticed, his supply of feathers was untouched and he was able to take advantage of the situation and establish himself as a pillow manufacturer. Soon he was able to move the operations out of his garage and into a true manufacturing plant.

In 1954 Bernard's 16-year-old son, Leo, began learning the business. After school, he worked in the factory, cutting fabric, and accompanied his father on visits to department stores on open buying days. He joined the company full-time in 1958. In 1964 Leo, still in his 20s, took over the business from his father and began to expand it. Factories in Los Angeles and Chicago were opened. A third generation, in the form of Leo's sons, were soon learning the business as well. The eldest, Jeff Hollander, began helping out on weekends when he was just six, counting the change in the soft drink machines and sorting canceled checks. After attending the University of Pennsylvania's Wharton School of Business, he worked briefly for a Washington, D.C., advertising agency. In 1981 he agreed to

---

Company Perspectives:

At Hollander the theme Live comfortably guides everything we do . . . down to the tiniest detail.

---

come to work for the family business at a salary less than half of what he made at the ad agency, but he correctly surmised that he had a greater chance for advancement working for his father.

The 1980s brought major changes to the bedding industry, in particular bed pillows, which for years had been dominated by a dozen strong regional companies. A wave of consolidation swept through the industry, led by Pillowtex Corp., which by the end of the decade had a 50 percent market share in pillows. When the shakeout was complete only four national manufacturers and a handful of weak regional companies remained. Hollander, by attending to its own business and choosing not to get caught up in the acquisition mania of this period, was one of the national survivors. But unlike some of its larger rivals it had not accumulated massive debt loads buying up the competition, a decision that over the course of the ensuing decade would lead to the demise of some.

One of the most important steps Hollander took in the 1980s was to start manufacturing offshore in Asia, years before it became a standard approach by U.S manufacturers. Because it was becoming increasingly difficult to find companies in the United States to do detail work such as hand sewing and double-needle sewing, Hollander turned to China, establishing an early presence in a country that would be destined to play a major role in the future of textiles.

Broader Product Lines in the 1980s

In 1989 and 1990 Hollander relocated its corporate headquarters from Newark, New Jersey, to Boca Raton, Florida, and later moved its product testing lab to the new location. At this stage, the company remained very much a private-label pillow company, well established with mass merchants such as Kmart, Wal-Mart, Sam's Wholesale, and Price Club. The company was dominant at the low price point, roughly $6, controlling about 40 percent of the synthetic pillow market, but with better stores Hollander's sterling reputation as a low-end supplier was not an advantage and the company did little business at higher-price point, higher-margin merchandise. Because there was less competition in the bedding industry in the wake of consolidation, both in terms of manufacturers and retailers, Hollander saw an opportunity to broaden its approach. No longer content to compete on price alone, the company now wanted to upgrade its styling and offer higher-end merchandise, thus becoming a total resource for its customers. A line of natural-fill comforters was introduced in 1989, followed by more expensive duvet covers. New synthetic fillings as well as feather and down were used in pillows to produce more upscale products to trade-up customers. Moreover, the company took advantage of its strong position in pillows to grow its mattress pad business. The company's decorative bedding products also were upgraded with the hiring of a print stylist. One of the results of this effort was new sheets added to an expanded line of decorative bedding ensembles, in

order to provide low-price point ensembles with a fashion look. To support this aggressive approach to expanding its product lines, Hollander added its manufacturing capacity in down and feather processing by opening a California plant, and increased mattress pad quilting, and cutting and sewing operations.

By 1993 Hollander was generating around $140 million in annual sales, the result of five years of a 25 to 30 percent growth rate. Because the pillow business was mature, the company decided that rather than slug it out with the competition in taking away market share it would attempt to grow its fashion bedding business. To jumpstart this effort, Hollander acquired the assets of Countess York, a bed covering manufacturer that had been forced into Chapter 11 bankruptcy. Hollander's business was now restructured into two divisions: basic bedding and decorative bedding, which consisted of the Countess York line of comforters, bedspreads, comforter sets, window coverings, sheets and pillow cases, as well as the Cornucopia Cache line of decorative pillows. To keep pace with the demands of its expanded product offerings, Hollander also invested about $1 million to bolster quality control, including the purchase of inspection machines, computerized color matching, and a statistical record-keeping machine. A new director of quality assurance was brought in to implement a formal quality control program that was rolled out to all of Hollander's manufacturing operations.

The Countess York line failed to catch on with retailers, prompting Hollander to scrap the line and in February 1993 hire a respected designer, Terry Dikomeit, to start a line from scratch. In a matter of just two months, Dikomeit designed and unveiled to buyers a line of fully coordinated ensembles that received favorable reviews from retailers. Department stores continued to see Hollander as a mass-merchant vendor and shied away, but Dikomeit's reputation in the industry was strong enough to begin breaking down some resistance. Specialty stores, on the other hand, had no such reservations and embraced Hollander's new emphasis. But in keeping with its experience in mass merchandising, Hollander opted to hold the line on pricing, giving up the final markup points in favor of setting prices that would result in high volumes. The Countess York label would later be revived as a mass-market line.

Stepped-Up Licensing in the Late 1990s

In July 1998 Hollander became involved with juvenile bedding licensing by acquiring the rights to Hank Player, a sports apparel maker. Several months later the company hired a new vice-president of sales for fashion bedding, Tom McCaffrey, who had successfully headed The Bibb Co.'s juvenile line. Later in 1999 Hollander added licenses for the classic patchwork dolls Raggedy Ann and Andy, and Rocky and Bullwinkle, the 1960s television cartoon characters that were about to be revived as a motion picture. In addition, Hollander signed a licensing agreement with major league baseball to produce juvenile bedding designs for the mass merchants, warehouse clubs, off-price retailers, toy chains, catalogs, and baseball team stores. Hollander added Todd Parr and its "Silly City" concept as a juvenile bedding license in 2000. Although Raggedy Ann and Andy, and to a lesser extent Todd Parr and Hanker, did well, the Rocky and Bullwinkle license proved disappointing, and the baseball design did not live up to expectations. Because

Key Dates:

1953: The company is founded by Bernard Hollander in New Jersey.
1964: Leonard Hollander succeeds his father as company head.
1989: Corporate headquarters are moved to Boca Raton, Florida.
1992: The company moves into the fashion bedding category.
2000: The Beauty Rest license is acquired.
2004: The Hollander brand is launched.

the major licenses commanded high royalties and major guarantees by licensors, Hollander soured on the hit-or-miss nature of this segment. Furthermore, the company's non-licensed bedding generated about 80 percent of its juvenile business. As a result, McCaffrey was let go and Hollander scaled back its juvenile licensing efforts.

The basic bedding division also became involved in licensing. It signed a licensing agreement with the U.K.-based fashion and home furnishing company Laura Ashley and enjoyed good success. Then in 2000 Hollander signed an agreement with major mattress manufacturer Simmons Company to produce a collection of down pillows, comforters, and featherbeds under the well-known Beauty Rest label. In 2002 Hollander acquired the bedding license from designer Karen Neuburger.

While pursuing licensing opportunities, Hollander also bolstered its manufacturing capabilities overseas. It opened a factory in Auma, Germany, located in the former East Germany, to produce pillows and comforters for the European market. Hollander also began manufacturing in mainland China in 2001, opening five factories in Huangzou. The company added to its presence in China two years later with the opening of an office in Shanghai, a city that was emerging as a hub for business in China.

The bedding industry had seen a number of changes during the 1990s and early years of the new century. Pillowtex, once the industry leader, collapsed, its assets sold off in bankruptcy court, leaving just two 1950s-era pillow manufacturers left

standing: Hollander, the market leader in terms of volume, and Pacific Coast Feather Company, the market leader in terms of revenues. While both companies were successful, Pacific Coast made the wise choice of building its own brand rather than relying on private branding and licensing. Hollander now played catch-up in this area. When Bed Bath & Beyond approached the company in October 2002 about producing a fiberbed product, Hollander took advantage of the opportunity by arranging to sell the product under a new Hollander label rather than as a Bed Bath & Beyond product.

For the first time in its history, Hollander hired a marketing firm and a public relations firm to represent it and help build its own brand. It spent more than $1 million advertising in trade publications and developing in-store displays, and also devoted time to renegotiating a number of private-label agreements in preparation for the 2004 launch of Hollander's own line of branded bedding products. The Hollander brand got off to a good start, but whether conflicts would develop with private-label or license customers, who now became competitors as well, remained to be seen.

Principal Divisions

Basic Bedding; Fashion Bedding; Designer Bedding.

Principal Competitors

Dan River Inc.; Pacific Coast Feather Company; Springs Industries, Inc.; WestPoint Stevens Inc.

Further Reading

Adler, Carlye, "Soft Branding," *Fortune Small Business,* September 2004, p. 79.

Bernard, Sharyn K., "Beyond Basics: Hollander Home Fashions Seeks to Diversify and Grow As a Better Bedding Resource," *HFD—The Weekly Home Furnishings Newspaper,* June 24, 1991, p. 44.

DesMarteau, Kathleen, "Hollander's Home Run," *Bobbin,* September 1997, p. 20.

Goldbogen, Jessica, "Hollander Seeks the Spotlight After 50 Years," *HFN—The Weekly Newspaper for the Home Furnishing Network,* November 4, 2002, p. 22.

Salisbury, Susan, "Boca Raton, Fla., Bedding Maker's Leaders Plan to Start Promoting Company," *Palm Beach Post,* February 24, 2003.

—Ed Dinger

Industrie Zignago Santa Margherita S.p.A.

Via Ita Marzotto 8
Fossalta Di Portogruaro
I-30025 VE
Italy
Telephone: +39 0421 246111
Fax: +39 0421 246246
Web site: http://www.zignago.com

Public Company
Incorporated: 1940 as Societa Fondaiaria Agro
    Alimentare SFAI
Employees: 1,684
Sales: EUR 258.1 million (2003)
Stock Exchanges: Borsa Italiana
Ticker Symbol: IZ
NAIC: 327211 Flat Glass Manufacturing; 312130
    Wineries; 313312 Textile and Fabric Finishing
    (Except Broadwoven Fabric) Mills; 551112 Offices of
    Other Holding Companies

Mini-conglomerate Industrie Zignago Santa Margherita S.p.A. operates in three primary sectors: glass, textiles, and wine. The company is one of Italy's largest wine producers and distributors through its Santa Margherita subsidiary. Santa Margherita operates wineries throughout Italy, including Torreslla in the Veneto region; Kettmeir, in Trentino Alto Adige; Ca' del Bosco, in the Lombard region; and Chianti Classico wines at the Lamole and Vistarenni wineries in Tuscany. The company also produces fine and sparkling wines in Veneto and Trentino Alto Adige. Santa Margherita sells some 15 million bottles per year; the export market accounts for 55 percent of the wine division's sales. Zignago's glass operations include Zignago Vetro in Italy and Verreries Brosse in France. These subsidiaries produce bottles and glass containers for the food, beverage, cosmetic, pharmaceutical, and other industries. Zignago Vetro is Italy's leading producer of glass food packaging products, which account for 40 percent of the division's sales. Zignago Vetro and Verreries Brosse also combine to form the world's fifth largest producer of perfume bottles—including the Brosse-designed Chanel No. 5 bottle. Zignago's third division focuses on the high-end linen segment of the textile market. Linificio e Canapificio Nazionale, the group's textile operation, is the second largest producer of wet and dry spun linen in Europe, producing up to 4,300 tons per year. Zignago also has a number of minor investments in other companies. Zignago itself is controlled by the Marzotto and Dona dalle Rose families. Zignago and Marzotto, owner of designer names such as Valentino, Armani, Hugo Boss, and others, have been moving to combine their operations.

Textile Beginnings in the 19th Century

Formed in 1940, Industrie Zignago Santa Margherita included operations with origins stretching back to the mid-19th century. Yet the prevailing influence in Zignago's development remained Italy's prominent Marzotto textile family. As members of the Italian nobility, the Marzotto family played a major role in northern Italy's industrial growth, particularly in establishing the region's dominance in the textiles industry, in the 19th century. The family's first textiles venture came in 1836, when Luigi Marzotto founded a woolens mill in Valdagno.

The Marzotto mill grew strongly under Luigi Marzotto and son Gaetano, who took over in 1842, and by 1880 the company had set up a second plant, in Maglio. Gaetono's son Vittorio Emanuele later joined the family firm and established a strong exports business. The company was divided up in 1910, with Vittorio Emanuele taking over the original Valdagno plant. Vittorio was joined by his son, Gaetano, Jr., who took over as head of the company in 1921.

Founding a Mini-Conglomerate in the 1940s

The younger Marzotto received credit for transforming the family linen business from a relatively small manufacturing operation to one of Italy's leading textiles companies. Marzotto stepped up the group's exports, and by the outbreak of World War II, the company's linens and wools reached across Europe, including Eastern Europe, and to Latin America and elsewhere.

Marzotto also began developing a variety of other interests, such as the launch of a hotel chain, Jolly Hotels, in order to provide himself with accommodations during his many business trips across Italy. Another major investment came in the mid-1930s, when Gaetano sought a degree of vertical integration for the company's textiles business. In 1935, Gaetano bought a 1,000-hectare farm from the noble Stucky family. The purchase enabled Marzotto to enter sheep-raising and other agricultural pursuits with the stated purpose of developing a range of consumer-oriented products.

Marzotto created a new business, Societa Fondaiaria Agro Alimentare SFAI, in order to oversee the farm's various operations. These ranged from livestock breeding to dairy products and sugar production. The Stucky estate also included a 140-hectare vineyard, Santa Margherita.

In the years following World War II, SFAI adopted a new holding company structure for its various holdings. The range of the company's operations continued to expand over the next decades. An offshoot of the group's other consumer-oriented products businesses was an entry into packaging. That business became known as Zignago Vetro, and rose to become a leading Italian and European producer of glass packaging.

Through Santa Margherita, meanwhile, SFAI emerged as one of Italy's leading wine groups. A part of its success came through its willingness to develop new wine varieties. In the 1950s and early 1960s, for example, the company began experimenting with adapting French champagne-making techniques to the Trentino-Alto Adige region's Pinot Grigio grapes. The result of these experiments was the launch of a new sparkling wine variety, Pinot Grigio, which became an instant bestseller in Italy.

Three-Pronged Strategy in the 1990s

By the end of the 1980s, Santa Margherita, which was regrouped as a separate company, Santa Margherita S.p.A., had gained a leading share in Italy's wine market, particularly among the country's growing "modern" wine segment. One of Santa Margherita's modern wines was its Chardonnay, introduced in 1981. In 1984, the company founded a new winery, Cantine Torresella, in order to produce Veneto-region wine varieties. Two years later, the company acquired Kettmeir S.p.A., in the South Tyrol region.

SFAI itself began a process of transformation during the 1980s. The holding company listed its stock on the Borsa

Italiana in 1986, and changed its name to Industrie Zignago Santa Margherita S.p.A. Majority control of Zignago's stock nonetheless remained under control of the Marzotto family and partner and fellow nobles the Dona dalle Rosa family. Over the next decade and a half, Zignago began a refocusing effort around a triple core of Wine, Textiles, and Glass. As part of its new strategy, the company sold off its noncore holdings, a process completed, in large part, by the mid-1990s.

During this period, Zignago's major shareholder, Marzotto, then under leadership of Pietro Marzotto, was undergoing its own transformation from one of Italy's leading textiles companies to one of the world's leading luxury branded clothing stables, starting with the purchase of Germany's Hugo Boss in 1991. At the same time, however, Marzotto had inaugurated a new vertical integration strategy designed to give the company complete control over the entire chain of wool and wool clothing production. This effort led Marzotto to make a number of acquisitions, including that of Linificio e Canapificio Nazionale in 1985.

Linificio e Canapificio stemmed from an 1873 merger that brought together two small linen companies in the village of Adda. Cassano d'Adda specialized in producing linen and hemp using the dry process, while Fara Gera d'Adda specialized in production based on wet spinning. The new company went public soon after, with a listing on the Borsa Italiana in 1876.

Linificio grew strongly, emerging as a regional and then national leader. Acquisitions formed a large part of the company's growth, and by the early 1920s, Linificio had established itself as the country's dominant linen and hemp yarn producer. At its height in the 1930s, Linificio controlled some 75 percent of the country's market.

Hit hard by the development of synthetic textiles in the decades following World War II, Linificio found new life in a diversification move in the 1980s. In 1984, the company decided to leverage its experience in the spinning industry by acquiring Linimpianti. That purchase enabled Linificio to begin manufacturing and distributing spinning, hackling, and related equipment.

Taking the Lead in the 2000s

Linificio also sought to reduce its manufacturing reliance on the Italian market. The company made a first step internationally with the purchase of France's Paul Le Bland et fils, based in Lille, in 1989. In the early 1990s, the company took a new step, opening a joint venture production subsidiary, Filin S.A., in Tunisia in 1993. By the end of the decade, Linificio expanded its production focus with the creation of UAB Lietlinen, in Lithuania. That company began production in 2002.

By then, Marzotto had grown to include fashion powerhouse Valentino, acquired in 2002. Fears of a possible takeover attempt for the company, however, led its board to propose a merger with Zignago, in which the Marzotto family-controlled holding company would pay EUR 435 million for the textile and fashion group. That plan, launched by Pietro Marzotto, was soon vetoed by other Marzotto family members.

Instead, Marzotto transferred only the struggling Linificio to Zignago in 2003. The new division then absorbed the existing

Key Dates:

1935: Gaetano Marzotto acquires a 1,000-hectare farm in Italy, including the 140-hectare Santa Margherita vineyard.

1940: The Societa Fondaiaria Agro Alimentare SFAI is formed to exploit agricultural and consumer products.

1961: Santa Margherita launches the Pinot Grigio sparkling wine.

1984: Santa Margherita establishes Cantine Torresella in the Veneto region.

1985: Marzotto S.p.A. acquires Linificio e Canapificio Nazionale.

1986: SFAI goes public and changes its name to Industrie Zignago Santa Margherita; the company begins shedding diversified operations to focus on the three-pronged core of Wine, Glass, and Textiles; Santa Margherita acquires Ketmeir S.p.A.

1989: Linificio acquires Paul Le Blan in Lille, France.

1993: Linificio establishes the joint venture production subsidiary Filin in Tunisia.

2000: Linificio forms a production subsidiary in Lithuania.

2001: Zignago Vetro acquires Verreries Brosse in France.

2003: Zignago acquires Linificio.

Zignago Tessile, retaining the Linificio name. The merger allowed Zignago to claim a clear leadership position in the Italian linen market.

The company's wine division also had grown strongly into the mid-2000s, notably with the acquisitions of Ca' del Bosco, in the province of Brescia, and Fattoria Pile e Lamole, based in the Chianti area of the Florence region, and another Chianti-region vineyard, Fattoria Vistarenni. Santa Margherita also emerged as a leading Italian wine exporter, pursuing markets in the United States, United Kingdom, Japan, and Germany, among others. By the mid-2000s, exports accounted for nearly 55 percent of Zignago's wine business.

Zignago capped its success in wine and textiles with growth in its third core business as well. In 2001, Zignago Vetro grew through the purchase of Verreries Brosse, based in Vieux Rouen, France. Brosse had been founded in 1854, and had developed a specialty as a producer of perfume bottles. Among Brosse's many triumphs was the creation of the bottle for the famed Chanel No. 5 in 1921. The addition of Brosse enabled Zignago to claim the leading position in Italy and a spot among the world's top five producers of cosmetic and perfume bottles. Zignago had successfully woven a place for itself in the Italian and international markets in the new century.

Principal Subsidiaries

Zignago Vetro S.p.A.; Verreries Brosse S.A.S.; Attività Industriali Friuli S.R.L.; Santa Margherita S.p.A.; Linificio e Canapificio Nazionale S.p.A.; Tessile S.p.A.; Multitecno S.R.L.; P.A.I.F.A. Holding B.V.; Villanova S.R.L.; Prind S.p.A.

Principal Competitors

Boero Bartolomeo S.p.A.; CALP Cristalleria Artistica La Piana S.p.A.; Cofina SGPS, S.A.; Dalmine S.p.A.; Danieli & C. Officine Meccaniche S.p.A.; Davide Campari-Milano S.p.A.; Industria Macchine Automatiche S.p.A.; Schoeller Eitorf AG; Sol S.p.A.

Further Reading

"Marzotto Restructures," *WWD,* September 9, 2002, p. 2.

O'Brian, Heather, "Italian Luxury Merger on the Table," *Daily Deal,* September 9, 2002.

"Zignano Vetro," *Glass,* March 2002, p. 42.

—M.L. Cohen

International Shipbreaking Ltd. L.L.C.

P.O. Box 6048
Brownsville, Texas 78523-6048
U.S.A.
Telephone: 956-831-2299

Private Company
Incorporated: 1995
Sales: $40 million (2004 est.)
NAIC: 336611 Ship Building and Repairing

International Shipbreaking Ltd. L.L.C. (ISL) is a Brownsville, Texas, company that dismantles obsolete maritime vessels and equipment for recycling. Privately owned, ISL is the largest and most technically advanced of the handful of companies providing shipbreaking services. Its 43-acre yard is able to accommodate vessels as long as 1,000 feet and as wide as 140 feet, and can handle as many as nine vessels at one time. While the competition continues to rely on welding torches to carve out portions of a ship, ISL uses metal shears. It also uses an onboard smelter to melt aluminum, rather than haul the material away in unwieldy and dangerous pieces. Dangerous substances such as PCBs and asbestos are removed by the company's own trucks, unlike other shipbreakers that contract out the work. Taking apart a vessel is a painstaking process. After all dangerous toxins are removed by workers wearing biohazard suits, scores of cutters using torches and shears whittle down the superstructure, and the pieces are removed by cranes using large magnets. The resulting gutted hull, called the "canoe" in the business, is removed from the water, and carved up, and the scrap metal is sold all over the world to recycling mills. Over the years, the industry has come under fire for dangerous work conditions, which resulted in a number of worker deaths, and the reckless handling of hazardous materials. ISL is in the forefront of improving shipbreaking practices and improving the industry's image. Any diesel fuel recovered in vessels is properly recycled, freshly cleaned jumpsuits are issued to workers each day, and management makes sure that water supplemented with electrolytes is available to keep workers hydrated.

World War II-Era Ships Fueling Shipbreaking Industry

The United States turned out hundreds of vessels of all types to support the war effort of the Allies during World War II. When the conflict ended many of the yards that built these ships began scrapping them. More than 2,200 ships were retained to make up the U.S. National Defense Reserve Fleet, which was docked at a dozen harbors. Over the years the country would occasionally find uses for the ships. From 1955 to 1964 the Department of Agriculture stored grain on 600 of them, and also in the 1950s, when the Suez Canal was temporarily closed, the government activated 19 tankers and 223 cargo ships to alleviate the problems caused by shipping delays. During the 1960s, 18 ships returned to service during the 1961 crisis in Berlin. The Soviet Union had attempted to cut off the Western-controlled section of Berlin from the outside world, forcing the United States and its allies to resupply the beleaguered city through the air, an effort that required maritime support. In addition, during the Vietnam War the United States brought 172 ships back into military service. During the 1970s a large number of merchant vessels in the Reserve Fleet reached retirement age, which led to the rise in the number of shipbreaking companies, half a dozen of which were located in Brownsville. This supply of scrap lasted until the mid-1980s, when shipbreaking activities slowed dramatically. Hundreds of World War II-era vessels still remained, rusting in ports around the country, now less a Reserve Fleet than a ghost fleet. With the fall of the Soviet Union and the end of the Cold War, the U.S. Government made more ships available for recycling in 1991, which led to a resurgence in shipbreaking.

Founding the Company in the Mid-1990s

International Shipbreaking was established in Brownsville in 1995 by New Yorker Kevin McCabe and two partners. A city of 100,000, Brownsville was an attractive site for shipbreaking for a number of reasons. It was situated near an artificial deepwater channel, built in 1934, that led 17 miles from the Rio Grande to the Gulf of Mexico and was home to many of the vessels that comprised the ghost fleet. The port's proximity to the Mexican border gave it ready access to cheap, unsophisticated immigrant labor and to the railways that led to southern

Key Dates:

1995: The company is formed.
1997: The shipbreaking industry is rocked by investigative newspaper reports.
1999: The company is awarded a contract in a pilot program.
2001: Congress mandates the dismantling of the ''Ghost Fleet.''

U.S. and Mexican mills, major customers for scrap steel. Brownsville's moderate climate allowed for year-round operation and its isolation, which made it ideal to bring illegal drugs and laundered money into the United States, also shielded shipbreakers from regulatory interference. In the words of a Pulitzer Prize-winning series published by the *Baltimore Sun* in 1997, ''A businessman got left alone in Brownsville. It's a long way across wide-open, flat scrubland to the rest of Texas. State environmental regulators don't find their way down from Austin very often. The official in charge of PCB enforcement for the Environmental Protection Agency is based in Dallas, several hundred miles away, and went years without coming here. The two-man office of the Occupational Safety and Health Administration, responsible for all of south Texas, is a three-hour drive away, in Corpus Christi.''

McCabe left a job with a New York City securities company to become involved in shipbreaking. He and his partners raised $2 million to enter the business, supplemented by nearly $500,000 in incentives and loan guarantees provided by the Brownsville Economic Development Council. It was a capital-intensive business, requiring money not only for an initial outlay for equipment, but also to purchase vessels to dismantle, procure insurance, and pay towing costs. In October 1995 ISL became operational after landing its first decommissioning project with the U.S. Navy, a job dismantling two aging tankers, The Yukon and the U.S.S. Marias. ISL was only one of seven companies certified by the Defense Department to do this kind of work. With about 80 employees the company first took apart the Yukon, which provided 6,900 tons of scrap steel, 75 tons of nonferrous metals, and 200 tons of reusable items such as generators, engines, winches, tubing, and even doors, chairs, refrigerators, and copy machines. Only a handful of items from the Yukon, and later the Marias, were sold for their nostalgic value, but that would change with ISL's third project, dismantling the U.S.S. Iwo Jima. This aircraft carrier had served during the Vietnam War and in 1970 retrieved the three astronauts of the ill-fated Apollo 13 mission that limped home from the moon after its craft was damaged. The Texas Air Museum raised the money to purchase the entire bridge and island (the section of the carrier above the main deck) of the Iwo Jima. ISL first tried, in the summer of 1996, to remove the section using a crane, but finally had to resort to cutting the unit into 16 sections, which were then shipped and reassembled at the museum's grounds in Rio Hondo, Texas.

ISL started strongly, building its workforce to 170 in 1997, but then fortunes began to change. Scrap steel prices that peaked at $145 a ton began a two-year slide, bottoming out in 1999 at $70 a ton. But perhaps even more problematic was the adverse publicity that ISL and the entire shipbreaking industry received upon the publication of the *Baltimore Sun* investigative series. ISL was spotlighted, as the newspaper chronicled the death of one immigrant worker, 43-year-old Raul Mendoza. According to writers Will Englund and Gary Cohn, Mendoza was paid $250 a week but his family said he had to kick back $50 to the yard superintendent. On the money that remained he supported his family in Brownsville and helped his parents in Mexico. In December 1995 he was working in the dark, below deck, on the Yukon without a safety harness, attempting to drain water by cutting a hole in a compartment. He decided to cut a second hole on the other side of the tank, but when he walked over a beam he disappeared in the dark. All his partner heard was a scream. Mendoza suffered a broken pelvis, a lacerated leg, and internal bleeding. He died two days later.

ISL maintained that it had a substantial safety program, but to make matters worse, in December 1996, as the *Sun* series was being researched, another worker, 59-year-old Maximino Chavez, was killed. He was walking across the noisy yard when a cutter was torching through a bulkhead of the Iwo Jima. A one-ton section of iron fell to the ground and struck Chavez in the head. He died in the hospital several hours later. The company was faulted for not using braces to hold debris in place. The *Sun* also pointed out the practice of ISL workers who burned the PCB insulation off electrical cables rather than properly dispose of the hazardous material in a designated landfill. Aside from exposure to PCBs, workers were exposed to asbestos dust without the benefit of protection.

But ISL was not alone among shipbreakers to be scrutinized by the newspaper. The entire industry received scathing treatment, with a number of other incidents reported: fires, pollution, and accidents in Baltimore; the death of a worker without a safety harness in Chesapeake, Virginia; the exposure of workers in Richmond, Virginia, to lead, cadmium, and copper fumes; the death of one worker and another badly burned in accidents that occurred in Wilmington, North Carolina; major safety violations at Quonset Point, Rhode Island; workers exposed to asbestos in Terminal Island, California, and told to lie to government regulators; toxic substances dumped into San Francisco Bay by an area yard; and also in Brownsville, the explosion of a 30-foot oxygen tank in another shipbreaking yard. The adverse publicity led to the convening of a Defense Department review panel, which would recommend increased government oversight and lead to Congress establishing a Ship Disposal Project in the Navy to revisit the decommissioning process.

Industry Crippled in the Late 1990s

Because of a bad reputation and poor scrap steel prices, the shipbreaking industry was all but ruined by 1998. From 1997 to 1999, ISL lost more than $3 million. Along the way, one of McCabe's partners pulled out. The company was on the verge of bankruptcy when McCabe renewed his commitment to the venture, investing another $2.25 million. While others in the industry were retrenching, he was buying another 16 acres of land and adding high-tech equipment including giant metal shears that worked much faster than welding torches and reduced labor costs. The company also acquired high-temperature smelters to melt aluminum on the decks of ships being dismantled.

Prospects began to improve in September 1999 when the Navy launched a pilot program to safely scrap ships in the United States. ISL was one of four out of 15 applicants to be awarded a contract. The project, to scrap the U.S.S. Bagley, was worth $1.81 million. ISL was the only one of the shipbreakers actively involved at the time in dismantling operations: three ships for the Navy and another for the U.S. Maritime Administration, an arm of the transportation department.

Good news continued for the company in 2001 when Congress passed legislation mandating that the 130-vessel ghost fleet be dismantled by 2006. Over the next three years the Maritime Administration spent $41 million on the project, of which more than $5 million went to ISL, the largest amount received by any shipbreaking firm. Indeed, by 2004 ISL emerged as the industry leader, the most technologically advanced company, offering much improved safety conditions and environmentally sound practices. It was well positioned to take full advantage of the opportunities presented by the ghost fleet, which would see another 45 ships added to its ranks in the next few years.

Although shipbreakers depended heavily on government contracts, there was also the possibility of increased private-sector work due to the phasing out of single-hulled tankers by the oil industry. In 2002, ISL generated some $8 million in revenues, and in 2004 the company was expected to do $40 million in business. There were some caveats, however. The Maritime Administration's budget was cut in half in 2004, from $31 million to $16.2 million. Well aware that the government was not a guaranteed revenue stream, McCabe told *Fortune Small Business* in October 2004 that "on years" and "off years" were to be expected. "We're not going for home runs," he explained. "Think of it as a single game."

Principal Competitors

Baltimore Marine Industries Inc.; Earl Industries, L.L.C.; Gulf Copper Ship Repair, Inc.; Todd Shipyards Corporation.

Further Reading

Cohn, Gary, and Will Englund, "The Curious Captains of a Reckless Industry," *Baltimore Sun,* December 8, 1997.
——, "Scrapping Ships, Sacrificing Men," *Baltimore Sun,* December 7, 1997.
——, " 'You're Going to Die Anyway,' " *Baltimore Sun,* December 7, 1997.
Stewart, Christopher S., "Ship Breaking: An Upstart Is Revolutionizing the Arcane, Dangerous Business of Boat Recycling," *Fortune Small Business,* October 1, 2004, p. 70.

—Ed Dinger

Ipiranga S.A.

Rua Francisco Eugenio 329
Rio de Janeiro 20948-900 RJ
Brazil
Telephone: +55 21 2574 5591
Fax: +55 21 2569 4836
Web site: http://www.ipiranga.com.br

Public Company
Incorporated: 1933
Employees: 1,588
Sales: BRL 21.29 billion ($6.93 billion) (2003)
Stock Exchanges: Bolsa de Valores do Rio de Janeiro
Ticker Symbol: PTIP
NAIC: 324110 Petroleum Refineries; 424720 Petroleum
and Petroleum Products Merchant Wholesalers
(Except Bulk Stations and Terminals); 424710
Petroleum Bulk Stations and Terminals; 447110
Gasoline Stations with Convenience Stores

One of Brazil's largest privately held companies, Ipiranga S.A. focuses on the domestic oil and petrochemical sectors. The company operates through the following primary divisions: Companhia Brasileira de Petróleo Ipiranga (CBPI); Distribuidora de Produtos de Petróleo Ipiranga (DPPI); Refinaria de Petróleo Ipiranga S.A. (RPISA); Ipiranga Petroquímica; Ipiranga Comercial Química; and others. Ipiranga also holds stakes in rival Copesul, among others. The company is one of Brazil's top three oil refiners—although far smaller than state-owned Petrobrás, which has long operated a near-monopoly on the country's refining market. Ipiranga is also in the top three in the distribution market, particularly through its network of nearly 3,500 Ipiranga gasoline stations. The company's active implementation of a franchising strategy, adding a variety of new services and amenities, such as convenience stores and the like, in its service stations, has contributed strongly to that operation; these services account for as much as 15 percent of the group's total sales, which topped BRL 21 billion ($6.9 billion) in 2003. Unable to compete with Petrobrás in the refined oil market, Ipiranga has shifted its focus to lubricants and related products, and also has targeted expansion in the GNV (vehicular natural gas) arena. Through Ipiranga Petroquimica, the company is a leading Brazilian producer of petroleum derivatives, such as polypropylene, solvents, and asphalt, among other products. Although the Ipiranga holding company remains privately held (and owned in part by the founding families), the company's DPPI, CBPI, and RPISA subsidiaries are all listed on the Brazilian stock exchange, Bolsa de Valores do Rio de Janeiro.

Founding Brazilian Refiner in the 1930s

In 1937, a group of Brazilian, Uruguyan, and Argentinean entrepreneurs, including Joao Francisco Tellechea, Eustáquio Ormazabaal, Herr Ribeiro de Matos, Oscar Germano Pereira, Manuel Moralles, and Raul Aguiar, joined to build Brazil's first oil refinery in Uruguaiana, the state of Rio Grande. The group's project had in fact been launched as a Brazilian-Argentinean partnership in 1933, as Destilaria Rio Grandense de Petróleo S/A, with the plan to distill petroleum products using imported refined oil from Argentina. Yet their plans were quickly thwarted when the Argentinean government passed legislation prohibiting oil exports.

Instead, the group took on partners in Uruguay and built their own refinery on the Ipiranga River. The company took on the name of Ipiranga S/A Cia. Brasileira de Petróleo and production began in 1937, and included gasoline and diesel oil, as well as kerosene and fuel oil. The latter two petroleum derivatives met with only a limited market, however, because of the predominance of wood-burning stoves and furnaces in the largely nonindustrialized region. Instead, the company used its fuel oil for the production of oil-based lubricants, and began exporting its kerosene production.

In 1938, however, the Brazilian government nationalized the country's oil industry and declared that only Brazilian citizens were to be allowed to own shares in the country's oil refineries. Ipiranga's shareholder group was forced to reorganize. Joao Francisco Tellechea and Eustáquio Ormazabaal remained primary shareholders, and the group's Argentinean and Uruguayan partners transferred their shares to Rio de Janeiro lawyer Joao

Company Perspectives:

The main mission of Companhia Brasileira de Petroleo Ipiranga S.A. is to produce and commercialize petroleum products and to provide service with maximum efficiency, satisfying market demands while respecting safety, the environment and occupation health.

Pedro Gouvêa Vieira. These three families were to remain in control of the company into the next century.

The outbreak of World War II cut short the company's supply of crude oil, and by 1942, with Brazil's entry into the war, the company's refinery operations were brought to a standstill. In 1943, however, the Brazilian government asked Ipiranga to begin developing a solvent specifically for use in the rubber industry. In this way, Ipiranga was able to reduce the country's reliance on imports. Ipiranga continued developing other petrochemical products. In 1948, for example, the company began producing sulfuric acid as a byproduct of the refining process. The company also began producing phosphate-based fertilizers and asphalt.

The end of the war had brought new engine technologies requiring higher octane fuel than that capable of being produced in the Ipiranga refinery. The company began construction on a modern refinery, which was opened to some fanfare in 1953. Just months later, however, the Brazilian government passed new legislation creating Petrobrás, the state-owned oil monopoly. Production at Ipiranga's refinery, therefore, was placed under a strict restriction of just 9,300 barrels per day.

During this period, as well, the company began developing its brand identity, launching the first Ipiranga brand campaign in 1955. The company had by then begun to supply gasoline to a number of service stations in the region. After the Brazilian government placed new restrictions on this sector, preventing refineries from selling directly to service stations, Ipiranga created a new company, Distribuidora de Produtos de Petróleo Ipiranga, or DPPI, in 1957.

DPPI took on greater importance for the company just two years later when it acquired the Brazilian operations of the United States' Gulf Oil Co. That purchase gave Ipiranga a network of 500 service stations. The purchase, for $4 million, marked the first time a domestic company had acquired a foreign-owned company in Brazil.

Ipiranga continued adding to its operations through the 1950s and into the 1960s. In 1958, the company created a new holding company, Icisa, for a number of its non-oil operations, which by then included production cans and oil drums, floor wax, and other products. In the 1960s and 1970s, the company entered sectors such as hotel operation, fishing, and the transport market.

Petrochemicals in the 1970s

Yet Ipiranga's core remained focused on oil and oil derivatives. In 1961, the company opened a new asphalt production plant, then inaugurated a new solvents facility three years later. In 1966, Ipiranga established a fertilizer subsidiary, Fertisul S.A. The company boosted its distribution wing with the purchase of Sociedade Abastecedora de Gasolina e Oleos, or SAGOL, in 1970. The following year, Ipiranga acquired ASSFRIO Asfalto Frio Ltda., which later changed its name to Ipiranga Asfaltos S.A., becoming the group's main asphalt operation.

In the 1970s, Ipiranga launched its entry into the petrochemicals sector, building two new distillation units at its refinery, including its own catalytic cracker. In 1976, the company joined with Germany's Hoescht and Brazilian government-owned Petroquisa to form Polisul Petroquímica S.A. in Triunfo, in South Brazil. That company later developed into Ipiranga's dedicated petrochemicals unit, Ipiranga Petroquimica. The Polisul facility began production in 1982. During the decade, production increased from an initial capacity of 60,000 tons per year to more than 100,000 tons per year in 1986. By 1990, with the addition of a second production unit, Polisul's capacity jumped to 220,000 tons per year.

The importance of petrochemicals to Ipiranga's operations was recognized in 1991, with the creation of subsidiary Ipiranga Comercial Química, devoted to the distribution of the group's petrochemicals production. In 1992, Ipiranga and Hoechst bought out Petroquisa's stake in Polisul, with each taking a 50 percent holding. After opening a third production unit in 1996, raising production to 350,000 tons per year, Hoechst sold its half of Polisul to Ipiranga, which then renamed the subsidiary as Ipiranga Petroquimica. By then, Ipiranga Petroquimica had become the first in Brazil to launch production of high-density polyethylene.

Ipiranga's distribution subsidiary also had grown strongly during the decade. In 1991, Ipiranga became the first in Brazil to begin offering GNV filling services at its service stations. The number of GNV-equipped stations remained limited, however. Yet Ipiranga's own network grew significantly in 1993, when the company acquired ArcoBrasil and its operating subsidiary Companhia Atlantic de Petroleo, the Brazilian distribution operations of the United States' Atlantic Richfield Co. The acquisition, which cost Ipiranga some $250 million, gave it control of Arco's 2,600 franchised service stations in Brazil, as well as logistics support operations. The acquisition also gave Ipiranga control of Arco's lubricating oil production facility and its grease production plant, the largest in Brazil. The purchase doubled Ipiranga's network of service stations and its share of the Brazilian service station market, and catapulted it from sixth place to third place among the country's leading gasoline distributors. Ipiranga continued to add to its network, and by 2004, the company operated more than 5,600 service stations throughout Brazil.

Potential Petrobrás Target in the Early 21st Century

The deregulation and liberalization of Brazil's oil market, launched in the early 1990s, became fact in 1997 when the government eliminated the longstanding monopoly of its Petrobrás wing. Ipiranga quickly took advantage of the new market freedom, setting up a new subsidiary, Unidade de Novos Negócios (UNN), for its future oil and gas exploration interests, in 1998. The first of these came that same year, when the company joined in a consortium exploiting the BAS 97 and BCAM 1 oil fields in the south of Bahia.

Key Dates:

1933: Brazilians Joao Francisco Tellechea and Eustáquio Ormazabaal join with Argentinean investors to found an oil products distillery in Rio Grande.

1937: After taking on Uruguayan investors, the group instead founds an oil refinery on Brazil's Ipiranga River, the first in the country.

1938: The Brazilian government nationalizes oil production, and foreign investors are forced to exit the holding.

1943: The company begins producing solvents for the rubber industry after cuts in oil supplies force a shutdown of the refinery.

1948: Production of asphalt, sulfuric acid, and phosphate fertilizers is launched.

1957: The company establishes the DPPI distribution subsidiary to operate service stations.

1959: The company acquires Gulf Corp.'s Brazilian service station network.

1961: The company opens a new asphalt production plant.

1964: The company opens a new solvents production plant.

1970: DPPI acquires the SAGOL service station group.

1974: The company enters the petrochemicals market with the launch of a catalytic cracking facility.

1976: The joint venture petrochemicals company, Polisul, is founded.

1982: Polisul launches production in Triunfo.

1986: Polisul production expands to 100,000 tons per year.

1991: A new chemicals distribution subsidiary, Ipiranga Comercial Quimica, is created.

1993: The company acquires Atlantic Richfield's Brazilian service station network, and becomes the third largest operator in the country.

1995: The company becomes the first to launch production of polypropylene in Brazil.

1998: The company begins oil and gas exploration and production operations.

2000: The company launches a restructuring in order to simplify its holding structure.

2002: The company announces plans to merge its two distribution subsidiaries, CBPI and DPPI.

2003: The company announces its decision to exit oil and gas production and instead concentrate on the end-products market.

2004: Petrobrás announces its potential interest in acquiring Ipiranga.

In 1999, Ipiranga became a founding member of TSB—Transportadora Sulbrasileira de Gás, the consortium set up to build and operate a gas pipeline connecting Uruguaiana to Porto Alegre. Ipiranga's partners in the venture included Gaspetro, REPSOL-YPF, Total Petróleo, and Techint.

Ipiranga continued seeking out new oil and gas exploration activities at the dawn of the 21st century, signing on to several new projects by 2001. The company also joined in on a consortium building a thermoelectric power plant supplying energy to the fast-growing petrochemical industry in Triunfo.

Ipiranga began restructuring its operations in the early 2000s, simplifying its organization in order to attract new investment capital. The company also decided to pull out of upstream operations such as oil and gas exploration, and instead invest in developing its production of lubricants and GNV, both fast-growing markets in the approach to the mid-2000s. In the lubricants sector, the company hoped to boost its market share from 16 percent to 23 percent by the end of the decade. End products also took on a greater focus in the group's petrochemicals wing, which indicated its intention to begin distributing chemical products for pharmaceutical, cosmetics, and human and animal food sectors.

By 2004, however, Ipiranga's strong petrochemicals operations had attracted the interest of state-owned Petrobrás. After a long series of divestments in the early to mid-1990s, Petrobrás was in the process of reversing course, seeking to join a global petrochemicals industry trend toward greater vertical integration. Ipiranga appeared to be a natural choice for Petrobrás's new expansion aims. Nonetheless, the strong hold of Ipiranga's founding families on the group's shares appeared to shield the company from a hostile takeover attempt. After 70 years, Ipiranga remained one of Brazil's leading privately controlled oil and petrochemicals companies.

Principal Subsidiaries

Ipiranga Quimica; Ipiranga Petroquimica; EMCA.

Principal Competitors

Exxon Mobil Corporation; Royal Dutch Petroleum Co.; Eastern Oil Joint Stock Co.; BP PLC; Petrom S.A.; Sinopec Qilu Petrochemical Company Ltd.; SOCAR; ChevronTexaco Corporation; Petrobrás Distribuidora S.A.; Royal Dutch/Shell Group; Repsol YPF S.A.; El Paso Corporation; Venezuelan National Petroleum Co.

Further Reading

Benedict, Roger, "Atlantic Richfield Co. Decides to Pull Out of Products Marketing Operations in Brazil," *Oil Daily,* October 12, 1993, p. 1.

Goldeen, Joe, "Ipiranga Bets on GNV and Lubricants," *Jornal do Comercio,* June 25, 2003.

"Ipiranga Pulling Out of Upstream," *LatAm Energy,* August 13, 2003, p. 12.

Kepp, Michael, "Petrobrás Oils Its Acquisition Wheels," *Daily Deal,* March 15, 2004.

Matthews, Chris, et al., "Ipiranga Posts US$38mn Net Profits in HI," *The America's Intelligence Wire,* August 13, 2004.

Miller, Jason, "Ipiranga to Increase Lubricants Sales," *Jornal do Comercio,* July 22, 2003.

"Unification of Ipiranga Begins," *Chemical Business Newsbase,* March 25, 2002.

—M.L. Cohen

>KNIGHT RIDDER>

Knight Ridder, Inc.

50 W. San Fernando Street, Suite 1500
San Jose, California 95113
U.S.A.
Telephone: (408) 938-7700
Fax: (408) 938-7766
Web site: http://www.kri.com

Public Company
Incorporated: 1974 as Knight-Ridder Newspapers, Inc.
Employees: 18,000
Sales: $2.9 billion (2003)
Stock Exchanges: New York
Ticker Symbol: KRI
NAIC: 511110 Newspaper Publishers; 516110 Internet
   Publishing and Broadcasting; 519110 Newspaper
   Syndicates

Knight Ridder, Inc. is the second largest newspaper publisher in the United States, with 31 daily and 26 nondaily newspapers in 28 U.S. markets, including the well known and prize-winning *Detroit Free Press, Miami Herald, Philadelphia Inquirer,* and *San Jose Mercury News.* Knight Ridder's newspapers have won 84 Pulitzer Prizes, and its online news service with the Tribune Company has become equally respected and used by millions around the world. Second only to the Gannett Company, Inc., the U.S.'s largest newspaper publisher with more than 100 dailies (including the most widely read domestic paper, *USA Today*) and 500 nondaily papers, Knight Ridder has not given up hope of one day equaling its $7 billion rival.

Two Destinies: 1890s to 1940

What is today's Knight Ridder empire began as two separate newspaper groups which merged in 1974. The Ridder group originated in 1875 with the publication of the *Catholic News,* based in New York City. A second publication was acquired in 1892 when Herman Ridder purchased the *Staats-Zeitung,* the nation's largest German-language paper, also based in New York. The Knight group began in 1903 when Charles Landon (C.L.) Knight bought the *Akron Beacon Journal,* in Ohio, which

the company still owns. Knight soon bought two smaller Ohio newspapers, the *Springfield Sun* and the *Massillon Independent.*

Knight, considered a brilliant writer, began training his son John at an early age to replace him. John S. Knight worked as copy boy and reporter, then went to college and fought in World War I. In 1919 at age 25, he joined the *Beacon Journal*'s staff and became managing editor in 1925. He carefully observed the operations of better newspapers and applied his insights to the *Beacon Journal.* C.L. Knight died in 1933, in the depths of the Great Depression, leaving an estate of $515,000 and debts of $800,000 to his sons, John S. and James L. Knight. The *Beacon Journal* faced stiff competition from another Akron paper, the *Times-Press,* owned by Scripps-Howard, while the Great Depression was at its most severe. John Knight froze family earnings and took on the *Times-Press,* running more news and features than his competitor to win over readers. He paid off the *Beacon Journal*'s debts within four years, and made it Akron's leading newspaper.

John Knight's first major test as publisher came during a 1936 Akron rubber strike. Rubber was the city's major industry, and as the strike dragged on, money and advertising dried up. The *Times-Press* cut back on editorial pages, but Knight increased local news coverage and won readers from the *Times-Press.* When the strike ended, he kept the readers and won new advertising.

On October 15, 1937 John Knight became president and publisher of the *Miami Herald,* after purchasing it for $2.25 million. The business side of the paper had been run poorly before the Knights bought it, so James Knight, who had studied the business and production side of newspaper publishing, became operations manager. The Knights' first move was to distance the paper from the Miami political establishment, with whom it had close ties. The *Herald* had two competitors; the Knights soon bought one, the *Miami Tribune,* which had been losing money. For a cost of $600,000 plus the *Massillon Independent,* the Knights bought the *Tribune,* eliminating a competitor and acquiring the *Tribune*'s building, new printing press, and other equipment. Knight closed the *Tribune* on December 1, 1937, taking six of the paper's best people with him.

The Knights added more photographs, comics, and new columnists to the *Herald.* In the next two years two local stories—a kidnapping case and a controversy over pasteurized milk—received national attention and won 14,000 new readers. Having turned the *Miami Herald* around, the Knights bought another paper, the *Detroit Free Press,* in 1940.

World War II Era Expansion: 1941–60

In 1941 Knight Newspapers, Inc. was incorporated in Ohio. World War II found German submarines off the Florida coast driving away tourists and the business that had supported the *Herald.* The paper lost much of its staff to the army, but several large military bases were set up in the Miami area, and the soldiers boosted the *Herald*'s circulation again. Lee Hills was brought in as news editor. He immediately recruited talented journalists from other Florida papers to make up for the staff the *Herald* had lost to the war effort. When a serious newsprint shortage created problems toward the end of the war, Hills and James Knight decided to cut advertising and circulation outside the Miami metropolitan area rather than editorial content, which wrested a large number of readers from its remaining competitor, the *Miami News.*

In 1944 the Knights bought the *Chicago Daily News* for $3 million and took on the paper's $12 million in debt. The *Daily News* had won a reputation for having the most thorough foreign news section of any Chicago paper, but John Knight found the stories too long and poorly written. He ordered the stories be more succinct, creating a brief storm of protest among some writers and readers.

The population of Dade County, Florida, nearly doubled in the years from 1940 to 1950 and the *Herald*'s circulation grew from 86,313 in 1941 to 175,985 in 1951. In 1946 Lee Hills began the *Clipper Edition,* a streamlined version of the *Herald* distributed in 23 Latin American countries. The paper won prestige and readership in Latin America, while the *Herald*'s Miami edition began to specialize in coverage of Latin America. Because of these early efforts, the paper is considered by many to have the best Latin American coverage of any U.S. newspaper.

In 1948 the *Herald*'s printers began a lengthy, sometimes violent strike over wages and the length of their work week. They were among the best paid printers in the country but wanted to receive the same wages for working 35 hours as they were getting for working 40. The strike dragged on, and on

October 1, 1949 the paper's newsprint warehouse burned down in a mysterious fire. Because of the strike, the *Herald* experimented with alternative production methods and ended up with production methods years ahead of those at most other papers.

Changing Times: 1950–69

In 1950 the paper won its first Pulitzer Prize for fighting government corruption in southern Florida. The next year Hills became executive editor of the *Herald* and the *Detroit Free Press.* He encouraged individual style and quality writing, drawing a large number of excellent reporters and columnists from other papers. In 1955 Knight bought the *Charlotte Observer,* in North Carolina, and went on to purchase its rival, the *Charlotte News,* in 1959. In the same year, the Knights sold the *Chicago Daily News* to Marshall Field for $17 million.

In 1960 Knight took a gamble and built a $30 million building containing offices and printing presses for the *Miami Herald.* At the time it was the biggest building in Florida and the most extensive newspaper printing plant ever built. It reflected the Knights' belief that the *Herald*—and Miami—would continue to grow, which they did.

As the group grew larger, the Knights wanted to increase financial coordination among the newspapers. At the suggestion of Lee Hills, the Knights formed an executive committee in 1960 to undertake quarterly reviews of the operations of the Knight newspapers. They also hired finance man Alvah H. Chapman, Jr., as James Knight's assistant; he rose within ten years to be president of the *Herald* and executive vice-president of Knight Newspapers. He introduced computers for administration, layout, typesetting, and production; and for improving the circulation, advertising, and business departments. Chapman mandated budgeting at all Knight newspapers, which was rarely done at small and medium-sized newspapers.

Knight Newspapers began an aggressive acquisition campaign during the same period, looking for newspapers in growing cities with at least 50,000 inhabitants. The *Tallahassee Democrat,* in Florida, was added to the group in 1965, and in 1969 the son of Moses Annenberg (the former *Miami Tribune* owner who had sold his paper to the Knights), Walter Annenberg, sold the *Philadelphia News* and the *Philadelphia Inquirer* to Knight Newspapers for $55 million. Additional papers bought by Knight in 1969 continued the company's strategy of owning more than one newspaper in a market, often eliminating competition.

By the end of the 1960s Knight's combined daily circulation had risen to 2.2 million and the company made $12.7 million in profit on revenues of $162.8 million, largely on rising advertising earnings. Knight was considered a well-managed, highly profitable, and very aggressive newspaper group, although its editorial content was not always top quality. In 1969 Knight Newspapers, Inc. went public, the first offering immediately selling out at $30 a share.

A Shift in Priorities: 1970s

Knight acquired five more dailies in 1973: the *Lexington Herald* and the *Lexington Leader,* both in Kentucky; the *Colum-*

Key Dates:

1875: Herman Ridder begins publishing the *Catholic News* in New York.
1892: Ridder buys *Die Staats-Zeitung,* the leading German-language newspaper in the United States.
1903: C.L. Knight buys the Ohio-based *Akron Beacon Journal.*
1937: John Knight purchases the *Miami Herald.*
1940: The *Detroit Free Press* is added to the Knight holdings.
1941: Knight Newspapers, Inc. is incorporated in Ohio.
1942: Ridder Publications is incorporated in Delaware.
1950: The *Miami Herald* wins its first Pulitzer Prize.
1969: Both Knight and Ridder go public to raise funds for expansion.
1974: Knight and Ridder merge to become Knight-Ridder Newspapers, Inc. (the hyphen was eventually removed from the name).
1976: The company is renamed Knight-Ridder, Inc.
1986: Knight-Ridder acquires the South Carolina-based Star-Record Company.
1993: The *San Jose Mercury News* becomes the first newspaper to go online through Web server AOL.
1998: The company relocates its headquarters from Miami to the Silicon Valley.
2000: Knight Ridder begins supplying Yahoo!'s server with news banners and headlines.
2004: A Knight Ridder publication (the *Miami Herald*) wins the company's 84th Pulitzer Prize.

bus Ledger and the *Columbus Enquirer,* both in Georgia; and the *Bradenton Herald* in Florida.

Herman Ridder, founder of the Ridder group, had worked his way up through the ranks at the *Staats-Zeitung* after its purchase in 1892. He was a founder and president of the Associated Press and an early supporter of the American Newspaper Publishers Association, becoming its president in 1907. His sons Bernard, Joseph, and Victor bought the *New York Journal of Commerce* and the *St. Paul Dispatch-Pioneer Press* in 1927. Ridder Publications was incorporated in Delaware in 1942.

After World War II the company expanded westward in search of well-priced properties in growing markets. They bought the *Long Beach Press-Telegram, Long Beach Independent, San Jose Mercury News,* and the *Pasadena Star News,* all in California, as well as some smaller California papers; a 65 percent stake in the *Seattle Times,* in Washington; the Gary *Post Tribune* in Indiana; and radio and television station WCCO, in Minneapolis, Minnesota. The *San Jose Mercury News* was the most profitable Ridder publication. The company bought the Boulder *Daily Camera* in Colorado in 1969 and the *Wichita Eagle* and Beacon Publishing Company of Kansas in 1973.

Ridder's 1973 earnings were $14.3 million on revenue of $166 million while Knight's 1973 earnings were $22.1 million on revenue of $341.9 million. Their merger grew out of talks between friends Lee Hills and Bernard Ridder, Jr., grandson of

Herman Ridder, who were interested in expansion. Influenced by the success of the rival Gannett group, both Knight and Ridder had gone public in 1969 to raise capital for acquisitions. The groups described the potential benefits of a merger to their stockholders as "a broader and more diversified income base, greater newspaper size, mix and geographical distribution, and a stronger balance sheet." The merger was accomplished through an exchange of stock, and five Ridder representatives joined ten from Knight Newspapers, to form Knight-Ridder's board of directors.

The Knight group had focused on the South and East, while Ridder had focused on the West and Midwest. At the time of the merger Knight owned 16 dailies in seven states, while Ridder owned or had a substantial interest in 19 dailies in ten states. The Ridder dailies were all in exclusive markets, while the Knight's three largest revenue yielders—in Miami, Detroit, and Philadelphia—all faced competition. At the time of the merger *Time* magazine reported (July 22, 1974) that in general, "the Ridder papers do not have the heft and influence of the Knight dailies."

When the groups merged on November 30, 1974, Ridder became a wholly owned subsidiary of Knight, and the renamed Knight-Ridder Newspapers, Inc. became the largest newspaper company in the United States with newspapers from coast to coast. The new company had 35 newspapers in 25 cities, combined circulation averaging 3.8 million daily and 4.2 million on Sunday, total assets of $465 million, and profits of $36 million. Other large companies published newspapers but were diversified, while Knight-Ridder focused on newspapers alone (both had agreed to sell noncore holdings as part of the Federal Communications Commission's conditions for merging). The new company continued to give its newspapers editorial autonomy while maintaining strict central control of business operations with papers organized into three groups along geographical lines.

In 1976 Knight-Ridder Newspapers, Inc. became Knight-Ridder, Inc. Alvah H. Chapman, Jr., was elected chief executive officer succeeding Lee Hills, and Bernard H. Ridder, Jr., was elected chairman of the executive committee succeeding James L. Knight, who resigned. James Knight died in 1991 at the age of 81. John Knight also retired as editorial chairman in 1976. He died in 1981 at the age of 81. Lee Hills took his place until 1979 when he retired and Bernard H. Ridder, Jr., succeeded him.

The Perils of Diversification: 1980s

While other media companies went on newspaper-buying binges, Knight-Ridder watched from the sidelines, believing newspapers were a mature market. Knight-Ridder instead moved into other areas, buying radio stations and entering the cable television market in 1981. In addition, the company started Viewdata Corporation, which offered news and financial services on home computers. The company also moved into computer-based graphics services; the Knight-Ridder Graphics Network went online in October 1985, at first servicing only newspapers in the group. It began to offer a full-scale daily service to papers outside Knight-Ridder in 1986. Within a year it was used by 28 of the chain's newspapers and had 110 outside subscribers in North America and Europe. Subscribing newspapers paid $50 to $300 a month, depending on their circulation, for the privilege of using the system.

Viewdata, however, did not fare well and was closed in 1986 after losing $50 million. By this time Knight-Ridder returned to its roots by acquiring the six-paper State-Record Company, based in Columbia, South Carolina, for $311 million. By the later years of the decade, many felt Knight-Ridder had lost touch with its readers. Hispanics accounted for half the population of the Miami area, but only 20 percent of them read the *Miami Herald.* In 1986 several of the *Herald*'s offices were closed. The following year, the company undertook a cost-cutting campaign headed by P. Anthony Ridder, president of the newspaper division, and redesigned the Spanish version of the *Miami Herald,* to win Hispanic readership.

By 1988 Knight-Ridder's business information services division was growing three times as fast as its newspapers, which prompted the $353 million purchase of Dialog Information Services, Inc. The same year James Batten was appointed CEO, replacing Alvah Chapman, and Anthony (Tony) Ridder became president. In 1989, however, the company's debt approached $1 billion and Batten sold the company's broadcasting group and the *Pasadena Morning Star News,* netting $425 million. Still, the company was sufficiently wary of a takeover for its shareholders to vote a ''quality of journalism'' amendment to prevent a buyout by a media baron such as Rupert Murdoch.

New Frontiers: 1990s

Under Batten and Ridder's leadership in the early and mid-1990s, Knight-Ridder refocused on newspapers and business information services by making additional divestments. The company stayed away from costly bleeding-edge gambles similar to Viewdata, working instead to extend its core businesses. One such move was the partnership of Knight-Ridder's *San Jose Mercury News* and online service provider America Online (AOL) in 1993, making the *Mercury News* the first newspaper in the country to offer its readers an online version of its paper. The flat rate service offered news and features from the paper, advertising, and bulletin boards for messaging. A similar venture was developed for the *Detroit Free Press,* this time in partnership with AOL's rival CompuServe. Knight-Ridder hoped to have all of its papers online within a few years.

In its business information services division, Knight-Ridder was disappointed with Dialog's lackluster growth of 10 percent a year. To remedy the situation, the company adopted two strategies—geographic growth and user growth. In 1993 it acquired Data-Star, a European online service, from the Swiss engineering company Motor-Columbus. In its first year under Knight-Ridder, Data-Star helped boost Dialog's revenue 19 percent over 1992. In 1994 the company moved into the Canadian market through a joint venture with Southam, Inc. called Infomart DIALOG. The company's three online services—DIALOG, Data-Star, and Infomart DIALOG—were then grouped within the newly named Knight-Ridder Information, Inc. (KRII), replacing Dialog Information Services. With regard to the second strategy, KRII's services were used primarily by librarians and other information specialists who had mastered the complex and powerful software of its services. In order to expand the potential user base, KRII began to develop user-friendly interfaces for the services to attract a broader client base.

In early 1995 Tony Ridder took over as CEO and assumed the title of chairman upon Batten's death. Ridder began

revamping the company, selling off its noncore assets such as the *Journal of Commerce* to Britain's Economist Group for $115 million and its financial newswire after it failed to compete successfully with rivals Reuters, Dow Jones, and Bloomberg Financial News. Next Knight-Ridder made another significant divestment—this one outside the business information sector—when it sold its stake in TKR Cable to its partner Tele-Communications Inc. for about $420 million in cash and stock.

With the newspaper division more important than ever to Knight-Ridder's future, the company initiated a two-year, $120 million modernization of the *Miami Herald*'s main plant and spent $360 million to acquire four daily newspapers in the San Francisco Bay area from Lehser Communications, Inc. The acquired papers had a combined circulation of 190,000 daily and 206,000 on Sunday. In 1997 Knight-Ridder bought four additional papers from the Walt Disney Company, sold its KRII division, and decided to move its headquarters to the Silicon Valley area in San Jose, California. The move was completed in 1998, the same year Knight-Ridder joined competitors Gannett and the Tribune Company to create Classified Ventures, an online automotive and real estate classifieds service.

In 1998 Knight Ridder was recognized as a ''Web pioneer'' and earned the top slot on the *InformationWeek* 500, the IT magazine's annual poll of businesses with the most innovative use of technology. Knight Ridder had not only been the first major newspaper publisher to put one of its papers online (the *San Jose Mercury News* in 1993), but was also the first to get versions of all of its newspapers on the Web. Knight Ridder bested a wide range of billion-dollar firms to earn the *InformationWeek* honor, including rival Gannett, as well as multinational giants Coca-Cola Company, Philip Morris, and IBM.

The following year, 1999, the company formed KnightRidder.com to oversee its burgeoning online services and web operations, which included another joint venture with the Tribune Company, this one to create CareerBuilder, an online job search service. Knight Ridder finished the century with revenues topping $3.2 billion.

Frugality and Reorganization: 2000s

In the new millennium Knight Ridder continued to focus on the Internet and its ever increasing opportunities. In 2000 the company reached an agreement with Yahoo!, the huge Internet search engine, to provide banners of top news stories on its pages. The following year KnightRidder.com was renamed Knight Ridder Digital and Chairman and CEO Ridder began tightening the firm's belt, reducing its workforce and instituting cost-cutting measures across the board. By the end of the year, Knight Ridder still retained its rank as the world's second largest newspaper company, with 31 dailies in 28 U.S. markets, and readership of 8.5 million daily and 12.6 million on Sunday.

In 2003 the web-savvy Knight Ridder was struck by a virus that shut down its newspaper sites for several hours. The company's IT team, however, had the sites back online by day's end, proving why Knight Ridder's Digital unit was hitting its projections and posting strong earnings. The company finished the year with overall operating revenues of just under $2.9 billion, slightly less than the previous year due to several factors, including weaker advertising rates. Knight Ridder Digital, however, contributed a profit of $15.2 million and revenues were up 44 percent from 2002.

The following year, 2004, Knight Ridder bought Star Publications and was poised for further acquisitions should complementary businesses become available. Chief Executive Ridder, who was nearing retirement age, concentrated on leaving Knight Ridder as a publishing powerhouse in terms of both product and profit. While he had been increasingly criticized in the new century for putting profits ahead of journalistic integrity, Ridder was determined to have both. Goals for the remainder of the decade included acquiring additional newspapers in underserved areas, keeping operating costs down, and increasing national readership not only through Pulitzer Prize-winning journalism (the *Miami Herald* earned its 18th Pulitzer and the company its 84th in 2004), but by reaching out to younger and minority readers as well.

Principal Divisions

Aberdeen (SD) American News Company; Akron (OH) Journal Publishing Company; Belleville (IL) News-Democrat; Biloxi (MI) Sun Herald; Bradenton (FL) Herald; Charlotte (SC) Observer; Columbia (SC) State; Columbus (GA) Ledger Enquirer; Contra Costa (CA) Newspapers Inc.; Detroit (MI) Free Press; Fort Wayne (IN) News Sentinel; Duluth (MN) News Tribune; Florida Keys Keynoter; Fort Worth (TX) Star-Telegram; Grand Forks (ND) Herald; Kansas City Star; Lexington (KY) Herald-Leader; Macon (GA) Telegraph; Miami (FL) Herald; Monterey County (CA) Herald; Myrtle Beach (SC) Sun News; Olathe (KS) News; Philadelphia (PA) Newspapers Inc.; St. Paul (MN) Pioneer Press; San Jose (CA) Mercury News Inc.; San Luis Obispo (CA) Tribune; State College (PA) Centre Daily Times; Tallahassee (FL) Democrat; Wichita (KS) Eagle; Wilkes-Barre (PA) Times Leader.

Principal Operating Units

Knight Ridder Digital; Knight Ridder Shared Services; Knight Ridder/Tribune News Information Services; Knight Ridder Washington Bureau; Knight Ridder Newspaper Division.

Principal Competitors

Cox Enterprises, Inc.; Dow Jones & Company, Inc.; Gannett Company, Inc.; New York Times Company; News Corporation Ltd.; Tribune Company.

Further Reading

Brach, Abby, "*InformationWeek* Names Knight Ridder Most Innovative User of Technology," *InformationWeek,* September 16, 1998.
DeGeorge, Gail, "Knight Ridder: Running Hard, but Staying in Place," *Business Week,* February 26, 1996.
DeGeorge, Gail, and Veronica N. Byrd, "Knight Ridder: Once Burned, and the Memory Lingers," *Business Week,* April 11, 1994.
"Dynastic Ridder Clan Gathers—40 Strong," *Editor & Publisher,* April 19, 1969.
Jones, Tim, "For Newspapers, a Bundle of Woes," *Chicago Tribune,* October 29, 1995, p. 1.
"Knight Ridder Will Become Largest All-Newspaper Firm," *Editor & Publisher,* November 16, 1974.
Leonard, Devin, "Tony Ridder Just Can't Win," *Fortune,* December 24, 2001, p. 99.
Moses, Lucia, "Tony Ridder Still Loves His Job," *Editor & Publisher,* February 1, 2004.
"Newspaper Story," *Forbes,* August 29, 1994, p. 284.
"Publisher Who Built Newspaper Empire Dies at 85," *Knight Ridder/Tribune News Service,* May 11, 2002.
Sandoval, Ricardo, "Knight Ridder Buys Four Lesher Papers in San Francisco Bay Area," *San Jose Mercury News,* August 29, 1995.
Smiley, Nixon, *Knights of the Fourth Estate: The Story of the Miami Herald,* Miami, Fla.: E.A. Seemann Publishing, 1974.
Whited, Charles, *Knight: A Publisher in the Tumultuous Century,* New York: E.P. Dutton, 1988.

—Scott M. Lewis
—updates: David E. Salamie, Nelson Rhodes

Lancair International, Inc.

2244 Airport Way
Redmond, Oregon 97756
U.S.A.
Telephone: (541) 923-2244
Fax: (541) 923-2255
Web site: http://www.lancair-kits.com

Private Company
Incorporated: 1991
Employees: 70
Sales: $15 million (2004 est.)
NAIC: 336411 Aircraft Manufacturing

Lancair International, Inc. (pronounced ''Lance air'') is a leading manufacturer of kit planes. The company has sold about 1,900 kits in 34 countries; hundreds of these sporty aircraft have been completed and are flying. Lancair International takes orders for an average of 100 kits per year, at $100,000 or so each.

The company developed in the 1980s as advances in composites materials technology met a void in the market when conventional aircraft manufacturers stopped producing smaller planes. Bringing the two together was company founder Lance Neibauer, who combined his talents in both visual design and his passion for aviation to shape fiberglass into a masterpiece. The Lancair 320 has even been featured in an exhibit at the Museum of Modern Art in New York City.

Lancair International, the kit plane manufacturer, is a separate company from The Lancair Company of Bend, Oregon, which produces fully completed aircraft. (The two were both founded by Lance Neibauer.)

Origins

Lance Neibauer was a successful graphic artist when he decided to follow his love of airplanes in the late 1970s, reports *Oregon Business.* Neibauer had been flying since childhood and came from an aeronautical family. His uncle had founded Meyers Aircraft Corp., which became part of Rockwell International Inc.

Neibauer had studied sculpture among other arts at Michigan State University. He became captivated with the possibilities of composite materials—fiberglass (later Kevlar) or carbon fiber held together with epoxy—just as they were revolutionizing homebuilt aircraft design.

Around this time, conventional aircraft manufacturers were being crushed by massive product liability lawsuits, and they abandoned the market for smaller, relatively inexpensive aircraft. The homebuilt industry had started with designers selling plans for perhaps $50, leaving the builder to scrounge the necessary parts, recalled *Air Progress* in 1988. The idea of ready-to-assemble kits appealed to a large number of prospective aircraft owners. To be classified as a homebuilt, or experimental aircraft, buyers had to build at least 51 percent of the plane, transferring the bulk of the liability to them.

According to *Air Progress,* Neibauer began working on his own kit design in 1981. He then spent a year building the prototype after setting up a 1,100-square-foot workshop in southern California. The airplane first flew on June 20, 1984, noted *Air Progress.*

After some reworking it was unveiled in 1985 as the Lancair 200. In a 1988 *Air Progress* interview, Neibauer suggested that the early kits cost about $18,000. By this time, Neibauer was offering the option for customers to build their kits inside the Lancair factory. (In 2003, the fee for up to 18 weeks of access to tooling, etc. was $4,000 per week.)

In the same interview, Neibauer credited his company's streamlined management structure for its initial success. ''We don't keep a top-heavy company . . . everybody just works their tails off.'' He also acknowledged technical assistance from the likes of DuPont and noted composite engineer Martin Hollman.

New Designs for the 1990s

The first Lancair found an enthusiastic reception among pilots looking for a high-performance, cross-country touring machine.

The two-place Lancair 320 and 360 followed. Next was a four-seat version, the Lancair IV, and a pressurized variant. In February 1991, the Lancair IV shattered the speed record for planes in its class by averaging 360.3 mph between San Francisco and Denver.

By the end of 1990, Lancair had sold more than 600 kits, according to *Design News,* and 100 of them were flying. Neibauer told the *Portland Oregonian* Lancair had a 30 percent share of the kitplane market in the early 1990s. Advanced Composite Technology had begun building the kits under license, delivering its first model, a pressurized version of the Lancair IV, in 1990.

In 1992, Neibauer relocated his company from Santa Paula, California, to the town of Redmond in eastern Oregon. The operation had outgrown its southern California site; Redmond was chosen from among 200 candidates. Lancair at first employed 20 people at the new 27,000-square-foot plant next to Roberts Field. The company was incorporated as Lancair International, Incorporated. Another unit, Neico Aviation Inc., was created to market the planes.

Pilots raved about the Lancair's performance, responsiveness, and comfort. The Lancair 320 cruised at 265 mph. The Lancair IV-P first flew in November 1993; it was thought to be the first kit-built aircraft to have pressurization available as an option. The ES model debuted in 1993.

In 1995 the Lancair 320 was featured in a materials exhibit at New York's Museum of Modern Art. The company, which

then had 60 employees, was selling 200 kits a year and revenues were estimated at $8 million.

One of Lancair's kits sold for up to $28,000 and required, officially, 1,500 to 2,500 hours of build time. This price did not include engine or avionics, which could put the total cost in the $50,000 to $100,000 range. While they required a considerable commitment of labor on the part of the buyer before they could be flown, homebuilts were popular due to their lower cost and much higher performance than conventional aircraft.

As of August 1998, according to *Flight International,* Lancair had sold 1,400 kits, 300 of them the Lancair IV model. The Redmond factory then employed 40 people, reported the Associated Press.

By the late 1990s, Lancair had its eye on the certificated—or fully assembled—aircraft market. The Lancair Super ES, derived from the Lancair IV, was considered for this, but it was the Columbia 300 that was first approved by the FAA. A separate company, Pacific Aviation Composites USA, and later The Lancair Company, was created to develop production aircraft.

A Legacy Enduring Beyond 2000

Around 2000, Lancair International developed a line of side-by-side two-seat kitplanes under the Legacy name. These were essentially a return to the original concept featuring a redesigned, aerodynamically advanced wing.

Lancair International began 2001 with two new offerings. The company made available a 700-horsepower turboprop engine as an option for the IV-P kitplane. The company also began marketing kits for the CH-7 Kompress helicopter. Italy's Heli-Sport designed and built the helicopters, which were designed by Lamborghini Marcello Gandini, otherwise known for his work with Lamborghini automobiles.

The turbine engine IV-P became the basis of the Sentry, a high-performance type being tested for the military and racing market. The Mexican navy had bought nine other kits (Super ES, Legacy, and IV-P models) for use as trainers, noted *Flight International,* and was evaluating an armed variant of the Sentry as a patrol/attack aircraft.

Joseph C. Bartels, a lawyer from New Orleans, acquired Lancair in February 2003. He had come to Oregon in December 1992 to build his own IV-P, and then formed Aero Cool, LLC to supply air-conditioners for the type. Lancair International sold 68 kits in 2003, ten more than the previous year. The Lancair ES was popular enough to have spawned a miniature remote controlled scale model, made by Great Planes Model Manufacturing Co.

The Redmond plant was being expanded again. Lancair employed 70 people there and 100 at a parts-making operation in the Philippines, according to the *Associated Press.* Lancair rolled out a pressurized version of the ES kit in 2004. The company was taking orders for 100 planes a year.

Principal Operating Units

Kit Components Inc.; Lancair Avionics Inc.; Neico International, Inc.

Principal Competitors

Cirrus Design; Van's Aircraft.

Further Reading

Allen, Chris, "Cross-Country Runner," *Flight International,* November 7, 1990, pp. 40+.

Bak, David J., "Build Your Own Airplane," *Design News,* September 11, 1995, pp. 76+.

Dittrich, Virginia, "Aircraft Maker Chooses Redmond," *Oregon Business,* September 1991, pp. 13+.

EAA Aviation Center, "Busy Times at Lancair," January 2001, http://www.eaa.org/communications/eaanews/010105_lancair.html.

"Entrepreneur Enters Competitive World of Aircraft Building," *Associated Press Newswires,* April 28, 1998.

Fisher, Lawrence, "The Rising Popularity of Home-Built Planes," *New York Times,* Sec. 3, June 17, 1990, p. 11.

Garvey, William, and Rich Cox, "Kitplanes Grow Up," *Popular Mechanics,* August 1992, pp. 44+.

"Great Planes Lancair ES," *Model Airplane News,* October 2003, pp. 46+.

Gustafson, David A., "The Hot New Designers," *Air Progress,* November 1988, pp. 32–39, 56, 68–69.

Higdon, Dave, "Heli-Expo 2001: Lots of Rain Outside; Warm and Fuzzy Inside," *AVweb,* February 15, 2001, http://www.avweb.com/news/hai2002/184258-1.html.

Inman, Carla, "Form, Function and Flight," *Oregon Business,* October 1995, pp. 22–24.

"Lancair Aims Sentry Racer at Military Market," *Flight International,* October 1, 2002, p. 32.

"Lancair Claims Pressurisation Is World First," *Flight International,* November 10, 1993.

Lancair International, Inc., "History of Lancair," http://www.lancair-kits.com/history.html.

"Lancair Introduces the All New CFRP ES-Pressurized and ES-2 Door Models in June," *Advanced Materials & Composites News,* June 21, 2004.

"Lancair Secures ES Deal," *Flight International,* January 18, 1995, p. 19.

"Lance Neibauer Sells Lancair Kit Company to Joseph C. Bartels," *Weekly of Business Aviation,* February 3, 2003, p. 55.

Lert, P., "Lancair Comes of Age," *Air Progress,* December 1988, pp. 50+.

Max, Kevin, "Lancair: A Tale of Two Businesses," *Bulletin* (Bend, OR), September 22, 2002.

Norris, Guy, "Mexicans Study Lancair IV for Coastal Protection Role," *Flight International,* March 13, 2001, p. 34.

Phelan, Paul, "Building on Basics—Lancair IV," *Flight International,* August 5, 1998, p. 54.

"Redmond-Based Lancair Growing, Changing," *Associated Press Newswires,* July 5, 2004.

"Roberts Has Role in Opening," *Portland Oregonian,* March 4, 1992, p. B2.

Shotwell, Robert E., "Redmond Launches Kit-Plane Plant," *Portland Oregonian,* April 29, 1992, p. B2.

"Small Aircraft Take Flight with CAD," *Design News,* August 17, 1998, p. 57.

Warwick, Graham, "New-Entrant Blues; New Manufacturers Are Easing into Light Aircraft Production, Learning the Stock Lessons of the Arena: Stay Flexible and Ignore Delays," *Flight International,* June 17, 1998, p. 30.

—Frederick C. Ingram

LASERSCOPE

Laserscope

3070 Orchard Drive
San Jose, California 95134-2011
U.S.A.
Telephone: (408) 943-0636
Toll Free: (800) 356-9630
Fax: (408) 943-9630
Web site: http://www.laserscope.com

Public Company
Incorporated: 1984
Employees: 195
Sales: $57.4 million (2003)
Stock Exchanges: NASDAQ
Ticker Symbol: SCP
NAIC: 334511 Search, Detection, Navigation, Guidance, Aeronautical, and Nautical System and Instrument Manufacturing

Laserscope is a San Jose, California-based company that makes medical laser systems for a variety of uses. One of Laserscope's newer systems treats benign prostatic hyperplasia, a urological disorder that involves the enlargement of the prostate gland and mostly strikes men over the age of 50. Laserscope also offers systems with aesthetic applications, such as the removal of wrinkles, leg and facial veins, and unwanted hair. To a lesser degree the company's lasers find uses in such markets as ear, nose, and throat surgery; general surgery; gynecology; and photodynamic therapy. In addition, Laserscope sells products used by its systems: disposable optical fibers, side-firing devices, individual custom hand pieces required in some surgical applications, scanning devices, micromanipulators for microscopic surgery, and other accessories and procedure-specific kits. Laserscope products are sold through the company's own sales force in the United States, France, and the United Kingdom, and marketed to the rest of the world through distributors. Laserscope is a public company, trading on the NASDAQ.

Use of Medical Lasers Dating to the 1960s

The word laser is an acronym that stands for Light Amplification by the Stimulated Emission of Radiation, a concept conceived by Albert Einstein in 1917. It was not until 1954 that researchers in Bell Laboratories took the first major step in making the idea a reality, producing stimulated emissions of microwave radiation, or MASER. In 1958 the first theoretical plans for building a viable light laser were published and two years later the first laser, using a ruby rod, was built. Soon researchers began to study the effects of lasers on biologic systems in the hope of finding medical applications. The only medical application found for the ruby laser was in retinal surgery, which began in the mid-1960s. More advanced lasers were developed and by the late 1970s some researchers found uses in non-ophthalmic procedures, but it was not until the early 1980s that lasers were compact and powerful enough to appear widely in hospitals as well as some physicians' offices. These continuous wave lasers, however, were far from precise and could easily cause heat injury to normal tissue. This problem was resolved in the late 1980s with the introduction of pulsed dye lasers, which were more discriminating, allowing the devices to be selective enough, for example, to remove port wine stains on patients. The advent of scanning devices in the early 1990s brought computer control to the use of laser beams in surgery, opening a wide range of medical applications.

Laserscope was founded in a small Santa Clara office in 1982. Its founder investors included Dr. David B. Apfelberg, a plastic surgeon and the head of the Palo Alto Medical Foundation Laser Center; Dr. Rodney Perkins, a specialist in otologic surgery who became Laserscope's chairman; and Robert J. Pressley, who held a Ph.D. in physics and had headed research and development at Holobeam, which manufactured commercial lasers, and previously founded XMR, Inc., another maker of laser systems. Laserscope started out with $250,000 in the bank. Over the next four years the company raised another $20 million in seed money. Investors included venture capital funds Sierra Ventures and Technology Funding Partners. After two years of development, Laserscope's first product, the KTP/532, marketed as part of the Omniplus system, was introduced in 1984.

The Omniplus used a crystal system developed by Du Pont Co. that allowed the laser to be used in several different surgical applications, from removing birthmarks to tumors. In July 1986 Du Pont and Laserscope forged an alliance, with Du Pont buying an unspecified minority interest. According to a Du Pont spokesman, the amount invested was ''more than $1 million and less than $10 million.'' The hope was that with the backing of a major corporation Laserscope would be able to grow more rapidly. Aside from cash, Du Pont, which also took a position on Laserscope's board of directors, provided help in research, development, manufacturing, and marketing. For Du Pont, the alliance with Laserscope was part of an effort to strengthen its position in the medical industry.

Late 1980s Enthusiasm for the Company

Although Omniplus was versatile, it was expensive, costing around $130,000, and despite Du Pont's support there were serious doubts about Laserscope's strategy, given that the industry was moving toward the development of lower-cost devices that physicians could purchase. Already there were units in the $20,000 range. Nevertheless, buyers lined up, as revenues grew from $11 million in 1988 to $20 million in 1989, and investors remained enthusiastic about the company's prospects, which were soon buoyed by the introduction of a more advanced laser system, the KTP/YAG. In late 1989 the company went public. The target price for the initial stock offering was from $6.50 to $8 per share, but demand was strong enough that the price was boosted to $9. Laserscope had carved out a leadership position in the general surgery market of the medical laser industry, with its systems used in dermatology as well as gynecology, and ear, nose, and throat surgery. Hospitals also were buying units, looking to become involved in laparoscopic gallbladder surgery, which was becoming prevalent. In 1990 revenues surged to $54 million and the price of its stock reached $31.50 a share. As a result, the company outgrew its space. Laserscope had employed just 50 people in 1986 but by the end of 1990 it had a staff of 250, necessitating a move from its Santa Clara location to a new headquarters in San Jose. Also during 1990 Du Pont decided to cash out after holding its investment in Laserscope for three years. Du Pont made a 25 percent return, but it left a lot of money on the table, selling when Laserscope was priced at $20.50 per share, well below its peak.

Laserscope appeared to be flying high at this stage, but a recession and other factors combined to put a halt to its growth in the early 1990s. Aside from customers cutting back during poor economic times, Laserscope was hurt by new Medicare guidelines on capital spending that made hospitals reluctant to make major capital expenditures, and the decision by many doctors to use electrocautery devices, a decades-old technology, for gallbladder surgery rather than lasers. Although initially enthusiastic about the new laser devices, doctors had come to

realize that the much cheaper, already installed electrocautery devices performed as well as lasers in this particular application. Nevertheless, management remained optimistic about the future, contending that Laserscope was in better shape than its competition and that it was taking important steps to resume its prior pattern of growth. It signed agreements with distributors overseas in an effort to increase international sales from 5 percent of total revenues to about half. Laserscope hired more clinical consultants to train surgeons on how to use lasers and added more annual training seminars. It also spent heavily on research and development of new products. In 1991 the company introduced a product to perform surgery on herniated spinal discs.

As conditions worsened in 1991, however, the company was forced to take more drastic steps. In October of that year, it laid off about 15 percent of the workforce, 38 out of 260 employees. Within months, Laserscope's CEO, Herbert Taus, retired. Chairman Perkins stepped in as CEO on an interim basis while the company searched for a replacement. In the meantime, the board instituted a shareholders' rights plan to help stave off any takeover attempts. In late December 1991, Laserscope named a new president, as Perkins remained chief executive—at least in name. Taking over was Robert McCormick, the former marketing head of Acuson Corp., who was instrumental in the ultrasound manufacturer increasing sales from $3 million to $280 million. McCormick laid out a new strategy to return the company to profitability after three straight losing quarters. As his predecessor had proposed, McCormick wanted to increase foreign sales and boost training efforts. He also wanted to explore new surgical markets in plastic surgery and dermatology, and was willing to develop non-laser surgical devices, taking the position that Laserscope, despite its name, was in essence a surgical systems company and did not have to limit itself to laser products.

Over the next few years, Laserscope made some progress in its strategy. In 1992 it won approval from the U.S. Food and Drug Administration to sell a laser device for cosmetic surgery and one for use in prostate disease, and it also developed a new laser system used in combination with a photosensitive drug to destroy cancerous cells. In 1995 Laserscope introduced SmartScan, the first laser system designed for surgical and dermatological procedures performed in an office or outpatient center. Laserscope also took steps to grow its international business, but earnings continued to languish and investors lost faith in the company. The price of its stock fell to $2 per share in 1995.

Prospects appeared brighter for Laserscope in 1996 when it acquired Heraeus Surgical, Inc. for $2 million in cash and some 4.6 million shares of common stock. The Milpitas, California-based company manufactured lasers used by dermatologists, a thriving segment of the laser industry. In addition, Heraeus offered some diversity because it also sold operating room products such as lighting systems, surgical tables, centralized smoke evacuation systems, and ceiling-mounted equipment management systems. Because Heraeus was a subsidiary of a German company, Heraeus MED GmbH, it also brought with it some international distribution channels. The two companies' laser technologies were compatible and by combining operations it was expected that Laserscope could trim as much as $5 million a year in operating expenses.

Key Dates:

1982: The company is founded.
1987: The first product is developed.
1989: The company is taken public.
1996: Heraeus Surgical, Inc. is acquired.
1999: Eric Reuter is named CEO.
2002: The company enters the urology market.

Late 1980s Change in Leadership

As a result of the Heraeus acquisition, Laserscope generated record revenues in 1997, totaling nearly $64 million, but the company continued to post net losses, much of it related to the company's Ascent Medical Systems group of non-laser products for operating and treatment rooms. The following year saw revenues drop 14 percent to $52.7 million, which led to a net loss of $9.7 million, a stock price hovering around $1, and the hiring of a new chief executive. In June 1999 38-year-old Eric Reuter was named Laserscope's new president and CEO. He had joined the company in September 1996 as vice-president of Research and Development. After earning degrees in mechanical engineering and materials sciences from the University of California at Davis, he completed the Stanford Executive Program in Product Development and Manufacturing Strategy. He became a mechanical engineer and program manager at Siemens Medical Systems, and later held an engineering management position at the Stanford Linear Accelerator Center at Stanford University.

With Reuter at the helm, Laserscope once again attempted to engineer a turnaround after nearly a decade of floundering. Over the next few years Laserscope raised additional funds, sold off a German subsidiary and unprofitable businesses such as Ascent Medical Systems, and began to focus its research efforts on products with long-term potential. Revenues dipped to $35 million in 2001 before the company's balance sheet began to reflect the changes made by the new management team. An important step was the 2002 launch of a new laser treatment to treat benign prostatic hyperplasia (BPH). Also of major importance was the signing of an exclusive distribution agreement with McKesson Medical, which more than doubled the sale of Laserscope products from 2001 to 2002. Laserscope saw revenues improve to $43.1 million while posting net income of $323,000. Moreover, Laserscope was on the verge of realizing even greater prosperity

as demographics began to favor the company's line of medical laser systems. With baby boomers aging and willing to spend money on looking younger, demand was growing for Laserscope's laser systems for aesthetic applications. In addition, the aging population also played to the company's strength in the BPH market. In 2002 some 180,000 men in the United States alone were surgically treated for the condition, a number that was expected to double over the next five years. The upside was even greater, because 90 percent of the men suffering from BPH were using medication rather than surgery. Moreover, only about 20 percent of men sought treatment of any sort. With the number of older men increasing in the population and a larger percentage opting for surgery rather than expensive prescription drugs year after year with no guaranteed result, the potential for the BPH market to become a cash cow for Laserscope increased in probability. In 2003 Laserscope recorded revenues of $57.4 million and a $2.5 million net profit. Many doctors were still resistant to the laser treatment, which was considered the best solution for BPH, but investors were already factoring in the likelihood that the laser option would soon win out. They bid up the price of Laserscope stock just as they had 15 years earlier. But whether the company would finally realize its promise remained an unanswered question.

Principal Subsidiaries

Laserscope France S.A.; Laserscope (U.K.) Ltd.; Lasercare.

Principal Competitors

Candela Corporation; Lumenis Ltd.; Palomar Medical Technologies, Inc.

Further Reading

Aragon, Lawrence, "Laserscope Tries to Heat Up Once-Hot Laser Market," *Business Journal,* September 23, 1991, p. 1.

Atkinson, Bill, "DuPont Sees Laserscope As Road to Medical Equipment Sales," *Business Journal,* July 28, 1986, p. 6.

Baum, L. Frank, "Turnaround Time for Laserscope," *Equities,* October-December 2002, p. 27.

Greenberg, Hank, "After Getting Zapped, Can Laserscope Start Shining Again," *San Francisco Chronicle,* May 29, 1996, p. D1.

Kruger, Daniel, "Laser Burn," *Forbes,* June 7, 2004, p. 216.

Shinkle, Kirk, "Laserscope Inc. San Jose, California; Its Prostate Treatment Accelerates Growth," *Investor's Business Daily,* November 24, 2003, p. A06.

—Ed Dinger

Le Cordon Bleu S.A.

8 rue Léon Delhomme
75015 Paris
France
Telephone: 33 (0) 1 53 68 25 50
Fax: 33 (0) 1 48 56 03 96

40 Enterprise Avenue
Secaucus, New Jersey 07094
U.S.A.
Telephone: (201) 617-5221
Toll Free: (800) 457-2433
Fax: (201) 617-1914
Web site: http://www.cordonbleu.net

Private Company
Incorporated: 1896
Employees: 200
NAIC: 611519 Other Technical and Trade Schools

Le Cordon Bleu S.A. has 25 institutes in 15 countries. Students from more than 75 countries enroll each year to earn their Grand Diplôme, which prepares them to become world class master chefs at the world's best restaurants. In addition to its courses, Le Cordon Bleu markets culinary publications, videocassettes, a television series, and gourmet products, cooking equipment, and table settings, and accessories with its sister company, Pierre Deux-French Country, in Japan and the United States. Le Cordon Bleu Australia offers undergraduate and graduate business degrees in several hospitality disciplines, such as International Hotel and Resort Management and International Hospitality and Restaurant Business and a Master of Arts in Gastronomy.

1895–1984: The Establishment of the Cordon Bleu Paris

In 1895, Marthe Distel, a French journalist, launched a weekly publication, *La Cuisinière Cordon Bleu.* The great chefs of Paris wrote for the magazine, namely recipes and descriptions of ingredients, exact methods of preparation, and the history of dishes.

These articles combined to form the basis during the next 70 years for what became the largest recipe collection in the world. The following year, in 1896, Le Cordon Bleu, a free school for subscribers to the magazine, opened its doors in Paris with the first cooking demonstration to take place on an electric stove.

The name for Distel's venture deliberately recalled a 16th-century knightly tradition of spectacular feasts in France. In 1578, King Henri III of France had created L'Ordre du Saint Esprit, the Order of the Holy Spirit, whose knights were named Cordon Bleu because they wore a blue ribbon from which hung the cross of the Holy Spirit. The order's feasts became legendary, and the expression "Cordon Bleu" entered the French language to mean an outstanding chef.

Le Cordon Bleu school expanded and its reputation grew. As early as 1897, it attracted its first Russian student. The first Japanese student joined the school in 1905. During the 1920s, *Le Cordon Bleu* magazine was translated into Spanish and published in Argentina. In 1927, the *Daily Mail* of London referred to the school's "Babel of nationalities."

In the 1930s, Le Cordon Bleu's store began to sell canned goods of pastry ingredients and main dishes that had been prepared at the school, and in 1937 Le Cordon Bleu opened a restaurant in Paris. After World War II, Le Cordon Bleu was accredited by the United States for professionally retraining soldiers, and Julia Child, the first person to teach French cuisine on American television, earned her *toque* from Le Cordon Bleu on the GI Bill. By the 1950s, Le Cordon Bleu represented the highest level of culinary training, the elevation of well-known and regional cuisine to *haute cuisine*, and the codification of the culinary techniques necessary to produce French cuisine and pastry.

From the start, Le Cordon Bleu's method emphasized individual hands-on experience and personal discovery in the kitchen. Over time, the school's "classic program," consisting of demonstrations and classes under the direction of Le Cordon Bleu master chefs, evolved. At the first level, students learned how to prepare ingredients, blend sauces, and put together a few simple dishes, such as boeuf bourgignon and sole à la normande. Intermediate classes studied the culinary differences among the French provinces and focused on more elaborate dishes, such as baron de lapereau rôti aux mirabelles, a rabbit dish with yellow plums from northeast France. The Superior Cuisine classes encompassed the style of a chef's preparation and presentation. In nine months, students could earn their Grand Diplôme, which was recognized worldwide by culinary professionals. Le Cordon Bleu also began to publish cookbooks for amateurs and professionals.

1984–91: Creating an International Presence in Culinary Instruction

In 1984, André J. Cointreau, a descendent of both the Cointreau and Rémy Martin dynasties, acquired Le Cordon Bleu Paris and began an era of unprecedented change for the school. The school moved to rue Leon Delhomme in Paris in 1988 and introduced English translation in its non-diploma classes. Le Cordon Bleu also branched out into advertising endorsements and commercial promotions. Cointreau's wife, Hedwidge Cointreau de Bouteville, owned the Pierre Deux, an expensive Provençal home furnishings company, and her business began to sell Le Cordon Bleu's cookbooks and other kitchen wares.

Having improved and updated Le Cordon Bleu Paris, Cointreau embarked on the acquisition of other cooking schools. In 1988, he acquired Eleanor's Cuisine Française, an eight-year-old Ottawa school founded by Eleanor Orser, a graduate of Le Cordon Bleu in Paris. The association opened the doors of the school to students from across North America, who could now complete the first level of the school's three-part "classic cycle" of instruction in Canada and in English. After a 12-week course, and after passing the required examination, students received a certificate.

In 1990, Cointreau also acquired the Cordon Bleu School of Cookery in London and renamed it Le Cordon Bleu. This school had been founded as Le Petit Cordon Bleu Culinary School in 1933 by Rosemary Hume and Dione Lucas, graduates of Le Cordon Bleu in Paris. In 1935, Hume and Lucas's school also opened a restaurant staffed by students. Dione Lucas wrote *The Cordon Bleu Cook Book*, which introduced Americans to the techniques and traditions of French cooking.

The London school closed during World War II and reopened in 1945. When it reopened, Constance Spry became one of its owners, and its name changed to the Constance Spry Cordon Bleu School of Cookery. When Queen Elizabeth II was coronated in 1952, the students of the Cordon Bleu School of Cookery catered the lunch for the occasion, inventing "Coronation Chicken," made with curried mayonnaise. In 1963, the Penguin *Cordon Bleu Cookery Book* became an immediate best seller in the United Kingdom. Soon after Cointreau purchased Le Cordon Bleu London, he initiated a massive renovation in which the school's tiny cooking stations were replaced with big airy rooms featuring shiny stainless steel equipment.

In 1991, Le Cordon Bleu opened a branch in Tokyo after realizing that 20 percent of the students in its Paris classes were Japanese. Bringing the atmosphere of Paris to the exclusive residential and shopping district of Daikanyama required several years of planning. Most of the Tokyo school's interior furnishings and equipment, including the elegant chairs in the reception area and the huge mirrors that gave students overhead views of demonstrations, were identical to those at the Paris school and at its London and Ottawa branches. Cooking materials and ingredients, too, were imported from France to be as authentic as possible.

In 1993, Le Cordon Bleu Adelaide opened, introducing another continent to the school's century of tradition. Three years later, the government of New South Wales asked the school to train its cooking and hotel staff for the 2000 Olympic Games held that year in Sydney. Later in the decade, the Australian branch of the international cooking school expanded its curriculum to include undergraduate and graduate degree programs. Students could earn a bachelor of business in international restaurant and catering management, international hotel and resort management, or international convention and event management. More advanced students could earn an M.B.A. in international hotel and restaurant management or a master of arts in gastronomy.

The average age of the students earning a degree at Le Cordon Bleu schools was 25. A large number came directly from various undergraduate studies, although there were also a significant number of professionals with backgrounds as diverse as banking, the arts, and advertising. The ratio of men to women was approximately even. Graduates worked toward careers in professional kitchens, catering, restaurant and hotel management, journalism, consulting, food service, food styling, and education. All wore the crisp white apron and hat stamped with Le Cordon Bleu's emblem, known as the "whites," even amateurs in one-day classes.

Le Cordon Bleu also began to develop in other directions to strengthen its international presence in the 1990s. In 1991, it released *Le Cordon Bleu at Home*, written in English and intended for the American market, and including recipes at its basic, intermediate, and superior levels of training. The cookbook, the school's first in a language other than French, was accompanied by a series of videos of Cordon Bleu chefs preparing menus. It was true to Le Cordon Bleu standards and traditions, but with some changes. Respecting the American bias against heavy French cooking, and the American desire not to pass the entire day in the kitchen, its recipes were lower in fat and easier to prepare.

1994–2004: An Increasing Presence Throughout the Culinary and Hospitality Industries

In 1994, Le Cordon Bleu partnered with the Royal Viking Line in a chef exchange program, sending guest chefs on board

Key Dates:

1896: The first cooking demonstration takes place at Le Cordon Bleu in Paris.
1933: The London-based Cordon Bleu School of Cookery begins operations.
1984: André J. Cointreau purchases Le Cordon Bleu in Paris.
1988: Le Cordon Bleu opens a school in Ottawa, Canada.
1990: Le Cordon Bleu purchases the London Cordon Bleu School of Cookery.
1991: The Tokyo branch of Le Cordon Bleu opens.
1993: Le Cordon Bleu opens a school in Adelaide, Australia.
2000: Le Cordon Bleu enters into an exclusive agreement with Career Education Corp.
2003: Le Cordon Bleu opens its first institute in Mexico.
2004: The company launches a line of Le Cordon Bleu knives by Wusthof in Canada.

cruise ships to plan menus and host on-board culinary presentations. In return, Royal Viking chefs visited Le Cordon Bleu as guest instructors. Six years later, in 2000, Le Cordon Bleu opened Signatures, its first dining establishment aboard a Radisson-owned cruise ship.

A partnership with T-Fal Corp. in 1999 also led to other marketing activities, such as the joint development of new cookware concepts, the exchange of technical expertise, and recipe development. After testing T-Fal top-of-the-line Integral non-stick cookware at its London school for more than a year, Le Cordon Bleu began to use T-Fal cookware throughout the world in its training programs and lent its name and endorsement to the cookware company's product line.

In 2000, Le Cordon Bleu purchased the $1.4 million home of the defunct Le Cercle Universitaire d'Ottawa gourmet dining club as the new home for its Canadian cooking school and North American headquarters. According to Cointreau, in an article in the *Ottawa Citizen*, he chose the Canadian city because of its sophistication and European feel and because "it's bilingual, and its people are very tolerant and open-minded." In 2001, Le Cordon Bleu opened its first North American restaurant, Signatures, at Le Cordon Bleu Culinary Arts Institute in Ottawa. The restaurant won an epicurean award for best service in the national capital region at the 17th annual Wine and Food Show in Ottawa in 2002. It also earned a second place medal for best wine list matched to the menu.

Also in 2000, Le Cordon Bleu partnered with Career Education Corp. (CEC), a company that bought up private vocational schools in the United States. CEC blended the curriculum of Le Cordon Bleu into that of its existing culinary schools: the Southern California School of Culinary Arts of Pasadena, California; the Western Culinary Institute of Portland, Oregon; the International Culinary Academy of Pittsburgh, Pennsylvania; the Scottsdale Culinary institute of Scottsdale, Arizona; and the Midwest Culinary Academy of Mendota Heights, Minnesota.

Other school openings followed. In 2002, Le Cordon Bleu opened its first institute in Korea at the Sookmyung Women's University in Seoul. In 2003, it opened Le Cordon Bleu Instituto de Gastronomia in the former French Embassy in Mexico City. An application restaurant called Marianne, after La Marianne, one of the symbols of France since the Revolution, opened alongside the school to offer education in five domains: bar management, sommellerie, banquet/bakery management, restaurant management, and service administration. Other schools opened in Peru, Lebanon, India, Indonesia, Israel, Taiwan, and elsewhere until, by 2004, there were 25 schools in 15 countries.

As Le Cordon Bleu embarked on its second century, its overall growth as an institution led to its increasing international perspective and presence and to expansion into other areas of the culinary and hospitality industries. It opened bakeries, cafés, bistros, and restaurants in Australia, Korea, and Japan and partnered with Wüsthof of Solingen, Germany, one of the world's premiere manufacturers of precision forged cutlery, to introduce a line of forged knives with Le Cordon Bleu's logo. Looking to the future, Le Cordon Bleu expected to remain a vital and active member of the international business and culinary communities.

Principal Competitors

California School of Culinary Arts; Chicago School of Culinary Arts.

Further Reading

"The Cordon Blues: Why U.K. Regulators Rejected the Famed French Cooking School's Trademark Claims," *Marketing Magazine*, August 5, 1996, p. 21.

Julian, Sheryl, "Going Back to London's Cordon Bleu: The London School Has Changed and So Have Its Students," *Boston Globe*, May 17, 2000, p. E1.

Lawnham, Patrick, "Gastronomes Given Food for Serious Thought," *Australian*, December 11, 2002, p. 36.

Obra, Joan, "Chef's School Gains an Edge from French Connection," *Oregonian*, July 6, 2001, p. B1.

Ostman, Eleanor, "'Le Cordon Bleu at Home,' Brings Cooking Lessons to You," *Houston Chronicle*, December 11, 1991, p. 1.

Prentice, Michael, "Home on the Range: Cordon Bleu Settles in Ottawa," *Ottawa Citizen*, April 26, 2001, p. D3.

Schilling, Mark, "Le Cordon Bleu Takes Its Kitchens East," *Wall Street Journal*, September 12, 1991, p. A16.

—Carrie Rothburd

Level 3 Communications, Inc.

1025 Eldorado Boulevard
Broomfield, Colorado 80021
U.S.A.
Telephone: (720) 888-1000
Fax: (720) 888-5422
Web site: http://www.level3.com

Public Company
Incorporated: 1998
Employees: 4,650
Sales: $4.02 billion (2003)
Stock Exchanges: NASDAQ
Ticker Symbol: LVLT
NAIC: 541512 Computer System Design Services;
234920 Power and Communication Transmission Line
Construction

Level 3 Communications, Inc. operates one of the largest communications and Internet networks in the world. The company's network, which utilizes advanced optical and Internet Protocol technologies, encompasses approximately 23,000 miles of fiber in North America and Europe. In North America, Level 3's network covers nearly 19,000 miles, connecting 72 markets. In Europe, the company's network connects 20 markets, covering roughly 3,600 miles. Level 3 ranks as one of the largest providers of wholesale dial-up service to Internet service providers (ISPs) and as a primary provider of Internet connectivity for millions of broadband subscribers. Of the six largest ISPs in the United States, five use Level 3's network. Additionally, nine of the ten largest telecommunications companies in the world use Level 3's network. Level 3 also operates as a reseller of software to corporate clientele through its information services business segment, which manages sales offices in 30 countries that serve more than 8,000 customers.

Origins

Level 3 sprang from the bounty produced by another company, the immensely successful and prolific Peter Kiewit Sons' Inc. Level 3's former parent began as a masonry business founded in 1884 in Omaha, Nebraska, by Peter Kiewit, the son of Dutch immigrants. Shortly after 1900, the masonry company had evolved into a general contracting firm, with Peter Kiewit and two of his six sons taking on small construction projects for Omaha residences and businesses. This foray into construction marked the beginning of one of the most active construction companies in the United States. During the 1930s, Peter Kiewit Sons' began focusing on large-scale construction projects, entering the segment of the construction industry that would make the company a towering force. As the decades passed, Peter Kiewit Sons' completed massive construction projects such as the Fort McHenry Tunnel beneath Baltimore Harbor, the Flaming Gorge Dam in Utah, and nearly all of the Interstate Highway System in the western United States, among numerous other high-profile projects.

Success in the large-scale construction industry turned Peter Kiewit Sons' into a multi-billion-in-sales company. The company was generating so much cash on an annual basis that it literally had more money than it knew what to do with, thus leading to its diversification into non-construction businesses. Peter Kiewit Sons' delved into a range of businesses, developing interests in coal mining, toll roads, newspaper publishing, and cable television, among others. This foray into diverse businesses engendered the assets that gave birth to Level 3, whose origins were rooted in the 1980s, when Walter Scott was beginning his tenure as chief executive officer of Peter Kiewit Sons'.

Walter Scott was appointed chief executive officer in 1979, succeeding the five-decade reign of command of Peter Kiewit, the youngest of the founder's six sons. Scott's character and influence were significantly important to the promotion of Level 3, giving the company legitimacy and credibility within the financial community, a standing the company would need because of the costly nature of its work. Scott, who joined Peter Kiewit shortly after World War II, was held in extremely high regard in Omaha—home to five *Fortune* 500 companies—enjoying as much popularity among the city's residents as the "Oracle of Omaha," famed investor Warren Buffett. Many residents of Omaha would invest heavily in Level 3, as would those outside Nebraska, primarily because of their faith in Scott. Investors also were encouraged by the presence of Level 3's other architect, Jim

Crowe, who arguably ranked as the single most important individual in Level 3's conception and development.

Scott and Crowe were both construction-minded executives. Scott was an industry veteran who presided over one of the most accomplished building concerns in the world. Crowe joined Peter Kiewit Son's after leaving Morrison Knudsen, a giant construction firm. Despite their backgrounds, both executives staked their futures on the telecommunications industry, the realm in which Level 3 sought to thrive. The change in their professional lives drew its impetus from Crowe, who spearheaded Peter Kiewit Sons' diversification into telecommunications during the 1980s. At Crowe's urging, Scott agreed to buy Metropolitan Fiber Systems, a company that built circuit-switch and fiber-optic networks for telephone companies. By 1987, after the acquisition was renamed MFS, Crowe had begun building his own networks and quickly made MFS one of the nation's largest competitive local-exchange carriers, or CLECs.

Mid-1990s: The Stage Is Set for Level 3

The rapid rise of MFS prompted Peter Kiewit Sons' to give its subsidiary its own freedom to grow. In 1993, MFS was spun off as a separate company and taken public, with Crowe appointed as its leader. The future of the company was changed significantly a short time later, after Scott attended an exclusive, biennial gathering hosted by Warren Buffett. Bill Gates, the cofounder of Microsoft Corporation, gave a speech in front of the 50 guests, stressing the revolutionary nature of the Internet and how his company was responding to the advent of the Internet age. Gates also remarked that the new technological advance could render the business of traditional telephone companies obsolete, a comment that pricked Scott's ears. ''Yes, Bill's talk is probably what got us thinking about the Internet,'' he reflected in a July 22, 2002 interview with *Telephony*.

After the gathering of Buffett intimates, Scott and Crowe decided they wanted to find a business that was involved in the infrastructure of the Internet and join that company with MFS. In April 1996, the pair found such a company, UUNet, an ''Internet backbone'' company they acquired for $2 billion, the highest amount paid for an Internet-related company at the time. If there were any skeptics who raised an eyebrow at the price paid by MFS, their jaws would have dropped several months later when WorldCom entered the picture. Bernie Ebbers, the CEO of WorldCom, perceived MFS's acquisition of UUNet as a threat to his company, a threat he dispatched in August 1996 by offering to acquire MFS. The transaction was concluded in December 1996, when WorldCom acquired MFS in an all-stock acquisition valued at $14.3 billion.

The stakes were high in telecommunications in the 1990s, with interest and investment invigorated by the development of technology possessing enormous potential. Bernie Ebbers could not let MFS usurp his own efforts at building the nation's premier network, nor could Scott and Crowe turn their backs on the possibilities available in the industry they had adopted as their proving ground. Crowe wanted to build a new company patterned after MFS, but unlike MFS, which was involved in conventional circuit-switch networks, Crowe's new company would focus on constructing a fiber-optic-only network based on Internet protocol—the language by which the signal was sent.

With Scott's blessing, Crowe's new venture was organized within Kiewit Diversified Group (KDG), which comprised all of Peter Kiewit Sons' businesses and investments in non-construction areas. Crowe began building his start-up company in mid-1997, enlisting the help of 18 former MFS executives whom he recruited from WorldCom. His first objective, under the guidance of Scott, was to sell KDG's non-telecommunications assets to provide the start-up capital for building an expensive and vast fiber-optic network. Crowe's company was a start-up, but one with enormous financial resources behind it from the start, putting it in an entirely different league from other venture-backed, start-up enterprises. By the beginning of 1998, the sale of KDG's non-telecommunications business provided Crowe with roughly $2 billion in seed money. He also had another $1 billion in non-telecommunications assets to be sold at a later date, businesses that in the meantime would provide the start-up venture with a source of cash flow.

Level 3 Becoming a Separate Company: 1998

As with MFS, Scott and Crowe believed it would be best to separate KDG from the construction company. The name Level 3 Communications, Inc. was chosen, a reference to the seven-layer Open Systems Interconnect network model—a framework for international standards in computer network architecture. Crowe and his executive team were focused on the lowest three layers, or levels; the bottom layer being the physical fiber itself, followed by the optical layer, or signal, and the network layer, the language by which the signal was sent. On April 1, 1998, Level 3 began trading on the NASDAQ National Market.

Crowe faced a daunting challenge as he set out, charged with completing a project whose scale rivaled that of Peter Kiewit Sons' largest construction projects. His goal was to build a worldwide network, an objective to be reached in stages, with the first stage of the global plan calling for the creation of a network in North America. Level 3's network, as it was constructed, featured built-in flexibility, with fiber run through buried conduit that allowed for easy upgrades, enabling the company to incorporate advances in fiber technology. ''Our design goal is not to try to guess where design technology will take us five years from now,'' Crowe explained in a February 2, 1998 interview with *Telephony*. ''Our goal is to build a network that can accommodate unprecedented technological change,'' he added.

Crowe threw himself into the mammoth task at hand. He secured rights of way from railroad companies and ordered legions of employees to dig trenches and lay cable, efforts that quickly exhausted billions of dollars in capital. As the herculean task of constructing the first section of the global network was

Key Dates:

1980s: Construction giant Peter Kiewit Sons' diversifies into telecommunications, creating the business foundation for Level 3.

1993: MFS, constituting Peter Kiewit Sons' telecommunications interests, is spun off as a public company.

1996: MFS acquires UUNet, a deal that attracts the attention of WorldCom, which purchases MFS for $14 billion before the end of the year.

1997: The basis of Level 3 is formed through a Peter Kiewit Sons' subsidiary, Kiewit Diversified Group.

1998: Level 3 begins trading on the NASDAQ National Market.

2000: Level 3 begins to experience profound difficulties.

2002: Level 3 acquires Software Spectrum, Inc. and CorpSoft, Inc.

2003: Level 3 acquires Genuity, Inc.

underway, Level 3 moved its headquarters from Omaha to Broomfield, Colorado, where a greater supply of qualified engineers could be found. After 30 months of working furiously to establish a network, Level 3 completed its first section, a 16,000-mile network that spread across North America.

Disaster at the Turn of the Century

Investors, particularly those in Omaha who had made a fortune from investing in MFS, flocked to Level 3. By March 2000, the company's stock was trading for $130 per share. Its market capitalization stood at a monstrous $44 billion—$4 billion more than the market capitalization of General Motors. In the blossoming new sector of Internet-related business, Level 3 ranked as one of the most powerful forces in the world, embodying what the business press hailed as the advent of the "new" economy. Unfortunately for Level 3, the promise of a new era in business quickly faded, as the dot-com sector suffered a spectacular collapse, leading to the ruin of scores of companies and staggering losses in the financial community.

Level 3 began to experience the first tremors of the coming catastrophe in the spring of 2000. The company's biggest customers, ISPs and CLECs, began to falter, causing Level 3's sales to wilt. Further, large, established telecommunications companies such as AT&T and Sprint were expanding their broadband capacity. These industry veterans were joined by new companies such as Global Crossing, Williams, and Broadwing, who were building their own new networks. The result was a glut of capacity that greatly diminished the value of Crowe's impressive new network, as wholesale prices for using Level 3's expensive, fiber-optic lines plunged. No one doubted the technological quality of Crowe's network, "but it's like a great racetrack," an analyst explained in a July 22, 2002 interview with *Fortune*. "You still need the fans. You still need the customers. And companies like AT&T and Qwest started with customers."

Level 3's stock value decreased dramatically as the dot-com bubble burst. The company's share price plummeted from $130

to $13, eventually dropping to $3 by 2002. Investors, particularly those in Omaha, lost enormous amounts of money because of Level 3's downward slide, losses that represented billions, not millions, of dollars—"There are hundreds, probably thousands of investors in Omaha who have suffered combined losses in Level 3 stock equal to tens of billions of dollars," wrote reporter Andy Serwer in a July 22, 2002 *Fortune* article.

The severity of the losses was stunning, but there was hope that Level 3 ultimately could realize the full financial potential of its impressive fiber-optic network. While numerous other Internet-oriented businesses collapsed during the meltdown at the turn of the century, Level 3 survived—a feat industry optimists applauded. The company was incurring substantial losses, posting a deficit of more than $1 billion in 2002, and awash in debt, hobbled by interest payments from roughly $7 billion of debt, but it was alive and in business. Crowe, despite the precarious financial state of the company, pressed forward, acquiring Software Spectrum, Inc. and CorpSoft, Inc. in 2002. Theses acquisitions helped form the company's information services business segment, which sold software to the company's corporate clientele and became a producer of a significant amount of revenue for Level 3. Crowe also capitalized on the misfortune of others, acquiring valuable assets from failing telecommunications companies for pennies on the dollar. One such deal was completed in February 2003, when Level 3 acquired Genuity, Inc., a bankrupt former Verizon subsidiary that operated a network used by Verizon and America Online.

As Level 3 prepared for the future, the success of the company hung in the balance. Much remained to be determined about the true worth of the company's sophisticated network spanning North America and Europe. In the years ahead, the investors who held on to their stock during Level 3's downward spiral would discover the wisdom of their choice, as Scott and Crowe sought to return the luster to their professional reputations.

Principal Subsidiaries

Software Spectrum, Inc.; CorpSoft, Inc.; (i)Structure, LLC.

Principal Competitors

Global Crossing Ltd.; Qwest Communications International Inc.; WiTel Communications Group, Inc.; MCI, Inc.; Sprint Corporation; France Telecom SA; Deutsche Telekom AG; AT&T Corp.

Further Reading

Bryer, Amy, "Rocky Times at Level 3," *Denver Business Journal,* May 11, 2001, p. 1A.

Carter, Wayne, "Reborn for the Future," *Telephony,* February 2, 1998, p. 42.

——, "Unfinished Business," *Telephony,* January 26, 1998, p. 7.

Kruger, Daniel, "A Lower Level," *Forbes,* July 5, 2004, p. 150.

Salkever, Alex, "A Fine Line for Level 3," *Business Week Online,* September 8, 2003, p. 32.

Serwer, Andy, "The Inside Story of Level 3," *Fortune,* July 22, 2002, p. 130.

—Jeffrey L. Covell

Linde AG

Abraham Lincoln Strasse 21
65189 Wiesbaden
Germany
Telephone: +49-611-770-0
Fax: +49-611-770-269
Web site: http://www.linde.de

Public Company
Incorporated: 1879 as Gesellschaft für Linde's
 Eismaschinen
Employees: 46,662
Sales: $11.28 billion (2003)
Stock Exchanges: German OTC
Ticker Symbol: LIN; LNAGF
NAIC: 237990 Other Heavy and Civil Engineering
 Construction; 325120 Industrial Gas Manufacturing;
 325188 All Other Inorganic Chemical Manufacturing;
 333924 Industrial Truck, Tractor, Trailer, and Stacker
 Machinery Manufacturing; 333994 Industrial Process
 Furnace and Oven Manufacturing; 336111
 Automobile Manufacturing; 541330 Engineering
 Services; 551112 Offices of Other Holding Companies

Linde AG, an international technology company, operates in two business segments: Gas and Engineering and Materials Handling. The company produces industrial and medical gases, develops plants for gas production, and is one of the biggest manufacturers of industrial trucks in the world. In 2004, Linde exited the refrigeration business, in which it had been Europe's market leader.

A Century of Business: 1875–1985

Carl von Linde invented his refrigeration machine in 1875, and formed his own company four years later. For the next 100-plus years, Linde AG was involved in a wide variety of engineering endeavors, from manufacturing refrigeration and air conditioning systems to the production of rare gases and the construction of an array of industrial plants.

Linde was born in Berndorf on June 11, 1842. He became professor of mechanical engineering at the College of Technology in Munich at the age of 26 and retained that position until he was 68. Linde made the most of his time spent at the school and undertook research in the areas of refrigeration and air and gas liquefaction processes. For the first ten years of his company's existence, Linde took a sabbatical from teaching and was its sole director. After the firm was well on its way to success, however, Linde returned and directed its operations from the college. He died on November 16, 1934.

By the mid-1980s, Linde consisted of four divisions managed by the executive board of directors in Wiesbaden: the refrigeration and shop equipment division; the industrial gases division; the process plant engineering and construction division; and the hydraulic and materials handling equipment division. The divisional breakdown of the company did not formally occur until 1972, but those operations traditionally followed separate paths of development.

Linde's first scientific breakthrough, which occurred in 1875, was an ammonia compression machine used for manufacturing ice. Four years later, Linde founded Gesellschaft für Linde's Eismaschinen. Initially, orders for refrigeration machines were "almost distressingly slow." Looking for possible business alternatives, his solution was to engineer and supply ice factories in which his refrigeration machines would be installed. By 1890, over 700 of his machines were employed in 445 breweries across Western Europe.

Soon thereafter, the company changed its emphasis from planning ice factories to building and operating cold stores. Linde cofounded Gesellschaft für Markt-und Kühlhallen in Berlin to use his refrigeration technology and expand the cold stores operations. Yet, for over 50 years, even though other firms purchased Linde's refrigeration systems, and most of the company's ice factories had been sold, the cold storage operations were never a financial success. As a result, Linde sold all of its holdings in that area during 1982 and 1983.

It was only after 1920 that the company's sales of refrigeration equipment skyrocketed, due primarily to the acquisition of two major competitors. Industriegas GmbH, located in

Mannheim, designed oxygen generators. The value of the purchase for Linde, however, was in the Industriegas subsidiary, Maschinenfabrik Sürth. Sürth, situated near Cologne, was well-known as the first German company to manufacture transportation containers for compressed and liquefied gases, and also for the production of various components for refrigeration units. The second significant acquisition was Kulmöbelwerk G.H. Walb and Company of Mainz-Kostheim, a manufacturer of large commercial items such as refrigerated grocery counters.

After their assimilation by Linde, and throughout the 1930s, the Sürth works built components and systems units for commercial refrigeration, while G.H. Walb made smaller units and domestic products. Commercial production continued through World War II, although these plants were required to provide mining and compression units to the armed forces. Near the end of the war, both the Sürth and the G.H. Walb works were entirely destroyed. By 1949, however, a new machine shop had been built at the Sürth facility, and by 1960 the operation had been completely reconstructed. Soon afterwards, Linde established its entire refrigeration engineering department at this factory. The branches at Sürth and G.H. Walb were then combined in 1964 to form the refrigeration and shop equipment division of the 1980s.

Carl von Linde's 1895 invention for producing liquid air led to the growth of the TVT München division of process plant engineering and construction. In addition, his related research with other rare gases laid the groundwork for what became the industrial gases division. The separation of these divisions was more for administrative purposes than for anything else, since their operations significantly overlapped.

Linde's initial plan was systematically to improve the design and production of air liquefiers, and he devoted much of his time in Munich to the development of new gas liquefaction processes. During 1903, the company built the first production plant for purified oxygen and successfully produced pure nitrogen. Linde also built the first double-column rectifier, which allowed pure oxygen and nitrogen to be produced in the same apparatus without using any extra energy; this breakthrough occurred in 1912.

During this time, Linde also built gas production plants in Düsseldorf, Mülheim, Nürnberg, and Dresden. Expanding throughout Europe, the company built plants in Antwerp, Toulouse, Paris, Barcelona, Stockholm, Vienna, and London. In 1907 Linde established the Linde Air Products Company in Cleveland, Ohio. (This plant was extremely successful; eventually acquired by Union Carbide, and known as the Linde division in the mid-1980s.)

Until World War II, Linde was deeply involved in expanding its existing plants. During the war, however, both the plant engineering and construction and industrial gases facilities within Germany were heavily damaged; as a result, they had difficulty re-establishing their operations both at home and abroad. However, the economic prosperity in West Germany during the late 1950s and early 1960s led to a rise in domestic demand for liquid oxygen and nitrogen, and contracts with former partners overseas were also renewed.

Linde built the world's first heavy water nuclear energy plant in 1955 and the first system to separate radioactive elements from nuclear reactor gases in 1959. It also constructed, in 1964, the world's largest air separation unit in West Germany; two years later the company built the world's largest ammonia-synthesis plant in the United States; in 1970, it devised Europe's most extensive helium refrigeration system.

The Güldner Aschaffenburg division had its beginnings very early in the century when Linde needed engines to drive the refrigeration machines his firm was manufacturing. He formed a partnership with Dr. Hugo Güldner, a chief design engineer, and Dr. Georg von Krauss, a locomotive manufacturer. The first diesel engines were built at the Güldner works in 1907; by this time, Linde controlled the majority of company stock.

During World War I, the factory was retooled entirely for the war effort, manufacturing iron shells, motor vehicles and aircraft engines. The company recovered quickly in the 1920s, and expanded its product line to include engines for agricultural equipment and components for the repair of locomotives, railcars, and boats. The Güldner facilities were taken over completely by Linde in 1929 and thereafter concentrated on producing small diesel engines and tractors.

The plant in Aschaffenburg was totally destroyed during an Allied air raid in World War II, but the works were fully functional once again by 1950. A new era for the company began in 1955 with the production of the Hydrocar, a platform truck with hydrostatic transmission. Linde then acquired the hydraulics department of Gusswerk Paul Saalmann & Sohne in 1958. By 1969, the Aschaffenburg factory discontinued the production of tractors and diesel engines and concentrated entirely on forklift trucks and hydraulic equipment. Acquisitions followed. Linde purchased a Hamburg-based company in 1973. Then the company looked outside its borders, acquiring the majority share of an American Company in 1977 and taking over France's largest forklift manufacturer in 1984.

A number of important developments occurred during the first half of the 1980s. The refrigeration and shop equipment division designed its units for energy conservation as well as individually customizing them to match contemporary store styles throughout the world. The product line covered a comprehensive selection of refrigerated and freezer display cases, refrigeration systems, and energy monitoring and control systems. Besides the impressive growth in orders from Arab countries, industrial users, whose needs ranged from switchgears and transformers to computer rooms and brewery storage, also contributed to increased profits for Linde.

Much of the innovative research in the utilization of wastewater and sewage was conducted at Linde's process plant engineering and construction division. The new techniques it developed during the beginning of the 1980s included the highly

Key Dates:

1875: Carl von Linde invents an ammonia compression machine used to manufacture ice.
1879: Gesellschaft für Linde's Eismaschinen is founded.
1903: Company builds first production plant for purified oxygen.
1912: Company constructs device to simultaneously produce oxygen and nitrogen.
1914: Manufacturing is altered due to World War I.
1920: Acquisition of competitors elevates refrigeration business.
1945: Company sustains heavy damage during World War II.
1955: Linde begins Hydrocar production.
1959: Company builds first system to separate radioactive elements from nuclear gases.
1969: Linde stops tractor production to concentrate on forklifts.
1979: Linde marks 100th anniversary.
2000: Company buys AGA AB, becoming Europe's second largest industrial gas group.
2004: Company exits refrigeration business.

economical DS process for storing and utilizing sewage sludge and the Laran process for anaerobic decomposition of contaminated wastewaters. Additional environmental protection research was conducted in the purification of flue gases, including the mechanism known as smokestack "scrubbers."

The industrial gases division maintained a strong market position: stricter environmental protection measures in many countries led to increased use of oxygen in the steel industry, at foundries, and in the manufacture of electrodes; the wastewater purification field grew sizably in the past decade; and demand for high-purity gases increased dramatically in the semiconductor and glass-fiber industries.

The improvement in the Güldner Aschaffenburg division's sales, due largely to new drive and transmission systems which had been developed in recent years, had been mostly in the form of exports to foreign companies manufacturing agricultural and construction equipment. In addition, in 1985 this division also produced a small, three-ton capacity, forklift truck which helped to increase sales. However, continued growth in this area was limited due to competition, lower prices, and a worldwide overcapacity.

The breakdown of division size in terms of sales during the mid-1980s was refrigeration and shop equipment, 19 percent; process plant engineering and construction, 25 percent; industrial gases, 21 percent; and hydraulics and materials handling, 35 percent. Linde's long-term goals were to increase inventory turnover, maintain nearly full employment of its facilities, and retain the company's reputation as a world leader in the construction industry.

Gas on the Rise: The Mid-1980s to 2000

During the late 1980s, faced with an increasingly competitive environment for its refrigeration business, Linde implemented plant modernization. Its materials handling business

received a boost through the purchase of Lansing in Great Britain, in 1989.

In 1991, Linde ranked 334th in sales among the world's industrial companies, with sales of $4.17 billion and profits of $147 million. The opening of relations between East and West had afforded business opportunities for Linde. Plant construction took place in the former Soviet Union, Eastern Germany, Poland, and Romania. Plants were also established in China. To the west, Linde expanded its U.S. operations.

Despite the global reach, in 1997, the *Economist* wrote of Linde, it is "Old Germany: a conglomerate that makes machine tools, gases, fork-lifts and refrigeration equipment." Viewed as a producer of some of the world's best products, it was seen as reticent to make revelations about itself to those beyond its borders. This despite half of its production was done outside Germany and nearly two-thirds of its $5 billion in sales were international. Top officers were engineers who focused on product above all else.

A build-up of its gas business during the late 1990s came via acquisitions and culminated with the purchase of Sweden-based AGA AB in early 2000. Established in 1904, AGA had for much of its history been a diversified company. International competition forced change, and the company limited itself to the gas business beginning in the 1980s. In 1999, AGA held a strong market position in Europe and North and South America. Its sales volume was EUR 1.6 billion. Employees numbered 9,500.

The acquisition resulted in the formation of the second largest industrial gas group in Europe, holding about one-quarter of the market. The AGA purchase also boosted Linde's Latin American market share of industrial gases to 20 percent.

According to an April 2002 *Chemical Week* article, Linde ranked fourth among major worldwide industrial gas producers, tied with Air Products and Chemicals, and behind Air Liquide, BOC, and Praxair.

"The Aga deal represents a substantial expansion of Linde's business, but it is much smaller than the very ambitious plans that the company was negotiating in 1999 and early 2000. Linde had hoped to take control of fellow German gases group Messer, and it was also poised to acquire most of BOC's U.S. gases business that Air Liquide and Air Products were expected to divest to win regulatory approval for their proposed joint takeover of BOC. Antitrust concerns had sunk all these deals except Aga by mid-2000," wrote Natasha Alperowicz and David Hunter for *Chemical Week*.

Growing Niches: 2001–04

The $3.8 billion price tag for AGA put a hold on any large acquisitions by Linde for the next few years. *Chemical Week* reported the company would concentrate on reducing debt and increasing sales in the high-growth markets of healthcare and hydrogen production.

Linde's healthcare operation was its fastest growing business, with the majority of sales to hospitals (56 percent) and home respiratory services (28 percent). But Linde's inhaled nitrogen oxide (INO) business, begun in 2001 in the United States, for the treatment of newborns with respiratory problems, was sky-rocketing. Hydrogen sales to the refining and petrochemical industry were on the upswing. The company was solidly positioned in the growing hydrogen vehicle fuel market as well.

Linde was challenged by the economic conditions in Europe during 2003. In light of this, the company focused on internal improvements while extending itself further out into the global marketplace.

In the spring of 2004, Linde sold its refrigeration business to the U.S.-based Carrier Corporation. The deal closed in September 2004, bringing to an end the business line on which it was founded. The sale freed up Linde to focus on the future of Gas and Engineering and Material Handling, both profitable and world leading business segments.

Principal Subsidiaries

Linde Gas Austria; Linde Gas Pty. Ltd.; Linde Gas Brazil; PanGas; Linde Gas Columbia; Linde Technoplyn; AGA Linde HealthCare GmbH & Co. KG; Tega-Technische Gase und Gasetechnik GmbH; Linde Gas Denmark; Abello Linde Spain; Linde Gas France; Linde Gas Finland; Linde Gas Great Britain (U.K.); Linde Gas Ungarn AG; Linde Gas Italy; Linde Gas Mexico; Linde Gas Norway; Linde Gas Poland; Linde Gas Puerto Rico; AGA S.A.; Linde Gas Chile; Linde Gas Romania; AGA AB; Linde Gas USA; AGA Gas C.A.; Linde Kyrotechnik AG; Linde-KCA-Dresden GmbH; Selas-Linde GmbH; Societe of Application des Techniques Linde S.A.R.L.; Linde Impianti Italia S.p.A. (Italy); Linde Engineering USA; Linde Fordeertechnik GmbH; Linde Material Handling Pty. Ltd.; Linde Lansing Fordertechnik AG; Linde Xiamen Gabelstaplergesellschaft mbH; Linde Material Handling Czech Republic; Linde Material Handling Iberica, S.A.; Fenwick-Linde France; Linde Material Handling Great Britain (U.K.); Linde Guldner Italiana S.p.A. (Italy); Linde Milenz Truck A.B.; Linde Lift Truck Corporation; STILL GmbH.

Principal Competitors

Hussmann International; L'Air Liquide SA; NACCO Industries, Inc.

Further Reading

"AGA Forms Alliance with Linde AG for Air Separation," *Dow Jones Newswire*, June 18, 1997.

Alperowizc, Natasha, "Linde and Carbide to Supply PE and PP Plants in Ukraine," *Chemical Week*, January 22, 1992, p. 16.

——, "Samsung/Linde Clinch Jilin Cracker, Firms Bid for Maoming EO/EG," *Chemical Week*, September 31, 1992, p. 32.

"Badger Combines Linde/Mobil MTBE Processes," *European Chemical News*, August 19, 1991, p. 22.

"BASF Approves Linde Bid for Antwerp Cracker," *European Chemical News*, October 29, 1990, p. 33.

"Business Brief: Praxair Inc.," *Wall Street Journal*, January 19, 1996.

Chynoweth, Emma, "Linde Ready to Offer Propane Dehydrogenation Technology," *Chemical Week*, October 17, 1990, p. 20.

"Cuts at Linde," *Process Engineering*, January 2003, p. 2.

Geburtstag Carl von Linde: 1842–1943. Wiesbaden: Linde AG, 1992.

Hunter, David, and Natasha Alperowicz, "Linde Gets the Measure of Its Gases," *Chemical Week*, April 10, 1002, pp. 37+.

Linde: 1879–1979. Wiesbaden: Linde AG, 1979.

"Linde Bids for AGA of Sweden," *Wall Street Journal Europe*, August 17, 1999, p. 8.

"Linde Confirms Bids for BOC Assets," *Chemical Week*, March 29, 2000, p. 27.

"Millenium Sells LaPorte Plant to Linde for $122.5 MM in Cash," *Chemical Market Reporter*, November 23, 1998, p. 1.

"Neighbors: German Industry," *Economist*, December 20, 1997, pp. 99+.

Roberts, Micheal, "Linde Claims First Victory in Race for Tega," *Chemical Week*, August 1, 1990, p. 7.

——, "Linde Tries to Block Tega Berlin Sale to L'Air Liquide," *Chemical Week*, August 29, 1990, p. 14.

—update: Kathleen Peippo

Mag Instrument, Inc.

1635 South Sacramento Avenue
P.O. Box 50600
Ontario, California 91761
U.S.A.
Telephone: (909) 947-1006
Toll Free: (800) 289-6241
Fax: (909) 947-3116
Web site: http://www.maglite.com

Private Company
Incorporated: 1974 as Mag Instrument, Inc.
Employees: 900
Sales: $150 million (2003 est.)
NAIC: 335129 Other Lighting Equipment Manufacturing

Mag Instrument, Inc. is a producer of high-quality flashlights under the Maglite brand. A believer in the American dream, company founder Anthony Maglica has kept manufacturing inside the United States, thanks in part to extensive use of automation. The company began work on a new facility in Ontario, California, in 2004. The flashlights are exported to more than 85 countries around the world; one-quarter of sales come from outside the United States.

Origins

Company founder Anthony Maglica was born in New York City in 1930, at the beginning of the Great Depression. He moved with his mother to her homeland of Croatia at age two. He was eventually trained as a machinist in Europe.

In 1950, Maglica returned to the United States with little knowledge of English but ample faith in the free enterprise system. According to the *Business Press* of California, he was unable to find anything but sewing work in New York City, so he moved west. He operated a lathe for Long Beach-based Pacific Valve Co. and then A.O. Smith Water Products Co., an East Los Angeles manufacturer of water heaters.

In 1955 he set up a small job shop in his garage in Los Angeles as a side venture. His start-up capital was the $125 he had saved, just enough for a down payment on a $1,000 lathe.

The business was incorporated on September 25, 1974, as Mag Instrument, Inc. By this time, Maglica was producing artillery shells. He also was making components for a flashlight manufacturer. Dismayed by the poor quality of their product, in 1976 he decided to build a better flashlight. At the time, most were cheap and virtually disposable.

After three years, Maglica came up with a design that was tough and durable, with anodized aluminum housing rather than plastic. Called the Maglite, it was initially marketed toward law enforcement and rescue personnel. The flashlight also was designed to be attractive to civilians. Sportsmen were another early target market.

The Maglite, introduced in 1979, was a critical and commercial success. It won numerous accolades from product design circles as it made its way into home improvement chains and department stores. The Maglite Rechargeable Flashlight System (Mag Charger) was introduced in 1982.

That year, Maglica relocated the firm, which then had 80 employees, to a new 126,000-square-foot factory in Ontario, California, about 50 miles east of Los Angeles. Using his tooling experience, Maglica designed the machinery for the plant himself.

Defending Its Trademarks in the 1980s

According to California's *Business Press,* a 1984 lawsuit against U.S. retailers who had imported cheap knock-offs of the Maglite flashlights was a turning point for the company in more ways than one. While Mag won the suit, instead of pursuing a cash award, Maglica had the retailers buy five Mag flashlights for every imported copy they had sold. This was an effective way to gain a great deal of shelf space, as the merchants included Sears, Roebuck & Co. and Kmart Corporation.

The original Maglite ran on D cells. In 1984 the company unveiled a smaller flashlight called the Mini Maglite, which ran on AA batteries. A still smaller AAA version came out three years later. The keyring-sized Solitaire flashlight was introduced in 1988. In the mid-1980s, Maglica also developed underwater lighting for eminent sea explorer Jacques Cousteau.

In 1987 the company won $3.1 million in a copyright infringement suit against Streamlight, Inc. Another judgment celebration. They reinforced the "thousand points of light" theme. He also supplied them for the younger Bush's inauguration in 2001. Audience members lit the lights as part of a grand finale.

Exporting in the 1990s

Although an impassioned advocate for U.S. manufacturing, Maglica remained sensitive to the situation in the former Yugoslavia where he was raised. In 1994, Mag donated 40,000 flashlights inscribed with "Remember Sarajevo" for the closing ceremonies at the Lillehammer Winter Olympics. In 1997, Maglica established the nonprofit Maglite Foundation in Croatia. Its mission was the environmental cleanup of the region, particularly on the island of Zlarin, where Maglica grew up.

Mag entered the European market in 1995. The flashlights fared well even in Germany, known for its "over-engineered" products. They also were accepted in quality-conscious Japan. Total sales were reported at about $240 million per year.

The company was soon looking to expand its manufacturing space. It sought to take over the coating process done to the aluminum flashlights by a Kalamazoo, Michigan company.

Continued Growth in the Early 2000s

In the first years of the new millennium, Mag Instrument employed 850 people and had 450,000 square feet of manufacturing space scattered across 11 buildings. In November 1999, Mag began leasing another, 300,000-square-foot facility as a stopgap measure to meet increasing demand.

The flashlights were sold in more than 85 countries; exports accounted for 25 percent of total sales, which were reported at between $100 million and $250 million in various sources. The company was valued at $775 million, Maglica's attorney told Ontario's *Business Press* in 2000 after settling a palimony suit brought by Maglica's longtime companion. The *Business Press* added that the company had produced 39 million flashlights the year before.

In 2003, Mag won a rare monetary award ($113,000) against a Japanese manufacturer, Asahi Electric Corp., which was found to have infringed upon Mag's patent. The 17-year patent on Mag's flashlight, however, was due to expire in March 2005. U.S. Representative Joe Baca was sponsoring a bill to extend the patent for two more years. According to the *Business Press* of California, part of Mag's appeal was an eight-year gap after the request of a renewal in 1995 in which Mag had no patent protection.

soon followed against Kassnar Imports, Inc. ($2.75 million, 1989) and The Brinkmann Corporation ($1.2 million, 1990). More imitations by potential competitors—some 50 different companies around the world—would follow. Mag spent $17 million from 1986 to 1989 to fight cheap knock-offs. This was more than three times the company's advertising budget, noted the *Wall Street Journal.*

It was often difficult to collect on such judgments, as manufacturers who lost suits were prone to declaring bankruptcy. Nevertheless, Mag spent millions to aggressively defend its trademarks for the design and manufacturing process of its flashlights. According to *Management Review,* the United States lagged behind other countries in protecting design features. In 1997, however, the "shape, style and overall appearance" of its Mini Maglite flashlights received copyright protection, followed by the other designs in 2003.

Inc. magazine reported revenues were in the range of $70 million in 1989. *ADWEEK* mentioned reports the company held a 25 percent share of a U.S. flashlight market worth $400 million. Mag ended the decade with about 500 employees. Maglica was committed to keeping manufacturing operations in the United States. Extensive use of automation on the factory floor helped keep costs down.

A loyal Republican, Maglica donated 40,000 Mini Maglite flashlights for President George H.W. Bush's 1989 inauguration

The company began construction of a new $80 million, 700,000-square-foot facility in 2004. It was expected to house a total of 2,400 employees after its scheduled opening in 2006. The company's long-term goal was to increase exports to at least half of total sales.

Principal Competitors

The Black & Decker Corporation; Dorcy International; Energizer Holdings, Inc.; First Alert/Powermate, Inc.; Garrity Industries, Inc.; Rayovac Corporation.

Further Reading

Ascenzi, Joseph, "With Palimony Suit Over, Mag Instrument to Shine," *Business Press* (Ontario), March 20, 2000, p. 6.

Barrier, Michael, "Why a Quality Pacesetter Chooses to Hide His Light Under a Bushel—Tony Maglica, Flashlight Manufacturer," *Nation's Business,* June 1991.

Benson, Don, "Mag-Lite Shines On; Ontario Center for Expansion; Planning Commission Approves Proposal to Double the Size of Plant," *Business Press* (Ontario), March 29, 1999, p. 3.

Brown, Paul B., "Magnificent Obsession; Company Founder Obsesses Over Quality Control and Spends Millions on Patent Protection, All to Keep His Product Unique," *Inc.,* August 1989.

Chacon, Robert, "$2 Mil. Judgment Shines Light on Family Affairs," *Business Press* (Ontario), July 22, 2002, p. 4.

Emshwiller, John R., "Copycat Flashlight Firms Are Hit by Battery of Suits," *Wall Street Journal,* Enterprise Sec., August 22, 1989.

Eventov, Adam, "Anthony Maglica; Mag-Lite Creator Finds His Personal Life in Unwanted Spotlight," *Business Press* (Ontario), August 16, 1999, p. 16.

——, "Growing Demand Forces Mag-Lite Maker into Lease," *Business Press* (Ontario), November 15, 1999, p. 3.

Hammond, Teena, "Is It Lights Out for Mag-Lite Maker?," *Business Press* (Ontario), August 12, 1996, p. 1.

Herrera, Paul, "Mag Outlines Growth Plan," *Press-Enterprise,* August 26, 2004, p. D1.

"High-End Flashlights Hot," *MMR,* July 29, 2002, p. 45.

Hinsberg, Pat, "Mag Instrument Lights Up Grey-L.A.," *ADWEEK,* Eastern ed., April 10, 1989, p. 2.

Mag Instrument, Inc., "Anthony Maglica and Mag Instrument—An American Success Story," August 25, 2004.

"Mag Wins Lawsuit," *Ontario Business Press,* Business Briefs, January 27, 2003.

Messinger, Rob, "Maker of Popular Mag-Lite Likely to Stay in Ontario," *Business Press* (Ontario), November 18, 1996, p. 7.

——, "Ontario Sweetens the Pot for Growth-Minded Mag," *Business Press* (Ontario), November 25, 1996, p. 4.

Park, Carol, "Ontario, Calif.-Based Flashlight Maker Seeks Patent Protection," *Business Press* (San Bernardino), October 4, 2004.

Powers, Kemp, "Anthony Maglica: Mag Instrument," *Fortune Small Business,* September 1, 2004, http://www.fortune.com/fortune/smallbusiness/articles/0,15114,681497,00.html.

Reynolds, Larry, "Is Your Product Design Really Protected?," *Management Review,* August 1, 1991, p. 36.

—Frederick C. Ingram

Manhattan Associates, Inc.

2300 Windy Ridge Parkway
Atlanta, Georgia 30339
U.S.A.
Telephone: (770) 955-7070
Fax: (770) 955-0302
Web site: http://www.manhattanassociates.com

Public Company
Incorporated: 1990 as Manhattan Associates Software,
    L.L.C.
Employees: 1,117
Sales: $196.81 million (2003)
Stock Exchanges: NASDAQ
Ticker Symbol: MANH
NAIC: 511210 Software Publishers

Manhattan Associates, Inc. helps companies navigate their products through the supply chain, providing technology-based solutions to improve the efficiency of the distribution and transportation of goods. Manhattan's software, hardware, and services coordinate the flow of information among manufacturers, distributors, retailers, suppliers, transportation providers, and consumers. The company operates in eight markets, serving nearly 1,000 clients in the consumer goods, food, government, high-technology, industrial, life sciences, retail, and third-party logistics industries. Manhattan operates internationally through offices in the United Kingdom, The Netherlands, Germany, and Asia, generating nearly a fifth of total sales from its overseas business.

Origins

As the 1980s began, the U.S. textile industry faced a daunting challenge. Global competition had intensified, with many foreign manufacturers selling their apparel for prices that undercut the capabilities of most domestic producers. The U.S. manufacturers needed to find a way to beat back the ever encroaching presence of overseas competitors. They needed a solution that would enable them to compete effectively. The problem was widespread and it was growing worse, prompting the industry as a whole to take action. Midway through the decade, studies were begun that brought together experts from a number of different fields. The studies were part of an industrywide initiative focusing on the supply chain, the various steps a product took to get from a manufacturer to a customer. The national undertaking hoped to lower the cost of goods sold by increasing the efficiency of the supply chain. ''Quick Response'' was the result of the inquiry.

Quick Response relied on technology to give U.S. clothing manufacturers an advantage over foreign competition. Through the use of technology, the flow of information among manufacturers, distributors, and retailers was improved substantially, allowing retailers to inform manufacturers and distributors of what merchandise they needed more rapidly. Manufacturers and distributors, for their part, were able to restock retailers more efficiently. The reduction in idle inventory enabled textile product retailers to reduce the cost of goods sold, making the industrywide initiative a success.

Manhattan's four founders were involved in the studies that produced Quick Response. The founding group was led by Alan J. Dabbiere, the individual who would lead the company during its first decade of existence. Dabbiere participated in Quick Response pilot projects as part of his job at Kurt Salmon Associates, a management consulting firm he joined in 1986. Kurt Salmon, which specialized in consumer products manufacturing and retailing in its consultancy work, served as an instrumental contributor in developing the blueprint for Quick Response and its counterpart, Efficient Consumer Response, a system for improving efficiency in the food and grocery industry's supply chain. Dabbiere represented an integral component of Kurt Salmon's efforts. He was joined in founding Manhattan by three technology-oriented executives from Infosys Technologies Limited, an India-based software development company founded in 1981. When Infosys opened its first international office in the United States in 1987, Deepak Raghavan, Deepak M.J. Rao, and Ponnambalam Muthiah joined the company. In the years preceding the formation of Manhattan, Raghavan and Muthiah both worked as senior software engineers, specializing in the design and use of information systems for the apparel manufacturing industry. Rao, who performed the duties of an assistant project manager at Infosys, specialized in the design and use of information systems for the banking industry.

Company Perspectives:

Large or small, global or local, established or newcomer . . . if you're in business today, you're under pressure to be efficient, cost-effective and competitively astute. The old days of going out to the warehouse, picking products off the shelves and shipping customers a month's worth of inventory are gone. Today, advanced capabilities, automated operations, accelerated responsiveness and a rapid return on investment differentiate those who succeed from those who do not.

The four founders gathered in Manhattan Beach, California, as the new decade began. Their interest in enhancing supply-chain execution centered on one part of the complex process that carried a product from manufacturer to customer: the warehouse. They believed that distribution centers offered an ideal way to demonstrate what information technology solutions could deliver in efficiency to the supply chain. Manhattan Associates Software, L.L.C. was formed in 1990 to bring their idea to the marketplace. Dabbiere became the new company's president and chief executive officer, Raghavan its chief technology officer, Rao a vice-president, and Muthiah a vice-president.

PkMS Software Driving Growth in the 1990s

Manhattan was a new company in a new field, one in which the company would come to dominate. Its first software product aided customers in complying with the shipping-label specifications of retailers. Manhattan signed its first client in 1991, beginning a steady march that saw the company develop quickly. The centerpiece of the company's business was a warehouse management system, Manhattan's proprietary PkMS, which was developed not long after the company was founded. PkMS, a flexible, modular software system that controlled the efficient movement of goods through the supply chain, drove Manhattan's physical and financial growth throughout the 1990s. By using PkMS, a company could manage the checklist of tasks assigned to a distribution center. PkMS managed receiving stock, locating stock, picking stock, verifying orders, and packing and shipping product, orchestrating, in an efficient manner, the complex dance of packages moving in and out of a warehouse. The benefits to the customer were as numerous as the number of tasks that fell under the purview of PkMS. Inventory turnover increased, inventory accuracy improved, response time decreased, labor productivity increased, and customer service improved, yielding advances in efficiency that translated into reduced costs and increased profits for the customer.

Manhattan's solutions resolved some of the most pressing problems challenging U.S. textile manufacturers, distributors, and retailers. The idea that began in Manhattan Beach flowered into a growing financial enterprise. By 1993, Manhattan had developed into a $3.3 million company. The following year, when it signed its 50th customer to license PkMS, the company nearly doubled its sales, generating $6.5 million in revenue. In 1995, a year that marked the arrival of the company's 25th employee, Manhattan relocated from the beach that gave it its name and settled in Atlanta, Georgia. Sales during the year leaped upward again, reaching $11.2 million. After a modest gain to $14.4 million in 1996, Manhattan recorded a remarkable surge in financial growth in 1997, more than doubling its sales to $32.4 million. By this point, the Dabbiere-led venture was contemplating its debut on Wall Street.

By the end of 1997, Manhattan had made its mark in the warehouse management system sector of supply-chain execution. The company added 56 new clients during the year, giving it a customer base of more than 250 companies. These customers, who reflected Manhattan's diversification beyond the apparel industry, included members of the consumer products and the foodservice and grocery industries. Calvin Klein, Dean Foods, Mikasa, SEIKO Corporation of America, and Patagonia were PkMS licensees, each finding rewards in using Manhattan's software system to manage their distribution centers. The company's payroll swelled, particularly in 1997, when the number of Manhattan employees shot up from 88 to more than 200. In October 1997, Dabbiere made room for the robust growth of the company by announcing that Manhattan was relocating its headquarters to another facility in Atlanta that was more than three times the size of the company's existing headquarters. To Dabbiere and his colleagues, the strident growth of the company suggested more than a move to larger quarters. The time had come for Manhattan's end as a limited liability company and its debut as a publicly traded company.

Initial Public Offering of Stock in 1998

Dabbiere and his team prepared for Manhattan's initial public offering (IPO) of stock, desiring to take advantage of the company's strong position. Manhattan's PkMS was the only warehouse management system designed exclusively for manufacturers and distributors who shipped to retail and grocery. After acquiring Performance Analysis Corporation, whose software helped determine the optimal storage location for inventory within a distribution center, Manhattan filed for an IPO in the spring of 1998. Manhattan Associates, Inc. was formed to acquire the assets of Manhattan Associates Software, L.L.C., leading to the sale of 3.5 million shares of stock on the NASDAQ at $15 per share.

Dabbiere quickly made advances after Manhattan's IPO. In July 1998, the company announced the formation of a subsidiary in the United Kingdom, an office near Heathrow Airport in Stockley Park. By this point, the company already enjoyed a European customer base, serving Revlon, Warnaco, Ocular Sciences, and Venator Group's European Footlocker. The subsidiary was formed to provide better support to Manhattan's existing clients and to cultivate additional European customers. The year of Manhattan's public debut also saw it become the first company to guarantee ongoing compliance with the stringent and specific guidelines demanded by the leading 100 retailers in the United States. Dabbiere also tapped into one of the strengths of his former employer in 1998, agreeing in September to acquire DCMS, the Distribution Center Management Systems software product developed by Kurt Salmon. By the end of the year, Manhattan boasted more than 350 customers operating in more than 750 sites worldwide.

As Manhattan concluded its first decade of business, the company was demonstrating surging growth. Fruit of the Loom became the 100th customer to install PkMS in 1999, representing a 56 percent increase from the previous year in the

Key Dates:

1990: Manhattan Associates Software, L.L.C. is formed in Manhattan Beach, California.
1995: The company relocates to Atlanta, Georgia.
1998: The company completes its initial public offering of stock, becoming Manhattan Associates, Inc. in the process.
2000: Manhattan acquires Intrepa, L.L.C.
2002: Manhattan acquires Logistics.com, Inc.

number of new clients secured. To help manage this growth, which saw sales increase to $85.2 million for the year, Dabbiere looked for outside help, announcing the appointment of Richard M. Haddrill as president and chief executive officer in October 1999. Dabbiere took the title of chairman, leaving the day-to-day management of the company to Haddrill, who had spent the previous three years serving as president and chief executive officer of Powerhouse Technologies, Inc., a $250 million diversified gaming technology company.

Under Haddrill's leadership, Manhattan celebrated its tenth anniversary and plotted its course for the new decade ahead. Late in the company's anniversary year, it acquired a Mishawaka, Indiana-based company named Intrepa L.L.C., a developer of transportation and distribution applications with more than 100 employees and seven offices in the United States. Intrepa served more than 250 customers in the healthcare, automotive, publishing, and industrial wholesale industries, counting Nissan, Dupont Merck, Gerber Products, and Novartis as some of its better-known clientele. The $30 million transaction was expected to add between $14 million and $18 million to Manhattan's revenue volume, giving the company more than 750 customers in 11 markets. "Intrepa LLC's current technology, broad solution footprint, deep domain expertise, and an impressive client list were key drivers behind our decision to acquire Intrepa," Haddrill remarked in a December 2000 interview with *Manufacturing Systems*.

The early years of the decade marked a serious decline in technology spending, making for a bleak start to the 21st century for many software companies. Manhattan was insulated somewhat from the downturn because of its focus on warehousing. In tight economic times, companies could not afford to have their warehouses in disarray. "Warehouse software is a less discretionary purchase than other areas of technology," an analyst explained in a December 3, 2001 interview with *Investor's Business Daily*. "Customers tend to invest in such software when they have some kind of significant problem. It's not just a matter of getting to the next level of performance." Manhattan's advantageous position as a warehouse specialist in the broader supply-chain software field helped the company record impressive growth while others suffered from the downturn. The company expanded into Germany and France in 2001, ending the year with more than $138 million in revenue. Manhattan's focus on warehousing shielded it from the worst of a recessive economy, but the company's niche in the supply-chain software field also was threatening to become a detriment. The dynamics of the supply-chain execution industry were changing. Manhattan, the "king of warehouse management,"

according to the January 17, 2003 issue of *Investor's Business Daily,* needed to widen the scope of its kingdom.

A More Comprehensive Manhattan Emerging in 2002

Competition within the supply-chain execution industry was taking on a new dimension. Companies larger than Manhattan, competitors such as Manugistics Group Inc., I2 Technologies Inc., and SAP AG, were encroaching on Manhattan's warehouse niche. Each of the three companies offered a wider range of business software than Manhattan, offering their customers a more comprehensive solution to problems along the supply chain. Haddrill needed to extend Manhattan's reach, and in November 2002 he announced a deal that expanded the services the company could provide to its customers. Manhattan agreed to acquire Logistics.com, Inc., a Burlington, Massachusetts-based logistics planning and execution firm. Logistics.com developed software to help trucking and rail companies handle routing and planning, offering three products: OptiManage, a comprehensive transportation management solution for shippers; OptiBid, a procurement solution for shippers; and OptiYield, a decision support and optimization solution for carriers. The acquisition of Logistics.com moved Manhattan out of the warehouse, giving the company the capability to address problems in both distribution and transportation.

As Manhattan reshaped itself from a warehouse management software provider to a broader supply-chain execution provider, changes in leadership set the stage for the company's future. In May 2003, Dabbiere announced he was leaving the company to devote more time to his family. Less than a year later, Haddrill announced he was leaving as well, which led to the appointment of Peter F. Sinisgalli as chief executive officer in July 2004. Under Sinisgalli's stewardship, Manhattan was expected to continue expanding its involvement along the supply chain, as the company endeavored to be not only the king of the warehouse but a dominant player in the supply-chain execution industry as well.

Principal Subsidiaries

Manhattan Associates Software, L.L.C.; Manhattan Associates, Ltd.; Manhattan Associates Europe, B.V.; Manhattan Associates, Pty Ltd.; Manhattan Associates (India) Development Centre Private Limited.

Principal Competitors

Retek, Inc.; Manugistics Group, Inc.; i2 Technologies, Inc.; SAP AG; RedPrairie Corporation; Catalyst International, Inc.

Further Reading

Armbruster, William, "Dabbiere Steps Down As Chairman of Manhattan Associates," *Journal of Commerce Online,* May 22, 2003, p. 15.
Grugal, Robin M., "Manhattan Associates Inc.," *Investor's Business Daily,* December 3, 2001, p. A10.
Hickey, Kathleen, "Sinisgalli to Manhattan Associates," *Traffic World,* March 8, 2004, p. 19.
Michel, Roberto, "Manhattan Associates Acquires Intrepa," *Manufacturing Systems,* December 2000, p. 15.
"Warehouse Software Gets Bigger Inventory of Major Competitors," *Investor's Business Daily,* January 17, 2003, p. A5.

—Jeffrey L. Covell

Marzotto S.p.A.

Largo S. Margherita, 1
36078 Valdagno
Vicenze
Italy
Telephone: (39) 445 42 94 11
Fax: (39) 445 42 76 30
Web site: http://www.marzotto.it

Public Company
Founded: 1836
Employees: 11,077
Sales: EUR 1.73 billion ($2.16 billion) (2003)
Stock Exchanges: Borsa Italiana
Ticker Symbol: MZ
NAIC: 313210 Broadwoven Fabric Mills; 313111 Yarn
    Spinning Mills; 313249 Other Knit Fabric and Lace
    Mills; 314121 Curtain and Drapery Mills; 314129
    Other Household Textile Product Mills; 315222
    Men's and Boys' Cut and Sew Suit, Coat, and
    Overcoat Manufacturing; 315224 Men's and Boys'
    Cut and Sew Trouser, Slack, and Jean Manufacturing;
    315228 Men's and Boys' Cut and Sew Other
    Outerwear Manufacturing; 315232 Women's and
    Girls' Cut and Sew Blouse and Shirt Manufacturing;
    315233 Women's and Girls' Cut and Sew Dress
    Manufacturing; 315234 Women's and Girls' Cut and
    Sew Suit, Coat, Tailored Jacket, and Skirt
    Manufacturing; 315999 Other Apparel Accessories
    and Other Apparel Manufacturing

Marzotto S.p.A. has transformed itself from a textiles-focused company to a brand-centered stable of designer clothing labels. Long Italy's leading textile producer, Marzotto is now one of its biggest designer name groups, steering the dual flagships of Hugo Boss, acquired in 1991, and Valentino, acquired in 2002. The company also produces clothing under the Marlboro Classics label, under license from Philip Morris. Hugo Boss represents the company's largest single holding, producing 60.5 percent of the group's EUR 1.73 billion ($2.16 billion) in sales in 2003. Valentino, which added 8.7 percent to the group's revenues that year, is expected to grow strongly, especially with the 2003 launch of the new Red youth-oriented fashion line. The Marlboro Classic line adds 8.3 percent to group sales. An additional 12.7 percent of sales are generated through the company's other labels, including Arezie, Borgofiori, Lebole, and Principe, and its licenses for Gianfranco Ferré and Missoni. In 2003 the company sold off the bulk of its textiles production, grouped under subsidiary Linificio e Canapificio Nazionale to another Marzotto family holding, Zignago. Textiles, including wool and linen, accounted for nearly 14 percent of Marzotto's revenues in 2003. The Marzotto family remains the company's largest shareholder.

Mid-19th-Century Origins and Early 20th-Century Development

The firm was founded in the town of Valdagno in 1836, before the collection of independent states later known as Italy had even achieved nationhood. Members of the nobility, the Marzottos were by no means poor; Luigi Marzotto established his woolens mill with a capital of 2,000 Venetian Lire, the equivalent of nearly $100,000 in the mid-1990s. He handed the business over to son Gaetano in 1842. The unification of the kingdom of Italy in 1861 opened new markets to the company, and its location in the northeastern region of the nation—which made the transition from an agrarian to an industrial economy more quickly than southern Italy—gave it an advantage over its competitors to the south. By 1866, 200 employees worked the company's carding, spinning, and dyeing machines and weaving looms. An 1880 expansion took the Marzottos to nearby Maglio, where Gaetano built a new spinning factory. The wool industry had by this time become one of Italy's largest, in terms of both employment and production, and enjoyed protective tariffs of up to 40 percent in the waning years of the 19th century.

By the beginning of the 20th century, Marzotto's payroll had risen to more than 1,200. When Gaetano died in 1910, the company was split in two; son Vittorio Emanuele, who has been credited with leading the company into the export business, inherited the Valdagno operations, while Gaetano's grandsons took over the Maglio mill. Despite inflation, high unemployment, and rampant strikes in the period between the two world wars, the Marzotto group continued to grow. In fact, Vittorio was able to open another worsted wool mill during this period. By the time Gaetano Marzotto, Jr., inherited the Valdagno mill from his father in 1921, the company employed more than 2,000.

A company history characterizes Gaetano, Jr., as "an authentic founder of the family business." His efforts at modernization and expansion during the fascist-dominated 1920s strengthened the company to the extent that it not only survived the Great Depression without being nationalized, but also reacquired the family mill in Maglio. The leader capitalized on continental textile manufacturers' difficulties during this period, expanding exports to Eastern Europe, Latin America, and throughout the Mediterranean region. Experiencing difficulty in finding suitable lodgings during his nationwide travels, Gaetano, Jr., also established the Jolly hotel chain, which the Marzotto family would continue to own and operate throughout the 20th century.

Transformation Beginning in the 1950s, Accelerating in the 1970s

Although the company came under government control during World War II, Gaetano resumed ownership at the conflict's end. He capitalized on Italy's "economic miracle"—a period of currency stabilization and exuberant industrial growth from the mid-1940s to the mid-1960s—by diversifying into the manufacture of traditionally styled, private-label menswear during an early 1950s downturn in the core textile business. Although inflation and subsequent wage indexing (quarterly increases that corresponded to the rate of inflation) regularly increased hourly pay, worker unrest began in the late 1960s and continued throughout much of the 1970s. In 1969, striking laborers demolished a statue of patriarch Gaetano Marzotto in the middle of what had become the "company town" of Valdagno.

When Gaetano, Jr., died in 1972, his son Giannino and grandson Pietro inherited an essentially healthy but outdated business. Modernization, both of production and management techniques, intensified under Marzotto's fifth generation of family management. "Stagflation"—slow economic growth combined with hyperinflation—brought a sense of urgency to these efforts. Whereas increases in employment levels had previously been a positive indication of the textile group's condition, high labor expenses made a fat payroll a distinct disadvantage in the 1970s and beyond. Pietro reduced employment from 9,000 in 1976 to 4,500 by 1986 and simultaneously managed to refurbish the company's plants without incurring excessive debt. Having gone public in 1961, the company issued voting shares in 1981. Marzotto started selling its private-label apparel to retailers in the United States in 1973 and by 1985, when the

parent company established an American subsidiary, two-fifths of its ITL 402 billion sales were made outside Italy.

Geographic and Product Diversification Via Acquisition Beginning in the Mid-1980s

The gradual, yet cumulatively revolutionary strategy that unfolded at Marzotto over the decade from 1985 to 1995 incorporated three key goals: reduction of overheads, upmarket expansion in apparel, and elimination of noncore or loss-plagued operations. These objectives were achieved through acquisitions, divestments, restructuring, and internal development.

In a March 1988 interview with *WWD*'s Mark Ganem, Pietro likened his corporate acquisition strategy to a moderate diet, noting, "Even after the best dinner, a big dessert can ruin everything." To illustrate, the company acquired the FinBassetti Group, including its controlling interest in Linificio e Canapificio Nazionale, in 1985, but waited two years while integrating those operations before making a second purchase. The 1987 acquisition of Italy's Lanerossi increased Marzotto's total revenues by more than 72 percent, from ITL 402 billion in 1985 to ITL 691.5 billion in 1986. The ITL 168 billion purchase, which catapulted Marzotto to the top of Italy's textile and apparel heap, was made over bids by such competitors as Benetton, the Bertrand Group, and Cotonificio Cantoni. Furthermore, the addition of Lanerossi made Marzotto Europe's first fully integrated wool producer, incorporating everything "from the sheep to the suit," as Textiles General Manager Elio Lora Lamia told *Daily News Record*'s Elizabeth Chute. Marzotto also acquired France's Le Blan & Fils, a yarn manufacturer, in 1989 and the Biella, Italy-based Guabello wool mill in 1991.

Internal growth was robust as well; even if acquisitions were excluded, revenue increases averaged more than 12 percent from 1983 to 1987. Sales flattened at about ITL 1.5 trillion throughout the remainder of the decade, however, and net income actually declined from ITL 59.7 billion in 1988 to ITL 45.4 billion in 1990.

Marzotto also began to gradually shift its image upmarket in the mid-1980s by launching its own moderately priced men's fashion label, Principe by Marzotto. The company first penetrated the designer market with the 1986 launch of Missoni Uomo, later adding Laura Biagiotti and Gianfranco Ferre to its stable of licensed and house designers. A major turning point in this realm came in 1991, when Marzotto paid Japanese investor Akira Akagi ITL 200 billion ($165 million) for a controlling interest in Hugo Boss, Germany's largest manufacturer of menswear. The Hugo Boss purchase was considered a threefold success: It extended Marzotto's global reach, further strengthened its primary textiles business, and added a widely recognized, high-end brand.

Difficult trading conditions in the Italian economy as well as the global apparel market continued to depress Marzotto's fiscal results in the early years of the decade. Sales increased a cumulative 71 percent, from ITL 1.4 trillion in 1990 to ITL 2.4 trillion ($1.5 billion) in 1995, but net income only rose about 25 percent, from ITL 40.1 billion to ITL 50.1 billion ($32 million).

In response to this tough environment, Marzotto announced in 1992 that it would endeavor to transfer 40 percent of its

---

Key Dates:

1836: Luigi Marzotto founds a woolens mill in Valdagno in 1836.

1880: Marzotto opens a spinning factory in Maglio.

1910: The company is split in two and Vittorio Emanuele Marzotto takes over the Valdagno business, which begins international exports in the 1920s.

1950s: The company diversifies in the manufacturing of private-label menswear.

1961: The company goes public with a listing on the Borsa Italiana (Milan exchange).

1973: The company begins sales of private-label clothing to the United States.

1985: A U.S. subsidiary is established.

1985: Linificio e Canapificio Nazionale is acquired.

1987: The company acquires Lanerossi, becoming the leading Italian textiles group.

1991: Hugo Boss, the largest menswear maker in Germany, is acquired.

1994: The company acquires 90 percent of Czechoslovakia's Nuova Mosilana woolen mill.

1997: Proposed merger with HPI collapses.

2000: The company acquires 84.4 percent of Litekas and Calw, a Lithuanian wool garments manufacturer.

2002: The company acquires Valentino from HPI.

2003: The company sells Linificio e Canapificio Nazionale to Zignago, another Marzotto family holding, as part of refocusing as a luxury fashion group.

2004: Valentino returns to profitability.

---

clothing production overseas in order to reduce labor costs. The revelation that the company would relinquish the unique reputation enjoyed by luxury products ''Made in Italy'' came as a surprise to many observers. Marzotto cut about 600 jobs in its home country that year, closed a domestic clothing plant in 1993, and completed the purchase of a 90 percent stake in Czechoslovakia's Nuova Mosilana woolen mill in 1994.

Refocusing As a Designer Clothing Group for the New Century

The company's grandest move to date came in the spring of 1997, when it announced that it would merge with compatriot HPI to form the world's largest designer clothing manufacturer, Gruppo Industriale Marzotto. The ITL 8 trillion ($4.7 billion) conglomerate would carry names such as Giorgio Armani, Valentino, Calvin Klein, Hugo Boss, and Gianfranco Ferré, and pose formidable competition to giants of the global luxury goods market including France's LVMH Moet Hennessy Louis Vuitton. Marzotto would have owned 12.4 percent of the new company, whose other leading stakeholders would have included Mediobanca (10.5 percent) and Fiat (17.3 percent). But by May 1997, Pietro Marzotto—slated to serve as the new entity's chairman—abruptly pulled out of the deal, citing concerns over strategy, investment policies, and capitalization.

The collapse of the HPI deal led to a shakeup within the Marzotto family, leading Pietro Marzotto to step down as chief executive and turn day-to-day operations over to Jean de Jaeger, who two years previous had become the first non-Marzotto to be promoted to the chief executive office. With nearly 30 years at the company to his credit, the Belgian de Jaeger advanced to executive deputy chairman. Pietro Marzotto nonetheless remained the group's majority shareholder and continued as chairman in charge of corporate strategy.

In 2000, Marzotto joined the de-localization trend in the European textiles industry, purchasing an 84.4 percent stake in Litekas and Calw, a Lithuanian wool garments manufacturer. The acquisition permitted the company to shift part of its textiles production to that lower-cost market.

Yet Marzotto's interest in textiles was beginning to wane. Rising competition from the Far East had sapped most of the profitability from all but the highest-end of the textiles market. Marzotto had continued building up its stable of designer labels and licenses, despite the failure of the HPI merger.

The turning point for the company's new strategy came in 2002, when Marzotto bought out Valentino, which had been struggling under HPI. The price of the acquisition came to $210 million, including nearly $180 million in debt. Marzotto quickly set to work putting together a turnaround strategy for Valentino. Over the next two years, the company worked at revitalizing its ready-to-wear line. In 2003, Valentino launched a new label, Red, designed to capture a share of the fast-growing youth market.

Meanwhile, a new shakeup was taking place within Marzotto itself. In 2002, Pietro Marzotto launched an effort, ostensibly to protect the group from a hostile takeover, whereby the family's Zignago holding company would acquire Marzotto S.p.A. Yet a group of Marzotto family members formed a pact to block the move. In response, Pietro Marzotto announced his decision to retire.

In 2003, however, Marzotto carried out a more limited transfer of its operations, selling its main textiles subsidiary, Linificio e Canapificio Nazionale, to Zignago. Refocused as a fashion house, Marzotto quickly saw results. By the end of 2003, Valentino, which had been losing money under HPI, had returned to profits. The company also saw strong growth at its flagship Hugo Boss subsidiary. With profits surging and sales gaining steadily, Marzotto set its sights on expanding its stable of fashion labels in the new century.

Principal Subsidiaries

Marzotto International N.V. (Netherlands); Marzotto (U.S.A.) Corp.; Alicante S.p.A.; Marzotto France S.a.r.l.; Magnolia S.p.A. (99.81%); Larix S.p.A.; Lanificio Guabello S.p.A. (95.7%); Marzotto International Factor S.p.A. (80%); Nova Mosilana A.S. (Czech Republic); Vincenzo Zucchi S.p.A. (25%); Mascioni S.p.A. (28.3%); Hugo Boss Australia Pty. (35.25%); Lininpianti S.p.A. (44.26%); Paul Le Blan et Fils S.A. (France; 44.26%); Filature de Lin Filin S.A. (Spain; 22.13%).

Principal Competitors

Industria de Diseno Textil S.A.; The Gap Inc.; Hennes & Mauritz AB; Benetton Group S.p.A.; Vivarte; Gruppo Coin S.p.A.;

Kiabi S.A.; La Redoute; Charles Vogele Holding AG; Peek und Cloppenburg KG; Somfy International S.A; Cortefiel S.A.; Mango S.A.

Further Reading

Bannon, Lisa, ''Marzotto Automated Dyehouse Replaces 3,'' *Daily News Record,* June 7, 1989, p. 7.

——, ''Marzotto Planning to Buy U.S. Clothing Manufacturer,'' *Daily News Record,* December 7, 1988, pp. 2–3.

Chute, Elizabeth, ''Marzotto: 150; Lanerossi: 1; Ferre: 000.1,'' *Daily News Record,* January 4, 1988, pp. A50–A51.

Conti, Samantha, ''For Marzotto's CEO: Timing Is Money,'' *Daily News Record,* November 19, 1996, p. 5.

——, ''Italians Streamline for Harder Times,'' *WWD,* February 26, 1997, pp. S10–S11.

——, ''Marzotto Plans to Hit Acquisition Trail,'' *Daily News Record,* May 28, 1997, p. COV.

Forden, Sara Gay, ''Marzotto Makes a Move on Eastern Europe,'' *WWD,* October 21, 1992, p. 23.

——, ''Marzotto to the Market and the Market to Marzotto,'' *Daily News Record,* June 20, 1994, pp. 16–17.

——, ''More Italy Producers Look Offshore for Less-Expensive Manufacturing,'' *Daily News Record,* June 29, 1992, p. 6.

Forden, Sara Gay, and Samantha Conti, ''End of the Affair: Marzotto-HPI Deal Suddenly Called Off,'' *WWD,* May 5, 1997, pp. 1–2.

Ganem, Mark, ''Marzotto 'Designs' a Future,'' *WWD,* March 30, 1988, p. 50.

Gellers, Stan, ''De Jaeger to Become CEO of Marzotto SpA on Jan. 1,'' *Daily News Record,* September 27, 1995, p. 2.

——, ''Sighs of Relief in U.S. Market As Marzotto-HPI Merger Falters,'' *Daily News Record,* May 7, 1997, p. 1.

Gellers, Stan, Samantha Conti, and Miles Socha, ''U.S. Retailers Give Marzotto, HPI Merger a Thumbs-Up,'' *Daily News Record,* March 12, 1997, pp. COV.

Kaiser, Amanda, ''Marzotto Sees Valentino Turnaround,'' *WWD,* November 24, 2003, p. 3.

''A New Breed for the New Money,'' *Economist,* March 15, 1986, pp. 71–72.

''Tailoring Marzotto's Future in the Luxury Arena,'' *WWD,* December 4, 2002, p. 17.

Wilson, Eric, ''Valentino Rejuvenation on Track,'' *WWD,* October 30, 2003, p. 3.

Zargani, Luisa, ''Boss, Textiles Help Marzotto Triple Profit,'' *Daily News Record,* September 20, 2004, p. 8.

—April Dougal Gasbarre
—update: M.L. Cohen

Medtronic, Inc.

710 Medtronic Parkway
Minneapolis, Minnesota 55432-5604
U.S.A.
Telephone: (763) 514-4000
Fax: (763) 514-4879
Web site: http://www.medtronic.com

Public Company
Incorporated: 1957
Employees: 31,000
Sales: $9.09 billion (2004)
Stock Exchanges: New York
Ticker Symbol: MDT
NAIC: 334510 Electromedical and Electrotherapeutic
Apparatus Manufacturing; 339113 Surgical Appliance
and Supplies Manufacturing; 339112 Surgical and
Medical Instrument Manufacturing

Medtronic, Inc. is the world's leading medical technology company, controlling more than half of the $8 billion global heart-pacing market, which includes pacemakers and defibrillators. The company's products and services also include implantable neurological pain, tremor, spasticity, and incontinence management systems; heart valves; catheters and stents for angioplasty; implantable drug administration systems; hydrocephalic shunts; autotransfusion equipment; disposable devices for handling and monitoring blood during surgery; and instruments and devices used in surgical procedures of the head and spine and by ear, nose, and throat physicians. Headquartered in Minneapolis, Minnesota, the company conducts business in more than 120 countries; some two-thirds of revenues are generated domestically, with 20 percent originating in Europe and 10 percent in the Asia-Pacific region.

Early History

Medtronic was founded as an outgrowth of Earl Bakken's part-time work at Minneapolis's Northwestern Hospital. Although much of his time was consumed with graduate studies in electrical engineering, Bakken found time to repair the centrifuges, electrocardiograph machines, and other intricate electronic equipment at the hospital. Bakken and his brother-in-law, Palmer Hermundslie, surmised that they could make a living at repairing medical equipment. In 1949 Bakken quit school, and Hermundslie left his job at a local lumber company so that they could form the medical equipment repair service they dubbed "Medtronic."

Bakken and Hermundslie initially worked out of a small garage in Minneapolis. During Medtronic's difficult first year, there was one month the business grossed a meager eight dollars. In 1950, however, the partners contracted as sales representatives for the Sanborn Company, the Gilford Instrument Company, and Advanced Instruments, Inc. In the early part of the decade more than half of their sales in the five-state region around Minneapolis came from selling the merchandise of the other companies.

As Bakken gained experience with medical professionals and their instruments, he was called upon to advise them in their experiments. Over the course of Medtronic's first decade Bakken built nearly 100 custom-made—often single-use—devices for medical research. Soon Medtronic was manufacturing several medical research products, including two types of defibrillators, as well as forceps, an animal respirator, a cardiac rate monitor, and a physiologic stimulator.

Advent of the Pacemaker

Medtronic's history became inextricably connected to the history of open-heart surgery. Electrically stimulated pacemaking had taken off in the 1950s when several physicians developed external machines that extended the lives of patients who otherwise would have died. These early pacemakers, however, had several disadvantages. The high-voltage electrodes they used often burned patients' skin, the devices were large and unmanageable, and they had to be plugged into the wall, thus restricting patients' mobility and making power failures life-threatening events.

During the late 1950s Dr. C. Walton Lillehei, a pioneer of open-heart surgery at the University of Minnesota Medical School, was researching a battery-powered device that would

Company Perspectives:

Mission: To contribute to human welfare by application of biomedical engineering in the research, design, manufacture, and sale of instruments or appliances that alleviate pain, restore health, and extend life; to direct our growth in the areas of biomedical engineering where we display maximum strength and ability; to gather people and facilities that tend to augment these areas; to continuously build on these areas through education and knowledge assimilation; to avoid participation in areas where we cannot make unique and worthy contributions; to strive without reserve for the greatest possible reliability and quality in our products; to be the unsurpassed standard of comparison and to be recognized as a company of dedication, honesty, integrity, and service; to make a fair profit on current operations to meet our obligations, sustain our growth, and reach our goals; to recognize the personal worth of employees by providing an employment framework that allows personal satisfaction in work accomplished, security, advancement opportunity, and means to share in the company's success; to maintain good citizenship as a company.

conduct a mild electric shock to the surface of a patient's heart in order to combat the heart block that caused fatalities in about 10 percent of open-heart surgeries. In 1957 Lillehei asked Bakken, who worked part-time repairing medical electronics at the school, to design an appropriate device. Within six weeks Bakken returned to Lillehei with the world's first transistorized, battery-operated, wearable pacemaker. By the end of the decade use of the devices had extended beyond the United States to Canada, Australia, Cuba, Europe, Africa, and South America. Bakken's invention was honored by the National Society of Professional Engineers as one of ten outstanding engineering products for the period from 1954 to 1984, and Medtronic earned a reputation as a front-running producer of biomedical engineering devices.

The partnership between electronics and cardiac research continued to advance open-heart surgery—and Medtronic—throughout the 1950s. Dr. Samuel Hunter of St. Joseph's Hospital research laboratory in St. Paul, Minnesota, worked with Norman Roth, an electrical engineer at Medtronic, to create the so-called Hunter-Roth electrode, which required about 70 percent less current than Bakken's pacemaker system. In 1958 Dr. William Chardack and electrical engineer Wilson Greatbatch built the first implantable pacemaker in the United States. The device, which incorporated the Hunter-Roth bipolar wire lead, was first successfully implanted in a human in 1960. By October of that year Medtronic had purchased the exclusive rights to produce and market what was called the "Chardack-Greatbatch implantable pulse generator."

Rapid Growth in the 1960s

The growing company organized its distribution outside the United States and Canada through the employment of the Picker International Corporation of White Plains, New York. Picker specialized in electrical medical equipment sales and had an inter-

national network of 72 foreign sales offices. Fourteen Medtronic sales representatives covered the United States and Canada beginning in 1960. The company introduced several products that year, including the Telecor heart monitor; the Cardiac Sentinel, an alarm that automatically summoned aid when a patient's heart rate became critical and stimulated the heart; and the Coagulation Generator, which stanched bleeding during surgery.

The growing product line and increasing demand required that the company move to a new, larger facility in 1961. Despite Medtronic's dramatic sales increases—from $180,000 to more than $500,000 from 1960 to 1962—the company incurred losses during the same period. Expenses, such as the appointment of Picker International, the cost of building a new headquarters, new product research, and attendance at major medical and engineering conventions, increased faster than sales. Early in 1962 the company eased its financial tensions through a bond offering of $200,000 and a $100,000 bank loan. The credit helped Medtronic turn a profit of $17,000 for the first three months of fiscal 1962.

Research continued throughout the 1960s on Medtronic's most important product, the implantable pacemaker. Enhancing the company's pacemaker sales was the introduction of Medicare in 1965, which provided U.S. government funding of healthcare for citizens over the age of 65 and thus increased the use of pacemakers. Among Medtronic's new pacemaker products was an endocardial catheter, a wire lead inserted through the jugular vein to the heart. When pacemakers with this "transvenous" lead were introduced to the market in 1965, they seized a substantial portion of pacemaker sales. In the mid-1960s Medtronic also introduced external and implantable pacemakers that compensated for irregular heartbeats.

New product introductions and pacemaker improvements helped sales surge to more than $12 million by the end of the 1967–68 fiscal year. Profits increased dramatically as well, exceeding $1 million that year. Medtronic established a European Service Center in 1967 to provide technical support for the continent, which generated 80 percent of overseas sales. In late 1969 Medtronic formed its own international division to accommodate direct European sales. In 1970 the company was able to drop its contract with Picker International and control international sales, which accounted for 30 percent of total sales by that time. Direct sales offices were established in 19 countries, and technical centers and manufacturing plants were erected in primary markets.

Medtronic also gained control of its primary North American distributors during the late 1960s and early 1970s. In 1968 the company purchased John Hay & Company, Ltd., a medical sales organization headquartered in Vancouver, British Columbia. The A.F. Morrison Company was acquired the following year, and by 1973 Medtronic accomplished complete jurisdiction over its North American sales with the purchase of the Medical Specialty Company and Corvek Medical Equipment.

Continued Growth Through the 1970s

Medtronic reached several milestones during the 1970s. The company surpassed $100 million in annual sales in 1975, and in 1977 Medtronic stock was listed on the New York Stock Exchange. Globally Medtronic commanded a market share of

---

Key Dates:

1949: Earl Bakken and Palmer Hermundslie form a partnership called Medtronic to service and repair medical equipment.

1957: Bakken develops the world's first small, wearable, battery-operated external pacemaker; company is incorporated as Medtronic, Inc.

1960: Medtronic purchases the exclusive rights to produce and market an implantable pacemaker known as the "Chardack-Greatbatch implantable pulse generator."

1969: An international division is formed to accommodate direct European sales.

1976: Neurological Division is established.

1977: Medtronic stock is listed on the New York Stock Exchange; company establishes its Heart Valves Division and introduces the Medtronic Hall mechanical heart valve.

1981: The Spectrax SXT programmable pacemaker is introduced.

1985: The Activitrax "rate-responsive" pacemaker makes its debut.

1993: Medtronic introduces the PCD defibrillator.

1998: Physio-Control International Corporation, maker of external defibrillators, is acquired.

1999: Medtronic acquires Sofamor Danek Group, Arterial Vascular Engineering, and Xomed Surgical Products.

2001: MiniMed Inc., producer of devices for patients with diabetes, is acquired; company introduces InSync, the first electrical device for treating congestive heart failure.

---

35 percent in the pacemaker category. By the end of the decade, Medtronic's annual sales exceeded $200 million. The company also began to diversify into other medical fields and regions. In 1976 Medtronic established its Neurological Division, which developed products to help relieve chronic and acute pain. A year later Medtronic founded its Heart Valves Division and launched the Hall mechanical heart valve. The company also established a headquarters in Latin America, as well as one in Europe. Manufacturing facilities in Puerto Rico, Canada, and France followed. By the end of the decade Medtronic had made its first major acquisition, Medical Data Systems, an Ann Arbor, Michigan, nuclear imaging company.

Medtronic remained primarily a pacemaker company, however, and cardiovascular products developed for the diagnosis and treatment of heart disease included a nuclear-powered pacemaker. Medtronic's pacemakers were also made smaller, more resilient, and more reliable during the decade. The company consolidated pacemaker production vertically through the creation of Micro-Rel, Inc., a manufacturer of hybrid circuits, and the acquisition of Energy Technology—later renamed Promeon—a producer of lithium batteries. Other cardiovascular equipment developed in the 1970s helped physicians diagnose patients instantaneously and monitor them by telephone. Cardiovascular products contributed the bulk of Medtronic's sales.

Despite the company's success, the 1970s was not a trouble-free decade for Medtronic. Like many U.S. companies, Medtronic was affected by high inflation during the late 1970s. Tougher regulatory policies instituted by the U.S. Nuclear Regulatory Commission and the Food and Drug Administration also increased research costs through requirements for tougher clinical and follow-up testing. In 1976 Medtronic was forced to issue its first major product recall after the company discovered a technical flaw with the Xytron pacemaker. Medtronic's U.S. market share subsequently fell from 60 percent to 40 percent.

Medtronic experienced several leadership changes during the 1970s. In 1974 Bakken gave up the day-to-day responsibilities of the presidency to become chairman of the board. Thomas E. Holloran replaced him for two years, followed by Dale R. Olseth, who was elected president and chief executive officer.

Diversification in the 1980s

In the 1980s Medtronic sought to expand its product line further while keeping its strong emphasis on pacemakers. Routine reinvestment of more than 8 percent of annual revenues during the decade fueled research and development of new and improved medical devices, and by 1981 annual sales reached another milestone—the $300 million mark. William R. Wallin was named president and CEO in 1985, and diversification became a corporate goal.

Computer technology helped Medtronic develop pacemakers that catered to a patient's particular requirements. The Spectrax SXT, a programmable pacemaker that could be reprogrammed after the initial implantation without performing surgery, led the market soon after its release in 1981. In 1985 the Activitrax pacemaker was the first such device to automatically adjust the rate of heart stimulation in accordance with the rate of activity. After its introduction to the market in 1986, the Activitrax quickly claimed 20 percent of the pacemaker category. That same year Medtronic solidified its position in this market for "rate-responsive pacing" with the purchase of Biotech of Bologna, Italy, and Vitatron of Dieren in the Netherlands. Breakthrough products in the late 1980s included CapSure steroid leads, which were designed to ease tissue inflammation, and Synergyst pacemakers, which united dual chamber and rate-responsive pacing.

Medtronic expanded into the fields of cardiac surgery and vascular therapies in the late 1980s through new products and acquisitions. Among the product lines new to Medtronic were tissue heart values, coronary angioplasty catheters, and tissue heart valves. Among the companies Medtronic acquired were Johnson & Johnson Cardiovascular, which produced the industry leading Maxima membrane oxygenator, a device used during open-heart surgery to reoxygenate blood, and Versaflex Delivery Systems, Inc., a company that made coronary angioplasty catheters. The company also began to develop neurological and drug delivery services, including the SynchroMed Drug Delivery System, the first implantable and programmable drug delivery system. Neurological devices introduced in the late 1980s included the Selectra and ComfortWave electrical nerve stimulators, used to treat sprains and back pain. La Jolla Technology, Inc., another producer of electrical nerve stimulators, was acquired in 1987 to strengthen Medtronic's position in this industry.

Medtronic's rapid growth and expansion, however, was not without setbacks. In 1983 Medtronic voluntarily recalled a new pacemaker lead when it recorded relatively high failure rates in clinical tests. These disadvantages resulted in slowed pacemaker sales, and in 1985 Medtronic reported its first year without an increase in sales and earnings. Medtronic was also involved in expensive patent litigation with such large medical manufacturers as Eli Lilly & Co. and Siemens AG during the decade.

Despite a few bumps in the road, Medtronic was able to increase its annual sales from $300 million in 1981 to $755 million in 1988 through numerous acquisitions and the development of new technologies. By the end of the decade, Medtronic had moved beyond its position as a pacemaker manufacturer and had become a major medical technology corporation.

Continuing Expansion in the Early 1990s

In 1991 William W. George became president and CEO, succeeding Wallin, who became chairman of the board, and Medtronic's total sales exceeded $1 billion. Medtronic had developed six primary areas of expertise by the early 1990s: bradycardia pacing, tachyarrhythmia management, heart valves, and cardiopulmonary, interventional vascular, and neurological devices. In 1992 the company's international sales contributed 40 percent of total revenues, justifying new facilities and expanded operations in Japan, China, and Eastern Europe, as well as increased focus on such developing nations as India and China and on countries in Latin America and Africa.

Continuing with its diversification strategy, Medtronic acquired a number of companies during the first half of the decade, including TUR, a German pacemaker manufacturer; Bio-Medicus, Inc., the world's largest maker of centrifugal blood pumps; PS Medical, Inc., a maker of shunts, devices designed to prevent fluid buildup in the brain; and DLP, Inc., which developed cardiac cannulae used in surgery. These acquisitions helped solidify Medtronic's lead in the area of medical technology and advanced the company's presence in new fields. In 1995, according to the *Minneapolis Star Tribune*, Medtronic had a 49 percent share of the conventional pacemaker market, 32 percent of the implantable defibrillator market, and 75 percent in nerve-related devices.

Medtronic stepped up its product development cycles and continued to feed its research and development budget—the company spent about 11 percent of total revenues on research and development in 1995, up from 9.4 percent in 1990—to survive in the increasingly competitive medical technology marketplace. The Thera line of pacemakers took about 27 months from final design to market introduction, about half the pacemaker design cycle of the mid-1980s. Medtronic's focus on product development resulted in a number of pioneering devices during the first part of the decade, including the PCD defibrillator (1993), the Jewel implantable cardioverter-defibrillator, implantable Transvene taccharrhythmia leads, the Model 9790 pacemaker programmer, and additional models of the SynchroMed Drug Delivery System, including one for the treatment of chronic spasticity.

Accelerated Development in the Late 1990s

In the second half of the decade, Medtronic adopted an increasingly aggressive expansion strategy to survive in the medical product field, which had been consolidated into a handful of large medical technology companies. The pacemaker category, Medtronic's core business, was expected to slow in growth, and the company intended to stave off declining profits through diversification. Medtronic's revenues exceeded $2 billion in 1996, and the company continued its acquisition and new product introduction efforts. In 1995 Medtronic added Micro Interventional Systems, Inc., a developer of catheters designed to treat stroke victims, to its neurological division. A year later the company acquired Synectics Medical AB of Sweden, which made systems for gastroenterology, urology, and sleep apnea; InStent, a stent manufacturer; and AneuRx, a maker of endovascular stented grafts. Between 1996 and 1998 Medtronic introduced a number of new products, including the Micro Jewel II, an implantable cardioverter-defibrillator; the Wiktor Prime coronary stent, designed to support the walls of a coronary artery; and the Activa Tremor Control System, which helped treat tremors associated with Parkinson's disease.

Amid the flurry of sales growth—during the second quarter of fiscal 1997, Medtronic's pacemaker sales grew 9 percent, implantable defibrillator sales increased 27 percent, and its neurological product sales grew more than 60 percent—the company's vascular operations, which included catheters and stents, were not doing as well as the company had hoped. Although the coronary stent market was growing rapidly, Medtronic was unable to successfully market stents, and as a result the company was forced in early 1998 to take its first business-related charge since 1985. The company also announced plans to close eight manufacturing plants and downsize its staff by 600 employees.

Medtronic was also losing market share in the defibrillator category to strong competition, particularly from Guidant Corporation, which offered a technologically advanced dual-chamber defibrillator that grabbed about 25 percent of the U.S. defibrillator market soon after its introduction in 1998. Medtronic was the leader in the $1.8 billion global defibrillator industry, which was growing at the breakneck rate of about 30 percent a year, but according to Sanford Bernstein & Co.'s Kenneth Abramowitz, as reported in the *Wall Street Journal*, in the United States Medtronic held some 40 to 45 percent of the market, while Guidant had a share of 45 to 50 percent. Medtronic fought back in September 1998, however, by acquiring Physio-Control International Corporation, a maker of external defibrillators, in its largest acquisition to that date.

Medtronic's problems were relatively minor in comparison to its outstanding growth in 1998. Medtronic acquired Avecor Cardiovascular, Inc. to expand its cardiac surgery operation, and Midas Rex LP, a maker of pneumatic instruments for neurological surgery. Through its acquisitions Medtronic grew by 45 percent in 1998. Medtronic also opened a new pacemaker manufacturing facility in Europe in that year and was honored as one of the 100 best companies to work for by *Fortune* magazine.

As Medtronic entered its 50th anniversary year in 1999, the company showed no signs of slowing down. Among the new products introduced by the company were the Medtronic.Kappa 700, a series of pacemakers designed to adapt automatically to patient needs; the InSync stimulator, a device used to treat heart failure; and the Gem implantable defibrillator series. By the close of fiscal 1999, which ended in April, Medtronic had acquired two more companies in two huge stock-swap transactions. Sofamor Danek Group, Inc., the leader in spinal disorder treatment and cranial surgery (acquired for about $3.6 billion), significantly boosted Medtronic's neurology division, and according to *Health Industry Today,* the $4.3 billion purchase of Arterial Vascular Engineering, Inc., increased Medtronic's market share to a commanding 40 percent of the $3.5 billion global market in coronary stents.

Medtronic reported that fiscal 1999 represented the company's 14th consecutive year of increased revenues, with nearly one-third of its revenue attributed to operations in Europe, Africa, and the Middle East. Not only was Medtronic enjoying increased sales but the company was also leading the pack in terms of product development. According to the U.S. Patent and Trademark Office, Medtronic was issued the most medical device patents in the world from 1969 to September 1998; to remain competitive in the aggressive medical device industry, Medtronic planned to invest nearly $500 million in research and development in fiscal 2000.

As Medtronic approached the new millennium, the company continued to strengthen its four primary product platforms: cardiac rhythm management, neurological and spinal surgery, vascular devices, and cardiac surgery. In November 1999 Medtronic acquired Xomed Surgical Products, Inc., the leading manufacturer of surgical products used to treat ear, nose, and throat problems, for approximately $800 million. This acquisition, according to Medtronic, was aimed at positioning the company as the global market leader in the ear, nose, and throat category. Revenues for fiscal 2000 surpassed the $5 billion mark for the first time.

Reaching New Heights in the Early 2000s

In April 2001 George retired as CEO. In his ten years at the helm, Medtronic's revenues grew from around $1 billion to $5.55 billion, earnings jumped from $133 million to $1.3 billion, and the firm's market value leaped from $3.3 billion to $54 billion; he had also transformed the firm from primarily a manufacturer of pacemakers to a diversified medical technology company. Succeeding George was Arthur D. Collins, Jr., who had served as president since 1996 and had played a significant role in assimilating the many businesses acquired during the late 1990s. George remained on the company board as chairman for one more year, until April 2002, whereupon Collins was elected to that position as well.

Collins's first year at the helm was noteworthy for Medtronic's entrance into two new sectors: devices to treat diabetes and congestive heart failure, both of which were chronic diseases affecting millions of patients around the world. In August 2001 the company spent $3.8 billion in cash for MiniMed Inc. and a related company called Medical Research Group, Inc. (later combined as Medtronic MiniMed). Northridge, California-based MiniMed was the leading U.S. producer of insulin infusion pumps for patients with diabetes, and also produced glucose monitors. Medical Research Group was working to develop both an implantable insulin pump and a fully implanted glucose sensor, hoping that these two devices,

working together, could work as a sort of artificial pancreas. Also during 2001 Medtronic introduced InSync, the first electrical device ever approved for treating patients with congestive heart failure. InSync was designed to resynchronize the beating of an otherwise weakened and uncoordinated heart muscle.

Acquisitions and new product introductions continued in 2002. In April Medtronic paid $328.6 million for VidaMed, Inc., maker of a transurethral needle ablation system for treating enlarged prostate glands nonsurgically. Medtronic also acquired Spinal Dynamic Corporation (SDC) in a $254.3 million transaction completed in October 2002. SDC was developing an artificial disc as a replacement for a degenerated cervical disc, with the purported advantages including a shorter recovery time after spinal surgery and increased neck mobility. Among the new products debuting that year were the InSync ICD, which not only resynchronized the beating of a diseased heart but also provided a defibrillator backup; and InFuse, a genetically engineered bone-growth product used in spinal fusion surgery. Also introduced was Medtronic CareLink, an Internet-based network that enabled patients to send data from their implanted defibrillators to their doctors, thereby reducing the number of necessary office visits.

Earnings were negatively affected in 2002 when Medtronic agreed to pay Boston Scientific Corporation $175 million to settle several patent-infringement lawsuits involving coronary stents. In another case involving stent patents owned by Cordis Corporation, a subsidiary of Johnson & Johnson, Medtronic was in the process of appealing a $271 million jury verdict—a case that appeared headed to the U.S. Supreme Court. Further uncertainty arose in September 2003 when the U.S. Department of Justice notified Medtronic that its Medtronic Sofamor Danek spinal surgery unit was the subject of an investigation into allegations of illegal kickbacks to physicians.

Medtronic enjoyed its best year ever in fiscal 2004. Net income fell just short of $2 billion, reaching $1.96 billion, while revenues of $9.09 billion represented an 18 percent increase over the previous year's total. The year ended with both good and bad news. On the one hand, Medtronic received U.S. Food and Drug Administration approval of its EnPulse system, the first fully automatic pacemaker for hearts that beat too slowly. On the other, the company announced that it was recalling 1,800 implanted heart defibrillators after some of them malfunctioned and may have caused the deaths of four patients. Medtronic was also attempting to regain lost ground in its vascular business, which had seen competitors surge ahead by introducing drug-coated stents designed to prevent reblockage of coronary arteries. Medtronic entered into a joint venture with Abbott Laboratories to develop a Medtronic stent coated with an Abbott drug. The company hoped to introduce the product to the U.S. market by the end of 2005.

Principal Subsidiaries

Medtronic Asia, Ltd.; Medtronic AVE, Inc.; Medtronic Europe Sàrl (Switzerland); Medtronic International, Ltd.; Medtronic Limited (U.K.); Medtronic MiniMed, Inc.; Medtronic of Canada, Ltd.; Medtronic Physio-Control International, Inc.; Medtronic Sofamor Danek, Inc.; Medtronic Xomed, Inc.; Vitatron N.V. (Netherlands).

Principal Operating Units

Cardiac Rhythm Management (CRM); Spinal, Ear, Nose and Throat (ENT) and Surgical Navigation Technologies (SNT); Neurological and Diabetes; Vascular; Cardiac Surgery.

Principal Competitors

Guidant Corporation; St. Jude Medical, Inc.; Johnson & Johnson; Zimmer Holdings, Inc.; Boston Scientific Corporation; Stryker Corporation; Edwards Lifesciences Corporation.

Further Reading

Alexander, Steve, "New Product Machine," *Minneapolis Star Tribune,* June 5, 1995, p. D1.

Arndt, Michael, "High Tech—and Handcrafted: Despite a Recent Recall, Medtronic Sets the Quality Standard for Heart Care," *Business Week,* July 5, 2004, p. 86.

Barshay, Jill J., "Medical Devices," *Minneapolis Star Tribune,* September 22, 1998, p. D1.

Black, Sam, "Collins Ready to Take Helm," *Minneapolis-St. Paul CityBusiness,* April 27, 2001, pp. 1, 40.

Burton, Thomas M., "Medtronic's Stock Price Falls 10% on Warning of Earnings Shortfall," *Wall Street Journal,* August 7, 1998, p. B5.

——, "Medtronic to Buy MiniMed and Medical Research," *Wall Street Journal,* May 31, 2001, p. A3.

——, "Medtronic to Name Collins to Succeed George As CEO," *Wall Street Journal,* August 24, 2000, p. B4.

Dubashi, Jagannath, "Change of Pace," *Financial World,* March 17, 1992, pp. 26–27.

Fiedler, Terry, "Medtronic Bucks the Trend," *Minneapolis Star Tribune,* December 16, 2002, p. 1D.

Lau, Gloria, "Companies in the News—Device Maker Medtronic Inc. Steps Up Defibrillator Efforts," *Investor's Business Daily,* July 21, 1998, p. A33.

Mathews, Anna Wilde, and Thomas M. Burton, "Invasive Procedure: After Medtronic Lobbying Push, the FDA Had Change of Heart," *Wall Street Journal,* July 9, 2004, pp. A1+.

Medtronic Beginnings, Minneapolis: Medtronic, Inc., 1993.

McLean, Bethany, "How Smart Is Medtronic Really?," *Fortune,* October 25, 1999, pp. 173–74+.

Moore, Michael P., "The Genesis of Minnesota's Medical Alley," *University of Minnesota Medical Bulletin,* Winter 1992, pp. 7-13.

Nelson, Glen D., "A Brief History of Cardiac Pacing," *Texas Heart Institute Journal,* vol. 20, 1993, pp. 12–18.

Royer, Mary-Paige, "Picking Up the Pace," *Corporate Report-Minnesota,* December 1989, pp. 46+.

Sherer, Paul M., "Medtronic Has Fans, but Doubters, Too," *Wall Street Journal,* December 31, 1998, p. C1.

Stevens, Tim, "Heart and Soul," *Industry Week,* May 4, 1998, pp. 44+.

The Story of Medtronic, Minneapolis: Medtronic, Inc., 1997.

Toward Man's Full Life, Minneapolis: Medtronic, Inc., 1990.

Veverka, Mark, "Plugged In: Acquisition Indigestion Could Cause Pacemaker King Medtronic to Skip a Beat," *Barron's,* September 20, 1999, pp. 57–58.

Whitford, David, "A Human Place to Work," *Fortune,* January 8, 2001, pp. 108–112+.

—April Dougal Gasbarre
—updates: Mariko Fujinaka, David E. Salamie

National Journal Group Inc.

1501 M Street, NW
Suite 300
Washington, D.C. 20005
U.S.A.
Telephone: (202) 739-8400
Fax: (202) 833-8069
Web site: http://www.nationaljournal.com

Private Company
Founded: 1969
Employees: 200
Sales: $30 million (2003 est.)
NAIC: 511120 Periodical Publishers

National Journal Group Inc. (NJ), based in Washington, D.C., is a nonpartisan publisher of daily, weekly, and monthly magazines and newsletters, as well as books and directories, devoted to politics and government, targeting a professional audience. Some of the company's material is also available online. NJ's flagship publication is *National Journal,* a weekly magazine that is best known for in-depth coverage on select topics. It is geared toward an exclusive audience, one willing to pay $1,700 for a yearly subscription. Published monthly, *Government Executive* caters to senior federal managers. In addition, a companion web site offers daily news updates. Daily publications include *CongressDaily,* a news service serving the U.S. Congress; the *Hotline,* offering inside information on politics and campaigns; *American Health Line,* which provides news regarding the business, policy, and politics of the healthcare industry; and *Technology Daily,* devoted to news about the policy and politics of information technology. NJ's book publishing efforts include *The Almanac of American Politics,* an encyclopedic look at politicians and politics. Directories include *The Capital Source,* a listing of some 6,500 important people and organizations in the nation's capital, and *The Federal Technology Source,* which provides the names of the most important people and organizations involved in technology at the federal level. Sister publications include *Government Exec-*

utive and the venerable *Atlantic Monthly.* NJ is owned by Washington, D.C., native and millionaire David G. Bradley.

Roots Dating to the Late 1960s

The *National Journal* magazine was founded in 1969 by 30-year-old New York attorney Anthony Carder Stout and New York investment banker Randy Smith, their goal to publish a magazine that covered the executive branch in much the same way *Congressional Quarterly* reported on Congress. The narrow focus did not work, however, and after spending a great deal of money, Smith walked away from the venture in 1975. At this point Stout hired John Fox Sullivan from *Newsweek* to serve as publisher, and *National Journal* now began to find a workable formula. Perhaps the most important step was to drop the original idea of focusing on the executive branch, expanding the magazine's purview to include all aspects of the federal government. Sullivan also determined that the best approach was to be nonpartisan and nonideological. As he explained to *Columbia Journalism Review* in a 2002 profile, the goal was not to be an encyclopedia: "We would pick and choose. We would be forward-looking—not what happened last week, but what might happen next year, the next ten years. We would write about issues in depth. But we would never say who should win this game. At most we would write about who was behind it, and what their strategies were." In 1977 *National Journal* adopted a new design for its cover, featuring a maroon background with white typeface, a look that would remain unchanged for the next 20 years.

Despite the many improvements Sullivan brought to the magazine, it failed to make the grade as a commercial property. In 1986 Stout decided to sell *National Journal* to Times Mirror Co. His Government Publishing Corp. owned 80 percent of *National Journal,* while the balance was owned by the *Washington Post,* which subsequently sold its interest to the new owner as well. Times Mirror was the media empire spawned by the *Los Angeles Times.* In the 1960s it branched into specialized publishing adding Year Book Medical Publishers and art book publisher Harry B. Abrams, as well as magazines *Popular Science, Outdoor Life, Golf Magazine,* and *Ski Magazine.* The company also added cable television operations, followed later by individual television stations. Other newspapers, such as the *Dallas Times Herald,* Long Island's *Newsday,* the *Hartford Courant,* the *Denver Post,* and the *Baltimore Sun* were acquired in the 1970s and 1980s. In addition, Times Mirror acquired the 100-year-old *Sporting News* and became involved in the medical information field. With revenues approaching $3 billion and profits exceeding $400 million by the mid-1980s, the $10 million purchase of obscure *National Journal* and other assets of Government Publishing Corp. caused little stir. The publication had a circulation of around 5,000, but although little known to the general public it did carry some clout with influential people in both the upper reaches of business and the national government. For Times-Mirror it was essentially a prestige buy, one that was not expected to have much of an impact on the bottom line. The magazine's management stayed on board and no significant changes were made. Stout remained the head of the magazine's board for another three years and Sullivan continued on as publisher.

During the decade that Times Mirror owned *National Journal,* other assets were added, resulting in the creation of National Journal Group to act as a holding company. Monthly *Government Executive* was purchased and brought into the fold. *CongressDaily,* a twice-daily fax newsletter service covering the House of Representatives and the U.S. Senate was launched in 1991, but not without some controversy. NJ and Times-Mirror were sued by Alexandria, Virginia-based Bulletin Broadfaxing Network Inc., which alleged NJ had committed fraud and misappropriated trade secrets. Bulletin had been created a year earlier and launched a daily fax newsletter covering the White House and federal government called the *White House Bulletin.* According to Bulletin, in the fall of 1990 it was in the process of developing a second fax publication to cover Congress and Capital Hill when an NJ official made buyout overtures. During the subsequent negotiations, Bulletin allegedly discussed in detail its plans for *Congressional Bulletin* with Sullivan and other NJ officials. A deal to acquire Bulletin was tentatively arranged and only awaited approval from Times Mirror, but in the end Times Mirror decided that because of poor economic conditions it was putting a temporary halt to any further acquisitions. The company's newspaper segment was hit particularly hard, leading to a 40 percent drop in net income for the year. Unable to acquire Bulletin, NJ opted to launch its own congressional fax publication, which prompted Bulletin to sue. In the end there was little the small company could do to stop NJ's *CongressDaily* venture. Not only did Bulletin have to take on giant Times Mirror, the truth was that fax technology was hardly new and other Times Mirror publications were already producing fax publications.

Parent Company Struggling in the Early 1990s

Times Mirror continued to struggle in the early 1990s. It suffered a net loss of more than $66 million in 1992, the first

loss in three decades. The company named a new chairman in 1995: Mark Willes, who had been vice-chairman at General Mills and a specialist in slashing costs. Over the next two years he cut the workforce, eliminated the evening edition of the *Baltimore Sun,* and closed down Long Island *Newsday*'s attempt to establish a New York City edition. *National Journal* also was tightly controlled on the cost side, an approach that limited the level of editorial talent the magazine could afford to hire. As was the case when Times Mirror purchased *National Journal* the sale of National Journal Group in 1997 to David G. Bradley was not noticed by the general public.

Bradley was an unlikely media mogul. He was born in Washington, D.C., in 1953, and early on developed an interest in politics, in particular Republican politics. His lofty goal was to become a senator by the age of 30. He got a taste for the government from the highest level when at the age of 18 he was employed by Richard Nixon's presidential campaign of 1972, earning $60 a week working for the Committee to Re-Elect the President, which would gain notoriety from the Watergate scandal, leading to Nixon's resignation from office. Before that moment, however, Bradley would serve as an intern in the Nixon White House while earning a B.A. in political science at Swarthmore College. He later earned an M.B.A. from Harvard University as well as a law degree from Georgetown University. In 1979 Bradley launched a for-profit research firm, the Advisory Board, starting out with four Princess telephones and four card tables in his mother's apartment in the Watergate building. The company had an open-ended mission to conduct any kind of research for any company in any industry. His underlying goal was to build a business that he could then sell for a few million dollars, enough to launch his political career.

Bradley's plan did not pan out as hoped, however. His business model was too broad and unworkable and far from getting rich, after four years of hard work he was still only making $25,000 a year. Instead of selling the company quickly he devoted some 15 years of his life laboring long hours to finally make something of his business. He built up a slate of major corporate clients, becoming a wealthy man, but his political ambitions in the meantime had long been neglected.

According to *Columbia Journalism Review,* it was during a 13-hour flight to Vietnam that Bradley, now 40 years of age, found the time for some soul searching: "I looked older. I was living in D.C., which had no elected senators. I wasn't a Republican anymore. I was never going to be a senator." During the trip he also bought a magazine, which led to the inspiration that he could indulge his interest in politics through publishing. As he put it, "If I couldn't take the course, then at least I could audit it." Upon his return to the United States, Bradley contacted a magazine broker, Rick LePere, to inquire about purchasing the *New Republic,* his favorite magazine, but was disappointed to learn that Barbra Streisand had recently bid $25 million for the publication, a price higher than he was willing to pay. But Times Mirror soon decided to put NJ on the block, and Sullivan contacted LePere about finding a suitable buyer. LePere brought in Bradley and an $11 million purchase price was agreed to. At the time, NJ was generating $18 million in annual revenues.

To serve as editor-in-chief at *National Journal,* Bradley hired Michael Kelly, who had recently been fired as the editor

Key Dates:

1969: *National Journal* is founded by Randy Smith and Anthony Stout.
1975: John Fox Sullivan is named publisher.
1986: Times Mirror Co. acquires the magazine.
1997: David G. Bradley acquires National Journal Group.
1999: Bradley buys the *Atlantic Monthly.*

of the *New Republic.* Initially Kelly had misgivings about even meeting with Bradley, about whom nobody in the publishing world knew anything. But after conversing for a dozen hours over the course of two days, Kelly agreed to become a columnist for the magazine and gradually assumed increasing responsibility with the direction of the publication as well as influencing Bradley in developing his new dream, building a profitable empire out of NJ.

Increasing Wealth for Bradley in the Late 1990s

In 1999 Bradley spun off a part of Advisory Board into a separate company called the Corporate Executive Board, which he then took public, realizing $142 million from the ensuing stock offering. Flush with cash, Bradley was able to continue pouring money into NJ. During the first 18 months of Bradley's ownership, the editorial budget of *National Journal* was bumped by 60 percent and the magazine began to attract brand name talent, such as legal analyst Stuart Taylor, former *Washington Post* press critic William Powers, and former *Baltimore Sun* White House reporter Carl Cannon.

Bradley also used some of his new wealth in 1999 to acquire the 140-year-old *Atlantic Monthly* for $10 million from real estate magnate and publisher Mortimer Zuckerman. With ties to Henry Wadsworth Longfellow, Ralph Waldo Emerson, and Oliver Wendell Holmes, Sr., *Atlantic* was without doubt a prestigious magazine, but one which during the 20 years Zuckerman owned was little more than a break-even affair—losing

$500,000 in a poor year and earning about $500,000 in a good year. Although *Atlantic* would not become part of NJ, its luster increased Bradley's profile and in turn the small media empire he was attempting to grow out of NJ. He also installed Kelly as the magazine's new editor, and as he had done with *National Journal,* he increased the editorial budget, doubling it so that Kelly was able to redesign the magazine and offer contracts to some 25 new writers.

By 2003, after several years of investing heavily, Bradley had produced strong results for NJ under his watch, as virtually everything—staff, circulation, revenues, and profits—had doubled in size. Michael Kelly was replaced as *Atlantic*'s editor and died in 2003. One of the ideas he and Bradley had discussed since the start of their collaboration was to launch a new weekly authoritative magazine in the mold of the *Economist,* targeting an elite audience in much the same way *National Journal* did. But whether that would be the next major step taken by NJ remained to be seen.

Principal Operating Units

National Journal; Government Executive; Hotline; American Health Line; Technology Daily; CongressDaily.

Principal Competitors

The Economist Group Ltd.; Times Publishing Company; The Washington Post Company.

Further Reading

Adams, Lorraine, Warren Strobel, and Kate O'Beirne, ''The Magazine of Restoration Washington,'' *Columbia Journalism Review,* September/October 2002, p. 28.
Sherman, Scott, ''Going Long, Going Deep,'' *Columbia Journalism Review,* November/December 2002, p. 48.
Whitford, David, ''Adventures in Publishing,'' *Fortune Small Business,* September 2001, p. 34.

—Ed Dinger

NeighborCare, Inc.

601 East Pratt Street, 3rd Floor
Baltimore, Maryland 21202-3123
U.S.A.
Telephone: (410) 528-7300
Fax: (410) 528-7473
Web site: http://www.neighborcare.com

Public Company
Incorporated: 1985 as Genesis Health Ventures, Inc.
Employees: 5,900
Sales: $1.44 billion (2004)
Stock Exchanges: NASDAQ
Ticker Symbol: NCRX
NAIC: 422210 Drugs and Druggists' Sundries
   Wholesalers; 446110 Pharmacies and Drug Stores;
   423450 Medical, Dental, and Hospital Equipment and
   Supplies Merchant Wholesalers

NeighborCare, Inc. is one of the largest providers of institutional pharmacy services in the United States. The company serves long-term-care facilities in 32 states and the District of Columbia that collectively have approximately 260,000 beds. These facilities include long-term-care and skilled nursing facilities, specialty hospitals, assisted and independent living communities, and other group settings. NeighborCare's pharmacy operations include 62 institutional pharmacies, 32 community-based professional retail pharmacies, and 20 onsite pharmacies that are located in customers' facilities. In addition, the company runs 16 home infusion, respiratory, and home medical equipment distribution centers.

NeighborCare was known as Genesis Health Ventures, Inc. from its founding in 1985 through November 2003, during which time the company was also a provider of integrated healthcare services through nursing homes and assisted-living facilities. The latter business was spun off into a public company called Genesis HealthCare Corporation in December 2003, at which point the firm adopted the name NeighborCare, Inc. and began concentrating solely on institutional pharmacy services.

Innovations in Senior Care in the 1980s

Michael R. Walker and Richard R. Howard were already veterans of the nursing home industry when they founded Genesis Health Ventures, Inc. in 1985. They had worked together since the 1970s, building up two $100 million nursing home chains, as well as their own reputations in the industry. When these chains were bought up by industry heavyweights Beverly Enterprises and HCR, Inc., Walker and Howard decided to go into business for themselves, setting up operations in an old furniture and dry goods store in the small town of Kennett Square outside Philadelphia. Their reputations served them well. On the first day of operation, the company was able to arrange some $32 million in loans.

Setting out to build a nursing home chain with a difference, Walker and Howard used these loans to purchase nursing home facilities in Connecticut and southwestern Massachusetts. At the time, the prevailing culture among nursing homes was to provide long-term custodial care, typically on a fee-for-service basis. Walker and Howard, however, looked toward building a health services network, focused on providing geriatric care, that would emphasize rehabilitative services. "No one wants to end up in a nursing home," Walker told *Institutional Investor,* and that belief provided the cornerstone for the company's growth. Through rehabilitative therapy and services, patients were encouraged to return home—or to less care-intensive facilities—and to independent lives. Genesis offered a program of clinical intervention and managed care that emphasized the restoration of functional ability. This, the company reasoned, would be good for its patients, and for its bottom line. The typical nursing home was expensive to operate, and long-term care provided only low profit margins.

Managed care was still relatively unknown in the healthcare industry, and nearly unheard of in the geriatric market. However, the projected growth of the elderly population, with forecasts of 35 million by the end of the century and nearly 60 million by the year 2025, signaled the need to control costs among the very population most in need of medical services. From the start, Genesis set out to control its own costs. Rather than contracting out for its network support services, such as pharmacy services, home medical equipment, and rehabilitation

Company Perspectives:

Over the years, NeighborCare's success has stemmed from our core philosophy of providing the highest quality health care services in the marketplace. Delivering pharmacy, infusion, medical supplies and equipment, oxygen, respiratory medications, services and more, in the most cost effective way and in a clinically appropriate manner, is the NeighborCare trademark. This strategy is further enhanced by NeighborCare's ability to provide care across a variety of settings from home to long term care, from the physician's office to an assisted living facility or to our customers in retail pharmacies.

therapy, the company instead focused on acquiring these services and their higher profit margins. As clients were discharged from the company's nursing homes, they could be retained within the company's network of other services. In 1986 Genesis made the first of many acquisitions, acquiring the Speech & Hearing Network, which was renamed Team Rehabilitation.

By 1990 the company had more than 30 facilities in its network, with 4,500 long-term beds, generating revenues of nearly $145 million. Genesis continued to expand its services network through carefully planned acquisitions. One important consideration was a proposed acquisition's proximity to other facilities in the company's managed care network. "If you own a pharmacy in Pennsylvania and a nursing home in North Carolina, you can't share information," Walker told the *Baltimore Sun*, "But if I have a pharmacy, a physical therapist, a physician in the same place, guess what? They can all get together once a week to discuss the patient's health and get that person out of long-term care."

Genesis next moved to expand into pharmacy and medical supply services—where profit margins ranged from 10 to 15 percent as opposed to the 3 to 5 percent available on nursing homes—acquiring Accredited Surgical Companies, Inc. and Drug Lane Pharmacies, Inc., both of which repackaged and sold drugs. The two companies were combined to form the ASCO Healthcare, Inc. subsidiary, which was expanded into a full-service medical supply company that supplied not only the Genesis network, but outside nursing homes as well. Genesis also expanded its business by entering a management agreement for providing life-care services at continuous-care retirement centers, and by opening a physician-staffed outpatient clinic.

Growth in the Early to Mid-1990s

Genesis went public in 1991, selling 1.8 million shares and raising $13.5 million, which the company used to pay down some $12.6 million in debt. By then, Genesis operated 42 geriatric-care facilities, managed 13 life-care communities, and held service contracts with more than 140 independent healthcare providers. The company continued to pursue acquisitions, purchasing Concord Healthcare Corp. and Total Care Systems, which helped boost the company's revenues to $171.5 million for its 1991 fiscal year. Genesis, which had been profitable since its formation, posted net income of nearly $3.3 million for the

year. Genesis also took another step toward completing its network by developing a subsidiary called Physician Services. This addition allowed Genesis to become the first and only company in its industry to employ its own primary care physicians for its customers.

The following year, the ASCO subsidiary expanded, acquiring Suburban Medical Services for $9 million. The company opened a second rehabilitative outpatient clinic in order to serve customers discharged from its nursing homes; at the same time, the company moved to extend its services with the construction of an assisted-living facility located next to its geriatric facility in Wilkes-Barre, Pennsylvania. At the end of 1992, Genesis posted a second public offering, of 2.5 million shares at $13 per share, setting the stage for the next phase in the company's growth. By then, the company's revenues neared $200 million, while net profits climbed to $7.4 million.

The next year, 1993, proved to be pivotal in the company's development. Genesis expanded its ASCO subsidiary with the purchase of a home healthcare company and the acquisition of Health Concepts and Services, Inc., a provider of nursing home staff training and services based in Baltimore. By then, ASCO's revenues had climbed to $80 million, with 80 percent of those sales coming from outside the Genesis network. Within Genesis, the company established its Functional Evaluation & Treatment Unit, later known as the Full Potential process. This unit provided a geriatric assessment program for evaluating and placing patients. Based on physician-directed teams including registered nurses; nurse practitioners; physical, occupational, recreational, and speech therapists; social workers; and dietitians, the unit worked with patients and their families, as well as community and network resources, to develop realistic rehabilitation goals and care plans designed to achieve those goals.

Until 1993, Genesis's emphasis had been on expanding the scope of its network services; however, calls for healthcare reform from the newly inaugurated Clinton administration led Genesis to shift its focus. One expected consequence of healthcare reforms in general—and the inevitable reforms to the Medicare/Medicaid system for the company's core geriatric clients—would be abolition of the old fee-for-service healthcare plans in favor of prepaid, bulk rate plans. With competition for prepayments expected to be intense, Genesis moved to create a critical mass of nursing homes and geriatric facilities that would enable it to compete more strongly for contracts, especially government contracts. In October 1993, the company announced the largest acquisition in its history, with the $205 million purchase of Meridian Healthcare, the largest nursing home operator in Maryland. Genesis added Meridian's 36 geriatric-care facilities to the 58 already in the company's network, nearly doubling its revenues, from $220 million in 1993 to nearly $400 million in 1994. Maryland then became the company's largest market, surpassing Massachusetts. The Meridian acquisition also meant that Genesis would be able to expand its range of services into Maryland, where Genesis was by then the state's largest senior care provider, controlling costs by achieving economies of scale.

The Meridian acquisition was the first in a flurry of new acquisitions. In a move to expand into the burgeoning home healthcare market, Genesis purchased a 14 percent share in a

Key Dates:

1985: Michael R. Walker and Richard R. Howard found Genesis Health Ventures, Inc. to build a nursing home chain.

1990: Company expands into pharmacy and medical supply services through acquisitions of Accredited Surgical Companies, Inc. and Drug Lane Pharmacies, Inc., which were combined to form ASCO Healthcare, Inc.

1991: Genesis goes public.

1993: Meridian Healthcare, the largest nursing home operator in Maryland, is acquired.

1996: Genesis acquires Baltimore-based NeighborCare Pharmacies, Inc. and Geriatric & Medical Companies, Inc., operator of 27 nursing homes in New Jersey and Pennsylvania; Genesis's institutional pharmacy and related services operations subsequently begin operating under the NeighborCare name.

1997: Genesis joins with two investment boutiques to acquire the Multicare Companies, operator of 155 nursing homes in the northeastern United States.

1998: Multicare's Scotchwood Services is integrated into NeighborCare, and NeighborCare also acquires Vitalink Pharmacy Service, Inc.

2000: Cuts in Medicare payments lead to huge losses and bankruptcy filing for both Genesis and Multicare.

2001: Genesis emerges from bankruptcy, having merged with Multicare.

2003: Elder care operations are spun off to shareholders as separate company, Genesis HealthCare Corporation; the company, now focused exclusively on institutional pharmacy services, changes its name to NeighborCare, Inc.

2004: Omnicare, Inc. launches a hostile takeover of NeighborCare.

partnership corporation acquiring Baltimore's Visiting Nurse Association. The company also entered a strategic alliance with Horizon Healthcare to provide pharmacy services in the New England region. By 1995, the company had successfully absorbed Meridian's operations under the Genesis banner, gaining recognition as well for its policy of maintaining both existing management and staff, ensuring continuity of client care. This policy served the company well as it sought further acquisitions.

After acquiring Pennsylvania-based TherapyCare Systems LP for $7 million in April 1995, Genesis, through ASCO, bolstered its home healthcare business in June of that year with the $2 million acquisition of Baltimore-based Eastern Medical Supplies, Inc., and that company's Eastern Rehab Services, Inc., affiliate. The new acquisitions, which generated about $3.5 million in annual revenues through the sale and rental of home medical equipment and respiratory rehabilitation equipment, provided Genesis with increased access to the home health market through hospital affiliations, hospice contracts, and two retail stores. Helping to fuel the company's expansion was a new public offering that raised nearly $52 million, enabling Genesis to pay down debt associated with the Meridian acquisition.

By August 1995, Genesis announced its next large acquisition, agreeing to pay $82.5 million for McKerley Health Care Centers, the largest nursing home chain in New Hampshire. A principal factor in the family-owned chain's decision to sell to Genesis was the company's treatment of its Meridian employees: All of that company's managers, executives, and staff had kept their jobs, while new jobs had been created, and two of Meridian's executives had been promoted to key executive positions within Genesis itself. The acquisition of McKerley added 15 owned or leased geriatric care facilities, with 1,500 beds and some 1,500 employees.

At the beginning of 1996, with 1995 revenues of $487 million and net income of nearly $24 million, Genesis made plans to build a new, $16 million, 100,000-square-foot headquarters in Kennett Square. At the same time, the company consolidated its operations, bringing its core businesses under the trademarked brand name Genesis ElderCare. Genesis Health Ventures, Inc., was kept on as the company's legal name, and the name under which it traded on the New York Stock Exchange.

Genesis's acquisition drive continued through 1996. In June the company purchased Baltimore-based NeighborCare Pharmacies, Inc. for $57.3 million. NeighborCare supplied drugs to nursing homes, operated pharmacies in physician offices, and provided infusion therapy treatments in homes and nursing homes. Genesis subsequently adopted NeighborCare as the name for all of its institutional pharmacy and related services operations. In July 1996 Genesis paid New York-based National Health Care Affiliates, Inc. $133.6 million to acquire 17 elder care facilities in Florida, Virginia, and Connecticut, adding more than 2,500 beds, as well as a rehabilitation therapy business and a nutritional therapy business. In keeping with its focus on its core markets, Genesis also sold several Indiana nursing homes acquired through its Meridian purchase.

In October 1996 Genesis made its largest acquisition to date, paying $223 million to acquire Geriatric & Medical Companies, Inc., which, with 27 nursing homes, added another 3,500 beds to Genesis's New Jersey and Pennsylvania networks. By the end of its 1996 fiscal year, Genesis had boosted its revenues to $671.5 million and posted net income of $37.2 million.

Genesis added to its nursing home operations in October 1997 when it joined with two investment boutiques, Cypress Group and Texas Pacific Group, to acquire the Multicare Companies, in a $1.4 billion deal. Genesis took a 42 percent stake in the acquired company, based in Hackensack, New Jersey. Multicare operated 155 nursing homes throughout the northeastern United States with 16,000 beds, which gave Genesis a total of more than 38,000 beds, making it one of the three or four largest owner/managers of nursing homes in the country.

Multicare also owned Edison, New Jersey-based Scotchwood Services, provider of long-term-care pharmacy, infusion therapy, and consulting services in seven states. In early 1998 Scotchwood was integrated into NeighborCare, extending the latter's reach to 13 states, including four new ones: Illinois, Ohio, West Virginia, and Wisconsin. NeighborCare grew still larger through the August 1998 acquisition of Vitalink Pharmacy Service, Inc. for $594.2 million in cash and stock and the assumption of $90 million in debt. Following the integration of Vitalink, NeighborCare operated more than 100 institutional and retail pharmacies in 25 states, from Florida to New England as well as in the Midwest and on the West Coast. The combined operations had annual revenue of approximately $900 million—about half of parent company Genesis's overall revenues.

Bankruptcy Under Weight of Medicare Cutbacks: 2000–01

In July 1998 Medicare began implementing a change in the way it paid nursing homes and other long-term-care facilities that was mandated in the federal Balanced Budget Act of 1997. In place of the old system that reimbursed providers for actual costs incurred, the new system paid facilities per-diem rates based on the basic level of care a patient required. Genesis began feeling the effects of the Medicare cutbacks in fiscal 1998, when it posted a net loss of $24.2 million on revenue of $1.41 billion. The following year was even worse: $270.6 million in the red on revenue of $1.87 billion. In June 2000 both Genesis and Multicare joined a wave of industry bankruptcies when they filed for Chapter 11 protection under a $1.5 billion debt load.

In October 2001 Genesis emerged from bankruptcy through a reorganization plan in which it merged with Multicare. The companies' bank lenders received about $220 million in cash, $242.6 million in senior notes, about 93 percent of the new common stock, and about $40 million in preferred stock. Unsecured creditors got about 7 percent of the new common stock, while the previous common stockholders of the companies, as is typical in Chapter 11 reorganization plans, received nothing. The companies' nursing homes continued to operate throughout the bankruptcy.

Company Split, Emergence of NeighborCare: 2003

In May 2002 cofounder Walker stepped down as CEO in order to focus full-time on lobbying the U.S. government to better fund long-term care. Robert H. Fish, a board member and a partner in a California healthcare consulting firm, was named interim CEO. Fish announced two months later that Genesis had agreed to acquire Cleveland-based NCS Healthcare Inc., the fourth largest institutional pharmacy provider in the country, for about $346 million in stock and assumed debt. The deal would have enabled NeighborCare to move from third to second place in the industry. But Omnicare, Inc., the number one institutional pharmacy provider, stepped in with a much larger offer, and Genesis was forced to end its bid that December.

In the meantime, as this takeover battle was playing itself out, Genesis hired two investment banks to explore the sale or spinoff of its nursing home and assisted living operations in order to focus exclusively on the faster-growing NeighborCare unit. In February 2003 the company announced that it planned to spin off the elder care business to shareholders as a separate publicly traded company. In July, John L. Arlotta came onboard as vice-chairman. Arlotta, with more than 30 years of experience in the pharmacy services industry, had most recently been president and chief operating officer of Carmark Pharmaceutical Services, a leading provider of drug benefit services to health plans, corporations, and insurance companies. On December 1, 2003, Genesis completed the spinoff of its elder care business, which began operating as Genesis HealthCare Corporation. The original Genesis changed its name to NeighborCare, Inc., with corporate headquarters in Baltimore. Arlotta took over leadership of NeighborCare as chairman and CEO.

NeighborCare had barely completed this separation when Omnicare stepped forward with an unsolicited takeover bid. Late in March, Omnicare made a private approach about a takeover but was quickly rebuffed. The firm then took its bid public two months later, offering $30 per share for NeighborCare, a substantial premium over what the stock had been trading for and amounting to a $1.5 billion bid. NeighborCare blasted the proposed transaction as "blatantly opportunistic" and rejected the approach again, prompting Omnicare to turn hostile with a tender offer. NeighborCare continued to oppose the takeover, calling the offer financially inadequate and insisting that shareholders would be better off allowing the company's operational plan to go forward. Into late 2004, Omnicare extended the deadline for its tender offer several times as the Federal Trade Commission (FTC) reviewed the deal to determine whether it was permissible under antitrust laws. How the FTC ruled was expected to play a major role in whether the deal moved forward.

Principal Subsidiaries

Accumed, Inc.; ASCO Healthcare, Inc.; CareCard, Inc.; Concord Pharmacy Services, Inc.; Delco Apothecary, Inc.; Eastern Medical Supplies, Inc.; Encare of Massachusetts, Inc.; Horizon Medical Equipment and Supply, Inc.; Institutional Health Care Services, Inc.; The Medical Centre, LLC; Medical Services Group, Inc.; NeighborCare Pharmacies, Inc.; Professional Pharmacy Services, Inc.; Quest Total Care Pharmacy.

Principal Competitors

Omnicare, Inc.; PharMerica, Inc.

Further Reading

Anders, George, "Genesis Group Agrees to Buy Multicare Cos.," *Wall Street Journal*, June 17, 1997, p. A3.

Atkinson, Bill, "Baltimore's NeighborCare Urges Shareholders to Reject Rival's Buyout Offer," *Baltimore Sun*, June 16, 2004.

——, "NeighborCare to Be Bought by Pa. Chain," *Baltimore Sun*, April 23, 1996, p. 1C.

Berman, Dennis K., "Omnicare Makes $1.5 Billion Bid to Acquire Rival NeighborCare," *Wall Street Journal*, May 25, 2004, p. C5.

Brin, Dinah Wisenberg, "Omnicare Shows Its Hunger to Grow," *Wall Street Journal*, July 21, 2004.

Brooke, Bob, "Genesis Project Marks New Beginning for Downtown," *Philadelphia Business Journal*, January 12, 1996, p. 23.

Fahey, Tom, "McKerley Sought Sale," *Union Leader*, August 23, 1996.

"Genesis Health Ventures," *Institutional Investor*, July 1994, p. S22.

George, John, "Elder Care Network Part of Genesis Plan," *Philadelphia Business Journal*, October 10, 1997, pp. B2, B10.

——, "Genesis Nursing $30 Million Shortfall," *Philadelphia Business Journal*, March 19, 1999, pp. 1+.

Goldstein, Josh, "One of Nation's Biggest Nursing Home Operators to Break into Two Companies," *Philadelphia Inquirer*, February 13, 2003.

——, "Pennsylvania's Genesis Health Ventures to Split Nursing Home, Pharmacy Units," *Philadelphia Inquirer,* December 1, 2003.

——, "Philadelphia-Area Nursing-Home Chain's CEO Resigns," *Philadelphia Inquirer,* May 29, 2002.

Jones, John A., "Genesis Expands Geriatric Network by Acquiring Meridian," *Investor's Business Daily,* March 28, 1994, p. 40.

——, "Genesis Health Is Set up to Manage Care for the Elderly," *Investor's Business Daily,* February 12, 1996, p. A33.

Mehta, Stephanie N., "Genesis Health to Acquire Vitalink for $594.2 Million in Cash, Stock," *Wall Street Journal,* April 28, 1998, p. B4.

Meisol, Patrick, "With Acquisition of Meridian, Genesis Health Nears Goal of Regional Domination," *Baltimore Sun,* October 3, 1993.

Pallarito, Karen, "CFO's Creative Solutions Win Cain Bros. Award," *Modern Healthcare,* September 9, 1996, p. 44.

Salganik, M. William, "Baltimore Pharmaceutical Supplier NeighborCare Posts Loss in Fighting Buyout," *Baltimore Sun,* August 5, 2004.

——, "Pharmacy Chain to Spin Off from Parent, Find Base in Baltimore," *Baltimore Sun,* November 18, 2003.

Saphir, Ann, "Genesis Joins Rush to Bankruptcy," *Modern Healthcare,* June 26, 2000, p. 8.

Vincent, Dale, "McKerley Health Care Chain Sold for $82.5M," *Union Leader,* August 22, 1995, p. A1.

—M.L. Cohen
—update: David E. Salamie

NGK

NGK Insulators Ltd.

2-56 Sudacho, Mizuho-ku
Nagoya
467-8530
Japan
Telephone: +81 528727171
Fax: +81 528727690
Web site: http://www.ngk.co.jp

Public Company
Incorporated: 1919
Employees: 3,556
Sales: ¥251.32 billion ($2.37 billion) (2004)
Stock Exchanges: Tokyo Nagoya Osaka Sapporo
NAIC: 335932 Noncurrent-Carrying Wiring Device
 Manufacturing; 333298 All Other Industrial
 Machinery Manufacturing; 335312 Motor and
 Generator Manufacturing

Based in Nagoya, Japan, NGK Insulators Ltd. is one of the world's leading producers of electrical insulators and industrial ceramics components, as well as a range of other power distribution, ceramics, and electronics products. The company's Insulator division specializes in the manufacturing of large-scale insulators for electricity transmission cables—such as its 11.5-meter-long ultrahigh voltage bushing shell, which can reach a diameter of 1.6 meters, making it the world's largest object crafted from porcelain. The company also produces related products, such as line arresters and insulator washing equipment. Other products in this division include power distribution products and components and sodium sulfur batteries. NGK's Ceramics division produces the Honeyceram line of ceramics-based automotive exhaust purification components, as well as ceramic membrane filters for the chemicals industries, and refractories for the industrial heating market. NGK's Engineering division leverages its insulator technologies for use in plant engineering designs and projects such as sewage and water treatment systems. NGK's Electronics business produces ceramics-based components for the electronics and semiconductor industries. Last, the company's Specialty Metals and Precision Casting & Molds divisions makes components based on beryllium-copper alloys. Founded in 1919, NGK operates subsidiaries and affiliate companies in 57 countries. Manufacturing of crucial technologies remains concentrated in Japan, which also accounts for some 80 percent of the company's sales. NGK also operates manufacturing facilities in the United States, China, Malaysia, Australia, Belgium, Canada, the United Kingdom, Germany, France, India, Indonesia, South Africa, and Thailand. The company is listed on the Tokyo Stock Exchange. Sales in its 2004 fiscal year topped ¥251 billion ($2.3 billion).

Insulator Offshoot in the 1920s

NGK Insulators stemmed from an import-export business established by Baron Ichizaemon Morimura in 1876. Initially, Morimura focused on shipments of porcelain china, which were distributed through a wholesale and retail shop the company opened in New York City. The rise in demand for Japanese china encouraged Morimura-kumi, as the company was called, to establish its own porcelain production operation in order to ensure the high quality of its products. That company, called Nippon Toki Gomei Kaisha, began production in the village of Noritake in 1904. The company's china products adopted the Noritake name, and their popularity later led Nippon Toki (also known as Nihon Touki) to change its name to Noritake as well.

The Noritake company soon began investigating developing technologies to extend the uses of its ceramics production. The growing use of electricity and electrical products had produced the demand for new components, such as insulators for high-voltage transmission lines. In 1906, Nippon Toki began researching means of adapting ceramics as insulators. By 1909, the company had completed its first generation of ceramics insulators.

Over the next decade, Nippon Toki continued to develop its ceramics technologies, improving the performance of its insulators. At the same time, the market for its insulators grew strongly, as demand for electrical power surged in Japan. This development led Nippon Toki to create a dedicated company for its insulator division in 1919. The new company took the name of NGK Insulators Ltd.

Company Perspectives:

In the rapidly changing business world of the 21st century, only a limited number of outstanding companies will survive. We are entering this age of changing business structures with value creation as a driving force in new untapped markets.

We have set new action guidelines which focus on four principal concepts: "Speedy," referring to speedy management, "Timely," meaning concentration on development, "Lean," aiming at highly-efficient management, and "Green," green management (consideration for our environment). By incorporating these principles, we strive to make NGK a company of excellence based on global standards.

Profile: Despite a surge in the severity of competition on the global stage, NGK, in line with its commitment to being a company of excellence based on global standards, is steadily evolving to fulfill its corporate mission to constantly provide value to clients, shareholders, employees and society as a whole. Firmly grounded in distinctive ceramics technology, NGK continues to make its presence felt across the "Triple-E" business domains of Energy, Ecology and Electronics.

Over the next decade, NGK developed ceramics technology capable of providing insulation support for the new class of 1000 kV ultra-high voltage transmission systems. As part of that effort, the company built a testing facility for the new range of insulators in 1929. In this way, NGK was able to develop methods of increasing the scale of its ceramic insulators, culminating in the fabrication of a world-leading 11.5-meter transmission bushing in 1995.

NGK also began developing other markets for its ceramics technologies. The company began producing ceramics-based corrosion-resistant components and equipment in the early 1930s. NGK also launched the production of components for sewage treatment and filtration systems. The company became a supplier to the automotive industry early on as well, in particular through its production of ceramic spark plugs. That operation grew sufficiently to be spun off as a separate company in 1936, as NGK Spark Plug Co. The importance of the company's products during the war years led NGK to build a second factory, in Handa, in Aichi in 1942.

International Expansion in the 1960s

NGK diversified its business somewhat in the 1950s, launching the production of beryllium-copper alloy-based components. Nonetheless, insulators remained the company's core business. In the decades following World War II, NGK emerged as a world-leading producer of electrical insulators. The development was helped by the construction of a new factory in Komaki in 1962, and the opening of a new High Voltage Laboratory the following year.

NGK turned to the international market for the next phase in its growth. In 1965, the company launched its first foreign subsidiary, founding NGK Insulators of America. This was followed by the creation of a Canadian subsidiary, NGK Insula-

tors of Canada, in 1968. In 1973, the company teamed up with General Electric to form U.S.-based Locke Insulators Inc. NGK next turned to Europe, forming subsidiaries in Germany in 1976 and Belgium in 1978. These subsidiaries were merged the following year.

During this time, NGK also had begun developing new products. In 1971, the company created a new subsidiary for the production of ceramics-based electronics components. The company also extended its ceramics technology to the automotive industry again, developing its Honeyceram filtration catalyst. Launched in 1976, Honeyceram—which was patterned after honeycombs—quickly set a standard in the emerging market for catalytic converters.

The wide adoption of the Honeyceram catalyst led NGK to establish a dedicated manufacturing facility in Europe as well, with the creation of NGK Ceramics Europe, in Belgium, in 1985. The following year, the company extended its beryllium-copper operations to North America, with the purchase of Cabot Corp. in the United States. That business then became known as NGK Metals Corporation.

The widespread adoption of catalytic converters in the U.S. market in the 1980s encouraged NGK to set up a dedicated manufacturing presence in that market as well, and in 1988 the company launched a new subsidiary, NGK Ceramics USA, in order to produce the Honeyceram system for the U.S. market.

In another international move, NGK founded the PT Wika-NGK Insulators joint venture to begin producing insulators in Indonesia in 1987. Another joint venture that year, with ASEA Brown Boveri AG, created Nastech Corp. in Japan, dedicated to the development and production of sodium sulfur (NAS) batteries. The company began testing its first prototype NAS battery in 1992.

World Leader in Insulators in the New Century

NGK's expansion continued throughout the 1990s and into the next century. In 1990, the company created a new subsidiary, NGK Okhotsk, in order to produce ferrite components for magnetic heads. Another new subsidiary was NGK Filtech, launched in 1991 in order to develop and manufacture filtering membrane components. In 1993, NGK traveled to Australia, setting up the NGK Stanger joint venture, which began manufacturing power distribution automation components and systems. Closer to its core business, the company opened a new U.S. subsidiary, NGK-Locke Polymer Insulators, extending its insulators business.

By the mid-1990s, NGK's Honeyceram was a world-leading catalytic converter element, with sales of more than 200 million pieces. In 1996, the company extended the manufacturing network for that product with a new subsidiary in Indonesia. That year, as well, NGK launched production of insulators at a new manufacturing plant in China. The company added another Indonesian subsidiary in 1997, with the creation of Siam NGK Technocera, dedicated to the production of kiln furniture for NGK's and others' ceramics manufacturing operations.

A new foreign extension for the company came in 2000, when NGK launched Honeyceram production in South Africa. The

Key Dates:

1906: Nippon Touki Gomei Kaisha (later Noritake) begins development of ceramics-based insulators.
1909: The first ceramic insulators are launched.
1919: The dedicated ceramic insulators business, NGK Insulators Ltd., is created.
1958: NGK begins production of beryllium-copper alloy components.
1965: NGK opens its first foreign subsidiary in the United States.
1968: A Canadian subsidiary is established.
1976: A European subsidiary in Germany is created; the Honeyceram catalyst for catalytic converters is launched.
1985: A Honeyceram production subsidiary is created in Belgium.
1988: Honeyceram production is launched in the United States.
1993: The NGK Stanger joint venture in Australia is created.
1995: NGK builds the world's largest ceramics-based bushing at 11.5 meters.
1996: Production begins in China.
2000: A Honeyceram production subsidiary is founded in South Africa.
2001: The company begins a glass-lined insulation partnership with De Deitrich in France.
2004: NGK announces plans to build new production sites in China, Poland, and the United States.

following year, NGK formed a cooperation agreement with France's De Dietrich in order to produce glass-lined insulation systems. Also that year, NGK formed two new subsidiaries in China's Suzhou, one for the production of Honeyceram catalysts, and the other to expand its kiln furniture business. By then, sales of Honeyceram had topped 500 million units worldwide.

The early 2000s marked a difficult period for NGK. The company's exposure to the electronics and information technology market left it vulnerable to the sector's collapse. The company, which despite its international scope, continued to generate some 80 percent of its revenues in Japan, also was hurt by the country's slow economic growth. Nonetheless, as it approached the mid-decade, NGK appeared to be on its way to regaining its momentum. NGK also began preparing for further expansion, launching plans to open new manufacturing sites in Poland,

China, and the United States. With nearly 100 years of ceramics technology behind it, NGK expected to remain a world leader in the ceramics insulator market in the 21st century.

Principal Subsidiaries

Akechi Insulators Co., Ltd.; Chubu Energys Corporation; FM Industries, Inc.; Kansai Energys Corporation; Koshin Electronics Co., Ltd.; Kyusyu Energys Corporation; Locke Insulators, Inc.; M-Elec Company; NGK Adrec Co., Ltd.; NGK Berylco France; NGK Berylco U.K. Ltd.; NGK Building Service, Ltd.; NGK Ceramics Europe S.A.; NGK Ceramics Polska Sp. z.o.o.; NGK Ceramics South Africa (Pty) Ltd.; NGK Ceramics Suzhou Co., Ltd. (China); NGK Chem-Tech, Ltd.; NGK Deutsche Berylco GmbH; NGK Europe GmbH; NGK Europe S.A.; NGK Expert Co., Ltd.; NGK Filtech, Ltd.; NGK Insulators of Canada, Ltd.; NGK Insulators Tangshan Co., Ltd.; NGK Kilntech Corporation; NGK Life Co., Ltd.; NGK Logistics, Ltd.; NGK Mettex Corporation; NGK North America, Inc.; NGK Okhotsk, Ltd.; NGK Optoceramics Co., Ltd.; NGK Printer Ceramics Co., Ltd.; NGK Sports Planning Co., Ltd.; NGK Technica, Ltd.; NGK Technocera Suzhou Co., Ltd. (China); NGK-E Solution, Ltd.; North America; P.T. NGK Ceramics (Indonesia); PT WIKA-NGK (Malaysia); Siam NGK Technocera Co., Ltd. (Thailand); Soritsu Electronics Co., Ltd.; Soshin Electronics (HK) Ltd. (Hong Kong); Soshin Electronics of America Inc.; Sosyo Sales Co., Ltd.; Tajimi Country Club Co., Ltd.; Tohoku Energys Corporation; Tokai Energys Corporation.

Principal Competitors

Shanghai Nanyang Sunlight Cable Co.; AREVA Group; Adolf Wurth GmbH und Company KG; Philips France; NetVersant Solutions Inc.; Harbin Cable Factory; Fuji Electric Co., Ltd.; Kubota Corporation; Sumitomo Metal Industries, Ltd.; Zhengzhou Cable Group Company Ltd.; Aberdare Cables Proprietary Ltd.; Rittal Corporation; LEONI AG.

Further Reading

"Final US Ruling Says Japanese Firm NGK Is Dumping Its Insulators," *Knight Ridder/Tribune Business News,* December 3, 2003.
"NGK Insulators to Produce Insulators in China," *Asian Economic News,* August 31, 1998.
"NGK Insulators to Set Up 2 Subsidiaries in China," *Asian Economic News,* December 24, 2001.
Oba, Tokiko, "NGK Insulators Poised for Fast Recovery," *Yomiuri Shimbun,* January 5, 2004.

—M.L. Cohen

Niman Ranch, Inc.

1025 East 12th Street
Oakland, California 94606
U.S.A.
Telephone: (510) 808-0340
Fax: (510) 808-0339
Web site: http://www.nimanranch.com

Private Company
Founded: 1969
Employees: 110
Sales: $31 million (2002 est.)
NAIC: 311611 Animal, Except Poultry, Slaughtering

Niman Ranch, Inc. works with more than 300 independent family farmers who raise livestock according to the company's strict protocols: They must meet Niman Ranch's environmental standards, use approved genetics, keep careful health records, and pass the company's regular inspections. Niman Ranch ranches its own cattle on 1,000 acres of rolling hills in the Point Reyes National Seashore, marketing its processed beef nationwide, along with sustainable beef raised by close to 50 other cattle producers throughout the West. The company's pork comes from 260-odd Midwestern hog farmers. Niman meats are available through the company's web site, via stores, and from third-party mail-order sources.

1969–77: Hobby Becomes a Specialty Business

Bill Niman began keeping pigs, goats, and chickens in 1969 on 11 acres of land that he bought for $18,000 in Bolinas, California, a coastal town an hour north of the Golden Gate Bridge in Marin County. At the time, he was an elementary school teacher with an interest in old-fashioned techniques of animal husbandry. Niman fed his animals outdated yogurt and spent barley from Anchor Steam Brewery and allowed them to range freely. Later, his first wife bartered tutoring services for a few head of cattle, and the couple began to sell its meat to neighbors and local businesses. "We learned an inch at a time," Niman recalled in a 2003 *Forbes* article.

From the beginning, Niman's husbandry practices focused on sustainability and ecological stewardship. "A couple of communes started up in Bolinas . . . people were very interested in self-sufficiency," he explained in the *San Francisco Business Times* in 2002. Unlike most livestock companies, which crammed their animals into feed lots without ever grazing and rushed them to slaughter at little more than a year of age—before they were fully mature—Niman gave his animals plenty of space to roam for close to two years.

"The whole idea in raising any grazing animal is to convert naturally growing grass and forage into proteins humans can eat," Niman stated in the *San Francisco Business Times*. Young calves received their mother's milk for the first two months and were weaned by seven months. For the next 14 to 18 months, they grazed on high-quality clover and hay (grasses which were about to go to seed and contained the most stored energy). When they reached 800–900 pounds, they were moved to feedlots where they were fed a ration of sugar beet pulp, cane molasses, corn, barley, wheat, and soy meal for an average of 140 days or until they were about 20 to 24 months of age.

Niman also refused to administer unnecessary hormones, chemicals, or feed additives to his cattle and other livestock. The use of antibiotic feed had become accepted practice in the United States by the 1970s in response to the crowded, disease-promoting conditions of the industrialized stock industry. In addition, administering sub-therapeutic antibiotics to animals promoted growth, bringing livestock to market faster. However, there was ongoing debate as to whether antibiotic resistance in animals can be transferred to humans.

Finally, Niman differed from other meat producers in the way in which he prepared his meat for market, going against the livestock industry's productionist model that emphasized efficiency. After slaughter, his cattle were "shrouded," following an old-fashioned and uncommon practice of wrapping the carcass in a salted cloth for five days to draw out excess moisture. Shrouding reduces carcass weight by about 10 percent. The meat was then aged up to one month. By contrast, most commercial meat was slaughtered, almost immediately butchered, and sealed in Cry-O-Vac bags in order to retain as much moisture as possible.

1978–97: Niman-Schell Meats Gradually Expands

In 1978, Niman took on a partner, Orville Schell, a journalist and early critic of the mass production methods of the meat industry, who that year wrote a book called *Modern Meat*. The company became Niman-Schell Meats. As word spread of Niman-Schell's tasty, naturally raised meat, the business grew from supplying neighbors to providing restaurants in California and beyond with meat. The two men increased the company acreage and hired a ranch hand, but Niman still had to work construction jobs to make ends meet. Niman realized he could not sustain a pork business since soybean and cornmeal feed difficult to transport. So in 1979, he switched to cattle alone. ''We raised more and more beef cattle as we got more land,'' he recalled in the *San Francisco Business Times*. The 11 acres became 200, and Niman-Schell became a USDA processing entity.

However, the 1980s were a tough time for Niman-Schell. With an 18 percent mortgage on its acreage, the company struggled to make payments. Fortunately, the federal government decided to acquire its land through the laws of eminent domain in 1984; the condemned land became part of the Point Reyes National Seashore, and Niman and his partner received $1.3 million for the property. They also retained the right to graze their cattle on the land for the rest of their life for the cost of property taxes, or $3,000 per month in rent.

Between 1980 and 1997, beef consumption fell from 72 pounds per person per year to 63 pounds as eating less or no red meat became associated with living a healthier lifestyle. However, during this same time, sales of Niman Ranch and other branded beef were actually increasing. Only a few million pounds of branded beef sold in 1979—more then 480 million in 1998. This increase was due to the enthusiasm of chefs throughout the country for the taste of cattle raised according to old-fashioned methods as well as to the introduction of branded beef offerings and value-added beef products such as marinated strips, fully prepared pot roast, and breaded and seasoned country-fried steaks.

In 1989, Niman-Schell also began to sell free-ranging, naturally fed lamb when he met sheep ranchers in the Sacramento Valley who shared his views on low-tech agriculture, who started selling their meat to him for distribution. In 1997, the company also began to sell pork products from hogs raised by Midwestern family farmers who agreed to the company's strict protocols. The move was a boon for the small, family hog farm, which was having difficulty surviving the late 1990s. Vertical integration and concentration in hog production had made difficult financial times for hog farmers, and the decline in the number of small hog farms accelerated in late 1998 and early 1999 when hog prices hit historic lows.

1997–2004: Steady Growth, New Alliances, and a National Reputation

Niman Schell became Niman-McConnell LLC in 1997, when Schell left the company to become dean of the University of California-Berkeley's School of Journalism, and two new investors, Rob Hurlbut and Mike McConnell, joined Niman Ranch. That same year, it hired a full-time controller as business began to speed up. The company had sales of about $3 million in 1997. By 1998, that figure was at about $5 million. Business doubled in 1999 and again in 2000 to put the company's sales in the range of $20 million annually. Hog slaughter more than doubled to 980 a week in 1999. The company, then a confederation of 30 ranchers, added a web site that informed customers where they could buy Niman meats. It was the first effort at publicity.

In April 2000, Niman Ranch joined Freshnex, an online marketplace that enabled restaurants and grocers to buy fresh foods in bulk at reduced shipping costs. Still the company required an employee who arrived at 4 a.m. each day to transcribe the 100-odd orders left by chefs on the company's answering machine the night before. Niman had become the meat of choice of top restaurants nationwide; in fact, even restaurants that did not buy from Niman claimed that they did as consumers came to recognize the outstanding taste of its free-ranging meats.

A strategic alliance formed between Niman and Chipotle Mexican Foods, a chain of fast-food restaurants owned by Illinois-based McDonald's Corporation since 1998. Chief executive officer of Chipotle, Steve Ellis, saw the arrangement as one of redefining fast food and its ingredients to focus on food quality and social responsibility. In 2001, the company became Niman Ranch, Inc. By 2002, it was supplying 20,000 pounds of pork a week to Chipotle and adding additional hog farms to its network to meet demand.

Sales doubled again in the late 1990s and early years of the new century to reach about $31 million in 2002 even as Americans were eating about 4 percent less red meat per person beginning in 2001. Niman Ranch had become a visible advocate for agricultural sustainability, a living wage for farmers, and a healthier and more humane ranching process. The company now marketed meats for 200 hog farmers, 45 cattle ranchers, and five lamb ranchers nationwide.

In 2003, Niman Ranch was slaughtering about 2,700 hogs a week when it received $350,000 from the USDA for product development, marketing, and hog purchases. The money went toward recruiting another 100 to 150 hog farmers who would bring with them another 1,000 head a week. Cattle, raised by Niman's network of 45 small West Coast ranchers, many in Marin and Sonoma counties, were slaughtered at the rate of 150 to 175 per week. (Large commercial operations slaughtered as many as 400 animals per hour.) These ranchers raised the cattle until they were one year old, at which time, Niman finished them on grain in feedlots in Idaho. Carcasses were transported back for butchering at the company's facility in East Oakland, purchased in 1999.

By the first years of the new century, organic beef represented 1 percent of the national beef market. Niman, whose own meats were not yet organic because the grain the company fed its livestock was not certified organic, wanted its meat to be still

Key Dates:

1969: Bill Niman founds a part-time livestock operation.
1978: Orville Schell joins Niman as a partner; company is named Niman-Schell Meats.
1979: Niman-Schell Meats switches to raising only cattle.
1989: Niman-Schell begins to sell free-ranging, naturally fed lamb.
1997: Schell leaves the company, which is renamed Niman-McConnell LLC.
1999: The company launches its web site.
2000: Niman Ranch joins Freshnex for marketing its meats.
2001: The company forms a strategic alliance with Chipotle Mexican Foods; changes its name to Niman Ranch, Inc.

more pure—completely natural, organic, and certified. Bill Niman commented in 2000 in the *Wine Spectator* that his company would accept no halfway measures in going organic. ''It will have to be all organic or none at all because we want to be what we say we are. That's why we feed out cattle in our own lots [by our] own employees. . . .''

Whatever direction Niman Ranch would take next, its decisions were dictated by the principles of sustainability, responsibility, and good taste that had guided it all along. As Bill Niman said in a 2004 *Beef* article, ''When you have your name on it, you focus on the eating quality, tenderness and flavor. You can get today's consumer to try something one time, and it better be a good experience or they won't try it again.''

Principal Subsidiaries

Niman Ranch Pork Co.

Principal Competitors

BC Natural Foods, LLC; Laura's Lean Beef Company; Maverick Ranch Association, Inc.; Cooperative Regions of Organic Producers Pool.

Further Reading

Bittman, Mark, ''The Master of Meat,'' *Wine Spectator*, November 2000, p. 16.
Brown, Steven E.F., ''Ahead of the Herd,'' *San Francisco Business Times*, February 15, 2002. p. 34.
Dolan, Kerry A., ''One Man's Meat,'' *Forbes*, March 17, 2003, p. 162.
Gordon, Kindra, ''What's in a Name?'' *Beef*, August 2004, p. 19.
Robbins, Jim, ''Balancing Cattle, Land and Ledgers,'' *New York Times*, October 8, 2003, p. F8.

—Carrie Rothburd

Nintendo Company, Ltd.

11-1 Kamitoba-Hokodate-cho
Minami-ku
Kyoto 601-8501
Japan
Telephone: (075) 601-8501
Toll Free: (800) 633-3236
Fax: (075) 662-9620
Web site: http://www.nintendo.co.jp

Public Company
Incorporated: 1889 as Marufuku Company, Ltd.
Employees: 2,977
Sales: ¥509.84 billion ($4.86 billion) (2004)
Stock Exchanges: Tokyo
Ticker Symbol: NTDOY
NAIC: 339932 Games, Toys, and Children's Vehicle
    Manufacturing; 421920 Electronic Games
    Wholesaling

Nintendo Company, Ltd. is known worldwide for Mario, Zelda, Luigi, Donkey Kong, and hundreds of Pokémon "pocket monster" characters. Nintendo's Game Boy handheld gaming systems (the Game Boy Advance PS is the latest version) have ruled the market since their debut, and its gaming console, the GameCube, overtook Xbox as the second most popular console after Sony's PlayStation 2. Though Sony has dominated the console market, Nintendo's Game Boy Advance and new Nintendo DS lead the handheld market, despite the introduction of Sony's PSP (PlayStation Portable). As its GameCube and Nintendo DS gain market share, Nintendo remains the interactive game leader for its graphics and innovation, and designer Shigeru Miyamoto's slew of popular animated characters.

A Playing Card Company: 1880s to Early 1960s

Nintendo was founded as Marufuku Company, Ltd. in Kyoto, Japan, in 1889 by Fusajiro Yamauchi. Marufuku made playing cards for the Japanese game of Hanafuda, believed to have its origin from Tarot cards. In 1907 Marufuku introduced the first Western-style playing cards in Japan. Marufuku initially made the cards for Russian prisoners of war during the Russo-Japanese War of 1904–05, when the soldiers wore out the decks they had brought from Russia.

Between 1907 and World War II Marufuku solidified its status in the playing card business. World War I, in which Japan fought on the side of the Allies, did not affect business in any remarkable way. In 1925, however, Marufuku began exporting Hanafuda cards to Japanese communities in South America, Korea, and Australia. From 1925 to 1928 Marufuku developed new marketing strategies to place its products in tobacco shops, complemented by aggressive, more Westernized advertising.

World War II devastated the Japanese economy and delivered a hard blow even to the previously modest but stable home amusement market. The playing card industry and Marufuku, though, fared far better than most. In the austere postwar climate, when entertainment had to be cheap and simple, the demand for playing cards only decreased slightly. Marufuku's manufacturing plant had not been damaged much in the war, and the company thrived in the succeeding years.

Hiroshi Yamauchi, great-grandson of Marufuku's founder, became president in 1950, embarking on a wide-ranging program to modernize and rationalize the way his family's company was run. In 1952 Marufuku consolidated its factories, which had been scattered throughout Kyoto. In 1951 Yamauchi changed the company name to one more appropriate to the leisure industry; he called it the Nintendo Playing Card Company, Ltd. In Japanese, the word "Nintendo" has a proverbial meaning loosely translated as, "You work hard but, in the end, it's in heaven's hands."

Business boomed in the postwar era. In 1953 Yamauchi responded to a shortage in playing-card-quality paper by challenging his company to develop plastic playing cards. After initial difficulties in printing and coating the plastic cards, Nintendo started mass production. In 1959 Nintendo reached an agreement with Walt Disney Company and released playing cards imprinted with Disney cartoon characters. By 1962 business was so good that Nintendo decided to go public, listing stock on the Osaka and Kyoto stock exchanges.

Diversification: 1960s to Early 1980s

In the 1960s Nintendo began a drive towards diversification and innovation, which eventually led to it becoming a household word in the late 1980s. In 1963 the company augmented its product line by marketing board games as well as playing cards. By 1969 the game department was so successful a new game production plant was built in Uji city, a suburb of Kyoto. In 1970 Nintendo introduced electronic technology for the first time in Japan with its Beam Gun Series. An especially popular example of this technology was the laser clay pigeon shooting system, introduced in 1973, in which arcade players aimed beams of light at targets projected on a small movie screen. By 1974, Nintendo was exporting this and other projection-based games to the United States and Europe.

In the next few years, arcade game technology made remarkable strides, with Nintendo in the vanguard. In 1975, in cooperation with Mitsubishi Electric, Nintendo developed a video game system using a video player—a technology made more complex the next year when a microprocessor was added to the system. By 1977 this technology was being marketed as part of the first, relatively unsophisticated generation of home video games.

In the amusement arcade Nintendo's games were beginning to feature higher levels of technology. In 1978 Nintendo developed and started selling coin-operated video games using microcomputers. This innovation, which in 1981 resulted in such arcade hits as Donkey Kong, gave arcade video games the complex graphics and stereo sound Nintendo would later market for home use.

As the 1980s began Nintendo started selling the Game and Watch product line—a handheld series of electronic games such as football, with liquid crystals and digital quartz microhardware. By this time, Nintendo found its export business required a firmer foothold in the United States and established Nintendo of America, Inc., a wholly owned subsidiary, in New York City. In 1982 the U.S. office was moved to Redmond, Washington, and established there with an operating capital of $600,000. As the 1980s progressed, the company focused on the development and marketing of home video technology. A new plant was built in 1983 in Uji city to meet the production

requirements of Nintendo's new flagship product, Famicom (short for the "family computer"). Famicom, which allowed arcade-quality video games to be played at home, came to be played in more than 35 percent of Japan's households.

With Famicom swiftly selling in Japan, Nintendo began exporting it to the United States. In 1985, however, when Nintendo was ready to enter U.S. homes, the home video market seemed all but tapped out. The United States had experienced a dramatic home video boom in the late 1970s and early 1980s, but by mid-decade this boom had ended, leaving the U.S. industry with hundreds of millions of dollars in losses. The sales of the U.S. home video industry had plummeted from a $3 billion peak in 1983 to a $100 million trough in 1985. These figures did not daunt Nintendo, which quietly test marketed its games during the darkest depths of the U.S. slump. The response was enthusiastic. Nintendo concluded that the problems in the U.S. home video market were caused by an excess of uninspiring, low-quality games that had flooded the market and disenchanted customers.

Seizing Opportunities: Middle and Late 1980s

Nintendo came to the United States in full force in 1985 with its American version of the Famicom, renamed the Nintendo Entertainment System (NES). First year profits were astounding, and the skillfully managed demand of the U.S. market showed few signs of softening from its introduction to the end of the decade. NES hardware was similar to its Japanese precursor, the Famicom, consisting of a Nintendo control deck, hand controls, and the game cartridges themselves. The control deck sported an eight-bit computer that generated stereo sound and images in 52 colors. It hooked up with the purchaser's television set to allow the viewer to play a complex video game—which could take up to 70 hours to complete—by manipulating a joystick that controlled movement in two dimensions.

The NES control deck was sold at close to cost, about $100, to place it in as many homes as possible. Nintendo then made a profit by selling its own game cartridges at $25 to $45 each by arranging lucrative licensing agreements with computer software manufacturers who were eager to get a piece of Nintendo's pie by creating software for NES games. From the very beginning of its U.S. home video foray, Nintendo gained customer loyalty and enthusiasm by producing or licensing sophisticated, challenging, and surprising software for its NES. By 1989, this practice had translated into an almost 80-percent share of the $3.4 billion home video game market. But the business strategies that brought Nintendo to its position of dominance soon came under intense scrutiny. Stymied competitors, the U.S. government, and Nintendo's own licensees—who found Nintendo's mode of granting licenses for game software could soak up as much as 50 percent of their profits—all came to regard Nintendo's trade practices with a suspicion that led to widely publicized litigation.

Nintendo and most industry analysts maintained that a lack of quality control killed the first home video craze in the early 1980s. To avoid making the same mistake, Nintendo erected a demanding series of market controls. Each of its licensees was limited to developing only six new game titles a year. Nintendo manufactured its own patented game cartridges and required would-be software programmers to buy the cartridges in batches of 10,000

Key Dates:

1889: Marufuku Company, Ltd. is founded in Japan by Fusajiro Yamauchi.
1907: Marufuku introduces Western-styled playing cards.
1933: Yamauchi forms Yamauchi Nintendo & Company, Ltd.
1951: The company is renamed Nintendo Playing Card Company.
1959: Nintendo signs an agreement with Disney to market themed playing cards.
1963: The firm's name is shortened to Nintendo Company, Ltd.
1969: A new manufacturing plant is built outside Kyoto.
1975: With Mitsubishi, Nintendo designs the first video game with electronic video recording.
1978: First coin-operated video machines are sold.
1980: Nintendo of America is established in Redmond, Washington.
1983: Famicom, Nintendo's first game console, is launched in Japan.
1986: Famicom, marketed as the Nintendo Gaming System, is introduced in the United States.

1989: Nintendo brings out its handheld Game Boy.
1991: Super NES gaming system is introduced in the United States.
1994: Sony launches Playstation; Nintendo debuts Super Game Boy.
1996: Nintendo 64 is introduced first in Japan, then the United States.
1998: *Pokémon* and *The Legend of Zelda* are launched in the United States.
2000: Sony launches the PlayStation 2 entertainment system.
2001: Microsoft introduces Xbox and Nintendo's long awaited GameCube debuts.
2002: Game Boy Advance reaches sales of over 25 million worldwide.
2003: Nintendo buys a minority stake in Bandai Company.
2004: Nintendo DS is released first in North America, then in Japan.

and then to assume full responsibility for reselling the game cartridges after they had been programmed by the licensee.

To make certain hardware competitors and software licensees would not try to circumvent Nintendo's control, Nintendo included a security chip in each game cartridge. Games programmed on cartridges lacking this microchip appeared scrambled when played. Nintendo reserved the right to modify games or to forbid a licensee's attempts to market a game deemed unsatisfactory by Nintendo evaluations. When a licensee's game gained approval, the developer had to wait two years before selling a version of its game to Nintendo's competitors. Because of these safeguards, the quality of Nintendo-compatible software remained high.

For the remainder of the decades, the company concentrated on popularizing its existing products and developing new ones. In Japan Nintendo developed and began selling a Family Computer Disk Drive System, which hit the mature Japanese market in 1986. The way this new product expanded communications capabilities of the Famicom was dramatically showcased in 1987, when Nintendo organized a nationwide Family Computer Golf Tournament in Japan. Players throughout the country used modems, public telephone lines, and disc facsimile technology to compete against each other from their own living rooms in Nintendo's home video game version of golf.

In 1988 Nintendo began publishing *Nintendo Power* magazine for its U.S. customers. This magazine, aimed at adolescents, was filled with game-playing tips and announcements concerning recently developed games and hardware. For those times when *Nintendo Power* could not help a frustrated game player, Nintendo introduced a 20-hour telephone bank with advice from 300 game counselors.

Further public relations efforts included a deal with Ralston Purina Company in May 1989 to market a citrus-flavored Nintendo Cereal System, featuring edible versions of the heroes

from its video games. In 1989 Nintendo also teamed up with PepsiCo and nationwide toy retailer Toys 'R' Us for special joint promotions and in-store displays. Nintendo spent $60 million on U.S. advertising during the year.

In 1989 Nintendo also returned to the handheld electronic game market it had created a decade earlier. The battery-operated Game Boy, about the size of a paperback book, featured interchangeable game cartridges, stereo sound, and complex dot-matrix graphics. In Japan Nintendo unveiled a new 16-bit advanced version of the Famicom, dubbed the Super Family Computer. Its more complex electronics meant more challenging games, more interesting graphics, and more realistic sound. Nintendo waited to release the U.S. version of the 16-bit machine until it felt the market was ready.

A New Game Forming: Early 1990s

In the early 1990s the continued success of Sega Enterprises, Ltd. gave Nintendo its first real competitor. It was Sega's 16-bit Genesis System that led Nintendo to upgrade its eight-bit machinery. Sega's growing product line and state-of-the art programs rivaled those of Nintendo and offered buyers an alternative video game system. Nintendo was not easily vanquished, however. Many industry observers saw Nintendo as the "next Disney," and a survey of school children found that the Mario character was more popular than Mickey Mouse. Although video game sales slowed in 1990, growing less than half as fast as they had the previous year, Nintendo's sales increased by 63 percent. When U.S. video game sales reached $4.2 billion by 1991, Nintendo products accounted for $3.2 billion.

In the summer of 1992 Japan's Capcom Company released *Street Fighter II* for Nintendo which was an immediate success. Also in 1992, Nintendo produced *Super Mario Paint*, a drawing program featuring the company's star character, a game based on the Road Runner cartoon character, a sequel to its very popular Zelda character, called *The Legend of Zelda: A Link to the Past.* Nintendo hoped eventually to raise its U.S. household penetration rate from 17 percent to the 35 percent it had achieved in Japan and mirror the ten-to-one software-to-hardware ratio it had achieved in its home country.

Nintendo's exports to the United States had grown eightfold from 1987 to 1991, and the company held 60 percent of the 16-bit U.S. market at the end of 1992. Yet Sega's comparative advertising, begun in 1990, pried open Nintendo's grip on consumers. Sega branded Nintendo's games as children's toys, and Nintendo of America failed to respond to the ploy. Nintendo's U.S. market share fell to 37 percent by the end of 1993. Jeopardy continued into 1994 when a new generation of machines hit the market.

Sega's and Sony's new game consoles were 32-bit systems utilizing CD-ROM disk drives. Sega's Saturn and Sony's PlayStation had inherently large storage capacities, thanks to the CD-ROMs, but were considered sluggish. Nintendo, on the other hand used much faster but more expensive silicon storage cartridges. Instead of matching the moves of its competitors, Nintendo concentrated on developing, in partnership with California-based Silicon Graphics, Inc., a 64-bit processor with superior capabilities.

Faced with consumer desertions to the 32-bit machines, Nintendo tried to extend the life of its 16-bit Super Nintendo System by bringing out hot games. *Donkey Kong Country*, which had been designed for the 64-bit system, was released in a 16-bit format and became the bestselling game of 1994.

Since consoles needed games, Sega, Sony, and Nintendo spent millions each year on software development. Independently produced games continued to generate the bulk of Nintendo's revenue in this important area, with in-house software only bringing in about 35 percent of sales. In 1995, pressed by the need to produce software for its new machine, Nintendo purchased a 25 percent stake in Rare Ltd., a U.K.-based developer. This was Nintendo's first investment in a software maker outside of Japan.

Nintendo's promise of a cheaper and more exciting video gaming system by early 1996 dampened Saturn and PlayStation sales somewhat during the 1995 Christmas season. Nevertheless, Sega passed Nintendo in terms of total sales for the first time in the fiscal year ending March 1996. Nintendo's consolidated sales fell 15 percent and operating profits fell 24 percent. The 32-bit machines, the economic recession in the important Japanese market, and the defection of independent software producers to the competition contributed to Nintendo's downward spiral.

Nintendo 64 (N64) finally hit the market in 1996. Japanese consumers were eager to check out the new system. "With preordering rampant and queues outside the stores, some 300,000 Nintendo 64 machines were snapped up by eager addicts on the first day," stated an August 1996 article in the *Economist.* Anticipating the U.S. release, Sega and Sony cut the prices on their 32-bit units.

The N64 Japanese launch got off to a fast start but stalled just as quickly: only a few games were ready for the format. Nintendo had backpedaled on the N64 release date a number of times, which frustrated independent software makers and led to the defection of some important developers to Sony. Further

complicating matters was the complexity of programming required for the N64 software and programmers' frustration with the limited storage capacity of the cartridges compared to the CDs used by the competition. Another factor in the mix, one which was not there during Nintendo's glory days, was the personal computer (PC). PC makers were fabricating increasingly sophisticated games, drawing talent from the software developer pool and eating into the market.

Difficulties aside, Nintendo continued to live up to its reputation for quality software and produced another blockbuster game. "This is probably the most perfectly crafted video game ever," wrote Neil Gross in *Business Week* (October 14, 1996). Shigeru Miyamoto, the designer of the original 8-bit Mario game, scored big with *Super Mario 64.*

Mario's fluid movements through dazzling three-dimensional graphics set the game apart from earlier versions and from competing 32-bit games. Sony and Sega, on the other hand, were not just waiting for Nintendo to rack up points. Sega was the first to release a web-browsing device, and Sony was way ahead of the pack in number of games available. Nintendo continued to feel the pinch and recorded its third straight year of declining financial results in the fiscal year ending March 1996.

In the first half of 1996 sales of the 16-bit Super Nintendo machines and related software plummeted. Sales generated by the new system, due in part to the lack of software, did not pick up all the slack. In September 1996 Nintendo 64 (N64), with eight titles on hand, hit North American shelves; by June 1997, 2.6 million machines had been sold, capturing half of the market. An additional 2.7 million had been sold elsewhere in the world. Revenues for fiscal 1997 were up 18 percent to $3.5 billion; earnings reached $54 million.

Sony, the market leader, had more than 11 million PlayStations in the hands of consumers worldwide and carried 150 game titles. Nintendo 64 offered just 17 titles for play. The importance of the software lay most clearly in its profitability. Nintendo's margins for hardware were usually under 5 percent while software yielded margins of nearly 45 percent. Software produced more than 50 percent of the company's profits. Aware of the dilemma it faced, Nintendo of America's chairman personally solicited the services of U.S. software developers.

In an effort to boost capacity, a sticking point with the game makers, Nintendo put an N64 peripheral in the pipeline. The DD64, a magnetic disk drive, was to also contain a communications device. Nintendo was headed in the right direction, but the progress was slow; however, sales and profits were boosted in 1997 by Pokémon (short for "pocket monster"), a new game played on Nintendo's handheld Game Boy machines. Nevertheless, the year was marked by a delay in the launch of the new DD64 hardware platform and the botched delivery of *Yoshi's Story,* a much ballyhooed software title.

From the 20th to the 21st Century: 1998 to 2001

Nintendo came back in early 1998 with the introduction of the Game Boy Camera, a digital offering that sold for $50 and attached to the Game Boy machine. Nintendo sold more than 700,000 of the units in its first five weeks on the Japanese market. Solidifying its dominance in the handheld market,

Nintendo also released Game Boy Color and Pokémon Pikachu, a virtual pet. (The Pokémon game had spawned a multibillion-dollar industry of related merchandise.) *GoldenEye 007*, based on the latest James Bond movie, was another hit for Nintendo in 1998, winning the prestigious "Game of the Year" award from the Academy of Interactive Art (AIA). *GoldenEye* helped fuel fiscal sales of $4.42 billion for 1998.

In late 1998 as Sega introduced its 128-bit Dreamcast in Japan, Nintendo spent millions on the rollout of *The Legend of Zelda: Ocarina of Time*. The game enthralled millions around the planet, achieving record sales and winning Nintendo the AIA "Game of the Year" award for the second year in a row. In addition to *Zelda* and *GoldenEye,* perennial favorite Pokémon was back in 1999 with *Pokémon Pinball* and *Pokémon Yellow* for Game Boy, and *Pokémon Snap* for N64. The Pokémon craze continued to sweep Asia and the United States, and Nintendo had no shortage of titles to sustain the hysteria. Sales for fiscal 1999 reached $4.73 billion, a healthy increase from the previous year's figures.

Sega's Dreamcast, which processed data more quickly than both PlayStation and N64 and was capable of producing more lifelike graphics, hit the United States in late 1999. Nintendo countered by releasing a slew of new N64 titles including *Mario Golf, Mario Party, Super Smash Bros., Donkey Kong 64, Racer,* and others. The new century a few months later brought several milestones for Nintendo, including the sale of its one-hundred millionth Game Boy, the release of *The Legend of Zelda: Majora's Mask* and *Pokémon Stadium* for N64, and *Pokémon Gold* and *Silver* for Game Boy Color.

Not to be outdone, Sony's new PlayStation 2, which it categorized as a home entertainment system, was even faster than Dreamcast and produced images with graphic quality similar to animated movies. Not just a game console, the PlayStation 2 accommodated movies and games recorded on DVDs (digital video disks). Breaking with industry convention, the console also played games produced for the original PlayStation. With PlayStation 2 flying off the shelves, Nintendo knew its new console had to be spectacular. The company partnered with ArtX and IBM for specially designed microchips for speed and graphics, and signed an agreement with Matsushita Electric Industrial Company, Inc., known for its Panasonic work, to create the media system for the new console, code named Dolphin (later christened GameCube).

By the following year, 2001, both Mario and Donkey Kong celebrated their 20th anniversaries and were featured in new games for the introduction of Game Boy Advance, which debuted in Japan in March 2001 at the end of the fiscal year. Revenues had fallen sharply, however, to just over $3.7 billion with Sony's PlayStation 2 dominating the console and software markets. Nintendo countered with the release of Game Boy Advance in the United States in June 2001 to much acclaim, though the gaming market declined dramatically after the terrorist attacks of September 11, 2001. All of the major players in the gaming industry lost sales, but geared up for a fresh start in 2002.

A New Era: 2002 and Beyond

At the beginning of 2002 Nintendo faced a changing of the guard: Hiroshi Yamauchi stepped down after 52 years of run-ning the company and was succeeded by Satoru Iwata, a software developer. Iwata had only joined Nintendo two years earlier but had been developing games for the company for decades. Despite the retirement of Yamauchi, it was business as usual at Nintendo: its phenomenally popular Game Boy Advance continued to attract new players and sales had reached more than 25 million handheld units. Then came the launch of its long anticipated GameCube and several games to go with it, including *Super Mario Sunshine*. Other bestselling games released during the year included *Mario Party 4, Eternal Darkness,* and the well-received *Metroid Prime*.

While the GameCube was intended for players of all ages, Nintendo had succeeded in attracting teens and a more mature audience with titles such as the *Diehard* games (based on the movies starring Bruce Willis) and *Resident Evil* series. Nintendo's legendary game designer, Shigeru Miyamoto, commented to *Japan, Inc.* (June 2003), "We always get Sony and others saying that Nintendo is for children, but it really isn't," he insisted. "People are becoming better at games; the players have grown up, and the company has to do the same. . . . It's about producing a formula that works everywhere around the world." Miyamoto continued to create new adventures for his most famous characters, including Zelda, Donkey Kong, and Mario, following the same mantra for more than 20 years, "Behind every door, a surprise."

In 2003 Nintendo launched its new Game Boy Advance SP, with a new flip top and an illuminated screen. Units flew off the shelves of toy stores, yet Nintendo soon suffered unexpected losses due to fluctuations with the yen. To bolster its bottom line the company slashed prices, and prepared to go big into China's lucrative video game market before rivals Sony and Microsoft. By offering the Chinese a lower priced version of its GameCube, Nintendo hoped to eclipse sales of both PlayStation 2 and Xbox. In addition, Nintendo bought a 3 percent stake in Japanese software developer and toy manufacturer Bandai Company. Though Bandai officials denied any future partnerships or deals were in the works with Nintendo, its development deal with Mattel was due to expire at the end of the year. Nintendo finished the year with sales of $4.2 billion, but net income plunged to $561.3 million, down from 2002's $802.5 million.

In 2004 Nintendo initiated several moves to steal customers from rival Sony—it lowered the price of its incredibly popular Game Boy Advance system, released two new *Pokémon* titles (*FireRed* and *LeafGreen*), and brought out its next generation handheld game, the Nintendo DS (DS stood for dual-screen). The DS took mobile gaming to a new level: it was wireless, had surround-sound, excellent graphics, and voice recognition; it was compatible with Game Boy Advance and its library of games; and it had two screens instead of one. The company had high expectations for the Nintendo DS, believing it would take gaming to a totally different level. Designer Miyamoto (whose Mario had sold 170 million games to date), confirmed this in an interview with *Game Developer* magazine (June-July 2004): "We didn't make the DS because we wanted to make our console games portable, or because we wanted to make our Game Boy Advance games more gorgeous. We really wanted to create the DS so people could [play] completely new styles of games no one has ever experienced before." The DS had already created a buzz in the industry by the time of its release, and had signed hundreds of game designers willing to create DS adventures.

While Sony's console sales eclipsed those of Nintendo and Microsoft, the latter's XBox was considered the most sophisticated in terms of graphics and had Microsoft's clout and billions behind it. Nintendo's hardware products—GameCube, Game Boy Advance SP, and the new DS—continued to attract new fans as well as loyalists. The company's imaginative games and characters, however, remained as popular as ever. "We see these characters as ageless," George Harrison, senior vice-president of marketing and corporate communications at Nintendo of America, had commented to *Brandweek* (January 7, 2002). "There is a huge following with people who have played Nintendo games since the 1980s. They are not at all embarrassed to play *Luigi's Mansion, Mario Cart,* and *Super Smash Brothers.*" Harrison was right on the mark; Nintendo's fans bought new games featuring their favorite characters again and again, and as Nintendo hoped, bought the next generation consoles or handhelds necessary to play them.

In the gaming wars of the mid-2000s Sony remained the undisputed king of consoles with its PlayStation 2, but Nintendo had gained ground on Microsoft's Xbox, enough to claim it had edged Xbox out of the number two slot. In the handheld arena, however, Nintendo was still the market leader with its perennially popular Game Boy and the new DS despite Sony's launch of the PSP (PlayStation Portable). "The key to success in our industry is no secret," Harrison told *Wireless News* (September 30, 2004), "when you offer great interactive entertainment at a great price, players respond in droves." These "droves" took Nintendo's sales to $4.7 billion for 2004, and this figure did not include sales of the new Nintendo DS, which was earning raves from the gaming industry. Not to be outdone, Sony's new handheld PSP hit stores in early 2005.

Principal Subsidiaries

Nintendo of America, Inc. (U.S.A.); Nintendo of Australia Pty, Ltd.; Nintendo of Canada, Ltd.; Nintendo Espana, S.A. (Spain); Nintendo France; Nintendo of Europe GmbH (Germany); Nintendo Hong Kong Limited; Nintendo Netherlands B.V.; Nintendo UK Entertainment Ltd.; Pokémon Company.

Principal Competitors

Microsoft Corporation; Sega Corporation; Sony Corporation.

Further Reading

Abrahams, Paul, "All's Fair in Console War: Sony Claims Its PlayStation 2 Has Triumphed in the Games Market," *Financial Times,* May 28, 2002, p. 30.
——, "Nintendo's Errors Could Well End Up Costing It the Game," *Financial Times,* October 17, 1998, p. 21.
Alexander, Steve, "The New 128-Bit Consoles: A Whole New Game," *Star Tribune* (Minneapolis), May 14, 1999, pp. D1–D2.
Brandt, Richard, "Clash of the Titans," *Business Week,* September 7, 1992.
Browder, Seanna, Steven B. Brull, and Andy Reinhardt, "Nintendo: At the Top of Its Game," *Business Week,* June 9, 1997, pp. 72–73.
Brown, Eryn, "Sony's Big Bazooka: PlayStation Is Blowing Away Its Competitors," *Fortune,* December 30, 2002, p. 111.
Carlton, Jim, "U.S. Retail Sales of Video Games Up 32% for Year," *Wall Street Journal,* November 6, 1998, p. B6.
Dawley, Heidi, and Paul M. Eng, "Killer Instinct for Hire," *Business Week,* May 29, 1995, pp. 91–92.
Dvorak, Phred, "Sony, Nintendo Unveil Handheld Rival Players," *Wall Street Journal,* May 12, 2004, p. 1.
Gross, Neil, "Infinitely Cool in 64 Bits," *Business Week,* October 14, 1996, p. 134.
Gross, Neil, and Robert D. Hof, "Nintendo's Yamauchi: No More Playing Around," *Business Week,* February 21, 1994, p. 71.
"Hasbro to Handle Pokémon in U.S.," *Advertising Age,* June 1, 1998, p. 44.
Hein, Kenneth, "Nintendo Grows Up," *Brandweek,* January 7, 2002, p. 12.
Heyamoto, Lisa, "President of Game Maker Steps Down," *Knight Ridder/Tribune News Service,* May 25, 2002.
Jackson, David S., "The Spielberg of Video Games," *Time,* May 20, 1996, p. 53.
Johansen-Berg, Kate, "A Game of Two Halves," *In-Store Marketing,* July 2002, p. 18.
Kharif, Olga, "The Video Wars Explode Online," *Business Week Online,* December 11, 2002.
King, Sharon R., "Mania for 'Pocket Monsters' Yields Billions for Nintendo," *New York Times,* April 26, 1999, pp. A1.
Konish, Nancy, "Video Game Giants Are Neck and Neck for the Profit," *Electronic Design,* September 14, 1998, p. 32A.
Krantz, Michael, "Super Mario's Dazzling Comeback," *Time,* May 20, 1996, pp. 52–54.
Kunii, Irene M., "Sega: We're Going to Blow Them Out of the Water," *Business Week,* December 7, 1998, p. 108.
——, "Smile, You're on Candid Game Boy," *Business Week,* April 27, 1998, p. 8.
Lefton, Terry, "Zelda Returns with $10M," *Brandweek,* October 19, 1998, p. 8.
Lewis, Leo, "Game Over? Mario, Donkey Kong, and Pokémon Are the Superstars Who Shaped Nintendo's Past. . .," *Japan, Inc.,* June 2003, p. 38.
Lewis, Peter, "Hand-to-Hand Combat," *Fortune,* May 31, 2004, p. 60.
Martinez, Michael J., "Let the (Video) Games Begin," *Kiplinger's Personal Finance,* December 2001, p. 30.
McGill, Douglas C., "Nintendo Scores Big," *New York Times,* December 4, 1988.
Moffat, Susan, "Can Nintendo Keep Winning?," *Fortune,* November 5, 1990.
Moledina, Jamil, "Doing Mushrooms, Miramoto Style," *Game Developer,* June-July 2004, p. 24.
——, "When Handhelds Collide," *Game Developer,* June-July 2004, p. 6.
Nakamoto, Michiyo, "Competition Continues to Squeeze Nintendo," *Financial Times,* May 23, 1996, p. 36.
——, "Move to New Technology Hurts Nintendo," *Financial Times,* November 6, 1996, p. 34.
——, "Sales of New Game Lift Nintendo," *Financial Times,* November 14, 1997, p. 22.
"Nintendo New Game Boy Will Knock Your Lights Out!," *PC Magazine,* March 17, 2003.
"Nintendo Wakes Up," *Economist,* August 3, 1996, pp. 55–56.
"Nintendo Unveils New Game Boy Advance SP," *PC Magazine,* January 7, 2003.
"Now, the Latest Beepings from Video-Game Land," *Money,* July 1991.
O'Brien, Soledad, "Japanese Videomaker Nintendo Buys Stake in Domestic Rival Bandai," *America's Intelligence Wire,* October 22, 2003.

''*Pokémon FireRed* and *Pokémon LeafGreen* Combine to Heat Up Sales,'' *Wireless News,* September 30, 2004.

Quittner, Josh, ''The Box Meets the Cube,'' *Time,* November 19, 2001, p. 145.

Takahashi, Dean, ''Nintendo Is Top Scorer in Game Sales, But Sony Sees Bigger Hardware Growth,'' *Wall Street Journal,* January 19, 1999, p. B6.

''A Video Game War That's Just Dandy for Everyone,'' *Business Week,* March 4, 2002, p. 54.

—Rene Steinke and Mary McNulty
—updates: Kathleen Peippo, Nelson Rhodes

Nordstrom, Inc.

1617 Sixth Avenue
Seattle, Washington 98101-1742
U.S.A.
Telephone: (206) 628-2111
Toll Free: (888) 282-6060
Fax: (206) 628-1795
Web site: http://www.nordstorm.com

Public Company
Incorporated: 1901 as Wallin & Nordstrom
Employees: 46,000
Sales: $6.49 billion (2003)
Stock Exchanges: New York
Ticker Symbol: JWN
NAIC: 452110 Department Stores; 448140 Family
    Clothing Stores; 448210 Shoe Stores; 454110
    Electronic Shopping and Mail-Order Houses

Nordstrom, Inc. was started in 1901 as a single shoe store in Seattle, Washington, that was opened by two Swedish immigrants. From those origins, the family-run enterprise expanded into a 180-outlet, 27-state chain, which tallied $6.49 billion in sales in 2003. In addition to more than 90 flagship Nordstrom department stores, the company also operates about 50 Nordstrom Rack outlet stores in the United States and around 35 Façonnable boutiques, most of which are located in Europe. Catalog and Internet sales are generated through the Nordstrom Direct unit. Carefully supervised expansion, tight family management, wide selection, and attentive customer service have long been the hallmarks of Seattle-based Nordstrom, one of the largest independent fashion specialty retailers in the United States. Members of the founding Nordstrom family continue to own about 20 percent of the company's stock.

Opening of Small Shoe Store in 1901

John W. Nordstrom, a 16-year-old Swede, arrived in Minnesota in 1887 with $5 to his name and, after working his way across the United States, settled briefly in Seattle. In 1897 he headed north to Alaska in search of gold. He found it. In 1899,

$13,000 richer, Nordstrom moved back to Seattle, where he opened a shoe store with Carl Wallin, a shoemaker he had met in Alaska. On its first day of business in 1901, Wallin & Nordstrom sold $12.50 in shoes.

Business quickly picked up. By 1905 annual sales increased to $80,000. The business continued to grow, and in 1923 the partners opened a second store in Seattle. By 1928, however, 57-year-old John Nordstrom had decided to retire from the shoe business, and passed on his share to his sons Everett and Elmer. Carl Wallin retired the following year and likewise sold his share to the next generation of Nordstroms. In 1930 the shoe stores were renamed Nordstrom's. In 1933 John Nordstrom's youngest son, Lloyd, joined the partnership.

The business that John Nordstrom left was substantially larger than the one he started back in 1901. It was up to the next generation of Nordstroms, however, to build on their father's success. In 1929 the Nordstrom brothers doubled the size of their downtown Seattle store. In 1930, despite the onset of the Great Depression, the two stores made $250,000 in sales. The shoe stores survived the Depression, but faced another severe threat during World War II, when leather rationing prohibited U.S. consumers from buying more than three pairs of shoes per year. The Nordstrom brothers had to search nationwide for supplies of shoes.

Expansion and Diversification in the 1950s and 1960s

In the postwar decades, the Nordstrom brothers built the company into the largest independent shoe chain in the United States. In 1950 the Nordstroms opened two new shoe stores: one in Portland, Oregon, and one in a Seattle suburb—the latter located at Northgate Mall, the nation's first shopping mall. Nine years later, Nordstrom remodeled its Seattle flagship store, and stocked it with 100,000 pairs of shoes—the biggest inventory in the country. By 1961 Nordstrom operated eight shoe stores and 13 leased shoe departments in Washington, Oregon, and California. That year, the firm grossed $12 million in sales and had 600 employees on its payroll.

In the early 1960s, the Nordstrom brothers came to a crossroads of sorts. Spurred by their success, they were convinced that their business could expand. The brothers were unsure whether they should simply expand their shoe business to the East and South or branch out into other areas of retailing. The brothers chose to diversify, and purchased Best Apparel, a Seattle-based women's clothing store, in 1963. With the addition of apparel outlets, the company expanded rapidly. In 1965 the Nordstroms opened a new Best Apparel store adjacent to a Nordstrom shoe store in suburban Seattle. In 1966 the company acquired a Portland retail fashion outlet, Nicholas Ungar, and merged it with the Nordstrom shoe store in Portland, which was renamed Nordstrom Best.

In the late 1960s, the modern Nordstrom department store began to take shape. Between 1965 and 1968, the company opened five stores that combined apparel and shoes. In 1967, when annual sales had reached $40 million, the chain's name was changed to Nordstrom Best. The firm diversified further in these years, as Nordstrom Best began to sell men's and children's clothing as well.

Third Generation Took Control in 1970

In 1968 Everett Nordstrom turned 65, and he and his two brothers decided to turn over the reins of the company to the next generation of Nordstroms. Five men—Everett's son Bruce, Elmer's sons James and John, Lloyd's son-in-law John A. McMillan, and family friend Robert E. Bender—took control of the company.

In August 1971 the company went public, offering Nordstrom Best stock on the over-the-counter market. Family members retained a majority of the stock, however. In 1971 Nordstrom earned $3.5 million on sales of $80 million. In 1973, when sales first topped $100 million, the company changed its name to Nordstrom, Inc. That same year saw the opening of the first Nordstrom Rack, an outlet store used to move old inventories at discount prices. It was located in the basement of the downtown Seattle store.

The firm continued to grow steadily throughout the 1970s by opening new stores, increasing volume in existing stores, and diversifying. In 1974 annual sales hit $130 million. The following year, Nordstrom bought three stores in Alaska. In 1976 the firm launched a new division, Place Two, which featured, in smaller stores, a selected offering of men's and women's apparel and shoes. By 1977 Nordstrom operated 24 stores, which generated sales of $246 million.

In 1978 Nordstrom expanded into the southern California market, opening an outlet in Orange County. That year, the firm reaped $13.5 million in earnings on nearly $300 million in sales. Buoyed by the success, Nordstrom's executives charted an aggressive expansion program, and began to open bigger stores in California. Their late 1970s confidence presaged a decade of phenomenal, but controlled, growth.

Rapid Growth in Early 1980s Fueled by Legendary Customer Service

By 1980 Nordstrom was the third largest specialty retailer in the country, ranking behind only Saks Fifth Avenue and Lord & Taylor. That year, the firm operated 31 stores in California, Washington, Oregon, Utah, Montana, and Alaska. In 1980 a new expansion plan called for 25 new stores to be added in the 1980s, and the Nordstroms projected that both earnings and total square footage would double by 1985.

The projection was not sufficiently optimistic. In 1980 sales hit $407 million, and in the next few years, sales and earnings continued to rise substantially. Between 1980 and 1983, when sales jumped to $787 million, earnings more than doubled, going from $19.7 million to $40.2 million. In 1982 Nordstrom established Nordstrom Rack as its third division, now consisting of a string of outlet stores. The chain's biggest growth area, however, was in the huge California market. By 1984 there were seven Nordstrom stores in that state. Five years later, Nordstrom had 22 full-size stores in California.

Nordstrom increasingly came to be recognized as an efficient, upscale, full-service department store. Its aggressive customer service plainly brought results. The firm consistently maintained the highest sales per square foot of retail space ratios in the industry, nearly twice those of other department stores.

Nordstrom's success was due to a variety of factors. Throughout its existence, shoes accounted for a good deal of the firm's sales—about 18 percent in 1989. In most fashion and apparel stores, shoes constitute a smaller percentage of sales. In addition Nordstrom consistently maintained huge inventories and selection, which were usually twice the size of other department stores. In the mid-1980s, a typical outlet stocked 75,000 pairs of shoes, 5,000 men's dress shirts, and 7,000 ties. Moreover, a decentralized corporate structure allowed local buyers, who knew their customers' needs, to make inventory selections.

Most significantly, though, Nordstrom's management encouraged the development of an aggressive sales force. The vast majority of Nordstrom clerks worked on commission, and the average salesperson earned $24,000 annually. Managers generally promoted from within the ranks of salespeople, which intensified the desire to sell.

In the 1980s the firm's customer service became legendary, as tales of heroic efforts by salespeople became legion: clerks were known to pay shoppers' parking tickets, rush deliveries to offices, unquestioningly accept returns, lend cash to strapped customers, and to send tailors to customers' homes. Salespeople received constant pep talks from management, and motivational exercises were a routine part of life at Nordstrom. Nordstrom also created an extremely customer-friendly environment.

Key Dates:

1901: John W. Nordstrom opens a shoe store in Seattle with Carl Wallin, called Wallin & Nordstrom.

1923: Second store is opened in Seattle.

1928: Nordstrom retires and sells his share in the firm to his sons Everett and Elmer.

1929: Wallin retires and also sells his shares to the Nordstrom sons.

1930: The shoe stores are renamed Nordstrom's.

1933: A third son, Lloyd, joins the firm.

1950: Two new shoe stores are opened, one in Portland, Oregon, and one in a Seattle suburb.

1963: Best Apparel, a Seattle-based women's clothing store, is acquired.

1966: The Nordstrom's shoe store in Portland begins selling clothing as well, adopting the name Nordstrom Best, which is soon the name of the company and all of its outlets.

1968: Third generation of Nordstroms take over management command.

1971: Nordstrom Best goes public.

1973: Company changes its name to Nordstrom, Inc.; first Nordstrom Rack opens.

1978: Opening of a store in Orange County, California, marks the first move outside the Northwest.

1985: Revenues surpass the $1 billion mark.

1988: First East Coast store opens in McLean, Virginia.

1991: First Midwest store opens in the Chicago suburb of Oak Brook, Illinois.

1995: The third-generation Nordstrom managers retire; non-family-member John Whitacre becomes chairman, while six fourth-generation family members become copresidents.

2000: Whitacre is ousted; Bruce Nordstrom is named chairman, Blake Nordstrom, president; Nordstrom acquires Façonnable S.A.

Many stores had free coat check service, concierges, and piano players who serenaded shoppers.

As the economy boomed in the 1980s, Nordstrom's figures climbed apace. In 1985 sales first topped $1 billion, as they jumped to $1.3 billion. In 1987 the firm reaped profits of $92.7 million on sales of $1.92 billion.

Began Eastward Expansion in the Mid-1980s

Nordstrom's growth in the latter half of the 1980s stemmed from a combination of expansion into new territories and the creation of larger stores in existing Nordstrom territory. In 1986, when the firm operated 53 stores in six western states, Nordstrom began to turn its sights to the East. In March 1988, Nordstrom opened its first store on the East Coast, a 238,000-square-foot facility in McLean, Virginia, just outside Washington, D.C. On its first day, the store racked up more than $1 million in sales. Over the first year, the store brought in $100 million in sales.

The same year, Nordstrom expanded on the West Coast as well, opening its biggest store, a 350,000-square-foot facility in downtown San Francisco. The lavish San Francisco store featured 103 different brands of champagne, 16 varieties of chilled vodka, and a health spa, among other luxurious amenities.

By the end of 1988, Nordstrom had 21,000 employees toiling in its 58 stores. Together they persuaded customers to buy $2.3 billion worth of goods in 1988, and earned profits of $123 million for the corporation.

Expansion in other areas of the East continued in the late 1980s. In 1989 Nordstrom opened a second store in the Washington, D.C., area—in the Pentagon City Mall. That same year the firm also opened outlets in Sacramento and Brea, California. Capping the decade, the company won the National Retail Merchants Association's Gold Medal. Clearly, Nordstrom had become a paragon of retailing success. Envious of its market share and sales figures, many competitors began to imitate its strategies of large inventory and lavish customer service.

Nordstrom continued to rely on its aggressive sales staff, but the corporate policy of encouraging clerks to go out of their way to make sales caused the company some grief. The employees' union (which was later decertified) complained about the pressure on employees to sell. In late 1989 a group of unionized employees charged that they were not being paid for performing extra services to customers.

In February 1990, after a three-month investigation, the Washington State Department of Labor & Industries alleged that the company had systematically violated state laws by failing to pay employees for a variety of duties, such as delivering merchandise and doing inventory work. The agency ordered Nordstrom to change its compensation and record-keeping procedures, and to pay back wages to some of Nordstrom's 30,000 employees. Soon after, the firm created a $15 million reserve to pay back-wage claims. The company, however, remained a target of class-action lawsuits on these matters, which were finally settled out of court in early 1993 when Nordstrom agreed to pay a set percentage of compensation to employees who worked at Nordstrom from 1987 to 1990. The settlement cost the company between $20 million and $30 million.

Other unforeseen events in 1989 and 1990 hit the company as well. The San Francisco earthquake of 1989 took a significant bite out of retail sales in the San Francisco Bay area. The general nationwide downturn in retailing hurt the company more, however. In September 1990, Nordstrom, then a 61-store company, announced it would cut costs by 3 to 12 percent and laid off some personnel. In the fourth quarter of 1989, Nordstrom's earnings dropped 34 percent from the previous year. Earnings fell about 7 percent for the entire year, from $123.3 million in 1988 to $115 million in 1989; sales, however, increased nearly 15 percent in that year, from $2.33 billion to $2.67 billion.

Slower Growth in the 1990s

In the early 1990s, Bruce, James, and John Nordstrom, John McMillan, and Robert Bender collectively still owned a 40 percent stock interest and continued to maintain tight control of the company. Although Nordstrom suffered from the recession of the early 1990s, it continued to expand and open new stores in the East and Midwest. In September 1990, Nordstrom launched its first store in the metropolitan New York area, in Paramus,

New Jersey. In April 1991 Nordstrom debuted its first Midwest store—in Oak Brook, Illinois, a Chicago suburb. In typical Nordstrom style, the store unveiled featuring 125,000 pairs of shoes, a concierge, an espresso bar, and a wood-paneled English-style pub. In 1991 the company also opened stores in Riverside, California; Edison, New Jersey; and Bethesda, Maryland.

Sales and earnings rebounded a fraction in 1990. Sales rose 8 percent to $2.89 billion, and profits rose a minuscule 0.7 percent to $115.8 million. In 1990 women's apparel and accessories accounted for 59 percent of Nordstrom's total sales; men's apparel accounted for 16 percent; and shoes—still a company mainstay—constituted 19 percent of all sales.

Such single-digit growth became the norm for Nordstrom throughout the early and mid-1990s, as sales grew sluggish thanks in large part to fluctuations in demand for women's apparel and the severe recession in southern California, where more than half of the company's total store square footage was located in the early years of the decade. The double-digit growth of the 1980s was gone—in fact, the sales increases of the 1990s were largely attributable to new store openings, with same-store sales (that is, sales at stores open more than a year) flat.

Largely shying away from the troubled California market, Nordstrom increasingly sought out new territory for expansion, particularly in the Midwest, South, and Northeast. In 1996 alone, the Philadelphia, Dallas, Denver, and Detroit metropolitan areas were added to the Nordstrom empire through new store openings. While it continued its steady expansion, Nordstrom also made a number of moves indicative of a company in something of a transition. Nordstrom produced its first mail-order catalog in the early 1990s, opened the first Nordstrom Factory Direct store near Philadelphia in 1993, and launched a proprietary Visa card in 1994. Also in 1993, the company opened a men's boutique in New York called Façonnable (pronounced fa-so-na-bleh) in partnership with the French firm Façonnable S.A. Nordstrom had been the exclusive U.S. distributor of Façonnable's line of upscale men's and women's apparel and accessories since 1989.

Meanwhile, with net earnings slipping somewhat (from 5.3 percent in 1988 to 3.91 percent in 1993), Nordstrom sought to cut costs, in particular its selling, general, and administrative costs, which accounted for 26.4 percent of sales in 1992. This relatively high figure resulted from Nordstrom's generous employee incentive program that fueled the company's reputation for customer service. By 1995, however, these costs had actually increased to 27.2 percent of sales, while net earnings improved only slightly to 4.01 percent.

Although considered innovative in many areas, Nordstrom had stayed away from large investments in systems technology prior to the mid-1990s. In 1995 a new information system was installed, along with a new system for personnel, payroll, and benefits processing. Most importantly, Nordstrom's first inventory control system rolled out that same year in southern California, with companywide rollout the following year. Although the status of an item throughout all stores could be checked using the system, Nordstrom maintained its traditional decentralized buying, bucking an industry trend toward centralization.

Perhaps the most significant transition took place in the management arena late in 1995, when Nordstrom's four

cochairmen—Bruce, James, and John Nordstrom and John McMillan—retired. This third generation of Nordstroms to lead the company were replaced by former copresidents Ray Johnson and John Whitacre, who became the new cochairmen (although Johnson subsequently retired in September 1996), and were in turn replaced in the copresidency by six fourth-generation family members—Bill, Blake, Dan, Erik, Jim A., and Pete Nordstrom—all in their early 30s. The new management team faced the difficult task of taking over in the hypercompetitive and sluggish sales environment of the mid-1990s as well as attempting to maintain Nordstrom's position as one of the top upscale retailers in the country.

Between 1997 and 1999 the company opened another ten new Nordstrom stores, adding 3.7 million square feet to the chain total. Among these was a new flagship store in downtown Seattle, which opened in August 1998 as a renovation of the historic Frederick & Nelson building, the flagship location for the Frederick & Nelson department store chain, founded in 1890. The states receiving their first Nordstrom store during the late 1990s were Arizona, Connecticut, Georgia, Kansas, Ohio, and Rhode Island. By 2000, there were 77 full-line Nordstrom stores, 38 Nordstrom Racks, and 23 Façonnable boutiques. Late in 1998 the company launched its online store at nordstrom.com. Nordstrom stock began trading on the New York Stock Exchange in June 1999.

Unfortunately, Nordstrom's struggles continued during this period. Many customers began viewing its merchandise as being too formal and neither keeping up with the latest lifestyle changes nor offering pacesetting fashions. In addition the unwieldy six-person copresidency inhibited rapid decision-making, and Nordstrom was well behind its competitors in making full use of information technology systems. In February 2000 Whitacre dismantled the copresidency, reassigning five of the Nordstrom cousins to line-management jobs. On the merchandise front, the company introduced new high-margin, private-label fashion lines for women, and centralized purchasing was instituted in order to provide a consistent chainwide merchandise look and to increase leverage with vendors. Along the same lines, regionally created advertising was replaced with the firm's first national television campaign to create a consistent Nordstrom image. Finally, the company's outdated computer systems began to be upgraded to more easily track merchandise and collect data on customer trends.

Return of Family Management, Early 2000s

The merchandising changes, however, quickly backfired. The overhaul, backed by an advertising campaign with the tag line "Reinvent Yourself," emphasized more youthful fashions that were appealing to 20-somethings but that alienated Nordstrom's core baby-boomer shoppers. Sales remained lackluster and earnings were down, leading to Whitacre's ouster in an August 2000 management shakeup. Bruce Nordstrom came out of retirement to take over the chairman's position, while his son Blake assumed the day-to-day reins as president. Blake Nordstrom, one of the former copresidents, had most recently been in charge of Nordstrom Rack. These developments occurred during one of Nordstrom's least profitable years in some time, as net income for fiscal 2000 totaled just $101.9 million on sales of $5.53 billion. Same-store sales increased just 0.3 percent over the previous year's sales. Also in 2000, Nordstrom acquired Façonnable S.A. for about $170 million, gaining full control of the Façonnable brand and the 53 Façonnable boutiques located around the world, mainly in Europe.

The new management team, attempting to turn the retailer's fortunes around, had the further problem of an economic downturn to deal with. After a brief upturn, same-store sales began falling in August 2001, leading the company to lay off as many as 2,500 employees late in the year as part of a cost-cutting initiative. Nordstrom also held its first-ever fall clearance sale to try to reduce excess inventories (unlike most competitors, who conducted regular sales, Nordstrom had traditionally held few promotions: two half-yearly sales for men and women, and an anniversary sale in July). Same-store sales fell 2.9 percent for the year, while net sales increased just 1.2 percent, despite the opening of four Nordstrom department stores and eight Nordstrom Racks. During the early 2000s, new store openings for the Nordstrom flagship centered on the Sun Belt, including the first locations in Florida and several additional ones in Texas. The number of store openings, however, was cut back from what had been perceived as an overly aggressive plan during the Whitacre era.

By 2003 Nordstrom appeared to have regained its lost luster through cost containment, technology initiatives, and a refocusing on its niche: luxury goods at affordable prices. Some analysts considered technology to be the key component, particularly a new state-of-the-art merchandising system, which began to be rolled out in 2002. The system could track sales minute by minute throughout its stores, enabling Nordstrom to reduce markdowns and better target its offerings to customers. On the merchandise side, the retailer began introducing edgier fashion offerings in a department called "via C," in an attempt to leverage its core customer base, which was younger and had a wider age range than its main competitors, Neiman-Marcus Co. and Saks Incorporated. Nordstrom enjoyed its most profitable year ever in 2003: $242.8 million in net income on record revenues of $6.49 billion. Same-store sales rose 4.3 percent, Nordstrom's best performance in ten years. Nordstrom hoped to maintain this forward momentum by continuing to roll out its technology initiatives, keeping a tight rein on expenses, and eschewing large investments in new real estate—only 11 new stores were slated for opening from 2004 through 2008—in favor of sprucing up existing stores and maximizing sales per square foot. The latter was already on the rise, increasing from $319 a square foot in 2002 to $327 in 2003, but were a far cry from industry leader Neiman Marcus's figure of $466 a square foot.

Principal Subsidiaries

Nordstrom fsb; Nordstrom Credit Card Receivables, LLC; Nordstrom Credit, Inc.; Nordstrom Private Label Receivables, LLC; Nordstrom Distribution, Inc.; N2HC, Inc.; Nordstrom International Limited; Nordstrom European Capital Group (France).

Principal Competitors

Saks Incorporated; Neiman-Marcus Co.; Dillard's, Inc.; The May Department Stores Company; Federated Department Stores, Inc.; J.C. Penney Corporation, Inc.; Sears, Roebuck and Co.

Further Reading

Bergmann, Joan, "Nordstrom Gets the Gold," *Stores,* January 1990.

Blumenthal, Robin Goldwyn, "Fashion Victim: A Hipper Nordstrom Is Trying to Tailor a Comeback, and It Just Might Succeed," *Barron's,* April 3, 2000, pp. 20, 22.

Browder, Seanna, "Great Service Wasn't Enough," *Business Week,* April 19, 1999, pp. 126–27.

Byron, Ellen, "Nordstrom Regains Its Luster: Challenge Awaits As Rivals Encroach on Image of Affordable Luxury," *Wall Street Journal,* August 19, 2004, p. B2.

De Voss, David, "The Rise and Rise of Nordstrom," *Lear's,* October 1989.

"Down the Tube: Nordstrom," *Economist,* June 5, 1993, p. 80.

Falum, Susan C., "At Nordstrom Stores, Service Comes First—But at a Big Price," *Wall Street Journal,* February 20, 1990.

Greenwald, John, "Losing Its Luster: Despite Exquisite Service, Nordstrom Has Suffered a Profit Slump," *Time,* March 24, 1997, pp. 64 +.

Hamilton, Joan O'C., and Amy Dunkin, "Why Rivals Are Quaking As Nordstrom Heads East," *Business Week,* June 15, 1987, p. 99.

Holmes, Stanley, "Can the Nordstroms Find the Right Style?," *Business Week,* July 30, 2001, pp. 59, 62.

Kossen, Bill, "A Good Fit? Northwest Retail Giant Attempts to Stay Nimble As It Tries to Bounce Back," *Seattle Times,* May 29, 2001, p. C1.

——, "Success Came a Step at a Time," *Seattle Times,* May 29, 2001, p. A1.

Lee, Louise, "Nordstrom Cleans Out Its Closets," *Business Week,* May 22, 2000, pp. 105–106, 108.

Lubove, Seth, "Don't Listen to the Boss, Listen to the Customer," *Forbes,* December 4, 1995, p. 45.

McAllister, Robert, "Nordstrom Tightens Its Belt for the Long Haul," *Footwear News,* September 6, 1993, p. 1.

Merrick, Amy, "Nordstrom Accelerates Plans to Straighten Out Business," *Wall Street Journal,* October 19, 2001, p. B4.

Moin, David, "A Big Job Ahead: Top Nordstrom Execs Map Rebuilding Plan," *WWD,* December 7, 2000, p. 1.

——, "Shakeup in Seattle: CEO Out, Family Back at Nordstrom Helm," *WWD,* September 1, 2000, p. 1.

Mulady, Kathy, "Back in the Family: Fourth Generation Takes Control After a Brief Change in Company Leadership," *Seattle Post-Intelligencer,* June 27, 2001, p. D1.

——, "Still in Style: From Small Shoe Store to Upscale Retailer, Company Has Kept Founder's Values," *Seattle Post-Intelligencer,* June 25, 2001, p. E1.

——, "A Time of Change: Company Makes Huge Leaps with Expansion, Public Stock Offering," *Seattle Post-Intelligencer,* June 26, 2001, p. D1.

Nordstrom, John W., *The Immigrant in 1887,* Seattle: Dogwood Press, 1950, 55 p.

Palmeri, Christopher, "Filling Big Shoes," *Forbes,* November 15, 1999, pp. 170, 172.

Schwadel, Francine, "Nordstrom's Push East Will Test Its Renown for the Best in Service," *Wall Street Journal,* August 1, 1989.

Solomon, Charlene Marmer, "Nightmare at Nordstrom," *Personnel Journal,* September 1990.

Spector, Robert, and Patrick D. McCarthy, *The Nordstrom Way: The Inside Story of America's #1 Customer Service Company,* 2nd edition, New York: Wiley, 2000, 244 p.

Spurgeon, Devon, "In Return to Power, the Nordstrom Family Finds a Pile of Problems," *Wall Street Journal,* September 8, 2000, p. B1.

Stevenson, Richard W., "Watch Out Macy's, Here Comes Nordstrom," *New York Times Magazine,* August 27, 1989.

Yang, Dori Jones, "Nordstrom's Gang of Four," *Business Week,* June 15, 1992, pp. 122–23.

Yang, Dori Jones, and Laura Zinn, "Will 'the Nordstrom Way' Travel Well?," *Business Week,* September 3, 1990, p. 82.

—Daniel Gross
—update: David E. Salamie

Oracle Corporation

500 Oracle Parkway
Redwood Shores, California 94065
U.S.A.
Telephone: (650) 506-7000
Fax: (650) 506-7200
Web site: http://www.oracle.com

Public Company
Incorporated: 1977 as System Development Laboratories
Employees: 41,650
Sales: $10.2 billion (2004)
Stock Exchanges: NASDAQ
Ticker Symbol: ORCL
NAIC: 511210 Software Publishers; 514210 Data
    Processing Services

Oracle Corporation is the number one supplier of information management software, and the second largest independent software firm in the world. Government agencies and corporations, large and small, use Oracle's database management software for an ever increasing range of business applications. Oracle also provides an array of services, from product support to consulting and educational tools in its quest to provide innovative global business solutions. Oracle continually updates its proprietary software, researches and develops new applications, and even publishes two magazines—the aptly named *Oracle* and *Profit*—to supply its customers with the latest and best data collection and management systems possible.

Databases for the CIA: 1977–81

Oracle Corporation traces its roots to 1977 when two computer programmers, Lawrence J. Ellison and Robert N. Miner, teamed up to start a new software firm. Ellison had been a vice-president of systems development at Omex Corporation and a member of a pioneering team at Amdahl Corporation, which developed the first IBM-compatible mainframe computer. Miner had served as Ellison's former supervisor at another computer company, Ampex Corporation. Both men had signifi-

cant experience designing customized database programs for government agencies, and the pair persuaded the Central Intelligence Agency (CIA) to let them pick up a lapsed $50,000 contract to build a special database program. Ellison and Miner then pooled $1,500 in savings to rent office space in Belmont, California, and start Oracle for the purpose of developing and marketing database management systems (DBMS) software. Ellison became president and chief executive and took charge of sales and marketing for the new company, while Miner supervised software development. The pair of entrepreneurs sought out well known private venture capitalist Donald L. Lucas to become chairman of the board.

While working on the CIA project, Ellison continued monitoring technical documents published by IBM, a practice he had established while working as a programmer at Amdahl. Ellison noticed the computer giant was interested in new types of speedy, efficient, and versatile database programs, called relational databases, that were projected to one day allow computer users to retrieve corporate data from almost any form. What was expected to make this possible was an IBM innovation called the Structured Query Language (SQL), a computer language that would tell a relational database what to retrieve and how to display it.

Banking on what later proved to be a correct hunch—that IBM would incorporate the new relational database and SQL into future computers—Ellison and Miner set out to provide a similar program for digital minicomputers and other types of machines. In 1978 Miner developed the Oracle RDBMS (relational database management system), the world's first relational database using SQL, which would allow organizations to use different-sized computers from different manufacturers but use standardized software. A year after its pioneering development, Oracle became the first company to commercially offer a relational database management system, two years before IBM debuted its own RDBMS system.

After its initial innovation, Oracle quickly became profitable and by 1982 the company, then with 24 employees and a mainframe and minicomputer customer base of 75, reported annual revenues of nearly $2.5 million. In the same year, the company expanded internationally with the creation of Oracle Denmark.

Company Perspectives:

For nearly 30 years, Oracle has been building and refining a technology platform that delivers the highest-quality information while reducing your cost of doing business. Because if your information systems can create and manage high-quality data, your employees can improve their efficiency, make better decisions, and measure their success. We operate our business on four key principles—Simplify: Speed information delivery with integrated systems and a single database; Standardize: Reduce cost and maintenance cycles with open, easily available components; Automate: Improve operational efficiency with technology and best practices; Innovate: Drive your business forward in new ways with Oracle architecture. By adhering to these principles, Oracle has saved more than US$1 billion—so far. And customers are saving, too, by improving their ability to use information and IT as strategic assets.

About one-fourth of 1982 revenues were poured back into research and development, leading to a 1983 Oracle innovation, the first commercially available portable RDBMS. The portable RDBMS enabled companies to run their DBMS on a range of hardware and operating systems—including mainframes, minicomputers, workstations, and personal computers—and helped Oracle double revenues to over $5 million in 1983.

Expansion, Competition, Going Public: 1984–86

By the early 1980s Oracle began jousting with new entrants in the DBMS market. However, the company's reputation for innovations and its aggressive advertising style, which mentioned competitors' products by name, helped to push Oracle's sales upward. By 1985 the company brought in more than $23 million in revenues. The following year annual sales more than doubled to a record $55.4 million.

The year 1986 proved to be transitional and historic for Oracle in a number of respects. In March, Oracle made its first public offering of stock, selling one million common shares, then lauded itself as the fastest-growing software company in the world, having recorded 100 percent-or-better growth in revenues in eight of its first nine years. Much of this growth came from Oracle's targeted end users—multinational companies with a variety of what had previously been incompatible computer systems. By 1986 Oracle's customer base had grown to include 2,000 mainframe and minicomputer users represented by major international firms operating in such fields as the aerospace, automotive, pharmaceutical, and computer manufacturing industries, as well as a variety of government organizations.

To serve these customers, by 1986 Oracle had established 17 international marketing subsidiaries based in Australia, Canada, China, Europe, and the United Kingdom to market its products in a total of 39 countries. By the same time Oracle had also expanded the scope of its business operations to include related customer support, education, and consulting services. One of the principal reasons for Oracle's success was the 1986 emergence of SQL as the industry's standard language for relational database management systems, which in turn led to increased market acceptance of Oracle's SQL-compatible RDBMS.

In 1986 Oracle expanded its RDBMS product line and debuted another industry first, a distributed DBMS based on the company's SQL*Star software. Under the distributed system, computer users could access data stored on a network of computers in the same way and with the same ease as if all a network's information were stored on one computer. Although initially limited to operating principally on IBM and IBM-compatible computers, the Oracle SQL*Star software was the first commercially available software of its kind and was soon expanded to include dozens of additional computer brands and models.

Setting the Standard: 1987–90

By 1987 Oracle had emerged as the relational DBMS choice of most major computer manufacturers, allowing the company to expand the scope of hardware brands on which its products could operate. Largely as a result of such acceptance, Oracle achieved two major milestones in 1987 by topping $100 million in sales and becoming the world's largest database management software company with more than 4,500 end users in 55 countries.

During the late 1980s Oracle expanded its development, sales, and support partnerships with computer hardware manufacturers. Its partnerships with software manufacturers also began to blossom, and in 1987 the number of software companies using Oracle products grew fivefold. In order to maximize the benefits of these partnerships, Oracle established its VAR (Value-Added Reseller) Alliance Program, aimed at building cooperative selling and product-planning alliances with other software manufacturers.

Oracle continued its tradition of innovation and firsts in 1988 when it introduced a line of accounting programs for corporate bookkeeping, including a database for personal computers to work in conjunction with the Lotus Development Corporation's top-selling Lotus 1-2-3 spreadsheet program. The company also introduced its Oracle Transaction Process Subsystem (TPS), a software package designed to speed processing of financial transactions. Oracle's TPS opened a new market niche for the company, targeting customers such as banks needing to process large numbers of financial transactions in a short period of time.

In 1988 Oracle unveiled its initial family of computer-aided systems engineering (CASE) application development tools, including its CASE Dictionary, a multiuser shared repository for items pertaining to a computer application development project; and CASE Designer products, a graphical "workbench" of computer tools that enabled computer application analysts and designers to develop diagrams directly on a computer screen and automatically update the CASE Dictionary.

During Oracle's first decade of operations its relational database system was expanded for use on about 80 different hardware systems. Extending its alliances with hardware manufacturers, Oracle introduced its first version of a database management system program to run on Macintosh personal computers in 1988. The company also formed a new subsidiary, Oracle Complex Systems Corporation (OCSC), adding systems-

Key Dates:

1977: System Development Laboratories, the precursor to Oracle, is founded.
1978: The Oracle Relational Database Manager Program is developed.
1982: Oracle forms its first international subsidiary, Oracle Denmark.
1983: The company becomes Oracle Corporation.
1986: Oracle goes public on NASDAQ and debuts its SQL*Star software.
1987: Oracle ranks as the world's largest database management software company.
1991: The company experiences its first fiscal loss.
1992: Nippon Steel Corporation buys a stake in Oracle Japan; Oracle7 makes its debut.
1997: Network Computer Inc. is established.
1999: Oracle Japan goes public.
2000: Oracle E-Business Suite 11i and Technology Network (OTN) Xchange are introduced.
2001: Oracle's database system is the first to pass nine industry standard security evaluations.
2003: Oracle attempts a hostile takeover of rival PeopleSoft.
2004: Department of Justice files multiple antitrust lawsuits to prevent Oracle's takeover of PeopleSoft.

integration services to its line of customer services. Shortly after the subsidiary was formed, OCSC purchased Falcon Systems, Inc., a systems integrator company.

In 1989 Oracle's emergence as a major player in the software industry was recognized by Standard & Poor Corporation, which added Oracle to its index of 500 stocks. Additionally, Oracle relocated from Belmont to a new, larger office complex in nearby Redwood Shores, California. Seeking to break into new markets, Oracle formed a wholly owned subsidiary, Oracle Data Publishing, in December 1989 to develop and sell reference material and other information in electronic form. Oracle closed its books on the 1980s posting annual revenues of $584 million, netting $82 million in profit.

Oracle Stumbles: 1990–92

Oracle entered the 1990s anticipating continued high growth and in January 1990 the company decided to seek $100 million in public financing to support its expansion. But the company's expectations were misplaced and its image as a darling of Wall Street soon began to tarnish. In March 1990 Oracle announced a record 54 percent jump in quarterly revenues but a paltry 1 percent rise in net earnings. The company's first flat earnings quarter, attributed to an accounting glitch, shook Wall Street out of its long love affair with Oracle; the day after the earnings announcement the company's stock plummeted $7.88 to $17.50 in record one-day volume with nearly 21 million of the company's 129 million shares changing hands.

In April 1990 a dozen shareholders brought suit against Oracle, charging the company had made false and misleading earnings forecasts. On the heels of this lawsuit, Oracle announced it would conduct an internal audit and immediately restructure its management team with Lawrence Ellison assuming the additional post of chairman, while Lucas remained a director. Oracle also formed a separate domestic operating subsidiary, Oracle USA, aimed at addressing its domestic management and financial problems, which the company attributed to poor earnings. Gary D. Kennedy was named president of the new subsidiary.

For the fiscal year ending May 31, 1990, Oracle initially posted record sales of $970.8 million and profits of $117.4 million; but these results were below Oracle's own estimates. The company's stock price fell to $19.88 then plunged to $11.62 in August after an internal audit forced the company to restate earnings for three of its four fiscal quarters. As a result, Oracle negotiated a $250 million revolving line of credit from a bank syndicate. A few weeks later the company reported its first-ever quarterly loss of nearly $36 million with expenses outpacing revenues by 20 percent; the stock tumbled once again, having lost more than $2.7 billion in market value in six months.

In response to widespread criticism concerning overzealous sales techniques, accounting methods, poor management controls, and miscalculations of market strength, Oracle underwent another management shakeup. After less than four months on the job, Kennedy was replaced as president of Oracle USA by Michael S. Fields, a company vice-president. Oracle also moved to reduce its annual growth rate goals from 50 to 25 percent; laid off 10 percent of its domestic workforce of 4,000; consolidated Oracle USA's financial and administrative operations; and folded various international units into a single division.

Despite Oracle's most turbulent year in its history, 1990 was not without its firsts—with communism bowing out in Eastern Europe, Oracle formed an Eastern European subsidiary to serve its first customer sites in Bulgaria, Czechoslovakia, Hungary, Poland, Romania, and what was then the Soviet Union. Chief Executive Ellison was also lauded for his accomplishments, being named Entrepreneur of the Year for 1990 by the Harvard School of Business. Oracle began 1991, however, on a sour note—reporting quarterly losses of $6.7 million in early January despite a 29 percent increase in revenue. The report again sent shock waves rippling through Wall Street, and Oracle's stock fell to $6.62. By the middle of January 1991 Oracle's bankers had cut the company's line of credit from $170 million to $80 million while granting the company much-relaxed loan covenants.

Oracle announced in March 1991 it would restate prior financial results because of accounting errors and named a new chief financial officer, Jeffrey Henley. As part of its restatement, Oracle adopted a change in accounting methods requiring sales be booked when software was delivered, not when a contract was signed as previously allowed. Oracle's restatement of 1990 figures lowered annual revenue more than $50 million to $916 million and decreased earnings to $80 million. The increased need to use reserve funds for accounts receivable put Oracle in violation of its loan agreements and for the second time in as many fiscal quarters the company sought a waiver of loan requirements.

Oracle's sales growth continued to decline from previous years and the company finally admitted it had expanded too rapidly. For 1991 Oracle topped the $1 billion sales plateau for the first time in history and at the same time posted its first annual loss of $12.4 million. In October the company secured a new $100 million revolving line of credit from another bank syndicate. Two months later Oracle negotiated an agreement for $80 million in financing from Nippon Steel Corporation, which also agreed to sell Oracle products in Japan. In return, Nippon was given rights to purchase as much as 25 percent of Oracle's marketing subsidiary in Japan, duly named Oracle Japan.

By the end of its 1992 fiscal year, Oracle's balance sheet had improved as sales inched modestly upward and earnings rebounded, with the company reaching $1.18 billion in sales and $61.5 million in profits. Oracle entered 1993 with no bank debt, solid long-term financing in place, and in an improved financial position controlled by a revamped management team. Ellison told *Forbes* magazine in 1991: "You pay a price for growing too rapidly."

Oracle 7 and the Promise of Interactive TV: 1993–95

The release of Oracle 7 in the early 1990s seemed to signal the end of Oracle's brief taste of corporate mortality. The program supported a larger number of users than previous versions, handled more transactions, allowed data to be shared between multiple computers across a network, and improved application development features. It won industry praise, and in 1993 Ellison began talking up Oracle's role in a new technology to expand the role of databases even further. In a partnership with British Telecom and Apple Computer, Oracle used its software to deliver video on demand to a test group of interactive TV users in Great Britain.

By early 1994 Ellison's new push to develop a consumer market for Oracle's databases had evolved into the "media server alliance," in which the company's Oracle Media Server would be the database engine supplying interactive TV viewers with, for example, movies ordered through a library of digital multimedia. The hardware motor for this future super media service would be massive parallel computers made by nCube, a company in which Ellison was the principal shareholder. With his typical ebullience, Ellison declared, "I believe the sheer impact of the interactive network into the home will rival that of the electric light, the telephone, and the television."

By mid-1994 Oracle's sales had reached $2 billion, its consulting services accounted for a healthy 20 percent of sales, and it fueled corporate America's switch from the mainframe to the client/server computing model. The year also saw the release of Oracle 7's version 7.1, an improved program that supported slow or unreliable network environments; the copying of data between different locations; and the processing of data on multiple processors—an application increasingly favored in the so-called "data warehouses" used by large corporations. To serve the data warehouse market better, in 1995 Oracle acquired the product line of Information Resources, Inc. (IRI), whose online analytical processing (or OLAP) software enabled users to perform sophisticated business analyses in data warehouses. IRI's products also allowed users to incorporate video into their data warehouses, and when Oracle released version 3 of Oracle 7 in late 1995, these new video and data-crunching capabilities enhanced its claim of having the most

powerful and most multimedia-ready database product on the market.

With its share of the data management market now at 40 percent, Oracle unveiled Oracle Workgroup/2000, a forerunner of Oracle 8 to enable users to run and access databases on laptops as well as larger computers. By retooling its products to work with smaller computers, Oracle hoped to exploit the transition underway to more localized client/server computing environments: because these client and server computers were by definition more numerous than the huge and expensive mainframe computers, Oracle stood ready to enjoy a potentially vast increase in sales. Oracle's traditional rivals, Sybase and Informix, were dropping back in market share, and Microsoft—whose enormous resources enabled it to absorb the cost of pricing its own database programs below its competitors—was positioning its SQL Server database to eventually compete head on with Oracle.

The Network Computer and Oracle 8: 1996–97

As Oracle readied Oracle 8 for release, it introduced its WebSystem software in late 1995 to take advantage of the growing popularity of the Internet and its small-scale in-house cousins, the corporate intranet. WebSystem promised to enable corporations to organize and distribute their data over the Internet. With Oracle's revenues topping $4 billion, in May 1996 Ellison took on the "Wintel" (Microsoft Windows software plus Intel's processing hardware) monolith by unveiling the "Network Computer" (NC). Joining with such partners as Sun Microsystems and Netscape, Ellison offered to free corporations from the costly upgrades Intel and Microsoft forced on them with every new release of Windows and the x86 family of processors. Using Ellison's $500 NC—a kind of stripped-down PC with no hard drive and therefore no applications—data and applications could be stored and accessed as needed via the World Wide Web or remote server computers, equipped, naturally, with Oracle's databases. Since corporations would no longer have to buy storage and applications for each computer, they could save millions with no loss in functionality, and Oracle would have a vast new market for its database products. By late 1996 this strategy had evolved into the "Network Computing Architecture," a complicated new three-tier world for corporate computing consisting of a client computer (the computer accessed by the user), an applications (such as word processing software) server, and a database server.

In June 1997 Oracle 8 was launched with much fanfare, and combined Oracle's longtime relational database features and bundled with new technology related to the Network Computer project. With annual sales of $5.7 billion, a ten-year annual growth rate of 30 percent, and 50 percent of the world's relational database market, Oracle seemed to be in a position to confidently believe Oracle 8 and the NC heralded "nothing less than a new era in computing." Since Ellison's announcement of the inexpensive NC a year before, however, rivals Microsoft and Intel had reacted quickly to the Oracle/Sun/Netscape threat. Microsoft had purchased WebTV, a manufacturer of an NC-like computer-television hybrid that had actually come to market, and Intel had slashed processor prices to bring powerful full-featured personal computers below the $1,000 price mark. Since Oracle's NC computers were not scheduled to reach users until late 1997 at the earliest, Ellison's multimillion-dollar NC marketing campaign seemed premature.

Because the Asian and Pacific Rim countries accounted for 15 percent of Oracle's sales and were its fastest-growing market, when their economies began to collapse in late 1997 Oracle felt the brunt. In December 1997 Ellison announced Oracle's earnings, though still expanding at a 35 percent annual rate, would be lower than projected. A record 172 million Oracle shares changed hands on the news, sending Oracle's stock price down 30 percent and wiping out more than $9 billion in equity.

Speaking Softer: 1998–2001

Ellison took a conciliatory tone in a press conference in early 1998 when he admitted Oracle had erred in talking up the NC before the product had been realized. "We just could not deliver network computing," he admitted. Oracle's public statements began to focus less on the NC and more on other products such as its first database with Java support and its updated database management software, Oracle 8. While Oracle 8 experienced increasing competition from Microsoft's SQL Server database product, it nevertheless won several IT awards. In mid-1998 Oracle released an updated Oracle 8 to meet the Microsoft challenge head on. At the close of its 1998 fiscal year in May, Oracle could take solace in quarterly sales of $2.4 billion—a 26 percent increase over the previous year.

In 1999 Oracle teamed up with Hewlett-Packard Company to integrate the computer giant's e-business applications with its database management software, and partnered with Ford Motor Company to form AutoXchange, an Internet-based purchasing program. AutoXchange's design connected Ford and its numerous suppliers, who would pay fees based on the size and volume of their transactions. Oracle and Ford projected these fees could top $1 billion in less than two years; the two firms intended to split any earnings.

In early 2000 Oracle established multiple joint ventures, including one with Texas-based Entrust Technologies, Inc. for a new database program called Oracle Advanced Security. The program included the latest technological advances in online encryption and authentication. Other partnerships involved Novistar, which teamed up with Oracle to provide broad-based e-business software to the energy industry, and Sears Roebuck & Company and Carrefour S.A. signed with Oracle to produce a worldwide business-to-business e-commerce marketplace for retailers. Called GlobalNet-Exchange, the Internet system was intended to replace the electronic data interchange (EDI) used by retailers. Sears CEO and Chairman Arthur Martinez commented to *Women's Wear Daily* (February 29, 2000), "This is a revolution in retail. It will forever redefine supply-chain processes, increase collaboration with suppliers and reduce supply-chain costs." Sears and Carrefour owned majority stakes in GlobalNet-Exchange, Oracle held only a minority share of the startup.

Oracle finished fiscal 2000 with revenues of $10.2 billion and earnings at an all-time high of $6.3 billion due to an extra $4 billion from selling shares in Oracle Japan. By the following year, Oracle prospered like its former self of the 1980s with soaring sales, new product releases, and a myriad of new ventures both in the United States and abroad. The company finished the year with sales close to $11 billion and $2.6 billion in earnings.

Courting Controversy: 2002 and Beyond

For the early 2000s Oracle concentrated on doing what it did best: creating new software management systems for the world's businesses. In 2001 the company's Oracle Small Business Suite was considered "Best of the Web" by *Forbes* magazine; while *Pipeline* magazine declared Oracle the "Best International IT Company" of the year. Ellison received an award himself in 2002 from the Executive Club of Chicago, which deemed him International Executive of the Year. Honors and awards aside, Oracle was determined to stay at the top of its game; to this end, the company increased its research and development spending from 11 percent in 2002 (just under $1.1 billion on revenues of $9.7 billion) to 13 percent in 2004 (almost $1.3 billion), which it considered "essential to maintaining our competitive position."

Another facet of Oracle's competitive edge was its consulting and educational businesses, which were not faring as well as hoped. Oracle, however, could afford to give these segments time to develop further, since its software division (both new product licensing and updates) continued to bring in the lion's share of revenues at 73 percent for 2002 ($7.1 billion), 76 percent for 2003 ($7.2 billion), and 79 percent ($8.1 billion) for 2004.

In mid-2003 Oracle initiated a hostile takeover of PeopleSoft Inc. for $5.1 billion. The Pleasanton, California-based PeopleSoft, was in the process of acquiring J.D. Edwards & Company and was not amused by Oracle's takeover bid, no matter how attractive the offer. For its part, Oracle raised its offer several times in the succeeding months, to as high as $9.4 billion, only to be met by a storm of controversy. Few, it seemed, save Ellison were in favor of the takeover— shareholders of both firms were unhappy and the Department of Justice got involved over antitrust issues. By the end of 2003, Ellison appeared determined to win the battle whatever the cost. This single-mindedness echoed the hubris of the last decade when Oracle went from being the darling of Wall Street to a pariah. Stock prices fluctuated from a low of $10.53 in the third quarter to a high of $13.26 in the fourth, and year-end revenues fell for the second year in a row to $9.5 billion.

In 2004 most mentions of Oracle were followed by comments over its bid to buy PeopleSoft. Despite the imbroglio, however, it was business as usual. Other innovations included the latest version of its database management software, Oracle 10g, which was released with built-in self-diagnostics and fine-tuning measures. Oracle 10g, like its predecessors, won awards from a number of IT magazines and organizations. Oracle Customer DataHub was also making news as the first program capable of providing a single customer view from several different databanks. In addition, Oracle partnered with Dell Inc. to have its database software bundled with Dell's PowerEdge servers for small and midsized companies, and with bitter rival Microsoft for limited integration between Oracle 10g and Windows.

In late 2004 Oracle was still hoping to bring PeopleSoft into its fold. Not only were there injunctions and suits in the way, but

PeopleSoft had poison pill measures in place. While awaiting a resolution, Oracle shuffled its top management by separating the roles of CEO and chairman. Ellison remained chief executive and a director, while Executive Vice-President and CFO Jeff Henley, who had been with the company since 1991, moved up to chairmanship. Further, after three years of falling revenues, Oracle rebounded in fiscal 2004 with sales of $10.2 billion and earnings of $2.7 billion, with stock prices reaching a high of $14.89 in the third quarter to a low of $11.23 in the fourth quarter.

Oracle was in flux in late 2004 and early 2005; acquiring PeopleSoft would add dramatically to its software capabilities but at a very steep price. Oracle already had 55 marketing and sales offices throughout the United States and 70 international locations; if combined with PeopleSoft the assets of the two companies would indeed control a significantly larger portion of the database management and related software markets.

Principal Subsidiaries

Datalogix International, Inc.; Oracle Credit Corporation; Oracle China, Inc.; Oracle Corporation Canada, Inc.; Oracle Corporation Ireland Ltd.; Oracle Corporation Japan; Oracle Corporation United Kingdom Limited (U.K.); Oracle Danmark ApS; Oracle Deutschland GmbH (Germany); Oracle do Brasil (Brazil); Oracle France S.A.; Oracle Corporation South Africa Proprietary Ltd.; Oracle Iberica S.R.L.; Oracle Kft; Oracle Mexico S.A. de C.V.; Oracle Nederland B.V. (Netherlands); Oracle Norge A.S. (Norway); Oracle Portugal Sistemas de Informacao Lda.; Oracle Publishing; Oracle Svenska AB (Sweden); Oracle Systems China (Hong Kong) Limited.

Principal Competitors

IBM Corporation; Microsoft Corporation; Borland Software Corporation; Business Objects S.A.; Cognos Incorporated; Hyperion Solutions Corporation; NCR Corporation; PeopleSoft, Inc.

Further Reading

Brandt, Richard, and Evan I. Schwartz, "The Selling Frenzy That Nearly Undid Oracle," *Business Week,* December 3, 1990.

Cook, William J., "Shifting into the Fast Lane," *U.S. News & World Report,* January 23, 1995, p. 52.

Couretas, John, and Aaron Robinson, "GM, Ford to Do More Purchasing on Web," *Crain's Detroit Business,* November 8, 1999, p. 7.

Hatlestad, Luc, "The Greatest Show on Earth," *Red Herring,* August 1997.

Maloney, Janice, "Larry Ellison Is Captain Ahab and Bill Gates Is Moby Dick," *Fortune,* October 28, 1996.

Markoff, John, "Silicon Duo to Take on Microsoft," *International Herald Tribune,* December 14, 1998.

"Microsoft, Oracle Work on Integration Issues," May 24, 2004, p. 95.

O'Brien, Jennifer M., "HP e-Speaks, Resellers Listen," *Computer Dealer News,* September 3, 1999, p. 1.

"Oracle, Dell Bundle in Search of SMB Market," *eWeek,* April 6, 2004.

"Oracle in Overdrive," *Business Week,* June 28, 2004, p. 57.

"Oracle Profit Rises As Margin Grows," *Wall Street Journal,* June 16, 2004, p. A3.

"Oracle's Net Gained 16% in Quarter," *Wall Street Journal,* September 15, 2004, p. A3.

Perkins, Anthony, "Oracle CEO Larry Ellison on Building the Multimedia Library," *Red Herring,* May 1994.

Pita, Julia, "The Arrogance Was Unnecessary," *Forbes,* September 2, 1991.

"Return of the Prophet," *Economist,* June 28, 1997, p. 66.

Ryan, Thomas J., "Sears, Carrefour Join in Venture with Oracle," *Women's Wear Daily,* February 29, 2000, p. 2.

Schlender, Brenton R., "Software Tiger: Oracle Spurs Its Fast Growth with Aggressive Style," *Wall Street Journal,* May 31, 1989.

—Roger W. Rouland
—updates: Paul S. Bodine, Nelson Rhodes

OUTDOOR RESEARCH

DESIGNED BY ADVENTURE

Outdoor Research, Incorporated

2203 First Avenue South
Seattle, Washington 98134
U.S.A.
Telephone: (206) 467-8197
Fax: (206) 467-0374
Web site: http://www.orgear.com

Private Company
Incorporated: 1981
Employees: 200
Sales: $30.4 million (2003)
NAIC: 339920 Sporting and Athletic Goods Manufacturing

Outdoor Research, Incorporated designs and manufactures gear for use in the outdoors, marketing products such as gloves and mitts, gaiters, technical apparel, stuff sacks, and other accessories used in mountaineering. Outdoor Research, whose products bear the ''OR'' label, is regarded as a technical outfitter, renowned for producing high-performance equipment. The company designs gear for both men and women. Outdoor Research operates one retail outlet in Seattle and distributes to retailers throughout the world.

Origins

''Seattle,'' an industry analyst observed in the August 21, 1995 issue of the *Seattle Post-Intelligencer,* ''is the Silicon Valley of the outdoor industry.'' More than a decade before Silicon Valley became the epicenter of development and manufacture for the computer industry, Seattle represented the heart of design and production of equipment for outdoor enthusiasts. The region was littered with companies devoted to making equipment and clothing for use in the back-country, a list that included: JanSport, a backpack maker; Cascade Designs, a sleeping bag maker; K2, a ski boot and apparel maker; Recreational Equipment Inc. (REI), a mountaineering co-op retailer; and REI's subsidiary, Mountain Safety Research, which made equipment and accessories. The pack of outdoor gear companies in western Washington included sundry other wilderness outfitters, all descendants of the gold-rush suppliers that equipped fortune seekers headed to Alaska in the late 19th

century. Among the numerous companies devoted to the outdoors was Outdoor Research, a small company that reflected the personality of its founder, Ron Gregg.

Mountaineering and backpacking began to attract widespread attention during the 1970s, enjoying a substantial boost in popularity that enticed thousands to take to the mountains, including a young physicist in Seattle, Ron Gregg. Gregg was working on his doctorate in applied physics during the 1970s, when he first began to develop a passion for mountain climbing and kayaking.

At the end of the decade, one of Gregg's sojourns in the wilderness led him to start a career as an inventor and entrepreneur. Gregg and a friend had decided to climb the highest mountain in North America, picking a little-traveled route up the Taylor Spur to reach the 20,320-foot summit of Mount McKinley. The mountain, also known by its native name, Denali, rose above all other peaks in the Alaska Range, flanked by five giant glaciers and myriad icefalls that offered a supreme test of the effectiveness of mountaineering gear. Gregg, on his trip up the mountain, experienced what poorly designed gear could do to a climber. Snow was crammed under his gaiters, the fabric climbers used to cover their boots from their instep to below the knee. His cold feet became wet, but his discomfort paled against the problem affecting his friend. Gregg's climbing partner's feet became frostbitten, a condition caused by the poorly designed overboots he wore. Gregg's friend was airlifted off Mt. Denali and Gregg never made it to the summit.

Gregg reacted to the calamity in Alaska when he returned to Seattle. He began designing a new type of gaiter in 1980. At the time, he was employed as a physicist at Terra Technology, a manufacturer of seismic instruments. It was a job for which he had little passion, certainly not when compared with his enthusiasm for mountaineering. He worked on his gaiter design in his basement, eventually producing one with cords that crisscrossed the instep to keep the fabric snug across the boot and pant leg. His satisfaction at the result led to the formation of a company to manufacture and distribute the innovation. Outdoor Research became that company, established in 1981.

Gregg's entry into the outdoor equipment industry occurred after the mountaineering and backpacking boom period had been going on for a decade. The spike in popularity gave Gregg an ever increasing base of potential customers, but it also meant he was subject to intense competition, as the ranks of companies focused on the outdoor industry swelled. Gregg was aided in this regard by the narrow scope of his business. Outdoor Research did not make tents, or backpacks, or sleeping bags, or other gear that occupied the interests of most outdoor companies. The company focused on "the little things," as Gregg remarked in a March 20, 1997 interview with the *Seattle Times,* designing and making "items most people don't give a second thought to until they wish they had," as the Seattle newspaper noted.

The company's second product typified the niche it chose for itself. Shortly after finishing work on his gaiters, Gregg, disillusioned with his job at Terra Technology, began making first-aid kits for backpackers. Gregg's version of a first-aid kit was made with cloth, featuring numerous pockets to help keep items organized. The design was practical, a hallmark of Outdoor Research's products, and it won the business of enthusiasts who appreciated the thinking behind the product. In 1982, REI, whose mailed catalogs were dog-eared by back-country enthusiasts in search of equipment, agreed to include Gregg's first-aid kit in its catalog, but the retail co-op gave the Outdoor Research product only a modicum of visibility. REI put the kit on the back cover of its catalog. Within days, the first order of Outdoor Research's 1,000 first-aid kits sold out.

A year after the introduction of the first-aid kit, Outdoor Research was still a homespun business. Gregg, 34 years old at the time, was in his basement, handling invoices and stuffing Band-Aids into his kits. Joining him was Randy King, a future vice-president and minority owner in Outdoor Research who came to Gregg's aid in 1983. As the company developed, Gregg served as its designer while King focused on the business aspects of running Outdoor Research. Together, the pair guided the company in their respective roles as it moved out of Gregg's basement and into a more expansive setting, occupying a building south of downtown Seattle. The relocation reflected the growing regard for Outdoor Research, whose products, bearing the "OR" label, came to symbolize innovative quality to mountaineers. Outdoor Research was built on the reputation of its products, and that quality of the company was drawn directly from Gregg.

Gregg preached function over style. "My design goal is 'no-frills,'" Gregg explained in a March 20, 1997 interview with the *Seattle Times.* "Our basic success is not because we made products people wanted. OR makes products that perform in ways people didn't think they could," he said. "I've never been motivated to design gear that was particularly stylish or sexy looking," he remarked a year later in a July 3, 1998 interview with *Puget Sound Business Journal.* Outdoor Research, as an expression of Gregg's personality, was devoted to making superior products no matter the look of the product or how small the market for the product.

After the success of OR gaiters and the OR first-aid kit, the company continued to focus on "the little things" that were nonetheless vitally important to people who used them. The company made waterproof overmitts, gloves, casings to keep water bottles from freezing, crampon pouches, and a number of other accessories, all designed with practicality in the forefront and with style as less than an afterthought. The company developed a small but loyal base of customers who gave the OR brand a "utilitarian chic," as the *Seattle Times* called it in a March 20, 1997 article.

Growth Fueled by the Introduction of the Seattle Sombrero in the 1980s

Outdoor Research, with Gregg as its lead designer, made a variety of highly functional accessories and gear during its formative decade. The company also introduced its first widely popular product during the decade, an item that became its signal financial success. The Seattle Sombrero, a Gore-Tex hat with a Velcro-stripped crown, possessed the functional qualities of a Gregg-designed product, but its popularity outside the mountaineering community almost ran counter to Gregg's ethos. The hat, which looked more like a fedora than a sombrero, was fashionable, the first and only product with an OR label that drew admiring eyes in the streets of downtown Seattle rather than in the mountain ranges that flanked the city.

Sales of the Seattle Sombrero hat drove Outdoor Research's financial growth. In 1986, the company was ranked by *Inc.* as number 270 on the magazine's annual list of the 500 fastest-growing, privately held companies in the country. Annual sales in the year preceding *Inc.*'s recognition stood at $1.1 million, a total that would grow to nearly $5 million by the beginning of the 1990s. Hat sales fueled much of the company's growth, but Outdoor Research also possessed strength in other categories, deriving substantial revenue from its coveted gaiters and mittens.

Outdoor Research added to its product line as its sales increased, but only after rigorous testing. The company never tried to exploit the strength of its brand name by introducing a stream of new products whose sole purpose was to increase sales. The company moved methodically, rarely straying from the type of technical gear that defined it. In 1993, for example, Gregg climbed Mount Aconcagua in Argentina to test the company's Flex-Tex line, which was made with Spandura, a combination of DuPont's Condura nylon, Lycra spandex, and Supplex nylon. Growth for growth's sake was never the objective at Outdoor Research, but the company did demonstrate a desire to expand, particularly in the late 1990s.

Exploring New Business Opportunities in the Late 1990s

New markets and new business opportunities were embraced as the company neared its 20th anniversary. In 1998, Outdoor Research announced that it was opening its first retail store, a 2,200-square-foot shop built on the street level of the company's corporate headquarters. "It's not our intention to compete with REI or other retailers," the company's sales and marketing manager explained in a July 3, 1998 interview with

---

Key Dates:

1981: Outdoor Research is founded.
1986: Outdoor Research is ranked as one of the eight fastest-growing private companies in Washington state.
1998: The first Outdoor Research retail store is opened, concurrent with the debut of a line of women's apparel.
2003: Dan Nordstrom purchases Outdoor Research, becoming its president and chief executive officer.

Puget Sound Business Journal. "We want to increase our awareness in the Puget Sound region and offer consumers an opportunity to buy anything we make." The foray into the retail sector represented a new business frontier for Outdoor Research, a move made while the company prepared to enter another new business. In May 1998, the company signed a licensing agreement with Wild Roses, a Swiss, technical-apparel company founded by female alpinist Dode Kunz. Through its partnership with Wild Roses, Outdoor Research planned to enter the women's clothing market with the introduction of OR jackets and pants designed specifically for women. The women's line debuted at the Outdoor Retail Summer Market trade show in August 1998, with distribution in North America, Australia, and New Zealand slated for the fall of 1999.

Gregg, "whose porcupine mustache, high cheeks, and denim-colored eyes make him seem like a mountaineer straight out of central casting," as the March 20, 1997 issue of the *Seattle Times* noted, was the personification of Outdoor Research. The company took its ideals from its founder. Consequently, his death in 2003 represented not only a personal tragedy but it also threatened to strip Outdoor Research of its spirit, of its singular focus on making high-performance gear. On March 17, 2003, Gregg died in an avalanche in the Kokanee Glacier Provincial Park near Nelson, British Columbia, Canada. The skiing party he was with was buried by several feet of snow. Three of the six people in the group were swept away by the avalanche, and one managed to dig himself free, but Gregg and Washington state's assistant attorney general, James Schmid, were dead when their companions reached them.

Gregg's brother, Bob Gregg, served as interim president as employees at Outdoor Research mourned the loss of their founder. The company's future was uncertain for several weeks before someone stepped in to take permanent control of the company. In June 2003, the company was purchased for an undisclosed sum by Dan Nordstrom, a member of Seattle's wealthy retail family who managed the $6.5 billion department store chain Nordstrom, Inc. Nordstrom bought the company because he believed there was an opportunity "to build the company while at the same time retaining its reputation as an innovative maker of mountaineering equipment," as the June 4, 2003 issue of the *Seattle Post-Intelligencer* reported. The effect of Nordstrom's influence on Outdoor Research remained to be determined in the years ahead, but the legacy of innovation and craftsmanship left by Gregg gave the company's new president and chief executive officer a worthy blueprint to follow.

Principal Subsidiaries

Outdoor Research-Retail Store.

Principal Competitors

Patagonia; The North Face, Inc.; K2 Inc.

Further Reading

"Building Its Success on Practicality Outdoor Research Sells What You'd Never Think of," *Seattle Times,* March 20, 1997, p. C1.

Castro, Hector, "Two Local Skiers Swept Away; Outdoor Gear Company Founder, State Attorney Die in Avalanche," *Seattle Post-Intelligencer,* March 19, 2003, p. B1.

Cook, John, "Dan Nordstrom Buys Outdoor Research, Leaderless Company Gets Fresh Start," *Seattle Post-Intelligencer,* June 4, 2003, p. E1.

Kim, Nancy J., "Indoor Adventure," *Puget Sound Business Journal,* July 3, 1998, p. 10.

Lustigman, Alyssa, "Spandura Collection Passes Rugged Test," *Sporting Goods Business,* February 1993, p. 24.

—Jeffrey L. Covell

Outrigger Enterprises, Inc.

2375 Kuhio Avenue
Honolulu, Hawaii 96815
U.S.A.
Telephone: (808) 921-6600
Toll Free: (800) OUTRIGGER; (800) 688-7444
Fax: (808) 921-6600
Web site: http://www.outrigger.com

Private Company
Incorporated: 1953
Employees: 3,000
Sales: $400 million (2002 est.)
NAIC: 721110 Hotels (Except Casino Hotels) and
    Motels; 721199 All Other Traveler Accommodation

Outrigger Enterprises, Inc. is a leading vacation lodging company in the Pacific. It operates two main hotel brands, Outrigger Hotels & Resorts and OHANA Hotels & Resorts. Outrigger also has a marketing agreement with timeshare leader Fairfield Resorts. The company was built by the Kelley family, pioneers of affordable vacation accommodations in Hawaii.

Based in Honolulu, Outrigger owns or manages more than 12,000 hotel rooms and condominium units throughout Hawaii and the South Pacific. The company's Outrigger Properties division owns one-quarter of all the hotel rooms in Waikiki Beach, including two of seven beachfront hotels. An affiliate, Outrigger Lodging Services, operates nearly two dozen properties in the mainland United States.

Origins

Roy C. Kelley, a trained architect from California, moved to Hawaii in September 1929 with his new bride, Estelle. Ironically, they arrived on Black Friday, the day of the stock market crash that launched the Great Depression.

Kelley designed a number of historic buildings in Honolulu while under the employ of architect C.W. Dickey, including the main building of the Halekulani Hotel. By 1938, he was working exclusively for himself, chiefly designing residences.

The Kelleys began building and acquiring apartments in the 1930s. Their first hotel was The Islander on Seaside Avenue in Waikiki. Opened in 1947, it was Hawaii's first new hotel in 20 years. It had 33 rooms on four stories; a penthouse was added later. Although there were already a few hotels in Hawaii—the Royal Hawaiian, the Moana, and the Halekulani—The Islander catered to a more budget-conscious crowd. Rooms started at $7.50 a night.

According to *Kelleys of the Outrigger,* a history of the Kelley clan by John McDermott, the 20-unit Willard Inn was acquired for $2 million in 1949. Construction of the 100-room, six-story Edgewater Hotel soon followed. The Edgewater was Waikiki's first hotel with a swimming pool. It was later doubled in size.

Roy and Estelle Kelley were known for being actively involved in the management of the hotels. Roy Kelley kept an office next to the lobby of the Edgewater; it was moved to the new Reef Hotel after it was completed in 1955. Ten stories tall, the Reef was the first high rise in Waikiki. The 18-story Reef Towers was soon erected across the street.

The Kelleys kept the management hierarchy extremely flat, which helped reduce overhead. They also could build hotels cheaper than anyone else, owing in part to Roy Kelley's design skills. By 1962, records *Kelleys of the Outrigger,* the enterprise had 3,000 rooms in ten hotels.

Outrigger Waikiki Opening in 1967

The Outrigger Waikiki opened in 1967 at the site of the Outrigger Canoe Club, next to the famous Royal Hawaiian Hotel (then the star property of the Matson cruise line). The Outrigger was built with the help of equity partners, including Bob MacGregor, who served as its president for three years. The Outrigger East, Outrigger West, and Coral Reef hotels were soon added on property acquired in the Outrigger Waikiki deal.

In 1969, Roy Kelley sold the Edgewater, the Reef, and the Reef Towers to Cinerama Group. This left the Kelleys with four hotels: the Edgewater Lanais, the Islander, the Coral Seas, and the Outrigger Waikiki, notes McDermott. They were already building five more hotels with a total of 2,000 rooms.

As Dr. Richard Kelley, son of the company founders, told
McDermott, Cinerama ended up issuing the Kelleys stock in
lieu of payments after the Hawaiian tourism business fell off
in the 1970s. The family amassed a 50 percent ownership in
Cinerama after buying out other shareholders. They eventually
traded this interest for the hotels they had sold.

Gross sales were $20 million in 1982, reported *Hawaii Busi-
ness.* In that year, the Kelleys acquired the 626-room Prince
Kuhio Hotel for $40 million. It was elegant but had been unable
to turn a profit at its location away from the beach. The Malia
was acquired in 1984. Another hotel, the Hobron, was bought at
a bankruptcy auction in 1986 for $24 million.

Dr. Richard Kelley was named the company's CEO and
chairman in 1989 after serving as president for nearly two decades. He had left the practice of medicine in 1970 after working
as a pathologist for Queens Hospital. Dr. Kelley then began
running the Outrigger hotels (the Outrigger East and Outrigger
West were added). His father, he told McDermott, retained
oversight of the Waikiki Village, the Coral Seas, and the Reef
Lanai. (Roy Kelley and his wife Estelle died in 1997 and 1998,
respectively.) Bill Forman, head of the Cinerama Group (then
half-owned by the Kelleys), ran the hotels that his movie chain
had acquired. These three divisions were merged after the
Kelleys took back ownership of the Cinerama hotels in 1984.

Outrigger had 6,400 rooms in 18 hotels in 1986, recorded
Pacific Business News. A major renovation project was underway at many of the properties. The reservations system
needed to be updated as well. A new $1.5 million computer
system was installed in 1989. It was named STELLEX after
Estelle Kelley, who had originally managed reservations on
slips of paper.

Six hotels were sold off to Japanese investors in 1989: the
Outrigger Surf East, the Outrigger Waikiki Surf, the Outrigger
Waikiki Surf West, the Outrigger Malia, the Outrigger Hobron,
and the Outrigger Maile Court. Outrigger retained a ten-year
management contract on each of them.

Beyond Oahu in 1989

By the end of the decade, the company had ventured onto the
mainland. It was managing five hotels in Fort Worth, one of
which was company-owned. These were operated through
Outrigger Lodging Services, a 50–50 joint venture with hospitality executive John Fitts. The mainland was an attractive place
for expansion as hotels there could be acquired for half the cost
per room as Hawaiian ones.

Outrigger expanded to the Big Island in 1989, obtaining a
management contract for the Royal Waikoloan Hotel after
buying an interest in the hotel. Outrigger began operating its
second neighbor island hotel in 1993 after it acquired the Kauai
Hilton, which was renamed the Outrigger Kauai Beach.

According to *Hotel & Motel Management,* annual revenues
were about $165 million a year at the time. The Outrigger's
hotel shops accounted for $13 million of sales. Outrigger en-
tered the 1990s with a $3 advertising campaign focused on the
affordability of vacationing in Hawaii.

Revenues were $275 million in 1994, reported *Hotel &
Motel Management.* During the year, the reservation offices and
the office of Chairman Dr. Richard Kelley were moved to
Denver. In 1998, the company built a hotel at Denver International Airport under the Hilton Garden Inn brand.

Restructuring Under a Holding Company in 1995

The business was renamed Outrigger Enterprises, Inc. as it
shifted to a holding company structure in 1995. (It had been
formally known as Hotel Operating Company of Hawaii, Ltd.
for the previous nine years.) Outrigger Enterprises had three
main divisions: Outrigger Hotels & Resorts, Outrigger Properties, and an investments division.

The first international hotel, Outrigger Marshall Islands, was
opened in July 1996. Properties throughout Polynesia followed.
Outrigger gave up the Marshall Islands management contract in
2003, however.

Outrigger continued to develop properties in Waikiki. It
reclaimed its lease on the Holiday Isle, upgraded it, and reopened it in 1997 as the 287-room Outrigger Islander Waikiki,
reported *Travel Agent* (it was renamed the Ohana Islander
Waikiki in 2003).

Travel from Japan and Korea suffered as a result of the
Asian financial crisis of 1997. Outrigger responded by spending
millions to market its Big Kahuna vacations program to U.S.
travelers.

Launching OHANA in 1999

A new, moderately priced brand, OHANA Hotels & Resorts,
was introduced in December 1999 with 15 of Outrigger's
Waikiki hotels. (*Ohana* is the Hawaiian word for family.) In the
same year, the company bought what would become (for a few
years) its flagship property, the Outrigger Wailea Resort on
Maui, and opened a 600-room hotel in Guam. A Fiji hotel
followed in 2000. A spokesperson told *Hawaii Business* the
company prided itself on making the vacation experience localized and true to the histories of each of these new islands.

Key Dates:

1947: The Kelley family opens The Islander hotel in Waikiki.
1951: The six-story Edgewater Hotel opens.
1955: The Reef Hotel opens.
1967: The Outrigger Waikiki opens.
1984: The properties are consolidated into Outrigger Hotels Hawaii.
1989: The first hotels on a neighbor island and on the mainland are opened.
1995: A holding company structure is adopted.
1999: The OHANA Hotels & Resorts economy brand is launched.
2005: Construction slated to begin on $460 million Waikiki Beach Walk.

Outrigger opened a property in Tahiti around 1999 but withdrew from that market.

Dr. Charles Kelly, grandson of the founders, followed in his father's footsteps when he left medicine to join the family business in 2002. His initial focus was promoting the resorts at Wailea and Waikoloa Beach to the medical meetings community.

According to *Hawaii Business,* Outrigger Enterprises had gross sales of $400 million in 2002. During the year, the company began a strategic alliance with timeshare resort leader Fairfield Resorts. Outrigger benefited from a partnership with one of the strongest national players in the timeshare business, while Fairfield gained entry into the Hawaiian market.

Developments at Home and on the Horizon

Development of the $460 million, 7.7-acre Waikiki Beach Walk was scheduled to begin in 2005. Six hotels were being torn down to make room for this retail, entertainment, and lodging development. The first of two phases was to be completed by early 2007.

Rather than develop its own new high-rise hotel at the Beach Walk, Outrigger had put the property up for sale to fund expansion in other geographic areas. It also was selling the Waikoloa and Wailea hotels it operated under the Marriott brand. These had been acquired with an eye to gaining ground in the meetings and conventions market, which collapsed after 9/11.

Outrigger then shifted its focus in Hawaii to Oahu. It spent $20 million to upgrade the 530-room Outrigger Waikiki. The Outrigger Reef was also due for a renovation to begin at the end of 2005.

The company was ahead of schedule on its goal of having 20 properties in Australia by 2005, reported *Travel Agent* magazine in 2004. Outrigger also aimed to add a handful of properties to its first location in New Zealand.

Principal Divisions

Outrigger Hotels & Resorts; Outrigger Properties.

Principal Operating Units

Outrigger Hotels & Resorts; OHANA Hotels & Resorts; Outrigger's Condominium Collection; Outrigger Resort Club by Fairfield.

Principal Competitors

Aston Hotels & Resorts; Castle Hotels & Resorts; Marc Resorts Hawaii; Radisson Hotels & Resorts; Starwood Hotels & Resorts.

Further Reading

Andorka, Frank H., Jr., "Outrigger Courts Families with New Ohana Brand," *Hotel & Motel Management,* July 5, 1999, pp. 1+.

Barseghian, Tina, "Outrigger Voices So. Pacific Presence," *Leisure Travel News,* February 14, 2000, p. 20.

Choo, David K., "The Kelley Girl," *Hawaii Business,* November 2002, p. 11.

Cruz, Cathy S., "20 Years Ago . . . ," *Hawaii Business,* March 2003, p. 51.

Diamond, Craig, "Physician Gives Up Practice to Promote Meetings to His Family's Hotels," *Meeting News,* January 28, 2002, p. 16.

Foster, Camie, "Outrigger Charts Pacific Course," *Travel Agent,* March 29, 2004, pp. 40–42.

——, "Power in the Pacific," *Travel Agent,* October 7, 2002, pp. 78–86.

——, "Separate But Spectacular," *Travel Agent,* August 6, 2001, p. 123.

Gillingham, Paula, "Outrigger Has No Reservations About High-Tech Advances," *Pacific Business News,* August 3, 1998, p. 16.

Jacobs, Judy, "Outrigger Sale Signals Shift in Group Focus," *Meeting News,* July 12, 2004.

"The Kelleys of Waikiki," *Hawaii Business,* March 1983.

Long, Dina, "Outrigger, Fitts Form Lodging Management Firm," *Tour & Travel News,* November 14, 1988, p. 22.

——, "Outrigger Highlights Hotel Pricing in New Campaign," *Tour & Travel News,* April 9, 1990, p. 30.

Mac Dermott, Kathy, "Hawaiian Group to Run NZ Resort," *Australian Financial Review,* December 12, 2002, p. 42.

——, "Outrigger Spreads Its Wings," *Australian Financial Review,* September 16, 2003, p. 56.

McDermott, John and Bobbye, "Outrigger Hotels: Steady As It Grows," *Hotel & Motel Management,* January 9, 1995, pp. 4+.

McDermott, John W., *Kelleys of the Outrigger,* Honolulu, Hawaii: ORAFA Publishing Company, 1990.

Outrigger Enterprises, Inc., "The Story of Outrigger Hotels & Resorts," Honolulu: Outrigger Enterprises, Inc., 2004.

"Outrigger Puts Millions into Marketing," *Leisure Travel News,* June 15, 1998, p. 30.

"Outrigger Reaches Out," *Travel Agent,* Hawaii Supplement, June 16, 1997, p. 4.

"Outrigger Upgrading Hotels, Wooing the More Affluent," *Pacific Business News,* April 7, 1986, p. B19.

Paris, Ellen, "Outrigger Hotels Has Taken Its Advertising Business to the Mainland," *Hawaii Investor,* August 1, 1993, p. 43.

Parker, Wayne, "Paradise Is the Pacific," *Hawaii Business,* February 1998, pp. 30+.

Rebchook, John, "Outrigger Hotel Lands at DIA; Resort Company Will Break Ground Today on First Mainland Inn," *Rocky Mountain News,* April 14, 1998, p. 2B.

Smith, Rod, "Carey Taking Outrigger in New Direction," *Pacific Business News,* February 20, 1989, p. 1.

Sommerfeld, Jeff, "Outrigger Takes Helm at Top Port Douglas Resort," *Courier-Mail* (Queensland, Australia), December 7, 2001, p. 40.

White, John Wythe, "Outrigger's Pacific Odyssey," *Hawaii Business,* November 2000, pp. 31+.

—Frederick C. Ingram

Pacific Coast Feather Company

1964 4th Avenue South
Seattle, Washington 98134
U.S.A.
Telephone: (206) 624-1057
Fax: (206) 625-9782
Web site: http://www.pacificcoast.com

Private Company
Founded: 1924
Employees: 2,400
Sales: $350 million (2003 est.)
NAIC: 314129 Other Household Textile and Product Mills

Privately owned, Seattle-based Pacific Coast Feather Company (PCF) is the market leader in the pillow and down comforter industry, selling products under its own name and other labels, such as Sealy, Calvin Klein, and Dockers. The company maintains manufacturing facilities throughout the United States, Canada, and China, as well as a showroom in midtown Manhattan. In addition to pillows and comforters, PCF offers feather beds, covers, protectors, and pillow shams. PCF is owned by the Hanauer family. Gerard ''Jerry'' Hanauer serves as co-chairman and his son Nick Hanauer acts as chief executive officer and co-chairman.

Family Ties to Feathers
Dating to 18th Century Germany

The Hanauer family became involved in the feather and pillow business when Jerry Hanauer's grandfather, Joseph Hanauer, founded Cannstatter Bed Feather Company in Stuttgart, Germany, in 1884. Because the Hanauers were Jewish, they were looking to flee Nazi Germany during the 1930s. Fritz Hanauer, Jerry Hanauer's second cousin, wrote to a number of feather companies in the United States. Seattle's Pacific Coast Feather Company replied, saying it had a job for him. The company had been founded in 1924 by F.W. Cutler and a Mr. Van Faklenburg but was now suffering through hard times. When Fritz Hanauer joined the company in 1939 he started out washing chicken feathers. Nevertheless he encouraged his cousin Sigmund, Jerry's father, to relocate to Seattle. Due to

problems leaving Europe during the early months of World War II, it was not until 1940 that Gerard's family managed to make it to America's Northwest. By this time Pacific Feather had gone bankrupt, and Fritz had acquired the business. Upon his arrival, Sigmund bought a partnership stake from his cousin. After World War II was over Fritz Hanauer decided to return to Germany, and Sigmund bought him out, becoming sole owner.

Under the management of the Hanauer family, PCF focused its efforts on serving the Pacific Northwest. At the same time, the pillow industry underwent a revolutionary change following the 1941 introduction of Dacron, which could serve as a substitute filler for feathers.

In 1953 PCF opened a plant in Kinston, North Carolina, to produce Dacron for use in clothing and pillows, and two years later the company began manufacturing its own polyester pillow. During this period, while PCF was content to be a small regional player, national pillow manufacturers emerged, including Purofied Down Products and Dallas-based Pillowtex.

A third generation of the Hanauer family became involved in the pillow business in 1965 when Jerry Hanauer joined the company, forgoing a financial career in New York City. At the time, PCF was generating annual sales of only around $850,000. In 1972 he succeeded his father, who died two years later. By now Purofied and Pillowtex were large enough to feel threatened by the very existence of PCF, prompting Hanauer to look for a niche in which PCF would be able to compete. He found it in down comforters, supplying Scandia Down, which during the late 1970s and into the 1980s aggressively expanded across the country. PCF took advantage of the retailer's success to begin competing with its larger rivals on a national basis.

By now a fourth generation of the Hanauer family, in the form of Jerry's sons Nick and Joff Hanauer, were very much involved in growing the business. They were instrumental in revamping the company's manufacturing operations and marketing strategies. Instead of following the industry practice of supplying products under the retailer's brand name, PCF began building up Pacific Coast Feather as a quality brand. Sales grew to $22 million in 1985, and the company's success attracted the attention of Pillowtex, which attempted to buy PCF for $16 million. Hanauer turned down the bid and when asked to name his price quoted a figure so high that Pillowtex walked away. During the 1980s Pillowtex acquired five other companies as it grew into a dominant market leader and expanded into areas such as mattress pads. PCF in the meantime established manufacturing operations in Maquoketa, Iowa, in 1984; Lebanon, Pennsylvania, in 1986; Pico Rivera, California, in 1988; and Marysville, Washington, in 1989. It also established Pacific Coast Feather Cushion in Los Angeles in 1988. Purofied, on the other hand, began to struggle, filing for Chapter 11 bankruptcy protection in 1984 and closing its Brooklyn manufacturing plants. Several years later Purofied filed again and this time went out of business.

Consolidation in the Pillow Industry in the 1980s

PCF and Pillowtex began pursuing opposite strategies in the 1980s. The latter diversified its product offerings and used its size advantageously, pursuing a strategy akin to a virus: Once able to sell one of its products to a retailer, the company then maneuvered to elbow out all of its competitors by inducing the retailer to buy the entire Pillowtex line. As a result there was a significant shakeout in the pillow industry, which saw a dozen healthy regional companies reduced to just four national rivals and several regional competitors struggling to hang on. Because of its relationship with Scandia Down, PCF was one of the national players that emerged. In 1988 sales reached $55 million. At this point, Pillowtex had a 50 percent market share in pillows and 40 percent in down comforters.

To compete with Pillowtex, PCF narrowed its focus. Rather than diversify like Pillowtex and another rival, Hollander Home Fashions Corp., PCF trimmed its offerings to just pillows and comforters. Eschewing a merchandising approach that was commodity-driven based on price, which would have directly pitted PCF against Pillowtex in a game it could not hope to win, PCF concentrated on designing quality pillows and comforters to compete with Pillowtex on terms of its own choosing. PCF even conducted tests on Pillowtex products, as well as the pillows and comforters of other competitors, and learned that they did not meet the specifications listed on the packaging. Rather than take advantage of this research to convince retailers to switch to PCF, the company decided instead to build on its own reputation for quality. A major innovation was the introduction of the ComfortLock comforter, which employed a U-shaped stitch along the perimeter of the bed to prevent the common problem of down drifting to the sides and bottom. PCF patented the stitch in 1994, prompting a complaint from Pillowtex, which maintained that something as simple as a stitch was not patentable. Three years later, however, the U.S. Patent Office reaffirmed its decision.

Initially, PCF attempted to convince retailers to buy its pillows and comforters because of their high quality, but quickly realized that the retailers were more interested in profitability than anything else. The company had to learn now to use the quality of its products to make more money for its customers. By focusing on just pillows and comforters, PCF, despite being much smaller than Pillowtex, was able to bring more resources to bear on their product lines. PCF helped to educate both retailers and customers. All too often, retailers offered a wide range of choices at the low-end price points while offering only a small number of products priced at the upper range. The PCF approach was to convince retailers to reorganize their shelf space and reallocate their inventory dollars by offering products at price points that were evenly spaced out, creating what the company called a vertical hierarchy of quality, value, and benefits. Customers who came into the store to buy the cheapest pillow possible did not require a dozen choices: They would buy the cheapest pillow if only one was available. By offering so many options at the lowest price point—and providing the least amount of profit—retailers simply encouraged customers to buy a less expensive product that did not necessarily serve their needs. By offering a range of products in terms of quality and price, customers would trade up. The more expensive the pillow, the more health benefits it offered and the longer it would last. Thus the product mix on the retailer's shelves told a compelling story to the customer: In short, the higher the price, the smarter the purchase. The result was that retailers now made higher profits and were pleased to do business with PCF.

In 1991 PCF controlled a 10 percent share of the pillow market and 17 percent in down comforters. Over the course of the 1990s the company enjoyed strong growth, as it increased its sales of pillows and comforters while adding a limited number of new products. Unlike its rivals, however, PCF would not wander far afield and offer items such as bath towels: It was content to stick to bedding. In 1993 it established a new division and brand, National Sleep Products, to market its pillows and comforters that relied on synthetic materials rather than feathers. Because PCF was so well associated with feathers, it was having difficulty marketing polyester pillows under the Pacific Coast label. The goal now was to create a synthetic product line that followed a strategy similar to that of the company's feather pillows and comforters, with products under the new name falling in a range of price points.

Expanding Market Share in the 1990s

PCF sales totaled $60 million in 1993, $106 million in 1996, and $127 million in 1997, as the company continued to focus on pillows and comforters and promoting the Pacific Coast brand. Pillowtex, on the other hand, expanded into blankets, acquiring a number of blanket companies as well as the blanket business of Fieldcrest Cannon. In 1997 Pillowtex paid $400 million in cash and stock and assumed some $300 million in debt to acquire the rest of Fieldcrest Cannon. Although the deal turned Pillowtex into an industry giant, it became a lumbering one. Sensing that Pillowtex was not paying close enough attention to its pillow and comforter business, PCF increased its spending on marketing to take advantage of the situation. Within two years, PCF's market share in pillows grew to 21 percent while it controlled a similar share in the comforter market. Also in 1997 PCF set itself up for increased growth by reaching an agreement with mattress powerhouse Sealy to produce Sealy branded pillows, down comforters, and synthetic-fill comforters and mattress pads. It was PCF's first licensed deal and opened the door to future licensing arrangements with Calvin Klein and

```
┌─────────────────────────────────────────────────┐
│                  Key Dates:                      │
│                                                  │
│ 1884:  The Hanauer family becomes involved in    │
│        the feather and pillow business in        │
│        Germany.                                  │
│ 1924:  Pacific Coast Feather Company is founded. │
│ 1940:  The Hanauer brothers acquire Pacific      │
│        Coast Feather Company.                    │
│ 1972:  Jerry Hanauer succeeds his father as CEO. │
│ 1994:  The company patents the U-shaped stitch   │
│        in comforters.                            │
│ 2000:  The company becomes the market leader in  │
│        pillows and comforters.                   │
│ 2003:  Nick Hanauer is named CEO and co-chairman.│
└─────────────────────────────────────────────────┘
```

Dockers. At the same time, the company continued to heavily promote its own Pacific Coast Feather brand.

During the 1990s PCF opened manufacturing plants in Hebron, Kentucky, in 1997, and Henderson, North Carolina, in 1999. In addition, it launched Pacific Coast Feather Canada in Toronto in 1992, and in 1998 started a mattress pad business in Wayne, Nebraska, called Restful Nights. By the end of the 1990s PCF was generating sales around $245 million. As it enjoyed robust growth, however, PCF experienced some changes in the top ranks of management. Tragically, in 1998 Joff Hanauer was killed in an automobile accident. In 1999 Jerry Hanauer, now in his 70s, relinquished the CEO position to Roy Clothier, a longtime officer of the company. According to Hanauer, Clothier had been instrumental in the rapid rise and maintained, ''All we're doing here is making factual what has been reality.'' Clothier joined the company in 1981 as chief financial officer, was named chief operating officer in 1988, and added the presidency in 1993. Having a nonfamily member in a top post was a conscious decision by Hanauer, who believed that executive talent would shy away from a company if they felt that opportunity for advancement was limited.

In 1999 PCF acquired Southern Quilters, a North Carolina subcontract manufacturer. The deal added 250,000 square feet of plant space to PCF, an important factor in the company's effort to further its growth. Also in 1999, PCF established a new home fashions division to offer duvet covers, and coordinated dust ruffles, pillow shams, and sheets. Nevertheless, the focus of the company remained on pillows and comforters. In 2000 PCF eclipsed Pillowtex as the market leader in pillows and comforters. Losing more than $300 million in 1999 and 2000, Pillowtex filed for Chapter 11 bankruptcy protection in November 2000. Some 20 years after Pillowtex's attempt to acquire PCF, the roles were reversed: in 2002 PCF attempted to buy part of Pillowtex, but the rival's management team refused, insisting on a sale of the entire company. Eventually the assets were sold off in bankruptcy court.

With the downfall of Pillowtex, PCF solidified its position as the leading pillow and comforter manufacturer. With sales topping the $300 million mark, PCF moved into a larger showroom space in Manhattan in 2001 to help support the company's growth in a number of areas. Although it was now the number one company in its industry, PCF was determined not be become complacent but to retain a spirit of innovation, despite a change in leadership. In May 2003 Clothier died of liver disease at the age of 64. He was replaced as president by Eric Moen, who joined the company in 1989 after working for several fashion sportswear companies. Nick Hanauer was named CEO and co-chairman of the board.

PCF's pattern of growth fell off, due to the effects of a poor economy and trouble in the bedding industry that caused struggling companies to slash prices in hopes of hanging on. ''Having your competitors in financial trouble is always bad, because companies in bankruptcy can behave irrationally,'' Nick Hanauer explained to the *Puget Sound Business Journal* in June 2004. ''The industry becomes the victim of the stupidest, most irrational players.'' The industry was also likely on the verge of a sea change. Unlike other textile companies that moved all of their manufacturing operations offshore, companies that produced feather pillows and comforters continued to produce them domestically because feathers had to be transported compressed into bricks. For years, China had been the leading producer of duck and goose feathers and down, as well as the manufacturer of most comforter shells, which were then filled and finished elsewhere—primarily due to tariffs and taxes imposed on goods manufactured in China because the country was not a member of the World Trade Organization (WTO). PCF, which was the largest Western consumer of Chinese feathers and down in China, maintained a presence in the country, but with the admittance of China to the WTO in 2001, it became clear that China would now be competitive in the bedding industry. It was very likely that within the next decade all of PCF's manufacturing would move from the United States and Canada to China, leaving PCF as more a marketing and distribution company than a manufacturer. The impact of such a change on the quality of products and speed of distribution, not to mention the 2,400 people employed in PCF factories across the United States, remained to be seen.

Principal Subsidiaries

Pacific Coast Feather Cushion; Pacific Coast Feather Canada, Inc.; Restful Nights.

Principal Competitors

Hollander Home Fashions Corp.; Spring Industries, Inc.; Westpoint Stevens Inc.

Further Reading

''Pillow Fight: How a Domestic Rival Knocked the Stuffing Out of Pillowtex,'' *Business, North Carolina,* December 1, 2003, p. 50.

Ramsey, Bruce, ''The Feather Trade, Lightly Seattle Firm Sews Up a Soft Market,'' *Seattle Post-Intelligencer,* May 28, 1997, p. B4.

Schwartz, Donna Boyle, ''Pacific Coast Feather Flies High in Competitive Down Bedding,'' *HFD-The Weekly Home Furnishings Newspaper,* June 17, 1991, p. 53.

Wattman, Karla, ''Hanauer Power,'' *HFD-The Weekly Home Furnishings Newspaper,* September 6, 1993, p. 27.

—Ed Dinger

PepsiAmericas, Inc.

4000 Dain Rauscher Plaza
60 South Sixth Street
Minneapolis, Minnesota 55402
U.S.A.
Telephone: (612) 661-4000
Fax: (612) 661-3737
Web site: http://www.pepsiamericas.com

Public Company
Incorporated: 1962 as Illinois Central Industries, Inc.
Employees: 14,500
Sales: $3.2 billion (2003)
Stock Exchanges: New York
Ticker Symbol: PAS
NAIC: 312111 Soft Drink Manufacturing; 333415 Air
    Conditioning and Warm Air Heating Equipment and
    Commercial and Industrial Refrigeration Equipment
    Manufacturing; 811112 Automotive Exhaust System
    Repair

PepsiAmericas, Inc. is the result of the merger of the second- and third-largest bottlers in the Pepsi system. Predecessor Whitman Corporation, known until 1988 as IC Industries, owned and operated the largest independent Pepsi bottler company, the largest franchise for car services, and one of the leading manufacturers of refrigerators in the world, along with several other manufacturing divisions. The company, which began as a railroad operation, divested itself of non-bottling businesses completely in 1997. Whitman acquired PepsiAmericas, Inc. in 2000, and took the smaller company's name the following year.

Running the Rails: 1850s–1960s

Whitman has a company history dating back to 1851, when a group of European bankers decided to take advantage of the growing railroad business in the United States. Initially, the railroad, named the Illinois Central, was operated only inside Illinois, but just after the U.S. Civil War the company began a vigorous expansion plan, incorporating more than 200 railroads into its system. By 1867 the railroad had crossed the Mississippi into Iowa, eventually stretching southward through Kentucky, Tennessee, Arkansas, Alabama, Mississippi, and on to New Orleans. Additional Illinois Central lines ran to South Dakota, Minnesota, Wisconsin, Indiana, Missouri, and Nebraska. For more than a hundred years the Illinois Central Railroad hauled freight and passengers up and down the Mississippi Valley and throughout the northern portion of the Midwest.

On August 31, 1962, the railroad was incorporated as Illinois Central Industries, Inc. Under William Johnson's leadership the company had a new goal—diversification. The Johnson blueprint called for the building of a consumer and commercial products conglomerate by using company cash and stock to buy other businesses, and company tax credits to shelter their earnings. With the single-mindedness typical of its president, the company began methodically to work toward that end.

The first dramatic step was taken in 1968 when the company ventured into the non-rail business, purchasing the Abex Corporation. Formerly known as American Brake Shoe and Foundry, the company produced brakes, wheels and couplings for railroad cars, brake linings for cars and trucks, hydraulic systems for airplanes and ships, and specialty metal castings for industrial uses such as sugar mills and locomotives.

Diversification Drives Train: 1970s to Early 1990s

Sixteen years after this initial acquisition, Johnson bought the Pneumo Corporation, a Boston-based aerospace, food, and drug company, for $593 million. The Pneumo purchase was viewed as a means of increasing overall revenue. The subsidiary also provided income from its military contracts, and gave credence to Johnson's theory of growth through acquisition. Over a year later he orchestrated the merger of Abex and Pneumo, forming the Pneumo Abex Corporation.

In 1970 Illinois Central Industries diversified into the real estate business by becoming a major partner in the Illinois Center. The Center, a complex of office buildings, hotels, and condominiums, sprawled across 83 acres of lakefront property in downtown Chicago. In another real estate transaction, the company sold land it owned in New Orleans so that the city could build its

Company Perspectives:

Our vision is to be, by all relevant measures, the best performing beverage company worldwide. Mission. At first glance, PepsiAmericas' mission seems straightforward—"We make, sell and deliver beverages." But, in the competitive bottling industry, it takes a commitment to excellent service, preferred products, strong external relationships and keen business strategy to be the world's third largest bottling company.

athletic stadium, called the Superdome, on the site. Illinois Central Industries maintained ownership of 11 adjoining acres for future developments that included the Hyatt Regency hotel. The company would also develop an array of industrial parks in or near Fort Lauderdale, Memphis, and New Orleans.

This diversification toward real estate came at a time of increasing debate over what role the traditional railroad business should play in the evolving structure of the company. The faltering railway operations, on the one hand, were aided by a merger with the Gulf, Mobile, and Ohio Railroad, which was a combination of several railroads including: the Gulf, Mobile, and Northern, the Mobile and Ohio, and the Chicago and Alton. The merger was formally completed on August 10, 1972, and the new line was named the Illinois Central Gulf Railroad by the parent company.

The sale of some of the company's prime property, on the other hand, indicated movement away from continuing the railroad business. Indeed, by the late 1970s Johnson vacillated back and forth, placing the railroad for sale on the market and then removing it. Eventually, the piecemeal sale of the line proved immensely profitable and solidified Johnson's reputation as an astute businessman.

When the railroad was first placed on the market, no serious purchaser stepped forward, mainly because Johnson had let the railroad deteriorate through lack of maintenance. Johnson then decided to dismantle the line and sell it part by part. This process was greatly aided by capital improvements and rail deregulation during the mid-1980s, and Johnson netted handsome profits for his company.

As Johnson's strategy of diversification unfolded, the company changed its name in 1975 to IC Industries, Inc. Three areas of business were identified as important and company acquisitions fell into these categories: consumer products, commercial products, and railroad activities. The holding company was structured around decentralized management and a growing list of subsidiaries that maintained primarily autonomous operations.

In the consumer products group, a 1978 acquisition brought in the Pet Company, the St. Louis, Missouri, firm that produced evaporated milk. Expansion into a variety of food products followed, including Whitman Chocolates and Old El Paso, the best selling brand of Mexican foods in the United States. By the early 1990s, the enterprise had grown to 30 owned and eight leased manufacturing plants located in the United States and six foreign countries.

The Hussmann Corporation, a manufacturer of refrigeration equipment for food retailers and processors, composed an important branch of IC's commercial products group. In the early part of the 1980s Hussmann suffered a slump in sales and profits, but by 1984 the subsidiary regained its profitable standing and earned about $44 million before taxes. Later that same year, Hussmann acquired Riordan Holdings, Ltd., a London-based producer of food refrigeration equipment, which served to heighten Hussmann's overseas profile. By the early 1990s there were 20 Hussmann-owned and ten leased manufacturing facilities in the United States, Mexico, the United Kingdom, and Canada, as well as three owned and 95 leased branch facilities in these same countries (excluding Mexico) that sold, installed, and maintained Hussmann products.

In the early 1990s, the Pneumo Abex Corporation manufactured products that fell into three basic components: aerospace, industrial, and fluid power products. There was stiff competition, particularly in the aerospace business, but IC regarded the competition as a challenge to invest more of its dollars and technology in the field, enabling it to compete with larger firms such as Cleveland Pneumatic Company. Industrial products included braking materials for the automotive original equipment and replacement outlets, and safety equipment for recreational vehicles, trucks, and automobiles. Products were manufactured for use in mining, earthmoving, steel making, and food processing, to name a few. Canadian and U.S. railroads were markets for the iron and composition brake shoes, cast steel wheels, and custom-made track work manufactured by Pneumo Abex. Fluid power products included complete hydraulic systems used in construction and mobile equipment, industrial and marine machinery, materials-handling equipment, offshore drilling, and nuclear power plants. This division also manufactured products for aerospace and general aviation markets from 33 plants in the United States and 16 abroad.

When market analysts examined William Johnson's formula for corporate success, which entailed pruning acquisitions of all but their most profitable divisions, they most often looked to Pet, the largest subsidiary in Whitman's $1.8 billion consumer division of the early 1990s. One year following the acquisition of Pet, its pretax profits almost tripled to an estimated $85 million in 1984, on a revenue increase of 33 percent. Part of Johnson's carefully crafted plan involved selling low-return operations. Over one six-year period, 22 of Pet's units, with sales totaling $400 million, were sold in order to funnel money into Pet's more profitable products.

Pepsi-Cola General Bottlers was the second largest franchise bottler of Pepsi-Cola beverages in the United States, in the early 1990s, claiming the greatest share of the soft drink market in Chicago, Cincinnati, Kansas City, and Louisville. This branch of Whitman's consumer products group also handled other soft drinks, including Dad's Root Beer, 7-Up, Dr. Pepper, Orange Crush, Canada Dry, and Hawaiian Punch. In 1984 Pepsi General garnered only minimal profits, partly because of heavily discounted prices and partly because both Pepsi-Cola and Coca-Cola introduced new products to the consumer. However, for the next two years Pepsi General's sales growth averaged 7 percent, outstripping the industry's as a whole.

Another of Whitman's major consumer product holdings was Midas International, a company that made and installed automotive exhaust, suspension, and braking systems through approximately 2,000 franchised and company-owned Midas shops in the United States, Canada, England, France, Australia, Belgium, Germany, Austria, Panama, and Mexico, in the early 1990s. Originally specializing in replacement mufflers, Midas had broadened its range to include repairing and replacing brakes and shock absorbers at about 95 percent of its outlets. The expansion of services accounted for an estimated 9 percent profit growth shown during 1985 through 1986.

When Johnson retired in 1987, the new leadership was committed to continuing his strategy for the company. Under Chairman Karl D. Bays, IC Industries changed its name to Whitman Corporation in 1988 to emphasize its focus on consumer goods and services. Part of this strategy included selling over 65 companies, such as the Pneumo Abex aerospace operation and spinning off the remnants of its Illinois Central Railroad holdings to shareholders. Management also decided to sell most of its real estate holdings. Yet during the same time, Bays went on an acquisition rampage and purchased nearly 100 new companies, including Orval Kent salad products and Van de Kamp's frozen seafood products. When Bays died in November 1989, Whitman was well on its way toward a reorganization of its product lines.

Whitman's board of directors appointed James W. Cozad, an Amoco vice-chairman, to take Bays's place. Cozad was determined to transform Whitman into an even tighter organization, and immediately announced another restructuring of the company. His strategy was to encourage Whitman's growth by focusing on Pet Inc., Pepsi-Cola General Bottlers, and Midas International, while selling Hussmann and its manufacturing facilities for supermarket refrigerators. But sales for both Pet and Hussmann decreased substantially due to greater market competition, and Cozad was forced to take Hussmann off the market when no acceptable offer to purchase it was forthcoming.

Undismayed, Cozad embarked on a new reorganization strategy. He decided to concentrate on just three businesses, Pepsi-Cola Bottlers, Midas International, and Hussmann refrigerators. As a result, Whitman spun off Pet Inc. to its shareholders and lost such well-known brands as Old El Paso, Progresso, and Whitman Chocolates. At the same time, the company eliminated a significant number of jobs in order to reduce its long-term debt of $1.9 billion.

When Whitman changed leadership in 1992, with Bruce Chelberg replacing Cozad, there was no disruption in the development of the company. Chelberg put all his energy into developing the three core businesses of Whitman. Hussmann upgraded its operations throughout its domestic and foreign facilities. Pepsi-Cola General Bottlers doubled production capacity at its Chicago plant, installed state-of-the-art canning equipment, and entered into a joint venture with Grayson Mountain Water to produce a new one-calorie beverage. Midas International continued to expand its international car service network with new outlets in Mexico and Europe.

Under Chelberg's direction, all of Whitman's holdings fared well. Pepsi-Cola's operating profit increasing by 18 percent in 1993, led by its core brands of Pepsi-Cola and Diet Pepsi. Midas operating profits for 1993 were up 7 percent from the previous year, with sales steadily increasing in Mexico. Hussmann operating profits were down, but demand for supermarket refrigerators appeared to be on the rise in Britain, Mexico, and Canada. With its operations so successfully diversified, profitability seemed likely for Whitman as it headed toward the last years of the 20th century even if one or even two of its core businesses began to exhibit problems.

Tightened Focus: Mid-1990s to 2004

Whitman's 1996 sales rose 5.6 percent, to $3.1 billion. Net income climbed to $139.4 million from $133.5 million in the prior year. It was the fifth consecutive year of sales and earnings records for the company. Pepsi General Bottlers' operating profits were up in the United States but losses continued in Poland, a territory in development since 1995. Midas International's operating profits were also down, due to slow domestic retail and wholesale action and increased operating expenses. Hussmann Corporation's sales exceeded $1 billion for the first time on a strong domestic demand for supermarket equipment and improvement on the Mexican front.

In June 1997, the company announced plans to spin off Hussmann Corporation and Midas International to shareholders. Hussmann was the world's largest supplier of refrigeration systems for the food industry and operated in nine countries. Midas International was the world's largest automotive service operation with more than 2,500 stores in 17 countries.

Whitman would thereafter concentrate on the beverage business that brought in half of sales and more than half of operating income. Pepsi General Bottlers was the world's largest independent Pepsi-Cola franchisee with about 12 percent of U.S. volume and distribution rights in Poland, Russia, and the Baltics.

In January 1999, PepsiCo announced a realignment agreement of bottling territories. Whitman Corporation would become a master Pepsi-Cola bottler gaining territories in Illinois, Indiana, Missouri, Ohio, the Czech Republic, the Slovak Republic, Hungary, and Poland. Those businesses generated revenue of about $540 million in the United States and $180 million in central Europe, in 1998. Whitman, in turn, would transfer operations in Virginia, West Virginia, and Russia to PepsiCo, assume liabilities for domestic territory gained, and pay cash for the international business.

As part of the agreement, U.S. PepsiCo would transfer back its 20 percent stake in Whitman's Pepsi-Cola General Bottlers, but would ultimately hold a 40 percent stake in the newly created shares of Whitman Corporation. The transaction would boost Whitman's percentage of U.S. can-and-bottle volume to 17 percent and more than quadruple its international bottle volume.

In August 2000, Whitman, the second largest Pepsi bottler in the U.S. and one of five anchor bottlers for PepsiCo, announced plans to buy out PepsiAmericas, Inc., the nation's third largest Pepsi bottler. PepsiAmericas, formed from independent bottlers Delta Beverage, Pepsi-Cola Puerto Rico, and Dakota Beverage, had sales of $576 million versus Whitman's approximately $2.4 billion. The deal would give Whitman new territory in the south, the Dakotas, and the Caribbean.

In November, Whitman acquired PepsiAmericas for $331.7 million, boosting Whitman's U.S. market share. But its numbers still added up to less than half the 55 percent share held by Pepsi Bottling Group Inc.—a 1999 spinoff from PepsiCo.

According to *Crain's Chicago Business*, analysts liked the move by Whitman, but the proposed action did little to drive up its stock, which was down about 46 percent from its December 1998 peak. Other bottlers' shares had been off as well, partly due to a sales drop linked to a 1999 boost in prices.

In January 2001, Whitman changed its name to Pepsi-Americas, Inc. In November, PepsiAmericas' former chairman and CEO Robert C. Pohlad succeeded Chelberg as head of the company. PepsiAmericas ended the year by expanding its operations to Barbados, but there was another task underlying these highlights.

"After the merger, we needed to integrate three separate companies into one cohesive business," PepsiAmericas Chairman and CEO Pohlad explained in a May 2004 *Beverage Industry* article. "It involved integrating strategies, systems and culture. In 2003 our hard work paid off and we began to see positive results from a cost, pricing, volume mix and systems perspective. Everything began to click."

On the year, the company succeeded in improving earnings per share, return on invested capital, and bringing international operations to profitability. PepsiAmericas, thanks to a Pepsi-preferring triangle formed by Cleveland, Fargo, and New Orleans, distributed nearly 19 percent of all Pepsi-Cola products sold in the United States. And internationally, the company made strides though greater recognition of consumer preferences and operating improvements.

Principal Competitors

Coca-Cola Enterprises; Dr. Pepper/Seven-Up Bottling.

Further Reading

Byrne, Harlan S., "Foreign Focus," *Barron's*, August 14, 1995, p. 20.

"Carlson Awarded Three Accounts," *Travel Weekly*, May 24, 1993, p. 59.

Gallun, Alby F., "Buyout Gives Whitman's Stock No Pop," *Crain's Chicago Business*, August 28, 2000, p. 4.

A History of Whitman Corporation, Rolling Meadows, Ill.: Whitman Corporation, 1992.

Johnson, William B., *IC Industries,* New York: Newcomen Society, 1973.

Kimelman, John, "Willamette Approves Another Linerboard Machine," *Pulp & Paper,* January 1993, p. 21.

"Knocking It Out of the Park: PepsiAmericas' Strategy Is Driving in Runs," *Beverage Industry*, May 2004, pp. 36+.

"PepsiCo Reaches Agreement with Whitman Corporation to Form Master Pepsi Bottler," *PR Newswire*, January 25, 1999.

"The Pros Point to Six Stocks for This Uncertain Market," *Money*, June 1992, p. 49.

Prince, Greg W., "Whitman-Pepsi Americas 2000: That's the Consolidation Ticket," *Beverage World*," September 15, 2000, p. 12.

Therrien, Lois, "Whitman Is Still Trying to Balance Its Diet," *Business Week,* September 3, 1990, pp. 72–73.

Waters, Jennifer, "Whitman Spinoffs Could Put Fizz in Pepsi Bottler," *Crain's Chicago Business,* September 1, 1997, p. 4.

"Whitman Announces Completion of Toma Acquisition," *PR Newswire*, December 6, 1999.

"Whitman Company Report," *Morgan Stanley & Co., Inc.*, February 16, 1996.

"Whitman Company Report," *CS First Boston*, May 10, 1996.

"Whitman Corporation Announces Record Sales and Earnings," *PR Newswire*, January 16, 1997.

"Whitman Corporation Announces Spin-Off," *PR Newswire*, June 23, 1997.

"Whitman Deal Links Up Pepsi Bottlers," *Mergers & Acquisitions Journal*, October 2000, p. 20.

"Willamette Industries: Making the Grade," *Financial World*, December 8, 1992, p. 19.

—updates: Thomas Derdak, Kathleen Peippo

Pilot Air Freight Corp.

314 N. Middletown Road
Lima, Pennsylvania 19037
U.S.A.
Telephone: (610) 891-8100
Toll Free: (800) 447-4568
Fax: (610) 565-4267
Web site: http://www.pilotair.com

Private Company
Incorporated: 1970
Employees: 1,500
Sales: $250.2 million (2003)
NAIC: 541614 Process, Physical Distribution, and
Logistics Consulting Services

Pilot Air Freight Corp. is a leading U.S. freight forwarder and the largest privately owned forwarder in the world. Traditionally, it has specialized in heavy commercial cargo. Pilot operates through a network of 65 stations. It has a strongly domestic focus; international freight makes up 15 percent of business. The company's non-asset-based business model has been validated in several economical downturns. Pilot aims to set itself apart through flexibility and superior customer service.

Origins

Pilot Air Freight began operations in 1970 at the Philadelphia International Airport. Freight forwarders like Pilot did not own their own aircraft, but booked available cargo space on passenger and freight airlines. One newspaper likened it to a "travel agency" for cargo.

The company's future CEO John Edwards started with Pilot by opening the firm's branch in Buffalo, New York, in 1972. He became Pilot's president and CEO in 1979. Edwards was a native of Buffalo, New York. He owned the company, then called Pilot Air Freight Inc., through a partnership with two of his cousins.

Franchised Growth in the 1980s

Revenues reached $1 million in 1974, according to the *Philadelphia Business Journal.* By 1979, sales were $7 million. After the Federal Trade Commission ruled that Pilot's "agencies" in Boston, Chicago, and Los Angeles were in fact franchises, the company began building a proper franchise network. This led to rapid growth. Revenues were approaching $12 million in 1980.

In late 1983, Pilot created a subsidiary to form international joint ventures. By 1985, the company had 55 franchises and sales of about $55 million. Sales were $78 million in fiscal 1986. One analyst ranked it the fifth largest player in the heavy cargo industry. In 1987, Pilot tried to acquire publicly traded Northern Air Freight Inc. of Seattle, but was rebuffed.

The Pilot Perishables joint venture was launched in the mid-1980s with Flying Fresh International of San Francisco. The door-to-door service shepherded fresh fruits, vegetables, seafood, and meat through the customs process.

Former Braniff Inc. President Ron Ridgeway opened Pilot's Dallas franchise, one of the company's largest, in 1987. By 1989, Pilot had revenues of about $80 million a year, with perhaps 10 percent of that from international business. Pilot had 62 agents in the United States, 70 percent of them franchised, and 16 in foreign countries.

New Horizons, New Leadership in the 1990s

Pilot initiated a quality program in 1990, when sales were $90 million. The company signed up its first international franchisee, RMF Ireland Ltd., early in the year. Pilot pitched its flexibility as a main selling point, noted an article in *Sales & Marketing Management* on long-term sales efforts. Besides embracing heavier shipments, the company offered 24/7 pickups and deliveries, making it ideal for plants running two or three shifts a day.

By focusing on after-hours customer service, Pilot was able to develop a niche in the sports business, reported the *Journal*

Company Perspectives:

As your transportation and logistics expert, we equip you with everything you need to move your cargo—delivering your shipments by air, land or sea anywhere in the world.

We offer customized logistics solutions for just-in-time delivery—like our Merge and Deliver service and our Inbound Logistics Service, to control your inbound product flow.

At Pilot, we focus on every shipment and we pledge to you the highest level of on-time performance, reliability and cost effectiveness.

Key Dates:

1970: Pilot Air Freight is founded.
1979: Franchising begins.
1994: Richard Phillips acquires half of the company and becomes chairman.
1995: Revenues exceed $100 million.
1996: The PACE online shipping management system is implemented.
2001: Pilot begins home deliveries.
2003: Richard Phillips becomes the sole owner.
2004: Pilot forms World Freight Alliance.

---

of Commerce. It was the official forwarder of major league baseball umpires, whose uniforms had to be shipped overnight to various stadiums across North America, sometimes through customs.

The involvement in baseball, which began in the late 1980s, led to finding a new leader. Richard Phillips, a trial attorney by profession and lawyer for the Major League Umpires Association, became Pilot's counsel in 1990. He was named chairman of the company in 1994 after orchestrating a restructuring and refinancing program and acquiring a 50 percent share of the company. In 1995, Phillips replaced John J. Edwards as president and chief executive officer.

Support for the Gulf War was also a significant boost to business in the early 1990s. Pilot was already the military's largest civilian forwarder, noted the *St. Louis Post-Dispatch.*

Revenues were $78 million in 1993, though the company lost about $3 million. Revenues grew to $94 million in 1994, producing a profit of $4 million. Next-day business made up half of sales and 60 percent of Pilot's shipments weighed more than 300 pounds, noted *AirCommerce.* Pilot reported another banner year in 1995, as revenues exceeded $100 million. International business boomed, and import revenues more than doubled. A sea freight division, Pilot Marine Services, was formed during the year.

In early 1996, Pilot implemented a dial-up shipment management system called PACE. Two years later, the company signed on to have Seattle's ITM Corp. supply a web-based scheduling system. In 1999, Pilot deployed a "Shipping Verification" system designed with North Wales, Pennsylvania-based Integrated Productivity Systems, Inc.

Pilot opened more stations in the southeastern United States in the late 1990s to attract manufacturing-related shipments, reported *Journal of Commerce.* The company was enjoying continued double-digit growth domestically.

2000 and Beyond

Business boomed for Pilot even during the slow economy after 2000. The company had about 1,500 employees and 65 stations in the United States. The biggest ones were in Boston, Los Angeles, and Atlanta. In late 2001, the company opened a new 8,040-square-foot warehouse facility near Baltimore, Maryland.

Revenues were $217 million in 2002 and business was growing at an enormous rate. Booming catalog and internet shopping contributed; Pilot officially launched a home delivery service early in the year. The company already had made 11,000 home deliveries for customers such as Sharper Image and QVC in 2001. Pilot embraced items that were too heavy for UPS.

Home delivery gave Pilot the opportunity to offer more levels of service. Phillips told *Air Cargo World* the company could even assemble items such as treadmills in buyers' homes.

There was also the military-related business. Phillips told the *Journal of Commerce* in April 2003 the company was shipping more than two million pounds a month from California to Delaware for the Department of Defense.

Company Chairman, President, and CEO Richard G. Phillips became Pilot's sole owner in January 2003 after buying out his partners. He had previously owned 50 percent of stock.

Buoyed by Iraq-related military shipments, Pilot posted a record year in 2003, with 839,423 shipments, up 26 percent, that totaled 420.3 million pounds in weight. Sales reached $250 million. Shipping for Internet purchases continued to be a positive factor.

A New Alliance in 2004

To match the global capabilities of large forwarders like DHL's AEI Danzas, Pilot formed a global alliance with 50 other independent forwarders around the world. Pilot was the only U.S. member of the World Freight Alliance, which included Aramex in the Mideast, EAS Transportation in China, Two Way Forwarding and Logistics in Ireland, and Cargo Partners in Eastern Europe, reported *Traffic World.* Many of these partners had been left without a U.S. connection after DHL acquired Airborne Express. The alliance began operations in December 2003. Pilot opened a station in the Pacific Rim hub of Honolulu in early 2004.

Principal Competitors

BAX Global Inc.; DHL Worldwide Express Network S.A./N.V.; EGL Eagle Global Logistics; Exel Global Logistics; Menlo Worldwide Forwarding.

Further Reading

Allen, Margaret, " 'Travel Agency for Cargo' Thrives at D/FW," *Dallas Business Journal*, December 14, 2001, p. 21.

Anderson, Betsy, "A Delco Freight Forwarder Joins the 'Desert Express,' " *Philadelphia Inquirer,* January 14, 1991, p. D1.

Armbruster, William, "Q&A with Richard Phillips, Chief Executive, Pilot Air Freight," *Journal of Commerce,* April 7-13, 2003.

"Baltimore-Based Pilot Air Freight Prospers During Worst Business Slowdown in Years," *Daily Record* (Baltimore), November 30, 2001.

Barnett, Chris, "Flying Right; Large Firms Overcome Obstacles," *Journal of Commerce,* January 19, 1999, p. 10A.

Bennett, Elizabeth, "Pilot Air Is Flying High," *Philadelphia Business Journal,* March 30, 2001, p. 17.

Binzen, Peter, "When Freight Company Was Nearly Out, He Hit a Home Run," *Philadelphia Inquirer,* April 4, 1994, p. C3.

Cassidy, William B., "Pilot Plugs in ITM; Forwarder Signs with Internet Service to Offer Shippers Online Booking, Tracking," *Traffic World,* March 2, 1998, p. 44.

Cullen, David, "Fleets Online," *Fleet Owner,* December 1999.

Diamond, Jonathan, "Pilot Air Freight Flying with Franchises," *Philadelphia Business Journal,* July 29, 1985, pp. 29 +.

Everett, Martin, " 'This Is the Ultimate in Selling'; Risking All for a Deal That Takes Months to Close Isn't for Everyone, But Marketers Are Finding It Pays to Master the Art," *Sales & Marketing Management,* August 1, 1989, p. 28.

Faust, Fred, "TWA Sues Freight Forwarder Over Trademarks," *St. Louis Post-Dispatch,* November 4, 1996, p. 4.

Flannery, William, "Air Lift Freight Firms Moving Good for War Effort," *St. Louis Post-Dispatch,* February 3, 1991, p. 1E.

"Forwarder Offers On-Time Guarantee," *Logistics Management & Distribution Report,* March 1, 2001, p. 26.

Frasher, Steven, "Ontario, Calif., Air Freight Company Reaps Big Gains from Iraqi War Buildup," *Business Press,* May 26, 2003.

Keane, Angela, "Forwarding's New Alliance," *Traffic World,* February 23, 2004, p. 29.

Krause, Kristin S., "Homeward Bound: Air Freight Forwarders Apply Air Freight Precision to Heavyweight Home Deliveries," *Traffic World,* March 11, 2002, p. 13.

Lane, Polly, "Seattle-Based Freight-Forwarding Business Caters to Customers' Needs," *Seattle Times,* April 8, 1999.

Lehren, Andrew W., "Pilot Air Freight Expands Cargo, Sales Operations," *Philadelphia Business Journal,* June 27, 1988, p. 12B.

——, "Pilot Air Gets Contract, Searches for Acquisition," *Philadelphia Business Journal,* March 30, 1987, pp. 16 +.

Marzec, Michael, "Flying High on Nationwide Success; Pilot Air Freight Launches Franchises in More Than 55 Cities Since 1979," *Business First of Buffalo,* September 2, 1985, p. 9.

Mate, Paula, "Freight Forwarder Expands to Meet Growing Market," *Journal of Commerce,* February 6, 1989, p. 5B.

Page, Paul, "Piloting Pilot: Contrary and Controversial, Richie Phillips Has a Growth Strategy in a Decidedly Downbeat Air Forwarding Market," *Air Cargo World,* April 2003, pp. 12 +.

"Phillips Consolidates Pilot Air Freight Ownership," *Journal of Commerce Online,* January 20, 2003.

"Phillips Takes Top Management Posts at Forwarder Pilot Air," *Traffic World,* April 24, 1995, p. 23.

"Pilot Air Freight: Business Is Healthy and Growing," *AirCommerce,* February 27, 1995, p. 17A.

"Pilot Air Freight Enjoys Record Growth in 1995," *AirCommerce,* February 26, 1996, p. 15A.

"Pilot Air Freight Names Chairman, Secures $8 Million in New Credit," *Journal of Commerce,* February 16, 1994, p. 3B.

"Pilot Air Freight Posts Record Quarter," *Journal of Commerce Online,* January 28, 2004.

"Pilot Is Benefiting from DHL/Airborne Deal," *Logistics Today,* June 2004, p. 51.

"Pilot Seizes Growth Opportunity," *Logistics Today,* March 2004, p. 42.

"The Quality Crusaders: Carriers Have Been Busy Hiring Managers Specifically to Make Quality a Part of Their Corporate Culture," *Chilton's Distribution,* August 1990, pp. 94 +.

Robinson, Duncan, "Pilot Helps Major Leagues Meet Schedules; Forwarder Finds Niche in Sports," *Journal of Commerce,* March 5, 1990, p. 13B.

Solomon, Mark, "Mutiny Aboard the Good Ship Pilot," *Journal of Commerce,* December 28, 1992, p. 12.

Thompson, Kevin D., "Forwarding Perishables; New Venture Helps Shippers Avoid Risks," *Journal of Commerce,* October 15, 1986, p. 7A.

—Frederick C. Ingram

The Procter & Gamble Company

One Procter & Gamble Plaza
Cincinnati, Ohio 45202-3315
U.S.A.
Telephone: (513) 983-1100
Fax: (513) 983-9369
Web site: http://www.pg.com

Public Company
Incorporated: 1890
Employees: 110,000
Sales: $51.41 billion (2004)
Stock Exchanges: New York National (NSX) Amsterdam
    Paris Basel Geneva Lausanne Zürich Frankfurt
    Brussels
Ticker Symbol: PG
NAIC: 311111 Dog and Cat Food Manufacturing; 311919
    Other Snack Food Manufacturing; 311920 Coffee and
    Tea Manufacturing; 322291 Sanitary Paper Product
    Manufacturing; 325412 Pharmaceutical Preparation
    Manufacturing; 325611 Soap and Other Detergent
    Manufacturing; 325612 Polish and Other Sanitation
    Good Manufacturing; 325620 Toilet Preparation
    Manufacturing; 339994 Broom, Brush, and Mop
    Manufacturing

The Procter & Gamble Company (P&G) is a giant in the area of consumer goods. The leading maker of household products in the United States, P&G has operations in nearly 80 countries around the world and markets its nearly 300 brands in more than 160 countries; more than half of the company's revenues are derived overseas. Among its products, which fall into the main categories of fabric care, home care, beauty care, baby care, family care, health care, snacks, and beverages, are 16 that generate more than $1 billion in annual revenues: Actonel (osteoporosis treatment); Always (feminine protection); Ariel, Downy, and Tide (laundry care); Bounty (paper towels); Charmin (bathroom tissue); Crest (toothpaste); Folgers (coffee); Head & Shoulders, Pantene, and Wella (hair care); Iams (pet food); Olay (skin care); Pampers (diapers); and Pringles (snacks). Committed to remaining the leader in its markets, P&G is one of the most aggressive marketers and is the largest advertiser in the world. Many innovations that are now common practices in corporate America—including extensive market research, the brand-management system, and employee profit-sharing programs—were first developed at Procter & Gamble.

1837 Launch: Maker of Candles and Soap

In 1837 William Procter and James Gamble formed Procter & Gamble, a partnership in Cincinnati, Ohio, to manufacture and sell candles and soap. Both men had emigrated from the United Kingdom. William Procter had emigrated from England in 1832 after his woolens shop in London was destroyed by fire and burglary; Gamble came from Ireland as a boy in 1819 when famine struck his native land. Both men settled in Cincinnati, then nicknamed "Porkopolis" for its booming hog-butchering trade. The suggestion for the partnership apparently came from their mutual father-in-law, Alexander Norris, who pointed out that Gamble's trade, soap making, and Procter's trade, candle making, both required use of lye, which was made from animal fat and wood ashes.

Procter & Gamble first operated out of a storeroom at Main and Sixth streets. Procter ran the store while Gamble ran the manufacturing operation, which at that time consisted of a wooden kettle with a cast-iron bottom set up behind the shop. Early each morning Gamble visited houses, hotels, and steamboats collecting ash and meat scraps, bartering soap cakes for the raw materials. Candles were Procter & Gamble's most important product at that time.

Procter & Gamble was in competition with at least 14 other manufacturers in its early years, but the enterprising partners soon expanded their operations throughout neighboring Hamilton and Butler counties. Cincinnati's location on the Ohio River proved advantageous as the company began sending its goods downriver. In 1848 Cincinnati was also linked to the major cities of the East via rail, and Procter & Gamble grew.

Around 1851, when P&G shipments were moving up and down the river and across the country by rail, the company's famous moon-and-stars symbol was created. Because many people were illiterate at this time, trademarks were used to distinguish one company's products from another's. Company lore asserts that the symbol was first drawn as a simple cross on boxes of Procter & Gamble's Star brand candles by dockhands so that they would be easily identifiable when they arrived at their destinations. Another shipper later replaced the cross with an encircled star, and eventually William Procter added the familiar 13 stars, representing the original 13 U.S. colonies, and the man in the moon.

The moon-and-stars trademark became a symbol of quality to Procter & Gamble's base of loyal customers. In the days before advertising, trademarks were a product's principal means of identification, and in 1875 when a Chicago soap maker began using an almost-identical symbol, P&G sued and won. The emblem, which was registered with the U.S. Patent Office in 1882, changed slightly over the years until 1930, when Cincinnati sculptor Ernest Bruce Haswell developed its modern-day form.

During the 1850s Procter & Gamble's business grew rapidly. In the early part of the decade the company moved its operations to a bigger factory. The new location gave the company better access to shipping routes and stockyards where hogs were slaughtered. In 1854 the company leased an office building in downtown Cincinnati. Procter managed sales and bookkeeping and Gamble continued to run the manufacturing. By the end of the decade, the company's annual sales were more than $1 million, and Procter & Gamble employed about 80 people.

Prospering During the Civil War

Procter & Gamble's operations were heavily dependent upon rosin—derived from pine sap—which was supplied from the South. In 1860, on the brink of the Civil War, two young cousins, James Norris Gamble and William Alexander Procter (sons of the founders), traveled to New Orleans to buy as much rosin as they could, procuring a large supply at the bargain price of $1 a barrel. When wartime shortages forced competitors to cut production, Procter & Gamble prospered. The company supplied the Union Army with soap and candles, and the moon and stars became a familiar symbol with Union soldiers.

Although Procter & Gamble had foreseen the wartime scarcities, as time wore on, its stockpile of raw materials shrank. In order to keep up full production the company had to find new ways of manufacturing. Until 1863 lard stearin was used to produce the stearic acid for candle making. With lard expensive and in short supply, a new method was discovered to produce the stearic acid using tallow. What lard and lard stearin was available was instead developed into a cooking compound. The same process was later adapted to create Crisco, the first all-vegetable shortening. When P&G's supply of rosin ran out toward the end of the war, the company experimented with silicate of soda as a substitute, which later became a key ingredient in modern soaps and detergents.

Launching Ivory Soap in 1878

After the war Procter & Gamble expanded and updated its facilities. In 1869 the transcontinental railroad linked the two coasts and opened still more markets to Procter & Gamble. In 1875 the company hired its first full-time chemist to work with James Gamble on new products, including a soap that was equal in quality to expensive castile soaps, but which could be produced less expensively. In 1878 Procter & Gamble's White Soap hit the market and catapulted P&G to the forefront of its industry.

The most distinctive characteristic of the product, soon renamed Ivory soap, was developed by chance. A worker accidentally left a soap mixer on during his lunch break, causing more air than usual to be mixed in. Before long Procter & Gamble was receiving orders for "the floating soap." Although the office was at first perplexed, the confusion was soon cleared up, and P&G's formula for White Soap changed permanently.

Harley Procter, William Procter's son, developed the new soap's potential. Harley Procter was inspired to rename the soap by Psalm 45: "all thy garments smell of myrrh, and aloes, and cassia, out of the ivory palaces whereby they have made thee glad." Procter devoted himself to the success of the new product and convinced the board of directors to advertise Ivory. Advertising was risky at the time; most advertisements were placed by disreputable manufacturers. Nevertheless, in 1882 the company approved an $11,000 annual advertising budget. The slogan "$99\frac{44}{100}$% pure" was a welcome dose of sobriety amidst the generally outlandish advertising claims of the day. Procter, committed to the excellence of the company's products, had them analyzed and improved even before they went to market. This practice was the origin of P&G's superior product development. Procter believed that "advertising alone couldn't make a product successful—it was merely evidence of a manufacturer's faith in the merit of the article."

The success of Ivory and the ability of Procter & Gamble to spread its message further through the use of national advertising caused the company to grow rapidly in the 1880s. In 1886 P&G opened its new Ivorydale plant on the edge of Cincinnati to keep up with demand. In 1890 James N. Gamble hired a chemist, Harley James Morrison, to set up a laboratory at Ivorydale and improve the quality and consistency of Procter & Gamble's products. P&G soon introduced another successful brand: Lenox soap. Marketed as a heavier-duty product, the yellow soap helped P&G reach sales of more than $3 million by 1889.

The 1880s saw labor unrest at many American companies, including Procter & Gamble, which experienced a number of strikes and demonstrations. Thereafter, the company sought to avert labor problems before they became significant. Behind P&G's labor policies was a founder's grandson, William Cooper Procter. William Cooper Procter had joined the company in 1883 after his father, William Alexander Procter, requested that

---

Key Dates:

1837: William Procter and James Gamble form Procter & Gamble, a partnership in Cincinnati, Ohio, to manufacture and sell candles and soap.

c. 1851: Company's famous moon-and-stars symbol is created.

1878: P&G introduces White Soap, soon renamed Ivory.

1890: The Procter & Gamble Company is incorporated.

1911: Crisco, the first all-vegetable shortening, debuts.

1931: Brand management system is formally introduced.

1946: P&G introduces Tide laundry detergent.

1955: Crest toothpaste makes its debut.

1957: Charmin Paper Company is acquired.

1961: Test marketing of Pampers disposable diapers begins.

1963: Company acquires the Folgers coffee brand.

1982: Norwich-Eaton Pharmaceuticals is acquired.

1985: P&G purchases Richardson-Vicks Company, owner of the Vicks, NyQuil, and Oil of Olay brands.

1988: Noxell Corporation, maker of Noxema products and Cover Girl cosmetics, is acquired.

1991: Max Factor and Betrix cosmetic and fragrance lines are bought from Revlon, Inc.

1992: Pantene Pro-V shampoo is introduced.

1993: Major restructuring is launched, involving 13,000 job cuts and 30 plant closures.

1997: Company acquires Tambrands, Inc., maker of the Tampax line of tampons.

1998: Organization 2005 restructuring is launched.

1999: Premium pet food maker Iams Company is purchased.

2001: P&G acquires the Clairol hair-care business from Bristol-Myers Squibb Company.

2002: Jif peanut butter and Crisco shortening brands are divested.

2003: Company acquires a controlling interest in German hair-care firm Wella AG.

---

he return from the College of New Jersey (now Princeton University) just one month before graduation to help with the company's affairs. Procter learned the business from the ground up, starting in the soap factory.

Introducing Innovative Employee Benefits

In 1885 the young Procter recommended that the workers be given Saturday afternoons off, and the company's management agreed. Nevertheless, there were 14 strikes over the next two years. In 1887 the company implemented a profit-sharing plan in order to intertwine the employees' interests with those of the company. Although the semiannual dividends were received enthusiastically by employees, that enthusiasm rarely found its way back into the workplace. The next year William Cooper Procter recommended tying the bonuses to employee performance, which produced better results.

In 1890 The Procter & Gamble Company was incorporated, with William Alexander Procter as its first president. Two years

later the company implemented an employee stock-purchase program, which in 1903 was tied to the profit-sharing plan. By 1915 about 61 percent of the company's employees were participating. The company introduced a revolutionary sickness-disability program for its workers in 1915, and implemented an eight-hour workday in 1918. Procter & Gamble has been recognized as a leader in employee-benefit programs ever since.

Meanwhile, new soaps, including P&G White Naphtha, which was introduced in 1902, kept P&G at the forefront of the cleaning-products industry. In 1904 the company opened its second plant, in Kansas City, Missouri, followed by Port Ivory on Staten Island, New York. In 1907 William Cooper Procter became president of the company after his father's death.

Procter & Gamble soon began experimenting with a hydrogenation process which combined liquid cottonseed oil with solid cottonseed oil. After several years of research, Procter & Gamble patented the procedure, and in 1911 Crisco was introduced to the public. Backed by a strong advertising budget, Crisco sales took off.

World War I brought shortages, but Procter & Gamble management had again foreseen the crisis and had stockpiled raw materials. William Cooper Procter was also active in the wartime fundraising effort.

During the 1920s the flurry of new products continued. Ivory Flakes came out in 1919. Chipso soap flakes for industrial laundry machines were introduced in 1921. In 1926 Camay was introduced and three years later Oxydol joined the P&G line of cleaning products. The company's market research became more sophisticated when P&G chemist F.W. Blair began a six-month tour of U.S. kitchens and laundry rooms to assess the effectiveness of Procter & Gamble's products in practical use and to recommend improvements. After Blair returned, the economic-research department under D. Paul Smelser began a careful study of consumer behavior. Market research complemented Procter & Gamble's laboratories and home economics department in bringing new technology to market.

Soon after Richard R. Deupree became president of the company in 1930, synthetic soap products hit the market. In 1933 Dreft, the first synthetic detergent for home use, was introduced, followed by the first synthetic hair shampoo, Drene, in 1934. Further improvements in synthetics resulted in a host of new products years later.

Debut of Brand Management in 1931

In 1931 Neil McElroy, a former promotions manager who had spent time in England and had an up-close view of Procter & Gamble's rival Unilever, suggested a system of "one man—one brand." In effect, each brand would operate as a separate business, competing with the products of other firms as well as those of Procter & Gamble. The system would include a brand assistant who would execute the policies of the brand manager and would be primed for the top job. Brand management became a fixture at Procter & Gamble, and was widely copied by other companies.

The Great Depression caused hardship for many U.S. corporations as well as for individuals, but Procter & Gamble emerged virtually unscathed. Radio took Procter & Gamble's message into more homes than ever. In 1933 Procter & Gamble became a key sponsor of radio's daytime serials, soon known as ''soap operas.'' In 1935 Procter & Gamble spent $2 million on national radio sponsorship, and by 1937 the amount was $4.5 million. In 1939 Procter & Gamble had 21 programs on the air and spent $9 million. That year P&G advertised on television for the first time, when Red Barber plugged Ivory soap during the first television broadcast of a major league baseball game.

In 1940 Procter & Gamble's packaging expertise was given military applications when the government asked the company to oversee the construction and operation of ordinance plants. Procter & Gamble Defense Corporation operated as a subsidiary and filled government contracts for 60-millimeter mortar shells. Glycerin also became key to the war effort for its uses in explosives and medicine, and Procter & Gamble was one of the largest manufacturers of that product.

Postwar Growth Fueled by Tide

After World War II the availability of raw materials and new consumer attitudes set the stage for unprecedented growth. Procter & Gamble's postwar miracle was Tide, a synthetic detergent that, together with home automatic washing machines, revolutionized the way people washed their clothes. The company was not ready for the consumer demand for heavy-duty detergent when it introduced the product in 1946; within two years Tide, backed by a $21 million advertising budget, was the number one laundry detergent, outselling even the company's own Oxydol and Duz. Despite its premium price, Tide remained the number one laundry detergent into the 21st century. In 1950 Cheer was introduced as bluing detergent, and over the years other laundry products were also marketed: Dash in 1954, Downy in 1960, Bold in 1965, Ariel (an overseas brand) in 1967, Era in 1972, and Solo in 1979.

The 1950s were highly profitable for the company. In 1955, after five years of research, Procter & Gamble firmly established itself in the toiletries business with Crest toothpaste. Researchers at the company and at Indiana University developed the toothpaste using stannous fluoride—a compound of fluorine and tin—which could substantially reduce cavities. In 1960 the American Dental Association endorsed Crest, and the product was on its way to becoming the country's number one toothpaste, nudging past Colgate in 1962.

Procter & Gamble began acquiring smaller companies aggressively in the mid-1950s. In 1955 it bought the Lexington, Kentucky-based nut company W.T. Young Foods, and acquired Nebraska Consolidated Mills Company, owner of the Duncan Hines product line, a year later. In 1957 the Charmin Paper Company and the Clorox Chemical Company were also acquired.

In 1957 Neil McElroy, who had become Procter & Gamble president in 1948, left the company to serve as secretary of defense in President Dwight D. Eisenhower's cabinet. He was replaced by Howard Morgens who, like his predecessor, had climbed the corporate ladder from the advertising side. In 1959 McElroy returned to Procter & Gamble as chairman and remained in that position until 1971, when Morgens succeeded him. Morgens remained CEO until 1974.

Paper Products Push Included Pampers

Morgens oversaw Procter & Gamble's full-scale entry into the paper-goods markets. A new process developed in the late 1950s for drying wood pulp led to the introduction of White Cloud toilet paper in 1958, and Puffs tissues in 1960. Procter & Gamble's Charmin brand of toilet paper was also made softer.

Procter & Gamble's paper-products offensive culminated in the 1961 test marketing of Pampers disposable diapers. The idea for Pampers came from a Procter & Gamble researcher, Vic Mills, who was inspired while changing an infant grandchild's diapers in 1956. The product consisted of three parts: a leak-proof outer plastic shell, several absorbent layers, and a porous film that let moisture pass through into the absorbent layers, but kept it from coming back. Test market results showed that parents liked the diapers, but disliked the 10 cents-per-Pamper price. Procter & Gamble reduced the price to six cents and implemented a sales strategy emphasizing the product's price. Pamper's three-layer design was a phenomenal success, and within 20 years disposable diapers had gone from less than 1 percent to more than 75 percent of all diapers changed in the United States. Procter & Gamble improved the technology over the years, and added a premium brand, Luvs, in 1976.

The company expanded its food business by entering the coffee market through the 1963 acquisition of the Folgers brand and by introducing the stackable Pringles potato chips, which were shipped in resealable cans, in 1968. P&G, however, had to contend with charges from the Federal Trade Commission that both its Folgers and Clorox acquisitions violated antitrust statutes. In a case that found its way to the Supreme Court, Procter & Gamble was finally forced to divest Clorox in 1967. The Folgers action was dismissed after Procter & Gamble agreed not to make any more grocery acquisitions for seven years, and coffee acquisitions for ten years.

In the late 1960s public attention to water pollution focused on phosphates, a key group of ingredients in soap products. After initial resistance, Procter & Gamble, along with other soap makers, drastically reduced the use of phosphates in its products.

In 1974 Edward G. Harness became chairman and CEO of Procter & Gamble and the company continued its strong growth. Many familiar products were improved during the 1970s, and new ones were added as well, including Bounce fabric softener for the dryer in 1972 and Sure antiperspirant and Coast soap in 1974.

In 1977, after three years of test marketing, Procter & Gamble introduced Rely tampons, which were rapidly accepted in the market as a result of their ''super-absorbent'' qualities. In 1980, however, the Centers for Disease Control (CDC) published a report showing a statistical link between the use of Rely and a rare but often fatal disease known as toxic shock syndrome (TSS). In September 1980 the company suspended further sales of Rely tampons, taking a $75 million write-off on the product.

Ironically, P&G was able to capitalize on the resurgence of feminine napkins after the TSS scare. The company's Always brand pads quickly garnered market share, and by 1990 Always was the top sanitary napkin, with over one-fourth of the market.

Food and OTC Drug Acquisitions in the Early 1980s

In 1981 John G. Smale became CEO of Procter & Gamble. He had been president since 1974. Smale led the company further into the grocery business through a number of acquisitions, including Ben Hill Griffin citrus products. The company also entered the over-the-counter (OTC) drug market with the 1982 purchase of Norwich-Eaton Pharmaceuticals, makers of Pepto Bismol and Chloraseptic. The company completed its biggest purchase in 1985, with the acquisition of the Richardson-Vicks Company, maker of Vicks respiratory care products, NyQuil cold remedies, and Oil of Olay skin care products, for $1.2 billion; and bought the motion-sickness treatment Dramamine and the laxative Metamucil from G.D. Searle & Co. These purchases made Procter & Gamble a leader in over-the-counter drug sales.

In 1985, unable to squelch perennial rumors linking Procter & Gamble's famous moon-and-stars logo to Satanism, the company reluctantly removed the logo from product packages. The logo began to reappear on some packages in the early 1990s, and the company continued to use the trademark on corporate stationary and on its building.

During fiscal 1985, Procter & Gamble experienced its first decline in earnings since 1953. Analysts maintained that Procter & Gamble's corporate structure had failed to respond to important changes in consumer shopping patterns and that the company's standard practice of extensive market research slowed its reaction to the rapidly changing market. The mass-marketing practices that had served Procter & Gamble so well in the past lost their punch as broadcast television viewership fell from 92 percent to 67 percent in the mid-1980s. Many large companies responded to the challenge of cable TV and increasingly market-specific media with appropriately targeted "micro-marketing" techniques, and Procter & Gamble was forced to rethink its marketing strategy. In the late 1980s Procter & Gamble diversified its advertising, reducing its reliance on network television. Computerized market research including point-of-sale scanning also provided the most up-to-date information on consumer buying trends.

In 1987 the company restructured its brand-management system into a "matrix system." Category managers became responsible for several brands, making them sensitive to the profits of other Procter & Gamble products in their areas. Procter & Gamble brands continued to compete against one another, but far less actively. The restructuring also eliminated certain layers of management, quickening the decision-making process. The company became more aware of profitability than in the past. A company spokesperson summed it up for *Business Week:* "before it had been share, share, share. We get the share and the profits will follow." In the later 1980s, Procter & Gamble was no longer willing to settle just for market share.

In the late 1980s healthcare products were one of the fastest-growing markets as the U.S. population grew both older and more health conscious. To serve this market, Procter & Gamble's OTC drug group, which had been built up earlier in the decade, entered a number of joint ventures in pharmaceuticals. Procter & Gamble teamed up with the Syntex Corporation to formulate an OTC version of its best-selling antiarthritic, Naprosyn. Cooperative deals were also struck with the Dutch

Gist-Brocades Company for its De-Nol ulcer medicine; UpJohn for its anti-baldness drug, Minoxidil; and Triton Bioscience and Cetus for a synthetic interferon.

Noxell and Blendax Acquisitions in 1988

In September 1988 Procter & Gamble made its first move into the cosmetics business with the purchase of Noxell Corporation, maker of Noxema products and Cover Girl cosmetics, in a $1.3 billion stock swap. Procter & Gamble also planned to further develop its international operations. In 1988 the company acquired Blendax, a European health- and beauty-care goods manufacturer. The Bain de Soleil sun care-product line was also purchased that year. By 1989 foreign markets accounted for nearly 40 percent of group sales, up from 14 percent in 1985.

P&G's brand equity was threatened by the weak economy and resultant consumer interest in value in the late 1980s and early 1990s. This value orientation resulted in stronger performance by private labels, especially in health and beauty aids. Private labels' market share of that segment grew 50 percent between 1982 and 1992, to 4.5 percent.

To combat the trend, P&G inaugurated "Every Day Low Pricing" (EDLP) for 50 to 60 percent of its products, including Pampers and Luvs diapers, Cascade dish soap, and Jif peanut butter. The pricing strategy was good for consumers, but was compensated for with lower promotion deals for wholesalers. Some retailers objected to P&G's cut in promotional kickbacks to the point of actually dropping products, but others welcomed the value-conscious positioning. P&G redirected the money it saved from trade promotions for direct marketing efforts that helped bring coupon and sample programs to targeted groups for brands with narrow customer bases such as Pampers, Clearasil, and Oil of Olay.

In the 1990s Procter & Gamble also hopped on the so-called "green" bandwagon of environmental marketing. It reduced packaging by offering concentrated formulations of products in smaller packages and refill packs on 38 brands in 17 countries.

While P&G expanded its presence in cosmetics and fragrances through the July 1991 acquisition of the worldwide Max Factor and Betrix lines from Revlon, Inc. for $1.03 billion, it also divested holdings in some areas it had outgrown. In 1992 the corporation sold about one-half of its Cellulose & Specialties pulp business to Weyerhaeuser Co. for $600 million. While vertical integration had benefitted P&G's paper products in the past, the forestry business had become unprofitable and distracting by the 1990s. The corporation also sold an Italian coffee business in 1992 to focus on a core of European brands. P&G hoped to introduce products with pan-European packaging, branding, and advertising to capture more of the region's well-established markets. Meanwhile, Pantene Pro-V was introduced in 1992 and quickly became the fastest growing shampoo in the world.

Major Restructurings and Acquisitions in the Mid- to Late 1990s

Company sales surpassed the $30 billion mark in 1993. Under the leadership of Chairman and CEO Edwin L. Artzt and

President John E. Pepper, Procter & Gamble that year launched a major restructuring effort aimed at making the company's brand-name products more price-competitive with private label and generic brands, bringing products to market faster, and improving overall profitability. The program involved severe cost-cutting, including the closure of 30 plants around the world and elimination of 13,000 jobs, or 12 percent of P&G's total workforce. Culminated in 1997, the $2.4 billion program resulted in annual after-tax savings of more than $600 million. It also helped to increase Procter & Gamble's net earnings margin from 7.3 percent in 1994 to 10.2 percent in 1998.

During the restructuring period, the company continued its brisk acquisitions pace. In 1994 P&G entered the European tissue and towel market through the purchase of Vereinigte Papierwerke Schickedanz AG's European tissue unit, and added the prestige fragrance business of Giorgio Beverly Hills, Inc. That year also saw Procter & Gamble reenter the South African market following the lifting of U.S. sanctions. The company altered its geographic management structure the following year. P&G had divided its operations into United States and International, but would now organize around four regions—North America, Latin America, Asia, and Europe/Middle East/Africa. In July 1995 Artzt retired, and was replaced as chairman and CEO by Pepper. Durk I. Jager was named president and chief operating officer.

In 1996 Procter & Gamble purchased the Eagle Snacks brand line from Anheuser-Busch, the U.S. baby wipes brand Baby Fresh, and Latin American brands Lavan San household cleaner and Magia Blanca bleach. In celebration of the 50th anniversary of Tide's introduction, the company held a "Dirtiest Kid in America" contest. Also in 1996 P&G received U.S. Food & Drug Administration (FDA) approval to use olestra, a controversial fat substitute, in snacks and crackers. The company had developed olestra after 25 years of research and at a cost of $250 million. The FDA go-ahead came after an eight-year investigation and included a stipulation that foods containing the substitute include a warning label about possible gastrointestinal side effects. P&G soon began test-marketing Fat Free Pringles, Fat Free Ritz, and other products made using olestra. No product containing olestra ever caught on in the market, however, and olestra was eventually considered one of the company's biggest product failures ever.

In July 1997 Procter & Gamble spent about $1.84 billion in cash to acquire Tambrands, Inc. and the Tampax line of tampons, thereby solidifying its number one position worldwide in feminine products. The company sold its Duncan Hines baking mix line to Aurora Foods of Ohio for $445 million in 1998.

In September 1998 P&G announced a new restructuring initiative, dubbed Organization 2005. In 1996 the company had set a goal of doubling sales from the $35 billion of 1996 to $70 billion by 2005. But sales stood at just $37.15 billion by 1998, only a 4 percent increase over the previous year—when 7 percent increases were needed each year. A key element of this restructuring was a shift from an organization centered around the four geographic regions established in 1995 to one centered on seven global business units based on product lines: Baby Care, Beauty Care, Fabric & Home Care, Feminine Protection, Food & Beverage, Health Care & Corporate New Ventures, and

Tissues & Towels. According to a company press release announcing the new structure, "This change will drive greater innovation and speed by centering strategy and profit responsibility globally on brands, rather than on geographies." Jager would be the person leading the reorganization, as it was announced at the same time that he would become president and CEO on January 1, 1999, with Pepper remaining chairman only until September 1, 1999, when Jager would also assume that position.

In June 1999 Jager extended the Organization 2005 restructuring to include several new initiatives. The company said that by 2005 it would eliminate 15,000 jobs, shutter about ten factories, and record restructuring costs of $1.9 billion. The aims were to increase innovation, get new products to the market faster, and accelerate both revenue and profit growth.

In the meantime, P&G remained on the lookout for acquisitions and completed two significant ones in the latter months of 1999. In its biggest deal yet, Procter & Gamble laid out $2.22 billion in cash for the Iams Company, one of the leading makers of premium pet food in the United States, with annual global sales of approximately $800 million. P&G next acquired Recovery Engineering, Inc. for about $265 million. Based in Minneapolis, Recovery produced the fast-growing PUR brand of water-filter products, achieving $80 million in sales in 1998. Among new products introduced in 1999 was Swiffer, an electrostatic dusting mop that was part of a new category of household product: quick cleaning. The Swiffer line went on to become one of P&G's fastest-growing brands of the early 2000s. Also debuting in 1999 were Febreze, a spray used to eliminate odors in fabrics, and Dryel, a home dry-cleaning kit.

Early 2000s: Further Restructuring, Hair-Care Acquisitions

Early in 2000 Procter & Gamble placed itself in the middle of a major takeover battle in the pharmaceutical industry. Late in the previous year, Warner-Lambert Company had agreed to a nearly $70 billion merger with American Home Products Corporation (AHP). Pfizer Inc. quickly stepped in with a hostile bid for Warner-Lambert that exceeded AHP's offer. Warner-Lambert attempted to fend off Pfizer, bringing P&G into the picture in January 2000 to discuss a three-way deal involving AHP. But Jager was forced to abandon the white knight maneuver, which would have been a huge and risky move into the drug business, when word leaked out to the press and the company's stock price plummeted. Around this same time, Jager reportedly approached the Gillette Company, best known for its razors, about a takeover but was quickly rebuffed.

In June 2000, after the company issued its third profit warning in a year, Jager resigned. Taking over as president and CEO was A.G. Lafley, who had joined the company in June 1977 as a brand assistant for Joy and had most recently been in charge of the global beauty care unit. At the same time, Pepper returned to the company board as chairman. Lafley slowed down the rush to get products to market in order to make sure that they received the proper marketing support, while at the same time focusing more of the company's resources on shoring up its big core brands—the top dozen or so products, each of which brought in more than $1 billion in global revenues annually.

Among other developments in 2000, the Oil of Olay brand was renamed simply Olay in an effort to dispel the perception that the product was greasy. As part of an ongoing effort to focus on a smaller number of core brands, P&G sold Clearasil, the acne-treatment brand, to Boots PLC for about $340 million. The company also received FDA approval for Actonel, a prescription treatment for osteoporosis. Aided by a marketing partnership with Aventis, P&G was able to achieve $1 billion in annual Actonel sales by fiscal 2004.

Extending its 1999 restructuring still further, P&G announced in March 2001 that it would shed several thousand additional jobs over the following three years and double the amount of money it would spend to fix its operational problems. By the end of fiscal 2003, when the restructuring was declared to be complete, Procter & Gamble had cut about 21,600 jobs and incurred total before-tax charges of $4.85 billion. In the meantime, the company's fiscal 2001 results clearly showed the dismal state of affairs at that time: Sales fell nearly 2 percent to $39.24 billion, while net income plunged 17.5 percent to $2.92 billion thanks to after-tax restructuring charges of $1.48 billion.

In March 2001 Procter & Gamble reached an agreement with the Coca-Cola Company to create a $4 billion joint venture designed to join Coke's Minute Maid brand and distribution network with P&G's Pringles chips and Sunny Delight drink brands. But Coca-Cola pulled out of the deal just a few months later, having decided to try to build the Minute Maid brand on its own. Despite this setback, P&G succeeded in paring back its ever more marginal food business by selling the Jif peanut butter and Crisco shortening brands to the J.M. Smucker Company. The deal, completed in May 2002, was valued at about $900 million. In November 2001, meantime, P&G consummated its largest acquisition yet, buying the Clairol hair-care business from Bristol-Myers Squibb Company for nearly $5 billion in cash. The deal melded well with P&G's goal of securing faster-growing, more profitable product areas, such as beauty and hair care. Also acquired in 2001 was Dr. John's SpinBrush, maker of a battery-powered toothbrush featuring spinning bristles that at $5 was much cheaper than existing electric toothbrushes. Soon thereafter, the newly named Crest SpinBrush was successfully launched. Also brought out in 2001 were Crest Whitestrips, a tooth whitening product. These two new products helped increase global sales of the Crest brand by 50 percent, propelling it past the $1 billion mark during fiscal 2002.

In July 2002 Pepper again retired, and Lafley took on the additional post of chairman. Results for the fiscal year ending in June 2003 provided strong evidence that Lafley had engineered a remarkable turnaround. In its best performance in nearly a decade, Procter & Gamble posted an 8 percent increase in net sales, to $43.38 billion, and a 19 percent jump in net earnings, to $5.19 billion. P&G built on these results with another blockbuster acquisition—once again the largest in company history. In September 2003 the company acquired a controlling interest in Wella AG for $6.27 billion. Based in Germany, Wella was a leading maker of professional hair-care products with 2002 revenues of $3.6 billion. The deal provided P&G with an entrée into the salon market, where about half of Wella's sales were generated. Procter & Gamble also bolstered its dental care line by acquiring the Glide brand of dental floss from W.L. Gore & Associates, Inc. In September 2003, under a marketing and distribution agreement with AstraZeneca PLC, P&G began selling Prilosec OTC, an over-the-counter version of AstraZeneca's blockbuster heartburn medication, Prilosec.

In April 2004 Procter & Gamble reached an agreement to sell its Sunny Delight and Punica drinks businesses to J.W. Childs Associates LP, a private-equity firm in Boston. This further paring of the foods business left P&G with just two main food brands, Pringles and Folgers. The snacks and beverages unit accounted for only 7 percent of the company's total revenues in fiscal 2004. At the beginning of fiscal 2005 P&G realigned its business units, shifting its five previous units into three: global beauty care; global health, baby, and family care; and global household care. Pringles and Folgers were placed within the latter unit.

Sales for fiscal 2004 surged 19 percent, surpassing the $50 billion mark for the first time. Net earnings jumped 25 percent, hitting $6.48 billion. The newly invigorated company continued its streak of paying dividends without interruption since its 1890 incorporation, and it also increased its dividend for the 48th straight year.

Principal Subsidiaries

Cosmopolitan Cosmetics GmbH (Germany); The Folger Coffee Company; Giorgio Beverly Hills, Inc.; The Iams Company; Max Factor & Co.; Noxell Corporation; Olay Company, Inc.; P&G-Clairol, Inc.; Procter & Gamble Pharmaceuticals, Inc.; PUR Water Purification Products, Inc.; Tambrands Inc.; Vick International Corporation; Vidal Sassoon Co.; Procter & Gamble Australia Proprietary Limited; Procter & Gamble Inc. (Canada); Procter & Gamble France S.N.C.; Wella AG (Germany); Procter & Gamble India Holdings, Inc.; Procter & Gamble Italia, S.p.A. (Italy); Procter & Gamble Nederland B.V. (Netherlands); Procter & Gamble Switzerland SARL; Procter & Gamble Limited (U.K.); Thomas Hedley & Co. Limited (U.K.); Yardley of London Ltd. (U.K.).

Principal Operating Units

Global Beauty Care; Global Health, Baby, and Family Care; Global Household Care.

Principal Competitors

Unilever; Johnson & Johnson; Kimberly-Clark Corporation; Sara Lee Corporation; Kraft Foods Inc.; L'Oreal SA; Colgate-Palmolive Company.

Further Reading

Berner, Robert, "Why P&G's Smile Is So Bright," *Business Week,* August 12, 2002, pp. 58–60.

Berner, Robert, and Gerry Khermouch, "The Tide Is Turning at P&G," *Business Week,* April 8, 2002, p. 44.

Berner, Robert, Nanette Byrnes, and Wendy Zellner, "P&G Has Rivals in a Wringer," *Business Week,* October 4, 2004, p. 74.

Branch, Shelly, "P&G to Buy Iams," *Wall Street Journal,* August 12, 1999, p. B1.

Brooker, Katrina, "Can Procter & Gamble Change Its Culture, Protect Its Market Share, and Find the Next Tide?," *Fortune,* April 26, 1999, pp. 146–50, 152.

——, "The Un-CEO," *Fortune,* September 16, 2002, pp. 88–92, 96.

Canedy, Dana, "A Prescription to Keep P&G Growing Strong: Big Household Name Tries to Be a Drugstore, Too," *New York Times,* November 4, 1997, p. D1.

Deogun, Nikhil, and Emily Nelson, "Stirring Giant: P&G Is on the Move," *Wall Street Journal,* January 24, 2000, pp. A1+.

Dumaine, Brian, "P&G Rewrites the Marketing Rules," *Fortune,* November 6, 1989, pp. 34+.

Dyer, Davis, Frederick Dalzell, and Rowena Olegario, *Rising Tide: Lessons from 165 Years of Brand Building at Procter & Gamble,* Boston: Harvard Business School Press, 2004, 496 p.

Eisenberg, Daniel, "A Healthy Gamble," *Time,* September 16, 2002, pp. 46–48.

Ellison, Sarah, "P&G Lays Out Wella Strategy," *Wall Street Journal,* March 19, 2003, p. B3.

Galuszka, Peter, and Ellen Neuborne, "P&G's Hottest New Product: P&G," *Business Week,* October 5, 1998, pp. 92+.

Henkoff, Ronald, "P&G: New and Improved!," *Fortune,* October 14, 1996, pp. 151+.

"The House That Ivory Built: 150 Years of Procter & Gamble," *Advertising Age,* August 20, 1987.

"Jager's Gamble," *Economist,* October 30, 1999, p. 75.

Johnson, Bradley, "Retailers Accepting P&G Low Pricing," *Advertising Age,* June 22, 1992, p. 36.

Kirk, Jim, "The New Status Symbols; New Values Drive Private-Label Sales," *Adweek* (Eastern Ed.), October 5, 1992, pp. 38–44.

Laing, Jonathan R., "New and Improved: Procter & Gamble Fights to Keep Its Place on the Top Shelf," *Barron's,* November 29, 1993, pp. 8–9, 22, 24, 26.

Lawrence, Jennifer, "Jager: New P&G Pricing Builds Brands," *Advertising Age,* June 29, 1992, pp. 13, 49.

——, "Laundry Soap Marketers See the Value of 'Value!,'" *Advertising Age,* September 21, 1992, pp. 3, 56.

Lenzner, Robert, and Carrie Shook, "The Battle of the Bottoms," *Forbes,* March 24, 1997, pp. 98+.

Levin, Gary, "P&G Tells Shops: Direct Marketing Is Important to Us," *Advertising Age,* June 22, 1992, pp. 3, 35.

Lief, Alfred, *It Floats: The Story of Procter & Gamble,* New York: Rinehart & Company, 1958, 338 p.

Miller, Cyndee, "Moves by P&G, Heinz Rekindle Fears That Brands Are in Danger," *Marketing News,* June 8, 1992, pp. 1, 15.

Mitchell, Alan, "The Dawn of a Cultural Revolution," *Management Today,* March 1998, pp. 42–44, 46, 48.

Nelson, Emily, "P&G Agrees to Pay $4.95 Billion for Bristol-Myers's Clairol Unit," *Wall Street Journal,* May 22, 2001, p. B7.

——, "Rallying the Troops at P&G: New CEO Lafley Aims to End Upheaval by Revamping Program of Globalization," *Wall Street Journal,* August 31, 2000, p. B1.

P&G: A Company History, Cincinnati, Ohio: The Procter & Gamble Company, 2004, 17 p.

"P&G's New New-Product Onslaught," *Business Week,* October 1, 1979, p. 76.

Parker-Pope, Tara, "New CEO Preaches Rebellion for P&G's 'Cult,' " *Wall Street Journal,* December 11, 1998, p. B1.

——, "P&G, in Effort to Give Sales a Boost, Plans to Revamp Corporate Structure," *Wall Street Journal,* September 2, 1998, p. B6.

——, "P&G Targets Textiles Tide Can't Clean," *Wall Street Journal,* April 29, 1998, pp. B1, B4.

Parker-Pope, Tara, and Joann S. Lublin, "P&G Will Make Jager CEO Ahead of Schedule," *Wall Street Journal,* September 10, 1998, pp. B1, B8.

Parker-Pope, Tara, and Jonathan Friedland, "P&G Calls the Cops As It Strives to Expand Sales in Latin America," *Wall Street Journal,* March 20, 1998, pp. A1, A9.

Procter & Gamble: The House That Ivory Built, by the editors of Advertising Age, Lincolnwood, Ill.: NTC Business Books, 1988, 234 p.

"Procter & Gamble's Profit Problem-Food," *Business Week,* January 26, 1981, p. 52.

"Procter's Gamble," *Economist,* July 25, 1992, pp. 61–62.

Rice, Faye, "The King of Suds Reigns Again," *Fortune,* August 4, 1986, pp. 130+.

Saporito, Bill, "Behind the Tumult at P&G," *Fortune,* March 7, 1994, pp. 74+.

——, "Procter & Gamble's Comeback Plan," *Fortune,* February 4, 1985, pp. 30+.

Schiller, Zachary, "And Now, a Show from Your Sponsor," *Business Week,* May 22, 1995, pp. 100+.

——, "Ed Artzt's Elbow Grease Has P&G Shining," *Business Week,* October 10, 1994, pp. 84+.

——, "Make It Simple," *Business Week,* September 9, 1996, pp. 96+.

——, "The Marketing Revolution at Procter & Gamble," *Business Week,* July 25, 1988, pp. 72+.

——, "No More Mr. Nice Guy at P&G—Not by a Long Shot," *Business Week,* February 3, 1992, pp. 54+.

——, "P&G's Worldly New Boss Wants a More Worldly Company," *Business Week,* October 30, 1989, pp. 40+.

——, "Procter & Gamble Hits Back: Its Dramatic Overhaul Takes Aim at High Costs—and Low-Price Rivals," *Business Week,* July 19, 1993, pp. 20+.

Schisgall, Oscar, *Eyes on Tomorrow: Evolution of Procter & Gamble,* Chicago: J.G. Ferguson Publishing Co., 1981, 295 p.

Sellers, Patricia, "P&G: Teaching an Old Dog New Tricks," *Fortune,* May 31, 2004, pp. 166–68+.

Swasy, Alecia, *Soap Opera: The Inside Story of Procter & Gamble,* New York: Times Books, 1993, 378 p.

Vanderwicken, Peter, "P&G's Secret Ingredient," *Fortune,* July 1974, p. 75.

Weinstein, Steve, "Will Procter's Gamble Work?," *Progressive Grocer,* July 1992, pp. 36–40.

"Why Procter & Gamble Is Playing It Even Tougher," *Business Week,* July 18, 1983, pp. 176+.

Wilsher, Peter, "Diverse and Perverse," *Management Today,* July 1992, pp. 32–35.

—Thomas M. Tucker
—updates: April S. Dougal, David E. Salamie

PVC Container Corporation

2 Industrial Way West
Eatontown, New Jersey 07724-2202
U.S.A.
Telephone: (732) 542-0060
Fax: (732) 542-7706
Web site: http://www.pvcc.com

Public Company
Incorporated: 1968
Employees: 594
Sales: $90.4 million (2003)
Stock Exchanges: Over the Counter (OTC)
Ticker Symbol: PVCC
NAIC: 326160 Plastics Bottle Manufacturing

PVC Container Corporation manufactures plastic bottles and containers from a variety of resins, including polyvinyl chloride (PVC), high-density polyethylene (HDPE), polypropylene (PP), and polyethylene terephthalate (PET). The Eatontown, New Jersey-based company does business through four subsidiaries. Novapak Corporation produces specialty bottles and containers for the automotive, beverage, chemical, food, household, and personal care sectors. Airopak Corporation uses a fluorine mixture rather than air in its blow molded technology to make a line of containers suitable for the lawn and garden and industrial chemical markets. Marpac Industries Inc. designs and produces containers with complex shapes such as automotive fluid reservoirs, toner copier containers, and medical diagnostic equipment. The fourth PVC subsidiary, Novatec Plastics Corporation, manufactures the compounds used by the other subsidiaries and also sells its selection of 500 rigid vinyl compounds to outside customers. PVC's manufacturing and warehousing facilities are located in Hazleton, Pennsylvania; Paris, Illinois; Manchester, Pennsylvania; Walterboro, South Carolina; Philmont, New York; and Kingston, New York. Traded over the counter, PVC is majority owned by Kirtland Capital.

Forming the Company in the Late 1960s

PVC was formed as a public corporation in June 1968 by three men: a blow molder involved in making packaging for Eli Lilly Pharmaceuticals, a lawyer, and a financial advisor. The plan was to concentrate exclusively on using PVC and blow mold technology to make plastic containers. PVC had been a commercially used polymer for 40 years, although it was discovered by accident as early as 1838 by Henri Victor Regnault. The substance had been formed when vinyl chloride in a flask had been exposed to sunlight, resulting in a solid white substance. In the early 1900s attempts were made to use it to make commercial products, but PVC proved unpredictable and difficult to work with. It was not until 1936 when Waldo Semon, working for B.F. Goodrich, discovered the proper additives needed to plasticize PVC that the polymer became a viable material. It soon found a wide range of commercial applications, such as building materials, plumbing and piping, record albums, clothing, upholstery, and plastic containers.

PVC Container Corporation became operational in 1969 with the opening of a 30,000-square-foot, Eatontown, New Jersey plant. Using extrusion blow mold technology, the company initially produced PVC bottles ranging in size from four to 16 ounces. In 1972, after the company had established itself in the marketplace, it expanded the maximum size of the bottle it could produce to 48 ounces. As the business grew the Eatontown plant expanded, adding an additional 20,000 square feet in 1975, and another 20,000 square feet five years later. In 1978 Rimer Anstalt, a Lichtenstein-based private investment firm, acquired a controlling interest in the company, but Rimer was content to remain in the background as a passive investor and allow the company's management team to run the business.

Moving Beyond PVC Material in the 1980s

After a dozen years in operation, PVC began to broaden its reach during the 1980s. In 1981 it began producing HDPE bottles. The year also was marked by the arrival of Phillip L. Friedman, who would lead the company for the next quarter-century. Friedman was in his early 30s when he became president and chief executive and financial officer. During the previous 12 years he worked for Hooker Chemical Corporation, which would become Occidental Chemical Corporation, an important provider of PVC resins and compounds. After seven years at Hooker, Friedman rose to the rank of manager of business development and director of commercial development for the polyvinyl chloride plastics division. With Friedman at the helm, PVC in 1982 reached a major turning point when it established its own source of raw materials by forming Novatec Plastics & Chemicals Division to produce PVC compound and PVC alloys used in blow molding, profile/sheet/film extrusion, and injection molding. The decision to form Novatec was also shrewd because there was little competition in the compound supply market. In short order, Novatec became the third largest supplier of PVC bottle compounds. In 1985 PVC once again increased its maximum bottle size, this time to 64 ounces. At the close of the decade business was strong enough that the company moved into a new plant in Eatontown, 106,000 square feet in size. Moreover, the new facility featured its own decorating capabilities. Also of note during the late 1980s, in the final months of 1988, PVC came close to being sold to an unnamed third party for approximately $14 million. By mid-December 1988 the discussions were terminated, however.

In 1992 PVC took initial steps to move into the PET bottle sector by forging an alliance with a Canadian company, Kantrail Plastics. Kantrail had several years of experience producing PET containers for the Canadian market. Not only did PVC gain access to Kantrail's PET expertise, it also gained the exclusive rights to market Kantrail bottles in the United States. Although PVC remained devoted to the use of polyvinyl chloride, the material had come under increasing criticism in recent years because of safety and ecological concerns, making it a prudent step to branch into the PET market. Initially, PVC marketed a handful of oval bottles, water bottles, and a one-liter vegetable bottle. The company made a major commitment to the PET injection stretch blow molding business in 1996. Not only did it add 35,000 square feet of space to its Eatontown plant for PET production, it also built a $5.5 million, 60,000-square-foot factory in Walterboro, South Carolina, capable of making all of the company's product lines in addition to PET bottles. The South Carolina site was chosen because it was close to a major longtime PVC customer and also supported a company effort to grow the business regionally. Earlier, in 1993, PVC opened a 62,000-square-foot plant in Paris, Illinois, with the capability of producing the entire company product line for the Midwest markets. A year later that company line would expand to include containers as large as 2½ gallons.

During the first half of the 1990s PVC added other capabilities in addition to PET production. In 1992 the company added tri-layer blow molding to make use of polycarbonate. PVC achieved some diversity in 1994 when it paid $15.7 million to acquire Airopak Corporation, a Manchester, Pennsylvania-

based company that used blow molding technology to produce in-line fluorinated HDPE containers, suited for ultra-clean and solvent-based products. Finally, in 1995 PVC added PP bottles to its product line. In a short period of time PVC had expanded well beyond polyvinyl chloride, but because the company used PVC as part of its name, it lost some potential customers who looked elsewhere when they needed products made from PET, PP, HDPE, or other materials. There was talk of changing the company's name to something less restrictive, such as PVCC Corp., drawing on the stock's NASDAQ ticker symbol, but nothing ever came of the idea.

Revenues grew from $29.5 million in fiscal 1991 to $53.9 million in fiscal 1995. During this period net income also increased from $1.1 million to $1.6 million. Although PVC had enjoyed steady growth, it possessed a great deal of untapped potential that was not being realized under the ownership of Anstalt Rimer. In December 1996 a new majority owner took over, Kirtland Capital Partners, a Cleveland area private investment group originally formed in 1977 as Chagrin Valley Company Ltd. to do leveraged buyouts of companies. It was recapitalized in 1981 and took the Kirtland name in 1984 after a number of investors were added. Kirtland believed in long-term investments, making sure that companies were adequately capitalized, and working with management teams to help grow the businesses. Kirtland paid $17.5 million for a 63 percent interest in PVC and left in place the company's management team, which the new owner believed was "high caliber." Kirtland's managing partner, Raymond A. Lancaster, told the press at the time of the closing, "We see a lot of growth opportunities for this company."

In 1997 Novapak was created to produce high-margin specialty products, provide more diversity, and better position the company for steady growth. A balanced slate of product offerings helped PVC to achieve stability despite changing conditions. In fiscal 1997, for instance, demand was softer than expected for the company's general line of plastic bottles, but the difference was made up by increased demand for Airopak's specialty containers and Novatec's plastic compounds. As a result, the company was able to show improvement over the previous year, with sales totaling $58.4 million and net income $2.25 million, a slight decrease over the previous year.

With Kirtland's backing, PVC completed a pair of acquisitions in 1998 as part of an effort to expand the company's plastic bottle business by both internal and external means. In March of that year it bought the plastic container assets of McKechnie Investments Inc., picking up a 100,000-square-foot plant in Philmont, New York. McKechnie used extrusion blow mold technology to produce narrow-neck and wide-mouth bottles in a range of sizes using PVC, PP, HDPE, and low-density polyethylene, serving the toiletry, cosmetic, and specialty and household chemical markets. The acquisition also brought with it about $17 million in sales. Later in 1998 PVC exchanged $12 million in stock to acquire Marpac Industries Inc., a specialty container maker with plants in Ardmore, Oklahoma, and Kingston, New York. Generating some $10 million in annual sales, Marpac used lower-cavitation technical blow molding to serve the office machinery market with PP and PET bottles, containers, cartridges, double-wall cases, flexible spouts, and dis-

```
┌─────────────────────────────────────────────┐
│                                              │
│                 Key Dates:                   │
│                                              │
│  1968:  The company is formed.               │
│  1979:  Rimer Anstalt becomes majority owner.│
│  1982:  Novatec is formed.                   │
│  1993:  A plant is opened in Paris, Illinois.│
│  1994:  Airopak Corporation is acquired.     │
│  1996:  Kirtland Capital Partners acquires a │
│         majority stake.                      │
│  1998:  Marpac Industries is acquired.       │
│  2004:  Phillip Friedman steps downs as CEO. │
│                                              │
└─────────────────────────────────────────────┘
```

pensers. The Marpac assets were folded into the Airopak division. PVC also grew internally in 1998. It opened a new 160,000-square-foot plant in Hazleton, Pennsylvania, to produce PVC and PET bottles. The Paris, Illinois facility more than doubled in size to 130,000 square feet and added stretch blow molded capabilities. In addition, Airopak introduced dual-layer, co-extrusion in-line fluorination of bottles. As a result of expansion on a number of fronts, sales grew to $69.7 million in fiscal 1998 and $89.9 million in 1999. Net income, however, trailed off, dropping to $1.9 million in 1998 and $1.7 million in 1999.

New Century Bringing Challenging Conditions

Changing business conditions hindered PVC's growth at the start of the new century. The price of resins rose quickly, adversely impacting margins. In addition, the company faced increased competition. Although revenues grew to $94.8 million in fiscal 2000, the company lost nearly $1.2 million. To help in overcoming these challenges, PVC closed the Ardmore plant and cut employment by 7 percent, eliminating 50 out of 650 positions. It also instituted a "Challenge 2000" program, which encouraged employees to offer ideas on ways to reduce waste, lower costs, and improve quality.

Although the company did a better job in controlling costs and the price of resins fell, business continued to slide in fiscal 2001 as weak demand in both containers and compounds resulted from an economy lapsing into recession. Sales dipped below $90 million and the company lost another $1.1 million.

Sales continued to fall in 2002, reaching $84 million, but PVC was able to squeeze out a net profit of $261,445.

PVC initiated a comprehensive strategic plan in 2002, part of which included the integration of the Airopak, Marpac, and Novapak sales and marketing operations. As the close of fiscal 2003 approached, when the company would see sales rebound somewhat to $90.4 million and net income to $872,552, more drastic measures were contemplated. PVC hired Minneapolis-based U.S. Bancorp Piper Jaffray Inc. to help it explore alternatives, including the possible sale of the company. Although PVC was regarded as a well-run business, it suffered from a lack of size. After weighing the options, in February 2004 Friedman announced that it would not pursue any of the proposals that resulted from the process and elected to stay the course. One significant change took place several months later in September 2004 when Friedman announced that he was stepping down as the company's president and CEO, although he would stay on as chairman of the board. He was replaced by William J. Bergen, a former vice-president and general manager for the Plastics Americas Business Unit of Alcan Inc.

Principal Subsidiaries

Novatec Plastics Corporation; Novapak Corporation; Airopak Corporation; Marpac Industries Inc.

Principal Competitors

Owens-Illinois, Inc.; Silgan Holdings Inc.; PolyOne Corporation; Georgia Gulf Corporation.

Further Reading

Baird, Kristen, "Kirtland to Acquire Container Company," *Crain's Cleveland Business,* December 16, 1996, p. 2.

Pryweller, Joseph, "PVC Container Mulls Options, May Be Sold," *Plastics News,* May 26, 2003, p. 1.

Smith, Sarah S., "PVC Container Acquires Marpac," *Plastics News,* September 14, 1998, p. 1.

——, "PVC Container Buys Bottle Unit of McKechnie's," *Plastics News,* April 6, 1998, p. 1.

—Ed Dinger

Quilmes Industrial (QUINSA) S.A.

Teniente General Perón 667
Buenos Aires, C.F. 1038
Argentina
Telephone: (54) (11) 4321-2700
Fax: (54) (11) 4394-2310
Web site: http://www.Quinsa.com

Public Company
Incorporated: 1888 as Brasserie Argentine Quilmes S.A.
Employees: 6,234
Sales: $648.5 million (2003)
Stock Exchanges: Bourse de Luxembourg New York
Ticker Symbols: QUIN.LU; QUINp.LU; LQU
NAIC: 312111 Soft Drink Manufacturing; 312112 Bottled
    Water Manufacturing; 312120 Breweries; 551112
    Offices of Other Holding Companies

Quilmes Industrial (QUINSA) S.A. is a Luxembourg-based holding company that, through its principal subsidiary, dominates the production and sale of beer in Argentina, Bolivia, Paraguay, and Uruguay. The same subsidiary also takes part in a joint venture producing and marketing mineral water in Argentina. A subsidiary of this subsidiary controls the two largest bottlers and producers of PepsiCo Inc. beverages in Argentina. Although incorporated in Luxembourg, Quinsa is administered from Buenos Aires, where it maintains its executive offices.

A Century of Beermaking: 1890–1989

Born in Germany, Peter Frederick Otto Bemberg first came to Argentina in 1850 and, aided by marriage into the well-connected Ocampo family, successfully took part in ventures exploiting the young nation's rich natural resources. He was also a financier who based his operations in Paris. Two years prior to establishing a brewery in the city of Quilmes in the province of Buenos Aires in 1890, he and his son Otto Sebastián Bemberg incorporated the business in Paris. Quilmes quickly dominated the beer market in Argentina, with branches in all major cities. It acquired several more breweries, among them

Schlau in Rosario (1907) and Palermo in Buenos Aires (1916). Later additions included Norte in Tucumán and Maltería de Los Andes in Mendoza during the 1940s. The enterprise manufactured the first malt using Argentine barley in 1921, and this enterprise supplied not only the company's own breweries but practically the entire national beer industry. At the same time, and with the same objective of import substitution, the first bottle-cap factory in Argentina was established at Quilmes to replace cork stoppers. Associated companies produced ice, carbonic gas, and soft drinks. Among the carbonated sodas that it produced was a very popular orange drink, Naranja Bilz. This line of business disappeared in the 1970s.

Beverages were only one part of the activities of the Bemberg group. The family-owned string of enterprises included a large bank, railroads, streetcar lines, bread and cheese factories, textile mills, cattle ranches, and forestry stations. Otto Sebastián Bemberg remained in Paris, and his five children married French spouses. In 1947–48, however, under the authoritarian rule of President Juan Perón, the government confiscated all the Bemberg-dominated holdings, consisting of 33 companies and including 250,000 acres of land (although the legal process of expropriation was not completed until 1954). According to family lore, this action was taken because the Bembergs snubbed the president's charismatic wife, Eva Duarte Peron, when she visited Paris and sought to stay at their mansion as a house guest. The breweries were turned over to a labor federation, with the Quilmes plant becoming Cervecería y Maltería Argentina E.N.

Peron was overthrown by a military junta in 1955, and the Bemberg properties were returned in 1959. Cervecería y Maltería Quilmes S.A. now became a unit of Enterprises Quilmes S.A., a Bemberg-controlled holding company founded in 1952 and registered in Luxembourg. In the next two decades, several Quilmes breweries were closed, including Palmero in 1977 and Schlau in 1978, as beer drinking in Argentina fell by almost two-thirds per capita. In 1980 Quilmes, which held almost 70 percent of the remaining national beer market, began a radio and television advertising campaign, heavy on music, aimed at persuading Argentinians—particularly youths—to drink the beverage all year round, instead of only during the

Key Dates:

1890: Peter Frederick Otto Bemberg and his son open a brewery in the city of Quilmes.
1948: The Bemberg breweries and other family properties are confiscated by the government.
1959: The breweries and other properties are returned to Bemberg family ownership.
1980: Cervecería y Maltería Quilmes S.A. holds about 70 percent of the national beer market.
1989: Incorporated in Luxembourg, the company becomes Quilmes Industrial (QUINSA) S.A.
1995: The company's production of beer has increased fourfold in a decade.
2000: Quinsa's net sales peak at $955.1 million.
2003: A Brazilian brewer, AmBev, purchases a potentially controlling share of Quinsa.

summer. This accented a trend that began as early as the 1930s, when Argentine beermakers first started featuring young people in their ads, generally engaged in sporting activities such as tennis and horseback riding.

In 1984 Quilmes sold a 15 percent interest in the enterprise to Heineken N.V. The cash helped the company finance a renovation of the Norte and Andes breweries and to build a new $36 million plant in Corrientes. The following year, the company chairman, a great-grandson of the founder, went outside the family for the first time in hiring a chief executive: Norberto Morita, the Argentine-born son of Japanese parents. In this period Cervecería y Maltería Quilmes and three other beverage units in Uruguay and Paraguay were subsidiaries of Quilmes International (Bermuda) Ltd., the industrial arm of Enterprises Quilmes. The Uruguay plant produced a beer named Pilsen; the two in Paraguay made Pilsen, Bremen, and Bavaria. Quilmes also was importing Heineken for distribution and sale. (It manufactured Heineken in Argentina from 1997 to 2003.)

Expansion in the 1990s

Quilmes Industrial (QUINSA) S.A. was established as a separate Luxembourg-incorporated company in 1989, when the brewing interests of Enterprises Quilmes were spun off from the rest of the latter's business interests, which were chiefly financial. All the operating subsidiaries of Quinsa continued to be held through Quilmes International (Bermuda), or QI(B). In 1991 a brewery was built and brought on line in Santiago, Chile, at a cost of $30 million. The following year a big brewery entered production in Zarate, Buenos Aires, at a cost of $71 million. This facility was expanded in 1994 to double its capacity, at a cost of $53.5 million. Also in 1994, a new malt factory and a new mineral water plant began production. A new, larger Paraguayan brewery opened in 1995. During 1995–96 Quinsa acquired two breweries in Bolivia, and the following year it purchased Cervecería Bieckert S.A., the oldest brewery in Argentina. The company introduced Liberty, Argentina's first alcohol-free beer, in 1993, and a light beer in 1997. It began exporting Quilmes to the European Union in 1998 and the United States in 1999.

By this time Quilmes held nearly 80 percent of a beer market that had more than quadrupled per capita since 1982. Production grew fourfold between 1985 and 1995, net sales soared from $271 million in 1990 to $754 million in 1994, and profit rose from $16.1 million to $86.7 million during the same period. The company invested $300 million in new plants between 1992 and 1995 without having to borrow money, and 60 percent of its productive capacity was now in facilities less than six years old.

Quinsa was soon to find itself in crisis, however. Brazil's Companhia Cervejaria Brahma began trucking bottles of its Brahma-label beer into Argentina in 1992, then, in 1994, built its own brewery in Argentina, mounted a strong marketing campaign, and offered big price discounts. Compania de Cervecerías Unidas S.A. (CCU), a Chilean company allied with a German brewery, acquired several local and regional Argentine beermakers and, in 1996, began producing and distributing Budweiser under license. Another challenger was Germany's Warsteiner Brauerei Hans Cramer GmbH, which entered the Argentine market with two premium beers, Isenbeck and Warsteiner. Quilmes's Chilean venture was continuing to lose money, and its label there, Becker, held only one-eighth of the market. Even worse, Argentine beer consumption peaked in 1997, after which the economy fell into recession. In 2000 the Brazilian challenge became even more serious, with the merger of Brahma and archrival Companhia Antarctica Paulista Industria Brasileira de Bebidas e Conexos to form Companhia de Bebidas das Americas (AmBev), the world's third largest brewer. Quinsa's net sales peaked at $955.1 million in 2000.

Quinsa, in 1999, brought in Perrier Vittel S.A. as partner in its mineral water venture, Eco de los Andes, and agreed to import and distribute its Perrier and Nestlé Pureza Vital brands. In the same year it purchased 51 percent of Buenos Aires Embotelladora S.A. (Baesa), the largest PepsiCo bottling and distributing franchise in Argentina, for $80.6 million. Aside from returning Quilmes to the carbonated soft-drink business, the Baesa acquisition brought with it distribution of Baesa's mineral water label, Glaciar. When Quinsa bought PepsiCo's second largest Argentine bottling franchise, Embotelladoras del Interior S.A. (Edisa), in 2000 for $36.5 million, it added another mineral water brand, Villa de los Arroyos. Quinsa also raised its share of Baesa to 98 percent in that year. Baesa and Edisa became the soft-drink division of Cervecería y Maltería Quilmes.

New Century, New Alliance

As Argentina's recession worsened, the government found itself unable to make payments on its sizable debt and defaulted, causing the national currency—the peso—to fall from parity with the dollar to a value of less than one-third of the dollar. Accordingly, private firms such as Quinsa saw their dollar-denominated debt more than triple while their sales faltered because of the recession and a 40 percent inflation rate resulting from peso devaluation. Quinsa's owners—still chiefly the Bemberg, Montalembert, and de Ganay heirs of the founder—turned to rival AmBev for support, selling it what appeared to be a future controlling share in the business.

In the first stage of the deal, agreed upon in 2002 and completed in January 2003, AmBev in effect turned over its businesses in Argentina, Bolivia, Paraguay, and Uruguay to Quinsa in exchange for new nonvoting class B shares in the company. It also bought existing Class A shares from Beverage Associates Corp. (BAC), a company based in the British Virgin Islands and organized by Bemberg descendants that held most of these voting shares, for $346.4 million. This transaction gave AmBev 38.6 percent of Quinsa's voting shares, with BAC continuing to hold 53.5 percent and holders of publicly traded shares the remainder. Counting Class B shares, AmBev now owned, at a price of about $700 million, 49 percent of Quinsa, while BAC owned 30 percent. AmBev executives received half the seats on the ten-member board of Quinsa directors but left its executives in charge of operations. In the second stage of the deal, BAC received a recurring put option to sell its remaining Quinsa shares to AmBev between 2003 and 2009, while AmBev won a call option enabling it to buy BAC's shares beginning in 2009, making payment in newly issued AmBev stock and essentially allowing it to take over Quinsa at a 15 percent discount.

Commenting on the deal, a banker who was involved told John Barham of *LatinFinance,* "The concept is that you want to do the exchange [of shares] at a value the companies are worth at that time, not now. Beer companies' values are related to how much cash they generate. This stresses that BAC feels there is a lot of upside left in the company. . . . This structure ensures that if things get better in Argentina, Quilmes will be sold for a lot of money. If things have not improved, AmBev will not have to pay a high price."

After losing $135.9 million in 2002, Quinsa rebounded in 2003 with an increase of about one-third in sales and net profit of $36.8 million. Of its net sales, 75 percent was attributable to sales of beer and 43 percent to beer sales in Argentina. Quilmes's five Argentine breweries held an 80 percent share of the domestic market, with its leading brand, Quilmes Cristal, holding a 46 percent national share. The Argentine subsidiary also had two malting plants. The Bolivian subsidiary had five breweries and an estimated 97 percent market share in the country. The Paraguayan subsidiary's brewery produced Pilsen and several other labels and held 94 percent of the national market. Prior to being spun off to a separate company also owned by QI(B), the Uruguayan brewery held 98.5 percent of the national market with Pilsen and several other beers. The Chilean brewery's beers, Becker and Báltica, held only 10 percent of the market there. Baesa controlled 88 percent of the production and sale of PepsiCo carbonated soft drinks in Ar-

gentina and was also the only PepsiCo bottler and distributor in Uruguay.

In September 2003 Quinsa completed the restructuring of company debt, which belonged in large part to Cervecería y Maltería Quilmes, by extending the maturities of $232.6 million in bank loans from 2004 to 2009. In all, the long-term debt was $329.2 million. In June 2004, Quinsa owned 87.6 percent of Quilmes International Bermuda, with AmBev and BAC owning the remainder. (BAC had bought Heineken's 15 percent share in January 2003 for $102.7 million.) QI(B) held virtually all of Cervecería y Maltería Quilmes and controlling interests in the other beer subsidiaries and 49 percent of Eco de los Andes.

Principal Subsidiaries

Cervecería Boliviana Nacional S.A. (Bolivia); Cervecería Chile S.A.; Cervecería Paraguay S.A. (Paraguay); Cervecería y Maltería Quilmes S.A.I.C.A. y G.; Quilmes International (Bermuda) Ltd. (Bermuda); Seven Up Consesiones S.A.I. y C.

Principal Competitors

Coca-Cola de Argentina S.A.; Compania de Cervecerías Unidas S.A.; Warsteiner Brauerei Hans Cramer GmbH.

Further Reading

"Argentine Beer Giant Buys Baesa," *Beverage World International,* September-October 1999, p. 14.

Barham, John, "A Battle of Beer Giants Brews in Argentina," *Financial Times,* December 18, 1992, p. 20.

——, "El destape de Pepsi," *América economia,* March 1994, p. 30.

——, "Selling Well When Things Are Low," *LatinFinance,* June 2002, p. 51.

"La casa Bemberg," *Apertura,* September 1989, pp. 46–50.

Millman, Joel, "The Revenge on Eva Peron," *Forbes,* May 9, 1994, pp. 94, 96.

Pilling, David, "Argentine Brewer Aims to Tap Latin American Neighbours," *Financial Times,* November 24, 1995, p. 31.

Quintana, Daniel Pedro, "200 Años de Cervezas Argentinas," *Todo es historia,* February 2001, pp. 60–62.

Sainz, Alfredo, "Como hacen para bajar a Quilmes," *Mercado,* May 2000, pp. 54–56, 58.

Vera, Hector, "Marca a marca," *América economia,* December 2, 1999, pp. 26, 28.

—Robert Halasz

Radio One, Inc.

5900 Princess Garden Parkway, 7th Floor
Lanham, Maryland 20706
U.S.A.
Telephone: (301) 306-1111
Fax: (301) 306-9426
Web site: http://www.radio-one.com

Public Company
Incorporated: 1980 as Almic Broadcasting
Employees: 1,740
Sales: $303.2 million (2003)
Stock Exchanges: NASDAQ
Ticker Symbol: ROIA
NAIC: 515111 Radio Networks

Radio One, Inc. is the largest broadcasting company targeting African American audiences in the United States. The publicly traded company, based in Lanham, Maryland, owns and operates 70 radio stations, making it the seventh largest radio broadcasting company in the country. Major markets served include Atlanta, Baltimore, Boston, Cincinnati, Cleveland, Columbus, Dallas, Detroit, Houston, Los Angeles, Miami, Minneapolis, Philadelphia, St. Louis, and Washington, D.C. In addition, Radio One programs ''XM 169 The Power'' for XM Satellite Radio, and partners with Comcast Corporation on a cable television channel targeting African Americans. Radio One is majority-owned by founder Catherine Hughes, the company's chairperson, and her son Alfred C. Liggins III, who serves as president and chief executive officer.

Founder's Radio Career Beginning in the 1970s

Hughes was born Catherine Elizabeth Woods in Omaha, Nebraska, in 1947, the child of academically oriented, African American parents. Her father was the first African American to earn an accounting degree from Creighton University, her mother earned a master's degree in social work, and her mother's father founded Piney Woods Country Life School, a Mississippi private boarding school for African Americans. Hughes herself became the first African American to attend Omaha's Duchesne Academy of the Sacred Heart. Although as a child she was known to carry a transistor radio everywhere she went, she was a good student. When she was 16, however, Hughes became pregnant, at a time when there was a greater stigma attached to teenage pregnancy. After her mother kicked her out of the house, Hughes married the father of her child, Alfred Liggins, Jr., but they were divorced after two years and she had to raise her son on her own while finishing high school. She went on to college, with stints at Creighton and the University of Nebraska, Omaha, but she dropped out before receiving a degree to pursue a radio career. While attending college she took a job in 1969 with a black radio station in Omaha, KOWH, where she performed well at a number of tasks and came to the attention of Tony Brown, the founder of Washington, D.C.'s Howard University's School of Communication. He first took her on as an administrative assistant in 1971 but soon made her a sales director at the school radio station, WHUR-FM. Within two years she was named general manager of the station.

During her time at WHUR, Hughes developed a highly popular format called the *Quiet Storm,* a late-night show that played urban contemporary love ballads. She was frustrated that university officials would not license the concept to other stations, not believing that Quiet Storm possessed staying power. The station was wrong, as Quiet Storm would become a mainstay around the country, the most listened to nighttime radio format. In the word of Hughes, ''They basically threw a million-dollar baby out the window.'' Moreover, the experience created a desire in her to find a way to gain total control of her ideas and career. In 1978 Hughes became president and general manager at a new Washington, D.C. gospel radio station, WYCB-AM. Her stay was short, just six months, but Hughes learned how to grow a station from scratch. She decided, along with her second husband, Dewey Hughes, to buy and operate her own radio station.

The couple cobbled together $100,000 from their savings and $450,000 from investors, including $300,000 from Syndicated Communications Inc. (Syncom), an African American-owned venture capital firm that invested in African American-owned media. Although an experienced broadcaster, Hughes was naive about many aspects of business. When Syncom principals Herb

Company Perspectives:

Our strategy is to expand within our existing markets and into new markets that have a significant African-American presence.

Wilkins and Terry Jones initially asked her about her business plan, Hughes replied, "My plan is to become successful in business." Although embarrassed, she succeeded in getting their support. But she still fell short of the money she needed and turned to the banks for a loan. She was rejected by more than 30 banks before a Puerto Rican female loan officer, during her first week at Chemical Bank Corp., agreed to lend her $600,000. In 1980 Hughes and her husband started Almic Broadcasting, which a decade later would become known as Radio One.

The new company paid $950,000 for a Washington, D.C. 1,000-watt AM station, WOL, which could be acquired cheaply because it had recently been involved in a payola scandal. Against the advice of her backers, Hughes converted WOL to a 24-hour talk and news format, the first of its kind aimed at an African American audience. Although in the long run, she would be proven correct that there was indeed a market for such a station, Hughes did not understand that the talk format was the most expensive to operate, and WOL struggled for years to turn a profit. Hughes and her husband soon had difficulty meeting the monthly debt payments. To keep the station afloat, the couple lost their house and car, and Hughes even sold a rare family heirloom, a white-gold pocket watch made by slaves, which fetched $50,000. Finally the station cost her her marriage. Hughes's husband insisted that she either move to California, where he hoped to break into the music business, or they get a divorce. She chose to file for divorce and bought out his share of the business.

Struggles in the 1980s

Hughes endured considerable hardship as she nurtured Radio One to profitability, though she also found the challenge exhilarating. She drummed up advertising by going door to door to area merchants, and kept creditors at bay by making sure to at least send in a token amount of money along with a note explaining her situation. She filled in at the station as much as possible, running the switchboard, and picking up talk show guests in an old Chevy Nova. She and her son began to live out of the office, cooking on a hot plate and showering at the homes of friends. In 1982, after she had run the station for 14 months, the bank insisted that she would have to begin playing music or face foreclosure. They eventually reached a compromise that allowed WOL to keep the morning drive as a news, talk, and information show, but the bank refused to pay a salary for the slot. To get around the stricture, Hughes became the unpaid host of the show. According to *Broadcasting Cable,* "In her days as a talk-show host, Hughes was a firebrand in Washington's black community. Politicians picked her show to make major pronouncements. She led the criticism against then mayor Marion Barry's imprisonment on drug charges and organized a much publicized protest against the *Washington Post* for featuring a black rapper accused of murder on its first cover. She refused a

grant—Maryland's first to a minority owned company—to protest the General Assembly's plans to expel a black state senator accused of ethics violations. And she faced charges of anti-Semitism and prejudice against whites and Hispanics.''

In 1986 WOL finally turned the corner and became a profitable station. In that same year, Hughes attempted to buy a second radio station, WKYS, by forming a "community corporation," which managed to raise only $500,000, an effort that fell short. In 1987 Hughes succeeded in adding another property, buying WMMJ for $7.5 million. It became Radio One's first FM station, and was also the first FM station on the East Coast to adopt an urban adult contemporary format. Once again Hughes had to contend with input from the banks that financed the deal. At their insistence, in an effort to attract a white audience, the station installed the Evergreen computer system that programmed the station with music from mainstream white artists such as Barbra Streisand, Barry Manilow, and Neil Diamond. After watching the ratings decline for some 18 months, Hughes pulled the plug on Evergreen and began to rebuild the station's audience.

By now Hughes was being assisted by her son, Alfred C. Liggins III, whom she had been grooming to become a hardworking entrepreneur since childhood. When he was just 12 years old she made him take a job cleaning rabbit cages at a pet store. After he graduated from high school, he wanted to get involved in the record business, but she convinced him it was a better idea to work for the family business that he could one day take over. Therefore, in 1985 he became a salesman for WOL, but he was paid no salary, forced to survive on commissions alone. As a result, he learned how to work with advertisers and found ways to drive their businesses while growing his own. In 1993 he succeeded his mother as chief executive, although she remained heavily involved as the company's chairperson. During the early 1990s she also retired from her daily talk show, which she had only taken on as a necessity.

Radio One benefited from legislation in 1992 that loosened ownership restrictions in radio. Under the so-called duopoly rule, you could now own two AM and two FM stations in the same market. At the cost of $4.7 million Radio One acquired Baltimore's WWIN-AM and sister station WWIN-FM from respected African American broadcaster Ragan Henry. A year later Radio One added two more Baltimore stations, WERQ-FM and WOLB-AM, for approximately $9 million. The company's acquisition strategy was simple yet effective: Buy underperforming stations on the cheap in the top 30 markets for African American listeners, then turn them around. By 1994 Radio One generated $17.6 million in revenues.

Radio One added to its portfolio of radio stations in 1995 with two purchases. It paid some $34 million for WKYS-FM, a Washington, D.C. station that the company had failed to buy in a 1990 attempt and resulted in the loss of a $200,000 deposit. Radio One also entered the Atlanta market with the $4.5 million acquisition of WHTA-FM. Revenues reached $23.7 million in 1996 and improved to $32.4 million a year later, and $46.1 million in 1998. Although the company posted net losses in two of those years, broadcast cash flow, an important measure in the industry, showed strong growth, improving from $9.8 million in 1996 to $13.5 million in 1997, and $21.6 million in 1998.

```
┌─────────────────────────────────────────────────────────┐
│                  Key Dates:                             │
│                                                         │
│  1980:  The first radio station is acquired.            │
│  1987:  The second station is acquired.                 │
│  1993:  The founder's son succeeds her as chief executive.│
│  1999:  The company is taken public.                    │
│  2000:  A dozen Clear Channel stations are acquired.    │
│  2004:  A joint venture is formed with Comcast to launch a│
│         cable TV network.                               │
└─────────────────────────────────────────────────────────┘
```

Ownership rules were loosened even further with the passage of the Telecommunications Act of 1996, which allowed ownership of more local stations and eliminated the cap on the number of stations a company could own nationally. Although Hughes expressed concerns that deregulation would lead to just a handful of companies controlling hundreds of radio stations, making it even more difficult for minorities and women to become owners, she also knew that if Radio One was to survive it had to continue to grow. During the second half of the 1990s the company went on an acquisition binge, adding stations and entering new markets. The company, in 1996, also moved its corporate offices from Washington, D.C., to the Maryland suburb of Lanham. In 1997 Radio One paid $20 million to buy WPHI-FM to enter the Philadelphia, Pennsylvania market. A year later the company completed several acquisitions, including the $3.8 million purchase of WYCB-AM, a Washington, D.C. station; two San Francisco stations at the cost of $22 million; the $26.5 million purchase of Detroit's WWBR-FM; and the $34.2 million acquisition of Bell Broadcasting Company, which brought with it three more Detroit radio stations. Furthermore, during 1998 the company began taking steps to go public, an idea that had been taking shape for several years.

Rapid Growth in the Late 1990s

It was a watershed year for Radio One in 1999. The company added a bevy of stations to its portfolio, including single operations in Atlanta, WAMJ-FM; St. Louis, WFUN-FM; and Boston, WBOT-FM. The company also bought a pair of Cleveland stations, WENZ-AM and WERE-AM, and three Richmond stations, WKJS-FM, WARV-FM, and WDYL-FM. To help finance these deals Radio One completed an initial public offering of stock in May 1999, underwritten by Credit Suisse First Boston, Bear, Stearns & Co. Inc., BT Alex. Brown, Banc of America Securities, and Prudential Securities. The company netted $172 million, the most ever by an African American company. Hughes also held the distinction of becoming the first African American woman to serve as chairman of a publicly traded company. Not only was the company able to pay down a considerable portion of its debt, it was now in a better position to borrow money under better conditions, and to use stock to make acquisitions and reward employees. Radio One soon returned to the markets for a secondary offering, grossing another $77 million.

The buying binge continued for Radio One in 2000. It paid $1.3 billion to Clear Channel Communications, the broadcast giant that needed to divest some stations because of antitrust concerns, to acquire 12 stations in six markets: Cleveland, Los Angeles, Houston, Dallas, Miami, and Greenville, South Carolina. Also in 2000 Radio One paid $40 million to acquire three Indianapolis radio stations and a low-powered TV station from Shirk Inc., as well as six radio stations in Charlotte, North Carolina, and Augusta, Georgia, from Davis Broadcasting for $24 million in cash and stock. Because of its broader footprint, Radio One was now able to offer package deals to advertisers looking to reach the urban market on a national basis. To handle this business, the company formed a small national sales staff operating out of Washington and Detroit. Because it was now emerging as a major player in the radio industry, Radio One also attracted the attention of ABC Radio Networks, which in 2001 established an alliance with the company and ABC's Urban Advantage Network (UAB), geared toward the African American market. By devoting some of its commercial time to UAN, Radio One increased its national penetration, and UAN was now able to reach 93 percent of the African American market.

The impact of adding 21 radio stations in 2000 was evident on Radio One's balance sheet. Revenues grew to $155.7 million in 2000, almost double the $81.7 million generated a year before. In 2001, with a full year of contribution from the new stations, that total grew to $243.8 million. Also during the year, Radio One bought 15 stations from Blue Chip Broadcasting Inc. for $135 million in cash and stock. New stations included one in Minneapolis, a pair in Cincinnati, three in Columbus, four in Dayton, and six in Louisville. In addition, Radio One adjusted the mix of its portfolio in 2001 by selling a few stations, including WDLY-FM in Richmond, WJMZ-FM and WPEK-FM in South Carolina, and WARV-FM in Virginia.

Not content to merely own and operate a string of radio stations, Liggins harbored a goal of building a media company with wider scope. Acquiring a low-powered television station with cable penetration was in keeping with this goal, as was striking a deal in 2002 with XM Satellite Radio Holdings Inc. to provide a channel on the nationwide subscription-based radio service. But Liggins's dream was to launch an African American targeted cable television station to rival Black Entertainment Network. In 1999 he had realized that while Hispanics had several channels, African Americans had just one station, BET, aimed at them. He began seeking partners and finally found one in Comcast Corporation. The two companies agreed to establish TV One L.L.C., a cable TV network, 40 percent owned by Radio One, that would target an older and more affluent age group than BET, 25-to-54. Whether TV One would begin a new chapter for Radio One, marking a seminal point in its growth as an African American media empire, remained to be seen, however.

Principal Subsidiaries

Bell Broadcasting Company; Radio One Licenses, L.L.C.; Satellite One, L.L.C.

Principal Competitors

Clear Channel Communications, Inc.; Cumulus Media Inc.; Infinity Broadcasting Corporation.

Further Reading

Alexander, Keith L., "Quiet Storm," *Emerge,* September 1999, p. 44.

Bachman, Katy, "We Are Family," *Mediaweek,* August 23, 1999, p. 16.

Boorstin, Julia, "Catherine Hughes: Radio One," *Forbes Small Business,* September 2004, pp. 100 + .

Clarke, Robyn D., "High-Frequency Profits," *Black Enterprise,* June 2000, p. 130.

Clarke, Robyn D., and Derek T. Dingle, "The New Blood," *Black Enterprise,* June 1999, p. 161.

Ghosh, Chandrani, "The Comeback Queen," *Forbes,* September 20, 1999, p. 86.

"Mother/Son Makes Radio One," *Broadcasting Cable,* August 30, 1999, p. 14.

Stark, Phyllis, "Radio One Owner CEO Building an Empire," *Billboard,* January 14, 1995, p. 61.

Yang, Catherine, "BET Say Hello to the Competition," *Business Week,* January 26, 2004, p. 86.

—Ed Dinger

Reed & Barton Corporation

144 W. Britannia Street
Taunton, Massachusetts 02780
U.S.A
Telephone: (508) 824-6611
Fax: (508) 822-7269
Web site: http://www.reedandbarton.com

Private Company
Founded: 1824 as Babbitt & Crossman
NAIC: 339912 Silver and Plated Ware Manufacturing

Family owned, Reed & Barton Corporation is one of the oldest silversmiths in the United States, its roots dating back to 1824. Over the years, Reed & Barton has evolved into a diversified tabletop company composed of several divisions. The Reed & Barton Silversmiths division continues to produce a wide range of fine sterling silver, silverplated, and stainless steel tableware and gifts, including flatware, serveware, and holloware, as well as picture frames, Christmas ornaments, baby gifts, and musicals. The Reed & Barton Handcrafted Chests division is the world's largest maker of wooden jewelry boxes and flatware chests. In addition, it offers protective rolls and storage bags for flatware and holloware, cigar humidors, and pen chests. The result of a 1990s acquisition, Miller Rogaska Crystal by Reed & Barton produces handcrafted crystal, including stemware, barware, and giftware. Another acquisition, the Sheffield Silver Company, forms the basis of Reed & Barton: The Sheffield Collection. This division concentrates on holloware and silverplated tableware, offering products such as serving trays, wine coolers, candleware, and napkin rings. The R&B EveryDay division produces high-quality stainless steel flatware intended for everyday use. Reed & Barton also acts as the exclusive U.S. distributor for Belleek Fine Parian China, Ireland's oldest pottery, and Aynsley Fine English Bone China, a renowned, 200-year-old company that has supplied tableware to England's royalty. Reed & Barton maintains its headquarters in Taunton, Massachusetts, once known as ''Silver City'' because of the number of silver companies operating there. Reed & Barton products are sold in department stores and specialty shops, and the company also operates several retail stores.

Founding the Company in the Early 1800s

The man responsible for the founding of Reed & Barton, Isaac Babbitt, never worked with silver. He first employed pewter—an alloy composed of lead and tin and used to make everyday items such as tankards and dishes. Babbitt, who ran a pewter shop in Taunton, Massachusetts, then found a way to emulate a white metal alloy made from tin, antimony, and copper called Britannia metal, used by the British in the making of flatware and holloware sold in the United States. In 1824 he joined forces with Taunton jeweler William Crossman, forming a company named Babbitt & Crossman to produce their own Britannia tableware. Over the next two decades the company added associates and periodically amended its name, becoming Babbitt, Crossman & Company in 1827, Crossman West & Leonard two years later, and the Taunton Britannia Manufacturing company in 1830. Along the way, Henry G. Reed and Charles E. Barton, friends and fellow craftsmen, came to work at the firm. When the business failed in 1834, following years of steady growth, Reed and Barton, just in their 20s, stepped in to buy it. In 1837 the company was renamed Leonard, Reed & Barton, then in 1840 it assumed its modern name, Reed & Barton. The two men would run the business together for three decades. After Barton died of a heart attack in 1867, Reed carried on, but as a tribute to his longtime friend he decided to retain Barton in the company's name. Ownership of the firm would be passed down through the Reed family.

By the mid-1800s Britannia fell out of favor as a tableware material, supplanted by a new substitute for the prohibitively expensive silver. Sheffield Plate, developed in the 1740s, fused sterling silver to a plate of copper, but in 1840 this technology was superseded by electroplating, which deposited a thin layer of silver on a base metal, copper and later nickel, to produce items with a pure silver appearance. Electroplated silver gave consumers the look they wanted at a reasonable price, and as a result, by the early 1850s the new metal replaced both Sheffield Plate and Britannia metal as the flatware material of choice. Reed & Barton followed the market, and thus became involved in silver for the first time and a pioneer in the practice of silverplating. But silverplate would soon find competition from an unsuspected corner: sterling silver itself. In 1859 the legendary Comstock Lode of silver was discovered and once mining operations in the area were up to speed, silver flooded the market, bringing down prices to the point at which there was little difference between the price of items made from silverplate and actual sterling, which now became the material preferred in wedding gifts. Reed & Barton turned to sterling manufacturing in 1889 and by the end of the century committed an entire factory building to its production.

Maintaining Reputation for Quality: Early 20th Century Through Post-World War II Era

With the start of the 20th century, Reed & Barton underwent a change in leadership, following the 1901 death of Henry Reed at the age of 91. He was replaced by his son-in-law, William B.H. Dowse. By now, after decades of strong marketing efforts, Reed & Barton had developed a reputation for quality craftsmanship and fine design work, especially in sterling. The company's first patented flatware pattern, "Roman Medallion," was introduced in 1868. The firm's work was recognized in 1876 at the Philadelphia Centennial Exhibition, which awarded it a medal of excellence for its entry, an exquisite vase called "The Progress Vase." Later, the U.S. Navy would commission Reed & Barton to fashion ceremonial sterling services for several battleships, including the *Arizona, California, Minnesota, Montana, South Dakota,* and *Utah.* Several years after Dowse took over, in 1908, Reed & Barton introduced what would become its signature flatware pattern, "Francis I," which remains the company's most enduring design. It was so well regarded, in fact, that in 1924 a Francis I sterling silver dinner service won a million-dollar award from India's Maharajah of Barwani.

In 1923 Dowse was succeeded as Reed & Barton's president by his son-in-law, Sinclair Weeks, Sr. He would run the company for nearly half a century. During his tenure the company became involved in producing stainless steel flatware, a move born out of duty rather than design. During the first half of the 1940s, to fulfill its part in World War II, Reed & Barton switched from making silver tableware for civilians to producing flatware and holloware for the armed forces made out of stainless steel. A shiny, rust-resistant alloy invented in the early years of the century, stainless steel was originally used in such applications as cannon barrels and airplane engines before finding more mundane uses. In addition to tableware, Reed & Barton relied on stainless steel to produce surgical instruments for the Army Medical Corps. Following the war, the company continued to produce stainless steel tableware, which over the next half century would contribute increasingly to the balance sheet. But during the postwar years after servicemen returned home, married, and produced the Baby Boom generation, Reed & Barton's business remained very much devoted to the production of sterling silver items, the sales of which were spurred by a strong economy and the large number of weddings and christenings that took place during this period.

Battling the Practice of Deep Discounting in the 1970s–80s

In 1971 Sinclair Weeks, Sr., was succeeded as president by his son, Sinclair Weeks, Jr., who five years later would also take on the title of chief executive officer. During his tenure, Reed & Barton acquired the Sheffield Silver Company, founded in 1908 and well respected as a maker of fine silverplated holloware, especially its casseroles and bakers. The younger Weeks also took over during a period of unpredictable silver prices, due to rampant speculation. The result was that the public was uncertain about the true value of silver and there was confusion in the marketplace. The situation was complicated by the practice of deep discounting in the U.S. silver flatware industry. Manufacturers maintained high suggested prices but sold their wares to retailers at realistic levels. The retailers would then advertise a deep discount on the products, based on the inflated manufacturer's suggested retail price, in an effort to lure customers. It was a successful practice, but it soon got out of hand. Late in 1979 silver bullion prices jumped from $5 an ounce to more than $48 an ounce in early 1980. Retailers took advantage of their inventories, purchased before the escalation in silver prices, to offer 50 percent discounts. Then the silver market crashed, as did consumer demand for flatware, and the dependence on deep discounting became even more extreme. Reed & Barton's manufacturing rivals opted to name their suggested retail prices in order to allow retailers to advertise discounts as high as 85 percent. To Reed & Barton the practice amounted to false advertising intended to mislead consumers into making uninformed decisions. To bring sanity to the situation, Reed & Barton decided to stop issuing a suggested retail price list, but retailers refused to comply and insisted the company reinstate a price list. Reed & Barton finally agreed, issuing a list that would allow retailers to mark down its merchandise by some 25 percent. Some in the industry soon followed Reed & Barton's lead, but others continued to abuse the discounting practice. In March 1982 Reed & Barton sued five competitors in federal court, charging "false advertising concerning the price of their products." The resulting publicity helped to at least convince retailers to pull back on the use of deep discounting.

Aside from the deep discounting flap, the 1980s represented a period of significant change for Reed & Barton. The decade began strongly, with the company making the single largest order in its history: the 3,318 piece sterling service purchased by the Saudi Arabian government. The set included 50 custom sterling items, and ten four-foot and five-foot sterling platters for carrying roasted lambs. But silver was falling in popularity with the general public, forcing Reed & Barton to diversify. A housewares division was formed to broaden the product line. The company also began focusing more attention on stainless steel, which was increasing in popularity with consumers. As a result, Reed & Barton added breadth to the range of its price points, straying from its traditional perch at the high end of the market to the moderate range. The company also took steps to beef up its marketing efforts, especially in the bridal registry area.

By the mid-1980s, Reed & Barton had isolated a number of areas that offered strong potential: silverplated holloware, flat-

Key Dates:

1824: The company is founded as Babbitt & Crossman to produce Britannia metal items.
1834: Henry Reed and Charles Barton acquire the firm.
1867: Barton dies but the company retains his name.
1889: The firm begins sterling silver manufacturing.
1901: Reed dies.
1908: The company's signature Francis I pattern is introduced.
1941: The United States enters World War II; Reed & Barton turns to stainless steel flatware production.
1980: The Saudi Arabian government places the largest order in company history.
1996: Reed & Barton produces Olympic medals.
1998: Reed & Barton redesigns the Davis Cup.
1999: Reed & Barton marks its 175th anniversary.

ware, sterling flatware, stainless flatware, and giftware. Reed & Barton also was beginning to become less of a manufacturer and more of a product developer, distributor, and marketer. To remain competitive in the stainless steel arena, by the 1990s it ceased manufacturing these products in Taunton and began outsourcing to Asia, resulting in a steady drop in the number of people employed in Massachusetts. But at the same time it added products such as Christmas ornaments, jewelry, porcelain statues, and engravables. In the late 1980s Reed & Barton also took a stab at the mass-market flatware business, introducing a line of stainless and plastic-handled flatware. To protect the value of the Reed & Barton brand name, however, the products would assume the Savvy label. Manufacturing would be handled by a Connecticut company, with Reed & Barton providing the marketing and distribution.

The 1980s also saw changes in the top ranks of management. In September 1987 Albert D. Krebel, the president and CEO of Farberware Corp., replaced Weeks as president and CEO at Reed & Barton. Weeks stayed on as chairman, however. For Krebel it was a return to the silver industry, where he had more than 20 years of experience, working in sales and marketing and holding management positions at Gorham Silver Co., International Silver Co., and Wallace Silversmiths.

Product Diversification Along with Commitment to Tradition in the 1990s and Beyond

Under Krebel, Reed & Barton continued its efforts at diversification in the 1990s. Early in the decade, the company entered into a new product development joint venture with Swid Powell, a tabletop specialist. As a result of the collaboration, Reed & Barton began manufacturing and distributing architecturally designed serveware products. Next, Reed & Barton came to an agreement with the Ralph Lauren Home Collections to act as a licensee to produce sterling silver, silverplate, and stainless steel flatware, which would be sold in the same retail outlets as Ralph Lauren's china and crystal tabletop products. In

the 1990s other licensing deals would follow, including agreements with Waterford and Royal Doulton. The company also became involved in crystal. In 1993 it became the exclusive distributor of Val Saint Lambert Crystal's high-end tabletop lines in the United States, Canada, and Mexico. Reed & Barton also added the North American distribution rights for Aynsley china, Belleek china, and Galway crystal. Moreover, the company became involved in crystal manufacturing with the 1996 purchase of Miller Rogaska Crystal Co., maker of mid-range to upper-priced crystal stemware, barware, and giftware.

Reed & Barton reached a watershed moment in 1996 when sales of its stainless steel flatware outpaced sterling silver flatware for the first time. Nevertheless, the company continued to offer its time-tested sterling silver designs and continued to maintain a reputation for contemporary craftsmanship. Reed & Barton was selected by The Atlanta Committee for the Olympic Games to manufacture the gold, silver, and bronze medals for the 1996 Olympic Games. This contract was prestigious and highly coveted, and was the culmination of an established relationship between Reed & Barton and the committee. Already the company had been named a licensee of Olympic Games merchandise, granted the exclusive rights to market sterling silver, silverplate, goldplate, and wood giftware. In addition to producing 2,600 competition medals, Reed & Barton would make the wooden cases for them and also produce 30,000 commemorative medals to be given to dignitaries and others associated with the games. Reed & Barton's reputation also would be recognized, and enhanced, in 1998 when the company was chosen to redesign the Davis Cup, awarded annually in an international team tennis tournament.

Reed & Barton marked its 175th anniversary in 1999 by launching its first web site, but the company entered the new century committed to maintaining its tradition and the value of its brand by not venturing too far afield from the position in the high end of the market it had carved out over the years.

Principal Divisions

Reed & Barton Silversmiths; Reed & Barton Handcrafted Chests; Miller Rogaska Crystal; Sheffield Silver Company; R&B EveryDay.

Principal Competitors

Oneida Ltd.; Mikasa, Inc.; Syratech Corporation; Lunt Silversmith, Inc.

Further Reading

Schorow, Stephanie, "Tannon's 175-Year-Old Reed & Barton Still Brings Elegance to the Table," *Boston Herald,* June 2, 1999, p. 56.

Schwartz, Meredith, "Reed & Barton Turns 175," *Gifts & Decorative Accessories,* October 1999, p. 170.

Silk, Alvin, J., *Sterling Seasons—The Reed & Barton Story,* Taunton, Mass.: Reed & Barton Corporation, 1999.

"The Silverware Price Wars," *Business Week,* March 29, 1982, p. 160.

—Ed Dinger

Renault Argentina S.A.

Fray Justo Santa Maria de Oro 17
Buenos Aires, C.F. C1414CWT
Argentina
Telephone: (54) (11) 4778-2000
Toll Free: 0-810-666-7362
Fax: (54) (11) 4778-2023; (54) (11) 4778-2158
Web site: http://www.renault.com.ar

Public Company
Incorporated: 1955 as Industrias Kaiser Argentina
    S.A.I.C.P.
Employees: 1,329
Sales: ARS 856.77 million ($290.43 million) (2003)
Stock Exchanges: Bolsa de Comercio de Buenos Aires
Ticker Symbol: RENO
NAIC: 336111 Automobile Manufacturing; Light Truck
    and Utility Vehicle Manufacturing; 522220 Sales
    Financing; 524126 Direct Property and Casualty
    Insurance Carriers

Of Argentina's ten automakers, almost all are closely held subsidiaries or affiliates of their American, European, or Japanese parent organizations. The exception is Renault Argentina S.A., which is traded on the Buenos Aires stock exchange. Once the nation's largest automobile manufacturer, this company now ranks in the middle of the pack, struggling to sell new Renaults and Nissans in a nation badly mauled by economic crisis. Through subsidiaries, Renault Argentina also is engaged in vehicle financing and insurance.

Kaiser-Frazers, Nash Ramblers, and Renaults: 1955–79

Renault Argentina had its start as Industrias Kaiser Argentina S.A.I.C.P. (IKA), a joint venture of the Kaiser-Frazer Automobile Co. and an Argentine government ministry. Like other U.S.-based independent car companies competing with the Big Three in the wake of World War II, Kaiser-Frazer led a precarious existence. In 1955, shortly before halting all passenger car production in the United States, Kaiser-Frazer invested funds and idle equipment in an Argentine motor assembly plant built in Santa Isabel, on the outskirts of Córdoba. Thousands of Argentines participated in a public offering of shares of stock, which was oversubscribed.

Production began in 1956 and peaked in 1965, when 55,269 vehicles were assembled there, or 28 percent of Argentina's total production. About a third were Kaiser-Frazer automobiles and jeeps; the other two-thirds were Nash Ramblers and (from 1960) Renaults produced under license. With 8,500 employees, IKA was the nation's largest single automobile manufacturer. In early 1967 the company rolled out a new model, the Torino, on the base of the Rambler American 440. Furnished with the first industrial-scale engine designed totally in Argentina, the Torino became a classic.

Later in 1967, French-based Regie Nationale des Usines Renault assumed control of the company by purchasing a large percentage of the shares of stock and changed its name to IKA Renault S.A.I.C.F., which was changed to Renault Argentina S.A. in 1975. IKA Renault held 19 percent of the domestic auto market in fiscal 1971–72 but was struggling to make a profit. It had to refinance its debts to European creditors in 1972, receiving a $64 million infusion. The Renault 12, launched in 1971, became the best-selling model in Argentina during the early 1970s and remained so throughout the decade. Others were the R4 (dating from 1963), and R6 (1970), the Torino, and commercial vehicles. Political instability made the 1970s a difficult decade in Argentina, but the 32,861 vehicles that the company sold in 1978 represented 22 percent of the national total. Under the Renault Argentina banner was also Filiales Industriales, a group of seven companies annually producing the equivalent of $100 million a year worth of cables, forged parts, foundry steel and aluminum, dies, and polyurethane seats.

Renault Argentina in the 1980s

Renault Argentina began the new decade doing even better. In 1980, a boom year in which the auto industry sold 250,000 cars, the company raised its share to almost 24 percent. The Renault 12 still topped all models, and the following year the company presented a new, larger version with a two-liter en-

Key Dates:

1955: U.S. industrialist Henry J. Kaiser establishes an auto assembly plant in Argentina.
1960: Industias Kaiser Argentina (IKA) begins assembling Renault autos under license.
1965: IKA is Argentina's leading automobile producer.
1967: IKA rolls out the Torino—built with an Argentine-designed engine, it becomes a classic; Renault purchases a controlling interest in IKA, which becomes IKA Renault.
1971: The Renault 12, Argentina's best-selling car in this decade, is introduced.
1975: IKA Renault is renamed Renault Argentina S.A.
1984: Renault Argentina holds one-third of the Argentine automobile market.
1991: Buffeted by a sour national economy, the company has lost $300 million in three years.
1992: Manuel Fernando Antelo assumes control of the company, which is renamed Ciadea.
1994: Ciadea has enjoyed three consecutive years of healthy profits.
1997: Antelo sells most of his shares in Ciadea, which is renamed Renault Argentina.
2001: The company drops from second to fourth place among Argentine automakers.

gine, the Renault 18. Renault Argentina was enjoying what economists call a "virtuous circle": Gains in production efficiency had lowered its costs, allowing it to lower its prices, which raised demand and thus production, yielding still lower costs per unit. Competing against models such as the Ford Taurus 81 and the Peugeot 504, the Renault 18 filled a gap—medium-large autos—in the Renault line and helped the company leap into first place in the first half of 1984, with a third of the domestic market. Other new models were the Coupe Fuego (1982) and the 1.4-liter-engine Renault 11 (1984).

Renault Argentina reached its maximum size in this period. The Santa Isabel plant consisted of five principal areas—mechanics, pressing, assembly, painting, and mounting—occupying 300,000 square meters (about three million square feet) on 237 hectares (585 acres) of land. Three nearby affiliates provided a variety of components, some of them exported abroad. Three others did the same from the city of Buenos Aires, Tandil; Buenos Aires; and Villa Mercedes, San Luis. The seventh produced gearboxes in Los Andes, Chile, a few miles from the Argentine frontier. Some 13 affiliated auto dealers were selling Renault Argentina cars in five provinces. Four insurance companies were associates, as was Asorte, a service company.

Renault Argentina remained the leading automaker in 1985, when it ranked 13th highest in the nation in sales, but it lost money that year. The later part of the decade was even worse. Its finances mismanaged, Argentina was stricken by hyperinflation, and Renault Argentina had difficulty converting the increasingly worthless austral notes of its customers into hard currency. The company lost some $300 million between 1988 and 1991, resulting in a shakeup at the top.

Mixed Results in the 1990s

A new era for Argentine automaking began after Carlos Menem assumed the presidency in 1989. The network of government measures intended to protect the domestic industry came to an end, including a law that required 90 percent of all components to be manufactured within the country. As a result Renault Argentina reduced its high level of vertical integration, selling off most of its subsidiaries, although it retained and even expanded its profitable forging and die-making facilities. Employment fell from 10,000 to 6,000, and the number of models was cut from eight to three.

These cost-cutting measures enabled Renault Argentina to make a healthy profit in 1992, but, since the company had lost nearly $200 million the previous year, the parent firm in Paris had already decided to cut itself loose from Argentina. The beneficiary was an obscure auto parts manufacturer named Manuel Fernando Antelo, who purchased two-thirds of Renault Argentina on remarkably generous terms. According to journalist Luis Majul, Antelo was required to pay parent Renault only if there were profits, and he secured a bank loan for this purpose that accepted the shares he was buying as collateral. Moreover, Paris-based Renault contributed $100 million and took out $75 million in bonds to help the enterprise. Renault Argentina took a new name, that of Compania Interamericana de Automoviles S.A. (Ciadea). According to the terms of the agreement, Antelo was actually buying two-thirds of a new holding company, Compagnie Financiere pour l'Amerique Latine (COFAL), with parent Renault retaining the other third. COFAL held 72.3 percent of Ciadea, with the remainder publicly traded in Buenos Aires.

Antelo cut costs further by reducing the number of managers from 85 to 40 and the number of levels between the top and bottom positions from nine to five. He closed the plant during a dispute with suppliers and also when demand was low. In 1993 and 1994 Ciadea was the most profitable of all Argentine automakers, earning more than $100 million each year. It produced 106,000 units, or 26 percent of the domestic market, in 1994, ranking second to Sevel Argentina S.A., which was assembling Fiat and Peugeot cars. Ciadea was introducing a new model every 18 months, with the most popular ones being the Renault 9, which was the best-selling car in Argentina in 1994. The Renault 12 and 18 were retired that year, with the Renault 19 replacing the latter. Another success was the Trafic, a light truck that became the leader in its category. Also in 1994, Ciadea took a 10 percent interest in GMAC de Argentina S.A., which was engaged in the financing of car loans. A well-tailored man-about-town with a penchant for non-automotive models half his age, Antelo relished his success, was constantly trailed by paparazzi, and opened a pub, Museo Renault, in a mansion located in one of the most elegant neighborhoods of Buenos Aires.

The following year was one of recession. It saw a drop of 35 percent in Argentine autos sold, and Ciadea's production fell by even more, to 64,520, or 25 percent of the total. The company responded by cutting employment by 1,500, to 5,800, reducing its prices by an average of 20 percent, and introducing new models, including the mid-sized Mégane and the subcompact Clio. Ciadea even arranged to pay the interest on auto loans for the first year and a half. These measures kept the company from losing much market share, but its profit fell to only $6 million in 1997. At this point Antelo sold most of his shares back to the parent firm, which restored the Renault Argentina name for its affiliate. Although no longer in charge, he retained the title of chairman of the board.

Downsizing in the New Millennium

Renault Argentina ranked fourth in revenue among automakers in 1997, rose to second in 1998 (with record sales of $1.39 billion), and retained that ranking in 1999 and 2000. But in 2001 it fell to fourth place, and in 2002, to fifth place. The company chose to give priority to its finances and to cut production and staff as the economic downturn in Argentina turned into a crisis culminating in the devaluation of the peso at the end of 2001. That year the parent firm contributed $300 million to assure the survival of its affiliate. Like other companies, Renault Argentina was swamped in red ink, but it received an additional $160 million from parent Renault in January 2003 to allow it to pacify its bank creditors. The company lost another ARS 209.31 million (about $71 million) in 2003 and ended the year with debt of ARS 815.64 million (about $276 million). During the first half of 2004, however, the company made a small profit. Renault Argentina's principal shareholders were COFAL, 61 percent, and Renault Holding AG, 17 percent.

In late 2003 Renault Argentina was operating at only 15 percent of plant capacity—the average for the entire industry—and was turning out only about 100 cars a day. The company had stopped making the Trafic in 2002, was operating just three days a week, and was employing only 950 people. Production came to 15,540 vehicles. Domestic retail sales of Renaults totaled 14,718, or 11 percent of the total. Another 5,435 units were exported. The compact Clio, in a new version, represented about 60 percent of Renault Argentina's sales. The company also introduced new versions of the light truck Master and presented a special edition of the medium-sized Scenic. The rest of the line consisted of the medium-sized Mégane and Laguna and the Kangoo, which appeared as a compact model in 1998, the Express pickup, and a limited-edition Dynamique for young drivers. Renault also became the exclusive distributor of Nissan cars in Argentina after the parent organization bought 37 percent of the Japanese automaker in 2001. A $20 million investment was made for advertising and the development of a network of 26 concessionaires with 43 points of sale. In 2003 Renault sold 1,656 Nissans. The Nissan line in Argentina consisted of the sports utility Pathfinder, X-Terra, and X-Trail, and the pickups PU Frontier 4x2 and 4x4.

By this time Renault Argentina's Santa Isabel plant had grown to about 400,000 square meters. It was divided into several areas, such as stamping and welding, painting, and assembling for manufacturing, industrial logistics, engineering, and quality control for service, and human resources, sales, finance, and commercial for administration. Some 30 industrial robots were in operation. The plant was capable of turning out 640 vehicles per day. More than two million vehicles had been produced since 1956.

Principal Subsidiaries

Centro S.A. (60%); Centro Automotores S.A.; Centro del Norte S.A.C.I. y F. (51%); Centro Posadas S.A.; Cormasa S.A.; Industria de Conjuntos Mecanicos Aconcagua S.A. (Chile; 97%); Metalurgica Tandil S.A. (98%); Plan Rumbo S.A. de Ahorro para Fines Determinados.

Principal Competitors

Ford Argentina S.A.; General Motors de Argentina S.A.; Peugeot Citroen Argentina S.A.; Volkswagen Argentina S.A.

Further Reading

"Autos: La ofensiva de Renault," *Mercado,* December 9, 1984, pp. 40–43.

"Las buenas nuevas de IKA-Renault," *Mercado,* October 26, 1972, pp. 49, 51, 54.

Burt, Tim, and David Owen, "La apuesta global de Renault," *Mercado,* July 2000, pp. 169–71.

Doman, Matthew, "Marcha impecable," *América economia,* August 1995, pp. 28–29.

Franchini, Matias, "Renault, la salud antes que el liderazgo en ventas," *Mercado,* November 2003, pp. 28–30.

"IKA Renault a toda marcha," *Mercado,* November 15, 1973, pp. 41–44.

McDonald, Norbert, "Henry J. Kaiser and the Establishment of the Automobile Industry in Argentina," *Business History,* July 1988, pp. 329–45.

McElroy, John, "Heavy Metal: Renault Argentina Would Like to Become Your Die Maker," *Automotive Industries,* August 1991, p. 18.

"Modelos para todos los gustos," *Mercado,* May 1996, pp. 52–54.

Mujal, Luis, *Los nuevos ricos de la Argentina,* Buenos Aires: Editorial Sudamericana, 2nd ed., 1997, pp. 103–69.

"Renault Argentina acelera la marcha," *Mercado,* July 19, 1979, pp. 45–48.

Silveti, Edgardo A., "El desafio de Renault," *Mercado,* April 9, 1981, pp. 36–39.

Stok, Gustavo, "El sobreviviente," *América economia,* November 1997, pp. 48–49.

Wong, Wailin, "Renault Argentina Takes It Slow While Driving Road to Recovery," *Wall Street Journal,* December 24, 2003.

—Robert Halasz

Robert W. Baird & Co. Incorporated

777 East Wisconsin Avenue
P.O. Box 0672
Milwaukee, Wisconsin 53201-0672
U.S.A.
Telephone: (414) 765-3500
Toll Free: (800) RWBAIRD; (800) 792-2473
Fax: (414) 765-3633
Web site: http://www.rwbaird.com

Private Company
Founded: 1919 as The First Wisconsin Company
Employees: 2,320
Operating Revenues: $544 million (2003 est.)
NAIC: 523920 Portfolio Management

Robert W. Baird & Co. Incorporated, established and still based in the heart of the Midwest, extended its reach throughout the United States and into Europe while under the wing of giant insurer Northwestern Mutual. Once again operating as an independent company, Baird offers services in wealth management, investment banking, private equity, and asset management.

Firmly Rooted in the Midwest: 1919–70s

The First Wisconsin Company—forerunner of Robert W. Baird & Co. Incorporated—was founded in 1919 as the securities arm of the First Wisconsin National Bank. Robert Wilson Baird was named lead partner and then served as president for nearly three decades.

The 1929 stock market crash led to the separation of banks from the security business. Consequently, First Wisconsin Company split off in 1934 as the Securities Company of Milwaukee Incorporated. Five years later, the firm took the name The Wisconsin Company.

In 1943, The Wisconsin Company began publishing its annual "Financial Briefs," which would gain recognition and respect for its quality research. In 1948, the company purchased a seat on the New York Stock Exchange (NYSE), becoming the first Wisconsin brokerage to do so. Keeping with NYSE tradition, The Wisconsin Company took the name of its lead partner, becoming Robert W. Baird and Company.

Baird stepped aside as the president of the company that same year. William Brand served as president until 1957, when Clarence Bickel stepped in as the company's third president. Growth during the 1960s and 1970s necessitated ever larger facilities. Leading the charge were Carl Wilson, named president in 1965, followed by Brenton H. Rupple in 1973, and G. Frederick Kasten in 1979.

The 1970s were marked by the creation of a new department, Public Finance. Public Wisconsin bonds proved to be an instant hit for Baird. During the 1980s Baird became Wisconsin's top investment banker but lost its independence.

Under Another Wing: 1980s–90s

In 1982, Baird joined the Northwestern Mutual family of companies. Formed in 1857, the life insurance company was among the country's ten largest, known as "The Quiet Company" and for its tenacious hold to tradition. But the challenges of the early 1980s, including proposed changes in tax laws, climbing interest rates, and the AIDS crisis, forced a rethinking. The acquisition of Robert W. Baird and Company was part of its move toward diversification.

Northwestern Mutual bought 65 percent of Baird in the deal. In 1985 employees relinquished another 15 percent of their holdings to Northwestern Mutual "to help the insurance company manage its tax burden," according to the *Business Journal—Milwaukee.*

When the stock market crashed in October 1987, Baird, unlike many other firms, was quick to recover, experiencing just one month of losses—the only one recorded in its history. The effects of the crash lingered through 1990. But Milwaukee brokerage houses experienced a banner year in 1991.

"It was hard not to have a good year in 1991," wrote Peter Kendall for the *Business Journal—Milwaukee.* "Interest rates plunged, stocks leaped to a record even before the Persian Gulf

Company Perspectives:

The foundation of any successful business is built upon a strong culture—on shared values of honesty, integrity, genuine concern for clients, and respect for associates. The Baird Way remains central to our ability to enjoy the quality client partnerships and high performance standards that have always been Baird traditions.

War was won, bonds went along for the ride and corporations came to the market to fill up on low cost capital.''

Baird easily outpaced all previous years, aided by the dismantling of a rival brokerage, which had seen staff lost to the offices of its Chicago-based parent company. Kemper Securities Inc. had consolidated five separate subsidiaries in 1991, including Milwaukee-based Blunt Ellis & Loewi Inc.

Baird dominated in state initial public offerings, participating in six of the seven made during the year, and captured eight other corporate finance offerings. The combined value was $800 million.

The firm was also the leader in underwritings by Wisconsin municipalities and government agencies. Institutional accounts also saw an increase as did managed accounts, a business segment established in 1989.

During 1992, Baird began picking up coverage of smaller local issues, hoping to ''enhance its image as the leader in the region,'' according to Kendall. The move was also an effort to position itself to pull in business down the road from the companies it researched.

Baird marked its 75th year in 1994, a time when the stock market was experiencing huge mood swings—rising then falling then rising again. Kasten, meanwhile, had increased the number of office locations, the number of financial advisors, and the number of financial advisors serving institutions by more than four times. Baird had become the leader of its marketplace for corporate and public finance.

The firm had expanded outside its stronghold of Wisconsin, opening, for example, a public finance office in Chicago early in 1994. Then in 1995, Baird entered the Chicago investment banking arena, on the lookout for merger and acquisition, consulting, and underwriting opportunities. At the time a number of players in the market had internal distractions, leaving a crack in the door to the competitive market.

''But Frederick Kasten, Baird's president and chief executive officer, doesn't claim to have a crystal ball,'' wrote John Banker for the *Business Journal—Milwaukee*. ''We don't follow a strategy of taking advantage of the ebbs and flows in the market place,'' Kasten said. ''We're driven by one factor—to do what's right for our clients.''

Baird lured investment bankers from the Chicago office of Kidder, Peabody & Co., including director of investment banking Paul E. Purcell, to aid the cause, but they would have a

formidable task. In addition to regional players, Wall Street firms roamed the Chicago market.

Baird moved into new markets in 1997, bringing investment banking to Florida and Texas and announcing plans to open a brokerage and sell research on American companies though a London-based office. That year, a $10 million private offering raised the level of employee ownership to 36 percent. Northwestern Mutual continued to control the company, holding the remaining 64 percent. The company was valued at $165 million.

The move was prompted by increasing demand for equity ownership for the recruitment and retention of employees. Salaries and bonuses were no longer enough to satisfy brokerage employees. Baird needed to up the ante to compete with firms already offering greater ownership opportunities. Other firms had moved into the public arena following such an increase in employee ownership. But Northwestern Mutual, which held a majority of seats on the board of holding company Baird Financial Corp., maintained it had no plans to sell off the remainder of the company to employees in the near future, according to the *Business Journal—Milwaukee*.

In 1999, Paul E. Purcell was tapped to succeed Kasten, in 2000, as CEO. Kasten had helped Baird ''grow from a medium-sized brokerage firm to one of the largest regional firms in the country,'' according to the *Milwaukee Journal Sentinel*. Coming aboard in 1963 as a capital goods analyst, Kasten had served as CEO since 1980. His father, grandfather, and great-grandfather all had been the top executive of Firstar Corp., a company his great-grandfather helped organize. His successor, Purcell, had been named chief operating officer in January 1997 and president in January 1998. ''I love Baird; the people are great and we're going to continue to build it the way it's been built for the last 50 years,'' Purcell told Kathleen Gallagher of the *Milwaukee Journal Sentinel*.

In 1999, Baird acquired the United Kingdom's Granville PLC. The independent investment bank had offices in Hamburg, Paris, and Barcelona, in addition to its London headquarters. The company was established in the early 1970s to introduce institutional investment into private companies, according to the *Financial Times*. Its original name was Nightingale, after one of the three founding partners. Robin Hodgson, chair and one of the three, gave the company his middle name when he retired in the late 1970s. The third partner, Nicolas Moy, remained with the company. Longtime investors were the pension funds of the Post Office, British Telecommunications & BG, and Friends Provident, sharing nearly 42 percent of Granville.

Regaining Independence: 2000–04

In 2000, Baird Advisors was formed, specializing in fixed money management, and bringing more new blood into the company. Northwestern Mutual planned to grant more employee ownership in 2001. Since 1997, the time of the last increase in ownership, the firm had boosted the number of financial advisors from 614 to more than 780; expanded services from 11 to 16 states; acquired Granville; and brought in some of the top talent in the industry.

In addition to an increase in employee ownership to nearly 45 percent, there would be some relationship changes between

Key Dates:

1919: The First Wisconsin Company is established as a securities arm of the First Wisconsin National Bank.
1934: The company is separated from the bank and renamed Securities Company of Milwaukee Incorporated.
1939: The company modifies its name to The Wisconsin Company.
1948: The company lists on the New York Stock Exchange as Robert W. Baird and Company.
1957: The third president is appointed.
1963: Company growth drives a move to new offices.
1979: G. Frederick Kasten is named president.
1982: Northwestern Mutual purchases majority control of Baird.
1999: Granville PLC is acquired.
2001: Employees increase ownership to nearly 45 percent.
2004: Baird returns to independent status as an employee-owned company.

the two companies. According to the *Milwaukee Journal Sentinel,* beginning in 2002, Northwestern Mutual was to make an internal subsidiary its exclusive broker/dealer for selling mutual funds and other securities: 4,500 of its agents had been licensed to sell investment products through Baird. The 9 percent of the company to be moved to employee ownership had an estimated value of about $27 million.

Baird Holding Company recorded its second best year in 2003 with net revenue of $544 million, up 4 percent from 2002's $524 million. It was the best year since 2000. The industry as a whole had been declining since that record-breaking year, off 40 percent from its peak. But Baird had experienced just a 6 percent decline.

In 2004, Baird regained its independence as an employee-owned company. Baird had helped Northwestern Mutual move into the investment products market, but the insurance company had developed its own investment services division. Northwestern Mutual would finance 80 percent of the purchase by Baird employees, and a contract with Baird for security transactions

would continue though 2005, according to the *Wisconsin State Journal.*

As for Baird's future, said Purcell in a *PR Newswire* release: "In a very competitive industry, Baird has a great advantage because we are an employee-owned, fully independent company. We feel very strongly that Baird is a special place and others seem to agree, including FORTUNE magazine, which named Baird one of the '100 Best Companies to Work For' in 2004."

Principal Subsidiaries

Robert W. Baird & Co.; Robert W. Baird Group Ltd.

Principal Competitors

Jefferies Group, Inc.; Piper Jaffray Companies Inc.; Raymond James Financial.

Further Reading

"Baird Completes Buyback Transaction, Becomes Employee-Owned Firm," *PR Newswire,* May 13, 2004, p. 1.

"Baird Realignment Facilitates Increased Associate Ownership," *PR Newswire,* April 10, 2001, p. 1.

Banker, John, "Baird's Chicago Foray: Good Timing or a Risky Move?," *Business Journal—Milwaukee,* May 27, 1995, p. 9.

Gallagher, Kathleen, "Kasten, Architect of Baird's Growth, to Step Down As CEO," *Milwaukee Journal Sentinel,* February 23, 1999, p. 1.

——, "NML Agrees to Deal with Baird," *Milwaukee Journal Sentinel,* April 11, 2001, p. 1D.

Harris, Clay, "Baird Buys Granville for L37m," *Financial Times,* October 12, 1999, p. 29.

Hoeschen, Brad, "Baird Increases Ownership Stake," *Business Journal—Milwaukee,* February 27, 1998, p. 1.

Kendall, Peter, "As Baird Picks Up Neglected Stocks, Kemper Boasts Firepower," *Business Journal—Milwaukee,* July 25, 1992, p. 7.

——, "Stockbrokers Are Singing the Praises of 1991," *Business Journal—Milwaukee,* January 13, 1992, p. 1.

Newman, Judy, "Baird Employees to Buy Rest of Firm from Northwestern," *Wisconsin State Journal,* April 22, 2004, p. E1.

—Kathleen Peippo

Rolls-Royce Group PLC

65 Buckingham Gate
London
SE1E 6AT
United Kingdom
Telephone: +44 20 7222 9020
Fax: +44 20 7227 9170
Web site: http://www.rolls-royce.com

Public Company
Incorporated: 1884 as F.H. Royce and Company
Employees: 36,100
Sales: £6 billion ($11.12 billion) (2003)
Stock Exchanges: London
Ticker Symbol: RYCEY
NAIC: 333611 Turbine and Turbine Generator Set Unit
   Manufacturing; 335312 Motor and Generator
   Manufacturing; 336412 Aircraft Engine and Engine
   Parts Manufacturing

Rolls-Royce Group PLC is flying high in the 2000s. The London-based company, most famously linked to its former luxury car division, is one of the world's top manufacturers of high-power gas turbine engines for the aviation industry. Rolls-Royce has gained prominence in this cutthroat global market through its development of proprietary technology that allows a single-engine model to be adapted in order to build more powerful, and more economical, aircraft engines. The company's early 21st century engine designs, led by the Trent 900 and the Trent 1000, launched in 2003, are expected to take the company to the number one spot in the industry. The company has seen especially strong sales in the Asian market, including a $1 billion order from Japan's All Nippon Airways and a $450 million order from China Eastern Airlines in October 2004. Altogether, Rolls-Royce counts some 500 airlines, 4,000 corporate and utility aircraft and helicopter operators, more than 200 armed forces and navies, and more than 2,000 marine clients among its customers. With an installed base of nearly 55,000 engines, Rolls-Royce's maintenance and repair services accounts for some 50 percent of the group's nearly £6 billion ($11

billion) revenues in 2003. Rolls-Royce also has successfully balanced its operations in the cyclical aerospace market with the development of its industrial power division, which represents about 40 percent of the company's sales. Rolls-Royce is listed on the London Stock Exchange.

Late 19th-Century Origins

The origins of Rolls-Royce date back to its founder, Sir Frederick Henry Royce, born in March 1863 in Lincolnshire, England. His rags to riches story began when as a youth he went to London to sell newspapers for W.H. Smith on a street corner. In 1872, the year of his father's death, young Henry found himself in financial straits and augmented his newspaper selling job with work as a telegraph messenger. Five years later Royce got a job as an apprentice in a railway works near Peterborough, where he learned the basics of modern engineering. In 1880, he graduated to becoming a tester with the Electric Light and Power Company in London, and he studied the principles of electrical engineering in his spare time. In 1884 Royce and his friend Ernest Claremont began a small electrical and mechanical engineering workshop, F.H. Royce and Company, on Cooke Street in Manchester.

Business was slow and difficult at first, but before long the company became known for its electrical dynamos and cranes. Sales rose from £6,000 in 1897 to £20,000 in 1899. That year, the company's name was changed to the Royce Company, and its capital base was increased to £30,000 to finance a new factory at Trafford Park, Manchester.

By 1902, Britain's nascent motorcar industry caught the industrious Royce's eye. He bought a secondhand French Decauville, stripped it down to its parts, and studied the vehicle. Applying what would now be called ''reverse engineering,'' he set about building his own auto based on the Decauville. The result was a two-cylinder, ten-horsepower model not much different from the French original. The first model produced from the Cooke Street works emerged in 1904, in time to catch interest from another Decauville enthusiast of the day, Charles Rolls.

Born in 1877, Charles Stewart Rolls came from a far more privileged background than Royce. After studying at Eton and

Company Perspectives:

Rolls-Royce is a world leading power systems business, meeting the needs of customers, shareholders and employees for the next century. We provide cost-effectively engineered products and services to commercial and military customers in propulsion, electrical power and materials handling markets around the world. Customers from the world's leading airlines to executive jet operators rely on our powerful range of commercial aero engines and global support network. Military customers benefit from engines for helicopters, fast jets, trainers and transport aircraft, as well as naval vessels. We provide power utilities and independent operators with innovative solutions to their electrical generation, transmission and distribution needs and serve customers in industrial, marine and nuclear engineering markets.

Cambridge, he traveled around the Continent in the early 1890s, developing an interest in the motor car, which was then becoming popular in France. Once back in Britain, Rolls became a motorcar dealer in 1903. He sold mostly continental models, but with his dealership in fashionable Brook Street, London, and a repair shop in nearby Fulham, Rolls soon came to know the British car market well.

Forming Rolls-Royce in 1904

Rolls's interest in becoming a dealer of British automobiles led him to Royce's new line. The two men met, and a deal was finally struck for C.S. Rolls and Co. to become the exclusive dealer for Royce. Their December 23, 1904 agreement stipulated all cars sold by their arrangement were to be called ''Rolls-Royce.'' Four models went into production: the twin-cylinder, ten-horsepower; the three-cylinder, 15-horsepower; the four-cylinder, 20-horsepower; and the six-cylinder, 30-horsepower. All the vehicle engines shared a series of parts—pistons and rings, valves, connecting rods, springs and bearings, among others.

In 1905, the first year of production, Rolls-Royce's four types of vehicles ranged in price from £395 to £890 and, therefore, were purchased only by the wealthy. Expansion of the motorcar market at this time tended to focus on innovations in engine design. In 1905, Rolls-Royce introduced its eight-cylinder, V8 engine, regarded by motoring enthusiasts as innovative for the smoother, quieter ride it allowed.

In 1906 Rolls-Royce introduced the 40/50 model, or the Silver Ghost, named for its metallic appearance and its engine that was ''quiet as a ghost.'' Some British journalists called it ''the best car in the world.'' Orders for this and earlier models climbed steadily that year, and this brought about the expansion of the company to a new factory in Derby. To fund the new plant, a subscription of new shares worth £100,000 was offered on the stock market in December 1906 under a new name: Rolls-Royce Limited. The subscription named Royce as chief engineer and works director, and Rolls as technical managing director. Ernest Claremont was appointed to chair the company.

The Derby factory opened on July 9, 1908, amid much pageantry. Proof that the new Silver Ghost was to be a success

came in 1911 when the Indian government ordered eight new models for use by King George V and his entourage during the Delhi Durbar that year.

Around this time, Rolls began to distance himself from the car company as both his fame and outside interests grew. He resigned as technical managing director and became a consultant to Rolls-Royce in April 1910. Three months later, Rolls was tragically killed when his Wright biplane crashed. As a symbol of mourning, the intertwined ''RR'' logo on the Rolls-Royce radiator plate was changed from red to black. Soon thereafter the workaholic Royce fell seriously ill from exhaustion, and he spent much of 1912 convalescing. In time, Royce took a home in the south of France and reduced his shop floor work—but not his design contributions—to conserve his health.

Expansion into Aircraft Engines During World War I

Day-to-day responsibility of Rolls-Royce Limited then passed to Claude Johnson, who reaffirmed the longtime company commitment to producing and perfecting one model. For a company building luxury cars, the benefits of military procurement beginning at the outbreak of World War I were not immediately apparent. But, in 1914, Rolls-Royce found itself in demand to produce chassis for armored fighting vehicles, and Rolls-Royce cars soon became widely used as staff cars for the British Army.

During this time Rolls-Royce also was called upon to design aircraft engines to help with the war effort. The company's association with aviation propulsion had begun earlier. In fact, the original 1906 agreement between Rolls and Royce had mentioned in the first paragraph that the company had a wide mandate to provide propulsion on land, at sea, and in the air. Furthermore, Royce had served as a consultant to the Royal Aircraft Factory at Farnborough. Outside of this early interest in aviation, however, which Royce shared with Rolls, actual production of aero engines did not begin until the onset of World War I.

In early 1915, Royce led a team of engineers in working out a design. Within three days of the war's outbreak, Royce was poring over plans for a 200-horsepower aero engine. Some of the technology—crankshaft, connecting rods, geartrains—were borrowed from the Silver Ghost motorcar engine. But more pistons were required—12 in all. Thus was born the 60 degree V12 engine that became the prototype for all machinery produced by Rolls-Royce after 1918.

Testing of a 225-horsepower aero engine had begun at Derby. By 1916, the engine went into production. It was named the Eagle and was put into wartime service beginning in 1916 at 250 horsepower in size. By 1918, the Mark VIII form had risen in size to 365 horsepower. Two other engines, the Hawk and the Falcon, had been designed by Royce from his home in the south of France and relayed to his production team in Derby for manufacture. In total, 5,000 Rolls-Royce aero engines were made during World War I, accounting for nearly half the air horsepower used by Allied forces. By the late 1920s, the company derived more profit from the manufacture of aero engines than it did from making cars.

Producing aero engines also had applications for developing motorcar engines. In 1924, for example, Rolls-Royce intro-

<table>
<tr><td colspan="2">Key Dates:</td></tr>
</table>

1884:	Frederick Henry Royce founds F.H. Royce and Company in Manchester, England.
1904:	Royce builds his first automobile, and reaches a sales agreement with Charles Stewart Rolls to sell ''Rolls-Royce'' cars.
1915:	The company begins production of aircraft engines.
1931:	The company acquires Bentley Motor Ltd.
1940:	The gas turbine aircraft engine is developed.
1966:	The rival British aircraft maker Bristol-Siddley Engines is acquired.
1971:	Facing bankruptcy, Rolls-Royce is nationalized by the British government; the automotive division is split off and later acquired by Vickers PLC.
1987:	Rolls-Royce is privatized with a listing on the London Stock Exchange.
1989:	The company acquires Northern Engineering Industries, which produces industrial power plants, as part of a diversification effort; the first in the Trent engine series for widebody planes is launched.
1992:	The company launches a restructuring effort, cutting 20,000 jobs over four years.
1995:	The company acquires Allison Engine Company in the United States in order to establish a U.S. presence.
1999:	The company acquires National Airmotive, in California, boosting its services division to 50 percent of revenues; Vickers PLC (minus the Rolls-Royce car division, sold to Volkswagen) is acquired and becomes the world's leading marine power system producer.
2004:	The company wins a $1 billion order from All Nippon Airways in Japan and a $450 million order from China Eastern Airlines.

duced front wheel brakes to its cars, as well as power assistance through a gearbox driven servo. The interwar years also signaled a departure from the company's practice of producing only one car model. In 1922, the 3.5-liter, 20-horsepower model was introduced. In 1925, the ''New Phantom'' succeeded the Silver Ghost. Although its larger seven-liter engine had overhead valves rather than side valves, the chassis and the running gear were the same as those used on the Silver Ghost.

Over the next ten years, Rolls-Royce continued to manufacture automobiles for an increasingly exclusive and wealthy clientele. In 1931, the company purchased Bentley Motor Ltd., a consistently undercapitalized English manufacturer of high-performance automobiles. Royce, who was conferred a baronetcy in 1930, died in 1933.

Just before the outbreak of World War II, the Phantom II was replaced by the Phantom III. The new model was driven by a V12 engine, the most powerful yet. Without Royce to oversee its introduction, however, the Phantom III production had been expensive. This led in 1937 to the company's consideration of rationalizing its design and production facilities to contain expanding operating costs.

Before his death in 1933, Royce had set about designing a new generation of aero engines that surpassed 1,000 horsepower in size. The result was the PV12, a 27-liter engine eventually named the Merlin. The Merlin was first used by the Royal Air Force in 1937. Two years later, the aero engine could maintain 1,000 horsepower to 16,000 feet. Impressed with its design and output, the Royal Air Force agreed to help fund the development of three fighter planes designed around the Merlin—the Fairey Battle Bomber, the Hurricane, and the Spitfire. All performed with memorable accuracy in the famed Battle of Britain during World War II. Innovations to the engine during this time ensured it could attain 1,000 horsepower at more than twice the original altitude, 47,000 by the war's end. Activity during World War II had greatly expanded Rolls-Royce. Factories at Crewe and Glasgow, Scotland, had been opened. By 1945, the company employed significantly more than 50,000 people.

Ernest Hives, who served as CEO of Rolls-Royce from 1936 to 1957, decided in 1945 that the future of the company lay in continuing to produce aero engines. He guided the company's conversion from piston turbine engines to the new gas turbine engine designed by Stanley Hooker and Frank Whittle in 1940. Car production was moved from Derby to Crewe so that the Derby facilities could work almost exclusively on developing the gas turbine aero engine for the civil aviation industry.

An early customer of the Merlin engine was the Canadair DC4M, a Canadian-built aircraft. The introduction of a military engine in a civil aircraft took some tinkering before it was done successfully. Rolls-Royce used its experience to judge just how different commercial engine expectations were from military ones. In 1953, Rolls-Royce introduced the Dart propjet engine for the Vickers Viscount. This new engine had a centrifugal design and had taken over from the Merlin 60 series of engines. The last Dart engine was built in 1986, ending nearly 40 years of production.

Rolls-Royce also introduced the turbojet engine in the form of the AJ65 model, or the Avon, which powered the world's first commercial jetliner, de Havilland's Comet, as well as the Canberra, Hunter, and Lightning. The company's second wholly civil aero engine was the RB141, or Medway, launched in 1959. It served the BEA and BOAC airlines for a few years before it was replaced by the Spey, a smaller version. Aside from being used in the BAC One Eleven, Fokker F28, and Gulfstream II and III, the Spey made its way across the Atlantic into the American LTV A7 military aircraft.

Competition and Nationalization: 1960–70s

Hives was succeeded by Sir Denning Pearson in the late 1950s. Pearson was determined to penetrate the important American airliner market, but was rebuffed by fierce competition from Pratt & Whitney and General Electric (GE). In 1966 Rolls-Royce effectively consolidated the British aircraft engine industry with the acquisition of its top domestic rival, Bristol-Siddley Engines. Two years later, the company won a key order from Lockheed to build an engine for the TriStar plane. Although the contract seemed a major coup at the time, development of this powerful new engine, dubbed the RB211, consumed far more time and money than Rolls-Royce had anticipated—so much so that in February 1971 the company faced bankruptcy and was subsequently nationalized by the British government. To reduce costs, the company spun off its carmaking division into a separate company, Rolls-Royce Motor Cars Ltd., which eventually became a subsidiary of Vickers PLC. Both companies continued to use the Rolls-Royce name and the distinctive RR symbol.

At the same time, development of the RB211 engine under the engineering leadership of Sir Stanley Hooker continued apace. By 1972, the RB211 went into production for use in the TriStar aircraft. Although it had been costly to develop, it was very adaptable and modified for uses large and (relatively) small. In 1987, Rolls-Royce announced that 75 percent of customers for the new Boeing 757 airliner had chosen the RB211 engines for propulsion. The RB211 was even used in landbased and off-shore installations, mainly by the oil and natural gas industries in drilling operations. On the military engine side of operations, Rolls-Royce took part in the three-nation Turbo-Union RB199 engine development for the Tornado aircraft during the mid-1980s. The company also provided Pegasus vectored-thrust engines for the British V-Stol Harrier aircraft, used primarily by the Royal Air Force.

Under the chairmanship of Frank Tombs from 1985 until 1992, Rolls-Royce reemerged on the London Stock Exchange in May 1987, securing more than two million shareholders in the process. Many were from overseas, primarily Americans. By the end of 1988, a more hopeful business climate produced an order book for Rolls-Royce of £4.1 billion, compared with the £2.7 billion a year earlier. Sales for the company were slightly down, however, on 1987 figures, as were the operating profits, at £333 million.

In 1988, the company launched the RB211-524L civil turbofan engine. In addition, Rolls-Royce signed an agreement to provide the European Fighter Aircraft, a three-member European military production project, with the EJ200 engine. The company had a 33 percent stake in the project.

After its refloatation, Rolls-Royce set about diversifying away from its sole emphasis on aero engines. To that end, in May 1989, the company merged with Northern Engineering Industries PLC (NEI), which designed and constructed capital plant and equipment, particularly for the power generation industry. That year Frank Turner, director of civil engineers at Rolls-Royce, welcomed the diversification, which ensured the company would now derive 35 percent of its sales from non-aero engine business. He commented: "Through the sixteen years of state ownership, we were constrained . . . in obtaining approval for anything new. In effect, our gun arm was strapped. We found ourselves only able to react to the initiatives of our competitors, and then only when it was very late in the day."

The company announced in 1989 the formation of a joint venture between NEI and Asea Brown Boveri, the Swiss-based engineering group. The venture, NEI ABB Gas Turbines Ltd., was to be based in Newcastle in northern England. In the same year, Rolls-Royce introduced a new incarnation of the RB211 dubbed the Trent engine, to carry it into the new decade. The

Trent helped Rolls-Royce capture important orders for wide-body aircraft, such as the McDonnell Douglas-11 and the Airbus 330. Boeing subsequently announced that it would carry the Trent engines on its 767-X aircraft.

Early 1990s Recession Driving Reorganization

A stunning array of problems greeted Rolls-Royce and its rivals in the 1990s. The disruption of the global airline industry from the Persian Gulf conflict battered the airline industry and its suppliers in the early 1990s. Due to an embargo, NEI had to postpone the sale of four steam-turbine generators to the aggressor, Iraq. With a deepening global recession came reduced air travel. Loss-plagued civil airlines cautiously postponed or canceled new plane orders, forcing the three largest aerospace engine manufacturers into what one analyst called "suicidal price competition." Once the Gulf War was settled, leading nations around the world resumed downsizing their military budgets, slashing new aircraft orders. Sales for Rolls-Royce in 1991 fell 4 percent to £3.51, and pretax profits fell more sharply to £51 million, compared with £176 million a year earlier.

Better times appeared to be on Rolls-Royce's horizon, however, as the company's order book rose to record levels on the success of its Trent engine. In fact, the company's share of the civil aviation market had grown from 10 percent at the time of its refloatation in 1987 to 23 percent at the beginning of 1993. That same year, the company opened what it claimed was the world's largest airline engine testing facility, a £20 million ($30 million) test cell that was as big as a soccer field.

Sir Ralph Robins, who capped a lifetime career at Rolls-Royce with his advancement from CEO to chairman in 1992, realized that the company would not simply grow its way out of the industrywide crisis. He continued a reorganization set in motion by his predecessor, targeting across-the-board cost cuts. The company reduced development time by involving design and production engineers in the entire process and embarked on strategic joint ventures to pare research and development costs. The employee rolls received the most drastic surgery; the workforce was cut by more than one-third, from nearly 65,000 in 1989 to 42,600 by the end of 1996.

Robins's strategies for winning increased market share—and with it sales and profits—included emphases on the aftermarket segment, the fast-growing Asia-Pacific market, and the new class of super jumbo jets. Since price competition among the big-three aero engine makers had slashed that segment's profitability, Rolls-Royce focused on providing higher-margin parts and service to the world's airlines, hoping to double that business by the turn of the 21st century. Emphasis on sales to Asian airlines paid off handsomely; by the mid-1990s, the company had captured one-third of China's aero engine orders. Its Trent 800 became the engine of choice for Boeing 777s sold to Southeast Asian airlines, giving it a 32 percent share of the market for powering that model worldwide. The $525 million acquisition of U.S.-based Allison Engine Company boosted Rolls-Royce's presence in that still vital market, prompting the parent company to expect a $1.5 billion contract to retrofit U,S, Air Force B52s.

The company's £400 million investment in the next-generation Trent mega-thrust engines (80,000 pounds and up)

also proved sound. Rolls-Royce emerged with the industry's lightest, most fuel-efficient engine made for the super jumbo jets being designed by Boeing Co. These massive planes were expected to ferry up to 550 passengers as far as 10,000 miles at a stretch. Rolls-Royce hoped to power 50 percent of the 1,200 of these giant planes projected to be built by the middle of the 2010s.

Following a pretax loss of £184 million on revenues of £3.6 billion in 1992, revenues rose slightly, to £3.6 billion in 1995, but the company achieved a pretax profit of £175 million. Results for 1996 were adversely affected by the company's decision to divest its steam power generation interests; costs related to the sale pushed Rolls-Royce to a pretax loss of £28 million, but Sir Robins noted that ongoing holdings chalked up an operating profit of £242 million on the year. Despite the less-than-stellar bottom-line results, top executives were upbeat about the company's future prospects. Robins was expected to retire in 1998 and be succeeded by CEO John Rose.

21st-Century Leader

In the late 1990s, Rolls-Royce's more powerful, more economic aircraft engines were winning an increasing share of the global market. By the early 2000s, the company was able to boast of a market share approaching 25 percent. The company's ability to adapt its single Trent engine platform gave it a distinct advantage over competitors such as GE, which took the far more costly approach of designing new engines from scratch. Rolls-Royce's engines were also smaller and more fuel-efficient, and quickly became the engine of choice in the emerging new market for large-capacity aircraft.

Providing maintenance and repair services to the more than 54,000 Rolls-Royce aircraft engines on the market became a particularly important source of revenue for the company in the 2000s. Airlines increasingly sought to outsource their service and repair operations, and Rolls-Royce responded by expanding its capacity in this area. As part of that effort, the company acquired National Airmotive, based in California, one of the region's largest aircraft and overhaul providers. Rolls-Royce Engine Services, as the services division was called, rose to represent nearly 50 percent of the group's revenues by 2004.

Rolls-Royce also boosted its non-aircraft divisions at the end of the 20th century. In 1999 the company made two important acquisitions. The first came with the purchase of full control of its joint venture with Cooper Energy Services, boosting the company's industrial power operations with the venture's rotating compression equipment. The second came with the purchase of Vickers PLC, which had sold off the Rolls-Royce car division to Volkswagen in 1998, while the Rolls-Royce brand was transferred to BMW. The acquisition of Vickers transformed Rolls-Royce into a world leader in the production of marine gas turbine and other power systems.

By 2004, Rolls-Royce appeared set to take the number one spot in the global aircraft engine industry. The company's clear technology advantage had enabled it to outpace its rivals, in particular the joint venture between the United States' GE and Pratt & Whitney.

The September 11, 2001 terrorist attacks on the United States played a role in Rolls-Royce's success. As the aircraft markets in North America and Europe slumped—with thousands of aircraft remaining grounded into the mid-2000s—the Asian markets were taking off. With economies rising, and the need to transport a population numbering in the billions, the aircraft industry's hopes turned to this part of the world. The arrival of new and large aircraft, such as the Boeing 777, and the development of still larger aircraft, such as the massive Airbus 380–800, stimulated a demand for more powerful, yet more fuel-efficient, engines.

Rolls-Royce's technology advantage helped it to secure an increasing number of contracts in the Asian region. The launch of a new generation of Trent engines, the Trent 900 and Trent 1000, helped the company win a number of high-profile orders. In October 2004 alone, the group scored a contract to supply 50 engines to Japan's All Nippon Airways, worth $1 billion, and a second contract, worth $450 million, to supply China Eastern Airlines, that country's third largest airline. With an order book worth some £19 billion ($31 billion), Rolls-Royce soared into the new century.

Principal Subsidiaries

Rolls E.L. Turbofans Limited; Rolls-Royce Aero Engine Services Limited; Rolls-Royce Commercial Aero Engines Limited; Rolls-Royce Engine Controls Limited; Rolls-Royce International Support Services Limited; Rolls-Royce Military Aero Engines Limited; Sawley Packaging Company Limited; Allen Power Engineering Limited; Clarke Chapman Limited; Cochran Boilers Limited; International Combustion Limited; NEI Brantford International Limited (51%); NEI Overseas Holdings Limited; Parsons Power Generation Systems Limited; Peebles Electric Limited; Reyrolle Limited; Reyrolle Projects Limited; Rolls-Royce and Associates Limited; Rolls-Royce Industrial & Marie Gas Turbines Limited; Rolls-Royce Industrial & Marine Power Limited; Rolls-Royce Industrial Power (India) Limited; Rolls-Royce Industrial Power (Overseas Projects) Limited; Rolls-Royce Industrial Power Systems Limited; Rolls-Royce Materials Handling Limited; Rolls-Royce Nuclear Engineering Limited; Rolls-Royce Nuclear Engineering Services Limited; Rolls-Royce Power Engineering PLC; Rolls-Royce Power Generation Limited; Rolls-Royce Transmission & Distribution Limited; R-R Industrial Controls Limited; Thompson Kennicott Limited; Middle East Equity Partners Limited; Rolls-Royce & Partners Finance Limited; Rolls-Royce Capital Limited; Rolls-Royce International Limited; Rolls-Royce Leasing Limited; Rolls-Royce Overseas Holdings Limited; RRPF Engine Leasing Limited; RRPF Engine Leasing (No. 2) Limited; Motores Rolls-Royce Limitada (Brazil); Rolls-Royce Technical Support SARL (France); Allison Engine Company, Inc. (U.S.A.); Rolls-Royce Industrial Power (Pacific) Limited (Australia); Bristol Aerospace Limited (Canada); Ferranti-Packard Transformers Limited (Canada); Parsons Turbine Generators Canada Limited (Canada); Rolls-Royce Canada Limited; Rolls-Royce Gas Turbines Engines (Canada) Inc.; Rolls-Royce Holdings Canada Inc.; Rolls-Royce Industries Canada Inc.; Fushun & Reyrolle Bushing Co. Limited (China; 50.4%); Caillard S.A. (France); Ferranti-Packard de Mexico S.A. de C.V.; Rolls-Royce Industrial Power (New Zealand) Limited; NEI Africa Holdings Limited (South Africa; 60.33%); Northern Engineering Industries Africa Limited (South Africa; 56.36%); Rolls-

Royce Industrial & Marine Power Inc. (U.S.A.); Cutler Hammer Zambia Limited; NEI Zambia Limited; NEI Holdings Zimbabwe (Private) Limited; Rolls-Royce of Australia Pty. Limited; Nightingale Insurance Limited; Rolls-Royce & Partners Finance (Netherlands) B.V.; Rolls-Royce International Turbines (Saudi Arabia) Limited (51%); Rolls-Royce North America Inc. (U.S.A.); Rolls-Royce Inc. (U.S.A.); Rolls-Royce Capital Inc. (U.S.A.); Rolls-Royce Turbomeca Limited (50%); Rolls Smiths Engine Controls Limited (50%); Turbo-Union Limited (40%); Clarke Chapman Portia Port Services Limited (50%); Cooper Rolls Limited (50%); Derby Cogeneration Limited (50%); Rolls Laval Heat Exchangers Limited (50%); Rolls Wood Group (Repair & Overhauls) Limited (50%); Viking Power Limited (50%); Xian XR Aero Components Co Limited (China; 49%); BMW Rolls-Royce GmbH (Germany; 49.5%); EUROJET Turbo GmbH (Germany; 33%); MTU, Turbomeca, Rolls-Royce GmbH (Germany; 33.3%); Hong Kong Aero Engine Services Limited (50%); Industria de Turbo Propulsores S.A. (Spain; 45%); IAE International Aero Engines AG (Switzerland; 30%); Williams-Rolls Inc. (U.S.A.; 15%); Cooper, Rolls Corporation (Canada; 50%); Bellis India Limited (40%); Easun Reyrolle Relays and Devices Limited (India; 25%); RPG-RR Power Engineering Private Limited (India; 50%); EPE Reyrolle (Malaysia) Sdn. Bhd. (50%); Cooper Rolls Incorporated (U.S.A.; 50%); Sama Leasing Company Limited (Cayman Islands; 50%); RS Leasing Limited (50%); Aircraft Financing and Trading Holdings B.V. (Netherlands; 50%); Middle East Propulsion Company Limited (Saudi Arabia; 16.6%); R-H Component Technologies, L.C. (U.S.A.; 50%).

Principal Competitors

Aviation Industries Corporation of China I; Siemens AG; Siemens Westinghouse Power Corp.; Shenyang Liming Aero-Engine Group Corp.; General Electric Co. Power Systems; Dresser-Rand Co.; MAN AG; Solar Turbines Inc.; Harbin Steam Turbine Factory; Ingersoll-Rand Company Ltd.; Porsche Holding Ges GmbH.

Further Reading

Bangsberg, P.T., "Rolls-Royce Gearing Up to Sell More Aircraft Engines to China," *Journal of Commerce and Commercial,* November 18, 1993, p. 3B.

Banks, Howard, "Rolls on a Roll," *Forbes,* October 7, 1996, pp. 118–19.

Bird, Anthony, and Ian Hallows, *The Rolls Royce Motor Car,* London: B.T. Batsford Ltd., 1972.

Cavendish, Richard, "The Birth of Rolls Royce," *History Today,* May 2004, p. 60.

"Fighting the Flab: Rolls-Royce," *Economist,* April 3, 1993, pp. 58–59.

Flint, Perry, "No More 'Three On A Wing,' " *Air Transport World,* August 1996, pp. 58–62.

Foster, Geoffrey, "Three Over Thirty," *Management Today,* May 1996, pp. 64–66.

Gray, Robert, *Rolls on the Rocks: The History of Rolls-Royce,* Salisbury, England: Compton Press Ltd., 1971.

Gunston, Bill, *Rolls-Royce Aero Engines,* Wellingborough, England: Patrick Stephens, 1989.

Hodson, Roy, "The Eligible Engineer," *International Management,* February 1992, pp. 30–32.

House, Richard, "Sir Ralph Robins of Rolls-Royce: An Astonishing Turn of Speed," *Institutional Investor,* July 1996, pp. 23–24.

Jamaluddin Muhammad, "Rolls-Royce Stamps Its Power on Land, Air and Sea," *Bernama: The Malaysian News Agency,* July 5, 2004.

Johnson, Claude Goodman, *The Early History of Motoring,* London: Burrow, n.d.

Kay, William, "On a Rolls," *Barron's,* July 16, 1990, pp. 18–19.

"Knocking Engineers into New Shape," *Economist,* April 15, 1989, pp. 67–68.

Kositchotethana, Boonsong, "Rolls-Royce Looks to Soar with Asia-Pacific," *Bangkok Post,* March 3, 2003.

Lloyd, R. Ian, *Rolls-Royce, The Years of Endeavour,* London: Macmillan Press, 1978.

Morgan, Bryan, *The Rolls-Royce Story,* London: Collins, 1971.

Reed, Arthur, "Rolls's Post-Trent Planning," *Air Transport World,* November 1993, pp. 83–84.

Robotham, William Arthur, *Silver Ghosts & Silver Dawn,* London: Constable, 1970.

Rowland, John, *The Rolls-Royce Men: The Story of Charles Rolls and Henry Royce,* London: Lutterworth Press, 1969.

Sezer, Murad, "ANA Picks Rolls-Royce Engines for 50 Boeing 7E7 Planes," *CBS Marketwatch,* October 13, 2004.

Smart, Tim, "Clash of the Flying Titans," *Business Week,* November 22, 1993, pp. 64–66.

Verchere, Ian, "Rolls-Royce Runs Leaner and Meaner," *Interavia,* January 1992, pp. 33–37.

—Etan Vlessing
—updates: April Dougal Gasbarre, M.L. Cohen

Schott Brothers, Inc.

382 Fayette Street
Perth Amboy, New Jersey 08861
U.S.A.
Telephone: (732) 442-2486
Fax: (732) 442-6666
Web sites: http://www.schottnyc.com

Private Company
Founded: 1913 as Schott Bros.
Employees: 100
Sales: $6.5 million (2003)
NAIC: 315211 Men's and Boys' Cut and Sew Apparel
   Contractors (pt); 315222 Men's and Boys' Cut and
   Sew Suit, Coat, and Overcoat Manufacturing; 315234
   Women's and Girls; Cut and Sew Suit, Coat, Tailored
   Jacket, and Skirt Manufacturing; 315999 Other Apparel
   Accessories and Other Apparel Manufacturing (pt)

Schott Brothers, Inc. is one of the largest manufacturers of American-made men's and women's outerwear. The company is most well known for its tradition of creating quality leather jackets, especially the Schott "Perfecto." The "Perfecto" is the original biker jacket made famous by actor Marlon Brando in the 1950s classic film *The Wild Ones*. Schott's signature apparel is manufactured at the 250,000-square-foot company headquarters in Perth Amboy, New Jersey. Schott sells its handmade quality jackets and accessories worldwide. The company product line has evolved from the original sheepskin-lined raincoats sold door-to-door in New York City, to more than 100 different garments and accessories in men's and women's outerwear and sportswear lines, which are sold in retail stores and through the Internet. The company produces and sells approximately 350,000 to 400,000 apparel items annually.

Four generations of the Schott family have been involved in overseeing the privately owned specialty apparel business. The family has made it a priority to maintain the commitment to handcrafted quality intended by founder Irving Schott. In addition to the traditional leather outerwear created by Schott, the company produces wool peacoats, as well as jackets made from corduroy, down, and sateen. Schott's clothing lines include retro, motorcycle, American classic, military, wool, nylon, and women's lines.

A Humble Beginning: 1913–20s

In 1913, Irving Schott, son of Russian immigrants, founded Schott Bros. with his brother Jack. Their first humble workspace was in the basement of a tenement building on Manhattan's Lower East Side. There they hand cut and sewed sheepskin-lined raincoats, which were sold door-to-door. According to the creators, durability and functionality were the primary features of their high quality, handcrafted jackets.

Two years later the brothers had generated enough business to move to a manufacturing site in Staten Island. That same year Irving gave the brand name "Perfecto" to Schott Bros. leather jackets. The "Perfecto" name referred to Irving's favorite Cuban cigars, which were a regular accessory of the company founder. Schott's Perfecto jacket would be recognized as the finest American-made leather jacket for more than 30 years.

In the 1920s Irving and Jack were recognized as innovators in the apparel industry. First they revolutionized American-made outerwear by being the first in the industry to sew a zipper on a jacket. They also benefited from the emergence and growing popularity of motorcycles. In 1928 Irving had a vision of what would become an American classic when he designed and produced the first motorcycle jacket. Wool linings made it warmer, heavy grade leather made it protective when necessary, and a zipper made it more wind and weather resistant. That classic leather jacket sold for just $5.50 at a Harley Davidson dealer on Long Island. According to the Schott web site, "The Perfecto was durable, rugged, and immediately embraced. To this new generation of 'bikers,' the Perfecto was a symbol of the excitement, adventure and danger that fueled their fascination with motorcycles." To accommodate sales growth, Schott Bros. moved its manufacturing operation to South Amboy, New Jersey.

Outfitting the Military: 1930s–40s

Schott Bros. quality was recognized by the U.S. Air Force prior to World War II. The company was commissioned to design and manufacture "bomber jackets" for Air Force pilots. In addition, Schott Bros. became a major supplier of the U.S. military forces fighting abroad with nylon flyers for the Air Force and pea coats for the Navy. A tradition of providing for the American military forces was begun, and it continued for 60 years.

In 1940 Schott again moved its manufacturing business—design, production and storage—this time to nearby Perth Amboy, New Jersey. By 1947 a second generation joined in managing the business—Irving's son Mel.

Big Screen Exposure: 1950s

Schott Bros. apparel made its big screen debut in 1954 when Marlon Brando wore a Perfecto jacket in the cult classic *The Wild Ones*. The Perfecto gained national exposure and instant popularity, but sales declined because school districts banned the jackets due to their association with youth rebelliousness. By that time the Schotts had decided to reserve the Perfecto label for only their finest motorcycle jackets. Sales figures soon turned around for the Perfecto jacket, however. The following year, sales increased after the death of James Dean; the "hood" who often donned a Perfecto, "catapulted the motorcycle jacket back in vogue," according to the Schott web site. The jacket retailed for $49.

Up until the 1960s, the Schott family's focus was on the production side of the business. Irving prided himself on knowing how to operate and repair every machine and tool in the factory. When Milton Perlman joined the company in the 1960s, however, Schott Bros. began to develop a vision that revolved around sales. Perlman was very involved in the business outside of the shop. He would visit stores that sold Schott apparel, listen to their feedback, and respond to it. Perlman's sales vision helped place Schott Bros. on a growth curve for several decades.

Developing Sales Markets: 1960s–80s

Along with Mel Schott, Perlman worked to develop new sales markets for Schott outerwear throughout the United States and abroad. By 1963 the company began marketing the Perfecto jacket in Europe. At home American teens and young adults could be seen in Schott's leather and fringe style vests. It was the 60s, and Schott was part of the unique fashion scene. Perlman also helped the company design and introduce the western leather fringe jacket as well as non-leather jackets. Because the fringe on the popular western jackets had to be cut by hand, the company soon invested in an automated fringe machine.

By the mid-1980s, Mel's son Michael and daughter Roz were on board with the family business, beginning a new generation of family leadership. In 1985 the company moved to

a new location in Perth Amboy, a 250,000-square-foot building on Lehigh Street. It was the size of four square blocks. The following year Mel became president of Schott Bros., while 94-year-old Irving retained his title as chairman and CEO. Six years later Irving died, just months from his 100th birthday.

"It's hard to pinpoint exactly when black leather went from outlaw to chic," wrote Robin Updike in the *Baltimore Sun*. But that acceptance of an expanding leather jacket market would benefit Schott Bros. even though there were significantly more companies in the United States and abroad competing for leather consumers. Schott was committed to its history of quality handcrafted jackets made from the finest leather. That unwavering commitment to quality helped Schott maintain sales despite competition from inexpensive imports.

Expanding Globally: 1990s

By 1993 Schott Bros. had reached $60 million in sales worldwide. In addition to benefiting from worldwide distribution of its apparel through specialty stores on nearly every continent, Schott also gained from relationships with licensees in several countries. In the company's 80th year, Schott Bros. boasted 500 employees worldwide, who had helped produce 350,000 jackets. The Perfecto's price tag had grown to $300.

New apparel lines and a broader distribution market helped Schott achieve sales growth in the 90s. The company also introduced lines of handbags, belts, classically designed travel bags, and even Schott Perfecto school supplies. In addition, Schott brought back the traditional naval peacoat, but with a modern twist. The peacoat came in a variety of colors, rather than just the traditional navy blue. The classic melton wool naval peacoat was Schott's top seller in 1994. The company offered consumers a leather peacoat as well.

In 1994 Schott Bros. was again commissioned to supply the U.S. military. The Department of Defense contracted with Schott Bros. to manufacture jackets for the Air Force. The company unveiled its first women's line in 1997. The new line was the Rose Schott Collection, named for Irving's wife. Schott also expanded outerwear fabric selection, using wearnyl, fleece, and kings wool. Branching out beyond just the leather jacket market helped the company weather the cyclical nature of the leather industry. Because Schott had diversified over the years, the ups and downs of the leather market did not exert such a big impact on its bottom line.

Schott Bros. took a brief foray into the urban hip-hop market in 1998 when it acquired U.B. TUFF, a manufacturer of urban sportswear and outerwear for men and boys. It was Schott Bros. first acquisition, but it did not last long. The enterprise, which targeted a lower price customer base, quickly dissolved not long after it began.

During the late 1990s Schott began to broaden the production line through overseas manufacturing. Some garments just could not be produced at a competitive price in the U.S. plant. Nylon jackets, for example, were more labor intensive and less costly to produce abroad. The availability and quality of raw materials also had an impact on what Schott produced at home. The company put procedures in place to maintain the Schott standard of quality and attention to detail regardless of where the item was created. Generally, the apparel produced overseas

Key Dates:

1913: Schott Bros. is founded by Irving and Jack Schott.
1915: Company opens manufacturing facility in Staten Island; puts "Perfecto" label on outerwear.
1925: Irving Schott is the first clothier to sew a zipper on a jacket.
1928: Schott Bros. designs the first leather motorcycle jacket; manufacturing facility moves to South Amboy, New Jersey.
1930: Schott Bros. supplies "bomber jackets" to World War II pilots.
1940: Manufacturing moves to Perth Amboy, New Jersey.
1954: Schott motorcycle jackets are popularized by Marlon Brando in *The Wild Ones*.
1963: Schott Bros. begins selling "Perfecto" jackets in Europe.
1985: Company moves to 250,000-square-foot facility in Perth Amboy.
1993: Schott introduces classic naval pea coats.
1997: Company adds its first line exclusively for women.
1998: Company acquires U.B. TUFF.
2003: Schott re-releases limited edition replica of original "Perfecto" jacket.

were items new to the Schott collection. The company was committed, however, that its classic and signature styles would always be produced in the United States to ensure strict adherence to quality. Schott built relationships with licensees and manufacturing partners in Germany, France, China, and South America, and more recently in Russia.

Making Gains Abroad: 2000 and Beyond

In 2002 Schott Bros. began selling online. Because the Schott collection had grown so broad, the Internet store was one way for the company to make its entire line available to new and returning loyal customers. Most retail stores carried only a portion of the Schott Bros. apparel collection. Internet sales became a small but growing percentage of the company's sales. The Internet was also a way for Schott to connect with its customers. The home page linked to a Blog section where visitors were invited to "share the great things that have happened to you in a Schott jacket. . . ."

The Schott Bros. brand had grown in popularity worldwide, especially in Europe where consumers often had a greater appreciation for the classic American styles. Brand recognition and sales were frequently higher in Europe and Asia than in the United States. In Japan, Schott Bros.' reversible sheepskin coat won first place in the "hot fashion contest" at the U.S. Apparel Show in Tokyo in 2002. It was part of the International Fashion Fair, the largest fashion trade show in Japan. The coat scored high both on design and material.

While Schott Bros. expanded its product line to include suede shirts and leather pants, the company regularly brought back replicas of vintage top sellers. In 2003 Schott re-released a limited edition replica of the original Perfecto jacket, a top-of-the-line motorcycle jacket made entirely in the United States. Despite the price tag of $475, sales were strong.

By 2004 more than half of Schott's production still took place domestically, where the company could turn out the products faster and the Schott family could be directly involved in the daily manufacturing process. Exports continued as a large percentage of Schott's annual sales. The Schott family's third and fourth generations were successfully managing and nurturing Irving's venture—with Roz Schott as president; her son Jason as chief marketing officer; Steve Conlin (Mel's son-in-law) as chief executive officer; and Michael's son Oren as chief production officer. (Michael Schott died in 1997 of pancreatic cancer. He had been company president since 1994.) Family members remained committed to knowing every facet of the business, just as great grandfather Irving had. They appeared to possess that same commitment to quality and attention to detail of their company founder.

For 2005, the company refocused outerwear lines into Schott Luxe, for better men's stores; Schott West, western wear; and Schott Work, work wear. The streamlined product lines were developed for a fall 2005 release. The leather jacket market remained strong for Schott, with sales up 15 percent in 2004. The company also planned to move to a smaller, newer facility in Elizabeth, New Jersey, just ten miles from the current headquarters. The company sold its 100-year-old building as part of a city redevelopment project.

Principal Subsidiaries

Schott NYC Corp.

Principal Competitors

Vanson; Marc New York; Energie.

Further Reading

Czabala, Nancy, "It's Schott to Be Good" *Apparel Industry Magazine, Atlanta*, January 1997, Vol. 58 , Issue 1, pp. 14–16.
Hermann, Valli, "The Peacoat Resurfaces on a New Wave of Popularity," *Austin American Statesman*," December 1, 1994, p. E10.
"The History of Schott NYC," http://www.in2schott.dk.history.htm.
Interview with Jason Schott, Chief Marketing Officer, November 2004.
Johnson, Marylin, "Falling for a Classic: Navy-Inspired Peacoat Makes a Casual Statement," *Houston Chronicle*, November 29, 2001, p. 3.
Klara, Robert, "How to Be a Tough Guy (In One Easy Purchase)," *US Airways Inflight Magazine*, December 2004.
"Michael Schott (Obituary)," *Women's Wear Daily,* March 7, 1997, p. 24.
Parola, Robert, "Hot Schott," *Daily News Record,* January 23, 1989, p. 22.
"U.B. Tuff Acquired by Schott Bros.," *Business Wire New York,* July 16, 1998, p. 1.
Updike, Robin, "Black Leather, Long the Mark of the Wild Ones, Can Now Be Seen at the Opera," *Baltimore Sun*, November 25, 1993, p. 7F.

—Mary Heer-Forsberg

SDL PLC

Globe House, Clivemont Road
Maidenhead
SL6 7DY
United Kingdom
Telephone: +44 1628 410100
Fax: +44 1628 410505
Web site: http://www.sdlintl.com

Public Company
Incorporated: 1992
Employees: 1,174
Sales: £64.38 million (2003)
Stock Exchanges: London
Ticker Symbol: SDLLF
NAIC: 518111 Internet Service Providers

SDL PLC is one of the world's leading localization services providers to businesses seeking a global market presence. SDL's localization services involve translating and adapting such materials as user interfaces, web sites, help files, and other documentation, as well as sales, training, and marketing materials for local markets. SDL has been particularly active in developing automated translation software, such as its Knowledge-based Translation System (''KbTS''), launched in 2004, which promises to automate as much as 80 percent of translation work, with the remainder to be polished by the company's pool of some 2,000 onsite and freelance translators. SDL also provides ''internationalization'' services, such as the re-engineering of software to meet specific country-based computer platforms. SDL operates more than 40 offices in its primary markets in the United Kingdom, the rest of Europe, and the United States. The United States is the company's largest single market, at approximately one-third of total sales, while Europe, apart from the United Kingdom, provides more than one-third of sales as well. The company also operates offices in Asia, Central and South America, and Canada and Mexico. SDL has successfully taken advantage of the worldwide boom in Internet activity, nearly quadrupling its sales, to £64 million in 2003, since its initial public offering on the London Stock Exchange in 1999. SDL is led by founder, Chairman, and CEO Mark Lancaster.

Recognizing a Niche in the Early 1990s

Mark Lancaster was working as international development director at the United Kingdom's Ashton Tate in the early 1990s when he recognized the potential for a new type of service: providing localization services to the increasingly global marketplace. As corporations expanded from country-specific businesses to multinational operations, they were often confronted with the need to adapt their sales and marketing materials, documentation, product brochures, and even the products themselves, to their new foreign market. Faced with the complexity of the task—particularly for companies active in many different markets—corporations increasingly sought to outsource their localization needs. At the same time, the rise of the Internet introduced the need to develop a new type of multinational marketing tool, with web sites tailored for specific languages, cultures, operating platforms, and the like.

Lancaster founded SDL in 1992, initially to provide localization services for software developers. Translation played an integral part of the company's operations from the beginning. SDL quickly extended the scope of its operations, however, and in 1994 the company began investing in multimedia studios and developing a range of multimedia and design production techniques that enabled it to win contracts from such multimedia giants as Sony Corporation, for whom SDL began developing localized versions of popular Sony PlayStation games, and the Disney Company.

In 1995, SDL expanded its translation services with the acquisition of Amphion Solutions Ltd. That purchase brought SDL Amphion's leading-edge translation memory software, called Amptran. Translation memory software promised the increasing automation of translation tasks—such as the revision of software materials from previous versions—essentially by memorizing and then recognizing key words and phrases. In this way, the need for human input could gradually be reduced—also reducing the cost of translation.

With its multinational client base, SDL quickly began expanding into the international market. In 1995, the company opened its first branch office in France. The following year, the company entered the United States and Japan.

Company Perspectives:

Our mission is enabling global business. We have built our business on the following principles: Quality processes; Customer partnerships; Professionalism across all activities; Energetic investment in staff development; Support for different cultures and communities.

Key Dates:

1992: Mark Lancaster founds SDL in order to exploit the newly developing localization niche.

1993: The company begins developing multimedia and production technologies.

1995: Amphion Solutions Ltd. is acquired; the first French office is opened.

1996: Offices are opened in Japan and the United States.

1997: The company acquires Sheffield, England-based Polylang.

1999: SDL goes public on the London Stock Exchange; International Translation and Publishing Limited is acquired.

2000: The company acquires ATR Information AB, based in Sweden.

2001: The company acquires three companies from Sykes International, including its first U.S. production operation in Boulder, Colorado; the company also acquires Transparent Language Inc. (U.S.A.).

2002: The company acquires rival Alpnet in the United States.

2003: The company acquires Lomac in Russia to gain access to Eastern and Central European markets.

2004: The company debuts new software technology, KbTS, for Knowledge-based Translation System.

In order to continue its expansion, SDL turned to investment group Friends Ivory & Sime Private Equity, which provided the company with a £1 million capital injection in 1997. SDL then made a new acquisition, paying £1.4 million to acquire Sheffield, England-based Polylang. That purchase boosted SDL's capacity for localization services, as well as added Polylang's (renamed as SDL Sheffield Ltd.) web site development capability.

In 1998, SDL once again turned to the private investment market, now raising another £1.1 million through Friends Ivory & Sime and through JO Hambro. The company then used the investment to step up development of its own in-house software translation technologies. This resulted in the launch of SDLX, a 32-bit translation memory software package featuring "fuzzy logic," in 1999, followed by SDL WebFlow, in 2000.

Localization Leader in the 2000s

By then, SDL had established 12 branch offices in seven countries—including China, where SDL opened an office in 1999. That year marked a new milestone for the company, when it listed its shares on the London Stock Exchange. Enthusiasm for the company's technology, and for the prospective growth in the localization services sector, helped propel the company's shares from an initial price of 134p to a peak of more than 800p at the height of the tech stock craze of the early 2000s. SDL's performance seemed to bear out its stock price, as the company doubled its sales in 1999 over the previous year to more than £21 million.

Backed by its public listing, SDL began a series of takeovers in the early 2000s that enabled it to emerge as a leader in the worldwide localization market. A major step forward came in April 2000, when the company reached an agreement to acquire money-losing International Translation and Publishing Limited (ITP) for £14 million ($22 million). The acquisition helped boost SDL's international presence, with offices in Ireland, Spain, Italy, and Hungary, among others.

As Lancaster told *Language Technology News:* "Following the launch of SDLWebflow in January, SDL has received significant interest from global corporations who recognize the necessity for multilingual Web sites and require an efficient means of maintaining quality content in international markets. The acquisition of ITP allows the company to not only supply the leading technology available in the market but also to maintain existing and new clients' globalization demands and to provide an excellent platform to launch new workflow technology in the near future."

SDL successfully restored the ITP operations to profitability within months after integrating it into its organization. SDL's acquisition spree continued through 2000, with the purchase of

ATR Information AB, based in Sweden, giving SDL access to the Scandinavian market. At the beginning of 2001 the company bought three localization companies from Sykes Technologies Inc. Paying slightly more than $500,000, SDL gained new offices in Boulder, Colorado, marking the company's first production capacity in the United States, and in Edinburgh and Belgium. Soon after, the company paid $9 million to acquire U.S.-based Transparent Language Inc. and its Transcend Machine Translation software technology. By the end of 2001, the company's revenues had doubled again, topping £42 million.

The beginning of 2002 brought the next milestone in SDL's expansion—in January of that year the company completed the acquisition of its chief U.S. rival Alpnet, paying $7 million. The deal doubled SDL's size, giving it critical mass in the highly fragmented translation and localization market. SDL now claimed a leading stake as one of the four large-scale localization specialists.

SDL continued to seek out new business areas in 2003, buying up Russia-based Lomac, a leading provider of translation, software, electronic technical document publishing, and web site content in development. That purchase strengthened SDL's presence in the Eastern and Central European markets. By the end of that year, SDL's growth efforts had paid off, with sales topping £64 million.

Amid its acquisition drive, SDL also had been preparing its next-generation software technology. That package debuted in July 2004 as KbTS, for Knowledge-based Translation System. The new software promised to cut translation costs as much as 60 percent by automating as much as 80 to 90 percent of the translation process—as compared with just 40 percent for rival products. While the new system retained a need for real-time translators, whose job consisted, in large part, of polishing the machine-translated document, it also promised to double and even triple an individual translator's output. The launch of KbTS clearly established SDL as the global localization services leader.

Principal Subsidiaries

Alpnet Inc. (U.S.A.); Bengbu Alpnet Technology Co. Ltd. (China); Lomac CZ S.R.O. (Czech Republic); Lomac d.o.o. Ljubljana (Slovenia); Lomac d.o.o. Zagreb (Croatia); Lomac Elite S.R.L. (Romania); Lomac Magyarorszag Szolgaltato Kft. (Hungary); Lomac Sp. z.o.o. (Poland); SDL Global Solutions (Ireland) Limited; SDL International (Canada) Inc.; SDL International Belgium N.V.; SDL International Nederland B.V. (The Netherlands); SDL Italia S.R.L.; SDL Japan KK; SDL Multilingual Services GmbH & Co. KG; SDL Multi-Lingual Solutions (Singapore) PTE Ltd.; SDL Sheffield Limited; SDL Spain SL; SDL Sweden AB; SDL Technology Centre Limited (Ireland); Software & Documentation Localizations France S.A.R.L.

Principal Competitors

Brown Global Solutions; Lionbridge.

Further Reading

"Another Year of Progress for SDL," *Sheffield Star,* March 7, 2002.

Brock, Chris, "The Border Patrol," *New Media Creative,* July 2001, p. 50.

Essick, Kristi, Boris Grondahl, James Ledbetter, and Rick Wray, "Europe's Five Rising Stars," *Industry Standard,* May 21, 2001, p. 53.

Freeborn, Tim, "SDL Minds Its Language," *Shares Magazine,* July 1, 2004.

"SDL Acquires ITP," *Language Technology News,* April 7, 2000.

"SDL Agrees to Merger with Alpnet," *New Media Age,* December 20, 2001, p. 14.

"SDL Looks a Winner for the Long Term," *Daily Telegraph,* March 9, 2002.

"Speaking Your Language," *Money Observer,* November 2003.

—M.L. Cohen

Seddon Group Ltd.

Plodder Lane, Edge Fold
Bolton
Lancashire
United Kingdom
Telephone: +44 161 790 8531
Fax: +44 161 790 1922
Web site: http://www.seddongroup.co.uk

Private Company
Incorporated: 1920 as G&J Seddon Limited
Employees: 1,470
Sales: £291.5 million ($521 million) (2003)
NAIC: 236115 New Single-Family Housing Construction (Except Operative Builders); 236116 New Multi-Family Housing Construction (Except Operative Builders); 236117 New Housing Operative Builders; 236210 Industrial Building Construction; 236220 Commercial and Institutional Building Construction; 238320 Paint and Wall Covering Contractors; 423140 Motor Vehicle Part (Used) Merchant Wholesalers; 423830 Industrial Machinery and Equipment Merchant Wholesalers; 441120 Used Car Dealers; 811111 General Automotive Repair

Seddon Group Ltd. is one of the top family-owned construction businesses in the United Kingdom and is active in the new construction sector as well as in the market for refurbishment and renovation, including painting. The company serves the private, commercial, industrial, retail, and government sectors. The group operates through a number of subsidiary businesses. G&J Seddon Limited is the company's oldest component, dating back to the Seddon Group's founding in 1897. This company focuses on the Northwest England market, and provides new build, repair, refurbishment, and maintenance services, as well as design and build, joint venture, and speculative development projects. J&S Seddon Limited operates through branch offices in Birmingham, Derby, Stoke, Normanton, and Chester, providing the group's construction services to the national market. Its J&S Seddon painting subsidiary offers a full range of painting and painting maintenance and repairs throughout England. Jotcham & Kendall Ltd. focuses its construction on the area around Wotton-under-Edge, close to Bristol, where it has been in business since 1650. The company also operates Chestergate Seddon, which concentrates its construction operations on the British northwest region. In the early 1990s, Seddon launched a new housing development subsidiary, Seddon Homes, based in Cheshire. The company also operates a Plant Engineering subsidiary, providing equipment sales, parts, and repair services; that subsidiary also manufactures construction equipment under the Seddon Johnson brand. Seddon Group also operates Winget, a maker of site dumpers and cement mixers, and Seddon District Garage Limited, which provides automobile repair services as well as sales of used light commercial vehicles. Last, Seddon Group has entered the rapidly growing British market for private daycare facilities, through its Nu Nu Ltd. subsidiary. Seddon Group, now under the leadership of the fourth generation of the founding Seddon family, posted sales of £291 million ($521 million) in 2003. In 2004, the group moved to new headquarters in Bolton, Lancashire.

Laying the Foundation at the End of the 19th Century

Brothers George and John Seddon laid the foundation for the future Seddon Group when they went into business together as bricklayers in 1897. The brothers at first focused on their local market in Little Hulton, in Worsley. Over the following decades, however, the Seddons gained a reputation for quality work, and gradually expanded their range of operations to the Manchester area and later throughout the British northwestern region. By 1920, the company's growth led it to incorporate formally as G&J Seddon Limited.

At first, the Seddon company focused on bricklaying, becoming one of the region's most prominent and well respected businesses. Seddon's extension into full-scale construction began in the early 1930s, with the formation of a second company, J&S Seddon (Building) Limited, founded in the Potteries in 1932. The company soon began competing for large-scale public housing and public works projects, winning a large number of projects through the 1940s and 1950s. Government contracts,

Company Perspectives:

Company Vision: As a long established, traditional family owned construction Company, G & J Seddon Limited is planning for the future. Building on our financial stability and proven track record we will identify new opportunities to deliver quality buildings and services for the benefit of our customers and employees. We will maintain our valued workforce of highly qualified and well motivated professionals, providing sustainable employment, training and professional development. Our long term future will be secured by generating profitable business. Using modern management techniques and the latest thinking in construction will ensure that we enhance our position as a leading contractor within the industry.

Key Dates:

1897: George and John Seddon begin a bricklaying business in Little Hulton, near Manchester, England.
1920: The company is incorporated as G&J Seddon Limited.
1932: The contract construction business, J&S Seddon, is created.
1951: The plant engineering business, Seddons (Plant & Engineers) Ltd., is created; a branch office in Stoke-on-Trent is opened.
1957: The Stoke-on-Trent office becomes a separate subsidiary, Seddon Stoke.
1958: The District Garage, providing automotive service and used vehicle sales, is established.
1968: Jotcham & Kendall, originally founded in 1680, is acquired.
1982: The Seddon Group is created as a holding company for family businesses.
1986: Winget, manufacturer of site dumpers and cement mixers, is acquired.
1989: Viceroy Developments, a multi-site developer, is created.
1992: Seddon Homes, a developer of residential homes, is launched; Chestergate Seddon is launched.
1999: The company enters project management with the creation of Chestergate Health; the company enters the nursery and daycare business with Nu Nu Ltd.
2001: The property conversion subsidiary Seddon Regeneration Ltd. is created.
2004: The company moves to new headquarters in Bolton.

including from national, regional, and local governments, remained a mainstay of the Seddon company's operations into the next century. During this period, John Seddon's three sons joined the company and eventually took over its leadership.

The new generation also saw opportunities for further growth for the company. In the 1950s, Seddon began to expand both geographically and through diversifying its operations. By the beginning of that decade, the company had opened its first branch office, in Stoke-on-Trent. The company grew rapidly in that market as well, and by 1957 the Stoke office was established as a separate company, Seddon Stoke.

Meanwhile, Seddon had been developing a side business in plant engineering. In the late 1940s and early 1950s the company began operating an auxiliary site in Bolton providing plant services, including parts, maintenance, and repairs, for its growing fleet of construction vehicles and its growing inventory of construction equipment. By 1951, that operation had been developed into a full-fledged company, Seddons (Plant & Engineers) Ltd., which then began providing plant and fleet services to the wider Bolton construction market.

The Plant Engineering subsidiary soon developed into an important part of Seddon's business. Over the following decades, Seddon expanded the company, establishing a national network and becoming a major player in its sector in the United Kingdom. As part of that expansion, Seddon also began manufacturing its own construction equipment, marketed under the Seddon Johnson brand. A similar extension to the company's business came in 1958. In that year, the company launched an automotive repair business, District Garage in Bolton. That business also began selling used light commercial vehicles.

Regrouping in the 1980s

Seddon's first external growth move came in the late 1960s, with the acquisition of Jotcham & Kendall in 1968. That company traced its origins back to 1680, when John and Richard Jotcham were employed to work on the St. James Church in Charfield, near Wotton-under-Edge. The Jotcham family remained in the building trade into the 1900s. In the 1930s, then company head Harry Jotcham began working in an association with a local architect, Kendall. The pair formed a partnership,

and the company became known as Jotcham & Kendall. Placed under Seddon's J&S Seddon building contractors operation, Jotcham & Kendall remained one of the United Kingdom's oldest operating building companies.

A new generation of Seddons—John, George, Christopher, and David—arrived to take the helm of the company, with John Seddon assuming the chairman's spot in 1979. The third generation was to expand the family business significantly over the next two decades. By the 2000s, Seddon emerged as one of the United Kingdom's leading family-controlled construction groups. As part of that process, the company restructured its various holdings in 1982, creating a single holding company, Seddon Group.

The 1980s proved a time of significant expansion for the company—at least until the crash of the U.K. housing and construction markets at the end of the decade. Among Seddon's growth moves during this period was its acquisition of Winget in 1986. Winget, a leading U.K. manufacturer of site dumpers and cement mixers, enhanced the group's plant engineering operation with its strong brand name.

In the late 1980s, the company continued its restructuring, placing its J&S Seddon (Building) operation under Seddon Stoke. That business was joined by the company's rapidly growing painting operation, J&S Seddon (Painting) Ltd. Another company launched that year was the multi-site developer Viceroy Developments. Seddon's operation now included not only its core contract construction business, but a fast-growing speculative development segment as well.

Fourth-Generation Family Business in the 2000s

Despite the crisis in the construction and housing sectors in the early 1990s, Seddon continued to grow, in part by seeking out new areas of operations. Seddon extended its development business to the residential homes sector, launching Seddon Homes in 1992. The company, formed in Sandbach, Cheshire, targeted the higher end of the new home market. Another development vehicle, Chestergate Seddon, was formed in 1992, followed by Seddon Waterfold in 1994.

Seddon also joined the trend among building groups to provide services beyond traditional construction activities. The company began offering project management service in 1999. The new operation was placed into a new subsidiary, Chestergate Health Ltd.

In that year, as well, Seddon entered another promising field, that of the construction and operation of private nursery and daycare facilities. That sector, fueled by the buoyant British economy, experienced rapid growth in the early 2000s.

Seddon spotted another growth opportunity in the early 2000s, that of the renovation of existing homes and the conversion of existing buildings into residential properties. In 2001, the company created a new subsidiary for this business, Seddon Regeneration Ltd.

By then, Seddon had introduced the fourth generation of Seddons—Stuart, Jonathan, and Steve—into the company's leadership. With its operations now reaching across most of England and Wales, Seddon had outgrown its original Little Hulton site. In 2004, the company moved to new headquarters in nearby Bolton, which also permitted the company to group most of its operations, including the plant and engineering, District Garage, and Winget businesses in a single location. Seddon had laid a strong foundation for success in the new century.

Principal Subsidiaries

Chestergate Seddon Ltd.; District Garage Ltd.; G&J Seddon Ltd.; Seddon (Stoke) Ltd.; J&S Seddon (Building); J&S Seddon (Painting); Jotcham & Kendall Ltd.; Seddon Homes Ltd.; Seddons (Plant & Engineers) Ltd.; Winget Ltd.

Principal Competitors

George Wimpey PLC; Taylor Woodrow PLC; Barratt Developments PLC; Kier Group PLC; Berkeley Group PLC; Tarmac Ltd.

Further Reading

"First Sale for Seddon," *This Is Lancashire,* November 11, 2003.
Jones, David, "Firm's £16m Contract for University Facelift," *Daily Post,* February 22, 2002, p. 20.
"Major Office Scheme Launched," *This Is Lancashire,* August 15, 2003.
"Seddon Snaps Up Contractor," *Contract Flooring Journal,* June 2003, p. 24.

—M.L. Cohen

Sideco Americana S.A.

Carlos Maria Della Paciera 299
Buenos Aires, C.F. C1001ADA
Argentina
Telephone: (54) (11) 4319-3800
Fax: (54) (11) 4319-3860
Web site: http://www.sideco.com.ar

Public Company
Incorporated: 1961 as Demaco S.A.
Employees: 2,900
Sales: ARS 759.58 million ($257.48 million) (2003)
Stock Exchanges: Bolsa de Comercio de Buenos Aires
Ticker Symbol: SIDE
NAIC: 221111 Hydroelectric Power Generation; 221112
    Fossil Fuel Electric Power Generation; 221121
    Electric Bulk Power Transmission and Control;
    221210 Natural Gas Distribution; 221320 Sewage
    Treatment Facilities; 236116 New Multi-Family
    Housing Construction (Except Operative Builders);
    488490 Other Support Activities for Road
    Transportation; 541330 Engineering Services; 551112
    Offices of Other Holding Companies; 562111 Solid
    Waste Collection; 562212 Solid Waste Landfills

Sideco Americana S.A. is an Argentine holding company engaged in public services and infrastructure development, by means of subsidiaries and affiliates, in five areas: engineering and construction, toll roads and highways, environmental services, generation and transmission of electricity, and real estate development. It is the largest enterprise in Socma (Sociedad Macri S.A.), the holding company established by Francisco Macri, an Italian immigrant who rose from poverty to become one of Argentina's wealthiest men. As the nation's economy has weakened, Sideco has increasingly turned to Brazil for business.

Construction Firm and Public Works Contractor: 1961–89

Francisco Macri was born in 1930 in Rome and emigrated from there with his brother and sister to Argentina in 1949,

where they reunited with their father, who had settled earlier in Buenos Aires. Francisco found work as a bricklayer and studied engineering at night for two years. During the mid-1950s he became a subcontractor for construction jobs and road work, and in 1961 he and two others established Demaco S.A., a construction firm that built small homes cheaply. Demaco's big break was a contract to build the structures that housed pressure pumps for a gas pipeline stretching between Patagonia and Buenos Aires. Next, Demaco became a subcontractor for Impresit, a subsidiary of Fiat Argentina S.A. that was making silos in Mar de Plata. The company took the name Impresit Sideco (standing for silos of Demaco) in 1969.

Between 1971 and 1979 Impresit Sideco and other Macri companies took part in more than 30 public works projects expending a total of $1.8 billion. Its construction work included a bridge between Argentina and Paraguay and several residential towers in Buenos Aires. Eventually it was renamed Sideco Americana S.A. By 1976, when various Macri companies were placed within the holding company Sociedad Macri (Socma), Sideco was active in several South American countries, participating in industrial projects. Manliba S.A. and Aseo S.A., which would later be integrated into Sideco, were involved in sanitation projects, and Iecsa S.A., also later integrated into Sideco, was assembling electromechanical devices and instruments. By 1985 Sideco ranked 53rd in size among Argentine enterprises. Economic recession in the late 1980s, however, created deficits that significantly reduced its opportunities to gain government contracts for the public construction work that was its bread and butter.

Benefiting from Privatization in the 1990s

The years following the election of Carlos Menem to the presidency in 1989 brought about an enormous change in Argentina's economy. Sideco and other units of the Macri empire took an active part in the bidding for state-owned enterprises being privatized by the new administration. By means of several strategic alliances formed to bid on public sector concessions, Sideco acquired, in 1990, the right to operate and maintain a system of toll roads through Servicios Viales S.A. Concesionaria de Rutas por Peaje, a 77 percent-owned subsidiary that took in three highways north of Buenos Aires. Upgrading of the 1,173-

Key Dates:

1961: Demaco S.A., a builder of small homes, is founded.
1969: Demaco becomes Impresit Sideco, a firm building silos in Mar del Plata.
1976: Now Sideco Americana, the firm is working on many large-scale public works projects.
1990: Sideco wins the right to operate and maintain a system of Argentine toll roads.
1992: Sideco takes a stake in three natural gas distribution companies but later sells out; the company begins a residential housing development.
1994: Sideco becomes Argentina's largest toll road operator; the company holds shares in four privatized electrical transmission and distribution companies; the company acquires four companies involved in garbage and industrial waste collection, in addition to Iecsa, which provides engineering and construction services.
1997: Sideco has grown sixfold since 1992 and has 14 subsidiaries; the company takes a majority stake in the nation's privatized postal service.
1999: With the addition of Correo Argentino, Sideco's revenues reach $1.6 billion a year.
2000: Debt-ridden Correo Argentino stops making concession payments to the government.
2002: Sideco defaults on its debts, which are restructured the following year.
2003: Correo Argentino is seized and renationalized by the government.

kilometer (729-mile) network by the concession partners was completed in 1996. In 1994, Sideco took a one-third interest in Autopistas del Sol S.A. and thereby became Argentina's largest toll highway concessionaire. Autopistas del Sol, the busiest single such concession, encompassed the chief peripheral route bypassing Buenos Aires. Sideco also built a toll bridge extending over the Paraná River east of Rosario. A few years later Sideco's Brazilian subsidiary won a concession to build, maintain, and operate toll roads in the state of Paraná, and in 2000 it signed a contract to do the same in the state of Sao Paulo.

In 1992, Sideco entered the privatized field of natural gas distribution by taking a stake in three companies, but it reduced its interests in this field in 1997 and sold its shares in the three to Societé Italiana per il Gas S.p.A. for $182.5 million in 2000. Sideco was and remained involved, however, in the privatized electrical power market through various consortiums formed to obtain concessions to construct, operate, and maintain transmission and generation facilities. Between 1991 and 1994 it took shares in four such companies, the most important being Lineas de Transmisión del Litoral S.A. (Litsa), and Central Térmica San Miguel de Tucumán S.A. In addition, through Profingas S.A., it agreed in 1998 to construct a natural gas pipeline—later completed—that would distribute natural gas to certain municipalities in the state of Cordoba.

Sideco's participation in providing municipal solid waste and industrial waste services dated back to 1983 but gained

impetus in 1994, when it acquired from Socma the latter's holdings in Manliba, Aseo, Saframa S.A., and Transmetro S.A. Manliba, the most important, was, until 1997, the concessionaire for the largest portion of the garbage collected in Buenos Aires. As part of a strategy of intensifying its activity in industrial waste services and expanding to the area of hazardous waste services, Sideco, in late 1995, began operating industrial waste management services in Brazil through an indirect interest in Sistemas Ambientais Comercio Ltda. (Sasa). By 1997 Sideco was conducting its waste management businesses jointly with a subsidiary of Waste Management, Inc., the world's leading company in the field in terms of revenue. This subsidiary, Waste Management International, purchased, with Sideco Americana, 80 percent of Enterpa Ambiental S.A., Brazil's largest solid waste collection and disposal company, in 1998. This company, which later became Qualix Servicios Ambientales (and still later Qualix S.A.) was responsible for 30 percent of garbage collection and 50 percent of sanitary fill in Sao Paulo, Brazil's largest city. In 2000 Sideco exchanged its share of Sasa for Waste Management's stake in the company controlling Enterpa.

Also in 1994, Sideco acquired Socma's interest in Iecsa. This subsidiary, now engaged in the design, construction, and maintenance of industrial plants, telecommunications projects, highways, and other projects requiring the joint application of basic and integrated engineering, had dedicated itself to the telecommunications sector but, beginning in 1995, diversified its activities to include a focus on oil, gas, petrochemicals, refineries, and other high-technology construction. It also continued to engage in telecommunications construction in Chile, where it became active in 1990. In addition, to capitalize on favorable conditions of economic stability and increased credit availability, Sideco selectively extended its activities to housing development between 1992 and 1996, when it established Creaurbán S.A. By the end of 1999 this subsidiary had completed three residential projects in the Buenos Aires metropolitan area and was at work on three more.

The transformation of Sideco Americana into a concessionaire required better management and a break with corporate culture geared to deal with one client only—the state. Speaking to Rasul Ferro of *America economia* in 1997, Executive Vice-President Luis Graziani said, "At the highest management levels there were very few functionaries of the traditional structure of the construction enterprise that had the elasticity to adapt themselves to the new reality. . . . Today, Sideco's clients are people, they have faces, they have names, they have complaints, they demand quality. A gigantic change of mentality was needed. . . . There were moments in which one had to cut loose people who had been with the enterprise for many years; this creates traumatic situations, generates doubts, instability." The period of transition lasted for about a year and a half. By 1997 Sideco was a conglomerate with 14 subsidiaries and annual revenue of about $600 million, or six times its size in 1992.

During 1997 Socma entered a new field by taking a 73.5 percent share of a 30-year concession to operate Empresa Nacional de Correos y Telegrafos S.A. (Encotesa), the national postal service. What was described as "peripheral privatization" had, since about 1980, eliminated Encotesa's more profitable areas, leaving annual revenues approaching $500 million, but also more than 20,000 employees to pay, an operating deficit of $23.2 million in 1996, and a debt of $258 million. Nevertheless, Socma and its partners agreed to pay $103.2 million a year for the concession to operate the system, which was renamed Correo Argentino S.A. Sideco took a one-third share of the enterprise, while Itron S.A., a Socma company founded in 1983 and dedicated to information and communications, took 40 percent.

Itron soon turned over its holding in Correo Argentino to Sideco. The new company inherited about 1,500 branches and some 4,000 other points of sale in other locations, and it pledged to spend $250 million upgrading postal service, including installing a new British-imported system expected to save postal workers at least an hour a day in manual sorting and a new processing facility—which was built at a cost of $40 million—outside Buenos Aires to handle 85 percent of the mail. It also pledged to establish a new telecommunications network to integrate the branches in order to allow them to offer services such as telegrams via the Internet and instant money transfers (through an existing Sideco service, Pago Fácil). Among Correo Argentino's technological innovations were a web site for writing and distributing messages and software that allowed small businesses and professionals to send, by personal computer, formatted documents. The former outside points of sale were converted to franchised units offering most postal services in such locations as copy shops, bookstores, and telephone kiosks. Correo Argentino also franchised space in its branches for the sale of books, stationery, office supplies, gift and philately items, and special services.

Postal and Other 21st-Century Woes

Sideco had consolidated sales of $999.2 million in 1998, when it recorded net income of $26.2 million. With the addition of Correo Argentino, revenue reached $1.6 billion a year. Sideco's debt ballooned, however, from $176.2 million at the end of 1997 to $692.5 million in September 1999 as Correo Argentino remained submerged in red ink, even though labor costs had been reduced by cutting employment to 13,000. The company lost about $50 million in 1997 and continued to lose money in subsequent years. Macri tried vainly to persuade the government to renegotiate the concession contract and finally stopped making payments in 2000, when a new, unfriendly administration had taken power.

Three days before leaving office in December 1999, Menem had awarded to Correo Argentino all of the nation's Internet domains, in return for an annual payment of $50 million. The incoming president annulled this measure and also wounded Sideco by cutting highway tolls by 8 percent. His successor refused to allow Correo Argentino to merge with Organización Coordinadora Argentina (Oca), its chief competitor. The company was seized in November 2003 for nonpayment of debt and renationalized. Another blow to Sideco at this time was the termination of the Servicios Viales toll road concession. In addition, Macri's son Mauricio failed in his bid to become mayor of Buenos Aires, losing to a candidate backed by President Nestor Kirchner.

When Argentina defaulted on its debts in late 2001, the value of the national currency, formerly at parity with the dollar, fell to less than 30 cents. Sideco's dollar-denominated debt suddenly increased by more than threefold, leading to a similar default. With the national economy in deep recession, all of Sideco's important Argentine holdings lost money in 2002, as did Qualix in Brazil, in which Sideco held a 48 percent stake. The company made a profit, however, on its Brazilian road concessions. Also in that year it took a 34 percent share in Socma Alimentos do Brasil Ltda., a food products manufacturer. In addition, Iecsa had secured a share of private telecommunication systems in southern Brazil. By this time some 65 percent of Sideco's revenue was coming from Brazil.

With the loss of Correo Argentino, Sideco's revenues for 2003 fell from ARS 1.23 billion ($416.95 million) to ARS 759.58 million ($257.48 million). Of this total, the company's Brazilian enterprises accounted for 63 percent. Sideco lost ARS 286 million ($96.9 million), but this sum was about a third less than in 2002, and its long-term debt was reduced by a restructuring agreement with its creditors, followed by an issue of new debentures in 2004. Seemingly unfazed by its troubles, the company was seeking to win contracts for such infrastructure projects as roadwork in Bolivia and the construction of high-tension electricity lines between Bolivia and Brazil. Sideco executives traveled to China in the summer of 2004 to seek financing for such projects.

Principal Subsidiaries

Aseo S.A. (89%); Creaurbán S.A.; Iecsa S.A. (98%); Manliba S.A. (89%); Profingas S.A. (98%); Saframa S.A.; Servicios Viales (77%); Sideco Brasil Ltda. (Brazil; 67%); Urugua-I S.A. (50.2%).

Further Reading

Biacchi, Mario, "El cartero electronico," *Mercado,* September 1997, pp. 95–96.
Canton, Marcelo, "El Correo recorto sueldos por 650.000 pesos mensuales," *Clarín,* November 30, 2003, p. 18.
Esquivel, Natacha, "Macri cambia de perfil," *Mercado,* January 2000, pp. 56–58, 60.
Ferro, Raul, "Demoler y reconstruir," *América economia,* July, 1997, pp. 40, 42, 44.
Friedland, Jonathan, "Argentina's Macri Takes on Post Office," *Wall Street Journal,* September 8, 1997, p. A15.
Galeano, Pablo, "Franquicias en estereo," *Apertura,* August 2000, pp. 23–25.
Majul, Luis, *Los dueños de la Argentina* (5th ed.), Buenos Aires: Editorial Sudamerica, 5th ed., 1995.
Mandel-Campbell, Andrea, "Putting a New Stamp on the Postal Service," *Financial Times,* September 10, 1998, p. 24.
Pipano, Pablo, "Un cartero del siglo XXI," *Mercado,* June 2001, pp. 73, 75.
"Postales argentinas," *Mercado,* July 1997, pp. 75–76, 78.
"Socma: Treinta anos despues," *Mercado,* July 15, 1982, pp. 54–55.
Stok, Gustavo, "Macri, otra vez," *América economia,* September 10–23, 2004, p. 19.

—Robert Halasz

Skalli Group

46 avenue Kleber
F-75116 Paris
France
Telephone: 33 (1) 56 26 12 00
Fax: 33 (1) 56 26 12 09
Web site: http://www.vinskalli.com

Private Company
Founded: 1964
Sales: $482.8 million (2003)
NAIC: 311422 Specialty Canning; 311823 Dry Pasta
Manufacturing; 312130 Wineries

Skalli Group, one of the pioneers in producing branded varietally labeled wines, has been in the grain and wine business for three generations. Beginning in the late 1970s, the company began to organize the planting of new Languedoc varieties such as chardonnay and cabernet sauvignon. In southern France, the Skalli Group owns Les Vins Skalli whose brands are Fortant, Reserve F, and Robert Skalli varietals. In the United States, the Skalli Group owns St. Supery Vineyards & Winery.

1930s–70s: An Empire in Grain and Wine

The Skalli story begins in Algeria, near Oran, in the 1930s with Robert-Elie Skalli. The Skallis were *pieds noirs* French vineyardists, who first came to Algeria after phylloxrea devastated French vineyards in the 1870s. Robert Skalli built an empire in grain and wine. He established Rivoire et Carret, one of Europe's largest producers of cereal products, and purchased a flour mill in Marseilles and several wine cellars in France, including one in Sete. Skalli also began planting South-of-France varietal grapes such as carignane, alicante, grenache, and cinsault in Algeria and adapted vinification methods to take into account the North African climate.

By 1938, Algeria had close to a million acres of vineyards. By the 1950s, France depended heavily on Algerian vineyards for its everyday blended red table wines. After World War II,

Robert-Elie's son, Francis, took over operations of the family business (which included Rivoire et Carret; Lustucru, France's second largest pasta company; Taureau Aile rice; and a vineyard in Corsica) and began blending vines from the Oran vineyards with those from Mostaganem. In 1944, he established some of his own Algerian vineyards. By 1964, these vineyards totaled more than 600,000 acres, and Francis Skalli had begun a producer-partnership with other growers that prefigured his son's cooperative relationship with growers in France two decades later.

The Algerian war of independence eventually caused the *pieds noirs* to leave the country and return to Europe. The Skalli family relocated to the Languedoc region of southern France in 1964, the year that Francis Skalli died and two years after Algeria gained its independence.

Languedoc-Roussillon stretches along the Mediterranean coast approximately from Provence westward to the Spanish border. It is a huge vineyard area, comprising 400,000 hectares or about one million acres of cultivated land. But, by the end of the 1970s, the Languedoc region of France was producing inferior wines. Until 1982, the Skalli cellar in Sete purchased cheap, local wines that it used for blending *vins de table*.

Robert Skalli, son of Francis, took over the family's food conglomerate in 1975. In 1977, he traveled to California to study with some of the state's top winemakers—Robert Mondavi, Michael Reno of Domaine Chandon, and Bernard Portet of Claude Duval. California winemakers had pioneered the concept of varietals in the 1950s and 1960s in order to set themselves apart from France, and to avoid being sued for using a French regional name for their wine. Skalli's visit to California convinced him that varietal wines were viable in France. He began to view the Languedoc as a new world wine region.

1980s–90s: A New Base of Business in Varietal Wines

After the European Union took action to dry up the Languedoc, offering growers premiums for ripping up their grapes and abandoning viniculture, Skalli organized dozens of meetings. He convinced winegrowers in the departments of Aude, Herault, Gard, and Pyrenees-Orientales to tear up their inferior wines and replant their vineyards with cultivars then in demand—Cabernet Sauvignon, Merlot, and Chardonnay—to produce clean, sound wines at affordable prices. "We were pretty convincing," he recalled in a 1999 *Wall Street Journal* article. "We said, 'What's your market? The European Community, which accounts for 30 percent of your business, buys your wine for distillation. One day, after the surplus wines have been ripped up, the European Community will stop buying your wine because it will have found a balance between offer and demand. So you'll make *vin de table* at cut-rate prices, which interests nobody and which will no longer be subsidized by the European Community.' "

French tradition dictates that a wine be named after its region of origin instead of the grapes from which it was made (chablis instead of chardonnay). But Skalli named his wines in the New World way. "I discovered varietal wines with Robert Mondavi one afternoon in 1972 at age 22," Skalli explained in a 1998 *Toronto Sun* article. Varietals were more sophisticated than *vins de table*, but less subtle than high-end *appellation d'origine controlée* (AOC) wines; they became France's new mid-range market.

Skalli started with three growers and a cooperative. Initially his replanting project suspended production for three years, during which time Skalli Fortant, Skalli's wine division, provided support to growers through financing. Grower contracts took one of three forms: a one-year contract to explore the potential for a long-term relationship; a five-year agreement specifying grape variety and cultivation techniques; or a ten-year exclusive contract putting production under Fortant's direction and access. In 1983, the company introduced its Fortant varietals. By 1999, Skalli, working with 150 growers, including half a dozen coops, exported 65 percent of his wine to 25 countries.

In 1981, the company began looking for Napa Valley land to expand its vineyards, and in 1982 Skalli purchased the Dollarhide Ranch in Pope Valley for $3 million. By 1986, Skalli's new World vineyards were producing a limited supply of wine. The company released its first Atkinson Manor wine in 1989. The Dollarhide Ranch later became the St. Supery Vineyards & Winery. When complete, the St. Supery Wine Discovery Centre had a self-directed tour in a one-acre demonstration vineyard where visitors could pick leaves and taste grapes.

Beginning in the mid-1980s, many millions of bottles of varietal wines from Languedoc-Roussillon began to arrive in the United States. The Languedoc's economies of scale, fertile

soils, and favorable climate meant that these wines were priced extremely competitively. In the late 1980s, Skalli S.A. entered the wine business as a *negociant*, or broker, producing 600,000 cases of varietal wines a year, cabernet sauvignons, chardonnays, merlots, sauvignon blancs and syrahs, under the Fortant de France label. In 1987, the French *Institut National des Appellation d'Origine* created the "Vin de Pays d'Oc" appellation for varietal wines from the Languedoc. Vins de Pays are several ranks below AOC and subject to less stringent regulations.

In 1992, Fortant de France wines arrived on the Australian market. From 1993 to 1998, French sales of varietals went from six million to 29 million cases, and, while overall wine consumption in France was down, domestic sales of varietals jumped 44 percent from 1994 to 1995 and increased an additional 30 percent in 1996. Fortant de France was the leader among French varietal wines by 1998, with 30 percent of the market and $80 million in sales. The company exported 65 percent of its production to 25 countries.

2000s: A Focus on the Medium- and High-Quality Wine Market

By 2000, *vins de cépage*, or varietals, comprised the fastest growing segment of the French wine market. Production had nearly tripled during the 1990s, leaping to 51.2 million gallons from 5.5 million gallons. Fortant de France had reached 2.5 million cases in sales in its first ten years (from 1987 to 1997). Skalli employed a team of enologists and agronomists and had two vinification cellars and a barrel-aging cellar. In 2000, it was the fourth largest company in the Skalli Group.

In the new millennium, Skalli Group determined to focus its business on wine and abandon its other division. After acquiring the distribution networks of Caves de Notre-Dame and those of wine dealer Sefivins in Chateauneuf-du-Pape in 2001, Skalli Group announced its intended restructuring with plans to sell its pasta and rice businesses. Panzani, the leading French pasta group, bought the fresh pasta, sauces, and rice business of Lustucru, France's number one fresh pasta and rice company in 2002; however, owing to a ruling by France's competition authority, the dry pasta, semolina, and couscous business had to remain in the hands of the Skalli Group. This business became part of a new company, Pasta Corp.

The company also embarked upon its strategy to make Skalli wines a major player in France's medium- and high-quality wines market. This plan began with the withdrawal of Skalli's wines from supermarkets, making them available only in restaurants and specialty wine shops. It also focused on sale of its branded wines in the United Kingdom in 2002 in an attempt to increase the French share of the British wine market, and on its direct-to-consumer sales in the United States.

By 2003, Skalli had 2,500 hectares of vineyards under contract. It comprised approximately 150 growers working 17,500 acres of vineyards, six coops, and exported 65 percent of its wine, marketed under the Fortant de France (renamed Fortant in 2004), Robert Skalli, and F brands, to 25 countries.

As consumers and producers had become more confident, the company's range of experimentation had broadened. To

original chardonnay, cabernet sauvignon, cabernet blanc, and merlot, and the company looked forward to continued growth and marketing new wines.

Key Dates:	
1964:	The Skalli family relocates to southern France.
1975:	Robert Skalli takes over the family business.
1977:	Robert Skalli studies wine-making in California.
1981:	Skalli purchases the St. Supery Vineyards in Napa Valley.
1987:	''Vin de Pays d'Oc'' appellation is created; Fortant de France label is launched.
1990:	Skalli renovates its aging cellars.
1998:	Skalli introduces its premium varietals in the United States.
2003:	Phillippe Giraudon takes over general management of Vins Skalli; Robert Skalli assumes oversight of Groupe Skalli Family Wines.
2004:	Fortant de France changes its name to Fortant.

Principal Subsidiaries

Skalli-Fortant de France UK Limited.

Further Reading

Braude, Jonathan, ''Panzani Adds Pasta Helping,'' *Daily Deal*, September 14, 2002.

''French Grapes Fill Thirsty Niche,'' *New York Daily News*, October 15, 1999, p. 84.

Friedrich, Jaqueline, ''New Wine in Old Vineyards,'' *Wall Street Journal*, March 26, 1999, p. 13.

——, ''One Man's Brave New World of Wine,'' *Wall Street Journal*, February 9, 1999, p. 1.

Frost, M., ''Trust the French Winemakers to Move in on a Good Aussie Tradition,'' *Courier Mail*, June 20, 1998, p. 6.

Simmell, Gordon, ''Skalli Unveils Premium Wines,'' *Toronto Sun*, June 21, 1998, p. 76.

Thomas, Dana, and Rana Dogar, ''It's All in the Grapes,'' *Newsweek*, September 7, 1998, p. 46.

''Variety Is the Spice of Life,'' *Off License News*, June 13, 2003, p. 12.

—Carrie Rothburd

accommodate this expansion, in 2003 the company underwent reorganization: Phillippe Giraudon took over general management of Vins Skalli, while Robert Skalli assumed oversight of Skalli Group Family Wines, producer of premium cabernet and chardonnay from top growers. By 2004, grapes such as syrah, grenache, muscat, viognier, and mourvedre had joined the

Société Norbert Dentressangle S.A.

BP 98, Les Pierelles, Beausembla
Saint Vallier sur Rhone
F-26241 Cedex
France
Telephone: +33 4 75 23 25 26
Fax: +33 4 75 03 18 7733 4 75 23 22 20
Web site: http://www.norbert-dentressangle.com

Public Company
Incorporated: 1978
Employees: 11,750
Sales: EUR 1.22 billion ($1.5 billion) (2003)
Stock Exchanges: Euronext Paris
Ticker Symbol: GND
NAIC: 484121 General Freight Trucking, Long-Distance,
    Truckload

Société Norbert Dentressangle S.A., named after the company's founder, is one of France's top three freight trucking and logistics groups. The group has a decidedly international focus, with fully 65 percent of its traffic serving foreign destinations. The English Channel has long been a central part of Norbert Dentressangle's operations, and at 650 crossings daily, the company is the leading European company on this route. Positioned in the United Kingdom since 1978, Dentressangle is also one of the top two transporters in that market. Norbert Dentressangle serves most of Western Europe through its network of 190 agencies and fleet of more than 4,500 tractors. The company also has been expanding its operations to include the new Eastern Europe members of the European Union. Nonetheless, France remains the company's primary market, accounting for 56 percent of its revenues, which topped EUR 1.2 billion ($1.5 billion) in 2003. Transporting of conditioned goods represents 61 percent of the company's sales. Since the early 2000s, Norbert Dentressangle has adopted a strategy of expansion into the logistics services sector. The company has grown rapidly in this area, and by the end of 2003, logistics services, including warehousing and fleet rentals, accounted for 39 percent of the company's sales and much of the company's revenue growth.

Norbert Dentressangle is listed on the Euronext Paris stock exchange. The Dentressangle family remains primary shareholder, controlling nearly 68 percent of the stock; the company's employees own an additional 28 percent of the company's shares. Norbert Dentressangle continues to be led by founder and Chairman Norbert Dentressangle.

Channel Transport Pioneer in the 1970s

Georges and Therese Dentressangle established a small trucking firm in France's Ardeche region shortly after World War II. In 1966, the couple moved the business to the town of Saint Vallier, in the Rhone Valley region not far from Lyons.

The Dentressangles were joined by their son, Norbert, in 1974. As Dentressangle himself told *L'Entreprise:* "They pushed me to join the business rather than starting a long course of study." The younger Dentressangle proved a natural at organizing transport traffic and working with the company's clientele. Into the mid-1970s, Dentressangle had become interested in developing the family company's international business—and the potential held in the growing demand from England for the wines and cheese and other products of the Rhone Valley.

By the end of the decade, Dentressangle set himself a new objective: that of becoming a leading transporter across the English Channel. In order to put this plan in action, Dentressangle went to England in 1978, and established ND European Transport in the Leytonstone section of east London. Rather than place his parents' business at risk, Dentressangle set up the new company as a separate operation.

From the outset, Dentressangle was determined to develop his company into the leading transporter connecting the French and British markets. As Dentressangle told the *Financial Times:* "I understood that the market for commercial exchanges between different countries, especially between the UK and France, was an important development." Elaborating, he said, "I understood that the market was difficult because of the insularity of the UK and the geographic barrier. Also there was an imbalance of trade in the two directions with much more traffic moving towards the UK. That is why I created my first

Company Perspectives:

With 180 agencies in Europe, all operating to the same quality standards, Groupe Norbert Dentressangle has a truly European network and can provide you with: a broad range of transport possibilities to and from every country in Europe; ideal logistics solutions for every country.

company in the UK: to build up market share for the return journey.'' Yet developing the market proved difficult, as Dentressangle continued: ''At the beginning, it was very difficult, we needed a lot of tenacity and courage—but the UK is a country with which it is very interesting to work.''

By 1979, Dentressangle had decided to focus his business on a route connecting Saint Vallier and London. For this, he created a second business, Société Norbert Dentressangle, in Saint Vallier. The new company then took over the fleet and operations of the original family-owned company. Dentressangle also set out to build an agency network, bringing his fleet closer to potential customers. Focusing at first on the market for conditioned products, especially fruits and vegetables from France to England, Dentressangle began expanding the fleet in the 1980s to offer built tanker and refrigerated transports as well. The company also began offering storage and warehousing services, opening its first warehouse in Saint Rambert d'Albon, also near Lyons. By 1988, the company's sales had topped FRF 800 million (approximately $125 million).

Rapid Growth in the 1990s

The run up to European economic unification and the prospect of the elimination of trade barriers slated for 1992 led to the first wave of consolidation in the heavily fragmented European trucking and logistics sectors in the late 1980s. Dentressangle quickly positioned itself as one of the more ambitious consolidators, and in 1988 the company launched its first series of acquisitions.

In that year the company acquired Saint Uze-based Romulus, then Philibert & Sylvestre, based in Chanas. Yet these proved the first of many purchases completed over that year and the next, and included Volutrans, Bianco, and Bellmas, among others. By 1990, the company had topped FRF 1 billion in revenues.

Dentressangle's acquisition drive continued into the early 1990s as it moved to build on its growing status as a French and European trucking leader. By 1993, the company had completed some 25 acquisitions, boosting its sales to nearly FRF 2 billion. Among the company's most important purchases during this period was its acquisition of Translittoral, which specialized in trucking across the English Channel. With that purchase, Dentressangle established its position as the leading cross-channel trucking group, with 85,000 crosses per year.

The opening of the Channel Tunnel in 1994 gave another boost to the company, which boasted of becoming the first to send a truck through the tunnel. By the end of the decade, the company's Channel Tunnel business included more than 650 crossings per day. Unlike many of its competitors, which preferred to focus on ferry crossings, Dentressangle embraced the new connection between the French and British coasts, and shifted a large percentage of its traffic to the Channel Tunnel link.

Dentressangle went public in 1994, listing its shares on the Paris Stock Exchange's secondary market. The Dentressangle family nonetheless maintained strong control of the group, through its holding company Financiere Dentressangle, which maintained close to two-thirds of the group's shares. Another major shareholding block was formed by the company's employees, some 42 percent of which acquired shares. Altogether, the employee shareholders represented another 28 percent of the group's stock.

Changing Focus in the New Century

The latter half of the 1990s saw Norbert Dentressangle grow along two complementary lines. The first of these was the group's decision to enter the logistics sector—itself fast converging with the trucking sector as more companies sought to provide a broader scale of services to companies seeking to outsource more and more of their warehousing, transportation, and distribution needs. In 1995, Norbert Dentressangle set up its own dedicated logistics division.

Dentressangle's extension into logistics went hand in hand with its other major growth initiative—that of developing a truly European network of operations. From its leading position on the French and British route, and its leading position as a trucking operator within both national markets, Dentressangle began building up a European-wide presence. The company moved south, to Portugal, establishing subsidiary ND Portugal in 1995. The company also strengthened its operations in the United Kingdom that year, acquiring OTA International, serving western England, and Sheddick Transport, based in Wales. The following year, Dentressangle added Freeflag in England as well.

Spain came within the company's sphere of operations with the acquisition of Navamar in 1996. The company also began its first shipments to the Eastern Europe markets that year. In France, the company acquired Confluent and UTL the following year, a move that boosted the company into the top ranks of the country's transport logistics operators. Also in 1997, the company added its first operations in Eastern Europe, with the purchase of Hungary's Deltasped. By the end of that year, the company's sales had topped FRF 3 billion ($500 million).

Continued acquisitions enabled the group to top FRF 4 billion by the end of 1998. Among the company's purchases were international groupage company AJG, based in Britain, and Seroul in France. Dentressangle also deepened its expertise through the addition of temperature control specialists Mani and bulk products operator Thier. The latter acquisition also enabled the company to enter Germany's transport market. Also in 1998, the company shifted its stock listing to the Paris bourse's main board. By then, Dentressangle's share price had nearly tripled.

Dentressangle adopted a growth objective in 1999, with plans to achieve sales of EUR 1 billion by 2002. As part of this objective, the company began to step up its logistics operations. Acquisitions again played an important role in the company's strategy. At the end of 1999, Dentressangle acquired 60 percent of Via Location, a specialist in industrial vehicle rentals with

---

Key Dates:

1966: Georges and Therese Dentressangle move their trucking business, originally established after World War II, to Saint Vallier, in the Rhone Valley region.

1974: Son Norbert Dentressangle joins the family business.

1978: Norbert Dentressangle decides to set up a separate trucking business in England serving the French-English market.

1979: A second company is established in the Rhone Valley and business focuses on the Saint Vallier-London route.

1980: The first warehouse opens.

1988: An acquisition drive is launched, starting with Transport Romulus and Philibert & Sylvester.

1993: The company acquires Translittoral, becoming the leader of the cross-channel transport market.

1994: The company goes public with a listing on the Paris Stock Exchange's secondary market.

1995: A dedicated logistics division is established; a subsidiary is opened in Portugal.

1996: The company acquires Freeflag (England) and Navamar (Spain).

1998: The company enters Germany with the purchase of Thier; its listing is transferred to the Paris main board.

1999: The company acquires Soluzione Logistica, in Italy, establishing ND Italia.

2002: The company acquires Van Mierlo in The Netherlands.

2003: The company acquires Cidem in Italy.

2004: The company announces plans to enter China by 2005.

---

sales of nearly EUR 100 million. The following year, the company entered the Italian transport and logistics market with the purchase of Soluzione Logistica, which focused on that country's prominent textiles and clothing sectors.

In 2001, Dentressangle bought up Savam, formerly held by Rentokil Initial, which focused on large-volume, low-density transports. A year later, the company expanded its presence on the North Sea with the acquisition of The Netherlands' Van Mierlo. That purchase also backed up the group's winning The Netherlands and Belgium logistics contract for home furnishings giant Ikea. In France, where Dentressangle already provided logistics services to Ikea, the company deepened its logistics operations through the purchase of money-losing Stockalliance. That company, despite its losses, brought Dentressangle a complementary network of 20 warehouse sites across France.

By the end of 2003, the company's logistics operations already claimed 39 percent of its total revenues of more than EUR 1.2 billion. Adding to that growth was the group's latest acquisition in Italy, of Milan's Cidem, adding four more warehouse sites in that country.

Dentressangle continued to set ambitious growth targets for itself into the middle of the decade. Despite the sluggish European economy, the company planned to continue to seek out growth opportunities in the region, most notably in the logistics market. At the same time, the company announced its interest in expanding beyond Europe for the first time, with plans to extend into China as early as 2005. Under the leadership of Norbert Dentressangle himself, the company was en route to becoming a global logistics and transport leader.

Principal Competitors

United Parcel Service of America Inc.; FedEx Corporation; Stinnes AG; ICA Detaljhandel AB; Exel PLC; SNCF Participations; Kuhne und Nagel International AG; SCHENKER AG; Bidvest Group Ltd.; Posten Logistik AB; System Alliance GmbH; Hays PLC; John Swire and Sons Ltd.

Further Reading

"Il a fait de son nom une marque," *L'Entreprise,* May 30, 2002.
Morris, Lucie, "Norbert Starts a Lorry Exodus Over Brown's Budget Rises," *Daily Mail,* April 6, 1999, p. 19.
"Norbert Dentressangle veut croître plus vite dans la logistique," *Les Echos,* September 24, 2004.
"Norbert Dentressangle veut s'implanter en Chine d'ici à 2005," *Les Echos,* May 27, 2004.
Owen, David, "Unfashionable at the Start," *Financial Times,* May 5, 1998, p. 3.

—M.L. Cohen

Spectrum Control, Inc.

8031 Avonia Road
Fairview, Pennsylvania 16415
U.S.A.
Telephone: (814) 474-2207
Fax: (814) 474-2208
Web site: http://www.spectrumcontrol.com

Public Company
Incorporated: 1968
Employees: 864
Sales: $62.98 million (2003)
Stock Exchanges: NASDAQ
Ticker Symbol: SPEC
NAIC: 334419 Other Electronic Component
 Manufacturing

Based near Erie, Pennsylvania, Spectrum Control, Inc. designs and manufactures electronic control components and systems that shield sensitive electronics from electromagnetic, radio-frequency, or microwave interference. Spectrum's business is organized into three groups: signal integrity products, power integrity products and management systems, and frequency control products. The signal integrity segment offers low-pass EMI filters, surface mount EMI filters, and specialty ceramic capacitors. Power integrity products include power line filters, power entry modules, multisection filters, power terminal blocks, and custom power filter assemblies, while power management systems include power distribution units, remote power management systems, fuse interface panels, breaker interface panels, and customer power distribution systems. The frequency control products group makes ceramic resonators and bandpass filters, ceramic patch antennas, duplexers, lumped element filters, cavity filters, waveguide filters, as well as related products and systems. In addition, Spectrum offers product design, testing, and custom assembly services. Signal integrity products generate 70 percent of the company's sales, followed by power integrity products and management systems with 19 percent, and frequency control products with 11 percent. The telecommunications and military/aerospace industries combine to account for more than 70 percent

of Spectrum's sales. Major customers include Motorola, Lucent Technologies, Nokia, Ericsson, Marconi, Raytheon, Lockheed Martin, and Sun Microsystems. Spectrum is a public company, trading on the NASDAQ.

Founding the Company in the Late 1960s

Spectrum was founded in Erie in 1968 by three engineers, colleagues at Erie Technical Products Inc.: Thomas L. Venable, Glenn L. Warnhuis, and John R. Lane. They cobbled together $300,000 in seed money and started Spectrum Control in a former hardware store to make sophisticated electronic filters to prevent interference. Venable and Warnhuis did the design work, while Lane was responsible for marketing. Over the course of the next 15 years Spectrum grew steadily, moving out of the old hardware store to occupy four manufacturing plants. The number of customers grew to 1,500, including such corporate giants as IBM and Hewlett-Packard. The company also went public, raising money to fuel its growth. By 1985 annual sales had reached $22 million.

But with growth came challenges. Early on Spectrum had few employees and little difficulty in dealing with quality control. The larger the company became, the more concessions were made in the area of quality control. Spectrum became complacent, lapsing into accepting a certain number of defective products, a policy better known as acceptable quality levels or AQLs. A batch of filters would be sampled, and so long as the percentage of bad units were within a target range, the lot was shipped. Only if a batch had too many rejects would it be subjected to an expensive individual inspection process. Customers accepted the situation for a time, but in the early 1980s major customers began adopting the concept of zero defects in the components they bought. Quality control now became an overriding issue at Spectrum, one on which the future of the company hinged.

Spectrum's management team considered but dismissed the use of Japanese quality techniques, opting instead to pursue the ideas of management consultant Philip Crosby, the former director of quality for ITT Corp. Venable and 16 Spectrum employees spent five days at the headquarters of Philip Crosby

---

Company Perspectives:

Using a solutions-oriented approach, we provide products tailored to meet our customers' specific needs by anticipating and solving their systems architecture and performance problems. We combine engineering expertise, design and testing capabilities, vertically integrated manufacturing processes and flexible production schedules to provide custom solutions to our customers.

Associates Inc. in Winter Park, Florida, to learn in depth Crosby's concepts about achieving quality. Each night, according to Venable, the team drank beer and reviewed what they had learned that day and considered how it could be applied to real-world situations at home. At the very least, by the end of their time in Florida, Venable and his team had thoroughly rejected the idea of AQLs and now believed that the goal of achieving zero defects was worthwhile and pursuable, given a realistic structure. In Erie a program was implemented and training given to every employee. Many of the necessary changes were accomplished quickly and provided immediate payoffs, while some proved stubborn and required months of troubleshooting. But in the end, the Spectrum program was a success, resulting in significant savings each year. As a way to get employees invested in the program, about half of the realized savings were contributed to a profit-sharing plan.

Failed Attempt at Diversification in the 1980s

For almost 20 years Spectrum was content to focus on its narrow area of interest. Then in November 1986 it made an effort to diversify by acquiring San Fernando, California-based SFE Technologies, maker of electronic components, for $7 million in cash and the assumption of debt. At this stage Spectrum was generating annual revenues of $27 million and earnings of $3 million. The SFE purchase moved Spectrum into new product lines such as multilayer ceramic and wound-film capacitors, magnetic components, and quartz-crystal frequency-control devices. As a result of the acquisition, Spectrum picked up manufacturing facilities in San Fernando, Tucson, Arizona, New Orleans, and Schwabach, West Germany, and sales offices in England and The Netherlands. The German plant was of particular importance because it allowed Spectrum to shift the manufacture of some products that sold well in West Germany to the new location.

The SFE acquisition proved to be a poor decision, however. Adding new product lines simply caused Spectrum to lose focus. Only the West German business succeeded. After recording net income of $3.32 million in 1986, Spectrum saw profits drop to just $30,000 a year later, followed by losses of $3.61 million in 1988 and $850,000 in 1989. As the company continued to lose money in 1990, in April of that year Venable was replaced as president and chief executive officer by 47-year-old J.L. "Jack" Johnston. Venable stayed on as chairman but at the end of 1990 he left the company to pursue other business opportunities. Johnston brought with him more than 20 years of managerial experience in the electronics industry. He spent 18 years at Erie Technological Products and successor Murata Erie

North America, serving in a number of executive roles. He then joined Allen Bradley Company, serving as the general manager of the Electronic Components Division. Replacing Venable as chairman of the board was Gerald A. Ryan, a graduate of the Massachusetts Institute of Technology who had been a director of the company since its inception.

Johnston quickly took steps to return Spectrum to its core business of EMI/FRI filters, connectors, and capacitors, and to cut the company's losses. Unable to spin off or sell its Tucson subsidiary, Polytronics Inc., he opted to simply close down the operation, which was draining resources. In addition, a plant in Valencia, California, was closed because its work could be handled in Erie. In April 1991 Spectrum sold its gasket and shielding business to MAJR Products. These moves caused sales to decline from $32 million in 1990 to $26.8 million in 1991, but the company was now on a better footing to realize future growth. After losing $691,000 in 1991, Spectrum returned to profitability in 1992, posting net income of $1.4 million on sales of $31.6 million. Over the next four years the company enjoyed steady growth while it continued to take steps to refine its business mix. The German subsidiary shut down its manufacturing operations in 1993 and 1994 and was converted into a distributor of Spectrum products to the European market. Although emphasizing cost controls, Johnston was willing to spend money in some cases. In 1992 Spectrum bought assets—inventory, tooling, drawings, and customer order backlog—for the electronic filter products produced by Murata Erie North America, Ltd. Spectrum's sales grew to $41.3 million in 1993, $43.7 million in 1994, and $49.3 million in 1995. Net income during this period ranged from $5 million in 1993 to approximately $3 million in 1995.

Spectrum suffered a significant setback in December 1996 when Johnston died following heart surgery. While the board started the search for a new chief executive, an executive committee was formed to run the company on a temporary basis. One of the members, Richard A. Southworth, vice-president and general manager of the filter products group, would emerge as the board's choice to succeed Johnston. After graduating from Gannon University, where he studied Mechanical Engineering and Mathematics, Southworth had worked for Philips Components, Murta Erie North America, and Erie Technological Products. He joined Spectrum in 1991 as vice-president and general manager of the company's electromagnetic division.

In 1996 sales rose to $57.3 million and net income totaled $3.4 million, the result of increased demand from the telecommunications industry. When sales to this sector fell off in 1997, Spectrum saw its revenues recede to $56.5 million, although net income improved to nearly $4 million. With the business now on a sound footing, Spectrum was ready to once again use external means to add products and enter new markets. In April 1998 it paid approximately $1.1 million to acquire virtually all of privately held Republic Electronics Corp., a Wilkes-Barre, Pennsylvania-based electronics company that made subminiature ceramic capacitors used in telecommunications and microwave applications. Products included temperature compensating capacitors, single-layer microwave capacitors, high-voltage capacitors, switch-mode capacitors, and high Q capacitors. Republic brought with it only about $2 million in annual sales, but it provided Spectrum with a customer base in the capacitor segment on which

Key Dates:

1968: The company is incorporated.
1986: SFE Technologies is acquired.
1990: CEO Thomas Venable is replaced by Jack Johnston.
1996: Johnston dies following heart surgery.
2001: Recession leads to major layoffs and plant closings.

to build. Also in 1998 Spectrum established a control products division. To bolster this new area Spectrum acquired Wesson, Mississippi-based Potter Production Corporation at a cost of $3 million. Potter manufactured power filter and power distribution products, including electromagnetic interference and radio frequency interference power filters, power line filters, facility filters, magnetic resonance interference filters, power distribution products, and power management, conditioning, and surge suppression products. Potter generated about $8 million in annual sales. As was the case with the Republic acquisition, the addition of Potter provided Spectrum with a footprint in new product lines and expanded the customer base.

Boom Times in the Late 1990s

The Republic and Potter acquisitions would not add much to the balance sheet in 1998. Although the electronic components market did not experience the best of years, Spectrum still managed to improve sales to $59.9 million and hold steady on net income, which fell slightly to $3.93 million. The 1998 acquisitions would pay off more obviously in 1999 when Spectrum began to experience a major surge in business as the U.S. economy and the telecommunications industry enjoyed boom times. Spectrum also completed another acquisition to grow the business further, paying more than $20 million for the Signal Conditioning Products division of electronics giant AMP Incorporated. Manufacturing a full line of EMI filters, filtered arrays, filtered connectors, and related products, Signal helped to solidify Spectrum's position as a major player in EMI filter products.

The Signal acquisition came early enough in 1999 that it made a major contribution to Spectrum's balance sheet that year. Revenues grew to more than $97.7 million and net income increased to $5.5 million. Continued demand from telecommunications customers resulted in greater growth in 2000. To pay off some of the debt incurred from its recent acquisitions, Spectrum made a secondary offering of stock, netting $27.8 million. The timing proved to be ideal, as the company was in the midst of enjoying a record year. Revenues in 2000 jumped to $132.6 million and net income grew to $9.5 million. To keep up with demand, Spectrum had expanded its manufacturing capabilities

in Mexico and Wesson and hired hundreds of new workers. Then in early 2001 the bubble burst in the telecom sector, which accounted for some 60 percent of Spectrum's sales. Spectrum also was hurt by inventory buildups by telecommunications equipment companies. While they cleared their inventories, Spectrum was left with a maximum of capacity and a minimum of demand for its products.

Spectrum took immediate steps to cut costs in order to weather the storm. It eliminated 700 jobs, close to 40 percent of its workforce, and shut down a pair of Pennsylvania plants. By the close of this difficult year, Spectrum saw sales plummet to $89.3 million while recording a loss of nearly $3 million. Sales continued to fall in 2002, declining to $57.2 million, but cost-cutting measures paid off as the company lost only $737,000 for the year. Spectrum was also strong enough financially that it could afford to invest in the future when business conditions rebounded. In July 2002 it paid $6.5 million to pick up FSY Microwave, Inc., a Maryland company that designed and manufactured microwave filters. Spectrum also built a new plant in China, which it hoped would add business from the promising Asian market.

The addition of FSY helped Spectrum to reverse the trend on declining sales in 2003. Revenues approached $63 million and the company returned to profitability for the year, posting net income of $854,000. Spectrum benefited from improving conditions in the telecommunications industry in 2004 and it appeared that the company was in the midst of a significant rebound. It also was well positioned for sustained, long-term growth.

Principal Subsidiaries

Spectrum Control, Inc.; Spectrum Engineering International, Inc.; Spectrum Control Technology; Spectrum FSY Microwave, Inc.

Principal Competitors

Amphenol Corporation; AVX Corporation; Maxwell Technologies, Inc.

Further Reading

Brown, Paul B., "The Eternal Second Act," *Inc.,* June 1988, p. 119.
Panepento, Peter, "Spectrum Control of Fairview, Pa., Lays Off 40 Amid Telecom Turndown," *Erie Times-News,* June 29, 2001.
Stouffer, Paul W., "Cashing in on Clutter," *Barron's National Business and Financial Weekly,* November 17, 1986, p. 56.
Waters, Craig R., "Quality Begins at Home," *Inc.,* August 1985, p. 68.

—Ed Dinger

SRC Holdings Corporation

650 N. Broadview Place
Springfield, Missouri 65802
U.S.A.
Telephone: (417) 862-3501
Fax: (417) 864-0625
Web site: http://www.srcreman.com

Private Company
Incorporated: 1982
Employees: 800
Sales: $140 million (2004 est.)
NAIC: 335312 Motor and Generator Manufacturing

SRC Holdings Corporation owns SRC Remanufacturing and more than 20 other businesses. Most are related to the company's original specialty of rebuilding engines, generators, and other components. The company counts 20 original equipment manufacturers (OEMs) among its customers.

One of SRC's enterprises markets tours and books for those interested in SRC's famously entrepreneurial culture. CEO Jack Stack is an author of books espousing the attributes of openness and ownership; *Business Week* has described the company itself as a "management Mecca."

Origins

The tale of SRC Holdings Corporation begins in 1974, records the *Wall Street Journal,* when International Harvester Co. formed its International Harvester ReNew Center repair division. The unit remanufactured diesel engines, transmissions, and torque converters for Harvester's construction equipment division, according to *Diesel Progress.* It was later known by the names Springfield Remanufacturing Corp. and Springfield Remanufacturing Center Corp.

Jack Stack was assigned to the unit, based in the Ozarks community of Springfield, Missouri, in January 1979. Then called Springfield ReManufacturing, the factory was tottering on the edge of bankruptcy, losing $2 million a year on sales of $26 million. As its name suggests, the company's business was

disassembling and rebuilding diesel engines, water pumps, and other components.

Before coming to Springfield, Stack worked his way up from the proverbial mailroom to become responsible for 2,000 employees as superintendent of the machining division at Harvester's factory in Melrose Park, Illinois.

Approaching business as a game, the heart of Stack's method was to involve employees in the outcome. "It's much more than a metaphor," Stack later told *Personnel Journal.* "If you look at all the characteristics of a game and you look at all the characteristics of a business, you see that they're almost the same." He fostered a sense of competition between foremen at his Illinois assignment, and brought a similar approach to Springfield.

Stack set up productivity contests to get the plant on its feet. A sense of teambuilding and ownership as well as competition was encouraged. As Stack later wrote in *National Productivity Review,* SRC enthusiastically fielded teams against other companies at community events such as relay races.

1982 Management Buyout

By 1981, Springfield ReManufacturing was managing to turn a $1 million profit. International Harvester demanded that the Springfield plant cut production by two-thirds, however, as the parent company reeled from the effects of a recession on farm and construction equipment. Stack balked at the prospects of layoffs for the Springfield, Missouri community (the plant then employed about 120 people). He and a dozen fellow managers kept the plant running, and eventually bought it out. A new entity, SRC Holdings Corporation, was formed on December 27, 1982, to carry out the acquisition.

According to *strategy + business* magazine, it had taken two years to arrange financing. Stack, then just in his early 30s, was in charge of rounding up investors. Stack managed to seal the deal in spite of a competing bid from Dresser Industries Inc., which fell through at the last minute. Dresser was able to acquire Harvester's construction equipment business, noted *Inc.,* which accounted for 60 percent of SRC's revenues at the time. *Inc.* also observed that SRC decided to supply original

Company Perspectives:

Springfield ReManufacturing Corporation (SRC) has been at the forefront of the remanufacturing industry since the early 1980s when founder Jack Stack, known internationally for his development of The Great Game of Business, spearheaded an employee buyout of International Harvester's remanufacturing facilities.

Through the years we have evolved into several unique companies, each specializing in different remanufactured components for automobiles, commercial trucks, agricultural equipment and construction vehicles. Our growth and success can be attributed to quality control, warranty-backed products and an efficiency of production that generally flows from employee owned companies.

Our people make them better. That's not an idle boast. It's a statement of fact that has become our slogan and our legacy in the remanufacturing industry.

Key Dates:

1974: International Harvester ReNew Center is formed in Springfield, Missouri.
1982: Plant managers lead the buyout of Springfield Re-Manufacturing.
1986: A turnaround is in evidence; annual sales amount to $42 million.
1990: Great Game of Business, Inc. is formed to market business literature and tours.
2000: SRC has 22 subsidiaries and sales of $150 million.

equipment manufacturers (OEMs) exclusively. After becoming independent, notes *Diesel Progress,* SRC entered the on-road engine market with a General Motors product and began remanufacturing engines or components for Allis-Chalmers, Thermo King, Komatsu, Mercedes-Benz, Iveco, Isuzu, Nissan, Mitsubishi, and Ford-New Holland.

What SRC's management had acquired, noted *strategy+business,* was a company with a monstrous debt-to-equity ratio of 89:1. The company was bought with $9 million, mostly borrowed, which had to be repaid at credit card interest rates (18 percent).

An employee stock ownership plan (ESOP) was set up, making it the largest single shareholder, with 31 percent of shares. Stack owned 19 percent of the company.

To foster a team dynamic, the company styled its weekly division meetings as "huddles." Department heads then shared the numbers with their employees at "chalk talks," where game plans were worked out. Workers and management gathered after work at nearby Joann's Expressway Lounge, noted *Inc.* in a 1986 profile.

The company measured everything, not just production, but also such categories as housekeeping and employee morale. One bonus was aptly named "Skip the Praise, Give Us the Raise" (STP-GUTR). In its first 20 years, Stack told *Inc.* magazine, the company introduced nearly two dozen different incentive programs tied to a wide array of performance targets.

Mid-1980s Turnaround

The turnaround was remarkable, according to *strategy+business.* Share price rose 13,000 percent by fiscal 1986. Annual sales were up to $42 million after growing 30 percent per year.

It was not all smooth sailing. In December 1986, General Motors canceled an order for 5,000 engines, representing 40 percent of business for the upcoming year. SRC scrambled to introduce a number of new product lines to avoid laying people off, Stack told *Inc.*

Preaching openness and financial literacy, Stack required workers of all stripes to read profit and loss statements. Along the way, he became something of a management guru, publishing *The Great Game of Business* in 1992 and *A Stake in the Outcome* ten years later. Some referred to the practice as "open management." Stack later described it this way to the trade publication *Modern Casting:* "The best, most efficient, most profitable way to operate a business is to give everybody in the company a voice in saying how the company is run and a stake in the financial outcome, good or bad."

Diversification in the 1980s and 1990s

SRC ended the 1980s with sales of $50 million a year and 475 employees. To guard against the cyclical nature of the truck business, SRC had begun to diversify in 1985, branching out into automobile engines. The company developed its own business incubator for entrepreneurial employees, offering to fund 80 percent of the cost of launching viable start-ups. By 1995, this had given rise to about a dozen new companies, including Megavolt (manufacturer of generators, alternators, and starters) and NewStream Enterprises (engine rebuilding kits).

One of these, Engines Plus, was founded in 1986 with just $60,000. It specialized in rebuilding oil coolers. Its sales reached $7 million in the early 1990s. The Engines Plus unit sold its original oil cooler business to SRC Heavy Duty around 2004 in order to focus on producing small industrial power generators.

Stack was becoming more visible as a business leadership visionary. *Inc.* had named him CEO of its executive "Dream Team." He began giving summer lectures at MIT's Sloan School of Management around 1992. By the mid-1990s, reported *Business Week,* 2,400 people had made the pilgrimage to Springfield to study the company's open-book management. Company sales were about $104 million at the time, and there were 700 employees. SRC had earlier formed The Great Game of Business to market a two-day seminar and company tour as well as Stack's books, videos, and consulting—it alone was doing nearly $2 million a year worth of business.

A 50–50 joint venture was formed in 1998 with Deere & Co. ReGen Technologies L.L.C. remanufactured diesel engines for John Deere's agricultural and construction equipment.

Still Growing After 2000

At the turn of the millennium, SRC Holdings owned 22 companies and had sales of about $150 million a year. The company aimed for 15 percent as a manageable annual growth target, Stack told *Inc.*

In 2002 *Business Week* praised Stack as someone whose attention to relationships, openness, and focus on real results provided a positive example in contrast to the greed-driven debacles at Enron and the excesses of the dot-com bubble. Stack eschewed corner offices, corporate jets, and other executive trappings, observed *Business Week.*

President George W. Bush made a campaign stop at SRC Automotive in Springfield in February 2004. Bush used the visit to speak about the benefits of tax relief for the economy.

Principal Divisions

SRC Heavy Duty; ReGen Technologies, L.L.C.; Megavolt; SRC Automotive; Avatar Components Corporation; New-Stream Enterprises; Encore Inc.; The Great Game of Business, Inc.; SRC of Canada, Inc.; Engines Plus Incorporated; CCRC.

Principal Competitors

Detroit Diesel Remanufacturing; Jasper Engines and Transmissions; Marshall Engines; Williams Technologies, Inc.

Further Reading

Albrinck, Jill, Jennifer Hornery, David Kletter, and Gary Neilson, "Adventures in Corporate Venturing," *s + b,* First Quarter 2001.

Anfuso, Dawn, "Turning Business into a Game," *Personnel Journal,* March 1, 1995, p. 50.

Ballen, Kate, "John P. Stack (Springfield ReManufacturing Center)," *Fortune,* June 8, 1987, p. 82.

Burlingham, Bo, "Being the Boss; Company CEO Tells Why He Hates the Traditional Relationship Between Workers and Bosses, and Explains His Solution," *Inc.,* October 1989.

Byrne, John A., "After Enron: The Ideal Corporation; Following the Abuses of the '90s, Executives Are Learning That Trust, Integrity, and Fairness Do Matter—And Are Crucial to the Bottom Line," *Business Week,* August 26, 2002, p. 68.

——, "Management Meccas: Everyone Seems to Be Studying U.S. Corporate Stars," *Business Week,* September 18, 1995, p. 122.

Case, John, "No More 'Etch A Sketch' Planning," *Inc.,* December 1, 2001.

"Deere & Co. in Venture to Remanufacture Diesel Engines," *Dow Jones News Service,* January 15, 1998.

Denton, D. Keith, "Hitler's Secret, Einstein's Fear: Using Enemies to Empower Teams and Organizations," *Competitiveness Review,* January 1, 2000, pp. 209–18.

"Get Huddling," *Management Today,* April 1, 2000, p. 20.

Kanicki, David P., "Communication: The Key to Winning in the 'Great Game,' " *Modern Casting,* December 1, 1998.

Kleiner, Art, "Jack Stack's Story Is an Open Book," *strategy + business,* Special Issue: Profiles in Strategy, Fall 2004, pp. 48–57.

Menefee, Constance, "Measure Morale and Improve It," *Cincinnati Post,* April 22, 1997, p. 1C.

O'Brien, Timothy, "Company Wins Workers' Loyalty by Opening Its Books," *Wall Street Journal,* December 20, 1993, p. B1.

Osenga, Mike, "Targeting the OEM Side of the Aftermarket, Product Support vs. Aftermarket; SRC Finds Unique and Growing Niche in Rebuilding for OEMs," *Diesel Progress,* North American ed., November 2001.

Rhodes, Lucien, and Patricia Amend, "The Turnaround; How a Dying Division of International Harvester Became One of America's Most Competitive Small Companies," *Inc.,* August 1986, pp. 42–48.

Ross, Sherwood, "Inexperienced Job Seekers Can Aim Higher in Tight Market," *Reuters News,* March 8, 1999.

Stack, Jack, *The Great Game of Business,* New York: Doubleday, 1992; Currency, 1994.

——, "The Next in Line," *Inc.,* April 1998.

——, "Springfield ReManufacturing Bought the Company and Learned to Play the Game of Open-Book Management," *National Productivity Review,* December 22, 1993, p. 39.

Stack, Jack, and Bo Burlingham, *A Stake in the Outcome: Building a Culture of Ownership for the Long-Term Success of Your Business,* New York: Doubleday, 2002; Currency, 2003.

Walters, Laurel Shaper, "Opening Up Books to Employees Boosts Profits," *Christian Science Monitor,* March 25, 1996, p. 9.

—Frederick C. Ingram

Stratasys, Inc.

14950 Martin Drive
Eden Prairie, Minnesota 55344-2020
U.S.A.
Telephone: (952) 937-3000
Toll Free: (888) 0480-3548
Fax: (952) 937-0070
Web site: http://www.stratasys.com

Public Company
Incorporated: 1989
Employees: 229
Sales: $50.9 million (2003)
Stock Exchanges: NASDAQ
Ticker Symbol: SSYS
NAIC: 334119 Other Computer Peripheral Equipment
   Manufacturing

Based in Eden Prairie, Minnesota, Stratasys, Inc. manufactures rapid prototyping (RP) machines that produce physical models from computer designs using the company's patented fused deposition modeling (FDM) technology. Although engineers and designers have benefited greatly from the introduction of computer-aided design (CAD), they still need a physical copy in order to check the viability of their ideas. Thus designers would have to devote days, and sometimes weeks, making models by hand, often out of wood. With the introduction of RP machines, such as those made by Stratasys, CAD designs could be turned into a prototype in a matter of hours, available in a variety of materials. FDM technology relies on a high-speed robotic arm and an extruding head, in effect a glue gun, to spray melted thermoplastic filament. Relying on CAD coding, the gun moves over a platform, plotting small dots of plastic to create a model from the bottom up in a thermally controlled modeling chamber. Early RP machines were expensive and had a limited market. Although Stratasys continues to make high-end products, the company has enjoyed success with RP machines, billed as 3-D printers, that cost less than $25,000, making the technology available to a much wider range of customers, including schools. Because the machines require no special venting or chemical post-processing they are also suitable for office use. Moreover, they require little monitoring, allowing designers to accomplish other tasks while a prototype is created. Stratasys offers a variety of modeling material, including ABS (acrylonitrile, butadiene, and styrene), which is strong and thermal-resistant and used in commercial products such as toys and cell phones; ABSi, a translucent, higher-grade ABS; polycarbonate, a durable thermoplastic material; PC-ISO, a translucent polycarbonate appropriate for a number of medical applications; and polyphenylsufone, a thermoplastic material used to produce prototype parts for the automotive, aerospace, and chemical handling industries. Stratasys is a public company trading on the NASDAQ.

Company Origins Dating to the Late 1980s

Stratasys was founded by the husband and wife team of S. Scott Crump and Lisa H. Crump. He grew up in Connecticut, the son of a chemical engineer who was also a successful entrepreneur. Like his father, Crump was interested in both technology and business, and because of his father's belief that the children should make their own way in the world he became involved in business at an early age. When he was just 14 he traded for a broken-down car that he fixed up for his mother so she could drive him on his newspaper route. He then bought several Volkswagens that he refurbished and resold as a way to earn pocket money. He studied mechanical engineering at Washington State University and then in 1982 moved to Minneapolis to help found IDEA, Inc., which manufactured force, load, and pressure transducers. Ever the tinkerer, Crump in 1988 decided to make a toy frog for his young daughter using a glue gun loaded with a mixture of polyethylene and candle wax. His idea was to create the shape layer by layer. He then thought of a way to automate the process, spent $10,000 on digital-plotting equipment, and devoted countless weekend hours on the project. In 1989 he patented Fused Deposition Modeling technology. Along the way, his wife insisted that he either turn his obsession into a business or give it up. The couple founded the company in 1988 and in August of the following year they incorporated Stratasys in Delaware.

From the start Stratasys attracted attention because of its relatively low-cost product, offering a 3-D modeler for $130,000

($178,000 with a Silicon Graphics workstation). The company found no buyers for this early product and now looked to develop larger RP machines suited to the marketplace, selling to major corporate customers such as General Motors, 3M, and Pratt & Whitney who could afford a hefty price tag. To build five of these machines, roughly the size of a refrigerator, Crump raised $264,000 by liquidating family assets and sold a 35 percent stake in Stratasys in exchange for $1.2 million in venture capital. In April 1992 Stratasys sold its first product, the 3D Modeler. A year later, in June 1993, the company introduced its second product, the Benchtop.

To raise more capital, Stratasys went public in October 1994. With Jersey City, New Jersey-based M.H. Meyerson & Co., Inc. acting as the sole underwriter, the company sold 1.38 million shares of common stock at $5 per share, netting approximately $5.7 million. The funds were earmarked to expand the company's engineering capabilities in order to add features and applications to its RP products, as well as for marketing and sales.

IBM Co-Development Deal in the Mid-1980s

The cash, and the availability of stock, also came in handy a few months later when Stratasys paid $500,000 and issued 500,000 shares of stock to IBM for its RP technology. IBM had been developing a small 3-D printer that relied on an extrusion system very similar to Crump's patented FDM technology. The only major difference was the feeding system, which relied on plastic wafers. Because taking on IBM in court over patent violations would be expensive and counterproductive, Stratasys instead offered to co-develop a 3-D printer, which led to the January 1995 purchase of IBM technology. Moreover, with IBM owning a stake, Stratasys hoped to significantly increase its business opportunities.

The result of the co-development deal with IBM was the 1996 introduction of the Genisys 3-D printer. Priced around $50,000, it was the first RP machine costing less than $100,000. The product found a receptive market and enjoyed strong de- mand in the first year, but a number of problems with the system soon became apparent and sales dried up. One problem was contaminated wafers that did not melt properly, leaving pebbles that jammed the nozzle on the extruder. A change in suppliers corrected the problem, but Genisys also had difficulties with the wafer loader jamming and the modeling platform colliding with the nozzle. Models as they cooled also had a tendency to curl along the edges. After selling 150 units, Stratasys halted pro- duction of the Genisys in 1998. Major problems were corrected and the product returned to the market in April 1999 as GenisysXs. In the meantime the company also would begin a $10 million effort to completely redesign its benchtop modeler.

On other fronts, in November 1997 Stratasys received clearance from the Food and Drug Administration for its

MedModeler system, which served the medical market by pro- ducing anatomical parts from MRI and CT scans. In January 1998 Stratasys introduced its next product. Rather than a benchtop modeler like Genisys, the company now offered a large envelope RP system, the FDM Quantum, the second largest in the industry. It was the size of a small shed, measuring $84 \times 76 \times 39$ inches. But like Genisys, Quantum could be net- worked and used by a number of users, and operated un- attended. It also featured a new motion system, MagnaDrive, that moved the extrusion tip on an air cushion and controlled it by an electromagnetic homing device. Not only was the system more accurate, it also involved less moving parts and required less maintenance.

Stratasys acquired new RP technology in December 1998 from a private research and development company at a cost of $6.5 million in cash and stock. Stratasys also was spending far more than the industry average on its own R&D efforts. One of its innovations was WaterWorks, part of the 1999 launch of the FDM 3000 system. WaterWorks allowed completed models to be immersed in a water-based solution to remove supports. The need for post-processing work was eliminated and designers were presented with a cleaned prototype.

Stratasys enjoyed strong growth in the mid-1990s, with revenues growing from $10.3 million in 1995 to $29.6 million in 1997, but problems with Genisys and slumping sales in Europe blunted the company's momentum for the next few years. Revenues reached $37.6 million in 1999 and stalled. Sales totaled $35.6 million in 2000, $37.6 million in 2001, and $39.8 million in 2002. Net income during this period ranged from $988,000 in 2000 to $3.1 million in 2002. But a series of new product offerings was starting to have a positive impact on the company's fortunes.

In 2000 Stratasys introduced Prodigy, a modeler that filled a market niche, both in terms of price and performance, situated between the Genisys and the high-end machines. Like other Stratasys products, it could be networked and used nontoxic materials which required no special venting. Capable of making prototypes $8 \times 8 \times 12$ inches, Prodigy also offered three differ- ent layer thicknesses. Late in 2000 Stratasys released FDM Maxum, a big envelope modeler that used the company's MagnaDrive technology as well as the WaterWorks support system, and was 50 percent faster than the company's previous products. It also relied on Insight, a new preprocessing software developed by Stratasys to replace the QuickSlice software the company had been using since 1993. Insight saved time as well as material and was capable of building more than one smaller model simultaneously. It also provided status updates on elapsed time, time remaining, and the amount of material used. Users could be paged or notified by email when a job was interrupted or completed.

Responding to customer input, in 2001 Stratasys introduced Titan, a system that created prototypes from polycarbonate to create a functional prototype. In addition, Titan could use two other high-performance materials: polyphenylsulfone and ABS plastic. These materials were high-impact-strength manufacturing-grade plastic, resistant to high temperatures, fire retardant, possessed sterilization capabilities, and were resistant to oil, gasoline,

Key Dates:

1989: The company is incorporated.
1992: The first product is shipped.
1994: The company is taken public.
1995: Acquisition of IBM technology leads to the Genisys product.
2002: The Dimension system is introduced.
2004: Stratasys becomes a market leader.

chemicals, and acid. As a result, the models produced by Titan could be subjected to rigorous real-world testing.

Introducing Dimension in 2002

In February 2002, the money and time invested in reengineering Genisys led to the introduction of Dimension and the retirement of the older benchtop modeler. The IBM wafer system was replaced by a spool of plastic filament that was fed through a heated rod before reaching the nozzle. A number of expensive parts were eliminated by adopting this simple mechanism, which also greatly enhanced reliability. Moreover, Stratasys was able to price Dimension at less than $30,000, the least expensive product in the RP and 3D printing markets. In addition to being small, easy to use, and capable of being networked, Dimension used ABS plastic, making the models it produced functional and suitable for testing. As a result of its low price and capabilities, Dimension brought RP technology to a new and much larger base of customers, from small companies to high schools, who previously could not even have thought about in-house modeling.

With the launch of Dimension, Stratasys regained the momentum it had lost from its last attempt at bringing a benchtop modeler to the market. Investors took notice and bought shares of Stratasys stock, significantly bidding up its price. In November 2003 the company implemented a three-for-two stock split, a move that increased the number of outstanding shares to 10.2 million. The company's R&D efforts also continued to pay off as other new and enhanced products were introduced. A month after the release of Dimension, the company introduced Prodigy Plus, which brought WaterWorks and the InSight software to the Prodigy platform. In 2003 Stratasys introduced FDM Vantage, which extended the Titan design platform by adding polycarbonate and ABS as modeling materials. Also in 2003 the company joined forces with New Jersey-based Objet Geometries Ltd. to distribute that company's Eden333 RP system in North America. This system relied on an inkjet technology to create UV-cured resin to build ultra high-resolution models. Although not durable enough for functional testing, these prototypes were suitable for fit and form evaluation. The introduction

of Eden333 further expanded the market for RP systems in North America and gave the Stratasys distribution channel a wider range of capabilities to offer customers.

Improvements on Titan also were offered in 2003, with build speeds increasing by 50 percent. Sales were strong that year, improving by more than 20 percent over 2002 to $50.9 million. Net income almost doubled, from $3.1 million to slightly less than $6.2 million. According to statistics prepared by Wohlers Associates Inc., Stratasys, with its focus on low-end systems, became the market leader in the RP industry in 2003, shipping nearly half of all RP systems. In addition, for the first time Stratasys accounted for the largest installed base of RP systems worldwide.

In 2004 Stratasys introduced Dimension SST, which added an enhanced automatic soluble support system and also was capable of producing more complex models and prototypes. It was priced at $34,900, and the price on Dimension was lowered to $24,900, bringing RP technology to even more potential customers. The company continued to serve the higher-end of the RP market as well. In 2004 it introduced three variations of its Vantage system, ranging in price from $99,000 to $195,000. But it was clear that the future of the company lay with the low-end machines. A unit intended to crack the $20,000 barrier was in development, a move that made the idea of desktop 3-D printers accompanying CAD design stations seem almost as commonplace as desktop inkjet and laser printers bundled with personal computers.

Principal Subsidiaries

Stratasys GmbH; Stratasys Foreign Sales Corporation.

Principal Competitors

3D Systems Corporation; Dassault Systèmes S.A.; Delcam PLC.

Further Reading

DeGaspari, John, "Rapid Evolution: New Materials and Process Improvements Are Stretching the Boundaries of Prototyping Techniques," *Mechanical Engineering—CIME,* March 2002, p. 48.

Much, Marilyn, "Eden Prairie, Minnesota Manufacturer Known for Quality, Adaptability," *Investor's Business Daily,* April 22, 2003, p. A10.

Nelson, Brett, "Almost Out of the Woods," *Forbes,* September 20, 2004, p. 208.

St. Anthony, Neal, "Stratasys Breaks the Mold in Computer-Aided Design," *Star Tribune,* March 28, 2003, p. 1D.

Suzukamo, Leslie Brooks, "Eden Prairie, Minn.-Based 3-D Printer Maker Reports 19 Percent Earnings Boost," *Saint Paul Pioneer Press,* July 29, 2003.

—Ed Dinger

Tilley Endurables

Tilley Endurables, Inc.

900 Don Mills Road
Toronto, Ontario M3C 1V6
Canada
Telephone: (414) 441-6141
Toll Free: (800) 363-8737
Fax: (414) 444-3860
Web site: http://www.tilley.com

Private Company
Incorporated: 1984
Employees: 215
Sales: $25 million (2004 est.)
NAIC: 315991 Hat, Cap, and Millinery Manufacturing;
    315299 All Other Cut and Sew Apparel
    Manufacturing; 448190 Other Clothing Stores

Tilley Endurables, Inc. specializes in clothing for the adventurer. The company has five retail stores in Canada, including three in Toronto and one each in Montreal and Vancouver. All clothing items, with the exception of their "unholey" socks, are manufactured in Toronto. Tilley hats and classic shorts and some other items come with a lifetime warranty. Hats bear the washing instructions: "Give 'em hell." Tilley products are sold by more than 2,000 associated retailers in 17 countries, including Australia, Belgium, Canada, Chile, Ireland, Finland, Japan, The Netherlands, New Zealand, Singapore, St. Martin, Sweden, Turkey, and the United Kingdom, and by 1,500 retailers in the United States. Tilley products also can be purchased via mail order and online.

1980–87: Quest for the Perfect Hat

In 1980, on a whim, Alexander Tilley, an amateur yachtsman and art dealer who liked to sail Lake Ontario in all weather, decided to make himself the perfect hat. Alex Tilley wanted his sailor's hat to float, tie under the chin, stand up to the harshest weather, launder, look classic, and wear comfortably. Tilley located a milliner through the yellow pages who agreed to sew a hat for him, but then ran into problems. "The canvas I wanted to

use was so tough that needles couldn't go through it and it shrank when it got wet," he recalled in a 1989 *Boston Globe* article.

After experimenting, Tilley discovered that he could preshrink the canvas by boiling and steaming it and eventually completed his hat. A sailing trip to Belize with his two daughters yielded the final design; the hat had an adjustable, tuckaway, back-of-the-head wind cord. In 1986, Tilley added a layer of foam in the sweatband and closed-cell foam in the crown for flotation and sun protection.

Tilley was notable for his vibrant personality and relaxed approach to business, although by his own and others' estimation, he had neither the background nor the talent for running a successful company. It had taken him six years to earn a three-year undergraduate degree at the University of British Columbia, and he later flunked out of York University's M.B.A. program. His checkered career included working in a bank until informed that he was "too full of piss and vinegar to survive in banking," according to a 1990 *Record* article, and being fired "for sheer incompetence" from his sales job at Bell Canada. He later set up a tutoring business which went broke after 22 months, after which he spent a year selling printing presses. In the late 1970s, he opened Fine Art Consultants of Canada Ltd., which operated two "artmobiles" that sold and rented Canadian art.

But Tilley's prototype hats were admired by other sailors, and Tilley turned out to have a genius for marketing. He began to sell his hats from home for slightly above cost. His fledgling business got a boost in September 1980 when *Yachting*, a leading U.S. sailing magazine, wrote an editorial on the hat. Strong sales at the Toronto International Boat Show further helped the new business. In January 1984, Tilley founded Tilley Endurables and began to sell his hats via mail order from the basement of his Toronto home. "I had the perfect hat, conceived in frustration and created out of necessity, but it was so expensive to make that the only way I could sell it was by mail order," according to Tilley in the *Boston Globe*. Soon he had sold 20,000 hats, often trading hats as payment for magazine advertisements.

Shortly thereafter, Tilley abandoned his art rental business and added a line of yachting shorts. The garment had strong and capacious pockets that could carry a six pack, as Tilley liked to boast. But it was ''so well designed, [it was] a failure,'' according to Tilley in the *Record* article because of the cost of making the garment. The company donated its unsold stock of shorts to Canada's America's Cup team, leading, ironically, to fresh demand for the shorts.

Skirts and pants with ''anti-pickpocket'' security and secret pockets followed in 1985, all advertised as being the best adventure and travel clothing available and all selling a lifestyle modeled by Alex Tilley. Tilley hats were worn by the Canadian sailing team at the Los Angeles Olympics in 1984. The Ontario pavilion at Expo 86 selected the hat to be presented to the VIP of the day during the exhibition. Operation Raleigh, a program for young adventurers, presented Prince Andrew with his own Tilley when he visited Expo.

All items of Tilley clothing were made of what Tilley called ''adventure cloth, a blend of cotton and polyester fibers originally developed for the uniforms of GIs fighting in Vietnam. The fabric was easy to wash and cool to wear, even in the tropics. All items were manufactured in Canada, ''[a]nd will remain so,'' Tilley announced in *Northern Ontario Business* in 1988. The position was ''. . . a matter of honour. Also I get to keep my eye on it. And I am a fussy bugger. One supplier called me a 'fusspot' in print and I was delighted. . . . Everything we do is an attempt to make the best in the world.''

In 1987, Tilley Endurables moved into its headquarters and manufacturing plant on Don Mills Road. By the late 1980s, the broad-brimmed, brass-grommetted, sturdy canvas Tilley hat had become something of a fad and Tilley a renowned figure among enthusiastic customers. Each hat came with a four-page owner's manual and a lifetime guarantee and a two-year, all-peril, 50-percent deductible Hat Insurance Policy. Both the hat and classic shorts were guaranteed for life. The company would replace any hat either found defective or worn out. From 1980 to 1988, Tilley doubled the number of stores carrying its products each year until, by 1988, more than 50 stores carried Tilley clothing. In 1987, sales were reportedly closing in on $5 million, and by 1988 there were seven Tilley stores in Canada, of which Tilley owned two. In 1989, Tilley was selling about 100,000 hats a year. In 1990, the company reported a profit of $1 million on sales of $8 million. By 1992, Tilley products filled a 64-page catalogue.

1987–93: Financial Hard Times Followed by Reasoned Expansion

But the company continued to wade through hard times financially. In 1987, it almost went bankrupt after a failed expansion in Boston and Aspen. Tilley, whom others described as financially naive, mistakenly believed that he could use the same approach to sales in the United States—where his hat was virtually unknown—as he had in Toronto. Tilley Endurables' finances led Tilley to enter into a shareholders' agreement with Dennis Hails in 1989 after Tilley had trouble paying Hails Interiors for its work decorating the company's offices. Hails had offered to join the company under a management contract. and lent the company $200,000. Without being asked, Tilley gave Hails 50 percent of the company's shares for nothing and made him vice-president in charge of day-to-day operations. Tilley oversaw product design, marketing, and the company's catalogue.

Hails moved aggressively to eliminate costs and staff and closed the company's Boston store. However, by 1991, the relationship between the two men had soured, and they stopped talking to one another. The company—with net income of $700,000 on sales of $8.6 million—was paralyzed. Tilley filed a lawsuit against Hails, asserting that Hails had tried to prevent him from fulfilling his role in management. The dispute went to a court that applied the winding-up section of the Ontario Business Corporations Act which permitted the judge to find any solution to keep a viable company going. The court ordered Hails to sell his shares to Tilley.

The following year, Tilley brought two veteran retailers on board to handle day-to-day operations of his three retail outlets and mail-order business. Philip Davson became chief financial officer and Jim McKinney became general manager. ''My 'child' has been maimed over the last four years,'' he was quoted in the 1992 *Financial Post* article. ''Now we are adding fine people to make it whole again. . . .'' The company began a small, low-budget retail operation in Buffalo, duplicating the way Tilley had gotten into retail in Canada.

Sales for Tilley Endurables climbed 30 percent in 1992, reaching more than $10 million with profits of close to $750,000, and by 1993, Tilley Endurables was selling about 4,000 Tilley hats each week compared to 2,500 hats weekly just one year earlier. Its classic pants and classic shorts accounted for roughly half of the business. The company had 100 employees, five company-owned stores, and sold through close to 125 other retail outlets across Canada. About $2 million in business came from its Buffalo store and warehouse annually. Sir Edmund Hillary, Pierre Trudeau, and Paul Newman were just a few of the famous heads that had donned Tilley hats.

Mid-1990s–2004: Advertising a New Image and New Items

Advertising for Tilley Endurables targeted upscale, white, well-educated, and well-off customers; it was done mainly in-house, featuring Tilley and real customers who offered testimonials to Tilley Products. The company catalogue, which won the 1994 Gold Award from *Catalog Age*, also featured Tilley and customers. In an unconventional move in 1993, a move some employees disapproved of, these ads also began to display the footnote: ''We do not welcome to our company-owned stores those who make or promote tobacco products.''

Tilley defended his company's position in the press, which he did not see as contradicting his firm commitment to customer service. This commitment included the company's lifetime warranty on any item and such additional services as ''personalized

Key Dates:

1980: Tilley Endurables is founded by Alex Tilley.
1984: The company begins manufacturing and retailing travel and adventure clothing.
1987: The company moves into its headquarters in Toronto and opens a distribution center in New York State.
1989: Alex Tilley enters into a shareholders' agreement with Dennis Hails.
1991: Tilley buys back Hails's share of the company.
1994: The company's catalogue wins an award from *Catalog Age*.
1999: Allison Tilley joins the company.

travel advice'': detailed information on travel destinations, including entry requirements, health guidelines, local laws, and currency. At the company's flagship Don Mills store in Toronto, next door to its manufacturing plant, customers were greeted with a mug of coffee and cookies, and fact sheets for every country in the world were on display.

By 1996, Tilley had expanded to markets in Australia, Japan, Great Britain, and New Zealand, but despite its 700,000 North American customers, the company's image and items needed updating. That year a new team of designers came on board who worked to improve the fit or design of Tilley's existing 70 products, develop new styles and colors, experiment with innovative fabrics, and add new products to attract a younger following. ''[T]he clothes we currently have should be more desirable. If you can wear them on a date, they work,'' said Tilley in a 1997 *Record* article. In 1997, it relaunched its web site—first introduced in 1995—with ordering capabilities.

By April 1998, Tilley had added more than a dozen new items, including polo and rugby shirts. Ironically, however, in the late 1990s, it became trendy for young people to embrace hiking, exploring, bird watching, golfing, gardening, and other activities formerly linked with older people, and the company found that its traditional products—plaid shirts, khaki, and cargo pants—fell suddenly into the younger set's favor.

With $22 million in revenues in 1999 and 195 employees in Canada, the United Kingdom, and the United States, Tilley doubled the size of its Buffalo facility, increasing warehouse space and opening a new retail showroom. Its hat, which now sold in four colors and six styles, accounted for 30 percent of business. Tilley products—including 200,000 hats a year—sold in 14 countries through a network of more than 1,300 retailers. The company's main problem was that it could not make its products as fast as it intended.

Daughter Allison Tilley joined the family firm in 1999 as vice-president of marketing and merchandising with plans to update the firm's image and introduce her own line of women's clothing. As her first order of business, she set about redesigning the catalogue. One of the elements she brought back was customer testimonials and photographs and pictures of Tilley and family, which had been excised sometime in the late 1990s. ''My dad's personality is back in the book and so is mine. We have very loyal customers—400,000 of them—and they missed that in the old catalog,'' she said in a 2000 issue of *Catalog Age*. Although she continued to appear in the catalogue, by 2002, Allison had dropped out of the business to move to Hawaii to be with her housepainter paramour.

However, the company still continued to grow as branded adventure clothing increasingly attracted customers with its name and quality and associated lifestyle. In addition to true travel adventurers, many Tilley customers were people whose usual habitat was the urban jungle, and who traveled in jeeps and SUVs to drive downtown. In 2003, these people purchased 250,000 hats a year. In 2004, the company introduced its Different Drummer Legends line of jackets, vests, pants, shorts, and shirts, which were guaranteed for life, and began to manufacture items made of hemp, called by Tilley, Nature's Performance Fabric. Alex Tilley, proud and optimistic as ever about his company's products and future, said in a 2002 *Style* article: ''People who sell our things often realize they have a product that is sought after and relatively unique. . . . Once the word gets around that they sell Tilley, they attract new customers.''

Principal Competitors

Recreational Equipment, Inc.; L.L. Bean, Inc.; Patagonia.

Further Reading

Bernstein, Claire, ''Breakups Can Be Difficult in the Business World, Too,'' *Toronto Star*, March 30, 1992, p. B3.

Davis, William A., ''Hats off to Gear That Helps Travelers,'' *Boston Globe*, November 5, 1989, p. B1.

Eglinton, Rick, ''Tilley's Tale: Design Endures,'' *Toronto Star*, February 18, 2001, p. E5.

Evans, Mark, ''Adventures of the Unsinkable Alex Tilley,'' *Financial Post*, June 1, 1992, p. S16.

Gilhula, Vicki, ''Former Sudburian Tops in Hats,'' *Northern Ontario Business*, February 1988, p. 46.

Habib, Marlene, ''Tilley Sets Sights on Younger Market,'' *Record*, December 11, 1997, p. F1.

Loney, Sydney, ''An Enduring Adventure,'' *Style*, November 2002, p. 30.

Stegmann, Diane, ''Tilley Junior Redesigns Tilley Endurables,'' *Catalog Age*, July 2000, p. 22.

Strathdee, Mike, ''Garment Guru Shares Secrets,'' *Record*, November 30, 1990, p. A1.

—Carrie Rothburd

Viacom Inc.

1515 Broadway
New York, New York 10036
U.S.A.
Telephone: (212) 258-6000
Fax: (212) 258-6464
Web site: http://www.viacom.com

Public Company
Incorporated: 1971
Employees: 122,770
Sales: $26.6 billion (2003)
Stock Exchanges: New York
Ticker Symbol: VIA
NAIC: 5152210 Cable & Other Subscription
    Programming; 512110 Motion Picture and Video
    Production; 518111 Internet Services Providers;
    532230 Video Tape and Disc Rental; 511130 Book
    Publishers: 551112 Offices of Other Holding
    Companies; 713110 Amusement and Theme Parks

One of the largest media companies in the world, Viacom Inc. operates numerous subsidiaries in six segments: cable networks; television; radio; outdoor; entertainment; and video. Well known to cable viewers are MTV, Nickelodeon, Nick at Night, VH1, and Showtime. Television holdings include the CBS and UPN television networks, King World Productions, and Paramount Television. Infinity Radio owns and operates a wealth of radio stations. The entertainment segment includes: Paramount Pictures, a producer and distributor of motion pictures since 1912; venerable publisher Simon & Schuster; and Paramount Parks' theme attractions. Viacom Outdoor is engaged in display advertising. Blockbuster Inc. operates and franchises video stores around the globe.

1970s Formation

Viacom was formed by the Central Broadcasting System (CBS) in the summer of 1970 to comply with regulations by the U.S. Federal Communications Commission (FCC) barring tele-vision networks from owning cable TV systems or from syndicating their own programs in the United States. It formally became a separate company in 1971 when CBS distributed Viacom's stock to its stockholders at the rate of one share for every seven shares of CBS stock.

Viacom began with 70,000 stockholders and yearly sales of $19.8 million. It had about 90,000 cable subscribers, making it one of the largest cable operators in the United States. It also had an enviable stable of popular, previously-run CBS television series, including *I Love Lucy,* available for syndication, which accounted for a sizable percentage of Viacom's income.

By 1973 there were about 2,800 cable systems in the United States, with about 7.5 million subscribers. This market fragmentation, along with the lack of an infrastructure in many communities and tough federal regulations, slowed the development of cable television. In 1973, Viacom had 47,000 subscribers on Long Island, New York, but a drive to find 2,000 more added only 250.

In 1976, to compete with Home Box Office (HBO), the leading outlet for films in cable, Viacom established the Showtime movie network, which sought to provide its audience with feature films recently released in theaters. Viacom retained half interest in the network while Warner Amex owned the other half. Despite a federal ruling that removed many restrictions on the choice of movies and sports available on pay-TV during this time and allowed a wider variety of programming, Showtime lost $825,000 in 1977. Nevertheless, Viacom earned $5.5 million that year on sales of $58.5 million. Most of the company's earnings represented sales of television series, but it also reflected the growth of its own cable systems, which at this time had about 350,000 subscribers.

Showtime continued to compete aggressively with HBO. In 1977 it began transmitting its programming to local cable stations via satellite, at a cost of $1.2 million a year. The following year it worked out a deal with Teleprompter Corp., then the largest cable systems operator in the United States, with the result that Teleprompter offered its customers Showtime rather than HBO. Showtime also began offering a service channel called Front Row. Dedicated to family programming, including classic movies and children's shows, Front Row cost consumers

Company Perspectives:

Viacom is a leading global media company, with preeminent positions in broadcast and cable television, radio, outdoor advertising, and online. With programming that appeals to audiences in every demographic category across virtually all media, the company is a leader in the creation, promotion, and distribution of entertainment, news, sports, music, and comedy.

less than $5 a month and was aimed at smaller cable systems where subscribers could not afford a full-time pay-TV service.

Viacom's forays into the production of original programming in the late 1970s and early 1980s had mixed results. Competition was stiff, the odds of producing a successful television series or film were long, and Viacom experienced several failures. The *Lazarus Syndrome* and *Dear Detective* series were failures, and CBS canceled *Nurse* after 14 episodes.

Growth Through Acquisition in the 1980s

Cable systems were a capital-intensive business, and Viacom constantly invested money in building its cable infrastructure—spending $65 million in 1981 alone, for example. In the early 1980s Viacom started on a program of rapid growth across a range of media categories. Company President Terrence A. Elkes told *Business Week* that Viacom hoped to become a billion-dollar company in three to five years. Because management felt that cable operations were not a strong enough engine for that growth, Viacom looked to communications and entertainment. In 1981 it bought Chicago radio station WLAK-FM for $8 million and disclosed its minority stake in Cable Health Network, a new advertiser-supported cable service. It also bought Video Corp. of America for $16 million. That firm's video production equipment stood to save Viacom a great deal of money on production costs.

While its increased size would give Viacom clout with advertisers and advertising agencies, some industry analysts believed that the acquisitions were partly intended to discourage takeover attempts. Buying radio and TV stations increased the firm's debt, and added broadcast licenses to Viacom's portfolio. The transfer of such licenses was a laborious process overseen by the FCC, thereby slowing down attempts to act quickly in taking over a company.

By 1982 Showtime had 3.4 million subscribers, earning about $10 million on sales of $140 million, and was seeking to distinguish itself from other pay-TV sources by offering its own series of programs. While Viacom had sales of about $210 million, syndication still accounted for a large percentage of Viacom's profits, 45 percent in 1982. The growth rate of syndication had declined, however, while that for cable had increased, and by 1982 Viacom had added 450,000 subscribers to the 90,000 it inherited from CBS, making it the ninth largest cable operator in the United States.

However, a decline in pay-TV's popularity began in 1984, and growth in the industry was virtually halted. In early 1984,

Showtime became a sister station to Warner Amex's The Movie Channel in a move calculated to increase sales for both of them. HBO and its sister channel Cinemax were being offered on 5,000 of the 5,800 cable systems in the United States, while Showtime or The Movie Channel were available on 2,700. Besides having a far larger share of the market, HBO already featured many of the films shown by Showtime and The Movie Channel, removing some of the incentive for subscribing to both groups of services. That year Viacom earned $30.9 million on revenue of $320 million.

In September 1985, Viacom purchased the MTV Networks and the other half interest in Showtime from Warner Communications, a company that needed cash because its cable interests were suffering in the unfavorable market. As part of the deal Viacom paid Warner $500 million in cash and $18 million in stock warrants. Viacom also offered $33.50 a share for the one-third of MTV stock that was publicly held. The year before Viacom bought it, MTV had made $11.9 million on sales of $109.5 million. Again, these purchases increased Viacom's debt load, making it less attractive for a takeover.

The MTV Networks included MTV, a popular music video channel; Nickelodeon, a channel geared towards children; and VH-1, a music video channel geared toward an older audience than that of MTV. The most valuable property in the MTV Network was MTV itself. Its quick pace and flashy graphics were becoming highly influential in the media, and its young audience was a chief target of advertisers.

Established by Warner Amex in 1979 in response to a need for children's cable programming, Nickelodeon had not achieved any notable success until acquired by Viacom. Viacom quickly revamped Nickelodeon, giving it the slick, flashy look of MTV and unique programming that both appealed to children and distinguished the network from such competitors as The Disney Channel. Viacom also introduced "Nick at Night," a block of classic sitcoms aired late in the evening, popular among an adult audience. In the next few years Nickelodeon went from being the least popular channel on basic cable to the most popular.

However, Showtime lost about 300,000 customers between March 1985 and March 1986, and cash flow dropped dramatically. In 1986 Showtime embarked on an expensive and risky attempt to gain market share. While Showtime and arch-rival HBO had each featured exclusive presentations of some films, many films were shown on both networks. In order to eliminate this duplication, Showtime gained exclusive rights to several popular films and guaranteed its customers a new film, unavailable on other movie channels, every week. However, Showtime's move increased the price of acquiring even limited rights to a film at a time when many industry observers felt that the price of buying films for pay-TV should be decreasing since the popularity of video cassette recorders had lowered their worth. Consequently, the cost of programming was raised, and Showtime was forced to increase marketing expenditures to make certain potential viewers were aware of the new policy.

Weakened by the $2 billion debt load it incurred, in part, to scare off unfriendly buyers, Viacom lost $9.9 million on sales of $919.2 million in 1986 and, ironically, became a takeover

Key Dates:

1970: Viacom is formed by the Central Broadcasting System (CBS).
1971: Formally made a separate company, Viacom becomes one of the largest cable firms in the United States.
1973: Fragmentation in the cable industry inhibits growth.
1976: Company establishes Showtime movie network to compete with Home Box Office (HBO).
1981: Company invests $65 million in cable infrastructure.
1985: Company purchases MTV Networks.
1986: Debt-weakened Viacom is purchased by Sumner M. Redstone.
1989: Viacom files lawsuit against HBO.
1994: Company purchases Paramount and Blockbuster.
1996: Viacom spins off cable systems.
2000: Viacom buys CBS Corporation.
2004: Redstone announces intention to step down as CEO.

target. First Carl Icahn made an attempt to buy the company, and then a management buyout led by Terrence Elkes failed. Finally, after a six-month battle, Sumner M. Redstone, president of the National Amusements Inc. movie theater chain, bought Viacom for about $3.4 billion in March 1986. Some industry analysts felt that he had vastly overpaid, but Redstone believed Viacom had strong growth potential. Aside from its cable properties and syndication rights that now included the popular series *The Cosby Show,* Viacom owned five television and eight radio stations in major markets.

Redstone had already built National Amusements, the family business, from 50 drive-in movie theaters to a modern chain with 350 screens. Now faced with the task of turning Showtime around, he brought in Frank Biondi, former chief executive of HBO, who began organizing the company's many units into a cooperative workforce. Biondi in turn brought in HBO executive Winston Cox to run the network, and Cox immediately doubled Showtime's marketing budget. Showtime also obtained exclusive contracts with Paramount Pictures and Walt Disney films, which included the rights to air seven of the top ten films of 1986.

Turning Viacom Around in the Late 1980s

Redstone's banks were demanding $450 million in interest in the first two years following the takeover, but several fortuitous events aided him in paying off this debt. Shortly after the buyout Viacom began to earn millions from television stations wanting to show reruns of *The Cosby Show.* Furthermore, when Congress deregulated cable in 1987, prices for cable franchises soared. When Redstone sold some of Viacom's assets to help pay off its debt, he was thus able to get large sums for them. In February 1989 Viacom's Long Island and suburban Cleveland cable systems were sold to Cablevision Systems Corp. for $545 million, or about 20 times their annual cash flow. Cablevision also bought a 5 percent stake in Showtime for $25 million, giving it a tangible interest in the channel's success. Further, after Redstone restruc-

tured MTV and installed a more aggressive advertising-sales staff, MTV experienced continued growth, against the expectations of many industry analysts. In 1989, for example, the MTV Networks won 15 percent of all dollars spent on cable advertising. MTV was expanding throughout the world, broadcasting to Western Europe, Japan, Australia, and large portions of Latin America, with plans to further expand into Eastern Europe, Poland, Brazil, Israel, and New Zealand.

These successes enabled Redstone and Biondi to significantly cut Viacom's debt by September 1989 and negotiate more favorable terms on its loans. Even so, it was rough going at first, and Viacom lost $154.4 million in 1987, though its sales increased to about $1 billion.

Under its new leadership Viacom branched out. Along with Hearst Corp. and Capital Cities/ABC Inc. it introduced Lifetime, a channel geared towards women. It also started its own production operations in 1989, Viacom Pictures, which produced about ten feature films in 1989 at a cost of about $4 million a film. These films first appeared on Showtime. Viacom's television productions also achieved success after years of mixed results. Viacom produced the hit series *Matlock* for NBC and *Jake and the Fatman* for CBS. It also added the rights for *A Different World* and *Roseanne* to its rerun stable. In addition, Viacom continued to spend heavily on new and acquired productions for Nickelodeon and MTV.

In October 1989, Viacom sold 50 percent of Showtime to TCI, a cable systems operator, for $225 million. TCI had six million subscribers, and Viacom hoped the purchase would give TCI increased incentive to market Showtime, thus giving the network a wider distribution.

By 1989 Viacom owned five television stations, 14 cable franchises, and nine radio stations. In November of that year the company bought five more radio stations for $121 million. Sales for the year were about $1.4 billion, with profits of $369 million. In 1990, Viacom introduced a plan that halved the cost of Showtime, but forced cable operators to dramatically increase the number of subscriptions to it. This strategy was designed to increase Showtime's market share at a time when many consumers were starting to feel that pay-TV channels were no longer worth their price.

Several months after HBO introduced its Comedy Channel in 1989, Viacom began transmitting HA!, a channel similar in format. Both channels provided comedy programs, but HA! primarily showed episodes of old sitcoms, while the Comedy Channel showed excerpts from sitcoms, movies, and stand-up comedy routines. Both channels started with subscriber bases in the low millions, and most industry analysts believed that only one of them would survive; Viacom management expected to lose as much as $100 million over a three-year period before HA! broke even. The two companies considered merging their comedy offerings, but HBO parent Time Warner would only move forward with the idea if Viacom agreed to settle its $2.4 billion antitrust suit against HBO.

Showtime had filed the lawsuit in 1989, alleging that HBO was trying to put Showtime out of business by intimidating cable systems that carried Showtime and by trying to corner the market on Hollywood films to prevent competitors from airing them. The suit attracted wide attention and generated much negative publicity for the cable industry.

In August 1992 the suit was finally settled out of court, after having cost both sides tens of millions of dollars in legal fees. Time Warner agreed to pay Viacom $75 million and buy a Viacom cable system in Milwaukee for $95 million, about $10 million more than its estimated worth at the time. Time Warner also agreed to more widely distribute Showtime and The Movie Channel on Time Warner's cable systems, the second largest in the United States. Furthermore, the two sides also agreed to a joint marketing campaign to revive the image of cable, which had suffered since deregulation. Also during this time, in a move that surprised many industry analysts, HBO and Viacom agreed to merge their struggling comedy networks, HA! and the Comedy Channel, into one network, Comedy Central, which ultimately experienced great success.

Overall, Viacom appeared to be thriving. In 1993 the company's net income reached $66 million, earned on revenues of $1.9 billion. Nickelodeon, meanwhile, was going to 57.4 million homes, and was watched by more children between ages two and 11 than the children's programming on all four major networks combined. While Nickelodeon's earnings were not reported separately, the *Wall Street Journal* estimated its profits as $76 million in 1992 on sales of $190 million. However, by the mid-1990s, Redstone was ready for a new challenge. The 70-year-old media mogul found it by expanding Viacom into the motion picture and video rental markets.

In July 1994 Viacom purchased Paramount Communications Inc., one of the world's largest and oldest producers of motion pictures and television shows. The deal, which cost approximately $8 billion, elevated Viacom to the fifth largest media company in the world. The acquisition vastly expanded the company's presence in the entertainment business, giving it a motion picture library that included the classics *The Ten Commandments* and *The Godfather* and an entre into the premier movie market. Moreover, in the Paramount deal Viacom gained ownership of Simon & Schuster, Inc., one of the world's largest book publishers.

Later that same year, the company again expanded into a new segment of the entertainment industry by acquiring Blockbuster, the owner, operator, and franchiser of thousands of video and music stores. The Blockbuster group of subsidiaries was one of Viacom's most quickly growing enterprises; by 1997, Blockbuster boasted 60 million cardholders worldwide and over 6,000 music and video stores.

Viacom's acquisition of Paramount and Blockbuster gave the company thriving new enterprises, but left the company in significant debt. To both relieve that debt and focus the company's energies, Viacom divested itself of several segments of its business. In 1995 the company sold the operations of Madison Square Garden to a partnership of ITT Corp. and Cablevision Systems Corp. for $1.07 billion. In 1996, the company spun off its cable systems in a deal with TCI. Although the split-off represented a break with Viacom's origins as a cable provider, the deal relieved the company of $1.7 billion in debt. The following year, Viacom left the radio broadcasting business by selling its ten radio stations to Evergreen Media Corporation.

The approximately $1.1 billion deal reduced Viacom's debt even further.

Although Viacom was no longer a cable service provider, and it had expanded into the motion picture and video rental market, its cable networks remained a significant portion of its business. MTV Networks, which included MTV, Nickelodeon, and VH1, accounted for almost $625 million in operating profits in 1997, approximately 32 percent of Viacom's estimated earnings for the year.

By June 1998, Viacom had more than recovered from the hit it had taken from the Blockbuster purchase. Stock equaled its 1995 high, a joint production of the movie *Titanic* had seen spectacular box office receipts, and the sell-off of most of Simon & Schuster book publishing operations brought in $4.6 billion. A new strategy for Blockbuster drove up its sagging market share. Furthermore, Viacom had been on a global expansion drive, selling broadcast rights to Paramount's film library, for example. MTV was becoming an international brand as well.

Creating Synergy: 1999–2004

In 1999, Redstone held about $9 billion worth of Viacom shares. The company's stock had outshined rivals Time Warner, Disney, and News Corp. That year, Viacom announced plans to buy out CBS Corporation for $37 billion in stock. The heydays of network television were in the past. CBS's cash flow for the year would come from cable, radio, stations, and billboards. Cable ranked first among profitable segments of the entertainment business during the decade, with radio close behind.

CBS had made an early stab into cable in 1981, but the effort tanked. The "Tiffany Network" steered away from the medium after that while its direct competitors, ABC, NBC, and Fox, made inroads. The tide turned thanks to CEO Mel Karmazin and his predecessor Michael Jordan. "Not until 1997 did Jordan and Karmazin lead CBS back into cable by buying two music channels, the Nashville Network and County Music Television, for $1.5 billion," Marc Gunther wrote for *Fortune*.

Redstone had his eye on those channels and proposed an exchange of Viacom television stations for the country channels. But Karmazin convinced Redstone of the synergistic benefits of merging the two media giants and the deal was completed in May 2000. Redstone relinquished "effective operating control" of the merged company to Karmazin, according to the *Wall Street Journal* in 2003. Wall Street applauded the move, respectful of Karmazin's record in financial management and operational details as head of CBS.

But a few years down the road, it became less and less likely that Karmazin would succeed Redstone. Not only did the pair have an uneasy relationship, but Karmazin failed to meet earnings targets from 2001 to 2003. Moreover, Redstone wanted back some of the power he had relinquished.

Despite the three-year deal they arrived at in 2003, in June 2004 Karmazin resigned.

Redstone named MTV's Tom Freston and CBS's Leslie Moonves co-presidents, setting up a competition between them for his heir apparent.

Television, radio, and outdoor segments reported to Moonves and cable networks, entertainment, and video, to Freston. Television had produced 29 percent of Viacom's 2003 consolidated revenues; followed by video, 22 percent; cable networks, 21 percent; entertainment, 15 percent; radio, 8 percent; and outdoor, 5 percent.

Significantly, Redstone was prepared to finally step down as CEO, something he said he would do within the next three years. Gunther wrote for *Fortune*, "Until now the 81-year-old Redstone had stubbornly refused to set a date for his retirement. No one can force him out, because he controls 71% of the shareholder votes at $27 billion-a-year Viacom."

Principal Subsidiaries

Blockbuster Videos, Inc.; Paramount Pictures; Paramount Home Entertainment; Simon & Schuster; MTV Networks; Showtime Networks Inc.; VH1 Inc.; BET; The CBS Television Network; United Paramount Network; Infinity Broadcasting; Paramount Television; Paramount Parks.

Principal Competitors

News Corp.; Time Warner; Walt Disney.

Further Reading

Atlas, Riva, "Paramount, Anyone?" *Forbes*, May 23, 1994, p. 264.

Berkowitz, Harry, "Company President Leaves, Karmazin Steps Down at Viacom, Surprise Resignation Follows Often-Rocky Relationship with CEO Redstone," *Newsday*, June 2, 2004, p. A2.

Flint, Joe, "Final Cut: Karmazin Leaves Post, Ending a Stormy Marriage," *Wall Street Journal*, June 2, 2004.

Gubernick, Lisa, "Sumner Redstone Scores Again," *Forbes*, October 31, 1988.

Gunther, Marc, "Behind the Shakeup at Viacom," *Fortune*, June 28, 2004, p. 34.

——, "This Gang Controls Your Kids' Brains," *Fortune*, October 27, 1997, pp. 172–78.

——, "Sumner ♡ Mel: CBS, Viacom, and the Triumph of Cable," *Fortune*, October 11, 1999, pp. 54+.

——, "Viacom: Redstone's Remarkable Ride to the Top," *Fortune*, April 26, 1999, pp. 130+.

"How Much for Ads on Children's TV? A Million and a Half Dollars, If They Violate F.C.C. Rules," *New York Times*, October 22, 2004.

Impoco, Jim, "America's Hippest Grandpa," *U.S. News & World Report*, September 27, 1993, p. 67.

Lazaroff, Leon, "Viacom Prepares to Battle FCC over $550,000 Indecency Fine," *Knight-Ridder Tribune Business News*, November 10, 2004.

Lenzner, Robert, and Peter Newcomb, "The Vindication of Sumner Redstone," *Forbes*, June 15, 1998, pp. 50+.

Lieberman, David, "Is Viacom Ready to Channel the World?" *Business Week*, December 18, 1989.

Peers, Martin, "Leading the News: Viacom Is Near Deal to Retain Top Management," *Wall Street Journal*, March 20, 2003, p. A3

"Viacom's Risky Quest for Growth," *Business Week*, June 21, 1982.

—Scott M. Lewis
—updates: Susan Windisch Brown, Kathleen Peippo

Viasystems Group, Inc.

101 S. Hanley Road, Suite 400
St. Louis, Missouri 63105
U.S.A.
Telephone: (314) 727-2087
Fax: (314) 746-2233
Web site: http://www.viasystems.com

Private Company
Incorporated: 1996 as Circo Craft Holding Company
Employees: 22,400
Sales: $751.5 million (2003)
NAIC: 334412 Printed Circuit Board Manufacturing

Viasystems Group, Inc. is a St. Louis-based provider of electronics manufacturing services (EMS) to original equipment manufacturers (OEMs). It primarily serves the telecommunications, automotive, computer, industrial, and consumer industries. The company operates 18 plants and other facilities located in the United States, Canada, China, France, Ireland, Italy, The Netherlands, and the United Kingdom. Products and services offered by Viasystems include the design and building of printed circuit boards, backpanel assemblies that connect printed circuit boards, thermal management equipment, wire harnesses and customer cable assemblies, and electromechanical enclosure systems such as equipment racks, cabinets, shelters, and walk-in cabins. Viasystems also helps customers with the procurement and management of materials, and with the assembly, integration, and testing of their products and complete systems. Major customers include General Electric, Delphi, Lucent, and Siemens.

Forming the Company in the Mid-1990s

Viasystems was incorporated in August 1996 as Circo Craft Holding Company to acquire Circo Craft Co. Inc., Canada's leading independent manufacturer of printed circuit boards, and the board business of Lucent Technologies. The money, some $330 million, was provided by the Dallas investment firm of Hicks, Muse, Tate & Furst Incorporated and the St. Louis-area investment and management services firm of Mills & Partners,

Inc. The heads of the two companies had worked together on two prior ventures. Hicks, then operating under the Hicks & Haas name, burst onto the scene as a top leveraged buyout firm in the 1980s with the purchase of Dr. Pepper Co., which was then merged with Seven-Up Co. In 1989 Hicks teamed up with the chairman and chief executive officer of Mills & Partners, James N. Mills, to acquire Thermadyne Industries and other companies, forming Thermadyne Holdings. Mills served as chief executive officer and chairman of the board of the diversified manufacturer of cutting and welding products, wear-resistant products, and commercial and industrial floor cleaning equipment.

In 1993 Hicks and Mills again joined forces to buy Berg Electronics Corp. With Mills again taking over as CEO and chairman, Berg then completed nine strategic acquisitions to make itself into a global maker of electronic connectors for printed circuit boards as well as cable assembly products for computer and telecommunications customers. The partners then took Berg public in 1996. The October 1996 purchase of Circo Craft by Hicks and Mills was the first step in a bid to transfer Berg's success in the connector business to the printed-circuit board segment. Rather than fold the Circo and former Lucent assets into Berg, the partners opted to form a separate company. Circuit board makers were not generally embraced by investors and it was feared that shareholder value might be compromised by muddying Berg's business mix.

In January 1997 the Viasystems name was adopted and James Mills took over as CEO and chairman of the new concern. The strategy was to adopt the successful "buy and build" formula he had applied at Berg, with the aim of becoming a dominant global player in the PCB area and taking the company public. Already Viasystems was the second largest bare-board maker in the world and a force to be reckoned with in backpanel assemblies. It also had a number of acquisitions lined up to grow the company even larger and spread its global presence. In April 1997 Viasystems added Forward Group PLC, a major U.K. manufacturer of printed circuit boards with plants in England, Scotland, and South Africa. Subsequently another U.K.-based PCB manufacturer, Interconnection Systems Limited, was purchased. These deals greatly enhanced Viasystems' ability to serve the important European market. At this stage, the company also was taking steps to add plants in Mexico and establish a presence in Asia, as well as to fill in gaps in the U.S. market with the construction of facilities on both coasts. At the end of its first year of operation, Viasystems posted revenues of $795.3 million and a loss of $327.5 million.

Global Aspirations in the Late 1990s

Viasystems continued to expand through acquisitions in 1998. In January of that year it bought a PCB production facility in Sweden from Ericsson Telecom AB and a month later added Mommers Print Service B.V., a PCB company based in The Netherlands. Zincocelere S.p.A., an Italian PCB manufacturer with facilities in both Italy and England, was added in March. After this spate of activity, Mills declared that he was satisfied with the company's European footprint. Viasystems' European operations were then consolidated and structured into three business groups: Commercial Products, to serve customers primarily involved in the automotive, computers, datacom, industrial and instrumentation, and mobile telecommunications industries; Technology Products, to build PCBs and backpanels for high-end applications such as computer processing units and servers; and Special Products, to fabricate high-performance products primarily for defense and aerospace applications. Now that Viasystems had manufacturing facilities spread across North America and Europe, Mills hoped to focus next on Asia, thus establishing a global presence. Revenues for 1998 topped the $1 billion mark, and the company cut its net loss to $88 million.

The final step in Viasystems' global ambitions was taken in August 1999 when it paid $325 million to acquire the Kalex PCB manufacturing division of Termbray Industries International Holdings Ltd. Viasystems received two vertically integrated operations in China with a combined production capacity exceeding 15 million square feet, capable of producing double-sided and multilayer PCBs. As a result, Viasystems was now a true global PCB manufacturer, but it also was looking to evolve into a full-service CEM, thus making it a more valuable play when the company was ultimately taken public. For the year Viasystems grew sales to $1.1 million and recorded another sizable loss totaling $726.3 million.

Viasystems filed for an initial public offering (IPO) of stock in early 2000. In conjunction with the offering the company planned to acquired the wire-harness business of International Wire Inc. for $210 million. In the meantime, in keeping with its plan to become a global, full-service CEM, it acquired the cable assembly and power supply business of U.K.-based Marconi PLC at a cost of $115 million. With Morgan Stanley Dean Witter serving as the lead underwriter, Viasystems completed its IPO in April 2000. Although the price range was announced at $16–$19, the company was able to fetch $21 a share. As a result, the company netted $873 million, instead of the $500 million it had originally hoped to raise. About $500 million was earmarked to pay down a $950 million debt load. Investor

enthusiasm quickly waned, however, as it did with many technology stocks at the time. Viasystems dipped as low as $8 a share, although it rebounded to the $16 range, putting the company in a difficult position to return to the market for additional funds to aid in its quest to surpass San Jose-based Sanmina Corp. as the largest CEM. In October 2000 Viasystems canceled a secondary offering in which it hoped to sell another 17 million shares to the public.

Despite canceling its offering, Viasystems did make several more acquisitions in 2000, including Top Line Electronics Corporation, a San Jose CEM; Lucent Technologies' Global Provisioning Center in Rouen, France, a fully integrated builder of PCBs for the radio telecommunications and transmission market; Laughlin-Witt Group, Inc., a CEM with plants in Orange County, California, and Beaverton, Oregon; and Accutec, an Oak Creek, Wisconsin, company involved in the metal enclosure business. Viasystems also built a 150,000-square-foot plant in Shanghai. The addition of these assets helped to boost Viasystems' revenues to more than $1.6 billion in 2000. But the company also posted another net loss of $136 million.

At the start of 2001 Mills was upbeat in the press about the state of Viasystems and its progress in becoming something of a one-stop CEM, but within a few weeks the prospects for the company quickly soured. A slowing economy had hurt all of the technology sector, leading to a sudden drop in orders. Some 1,700 jobs in North America and another 250 in Europe were soon eliminated and a good bit of work was transferred to the Chinese plants, where workers earned $1.66 compared with $18 an hour in Viasystems' Richmond plant. The company also cut back on its capital expenditures for the year, although management felt it was still a good idea to spend as much as $70 million to upgrade facilities in China. By June Viasystems was announcing that it would close plants in Richmond, Virginia, and in Puerto Rico. In July, Hicks agreed to commit to providing another $100 million in funds to help the situation, then two weeks later a shakeup took place in the upper ranks of management. James Mills stepped down as CEO, replaced by Viasystems' chief financial officer and Mills & Partners' president and chief operating officer, David Sindelar. A company spokesman insisted that Mills had not been forced out; rather, the 44-year-old Sindelar was simply ready to tackle more responsibility.

Mills remained as chairman of the company, and although that reassured investors that Viasystems was not making any radical changes, it did not prevent analysts from criticizing Mills. According to a 2001 article in *EBN,* "industry observers say a series of missteps by Mills in executing Viasystems' dual PCB fabrication and EMS identities has put the company behind the eight ball. . . . Some observers say Viasystems' troubles started when the company began expanding its global footprint to low-cost Asian and higher-cost European sites. Some analysts said the company bought manufacturing plants that were not viable and added to its debts." There was also speculation that Viasystems had made itself an attractive takeover target for an EMS company that wanted to establish itself in Asia.

Collapsing Sales in the Early 2000s

Sales in 2001 fell to $1.2 billion while the company's net loss grew to more than $500 million. All told, Viasystems owed more

```
┌─────────────────────────────────────────────┐
│              Key Dates:                      │
│                                              │
│ 1996:  The company is formed.                │
│ 1997:  The Viasystems name is adopted.       │
│ 2000:  The company is taken public.          │
│ 2002:  The company files for Chapter 11      │
│        bankruptcy protection.                │
│                                              │
└─────────────────────────────────────────────┘
```

than $1 billion. Moreover, the price of Viasystems' stock fell below $1 on November 20 and after a month at this level it faced the prospect of being delisted by the New York Stock Exchange. In February 2002 Mills retired as chairman. By April the stock was delisted and the company resorted to the OTC Bulletin Board, the electronic exchange operated by the NASDAQ. To help in its efforts to reduce its debt and recapitalize, it hired a New York investment-advisory firm, Rothschild Inc. In October 2002 Viasystems filed a prepackaged bankruptcy restructuring plan that would eliminate $720 million in debt. As part of the plan, the company would be taken private, with its public debt replaced with privately held common and preferred stock.

Viasystems emerged from Chapter 11 bankruptcy protection in 2003. What kept the company afloat was its Chinese operations, where most production was shifted in order to cut costs. In 2003 Viasystems managed to generate revenues of only $751.5 million. In March 2004 it filed plans to conduct another IPO of stock, in hopes of raising $275 million. There were some positive trends emerging in the telecommunications industry that could bode well for the company's future, but the company's business remained extremely competitive, requiring a great deal of capital, and subject to severe price swings. The timing for an offering appeared right, but there were some questions about the long-term viability of the company. By July, amid fluctuating market conditions, management decided to withdraw the stock offering, opting instead for a private placement to current shareholders.

But the success of that effort, as well as the future of the company, remained very much in doubt.

Principal Subsidiaries

Viasystems, Inc.; Viasystems International, Inc.; Shanghai Viasystems EMS Co. Ltd. (China); Kalex Printed Circuit Board Limited (Hong Kong); Kalex EMS (Hong Kong) Company Ltd.

Principal Competitors

Flextronics International Ltd.; Sanmina-SCI Corporation; Solectron Corporation.

Further Reading

Elliot, Heidi, "Viasystems' Next Stop: Asia," *Electronic News,* March 23, 1998, p. 46.

Feldstein, Mary Jo, "Clayton, Mo.-Based Electronics Maker Plans Yet Another IPO," *St. Louis Post-Dispatch,* March 18, 2004.

McKeefry, Hailey Lynne, "Viasystems Scores Via Vertical Integration," *EBN,* January 1, 2001, p. 72.

Richtmyer, Richard, "Viasystems Plugs in Winning Formula," *Electronic Buyers' News,* August 9, 1999, p. 4.

Sender, Henny, "Why China Is Viasystems' Salvation," *Wall Street Journal,* December 5, 2003, p. C7.

Serant, Claire, "Is Viasystems' Restructuring Enough?," *EBN,* February 26, 2001, p. 85.

——, "Viasystems Fights Back After IPO Woes," *Electronic Buyers' News,* June 19, 2000, p. 74.

Sheerin, Matthew, "Viasystems: 'We're a CEM'—In IPO Filing, PCB Maker Maps Plan to Expand Its Offerings," *Electronic Buyers' News,* January 17, 2000, p. 1.

Waurzyniak, Patrick, "Berg Team Building Board Empire," *Electronic Buyers' News,* March 3, 1997, p. 1.

Waurzyniak, Patrick, and Matthew Sheerin, " 'Buy and Build' Plan Propels Board Maker," *Electronic Buyers' News,* May 12, 1997, p. 1.

—Ed Dinger

Vidrala S.A.

Barrio Munegazo 22
Llodio
E-01400
Spain
Telephone: +34 94 671 97 10
Fax: +34 94 671 97 17
Web site: http://www.vidrala.com

Public Company
Incorporated: 1965 as Vidrieras de Alava S.A.
Employees: 642
Sales: EUR 147.17 million ($157.5 million) (2003)
Stock Exchanges: Bolsa de Madrid
Ticker Symbol: VID.MC
NAIC: 327213 Glass Container Manufacturing; 423840
   Industrial Supplies Merchant Wholesalers

Vidrala S.A. is the second largest producer of hollow glass containers in Spain and Portugal, and is the largest independent producer in those markets. Based in Spain's Basque regions—where the company is close to the main wine-making regions of Spain and France—Vidrala produces some 600 different products spanning the wine and fruit juice sectors, as well as the soft drink, beer, other alcoholic beverages, preserves, vinegar, and related market segments. The company is also Spain's leading manufacturer of bottles for olive oil. Part of Vidrala's success has been a longstanding commitment to investment. In an industry where market share and sales growth are directly related to capacity, Vidrala has made steady increases in its production capacity since the mid-1980s. The company now operates a total of five furnaces in Spain, including three at the main Vidrala headquarters site in Llodio, the state of Alava, and two at subsidiary Crisnova's plant Caudete, in Albacete. Together, these plants give Vidrala production levels of more than 450,000 tons per year in Spain alone. Since 2003, Vidrala also has extended its operations to Portugal, where it acquired glassmaker Ricardo Gallo, in Marinha Grande. That acquisition boosted Vidrala's total production past 600,000 tons per year. The addition of Gallo also raised Vidrala's profile in the Iberian market, giving it a 20 percent share of the hollow glass market. Vidrala is listed on the Bolsa de Madrid and is controlled by the Delclaux family. In 2003, the company posted sales of EUR 147 million ($157 million).

Making Glass in the 1960s

Originally from the village of Galgan, in France's Pyrenées mountains, the Delclaux family had been involved in Spain's glassmaking industry for more than 100 years prior to the founding of Vidrala in 1965. The founder of the family's Spanish branch was Louis Delclaux, who, at the age of 20, immigrated to Spain in 1840. Delclaux settled in the town of Llodio, in the Alava region, and became one of the first to use the region's peat deposits to fuel a high-temperature furnace. Delclaux quickly became one of the region's most prominent industrialists.

The family's introduction to the glassmaking industry came through Delclaux's son, Isidoro Delclaux Ibarzabal, born in 1858, who made use of the family's furnaces to extend its production from metals to glass. Delclaux interests in particular went toward the production of flat glass for the growing photographic market. Delclaux also established La Verdad, a distributor of the family's and others glass and metal products. The next generation of Delclaux, Isidoro Delclaux Aróstegui, born in 1894, continued to build up the family's business.

By the second half of the 20th century, the Delclaux family's holdings encompassed a variety of glass and related companies, such as Vidrieras de Arte, Vidrieras de Llodio, Valca, Argón (later known as Praxair), Delta Eléctrica, Financiera Española, Tuvos Reunidos, and others. Another of the family's holdings was Vidrieras de Alava, under which was grouped the company's flat glass operations.

Founded in Llodio in 1965, Vidrieras de Alava brought the family into the production of glass bottles. The new company built its first furnace, and launched production in 1966. Total annual output at the new plant stood at just 25,000 tons per year.

The company quickly expanded its range of bottle types from an initial set of 12 as its production increased to meet the

Key Dates:

1965: Vidrieras de Alava is created by the Delclaux family in Llodio, Spain, in order to produce glass bottles; the family's flat glass manufacturing operations also are incorporated.
1966: Production begins at the first kiln.
1967: The company first exports sales to France.
1977: Lightweight glass bottles are launched.
1981: The company changes its name to Vidrala.
1985: Vidrala lists on the Bolsa de Madrid and Bilbao stock exchange; the flat glass operations are sold to Guardian Industries; a new subsidiary, Crisnova, is created in Albacette.
1989: The first Crisnova kiln begins production.
1995: The company installs the third kiln at the Llodio plant.
1999: The company launches production at its second Crisnova plant.
2003: The company acquires Ricardo Gallo of Portugal, increasing production capacity to 600,000 tons per year.
2004: A EUR 25 million investment program is launched in order to expand capacity in Spain and build a new central warehouse in Portugal.

strong demand for bottles in the period. Vidrieras de Alava also turned early to the foreign market, launching exports in 1967. The French wine industry became a particularly important market for the company, and Vidrieras de Alava supported its international growth with the construction of a second furnace at the Llodio site.

The company's proximity to France's wine growers helped its own growth over the next decade. This was particularly true given the relatively high costs and complexities of shipping glass bottles, and glass in general. Profits depended strongly on reducing the costs of transporting bottles, which in turn encouraged the development of a predominantly local, fragmented glass industry in Spain and throughout much of Europe.

In 1977, however, the company introduced a new range of bottles based on its development of lightweight glass. This technological development enabled Vidrieras de Alava to emerge as one of Spain's top bottle makers, and the company's sales expanded nationwide. The company continued to invest in developing new technologies and in 1981 began converting its furnaces with new energy savings technology. This enabled the company to slash its operating costs by some 50 percent. In that year, as well, the company changed its name to Vidrala.

Continued investment in improving and expanding its production capacity enabled Vidrala to gain an increasing share of the Spanish bottle market during the 1980s. In 1985, Vidrala went public, listing its shares on the Bolsa de Madrid and Bilbao stock exchange. The Delclaux family, which had sold its flat glass manufacturing operations to the United States' Guardian Industries that year, nonetheless retained control of Vidrala.

The public offering enabled the company to invest in its first expansion beyond the Basque region, with the creation of a subsidiary, Crisnova, in Albacete in Spain's southeast central region. Construction began on the new company's facility, with a state-of-the-art furnace. When production began in 1989, the Albacete plant featured among Europe's most modern glassmaking facilities. The Crisnova site added production capacity of 95,000 tons per year to Vidrala's Llodio plant's 130,000 tons per year.

By the early 1990s, Vidrala had claimed the number three spot among Spain's glass bottle manufacturers with a 14 percent market share. It was also the only glass bottle maker in the Basque region, giving it leadership status at home. While the overall glass industry grew only slowly during the economic difficulties at the beginning of the 1990s, Vidrala's technology investments and proximity to key markets enabled it to outpace its competitors. After a drop in sales in 1992, the company rebounded, with revenues nearing ESP 10 billion in 1993.

Investing in Leadership for the 2000s

Vidrala continued to gain despite the lingering recession into the mid-1990s, in part by leveraging its location in the Basque region to step up its exports to France. By then, France represented nearly 25 percent of Vidrala's sales. The company's plants also were operating at full capacity as the European market experienced a shortage in hollow glass.

Vidrala quickly recognized the potential for rapid market share gains to be had through an increase in its production. This led the company to construct a third kiln at the Llodio plant in 1995. Production at the new kiln was underway by the end of that year, adding full production potential of 110,000 tons per year. This brought the company's total production capacity to 340,000 tons per year. The boost in production enabled the company to post strong increases in its sales—in Spain, its sales rose by 18 percent by 1996, while in France, Vidrala marked a sales increase of 51 percent. The company ramped up to full production at the new kiln in 1997.

By then, the company had begun plans to expand its capacity again, this time through its Crisnova subsidiary. In 1998, the company launched construction of a second kiln at the Albacete site. Designed to add another 110,000 tons per year to the group's total output, the new kiln was brought online by mid-1999. The increase in production, to 450,000 tons per year, enabled the company to post strong revenue gains, with sales topping EUR 114 million in 1999, and rising to EUR 126 million by 2001.

The European glass market remained highly fragmented into the 2000s. Yet the first signs of a consolidation of the market—similar to that of the United States, which resulted in the creation of just three dominant groups in the 1980s—had begun to appear. Although a major player in the Spanish market, Vidrala remained tiny in the overall European market. The company was forced to seek means of gaining critical mass in order to protect its domestic position. As it moved toward the mid-1990s, the company began considering its options, such as extending its reach beyond Europe and into the Latin American or North African markets. The company also had the option of allowing itself to be acquired by a larger group.

Yet Vidrala's first external expansion effort kept it close to home. In 2003, the company reached an agreement to acquire leading Portuguese-based bottle maker Ricardo Gallo. Based in Marinha Grande, Gallo had been founded in 1899, and, with two kilns of its own, had built up an annual production capacity of 150,000 tons. Gallo also operated five warehouses located throughout Portugal. The merger of Gallo's operations into Vidrala gave the Spanish company control of 20 percent of the Iberian Peninsula's glass bottle market, and the second place position in Spain itself.

In 2004, the company launched a EUR 25 million investment program. Approximately EUR 15 million was earmarked for improvements at the Llodio plant, particularly in expanding the third kiln's production capacity by 10 percent in order to meet rising demand. Vidrala also began construction of a new, centralized warehouse in Portugal in order to replace Gallo's previous warehouse network. Vidrala, which had earned a reputation as the most efficient glass bottle maker in Europe—and one of the most efficient in the world—remained true to its longstanding commitment to investing in its growth.

Principal Subsidiaries

Crisnova S.A.

Principal Competitors

Ball Plastic Container Div.; Groupe Danone; Schott Glas; Owens-Illinois Inc.; OSRAM GmbH; Saint-Gobain Container Inc.; El Nasr Glass and Crystal Co.; Saint-Gobain Cristaleria S.A.; Rexam Beverage Packaging AB; Arc International.

Further Reading

"Furnace Rebuild," *Glass,* October 2003, p. 266.
"Growing Vidrala," *Glass,* April 2004.
"Vidrala Announces Transparency Measures," *Glass,* May 2003, p. 108.
"Vidrala," *Glass,* August 2002, p. 209.
"Vidrala investira 25 millions au Pays Basque et dans sa filiale Ricardo Gallo," *Expansion,* 23 June 2004.

—M.L. Cohen

VOLVO

AB Volvo

S-405 08
Göteborg
Sweden
Telephone: (31) 66 00 00
Fax: (31) 54 57 72
Web site: http://www.volvo.com

Public Company
Incorporated: 1915 as a subsidiary of AB Svenska
    Kullagerfabriken (SKF)
Employees: 75,740
Sales: EUR 19.15 billion ($24.12 billion) (2003)
Stock Exchanges: Stockholm NASDAQ
Ticker Symbol: VOLV; VOLVY
NAIC: 336120 Heavy Duty Truck Manufacturing; 333120
    Construction Machinery Manufacturing; 333618 Other
    Engine Equipment Manufacturing; 336412 Aircraft
    Engine and Engine Parts Manufacturing

The largest company in Sweden in revenue terms and the biggest employer in that nation's private sector, AB Volvo is one of the world's largest manufacturers of heavy-duty trucks and buses. The firm's truck operations, which include Volvo Trucks, Renault Trucks, and Mack Trucks, produced nearly 156,000 trucks during 2003. In buses, where Volvo holds the number two position worldwide, production topped 7,800. In addition, Volvo is the world's largest manufacturer of heavy diesel engines and the fourth largest producer of construction equipment, produces engines for leisure boats and power generating equipment, and makes components for aircraft and rocket engines. The company sold its Volvo automaking business to Ford Motor Company in March 1999 in order to focus on commercial vehicles.

Early History

Volvo began as a subsidiary of AB Svenska Kullagerfabriken (SKF), a large Swedish industrial company. In 1914 Scania Vabis ceased production of what had been Sweden's only domestically built automobile to concentrate on more profitable trucks. A year later, with the encouragement of the Swedish Association of Engineers and Architects, SKF began a confidential study of the feasibility of manufacturing its own car. Assar Gabrielsson and Gustav Larson started the project. Gabrielsson, who had represented SKF in France and the United States, was a ball bearing salesperson who had closely studied American automobiles. Larson was an engineer with substantial experience in Britain, having worked for the English company White & Poppe.

SKF named the secret project Volvo—Latin for "I roll"—a dormant product name the company had introduced in 1915 for a line of ball bearings. Independently incorporated in 1915, hence the title *aktiebolaget,* or "AB," the venture itself was only informally associated with SKF. The primary owners were Larson and Gabrielsson.

After agonizing over dozens of designs, the two partners settled on a simple model that would negotiate Swedish roads, with their snow, mud, steep hills, and millions of potholes, especially well. The original design, a car called the GL, or "Larson," was assembled at an abandoned SKF ball bearing factory at Hisingen, near Göteborg, from parts ordered out of various supplier catalogs from throughout Europe and the United States.

The first production model, an öV4, later called the "Jakob," rolled out of the factory on April 14, 1927. To the horror of all involved, it was discovered that the differential had been misconnected, resulting in a car that had three gears in reverse and only one gear for forward motion. The mistake took only ten minutes to correct and Volvo survived the comical episode.

With 60 workers turning out five cars a week, the company proceeded with plans to manufacture a truck. The first truck model, introduced in 1928, was, in fact, from a design that predated the GL by four months. Volvo trucks, equipped with in-line six-cylinder engines, became extremely popular. Whereas auto sales remained slow and their profits only marginal, the truck models consistently sold out. Profits from truck sales financed the operation for the next 20 years.

Company Perspectives:

Volvo Group Mission Statement: By creating value for our customers, we create value for our shareholders.

We use our expertise to create transport-related products and services of superior quality, safety and environmental care for demanding customers in selected segments.

We work with energy, passion, and respect for the individual.

Volvo's cars and trucks were extremely sturdy and, by many measures, better assembled than American and other European models. In what was the most effective advertising of the day, Volvo models won several speed and endurance tests, racing across Sweden and speeding from Moscow to Leningrad, and later winning contests in Monte Carlo and Argentina. Because both Larson and Gabrielsson detested automobile contests, however, Volvo refused to sponsor racers.

Volvo introduced a six-cylinder model, the PV651, in 1929, which proved highly successful with the lucrative taxicab market, and a larger version was soon planned. The following year, with the introduction of several new models and strong sales, Volvo purchased a controlling interest in its engine manufacturer, Pentaverken, located in Skövde. The company also purchased the Hisingen plant from SKF.

Challenges During the Great Depression and World War II

As the economy ground to a halt from the effects of the Great Depression, car sales slumped. General Motors Corporation (GM), which had a Chevrolet plant in Stockholm at the time, attacked Volvo for being, in effect, "kit made." The company conducted a quick study that revealed that its cars were about 90 percent domestic content. Thus, it hit back at GM, advertising its products as "the *Swedish* cars."

Such competition kept Volvo on the alert, constantly studying other manufacturers. In 1935 it brought out a revolutionary new design: the PV36 Carioca, a streamlined art deco model, named for a popular South American dance. Later that year, the company took full control of Pentaverken and, achieving its full independence from SKF, its stock was floated on the Stockholm exchange.

While the company was introducing variations on the PV36, growing hostilities in Europe began to interrupt fuel supplies. In response, Volvo developed a means of manufacturing a combustible gas from charcoal in 1939. By this time, however, the government was prohibiting the operation of private cars. Despite the lack of crucial foreign components, Volvo continued production of cars and trucks, though mostly for military use. The company pressed on with new civilian designs in anticipation of the end of the war. Meanwhile, in 1942, Volvo took control of Svenska Flygmotor AB, a precision engineering company, and Köpings Mekaniska Verkstad AB, a gear and gearbox manufacturer.

In 1944 Volvo began taking orders for its long-awaited new model, the PV444—priced at SEK 4800, the same as the 1927

öV4—although actual production had to wait until the end of the war the following summer. By then, however, an engineering strike crippled production, and gasoline was still under strict ration. Plans to introduce another model, the PV60, were similarly delayed in 1946 when a sheet metal supplier could not be lined up.

By 1947 these problems were alleviated, and production began, albeit slowly. Volvo now had a domestic competitor, Scania, which resumed automobile manufacturing after the war as a unit of Svenska Aeroplan Aktiebolaget (SAAB), an aircraft manufacturer. By 1948 car sales exceeded truck and bus sales for the first time, and by 1950, Volvo employed 6,000 people and had turned out more than 100,000 vehicles, including 20,000 for export.

The 1950s and 1960s: New Models and Markets

Gustav Larson retired from active involvement with Volvo in 1952 but continued to serve the company as an advisor. The following year, the company introduced the Duett, the first of many family estate cars designed for work and leisure. In 1954 Volvo had built a new truck factory in Göteborg, increasing annual production capacity to 15,000 vehicles, and had introduced fuel injection systems and turbochargers on its diesel engines.

In 1955 Volvo rolled out a small convertible with a plastic body and puncture proof tires called the Sport. Sales languished, however, and production was halted after only 67 had been produced. Volvo had better luck the next year with the Amazon, a welded frame sedan that borrowed heavily from other European models of the day. Later that year, Assar Gabrielsson also retired. He was succeeded by Gunnar Engellau, the head of Volvo Flygmotor.

Engellau took Volvo's helm at the height of the Suez Canal Crisis when all shipping, including oil, was refused passage. The resulting oil shortage in Sweden caused a severe drop in automobile sales. Engellau gambled that the crisis would be resolved within months, and he began laying plans for a major expansion, deciding to boldly go after export markets, especially the huge American market. Engellau was correct, and when the crisis subsided, Volvo was ready to meet the demand for new cars.

By 1959, with more than 15,000 employees, Volvo broke ground on a massive new production facility at Torslanda, near Hisingen. The following year, the company introduced a new sports car, the P1800. The car was prominently featured in the British television series *The Saint*. In fact, the car was even driven in private life by the star of the series, Roger Moore.

As other models in the product line were improved with ergonomically designed seats and new safety features—including the introduction of three-point safety belts as standard equipment in 1959—Volvo offered a revolutionary five-year engine guarantee that included coverage for damage resulting from accidents. The Swedish insurance industry, with government backing, sued Volvo for infringing on its business but, after four years of litigation, lost.

In 1963 Volvo opened a plant in Halifax, Nova Scotia, for the assembly of cars for the North American market. The initial 1956 introduction of the PV444 in the United States had been

---

Key Dates:

1915: The Swedish firm Svenska Kullagerfabriken (SKF) forms a subsidiary called AB Volvo to investigate the manufacturing of cars.

1927: Production of Volvo cars begins at a factory in Göteborg.

1928: First Volvo truck model rolls off the assembly line.

1935: Company gains full independence from SKF, and its stock is listed on the Stockholm exchange.

1964: New assembly plants open: for cars in Torslanda; for trucks near Brussels, Belgium.

1965: New auto assembly plant opens in Ghent, Belgium.

1990: Complex alliance is entered into with Renault.

1994: Following an aborted merger, the alliance with Renault is dissolved.

1995: Volvo Construction Equipment is created after Volvo buys out former joint venture partner.

1997: Company gains full control of a former joint venture in heavy trucks with GM, which is renamed Volvo Trucks North America, Inc.

1999: Volvo sells its automobile business to Ford Motor Company for $6.45 billion in order to concentrate on commercial vehicles; company reaches agreement to acquire rival truckmaker Scania AB for EUR 7 billion ($7.53 billion).

2000: European Commission blocks the Scania takeover on anticompetitive grounds.

2001: Volvo acquires Renault S.A.'s heavy-truck business, including Mack Trucks, in exchange for a 15 percent stake in Volvo.

---

met with indifference, as most Americans still favored large, stylish vehicles such as the Buick Roadmaster. But despite its plain appearance, the PV444 was extremely well built. Subsequent models, such as the PV544, featured larger engines and windows and many new accessories. Furthermore, the company began sponsoring auto races.

The Torslanda plant, with an annual production capacity of 200,000 vehicles, opened in 1964. But the Swedish government's decision not to join the European Economic Community stood to lock out Volvo sales on the continent because of import duties. In response, the company established an assembly plant at Ghent, Belgium, where Volvo cars would be exempt from import taxes. During this time, Volvo continued to improve its truck lines, rolling out its most powerful rig, the L495 Titan. This was followed by the tilt-cab L4571 Raske-Tiptop. In addition, a truck production plant opened in Alsemberg, near Brussels, Belgium, in 1964.

In 1966, the year before Sweden switched to right-lane driving, Volvo hit the market with a highly practical new sedan, the Volvo 144. Fitted with state-of-the-art safety features, including new safety belts and a new braking system, the 144 won Sweden's Car of the Year award. This model and its variations were especially popular in the United States, where—despite strong competition from Ford Motor Company's new Mustang—the car sold for $2,995. As sales jumped by 70

percent in Britain, Volvo established another assembly plant in 1968, this one in Malaysia. Truck assembly operations began in Australia that same year. Meanwhile, in Sweden, Volvo's new Amazon model was leading sales. In 1969 Volvo purchased Svenska Stålpressnings AB, which had supplied car bodies to Volvo since 1927. The following year, plans were laid for a new research and development division, the Volvo Technical Centre, which Volvo funded with between 4 and 5 percent of its sales. The VTC, as it was called, began testing hundreds of new safety features that quickly established Volvo as the world leader in automobile safety.

Joint Ventures and Merger Talks in the 1970s

In 1971 Gunnar Engellau retired and was succeeded by Pehr G. Gyllenhammar. Also that year, Volvo employees gained board representation. As part of a ten-year plan to maintain its feverish growth rates of the 1960s, Volvo attempted several industrial associations. The first of these occurred in 1972, when the company acquired a 33 percent interest in the Dutch auto manufacturer DAF. The company then forged links with Renault and Peugeot. While this substantially increased Volvo's production capacity within the European community, the company still regarded the United States as its largest market, bigger even than Sweden.

While auto sales were hurt severely by the oil crisis of 1973–74, its inflationary effects quickly tied up consumers' funds. This only hastened Volvo's need to find new growth markets. During this time, Volvo introduced two new models: the 265 and the DAF-built 66. In 1975 Volvo assumed greater control of DAF's auto business and changed the name of the company to Volvo Car B.V.

In 1977 Volvo proposed a merger with its Swedish rival Saab-Scania AB. While the combination would have produced one of Europe's largest industrial operations, effectively locking up the domestic market, Saab did not share Volvo's enthusiasm for the deal and allowed the matter to be dropped entirely. Volvo next turned to Norway, where it had hoped to establish a relationship with the state oil industry and therefore tie Volvo sales to the rising fortunes of the North Sea oil business. But Volvo shareholders rejected the ill-conceived proposal even before the Norwegians had a chance to say no. Volvo nevertheless managed to move into the oil industry another way, acquiring Beijerinvest Group, a Swedish company with interests in oil, food, finance, and trading, in 1978.

Meanwhile, Volvo restructured its operations, converting the car operation into a separate subsidiary. In 1979, with production at an all-time peak, Volvo turned out its four millionth car. It also established a closer relationship with Renault, combining research and product development and selling the French carmaker a 9.9 percent interest in Volvo Car Corporation. Volvo's sales began to rise at this point, causing an increase in share values that sustained a new share issue, followed by two more in 1981 and 1982.

Stronger Sales in the 1980s

Volvo owed much of its strength to its reputation for quality, its 1980 introduction of the first turbocharged auto, the 240, and modifications to the popular 340. Furthermore, in 1982, a top-of-the-line sedan known as the Volvo 760 was introduced and became a symbol for Volvo quality and safety. The 240, the 340, and the 760 designs represented the ideal range for the market.

In 1981 the Dutch government exercised its option to repurchase a majority in Volvo Car B.V., increasing its interest to 70 percent and thereby reducing Volvo's to 30 percent. During this time, Volvo continued its elaborate and expensive experiments with light components and new safety options. Many of these, tried on a series of test-bed vehicles, found their way into new variations of the 300 and 700 series cars. Also in 1981, U.S. truckmaker White Motor Corporation was acquired.

By 1985, Roger Holtback was promoted to head of the Volvo Car Corporation, and Håkan Frisinger was named president of AB Volvo. Under Frisinger's leadership, the company began planning a new production facility in Uddevalla, 80 kilometers northwest of Göteborg. In addition, the Dutch subsidiary introduced a new 400 series compact car.

Catalytic converters, which the company began installing in 1976, became standard on most European models in 1986. New child safety options were also incorporated into Volvo designs as were a variety of electronic sensors and controls.

Volvo's sales were extremely strong during the mid-1980s, due primarily to a devaluation in the Swedish krona. Output continued to rise until 1988, when production targets were ruined by a three-week strike. A few months later, the Uddevalla plant went on line, allowing the company to renovate the Torslanda facility, but too late to make up for lost time.

In the meantime, several acquisitions were completed during the second half of the decade. In 1986 Volvo acquired GM Heavy Truck Corp., which had an extensive dealer network in the United States and a strong presence in Canada as well. Also that year, the company bought a little more than 25 percent of the shares of two pharmaceutical companies, Pharmacia and Sonesson. The U.K. busmaker Leyland Bus Group Ltd. was acquired two years later.

The Early to Mid-1990s: Struggling to Survive

By 1990, Sweden's currency had rebounded, causing export sales to slow. The squeeze was too much for many Swedish companies to bear. In fact, in an effort to stay alive, Saab concluded a deal with General Motors in which GM gained effective control of the company. Volvo responded by entering into a complex agreement with Renault—based on a cross-ownership structure—to share the increasingly high costs of research and product development. As part of a wider reorganization, marketing responsibilities were transferred from regional sales offices back to Göteborg. Volvo's food and pharmaceutical interests were consolidated into Procordia AB, a government-controlled holding company, in exchange for a stake in Procordia. Dissatisfied with these events, Holtback resigned in protest and was replaced by Björn Ahlström, head of North American operations.

Volvo concluded a deal with Mitsubishi in 1991 in which the Japanese manufacturer would take a one-third interest in the Dutch facility, allowing Mitsubishi to manufacture parts for cars it intended to assemble in Europe. The deal outraged many, including some at Renault, which resented Mitsubishi's attempts to enter the French market. The alliances also indicated that Volvo management believed it could not survive on its own.

In 1990 and 1991, Volvo introduced two new models, the 940/960 and the five-cylinder 850, which had taken more than seven years to develop. The company had spent $2 billion to modernize its plants and develop the new models. The company once again swept a series of quality and safety awards for its automobiles, and the high marks it received from automotive critics and government agencies had a considerable effect on sales. Those able to purchase one chose a Volvo because they believed it to be the safest car available. This fact was not lost upon Volvo's marketing department. In the United States, where there were millions of young, upwardly mobile families, Volvo's reputation for safety was made the primary message of ad campaigns. As a result, the boxy Volvo gained an almost unshakable reputation for being the car of choice among America's "yuppies."

As economic downturns plagued Sweden, the government was faced with the precariousness of several of the country's lines of business and the possible loss of its automobile industry. To bolster the position of Swedish enterprises, the government introduced reforms to labor policies that had previously prevented Volvo and other companies from enforcing stricter absenteeism policies. This, combined with cost-cutting measures and the rationalization of the product line—dropping such models as the 760—helped to shore up Volvo's position. Nevertheless, the company faced difficult times.

In 1992 Volvo reported a loss of $469 million. Although sales rose by more than $1.6 billion the following year, the company still suffered a loss of $416 million. Hoping to strengthen itself by increasing its connections with Renault, the company worked on a merger in 1993. At the last minute, Volvo board members voted down the deal when they realized their CEO Pehr Gyllenhammar had agreed to a provision giving the French government the right to increase their ownership of the merged company beyond the 65 percent already in the contract. Gyllenhammar resigned, and Sören Gyll took over as chief executive officer. The alliance with Renault was subsequently dissolved in February 1994.

Gyll pointed Volvo in a new direction: The company would go it alone and refocus on its vehicle and engine manufacturing. The Swedish government had divested Procordia in 1993, and BCP, the consumer products group, became a subsidiary of the Volvo Group. By the end of 1994 Volvo had sold this subsidiary and within a couple years had sold its pharmaceutical interests, a financial brokerage, and its food and brewing businesses. Proceeds from these sales returned Volvo to profitability, reduced the company's debt from $2 billion to $100 million, and enabled the company to buy out its joint venture with Clark Company, the VME Group, which was subsequently renamed Volvo Construction Equipment.

Part of Gyll's plan for Volvo was sculpting a new image and market niche. With baby boomers aging, the demographics did not favor the safe, reliable cars bought by families with children. In 1986, at the height of its appeal in the United States, Volvo had sold more than 111,000 cars. By 1995, the company was selling fewer than 88,000 cars in the United States. Volvo decided to move into a more upscale market, with sporty and luxury models that would appeal to empty-nest boomers. The strategy met with a mixed response from analysts, some of whom felt Volvo needed the new racier image to compete and others who claimed consumers were confused by the apparent contradiction between "safety" and "excitement."

From Cars to Commercial Vehicles Under New Leader: Late 1990s and Early 2000s

In early 1997 Gyll suddenly stepped down from the CEO position and was replaced by Leif Johansson. A veteran of the Swedish appliance manufacturer Electrolux, Johansson continued Volvo on its course toward selling more upscale cars. Although Volvo had already introduced more stylish sedans and wagons redesigned from the old 850s, in 1997 it began selling the C70 coupe and convertible. Its price placed it in direct competition with other luxury coupes, like Mercedes' CLK. To foster its new image, Volvo described the C70 in advertisements as the car that "will move you in ways Volvo never has."

Volvo brought in $95 million in 1997 with the sale of its 11 percent interest in Renault. The company also bolstered its construction equipment subsidiary by acquiring Champion Road Machinery Limited, a Canadian producer of graders and other road construction and maintenance machinery. In addition, it gained full control of the former joint venture with GM called Volvo GM Heavy Truck Corporation, which was then renamed Volvo Trucks North America, Inc. The following year the company divested its remaining shares in Pharmacia & Upjohn. Also in 1998 Volvo added to its racier fleet of cars with the S80, a luxury sedan. In July 1998 the company spent $500 million to acquire Samsung Heavy Industries' construction equipment business, whose main product line was excavators. The acquired operation became part of a newly formed South Korean subsidiary, Volvo Construction Equipment Korea Co. Ltd. Late in the year, after the Asian financial crisis crippled demand in that region, Volvo announced the layoff of 6,000 workers, or more than 7 percent of its global workforce.

The following year proved to be one of the most momentous in Volvo history. In January 1999 the firm purchased a 13 percent stake in Scania AB as a first step in an attempted takeover aiming at merging the two firms' truck divisions (Scania and Saab had been split apart from the former Saab-Scania in 1995). Then, centering the company's future firmly in the commercial vehicle sector and bowing to the increasing forces for global consolidation, Johansson engineered the sale of the Volvo automobile business to Ford. In this historic deal, completed in March 1999, Ford paid $6.45 billion for the Volvo brand and plants in Sweden, Belgium, and the Netherlands. Volvo could continue to use the Volvo name on heavy-duty trucks but gave Ford the rights to use it on cars and light and medium trucks.

Johansson next set about completing the takeover of Scania. In April he increased Volvo's stake in its Swedish rival to 20 percent. After months of sometimes heated negotiations, Volvo reached an agreement in August 1999 to acquire Scania for

EUR 7 billion ($7.53 billion) in cash and stock. By early 2000 Volvo had increased its Scania stake to 45.5 percent, but two months later was forced to abandon the takeover when the European Commission, the European Union's antitrust authority, blocked the deal, citing concerns that Volvo would control too great a share of the truck markets in Sweden, Norway, and Finland. The commission later ordered Volvo to divest its stake in Scania by April 23, 2004.

Even before the Scania deal was officially scuttled, Volvo was pursuing two other avenues for growth, only one of which would prove successful. In December 1999 the company entered into an alliance with Mitsubishi Motors Corporation of Japan to cooperate in the development, production, and marketing of trucks and buses. Volvo also acquired a 5 percent stake in the Japanese company. But just a few months later, Daimler-Chrysler AG announced plans to buy a 34 percent stake in Mitsubishi, and this eventually led to the dissolution of the nascent alliance and the sale of Volvo's Mitsubishi stake.

In April 2000, meanwhile, Volvo reached an agreement to acquire Renault S.A.'s heavy-truck business, which included the France-based Renault Véhicules Industriels and the U.S.-based Mack Trucks, Inc. This deal was completed in January 2001 as a stock swap valued at EUR 1.7 billion ($1.59 billion) through which Renault acquired a 15 percent interest in Volvo. Renault also bought an additional 5 percent stake on the open market, making it Volvo's largest shareholder, and gained two seats on the Volvo board of directors. The deal made Volvo Europe's largest, North America's second largest, and the world's second largest manufacturer of heavy trucks. Despite finally being able to complete a significant acquisition, 2001 was a bleak year for Volvo overall. The global economic downturn hit the company's truck, bus, and construction equipment operations hard, leading to a net loss of EUR 159 million ($140 million) on revenues of EUR 19.33 billion ($18.06 billion).

As Volvo returned to modest profitability over the next two years, still weighed down by a far-from-robust global economy, it began realizing cost savings from integrating various aspects of its enlarged trucks business, which continued to produce models under three brands: Volvo, Renault, and Mack. In addition to introducing several new models, the Volvo Trucks unit began production at new plants in Russia and China in 2003. In March of the following year Volvo entered into an agreement with China National Heavy Truck Corporation and First Automotive Works Corporation to build a $200 billion heavy engine plant in eastern China. Volvo's revenues in China were expected to reach $800 million in 2004, double the total from the previous year. In addition to pursuing growth in the rapidly expanding markets of east Asia, Volvo was also aiming to significantly enlarge its construction equipment business, which ranked third worldwide, trailing only Caterpillar Inc. and Komatsu Ltd. The company hoped to increase the percentage of overall revenues generated by this business from 13 percent to about 20 percent and to eventually gain at least the number two global position. Another important development in 2004 was the divestment of the company's stake in Scania. Volvo first sold its Scania B shares to Deutsche Bank AG for about SEK 15 billion. Then the company's 27.3 million Scania A shares were transferred to a newly formed subsidiary, Ainax AB, and then Volvo spun off its shares in Ainax to shareholders. The proceeds from this divestment provided additional funds for Volvo to pursue further opportunities to bolster its operations through acquisitions.

Principal Subsidiaries

Volvo Global Trucks AB; Volvo Lastvagnar AB; Volvo Lastvagnar Sverige AB; Volvo Finland AB; Volvo Trucks (Deutschland) GmbH (Germany); Volvo Europa Truck NV (Belgium); Volvo Trucks (Schweiz) AG (Switzerland); Volvo Truck España SA (Spain); Volvo Truck and Bus Limited (U.K.); Volvo Trucks Canada Inc.; Volvo Trucks de Mexico; Volvo East Asia (Pte) Ltd. (Singapore); Volvo Truck Korea Ltd. (South Korea); Volvo Truck Australia Pty Ltd.; Volvo India Ltd.; France Véhicules Industriels (France); Renault Trucks UK Ltd.; Renault Trucks Nederland BV (Netherlands); Renault VI Belgique (Belgium); Renault Trucks Deutschland GmbH (Germany); Renault Véhicules Industriels Suisse (Switzerland); Renault V I España SA (Spain); Renault Trucks, España (Spain); Renault Trucks Italia SpA (Italy); Renault Trucks Osterreich GmbH (Austria); Mack Tracks Inc. (U.S.A.); Mack Canada; Mack Leasing System, Inc. (U.S.A.); Volvo Trucks North America, Inc. (U.S.A.); Volvo Truck & Bus Ltd. (U.K.); Volvo Bussar AB; Säffle Karosseri AB; Acrivia AB; Carrus Oy (Finland); Volvo Busse Deutschland GmbH (Germany); Volvo Construction Equipment NV (Netherlands); Volvo Wheel Loaders AB; Volvo Construction Equipment Components AB; Volvo Articulated Haulers AB; Volvo Construction Equipment SA (Belgium); Volvo Construction Equipment Europe Ltd. (U.K.); Volvo Construction Equipment Europe GmbH (Germany); Volvo Compact Service Equipment GmbH (Germany); Volvo Motor Graders, Ltd. (Canada); Volvo Construction Equipment North America Inc. (U.S.A.); Volvo Construction Equipment Korea Co. Ltd. (South Korea); AB Volvo Penta; Volvo Penta Norden AB; Volvo Penta Europe AB; Volvo Penta Central Europe GmbH (Germany); Wuxi da Hao Power, Co Ltd. (China; 70%); Volvo Penta of The Americas, Inc. (U.S.A.); Volvo Aero AB; Volvo Aero Engine Services AB; Volvo Aero Support AB; Volvo Aero Norge AB (Norway); Volvo Aero North America Inc. (U.S.A.); Volvo Powertrain AB; Volvo Parts AB.

Principal Divisions

Volvo Trucks; Renault Trucks; Mack Trucks; Volvo Buses; Volvo Construction Equipment; Volvo Penta; Volvo Aero; Volvo Financial Services.

Principal Competitors

DaimlerChrysler AG; PACCAR Inc.; Navistar International Corporation; Scania AB; Caterpillar Inc.; Komatsu Ltd.; Cummins, Inc.

Further Reading

Ahmad, Izham, "Sweden's Volvo Looks to China to Increase Its Sale of Big Trucks," *Wall Street Journal,* October 6, 2004, p. B2B.

Berman, Phyllis, "Stretching the Platform," *Forbes,* December 19, 1994, pp. 197–200.

Berss, Marcia, "The Master Builder," *Forbes,* November 19, 1984, pp. 242+.

Brown-Humes, Christopher, "Back to Earth with a Bump," *Financial Times,* September 21, 2000.

——, "Volvo's Route Around an Industry Pile-Up," *Financial Times,* March 31, 2000, p. 19.

Coleman, Brian, and Almar Latour, "A Boxy Prize: Safe, Little Volvo Becomes Hot Car in Takeover Derby," *Wall Street Journal Europe,* January 22, 1999, p. 1.

Dwyer, Paula, "Why Volvo Kissed Renault Goodbye," *Business Week,* December 20, 1993, pp. 54+.

"For Volvo, a Shift Away from Autos," *Business Week,* May 25, 1981, p. 75.

Holstein, William J., "Volvo Can't Play It Safe," *U.S. News and World Report,* July 27, 1998, pp. 40–42.

"How Volvo Is Beating the Auto Slump," *Business Week,* December 13, 1982, pp. 38+.

Kapstein, Jonathan, "Volvo's New Shock Absorbers Are Doing the Job," *Business Week,* March 20, 1989, pp. 120D+.

Latour, Altour, "Swedish Surprise: Volvo Chief Thrives on Contradictions," *Wall Street Journal Europe,* February 1, 1999, p. 1.

——, "Volvo Agrees to Acquire Rival Scania for $7.53 Billion," *Wall Street Journal,* August 9, 1999, p. A13.

Lindh, Björn-Eric, *Volvo: Cars from the '20s to the '90s,* (commissioned by Volvo), Förlagshuset Norden AB, 1990.

Mackintosh, James, "Life After Cars Proves a Hard Road for Volvo," *Financial Times,* September 17, 2003, p. 16.

Olsson, Christer, *Volvo: Sixty Years of Truckmaking,* (commissioned by Volvo), Förlagshuset Norden AB, 1990.

Osterland, Andrew, "Volvo: Swedish for Undervalued," *Financial World,* January 2, 1996, p. 20.

Simison, Robert L., Brian Coleman, and Almar Latour, "Ford to Pay $6.47 Billion in Volvo Deal," *Wall Street Journal,* January 29, 1999, p. A3.

Taylor, Alex, "Too Slow for the Fast Lane? Volvo and Saab," *Fortune,* July 21, 1997, pp. 68–73.

Tinnin, David B., "Volvo Grabs for Growth—Again," *Fortune,* December 29, 1980, p. 53.

"Volvo Searching Hard for Relief," *New York Times,* June 12, 1991.

"Volvo's U.S. Chief Quits in Response to Reorganization," *Wall Street Journal,* October 1, 1990.

Woodruff, David, and Almar Latour, "Volvo to Buy Renault's Heavy-Truck Business," *Wall Street Journal,* April 26, 2000, p. A18.

—John Simley
—updates: Susan Windisch Brown, David E. Salamie

Warners' Stellian Inc.

60 West Sycamore
St. Paul, Minnesota 55117
U.S.A.
Telephone: (651) 222-0011
Fax: (651) 726-1680
Web site: http://www.warnerstellian.com

Private Company
Founded: 1951 as Stellian Company
Employees: 235
Sales: $55 million (2003 est.)
NAIC: 443111 Household Appliance Stores

Headquartered in St. Paul, Minnesota, Warners' Stellian Inc. is the state's largest independent major appliance retail business. The family-owned and operated company has a name that is synonymous with quality and service throughout the Minneapolis and St. Paul metropolitan area. In its more than 50 years, Warners' Stellian has grown from one 3,000-square-foot store using an open pickup truck for deliveries, to six showrooms strategically covering every corner of the Twin Cities market and a fleet of 25 branded delivery trucks that criss-cross the seven-county metro area daily.

The private company is owned in partnership by the nine children of longtime owner Jim Warner. They maintain a corporate philosophy that promises customers, ''We will work harder than the competition to earn customers' business by offering the best product selection, in the most innovative showrooms presented by the best-trained sales staff, and delivering unsurpassed customer service. We strive to be the best value added choice for the consumer. By keeping the customer our #1 priority they have become our most effective form of advertising . . . they become our advocates.'' That formula has helped the company achieve steady, controlled growth, averaging approximately 10 percent increases year over year.

Warners' Stellian's reputation for service and extensive product selection ensures a competitive edge over national appliance retailers who are the company's primary competitors.

Their extensive selection includes well-known brands like Amana, Frigidaire, GE, Jenn-Air, Kitchenaid, Maytag, and Whirlpool, as well as specialty brands Asko, Avanti, Best, Bosch, Broan, Dacor, Fisher & Paykel, GE Monogram, Independent, LG, Marvel, Miele, Sub-Zero, Thermador, U-Line, Viking, and Wolf. Warners' Stellian offers it all—more than 400 products in air conditioning, cooking, dishwashers, freezers, laundry, microwaves, refrigerators, dehumidifiers, and other specialty products.

The Stellian Company: 1950s–60s

The company's roots were planted in 1951, when Steve and Lillian Farkas opened the Stellian Company, an appliance store at a busy intersection just a few blocks north of the St. Paul city limits. The husband/wife owners combined their names to establish Stellian as the company name. A few years later the business needed a larger space, which the owners found across the street of that same intersection in a brand new multi-store retail space. It was an ideal location at the edge of the emerging new growth first-ring suburbs of St. Paul.

In 1955, then 25-year-old Jim Warner joined the business as a bookkeeper. On Jim's first day he was thrust into the role of salesperson when he found himself alone in the store for several hours. He remembers being apologetic to a customer who taught him something about ovens that day. It was not long before Jim's sales skills drew him away from the books and onto the sales floor. Jim eventually earned titles such as office manager and sales manager, though he laughed about it later, recalling that he really only managed himself.

In the early years there were numerous small appliance stores scattered throughout the growing metropolitan area. There was even a Stellian competitor on the opposite corner of that busy intersection. But at that time, dealers generally carried just one brand. Stellian carried Frigidaire. General Electric products were sold across the street.

From the start, Stellian made customer service a top priority, offering free delivery and installation of new appliances, as well as recycling of old appliances. In those days, deliveries were made in an open pickup truck that doubled as a service vehicle.

Company Perspectives:

Warners' Stellian is a team of dedicated professionals striving to be the preferred choice for home appliances by creating experiences so compelling that customer satisfaction and loyalty is assured.

The business grew steadily, thanks in part to its ideal location at the edge of the rapidly growing suburbs of Roseville and Falcon Heights.

Profit margins for the Stellian Company waned in the late 1960s, causing the owners to expand product selection into carpeting, dinette sets, chainsaws, snow blowers, televisions, and more. Getting away from the store's original vision of specializing in appliances ultimately put a strain on the business. It became difficult for salespeople to become knowledgeable about such a wide variety of products, and even harder for the service department to manage repairs for all those products.

Warners Take Ownership: 1970s

After a few years of little or no growth in the company, Jim Warner and his nephew Rick purchased the business from Farkas in 1971. Jim and Rick renamed the business Warners' Stellian, and streamlined the product selection back to just appliances and televisions. They kept the Stellian name because it was well known in the business, due in part to the fact that the previous owner had done a substantial amount of advertising. They also phased out the service department, liquidated the parts business, and sold off the carpeting and furniture inventory, selling the last of the snow blowers on a hot, humid June day.

Jim became sole owner of the company in 1979 when he purchased his partner's portion of the business. During the 1980s, Warners' Stellian saw more competition from big, national chains including Sears, Kennedy-Cohen, and Kmart, but the small dealer showed steady sales growth. From the mid-1970s through the mid-1980s approximately 15 to 20 small appliance retailers in St. Paul went out of business. Warners' Stellian survived due to its ideal location, strong company identity, and loyal customer base won over by years of great service.

During the 1970s and 80s all of Jim and his wife Nonie's nine children worked at the store, doing everything from cleaning used appliances for resale to making deliveries. Several went away to college and returned later to join the family business. By the late 1980s, five sons and daughter Carla were invested members of the Warners' Stellian management team.

As in any small business, owners often cut corners where possible to save on expenses. Jim Warner was no different. Knowing he had the muscles of his nine children available, he leased inexpensive warehouse space at the Minnesota State Fairgrounds, just blocks from the store. Unfortunately, during the 10 days of the state fair each year, Warner had to move the stock out or have a state fair inventory sale. He was later able to secure enough inventory space in an offsite state fair building and avoid the late summer appliance shuffling.

Beginning to Expand: Late 1980s

By 1987 Warners' Stellian had about $2 million in annual sales. That year the company acquired Richfield Appliance, located in a suburb on the south side of neighboring Minneapolis. Though Jim Warner was not looking to expand, he bought the aging store at the urging of his children, who were at the time actively involved in running the company. The second generation cleaned and remodeled the store in keeping with the Warners' Stellian standard. As Jim Warner explains, "We've never been into running off with the profits. We've always been of the mind to put a lot of money back into the business." From clean restrooms to flawless carpeting to shiny windows, appearance of the stores and products had always been a priority at Warners' Stellian. Within a few years, the Richfield store was earning a profit and securing a new, loyal customer base for the company in Minneapolis and communities to the south and west. The store eventually brought in about a third of the sales revenue of the flagship St. Paul store.

In 1993 Warners' Stellian expanded its market presence further south to keep pace with rapidly widening suburban growth. The company opened a third store in the southern suburb of Apple Valley. With three stores to serve, Warners' Stellian soon outgrew its warehouse space at the fairgrounds. In 1996 the company built and moved to a new corporate headquarters and warehouse facility near downtown St. Paul. The new facility housed Warners' Stellian's customer service, advertising, purchasing, and logistics delivery divisions. With three active showrooms, the company by 1999 saw sales grow to approximately $15 million.

As the second generation of Warners joined in managing the company, Jim gradually turned over ownership to them. Eventually, he officially retired. All nine siblings became joint owners of the growing business, and six were equal partners involved in the company's daily operations.

Targeting New Markets and Builders: Late 1990s

By 2000, the company had to add about 30,000 additional square feet of warehouse space onto the four-year-old headquarters facility to accommodate dramatic corporate growth. That same year the Warners opened another 12,000-square-foot showroom, this one in the hot growth outer suburb of Maple Grove to the northwest. It was followed two years later by a comparable store in an equally burgeoning southeastern suburb, Woodbury. Sales volume for the five stores continued on a steady growth curve, resulting in the company doubling its sales volume from 1998–2003.

During that time the company stepped up efforts to pursue more business from the builder/remodeler sector by adding a division to service builders, designers, and architects. In just a few years the staff of that department grew from one employee to six. In addition, to increase networking opportunities with that market sector, the company joined a number of local organizations of designers, architects, and builders. The results began to show as the percentage of business generated from designers, builders, and remodelers showed steady improvement.

Because Warners' Stellian was Minnesota's largest independent retailer, its showrooms were often the place where new and

Key Dates:

1951: Company is founded by Steve and Lillian Farkas.
1955: Jim Warner begins work for Stellian Company.
1971: Jim and Rick Warner purchase business, rename it Warners' Stellian.
1979: Jim Warner becomes sole owner.
1987: Warners' Stellian purchases Richfield Appliance.
1993: A third showroom is opened in Apple Valley.
1996: Warners' Stellian builds new corporate headquarters/warehouse facility in St. Paul.
2000: Headquarters is expanded for more warehouse space; fourth showroom opens in Maple Grove.
2001: Jim Warner officially retires; six children assume leadership.
2002: Fifth showroom/store opens, in Woodbury.
2004: Showcase showroom opens in Edina; company plans to break ground for new corporate headquarters in 2005.

innovative specialty products made their debut. Such was the case when Warners' Stellian showcased the LC internet/multi-media refrigerator. It was never a big seller, but grabbed a few headlines for the company at the time. In addition, Warners' Stellian's buying power was enhanced by membership in Nationwide, a national buying group in the appliance industry.

Industry Innovators: 2004 and Beyond

The company made headlines again in 2004 when it opened a state-of-the-art showcase showroom in Edina, in one of the metro area's most trendy and upscale shopping areas. Carla had wanted to create something unique in the industry, so she spent several months traveling around the country to survey the showrooms of businesses in other markets. The result was a new kind of store. To create the new showroom, she enlisted the services of a local design firm to help create 18 original kitchen vignettes using Warners' appliances, surrounded by all different combinations of flooring, counters, cabinets, lighting products, and even wall decor.

The initial results were dramatic. The store was extremely popular with customers throughout the metro area, not just in the Edina area. First-year sales figures for the new store were very strong. In addition to attracting interested local and national vendors and business peers, the Edina showroom garnered Warners' Stellian recognition within the industry. Cooking classes and culinary demonstrations were scheduled in the showroom regularly to increase the company's exposure to a younger market, which included designers and culinary school students.

The year 2004 was also one for showroom facelifts in Apple Valley and St. Paul. The flagship St. Paul store was enlarged to nearly 10,000 square feet. The company also converted the Minneapolis (Richfield) store into an Outlet Center for new merchandise as well as ''scratch and dent'' type inventory, all with full factory warranties. Long-term plans called for the flagship store to adopt the kitchen vignette theme of the Edina showroom.

Need for more warehouse space to keep pace with a steadily growing sales volume prompted Warners' Stellian to plan an-

other move. In mid-2004 the company signed a purchase agreement with the St. Paul Port Authority to purchase an eight-acre plot in St. Paul's Great Northern Business Park, near downtown St. Paul. The new 120,000-square-foot facility would house the corporate headquarters and warehouse inventory for the company's six stores, more than doubling current capacity. Estimated cost for the new facility was $6 million. Groundbreaking was set to begin the spring of 2005, with completion by early 2006. Warner's purchased the land for $1, benefiting from the city's economic development incentives. The company planned to add 80 new jobs over the next ten years.

A Model for Family Businesses

Family businesses passed from one generation to the next often did not have high success rates. The passion of the founder, for example, does not necessarily transfer to the second generation. Such did not appear to be the case at Warners' Stellian, where a third generation was already on staff. Jim Warner was in awe of where his children had taken his small appliance business, and Carla Warner credited her father's firm foundation for modern-day success. ''He taught us how to treat the customer,'' she explained. ''Exceptional customer service is the key.'' The company slogan ''We're working harder to earn your business'' was evident to savvy consumers, who appreciated Warners' Stellian's ''hassle free'' buying experience, from the store visit to proper installation of their new appliance. Each purchase over $399 included free metro area delivery, free recycling of the old appliance, and arrangement for professional installation when necessary.

Looking ahead, the Warners hoped to open two more stores by 2009, possibly expanding their market further into southern and central Minnesota. They also planned to continue efforts to increase business done with builders, architects, and designers. The company web site was also being updated to enable online buying in the near future.

The company was unique in the industry in that it had an in-house staff for delivery and installation, its customers included both retail and builder segments, and the sales force was 50/50 men and women—highly unusual in the appliance industry. In addition, Warners' Stellian had low employee turnover. Many had been with the business more than ten years, and were like family.

Perhaps most unusual was the fact that the six siblings had been able to share management of the company so smoothly. Having a close-knit family with mutual respect among members had helped this company grow and prosper. In addition to earning a local reputation as a strong family company with a high degree of integrity, Warners' Stellian had a long history of being extremely generous and philanthropic within the St. Paul and Minneapolis communities.

Principal Subsidiaries

Warner Management; Warner Properties.

Principal Competitors

Sears, Roebuck and Co.; Guyers' Builders Supply Inc.; Best Buy Co., Inc.; The Home Depot, Inc.

Further Reading

Black, Sam, ''Warner's Stellian to Build Bigger HQ in St. Paul,'' *Business Journal (Minneapolis/St. Paul)* July 19, 2004.

Broom, Brenda, ''Appliance Specialist,'' *Furnishings Magazine*, 2004.

Firestone, Mary, ''Warner's Stellian Is Bucking the Trend Towards Huge National Appliance Retailers,'' *Twin Cities Business Monthly*, February 2003, p. 31.

''Minnesota Trendsetters: Warner's Stellian—The Warner Family,'' *Minnesota Monthly*, July 2004, p. 213.

Pond, Doug, ''Warners' Stellian: More Than a Flash in the Clan,*'' CFG Update* [CFG Insurance], May–June 2003, pp. 12–14.

—Mary Heer-Forsberg

WellChoice, Inc.

11 West 42nd Street
New York, New York 10036
U.S.A.
Telephone: (212) 476-7800
Fax: (212) 476-1281
Web site: http://www.wellchoice.com

Public Company
Incorporated: 2002
Employees: 5,400
Sales: $5.38 billion (2003)
Stock Exchanges: New York
Ticker Symbol: WC
NAIC: 524114 Direct Health and Medical Insurance
 Carriers

WellChoice, Inc. is the parent company of the largest health insurer in New York State, serving nearly five million members. The company's service area includes the New York metropolitan area, parts of upstate New York, and 16 counties in New Jersey. In most of WellChoice's New York markets it has the exclusive right to use the Blue Cross and Blue Shield names. The company serves large groups of more than 500 employees, including employees of New York City and New York State, smaller groups of employees, and individuals.

The Beginnings of Blue Cross and Blue Shield

WellChoice was incorporated nearly 70 years after the business it represented was formed. The company's roots stretch to the beginning of prepaid healthcare coverage in the United States, back to the formation of Blue Cross and Blue Shield, two organizations often referred to as "the Blues."

The two organizations sprang from different parts of the country, each seeking to provide different yet related services to workers. The concept underpinning Blue Shield emerged at the turn of the 20th century, when the owners of lumber and mining camps in the Pacific Northwest began paying monthly fees to groups of physicians for medical care. These early programs,

which helped cover the expense of physicians' services, eventually evolved into a structured organization, Blue Shield, which was established in California in 1939. Blue Cross, by contrast, sought to help cover the cost of hospital care, a concept first developed by a superintendent of schools in Dallas, Texas, named Justin Ford Kimball. Kimball's interest was in helping teachers pay for hospital bills by pooling their monthly payments to pay for hospital care. In 1929, he introduced a plan to guarantee schoolteachers 21 days of hospital care at Baylor University Hospital for a $6 monthly fee. Kimball enrolled 1,300 teachers in his health plan the first year. A decade later, there were three million people covered by the prepaid hospital plan devised by Kimball.

The idea of sharing risk—the essence of both concepts that grew into Blue Shield and Blue Cross—spread across the country, fueling the development of the Blues into national organizations. In 1939, five years after it first appeared in Minnesota, the Blue Cross symbol was officially adopted as the national emblem for prepaid hospital care programs tailored after Kimball's Baylor program. That same year, the head of the Blue Shield Plan in Buffalo, New York, commissioned artwork combining a serpent and the U.S. Army Medical Corps insignia, creating the Blue Shield symbol. Under these two brands, the two organizations grew, their stature increasing as regions across the country embraced the idea of prepaid hospital care and prepaid physician care.

News of the prepaid hospital care concept developed by Kimball reached Albany, New York, in 1934. A group of individuals decided to form its own version of the Baylor program in Albany, typifying the manner in which Kimball's idea evolved into a national movement called Blue Cross. The Albany group created a prepayment plan designed to provide hospital services for group members, calling their organization The Associated Hospital Service of the Capital District, a precursor to WellChoice. The Associated Hospital Service opened its first office in 1935, expanding, under the Blue Cross emblem, into 13 counties by the end of the year.

As it did throughout the country, Blue Cross grew in stature in New York as the decades passed. Its membership eclipsed 300,000 by the beginning of the 1950s. Midway through the decade, in an influential confirmation of the program's worth, New York state employees and federal employees became Blue Cross members. By the 1970s, the ranks of Blue Cross members reached 500,000. Blue Shield, meanwhile, expanded in New York and elsewhere in much the same manner as Blue Cross. Separately, the two national organizations grew region by region. In New York, there were several geographically distinct entities whose work was performed under the Blue Cross and Blue Shield banners. Soon, the family of associate Blue Cross and Blue Shield entities would come together, adding cohesion and structure to a fragmented collection of healthcare insurers.

Forming an Empire in 1985

The grassroots movements begun to help lumberjacks and teachers reached a milestone in their maturation in the early 1980s. In 1982, the Blue Cross Association and the National Association of Blue Shield Plans merged. Their union created the Blue Cross and Blue Shield Association, which led regional constituents of each organization to ally with their counterparts. In New York, the melding process occurred in 1985, when Blue Cross of Northeastern New York merged with Blue Cross and Blue Shield of Greater New York, creating the basis of WellChoice, Empire BlueCross BlueShield.

Empire suffered a tortuous first decade of existence. The state-owned insurer was beset with a host of problems, including mounting debt, soaring management and administrative costs, and consumer dissatisfaction. Empire's difficulties intensified during the early 1990s, as the company struggled mightily to stay financially afloat. Between 1992 and 1995, the organization's statewide market share, as measured by premium revenues, plummeted from 34 percent to 19 percent. Partway through the slide, the company's collapse was avoided by the intervention of the state in 1993, but it remained plagued with problems. Empire needed a permanent cure for its ailments, not a temporary treatment.

A new leader was hired in 1994 to spearhead Empire's turnaround. Michael A. Stocker joined Empire as its new chief executive officer in 1994, ushering in an era of great change in New York's healthcare insurance industry. Before joining Empire, Stocker served as president of CIGNA Healthplans, a position he accepted after serving as executive vice-president and general manager of U.S. Healthcare, Inc.'s New York market from 1985 to 1992. A graduate of the University of Notre Dame who received his medical degree from the Medical College of Wisconsin, Stocker took control of Empire at a pivotal period in the organization's history. Empire was bleed-

ing money and losing customers. It was Stocker's challenge to reverse the company's fortunes. As he did so, he left behind him an enduring legacy, one that forever changed the nature of Blue Cross and Blue Shield in New York.

A Bold Announcement in 1996

Stocker began to make changes that soon were evident in Empire's financial performance. The administrative and managerial functions of the company were made more efficient, helping Empire record $28.7 million in net income in 1996, one year after it posted a $19 million loss. Stocker's ultimate objective was much more profound in its implications than a reorganization, however. Stocker wanted to change Empire's status as a nonprofit organization into a for-profit corporation, proposing to radically alter the structure that had defined the company for six decades.

The first signs of Stocker's desire to change Empire into a for-profit concern appeared in early 1996. The company established two for-profit subsidiaries as a way to gain access to equity capital. Opposition to the idea of the state-owned Empire becoming a private-sector company, which hounded Stocker for years, quickly followed the formation of the two subsidiaries. Consumer groups were worried that profitable components of Empire's business would be plucked away from the company, thereby diluting its value. Stocker responded by announcing that Empire's board acknowledged the public's concern over the disposition of the organization's charitable assets. He promised, as quoted in the September 30, 1996 issue of *Modern Healthcare,* to "meet that issue head on." His solution, revealed in September 1996, was to seek full for-profit status for Empire and to create a new not-for-profit foundation endowed with the estimated market value of Empire to support the uninsured, under-insured, and hospitals. His declaration marked the beginning of a battle that dragged on into the 21st century.

Stocker's pressing need to convert to for-profit status drew its exigency from the market conditions affecting Empire. Stocker inherited a company that increasingly found itself competing against for-profit firms, which, he argued, left Empire at a disadvantage because it could not tap into equity markets to raise the capital needed to expand, buy new technology, and compete effectively for customers. Further, the deregulation of New York's inpatient hospital rates, scheduled to go into effect January 1, 1997, portended disaster for the state-owned insurer. Empire, as a last-resort insurer, received a 13 percent discount on hospital rates, but the deregulation of rates promised to strip the company of its discount. Roughly 60 percent of Empire's business was derived from traditional indemnity insurance contracts. These contracts, according to a report by New York's Special Advisory Review Panel, "may become obsolete" after deregulation. Stocker was convinced that Empire's long-term health could be ensured only by converting into a publicly traded company, but the road toward that goal was strewn with formidable obstacles.

Empire's efforts to complete an initial public offering of stock in 1997 stalled. The company needed permission from a host of agencies and departments to clear regulatory and approval hurdles, including the state attorney general's office, the New York Department of Insurance, the state Supreme Court,

Key Dates:

1929: A Baylor University official develops the prepaid healthcare concept that will become known as Blue Cross.

1934: The Associated Hospital Service of the Capital District is formed, a predecessor of WellChoice.

1985: Three years after Blue Cross and Blue Shield merge, the merger of several entities in New York creates Empire BlueCross BlueShield.

1994: Michael A. Stocker is named chief executive officer of Empire BlueCross BlueShield.

1996: Stocker announces that he wants to seek for-profit status for Empire BlueCross BlueShield.

2002: WellChoice, the parent company of Empire BlueCross BlueShield, completes its initial public offering of stock.

2004: Discussions of a merger with Oxford Health Plans are terminated.

and the Securities and Exchange Commission (SEC). There was also uncertainty about the legality of Empire's conversion proposal, which eventually required the passage of a new law by the New York State Legislature. After failing in 1997, Empire tried again to push its case forward in 1999, filing, through its parent company HealthChoice, a proposed plan of restructuring with the Department of Insurance. At the end of December 1999, the Superintendent of Insurance approved the plan with some modification, but the plan was never implemented.

Empire's biggest foe at the dawn of the 21st century was Eliot Spitzer, New York's Attorney General. Spitzer maintained that Empire's plan for conversion was illegal. While Stocker and his executive team took up their case with Spitzer, Empire argued for new legislation to be passed to permit its conversion. Company officials appeared before lawmakers in 2000 and were rebuffed; they pleaded their case again in the spring of 2001. Stocker, after nearly five years of waiting for approval, was frustrated. In an April 6, 2001 interview with *Long Island Business News,* he stated: "Every day that our conversion is delayed and Empire is prevented from competing in a level playing field with its for-profit competitors, the value of the foundation is also put at risk. If we do not restructure, it will not only jeopardize Empire's continued viability, but it will also increase the likelihood that a significant public benefit that belongs to the state will be dissipated."

Empire promised to compensate the public by contributing the estimated value of the company, $1 billion, to one foundation that would help those in need and a second foundation that would support hospitals. Spitzer opposed such a plan, vowing to fight the conversion in court unless legislatures changed the law. In August 2001, the impatience of the company was expressed in a full-page advertisement in the *New York Times,* a sentiment delivered in an open letter to New York Governor George Pataki and the state's legislative leaders. As quoted in the August 27, 2001 issue of *National Underwriter Life & Health-Financial Services,* the advertisement read: "Empire has had 10 public hearings on this issue. The only significant

reason we can see for a delay at this point is an inability to agree on how to divide the foundation's income. This is not an issue Empire can resolve, only you can resolve it. If you cannot agree on how to divide the $1 billion in foundation proceeds, then let the legislation pass, create one or more foundations, and let the foundation boards make the decision."

A New Era Beginning in 2002

After nearly six years of trying to change its status, Empire prevailed in 2002. In January, Governor Pataki signed legislation that gave HealthChoice the right to convert to a for-profit company. As the company prepared for its initial public offering (IPO), it formed WellChoice in August 2002 as the new parent company for its future as a for-profit enterprise. In November 2002, WellChoice completed its IPO, selling 16.7 million common shares and raising $417.3 million in net proceeds. The company was denied the first reward of its conversion, however, barring Stocker from gaining what he had been pursuing for six years. Consumer activists, represented by an advocacy group named Consumers Union, filed a lawsuit alleging the state law signed by Governor Pataki in January 2002 was unconstitutional because it was passed, as reported in the October 2, 2003 issue of *A.M. Best Newswire,* "strictly for the benefit of a single corporation." Consequently, state Supreme Court Judge Ira Gammerman froze the IPO proceeds in escrow until the consumers' lawsuit was resolved.

As WellChoice plotted its course in its new guise, the company faced a future that promised to include events peculiar to its new status as a for-profit enterprise. The Empire of old could not contemplate the actions WellChoice could entertain. One such event appeared likely to happen in April 2004, when WellChoice and Oxford Health Plans began discussing a possible merger. Oxford Health boasted 1.55 million members in New York and greater metropolitan areas in New Jersey, Connecticut, Delaware, and eastern parts of Pennsylvania. Although the discussions fell apart by the end of the month, the proposed merger hinted at similar actions in WellChoice's future. The remainder of the decade promised to see a more aggressive WellChoice, as the company developed and exercised its new corporate muscle as a for-profit company.

Principal Subsidiaries

EHC Benefits Agency, Inc.; Empire HealthChoice Assurance, Inc.; Empire HealthChoice HMO, Inc.; WellChoice Holdings of New York, Inc.; WellChoice Insurance of New Jersey, Inc.

Principal Competitors

UnitedHealth Group Incorporated; Aetna Inc.; Oxford Health Plans, Inc.; Health Insurance Plan of Greater New York; HealthNow New York, Inc.; Capital District Physicians' Health Plan, Inc.

Further Reading

Bell, Allison, "Empire Pleads with New York Officials to Enact Conversion Legislation," *National Underwriter Life & Health-Financial Services Edition,* August 27, 2001, p. 3.

Benson, Barbara, ''Empire IPO Languishes As State Dallies,'' *Crain's New York Business,* March 17, 1997, p. 1.

''Empire Blue Cross Continues Quest to Become for-Profit Co.,'' *Long Island Business News,* April 6, 2001, p. 12B.

Gross, Daniel, ''Empire Ends Up in Manhattan, B'klyn,'' *Crain's New York Business,* January 14, 2002, p. 22.

''Legal Brawl Could Kill WellChoice Oxford,'' *Investment Dealers' Digest,* April 19, 2004.

Levick, Diane, ''Oxford Health Plans' Stock Climbs 15 Percent on WellChoice Acquisition News,'' *Hartford Courant,* April 6, 2004, p. B4.

Lipowicz, Alice, ''The New Empire Won't Be Built in a Day,'' *Crain's New York Business,* September 30, 1996, p. 4.

Messina, Judith, ''Empire's No-Win Victory on Conversion,'' *Crain's New York Business,* February 7, 2000, p. 22.

——, ''Improved Empire Sees Value Soar,'' *Crain's New York Business,* May 27, 2002, p. 1.

Morse, Andrew, ''WellChoice Ends Oxford Talks,'' *Daily Deal,* April 23, 2004, p. 3.

''N.Y. Court Rejects Motion to Dismiss Suit Against WellChoice,'' *A.M. Best Newswire,* October 2, 2003.

Pallarito, Karen, ''Empire Blues' for-Profit Move Avoids Brewing Flap,'' *Modern Healthcare,* September 30, 1996, p. 2.

Sisson, Mary, ''WellChoice Earns Clean Bill of Health,'' *Crain's New York Business,* November 24, 2003, p. 3.

''Some Speculate That WellChoice and Oxford Could Merge,'' *A.M. Best Newswire,* April 6, 2004, p. 32.

—Jeffrey L. Covell

Westcon Group, Inc.

520 White Plains Road, Suite 100
Tarrytown, New York 10591-5167
U.S.A.
Telephone: (914) 829-7000
Fax: (914) 829-7137
Web site: http://www.westcongroup.com

Private Company
Incorporated: 1985
Employees: 1,000
Sales: $1.85 billion (2004)
NAIC: 541512 Computer Systems Design Services

Majority owned by South Africa-based Datatec Ltd., Westcon Group, Inc. is a global channel provider of networking technology. Through its divisions, Westcon, Comstor, and Voda One, the company offers products and services for convergence technology, remote access, Internet and e-business, virtual private networks, videoconferencing, wireless connectivity, and network security. With its headquarters located in Tarrytown, New York, the company does business through three divisions: Comstor, Westcon, and Voda One, specialty distributors for major manufacturers. The largest is Comstor, devoted primarily to selling Cisco products to some 45 countries around the world. Other vendors include Adtran, Inc., Proxim Corporation, RSA Security, Inc., and Symbol Technologies. The Westcon division focuses on the sale of Nortel Networks and security products, and its portfolio includes Check Point Software Technologies Ltd., Extreme Networks, Inc., Nokia Networks, Symantec Corporation, 3Com Corporation, and many others. The division serves some 65 countries. Westcon Group's Voda One division is primarily focused on distributing products manufactured by Avaya; the division also handles vendors such as MCK Communications, Inc., NICE systems, Plantronics, Inc., and Spectralink Corporation, among others, selling to customers in the United States.

Founding the Company in the Mid-1990s

Westcon was founded in June 1985 by Thomas Dolan, Philip Raffiani, and Roman Michalowski. Dolan, a former Ma-

rine with an engineering degree from Tulane University, was the manager of systems development at cosmetic giant Avon Products, Inc. He joined forces with Raffiani, an expert in IBM mainframe systems, and Michalowski to become involved in the fast-growing world of personal computing networking. It was a time of great flux, as companies began to realize the potential of linking personal computers into a local area network (LAN), a drastic change from the mainframe computer model that companies had been following for decades. Dolan recognized that because there was little standardization between systems, major businesses would need to find a way to communicate with one another electronically. Westcon was created to serve the LAN market, and started out as just a four-person operation located in Eastchester, New York. Michalowski served as chief executive officer, with Dolan in charge of worldwide sales and marketing and Raffiani as general manager.

Westcon was an early believer in the potential of Ethernet run over the twisted pair wiring of a telephone system rather than coaxial cable. Using cable, a LAN was limited in terms of distance, a problem not inherent with twisted pairs. Westcon's founders were so convinced that Ethernet over twisted pairs would take off that they mortgaged their homes to purchase $1 million of SynOptics products. With SynOptics products stored throughout its headquarters, the small Westcon staff quickly began moving the inventory by phone. Westcon became one of the first companies, if not the first, to sign a distribution agreement with SynOptics. Westcon was one of a number of small distributors that changed the way computer products were sold, a shift away from first-tier, authorized vendors to aggressive second-tier value-added distributors willing to take chances. More than just selling products, they were willing to offer technical support and training, as well as provide marketing and even financing, which helped many small businesses to upgrade their technology infrastructures, leading to increased growth.

The next major product to impact the evolution of Westcon was the router, which grew in importance with the deregulation of telephone service in the United States that led to lower long distance service prices. Dolan told *CRN* in 2002, "We recognized that meant people would be much more interested in high-speed connections from office to branch and from branch to home. We threw everything we had into getting into routers and the router marketplace. And that paid off very well for us.''

Bolstering Customer Service in the Early 1990s

Westcon provided product training from the start, becoming one of the first authorized Novell Inc. training centers. Over the next several years the company added certified training programs for products manufactured by SynOptics, Eicon Technologies, and Lotus Development Corp., as well as training for Microsoft applications. Training was an important component in the company's continued success, even though it accounted for just 10 percent of Westcon's business. In the early 1990s, Westcon also began to differentiate itself from the competition by bolstering its service capabilities, helping customers to find better ways to solve problems—especially in high-end networking. In this way, potential customers knew that they would receive more than just a product when they bought from Westcon. The company also tried to narrow its focus by concentrating on a limited number of product lines—such as SynOptics (which became Bay Networks Inc. and was later bought by Nortel Networks)—which it could then support in depth.

By 1995 the company was doing more than $150 million in annual sales and ready to embark on a major growth spurt. Over the next five years, revenues would grow tenfold and the company would extend its reach around the world. In 1995 the company took steps to expand its business to the West Coast. Soon it was setting its sights overseas. After already setting up an operation in Canada, Westcon in 1996 established an Australian subsidiary to sell its full line of products in the Australian market. Also in 1996, Westcon Inc. became known as Westcon Group, Inc.

Westcon Group reached a watershed moment in 1997. By this stage, the company had enjoyed success by primarily distributing and supporting SynOptics networking products, generating around $190 million in sales. The management team now considered whether it should continue to concentrate on networking or broaden its purview. The decision was to remain committed to networking products, albeit on a global basis. It would turn out to be a wise choice. In order to expand its presence worldwide, Westcon Group put itself on the block and began looking for a partner, considering a dozen possible suitors, most of them U.S.-based, before settling on Datatec, a South African international networking and distribution company founded in 1986. In June 1998 Datatec acquired a 92.5 percent interest in Westcon Group in a deal valued at $160 million. For Datatec, the Westcon Group acquisition gave it entry to the largest IT market in the world, which was imperative if it was to become a truly global concern. Westcon Group, on the other hand, gained access to the kind of capital needed to nurture its own global ambitions. Rather than pursuing the risky strategy of building operations from scratch, Westcon Group could now buy into new markets and pick up established vendor relationships.

With Datatec's backing, Westcon was able to upgrade MIS systems in the United States and Canada, move into new offices in Tarrytown, New York, and enter new product lines through acquisitions. Given the speed at which the industry was changing, Westcon Group targeted companies that offered a similar infrastructure in order to effect a necessarily prompt transition. Through a pair of acquisitions, Westcon Group became a specialty distributor of products made by Cisco Systems Inc. In September 1998 RBR Group Limited—distributor of Cisco products in the United Kingdom—was added, followed by the August 1999, $95 million acquisition of Comstor.net, which distributed Cisco products in the United States. Comstor, founded in Chantilly, Virginia, in 1986 and acquired by GE Capital IT Solutions ten years later, did $500 million in annual sales. As a result of these transactions, Westcon was a global company doing $1.5 billion in business, divided between two divisions. More important, it represented the four networking giants, Cisco, Nortel, Lucent Technologies, and 3Com Corp. The company's growth also was enhanced when these major vendors elected to cut down on their global distribution channels.

Westcon Group's Voda One division grew out of a pair of acquisitions in 2000: Omaha, Nebraska-based Inacom Communications, Inc., a subsidiary of bankrupt Inacom Corp., and Pittsburgh, Pennsylvania-based CCA Technologies, Inc., both of which distributed Lucent Technologies voice products. These additions made Westcon the largest Lucent voice distributor in the industry with some $225 million in annual sales. A few months later, Lucent spun off the voice business, which took on the name Avaya, Inc. All told, Westcon Group acquisitions made since its sale to Datatec provided diversity as the company moved into areas complementing the networking business, such as security and voice-over-IP (internet protocol). As a result of representing both data and voice products, Westcon Group also would be well positioned to become involved in convergence, the concept of carrying both data and voice over a network, as well as such emerging technologies as optical networking and storage. The key, as had been the case from the beginning, would be to add value to the equation.

Challenging Conditions in the New Century

Westcon Group underwent some management changes at the start of the new century. In November 2000, Michalowski stepped down as CEO, turning over the reins to Dolan, who in 2001 would be succeeded by Alan Marc Smith. A former SynOptics executive, Smith joined Westcon Group in February 1997 as director of business development and planning. A year later, he became the company's chief executive officer. Before resigning as CEO, Dolan prepared to take Westcon public in 2001 but the initial public offering (IPO) of stock was pulled as the economy began to falter. Management believed that the market was not assigning a proper value to the company, which had sufficient cash in hand and was a profitable concern. The decision was to wait until conditions improved.

At first, Westcon Group was much less affected by the poor economy than other technology companies. Revenues topped the $2 billion mark in 2001, and although there was a reduction in headcount, it was achieved mostly through attrition. With the tech sector continuing to struggle, the next two years would see a drop in sales, to $1.69 billion in 2002 and $1.65 billion in 2003, before the company began to enjoy a noticeable rebound.

Key Dates:

1985: The company is founded.
1998: Datatec Ltd. acquires the company.
1999: The company begins distributing Cisco products.
2000: The company begins distributing Avaya products.

Despite a downturn in business, Westcon Group remained strong enough to take advantage of conditions to grow by way of acquisition. Early in 2002 it reached a tentative agreement to buy Netherlands-based Landis Group N.V., a deal that would strengthen Westcon's position in Europe, adding locations in Austria, Belgium, Denmark, France, Germany, The Netherlands, Norway, Spain, Sweden, and the United Kingdom. By March, however, after two months of due diligence, Westcon Group announced that it was pulling out of the deal. A month later the acquisition was again in play, but this time Landis's U.K. assets were not included, since Westcon Group already possessed a strong operation in the U.K. market.

In 2004 Westcon Group took steps to become something of a one-stop shop for networking and convergence, which management believed was the next revolution in networking. Westcon Group introduced the Convergence Edge program to help solution providers sell convergence by providing training, services, marketing, and sales support of IP telephony solutions. A number of symposiums were then held around the country to promote the company's convergence services.

In 2004, as sales picked up, Westcon Group also revived its plan to go public, but it would do so without Smith at its head. He resigned in May 2004, replaced by Dolan. Both Smith and the company portrayed his departure as the completion of a task Smith had undertaken to grow the company to a global busi-

ness. But according to *Computer Reseller News,* a "source close to Westcon Group said Smith may have left because he wanted to have more control in the company." Whatever the truth of the matter, his leaving was not expected to have any impact on the company's planned $115 million IPO. Some of the proceeds were to be used to pay off debts to Datatec, with the rest earmarked for working capital and general corporate purposes, such as additional acquisitions and the expansion of existing operations. By the autumn of 2004 the company had not yet pulled the trigger on the offering, which had been expected to take place in the first half of the year; there was every reason to believe, however, that the IPO would occur when conditions proved favorable.

Principal Divisions

Westcon; Comstor; Voda One.

Principal Competitors

Ingram Micro; ScanSource, Inc.; Tech Data Corporation.

Further Reading

Campbell, Scott, "Distribution Grows Up," *CRN,* June 13, 2002.

Franse, Karen, "Westcon Eyes Expansion," *VARBusiness,* July 19, 1999, p. 75.

Haber, Lynn, "At Bat: A Distribution Slugger," *Computer Reseller News,* February 14, 1994, p. 136.

Hooper, Larry, "Westcon Chooses Depth, Not Breadth, to Sustain Growth," *CRN,* February 3, 2003, p 52.

Pereira, Pedro, "Going Global—Westcon Is Foundation for DataTec's Worldwide Distribution Strategy," *Computer Reseller News,* June 22, 1998, p. 6.

——, "The Westcon Way," *Computer Reseller News,* March 27, 1995, p. 167.

—Ed Dinger

Zones, Inc.

1102 15th Street Southwest, Suite 102
Auburn, Washington 98001
U.S.A.
Telephone: (253) 205-30000
Fax: (253) 205-2558
Web site: http://www.zones.com

Public Company
Incorporated: 1988 as Multiple Zones International, Inc.
Employees: 527
Sales: $460.77 million (2003)
Stock Exchanges: NASDAQ
Ticker Symbol: ZONS
NAIC: 454113 Mail-Order Houses

Zones, Inc. is a direct marketer of information technology products to small-to-medium sized businesses and the public sector. Zones sells its products through catalogs, the Internet, and legions of account executives. The company began by selling primarily Mac software to consumers—something Zones still does through an inbound call center—but during the late 1990s the company shifted its market focus to corporate customers. Zones sells more than 150,000 products made by manufacturers such as Apple, Cisco, Epson, Hewlett Packard, IBM, Microsoft, and Sony, among others. The company's facilities in the Pacific Northwest are complemented by a distribution center in Wilmington, Ohio.

Origins

Zones recorded electric growth during its formative years, quickly emerging as one of the fastest growing companies in the country during the 1990s. The company sprang from modest beginnings, however, starting out with six employees who occupied a 5,000-square-foot warehouse east of Seattle, Washington. Joining the six employees was the person who hired them, Sadrudin Kabani. Kabani, who led the company during its first six years in business, incorporated his company in late 1988, christening it "Multiple Zones International, Inc.," its corporate title throughout the 1990s. Kabani's strategy—to sell com-

puter software and hardware by mail-order—would not have struck the casual observer as a recipe for exponential financial growth, particularly during the late 1980s when the computer industry had yet to demonstrate much substantial growth itself. Zones grew explosively, nonetheless, generating $11 million in sales in 1989, $22 million in 1990, and $48 million in 1991.

Direct marketers such as Zones were positioned ideally to reap the rewards of the computer industry's phenomenal growth. Without the overhead of traditional retailers, direct marketers were able to sell products at a lower price than retailers who had to pay for prime real estate and attractive store design. Further, computer shoppers proved to be especially price conscious, employing a purchasing strategy that fit perfectly with the business strategies employed by entrepreneurs such as Kabani. Many consumers chose to visit a retail shop to look at a product before returning home to place an order for the same product with a direct marketer. Accordingly, Zones enjoyed an advantage in an incredibly fertile market, one that Kabani and his successors exploited with great success.

Zones's business orientation underwent several distinct changes during the course of the company's development, as it rethought its address to the computer market to maximize growth opportunities. Initially, the company focused on selling software, particularly software designed for Apple Computer, Inc.'s Macintosh (Mac) systems. Much of the company's growth early on, when annual sales more than doubled every year, was derived from the sale of Mac software. Kabani placed advertisements in consumer magazines such as *Macworld*, *MacUser*, and *MacWeek*, offering readers a selection of software and hardware, but mostly software, at discount prices. His business flourished, attracting the attention of a local entrepreneur, Firoz Lalji. Lalji, a Ugandan with a degree from the London School of Economics, started a chain of camera stores named Kits Cameras, Inc. in 1981, a business that recorded robust growth. Kits Cameras enriched Lalji, giving him the financial resources to invest in the success of other entrepreneurs. In 1990, when Zones was just beginning to attract attention, Lalji purchased half the company. Initially, Lalji remained in the background, letting Kabani run the company, but before the end of the decade Lalji made his presence

---

Company Perspectives:

The company is dedicated to creating a learning community of empowered individuals to serve its customers with integrity, commitment and passion. It strives to achieve this by stimulating a positive and collaborative workplace environment, delivering high speed and quality service to its customers, and adapting to external changes with flexibility, innovation and leading edge technology.

---

known, taking firm control of Zones and transforming the nature of its business.

Strong Growth During the 1990s

When Lalji made his initial investment, the most daunting problem facing Zones was how to expand fast enough to keep up with the volume of business the company was generating. After reaching $78 million in 1992, the company's revenues swelled to $113 million in 1994 and skyrocketed to $242 million the following year. The vigorous financial growth stretched the company's ability to find qualified new employees and dictated numerous moves to new, larger facilities. Zones, during the first half of the 1990s, appeared to be always on the move, barely able to settle into new headquarters before its growth necessitated another relocation. In 1991, the company moved out of its original 5,000-square-foot facility and established itself in a 26,000-square-foot building. In early 1994, the company was forced to move again, signing a lease for a 45,000-square-foot facility. Roughly two years later, as its sales neared $500 million, the company felt the constraints of its 45,000-square-foot headquarters and leased an entire seven-story building.

The forces driving Zones's physical expansion drew their power from the evolution of the company. Kabani began increasing the company's offering of computer hardware in 1992, not long after he began developing business in Europe and Asia, where the software market was growing at twice the rate of the U.S. market. By 1993, Zones had licensed affiliates in eight foreign countries—Denmark, Sweden, Norway, Switzerland, Belgium, Japan, and Hong Kong—and two company-owned offices in France and England. Customers in these countries, as well as those in the United States, were solicited not only through multi-page advertisements in consumer magazines but also through two publications produced by Zones, the *Mac Zone*, introduced in 1990, and the *PC Zone*, introduced in 1992. The publications, which were issued on a monthly basis by 1995, represented the essence of Zones's function in the computer market.

Kabani, in a June 18, 1993 interview with *Puget Sound Business Journal*, described his company as "the conduit between manufacturers and customers." More accurately, Zones represented a filter more than a conduit, with the company's staff responsible for determining how the manufacturer was presented to the customer. By the early 1990s, there were at least 30,000 products that Zones potentially could offer in its mail-order catalogs, but the company vetted the field, only including a product in its mailings after it gained the approval of

its product-review staff. Zones, through the *Mac Zone* and the *PC Zone*, never offered more than 5,000 products during the early 1990s. The company's vice-president of business development, in a May 21, 1993 interview with *Puget Sound Business Journal*, explained, "The vendor will know their product, but we know what will sell to our customers." Kabani added his views in the same publication on June 18, 1993, saying, "It has to fit our customers' needs. If it doesn't fit, it can't be in (the company catalogs), even if they try to pay for it."

Zones flourished during the mid-1990s. The company's sales demonstrated vigorous growth as it successfully increased hardware sales. In 1994, after two years of ramping up hardware sales, Zones generated 53 percent of its revenue from the sale of hardware. By 1996, the company derived 82 percent of its business from hardware sales. Zones had less success, however, in penetrating the market for Windows-based software and hardware. The competition in the PC market was more intense and more complex than the market for Mac products. "On the Mac side," Zones's head of corporate relations said in an August 8, 1997 interview with *Puget Sound Business Journal*, "we're one of three large resellers that dominate about half of the market. But on the PC side, it's much more competitive and there are many more channels of distribution. There are integrators, value-added resellers, resellers, and superstores. It's a long list."

Stumbling in the Late 1990s

When Apple Computer began to falter at the beginning of the late 1990s, Zones felt the sting of its over-dependence on Mac software and hardware. The company's sales, which had been making annual leaps upwards, flattened. To inject new vitality in the company, a new chief executive officer and president was hired. John DeFeo took over management of Zones in January 1997 and attempted to help the company contend with problems associated with its rapid growth and its inability to achieve satisfactory results in the PC market. "The company was managing itself by looking in the rear view mirror," DeFeo remarked in an August 8, 1997 interview with *Puget Sound Business Journal*. "We have to learn to look through the windshield and look at the road ahead and react to what we see coming as opposed to what's already happened."

Zones did change its perspective, but DeFeo was not the agent of change. He spent a little more than a year in charge of the company, achieving $490 million in sales at the end of 1997—only a marginal increase over the $457 million generated the previous year. The company's stock, which had been trading at $28 per share in late 1996, plunged to $4.25 per share by the summer of 1997. New, comprehensive changes were needed to help Zones adapt to the changing dynamics of its market, and the person to initiate such change was Firoz Lalji.

Lalji Taking Command in 1998

Lalji built Kits Cameras into an eight-state, 145-unit chain by the end of 1997, the year he left the company to take active control over his investment in Zones. Lalji was appointed president and chief executive officer of Zones in March 1998, beginning a tenure that ushered in profound changes for the company. Lalji gave Zones a new business model that started to dictate the company's actions in 1999. At the time, the com-

Key Dates:

1988: Zones is founded.
1990: Firoz Lalji acquires 50 percent of Zones.
1990: The *Mac Zone* is distributed to potential customers.
1992: The *PC Zone* is first published.
1998: Lalji is appointed president and chief executive officer of Zones.
1999: Zones begins to focus on corporate clientele.
2002: Lalji promises to make Zones a $1 billion-in-sales company by 2005.

pany's financial performance stood in sharp contrast to its record of growth throughout the decade. After years of exponential sales growth, Zones's financial progress was halted. Annual revenue, which jumped from $113 million in 1994 to $242 million in 1995 and to $457 million in 1996, rested at $487 million in 1999. Worse, the company was no longer profitable, posting a $6.6 million loss in 1999. For the next several years, Zones continued to record lackluster financial results, but a new version of the company was being built to fundamentally correct its problems.

Beginning in 1999, Lalji started to move the company away from consumer sales and focused on serving small-to-medium sized businesses. The company severed its business ties overseas in 1999, divesting majority control over operations in Germany, Austria, Switzerland, Mexico, the United Kingdom, France, and elsewhere. Zones did not entirely abandon consumer sales, but the future of the company as envisioned by Lalji was as a business-to-business, or B2B, company. The change in the company's market posture took time; the financial merits of the switch in focus were not immediately evident. When Zones brokered an agreement with Microsoft in 2000, however, Lalji's vision offered its first tangible evidence of success. The company's stock value more than doubled when it was selected by Microsoft to be the computer behemoth's primary supplier of computer products and distribution services to its 20,000 U.S.-based employees.

Thanks in large part to the arrangement with Microsoft, Zones's sales swelled to $634 million in 2000, but the company's turnaround was not completed with one deal. Further, Microsoft did not typify the type of customer Lalji was pursuing—though the boost to Zones's business was welcomed by Lalji. Instead of targeting multibillion-dollar companies, Lalji was after the 500,000 U.S. businesses with between 50 and 1,000 employees, the market for which was highly fragmented. No competitor in the $100 billion market controlled more than a 5 percent share.

The financial benefits from the company's new strategy were slow to materialize because corporate customers typically replaced their computers every three years. In 1999, the pur-

chasing cycle was reset, with a wave of purchases during the year signifying the arrival of the next wave in 2002. Recessive economic conditions, however, reduced technology spending, delaying the industry's historical cycle metrics. The first positive evidence that Lalji's strategy was working arrived in 2003.

Zones lost money in 2000, 2001, and 2002. Sales at the end of 2002 were $414 million, substantially below the total recorded six years earlier. In 2003, the first signs of a turnaround were on display. Sales increased to $460 million and the company returned to profitability, posting $1.5 million in net income. Lalji was encouraged by the results. Technology spending in the corporate sector was increasing, and Zones had established more than a foothold in the B2B market. Lalji, convinced he was on the right track, announced plans to make Zones a $1 billion-in-sales company by 2005. The goal was decidedly ambitious, requiring the company to more than double its sales in two years. Lalji's success in achieving his goal would be measured in Zones's ability to firmly establish itself as a dominant direct marketer of hardware and software to corporate clients.

Principal Subsidiaries

ZCS; CPCS; Zones Corporate Solutions.

Principal Competitors

CDW Corporation; PC Connection, Inc.; Insight Enterprises, Inc.; PC Mall, Inc.; Apple Computers, Inc.; Systemax Inc.; Dell Inc.; Hewlett Packard Company; International Business Machines Corporation.

Further Reading

Baker, M. Sharon, "Multiple Markets Vex Multiple Zones," *Puget Sound Business Journal,* August 8, 1997, p. 1.
——, Multiple Zones IPO Filing Offers Some Surprises," *Puget Sound Business Journal,* May 17, 1996, p. 3.
——, "Multiple Zones Readying IPO," *Puget Sound Business Journal,* April 19, 1996, p. 1.
Bowman, Robert, "Keeping Service Up to Speed," *Distribution,* June 1993, p. 52.
"Multiple Zones Swings on Microsoft Deal," *Puget Sound Business Journal,* March 31, 2000, p. 20.
Park, Clayton, "Fast-Growing Multiple Zones Tests Selling Via CD," *Puget Sound Business Journal,* November 12, 1993, p. 15.
——, "Multiple Carving Solid Niche in Mail-Order Software Sales," *Puget Sound Business Journal,* June 18, 1993, p. 50.
——, "Multiple Zones Goes Abroad with Software-Catalog Clones," *Puget Sound Business Journal,* May 21, 1993, p. 12.
"Q1 2004 Zones Inc. Earnings Conference Call," *America's Intelligence Wire,* April 30, 2004, p. 4.
Tice, Carol, "Multiple Zones Focusing on Its B2B Business," *Puget Sound Business Journal,* September 8, 2000, p. 5.
——, "Zones Targets Profitability with B2B Strategy," *Puget Sound Business Journal,* June 28, 2002, p. 26.

—Jeffrey L. Covell

INDEX TO COMPANIES

Index to Companies

Listings in this index are arranged in alphabetical order under the company name. Company names beginning with a letter or proper name such as Eli Lilly & Co. will be found under the first letter of the company name. Definite articles (The, Le, La) are ignored for alphabetical purposes as are forms of incorporation that precede the company name (AB, NV). Company names printed in bold type have full, historical essays on the page numbers appearing in bold. Updates to entries that appeared in earlier volumes are signified by the notation (**upd.**). Company names in light type are references within an essay to that company, not full historical essays. This index is cumulative with volume numbers printed in bold type.

A & A Die Casting Company, **25** 312
A and A Limousine Renting, Inc., **26** 62
A & A Medical Supply, **61** 206
A & C Black Ltd., **7** 165
A&E Plastics, **12** 377
A&E Television Networks, 32 3–7
A. & J. McKenna, **13** 295
A&K Petroleum Company. *See* Kerr-McGee Corporation.
A & M Instrument Co., **9** 323
A&M Records, **23** 389
A&N Foods Co., **II** 553
A&P. *See* The Great Atlantic & Pacific Tea Company, Inc.
A&P Water and Sewer Supplies, Inc., **6** 487
A. and T. McKenna Brass and Copper Works, **13** 295
A & W Brands, Inc., 25 3–5; **57** 227; **58** 384
A-dec, Inc., 53 3–5
á la Zing, **62** 259
A-1 Supply, **10** 375. *See also* International Game Technology.
A-R Technologies, **48** 275
A.A. Mathews. *See* CRSS Inc.
A. Ahlström Oy. *See* Ahlstrom Corporation.
A.B. Chance Industries Co., Inc., **31** 259
A.B.Dick Company, 28 6–8
A.B. Hemmings, Ltd., **13** 51
A.B. Leasing Corp., **13** 111–12
A-B Nippondenso, **III** 593
A.B. Watley Group Inc., 45 3–5
A-BEC Mobility, **11** 487
A.C. Delco, **26** 347, 349
A.C. Moore Arts & Crafts, Inc., 30 3–5
A.C. Nielsen Company, 13 3–5. *See also* ACNielsen Corporation.
A.C. Wickman, **13** 296
A.D. International (Australia) Pty. Ltd., **10** 272
A/E/C/ Systems International, **27** 362
A.E. Fitkin & Company, **6** 592–93; **50** 37
A.E. Gutman, **16** 486

A.E. Lottes, **29** 86
A.G. Becker, **11** 318; **20** 260
A.G. Edwards, Inc., 8 3–5; **19** 502; **32** 17–21 (**upd.**)
A.G. Industries, Inc., **7** 24
A.G. Morris, **12** 427
A.G. Spalding & Bros., Inc., **24** 402–03
A.G. Stanley Ltd. *See* The Boots Company PLC.
A.H. Belo Corporation, 10 3–5; **28** 367, 369; **30** 13–17 (**upd.**)
A.H. Robins Co., **10** 70; **12** 188; **16** 438; **50** 538
A. Hirsh & Son, **30** 408
A. Hölscher GmbH, **53** 195
A. Johnson & Co. *See* Axel Johnson Group.
A.L. Laboratories Inc., **12** 3
A.L. Pharma Inc., 12 3–5. *See also* Alpharma Inc.
A.L. Van Houtte Inc. *See* Van Houtte Inc.
A. Lambert International Inc., **16** 80
A. Leon Capel and Sons, Inc. *See* Capel Incorporated.
A.M. Castle & Co., 25 6–8
A. Michel et Cie., **49** 84
A. Moksel AG, 59 3–6
A.O. Smith Corporation, 7 139; **22** 181, **11** 3–6; **24** 499; **40** 3–8 (**upd.**)
A.P. Green Refractories, **22** 285
A.P. Møller - Maersk A/S, 57 3–6
A.P. Orleans, Inc. of New Jersey, **62** 262
A.S. Abell Co., **IV** 678
A.S. Watson & Company, **18** 254
A.S. Yakovlev Design Bureau, 15 3–6
A. Schilling & Company. *See* McCormick & Company, Incorporated.
A. Schulman, Inc., 8 6–8; **49** 3–7 (**upd.**)
A. Sulka & Co., **29** 457
A.T. Cross Company, 17 3–5; **49** 8–12 (**upd.**)
A.T. Massey Coal Company, Inc., **34** 164; **57** 236
A.T. Mays, **55** 90
A-T-O Inc. *See* Figgie International, Inc.

A.W. Baulderstone Holdings Pty. Ltd., **55** 62
A.W. Faber-Castell Unternehmensverwaltung GmbH & Co., 51 3–6
A.W. Sijthoff, **14** 555
A-Z International Companies, **III** 569; **20** 361
AA Distributors, **22** 14
AA Energy Corp., **I** 91
AAA Development Corp., **17** 238
AADC Holding Company, Inc., **62** 347
AAE Ahaus Alstatter Eisenbahn Holding AG, **25** 171
AAF-McQuay Incorporated, 26 3–5
AAI Corporation, **37** 399
Aai.FosterGrant, Inc., **60** 131, 133
AAON, Inc., 22 3–6
AAPT, 54 355–57
AAR Corp., 28 3–5
Aardman Animations Ltd., 43 143; **61** 3–5
Aaron Brothers, Inc., **17** 320, 322
Aaron Rents, Inc., 14 3–5; **33** 368; **35** 3–6 (**upd.**)
AARP, 27 3–5
Aasche Transportation, **27** 404
AASE SARL, **53** 32
Aastrom Biosciences, Inc., **13** 161
AAV Cos., **13** 48; **41** 22
Aavant Health Management Group, Inc., **11** 394
Aavid Thermal Technologies, Inc., 29 3–6
AB Capital & Investment Corporation, **23** 381
AB Ingredients Limited, **41** 32
AB Metal Pty Ltd, **62** 331
AB-PT. *See* American Broadcasting-Paramount Theatres, Inc.
ABA. *See* Aktiebolaget Aerotransport.
Abacus Direct Corporation, **46** 156
ABACUS International Holdings Ltd., **26** 429

Abana Pharmaceuticals, **24** 257
Abar Staffing, **25** 434
Abatix Corp., 57 7–9
ABB Asea Brown Boveri Ltd., II 1–4,
   13; **III** 427, 466, 631–32; **IV** 109, 204,
   300; **15** 483; **22** 7–12 (upd.), 64, 288;
   28 39; **34** 132. *See also* ABB Ltd.
ABB Hafo AB. *See* Mitel Corp.
ABB Ltd., 65 3–10 (upd.)
ABB RDM Service, **41** 326
Abba Seafood AB, **18** 396
Abbatoir St.-Valerien Inc., **II** 652
Abbey Business Consultants, **14** 36
Abbey Home Entertainment, **23** 391
Abbey Life Group PLC, **II** 309
Abbey Medical, Inc., **11** 486; **13** 366–67
Abbey National plc, 10 6–8; **39** 3–6
   (upd.)
Abbey Road Building Society, **10** 6–7
Abbott Laboratories, I 619–21, 686, 690,
   705; **II** 539; **10** 70, 78, 126; **11** 7–9
   (upd.), 91, 494; **12** 4; **14** 98, 389; **22** 75;
   25 55; **36** 38–39; **40** 9–13 (upd.); **46**
   394–95; **50** 538; **63** 206–07
ABC Appliance, Inc., 10 9–11
ABC Carpet & Home Co. Inc., 26 6–8
ABC Family Worldwide, Inc., 52 3–6, 84
ABC, Inc., **II** 129–33; **III** 214, 251–52; **17**
   150; **XVIII** 65; **19** 201; **21** 25; **24**
   516–17; **32** 3; **51** 218–19. *See also*
   Capital Cities/ABC Inc.
ABC Markets, **17** 558
ABC Rail Products Corporation, 18 3–5
ABC Stores. *See* MNS, Ltd.
ABC Supply Co., Inc., 22 13–16
ABC Treadco, **19** 455
ABECOR. *See* Associated Banks of Europe
   Corp.
Abeille Vie. *See* Aviva.
Les Abeilles International SA, **60** 149
Abell-Howe Construction Inc., **42** 434
Abelle Limited, **63** 182, 184
Abercrombie & Fitch Co., 15 7–9; **17**
   369; **25** 90; **35** 7–10 (upd.)
Abertis Infraestructuras, S.A., 65 11–13
ABF. *See* Associated British Foods PLC.
ABF Freight System, Inc., **16** 39–41
ABI. *See* American Furniture Company,
   Inc.
Abigail Adams National Bancorp, Inc.,
   23 3–5
Abilis, **49** 222
Abington Shoe Company. *See* The
   Timberland Company.
Abiomed, Inc., 47 3–6
Abita Springs Water Co., **58** 373
Abitec Corporation, **41** 32–33
Abitibi-Consolidated, Inc., 25 9–13
   (upd.); **26** 445; **63** 314–15
Abitibi-Price Inc., IV 245–47, 721; **9** 391
ABM Industries Incorporated, 25 14–16
   (upd.); **51** 295
ABN. *See* Algemene Bank Nederland N.V.
ABN AMRO Holding, N.V., 39 295; **50**
   3–7
Above The Belt, Inc., **16** 37
AboveNet, Inc., **61** 210, 213
ABR Foods, **II** 466
Abrafract Abrasives. *See* Carbo PLC.
Abraham & Straus, **9** 209; **31** 192
Abrams Industries Inc., 23 6–8
ABS Pump AB, **53** 85
Absolut Company, **31** 458, 460

Abu Dhabi National Oil Company, IV
   363–64, 476; **45** 6–9 (upd.)
AC Design Inc., **22** 196
AC Humko Corporation, **41** 32–33
AC Roma SpA, **44** 388
ACA Corporation, **25** 368
Academic Press. *See* Reed Elsevier.
Academy of Television Arts & Sciences,
   Inc., 55 3–5
Academy Sports & Outdoors, 27 6–8
Acadia Entities, **24** 456
Acadia Investors, **23** 99
Acadia Partners, **21** 92
Acadian Ambulance & Air Med
   Services, Inc., 39 7–10
Accel, S.A. de C.V., **51** 115–17
Accenture Ltd., **59** 130
Access Dynamics Inc., **17** 255
Access Graphics Technology Inc., **13** 128
Accessory Network Group, Inc., **8** 219
Acclaim Entertainment Inc., 13 115; **24**
   3–8, 538
ACCO World Corporation, 7 3–5; **12**
   264; **51** 7–10 (upd.)
Accolade Inc., **35** 227
Accor SA, 10 12–14; **13** 364; **27** 9–12
   (upd.); **48** 199; **49** 126; **53** 301; **56** 248;
   59 361
Accord Energy, **18** 367; **49** 120
Accres Uitgevers B.V., **51** 328
Acctex Information Systems, **17** 468
Accudata Inc., **64** 237
Accuralite Company, **10** 492
AccuRead Limited, **42** 165, 167
Accuscan, Inc., **14** 380
AccuStaff Inc. *See* MPS Group, Inc.
ACE Cash Express, Inc., 33 3–6
Ace Comb Company, **12** 216
Ace Hardware Corporation, 12 6–8; **35**
   11–14 (upd.)
ACE Limited, **45** 109
Ace Medical Company, **30** 164
Ace Novelty Company, **26** 374
Acer Inc., 10 257; **16** 3–6; **47** 385
Acer Sertek, **24** 31
Aceralia, **42** 414
Acerinox, **59** 226
Aceros Fortuna S.A. de C.V., **13** 141
Acesa. *See* Abertis Infraestructuras, S.A.
Aceto Corp., 38 3–5
ACF Industries, **30** 282
ACG. *See* American Cotton Growers
   Association.
Achatz GmbH Bauunternehmung, **55** 62
Achiever Computers Pty Ltd, **56** 155
ACI. *See* Advance Circuits Inc.
ACI Holdings Inc., **I** 91; **28** 24
ACI Ltd., **29** 478
Aciéries de Ploërmel, **16** 514
Aciéries Réunies de Burbach-Eich-
   Dudelange S.A. *See* ARBED S.A.
Acker Drill Company, **26** 70
Ackerley Communications, Inc., 9 3–5;
   50 95
Acklin Stamping Company, **8** 515
ACL. *See* Automotive Components
   Limited.
ACLC. *See* Allegheny County Light
   Company.
ACLU. *See* American Civil Liberties
   Union (ACLU).
ACM. *See* Advanced Custom Molders, Inc.
Acme Brick Company, **19** 231–32
Acme Can Co., **13** 188

Acme-Cleveland Corp., 13 6–8
Acme Cotton Products, **13** 366
Acme-Delta Company, **11** 411
Acme Fast Freight Inc., **27** 473
Acme Market. *See* American Stores
   Company.
Acme Newspictures, **25** 507
Acme Quilting Co., Inc., **19** 304
Acme Screw Products, **14** 181
ACMI, **21** 118–19
ACNielsen Corporation, 38 6–9 (upd.);
   61 81
Acordis, **41** 10
Acorn Financial Corp., **15** 328
Acorn Products, Inc., 55 6–9
Acova S.A., **26** 4
Acquired Systems Enhancement
   Corporation, **24** 31
ACR. *See* American Capital and Research
   Corp.
AcroMed Corporation, **30** 164
ACS. *See* Affiliated Computer Services,
   Inc.
Acsys, Inc., 44 3–5
ACT Group, **45** 280
ACT Inc, **50** 48
ACT Research Center Inc., **56** 238
Act III Theatres, **25** 453
Actava Group, **14** 332
Action, **6** 393
Action Furniture by Lane, **17** 183
Action Gaming Inc., **44** 337
Action Labs Inc., **37** 285
Action Performance Companies, Inc., 27
   13–15; **32** 344; **37** 319
Action Temporary Services, **29** 273
Active Apparel Group. *See* Everlast
   Worldwide Inc.
Activenture Corporation, **16** 253; **43** 209
Actividades de Construcción y Servicios
   S.A. (ACS), **55** 179
Activision, Inc., 24 3; **32** 8–11
Acuity Brands, Inc., **54** 255
Acumos, **11** 57
Acushnet Company, 64 3–5
Acuson Corporation, 10 15–17; **36** 3–6
   (upd.)
ACX Technologies, **13** 11; **36** 15
Acxiom Corporation, 35 15–18
AD-AM Gas Company, **11** 28
AD South Africa, Inc., **60** 34
Ad Vantage Computer Systems Inc., **58**
   273
Adage Systems International, Inc., **19** 438
Adam, Meldrum & Anderson Company
   (AM&A), **16** 61–62; **50** 107
Adam Opel AG, 7 6–8; **11** 549; **18** 125;
   21 3–7 (upd.); **61** 6–11 (upd.)
Adams Childrenswear. *See* Sears plc.
Adams Golf, Inc., 37 3–5; **45** 76
Adams Industries, **19** 414
Adams/Cates Company, **21** 257
Adanac General Insurance Company, **13** 63
Adaptec, Inc., 11 56; **31** 3–6
Adaptive Data Systems, **25** 531
Adar Associates, Inc. *See* Scientific-
   Atlanta, Inc.
ADC of Greater Kansas City, Inc., **22** 443
ADC Telecommunications, Inc., 10
   18–21; **30** 6–9 (upd.); **44** 69
Addison Communications Plc, **45** 272
Addison Corporation, **31** 399
Addison Structural Services, Inc., **26** 433
Addison Wesley, **IV** 659

Addressograph-Multigraph, **11** 494
Adecco S.A., **26** 240; **35** 441–42; **36** 7–11 (upd.)
Adeletom Aviation L.L.C., **61** 100
Adelphia Communications Corporation, 17 6–8; **52** 7–10 (upd.)
Ademco. *See* Alarm Device Manufacturing Company.
Adero Inc., **45** 202
ADESA Corporation, **34** 286
Adesso-Madden, Inc., **37** 372
ADI Group Limited. *See* AHL Services, Inc.
Adia S.A., **6** 9–11; **9** 327. *See also* Adecco S.A.
Adiainvest S.A. *See* Adecco S.A.
adidas AG, **8** 392–93; **13** 513; **14** 6–9; **17** 244; **22** 202; **23** 472, 474; **25** 205, 207; **36** 344, 346
adidas-Salomon AG, **33** 7–11 (upd.)
Adirondack Industries, **24** 403
Adjusters Auto Rental Inc. **16** 380
Adler, **23** 219
Adler and Shaykin, **11** 556–57
Adler Line. *See* Transatlantische Dampfschiffahrts Gesellschaft.
Adley Express, **14** 567
ADM. *See* Archer-Daniels-Midland Co.
Administaff, Inc., **52** 11–13
Administracion Corporativa y Mercantil, S.A. de C.V., **37** 178
Admiral Co. *See* Maytag Corporation.
ADNOC. *See* Abu Dhabi National Oil Company.
Adobe Systems Incorporated, **10** 22–24; **15** 149; **20** 46, 237; **33** 12–16 (upd.); **43** 151
Adolf Würth GmbH & Co. KG, **49** 13–15
Adolph Coors Company, **I** 236–38, 273; **13** 9–11 (upd.); **18** 72; **26** 303, 306; **34** 37; **36** 12–16 (upd.); **44** 198; **59** 68
Adolphe Lafont, **17** 210
Adonis Radio Corp., **9** 320
Adorence, **16** 482
ADP. *See* Automatic Data Processing, Inc.
Adria Produtos Alimenticios, Ltda., **12** 411
Adria Steamship Company, **6** 425
Adrian Hope and Company, **14** 46
Adrienne Vittadini, **15** 291
ADS. *See* Aerospace Display Systems.
Adsega, **II** 677
Adstaff Associates, Ltd., **26** 240
Adsteam, **60** 101
ADT Ltd., **26** 410; **28** 486; **63** 403
ADT Security Services, Inc., **44** 6–9 (upd.)
ADT Security Systems, Inc., **12** 9–11
Adtel, Inc., **10** 358
Adtran Inc., **22** 17–20
Adtranz **34** 128, 132–33, 136; **42** 45. *See also* ABB Ltd.
Advacel, **18** 20; **43** 17
Advance Auto Parts, Inc., **57** 10–12
Advance Chemical Company, **25** 15
Advance Circuits Inc., **49** 234
Advance Foundry, **14** 42
Advance Gems & Jewelry Co., Ltd., **62** 371
Advance/Newhouse Communications, **42** 114
Advance Publications Inc., **IV** 581–84; **13** 178, 180, 429; **19** 3–7 (upd.); **31** 376, 378; **59** 132–33

Advance-Rumely Thresher Co., **13** 16
Advance Transformer Co., **13** 397
Advanced Aerodynamics & Structures Inc. *See* Mooney Aerospace Group Ltd.
Advanced Casino Systems Corporation, **21** 277
Advanced Circuits Inc., **67** 3–5
Advanced Colortech Inc., **56** 238
Advanced Communications Engineering. *See* Scientific-Atlanta, Inc.
Advanced Communications Inc. *See* Metrocall, Inc.
Advanced Custom Molders, Inc., **17** 533
Advanced Data Management Group S.A., **23** 212
Advanced Entertainment Group, **10** 286
Advanced Fiberoptic Technologies, **30** 267
Advanced Fibre Communications, Inc., 63 3–5
Advanced Gravis, **28** 244
Advanced Logic Research, Inc., **27** 169
Advanced Marine Enterprises, Inc., **18** 370
Advanced Marketing Services, Inc., **24** 354; **34** 3–6
Advanced Medical Technologies, **III** 512
Advanced Metal Technologies Inc., **17** 234
Advanced Metallurgy, Inc., **29** 460
Advanced Micro Devices, Inc., **6** 215–17; **9** 115; **10** 367; **11** 308; **16** 316; **18** 18–19, 382; **19** 312; **20** 175; **30** 10–12 (upd.); **32** 498; **43** 15–16; **47** 384
Advanced MobilComm, **10** 432
Advanced Parking Systems Ltd., **58** 184
Advanced Plasma Systems, Inc., **48** 299
Advanced Pollution Instrumentation Inc., **62** 362
Advanced Structures, Inc., **18** 163
Advanced System Applications, **11** 395
Advanced Technology Laboratories, Inc., **9** 6–8
Advanced Telecommunications Corporation, **8** 311
Advanced Tissue Sciences Inc., **41** 377
Advanced Web Technologies, **22** 357
AdvanceMed LLC, **45** 146
AdvancePCS, Inc., **63** 336
Advanstar Communications, Inc., **27** 361; **57** 13–17
Advanta Corporation, **8** 9–11; **11** 123; **38** 10–14 (upd.)
Advanta Partners, LP, **42** 322
Advantage Company, **8** 311; **27** 306
The Advantage Group, Inc., **25** 185–86
Advantage Health Plans, Inc., **11** 379
Advantage Health Systems, Inc., **25** 383
Advantage Insurers, Inc., **25** 185, 187
Advantage Publishers Group, **34** 5
Advantest Corporation, **39** 350, 353
Advantica Restaurant Group, Inc., **27** 16–19 (upd.); **29** 150
Advantra International NV. *See* Punch International N.V.
Advent Corporation, **22** 97
Adventist Health, **53** 6–8
Advertising Unlimited, Inc., **10** 461
Advo, Inc., **6** 12–14; **53** 9–13 (upd.)
Advocat Inc., **46** 3–5
AEA. *See* United Kingdom Atomic Energy Authority.
AEA Investors Inc., **II** 628; **13** 97; **22** 169, 171; **28** 380; **30** 328
AEG A.G., **I** 151, 193, **409–11**; **6** 489; **IX** 11; **14** 169; **15** 142; **23** 495; **34** 131–32
AEG Hausgeräte, **53** 128

Aegek S.A., **64** 6–8
Aegis Group plc, **6** 15–16
Aegis Insurance Co., **III** 273
AEGON N.V., **III** 177–79, 201, 273; **33** 418–20; **50** 8–12 (upd.); **52** 288; **63** 166; **64** 171. *See also* Transamerica–An AEGON Company
AEI Music Network Inc., **35** 19–21
AEL Ventures Ltd., **9** 512
Aeneas Venture Corp., **26** 502
AEON Group, **V** 96–99; **11** 498–99; **31** 430–31; **37** 227; **56** 202
AEP. *See* American Electric Power Company.
AEP Industries, Inc., **36** 17–19
AEP-Span, **8** 546
Aer Lingus Group plc, **6** 59; **12** 367–68; **34** 7–10; **35** 382–84; **36** 230–31
Aera Energy LLC, **41** 359
Aérazur, **36** 529
Aerial Communications Inc., **31** 452
Aeritalia, **I** 467
Aero Engines, **9** 418
Aero International (Regional) SAS, **24** 88
Aero International Inc., **14** 43
Aero Mayflower Transit Company. *See* Mayflower Group Inc.
Aero O/Y. *See* Finnair Oy.
Aeroflot—Russian International Airlines, **I** 118; **6** 57–59; **14** 73; **27** 475; **29** 7–10 (upd.)
Aerojet, **8** 206, 208
Aerojet-General Corp., **9** 266; **63** 6–9
Aerolíneas Argentinas S.A., **33** 17–19
Aeroméxico, **20** 168
Aeromotive Systems Co., **55** 31
Aeronautics Leasing, Inc., **39** 33
Aeronca Inc., **46** 6–8; **48** 274
Aeropharm Technology, Inc., **63** 233–34
Aéroports de Paris, **33** 20–22
Aeroquip Corporation, **III** 640–42; **16** 7–9. *See also* Eaton Corporation.
Aerosance Inc., **62** 362
Aerospace Display Systems, **36** 158
Aerospace International Services, **41** 38
Aerospace Products International, Inc., **49** 141
The Aérospatiale Group, **I** 46, 50, 74, 94; **7** 9–12; **12** 190–91; **14** 72; **21** 8–11 (upd.); **24** 84–86, 88–89; **26** 179. *See also* European Aeronautic Defence and Space Company EADS N.V.
Aerostar, **33** 359–61
The AES Corporation, **10** 25–27; **13** 12–15 (upd.); **24** 359; **53** 14–18 (upd.); **65** 119
Aetna, Inc., **20** 59; **21** 12–16 (upd.), 95; **22** 139, 142–43; **30** 364; **63** 10–16 (upd.)
Aetna Life and Casualty Company, **III** 180–82, 209, 223, 226, 236, 254, 296, 298, 305, 313, 329; **10** 75–76; **12** 367; **15** 26; **23** 135; **40** 199
Aetna National Bank, **13** 466
AF Insurance Agency, **44** 33
AFC. *See* Advanced Fibre Communications, Inc.
AFC Enterprises, Inc., **32** 12–16 (upd.); **36** 517, 520; **54** 373
AFE Ltd., **IV** 241
Affiliated Computer Services, Inc., **61** 12–16
Affiliated Foods Inc., **53** 19–21
Affiliated Hospital Products Inc., **37** 400

Affiliated Music Publishing, **22** 193
Affiliated Paper Companies, Inc., **31** 359, 361
Affiliated Physicians Network, Inc., **45** 194
Affiliated Publications, Inc., **7** 13–16; **19** 285; **61** 241
Affinity Group Holding Inc., **56** 3–6
Affordable Inns, **13** 364
AFG Industries Inc., **I** 483; **9** 248; **48** 42
AFIA, **22** 143; **45** 104, 108
Afianzadora Insurgentes Serfin, **19** 190
AFK Sistema, **59** 300
AFL. *See* American Football League.
AFLAC Incorporated, **10** 28–30 (upd.); **38** 15–19 (upd.)
AFP. *See* Australian Forest Products.
AFRA Enterprises Inc., **26** 102
AFRAM Carriers, Inc. *See* Kirby Corporation.
African Rainbow Minerals, **63** 185
Africare, **59** 7–10
AFT. *See* Advanced Fiberoptic Technologies.
After Hours Formalwear Inc., **60** 3–5
AFW Fabric Corp., **16** 124
AG&E. *See* American Electric Power Company.
AG Barr plc, **64** 9–12
Ag-Chem Equipment Company, Inc., **17** 9–11. *See also* AGCO Corporation.
AG Communication Systems Corporation, **15** 194; **43** 446
Ag Services of America, Inc., **59** 11–13
Agan Chemical Manufacturers Ltd., **25** 266–67
Agape S.p.A., **57** 82–83
Agar Manufacturing Company, **8** 2
Agatha Christie Ltd., **31** 63 67
AGCO Corp., **13** 16–18; **67** 6–10 (upd.)
Age International, Inc., **62** 347
Agefi, **34** 13
AGEL&P. *See* Albuquerque Gas, Electric Light and Power Company.
Agence France-Presse, **34** 11–14
Agency, **6** 393
Agency Rent-A-Car, **16** 379
Agere Systems Inc., **61** 17–19
AGF. *See* Assurances Generales de France.
Agfa Gevaert Group N.V., **III** 487; **18** 50, 184–86; **26** 540–41; **50** 90; **59** 14–16
Aggregate Industries plc, **36** 20–22
Aggreko Plc, **45** 10–13
AGI Industries, **57** 208–09
Agiba Petroleum, **IV** 414
Agie Charmilles, **61** 106, 108
Agilent Technologies Inc., **38** 20–23; **63** 33–34
Agip SpA. *See* Ente Nazionale Idrocarburi
Agiv AG, **39** 40–41; **51** 25
Agnew Gold Mining Company (Pty) Ltd., **62** 164
Agouron Pharmaceuticals, Inc., **38** 365
Agr. *See* Artes Grafica Rioplatense S.A.
Agra Europe Limited, **58** 191
AGRANA, **27** 436, 439
Agri-Foods, Inc., **60** 256
Agri-Insurance Company, Ltd., **63** 23
AgriBank FCB, **8** 489
Agribrands International, Inc., **40** 89
Agrico Chemical Company. *See* The Williams Companies.
Agricole de Roquefort et Maria Grimal, **23** 219

Agricultural Minerals and Chemicals Inc., **13** 504
Agrifull, **22** 380
Agrigenetics, Inc. *See* Mycogen Corporation.
Agrilusa, Agro-Industria, **51** 54
Agrobios S.A., **23** 172
Agroferm Hungarian Japanese Fermentation Industry, **III** 43
Agrologica, **51** 54
Agromán S.A., **40** 218
AGTL. *See* Alberta Gas Trunk Line Company, Ltd.
Agua de la Falda S.A., **38** 231
Agua Pura Water Company, **24** 467
Agusta S.p.A., **46** 66
Agway, Inc., **7** 17–18; **21** 17–19 (upd.); **36** 440
Aherns Holding, **60** 100
AHL Services, Inc., **26** 149; **27** 20–23; **45** 379
Ahlstrom Corporation, **53** 22–25
Ahmanson. *See* H.F. Ahmanson & Company.
AHMSA. *See* Altos Hornos de México, S.A. de C.V.
Ahold. *See* Koninklijke Ahold NV.
AHP. *See* American Home Products Corporation.
AHS. *See* American Hospital Supply Corporation.
AHSC Holdings Corp. *See* Alco Health Services Corporation.
Ahtna AGA Security, Inc., **14** 541
AI Automotive, **24** 204
AIC. *See* Allied Import Company.
AICA, **16** 421; **43** 308
AICPA. *See* The American Institute of Certified Public Accountants.
Aid Auto, **18** 144
Aida Corporation, **11** 504
AIG. *See* American International Group, Inc.
AIG Global Real Estate Investment Corp., **54** 225
AIG/Lincoln International L.L.C., **54** 225
Aigner. *See* Etienne Aigner AG.
Aiken Stores, Inc., **14** 92
Aikenhead's Home Improvement Warehouse, **18** 240; **26** 306
AIL Technologies, **46** 160
AIM Create Co., Ltd. *See* Marui Co., Ltd.
AIM Management Group Inc., **65** 43–45
AIMCO. *See* Apartment Investment and Management Company.
Ainsworth Gaming Technologies, **54** 15
Ainsworth National, **14** 528
AIP. *See* Amorim Investimentos e Participaço.
Air & Water Technologies Corporation, **6** 441–42. *See also* Aqua Alliance Inc.
Air BP, **7** 141
Air By Pleasant, **62** 276
Air Canada, **6** 60–62; **23** 9–12 (upd.); **29** 302; **36** 230; **59** 17–22 (upd.)
Air China, **46** 9–11
Air Compak, **12** 182
Air de Cologne, **27** 474
Air Express International Corporation, **13** 19–20; **40** 138; **46** 71
Air France, **8** 313; **12** 190; **24** 86; **27** 26; **33** 21, 50, 377; **63** 17. *See also* Groupe Air France; Societe Air France.
Air Global International, **55** 30

Air-India Limited, **6** 63–64; **27** 24–26 (upd.); **41** 336–37; **63** 17–18; **65** 14
Air Inter. *See* Groupe Air France.
Air Inuit, **56** 38–39
Air Jamaica Limited, **54** 3–6
Air La Carte Inc., **13** 48
Air Lanka Catering Services Ltd. *See* Thai Airways International.
Air Liberté, **6** 208
Air Liquide. *See* L'Air Liquide SA.
Air London International, **36** 190
Air Mauritius Ltd., **63** 17–19
Air Methods Corporation, **53** 26–29
Air Midwest, Inc., **11** 299
Air New Zealand Limited, **14** 10–12; **24** 399–400; **27** 475; **38** 24–27 (upd.)
Air NorTerra Inc., **56** 39
Air Pacific, **24** 396, 400
Air Products and Chemicals, Inc., **I** 297–99, 315, 358, 674; **10** 31–33 (upd.); **11** 403; **14** 125; **54** 10
Air Pub S.à.r.l., **64** 359
Air Russia, **24** 400
Air Sahara Limited, **65** 14–16
Air Sea Broker AG, **47** 286–87
Air Southwest Co. *See* Southwest Airlines Co.
Air Taser, Inc. *See* Taser International, Inc.
Air Transport International LLC, **58** 43
Air Wisconsin Airlines Corporation, **55** 10–12
Airborne Freight Corporation, **6** 345–47 345; **13** 19; **14** 517; **18** 177; **34** 15–18 (upd.); **46** 72
Airbus Industrie, **7** 9–11, 504; **9** 418; **10** 164; **13** 356; **21** 8; **24** 84–89; **34** 128, 135; **48** 219. *See also* G.I.E. Airbus Industrie.
AirCal, **I** 91
Airco, **25** 81–82; **26** 94
Aircraft Modular Products, **30** 73
Aircraft Turbine Center, Inc., **28** 3
Airex Corporation, **16** 337
AirFoyle Ltd., **53** 50
Airgas, Inc., **54** 7–10
Airguard Industries, Inc., **17** 104, 106; **61** 66
AirLib. *See* Société d'Exploitation AOM.
Airline Interiors Inc., **41** 368–69
Airlines of Britain Holdings, **34** 398; **38** 105–06
Airlink, **24** 396
Airmark Plastics Corp., **18** 497–98
Airopak Corporation. *See* PVC Container Corporation.
Airpax Electronics, Inc., **13** 398
Airport Leather Concessions LLC, **58** 369
Airrest S.A., **64** 359
Airshop Ltd., **25** 246
Airstream. *See* Thor Industries, Inc.
AirTouch Communications, **11** 10–12. *See also* Vodafone Group PLC.
Airtours Plc, **27** 27–29, 90, 92
AirTran Holdings, Inc., **22** 21–23; **28** 266; **33** 302; **34** 32; **55** 10–11
AirWair Ltd., **23** 399, 401–02
AirWays Corporation. *See* AirTran Holdings, Inc.
Aisin Seiki Co., Ltd., **III** 415–16; **14** 64; **48** 3–5 (upd.)
AIT Worldwide, **47** 286–87
Aitchison & Colegrave. *See* Bradford & Bingley PLC.
Aitken, Inc., **26** 433

AITS. *See* American International Travel Service.

Aiuruoca, **25** 85

Aiwa Co., Ltd., 28 360; **30 18–20**

Ajax Iron Works, **II** 16

Ajax Repair & Supply, **58** 75

Ajinomoto Co., Inc., II 463–64, 475; **III** 705; **28 9–11 (upd.)**

AJS Auto Parts Inc., **15** 246

AK Steel Holding Corporation, 19 8–9; 41 3–6 (upd.)

Akane Securities Co. Ltd., **II** 443

Akashic Memories, **11** 234

Akemi, **17** 310; **24** 160

Aker RGI, **32** 99

AKG Acoustics GmbH, 62 3–6

AKH Co. Inc., **20** 63

Akin, Gump, Strauss, Hauer & Feld, L.L.P., 18 366; **33 23–25; 47** 140

Akorn, Inc., 32 22–24

Akro-Mills Inc., **19** 277–78

Akron Brass Manufacturing Co., **9** 419

Akron Extruders Inc., **53** 230

Akroyd & Smithers, **14** 419

Aktiebolaget Electrolux, 22 24–28 (upd.). *See also* Electrolux A.B.

Aktiebolaget SKF, III 622–25; 38 28–33 (upd.)

Aktieselskabet Dampskibsselskabet Svendborg, **57** 3, 5

Akzo Nobel N.V., 13 21–23, 545; **14** 27; **16** 69, 462; **21** 466; **41 7–10 (upd.); 52** 410

Al Copeland Enterprises, Inc., **7 26–28; 32** 13–15

Alaadin Middle East-Ersan, **IV** 564

Alabama Bancorp., **17** 152

Alabama Farmers Cooperative, Inc., 63 20–22

Alabama Gas Corporation, **21** 207–08

Alabama Power Company, **38** 445, 447–48

Alabama Shipyards Inc., **21** 39–40

Aladdin Industries, **16** 487

Aladdin Mills Inc., **19** 276; **63** 300

Alagasco, **21** 207–08

Alagroup, **45** 337

Alain Afflelou SA, 53 30–32

Alain Manoukian. *See* Groupe Alain Manoukian.

Alamac Knit Fabrics, Inc., **16** 533–34; **21** 192

Alamito Company, **6** 590

Alamo Engine Company, **8** 514

Alamo Group Inc., 32 25–28

Alamo Rent A Car, Inc., 6 348–50; 24 9–12 (upd.); 25 93; **26** 409

Alania, **24** 88

ALANTEC Corporation, **25** 162

ALARIS Medical Systems, Inc., 65 17–20

Alarm Device Manufacturing Company, **9** 413–15

Alaron Inc., **16** 357

Alascom, **26** 358. *See also* Pacific Telecom, Inc.

Alaska Air Group, Inc., 6 65–67; 11 50; **29 11–14 (upd.); 48** 219

Alaska Commercial Company, **12** 363

Alaska Hydro-Train, **6** 382; **9** 510

Alaska Junk Co., **19** 380

Alaska Native Wireless LLC, **60** 264

Alaska Railroad Corporation, 60 6–9

Alaska Steel Co., **19** 381

Alatas Mammoet, **26** 279

Alba Foods, **27** 197; **43** 218

Alba-Waldensian, Inc., 30 21–23

Albany Cheese, **23** 219

Albany International Corporation, 8 12–14; 51 11–14 (upd.)

Albaugh Inc., **62** 19

Albemarle Corporation, 59 23–25

Albert E. Reed & Co. Ltd. *See* Reed International PLC.

The Albert Fisher Group plc, 41 11–13

Albert Heijn NV, **II** 641–42; **38** 200, 202

Albert Nipon, Inc., **8** 323

Albert Willcox & Co., **14** 278

Alberta Energy Company Ltd., 16 10–12; 43 3–6 (upd.)

Alberta Gas Trunk Line Company, Ltd. *See* Nova Corporation of Alberta.

Alberto-Culver Company, II 641–42; **8 15–17; 36 23–27 (upd.); 60** 258

Albertson's, Inc., II 601–03, 604–05, 637; **7 19–22 (upd.); 8** 474; **15** 178, 480; **16** 249; **18** 8; **22** 38; **27** 247, 290, 292; **30 24–28 (upd.); 33** 306; **40** 366; **65 21–26 (upd.)**

Albion Industries, Inc., **16** 357

Albright & Wilson Ltd., **12** 351; **16** 461; **38** 378, 380; **50** 282; **59** 25

Albuquerque Gas & Electric Company. *See* Public Service Company of New Mexico.

Albuquerque Gas, Electric Light and Power Company, **6** 561–62

Alcan Aluminium Limited, IV 9–13, 14, 59, 154–55; **9** 512; **14** 35; **31 7–12 (upd.); 45** 337

Alcan Inc., **60** 338

Alcatel Alsthom Compagnie Générale d'Electricité, 6 304; **7** 9; **9 9–11**, 32; **11** 59, 198; **15** 125; **17** 353; **18** 155; **19** 164, 166; **21** 233

Alcatel S.A., 36 28–31 (upd.); 42 375–76; **52** 332, 334; **53** 237; **54** 264; **57** 409

Alchem Capital Corp., **8** 141, 143

Alchem Plastics, **19** 414

Alco Capital Group, Inc., **27** 288

Alco Health Services Corporation, III 9–10. *See also* AmeriSource Health Corporation.

Alco Office Products Inc., **24** 362

Alco Standard Corporation, I 412–13; 9 261; **16** 473–74

ALCO Trade Show Services, **26** 102

Alcoa Inc., 56 7–11 (upd.)

Alcon Laboratories, **10** 46, 48; **30 30–31**

Alden Merrell Corporation, **23** 169

Aldi Group, 11 240; **13 24–26; 17** 125

Aldila Inc., 46 12–14

Aldine Press, **10** 34

Aldiscon, **37** 232

Aldus Corporation, 10 34–36

Alenia, **7** 9, 11

Alert Centre Inc., **32** 373

Alert Management Systems Inc., **12** 380

Alessio Tubi, **IV** 228

Alestra, **19** 12

Alex & Ivy, **10** 166–68

Alex Lee Inc., 18 6–9; 44 10–14 (upd.)

Alexander & Alexander Services Inc., 10 37–39; 13 476

Alexander & Baldwin, Inc., 10 40–42; 29 307; **40 14–19 (upd.)**

Alexander and Lord, **13** 482

Alexander Hamilton Life Insurance Co., **II** 420; **29** 256

Alexander Howden Group, **10** 38–39

Alexander-Schroder Lumber Company, **18** 514

Alexander Smith, Inc., **19** 275

Alexander's, Inc., 10 282; **12** 221; **26** 111; **45 14–16**

Alexandria Petroleum Co., **51** 113

Alexis Lichine, **III** 43

Alfa Corporation, 59 210; **60 10–12**

Alfa-Laval AB, III 417–21; 8 376; **53** 328; **64 13–18 (upd.)**

Alfa Romeo, I 163, 167; **11** 102, 104, 139, 205; **13 27–29**, 218–19; **36 32–35 (upd.)**, 196–97

Alfa, S.A. de C.V., 11 386; **19 10–12; 37** 176

Alfa Trading Company, **23** 358

Alfalfa's Markets, **19** 500–02

alfi Zitzmann, **60** 364

Alfred A. Knopf, Inc., 13 428, 429; **31** 376–79

Alfred Bullows & Sons, Ltd., **21** 64

Alfred Dunhill Limited, **19** 369; **27** 487–89

Alfred Marks Bureau, Ltd. *See* Adia S.A.

Alfred McAlpine plc, **51** 138

Alfred Ritter GmbH & Co. KG, 58 3–7

Alfried Krupp von Bohlen und Halbach Foundation, **IV** 89

ALG. *See* Arkla, Inc.

Alga, **24** 83

Algamar, S.A., 64 91

Algemeen Burgerlijk Pensioenfonds, **26** 421

Algemeen Dagblad BV, **53** 273

Algemene Bank Nederland N.V., II 183–84, 185, 239, 527

Algo Group Inc., 24 13–15

Algoma Steel Corp., **8** 544–45

Algonquin Energy, Inc., **6** 487

Algonquin Gas Transmission Company, **6** 486; **14** 124–26

ALI. *See* Aeronautics Leasing, Inc.

Aliança Florestal-Sociedade para o Desenvolvimento Agro-Florestal, S.A., **60** 156

Alicia S.A. *See* Arcor S.A.I.C.

Alico, Inc., 63 23–25

Alidata SpA. *See* Alitalia—Linee Aeree Italiana, S.P.A.

Aligro Inc., **II** 664

Alimenta (USA), Inc., **17** 207

Alimentos Indal S.A., **66** 9

Alimondo, **17** 505

Alitalia—Linee Aeree Italiana, S.p.A., 6 68–69; 24 311; **29 15–17 (upd.)**

Alkor-Oerlikon Plastic GmbH, **7** 141

All American Airways. *See* USAir Group, Inc.

All American Communications Inc., 20 3–7; 25 138

All American Gourmet Co., **12** 178, 199

All American Sports Co., **22** 458–59

All British Escarpment Company LTD, **25** 430

All-Clad Metalcrafters Inc., **34** 493, 496–97

The All England Lawn Tennis & Croquet Club, 54 11–13

All-Glass Aquarium Co., Inc., **58** 60

All Nippon Airways Co., Ltd., I 106; **6 70–71** 118, 427; **16** 168; **24** 326; **33 50–51; 38 34–37 (upd.)**

All Seasons Vehicles, Inc. *See* ASV, Inc.

All Woods, Inc., **18** 514
Allami Biztosito, **III** 209; **15** 30
Allcom, **16** 392
Alldays plc, 49 16–19
Allders plc, 37 6–8
Alleanza Assicurazioni S.p.A., 65 27–29
Alleghany Corporation, 10 43–45; 19 319; **22** 494; **60 13–16 (upd.)**
Allegheny Airlines. *See* USAir Group, Inc.; US Airways Group, Inc.
Allegheny Beverage Corp., **7** 472–73
Allegheny County Light Company, **6** 483–84
Allegheny Energy, Inc., 38 38–41 (upd.)
Allegheny International, Inc., **8** 545; **9** 484; **22** 3, 436
Allegheny Ludlum Corporation, 8 18–20; 9 484; **21** 489
Allegheny Power System, Inc., V 543–45. *See also* Allegheny Energy, Inc.
Allegheny Steel and Iron Company, **9** 484
Allegiance Life Insurance Company, **22** 268; **50** 122
Allegis, Inc. *See* United Airlines.
Allegmeine Transpotmittel Aktiengesellschaft, **6** 394; **25** 169
Allegretti & Co., **22** 26
Allen & Co., **12** 496; **13** 366; **25** 270
Allen & Ginter, **12** 108
Allen-Bradley Co., **I** 80; **III** 593; **11** 429–30; **17** 478; **22** 373; **23** 211
Allen-Edmonds Shoe Corporation, 61 20–23
Allen Foods, Inc., 60 17–19
Allen Organ Company, 33 26–29
Allen-Stuart Equipment Company, **49** 160
Allen Systems Group, Inc., 59 26–28
Allen Tank Ltd., **21** 499
Allen's Convenience Stores, Inc., **17** 170
Allergan, Inc., 10 46–49; 23 196; **30 29–33 (upd.)**
Allforms Packaging Corp., **13** 442
Allgemeine Elektricitäts-Gesellschaft. *See* AEG A.G.
Allgemeine Handelsgesellschaft der Verbraucher AG. *See* AVA AG.
Allgemeine Schweizerische Uhrenindustrie, **26** 480
Allhabo AB, **53** 85
Allia S.A., **51** 324
Alliance Amusement Company, **10** 319
Alliance Assurance Company, **III** 369–73; **55** 333
Alliance Atlantis Communications Inc., 35 69; **39 11–14**
Alliance Capital Management Holding L.P., 22 189; **63 26–28**
Alliance de Sud, **53** 301
Alliance Entertainment Corp., 17 12–14; 35 430
Alliance Gaming Corp., **15** 539; **24** 36
Alliance Manufacturing Co., **13** 397
Alliance Packaging, **13** 443
Alliance Paper Group, **IV** 316
AllianceWare, Inc., **16** 321
Alliant Energy Corp., **39** 261
Alliant Techsystems Inc., 8 21–23; 30 34–37 (upd.)
Allianz AG, 57 18–24 (upd.), 112–13; **60** 110; **63** 45, 47
Allianz AG Holding, I 426; **III 183–86,** 200, 250, 252, 299–301, 347–48, 373, 377, 393; **14** 169–70; **15 10–14 (upd.); 51** 23

Allied Bakeries Limited. *See* Greggs PLC.
Allied Chemical, **8** 526; **9** 521–22; **22** 5. *See also* General Chemical Corp.
Allied Chemical & Dye Corp., **7** 262; **9** 154; **22** 29
Allied Color Industries, **8** 347
Allied Communications Group, **18** 77; **22** 297
Allied Construction Products, **17** 384
Allied Corporation, **6** 599; **7** 356; **9** 134; **11** 435; **24** 164; **25** 224; **31** 135. *See also* AlliedSignal Inc.
The Allied Defense Group, Inc., 65 30–33
Allied Department Stores, **50** 106
Allied Distributing Co., **12** 106
Allied Domecq PLC, 24 220; **29 18–20,** 85; **52** 416; **54** 229; **59** 256
Allied Dunbar, **I** 427
Allied Engineering Co., **8** 177
Allied Fibers, **19** 275
Allied Food Markets, **II** 662
Allied Gas Company, **6** 529
Allied Grape Growers, **I** 261
Allied Health and Scientific Products Company, **8** 215
Allied Healthcare Products, Inc., 24 16–19
Allied Holdings, Inc., **24** 411
Allied Irish Banks, plc, 16 13–15; 43 7–10 (upd.)
Allied Leisure, **40** 296–98
Allied-Lyons plc, I 215–16, 438; **9** 100; **10** 170; **13** 258; **21** 228, 323; **29** 18, 84; **50** 200. *See also* Carlsberg A/S.
Allied Maintenance Corp., **I** 514
Allied Mills, Inc., **10** 249; **13** 186; **43** 121
Allied Pipe & Tube Corporation, **63** 403
Allied Plywood Corporation, **12** 397
Allied Products Corporation, 21 20–22
Allied Radio, **19** 310
Allied Safety, Inc. *See* W.W. Grainger, Inc.
Allied Shoe Corp., **22** 213
Allied-Signal Corp., I 414–16; 6 599–600; **9** 519; **11** 435, 444; **13** 227; **16** 436; **17** 20; **21** 200, 396–97; **40** 35; **43** 320. *See also* AlliedSignal, Inc.
Allied Signal Engines, 9 12–15
Allied Steel and Conveyors, **18** 493
Allied Stores Corporation, **II** 611–12; **9** 211; **10** 282; **13** 43; **15** 94, 274; **16** 60; **22** 110; **23** 59–60; **25** 249; **31** 192; **37**
Allied Structural Steel Company, **10** 44
Allied Supermarkets, Inc., **7** 570; **28** 511
Allied Suppliers, **II** 609; **50** 401
Allied Telephone Company. *See* Alltel Corporation.
Allied Towers Merchants Ltd., **II** 649
Allied Van Lines Inc., **6** 412, 414; **14** 37. *See also* Allied Worldwide, Inc.
Allied Waste Industries, Inc., 50 13–16
Allied Worldwide, Inc., 49 20–23
AlliedSignal Inc., 22 29–32 (upd.); 29 408; **31** 154; **37** 158; **50** 234
Allis Chalmers Corporation, **I** 163; **III** 543–44; **9** 17; **11** 104; **13** 16–17, 563; **21** 502–03; **22** 380; **50** 196
Allis-Gleaner Corp. *See* AGCO Corp.
Allison Engine Company, **21** 436
Allison Engineering Company. *See* Rolls-Royce Allison.
Allison Gas Turbine Division, 9 16–19, 417; **10** 537; **11** 473

Allmanna Svenska Elektriska Aktiebolaget. *See* ABB Ltd.
Allmänna Telefonaktiebolaget L.M. Ericsson. *See* Telefonaktiebolaget L.M. Ericsson.
Allmerica Financial Corporation, 63 29–31
Allnet, **10** 19
Allo Pro, **III** 633
Allor Leasing Corp., **9** 323
Allou Health & Beauty Care, Inc., 28 12–14
Alloy & Stainless, Inc., **IV** 228
Alloy, Inc., 55 13–15
Allparts, Inc., **51** 307
Allserve Inc., **25** 367
Allsport plc., **31** 216, 218
The Allstate Corporation, III 259, 294; **10 50–52; 13** 539; **21** 96–97; **22** 495; **23** 286–87; **25** 155; **27 30–33 (upd.); 29** 397; **49** 332
ALLTEL Corporation, 6 299–301; 16 318; **20** 440; **46 15–19 (upd.); 54** 63, 108
Alltrans Group, **27** 472
Alltrista Corporation, 30 38–41
Allwaste, Inc., 18 10–13
Allweiler, **58** 67
Alma Media Group, **52** 51
Almac Electronics Corporation, **10** 113; **50** 42
Almac's Inc., **17** 558–59
Almacenes de Baja y Media, **39** 201, 204
Almaden Vineyards, **13** 134; **34** 89
Almanacksförlaget AB, **51** 328
Almanij NV, 44 15–18. *See also* Algemeene Maatschappij voor Nijverheidskrediet.
Almay, Inc. *See* Revlon Inc.
Almeida Banking House. *See* Banco Bradesco S.A.
Almys, **24** 461
ALNM. *See* Ayres, Lewis, Norris & May.
Aloe Vera of America, **17** 187
Aloha Airlines, Incorporated, 9 271–72; **21** 142; **24 20–22**
ALP. *See* Associated London Properties.
Alp Sport Sandals, **22** 173
Alpex, S.A. de C.V., **19** 12
Alpha Beta Co., **II** 605, 625, 653; **17** 559
Alpha Engineering Group, Inc., **16** 259–60
Alpha Healthcare Ltd., **25** 455
Alpha Processor Inc., **41** 349
Alpha Technical Systems, **19** 279
Alphaform, **40** 214–15
Alphanumeric Publication Systems, Inc., **26** 518
Alpharma Inc., 35 22–26 (upd.)
Alphonse Allard Inc., **II** 652; **51** 303
Alpine Electronics, Inc., 13 30–31
Alpine Gaming. *See* Century Casinos, Inc.
Alpine Lace Brands, Inc., 18 14–16
Alpine Securities Corporation, **22** 5
Alpnet Inc. *See* SDL PLC.
Alpre, **19** 192
Alps Electric Co., Ltd., II 5–6; 13 30; **44 19–21 (upd.)**
Alric Packing, **II** 466
Alrosa Company Ltd., 62 7–11
Alsco. *See* Steiner Corporation.
Alsen-Breitenbury, **III** 702
ALSO Holding AG, **29** 419, 422
Alsons Corp., **III** 571; **20** 362
Alsthom, **II** 12

Alsthom-Atlantique, **9** 9
Alta Dena, **25** 83, 85
Alta Electric Company, **25** 15
ALTA Health Strategies, Inc., **11** 113
Alta Vista Company, **50** 228
Altamil Corp., **IV** 137
Altana AG, **23** 498
AltaSteel Ltd., **51** 352
AltaVista Company, 43 11–13
ALTEC International, **21** 107–09
Altenburg & Gooding, **22** 428
Altera Corporation, 18 17–20; 43 14–18 (upd.); 47 384
Alternative Living Services. *See* Alterra Healthcare Corporation.
Alternative Tentacles Records, 66 3–6
Alternative Youth Services, Inc., **29** 399–400
Alterra Healthcare Corporation, 42 3–5
Altex, **19** 192–93
Althouse Chemical Company, **9** 153
Altiris, Inc., 65 34–36
Altman Weil Pensa, **29** 237
Alton & Eastern Railroad Company, **6** 504
Alton Towers, **55** 378
Altos Computer Systems, **10** 362
Altos Hornos de México, S.A. de C.V., 13 144; **19** 220; **39** 188; **42 6–8**
Altra Broadband Inc., **63** 34
Altran Technologies, 51 15–18
Altron Incorporated, 20 8–10
Altura Energy Ltd., **41** 359
Aluar. *See* Aluminios Argentinos.
Aluma Systems Corp., **9** 512; **22** 14
Alumalsa. *See* Aluminoy y Aleaciones S.A.
Alumax Inc., **I** 508; **III** 758; **8** 505–06; **22** 286; **56** 11
Aluminios Argentinos, **26** 433
Aluminoy y Aleaciones S.A., **63** 303
Aluminum Company of America, IV 14–16, 56, 59, 121–22, 131, 173, 703; **19** 240, 292; **20 11–14 (upd.); 22** 455; **42** 438; **52** 71. *See also* Alcoa Inc.
Aluminum Forge Co., **IV** 137
Aluminum Rolling Mills, **17** 280
Aluminum Sales Corporation, **12** 346
Alupak, A.G., **12** 377
Alvic Group, **20** 363
Alvin Ailey Dance Foundation, Inc., 52 14–17
Alvis Plc, 47 7–9
Alyeska Pipeline Service Co., **IV** 571; **14** 542; **24** 521
ALZA Corporation, 10 53–55; 36 36–39 (upd.); 40 11; **41** 200–01
Alzouman Aviation, **56** 148
AM Acquisition Inc., **8** 559–60
AM Cosmetics, Inc., **31** 89
Am-Safe, Inc., **16** 357
AM-TEX Corp., Inc., **12** 443
Amagasaki Spinners Ltd. *See* Unitika Ltd.
Amalgamaize Co., **14** 18
Amalgamated Bank, 60 20–22
Amalgamated Dental International, **10** 271–72
Amalgamated Distilled Products, **II** 609
Amalgamated Press, **7** 244, 342
Amalgamated Sugar Co., **14** 18; **19** 467–68
Amana Refrigeration Company, **18** 226; **38** 374; **42** 159
Amaray International Corporation, **12** 264
Amarillo Gas Company. *See* Atmos Energy Corporation.

Amarillo Railcar Services, **6** 580
Amati Communications Corporation, **57** 409
Amax Gold, **36** 316
AMAX Inc., I 508; **IV 17–19,** 46, 139, 171, 239, 387; **12** 244; **22** 106, 286. *See also* Cyprus Amex.
Amazon.com, Inc., 25 17–19; 56 12–15 (upd.)
AMB Generali Holding AG, 51 19–23
AMB Property Corporation, 57 25–27
Ambac Financial Group, Inc., 65 37–39
AmBase Corp., **III** 264
Amber's Stores, Inc., **17** 360
Amberg Hospach AG, **49** 436
AmBev. *See* Companhia de Bebidas das Américas.
Amblin Entertainment, 21 23–27; 33 431
AMBRA, Inc., **48** 209
AMC Entertainment Inc., 12 12–14; 14 87; **21** 362; **23** 126; **35 27–29 (upd.); 59** 342
AMCA International Corporation, **7** 513; **8** 545; **10** 329; **23** 299
AMCC. *See* Applied Micro Circuits Corporation.
Amcell. *See* American Cellular Network.
AMCO, Inc., **13** 159
AMCOL International Corporation, 59 29–33 (upd.)
Amcor Limited, IV 248–50; 19 13–16 (upd.)
AMCORE Financial Inc., 44 22–26
Amcraft Building Products Co., Inc., **22** 15
AMD. *See* Advanced Micro Devices, Inc.
Amdahl Corporation, III 109–11, 140; **12** 238; **13** 202; **14 13–16 (upd.); 16** 194, 225–26; **22** 293; **25** 87; **40 20–25 (upd.); 42** 147. *See also* Fujitsu Limited.
Amdocs Ltd., 47 10–12
AME Finanziaria, **IV** 587; **19** 19; **54** 20
Amec Spie S.A., I 568; **36** 322; **49** 65; **57 28–31**
Amedysis, Inc., 53 33–36
Amer Group plc, 24 530; **41 14–16**
Amer Sport, **22** 202
Amerace Corporation, **54** 373
Amerada Hess Corporation, IV 365–67, 400, 454, 522, 571, 658; **11** 353; **21 28–31 (upd.); 24** 521; **55 16–20 (upd.)**
AMERCO, 6 351–52; 67 11–14 (upd.)
Ameren Corporation, 60 23–27 (upd.)
AmerGen Energy LLC, **49** 65, 67
Ameri-Kart Corp., **19** 277, 279
America Latina Companhia de Seguros, **III** 289
America Online, Inc., 10 56–58, 237; **13** 147; **15** 54, 265, 321; **18** 24; **19** 41; **22** 52, 519, 522; **26 16–20 (upd.); 27** 20, 106, 301, 430, 517–18; **29** 143, 227; **32** 163; **33** 254; **34** 361; **35** 304, 306; **38** 269–71; **49** 311–12; **54** 74; **63** 393. *See also* CompuServe Interactive Services, Inc.; AOL Time Warner Inc.
America Publishing Company, **18** 213
America Today, **13** 545
America Unplugged, **18** 77
America West Airlines, 6 72–74, 121
America West Express, **32** 334
America West Holdings Corporation, 34 22–26 (upd.)
America's Car-Mart, Inc., 64 19–21

America's Favorite Chicken Company, Inc., 7 26–28. *See also* AFC Enterprises, Inc.
American & Efird, Inc., **12** 501; **23** 260
American Acquisitions, Inc., **49** 279
American Air Conditioning, **25** 15
American Air Filter, **26** 3–4
American Airlines, I 89–91, 97, 106, 115, 118, 124–26, 130, 132, 530; **6 75–77 (upd.); 9** 271–72; **11** 279; **12** 190, 192, 379, 381, 487, 13 173; **14** 73; **16** 146; **18** 73; **21** 141, 143; **24** 21, 399–400; **25** 90–91, 403, 421–22; **26** 427–28, 441; **31** 103, 306; **33** 270, 302; **34** 118; **38** 105; **55** 10–11. *See also* AMR Corporation.
American Allsafe Co., **8** 386
American Association of Retired Persons. *See* AARP.
American Austin Quality Foods Inc., **44** 40
American Automar Inc., **12** 29
American Automated, **11** 111
American Aviation Manufacturing Corp., **15** 246
American Axle & Manufacturing Holdings, Inc., 67 15–17
American Bakeries Company, **12** 275–76
American Bancorp, **11** 295
American Bancshares, Inc., **11** 457
American Bank, **9** 474–75
American Bank of Vicksburg, **14** 41
American Bankcorp, Inc., **8** 188
American Banker/Bond Buyer, **8** 526
American Banknote Corporation, 30 42–45
American Bar Association, 35 30–33
American Barge and Towing Company, **11** 194
American Beauty Cover Company, **12** 472
American Beef Packers, Inc., **16** 473
American Beet Sugar Company, **11** 13–14
American Beryllium Co., Inc., **9** 323
American Biltrite Inc., 16 16–18; 18 116, 118; **43 19–22 (upd.)**
American Biodyne Inc., **9** 348
American Biomedical Corporation, **11** 333
American Bottling, **49** 78
American Box Board Company, **12** 376
American Box Co., **IV** 137
American Brands, Inc., V 395–97; 7 3–4; **9** 408; **12** 87, 344; **14** 95, 271–72; **16** 108, 110, 242; **19** 168–69; **38** 169; **49** 150–51, 153. *See also* Fortune Brands, Inc.
American Broadcasting Co., **25** 418. *See also* ABC, Inc.; Capital Cities/ABC Inc.
American Builders & Contractors Supply Co. *See* ABC Supply Co., Inc.
American Builders, Inc., **8** 436
American Building Maintenance Industries, Inc., 6 17–19. *See also* ABM Industries Incorporated.
American Bus Lines Inc., **24** 118
American Business Information, Inc., 18 21–25
American Business Interiors. *See* American Furniture Company, Inc.
American Business Products, Inc., 20 15–17
American Cabinet Hardware Corp. *See* Amerock Corporation.
American Cable Systems, Inc. *See* Comcast Corporation.
American Cablesystems, **7** 99

American Can Co., **8** 476; **10** 130; **11** 29; **12** 408; **13** 255; **15** 127–28; **17** 106; **23** 98; **49** 293. *See also* Primerica Corp.

The American Cancer Society, 24 23–25

American Capital and Research Corp., **28** 201

American Carbide Corporation, **7** 584

American Cast Iron Pipe Company, 50 17–20

American Cellular Corporation, **63** 131–32

American Cellular Network, **7** 91; **24** 122

American Cement Co. *See* Giant Cement Holding, Inc.

American Chrome, **III** 699

American Civil Liberties Union (ACLU), 60 28–31

American Classic Voyages Company, 22 340, 27 34–37

American Clay Forming Company, **8** 178

American Clip Company, **7** 3

American Coin Merchandising, Inc., 28 15–17

American Colloid Co., 13 32–35. *See* AMCOL International Corporation.

American Colonial Insurance Company, **44** 356

American Commercial Lines Inc., **22** 164, 166–67

American Commonwealths Power Corporation, **6** 579

American Community Grocers, **II** 670

American Computer Systems. *See* American Software Inc.

American Construction Lending Services, Inc., **39** 380, 382

American Cotton Cooperative Association, **17** 207; **33** 85

American Cotton Growers Association, **57** 283

American Council on Education, **12** 141

American Courier Express, Inc., **24** 126

American Crayon Company, **12** 115

American Crystal Sugar Company, 7 377; **11** 13–15; **32** 29–33 (upd.)

American Cyanamid, I 300–02; 8 24–26 (upd.); **10** 269; **11** 494; **13** 231–32; **14** 254, 256; **16** 68; **22** 147; **27** 115–16; **50** 248, 250

American Dairy Queen Corporation, **10** 373

American Data Technology, Inc., **11** 111

American Digital Communications, Inc., **33** 329

American Diversified Foods, Inc., **14** 351

American Drew, Inc., **12** 301

American Drug Company, **13** 367

American Eagle Airlines, Inc., **28** 22

American Eagle Outfitters, Inc., 14 427; **24** 26–28; **25** 121; **55** 21–24 (upd.)

American Education Press, **10** 479

American Electric Company, **12** 193; **22** 10; **54** 371–73

American Electric Power Company, V 546–49; **6** 449, 524; **11** 516; **45** 17–21 (upd.)

American Emulsions Co., **8** 455

American Encaustic Tiling Co., **22** 170

American Energy Management Inc., **39** 261

American Envelope Co., **28** 251

American Equipment Co., **I** 571

American Express Company, I 480, 614; **II** 108, 176, 309, 380–82, 395–99, 450–52, 544; **III** 319, 340, 389; **6** 409;

8 118; **9** 335, 343, 468–69, 538; **10** 44–45, **59–64 (upd.);** **11** 41, 416–17, 532; **12** 533; **14** 106; **15** 50; **18** 60, 112, 516, 543; **21** 97; **23** 229; **26** 516; **33** 394–96; **38 42–48 (upd.);** **52** 13

American Factors, Ltd. *See* Amfac/JMB Hawaii L.L.C.

American Family Corporation, III 187–89. *See also* AFLAC Inc.

American Family Life Insurance Company, **33** 407

American Family Publishers, **23** 393–94

American Feldmühle Corp., **II** 51; **21** 330

American Financial Corporation, III 190–92, 221; **8** 537; **9** 452; **18** 549

American Financial Group Inc., 48 6–10 (upd.)

American Fine Wire, Inc., **33** 248

American First National Supermarkets, **16** 313

American Fitness Centers, **25** 40

American Fitness Products, Inc., **47** 128

American Flange, **30** 397

American Flavor & Fragrance Company, **9** 154

American Flyer Trains, **16** 336–37

American Foods Group, 43 23–27

American Football League, **29** 346

American Foreign Insurance Association. *See* AFIA.

American Freightways Corporation, **42** 141

American Fructose Corp., **14** 18–19

American Fur Company, **25** 220

American Furniture Company, Inc., 12 300; **21 32–34**

American Gaming and Electronics, Inc., **43** 461

American Gas & Electric. *See* American Electric Power Company.

American General Capital Corp., **I** 614

American General Corporation, III 193–94; 10 65–67 (upd.); **11** 16; **46 20–23 (upd.);** **47** 15

American General Finance Corp., 11 16–17

American Golf Corporation, 45 22–24

American Gramaphone LLC, 52 18–20

American Graphics, **23** 100

American Greetings Corporation, 7 23–25; **12** 207–08; **15** 507; **16** 256; **21** 426–28; **22 33–36 (upd.);** **59 34–39 (upd.);** **61** 336

American Grinder and Manufacturing Company, **9** 26

American Hardware & Supply Company. *See* TruServ Corporation.

American Hawaii Cruises, **27** 34

American Health & Life Insurance Company, **27** 47

American Healthcorp Inc., **48** 25

American Healthways, Inc., 65 40–42

American Heritage Savings, **II** 420

American Hoechst Corporation. *See* Hoechst Celanese Corporation.

American Hoist & Derrick Co., **8** 544

American Home Mortgage Holdings, Inc., 46 24–26

American Home Patients Centers Inc., **46** 4

American Home Products, I 622–24, 631, 676–77, 696, 700; **8** 282–83; **10 68–70 (upd.),** 528; **11** 35; **15** 64–65; **16** 191, 438; **21** 466; **24** 288; **25** 477; **36** 87; **38** 365; **49** 349–50. *See also* Wyeth.

American Home Publishing Co., Inc., **14** 460

American Home Shield. *See* ServiceMaster Inc.

American Home Video, **9** 186

American Homestar Corporation, 18 26–29; 41 17–20 (upd.)

American Homeware Inc., **15** 501

American Hospital Association, **10** 159

American Hospital Supply Co., **III** 80; **11** 459, 486; **19** 103; **21** 118; **30** 496; **53** 345

American Hydron, **13** 366; **25** 55

American I.G. Chemical Corporation. *See* GAF Corporation.

American Impacts Corporation, **8** 464

American Improved Cements. *See* Giant Cement Holding, Inc.

American Independent Oil Co. *See* Aminoil, Inc.

American Information Services, Inc., **11** 111

American Institute of Certified Public Accountants (AICPA), 44 27–30

American Institutional Products, Inc., **18** 246

American Instrument Co., **13** 233

American International Airways, Inc., **17** 318; **22** 311

American International Group, Inc., III 195–98, 200; **10** 39; **11** 532–33; **15 15–19 (upd.);** **18** 159; **45** 109; **46** 20; **47 13–19 (upd.);** **48** 219; **63** 175

American Isuzu Motors, Inc. *See* Isuzu Motors, Ltd.

American Italian Pasta Company, 27 38–40

American Janitor Service, **25** 15

American Jet Industries, **7** 205

American Ka-Ro, **8** 476

American Knitting Mills of Miami, Inc., **22** 213

American La-France, **10** 296

American Land Cruiser Company. *See* Cruise America Inc.

American Lawyer Media Holdings, Inc., 32 34–37

American Learning Corporation, **7** 168

American Light and Traction. *See* MCN Corporation.

American Lightwave Systems, Inc., **10** 19

American Limousine Corp., **26** 62

American Linen Supply Company. *See* Steiner Corporation.

American Locker Group Incorporated, 34 19–21

American Lung Association, 48 11–14

American Machine and Foundry Co., **7** 211–13; **11** 397; **25** 197

American Machine and Metals, **9** 23

American Machine and Tool Co., Inc., **57** 160

American Machinery and Foundry, Inc., **57** 85

American Maize-Products Co., 14 17–20; 23 464

American Management Systems, Inc., 11 18–20

American Materials & Technologies Corporation, **27** 117

American Media, Inc., 27 41–44

American Medical Association, 39 15–18

American Medical Holdings, **55** 370

American Medical International, Inc., III 73–75, 79; 14 232

American Medical Optics, 25 55

American Medical Response, Inc., 39 19–22

American Medical Services, II 679–80; 14 209

American Medicorp, Inc., 14 432; 24 230

American Melamine, 27 317

American Merchandising Associates Inc., 14 411

American Metal Climax, Inc. See AMAX.

American Metals and Alloys, Inc., 19 432

American Metals Corp., III 569; 20 361

American Micro Devices, Inc., 16 549

The American Mineral Spirits Company, 8 99–100

American Modern Insurance Group. See The Midland Company.

American Motors Corp., I 135–37; 8 373; 10 262, 264; 18 493; 26 403

American Multi-Cinema. See AMC Entertainment Inc.

American National Bank, 13 221–22

American National Can Co., IV 175

American National General Agencies Inc., III 221; 14 109; 37 85

American National Insurance Company, 8 27–29; 27 45–48 (upd.); 39 158

American Natural Resources Co., 13 416

American Natural Snacks Inc., 29 480

American Oil Co., 7 101; 14 22

American Olean Tile Company, III 424; 22 48, 170

American Optical Co., 7 436; 38 363–64

American Overseas Airlines, 12 380

American Pad & Paper Company, 20 18–21

American Paging, 9 494–96

American Paper Box Company, 12 376

American Patriot Insurance, 22 15

American Payment Systems, Inc., 21 514

American Petrofina, Inc., 7 179–80; 19 11

American Pfauter, 24 186

American Phone Centers, Inc., 21 135

American Pop Corn Company, 59 40–43

American Port Services (Amports), 45 29

American Power & Light Co., 6 545, 596–97; 12 542; 49 143

American Power Conversion Corporation, 24 29–31; 67 18–20 (upd.)

American Premier Underwriters, Inc., 10 71–74; 48 9

American Prepaid Professional Services, Inc. See CompDent Corporation.

American President Companies Ltd., 6 353–55; 54 274. See also APL Limited.

American Printing House for the Blind, 26 13–15

American Prospecting Equipment Co., 49 174

American Public Automotive Group, 37 115

American Publishing Co., 24 222; 62 188

American Re Corporation, 10 75–77; 35 34–37 (upd.); 46 303; 63 13–14, 411–12

American Recreation Company Holdings, Inc., 16 53; 44 53–54

American Red Cross, 40 26–29

American Refrigeration Products S.A, 7 429

American Research and Development Corp., 19 103

American Residential Mortgage Corporation, 8 30–31

American Residential Services, 33 141

American Retirement Corporation, 42 9–12; 43 46

American Rice, Inc., 17 161–62; 33 30–33

American Rug Craftsmen, 19 275

American Safety Razor Company, 20 22–24

American Salt Co., 12 199

American Satellite Co., 15 195

American Savings & Loan, 10 117

American Savings Bank, 9 276; 17 528, 531

American Sealants Company. See Loctite Corporation.

American Seating Co., I 447; 21 33

American Seaway Foods, Inc, 9 451

American Securities Capital Partners, 59 13

American Service Corporation, 19 223

American Shipbuilding, 18 318

American Ships Ltd., 50 209

American Skiing Company, 28 18–21; 31 67, 229

American Sky Broadcasting, 27 305; 35 156

American Smelting and Refining Co. See ASARCO.

The American Society of Composers, Authors and Publishers (ASCAP), 29 21–24

American Software Inc., 22 214; 25 20–22

American Southern Insurance Co., 17 196

American Standard Companies Inc., III 663–65; 19 455; 22 4, 6; 28 486; 30 46–50 (upd.); 40 452

American States Water Company, 46 27–30

American Steamship Company, 6 394–95; 25 168, 170

American Steel & Wire Co., 13 97–98; 40 70, 72

American Steel Foundries, 7 29–30

American Stock Exchange, 10 416–17; 54 242

American Stores Company, II 604–06; 12 63, 333; 13 395; 17 559; 18 89; 22 37–40 (upd.); 25 297; 27 290–92; 30 24, 26–27. See also Albertson's, Inc.

American Sugar Refining Company. See Domino Sugar Corporation.

American Sumatra Tobacco Corp., 15 138

American Superconductor Corporation, 41 141

American Surety Co., 26 486

American Systems Technologies, Inc., 18 5

American Teaching Aids Inc., 19 405

American Technical Ceramics Corp., 67 21–23

American Technical Services Company. See American Building Maintenance Industries, Inc.; ABM Industries Incorporated.

American Telephone and Telegraph Company. See AT&T.

American Television and Communications Corp., IV 675; 7 528–30; 18 65

American Textile Co., III 571; 20 362

American Thermos Bottle Company. See Thermos Company.

American Threshold, 50 123

American Tile Supply Company, 19 233

American Tissue Company, 29 136

American Tobacco Co., 14 77, 79; 15 137–38; 16 242; 18 416; 27 128–29; 33 82; 43 126; 50 116–17, 119, 259–60. See also American Brands Inc., B.A.T. Industries PLC.; Fortune Brands, Inc.

American Tool Companies, Inc., 52 270

American Tool Company, 13 563

American Totalisator Corporation, 10 319–20

American Tourister, Inc., 10 350; 13 451, 453; 16 19–21. See also Samsonite Corporation.

American Tower Corporation, 33 34–38

American Tractor Corporation, 10 379

American Trading and Production Corporation, 7 101

American Trans Air, 34 31

American Transitional Hospitals, Ltd., 65 307

American Transport Lines, 6 384

Amcrican Twist Drill Co., 23 82

American Vanguard Corporation, 47 20–22

American VIP Limousine, Inc., 26 62

American Water Works Company, Inc., 6 443–45; 26 451; 38 49–52 (upd.)

American Wood Reduction Company, 14 174

American Woodmark Corporation, 31 13–16

American Yard Products, 22 26, 28

American Yearbook Company, 7 255; 25 252

American-Strevell Inc., II 625

Americana Entertainment Group, Inc., 19 435

Americana Foods, Inc., 17 474–75

Americana Healthcare Corp., 15 522

Americana Ships Ltd., 50 210

Americom, 61 272

Ameridrive, 58 67

AmeriFirst Bank, 11 258

Amerifirst Federal Savings, 10 340

AmeriGas Partners, L.P., 12 498, 500; 56 36

Amerihost Properties, Inc., 30 51–53

AmeriKing Corp., 36 309

Amerimark Inc., II 682

Amerin Corporation. See Radian Group Inc.

AmeriServe Food Distribution. See Holberg Industries, Inc.

Amerisex, 64 198

AmeriSource Health Corporation, 37 9–11 (upd.)

AmerisourceBergen Corporation, 64 22–28 (upd.)

Ameristar Casinos, Inc., 33 39–42

AmeriSteel Corp., 59 202

AmeriSuites, 52 281

Amerisystems, 8 328

Ameritech Corporation, V 265–68; 6 248; 7 118; 10 431; 11 382; 12 137; 14 252–53, 257, 259–61, 364; 15 197; 18 30–34 (upd.); 25 499; 41 288–90; 43 447; 44 49

Ameritech Illinois. See Illinois Bell Telephone Company.

Ameritrade Holding Corporation, 34 27–30

Ameritrust Corporation, 9 476

Ameriwood Industries International Corp., **17** 15–17; **59** 164
Amerock Corporation, **13** 41; **53** 37–40
Ameron International Corporation, **67** 24–26
Amerop Sugar Corporation, **60** 96
Amersham PLC, **50** 21–25; **63** 166
Ames Department Stores, Inc., **9** 20–22; **10** 497; **15** 88; **30** 54–57 (upd.)
Ametek Inc., **9** 23–25; **12** 88; **38** 169
N.V. Amev, **III** 199–202
AMEX. *See* American Stock Exchange.
Amey Plc, **47** 23–25; **49** 320
AMF. *See* American Machinery and Foundry, Inc.
AMF Bowling, Inc., **19** 312; **23** 450; **40** 30–33
Amfac Inc., **I** 417–18, 566; **10** 42; **23** 320
Amfac/JMB Hawaii L.L.C., **24** 32–35 (upd.)
AMFM Inc., **35** 221, 245, 248; **37** 104; **41** 384
Amgen, Inc., **8** 216–17; **10** 78–81; **13** 240; **14** 255; **21** 320; **30** 58–61 (upd.); **38** 204; **50** 248, 250, 538; **54** 111
Amherst Coal Co., **7** 309
AMI. *See* Advanced Metallurgy, Inc.
Amiga Corporation, **7** 96
Aminoil, Inc. *See* American Independent Oil Co.
Amisys Managed Care Information Systems, **16** 94
Amitron S.A., **10** 113; **50** 43
Amity Leather Products Company. *See* AR Accessories Group, Inc.
AMK Corporation, **7** 85; **21** 111
Amkor, **23** 17
AMLI Realty Company, **33** 418, 420
Amling Co., **25** 89
Ammirati Puris Lintas, **14** 316; **22** 294
Amnesty International, **50** 26–29
Amoco Corporation, **IV** 368–71, 412, 424–25, 453, 525; **7** 107, 443; **10** 83–84; **11** 441; **12** 18; **14** 21–25 (upd.), 494; **18** 365; **19** 297; **26** 369. *See also* BP p.l.c.
AMOR 14 Corporation, **64** 95
Amorim Investimentos e Participaço, **48** 117, 119
Amorim Revestimentos, **48** 118
Amoskeag Company, [**8** 32–33; **9** 213–14, 217; **31** 199
Amot Controls Corporation, **15** 404; **50** 394
AMP, Inc., **II** 7–8; **11** 319; **13** 344; **14** 26–28 (upd.); **17** 274; **22** 542; **28** 486; **36** 158; **54** 239; **63** 404
Ampacet Corporation, **67** 27–29
Ampad Holding Corporation. *See* American Pad & Paper Company.
AMPAL. *See* American-Palestine Trading Corp.
AMPCO Auto Parks, Inc. *See* American Building Maintenance Industries, Inc.; ABM Industries Incorporated.
Ampeg Company, **48** 353
AMPEP, **III** 625
Ampex Corporation, **17** 18–20
Amphenol Corporation, **40** 34–37
Ampol Petroleum Ltd., **III** 729; **27** 473
Ampro, **25** 504–05
AMR. *See* American Medical Response, Inc.
AMR Combs Inc., **36** 190

AMR Corporation, **8** 315; **22** 252; **26** 427–28; **28** 22–26 (upd.); **29** 409; **33** 19; **34** 119; **52** 21–26 (upd.); **54** 4
AMR Information Services, **9** 95
Amram's Distributing Limited, **12** 425
AMRE, **III** 211
AMREP Corporation, **21** 35–37; **24** 78
Amro. *See* Amsterdam-Rotterdam Bank N.V.
Amrop International Australasia, **34** 249
AMS. *See* Advanced Marketing Services, Inc.
Amsbra Limited, **62** 48
Amscan Holdings, Inc., **61** 24–26
Amsco International, **29** 450
Amserve Ltd., **48** 23
AmSouth Bancorporation, **12** 15–17; **48** 15–18 (upd.)
Amstar Corp., **14** 18
Amstar Sugar Corporation, **7** 466–67; **26** 122
Amsted Industries Incorporated, **7** 29–31; **66** 27
Amsterdam-Rotterdam Bank N.V., **II** 185–86; **14** 169; **17** 324
Amstrad plc, **III** 112–14; **48** 19–23 (upd.)
AmSurg Corporation, **48** 24–27
AMT. *See* American Machine and Tool Co., Inc.; American Materials & Technologies Corporation.
Amtech. *See* American Building Maintenance Industries, Inc.; ABM Industries Incorporated.
Amtech Systems Corporation, **11** 65; **27** 405
Amtel, Inc., **8** 545; **10** 136
Amtorg, **13** 365
Amtrak. *See* The National Railroad Passenger Corporation.
Amtran, Inc., **34** 31–33
AmTrans. *See* American Transport Lines.
Amurol Confections Company, **58** 378
Amvac Chemical Corporation, **47** 20
Amvent Inc., **25** 120
AMVESCAP PLC, **65** 43–45
Amway Corporation, **III** 11–14; **13** 36–39 (upd.); **17** 186; **18** 67, 164; **20** 435; **23** 509; **29** 493; **30** 62–66 (upd.); **31** 327
Amylin Pharmaceuticals, Inc., **67** 30–32
ANA. *See* All Nippon Airways Co., Ltd.
Anacomp, Inc., **11** 19
Anaconda Aluminum, **11** 38
Anaconda Co., **7** 261–63
Anaconda-Jurden Associates, **8** 415
Anadarko Petroleum Corporation, **10** 82–84; **52** 27–30 (upd.); **65** 316–17
Anadex, Inc., **18** 435–36
Anaheim Angels Baseball Club, Inc., **53** 41–44
Anaheim Imaging, **19** 336
Analog Devices, Inc., **10** 85–87; **18** 20; **19** 67; **38** 54; **43** 17, 311; **47** 384
Analogic Corporation, **23** 13–16
Analysts International Corporation, **36** 40–42
Analytic Sciences Corporation, **10** 88–90; **13** 417
Analytical Nursing Management Corporation (ANMC). *See* Amedisys, Inc.
Analytical Science Laboratories Inc., **58** 134

Analytical Surveys, Inc., **33** 43–45
Anam Group, **21** 239; **23** 17–19
Anarad, Inc., **18** 515
Anaren Microwave, Inc., **33** 46–48
Anchor Bancorp, Inc., **10** 91–93
Anchor Brake Shoe, **18** 5
Anchor Brewing Company, **47** 26–28
Anchor Corporation, **12** 525
Anchor Gaming, **24** 36–39; **41** 216
Anchor Hocking Glassware, **13** 40–42; **14** 483; **26** 353; **49** 253; **53** 39
Anchor Motor Freight, Inc., **12** 309–10
Anchor National Financial Services, Inc., **11** 482
Anchor National Life Insurance Company, **11** 482
Anders Wilhelmsen & Co., **22** 471
Andersen Consulting, **38** 430
Andersen Corporation, **9** 344; **10** 94–95; **11** 305; **22** 346; **39** 324
Andersen Worldwide, **29** 25–28 (upd.); **57** 165
Anderson Animal Hospital, Inc., **58** 354
Anderson Box Co., **8** 267
The Anderson-DuBose Company, **60** 32–34
Anderson Exploration Ltd., **61** 75
Anderson, Greenwood & Co., **11** 225–26
Anderson Packaging, Inc., **64** 27
Anderson Testing Company, Inc., **6** 441
The Andersons, Inc., **31** 17–21
Andlinger & Co., **60** 132
Andreas Christ, **26** 243
Andreas Stihl AG & Co. KG, **16** 22–24; **59** 44–47 (upd.)
Andrew Corporation, **10** 96–98; **32** 38–41 (upd.)
Andrew Jergens Co., **25** 56
Andrews Group, Inc., **10** 402
Andrews McMeel Universal, **40** 38–41
Andrews Office Supply and Equipment Co., **25** 500
Andritz AG, **27** 269; **51** 24–26
Andrx Corporation, **55** 25–27
Anfor, **IV** 249–50
Angele Ghigi, **II** 475
Angelica Corporation, **15** 20–22; **43** 28–31 (upd.); **61** 206
Angelo's Supermarkets, Inc., **II** 674
ANGI Ltd., **11** 28
Angle Steel, **25** 261
Anglian Water Plc, **38** 51
Anglo-Abrasives Ltd. *See* Carbo PLC.
Anglo-American Clays Corp., **IV** 346
Anglo American Corporation of South Africa Limited, **IV** 20–23, 56–57, 64–68, 79–80, 90, 92, 94–96, 118–20, 191, 239–40; **7** 121–23, 125; **16** 25–30 (upd.), 292; **21** 211, 354; **22** 233; **28** 88, 93; **49** 232–34
Anglo American Industrial Corporation, **59** 224–25
Anglo American PLC, **50** 30–36 (upd.)
Anglo-American Telegraph Company Ltd., **25** 98
Anglo-Canadian Telephone Company of Montreal. *See* British Columbia Telephone Company.
Anglo-Celtic Watch Company, **25** 430
Anglo Company, Ltd., **9** 363
Anglo-Dutch Unilever group, **9** 317
Anglo Energy, Ltd., **9** 364
Anglo-Iranian Oil Co., **7** 141
Anglo-Lautaro Nitrate Corporation, **9** 363

Anglo-Persian Oil Co., **7** 140
Anglovaal Industries Ltd., **20** 263
Anheuser-Busch Companies, Inc., I
  217–19, 236–37, 254–55, 258, 265,
  269–70, 290–91, 598; **IV** 624; **9** 100;
  10 99–101 (upd.), 130; **11** 421; **12**
  337–38; **13** 5, 10, 258, 366; **15** 429; **17**
  256; **18** 65, 70, 72–73, 499, 501; **19**
  221, 223; **21** 229, 319–20; **22** 421; **23**
  403; **25** 281–82, 368; **26** 432; **29** 84–85;
  29 218; **31** 381, 383; **34 34–37 (upd.)**;
  36 12–15, 163; **59** 97, 352; **63** 229
ANI America Inc., **62** 331
Anker BV, 53 45–47
ANMC. *See* Amedisys, Inc.
Ann Street Group Ltd., **61** 44–46
Anne Klein & Co., **15** 145–46; **24** 299; **40**
  277–78; **56** 90
Anneplas, **25** 464
Annie's Homegrown, Inc., 59 48–50
AnnTaylor Stores Corporation, 13
  43–45; **15** 9; **25** 120–22; **37 12–15**
  (upd.); **67 33–37 (upd.)**
Annuaries Marcotte Ltd., **10** 461
Anocout Engineering Co., **23** 82
ANR Pipeline Co., 17 21–23; 31 119
Ansa Software, **9** 81
Ansbacher-Siegle Corp., **13** 460
The Anschutz Corporation, 12 18–20; 36
  43–47 (upd.); **37** 312
Ansco & Associates, LLC, **57** 119
Ansell Ltd., 60 35–38 (upd.)
Ansell Ltd., 60 35–38 (upd.)
Ansell Rubber Company, **10** 445
Anselmo L. Morvillo S.A., **19** 336
Ansett Airlines, **6** 73; **14** 11; **27** 475
Ansett Australia, **24** 398, 400; **26** 113
Ansett Transport Industries Limited, **V**
  523–25; **27** 473
Ansoft Corporation, 63 32–34
ANSYS Technologies Inc., **48** 410
Antalis, **34** 38, 40
Antares Alliance Group, **14** 15
Antares Capital Corp., **53** 213
Antares Electronics, Inc., **10** 257
Ante Corp., **22** 222
Antenna Company, **32** 40
Anteon Corporation, 57 32–34
ANTEX. *See* American National Life
  Insurance Company of Texas.
Anthem Electronics, Inc., 13 46–47; 17
  276
Anthem P&C Holdings, **15** 257
Anthes Industries Inc., **9** 512
Anthony & Sylvan Pools Corporation,
  56 16–18
Anthony Industries Inc. *See* K2 Inc.
Anthony Stumpf Publishing Company, **10**
  460
Anthropologie, **14** 524–25
Antinori. *See* Marchesi Antinori SRL.
The Antioch Company, 40 42–45
Antique Street Lamps, **19** 212
ANTK Tupolev. *See* Aviacionny Nauchno-
  Tehnicheskii Komplex im. A.N.
  Tupoleva.
Antofagasta plc, 65 46–49
Antonio Puig, S.A. *See* Puig Beauty and
  Fashion Group S.L.
Antonov Design Bureau, 53 48–51
ANZ. *See* Australia and New Zealand
  Banking Group Limited.
ANZ Securities, **24** 400
AO Sidanco, **45** 50

AO VimpelCom, **59** 300
AOE Plastic GmbH, **7** 141
Aohata Corporation, **57** 202, 204
Aoki Corporation, **9** 547, 549; **29** 508
AOL Time Warner Inc., 45 201; **47** 271;
  57 35–44 (upd.)
Aon Corporation, III 203–05; 22 495; **45**
  25–28 (upd.); **50** 267, 433
AP. *See* The Associated Press.
AP&L. *See* American Power & Light Co.
AP Bank, Ltd., **13** 439
AP-Dow Jones/Telerate Company, **10** 277
AP Support Services, **25** 13
Apache Corporation, 10 102–04; 11 28;
  18 366; **32 42–46 (upd.)**
Apache Energy Ltd., **25** 471
APACHE Medical Systems, Inc., **16** 94
Apanage GmbH & Co. KG, **53** 195
Apartment Furniture Rental, **26** 102
Apartment Investment and Management
  Company, 49 24–26
Apasco S.A. de C.V., 51 27–29
APB. *See* Atlantic Premium Brands, Ltd.
APCOA/Standard Parking. *See* Holberg
  Industries, Inc.
Apex, **17** 363
Apex Digital, Inc., 63 35–37
Apex Financial Corp., **8** 10
Apex Oil, **37** 310–11
Apex One Inc., **31** 137
APH. *See* American Printing House for the
  Blind.
APi Group, Inc., 56 238; **64 29–32**
APL Corporation, **9** 346
APL Limited, 41 399; **61 27–30 (upd.)**
Aplex Industries, Inc., **26** 363
Apline Guild, **12** 173
Aplix, **19** 477
APM Ltd. *See* Amcor Limited
APN. *See* Affiliated Physicians Network,
  Inc.
Apogee Enterprises, Inc., 8 34–36; 22
  347
Apogee Sound International LLC, **62** 39
Apollo Advisors L.P., **16** 37; **26** 500, 502;
  43 438
Apollo Apparel Partners, L.P., **12** 431
Apollo Computer, **9** 471; **11** 284
Apollo Group, Inc., 24 40–42
Apollo Heating & Air Conditioning Inc.,
  15 411
Apollo Investment Fund Ltd., **31** 211; **39**
  174
Apollo Ski Partners LP of New York, **11**
  543, 545
Apothekernes Laboratorium A.S., **12** 3–5
Appalachian Computer Services, **11** 112
Appalachian Travel Services, Inc., **25** 185,
  187
Appetifrais S.A., **51** 54
Applause Inc., 17 461; **24 43–46**
Apple Bank for Savings, 59 51–53
Apple Computer, Inc., II 6, 62, 103, 107,
  124; **III 115–16**, 121, 149, 172; **6**
  218–20 (upd.), 222, 225, 231, 244, 248,
  254–58, 260, 289; **8** 138; **9** 166,
  170–71, 368, 464; **10** 22–23, 34, 57,
  233, 235, 404, 458–59, 518–19; **11** 45,
  50, 57, 62, 490; **12** 139, 183, 335, 449,
  455, 470; **13** 90, 388, 482; **16** 195,
  367–68, 372, 417–18; **18** 93, 511, 521;
  20 31; **21** 391; **23** 209; **24** 370; **25**
  299–300, 348, 530–31; **28** 244–45; **33**

12–14; **34** 512; **36 48–51 (upd.)**, 168;
  38 69
Apple Orthodontix, Inc., **35** 325
Apple South, Inc., **21** 362; **35** 39. *See also*
  Avado Brands, Inc.
Applebee's International Inc., 14 29–31;
  19 258; **20** 159; **21** 362; **31** 40; **35**
  38–41 (upd.)
Appleton Papers, **I** 426
Appleton Wire Works Corp., **8** 13
Appliance Recycling Centers of America,
  Inc., 42 13–16
Applica Incorporated, 43 32–36 (upd.)
Applied Beverage Systems Ltd., **21** 339
Applied Biomedical Corp., **47** 4
Applied Bioscience International, Inc., 10
  105–07
Applied Color Systems, **III** 424
Applied Communications, Inc., **6** 280; **11**
  151; **25** 496; **29 477–79**
Applied Data Research, Inc., **18** 31–32
Applied Digital Data Systems Inc., **9** 514
Applied Engineering Services, Inc. *See* The
  AES Corporation.
Applied Films Corporation, 12 121; **35**
  148; **48 28–31**
Applied Industrial Materials Corporation,
  22 544, 547
Applied Komatsu Technology, Inc., **10** 109
Applied Laser Systems, **31** 124
Applied Learning International, **IV** 680
Applied Materials, Inc., 10 108–09; 18
  382–84; **46 31–34 (upd.)**
Applied Micro Circuits Corporation, 38
  53–55
Applied Network Technology, Inc., **25** 162
Applied Power Inc., 9 26–28; 32 47–51
  (upd.)
Applied Programming Technologies, Inc.,
  12 61
Applied Solar Energy, **8** 26
Applied Technology Corp., **11** 87
Applied Thermal Technologies, Inc., **29** 5
Approvisionnement Atlantique, **II** 652; **51**
  303
Apria Healthcare Inc., **43** 266
Aprilia SpA, 17 24–26
APS. *See* Arizona Public Service
  Company.
APS Healthcare, **17** 166, 168
APSA, **63** 214
Apura GmbH, **IV** 325
APUTCO, **6** 383
Aqua Alliance Inc., 32 52–54 (upd.)
Aqua Cool Pure Bottled Water, **52** 188
Aqua de Oro Venture, **58** 23
Aquafin N.V., **12** 443; **38** 427
Aquarium Supply Co., **12** 230
Aquarius Group. *See* Club Mediterranee
  SA.
Aquarius Platinum Ltd., 63 38–40
Aquatech, **53** 232
Aquila Energy Corp., **6** 593
Aquila, Inc., 50 37–40 (upd.)
Aquitaine. *See* Société Nationale des
  Petroles d'Aquitaine.
AR Accessories Group, Inc., 23 20–22
AR-TIK Systems, Inc., **10** 372
ARA Services, II 607–08; 21 507; **25** 181.
  See also Aramark.
Arab Japanese Insurance Co., **III** 296
Arab-Israel Bank Ltd., **60** 50
Arabian American Oil Co. *See* Saudi
  Arabian Oil Co.

Arabian Gulf Oil Company. *See* Natinal Oil Corporation.
Arabian Investment Banking Corp., **15** 94; **26** 53; **47** 361
Aracruz Celulose S.A., 57 45–47
Aral AG, 62 12–15
ARAMARK Corporation, 13 48–50; **16** 228; **21** 114–15; **35** 415; **41** 21–24
Aramco. *See* Arabian American Oil Co.; Saudi Arabian Oil Company.
Aramis Inc., **30** 191
Arandell Corporation, 37 16–18
Arapuã. *See* Lojas Arapuã S.A.
Aratex Inc., **13** 49
ARBED S.A., IV 24–27, 53; **22** 41–45 (upd.); **26** 83; **42** 414
Arbeitsgemeinschaft der öffentlich-rechtlichen Rundfunkanstalten der Bundesrepublick. *See* ARD.
The Arbitron Company, 10 255, 359; **13** 5; **38** 56–61
Arbor Acres, **13** 103
Arbor Drugs Inc., 12 21–23. *See also* CVS Corporation.
Arbor International, **18** 542
Arbor Living Centers Inc., **6** 478
Arby's Inc., II 614; **8** 536–37; **14** 32–34, 351; **58** 323
ARC. *See* American Rug Craftsmen.
ARC International Corporation, **27** 57
ARC Materials Corp., **III** 688
ARC Propulsion, **13** 462
ARCA. *See* Appliance Recycling Centers of America, Inc.
Arcadia Company, **14** 138
Arcadia Group plc, 28 27–30 (upd.), 95–96
Arcadia Partners, **17** 321
Arcadian Corporation, **18** 433; **27** 317–18
Arcadian Marine Service, Inc., **6** 530
Arcadis NV, 26 21–24
Arcata Corporation, **12** 413
Arcata National Corp., **9** 305
Arcelor S.A., **65** 311
ARCH Air Medical Service, Inc., **53** 29
Arch Mineral Corporation, 7 32–34
Arch Petroleum Inc., **39** 331
Arch Wireless, Inc., 39 23–26; **41** 265, 267
Archbold Container Co., **35** 390
Archbold Ladder Co., **12** 433
Archer-Daniels-Midland Co., I 419–21; **7** 432–33, 241 **8** 53; **11** 21–23 (upd.); **17** 207; **22** 85, 426; **23** 384; **25** 241; **31** 234; **32** 55–59 (upd.)
Archer Management Services Inc., **24** 360
Archibald Candy Corporation, **36** 309
Archie Comics Publications, Inc., 63 41–44
Archipelago RediBook, **48** 226, 228
Archstone-Smith Trust, 49 27–30
Archway Cookies, Inc., 29 29–31
ArcLight, LLC, **50** 123
ARCO. *See* Atlantic Richfield Company.
ARCO Chemical Company, 10 110–11
ARCO Comfort Products Co., **26** 4
Arco Electronics, **9** 323
Arco Pharmaceuticals, Inc., **31** 346
Arcon Corporation, **26** 287
Arcor S.A.I.C., 66 7–9
Arctco, Inc., 12 400–01; **16** 31–34; **35** 349, 351
Arctic Alaska Fisheries Corporation, **14** 515; **50** 493–94

Arctic Cat Inc., 40 46–50 (upd.)
Arctic Enterprises, **34** 44
Arctic Slope Regional Corporation, 38 62–65
ARD, 41 25–29
Ardal og Sunndal Verk AS, **10** 439
Arden Group, Inc., 29 32–35
Ardent Risk Services, Inc. *See* General Re Corporation.
Ardent Software Inc., **59** 54–55
Argenbright Security Inc. *See* Securicor Plc.
Argentaria Caja Postal y Banco Hipotecario S.A. *See* Banco Bilbao Vizcaya Argentaria S.A.
Argentine National Bank, **14** 46
Argon Medical, **12** 327
Argonaut, **10** 520–22
Argos, **I** 426; **22** 72; **50** 117
Argos Retail Group, **47** 165, 169
Argos Soditic, **43** 147, 149
Argosy Gaming Company, 21 38–41
Argosy Group LP, **27** 197
Argus Corp., **IV** 611
Argus Energy, **7** 538
Argus Motor Company, **16** 7
Arguss Communications, Inc., **57** 120
Argyle Television Inc., **19** 204
Argyll Group PLC, I 241; **II** 609–10, 656; **12** 152–53; **24** 418. *See also* Safeway PLC.
Aria Communications, Inc. *See* Ascend Communications, Inc.
Ariba, Inc., 38 432; **57** 48–51
Ariel Capital Management, **28** 421
Ariens Company, 48 32–34
Aries Technology, **25** 305
Ariete S.P.A. *See* De'Longhi S.p.A.
Aris Industries, Inc., 15 275; **16** 35–38
Arista Laboratories Inc., **51** 249, 251
Aristech Chemical Corp., **12** 342
Aristocrat Leisure Limited, 54 14–16
The Aristotle Corporation, 62 16–18
Arizona Airways, **22** 219
Arizona Daily Star, **58** 282
Arizona Edison Co., **6** 545
Arizona Growth Capital, Inc., **18** 513
AriZona Iced Tea. *See* Ferolito, Vultaggio & Sons.
Arizona One, **24** 455
Arizona Public Service Company, **6** 545–47; **19** 376, 412; **26** 359; **28** 425–26; **54** 290
Arizona Refrigeration Supplies, **14** 297–98
Arjo Wiggins Appleton p.l.c., 13 458; **27** 513; **34** 38–40
Ark Restaurants Corp., 20 25–27
Arkansas Best Corporation, 16 39–41; **19** 455; **42** 410
Arkansas Louisiana Gas Company. *See* Arkla, Inc.
Arkia, **23** 184, 186–87
Arkla, Inc., V 550–51; **11** 441
Arla Foods amba, 48 35–38
Arlington Securities plc, **24** 84, 87–89
Arlon, Inc., **28** 42, 45
Armani. *See* Giorgio Armani S.p.A.
Armaturindistri, **III** 569
Armco Inc., IV 28–30; **10** 448; **11** 5, 255; **12** 353; **19** 8; **26** 407; **30** 282–83; **41** 3, 5; **54** 247–48. *See also* AK Steel.
Armement Sapmer Distribution, **60** 149
Armin Corporation. *See* Tyco International Ltd.

Armor All Products Corp., 12 333; **15** 507; **16** 42–44; **22** 148; **26** 349; **47** 235
Armor Elevator, **11** 5
Armor Holdings, Inc., 27 49–51
Armour. *See* Tommy Armour Golf Co.
Armour & Company, **8** 144; **12** 198; **13** 21, 506; **23** 173; **55** 365
Armour-Dial, **8** 144; **23** 173–74
Armour Food Co., **12** 370; **13** 270
Armstrong Air Conditioning Inc. *See* Lennox International Inc.
Armstrong Tire Co., **15** 355
Armstrong World Industries, Inc., III 422–24; **9** 466; **12** 474–75; **22** 46–50 (upd.), 170–71; **26** 507; **53** 175–76; **59** 381–82
Armtek, **7** 297
Army and Air Force Exchange Service, 39 27–29
Army Cooperative Fire Insurance Company, **10** 541
Army Ordnance, **19** 430
Army Signal Corps Laboratories, **10** 96
Arnold & Porter, 35 42–44
Arnold Clark Automobiles Ltd., 60 39–41
Arnold Communications, **25** 381
Arnold Electric Company, **17** 213
Arnold Industries Inc., **35** 297
Arnold, Schwinn & Company. *See* Schwinn Cycle and Fitness L.P.
Arnold Thomas Co., **9** 411
Arnoldo Mondadori Editore S.p.A., IV 585–88; **19** 17–21 (upd.); **54** 17–23 (upd.)
Arnott's Ltd., II 481; **26** 57–59; **66** 10–12
Aro Corp., **III** 527; **14** 477, 508; **15** 225
Aromat Corporation, **III** 710; **7** 303
Aromatic Industries, **18** 69
Arrendadora del Norte, S.A. de C.V., **51** 150
Arrosto Coffee Company, **25** 263
Arrow Air Holdings Corporation, 55 28–30
Arrow Electronics, Inc., 10 112–14; **13** 47; **19** 310–11, 313; **29** 414; **30** 175; **50** 41–44 (upd.)
Arrow Freight Corporation, **58** 23
Arrow Furniture Co., **21** 32
Arrow Pacific Plastics, **48** 334
Arrow Shirt Co., **24** 384
Arrowhead Mills Inc., **27** 197–98; **43** 218–19
Arsam Investment Co., **26** 261
Arsynco, Inc., **38** 4
The Art Institute of Chicago, 29 36–38
Art Van Furniture, Inc., 28 31–33
Artal Luxembourg SA, **33** 446, 449
Artal NV, **40** 51
Artear S.A. *See* Grupo Clarín S.A.
Artec, **12** 297
Artech Digital Entertainments, Inc., **15** 133
Artek Systems Corporation, **13** 194
Artémis Group, **27** 513
Artes Grafica Rioplatense S.A., **67** 202
Artesian Manufacturing and Bottling Company, **9** 177
Artesian Resources Corporation, **45** 277
Artesyn Solutions Inc., **48** 369
Artesyn Technologies Inc., 46 35–38 (upd.)
Artex Enterprises, **7** 256; **25** 167, 253

Arthur Andersen & Company, Société Coopérative, **10** 115–17, 174; **16** 92; **25** 358; **29** 392; **46** 186. *See also* Andersen Worldwide.

Arthur D. Little, Inc., 35 45–48

Arthur H. Fulton, Inc., **42** 363

Arthur Murray International, Inc., 32 60–62

Arthur Rank Organisation, **25** 328

Arthur Young & Company, **10** 386; **19** 311; **33** 235. *See also* Ernst & Young.

Artisan Entertainment Inc., 32 63–66 (upd.)

Artisan Life Insurance Cooperative, **24** 104

Artisoft, Inc., **18** 143

Artistic Direct, Inc., **37** 108

Artists & Writers Press, Inc., **13** 560

Artists Management Group, **38** 164

ArtMold Products Corporation, **26** 342

Artra Group Inc., **40** 119–20

Arts and Entertainment Network. *See* A&E Television Networks.

Arundel Corp, **46** 196

Arval. *See* PHH Arval.

Arvin Industries, Inc., 8 37–40. *See also* ArvinMeritor, Inc.

ArvinMeritor, Inc., 54 24–28 (upd.)

ASA Holdings, **47** 30

Asahi Breweries, Ltd., I 220–21, 282, 520; **13** 454; **20** 28–30 (upd.); **21** 230, 319–20; **26** 456; **36** 404–05; **50** 201–02; **52** 31–34 (upd.); **63** 229

Asahi Chemical Industry Co., **I** 221

Asahi Corporation, **16** 84; **40** 93

Asahi Denka Kogyo KK, 64 33–35

Asahi Glass Company, Ltd., III 666–68; **11** 234–35; **48** 39–42 (upd.)

Asahi Komag Co., Ltd., **11** 234

Asahi Kyoei Co., **I** 221

Asahi Medix Co., Ltd., **36** 420

Asahi National Broadcasting Company, Ltd., 9 29–31

Asahi Real Estate Facilities Co., Ltd., **6** 427

Asahi Shimbun, **9** 29–30

Asanté Technologies, Inc., 20 31–33

ASARCO Incorporated, IV 31–34; **40** 220–22, 411

ASB Agency, Inc., **10** 92

ASB Air, **47** 286–87

Asbury Associates Inc., **22** 354–55

Asbury Automotive Group Inc., 26 501; **60 42–44**

ASC, Inc., 55 31–34

ASCAP. *See* The American Society of Composers, Authors and Publishers.

Ascend Communications, Inc., 24 47–51; **34** 258

Ascension Health, **61** 206

Ascential Software Corporation, 59 54–57

ASCO Healthcare, Inc., **18** 195–97

Asco Products, Inc., **22** 413

Ascom AG, 9 32–34; 15 125

Ascotts, **19** 122

ASCP. *See* American Securities Capital Partners.

ASD, **IV** 228

ASD Specialty Healthcare, Inc., **64** 27

ASDA Group Ltd., **II** 611–12, 513, 629; **11** 240; **28** 34–36 (upd.); **63** 431; **64** 36–38 (upd.)

ASEA AB. *See* ABB Ltd.

Asepak Corp., **16** 339

A.B. Asesores Bursatiles, **III** 197–98; **15** 18

ASF. *See* American Steel Foundries.

ASG. *See* Allen Systems Group, Inc.

Asgrow Florida Company, **13** 503

Asgrow Seed Co., **29** 435; **41** 306

Ash Company, **10** 271

Ash Resources Ltd., **31** 398–99

Ashanti Goldfields Company Limited, 43 37–40

Ashbourne PLC, **25** 455

Ashland Inc., 19 22–25; **27** 316, 318; **50** 45–50 (upd.)

Ashland Oil, Inc., IV 71, 198, 366, 372–74, 472, 658; **7** 32–33; **8** 99; **9** 108; **18** 279. *See also* Marathon.

Ashley Furniture Industries, Inc., 35 49–51

Ashtead Group plc, 34 41–43

Ashton-Tate Corporation, **9** 81–82; **10** 504–05

Ashworth, Inc., 26 25–28

Asia Oil Co., Ltd., **IV** 404, 476; **53** 115

Asia Pacific Breweries Limited, 59 58–60

Asia Pulp & Paper, **38** 227

Asia Shuang He Sheng Five Star Beer Co., Ltd., **49** 418

Asia Television, **IV** 718; **38** 320

Asia Terminals Ltd., **IV** 718; **38** 319

AsiaInfo Holdings, Inc., 43 41–44

Asiamerica Equities Ltd. *See* Mercer International.

Asian Football Confederation, **27** 150

Asiana Airlines, Inc., 24 400; **46 39–42**

ASICS Corporation, 24 404; **57 52–55**

ASK Group, Inc., 9 35–37; **25** 34

Ask Jeeves, Inc., 65 50–52

Ask Mr. Foster Agency, **22** 127; **26** 308; **55** 90

Asland SA, **III** 705, 740

ASMI. *See* Acer Semiconductor Manufacturing Inc.

ASML Holding N.V., 50 51–54

Aso Cement, **III** 705

Aspect Telecommunications Corporation, 16 392–93; **22 51–53**

ASPECTA Global Group AG, **53** 162

Aspen Imaging International, Inc., **17** 384

Aspen Mountain Gas Co., **6** 568

Aspen Skiing Company, 15 23–26, 234; **43** 438

Aspen Systems, **14** 555

Asplundh Tree Expert Co., 20 34–36; **59 61–65 (upd.)**

Asprofos S.A., **64** 177

Asset Management Company, **25** 86

Asset Marketing Inc. *See* Commercial Financial Services, Inc.

Assicurazioni Generali SpA, III 206–09, 211, 296, 298; **14** 85; **15** 27–31 (upd.); **51** 19, 23; **65** 27–28

Assisted Living Concepts, Inc., 43 45–47

Associate Venture Investors, **16** 418

Associated Book Publishers, **8** 527

Associated British Foods plc, II 465–66, 565, 609; **11** 526; **13** 51–53 (upd.); **24** 475; **41** 30–33 (upd.)

Associated British Ports Holdings Plc, 45 29–32

Associated Bulk Carriers Ltd., **38** 345

Associated Communications Companies, **7** 78; **23** 479

Associated Container Transportation, **23** 161

Associated Cooperative Investment Trust Ltd. *See* Hammerson plc.

Associated Dry Goods Corp., **V** 134; **12** 54–55; **24** 298; **63** 259

Associated Estates Realty Corporation, 25 23–25

Associated Fire Marine Insurance Co., **26** 486

Associated Food Holdings Ltd., **II** 628

Associated Fresh Foods, **II** 611–12; **48** 37

Associated Gas & Electric Company, **6** 534; **14** 124. *See also* General Public Utilities Corporation.

Associated Gas Services, Inc., **11** 28

Associated Grocers, Incorporated, 9 38–40; 19 301; **31 22–26 (upd.)**

Associated Grocers of Arizona, **II** 625

Associated Grocers of Colorado, **II** 670

The Associated Group, **10** 45

Associated Hospital Service of New York. *See* Empire Blue Cross and Blue Shield.

Associated Inns and Restaurants Company of America, **14** 106; **25** 309; **26** 459

Associated International Insurance Co. *See* Gryphon Holdings, Inc.

Associated Lead Manufacturers Ltd. *See* Cookson Group plc.

Associated London Properties. *See* Land Securities PLC.

Associated Madison Insurance, **I** 614

Associated Merchandisers, Inc., **27** 246

Associated Merchandising Corp., **16** 215

Associated Milk Producers, Inc., 11 24–26; 48 43–46 (upd.)

Associated Natural Gas Corporation, 11 27–28

Associated Newspapers Holdings P.L.C., **19** 118, 120; **37** 121

Associated Octel Company Limited, **10** 290

The Associated Press, 7 158; **10** 277; **13** 54–56; **25** 506; **31** 27–30 (upd.); **34** 11

Associated Publishing Company, **19** 201

Associated Pulp & Paper Mills, **IV** 328

Associated Sales Agency, **16** 389

Associated Spring Co., **13** 73

Associated Stationers, **14** 521, 523

Associated Television, **7** 78

Associates First Capital Corporation, **22** 207; **59** 126

Association des Centres Distributeurs E. Leclerc, 37 19–21

Association of Junior Leagues International Inc., 60 45–47

Assurances du Groupe de Paris, **III** 211

Assurances Générales de France, III 351; **27** 513; **42** 151; **51** 23; **57** 23; **63 45–48**

AST Holding Corp. *See* American Standard Companies, Inc.

AST Research, Inc., 9 41–43; **10** 459, 518–19; **12** 470; **18** 260

Astakos Terminal S.A., **64** 8

Astech, **18** 370

Asteroid, **IV** 97

Astley & Pearce, **10** 277

Aston Brooke Software, **14** 392

Aston Villa plc, 41 34–36

Astor Holdings Inc., **22** 32

Astoria Financial Corporation, 44 31–34; 46 316

Astra. *See* PT Astra International Tbk.

Astra AB, I 625–26, 635, 651; **11** 290; **20 37–40 (upd.); 34** 282, 284

Astra Resources, **12** 543

AstraZeneca PLC, 50 55–60 (upd.); 53 290; **55** 27
Astrium N.V., **52** 113
Astrolink International LLC, **54** 406–07
Astronics Corporation, 35 52–54
Astrotech Space Operations, L.P., **11** 429; **37** 365
Astrum International Corp., **12** 88; **13** 453; **16** 20–21; **43** 355
Asur. *See* Grupo Aeropuerto del Sureste, S.A. de C.V.
ASV, Inc., 34 44–47; 66 13–15 (upd.)
ASW. *See* American Steel & Wire Corp.
Asylum Records, **23** 33; **26** 150
AT&E Corp., **17** 430
AT&T Bell Laboratories, Inc., 13 57–59; 22 17
AT&T Corp., III 149, 160, 167; **V 259–64; 7** 88, 118–19, 146, 288–89, 333; **8** 310–11; **9** 32, 43, 106–07, 138, 320, 321, 344, 478–80, 495, 514; **10** 19, 58, 87, 97, 175, 202–03, 277–78, 286, 431, 433, 455–57; **11** 10, 59, 91, 183, 185, 196, 198, 302, 395, 500–01; **12** 9, 135–36, 162; **13** 212–13, 326, 402; **14** 95, 251–53, 257–61, 318, 336–37, 345, 347, 354, 363–64; **15** 125–26, 455; **16** 223, 318, 368, 467; **18** 30, 32, 74, 76, 111–12, 155, 164–65, 368, 516–18, 569–70; **19** 12, 41; **20** 34, 313; **21** 70, 200–01, 514; **22** 51; **23** 135; **25** 100, 256, 301, 495–99; **26** 187, 225, 431, 520; **27** 363; **28** 242; **29** 59, 39–45 **(upd.); 30** 99, 339; **33** 34–35, 37, 91, 93–94; **34** 257–59; **38** 269–70, 416; **42** 224; **43** 50, 222, 443; **44** 47; **46** 373; **47** 319–20; **49** 70, 346–47; **50** 299–300, 318; **54** 29–31, 68–69; **59** 128, 399, 401; **61** 17
AT&T Istel Ltd., 14 35–36
AT&T Microelectronics, **63** 397
AT&T Wireless Services, Inc., 54 29–32 (upd.), 313; **63** 131–32
At Home Corporation, 43 48–51
Atanor S.A., 62 19–22
Atari Corporation, 9 44–47; 10 284, 482, 485; **13** 472; **23 23–26 (upd.); 32** 8; **66 16–20 (upd.)**
ATAS International, **26** 527, 530
ATC, **13** 280
ATC Healthcare Inc., 64 39–42
Atchison Casting Corporation, 24 144; **39 30–32**
ATCO Ltd., **13** 132
ATD Group, **10** 113; **50** 43
ATE Investment, **6** 449
Atelier de Construction Electrique de Delle, **9** 9
ATEQ Corp., **III** 533
Atex, Inc., **10** 34
Athalon Products, Ltd., **10** 181; **12** 313
Athena Assurances, **27** 513, 515
Athena Neuroscience, **63** 142
Athenia Steel Co., **13** 369
Athern, **16** 337
Athlete's Foot Inc., **29** 186; **54** 306, 308; **67** 204–05
Athletic Attic, **19** 230
Athletic Shoe Company, **17** 243
Athletic Textile Company, Inc., **13** 532
Athletic X-Press, **14** 293
The Athletics Investment Group, 62 23–26
Athleticum Sportmarket, **48** 279

Athol Machine Co., **13** 301
ATI Technologies Inc., **54** 269–71
Atkins Nutritionals, Inc., 58 8–10
ATL Group, **65** 304
Atlalait, **19** 50
Atlanta Gas Light Company, 6 446–48; 23 27–30 (upd.)
Atlanta-LaSalle Corporation, **43** 54
Atlanta National Bank, **16** 521
Atlanta National League Baseball Club, Inc., 43 52–55
Atlantic & Pacific Tea Company (A&P). *See* Great Atlantic & Pacific Tea Company, Inc.
Atlantic Acceptance Corporation, **7** 95
Atlantic Airways, **52** 167
Atlantic American Corporation, 23 413; **44 35–37**
Atlantic Auto Finance Corp. *See* United Auto Group, Inc.
Atlantic Cellular, **43** 341
Atlantic Coast Airlines Holdings, Inc., 55 35–37
Atlantic Coast Carton Company, **19** 77
Atlantic Coast Line Railroad Company. *See* CSX Corporation.
Atlantic Computers, **14** 35
Atlantic Container Lines Ltd., **23** 161
Atlantic Energy, Inc., 6 449–50
Atlantic Envelope Company, **54** 251–52, 255
The Atlantic Group, 23 31–33
Atlantic Mills, **27** 188
Atlantic Mutual, **41** 65
Atlantic Precision Instrument Company, **13** 234
Atlantic Precision Works, **9** 72
Atlantic Premium Brands, Ltd., 57 56–58
Atlantic Records Group, **18** 458; **26** 150; **64** 115
Atlantic Refining Co. *See* Atlantic Richfield Company.
Atlantic Research Corporation, **13** 462; **54** 330–31
Atlantic Richfield Company, IV 375–77, 379, 435, 454, 456–57, 467, 494, 522, 536, 571; **7** 57, 108, 537–38, 558–59; **8** 184, 416; **10** 110; **13** 13; **19** 175; **24** 521, 524; **26** 4, 372; **31 31–34 (upd.);** 40 358; **45** 49, 55, 252; **63** 113
Atlantic Sea Products, **13** 103
The Atlantic Seaboard Dispatch. *See* GATX.
Atlantic Securities Ltd., **II** 223
Atlantic Southeast Airlines, Inc., 26 439; **47 29–31**
Atlantic Southern Properties, Inc., **6** 449–50
Atlantic Transport Company, **19** 198
Atlantic Wholesalers, **II** 631
Atlantis Energy Inc., **44** 182
Atlantis Group, Inc., **17** 16; **19** 50, 390
Atlantis Resort and Casino. *See* Sun International Hotels Limited.
Atlas Air, Inc., 39 33–35
Atlas Air Worldwide Holdings, Inc., **60** 238
Atlas America, Inc., **42** 311
Atlas Cement Company, **31** 252
Atlas Copco AB, III 425–27, 480; **28 37–41 (upd.); 63** 211
Atlas Eléctrica S.A., **22** 27
Atlas Hotels, Inc., **V** 164

Atlas Plastics, **19** 414
Atlas Securities, **47** 160
Atlas Tag & Label, **9** 72
Atlas Van Lines, Inc., 14 37–39
Atlas Ventures, **25** 96
Atlatec SA de CV, **39** 192
Atle Byrnestad, **6** 368; **27** 92
Atmel Corporation, 17 32–34; 19 313
Atmos Energy Corporation, 43 56–58
Atmospherix Ltd. *See* Blyth Industries, Inc.
Atochem S.A., I 303–04, 676. *See also* Total-Fina-Elf.
AtoHaas Americas, **26** 425
Atomic Austria GmbH, **41** 14–16
ATR, **7** 9, 11
ATS. *See* Magasins Armand Thiéry et Sigrand.
ATT Microelectrica España, **V** 339
Attachmate Corporation, 11 520; **56 19–21**
ATTC Manufacturing Inc., **48** 5
Attica Enterprises S.A., 64 43–45
Atvidabergs Industrier, **25** 463
Atwater McMillian. *See* St. Paul Companies, Inc.
Atwood Mobil Products, 53 52–55
Atwood Resources Inc., **17** 372
ATX Technologies, Inc., **32** 374
ATx Telecom Systems Inc., **31** 124
Au Bon Marché, **26** 160
Au Bon Pain Co., Inc., 18 35–38; 44 327
AU Optronics Corporation, 67 38–40, 53
Au Printemps S.A., V 9–11; 17 124; **41** 114. *See also* Pinault-Printemps-Redoute S.A.
Auchan, 10 205; **23** 230; **27** 94; **37 22–24; 39** 183–85; **54** 219–20
Auctentia Subastas S.L., **60** 146
Audifon U.K. Ltd., **56** 338
Audio Accessories, Inc., **37** 301
Audio Development Company, **10** 18
Audio International Inc., **36** 159
Audio King Corporation, 24 52–54
Audio/Video Affiliates, Inc., **10** 468–69
Audiofina, **44** 377
Audiovox Corporation, 34 48–50
Audits & Surveys Worldwide Inc., **28** 501, 504
Auerhahn, **60** 364
Augat Inc., **54** 373
Aughton Group, **II** 466
August Max Woman. *See* The United States Shoe Corporation.
August Schell Brewing Company Inc., 22 421; **59 66–69**
August Storck KG, 66 21–23
Ault Incorporated, 34 51–54
Aunt Fanny's Bakery, **7** 429
Auntie Anne's, Inc., 35 55–57
Aura Books plc, **34** 5
Aurea Concesiones de Infraestructuras SA, **55** 182. *See also* Abertis Infraestructuras, S.A.
Aurec Information and Directory Systems. *See* Amdocs Ltd.
Aurigene Discovery Technologies Limited, **59** 168
AurionGold Limited, **61** 293
Aurora Casket Company, Inc., 56 22–24
Aurora Dairy Corporation, **37** 195, 198
Aurora Foods Inc., 26 384; **32 67–69**
Aurora Systems, Inc., **21** 135
Aurrera S.A., **35** 459
Aurum Corp., **38** 431

Ausimont S.p.A., **8** 271; **61** 333
Ausplay, **13** 319
Aussedat-Rey, **IV** 288; **23** 366, 368
The Austin Company, 8 41–44
Austin Industries, **25** 402
Austin Nichols, **I** 261, 280–81
Austin Quality Foods, **36** 313
Austin Rover, **14** 321
Austins Steaks & Saloon, Inc. *See* WesterN
  SizzliN Corporation.
**Australia and New Zealand Banking
  Group Limited, II** 187–90; **52** 35–40
  (upd.)
Australia National Bank, Limited, **10** 170
Australian Airlines, **27** 475. *See also*
  Qantas Airways Limited.
Australian and Overseas
  Telecommunications Corporation. *See*
  Telecom Australia.
Australian Automotive Air, Pty. Ltd., **III**
  593
Australian Consolidated Investments,
  Limited, **10** 170
Australian Consolidated Press, **27** 42; **54**
  299
Australian Mutual Provident Society, **IV**
  61, 697
Australian Petroleum Pty. Ltd., **25** 471
Australian Tankerships Pty. Ltd., **25** 471
Australian Telecommunications
  Corporation, **6** 342
Australian Wheat Board. *See* AWB Ltd.
Austria Tabak, **55** 200
**Austrian Airlines AG (Österreichische
  Luftverkehrs AG), 27** 26; **33** 49–52; **34**
  398; **48** 258, 259
Austrian Star Gastronomie GmbH, **48** 63
Austro-Americana, **6** 425
Authentic Fitness Corp., 16 511; **20**
  41–43; **46** 450; **51** 30–33 **(upd.)**
Auto Avio Costruzione, **13** 219
Auto Ordnance Corporation, **19** 430–31
Auto Parts Wholesale, **26** 348
Auto Shack. *See* AutoZone, Inc.
Auto Value Associates, Inc., 25 26–28
Autobytel Inc., 47 32–34
Autocam Corporation, 51 34–36
Autodesk, Inc., 10 118–20
Autogrill SpA, 24 195; **49** 31–33
Autoliv, Inc., 41 369; **65** 53–55
**Autologic Information International,
  Inc., 20** 44–46; **26** 518–20
Automat, **II** 614
Automated Communications, Inc., **8** 311
Automated Design Systems, **25** 348
Automated Loss Prevention Systems, **11**
  445
Automated Security (Holdings) PLC, **11**
  444
Automatic Coil Corp., **33** 359, 361
Automatic Data Processing, Inc., III
  117–19; 9 48–51 **(upd.)**, 125, 173; **21**
  69; **46** 333; **47** 35–39 **(upd.)**
Automatic Liquid Packaging, **50** 122
Automatic Manufacturing Corporation, **10**
  319
Automatic Payrolls, Inc. *See* Automatic
  Data Processing, Inc.
Automatic Retailers of America, Inc., **II**
  607; **13** 48
Automatic Sprinkler Corp. of America. *See*
  Figgie International, Inc.
Automatic Toll Systems, **19** 111

Automatic Voting Machine Corporation.
  See American Locker Group
  Incorporated.
AutoMed Technologies, Inc., **64** 27
Automobiles Citroen, 7 35–38; **16** 420
**Automobili Lamborghini Holding S.p.A.,
  34** 55–58 **(upd.)**
Automobili Lamborghini S.p.A., 13
  60–62, 219
Automotive Components Limited, **10** 325;
  56 158
Automotive Diagnostics, **10** 492
Automotive Group. *See* Lear Seating
  Corporation.
Automotive Industries Holding Inc., **16** 323
AutoNation, Inc., 41 239; **50** 61–64
Autonet, **6** 435
Autonom Computer, **47** 36
Autophon AG, **9** 32
Autoroutes du Sud de la France SA, 55
  38–40
Autosite.com, **47** 34
Autotote Corporation, 20 47–49. *See also*
  Scientific Games Corporation.
Autoweb.com, **47** 34
AUTOWORKS Holdings, Inc., **24** 205
AutoZone, Inc., 9 52–54; **26** 348; **31**
  35–38 (upd.); 36 364; **57** 10–12
**AVA AG (Allgemeine
  Handelsgesellschaft der Verbraucher
  AG), 33** 53–56
Avado Brands, Inc., 31 39–42; **46** 234
Avalon Publishing Group. *See* Publishers
  Group, Inc.
AvalonBay Communities, Inc., 58 11–13
Avantel, **27** 304
Avaya Inc., **41** 287, 289–90
Avco. *See* Aviation Corp. of the Americas.
Avco Corp., **34** 433
Avco Financial Services Inc., 13 63–65
Avco National Bank, **II** 420
Avdel, **34** 433
Avecia Group PLC, 63 49–51
Avecor Cardiovascular Inc., **8** 347; **22** 360
Aveda Corporation, 24 55–57
Avedis Zildjian Co., 38 66–68
Avendt Group, Inc., **IV** 137
Avenor Inc., **25** 13
Aventis Pharmaceuticals, **34** 280, 283–84;
  38 378, 380; **63** 232, 235
Avery Dennison Corporation, IV
  251–54; 15 229, 401; **17** 27–31 **(upd.)**,
  445; **49** 34–40 **(upd.)**
AvestaPolarit, **49** 104
Avex Electronics Inc., **40** 68
Avfuel, **11** 538
Avgain Marine A/S, **7** 40; **41** 42
Avia Group International, Inc. *See* Reebok
  International Ltd.
**Aviacionny Nauchno-Tehnicheskii
  Komplex im. A.N. Tupoleva, 24** 58–60
AVIACO. *See* Aviacion y Comercio.
**Avianca Aerovías Nacionales de
  Colombia SA, 36** 52–55
Aviation Corp. of the Americas, **9** 497–99;
  11 261, 427; **12** 379, 383; **13** 64
Aviation Inventory Management Co., **28** 5
Aviation Power Supply, **II** 16
Aviation Sales Company, 41 37–39
Aviation Services West, Inc. *See* Scenic
  Airlines, Inc.
Avid Technology Inc., 38 69–73
Avimo, **47** 7–8
Avion Coach Corporation, **11** 363

**Avions Marcel Dassault-Breguet
  Aviation, I** 44–46; **7** 11; **7** 205; **8** 314.
  See also Groupe Dassault Aviation SA.
Avis Rent A Car, Inc., 6 356–58; **8** 33; **9**
  284; **10** 419; **16** 379–80; **22** 54–57
  (upd.), 524; **25** 93, 143, 420–22
Avisun Corp., **IV** 371
Aviva PLC, 50 65–68 **(upd.)**
Avnet Electronics Supply Co., **19** 311, 313
Avnet Inc., 9 55–57; **10** 112–13; **13** 47;
  50 41
Avocent Corporation, 65 56–58
Avon Products, Inc., III 15–16; **8** 329; **9**
  331; **11** 282, 366; **12** 314, 435; **13** 38;
  14 501–02; **17** 186; **19** 26–29 **(upd.)**,
  253; **21** 49, 51; **25** 292; 456; **27** 429; **30**
  64, 308–09; **46** 43–46 **(upd.)**
Avon Rubber plc, **23** 146
Avondale Industries, Inc., 7 39–41; **41**
  40–43 (upd.)
Avondale Mills, Inc., **8** 558–60; **9** 466
Avonmore Foods Plc, **59** 205
Avril Alimentaire SNC, **51** 54
Avro. *See* A.V. Roe & Company.
Avstar, **38** 72
Avtech Corp., **36** 159
AVTOVAZ Joint Stock Company, 65
  59–62
AVX Corporation, 21 329, 331; **67**
  21–22; **41–43**
AW Bruna Uitgevers BV, **53** 273
AW North Carolina Inc., **48** 5
AWA. *See* America West Holdings
  Corporation.
AWA Defence Industries (AWADI). *See*
  British Aerospace Defence Industries.
AwardTrack, Inc., **49** 423
AWB Ltd., 56 25–27
Awesome Transportation, Inc., **22** 549
Awrey Bakeries, Inc., 56 28–30
AXA Colonia Konzern AG, III 210–12;
  15 30; **21** 147; **27** 52–55; **49** 41–45
  (upd.)
AXA Financial, Inc., **63** 26–27
AXA UK plc, **64** 173
Axe-Houghton Associates Inc., **41** 208
Axel Johnson Group, I 553–55
Axel Springer Verlag AG, IV 589–91; **20**
  50–53 (upd.); 23 86; **35** 452; **54** 295
Axon Systems Inc., **7** 336
Ayala Plans, Inc., **58** 20
Aydin Corp., 19 30–32
Ayr-Way Stores, **27** 452
Ayres, Lewis, Norris & May, Inc., **54** 184
AYS. *See* Alternative Youth Services, Inc.
AZA Immobilien AG, **51** 196
Azcon Corporation, 23 34–36
Azerty, **25** 13
Azienda Generale Italiana Petroli. *See* Agip
  SpA.
AZL Resources, **7** 538
Aznar International, **14** 225
Azon Limited, **22** 282
AZP Group Inc., **6** 546
Aztar Corporation, 13 66–68
Azteca, **18** 211, 213

B&D. *See* Barker & Dobson.
B&G Foods, Inc., 40 51–54
B & K Steel Fabrications, Inc., **26** 432
B & L Insurance, Ltd., **51** 38
B&M Baked Beans, **40** 53
B & O. *See* Baltimore and Ohio Railroad.
B&Q plc. *See* Kingfisher plc.

B&S. *See* Binney & Smith Inc.
B.A.T. Industries PLC, **14** 77; **16** 242; **22** **70–73** (upd.); **25** 154–56; **29** 196; **63** 260–61. *See also* Brown & Williamson Tobacco Corporation
B. B. & R. Knight Brothers, **8** 200; **25** 164
B.B. Foods, **13** 244
B-Bar-B Corp., **16** 340
B.C. Rail Telecommunications, **6** 311
B.C. Sugar, **II** 664
B.C. Ziegler and Co. *See* The Ziegler Companies, Inc.
B. Dalton Bookseller Inc., **10** 136; **13** 545; **16** 160; **18** 136; **25** 29–31; **30** 68
B-E Holdings, **17** 60
B/E Aerospace, Inc., **30** 72–74
B.F. Goodrich Co. *See* The BFGoodrich Company.
B.F. Walker, Inc., **11** 354
B.I.C. America, **17** 15, 17
B.J.'s Wholesale, **12** 335
B.J. Alan Co., Inc., **67** 44–46
The B. Manischewitz Company, LLC, **31** **43–46**
B. Perini & Sons, Inc., **8** 418
B Ticino, **21** 350
B.V. Tabak Export & Import Compagnie, **12** 109
BA. *See* British Airways.
BAA plc, **10** 121–23; **29** 509, 511; **33** **57–61** (upd.); **37** 8
Bålforsens Kraft AB, **28** 444
Baan Company, **25** 32–34; **26** 496, 498
Babbage's, Inc., **10** 124–25
Babcock & Wilcox Co., **37** 242–45
Babcock International, **57** 142
BABE. *See* British Aerospace plc.
Baby Dairy Products, **48** 438
Baby Phat. *See* Phat Fashions LLC.
Baby Superstore, Inc., **15** 32–34; **57** 372
Babybird Co., Ltd. *See* Nagasakiya Co., Ltd.
BabyCenter.com, **37** 130
Babyliss, S.A., **17** 110
BAC. *See* Barclays American Corp.; Beverage Associates Corp.; British Aircraft Corporation.
Bacardi Limited, **18** 39–42; **63** 264, 266
Baccarat, **23** 241; **24** 61–63; **27** 421, 423
Bache & Company, **III** 340; **8** 349
Bachman Foods, **15** 139
Bachman Holdings, Inc., **14** 165; **34** 144–45
Bachman's Inc., **22** 58–60; **24** 513
Bachoco. *See* Industrias Bacholo, S.A. de C.V.
Back Bay Investments Ltd., **64** 217
Back Bay Restaurant Group, Inc., **20** **54–56**
Back Yard Burgers, Inc., **45** 33–36
Backer & Spielvogel, **12** 168; **14** 48–49; **22** 296
Backer Spielvogel Bates Worldwide **42** 329. *See also* Bates Worldwide, Inc.
Bacon's Information, Inc., **55** 289
Bacova Guild, Ltd., **17** 76
Bad Boy Worldwide Entertainment Group, **31** 269; **58** 14–17
Badak LNG Transport Inc., **56** 181
Baddour, Inc. *See* Fred's, Inc.
Badger Illuminating Company, **6** 601
Badger Meter, Inc., **22** 61–65
Badger Paper Mills, Inc., **15** 35–37
Badin-Defforey, **27** 93

BAe. *See* British Aerospace plc.
BAE Systems, **41** 412; **52** 114
BAFS. *See* Bangkok Aviation Fuel Services Ltd.
Bahamas Air Holdings Ltd., **66** 24–26
Bahlsen GmbH & Co. KG, **44** 38–41
Bailey, Banks & Biddle, **16** 559
Bailey Nurseries, Inc., **57** 59–61
Bailey's Pub and Grille. *See* Total Entertainment Restaurant Corporation.
Bain & Company, **9** 343; **21** 143; **55** **41–43**
Bain Capital, Inc., **14** 244–45; **16** 466; **20** 18; **24** 456, 482; **25** 254; **26** 184; **38** 107–09; **63** 133, 137–38
Baird, **7** 235, 237
Bairnco Corporation, **28** 42–45
Bajaj Auto Limited, **39** 36–38
BAKAB. *See* Bålforsens Kraft AB.
Bakelite Corp., **13** 231
Baker. *See* Michael Baker Corporation.
Baker and Botts, L.L.P., **28** 46–49
Baker & Hostetler LLP, **40** 55–58
Baker & McKenzie, **10** 126–28; **42** **17–20** (upd.)
Baker & Taylor Corporation, **16** 45–47; **43** 59–62 (upd.)
Baker Cummins Pharmaceuticals Inc., **11** 208
Baker Extract Co., **27** 299
Baker Hughes Incorporated, **III** 428–29; **11** 513; **22** 66–69 (upd.); **25** 74; **57** 62–66 (upd.); **59** 366; **63** 306
Baker Industries, Inc., **8** 476; **13** 124
Baker Oil Tools. *See* Baker Hughes Incorporated.
Baker-Raulang Co., **13** 385
Bakers Best Snack Food Corporation, **24** 241
Bakers Square. *See* VICORP Restaurants, Inc.
Bakersfield Savings and Loan, **10** 339
Bal-Sam India Holdings Ltd., **64** 95
Balance Bar Company, **32** 70–72
Balchem Corporation, **42** 21–23
Balco, Inc., **7** 479–80; **27** 415
Balcor, Inc., **10** 62
Bald Eagle Corporation, **45** 126
Baldor Electric Company, **21** 42–44
Baldwin & Lyons, Inc., **51** 37–39
Baldwin-Ehret-Hill Inc., **28** 42
Baldwin Filters, Inc., **17** 104
Baldwin Hardware Manufacturing Co. *See* Masco Corporation.
Baldwin-Montrose Chemical Co., Inc., **31** 110
Baldwin Piano & Organ Company, **16** 201; **18** 43–46
Baldwin Rubber Industries, **13** 79
Baldwin Technology Company, Inc., **25** **35–39**
Baldwin-United Corp., **III** 254, 293; **52** 243–44
Balfour Beatty Construction Ltd., **III** 433–34; **36** 56–60 (upd.); **58** 156–57
Balfour Company, L.G., **19** 451–52
Ball & Young Adhesives, **9** 92
Ball Corporation, **I** 597–98; **10** 129–31 (upd.); **13** 254, 256; **15** 129; **16** 123; **30** 38; **64** 86
The Ball Ground Reps, Inc., **26** 257
Ball Industries, Inc., **26** 539
Ball Stalker Inc., **14** 4
Ballantine Books, **13** 429; **31** 376–77, 379

Ballantyne of Omaha, Inc., **27** 56–58
Ballard Medical Products, **21** 45–48
Ballast Nedam Group, **24** 87–88
Ballet Makers-Europe, Ltd., **62** 59
Balli Group plc, **26** 527, 530
Bally Entertainment Corp., **19** 205, 207
Bally Gaming International, **15** 539
Bally Manufacturing Corporation, **III** **430–32**; **10** 375, 482; **12** 107; **15** 538–39; **17** 316–17, 443; **41** 214–15; **53** 364–65
Bally Total Fitness Holding Corp., **25** **40–42**
Bâloise-Holding, **40** 59–62
Baltek Corporation, **34** 59–61
Baltic Cable, **15** 521
Baltica, **27** 54
Baltika Brewery Joint Stock Company, **65** 63–66
Baltimar Overseas Limited, **25** 469
Baltimore & Ohio Railroad[see]CSX Corporation.
Baltimore Aircoil Company, Inc., **7** 30–31; **66** 27–29
Baltimore Gas and Electric Company, **V** **552–54**; **11** 388; **25** 43–46 (upd.)
Baltimore Orioles L.P., **66** 30–33
Baltimore Paper Box Company, **8** 102
Baltimore Technologies Plc, **42** 24–26
Baltino Foods, **13** 383
Balzers Process Systems GmbH, **48** 30
Banamex, **22** 285; **23** 170; **34** 81; **57** 170. *See also* Banco Nacional de Mexico; Grupo Financiero Banamex S.A.
Banana Boat Holding Corp., **15** 359
Banana Brothers, **31** 229
Banana Importers of Ireland, **38** 197
Banana Republic Inc., **25** 47–49; **31** 51–52
Banc Internacional d'Andorra-Banca Mora, **48** 51
Banc One Corporation, **9** 475; **10** 132–34; **11** 181. *See also* Bank One Corporation.
Banca Commerciale Italiana SpA, **II** **191–93**, 242, 271, 278, 295, 319; **17** 324; **50** 410
BancA Corp., **11** 305
Banca del Salento, **65** 73
Banca di Roma S.p.A., **65** 86, 88
Banca Esperia, **65** 230–31
Banca Fideuram SpA, **63** 52–54
Banca Intesa SpA, **65** 27, 29, 67–70
Banca Monte dei Paschi di Siena SpA, **65** 71–73
Banca Nazionale del Lavoro S.p.A., **65** 73
Banca Nazionale dell'Agricoltura, **II** 272
Banca Serfin. *See* Grupo Financiero Serfin, S.A.
Bancard Systems, **24** 395
BancBoston Capital, **48** 412
Bancen. *See* Banco del Centro S.A.
BancFinancial Services Corporation, **25** 187
BancMortgage Financial Corp., **25** 185, 187
Banco Alianca S.A., **19** 34
Banco Azteca, **19** 189
Banco Bilbao Vizcaya Argentaria S.A., **48** 47–51 (upd.)
Banco Bilbao Vizcaya, S.A., **II** 194–96
Banco Bradesco S.A., **13** 69–71; **19** 33
Banco Capitalizador de Monterrey, **19** 189

Banco Central, II 197–98; **56** 65. *See also* Banco Santander Central Hispano S.A.

Banco Central de Crédito. *See* Banco Itaú.

Banco Chemical (Portugal) S.A. *See* Chemical Banking Corp.

Banco Comercial, **19** 188

Banco Comercial de Puerto Rico, **41** 311

Banco Comercial Português, SA, 50 69–72

Banco Credito y Ahorro Ponceno, **41** 312

Banco da América, **19** 34

Banco de Comercio, S.A. *See* Grupo Financiero BBVA Bancomer S.A.

Banco de Credito Local, **48** 51

Banco de Credito y Servicio, **51** 151

Banco de Galicia y Buenos Aires, S.A., **63** 178–80

Banco de Londres, Mexico y Sudamerica. *See* Grupo Financiero Serfin, S.A.

Banco de Madrid, **40** 147

Banco de Mexico, **19** 189

Banco de Ponce, **41** 313

Banco del Centro S.A., **51** 150

Banco del Norte, **19** 189

Banco di Roma, **II**, 257, 271

Banco di Santo Spirito, **I** 467

Banco di Sicilia S.p.A., **65** 86, 88

Banco do Brasil S.A., II 199–200

Banco Español de Credito, **II** 198

Banco Espírito Santo e Comercial de Lisboa S.A., 15 38–40

Banco Federal de Crédito. *See* Banco Itaú.

Banco Frances y Brasiliero, **19** 34

Banco Industrial de Monterrey, **19** 189

Banco Itaú S.A., 19 33–35

Banco Mercantil del Norte, S.A., **51** 149

Banco Nacional de Mexico, **9** 333; **19** 188, 193

Banco Opportunity, **57** 67, 69

Banco Pinto de Mahalhães, **19** 34

Banco Popolar. *See* Popular, Inc.

Banco Português do Brasil S.A., **19** 34

Banco Santander Central Hispano S.A., 36 61–64 **(upd.); 42** 349; **63** 179

Banco Serfin, **34** 82

Banco Sul Americano S.A., **19** 34

Banco União Comercial, **19** 34

BancOhio National Bank in Columbus, **9** 475

Bancomer S.A., **19** 12; **48** 47. *See also* Grupo Financiero BBVA Bancomer S.A.

Bancorp Leasing, Inc., **14** 529

BancorpSouth, Inc., **14** 40–41

Bancrecer. *See* Banco de Credito y Servicio.

BancSystems Association Inc., **9** 475, 476

Bandag, Inc., 19 36–38, 454–56

Bandai Co., Ltd., 23 388; **25** 488; **38** 415; **55** 44–48; **61** 202; **67** 274

Bando McGlocklin Small Business Lending Corporation, **53** 222–24

Banesto. *See* Banco Español de Credito.

Banfi Products Corp., 36 65–67

Banfield, The Pet Hospital. *See* Medical Management International, Inc.

Bang & Olufsen Holding A/S, 37 25–28

Bangkok Airport Hotel. *See* Thai Airways International.

Bangkok Aviation Fuel Services Ltd. *See* Thai Airways International.

Bangladesh Krishi Bank, **31** 220

Bangor and Aroostook Railroad Company, **8** 33

Bangor Mills, **13** 169

Bangor Punta Alegre Sugar Corp., **30** 425

Banister Continental Corp. *See* BFC Construction Corporation.

Bank Austria AG, 23 37–39; **59** 239

Bank Brussels Lambert, II 201–03, 295, 407

Bank Central Asia, **18** 181; **62** 96, 98

Bank du Louvre, **27** 423

Bank für Elektrische Unternehmungen. *See* Elektrowatt AG.

Bank Hapoalim B.M., II 204–06; **25** 266, 268; **54** 33–37 **(upd.)**

Bank Hofmann, **21** 146–47

Bank Leumi le-Israel B.M., 25 268; **60** 48–51

Bank of America Corporation, 6 385; **9** 50, 123–24, 333, 536; **12** 106, 466; **14** 170; **18** 516; **22** 542; **25** 432; **26** 486; **46** 47–54 **(upd.); 47** 37

The Bank of Bishop and Co., Ltd., **11** 114

Bank of Boston Corporation, II 207–09; **7** 114; **12** 31; **13** 467; **14** 90. *See also* FleetBoston Financial Corporation.

Bank of Brandywine Valley, **25** 542

Bank of Britain, **14** 46–47

Bank of China, 63 55–57

Bank of Delaware, **25** 542

Bank of East Asia Ltd., 63 58–60

Bank of England, **10** 8, 336; **14** 45–46; **47** 227

Bank of Ireland, 16 13–14; **19** 198; **50** 73–76

Bank of Italy, **III** 209, 347; **8** 45

The Bank of Jacksonville, **9** 58

Bank of Lee County, **14** 40

Bank of Mexico Ltd., **19** 188

The Bank of Milwaukee, **14** 529

Bank of Mississippi, Inc., 14 40–41

Bank of Montreal, II 210–12, 231, 375; **26** 304; **46** 55–58 **(upd.)**

Bank of Nettleton, **14** 40

Bank of New England Corporation, II 213–15; **9** 229

Bank of New Orleans, **11** 106

Bank of New South Wales. *See* Westpac Banking Corporation.

Bank of New York Company, Inc., II 216–19, 247; **34** 82; **46** 59–63 **(upd.)**

Bank of North Mississippi, **14** 41

The Bank of Nova Scotia, II 220–23, 345; **59** 70–76 **(upd.)**

Bank of Oklahoma, **22** 4

The Bank of Scotland. *See* The Governor and Company of the Bank of Scotland.

Bank of Sherman, **14** 40

Bank of the Ohio Valley, **13** 221

Bank of the Philippine Islands, 58 18–20

Bank of Tokyo, Ltd., II 224–25, 276, 301, 341, 358; **12** 138; **16** 496, 498; **50** 498

Bank of Tokyo-Mitsubishi Ltd., 15 41–43 **(upd.)**, 431; **26** 454, 457; **38** 387

Bank of Tupelo, **14** 40

Bank of Wales, **10** 336, 338

Bank One Corporation, 36 68–75 **(upd.)**

Bank-R Systems Inc., **18** 517

BankAmerica Corporation, II 226–28, 436; **8** 45–48 **(upd.)**, 295, 469, 471; **13** 69; **17** 546; **18** 518; **25** 187; **26** 65; **47** 401; **61** 249. *See also* Bank of America.

BankAtlantic Bancorp, Inc., **66** 273

BankBoston. *See* FleetBoston Financial Corporation.

BankCard America, Inc., **24** 394

Bankers and Shippers Insurance Co., **III** 389

Bankers Corporation, **14** 473

Bankers Life and Casualty Co., **10** 247; **16** 207; **33** 110

Bankers Life Association. *See* Principal Mutual Life Insurance Company.

Bankers National Life Insurance Co., **10** 246

Bankers Trust Co., **38** 411

Bankers Trust New York Corporation, II 229–31; **10** 425; **11** 416; **12** 165, 209; **13** 188, 466; **17** 559; **19** 34; **22** 102; **25** 268

Bankhaus August Lenz AG, **65** 230, 232

Banknorth Group, Inc., 55 49–53

Bankruptcy Services LLC, **56** 112

Banksia Wines Ltd., **54** 227, 229

BankWatch, **37** 143, 145

Banner Aerospace, Inc., 14 42–44; **37** 29–32 **(upd.)**

Banner International, **13** 20

Banner Life Insurance Company, **III** 273; **24** 284

Banorte. *See* Grupo Financiero Banorte, S.A. de C.V.

Banpais. *See* Grupo Financiero Asemex-Banpais S.A.

BanPonce Corporation, **41** 312

Banque Bruxelles Lambert. *See* Bank Brussels Lambert.

Banque de Bruxelles. *See* Bank Brussels Lambert.

Banque de France, **14** 45–46

Banque de la Société Générale de Belgique. *See* Generale Bank.

Banque de Paris et des Pays-Bas, **10** 346; **19** 188–89; **33** 179

Banque Indosuez, **II** 429; **52** 361–62

Banque Internationale de Luxembourg, **42** 111

Banque Lambert. *See* Bank Brussels Lambert.

Banque Nationale de Paris S.A., II 232–34, 239; **III** 201, 392–94; **9** 148; **13** 203; **15** 309; **19** 51; **33** 119; **49** 382. *See also* BNP Paribas Group.

Banque Paribas. *See* BNP Paribas Group.

Banque Sanpaolo of France, **50** 410

La Banque Suisse et Française. *See* Crédit Commercial de France.

Banque Worms, **27** 514

Banta Corporation, 12 24–26; **19** 333; **32** 73–77 **(upd.)**

Bantam Ball Bearing Company, **13** 522

Bantam Doubleday Dell Publishing Group, **IV** 594; **13** 429; **15** 51; **27** 222; **31** 375–76, 378

Banyan Systems Inc., 25 50–52

Banyu Pharmaceutical Co., **11** 290; **34** 283

Baoshan Iron and Steel, **19** 220

BAP of New York, Inc., **15** 246

Bar Technologies, Inc., **26** 408

Barastoc Stockfeeds Pty Ltd., **62** 307

Barat. *See* Barclays PLC.

Barber Dental Supply Inc., **19** 291

Barberet & Blanc, **I** 677; **49** 350

Barcel, **19** 192

Barclay Furniture Co., **12** 300

Barclay White Inc., **38** 436

Barclays Business Credit, **13** 468

Barclays PLC, II 235–37, 239, 244, 308, 319, 333, 383, 422, 429; **IV** 23, 722; **7**

332–33; **8** 118; **11** 29–30; **17** 324–25; **20** 57–60 (upd.); **25** 101; **28** 167; **47** 227; **64** 46–50 (upd.)
BarclaysAmerican Mortgage Corporation, 11 29–30
Barco Manufacturing Co., **16** 8; **26** 541
Barco NV, 44 42–45
Barcolo Manufacturing, **15** 103; **26** 100
Barden Cablevision, **IV** 640; **26** 273
Bardon Group. *See* Aggregate Industries plc.
Bareco Products, **15** 352
Barefoot Inc., **23** 428, 431
Bari Shoes, Inc., **22** 213
Barilla G. e R. Fratelli S.p.A., 17 35–37; **50** 77–80 (upd.); **53** 243
Baring Brothers & Co., Ltd., **39** 5
Barings PLC, 14 45–47
Barker & Dobson, **II** 629; **47** 367
Barker and Company, Ltd., **13** 286
Barlow Rand Ltd., I 422–24
Barlow Specialty Advertising, Inc., **26** 341
Barmag AG, 39 39–42
Barneda Carton SA, **41** 326
Barnes & Noble, Inc., 10 135–37; **12** 172; **13** 494, 545; **14** 61–62; **15** 62; **16** 160; **17** 524; **23** 370; **25** 17, 29–30; **30** 67–71 (upd.); **41** 61; **43** 78, 408
Barnes Group, Inc., 13 72–74
Barnett Banks, Inc., 9 58–60
Barnett Brass & Copper Inc., **9** 543
Barnett Inc., 28 50–52
Barney's, Inc., 28 53–55; **36** 290, 292
Barnstead/Thermolyne Corporation, **14** 479–80
Baroid, **19** 467–68
Baron Industries Corporation, **53** 298
Baron Philippe de Rothschild S.A., 39 43–46
Barr. *See* AG Barr plc.
Barr & Stroud Ltd., **III** 727
Barr Laboratories, Inc., 26 29–31
Barracuda Technologies, **47** 7, 9
Barratt Developments plc, I 556–57; **56** 31–33 (upd.)
Barrett Business Services, Inc., 16 48–50
Barricini Foods Inc., **27** 197
Barrick Gold Corporation, 34 62–65; **38** 232
Barris Industries, Inc., **23** 225
Barry Callebaut AG, 29 46–48
Barry Wright Corporation, **9** 27; **32** 49
Barry's Jewelers. *See* Samuels Jewelers Incorporated.
Barsab Investment Trust. *See* South African Breweries Ltd.
Barsotti's, Inc. *See* Foster Wheeler Corp.
Bart Starr, **12** 284
Bartlett & Co., **33** 261
Barton & Ludwig, Inc., **21** 96
Barton Beers, Ltd., **29** 219
Barton Brands, **II** 609
Barton Incorporated, **13** 134; **24** 140; **34** 89
Barton Malow Company, 51 40–43
Barton Protective Services Inc., 53 56–58
Bartow Food Company, **25** 332
Barwig Medizinische Systeme. *See* OEC Medical Systems, Inc.
The Baseball Club of Seattle, LP, 50 81–85
Baseline, **58** 167
BASF Aktiengesellschaft, I 305–08, 309, 319, 346–47, 632, 638; **13** 75; **14** 308;

16 462; **18** 47–51 (upd.), 186, 234; **21** 544; **24** 75; **26** 305, 368; **27** 22; **28** 194; **41** 45; **50** 86–92 (upd.); **59** 31
Bashas' Inc., 33 62–64
Basic Resources, Inc. *See* Texas Utilities Company.
Basics, **14** 295
BASIS Information Technologies, Inc., **11** 112–13, 132
The Basketball Club of Seattle, LLC, 50 93–97
Basketball Properties Ltd, **53** 166
Baskin-Robbins Ice Cream Co., **7** 128, 372; **17** 474–75; **25** 366; **29** 18
Basle A.G., **8** 108–09
Bass Anglers Sportsman Society Inc., **52** 192
Bass Brewers Ltd., **15** 441; **29** 85
Bass Brothers Enterprises Inc., **28** 107; **36** 472
Bass Charington, **29** 84
Bass PLC, I 222–24; **III** 94–95; **9** 99, 425–26; **15** 44–47 (upd.); **16** 263; **23** 482; **24** 194; **33** 127; **35** 396; **38** 74–78 (upd.); **43** 226
Bass Pro Shops, Inc., 42 27–30
Bassett Boat Company, **30** 303
Bassett Furniture Industries, Inc., 18 52–55; **19** 275
Bassett Lowke Ltd., **60** 372
Bassett-Walker Inc. *See* VF Corporation.
Bassins Food Chain, **II** 649
BAT Industries plc, I 425–27, 605; **II** 628; **III** 185, 522; **9** 312; **23** 427; **30** 273. *See also* British American Tobacco PLC.
Bata Ltd., 62 27–30
Batavia Wine Company, **13** 134
Bateaux Parisiens, **29** 442
Bates, **16** 545
Bates Chemical Company, **9** 154
Bates Manufacturing Company, **10** 314
Bates Worldwide, Inc., 14 48–51; **26** 500; **33** 65–69 (upd.)
Batesville Casket Company, **10** 349–50
Bath & Body Works, **11** 41; **24** 237
Bath Industries Inc., **18** 117–18
Bath Iron Works Corporation, 12 27–29; **36** 76–79 (upd.)
Bath Plus Inc., **51** 196
Baton Rouge Gas Light Company. *See* Gulf States Utilities Company.
Battelle Laboratories, **25** 260
Battelle Memorial Institute, Inc., 10 138–40 *Cx Batten Barton Durstine .a Osborn $$Batten Barton Durstine & Osborn. *See* Omnicom Group Inc.
Battle Creek Food Company, **14** 557–58
Battle Mountain Gold Company, 23 40–42
Battlefield Equipment Rentals, **21** 499, 501
BATUS Inc., **9** 312; **18** 136; **30** 273; **63** 260
Baublys-Control Laser Corporation. *See* Excel Technology, Inc.
Baudhuin-Anderson Company, **8** 553
Bauer + Kunzi, **64** 226
Bauer Audio Visual, Inc., **24** 96
Bauer Nike Hockey Inc., **36** 347
Bauer Publishing Group, 7 42–43; **20** 53
Bauerly Companies, 61 31–33
Baume & Mercier, **27** 487, 489

Bausch & Lomb Inc., 7 44–47; **10** 46–47; **13** 365–66; **25** 22, 53–57 (upd.), 183; **30** 30; **42** 66; **65** 273–74
Bavaria SA, **36** 52
Bavarian Brewing Limited, **25** 280
Bavarian Specialty Foods, **13** 383
BAX Global, **58** 43
Baxter Healthcare, **36** 497–98
Baxter International Inc., I 627–29; **9** 346; **10** 141–43 (upd.), 198–99; **11** 459–60; **12** 325; **18** 469; **22** 361; **25** 82; **26** 433; **36** 92; **54** 42
Baxter Travenol, **21** 119; **24** 75
The Bay, **16** 216
Bay Area Review Course, Inc., **IV** 623
Bay Cities Transportation Company, **6** 382
Bay Colony Life Insurance Co., **III** 254
Bay Frontier Onoda Co. Ltd., **60** 301
Bay Harbour Management L.C., **28** 55
Bay Networks, Inc., **20** 33, 69; **26** 276; **36** 352
Bay Ridge Savings Bank, **10** 91
Bay Shipbuilding Corporation, **18** 320; **59** 274, 277
Bay State Gas Company, 38 79–82
Bay State Iron Manufacturing Co., **13** 16
Bay State Tap and Die Company, **13** 7
Bay West Paper Corporation. *See* Mosinee Paper Corporation.
Bayard SA, 49 46–49
BayBanks, Inc., 12 30–32
Bayer A.G., I 309–11, 319, 346–47, 350; **12** 364; **13** 75–77 (upd.); **14** 169; **16** 439; **18** 234; **21** 544; **22** 225; **41** 44–48 (upd.); **45** 255; **59** 15; **63** 352
Bayer S.p.A., **8** 179
Bayerische Hypotheken- und Wechsel-Bank AG, II 238–40. *See also* HVB Group.
Bayerische Landesbank, **14** 170; **47** 83
Bayerische Motoren Werke A.G., I 75, 138–40, 198; **11** 31–33 (upd.); **13** 30; **17** 25; **21** 441; **27** 20, 203; **38** 83–87 (upd.)
Bayerische Vereinsbank A.G., II 241–43; **III** 401. *See also* HVB Group.
Bayerische Wagnisbeteiligung GmbH, **27** 192
Bayerische Zellstoff, **IV** 325
Bayernwerk AG, V 555–58, 698–700; **23** 43–47 (upd.); **39** 57
Bayliner Marine Corporation, **22** 116
Bayou Steel Corporation, 31 47–49
Baystate Corporation, **12** 30
Baytree Investors Inc., **15** 87
Bayview Water Company, **45** 277
Bazaar & Novelty. *See* Stuart Entertainment Inc.
Bazar de l'Hotel de Ville, **19** 308
BBA. *See* Bush Boake Allen Inc.
BBAG Osterreichische Brau-Beteiligungs-AG, 38 88–90
BBC. *See* British Broadcasting Corp.
BBC Brown, Boveri Ltd. *See* ABB Ltd.
BBDO. *See* Batten Barton Durstine & Osborn.
BBDO Worldwide Network, **22** 394
BBGI. *See* Beasley Broadcast Group, Inc.
BBME. *See* British Bank of the Middle East.
BBN Corp., 19 39–42
BBO & Co., **14** 433
BBVA. *See* Banco Bilbao Vizcaya Argentaria S.A.

BC Development, **16** 481
BC Partners, **51** 322; **53** 138
BC Property Management Inc., **58** 23
BC TEL. *See* British Columbia Telephone Company.
BCal. *See* British Caledonian Airways.
BCC, **24** 266, 270
BCE, Inc., V **269–71**; **7** 333; **12** 413; **18** 32; **36** 351; **44** 46–50 (upd.)
BCI. *See* Banca Commerciale Italiana SpA.
Bcom3 Group, Inc., **40** 142
BCOP. *See* Boise Cascade Office Products.
BCP Corporation, **16** 228–29
BCPA. *See* British Commonwealth Pacific Airways.
BDB. *See* British Digital Broadcasting plc.
BDB Corp., **10** 136
BDDP. *See* Wells Rich Greene BDDP.
Be Free Inc., **49** 434
BEA. *See* Bank of East Asia Ltd.
BEA Systems, Inc., **36 80–83**
Beach Hill Investments Pty Ltd., **48** 427
Beach Patrol Inc., **29** 181
Beacon Communications Group, **23** 135
Beacon Education Management LLC. *See* Chancellor Beacon Academies, Inc.
Beacon Manufacturing Company, **19** 304–05
Beall-Ladymon, Inc., **24** 458
Bealls, **24** 456
Beamach Group Ltd., **17** 182–83
Beaman Corporation, **16** 96; **25** 390
Bean Fiberglass Inc., **15** 247
Bear Automotive Service Equipment Company, **10** 494
Bear Creek Corporation, **12 444–45**; **38 91–94**; **39** 361
Bear Instruments Inc., **48** 410
Bear Stearns Companies, Inc., **II 400–01**, 450; **10 144–45** (upd.), 382; **20** 313; **24** 272; **52 41–44** (upd.)
Bearings, Inc., **13 78–80**
Beasley Broadcast Group, Inc., **51 44–46**
Beasley Industries, Inc., **19** 125–26
Beatrice Company, **II 467–69**, 475; **9** 318; **12** 82, 87, 93; **13** 162–63, 452; **14** 149–50; **15** 213–14, 358; **16** 160, 396; **19** 290; **24** 273; **26** 476, 494; **28** 475; **42** 92; **62** 89–90. *See also* TLC Beatrice International Holdings, Inc.
Beatrice Foods, **21** 322–24, 507, 545; **25** 277–78; **38** 169; **43** 355
Beatrix Mines Ltd., **62** 164
Beauharnois Power Company, **6** 502
Beaulieu of America, **19** 276
Beauté Prestige International S.A. *See* Shiseido Company Limited.
BeautiControl Cosmetics, Inc., **21 49–52**
Beauty Biz Inc., **18** 230
Beauty Systems Group, Inc., **60** 260
Beazer Homes USA, Inc., **17 38–41**
Beazer Plc., **7** 209
bebe stores, inc., **31 50–52**
BEC Group Inc., **22** 35; **60** 133
BEC Ventures, **57** 124–25
Bechstein, **56** 299
Bechtel Group, Inc., **I 558–59**, 563; **6** 556; **13** 13; **24 64–67** (upd.); **25** 402; **52** 374
Beck & Gregg Hardware Co., **9** 253
Beck's North America, Inc. *See* Brauerei Beck & Co.
Becker Drill, Inc., **19** 247
Becker Group of Germany, **26** 231

Beckett Papers, **23 48–50**
Beckley-Cardy Co., **IV** 623–24; **57** 13
Beckman Coulter, Inc., **22 74–77**
Beckman Instruments, Inc., **14 52–54**; **16** 94
BECOL. *See* Belize Electric Company Limited.
Becton, Dickinson & Company, **I 630–31**; **11 34–36** (upd.); **36 84–89** (upd.); **42** 182–83; **52** 171
Bed Bath & Beyond Inc., **13 81–83**; **14** 61; **18** 239; **24** 292; **33** 384; **41 49–52** (upd.)
Bedcovers, Inc., **19** 304
Beddor Companies, **12** 25
Bedford Chemical, **8** 177
Bedford-Stuyvesant Restoration Corp., **II** 673
Bee Chemicals, **I** 372
Bee Discount, **26** 476
Bee Gee Shoe Corporation, **10** 281
Beech Aircraft Corporation, **II** 87; **8 49–52**, 313; **11** 411, 413; **27** 98; **38** 375; **46** 354
Beech Holdings Corp., **9** 94
Beech-Nut Nutrition Corporation, **21 53–56**; **46** 290; **51 47–51** (upd.)
Beecham Group PLC, **I** 668; **9** 264; **14** 53; **16** 438
Beechcroft Developments Ltd., **51** 173
Beechwood Insurance Agency, Inc., **14** 472
Beeck-Feinkost GmbH, **26** 59
ZAO BeeOnLine-Portal, **48** 419
Beerman Stores, Inc., **10** 281
Beers Construction Company, **38** 437
Behr-Manning Company, **8** 396
Behringwerke AG, **14** 255; **50** 249
BEI Technologies, Inc., **65 74–76**
Beiersdorf AG, **29 49–53**; **41 374–77**
Beijing Contact Lens Ltd., **25** 56
Beijing Dentsu, **16** 168
Beijing-Landauer, Ltd., **51** 210
Beijing Liyuan Co., **22** 487
Beijing Yanshan Petrochemical Company, **22** 263
Beijing ZF North Drive Systems Technical Co. Ltd., **48** 450
Beirao, Pinto, Silva and Co. *See* Banco Espírito Santo e Comercial de Lisboa S.A.
Bejam Group PLC, **II** 678; **33** 206–07
Bekins Company, **15 48–50**; **26** 197
Bel. *See* Fromageries Bel.
Bel Air Markets, **14** 397; **58** 290
Bel Fuse, Inc., **53 59–62**
Belco Oil & Gas Corp., **23** 219; **40 63–65**; **63** 440
Belcom Holding AG, **53** 323, 325
Belden Inc., **19 43–45**
Beldis, **23** 219
Beldoch Industries Corp., **17** 137–38
Belgacom, **6 302–04**; **63 371–72**
Belgian Rapid Access to Information Network Services, **6** 304
Belglas, **16** 420; **43** 307
Belgo Group plc, **31** 41
Belize Electric Company Limited, **47** 137
Belk Stores Services, Inc., **V 12–13**; **19 46–48** (upd.)
Bell Aerospace, **24** 442
Bell Aircraft Company, **11** 267; **13** 267
Bell and Howell Company, **9** 33, **61–64**; **11** 197; **14** 569; **15** 71; **29 54–58** (upd.), 159

Bell Atlantic Corporation, V **272–74**; **9** 171; **10** 232, 456; **11** 59, 87, 274; **12** 137; **13** 399; **18** 33; **25 58–62** (upd.), 91, 497; **27** 22, 365. *See also* Verizon Communications.
Bell Canada Enterprises Inc. *See* BCE, Inc.
Bell Canada International, Inc., **6 305–08**; **12** 413; **21** 308; **25** 102
Bell Communications Research, **13** 58; **25** 496. *See also* Telcordia Technologies, Inc.
Bell Fibre Products, **12** 377
Bell Helicopter Textron Inc., **46 64–67**
Bell Helmets Inc., **22** 458
Bell Industries, Inc., **13** 47; **18** 498; **19** 311; **47 40–43**
Bell Laboratories, **8** 157; **9** 171; **10** 108; **11** 327; **12** 61; **14** 52, 281–82; **23** 181; **34** 257–58. *See also* AT&T Bell Labroatories, Inc.
Bell Mountain Partnership, Ltd., **15** 26
Bell-Northern Research, Ltd. *See* BCE Inc.
Bell Pharmacal Labs, **12** 387
Bell Resources, **III** 729; **10** 170; **27** 473
Bell Sports Corporation, **16 51–53**; **44 51–54** (upd.)
Bell System, **7** 99, 333; **11** 500; **16** 392–93
Bell Telephone Manufacturing, **II** 13
Bellcore. *See* Telcordia Technologies, Inc.
Belle Alkali Co., **7** 308
Bellofram Corp., **14** 43
BellSouth Corporation, V **276–78**; **9** 171, 321; **10** 431, 501; **15** 197; **18** 23, 74, 76; **19** 254–55; **22** 19; **27** 20; **29 59–62** (upd.); **43** 447; **45** 390
Bellway Plc, **45 37–39**
Belmin Systems, **14** 36
Belmont Savings and Loan, **10** 339
Belo Corporation. *See* A.H. Belo Corporation
Beloit Corporation, **8** 243; **14 55–57**; **34** 358; **38** 224, 226–28
Beloit Tool Company. *See* Regal-Beloit Corporation.
Beloit Woodlands, **10** 380
Bemis Company, Inc., **8 53–55**; **26** 43
Ben & Jerry's Homemade, Inc., **10 146–48**; **35 58–62**
Ben Bridge Jeweler, Inc., **60 52–54**
Ben Franklin Retail Stores, Inc. *See* FoxMeyer Health Corporation.
Ben Franklin Savings & Trust, **10** 117
Ben Hill Griffin, **III** 53
Ben Line, **6** 398
Ben Myerson Candy Co., Inc., **26** 468
Ben Venue Laboratories Inc., **16** 439; **39** 73
Benchmark Capital, **49 50–52**; **57** 49
Benchmark Electronics, Inc., **40 66–69**
Benchmark Tape Systems Ltd, **62** 293
Benckiser Group, **37** 269
Benckiser N.V. *See* Reckitt Benckiser plc.
Bendick's of Mayfair. *See* August Storck KG.
Bendix Corporation, **I 141–43**; **7** 356; **8** 545; **9** 16–17; **10** 260, 279; **11** 138; **13** 356–57; **15** 284; **17** 564; **21** 416; **22** 31
Beneficial Corporation, **8 56–58**, 117; **10** 490
Beneficial Finance Company, **27** 428–29
Beneficial Standard Life, **10** 247
Benefit Consultants, Inc., **16** 145
Benefits Technologies, Inc., **52** 382
Benelli Arms S.p.A., **39** 151

Benesse Corporation, **13** 91, 93; **39** 49
Bénéteau SA, **55** 54–56
Benetton Group S.p.A., **8** 171; **10** 149–52; **15** 369; **18** 193; **25** 56; **49** 31; **63** 361–62; **67** 47–51 (upd.)
Benfield Greig Group plc, **53** 63–65
Benguet Corporation, **58** 21–24
Benihana, Inc., **18** 56–59
Benjamin Moore and Co., **13** 84–87; **38** 95–99 (upd.)
Benjamin Sheridan Corporation, **62** 82
Benlee, Inc., **51** 237
Benlox Holdings PLC, **16** 465
Benn Bros. plc, **IV** 687
Bennett Industries, Inc., **17** 371–73
Bennett's Smokehouse and Saloon, **19** 122; **29** 201
Bennigan's, **7** 336; **12** 373; **19** 286; **25** 181
Benpres Holdings, **56** 214
BenQ Corporation, **67** 52–54
Bensdorp, **29** 47
Benson & Hedges, Ltd. *See* Gallaher Limited.
Benson Wholesale Co., **II** 624
Bentalls, **37** 6, 8
Bentex Holding S.A., **48** 209
Bentley Laboratories, **22** 360
Bentley Mills, Inc., **8** 272
Bentley Motor Ltd., **21** 435
Bentley's Luggage Corp., **58** 370
Bentoel, PT, **62** 97
Benton International, Inc., **29** 376
Benton Oil and Gas Company, **47** 44–46
Bentwood Ltd., **62** 342
Benwood Iron Works, **17** 355
Bercy Management. *See* Elior SA.
Beresford International plc, **24** 335; **27** 159
Beretta. *See* Fabbrica D' Armi Pietro Beretta S.p.A.
Bergdorf Goodman Inc., **25** 177; **52** 45–48
Bergen Brunswig Corporation, **V** 14–16, 152; **13** 88–90 (upd.); **18** 97. *See also* AmerisourceBergen Corporation.
Berger Associates, Inc., **26** 233
Berger Bros Company, **62** 31–33
Berger Manufacturing Company, **26** 405
Berges electronic GmbH, **56** 357
Bergstrom Paper Company, **8** 413
Beringer Blass Wine Estates Ltd., **66** 34–37 (upd.)
Beringer Wine Estates Holdings, Inc., **22** 78–81; **36** 472. *See also* Beringer Blass Wine Estates Ltd.
Berisford International plc, **19** 492, 494
Berjaya Group Bhd., **22** 464–65; **57** 84; **67** 55–57
Berk Corp., **52** 193
Berkeley Farms, Inc., **46** 68–70
Berkey Photo Inc., **I** 447
Berkley Dean & Co., **15** 525
Berkley Petroleum Corporation, **52** 30
Berkline Corp., **17** 183; **20** 363; **39** 267
Berkshire Hathaway Inc., **III** 213–15; **18** 60–63 (upd.); **29** 191; **30** 411; **36** 191; **38** 98; **40** 196, 199, 398; **39** 232, 235; **42** 31–36 (upd.); **60** 52; **64** 140, 209
Berkshire Partners, **10** 393
Berkshire Realty Holdings, L.P., **49** 53–55
Berleca Ltd., **9** 395; **42** 269
Berlex Laboratories, Inc., **10** 214; **66** 38–40
Berli Jucker, **18** 180–82

BerlinDat Gesellschaft für Informationsverarbeitung und Systemtechnik GmbH, **39** 57
Berliner Stadtreinigungsbetriebe, **58** 25–28
Berliner Verkehrsbetriebe (BVG), **58** 29–31
Berlitz International, Inc., **IV** 643; **7** 286, 312; **13** 91–93; **39** 47–50 (upd.)
Berman Brothers Fur Co., **21** 525
Berman Buckskin, **21** 525
Bernard C. Harris Publishing Company, Inc., **39** 51–53
Bernard Chaus, Inc., **27** 59–61
Bernard Warschaw Insurance Sales Agency, Inc., **55** 128
Bernardin Ltd., **30** 39
Berndorf Austria, **44** 206
Berndorf Switzerland, **44** 206
Berner Nut Company, **64** 110
Bernheim-Meyer: A l'Innovation. *See* GIB Group.
Bernie Schulman's, **12** 132
Bernina Holding AG, **47** 47–50
Berrios Enterprises, **14** 236
Berry Bearing Company, **9** 254
Berry Petroleum Company, **47** 51–53
Berry Plastics Corporation, **21** 57–59
Bert L. Smokler & Company, **11** 257
Bertelsmann A.G., **IV** 592–94, 614–15; **10** 196; **15** 51–54 (upd.); **17** 399; **19** 285; **22** 194; **26** 19, 43; **30** 67, 70; **31** 375, 378; **43** 63–67 (upd.), 422; **44** 377; **54** 17, 21–22; **61** 88, 241
Bertelsmann Music Group, **52** 428
Bertolini's Authentic Trattorias, **30** 329
Bertram & Graf Gmbh, **28** 45
Bertucci's Corporation, **16** 54–56, 447; **64** 51–54 (upd.)
Berwick Industries, Inc., **35** 130–31
Berwind Corp., **14** 18
Beryl Corp., **26** 149
Beryllium Resources, **14** 80
Berzelius Umwelt-Service, **IV** 141
Besi, **26** 498
Besnier SA, **19** 49–51; **23** 217, 219; **24** 444–45; **25** 83, 85
Bess Mfg., **8** 510
Bessemer Capital Partners L.P., **15** 505
Best Buy Co., Inc., **9** 65–66; **10** 305; **17** 489; **18** 532–33; **19** 362; **23** 51–53 (upd.); **24** 52, 502; **29** 120, 123; **30** 464, 466; **38** 315; **62** 152; **63** 61–66 (upd.)
best energy GmbH, **39** 54, 57
Best Fabric Outlets, **16** 198
Best Holding Corporation. *See* Arkansas Best Corporation.
Best Manufacturing, **15** 490
Best Power, **24** 29
Best Products Inc., **19** 396–97
Best Read Guides Franchise Corp., **36** 341
Best Western, **14** 106; **25** 308
BestChoice Administrators, Inc., **51** 276–77
Bestfoods, **II** 496–97; **22** 82–86 (upd.)
Bestform Group Inc., **54** 403
Bestline Products, **17** 227
Bestmeat Company, **59** 3, 5
Bestop Inc., **16** 184
Bestway Distribution Services, Inc., **24** 126
Bestway Transportation, **14** 505
Beswick, **II** 17
BET Holdings, Inc., **18** 64–66; **22** 224; **25** 213; **34** 43

Beta West Properties, **25** 496–97
Beth Israel Medical Center. *See* Continuum Health Partners, Inc.
Bethesda Research Laboratories, Inc., **17** 287, 289
Bethlehem Steel Corporation, **IV** 35–37, 228, 572–73; **6** 540; **7** 48–51 (upd.), 447, 549–50; **11** 65; **12** 354; **13** 97, 157; **18** 378; **22** 285; **23** 305; **25** 45; **26** 405; **27** 62–66 (upd.); **50** 501–02
Betriebs- und Baugesellschaft GmbH, **53** 285
Better Brands Ltd., **32** 518–19
Betz Laboratories, Inc., **I** 312–13; **10** 153–55 (upd.); **15** 536
Beverage Associates Corp., **67** 317
Beverly Enterprises, Inc., **III** 76–77; **14** 242; **16** 57–59 (upd.); **25** 309
Beverly Hills Savings, **II** 420
Beverly Pest Control, **25** 15
Bevis Custom Furniture, Inc., **12** 263
Bevrachtingskantoor, **26** 280
Bewag AG, **38** 449; **39** 54–57; **57** 395, 397
Bezeq, **25** 266
BFC Construction Corporation, **25** 63–65
The BFGoodrich Company, **V** 231–33; **8** 80–81, 290; **9** 12, 96, 133; **10** 438; **11** 158; **19** 52–55 (upd.); **20** 260, 262; **21** 260; **23** 170; **25** 70; **30** 158; **31** 135; **61** 196. *See also* Goodrich Corporation.
BFI. *See* Browning-Ferris Industries, Inc.
BFP Holdings Corp. *See* Big Flower Press Holdings, Inc.
BG Freight Line Holding B.V., **30** 318
BG plc, **29** 104
BG&E. *See* Baltimore Gas and Electric Company.
BGC Finance, **II** 420
BGJ Enterprises, Inc. *See* Brown Printing Company.
BH Acquisition Corporation, **22** 439
Bharti Telecom, **16** 84
BHC Communications, Inc., **9** 119; **26** 32–34; **31** 109
BHP Billiton, **67** 58–64 (upd.)
BHP Steel of Australia, **18** 380
BHPC Marketing, Inc., **45** 41
Bhs plc, **16** 466; **17** 42–44, 334–35
BHV. *See* Bazar de l'Hotel de Ville.
Bi-Lo Inc., **II** 641; **V** 35; **16** 313
Biacore International AB, **25** 377
Bianchi, **13** 27
Bibb Co., **31** 199
Bibop-Carire S.p.A., **65** 86, 88
BIC Corporation, **8** 59–61; **20** 23; **23** 54–57 (upd.)
BICC PLC, **III** 433–34; **11** 520. *See also* Balfour Beatty plc.
BICE Med Grille, **16** 447
Bicoastal Corporation, **II** 9–11
Bicycle Holding, Inc. *See* United States Playing Card Company.
Bidermann Industries, **22** 122; **41** 129
Biederman & Company, **14** 160
Biedermann Motech, **37** 112
Bieffe, **16** 52
Bierbrauerei Wilhelm Remmer, **9** 86
Biesemeyer Manufacturing Corporation, **26** 363
Biffa Waste Services Ltd. *See* Severn Trent PLC.

Big B, Inc., 17 45–47
Big Bear Stores Co., 13 94–96
Big D Construction Corporation, **42** 432
Big Dog Holdings, Inc., 45 40–42
Big Entertainment, Inc., **58** 164
Big 5 Sporting Goods Corporation, 12 477; **55** 57–59
Big Flower Press Holdings, Inc., 21 60–62; **32** 465–66
Big Foot Cattle Co., **14** 537
Big Guns, Inc., **51** 229
Big Horn Mining Co., **8** 423
Big Idea Productions, Inc., 49 56–59
Big Lots, Inc., 50 98–101
Big M, **8** 409–10
Big O Tires, Inc., 20 61–63
Big Rivers Electric Corporation, 11 37–39
Big Sky Western Bank, **35** 197, 199
Big V Supermarkets, Inc., 25 66–68
Big Y Foods, Inc., 23 169; **53** 66–68
Bigelow-Sanford, Inc., **31** 199
BII. See Banana Importers of Ireland.
Bike Athletics, **23** 449
BIL, **54** 366–68. See also Brierley Investments.
Bilfinger & Berger AG, I 560–61; **55** 60–63 (upd.)
Bill & Melinda Gates Foundation, 41 53–55, 119
Bill Acceptance Corporation Ltd., **48** 427
Bill Blass Ltd., 32 78–80
Bill France Racing, **19** 222
Bill's Casino, **9** 426
Billabong International Ltd., 44 55–58
Billboard Publications, Inc., **7** 15
Billing Concepts Corp., 26 35–38
Billiton International, **IV** 532; **22** 237
BillPoint Inc., **58** 266
Bilsom, **40** 96–97
Bilt-Rite Chase-Pitkin, Inc., **41** 416
Biltwell Company, **8** 249
Bimar Foods Inc., **19** 192
Bimbo Bakeries USA, **29** 341
Bimbo, S.A., **36** 162, 164
Bin Zayed Group, **55** 54, 56
Binderline Development, Inc., **22** 175
Bindley Western Industries, Inc., 9 67–69; **50** 123
The Bing Group, 60 55–58
Bingham Dana LLP, 43 68–71
Binghamton Container Company, **8** 102
Bingo Express Co., Ltd., **64** 290
Bingo King. See Stuart Entertainment Inc.
Binks Sames Corporation, 21 63–66
Binney & Smith Inc., 25 69–72; **58** 313
Binnie & Partners, **22** 89
Binter Canarias. See Iberia.
Bio-Clinic, **11** 486–87
Bio-Dental Technologies Corporation, **46** 466
Bio-Dynamics, Inc., **10** 105, 107; **37** 111
Bio Foods Inc. See Balance Bar Company.
Bio Synthetics, Inc., **21** 386
Biodevelopment Laboratories, Inc., **35** 47
Biogen Inc., 14 58–60; **36** 90–93 (upd.)
Bioindustrias, **19** 475
bioKinetics, **64** 18
Biokyowa, **III** 43; **48** 250
Biomedical Reference Laboratories of North Carolina, **11** 424
Biomega Corp., **18** 422
Biomet, Inc., 10 156–58
Bionaire, Inc., **19** 360

BioScience Communications, **62** 115
Bioscot, Ltd., **63** 351
Biovail Corporation, 47 54–56
Biralo Pty Ltd., **48** 427
Bird & Sons, **22** 14
Bird Corporation, 19 56–58
Birdair, Inc., **35** 99–100
Birds Eye, **32** 474
Birdsall, Inc., **6** 529, 531
Bireley's, **22** 515
Birkbeck, **10** 6
Birkenstock Footprint Sandals, Inc., 12 33–35; **42** 37–40 (upd.)
Birmingham & Midland Bank. See Midland Bank plc.
Birmingham Slag Company, **7** 572–73, 575
Birmingham Steel Corporation, 13 97–98; **18** 379–80; **19** 380; **40** 70–73 (upd.)
Birra Moretti, **25** 281–82
Birra Peroni S.p.A., **59** 357
Biscayne Bank. See Banco Espírito Santo e Comercial de Lisboa S.A.
Biscayne Federal Savings and Loan Association, **11** 481
Bishop & Co. Savings Bank, **11** 114
Bishop National Bank of Hawaii, **11** 114
BISSELL, Inc., 9 70–72; **30** 75–78 (upd.)
Disset Gold Mining Company, **63** 182–83
Bit LLC, **59** 303
Bit Software, Inc., **12** 62
Bitco Corporation, **58** 258
Bits & Pieces, **26** 439
Bitumen & Oil Refineries (Australia) Ltd. See Boral Limited.
Bituminous Casualty Corporation, **58** 258–59
Bivac International, **55** 79
BIW. See Bath Iron Works.
BIZ Enterprises, **23** 390
Bizarro e Milho, Lda., **64** 91
BizBuyer.com, **39** 25
Bizimgaz Ticaret Ve Sanayi A.S., **55** 346
Bizmark, **13** 176
BizMart, **6** 244–45; **8** 404–05
BJ Services Company, 15 534, 536; **25** 73–75
BJ's Pizza & Grill, **44** 85
BJ's Restaurant & Brewhouse, **44** 85
BJ's Wholesale Club, **12** 221; **13** 547–49; **33** 198
BJK&E. See Bozell Worldwide Inc.
BK Tag, **28** 157
BK Vision AG, **52** 357
BL Systems. See AT&T Istel Ltd.
BL Universal PLC, **47** 168
The Black & Decker Corporation, III 435–37, 628, 665; **8** 332, 349; **15** 417–18; **16** 384; **17** 215; **20** 64–68 (upd.); **22** 334; **43** 101, 289; **59** 271; **67** 65–70 (upd.)
Black & Veatch LLP, 22 87–90
Black Box Corporation, 20 69–71
Black Clawson Company, **24** 478
Black Diamond Equipment, Ltd., 62 34–37
Black Entertainment Television. See BET Holdings, Inc.
Black Hawk Broadcasting Group, **10** 29; **38** 17
Black Hills Corporation, 20 72–74
Black Pearl Software, Inc., **39** 396
BlackBerry. See Research in Motion Ltd.

Blackfoot Telecommunications Group, 60 59–62
Blackhawk Holdings, Inc. See PW Eagle Inc.
Blackhorse Agencies, **II** 309; **47** 227
Blacks Leisure Group plc, 39 58–60
The Blackstone Group, **II** 434, 444; **IV** 718; **11** 177, 179; **13** 170; **17** 238, 443; **22** 404, 416; **26** 408; **37** 309, 311; **61** 208
Blackstone Hotel Acquisition Co., **24** 195
Blaine Construction Company. See The Yates Companies, Inc.
Blair Corporation, 25 76–78; **31** 53–55
Blandburgh Ltd., **63** 77
Blanes, S.A. de C.V., **34** 197
BLC Insurance Co., **III** 330
BLD Europe, **16** 168
Blendax, **III** 53; **8** 434; **26** 384
Blessings Corp., 14 550; **19** 59–61
Blimpie International, Inc., 15 55–57; **17** 501; **32** 444; **49** 60–64 (upd.)
Bliss Manufacturing Co., **17** 234–35
Blitz-Weinhart Brewing, **18** 71–72; **50** 112, 114
Bloch & Guggenheimer, Inc., **40** 51–52
Block Drug Company, Inc., 8 62–64; **27** 67–70 (upd.)
Block Financial Corporation, **17** 265; **29** 227
Block Management, **29** 226
Block Medical, Inc., **10** 351
Blockbuster Inc., 9 73–75, 361; **11** 556–58; **12** 43, 515; **13** 494; **18** 64, 66; **19** 417; **23** 88, 503; **25** 208–10, 222; **26** 409; **28** 296; **29** 504; **31** 56–60 (upd.), 339–40; **50** 61. See also Viacom Inc.
Blockson Chemical, **I** 380; **13** 379
Blodgett Holdings, Inc., 61 34–37 (upd.)
Blohm Maschinenbau GmbH, **60** 193
Blonder Tongue Laboratories, Inc., 48 52–55
Bloomberg L.P., 18 24; **21** 67–71; **63** 326
Bloomingdale's Inc., 9 209, 393; **10** 487; **12** 36–38, 307, 403–04; **16** 328; **23** 210; **25** 257; **31** 190
Blount International, Inc., 12 39–41; **24** 78; **26** 117, 119, 363; **48** 56–60 (upd.)
Blow-ko Ltd., **60** 372
BLP Group Companies. See Boron, LePore & Associates, Inc.
BLT Ventures, **25** 270
Blue, **62** 115
Blue Arrow PLC, **9** 327; **30** 300
Blue Bell Creameries L.P., 30 79–81
Blue Bell, Inc., **V** 390–91; **12** 205; **17** 512
Blue Bell Mattress Company, **58** 63
Blue Bird Corporation, 35 63–66
Blue Bunny Ice Cream. See Wells' Dairy, Inc.
Blue Byte, **41** 409
Blue Chip Stamps, **30** 412
Blue Circle Industries PLC, III 669–71, 702. See also Lafarge Cement UK.
Blue Cross and Blue Shield Association, 10 159–61; **14** 84
Blue Cross and Blue Shield Mutual of Northern Ohio, **12** 176
Blue Cross and Blue Shield of Colorado, **11** 175
Blue Cross and Blue Shield of Greater New York, **III** 245–46
Blue Cross and Blue Shield of Minnesota, **65** 41–42

Blue Cross and Blue Shield of Ohio, **15** 114
Blue Cross Blue Shield of Michigan, **12** 22
Blue Cross of California, **25** 525
Blue Cross of Northeastern New York, **III** 245–46
Blue Diamond Growers, 28 56–58
Blue Dot Services, **37** 280, 283
Blue Line Distributing, **7** 278–79
Blue Martini Software, Inc., 59 77–80
Blue Mountain Arts, Inc., 29 63–66
Blue Mountain Springs Ltd., **48** 97
Blue Nile Inc., 61 38–40
Blue Rhino Corporation, 56 34–37
Blue Ribbon Packing Company, **57** 57
Blue Ribbon Sports. See Nike, Inc.
Blue Ridge Lumber Ltd., **16** 11
Blue Shield of California, **25** 527
Blue Square Israel Ltd., 41 56–58
Blue Tee Corporation, **23** 34, 36
Blue Water Food Service, **13** 244
Bluebird Inc., **10** 443
Bluefly, Inc., 60 63–65
BlueScope Steel Limited, **62** 55
Bluewin AG, **58** 337
Blumberg Communications Inc., **24** 96
Blyth and Co., **13** 448, 529
Blyth Industries, Inc., 18 67–69
BM-Telecom, **59** 303
BMC Forestry Corporation, **58** 23
BMC Industries, Inc., 17 48–51; 59 81–86 (upd.)
BMC Real Estate, Inc., **62** 55
BMC Software, Inc., 14 391; **55 64–67; 58** 295
bmd wireless AG, **63** 204
BMG/Music, **37** 192–93. See also Bertelsmann AG.
BMHC. See Building Materials Holding Corporation.
BMI. See Broadcast Music Inc.
BMI Systems Inc., **12** 174
BMML, Confecçoes, Lda., **64** 91
BMO Corp., **III** 209
BMO Nesbitt Burns, **46** 55
BMS Laboratories Ltd., **59** 168
BMW. See Bayerische Motoren Werke.
BNA. See Banca Nazionale dell'Agricoltura; Bureau of National Affairs, Inc.
BNCI. See Banque Nationale Pour le Commerce et l'Industrie.
BNE. See Bank of New England Corp.
BNG, Inc., **19** 487
BNL. See Banca Nazionale del Lavoro S.p.A.
BNP Paribas Group, 36 94–97 (upd.); 42 349
BNS Acquisitions, **26** 247
Boa Shoe Company, **42** 325
Oy Board International AB, **56** 255
Boart Longyear Company, 26 39–42, 69
Boatmen's Bancshares Inc., 15 58–60
BoatsDirect.com, **37** 398
Bob Evans Farms, Inc., 9 76–79; 10 259; **35** 83–84; **63 67–72 (upd.)**
Bob's Red Mill Natural Foods, Inc., 63 73–75
Bobbie Brooks Inc., **17** 384
Bobbs-Merrill, **11** 198
Bobit Publishing Company, 55 68–70
Bobro Products. See BWP Distributors.
BOC Group plc, I 314–16, 358; **11** 402; **12** 500; **25 79–82 (upd.); 63** 56

Boca Resorts, Inc., 37 33–36
BOCAP Corp., **37** 372
Bock Bearing Co., **8** 530
BOCM Fish Feed Group, **56** 257
Boddington, **21** 247
Bodegas y Vinedos Penaflor S.A. See Penaflor S.A.
Bodeker Drug Company, **16** 399
Bodum Design Group AG, 47 57–59
The Body Shop International plc, 11 40–42; 53 69–72 (upd.)
Bodycote International PLC, 63 76–78
Boehringer Gastro Profi, **60** 364
Boehringer Ingelheim GmbH. See C.H. Boehringer Sohn.
Boehringer Mannheim Companies, **37** 111–12
The Boeing Company, I 47–49, 195, 511, 530; **II** 62, 442; **6** 130, 327; **7** 11, 456, 504; **8** 81, 313, 315; **9** 12, 18, 128, 194, 206, 232, 396, 416–17, 458–60, 498; **10 162–65 (upd.),** 262, 316, 369, 536; **11** 164, 267, 277–79, 363, 427; **12** 180, 190–91, 380; **13** 356–58; **21** 140, 143, 436; **24** 21, 84, 85–86, 88–89, 442; **25** 34, 224, 430–31; **26** 117; **28** 195, 225; **32 81–87 (upd.); 36** 122, 190; **38** 372; **48** 218–20; **50** 367
Bofors Nobel Inc., **9** 380–81; **13** 22
Bogen Communications International, Inc., 62 38–41
Bohemia, Inc., 13 99–101; 31 467
Bohm-Allen Jewelry, **12** 112
Bohn Aluminum & Brass, **10** 439
Boise Cascade Corporation, IV 255–56, 333; **6** 577; **7** 356; **8 65–67 (upd.),** 477; **15** 229; **16** 510; **19** 269, 445–46; **22** 154; **31** 13; **32 88–92 (upd.); 36** 509; **37** 140; **52** 55
Bolands Ltd., **II** 649
Bolar Pharmaceutical Co., **16** 529
Boley G.m.b.H., **21** 123
Bolles & Houghton, **10** 355
Bollinger Shipyards, Inc., 61 41–43
Bollore, S.A., **65** 266–67
The Bolsa Chica Company, **8** 300
BolsWessanen N.V. See Koninklijke Wessanen nv.
Bolt, Beranek & Newman Inc., **26** 520
Bolt Security, **32** 373
Bolthouse Farms, Inc., **54** 257
BOMAG, **8** 544, 546
Bombadier Defence Services UK, **41** 412
Bombardier Aerospace Group, **36** 190–91
Bombardier, Inc., **12** 400–01; **16** 78; **25** 423; **27** 281, 284; **34** 118–19; **35** 350–51; **42 41–46 (upd.)**
The Bombay Company, Inc., 10 166–68; 27 429
Bon Appetit Holding AG, II 656; **48 61–63**
Bon Dente International Inc., **39** 320
The Bon Marché, Inc., 9 209; **19** 88, 306, 309; **23 58–60; 26** 158, 160
Bon Secours Health System, Inc., 24 68–71
The Bon-Ton Stores, Inc., 16 60–62; 50 106–10 (upd.); 63 144, 148
Bonanza, **7** 336; **10** 331; **15** 361–63
Bonanza Steakhouse, **17** 320
Bonaventura, **IV** 611
Bond Brewing International, **23** 405
Bond Corporation Holdings Limited, 10 169–71; 54 228

Bondex International, **8** 456
Bonduel Pickling Co. Inc., **25** 517
Bonduelle SA, 51 52–54
Bongrain SA, 19 50; **23** 217, 219; **25 83–85**
Boni & Liveright, **13** 428
Bonifiche Siele, **II** 272
Bonimart, **II** 649
Bonneville International Corporation, 29 67–70; 30 15
Bonneville Power Administration, 50 102–05
Bonnie Plant Farm, **63** 21
Bonnier AB, 52 49–52
Bonnier AB, 52 49–52
Bontrager Bicycles, **16** 495
Bonwit Teller, **13** 43; **17** 43; **54** 304–05
Book-Mart Press, Inc., **41** 111
Book-of-the-Month Club, Inc., 13 105–07
Booker plc, 13 102–04; 31 61–64 (upd.)
Booker Tate, **13** 102
Booklink Technologies, **26** 19
Bookmasters, **10** 136
Books-A-Million, Inc., 14 61–62; 16 161; **41 59–62 (upd.)**
Bookstop, **10** 136
Boole & Babbage, Inc., 25 86–88
Booth Bay, Ltd., **16** 37
Booth Creek Ski Holdings, Inc., 31 65–67
Booth, Inc., **II** 420
Bootprint Entertainment, **31** 240
The Boots Company PLC, I 668, 708; **II** 650; **V 17–19; 8** 548; **18** 51; **19** 122; **24 72–76 (upd.)**
Booz Allen & Hamilton Inc., 10 172–75
Boral Limited, III 672–74; 43 72–76 (upd.)
Borden Cabinet Corporation, **12** 296
Borden, Inc., II 470–73, 486, 498, 538, 545; **7** 127, 129, 380; **11** 173; **15** 490; **16** 43; **17** 56; **22** 84, **91–96 (upd.); 24** 273, 288; **27** 38, 40, 316, 318
Border Fine Arts, **11** 95
Border Television, **41** 352
Borders Group, Inc., 9 361; **10** 137; **15 61–62; 17** 522; **18** 286; **25** 17; **30** 69; **43 77–79 (upd.),** 408; **47** 211
Borders, Perrin and Norrander, **23** 480
Borealis A/S, **30** 205; **45** 8; **61** 346
Borg Instruments, **23** 494
Borg-Warner Australia, **47** 280
Borg-Warner Automotive, Inc., 14 63–66; 23 171; **32 93–97 (upd.)**
Borg-Warner Corporation, III 438–41; **13** 123–25; **14** 63, 65, 357, 541; **25** 74, 253; **41** 79. See also Burns International.
Borland International, Inc., 9 80–82; 10 237, 509, 519, 558; **15** 492; **25** 349; **38** 417
Borman's, Inc., **II** 638; **16** 249
Borneo Airways. See Malaysian Airlines System BHD.
Boron, LePore & Associates, Inc., 45 43–45
Borregaard Osterreich AG, **18** 395
Borror Corporation. See Dominion Homes, Inc.
Borsheim's, **III** 215; **18** 60
Borun Bros., **12** 477
Bosch. See Robert Bosch GmbH.
Boscov's Department Store, Inc., 31 68–70

Bose Corporation, 13 108–10; 36 98–101 (upd.)
Bosendorfer, L., Klavierfabrik, A.G., **12** 297
Bosert Industrial Supply. *See* W.W. Grainger, Inc..
Bossa, **55** 188
Bost Sports Clubs. *See* Town Sports International, Inc.
Boston Acoustics, Inc., 22 97–99
Boston and Maine Corporation, **16** 350
The Boston Beer Company, Inc., 18 70–73, 502; 22 422; 31 383; 50 111–15 (upd.)
Boston Celtics Limited Partnership, 14 67–69
Boston Chicken, Inc., **12** 42–44; **23** 266; **29** 170, 172. *See also* Boston Market Corporation.
The Boston Consulting Group, 9 343; **18** 70; **22** 193; **58 32–35**
Boston Corp., **25** 66
Boston Distributors, **9** 453
Boston Edison Company, 12 45–47
Boston Educational Research, **27** 373
Boston Garden Arena Corporation, **14** 67
Boston Gas Company, **6** 486–88
Boston Globe, **7** 13–16
Boston Herald, **7** 15
Boston Market Corporation, 48 64–67 (upd.); 63 280, 284–85
Boston National Bank, **13** 465
Boston Popcorn Co., **27** 197–98; **43** 218
Boston Professional Hockey Association Inc., 39 61–63
Boston Properties, Inc., 22 100–02
Boston Scientific Corporation, 37 37–40
Boston Technology, **43** 117
Boston Ventures Management, Inc., **17** 444; **27** 41, 393; **54** 334, 337; **65** 374
Boston Whaler, Inc. *See* Reebok International Ltd.
Bostrom Seating, Inc., **23** 306
BOTAS. *See* Türkiye Petrolleri Anonim Ortakliği.
Botswana General Insurance Company, **22** 495
Bottu, **II** 475
BOTWEB, Inc., **39** 95
Bou-Matic, 62 42–44
Bougainville Copper Pty., **IV** 60–61
Boulanger, **37** 22
Boulder Creek Steaks & Saloon, **16** 447
Boulder Natural Gas Company, **19** 411
Boulet Dru DuPuy Petit Group. *See* Wells Rich Greene BDDP.
Boulevard Bancorp, **12** 165
Boulton & Paul Ltd., **31** 398–400
Boundary Gas Inc., **6** 457; **54** 260
Boundary Healthcare, **12** 327
Bourbon. *See* Groupe Bourbon S.A.
Bourdon, **19** 49
Bourjois, **12** 57
Bouverat Industries, **51** 36
Bouygues S.A., I 562–64; 13 206; **23** 475–76; **24 77–80 (upd.); 31** 126, 128; **48** 204
Bovis Construction, **38** 344–45
Bovis Lend Lease, **52** 222
Bovis Ltd., **I** 588
Bow Bangles, **17** 101, 103
Bow Flex of America, Inc. *See* Direct Focus, Inc.
Bow Valley Energy Inc., **47** 397

Bowater PLC, IV 257–59; 8 483–84; **25** 13
Bowdens Media Monitoring Ltd., **55** 289
Bowers and Merena Galleries Inc., **48** 99
Bowery Savings Bank, **9** 173
Bowes Co., **II** 631
Bowling Green Wholesale, Inc. *See* Houchens Industries Inc.
Bowman Gum, Inc., **13** 520
Bowne & Co., Inc., 18 331–32; **23 61–64**
Bowthorpe plc, 33 70–72
Box Innards Inc., **13** 442
BoxCrow Cement Company, **8** 259
The Boy Scouts of America, 34 66–69
Boyd Bros. Transportation Inc., 39 64–66
Boyd Coffee Company, 53 73–75
Boyd Gaming Corporation, 43 80–82
The Boyds Collection, Ltd., 29 71–73
Boyer Brothers, Inc., **14** 17–18
Boyer's International, Inc., **20** 83
Boyles Bros. Drilling Company. *See* Christensen Boyles Corporation.
Boys Market, **17** 558–59
Bozell, Jacobs, Kenyon, and Eckhardt Inc. *See* True North Communications Inc.
Bozell Worldwide Inc., 25 89–91
Bozkurt, **27** 188
Bozzuto's, Inc., 13 111–12
BP Amoco plc, **31** 31, 34; **40** 358; **63** 113
BP Canada. *See* Talisman Energy Inc.
BP p.l.c., 45 46–56 (upd.), 409, 412; **61** 117, 346–47; **62** 12
BPB, **III** 736
BPD, **13** 356
BPI Communications, Inc., **7** 15; **19** 285; **27** 500; **61** 241
BR. *See* British Rail.
Braathens ASA, 47 60–62
Brabants Dagblad BV, **III** 199, 201; **53** 362
Brach and Brock Confections, Inc., 15 63–65; 29 47
Brad Foote Gear Works, **18** 453
Braden Manufacturing, **23** 299–301
Bradford & Bingley PLC, 65 77–80
Bradford Exchange Ltd. Inc., **21** 269
Bradlees Discount Department Store Company, II 666–67; **12 48–50; 24** 461
Bradley Air Services Ltd., 56 38–40
Bradley Lumber Company, **8** 430
Bradstreet Co. *See* The Dun & Bradstreet Corp.
Braegen Corp., **13** 127
Bragussa, **IV** 71
BRAINS. *See* Belgian Rapid Access to Information Network Services.
Brake Bros plc, 45 57–59
BRAL Reststoff-Bearbeitungs-GmbH, **58** 28
Bramalea Ltd., 9 83–85; 10 530–31
Brambles Industries Limited, 24 400; **42 47–50; 57** 258, 260
Bramco, **III** 600
Brand Companies, Inc., **9** 110; **11** 436
Branded Restaurant Group, Inc., **12** 372
Brandeis & Sons, **19** 511
BrandPartners Group, Inc., 58 36–38
Brandt Zwieback-Biskuits GmbH, **44** 40
Brandywine Asset Management, Inc., **33** 261
Brandywine Holdings Ltd., **45** 109

Brandywine Insurance Agency, Inc., **25** 540
Brandywine Iron Works and Nail Factory, **14** 323
Brandywine Valley Railroad Co., **14** 324
Braniff Airlines, **16** 274; **17** 504; **36** 231
Brannock Device Company, 48 68–70
Brascan Corporation, 25 281; **67 71–73**
Brasil Telecom Participaçoes S.A., 57 67–70; 63 378
Brass-Craft Manufacturing Co. *See* Masco Corporation.
Brass Eagle Inc., 34 70–72; 58 87–88
Braswell Motor Freight, **14** 567
Braud & Faucheux. *See* Manitou BF S.A.
Brauerei Beck & Co., 9 86–87; **33 73–76 (upd.)**
Braun GmbH, 17 214–15; **26** 335; **51 55–58**
Brauns Fashions Corporation. *See* Christopher & Banks Corporation.
Brazcot Limitada, **53** 344
Brazos Gas Compressing, **7** 345
Brazos Sportswear, Inc., 23 65–67
Breakthrough Software, **10** 507
Breckenridge-Remy, **18** 216
Breco Holding Company, **17** 558, 561
Bredel Exploitatie B.V., **8** 546
Breed Corp., **63** 224
BREED Technologies, Inc., **22** 31
Bremer Financial Corp., 45 60–63
Brenco Inc., **16** 514
Brenda Mines Ltd., **7** 399
Brennan College Services, **12** 173
Brenntag AG, 8 68–69, 496; **23 68–70 (upd.), 23** 453–54; **59** 387, 389–91
Brent Walker Ltd., **49** 450–51
Brentwood Associates Buyout Fund II LP, **44** 54
Brentwood Corporation, **61** 398
Bresler's Industries, Inc., **35** 121
Breslube Enterprises, **8** 464
Bresser Optik, **41** 264
Brewster Lines, **6** 410
Breyers Ice Cream Co. *See* Good Humor-Breyers.
BRI Bar Review Institute, Inc., **IV** 623; **12** 224
BRI International, **21** 425
Briarpatch, Inc., **12** 109
Briazz, Inc., 53 76–79
Bricorama, **23** 231
Bricotruc, **37** 259
Bridas S.A., **24** 522
Bridel, **19** 49–50; **25** 85
Bridge Communications Inc., **34** 442–43
The Bridge Group, **55** 41
Bridge Technology, Inc., **10** 395
Bridgeport Machines, Inc., 17 52–54
Bridgestone Americas Holding Inc., **64** 133
Bridgestone Corporation, V 234–35; **15** 355; **20** 262; **21 72–75 (upd.); 59 87–92 (upd.)**
Bridgestone/Firestone, **19** 454, 456
BridgeStreet Corporate Housing Worldwide Inc., **58** 194
Bridgewater Properties, Inc., **51** 229
Bridgeway Plan for Health, **6** 186
Bridgford Company, **13** 382
Bridgford Foods Corporation, 27 71–73
Brierly Investment Limited, **19** 156; **24** 399
Briggs and Lundy Lumber Cos., **14** 18
Briggs & Stratton Corporation, 8 70–73; 27 74–78 (upd.); 64 353, 355

Brigham's Inc., **15** 71
Bright Horizons Family Solutions, Inc.,
    31 71–73
Bright of America Inc., **12** 426
Bright Star Technologies, **13** 92; **15** 455;
    41 362
Brighter Vision Learning Adventures, **29**
    470, 472
Brighton & Hove Bus and Coach
    Company, **28** 155–56
Brighton Federal Savings and Loan Assoc.,
    II 420
Brightpoint, Inc., 18 74–77
Brightwork Development Inc., **25** 348
Briker, **23** 231
Brillianty Alrosa, **62** 9
Brillion Iron Works Inc., **23** 306
Brin's Oxygen Company Limited. *See*
    BOC Group plc.
The Brink's Company, IV 180–82; **19**
    319; **58 39–43 (upd.)**
Brinker International, Inc., 10 176–78;
    18 438; **38 100–03 (upd.)**
Brinson Partners Inc., **41** 198
BRIO AB, 24 81–83
Brio Technology, **25** 97
Brioche Pasquier S.A., 58 44–46
Briones Alonso y Martin, **42** 19
Brioni Roman Style S.p.A., 67 74–76
BRISA Auto-estradas de Portugal S.A.,
    64 55–58
Brisco Engineering, **41** 412
Bristol-Erickson, **13** 297
Bristol Gaming Corporation, **21** 298
Bristol Hotel Company, 23 71–73; 38 77
Bristol-Myers Squibb Company, III
    17–19; 7 255; **8** 210, 282–83; **9 88–91**
    (upd.); 10 70; **11** 289; **12** 126–27; **16**
    438; **21** 546; **25** 91, 253, 365; **32** 213;
    34 280, 282, 284; **37 41–45 (upd.); 50**
    538; **51** 223, 225; **58** 180; **59** 307; **63**
    234
Bristow Helicopter Group Ltd., **67** 101
Britannia Airways, **8** 525–26
Britannia Security Group PLC, **12** 10
Britannia Soft Drinks Limited, **38** 77
Britannica Software, **7** 168
Britannica.com, **39** 140, 144
Britches of Georgetowne, **10** 215–16
BRITE. *See* Granada Group PLC.
Brite Voice Systems, Inc., 20 75–78
BriteSmile, Inc., **35** 325
British & Commonwealth Shipping
    Company, **10** 277
British Aerospace plc, I 46, **50–53**, 55,
    74, 83, 132, 532; **7** 9, 11, 458–59; **8**
    315; **9** 499; **11** 413; **12** 191; **14** 36; **21**
    8, 443; **24 84–90 (upd.); 27** 474; **48** 81,
    274
British Airways plc, I 83, **92–95; 14**
    70–74 (upd.); 18 80; **22** 52; **24** 86, 311,
    396, 399–400; **26** 115; **27** 20–21, 466;
    28 25; **31** 103; **33** 270; **34** 398; **37** 232;
    38 104–05; **39** 137–38; **43 83–88**
    (upd.); 52 24–25; **63** 17–18
British American Cosmetics, **I** 427
British American Financial Services, **42**
    450
British American Tobacco PLC, 9 312;
    29 194–95; **34** 39; **49** 367, 369; **50**
    116–19 (upd.); 64 291
British and Foreign Steam Navigation
    Company, **23** 160

British and North American Royal Mail
    Steam Packet Company. *See* Cunard
    Line Ltd.
British-Borneo Oil & Gas PLC, 34
    73–75
British Broadcasting Corporation Ltd., 7
    52–55; 21 76–79 (upd.); 24 192; **39**
    198; **42** 114, 116
British Caledonian Airways, **I** 94–95
British Car Auctions, **14** 321
British Chrome, **III** 699
British Coal Corporation, IV 38–40; **50**
    282
British Columbia Packers, **II** 631–32
British Columbia Telephone Company, 6
    309–11
British Commonwealth Insurance, **III** 273
British Credit Trust, **10** 443
British Data Management, Ltd., **33** 212,
    214
British Digital Broadcasting plc, **24** 192,
    194
British Electric Traction Company. *See*
    Rentokil Initial Plc.
British Energy Plc, 19 391; **49 65–68.**
    See also British Nuclear Fuels PLC.
British European Airways. *See* Jersey
    European Airways (UK) Ltd.
British Gas plc, V 559–63; **6** 478–79; **11**
    97; **18** 365–67; **38** 408; **49** 120–21; **50**
    178. *See also* Centrica plc.
British Gauge and Instrument Company, **13**
    234
British General Post Office, **25** 99–100
British Home Stores PLC. *See* Storehouse
    PLC.
British Independent Television Enterprises
    Ltd. *See* Granada Group PLC.
British Insulated Callender's Cables
    Limited. *See* BICC PLC
British Interactive Broadcasting Ltd., **20** 79
British Land Plc, 10 6; **47** 168; **54 38–41**
British Leyland Motor Corporation, **13**
    286–87; **14** 35–36; **47** 8
British Linen Bank, **10** 336
British Midland plc, 34 398; **38 104–06**
British Motor Corporation, **7** 459; **13** 286
British Motor Holdings, **7** 459
British Newfoundland Corporation, **6** 502
British Nuclear Fuels PLC, 6 451–54; **13**
    458; **50** 281
British Nylon Spinners (BNS), **17** 118
British Oxygen Co. *See* BOC Group.
The British Petroleum Company plc, I
    241, 303; **II** 563; **IV** 61, 280, 363–64,
    378–80, 381–82, 412–13, 450–54, 456,
    466, 472, 486, 497–99, 505, 515,
    524–25, 531–32, 557; **6** 304; **7 56–59**
    (upd.), 140–41, 332–33, 516, 559; **9**
    490, 519; **11** 538; **14** 317; **16** 394,
    461–62; **19** 155, 391; **21 80–84 (upd.),**
    352; **25** 101; **26** 366, 369; **30** 86, 88; **47**
    393. *See also* BP p.l.c.
British Printing and Communications
    Corp., **IV** 623–24, 642; **7** 312; **12** 224
British Rail, **10** 122; **27** 474. *See also*
    British Railways Board.
British Railways, **6** 413
British Railways Board, V 421–24
British Road Services, **6** 413
British Satellite Broadcasting, **10** 170
British Shoe Corporation. *See* Sears plc.
British Sky Broadcasting Group plc, 20
    79–81; 24 192, 194; **60 66–69 (upd.)**

British Steel plc, IV 41–43, 128; **17** 481;
    19 62–65 (upd.), 391; **24** 302; **49** 98,
    101, 104; **59** 225
British Sugar plc, **13** 53; **41** 30, 32–33
British Telecommunications plc, I 83,
    330; **V 279–82; 7** 332–33; **8** 153; **9** 32;
    11 59, 185, 547; **15 66–70 (upd.),** 131;
    16 468; **18** 155, 345; **20** 81; **21** 233; **24**
    370; **25** 101–02, 301; **27** 304; **29** 44.
    See also BT Group plc.
British Thermoplastics and Rubber. *See*
    BTR plc.
British Timken Ltd., **8** 530
British Trimmings Ltd., **29** 133
British Twin Disc Ltd., **21** 504
British Vita plc, 9 92–93; **19** 413–15; **33**
    77–79 (upd.)
British World Airlines Ltd., 18 78–80
Britoil, **IV** 380; **21** 82
Britt Airways, **I** 118
Britt Lumber Co., Inc., **8** 348
Brittania Sportswear, **16** 509
Britvic Soft Drinks Limited, **38** 74, 77
BritWill Healthcare Corp., **25** 504
BRK Brands, Inc., **28** 134
BRK Electronics, **9** 414
Bro-Well, **17** 56
Broad, Inc., **11** 482
Broad River Power Company, **6** 575
Broadband Networks Inc., **36** 352
Broadbandtalentnet.com, **44** 164
Broadbase Software, Inc., **51** 181
Broadcast Music Inc., 23 74–77; 29
    22–23
Broadcast Technology Systems, Inc., **13**
    398
Broadcaster Press, **36** 341
Broadcom Corporation, 34 76–79; 36
    123
Broadcom Eireann Research, **7** 510
Broadcort Capital Corp., **13** 342
Broadgate Property Holdings Limited, **54**
    40
The Broadmoor Hotel, 30 82–85
BroadVision Inc., **18** 543; **38** 432
Broadway & Seymour Inc., **17** 264; **18** 112
Broadway.com, **58** 167
Broadway-Hale Stores, Inc., **12** 356
Broadway Stores, Inc., **31** 193
Brobeck, Phleger & Harrison, LLP, 31
    74–76
Brock Candy Company. *See* Brach and
    Brock Confections, Inc.
Brock Hotel Corp., **13** 472–73; **31** 94
Brock Residence Inn, **9** 426
Brockway Glass Co., **15** 128
Brockway Standard Holdings Corporation.
    See BWAY Corporation.
Broder Bros. Co., 38 107–09
Broderbund Software, Inc., 10 285; **13**
    113–16; 25 118; **29 74–78 (upd.)**
Les broderies Lesage, **49** 83
Brok SA, **54** 315, 317
Broken Hill Proprietary Company Ltd.,
    IV 44–47, 58, 61, 171, 484; **10** 170; **21**
    227; **22 103–08 (upd.); 26** 248; **50**
    199–202. *See also* BHP Billiton.
Bronson Laboratories, Inc., **34** 460
Bronson Pharmaceuticals, **24** 257
Brooke Bond, **32** 475
Brooke Group Ltd., 15 71–73. *See also*
    Vector Group Ltd.
Brooke Partners L.P., **11** 275
Brookfield Athletic Shoe Company, **17** 244

Brookfield International Inc., **35** 388
Brookfield Properties Inc., **67** 72
Brooklyn Union Gas, **6** 455–57; **27** 264–66
Brooks Brothers Inc., **13** 43; **22** 109–12; **24** 313, 316
Brooks Fashion, **29** 164
Brooks Fiber Communications, **41** 289–90
Brooks Fiber Properties, Inc., **27** 301, 307
Brooks, Harvey & Company, Inc., **16** 376
Brooks Shoe Manufacturing Co., **16** 546
Brooks Sports Inc., **32** 98–101
Brookshire Grocery Company, **16** 63–66
Brookstone, Inc., **II** 560; **12** 411; **18** 81–83
Brother Industries, Ltd., **13** 478; **14** 75–76
Brother International, **23** 212
Brothers Foods, **18** 7
Brothers Gourmet Coffees, Inc., **20** 82–85
Brotherton Chemicals, **29** 113
Broughton Foods Co., **17** 55–57
Brown & Bigelow, **27** 193
Brown & Brown, Inc., **41** 63–66
Brown & Haley, **23** 78–80
Brown & Root, Inc., **13** 117–19; **38** 481. See also Kellogg Brown & Root Inc.
Brown & Sharpe Manufacturing Co., **23** 81–84
Brown and Williamson Tobacco Corporation, **I** 426; **14** 77–79; **15** 72; **22** 72–73; **33** 80–83 (upd.)
Brown Boveri. See BBC Brown Boveri.
Brown Brothers Harriman & Co., **45** 64–67
Brown Cow West Corporation, **55** 360
Brown-Forman Corporation, **I** 225–27; **10** 179–82 (upd.); **12** 313; **18** 69; **38** 110–14 (upd.)
Brown Group, Inc., **V** 351–53; **9** 192; **10** 282; **16** 198; **20** 86–89 (upd.)
Brown Institute, **45** 87
Brown Jordan Co., **12** 301
Brown Printing Company, **26** 43–45
Brown-Service Insurance Company, **9** 507
Brown Shipbuilding Company. See Brown & Root, Inc.
Brown, Shipley & Co., Limited, **45** 65
Brown Shoe Co. See Brown Group, Inc.
Browning-Ferris Industries, Inc., **V** 749–53; **8** 562; **10** 33; **17** 552; **18** 10; **20** 90–93 (upd.); **23** 491; **33** 382; **46** 456; **50** 13–14
Browning International, **58** 147
Browning Manufacturing, **II** 19
Browning Telephone Corp., **14** 258
Broyhill Furniture Industries, Inc., **10** 183–85; **12** 308
BRS Ltd., **6** 412–13
Bruce Foods Corporation, **39** 67–69
Bruce Power LP, **49** 65, 67
Bruce's Furniture Stores, **14** 235
Bruckmann, Rosser, Sherill & Co., **27** 247; **40** 51
Bruegger's Corporation, **29** 171; **63** 79–82
Brugman, **27** 502
Brummer Seal Company, **14** 64
Bruno's Inc., **7** 60–62; **13** 404, 406; **23** 261; **26** 46–48 (upd.)
Brunswick Corporation, **III** 442–44, 599; **9** 67, 119; **10** 262; **17** 453; **21** 291; **22**

113–17 (upd.), 118; **30** 303; **40** 30; **45** 175
Brunswick Mining, **64** 297
The Brush Electric Light Company, **11** 387; **25** 44
Brush Electrical Machines, **III** 507–09
Brush Engineered Materials Inc., **67** 77–79
Brush Moore Newspaper, Inc., **8** 527
Brush Wellman Inc., **14** 80–82
Bruxeland S.P.R.L., **64** 91
Bryce Brothers, **12** 313
Brylane Inc., **29** 106–07; **64** 232
Bryn Mawr Stereo & Video, **30** 465
Brynwood Partners, **13** 19
BSA. See The Boy Scouts of America.
BSB, **IV** 653; **7** 392
BSC. See Birmingham Steel Corporation; British Steel Corporation.
BSH Bosch und Siemens Hausgeräte GmbH, **67** 80–84
BSkyB, **IV** 653; **7** 392; **29** 369, 371; **34** 85
BSN Groupe S.A., **II** 474–75, 544; **22** 458; **23** 448. See also Groupe Danone
BSN Medical, **41** 374, 377
BT Group plc, **49** 69–74 (upd.)
BTG, Inc., **45** 68–70; **57** 173
BTI Services, **9** 59
BTM. See British Tabulating Machine Company.
BTR Dunlop Holdings, Inc., **21** 432
BTR plc, **I** 428–30; **8** 397; **24** 88
BTR Siebe plc, **27** 79–81. See also Invensys PLC.
Bublitz Case Company, **55** 151
Buca, Inc., **38** 115–17
Buchanan Electric Steel Company, **8** 114
Buck Consultants, Inc., **32** 459; **55** 71–73
Buck Knives Inc., **48** 71–74
Buckaroo International. See Bugle Boy Industries, Inc.
Buckbee-Mears Company. See BMC Industries, Inc.
Buckeye Business Products Inc., **17** 384
Buckeye Technologies, Inc., **42** 51–54
Buckhorn, Inc., **19** 277–78
The Buckle, Inc., **18** 84–86
Buckley/DeCerchio New York, **25** 180
BUCON, Inc., **62** 55
Bucyrus Blades, Inc., **14** 81
Bucyrus-Erie Company, **7** 513
Bucyrus International, Inc., **17** 58–61
Bud Bailey Construction, **43** 400
Budapest Bank, **16** 14
The Budd Company, **8** 74–76; **20** 359
Buderus AG, **III** 694–95; **37** 46–49
Budgens Ltd., **57** 257; **59** 93–96
Budget Group, Inc., **25** 92–94
Budget Rent a Car Corporation, **6** 393; **9** 94–95; **22** 524; **24** 409; **25** 143; **39** 370; **41** 402
Budgetel Inn. See Marcus Corporation.
Budweiser, **18** 70
Budweiser Budvar, National Corporation, **59** 97–100
Budweiser Japan Co., **21** 320
Buena Vista Home Video. See The Walt Disney Company.
Buena Vista Music Group, **44** 164
Bufete Industrial, S.A. de C.V., **34** 80–82
Buffalo Forge Company, **7** 70–71
Buffalo News, **18** 60
Buffalo Paperboard, **19** 78
Buffalo Wild Wings, Inc., **56** 41–43

Buffets, Inc., **10** 186–87; **22** 465; **32** 102–04 (upd.)
Bugaboo Creek Steak House Inc., **19** 342
Bugatti Industries, **14** 321
Bugle Boy Industries, Inc., **18** 87–88
Buhrmann NV, **41** 67–69; **47** 90–91; **49** 440
Buick Motor Co. See General Motors Corporation.
Build-A-Bear Workshop Inc., **62** 45–48
Builders Emporium, **13** 169; **25** 535
Builders Square, **9** 400; **12** 345, 385; **14** 61; **16** 210; **31** 20; **35** 11, 13. See also Kmart Corporation.
Building Materials Holding Corporation, **52** 53–55
Building One Services Corporation. See Encompass Services Corporation.
Building Products of Canada Limited, **25** 232
Buitoni SpA, **II** 548; **17** 36; **50** 78
Bulgari S.p.A., **20** 94–97
Bulgheroni SpA, **27** 105
Bulkships, **27** 473
Bull. See Compagnie des Machines Bull S.A.
Bull Motors, **11** 5
Bull Run Corp., **24** 404
Bull S.A., **III** 122–23; **43** 89–91 (upd.)
Bull Tractor Company, **7** 534; **16** 178; **26** 492
Bull-Zenith, **25** 531
Bulldog Computer Products, **10** 519
Bulletin Broadfaxing Network Inc., **67** 257
Bulley & Andrews, LLC, **55** 74–76
Bullock's, **31** 191
Bulova Corporation, **12** 316–17, 453; **13** 120–22; **14** 501; **36** 325; **41** 70–73 (upd.)
Bumble Bee Seafoods L.L.C., **24** 114; **64** 59–61
Bundall Computers Pty Limited, **56** 155
Bundy Corporation, **17** 62–65, 480
Bunge Ltd., **62** 49–51
Bunte Candy, **12** 427
Bunzl plc, **IV** 260–62; **12** 264; **31** 77–80 (upd.)
Buquet, **19** 49
Burbank Aircraft Supply, Inc., **14** 42–43; **37** 29, 31
Burberry Ltd., **10** 122; **17** 66–68; **19** 181; **41** 74–76 (upd.); **47** 167, 169
Burda Holding GmbH. & Co., **20** 53; **23** 85–89
Burdines, Inc., **9** 209; **31** 192; **60** 70–73
Bureau de Recherches de Pétrole, **7** 481–83; **21** 203–04
The Bureau of National Affairs, Inc., **23** 90–93
Bureau Veritas SA, **55** 77–79
Burelle S.A., **23** 94–96
Burger and Aschenbrenner, **16** 486
Burger Boy Food-A-Rama, **8** 564
Burger King Corporation, **II** 613–15, 647; **7** 316; **8** 564; **9** 178; **10** 122; **13** 43, 553; **14** 25, 32, 212, 214, 452; **16** 95–97, 396; **17** 69–72 (upd.), 501; **18** 437; **21** 25, 362; **23** 505; **24** 140–41; **25** 228; **26** 284; **33** 240–41; **36** 517, 519; **56** 44–48 (upd.); **63** 282–84
Burgess, Anderson & Tate Inc., **25** 500
Bürhle, **17** 36; **50** 78
Burhmann-Tetterode, **22** 154
Buriot International, Inc., **53** 236

Burke Mills, Inc., 66 41–43
Burke Scaffolding Co., 9 512
BURLE Industries Inc., 11 444
Burlington Coat Factory Warehouse Corporation, 10 188–89; 60 74–76 (upd.)
Burlington Homes of New England, 14 138
Burlington Industries, Inc., V 354–55; 8 234; 9 231; 12 501; 17 73–76 (upd.), 304–05; 19 275
Burlington Mills Corporation, 12 117–18
Burlington Motor Holdings, 30 114
Burlington Northern Santa Fe Corporation, V 425–28; 10 190–91; 11 315; 12 145, 278; 27 82–89 (upd.); 28 495
Burlington Resources Inc., 10 190–92; 11 135; 12 144; 47 238
Burmah Castrol PLC, IV 381–84; 15 246; 30 86–91 (upd.)
Burnards, II 677
Burndy, 19 166
Burney Mountain Power, 64 95
Burns & Ricker, Inc., 40 51, 53
Burns & Wilcox Ltd., 6 290
Burns-Alton Corp., 21 154–55
Burns Companies, III 569; 20 360
Burns International Security Services, III 440; 13 123–25; 42 338. See also Securitas AB.
Burns International Services Corporation, 41 77–80 (upd.)
Burns Lumber Company, Inc., 61 254, 256
Burns, Philp & Company Ltd., 21 496–98; 63 83–86
Burnup & Sims, Inc., 19 254; 26 324
Burpee & Co. See W. Atlee Burpee & Co.
Burr-Brown Corporation, 19 66–68
Burris Industries, 14 303; 50 311
Burroughs Corp., III 165–66; 18 386, 542. See also Unisys Corporation.
Burroughs Mfg. Co., 16 321
Burrups Ltd., 18 331, 333; 47 243
Burry, II 560; 12 410
Burt's Bees, Inc., 58 47–50
The Burton Group plc, V 20–22. See also Arcadia Group plc.
Burton Rubber Processing, 8 347
Burton Snowboards Inc., 22 118–20, 460
Burtons Gold Medal Biscuits Limited, II 466; 13 53
Burwell Brick, 14 248
Busch Entertainment Corporation, 34 36
Bush Boake Allen Inc., 30 92–94; 38 247
Bush Brothers & Company, 45 71–73
Bush Hog, 21 20–22
Bush Industries, Inc., 20 98–100
Bush Terminal Company, 15 138
Business Communications Group, Inc. See Caribiner International, Inc.
The Business Depot, Ltd., 10 498; 55 353
Business Expansion Capital Corp., 12 42
Business Express Airlines, Inc., 28 22
Business Information Technology, Inc., 18 112
Business Men's Assurance Company of America, III 209; 13 476; 14 83–85; 15 30
Business Objects S.A., 25 95–97
Business Post Group plc, 46 71–73
Business Resources Corp., 23 489, 491
Business Science Computing, 14 36
Business Software Association, 10 35
Business Software Technology, 10 394

Business Wire, 25 240
Businessland Inc., III 153; 6 267; 10 235; 13 175–76, 277, 482
Busse Broadcasting Corporation, 7 200; 24 199
BUT S.A., 24 266, 270
Butler Bros., 21 96
Butler Cox PLC, 6 229
Butler Group, Inc., 30 310–11
Butler Manufacturing Company, 12 51–53; 43 130; 62 52–56 (upd.)
Butler Shoes, 16 560
Butterfield & Butterfield. See eBay Inc.
Butterfield & Swire. See Swire Pacific Ltd.
Butterick Co., Inc., 23 97–99
Buttrey Food & Drug Stores Co., 18 89–91
Butzbacher Weichenbau GmbH & Co. KG, 53 352
Buxton, 23 21
buy.com, Inc., 46 74–77
Buzzard Electrical & Plumbing Supply, 9 399; 16 186
BVA Investment Corp., 11 446–47
BWAY Corporation, 24 91–93
BWP Distributors, 29 86, 88
Byerly's, Inc. See Lund Food Holdings, Inc.
Byron Weston Company, 26 105

C&A, 40 74–77 (upd.)
C&A Brenninkmeyer KG, V 23–24
C&E Software, 10 507
C&G. See Cheltenham & Gloucester PLC.
C & G Systems, 19 442
C & H Distributors, Inc., 27 177
C&J Clark International Ltd., 52 56–59
C & O. See Chesapeake and Ohio Railway.
C&R Clothiers, 17 313
C&S Bank, 10 425–26
C&S Co., Ltd., 49 425, 427
C&S/Sovran Corporation, 10 425–27; 18 518; 26 453; 46 52
C & S Wholesale Grocers, Inc., 55 80–83
C&W. See Cable and Wireless plc.
C-COR.net Corp., 38 118–21
C-Cube Microsystems, Inc., 37 50–54; 43 221–22
C.A. Delaney Capital Management Ltd., 32 437
C.A. La Electricidad de Caracas, 53 18
C.A. Muer Corporation, 65 205
C.A.S. Sports Agency Inc., 22 460, 462
C.A. Swanson & Sons. See Vlasic Foods International Inc.
C.D. Haupt, IV 296; 19 226
C.E. Chappell & Sons, Inc., 16 61–62; 50 107
C.E.T. See Club Européen du Tourisme.
C.F. Burns and Son, Inc., 21 154
C.F. Hathaway Company, 12 522
C.F. Martin & Co., Inc., 42 55–58; 48 231
C.F. Mueller Co., 12 332; 47 234
C.F. Orvis Company. See The Orvis Company, Inc.
C.G. Conn, 7 286
C.H. Boehringer Sohn, 39 70–73
C.H. Heist Corporation, 24 111–13
C.H. Masland & Sons. See Masland Corporation.
C.H. Musselman Co., 7 429

C.H. Robinson, Inc., 8 379–80; 11 43–44; 23 357
C.H. Robinson Worldwide, Inc., 40 78–81 (upd.)
C.I. Traders Limited, 61 44–46
C. Itoh & Co., I 431–33; II 679; 7 529; 10 500; 17 124; 26 456. See also ITOCHU Corporation.
C.J. Lawrence, Morgan Grenfell Inc., II 429
C.J. Smith and Sons, 11 3
C.M. Aikman & Co., 13 168
C.M. Armstrong, Inc., 14 17
C.M. Barnes Company, 10 135
C.M. Life Insurance Company, 53 213
C.M. Page, 14 112
C-MAC Industries Inc., 48 369
C.O.M.B. Company, 18 131–33
C. Of Eko-Elda A.B.E.E., 64 177
C/P Utility Services Company, 14 138
C.P.T. Holding B.V., 56 152
C.P.U., Inc., 18 111–12
C.R. Anthony Company, 24 458
C.R. Bard, Inc., 9 96–98; 22 360–61; 65 81–85 (upd.)
C.R. Eggs, Inc., 25 332
C-Tec Corp. See Commonwealth Telephone Enterprises, Inc.
C.V. Gebroeders Pel, 7 429
C.W. Acquisitions, 27 288
C.W. Costello & Associates Inc., 31 131
C.W. Zumbiel Company, 11 422
C. Wuppesahl & Co. Assekuranzmakler, 25 538
CAA. See Creative Artists Agency LLC.
Cabana (Holdings) Ltd., 44 318
Cabela's Inc., 26 49–51
Cable & Wireless HKT, 30 95–98 (upd.)
Cable and Wireless plc, IV 695; V 283–86; 7 332–33; 11 547; 15 69, 521; 17 419; 18 253; 25 98–102 (upd.); 26 332; 27 307; 49 70, 73
Cable London, 25 497
Cable Management Advertising Control System, 25 497
Cable News Network, 9 30; 12 546
Cabletron Systems, Inc., 10 193–94; 10 511; 20 8; 24 183; 26 276
Cablevision Electronic Instruments, Inc., 32 105–07
Cablevision Systems Corporation, 7 63–65; 18 211; 30 99–103 (upd.), 106; 47 421; 67 369. See also Cablevision Electronic Instruments, Inc.
Cablex AG, 58 337
CABLO Metall-Recycling & Handel GmbH, 62 253
Cabot, Cabot & Forbes, 22 100
Cabot Corporation, 8 77–79; 29 79–82 (upd.)
Cabot Medical Corporation, 21 117, 119
Cabot-Morgan Real Estate Co., 16 159
Cabot Noble Inc., 18 503, 507; 50 457
Cabrera Vulcan Shoe Corp., 22 213
Cache Incorporated, 30 104–06
CACI International Inc., 21 85–87
Cacique, 24 237
Cactus Feeders, Inc., 63 120
Cadadia, II 641–42
Cadbury Schweppes PLC, II 476–78, 510, 512, 592; 9 178; 15 221; 22 513; 25 3, 5; 39 383, 385; 49 75–79 (upd.); 52 95; 57 250
CADCAM Technology Inc., 22 196

Caddell Construction Company, **12** 41
Cademartori, **23** 219
Cadence Design Systems, Inc., 10 118; **11 45–48**, 285, 490–91; **35** 346; **38** 188; **48 75–79 (upd.)**
Cadence Industries Corporation, **10** 401–02
Cadet Uniform Services Ltd., **21** 116
Cadillac Fairview Corporation Ltd., **61** 273, 275
Cadillac Plastic, **8** 347
Cadisys Corporation, **10** 119
Cadmus Communications Corporation, 16 531; **23 100–03**
CAE USA Inc., 8 519; **48 80–82**
Caere Corporation, 20 101–03
Caesar's Entertainment Inc., **62** 179
Caesars World, Inc., 6 199–202; 17 318
Caf'Casino, **12** 152
Café Express, **47** 443
Caffarel, **27** 105
Caffè Nero Group PLC, 63 87–89
Cagiva Group, **17** 24; **30** 172; **39** 37
Cagle's, Inc., 20 104–07
Cahners Business Information, 43 92–95
Cahners Publishing, **IV** 667; **12** 561; **17** 398; **22** 442
CAI Corp., **12** 79
Cains Marcelle Potato Chips Inc., **15** 139
Cains Pickles, Inc., **51** 232
Cairncom Pty Limited, **56** 155
Cairo Petroleum Refining Co., **51** 113
Caisse de dépôt et placement du Quebec, **II** 664
Caisse des Dépôts—Développement (C3D), **48** 107
Caisse Nationale de Crédit Agricole, **15** 38–39
Caithness Glass Limited, **38** 402
Cajun Bayou Distributors and Management, Inc., **19** 301
Cajun Electric Power Cooperative, Inc., **21** 470
CAK Universal Credit Corp., **32** 80
CAL. *See* China Airlines.
Cal Circuit Abco Inc., **13** 387
CAL Corporation, **21** 199, 201
Cal-Dive International Inc., **25** 104–05
Cal-Van Tools. *See* Chemi-Trol Chemical Co.
Cal/Ink, **13** 228
Cala, **17** 558
Calais Railroad Company, **16** 348
Calardu Pty Limited, **56** 155
Calavo Growers, Inc., 47 63–66
Calcast Ltd., **63** 304
Calcined Coke Corp., **IV** 402
Calcitherm Group, **24** 144
CalComp Inc., 13 126–29
Calcot Ltd., 33 84–87
Calder Race Course, Inc., **29** 118
Caldera Systems Inc., **38** 416, 420
Caldor Inc., 12 54–56, 508; **30** 57
Caledonian Airways. *See* British Caledonian Airways.
Caledonian Bank, **10** 337
Calgary Power Company. *See* TransAlta Utilities Corporation.
Calgene, Inc., **29** 330; **41** 155
Calgon Corporation, **16** 387; **34** 281
Calgon Vestal Laboratories, **37** 44
Calgon Water Management, **15** 154; **40** 176
Cali Realty. *See* Mack-Cali Realty Corporation.

California Automated Design, Inc., **11** 284
California Bank & Trust, **53** 378
California Cedar Products Company, 58 51–53
California Charter Inc., **24** 118
California Cheese, **24** 444
California Computer Products, Inc. *See* CalComp Inc.
California Dental Supply Co., **19** 289
California Design Studio, **31** 52
California Federal Bank, **22** 275
California Fruit Growers Exchange. *See* Sunkist Growers, Inc.
California Ink Company, **13** 227
California Institute of Technology, **9** 367
California Pacific, **22** 172
California Pizza Kitchen Inc., 15 74–76
California Plant Protection, **9** 408
California Portland Cement Co., **III** 718; **19** 69
California Pro Sports Inc., **24** 404
California Slim, **27** 197
California Sports, Inc., 56 49–52
California Steel Industries, Inc., IV 125; **67 85–87**
Caligen, **9** 92
Caligor. *See* Henry Schein Medical.
CALipso Sales Company, **62** 74
Call-Chronicle Newspapers, Inc., **IV** 678
Callaghan & Company, **8** 526
Callanan Industries, Inc., 60 77–79
Callaway Golf Company, 15 77–79; 16 109; **19** 430, 432; **23** 267, 474; **37** 4; **45 74–77 (upd.); 46** 13
Callaway Wines, **I** 264
Callon Petroleum Company, 47 67–69
Calloway's Nursery, Inc., **12** 200; **51 59–61**
Calmar Co., **12** 127
CalMat Co., 19 69–72
Calor Gas Ltd., **55** 346
Calor Group, **53** 166
Calpine Corporation, 36 102–04
Calspan SRL Corporation, **54** 395
Caltex Petroleum Corporation, IV 560, 562, 718; **7** 483; **19 73–75; 21** 204; **25** 471; **38** 320
Calumatic Group, **25** 82
Calumet Electric Company, **6** 532
Calvert Insurance Co. *See* Gryphon Holdings, Inc.
Calvin Klein, Inc., 9 203; **22 121–24; 25** 258; **27** 329; **32** 476; **55 84–88 (upd.)**
Calyx & Corolla Inc., **37** 162–63
Camargo Foods, **12** 531
Camas. *See* Aggregate Industries plc.
CamBar. *See* Cameron & Barkley Company.
Camber Corporation, **25** 405
Camberley Enterprises Limited, **59** 261
Cambex, **46** 164
Cambrex Corporation, 12 147–48; **16 67–69; 44 59–62 (upd.)**
Cambrian Wagon Works Ltd., **31** 369
Cambridge Applied Nutrition Toxicology and Biosciences Ltd., **10** 105
Cambridge Biotech Corp., **13** 241
Cambridge Electric Co., **14** 124, 126
Cambridge Gas Co., **14** 124
The Cambridge Instrument Company, **35** 272
Cambridge Interactive Systems Ltd., **10** 241

Cambridge SoundWorks, 36 101; Inc., **48 83–86**
Cambridge Steam Corp., **14** 124
Cambridge Technology Partners, Inc., 36 105–08
Cambridge Tool & Mfg. Co. Inc., **48** 268
Cambridge Water, **51** 389
Camden Wire Co., Inc., **7** 408; **31** 354–55
CAMECO, **IV** 436
Camelot Barthropp Ltd., **26** 62
Camelot Community Care, Inc., **64** 311
Camelot Group plc, **34** 140
Camelot Music, Inc., 26 52–54
Cameron & Barkley Company, 13 79; **28 59–61; 63** 288–89
Cameron Ashley Inc., **19** 57
Cameron-Brown Company, **10** 298
Cameron Iron Works, **II** 17
Camintonn, **9** 41–42
Campagnia della Fede Cattolica sotto l'Invocazione di San Paolo, **50** 407
Campbell Cereal Company. *See* Malt-O-Meal Company.
Campbell, Cowperthwait & Co., **17** 498
Campbell Hausfeld. *See* Scott Fetzer Company.
Campbell Industries, Inc., **11** 534
Campbell-Mithun-Esty, Inc., 13 516; **16 70–72**
Campbell Scientific, Inc., 51 62–65
Campbell Soup Company, II 479–81, 508, 684; **7 66–69 (upd.)**, 340; **10** 382; **11** 172; **18** 58; **25** 516; **26 55–59 (upd.); 33** 32; **43** 121; **44** 295; **64** 154
Campeau Corporation, V 25–28; 9 209, 211; **12** 36–37; **13** 43; **15** 94; **17** 560; **22** 110; **23** 60; **31** 192; **37** 13; **60** 72; **67** 34
Camping World, Inc., **56** 5
Campo Electronics, Appliances & Computers, Inc., 16 73–75
Campo Lindo, **25** 85
Campofrío Alimentación S.A, 18 247; **59 101–03**
CAMPSA. *See* Compañia Arrendataria del Monopolio de Petróleos Sociedad Anónima.
Campus Services, Inc., **12** 173
Canada Cable & Wire Company, **9** 11
Canada, Limited, **24** 143
Canada Packers Inc., II 482–85; 41 249
Canada Safeway Ltd., **II** 650, 654
Canada Surety Co., **26** 486
Canada Trust. *See* CT Financial Services Inc.
Canadair, Inc., 7 205; **13** 358; **16 76–78**
Canadian Ad-Check Services Inc., **26** 270
Canadian Airlines International Ltd., **6** 61–62, 101; **12** 192; **23** 10; **24** 400; **59** 20
The Canadian Broadcasting Corporation (CBC), 37 55–58
Canadian Electrolytic Zinc Ltd., **64** 297
Canadian Football League, **12** 457
Canadian Forest Products, **IV** 270. *See also* Canfor Corporation.
Canadian Freightways, Ltd., **48** 113
Canadian General Electric Co., **8** 544–45
Canadian Imperial Bank of Commerce, II 244–46; 7 26–28; **10** 8; **32** 12, 14; **61 47–51 (upd.)**
Canadian Industrial Alcohol Company Limited, **14** 141

Canadian Keyes Fibre Company, Limited of Nova Scotia, **9** 305

Canadian National Railway System, 6 359–62; **12** 278–79; **22** 444; **23** 10

Canadian Niagara Power Company, **47** 137

Canadian Odeon Theatres. *See* Cineplex Odeon Corporation.

Canadian Overseas Telecommunications Corporation, **25** 100

Canadian Pacific Limited, V 429–31; **8** 544–46

Canadian Pacific Railway Limited, 45 78–83 (upd.)

Canadian Steel Foundries, Ltd., **39** 31

Canadian Telephones and Supplies. *See* British Columbia Telephone Company.

Canadian Tire Corporation, Limited, **25** 144

Canadian Utilities Limited, 13 130–32; **56 53–56 (upd.)**

Canadian Vickers, **16** 76

Canal Bank, **11** 105

Canal Electric Co., **14** 125–26

Canal Plus, III 48; **7** 392; **10 195–97**, 345, 347; **23** 476; **29** 369, 371; **31** 330; **33** 181; **34 83–86 (upd.)**

CanalSatellite, **29** 369, 371

CanAmera Foods, **7** 82

Canandaigua Brands, Inc., 34 87–91 (upd.)

Canandaigua Wine Company, Inc., 13 133–35

Cananwill, **III** 344

Canary Wharf Group Plc, 30 107–09

Candela Corporation, 48 87–89

Candie's, Inc., 31 81–84

Candle Corporation, 64 62–65

Candle Corporation of America. *See* Blyth Industries, Inc.

Candle-Lite Inc., **61** 172

Candlewood Hotel Company, Inc., 41 81–83

Candy SpA. *See* Arcor S.A.I.C.

Canfor Corporation, 17 540; **42 59–61**

Cannapp Pty Limited, **56** 155

Cannell Communications, **25** 418

Cannon Design, 63 90–92

Cannon Express, Inc., 53 80–82

Cannon Mills, Co., **9** 214–16

Cannondale Corporation, 16 494; **21 88–90**; **26** 183, 412

Canon Inc., III 120–21; **9** 251; **10** 23; **13** 482; **15** 150; **18 92–95 (upd.)**, 186, 341–42, 383, 386–87; **24** 324; **26** 213; **33** 13; **43** 152, 283–84

Canpotex Ltd., **18** 432

Canrad-Hanovia, **27** 57

Canstar Sports Inc., 15 396–97; **16 79–81**

Canteen Corp., **II** 679–80; **13** 321

Cantel Corp., **11** 184; **18** 32; **20** 76; **30** 388

Canterbury Park Holding Corporation, 42 62–65

Canterra Energy Ltd., **47** 180

Cantine Giorgio Lungarotti S.R.L., 67 88–90

Canton Railway Corp., **IV** 718; **38** 320

Cantor Fitzgerald Securities Corporation, **10** 276–78

CanWest Global Communications Corporation, 35 67–70; **39** 13

Canyon Cafes, **31** 41

Cap Gemini Ernst & Young, 37 59–61

Cap Rock Energy Corporation, 6 580; **46 78–81**

Capacity of Texas, Inc., **33** 105–06

CAPCO. *See* Central Area Power Coordination Group; Custom Academic Publishing Company.

Capco Energy, Inc., **33** 296

Capcom Co., **7** 396

Cape and Vineyard Electric Co., **14** 124–25

Cape Cod-Cricket Lane, Inc., **8** 289

Cape Cod Potato Chip Company, Inc., **41** 233

Cape May Light and Power Company, **6** 449

Cape PLC, **22** 49

Capel Incorporated, 45 84–86

Capezio/Ballet Makers Inc., 62 57–59

AB Capital & Investment Corporation, **6** 108; **23** 381

Capital Advisors, Inc., **22** 4

Capital Bank N.A., **16** 162

Capital Cities/ABC Inc., II 129–31; **III** 214; **11** 331; **15** 464; **18** 60, 62–63, 329; **30** 490; **42** 31, 33–34; **56** 119; **63** 433, 436. *See also* ABC, Inc.

Capital Concrete Pipe Company, **14** 250

Capital Controls Co., Inc. *See* Severn Trent PLC.

Capital Distributing Co., **21** 37

Capital Factors, Inc., **54** 387

Capital-Gazette Communications, Inc., **12** 302

Capital Grille, **19** 342

Capital Group, **26** 187

Capital Holding Corporation, III 216–19. *See also* Providian Financial Corporation.

Capital Life Insurance Company, **11** 482–83

Capital Management Services. *See* CB Commercial Real Estate Services Group, Inc.

Capital One Financial Corporation, 18 535; **52 60–63**

Capital Radio plc, 35 71–73; **39** 199

Capital Trust Corp., **17** 498

Capitalia S.p.A., 65 86–89

Capitol-EMI, **11** 557

Capitol Film + TV International, **IV** 591

Capitol Films, **25** 270

Capitol Pack, Inc., **13** 350

Capitol Printing Ink Company, **13** 227–28

Capitol Publishing, **13** 560

Capitol Transamerica Corporation, **60** 16

Capseals, Ltd., **8** 476

Capstar, **62** 119

CapStar Hotel Company, 21 91–93

Capstone Pharmacy of Delaware, Inc., **64** 27

Captain D's, LLC, 59 104–06

Car-lac Electronic Industrial Sales Inc., **9** 420

Car Toys, Inc., 67 91–93

Car-X, **10** 415

Caraco Pharmaceutical Laboratories Inc., **57** 345–46

Caradco, Inc., **45** 216

Caradon plc, 18 561; **20 108–12 (upd.)**. *See also* Novar plc.

Carando Foods, **7** 174–75

Carat Group. *See* Aegis Group plc.

Caratti Sports, Ltd., **26** 184

Caraustar Industries, Inc., 19 76–78; **44 63–67 (upd.)**

Caravali, **13** 493–94

Caravelle Foods, **21** 500

The Carbide/Graphite Group, Inc., 40 82–84

Carbo PLC, 67 94–96 (upd.)

Carbocol, **IV** 417

Carboline Co., **8** 455

CarboMedics, **11** 458–60

Carbon Research Laboratories, **9** 517

Carbone Lorraine S.A., 33 88–90

La Carbonique, **23** 217, 219

Carborundum Company, 15 80–82. *See also* Carbo PLC.

Cardàpio, **29** 444

Cardell Corporation, **54** 239

Cardem Insurance Co., **III** 767; **22** 546

Cardiac Pacemakers, Inc., **11** 90; **11** 458; **22** 361

Cardinal Distributors Ltd., **II** 663

Cardinal Freight Carriers, Inc., **42** 365

Cardinal Health, Inc., 18 96–98; **50 120–23 (upd.)**

Cardinal Holdings Corporation, **65** 334

Cardiotronics Systems, Inc., **21** 47

Cardo AB, 49 156; **53 83–85**

Cardon-Phonocraft Company, **18** 492

Care Advantage, Inc., **25** 383

Care Group, **22** 276

Career Education Corporation, 45 87–89

Career Horizons Inc., **49** 265

CareerCom Corp., **25** 253

CareerStaff Unlimited Inc., **25** 455

Caremark International Inc., 10 143, **198–200**; **33** 185

Caremark Rx, Inc., 54 42–45 (upd.)

Carenes, SA, **12** 377

CareTel, Inc., **53** 209

CareUnit, Inc., **15** 123

CareWise, Inc., **36** 365, 367–68

Carey Diversified LLC. *See* W.P. Carey & Co. LLC.

Carey International, Inc., 26 60–63

Carey-McFall Corp. *See* Springs Industries, Inc.

Carey Straw Mill, **12** 376

S.A. CARFUEL, **12** 152

Cargill, Incorporated, II 517, **616–18**; **13 136–38 (upd.)**, 186, 351; **18** 378, 380; **21** 290, 500; **22** 85, 426; **25** 332; **31** 17, 20; **40 85–90 (upd.)**; **41** 306

Cargill Trust Co., **13** 467

Cargo Express, **16** 198

Cargo Furniture, **31** 436

Cargolux Airlines International S.A., 47 287; **49 80–82**

CARGOSUR. *See* Iberia.

Carhartt, Inc., 30 110–12

Caribiner International, Inc., 24 94–97

Caribou Coffee Company, Inc., 28 62–65

Carintusa Inc., **8** 271

Carisam International Corp., **29** 511

Caritas Foundation, **22** 411, 413

Carl Ed. Meyer GmbH, **48** 119

Carl I. Brown and Company, **48** 178

Carl Karcher Enterprises, Inc., **19** 435; **46** 94

Carl Marks & Co., **11** 260–61

Carl-Zeiss-Stiftung, III 445–47, 583; **33** 218; **34 92–97 (upd.)**

Carl's Jr. *See* CKE Restaurants, Inc.

Carl's Superstores, **9** 452
Carlin Foods Corporation, **62** 50
Carlin Gold Mining Company, **7** 386–87
Carling O'Keefe Ltd., **I** 229, 254, 269, 438–39; **7** 183; **12** 337; **26** 305
Carlisa S.A. *See* Arcor S.A.I.C.
Carlisle Companies Incorporated, 8 80–82
Carlisle Memory Products, **14** 535
Carlon, **13** 304–06
Carlova, Inc., **21** 54
Carlsberg A/S, 9 99–101; 29 83–85 (upd.)
Carlson Companies, Inc., 6 363–66; 22 125–29 (upd.); 26 147, 439–40; **27** 9, 11; **29** 200; **38** 387
Carlson Wagonlit Travel, 55 89–92
Carlton and United Breweries Ltd., I 228–29, 437–39; **7** 182–83. *See also* Foster's Group Limited
Carlton Cards Retail, Inc., **39** 87; **59** 34–35
Carlton Communications plc, 15 83–85; 23 111, 113; **24** 194; **50 124–27 (upd.); 52** 367
Carlton Foods Corporation, **57** 56–57
Carlton Investments L.P., **22** 514
The Carlyle Group, **11** 364; **14** 43; **16** 47; **21** 97; **30** 472; **43** 60; **49** 444
Carlyle Management Group, **63** 226
Carma Laboratories, Inc., 60 80–82
CarMax, Inc., 26 410; **29** 120, 123; **55 93–95; 65** 113
Carmeda AB, **10** 439
Carmichael Lynch Inc., 28 66–68
Carmike Cinemas, Inc., 14 86–88; 21 362; **37 62–65 (upd.)**
Carmine's Prime Meats, Inc., **35** 84
Carnation Company, II 486–89, 518, 548; **7** 339, 383, 429; **10** 382; **28** 311; **61** 138
Carnaud Basse-Indre, **IV** 228
Carnaud MetalBox, **13** 190; **20** 111; **32** 125–26; **49** 295
Carnegie Brothers & Co., Ltd., **9** 407
Carnegie Corporation of New York, 35 74–77; 45 403–05
Carnegie Foundation for the Advancement of Teaching, **12** 141
Carnegie Group, **41** 371–72
Carnival Corporation, 27 90–92 (upd.); 36 194
Carnival Cruise Lines, Inc., 6 367–68; 21 106; **22** 444–46, 470; **27** 27; **52** 297–98
Caro Produce and Institutional Foods, **31** 359–61
Carol's Shoe Corp., **22** 213
Carolco Pictures Inc., **III** 48; **10** 196
Carolina Biological Supply, **11** 424
Carolina Coach Co., **13** 397–98
Carolina Coin Caterers Corporation, **10** 222
Carolina Energies, Inc., **6** 576
Carolina First Corporation, 31 85–87
Carolina Freight Corporation, 6 369–72
Carolina Paper Board Corporation. *See* Caraustar Industries, Inc.
Carolina Power & Light Company, V 564–66; 23 104–07 (upd.)
Carolina Telephone and Telegraph Company, 10 201–03
Carolinas Capital Funds Group, **29** 132
Carolinas-Virginia Nuclear Power Association, **27** 130

Carpenter Investment and Development Corporation, **31** 279
Carpenter Technology Corporation, 13 139–41
CarpetMAX, **25** 320
Carpets International Plc., **8** 270–71
Carpro, Inc., **65** 127
CARQUEST Corporation, 26 348; **29 86–89**
Carr-Gottstein Foods Co., 17 77–80
Carr-Lowrey Glass Co., **13** 40
Carr-Union Line, **6** 397
Carrabba's Italian Grill, **12** 373–75
CarrAmerica Realty Corporation, 56 57–59
Carre Orban International, **34** 248
Carrefour SA, II 628; **8** 404–05; **10** 204–06; **12** 153; **19** 98, 309; **21** 225; **23** 230–32; 246–47, 364; **24** 475; **27** 207, **93–96 (upd.); 34** 198; **37** 21, 23; **63** 427; **64 66–69 (upd.)**
Carrera-Optyl Group, **54** 319–20
Carrera y Carrera, **52** 147, 149
The Carriage House Companies, Inc., 55 96–98
Carriage Services, Inc., 37 66–68
Carrier Access Corporation, 44 68–73
Carrier Corporation, 7 70–73; 13 507; **22** 6; **26** 4; **29** 216; **67** 239
Carrington Laboratories, **33** 282
Carrington Viyella, **44** 105
Carroll County Electric Company, **6** 511
Carroll Reed Ski Shops, Inc., **10** 215
Carroll's Foods, Inc., 7 477; **22** 368; **43** 382; **46 82–85**
Carrows, **27** 16, 19
Carry Machine Supply, Inc., **18** 513
The Carsey-Werner Company, L.L.C., 37 69–72
Carsmart.com, **47** 34
Carso Global Telecom S.A. de C.V., **34** 362
Carson, Inc., 31 88–90; 46 278
Carson Pirie Scott & Company, II 669; **9** 142; **15 86–88; 19** 324, 511–12; **41** 343–44; **63** 147
Carson Water Company, **19** 411
CART. *See* Championship Auto Racing Teams, Inc.
Carte Blanche, **9** 335
Cartem Wilco Group Inc., **59** 350
CarTemps USA. *See* Republic Industries, Inc.
Carter & Sons Freightways, Inc., **57** 278
Carter Hawley Hale Stores, V 29–32; 8 160; **12** 356; **15** 88; **16** 466; **17** 43, 523; **18** 488; **25** 177; **63** 259–60
Carter Holt Harvey Ltd., **IV** 280; **15** 229; **19** 155
Carter Lumber Company, 45 90–92
Carter Oil Company, **11** 353
Carter-Wallace, Inc., 8 83–86; 38 122–26 (upd.)
Carteret Savings Bank, **III** 263–64; **10** 340
Carterphone, **22** 17
Cartier, **27** 329, 487–89
Cartier Monde, IV 93; **29 90–92**
Cartier Refined Sugars Ltd., **II** 662–63
Cartiera F.A. Marsoni, **IV** 587
Cartiers Superfoods, **II** 678
Cartocor S.A. *See* Arcor S.A.I.C.
Carton Titan S.A. de C.V., **37** 176–77
Cartotech, Inc., **33** 44
Carvel Corporation, 35 78–81

Carver Pump Co., **19** 36
Cary-Davis Tug and Barge Company. *See* Puget Sound Tug and Barge Company.
CASA. *See* Construcciones Aeronauticas S.A.
Casa Bancária Almeida e Companhia. *See* Banco Bradesco S.A.
Casa Cuervo, S.A. de C.V., 31 91–93
Casa Ley, S.A. de C.V., **24** 416
Casa Saba. *See* Grupo Casa Saba, S.A. de C.V.
Casablanca Records, **23** 390
Casalee, Inc., **48** 406
Casarotto Security, **24** 510
Cascade Communications Corp., **16** 468; **20** 8; **24** 50
Cascade Corporation, 65 90–92
Cascade Fertilizers Ltd., **25** 232
Cascade Fiber, **13** 99
Cascade General, Inc., 65 93–95
Cascade Natural Gas Corporation, 6 568; **9 102–04**
Cascade Steel Rolling Mills, Inc., **19** 380–81
Cascades Paperboard International Inc., **66** 324
CasChem, Inc. *See* Cambrex Corporation.
Casco Northern Bank, 14 89–91
Casden Properties, **49** 26
Case Corporation. *See* CNH Global N.V.
Case Technologies, Inc., **11** 504
Casey's General Stores, Inc., 19 79–81
Cash & Go, Inc., **57** 139
Cash America International, Inc., 20 113–15; 33 4; **61 52–55 (upd.)**
Cash Wise Foods and Liquor, **30** 133
Casino, **10** 205; **23** 231; **26** 160; **27** 93–94
Casino America, Inc. *See* Isle of Capri Casinos, Inc.
Casino Frozen Foods, Inc., **16** 453
Casino Guichard-Perrachon S.A., 22 515; **37** 23; **54** 306–07; **59 107–10 (upd.)**
Casino USA, **16** 452
Casinos International Inc., **21** 300
CASIO Computer Co., Ltd., III 448–49, 455; **10** 57; **16 82–84 (upd.); 21** 123; **26** 18; **40 91–95 (upd.)**
Casite Intraco LLC, **56** 156–57
Caspian Pipeline Consortium, **47** 75
Cassa Risparmio Firenze, **50** 410
Cassandra Group, **42** 272
Cassco Ice & Cold Storage, Inc., **21** 534–35
CAST Inc., **18** 20; **43** 17
Cast-Matic Corporation, **16** 475
Castex, **13** 501
Castings, Inc., **29** 98
Castle & Cooke, Inc., II 490–92; 9 175–76; **10** 40; **20 116–19 (upd.); 24** 115. *See also* Dole Food Company, Inc.
Castle Cement, **31** 400
Castle Communications plc, **17** 13
Castle Harlan Investment Partners III, **36** 468, 471
Castle Rock Entertainment, **57** 35
Castle Rock Pictures, **23** 392
Castle Rubber Co., **17** 371
Castlemaine Tooheys, **10** 169–70
Castleton Thermostats. *See* Strix Ltd.
Castorama S.A., **37** 258–60. *See also* Groupe Castorama-Dubois Investissements.

Castro Convertibles. *See* Krause's Furniture, Inc.
Castrorama, **10** 205; **27** 95
Casual Corner Group, Inc., 25 121; **43 96–98**; **52** 229
Casual Male Retail Group, Inc., 52 64–66
Casual Wear Española, S.A., **64** 91
Caswell-Massey Co. Ltd., 51 66–69
CAT Scale Company, **49** 329–30
Catalina Lighting, Inc., 43 99–102 (upd.)
Catalina Marketing Corporation, 18 99–102
Catalogue Marketing, Inc., **17** 232
Catalyst Telecom, **29** 414–15
Catalytica Energy Systems, Inc., 44 74–77
Catalytica Pharmaceuticals Inc., **56** 95
Catamaran Cruisers, **29** 442
Catamount Petroleum Corp., **17** 121
Cataract, Inc., **34** 373
CATCO. *See* Crowley All Terrain Corporation.
Catellus Development Corporation, 24 98–101; **27** 88
Caterair International Corporation, **16** 396
Caterpillar Inc., III 450–53, 458, 463; **9** 310; **10** 274, 377, 381; **11** 473; **12** 90; **13** 513; **15 89–93 (upd.)**, 225; **16** 180, 309–10; **18** 125; **19** 293; **21** 173, 499–501, 503; **22** 542; **34** 44, 46–47; **52** 213–14; **63 93–99 (upd.)**
Cathay Insurance Co., **III** 221; **14** 109
Cathay Pacific Airways Limited, 6 78–80; **18** 114–15; **34 98–102 (upd.)**
Catherines Stores Corporation, 15 94–97; **38** 129
Cathodic Protection Services Co., **14** 325
Catholic Digest, **49** 48
Catholic Order of Foresters, 24 102–05
CatiCentre Ltd. Co, **48** 224
Cato Corporation, 14 92–94
Catteau S.A., **24** 475
Catterton Partners, **62** 137
Cattleman's, Inc., 20 120–22
Cattles plc, 58 54–56
Cattybrook Brick Company, **14** 249
CATV, **10** 319
Caudill Rowlett Scott. *See* CRSS Inc.
Caudle Engraving, **12** 471
Cavalcade Holdings, Inc., **53** 146
Cavallo Pipeline Company, **11** 441
Cavco Industries, Inc., 65 96–99
Cavendish International Holdings, **IV** 695
Cavenham Ltd., **7** 202–03; **28** 163
Caves Altovisto, **22** 344
Caves de Roquefort, **19** 51; **24** 445
Caviton Ltd. *See* Harvey Norman.
CB Commercial Real Estate Services Group, Inc., 21 94–98
CB&I, **7** 76–77
CB&Q. *See* Chicago, Burlington and Quincy Railroad Company.
CB&T. *See* Synovus Financial Corp.
CBE Technologies Inc., **39** 346
CBI Industries, Inc., 7 74–77; **22** 228; **48** 323
CBN. *See* The Christian Broadcasting Network, Inc.
CBN Cable Network, **13** 279–81
CBN Satellite Services, **13** 279
CBOT. *See* Chicago Board of Trade.
CBPI. *See* Companhia Brasileira de Petróleo Ipiranga.

CBR-HCI Construction Materials Corp., **31** 253
CBRL Group, Inc., 35 82–85 (upd.)
CBS Corporation, II 132–34; **III** 188; **IV** 623, 652, 675, 703; **6 157–60 (upd.)**; **11** 327; **12** 75, 561; **16** 201–02; **17** 150, 182; **19** 210, 426, 428; **21** 24; **24** 516–17; **25** 330, 418; **26** 102; **28 69–73 (upd.)**; **30** 269, 272; **36** 326; **43** 170–71. *See also* CBS Television Network.
CBS.MarketWatch.com, **49** 290
CBS Musical Instruments, **16** 201–02; **43** 170–71
CBS Radio Group, **37** 192; **48** 217
CBS Records, **22** 194; **23** 33; **28** 419
CBS Television Network, 66 44–48 (upd.)
CBSI. *See* Complete Business Solutions, Inc.
CBW Inc., **42** 129
CC Beverage Corporation, **48** 97
cc:Mail, Inc., **25** 300
CCA. *See* Container Corporation of America; Corrections Corporation of America.
CCA Industries, Inc., 53 86–89
CCAir Inc., **11** 300
CCB Financial Corp., **33** 293
CCC Franchising Corporation. *See* Primedex Health Systems, Inc.
CCG. *See* The Clark Construction Group, Inc.
CCH Computax, **7** 93–94
CCH Inc., 7 93; **14 95–97**; **33** 461
CCI Asia-Pacific Ltd., **27** 362
CCI Electronique, **10** 113; **50** 43
CCL Industries, Ltd., **15** 129
CCM Inc. *See* The Hockey Company.
CCM Sport Maska, Inc., **15** 396
CCN Group Ltd., **45** 154
CCP Insurance, Inc., **10** 248
CCR, Inc. *See* Rica Foods, Inc.
CCS Automation Systems Inc., **I** 124
CCT. *See* Crowley Caribbean Transport.
CD Titles, Inc., **22** 409
CDB Infotek Inc. *See* ChoicePoint Inc.
CDC. *See* Canada Development Corporation; Control Data Corporation.
CDG Books Canada Inc., **27** 224
CDI. *See* Centre de Dechets Industriels Group.
CDI Corporation, 6 139–41; **54 46–49 (upd.)**
CDMS. *See* Credit and Data Marketing Services.
CDR. *See* Consortium de Realisation.
CDR International, **13** 228
CDS Holding Corp., **22** 475
CDW Computer Centers, Inc., 16 85–87; **52 67–70 (upd.)**
CDX Audio Development, Inc., **18** 208
CE Consulting, **51** 17
CE-Minerals, **IV** 109
CEAG AG, **23** 498
Ceat Ltd., **20** 263
Cébé, **61** 191–92
CEC Entertainment, Inc., 31 94–98 (upd.)
Cecil Gee, **51** 253
Ceco Doors, **8** 544–46
Ceco Industries, Inc. *See* Robertson-Ceco Corporation.
CeCorr Inc., **47** 149

CECOS International, Inc. *See* Browning-Ferris Industries, Inc.
Cedar Fair, L.P., 22 130–32
Cedarapids, Inc., **11** 413; **38** 374, 376; **40** 432
Cedec S.A., **14** 43
Cederroth International AB, **8** 17; **36** 25–26
CEDIS, **12** 153
Cedric Chivers, **35** 243–44
Cegetel SA, **38** 300
CEIR, **10** 255
Celadon Group Inc., 30 113–16
Celanese Corp., I 317–19, 347; **19** 192; **54** 50, 52. *See also* Hoechst Celanese Corporation.
Celanese Mexicana, S.A. de C.V., 54 50–52
Celebrity Entertainment, Inc., **27** 43
Celebrity, Inc., 22 133–35, 472
Celeron Corporation, **20** 258, 262–63
Celestial Farms, **13** 383
Celestial Seasonings, Inc., 16 88–91; **49** 336. *See also* The Hain Celestial Group, Inc.
Celestica Inc., **65** 283–84
Celestron International, **41** 262–63
Celfor Tool Company. *See* Clark Equipment Company.
Celgene Corporation, 67 97–100
Celite Corporation, **7** 291; **10** 43, 45; **60** 16
Celite Mineracao do Nordeste Ltda, **51** 196
Cell Technology, Inc. *See* Air Methods Corporation.
Cell-Tel Monitoring, Inc., **46** 386
Cella Italian Wines, **10** 181
CellAccess Technology, Inc., **25** 162
CellLife International, **49** 280
Cellnet Data Systems, **11** 547; **22** 65
Cellstar Corporation, **18** 74
Cellu-Products Co., **14** 430
Cellular One, **9** 321
Cellular 2000. *See* Rural Cellular Corporation.
CellularOne. *See* Rural Cellular Corporation.
CellularVision, **13** 399
Celluloid Studios, **63** 422
Cellulose & Specialties, **8** 434
Cellulose du Pin, **19** 226–27
Celsius Energy Company, **6** 569
Celtrion, **62** 221
Cement Products, **46** 196
Cement Roadstone Holdings. *See* CRH PLC.
Cementhai Chemicals Co., **56** 322
Cementia, **III** 705
Cementos Apasco, S.A. de C.V., **51** 29
Cementos de Acapulco, S.A. de C.V., **51** 28
Cementos Portland Moctezuma, **21** 261
Cementos Veracruz, S.A. de C.V., **51** 27, 29
Cementownia Chelm, **31** 398, 400
CEMEX S.A. de C.V., 20 123–26; **51** 27–28; **59 111–16 (upd.)**
CEMIG. *See* Companhia Energética De Minas Gerais S.A.
Cemp Investments Ltd., **16** 79–80
Cemsto, **13** 545
CenCall Communications, **10** 433
Cenco, Inc., **10** 262–63; **35** 135
Cencor, **25** 432

Cendant Corporation, 41 363; **44 78–84
(upd.); 48** 234–35; **53** 274–75; **57** 380;
58 77; **61** 267
Cenex Cooperative, **21** 342
Cenex Harvest States Cooperative. *See*
CHS Inc.
Cenex Inc., **19** 160
Centaur Communications, **43** 204, 206
Centel Corporation, 6 312–15, 593; **9**
106, 480; **10** 203; **14** 258; **16** 318; **17** 7;
50 39
**Centennial Communications
Corporation, 39 74–76**
Centennial Technologies Inc., **48** 369
Center Co., Ltd., **48** 182
Center of Insurance, **51** 170
Center Rental & Sales Inc., **28** 387
**Centerior Energy Corporation, V
567–68**
CenterMark Properties, **57** 156
Centerra Corporation, **24** 79
Centertel, **18** 33
Centex Corporation, 8 87–89, 461; **11**
302; **23** 327; **29 93–96 (upd.)**
Centocor Inc., 14 98–100; 36 306
CenTrade, a.s., **64** 73
Central Alloy Steel Corporation. *See*
Republic Engineered Steels, Inc.
**Central and South West Corporation, V
569–70; 21** 197–98; **45** 21
Central Arizona Light & Power Company,
6 545
Central Asia Gas Pipeline Ltd, **24** 522
Central Bank of Scotland, **10** 337
Central Computer Systems Inc., **11** 65
Central Detallista, S.A. de C.V., **12** 154;
16 453
Central Electric & Gas Company. *See*
Centel Corporation.
Central Electric and Telephone Company,
Inc. *See* Centel Corporation.
Central Elevator Co., **19** 111
**Central European Media Enterprises
Ltd., 61 56–59**
Central Fiber Products Company, **12** 376
Central Florida Press, **23** 101
Central Freight Lines, Inc., **53** 249
**Central Garden & Pet Company, 23
108–10; 58 57–60 (upd.)**
**Central Hudson Gas And Electricity
Corporation, 6 458–60**
Central Illinois Public Service Company.
See CIPSCO Inc.
**Central Independent Television, 7
78–80; 15** 84; **23 111–14 (upd.); 50**
125
Central Indiana Power Company, **6** 556
Central Investment Corp., **12** 184
**Central Japan Railway Company, 43
103–06**
Central Maine Power, 6 461–64; 14 126
Central Mining and Investment Corp., **IV**
23, 79, 95–96, 524, 565
Central National Bank, **9** 475
Central National Bank & Trust Co., **13** 467
Central Nebraska Packing, **10** 250
Central Newspapers, Inc., 10 207–09
Central Ohio Mobile Power Wash. *See*
MPW Industrial Services, Inc.
Central Pacific Railroad, **13** 372
Central Park Bank of Buffalo, **11** 108
Central Parking Corporation, 18 103–05
Central Penn National Corp., **11** 295
Central Point Software, **10** 509

Central Public Service Corporation, **6** 447;
23 28
Central Public Utility Corp., **13** 397
Central Research Laboratories, **22** 194
Central Savings and Loan, **10** 339
Central Solvents & Chemicals Company, **8**
100
Central Songs, **22** 193
**Central Soya Company, Inc., 7 81–83;
31** 20; **36** 185, 187
**Central Sprinkler Corporation, 29
97–99**
Central States Indemnity, **18** 62
Central Supply Company. *See* Granite
Rock Company.
Central Telephone & Utilities Corporation.
See Centel Corporation.
Central Terminal Company, **6** 504
Central Textile, **16** 36
Central Trust Co., **11** 110
Central Union Telephone Company, **14**
251, 257
**Central Vermont Public Service
Corporation, 54 53–56**
Central West Public Service Company. *See*
Centel Corporation.
Centralab Inc., **13** 398
Centrale Verzorgingsdienst Cotrans N.V.,
12 443
Centran Corp., **9** 475
Centre de Dechets Industriels Group, **IV**
296; **19** 226
Centre Investissements et Loisirs, **48** 107
Centre Partners Management LLC, **18** 355;
24 482
Centrepoint Properties Ltd., **54** 116–17
Centrica plc, 29 100–05 (upd.)
Centron DPL Company, Inc., **25** 171
Centronics Corp., **16** 192
Centros Commerciales Pryca, **23** 246, 248
Centrum Communications Inc., **11** 520
CenTrust Federal Savings, **10** 340
Centura Software, **10** 244
Centuri Corporation, 54 57–59
Centurion Brick, **14** 250
Century Aluminum Company, 52 71–74
Century Bakery. *See* Dawn Food Products,
Inc.
Century Brewing Company. *See* Rainier
Brewing Company.
**Century Business Services, Inc., 52
75–78**
Century Casinos, Inc., 53 90–93
Century Cellular Network, Inc., **18** 74
**Century Communications Corp., 10
210–12; 52** 9
Century Data Systems, Inc., **13** 127
Century Electric Company, **13** 273
Century Finance, **25** 432
Century Hutchinson, Ltd., **13** 429
Century Manufacturing Company, **26** 363
Century Papers, Inc., **16** 387
Century Savings Assoc. of Kansas, **II** 420
Century Supply Corporation, **39** 346
**Century Telephone Enterprises, Inc., 9
105–07; 54 60–63 (upd.)**
Century Theatres, Inc., 31 99–101
Century Tool Co., **III** 569; **20** 360
Century 21 Real Estate, **II** 679; **11** 292; **21**
97; **25** 444; **59** 345; **61** 267
Century Wood Door Ltd., **63** 268
CenturyTel. *See* Century Telephone
Enterprises, Inc.
CEP Industrie, **55** 79

CEPA. *See* Consolidated Electric Power
Asia.
CEPAM, **21** 438
CEPCO. *See* Chugoku Electric Power
Company Inc.
Cephalon, Inc., 45 93–96
CEPSA. *See* Compañia Española de
Petroleos S.A.
Cera Trading Co. *See* Toto Ltd.
Ceradyne, Inc., 65 100–02
Ceramconsult AG, **51** 196
Ceramesh, **11** 361
Ceramic Art Company, **12** 312
Ceramic Supply Company, **8** 177
Ceramic Tile International, Inc., **53** 176
Cerberus Limited, **6** 490
Cerco S.A., **62** 51
Cereal and Fruit Products, **32** 519
Cereal Industries, **II** 466
Cereal Packaging, Ltd., **13** 294; **50** 294
Cereal Partners Worldwide, **10** 324; **13**
294; **36** 234, 237; **50** 295
Cereol SA, **36** 185; **62** 51
CERES, **55** 178
Cerestar, **36** 185, 187
Ceresucre, **36** 185
Ceridian Corporation, **10** 257; **38** 58
Cerner Corporation, 16 92–94
Cerro de Pasco Corp., **40** 411
Cerro Metal Products Company, **16** 357
CertainTeed Corporation, 16 8; **19** 58;
35 86–89
Certanium Alloys and Research Co., **9** 419
Certegy, Inc., 63 100–03
Certified Grocers of Florida, Inc., **15** 139
Certified Laboratories, **8** 385
Certified TV and Appliance Company, **9**
120
Certus International Corp., **10** 509
Cerulean, **51** 249, 251
Cerus, **23** 492
Cerveceria Cuahtémoc Moctezuma, **25** 281
Cerveceria Cuauhtemoc, **19** 10
Cerveceria Moctezuma, **23** 170
Cerveceria Polar, I 230–31. *See also*
Empresas Polar SA.
Ceska Nezavisla Televizni Spolecnost, **61**
56
Ceské aerolinie, a.s., 66 49–51
Cesky Telecom, a.s., 64 70–73
Cessna Aircraft Company, 8 49–51,
90–93, 313–14; **26** 117; **27 97–101
(upd.); 34** 431, 433; **36** 190; **44** 309
CET. *See* Compagnie Européenne de
Télésecurité.
CET 21, **61** 56, 58
Cetelem S.A., 21 99–102
Cetus Corp., **III** 53; **7** 427; **10** 78, 214; **41**
201; **50** 193
CF&I Steel Corporation, **8** 135
CF AirFreight, **6** 390; **25** 149
CF Braun, **13** 119
CF Holding Corporation, **12** 71
CFC Investment Company, **16** 104
CFM. *See* Compagnie Française du
Méthane.
CFP. *See* Compagnie Française des
Pétroles.
CFS Continental, Inc., **II** 675; **26** 504
CG&E. *See* Cincinnati Gas & Electric
Company.
CGE. *See* Alcatel Alsthom.
CGIP, **57** 380
CGM. *See* Compagnie Générale Maritime.

CGR Management Corporation, **51** 85
CH Mortgage Company I Ltd., **58** 84
Chace Precision Metals, Inc., **29** 460–61
Chaco Energy Corporation. *See* Texas
    Utilities Company.
Chadbourne & Parke, 36 109–12
Chadwick's of Boston, Ltd., 27 348; **29**
    106–08
Chalet Suisse International, Inc., **13** 362
Chalk Line Productions, Inc., **58** 124
Chalk's Ocean Airways. *See* Flying Boat,
    Inc.
Challenge Corp. Ltd. *See* Fletcher
    Challenge Ltd.
Challenger Airlines, **22** 219
Challenger Minerals Inc., **9** 267
Challenger Series, **55** 312
The Chalone Wine Group, Ltd., 36
    113–16
Chamberlain Group, Ltd., **23** 82
Chambers Corporation, **8** 298; **17** 548–49
Chambon Offshore International, **60** 149
Chambosse Brokerage Co., **29** 33
Champ Industries, Inc., **22** 15
Champalimaud, **36** 63
Champcork–Rolhas de Champanhe SA, **48**
    118
Champion Engineering Co., **III** 582
Champion Enterprises, Inc., 17 81–84;
    22 207
Champion Forge Co., **41** 366
Champion, Inc., **8** 459; **12** 457
Champion Industries, Inc., 28 74–76
Champion International Corporation,
    III 215; **IV** 263–65, 334; **12** 130; **15**
    229; **18** 62; **20 127–30 (upd.); 22** 352;
    26 444; **47** 189, 191
Champion Modular Restaurant Company,
    Inc. *See* Checkers Drive-Up Restaurants
    Inc.
Champion Productions, **56** 74
Champion Products Inc., **27** 194
Champion Spark Plug Co., **II** 17; **III** 593
Championship Auto Racing Teams, Inc.,
    37 73–75
Champlin Petroleum Company, **10** 83
Champps Americana, **27** 480–82
Champs Sports, **14** 293, 295. *See also*
    Venator Group Inc.
Chancellor Beacon Academies, Inc., 53
    94–97
Chancellor Media Corporation, 24
    106–10; 35 247
Chancery Law Publishing Ltd., **17** 272
Chandeleur Homes, Inc., **17** 83
The Chandris Group, **11** 377
Chanel SA, 12 57–59; 23 241; **49 83–86**
    (upd.)
Changchun Terumo Medical Products Co.
    Ltd., **48** 395
Channel Master Corporation, **15** 134
Channel One Communications Corp., **22**
    442
Channel Tunnel Group, **13** 206
Chansam Investments, **23** 388
Chantex Inc., **18** 519
Chantiers de l'Atlantique, **9** 9
Chaparral Steel Co., 8 522–24; **13**
    142–44; 18 379; **19** 380
Chapman Printing Company. *See*
    Champion Industries, Inc.
Chapman Valve Manufacturing Company,
    8 135
Chappel Music, **23** 389

Chapters Campus Bookstores Company, **58**
    187
Chapters Inc., **62** 153
Charan Industries Inc., **18** 519
Charan Toy Co., Inc., **18** 519
Chargeurs International, 6 373–75, 379;
    20 79; **21 103–06 (upd.); 29** 369, 371
Charise Charles Ltd., **9** 68
Charles B. Perkins Co., **II** 667; **24** 461
Charles Barker, plc, **25** 91
Charles D. Burnes Co., Inc. *See* The
    Holson Burnes Group, Inc.
Charles E. Smith Residential Realty Inc.,
    49 29
Charles Huston & Sons, **14** 323
Charles Krug Winery, **50** 387
Charles M. Schulz Creative Associates, **39**
    95
The Charles Machine Works, Inc., 64
    74–76
Charles of the Ritz Group Ltd., **64** 334
Charles Phillips & Co. Ltd., **II** 677
Charles R. McCormick Lumber Company,
    12 407
Charles Revson Inc. *See* Revlon Inc.
Charles River Laboratories
    International, Inc., 25 55; **42 66–69**
The Charles Schwab Corporation, II
    228; **8 94–96; 18** 552; **22** 52; **26 64–67**
    (upd.); 34 407; **38** 430; **59** 75
Charles Scribner's Sons, **7** 166
The Charles Stark Draper Laboratory,
    Inc., 35 90–92
Charlesbank Capital Partners LLC, **44** 54
Charleston Consolidated Railway, Gas and
    Electric Company, **6** 574
Charley Brothers, **II** 669
Charley's Eating & Drinking Saloon, **20** 54
Charlie Browns, **24** 269–70
Charlotte Russe Holding, Inc., 35 93–96
Charming Shoppes, Inc., 8 97–98; 38
    127–29; 39 287, 289; **64** 232
Charoen Pokphand Group, 62 60–63
Charrington United Breweries, **38** 76
Chart House Enterprises, Inc., II
    613–14; **17** 70, 71, **85–88; 56** 46
Chart Industries, Inc., 21 107–09
Charter Club, **9** 315
Charter Communications, Inc., 33 91–94
Charter Consolidated, **IV** 23, 119–20; **16**
    293; **49** 234
Charter Corp., **III** 254; **14** 460
Charter Golf, Inc. *See* Ashworth, Inc.
Charter Medical Corporation, **31** 356
Charter National Life Insurance Company,
    11 261
Charter Oak Capital Partners, **58** 88
Charter Oil Co., **II** 620; **12** 240
Charterhouse Japhet, **24** 269
ChartHouse International Learning
    Corporation, 49 87–89
Chartwell Associates, **9** 331
Chartwell Investments, **44** 54
Chartwell Land plc, **V** 106; **24** 266, 269
Chas. H. Tompkins Co., **16** 285–86
Chas. Levy Company LLC, 60 83–85
Chase Drier & Chemical Co., **8** 177
The Chase Manhattan Corporation, II
    247–49; III 248; **9** 124; **10** 61; **13**
    145–48 (upd.), 476; **14** 48, 103; **15**
    38–39; **16** 460; **17** 498; **23** 482; **36** 358;
    46 316. *See* J.P. Morgan Chase & Co.
Chase National Bank, **25** 114

Chaston Medical & Surgical Products, **13**
    366
Chateau Communities, Inc., 37 76–79
Chateau St. Jean, **22** 80
Chateau Souverain, **22** 80
Chateau Ste. Michelle Winery, **42** 245, 247
Chateaux St. Jacques, **24** 307
Chatham Technologies Inc., **38** 189
Chatillon. *See* John Chatillon & Sons Inc.
Chattanooga Gas Company, Inc., **6** 577
Chattanooga Gas Light Company, **6** 448;
    23 30
Chattanooga Medicine Company. *See*
    Chattem, Inc.
Chattem, Inc., 17 89–92
Chatto, Virago, Bodley Head & Jonathan
    Cape, Ltd., **13** 429; **31** 376
Chautauqua Airlines, Inc., 38 130–32
CHC Helicopter Corporation, 67 101–03
Check Express, **33** 4–5
Check Point Software Technologies Ltd.,
    20 238
Checker Auto Parts. *See* CSK Auto
    Corporation.
Checker Holding, **10** 370
Checker Motors Corp., **10** 369
Checkers Drive-Up Restaurants Inc., 14
    452; **16 95–98; 46** 98
CheckFree Corporation, **22** 522
Checkpoint Systems, Inc., 39 77–80
The Cheesecake Factory Inc., 17 93–96
Cheetham Salt Ltd., **62** 307
Chef Boyardee, **10** 70; **50** 538
Chef Francisco, **13** 383
Chelan Power Company, **6** 596
Chelsea GCA Realty, Inc., **27** 401
Chelsea Milling Company, 29 109–11
Chelsfield PLC, 67 104–06
Cheltenham & Gloucester PLC, 61
    60–62
Chem-Nuclear Systems, Inc., **9** 109–10
Chemcentral Corporation, 8 99–101
Chemdal Corp., **13** 34; **59** 31
Chemed Corporation, 13 149–50; 15
    409–11; **16** 386–87; **49** 307–08; **61** 314
Chemetron Process Equipment, Inc., **8** 545
Chemex Pharmaceuticals, Inc., **8** 63; **27** 69
Chemfab Corporation, 35 97–101
ChemFirst, Inc., **27** 316
Chemgas Holding BV, **41** 340
Chemgrout, **26** 42
Chemi-Trol Chemical Co., 16 99–101
Chemical Banking Corporation, II 234,
    250–52, 254; **9** 124, 361; **12** 15, 31; **13**
    49, 147, 411; **14 101–04 (upd.); 15** 39;
    21 138; **26** 453; **38** 253
Chemical Grouting Co. Ltd., **51** 179
Chemical Process Co., **7** 308
Chemical Products Company, **13** 295
Chemical Waste Management, Inc., 9
    108–10; 11 435–36
Chemicon International, Inc., **63** 353
Chemie Linz, **16** 439
Cheminor Drugs Limited, **59** 168
Chemins de fer de Paris à Lyon et à la
    Méditerranée, **6** 424
Chemins de fer du Midi, **6** 425
Chemische Werke Hüls GmbH. *See* Hüls
    A.G.
Chemise Lacoste, **9** 157
ChemLawn, **13** 199; **23** 428, 431; **34** 153
Chemmar Associates, Inc., **8** 271
Chemonics Industries–Fire-Trol, **17**
    161–62

Chemonics International–Consulting, **17** 161–62

Chempump, **8** 135

Chemquest Sdn Bhd, **57** 292, 294–95

Cheney Bigelow Wire Works, **13** 370

CHEP Pty Ltd., **42** 50

Cherokee Inc., 18 106–09

Cherry-Burrell Process Equipment, **8** 544–45

Cherry Hill Cheese, **7** 429

Cherry Lane Music Publishing Company, Inc., 62 64–67

Cherry-Levis Co., **26** 172

Chesapeake and Ohio Railroad, **10** 43; **13** 372. See also CSX Corporation.

Chesapeake Corporation, 8 102–04; 10 540; **25** 44; **30 117–20 (upd.)**

Chesapeake Microwave Technologies, Inc., **32** 41

Chesapeake Paperboard Company, **44** 66

Chesapeake Utilities Corporation, 56 60–62

Chesebrough-Pond's USA, Inc., 8 105–07; 9 319; **17** 224–25; **22** 123

Chessington World of Adventures, **55** 378

Chester Engineers, **10** 412

Cheung Kong (Holdings) Limited, IV 693–95; 18 252; **20 131–34 (upd.); 23** 278, 280; **49** 199. See also Hutchison Whampoa Ltd.

Chevignon, **44** 296

Chevrolet, **9** 17; **19** 221, 223; **21** 153; **26** 500

Chevron Corporation, IV 385–87; 9 391; **10** 119; **12** 20; **17** 121–22; **18** 365, 367; **19** 73, 75, **82–85 (upd.); 25** 444; **29** 385; **40** 354, 357–58; **41** 391, 394–95; **49** 121; **57** 152; **63** 310. See also ChevronTexaco Corporation.

Chevron U.K. Ltd., **15** 352

ChevronTexaco Corporation, 47 70–76 (upd.), 343; 63 104, 113

Chevy Chase Savings Bank, **13** 439

Chevy's, Inc., **33** 140

Chevy's Mexican Restaurants, **27** 226

ChexSystems, **22** 181

Cheyenne Software, Inc., 12 60–62; 25 348–49

CHF. See Chase, Harris, Forbes.

Chi-Chi's Inc., 13 151–53; 14 195; **25** 181; **51 70–73 (upd.)**

CHI Construction Company, **58** 84

Chiasso Inc., 53 98–100

Chiat/Day Inc. Advertising, 9 438; **11 49–52. See also TBWA/Chiat/Day.**

Chiba Gas Co. Ltd., **55** 375

Chiba Mitsukoshi Ltd., **56** 242

Chibu Electric Power Company, Incorporated, V 571–73

Chic by H.I.S, Inc., 20 135–37; 54 403

Chicago and North Western Holdings Corporation, 6 376–78

Chicago and Southern Airlines Inc. See Delta Air Lines, Inc.

Chicago Bears Football Club, Inc., 33 95–97

Chicago Board of Trade, 41 84–87

Chicago Bridge & Iron Company, **7** 74–77

Chicago Cutlery, **16** 234

Chicago Faucet Company, **49** 161, 163

Chicago Flexible Shaft Company, **9** 484

Chicago Heater Company, Inc., **8** 135

Chicago Magnet Wire Corp., **13** 397

Chicago Medical Equipment Co., **31** 255

Chicago Motor Club, **10** 126

Chicago Musical Instrument Company, **16** 238

Chicago National League Ball Club, Inc., 66 52–55

Chicago O'Hare Leather Concessions Joint Venture Inc., **58** 369

Chicago Pacific Corp., **III** 573; **12** 251; **22** 349; **23** 244; **34** 432

Chicago Pizza & Brewery, Inc., 44 85–88

Chicago Pneumatic Tool Co., **III** 427, 452; **7** 480; **26** 41; **28** 40

Chicago Rawhide Manufacturing Company, **8** 462–63

Chicago Rollerskate, **15** 395

Chicago Screw Co., **12** 344

Chicago Shipbuilding Company, **18** 318

Chicago Sun-Times, Inc., **62** 188

Chicago Times, **11** 251

Chicago Title and Trust Co., **10** 43–45

Chicago Title Corp., **54** 107

Chicago Tribune. See Tribune Company.

Chichibu Concrete Industry Co. Ltd., **60** 301

Chick-fil-A Inc., 23 115–18

Chicken of the Sea International, 24 114–16 (upd.)

Chico's FAS, Inc., 45 97–99; 60 348

Chicobel S.A. Belgique. See Leroux S.A.S.

Chief Auto Parts, **II** 661; **32** 416

Chieftain Development Company, Ltd., **16** 11

Child World Inc., **13** 166; **18** 524

Childers Products Co., **21** 108

Children's Book-of-the-Month Club, **13** 105

Children's Comprehensive Services, Inc., 42 70–72

Children's Discovery Centers of America. See Knowledge Learning Corporation.

Children's Hospitals and Clinics, Inc., 54 64–67

The Children's Place Retail Stores, Inc., 37 80–82

Children's Record Guild, **13** 105

Children's Television Workshop, **12** 495; **13** 560; **35** 75

Children's World Learning Centers, **II** 608; **13** 48

Children's World Ltd. See The Boots Company PLC.

ChildrenFirst, Inc., 59 117–20

Childtime Learning Centers, Inc., 34 103–06

Chiles Offshore Corporation, 9 111–13; 57 126; **59** 322

Chili's Grill & Bar, **10** 331; **12** 373–74; **19** 258; **20** 159

Chilton Corp., **25** 239; **27** 361

Chilton Publications. See Cahners Business Information.

Chimney Rock Winery, **48** 392

China Airlines, 34 107–10; 39 33–34

China Coast, **10** 322, 324; **16** 156, 158

China.com Corp., **49** 422

China Communications System Company, Inc. (Chinacom), **18** 34

China Development Corporation, **16** 4

China Eastern Airlines Co. Ltd., 31 102–04; 46 10

China Foreign Transportation Corporation, **6** 386

China International Capital Corp., **16** 377

China International Trade and Investment Corporation, **IV** 695; **6** 80; **18** 113, 253; **19** 156; **25** 101; **34** 100. See also CITIC Pacific Ltd.

China Life Insurance Company Limited, 65 103–05

China Light & Power, **6** 499; **23** 278–80

China Merchants International Holdings Co., Ltd., 52 79–82

China Mutual Steam Navigation Company Ltd., **6** 416

China National Aviation Company Ltd., **18** 115; **21** 140; **66** 192

China National Cereals, Oils & Foodstuffs Import and Export Corporation, **24** 359

China National Heavy Duty Truck Corporation, **21** 274

China National Machinery Import and Export Corporation, **8** 279

China National Petroleum Corporation, 18 483; **46 86–89**

China OceanShipping Company, **50** 187

China Resources (Shenyang) Snowflake Brewery Co., **21** 320

China Southern Airlines Company Ltd., 31 102; **33 98–100; 46** 10

China Telecom, 50 128–32

China Unicom, **47** 320–21

Chinese Electronics Import and Export Corp., **I** 535

Chinese Metallurgical Import and Export Corp., **IV** 61

Chinese Petroleum Corporation, IV 388–90, 493, 519; **31 105–108 (upd.)**

The Chinet Company, **30** 397

Chipcom, **16** 392

Chipotle Mexican Grill, Inc., 63 280, 284–85; **67 107–10**, 268

Chippewa Shoe, **19** 232

CHIPS and Technologies, Inc., 6 217; **9 114–17**

Chiquita Brands International, Inc., 7 84–86; 21 110–13 (upd.); 38 197; **60** 268

ChiRex, **38** 380

Chiro Tool Manufacturing Corp., **III** 629

Chiron Corporation, 7 427; **10 213–14; 36 117–20 (upd.); 45** 94

Chisholm Coal Company, **51** 352

Chisholm-Mingo Group, Inc., 41 88–90

Chitaka Foods International, **24** 365

Chittenden & Eastman Company, 58 61–64

Chiyoda Fire and Marine, **III** 404

Chock Full o'Nuts Corp., 17 97–100; 20 83

Chocoladefabriken Lindt & Sprüngli AG, 27 102–05; 30 220

Choice Hotels International Inc., 14 105–07; 26 460

ChoiceCare Corporation, **24** 231

ChoicePoint Inc., 31 358; **65 106–08**

Chorus Line Corporation, 25 247; **30 121–23**

Chotin Transportation Co., **6** 487

Chouinard Equipment. See Lost Arrow Inc.

Chris-Craft Industries, Inc., 9 118–19; 26 32; **31 109–12 (upd.); 46** 313

Christensen Boyles Corporation, 19 247; **26 68–71**

Christensen Company, **8** 397

Christiaensen, **26** 160

The Christian Broadcasting Network, Inc., 13 279; **52 83–85; 57** 392

Christian Dalloz SA, 40 96–98
Christian Dior S.A., 19 86–88; 23 237,
    242; **49 90–93 (upd.)**
Christian Salvesen Plc, 45 10, 100–03
The Christian Science Publishing
    Society, 55 99–102
Christian Supply Centers, Inc., **45** 352
Christiana Bank og Kredietklasse, **40** 336
Christie, Mitchell & Mitchell, **7** 344
Christie's International plc, 15 98–101;
    39 81–85 (upd.); 49 325
Christofle Orfevrerie, **44** 206
Christofle SA, 40 99–102
Christopher & Banks Corporation, 42
    73–75
Christopher Charters, Inc. *See* Kitty Hawk,
    Inc.
Chromalloy American Corp., **13** 461; **54**
    330
Chromalloy Gas Turbine Corp., **13** 462; **54**
    331
Chromatic Color, **13** 227–28
Chromcraft Revington, Inc., 15 102–05;
    26 100
Chromium Corporation, 52 103–05
Chrompack, Inc., **48** 410
The Chronicle Publishing Company,
    Inc., 23 119–22
Chronimed Inc., 26 72–75
Chronoservice, **27** 475
Chrysalis Group plc, 22 194; **40 103–06**
Chrysler Corporation, I 144–45, 504; **7**
    205, 461; **8** 74–75, 315, 505–07; **9** 118,
    349–51, 472; **10** 174, 198, 264–65, 290,
    317, 353, 430; **11 53–55 (upd.),**
    103–04, 429; **13** 61, 501, 555; **14** 321,
    367, 457; **16** 184, 322, 484; **17** 184; **18**
    173–74, 308, 493; **20** 359–60; **22** 52,
    55, 175, 330; **23** 352–54; **25** 89–91, 93,
    142–44, 329; **26** 403, 501; **31** 130; **36**
    34, 242; **38** 480–81; **43** 163–64; **47** 436;
    50 197. *See also* DaimlerChrysler AG
Chrysler Financial Company, LLC, **45** 262
CHS Inc., 60 86–89
CHT Steel Company Ltd., **51** 352
CH2M Hill Ltd., 22 136–38
Chubb Corporation, III 220–22, 368; **11**
    481; **14 108–10 (upd.); 29** 256; **37**
    83–87 (upd.); 45 109
Chubb, PLC, 50 133–36
Chubb Security plc, **44** 258
Chubu Electric Power Company, Inc., V
    571–73; 46 90–93 (upd.)
Chuck E. Cheese, **13** 472–74; **31** 94
Chugach Alaska Corporation, 60 90–93
Chugai Boyeki Co. Ltd., **44** 441
Chugai Pharmaceutical Co., Ltd., 8
    215–16; **10** 79; **50 137–40**
Chugai Shogyo Shimposha. *See* Nihon
    Keizai Shimbun, Inc.
Chugoku Electric Power Company Inc.,
    V 574–76; 53 101–04 (upd.)
Chugoku Funai Electric Company Ltd., **62**
    150
Chunghwa Picture Tubes, **23** 469
Chuo Rika Kogyo Corp., **56** 238
Chuo Trust & Banking Co. *See* Yasuda
    Trust and Banking Company, Limited.
Chupa Chups S.A., 38 133–35
Church & Company, **45** 342, 344
Church & Dwight Co., Inc., 29 112–15
Church and Tower Group, **19** 254
Church's Chicken, 7 26–28; **15** 345; **23**
    468; **32** 13–14; **66 56–59**

Churchill Downs Incorporated, 29
    116–19
Churchill Insurance Co. Ltd., **III** 404
CI Holdings, Limited, **53** 120
Cianbro Corporation, 14 111–13
Cianchette Brothers, Inc. *See* Cianbro
    Corporation.
Ciba-Geigy Ltd., I 632–34; IV 288; **8** 63,
    108–11 (upd.), 376–77; **9** 153, 441; **10**
    53–54, 213; **15** 229; **18** 51; **21** 386; **23**
    195–96; **25** 55; **27** 69; **28** 193, 195; **30**
    327; **36** 36, 119; **50** 90; **61** 226–27. *See*
    also Novartis AG.
CIBC. *See* Canadian Imperial Bank of
    Commerce.
CIBC Wood Gundy Securities Corp., **24**
    482
Ciber, Inc., 18 110–12
Ciby 2000, **24** 79
CIC. *See* Commercial Intertech
    Corporation.
CIC Investors #13 LP, **60** 130
CICI, **11** 184
Cie Continental d'Importation, **10** 249
Cie des Lampes, **9** 9
Cie Générale d'Electro-Ceramique, **9** 9
Cie.Generale des Eaux S.A., **24** 327
CIENA Corporation, 54 68–71
Cifra, S.A. de C.V., 8 556; **12 63–65; 26**
    524; **34** 197–98; **35** 320; **63** 430. *See*
    also Wal-Mart de Mexico, S.A. de C.V.
Cifunsa. *See* Compania Fundidora del
    Norte, S.A.
Ciga Group, **54** 345, 347
Cigarrera La Moderna, **21** 260; **22** 73
Cigarros la Tabacelera Mexicana
    (Cigatam), **21** 259
CIGNA Corporation, III 223–27; 10 30;
    11 243; **22 139–44 (upd.),** 269; **38** 18;
    45 104–10 (upd.)
CIGWELD, **19** 442
Cii-HB, **III** 678; **16** 122
Cilbarco, **II** 25
CILCORP Energy Services Inc., **60** 27
Cilva Holdings PLC, **6** 358
Cima, **14** 224–25
CIMA Precision Spring Europa, **55** 305–06
Cimaron Communications Corp., **38** 54
Cimarron Utilities Company, **6** 580
CIMCO Ltd., **21** 499–501
Cimeco S.A. *See* Grupo Clarín S.A.
Cimenteries CBR S.A., **23** 325, 327
Ciments Français, 40 107–10
Ciments Lafarge France/Quebec. *See*
    Lafarge Cement
Cimos, **7** 37
Cinar Corporation, 40 111–14
Cincinnati Bell, Inc., 6 316–18; 29 250,
    252
Cincinnati Electronics Corp., **II** 25
Cincinnati Financial Corporation, 16
    102–04; 44 89–92 (upd.)
Cincinnati Gas & Electric Company, 6
    465–68, 481–82
Cincinnati Milacron Inc., 12 66–69. *See*
    also Milacron, Inc.
Cincom Systems Inc., 15 106–08
Cine-Groupe, **35** 279
Cinecentrum, **IV** 591
Cinemark, **21** 362; **23** 125
CinemaSource, **58** 167
Cinemax, **IV** 675; **7** 222–24, 528–29; **23**
    276

Cineplex Odeon Corporation, II 145, **6**
    161–63; 14 87; **23 123–26 (upd.); 33**
    432
Cinerama Group, **67** 291
Cinnabon Inc., 13 435–37; 23 127–29; 32
    12, 15
Cinquième Saison, **38** 200, 202
Cinram International, Inc., 43 107–10
Cinsa. *See* Compania Industrial del Norte,
    S.A.
Cintas Corporation, 16 228; **21 114–16,**
    507; **30** 455; **51 74–77 (upd.)**
Cintra. *See* Concesiones de Infraestructuras
    de Transportes, S.A.; Corporacion
    Internacional de Aviacion, S.A. de C.V.
Cinven, **49** 451; **63** 49–50
Cipal-Parc Astérix, **27** 10
Ciprial S.A., **27** 260
CIPSCO Inc., 6 469–72, 505–06. *See*
    also Ameren Corporation.
CIR. *See* Compagnie Industriali Riunite
    S.p.A.
Circa Pharmaceuticals, **16** 529; **56** 375
Circle A Ginger Ale Company, **9** 177
Circle International Group Inc., **17** 216; **59**
    171
The Circle K Company, II 619–20; 7
    113–14, 372, 374; **20 138–40 (upd.); 25**
    125; **26** 447; **49** 17
Circle Plastics, **9** 323
Circon Corporation, 21 117–20
Circuit City Stores, Inc., 9 65–66,
    120–22; 10 235, 305–06, 334–35,
    468–69; **12** 335; **14** 61; **15** 215; **16** 73,
    75; **17** 489; **18** 533; **19** 362; **23** 51–53,
    363; **24** 52, 502; **26** 410; **29 120–24**
    (upd.); 30 464–65; **55** 93, 107; **63** 61;
    65 109–14 (upd.)
Circus Circus Enterprises, Inc., 6
    203–05; 19 377, 379
Circus Distribution, Inc. *See* DC Shoes,
    Inc.
Circus Knie, **29** 126
Circus World, **16** 389–90
Cirque du Soleil Inc., 29 125–28
Cirrus Design Corporation, 44 93–95
Cirrus Logic, Inc., 9 334; **11 56–57; 25**
    117; **48 90–93 (upd.)**
CIS Acquisition Corporation, **56** 134
CIS Mortgage Maker Ltd., **51** 89
Cisco Systems, Inc., 11 58–60, 520; **13**
    482; **16** 468; **19** 310; **20** 8, 33, 69, 237;
    25 499; **26** 276–77; **34 111–15 (upd.),**
    441, 444; **36** 300; **38** 430; **43** 251
Cise, **24** 79
Cisneros Group of Companies, 47 312;
    54 72–75
CIT Alcatel, **9** 9–10
CIT Financial Corp., **8** 117; **12** 207
CIT Group, Inc., **13** 446, 536; **63** 404
Citadel Communications Corporation,
    35 102–05
Citadel General, **III** 404
Citadel, Inc., **27** 46
CitFed Bancorp, Inc., 16 105–07
CITGO Petroleum Corporation, II
    660–61; **IV 391–93,** 508; **7** 491; **31**
    113–17 (upd.); 32 414, 416–17; **45** 252,
    254
Citibanc Group, Inc., **11** 456
Citibank, **III** 243, 340; **9** 124; **10** 150; **11**
    418; **13** 146; **14** 101; **23** 3–4, 482; **25**
    180, 542; **50** 6; **59** 121, 124–25. *See*
    also Citigroup Inc

Citibank of Mexico, **34** 82
CITIC Pacific Ltd., **16** 481; **18 113–15**; **20** 134. *See also* China International Trade and Investment Corporation.
Citicasters Inc., **23** 293–94
Citicorp, **II 253–55**; **III** 397; **7** 212–13; **8** 196; **9 123–26 (upd.)**, 441; **10** 463, 469; **11** 140; **12** 30, 310, 334; **13** 535; **14** 103, 108, 235; **15** 94, 146, 281; **17** 324, 559; **21** 69, 145; **22** 169, 406; **25** 198, 542. *See also* Citigroup Inc.
Cities Service Company, **12** 542; **22** 172
CitiFinancial, **59** 121, 125
Citifor, **19** 156
Citigroup Inc., **30 124–28 (upd.)**; **42** 332; **46** 316; **54** 143; **59 121–27 (upd.)**
Citivision PLC, **9** 75
Citizen Watch Co., Ltd., **III 454–56**, 549; **13** 121–22; **21 121–24 (upd.)**; **23** 212; **41** 71–82
Citizen's Federal Savings Bank, **10** 93
Citizen's Industrial Bank, **14** 529
Citizens Bank, **11** 105
Citizens Bank of Hamilton, **9** 475
Citizens Bank of Savannah, **10** 426
Citizens Building & Loan Association, **14** 191
Citizens Federal Savings and Loan Association, **9** 476
Citizens Financial Group, Inc., **12** 422; **42 76–80**
Citizens Gas Co., **6** 529
Citizens Gas Fuel Company. *See* MCN Corporation.
Citizens Gas Light Co., **6** 455
Citizens Gas Supply Corporation, **6** 527
Citizens Insurance Company of America, **63** 29
Citizens Mutual Savings Bank, **17** 529–30
Citizens National Bank, **13** 466; **25** 114; **41** 312
Citizens National Gas Company, **6** 527
Citizens Saving and Trust Company, **17** 356
Citizens Savings & Loan Association, **9** 173
Citizens Savings and Loan Society. *See* Citizens Mutual Savings Bank.
Citizens State Bank, **41** 178, 180
Citizens Telephone Company, **14** 257–58
Citizens Utilities Company, **7 87–89**; **37** 124–27
Citizens' Savings and Loan, **10** 339
Citrix Systems, Inc., **44 96–99**
Citroën. *See* Automobiles Citroen; PSA Peugeot Citroen S.A.
City and Suburban Telegraph Association. *See* Cincinnati Bell Inc.
City Capital Associates, **31** 211
City Centre Properties Ltd. *See* Land Securities PLC.
City Collection Company, Inc., **58** 184
City Finance Company, **10** 340; **11** 261
City Investing Co., **13** 363
City Light and Traction Company, **6** 593
City Light and Water Company, **6** 579
City Market Inc., **12** 112
City National Bank of Baton Rouge, **11** 107
City of Seattle Water Department, **12** 443
City of Westminster Assurance Company Ltd., **59** 246
The City Post Publishing Corp., **12** 359
City Public Service, **6 473–75**

City Savings, **10** 340
City Stores Company, **16** 207
Civic Drugs, **12** 21
Civic Parking LLC, **18** 105
Civil & Civic Contractors. *See* Lend Lease Corporation Ltd.
Civil Aviation Administration of China, **31** 102; **33** 98
Civil Service Employees Insurance Co., **III** 214
CJ Banks. *See* Christopher & Banks Corporation.
CJ Corporation, **62 68–70**
CKE Restaurants, Inc., **19 89–93**, 433, 435; **25** 389; **27** 19; **29** 203; **37** 349–51; **46 94–99 (upd.)**
CKS Group Inc. *See* marchFIRST, Inc.
CKS Inc., **23** 479
Clabir Corp., **12** 199
Claeys, **22** 379–80
Claire's Stores, Inc., **17 101–03**; **18** 411
Clairol, **III** 17–18; **17** 110
Clal Electronic Industries Ltd., **24** 429
Clal Group, **18** 154
CLAM Petroleum, **7** 282
Clancy Paul Inc., **13** 276
Clapp-Eastham Company. *See* GenRad, Inc.
Clara Candy, **15** 65
CLARCOR Inc., **17 104–07**; **56** 157; **61 63–67 (upd.)**
Claremont Technology Group Inc., **31** 131
Clariden Bank, **21** 146–47; **59** 142, 144
Claridge Group, **25** 266, 268
Clarify Corp., **38** 431
Clarion Company Ltd., **64 77–79**
Clarion Hotels and Resorts, **25** 309
Clark & McKenney Hardware Co. *See* Clarcor Inc.
Clark Bar Candy Company, **53** 304
The Clark Construction Group, Inc., **8 112–13**
Clark, Dietz & Associates-Engineers. *See* CRSS Inc.
Clark Equipment Company, **7** 513–14; **8 114–16**; **10** 265; **13** 500; **15** 226; **55** 221
Clark Estates Inc., **8** 13
Clark Filter, Inc., **17** 104
Clark Materials Handling Company, **7** 514
Clark Retail Enterprises Inc., **37** 311
Clark-Schwebel, Inc., **28** 195
Clarkins, Inc., **16** 35–36
Clarksburg Casket Co., **56** 23
CLASSA. *See* Compañia de Líneas Aéreas Subvencionadas S.A.
Classic FM plc, **39** 198–200
Classic Vacation Group, Inc., **46 100–03**
Claudel Roustand Galac, **19** 50
Claussen Pickle Co., **12** 371
Claxson Interactive Group, **54** 74
Clayco Construction Company, **41** 225–26
Clayton Brown Holding Company, **15** 232
Clayton Dubilier & Rice Inc., **25** 501; **29** 408; **40** 370; **49** 22
Clayton Homes Incorporated, **13 154–55**; **37** 77; **54 76–79 (upd.)**
Clayton-Marcus Co., **12** 300
Clayton/National Courier Systems, Inc., **24** 126
CLE. *See* Compagnie Laitière Européenne.
Cleancoal Terminal, **7** 582, 584
Clear Channel Communications, Inc., **23 130–32**, 294; **25** 418; **27** 278; **33** 322,

324; **35** 219–21, 233; **36** 422, 424; **37** 104–05
Clear Shield Inc., **17** 157, 159
Clearly Canadian Beverage Corporation, **48 94–97**
Clearwater Tissue Mills, Inc., **8** 430
Cleary, Gottlieb, Steen & Hamilton, **35 106–09**
Cleco Corporation, **37 88–91**
Clef, **IV** 125
Clemente Capital Inc., **25** 542
Clements Energy, Inc., **7** 376
Cleo Inc., **12** 207–09; **35** 131
Le Clerc, **21** 225–26
Cleve-Co Jig Boring Co., **23** 82
Cleveland and Western Coal Company, **7** 369
Cleveland-Cliffs Inc., **13 156–58**; **17** 355; **62 71–75 (upd.)**
Cleveland Cotton Products Co., **37** 393
Cleveland Electric Illuminating Company. *See* Centerior Energy Theodor.
Cleveland Fabric Centers, Inc. *See* Fabri-Centers of America Inc.
Cleveland Grinding Machine Co., **23** 82
Cleveland Indians Baseball Company, Inc., **37 92–94**
Cleveland Iron Mining Company. *See* Cleveland-Cliffs Inc.
Cleveland Pneumatic Co., **III** 512
Cleveland Precision Instruments, Inc., **23** 82
Cleveland Twist Drill Company. *See* Acme-Cleveland Corp.
Clevepak Corporation, **8** 229; **13** 442; **59** 349
Clevite Corporation, **14** 207
CLF Research, **16** 202; **43** 170
Click Messenger Service, Inc., **24** 126
ClickAgents.com, Inc., **49** 433
ClientLogic Corporation. *See* Onex Corporation.
Clif Bar Inc., **50 141–43**
Clifford & Wills, **12** 280–81
Clifford Chance LLP, **38 136–39**
Cliffs Corporation, **13** 157; **27** 224
Climaveneta Deutschland GmbH. *See* De'Longhi S.p.A.
Clinical Partners, Inc., **26** 74
Clinical Pathology Facility, Inc., **26** 391
Clinical Science Research Ltd., **10** 106
Clinique Laboratories, Inc., **30** 191
Clinton Cards plc, **39 86–88**
Clipper Group, **12** 439
Clipper, Inc., **IV** 597
Clipper Manufacturing Company, **7** 3
La Cloche d'Or, **25** 85
Clopay Corp., **34** 195
The Clorox Company, **III 20–22**, 52; **8** 433; **22 145–48 (upd.)**, 436; **26** 383
Close Brothers Group plc, **39 89–92**
Clothesline Corporation, **60** 65
The Clothestime, Inc., **20 141–44**
Clouterie et Tréfilerie des Flandres, **IV** 25–26
Clover Club, **44** 348
Clovis Water Co., **6** 580
Clow Water Systems Co., **55** 266
CLRP. *See* City of London Real Property Company Ltd.
CLSI Inc., **15** 372; **43** 182
Club Aurrera, **8** 556
Club Corporation of America, **26** 27
Club de Hockey Canadien Inc., **26** 305

Club Méditerranée S.A., 6 206–08; 21 125–28 (upd.); 27 10
Club Monaco Inc., **62** 284
ClubCorp, Inc., 33 101–04
Cluett Corporation, **22** 133
Cluett, Peabody & Co., Inc., **8** 567–68
Cluster Consulting, **51** 98
Clyde Iron Works, **8** 545
Clydesdale Group, **19** 390
CM&M Equilease, **7** 344
CM&P. *See* Cresap, McCormick and Paget.
CMAC Investment Corporation. *See* Radian Group Inc.
CMB Acier, **IV** 228
CMB Packaging SA, **8** 477; **49** 295
CMC. *See* Commercial Metals Company.
CME. *See* Campbell-Mithun-Esty, Inc.; Central European Media Enterprises Ltd.
CMGI, Inc., **43** 11, 13, 420, 422
CMI International, Inc., **27** 202, 204
CMIH. *See* China Merchants International Holdings Co., Ltd.
CML Group, Inc., 10 215–18; 22 382, 536; **38** 238
CMP Media Inc., 26 76–80; 28 504
CMP Properties Inc., **15** 122
CMS Energy Corporation, IV 23; **V 577–79; 8** 466; **14 114–16 (upd.)**
CMS Healthcare, **29** 412
CMT Enterprises, Inc., **22** 249
CN. *See* Canadian National Railway System.
CNA Financial Corporation, III 228–32, 339; **38 140–46 (upd.); 63** 174
CNB Bancshares Inc., **31** 207
CNBC, Inc., **28** 298
CNC Holding Corp., **13** 166
CNCA. *See* Caisse National de Crédit Agricole.
CNEP. *See* Comptoir National d'Escompte de Paris.
CNET Networks, Inc., 47 77–80
CNF Transportation. *See* Consolidated Freightways, Inc.
CNG. *See* Consolidated Natural Gas Company.
CNH Global N.V., 38 147–56 (upd.); 67 9
CNI. *See* Community Networks Inc.
CNN. *See* Cable News Network.
CNP. *See* Compagnie Nationale à Portefeuille.
CNPC. *See* China National Petroleum Corporation.
CNS, Inc., 20 145–47
CNTS. *See* Ceska Nezavisla Televizni Spolecnost.
Co-Counsel, Inc., **29** 364
Co-Op Blue Square Consumer Cooperative Society, **41** 56–58
Co-operative Group (CWS) Ltd., 51 86–89
Co-operative Insurance Society Ltd., **51** 89
Co-Steel International Ltd., **8** 523–24; **13** 142–43; **24** 144
Coach and Car Equipment Corp., **41** 369
Coach, Inc., 45 111–15 (upd.); 54 325–26
Coach Leatherware, **10** 219–21; **12** 559
Coach Specialties Co. *See* Fleetwood Enterprises, Inc.
Coach USA, Inc., 24 117–19; 30 431, 433; **55 103–06 (upd.)**
Coachmen Industries Inc., **21** 153; **39** 393

Coal India Ltd., IV 48–50; 44 100–03 (upd.)
Coalport, **12** 528
Coast American Corporation, **13** 216
Coast Consolidators, Inc., **14** 505
Coast to Coast Hardware. *See* TruServ Corporation.
Coast-to-Coast Stores, **12** 8
Coastal Coca-Cola Bottling Co., **10** 223
Coastal Container Line Inc., **30** 318
Coastal Corporation, IV 394–95; 7 553–54; **31 118–21 (upd.)**
Coastal Lumber, S.A., **18** 514
Coastal States Corporation, **11** 481
Coastal States Life Insurance Company, **11** 482
CoastAmerica Corp., **13** 176
Coastline Distribution, Inc., **52** 399
Coates/Lorilleux, **14** 308
Coats plc, V 356–58; 44 104–07 (upd.)
CoBank. *See* National Bank for Cooperatives.
Cobb & Branham, **14** 257
COBE Cardiovascular, Inc., 61 68–72
COBE Laboratories, Inc., 13 159–61; 22 360; **49** 156; **61** 70
Coberco. *See* Friesland Coberco Dairy Foods Holding N.V.
Cobham plc, 30 129–32
Coborn's, Inc., 30 133–35
Cobra Electronics Corporation, 14 117–19; 60 137
Cobra Golf Inc., 16 108–10; 23 474; **64** 5
Cobra Ventilation Products, **22** 229
Coburn Vision Care, **III** 727
Coca-Cola Bottling Co. Consolidated, 10 222–24; 15 299
Coca-Cola Bottling Company of Northern New England, Inc., **21** 319
The Coca-Cola Company, I 232–35; III 215; **7** 155, 383, 466; **8** 399; **9** 86, 177; **10** 130, 222–23, **225–28 (upd.); 11** 421, 450–51; **13** 284; **14** 18, 453; **15** 428; **17** 207; **18** 60, 62–63, 68, 467–68; **19** 391; **21** 337–39, 401; **23** 418–20; **24** 516; **25** 183; **27** 21, 150; **28** 271, 473; **29** 85; **31** 243; **32** 59, **111–16 (upd.); 40** 350–52; **42** 31, 34–35; **47** 289, 291; **67 111–17 (upd.)**
Coca-Cola Enterprises, Inc., 10 223; **13 162–64; 23** 455–57; **32** 115
Cochrane Corporation, **8** 135
Cochrane Foil Co., **15** 128
Cockburn & Campbell Ltd., **38** 501
Cockburn-Adelaide Cement, **31** 398, 400
Cockerill Sambre Group, IV 51–53; 22 44; **26 81–84 (upd.); 42** 416
Coco's, **27** 16, 19
Code Hennessey & Simmons Limited, **39** 358
Codec, **19** 328
Codelco. *See* Corporacion Nacional del Cobre de Chile.
Coelba. *See* Companhia de Electricidade da Bahia.
Coeur d'Alene Mines Corporation, 20 148–51
COFAL. *See* Compagnie financiere pour l'Amerique Latine.
Coffee Club Franchise B.V., **53** 221
Coffee People, Inc., **40** 152–54
Cofica, **21** 99
Cofitel SA, **25** 466
Coflexip S.A., 25 103–05

Cofresco Frischhalteprodukte GmbH & Co. KG, **53** 221
Cofroma, **23** 219
COGEMA Canada, **IV** 436
Cogeneracion Prat SA, **41** 325, 327
Cogeneration Development Corp., **42** 387–88
Cogent Communications Group, Inc., 55 107–10
Cogent Data Technologies, Inc., **31** 5
Cogentrix Energy, Inc., 10 229–31
Cogetex, **14** 225
Cogifer, S.A., **18** 4; **31** 156, 158
Cognex Corp., **22** 373
CogniSeis Development, Inc., **18** 513, 515
Cognitive Solutions, Inc., **18** 140
Cognizant Technology Solutions Corporation, 57 176–77; 59 128–30; 61 82
Cognos Inc., 11 78; **25** 97; **44 108–11**
Cohasset Savings Bank, **13** 468
Coherent, Inc., 31 122–25
Coherix Corporation, **48** 446
Cohn-Hall-Marx Co. *See* United Merchants & Manufacturers, Inc.
Cohoes Bancorp Inc., **41** 212
Cohu, Inc., 32 117–19
Coils Plus, Inc., **22** 4
Coinamatic Laundry Equipment, **II** 650
Coinmach Laundry Corporation, 20 152–54
Coinstar, Inc., 44 112–14
Coktel Vision, **15** 455
Colas S.A., 31 126–29
Colbert Television Sales, **9** 306
Colby Group Holdings Limited, **59** 261
Cold Spring Granite Company, 16 111–14; 67 118–22 (upd.)
Coldwater Creek Inc., 21 129–31
Coldwell Banker, **11** 292; **12** 97; **27** 32; **59** 345; **61** 267. *See also* CB Commercial Real Estate Services Group, Inc.; Sears, Roebuck and Co.
Cole Haan Holdings Incorporated, **36** 346
Cole National Corporation, 13 165–67, 391
Cole Sewell Corporation, **39** 322, 324
Cole's Craft Showcase, **13** 166
Coleco Industries, Inc., **18** 520; **21** 375
The Coleman Company, Inc., 9 127–29; 26 119; **28** 135, 247; **30 136–39 (upd.)**
Coleman Outdoor Products Inc., **21** 293
Colemans Ltd., **11** 241
Coles Book Stores Ltd., **7** 486, 488–89; **58** 185
Coles Express Inc., 15 109–11
Coles Myer Ltd., V 33–35; 18 286; **20 155–58 (upd.)**
Colex Data, **14** 556
Colfax Corporation, 58 65–67
Colgate-Palmolive Company, II 672; **III 23–26; IV** 285; **9** 291; **11** 219, 317; **14 120–23 (upd.);** 279; **17** 106; **25** 365; **27** 212–13, 390; **35 110–15 (upd.)**
Colgens, **22** 193
Collabra Software Inc., **15** 322
Collect-a-Can (Pty) Ltd., **57** 183
Collectors Universe, Inc., 48 98–100
College Construction Loan Insurance Assoc., **II** 455; **25** 427
College Entrance Examination Board, **12** 141
College Survival, Inc., **10** 357
Collegiate Arlington Sports Inc., **II** 652

Collins & Aikman Corporation, I 483; 13 168–70; 25 535; 41 91–95 (upd.)
Collins Industries, Inc., 33 105–07
Collins Stewart, 41 371–72
Colo-Macco. See CRSS Inc.
Cologne Re. See General Re Corporation; Kölnische Rückversicherungs-Gesellschaft AG.
Colombia Graphophone Company, 22 192
Colombo, 25 84
Colonia Insurance Company (UK) Ltd., III 273, 394; 49 43
Colonia Versicherung Aktiengesellschaft. See AXA Colonia Konzern AG.
Colonial Candle of Cape Cod, 18 69
Colonial Companies Inc., 52 381
Colonial Container, 8 359
Colonial Food Stores, 7 373
Colonial Healthcare Supply Co., 13 90
Colonial Life Insurance Company, 11 481
Colonial National Bank, 8 9; 38 10–12
Colonial National Leasing, Inc., 8 9
Colonial Packaging Corporation, 12 150
Colonial Penn Group Insurance Co., 11 262; 27 4
Colonial Properties Trust, 65 115–17
Colonial Rubber Works, 8 347
Colonial Sugar Refining Co. Ltd. See CSR Limited.
Colonial Williamsburg Foundation, 53 105–07
Colony Capital, Inc., 27 201
Colony Communications, 7 99
Colony Gift Corporation, Ltd., 18 67, 69
Color-Box, Inc., 8 103
Color Corporation of America, 8 553
Color Me Mine, 25 263
Color Tile, 31 435
Colorado Belle Casino. See Circus Circus Enterprises, Inc.
Colorado Electric Company. See Public Service Company of Colorado.
Colorado Fuel & Iron (CF&I), 14 369
Colorado Gaming & Entertainment Co., 21 335
Colorado Gathering & Processing Corporation, 11 27
Colorado MEDtech, Inc., 48 101–05
Colorado National Bank, 12 165
Colorado Technical University, Inc., 41 419
Colorfoto Inc., I 447
Coloroll, 44 148
Colorstrip, Inc., 63 272
Colortree. See National Envelope Corporation.
ColorTyme, Inc., 45 367
Colossal Pictures, 10 286
Colt, 19 430–31
Colt Industries Inc., I 434–36
Colt Pistol Factory, 9 416
COLT Telecom Group plc, 41 96–99
Colt's Manufacturing Company, Inc., 12 70–72
Coltec Industries Inc., 30 158; 32 96; 46 213; 52 158–59
Columbia Administration Software Publishing Corporation, 51 244
Columbia Artists Management, Inc., 52 199–200
Columbia Brewery, 25 281
Columbia Broadcasting System. See CBS Corporation.

Columbia Chemical Co. See PPG Industries, Inc.
Columbia Electric Street Railway, Light and Power Company, 6 575
Columbia Gas & Electric Company, 6 466. See also Columbia Gas System, Inc.
Columbia Gas Light Company, 6 574
Columbia Gas of New York, Inc., 6 536
The Columbia Gas System, Inc., V 580–82; 16 115–18 (upd.)
Columbia Gas Transmission Corporation, 6 467
Columbia General Life Insurance Company of Indiana, 11 378
Columbia Hat Company, 19 94
Columbia Insurance Co., III 214
Columbia Pictures Entertainment, Inc., II 135–37, 170, 234, 619; 10 227; 12 73; 21 360; 22 193; 25 139; 28 71. See also Columbia TriStar Motion Pictures Companies.
Columbia Railroad, Gas and Electric Company, 6 575
Columbia Records, 16 201; 26 150
Columbia Records Distribution Corp., 43 170
Columbia Sportswear Company, 19 94–96; 41 100–03 (upd.)
Columbia Steamship Company, 17 356
Columbia Transportation Co., 17 357
Columbia TriStar Motion Pictures Companies, 12 73–76 (upd.); 28 71
Columbia TriStar Television Distribution, 17 149
Columbia/HCA Healthcare Corporation, 13 90; 15 112–14; 22 409–10; 27 356
Columbian Carbon Company, 25 70–71
Columbian Chemicals Co., IV 179; 28 352, 356
Columbus & Southern Ohio Electric Company (CSO), 6 467, 481–82
Columbus Bank & Trust. See Synovus Financial Corp.
Columbus McKinnon Corporation, 37 95–98
Columbus Realty Trust, 26 378
Columbus Stainless, 59 226
Colwell Systems, 19 291; 22 181
Com Dev, Inc., 32 435
Com Ed. See Commonwealth Edison.
Com-Link 21, Inc., 8 310
Comair Holdings Inc., 13 171–73; 31 420; 34 116–20 (upd.)
Comalco Fabricators (Hong Kong) Ltd., III 758
Comalco Ltd., IV 59–61, 122, 191
Comark, 24 316; 25 417–18
Comat Services Pte. Ltd., 10 514
Comau, I 163
Combibloc Inc., 16 339
Combined International Corporation. See Aon Corporation
Combined Properties, Inc., 16 160
Combustion Engineering Group, 22 11; 25 534
Combustiveis Industriais e Domésticos. See CIDLA.
Comcast Corporation, 7 90–92; 9 428; 10 432–33; 17 148; 22 162; 24 120–24 (upd.); 27 342, 344; 49 175; 63 437
ComCore Semiconductor, Inc., 26 330
Comdata, 19 160
Comdial Corporation, 21 132–35

Comdisco, Inc., 9 130–32; 11 47, 86, 484, 490
Comerci. See Controladora Comercial Mexicana, S.A. de C.V.
Comercial Mexicana, S.A. See Controladora Comercial Mexicana, S.A. de C.V.
Comerica Incorporated, 40 115–17
Comesi San Luis S.A.I.C. See Siderar S.A.I.C.
Comet. See Kingfisher plc.
Comet American Marketing, 33 31
Comet Rice, Inc., 33 31
ComFed Bancorp, 11 29
Comfin, 60 96
COMFORCE Corporation, 40 118–20
Comfort Inns, 21 362
Comforto GmbH, 8 252; 39 206
Cominco Ltd., 37 99–102 55
Comision Federal de Electricidad de Mexico (CFE), 21 196–97
CommAir. See American Building Maintenance Industries, Inc.
Command Security Corporation, 57 71–73
Commander Foods, 8 409
Commander-Larabee Co., 25 242
Commemorative Brands Inc., 19 453
Commerce Clearing House, Inc., 7 93–94. See also CCH Inc.
Commerce.TV, 42 323
Commerce Union, 10 426
The CommerceBank of Washington, 53 378
CommerceConnect LLC, 56 73
Commercial Air Conditioning of Northern California, 25 15
Commercial Air Lines, Inc., 23 380
Commercial Aseguradora Suizo Americana, S.A., III 243
Commercial Chemical Company, 16 99
Commercial Credit Company, 8 117–19; 10 255–56; 15 464
Commercial Federal Corporation, 12 77–79; 62 76–80 (upd.)
Commercial Financial Services, Inc., 26 85–89
Commercial Intertech Corporation, 57 86
Commercial Life, III 243
Commercial Metals Company, 15 115–17; 42 81–84(upd.)
Commercial Motor Freight, Inc., 14 42
Commercial Realty Services Group, 21 257
Commercial Union plc, II 272, 308; III 233–35
Commerzbank A.G., II 256–58; 9 283; 14 170; 47 81–84 (upd.); 51 19, 23
Commerzbank AG, 57 113
Commerzfilm, IV 591
CommLink Corp., 17 264
Commodity Credit Corp., 11 24
Commodore Corporation, 8 229
Commodore International, Ltd., II 6; 7 95–97, 532; 9 46; 10 56, 284; 23 25; 26 16
Commonwealth Aluminium Corp., Ltd. See Comalco Ltd.
Commonwealth Brands, Inc., 51 170
Commonwealth Edison, V 583–85; 6 505, 529, 531; 12 548; 15 422; 48 163
Commonwealth Energy System, 14 124–26
Commonwealth Industrial Gases, 25 82

Commonwealth Industries, **III** 569; **11** 536; **20** 360

Commonwealth Insurance Co., **III** 264

Commonwealth Life and Accident Insurance Company, **27** 46–47

Commonwealth Life Insurance Co. *See* Providian Financial Corporation

Commonwealth Limousine Services, Ltd., **26** 62

Commonwealth Mortgage Assurance Co., **III** 344

Commonwealth Oil Refining Company, **7** 517; **45** 410

Commonwealth Power Railway and Light Company, **14** 134

Commonwealth Southern Corporation, **14** 134

Commonwealth Steel Company Ltd, **62** 331

Commonwealth Telephone Enterprises, Inc., 25 106–08

Commonwealth United Corp., **53** 364

CommQuest Technologies, **63** 199

Commtron, Inc. *See* AmerisourceBergen Corporation.

Communications and Systems Specialists, **18** 370

Communications Consultants, Inc., **16** 393

Communications Corp. of America, **25** 418

Communications Industries Inc., **25** 496

Communications Network Consultants, **29** 400

Communications Solutions Inc., **11** 520

Communications Technology Corp. (CTC), **13** 7–8

Community Coffee Co. L.L.C., 53 108–10

Community Direct, Inc., **7** 16

Community HealthCare Services, **6** 182

Community National Bank, **9** 474

Community Networks Inc., **45** 69

Community Newspapers, Inc., **45** 352

Community Power & Light Company, **6** 579–80

Community Psychiatric Centers, 15 118–20

Community Public Service Company, **6** 514

Comnet Corporation, **9** 347

Comp-U-Card of America, Inc. *See* CUC International Inc.

Compac Corp., **11** 535

Compagnia di Participazioni Assicurative ed Industriali S.p.A., **24** 341

Compagnie Bancaire, **21** 99–100

Compagnie d'Assurances Générales, **III** 391

Compagnie de Recherche et d'Exploitation du Pétrole du Sahara, **21** 203

Compagnie de Saint-Gobain, III 675–78, 704; **8** 395, 397; **15** 80; **16 119–23 (upd.)**; **19** 58, 226; **21** 222; **26** 446; **33** 338, 340; **35** 86, 88; **64 80–84 (upd.)**

Compagnie des Alpes, 48 106–08; 56 143, 145

Compagnie des Cristalleries de Baccarat. *See* Baccarat.

Compagnie des Machines Bull S.A., III 122–23, 154; **IV** 600; **12** 139; **25** 33. *See also* Bull S.A.; Groupe Bull.

Compagnie du Midi, **III** 209, 211

Compagnie Européenne de Publication, **IV** 614–16

Compagnie Européenne de Télésecurité, **32** 374

Compagnie Financier Richemont AG, **19** 367, 369–70

Compagnie Financiere Alcatel, **9** 10

Compagnie Financière Belge des Pétroles. *See* PetroFina S.A.

Compagnie Financiere De Bourbon, **60** 149

Compagnie Financière de Paribas, II 259–60; 21 99; **27** 138; **33** 339. *See also* BNP Paribas Group.

Compagnie Financière de Richemont AG, **29** 90

Compagnie Financière de Suez. *See* Suez Lyonnaise des Eaux.

Compagnie Financière du Groupe Victoire, **27** 54; **49** 44

Compagnie Financiere pour l'Amerique Latine, **67** 326

Compagnie Financière Richemont AG, **27** 487; **29** 91–92; **50 144–47**

Compagnie Financière Sucres et Denrées S.A., 60 94–96

Compagnie Française Chaufour Investissement, **27** 100

Compagnie Française de Manutention, **27** 295

Compagnie Française des Pétroles. *See* TOTAL S.A.

Compagnie Fromagère de la Vallée de l'Ance, **25** 84

Compagnie Générale d'Électricité, II 12–13; 9 9–10

Compagnie Generale de Cartons Ondules, **IV** 296; **19** 226

Compagnie Générale des Eaux. *See* Vivendi SA.

Compagnie Générale des Établissements Michelin, V 236–39; 19 508; **42 85–89 (upd.)**; **59** 87

Compagnie Générale Maritime et Financière, 6 379–81

Compagnie Industriali Riunite S.p.A., **IV** 587–88; **54** 21

Compagnie Industrielle de Matérials de Manutention, **27** 296

Compagnie Industrielle des Fillers. *See* L'Entreprise Jean Lefebvre.

Compagnie Internationale Express, **25** 120

Compagnie Laitière Européenne, **25** 83, 85

Compagnie Luxembourgeoise de Télédiffusion, **15** 54

Compagnie Monegasque du Banque, **65** 230, 232

Compagnie Nationale à Portefeuille, **29** 48

Compagnie Nationale de Navigation, **27** 515

Compagnie Parisienne de Garantie, **III** 211

Compagnie Transcontinentale de Reassurance, **57** 136

Compagnie Union des Assurances de Paris (UAP), **49** 44

Compal, **47** 152–53

Companhia Brasileira de Petróleo Ipiranga, **67** 216

Companhia de Bebidas das Américas, 57 74–77; 67 316

Companhia de Celulose do Caima, **14** 250

Companhia de Electricidade da Bahia, **49** 211

Companhia de Seguros Argos Fluminense, **III** 221

Companhia de Seguros Tranquilidade Vida, S.A. *See* Banco Espírito Santo e Comercial de Lisboa S.A.

Companhia Energética de Minas Gerais S.A., 53 18; **65 118–20**

Companhia Industrial de Papel Pirahy, **52** 301

Companhia Siderúrgica de Tubarao, **IV** 125

Companhia Siderúrgica Mannesmann S.A. *See* Mannesmann AG.

Companhia Vale do Rio Doce, IV 54–57; 43 111–14 (upd.); **67** 85–86

Compania Electro Metaluurgica, **67** 13

Compañía Española de Petróleos S.A. (Cepsa), IV 396–98; 56 63–66 (upd.)

Compania Fresnillo, **22** 286

Compania Fundidora del Norte, S.A., **54** 152

Compania General de Aceptaciones. *See* Financiera Aceptaciones.

Compania Hulera Euzkadi, **21** 260; **23** 170

Compania Industrial de San Cristobal, S.A. de C.V., **54** 186

Compania Industrial del Norte, S.A., **54** 152

Compañía Mexicana de Transportación Aérea, **20** 167

Compania Minera de Penoles. *See* Industrias Penoles, S.A. de C.V.

Compania Minera Las Torres, **22** 286

Compania Siderurgica Huachipato, **24** 209

Compañía Telefónica Nacional de España S.A. *See* Telefónica Nacional de España S.A.

Compaq Computer Corporation, III 124–25; 6 217, **221–23 (upd.)**; **9** 42–43, 166, 170–71, 472; **10** 87, 232–33, 366, 459, 518–19; **12** 61, 183, 335, 470; **13** 388, 483; **16** 4, 196, 367–68; **17** 274; **21** 123, 391; **22** 288; **25** 184, 239, 498, 531; **26 90–93 (upd.)**; **27** 365; **28** 191; **29** 439; **30** 12; **36** 384; **43** 13; **47** 153; **63** 123, 125. *See also* Hewlett-Packard Company.

Compart, **24** 341

Compass Airlines, **27** 475

Compass Design Automation, **16** 520

Compass Group PLC, 6 193; **24** 194; **27** 482; **34 121–24**

CompDent Corporation, 22 149–51

Compeda, Ltd., **10** 240

Competence ApS, **26** 240

Competrol Ltd., **22** 189

CompHealth Inc., 25 109–12

Complete Business Solutions, Inc., 31 130–33

Complete Post, **50** 126

Completion Bond Co., **26** 487

Components Agents Ltd., **10** 113; **50** 43

Composite Craft Inc., **I** 387

Composite Research & Management Co., **17** 528, 530

Comprehensive Care Corporation, 15 121–23

Compression Labs Inc., **10** 456; **16** 392, 394; **27** 365

Compressor Controls Corporation, **15** 404; **50** 394

Comptoir Général de la Photographie. *See* Gaumont SA.

Comptoir Métallurgique Luxembourgeois, **IV** 25

Comptoirs Modernes S.A., 19 97–99

Compton Foods, **II** 675

Compton's MultiMedia Publishing Group, Inc., **7** 165

Compton's New Media, Inc., **7** 168

Compu-Notes, Inc., **22** 413

CompuAdd Computer Corporation, 11 61–63

CompuChem Corporation, **11** 425

CompuCom Systems, Inc., 10 232–34, 474; **13** 176

CompuDyne Corporation, 51 78–81

Compumech Technologies, **19** 312

CompuPharm, Inc., **14** 210

CompUSA, Inc., 10 235–36; 35 116–18 (upd.)

Compuscript, Inc., **64** 27

CompuServe Incorporated, 9 268–70; 10 237–39; 12 562; **13** 147; **15** 265; **16** 467, 508; **26** 16; **29** 224, 226–27; **34** 361; **50** 329. See also America Online, Inc.

CompuServe Interactive Services, Inc., 27 106, **106–08 (upd.)**, 301, 307; **57** 42. See also AOL Time Warner Inc.

Computer Associates International, Inc., 6 224–26; 10 394; **12** 62; **14** 392; **27** 492; **49 94–97 (upd.)**

Computer City, **12** 470; **36** 387

The Computer Company, **11** 112

Computer Consoles Inc., **III** 164

Computer Data Systems, Inc., 14 127–29

The Computer Department, Ltd., **10** 89

Computer Discount Corporation. See Comdisco, Inc.

Computer Discount Warehouse. See CDW Computer Centers, Inc.

Computer Engineering Associates, **25** 303

Computer Factory, Inc., **13** 176

Computer Learning Centers, Inc., 26 94–96

Computer Network, **20** 237

Computer Peripheral Manufacturers Association, **13** 127

Computer Power, **6** 301

Computer Renaissance, Inc., **18** 207–8

Computer Resources Management, Inc., **26** 36

Computer Sciences Corporation, 6 25, **227–29; 13** 462; **15** 474; **18** 370

Computer Systems and Applications, **12** 442

Computer Systems Division (CDS), **13** 201

Computer Terminal Corporation, **11** 67–68

ComputerCity, **10** 235

ComputerCraft, **27** 163

Computerized Lodging Systems, Inc., **11** 275

Computerized Waste Systems, **46** 248

ComputerLand Corp., 9 116; **10** 233, 563; **12** 335; **13 174–76**, 277; **33** 341–42

Computervision Corporation, 7 498; **10 240–42; 11** 275; **13** 201

Compuware Corporation, 10 243–45; 30 140–43 (upd.); 38 482; **66 60–64 (upd.)**

CompX International, Inc., **19** 466, 468

Comsat Corporation, 13 341; **23 133–36; 28** 241; **29** 42

Comshare Inc., 23 137–39

Comstock Canada, **9** 301

Comstock Resources, Inc., 47 85–87

Comtec Information Systems Inc., **53** 374

Comtel Electronics, Inc., **22** 409

Comunicaciones Avanzados, S.A. de C.V., **39** 195

Comverse Technology, Inc., 15 124–26; 43 115–18 (upd.)

Comviq GSM AB, **26** 331–33

Con Ed. See Consolidated Edison, Inc.

Con-Ferro Paint and Varnish Company, **8** 553

ConAgra, Inc., II 493–95, 517, 585; **7** 432, 525; **8** 53, 499–500; **12 80–82 (upd.); 13** 138, 294, 350, 352; **14** 515; **17** 56, 240–41; **18** 247, 290; **21** 290; **23** 320; **25** 243, 278; **26** 172, 174; **36** 416; **42 90–94 (upd.); 50** 275, 295, 493; **55** 364–65; **64** 61

Conair Corp., 16 539; **17 108–10; 24** 131; **25** 56

Concept, Inc., **23** 154

Concepts Direct, Inc., 39 93–96

Concepts in Community Living, Inc., **43** 46

Concert Communications Company, **15** 69; **27** 304–05; **49** 72

Concesiones de Infraestructuras de Transportes, S.A., **40** 217

Concession Air, **16** 446

Concha y Toro. See Viña Concha y Toro S.A.

Concord Camera Corporation, 41 104–07

Concord EFS, Inc., 52 86–88

Concord Fabrics, Inc., 16 124–26

Concord Leasing, Inc., **51** 108

Concord Watch Company, S.A., **28** 291

Concorde Acceptance Corporation, **64** 20–21

Concorde Hotels, **27** 421

Concrete Safety Systems, Inc., **56** 332

Concretos Apasco, S.A. de C.V., **51** 28–29

Concurrent Logic, **17** 34

Condé Nast Publications, Inc., 13 177–81; 23 98; **59 131–34 (upd.)**

CONDEA Vista Company, **61** 113

Condor Systems Inc., **15** 530

Cone Communications, **25** 258

Cone Mills LLC, 8 120–22; 67 123–27 (upd.)

Conelectron, **13** 398

Conexant Systems, Inc., 36 121–25; 43 328

Confecciones Cuscatlecas, S.A. de C.V., **64** 142

Confectionaire, **25** 283

Confederacion Norte-Centromericana y del Caribe de Futbol, **27** 150

Confederacion Sudamericana de Futbol, **27** 150

Confederation Africaine de Football, **27** 150

Confederation Freezers, **21** 501

ConferencePlus, Inc., **57** 408–09

Confidata Corporation, **11** 111

Confiserie-Group Hofbauer, **27** 105

Confiseriefabrik Richterich & Co. Laufen. See Ricola Ltd.

Congas Engineering Canada Ltd., **6** 478

Congoleum Corp., 12 28; **16** 18; **18 116–19; 36** 77–78; **43** 19, 21; **63** 300

Congress Financial Corp., **13** 305–06; **19** 108; **27** 276

Congressional Information Services. See Reed Elsevier.

Conic, **9** 324

Conifer Records Ltd., **52** 429

Coniston Partners, **I** 130; **II** 680; **6** 130; **10** 302

Conn-Selmer, Inc., 55 111–14

Conn's, Inc., 67 128–30

CONNA Corp., **7** 113; **25** 125

Connect Group Corporation, **28** 242

Connecticut General Corporation. See CIGNA Corporation.

Connecticut Health Enterprises Network, **22** 425

Connecticut Light and Power Co., 13 182–84; 21 514; **48** 305

Connecticut Mutual Life Insurance Company, III 236–38, 254, 285

Connecticut National Bank, **13** 467

Connecticut River Banking Company, **13** 467

Connecticut Telephone Company. See Southern New England Telecommunications Corporation.

Connecticut Yankee Atomic Power Company, **21** 513

The Connection Group, Inc., **26** 257

Connectix Corporation, **28** 245

The Connell Company, 29 129–31

Conner Corp., **15** 327

Conner Peripherals, Inc., 6 230–32; 10 403, 459, 463–64, 519; **11** 56, 234; **18** 260

Connie Lee. See College Construction Loan Insurance Assoc.

Connoisseur Communications, **37** 104

Connolly Data Systems, **11** 66

Connolly Tool and Machine Company, **21** 215

Connors Bros. Income Fund, **II** 631–32; **64** 61

Connors Steel Co., **15** 116

Conoco Inc., IV 399–402; 6 539; **7** 346, 559; **8** 556; **11** 97, 400; **16 127–32 (upd.); 18** 366; **21** 29; **50** 178, 363; **63** 439

ConocoPhillips, 61 114; **63 104–15 (upd.)**

Conover Furniture Company, **10** 183

ConQuest Telecommunication Services Inc., **16** 319

Conquistador Films, **25** 270

Conrad Industries, Inc., 58 68–70

Conrad International Corporation, **62** 179

Conrail Inc., **22** 167, 376. See also Consolidated Rail Corporation.

Conran Associates, **17** 43

Conrock Co., **19** 70

Conseco Inc., 10 246–48; 15 257; **33 108–12 (upd.); 64** 396

Conshu Holdings, **24** 450

Conso International Corporation, 29 132–34

Consodata S.A., **47** 345, 347

CONSOL Energy Inc., 59 135–37

Consolidated Aircraft Corporation, **9** 16, 497

Consolidated Asset Management Company, Inc., **25** 204

Consolidated-Bathurst Inc., **26** 445

Consolidated Brands Inc., **14** 18

Consolidated Cigar Holdings, Inc., **15** 137–38; **27** 139–40; **28** 247

Consolidated Citrus Limited Partnership, **60** 189

Consolidated Coin Caterers Corporation, **10** 222

Consolidated Converting Co., **19** 109

Consolidated Copper Corp., **13** 503

Consolidated Delivery & Logistics, Inc., **24** 125–28
Consolidated Denison Mines Ltd., **8** 418
Consolidated Edison, Inc., V 586–89; **6** 456; **35** 479; **45** 116–20 (upd.)
Consolidated Electric & Gas, **6** 447; **23** 28
Consolidated Electric Power Asia, **38** 448
Consolidated Electric Supply Inc., **15** 385
Consolidated Electronics Industries Corp. (Conelco), **13** 397–98
Consolidated Foods Corp., **12** 159, 494; **29** 132
Consolidated Freightways Corporation, **V** 432–34; **6** 280, 388; **12** 278, 309; **13** 19; **14** 567; **21** 136–39 (upd.); **25** 148–50; **48** 109–13 (upd.)
Consolidated Gas Company. *See* Baltimore Gas and Electric Company.
Consolidated International, **50** 98
Consolidated National Life Insurance Co., **10** 246
Consolidated Natural Gas Company, V 590–91; **19** 100–02 (upd.); **54** 83
Consolidated Papers, Inc., 8 123–25; **36** 126–30 (upd.)
Consolidated Plantations Berhad, **36** 434–35
Consolidated Power & Light Company, **6** 580
Consolidated Power & Telephone Company, **11** 342
Consolidated Press Holdings, **8** 551; **37** 408–09
Consolidated Products, Inc., 14 130–32, 352
Consolidated Rail Corporation, V 435–37, 485; **10** 44; **12** 278; **14** 324; **29** 360; **35** 291. *See also* Conrail Inc.
Consolidated Restaurant Cos. *See* Landry's Restaurants, Inc.
Consolidated Rock Products Co., **19** 69
Consolidated Specialty Restaurants, Inc., **14** 131–32
Consolidated Stores Corp., **13** 543; **29** 311; **35** 254; **50** 98
Consolidated Theaters, Inc., **14** 87
Consolidated Tire Company, **20** 258
Consolidated Trust Inc., **22** 540
Consolidated TVX Mining Corporation, **61** 290
Consolidated Tyre Services Ltd., **IV** 241
Consolidated Vultee, **II** 32
Consolidation Coal Co., **8** 154, 346–47
Consolidation Services, **44** 10, 13
Consorcio G Grupo Dina, S.A. de C.V., **36** 131–33
Consorcio Siderurgica Amazonia Ltd. *See* Siderar S.A.I.C.
Consortium, **34** 373
Consortium de Realisation, **25** 329
Consortium De Realization SAS, **23** 392
Consoweld Corporation, **8** 124
Constar International Inc., 8 562; **13** 190; **32** 125; **64** 85–88
Constellation Energy Corporation, **24** 29
Constellation Enterprises Inc., **25** 46
Constinsouza, **25** 174
Constitution Insurance Company, **51** 143
Construcciones Aeronáuticas SA, **7** 9; **12** 190; **24** 88. *See also* European Aeronautic Defence and Space Company EADS N.V.
Construction DJL Inc., **23** 332–33
Constructora CAMSA, C.A., **56** 383

Consul GmbH, **51** 58
Consul Restaurant Corp., **13** 152
Consumer Access Limited, **24** 95
Consumer Products Company, **30** 39
Consumer Value Stores, **9** 67; **18** 199; **24** 290. *See also* CVS Corporation.
Consumer's Gas Co., **I** 264
ConsumerNet, **49** 422
Consumers Cooperative Association, **7** 174. *See also* Farmland Industries, Inc.
Consumers Distributing Co. Ltd., **II** 649, 652–53
Consumers Electric Light and Power, **6** 582
The Consumers Gas Company Ltd., 6 476–79; **43** 154. *See also* Enbridge Inc.
Consumers Mutual Gas Light Company. *See* Baltimore Gas and Electric Company.
Consumers Power Co., 14 133–36
Consumers Public Power District, **29** 352
Consumers Union, 26 97–99
Consumers Water Company, 14 137–39; **39** 329
Contact Software International Inc., **10** 509
Container Corporation of America, **V** 147; **8** 476; **26** 446
The Container Store, 36 134–36
Container Transport International, **III** 344
Contaminant Recovery Systems, Inc., **18** 162
CONTAQ Microsystems Inc., **48** 127
Conte S.A., **12** 262
Contech, **10** 493
Contel Corporation, **V** 296–98; **13** 212; **14** 259; **15** 192; **43** 447
Contempo Associates, **14** 105; **25** 307
Contempo Casuals, Inc. *See* The Wet Seal, Inc.
Contemporary Books, **22** 522
Content Technologies Inc., **42** 24–25
Contex Graphics Systems Inc., **24** 428
Conti-Carriers & Terminals Inc., **22** 167
Contico International, L.L.C., **51** 190
ContiCommodity Services, Inc., **10** 250–51
ContiGroup Companies, Inc., 43 119–22 (upd.)
Continental AG, V 240–43, 250–51, 256; **8** 212–14; **9** 248; **15** 355; **19** 508; **56** 67–72 (upd.)
Continental Airlines, Inc., I 96–98, 103, 118, 123–24, 129–30; **6** 105, 120–21, 129–30; **12** 381; **20** 84, 262; **21** 140–43 (upd.); **22** 80, 220; **25** 420, 423; **26** 439–40; **34** 398; **52** 89–94 (upd.)
Continental American Life Insurance Company, **7** 102
Continental Baking Co., **7** 320–21; **12** 276; **13** 427; **27** 309–10; **38** 252
Continental Bank Corporation, II 261–63, 285, 289, 348; **47** 231. *See also* Bank of America.
Continental Bio-Clinical Laboratories, **26** 391
Continental Cablevision, Inc., 7 98–100; **17** 148; **19** 201
Continental Can Co., Inc., 10 130; **13** 255; **15** 127–30; **24** 428; **26** 117, 449; **32** 125; **49** 293–94
Continental-Caoutchouc und Gutta-Percha Compagnie. *See* Continental AG.
Continental Carbon Co., **36** 146–48
Continental Care Group, **10** 252–53

Continental Casualty Co., **III** 228–32; **16** 204
Continental Cities Corp., **III** 344
Continental Corporation, III 239–44, 273; **10** 561; **12** 318; **15** 30; **38** 142
Continental Design, **58** 194
Continental Divide Insurance Co., **III** 214
Continental Electronics Corporation, **18** 513–14
Continental Emsco, **24** 305
Continental Equipment Company, **13** 225
Continental Express, **11** 299
Continental Fiber Drum, **8** 476
Continental Gas & Electric Corporation, **6** 511
Continental General Tire Corp., 23 140–42
Continental Grain Company, 10 249–51; **13** 185–87 (upd.); **30** 353, 355; **40** 87. *See also* ContiGroup Companies, Inc.
Continental Group Co., I 599–600; **8** 175, 424; **17** 106
Continental Hair Products, Inc. *See* Conair Corp.
Continental Health Affiliates, **17** 307
Continental Homes Inc., **26** 291; **58** 84
Continental Illinois Corp. *See* Continental Bank Corporation.
Continental Investment Corporation, **9** 507; **12** 463; **22** 541; **33** 407
Continental Medical Systems, Inc., 10 252–54; **11** 282; **14** 233; **25** 111; **33** 185
Continental Milling Company, **10** 250
Continental Modules, Inc., **45** 328
Continental Motors Corp., **10** 521–22
Continental Mutual Savings Bank, **17** 529
Continental Oil Co. *See* ConocoPhillips.
Continental Packaging Inc., **13** 255
Continental Plastic Containers, Inc., **25** 512
Continental Reinsurance, **11** 533
Continental Research Corporation, **22** 541
Continental Restaurant Systems, **12** 510
Continental Risk Services, **III** 243
Continental Scale Works, **14** 229–30
Continental Telephone Company, **9** 494–95; **11** 500. *See also* GTE Corporation.
Continental Wood Preservers, Inc., **12** 397
ContinueCare Corporation, **25** 41
Continuum Electro-Optics, Inc. *See* Excel Technology, Inc.
Continuum Health Partners, Inc., 60 97–99
Contran Corporation, **19** 467
Contrans Acquisitions, Inc., **14** 38
Contred Ltd., **20** 263
Control Data Corporation, III 126–28; **17** 49; **19** 110, 513–15; **25** 496; **30** 338; **38** 58; **46** 35
Control Data Systems, Inc., 8 117–18, 467; **10** 255–57, 359, 458–59; **11** 469; **16** 137
Control Systemation, Inc. *See* Excel Technology, Inc.
Controladora Comercial Mexicana, S.A. **de C.V., 36** 137–39
Controladora PROSA, **18** 516, 518
Controlled Materials and Equipment Transportation, **29** 354
Controlonics Corporation, **13** 195
Controls Company of America, **9** 67
Controlware GmbH, **22** 53
Convair, **9** 18, 498; **13** 357
Convenient Food Mart Inc., **7** 114; **25** 125

Convergent Technologies, **11** 519
Converse Inc., 9 133–36, 234; **12** 308; **31 134–38 (upd.),** 211
Conway Computer Group, **18** 370
Conwest Exploration Company Ltd., **16** 10, 12; **43** 3
Conycon. *See* Construcciones y Contratas.
Conzinc Riotinto of Australia. *See* CRA Limited.
Cook Bates Inc., **40** 347–48
Cook Data Services, Inc., **9** 73
Cook Standard Tool Co., **13** 369
Cooke Engineering Company, **13** 194
Cooker Restaurant Corporation, 20 159–61; 51 82–85 (upd.)
Cooking and Crafts Club, **13** 106
Cookson Group plc, III 679–82; 16 290; **44 115–20 (upd.);** **49** 234–35
CoolBrands International Inc., 35 119–22
Coolidge Mutual Savings Bank, **17** 529
Coop Schweiz Genossenschaftsverband, 48 114–16
Cooper Cameron Corporation, 20 162–66 (upd.); 58 71–75 (upd.)
Cooper Canada Ltd., **16** 80
The Cooper Companies, Inc., 39 97–100
Cooper Industries, Inc., II 14–17; 14 564; **19** 43, 45, 140; **30** 266; **44 121–25 (upd.);** **49** 159
Cooper Tire & Rubber Company, 8 126–28; 23 143–46 (upd.)
Cooper-Weymouth, **10** 412
Cooper's, Inc., **12** 283
Cooperative Business International, Inc., **60** 88
Cooperative Grange League Federation Exchange, **7** 17
Coopers & Lybrand, 9 137–38; 12 391; **25** 383. *See also* PricewaterhouseCoopers.
CooperVision, **7** 46; **25** 55
Coordinados Elite, S.A. de United Apparel Ventures, **62** 353
Coordinated Caribbean Transport. *See* Crowley Caribbean Transport.
Coors Company. *See* Adolph Coors Company.
Coorsh and Bittner, **7** 430
Coote & Jurgenson, **14** 64
Copart Inc., 23 147–49, 285, 287
Copeland Corp., **II** 20
Copeman Ridley, **13** 103
Coperion Holding GmbH, **61** 108
Copico, **44** 273
Copley Pharmaceuticals Inc., **13** 264
The Copley Press, Inc., 23 150–52
Copolymer Corporation, **9** 242
Copper Range Company, **7** 281–82
The Copps Corporation, 32 120–22; 58 320
Copycat Ltd., **8** 383
Cor Therapeutics, **47** 251
Coral Energy, **41** 359
Corange, Ltd., **37** 111–13
Corbett Canyon. *See* The Wine Group, Inc.
Corbett Enterprises Inc., **13** 270
Corbis Corporation, 31 139–42
Corby Distilleries Limited, 14 140–42
Corchos de Mérida S.A., **48** 349
Corco. *See* Commonwealth Oil Refining Company.
Corco, Inc. *See* Liqui-Box Corporation.

Corcoran & Riggs. *See* Riggs National Corporation.
The Corcoran Group, Inc., 58 76–78; 61 267
Cordant Technologies, **56** 11
Cordes, **56** 234
Cordiant plc. *See* Saatchi & Saatchi plc.
Cordis Corporation, 19 103–05; 36 306; **46 104–07 (upd.)**
Cordon & Gotch, **IV** 619
Cordon Bleu. *See* Le Cordon Bleu S.A.
Core Laboratories Inc., **I** 486; **11** 265
Corel Corporation, 15 131–33; 33 113–16 (upd.)
CoreStates Financial Corp, 17 111–15
CoreTek, Inc., **36** 353
Corfuerte S.A. de C.V., **23** 171
Corimon, **12** 218
Corinthian Broadcast Corporation, **10** 4
Corinthian Colleges, Inc., 39 101–04
Corio Inc., **38** 188, 432
Cork Asia Pacific. *See* McPherson's Ltd.
Cormetech. *See* Corning Inc.
Cornelia Insurance Agency. *See* Advantage Insurers, Inc.
Cornelius Nurseries, Inc., **51** 61
Cornell Corrections, **28** 255
Cornerstone Direct Marketing, **8** 385–86
Cornerstone Propane Partners, L.P., **37** 280, 283
Cornerstone Real Estate Advisors Inc., **53** 213
Cornerstone Title Company, **8** 461
Corning Clinical Laboratories, **26** 390–92
Corning Consumer Products Company, **27** 288
Corning Inc., III 683–85; 8 468; **11** 334; **13** 398; **22** 454; **25** 254; **30** 151–52; **44 126–30 (upd.)**
Coro International A.V.V., **39** 346
Coronet Industries, Inc., **14** 436
Corporacion Durango, S.A. de C.V., **37** 178
Corporacion Financiera Hipotecaria, **63** 213
Corporación Internacional de Aviación, S.A. de C.V. (Cintra), 20 167–69
Corporación Moctezuma, **21** 261
Corporacion Nacional del Cobre de Chile, 38 231; **40 121–23**
Corporacion Siderurgica Integral, **22** 44
Corporate Childcare Development, Inc. *See* Bright Horizons Family Solutions, Inc.
Corporate Express, Inc., 22 152–55, 531; **41** 67–69; **47 88–92 (upd.);** **49** 440
Corporate Intelligence, **55** 251
Corporate Microsystems, Inc., **10** 395
Corporate Partners, **12** 391
Corporate Software Inc., 9 139–41
CorporateFamily Solutions. *See* Bright Horizons Family Solutions, Inc.
Corporation for Public Broadcasting, 14 143–45; 47 259
Corporation Trust Co. *See* CCH Inc.
Corrado Passera, **IV** 588
Corral Midwest, Inc., **10** 333
CorrChoice, Inc. *See* Greif Inc.
Correctional Services Corporation, 30 144–46
Corrections Corporation of America, 23 153–55; 28 255; **63** 425
Correo Argentina S.A., **63** 179; **67** 348
Corrigan-McKinney Steel Company, **13** 157
Corrigan's, **16** 559

CorrLogic, Inc., **51** 81
Corroon & Black. *See* Willis Corroon Group Plc.
Corrosion Technologies de México SA de C V, **53** 285
Corrpro Companies, Inc., 20 170–73
CORT Business Services Corporation, 26 100–02
El Corte Inglés Group, 26 128–31 (upd.)
Cortec Corporation, **14** 430
Cortefiel S.A., 64 89–91
Corticeira Amorim, Sociedade Gestora de Participaço es Sociais, S.A., 48 117–20, 349
Corus Group plc, 49 98–105 (upd.)
Cory Bros & Co. Ltd., **31** 367, 369
Cory Components, **36** 158
Cory Environmental Ltd., **51** 130
Cory Food Services, Inc., **II** 608
Cory Orchard and Turf. *See* Chemi-Trol Chemical Co.
Cosco, Inc., **59** 164
Cosco Pacific, **20** 313
Cosi, Inc., 53 111–13
Cosmair Inc., 8 129–32; 12 404; **31** 418; **62** 282
Cosmar Corp., **37** 269–71
The Cosmetic Center, Inc., 22 156–58
Cosmetic Technology International, Inc., **22** 409
Cosmetics & More Inc., **64** 334
Cosmo Oil Co., Ltd., IV 403–04; 53 114–16 (upd.); **63** 308, 311
Cosmopolitan Cosmetics GmbH, **48** 420, 422
Cosmopolitan Productions, **IV** 626; **19** 203
Cosmos International, Inc., **51** 307
Cosmotel, **46** 401
Cosorzio Interprovinciale Vini, **10** 181
Cost Plus, Inc., 12 393; **27 109–11; 34** 337, 340
Cost-U-Less, Inc., 51 90–93
Costa Coffee, **63** 88
Costa Cruise Lines, **27** 29, 90, 92
Costa Rica International, Inc., **41** 329
Costain Civil Engineering Ltd., **13** 206
Costain Homes, **31** 386
Costco Wholesale Corporation, V 36; 10 206; **11** 240; **14** 393–95; **15** 470; **25** 235; **27** 95; **43 123–25 (upd.);** **63** 427, 430; **64** 68
Costruzioni Meccaniche Nazionalia, **13** 218
Cosway Corporation Berhad. *See* Berjaya Group Bhd.
Coto Centro Integral de Comercializacion S.A., 66 65–67
Cott Corporation, 9 291; **52 95–98**
Cotter & Company, V 37–38; 12 8. *See also* TruServ Corporation.
Cotter Corporation, **29** 488
Cotton Incorporated, 46 108–11
Cotton Producers Association. *See* Gold Kist Inc.
Coty, Inc., 36 140–42; 37 270
Coudert Brothers, 30 147–50
Coulee Region Organic Produce Pool. *See* Organic Valley.
Coulter Corporation. *See* Beckman Coulter, Inc.
Counsel Corp., **46** 3
Counselor Co., **14** 230
Country Fresh, Inc., **26** 449
Country Hedging, Inc., **60** 88
Country Kitchen International, **22** 127

Country Music Television, **11** 153
Country Seat Stores, Inc., **15** 87
Country Store of Concord, Inc., **10** 216
**Countrywide Credit Industries, Inc., 16
133–36**
County Catering Co., **13** 103
County Data Corporation, **18** 24
County Market, **II** 670
County Seat Stores Inc., II 669; **9**
142–43; **50** 455
Courage Brewing Group., **I** 229, 438–39
Courier Corporation, 41 108–12
Courir S.A., **39** 183–85
Courrèges Parfums, **III** 48; **8** 343
The Courseware Developers, **11** 19
Court Courier Systems, Inc., **24** 126
Court House Square, **10** 44
**Courtaulds plc, V 359–61; 17 116–19
(upd.); 33** 134; **41** 9; **52** 99, 101; **54** 326
Courts Plc, 45 121–24
Courtyard by Marriott, **9** 427
Cousins Mortgage and Equity Investments,
12 393
**Cousins Properties Incorporated, 65
121–23**
Covance Inc., 30 151–53
**Covanta Energy Corporation, 64 92–95
(upd.)**
Covantage, **11** 379
Covenant Life Insurance, **III** 314
Coventry Climax Engines, Ltd., **13** 286
Coventry Corporation, **17** 166, 168
Coventry Health Care, Inc., 59 138–40
Coventry Machinists Company, **7** 458
Coville Inc., **16** 353
Covington & Burling, 40 124–27
Covisint LLC. *See* Compuware
Corporation.
Covol Technologies Inc. *See* Headwaters
Incorporated.
Cowles Media Company, 23 156–58
Cox Cable Communications, Inc., **42** 114
Cox Enterprises, Inc., IV 595–97; 7 327;
9 74; **17** 148; **22 159–63 (upd.); 24**
120; **30** 217; **38** 307–08; **67 131–35
(upd.)**
Cox Medical Enterprises, Inc., **21** 47
Cox Newsprint, Inc., **25** 11
Cox Pharmaceuticals, **35** 25
Cox Woodlands Company, **25** 11
Coz Chemical Co., **21** 20, 22
CP. *See* Canadian Pacific Limited.
CP/AAON. *See* AAON, Inc.
CP National, **19** 412
CP Ships Holding, Inc., **45** 80; **50** 209–10
CPC International Inc., II 496–98; 27
40. *See also* Bestfoods.
CP8, **43** 89
CPI Corp., 38 157–60
CPL. *See* Carolina Power & Light
Company.
CR England, Inc., 63 116–18
CR2A Holding, **48** 402
CRA Limited, IV 58–61, 67, 192; **7** 124.
See also Rio Tinto plc.
Crabtree & Evelyn Ltd., **51** 67
Crabtree Electricals, **III** 503; **7** 210
**Cracker Barrel Old Country Store, Inc.,
10** 258–59. *See also* CBRL Group, Inc.
Craft House Corp., **8** 456
Craftique, Inc., **33** 350–51
Craftmade International, Inc., 44 131–33
Craftopia.com, **64** 185
Craig Bit Company, **13** 297

**Crain Communications, Inc., 12 83–86;
35 123–27 (upd.)**
Cram Company. *See* The George F. Cram
Company, Inc.
Cramer, Berkowitz & Co., 34 125–27
Cramer Electronics, **10** 112; **50** 41
Cranberry Canners, Inc. *See* Ocean Spray
Cranberries, Inc.
Crane & Co., Inc., 26 103–06; 30 42
Crane Carton Co., **44** 66
Crane Co., 8 133–36, 179; **24** 332; **30
154–58 (upd.)**
Crane Packing Company, **19** 311
Crane Supply Company, **8** 135
Cranston Mills, **13** 168
Cranswick plc, 40 128–30
Crate and Barrel, 9 144–46; 27 429; **36**
135. *See also* Euromarket Designs Inc.
Cravath, Swaine & Moore, 27 325; **43
126–28**
Crawford Door Försäljnings AB, **53** 85
Crawford Group, Inc., **17** 372
Crawford Supply Company, **6** 392
Cray Research, Inc., III 129–31; 10 256;
16 137–40 (upd.); 21 391; **22** 428; **29**
440
Crayfish Company, Ltd., **36** 153
Crazy Eddie Inc., **23** 373
Crazy Shirts, Inc., **45** 42
CRC Holdings Corp., **51** 217
CRD Total France, **IV** 560
Creaciones Victorio & Lucchino, **60** 246
Cream City Railway Company, **6** 601
Cream Wine Company, **48** 392
Creasy Co., **II** 682
Creative Artists Agency LLC, 10 228; **22**
297; **23** 512, 514; **32** 115; **38 161–64**
Creative Artists Associates, **43** 235
Creative BioMolecules, Inc., **29** 454
Creative Business Concepts, Inc., **39** 346
Creative Concepts in Advertising, **27** 194
Creative Displays, Inc., **27** 279
Creative Engineering Inc., **13** 472
Creative Food 'N Fun Co., **14** 29
Creative Forming, Inc., **8** 562
Creative Gems & Jewelry, Ltd., **62** 371
Creative Integration and Design Inc., **20**
146
Creative Memories, **40** 44
Creative Optics Inc., **61** 193
Creative Technologies Corp., **15** 401
Creative Technology Ltd., 48 83; **57
78–81**
Credit & Risk Management Associates,
Inc., **18** 170
**Credit Acceptance Corporation, 18
120–22**
Crédit Agricole, II 264–66, 355; **19** 51;
59 190, 193
Crédit Commercial de France, **25** 173
Crédit Communal de Belgique, **42** 111
Credit Immobilier, **7** 538
Crédit Local de France, **42** 111
Crédit Lyonnais, 6 396; **7** 12; **9 147–49;
19** 34, 51, 166; **21** 226; **25** 170, 329; **33
117–21 (upd.)**
Crédit National S.A., 9 150–52
Crédit Suisse Group, II 267–69, 369–70,
378–79, 402–04; **21 144–47 (upd.); 52**
354, 356–358; **59 141–47 (upd.)**. *See
also* Schweizerische Kreditanstalt.
Credit Union Federation, **48** 290
CrediThrift Financial, **11** 16
Credito Agrario, **65** 72

Credito Italiano, II 270–72
Credito Minero y Mercantil, S.A., **22** 285
Credito Provincial Hipotecario, **19** 189
Creditrust Corp., **42** 259
Cree Inc., 13 399; **53 117–20**
Crellin Holding, Inc., **8** 477
Crellin Plastics, **8** 13
Cremascoli Ortho Group, **61** 403
Cremonini S.p.A., 57 82–84
Crenlo Corp., **16** 180
Creo Inc., 48 121–24
Cresap, McCormick and Paget, **32** 458
Crescent Box & Printing Co., **13** 442
Crescent Capital, **44** 95
Crescent Niagara Corp., **II** 16
Crescent Real Estate Equities Company, **25**
454
Crescent Software Inc., **15** 373
Crescent Vert Company, Ltd., **II** 51; **21**
330
Crescent Washing Machine Company, **8**
298
Crescott, Inc., **15** 501
Crest Fruit Co., **17** 458
Crest Ridge Homes, Inc., **17** 83
Crest Service Company, **9** 364
Crestbrook Forest Industries Ltd., **IV** 285
Crestline, **60** 140
Crestmont Financial Corporation, **14** 472
Cresud S.A.C.I.F. y A., 63 119–21, 214
Creusot-Loire, **19** 166
Crevettes du Cameroun, **13** 244
CRH plc, 37 203, 206; **60** 77; **64 96–99**
Crimson Associates L.P., **26** 48
Crisnova S.A. *See* Vidrala S.A.
Crisoba. *See* Compania Industrial de San
Cristobal, S.A. de C.V.
Crist Partners, **34** 249
Cristalerias de Chile S.A., 67 136–38
Criterion Casualty Company, **10** 312
Criterion Life Insurance Company, **10** 311
Critical Care Concepts, **50** 123
Crocker National Bank, **13** 535
Crocker National Corporation, **12** 536
Crockett Container Corporation, **8** 268
Croda International Plc, 45 125–28
Croitex S.A., **26** 374
Crompton & Knowles Corp., I 633; **9
153–55**
**Crompton Corporation, 36 143–50
(upd.); 52** 305
CROPP. *See* Organic Valley.
Crosby Enterprises, **17** 19
Croscill Home Fashions, **8** 510
Croscill, Inc., 42 95–97
Crosman Corporation, 62 81–83
Cross & Trecker Corporation, **10** 330
Cross Company. *See* A.T. Cross Company.
Cross-Continent Auto Retailers, **26** 501
Cross Country Group, **25** 358
Cross Creek Apparel, Inc., **30** 400
Cross Pointe Paper Corporation, **26** 363
Cross/Tessitore & Associates, **16** 259
Cross Timbers Oil Company. *See* XTO
Energy, Inc.
Crossair AG. *See* Swiss International Air
Lines Ltd.
Crossfield Foods, **61** 133
Crossley Motors, Ltd., **13** 285
Crosspoint Venture Partners, **57** 49
Crothers Properties, Inc., **21** 500
Crouse-Hinds Co., **19** 45
Crowell-Collier Publishing Company, **7**
286

Crowell Publishing Company, **19** 266
Crowley Maritime Corporation, 6 382–84; 9 510–11; **28 77–80 (upd.)**
Crowley, Milner & Company, 19 106–08
Crown Advertising Agency. *See* King Kullen Grocery Co., Inc.
Crown America Corp., **13** 393
Crown Books Corporation, 14 61; **16** 159–61; **21 148–50; 41** 61
Crown Casino, **54** 299
Crown Central Petroleum Corporation, 7 101–03
Crown, Cork & Seal Company, Inc., I 601–03; 13 188–90 (upd.); 15 129; **17** 106; **24** 264; **30** 475; **32 123–27 (upd.); 64** 86–87
Crown Courier Systems, Inc., **24** 126
Crown Crafts, Inc., 16 141–43
Crown Drugs, **II** 673
Crown Equipment Corporation, 15 134–36
Crown House Engineering, **44** 148
Crown Media Holdings, Inc., 45 129–32
Crown Oil and Refining Company, **7** 101
Crown Packaging, **19** 155
Crown Pet Foods Ltd., **39** 356
Crown Point Ventures, **49** 316
Crown Publishing Group, **IV** 584; **13** 429; **31** 376, 379
Crown Radio, **17** 123–24; **41** 114
Crown Technical Systems, Inc., **37** 215
Crown Vantage Inc., 29 135–37
Crown Zellerbach Corporation, **8** 261; **24** 247
Crownx Inc. *See* Extendicare Health Services, Inc.
Crowson and Son Ltd., **23** 219
CRSS Inc., 6 142–44; 23 491
CRT, **51** 199
CRTC. *See* Canadian Radio-Television and Telecommunications Commission.
Cruise America Inc., 21 151–53
Cruise Associates, **22** 471
Crum & Forster Holdings, Inc., **III** 172; **6** 290; **26** 546; **57** 136
Crump E & S, **6** 290
Crupo Camino Real. *See* Real Turismo, S.A. de C.V.
Cruse Bekleidung GmbH & Co. KG, **53** 195
Crush International, **III** 53
Crushed Stone Sales Ltd., **IV** 241
Cruzan Rum Distillery, Ltd., **27** 478
Cruzcampo, **18** 501
Cruzeiro do Sul Airlines. *See* Varig, SA.
Cryenco Sciences Inc., **21** 109
CryoLife, Inc., 46 112–14
Crystal Brands, Inc., 9 156–58; 12 431
Crystal Market, **41** 174
Crystal Rock Water Co., **51** 396
Crystal SA. *See* Dalkia Holding.
Crystallex International Corporation, **61** 291
CS Crable Sportswear Inc., **23** 66
CS First Boston Inc., II 269, **402–04; 12** 209; **21** 146. *See also* Credit Suisse Group.
CS Holding. *See* Credit Suisse Group.
CS Life, **21** 146–47
CSA. *See* China Southern Airlines Company Ltd.
CSC. *See* Computer Sciences Corporation.
CSC Holdings, Inc., **32** 105
CSC Service Co Ltd., **62** 245

CSE Corp., **III** 214
Csemege, **53** 178
CSFB. *See* Financière Crédit Suisse-First Boston; Credit Suisse Group.
CSFBdirect Inc., **46** 55
CSG Information Services, **55** 250–51
CSI Computer Systems, **47** 36
CSK, **10** 482
CSK Auto Corporation, 38 165–67
CSM N.V., 65 124–27
CSO. *See* Columbus & Southern Ohio Electric Company.
CSR Limited, III 686–88; 28 81–84 (upd.)
CSR Rinker Materials Corp., **46** 197
CSS Industries, Inc., 35 128–31
CST Office Products, **15** 36; **42** 416
CSX Corporation, V 438–40, 485; **6** 340; **9** 59; **13** 462; **22 164–68 (upd.); 29** 360–61
CSY Agri-Processing, **7** 81–82
CT Financial Services Inc., **49** 397
CT&T. *See* Carolina Telephone and Telegraph Company.
CTA. *See* Comptoir des Textiles Artificielles.
CTA Makro Commercial Co., Ltd., **55** 347
CTB International Corporation, 43 129–31 (upd.)
CTG, Inc., 11 64–66
CTI, *See* Cosmetic Technology International, Inc.
CTR. *See* Compagnie Transcontinentale de Reassurance.
CTS Corporation, 19 104; **39 105–08**
CTV Network, **35** 69
C2B Technologies, **45** 201
CTX Mortgage Company, **8** 88
Cub Foods, **II** 669–70; **14** 411; **17** 302; **18** 505; **22** 327; **50** 455
Cuban American Oil Company, **8** 348
Cubic Corporation, 19 109–11
CUC International Inc., 16 144–46. *See also* Cendant Corporation.
Cudahy Corp., **12** 199
Cuisinart Corporation, 17 110; **24 129–32**
Culbro Corporation, 14 19; **15 137–39.** *See also* General Cigar Holdings, Inc.
Culinar Inc., **59** 364
Culinary Foods, Inc., **14** 516; **50** 493
Cullen/Frost Bankers, Inc., 25 113–16
Culligan International Company, 12 87–88, 346; **16** 20
Culligan Water Technologies, Inc., 38 168–70 (upd.)
Cullinet Software Corporation, **14** 390; **15** 108
Cullman Bros. *See* Culbro Corporation.
Culp, Inc., 29 138–40
Culter Industries, Inc., **22** 353
Culver Franchising System, Inc., 58 79–81
Cumberland Farms, Inc., 17 120–22; 26 450
Cumberland Federal Bancorporation, **13** 223; **31** 206
Cumberland Newspapers, **7** 389
Cumberland Packing Corporation, 26 107–09
Cummins Cogeneration Co. *See* Cogeneration Development Corp.
Cummins Engine Co., Inc., I 146–48, 186; **10** 273–74; **12 89–92 (upd.); 16**

297; **19** 293; **21** 503; **26** 256; **40 131–35 (upd.); 42** 387
Cummins Utility Supply, **58** 334
Cumo Sports, **16** 109
Cumulus Media Inc., 37 103–05
CUNA Mutual Group, 11 495; **62 84–87**
Cunard Line Ltd., 23 159–62; 27 90, 92; **36** 323; **38** 341, 344
CUNO Incorporated, 57 85–89
CurranCare, LLC, **50** 122
Current, Inc., 37 106–09
Currys Group PLC. *See* Dixons Group PLC.
Curtas Technologie SA, **58** 221
Curtice-Burns Foods, Inc., 7 17–18, **104–06; 21** 18, **154–57 (upd.)**
Curtin & Pease/Peneco, **27** 361
Curtis Circulation Co., **IV** 619
Curtis Homes, **22** 127
Curtis Industries, **13** 165
Curtis 1000 Inc. *See* American Business Products, Inc.
Curtis Restaurant Supply, **60** 160
Curtis Squire Inc., **18** 455
Curtiss-Wright Corporation, 7 263; **8** 49; **9** 14, 244, 341, 417; **10 260–63; 11** 427; **23** 340; **35 132–37 (upd.)**
Curver-Rubbermaid. *See* Newell Rubbermaid.
Curves International, Inc., 54 80–82
Cushman & Wakefield Inc., **58** 303
Custom Academic Publishing Company, **12** 174
Custom Building Products of California, Inc., **53** 176
Custom Chrome, Inc., 16 147–49
Custom Electronics, Inc., **9** 120
Custom Expressions, Inc., **7** 24; **22** 35
Custom Hoists, Inc., **17** 458
Custom, Ltd, **46** 197
Custom Organics, **8** 464
Custom Primers, **17** 288
Custom Publishing Group, **27** 361
Custom Technologies Corp., **19** 152
Custom Thermoform, **24** 512
Custom Tool and Manufacturing Company, **41** 366
Custom Transportation Services, Inc., **26** 62
Custom Woodwork & Plastics Inc., **36** 159
Customized Transportation Inc., **22** 164, 167
AB Custos, **25** 464
Cutisin, **55** 123
Cutler-Hammer Inc., **63** 401
Cutter & Buck Inc., 27 112–14
Cutter Precision Metals, Inc., **25** 7
CVC Capital Partners Limited, **49** 451; **54** 207
CVE Corporation, Inc., **24** 395
CVG Aviation, **34** 118
CVI Incorporated, **21** 108
CVN Companies, **9** 218
CVPS. *See* Central Vermont Public Service Corporation.
CVRD. *See* Companhia Vale do Rio Doce Ltd.
CVS Corporation, 32 166, 170; **34** 285; **45 133–38 (upd.); 63** 335–36
CWA. *See* City of Westminster Assurance Company Ltd.
CWM. *See* Chemical Waste Management, Inc.

CWP. *See* Custom Woodwork & Plastics Inc.
CWT Farms International Inc., **13** 103
CXT Inc., **33** 257
Cyber Communications Inc., **16** 168
CyberCash Inc., **18** 541, 543
Cybermedia, Inc., 25 117–19, 349
Cybernet Electronics Corp., **II** 51; **21** 330
Cybernex, **10** 463
Cybershield, Inc., **52** 103, 105
CyberSource Corp., **26** 441
CYBERTEK Corporation, **11** 395
CyberTrust Solutions Inc., **42** 24–25
Cybex International, Inc., 49 106–09
Cycle & Carriage Ltd., **20** 313; **56** 285
Cycle Video Inc., **7** 590
Cyclops Corporation, **10** 45; **13** 157
Cydsa. *See* Grupo Cydsa, S.A. de C.V.
Cygna Energy Services, **13** 367
Cygne Designs, Inc., 25 120–23; **37** 14
Cygnus Business Media, Inc., 56 73–77
Cymbal Co., Ltd. *See* Nagasakiya Co., Ltd.
Cynosure Inc., **11** 88
Cypress Amax Minerals Co., **13** 158; **22** 285–86
Cypress Insurance Co., **III** 214
Cypress Management Services, Inc., **64** 311
Cypress Semiconductor Corporation, 18 17, 383; **20 174–76**; **43** 14; **48 125–29** **(upd.)**
Cyprus Amax Coal Company, **35** 367
Cyprus Amax Minerals Company, 21 **158–61**
Cyprus Minerals Company, 7 107–09
Cyrix Corp., **10** 367; **26** 329
Cyrk Inc., 19 112–14; **21** 516; **33** 416
Cytec Industries Inc., 27 115–17
Czarnikow-Rionda Company, Inc., 32 **128–30**

D&B. *See* Dun & Bradstreet Corporation.
D&D Enterprises, Inc., **24** 96
D&F Industries, Inc., **17** 227; **41** 204
D&K Wholesale Drug, Inc., 14 146–48
D&N Systems, Inc., **10** 505
D&O Inc., **17** 363
D&W Computer Stores, **13** 176
D & W Food Stores, Inc., **8** 482; **27** 314
D Green (Electronics) Limited, **65** 141
D.B. Kaplan's, **26** 263
D.C. Heath & Co., **36** 273; **38** 374
D.C. National Bancorp, **10** 426
D. de Ricci-G. Selnet et Associes, **28** 141
d.e.m.o., **28** 345
D.E. Shaw & Co., **25** 17; **38** 269
D.E. Winebrenner Co., **7** 429
D.G. Calhoun, **12** 112
D.G. Yuengling & Son, Inc., 38 171–73
D.I. Manufacturing Inc., **37** 351
D.K. Gold, **17** 138
D.L. Rogers Group, **37** 363
D.L. Saslow Co., **19** 290
D.M. Nacional, **23** 170
D.R. Horton, Inc., 25 217; **26** 291; **58** **82–84**
D.W. Mikesell Co. *See* Mike-Sell's Inc.
Da Gama Textiles Company, **24** 450
D'Addario & Company, Inc. *See* J. D'Addario & Company, Inc.
Dade Reagents Inc., **19** 103
DADG. *See* Deutsch-Australische Dampfschiffs-Gesellschaft.

DAEDUK Techno Valley Company Ltd., **62** 174
Daewoo Group, III 457–59, 749; **18** **123–27 (upd.)**; **30** 185; **57 90–94 (upd.)**
DAF, **7** 566–67
Daffy's Inc., 26 110–12
NV Dagblad De Telegraaf. *See* N.V. Holdingmaatschappij De Telegraaf.
D'Agostino Supermarkets Inc., 19 **115–17**
Dagsbladunie, **IV** 611
DAH. *See* DeCrane Aircraft Holdings Inc.
Dahl Manufacturing, Inc., **17** 106
Dahlberg, Inc., **18** 207–08
Dahlonega Equipment and Supply Company, **12** 377
Dai-Ichi. *See also listings under* Daiichi.
Dai-Ichi Bank, **I** 511
Dai-Ichi Kangyo Asset Management Co. Ltd., **58** 235
Dai-Ichi Kangyo Bank Ltd., II 273–75, 325–26, 360–61, 374; **58** 228
Dai-Ichi Mokko Co., **III** 758
Dai-Ichi Mutual Life Insurance Co., **III** 277, 401; **25** 289; **26** 511; **38** 18
Dai Nippon. *See also listings under* Dainippon.
Dai Nippon Brewery Co., **I**, 282; **21** 319
Dai Nippon Ink and Chemicals, Inc., **54** 330
Dai Nippon Printing Co., Ltd., IV **598–600**; **57 95–99 (upd.)**
Dai Nippon Yuben Kai Kodansha. *See* Kodansha Ltd.
Daido Boeki, **24** 325
Daido Steel Co., Ltd., IV 62–63
The Daiei, Inc., V 39–40; **17 123–25** **(upd.)**; **18** 186, 285; **36** 418–19; **41** **113–16 (upd.)**
Daig Corporation, **43** 349–50
Daignault Rolland, **24** 404
Daihatsu Motor Company, Ltd., 7 **110–12**; **21 162–64 (upd.)**; **38** 415
Daiichi. *See also listings under* Dai-Ichi.
Daiichi Atomic Power Industry Group, **II** 22
Daikin Industries, Ltd., III 460–61
Daikyo Oil Co., Ltd., **IV** 403–04, 476; **53** 114
Daily Mail and General Trust plc, 19 **118–20**; **39** 198–99
Daily Press Inc., **IV** 684; **22** 522
The Daimaru, Inc., V 41–42, 130; **42** **98–100 (upd.)**
Daimler-Benz Aerospace AG, 16 150–52; **24** 84
Daimler-Benz AG, I 149–51, 186–87, 411, 549; **III** 750; **7** 219; **10** 261, 274; **11** 31; **12** 192, 342; **13** 30, 286, 414; **14** 169; **15 140–44 (upd.)**; **20** 312–13; **22** 11; **26** 481, 498
DaimlerChrysler Aerospace AG. *See* European Aeronautic Defence and Space Company EADS N.V.
DaimlerChrysler AG, 34 128–37 (upd.), 306; **57** 247; **64 100–07 (upd.)**
Dain Bosworth Inc., **15** 231–33, 486
Dain Rauscher Corporation, 35 138–41 **(upd.)**
Daini-Denden Incorporated, **12** 136–37
Daini-Denden Kikaku Company, Ltd., **II** 51. *See also* DDI Corporation.
Dainippon. *See also listings under* Dai-Nippon.

Dainippon Ink & Chemicals, Inc., **10** 466–67; **13** 308, 461; **17** 363; **28** 194
Daio Paper Corporation, IV 266–67
Dairy Crest Group plc, 32 131–33
Dairy Equipment Company, **62** 43
Dairy Farm Ice and Cold Storage Co., **IV** 700; **47** 176
Dairy Farm Management Services Ltd., **I** 471; **20** 312
Dairy Farmers of America Inc., **48** 45
Dairy Fresh, Inc., **26** 449
Dairy Mart Convenience Stores, Inc., 7 **113–15**; **17** 501; **25 124–27 (upd.)**
Dairy Queen. *See* International Dairy Queen, Inc.
Dairymen, Inc., **11** 24
Dairyworld Foods, **59** 364
Daishowa Paper Manufacturing Co., Ltd. IV 268–70, 326, 667; **17** 398; **57** **100–03 (upd.)**
Daisy/Cadnetix Inc., **6** 248; **24** 235
Daisy Manufacturing Company, Inc., **34** 72; **60** 291
Daisy Outdoor Products Inc., 58 85–88
Daisy Systems Corp., **11** 46, 284–85, 489
Daisytek International Corporation, 18 **128–30**
Daiwa Bank, Ltd., II 276–77, 347, 438; **26** 457; **39 109–11 (upd.)**
Daiwa Securities Company, Limited, II **405–06**; **9** 377
Daiwa Securities Group Inc., 55 115–18 **(upd.)**
Daka, Inc. *See* Unique Casual Restaurants, Inc.
Dakin Inc., **24** 44; **33** 415
Dakota Power Company, **6** 580; **20** 73
Dakotah Mills, **8** 558–59; **16** 353
Daksoft, Inc., **20** 74
Daktronics, Inc., 32 134–37
Dal-Tile International Inc., 22 46, 49, 169–71; **53** 175–76
Dale Carnegie Training, Inc., 28 85–87
Dale Electronics, **21** 519
Daleville & Middletown Telephone Company, **14** 258
Dalfort Corp., **15** 281
Dalgety PLC, II 499–500; **12** 411; **22** 147; **27** 258, 260. *See also* PIC International Group PLC
Dalian, **14** 556
Dalian Cement Factory, **III** 718
Dalian Dali Steel Works Co. Ltd., **53** 173
Dalian International Nordic Tire Co., **20** 263
Dalkia Holding, 66 68–70
D'Allaird's, **24** 315–16
Dallas Airmotive, **II** 16
Dallas Ceramic Co. *See* Dal-Tile International Inc.
Dallas Cowboys Football Club, Ltd., 33 **122–25**
Dallas-Fort Worth Suburban Newspapers, Inc., **10** 3
Dallas Semiconductor Corporation, 13 **191–93**; **31 143–46 (upd.)**
Daltex General Agency, Inc., **25** 115
Damark International, Inc., 18 **131–34**[see–als]Provell Inc.
Damart, **25** 523
Dameron-Pierson Co., **25** 500
Dames & Moore, Inc., 25 128–31. *See also* URS Corporation.
Damon, **21** 153

Damon Clinical Laboratories Inc., **26** 392
Damon Corp., **11** 334; **54** 57
Dan River Inc., 35 142–46
Dan's Supreme, **24** 528
Dana Alexander Inc., **27** 197; **43** 218
Dana Corporation, I 152–53; 10 264–66 (upd.); 23 170–71; **47** 376
Dana Design Ltd., **16** 297
Danaher Corporation, 7 116–17; 58 65
Danapak Holding Ltd., **11** 422
Danapak Riverwood Multipack A/S, **48** 344
Danbury Mint, **34** 370
Danbury Phamacal Inc., **31** 254
Danfoss A/S, **61** 322
Daniel Industries, Inc., 16 153–55
Daniel International Corp., **I** 570–71; **8** 192
Daniel James Insurance Group, **41** 64
Daniel P. Creed Co., Inc., **8** 386
Daniel's Jewelers, **16** 559
Danieli & C. Officine Meccaniche, **13** 98
Daniels Packaging, **12** 25
Daniels Pharmaceuticals, Inc., **24** 257
Danielson Holding Corporation, **64** 92
Danisco A/S, 44 134–37
Danish Aalborg, **27** 91
Danley Machine Corp., **I** 514
Danner Shoe Manufacturing Company, **18** 300; **61** 164
Dannon Co., Inc., 14 149–51
Danone Group, **25** 85; **35** 394, 397
Danray, **12** 135
Dansk Bioprotein, **IV** 406–07
Dansk International Designs Ltd., **10** 179, 181; **12** 313
Dansk Metal and Armaturindistri, **III** 569; **20** 361
Danske Bank Aktieselskab, 50 148–51
Danskin, Inc., 12 93–95; 15 358; **62** 88–92 (upd.)
Danville Resources, Inc., **13** 502
Danzas Group, V 441–43; 40 136–39 (upd.)
DAP, Inc., **12** 7; **18** 549
DAP Products Inc., **36** 396
Dara Michelle, **17** 101–03
D'Arcy Masius Benton & Bowles, Inc., 6 20–22; 26 187; **28** 137; **32 138–43 (upd.)**
Darden Restaurants, Inc., 16 156–58; 36 238; **44 138–42 (upd.)**
Darigold, Inc., 9 159–61
Darius International, Inc., **62** 296
Darling, Brown & Sharpe. *See* Brown & Sharpe Manufacturing Co.
Darracq, **7** 6
Darrell J. Sekin Transport Co., **17** 218
Dart & Kraft Financial Corp., **III** 610–11; **12** 310; **14** 547
Dart Group Corporation, II 645, 656, 667, 674; **12** 49; **15** 270; **16 159–62; 21** 148; **23** 370; **24** 418; **27** 158; **32** 168
Dart Industries, **9** 179–80. *See also* Premark International Inc.
Dart Transit Co., **13** 550
Dartex, **18** 434
Darty S.A., 27 118–20
Darvel Realty Trust, **14** 126
Darya-Varia Laboratoria, **18** 182
DASA. *See* Daimler-Benz Aerospace AG; Deutsche Aerospace Airbus.
Dashwood Industries, **19** 446

DASS Die andere SystemsentsorgungsGesellschaft mbH, **58** 28
Dassault Aviation SA, **21** 11
Dassault-Breguet. *See* Avions Marcel Dassault-Breguet Aviation.
Dassault Systèmes S.A., 25 132–34; 26 179. *See also* Groupe Dassault Aviation SA.
Dassler, **14** 6
Dastek Inc., **10** 464; **11** 234–35
DAT GmbH, **10** 514
Data Acquisition Systems, Inc., **16** 300
Data Architects, **14** 318
Data Base Management Inc., **11** 19
Data-Beam Corp., **25** 301
Data Broadcasting Corporation, 31 147–50
Data Card Corporation, **IV** 680; **58** 340
Data Force Inc., **11** 65
Data General Corporation, 8 137–40; 9 297; **10** 499; **12** 162; **13** 201; **16** 418; **20** 8
Data One Corporation, **11** 111
Data Preparation, Inc., **11** 112
Data Printer, Inc., **18** 435
Data Specialties Inc. *See* Zebra Technologies Corporation.
Data Structures Inc., **11** 65
Data Systems Technology, **11** 57; **38** 375
Data Technology Corp., **18** 510
Data 3 Systems, **9** 36
Datac plc, **18** 140
Datachecker Systems, **III** 164; **11** 150
Datacraft Corp., **II** 38
DataFocus, Inc., **18** 112
DataPath Systems, **64** 246
Datapoint Corporation, 11 67–70
Dataquest Inc., **10** 558; **21** 235, 237; **22** 51; **25** 347
Datas Incorporated. *See* Delta Air Lines, Inc.
Datascope Corporation, 39 112–14
Dataset Communications Inc., **23** 100
Datastream International Ltd., **10** 89; **13** 417
Datatec Ltd., **67** 392–94
DataTimes Corporation, **29** 58
Datavision Inc., **11** 444
Datec, **22** 17
Datek Online Holdings Corp., 32 144–46; 48 225–27
Datran, **11** 468
Datsun. *See* Nissan Motor Company, Ltd.
Datura Corp., **14** 391
Dauphin Deposit Corporation, 14 152–54
Dauphin Distribution Services. *See* Exel Logistics Ltd.
Daut + Rietz and Connectors Pontarlier, **19** 166
Dave & Buster's, Inc., 33 126–29
Davenport Mammoet Heavy Transport Inc., **26** 280
The Davey Tree Expert Company, 11 71–73
The David and Lucile Packard Foundation, 41 117–19
David B. Smith & Company, **13** 243
David Berg & Co., **14** 537
David Brown & Son. *See* Brown & Sharpe Manufacturing Co.
David Brown, Ltd., **10** 380
David Clark, **30** 357

David Crystal, Inc., **9** 156
David Hafler Company, **43** 323
The David J. Joseph Company, 14 155–56; **19** 380; **55** 347
David Jones Ltd., 60 100–02
David Kelley Design. *See* IDEO Inc.
David L. Babson & Company Inc., **53** 213
David Lloyd Leisure Ltd., **52** 412, 415–16
David S. Smith Ltd. *See* DS Smith Plc.
David Wilson Homes Ltd., **45** 442–43
David's Bridal, Inc., 33 130–32; 46 288
David's Supermarkets, **17** 180
Davide Campari-Milano S.p.A., 57 104–06
Davids. *See* Metcash Trading Ltd.
Davidson & Associates, **16** 146
Davidson & Leigh, **21** 94
Davidson Brothers Co., **19** 510
Davis & Geck, **27** 115
Davis Manufacturing Company, **10** 380
Davis Polk & Wardwell, 36 151–54
Davis Service Group PLC, 45 139–41; 49 374, 377
Davis-Standard Company, **9** 154; **36** 144
Davis Vision, Inc., **27** 209
Davis Wholesale Company, **9** 20
Davlyn Industries, Inc., **22** 487
Davox Corporation, **18** 31
Davy Bamag GmbH, **IV** 142
Davy McKee AG, **IV** 142
DAW Technologies, Inc., 25 135–37
Dawe's Laboratories, Inc., **12** 3
Dawn Food Products, Inc., 17 126–28
Dawson Holdings PLC, 43 132–34
Day & Zimmermann Inc., 6 579; **9** 162–64; **31 151–55 (upd.)**
Day Brite Lighting, **II** 19
Day-Glo Color Corp., **8** 456
Day International, **8** 347
Day-N-Nite, **II** 620
Day Runner, Inc., 14 157–58; 41 120–23 (upd.)
Day-Timers, Inc., **51** 9
Daybridge Learning Centers, **13** 49, 299
Dayco Products, **7** 297
Daylin Corporation, **46** 271
Days Inns of America, Inc., **III** 344; **11** 178; **13** 362, 364; **21** 362
Daystar International Inc., **11** 44
Daytex, Inc., **II** 669; **18** 505; **50** 455
Dayton Engineering Laboratories, **9** 416
Dayton Hudson Corporation, V 43–44; 8 35; **9** 360; **10** 136, 391–93, 409–10, 515–16; **13** 330; **14** 376; **16** 176, 559; **18** 108, 135–37 (upd.); **22** 59. *See also* Target Corporation.
Dayton Power & Light Company, **6** 467, 480–82
Daytron Mortgage Systems, **11** 485
Dazey Corp., **16** 384; **43** 289
DB. *See* Deutsche Bundesbahn.
DB Group, **59** 59–60
DB Reise & Touristik AG, **37** 250
DBA Holdings, Inc., **18** 24
DBMS Inc., **14** 390
DBS, **56** 363
DBT Online Inc. *See* ChoicePoint Inc.
DC Comics Inc., 25 138–41
DC Shoes, Inc., 60 103–05
DCA Advertising, **16** 168
DCA Food Industries, **27** 258–60, 299
DCE Consultants, **51** 17
DCL BioMedical, Inc., **11** 333
DCMS Holdings Inc., **7** 114; **25** 125

DDB Needham Worldwide, **14** 159–61; **22** 394

DDD Energy, Inc., **47** 348, 350

DDI Corporation, **7** 118–20; **13** 482; **21** 330–31

NV De Beer and Partners, **45** 386

De Beers Consolidated Mines Limited / De Beers Centenary AG, **IV** 64–68, 79, 94; **7** 121–26 (**upd.**); **16** 25–26, 29; **21** 345–46; **28** 88–94 (**upd.**); **50** 31, 34; **62** 7, 9–10

De Bono Industries, **24** 443

De Dietrich & Cie., **31** 156–59

De Grenswisselkantoren NV, **III** 201

de Havilland Aircraft Co., **III** 507–08; **7** 11. See also Bombardier Inc.

de Havilland Holdings, Ltd., **24** 85–86

De La Rue plc, **10** 267–69; **34** 138–43 (**upd.**); **46** 251

De Leuw, Cather & Company, **8** 416

De Paepe, **45** 386

De Streekkrant-De Weekkrantgroep NV, **48** 347

De Tomaso Industries, **11** 104; **50** 197

De Trey Gesellchaft, **10** 271

De Vito/Verdi, **26** 111

DEA Group, **23** 83

Dead Sea Works Ltd., **55** 229

Dealer Equipment and Services, **10** 492

Dealers Wholesale Inc., **56** 230

Dean & Barry Co., **8** 455

Dean & DeLuca, Inc., **36** 155–57

Dean Foods Company, **7** 127–29; **17** 56; **21** 157, 165–68 (**upd.**); **26** 447; **29** 434; **46** 70

Dean Witter, Discover & Co., **7** 213; **12** 96–98; **21** 97; **22** 405–07. See also Morgan Stanley Dean Witter & Company.

Dearborn Mid-West Conveyor Company, **56** 78–80

Dearborn Publishing Group, **42** 211

Death Row Records, **27** 121–23

Deb Shops, Inc., **16** 163–65

DeBartolo Realty Corp., **27** 401

Debenhams Plc, **28** 95–97; **39** 88

Debevoise & Plimpton, **39** 115–17

Debis, **26** 498

DeBoles Nutritional Foods Inc., **27** 197–98; **43** 218–19

Debron Investments Plc., **8** 271

DEC. See Digital Equipment Corp.

Decafin SpA, **26** 278, 280

Decathlon S.A., **39** 183–84

Decca Record Company Ltd., **23** 389

Dechert, **43** 135–38

Decision Systems Israel Ltd. (DSI), **21** 239

DecisionQuest, Inc., **25** 130

Decker, Howell & Co., **26** 451

Deckers Outdoor Corporation, **22** 172–74

Deco Industries, Inc., **18** 5

Deco Purchasing Company, **39** 211

Decolletage S.A. St.-Maurice, **14** 27

Decora Industries, Inc., **31** 160–62

DeCrane Aircraft Holdings Inc., **36** 158–60

Dee and Cee Toy Co., **25** 312

Dee Corporation plc, **II** 628–29, 642; **24** 269

Dee Zee Inc., **61** 173

Deep Ocean Services, L.L.C., **44** 203

Deep Rock Oil Company. See Kerr-McGee Corporation.

DeepFlex Production Partners, L.P., **21** 171

Deepsea Ventures, Inc., **IV** 152; **24** 358

DeepTech International Inc., **21** 169–71

Deepwater Light and Power Company, **6** 449

Deere & Company, **III** 462–64; **10** 377–78, 380; **11** 472; **13** 16–17, 267; **16** 179; **17** 533; **21** 172–76 (**upd.**); **22** 542; **26** 492; **42** 101–06 (**upd.**)

Deering Harvesting Machinery Company. See Navistar.

Deering Milliken & Co., **51** 12. See also Milliken & Co.

Def Jam Records, Inc., **23** 389, 391; **31** 269; **33** 373–75

Defense Technology Corporation of America, **27** 50

Defiance, Inc., **22** 175–78

Deflecta-Shield Corporation, **40** 299–300

Deft Software, Inc., **10** 505

Degussa Group, **IV** 69–72, 118

Degussa-Hüls AG, **32** 147–53 (**upd.**); **34** 209

Degussa-Metais, Catalisadores e Ceramica, Lda, **56** 127

DEKA Research & Development Corporation. See Segway LLC.

DeKalb AgResearch Inc., **9** 411; **41** 304–06

Dekalb Energy Company, **18** 366

DeKalb Farmers Market, **23** 263–64

DeKalb Genetics Corporation, **17** 129–31; **29** 330

DeKalb Office Supply, **25** 500

DeKuyper, **58** 194

Del Laboratories, Inc., **28** 98–100

Del Mar Avionics, **26** 491

Del Monte Corporation, **7** 130–32; **12** 439; **14** 287; **25** 234

Del Monte Foods Company, **23** 163–66 (**upd.**); **36** 472; **38** 198

Del Taco, Inc., **58** 89–92

Del Webb Corporation, **14** 162–64; **17** 186–87; **19** 377–78; **26** 291

Delafield, Harvey, Tabrell, Inc., **17** 498

Delafield Industries, **12** 418

Delaware and Hudson Railway Company, Inc., **16** 350; **45** 78

Delaware Charter Guarantee & Trust Co., **III** 330

Delaware Guarantee and Trust Co. See Wilmington Trust Company.

Delaware Management Holdings, **III** 386

Delaware North Companies Incorporated, **7** 133–36

Delchamps, Inc., **II** 638; **27** 247

Delco Electronics Corporation, **II** 32–35; **25** 223–24; **45** 142–43

Delek Investment & Properties Ltd., **45** 170

Delhaize "Le Lion" S.A., **II** 626; **15** 176; **27** 94; **44** 143–46

Delhi Gas Pipeline Corporation, **7** 551

Deli Universal NV, **13** 545; **66** 71–74

dELiA*s Inc., **29** 141–44

Delicato Vineyards, Inc., **50** 152–55

Delicious Foods, **13** 383

Delimaatschappij, **13** 545

Dell Computer Corporation, **9** 165–66; **10** 309, 459; **11** 62; **16** 5, 196; **24** 31; **25** 254; **27** 168; **31** 163–66 (**upd.**); **47** 323; **50** 92; **63** 122–26 (**upd.**), 153

Dell Distributing, **25** 483

Dell Publishing Co., **13** 560

Delmarva Properties, Inc., **8** 103; **30** 118

Delmas-Vieljeux. See Groupe Bolloré.

Deloitte & Touche, **9** 167–69, 423; **24** 29

Deloitte Touche Tohmatsu International, **29** 145–48 (**upd.**)

De'Longhi S.p.A., **66** 75–77

DeLorean Motor Co., **10** 117; **14** 321

DeLorme Publishing Company, Inc., **53** 121–23

Delphi Automotive Systems Corporation, **22** 52; **36** 243; **25** 223; **37** 429; **45** 142–44

Delphy Industries S.A.S., **53** 221

Delta and Pine Land Company, **21** 386; **33** 133–37; **59** 148–50

Delta Acceptance Corporation Limited, **13** 63

Delta Air Lines, Inc., **I** 91, 97, **99–100**, 102, 106, 120, 132; **6** 81–83 (**upd.**), 117, 131–32, 383; **12** 149, 381; **13** 171–72; **14** 73; **21** 141, 143; **22** 22; **25** 420, 422–23; **26** 439; **27** 20, 409; **33** 50–51, 377; **34** 116–17, 119; **39** 118–21 (**upd.**); **47** 29; **52** 90, 92–93

Delta Biologicals S.r.l., **11** 208

Delta Biotechnology Ltd., **25** 82

Delta Campground Management Corp., **33** 399

Delta Communications. See Reed Elsevier.

Delta Education, **29** 470, 472

Delta Faucet Co. See Masco Corporation.

Delta Health, Inc. See DVI, Inc.

Delta International Machinery Corp., **26** 361–63

Delta Lloyd, **III** 235

Delta Play, Ltd., **44** 261

Delta Pride Catfish Inc., **18** 247

Delta Queen Steamboat Company, **27** 34–35

Delta Resources Inc., **26** 519

Delta Savings Assoc. of Texas, **IV** 343

Delta Steamship Lines, **9** 425–26

Delta V Technologies, Inc., **33** 348

Delta Woodside Industries, Inc., **8** 141–43; **17** 329; **30** 159–61 (**upd.**); **42** 118

Deltak, L.L.C., **23** 300; **52** 139

Deltec, Inc., **56** 81–83

Deltic Timber Corporation, **32** 339, 341; **46** 115–17

Deluxe Corporation, **7** 137–39; **19** 291; **22** 179–82 (**upd.**); **37** 107–08

Deluxe Data, **18** 518

Deluxe Media Services Inc., **64** 320

Deluxe Upholstering Ltd., **14** 303

DEMCO, Inc., **60** 106–09

Demerara Company, **13** 102

Deming Company, **8** 135

Demko, **30** 469

DeMoulas / Market Basket Inc., **23** 167–69

Den Fujita, **9** 74

Den Norske Bank, **22** 275

Den Norske Stats Oljeselskap AS, **IV** 405–07, 486. See also Statoil ASA.

DenAmerica Corporation, **29** 149–51

Denault Ltd., **II** 651

Denbury Resources, Inc., **67** 139–41

Denby Group plc, **44** 147–50

Denison International plc, **46** 118–20

Denison Mines, Ltd., **12** 198

Denker & Goodwin, **17** 498

Denmark Tiscali A/S, **48** 398

Denney-Reyburn, **8** 360

Dennis Publishing Ltd., **62** 93–95
Dennison Manufacturing Company. *See* Avery Dennison Corporation.
Denny's Restaurants Inc., **II** 680; **12** 511; **13** 526; **27** 16–18; **50** 489
Denshi Media Services, **IV** 680
DENSO Corporation, **46** 121–26 (upd.)
Dental Benefits Insurance Company, **51** 276, 278
Dental Capital Corp., **19** 290
Dental Research, **25** 56
DentiCare, Inc., **22** 149
Dentists Management Corporation, **51** 276–78
Dentons Green Brewery, **21** 246
Dentsply International Inc., **10** 270–72
Dentsu Inc., **I** 9–11, 36, 38; **9** 30; **13** 204; **16** 166–69 (upd.); **25** 91; **40** 140–44 (upd.)
Denver & Rio Grande Railroad, **12** 18–19
Denver Chemical Company, **8** 84; **38** 124
Denver Gas & Electric Company. *See* Public Service Company of Colorado.
Denver Nuggets, **51** 94–97
Deocsa, **51** 389
DEP. *See* Hellenic Petroleum SA.
DEP Corporation, **20** 177–80; **34** 209
Department 56, Inc., **14** 165–67; **22** 59; **34** 144–47 (upd.)
Department of Currency and Coinage, **62** 248
Department Stores International, **I** 426; **22** 72; **50** 117
Deposit Guaranty Corporation, **17** 132–35
DePree Company, **17** 90–91
DePuy, Inc., **10** 156–57; **30** 162–65; **36** 306; **37** 110–13 (upd.)
Derby Cycle Corporation, **65** 297
Derby Outdoor, **27** 280
Deritend Computers, **14** 36
Dermablend, Inc., **31** 89
Derwent Publications, **8** 526
Des Moines Electric Light Company, **6** 504
DESA Industries, **8** 545
Desc, S.A. de C.V., **23** 170–72
Deschutes Brewery, Inc., **57** 107–09
Desco, **51** 120
Deseret Management Corporation, **29** 67
Deseret National Bank, **11** 118
Deseret Pharmaceutical Company, **21** 45
Design-Center Southwest, **19** 411
Design Trend, Inc., **37** 394
Designcraft Inc. *See* Sloan's Supermarkets Inc.
Designer Holdings Ltd., **20** 181–84; **22** 123
Designs, Inc. *See* Casual Male Retail Group, Inc.
Designtroupe, **60** 143–44
Desmonds Formalwear, **60** 5
DeSoto, Inc., **8** 553; **13** 471
Desoutter Brothers plc, **III** 427; **28** 40
Destec Energy, Inc., **12** 99–101; **49** 121
Det Danske Rengorings Selskab A/S, **49** 221
Detroit Ball Bearing Co., **13** 78
Detroit Chemical Coatings, **8** 553
Detroit City Gas Company. *See* MCN Corporation.
Detroit Diesel Corporation, **V** 494–95; **9** 18; **10** 273–75; **11** 471; **12** 90–91; **18** 308; **19** 292–94; **21** 503

The Detroit Edison Company, **V** 592–95; **7** 377–78; **14** 135; **18** 320. *See also* DTE Energy Co.
Detroit-Graphite Company, **8** 553
The Detroit Lions, Inc., **55** 119–21
The Detroit Pistons Basketball Company, **41** 124–27
Detroit Red Wings, **7** 278–79; **24** 293; **37** 207; **46** 127
Detroit Stoker Company, **37** 399–401
Detroit Tigers Baseball Club, Inc., **24** 293; **37** 207; **46** 127–30
Dettmers Industries Inc., **36** 159–60
Deutsch-Australische Dampfschiffs-Gesellschaft, **6** 398
Deutsch, Inc., **42** 107–10
Deutsche Aerospace Airbus, **7** 9, 11; **12** 190–91; **21** 8; **52** 113–14
Deutsche BA, **14** 73; **24** 400; **26** 115
Deutsche Babcock AG, **III** 465–66
Deutsche Bahn AG, **37** 250, 253; **46** 131–35 (upd.); **59** 387, 390–91
Deutsche Bank AG, **I** 151, 549; **II** 278–80; **14** 168–71 (upd.); **15** 13; **16** 364–65; **17** 324; **21** 147, **34** 29; **40** 145–51 (upd.); **47** 81–84; **49** 44
Deutsche Börse AG, **37** 131–32; **59** 151–55
Deutsche BP Aktiengesellschaft, **7** 140–43; **62** 12, 14
Deutsche Bundespost Telekom, **V** 287–90; **18** 155. *See also* Deutsche Telekom AG
Deutsche Bundesbahn, **V** 444–47; **6** 424–26
Deutsche Erdol Aktiengesellschaft, **7** 140
Deutsche Grammophon Gesellschaft, **23** 389
Deutsche Herold, **49** 44
Deutsche Kreditbank, **14** 170
Deutsche Lufthansa Aktiengesellschaft, **I** 110–11, 120; **6** 59–60, 69, 95–96, 386; **12** 191; **25** 159; **26** 113–16 (upd.); **27** 465; **33** 49; **36** 426; **48** 258
Deutsche Petroleum-Verkaufsgesellschaft mbH, **7** 140
Deutsche Post AG, **29** 152–58; **40** 138; **63** 418
Deutsche Reichsbahn. *See* Deutsche Bundesbahn.
Deutsche Shell, **7** 140
Deutsche Steinkohle AG, **60** 250
Deutsche Telekom AG, **18** 155; **25** 102; **38** 296; **48** 130–35 (upd.)
Deutsche Verlags-Anstalt GmbH, **66** 123
Deutsche Vermögensberatung AG, **51** 19, 23
Deutsche Wagnisfinanzierung, **47** 83
Deutscher Kommunal-Verlag Dr. Naujoks & Behrendt, **14** 556
Deutscher Ring, **40** 61
Deutz AG, **39** 122–26
Deutz-Allis. *See* AGCO Corp.
Deutz Farm Equipment, **13** 17
Devanlay SA, **48** 279
Devcon Corporation, **III** 519; **22** 282
Deveaux S.A., **41** 128–30
Developer's Mortgage Corp., **16** 347
Devenish, **21** 247
DeVilbiss Company, **8** 230
DeVilbiss Health Care, Inc., **11** 488
Deville, **27** 421
Devoe & Raynolds Co., **12** 217
Devoke Company, **18** 362

Devon Energy Corporation, **22** 304; **61** 73–75
Devro plc, **55** 122–24
DeVry Incorporated, **9** 63; **29** 56, 159–61
Dewey Ballantine LLP, **48** 136–39
Dex Media, Inc., **65** 128–30
Dexer Corporation, **41** 10
Dexia Group, **42** 111–13
The Dexter Corporation, **I** 320–22; **12** 102–04 (upd.); **17** 287; **52** 183. *See also* Invitrogen Corporation.
Dexter Lock Company, **45** 269
Dexter Shoe, **18** 60, 63
DFS Group Ltd., **I** 35; **33** 276; **66** 78–80
DFW Printing Company, **10** 3
DG&E. *See* Denver Gas & Electric Company.
DG Bank, **33** 358
DGS SpA, **62** 100
DH Compounding, **8** 347
DH Technology, Inc., **18** 138–40
Dharma Juice, **31** 350
DHI Corp., **II** 680
DHJ Industries, Inc., **12** 118
DHL Worldwide Express, **6** 385–87; **18** 177, 316; **24** 133–36 (upd.); **26** 441; **27** 471, 475; **29** 152
Di Giorgio Corp., **II** 602; **12** 105–07; **24** 528–29
Di-Rite Company, **11** 534
Diageo plc, **24** 137–41 (upd.); **25** 411; **29** 19; **31** 92; **34** 89; **36** 404; **42** 223; **56** 46, 48; **61** 323, 325
Diagnostic Health Corporation, **14** 233
Diagnostic Imaging Services, Inc., **25** 384
Diagnostic/Retrieval Systems Inc. *See* DRS Technologies Inc.
Diagnostic Ventures Inc. *See* DVI, Inc.
Dial-A-Mattress Operating Corporation, **32** 427; **46** 136–39
The Dial Corporation, **8** 144–46; **23** 173–75 (upd.); **29** 114; **32** 230; **34** 209
Dial Home Shopping Ltd., **28** 30
Dial-Net Inc., **27** 306
Dialight Corp., **13** 397–98
Dialog Information Services, Inc., **IV** 630
Dialogic Corporation, **18** 141–43
Diamandis Communications Inc., **IV** 619, 678
Diamedix, **11** 207
Diamond Animal Health, Inc., **39** 216
Diamond Communications, **10** 288
Diamond Crystal Brands, Inc., **32** 274, 277
Diamond Electronics, **24** 510
Diamond Fields Resources Inc., **27** 457
Diamond Head Resources, Inc. *See* AAON, Inc.
Diamond International Corp., **13** 254–55; **26** 446
Diamond M Offshore Inc., **12** 318
Diamond Match Company, **14** 163
Diamond of California, **64** 108–11 (upd.)
Diamond Offshore Drilling, Inc., **36** 325; **43** 202
Diamond Park Fine Jewelers, **16** 559
Diamond Rug & Carpet Mills, **19** 276
Diamond Savings & Loan, **II** 420
Diamond Shamrock Corporation, **IV** 408–11, 481; **7** 34, 308–099, 345; **13** 118; **19** 177; **45** 411. *See also* Ultramar Diamond Shamrock Corporation.
Diamond Sparkler Manufacturing Co. Inc. *See* B.J. Alan Co., Inc.

Diamond-Star Motors Corporation, **9** 349–51
Diamond State Insurance Company, **63** 410–12
Diamond Walnut Growers, **7** 496–97
DiamondCluster International, Inc., 51 **98–101**
Dianatel, **18** 143
Diapositive, **44** 296
Diasonics Ultrasound, Inc., **27** 355
Diaxon A.B.E.E., **64** 177
Dibrell Brothers, Incorporated, 12 **108–10; 13** 492
dick clark productions, inc., 16 170–73
Dick Corporation, 64 112–14
Dick Simon Trucking, Inc. *See* Simon Transporation Services Inc.
Dick's Sporting Goods, Inc., 59 156–59
Dickerman, **8** 366
Dickson Forest Products, Inc., **15** 305
Dickstein Partners, L.P., **13** 261
Didier Lamarthe, **17** 210
Didier-Werke AG, **IV** 232; **53** 285
Diebold, Incorporated, 7 144–46; 22 **183–87 (upd.)**
Diedrich Coffee, Inc., 40 152–54
Diehl Manufacturing Co., **II** 9
Dierbergs Markets Inc., 63 127–29
Diesel Nacional, S.A. *See* Consorcio G Grupo Dina, S.A. de C.V.
Diesel SpA, 40 155–57; 63 361–62
Diesel United Co., **III** 533
Diet Center, **10** 383
Dieter Hein Co., **14** 537
Dietrich & Cie. *See* De Dietrich & Cie.
Dietrich Corp., **II** 512; **15** 221; **51** 158
DiFeo Automotive Group, **26** 500–01
Diffusion Immobilier. *See* Union Financière de France Banque.
DiFranza Williamson, **6** 40
DIG Acquisition Corp., **12** 107
Digex, Inc., 45 201; **46 140–43**
Digi International Inc., 9 170–72; 20 237; **67** 55–56
Digicom, **22** 17
Digidesign Inc., **38** 70, 72
DiGiorgio Corporation, **25** 421
Digital City, Inc., **22** 522; **63** 393
Digital Data Systems Company, **11** 408
Digital Directory Assistance, **18** 24
Digital Entertainment Network, **42** 272
Digital Equipment Corporation, II 62, 108; **III 132–35**, 142, 149, 166; **6** **233–36 (upd.)**; **8** 137–39, 519; **9** 35, 43, 57, 166, 170–71, 514; **10** 22–23, 34, 86, 242, 361, 463, 477; **11** 46, 86–88, 274, 491, 518–19; **12** 147, 162, 470; **13** 127, 202, 482; **14** 318; **15** 108; **16** 394, 418; **18** 143, 345; **19** 310; **21** 123; **25** 499; **26** 90, 93; **34** 441–43; **36** 81, 287; **43** 13; **45** 201; **50** 227
Digital Marketing, Inc., **22** 357
Digital Research in Electronic Acoustics and Music S.A., **17** 34
Digital River, Inc., 50 156–59
Digitech, **19** 414
Digitel, **63** 380
Dii Group Inc., **38** 188–89
Dill Enterprises, Inc., **14** 18
Dillard Department Stores, Inc., V **45–47; 10** 488; **11** 349; **12** 64; **13** 544–45; **16 174–77 (upd.)**, 559; **19** 48, 324; **27** 61; **63** 261
Dillard Paper Company, 11 74–76

Dillingham Construction Corporation, 44 151–54 (upd.)
Dillingham Corp., I 565–66
Dillingham Holdings Inc., **9** 511
Dillon Companies Inc., II 645; **12** 111–13; **15** 267; **22** 194
Dillon Paper, **IV** 288
Dillon, Read, and Co., Inc., **11** 53; **20** 259; **24** 66
Dillons, **59** 230
DiMark, Inc., **63** 189
Dime Bancorp, **44** 32–33; **46** 316
Dime Banking and Loan Association of Rochester, **10** 91
Dime Savings Bank of New York, F.S.B., 9 173–74
Dimeling, Schreiber & Park, **11** 63; **44** 309
Dimension Films, **64** 285
Dimensions in Sport, Ltd., **37** 5
Dimeric Development Corporation, **14** 392
DIMON Inc., 12 110; **27 124–27**
Dina. *See* Consorcio G Grupo Dina, S.A. de C.V.
Dinamica, S.A., **19** 12
Dine S.A., **23** 170–72
Dineen Mechanical Contractors, Inc., **48** 238
Diners Club, **6** 62; **9** 335
Dinner Bell Foods, Inc., **11** 93
Dionex Corporation, 46 144–46
Dior. *See* Christian Dior S.A.
Dippin' Dots, Inc., 56 84–86
Dirección General de Correos y Telecomunicaciónes. *See* Telefónica Nacional de España S.A.
Direct Container Lines, **14** 505
Direct Focus, Inc., 47 93–95
Direct Friends, **25** 91
Direct Line, **12** 422
Direct Mail Services Pty. Ltd., **10** 461
Direct Marketing Technology Inc., **19** 184
Direct Merchants Credit Card Bank, N.A., **56** 224
Direct Transit, Inc., **42** 364
Direction of Coins and Medals, **62** 248
DirectLine Insurance, **22** 52
Directorate General of **Telecommunications, 7 147–49**
DIRECTV, Inc., 21 70; **35** 156, 158–59; **38 174–77**
Dirki S.A., **64** 8
Disc Go Round, **18** 207, 209
Disc Manufacturing, Inc., **15** 378
Disclosure, Inc., **18** 24
Disco SA, **V** 11; **19** 308–09
Discount Auto Parts, Inc., 18 144–46; 26 348; **57** 12
Discount Corporation, **12** 565
Discount Drug Mart, Inc., 14 172–73
Discount Investment Corporation Ltd., **24** 429
Discount Labels, Inc., **20** 15
Discount Tire Co., **19** 294; **20** 263
Discover, **9** 335; **12** 97
Discovery Communications, Inc., 42 **114–17**
Discovery Partners International, Inc., 58 93–95
Discovery Toys, Inc., **19** 28
Discovery Zone, **31** 97
Discreet Logic Inc., 20 185–87
Disctronics, Ltd., **15** 380
Disney. *See* The Walt Disney Company.
Disneyland Paris. *See* Euro Disney S.C.A.

Disnorte, **51** 389
Dispatch Communications, **10** 432
Displayco Midwest Inc., **8** 103
Distillers Co. plc, I 239–41, 252, 263, 284–85; **II** 609–10; **43** 214. *See also* Diageo PLC.
Distinctive Printing and Packaging Co., **8** 103
Distinctive Software Inc., **10** 285
Distribuidora Bega, S.A. de C.V., **31** 92
Distribuidora de Produtos de Petróleo Ipiranga, **67** 216–17
Distribution Centers Incorporated. *See* Exel Logistics Ltd.
Distribution Centre Sdn. Bhd., **62** 268
Distribution Services, Inc., **10** 287
Distribution Solutions International, Inc., **24** 126
District News Co., **II** 607
Distrigas, **IV** 425
DITAS. *See* Türkiye Petrolleri Anonim Ortakliği.
Divani & Divani. *See* Industrie Natuzzi S.p.A.
Divco-Wayne Corp., **17** 82
DIVE!, **26** 264
Diversey Corp., **I** 275, 333; **13** 150, 199; **26** 305–06; **32** 476
Diversified Agency Services, **I** 32
Diversified Foods Inc., **25** 179
Diversified Retailing Co., **III** 214
Diversified Services, **9** 95
Diversion Entertainment, Inc., **58** 124
Diversity Consultants Inc., **32** 459
Divesco Inc., **58** 333
DiviCom, **43** 221–22
Dixie Airline, **25** 420
Dixie Bearings, Inc., **13** 78
Dixie Carriers, Inc., **18** 277
Dixie Container Corporation, **12** 377
Dixie Crystals Brands, Inc., **32** 277
The Dixie Group, Inc., 20 188–90
Dixie Hi-Fi, **9** 120–21
Dixie-Narco Inc., **III** 573; **22** 349
Dixie Offshore Transportation Company. *See* Kirby Corporation.
Dixie Power & Light Company, **6** 514
Dixie Yarns, Inc., **9** 466; **19** 305
Dixieland Food Stores, **II** 624
Dixieline. *See* Lanoga Corporation.
Dixon Industries, Inc., 26 117–19; 48 59
Dixon Ticonderoga Company, 12 114–16
Dixons Group plc, V 48–50; 9 65; **10** 45, 306; **19 121–24 (upd.); 23** 52; **24** 269–70; **49 110–13 (upd.)**
DIY Home Warehouse, **16** 210
DJ Moldings Corp., **18** 276
DJ Pharma, Inc., **47** 56
Djarum PT, 62 96–98
Djedi Holding SA, **23** 242
DKB. *See* Dai-Ichi Kangyo Bank Ltd.
DKNY. *See* Donna Karan International Inc.
Dl Radiators France S.A.R.L. *See* De'Longhi S.p.A.
DLC. *See* Duquesne Light Company.
DLJ. *See* Donaldson, Lufkin & Jenrette.
DLJ Merchant Banking Partners II, **21** 188; **36** 158–59
DLL. *See* David Lloyd Leisure Ltd.
DM Associates Limited Partnership, **25** 127
DMA, **18** 510
DMAX-Ltd., **57** 190

DMB&B. *See* D'Arcy Masius Benton & Bowles.
dmc2 Italia SrL, **56** 127
DMGT. *See* Daily Mail and General Trust.
DMI Furniture, Inc., 44 132; **46 147–50**
DMP Mineralöl Petrochemie GmbH, **IV** 487
DMV Stainless, **54** 393
DNATA, **39** 137, 139
DNN Galvanizing Limited Partnership, **24** 144
DNP DENMARK A/S, **IV** 600
Do It All, **24** 75
Do it Best Corporation, 30 166–70
Dobbs House, **21** 54
Dobbs Houses Inc., **15** 87
Dobrolet. *See* Aeroflot.
Dobson Communications Corporation, 63 130–32
Dobson Park Industries, **38** 227
Doc Green's Gourmet Salads Inc., **64** 327, 329
Doc Holliday's Pawnbrokers and Jewelers, Inc., **61** 55
Docks de France, **37** 23; **39** 183–84
Doctor's Associates Inc., 67 142–45 (upd.)
The Doctors' Company, 55 125–28
Documentation Resources, **11** 65
Documentum, Inc., 46 151–53
DOD Electronics Corp., **15** 215
Dodd, Mead & Co., **14** 498
Dodge & Day. *See* Day & Zimmermann, Inc.
The Dodge Group, **11** 78
Dodge Manufacturing Company, **9** 440
Dodge Motor Company, **20** 259
Doduco Corporation, **29** 460–61
Doe Run Company, **12** 244
Doeflex PLC, **33** 79
Dofasco Inc., IV 73–74; 24 142–44 (upd.)
Dogi International Fabrics S.A., 52 99–102
Doherty, Mann & Olshan. *See* Wells Rich Greene BDDP.
Dolan Design, Inc., **44** 133
Dolby Laboratories Inc., 20 191–93
Dolce & Gabbana SpA, 61 192–93; **62 99–101**
Dole Corporation, **44** 152
Dole Food Company, Inc., II 491–92; **9 175–76; 20** 116; **31 167–70 (upd.)**
Dollar Bills, Inc. *See* Dollar Tree Stores, Inc.
Dollar Express Inc., **62** 104
Dollar General, **26** 533
Dollar Thrifty Automotive Group, Inc., 25 92, **142–45**
Dollar Tree Stores, Inc., 16 161; **23 176–78; 62 102–05 (upd.)**
Dollfus Mieg & Cie. *See* Groupe DMC.
Dollond & Aitchison Group, **49** 151–52
Dolmar GmbH, **59** 272
Dolomite Franchi SpA, **53** 285
Dolphin Book Club, **13** 106
Dolphin Services, Inc., **44** 203
Dom Perignon, **25** 258
Domaine Carneros, **43** 401
Domaines Barons de Rothschild, **36** 113, 115
Doman Industries Limited, 59 160–62
Dombrico, Inc., **8** 545
Domco Industries, **19** 407

Dome Petroleum, Ltd., **IV** 371, 401, 494; **12** 364
Dominick International Corp., **12** 131
Dominick's Finer Foods, Inc., 9 451; **13** 25, 516; **17** 558, 560–61; **56 87–89**
Dominion Bond Rating Service Ltd., **65** 244
Dominion Bridge Company, Limited, **8** 544
Dominion Dairies, **7** 429
Dominion Engineering Works Ltd., **8** 544
Dominion Foils Ltd., **17** 280
Dominion Hoist & Shovel Co., **8** 544
Dominion Homes, Inc., 19 125–27
Dominion Industries Ltd., **15** 229
Dominion Mushroom Co., **II** 649–50
Dominion Resources, Inc., V 596–99; 54 83–87 (upd.); 60 152
Dominion Salt Ltd., **62** 307
Dominion Stores Ltd., **II** 650, 652
Dominion Terminal Associates, **IV** 171; **7** 582, 584
Dominion Textile Inc., 8 559–60; **12 117–19**
Domino S.p.A., **51** 324
Domino Sugar Corporation, 26 120–22; 42 370
Domino Supermarkets, **24** 528
Domino's, Inc., 7 150–53; 9 74; **12** 123; **15** 344, 346; **16** 447; **21 177–81 (upd.); 22** 353; **24** 295; **25** 179–80, 227–28; **26** 177; **33** 388; **37** 208; **63 133–39 (upd.)**
Domtar Inc., IV 271–73
Don Canham Enterprises. *See* School-Tech, Inc.
Don Massey Cadillac, Inc., 37 114–16
Don's Foods, Inc., **26** 164
Donaldson Company, Inc., 16 178–81; 49 114–18 (upd.)
Donaldson, Lufkin & Jenrette, Inc., 9 115, 142, 360–61; **18** 68; **22 188–91; 26** 348; **35** 247; **41** 197; **57** 16; **59** 143; **63** 26
Donaldson's Department Stores, **15** 274
Donatos Pizzeria Corporation, 58 96–98; 63 284–85
Dong Guan Highsonic Electronic Products Company, **62** 150
Dong Yang Department Store Company, **62** 174
Dong-Myung Industrial Company Ltd., **64** 270
Dongguan Shilong Kyocera Optics Co., Ltd., **21** 331
Dongguan Xinda Giftware Co. Ltd., **60** 372
Dongil Frozen Foods Co., **II** 553
Dönkasan, **55** 188
Donn, Inc., **18** 162
Donna Karan Company, 15 145–47; 24 299; **25** 294, 523
Donna Karan International Inc., 56 90–93 (upd.)
Donnellon McCarthy Inc., **12** 184
Donnelly Coated Corporation, **48** 28
Donnelly Corporation, 12 120–22; 35 147–50 (upd.)
Donnkenny, Inc., 17 136–38
Donohue Inc., **12** 412
Donohue Meehan Publishing Co., **27** 362
Donruss Leaf Inc., **19** 386
Donruss Playoff L.P., 66 81–84
Donzi Marine Corp., **III** 600
Dorel Industries Inc., 59 163–65
Dorenbecher Properties, **19** 381

Doric Corp., **19** 290
Dorling Kindersley Holdings plc, 20 194–96
Dorman Products of America, Ltd., **51** 307
Dorman's, Inc., **27** 291
Dorney Park, **22** 130
Dornier GmbH, **I** 151; **15** 142; **34** 131; **52** 113
Dorothy Hamill International, **13** 279, 281
Dorr-Oliver Inc., **35** 134–35
Dorset Capital, **49** 189
Dorsey & Whitney LLP, 47 96–99
Doskocil Companies, Inc., 12 123–25. *See also* Foodbrands America, Inc.
Dot Wireless Inc., **46** 422
Doty Agency, Inc., **41** 178, 180
Double A Products Co., **23** 82–83
DoubleClick Inc., 46 154–57; 49 423, 432
Doubleday Book Shops, Inc., **10** 136; **25** 31; **30** 68
Doubleday-Dell, **IV** 594, 636
Doubletree Corporation, 21 182–85; 41 81–82; **62** 179
Doughty Handson, **49** 163
Douglas & Lomason Company, 16 182–85
Douglas Aircraft Co., **I** 195; **9** 12, 18, 206; **13** 48; **16** 77; **21** 141; **24** 375
Douglas Dynamics L.L.C., **41** 3
Doulton Glass Industries Ltd., **IV** 659
Douwe Egberts, **II** 572; **54** 324–25
Dove International, **7** 299–300
Dover Corporation, III 467–69; 28 101–05 (upd.)
Dover Downs Entertainment, Inc., 43 139–41
Dover Publications Inc., 34 148–50; 41 111
Dovrat Shrem, **15** 470
The Dow Chemical Company, I 323–25, 334, 341–42, 360, 370–71, 708; **8 147–50 (upd.),** 153, 261–62, 548; **9** 500–1; **10** 289; **11** 271; **12** 99–100, 254, 364; **14** 114, 217; **16** 99; **18** 279; **21** 387; **28** 411; **38** 187; **50 160–64 (upd.)**
Dow Corning. *See* Corning Inc.; Dow Chemical Co.; Wright Medical Group, Inc.
Dow Jones & Company, Inc., IV 601–03, 654, 656, 670, 678; **7** 99; **10** 276–78, 407; **13** 55; **15** 335–36; **19 128–31 (upd.),** 204; **21** 68–70; **23** 157; **47 100–04 (upd.)**
Dow Jones Telerate, Inc., 10 276–78
DOW Stereo/Video Inc., **30** 466
DowElanco, **21** 385, 387
Dowell Schlumberger. *See* Schlumberger Limited.
Down River International, Inc., **15** 188
Downe Communications, Inc., **14** 460
Downingtown Paper Company, **8** 476
Downyflake Foods, **7** 429
Dowty Aerospace, **17** 480
Dowty Group plc, **58** 345
Doyle Dane Bernbach. *See* Omnicom Group Inc.
Doyle Hotel Group, **64** 216
DP&L. *See* Dayton Power & Light Company.
DPF, Inc., **12** 275; **38** 250–51
DPL Inc., 6 480–82
DPPI. *See* Distribuidora de Productos de Petróleo Ipiranga.
DQE, 6 483–85; 38 40

Dr. August Oetker KG, 51 102–06
Dr. E. Fresenius KG. *See* Fresenius
 Aktiengesellschaft.
Dr. Gerhard Mann Pharma, **25** 56
DR Holdings, Inc., **10** 242
Dr. Ing he F. Porsche GmbH, **13** 413–14
Dr. Karl Thomae GmbH, **39** 72–73
Dr. Martens, **23** 399, 401
Dr Pepper/Seven Up, Inc., 9 177–78; **32**
 154–57 (upd.); **57** 252
Dr. Reddy's Laboratories Ltd., 59
 166–69
The Dr. Robert C. Atkins Foundation, **58**
 8–9
Dr. Solomon's Software Ltd., **25** 349
Drackett Professional Products, 12
 126–28
DraftDirect Worldwide, **22** 297
Draftline Engineering Co., **22** 175
Dragados y Construcciones. *See* Grupo
 Dragados SA.
Dragon Genomics Co. Ltd., **62** 347
Dragon International, **18** 87
Dragonair. *See* Hong Kong Dragon
 Airlines Ltd.
Drake Beam Morin, Inc., IV 623; **44**
 155–57
Drake Steel Supply Co., **19** 343
Drallos Potato Company, **25** 332
Draper Corporation, **14** 219; **15** 384
Draw-Tite, Inc., **11** 535
DreamWorks SKG, 17 72; **21** 23, 26; **26**
 150, 188; **43** 142–46; **61** 3; **62** 68–69
The Drees Company, Inc., 41 131–33
Dreher Breweries, **24** 450
Dresden Papier GmbH, **64** 275
Dresdner Bank A.G., II 281–83; **III** 201,
 289, 401; **14** 169–70; **15** 13; **47** 81–84;
 57 20, 110–14 (upd.); **60** 110
Dresdner Kleinwort Wasserstein, 60
 110–13 (upd.)
Dresdner RCM Global Investors, **33** 128
The Dress Barn, Inc., 24 145–46
Dresser Industries, Inc., I 486; **III**
 470–73; **12** 539; **14** 325; **15** 225–26,
 468; **16** 310; **18** 219; **24** 208; **25** 188,
 191; **52** 214–216; **55 129–31** (upd.),
 194, 221; **62** 204
Dresser Power, **6** 555
Dressmaster GmbH, **53** 195
Drew Graphics, Inc., **13** 227–28
Drew Industries Inc., 28 106–08
Drewry Photocolor, **I** 447
Drexel Burnham Lambert Incorporated,
 II 407–09; **III** 254–55, 531; **7** 305; **8**
 327, 349, 388–90, 568; **9** 346; **12** 229;
 13 169, 299, 449; **14** 43; **15** 71, 281,
 464; **16** 535, 561; **20** 415; **22** 55, 189;
 24 273; **25** 313; **33** 253. *See also* New
 Street Capital Inc.
Drexel Heritage Furnishings Inc., III
 571; **11** 534; **12** 129–31; **20** 362; **39** 266
Dreyer's Grand Ice Cream, Inc., 10
 147–48; **17** 139–41; **30** 81; **35** 59–61
Dreyfus Interstate Development Corp., **11**
 257
DRH Cambridge Homes, Inc., **58** 84
DRI. *See* Dominion Resources, Inc.
Dribeck Importers Inc., **9** 87
Driefontein Consolidated (Pty.) Ltd., **62**
 164
Drip In Irrigation, **26** 494
Drogueros S.A., **39** 188
Drott Manufacturing Company, **10** 379

Drouot Group, **III** 211
Drs. Foster & Smith, Inc., 62 106–08
DRS Investment Group, **27** 370
DRS Technologies, Inc., 58 99–101
Drug Emporium, Inc., 12 132–34, 477
Drummond Lighterage. *See* Puget Sound
 Tug and Barge Company.
Drummonds' Bank, **12** 422
Druout, **I** 563; **24** 78
DryClean U.S.A., **14** 25
Dryden and Co., **III** 340
Drypers Corporation, 18 147–49
Drysdale Government Securities, **10** 117
DS Smith Plc, 61 76–79
DSC Communications Corporation, 9
 170; **12** 135–37; **63** 3–4
DSIC. *See* Diamond State Insurance
 Company.
DSL Group Ltd., **27** 49
DSM Melamine America, **27** 316–18
DSM N.V., I 326–27; **15** 229; **56 94–96**
 (upd.); **58** 324, 326
DST Alliance, **63** 386
DST Systems Inc., **6** 400–02; **26** 233
DTAG. *See* Dollar Thrifty Automotive
 Group, Inc.
DTE Energy Company, 20 197–201
 (upd.)
Du Mont Company, **8** 517
Du Pareil au Même, 43 147–49
Du Pont. *See* E.I. du Pont de Nemours &
 Co.
Du Pont Photomask, **IV** 600
Duane Reade Holding Corp., 21 186–88
Dublin Corporation, **50** 74
DuBois Chemicals Division, **13** 149–50;
 22 188; **26** 306
Ducati Motor Holding S.p.A., 17 24; **30**
 171–73; **36** 472
Duck Head Apparel Company, Inc., 8
 141–43; **30** 159; **42** 118–21
Duckback Products, Inc., **51** 190
Ducks Unlimited, **28** 306
Duckwall-ALCO Stores, Inc., 24 147–49
Duco Ltd., **25** 104–05
Ducommun Incorporated, 30 174–76
Ducros, **36** 185, 187–88
Dudley Jenkins Group Plc, **53** 362
Dudley Stationery Ltd., **25** 501
Duff & Phelps Credit Rating, **37** 143, 145
Duffy Meats, **27** 259
Duke Energy Corporation, V 600–02; **27**
 128–31 (upd.); **40** 354, 358; **63** 104,
 113
Duke Energy Field Services, Inc., **24** 379;
 40 354, 358
Duke Realty Corporation, 57 115–17
Dumes SA, **13** 206
Dumont Broadcasting Corporation, **7** 335
The Dun & Bradstreet Corporation, IV
 604–05, 643, 661; **8** 526; **9** 505; **10** 4,
 358; **13** 3–4; **19 132–34** (upd.); **38** 6;
 57 175; **59** 128; **61 80–84** (upd.)
Dun & Bradstreet Software Services
 Inc., 11 77–79; **43** 183
Dunavant Enterprises, Inc., 54 88–90
Dunbar-Stark Drillings, Inc., **19** 247
Duncan Toys Company, 55 132–35
Duncanson & Holt, Inc., **13** 539
Dundee Acquisition Corp., **19** 421
Dundee Bancorp, **36** 314
Dundee Cement Co., **III** 702; **8** 258–59
Dunfey Brothers Capital Group, **12** 368
Dunfey Hotels Corporation, **12** 367

Dunhill Staffing Systems, Inc., **52** 397–98
Dunkin' Donuts, **II** 619; **21** 323; **29** 18–19
Dunlop Coflexip Umbilicals Ltd. *See* Duco
 Ltd.
Dunlop Ltd., **25** 104
Dunlop Tire Corporation. *See* Sumitomo
 Rubber Industries, Ltd.
Dunn Bennett, **38** 401
Dunn Bros., **28** 63
Dunn-Edwards Corporation, 56 97–99
Dunn Manufacturing Company, **25** 74
Dunnes Stores Ltd., 58 102–04
Dunning Industries, **12** 109
Dunphy Holding Pty. Ltd., **64** 349
Dunwoodie Manufacturing Co., **17** 136
Duo-Bed Corp., **14** 435
Dupey Enterprises, Inc., **17** 320
Duplainville Transport, **19** 333–34
Duplex Products, Inc., 17 142–44, 445
Dupont. *See* E.I. du Pont de Nemours &
 Company.
Dupont Chamber Works, **6** 449
Duquesne Light Company, **6** 483–84
Duquesne Systems, **10** 394
Dura Automotive Systems Inc., **53** 55; **65**
 282, 284
Dura Convertible Systems, **13** 170
Duracell International Inc., 9 179–81; **12**
 559; **13** 433; **17** 31; **24** 274; **39** 336, 339
Duraflame Inc., **58** 52
Durametallic, 17 147; **21 189–91**
Durango-Mapimi Mining Co., **22** 284
Duravit AG, **51** 196
Duray, Inc., **12** 215
D'Urban, Inc., **41** 169
Duriron Company Inc., 17 145–47; **21**
 189, 191
Durkee Famous Foods, **7** 314; **8** 222; **17**
 106; **27** 297
Dürkopp Adler AG, 65 131–34
Duro-Matic Products Co., **51** 368
Dürr AG, 44 158–61
Durr-Fillauer Medical Inc., **13** 90; **18** 97;
 50 121
Dürrkopp Adler AG, **62** 132
Dutch Boy, **II** 649; **10** 434–35
Dutch Crude Oil Company. *See*
 Nederlandse Aardolie Maatschappij.
Dutch State Mines. *See* DSM N.V.
Dutchland Farms, **25** 124
Duttons Ltd., **24** 267
Duty Free International, Inc., 11 80–82.
 See also World Duty Free Americas,
 Inc.
Duval Corp., **7** 280; **25** 461
DVI, Inc., 51 107–09
DVM Pharmaceuticals Inc., **55** 233
DWG Corporation. *See* Triarc Companies,
 Inc.
Dyas B.V., **55** 347
Dyckerhoff AG, 35 151–54
Dycom Industries, Inc., 57 118–20
Dyersburg Corporation, 21 192–95
Dyke and Dryden, Ltd., **31** 417
Dylex Limited, 29 162–65
Dymed Corporation. *See* Palomar Medical
 Technologies, Inc.
DYMO. *See* Esselte Worldwide.
Dynaction S.A., 67 146–48
Dynalectric Co., **45** 146
DynaMark, Inc., **18** 168, 170, 516, 518
Dynamem Corporation, **22** 409
Dynamic Capital Corp., **16** 80
Dynamic Controls, **11** 202

Dynamic Foods, **53** 148
Dynamic Health Products Inc., **62** 296
Dynamic Homes, **61** 125–27
Dynamic Microprocessor Associated Inc., **10** 508
Dynamics Corporation of America, **39** 106
Dynamit Nobel AG, **III** 692–95; **16** 364; **18** 559
Dynamix, **15** 455
Dynapar, **7** 116–17
Dynaplast, **40** 214–15
Dynascan AK, **14** 118
Dynasty Footwear, Ltd., **18** 88
Dynatech Corporation, 13 194–96
Dynatron/Bondo Corporation, **8** 456
DynCorp, 45 145–47
Dynegy Inc., 47 70; **49 119–22 (upd.)**
Dyno Industrier AS, **13** 555
Dystrybucja, **41** 340

E&B Company, **9** 72
E&B Marine, Inc., **17** 542–43
E & H Utility Sales Inc., **6** 487
E. & J. Gallo Winery, I 242–44, 260; **7 154–56 (upd.)**; **15** 391; **28 109–11 (upd.)**, 223
E&M Laboratories, **18** 514
E & S Retail Ltd. *See* Powerhouse.
E! Entertainment Television Inc., 17 148–50; **24** 120, 123; **47** 78
E-mu Systems, Inc., **57** 78–79
E-Stamp Corporation, **34** 474
E-Systems, Inc., 9 182–85
E*Trade Financial Corporation, 60 114–17 (upd.)
E*Trade Group, Inc., 20 206–08; **38** 439; **45** 4
E-II Holdings Inc., **9** 449; **12** 87; **43** 355. *See also* Astrum International Corp.
E-Z Haul, **24** 409
E-Z Serve Corporation, 15 270; **17 169–71**
E A Rosengrens AB, **53** 158
E.B. Badger Co., **11** 413
E.B. Eddy Forest Products, **II** 631
E.C. Snodgrass Company, **14** 112
E.C. Steed, **13** 103
E. de Trey & Sons, **10** 270–71
E.F. Hutton Group, **II** 399, 450–51; **8** 139; **9** 469; **10** 63
E.F. Hutton LBO, **24** 148
E.H. Bindley & Company, **9** 67
E.I. du Pont de Nemours & Company, I 328–30, 334, 337–38, 343–44, 346–48, 351–53, 365, 377, 379, 383, 402–03, 545, 675; **IV** 371, 399, 401–02, 409, 481, 599; **7** 546; **8 151–54 (upd.)**, 485; **9** 154, 216, 352, 466; **10** 289; **11** 432; **12** 68, 365, 416–17; **13** 21, 124; **16** 127, 130, 201, 439, 461–62; **19** 11, 223; **21** 544; **22** 147, 260, 405; **24** 111, 388; **25** 152, 540; **26 123–27 (upd.)**; **34** 80, 283–84; **37** 111; **40** 370; **45** 246; **59** 135; **63** 108
E.J. Brach & Sons. *See* Brach and Brock Confections, Inc.
E.J. Longyear Company. *See* Boart Longyear Company.
E. Katz Special Advertising Agency. *See* Katz Communications, Inc.
E.M. Warburg Pincus & Co., **7** 305; **13** 176; **16** 319; **25** 313; **29** 262
E. Missel GmbH, **20** 363

E.On AG, 50 165–73 (upd.); **51** 217; **59** 391; **62** 14
E.piphany, Inc., 49 123–25
E.R.R. Enterprises, **44** 227
E. Rabinowe & Co., Inc., **13** 367
E. Rosen Co., **53** 303–04
E.S. International Holding S.A. *See* Banco Espírito Santo e Comercial de Lisboa S.A.
The E.W. Scripps Company, IV 606–09; **7 157–59 (upd.)**; **24** 122; **25** 507; **28 122–26 (upd.)**; **63** 186; **66 85–89 (upd.)**
EADS N.V. *See* European Aeronautic Defence and Space Company EADS N.V.
EADS SOCATA, 54 91–94
Eagel One Industries, **50** 49
Eagle Airways Ltd., **23** 161
Eagle Credit Corp., **10** 248
Eagle Distributing Co., **37** 351
Eagle Family Foods, Inc., **22** 95
Eagle Floor Care, Inc., **13** 501; **33** 392
Eagle Gaming, L.P., **16** 263; **43** 226
Eagle Global Logistics. *See* EGL, Inc.
Eagle Hardware & Garden, Inc., 9 399; **16 186–89**; **17** 539–40
Eagle Industries Inc., **8** 230; **22** 282; **25** 536
Eagle Managed Care Corp., **19** 354, 357; **63** 334
Eagle-Picher Industries, Inc., 8 155–58; **23 179–83 (upd.)**
Eagle Plastics, **19** 414
Eagle Sentry Inc., **32** 373
Eagle Star Insurance Co., **I** 426–27; **III** 185, 200
Eagle Thrifty Drug, **14** 397
Eagle Trading, **55** 24
Eagle Travel Ltd., **IV** 241
Earl Scheib, Inc., 32 158–61
Early American Insurance Co., **22** 230
Early Learning Centre, **39** 240, 242
Earth Resources Company, **17** 320
Earth Wise, Inc., **16** 90
Earth's Best, Inc., **21** 56; **36** 256
The Earthgrains Company, 36 161–65; **54** 326
EarthLink, Inc., 33 92; **36 166–68**; **38** 269
EAS. *See* Engineered Air Systems, Inc.; Executive Aircraft Services.
Easco Hand Tools, Inc., **7** 117
Easi-Set Industries, Inc., **56** 332
Eason Oil Company, **6** 578; **11** 198
East African External Communications Limited, **25** 100
East African Gold Mines Limited, **61** 293
East Hartford Trust Co., **13** 467
East Japan Railway Company, V 448–50; **66 90–94 (upd.)**
The East New York Savings Bank, **11** 108–09
East-West Airlines, **27** 475
East-West Federal Bank, **16** 484
East West Motor Express, Inc., **39** 377
Easter Enterprises. *See* Nash Finch Company.
Easter Seals, Inc., 58 105–07
Easterday Supply Company, **25** 15
Eastern Air Group Co., **31** 102
Eastern Airlines, I 66, 78, 90, 98–99, **101–03**, 116, 118, 123–25; **6** , 104–05; **8** 416; **9** 17–18, 80; **11** 268, 427; **12**

191, 487; **21** 142, 143; **23** 483; **26** 339, 439
Eastern Associated Coal Corp., **6** 487
Eastern Australia Airlines, **24** 396
Eastern Aviation Group, **23** 408
Eastern Carolina Bottling Company, **10** 223
The Eastern Company, 48 140–43
Eastern Electricity, **13** 485
Eastern Enterprises, 6 486–88
Eastern Indiana Gas Corporation, **6** 466
Eastern Kansas Utilities, **6** 511
Eastern Machine Screw Products Co., **13** 7
Eastern Market Beef Processing Corp., **20** 120
Eastern Pine Sales Corporation, **13** 249
Eastern Platinum Ltd. *See* Lonmin plc.
Eastern Shore Natural Gas Company, **56** 62
Eastern Software Distributors, Inc., **16** 125
Eastern States Farmers Exchange, **7** 17
Eastern Texas Electric. *See* Gulf States Utilities Company.
Eastern Torpedo Company, **25** 74
Eastern Wisconsin Power, **6** 604
Eastern Wisconsin Railway and Light Company, **6** 601
EastGroup Properties, Inc., 67 149–51
Eastman Chemical Company, 14 174–75; **25** 22; **38 178–81 (upd.)**
Eastman Christensen Company, **22** 68
Eastman House. *See* Chittenden & Eastman Company.
Eastman Kodak Company, III 474–77; **7 160–64 (upd.)**, 436–38; **8** 376–77; **9** 62, 231; **10** 24; **12** 342; **14** 174–75, 534; **16** 168, 449; **18** 184–86, 342, 510; **25** 153; **29** 370; **36 169–76 (upd.)**; **38** 178–79; **41** 104, 106; **43** 284; **45** 284; **61** 226–27
Eastmaque Gold Mines, Ltd., **7** 356
Easton Sports, Inc., 51 163; **66 95–97**
Eastover Mining, **27** 130
Eastpak, Inc., **30** 138
Eastport International Inc., **63** 318
Eastwynn Theatres, Inc., **37** 63
easyJet Airline Company Limited, 39 127–29; **52** 330
Eatco, Inc., **15** 246
Eateries, Inc., 33 138–40
Eaton, Cole & Burnham Company, **8** 134
Eaton Corporation, I 154–55, 186; **10 279–80 (upd.)**; **12** 547; **27** 100; **67 152–56 (upd.)**
Eaton Vance Corporation, 18 150–53
EAudio, Inc., **48** 92
EBA Holding S.A., **63** 180
EBASCO. *See* Electric Bond and Share Company.
eBay Inc., 32 162–65; **49** 51; **67 157–61 (upd.)**
EBCO, **55** 302
Eberhard Faber, **12** 115
Eberhard Foods, **8** 482
Eberhard Manufacturing Company, **48** 141
EBIC. *See* European Banks' International Co.
Ebiex S.A., **25** 312
EBS. *See* Electric Bond & Share Company; Electronic Bookshelf.
EBSCO Industries, Inc., 17 151–53; **40 158–61 (upd.)**
EC Comics, **25** 139
EC Erdolchemie GmbH, **7** 141

ECAD Inc., **48** 75

ECC. *See* Educational Credit Corporation.

ECC Group plc, III 689–91. *See also* English China Clays plc.

ECC International Corp., 42 122–24

Ecce, **41** 129

ECCO. *See* Adecco S.A.

Ecco Sko A/S, 62 109–11

Echlin Inc., I 156–57; 11 83–85 (upd.); 15 310

Echo Bay Mines Ltd., IV 75–77; 23 40; **38 182–85 (upd.)**

Les Echos, **IV** 659

EchoStar Communications Corporation, 35 155–59

EchoStar Satellite Corp., **39** 400

ECI Telecom Ltd., 18 154–56

Eckerd Corporation, 9 186–87; 18 272; **24** 263; **43** 247; **63** 335–36. *See also* J.C. Penney Company, Inc.

Eckes AG, 56 100–03

ECL, **16** 238

Eclipse Candles, Ltd., **18** 67, 69

Eclipse Telecommunications, Inc., **29** 252

Eco Hotels, **14** 107

Eco SA, **48** 224

Eco-Tech Company Inc., **60** 272

Ecoiffier, **56** 335

Ecolab Inc., I 331–33; 13 197–200 (upd.); 26 306; **34 151–56 (upd.)**, 205, 208

Ecology and Environment, Inc., 39 130–33

Econo Lodges of America, **25** 309

Econo-Travel Corporation, **13** 362

Economist Group, **15** 265

The Economist Group Ltd., 67 162–65

Economy Book Store, **10** 135

Economy Fire & Casualty, **22** 495

Ecopetrol. *See* Empresa Colombiana de Petróleos.

EcoSystems Software, Inc., **10** 245; **30** 142

EcoWater Systems, Inc., **16** 357

ECS S.A., 12 138–40

Ecton, Inc., **36** 5

Ecusta Corporation, **8** 414

ed bazinet international, inc., **34** 144–45

Edah, **13** 544–45

Eddie Bauer, Inc., 9 188–90; 9 316; **10** 489, 491; **11** 498; **25** 48; **27** 427, 429–30; **29** 278; **36 177–81 (upd.)**

Eddy Bakeries, Inc., **12** 198

Eddy Paper Co., **II** 631

Edeka Zentrale A.G., II 621–23; 33 56; **47 105–07 (upd.)**

edel music AG, 44 162–65

Edelbrock Corporation, 37 117–19

Edelhoff AG & Co., **39** 415

Edelman, 62 112–15

Edenton Cotton Mills, **12** 503

EDF. *See* Electricité de France.

Edgars Consolidated Stores Ltd., 66 98–100

Edge Petroleum Corporation, 67 166–68

Edge Research, **25** 301

Edgell Communications Inc., **IV** 624

Edgewater Hotel and Casino. *See* Circus Circus Enterprises, Inc.

EDI, **26** 441

Edina Realty Inc., **13** 348

Edison Brothers Stores, Inc., 9 191–93; 17 369, 409; **33** 126–28

Edison Electric Co., **6** 572

Edison Electric Illuminating Co., **6** 595, 601; **14** 124

Edison Electric Illuminating Company of Boston, **12** 45

Edison Electric Light & Power, **6** 510

Edison Electric Light Co., **6** 565, 595; **11** 387; **12** 193; **50** 365

Edison General Electric Co., **12** 193; **14** 168; **26** 451

Edison International, 56 104–07 (upd.)

Edison Schools Inc., 37 120–23

Editions Dalloz, **IV** 615

Editions Jean-Baptiste Baillière, **25** 285

Editions Ramsay, **25** 174

Editorial Centro de Estudios Ramón Areces, S.A., **V** 52; **26** 130

Editorial Television, S.A. de C.V., 18 211, 213; **23** 417; **57 121–23**

Editoriale L'Espresso, **IV** 586–87

Editoriale Le Gazzette, **IV** 587

Edivisa. *See* Editorial Television, S.A. de C.V.

EDiX Corporation, **64** 191

EdK. *See* Edeka Zentrale A.G.

Edmark Corporation, 14 176–78; 41 134–37 (upd.)

EDO Corporation, 46 158–61

EdoWater Systems, Inc., **IV** 137

EDP Group. *See* Electricidade de Portugal, S.A.

Edrington Group, **63** 246

EDS. *See* Electronic Data Systems Corporation.

Education Association Mutual Assurance Company. *See* Horace Mann Educators Corporation.

The Education Finance Group, **33** 418, 420

Education Loan Processing, **53** 319

Education Management Corporation, 35 160–63

Education Systems Corporation, **7** 256; **25** 253

Educational & Recreational Services, Inc., **II** 607

Educational Broadcasting Corporation, 48 144–47

Educational Computer International, Inc. *See* ECC International Corp.

Educational Credit Corporation, 8 10; **38** 12

Educational Development Corporation. *See* National Heritage Academies, Inc.

Educational Loan Administration Group, Inc., **33** 420

Educational Publishing Corporation, **22** 519, 522

Educational Supply Company, **7** 255; **25** 252

Educational Testing Service, 12 141–43; 42 209–10, 290; **62 116–20 (upd.)**

Educor. *See* Naspers Ltd.

Educorp, Inc., **39** 103

Edumond Le Monnier S.p.A., **54** 22

EduQuest, **6** 245

EduServ Technologies, Inc., **33** 420

Edusoft Ltd., **40** 113

EduTrek International, Inc., **45** 88

Edw. C. Levy Co., 42 125–27

Edward D. Jones & Company L.P., 30 177–79; 66 101–04 (upd.)

Edward J. DeBartolo Corporation, 8 159–62

Edward P. Allis Company, **13** 16

Edward Smith & Company, **8** 553

Edwards & Jones, **11** 360

Edwards Food Warehouse, **II** 642

Edwards George and Co., **III** 283

Edwards Theatres Circuit, Inc., 31 171–73; 59 341–42

Edwardstone Partners, **14** 377

EEC Environmental, Inc., **16** 259

EEGSA. *See* Empresa Eléctrica de Guatemala S.A.

EEX Corporation, **65** 262

EFM Media Management, **23** 294

Efnadruck GmbH, **IV** 325

Efrat Future Technology Ltd. *See* Comverse Technology, Inc.

EFS National Bank, **52** 87

EFTEC, **32** 257

EG&G Incorporated, 8 163–65; 18 219; **22** 410; **29 166–69 (upd.)**

EGAM, **IV** 422

Egg plc, **48** 328

Egghead Inc., 9 194–95; 10 284

Egghead.com, Inc., 31 174–77 (upd.)

EGL, Inc., 59 170–73

EGPC. *See* Egyptian General Petroleum Corporation.

eGrail Inc., **62** 142

EgyptAir, 6 84–86; 27 132–35 (upd.)

Egyptian General Petroleum Corporation, IV 412–14; 32 45; **51 110–14 (upd.)**

EHAPE Einheitspreis Handels Gesellschaft mbH. *See* Kaufhalle AG.

eHow.com, **49** 290

Ehrlich-Rominger, **48** 204

Eiffage, 27 136–38

Eiffel Construction Metallique, **27** 138

800-JR Cigar, Inc., 27 139–41

84 Lumber Company, 9 196–97; 39 134–36 (upd.)

Eildon Electronics Ltd., **15** 385

Eileen Fisher Inc., 61 85–87

Einstein/Noah Bagel Corporation, 29 170–73; 44 313; **63** 81

eircom plc, 31 178–81 (upd.)

EIS, Inc., **45** 176, 179; **62** 115

Eisai Company, **13** 77

EJ Financial Enterprises Inc., **48** 308–09

Ek Chor China Motorcycle, **62** 63

Eka Nobel AB, **9** 380

Ekco Group, Inc., 12 377; 16 190–93

Eko-Elda A.B.E.E., **64** 177

Ekoterm CR. *See* Dalkia Holding.

EKT, Inc., **44** 4

El Al Israel Airlines Ltd., 23 184–87

El Camino Resources International, Inc., 11 86–88

El Chico Restaurants, Inc., 19 135–38; 36 162–63

El Corte Inglés, S.A., V 51–53; 26 128–31 (upd.)

El Dorado Investment Company, **6** 546–47

El-Mel-Parts Ltd., **21** 499

El Nasr Petroleum Co., **51** 113

El Paso Corporation, 66 63 440; **105–08 (upd.)**

El Paso Electric Company, 21 196–98

El Paso Healthcare System, Ltd., **15** 112; **35** 215

El Paso Natural Gas Company, 10 190; **11** 28; **12 144–46; 19** 411; **27** 86. *See also* El Paso Corporation.

El Pollo Loco, **II** 680; **27** 16–18

El Portal Group, Inc., **58** 370

El Taco, **7** 505

Elamex, S.A. de C.V., **51** 115–17
Elan Corporation PLC, **10** 54; **63** 140–43
Elan Ski Company, **22** 483
Elanco Animal Health, **47** 112
Elano Corporation, **14** 179–81
Elantis, **48** 290
Elastic Reality Inc., **38** 70
Elcat Company, **17** 91
Elco Corporation, **21** 329, 331
Elco Industries Inc., **22** 282
The Elder-Beerman Stores Corp., **10** 281–83; **19** 362; **63** 144–48 (upd.)
Elder Dempster Line, **6** 416–17
Elders IXL Ltd., **I** 264, 437–39, 592–93; **7** 182–83; **21** 227; **26** 305; **28** 201; **50** 199
Elders Keep, **13** 440
Eldorado Gold Corporation, **22** 237
ele Corporation, **23** 251
Electra Corp., **III** 569; **20** 361–62
Electra/Midland Corp., **13** 398
Electrabel N.V., **67** 169–71
Electric Boat Co. *See* General Dynamics Corporation.
Electric Bond & Share Company, **6** 596
Electric Clearinghouse, Inc., **18** 365, 367
Electric Energy, Inc., **6** 470, 505
Electric Fuels Corp. *See* Florida Progress Corporation.
Electric Light and Power Company, **6** 483
Electric Light Company of Atlantic City. *See* Atlantic Energy, Inc.
Electric Lightwave, Inc., **37** 124–27
Electric Storage Battery Co., **39** 338
Electric Transit, Inc., **37** 399–400
Electricidade de Portugal, S.A., **47** 108–11; **49** 211
Electricité de France, **V** 603–05, 626–28; **41** 138–41 (upd.)
Electricity Generating Authority of Thailand (EGAT), **56** 108–10
Electricity Metering Distribucion, S.A. DE C.V., **64** 205
Electro-Flo, Inc., **9** 27
Electro Metallurgical Co., **11** 402
Electro-Motive Engineering Company, **10** 273
Electro Refractories and Abrasives Company, **8** 178
Electro Rent Corporation, **58** 108–10
Electro String Instrument Corporation, **16** 201; **43** 169
Electrocomponents PLC, **50** 174–77
Electrolux AB, **53** 124–29 (upd.); **63** 211
Electrolux Group, **III** 478–81; **11** 439; **12** 158–59, 250; **13** 562, 564; **17** 353; **21** 383. *See also* Aktiebolaget Electrolux.
Electromagnetic Sciences Inc., **21** 199–201
Electromedics, **11** 460
Electronic Arts Inc., **10** 284–86; **13** 115; **29** 76; **35** 227
Electronic Banking Systems, **9** 173
Electronic Book Technologies, Inc., **26** 216
29 427
Electronic Data Systems Corporation, **III** 136–38; **6** 226; **9** 36; **10** 325, 327; **11** 62, 123, 131; **13** 482; **14** 15, 318; **22** 266; **27** 380; **28** 112–16 (upd.); 241; **XXIX** 375; **36** 242; **49** 116, 311, 313; **64** 150. *See also* Perot Systems Corporation.
Electronic Engineering Co., **16** 393

Electronic Hair Styling, Inc., **41** 228
Electronic Processing Inc. *See* EPIQ Systems, Inc.
Electronic Tool Company, **16** 100
Electronics Corp. of Israel Ltd. *See* ECI Telecom Ltd.
Electronics for Imaging, Inc., **15** 148–50; **43** 150–53 (upd.)
Electrowatt Ltd., **21** 146–47
Elekom, **31** 176
Elektra. *See* Grupo Elektra, S.A. de C.V.
Elektra Entertainment Group, **64** 115–18
Elektra Records, **III** 480; **23** 33
Elektriska Aktiebolaget. *See* ABB Asea Brown Boveri Ltd.
Elektrizitäts-Gesellschaft Laufenburg, **6** 490
Elektrizitätswerk Wesertal GmbH, **30** 206
Elektrocieplownie Warszawskie S.A., **57** 395, 397
Elektrowatt AG, **6** 489–91
Elementis plc, **40** 162–68 (upd.)
Eletropaulo Metropolitana, **53** 18
Eletson Corp., **13** 374
Elettra Broadcasting Corporation, **14** 509
Elettrofinanziaria Spa, **9** 152
Elf Aquitaine SA, **21** 202–06 (upd.); **23** 236, 238; **24** 494; **25** 104; **26** 369, 425; **49** 349–51; **50** 179–80, 479, 484; **61** 238. *See also* Société Nationale Elf Aquitaine.
Elfa International, **36** 134–35
Elgin Blenders, Inc., **7** 128
Elgin Exploration, Inc., **19** 247; **26** 70
Eli Lilly and Company, **I** 645–47; **8** 168, 209; **9** 89–90; **10** 535; **11** 9, 89–91 (upd.), 458, 460; **12** 187, 278, 333; **14** 99–100, 259; **17** 437; **18** 420, 422; **19** 105; **21** 387; **26** 31; **32** 212; **44** 175; **45** 382; **47** 112–16 (upd.), 221, 236; **50** 139
Eli Witt Company, **15** 137, 139; **43** 205
Elior SA, **49** 126–28
Elite Acquisitions, Inc., **65** 150
Elite Microelectronics, **9** 116
Elizabeth Arden, Inc., **III** 48; **8** 166–68, 344; **9** 201–02, 428, 449; **11** 90; **12** 314; **30** 188; **32** 476; **40** 169–72 (upd.); **47** 113
Eljer Industries, Inc., **II** 420; **24** 150–52
ElkCorp, **52** 103–05
Elke Corporation, **10** 514
Elkjop ASA, **49** 113
Elko-Lamoille Power Company, **11** 343
Ellanef Manufacturing Corp., **48** 274
Ellen Tracy, Inc., **55** 136–38
Ellenville Electric Company, **6** 459
Ellerbe Becket, **41** 142–45
Ellesse International S.p.A. *See* Reebok International Ltd.
Ellett Brothers, Inc., **17** 154–56
Ellington Recycling Center, **12** 377
Elliot Group Limited, **45** 139–40
Elliott Automation, **13** 225
Elliott Bay Design Group, **22** 276
Elliott Paint and Varnish, **8** 553
Ellipse Programmes, **48** 164–65
Ellis & Everard, **41** 341
Ellis-Don Ltd., **38** 481
Ellis Paperboard Products Inc., **13** 442
Ellis Park Race Course, **29** 118
Ellisco Co., **35** 130
Ellos A.B., **II** 640

Elmendorf Board, **IV** 343
Elmer's Products, Inc. *See* Borden, Inc.
Elmer's Restaurants, Inc., **42** 128–30
Elmo Semiconductor Corp., **48** 246
Elphinstone, **21** 501
Elrick Industries, Inc., **19** 278
Elscint Ltd., **20** 202–05
Elsevier NV, **IV** 610–11, 643, 659; **7** 244; **14** 555–56; **17** 396, 399. *See also* Reed Elsevier.
Elsinore Corporation, **36** 158; **48** 148–51
Eltra Corporation, **I** 416; **22** 31; **31** 135
Eltron International Inc., **53** 374
Elvirasminde A/S. *See* August Storck KG.
Elvis Presley Enterprises, Inc., **61** 88–90
ELYO, **42** 387–88
eMachines, Inc., **63** 155
Email Ltd., **62** 331
EMAP plc, **35** 71–72, 164–66, 242–44
Embankment Trust Ltd., **IV** 659
Embassy Suites, **9** 425; **24** 253
Embedded Support Tools Corporation, **37** 419, 421
Embers America Restaurants, **30** 180–82
Embotelladora Central, S.A., **47** 291
Embraer. *See* Empresa Brasileira de Aeronáutica S.A.
Embraer-Liebherr Equipamentos do Brasil S.A., **64** 241
EMC Corporation, **12** 147–49; **20** 8; **46** 162–66 (upd.)
EMC Technology Services, Inc., **30** 469
Emco, **III** 569; **20** 361
EMCOR Group Inc., **60** 118–21
EMD Holding, Inc., **64** 205
EMD Technologies, **27** 21; **40** 67
Emerald Technology, Inc., **10** 97
Emerson, **46** 167–71 (upd.)
Emerson-Brantingham Company, **10** 378
Emerson Electric Co., **II** 18–21, 92; **8** 298; **12** 248; **13** 225; **14** 357; **15** 405–06; **21** 43; **22** 64; **25** 530; **36** 400; **61** 96, 98
Emerson Foote, Inc., **25** 90
Emerson Radio Corp., **30** 183–86
Emery Air Freight Corporation, **6** 386, 388–91; **18** 177. *See also* Emery Worldwide Airlines.
Emery Worldwide Airlines, Inc., **21** 139; **25** 146–50 (upd.)
Emge Packing Co., Inc., **11** 92–93
Emhart Corp., **III** 437; **8** 332; **20** 67; **67** 67
EMI Group plc, **22** 192–95 (upd.); **24** 485; **26** 188, 314; **52** 428
Emigrant Savings Bank, **59** 174–76
Emil Moestue as, **51** 328
The Emirates Group, **24** 400; **39** 137–39
Emmis Communications Corporation, **47** 117–21
Empain, **18** 472; **19** 165
Empaques de Carton Titan, **19** 10–11
Empex Hose, **19** 37
Empi, Inc., **27** 132–35
Empire Blue Cross and Blue Shield, **III** 245–46. *See also* WellChoice, Inc.
Empire-Cliffs Partnership, **62** 74
Empire Family Restaurants Inc., **15** 362
Empire Hanna Coal Co., Ltd., **8** 346
Empire Iron Mining Partnership, **62** 74
Empire of America, **11** 110
Empire of Carolina Inc., **66** 370
Empire Savings, Building & Loan Association, **8** 424
Empire State Pickling Company, **21** 155

Empire Steel Castings, Inc., **39** 31–32
Empire Stores, **19** 309
Employee Solutions, Inc., 18 157–60
employeesavings.com, **39** 25
Employers General Insurance Group, **58** 259
Employers Insurance of Wausau, **59** 264
Employers' Liability Assurance, **III** 235
Employer's Overload, **25** 432
Employers Reinsurance Corp., **II** 31; **12** 197
Emporsil-Empresa Portuguesa de Silvicultura, Lda, **60** 156
Empresa Brasileira de Aeronáutica S.A. (Embraer), 36 182–84
Empresa Colombiana de Petróleos, IV 415–18
Empresa Constructora SA, **55** 182
Empresa de Obras y Montajes Ovalle Moore, S.A., **34** 81
Empresa Eléctrica de Guatemala S.A., **49** 211
Empresa Nacional de Telecomunicaciones, **63** 375
Empresas Emel S.A., **41** 316
Empresas Frisco, **21** 259
Empresas ICA, **34** 82
Empresas ICA Sociedad Controladora, S.A. de C.V., 41 146–49
Empresas La Moderna, **21** 413; **29** 435
Empresas Polar SA, 55 139–41 (upd.)
Empresas Tolteca, **20** 123
Emprise Corporation, **7** 134–35
EMS-Chemie Holding AG, **III** 760; **32** 257
EMS Technologies, Inc., **21** 199, 201; **22** 173
Enbridge Inc., 43 154–58
ENCAD, Incorporated, 25 151–53
Encompass Services Corporation, 33 141–44
Encon Safety Products, Inc., **45** 424
Encor Inc., **47** 396
Encore Computer Corporation, 13 201–02
Encore Distributors Inc., **17** 12–13
Encryption Technology Corporation, **23** 102
Encyclopedia Britannica, Inc., 7 165–68; 12 435, 554–55; **16** 252; **39 140–44 (upd.); 43** 208
Endata, Inc., **11** 112
Endemol Entertainment Holding NV, 46 172–74; 53 154
ENDESA S.A., V 606–08; 46 175–79 (upd.); 49 210–11
Endevco Inc., **11** 28
Endicott Trust Company, **11** 110
Endo Vascular Technologies, Inc., **11** 460
ENDOlap, Inc., **50** 122
Endovations, Inc., **21** 47
ENECO. *See* Empresa Nacional Electrica de Cordoba.
Enerchange LLC, **18** 366
Enercon, Inc., **6** 25
Energas Company, **43** 56–57
Energen Corporation, 6 583; **21 207–09**
Energieversorgung Ostbayern AG, **23** 47
Energis plc, 44 363; **47 122–25**
Energizer Holdings, Inc., 9 180; **32 171–74; 39** 336, 339; **60** 349, 352
Energy & Minerals, Inc., **42** 354
Energy Absorption Systems, Inc., **15** 378
Energy Atlantic, LLC. *See* Maine & Maritimes Corporation.

Energy Biosystems Corp., **15** 352
Energy Coatings Co., **14** 325
Energy Electromechanical Projects S.A., **64** 8
Energy Film Library, **31** 216, 218
Energy Foundation, **34** 386
The Energy Group, **26** 359
Energy Increments Inc., **19** 411
Energy National, Inc., **27** 485
Energy Resources, **27** 216
Energy Steel Corporation, **19** 472
Energy Systems Group, Inc., **13** 489
Energy Transportation Systems, Inc., **27** 88
Energy Ventures, Inc., **49** 181
Energyline Systems, **26** 5
EnergyOne, **19** 487
Enerplus Resources, **21** 500
Enesco Corporation, 11 94–96; 15 475, 477–78
Enet S.A., **64** 8
Enforcer Products, Inc., **54** 254
Engelhard Corporation, IV 23, **78–80; 16** 28; **21 210–14 (upd.); 50** 33
Engen, **IV** 93; **22** 236
Engenio Information Technologies, Inc., **64** 246
Engineered Support Systems, Inc., 59 177–80
Engineering Company, **9** 16
Engineering for the Petroleum and Process Industries, **IV** 414
Engineering Plastics, Ltd., **8** 377
Engineering Systems, Inc., **54** 182
Engineers & Fabricators, Inc., **18** 513
England Corsair Furniture, **14** 302
Engle Homes, Inc., 46 180–82
Engles Management Corp., **26** 448
English China Clays Ltd., III 689–91; **15 151–54 (upd.); 36** 20; **40 173–77 (upd.)**
English Electric Co., **24** 85
Engraph, Inc., 12 150–51
Enhanced Derm Technologies, **50** 122
Enhanced Services Billing, Inc. *See* Billing Concepts Corp.
ENI. *See* Ente Nazionale Idrocarburi.
ENI S.p.A., **34** 75; **61** 236, 238
Enimont, **IV** 422, 525
Ennis Business Forms, Inc., 21 215–17
Enocell Oy, **IV** 277
The Enoch F. Bills Co., **25** 365
Enogex, Inc., **6** 539–40
Enova Corporation. *See* Sempra Energy.
ENPAC Corporation, **18** 162
Enquirer/Star Group, Inc., 10 287–88; 12 358. *See also* American Media, Inc.
Enrich International, Inc., 33 145–48; 37 340, 342
Enron Corporation, V 609–10; **6** 457, 593; **18** 365; **19 139–41,** 162, 487; **27** 266; **34** 82; **46 183–86 (upd.); 49** 121–22; **54** 86; **59** 217
ENSCO International Incorporated, 57 124–26
Enserch Corp., V 611–13. *See also* Texas Utilities.
Ensign Oil Company, **9** 490
Enskilda S.A., **II** 352–53
Enso-Gutzeit Oy, IV 274–77; 17 539. *See also* Stora Enso Oyj
ENSTAR Corporation, **11** 441
Enstar Group Inc., **13** 299
Ensys Environmental Products, Inc., **10** 107
Ente Nazionale Idrocarburi, IV 419–22

Ente Nazionale per l'Energia Elettrica, V 614–17
Entenmann's Bakery, **35** 415; **38** 364
Entercom Communications Corporation, 48 272; **58 111–12**
Entergy Corporation, V 618–20; 6 496–97; **45 148–51 (upd.)**
Enterprise Development Company, **15** 413
Enterprise Electronics Corporation, **18** 513–15
Enterprise Federal Savings & Loan, **21** 524
Enterprise Inns plc, 59 181–83
Enterprise Integration Technologies, **18** 541
Enterprise Leasing, 6 392–93
Enterprise Metals Pty. Ltd., **IV** 61
Enterprise Oil plc, 11 97–99; 50 178–82 (upd.)
Enterprise Rent-A-Car, Inc., **16** 380; **33** 192
Enterra Corp., **25** 546
Entertainment Publications, **16** 146
Entertainment UK, **24** 266, 269
Entertainment Zone, Inc., **15** 212
Entex Information Services, **24** 29
Entity Software, **11** 469
Entrada Industries Incorporated, **6** 568–69; **26** 387
Entravision Communications Corporation, 41 150–52
Entré Computer Centers, **13** 175
Entreprise Nationale Sonatrach, IV 423–25; 10 83–84; **12** 145. *See also* Sonatrach.
Entrust Financial Corp., **16** 347
Envergure, **27** 421
Envirex, **11** 361
Envirocal Inc., **60** 223
Envirodrill Services, Inc., **19** 247
Envirodyne Industries, Inc., 17 157–60
EnviroLease, Inc., **25** 171
ENVIRON International Corporation, **10** 106
Environmental Defense Fund, **9** 305
Environmental Industries, Inc., 31 182–85
Environmental Mediation, Inc., **47** 20
Environmental Planning & Research. *See* CRSS Inc.
Environmental Research and Technology, Inc., **23** 135
Environmental Systems Corporation, **9** 109
Environmental Systems Research Institute Inc. (ESRI), 62 121–24
Environmental Technologies Group, LLC, **56** 161
Environmental Testing and Certification Corporation, **10** 106–07
Environmentals Incorporated. *See* Angelica Corporation.
Envirosciences Pty. Ltd., **16** 260
EnviroSource Inc., **63** 237
Envision Corporation, **24** 96
Enwright Environmental Consulting Laboratories, **9** 110
Enzafruit Worldwide, **38** 202
Enzo Biochem, Inc., 41 153–55
Enzyme Bio-Systems, Ltd., **21** 386
Eon Labs, Inc., 67 172–74
Eon Systems, **38** 409
l'Epargne, **12** 152
EPE Technologies, **18** 473
EPI. *See* Essentially Pure Ingredients.
EPI Group Limited, **26** 137
Epic Express, **48** 113

Epic Systems Corporation, 62 125–28
Les Epiceries Presto Limitée, **II** 651
Epiphone, **16** 238–39
EPIQ Systems, Inc., 56 111–13
Epoch Software, Plc, **49** 290
Epoch Systems Inc., **9** 140; **12** 149
ePOWER International, **33** 3, 6
Eppler, Guerin & Turner, Inc., **III** 330
Epson, **18** 386–87, 435
Equant N.V., 52 106–08
EQUICOR-Equitable HCA Corp., **III** 80,
   226; **45** 104, 109
Equicor Group Ltd., **29** 343
Equifax, Inc., 6 23–25; 25 182, 358; **28
   117–21 (upd.); 63** 100, 102; **65** 106–08
Equilink Licensing Group, **22** 458
Equilon Enterprises LLC, **41** 359, 395
Equinox Systems. *See* Avocent
   Corporation.
Equistar Chemicals, LP, **45** 252, 254
EquiStar Hotel Investors L.P. *See* CapStar
   Hotel Co.
Equitable Bancorporation, **12** 329
Equitable Equipment Company, **7** 540
**Equitable Life Assurance Society of the
   United States, III** 80, 229, 237,
   247–49, 274, 289, 291, 305–06, 316,
   329, 359; **13** 539; **19** 324, 511; **22**
   188–90; **23** 370, 482; **27** 46; **61** 249
**Equitable Resources, Inc., 6 492–94; 54
   95–98 (upd.); 63** 440
Equitas, **22** 315
Equitec Financial Group, **11** 483
Equitex Inc., **16** 431
Equity & Law, **III** 211
Equity Corp. International, **51** 332
Equity Corporation, **6** 599; **37** 67–68
Equity Group Investment, Inc., **22** 339
Equity Marketing, Inc., 26 136–38
**Equity Office Properties Trust, 54
   99–102**
Equity Residential, 49 55, **129–32; 54**
   100
Equity Title Services Company, **13** 348
Equivalent Company, **12** 421
Equus Capital Corp., **23** 65
**Equus Computer Systems, Inc., 49
   133–35**
Equus II Inc., **18** 11
ERA, **61** 267
Eram SA, 51 118–20
ERAP. *See* Entreprise de Recherches et
   d'Activités Pétrolières.
EraSoft Technologies, **27** 492
Ercea, **41** 128–29
ERCO Systems Group, **16** 461–63
Ercon Corp., **49** 181
ERDA Inc., **36** 160
ERE Yarmouth, **57** 234
**ERGO Versicherungsgruppe AG, 44
   166–69,** 443
**Erickson Retirement Communities, 57
   127–30**
Ericson Yachts, **10** 215
Ericsson, **9** 32–33; **11** 196, 501; **17** 33,
   353; **18** 74; **47** 321; **53** 126–28; **61** 137;
   63 211. *See also* Telefonaktiebolaget LM
   Ericsson.
Eridania Béghin-Say S.A., 14 17, 19; **36
   185–88**
Erie County Bank, **9** 474
Erie Indemnity Company, 35 167–69
Erie Scientific Company, **14** 479–80
ERIM International Inc., **54** 396

Erisco Managed Care Technologies, **57** 176
ERKA. *See* Reichs Kredit-Gesellschaft
   mbH.
ERLY Industries Inc., 17 161–62; 33
   30–31
Ermenegildo Zegna SpA, 63 149–52
Ernest Jones (Jewelers) Plc, **61** 326
Ernie Ball, Inc., 56 114–16
Ernst & Young, 9 198–200, 309, 311; **10**
   115; **25** 358; **29 174–77 (upd.),** 236,
   392
Ernst Göhner Foundation, **47** 286–87
Ernst, Homans, Ware & Keelips, **37** 224
Erol's, **9** 74; **11** 556
Eroski. *See* Grupo Eroski
ERPI, **7** 167
Ersco Corporation, **17** 310; **24** 160
The Ertl Company, **37** 318
Erving Healthcare, **13** 150
ES&A. *See* English, Scottish and
   Australian Bank Ltd.
Esaote Biomedica, **29** 298
ESB Inc., **IV** 112; **18** 488
Esbjerg Thermoplast, **9** 92
Escada AG, **14** 467
Escalade, Incorporated, 19 142–44
Escan, **22** 354
Eschweiler Bergwerks-Verein AG, **IV**
   25–26, 193
ESCO Electronics Corporation, **17** 246,
   248; **24** 425
Esco Trading, **10** 482
Escota SA, **55** 40
Escotel Mobile Communications, **18** 180
Esdon de Castro, **8** 137
ESGO B.V., **49** 222
ESI Energy, Inc. *See* FPL Group Inc.
Eskay Screw Corporation, **11** 536
Eskimo Pie Corporation, 21 218–20; 35
   119, 121
Esmark, Inc., **12** 93; **15** 357; **19** 290; **62**
   89, 91
Esmerk Group, **51** 328
Espírito Santo. *See* Banco Espírito Santo e
   Comercial de Lisboa S.A.
ESPN, Inc., 24 516; **56 117–22; 63** 437
Esporta plc, 35 170–72
**Esprit de Corp., 8 169–72; 29 178–82
   (upd.)**
Esquire Education Group, **12** 173
Esquire Inc., **I** 453; **IV** 672; **13** 178; **19**
   405
ESS Technology, Inc., 22 196–98
Essanelle Salon Co., **18** 455
Essantee Theatres, Inc., **14** 86
Essef Corporation, 18 161–63; 56 17
Esselte, 64 119–21
**Esselte Leitz GmbH & Co. KG, 48
   152–55**
**Esselte Pendaflex Corporation, 11
   100–01**
**Essence Communications, Inc., 24
   153–55**
Essentially Pure Ingredients, **49** 275–76
Essex International Ltd., **19** 452
Essex Outfitters Inc., **9** 394; **42** 268–69
Essilor International, 18 392; **21 221–23;
   40** 96–98
Esso Petroleum, **I** 52; **II** 628; **7** 140; **11**
   97; **13** 558; **24** 86; **25** 229, 231–32. *See
   also* Exxon Corporation; Imperial Oil
   Limited; Standard Oil Company of New
   Jersey.
Essroc Corporation, **40** 108

Estat Telecom Group plc, **31** 180
Estech, Inc., **19** 290
Estee Corp., **27** 197; **43** 218
The Estée Lauder Companies Inc., 8
   131; **9 201–04; 11** 41; **24** 55; **30
   187–91 (upd.)**
**Esterline Technologies Corp., 15 155–57;
   53** 353
Estes Industries Inc. *See* Centuri
   Corporation.
Estronicks, Inc., **19** 290
ETA Systems, Inc., **10** 256–57
Etablissement Mesnel, **I** 202
Etablissements Badin-Defforey, **19** 98
Etablissements Bourgogne et Grasset, **66**
   251
Etablissements Braud. *See* Manitou BF
   S.A.
**Etablissements Economiques du Casino
   Guichard, Perrachon et ie, S.C.A., 12
   152–54; 16** 452. *See also* Casino
   Guichard-Perrachon S.A.
Etablissements Robert Ouvrie S.A., **22** 436
Etam Developpement SA, 35 308; **44
   170–72**
ETBD. *See* Europe Through the Back
   Door.
Eteq Microsystems, **9** 116
**Eternal Word Television Network, Inc.,
   57 131–34**
Ethan Allen Interiors, Inc., 10 184; **12**
   307; **12 155–57; 39 145–48 (upd.)**
Ethical Personal Care Products, Ltd., **17**
   108
Ethicon, Inc., 10 213; **23 188–90**
Ethyl Corp., I 334–36, 342; **10 289–91
   (upd.); 14** 217; **52** 349; **59** 23–24
Etienne Aigner AG, 14 224; **52 109–12**
Etimex Kunststoffwerke GmbH, **7** 141
Etkin Skanska, **38** 437
Étoile Commerciale S.A., **51** 143
Etos, **II** 641
EToys, Inc., 37 128–30
ETPM Entrêpose, **IV** 468
ETS. *See* Educational Testing Service.
Euclid Chemical Co., **8** 455–56
Euclid Crane & Hoist Co., **13** 385
Euralux, **III** 209
The Eureka Company, 12 158–60; 15
   416. *See also* White Consolidated
   Industries Inc.
Eureka Technology, **18** 20; **43** 17
Eureka X-Ray Tube, Inc., **10** 272
Eurex, **41** 84, 87
Euris, **22** 365; **54** 306–07
**Euro Disney S.C.A., 58 113–16 (upd.);
   63** 435
Euro Disneyland SCA, 20 209–12
Euro Exhausts, **54** 206
Euro RSCG Worldwide S.A., 10 345,
   347; **13 203–05; 16** 168; **33** 181
Eurobase, **50** 48
Eurocom S.A. *See* Euro RSCG Worldwide
   S.A.
Eurocopter SA, **7** 9, 11; **21** 8
EuroCross, **48** 381
Eurodis, **46** 71
EuroDollar Rent A Car. *See* Republic
   Industries, Inc.
Eurofighter Jagdflugzeug GmbH, **24** 84
Eurofilter Airfilters Ltd., **17** 106
Euroforum BV, **58** 191
Eurogroup, **V** 65
Euroimpex, **18** 163

Euromarché SA, **10** 205; **19** 308–09; **23** 231; **27** 94–95
Euromarket Designs Inc., 9 144; **31 186–89 (upd.); 34** 324, 327
Euromissile Dynamics Group, **7** 9; **24** 84
Euromoney Publications, **19** 118, 120
Euronda, **IV** 296; **19** 226
Euronext Paris S.A., 37 131–33
Euronova S.R.L., **15** 340
Europa Discount Sud-Ouest, **23** 248
Europaischen Tanklager- und Transport AG, **7** 141
Europate, S.A., **36** 162–63
Europcar Chauffeur Drive U.K. International, **26** 62
Europcar International Corporation, Limited, **25** 142, 144, **27** 9, 11
Europcar Interrent, **10** 419
Europe Computer Systems. *See* ECS S.A.
Europe Craft Imports, Inc., **16** 37
Europe Publications, **44** 416
Europe Through the Back Door Inc., 65 135–38
European Acquisition Capital, **53** 46
European Aeronautic Defence and Space Company EADS N.V., 34 128, 135; **52 113–16 (upd.); 54** 91
European-American Bank & Trust Company, **14** 169
European Gas Turbines, **13** 356
European Health Spa, **46** 431
European Investment Bank, 66 109–11
European Retail Alliance (ERA), **12** 152–53
European Silicon Structures, **17** 34
European Software Company, **25** 87
Europene du Zirconium (Cezus), **21** 491
Europensiones, **III** 348
Europoligrafico SpA, **41** 326
Europspace Technische Entwicklungen, **51** 17
Eurosar S.A., **25** 455
Eurotech BV, **25** 101
Eurotechnique, **III** 678; **16** 122
Eurotel Praha, spol. s.r.o., **64** 73
Eurotunnel Group, 37 134–38 (upd.)
Eurotunnel PLC, 13 206–08
Eurovida, **III** 348
Euthenics Systems Corp. *See* Michael Baker Corporation.
Euvia Media AG & Co., **54** 295, 297
EVA Airways Corporation, 13 211; **51 121–23**
Evac International Ltd, **51** 324
Evaluation Associates, LLC. *See* Milliman USA.
Evans & Sutherland Computer Corporation, 19 145–49
Evans Drumhead Company, **48** 232
Evans, Inc., 30 192–94
Evans Products Co., **13** 249–50, 550
Evans Rents, **26** 101
Evansville Paint & Varnish Co. *See* Red Spot Paint & Varnish Co.
Evansville Veneer and Lumber Co., **12** 296
Evelyn Wood, Inc., **7** 165, 168
Evence Coppée, **III** 704–05
Evenflo Companies, Inc., **19** 144; **54** 73
Ever Ready Ltd., **7** 209; **9** 179–80; **30** 231
Everan Capital Corp., **15** 257
Evercore Capital Partners, **59** 383
Everdream Corporation, **59** 12
Everest & Jennings, **11** 200
Everett Pulp & Paper Company, **17** 440

Everex Systems, Inc., **12** 162; **16 194–96**
Everfresh Beverages Inc., **26** 326
Evergenius, **13** 210
Evergreen Air Cargo Service Co., **51** 123
Evergreen Healthcare, Inc., **14** 210
Evergreen International Aviation, Inc., 53 130–33
Evergreen Marine Corporation (Taiwan) Ltd., 13 209–11; 50 183–89 (upd.)
Evergreen Media Corporation, **24** 106
Evergreen Resources, Inc., **11** 28
Everlast Worldwide Inc., 47 126–29
Everlaurel, **13** 210
Everready Battery Co., **13** 433; **39** 338
Everyday Learning Corporation, **22** 519, 522
Everything for the Office, **22** 154
Everything Yogurt, **25** 180
Everything's A Dollar Inc. (EAD), **13** 541–43
EVI, Inc., **39** 416
Evinrude Outboard Motor Company, **27** 75
Evity, Inc., **55** 67
EWTN. *See* Eternal Word Television Network, Inc.
Ex-Lax Inc., **15** 138–39
Exabyte Corporation, 12 161–63; 26 256; **40 178–81 (upd.)**
Exactis.com Inc., **49** 423
ExamOne World Wide, **48** 256
Exar Corp., 14 182–84
Exatec A/S, **10** 113; **50** 43
Exbud, **38** 437
Excaliber, **6** 205
EXCEL Communications Inc., 18 164–67
Excel Corporation, **11** 92–93; **13** 138, 351; **54** 168
Excel Industries Inc., **53** 55
Excel Mining Systems, Inc., **13** 98
Excel Technology, Inc., 65 139–42
Excelsior Life Insurance Co., **21** 14
Excelsior Printing Company, **26** 105
Excerpta Medica International. *See* Reed Elsevier
Excite, Inc., **22** 519; **27** 517. *See also* At Home Corporation.
Exco International, **10** 277
Execu-Fit Health Programs, **11** 379
Executive Aircraft Services, **27** 21
Executive Airlines, Inc., **28** 22
Executive Fund Life Insurance Company, **27** 47
Executive Gallery, Inc., **12** 264
Executive Income Life Insurance Co., **10** 246
Executive Jet, Inc., 36 189–91; 42 35
Executive Life Insurance Co., **III** 253–55; **11** 483
Executive Money Management, **57** 269
Executive Risk Inc., **37** 86
Executive Systems, Inc., **11** 18
Executone Information Systems, Inc., 13 212–14; 15 195
ExecuTrain. *See* International Data Group, Inc.
Executrans, Inc., **21** 96
Exel Logistics Ltd., **6** 412, 414
Exel Ltd., **13** 150
Exel plc, 51 124–30 (upd.)
Exelon Corporation, 48 156–63 (upd.); 49 65
Exeter & Hampton Electric Company, **37** 406

Exide Electronics Group, Inc., 9 10; **20 213–15; 24** 29
Exmark Manufacturing Company, Inc., **26** 494
Exp@nets, **37** 280, 283
Expand SA, 48 164–66
Expedia, Inc., 46 101, 103; **47** 421; **58 117–21**
Expeditors International of Washington Inc., 17 163–65
Experian Information Solutions Inc., 28 120; **45 152–55**
Experian Ltd., **47** 165, 168–69
Explorer Motor Home Corp., **16** 296
Export & Domestic Can Co., **15** 127
Express Airlines, Inc., **28** 266
Express Baggage Reclaim Services Limited, **27** 21
Express Gifts Ltd., **60** 122
Express Newspapers plc, **IV** 687; **28** 503
Express Rent-a-Tire, Ltd., **20** 113
Express Scripts Inc., 17 166–68; 44 173–76 (upd.)
Expression Homes, **22** 205, 207
ExpressJet Holdings Inc., **52** 89, 93
Exsa, **55** 188
ExSample Media BV, **53** 362
Extel Financial Ltd., **IV** 687
Extended Stay America, Inc., 41 156–58
Extendicare Health Services, Inc., 6 181–83
Extron International Inc., **16** 538; **43** 33
EXX Inc., 40 334; **65 143–45**
Exxon Corporation, I 364; **II** 62, 431, 451; **IV 426–30; 7 169–73 (upd.),** 230, 538, 559; **9** 440–41; **11** 353; **14** 24–25, 291, 494; **12** 348; **16** 489, 548; **20** 262; **23** 317; **25** 229–30; **26** 102, 369; **27** 217; **32 175–82 (upd.); 45** 54
Exxon Mobil Corporation, 40 358; **50** 29; **54** 380, 385; **63** 104, 113; **67 175–86 (upd.)**
Eyckeler & Malt AG, **59** 4–5
Eye Masters Ltd., **23** 329
Eyeful Home Co., **III** 758
Eyes Multimedia Productions Inc., **51** 286–87
EZ Paintr Corporation, **9** 374
Ezaki Glico Company Ltd., **61** 223
EZCORP Inc., 43 159–61; 61 53, 55
EZPor Corporation, **12** 377

F. & F. Koenigkramer Company, **10** 272
F&G International Insurance, **III** 397
F & J Meat Packers, Inc., **22** 548–49
F & M Distributors, **12** 132
F&N Foods Ltd., **54** 116–17
F & R Builders, Inc., **11** 257
F.A. Computer Technologies, Inc., **12** 60
F.A.O. Schwarz. *See* FAO Schwarz
F.B. McFarren, Ltd., **21** 499–500
F.C. Internazionale Milano SpA, **44** 387
F.E. Compton Company, **7** 167
F. Egger Co., **22** 49
F.H. Tomkins Buckle Company Ltd., **11** 525
F. Hoffmann-La Roche & Co. A.G., I 642–44, 657, 685, 693, 710; **7** 427; **9** 264; **10** 80, 549; **11** 424–25; **14** 406; **32** 211–12; **50 190–93 (upd.)**
F.K.I. Babcock, **III** 466
F. Kanematsu & Co., Ltd. *See* Kanematsu Corporation.
F.N. Herstal. *See* Groupe Herstal S.A.

F.W. Means & Company, **11** 337

F.W. Sickles Company, **10** 319

F.W. Woolworth & Co. Ltd. *See* Kingfisher plc.

F.W. Woolworth Co. *See* Woolworth Corporation.

F.X. Matt Brewing Co., **18** 72; **50** 114

F.X. Schmid Vereinigte Münchener Spielkartenfabriken GmbH & Co. KG, **64** 325

Fab-Asia, Inc., **22** 354–55

Fab Industries, Inc., 27 142–44

Fab 9, **26** 431

Fabbrica D' Armi Pietro Beretta S.p.A., 39 149–51

Fabco Automotive Corp., **23** 306; **27** 203

Faber-Castell. *See* A.W. Faber-Castell Unternehmensverwaltung GmbH & Co.

Fabergé, Inc., **III** 48; **8** 168, 344; **11** 90; **47** 114

Fabio Perini S.p.A., **60** 193

Fabri-Centers of America Inc., 15 329; 16 197–99; 18 223; 43 291

Fabtek Inc., **48** 59

Facet International, **61** 66

Facom S.A., 32 183–85; 37 143, 145

Façonnable S.A., **67** 279–80

Facts on File, Inc., **14** 96–97; **22** 443

FAE Fluid Air Energy SA, **49** 162–63

Fafnir Bearing Company, **13** 523

FAG—Kugelfischer Georg Schäfer AG, 11 84; **47** 280; **62** 129–32; **65** 134

Fagerdala World Foams, **54** 360–61

FAI, **III** 545–46

Failsafe, **14** 35

Fair Grounds Corporation, 44 177–80

Fair, Isaac and Company, 18 168–71, 516, 518

Fairbanks Morse Co., **12** 71

Fairchild Aircraft, Inc., 9 205–08, 460; **11** 278

Fairchild Camera and Instrument Corp., **III** 141, 455, 618; **7** 531; **10** 108; **11** 503; **13** 323–24; **17** 418; **21** 122

Fairchild Communications Service, **8** 328

The Fairchild Corporation, **37** 30

Fairchild Dornier GmbH, 48 167–71 (upd.)

Fairchild Industries, **14** 43; **15** 195; **34** 117

Fairchild Publications, **59** 133–34

Fairchild Semiconductor Corporation, **II** 63–65; **10** 365–66; **16** 332; **41** 201

Fairclough Construction Group plc, I 567–68

Fairey Industries Ltd., **IV** 659

Fairfax Financial Holdings Limited, 57 135–37

Fairfield Communities, Inc., 36 192–95

The Fairfield Group, **33** 259–60

Fairfield Manufacturing Co., **14** 43

Fairfield Publishing, **13** 165

Fairfield Resorts. *See* Outrigger Enterprises, Inc.

Fairmont Foods Co., **7** 430; **15** 139

Fairmont Hotels and Resorts Inc., **45** 80

Fairmont Insurance Co., **26** 487

Fairmount Glass Company, **8** 267

Fairport Machine Shop, Inc., **17** 357

Fairway Marketing Group, Inc., **24** 394

Fairway Outdoor Advertising, Inc., **36** 340, 342

Faiveley S.A., 39 152–54

Falcon Drilling Co. *See* Transocean Sedco Forex Inc.

Falcon Microsystems, Inc., **57** 172–73

Falcon Products, Inc., 33 149–51

Falcon Seaboard Inc., **7** 309

Falconbridge Limited, 49 136–39

Falley's, Inc., **17** 558, 560–61

Falls Financial Inc., **13** 223; **31** 206

Falls National Bank of Niagara Falls, **11** 108

Falls Rubber Company, **8** 126

FAME Plastics, Inc., **18** 162

Family Bookstores, **24** 548. *See also* Family Christian Stores, Inc.

Family Channel. *See* International Family Entertainment Inc.

Family Christian Stores, Inc., 51 131–34

Family Dollar Stores, Inc., 13 215–17; 62 133–36 (upd.)

Family Golf Centers, Inc., 29 183–85

Family Mart Group, **V** 188; **36** 418, 420

Family Preservation Services, Inc., **64** 311

Family Restaurants, Inc., **14** 194

Family Steak Houses of Florida, Inc., **15** 420

Famous Amos Chocolate Chip Cookie Corporation, **27** 332

Famous Atlantic Fish Company, **20** 5

Famous-Barr, **46** 288

Famous Dave's of America, Inc., 40 182–84 4

Famous Restaurants Inc., **33** 139–40

FAN, **13** 370

Fanafel Ltda., **62** 348, 350

Fancom Holding B.V., **43** 130

Fannie Mae, 45 156–59 (upd.); 54 122–24

Fannie May Candy Shops Inc., **36** 309

Fansteel Inc., 19 150–52

Fantastic Sam's, **26** 476

Fanthing Electrical Corp., **44** 132

Fantle's Drug Stores, **16** 160

Fanuc Ltd., III 482–83; 17 172–74 (upd.)

Fanzz, **29** 282

FAO Schwarz, 46 187–90; 62 208

Faprena, **25** 85

Far Eastern Air Transport, Inc., **23** 380

Far Eastern Bank, **56** 363

Faraday National Corporation, **10** 269

Farah Incorporated, 24 156–58

Farben. *See* I.G. Farbenindustrie AG.

Farberware, Inc., **27** 287–88

Farbro Corp., **45** 15

Farbwerke Hoechst A.G., **13** 262

FAREC Fahrzeugrecycling GmbH, **58** 28

Farley Industries, **25** 166

Farley Northwest Industries Inc., I 440–41

Farley's & Sathers Candy Company, Inc., 15 190; **62 137–39**

Farm Credit Bank of St. Louis/St. Paul, **8** 489–90

Farm Electric Services Ltd., **6** 586

Farm Family Holdings, Inc., 39 155–58

Farm Fresh Catfish Company, **54** 167

Farm Fresh Foods, **25** 332

Farm Journal Corporation, 42 131–34

Farm Power Laboratory, **6** 565; **50** 366

Farmcare Ltd., **51** 89

Farmer Bros. Co., 52 117–19

Farmer Jack, **16** 247; **44** 145

Farmers and Mechanics Bank of Georgetown, **13** 439

Farmers Insurance Group of Companies, 23 286; **25 154–56; 29** 397

Farmers National Bank & Trust Co., **9** 474

Farmers Petroleum, Inc., **48** 175

Farmland Foods, Inc., IV 474; **7** 17, **7** 174–75

Farmland Industries, Inc., 39 282; **48** 172–75

Farmstock Pty Ltd., **62** 307

Farrar, Straus and Giroux Inc., 15 158–60; 35 451

FAS Acquisition Co., **53** 142

FASC. *See* First Analysis Securities Corporation.

Fasco Consumer Products, **19** 360

Fashion Bar, Inc., **24** 457

Fashion Bug, **8** 97

Fashion Resource, Inc. *See* Tarrant Apparel Group.

Fasson. *See* Avery Dennison Corporation.

Fast Air, **31** 305

Fast Fare, **7** 102

Fastenal Company, 14 185–87; 42 135–38 (upd.)

FAT KAT, Inc., **51** 200, 203

Fata European Group, **IV** 187; **19** 348

Fatburger Corporation, 64 122–24

Fateco Förlag, **14** 556

FATS, Inc., **27** 156, 158

Faugere et Jutheau, **III** 283

Faultless Starch/Bon Ami Company, 55 142–45

Fauquet, **25** 85

Favorite Plastics, **19** 414

FAvS. *See* First Aviation Services Inc.

Fawcett Books, **13** 429

Fay's Inc., 17 175–77

Faydler Company, **60** 160

Fayette Tubular Products, **7** 116–17

Faygo Beverages Inc., 55 146–48

Fayva, **13** 359–61

Fazoli's Systems, Inc., 13 321; **27 145–47**

FB&T Corporation, **14** 154

FBC. *See* First Boston Corp.

FBO. *See* Film Booking Office of America.

FBR. *See* Friedman, Billings, Ramsey Group, Inc.

FBS Fuhrpark Business Service GmbH, **58** 28

FC Holdings, Inc., **26** 363

FCA Ltd. *See* Life Time Fitness, Inc.

FCC. *See* Federal Communications Commission.

FCI. *See* Framatome SA.

FDIC. *See* Federal Deposit Insurance Corp.

Feather Fine, **27** 361

Featherlite Inc., 28 127–29

Feature Enterprises Inc., **19** 452

FECR. *See* Florida East Coast Railway, L.L.C.

Fedders Corporation, 18 172–75; 43 162–67 (upd.)

Federal Barge Lines, **6** 487

Federal Bicycle Corporation of America, **11** 3

Federal Cartridge, **26** 363

Federal Coca-Cola Bottling Co., **10** 222

Federal Deposit Insurance Corp., **12** 30, 79

Federal Express Corporation, II 620; **V 451–53; 6** 385–86, 389; **12** 180, 192; **13** 19; **14** 517; **17** 504–05; **18** 315–17, 368, 370; **24** 22, 133; **25** 148; **26** 441; **27** 20, 22, 471, 475; **39** 33, 35; **41** 245–47; **63** 415. *See also* FedEx Corporation.

Federal Home Life Insurance Co., **IV** 623

Federal Home Loan Mortgage Corp., **18** 168; **25** 427. *See also* Freddie Mac.

Federal Insurance Co., **III** 220–21; **14** 108–109; **37** 83–85

Federal Laboratories, **57** 230

Federal Light and Traction Company, **6** 561–62

Federal-Mogul Corporation, I 158–60; 10 292–94 (upd.); 26 139–43 (upd.)

Federal National Mortgage Association, II 410–11; 18 168; **25** 427. *See also* Fannie Mae.

Federal Pacific Electric, **9** 440

Federal Packaging and Partition Co., **8** 476

Federal Packaging Corp., **19** 78

Federal Paper Board Company, Inc., 8 173–75; 15 229; **47** 189

Federal Power, **18** 473

Federal Prison Industries, Inc., 34 157–60

Federal Reserve Bank of New York, **21** 68

Federal Savings and Loan Insurance Corp., **16** 346

Federal Signal Corp., 10 295–97

Federal Trade Commission, **6** 260; **9** 370

Federated Department Stores Inc., 9 209–12; 10 282; **11** 349; **12** 37, 523; **13** 43, 260; **15** 88; **16** 61, 206; **17** 560; **18** 523; **22** 406; **23** 60; **27** 346–48; **30** 379; **31 190–94 (upd.); 35** 368; **36** 201, 204; **37** 13; **50** 107; **60** 70; **63** 145, 259, 263

Federated Development Company, **8** 349

Federated Livestock Corporation, **64** 306

Fédération Internationale de Football Association, 27 148–51

Federation Nationale d'Achats des Cadres. *See* FNAC.

FedEx Corporation, 18 128, **176–79 (upd.)**, 535; **33** 20, 22; **34** 474; **42 139–44 (upd.); 46** 71

FEE Technology, **29** 461–62

Feed-Rite Controls, Inc., **16** 270

Feed-Rite, Inc., **62** 307

Feffer & Simons, **16** 46

Feikes & Sohn KG, **IV** 325

Felco. *See* Farmers Regional Cooperative.

Feld Entertainment, Inc., 32 186–89 (upd.)

Feldmühle Nobel AG, III 692–95; IV 142, 325, 337; **36** 449. *See also* Metallgesellschaft.

Felixstowe Ltd., **18** 254

Fellowes Manufacturing Company, 28 130–32

Felten & Guilleaume, **IV** 25

Femsa, **19** 473. *See also* Formento Económico Mexicano, S.A. de C.V.

Femtech, **8** 513

Fendall Company, **40** 96, 98

Fendel Schiffahrts-Aktiengesellschaft, **6** 426

Fender Musical Instruments Company, 16 200–02; 43 168–72 (upd.)

Fendi S.p.A., **45** 344

Fenicia S.A., **22** 320; **61** 175

Fenn, Wright & Manson, **25** 121–22

Fenton Hill American Limited, **29** 510

Fenway Partners, **47** 361

Fenwick & West LLP, 34 161–63, 512

Ferembal S.A., **25** 512

Ferfin, **24** 341

Fergus Brush Electric Company, **18** 402

Ferguson Enterprises, **64** 409, 411

Ferguson Machine Co., **8** 135

Ferguson Manufacturing Company, **25** 164

Fermec Manufacturing Limited, **40** 432

Fermentaciones Mexicanas S.A. de C.V., **III** 43; **48** 250

Fernando Roqué, **6** 404; **26** 243

Ferolito, Vultaggio & Sons, 27 152–55

Ferragamo, **63** 151

Ferranti Business Communications, **20** 75

Ferrari S.p.A., 13 218–20; 36 196–200 (upd.)

Ferrellgas Partners, L.P., 35 173–75

Ferrero SpA, 54 103–05

Ferrier Hodgson, **10** 170

Ferris Industries, **64** 355

Ferro Corporation, 8 176–79; 9 10; **56 123–28 (upd.)**

Ferro Engineering Co., **17** 357

Ferrocarril del Noreste, S.A. de C.V. *See* Grupo Transportación Ferroviaria Mexicana, S.A. de C.V.

Ferrolux Metals Co., **63** 360

Ferrovial. *See* Grupo Ferrovail

Ferroxcube Corp. of America, **13** 397

Ferrum Inc., **24** 144

Ferruzzi Agricola Finanziario, **7** 81–83

Ferruzzi Finanziaria S.p.A., **24** 341; **36** 186

Fertisere SAS, **58** 221

Fetzer Vineyards, **10** 182

FFI Fragrances. *See* Elizabeth Arden, Inc.

FFM Bhd, **57** 292–95

FHP International Corporation, 6 184–86; 17 166, 168; **44** 174

Fiamm Technologies. *See* Valeo.

Fianzas Monterrey, **19** 189

Fiat SpA, I 161–63, 459–60, 466, 479; **9** 10; **11 102–04 (upd.)**, 139; **13** 17, 27–29, 218–20; **16** 322; **17** 24; **22** 379–81; **36** 32–34, 196–97, 199, 240, 243; **50 194–98 (upd.)**

Fibamex, **17** 106

Fibanc SA, **65** 230, 232

Fibar, **44** 261

Fiber Chemical Corporation, **7** 308

Fiberglas Canada, **III** 722

Fiberite, Inc., **27** 117; **28** 195

FiberMark, Inc., 37 139–42; 53 24

Fibermux Corporation, **10** 19; **30** 7

Fibic Corp., **18** 118

Fibreboard Corporation, 12 318; **14** 110; **16 203–05**

FibreChem, Inc., **8** 347

Fibro Tambor, S.A. de C.V., **8** 476

Fichet-Bauche SA, **53** 158

Fichtel & Sachs AG, **III** 566; **14** 328; **38** 299

Fidelco Capital Group, **10** 420

Fidelio Software GmbH, **18** 335, 337

Fidelity Exploration & Production Company, **42** 249, 253

Fidelity Federal Savings and Loan, **II** 420

Fidelity Investments Inc., II 412–13; 8 194; **9** 239; **14 188–90 (upd.); 18** 552; **19** 113; **21** 147; **22** 52. *See also* FMR Corp.

Fidelity Leasing Corporation, **42** 312–13

Fidelity National Financial Inc., 54 106–08

Fidelity National Title, **19** 92

Fidelity Oil Group, **7** 324

Fidenas Investment Ltd., **30** 185

Fides Holding, **21** 146

Field Corporation, **18** 355

Field Enterprises Educational Corporation, **16** 252; **26** 15; **43** 208

Field Enterprises, Inc., **12** 554

Field Group plc, **30** 120

Field Limited Partnership, **22** 441

Field Oy, **10** 113; **50** 43

Fieldale Farms Corporation, 23 191–93; 25 185–86

Fieldco Guide Dog Foundation, **42** 207

Fieldcrest Cannon, Inc., 8 32–33; **9 213–17; 16** 535; **19** 276, 305; **31 195–200 (upd.); 41** 299–301

Fieldstone Cabinetry, **III** 571; **20** 362

Fielmann AG, 31 201–03

Fiesta Restaurants Inc., **33** 139–40

FIFA. *See* Fédération Internationale de Football Association.

Fifa International, **39** 58

Fifth Generation Systems Inc., **10** 509

Fifth Third Bancorp, 9 475; **11** 466; **13 221–23; 31 204–08 (upd.)**

50-Off Stores, **23** 177. *See also* LOT$OFF Corporation.

Le Figaro. See Société du Figaro S.A.

Figgie International Inc., 7 176–78; 24 403–04

Figi's Inc., **9** 218, 220

FII Limited, **38** 197

Fil-Mag Group, **29** 461

Fila Holding S.p.A., 20 216–18; 39 60; **52 120–24 (upd.)**

Filene's. *See* The May Department Stores Company.

Filene's Basement. *See* Value City Department Stores, Inc.

FileNet Corporation, 62 140–43

Filergie S.A., **15** 355

Filipacchi Medias S.A. *See* Hachette Filipacchi Medias S.A.

Filiz Lastex, S.A., **15** 386

Filles S.A. de C.V., **7** 115; **25** 126

Film Roman, Inc., 58 122–24

Films for the Humanities, Inc., **22** 441

Filofax Inc., **41** 120, 123

Filter Queen-Canada, **17** 234

Filterfresh Corporation, **39** 409

Filtertek, Inc., **24** 425

Filtrona International Ltd., **31** 77

Filtros Baldwin de Mexico, **17** 106

Filtros Continental, **17** 106

Fimalac S.A., 37 143–45

Fimaser, **21** 101

Fimestic, **21** 101

FINA, Inc., 7 179–81; 26 368

Finaler. *See* Leroux S.A.S.

Finalrealm Limited, **42** 404

Finance Oil Corp., **49** 304

Financial Computer Services, Inc., **11** 111

Financial Data Services, Inc., **11** 111

Financial Network Marketing Company, **11** 482

Financial News Network, Inc., **25** 507; **31** 147

Financial Performance Corporation. *See* BrandPartners Group, Inc.

Financial Security Assurance Inc., **25** 497

Financial Services Corp., **III** 306–07

Financial Services Corporation of Michigan, **11** 163

Financial Systems, Inc., **11** 111

Financial Technologies International, **17** 497

The Financial Times Group, **46** 337

Financiera Aceptaciones, **19** 189

Financière Leroux. *See* Leroux S.A.S.
Financière Saint Dominique, **9** 151–52
Finast. *See* First National Supermarkets, Inc.
Find-A-Home Service, Inc., **21** 96
Findel plc, 60 122–24
Findlays Spring Natural Mineral Water, **64** 11
Findomestic, **21** 101
Findorff. *See* J.H. Findorff and Son, Inc.
Fine Art Developments Ltd., **15** 340
Fine Fare, **II** 609, 628–29
Fine Fragrances, **22** 213
Finesco, LLC, **37** 200–01
Finevest Services Inc., **15** 526
Fingerhut Companies, Inc., V 148; **9** 218–20; **15** 401; **18** 133; **31** 190; **34** 232; **36** 201–05 (upd.); **37** 130; **56** 226
Fininvest Group
Fininvest S.p.A., **IV** 587–88; **54** 17, 21, 23; **65** 230–31
The Finish Line, Inc., 29 186–88
FinishMaster, Inc., 17 310–11; **24** 159–61
Finlay Enterprises, Inc., 16 206–08
Finmeccanica S.p.A., **13** 28; **23** 83; **36** 34; **50** 197; **52** 115
Finnair Oy, 6 87–89; **25** 157–60 (upd.); **33** 50; **61** 91–95 (upd.)
Finnforest Oy, **IV** 316
Finnigan Corporation, **11** 513
Finsa, **II** 196
FinSer Capital Corporation, **17** 262
Finsider, **IV** 125
Firan Motor Coach, Inc., **17** 83
Firearms Training Systems, Inc., 27 156–58
Fireman's Fund Insurance Company, III 214, 250–52, 263
Firestone Tire and Rubber Co., **8** 80; **9** 247; **15** 355; **17** 182; **18** 320; **20** 259–62; **50** 316. *See also* Bridgestone Corporation.
Firma Hamburger Kaffee-Import- Geschäft Emil Tengelmann. *See* Tengelmann Group.
Firma Huter Vorfertigung GmbH, **49** 163
Firmenich International S.A., 60 125–27
FirmLogic, L.P., **52** 423
The First, **10** 340
First & 42nd, **62** 115
First Acadiana National Bank, **11** 107
First Air. *See* Bradley Air Services Ltd.
First Albany Companies Inc., 37 146–48
First Alert, Inc., 28 133–35
First American. *See* Bremer Financial Corp.
First American Bank Corporation, **8** 188; **41** 178
The First American Corporation, 52 125–27
First American Media, Inc., **24** 199
First American National Bank, **19** 378
First American National Bank-Eastern, **11** 111
First Analysis Securities Corporation, **22** 5
First and Merchants, **10** 426
First Atlanta Corporation, **16** 523
First Atlantic Capital, Ltd., **28** 340, 342
First Aviation Services Inc., 49 140–42
First Bancard, Inc., **11** 106
First BanCorporation, **13** 467
First Bank of Savannah, **16** 522

First Bank System Inc., 11 130; **12** 164–66; **13** 347–48; **24** 393. *See also* U.S. Bancorp
First Boston Corp., **II** 426, 434, 441; **9** 378, 386; **12** 439; **13** 152, 342. *See also* CSFB.
First Brands Corporation, 8 180–82; **16** 44
First Capital Financial, **8** 229
First Carolina Investors Inc., **17** 357
First Cash Financial Services, Inc., 57 138–40; **61** 53, 55
First Chicago Corporation, II 284–87. *See also* Bank One Corporation.
First Chicago Venture Capital, **24** 516
First Choice Holidays PLC, 40 185–87, 284–85
First Cincinnati, Inc., **41** 133
First Commerce Bancshares, Inc., 15 161–63
First Commerce Corporation, 11 105–07
First Commercial Savings and Loan, **10** 340
First Constitution Financial Corporation. *See* The Aristotle Corporation.
First Consumers National Bank, **10** 491; **27** 429
First Data Corporation, 10 63; **18** 516–18, 537; **24** 393 **30** 195–98 (upd.); **46** 250; **54** 413
First Data Management Company of Oklahoma City, **11** 112
First Delaware Life Insurance Co., **III** 254
First Deposit Corp.,. *See* Providian Financial Corporation.
First Empire State Corporation, 11 108–10
First Executive Corporation, III 253–55
First Express, **48** 177
First Federal Savings & Loan Assoc., **IV** 343; **9** 173
First Federal Savings and Loan Association of Crisp County, **10** 92
First Federal Savings and Loan Association of Hamburg, **10** 91
First Federal Savings and Loan Association of Fort Myers, **9** 476
First Federal Savings and Loan Association of Kalamazoo, **9** 482
First Federal Savings Bank of Brunswick, **10** 92
First Fidelity Bank, N.A., New Jersey, 9 221–23
First Fidelity Bank of Rockville, **13** 440
First Financial Insurance, **41** 178
First Financial Management Corporation, 11 111–13; **18** 542; **25** 183; **30** 195
First Florida Banks, **9** 59
First Hawaiian, Inc., 11 114–16
FIRST HEALTH Strategies, **11** 113
First Healthcare, **14** 242
First Heights, fsa, **8** 437
First Hospital Corp., **15** 122
First Industrial Realty Trust, Inc., 65 146–48
First Insurance Agency, Inc., **17** 527
First International Computer, Inc., 56 129–31
First Interstate Bancorp, II 228, 288–90; **8** 295; **9** 334; **17** 546
First Investment Advisors, **11** 106
First Investors Management Corp., **11** 106

First Leisure Corporation plc. *See* Esporta plc.
First Liberty Financial Corporation, **11** 457
First Line Insurance Services, Inc., **8** 436
First Madison Bank, **14** 192
First Maryland Bancorp, **16** 14
First Mississippi Corporation, 8 183–86. *See also* ChemFirst, Inc.
First Mississippi National, **14** 41
First National Bank, **10** 298; **13** 467
First National Bank and Trust Company, **22** 4
First National Bank and Trust Company of Kalamazoo, **8** 187–88
First National Bank in Albuquerque, **11** 119
First National Bank of Akron, **9** 475
First National Bank of Allentown, **11** 296
First National Bank of Atlanta, **16** 522
First National Bank of Boston, **12** 310; **13** 446
First National Bank of Carrollton, **9** 475
First National Bank of Commerce, **11** 106
First National Bank of Harrington, Delaware. *See* J.C. Penny National Bank.
First National Bank of Hartford, **13** 466
First National Bank of Hawaii, **11** 114
First National Bank of Highland, **11** 109
First National Bank of Houma, **21** 522
The First National Bank of Lafayette, **11** 107
First National Bank of Minneapolis, **22** 426–27
First National Bank of Salt Lake, **11** 118
First National Bank of Seattle, **8** 469–70
First National Bankshares, Inc., **21** 524
First National City Bank, **9** 124; **16** 13
First National Holding Corporation, **16** 522
First National Supermarkets, Inc., **II** 641–42; **9** 452
First Nations Gaming, Ltd., **44** 334
First Nationwide Bank, 8 30; **14** 191–93
First Nationwide Holdings Inc., **28** 246
First New England Bankshares Corp., **13** 467
First Nitrogen, Inc., **8** 184
First Nuclear Corporation, **49** 411
First of America Bank Corporation, 8 187–89
First of America Bank-Monroe, **9** 476
First Omni Bank NA, **16** 14; **18** 518; **43** 8
First Options of Chicago, Inc., **51** 148
First Pacific Company Limited, 18 180–82
First Physician Care, Inc., **36** 367
First Pick Stores, **12** 458
First Private Power Corporation, **56** 215
First Quench Retailing Ltd., **52** 416
First Railroad and Banking Company, **11** 111
First Republic Corp.,; **14** 483
First RepublicBank Corporation, **II** 337; **10** 425–26
First Savings and Loan, **10** 339
First Seattle Dexter Horton National Bank, **8** 470
First Security Bank of Missoula, **35** 197–99
First Security Corporation, 11 117–19; **38** 491
First Signature Bank and Trust Co., **III** 268
First Sport Ltd., **39** 60

1st State Bank & Trust, **9** 474

First State Bank Southwest Indiana, **41** 178–79

First SunAmerican Life Insurance Company, **11** 482

First Team Sports, Inc., 15 396–97; **22 202–04**

First Tennessee National Corporation, 11 120–21; **48 176–79 (upd.)**

First Trust Bank, **16** 14

First Union Corporation, 10 298–300; **24** 482; **37** 148; **57** 415. *See also* Wachovia Corporation.

First USA, Inc., 11 122–24

First USA Paymentech, **24** 393

First Variable Life, **59** 246

First Virginia Banks, Inc., 11 125–26

First Women's Bank of New York, **23** 3

First Worth Corporation, **19** 232

The First Years Inc., 46 191–94

FirstAir Inc., **48** 113

Firstar Corporation, 11 127–29; **33 152–55 (upd.)**

FirstBancorp., **13** 467

FirstGroup plc, **38** 321

FirstMiss, Inc., **8** 185

FirstPage USA Inc., **41** 265

Firth Carpet, **19** 275

Fischbach Corp., **III** 198; **8** 536–37

FISCOT, **10** 337

Fiserv Inc., 11 130–32; **33 156–60 (upd.)**

Fish & Neave, 54 109–12

Fisher & Company, **9** 16

Fisher Broadcasting Co., **15** 164

Fisher-Camuto Corp., **14** 441

Fisher Companies, Inc., 15 164–66

Fisher Controls International, LLC, 13 224–26; **15** 405, 407; **29** 330; **46** 171; **61 96–99 (upd.)**

Fisher Foods, Inc., **II** 602; **9** 451, 452; **13** 237; **41** 11, 13

Fisher Nut, **14** 275

Fisher-Price Inc., 12 167–69; bf]XIII 317; **25** 314, 380; **32 190–94 (upd.)**; **61** 201–03

Fisher Scientific International Inc., 24 162–66; **25** 260

Fishers Agricultural Holdings, **II** 466

Fiskars Corporation, 33 161–64; **60** 351

Fiskeby Board AB, **48** 344

Fisons plc, 9 224–27; **23 194–97 (upd.)**

Fitch IBCA Inc., **37** 143, 145

Fitch Investor Services, **65** 243–44

Fitch Lovell PLC, **13** 103

Fitchburg Gas and Electric Light, **37** 406

Fitzsimmons Stores Inc., **16** 452

Fitzwilton Public Limited Company, **12** 529; **34** 496

Five Bros. Inc., **19** 456

Five Star Entertainment Inc., **28** 241

Five Star Group, Inc., **64** 166

546274 Alberta Ltd., **48** 97

FKI Plc, 57 141–44

FKM Advertising, **27** 280

FL Industries Holdings, Inc., **11** 516

Flagler Development Company, **59** 184–85

Flagship Resources, **22** 495

Flagstar Companies, Inc., 10 301–03; **29** 150. *See also* Advantica Restaurant Group, Inc.

Flagstone Hospitality Management LLC, **58** 194

Flair Corporation, **18** 467

Flair Fold, **25** 11

Flambeau Products Corporation, **55** 132

Flanders Corporation, 65 149–51

Flanigan's Enterprises, Inc., 60 128–30

Flapdoodles, **15** 291

Flashes Publishers, Inc., **36** 341

Flatbush Gas Co., **6** 455–56

Flatiron Mandolin Company, **16** 239

Flatow, Moore, Bryan, and Fairburn, **21** 33

Flavors Holdings Inc., **38** 294

Fleck Controls, Inc., **26** 361, 363

Fleer Corporation, 10 402; **13** 519; **15** 167–69; **19** 386; **34** 447; **37** 295

Fleet Aerospace Corporation. *See* Magellan Aerospace Corporation.

Fleet Call, Inc., **10** 431–32

Fleet Equity Partners, **62** 325, 327

Fleet Financial Group, Inc., IV 687; **9** 228–30; **12** 31; **13** 468; **18** 535; **38** 13, 393

Fleet Holdings, **28** 503

FleetBoston Financial Corporation, 36 206–14 (upd.)

Fleetway, **7** 244

Fleetwood Enterprises, Inc., III 484–85; **13** 155; **17** 83; **21** 153; **22 205–08 (upd.)**; **33** 399

Fleming Chinese Restaurants Inc., **37** 297

Fleming Companies, Inc., II 624–25, 671; **7** 450; **12** 107, 125; **13** 335–37; **17 178–81 (upd.)**; **18** 506–07; **23** 407; **24** 529; **26** 449; **28** 152, 154; **31** 25; **34** 198; **50** 457

Fleming Foodservice, **26** 504

Fletcher Challenge Ltd., IV 250, 278–80; **19 153–57 (upd.)**; **25** 12; **63** 315

Fletcher Pacific Construction Co. Ltd., **64** 113

Fleury Michon S.A., 39 159–61

Flex Elektrowerkzeuge GmbH, **26** 363

Flex Interim, **16** 421; **43** 308

Flex-O-Lite, **14** 325

Flexi-Van Corporations, **II** 492; **20** 118

Flexsteel Industries Inc., 15 170–72; **41 159–62 (upd.)**

Flextronics International Ltd., 12 451; **38 186–89**

Flexys, **16** 462

FLGI Holding Company, **10** 321

Flick Industrial Group. *See* Feldmühle Nobel AG.

Flight One Logistics, Inc., **22** 311

Flight Refuelling Limited. *See* Cobham plc.

FlightSafety International, Inc., 9 231–33; **29 189–92 (upd.)**

Flint Ink Corporation, 13 227–29; **41 163–66 (upd.)**

Flip Chip Technologies, LLC, **33** 248

Flo-Pak, Inc., **57** 160

Florafax International, Inc., **37** 162

Floral City Furniture Company, **14** 302–03; **50** 309–10

Flori Roberts, Inc., **11** 208

Florida Crystals Inc., 35 176–78

Florida Cypress Gardens, Inc., **IV** 623

Florida Distillers Company, **27** 479

Florida East Coast Industries, Inc., 59 184–86

Florida East Coast Railway, L.L.C., **8** 486–87; **12** 278; **59** 184

Florida Flavors, **44** 137

Florida Frozen Foods, **13** 244

Florida Gaming Corporation, 47 130–33

Florida Gas Co., **15** 129

Florida Gas Transmission Company, **6** 578

Florida Panthers Hockey Club, Ltd., **37** 33, 35

Florida Power & Light Company. *See* FPL Group, Inc.

Florida Presbyterian College, **9** 187

Florida Progress Corp., V 621–22; **23 198–200 (upd.)**

Florida Rock Industries, Inc., 23 326; **46 195–97**

Florida Steel Corp., **14** 156

Florida's Natural Growers, 45 160–62

FloridaGulf Airlines, **11** 300

Florimex Verwaltungsgesellschaft mbH, **12** 109

Florists' Transworld Delivery, Inc., 28 136–38

Florsheim Shoe Group Inc., 9 135, **234–36**; **12** 308; **16** 546; **31 209–12 (upd.)**

Flour City International, Inc., 44 181–83

Flow International Corporation, 56 132–34

Flow Laboratories, **14** 98

Flow Measurement, **26** 293

Flower Time, Inc., **12** 179, 200

Flowers Industries, Inc., 12 170–71; **35 179–82 (upd.)**. *See also* Keebler Foods Company.

Flowserve Corporation, 33 165–68

Floyd West & Co., **6** 290

Fluent, Inc., **29** 4–6

Fluf N'Stuf, Inc., **12** 425

Fluke Corporation, 15 173–75

Flunch, **37** 22

Fluor Corporation, I 569–71, 586; **8 190–93 (upd.)**; **12** 244; **26** 433; **34 164–69 (upd.)**; **57** 237–38

Fluor Daniel Inc., **41** 148

The Fluorocarbon Company. *See* Furon Company.

Flushing Federal Savings & Loan Association, **16** 346

FlyBE. *See* Jersey European Airways (UK) Ltd.

Flying Boat, Inc. (Chalk's Ocean Airways), 56 135–37

Flying Colors Toys Inc., **52** 193

Flying Fruit Fantasy, USA, Inc., **57** 56–57

Flying J Inc., 19 158–60

Flying Tiger Line, **6** 388; **25** 146; **39** 33

FMC Corp., I 442–44, 679; **11 133–35 (upd.)**; **14** 457; **22** 415; **30** 471; **47** 238

FMR Corp., 8 194–96; **14** 188; **22** 413; **30** 331; **32 195–200 (upd.)**

FMXI, Inc. *See* Foamex International Inc.

FN Manufacturing Co., **12** 71

FNAC, 21 224–26; **26** 160

Flo-Pak, Inc., **57** 160

FNC Comercio, **III** 221

FNCB. *See* First National City Bank of New York.

FNH USA, Inc., **58** 147

FNK. *See* Finance Oil Corp.

FNMA. *See* Federal National Mortgage Association.

FNN. *See* Financial News Network.

Foamex International Inc., 17 182–85; **26** 500

Focal Surgery, Inc., **27** 355

FOCUS, **44** 402

Fodor's Travel Guides, **13** 429

Fog Cutter Capital Group Inc., **64** 124

Fogdog Inc., **36** 347

Fokker. *See* N.V. Koninklijke Nederlandse Vliegtuigenfabriek Fokker.

Fokker Aircraft Corporation of America, **9** 16

Foley & Lardner, 28 139–42

Folksamerica Holding Company, Inc., **48** 431

Follett Corporation, 12 172–74; 16 47; **39 162–65 (upd.); 43** 61

Follis DeVito Verdi. *See* De Vito/Verdi.

Follum Fabrikker, **63** 314

Fomento de Valores, S.A. de C.V., **23** 170

Fomento Economico Mexicano, S.A. de C.V. *See* Femsa.

Fonda Group, **36** 462

Fondazione Cassa di Risparmio di Venezia, **50** 408

Fondiaria Group, **III** 351

Fonterra Co-Operative Group Ltd., 58 125–27

Food City, **II** 649–50

The Food Emporium, 64 125–27

Food Fair, **19** 480

Food 4 Less Supermarkets, Inc., **II** 624; **17** 558–61

Food Giant, **II** 670

Food Ingredients Technologies, **25** 367

Food King, **20** 306

Food Lion LLC, II 626–27; 7 450; **15 176–78 (upd.),** 270; **18** 8; **21** 508; **33** 306; **44** 145; **66 112–15 (upd.)**

Food Machinery Corp. *See* FMC Corp.

Food Source, **58** 290

Food Town Inc., **II** 626–27

Food World, **26** 46; **31** 372

Foodarama Supermarkets, Inc., 28 143–45

FoodBrands America, Inc., 21 290; **22** 510; **23 201–04.** *See also* Doskocil Companies, Inc.

FoodLand Distributors, **II** 625, 645, 682

Foodmaker, Inc., 13 152; **14 194–96**

Foodstuffs, **9** 144

Foodtown, **II** 626; **V** 35; **15** 177; **24** 528

FoodUSA.com, **43** 24

Foodways National, Inc., **12** 531; **13** 383

Foot Locker. *See* Venator Group Inc.

Footaction. *See* Footstar, Incorporated.

Foote, Cone & Belding Worldwide, I 12–15, 28, 34; **11** 51; **13** 517; **22** 395; **25** 90–91; **66 116–20 (upd.)**

Foote Mineral Company, **7** 386–87

Footquarters, **14** 293, 295

Footstar, Incorporated, 24 167–69

Foracon Maschinen und Anlagenbau GmbH & Co., **56** 134

Forbes Inc., 30 199–201

The Ford Foundation, 34 170–72; 52 200–01

Ford Motor Company, I 164–68; III 515, 603; **7** 377, 461, 520–21; **8** 70, 74–75, 117, 372–73, 375, 505–06; **9** 94, 118, 126, 190, 283–84, 325, 341–43; **10** 32, 241, 260, 264–65, 279–80, 290, 353, 407, 430, 460, 465; **11** 53–54, 103–04, **136–40 (upd.),** 263, 326, 339, 350, 528–29; **12** 68, 91, 294, 311; **13** 28, 219, 285, 287, 345, 555; **14** 191–92; **15** 91, 171, 513, 515; **16** 321–22; **17** 183, 303–04; **18** 112, 308, 319; **19** 11, 125, 221, 223, 482, 484; **20** 359; **21** 153, 200, 503; **22** 175, 380–81; **23** 143, 339–41, 434; **24** 12; 25 90, 93, 142–43, 224, 226, 358; **26** 176, 452, 501; **27** 20, 202; **29** 265; **34** 133–34, 136, 303, 305; **36** 34, 180, 198, **215–21 (upd.),**

242–43; **38** 86, 458–59; **40** 134; **41** 280–81; **54** 207; **59** 90; **63** 302, 304; **64 128–34 (upd.)**

Ford Motor Company, S.A. de C.V., 20 219–21

Ford New Holland, Inc. *See* New Holland N.V.

Fording Inc., **45** 80

FORE Systems, Inc., 25 161–63; 33 289

Forefront Communications, **22** 194

Forefront Petroleum Company, **60** 160

Foreign & Colonial, **64** 303

Foremost-McKesson Inc. *See* McKesson Corporation.

Foremost Warehouse Corp., **14** 372

Forest City Auto Parts, **23** 491

Forest City Enterprises, Inc., 16 209–11; 52 128–31 (upd.)

Forest City Ratner Companies, **17** 318

Forest E. Olson, Inc., **21** 96

Forest Laboratories, Inc., 11 141–43; 47 55; **52 132–36 (upd.)**

Forest Oil Corporation, 19 161–63

Forestry Corporation of New Zealand, **19** 156

Företagsfinans, **25** 464

Forethought Group, Inc., **10** 350

Forever Living Products International Inc., 17 186–88

Forge Books. *See* Tom Doherty Associates Inc.

Forjas Metalicas, S.A. de C.V. (Formet), **44** 193

Formento Económico Mexicano, S.A. de C.V., **25** 279, 281

Formica Corporation, 10 269; **13 230–32**

Forming Technology Co., **III** 569; **20** 361

Formonix, **20** 101

Formosa Plastics Corporation, 11 159; **14 197–99; 16** 194, 196; **31** 108, **58 128–31 (upd.)**

Formtec Inc., **62** 350

Formulabs, Inc., **52** 307

Formule 1, **13** 364; **27** 10

Forney Fiber Company, **8** 475

Forrester Research, Inc., 54 113–15

Forstmann Little & Co., I 483; **7** 206; **10** 321; **12** 344, 562; **14** 166; **16** 322; **19** 372–73, 432; **22** 32, 60; **30** 426; **34** 145, 448; **36** 523; **38** 190–92; **54** 372

Fort Bend Utilities Company, **12** 269

Fort Garry Brewery, **26** 304

Fort Howard Corporation, 8 197–99; 15 305; **22** 209. *See also* Fort James Corporation.

Fort James Corporation, 22 209–12 (upd.); 29 136

Fort Mill Manufacturing Co. *See* Springs Industries, Inc.

Forte Plc, **15** 46; **16** 446; **24** 195; **29** 443; **64** 340

Fortis, Inc., 15 179–82; 47 134–37 (upd.); 50 4–6

Fortum Corporation, 30 202–07 (upd.)

Fortun Foods, **26** 59

Fortune Brands, Inc., 19 168; **29 193–97 (upd.); 45** 269; **49** 153; **51** 7; **58** 194, 196; **64** 3

Fortune Enterprises, **12** 60

Fortunoff Fine Jewelry and Silverware Inc., 26 144–46

Forum Cafeterias, **19** 299–300

Fosgate Electronics, **43** 322

Foss Maritime Co., **9** 509, 511

Fossil, Inc., 17 189–91

Foster & Kleiser, **7** 335; **14** 331

Foster Forbes, **16** 123

Foster Grant. *See* FosterGrant, Inc.

Foster Management Co., **11** 366–67

Foster Medical Corp., **11** 282

Foster Poultry Farms, 32 201–04

Foster-Probyn Ltd., **38** 501

Foster Sand & Gravel, **14** 112

Foster Wheeler Corporation, 6 145–47; 23 205–08 (upd.); 25 82

Foster's Group Limited, 7 182–84; 21 227–30 (upd.); 26 303, 305–06; **36** 15; **50 199–203 (upd.),** 261

FosterGrant, Inc., 60 131–34

Fougerolle, **27** 136, 138

Foundation Computer Systems, Inc., **13** 201

Foundation Fieldbus, **22** 373

Foundation Health Corporation, 11 174; **12 175–77**

Founders Equity Inc., **14** 235

Founders of American Investment Corp., **15** 247

Fountain Powerboats Industries, Inc., 28 146–48

Four Media Co., **33** 403

Four Paws Products, Ltd., **58** 60

Four Queens Hotel and Casino. *See* The Elsinore Corporation.

Four Seasons Hotels Inc., 9 237–38; 29 198–200 (upd.)

Four-Ten Corporation, **58** 378

Four Winds, **21** 153

4Kids Entertainment Inc., 59 187–89

Fournier Furniture, Inc., **12** 301

4P, **30** 396–98

Fourth Financial Corporation, 11 144–46; 15 60

Fowler, Roenau & Geary, LLC, **37** 224

Fox and Hound English Pub and Grille. *See* Total Entertainment Restaurant Corporation.

Fox & Jacobs, **8** 87

Fox Broadcasting Company, **II** 156; **9** 428; **21** 25, 360; **24** 517; **25** 174, 417–18

Fox Children's Network, **21** 26

Fox Entertainment Group, Inc., 43 173–76; 52 4–5

Fox Family Worldwide, Inc., 24 170–72; 63 437. *See also* ABC Family Worldwide, Inc.

Fox Film Corp. *See* Twentieth Century Fox Film Corporation.

Fox Grocery Co., **II** 682

Fox, Inc., **12** 359; **25** 490

Fox Network, **29** 426

Fox Paine & Company L.L.C., **63** 410, 412

Fox Paper Company, **8** 102

Fox-Vliet Drug Company, **16** 212

Foxboro Company, 13 233–35; 27 81

Foxconn International, Inc. *See* Hon Hai Precision Industry Co., Ltd.

FoxMeyer Health Corporation, 8 55; **16 212–14**

Foxmoor, **29** 163

Foxx Hy-Reach, **28** 387

Foxy Products, Inc., **60** 287

FP&L. *See* Florida Power & Light Co.

FPA Corporation. *See* Orleans Homebuilders, Inc.

FPK LLC, **26** 343

FPL Group, Inc., V 623–25; 45 150; **49 143–46 (upd.)**

FR Corp., **18** 340; **43** 282
Fracmaster Ltd., **55** 294
Fragrance Corporation of America, Ltd., **53** 88
Fragrance Express Inc., **37** 271
Framatome SA, **9** 10; **19 164–67**
Framingham Electric Company, **12** 45
Franc-Or Resources, **38** 231–32
France-Loisirs, **IV** 615–16, 619
France Quick, **12** 152; **26** 160–61; **27** 10
France Télécom Group, **V 291–93**, 471; **9** 32; **14** 489; **18** 33; **21 231–34** (upd.); **25** 96, 102; **34** 13; **47** 214; **52** 108; **63** 375–77
Franchise Associates, Inc., **17** 238
Franchise Business Systems, Inc., **18** 207
Franchise Finance Corp. of America, **19** 159; **37** 351
Francis H. Leggett & Co., **24** 527
Franciscan Vineyards, Inc., **34** 89
Franco-Américaine de Constructions Atomiques, **19** 165
Frank & Pignard SA, **51** 35
Frank & Schulte GmbH, **8** 496
Frank Dry Goods Company, **9** 121
Frank H. Nott Inc., **14** 156
Frank Holton Company, **55** 149, 151
Frank J. Rooney, Inc., **8** 87
Frank J. Zamboni & Co., Inc., **34 173–76**
Frank Russell Company, **45** 316; **46 198–200**
Frank Schaffer Publications, **19** 405; **29** 470, 472
Frank W. Horner, Ltd., **38** 123
Frank's Nursery & Crafts, Inc., **12 178–79**, 198–200
Frankel & Co., **39 166–69**
Frankenberry, Laughlin & Constable, **9** 393
Frankford-Quaker Grocery Co., **II** 625
Frankfurter Allgemeine Zeitung GmbH, **66 121–24**
Franklin Assurances, **III** 211
Franklin Brass Manufacturing Company, **20** 363
Franklin Coach, **56** 223
Franklin Container Corp., **IV** 312; **19** 267
Franklin Corp., **14** 130; **41** 388
Franklin Covey Company, **37 149–52** (upd.)
Franklin Electric Company, Inc., **43 177–80**
Franklin Electronic Publishers, Inc., **23 209–13**
Franklin Mint, **9** 428; **37** 337–38
Franklin Mutual Advisors LLC, **52** 119, 172
Franklin National Bank, **9** 536
Franklin Plastics, **19** 414
Franklin Quest Co., **11 147–49**; **41** 121. See also Franklin Covey Company.
Franklin Research & Development, **11** 41
Franklin Resources, Inc., **9 239–40**
Franklin Sports, Inc., **17** 243
Franklin Steamship Corp., **8** 346
Frans Maas Beheer BV, **14** 568
Franzia. See The Wine Group, Inc.
Fraser & Chalmers, **13** 16
Fraser & Neave Ltd., **54 116–18**; **59** 58–59
Fray Data International, **14** 319
Frazer & Jones, **48** 141
Fred Campbell Auto Supply, **26** 347

Fred Meyer Stores, Inc., **II** 669; **V 54–56**; **18** 505; **20 222–25** (upd.); **35** 370; **50** 455; **64 135–39** (upd.)
Fred Sammons Company of Chicago, **30** 77
Fred Schmid Appliance & T.V. Co., Inc., **10** 305; **18** 532
Fred Usinger Inc., **54 119–21**
The Fred W. Albrecht Grocery Co., **13 236–38**
Fred Weber, Inc., **61 100–02**
Fred's, Inc., **23 214–16**; **62 144–47** (upd.)
Freddie Mac, **54 122–25**
Fredelle, **14** 295
Frederick & Nelson, **17** 462
Frederick Atkins Inc., **16 215–17**
Frederick Bayer & Company, **22** 225
Frederick Gas Company, **19** 487
Frederick Manufacturing Corporation, **26** 119; **48** 59
Frederick's of Hollywood Inc., **16 218–20**; **25** 521; **59 190–93** (upd.)
Fredrickson Motor Express, **57** 277
Free-lance Uitzendburo, **26** 240
Freeborn Farms, **13** 244
Freedom Communications, Inc., **36 222–25**
Freedom Group Inc., **42** 10–11
Freedom Technology, **11** 486
Freeman Chemical Corporation, **61** 111–12
Freeman, Spogli & Co., **17** 366; **18** 90; **32** 12, 15; **35** 276; **36** 358–59; **47** 142–43; **57** 11, 242
Freemans. See Sears plc.
FreeMark Communications, **38** 269
Freeport-McMoRan Copper & Gold, Inc., **IV 81–84**; **7 185–89** (upd.); **16** 29; **23** 40; **57 145–50** (upd.)
Freeport Power, **38** 448
Freezer Queen Foods, Inc., **21** 509
Freezer Shirt Corporation, **8** 406
Freight Car Services, Inc., **23** 306
Freight Outlet, **17** 297
Frejlack Ice Cream Co., **II** 646; **7** 317
Fremont Canning Company, **7** 196
Fremont Group, **21** 97
Fremont Investors, **30** 268
Fremont Partners, **24** 265
Fremont Savings Bank, **9** 474–75
French Connection Group plc, **41 167–69**
French Fragrances, Inc., **22 213–15**; **40** 170. See also Elizabeth Arden, Inc.
French Kier, **I** 568
French Quarter Coffee Co., **27** 480–81
Frequency Electronics, Inc., **61 103–05**
Frequency Sources Inc., **9** 324
Fresenius AG, **22** 360; **49 155–56**; **56 138–42**
Fresh America Corporation, **20 226–28**
Fresh Choice, Inc., **20 229–32**
Fresh Enterprises, Inc., **66 125–27**
Fresh Fields, **19** 501
Fresh Foods, Inc., **25** 391; **29 201–03**
Fresh Start Bakeries, **26** 58
Freshbake Foods Group PLC, **II** 481; **7** 68; **25** 518; **26** 57
Fretter, Inc., **9** 65; **10** 9–10, **304–06**, 502; **19** 124; **23** 52
Freudenberg & Co., **41 170–73**
Friction Products Co., **59** 222
Frictiontech Inc., **11** 84
Friday's Front Row Sports Grill, **22** 128

Friden, Inc., **30** 418; **53** 237
Fried, Frank, Harris, Shriver & Jacobson, **35 183–86**
Fried. Krupp GmbH, **IV 85–89**, 104, 128, 203, 206, 222, 234. See also Thyssen Krupp AG.
Friede Goldman Halter, **61** 43
Friedman, Billings, Ramsey Group, Inc., **53 134–37**
Friedman's Inc., **29 204–06**
Friedrich Grohe AG & Co. KG, **53 138–41**
Friendly Hotels PLC, **14** 107
Friendly Ice Cream Corp., **15** 221; **30 208–10**
Friesland Coberco Dairy Foods Holding N.V., **59 194–96**
Frigidaire Home Products, **13** 564; **19** 361; **22** 28, **216–18**, 349
Frigoscandia AB, **57** 300
Frisby P.M.C. Incorporated, **16** 475
Frisch's Restaurants, Inc., **35 187–89**
Frisdranken Industries Winters B.V., **22** 515
Frito-Lay Company, **22** 95; **32 205–10**; **44** 348
Fritz Companies, Inc., **12 180–82**
Fritz Gegauf AG. See Bernina Holding AG.
Fritz W. Glitsch and Sons, Inc. See Glitsch International, Inc.
Frolic, **16** 545
Frolich Intercon International, **57** 174
Fromagerie d'Illoud. See Bongrain SA.
La Fromagerie du Velay, **25** 85
Fromagerie Paul Renard, **25** 85
Fromageries Bel, **19** 51; **23 217–19**; **25** 83–84
Fromageries des Chaumes, **25** 84
Fromarsac, **25** 84
Frome Broken Hill Co., **IV** 59
Front Range Pipeline LLC, **60** 88
Frontec, **13** 132
Frontenac Co., **24** 45
Frontier Airlines, Inc., **I** 103, 118, 124, 129–30; **11** 298; **22 219–21**; **25** 421; **26** 439–40; **39** 33
Frontier Communications, **32** 216, 218
Frontier Corp., **16 221–23**; **18** 164
Frontier Electronics, **19** 311
Frontier Expeditors, Inc., **12** 363
Frontier Pacific Insurance Company, **21** 263
Frontier Vision Partners L.P., **52** 9
FrontLine Capital Group, **47** 330–31
Frontline Ltd., **45 163–65**
Frontstep Inc., **55** 258
Frosch Touristik, **27** 29
Frost & Sullivan, Inc., **53 142–44**
Frost National Bank. See Cullen/Frost Bankers, Inc.
Frozen Food Express Industries, Inc., **20 233–35**; **27** 404
Fru-Con Holding Corporation, **I** 561; **55** 62
Fruehauf Corp., **I 169–70**, 480; **7** 259–60, 513–14; **27** 202–03, 251; **40** 432
Fruit of the Loom, Inc., **8 200–02**; **16** 535; **25 164–67** (upd.); **54** 403
The Frustum Group Inc., **45** 280
Fruth Pharmacy, Inc., **66 128–30**
Fry's Food Stores, **12** 112
Frye Copy Systems, **6** 599
Frymaster Corporation, **27 159–62**

FSA Corporation, **25** 349

FSI International, Inc., 17 192–94. *See also* FlightSafety International, Inc.

FSP. *See* Frank Schaffer Publications.

FT Freeport Indonesia, **57** 145

FTD, **26** 344. *See also* Florists Transworld Delivery, Inc.

F3 Software Corp., **15** 474

FTP Software, Inc., 20 236–38

Fubu, 29 207–09

Fuddruckers, **27** 480–82

Fuel Pipeline Transportation Ltd. *See* Thai Airways International.

Fuel Resources Development Co., **6** 558–59

Fuel Resources Inc., **6** 457

FuelMaker Corporation, **6** 569

Fuji Bank, Ltd., II 291–93, 360–61, 391, 422, 459, 554; **17** 556–57; **24** 324; **26** 455; **58** 228

Fuji Electric Co., Ltd., II 22–23, 98, 103; **13** 356; **18** 511; **22** 373; **42** 145; **48** **180–82 (upd.)**

Fuji Gen-Gakki, **16** 202; **43** 171

Fuji Heavy Industries, **I** 207; **9** 294; **12** 400; **13** 499–501; **23** 290; **36** 240, 243; **64** 151

Fuji Kaolin Co. *See* English China Clays Ltd.

Fuji Photo Film Co., Ltd., III 486–89; 7 162; **18** 94, 183–87 **(upd.)**, 341 42; **36** 172, 174; **43** 284

Fuji Photo Film USA, Inc., **45** 284

Fuji Seito, **I** 511

Fuji Television, **7** 249; **9** 29

Fuji Xerox. *See* Xerox Corporation.

Fujian Hualong Carburetor, **13** 555

Fujisawa Pharmaceutical Company, Ltd., I 635–36; 58 132–34 (upd.)

Fujitsu-ICL Systems Inc., 11 150–51

Fujitsu Limited, I 455, 541; **III 139–41**, 164, 482; **6** 217, 240–42; **10** 238; **11** 308, 542; **13** 482; **14** 512; **16** 139, **224–27 (upd.)**; **17** 172; **21** 390; **27** 107; **40** 145–50 **(upd.)**; **43** 285; **50** 156

Fujitsu Takamisawa, **28** 131

Fukuoka Mitsukoshi Ltd., **56** 242

Fukuoka Paper Co., Ltd., **IV** 285

Fukutake Publishing Co., Ltd., **13** 91, 93

Ful-O-Pep, **10** 250

Fulbright & Jaworski L.L.P., 22 4; **47** **138–41**

Fulcrum Communications, **10** 19

The Fulfillment Corporation of America, **21** 37

Fulham Brothers, **13** 244

Fullbright & Jaworski, **28** 48

Fuller Co., **6** 395–96; **25** 169–70

Fuller Smith & Turner P.L.C., 38 **193–95**

Fulton Bank, **14** 40

Fulton Co., **III** 569; **20** 361

Fulton Manufacturing Co., **11** 535

Fulton Municipal Gas Company, **6** 455

Fulton Performance Products, Inc., **11** 535

Funai Electric Company Ltd., 62 148–50

Funco, Inc., 20 239–41

Fund American Companies. *See* White Mountains Insurance Group, Ltd.

Fundimensions, **16** 337

Funk & Wagnalls, **22** 441

Funnel Cake Factory, **24** 241

Funtastic Limited, **52** 193

Fuqua Enterprises, Inc., 17 195–98

Fuqua Industries Inc., I 445–47; 8 545; **12** 251; **14** 86; **37** 62; **57** 376–77

Furnishings International Inc., **20** 359, 363; **39** 267

Furniture Brands International, Inc., 31 246, 248; **39 170–75 (upd.)**

The Furniture Center, Inc., **14** 236

Furon Company, 28 149–51

Furr's Restaurant Group, Inc., 53 **145–48**

Furr's Supermarkets, Inc., II 601; **28** **152–54**

Furst Group, **17** 106

Furukawa Electric Co., Ltd., III 490–92; **15** 514; **22** 44

Futronix Corporation, **17** 276

Future Diagnostics, Inc., **25** 384

Future Graphics, **18** 387

Future Now, Inc., 6 245; **12 183–85**

Future Shop Ltd., 62 151–53; 63 63

FutureCare, **50** 123

Futurestep, Inc., **34** 247, 249

FWD Corporation, **7** 513

FX Coughlin Inc., **51** 130

Fyffes Plc, 38 196–99, 201

Fytek, S.A. de C.V., **66** 42

G&G Shops, Inc., **8** 425–26

G&K Services, Inc., 16 228–30; 21 115

G&L Inc., **16** 202; **43** 170

G&R Pasta Co., Inc., **II** 512

G.B. Lewis Company, **8** 359

G. Bruss GmbH and Co. KG, **26** 141

G.C. Industries, **52** 186

G.C. Murphy Company, **9** 21

G.C. Smith, **I** 423

G.D. Searle & Co., I 686–89; III 53; **8** 398, 434; **10** 54; **12 186–89 (upd.)**; **16** 527; **26** 108, 383; **29** 331; **34 177–82** **(upd.)**; **56** 373, 375

G. Felsenthal & Sons, **17** 106

G.H. Bass & Co., **15** 406; **24** 383

G.H. Besselaar Associates, **30** 151

G.H. Rinck NV, **V** 49; **19** 122–23; **49** 111

G. Heileman Brewing Co., I 253–55, 270; **10** 169–70; **12** 338; **18** 501; **23** 403, 405

G.I.E. Airbus Industrie, I

G.I. Joe's, Inc., 30 221–23 41–43, 49–52, 55–56, 70, 72, 74–76, 107, 111, 116, 121; **9** 458, 460; **11** 279, 363; **12** **190–92 (upd.)**

G-III Apparel Group, Ltd., 22 222–24

G.J. Coles & Coy. Ltd., **20** 155

G.L. Kelty & Co., **13** 168

G.L. Rexroth GmbH, **III** 566; **38** 298, 300

G. Leblanc Corporation, 55 149–52

G.M. Pfaff AG, **30** 419–20

G.P. Group, **12** 358

G.R. Foods, Inc. *See* Ground Round, Inc.

G.R. Herberger's Department Stores, **19** 324–25; **41** 343–44

G.S. Blodgett Corporation, 15 183–85; **22** 350. *See also* Blodgett Holdings, Inc.

Gabelli Asset Management Inc., **13** 561; **30 211–14**. *See also* Lynch Corporation.

Gables Residential Trust, 49 147–49

GAC. *See* The Goodyear Tire & Rubber Company.

GAC Holdings L.P., **7** 204; **28** 164

Gadzooks, Inc., 18 188–90; 33 203

GAF, I 337–40, 549; **8** 180; **9** 518; **18** 215; **22** 14, **225–29 (upd.)**; **25** 464

Gage Marketing Group, 26 147–49; 27 21

Gaggenau Hausgeräte GmbH, **67** 81

Gagliardi Brothers, **13** 383

Gaiam, Inc., 41 174–77

Gain Technology, Inc., **10** 505

Gaines Furniture Manufacturing, Inc., **43** 315

Gainsco, Inc., 22 230–32

GalaGen Inc., **65** 216

Galas Harland, S.A., **17** 266, 268

Galavision, Inc., **24** 515–17; **54** 72

Galaxy Carpet Mills Inc., **19** 276; **63** 300

Galaxy Energies Inc., **11** 28

Galaxy Nutritional Foods, Inc., 58 **135–37**

Galbreath Escott, **16** 474

The Gale Group, Inc., **34** 437

Gale Research Inc., **8** 526; **23** 440

Galen Health Care, **15** 112; **35** 215–16

Galen Laboratories, **13** 160

Galerías Preciados, **26** 130

Galeries Lafayette S.A., V 57–59; 23 **220–23 (upd.)**

Galey & Lord, Inc., 20 242–45; 66 **131–34 (upd.)**

Gallaher Group Plc, 49 150–54 (upd.)

Gallaher Limited, V 398–400; 19 168–71 **(upd.); 29** 195

Gallatin Steel Company, **18** 380; **24** 144

Galleria Shooting Team, **62** 174

Gallo Winery. *See* E. & J. Gallo Winery.

Gallop Johnson & Neuman, L.C., **26** 348

The Gallup Organization, 37 153–56; 41 196–97

Galoob Toys. *See* Lewis Galoob Toys Inc.

GALP, **48** 117, 119

Galveston *Daily News*, **10** 3

GALVSTAR, L.P., **26** 530

Galyan's Trading Company, Inc., 47 **142–44**

Gamax Holding, **65** 230, 232

Gamble-Skogmo Inc., **13** 169; **25** 535

The Gambrinus Company, 29 219; **40** **188–90**

Gambro AB, 13 159–61, 327–28; **49** **155–57; 63** 211

Gamebusters, **41** 409

Gamesa, **19** 192

GameTime, Inc., **19** 387; **27** 370–71

GAMI. *See* Great American Management and Investment, Inc.

Gamlestaden, **9** 381–82

Gamma Capital Corp., **24** 3

Gammalink, **18** 143

Gander Mountain, Inc., 20 246–48

Gannett Co., Inc.,

Gannett Company, Inc., IV 612–13, 629–30; **7 190–92 (upd.); 9** 3; **18** 63; **23** 157–58, 293; **24** 224; **25** 371; **30** **215–17 (upd.); 32** 354–55; **41** 197–98; **63** 394; **66 135–38 (upd.)**

Gannett Supply, **17** 282

Gantos, Inc., 17 199–201

The Gap, Inc., V 60–62; 9 142, 360; **11** 499; **18 191–94 (upd.); 24** 27; **25** 47–48; **31** 51–52; **55 153–57 (upd.)**

GAR Holdings, **19** 78

Garamond Press, **23** 100

Garan, Inc., 16 231–33; 64 140–43 **(upd.)**

Garanti Bank, **65** 69

Garantie Mutuelle des Fonctionnaires, **21** 225

Garden Botanika, **11** 41

Garden City Newspapers Inc., **38** 308

Garden Escape, **26** 441

Garden Fresh Restaurant Corporation, **31 213–15**

Garden of Eatin' Inc., **27** 198; **43** 218–19

Garden Ridge Corporation, **27 163–65**

Garden State BancShares, Inc., **14** 472

Garden State Life Insurance Company, **10** 312; **27** 47–48

Garden State Paper, **38** 307–08

Gardenburger, Inc., **33 169–71**

Gardener's Eden, **17** 548–49

Gardner & Harvey Container Corporation, **8** 267

Gardner Advertising. *See* Wells Rich Green BDDP.

Gardner Cryogenics, **13** 140

Gardner Denver, Inc., **49 158–60**

Gardner Merchant Ltd., **11** 325; **29** 442–44

Gardner Rubber Co. *See* Tillotson Corp.

Garelick Farms, Inc., **26** 449

Garfield Weston, **13** 51

Garfinckel, Brooks Brothers, Miller & Rhodes, Inc., **15** 94; **22** 110

Garfinckels, **37** 12

Garland Publishing, **44** 416

Garland-Compton, **42** 328

Garmin Ltd., **60 135–37**

Garrett, **9** 18; **11** 472

Garrett & Company, **27** 326

Garrett AiResearch, **9** 18

Garrick Investment Holdings Ltd., **16** 293

Garrido y Compania, Inc., **26** 448

Gart Sports Company, **24 173–75**

Gartner Group, Inc., **21 235–37**; **25** 22; **57** 176–77

Garuda Indonesia, **6 90–91**; **58 138–41 (upd.)**

Gary Fisher Mountain Bike Company, **16** 494

Gary Industries, **7** 4

Gary-Williams Energy Corporation, **19** 177

Gas Energy Inc., **6** 457

Gas Light and Coke Company. *See* British Gas plc.

Gas Light Company. *See* Baltimore Gas and Electric Company.

Gas Natural, **49** 211

Gas Service Company, **6** 593; **12** 542; **50** 38

Gas Tech, Inc., **11** 513

Gas Utilities Company, **6** 471

Gastar Co. Ltd., **55** 375

Gaston Paper Stock Co., Inc., **8** 476

Gasunie. *See* N.V. Nederlandse Gasunie.

GATC. *See* General American Tank Car Company.

Gate City Company, **6** 446

The Gates Corporation, **9 241–43**

Gates Distribution Company, **12** 60

Gates Radio Co., **II** 37

Gates Rubber, **26** 349

Gates/FA Distributing Inc., **29** 413–14

Gateway Books, **14** 61

Gateway Corporation Ltd., **II** 612, **628–30**, 638, 642; **10** 442; **16** 249; **25** 119. *See also* Somerfield plc.

Gateway Foodmarkets Ltd., **II** 628; **13** 26

Gateway, Inc., **27 166–69 (upd.)**; **63 153–58 (upd.)**

Gateway International Motorsports Corporation, Inc., **43** 139–40

Gateway State Bank, **39** 381–82

Gateway Technologies, Inc., **46** 387

Gateway 2000, Inc., **10 307–09**; **11** 240; **22** 99; **24** 31; **25** 531. *See also* Gateway, Inc.

Gatliff Coal Co., **6** 583

Gattini, **40** 215

Gatwick Handling, **28** 157

GATX, **6 394–96**; **25 168–71 (upd.)**; **47** 298

Gaultier. *See* Groupe Jean-Paul Gaultier.

Gaumont SA, **25 172–75**; **29 369–71**

Gaya Motor, P.T. **23** 290

Gaylord Brothers', **60** 109

Gaylord Container Corporation, **8 203–05**; **24** 92

Gaylord Entertainment Company, **11 152–54**; **36 226–29 (upd.)**; **38** 456

Gaymer Group, **25** 82

Gaz de France, **IV** 425; **V 626–28**; **38** 407; **40 191–95 (upd.)**

Gazelle Graphics Systems, **28** 244

Gazprom, **18** 50; **30** 205. *See also* OAO Gazprom.

GB Foods Inc., **19** 92

GB-Inno-BM. *See* GIB Group.

GB s.a. *See* GIB Group.

GB Stores, Inc., **14** 427

gbav Gesellschaft für Boden- und Abfallverwertung, **58** 28

GC Companies, Inc., **25 176–78**

GCFC. *See* General Cinema Finance Co.

GD Express Worldwide, **27** 472, 475; **30** 463

GDE Systems, Inc., **17** 492

GDF. *See* Gaz de France.

GDS, **29** 412

GE. *See* General Electric Company.

GE Aircraft Engines, **9** 244–46

GE Capital Aviation Services, **36 230–33**

GE Capital Corporation, **29** 428, 430; **63** 165

GE Capital Services, **27** 276; **49** 240

GE SeaCo SRL, **29** 428, 431

GEA AG, **27 170–74**

GEAC Computer Corporation Ltd., **43 181–85**

Geant Casino, **12** 152

Gear Products, Inc., **48** 59

Geberit AG, **49 161–64**

Gebrüder Hepp, **60** 364

Gebrüder Sulzer Aktiengesellschaft. *See* Sulzer Brothers Limited.

GEC. *See* General Electric Company.

GECAS. *See* GE Capital Aviation Services.

Gecina SA, **42 151–53**

Geco Mines Ltd., **64** 297

Gedney. *See* M.A. Gedney Co.

Geerlings & Wade, Inc., **45 166–68**

Geest Plc, **38** 198, **200–02**

Gefco SA, **54 126–28**

Geffen Records Inc., **21** 26; **23** 33; **26** 150–52; **43** 143

GEHE AG, **27 175–78**

Gehl Company, **19 172–74**

GEICO Corporation, **III** 214, 248, 252, 273, 448; **10 310–12**; **18** 60, 61, 63; **40 196–99 (upd.)**; **42** 31–34

Geiger Bros., **60 138–41**

Gelco Corporation, **53** 275

Gelco Express, **18** 177

Gelco Truck Services, **19** 293

Gelsenberg AG, **7** 141

Gelson's, **29** 32

Gem State Utilities. *See* Pacific Telecom, Inc.

Gemaire Distributors, Inc., **52** 398–99

GemChem, Inc., **47** 20

Gemco, **17** 366

Gemcolite Company, **8** 178

Gemeinhardt Co., **16** 201; **43** 170

Gemina S.p.A., **52** 121–22

Gemini Group Limited Partnership, **23** 10

Gemini Industries, **17** 215

Gemini Sound Products Corporation, **58 142–44**

Gemplus International S.A., **18** 543; **64 144–47**

Gemstar-TV Guide International, **43** 431

Gen-Probe, Inc., **50** 138–39

Gen-X Technologies Inc, **53** 285

GenCare Health Systems, **17** 166–67

Gencor Ltd., **I** 423; **IV 90–93**, 95; **22 233–37 (upd.)**; **49** 353. *See also* Gold Fields Ltd.

GenCorp Inc., **8** 206–08; **9 247–49**; **13** 381; **59** 324; **63** 6

Gendex Corp., **10** 270, 272

Gene Upton Co., **13** 166

Genencor International Inc., **44** 134, 136

Genender International Incorporated, **31** 52

Genentech Inc., **I** 637–38; **III** 43; **8 209–11 (upd.)**, 216–17; **10** 78, 80, 142, 199; **17** 289; **29** 386; **30** 164; **32 211–15 (upd.)**; **37** 112; **38** 204, 206; **41** 153, 155

General Accident plc, **III 256–57**, 350. *See also* Aviva PLC.

General American Tank Car Company. *See* GATX Corporation.

General Aniline and Film Corporation. *See* GAF Corporation.

General Aquatics, Inc., **16** 297; **56** 16–17

General Atlantic Partners, **25** 34; **26** 94

General Atomics, **57 151–54**

General Aviation Corp., **9** 16

General Bearing Corporation, **45 169–71**

General Binding Corporation, **10 313–14**

General Bussan Kaisha, Ltd. *See* TonenGeneral Sekiyu K.K.

General Cable Corporation, **7** 288; **8** 367; **18** 549; **40 200–03**

General Casualty Co., **III** 404

The General Chemical Group Inc., **22** 29, 115, 193, 349, 541; **29** 114; **37 157–60**

General Cigar Holdings, Inc., **27** 139–40; **43** 204–05; **66 139–42 (upd.)**

General Cinema Corporation, **I 245–46**; **IV** 624; **12** 12–13, 226, 356; **14** 87; **19** 362; **26** 468; **27** 481. *See also* GC Companies, Inc.

General Corporation, **9** 173

General DataComm Industries, Inc., **14 200–02**

General Diaper Corporation, **14** 550

General Dynamics Corporation, **I 57–60**, 62, 71, 74, 77, 482, 525, 527, 597; **6** 229; **7** 520; **8** 51, 92, 315, 338; **9** 206, 323, 417–18, 498; **10 315–18 (upd.)**, 522, 527; **11** 67, 165, 269, 278, 364; **13** 374; **16** 77–78; **18** 62, 554; **27** 100; **30** 471; **36** 76, 78–79; **40 204–10 (upd.)**

General Electric Capital Aviation Services, **48** 218–19

General Electric Capital Corporation, **15** 257, 282; **19** 190; **59** 265, 268

General Electric Company, II 27–31, 143, 151–52, 330, 349, 431, 604; III 340, 437, 440, 443, 475, 483, 502, 526, 614; **6** 452, 517; **7** 161, 456, 520, 532; **8** 157, 262, 332, 377; **9** 14–18, 27, 128, 162, 244, 246, 352–53, 417–18, 439, 514; **10** 16, 241, 536–37; **11** 46, 313, 318, 422, 472, 490; **12** 68, 190, **193–97 (upd.)**, 247, 250, 252, 544–45; **13** 30, 124, 326, 396, 398, 501, 529, 554, 563–64; **15** 196, 285, 380, 403, 467; **17** 149, 173, 272; **18** 228, 369; **19** 110, 164–66, 210, 335; **20** 8, 152; **22** 37, 218, 406; **23** 181; **26** 371; **28** 4–5, 8; **30** 490; **31** 123; **34 183–90 (upd.)**; **41** 366; **43** 447, 466; **45** 17, 19, 117; **47** 351; **50** 233, 392; **51** 184; **57** 309–10, 319, 334; **61** 227; **63 159–68 (upd.)**, 436

General Electric Company, PLC, I 423; II 24–26; **9** 9–10; **13** 356; **20** 290; **24** 87; **42** 373, 377. *See also* Marconi plc.

General Electric Credit Corporation, **19** 293; **20** 42

General Electric International Mexico, S.A. de C.V., **51** 116

General Electric Mortgage Insurance Company, **52** 244

General Electric Railcar Wheel and Parts Services Corporation, **18** 4

General Electric Venture Capital Corporation, **9** 140; **10** 108

General Elevator Corporation, **25** 15

General Export Iron and Metals Company, **15** 116

General Felt Industries Inc., I 202; **14** 300; **17** 182–83

General Finance Corp., III 232; **11** 16

General Finance Service Corp., **11** 447

General Fire Extinguisher Co. *See* Grinnell Corp.

General Foods Corp., **1** 608, 712; II 530–34, 557, 569; V 407; **7** 272–74; **10** 551; **12** 167, 372; **18** 416, 419; **25** 517; **26** 251; **44** 341

General Foods, Ltd., **7** 577

General Furniture Leasing. *See* CORT Business Services Corporation.

General Glass Corporation, **13** 40

General Growth Properties, Inc., **57 155–57**

General Host Corporation, **7** 372; **12** 178–79, **198–200**, 275; **15** 362; **17** 230–31

General Housewares Corporation, **16 234–36**; **18** 69

General Injectables and Vaccines Inc., **54** 188

General Instrument Corporation, **10 319–21**; **17** 33; **34** 298; **54** 68

General Insurance Co. of America. *See* SAFECO Corporation.

General Leisure, **16** 33

General Maritime Corporation, **59 197–99**

General Medical Corp., **18** 469

General Merchandise Services, Inc., **15** 480

General Mills, Inc., II 501–03, 525, 556, 576, 684; **7** 547; **8** 53–54; **9** 156, 189–90, 291; **10** 177, **322–24 (upd.)**; **11** 15, 497–98; **12** 167–68, 275; **13** 244, 293–94, 408, 516; **15** 189; **16** 71, 156–58, 337; **18** 225, 523; **22** 337–38; **25** 90, 241, 243, 253; **30** 286; **31** 429–31; **33** 359; **36** 179–80, **234–39**

(upd.); **44** 138–40; **50** 293–96; **62** 269; **63** 250, 252

General Motors Acceptance Corporation, **21** 146; **22** 55

General Motors Corporation, I 171–73; II 32–35; III 442, 458, 482–83, 536, 563, 581, 760; **6** 256, 336, 356, 358; **7** 6–8, 427, 461–64, 513, 565, 567, 599; **8** 151–52, 505–07; **9** 16–18, 36, 283, 293–95, 341, 343, 344, 439, 487–89; **10** 198, 232, 262, 264, 273–74, 279–80, 288–89, **325–27 (upd.)**, 419–20, 429, 460, 537; **11** 5, 29, 53, 339, 350, 427–29, 437–39, 471–72, 528, 530; **12** 90, 160, 309, 311; **13** 109, 124, 179, 344–45, 357; **16** 321–22, 436, 484; **17** 173, 184, 304; **18** 125–26, 168, 308; **19** 293–94, 482, 484; **21** 3, 6, 444; **22** 169, 175, 216; **23** 267–69, 288–91, 340, 459–61; **25** 142–43, 149, 223–24, 300; **29** 375, 407–08; **34** 133–35, 303; **36** 32, **240–44 (upd.)**, 298; **38** 458, 461; **43** 319; **45** 142, 170; **50** 197, 376; **51** 34; **55** 326; **56** 284; **57** 92, 189; **59** 393, 395–96; **62** 180–81; **63** 302, 304; **64** 148–53 (upd.); **65** 59, 62

General Nutrition Companies, Inc., **11 155–57**; **24** 480; **29 210–14 (upd.)**; **31** 347; **37** 340, 342; **45** 210; **63** 331, 335

General Office Products Co., **25** 500

General Packing Service, Inc., **19** 78

General Parts Inc., **29** 86

General Petroleum Authority. *See* Egyptian General Petroleum Corporation.

General Physics Corporation, **13** 367; **64** 166

General Portland Cement Co., III 704–05; **17** 497

General Portland Inc., **28** 229

General Printing Ink Corp. *See* Sequa Corp.

General Public Utilities Corporation, V 629–31; **6** 484, 534, 579–80; **11** 388; **20** 73. *See also* GPU, Inc.

General Radio Company. *See* GenRad, Inc.

General Railway Signal Company. *See* General Signal Corporation.

General Re Corporation, III 258–59, 276; **24 176–78 (upd.)**; **42** 31, 35

General Rent A Car, **25** 142–43

General Research Corp., **14** 98

General Sekiyu K.K., IV 431–33, 555; **16** 490. *See also* TonenGeneral Sekiyu K.K.

General Signal Corporation, **9 250–52**; **11** 232

General Spring Products, **16** 321

General Steel Industries Inc., **14** 324

General Supermarkets, II 673

General Telephone and Electronics Corp. *See* GTE Corporation.

General Telephone Corporation. *See* GTE Corporation.

General Time Corporation, **16** 483

General Tire, Inc., **8** 206–08, **212–14**; **9** 247–48; **20** 260, 262; **22** 219; **56** 71; **59** 324

General Transistor Corporation, **10** 319

General Turbine Systems, **58** 75

General Utilities Company, **6** 555

General Waterworks Corporation, **40** 449

Generale Bank, II **294–95**

Générale Biscuit S.A., II 475

Générale de Banque, **36** 458

Générale de Mécanique Aéronautique, I 46

Générale de Restauration, **49** 126

Générale des Eaux Group, V **632–34**; **21** 226. *See* Vivendi Universal S.A.

Generale du Jouet, **16** 428

Générale Occidentale, II 475; IV 614–16

Générale Restauration S.A., **34** 123

Generali. *See* Assicurazioni Generali.

Génération Y2K, **35** 204, 207

Genesco Inc., **14** 501; **17 202–06**; **27** 59

Genesee & Wyoming Inc., **27 179–81**

Genesee Brewing Co., **18** 72; **50** 114

Genesee Iron Works. *See* Wickes Inc.

Genesis Health Ventures, Inc., **18 195–97**; **25** 310. *See also* NeighborCare,Inc.

Genesse Hispania, **60** 246

Genetic Anomalies, Inc., **39** 395

Genetics Institute, Inc., **8 215–18**; **10** 70, 78–80; **50** 538

Geneva Metal Wheel Company, **20** 261

Geneva Pharmaceuticals, Inc., **8** 549; **22** 37, 40

Geneva Rubber Co., **17** 373

Geneva Steel, **7 193–95**

Geneve Corporation, **62** 16

GENEX Services, Inc., **52** 379

Genix Group. *See* MCN Corporation.

Genmar Holdings, Inc., **45 172–75**

Genoc Chartering Ltd, **60** 96

Genosys Biotechnologies, Inc., **36** 431

Genovese Drug Stores, Inc., **18 198–200**; **21** 187; **32** 170; **43** 249

Genpack Corporation, **21** 58

GenRad, Inc., **24 179–83**

GenSet, **19** 442

Genstar, **22** 14; **23** 327

Genstar Gypsum Products Co., IV 273

Genstar Rental Electronics, Inc., **58** 110

Genstar Stone Products Co., **15** 154; **40** 176

GenSys Power Ltd., **64** 404

GenTek Inc., **37** 157; **41** 236

Gentex Corporation, **26 153–57**; **35** 148–49

Gentex Optics, **17** 50; **18** 392

Genting Bhd., **65 152–55**

GenTrac, **24** 257

Gentry Associates, Inc., **14** 378

Gentry International, **47** 234

Genty-Cathiard, **39** 183–84; **54** 306

Genuardi's Family Markets, Inc., **35 190–92**

Genuin Golf & Dress of America, Inc., **32** 447

Genuine Parts Company, **9 253–55**; **45 176–79 (upd.)**

Genung's, II 673

Genus, **18** 382–83

Genzyme Corporation, **13 239–42**; **38 203–07 (upd.)**; **47** 4

Genzyme Transgenics Corp., **37** 44

Geo. H. McFadden & Bro., **54** 89

GEO SA, **58** 218

Geo Space Corporation, **18** 513

GEO Specialty Chemicals, Inc., **27** 117

geobra Brandstätter GmbH & Co. KG, **48 183–86**

Geodis S.A., **67 187–90**

Geographics, Inc., **25** 183

Geomarine Systems, **11** 202

The Geon Company, **11 158–61**

Geon Industries, Inc. *See* Johnston Industries, Inc.

GeoQuest Systems Inc., **17** 419

Georesources, Inc., **19** 247

Georg Fischer AG Schaffhausen, **38** 214; **61 106–09**

Georg Neumann GmbH, **66** 288

George A. Hormel and Company, **II 504–06**; **7** 547; **12** 123–24; **18** 244. *See also* Hormel Foods Corporation.

George A. Touche & Co., **9** 167

George Booker & Co., **13** 102

George Buckton & Sons Limited, **40** 129

The George F. Cram Company, Inc., **55 158–60**

George H. Dentler & Sons, **7** 429

The George Hyman Construction Company, **8** 112–13; **25** 403

George J. Ball, Inc., **27** 507

George K. Baum & Company, **25** 433

George P. Johnson Company, **60 142–44**

George R. Rich Manufacturing Company. *See* Clark Equipment Company.

George S. May International Company, **55 161–63**

George Smith Financial Corporation, **21** 257

George Weston Limited, **II 631–32**; **36 245–48 (upd.)**; **41** 30, 33

George Wimpey plc, **12 201–03**; **28** 450; **51 135–38 (upd.)**

Georges Renault SA, **III** 427; **28** 40

Georgetown Group, Inc., **26** 187

Georgetown Steel Corp., **IV** 228

Georgia Carpet Outlets, **25** 320

Georgia Cotton Producers Association. *See* Gold Kist Inc.

Georgia Federal Bank, **I** 447; **11** 112–13; **30** 196

Georgia Gulf Corporation, **9 256–58**; **61 110–13 (upd.)**

Georgia Hardwood Lumber Co.,. *See* Georgia-Pacific Corporation

Georgia Kraft Co., **8** 267–68

Georgia Natural Gas Corporation, **6** 447–48

Georgia-Pacific Corporation, **IV 281–83**, 288, 304, 345, 358; **9** 256–58, **259–62 (upd.)**; **12** 19, 377; **15** 229; **22** 415, 489; **31** 314; **44** 66; **47 145–51 (upd.)**; **51** 284; **61** 110–11

Georgia Power & Light Co., **6** 447, 537; **23** 28; **27** 20

Georgia Power Company, **38** 446–48; **49** 145

Georgia Railway and Electric Company, **6** 446–47; **23** 28

Georgie Pie, **V** 35

GeoScience Corporation, **18** 515; **44** 422

Geosource Inc., **21** 14; **22** 189

Geotec Boyles Brothers, S.A., **19** 247

Geotecnia y Cimientos SA, **55** 182

Geotek Communications Inc., **21 238–40**

GeoTel Communications Corp., **34** 114

Geothermal Resources International, **11** 271

GeoVideo Networks, **34** 259

Geoworks Corporation, **25** 509

Geraghty & Miller Inc., **26** 23

Gerald Stevens, Inc., **37 161–63**

Gérard, **25** 84

Gerber Products Company, **II** 481; **III** 19; **7 196–98**, 547; **9** 90; **11** 173; **21** 53–55, **241–44 (upd)**; **25** 366; **34** 103; **36** 256

Gerber Scientific, Inc., **12 204–06**

Gerbes Super Markets, Inc., **12** 112

Gerbo Telecommunicacoes e Servicos Ltda., **32** 40

Gerdau S.A., **59 200–03**

Geren Associates. *See* CRSS Inc.

Geriatrics Inc., **13** 49

Gericom AG, **47 152–54**

Gerling-Konzern Versicherungs-Beteiligungs-Aktiengesellschaft, **51 139–43**

Germaine Monteil Cosmetiques Corp., **I** 426

German American Bancorp, **41 178–80**

German-American Car Company. *See* GATX.

The German Society. *See* The Legal Aid Society.

GERPI, **51** 16

Gerrard Group, **61** 270, 272

Gerresheimer Glas AG, **43 186–89**

Gerrity Oil & Gas Corporation, **11** 28; **24** 379–80

Gerry Weber International AG, **63 169–72**

GESA. *See* General Europea S.A.

Gesbancaya, **II** 196

Geschmay Group, **51** 14

GET Manufacturing Inc., **36** 300

Getchell Gold Corporation, **61** 292

Getronics NV, **39 176–78**

Getty Images, Inc., **31 216–18**

Getty Oil Co., **6** 457; **8** 526; **11** 27; **17** 501; **18** 488; **27** 216; **47** 436. *See also* ChevronTexaco.

Getz Corp., **IV** 137

Gevaert. *See* Agfa Gevaert Group N.V.

Gevity HR, Inc., **63 173–77**

Geyser Peak Winery, **58** 196

GFI Informatique SA, **49 165–68**

GfK Aktiengesellschaft, **49 169–72**

GFL Mining Services Ltd., **62** 164

GFS. *See* Gordon Food Service Inc.

GFS Realty Inc., **II** 633

GGT Group, **44** 198

GHI, **28** 155, 157

Ghirardelli Chocolate Company, **24** 480; **27** 105; **30 218–20**

GI Communications, **10** 321

GI Export Corp. *See* Johnston Industries, Inc.

GIAG, **16** 122

Gianni Versace SpA, **22 238–40**

Giant Bicycle Inc., **19** 384

Giant Cement Holding, Inc., **23 224–26**

Giant Eagle, Inc., **12** 390–91; **13** 237

Giant Food, Inc., **II 633–35**, 656; **13** 282, 284; **15** 532; **16** 313; **22 241–44 (upd.)**; **24** 462; **60** 307

Giant Industries, Inc., **19 175–77**; **61 114–18 (upd.)**

Giant Resources, **III** 729

Giant Stores, Inc., **7** 113; **25** 124

Giant TC, Inc. *See* Campo Electronics, Appliances & Computers, Inc.

Giant Tire & Rubber Company, **8** 126

Giant-Vac Manufacturing Inc., **64** 355

Giant Video Corporation, **29** 503

Giant Wholesale, **II** 625

GIB Group, **V 63–66**; **22** 478; **23** 231; **26 158–62 (upd.)**

Gibbons, Green, van Amerongen Ltd., **II** 605; **9** 94; **12** 28; **19** 360

Gibbs Construction, **25** 404

GIBCO Corp., **17** 287, 289

Gibraltar Casualty Co., **III** 340

Gibraltar Steel Corporation, **37 164–67**

Gibson, Dunn & Crutcher LLP, **36 249–52**; **37** 292

Gibson Greetings, Inc., **7** 24; **12 207–10**; **16** 256; **21** 426–28; **22** 34–35; **59** 35, 37

Gibson Guitar Corp., **16 237–40**

Gibson McDonald Furniture Co., **14** 236

GIC. *See* The Goodyear Tire & Rubber Company.

Giddings & Lewis, Inc., **8** 545–46; **10 328–30**; **23** 299; **28** 455

Giftmaster Inc., **26** 439–40

Gil-Wel Manufacturing Company, **17** 440

Gilbane, Inc., **34 191–93**

Gilbert & John Greenall Limited, **21** 246

Gilbert Lane Personnel, Inc., **9** 326

Gildon Metal Enterprises, **7** 96

Gilead Sciences, Inc., **54 129–31**

Gilkey Bros. *See* Puget Sound Tug and Barge Company.

Gill Interprovincial Lines, **27** 473

Gillett Holdings, Inc., **7 199–201**; **11** 543, 545; **43** 437–38

The Gillette Company, **III 27–30**, 114, 215; **8** 59–60; **9** 381, 413; **17** 104–05; **18** 60, 62, 215, 228; **20 249–53 (upd.)**; **23** 54–57; **26** 334; **28** 247; **39** 336; **51** 57; **52** 269

Gilliam Furniture Inc., **12** 475

Gilliam Manufacturing Co., **8** 530

Gilliam S.A., **61** 104

Gilman Paper Co., **37** 178

Gilmore Steel Corporation. *See* Oregon Steel Mills, Inc.

Gilroy Foods, **27** 299

Gimbel Brothers, Inc. *See* Saks Holdings, Inc.

Gimbel's Department Store, **I** 426–27; **8** 59; **22** 72; **50** 117–18

Gindick Productions, **6** 28

Gingiss Group, **60** 5

Ginn & Co., **IV** 672; **19** 405

Ginnie Mae. *See* Government National Mortgage Association.

Gino's East, **21** 362

Ginsber Beer Group, **15** 47; **38** 77

Giorgio Armani S.p.A., **45 180–83**

Giorgio Beverly Hills, Inc., **26** 384

Girbaud, **17** 513; **31** 261

Girl Scouts of the USA, **35 193–96**

Giro Sport Designs International Inc., **16** 53; **44** 53–54

Girod, **19** 50

Girsa S.A., **23** 170

Girvin, Inc., **16** 297

Gist-Brocades Co., **III** 53; **26** 384

Git-n-Go Corporation, **60** 160

The Gitano Group, Inc., **8 219–21**; **20** 136 **25** 167; **37** 81

Givaudan SA, **43 190–93**

GIW Industries Inc., **62** 217

GJM International Ltd., **25** 121–22

GK Technologies Incorporated, **10** 547

GKH Partners, **29** 295

GKN plc, **III 493–96**; **38 208–13 (upd.)**; **42** 47; **47** 7, 9, 279–80

Glacier Bancorp, Inc., **35 197–200**

Glacier Park Co., **10** 191

Glacier Water Services, Inc., **47 155–58**

Glamar Group plc, **14** 224

Glamis Gold, Ltd., **54 132–35**

Glamor Shops, Inc., **14** 93

Glanbia plc, **38** 196, 198; **59 204–07**, 364

Glass Glover Plc, **52** 419
Glasstite, Inc., **33** 360–61
GlasTec, **II** 420
Glastron. *See* Genmar Holdings, Inc.
Glatfelter Wood Pulp Company, **8** 413
Glaxo Holdings plc, I 639–41, 643, 668, 675, 693; **9 263–65** (upd.); **10** 551; **11** 173; **20** 39; **26** 31; **34** 284; **38** 365; **50** 56; **54** 130
GlaxoSmithKline plc, 46 201–08 (upd.)
Gleason Corporation, 24 184–87
Glen & Co, **I** 453
Glen Alden Corp., **15** 247
Glen-Gery Corporation, **14** 249
Glen Line, **6** 416
Glencairn Ltd., **25** 418
Glencore International AG, **52** 71, 73
The Glenlyte Group, **29** 469
Glenlyte Thomas Group LLC, **29** 466
Glenn Advertising Agency, **25** 90
Glenn Pleass Holdings Pty. Ltd., **21** 339
GLF-Eastern States Association, **7** 17
The Glidden Company, I 353; **8 222–24; 21** 545
Glimcher Co., **26** 262
Glitsch International, Inc. *See* Foster Wheeler Corp.
Global Access, **31** 469
Global Apparel Sourcing Ltd., **22** 223
Global Berry Farms LLC, 62 154–56
Global BMC (Mauritius) Holdings Ltd., **62** 55
Global Communications of New York, Inc., **45** 261
Global Crossing Ltd., 32 216–19
Global Engineering Company, **9** 266
Global Health Care Partners, **42** 68
Global Industries, Ltd., 37 168–72
Global Information Solutions, **34** 257
Global Interactive Communications Corporation, **28** 242
Global Marine Inc., 9 266–67; 11 87
Global One, **52** 108
Global Outdoors, Inc., 49 173–76
Global Petroleum Albania S.A./Elda Petroleum Sh.P.K., **64** 177
Global Power Equipment Group Inc., 52 137–39
Global Switch International Ltd., **67** 104–05
Global TeleSystems, Inc., **59** 208, 210. *See also* Global Crossing Ltd.
Global Transport Organization, **6** 383
Global Vacations Group. *See* Classic Vacation Group, Inc.
Global Van Lines. *See* Allied Worldwide, Inc.
GlobalCom Telecommunications, Inc., **24** 122
GlobaLex, **28** 141
Globalia, **53** 301
GlobalSantaFe Corporation, 48 187–92 (upd.)
Globalstar Telecommunications Limited, **54** 233
GLOBALT, Inc., **52** 339
Globe Business Furniture, **39** 207
Globe Feather & Down, **19** 304
Globe Newspaper Co., **7** 15
Globe Pequot Press, **36** 339, 341
Globe Steel Abrasive Co., **17** 371
Globe Telegraph and Trust Company, **25** 99
Globelle Corp., **43** 368

Globenet, **57** 67, 69
Globetrotter Communications, **7** 199
Globo, **18** 211
Glock Ges.m.b.H., 42 154–56
Gloria Jean's Gourmet Coffees, **20** 83
La Gloria Oil and Gas Company, **7** 102
Glosser Brothers, **13** 394
Glotel plc, 53 149–51
Gloucester Cold Storage and Warehouse Company, **13** 243
Glow-Tec International Company Ltd., **65** 343
Glowlite Corporation, **48** 359
Glycomed Inc., **13** 241; **47** 222
Glyn, Mills and Co., **12** 422
GM. *See* General Motors Corporation.
GM Hughes Electronics Corporation, II 32–36; 10 325. *See also* Hughes Electronics Corporation.
GMARA, **II** 608
GMR Properties, **21** 257
GNB International Battery Group, **10** 445
GNC. *See* General Nutrition Companies, Inc.
GND Holdings Corp., **7** 204; **28** 164
GNMA. *See* Government National Mortgage Association.
Gnôme & Rhône, **46** 369
The Go-Ahead Group Plc, 28 155–57
Go Fly Ltd., **39** 128
Go Gro Industries, Ltd., **43** 99
Go Sport. *See* Groupe Go Sport S.A.
Go-Video, Inc. *See* Sensory Science Corporation.
Goal Systems International Inc., **10** 394
Godfather's Pizza Incorporated, 11 50; **12** 123; **14** 351; **17** 86; **25 179–81**
Godfrey Co., **II** 625
Godfrey L. Cabot, Inc., **8** 77
Godiva Chocolatier, Inc., 64 154–57
Godsell, **10** 277
Godtfred Kristiansen, **13** 310–11
Goelitz Confectionary. *See* Herman Goelitz, Inc.
GOFAMCLO, Inc., **64** 160
Goggin Truck Line, **57** 277
GoGo Tours, Inc., **56** 203–04
Göhner AG, **6** 491
Gokey Company, **10** 216; **28** 339
Gold Bond Stamp Company. *See* Carlson Companies, Inc.
Gold Exploration and Mining Co. Limited Partnership, **13** 503
Gold Fields Ltd., IV 94–97; 62 157–64 (upd.)
Gold Kist Inc., 7 432; **17 207–09; 26 166–68**
Gold Lance Inc., **19** 451–52
Gold Lion, **20** 263
Gold Prospectors' Association of America, **49** 173
Gold Star Chili, Inc., **62** 325–26
Gold'n Plump Poultry, 54 136–38
Gold's Gym Enterprises, **25** 450
Goldblatt's Department Stores, **15** 240–42
Golden Bear International, **33** 103; **42** 433; **45** 300
Golden Belt Manufacturing Co., 16 241–43
Golden Books Family Entertainment, Inc., 28 158–61
Golden Circle Financial Services, **15** 328
Golden Corral Corporation, 10 331–33; 66 143–46 (upd.)

Golden Enterprises, Inc., 26 163–65
Golden Gate Airlines, **25** 421
Golden Gates Disposal & Recycling Co., **60** 224
Golden Grain Macaroni Co., **II** 560; **12** 411; **30** 219; **34** 366
Golden Moores Finance Company, **48** 286
Golden Nugget, Inc. *See* Mirage Resorts, Incorporated.
Golden Ocean Group, **45** 164
Golden Partners, **10** 333
Golden Peanut Company, **17** 207
Golden Poultry Company, **26** 168
Golden Press, Inc., **13** 559–61
Golden Road Motor Inn, Inc. *See* Monarch Casino & Resort, Inc.
Golden Sea Produce, **10** 439
Golden Skillet, **10** 373
Golden State Foods Corporation, 32 220–22
Golden State Newsprint Co. Inc., **IV** 296; **19** 226; **23** 225
Golden State Vintners, Inc., 33 172–74
Golden Telecom, Inc., 59 208–11
Golden West Financial Corporation, 47 159–61
Golden West Homes, **15** 328
Golden West Publishing Corp., **38** 307–08
Golden Youth, **17** 227
Goldenberg Group, Inc., **12** 396
Goldfield Corp., **12** 198
Goldfine's Inc., **16** 36
Goldline Laboratories Inc., **11** 208
The Goldman Sachs Group Inc., II 11, 268, 326, 361, **414–16**, 432, 434, 448; **IV** 611; **9** 378, 441; **10** 423; **12** 405; **13** 95, 448, 554; **15** 397; **16** 195; **20 254–57 (upd.)**, 258; **21** 146; **22** 427–28; **26** 456; **27** 317; **29** 508; **36** 190–91; **38** 289, 291; **51** 358–59, 61; **51 144–48 (upd.)**
Goldner Hawn Johnson & Morrison Inc., **48** 412
Goldome Savings Bank, **11** 110; **17** 488
Goldsmith's, **9** 209
Goldstar Co., Ltd., II 53–54; **12 211–13; 13** 213; **30** 184; **43** 428
Goldwin Golf, **45** 76
Goldwyn Films. *See* Metro-Goldwyn-Mayer Inc.
Goleta National Bank, **33** 5
Golf Card International, **56** 5
Golf Day, **22** 517
The Golub Corporation, 26 169–71
Gomoljak, **14** 250
Gonnella Baking Company, 40 211–13
The Good Guys!, Inc., 10 334–35; 30 224–27 (upd.)
The Good Humor-Breyers Ice Cream Company, 14 203–05; 15 222; **17** 140–41; **32** 474, 476
Good Natural Café, **27** 481
Good Times Restaurants Inc., **8** 303; **63** 370
Good Vibrations, Inc., **28** 345
Good Weather International Inc., **III** 221; **14** 109
Goodbody & Company, **22** 428
Goodbody James Capel, **16** 14
Goodby, Berlin & Silverstein, **10** 484
Goodebodies, **11** 41
Goodfriend. *See* Goody's Family Clothing, Inc.
Goodman Bros. Mfg. Co., **14** 436

Goodman Fielder Ltd., 7 577; **44** 137; **52** 140–43; **63** 83, 85
Goodman Holding Company, 42 157–60
GoodMark Foods, Inc., 26 172–74
Goodrich Corporation, 46 209–13 (upd.)
Goodson Newspaper Group, **29** 262
GoodTimes Entertainment Ltd., **31** 238; **48 193–95**
Goodwill Industries International, Inc., **15** 511; **16** 244–46; **66 147–50 (upd.)**
Goodwin & Co., **12** 108
Goodwin, Dannenbaum, Littman & Wingfield, **16** 72
Goody Products, Inc., **12** 214–16; **60** 131–32
Goody's Family Clothing, Inc., **20** 265–67; **64 158–61 (upd.)**
The Goodyear Tire & Rubber Company, **V** 244–48; **8** 81, 291–92, 339; **9** 324; **10** 445; **16** 474; **19** 221, 223, 455; **20** 259–64 (upd.); **21** 72–74; **59** 87–89
Google, Inc., 50 204–07
Gordon B. Miller & Co., **7** 256; **25** 254
Gordon Food Service Inc., **8 225–27**; **39 179–82 (upd.)**
Gordon Jewelry Corporation, **16** 559, 561; **40** 472
Gordon Manufacturing Co., **11** 256
Gordon Publications. *See* Reed Elsevier.
Gordon S. Black Corporation, **41** 197–98
Gordon-Van Cheese Company, **8** 225
Gordy Company, **26** 314
Gorges Foodservice, Inc., **14** 516; **50** 493
Gorgonz Group, Inc., **64** 300
Gorham Silver, **12** 313
Gorilla Sports Club, **25** 42
Gorman Eckert & Co., **27** 299
The Gorman-Rupp Company, **18 201–03**; **57 158–61 (upd.)**
Gorton's, 13 243–44
The Gosho Co. *See* Kanematsu Corporation.
Goss Holdings, Inc., 43 194–97
Götabanken, **II** 353
Gothenburg Light & Power Company, **6** 580
Gothenburg Tramways Co., **II** 1
Gott Corp., **21** 293
Gottleib Group, **38** 437
Gottschalks, Inc., **18 204–06**; **26** 130
Gould Electronics, Inc., **11** 45; **13** 127, 201; **14 206–08**; **21** 43
Goulds Pumps Inc., 24 188–91
Gourmet Award Foods, **29** 480–81
Government Bond Department, **9** 369
Government Employees Insurance Company. *See* GEICO Corporation.
Government Technology Services Inc., **45** 69
Governor and Company of Adventurers of England. *See* Hudson's Bay Company.
The Governor and Company of the Bank of Scotland, 10 336–38
Goya Foods Inc., **22 245–47**; **24** 516
GP Group Acquisition Limited Partnership, **10** 288; **27** 41–42
GP Strategies Corporation, 64 162–66 (upd.)
GPAA. *See* Gold Prospectors' Association of America.
GPE. *See* General Precision Equipment Corporation.
GPI. *See* General Parts Inc.
GPI, **53** 46

GPM Gas Corporation, **40** 357–58
GPS Pool Supply, **29** 34
GPT, **15** 125
GPU. *See* General Public Utilities Corporation.
GPU, Inc., 27 182–85 (upd.)
Graber Industries, Inc. *See* Springs Industries, Inc.
Grace. *See* W.R. Grace & Co.
Grace Drilling Company, **9** 365
Grace-Sierra Horticultural Products Co., **22** 475
Graco Inc., **19 178–80**; **67 191–95 (upd.)**
Gradall Industries, Inc., **52** 196
Gradco Systems, Inc., **6** 290
Gradiaz, Annis & Co., **15** 138
Gradmann & Holler, **III** 283
Graf, **23** 219
Graficas e Instrumentos S.A., **13** 234
Graficas Monte Alban S.A., **47** 326
Graftek Press, Inc., **26** 44
Graham Brothers, **27** 267, 269
Graham Container Corp., **8** 477
Graham Corporation, 62 165–67
Gralla, **IV** 687
Grameen Bank, 31 219–22
Gramercy Pictures, **23** 391
Gramophone Company, **22** 192
Grampian Electricity Supply Company, **13** 457
Gran Central Corporation, **8** 487
Gran Dorado, **48** 315
Granada Group PLC, **II 138–40**; **17** 353; **24 192–95 (upd.)**, 269; **25** 270; **32** 404; **52** 367
Granada Royale Hometels, **9** 426
Granaria Holdings B.V., **23** 183; **66 151–53**
GranCare, Inc., **14 209–11**; **25** 310
Grand Bazaar Innovations Bon Marché, **13** 284; **26** 159–60
Grand Casinos, Inc., **20 268–70**; **21** 526; **25** 386
Grand Department Store, **19** 510
Grand Hotel Krasnapolsky N.V., 23 227–29
Grand Magasin de Nouveautés Fournier d'Annecy, **27** 93
Grand Metropolitan plc, **I** 247–49, 259, 261; **II** 608, 613–15; **9** 99; **13** 391; **14 212–15 (upd.)**; **15** 72; **17** 69, 71; **20** 452; **21** 401; **26** 58; **33** 276; **34** 121; **35** 438; **42** 223; **43** 215; **56** 46. *See also* Diageo plc.
Grand Ole Opry. *See* Gaylord Entertainment Company.
Grand Prix Association of Long Beach, Inc., **43** 139–40
Grand Rapids Carpet Sweeper Company, **9** 70
Grand Rapids Gas Light Company. *See* MCN Corporation.
Grand Rapids Wholesale Grocery Company, **8** 481
Grand Union Company, **II** 637, 662; **7 202–04**; **8** 410; **13** 394; **16** 249; **28 162–65 (upd.)**
Grand Valley Gas Company, **11** 28
Grand-Perret, **39** 152–53
Grandes Superficies S.A., **23** 247
Les Grands Magasins Au Bon Marché, **26** 159–60
GrandVision S.A., 43 198–200
Grandy's, **15** 345

Granger Associates, **12** 136
Gränges, **III** 480; **22** 27; **53** 127–28
Granite Broadcasting Corporation, 42 161–64
Granite City Steel Company, **12** 353
Granite Construction Incorporated, 61 119–21
Granite Furniture Co., **14** 235
Granite Rock Company, 26 175–78
Granite State Bankshares, Inc., 37 173–75
Grant Oil Tool Co., **III** 569; **20** 361
Grant Prideco, Inc., 57 162–64
Grant Thornton International, 57 165–67
Grantham, Mayo, Van Otterloo & Co. LLC, **24** 407
Grantree Corp., **14** 4; **33** 398
Granville PLC. *See* Robert W. Baird & Co. Incorporated.
Graphic Controls Corp., **IV** 678
Graphic Industries Inc., **25 182–84**; **36** 508
Graphic Research, Inc., **13** 344–45
Graphics Systems Software, **8** 519
Graphix Zone, **31** 238
Grass Valley Group, **8** 518, 520
Grasselli Chemical Company, **22** 225
Grasso Production Management Inc., **37** 289
Grattan Plc. *See* Otto-Versand (Gmbh & Co.).
The Graver Company, **16** 357
Gray Communications Systems, Inc., 24 196–200
Gray Line, **24** 118
Gray Matter Holdings, L.L.C., **64** 300
Gray, Siefert & Co., Inc., **10** 44; **33** 259–60
Graybar Electric Company, Inc., 54 139–42
Grays Harbor Mutual Savings Bank, **17** 530
Greaseater, Ltd., **8** 463–64
Great Alaska Tobacco Co., **17** 80
Great American Bagel and Coffee Co., **27** 482
Great American Broadcasting Inc., **18** 65–66; **22** 131; **23** 257–58
Great American Cookie Company. *See* Mrs. Fields' Original Cookies, Inc.
Great American Entertainment Company, **13** 279; **48** 194
Great American First Savings Bank of San Diego, **II** 420
Great American Insurance Company, **48** 9
Great American Lines Inc., **12** 29
Great American Management and Investment, Inc., **8 228–31**; **49** 130
Great American Reserve Insurance Co., **IV** 343; **10** 247
Great American Restaurants, **13** 321
The Great Atlantic & Pacific Tea Company, Inc., **II 636–38**, 629, 655–56, 666; **13** 25, 127, 237; **15** 259; **16** 63–64, 247–50 (upd.); **17** 106; **18** 6; **19** 479–80; **24** 417; **26** 463; **33** 434; **55 164–69 (upd.)**; **64** 125
Great Bagel and Coffee Co., **27** 480–81
Great Eastern Railway, **6** 424
Great Harvest Bread Company, 44 184–86
Great Lakes Bancorp, 8 232–33
Great Lakes Carbon Corporation, **12** 99

Great Lakes Chemical Corp., I 341–42;
8 262; **14 216–18 (upd.)**
Great Lakes Energy Corp., **39** 261
Great Lakes Steel Corp., **8** 346; **12** 352; **26**
528
Great Lakes Window, Inc., **12** 397
Great Land Seafoods, Inc., **II** 553
Great Northern Nekoosa Corp., **IV**
282–83; **9** 260–61; **47** 148
Great Northern Railway Company, **6** 596
Great Plains Energy Incorporated, 65
156–60 (upd.)
Great Plains Software Inc., **38** 432
Great Plains Transportation, **18** 226
Great River Oil and Gas Corporation, **61**
111
Great Shoshone & Twin Falls Water Power
Company, **12** 265
The Great Universal Stores plc, V
67–69; **15** 83; **17** 66, 68; **19 181–84**
(upd.); **41** 74, 76; **45** 152; **50** 124. *See*
also GUS plc.
Great-West Lifeco Inc., III 260–61; **21**
447. *See also* Power Corporation of
Canada.
The Great Western Auction House &
Clothing Store, **19** 261
Great Western Bank, **47** 160
Great Western Billiard Manufactory, **III**
442
Great Western Financial Corporation,
10 339–41
Great Western Foam Co., **17** 182
Great World Foods, Inc., **17** 93
Greatamerica Corp., **10** 419
Greater All American Markets, **II** 601; **7**
19
Greater Washington Investments, Inc., **15**
248
Greb Industries Ltd., **16** 79, 545
Grebner GmbH, **26** 21
Grede Foundries, Inc., 38 214–17
Greeley Beef Plant, **13** 350
Greeley Gas Company, **43** 56–57
Green Acquisition Co., **18** 107
Green Bay Food Company, **7** 127
The Green Bay Packers, Inc., 32 223–26
Green Capital Investors L.P., **23** 413–14
Green Giant, **14** 212, 214; **24** 140–41
Green Island Cement (Holdings) Ltd.
Group, **IV** 694–95
Green Line Investor Services, **18** 553
Green Mountain Coffee, Inc., 31 227–30
Green Power & Light Company. *See*
UtiliCorp United Inc.
Green River Electric Corporation, **11** 37
Green Siam Air Services Co., Ltd., **51** 123
Green Tree Financial Corporation, 11
162–63. *See also* Conseco, Inc.
The Greenalls Group PLC, 21 245–47
Greenbacks Inc., **62** 104
Greenberg Traurig, LLP, 65 161–63
The Greenbrier Companies, 19 185–87
Greene King plc, 31 223–26
Greene, Tweed & Company, 55 170–72
Greenfield Healthy Foods, **26** 58
Greenfield Industries Inc., **13** 8
Greenham Construction Materials, **38**
451–52
Greenman Brothers Inc. *See* Noodle
Kidoodle.
GreenPoint Financial Corp., 28 166–68
Greensboro Life Insurance Company, **11**
213

Greenville Tube Corporation, **21** 108
Greenwich Associates, **19** 117
Greenwood Mills, Inc., 14 219–21
Greenwood Publishing Group. *See* Reed
Elsevier.
Greenwood Trust Company, **18** 478
Greg Manning Auctions, Inc., 60 145–46
Greggs PLC, 65 164–66
Greif Inc., 15 186–88; **66 154–56 (upd.)**
Greiner Engineering Inc., **45** 421
Gresham Insurance Company Limited, **24**
285
GretagMacbeth Holdings AG, **18** 291
Gretel's Pretzels, **35** 56
Gretsch & Brenner, **55** 150
Grévin & Compagnie SA, 56 143–45
Grey Advertising, Inc., 6 26–28; **10** 69;
14 150; **22** 396; **25** 166, 381
Grey Global Group Inc., 66 157–61
(upd.)
Grey Wolf, Inc., 43 201–03
Greyhound Corp., I 448–50; **8** 144–45;
10 72; **12** 199; **16** 349; **22** 427; **23**
173–74; **27** 480; **42** 394
Greyhound Lines, Inc., 32 227–31
(upd.); **48** 319
Greyhound Temporary Services, **25** 432
Griffin Bacal, **25** 381
Griffin Land & Nurseries, Inc., 43
204–06
Griffin Pipe Products Co., **7** 30–31
Griffin Wheel Company, **7** 29–30
Griffon Corporation, 34 194–96
Griffon Cutlery Corp., **13** 166
Grigg, Elliot & Co., **14** 555
Grimes Aerospace, **22** 32
Grinnell Corp., 11 198; **13 245–47**; **63**
401, 403
Grist Mill Company, 15 189–91; **22** 338
Gristede Brothers, **23** 407; **24** 528, 29
Gristede's Sloan's, Inc., 31 231–33
GRM Industries Inc., **15** 247–48
Gro-Mor Company, **60** 160
Grocery Warehouse, **II** 602
Grogan-Cochran Land Company, **7** 345
Grohe. *See* Friedrich Grohe AG & Co. KG.
Grolier Inc., IV 619; **16 251–54**; **43**
207–11 (upd.)
Grolier Interactive, **41** 409
Grolsch. *See* Royal Grolsch NV.
Gross Brothers Laundry. *See* G&K
Services, Inc.
Gross Townsend Frank Hoffman, **6** 28
Grosskraftwerk Franken AG, **23** 47
Grossman's Inc., 13 248–50
Grosvenor Casinos Ltd., **64** 320
Ground Round, Inc., 21 248–51
Ground Services Inc., **13** 49
Group Arnault, **32** 146
Group 4 Falck A/S, 42 165–68, 338; **63**
425
Group Health Cooperative, 41 181–84
Group Hospitalization and Medical
Services, **10** 161
Group Lotus plc, **13** 357; **62** 268
Group Maeva SA, **48** 316
Group Maintenance America Corp. *See*
Encompass Services Corporation.
Group 1 Automotive, Inc., 52 144–46
Group Schneider S.A., **20** 214
Groupe AB, **19** 204
Groupe AG, **III** 201–02
Groupe Air France, 6 92–94. *See also*
Air France; Societe Air France.

Groupe Alain Manoukian, 55 173–75
Groupe André, 17 210–12. *See also*
Vivarte SA.
Groupe Arnault, **66** 244
Groupe Axime, **37** 232
Groupe Barrière SA, **48** 199
Groupe Bisset, **24** 510
Groupe Bolloré, 37 21; **67 196–99**
Groupe Bourbon S.A., 60 147–49
Groupe Bruxelles Lambert, **26** 368
Groupe Bull, 10 563–64; **12** 246; **21** 391;
34 517. *See also* Compagnie des
Machines Bull.
Groupe Casino. *See* Casino Guichard-
Perrachon S.A.
Groupe Castorama-Dubois
Investissements, 23 230–32
Groupe Danone, 14 150; **32 232–36**
(upd.); **55** 359; **65** 215–17
Le Groupe Darty, **24** 266, 270
Groupe Dassault Aviation SA, 26 179–82
(upd.); **42** 373, 376
Groupe de la Cité, IV 614–16, 617
Groupe DMC (Dollfus Mieg & Cie), 27
186–88
Groupe Fournier SA, 44 187–89
Groupe Go Sport S.A., 39 183–85; **54**
308
Groupe Guillin SA, 40 214–16
Groupe Herstal S.A., 58 145–48
Groupe Jean-Claude Darmon, 44 190–92
Groupe Jean Didier, **12** 413
Groupe Jean-Paul Gaultier, **34** 214
Groupe Lagardère S.A., 15 293; **21** 265,
267
Groupe Lapeyre S.A., 33 175–77
Groupe LDC. *See* L.D.C. S.A.
Groupe Legris Industries, 23 233–35
Groupe Les Echos, 25 283–85
Groupe Louis Dreyfus S.A., 60 150–53
Groupe Partouche SA, 48 196–99
Groupe Pechiney, **33** 89
Groupe Pinault-Printemps-Redoute, **19** 306,
309; **21** 224, 226
Groupe Poliet, 66 363–64
Groupe Poron, **35** 206
Groupe Promodès S.A., 19 326–28
Groupe Rallye, **39** 183–85
Groupe Rothschild, **22** 365
Groupe Rougier SA, 21 438–40
Groupe Roussin, **34** 13
Groupe Salvat, **IV** 619
Groupe SEB, 35 201–03
Groupe Sidel S.A., 21 252–55
Groupe Soufflet SA, 55 176–78; **65** 65
Groupe Tetra Laval, **53** 327
Groupe Victoire, **III** 394
Groupe Vidéotron Ltée., 20 271–73
Groupe Yves Saint Laurent, 23 236–39
Groupe Zannier S.A., 35 204–07
Groupement d'Achat AVP SAS, **58** 221
Groupement des Mousquetaires. *See* ITM
Entreprises SA.
Groupement Français pour l'Investissement
Immobilier, **42** 153
Groupement Laitier du Perche, **19** 50
Groupement pour le Financement de la
Construction. *See* Gecina SA.
GroupMAC. *See* Encompass Services
Corporation.
Groux Beverage Corporation, **11** 451
Grove Manufacturing Co., **9** 393
Grove Worldwide, Inc., **59** 274, 278
Grow Biz International, Inc., 18 207–10

Grow Group Inc., 12 217–19, 387–88; **59** 332

Growing Healthy Inc., **27** 197; **43** 218

Growth International, Inc., **17** 371

Grubb & Ellis Company, 21 256–58

Gruma, S.A. de C.V., 19 192; **31 234–36**

Grumman Corp., I 61–63, 67–68, 78, 84, 490, 511; **7** 205; **8** 51; **9** 17, 206–07, 417, 460; **10** 536; **11 164–67 (upd.)**, 363–65, 428; **15** 285; **28** 169

Grundig AG, **12** 162; **13** 402–03; **15** 514; **27 189–92**; **48** 383; **50** 299

Gruner + Jahr AG & Co., **7** 245; **22** 442; **23** 85

Gruntal & Co., L.L.C., 20 274–76

Gruntal Financial Corp., **III** 264

Grupo Acerero del Norte, S.A. de C.V., **22** 286; **42** 6

Grupo Aeropuerto del Sureste, S.A. de C.V., 48 200–02

Grupo Antarctica Paulista. *See* Companhia de Bebidas das Américas.

Grupo Banco Bilbao Vizcaya Argentaria S.A., **54** 147

Grupo Bimbo, S.A. de C.V., **31** 236

Grupo Bufete. *See* Bufete Industrial, S.A. de C.V.

Grupo Cabal S.A., **23** 166

Grupo Campi, S.A. de C.V., **39** 230

Grupo Carso, S.A. de C.V., 14 489; **21 259–61**; **63** 383

Grupo Casa Saba, S.A. de C.V., 39 186–89

Grupo Clarín S.A., 67 200–03

Grupo Corvi S.A. de C.V., **7** 115; **25** 126

Grupo Cruzcampo S.A., **34** 202

Grupo Cuervo, S.A. de C.V., **31** 91–92

Grupo Cydsa, S.A. de C.V., 39 190–93

Grupo de Ingenieria Ecologica, **16** 260

Grupo Dina. *See* Consorcio G Grupo Dina, S.A. de C.V.

Grupo Dragados SA, 55 179–82

Grupo DST, **41** 405–06

Grupo Editorial Random House Mondadori S.L., **54** 22

Grupo Elektra, S.A. de C.V., 39 194–97

Grupo Empresarial Angeles, **50** 373

Grupo Eroski, 64 167–70

Grupo Ferrovial, S.A., 40 217–19

Grupo Financiero Asemex-Banpais S.A., **51** 150

Grupo Financiero Banamex S.A., 27 304; **54 143–46**; **59** 121

Grupo Financiero Banorte, S.A. de C.V., 51 149–51

Grupo Financiero BBVA Bancomer S.A., 54 147–50

Grupo Financiero Galicia S.A., 63 178–81

Grupo Financiero Inbursa, **21** 259

Grupo Financiero Inverlat, S.A., **39** 188; **59** 74

Grupo Financiero Serfin, S.A., 19 188–90, 474; **36** 63

Grupo Gigante, S.A. de C.V., 34 197–99

Grupo Hecali, S.A., **39** 196

Grupo Herdez, S.A. de C.V., 35 208–10; **54** 167

Grupo Hermes, **24** 359

Grupo ICA, **52** 394

Grupo IMSA, S.A. de C.V., 44 193–96

Grupo Industrial Alfa, S.A. de C.V., **44** 332. *See also* Alfa, S.A. de C.V.

Grupo Industrial Atenquique, S.A. de C.V., **37** 176

Grupo Industrial Bimbo, 19 191–93; **29** 338

Grupo Industrial Durango, S.A. de C.V., 37 176–78

Grupo Industrial Maseca S.A. de C.V. (Gimsa). *See* Gruma, S.A. de C.V.

Grupo Industrial Saltillo, S.A. de C.V., 54 151–54

Grupo Irsa, **23** 171

Grupo Leche Pascual S.A., 59 212–14

Grupo Lladró S.A., 52 147–49

Grupo Martins, **59** 361

Grupo Mexico, S.A. de C.V., 40 220–23, 413

Grupo Modelo, S.A. de C.V., 29 218–20

Grupo Nacional Provincial, **22** 285

Grupo Pipsamex S.A., **37** 178

Grupo Portucel Soporcel, 60 154–56

Grupo Posadas, S.A. de C.V., 57 168–70

Grupo Protexa, **16** 210

Grupo Pulsar. *See* Pulsar Internacional S.A.

Grupo Quan, **19** 192–93

Grupo Salinas, **39** 196

Grupo Sanborns S.A. de C.V., **35** 118

Grupo Servia, S.A. de C.V., **50** 209

Grupo TACA, 38 218–20

Grupo Televisa, S.A., 9 429; **18 211–14**; **19** 10; **24** 515–17; **39** 188, 398; **54 155–58 (upd.)**; **57** 121

Grupo TMM, S.A. de C.V., 50 208–11

Grupo Transportación Ferroviaria Mexicana, S.A. de C.V., 47 162–64

Grupo Tribasa, **34** 82

Grupo Tudor, **IV** 471

Grupo Xtra, **39** 186, 188

Gruppo Banco di Napoli, **50** 410

Gruppo Buffetti S.p.A., **47** 345–46

Gruppo Coin S.p.A., 41 185–87

Gruppo Editoriale L'Espresso S.p.A., **54** 19–21

Gruppo GFT, **22** 123

Gruppo IRI, **V** 325–27

Gryphon Development, **24** 237

Gryphon Holdings, Inc., 21 262–64

GS Financial Services L.P., **51** 148

GSD&M Advertising, 44 197–200

GSG&T, **6** 495

GSG Holdings Ltd., **39** 87

GSI. *See* Geophysical Service, Inc.

GSI Acquisition Co. L.P., **17** 488

GSI Commerce, Inc., 67 204–06

GSR, Inc., **17** 338

GSU. *See* Gulf States Utilities Company.

GT Bicycles, 26 183–85, 412

GT Global Inc. *See* AMVESCAP PLC.

GT Interactive Software, 19 405; **31 237–41**. *See also* Infogrames Entertainment S.A.

GTE Corporation, V 294–98; **9** 49, 171, 478–80; **10** 19, 97, 431; **11** 500; **14** 259, 433; **15 192–97 (upd.)**; **18** 74, 111, 543; **22** 19; **25** 20–21, 91; **26** 520; **27** 302, 305; **46** 373; **50** 299. *See also* British Columbia Telephone Company; Verizon Communications.

GTE Northwest Inc., **37** 124–26

GTECH Holdings, Inc., **27** 381

GTI Corporation, **29** 461–62

GTM-Entrepose, **23** 332

GTM Group, **43** 450, 452; **54** 392

GTO. *See* Global Transport Organization.

GTS Duratek, Inc., **13** 367–68

GTSI. *See* Government Technology Services Inc.

GTSI Corp., 57 171–73

GU Markets, **55** 83

Guangzhou Kurabo Chemicals Co. Ltd., **61** 229

Guangzhou M. C. Packaging, **10** 130

Guangzhou Pearl River Piano Group Ltd., 49 177–79

Guangzhou Railway Corporation, **52** 43

Guarantee Reserve Life Insurance Company, **59** 246

Guaranty Bank & Trust Company, **13** 440

Guaranty Federal Bank, F.S.B., **31** 441

Guaranty Federal Savings & Loan Assoc., **IV** 343

Guaranty Properties Ltd., **11** 258

Guaranty Savings and Loan, **10** 339

Guaranty Trust Co. *See* J.P. Morgan & Co. Incorporated.

Guardforce Limited, **45** 378

Guardian Bank, **13** 468

Guardian Federal Savings and Loan Association, **10** 91

Guardian Financial Services, 64 171–74 (upd.)

Guardian Media Group plc, 53 152–55

Guardian Mortgage Company, **8** 460

Guardian Refrigerator Company. *See* Frigidaire Home Products.

Guardian Royal Exchange Plc, 11 168–70; **33** 319. *See also* Guardian Financial Services.

Gubor Schokoladen, **15** 221

Gucci Group N.V., 45 343–44; **50 212–16 (upd.)**; **54** 320; **57** 179

Guccio Gucci, S.p.A., 12 281; **15 198–200**; **27** 329; **57** 180

GUD Holdings, Ltd., **17** 106; **61** 66

Gudang Garam Tbk, PT, **62** 96–97

Guerbet Group, 46 214–16

Guerdon Homes, Inc., **41** 19

Guerlain, 23 240–42; **33** 272

Guess, Inc., 15 201–03; **17** 466; **23** 309; **24** 157; **27** 329

Guest, Keen and Nettlefolds plc. *See* GKN plc.

Guest Supply, Inc., 18 215–17

Guida, **63** 151

Guidant Corporation, 30 316; **37** 39; **43** 351; **58 149–51**

Guideoutdoors.com Inc., **36** 446

Guilbert S.A., 42 169–71; **55** 355

Guild Press, Inc., **13** 559

Guild Wineries, **13** 134; **34** 89

Guilford Industries, **8** 270–72

Guilford Mills Inc., 8 234–36; **40 224–27 (upd.)**

Guilford of Maine, Inc., **29** 246

Guilford Transportation Industries, Inc., **16** 348, 350

Guillemot Corporation, 41 188–91, 407, 409

Guillin. *See* Groupe Guillin SA

Guinness Mahon, **36** 231

Guinness Overseas Ltd., **25** 281

Guinness Peat Aviation, **10** 277; **36** 426

Guinness plc, I 250–52, 268, 272, 282; **II** 610; **9** 100, 449; **10** 399; **13** 454; **18** 62, 501; **29** 84; **33** 276; **36** 405–06. *See also* Diageo plc.

Guinness/UDV, 43 212–16 (upd.); **61** 324–25

Guitar Center, Inc., 29 221–23

Guittard Chocolate Company, 55 183–85
Gulco Industries, Inc., **11** 194
Gulf + Western Inc., I 451–53; IV 672; **7** 64; **10** 482; **13** 121, 169, 470; **25** 328, 535; **33** 3; **41** 71; **51** 165
Gulf + Western Industries, **22** 122. See also Paramount Communications.
Gulf Air Company, 27 25; **39** 137–38; **56 146–48**
Gulf Canada Ltd., **I** 262, 264; **IV** 721; **6** 478; **9** 391; **13** 557–58
Gulf Canada Resources Ltd., **63** 110
Gulf Caribbean Marine Lines, **6** 383
Gulf Coast Sportswear Inc., **23** 65
Gulf Energy Development, **22** 107
Gulf Engineering Co. Ltd., **IV** 131
Gulf Island Fabrication, Inc., 44 201–03
Gulf Marine & Maintenance Offshore Service Company, **22** 276
Gulf Oil Chemical Co., **13** 502
Gulf Oil Corp., **17** 121–22; **21** 494; **25** 444; **33** 253. See also Chevron.
Gulf Power Company, **38** 446, 448
Gulf Public Service Company, Inc, **6** 580; **37** 89
Gulf Resources & Chemical Corp., **15** 464
Gulf States Steel, **I** 491
Gulf States Utilities Company, 6 495–97; 12 99
GulfMark Offshore, Inc., 49 180–82
Gulfstream Aerospace Corporation, 7 205–06; 13 358; **24** 465; **28 169–72 (upd.); 36** 190–91
Gulfwind Marine USA, **30** 303
Gulistan Holdings Inc., **28** 219
Gulton Industries Inc., **7** 297; **19** 31
Gump's, **7** 286
Gunder & Associates, **12** 553
Gunderson, Inc. See The Greenbrier Companies.
Gunfred Group, **I** 387
Gunite Corporation, 23 306; **51 152–55**
The Gunlocke Company, 12 299; **13** 269; **23 243–45**
Gunnebo AB, 53 156–58
Gunnite, **27** 203
Gunther, S.A., **8** 477
Gupta, **15** 492
Gurwitch Bristow Products, LLC, **49** 285
GUS plc, 47 165–70 (upd.); 54 38, 40
Gustav Schickendanz KG. See Karstadt Quelle AG.
Gustin-Bacon Group, **16** 8
Guthy-Renker Corporation, 32 237–40
Gutteridge, Haskins & Davey, **22** 138
Gutzeit. See W. Gutzeit & Co.
Guy Degrenne SA, 44 204–07
Guy Motors, **13** 286
Guy Pease Associates, **34** 248
Guyenne et Gascogne, 23 246–48
Guyomarc'h, **39** 356
GVN Technologies, **63** 5
GW Utilities Ltd., **I** 264; **6** 478
Gwathmey Siegel & Associates Architects LLC, 26 186–88
GWC. See General Waterworks Corporation.
GWK GmbH, **45** 378
GWR Group plc, 39 198–200
Gymboree Corporation, 15 204–06
Gynecare Inc., **23** 190
Gynetics, Inc., **26** 31

H&D. See Hinde & Dauch Paper Company.
H&D Holdings, **64** 79
H&H Craft & Floral, **17** 322
H & H Plastics Co., **25** 312
H & R Block, Incorporated, 9 268–70; 25 434; **27** 106, 307; **29 224–28 (upd.); 48** 234, 236; **52** 316
H.B. Fenn and Company Ltd., **25** 485
H.B. Fuller Company, 8 237–40; 32 254–58 (upd.)
H.B. Nickerson & Sons Ltd., **14** 339
H.B. Tuttle and Company, **17** 355
H.B. Viney Company, Inc., **11** 211
H. Berlind Inc., **16** 388
H.C. Prange Co., **19** 511–12
H Curry & Sons. See Currys Group PLC.
H.D. Lee Company, Inc. See Lee Apparel Company, Inc.
H.D. Vest, Inc., 46 217–19
H. Douglas Barclay, **8** 296
H.E. Butt Grocery Company, 13 251–53; 32 259–62 (upd.); 33 307
H.E. Moss and Company Tankers Ltd., **23** 161
H.F. Ahmanson & Company, II 181–82; 10 342–44 (upd.); 28 167; **47** 160
H.F.T. Industrial Ltd., **62** 150
H.G. Anderson Equipment Corporation, **6** 441
H.H. Brown Shoe Company, **18** 60, **18** 62
H.H. Cutler Company, **17** 513
H.H. Robertson, Inc., **19** 366
H.H. West Co., **25** 501
H.I.G. Capital L.L.C., **30** 235
H.J. Heinz Company, II 450, 507–09, 547; **7** 382, 448, 576, 578; **8** 499; **10** 151; **11 171–73 (upd.); 12** 411, 529, 531–32; **13** 383; **21** 55, 500–01; **22** 147; **25** 517; **27** 197–98; **33** 446–49; **36 253–57 (upd.); 43** 217–18
H.J. Justin & Sons. See Justin Industries, Inc.
H.J. Russell & Company, 66 162–65
H.K. Ferguson Company, **7** 355
H.K. Porter Company, Inc., **19** 152
H.L. Green Company, Inc., **9** 448
H.L. Yoh Company. See Day & Zimmerman, Inc.
H. Lewis and Sons, **14** 294
H. Lundbeck A/S, 44 208–11
H.M. Byllesby & Company, Inc., **6** 539
H.M. Spalding Electric Light Plant, **6** 592; **50** 37
H. Miller & Sons, Inc., **11** 258
H N Norton Co., **11** 208
H.O. Houghton & Company, **10** 355
H.O. Systems, Inc., **47** 430
H-P. See Hewlett-Packard Co.
H.P. Foods, **II** 475
H.P. Hood, **7** 17–18
H. Salt Fish and Chips, **13** 320
H. Samuel Plc, **61** 326
H.T. Cherry Company, **12** 376
H.W. Johns Manufacturing Co. See Manville Corp.
H.W. Madison Co., **11** 211
H.W.S. Solutions, **21** 37
The H.W. Wilson Company, 17 152; **23** 440; **66 166–68**
H. Williams and Co., Ltd., **II** 678
Ha-Lo Industries, Inc., 27 193–95
Häagen-Dazs, **II** 631; **10** 147; **14** 212, 214; **19** 116; **24** 140, 141

Haake-Beck Brauerei AG, **9** 86
Haan Crafts Corporation, **62** 18
Haas, Baruch & Co. See Smart & Final, Inc.
Haas Publishing Companies, Inc., **22** 442
Haas Wheat & Partners, **15** 357; **65** 258–59
Habersham Bancorp, 25 185–87
Habitat for Humanity International, 36 258–61
Habitat/Mothercare PLC. See Storehouse PLC.
Hach Co., **14** 309; **18 218–21**
Hachette Filipacchi Medias S.A., 21 265–67; 33 310
Hachette S.A., IV 617–19; **10** 288; **11** 293; **12** 359; **16** 253–54; **17** 399; **21** 266; **22** 441–42; **23** 476; **43** 210. See also Matra-Hachette S.A.
Haci Omer Sabanci Holdings A.S., 55 186–89
Hacker-Pschorr Brau, **35** 331
Hackman Oyj Adp, 44 204, **212–15**
Hadco Corporation, 24 201–03
Haemocell, **11** 476
Haemonetics Corporation, 20 277–79
Haftpflichtverband der Deutschen Industrie Versicherung auf Gegenseitigkeit V.a.G. See HDI (Haftpflichtverband der Deutschen Industrie Versicherung auf Gegenseitigkeit V.a.G.).
Hagemeyer N.V., 18 180–82; **39 201–04; 45** 426; **54** 203
Hagemeyer North America, **63** 289
Haggar Corporation, 19 194–96; 24 158
Haggen Inc., 38 221–23
Hägglunds Vehicle AB, **47** 7, 9
Hahn Automotive Warehouse, Inc., 24 204–06
Hahn Department Stores. See Allied Stores Corp.
Hahn, Inc., **17** 9
Haier Group Corporation, 65 167–70
Haile Mines, Inc., **12** 253
The Hain Celestial Group, Inc., 43 217–20 (upd.)
Hain Food Group, Inc., I 514; **27 196–98; 36** 256
Hake Group, Inc. See Matrix Service Company.
Hakuhodo, Inc., 6 29–31; 16 167; **42 172–75 (upd.)**
Hakunetsusha & Company, **12** 483
HAL Inc., 9 271–73. See also Hawaiian Airlines, Inc.
Hale and Dorr, **31** 75
Hale-Halsell Company, 60 157–60
Haleko Hanseatisches Lebensmittel Kontor GmbH, **29** 500
Halewood, **21** 246
Half Price Books, Records, Magazines Inc., 37 179–82
Halfords Ltd., **24** 75
Halkin Holdings plc, **49** 338–39
Hall Bros. Co. See Hallmark Cards, Inc.
Hall, Kinion & Associates, Inc., 52 150–52
Hall Laboratories, Inc., **45** 209
Hall-Mark Electronics, **23** 490
La Halle aux Chaussures, **17** 210
Haller, Raymond & Brown, Inc., **II** 10
Hallhuber GmbH, **63** 361, 363
Halliburton Company, III 473, **497–500,** 617; **11** 505; **13** 118–19; **17** 417; **25**

188–92 (upd.); **55** 190–95 (upd.); **59** 378; **62** 201

Hallmark Cards, Inc., IV 620–21; **7** 23–25; **12** 207, 209; **16** 255–57 (upd.), 427; **18** 67, 69, 213; **21** 426–28; **22** 33, 36; **24** 44, 516–17; **25** 69, 71, 368; **28** 160; **29** 64; **39** 87; **40** 228–32 (upd.); **45** 131; **59** 34, 35, 37

Hallmark Chemical Corp., **8** 386

Hallmark Holdings, Inc., **51** 190

Hallmark Investment Corp., **21** 92

Hallmark Residential Group, Inc., **45** 221

Halo Lighting, **30** 266

Haloid Company. *See* Xerox Corporation.

Halsam Company, **25** 380

Halstead Industries, **26** 4; **52** 258

Halter Marine, **22** 276

Hambrecht & Quist Group, **10** 463, 504; **26** 66; **27** 447; **31** 349

Hambro American Bank & Trust Co., **11** 109

Hambro Countrywide Security, **32** 374

Hambros Bank, **16** 14; **27** 474; **43** 7

Hamburg-Amerikanische-Packetfahrt-Actien-Gesellschaft, **6** 397–98

Hamburgische Electricitaets-Werke AG, **57** 395, 397

Hamelin Group, Inc., **19** 415

Hamer Hammer Service, Inc., **11** 523

Hamersley Holdings, IV 59–61

Hamil Textiles Ltd. *See* Algo Group Inc.

Hamilton Beach/Proctor-Silex Inc., 7 369–70; **16** 384; **17** 213–15; **24** 435; **43** 289

Hamilton Group Limited, **15** 478

Hamilton Industries, Inc., **25** 261

Hamilton National Bank, **13** 465

Hamilton Oil Corp., IV 47; **22** 107

Hamilton Standard, **9** 417

Hamilton/Hall-Mark, **19** 313

Hamish Hamilton, IV 659; **8** 526

Hammacher Schlemmer & Company, 21 268–70; **26** 439–40

Hammarplast, **13** 493

Hammermill Paper Co., **23** 48–49

Hammers Plastic Recycling, **6** 441

Hammerson plc, IV 696–98; **26** 420; **40** 233–35

Hammery Furniture Company, **14** 302–03

Hammes Co., **38** 482

Hamming-Whitman Publishing Co., **13** 559

Hammonton Electric Light Company, **6** 449

Hampton Industries, Inc., 20 280–82

Hampton Inns, **9** 425–26

Hampton Roads Food, Inc., **25** 389

Hamworthy Engineering Ltd., **31** 367, 369

Han Comm Inc., **62** 174

Hancock Fabrics, Inc., 16 197–99; **18** 222–24

Hancock Holding Company, 15 207–09

Hancock Jaffe Laboratories, **11** 460

Hancock Park Associates. *See* Leslie's Poolmart, Inc.

Hancock Textile Co., Inc., **27** 291

Handleman Company, 15 210–12

Handspring Inc., 49 183–86

Handy & Harman, 23 249–52

Handy Andy Home Improvement Centers, Inc., **16** 210; **26** 160–61

Hanes Corp., **8** 202, 288; **25** 166

Hanes Holding Company, **11** 256; **48** 267

Hang Chong, **18** 114

Hang Seng Bank Ltd., 60 161–63

Hanger Orthopedic Group, Inc., 41 192–95

Haniel & Cie. GmbH, **27** 175

Hanjin Group. *See* Korean Ail Lines Co. Ltd.

Hanjin Shipping Co., Ltd., 50 217–21

Hankook Tyre Manufacturing Company, V 255–56; **19** 508

Hankuk Glass Industry Co., III 715

Hankyu Corporation, V 454–56; **23** 253–56 (upd.)

Hankyu Department Stores, Inc., V 70–71; **62** 168–71 (upd.)

Hanley Brick, **14** 250

Hanmi Financial Corporation, 66 169–71

Hanna Andersson Corp., 49 187–90

Hanna-Barbera Cartoons Inc., 7 306; **18** 65; **23** 257–59, 387; **25** 313; **33** 432

Hanna Mining Co., **8** 346–47

Hanna Ore Mining Company, **12** 352

Hannaford Bros. Co., 12 220–22

Hannen Brauerei GmbH, **9** 100

Hannifin Corporation. *See* Parker Hannifin Corporation.

HANNOVER International AG für Industrieversicherungen, **53** 162

Hannover Papier, **49** 353

Hanover Bank. *See* Manufacturers Hanover Corporation.

Hanover Compressor Company, 59 215–17

Hanover Direct, Inc., 36 262–65

Hanover Foods Corporation, 35 211–14

Hanover House, Inc., **24** 154

Hanover Insurance Company, **63** 29

Hansa Linie, **26** 279–80

Hansen Natural Corporation, 31 242–45

Hansgrohe AG, 56 149–52

Hansol Paper Co., **63** 315–16

Hanson Building Materials America Inc., 60 164–66

Hanson Industries, **44** 257

Hanson PLC, III 501–03, 506; IV 23, 94, 97, 169, 171, 173, 290; **7** 207–10 (upd.); **13** 478–79; **17** 39–40, 325; **23** 296–97; **27** 287–88; **30** 228–32 (upd.), 441; **37** 6–7, 205; **39** 345; **45** 332; **50** 57

Hansvedt Industries Inc., **25** 195

Hanwha Group, 62 172–75

Hapag-Lloyd Ag, 6 397–99; **42** 283

Happy Air Exchangers Ltd., **21** 499

Happy Kids Inc., 30 233–35

Haralambos Beverage Corporation, **11** 451

Harbert Corporation, 13 98; **14** 222–23

HARBIN Samick Corp., **56** 300

Harbison-Walker Refractories Company, 24 207–09

Harbor Group, **41** 262–63

Harbor Tug and Barge Co., **6** 382

Harborlite Corporation, **10** 45; **60** 16

Harbour Group, **24** 16

Harco, Inc., **37** 31

Harcourt Brace and Co., 12 223–26

Harcourt Brace Jovanovich, Inc., IV 622–24; **7** 312; **12** 224; **13** 106; **14** 177; **19** 404; **25** 177

Harcourt General, Inc., 12 226; **20** 283–87 (upd.); **25** 178; **49** 286; **57** 15

Harcros Investment Trust Ltd. *See* Harrisons & Crosfield PLC.

Hard Rock Cafe International, Inc., 12 227–29; **25** 387; **27** 201; **32** 241–45 (upd.); **37** 191; **41** 308; **64** 320

Hardee's Food Systems Inc., II 679; **7** 430; **8** 564; **9** 178; **15** 345; **16** 95; **19** 93; **23** 505; **27** 16–18; **46** 98

Hardin Stockton, **21** 96

Harding Lawson Associates Group, Inc., 16 258–60

Hardinge Inc., 25 193–95

Hardman Inc., III 699

Hardware Wholesalers Inc., **12** 8. *See also* Do it Best Corporation.

Hardy Oil & Gas, **34** 75

HARIBO GmbH & Co. KG, 44 216–19

Harima Shipbuilding & Engineering Co., Ltd., I 511; III 533

Harken Energy Corporation, **17** 169–70

Harland and Wolff Holdings plc, 19 197–200

Harlem Globetrotters International, Inc., 7 199, 335; **61** 122–24

Harlequin Enterprises Limited, IV 587, 590, 617, 619, 672; **19** 405; **29** 470–71, 473; **52** 153–56

Harley-Davidson, Inc., 7 211–14; **13** 513; **16** 147–49; **21** 153; **23** 299–301; **25** 22, 196–200 (upd.); **40** 31

Harleysville Group Inc., 37 183–86

Harman International Industries Inc., 15 213–15; **36** 101; **62** 5

Harmon Industries, Inc., 25 201–04

Harmon Publishing Company, **12** 231

Harmonic Inc., 43 221–23

Harmony Gold Mining Company Limited, 63 182–85

Harmsworth Brothers, **17** 396

Harmsworth Publishing, **19** 118, 120

Harnischfeger Industries, Inc., 8 241–44; **14** 56; **26** 355; **38** 224–28 (upd.)

Harold's Stores, Inc., 22 248–50

Harp Lager Ltd., **15** 442; **35** 395, 397

Harper Group Inc., 12 180; **13** 20; **17** 216–19

Harper House, Inc. *See* Day Runner, Inc.

Harper Robinson and Company, **17** 163

HarperCollins Publishers, 14 555–56; **15** 216–18; **23** 156, 210; **24** 546; **46** 196

Harpers, Inc., **12** 298; **48** 245

Harpo Inc., 28 173–75; **30** 270; **66** 172–75 (upd.)

Harrah's Entertainment, Inc., 9 425–27; **16** 261–63; **27** 200; **43** 224–28 (upd.); **62** 195

Harris & Harris Group, **59** 12

Harris Adacom Corporation B.V., **21** 239

Harris Bankcorp, **46** 55

Harris Corporation, II 37–39; **11** 46, 286, 490; **20** 288–92 (upd.); **27** 364

Harris-Emery Co., **19** 510

Harris Financial, Inc., **11** 482

Harris InfoSource International, Inc., **61** 83

Harris Interactive Inc., 41 196–99

Harris Laboratories, **14** 549

Harris Manufacturing Company, **25** 464

Harris Microwave Semiconductors, **14** 417

Harris Oil Company, **17** 170

Harris Pharmaceuticals Ltd., **11** 208

Harris Publications, **13** 179

Harris Publishing. *See* Bernard C. Harris Publishing Company, Inc.

Harris Queensway, **24** 269

Harris Teeter Inc., 23 260–62

Harris Transducer Corporation, **10** 319

Harrisons & Crosfield plc, III 696–700. *See also* Elementis plc.

Harrods Holdings, , 21 353; **45** 188; **47 171–74**

Harron Communications Corporation, **52** 9

Harrow Stores Ltd., **II** 677

Harry and David. *See* Bear Creek Corporation.

Harry N. Abrams, Inc., 58 152–55

Harry Winston Inc., 45 184–87

Harry's Farmers Market Inc., 23 263–66

Harry's Premium Snacks, **27** 197; **43** 218

Harsah Ceramics, **25** 267

Harsco Corporation, 8 245–47; 11 135; **30** 471. *See also* United Defense Industries, Inc.

Harshaw Chemical Company, **9** 154; **17** 363

Hart Press, **12** 25

Hart Schaffner & Marx. *See* Hartmarx Corporation.

Harte & Co., **7** 308

Harte-Hanks Communications, Inc., 17 220–22; 63 186–89 (upd.)

Harter Bank & Trust, **9** 474–75

Hartford Container Company, **8** 359

Hartford Electric Light Co., **13** 183

Hartford Financial Services Group, **41** 64

Hartford Fire Insurance, **11** 198

Hartford Group, **63** 47

Hartford Insurance Group, **22** 428

Hartford Life International Ltd., **63** 179

Hartford Machine Screw Co., **12** 344

Hartford National Bank and Trust Co., **13** 396

Hartford National Corporation, **13** 464, 466–67

Hartmann & Braun, **III** 566; **38** 299

Hartmann Elektronik GmbH, **61** 287

Hartmann Fibre, **12** 377

Hartmann Luggage, **12** 313

Hartmarx Corporation, 8 248–50; 25 258; **32 246–50 (upd.)**

The Hartstone Group plc, 14 224–26

The Hartz Mountain Corporation, 12 230–32; 46 220–23 (upd.)

Harvard Private Capital Group Inc., **26** 500, 502

Harvard Sports, Inc., **19** 144

Harvard Table Tennis, Inc., **19** 143–44

Harvard Ventures, **25** 358

Harvest Day, **27** 291

Harvest International, **III** 201

Harvest Partners, Inc., **40** 300; **52** 139

Harvest States Cooperative, **64** 307

Harvestore, **11** 5

Harvey & Thompson, **61** 53

Harvey Benjamin Fuller, **8** 237–38

Harvey Group, **19** 312

Harvey Hotel Corporation, **23** 71, 73

Harvey Norman Holdings Ltd., 56 153–55

Harveys Casino Resorts, 27 199–201

Harwood Homes, **31** 386

Harza Engineering Company, 14 227–28

Has.net, **48** 402

Hasbro, Inc., III 504–06; 7 305; **12** 168–69, 495; **13** 561; **16 264–68 (upd.);** **17** 243; **18** 520–21; **21** 375; **25** 313, 380–81, 487–89; **28** 159; **34** 369; **43** 229–34 (upd.); **52** 192–93, 206;

Haskel International, Inc., 59 218–20

Haslemere Estates, **26** 420

Hasler Holding AG, **9** 32

Hassenfeld Brothers Inc. *See* Hasbro, Inc.

Hasten Bancorp, **11** 371

Hastings Entertainment, Inc., 29 229–31

Hastings Filters, Inc., **17** 104

Hastings Manufacturing Company, 17 106; **56 156–58**

Hatch Grinding, **29** 86, 88

Hatersley & Davidson, **16** 80

Hatfield Jewelers, **30** 408

Hatteras Yachts Inc., **45** 175

Hattori Seiko Co., Ltd. *See* Seiko Corporation.

HAULOTTE, **51** 295

Hauni Maschinenbau AG, **60** 193

Hauser, Inc., 46 224–27

Hausted, Inc., **29** 451

Havas, SA, 10 195–96, **345–48; 13** 203–04; **33 178–82 (upd.); 34** 83. *See also* Vivendi Universal Publishing

Haverty Furniture Companies, Inc., 31 246–49

Havertys, **39** 174

Haviland Candy Co., **15** 325

Haw Par Corporation, **56** 362

Hawaii National Bank, **11** 114

Hawaii World, **62** 276

Hawaiian Airlines Inc., 9 271–73; **22** 251–53 (upd.); **24** 20–22; **26** 339. *See also* HAL Inc.

Hawaiian Electric Industries, Inc., 9 274–77

Hawaiian Tug & Barge, **9** 276

Hawk Corporation, 59 221–23

Hawk Model Co., **51** 368

Hawker Siddeley Group Public Limited Company, III 507–10; 8 51; **12** 190

Hawkins Chemical, Inc., 16 269–72

Hawley Group Limited, **12** 10

Hawley Products, **16** 20

Haworth Inc., 8 251–52; 27 434; **39 205–08 (upd.)**

Hawthorn Company, **8** 287

Hawthorn-Mellody, **11** 25

Hawthorne Appliance and Electronics, **10** 9–11

Haxton Foods Inc., **21** 155

Hay Group, **42** 329–30

Hayden Clinton National Bank, **11** 180

Hayden Publications, **27** 499

Hayes Aircraft Corp., **54** 283

Hayes Conyngham & Robinson, **24** 75

Hayes Corporation, 24 210–14; 53 381

Hayes Industries Inc., **16** 7

Hayes Lemmerz International, Inc., 27 202–04

Hayes Microcomputer Products, **9** 515

Hayes Wheel Company, **7** 258

Hayne, Miller & Swearingen, Inc., **22** 202

Hays Plc, 27 205–07

HAZCO International, Inc., **9** 110

Hazel-Atlas Glass Co., **15** 128

Hazelden Foundation, 28 176–79

Hazeltine, Inc., **II** 20

Hazelnut Growers of Oregon, **7** 496–97

Hazleton Laboratories Corp., **30** 151

Hazlewood Foods plc, 32 251–53

Hazzard and Associates, **34** 248

HBO. *See* Home Box Office Inc.

HCA—The Healthcare Company, 35 215–18 (upd.)

HCI. *See* Holland Chemical International.

HCI Construction, **61** 125, 127

HCI Direct, Inc., 55 196–98

HCI Distribution Company, **61** 125–26

HCL America, **10** 505

HCL Sybase, **10** 505

HCR Manor Care, **25** 306, 310

HCS Technology, **26** 496–97

HDI (Haftpflichtverband der Deutschen Industrie Versicherung auf Gegenseitigkeit V.a.G.), 53 159–63

HDM Worldwide Direct, **13** 204; **16** 168

HdP. *See* Holding di Partecipazioni Industriali S.p.A.

HDR Inc., 48 203–05

HDS. *See* Heartland Express, Inc.

Head N.V., 55 199–201

Head Sportswear International, **15** 368; **16** 296–97; **43** 374

Headrick Outdoor, **27** 280

Heads and Threads, **10** 43

Headwaters Incorporated, 56 159–62

Headway Corporate Resources, Inc., 40 236–38

Headway Technologies, Inc., **49** 392–93

Heald Machine Co., **12** 67

Healing Arts Publishing, Inc., **41** 177

Healix Health Services Inc., **48** 310

Health & Tennis Corp., **25** 40

Health and Diet Group, **29** 212

Health Care & Retirement Corporation, 22 254–56; **25** 306, 310

Health Care International, **13** 328

Health Development Corp., **46** 432

Health Maintenance Organization of Pennsylvania. *See* U.S. Healthcare, Inc.

Health Management Associates, Inc., 56 163–65

Health Management Center West, **17** 559

Health-Mor Inc. *See* HMI Industries.

Health O Meter Products Inc., 14 229–31; 15 307

Health Plan of America, **11** 379

Health Plan of Virginia, **III** 389

Health Products Inc., **I** 387

Health Risk Management, Inc., 24 215–17

Health Services Capital Corporation, **64** 27

Health Services, Inc., **10** 160

Health Systems International, Inc., 11 174–76; 25 527

Healthcare, L.L.C., **29** 412

HealthCare USA, **59** 139

HealthCo International, Inc., **19** 290

Healthdyne, Inc., **17** 306–09; **25** 82

Healthmagic, Inc., **29** 412

HealthRider Corporation, **38** 238

HealthRite, Inc., **45** 209

Healthshares L.L.C., **18** 370

Healthsource Inc., **22** 143; **45** 104, 109

HealthSouth Corporation, 33 183–86 (upd.)

HealthSouth Rehabilitation Corporation, 14 232–34; 25 111

Healthtex, Inc., 17 223–25, 513

HealthTrust, **III** 80; **15** 112; **35** 215, 217

Healthy Choice, **12** 531

Hearing Aid Specialists Pty Limited, **56** 338

The Hearst Corporation, IV 625–27; 12 358–59; **19 201–04 (upd.); 21** 404; **32** 3; **46 228–32 (upd.); 51** 218–20; **54** 17, 22, 74; **56** 119

Heartland Components, **III** 519; **22** 282

Heartland Express, Inc., 13 550–51; 18 225–27

Heartland Homes, Inc., **41** 19

Heartland Industrial Partners L.P., **41** 94

Heartland Securities Corp., **32** 145
Heartstream Inc., **18** 423
The Heat Group, 53 164–66
Heatcraft Inc., **8** 320–22
Heatilator Inc., **13** 269
Heating & Cooling Supply, Inc., **52** 398–99
Heavy Duty Parts, Inc., **19** 37
Hebdo Mag International, Inc. *See* Trader Classified Media N.V.
Hebei Longteng Paper Corporation, **63** 316
Hechinger Company, 12 233–36; 28 51
Heckett Technology Services Inc., **8** 246–47
Heckler & Koch GmbH, **24** 88
Hecla Mining Company, 17 363; **20** 149, **293–96**
Hede Nielsen A/S, **47** 219
Heekin Can Inc., 10 130; **13 254–56**
Heery International, Inc., 58 156–59
Hees International Bancorp Inc. *See* Brascan Corporation.
HEFCO, **17** 106
Hefei Rongshida Group Corporation, **22** 350
Hegenscheidt-MFD GmbH & Co. KG, **53** 352
HEI Investment Corp., **9** 276
HEICO Corporation, 15 380; **30 236–38; 66** 327
Heide Park, **55** 378
Heidelberger Druckmaschinen AG, 33 346; **40 239–41**
Heidelberger Zement AG, 23 325–26; **31 250–53**
Heidelburger Drueck, **III** 301
Heidemij. *See* Arcadis NV.
Heidi Bakery, **II** 633
Heidrick & Struggles International, Inc., 14 464; **28 180–82**
Heights of Texas, fsb, **8** 437
Heijmans N.V., 66 176–78
Heil Company, **28** 103
Heileman Brewing Co. *See* G. Heileman Brewing Co.
Heilig-Meyers Company, 14 235–37; 23 412, 414; **40 242–46 (upd.)**
Heim-Plan Unternehmensgruppe, **25** 455
Heimstatt Bauspar AG, **III** 401
Heineken N.V., I 256–58, 266, 288; **II** 642; **13 257–59 (upd.); 14** 35; **17** 256; **18** 72; **21** 319; **25** 21–22; **26** 305; **34 200–04 (upd.); 59** 58–59; **63** 229
Heinrich Bauer North America, **7** 42–43
Heinrich Bauer Verlag, **23** 85–86
Heinrich Koppers GmbH, **IV** 89
Heinz Co. *See* H.J. Heinz Company.
Heinz Deichert KG, **11** 95
Heinz Italia S.p.A., **15** 221
Heisey Glasswork Company, **19** 210
Heitman Properties, **60** 184
HEL&P. *See* Houston Electric Light & Power Company.
Helados La Menorquina S.A., **22** 515
Helen of Troy Corporation, 18 228–30
Helen's Arts & Crafts, **17** 321
Helena Rubenstein, Inc., **III** 48; **8** 343–44; **9** 201–02; **30** 188; **46** 277
Helene Curtis Industries, Inc., 8 253–54; 18 217; **22** 487; **28 183–85 (upd.); 32** 476
Helikopter Services Group AS, **67** 102
Heliotrope Studios, Inc., **39** 396
Helix Biocore, **11** 458

Hella KGaA Hueck & Co., 66 179–83
Hellenic Petroleum SA, 64 175–77
Heller, Ehrman, White & McAuliffe, 41 200–02
Heller Financial, Inc., **7** 213; **16** 37; **25** 198; **63** 165
Hellman & Friedman Capital Partners III, L.P., **57** 15
Hellman, Haas & Co. *See* Smart & Final, Inc.
Helly Hansen ASA, 18 396; **25 205–07**
Helme Products, Inc., **15** 139
Helmerich & Payne, Inc., 18 231–33
Helmsley Enterprises, Inc., 9 278–80; 39 209–12 (upd.)
Helmut Delhey, **6** 428
Helmuth Hardekopf Bunker GmbH, **7** 141
Help-U-Sell, Inc., **III** 304
Helzberg Diamonds, 18 60, 63; **40 247–49**
Hemelinger Aktienbrauerei, **9** 86
Hemex, **11** 458
Hemlo Gold Mines Inc., 9 281–82; 23 40, 42
Henderson Brothers Holdings, Inc., **37** 225
Henderson-Union Electric Cooperative, **11** 37
Henijean & Cie, **III** 283
Henkel KGaA, III 31–34, 45; **9** 382; **13** 197, 199; **22** 145, 257; **30** 291; **34** 153, **205–10 (upd.); 51** 223–25
Henkel Manco Inc., 22 257–59
Henkell & Söhnlein Sektkellereien KG, **51** 102, 105
Henley Drilling Company, **9** 364
The Henley Group, Inc., I 416; **III 511–12; 6** 599–600; **9** 298; **11** 435; **12** 325; **17** 20; **37** 158
Henlys Group plc, **35** 63, 65
Hennes & Mauritz AB, 29 232–34
Hennessy Company, **19** 272
Henney Motor Company, **12** 159
Henningsen Foods, Inc., **57** 202, 204
Henredon Furniture Industries, **III** 571; **11** 534; **20** 362; **39** 266
Henri Bendel Inc., **17** 203–04
Henry Broderick, Inc., **21** 96
Henry Denny & Sons, **27** 259
Henry Gordy International, Inc. *See* EXX Inc.
Henry Holt & Co., **IV** 622–23; **13** 105; **27** 223; **35** 451
Henry I. Siegel Co., **20** 136
Henry J. Kaiser Company, Ltd., **28** 200
Henry J. Tully Corporation, **13** 531
The Henry Jones Co-op Ltd., **7** 577
Henry Jones Foods, **7** 182; **11** 212
Henry L. Doherty & Company, **12** 542
Henry Lee Company, **16** 451, 453
Henry, Leonard & Thomas Inc., **9** 533
Henry Meadows, Ltd., **13** 286
Henry Modell & Company Inc., 32 263–65
Henry Pratt Company, **7** 30–31
Henry S. Miller Companies, **21** 257
Henry Schein, Inc., 29 298; **31 254–56**
Henry Willis & Co. *See* Willis Corroon Group Plc.
Hensley & Company, 64 178–80
HEPCO. *See* Hokkaido Electric Power Company Inc.
Hepworth plc, **44** 438
Her Majesty's Stationery Office, 7 215–18

Heraclio Fournier S.A., **62** 383–84
Heraeus Holding GmbH, IV 98–100, 118; **54 159–63 (upd.)**
Heraeus Surgical, Inc., **67** 228
Herald Publishing Company, **12** 150
Heralds of Liberty, **9** 506
Herbalife International, Inc., 17 226–29; 18 164; **41 203–06 (upd.)**
Herbert Clough Inc., **24** 176
Herbert W. Davis & Co., **III** 344
Herby's Foods, **36** 163
Herco Technology, **IV** 680
Hercules Inc., I 343–45, 347; **19** 11; **22 260–63 (upd.); 28** 195; **30** 36; **66 184–88 (upd.)**
Hercules Offshore Drilling, **28** 347–48
Hereford Paper and Allied Products Ltd., **14** 430
Herff Jones, **25** 254
Heritage Bankcorp, **9** 482
Heritage Federal Savings and Loan Association of Huntington, **10** 92
Heritage House of America Inc. *See* Humana Inc.
Heritage Media Group, **25** 418
Heritage Springfield, **14** 245
Heritage 21 Construction, **60** 56
Herley Industries, Inc., 33 187–89
Herman Goelitz, Inc., 28 186–88
Herman Miller, Inc., 8 251–52, **255–57; 39** 205–07
Herman's World of Sports, **II** 628–29; **15** 470; **16** 457; **43** 385
Hermann Pfauter Group, **24** 186
Hermès International S.A., 14 238–40; 34 211–14 (upd.); 49 83
Hermosillo, **51** 389
Herrburger Brooks P.L.C., **12** 297
Herrick, Waddell & Reed. *See* Waddell & Reed, Inc.
Herring-Hall-Marvin Safe Co. of Hamilton, Ohio, **7** 145
Hershey Foods Corporation, II 510–12; 7 300; **11** 15; **12** 480–81; **15** 63–64, **219–22 (upd.)**, 323; **27** 38–40; **30** 208–09; **51 156–60 (upd.); 53** 241
F.N. Herstal. *See* Groupe Herstal S.A.
Hertel AG, **13** 297
Hertie Waren- und Kaufhaus GmbH, V 72–74; 19 234, 237
Herts Pharmaceuticals, **17** 450; **41** 375–76
The Hertz Corporation, I 130; **6** 392–93; **9 283–85; 10** 419; **11** 494; **16** 379; **21** 151; **22** 524; **24** 409; **25** 143; **33 190–93 (upd.); 36** 215; **64** 128
Hertz-Penske Leasing. *See* Penske Corporation.
Hervillier, **27** 188
Heska Corporation, 39 213–16
Hespeler Hockey Inc., **22** 204
Hess. *See* Amerada Hess Corporation.
Hess Department Stores Inc., **16** 61–62; **19** 323–24; **41** 343; **50** 107
Hessische Ludwigs-Eisenbahn-Gesellschaft, **6** 424
Hesston Corporation, **13** 17; **22** 380
Hetteen Hoist & Derrick. *See* Polaris Industries Inc.
Heublein Inc., I 259–61, 281; **7** 266–67; **14** 214; **21** 314–15; **24** 140; **25** 177; **31** 92; **34** 89
Heuer. *See* TAG Heuer International SA.
Heuga Holdings B.V., **8** 271
Hewitt & Tuttle, **17** 355–56

Hewlett-Packard Company, II 62; **III** 142–43; **6** 237–39 **(upd.)**; **8** 139, 467; **9** 7, 35–36, 57, 115, 471; **10** 15, 34, 86, 232, 257, 363, 404, 459, 464, 499, 501; **11** 46, 234, 274, 284, 382, 491, 518; **12** 61, 147, 162, 183, 470; **13** 128, 326, 501; **14** 354; **15** 125; **16** 5, 139–40, 299, 301, 367, 394, 550; **18** 386–87, 434, 436, 571; **19** 515; **20** 8; **25** 96, 118, 151–53, 499, 531; **26** 177, 520; **27** 221; **28 189–92 (upd.)**; **33** 15; **36** 3, 81–82, 299–300; **38** 20, 187, 417–19; **41** 117, 288; **43** 294; **50 222–30 (upd.)**; **51** 150; **63** 33, 125, 153

Hexalon, **26** 420

Hexcel Corporation, 11 475; **27** 50; **28** 193–95

Heyer-Schulte, **26** 286

Heytesbury Party Ltd., **34** 422

HFC. *See* Household Finance Corporation.

HFS Inc., **21** 97; **22** 54, 56; **53** 275

HG Hawker Engineering Co. Ltd. *See* Hawker Siddeley Group PLC.

HGCC. *See* Hysol Grafil Composite Components Co.

HH Finch Ltd., **38** 501

HI. *See* Houston Industries Incorporated.

Hi-Bred Corn Company, **9** 410

Hi-Flier, Inc. *See* EXX Inc.

Hi-Lo Automotive, Inc., **26** 348–49

Hi Tech Consignments, **18** 208

Hi-Tek Polymers, Inc., **8** 554

Hibbett Sporting Goods, Inc., 26 189–91

Hibbing Taconite Company, **62** 74

Hibernia Corporation, 37 187–90

Hickman Coward & Wattles, **24** 444

Hickory Farms, Inc., 12 178, 199; **17** 230–32

Hickory Specialties, Inc., **63** 69, 71

Hickorycraft, **III** 571; **20** 362

Hicks & Greist, **6** 40

Hicks, Muse, Tate & Furst, Inc., **24** 106; **30** 220; **36** 423; **55** 202

Hicksgas Gifford, Inc., **6** 529

Hidden Creek Industries, Inc., **16** 397; **24** 498

HiFi Buys, **30** 465

Higgs International Ltd., **51** 130

High Integrity Systems, **51** 16

High Retail System Co. *See* Takashimaya Co., Limited.

Highgate Hotels, Inc., **21** 93

Highland Distillers Ltd., **60** 355

Highland Gold Ltd., **63** 182, 184

Highland Superstores, **9** 65–66; **10** 9–10, 304–05, 468; **23** 51–52

Highland Telephone Company, **6** 334

Highlander Publications, **38** 307–08

Highmark Inc., I 109; **27 208–11**

Highsmith Inc., 60 167–70

Highteam Public Relations Co. Ltd., **60** 143

Highveld Steel and Vanadium Corporation Limited, 59 224–27

Hilbun Poultry, **10** 250

Hildebrandt International, 29 235–38

Hilex Poly Co., Inc., **8** 477

Hill & Knowlton Inc. *See* WPP Group PLC.

Hill 50 Ltd., **63** 182, 184

Hill-Rom Company, **10** 349–50

Hill's Pet Nutrition, Inc., 14 123; **26** 207; **27** 212–14, 390. *See also* Colgate-Palmolive Company.

Hillard Oil and Gas Company, Inc., **11** 523

Hillards, PLC, **II** 678

Hillenbrand Industries, Inc., 10 349–51; 16 20

Hiller Aircraft Company, **9** 205; **48** 167

Hiller Group, **14** 286

Hillerich & Bradsby Company, Inc., 24 403; **51 161–64**

The Hillhaven Corporation, 14 241–43; 16 57, 515, 517; **25** 456

Hillos GmbH, **53** 169

Hills & Dales Railway Co. *See* Dayton Power & Light Company.

Hills Brothers Inc., **II** 548; **7** 383; **28** 311

Hills Pet Products, **III** 25

Hills Stores Company, 11 228; **13** 260–61; **21** 459; **30** 57

Hillsborough Holdings Corporation. *See* Walter Industries, Inc.

Hillsdale Machine & Tool Company, **8** 514

Hillsdown Holdings, PLC, IV 513–14; **24** 218–21 **(upd.)**; **28** 490; **41** 252

Hillside Industries Inc., **18** 118

Hilo Electric Light Company, **9** 276

Hilti AG, 53 167–69

Hilton Athletic Apparel, **16** 296–97

Hilton Group plc, 49 191–95 (upd.), 449–50

Hilton Hotels Corporation, III 91–93; 9 95, 426; **19 205–08 (upd.)**; **21** 91, 93, 182, 333, 363; **23** 482; **27** 10; **54** 345–46; **62 176–79 (upd.)**. *See also* Hilton Group plc.

Hilton International Co., **6** 385; **12** 489

Himley Brick, **14** 248

Himolene, Inc., **8** 181

Hinde & Dauch Paper Company, **19** 496

Hinds, Hayden & Eldredge, **10** 135

Hines Horticulture, Inc., 49 196–98

Hino Motors, Ltd., 7 219–21; 21 163, 271–74 **(upd.)**; **23** 288

Hinomaru Truck Co., **6** 428

HIP Health Plan, **22** 425

Hipercor, S.A., **V** 52; **26** 129

Hiram Walker Resources Ltd., I 262–64; 6 478; **18** 41

Hiram Walker-Consumers' Home Ltd. *See* Consumers' Gas Company Ltd.

Hiram Walker-Gooderham & Worts Ltd., **29** 18

Hire-Purchase Company of Ireland, **16** 13; **43** 7

Hiroshima Yakult Co., **25** 449

The Hirsh Company, **17** 279

Hirth-Krause Company. *See* Wolverine World Wide Inc.

Hirz, **25** 85

Hispanic Broadcasting Corporation, 35 219–22; **41** 383, 385

Hispanoil. *See* Hispanica de Petroleos.

History Book Club, **13** 105–06

Hit de Venezuela, **54** 73

HIT Entertainment PLC, 40 250–52

Hit or Miss. *See* The TJX Companies, Inc.

Hitachi, Ltd., **I** 454–55; **III** 140, 143, 464, 482; **7** 425; **9** 297; **11** 45, 308; **12** 237–39 **(upd.)**; **14** 201; **16** 139; **17** 353, 556; **18** 383; **19** 11; **21** 174–75, 390; **23** 53; **24** 324; **40 253–57 (upd.)**

Hitachi Metals, Ltd., IV 101–02

Hitachi Zosen Corporation, III 513–14; **8** 449; **53 170–73 (upd.)**

Hitchiner Manufacturing Co., Inc., 23 267–70

Hi3G, **63** 208

Hjalmar Blomqvist A.B., **II** 639

HL&P. *See* Houston Lighting and Power Company.

HLH Products, **7** 229

HMI Industries, Inc., 17 233–35

HMO-PA. *See* U.S. Healthcare, Inc.

HMSHost Corp., **49** 31; **63** 322

HMT Technology Corp., **IV** 102

HMV Group plc, 59 228–30; 64 304

Ho-Chunk Inc., 61 125–28

Hoan Products Ltd. *See* Lifetime Hoan Corporation.

HOB Entertainment, Inc., 37 191–94

Hobart Corporation. *See* KitchenAid, Inc; Whirlpool Corporation.

Hobart Manufacturing Company, **8** 298

Hobby Lobby Stores Inc., **17** 360

Hobson, Bates & Partners, Ltd., **14** 48

Hochschild, Kohn Department Stores, **II** 673

Hochtief AG, 14 298; **17** 376; **24** 88; **33** 194–97

The Hockey Company, 34 215–18

Hocking Glass Company, **13** 40

Hockleys Professional Limited, **55** 281

Hodenpyl-Walbridge & Company, **14** 134

Hodgart Consulting. *See* Hildebrandt International.

Hoechst AG, I 346–48, 605, 632, 669–70; **8** 262, 451–53; **13** 262–64; **18 234–37 (upd.)**, 401; **21** 544; **22** 32; **25** 376; **34** 284; **35** 455–57; **38** 380; **50** 420; **60** 132

Hoechst Celanese Corporation, 8 562; **11** 436; **12** 118; **13** 118, 262–65; **22** 278; **24** 151; **26** 108; **54** 51–52

Hoeganaes Corporation, **8** 274–75

Hoenig Group Inc., 41 207–09

Hoesch AG, IV 103–06

Hofbräubierzentrale GmbH Saarbrücken, **41** 222

Hoffman Enclosures Inc., **26** 361, 363

Hoffmann-La Roche & Co. *See* F. Hoffmann- La Roche & Co.

Hoffritz, **27** 288

Hofmann Herbold & Partner, **34** 249

Hogan & Hartson L.L.P., 44 220–23; 47 445–46

Hogatron, **60** 364

Hogue Cellars, **50** 520

Hohner. *See* Matth. Hohner AG.

Hojalata y Laminas S.A., **19** 10

Hojgaard & Schultz, **38** 436

HOK Group, Inc., 59 231–33

Hokkaido Electric Power Company Inc. (HEPCO), V 635–37; **58 160–63 (upd.)**

Hokkaido Forwarding, **6** 428

Hokuriku Electric Power Company, V 638–40

Hokuyo Sangyo Co., Ltd., **IV** 285

Holberg Industries, Inc., 36 266–69

Holbrook Grocery Co., **II** 682

Holcemca B.V., **51** 29

Holcim, Ltd., **51** 27, 29; **59** 111, 115

Holco BV, **41** 12

Holcroft & Company, **7** 521

Hold Everything, **17** 548–50

Holden Ltd., 62 180–83

Holden Meehan. *See* Bradford & Bingley PLC.

Holderbank Financière Glaris Ltd., III 701–02; **8** 258–59, 456; **39** 217. *See also* Holnam Inc

Holding di Partecipazioni Industriali S.p.A., **52** 120, 122
N.V. Holdingmaatschappij De Telegraaf, 23 271–73
Holec Control Systems, **26** 496
Holes-Webway Company, **40** 44
Holga, Inc., **13** 269
Holgate Toys, **25** 379–80
Holiday Corp., **16** 263; **22** 418; **38** 76; **43** 226
Holiday Inns, Inc., III 94–95; **6** 383; **9** 425–26; **10** 12; **11** 178, 242; **13** 362; **14** 106; **15** 44, 46; **16** 262; **18** 216; **21** 361–62; **23** 71; **24** 253; **25** 386; **27** 21. *See also* The Promus Cos., Inc.
Holiday Magic, Inc., **17** 227
Holiday Mart, **17** 124; **41** 114–15
Holiday Rambler Corporation, **7** 213; **25** 198
Holiday RV Superstores, Incorporated, 26 192–95
Holland & Barrett, **13** 103; **31** 346, 348
Holland & Holland, **49** 84
Holland & Knight LLP, 60 171–74
Holland America Line. *See* Carnival Corporation.
Holland Burgerville USA, 44 224–26
Holland Casino, **23** 229
Holland Chemical International, **59** 391
Holland Electro B.V., **17** 234
Holland Graphic Occasions, **64** 226
Holland Motor Express, **14** 505
Holland Studio Craft, **38** 402
Hollander Home Fashions Corp., 67 207–09
Hollandse Signaalapparaten, **13** 402; **50** 300
Holley Performance Products Inc., 52 157–60
Hollinger Hardware Limited. *See* Home Hardware Stores Limited.
Hollinger International, Inc., 24 222–25; **32** 358; **62** 184–88 **(upd.)**
Hollingsead International, Inc., **36** 158–60
Holloway-Staubach Corporation. *See* The Staubach Company.
Holly Corporation, 12 240–42; **61** 117
Holly Farms Corp., **7** 422–24; **23** 376–77
Holly Sugar Company. *See* Imperial Holly Corporation.
Hollywood Casino Corporation, 21 275–77
Hollywood Entertainment Corporation, 25 208–10; **29** 504; **31** 339
Hollywood Media Corporation, 58 164–68
Hollywood Park, Inc., 20 297–300
Hollywood Park Race Track, **29** 118
Hollywood Pictures, **II** 174; **30** 487
Holme Roberts & Owen LLP, 28 196–99
Holmen AB, 52 161–65 **(upd.)**
Holmes International. *See* Miller Industries, Inc.
Holnam Inc., III 702; **8** 258–60; **39** 217–20 **(upd.)**
Holophane Corporation, 19 209–12; **54** 255
Holson Burnes Group, Inc., 14 244–45
Holsten Brauerei AG, **35** 256, 258
Holt and Bugbee Company, 66 189–91
Holt, Rinehart and Winston, Inc., **IV** 623–24; **12** 224
Holt's Cigar Holdings, Inc., 42 176–78
Holthouse Furniture Corp., **14** 236

Holtzbrinck. *See* Verlagsgruppe Georg von Holtzbrinck.
Holvick Corp., **11** 65
Holvis AG, **15** 229
Holyman Sally Ltd., **29** 431
Holyoke Food Mart Inc., **19** 480
Holzer and Co., **III** 569; **20** 361
Homart Development Co., **57** 156
Home & Automobile Insurance Co., **III** 214
Home and Community Care, Inc., **43** 46
Home Box Office Inc., 7 222–24, 528–29; **10** 196; **18** 65; **23** 274–77 **(upd.)**, 500; **25** 498
Home Builders Supply, Inc. *See* Scotty's, Inc.
Home Centers of America, Inc., **18** 286
Home Choice Holdings, Inc., **33** 366–67
The Home Depot, Inc., V 75–76; **9** 400; **10** 235; **11** 384–86; **12** 7, 235, 345, 385; **13** 250, 548; **16** 187–88, 457; **17** 366; **18** 238–40 **(upd.)**; **19** 248, 250; **21** 356, 358; **22** 477; **23** 232; **26** 306; **27** 416, 481; **31** 20; **35** 11–13; **39** 134; **43** 385; **44** 332–33
Home Entertainment of Texas, Inc., **30** 466
Home Hardware Stores Ltd., 62 189–91
Home Insurance Company, III 262–64
Home Interiors & Gifts, Inc., 15 475, 477; **55** 202–04
Home Nutritional Services, **17** 308
Home Office Reference Laboratory, Inc., **22** 266
Home Oil Company Ltd., **I** 264; **6** 477–78
Home Products International, Inc., 18 492; **55** 205–07
Home Properties Co., Inc., **21** 95
Home Properties of New York, Inc., 42 179–81
Home Quarters Warehouse, Inc., **12** 233, 235
Home Savings of America, **16** 346; **28** 167; **47** 160
The Home School, Inc., **41** 111
Home Shopping Network, Inc., V 77–78; **9** 428; **18** 76; **24** 517; **25** 211–15 **(upd.)**; **26** 441; **33** 322. *See also* HSN.
Home Telephone and Telegraph Company, **10** 201
Home Telephone Company. *See* Rochester Telephone Corporation.
Home Vision Entertainment Inc., **31** 339–40
HomeBase, Inc., II 658; **13** 547–48; **33** 198–201 **(upd.)**
HomeBuyers Preferred, Inc., **51** 210
HomeChef, Inc. *See* Viking Range Corporation.
HomeClub Inc., **13** 547–48; **16** 187; **17** 366. *See also* HomeBase, Inc.
HomeFed Bank, **10** 340
Homegrocer.com Inc., **38** 223
Homelite, **21** 175
Homemade Ice Cream Company, **10** 371
Homemakers Furniture. *See* John M. Smyth Co.
HomeMax, Inc., **41** 20
Homes By Oakwood, Inc., **15** 328
Homeserve.net Ltd., **46** 72
Homestake Mining Company[ro12 243–45; **20** 72; **27** 456; **38** 229–32 **(upd.)**
Hometown Auto Retailers, Inc., 44 227–29

HomeTown Buffet, Inc., **19** 435; **22** 465. *See also* Buffets, Inc
Homette Corporation, **30** 423
Homewood Suites, **9** 425–26
Hominal Developments Inc., **9** 512
Hon Hai Precision Industry Co., Ltd., 59 234–36
Hon Industries Inc., 13 266–69; **23** 243–45
Honam Oil Refinery, **II** 53
Honda Giken Kogyo Kabushiki Kaisha. *See* Honda Motor Company Limited.
Honda Motor Company Limited, I 174–76; **7** 459; **8** 71–72; **9** 294, 340–42; **10** 352–54 **(upd.)**; **11** 33, 49–50, 352; **12** 122, 401; **13** 30; **16** 167; **17** 25; **21** 153; **23** 289–90, 338, 340; **25** 197–99; **27** 76; **29** 239–42 **(upd.)**; **34** 305–06; **36** 243; **55** 326; **59** 393–94, 397
Honey Bear Tree. *See* Furth Pharmacy. Inc.
Honeywell Inc., I 63; **II** 40–43; **8** 21; **9** 171, 324; **11** 198, 265; **12** 246–49 **(upd.)**; **13** 234, 499; **17** 33; **18** 341; **22** 373, 436; **23** 471; **29** 464; **30** 34; **33** 334, 337; **43** 284; **50** 231–35 **(upd.)**; **63** 161
Hong Kong Dragon Airlines Ltd., 18 114; **66** 192–94
Hong Kong Fortune, **62** 63
Hong Kong Industrial Co., Ltd., **25** 312
Hong Kong Island Line Co., **IV** 718
Hong Kong Mass Transit Railway Corp., **19** 111
Hong Kong Ming Wah Shipping Co., **52** 80
Hong Kong Resort Co., **IV** 718; **38** 320
Hong Kong Telecommunications Ltd., 6 319–21; **18** 114. *See also* Cable & Wireless HKT.
Hong Kong Telephone Company, **47** 177
Hong Leong Group Malaysia, **26** 3, 5
Hongkong & Kowloon Wharf & Godown Company, **20** 312
Hongkong and Shanghai Banking Corporation Limited, II 296–99; **17** 325; **18** 253; **25** 12. *See also* HSBC Holdings plc.
Hongkong Electric Company Ltd., 6 498–500; **20** 134
Hongkong Electric Holdings Ltd., 23 278–81 **(upd.)**; **47** 177
Hongkong Land Holdings Ltd., IV 699–701; **6** 498–99; **23** 280; **47** 175–78 **(upd.)**
Honolua Plantation Land Company, Inc., **29** 308
Honshu Paper Co., Ltd., IV 284–85, 292, 297, 321, 326; **57** 274–75
Hood Rubber Company, **15** 488–89
Hood Sailmakers, Inc., **10** 215
Hoogovens. *See* Koninklijke Nederlandsche Hoogovens en Staalfabricken NV.
Hook's Drug Stores, **9** 67
Hooker Corp., **19** 324
Hooker Furniture Corp. *See* Bassett Furniture Industries, Inc.
Hooper Holmes, Inc., 22 264–67
Hoorcomfort Nederland B.V., **56** 338
Hoosier Insurance Company, **51** 39
Hoosier Park L.P., **29** 118
Hooters of America, Inc., 18 241–43

The Hoover Company, **12** 158, **250–52**; **15** 416, 418; **21** 383; **30** 75, 78; **40** 258–62 (upd.)
Hoover Group Inc., **18** 11
Hoover Treated Wood Products, Inc., **12** 396
Hopkinsons Group. *See* Carbo PLC.
Hopkinton LNG Corp., **14** 126
Hopper Soliday and Co. Inc., **14** 154
Hops Restaurant Bar and Brewery, **31** 41; **46 233–36**
Hopwood & Company, **22** 427
Horace Mann Educators Corporation, **22 268–70**
Horizon Air Industries, Inc. *See* Alaska Air Group, Inc.
Horizon Corporation, **8** 348
Horizon Group Inc., **27** 221
Horizon Healthcare Corporation, **25** 456
Horizon Holidays, **14** 36
Horizon Industries, **19** 275
Horizon Lamps, Inc., **48** 299
Horizon Organic Holding Corporation, **37 195–99**
Horizon Travel Group, **8** 527
Horizon/CMS Healthcare Corp., **25** 111, 457; **33** 185
Horizons Laitiers, **25** 85
Hormel Foods Corporation, **18 244–47** (upd.); **54 164–69** (upd.); **59** 102
Horn Venture Partners, **22** 464
Hornbrook, Inc., **14** 112
Horne's, **16** 62
Horsehead Industries, Inc., **51 165–67**
Horseshoe Gaming Holding Corporation, **62 192–95**
Horsham Corp. *See* TrizecHahn.
Horst Breuer GmbH, **20** 363
Horst Salons Inc., **24** 56
Horten, **47** 107; **50** 117, 119
Hortifrut, S.A., **62** 154
Horton Homes, Inc., **25 216–18**
Hoshienu Pharmaceutical Co. Ltd., **58** 134
Hoshino Gakki Co. Ltd., **55 208–11**
Hosiery Corporation International. *See* HCI Direct, Inc.
Hospal SA, **49** 156
Hospital Central Services, Inc., **56 166–68**
Hospital Corporation of America, **III 78–80**; **15** 112; **23** 153; **27** 237; **53** 345. *See also* HCA - The Healthcare Company.
Hospital Cost Consultants, **11** 113
Hospital Management Associates, Inc. *See* Health Management Associates, Inc.
Hospital Products, Inc., **10** 534
Hospital Specialty Co., **37** 392
Hospitality Franchise Systems, Inc., **11 177–79**; **14** 106; **17** 236. *See also* Cendant Corporation.
Hospitality Worldwide Services, Inc., **26 196–98**
Hosposable Products, Inc. *See* Wyant Corporation.
Host Communications Inc., **24** 404
Host Marriott Corporation, **21** 366
Host Marriott Services Corp., **16** 446; **17** 95. *See also* HMSHost
Hot 'n Now, **16** 96–97
Hot Dog Construction Co., **12** 372
Hot Sam Co., **12** 179, 199. *See also* Mrs. Fields' Original Cookies, Inc.
Hot Shoppes Inc. *See* Marriott.

Hot Topic, Inc., **33 202–04**
Hotel Corporation of America, **16** 337
Hotel Corporation of India, **27** 26
Hotel Properties Ltd., **30** 107
Hotel Reservations Network, Inc., **47** 420
Hotels By Pleasant, **62** 276
HotRail Inc., **36** 124
HotWired, **45** 200
Houbigant, **37** 270
Houchens Industries Inc., **51 168–70**
Houghton Mifflin Company, **10 355–57**; **26** 215; **36 270–74** (upd.); **46** 441
Houlihan's Restaurant Group, **25** 546
Housatonic Power Co., **13** 182
House of Blues, **32** 241, 244
House of Fabrics, Inc., **16** 197–98; **18** 223; **21 278–80**
House of Fraser PLC, **21** 353; **37** 6, 8; **45 188–91**; **47** 173. *See also* Harrods Holdings.
House of Miniatures, **12** 264
House of Windsor, Inc., **9** 533
Household International, Inc., **II 417–20**, 605; **7** 569–70; **8** 117; **10** 419; **16** 487–88; **21 281–86** (upd.); **22** 38, 542; **24** 152
Household Rental Systems, **17** 234
Housing Development Finance Corporation, **20** 313
Housmex Inc., **23** 171
Houston Airport Leather Concessions LLC, **58** 369
Houston, Effler & Partners Inc., **9** 135
Houston Electric Light & Power Company, **44** 368
Houston Industries Incorporated, **V 641–44**; **7** 376. *See also* Reliant Energy Inc.
Houston International Teleport, Inc., **11** 184
Houston Oil & Minerals Corp., **11** 440–41
Houston Pipe Line Company, **45** 21
Hoveringham Group, **III** 753; **28** 450
Hoving Corp., **14** 501
Hovnanian Enterprises, Inc., **29 243–45**
Howard B. Stark Candy Co., **15** 325
Howard Flint Ink Company, **13** 227
Howard H. Sweet & Son, Inc., **14** 502
Howard Hughes Corporation, **63** 341
Howard Hughes Medical Institute, **39 221–24**
Howard Hughes Properties, Ltd., **17** 317
Howard Humphreys, **13** 119
Howard Johnson International, Inc., **7** 266; **11** 177–78; **15** 36; **16** 156; **17 236–39**; **25** 309; **52** 280–81. *See also* Prime Hospitality Corporation.
Howard Research and Development Corporation, **15** 412, 414
Howard, Smith & Levin, **40** 126
Howden. *See* Alexander Howden Group.
Howdy Company, **9** 177
Howe & Fant, Inc., **23** 82
Howe Sound Co., **12** 253
Howmedica, **29** 455
Howmet Corporation, **12 IV 253–55**; **22** 506
Hoyle Products, **62** 384
Hoyt Archery Company, **10** 216
HP. *See* Hewlett-Packard Company.
HPI Health Care Services, **49** 307–08
HQ Global Workplaces, Inc., **47** 331
HQ Office International, **8** 405; **23** 364
HRB Business Services, **29** 227

Hrubitz Oil Company, **12** 244
HSBC Holdings plc, **12 256–58**; **17** 323, 325–26; **26 199–204** (upd.); **60** 161–62
HSG. *See* Helikopter Services Group AS.
Hsiang-Li Investment Corp., **51** 123
HSN, **25** 411; **64 181–85** (upd.)
HSS Hire Service Group PLC, **45** 139–41
HTH, **12** 464
HTM Goedkoop, **26** 278–79; **55** 200
H2O Plus, **11** 41
Hua Bei Oxygen, **25** 82
Hua Yang Printing Holdings Co. Ltd., **60** 372
Hub Group, Inc., **26** 533; **38 233–35**
Hub Services, Inc., **18** 366
Hubbard Air Transport, **10** 162
Hubbard, Baker & Rice, **10** 126
Hubbard Broadcasting Inc., **24 226–28**
Hubbard Construction Co., **23** 332
Hubbell Incorporated, **9 286–87**; **31 257–59** (upd.)
Huck Manufacturing Company, **22** 506
Hudepohl-Schoenling Brewing Co., **18** 72; **50** 114
Hudson Automobile Company, **18** 492
The Hudson Bay Mining and Smelting Company, Limited, **12 259–61**; **13** 502–03; **16** 29
Hudson Foods Inc., **13 270–72**
Hudson Housewares Corp., **16** 389
Hudson I.C.S., **58** 53
Hudson Pharmaceutical Corp., **31** 347
Hudson River Bancorp, Inc., **41 210–13**
Hudson Software, **13** 481
Hudson's. *See* Target Corporation.
Hudson's Bay Company, **V 79–81**; **8** 525; **12** 361; **25 219–22** (upd.)
Hue International, **8** 324
Hueppe Duscha, **III** 571; **20** 362
Huffman Manufacturing Company, **7** 225–26
Huffy Bicycles Co., **19** 383
Huffy Corporation, **7 225–27**; **26** 184, 412; **30 239–42** (upd.)
Hugerot, **19** 50
Hugh O'Neill Auto Co., **12** 309
Hughes Air West, **25** 421
Hughes Aircraft Corporation, **7** 426–27; **9** 409; **10** 327; **13** 356, 398; **15** 528, 530; **21** 201; **23** 134; **24** 442; **25** 86, 223; **30** 175. *See also* GM Hughes Electronics Corporation.
Hughes Communications, Inc., **13** 398; **18** 211
Hughes Corp., **18** 535
Hughes Electronics Corporation, **25 223–25**; **36** 240, 243; **38** 175, 375; **46** 327; **54** 72, 74; **64** 151
Hughes Helicopter, **26** 431; **46** 65
Hughes Hubbard & Reed LLP, **44 230–32**
Hughes Markets, Inc., **22 271–73**
Hughes Network Systems Inc., **21** 239
Hughes Properties, Inc., **17** 317
Hughes Space and Communications Company, **33** 47–48
Hughes Supply, Inc., **14 246–47**; **39** 360
Hughes Television Network, **11** 184
Hughes Tool Co. *See* Baker Hughes Incorporated.
Hugo Boss AG, **48 206–09**
Hugo Neu Corporation, **19** 381–82
Hugo Stinnes GmbH, **8** 69, 494–95; **50** 168

Huhtamäki Oyj, 30 396, 398; **64 186–88**
HUK-Coburg, 58 169–73
The Hull Group, L.L.C., **51** 148
Hulman & Company, 44 233–36; 46 245
Hüls A.G., I 349–50; 25 82. *See also*
Degussa-Hüls AG.
Hulton, **17** 397
Hulton Getty, **31** 216–17
Human Services Computing, Inc. *See* Epic
Systems Corporation.
Humana Inc., III 81–83; 15 113; **24
229–32 (upd.); 35** 215–16; **53** 185; **54**
48
**The Humane Society of the United
States, 54 170–73**
Humanetics Corporation, **29** 213
Humanities Software, **39** 341
Humberside Sea & Land Services, **31** 367
Humble Oil & Refining Company, **13** 118;
14 291. *See also* Exxon.
Hummel Lanolin Corporation, **45** 126
Hummel-Reise, **44** 432
Hummer, Winblad Venture Partners, **36**
157
Hummingbird, **18** 313
Humongous Entertainment, Inc., **31**
238–40
Humps' n Horns, **55** 312
Hunco Ltd., **IV** 640; **26** 273
Hungarian-Soviet Civil Air Transport Joint
Stock Company. *See* Malæv Plc.
**Hungry Howie's Pizza and Subs, Inc., 25
226–28**
Hungry Minds, Inc. *See* John Wiley &
Sons, Inc.
**Hunt Consolidated, Inc., 27 215–18
(upd.)**
**Hunt Manufacturing Company, 12
262–64**
Hunt Oil Company, 7 228–30[ro. *See
also* Hunt Consolidated, Inc.
Hunt-Wesson, Inc., 17 240–42; 25 278
Hunter-Douglas, **8** 235
Hunter Fan Company, 13 273–75
**Huntingdon Life Sciences Group plc, 42
182–85**
Huntington Bancshares Inc., 11 180–82
**Huntington Learning Centers, Inc., 55
212–14**
Hunton & Williams, 35 223–26
**Huntsman Chemical Corporation, 8
261–63; 9** 305
Huntstown Power Company Ltd., **64** 404
Hupp Motor Car Company, **8** 74; **10** 261
Hurd & Houghton, **10** 355
Huron Steel Company, Inc., **16** 357
**Hurricane Hydrocarbons Ltd., 54
174–77**
Huse Food Group, **14** 352
Husky Energy Inc., 47 179–82; 49 203
Husky Oil Ltd., **IV** 695; **18** 253–54; **19**
159
Husqvarna AB, **53** 126–27
Husqvarna Forest & Garden Company, **13**
564
Hussmann Corporation, **I** 457–58; **7**
429–30; **10** 554; **13** 268; **22** 353–54; **67**
299
Hutcheson & Grundy, **29** 286
Hutchinson-Mapa, **IV** 560
**Hutchinson Technology Incorporated, 18
248–51; 63 190–94 (upd.)**
Hutchison Microtel, **11** 548

Hutchison Whampoa Limited, 18 114,
252–55; 25 101; **47** 181; **49 199–204
(upd.)**
Huth Inc., **56** 230
Huth Manufacturing Corporation, **10** 414
Hüttenwerke Kayser AG, **62** 253
Huttepain, **61** 155
Huttig Building Products, **31** 398, 400
Huttig Sash & Door Company, **8** 135
HVB Group, 59 237–44 (upd.)
Hvide Marine Incorporated, 22 274–76
HWI. *See* Hardware Wholesalers, Inc.
Hy-Form Products, Inc., **22** 175
Hy-Vee, Inc., 36 275–78; 42 432
Hyatt-Clark Industries Inc., **45** 170
Hyatt Corporation, III 96–97; 9 426; **16
273–75 (upd.); 22** 101; **23** 482; **48** 148;
64 393, 395
Hyatt Legal Services, **20** 435; **29** 226
Hyco-Cascade Pty. Ltd. *See* Cascade
Corporation.
**Hyde Athletic Industries, Inc., 17
243–45.** *See* Saucony Inc.
Hyde Company, A.L., **7** 116–17
Hyder Investments Ltd., **51** 173
Hyder plc, 34 219–21; 52 375
Hydra Computer Systems, Inc., **13** 201
Hydrac GmbH, **38** 300
Hydril Company, 46 237–39
Hydro-Aire Incorporated, **8** 135
Hydro Carbide Corp., **19** 152
Hydro-Carbon Light Company, **9** 127
Hydro Electric, **19** 389–90; **49** 363–64
Hydro-Electric Power Commission of
Ontario, **6** 541; **9** 461
Hydro Med Sciences, **13** 367
**Hydro-Quebéc, 6 501–03; 32 266–69
(upd.)**
Hydrocarbon Technologies, Inc., **56** 161
Hydrodynamic Cutting Services, **56** 134
Hyer Boot, **19** 232
Hygeia Sciences, Inc., **8** 85, 512
Hygrade Foods, **14** 536
Hygrade Operators Inc., **55** 20
Hylsa. *See* Hojalata y Laminas S.A.
Hylsamex, S.A. de C.V., 39 225–27
Hynix Semiconductor Inc., **56** 173
Hyper Shoppes, Inc., **II** 670; **18** 507; **50**
456–57
Hypercom Corporation, 27 219–21
**Hyperion Software Corporation, 22
277–79**
Hypermart USA, **8** 555–56
Hyplains Beef, **7** 175
Hypo-Bank. *See* Bayerische Hypotheken-
und Wechsel-Bank AG.
Hypobaruk, **III** 348
Hyponex Corp., **22** 475
Hyster Company, 17 246–48; 33 364
Hyster-Yale Materials Handling, Inc., **I**
424; **7** 369–71
Hyundai Group, I 207, 516; **III 515–17;
7 231–34 (upd.); 9** 350; **10** 404; **13** 280,
293–94; **23** 353; **25** 469; **29** 264, 266;
47 279; **56 169–73 (upd.); 64** 106

I Can't Believe It's Yogurt, Inc., **17** 474;
35 121
I Pellettieri d'Italia S.p.A., **45** 342
I. Appel, **30** 23
I.B. Kleinert Rubber Company, **37** 399
I.C. Isaacs & Company, 31 260–62
I.D. Systems, Inc., **11** 444
I-DIKA Milan SRL, **12** 182

I. Feldman Co., **31** 359
I.G. Farbenindustrie AG, **8** 108–09; **11** 7;
13 262; **21** 544; **26** 452; **59** 15. *See also*
BASF A.G.; Bayer A.G.; Hoechst A.G.
I.M. Pei & Associates, **I** 580; **41** 143. *See
also* Pei Cobb Freed & Partners
Architects LLP.
I. Magnin Inc., **8** 444; **15** 86; **24** 422; **30**
383; **31** 191, 193
I.N. Kote, **IV** 116; **19** 219
I.N. Tek, **IV** 116; **19** 219
I-X Corp., **22** 416
IAC/InterActiveCorp., **64** 181
Iacon, Inc., **49** 299, 301
IAL. *See* International Aeradio Limited.
IAM/Environmental, **18** 11
Iams Company, 26 205–07; 27 213
IAWS Group plc, 46 405; **49 205–08**
IBANCO, **26** 515
Ibanez. *See* Hoshino Gakki Co. Ltd.
IBC Group plc, **58** 189, 191
IBC Holdings Corporation, **12** 276
IBCA. *See* International Banking and
Credit Analysis.
Iberdrola, S.A., V 608; **47** 110; **49
209–12**
**Iberia Líneas Aéreas De España S.A., 6
95–97; 33** 18; **36 279–83 (upd.)**
IBERIABANK Corporation, 37 200–02
Iberpistas. *See* Abertis Infraestructuras,
S.A.
Iberswiss Catering. *See* Iberia.
IBH Holding AG, **7** 513
IBJ. *See* The Industrial Bank of Japan Ltd.
IBM. *See* International Business Machines
Corporation.
IBM Foods, Inc., **51** 280
IBP, Inc., II 515–17; 7 525; **21 287–90
(upd.); 23** 201
IBS Conversions Inc., **27** 492
Ibstock Brick Ltd., 37 203–06 (upd.)
Ibstock plc, 14 248–50
IC Designs, Inc., **48** 127
IC Industries Inc., I 456–58; 7 430; **10**
414, 553; **18** 3; **22** 197; **43** 217. *See also*
Whitman Corporation.
ICA AB, II 639–40
ICA Fluor Daniel, S. de R.L. de C.V., **41**
148
ICA Mortgage Corporation, **8** 30
Icahn Capital Corp., **35** 143
Icarus Consulting AG, **29** 376
ICEE-USA, **24** 240
Iceland Group plc, 33 205–07
Icelandair, 52 166–69
Icelandic Air, **49** 80
**ICF Kaiser International, Inc., 28
200–04**
ICH Corporation, **19** 468
Ichikoh Industries Ltd., **26** 154
ICI. *See* Imperial Chemical Industries plc.
ICI Canada, **22** 436
ICL plc, II 65, 81; **III** 141, 164; **6
240–42; 11** 150; **16** 226
ICM Mortgage Corporation, **8** 436
ICN Pharmaceuticals, Inc., 52 170–73
Icon Health & Fitness, Inc., 38 236–39
Icon International, **24** 445
iConcepts, Inc., **39** 95
Icot Corp., **18** 543
ICS. *See* International Care Services.
ICS, **26** 119
ID, Inc., **9** 193
id Software, **31** 237–38; **32** 9

Idaho Power Company, 12 265–67
IDB Communications Group, Inc., 11
  183–85; 20 48; **27** 301, 307
IDC, **25** 101
Ideal Basic Industries, **III** 701–02; **8**
  258–59; **12** 18
Ideal Corp., **23** 335
Ideal Loisirs Group, **23** 388
Ideas Publishing Group, **59** 134
IDEC Pharmaceuticals Corporation, **32** 214
Idemitso Petrochemicals, **8** 153
Idemitsu Kosan Co., Ltd., IV 434–36,
  476, 519; **49 213–16 (upd.); 63** 308,
  311–12
Identification Business, Inc., **18** 140
Identix Inc., 44 237–40
IDEO Inc., 65 171–73
IDEXX Laboratories, Inc., 23 282–84
IDG Books Worldwide, Inc., 27 222–24.
  See also International Data Group, Inc.
IDG Communications, Inc, **7** 238
IDG World Expo Corporation, **7** 239
IDI, **22** 365
IDI Temps, **34** 372
IDO. *See* Nippon Idou Tsushin.
Ido Bathroom Ltd., **51** 324
IDS Ltd., **22** 76
IDT Corporation, 34 222–24; 58 124; **63**
  44
IDX Systems Corporation, 64 189–92
IEC Electronics Corp., 42 186–88
Iecsa S.A. *See* Sideco Americana S.A.
IEL. *See* Industrial Equity Ltd.
IFC Disposables, Inc., **30** 496–98
IFF. *See* International Flavors &
  Fragrances Inc.
Ifil, **27** 515
IFM, **25** 85
Ifö Sanitär AB, **51** 324
IG. *See* Integrated Genetics.
IG Farben. *See* I.G. Farbenindustrie AG.
IG Holdings, **27** 430
IGA, **II** 624, 649, 668, 681–82; **7** 451; **15**
  479; **18** 6, 9; **25** 234
iGetSmart.com, Inc. *See* Workflow
  Management, Inc.
Iggesund Paperboard AB, **52** 161, 164
Igloo Products Corp., 21 291–93; 22 116
IGT-International, **10** 375–76
IGT-North America, **10** 375
IHI. *See* Ishikawajima Harima Heavy
  Industries.
IHOP Corporation, 17 249–51; 19 435,
  455; **58 174–77 (upd.)**
IIS, **26** 441
IJ Holdings Corp., **45** 173
IK Coach, Ltd., **23** 290
IKEA International A/S, V 82–84; 26
  161, **208–11 (upd.)**
IKON Office Solutions, Inc., 50 236–39
Il Fornaio (America) Corporation, 27
  225–28
Il Giornale, **13** 493
Ilaco, **26** 22
ILC Dover Inc., **63** 318
ILFC. *See* International Lease Finance
  Corporation.
Ilitch Holdings Inc., 37 207–210; 46 130
Illco Toy Co. USA, **12** 496
Illinois Bell Telephone Company, 14
  251–53; 18 30
Illinois Central Corporation, I 456; **8**
  410; **10** 553; **11 186–89**
Illinois Lock Company, **48** 142

Illinois Power Company, 6 470, **504–07;**
  49 119, 121
Illinois Steel Co., **8** 114
Illinois Terminal Company, **6** 504
Illinois Tool Works Inc., III 518–20; 22
  280–83 (upd.); 44 193
Illinois Traction Company, **6** 504
Illinova Energy Partners, **27** 247
Illuminet Holdings Inc., **47** 430
illycaffè SpA, 50 240–44
Ilwaco Telephone and Telegraph Company.
  See Pacific Telecom, Inc.
ILX Resorts Incorporated, 65 174–76
Ilyushin, **24** 60
IMA Bancard, Inc., **24** 395
Imabari, **25** 469
Image Business Systems Corp., **11** 66
Image Industries, Inc., **25** 320–21
Image Technologies Corporation, **12** 264
Imageline Inc., **25** 348
ImageTag Inc., **49** 290
Imaginarium Toy Centers, Inc., **57** 374
Imagine Entertainment, **43** 144
Imagine Foods, Inc., 50 245–47
Imagine Manufacturing Solutions Inc., **48**
  410
ImagiNet, **41** 97
Imaging Technologies, **25** 183
Imaje, S.A., **28** 104
IMAKE Software and Services, Inc , **49**
  423–24
IMall Inc., **26** 441
Imasa Group, **IV** 34
Imasco Limited, I 514; **II** 605; **V 401–02;**
  49 367–68
Imation Corporation, 20 301–04; 33 348;
  61 368. *See also* 3M Company.
Imatra Steel Oy Ab, 55 215–17
Imatran Voima Oy. *See also* Fortum
  Corporation
Imax Corporation, 21 362; **28 205–08;**
  46 422
IMC. *See* Intertec Marine Corporation.
IMC Fertilizer Group, Inc., 8 264–66
IMC Global Inc., **57** 149
Imcera Group, Inc., **8** 264, 266
ImClone Systems Inc., 58 178–81
IMCO Recycling, Incorporated, 32
  270–73
IMED Corp., **III** 511–12; **38** 364
Imerys S.A., 40 176, **263–66 (upd.)**
Imetal S.A., IV 107–09
IMG. *See* International Management
  Group.
Imhoff Industrie Holding GmbH, **53** 315
IMI plc, 9 288–89; 29 364
IMIWeb Bank, **50** 410
Imlo, **26** 22
Immeon Networks LLC, **54** 407
Immersion Corporation, **28** 245
Immobilier Batibail, **42** 152
Immunex Corporation, 8 26; **14 254–56;**
  50 421, **248–53 (upd.)**, 538
Immuno Therapeutics, Inc., **25** 382
Imo Industries Inc., 7 235–37; 27 229–32
  (upd.)
Imo Pump, **58** 67
Impala Platinum Holdings Ltd., **IV** 91–93;
  63 38–39
Impark Limited, **42** 433
IMPATH Inc., 45 192–94
Imperial and International Communications
  Limited, **25** 100

Imperial Airways. *See* British Overseas
  Airways Corporation.
Imperial Business Forms, **9** 72
Imperial Chemical Industries plc, I
  351–53; IV 698; **7** 209; **8** 179, 222,
  224; **9** 154, 288; **10** 436; **11** 97, 361; **12**
  347; **17** 118; **18** 50; **21** 544; **44** 116–17;
  49 268, 270; **50** 57, 90, 178–79, **50**
  254–58 (upd.); 63 49
Imperial Commodities Corporation. *See*
  Deli Universal NV.
Imperial Feather Company, **19** 304
Imperial Group Ltd., **III** 503; **7** 209; **17**
  238
Imperial Holly Corporation, 12 268–70.
  See also Imperial Sugar Company.
Imperial Japanese Government Steel
  Works, **17** 349–50
Imperial Metal Industries Ltd. *See* IMI plc.
Imperial Oil Limited, IV 437–39; 25
  229–33 (upd.);
Imperial Outdoor, **27** 280
Imperial Packing Co. *See* Beech-Nut
  Nutrition Corporation.
Imperial Paper, **13** 169
Imperial Parking Corporation, 58
  182–84
Imperial Premium Finance, **III** 264
Imperial Products, Inc., **62** 289
Imperial Savings Association, **8** 30–31
Imperial Sports, **19** 230
Imperial Sugar Company, 32 274–78
  (upd.); 54 168
Imperial Tobacco Company, **49** 153. *See
  also* B.A.T. Industries PLC.
Imperial Tobacco Group PLC, 50
  116–18, **259–63**
Implats. *See* Impala Platinum Holdings
  Ltd.
IMPO Import Parfumerien, **48** 116
Imported Auto Parts, Inc., **15** 246
Impressions Software, **15** 455
Imprimis, **8** 467
Impulse, **9** 122
Impulse Designs, **31** 435–36
IMRA America Inc., **48** 5
Imreg, **10** 473–74
IMRS. *See* Hyperion Software Corporation.
IMS Health, Inc., 57 174–78; 59 129–30
IMS International, Inc., **10** 105
IMX Pharmaceuticals, **59** 285
In Focus Systems, Inc., 22 287–90
In Home Health, Inc., **25** 306, 309–10
In-N-Out Burger, 19 213–15
In-Sink-Erator, II 19; **66 195–98**
INA Corporation, **III** 208, 223–25, 226; **11**
  481; **22** 269. *See also* CIGNA
  Corporation.
INA-Holding Schaeffler KG, **62** 129
InaCom Corporation, 13 176, **276–78;**
  19 471
Inalca S.p.A. *See* Cremonini S.p.A.
Incentive Group, **27** 269
Inchcape PLC, III 521–24; 16 276–80
  (upd.); 50 264–68 (upd.); 54 378; **59**
  260
INCO-Banco Indústria e Comércio de
  Santa Catarina, **13** 70
Inco Limited, IV 110–12; 39 338; **45**
  195–99 (upd.)
Incon Research Inc., **41** 198
InControl Inc., **11** 460
Incredible Universe, **12** 470; **17** 489; **36**
  387

Incyte Genomics, Inc., 52 174–77
Indemnity Insurance Company. *See*
  CIGNA Corporation.
Indentimat Corp., **14** 542
Independent Breweries Company, **9** 178
Independent Delivery Services, Inc., **37**
  409
Independent Election Corp. of America, **47**
  37
Independent Exhibitions Ltd., **27** 362
Independent Grocers Alliance. *See* IGA.
Independent Lock Co., **13** 166
Independent News & Media PLC, 61
  129–31
Independent Petrochemical, **14** 461
Independent Stave Company, **28** 223
Independent Torpedo Company, **25** 73
India Exotics, Inc., **22** 133
Indian Airlines Corporation. *See* Air-India.
Indian Airlines Ltd., 46 240–42
Indian Archery and Toy Corp., **19** 142–43
Indian Iron & Steel Company Ltd. *See*
  Steel Authority of India Ltd.
Indian Oil Corporation Ltd., IV 440–41,
  483; **48 210–13 (upd.)**
Indiana Bearings, Inc., **13** 78
Indiana Bell Telephone Company,
  Incorporated, 14 257–61; 18 30
Indiana Board and Filler Company, **12** 376
Indiana Electric Corporation, **6** 555
Indiana Energy, Inc., 27 233–36
Indiana Gaming Company, **21** 40
Indiana Gas & Water Company, **6** 556
Indiana Group, **I** 378
Indiana Parts and Warehouse, **29** 86, 88
Indiana Power Company, **6** 555
Indiana Protein Technologies, **55** 233
Indiana Tube Co., **23** 250
Indianapolis Air Pump Company, **8** 37
Indianapolis Brush Electric Light & Power
  Company, **6** 508
Indianapolis Cablevision, **6** 508–09
Indianapolis Light and Power Company, **6**
  508
Indianapolis Motor Speedway
  Corporation, 9 16; **46 243–46**
Indianapolis Power & Light Company, **6**
  508–09
Indianapolis Pump and Tube Company, **8**
  37
IndianOil Companies. *See* Indian Oil
  Corporation Ltd.
Indigo Books & Music Inc., 58 185–87
Indigo NV, 26 212–14, 540–41
The Inditex Group. *See* Industria de Diseño
  Textil S.A.
Indo Mobil Ltd., **48** 212
Indola Cosmetics B.V., **8** 16
Indresco, Inc., **22** 285; **52** 215
Induba, S.A. de C.V., **39** 230
Induban, **II** 196
Indura SA Industria Y Commercio, **25** 82
Industri Kapital, **27** 269
Industri Kapital 2000 Ltd., **64** 17
Industria de Diseño Textil S.A. (Inditex),
  64 193–95
Industrial & Commercial Bank, **56** 363
Industrial Air Products, **19** 380–81
Industrial Air Tool, **28** 387
Industrial Airsystems Inc., **56** 247
Industrial Bancorp, **9** 229
Industrial Bank of Japan, Ltd., II
  300–01, 310–11, 338, 369, 433, 459; **17**
  121; **58** 228

Industrial Bank of Scotland, **10** 337
Industrial Chemical and Equipment, **16** 271
Industrial Circuits, **IV** 680
Industrial Computer Corp., **11** 78
Industrial Development Corp. of Zambia
  Ltd., **IV** 239–41
Industrial Development Corporation, **57**
  185
Industrial Devices Inc., **48** 359
Industrial Equity Ltd., **17** 357
Industrial Exportadora Famian, S.A. de
  C.V., **62** 353
Industrial Gases Lagos, **25** 82
Industrial Instrument Company. *See*
  Foxboro Company.
Industrial Light & Magic, **12** 322; **50** 320
Industrial Mutual Insurance, **III** 264
Industrial National Bank, **9** 229
Industrial Powder Coatings, Inc., **16** 475
Industrial Publishing Company, **9** 413; **27**
  361
Industrial Resources, **6** 144
Industrial Services Group, Inc., **56** 161
Industrial Services of America, Inc., 46
  247–49
Industrial Shows of America, **27** 362
Industrial Tectonics Corp., **18** 276
Industrial Tires Limited, **65** 91
Industrial Trade & Consumer Shows Inc.
  See Maclean Hunter Publishing Limited.
Industrial Trust Co. of Wilmington, **25** 540
Industrial Trust Company, **9** 228
Industrias Bachoco, S.A. de C.V., 39
  228–31
Industrias del Atlantico SA, **47** 291
Industrias Nacobre, **21** 259
Industrias Negromex, **23** 170
Industrias Penoles, S.A. de C.V., 22
  284–86
Industrias Resistol S.A., **23** 170–71
Industrie Natuzzi S.p.A., 18 256–58
Industrie Zignago Santa Margherita
  S.p.A., 67 210–12, 246, 248
Les Industries Ling, **13** 443
Industriförvaltnings AB Kinnevik, **26**
  331–33; **36** 335
AB Industrivärden, **32** 397
Induyco. *See* Industrias y Confecciones,
  S.A.
Indy Lighting, **30** 266
Indy Racing League, **37** 74
Inelco Peripheriques, **10** 459
Inespo, **16** 322
Inexco Oil Co., **7** 282
Infineon Technologies AG, 50 269–73; 57
  323
Infinity Broadcasting Corporation, 11
  190–92; 22 97; **23** 510; **28** 72; **35** 232;
  48 214–17 (upd.)
Infinity Enterprises, Inc., **44** 4
Infinity Partners, **36** 160
INFLEX, S.A., **8** 247
Inflight Sales Group Limited, **11** 82; **29**
  511
InfoAsia, **28** 241
Infocom, **32** 8
Infogrames Entertainment S.A., 35
  227–30; 41 407; **66** 16, 19
Infonet Services Corporation, **27** 304. *See
  also* Belgacom.
Infoplan, **14** 36
Informa Group plc, 58 188–91
Informatics General Corporation, **11** 468;
  25 86

Information Access Company, 12
  560–62; **17 252–55; 34** 438. *See also*
  The Thomson Corporation.
Information and Communication Group, **14**
  555
Information Associates Inc., **11** 78
Information Builders, Inc., 14 16; **22**
  291–93
Information Consulting Group, **9** 345
Information, Dissemination and Retrieval
  Inc., **IV** 670
Information Holdings Inc., 47 183–86
Information International. *See* Autologic
  Information International, Inc.
Information Management Reporting
  Services. *See* Hyperion Software
  Corporation.
Information Management Science
  Associates, Inc., **13** 174
Information Please LLC, **26** 216
Information Resources, Inc., 10 358–60;
  13 4; **25** 366
Information Spectrum Inc., **57** 34
Informix Corporation, 10 361–64, 505;
  30 243–46 (upd.)
Infoseek Corporation, **27** 517; **30** 490
InfoSoft International, Inc. *See* Inso
  Corporation.
Infostrada S.p.A., **38** 300
Infosys Technologies Ltd., 38 240–43
Infotech Enterprises, Ltd., **33** 45
Infotechnology Inc., **25** 507–08
Infotel, Inc., **52** 342
Infun, S.A., **23** 269
ING Australia Limited, **52** 35, 39
ING, B.V., **14** 45, 47
Ing. C. Olivetti & C., S.p.A., III 144–46;
  10 499; **16** 122; **25** 33. *See also* Olivetti
  S.p.A
ING Groep N.V., **63** 15
Ingalls Quinn and Johnson, **9** 135
Ingalls Shipbuilding, Inc., 12 28, **271–73;**
  36 78–79; **41** 42
Ingear, **10** 216
Ingefico, S.A., **52** 301
Ingenico—Compagnie Industrielle et
  Financière d'Ingénierie, 46 250–52
Ingenious Designs Inc., **47** 420
Ingersoll-Rand Company, III 473,
  525–27; 10 262; **13** 27, 523; **15** 187,
  223–26 (upd.); 22 542; **33** 168; **34** 46;
  55 218–22 (upd.)
Ingka Holding B.V. *See* IKEA
  International A/S.
Ingleby Enterprises Inc. *See* Caribiner
  International, Inc.
Inglenook Vineyards, **13** 134; **34** 89
Ingles Markets, Inc., 20 305–08
Inglis Ltd. *See* Whirlpool Corporation.
Ingram Book Group, **30** 70
Ingram Industries, Inc., 10 518–19; **11**
  193–95; 13 90, 482; **49 217–20 (upd.);**
  52 178. *See also* Ingram Micro Inc.
Ingram Micro Inc., 24 29; **52 178–81**
AB Ingredients, **II** 466
Ingredients Technology Corp., **9** 154
Ingres Corporation, **9** 36–37; **25** 87
Ingwerson and Co., **II** 356
INH. *See* Instituto Nacional de
  Hidrocarboros.
Inha Works Ltd., **33** 164
INI. *See* Instituto Nacional de Industria.
Initial Electronics, **64** 198
Initial Security, 64 196–98

Initial Towel Supply. *See* Rentokil Initial Plc.
Inktomi Corporation, 41 98; **45 200–04**
Inland Container Corporation, IV 341–42; **7** 528; **8 267–69**
Inland Motors Corporation, **18** 291
Inland Paperboard and Packaging, Inc., **31** 438
Inland Pollution Control, **9** 110
Inland Steel Industries, Inc., IV 113–16, 158, 703; **7** 447; **13** 157; **15** 249–50; **17** 351; **19** 9, 216–20 **(upd.),** 311, 381; **23** 35; **30** 254; **40** 269, 381; **41** 4
Inland Valley, **23** 321
Inmac, Inc., **16** 373
Inmos Ltd., **11** 307; **29** 323
InnCOGEN Limited, **35** 480
The Inner-Tec Group, **64** 198
InnerCity Foods Joint Venture Company, **16** 97
Inno-BM, **26** 158, 161
Inno-France. *See* Societe des Grandes Entreprises de Distribution, Inno-France.
Innova International Corporation, **26** 333
Innovacom, **25** 96
Innovation, **26** 158
Innovative Marketing Systems. *See* Bloomberg L.P.
Innovative Pork Concepts, **7** 82
Innovative Products & Peripherals Corporation, **14** 379
Innovative Software Inc., **10** 362
Innovative Sports Systems, Inc., **15** 396
Innovative Valve Technologies Inc., **33** 167
Innovex Ltd., **21** 425
Inpaco, **16** 340
Inpacsa, **19** 226
Inprise/Borland Corporation, **33** 115
Input/Output, Inc., **11** 538
INS. *See* International News Service.
Insa, **55** 189
Insalaco Markets Inc., **13** 394
Inserra Supermarkets, 25 234–36
Insight Enterprises, Inc., 18 259–61
Insight Marques SARL IMS SA, **48** 224
Insilco Corporation, 12 472; **16 281–83;** **23** 212; **36** 469–70
Insley Manufacturing Co., **8** 545
Inso Corporation, 26 215–19; 36 273
Inspiration Resources Corporation, **12** 260; **13** 502–03
Inspirations PLC, **22** 129
Insta-Care Holdings Inc., **16** 59
Insta-Care Pharmacy Services, **9** 186
Instant Auto Insurance, **33** 3, 5
Instant Interiors Corporation, **26** 102
Instapak Corporation, **14** 429
Instinet Corporation, 34 225–27; 48 227–28
Institute de Development Industriel, **19** 87
Institute for Professional Development, **24** 40
Institute for Scientific Information, **8** 525, 528
Institution Food House. *See* Alex Lee Inc.
Institutional Financing Services, **23** 491
Instituto Bancario San Paolo di Torino, **50** 407
Instituto Nacional de Industria, I 459–61
Instromet International, **22** 65
Instrument Systems Corp. *See* Griffon Corporation.
Instrumentarium Corp., **13** 328; **25** 82

Instrumentation Laboratory Inc., **III** 511–12; **22** 75
Instrumentation Scientifique de Laboratoire, S.A., **15** 404; **50** 394
Insurance Auto Auctions, Inc., 23 148, **285–87**
Insurance Company of North America. *See* CIGNA Corporation.
Insurance Company of the Southeast, Ltd., **56** 165
Insurance Partners L.P., **15** 257
InSync Communications, **42** 425
Intabex Holdings Worldwide, S.A., **27** 126
Intalco Aluminum Corp., **12** 254
Intamin, **17** 443
Intarsia Corp., **38** 187
Intat Precision Inc., **48** 5
INTEC, **6** 428
Integra-A Hotel and Restaurant Company, **13** 473
Integral Corporation, **14** 381; **23** 446; **33** 331
Integrated Business Information Services, **13** 5
Integrated Computer Systems. *See* Learning Tree International Inc.
Integrated Defense Technologies,
Integrated Defense Technologies, Inc., 44 423; **54 178–80**
Integrated Genetics, **8** 210; **13** 239; **38** 204, 206
Integrated Health Services, Inc., **11** 282
Integrated Medical Systems Inc., **12** 333; **47** 236
Integrated Resources, Inc., **11** 483; **16** 54; **19** 393
Integrated Silicon Solutions, Inc., **18** 20; **43** 17; **47** 384
Integrated Software Systems Corporation, **11** 469
Integrated Systems Engineering, Inc., **51** 382
Integrated Systems Operations. *See* Xerox Corporation.
Integrated Systems Solutions Corp., **9** 284; **11** 395; **17** 264
Integrated Telecom Technologies, **14** 417
Integris Europe, **49** 382, 384
Integrity Inc., 44 241–43
Integrity Life Insurance, **III** 249
Intel Corporation, II 44–46, 62, 64; **9** 42–43, 57, 114–15, 165–66; **10 365–67 (upd.),** 477; **11** 62, 308, 328, 490, 503, 518, 520; **12** 61, 449; **13** 47; **16** 139–40, 146, 394; **17** 32–33; **18** 18, 260; **19** 310, 312; **20** 69, 175; **21** 36; **22** 542; **24** 233, 236, 371; **25** 418, 498; **26** 432; **27** 365–66; **34** 441; **36** 123, **284–88 (upd.);** **38** 71, 416; **41** 408; **43** 14–16; **47** 153; **50** 53–54, 225; **63** 123–24
Intelcom Support Services, Inc., **14** 334
Intelicom Solutions Corp., **6** 229
Intelig, **57** 67, 69
IntelliCorp, Inc., 9 310; **31** 298; **45 205–07**
Intelligent Electronics, Inc., 6 243–45; 12 184; **13** 176, 277
Intelligent Interactions Corp., **49** 421
Intelligent Software Ltd., **26** 275
Intelligraphics Inc., **33** 44
Intellimetrics Instrument Corporation, **16** 93
Intellisys, **48** 257

Inter American Aviation, Inc. *See* SkyWest, Inc.
Inter-American Satellite Television Network, **7** 391
Inter-City Gas Ltd., **19** 159
Inter-City Products Corporation, **52** 399
Inter-City Wholesale Electric Inc., **15** 385
Inter-Comm Telephone, Inc., **8** 310
Inter-Continental Hotels and Resorts, **38** 77
Inter-Europa Bank in Hungary, **50** 410
Inter-Island Airways, Ltd., **22** 251; **24** 20
Inter-Island Steam Navigation Co. *See* Hawaiian Airlines.
Inter Island Telephone. *See* Pacific Telecom, Inc.
Inter Link Foods PLC, 61 132–34
Inter-Ocean Corporation, **16** 103; **44** 90
Inter Parfums Inc., 35 235–38
Inter-Regional Financial Group, Inc., 15 231–33. *See also* Dain Rauscher Corporation.
Inter Techniek, **16** 421
Interactive Computer Design, Inc., **23** 489, 491
Interactive Media CCSP AG, **61** 350
Interactive Search Holding. *See* Ask Jeeves, Inc.
Interactive Systems, **7** 500
InterAd Holdings Ltd., **49** 422
Interamericana de Talleras SA de CV, **10** 415
Interbake Foods, **II** 631
InterBold, **7** 146; **11** 151
Interbrás, **IV** 503
Interbrew S.A., 16 397; **17 256–58; 25** 279, 282; **26** 306; **34** 202; **38** 74, 78; **50 274–79 (upd.);** **59** 299
Interceramic. *See* Internacional de Ceramica, S.A. de C.V.
Interchemical Corp., **13** 460
Intercity Food Services, Inc., **II** 663
Interco Incorporated, III 528–31; 9 133, 135, 192, 234–35; **10** 184; **12** 156, 306–08; **22** 49; **29** 294; **31** 136–37, 210; **39** 146; **51** 120. *See also* Furniture Brands International, Inc.
Intercontessa AG, **35** 401; **36** 294
Intercontinental Apparel, **8** 249
Intercontinental Electronics Corp. *See* IEC Electronics Corp.
Intercontinental Mortgage Company, **8** 436
Intercontinentale, **III** 404
Intercord, **22** 194
Intercorp Excelle Foods Inc., 64 199–201
Intercostal Steel Corp., **13** 97
Interdesign, **16** 421
InterDigital Communications Corporation, 61 135–37
Interdiscount/Radio TV Steiner AG, **48** 116
Interealty Corp., **43** 184
Interep National Radio Sales Inc., 35 231–34
Interessen Gemeinschaft Farbenwerke. *See* I.G. Farbenindustrie AG.
Interface Group, **13** 483
Interface, Inc., 8 270–72; 18 112; **29 246–49 (upd.)**
Interferon Sciences, Inc., **13** 366–67
InterFirst Bankcorp, Inc., **9** 482
Interglas S.A., **22** 515
Intergram, Inc., **27** 21
Intergraph Corporation, 6 246–49; 10 257; **24 233–36 (upd.); 53** 267

INTERIM Services, Inc., **9** 268, 270; **25** 434; **29** 224, 227. *See also* Spherion Corporation.

Interinvest S.A., **33** 19

Interlabor, **16** 420–21

Interlabor Interim, **43** 308

The Interlake Corporation, **8 273–75**; **38** 210

Interlake Steamship Company, **15** 302

Intermaco S.R.L., **43** 368

Intermagnetics General Corp., **9** 10

Intermarché, **35** 398, 401. *See also* ITM Entreprises SA.

Intermark, Inc., **12** 394; **34** 338–39

Intermec Corporation, **29** 414

Intermedia, **25** 499

Intermedics, **III** 633; **11** 458–59; **12** 325–26; **40** 66–67

Intermet Corporation, **32 279–82**

Intermodal Engineering Co. Ltd., **56** 181

Intermountain Health Care, Inc., **27 237–40**

Internacional de Ceramica, S.A. de C.V., **53 174–76**

International Aeradio Limited, **47** 352

International Aero Engines, **9** 418

International Agricultural Corporation, **8** 264–65

International Air Service Co., **24** 21

International Airline Support Group, Inc., **55 223–25**

International Alliance Services, Inc. *See* Century Business Services, Inc.

International Bank of Japan, **17** 122

International Banking and Credit Analysis (IBCA), **37** 144

International Banking Corp., **9** 123

International Banking Technologies, Inc., **11** 113

International Basic Economy Corporation, **13** 103

International Beauty Supply, Ltd. *See* L.L. Knickerbocker Co., Inc.

International Beverage Corporation. *See* Clearly Canadian Beverage Corporation.

International Brewing Holdings Pty., **21** 229; **50** 201

International Brotherhood of Teamsters, **37 211–14**

International Business Directories, Inc., **26** 484

International Business Machines Corporation, **I** 455, 534, 541; **II** 6, 44–45, 56, 62, 68, 70, 73, 86, 99, 107, 113, 134, 159, 211, 274, 326, 379, 397, 432, 440; **III** 147–49; **6 250–53 (upd.)**; **7** 145–46, 161; **8** 138–39, 466–67; **9** 36, 41–42, 48, 50, 114–15, 131, 139, 165–66, 170–71, 184, 194, 284, 296–97, 310, 327, 463–64; **10** 19, 22–24, 58, 119, 125, 161, 194, 232, 237, 243–44, 255–56, 309, 361–62, 366–67, 394, 456, 463, 474, 500–01, 505, 510, 512–13, 518–19, 542; **11** 19, 45, 50, 59, 61–62, 64–65, 68, 86–88, 150, 273–74, 285, 364, 395, 469, 485, 491, 494, 506, 519; **12** 61, 138–39, 147–49, 161–62, 183, 204, 238, 278, 335, 442, 450, 469–70, 484; **13** 47, 127, 174, 214, 326, 345, 387–88, 403, 482; **14** 13–15, 106, 268–69, 318, 354, 391, 401, 432–33, 446, 533; **15** 106, 440, 454–55, 491–92; **16** 4, 94, 140, 224–26, 301, 367–68, 372; **17** 353, 418, 532–34; **18** 94, 110, 112, 162, 250, 292, 305–07, 344, 434–36; **19** 41, 110, 310, 312, 437; **20** 237, 313; **21** 86, 391; **23** 135, 138, 209, 470; **24** 234; **25** 20–21, 34, 86–87, 96, 133–34, 149, 298–301, 356, 358, 530–32; **26** 90, 187, 275–76, 427, 429, 441, 540, 542; **28** 112; **29** 375, 414; **30** 247–51 (upd.); **34** 442–43; **36** 81–82, 171, 480–81; **38** 54–55, 250, 417; **43** 126–27; **46** 165; **47** 153; **49** 94; **57** 321; **63 195–201 (upd.)**; **64** 65

International Care Services. *See* Extendicare Health Services, Inc.

International Cellucotton Products Co. *See* Kimberly-Clark Corporation.

International Cementers Inc., **25** 74

International Communication Materials, Inc., **18** 387

International Computers. *See* ICL plc.

International Controls Corporation, **10 368–70**

International Corona Corporation, **12** 244

International Creative Management, Inc., **38** 161; **43 235–37**

International Dairy Queen, Inc., **7** 266; **10 371–74**; **39 232–36 (upd.)**

International Data Group, Inc., **7 238–40**; **12** 561; **25 237–40 (upd.)**; **27** 222

International Distillers & Vintners Ltd., **31** 92

International Engineering Company, Inc., **7** 355

International Enviroguard Systems, Inc., **57** 7–8

International Epicure, **12** 280

International Factoring Corp., **II** 436; **61** 249

International Family Entertainment Inc., **13 279–81**; **52** 85

International Finance Corp., **19** 192

International Financial Systems Limited, **62** 141

International Flavors & Fragrances Inc., **9 290–92**; **38 244–48 (upd.)**

International Fuel Cells Inc., **39** 394

International Game Technology, **10 375–76**; **24** 37 **25** 313; **41 214–16 (upd.)**; **54** 14–15

International Group, **13** 277

International Harvester Co., **III** 473; **10** 264, 280, 378, 380, 528; **13** 16; **17** 158; **22** 380; **67** 358. *See also* Navistar International Corporation.

International Home Foods, Inc., **42** 94; **64** 61

International Hotel Group, **59** 296

International House of Pancakes. *See* IHOP Corporation.

International Hydron, **10** 47; **13** 367

International Imaging Limited, **29** 58

International Industries, **17** 249

International Insurance Company of Hannover Ltd., **53** 162

International Lease Finance Corporation, **III** 198; **36** 231; **48 218–20**

International Light Metals Corp., **IV** 163

International MacGregor, **27** 269

International Management Group, **18 262–65**

International Marine Services, **22** 276

International Match, **12** 463

International Milling. *See* International Multifoods Corporation.

International Mineral & Chemical, Inc., **8** 265–66

International Minerals and Chemical Corporation, **19** 253

International Multifoods Corporation, **7 241–43**; **12** 125; **14** 515; **21** 289; **23** 203; **25 241–44 (upd.)**; **28** 238; **50** 493

International Music Co., **16** 202; **43** 171

International News Service, **IV** 626–27; **19** 203; **25** 507

International Nickel Co. of Canada, Ltd. *See* Inco Limited.

International Nutrition Laboratories, **14** 558

International Olympic Committee, **44 244–47**

International Organization of Consumers Unions, **26** 98

International Paper Company, **III** 764; **IV** 16, 245, **286–88**, 289, 326; **8** 267; **11** 76, 311; **15 227–30 (upd.)**; **16** 349; **17** 446; **23** 48–49, 366, 368; **25** 9; **26** 444; **30** 92, 94; **32** 91, 346; **47 187–92 (upd.)**; **63 267–69**

International Parts Corporation, **10** 414; **56** 230

International Periodical Distributors, **34** 5

International Permalite, **22** 229

International Petroleum Co., Ltd. *See* Standard Oil Co. of New Jersey.

International Pipeline Services, Inc., **51** 248

International Playing Card Company, **62** 384

International Playtex, Inc., **12** 93; **62** 88

International Power PLC, **50 280–85 (upd.)**

International Processing Corporation, **50** 123

International Products Corporation. *See* The Terlato Wine Group.

International Proteins Corporation, **21** 248

International Publishing Corp., **23** 350; **49** 407

International Raw Materials, Ltd., **31** 20

International Rectifier Corporation, **31 263–66**

International Roofing Company, **22** 13–14

International Sealants Corporation, **8** 333

International Shipbreaking Ltd. L.L.C., **67 213–15**

International Shipholding Corporation, Inc., **27 241–44**

International Silver Company, **12** 472; **14** 482–83

International SMC Ltd., **60** 278

International Specialty Products, Inc., **22** 225, 228–29

International Speedway Corporation, **19 221–23**; **32** 439

International Stores, **I** 427

International Supply Consortium, **13** 79

International Talent Group, **25** 281

International Talent Management, Inc. *See* Motown Records Company L.P.

International Telcell Group, **7** 336

International Telecommunications Satellite Organization, **46** 328

International Telephone & Telegraph Corporation, **I 462–64**; **II** 98–99, 166, 644–45, 684; **8** 157; **9** 10–11, 324; **10** 19, 44, 301; **11 196–99 (upd.)**, 337, 516; **12** 18; **13** 246; **14** 332, 488; **19**

131, 205, 208; **25** 100, 432; **46** 412; **63** 401

International Television Corporation Entertainment Group, **23** 391

International Thomson Organisation Ltd. *See* The Thomson Corporation.

International Thomson Organization Ltd., **23** 92

International Total Services, Inc., 37 215–18

International Utilities Corp., **6** 444

International Wind Systems, **6** 581

International Wine & Spirits Ltd., **9** 533

International Wire Works Corp., **8** 13

International Wireless Inc., **21** 261

Internationale Nederlanden Group, **24** 88

Internet Shopping Network, **26** 441

Interocean Management Corp., **9** 509–11

Interpac Belgium. *See* Belgacom.

Interpretive Data Systems Inc. *See* IDX Systems Corporation.

Interprovincial Pipe Line Ltd., **I** 264; **IV** 439; **25** 231. *See also* Enbridge Inc.

The Interpublic Group of Companies, Inc., I 16–18, 31, 36; **14** 315; **16** 70, 72, 167; **20** 5; **22** 294–97 (upd.); **23** 478; **28** 66–67; **32** 142; **42** 107; **51** 259

Interra Financial. *See* Dain Rauscher Corporation.

InterRedec, Inc., **17** 196

Interscience, **17** 271

Interscope Communications, Inc., **23** 389, 391; **27** 121

Interscope Music Group, 31 267–69

Intersec, Inc., **27** 21

Interstate & Ocean Transport, **6** 577

Interstate Assurance Company, **59** 246–47

Interstate Bakeries Corporation, 7 320; **12** 274–76; **27** 310; **38** 249–52 (upd.)

Interstate Brick Company, **6** 568–69

Interstate Electric Manufacturing Company. *See* McGraw Electric Company.

Interstate Finance Corp., **11** 16

Interstate Financial Corporation, **9** 475

Interstate Hotels & Resorts Inc., 58 192–94

Interstate Iron and Steel Company. *See* Republic Engineered Steels, Inc.

Interstate Logos, Inc., **27** 278

Interstate Paint Distributors, Inc., **13** 367

Interstate Power Company, **6** 555, 605; **18** 404

Interstate Properties Inc., **45** 15–16

Interstate Public Service Company, **6** 555

Interstate Supply Company. *See* McGraw Electric Company.

Interstate United Corporation, **II** 679; **13** 435

InterTAN, Inc. *See* Circuit City Stories, Inc.

Intertec Design, Inc., **34** 371–72

Intertec Publishing Corp., **22** 441

Intertechnique SA, **36** 530

Interturbine Holland, **19** 150

Intertype Corp., **II** 37

Intervideo TV Productions-A.B., **II** 640

Intervision Express, **24** 510

InterWest Partners, **16** 418

Intimate Brands, Inc., 24 237–39' **29** 357

InTouch Systems, Inc., **43** 118

Intrac Handelsgesellschaft mbH, **7** 142

Intraco Corp., **56** 157–58

Intrado Inc., 63 202–04

The Intrawest Corporation, 15 234–36; **31** 67; **43** 438

Intrepa L.L.C. *See* Manhattan Associates, Inc.

Intrepid Corporation, **16** 493

IntroGene B.V., **13** 241

Intuit Inc., 13 147; **14** 262–64; **23** 457; **33** 208–11 (upd.)

Invacare Corporation, 11 200–02, 486; **47** 193–98 (upd.)

Invenex Laboratories, **17** 287

Invensys PLC, 50 286–90 (upd.)

Invento Products Corporation, **21** 269

Invep S.p.A., **10** 150

Inverness Medical Innovations, Inc., 45 208; **63** 205–07

Inverness Medical Technology, Inc., **45** 210

Inversale, **9** 92

Inversiones Financieras del Sud S.A., **63** 120–21

INVESCO PLC. *See* AMVESCAP PLC.

Invesgen S.A., **26** 129

Investcorp SA, 15 200; **24** 195, 420; **25** 205, 207; **57** 179–82; **63** 49–50

Investimentos Itaú S.A., **19** 33

Investor AB, 63 208–11

Investors Bank and Trust Company, **18** 152

Investors Diversified Services, Inc., **II** 398; **8** 348–49; **10** 43–45, 59, 62; **21** 305; **25** 248, **38** 42

Investors Management Corp., **10** 331

Investors Overseas Services, **10** 368–69

InvestorsBancorp, **53** 222, 224

Investrónica S.A., **26** 129

Invista Capital Management, **III** 330

Invitrogen Corporation, 52 182–84

Invivo Corporation, 52 185–87

The Invus Group, Ltd., **33** 449

Iomega Corporation, 18 509–10; **21** 294–97

IONA Technologies plc, 43 238–41

Ionia S.A., **64** 379

Ionics, Incorporated, 52 188–90

Ionpure Technologies Corporation, **6** 486–88

Iowa Beef Packers, **21** 287

Iowa Beef Processors, **II** 516–17; **13** 351

Iowa Mold Tooling Co., Inc., **16** 475

Iowa Public Service Company, **6** 524–25

IP Gas Supply Company, **6** 506

IP Services, Inc., **IV** 597

IP Timberlands Ltd., **IV** 288

IP&L. *See* Illinois Power & Light Corporation.

Ipalco Enterprises, Inc., 6 508–09; **53** 18

IPC. *See* International Publishing Corp.

IPC Communications, Inc., **15** 196

IPC Magazines Limited, 7 244–47

IPD. *See* International Periodical Distributors.

IPEC Holdings Ltd., **27** 474–75

Iphotonics Inc., **48** 369

Ipiranga S.A., 67 216–18

Ipko-Amcor, **14** 225

IPL Energy Inc., **54** 354. *See also* Enbridge Inc.

IPS Praha a.s., **38** 437

IPS Publishing, **39** 341–42

IPSOA Editore, **14** 555

Ipsos SA, 24 355; **48** 221–24

Ipswich Bancshares Inc., **55** 52

iQuantic Buck, **55** 73

IQUE, Inc., **21** 194

Irby-Gilliland Company, **9** 127

Irdeto, **31** 330

Irex Corporation, **59** 382–83

IRI. *See* Instituto per la Ricostruzione Industriale.

Irideon, Inc., **35** 435

Iridian Asset Management LLC, **52** 172

Iris Associates, Inc., **25** 299, 301

Irish Agricultural Wholesale Society Ltd. *See* IAWS Group plc.

Irish Air. *See* Aer Lingus Group plc.

Irish Life & Permanent Plc, 59 245–47

Irish Life Assurance Company, **16** 14; **43** 7

Iron and Steel Industrial Corporation, **59** 224

Iron and Steel Press Company, **27** 360

Iron Cliffs Mining Company, **13** 156

Iron Mountain Forge, **13** 319

Iron Mountain, Inc., 33 212–14

Iron Ore Company of Canada, **8** 347

IronUnits LLC, **62** 74

Iroquois Gas Corporation, **6** 526

IRSA Inversiones y Representaciones S.A., 63 119–21, 212–15

Irvin Feld & Kenneth Feld Productions, Inc., 15 237–39. *See also* Feld Entertainment, Inc.

Irving Tanning Company, **17** 195

Irving Trust Coompany, **22** 55

Irwin Lehrhoff Associates, **11** 366

Irwin Toy Limited, 14 265–67

Isabela Shoe Corporation, **13** 360

Isagro S.p.A., **26** 425

Isbank. *See* Turkiye Is Bankasi A.S.

Iscor. *See* Iron and Steel Industrial Corporation.

Iscor Limited, 57 183–86

Isdin, **60** 246

Isetan Company Limited, V 85–87; 36 289–93 (upd.)

Ishikawajima-Harima Heavy Industries Co., Ltd., I 508, 511; **III** 532–33; **9** 293; **41** 41; **63** 223

Ishizaki Honten, **III** 715

Isis Distributed Systems, Inc., **10** 501

Island Air, **24** 22

Island Def Jam Music, **57** 359

The Island ECN, Inc., 48 225–29

Island Equipment Co., **19** 381

Island Pictures Corp., **23** 389

Island Records, **23** 389

Islands Restaurants, **17** 85–87

Isle of Capri Casinos, Inc., 33 41; **41** 217–19

Isosceles PLC, **II** 628–29; **24** 270; **47** 367–68

Isotec Communications Incorporated, **13** 213

Ispat Inland Inc., 40 267–72 (upd.), 381

Ispat International N.V., 30 252–54

Israel Chemicals Ltd., 55 226–29

ISS A/S, 49 221–23, 376

ISS International Service System, Inc., **8** 271

ISS Securitas, **42** 165, 167

ISSI. *See* Integrated Silicon Solutions Inc.

Istante Vesa s.r.l., **22** 239

Istituto Farmacologico Serono S.p.A. *See* Serono S.A.

Istituto Mobiliare Italiano S.p.A., **50** 407, 409

Istituto per la Ricostruzione Industriale S.p.A., I 465–67; **11** 203–06; **13** 28, 218

Isuzu Motors, Ltd., **7** 8, 219; **9 293–95**; **10** 354; **23 288–91 (upd.)**; **36** 240, 243; **57 187–91 (upd.)**; **64** 151
Isuzu Motors of Japan, **21** 6
IT Group, **28** 203
IT International, **V** 255
IT-Software Companies, **48** 402
Italcimenti Group, **40** 107–08
Italianni's, **22** 128
Italstate. *See* Societa per la Infrastrutture e l'Assetto del Territoria.
Italtel, **V** 326–27
Italware, **27** 94
Itaú. *See* Banco Itaú S.A.
Itaú Winterthur Seguradura S.A., **III** 404
Itaúsa. *See* Investimentos Itaú S.A.
Itek Corp., **I** 486; **11** 265
Itel Corporation, **9** 49, **296–99**; **15** 107; **22** 339; **26** 519; **47** 37
Items International Airwalk Inc., **17 259–61**
Ithaca Gas & Electric. *See* New York State Electric and Gas.
ITI Education Corporation, **29** 472
ITM Entreprises SA, **36 294–97**
Ito Gofuku Co. Ltd. *See* Matsuzakaya Company Limited.
Ito-Yokado Co., Ltd., **II** 661; **V 88–89**; **32** 414, 416–17; **42 189–92 (upd.)**
Itochu and Renown, Inc., **12** 281
ITOCHU Corporation, **19** 9; **32 283–87 (upd.)**; **34** 231; **42** 342; **63** 346
Itochu Housing, **38** 415
Itochu of Japan, **14** 550
Itoh. *See* C. Itoh & Co.
Itoham Foods Inc., **II** 518–19; **61 138–40 (upd.)**
Itokin, **III** 48
Itoman & Co., **26** 456
Itron, Inc., **64 202–05**
The Itsy Bitsy Entertainment Company, **51** 309
ITT, **21** 200; **24** 188, 405; **30** 101; **47** 103; **62** 179. *See also* International Telephone and Telegraph Corporation.
ITT Aerospace, **33** 48
ITT Automotive Inc. *See* Valeo.
ITT Educational Services, Inc., **33 215–17**
ITT Sheraton Corporation, **III 98–101**; **23** 484; **54** 345–47. *See also* Starwood Hotels & Resorts Worldwide, Inc.
ITT World Directories, **27** 498, 500
iTurf Inc., **29** 142–43
ITW. *See* Illinois Tool Works Inc.
ITW Devcon, **12** 7
IU International, **23** 40
IURA Edition, **14** 556
IV Therapy Associates, **16** 440
IVACO Industries Inc., **11** 207
Ivanhoe, Inc., **II** 662, 664; **57** 157
IVAX Corporation, **11 207–09**; **41** 420–21; **55 230–33 (upd.)**
IVC Industries, Inc., **45 208–11**
Ives Trains, **16** 336
iVillage Inc., **46** 232, **253–56**
Ivy and Mader Philatelic Auctions, Inc., **60** 146
Ivy Mortgage Corp., **39** 380, 382
Iwerks Entertainment, Inc., **33** 127; **34 228–30**
IXC Communications, Inc., **29 250–52**; **37** 127

IXI Ltd., **38** 418–19
IYG Holding Company of Japan, **7** 492; **32** 414, 417
The IZOD Gant Corporation, **24** 385
Izod Lacoste, **9** 156–57
Izukyu Corporation, **47** 408
Izumi Fudosan. *See* Sumitomo Reality & Development Co., Ltd.

J&E Davy, **16** 14
J&G Meakin, **12** 529
J & J Snack Foods Corporation, **24 240–42**
J&L Industrial Supply, **13** 297
J&L Steel. *See* Jones & Laughlin Steel Corp.
J & M Laboratories, **48** 299
J&R Electronics Inc., **26 224–26**
J&W Hardie Ltd., **62** 347
J. & W. Seligman & Co. Inc., **17** 498; **61 141–43**
J.A. Baldwin Manufacturing Company, **17** 106; **61** 65
J.A. Jones, Inc., **16 284–86**; **17** 377
J. Alexander's Corporation, **65 177–79**
J.B. Hudson & Son, **18** 136
J.B. Hunt Transport Services Inc., **12 277–79**; **15** 440; **26** 533; **50** 209; **63** 237
J.B. Lippincott & Company, **14** 554–56; **33** 460
J.B. McLean Publishing Co., Ltd. *See* Maclean Hunter Publishing Limited.
J.B. Williams Company, **8** 63
J.B. Wolters Publishing Company, **14** 554
J. Baker, Inc., **13** 361; **31 270–73**
J. Beres & Son, **24** 444–45
J Bibby & Sons, **I** 424
J Bibby Agriculture Limited, **13** 53
J. Boag & Son Limited, **57** 306
J. Bulova Company. *See* Bulova Corporation.
J. Byrons, **9** 186
J.C. Baxter Co., **15** 501
J.C. Hillary's, **20** 54
J.C. McCormic, Inc., **58** 334
J.C. Penney Company, Inc., **V 90–92**; **8** 288, 555; **9** 156, 210, 213, 219, 346–94; **10** 409, 490; **11** 349; **12** 111, 431, 522; **14** 62; **16** 37, 327–28; **17** 124, 175, 177, 366, 460; **18** 108, 136, 168, 200, **269–73 (upd.)**, 373, 478; **19** 300; **21** 24, 527; **25** 91, 254, 368; **26** 161; **27** 346, 429; **31** 260–61; **32** 166, 168–70; **39** 270; **41** 114–15; **43 245–50 (upd.)**
J.C. Potter Sausage Company, **57** 56–57
J. Crew Group Inc., **12 280–82**; **25** 48; **34 231–34 (upd.)**; **36** 472
J.D. Bassett Manufacturing Co. *See* Bassett Furniture Industries, Inc.
J.D. Edwards & Company, **14 268–70**; **38** 431
J.D. Power and Associates, **9** 166; **32 297–301**
J. D'Addario & Company, Inc., **48 230–33**
J.E. Nolan, **11** 486
J.E. Sirrine. *See* CRSS Inc.
J.E. Smith Box & Printing Co., **13** 441
J. Edward Connelly Associates, Inc., **22** 438
J. Evershed & Son, **13** 103
J.F. Corporation. *See* Isetan Company Limited.
J.F. Shea Co., Inc., **55 234–36**

J.H. Findorff and Son, Inc., **60 175–78**
J.H. Heafner Co., **20** 263
J.H. Westerbeke Corp. *See* Westerbeke Corporation.
J.H. Whitney & Company, **9** 250; **32** 100
J. Homestock. *See* R.H. Macy & Co.
J. Horner's, **48** 415
J.I.C. Group Limited, **61** 233
J.I. Case Company, **I** 148; **10 377–81**; **13** 17; **22** 380. *See also* CNH Global N.V.
JJ. Farmer Clothing Inc., **51** 320–21
J.J. Kenney Company, Inc., **51** 244
The J. Jill Group, Inc., **35 239–41**
J.K. Armsby Co., **7** 130–31
J.K. Starley and Company Ltd, **7** 458
J.L. Clark, Inc. *See* Clarcor Inc.
J.L. French Automotive Castings, Inc. *See* Onex Corporation.
J.L. Hudson Company. *See* Target Corporation.
J.L. Shiely Co. *See* English China Clays Ltd.
J.L. Wright Company, **25** 379
J. Levin & Co., Inc., **13** 367
J.M. Brunswick & Brothers, **III** 442
J.M. Douglas & Company Limited, **14** 141
J.M. Huber Corporation, **40** 68
J.M. Kohler Sons Company, **7** 269
The J.M. Smucker Company, **11 210–12**
J.M. Tull Metals Co., Inc., **IV** 116; **15** 250; **19** 219
J.M. Voith AG, **33 222–25**
J. Mandelbaum & Sons, **19** 510
J-Mar Associates, **31** 435–36
J.P. Heilwell Industries, **II** 420
J.P. Morgan & Co. Incorporated, **II 329–32**; **9** 386; **11** 421; **12** 165; **13** 13; **16** 25, 375; **19** 190; **26** 66, 500; **30 261–65 (upd.)**; **33** 464; **35** 74; **36** 151–53; **50** 30
J.P. Morgan Chase & Co., **38 253–59 (upd.)**
J.P. Stevens Inc., **8** 234; **12** 404; **16** 533–35; **17** 75; **19** 420; **27** 468–69; **28** 218; **62** 283
J.R. Brown & Sharpe. *See* Brown & Sharpe Manufacturing Co.
J.R. Geigy S.A., **8** 108–10; **39** 72
J.R. Simplot Company, **16 287–89**; **21** 508; **26** 309; **60 179–82 (upd.)**
J Sainsbury plc, **II 657–59**, 677–78; **10** 442; **11** 239, 241; **13 282–84 (upd.)**; **17** 42; **21** 335; **22** 241; **32** 253; **38 260–65 (upd.)**; **56** 316
J. Sears & Company. *See* Sears plc.
J. Spiegel and Company. *See* Spiegel, Inc.
J.U. Dickson Sawmill Inc. *See* Dickson Forest Products, Inc.
J.W. Bateson, **8** 87
J.W. Charles Financial Services Inc., **25** 542
J.W. Childs Associates, L.P., **46** 220; **64** 119
J.W. Childs Equity Partners LP, **40** 274
J.W. Foster and Sons, Inc. *See* Reebok International Ltd.
J.W. Spear, **25** 314
J.W. Wassall Ltd. *See* Wassall PLC.
J. Walter Thompson Co. *See* JWT Group Inc.
J. Weingarten Inc., **7** 203; **28** 163
J. Wiss & Sons Co., **II** 16
J.Z. Sales Corp., **16** 36
J. Zinmeister Co., **II** 682

Jabil Circuit, Inc., 36 298–301
Jacintoport Corporation, **7** 281
Jack Daniel Distillery, **10** 180
Jack Daniel's. *See* Brown-Forman Corporation.
Jack Eckerd Corp., **16** 160; **19** 467
Jack Frain Enterprises, **16** 471
Jack Henry and Associates, Inc., 17 262–65
Jack Houston Exploration Company, **7** 345
Jack in the Box, Inc. *See* Foodmaster, Inc.
Jack Schwartz Shoes, Inc., 18 266–68
Jackpot Enterprises Inc., 21 298–300; **24** 36
Jackson & Perkins. *See* Bear Creek Corporation.
Jackson Cushion Spring Co., **13** 397
Jackson Furniture of Danville, LLC, **48** 246
Jackson Hewitt, Inc., 48 234–36
Jackson Ice Cream Co., **12** 112
Jackson Mercantile Co. *See* Jitney-Jungle Stores of America, Inc.
Jackson National Life Insurance Company, 8 276–77; **48** 327
Jackson Purchase Electric Cooperative Corporation, **11** 37
Jaco Electronics, Inc., 19 311; **30** 255–57
Jacob Holm & Sons A/S, **22** 263
Jacob Leinenkugel Brewing Company, 12 338; **28** 209–11; **59** 68
Jacobs Brake Manufacturing Company, **7** 116–17
Jacobs Engineering Group Inc., 6 148–50; **26** 220–23 (upd.)
Jacobs Suchard (AG), **II** 520–22, 540, 569; **15** 64; **29** 46–47. *See also* Kraft Jacobs Suchard AG.
Jacobson Stores Inc., 21 301–03
Jacoby & Meyers, **20** 435
Jacor Communications, Inc., 23 292–95; **24** 108; **27** 339; **35** 220
Jacques Borel International, **II** 641; **10** 12; **49** 126
Jacques Chocolaterie S.A., **53** 315
Jacuzzi Inc., 7 207, 209; **23** 296–98
Jade Accessories, **14** 224
Jade KK, **25** 349
Jadepoint, **18** 79–80
Jafco Co. Ltd., **49** 433
Jafra Cosmetics, **15** 475, 477
Jagenberg AG, **9** 445–46; **14** 57
Jaguar Cars, Ltd., 11 140; **13** 219, 285–87, 414; **36** 198, 217; **64** 132. *See also* Ford Motor Company.
JAI Parabolic Spring Ltd., **III** 582
JAIX Leasing Company, **23** 306
JAKKS Pacific, Inc., 52 191–94
JAL. *See* Japan Air Lines.
Jalate Inc., 25 245–47
Jaluzot & Cie. *See* Pinault-Printemps-Redoute S.A.
Jamaica Gas Light Co., **6** 455
Jamaica Water Supply Company. *See* JWP Inc.
Jamar Company, **64** 30, 32
Jamba Juice Company, 47 199–202
James Bay Development Corporation, **6** 502
James Beattie plc, 43 242–44
James Burn/American, Inc., **17** 458
James C. Heintz Company, **19** 278
James Ericson, **III** 324
James Felt Realty, Inc., **21** 257

James Fison and Sons. *See* Fisons plc.
James G. Fast Company. *See* Angelica Corporation.
James Galt & Co. Ltd., **60** 124
James Hardie Industries N.V., 26 494; **56** 174–76
James Heekin and Company, **13** 254
James Industries, Inc., **61** 298
James McNaughton Ltd., **IV** 325
James Publishing Group, **17** 272
James R. Osgood & Company, **10** 356
James River Corporation of Virginia, IV 289–91; **8** 483; **22** 209; **29** 136. *See also* Fort James Corporation.
James Talcott, Inc., **11** 260–61
James Wellbeloved, **39** 354, 356
James Wholesale Company, **18** 7
Jamestown Insurance Co. Ltd., **55** 20
Jamestown Publishers, **22** 522
Jamesway Corporation, **13** 261; **23** 177
Jamie Scott, Inc., **27** 348
Jamieson & Co., **22** 428
Jan Bell Marketing Inc., **24** 335. *See also* Mayor's Jewelers, Inc.
Janata Bank, **31** 219
Janco Overseas Limited, **59** 261
Jane Jones Enterprises, **16** 422; **43** 309
Jane's Information Group, **8** 525
Janesville Electric, **6** 604
Janin, S.A., **36** 163
Janna Systems Inc., **38** 433
Janson Publications, **22** 522
N.V. Janssen M&L, **17** 147
JANT Pty. Ltd., **IV** 285
Jantzen Inc. *See* VF Corporation.
Janus Capital Group Inc., 6 401–02; **26** 233; **57** 192–94
Japan Advertising Ltd., **16** 166
Japan Airlines Company, Ltd., I 104–06; **6** 386, 427; **24** 399–400; **32** 288–92 (upd.); **49** 459
Japan Brewery. *See* Kirin Brewery Company, Limited.
Japan Broadcasting Corporation, 7 248–50; **9** 31
Japan Creative Tours Co., **I** 106
Japan Elanco Company, Ltd., **17** 437
Japan Energy Corporation, **13** 202; **14** 206, 208; **59** 375
Japan Food Corporation, **14** 288
Japan Leasing Corporation, 8 278–80; **11** 87
Japan Medico, **25** 431
Japan Pulp and Paper Company Limited, IV 292–93, 680
Japan Rifex Co., Ltd., **64** 261
Japan Telecom, **7** 118; **13** 482
Japan Telegraphic Communication Company (Nihon Denpo-Tsushin Sha), **16** 166
Japan Tobacco Inc., V 403–04; **30** 387; **46** 257–60 (upd.)
Japan Trustee Services Bank Ltd., **53** 322
Japan Try Co., **III** 758
Japan Vilene Company Ltd., **41** 170–72
Japanese Electronic Computer Co., **III** 140
Japanese National Railway, **43** 103
Japonica Partners, **9** 485
Jara Enterprises, Inc., **31** 276
Jarden Corporation, **62** 365, 381
Jardinay Manufacturing Corp., **24** 335
Jardine Matheson Holdings Limited, I 468–71; **18** 114; **20** 309–14 (upd.)
Jarvis plc, 39 237–39

Jas. D. Easton Archery. *See* Easton Sports, Inc.
Jas. I. Miller Co., **13** 491
Jason Incorporated, 23 299–301; **52** 138
Jasper Corporation, **III** 767; **22** 546. *See also* Kimball International, Inc.
JAT, **27** 475
Jato, **II** 652
Jauch & Hübener, **14** 279
Java-China-Japan Line, **6** 403–04; **26** 242
Java Software, **30** 453
Javelin Software Corporation, **10** 359
Jax, **9** 452
Jay Cooke and Co., **9** 370
Jay Jacobs, Inc., 15 243–45
Jay's Washateria, Inc., **7** 372
Jayco Inc., 13 288–90
Jazz Basketball Investors, Inc., 55 237–39
Jazzercise, Inc., 45 212–14
JB Oxford Holdings, Inc., 32 293–96
JB Pawn, Inc., **57** 139
JBA Holdings PLC, **43** 184
JBL, **22** 97
JCB, **14** 321
JCJL. *See* Java-China-Japan Line.
JCT Wireless Technology Company, **61** 233
JD Wetherspoon plc, 30 258–60
JDS Uniphase Corporation, 34 235–37
The Jean Coutu Group (PJC) Inc., 46 261–65
Jean-Jacques, **19** 50
Jean Lassale. *See* Seiko Corporation.
Jean Lincet, **19** 50
Jean-Philippe Fragrances, Inc. *See* Inter Parfums, Inc.
Jeanmarie Creations, Inc., **18** 67, 69
Jeanneau SA, **55** 56
Jefferies Group, Inc., 25 248–51
Jefferson Bancorp, Inc., **37** 201
Jefferson National Life Group, **10** 247
Jefferson-Pilot Corporation, 11 213–15; **29** 253–56 (upd.)
Jefferson Properties, Inc. *See* JPI.
Jefferson Smurfit Group plc, IV 294–96; **16** 122; **19** 224–27 (upd.); **49** 224–29 (upd.). *See also* Smurfit-Stone Container Corporation.
Jefferson Standard Life Insurance, **11** 213–14
Jefferson Ward, **12** 48–49
Jefferson Warrior Railroad Company, **III** 767; **22** 546
JEGTCO. *See* Japan Electricity Generation and Transmission Company (JEGTCO).
Jeld-Wen, Inc., 33 409; **45** 215–17
Jem Development, **17** 233
Jenkens & Gilchrist, P.C., 65 180–82
Jenn-Air Corporation. *See* Maytag Corporation.
Jennie-O Foods, **II** 506; **54** 166–67
Jennifer Convertibles, Inc., 31 274–76
Jenny Craig, Inc., 10 382–84; **12** 531; **29** 257–60 (upd.)
Jeno's, **13** 516; **26** 436
Jenoptik AG, 33 218–21; **53** 167
Jenson, Woodward & Lozier, Inc., **21** 96
JEORA Co., **IV** 564
Jepson Corporation, **8** 230
Jeri-Jo Knitwear, Inc., **27** 346, 348
Jerome Foods, Inc., **54** 168
Jerome Increase Case Machinery Company. *See* J.I. Case Company.

Jerrico Inc., **27** 145
Jerrold Corporation, **10** 319–20
Jerry Bassin Inc., **17** 12–14
Jerry's Famous Deli Inc., 24 243–45
Jerry's Restaurants, **13** 320
Jersey Central Power & Light Company, **27** 182
Jersey European Airways (UK) Ltd., 61 144–46
Jersey Standard. *See* Standard Oil Co. of New Jersey.
Jerusalem Post Publications Limited, **62** 188
Jervis B. Webb Company, 24 246–49
JESCO Inc. *See* The Yates Companies, Inc.
Jesse Jones Sausage Co. *See* GoodMark Foods, Inc.
Jet Airways (India) Private Limited, 65 14–15; **183–85**
Jet Set Corporation, **18** 513
JetBlue Airways Corporation, 44 248–50
Jetro Cash & Carry Enterprises Inc., 38 266–68
Jeumont-Schneider Industries, **9** 10
Jevic Transportation, Inc., **45** 448
Jewel Companies, Inc., **II** 605; **6** 531; **12** 63; **18** 89; **22** 38; **26** 476; **27** 291
Jewel Food Stores, **7** 127–28; **13** 25
JFD-Encino, **24** 243
JFE Steel Corporation, **67** 85
JFW Distributing Company. *See* Spartan Stores Inc.
JG Industries, Inc., 15 240–42
Jheri Redding Products, Inc., **17** 108
JHT, Inc., **39** 377
Jiamusi Combine Harvester Factory, **21** 175
Jiangsu General Ball & Roller Co., Ltd., **45** 170
JIB Group plc, **20** 313
Jiffy Auto Rental, **16** 380
Jiffy Convenience Stores, **II** 627
Jiffy Lube International, Inc., **IV** 490; **21** 541; **24** 339; **25** 443–45; **50** 353
Jiffy Mixes, **29** 109–10
Jiffy Packaging, **14** 430
Jiji, **16** 166
Jil Sander A.G., **45** 342, 344
Jillian's Entertainment Holdings, Inc., 40 273–75
Jim Beam Brands Worldwide, Inc., 14 271–73; 29 196; **58 194–96 (upd.)**
Jim Cole Enterprises, Inc., **19** 247
The Jim Henson Company, 23 302–04; 45 130
Jim Hjelm's Private Collection, Ltd. *See* JLM Couture, Inc.
The Jim Pattison Group, 37 219–22
Jim Walter Corporation. *See* Walter Industries, Inc.
Jimmy Carter Work Project. *See* Habitat for Humanity International.
Jintan Taionkei Co. *See* Terumo Corporation.
Jitney-Jungle Stores of America, Inc., 27 245–48
JJB Sports plc, 32 302–04
JLA Credit, **8** 279
JLG Industries, Inc., 52 195–97
JLL. *See* Jones Lang LaSalle Incorporated.
JLM Couture, Inc., 64 206–08
JMB Internacionale S.A., **25** 121
JMB Realty Corporation, IV 702–03. *See also* Amfac/JMB Hawaii L.L.C.

Jno. H. Swisher & Son. *See* Swisher International Group Inc.
JNR. *See* Japan National Railway.
Jo-Ann Fabrics and Crafts, **16** 197
Jo-Gal Shoe Company, Inc., **13** 360
Joanna Cotton Mills, **14** 220
Jobete Music. *See* Motown Records Company L.P.
JobWorks Agency, Inc., **16** 50
Jockey International, Inc., 12 283–85; 34 238–42 (upd.)
Joe Alexander Press, **12** 472; **36** 469
Joe's American Bar & Grill, **20** 54
Joe's Crab Shack, **15** 279
The Joffrey Ballet of Chicago, 52 198–202
Joh. A. Benckiser GmbH, **36** 140
John A. Frye Shoe Company, **V** 376; **8** 16; **26** 397–98; **36** 24
John A. Pratt and Associates, **22** 181
John Alden Life Insurance, **10** 340
John B. Sanfilippo & Son, Inc., 14 274–76
John Brown plc, I 572–74
John Carr Group, **31** 398–400
John Charcol. *See* Bradford & Bingley PLC.
John Chatillon & Sons Inc., **29** 460
John Crane International, **17** 480
John Crosland Company, **8** 88
The John D. and Catherine T. MacArthur Foundation, 34 243–46
John Deere. *See* Deere & Company.
John F. Jelke Company, **9** 318
John Fairfax Holdings Limited, 7 251–54
John H. Harland Company, 17 266–69
John H.R. Molson & Bros. *See* The Molson Companies Limited.
John Hancock Financial Services, Inc., 42 193–98 (upd.)
John Hancock Mutual Life Insurance Company, III 265–68, 332, 400; **IV** 283; **13** 530; **25** 528
John Holroyd & Co. of Great Britain, **7** 236
John Labatt Ltd., **8** 399; **16** 397; **17** 256–57. *See also* Labatt Brewing Company Limited.
John Laing plc, I 575–76, 588; **51 171–73 (upd.)**
John Lewis Partnership plc, V 93–95; 42 199–203 (upd.)
John M. Hart Company, **9** 304
John M. Smyth Co., **15** 282
John McConnell & Co., **13** 102
John Menzies plc, 39 240–43
John Morrell and Co., **21** 111
The John Nuveen Company, 21 304–06; 22 492, 494–95
John Oster Manufacturing Company. *See* Sunbeam-Oster.
John Paul Mitchell Systems, 24 250–52
John Pew & Company, **13** 243
John Q. Hammons Hotels, Inc., 24 253–55
John R. Figg, Inc., **II** 681
John Rogers Co., **9** 253
John Sands, **22** 35
John Schroeder Lumber Company, **25** 379
John Sexton & Co., **26** 503
John Strange Paper Company, **8** 358
John Swire & Sons Ltd. *See* Swire Pacific Ltd.

John W. Danforth Company, 48 237–39
John Wanamaker, **22** 110
John Wiley & Sons, Inc., 17 270–72; 65 186–90 (upd.)
John Yokley Company, **11** 194
John Zink Company, **22** 3–4; **25** 403
Johnny Rockets Group, Inc., 31 277–81
Johns Manville Corporation, 7 293; **11** 420; **19** 211–12; **61** 307–08; **64 209–14 (upd.)**
Johnsen, Jorgensen and Wettre, **14** 249
Johnson. *See* Axel Johnson Group.
Johnson & Higgins, 14 277–80
Johnson and Howe Furniture Corporation, **33** 151
Johnson & Johnson, III 35–37; IV 285, 722; **7** 45–46; **8 281–83 (upd.)**, 399, 511–12; **9** 89–90; **10** 47, 69, 78, 80, 534–35; **15** 357–58, 360; **16** 168, 440; **17** 104–05, 340, 342–43, 533; **19** 103, 105; **25** 55–56; **34** 280, 283–84; **36 302–07 (upd.)**; **37** 110–11, 113; **41** 154–55; **46** 104; **55** 122–23; **63** 205–06
Johnson Brothers, **12** 528
Johnson Controls, Inc., III 534–37; 13 398; **16** 184, 322; **26 227–32 (upd.); 59 248–54 (upd.)**
Johnson Engineering Corporation, **37** 365
Johnson Matthey PLC, II 390; **IV** 23, 117–20; **16** 28, 290–94 (upd.), 439; **49 230–35 (upd.); 50** 33
Johnson Products Co., Inc., **11** 208; **31** 89
Johnson Publishing Company, Inc., 27 361; **28 212–14**
Johnson Wax. *See* S.C. Johnson & Son, Inc.
Johnson Worldwide Associates, Inc., 24 530; **28 215–17**, 412
Johnsonville Sausage L.L.C., 63 216–19
Johnston Coca-Cola Bottling Company of Chattanooga, **13** 163–64
Johnston Industries, Inc., 15 246–48
Johnston, Lemon & Co., **53** 134
Johnston Press plc, 35 242–44
Johnston Sport Architecture Inc., **63** 91
Johnstown America Industries, Inc., 23 305–07
Johnstown Sanitary Dairy, **13** 393
Joint Environment for Digital Imaging, **50** 322
Joker S.A., **56** 103
Jolly Time. *See* American Pop Corn Company.
Jonathan Logan Inc., **13** 536
Jonell Shoe Manufacturing Corporation, **13** 360
Jones & Babson, Inc., **14** 85
Jones & Johnson, **14** 277
Jones & Laughlin Steel Corp., **I** 489–91; **IV** 228
Jones Apparel Group, Inc., 11 216–18; 27 60; **30** 310–11; **39 244–47 (upd.)**, 301, 303; **62** 284
Jones Brothers Tea Co., **7** 202
Jones, Day, Reavis & Pogue, 33 226–29
Jones Environmental, **11** 361
Jones Financial Companies, L.P. *See* Edward Jones.
Jones Intercable, Inc., 14 260; **17** 7; **21** 307–09; **24** 123; **25** 212
Jones Janitor Service, **25** 15
Jones Lang LaSalle Incorporated, 49 236–38

Jones Medical Industries, Inc., 24
256–58; **34** 460
Jones Motor Co., **10** 44
Jones-Rodolfo Corp. *See* Cutter & Buck,
Inc.
Jonkoping & Vulcan, **12** 462
Jordache Enterprises, Inc., 15 201–02;
23 308–10
The Jordan Co., **11** 261; **16** 149
Jordan Industries, Inc., 36 308–10
Jordan Valley Electric Cooperative, **12** 265
Jos. A. Bank Clothiers, Inc., II 560; **12**
411; **31 282–85**
The Joseph & Feiss Company, **48** 209
Joseph Leavitt Corporation, **9** 20
Joseph Littlejohn & Levy, **27** 204; **53** 241
Joseph Lumber Company, **25** 379
Joseph Malecki Corp., **24** 444–45
Joseph Schlitz Brewing Company, **25** 281
Joseph T. Ryerson & Son, Inc., 15
249–51; **19** 381. *See also* Ryerson Tull,
Inc.
Joseph Transportation Inc., **55** 347
Josephson International, **27** 392; **43** 235
Joshin Denki, **13** 481
Joshu Railway Company, **6** 431
Joshua's Christian Bookstores, **31** 435–36;
51 132
Josiah Wedgwood and Sons Limited. *See*
Waterford Wedgewood plc..
Jostens, Inc., 7 255–57; **25 252–55**
(upd.); **36** 470
Jotcham & Kendall Ltd. *See* Seddon Group
Ltd.
JOULÉ Inc., 58 197–200
Journal Register Company, 29 261–63
Journal Star Printing Company, **64** 237
Journey's End Corporation, **14** 107
Jove Publications, Inc., **IV** 623; **12** 224
Jovi, **II** 652
Joy Planning Co., **III** 533
Joy Technologies Inc., **II** 17; **26** 70; **38**
227
Joyce International, Inc., **16** 68
JP Foodservice Inc., **24** 445
JP Household Supply Co. Ltd., **IV** 293
JP Planning Co. Ltd., **IV** 293
JP Realty Inc., **57** 157
JPF Holdings, Inc. *See* U.S. Foodservice.
JPI, 49 239–41
JPS Automotive L.P., **17** 182–84
JPS Textile Group, Inc., 28 218–20
JPT Publishing, **8** 528
JR & F SA, **53** 32
JR Central, **43** 103
Jr. Food Stores, Inc., **51** 170
JR Tokai, **43** 103
JSC MMC Norilsk Nickel, 48 300–02
JT Aquisitions, **II** 661
JTL Corporation, **13** 162–63
JTN Acquisition Corp., **19** 233
JTS Corporation. *See* Atari Corporation.
Judel Glassware Co., Inc., **14** 502
The Judge Group, Inc., 51 174–76
Judson Dunaway Corp., **12** 127
Judson Steel Corp., **13** 97
Jugend & Volk, **14** 556
Juice Works, **26** 57
Jujamcyn, **24** 439
Jujo Paper Co., Ltd., IV 297–98
JuJu Media, Inc., **41** 385
Julius Baer Holding AG, 52 203–05
Julius Garfinckel & Co., Inc., **22** 110

Julius Meinl International AG, 53
177–80
Jumbo Food Stores. *See* Shoppers Food
Warehouse Corp.
Jumping-Jacks Shoes, Inc., **17** 390
Junghans Uhren, **10** 152
Juniper Networks, Inc., 43 251–55
Juno Lighting, Inc., 30 266–68
Juno Online Services, Inc., 38 269–72;
39 25–26
Juovo Pignone, **13** 356
Jupiter National, **15** 247–48; **19** 166
Jupiter Partners II, **62** 265
Jupiter Tyndall, **47** 84
Jurgensen's, **17** 558
Juristförlaget, **14** 556
Jurys Doyle Hotel Group plc, 64 215–17
Jusco Car Life Company, **23** 290
JUSCO Co., Ltd., V 96–99; **11** 498; **36**
419; **43** 386
Jusco Group, **31** 430
Just Born, Inc., 32 305–07
Just For Feet, Inc., 19 228–30
Just Squeezed, **31** 350
Just Toys, Inc., **29** 476
Justin Industries, Inc., 19 231–33
Juventus F.C. S.p.A, 44 387–88; **53**
181–83
JVC. *See* Victor Company of Japan, Ltd.
JW Aluminum Company, **22** 544
JW Bernard & Zn., **39** 203
JWD Group, Inc., **48** 238
JWP Inc., 9 300–02; **13** 176. *See also*
EMCOR Group Inc.
JWT Group Inc., I 19–21, 23. *See also*
WPP Group plc.
JZC. *See* John Zink Company.

K&B Inc., 12 286–88; **17** 244
K&F Manufacturing. *See* Fender Musical
Instruments.
K & G Men's Center, Inc., 21 310–12;
48 286
K&K Insurance Group, **26** 487
K&K Toys, Inc., **23** 176
K&M Associates L.P., **16** 18; **43** 19
K & R Warehouse Corporation, **9** 20
K-C Aviation, **III** 41; **16** 304; **43** 258
K-Graphics Inc., **16** 306; **43** 261
K-Group, **27** 261
K-H Corporation, **7** 260
K Shoes Ltd., **52** 57–58
K-Swiss, Inc., 33 243–45
K-tel International, Inc., 21 325–28
K-III Holdings. *See* Primedia Inc.
K.F. Kline Co., **7** 145; **22** 184
K.H.S. Musical Instrument Co. Ltd., **53**
214
K.H. Wheel Company, **27** 202
K. Hattori & Co., Ltd. *See* Seiko
Corporation.
k.k. Staatsbahnen, **6** 419
K Line. *See* Kawasaki Kisen Kaisha, Ltd.
K-Line Pharmaceuticals Ltd. *See* Taro
Phramaceutical Industries Ltd.
K.O. Lester Co., **31** 359, 361
K.P. American, **55** 305
K.W. Muth Company, **17** 305
KA Teletech, **27** 365
Ka Wah AMEV Insurance, **III** 200–01
Kabelvision AB, **26** 331–33
Kable News Company. *See* AMREP
Corporation.
Kable Printing Co., **13** 559

Kaepa, **16** 546
Kafte Inc., **28** 63
Kaga Forwarding Co., **6** 428
Kagle Home Health Care, **11** 282
Kagoshima Central Research Laboratory,
21 330
Kahan and Lessin, **II** 624–25
Kaiser + Kraft GmbH, **27** 175
Kaiser Aluminum & Chemical
Corporation, IV 121–23; **12** 377; **8**
348, 350; **22** 455; **50** 104. *See also* ICF
Kaiser International, Inc.
Kaiser Foundation Health Plan, Inc., 53
184–86
Kaiser Packaging, **12** 377
Kaiser Permanente Corp., **12** 175; **24** 231;
25 434, 527; **41** 183. *See also* Kaiser
Foundation Health Plan, Inc.
Kaiser Steel, **IV** 59
Kaiser's Kaffee Geschäft AG, **27** 461
Kajaani Oy, **IV** 350
Kajima Corporation, I 577–78; **51**
177–79
Kal Kan Foods, Inc., 22 298–300
Kalamazoo Limited, **50** 377
Kaldveer & Associates, **14** 228
Kaliningradnefteprodukt, **48** 378
Kalitta Group, **22** 311
Kalua Koi Corporation, **7** 281
Kaman Corporation, 12 289–92; **16** 202;
42 204–08 (upd.); **43** 171
Kamewa Group, **27** 494, 496
Kaminski/Engles Capital Corp. *See* Suiza
Foods Corporation.
Kammer Valves, A.G., **17** 147
Kampgrounds of America, Inc., 33
230–33
Kamps AG, 44 251–54
Kana Software, Inc., 51 180–83
Kanda Shokai, **16** 202; **43** 171
Kanders Florida Holdings, Inc., **27** 50
Kane Foods, **III** 43
Kane-Miller Corp., **12** 106
Kanebo, Ltd., 53 187–91
Kanematsu Corporation, IV 442–44; **24**
259–62 (upd.)
Kangaroo. *See* Seino Transportation
Company, Ltd.
Kanoldt, **24** 75
Kanpai Co. Ltd., **55** 375
The Kansai Electric Power Company,
Inc., V 645–48; **62 196–200 (upd.)**
Kansallis-Osake-Pankki, II 302–03
Kansas City Ingredient Technologies, Inc.,
49 261
Kansas City Power & Light Company, 6
510–12, 592; **12** 541–42; **50** 38. *See*
also Great Plains Energy Incorporated.
Kansas City Securities Corporation, **22** 541
Kansas City Southern Industries, Inc., 6
400–02; **26 233–36 (upd.)**; **29** 333; **47**
162; **50** 208–09; **57** 194
Kansas City White Goods Company. *See*
Angelica Corporation.
Kansas Fire & Casualty Co., **III** 214
Kansas Public Service Company, **12** 541
Kansas Utilities Company, **6** 580
The Kantar Group, **48** 442
Kanzaki Paper Manufacturing Co., **IV** 285,
293
Kao Corporation, III 38–39; **16** 168; **20**
315–17 (upd.); **51** 223–25
Kaolin Australia Pty Ltd. *See* English
China Clays Ltd.

Kapalua Land Company, Ltd., **29** 307–08
Kaplan Educational Centers, **12** 143
Kaplan, Inc., 42 209–12, 290
Kaplan Musical String Company, **48** 231
Kapok Computers, **47** 153
Karan Co. *See* Donna Karan Company.
Karastan Bigelow, **19** 276
Karl Kani Infinity, Inc., 49 242–45
Karl Schmidt Unisia, Inc., **56** 158
Karlsberg Brauerei GmbH & Co KG, 41 220–23
Karmelkorn Shoppes, Inc., **10** 371, 373; **39** 232, 235
Karrosseriewerke Weinsberg GmbH. *See* ASC, Inc.
Karstadt Aktiengesellschaft, V 100–02; 19 234–37 (upd.)
Karstadt Quelle AG, 57 195–201 (upd.)
Karsten Manufacturing Corporation, 51 184–86
Kasai Securities, **II** 434
Kasco Corporation, **28** 42, 45
Kash n' Karry Food Stores, Inc., 20 318–20; 44 145
Kashi Company, **50** 295
Kashima Chlorine & Alkali Co., Ltd., **64** 35
Kasmarov, **9** 18
Kaspare Cohn Commercial & Savings Bank. *See* Union Bank of California.
Kasper A.S.L., Ltd., 40 276–79
Kasuga Radio Company. *See* Kenwood Corporation.
Kat-Em International Inc., **16** 125
Katabami Kogyo Co. Ltd., **51** 179
Kate Spade LLC, **49** 285
Katharine Gibbs Schools Inc., **22** 442
Kathy's Ranch Markets, **19** 500–01
Katies, **V** 35
Kativo Chemical Industries Ltd., **8** 239; **32** 256
Katy Industries Inc., I 472–74; 14 483–84; **16** 282; **51 187–90 (upd.)**
Katz Communications, Inc., 6 32–34
Katz Media Group, Inc., 35 232, **245–48**
Kaufhalle AG, **V** 104; **23** 311; **41** 186–87
Kaufhof Warenhaus AG, V 103–05; 23 311–14 (upd.)
Kaufman and Broad Home Corporation, 8 284–86; 11 481–83. *See also* KB Home.
Kaufmann Department Stores, Inc. *See* The May Department Stores Company.
Kaufring AG, 35 249–52
Oy Kaukas Ab. *See* UPM-Kymmene
Kaukauna Cheese Inc., **23** 217, 219
Kauppiaitten Oy, **8** 293
Kawamata, **11** 350
Kawasaki Denki Seizo, **II** 22
Kawasaki Heavy Industries, Ltd., I 75; **III 538–40**, 756; **7** 232; **8** 72; **23** 290; **59** 397; **63 220–23 (upd.)**
Kawasaki Kisen Kaisha, Ltd., V 457–60; 56 177–81 (upd.)
Kawasaki Steel Corporation, IV 30, **124–25**, 154, 212–13; **13** 324; **19** 8
Kawecki Berylco Industries, **8** 78
Kawsmouth Electric Light Company. *See* Kansas City Power & Light Company.
Kay-Bee Toy Stores, 15 252–53; 16 389–90; **50** 99. *See also* KB Toys.
Kay Home Products, **17** 372
Kay Jewelers Inc., **61** 327
Kaydon Corporation, 18 274–76

Kaye, Scholer, Fierman, Hays & Handler, **47** 436
Kayex, **9** 251
Kaynar Manufacturing Company, **8** 366
Kayser Aluminum & Chemicals, **8** 229
Kayser Roth Corp., **8** 288; **22** 122
Kaytee Products Incorporated, **58** 60
KB Home, 45 218–22 (upd.)
AO KB Impuls, **48** 419
KB Investment Co., Ltd., **58** 208
KB Toys, 35 253–55 (upd.)
KBLCOM Incorporated, **V** 644
KC. *See* Kenneth Cole Productions, Inc.
KC Holdings, Inc., **11** 229–30
KCI Konecranes International, **27** 269
KCPL. *See* Kansas City Power & Light Company.
KCS Industries, **12** 25–26
KCSI. *See* Kansas City Southern Industries, Inc.
KCSR. *See* Kansas City Southern Railway.
KD Acquisition Corporation, **34** 103–04
KD Manitou, Inc. *See* Manitou BF S.A.
KDI Corporation, **56** 16–17
KDT Industries, Inc., **9** 20
Keane, Inc., 38 431; **56 182–86**
The Keds Corp., **37** 377, 379
Keebler Foods Company, 35 181; **36 311–13; 50** 295
Keefe Manufacturing Courtesy Coffee Company, **6** 392
Keegan Management Co., **27** 274
Keene Packaging Co., **28** 43
KEG Productions Ltd., **IV** 640; **26** 272
Keil Chemical Company, **8** 178
Keio Teito Electric Railway Company, V 461–62
The Keith Companies Inc., 54 181–84
Keith Prowse Music Publishing, **22** 193
Keithley Instruments Inc., 16 299–301; 48 445
Kelco, **34** 281
Kelda Group plc, 45 223–26
Keliher Hardware Company, **57** 8
Keller Builders, **43** 400
Keller-Dorian Graveurs, S.A., **17** 458
Kelley & Partners, Ltd., **14** 130
Kelley Drye & Warren LLP, 40 280–83
Kellock, **10** 336
Kellogg Brown & Root, Inc., 62 201–05 (upd.)
Kellogg Company, II 523–26, 530, 560; **12** 411; **13** 3, **291–94 (upd.); 15** 189; **18** 65, 225–26; **22** 336, 338; **25** 90; **27** 39; **29** 30, 110; **50 291–96 (upd.); 63** 249, 251–52
Kellogg Foundation, **41** 118
Kellwood Company, 8 287–89; 59 268; **62** 210
Kelly & Cohen, **10** 468
Kelly-Moore Paint Company, Inc., 56 99, **187–89**
Kelly Nason, Inc., **13** 203
Kelly Services, Inc., 6 35–37, 140; **9** 326; **16** 48; **25** 356, 432; **26 237–40 (upd.); 40** 236, 238; **49** 264–65
The Kelly-Springfield Tire Company, 8 290–92; 20 260, 263
Kelsey-Hayes Group of Companies, 7 258–60; 27 249–52 (upd.)
Kelso & Co., **12** 436; **19** 455; **21** 490; **33** 92; **63** 237
Kelty Pack, Inc., **10** 215
Kelvinator Inc., **17** 487

Kelvinator of India, Ltd., **59** 417
KemaNobel, **9** 380–81; **13** 22
Kemet Corp., 14 281–83
Kemi Oy, **IV** 316
Kemper Corporation, III 269–71, 339; **15 254–58 (upd.); 22** 495; **33** 111; **42** 451
Kemper Financial Services, **26** 234
Kemper Snowboards, **22** 460
Kendall International, Inc., IV 288; 11 219–21; 14 121; **15** 229; **28** 486
Kendall-Jackson Winery, Ltd., 28 111, **221–23**
Kenetech Corporation, 11 222–24
Kenhar Corporation. *See* Cascade Corporation.
Kenmore Air Harbor Inc., 65 191–93
Kennametal, Inc., 13 295–97
Kennecott Corporation, IV 192, 288, 576; **7 261–64; 10** 262; **12** 244; **27 253–57 (upd.); 35** 135; **38** 231. *See also* Rio Tinto PLC.
Kennedy Automatic Products Co., **16** 8
Kennedy-Wilson, Inc., 60 183–85
Kenner Parker Toys, Inc., **9** 156; **12** 168; **14** 266; **16** 337; **25** 488–89
Kenneth Cole Productions, Inc., 22 223; **25 256–58**
Kenneth O. Lester, Inc., **21** 508
Kenny Rogers' Roasters, **22** 464; **29** 342, 344
Kenroy International, Inc., **13** 274
Kensington Associates L.L.C., **60** 146
Kent Electronics Corporation, 17 273–76
Kentrox Industries, **30** 7
Kentucky Electric Steel, Inc., 31 286–88
Kentucky Fried Chicken, **III** 106; **7** 26–28, 433; **8** 563; **12** 42; **13** 336; **16** 97; **18** 8, 538; **19** 92; **21** 361; **22** 464; **23** 384, 504. *See also* KFC Corporation.
Kentucky Institution for the Education of the Blind. *See* American Printing House for the Blind.
Kentucky Utilities Company, 6 513–15; 11 37, 236–38; **51** 217
Kenwood Corporation, 19 360; **23** 53; **31 289–91**
Kenwood Silver Company, Inc., **31** 352
Kenyon & Eckhardt Advertising Agency, **25** 89–91
Kenyon Corp., **18** 276
Kenzo, **25** 122
Keo Cutters, Inc., **III** 569; **20** 360
Keolis SA, 51 191–93
Kepco. *See* Korea Electric Power Corporation; Kyushu Electric Power Company Inc.
Keppel Tatlee, **56** 363
Keramik Holding AG Laufen, 51 194–96
Kern County Land Co., **10** 379
Kernite SA, **8** 386
Kernkraftwerke Lippe-Ems, **V** 747
Kerr Concrete Pipe Company, **14** 250
Kerr Corporation, **14** 481
Kerr Drug Stores, **32** 170
Kerr Group Inc., 10 130; **24 263–65; 30** 39
Kerr-McGee Corporation, IV 445–47; 13 118; **22 301–04 (upd.); 63** 441
Kerry Group plc, 27 258–60
Kerry Properties Limited, 22 305–08; 24 388
Keski-Suomen Tukkukauppa Oy, **8** 293

Kesko Ltd (Kesko Oy), 8 293–94; **27** 261–63 **(upd.)**
Kessler Rehabilitation Corporation. *See* Select Medical Corporation.
Ketchikan Paper Company, **31** 316
Ketchum Communications Inc., 6 38–40
Kettle Chip Company (Australia), **26** 58
Kettle Foods Inc., 26 58; **48** 240–42
Kettle Restaurants, Inc., **29** 149
Kewanee Public Service Company, **6** 505
Kewaunee Scientific Corporation, 25 259–62
Kewpie Kabushiki Kaisha, 57 202–05
Key Computer Laboratories, Inc., **14** 15
Key Industries, Inc., **26** 342
Key Pharmaceuticals, Inc., **11** 207; **41** 419
Key Safety Systems, Inc., 63 224–26
Key Tronic Corporation, 14 284–86
KeyCorp, 8 295–97; **11** 110; **14** 90
Keyes Fibre Company, 9 303–05
KeyLabs, **65** 34–35
Keypage. *See* Rural Cellular Corporation.
KeySpan Energy Co., 27 264–66
Keystone Consolidated Industries, Inc., **19** 467
Keystone Foods Corporation, **10** 443
Keystone Frozen Foods, **17** 536
Keystone Health Plan West, Inc., **27** 211
Keystone Insurance and Investment Co., **12** 564
Keystone International, Inc., 11 225–27; **28** 486
Keystone Life Insurance Co., **III** 389; **33** 419
Keystone Paint and Varnish, **8** 553
Keystone Portland Cement Co., **23** 225
Keystone Savings and Loan, **II** 420
Keystone Tube Inc., **25** 8
Keytronics, **18** 541
KFC Corporation, 7 265–68; **10** 450; **21** 313–17 **(upd.)**; **23** 115, 117, 153; **32** 12–14; **58** 383–84
KFF Management, **37** 350
KHBB, **16** 72
KHD AG. *See* Klöckner-Humboldt-Deutz AG.
KHD Konzern, III 541–44
KHL. *See* Koninklijke Hollandsche Lloyd.
KI, **57** 206–09
Kia Motors Corporation, 12 293–95; **29** 264–67 **(upd.)**; **56** 173
Kiabi Europe, 37 22–23; **66** 199–201
Kian Dai Wools Co. Ltd., **53** 344
Kickers Worldwide, **35** 204, 207
Kidd, Kamm & Co., **21** 482
Kidde Inc., I 475–76; **23** 297; **39** 344–46
Kidde plc, 44 255–59 **(upd.)**; **50** 133–35
Kidder, Peabody & Co., **II** 31, 207, 430; **7** 310; **12** 197; **13** 465–67, 534; **16** 322; **22** 406
Kiddie Products, Inc. *See* The First Years Inc.
Kids ''R'' Us. *See* Toys ''R'' Us.
Kids Foot Locker, **14** 293, 295
Kidz Biz Ltd., **52** 193
Kiehl's Since 1851, Inc., 52 209–12
Kien, **13** 545
Kienzle Apparate GmbH, **III** 566; **38** 299
Kierulff Electronics, **10** 113; **50** 42
Kieser Verlag, **14** 555
Kiewit Diversified Group Inc. *See* Level 3 Communications, Inc.
Kiewit Materials. *See* Rinker Group Ltd.
Kiewit-Murdock Investment Corp., **15** 129

Kijkshop/Best-Sellers, **13** 545
Kikkoman Corporation, 14 287–89; **47** 203–06 **(upd.)**
Kilgore Federal Savings and Loan Assoc., **IV** 343
Killington, Ltd., **28** 21
Kilpatrick's Department Store, **19** 511
KIM Holdings, Inc., **66** 204
Kimball International, Inc., 12 296–98; **48** 243–47 **(upd.)**
Kimbell Inc., **II** 684
Kimberly-Clark Corporation, III 40–41; **IV** 254, 297–98, 329, 648, 665; **8** 282; **15** 357; **16** 302–05 **(upd.)**; **18** 147–49; **19** 284, 478; **22** 209; **43** 256–60 **(upd.)**; **52** 301–02; **54** 185, 187
Kimberly-Clark de México, S.A. de C.V., 54 185–87
Kimco Realty Corporation, 11 228–30
Kimowelt Medien, **39** 13
Kincaid Furniture Company, **14** 302–03
Kindai Golf Company, **32** 447
Kinden Corporation, **7** 303
Kinder Morgan, Inc., 45 227–30
KinderCare Learning Centers, Inc., 13 298–300; **34** 105; **35** 408
Kindergard Corporation, **57** 230
Kineret Acquisition Corp. *See* The Hain Celestial Group, Inc.
Kinetic Concepts, Inc., 20 321–23
King & Spalding, 23 315–18
The King Arthur Flour Company, 31 292–95
King Bearing, Inc., **13** 79
King Cullen, **II** 644
King Features Syndicate, **IV** 626; **19** 201, 203–04; **46** 232
King Folding Box Co., **13** 441
King Hickory, **17** 183
King Kullen Grocery Co., Inc., 15 259–61; **19** 481; **24** 528
King Pharmaceuticals, Inc., 54 188–90
King Ranch, Inc., 14 290–92; **60** 186–89 **(upd.)**
King-Seeley, **16** 487
King Soopers Inc., **12** 112–13
King World Productions, Inc., 9 306–08; **28** 174; **30** 269–72 **(upd.)**
King's Lynn Glass, **12** 528
Kingbird Media Group LLC, **26** 80
Kingfisher plc, V 106–09; **10** 498; **19** 123; **24** 266–71 **(upd.)**; **27** 118, 120; **28** 34, 36; **49** 112–13
Kings, **24** 528
Kings County Lighting Company, **6** 456
Kings County Research Laboratories, **11** 424
Kings Mills, Inc., **13** 532
Kings Super Markets, **24** 313, 316
Kingsin Line, **6** 397
Kingston Technology Corporation, 20 324–26; **38** 441
Kinki Nippon Railway Company Ltd., V 463–65
Kinki Piping Company Ltd., **60** 236
Kinko's Inc., 12 174; **16** 306–08; **18** 363–64; **43** 261–64 **(upd.)**
Kinnevik. *See* Industriförvaltnings AB Kinnevik.
Kinney Corporation, **23** 32; **24** 373
Kinney National Service Inc., **25** 140
Kinney Shoe Corp., 11 349; **14** 293–95
Kinney Tobacco Co., **12** 108
Kinoshita Sansho Steel Co., **I** 508

Kinpo Electronic, **23** 212
Kinross Gold Corporation, 36 314–16
Kinson Resources Inc., **27** 38
Kintana, Inc., **59** 295
Kintec Corp., **10** 97
Kirby. *See* Scott Fetzer Company.
Kirby Corporation, 18 277–79; **22** 275; **66** 202–04 **(upd.)**
Kirch Gruppe, **10** 196; **35** 452
KirchMedia GmbH & Co., **54** 295–98
KirchPayTV, **46** 402
Kirin Brewery Company, Limited, I 265–66, 282; **10** 78, 80; **13** 258, 454; **20** 28; **21** 318–21 **(upd.)**; **36** 404–05; **52** 31–32; **54** 227, 229–30; **57** 305; **63** 227–31 **(upd.)**
Kirk Stieff Company, **10** 181; **12** 313
Kirkland & Ellis LLP, 65 194–96
Kirkland Messina, Inc., **19** 392, 394
Kirsch Co., **II** 16
Kirschner Manufacturing Co., **16** 296
Kirshenbaum Bond + Partners, Inc., 57 210–12
Kirsten Modedesign GmbH & Co. KG, **53** 195
Kirtland Capital Partners, **67** 312–13
Kit Manufacturing Co., 18 280–82
Kita Consolidated, Ltd., **16** 142
Kitchell Corporation, 14 296–98
KitchenAid, 8 298–99
Kitchenbell, **III** 43
Kittery Electric Light Co., **14** 124
Kittinger, **10** 324
Kitty Hawk, Inc., 22 309–11
Kiwi International Airlines Inc., 20 327–29
Kiwi Packaging, **IV** 250
Kiwi Polish Co., **15** 507
KJJ. *See* Klaus J. Jacobs Holdings.
KJPCL. *See* Royal Interocean Lines.
KKR. *See* Kohlberg Kravis Roberts & Co.
KLA Instruments Corporation, 11 231–33; **20** 8
KLA-Tencor Corporation, 45 231–34 **(upd.)**
Klaus J. Jacobs Holdings, **29** 46–47
Klaus Steilmann GmbH & Co. KG, 53 192–95
KLC/New City Televentures, **25** 269
Klein Bicycles, **16** 495
Klein Sleep Products Inc., **32** 426
Kleiner, Perkins, Caufield & Byers, 10 15, 504; **14** 263; **16** 418; **27** 447; **53** 196–98
Kleinwort Benson Group PLC, II 421–23; **22** 55. *See also* Dresdner Kleinwort Wasserstein.
Klement's Sausage Company, 61 147–49
Kline Manufacturing, **II** 16
KLLM Transport Services, **27** 404
KLM Royal Dutch Airlines, **26** 33924 311, 396–97; **27** 474; **29** 15, 17; **33** 49, 51; **34** 397; **47** 60–61. *See also* Koninklijke Luftvaart Maatschappij N.V.
Klöckner-Humboldt-Deutz AG. *See* KHD Konzern.
Klöckner-Werke AG, IV 126–28; **19** 64; **39** 125; **58** 201–05 **(upd.)**
Klondike, **14** 205
Kloof Gold Mining Company Ltd., **62** 164
Klopman International, **12** 118
Klüber Lubrication München KG, **41** 170
Kluwer Publishers, **IV** 611; **14** 555
Klynveld Main Goerdeler, **10** 387

Klynveld Peat Marwick Goerdeler. *See* KPMG Worldwide.

KM&G. *See* Ketchum Communications Inc.

Kmart Canada Co., **25** 222

Kmart Corporation, **V** 35, **110–12**; **7** 61, 444; **9** 361, 400, 482; **10** 137, 410, 490, 497, 515–16; **12** 48, 54–55, 430, 477–78, 507–08; **13** 42, 260–61, 274, 317–18, 444, 446; **14** 192, 394; **15** 61–62, 210–11, 330–31, 470; **16** 35–37, 61, 187, 210, 447, 457; **17** 297, 460–61, 523–24; **18** 137, **283–87 (upd.)**, 477; **19** 511; **20** 155–56; **21** 73; **22** 258, 328; **23** 210, 329; **24** 322–23; **25** 121; **26** 348, 524; **27** 313, 429, 451, 481; **32** 169; **43** 77–78, 293, 385; **47 207–12 (upd.)**; **48** 331; **53** 146; **63** 429

Kmart Mexico, **36** 139

KMC Enterprises, Inc., **27** 274

KMI Corporation, **55** 302

KN. *See* Kühne & Nagel Group.

KN Energy. *See* Kinder Morgan, Inc.

Kna-Shoe Manufacturing Company, **14** 302; **50** 309

Knape & Vogt Manufacturing Company, **17 277–79**

Knapp Communications Corporation, **II** 656; **13** 180; **24** 418

Knapp-Monarch, **12** 251

Knauf, **III** 736

K'Nex Industries, Inc., 52 206–08

KNI Retail A/S, **12** 363

Knickerbocker Trust Company, **13** 465

Knife River Coal Mining Company, **7** 322–25

Knife River Corporation, **42** 249, 253

Knight-Ridder, Inc., **IV 628–30**, 670; **7** 327; **10** 407; **15 262–66 (upd.)**; **18** 323; **38** 307; **63** 394; **67 219–23 (upd.)**

Knight Transportation, Inc., 64 218–21

Knightsbridge Capital Corporation, **59** 192

Knightsbridge Partners, **26** 476

Knightway Promotions Ltd., **64** 346

KNILM, **24** 397

Knogo Corp., **11** 444; **39** 78

Knoll Group Inc., **I** 202; **14 299–301**

Knorr-Bremse, **11** 31

Knorr Co. *See* C.H. Knorr Co.

Knorr Foods Co., Ltd., **28** 10

Knott's Berry Farm, **18 288–90**; **22** 130

Knowledge Learning Corporation, **51 197–99**; **54** 191

Knowledge Systems Concepts, **11** 469

Knowledge Universe, Inc., 54 191–94, 215–16

KnowledgeWare Inc., **9 309–11**; **27** 491; **31 296–98 (upd.)**; **45** 206

Knox County Insurance, **41** 178

Knox Reeves Advertising Agency, **25** 90

Knoxville Glove Co., **34** 159

Knoxville Paper Box Co., Inc., **13** 442

KNP BT. *See* Buhrmann NV.

KNP Leykam, **49** 352, 354

KNSM. *See* Koninklijke Nederlandsche Stoomboot Maatschappij.

Knudsen & Sons, Inc., **11** 211

Knudsen Foods, **27** 330

Knutson Construction, **25** 331

KOA. *See* Kampgrounds of America, Inc.

Koala Corporation, 44 260–62

Kobacker Co., **18** 414–15

Kobe Hankyu Company Ltd., **62** 170

Kobe Shipbuilding & Engine Works, **II** 57

Kobe Steel, Ltd., **I** 511; **IV** 16, **129–31**, 212–13; **8** 242; **11** 234–35; **13** 297; **19 238–41 (upd.)**; **38** 225–26

Kobelco America Inc., **19** 241

Kobelco Middle East, **IV** 131

Kobold. *See* Vorwerk & Co.

Kobrand Corporation, **24** 308; **43** 402

Koç Holding A.S., **I** 478–80; **27** 188; **54 195–98 (upd.)**

Koch Enterprises, Inc., 29 215–17

Koch Industries, Inc., **IV** 448–49; **20 330–32 (upd.)**; **21** 108; **22** 3

Koch-Light Laboratories, **13** 239; **38** 203–04

Kockos Brothers, Inc., **II** 624

Kodak. *See* Eastman Kodak Company.

Kodansha Ltd., **IV** 631–33; **38 273–76 (upd.)**

Koehring Company, **8** 545; **23** 299

Koehring Cranes & Excavators, **7** 513

Koei Real Estate Ltd. *See* Takashimaya Co., Limited.

Koenig & Bauer AG, 64 222–26

Koenig Plastics Co., **19** 414

Kogaku Co., Ltd., **48** 295

Kohl's Corporation, **9 312–13**; **22** 72; **30 273–75 (upd.)**; **50** 117–18; **63** 146

Kohl's Food Stores, Inc., **I** 426–27; **16** 247, 249

Kohlberg & Co., **52** 159

Kohlberg Kravis Roberts & Co., **II** 370, 452, 468, 544, 645, 654, 656, 667; **7** 130, 132, 200; **9** 53, 180, 230, 469, 522; **10** 75–77, 302; **12** 559; **13** 163, 166, 363, 453; **14** 42; **15** 270; **18** 3; **19** 493; **22** 91, 441, 513; **23** 163; **24** 92, **272–74**, 416, 418; **25** 11, 278; **26** 46, 48, 352; **27** 11; **28** 389, 475; **30** 386; **32** 408; **33** 255; **35** 35; **38** 190; **40** 34, 36, 366; **43** 355; **44** 153; **45** 243; **49** 369; **56 190–94 (upd.)**

Kohler Company, **7 269–71**; **10** 119; **24** 150; **32 308–12 (upd.)**; **53** 176

Kohler Mix Specialties, Inc., **25** 333

Kohn Pedersen Fox Associates P.C., 57 213–16

Kokkola Chemicals Oy, **17** 362–63

Kokomo Gas and Fuel Company, **6** 533

Kokusai Kigyo Co. Ltd., **60** 301

Kolb-Lena, **25** 85

Kolker Chemical Works, Inc., **7** 308

The Koll Company, **8 300–02**; **21** 97; **25** 449

Kollmorgen Corporation, **18 291–94**

Kölnische Rückversicherungs- Gesellschaft AG, **24** 178

Komag, Inc., 11 234–35

Komatsu Ltd., **III** 453, 473, **545–46**; **15** 92; **16 309–11 (upd.)**; **52 213–17 (upd.)**

Kompass Allgemeine Vermögensberatung, **51** 23

Konan Camera Institute, **III** 487

Kone Corporation, **27 267–70**; **67** 8

Kongl. Elektriska Telegraf-Verket. *See* Swedish Telecom.

Konica Corporation, **III 547–50**; **30 276–81 (upd.)**; **43** 284

König Brauerei GmbH & Co. KG, 35 256–58 (upd.)

Koninklijke Ahold N.V., **II** 641–42; **12** 152–53; **16 312–14 (upd.)**

Koninklijke Bols Wessanen, N.V., **29** 480–81; **57** 105

Koninklijke Grolsch BV. *See* Royal Grolsch NV.

Koninklijke Hoogovens NV, **26** 527, 530. *See also* Koninklijke Nederlandsche Hoogovens en Staalfabrieken NV.

Koninklijke Java-China Paketvaart Lijnen. *See* Royal Interocean Lines.

NV Koninklijke KNP BT. *See* Buhrmann NV.

Koninklijke KPN N.V. *See* Royal KPN N.V.

Koninklijke Luchtvaart Maatschappij N.V., **I 107–09**, 119, 121; **6** 105, 109–10; **14** 73; **28 224–27 (upd.)**

Koninklijke Nederlandsche Hoogovens en Staalfabrieken NV, **IV 132–34**; **49** 98, 101

Koninklijke Nederlandsche Stoomboot Maatschappij, **26** 241

N.V. Koninklijke Nederlandse Vliegtuigenfabriek Fokker, **I 54–56**, 75, 82, 107, 115, 121–22; **28 327–30 (upd.)**

Koninklijke Nedlloyd Groep N.V., **6 403–05**

Koninklijke Nedlloyd N.V., **26 241–44 (upd.)**

Koninklijke Numico N.V. *See* Royal Numico N.V.

Koninklijke Paketvaart Maatschappij, **26** 242

Koninklijke Philips Electronics N.V., **50 297–302 (upd.)**

Koninklijke PTT Nederland NV, **V 299–301**; **27** 471–72, 475. *See also* Royal KPN NV.

Koninklijke Van Ommeren, **22** 275

Koninklijke Vendex KBB N.V. (Royal Vendex KBB N.V.), **62 206–09 (upd.)**

Koninklijke Wessanen nv, **II 527–29**; **54 199–204 (upd.)**

Koninklijke West-Indische Maildienst, **26** 242

Konishiroku Honten Co., Ltd., **III** 487, 547–49

Konrad Hornschuch AG, **31** 161–62

Koo Koo Roo, Inc., 25 263–65

Kookmin Bank, 58 206–08

Koop Nautic Holland, **41** 412

Koor Industries Ltd., **II 47–49**; **22** 501; **25 266–68 (upd.)**; **54** 363

Koors Perry & Associates, Inc., **24** 95

Koortrade, **II** 48

Kop-Coat, Inc., **8** 456

Kopin Corp., **13** 399

Köpings Mekaniska Verkstad, **26** 10

Koppel Steel, **26** 407

Koppers Industries, Inc., **I 354–56**; **6** 486; **17** 38–39; **26 245–48 (upd.)**

Koracorp Industries Inc., **16** 327

Körber AG, 60 190–94

Korea Automotive Fuel Systems Ltd., **13** 555

Korea Automotive Motor Corp., **16** 436; **43** 319

Korea Electric Power Corporation (Kepco), 56 195–98

Korea Ginseng Corporation. *See* KT&G Corporation.

Korea Independent Energy Corporation, **62** 175

Korea Steel Co., **III** 459

Korea Tobacco & Ginseng Corporation. *See* KT&G Corporation.

Korean Air Lines Co. Ltd., **6** 98–99; **24** 443; **27** 271–73 (upd.); **46** 40
Korean Development Bank, **III** 459
Korean Life Insurance Company, Ltd., **62** 175
Koret of California, Inc., **62** 210–13
Kori Kollo Corp., **23** 41
Korn/Ferry International, **34** 247–49
Koro Corp., **19** 414
Korrekt Gebäudereinigung, **16** 420; **43** 307
KorrVu, **14** 430
Kortbetalning Servo A.B., **II** 353
Kortgruppen Eurocard-Köpkort A.B., **II** 353
Korvettes, E.J., **14** 426
Kos Pharmaceuticals, Inc., **63** 232–35
Koss Corporation, **38** 277–79
Kosset Carpets, Ltd., **9** 467
Kotobukiya Co., Ltd., **V** 113–14; **56** 199–202 (upd.)
Kowa Metal Manufacturing Co., **III** 758
Koyland Ltd., **64** 217
KPM. See Koninklijke Paketvaart Maatschappij.
KPMG International, **29** 176; **33** 234–38 (upd.)
KPMG Worldwide, **7** 266; **10** 115, 385–87
KPN. See Koninklijke PTT Nederland N.V.
KPR Holdings Inc., **23** 203
Kraft Foods Inc., **II** 530–34, 556; **V** 407; **7** 272–77 (upd.), 339, 433, 547; **8** 399, 499; **9** 180, 290, 318; **11** 15; **12** 372, 532; **13** 408, 515, 517; **14** 204; **16** 88, 90; **17** 56; **18** 67, 246, 416, 419; **19** 51; **22** 82, 85; **23** 219, 384; **25** 366, 517; **26** 249, 251; **28** 479; **44** 342; **45** 235–44 (upd.); **48** 331; **63** 83, 86
Kraft Foodservice, **26** 504; **31** 359–60
Kraft Jacobs Suchard AG, **26** 249–52 (upd.)
Kraftco Corporation, **14** 204
KraftMaid Cabinetry, Inc., **20** 363; **39** 267
Kragen Auto Supply Co., **27** 291. See also CSK Auto Corporation.
Kramer, **III** 48
Kramer Guitar, **29** 222
Kramer Machine and Engineering Company, **26** 117
Krames Communications Co., **22** 441, 443
Kransco, **25** 314; **61** 392
Krasnapolsky Restaurant and Wintergarden Company Ltd., **23** 228
Kraus-Anderson, Incorporated, **36** 317–20
Krause Publications, Inc., **35** 259–61
Krause's Furniture, Inc., **27** 274–77
Krauss-Maffei AG, **I** 75; **III** 566; **14** 328; **38** 299
Kredietbank N.V., **II** 304–05; **59** 246
Kreditanstalt für Wiederaufbau, **29** 268–72
Kreher Steel Co., **25** 8
Krelitz Industries, Inc., **14** 147
Kresge Foundation. See Kmart Corporation.
Kreuger & Toll, **12** 462–63
Kreymborg, **13** 544–45
Krislex Knits, Inc., **8** 235
Krispy Kreme Doughnut Corporation, **21** 322–24; **61** 150–54 (upd.)
Kristall, **62** 10
Kroenke Sports Enterprises, **51** 97
Kroeze, **25** 82

The Kroger Company, **II** 605, 632, 643–45, 682; **7** 61; **12** 111–13; **13** 25, 237, 395; **15** 259, 267–70 (upd.), 449; **16** 63–64; **18** 6; **21** 323, 508; **22** 37; **24** 416; **25** 234; **28** 512; **30** 24, 27; **40** 366; **57** 324, 327; **64** 135; **65** 197–202 (upd.)
Kroll Inc., **57** 217–20
Krone AG, **33** 220
Kronos, Inc., **18** 295–97; **19** 468
Krovtex, **8** 80
Kroy Tanning Company, **17** 195
KRS Corporation, **57** 202–04
Krueger Insurance Company, **21** 257
Krueger International. See KI.
Kruger Inc., **17** 280–82
Kruidvat, **54** 265–67
Krumbhaar Chemical Inc., **14** 308
Krupp AG, **17** 214; **22** 364; **49** 53–55; **59** 390. See also Fried. Krupp GmbH; Thyssen Krupp AG.
Krupp Widia GmbH, **12** 66
Kruse International, **32** 162
The Krystal Company, **33** 239–42
KSB AG, **62** 214–18
KT&G Corporation, **62** 219–21
KT Contract Services, **24** 118
KTR. See Keio Teito Electric Railway Company.
K2 Inc., **16** 295–98; **22** 481, 483; **23** 474; **43** 389
KU Energy Corporation, **6** 513, 515; **11** 236–38
Kubota Corporation, **III** 551–53; **10** 404; **12** 91, 161; **21** 385–86; **24** 324; **39** 37; **40** 134
Kudelski Group SA, **44** 263–66
Kuehne & Nagel International AG, **V** 466–69; **53** 199–203 (upd.)
Kuhlman Corporation, **20** 333–35
Kühn + Bayer, **24** 165
Kühne & Nagel International AG, **V** 466–69
Kulicke and Soffa Industries, Inc., **33** 246–48
Kulka Smith Inc., **13** 398
Kumagai Gumi Co., **I** 579–80
Kumba Resources, **57** 183, 186
Kunkel Industries, **19** 143
Kunz-Holding GmbH & Co., **53** 216
Kuo International Ltd., **I** 566; **44** 153
Kuok Group, **28** 84; **57** 292, 294
Kuoni Travel Holding Ltd., **40** 284–86
The Kuppenheimer Company, **8** 248–50; **32** 247
Kurabo Industries Ltd., **61** 229
Kurt Möller Verlag, **7** 42
Kurushima Dockyard, **II** 339
Kurzweil Technologies, Inc., **51** 200–04
KUS. See Karl Schmidt Unisia, Inc.
The Kushner-Locke Company, **25** 269–71
Kuwait Airways, **27** 135
Kuwait Aviation Fueling Co., **55** 243
Kuwait Investment Office, **II** 198; **IV** 380, 452; **27** 206
Kuwait Petroleum Corporation, **IV** 450–52; **18** 234; **38** 424; **55** 240–43 (upd.)
Kvaerner ASA, **20** 313; **31** 367, 370; **36** 321–23
KW, Inc. See Coca-Cola Bottling Company of Northern New England, Inc.
Kwik-Fit Holdings plc, **54** 205–07

Kwik Save Group plc, **11** 239–41; **13** 26; **47** 368
Kwik Shop, Inc., **12** 112
Kwikasair Ltd., **27** 473
KWIM. See Koninklijke West-Indische Maildienst.
Kymmene Corporation, **IV** 299–303. See also UPM-Kymmene Corporation.
Kyocera Corporation, **II** 50–52; **7** 118; **21** 329–32 (upd.); **67** 41–42
Kyodo, **16** 166
Kyodo Dieworks Thailand Co., **III** 758
Kyodo Kako, **IV** 680
Kyodo Kokusan K.K., **21** 271
Kyoei Mutual Fire and Marine Insurance Co., **III** 273
Kyoei Steel, **59** 202
Kyosai Trust Co. See Yasuda Trust and Banking Company, Limited.
Kyotaru Co., **66** 270–71
Kyoto Ceramic Co., Ltd. See Kyocera Corporation.
Kyowa Hakko Kogyo Co., Ltd., **III** 42–43; **45** 94; **48** 248–50 (upd.)
Kyushu Electric Power Company Inc., **V** 649–51; **17** 349
Kywan Petroleum Ltd., **13** 556
KYZ International, **9** 427
KZO, **13** 21

L & G, **27** 291
L&H. See Lernout and Hauspie.
L. & H. Sales Co., **16** 389
L. and J.G. Stickley, Inc., **50** 303–05
L&W Supply Corp., **III** 764
L E Lundbergföretagen AB, **52** 161, 164
L-3 Communications Holdings, Inc., **48** 251–53; **54** 234
L.A. Dreyfus Company, **58** 378
L.A. Gear, Inc., **8** 303–06; **11** 349; **31** 413; **32** 313–17 (upd.)
L.A. Mex. See Checkers Drive-Up Restaurants Inc.
L.A. T Sportswear, Inc., **26** 257–59
L.B. Foster Company, **33** 255–58
L. Bosendorfer Klavierfabrik, A.G., **12** 297
L.D.C. SA, **61** 155–57
L.D. Canocéan, **25** 104
The L.D. Caulk Company, **10** 271
L. Fish, **14** 236
L.G. Balfour Company, **12** 472; **19** 451–52; **36** 469
L. Greif & Bro. Inc., **17** 203–05
L. Grossman and Sons. See Grossman's Inc.
L.J. Knowles & Bros., **9** 153
L.J. Melody & Co., **21** 97
L.K. Liggett Company, **24** 74
L. Kellenberger & Co. AG, **25** 194
L.L. Bean, Inc., **9** 190, 316; **10** 388–90; **12** 280; **19** 333; **21** 131; **22** 173; **25** 48, 206; **29** 278; **36** 180, 420; **38** 280–83 (upd.)
The L.L. Knickerbocker Co., Inc., **25** 272–75
L. Luria & Son, Inc., **19** 242–44
L.M. Ericsson, **II** 81–82, 365; **11** 46, 439; **14** 488. See also Telefonaktiebolaget LM Ericsson.
L-O-F Glass Co. See Libbey-Owens-Ford Glass Co.
L. Prang & Co., **12** 207
L.S. Holding, Inc., **60** 204

L.S. Starrett Company, 13 301–03; **64 227–30 (upd.)**
L.W. Pierce Co., Inc. *See* Pierce Leahy Corporation.
L.W. Singer, 13 429
La Banque Suisse et Française. *See* Crédit Commercial de France.
La Barge Mirrors, III 571; 20 362
La Cadena Investments, 64 364
La Cerus, IV 615
La Choy Food Products Inc., 17 241; **25 276–78**
La Cinq, IV 619
La Cloche d'Or, 25 85
La Crosse Telephone Corporation, 9 106
La Cruz del Campo S.A., 9 100
La Fromagerie du Velay, 25 85
La Grange Foundry, Inc., 39 31
La Halle aux Chaussures, 17 210
La Joya, 51 389
La Madeleine French Bakery & Café, 33 **249–51**
La Maison du Jambon, 58 218
La Martiniere Groupe, 58 152
La Oroya, 22 286
La Petite Academy, 13 299
La Pizza Loca Inc., 44 86
La Poste, V 270–72; **47 213–16 (upd.)**
The La Quinta Companies, 42 213–16 **(upd.)**
La Quinta Inns, Inc., 11 242–44; 21 362
La Redoute S.A., 19 306, 309
La Rinascente, 12 153
La-Ru Truck Rental Company, Inc., 16 386
La Ruche Meridionale, 12 153
La Senza Corporation, 66 205–07
La 7, 47 345, 347
La Societe Anonyme Francaise Holophane, 19 211
La Supercalor S.P.A. *See* De'Longhi S.p.A.
La Vie Claire, 13 103
La-Z-Boy Chair Company, 14 302–04; 31 248
La-Z-Boy Incorporated, 50 309–13 **(upd.)**
LAB. *See* Lloyd Aereo de Bolivia.
The Lab, Inc., 37 263
LaB Investing Co. L.L.C, 37 224
LaBakelite S.A., I 387
LaBarge Inc., 41 224–26
Labatt Brewing Company Limited, I 267–68; 18 72; **25 279–82 (upd.)**; 26 303, 306
Labatt U.S.A., 54 212–14
L'Abeille SA, 61 44–45
Labelcraft, Inc., 8 360
LaBelle Iron Works, 7 586
LabOne, Inc., 48 254–57
Labor Ready, Inc., 29 273–75
Labor W. *See* Sennheiser Electronic GmbH and Co. AG.
Laboratoire L. Lafon, 45 94
Laboratoires de Biologie Végétale Yves Rocher, 35 262–65
Laboratoires Goupil, III 48
Laboratoires Roche Posay, III 48
Laboratorio Chile S.A., 55 233
Laboratorios Elmor S.A., 55 233
Laboratorios Liade S.A., 24 75
Laboratorium Wennebostel. *See* Sennheiser Electronic GmbH and Co. AG.
Laboratory Corporation of America Holdings, 42 217–20 **(upd.)**
LaBranche & Co. Inc., 37 223–25

Labsphere, Inc., **48** 446
Labtronics, Inc., **49** 307–08
Lachine Rapids Hydraulic and Land Company, **6** 501
Laci Le Beau Tea, **49** 275–76
Lacks Enterprises Inc., 61 158–60
Laclede Steel Company, 15 271–73
Lacombe Electric. *See* Public Service Company of Colorado.
LaCrosse Footwear, Inc., 18 298–301; **161–65 (upd.)**
Lacto Ibérica, 23 219
Lactos, 25 85
Lacy Diversified Industries, Ltd., 24 159–61
Ladbroke Group PLC, II 141–42; 19 208; **21 333–36 (upd.)**; 42 64; 49 449–50. *See also* Hilton Group plc.
Ladd and Tilton, 14 527–28
LADD Furniture, Inc., 12 299–301; 23 244
Ladd Petroleum Corp., II 30
LADECO, 31 304. *See also* Iberia.
Ladenburg, Thalmann & Co. Inc., 17 346
Ladenso, IV 277
Ladish Co., Inc., 30 282–84
Lady Foot Locker, V 226; 14 293, 295
Lady Lee, 27 291
Laerdal Medical, 18 423
Lafarge Cement UK, 54 208–11 (upd.)
Lafarge Coppée S.A., III 703–05; 8 258; 10 422–23; 23 333; 59 111–12, 115; 64 380
Lafarge Corporation, 24 332; **28 228–31**
Lafayette Manufacturing Co., 12 296
Lafayette Radio Electronics Corporation, 9 121–22
Lafuma S.A., 39 248–50
LAG&E. *See* Los Angeles Gas and Electric Company.
LaGard Inc., 20 363
Lagardère Groupe SCA, 16 254; 24 84, 88; 34 83
Laidlaw Inc., 39 19, 21
Laidlaw Transportation, Inc., 6 410; 32 227, 231
Laing's Properties Ltd. *See* John Laing plc.
L'Air Liquide SA, I 357–59; 11 402; **47 217–20 (upd.)**
Laiterie Centrale Krompholtz, 25 84
Laiterie de la Vallée du Dropt, 25 84
Laiterie Ekabe, 19 50
SA Laiterie Walhorn Molkerel, 19 50
Laiteries Prairies de l'Orne, 19 50
Lake Erie Screw Corp., 11 534, 536
Lake Odessa Machine Products, 18 494
Lake Pacific Partners, LLC, 55 124
Lake Superior & Ishpeming Railroad Company, 62 74
Lake Superior Consolidated Mines Company, 17 355–56
Lake Superior Paper Industries, 26 363
Lakehead Pipe Line Partners, L.P., 43 155
Lakeland Industries, Inc., 45 245–48
Laker Airways, 24 399
Lakes Entertainment, Inc., 51 205–07
The Lakeside Publishing and Printing Co. *See* R.R. Donnelley & Sons Co.
Lakestone Systems, Inc., 11 469
Lakewood Animal Hospital, Inc., 58 354
Lalique, 55 309
Lam Research Corporation, IV 213; 11 245–47; 18 383; **31 299–302 (upd.)**

Lam Son Sugar Joint Stock Corporation (Lasuco), 60 195–97
Lamar Advertising Company, 27 278–80
The Lamaur Corporation, 41 227–29
Lamb Technicon Corp., I 486
Lamb Weston, Inc., 23 319–21
Lambda Electronics Inc., 32 411
Lambert Brothers, Inc., 7 573
Lambert Brussels Financial Corporation. *See* Drexel Burnham Lambert Incorporated.
Lambert Frères, 33 339
Lambert Kay Company, 8 84
Lambert Rivière, 41 340
Lamborghini. *See* Automobili Lamborghini S.p.A.
Lamkin Brothers, Inc., 8 386
Lamons Metal Gasket Co., 11 535
Lamontagne Ltd., II 651
Lamonts Apparel, Inc., 15 274–76
Lampadaires Feralux, Inc., 19 472
The Lamson & Sessions Co., 13 304–06; **61 166–70 (upd.)**
Lamson Corporation, 7 145; 49 159
Lan Chile S.A., 31 303–06; 33 ; 59 172
Lanca, 14 224
Lancair International, Inc., 67 224–26
Lancaster Colony Corporation, 8 307–09; 57 354–55; **61 171–74 (upd.)**
Lancaster Financial Ltd., 14 472
Lancaster National Bank, 9 475
Lancaster Press, 23 102
Lance, Inc., 14 305–07; **41 230–33 (upd.)**; 56 365–66
Lancel, 27 487, 489
Lancer Corporation, 21 337–39
Lancey Investissement SAS, 58 221
Lanchester Motor Company, Ltd., 13 286
Land O'Lakes, Inc., II 535–37; 7 339; 13 351; **21 340–43 (upd.)**
Land-O-Sun Dairies, L.L.C., 26 449
Land Securities PLC, IV 704–06; 49 246–50 **(upd.)**; 54 38
Landauer, Inc., 51 208–10
Lander Company, 21 54
Landis International, Inc., 10 105–06
Landmark Banks, 10 426
Landmark Business Products, Inc., 61 254
Landmark Communications, Inc., 12 302–05; 22 442; 52 401–02; **55 244–49 (upd.)**
Landmark Financial Services Inc., 11 447
Landmark Target Media, IV 597
Landmark Union Trust, 18 517
Landoll, Inc., 22 522
Landry's Restaurants, Inc., 15 277–79; **65 203–07 (upd.)**
Lands' End, Inc., 9 314–16; 12 280; 16 37; 19 333; 26 439; 27 374, 429; 29 276–79 **(upd.)**; 56 311, 313
Landstar System, Inc., 26 533; **63 236–38**
Lane Bryant, Inc., 64 231–33
The Lane Co., Inc., 12 306–08
Lane Drug Company, 12 132
Lane, Piper, and Jaffray, Inc. *See* Piper Jaffray Companies.
Lane Publishing Co., IV 676; 7 529
Laneco, Inc., II 682
Lang Exploratory Drilling, 26 42
Langdon Rieder Corp., 21 97
Lange International S.A., 15 462; 43 375–76
Langen Packaging Inc., 51 249, 251

Langenpac NV, **51** 249–50

Langford Labs, **8** 25

Lanier Business Products, Inc., **8** 407; **20** 290

Lanman Companies, Inc., **23** 101

Lannet Data Communications Ltd., **18** 345–46; **26** 275–77

Lanoga Corporation, 62 222–24

LAPE. *See* Líneas Aéreas Postales Españolas.

Lapeyre S.A. *See* Groupe Lapeyre S.A.

LaPine Technology, **II** 51; **21** 331

Lapp, **8** 229

Lara, **19** 192

Larami Corp., **14** 486

Lareco, **26** 22

Largardère Groupe, **43** 210

Largo Entertainment, **25** 329

Largo Music Publishing, **55** 250

Lariat Petroleum, **65** 262

Larousse Group. *See* Groupe de la Cité.

Larry Flynt Publishing Inc., 31 307–10

Larry H. Miller Group, 29 280–83

Larry's Food Products, **36** 163

Larsen Company, **7** 128

Larson Boats. *See* Genmar Holdings, Inc.

Las Vegas Gas Company, **19** 411

Las Vegas Sands, Inc., 50 306–08

LaSalle Investment Management, Inc., **49** 238

LaSalle Machine Tool, Inc., **13** 7–8

LaSalle Partners, **49** 28

LaSalle Steel Corporation, **28** 314

LaSalles & Koch Co., **8** 443

Lasco Shipping Co., **19** 380

Laser Tech Color, **21** 60

Lasercharge Pty Ltd, **18** 130

Laserscope, 67 227–29

LaserSoft, **24** 349

LaSiDo Inc., 58 209–11

Lasky's, **24** 269

Lasmo, **IV** 455, 499; **65** 316–17

Lason, Inc., 31 311–13

Lasuco. *See* Lam Son Sugar Joint Stock Corporation.

Latcom, Inc., **55** 302

Latham & Watkins, 33 252–54; 37 292

Latin Communications Group Inc., **41** 151

Latitude Communications, **22** 52

Latrobe Brewing Company, 25 281; **54 212–14**

Latrobe Steel Company, **8** 529–31

Lattice Semiconductor Corp., 16 315–17; 43 17

Lauda Air Luftfahrt AG, 48 258–60

Lauder Chemical, **17** 363

Laura Ashley Holdings plc, 13 307–09; 37 226–29 (upd.)

Laura Scudders, **7** 429; **44** 348

Laureate Enterprises Inc., **64** 190

Laurel Glen, **34** 3, 5

The Laurel Pub Company Limited, 59 255–57

Laurel Technologies Partnership, **58** 101

Laurent-Perrier SA, 42 221–23

Laurentian Group, **48** 290

Laurus N.V., 65 208–11

Lauson Engine Company, **8** 515

LaVista Equipment Supply Co., **14** 545; **60** 326

Lavold, **16** 421; **43** 308

Lawn Boy Inc., **7** 535–36; **8** 72; **26** 494

Lawrenceburg Gas Company, **6** 466

The Lawson Co., **7** 113; **25** 125

Lawson Inc., **41** 113, 115

Lawson Software, 38 284–88

Lawter International Inc., 14 308–10; 18 220

Lawyers Cooperative, **8** 527–28

Layer Five, **43** 252

Layne & Bowler Pump, **11** 5

Layne Christensen Company, 19 245–47; 26 71

Layton Homes Corporation, **30** 423

Lazard Freres & Co., **IV** 23, 79, 658–59; **7** 287, 446; **10** 399; **12** 165, 391, 547, 562

Lazard LLC, 38 289–92

Lazare Kaplan International Inc., 21 344–47

Lazio. *See* Societá Sportiva Lazio SpA.

LBO Holdings, **15** 459

LBS Communications, **6** 28

LCI International, Inc., 16 318–20

LCIE, **55** 79

LCP Hotels. *See* CapStar Hotel Co.

LDB Corporation, 53 204–06

LDC. *See* L.D.C. S.A.

LDCom Networks, **60** 151

LDDS-Metro Communications, Inc., 8 310–12

LDDS WorldCom, Inc., **16** 467–68

LDI. *See* Lacy Diversified Industries, Ltd.

LDMA-AU, Inc., **49** 173

LDS Health Services Corporation, **27** 237

Le Bon Marché. *See* Bon Marché.

Le Buffet System-Gastronomie, **V** 74

Le Chameau, **39** 250

Le Chateau Inc., 63 239–41

Le Clerc, **21** 225–26

Le Cordon Bleu S.A., II 609; **45** 88; **45** 88; **67 230–32**

Le Courviour S.A., **10** 351

Le Monde S.A., 33 308–10

Le Riche Group Ltd., **61** 44, 46

Le Rocher, Compagnie de Reassurance, **III** 340

Le Touquet's, SA, **48** 197

Lea & Perrins, **II** 475

Lea County Gas Co., **6** 580

Lea Lumber & Plywood Co., **12** 300

Lea Manufacturing, **23** 299

Leach McMicking, **13** 274

Leadra Design Inc., **59** 164

Leaf Candy Company, **64** 187

Leaf North America, **51** 159

Leahy & Co. *See* Pierce Leahy Corporation.

Lean Cuisine, **12** 531

LeapFrog Enterprises, Inc., 54 191, 193, **215–18; 61** 203

Lear Corporation, **17** 303, 305

Lear Inc., **8** 49, 51

Lear Romec Corp., **8** 135

Lear Seating Corporation, 16 321–23

Lear Siegler Holdings Corporation, **25** 431

Lear Siegler Inc., I 481–83; **8** 313; **13** 169, 358, 398; **19** 371–72; **30** 426; **44** 308

Learjet Inc., 8 313–16; 9 242; **27 281–85 (upd.)**

Learning Centers Inc., **51** 198

The Learning Company Inc., 24 275–78, 480; **29** 74, 77; **41** 409; **61** 202

Learning Tree International Inc., 24 279–82

LeaRonal, Inc., 23 322–24

Lease International SA, **6** 358

Leaseway Personnel Corp., **18** 159

Leaseway Transportation Corp., 12 309–11

Leatherback Industries, **22** 229

Leatherman Tool Group, Inc., 51 211–13

Lebhar-Friedman, Inc., 55 250–52

Leblanc Corporation. *See* G. Leblanc Corporation.

LeBoeuf, Lamb, Greene & MacRae, L.L.P., 29 284–86

Lebr Associates Inc., **25** 246

Lech Brewery, **24** 450

Leche Pascual Group. *See* Grupo Leche Pascual S.A.

Lechmere Inc., 10 391–93

Lechters, Inc., 11 248–50; 39 251–54 (upd.)

Leclerc. *See* Association des Centres Distributeurs E. Leclerc.

LeCroy Corporation, 41 234–37

Lectorum Publications, **29** 426

Ledcor Industries Limited, 46 266–69

Lederle Laboratories, **14** 254, 256, 423; **27** 115; **50** 248, 250

Lederle Standard Products, **26** 29

Ledesma Sociedad Anónima Agrícola Industrial, 62 225–27

Lee Ackerman Investment Company, **18** 513

Lee Apparel Company, Inc., 8 317–19; 17 512, 514

The Lee Company. *See* VF Corporation.

Lee Cooper Group Ltd., **49** 259

Lee Enterprises, Incorporated, 11 251–53; 47 120; **64 234–37 (upd.)**

Lee International, **24** 373

Lee National Corporation, **26** 234

Lee Optical, **13** 390

Lee Rubber and Tire Corp., **16** 8

Lee Way Holding Co., **14** 42

Lee's Famous Recipe Chicken, **58** 323

Leeann Chin, Inc., 30 285–88

Leeds & Northrup Company, **28** 484; **63** 401

Lees Carpets, **17** 76

Leewards Creative Crafts Inc., **17** 322

Lefrak Organization Inc., 8 357; **26 260–62**

Legacy Homes Ltd., **26** 290

Legal & General Group plc, III 272–73; **24 283–85 (upd.); 30** 494; **33** 319

The Legal Aid Society, 48 261–64

Legal Technologies, Inc., **15** 378

Legault and Masse, **II** 664

Legent Corporation, 10 394–96; 14 392

Legetojsfabrikken LEGO Billund A/S. *See* Lego A/S.

Legg Mason, Inc., 11 493; **33 259–62**

Leggett & Platt, Inc., 9 93; **11 254–56; 48 265–68 (upd.)**

Leggett Stores Inc., **19** 48

Lego A/S, 12 495; **13 310–13; 40 287–91 (upd.); 52** 206

Legrand SA, 21 348–50

Lehigh Acquisition Corp., **34** 286

Lehigh Portland Cement Company, 23 325–27; 31 252

Lehman Brothers, **14** 145; **22** 445; **25** 301; **38** 411; **48** 59

Lehman Merchant Bank Partners, **19** 324

Lehmer Company. *See* Centel Corporation.

Lehser Communications, Inc., **15** 265

Leica Camera AG, 35 266–69

Leica Microsystems Holdings GmbH, 35 270–73

Leigh-Mardon Security Group, **30** 44
Leighton Holdings Ltd., **19** 402
Leinenkugel Brewing Company. *See* Jacob Leinenkugel Brewing Company.
Leiner Health Products Inc., 34 250–52
The Leisure Company, **34** 22
Leisure Concepts, Inc., **59** 187–89
Leisure System Inc., **12** 359
Leitz. *See* Esselte Worldwide.
LeMaster Litho Supply, **13** 228
Lemmerz Holding GmbH, **27** 202, 204
Lemmon Co., **54** 363
Lempereur, **13** 297
Lend Lease Corporation Limited, IV 707–09; 17 283–86 (upd.); 47 410; **52 218–23 (upd.)**
Lender's Bagel, **32** 69
Lending Textiles, **29** 132
Lenel Systems International Inc., **24** 510
Lennar Corporation, 11 257–59
Lennon's, **II** 628
Lennox Industries, Inc., **22** 6
Lennox International Inc., 8 320–22; 28 232–36 (upd.)
Lenoir Furniture Corporation, **10** 183
Lenox, Inc., 10 179, 181; **12 312–13; 18** 69; **38** 113
Lens, Inc., **30** 267–68
LensCrafters Inc., 13 391; **17** 294; **23 328–30; 43** 199; **52** 227, 229
Lentheric, **I** 426
L'Entreprise Jean Lefebvre, 23 331–33
Leo Burnett Company, Inc., I 22–24, 25, 31, 37; **11** 51, 212; **12** 439; **20 336–39 (upd.)**
Leo d'Or Trading Co. Ltd., **56** 242
The Leo Group, **32** 140; **40** 140
Léon Gaumont et Cie. *See* Gaumont SA.
Leonard Bernstein Music Publishing Company, **23** 391
Leonard Development Group, **10** 508
Leonard Green & Partners LP, **12** 477–78; **24** 173
Leonard Machinery Corp., **16** 124
Leonard Parker Company, **26** 196
Leonard Silver, **14** 482
Leonardi Manufacturing, **48** 70
Leonardo Editore, **IV** 587
Leprino Foods Company, 28 237–39; 59 204
Lerner Plastics, **9** 323
Lernout and Hauspie, **51** 202
Leroux S.A.S., 65 212–14
Leroy Merlin SA, 23 230; **37** 24; **54 219–21**
Les Abeilles International SA, **60** 149
Les Boutiques San Francisco, Inc., 62 228–30
Les broderies Lesage, **49** 83
Les Echos. *See* Groupe Les Echos.
Les Grands Magasins Au Bon Marché: Etablissements Vaxelaire-Claes, **26** 159–60
Les Industries Ling, **13** 443
Les Papeteries du Limousin, **19** 227
Les Schwab Tire Centers, 50 314–16
Lesaffre et Compagnie, **52** 305
Lesco Inc., 19 248–50
The Leslie Fay Companies, Inc., 8 323–25
The Leslie Fay Company, Inc., 39 255–58 (upd.); 40 276–77
Leslie Paper, **IV** 288
Leslie's Poolmart, Inc., 18 302–04

Lesser-Goldman, **II** 18
Lester Ink and Coatings Company, **13** 228
Lester of Minnesota, Inc., **62** 55
Lestrem Group, **IV** 296; **19** 226
Létang et Rémy, **44** 205
Lettuce Entertain You Enterprises, **38** 103
Leucadia National Corporation, 6 396; **11** ; **25** 170 **260–62**
Leumi & Company Investment Bankers Ltd., **60** 50
Leuna-Werke AG, **7** 142
Leupold & Stevens, Inc., 52 224–26
Level Five Research, Inc., **22** 292
Level 13 Entertainment, Inc., **58** 124
Level 3 Communications, Inc., 67 233–35
Levenger Company, 63 242–45
Lever Brothers Company, 9 291, **317–19; 14** 314. *See also* Unilever.
Leverage Group, **51** 99
Levernz Shoe Co., **61** 22
Levi Strauss & Co., II 634, 669; **V 362–65; 9** 142; **12** 430; **16 324–28 (upd.),** 509, 511; **17** 512; **19** 196; **23** 422; **24** 158; **25** 47; **57** 283–84, 86
Leviathan Gas Pipeline Company, **21** 171
Levine, Huntley, Vick & Beaver, **6** 28
Leviton Manufacturing Co., Inc., **54** 372
Levitt Corp., **21** 471
Levitt Industries, **17** 331
Levitt Investment Company, **26** 102
Levitz Furniture Inc., 15 280–82; 23 412, 414
Levolor Hardware Group, **53** 37
Levtex Hotel Ventures, **21** 363
Levy. *See* Chas. Levy Company LLC.
Levy Home Entertainment, LLC, **60** 83, 85
Levy Restaurants L.P., 26 263–65
Lew Liberbaum & Co., **27** 197
The Lewin Group, Inc., **21** 425
Lewis and Marks, **16** 27; **50** 32
Lewis Batting Company, **11** 219
Lewis Galoob Toys Inc., 16 329–31
Lewis Group Ltd., **58** 54–55
Lewis Homes, **45** 221
Lewis Refrigeration Company, **21** 500
Lex Electronics, **10** 113; **50** 42
Lex Service plc, **19** 312; **50** 42
Lexecon, Inc., **26** 187
Lexington Furniture Industries, **III** 571; **20** 362
Lexington Ice Company, **6** 514
Lexington Utilities Company, **6** 514; **11** 237
LEXIS-NEXIS Group, 17 399; **18** 542; **21** 70; **31** 388, 393; **33 263–67**
Lexitron, **II** 87
Lexmark International, Inc., 9 116; **10** 519; **18 305–07; 30** 250
Leybold GmbH, **IV** 71; **48** 30
Leyland Motor Corporation, **7** 459
LF International, Inc., **59** 259
LFC Financial, **10** 339
LFC Holdings Corp. *See* Levitz Furniture Inc.
LFE Corp., **7** 297
LG&E Energy Corporation, 6 516–18; 18 366–67; **50** 172; **51 214–17 (upd.)**
LG Chemical Ltd., **26** 425
LG Electronics Inc., **13** 572, 575; **43** 428
LG Group, **18** 124; **34** 514, 517–18
LG Semiconductor, **56** 173
LGT Asset Management. *See* AMVESCAP PLC.

Lhomme S.A., **8** 477
Li & Fung Limited, 59 258–61
Liaison Agency, **31** 216–17
Lianozovo Dairy, **48** 438
Libbey Inc., 49 251–54
Libbey-Owens-Ford Company, **III** 640–42, 714–15, 731; **7** 292; **16** 7–9; **22** 434; **23** 83; **26** 353; **31** 355
Libeltex, **9** 92
Liber, **14** 556
Liberty Bank of Buffalo, **9** 229
Liberty Brokerage Investment Company, **10** 278
Liberty Can and Sign Company, **17** 105–06
The Liberty Corporation, 22 312–14
Liberty Gauge Company, **17** 213
Liberty Hardware Manufacturing Corporation, **20** 363
Liberty Life, **IV** 97
Liberty Livewire Corporation, 42 224–27
Liberty Media Corporation, 18 66; **19** 282; **25** 214; **34** 224; **42** 114, 224; **47** 414, 416, 418; **50 317–19**
Liberty Mutual Holding Company, 59 262–64
Liberty Mutual Insurance Group, **11** 379; **48** 271
Liberty Mutual Savings Bank, **17** 530
Liberty National Insurance Holding Company. *See* Torchmark Corporation.
Liberty National Life Insurance Co., **9** 506–07
Liberty Natural Gas Co., **11** 441
Liberty Property Trust, 57 221–23
Liberty Software, Inc., **17** 264
Liberty Surf UK, **48** 399
Liberty Tax Service, **48** 236
Liberty Travel, Inc., 56 203–06
Librairie Générale Francaise. *See* Hachette.
Librairie Larousse. *See* Groupe de la Cité.
Librairie Louis Hachette. *See* Hachette.
Librizol India Pvt. Ltd., **48** 212
Libyan National Oil Corporation, IV 453–55. *See also* National Oil Corporation.
Lieberman Enterprises, **24** 349
Liebert Corp., **II** 20
Liebherr Haushaltgerate GmbH, **65** 167
Liebherr-International AG, 64 238–42
Life Investors International Ltd., **III** 179; **12** 199
Life of Eire, **III** 273
Life Partners Group, Inc., **33** 111
Life Retail Stores. *See* Angelica Corporation.
Life Savers Corp., **7** 367; **21** 54
Life Science Research, Inc., **10** 105–07
Life Technologies, Inc., 17 287–89; 52 183–184
Life Time Fitness, Inc., 66 208–10
Life Uniform Shops. *See* Angelica Corporation.
Lifecycle, Inc., **25** 40
Lifeline Systems, Inc., 32 374; **53 207–09**
LifeLink, **11** 378
Lifemark Corp., **III** 74; **14** 232; **33** 183
LifeScan Inc., **63** 206
Lifestyle Fitness Clubs, **46** 432
Lifetime Corp., **29** 363–64
Lifetime Entertainment Services, 51 218–22
Lifetime Foam Products, Inc., **12** 439

Lifetime Hoan Corporation, **27 286–89**
Lifeway Foods, Inc., **65 215–17**
Ligand Pharmaceuticals Incorporated,
    10 48; **47 221–23**
Liggett & Meyers, **29** 195
Liggett-Ducat, **49** 153
Liggett Group Inc., **7** 105; **15** 71; **16** 242;
    37 295. *See also* Vector Group Inc.
Light & Power Company, **12** 265
Light Savers U.S.A., Inc. *See* Hospitality
    Worldwide Services, Inc.
Lightel Inc., **6** 311
Lighthouse, Ltd., **24** 95
Lil' Champ Food Stores, Inc., **36** 359
LILCO. *See* Long Island Lighting
    Company.
Lilia Limited, **17** 449
Lille Bonnières et Colombes, **37** 143–44
Lillian Vernon Corporation, **12 314–15**;
    35 274–77 (upd.)
Lillie Rubin, **30** 104–06
Lilliput Group plc, **11** 95; **15** 478
Lilly & Co. *See* Eli Lilly & Co.
Lilly Industries, **22** 437
Lily Tulip Co., **I** 611; **8** 198
Limhamns Golvindustri AB. *See* Tarkett
    Sommer AG.
The Limited, Inc., **V 115–16**; **9** 142; **12**
    280, 356; **15** 7, 9; **16** 219; **18** 193, 215,
    217, 410; **20 340–43 (upd.)**; **24** 237; **25**
    120–21, 123; **28** 344; **47** 142–43; **61**
    371; **64** 232
LIN Broadcasting Corp., **9 320–22**; **11**
    330
Lin Data Corp., **11** 234
Linamar Corporation, **18 308–10**
Lincare Holdings Inc., **43 265–67**
Lincoln American Life Insurance Co., **10**
    246
Lincoln Automotive, **26** 363
Lincoln Benefit Life Company, **10** 51
Lincoln Electric Co., **13 314–16**
Lincoln Electric Motor Works, **9** 439
Lincoln Federal Savings, **16** 106
Lincoln Income Life Insurance Co., **10** 246
Lincoln Liberty Life Insurance Co., **III** 254
Lincoln Marketing, Inc., **18** 518
Lincoln National Corporation, **III**
    274–77; **10** 44; **22** 144; **25 286–90**
    (upd.)
Lincoln Property Company, **8 326–28**;
    54 222–26 (upd.)
Lincoln Savings, **10** 340
Lincoln Savings & Loan, **9** 199
Lincoln Snacks Company, **24 286–88**
Lincoln Telephone & Telegraph
    Company, **14 311–13**
LinCom Corp., **8** 327
Lindal Cedar Homes, Inc., **29 287–89**
Linde AG, **I 581–83**; **9** 16, 516; **11**
    402–03; **25** 81; **48** 323; **67 236–39**
    (upd.)
Lindemans. *See* Southcorp Limited.
Lindex, **II** 640
Lindsay Manufacturing Co., **20 344–46**
Lindt & Sprüngli. *See* Chocoladefabriken
    Lindt & Sprüngli AG.
Linear Corporation Bhd, **66** 28
Linear Technology, Inc., **16 332–34**
Linens 'n Things, Inc., **13 81–82**; **24**
    289–92; **33** 384; **41** 50
Linfood Cash & Carry, **13** 103
Linfood Holdings Ltd., **II** 628–29
Ling Products, **12** 25

Ling-Temco-Vought. *See* LTV Corporation.
Lingerfelt Development Corporation, **57**
    223
Lingerie Time, **20** 143
Linguaphone Group, **43** 204, 206
Linificio e Canapificio Nazionale S.p.A.,
    67 210–11, 246–48
Link House Publications PLC, **IV** 687
Link Motor Supply Company, **26** 347
Linmark Westman International Limited,
    25 221–22
Linroz Manufacturing Company L.P., **25**
    245
LINT Company, **64** 237
Lintas: Worldwide, **14 314–16**
Lintott Engineering, Ltd., **10** 108
Linz, **16** 559
Lion Corporation, **III 44–45**; **51 223–26**
    (upd.)
Lion Manufacturing, **25** 40
Lion Match Company, **24** 450
Lion Nathan Limited, **54 227–30**, 342; **63**
    229
Lion's Head Brewery. *See* The Stroh
    Brewery Company.
Lionel L.L.C., **12 494**; **16 335–38**; **18** 524
Lionex Corporation, **13** 46
Lions Gate Entertainment Corporation,
    35 278–81
Liontech, **16** 337–38
Lippincott & Margulies, **III** 283
Lippincott-Raven Publishers, **14** 556
Lipschutz Bros., Inc., **29** 511
Lipson Alport Glass & Associates, **27** 195
Lipton. *See* Thomas J. Lipton Company.
Liqui-Box Corporation, **16 339–41**
Liquid Ag Systems Inc., **26** 494
Liquid Carbonic, **7** 74, 77
Liquid Gas Company Ltd., **60** 236
Liquid Holdings, Inc., **45** 168
Liquor Barn, **II** 656
Liquorland, **V** 35
Liquorsave, **II** 609–10
LIRCA, **III** 48
Liris, **23** 212
Listening Library Inc., **31** 379
Lister, **21** 503
Litehouse Inc., **60 198–201**
LiTel Communications, Inc., **16** 318
Lithia Motors, Inc., **41 238–40**
Lithonia Lighting, Inc., **54** 252, 254–55
LitleNet, **26** 441
Littelfuse, Inc., **26 266–69**
Little, Brown & Company, **IV** 675; **7** 528;
    10 355; **36** 270
Little Caesar Enterprises, Inc., **24**
    293–96 (upd.); **27** 481; **63** 133, 136–37.
    See also Ilitch Holdings Inc.
Little Caesar International, Inc., **7**
    278–79; **7** 278–79; **15** 344, 346; **16** 447;
    25 179, 227–28
Little General, **II** 620; **12** 179, 200
Little Giant Pump Company, **8** 515
Little League Baseball, Incorporated, **23**
    450
Little Leather Library, **13** 105
Little, Royal, bf]VIII 545; **13** 63
Little Switzerland, Inc., **19 451**; **60**
    202–04
Little Tikes Company, **12 169**; **13**
    317–19; **62 231–34 (upd.)**
Littlewoods Financial Services, **30** 494

Littlewoods plc, **V 117–19**; **24** 316; **42**
    228–32 (upd.)
Litton Industries Inc., **I 484–86**; **III** 473,
    732; **6** 599; **10** 537; **11 263–65 (upd.)**,
    435; **12** 248, 271–72, 538–40; **15** 287;
    19 31, 110, 290; **21** 86; **22** 436; **45** 306;
    48 383. *See also* Avondale Industries.
Litwin Engineers & Constructors, **8** 546
LIVE Entertainment Inc., **18** 64, 66; **20**
    347–49; **24** 349
LiveAquaria.com., **62** 108
Liverpool Daily Post & Echo Ltd., **49** 405
Liverpool Mexico S.A., **16** 216
Living Arts, Inc., **41** 174
Living Centers of America, **13** 49
Living Videotext, **10** 508
LivingWell Inc., **12** 326
Liz Claiborne, Inc., **8 329–31**; **16** 37, 61;
    25 258, **291–94 (upd.)**; **55** 136, 138
Lledo Collectibles Ltd., **60** 372
LLJ Distributing Company. *See* Spartan
    Stores Inc.
Lloyd Aereo de Bolivia, **6** 97
Lloyd Creative Staffing, **27** 21
Lloyd George Management, **18** 152
Lloyd Instruments, Ltd., **29** 460–61
Lloyd Italico, **III** 351
Lloyd Thompson Group plc, **20** 313
Lloyd Triestino company, **50** 187
Lloyd-Truax Ltd., **21** 499
Lloyd's Electronics, **14** 118
Lloyd's of London, **III 278–81**; **9** 297; **10**
    38; **11** 533; **22 315–19 (upd.)**
Lloyds Bank PLC, **II 306–09** 319, 334,
    358; **17** 324–25; **48** 373
Lloyds Chemists plc, **27** 177
Lloyds Life Assurance, **III** 351
Lloyds TSB Group plc, **39** 6; **47 224–29**
    (upd.); **61** 60, 62
LLP Group plc, **58** 189
LM Ericsson. *See* Telefonaktiebolaget LM
    Ericsson.
LMC Metals, **19** 380
LME. *See* Telefonaktiebolaget LM
    Ericsson.
LNM Group, **30** 252
Lo-Cost, **II** 609
Lo-Vaca Gathering Co., **7** 553
Loblaw Companies Limited, **II 631–32**;
    19 116; **43 268–72**; **51** 301. *See also*
    George Weston Limited.
Local Data, Inc., **10** 97
Lockhart Corporation, **12** 564
Lockheed Corporation, **I** 52, 54, 61, 63,
    64–66, 67–68, 71–72, 74, 76–77, 82,
    84, 90, 92–94, 100, 102, 107, 110, 113,
    121, 126, 195; **9** 12, 17–18, 272, 417,
    458–60, 501; **10** 262–63, 317, 536; **11**
    164, 166, **266–69 (upd.)**, 278–69,
    363–65; **12** 190; **13** 126, 128; **17** 306;
    21 140; **22** 506; **24** 87, 311, 375, 397;
    25 303, 347; **34** 371
Lockheed Martin Corporation, **15**
    283–86 (upd.); **21** 86; **24** 88; **29** 409;
    32 437; **33** 47–48; **38** 372, 376; **45** 306;
    48 251; **49** 345, 347; **54** 233; **61** 12, 15
Locksmith Publishing Corp., **56** 75
Lockwood Banc Group, Inc., **11** 306
Lockwood Greene Engineers, Inc., **17** 377
Lockwood National Bank, **25** 114
Lockwood Technology, Inc., **19** 179
Loctite Corporation, **8 332–34**; **30**
    289–91 (upd.); **34** 209
Lodding Engineering, **7** 521

Lodestar Group, **10** 19
Lodge Plus, Ltd., **25** 430
LodgeNet Entertainment Corporation,
    26 441; **28 240–42**
The Lodging Group, **12** 297; **48** 245
Loehmann's Inc., 24 297–99
Loew's, Inc., **31** 99
The Loewen Group, Inc., 16 342–44; 37
    67–68; **40 292–95 (upd.)**
Loewenstein Furniture Group, Inc., **21**
    531–33
Loews Cineplex Entertainment Corp., **37**
    64
Loews Corporation, I 487–88; 12 316–18
    (upd.), 418; **13** 120–21; **19** 362; **22** 73;
    25 177, 326–28; **36 324–28 (upd.); 41**
    70, 72
LOF Plastics, Inc. *See* Libbey-Owens-Ford.
Loffland Brothers Company, **9** 364
Logan's Roadhouse, Inc., 19 287–88; 22
    464; **29 290–92; 35** 84; **60 230–31**
Logic Modeling, **11** 491
Logica plc, 14 317–19; 37 230–33 (upd.)
Logicon Inc., 20 350–52; 45 68, 310
Logility, **25** 20, 22
Logistics.com, Inc. *See* Manhattan
    Associates, Inc.
Logistics Data Systems, **13** 4
Logistics Industries Corporation, **39** 77
Logistics Management Systems, Inc., **8** 33
Logitech International SA, 9 116; **28**
    243–45
Logo Athletic, Inc., **35** 363
Logo 7, Inc., **13** 533
Logon, Inc., **14** 377
Lohja Corporation, **61** 295
LoJack Corporation, 48 269–73
Lojas Arapuã S.A., 22 320–22; 61
    175–78 (upd.)
Loma Linda Foods, **14** 557–58
Lomak Petroleum, Inc., **24** 380
Lomas & Nettleton Financial Corporation,
    III 249; **11** 122
London & Hull, **III** 211
London & Midland Bank. *See* Midland
    Bank plc.
London & Overseas Freighters plc. *See*
    Frontline Ltd.
London & Rhodesia Mining & Land
    Company. *See* Lonrho Plc.
London and Scottish Marine Oil, **11** 98
London & Western Trust, **39** 90
London Assurance Corp., **55** 331
London Brick Co., **14** 249
London Brokers Ltd., **6** 290
London Buses Limited, **6** 406
London Cargo Group, **25** 82
London Central, **28** 155–56
London Drugs Ltd., 46 270–73
London East India Company, **12** 421
London Electricity, **12** 443; **41** 141
London Fog Industries, Inc., 16 61; **29**
    293–96
London General Omnibus Company, **6** 406
London Insurance Group, **III** 373; **36** 372
London International Group. *See* SSL
    International plc.
London Precision Machine & Tool, Ltd.,
    39 32
London Records, **23** 390
London Regional Transport, 6 406–08
London Rubber Co., **49** 380
London South Partnership, **25** 497

London Stock Exchange Limited, 34
    253–56; 37 131–33
London Transport, **19** 111
Londontown Manufacturing Company. *See*
    London Fog Industries, Inc.
Lone Star Brewing Co., **I** 255
Lone Star Funds, **59** 106
Lone Star Industries, **23** 326; **35** 154
Lone Star Steakhouse & Saloon, Inc., 21
    250; **51 227–29**
Lone Star Technologies, Inc., **22** 3
Lonely Planet Publications Pty Ltd., 55
    253–55
Long Distance Discount Services, Inc., **8**
    310; **27** 305
Long Distance/USA, **9** 479
Long Island Bancorp, Inc., 16 345–47;
    44 33
Long Island Cable Communication
    Development Company, **7** 63
Long Island College Hospital. *See*
    Continuum Health Partners, Inc.
Long Island Lighting Company, V
    652–54; 6 456; **27** 264
Long Island Power Authority, **27** 265
Long Island Rail Road, **35** 290
Long John Silver's, 57 224–29 (upd.)
Long John Silver's Restaurants Inc., 13
    320–22; 58 384
Long Lac Mineral Exploration, **9** 282
Long Life Fish Food Products, **12** 230
Long-Term Credit Bank of Japan, Ltd.,
    II 310–11, 338, 369
Long Valley Power Cooperative, **12** 265
The Longaberger Company, 12 319–21;
    44 267–70 (upd.)
Longchamps, Inc., **38** 385; **41** 388
LongHorn Steaks Inc., **19** 341
Longman Group Ltd., **IV** 611, 658
Longs Drug Stores Corporation, V 120;
    25 295–97 (upd.)
Longview Fibre Company, 8 335–37; 37
    234–37 (upd.)
Lonmin plc, 66 211–16 (upd.)
Lonrho Plc, 10 170; **21 351–55; 43** 38; **53**
    153, 202. *See also* Lonmin plc.
Loomis Armored Car Service Limited, **45**
    378
Loomis Fargo Group, **42** 338
Loomis Products, Inc., **64** 349
Loop One2, **53** 240
Loose Leaf Metals Co., Inc., **10** 314
Lor-Al, Inc., **17** 10
Loral Corporation, 7 9; **8 338–40; 9**
    323–25; 13 356; **15** 283, 285; **20** 262;
    47 319
Loral Space & Communications Ltd., 54
    231–35 (upd.)
Lord & Taylor, **13** 44; **14** 376; **15** 86; **18**
    137, 372; **21** 302
L'Oréal, III 46–49; 8 129–31; **341–44**
    (upd.); 11 41; **23** 238, 242; **31** 418; **46**
    274–79 (upd.); 52 211
Lorentzen & Wettre AB, **53** 85
Lorillard Industries, **V** 407, 417; **18** 416;
    22 73; **29** 195
Lorimar Telepictures, **II** 177; **25** 90–91,
    329
Loronix Inc., **24** 509
Los Angeles Drug Co., **12** 106
Los Angeles Lakers. *See* California Sports,
    Inc.
Los Lagos Corp., **12** 175
Loss Prevention Inc., **24** 509

Lost Arrow Inc., 22 323–25
LOT Polish Airlines (Polskie Linie
    Lotnicze S.A.), 33 268–71
LOT$OFF Corporation, 24 300–01
Lotus Cars Ltd., 14 320–22; 62 268
Lotus Development Corporation, 6
    254–56; 9 81, 140; **10** 24, 505; **12** 335;
    16 392, 394; **20** 238; **21** 86; **25 298–302**
    (upd.); 30 251; **38** 417; **63** 199
Lotus Publishing Corporation, **7** 239; **25**
    239
Louart Corporation, **29** 33–34
Loucks, Hoffman & Company, **8** 412
Loudcloud, Inc. *See* Opsware Inc.
Louis Allis, **15** 288
Louis Cruise Lines, **52** 298–99
Louis Dreyfus. *See* Groupe Louis Dreyfus
    S.A.
Louis Dreyfus Energy Corp., **28** 471
Louis Harris & Associates, Inc., **22** 188
Louis Kemp Seafood Company, **14** 515; **50**
    493
Louis Rich, Inc., **12** 372
Louis Vuitton, I 272; **III** 48; **8** 343; **10**
    397–99. *See also* LVMH Moët
    Hennessy Louis Vuitton SA.
Louisiana & Southern Life Insurance Co.,
    14 460
Louisiana Bank & Trust, **11** 106
Louisiana Corporation, **19** 301
Louisiana Energy Services, **27** 130
The Louisiana Land and Exploration
    Company, 7 280–83
Louisiana-Pacific Corporation, IV
    304–05; 16 203; **22** 491; **31 314–17**
    (upd.); 32 91; **59** 161
Louisville Gas and Electric Company, **49**
    120. *See also* LG&E Energy
    Corporation.
Louisville Home Telephone Company, **14**
    258
Loup River Public Power District, **29** 352
Louthan Manufacturing Company, **8** 178
LoVaca Gathering Company. *See* The
    Coastal Corporation.
Lovelace Truck Service, Inc., **14** 42
Loveman's, Inc., **19** 323
Lowe Group, **22** 294
Lowe's Companies, Inc., V 122–23; 11
    384; **12** 234, 345; **18** 239; **21** 324,
    356–58 (upd.); 27 416; **44** 333
Lowell Shoe, Inc., **13** 360
Löwenbräu, **II** 240
Lower Manhattan Development
    Corporation, **47** 360
Lowes Food Stores. *See* Alex Lee Inc.
Lowney/Moirs, **II** 512
Lowrance Electronics, Inc., 18 311–14
Lowrey's Meat Specialties, Inc., **21** 156
LPL Investment Group, **40** 35–36
LRV Corporation, **61** 173
LS Management, Inc., **51** 229
LSI. *See* Lear Siegler Inc.
LSI Logic Corporation, 13 323–25; 18
    382; **64 243–47**
LTR Industries, **52 301–03**
LTU Group Holding GmbH, 37 238–41
LTV Aerospace. *See* Vought Aircraft
    Industries, Inc.
The LTV Corporation, I 489–91; 7
    107–08; **8** 157, 315; **10** 419; **11** 166,
    364; **12** 124; **17** 357; **18** 110, 378; **19**
    466; **24 302–06 (upd.); 26** 406; **45** 306;
    52 254; **59** 282

The Lubrizol Corporation, I 360–62; 21 385–87; 30 292–95 (upd.)
Luby's Cafeteria's, Inc., 17 290–93; 19 301
Luby's, Inc., 42 233–38 (upd.)
Lucas Bols, II 642
Lucas Digital Ltd., 12 322
Lucas Industries Plc, III 554–57; 27 251
Lucas Ingredients, 27 258
Lucas-Milhaupt, Inc., 23 250
LucasArts Entertainment Company, 32 9
Lucasfilm Ltd., 9 368, 472; 12 322–24; 22 459; 34 350; 38 70; 50 320–23 (upd.)
LucasVarity plc, 27 249, 251
Lucchini, IV 228
Lucent Technologies Inc., 18 154, 180; 20 8; 22 19; 26 275, 277; 29 44, 414; 34 257–60; 36 122, 124; 41 289–90; 44 426; 48 92; 61 17; 63 203
Lucille Farms, Inc., 45 249–51
Lucky Brand Dungarees, 18 85
Lucky-Goldstar, II 53–54; 13 574. See also Goldstar Co., Ltd.
Lucky Stores Inc., II 605, 653; 6 355; 8 474; 12 48; 17 369, 559; 22 39; 27 290–93
Ludi Wap S.A., 41 409
Ludovico, 25 85
Lufkin Rule Co., II 16
Luftfahrzeug-Betriebs GmbH, 60 253
Lufthansa. See Deutsche Lufthansa Aktiengesellschaft.
The Luggage Company, 14 224
Luigino's, Inc., 64 248–50
Luitpold-Werk GmbH & Co., 56 303
Lukens Inc., 14 323–25; 27 65
LUKOIL. See OAO LUKOIL.
Lumac B.V., I 387
Lumbermens Building Centers. See Lanoga Corporation.
Lumbertown USA, 52 232
Lumex, Inc., 17 197
Lumidor Safety Products, 52 187
La Lumière Economique, II 79
Luminar Plc, 40 296–98
Lummus Crest, 26 496
Lunar Corporation, 29 297–99
Luncheon Voucher, 27 10
Lund Boat Co. See Genmar Holdings, Inc.
Lund Food Holdings, Inc., 22 326–28
Lund International Holdings, Inc., 40 299–301
Lundstrom Jewelers, 24 319
Lunenburg Sea Products Limited, 14 339
L'Unite Hermetique S.A., 8 515
Lunn Poly, 8 525–26
Lurgei, 6 599
LURGI. See Metallurgische Gesellschaft Aktiengesellschaft.
Lutèce, 20 26
Lutheran Brotherhood, 31 318–21
Luxair, 49 80
Luxor, 6 205; 17 353
Luxottica SpA, 17 294–96; 23 328; 43 96; 49 301; 52 227–30 (upd.); 54 320. See also Casual Corner Group, Inc.
LuxSonor Semiconductor Inc., 48 92
Luxury Linens, 13 81–82
Luzianne Blue Plate Foods. See Wm. B. Reily & Company Inc.
LVMH Moët Hennessy Louis Vuitton SA, I 272; 19 86; 24 137, 140; 33 272–77 (upd.); 45 344; 46 277; 49 90,

326; 51 234–35; 56 92; 61 323. See also Christian Dior S.A.
LXE Inc., 21 199–201
Lycos, 27 517; 37 384; 47 420. See also Terra Lycos, Inc.
Lydall, Inc., 64 251–54
Lykes Corp., 24 303
Lyn Knight Currency Auctions, Inc, 48 100
Lynch Corporation, 43 273–76; 301–02
Lynde Company, 16 269–71
Lynx Express Delivery, 6 412, 414
Lyondell Chemical Company, IV 456–57; 10 110; 45 252–55 (upd.)
Lyonnaise Communications, 10 196; 25 497
Lyonnaise des Eaux-Dumez, V 655–57; 23 332. See also Suez Lyonnaise des Eaux.
Lyons. See J. Lyons & Co. Ltd.
LyphoMed Inc., 17 287
Lysaght, 24 143
Lytag Ltd., 31 398–99

M & C Saatchi, 42 330
M&C Systems Co Ltd., 62 245
M&F Worldwide Corp., 38 293–95
M&G Group plc, 48 328
M and H Valve Co., 55 266
M&I Bank. See Marshall & Ilsley Corporation.
M&J Diesel Locomotive Filter Co., 17 106
M&M Limited, 7 299
M and M Manufacturing Company, 23 143
M&M/Mars, 14 48; 15 63–64; 21 219
M & S Computing. See Intergraph Corporation.
M&T Capital Corporation, 11 109
M/A Com Inc., 14 26–27
M-Cell Ltd., 31 329
M-I Drilling Fluids Co., III 473; 15 468
M-R Group plc, 31 312–13
M-real Oyj, 56 252–55 (upd.)
M-Web Holdings Ltd., 31 329–30
M.A. Bruder & Sons, Inc., 56 99, 189, 207–09
M.A. Gedney Co., 51 230–32
M.A. Hanna Company, 8 345–47; 12 352
M.B. McGerry, 21 94
M.D.C., 11 258
M.E.P.C. Ltd. See MEPC PLC.
M.F. Patterson Dental Supply Co. See Patterson Dental Co.
M/G Transport Inc. See The Midland Company.
M.G. Waldbaum Company, 25 332–33
M.H. McLean Wholesaler Grocery Company, 8 380
M.H. Meyerson & Co., Inc., 46 280–83
M.I. Schottenstein Homes Inc., 19 125–26
M.J. Brock Corporation, 8 460
M.J. Designs, Inc., 17 360
M.L.C. Partners Limited Partnership, 22 459
M. Loeb Ltd., II 652
M.M. Warburg. See SBC Warburg.
M.P. Burke PLC, 13 485–86
M.P. Pumps, Inc., 8 515
M. Polaner Inc., 10 70; 40 51–52; 50 538
M.S. Carriers, Inc., 42 363, 365
M. Shanken Communications, Inc., 50 324–27
M. Sobol, Inc., 28 12
M Stores Inc., II 664

M.T.G.I. Textile Manufacturers Group, 25 121
M.W. Carr, 14 245
M.W. Kellogg Co., 34 81; 62 204
Maakauppiaitten Oy, 8 293–94
Maatschappij tot Exploitatie van de Onderneming Krasnapolsky. See Grand Hotel Krasnapolsky N.V.
Maatschappij tot Exploitatie van Steenfabrieken Udenhout, voorheen Weyers, 14 249
Mabley & Carew, 10 282
Mac Frugal's Bargains - Closeouts Inc., 17 297–99
Mac-Gray Corporation, 44 271–73
Mac Publications LLC, 25 240
The Macallan Distillers Ltd., 63 246–48
MacAndrews & Forbes Holdings Inc., II 679; 9 129; 11 334; 28 246–49; 30 138; 38 293–94; 64 333
MacArthur Foundation. See The John D. and Catherine T. MacArthur Foundation.
Macau Telephone, 18 114
Macauley & Co. See Greif Inc.
MacCall Management, 19 158
MacDermid Incorporated, 32 318–21
MacDonald Companies, 15 87
MacDonald Dettwiler and Associates, 32 436
MacDonald, Halsted, and Laybourne, 10 127
Mace Security International, Inc., 57 230–32
The Macerich Company, 57 233–35
Macey Furniture Co., 7 493
Macfield Inc., 12 502; 62 374
MacFrugal's Bargains Close-Outs Inc., 29 312; 50 98
MacGregor Sporting Goods Inc., 22 115, 458; 23 449
Mach Performance, Inc., 28 147
Machine Vision International Inc., 10 232
Macintosh. See Apple Computer, Inc.
Mack-Cali Realty Corporation, 42 239–41
Mack Trucks, Inc., I 177–79; 9 416; 12 90; 22 329–32 (upd.); 61 179–83 (upd.)
Mack-Wayne Plastics, 42 439
Mackay Envelope Corporation, 45 256–59
MacKenzie & Co., II 361
Mackie Designs Inc., 30 406; 33 278–81
Maclean Hunter Publishing Limited, IV 638–40; 22 442; 23 98; 26 270–74 (upd.); 30 388
Maclin Co., 12 127
Macluan Capital Corporation, 49 196
The MacManus Group, 32 140; 40 140
MacMark Corp., 22 459
MacMarr Stores, II 654
Macmillan & Co. Ltd., 35 452
MacMillan Bloedel Limited, IV 306–09[ro; 9 391; 19 444, 446; 25 12; 26 445
Macmillan, Inc., 7 284–86; 9 63; 12 226; 13 91, 93; 17 399; 22 441–42; 23 350, 503; 25 484; 27 222–23
The MacNeal-Schwendler Corporation, 25 303–05
Macon Gas Company, 6 447; 23 28
Macon Kraft Co., 11 421
Macrodata, 18 87
Macromedia, Inc., 50 328–31; 61 124
MACSTEEL Monroe, Inc., 62 289

Macwhyte Company, **27** 415
Macy's. *See* R.H. Macy & Co., Inc.
Macy's California, **21** 129
Mad Dog Athletics, **19** 385
MADD. *See* Mothers Against Drunk Driving.
Madden's on Gull Lake, 52 231–34
Madeira Wine Company, S.A., 49 255–57
Maderin ECO S.A., **51** 6
Madge Networks N.V., 18 346; **26 275–77**
Madison & Sullivan, Inc., **10** 215
Madison Dearborn Partners LLC, **46** 289; **49** 197; **51** 131, 282, 284
Madison Financial Corp., **16** 145
Madison Foods, **14** 557
Madison Furniture Industries, **14** 436
Madison Gas and Electric Company, 6 605–06; **39 259–62**
Madison-Kipp Corporation, 58 213–16
Madison Resources, Inc., **13** 502
Madrange SA, 58 217–19
MAEFORT Hungarian Air Transport Joint Stock Company, **24** 310
Maersk Oile, **22** 167; **65** 316–17
Maersk Sealand. *See* A.P. Møller - Maersk A/S.
Maes Group Breweries, **II** 475
Maeva Group. *See* Club Mediterranee SA.
Mafco Holdings, Inc., **28** 248; **38** 293–95
Mag Instrument, Inc., 67 240–42
Magazine and Book Services, **13** 48
MagCorp, **28** 198
Magee Company, **31** 435–36
Magella Healthcare Corporation, **61** 284
Magellan Aerospace Corporation, 46 8; **48 274–76**
Magellan Corporation, **22** 403; **60** 137
Magic Chef Co. **8** 298. *See also* Maytag Corporation.
Magic City Food Products Company. *See* Golden Enterprises, Inc.
Magic Marker, **29** 372
Magic Pantry Foods, **10** 382
Magic Years Child Care, **51** 198
Magicsilk, Inc., **22** 133
MagicSoft Inc., **10** 557
Maglificio di Ponzano Veneto dei Fratelli Benetton. *See* Benetton.
Magma Copper Company, 7 287–90, 385–87; **22** 107
Magma Power Company, 11 270–72
Magna Computer Corporation, **12** 149; **13** 97
Magna Distribuidora Ltda., **43** 368
Magnaflux, **III** 519; **22** 282
Magnavox Co., **13** 398; **19** 393
MagneTek, Inc., 15 287–89; 41 241–44(upd.)
Magnetic Controls Company, **10** 18
Magnetic Peripherals Inc., **19** 513–14
Magnivision, **22** 35
La Magona d'Italia, **IV** 228
Magro, **48** 63
MAGroup Inc., **11** 123
Magyar Viscosa, **37** 428
Mahalo Air, **22** 252; **24** 22
Maharam Fabric, **8** 455
Mahir & Numan A.S., **48** 154
MAI PLC, **28** 504
MAI Systems Corporation, **10** 242; **11 273–76; 26** 497, 499
Maid-Rite Corporation, 62 235–38

Maidenform, Inc., 59 265–69 (upd.)
Maidenform Worldwide Inc., 20 352–55
Mail Boxes Etc., 18 315–17; 25 500; **41 245–48 (upd.).** *See also* U.S. Office Products Company.
Mail.com Inc., **38** 271
Mail Coups, Inc., **53** 13
Mail Finance, **53** 239
Mail Marketing Systems Inc., **53** 13
Mail-Well, Inc., 25 184; **28 250–52**
MailCoups, Inc., **53** 9
Mailson Ferreira da Nobrega, **II** 200
Mailtek, Inc., **18** 518
MAIN. *See* Mid-American Interpool Network.
Main Plaza Corporation, **25** 115
Main Street Advertising USA, **IV** 597
Maine & Maritimes Corporation, 56 210–13
Maine Central Railroad Company, 16 348–50
Mainline Industrial Distributors, Inc., **13** 79
Mainline Travel, **I** 114
Maison Blanche Department Stores Group, **35** 129
Maison de Schreiber and Aronson, **25** 283
Maison de Valérie, **19** 309
Maison Louis Jadot, 24 307–09
Majestic Contractors Ltd., **8** 419–20
Majestic Industries, Inc., **43** 459
Majestic Wine Warehouses Ltd., **II** 656
The Major Automotive Companies, Inc., 45 260–62
Major League Baseball, **12** 457
Major SA, **53** 179
Major Video Concepts, **6** 410
Major Video, Inc., **9** 74
Mak van Waay, **11** 453
Makepeace Preserving Co., **25** 365
Makita Corporation, 22 333–35; 59 270–73 (upd.)
Makivik Corporation, **56** 38–39
Makoff R&D Laboratories, **56** 375
Makovsky & Company, **12** 394
Makro Inc., **18** 286
Malama Pacific Corporation, **9** 276
Malapai Resources, **6** 546
Malayan Motor and General Underwriters, **III** 201
Malaysian Airlines System Berhad, 6 100–02; 29 300–03 (upd.)
Malaysian Sheet Glass, **III** 715
Malcolm Pirnie, Inc., 42 242–44
Malden Mills Industries, Inc., 16 351–53
Malév Plc, 24 310–12; 27 474; **29** 17
Malew Engineering, **51** 354
Malheur Cooperative Electric Association, **12** 265
Malibu, **25** 141
Mall.com, **38** 271
Mallard Bay Drilling, Inc., **28** 347–48
Malleable Iron Works, **II** 34
Mallinckrodt Group Inc., 8 85; **19** 28, **251–53; 63** 404
Malmö Aviation, **47** 61
Malmö Woodworking Factory. *See* Tarkett Sommer AG.
Malone & Hyde, Inc., **II** 625, 670–71; **9** 52–53; **14** 147; **18** 506; **50** 456–57
Malt-O-Meal Company, 15 189; **22 336–38; 63 249–53 (upd.)**
Malterie Soufflet. *See* Groupe Soufflet SA
Mama Fu's Noodle House, Inc., **64** 327–28

Mama's Concept, Inc., **51** 229
Mameco International, **8** 455
Mammoet Transport B.V., 26 241, **278–80**
Man Aktiengesellschaft, III 301, **561–63**
MAN Gutehoffnungshütte AG, **15** 226
Management and Training Corporation, 28 253–56
Management By Information Inc., **48** 307
Management Decision Systems, Inc., **10** 358
Management Recruiters International. *See* CDI Corp.
Management Science America, Inc., **11** 77; **25** 20
Manchester Board and Paper Co., **19** 77
Manchester United Football Club plc, 30 296–98; 44 388
Manco, Inc., **13** 166. *See also* Henkel Manco Inc.
Mancuso & Co., **22** 116
Mandabach & Simms, **6** 40
Mandalay Pictures, **35** 278–80
Mandalay Resort Group, 32 322–26 (upd.)
Mandarin, Inc., **33** 128
Mandarin Oriental Hotel Group International Ltd., **I** 471; **20** 312
Mandarin Oriental International Limited, **47** 177
Manetta Mills, Inc., **19** 304
Manhattan Associates, Inc., 67 243–45
Manhattan Bagel Inc., **63** 80
Manhattan Card Co., **18** 114
Manhattan Construction Company. *See* Rooney Brothers Co.
Manhattan Electrical Supply Co., **9** 517
Manhattan International Limousine Network Ltd., **26** 62
Manheim Auctions, Inc. *See* Cox Enterprises, Inc.
Manila Electric Company (Meralco), 56 214–16
Manischewitz Company. *See* B. Manischewitz Company.
Manistique Papers Inc., **17** 282
Manitoba Bridge and Engineering Works Ltd., **8** 544
Manitoba Rolling Mill Ltd., **8** 544
Manitoba Telecom Services, Inc., 61 184–87
Manitou BF S.A., 27 294–96
The Manitowoc Company, Inc., 18 318–21; 59 274–79 (upd.)
Mann Theatres Chain, **25** 177
Mann's Wine Company, Ltd., **14** 288
Mann's Wine Pub Co., Ltd., **47** 206
Mannatech Inc., 33 282–85
Mannesmann AG, III 564–67; 14 326–29 (upd.); 34 319; **38 296–301 (upd.); 54** 391, 393. *See also* Vodafone Group PLC.
Mannheim Steamroller. *See* American Gramophone LLC.
Manning, Selvage & Lee. *See* D'Arcy Masius Benton & Bowles, Inc.
Manor AG, **48** 279
Manor Care, Inc., 6 187–90; 14 105–07; **15** 522; **25 306–10 (upd.)**
Manor Healthcare Corporation, **26** 459
Manos Enterprises, **14** 87
Manpower, Inc., 9 326–27; 16 48; **25** 432; **30 299–302 (upd.); 40** 236, 238; **44** 157; **49** 264–65

Mantrec S.A., **27** 296

Mantua Metal Products. *See* Tyco Toys, Inc.

Manufactured Home Communities, Inc., **22** 339–41; **46** 378

Manufacturera Mexicana de Partes de Automoviles S.A., **56** 247

Manufacturers and Traders Trust Company, **11** 108–09

Manufacturers Casualty Insurance Co., **26** 486

Manufacturers Fire Insurance Co., **26** 486

Manufacturers Hanover Corporation, II **312–14; 9** 124; **11** 16, 54, 415; **13** 536; **14** 103; **16** 207; **17** 559; **22** 406; **26** 453; **38** 253. *See also* Chemical Bank.

Manufacturers National Bank of Detroit, **40** 116

Manufacturing Management Inc., **19** 381

Manville Corporation, III 706–09, 721; **7** **291–95 (upd.); 10** 43, 45; **11** 420–22. *See also* Johns Manville Corporation.

Manweb plc, **19** 389–90; **49** 363–64

MAP. *See* Marathon Ashland Petroleum LLC.

MAPCO Inc., IV 458–59; 26 234; **31** 469, 471

Mapelli Brothers Food Distribution Co., **13** 350

MAPICS, Inc., 55 256–58

Maple Grove Farms of Vermont, Inc., **40** 51–52

Maple Leaf Foods Inc., 41 249–53

Maple Leaf Mills, **41** 252

Maple Leaf Sports & Entertainment **Ltd., 61 188–90**

MAPP. *See* Mid-Continent Area Power Planner.

Mapra Industria e Comercio Ltda., **32** 40

MAR Associates, **48** 54

Mar-O-Bar Company, **7** 299

Marantha! Music, **14** 499

Marantz Co., **14** 118

Marathon Ashland Petroleum LLC, **49** 329–30; **50** 49

Marathon Insurance Co., **26** 486

Marathon Oil Co., **13** 458; **49** 328, 330. *See also* United States Steel Corp.

Marauder Company, **26** 433

Marblehead Communications, Inc., **23** 101

Marbodal, **12** 464

Marboro Books, Inc., **10** 136

Marbro Lamp Co., **III** 571; **20** 362

Marc's Big Boy. *See* The Marcus Corporation.

Marcade Group. *See* Aris Industries, Inc.

Marcam Coporation. *See* MAPICS, Inc.

Marceau Investments, **II** 356

March-Davis Bicycle Company, **19** 383

March of Dimes, 31 322–25

March Plasma Systems, Inc., **48** 299

Marchand, **13** 27

Marchesi Antinori SRL, 42 245–48

marchFIRST, Inc., 34 261–64

Marchland Holdings Ltd., **II** 649

Marchon Eyewear, **22** 123

Marciano Investments, Inc., **24** 157

Marcillat, **19** 49

Marco Acquisition Corporation, **62** 268

Marcolin S.p.A., 61 191–94; 62 100

Marcon Coating, Inc., **22** 347

Marconi plc, 33 286–90 (upd.)

The Marcus Corporation, 21 359–63

Marcy Fitness Products, Inc., **19** 142, 144

Maremont Corporation, **8** 39–40

Margarete Steiff GmbH, 23 334–37

Marge Carson, Inc., **III** 571; **20** 362

Margo's La Mode, **10** 281–82; **45** 15

Marico Acquisition Corporation, **8** 448, 450

Marie Brizard & Roger International **S.A., 22 342–44**

Marie Callender's Restaurant & Bakery, **Inc., 13** 66; **28 257–59**

Marina Mortgage Company, **46** 25

Marine Bank and Trust Co., **11** 105

Marine Computer Systems, **6** 242

Marine Harvest, **13** 103; **56** 257

Marine Manufacturing Corporation, **52** 406

Marine Midland Corp., **9** 475–76; **11** 108; **17** 325

Marine Transport Lines, Inc., **59** 323

Marine United Inc., **42** 361

Marinela, **19** 192–93

MarineMax, Inc., 30 303–05; 37 396

Marinette Marine Corporation, **59** 274, 278

Marion Brick, **14** 249

Marion Foods, Inc., **17** 434; **60** 268

Marion Laboratories Inc., I 648–49; 8 149; **9** 328–29; **16** 438; **50** 163

Marion Manufacturing, **9** 72

Marion Merrell Dow, Inc., 9 328–29 **(upd.)**

Marionet Corp., **IV** 680–81

Marionnaud Parfumeries SA, 51 233–35; **54** 265–66

Marisa Christina, Inc., 15 290–92; 25 245

Maritime Electric Company, Limited, **15** 182; **47** 136–37

Maritz Inc., 38 302–05

Mark Controls Corporation, **30** 157

Mark Cross, Inc., **17** 4–5

Mark Goldston, **8** 305

Mark IV Industries, Inc., 7 296–98; 21 418; **28 260–64 (upd.); 61** 66

Mark Travel Corporation, **30** 448

Mark Trouser, Inc., **17** 338

Markborough Properties, **V** 81; **8** 525; **25** 221

Market Development Corporation. *See* Spartan Stores Inc.

Market Growth Resources, **23** 480

Market National Bank, **13** 465

Marketing Data Systems, Inc., **18** 24

Marketing Equities International, **26** 136

MarketSpan Corp. *See* KeySpan Energy Co.

Marks and Spencer p.l.c., II 678; **V** **124–26; 10** 442; **17** 42, 124; **22** 109, 111; **24** 268, 270; **42 313–17 (upd.),** 474; **28** 96; **35** 308, 310; **41** 114; **42** 231; **61** 258–59, 261; **62** 342–43

Marks-Baer Inc., **11** 64

Marks Brothers Jewelers, Inc., 24 **318–20**

Marlene Industries Corp., **16** 36–37

Marley Co., **19** 360

Marley Holdings, L.P., **19** 246

Oy Marli Ab, **56** 103

Marman Products Company, **16** 8

The Marmon Group, IV 135–38; 16 **354–57 (upd.)**

Marmon-Perry Light Company, **6** 508

Marolf Dakota Farms, Inc., **18** 14–15

Marotte, **21** 438

Marpac Industries Inc. *See* PVC Container Corporation.

Marquam Commercial Brokerage Company, **21** 257

Marquette Electronics, Inc., 13 326–28

Marquis Who's Who, **17** 398

Marr S.p.A., 57 82–84

Marriner Group, **13** 175

Marriot Inc., **29** 442

Marriot Management Services, **29** 444

Marriott Corporation, II 608; **III** **102–03,** 248; **7** 474–75; **9** 95, 426; **15** 87; **17** 238; **18** 216; **19** 433–34; **21** 91, 364; **22** 131; **23** 436–38; **27** 334; **38** 386; **41** 82; **64** 340

Marriott International, Inc., 21 182, **364–67 (upd.); 29** 403, 406; **41** 156–58; **52** 415

Mars, Incorporated, 7 299–301; 22 298, 528; **40 302–05 (upd.)**

Marsh & McLennan Companies, Inc., **III 282–84; 10** 39; **14** 279; **45** 28, **263–67 (upd.); 53** 64

Marsh Supermarkets, Inc., 17 300–02

Marshall & Ilsley Corporation, 56 **217–20**

Marshall Amplification plc, 62 239–42

Marshall Die Casting, **13** 225

Marshall Field's, 8 33; **9** 213; **12** 283; **15** 86; **18** 488; **22** 72; **50** 117, 119; **61** 394, 396; **63** 242, 244, **254–63.** *See also* Target Corporation.

Marshall Industries, **19** 311

Marshalls Incorporated, 13 329–31; 14 62

Marship Tankers (Holdings) Ltd., **52** 329

Marstellar, **13** 204

Marstons, **57** 412–13

The Mart, **9** 120

Martank Shipping Holdings Ltd., **52** 329

Martek Biosciences Corporation, 65 **218–20**

Marten Transport, **27** 404

Martha Lane Adams, **27** 428

Martha Stewart Living Omnimedia, **L.L.C., 24 321–23; 47** 211

Martin & Pagenstecher GMBH, **24** 208

Martin-Baker Aircraft Company **Limited, 61 195–97**

Martin Band Instrument Company, **55** 149, 151

Martin Bros. Tobacco Co., **14** 19

Martin Collet, **19** 50

Martin Dunitz, **44** 416

Martin Gillet Co., **55** 96, 98

Martin Guitar Company. *See* C.F. Martin & Co., Inc.

Martin Hilti Foundation, **53** 167

Martin Industries, Inc., 44 274–77

Martin Marietta Corporation, I 67–69, 416; **IV** 163; **7** 356, 520; **8** 315; **9** 310; **10** 162, 199, 484; **11** 166, 277–78, 364; **12** 127, 290; **13** 327, 356; **15** 283; **17** 564; **18** 369; **19** 70; **22** 400; **28** 288. *See also* Lockheed Martin Corporation.

Martin Mathys, **8** 456

Martin Sorrell, **6** 54

Martin Theaters, **14** 86

Martin-Yale Industries, Inc., **19** 142–44

Martin Zippel Co., **16** 389

Martin's, **12** 221

Martindale-Hubbell, **17** 398

Martini & Rossi SpA, 18 41; **63 264–66**

Martinus Nijhoff, **14** 555; **25** 85

Martz Group, 56 221–23

Marubeni Corporation, 24 324–27 (upd.)

Marubeni K.K., I 492–95; **12** 147; **17** 556

Maruetsu, **17** 124; **41** 114

Marui Company Ltd., V 127; **62** 243–45 **(upd.)**

Marusa Co. Ltd., **51** 379

Maruti Udyog Ltd., **59** 393, 395–97

Maruzen Co., Limited, IV 403–04, 476, 554; **18** 322–24

Maruzen Oil Co., Ltd., **53** 114

Marvel Entertainment Group, Inc., 10 400–02; **18** 426, 520–21; **21** 404; **25** 141; **34** 449

Marvin & Leonard Advertising, **13** 511–12

Marvin H. Sugarman Productions Inc., **20** 48

Marvin Lumber & Cedar Company, 10 95; **22** 345–47

Marwick, Mitchell & Company, **10** 385

Marx, **12** 494

Mary Ann Co. Ltd., **V** 89

Mary Ann Restivo, Inc., **8** 323

Mary Ellen's, Inc., **11** 211

Mary Kathleen Uranium, **IV** 59–60

Mary Kay Corporation, 9 330–32; **12** 435; **15** 475, 477; **18** 67, 164; **21** 49, 51; **30** 306–09 **(upd.)**

Maryland Cup Company, **8** 197

Maryland Medical Laboratory Inc., **26** 391

Maryland National Corp., **11** 287

Maryland National Mortgage Corporation, **11** 121; **48** 177

Marzotto S.p.A., 20 356–58; **48** 206–07; **67** 246–49 **(upd.)**

Masayoshi Son, **13** 481–82

Maschinenfabrik Augsburg-Nürnberg. *See* M.A.N.

Masco Corporation, III 568–71; **11** 385, 534–35; **12** 129, 131, 344; **13** 338; **18** 68; **20** 359–63 **(upd.)**; **39** 263–68 **(upd.)**

Masco Optical, **13** 165

Mase Westpac Limited, **11** 418

Maserati. *See* Officine Alfieri Maserati S.p.A.

Mashantucket Pequot Gaming Enterprise Inc., 35 282–85

MASkargo Ltd. *See* Maladian Airlines System Bhd.

Masland Corporation, 17 303–05; **19** 408

Mason Best Co., **IV** 343

Masonite International Corporation, 63 267–69

Mass Rapid Transit Corp., **19** 111

Massachusetts Capital Resources Corp., **III** 314

Massachusetts Electric Company, **51** 265

Massachusetts Mutual Life Insurance Company, III 285–87, 305; **25** 528; **53** 210–13 **(upd.)**

Massachusetts Technology Development Corporation, **18** 570

Massachusetts's General Electric Company, **32** 267

Massey Energy Company, 57 236–38

MasTec, Inc., 55 259–63 **(upd.)**

Master Builders, **I** 673

Master Electric Company, **15** 134

Master Glass & Color, **24** 159–60

Master Lock Company, 45 268–71

Master Loom, **63** 151

Master Processing, **19** 37

Master Products, **14** 162

Master Shield Inc., **7** 116

Master Tank and Welding Company, **7** 541

Master Tek International, Inc., **47** 372

MasterBrand Industries Inc., **12** 344–45

MasterCard International, Inc., 9 333–35; **18** 337, 543; **25** 41; **26** 515; **41** 201; **61** 248

Mastercraft Homes, Inc., **11** 257

Masters-Jackson, **50** 49

Mastex Industries, **29** 132

Maszovlet. *See* Malév Plc.

Matador Records, **22** 194

Matairco, **9** 27

Matalan PLC, 49 258–60

Matane Pulp & Paper Company, **17** 281

Matchbox Toys Ltd., **12** 168

MatchLogic, Inc., **41** 198

Matco Tools, **7** 116

Material Management and Services Inc., **28** 61

Material Sciences Corporation, 54 331; **63** 270–73

Mathematica, Inc., **22** 291

Mather Metals, **III** 582

Mathews Conveyor Co., **14** 43

Matra, **IV** 617–19; **13** 356; **17** 354; **24** 88

Matra Aerospace Inc., **22** 402

Matra-Hachette S.A., 15 293–97 **(upd.)**; **21** 267. *See also* European Aeronautic Defence and Space Company EADS N.V.

Matria Healthcare, Inc., 17 306–09

Matrix Science Corp., **14** 27

Matrix Service Company, 65 221–23

Matsumoto Medical Instruments, Inc., **11** 476; **29** 455

Matsushita Electric Industrial Co., Ltd., II 55–56, 58, 61, 91–92, 102, 117–19, 361, 455; **10** 286, 389, 403, 432; **11** 487; **12** 448; **13** 398; **18** 18; **20** 81; **26** 511; **33** 432; **36** 399–400, 420; **64** 255–58 **(upd.)**

Matsushita Electric Works, Ltd., III 710–11; **7** 302–03 **(upd.)**; **12** 454; **16** 167; **27** 342

Matsushita Kotobuki Electronics Industries, Ltd., **10** 458–59

Matsuzakaya Company Ltd., V 129–31; **64** 259–62 **(upd.)**

Mattatuck Bank & Trust Co., **13** 467

Mattel, Inc., 7 304–07; **12** 168–69, 495; **13** 560–61; **15** 238; **16** 428; **17** 243; **18** 520–21; **25** 311–15 **(upd.)**, 381, 488; **27** 20, 373, 375; **28** 159; **29** 74, 78; **32** 187; **34** 369–70; **52** 192–93; **61** 198–203 **(upd.)**, 390, 392

Matth. Hohner AG, 53 214–17

Matthew Bender & Company, Inc., **IV** 677; **7** 94; **14** 97; **17** 486

Matthews International Corporation, 29 304–06

Matthews Paint Co., **22** 437

Matussière et Forest SA, 58 220–22

Maui Electric Company, **9** 276

Maui Land & Pineapple Company, Inc., 29 307–09

Maui Tacos International, Inc., **49** 60

Mauna Loa Macadamia Nut Corporation, 64 263–65

Maus Frères SA, 19 307; **48** 277–79

Maverick Tube Corporation, 59 280–83

Max & Erma's Restaurants Inc., 19 258–61

Max Factor & Co., **12** 314

Max-Grundig-Stiftung, **27** 190–91

Max Media Properties LLC, **25** 419

Max Television Co., **25** 418

Maxco Inc., 17 310–11; **24** 159, 160

Maxell Corp., **14** 534

Maxi-Papier-Markt, **10** 498; **24** 270

Maxi Vac, Inc., **9** 72

Maxicare Health Plans, Inc., III 84–86; **25** 316–19 **(upd.)**; **44** 174

Maxie's of America, **25** 389

The Maxim Group, 25 88, 320–22

Maxim Integrated Products, Inc., 16 358–60

MAXIMUS, Inc., 43 277–80

Maxis Software, **13** 115

Maxoptix Corporation, **10** 404

Maxpro Sports Inc., **22** 458

Maxpro Systems, **24** 509–10

Maxtor Corporation, 10 403–05, 459, 463–64

Maxus Energy Corporation, 7 308–10; **10** 191

Maxwell Communication Corporation plc, IV 611, 641–43; **7** 286, 311–13 **(upd.)**, 343; **10** 288; **13** 91–93; **23** 350; **39** 49; **47** 326; **49** 408

Maxwell Shoe Company, Inc., 30 310–12

Maxwell Travel Inc., **33** 396

MAXXAM Inc., 8 348–50

Maxxcom Inc., **63** 290–91

Maxxim Medical Inc., 12 325–27

May & Speh Inc., **35** 17

The May Department Stores Company, V 132–35; **8** 288; **11** 349; **12** 55, 507–08; **13** 42, 361; **15** 275; **16** 62, 160, 206–07; **18** 414–15; **19** 261–64 **(upd.)**; **23** 345; **27** 61, 291, 346, 348; **33** 471, 473; **46** 284–88 **(upd.)**; **60** 3; **63** 259–61, 263

May International. *See* George S. May International Company.

Mayer & Schweitzer, **26** 66

Mayer, Brown, Rowe & Maw, 47 230–32

Mayfield Dairy Farms, Inc., **7** 128

Mayflower Group Inc., 6 409–11; **15** 50

Mayo Foundation, 9 336–39; **13** 326; **34** 265–69 **(upd.)**

Mayor's Jewelers, Inc., 41 254–57

Mays + Red Spot Coatings, LLC, **55** 321

Maytag Corporation, III 572–73; **12** 252, 300; **21** 141; **22** 218, 348–51 **(upd.)**; **23** 244; **42** 159; **43** 166; **61** 36

Mazda Motor Corporation, II 4, 361; **9** 340–42; **11** 86; **13** 414; **16** 322; **23** 338–41 **(upd.)**; **36** 215; **63** 274–79 **(upd.)**; **64** 128, 133

Mazel Stores, Inc., 29 310–12

MB Group, **20** 108. *See also* Novar plc.

MBB. *See* Messerschmitt-Bölkow-Blohm.

MBC. *See* Middle East Broadcasting Centre, Ltd.

MBC Holding Company, 40 306–09

MBE. *See* Mail Boxes Etc.

MBG Marketing, **62** 154

MBNA Corporation, 11 123; **12** 328–30; **33** 291–94 **(upd.)**

MC Distribution Services, Inc., **35** 298

MCA Inc., II 143–45; **10** 286; **11** 557; **17** 317; **21** 23, 25–26; **22** 131, 194; **25** 411; **26** 151, 314; **33** 431; **52** 191; **64** 257. *See also* Universal Studios.

McAfee Associates. *See* Network Associates, Inc.

McAlister's Corporation, 66 217–19

MCall, **64** 57

The McAlpin Company, **19** 272
McAndrew & Forbes Holdings Inc., **23** 407; **26** 119
McArthur Glen Realty, **10** 122; **33** 59
MCC. *See* Maxwell Communications Corporation; Morris Communications Corporation.
McCain Foods, **41** 252
McCall Pattern Company, **22** 512; **23** 99
McCall Printing Co., **14** 460
McCall's Corp., **23** 393
McCann-Erickson Worldwide, **14** 315; **16** 167; **18** 68; **22** 294
McCann-Erickson Hakuhodo, Ltd., **42** 174
McCarthy Building Companies, Inc., 48 280–82
McCarthy Milling, **II** 631; **27** 245–47
McCaw Cellular Communications, Inc., 6 274, **322–24**; **7** 15; **9** 320–21; **10** 433; **15** 125, 196; **27** 341, 343–44; **29** 44, 61; **36** 514–15; **43** 447; **49** 71–72. *See also* AT&T Wireless Services, Inc.
McClain Industries, Inc., 51 236–38
McClatchy Newspapers, Inc., 23 156, 158, **342–44**
McCleary, Wallin and Crouse, **19** 274
McClintic-Marshall, **7** 49
The McCloskey Corporation, **8** 553
The McClure Syndicate, **25** 138
McColl-Frontenac Petroleum Inc., **IV** 439; **25** 232
McComb Manufacturing Co., **8** 287
McCormack & Dodge, **IV** 605; **11** 77
McCormick & Company, Incorporated, 7 314–16; **17** 104, 106; **21** 497; **27 297–300 (upd.)**; **36** 185, 188; **63** 84; **64** 414
McCormick & Schmick's, **31** 41
McCown De Leeuw & Co., **16** 510
McCoy Corporation, 58 223–25
McCracken Brooks, **23** 479; **25** 91
McCrory Stores, **9** 447–48
McCulloch Corp., **8** 348–49
McCullough Environmental Services, **12** 443
McDermott International, Inc., III 558–60; **37 242–46 (upd.)**
McDonald's Corporation, II 613–15 **646–48**; **7** 128, 266–67, 316, **317–19 (upd.)**, 435, 505–06; **8** 261–62, 564; **9** 74, 178, 290, 292, 305; **10** 122; **11** 82, 308; **12** 43, 180, 553; **13** 494; **14** 25, 32, 106, 195, 452–53; **16** 95–97, 289; **17** 69–71; **19** 85, 192, 214; **21** 25, 315, 362; **23** 505; **25** 179, 309, 387; **26 281–85 (upd.)**; **31** 278; **32** 442–44; **33** 240; **36** 517, 519–20; **39** 166, 168; **48** 67; **57** 83–84; **58** 79–81, 96; **63 280–86 (upd.)**
McDonnell Douglas Corporation, I 70–72, 76–77, 82, 84–85, 90, 105, 108, 111; **7** 456, 504; **8** 49–51, 315; **9** 18, 183, 206, 231, 271–72, 418, 458, 460; **10** 536; **11** 164–65, 267, **277–80 (upd.)**, 285, 363–65; **12** 190–91; **13** 356; **15** 283; **16** 78, 94; **18** 368; **32** 81, 83, 85; **63** 397
McDougal, Littell & Company, **10** 357
McDowell Energy Center, **6** 543
McDowell Furniture Company, **10** 183
McDuff, **10** 305
McElligott Wright Morrison and White, **12** 511
McFadden Holdings L.P., **27** 41

McGaughy, Marsha 584, **634–37**, 643, 656, 674; **10** 62; **12** 359; **13** 417; **18 325–30 (upd.)**; **26** 79; **27** 360
McGaw Inc., **11** 208
McGraw-Edison Co., **II** 17, 87
McGraw Electric Company. *See* Centel Corporation.
The McGraw-Hill Companies, Inc., IV 584, **634–37**, 643, 656, 674; **12** 359; **13** 417; **18 325–30 (upd.)**; **26** 79; **27** 360; **51 239–44 (upd.)**
McGregor Corporation, **6** 415; **26** 102
McGrew Color Graphics, **7** 430
MCI. *See* Manitou Costruzioni Industriali SRL; Melamine Chemicals, Inc.
MCI Communications Corporation, III 149, 684; **V 302–04**; **7** 118–19; **8** 310; **9** 171, 478–80; **10** 19, 80, 89, 97, 433, 500; **11** 59, 183, 185, 302, 409, 500; **12** 135–37; **13** 38; **14** 252–53, 260, 364; **15** 222; **16** 318; **18** 32, 112, 164–66, 569–70; **19** 255; **25** 358; **26** 102, 441; **27** 430; **29** 42; **46** 374; **49** 72–73
MCI WorldCom, Inc., 27 301–08 (upd.)
McIlhenny Company, 20 364–67
McIlwraith McEachern Limited, **27** 474
McJunkin Corporation, 13 79; **28** 61; **63 287–89**
McKechnie plc, 34 270–72
McKee Foods Corporation, 7 320–21; **27 309–11 (upd.)**
McKenna Metals Company, **13** 295–96
McKesson Corporation, I 496–98, 713; **II** 652; **8** 464; **9** 532; **11** 91; **12 331–33 (upd.)**; **16** 43; **18** 97; **37** 10; **41** 340; **47 233–37 (upd.)**
McKesson General Medical, **29** 299
McKinsey & Company, Inc., 9 343–45; **10** 175; **13** 138; **18** 68; **25** 34; **26** 161
McLain Grocery, **II** 625
McLane America, Inc., **29** 481
McLane Company, Inc., 8 556; **13 332–34**; **36** 269
McLaren Consolidated Cone Corp., **7** 366
McLean Clinic, **11** 379
McLeodUSA Incorporated, 32 327–30; **38** 192
McLouth Steel Products, **13** 158
MCM Electronics, **9** 420
McMahan's Furniture Co., **14** 236
MCMC. *See* Minneapolis Children's Medical Center.
McMenamins Pubs and Breweries, 65 224–26
McMoCo, **7** 187
McMoRan, **7** 185, 187
McMullen & Yee Publishing, **22** 442
McMurtry Manufacturing, **8** 553
MCN Corporation, 6 519–22; **13** 416; **17** 21–23; **45** 254
McNeil Corporation, **26** 363
McNeil Laboratories. *See* Johnson & Johnson
MCO Holdings Inc., **8** 348–49
MCorp, **10** 134; **11** 122
McPaper AG, **29** 152
McPherson's Ltd., 66 220–22
McQuay International. *See* AAF-McQuay Incorporated.
McRae's, Inc., **19** 324–25; **41** 343–44
MCS, Inc., **10** 412
MCSi, Inc., 41 258–60
MCT Dairies, Inc., **18** 14–16
McTeigue & Co., **14** 502

McWane Corporation, 55 264–66
McWhorter Inc., **8** 553; **27** 280
MD Distribution Inc., **15** 139
MD Foods (Mejeriselskabet Danmark Foods), **48** 35
MDC. *See* Mead Data Central, Inc.
MDC Partners Inc., 63 290–92
MDI Entertainment, LLC, **64** 346
MDP. *See* Madison Dearborn Partners LLC.
MDS/Bankmark, **10** 247
MDU Resources Group, Inc., 7 322–25; **42 249–53 (upd.)**
Mead & Mount Construction Company, **51** 41
The Mead Corporation, IV 310–13, 327, 329, 342–43; **8** 267; **9** 261; **10** 406; **11** 421–22; **17** 399; **19 265–69 (upd.)**; **20** 18; **33** 263, 265
Mead Data Central, Inc., 7 581; **10 406–08**. *See also* LEXIS-NEXIS Group.
Mead John & Co., **19** 103
Mead Packaging, **12** 151
Meade County Rural Electric Cooperative Corporation, **11** 37
Meade Instruments Corporation, 41 261–64
Meadow Gold Dairies, Inc., **II** 473
Meadowcraft, Inc., 29 313–15
Means Services, Inc., **II** 607
Measurex Corporation, **8** 243; **14** 56; **38** 227
Mebetoys, **25** 312
MEC. *See* Mitsubishi Estate Company, Limited.
MECA Software, Inc., **18** 363
Mecair, S.p.A., **17** 147
MECAR S.A. *See* The Allied Defense Group.
Mecca Bingo Ltd., **64** 320
Mecca Bookmakers, **49** 450
Mecca Leisure PLC, **12** 229; **32** 243
Meccano S.A., **52** 207
Mechanics Exchange Savings Bank, **9** 173
Mecklermedia Corporation, 24 328–30; **26** 441; **27** 360, 362
Meconic, **49** 230, 235
Medal Distributing Co., **9** 542
Medallion Pictures Corp., **9** 320
Medar, Inc., **17** 310–11
Medco Containment Services Inc., 9 346–48; **11** 291; **12** 333; **44** 175
Medeco Security Locks, Inc., **10** 350
Medford, Inc., **19** 467–68
Medi Mart Drug Store Company. *See* The Stop & Shop Companies, Inc.
Media Arts Group, Inc., 42 254–57
Media Exchange International, **25** 509
Media General, Inc., III 214; **7 326–28**; **18** 61; **23** 225; **38 306–09 (upd.)**
Media Groep West B.V., **23** 271
Media News Corporation, **25** 507
Media Play. *See* Musicland Stores Corporation.
MediaBay, **41** 61
Mediacom Inc., **25** 373
Mediamark Research, **28** 501, 504
Mediamatics, Inc., **26** 329
MediaOne Group Inc. *See* U S West, Inc.
Mediaplex, Inc., **49** 433
Mediaset SpA, 50 332–34
Media24. *See* Naspers Ltd.
Medic Computer Systems LLC, **16** 94; **45** 279–80

Medical Arts Press, Inc., **55** 353, 355
Medical Care America, Inc., **15** 112, 114; **35** 215–17
Medical China Publishing Limited, **51** 244
Medical Development Corp. *See* Cordis Corp.
Medical Development Services, Inc., **25** 307
Medical Economics Data, **23** 211
Medical Equipment Finance Corporation, **51** 108
Medical Indemnity of America, **10** 160
Medical Information Technology Inc., 64 266–69
Medical Innovations Corporation, **21** 46
Medical Learning Company, **51** 200, 203
Medical Management International, Inc., 65 227–29
Medical Marketing Group Inc., **9** 348
Medical Service Assoc. of Pennsylvania. *See* Pennsylvania Blue Shield.
Medical Tribune Group, **IV** 591; **20** 53
Medicare-Glaser, **17** 167
Medicine Bow Coal Company, **7** 33–34
Medicine Shoppe International. *See* Cardinal Health, Inc.
Medicis Pharmaceutical Corporation, 59 284–86
Medicor, Inc., **36** 496
Medicus Intercon International. *See* D'Arcy Masius Benton & Bowles, Inc.
Medifinancial Solutions, Inc., **18** 370
MedImmune, Inc., 35 286–89
Medinol Ltd., **37** 39
Mediobanca Banca di Credito Finanziario SpA, **11** 205; **65** 86, 88, 230–31
Mediocredito Toscano, **65** 72
Mediolanum S.p.A., 65 230–32
The Mediplex Group, Inc., **11** 282
Medis Health and Pharmaceuticals Services Inc., **II** 653
Medite Corporation, **19** 467–68
MEDITECH. *See* Medical Information Technology Inc.
Meditrust, 11 281–83
Medline Industries, Inc., 61 204–06
MedPartners, Inc., **36** 367. *See also* Caremark Rx, Inc.
Medtech, Ltd., **13** 60–62
Medtronic, Inc., 8 351–54; **11** 459; **18** 421; **19** 103; **22** 359–61; **26** 132; **30** 313–17 **(upd.)**; **37** 39; **43** 349; **67** 250–55 **(upd.)**
Medusa Corporation, **8** 135; **24** 331–33; **30** 156
Mega Bloks, Inc., 61 207–09
The MEGA Life and Health Insurance Co., **33** 418–20
MEGA Natural Gas Company, **11** 28
MegaBingo, Inc., **41** 273, 275
Megafoods Stores Inc., 13 335–37; **17** 560
Megahouse Corp., **55** 48
MegaKnowledge Inc., **45** 206
Megasong Publishing, **44** 164
Megasource, Inc., **16** 94
Meggitt PLC, 34 273–76; **48** 432, 434
MEGTEC Systems Inc., **54** 331
MEI Diversified Inc., **18** 455
Mei Foo Investments Ltd., **IV** 718; **38** 319
Meier & Frank Co., 23 345–47
Meierjohan-Wengler Inc., **56** 23
Meijer Incorporated, 7 329–31; **15** 449; **17** 302; **27** 312–15 **(upd.)**

Meiji Milk Products Company, Limited, II 538–39
Meiji Mutual Life Insurance Company, III 288–89
Meiji Seika Kaisha Ltd., II 540–41; **64** 270–72 **(upd.)**
Meinecke Muffler Company, **10** 415
Meineke Discount Muffler Shops, **38** 208
Meis of Illiana, **10** 282
Meisel. *See* Samuel Meisel & Co.
Meisenzahl Auto Parts, Inc., **24** 205
Meister, Lucious and Company, **13** 262
Meiwa Manufacturing Co., **III** 758
Mel Farr Automotive Group, 20 368–70
Melaleuca Inc., 31 326–28
Melamine Chemicals, Inc., 27 316–18
Melbourne Engineering Co., **23** 83
Meldisco. *See* Footstar, Incorporated.
Melitta Unternehmensgruppe Bentz KG, 53 218–21
Mello Smello. *See* The Miner Group International.
Mellon Bank Corporation, II 315–17, 342, 402; **9** 470; **13** 410–11; **18** 112
Mellon Financial Corporation, 42 76; **44** 278–82 **(upd.)**; **55** 71
Mellon Indemnity Corp., **24** 177
Mellon Stuart Building Services, Inc., **51** 248
Mellon-Stuart Co., I 584–85; **14** 334
Melmarkets, **24** 462
Meloy Laboratories, Inc., **11** 333
Melroe Company, **8** 115–16; **34** 46
Melville Corporation, V 136–38; **9** 192; **13** 82, 329–30; **14** 426; **15** 252–53;, **16** 390; **19** 449; **21** 526; **23** 176; **24** 167, 290; **35** 253; **57** 368. *See also* CVS Corporation.
Melvin Simon and Associates, Inc., 8 355–57; **26** 262. *See also* Simon Property Group, Inc.
MEM, **37** 270–71
Memco, **12** 48
Memorial Sloan-Kettering Cancer Center, 57 239–41
Memphis International Motorsports Corporation Inc., **43** 139–40
Memphis Retail Investors Limited Partnership, **62** 144
The Men's Wearhouse, Inc., 17 312–15; **21** 311; **48** 283–87 **(upd.)**
Menasha Corporation, 8 358–61; **59** 287–92 **(upd.)**
Menck, **8** 544
Mendocino Brewing Company, Inc., 60 205–07
The Mennen Company, **14** 122; **18** 69; **35** 113
Mental Health Programs Inc., **15** 122
The Mentholatum Company Inc., 32 331–33
Mentor Corporation, 26 286–88
Mentor Graphics Corporation, 8 519; **11** 46–47, **284–86**, 490; **13** 128
MEPC plc, IV 710–12
Mepco/Electra Inc., **13** 398
MeraBank, **6** 546
Meralco. *See* Manila Electric Company.
MERBCO, Inc., **33** 456
Mercantile Bancorporation Inc., **33** 155
Mercantile Bankshares Corp., 11 287–88
Mercantile Credit Co., **16** 13
Mercantile Estate and Property Corp. Ltd. *See* MEPC PLC.

Mercantile Stores Company, Inc., V 139; **19** 270–73 **(upd.)**
Mercator & Noordstar N.V., **40** 61
Mercator Software, **59** 54, 56
Mercedes Benz. *See* DaimlerChrysler AG
Mercer International Inc., 64 273–75
Merchant Bank Services, **18** 516, 518
Merchant Distributors, Inc., **20** 306
Merchants & Farmers Bank of Ecru, **14** 40
Merchants Bank & Trust Co., **21** 524
Merchants Distributors Inc. *See* Alex Lee Inc.
Merchants Home Delivery Service, **6** 414
Merchants National Bank, **9** 228; **14** 528; **17** 135
Merck & Co., Inc., I 650–52; **III** 299; **8** 154, 548; **10** 213; **11** 9, 90, **289–91** **(upd.)**; **12** 325, 333; **14** 58, 422; **15** 154; **16** 440; **20** 39, 59; **26** 126; **34** 280–85 **(upd.)**; **36** 91, 93, 305; **38** 380; **44** 175; **47** 236; **50** 56, 138–39; **58** 180–81; **63** 235
Mercury Air Group, Inc., 20 371–73
Mercury Asset Management (MAM), **14** 420; **40** 313
Mercury Communications, Ltd., 7 332–34; **10** 456; **11** 547–48; **25** 101–02; **27** 365
Mercury General Corporation, 25 323–25
Mercury, Inc., **8** 311
Mercury Interactive Corporation, 59 293–95
Mercury International Ltd., **51** 130
Mercury Mail, Inc., **22** 519, 522
Mercury Records, **13** 397; **23** 389, 391
Mercury Telecommunications Limited, **15** 67, 69
Mercy Air Service, Inc., **53** 29
Meredith Corporation, 11 292–94; **17** 394; **18** 239; **23** 393; **29** 316–19 **(upd.)**
Merfin International, **42** 53
Merial, **34** 284
Merico, Inc., **36** 161–64
Merida, **50** 445, 447
Meridian Bancorp, Inc., 11 295–97; **17** 111, 114
Meridian Emerging Markets Ltd., **25** 509
Meridian Gold, Incorporated, 47 238–40
Meridian Healthcare Ltd., **18** 197; **59** 168
Meridian Industrial Trust Inc., **57** 301
Meridian Investment and Development Corp., **22** 189
Meridian Oil Inc., **10** 190–91
Meridian Publishing, Inc., **28** 254
Merillat Industries Inc., 13 338–39
Merisel, Inc., 10 518–19; **12** 334–36; **13** 174, 176, 482
Merit Distribution Services, **13** 333
Merit Medical Systems, Inc., 29 320–22; **36** 497
Merit Tank Testing, Inc., **IV** 411
Merita/Cotton's Bakeries, **38** 251
Meritage Corporation, 26 289–92; **62** 327
MeritaNordbanken, **40** 336
Meritor Automotive Inc., **43** 328. *See also* ArvinMeritor Inc.
Merix Corporation, 36 329–31
Merkur Direktwerbegesellschaft, **29** 152
Merlin Gérin, **19** 165
Merpati Nusantara Airlines. *See* Garuda Indonesia.
Merrell, **22** 173

Merrell Dow, **16** 438
Merriam-Webster, Inc., **7** 165, 167; **23** 209–10; **39** 140, 143
Merrill Corporation, 18 331–34; 47 241–44 (upd.)
Merrill Gas Company, **9** 554
Merrill Lynch & Co., Inc., II 424–26; **III** 340, 440; **7** 130; **8** 94; **9** 125, 187, 239, 301, 386; **11** 29, 122, 348, 557; **13** 44, 125, **340–43 (upd.)**, 448–49, 512; **14** 65; **15** 463; **16** 195; **17** 137; **21** 68–70; **22** 404–06, 542; **23** 370; **25** 89–90, 329; **29** 295; **32** 14, 168; **40** 310–15 (upd.); **49** 130; **50** 419
Merrill Lynch Capital Partners, **47** 363
Merrill, Pickard, Anderson & Eyre IV, **11** 490
Merrill Publishing, **IV** 643; **7** 312; **9** 63; **29** 57
Merrimack Services Corp., **37** 303
Merry-Go-Round Enterprises, Inc., 8 362–64; 24 27
Merry Group. See Boral Limited.
Merry Maids. See ServiceMaster Inc.
Merryhill Schools, Inc., **37** 279
The Mersey Docks and Harbour Company, 30 318–20
Mervyn's California, **10** 409–10; **13** 526; **27** 452; **39** 269–71 (upd.). See also Target Corporation.
Merz + Co., **52** 135
Mesa Air Group, Inc., 32 334–37 (upd.)
Mesa Airlines, Inc., 11 298–300
Mesa Petroleum, **11** 441; **27** 217
Mesaba Holdings, Inc., 22 21; 28 265–67
Messerschmitt-Bölkow-Blohm GmbH., I 46, 51–52, 55, **73–75; 11** 267; **24** 86; **52** 113
Messner, Vetere, Berger, Carey, Schmetterer, **13** 204
Mesta Machine Co., **22** 415
Mestek, Inc., 10 411–13
Met Food Corp. See White Rose Food Corp.
Met-Mex Penoles. See Industrias Penoles, S.A. de C.V.
META Group, Inc., **37** 147
Metaframe Corp., **25** 312
Metal Box plc, I 604–06; 20 108. See also Novar plc.
Metal-Cal. See Avery Dennison Corporation.
Metal Casting Technology, Inc., **23** 267, 269
Metal Office Furniture Company, **7** 493
AB Metal Pty Ltd, **62** 331
Metalcorp Ltd, **62** 331
Metales y Contactos, **29** 461–62
Metaleurop S.A., 21 368–71
MetalExchange, **26** 530
Metall Mining Corp., **27** 456
Metallgesellschaft AG, IV 139–42, 229; **16 361–66 (upd.)**
MetalOptics Inc., **19** 212
Metalúrgica Gerdau. See Gerdau S.A.
Metalurgica Mexicana Penoles, S.A. See Industrias Penoles, S.A. de C.V.
Metaphase Technology, Inc., **10** 257
Metatec International, Inc., 47 245–48
Metcalf & Eddy Companies, Inc., **6** 441; **32** 52
Metcash Trading Ltd., 58 226–28
Meteor Film Productions, **23** 391
Meteor Industries Inc., 33 295–97

Methane Development Corporation, **6** 457
Methanex Corporation, 12 365; 19 155–56; **40 316–19**
Methode Electronics, Inc., 13 344–46
MetLife. See Metropolitan Life Insurance Company.
MetMor Financial, Inc., **III** 293; **52** 239–40
Meto AG, **39** 79
MetPath, Inc., **III** 684; **26** 390
Metra Corporation. See Wärtsilä Corporation.
Metra Steel, **19** 381
Metrastock Ltd., **34** 5
Metric Constructors, Inc., **16** 286
Metric Systems Corporation, **18** 513; **44** 420
Metris Companies Inc., 25 41; **56 224–27**
Metro AG, 23 311; **50 335–39**
Metro Distributors Inc., **14** 545
Metro-Goldwyn-Mayer Inc., 25 173, 253, **326–30 (upd.); 33** 120
Metro Holding AG, **38** 266
Metro Information Services, Inc., 36 **332–34**
Metro International SA, **36** 335
Metro-Mark Integrated Systems Inc., **11** 469
Metro-North Commuter Railroad Company, **35** 292
Metro Pacific, **18** 180, 182
Metro-Richelieu Inc., **II** 653
Metro Southwest Construction. See CRSS Inc.
Metro Support Services, Inc., **48** 171
Metrocall, Inc., 18 77; **39** 25; **41 265–68**
Metrol Security Services, Inc., **32** 373
Metroland Printing, Publishing and Distributing Ltd., **29** 471
Metromail Corp., **IV** 661; **18** 170; **38** 370
Metromedia Companies, 7 91, **335–37;** **14** 298–300
Metromedia Company, 61 210–14 (upd.)
Metronic AG, **64** 226
Metroplex, LLC, **51** 206
Metropolis Intercom, **67** 137–38
Metropolitan Baseball Club Inc., 39 **272–75**
Metropolitan Broadcasting Corporation, **7** 335
Metropolitan Clothing Co., **19** 362
Metropolitan Distributors, **9** 283
Metropolitan District Railway Company, **6** 406
Metropolitan Edison Company, **27** 182
Metropolitan Financial Corporation, 12 165; **13 347–49**
Metropolitan Furniture Leasing, **14** 4
Metropolitan Gas Light Co., **6** 455
Metropolitan Life Insurance Company, **II** 679; **III 290–94,** 313, 329, 337, 339–40; **IV** 283; **6** 256; **8** 326–27; **11** 482; **22** 266; **25** 300; **42** 194; **45** 249, 411; **52 235–41 (upd.); 54** 223–25
The Metropolitan Museum of Art, 55 **267–70**
Metropolitan Opera Association, Inc., 40 **320–23**
Metropolitan Railway, **6** 407
Metropolitan Reference Laboratories Inc., **26** 391
Metropolitan Tobacco Co., **15** 138
Metropolitan Transportation Authority, **35 290–92**

MetroRed, **57** 67, 69
Metrostar Management, **59** 199
METSA, Inc., **15** 363
Metsä-Serla Oy, IV 314–16, 318, 350. See also M-real Oyj.
Metsec plc, **57** 402
Metso Corporation, 30 321–25 (upd.)
Mettler-Toledo International Inc., 30 **326–28**
Mettler United States Inc., **9** 441
Metwest, **26** 391
Metz Baking Company, **36** 164
Metzdorf Advertising Agency, **30** 80
Metzeler Kautschuk, **15** 354
Mexican Metal Co. See Industrias Penoles, S.A. de C.V.
Mexican Restaurants, Inc., 41 269–71
Meyer Brothers Drug Company, **16** 212
Meyer Corporation, **27** 288
Meyerland Company, **19** 366
Meyers Motor Supply, **26** 347
Meyers Parking, **18** 104
The Meyne Company, **55** 74
Meyr Melnhof Karton AG, **41 325–27**
M4 Data (Holdings) Ltd., **62** 293
M40 Trains Ltd., **51** 173
MFS Communications Company, Inc., **11 301–03; 14** 253; **27** 301, 307
MG&E. See Madison Gas & Electric.
MG Holdings. See Mayflower Group Inc.
MG Ltd., **IV** 141
MGD Graphics Systems. See Goss Holdings, Inc.
MGIC Investment Corp., 45 320; **52** **242–44**
MGM. See McKesson General Medical.
MGM Grand Inc., 17 316–19; 18 336–37
MGM Mirage. See Mirage Resorts, Incorporated.
MGM Studios, **50** 125
MGM/UA Communications Company, II **146–50,** 408; **IV** 676; **12** 73, 316, 323; **15** 84; **17** 316. See also Metro-Goldwyn-Mayer Inc.
MGN. See Mirror Group Newspapers Ltd.
MGT Services Inc. See The Midland Company.
MH Alshaya Group, **28** 96
MH Media Monitoring Limited, **26** 270
MHI Group, Inc., **13** 356; **16** 344
MHS Holding Corp., **26** 101
MHT. See Manufacturers Hanover Trust Co.
MI. See Masco Corporation.
MI S.A., **66** 244
Mi-Tech Steel Inc., **63** 359–60
Miami Computer Supply Corporation. See MCSi, Inc.
Miami Power Corporation, **6** 466
Miami Subs Corp., **29** 342, 344
Micamold Electronics Manufacturing Corporation, **10** 319
Mich-Wis. See Michigan Wisconsin Pipe Line.
Michael Anthony Jewelers, Inc., 24 **334–36**
Michael Baker Corporation, 14 333–35; **51 245–48 (upd.)**
MICHAEL Business Systems Plc, **10** 257
Michael C. Fina Co., Inc., 52 245–47
Michael Foods, Inc., 25 331–34; 39 319–321
Michael Joseph, **IV** 659

Michael Page International plc, 45 272–74; **52** 317–18

Michael's Fair-Mart Food Stores, Inc., **19** 479

Michaels Stores, Inc., 17 320–22, 360; **25** 368

MichCon. *See* MCN Corporation.

Michelin. *See* Compagnie Générale des Établissements Michelin.

Michie Co., **33** 264–65

Michigan Automotive Compressor, Inc., **III** 638–39

Michigan Automotive Research Corporation, **23** 183

Michigan Bell Telephone Co., 14 336–38; **18** 30

Michigan Carpet Sweeper Company, **9** 70

Michigan Consolidated Gas Company. *See* MCN Corporation.

Michigan International Speedway. *See* Penske Corporation.

Michigan Livestock Exchange, **36** 442

Michigan Motor Freight Lines, **14** 567

Michigan National Corporation, 11 304–06; **18** 517

Michigan Oil Company, **18** 494

Michigan Packaging Company. *See* Greif Inc.

Michigan Seamless Tube Company. *See* Quanex Corporation.

Michigan Shoe Makers. *See* Wolverine World Wide Inc.

Michigan Spring Company, **17** 106

Michigan Steel Corporation, **12** 352

Michigan Tag Company, **9** 72

Michigan Wisconsin Pipe Line, **39** 260

Mick's Inc., **30** 329

Mickey Shorr Mobile Electronics, **10** 9–11

Micro Contract Manufacturing Inc., **44** 441

Micro D, Inc., **11** 194

Micro Decisionware, Inc., **10** 506

Micro Focus Inc., **27** 491

Micro Magic, Inc., **43** 254

Micro Metallics Corporation, **64** 297

Micro Peripherals, Inc., **18** 138

Micro Power Systems Inc., **14** 183

Micro Switch, **14** 284

Micro/Vest, **13** 175

Micro Warehouse, Inc., 16 371–73

MicroAge, Inc., 16 367–70; 29 414

Microamerica, **12** 334

Microban Products Company, **27** 288

MicroBilt Corporation, **11** 112

Microcar SA, **55** 54, 56

MicroClean Inc, **50** 49

Microcom, Inc., **26** 93; **50** 227

Microcomputer Asset Management Services, **9** 168

Microcomputer Systems, **22** 389

Microdot Inc., 8 365–68, 545

Microfral, **14** 216

MicroFridge, **44** 273

Micromass Ltd., **43** 455

Micromedex, **19** 268

Micron Technology, Inc., 11 307–09; 29 323–26 (upd.)

Micropolis Corp., **10** 403, 458, 463

MicroPro International Corp., **10** 556. *See also* The Learning Company Inc.

Microprocessor Systems, **13** 235

Microprose Inc., **24** 538

Micros Systems, Inc., 18 335–38

Microsensor Systems Inc., **43** 366

Microsoft Corporation, 6 257–60; 9 81, 140, 171, 195, 472; **10** 22, 34, 57, 87, 119, 237–38, 362–63, 408, 477, 484, 504, 557–58; **11** 59, 77–78, 306, 519–20; **12** 180, 335; **13** 115, 128, 147, 482, 509; **14** 262–64, 318; **15** 132–33, 321, 371, 483, 492, 511; **16** 4, 94, 367, 392, 394, 444; **18** 24, 64, 66, 306–7, 345, 349, 367, 541, 543; **19** 310; **20** 237; **21** 86; **24** 120, 233, 236, 371; **25** 21, 32, 34, 96, 117, 119, 184, 498–99, 509; **26** 17, 294–95, 441, 520; **27** 319–23 (upd.), 448, 517; **28** 245, 301; **29** 65, 439; **30** 391, 450; **33** 115–16, 210; **34** 443, 445, 513; **36** 384; **37** 383; **38** 71, 270–71, 416; **41** 53–54; **42** 424; **43** 240; **44** 97; **45** 200–02; **47** 419–21; **53** 252, 254; **54** 269–71; **58** 117–20; **63** 64, **293–97 (upd.);** **64** 78

Microtek, Inc., **22** 413

MicroUnity Systems Engineering Inc., **50** 53

Microware Surgical Instruments Corp., **IV** 137

Microwave Communications, Inc. *See* MCI Telecom.

Mid-America Capital Resources, Inc., **6** 508

Mid-America Dairymen, Inc., 7 338–40; **11** 24; **22** 95; **26** 448

Mid-America Interpool Network, **6** 506, 602

Mid-America Packaging, Inc., **8** 203

Mid-America Tag & Label, **8** 360

Mid Bus Inc., **33** 107

Mid-Central Fish and Frozen Foods Inc., **II** 675

Mid-Continent Computer Services, **11** 111

Mid-Continent Life Insurance Co., **23** 200

Mid-Continent Telephone Corporation. *See* Alltel Corporation.

Mid-Georgia Gas Company, **6** 448

Mid-Illinois Gas Co., **6** 529

Mid-Michigan Music Co., **60** 84

Mid-Pacific Airlines, **9** 271; **24** 21–22

Mid-Packaging Group Inc., **19** 78

Mid-South Towing, **6** 583

Mid-States Development, Inc., **18** 405

Mid-Valley Dairy, **14** 397

MidAmerican Communications Corporation, **8** 311

Midas Inc., 56 228–31 (upd.)

Midas International Corporation, 10 414–15, 554; **24** 337

MIDCO, **III** 340

Middle East Broadcasting Centre, Ltd., **25** 506, 508

Middle East Tube Co. Ltd., **25** 266

Middle South Utilities. *See* Entergy Corporation.

Middle West Corporation, **6** 469–70

Middle Wisconsin Power, **6** 604

The Middleby Corporation, 22 352–55; **61** 34

Middlesex Water Company, 45 275–78

Middleton Aerospace, **48** 275

The Middleton Doll Company, 53 222–25

Middleton Packaging, **12** 377

Middletown Manufacturing Co., Inc., **16** 321

Middletown National Bank, **13** 467

Midland Advertising & Design, Inc., **56** 332

Midland Bank plc, II 318–20; 9 505; **12** 257; **14** 169; **17 323–26 (upd.); 19** 198; **26** 202; **33** 395

Midland Brick, **14** 250

The Midland Company, 65 233–35

Midland Enterprises Inc., **6** 486–88

Midland Independent Newspaper plc, **23** 351

Midland International, **8** 56–57

Midland Investment Co., **II** 7

Midland National Bank, **11** 130

Midland-Ross Corporation, **14** 369

Midland Southwest Corp., **8** 347

Midland Steel Products Co., **13** 305–06

Midland United, **6** 556; **25** 89

Midland Utilities Company, **6** 532

Midlands Electricity, **13** 485

Midlantic Corp., **13** 411

Midlantic Hotels Ltd., **41** 83

Midrange Performance Group, **12** 149

Midway Airlines Corporation, 6 105, 120–21; **33 301–03**

Midway Games, Inc., 25 335–38

Midway Manufacturing Company, **15** 539

Midwest Agri-Commodities Company, **11** 15; **32** 29

Midwest Biscuit Company, **14** 306

Midwest Com of Indiana, Inc., **11** 112

Midwest Express Holdings, Inc., 35 293–95; **43** 258

Midwest Federal Savings & Loan Association, **11** 162–63

Midwest Financial Group, Inc., **8** 188

Midwest Foundry Co., **IV** 137

Midwest Grain Products, Inc., 49 261–63

Midwest Manufacturing, **12** 296

Midwest Realty Exchange, Inc., **21** 257

Midwest Resources Inc., 6 523–25

Midwest Staffing Systems, **27** 21

Midwest Steel Corporation, **13** 157

Midwest Suburban Publishing Inc., **62** 188

Midwest Synthetics, **8** 553

Midwinter, **12** 529

Miele & Cie. KG, 56 232–35

MIG Realty Advisors, Inc., **25** 23, 25

Miguel Galas S.A., **17** 268

MIH Limited, 31 329–32

Mikasa, Inc., 28 268–70

Mike-Sell's Inc., 15 298–300

Mikemitch Realty Corp., **16** 36

Mikohn Gaming Corporation, 39 276–79

Mikon, Ltd., **13** 345

Milac, **27** 259

Milacron, Inc., 53 226–30 (upd.)

Milan A.C., S.p.A., **44** 387

Milbank, Tweed, Hadley & McCloy, 27 324–27

Milchem, Inc., **63** 306

Mile-Hi Distributing, **64** 180

Miles Inc., **22** 148

Miles Kimball Co., **9** 393

Miles Laboratories, I 653–55, 674, 678; **14** 558

Milgram Food Stores Inc., **II** 682

Milgray Electronics Inc., **19** 311; **47** 41

Milk Producers, Inc., **11** 24

Milk Specialties Co., **12** 199

Mill-Power Supply Company, **27** 129–30

Millea Holdings Inc., 64 276–81 (upd.)

Millennium Chemicals Inc., **30** 231; **45** 252, 254

Millennium Pharmaceuticals, Inc., 47 249–52

Miller Automotive Group, **52** 146

Miller Brewing Company, I, 254–55, 257–58, **269–70,** 283, 290–91; **10** 100; **11** 421; **12 337–39 (upd.),** 372; **13** 258; **15** 429; **17** 256; **18** 70, 72, 418, 499, 501; **21** 230; **22** 199, 422; **26** 303, 306; **27** 374; **28** 209–10; **34** 36–37; **44** 342; **50** 202. *See also* SABMiller plc.
Miller Companies, **17** 182
Miller Container Corporation, **8** 102
Miller Exploration Company. *See* Edge Petroleum Corporation.
Miller Freeman, Inc., **IV** 687; **27** 362; **28** 501, 504
Miller Group Ltd., **22** 282
Miller Industries, Inc., 26 293–95
Miller, Mason and Dickenson, **III** 204–05
Miller Plant Farms, Inc., **51** 61
Miller Publishing Group, LLC, 57 242–44
Miller, Tabak, Hirsch & Co., **13** 394; **28** 164
Millet, **39** 250
Millet's Leisure. *See* Sears plc.
Millicom, **11** 547; **18** 254
Milliken & Co., V 366–68; **8** 270–71; **17 327–30 (upd.); 29** 246
Milliken, Tomlinson Co., **II** 682
Milliman USA, 66 223–26
Millipore Corporation, 9 396; **23** 284; **25 339–43; 43** 454
Mills Clothing, Inc. *See* The Buckle, Inc.
Millville Electric Light Company, **6** 449
Millway Foods, **25** 85
Milne & Craighead, **48** 113
Milne Fruit Products, Inc., **25** 366
Milnot Company, 46 289–91; 51 47
Milpark Drilling Fluids, Inc., **63** 306
Milsco Manufacturing Co., **23** 299, 300
Milton Bradley Company, 17 105; **21 372–75; 25** 380
Milton Light & Power Company, **12** 45
Milton Roy Co., **8** 135
Milupa S.A., **37** 341
Milwaukee Brewers Baseball Club, 37 247–49
Milwaukee Cheese Co. Inc., **25** 517
Milwaukee Electric Railway and Light Company, **6** 601–02, 604–05
Milwaukee Electric Tool, **28** 40
Minatome, **IV** 560
Mindpearl, **48** 381
Mindport, **31** 329
Mindset Corp., **42** 424–25
Mindspring Enterprises, Inc., **36** 168
Mine Safety Appliances Company, 31 333–35
The Miner Group International, 22 356–58
Minera Loma Blanca S.A., **56** 127
Mineral Point Public Service Company, **6** 604
Minerales y Metales, S.A. *See* Industrias Penoles, S.A. de C.V.
Minerals & Metals Trading Corporation of India Ltd., IV 143–44
Minerals and Resources Corporation Limited, **IV** 23; **13** 502; **50** 34. *See also* Minorco.
Minerals Technologies Inc., 11 310–12; 52 248–51 (upd.)
Minerec Corporation, **9** 363
Minerve, **6** 208
Minet Group, **III** 357; **22** 494–95
MiniScribe, Inc., **10** 404

Minitel, **21** 233
Minivator Ltd., **11** 486
Minneapolis Children's Medical Center, **54** 65
Minneapolis-Honeywell Regulator Co., **8** 21; **22** 427
Minneapolis Steel and Machinery Company, **21** 502
Minnehoma Insurance Company, **58** 260
Minnesota Brewing Company. *See* MBC Holding Company.
Minnesota Linseed Oil Co., **8** 552
Minnesota Mining & Manufacturing Company, I 387, **499–501; IV 8** 35, **369–71 (upd.); 11** 494; **13** 326; **22** 427; **25** 96, 372; **26 296–99 (upd.).** *See also* 3M Company.
Minnesota Paints, **8** 552–53
Minnesota Power & Light Company, 11 313–16
Minnesota Power, Inc., 34 286–91 (upd.)
Minnesota Sugar Company, **11** 13
Minnetonka Corp., **III** 25; **22** 122–23
Minntech Corporation, 22 359–61
Minn-Dak Farmers Cooperative, **32** 29
Minolta Co., Ltd., III 574–76; **18** 93, 186, **339–42 (upd.); 43 281–85 (upd.)**
Minorco, **IV** 97; **16** 28, 293
Minstar Inc., **11** 397; **15** 49; **45** 174
Minton China, **38** 401
The Minute Maid Company, 28 271–74, 473; **32** 116
Minuteman International Inc., 46 292–95
Minyard Food Stores, Inc., 33 304–07
Mippon Paper, **21** 546; **50** 58
Miracle Food Mart, **16** 247, 249–50
Miracle-Gro Products, Inc., **22** 474
Miraflores Designs Inc., **18** 216
Mirage Resorts, Incorporated, 6 209–12, **15** 238; **28 275–79 (upd.); 29** 127; **43** 82
Miraglia Inc., **57** 139
Miramax Film Corporation, 64 282–85
Mirant, **39** 54, 57
Mircali Asset Management, **III** 340
Mircor Inc., **12** 413
Mirror Group Newspapers plc, 7 341–43; 23 348–51 (upd.); 49 408; **61** 130
Misceramic Tile, Inc., **14** 42
Misr Airwork. *See* AirEgypt.
Misr Bank of Cairo, **27** 132
Misrair. *See* AirEgypt.
Miss Erika, Inc., **27** 346, 348
Miss Selfridge. *See* Sears plc.
Misset Publishers, **IV** 611
Mission Group. *See* SCEcorp.
Mission Jewelers, **30** 408
Mission Valley Fabrics, **57** 285
Mississippi Chemical Corporation, 8 183; **27** 316; **39 280–83**
Mississippi Gas Company, **6** 577
Mississippi Power Company, **38** 446–47
Mississippi River Corporation, **10** 44
Mississippi River Recycling, **31** 47, 49
Mississippi Valley Title Insurance Company, **58** 259–60
Missoula Bancshares, Inc., **35** 198–99
Missouri Book Co., **10** 136
Missouri Fur Company, **25** 220
Missouri Gaming Company, **21** 39
Missouri Gas & Electric Service Company, **6** 593

Missouri Pacific Railroad, **10** 43–44
Missouri Public Service Company. *See* UtiliCorp United Inc.
Missouri Utilities Company, **6** 580
Mist Assist, Inc. *See* Ballard Medical Products.
Mistik Beverages, **18** 71
Misys PLC, 45 279–81; 46 296–99
Mitchel & King Skates Ltd., **17** 244
Mitchell Energy and Development Corporation, 7 344–46; 61 75
Mitchell Home Savings and Loan, **13** 347
Mitchell International, **8** 526
Mitchells & Butlers PLC, 59 296–99
MiTek Industries Inc., **IV** 259
MiTek Wood Products, **IV** 305
Mitel Corporation, 15 131–32; **18 343–46**
MitNer Group, **7** 377
MITRE Corporation, 26 300–02
Mitre Sport U.K., **17** 204–05
MITROPA AG, 37 250–53
Mitsubishi Aircraft Co., **9** 349; **11** 164
Mitsubishi Bank, Ltd., II 321–22; **15** 41; **16** 496, 498; **50** 498. *See also* Bank of Tokyo-Mitsubishi Ltd.
Mitsubishi Chemical Corporation, 56 236–38 (upd.)
Mitsubishi Chemical Industries Ltd., I 363–64; **11** 207
Mitsubishi Corporation, I 261, **502–04; IV** 285, 518, 713; **6** 499; **7** 82, 233, 590; **9** 294; **12 340–43 (upd.); 17** 349, 556; **24** 359; **27** 511
Mitsubishi Electric Corporation, II 57–59, 68, 73, 94, 122; **18** 18; **23** 52–53; **43** 15; **44 283–87 (upd.)**
Mitsubishi Estate Company, Limited, IV 713–14; **58** 303; **61 215–18 (upd.)**
Mitsubishi Foods, **24** 114
Mitsubishi Group, **7** 377; **21** 390
Mitsubishi Heavy Industries, Ltd., III 577–79; **7 347–50 (upd.); 8** 51; **9** 349–50; **10** 33; **13** 507; **15** 92; **24** 359; **40 324–28 (upd.); 63** 95
Mitsubishi International Corp., **16** 462
Mitsubishi Kasei Corp., **14** 535
Mitsubishi Kasei Vinyl Company, **49** 5
Mitsubishi Materials Corporation, III 712–13; **38** 463
Mitsubishi Motors Corporation, 7 219; **8** 72, 374; **9** 349–51; **23 352–55 (upd.); 34** 128, 136; **57 245–49 (upd.); 64** 100
Mitsubishi Oil Co., Ltd., IV 460–62, 479, 492
Mitsubishi Rayon Co. Ltd., V 369–71
Mitsubishi Shipbuilding Co. Ltd., **9** 349
Mitsubishi Trust & Banking Corporation, II 323–24
Mitsui & Co., Ltd., 7 303; **13** 356; **24** 325, 488–89; **27** 337; **28 280–85 (upd.)**
Mitsui Bank, Ltd., II 325–27, 328, 372; **III** 295–97; **17** 556. *See also* Sumitomo Mitsui Banking Corporation.
Mitsui Bussan K.K., I 505–08; **II** 392; **III** 295–96; **9** 352–53. *See also* Mitsui & Co., Ltd.
Mitsui Group, **9** 352; **16** 84; **20** 310; **21** 72
Mitsui Light Metal Processing Co., **III** 758
Mitsui Marine and Fire Insurance Company, Limited, III 209, **295–96**
Mitsui Mining & Smelting Co., Ltd., IV 145–46, 147–48

Mitsui Mining Company, Limited, IV 147–49
Mitsui Mutual Life Insurance Company, III 297–98; **39** 284–86 (upd.)
Mitsui-no-Mori Co., Ltd., IV 716
Mitsui O.S.K. Lines, Ltd., V 473–76; **6** 398; **26** 278–80
Mitsui Petrochemical Industries, Ltd., I 390, 516; **9** 352–54
Mitsui Real Estate Development Co., Ltd., IV 715–16
Mitsui Toatsu, **9** 353–54
Mitsui Trust & Banking Company, Ltd., II 328
Mitsukoshi Ltd., I 508; V 142–44; **14** 502; **41** 114; **47** 391; **56** 239–42 (upd.)
Mity Enterprises, Inc., **38** 310–12
Mizuho Financial Group Inc., **58** 229–36 (upd.)
Mizuno Corporation, **25** 344–46
MJ Pharmaceuticals Ltd., **57** 346
MK-Ferguson Company, **7** 356
MLC. *See* Medical Learning Company.
MLC Ltd., IV 709; **52** 221–22
MLH&P. *See* Montreal Light, Heat & Power Company.
MLT Vacations Inc., **30** 446
MM Merchandising Munich, **54** 296–97
MMAR Group Inc., **19** 131
MMC Networks Inc., **38** 53, 55
MML Investors Services, III 286; **53** 213
MMS America Corp., **26** 317
MNC Financial. *See* MBNA Corporation.
MNC Financial Corp., **11** 447
MND Drilling, **7** 345
MNet, **11** 122
MNS, Ltd., **65** 236–38
Mo och Domsjö AB, IV 317–19. *See also* Holmen AB
MOB, **56** 335
Mobil Corporation, IV 93, 295, 363, 386, 401, 403, 406, 423, 428, 454, **463–65**, 466, 472–74, 486, 492, 504–05, 515, 517, 522, 531, 538–39, 545, 554–55, 564, 570–71; **6** 530; **7** 171, **351–54** (upd.); **8** 552–53; **9** 546; **10** 440; **12** 348; **16** 489; **17** 363, 415; **19** 140, 225, 297; **21** 376–80 (upd.); **24** 496, 521; **25** 232, 445; **26** 369; **32** 175, 179, 181; **45** 50; **50** 416. *See also* Exxon Mobil Corporation.
Mobil Oil Australia, **24** 399
Mobil Oil Indonesia, **56** 273
Mobile America Housing Corporation. *See* American Homestar Corporation.
Mobile Corporation, **25** 232
Mobile Mini, Inc., **21** 476; **58** 237–39
Mobile Telecommunications Technologies Corp., V 277–78; **16** 74; **18** 347–49
Mobile TeleSystems OJSC, **48** 419; **59** 300–03
Mobilefone, Inc., **25** 108
MobileMedia Corp., **39** 23, 24
MobileStar Network Corp., **26** 429
Mobu Company, **6** 431
Mobujidosha Bus Company, **6** 431
Mochida Pharaceutical Co. Ltd., II 553
Modar, **17** 279
Mode 1 Communications, Inc., **48** 305
Modell's Shoppers World, **16** 35–36
Modell's Sporting Goods. *See* Henry Modell & Company Inc.
Modeluxe Linge Services SA, **45** 139–40

Modem Media, **23** 479
Modern Furniture Rentals Inc., **14** 4; **27** 163
Modern Handling Methods Ltd., **21** 499
Modern Merchandising Inc., **19** 396
Modern Times Group AB, **36** 335–38
Modern Woodmen of America, **66** 227–29
Modernistic Industries Inc., **7** 589
Modine Manufacturing Company, **8** 372–75; **56** 243–47 (upd.)
Modis Professional Services. *See* MPS Group, Inc.
MoDo. *See* Mo och Domsjö AB.
MoDo Paper AB, **28** 446; **52** 164
Moe's Southwest Grill, LLC, **64** 327–28
Moen Incorporated, **12** 344–45
Moët-Hennessy, I 271–72; **10** 397–98; **23** 238, 240, 242. *See also* LVMH Moët Hennessy Louis Vuitton SA.
Mogen David. *See* The Wine Group, Inc.
The Mogul Metal Company. *See* Federal-Mogul Corporation.
Mohasco Corporation, **15** 102; **26** 100–01
Mohawk & Hudson Railroad, **9** 369
Mohawk Carpet Corp., **26** 101
Mohawk Industries, Inc., **19** 274–76; **31** 199; **63** 298–301 (upd.)
Mohawk Rubber Co. Ltd., V 256; **7** 116; **19** 508
Mohegan Tribal Gaming Authority, **37** 254–57
Mohr-Value Stores, **8** 555
Mojave Foods Corporation, **27** 299
Mojo MDA Group Ltd., **11** 50–51; **43** 412
Moksel. *See* A. Moskel AG.
Mokta. *See* Compagnie de Mokta.
MOL. *See* Mitsui O.S.K. Lines, Ltd.
Molabe S.A. Espagne. *See* Leroux S.A.S.
Molerway Freight Lines, Inc., **53** 250
Molex Incorporated, **11** 317–19; **14** 27; **54** 236–41 (upd.)
Molfino Hermanos SA, **59** 365
Molinera de México S.A. de C.V., **31** 236
Molinos Nacionales C.A., **7** 242–43; **25** 241
Molinos Río de la Plata S.A., **61** 219–21
Molins plc, **51** 249–51
Moll Plasticrafters, L.P., **17** 534
Molloy Manufacturing Co., III 569; **20** 360
Mölnlycke AB, **36** 26
The Molson Companies Limited, I 273–75, 333; **7** 183–84; **12** 338; **13** 150, 199; **21** 320; **23** 404; **25** 279; **26** 303–07 (upd.); **36** 15
Molycorp, IV 571; **24** 521
Momentus Group Ltd., **51** 99
Mon-Dak Chemical Inc., **16** 270
Mon-Valley Transportation Company, **11** 194
Mona Meyer McGrath & Gavin, **47** 97
MONACA. *See* Molinos Nacionales C.A.
Monaco Coach Corporation, **31** 336–38
Monadnock Paper Mills, Inc., **21** 381–84
Monarch Air Lines, **22** 219
Monarch Casino & Resort, Inc., **65** 239–41
Monarch Development Corporation, **38** 451–52
Monarch Foods, **26** 503
Mondadori. *See* Arnoldo Monadori Editore S.p.A.
Mondex International, **18** 543

Mondi Foods BV, **41** 12
Moneris Solutions Corp., **46** 55
Monet Jewelry, **9** 156–57
Money Access Service Corp., **11** 467
Money Management Associates, Inc., **53** 136
Monfort, Inc., **13** 350–52
Monitor Dynamics Inc., **24** 510
Monitor Group Inc., **33** 257
Monk-Austin Inc., **12** 110
Monmouth Pharmaceuticals Ltd., **16** 439
Monnaie de Paris, **62** 246–48
Monneret Industrie, **56** 335
Monogram Aerospace Fasteners, Inc., **11** 536
Monogram Models, **25** 312
Monogramme Confections, **6** 392
Monolithic Memories Inc., **16** 316–17, 549
Monon Corp., **13** 550
Monongahela Power, **38** 40
Monoprix. *See* Galeries Lafayette S.A.
Monro Muffler Brake, Inc., **24** 337–40
Monroe Savings Bank, **11** 109
Monsanto Company, I 365–67; **8** 398; **9** 318, 355–57 (upd.), 466; **12** 186; **13** 225; **16** 460–62; **17** 131; **18** 112; **22** 107; **23** 170–71; **26** 108; **29** 327–31 (upd.); **33** 135; **34** 179; **41** 306; **52** 312; **53** 261; **59** 149; **60** 227; **61** 97
Monsoon plc, **39** 287–89
Mont Blanc, **17** 5; **27** 487, 489
Montabert S.A., **15** 226
Montan TNT Pty Ltd., **27** 473
Montana Alimentaria S.p.A., **57** 82
Montana Coffee Traders, Inc., **60** 208–10
Montana-Dakota Utilities Co., **7** 322–23; **37** 281–82; **42** 249–50, 252
Montana Group, **54** 229
Montana Mills Bread Co., Inc., **61** 153
The Montana Power Company, **6** 566; **7** 322; **11** 320–22; **37** 280, 283; **44** 288–92 (upd.); **50** 367
Montana Refining Company, **12** 240–41
Montana Resources, Inc., IV 34
Montaup Electric Co., **14** 125
MontBell America, Inc., **29** 279
Monte Paschi Vita, **65** 71–72
Montedison S.p.A., I 368–69; **14** 17; **22** 262; **24** 341–44 (upd.); **36** 185–86, 188
Montefina, IV 499; **26** 367
Montell N.V., **24** 343
Monterey Homes Corporation. *See* Meritage Corporation.
Monterey Mfg. Co., **12** 439
Monterey Pasta Company, **58** 240–43
Monterey's Acquisition Corp., **41** 270
Monterey's Tex-Mex Cafes, **13** 473
Monterrey, Compania de Seguros sobre la Vida. *See* Seguros Monterrey.
Monterrey Group, **19** 10–11, 189
Montgomery Elevator Company, **27** 269
Montgomery Ward & Co., Incorporated, V 145–48; **8** 509; **9** 210; **10** 10, 116, 172, 305, 391, 393, 490–91; **12** 48, 309, 315, 335, 430; **13** 165; **15** 330, 470; **17** 460; **18** 477; **20** 263, **374–79** (upd.), 433; **22** 535; **25** 144; **27** 428–30; **43** 292
Montiel Corporation, **17** 321
Montinex, **24** 270
Montreal Engineering Company, **6** 585
Montreal Light, Heat & Power Consolidated, **6** 501–02
Montreal Mining Co., **17** 357

Montres Rolex S.A., **8** 477; **13** 353–55; **19** 452; **34** 292–95 (upd.)
Montrose Capital, **36** 358
Montrose Chemical Company, **9** 118, 119
Montupet S.A., **63 302–04**
Monumental Corp., **III** 179
Moody's Corporation, **IV** 605; **16** 506; **19** 133; **22** 189; **61** 81–83; **65** 242–44
Moody's Investors Service,
Moog Inc., **13** 356–58
Mooney Aerospace Group Ltd., **52 252–55**
Mooney Chemicals, Inc. *See* OM Group, Inc.
Moonlight Mushrooms, Inc. *See* Sylvan, Inc.
Moonstone Mountaineering, Inc., **29** 181
Moore and McCormack Co. Inc., **19** 40
Moore Corporation Limited, **IV** 644–46, 679; **15** 473; **16** 450; **36** 508
Moore Gardner & Associates, **22** 88
The Moore Group Ltd., **20** 363
Moore-Handley, Inc., **39 290–92**
Moore McCormack Resources Inc., **14** 455
Moore Medical Corp., **17 331–33**
Moquin Breuil. *See* Smoby International SA.
Moran Group Inc., **II** 682
Moran Health Care Group Ltd., **25** 455
Moran Towing Corporation, Inc., **15 301–03**
Morana, Inc., **9** 290
Moretti-Harrah Marble Co. *See* English China Clays Ltd.
Morgan & Banks Limited, **30** 460
Morgan Construction Company, **8** 448
Morgan Edwards, **II** 609
Morgan Engineering Co., **8** 545
Morgan Grampian Group, **IV** 687
Morgan Grenfell Group PLC, **II** 427–29; **59** 182–83, 255. *See also* Deutsche Bank AG.
The Morgan Group, Inc., **46 300–02**
Morgan Guaranty Trust Company. *See* J.P. Morgan & Co. Incorporated.
Morgan, J.P. & Co. Inc. *See* J.P. Morgan & Co. Incorporated.
Morgan, Lewis & Bockius LLP, **29 332–34**
Morgan, Lewis, Githens & Ahn, Inc., **6** 410
Morgan Schiff & Co., **29** 205
Morgan Stanley Dean Witter & Company, **33 311–14 (upd.)**; **38** 289, 291, 411
Morgan Stanley Group, Inc., **II 430–32**; **IV** 447, 714; **9** 386; **11** 258; **12** 529; **16** 374–78 (upd.); **18** 448–49; **20** 60, 363; **22** 404, 407; **25** 542; **30** 353–55; **34** 496; **36** 153
Moria Informatique, **6** 229
Morinaga & Co. Ltd., **61 222–25**
Morino Associates, **10** 394
Mormac Marine Group, **15** 302
Morning Star Technologies Inc., **24** 49
Morning Sun, Inc., **23** 66
Morningstar Storage Centers LLC, **52** 311
Morris Air, **24** 455
Morris Communications Corporation, **36 339–42**
Morris Motors, **7** 459
Morris Travel Services L.L.C., **26 308–11**
Morrison & Co. Ltd., **52** 221

Morrison Homes, Inc., **51** 138
Morrison Knudsen Corporation, **7 355–58**; **11** 401, 553; **28 286–90 (upd.)**; **33** 442; **50** 363. *See also* The Washington Companies.
Morrison Machine Products Inc., **25** 193
Morrison Restaurants Inc., **11 323–25**; **18** 464
Morse Equalizing Spring Company, **14** 63
Morse Industrial, **14** 64
Morse Shoe Inc., **13 359–61**
Mortgage Associates, **9** 229
Mortgage Guaranty Insurance Corp. *See* MGIC Investment Corp.
Mortgage Resources, Inc., **10** 91
Morton Foods, Inc., **27** 258
Morton International Inc., **9 358–59 (upd.)**, 500–01; **16** 436; **22** 505–06; **43** 319
Morton Thiokol Inc., **I 370–72**; **19** 508; **28** 253–54. *See also* Thiokol Corporation.
Morton's Restaurant Group, Inc., **28** 401; **30 329–31**
Mos Magnetics, **18** 140
MOS Technology, **7** 95
Mosby-Year Book, Inc., **IV** 678; **17** 486
Moseley, Hallgarten, Estabrook, and Weeden, **III** 389
Mosher Steel Company, **7** 540
Mosinee Paper Corporation, **15 304–06**. *See also* Wausau-Mosinee Paper Corporation.
Moskatel's, Inc., **17** 321
Moss Bros Group plc, **51 252–54**
Moss-Rouse Company, **15** 412
Mossgas, **IV** 93
Mossimo, Inc., **27 328–30**
Mostek Corp., **11** 307–08; **13** 191; **20** 175; **29** 323
Mostjet Ltd. *See* British World Airlines Ltd.
Móstoles Industrial S.A., **26** 129
Mostra Importaciones S.A., **34** 38, 40
Motel 6, **10** 13; **13 362–64**; **56 248–51 (upd.)**. *See also* Accor SA
Mother Karen's, **10** 216
Mothercare Stores, Inc., **16** 466
Mothercare UK Ltd., **17** 42–43, **334–36**
Mothers Against Drunk Driving (MADD), **51 255–58**
Mothers Work, Inc., **18 350–52**
Motif Inc., **22** 288
Motion Designs, **11** 486
Motion Factory, Inc., **38** 72
Motion Picture Association of America, **37** 353–54
Motion Picture Corporation of America, **25** 326, 329
Motiva Enterprises LLC, **41** 359, 395
MotivePower. *See* Wabtec Corporation.
The Motley Fool, Inc., **40 329–31**
Moto Photo, Inc., **45 282–84**
Moto S.p.A., **57** 84
Moto-Truc Co., **13** 385
Motor Cargo Industries, Inc., **35 296–99**; **58** 262
Motor Club of America Insurance Company, **44** 354
Motor Coaches Industries International Inc., **36** 132
Motor Parts Industries, Inc., **9** 363
Motor Wheel Corporation, **20** 261; **27** 202–04

Motorcar Parts & Accessories, Inc., **47 253–55**
Motoren-und-Turbinen-Union, **I** 151; **9** 418; **15** 142; **34** 128, 131, 133
Motorola, Inc., **II 60–62**; **7** 119, 494, 533; **8** 139; **9** 515; **10** 87, 365, 367, 431–33; **11** 45, 308, **326–29 (upd.)**, 381–82; **12** 136–37, 162; **13** 30, 356, 501; **17** 33, 193; **18** 18, 74, 76, 260, 382; **19** 391; **20** 8, 439; **22** 17, 19, 288, 542; **26** 431–32; **27** 20, 341–42, 344; **33** 47–48; **34** **296–302 (upd.)**; **38** 188; **43** 15; **44** 97, 357, 359; **45** 346, 348; **47** 318, 320, 385; **48** 270, 272
Motown Records Company L.P., **II** 145; **22** 194; **23** 389, 391; **26 312–14**
Mott's Inc., **57 250–53**
Moulinex S.A., **22 362–65**
Mound Metalcraft. *See* Tonka Corporation.
Mount. *See also* Mt.
Mount Hood Credit Life Insurance Agency, **14** 529
Mount Isa Mines, **IV** 61
Mount Vernon Group, **8** 14
Mount Washington Hotel. *See* MWH Preservation Limited Partnership.
Mountain Fuel Supply Company. *See* Questar Corporation.
Mountain Fuel Supply Company, **6** 568–69
Mountain Pass Canning Co., **7** 429
Mountain Safety Research, **18** 445–46
Mountain States Mortgage Centers, Inc., **29 335–37**
Mountain States Power Company. *See* PacifiCorp.
Mountain States Wholesale, **II** 602; **30** 25
Mountain Valley Indemnity Co., **44** 356
Mountain West Bank, **35** 197
Mountleigh PLC, **16** 465
Mouvement des Caisses Desjardins, **48 288–91**
Movado Group, Inc., **28 291–94**
Mövenpick Holdings, **63** 328
Movie Gallery, Inc., **31 339–41**
Movie Star Inc., **17 337–39**
Movies To Go, Inc., **9** 74; **31** 57
Movil@ccess, S.A. de C.V., **39** 25, 194
Moving Co. Ltd. *See* Marui Co., Ltd.
The Moving Picture Company, **15** 83; **50** 124, 126
The Mowry Co., **23** 102
MP3.com, **43** 109
MPB Corporation, **8** 529, 531
MPI. *See* Michael Page International plc.
MPS Group, Inc., **49 264–67**
MPW Industrial Services Group, Inc., **53 231–33**
Mr. Bricolage S.A., **37 258–60**
Mr. Coffee, Inc., **14** 229–31; **15 307–09**; **17** 215; **27** 275; **39** 406
Mr. D's Food Centers, **12** 112
Mr. Donut, **21** 323
Mr. Gasket Inc., **11** 84; **15 310–12**
Mr. Gatti's Inc., **15** 345; **53** 204–06
Mr. Goodbuys, **13** 545
Mr. M Food Stores, **7** 373
Mr. Maintenance, **25** 15
Mr. Payroll Corporation, **20** 113; **61** 52–54
MRD Gaming, **51** 206–07
M-real Oyj, **56 252–55 (upd.)**
MRJ Technology Solutions, **54** 396
MRN Radio Network, **19** 223
Mrs. Baird's Bakeries, **29 338–41**

Mrs. Fields' Original Cookies, Inc., 27 **331–35**
Mrs. Giles Country Kitchens, **63** 69, 71
Mrs. Paul's Kitchens. *See* Campbell Soup Company.
Mrs. Smith's Frozen Foods. *See* Kellogg Company
Mrs. Winner's Chicken & Biscuits, **58** 324
MS-Relais GmbH. *See* Matsushita Electric Works, Ltd.
MSAS Cargo International, **6** 415, 417
MSC. *See* Material Sciences Corporation.
MSE Corporation, **33** 44
MSI Data Corp., **10** 523; **15** 482
MSI Energy Services Inc., **56** 383
M6. *See* Métropole Télévision.
MSL Industries, **10** 44
MSNBC, **28** 301
MSP, Inc., **57** 231
MSR. *See* Mountain Safety Research.
MSU. *See* Middle South Utilities.
Mt. *See also* Mount.
Mt. Beacon Insurance Co., **26** 486
Mt. Carmel Public Utility Company, **6** 506
Mt. Goldsworthy Mining Associates, **IV** 47
Mt. Olive Pickle Company, Inc., 44 **293–95**
Mt. Summit Rural Telephone Company, **14** 258
Mt. Vernon Iron Works, **II** 14
Mt. West Group, **56** 383
MTC. *See* Management and Training Corporation.
MTel. *See* Mobile Telecommunications Technologies Corp.
MTG. *See* Modern Times Group AB.
MTM Entertainment Inc., **13** 279, 281
MTR Foods Ltd., 55 271–73
MTS Inc., 37 261–64
MTV, **31** 239
MTV Asia, **23** 390
MTVi Group, **37** 194
Muehlens KG, **48** 422
Mueller Co. *See* Tyco International Ltd.
Mueller Furniture Company, **8** 252; **39** 206
Mueller Industries, Inc., 7 359–61; 52 **256–60 (upd.)**
Muffler Corporation of America, **56** 230
Mukluk Freight Lines, **6** 383
Mule-Hide Products Co., **22** 15
Mullen Advertising Inc., 13 513; **51** **259–61**
Mullens & Co., **14** 419
Multex Systems, **21** 70
Multi-Color Corporation, 53 234–36
Multi Restaurants, **II** 664
Multibank Inc., **11** 281
Multicanal S.A., **67** 200–01
Multicare Companies. *See* NeighborCare, Inc.
Multicom Publishing Inc., **11** 294
Multiflex, Inc., **63** 318
Multilink, Inc., **27** 364–65
MultiMed, **11** 379
Multimedia Cablevision Inc. *See* Gannett Company, Inc.
Multimedia Games, Inc., 41 272–76
Multimedia, Inc., IV 591; **11 330–32; 30** 217
Multimedia Security Services, Inc., **32** 374
Multiplex, **67** 104–06
MultiScope Inc., **10** 508
Multitech International. *See* Acer Inc.
Multiview Cable, **24** 121

Munford, Inc., **17** 499
Munich Re (Münchener **Rückversicherungs-Gesellschaft** **Aktiengesellschaft in München), III** 202, **299–301**, 400–01; **35** 34, 37; **46** **303–07 (upd.)**; **63** 411–12
Munising Woodenware Company, **13** 156
Munksjö, **19** 227
Munsingwear, Inc., **22** 427; **25** 90; **27** 443, 445; **41** 291. *See also* PremiumWear, Inc.
Munson Transportation Inc., **18** 227
Munster and Leinster Bank Ltd., **16** 13
Mura Corporation, **23** 209
Murata, **37** 347
Murdock Madaus Schwabe, 26 315–19, 470
Murfin Inc., **8** 360
Murmic, Inc., **9** 120
Murphey Favre, Inc., **17** 528, 530
Murphy Family Farms Inc., 7 477; **21** 503; **22 366–68;** **46** 84
Murphy Oil Corporation, 7 362–64; 32 **338–41 (upd.)**
Murphy-Phoenix Company, **14** 122
Murphy's Pizza. *See* Papa Murphy's International, Inc.
Murray Inc., **19** 383
Murtaugh Light & Power Company, **12** 265
Muscatine Journal, **11** 251
Muse, Cordero, Chen, **41** 89
Musgrave Group Plc, 57 254–57; 58 102, 104; **59** 93
Music and Video Club, **24** 266, 270
Music-Appreciation Records, **13** 105
Music Corporation of America. *See* MCA Inc.
Music Go Round, **18** 207–09
Music Man Co., **16** 202; **43** 170; **56** 116
Music Plus, **9** 75
Musical America Publishing, Inc., **22** 441
Musician's Friend, **29** 221, 223
Musicland Stores Corporation, 9 **360–62; 11** 558; **19** 417; **37** 263; **38** **313–17 (upd.);** **63** 63
MusicNet, Inc., **53** 282
MusicNow, Inc. *See* Circuit City Stores, Inc.
Musitek, **16** 202; **43** 170
Muskegon Gas Company. *See* MCN Corporation.
Muskegon Wire, **55** 305
Mutual & Federal, **61** 270, 272
Mutual Benefit Life Insurance Company, **III** 243, **302–04**
Mutual Broadcasting System, **23** 509
Mutual Gaslight Company. *See* MCN Corporation.
Mutual Life Insurance Company of New **York, III 305–07**, 316, 321, 380
Mutual Marine Office Inc., **41** 284
Mutual of Omaha, **III** 365; **25** 89–90; **27** 47
Mutual Papers Co., **14** 522
Mutual Savings & Loan Association, **III** 215; **18** 60
Muzak, Inc., 7 90–91; **18 353–56; 35** 19–20
Muzzy-Lyon Company. *See* Federal-Mogul Corporation.
MVC. *See* Music and Video Club.
MVF. *See* Mission Valley Fabrics.
MVR Products Pte Limited, **47** 255

MWA. *See* Modern Woodmen of America.
MWH Preservation Limited Partnership, **65 245–48**
Mwinilunga Canneries Ltd., **IV** 241
MXL Industries, Inc., **13** 367; **64** 166
Myanmar Brewery Ltd., **59** 60
Myco-Sci, Inc. *See* Sylvan, Inc.
Mycogen Corporation, 21 385–87
Mycrom, **14** 36
Myer Emporium Ltd., **20** 156
Myers Industries, Inc., 19 277–79
Mygind International, **8** 477
Mylan Laboratories Inc., I 656–57; 20 **380–82 (upd.);** **59 304–08 (upd.)**
Myojo Cement Co. Ltd., **60** 301
Myrna Knitwear, Inc., **16** 231
Myrurgia S.A., **60** 246

N.A. Woodworth, **III** 519; **22** 282
N. Boynton & Co., **16** 534
N.C. Cameron & Sons, Ltd., **11** 95
N.C. Monroe Construction Company, **14** 112
N.E.M., **23** 228
N.E. Restaurant Co. Inc. *See* Bertucci's Corpration.
N.H. Geotech. *See* New Holland N.V.
N.L. Industries, **19** 212
N M Electronics, **II** 44
N M Rothschild & Sons Limited, 24 267; **39 293–95**
N. Shure Company, **15** 477
N.V. *see under first word of company name*
N.Y.P. Holdings Inc., **12** 360
Na Pali, S.A. *See* Quiksilver, Inc.
Naamloze Vennootschap tot Exploitatie van het Café Krasnapolsky. *See* Grand Hotel Krasnapolsky N.V.
Nabari Kintetsu Gas Company Ltd., **60** 236
Nabisco Brands, Inc., II 475, 512, **542–44;** **7** 128, 365–67; **12** 167; **25** 366. *See also* RJR Nabisco.
Nabisco Foods Group, 7 365–68 (upd.); **9** 318; **14** 48; **24** 358. *See also* Kraft Foods Inc.
Nabisco Holdings Corporation, **25** 181; **42** 408; **44** 342
Nabisco Ltd., **24** 288
Nabors Industries, Inc., 9 363–65
Nacamar Internet Services, **48** 398
NACCO Industries, Inc., 7 369–71; 17 213–15, 246, 248
Nacional de Drogas, S.A. de C.V., **39** 188
NACO Finance Corp., **33** 398
Naco-Nogales, **51** 389
Nadler Sportswear. *See* Donnkenny, Inc.
Naegele Outdoor Advertising Inc., **36** 340
Naf Naf SA, 44 296–98
NAFI Corp. *See* Chris-Craft Industries, Inc.
Nagasakiya Co., Ltd., V 149–51
Nagasco, Inc., **18** 366
Nagase & Co., Ltd., 8 376–78; 61 **226–30 (upd.)**
Nagase-Landauer, Ltd., **51** 210
Nagel Meat Markets and Packing House, **II** 643
Nagoya Mitsukoshi Ltd., **56** 242
NAI. *See* Natural Alternatives International, Inc.; Network Associates, Inc.
NAI Technologies, Inc., **58** 101
Naiman Co., **25** 449
Nairn Linoleum Co., **18** 116
Nakano Vinegar Co. Ltd., **26** 58

Nalco Chemical Corporation, I 373–75; **12** 346–48 (upd.)
Nalge Co., **14** 479–80
NAM. *See* Nederlandse Aardolie Maatschappij.
Nam Tai Electronics, Inc., **61** 231–34
Namibia Breweries Ltd., **33** 75
NAMM. *See* North American Medical Management Company, Inc.
Namor Productions, **58** 124
Namur Re S.A., **51** 143
Nan Ya Plastics Corp., **14** 197–98; **58** 130
NANA Regional Corporation, **7** 558
Nance Petroleum Corporation, **63** 347
Nanfang South China Motor Corp., **34** 132
Nantucket Allserve, Inc., **22** 369–71
Nantucket Corporation, **6** 226
Nantucket Mills, **12** 285; **34** 240
NAPA. *See* National Automotive Parts Association.
NAPC. *See* North American Philips Corp.
Napocor. *See* National Power Corporation.
NAPP Systems, Inc., **11** 253
Narragansett Electric Company, **51** 265
NAS. *See* National Audubon Society.
NASA. *See* National Aeronautics and Space Administration.
NASCAR. *See* National Association for Stock Car Auto Racing.
NASD, **54** 242–46 (upd.)
NASDAQ, **37** 132
Nash DeCamp Company, **23** 356–57
Nash Finch Company, **8** 379–81; **11** 43; **23** 356–58 (upd.); **40** 80; **65** 249–53 (upd.)
Nashua Corporation, **8** 382–84; **61** 280
The Nashville Network, **11** 153
Nashville Speedway USA, Inc., **43** 139–41
Naspers Ltd., **66** 230–32
NASRIN Services LLC, **64** 346
Nassau Gas Light Co., **6** 455
Nassco Holdings Inc., **36** 79
Nasu Nikon Co., Ltd., **48** 295
Nat Robbins, **37** 269–70
NaTec Ltd. *See* CRSS Inc.
Nathan's Famous, Inc., **29** 342–44
National, **10** 419
The National Academy of Television Arts & Sciences, **55** 3
National Acme Company. *See* Acme-Cleveland Corp.
National Advertising Company, **27** 280
National Aeronautics and Space Administration, **11** 201, 408; **12** 489; **37** 364–65
National Air Transport Co., **9** 416; **11** 427
National Airlines, **6** 388; **25** 146
National Allied Publications. *See* DC Comics Inc.
National Aluminum Company, **11** 38
National American Corporation, **33** 399
National Amusements Inc., **28** 295–97
National Association for Stock Car Auto Racing, **32** 342–44
National Association of Securities Dealers, Inc., **10** 416–18. *See also* NASD.
National Audubon Society, **26** 320–23
National Auto Credit, Inc., **16** 379–81
National Automotive Fibers, Inc. *See* Chris-Craft Industries, Inc.
National Automotive Parts Association, **26** 348
National Bancard Corporation, **11** 111–13

National Bancorp of Arizona, **12** 565
National Bank for Cooperatives, **8** 489–90
National Bank of Arizona, **53** 378
National Bank of Commerce, **9** 536; **11** 105–06; **13** 467
National Bank of Commerce Trust & Savings Association, **15** 161
National Bank of Greece, **41** 277–79
The National Bank of Jacksonville, **9** 58
National Bank of New Zealand, **II** 308; **19** 155
National Bank of Washington, **13** 440
National BankAmericard Inc. *See* Visa International.
National Basketball Association, **12** 457
National Beverage Corp., **26** 324–26; **55** 146. *See also* Faygo Beverages Inc.
National Binding Company, **8** 382
National BioSystems, **47** 37
National Bridge Company of Canada, Ltd., **8** 544
National Broadcasting Company, Inc., **II** 151–53; **6** 164–66 (upd.); **10** 173; **17** 149–50; **19** 201, 210; **21** 24; **23** 120; **28** 298–301 (upd.); **30** 99; **32** 3; **33** 324; **34** 186; **42** 161, 163. *See also* General Electric Company.
National Building Society, **10** 6–7
National Cable & Manufacturing Co., **13** 369
National Cable Television Association, **18** 64
National Can Corp., **I** 607–08; **13** 255
National Car Rental System, Inc., **10** 373, 419–20; **22** 524; **25** 93, 143. *See also* Republic Industries, Inc.
National Carriers, **6** 413–14
National Cash Register Company. *See* NCR Corporation.
National Cement Co., **35** 419
National Cheerleaders Association, **15** 516–18
National Chemsearch Corp. *See* NCH Corporation.
National Child Care Centers, Inc., **II** 607
National City Bancorporation, **56** 219
National City Bank, **9** 475
National City Corp., **9** 475; **15** 313–16
National Coach, **56** 223
National Comics Publications. *See* DC Comics Inc.
National Commercial Bank, **11** 108; **12** 422; **13** 476
National Components Industries, Inc., **13** 398
National Convenience Stores Incorporated, **7** 372–75; **20** 140
National Cranberry Association. *See* Ocean Spray Cranberries, Inc.
National Dairy Products Corp., **14** 204
National Data Corporation, **24** 393
National Demographics & Lifestyles Inc., **10** 461
National Discount Brokers Group, Inc., **28** 302–04
National Disinfectant Company. *See* NCH Corporation.
National Distillers and Chemical Corporation, **I** 376–78; **8** 439–41; **9** 231; **10** 181; **30** 441. *See also* Quantum Chemical Corp.
National Drive-In Grocery Corporation, **7** 372
National Drug Ltd., **II** 652

National Economic Research Associates, **III** 283
National Education Association, **9** 367
National Educational Corporation, **26** 95
National Educational Music Co. Ltd., **47** 256–58
National Electric Company, **11** 388
National Employers Life Assurance Co. Ltd., **13** 539
National Endowment for the Arts, **52** 15
National Enquirer, **10** 287–88
National Envelope Corporation, **32** 345–47
National Equipment Services, Inc., **57** 258–60
National Executive Service. *See* Carey International, Inc.
National Express Group PLC, **50** 340–42
National Express Laboratories, Inc., **10** 107
National Family Opinion. *See* NFO Worldwide, Inc.
National Farmers Organization, **53** 260
National Fence Manufacturing Co., Inc., **45** 327
National Fidelity Life Insurance Co., **10** 246
National Fidelity Life Insurance Co. of Kansas, **IV** 343
National Financial Partners Corp., **65** 254–56
National Fire & Marine Insurance Co., **III** 213–14; **42** 32
National Fire & Marine Insurance Co., **III** 213–14; **42** 32
National Football League, **12** 457; **29** 345–47; **37** 294
National Freight Corporation, **6** 412–13
National Fuel Gas Company, **6** 526–28
National Geographic Society, **9** 366–68; **30** 332–35 (upd.); **42** 115, 117
National Golf Properties, Inc. *See* American Golf Corporation
National Grape Co-operative Association, Inc., **20** 383–85
National Grid Company, **50** 280–81, 361–362
National Grid Group plc, **11** 399–400; **12** 349; **13** 484; **45** 298–99; **47** 122
National Grid Transco plc, **66** 283
National Grid USA, **51** 262–66 (upd.)
National Grocers of Ontario, **II** 631
National Guardian Corp., **18** 33
National Gypsum Company, **8** 43; **10** 421–24; **13** 169; **22** 48, 170; **25** 535
National Health Laboratories Incorporated, **11** 333–35. *See also* Laboratory Corporation of America Holdings.
National Heritage Academies, Inc., **60** 211–13
National Hockey League, **35** 300–03
National Home Centers, Inc., **44** 299–301
National Housing Systems, Inc., **18** 27
National ICEE Corporation, **24** 242
National Indemnity Co., **III** 213–14; **42** 32–33
National India Rubber Company, **9** 228
National Inking Appliance Company, **14** 52
National Instruments Corporation, **22** 372–74
National Integrity Life Insurance, **III** 249
National Intergroup, Inc., **V** 152–53; **12** 354; **16** 212. *See also* FoxMeyer Health Corporation.

National Iranian Oil Company, **IV** 466–68; **47** 342; **61 235–38 (upd.)**
National Journal Group Inc., **67 256–58**
National Key Company. *See* Cole National Corporation.
National Law Publishing Company, Inc., **32** 35
National Lead Co., **21** 489
National Leisure Group, **47** 421
National Liability and Fire Insurance Co., **III** 214
National Liberty Corp., **III** 218–19
National Life Insurance Co. of Canada, **III** 243
National Linen Service, **54** 251, 254
National Living Centers, **13** 49
National Lumber Co. *See* National Home Centers, Inc.
National Magazine Company Limited, **19** 201
National Marine Service, **6** 530
National Market System, **9** 369
National Media Corporation, **27 336–40**
National Medical Care, **22** 360
National Medical Enterprises, Inc., **III** 87–88; **10** 252; **14** 233; **33** 185. *See also* Tenet Healthcare Corporation.
National Mobility Corp., **30** 436
The National Motor Bearing Company. *See* Federal-Mogul Corporation.
The National Motor Club of America, Inc., **33** 418
National Mutual Life Assurance of Australasia, **III** 249
National Office Furniture, **12** 297
National Oil Corporation, **66 233–37 (upd.)**
National Oilwell, Inc., **54 247–50**
National Old Line Insurance Co., **III** 179
National Organization for Women, Inc., **55 274–76**
National Paper Co., **8** 476
National Parks Transportation Company, **25** 420–22
National Patent Development Corporation, **7** 45; **13 365–68**; **25** 54. *See also* GP Strategies Corporation.
National Periodical Publications. *See* DC Comics Inc.
National Permanent Mutual Benefit Building Society, **10** 6
National Petroleum Refiners of South Africa, **47** 340
National Pharmacies, **9** 346
National Picture & Frame Company, **24 345–47**
National Pig Development Co., **46** 84
National Postal Meter Company, **14** 52
National Power Corporation, **56** 214–15
National Power PLC, **11** 399–400; **12 349–51**; **13** 458, 484. *See also* International Power PLC.
National Presto Industries, Inc., **16 382–85**; **43 286–90 (upd.)**
National Processing, Inc., **24** 394
National Propane Corporation, **8** 535–37
National Public Radio, **19 280–82**; **47 259–62 (upd.)**
National Publishing Company, **41** 110
National Quotation Bureau, Inc., **14** 96–97
National R.V. Holdings, Inc., **32 348–51**
National Railroad Passenger Corporation (Amtrak), **22 375–78**; **66 238–42 (upd.)**

National Realty Trust. *See* NRT Incorporated.
National Record Mart, Inc., **29 348–50**
National Register Publishing Co., **17** 399; **23** 442
National Reinsurance Corporation. *See* General Re Corporation.
National Rent-A-Car, **6** 392–93
National Research Corporation, **8** 397
National Restaurants Management, Inc., **38** 385–87
National Revenue Corporation, **22** 181
National Rifle Association of America, **37 265–68**
National Rubber Machinery Corporation, **8** 298
National Sanitary Supply Co., **13** 149–50; **16 386–87**
National Satellite Paging, **18** 348
National School Studios, **7** 255; **25** 252
National Science Foundation, **9** 266
National Sea Products Ltd., **14 339–41**
National Security Containers LLC, **58** 238
National Semiconductor Corporation, **II 63–65**; **6 261–63**; **9** 297; **11** 45–46, 308, 463; **16** 332; **18** 18; **19** 312; **26 327–30 (upd.)**; **43** 15
National Service Industries, Inc., **11 336–38**; **54 251–55 (upd.)**
National Shoe Products Corp., **16** 17
National Slicing Machine Company, **19** 359
National-Southwire Aluminum Company, **11** 38; **12** 353
National Stamping & Electric Works, **12** 159
National Standard Co., **IV** 137; **13 369–71**
National Starch and Chemical Company, **32** 256–57; **49 268–70**
National Steel and Shipbuilding Company, **7** 356
National Steel Corporation, **I** 491; **IV** 163, 236–37, 572; **V** 152–53; **7** 549; **8** 346, 479–80; **11** 315; **12 352–54**; **14** 191; **16** 212; **23** 445; **26** 527–29; **28** 325. *See also* FoxMeyer Health Corporation.
National Student Marketing Corporation, **10** 385–86
National System Company, **9** 41; **11** 469
National Tea, **II** 631–32
National Technical Laboratories, **14** 52
National TechTeam, Inc., **41 280–83**
National Telecommunications of Austin, **8** 311
National Telephone and Telegraph Corporation. *See* British Columbia Telephone Company.
National Telephone Co., **7** 332, 508
National Thoroughbred Racing Association, **58 244–47**
National Trading Manufacturing, Inc., **22** 213
National Transcommunications Ltd. *See* NTL Inc.
National Union Electric Corporation, **12** 159
National Utilities & Industries Corporation, **9** 363
National Westminster Bank PLC, **II 333–35**; **13** 206
National Wine & Spirits, Inc., **49 271–74**

Nationale-Nederlanden N.V., **III 308–11**; **50** 11
Nationar, **9** 174
NationsBank Corporation, **10 425–27**; **11** 126; **13** 147; **18** 516, 518; **23** 455; **25** 91, 186; **26** 348, 453. *See also* Bank of America Corporation
NationsRent, **28** 388
Nationwide Cellular Service, Inc., **27** 305
Nationwide Credit, **11** 112
Nationwide Group, **25** 155
Nationwide Income Tax Service, **9** 326
Nationwide Logistics Corp., **14** 504
Nationwide Mutual Insurance Co., **26** 488
NATIOVIE, **II** 234
Native Plants, **III** 43
NATM Buying Corporation, **10** 9, 468
Natomas Company, **7** 309; **11** 271
Natref. *See* National Petroleum Refiners of South Africa.
Natrol, Inc., **49 275–78**
Natronag, **IV** 325
NatSteel Electronics Ltd., **48** 369
NatTeknik, **26** 333
Natudryl Manufacturing Company, **10** 271
Natural Alternatives International, Inc., **49 279–82**
Natural Gas Clearinghouse, **11** 355. *See also* NGC Corporation.
Natural Gas Corp., **19** 155
Natural Gas Pipeline Company, **6** 530, 543; **7** 344–45
Natural Gas Service of Arizona, **19** 411
Natural Selection Foods, **54 256–58**
Natural Wonders Inc., **14 342–44**
NaturaLife International, **26** 470
The Nature Company, **10** 215–16; **14** 343; **26** 439; **27** 429; **28** 306
The Nature Conservancy, **26** 323; **28 305–07**, 422
Nature's Sunshine Products, Inc., **15 317–19**; **26** 470; **27** 353; **33** 145
Nature's Way Products Inc., **26** 315
Naturipe Berry Growers, **62** 154
Natuzzi Group. *See* Industrie Natuzzi S.p.A.
NatWest Bancorp, **38** 393
NatWest Bank, **22** 52. *See also* National Westminster Bank PLC.
Naugles, **7** 506
Nautica Enterprises, Inc., **16** 61; **18 357–60**; **25** 258; **27** 60; **44 302–06 (upd.)**
Nautilus International, Inc., bf]XIII 532; **25** 40; **30** 161
Navaho Freight Line, **16** 41
Navajo LTL, Inc., **57** 277
Navajo Refining Company, **12** 240
Navajo Shippers, Inc., **42** 364
Navan Resources, **38** 231
Navarre Corporation, **22** 536; **24 348–51**
Navigant International, Inc., **47 263–66**
Navigation Mixte, **III** 348
Navire Cargo Gear, **27** 269
Navisant, Inc., **49** 424
Navistar International Corporation, **I 180–82**, 525, 527; **10 428–30 (upd.)**; **17** 327; **33** 254. *See also* International Harvester Co.
Navy Exchange Service Command, **31 342–45**
Navy Federal Credit Union, **33 315–17**
Naxon Utilities Corp., **19** 359

Naylor, Hutchinson, Vickers & Company. *See* Vickers PLC.

NBC **24** 516–17. *See also* National Broadcasting Company, Inc.

NBC Bankshares, Inc., **21** 524

NBC/Computer Services Corporation, **15** 163

NBD Bancorp, Inc., 9 476; **11 339–41**, 466. *See also* Bank One Corporation.

NBTY, Inc., 31 346–48

NCA Corporation, **9** 36, 57, 171

NCB. *See* National City Bank of New York.

NCC Industries, Inc., **59** 267

NCC L.P., **15** 139

NCH Corporation, 8 385–87

nChip, **38** 187–88

NCL Holdings. *See* Genting Bhd.

NCNB Corporation, II 336–37; **12** 519; **26** 453

NCO Group, Inc., 42 258–60

NCR Corporation, III 150–53; **IV** 298; **V** 263; **6 264–68 (upd.)**; **9** 416; **11** 62, 151, 542; **12** 162, 148, 246, 484; **16** 65; **29** 44; **30 336–41 (upd.)**; **36** 81

NCS. *See* Norstan, Inc.

NCS Healthcare Inc., **67** 262

NCTI (Noise Cancellation Technologies Inc.), **19** 483–84

nCube Corp., **14** 15; **22** 293

ND Marston, **III** 593

NDB. *See* National Discount Brokers Group, Inc.

NDL. *See* Norddeutscher Lloyd.

NEA. *See* Newspaper Enterprise Association.

Nearly Me, **25** 313

Neatherlin Homes Inc., **22** 547

Nebraska Bell Company, **14** 311

Nebraska Book Company, Inc., 65 257–59

Nebraska Cellular Telephone Company, **14** 312

Nebraska Furniture Mart, **III** 214–15; **18** 60–61, 63

Nebraska Light & Power Company, **6** 580

Nebraska Power Company, **25** 89

Nebraska Public Power District, 29 351–54

NEBS. *See* New England Business Services, Inc.

NEC Corporation, II 66–68, 73, 82, 91, 104, 361; **6** 287; **9** 42, 115; **10** 257, 366, 463, 500; **11** 46, 308, 490; **13** 482; **16** 139; **18** 382–83; **19** 391; **21 388–91 (upd.)**; **25** 82, 531; **36** 286, 299–300; **47** 320; **57 261–67 (upd.)**

Neckermann Versand AG. *See* Karstadt AG.

Nedcor, **61** 270–71

Nederland Line. *See* Stoomvaart Maatschappij Nederland.

Nederlander Organization, **24** 439

Nederlands Talen Institut, **13** 544

Nederlandsche Electriciteits Maatschappij. *See* N.E.M.

Nederlandsche Handel Maatschappij, **26** 242

Nederlandsche Heidenmaatschappij. *See* Arcadis NV.

Nederlandsche Kunstzijdebariek, **13** 21

Nederlandsche Stoomvart Maatschappij Oceaan, **6** 416

N.V. Nederlandse Gasunie, V 658–61; **38** 407

Nedlloyd Group. *See* Koninklijke Nedlloyd N.V.

NedMark Transportation Services. *See* Polar Air Cargo Inc.

Neeco, Inc., **9** 301

Needham Harper Worldwide. *See* Omnicom Group Inc.

Needlecraft, **II** 560; **12** 410

Needleworks, Inc., **23** 66

Neenah Printing, **8** 360

NEES. *See* New England Electric System.

Neff Corp., 32 352–53

Neff GmbH, **67** 81

Negromex, **23** 171–72

NEI. *See* Northern Engineering Industries PLC.

Neico International, Inc., **67** 226

NeighborCare, Inc., 67 259–63 (upd.)

Neighborhood Restaurants of America, **18** 241

Neilson/Cadbury, **II** 631

Neiman Bearings Co., **13** 78

The Neiman Marcus Group, Inc., 12 355–57; **15** 50, 86, 291; **17** 43; **21** 302; **25** 177–78; **27** 429; **49 283–87 (upd.)**; **52** 45–46

Neisner Brothers, Inc., **9** 20

NEL Equity Services Co., **III** 314

Nelson Bros., **14** 236

Nelson Entertainment Group, **47** 272

Nelson Publications, **22** 442

NEMF. *See* New England Motor Freight, Inc.

Neo Products Co., **37** 401

Neodata, **11** 293

Neopost S.A., 53 237–40

Neos, **21** 438

Neoterics Inc., **11** 65

Neozyme I Corp., **13** 240

Nepera, Inc., **16** 69

Neptun Maritime Oyj, **29** 431

Neptune Orient Lines Limited, 47 267–70; **61** 30

NER Auction Group, **23** 148

NERCO, Inc., 7 376–79

NES. *See* National Equipment Services, Inc.

Nesco Inc., **28** 6, 8

Nescott, Inc., **16** 36

Nespak SpA, **40** 214–15

Neste Oy, IV 469–71; **61** 346. *See also* Fortum Corporation

Nestlé S.A., II 486–89, **545–49**, 568–70; **6** 16; **7 380–84 (upd.)**; **8** 131, 498–500; **10** 47, 324; **11** 15, 205; **12** 480–81; **13** 294; **14** 214; **15** 63; **16** 168; **19** 50–51; **21** 55–56, 219; **22** 78, 80; **23** 219; **24** 388; **25** 21, 85, 366; **28 308–13 (upd.)**; **32** 115, 234; **36** 234, 237; **44** 351; **50** 295; **61** 261

Net Investment S.A., **63** 180

NetApp. *See* Network Appliance, Inc.

NetCom Systems AB, 26 331–33

NetCreations, **47** 345, 347

NetEffect Alliance, **58** 194

Netflix, Inc., 58 248–51

Netherlands Trading Co. *See* Nederlandse Handel Maatschappij.

NetHold B.V., **31** 330

NetLabs, **25** 117

NetMarket Company, **16** 146

NetPlane Systems, **36** 124

Netron, **II** 390

Netscape Communications Corporation, 15 320–22; **35 304–07 (upd.)**; **44** 97; **50 328–30**; **57** 37

NetStar Communications Inc., **24** 49; **35** 69

Nettingsdorfer, **19** 227

Nettle Creek Corporation, **19** 304

Netto, **11** 240

Net2Phone Inc., **34** 224

NetWest Securities, **25** 450

Network Appliance, Inc., 58 252–54

Network Associates, Inc., 25 119, **347–49**

Network Communications Associates, Inc., **11** 409

Network Solutions, Inc., **47** 430

Network Ten, **35** 68–69

Netzip Inc., **53** 282

Neuberger Berman Inc., 57 268–71

Neuer Markt, **59** 153

Neuro Navigational Corporation, **21** 47

Neutrogena Corporation, 17 340–44; **36** 305

Nevada Bell Telephone Company, 14 345–47

Nevada Community Bank, **11** 119

Nevada Natural Gas Pipe Line Co., **19** 411

Nevada Power Company, 11 342–44; **12** 265

Nevada Savings and Loan Association, **19** 412

Nevada Southern Gas Company, **19** 411

Nevada State Bank, **53** 378

Neversink Dyeing Company, **9** 153

Nevex Software Technologies, **42** 24, 26

New Access Communications, **43** 252

New America Publishing Inc., **10** 288

New Asahi Co., **I** 221

New Balance Athletic Shoe, Inc., 17 245; **25 350–52**; **35** 388

New Bauhinia Limited, **53** 333

New Bedford Gas & Edison Light Co., **14** 124–25

New Brunswick Scientific Co., Inc., 45 285–87

New Century Network, **13** 180; **19** 204, 285

New City Releasing, Inc., **25** 269

New CORT Holdings Corporation. *See* CORT Business Services Corporation.

New Daido Steel Co., Ltd., **IV** 62–63

New Dana Perfumes Company, 37 269–71

New Departure, **9** 17

New Dimension Software, Inc., **55** 67

New England Audio Company, Inc. *See* Tweeter Home Entertainment Group, Inc.

New England Business Services, Inc., 18 361–64

New England Confectionery Co., 15 323–25

New England CRInc, **8** 562

New England Electric System, V 662–64. *See also* National Grid USA.

New England Gas & Electric Association, **14** 124–25

New England Life Insurance Co., **III** 261

New England Motor Freight, Inc., **53** 250

New England Mutual Life Insurance Co., III 312–14

New England Network, Inc., **12** 31

New England Paper Tube Co., **54** 58

New England Power Association. *See* National Grid USA.

New Found Industries, Inc., **9** 465

New Galveston Company, Inc., **25** 116

New Hampshire Gas & Electric Co., **14** 124

New Hampton Goldfields Ltd., **63** 182, 184

New Hampton, Inc., **27** 429

New Haven District Telephone Company. *See* Southern New England Telecommunications Corporation.

New Haven Electric Co., **21** 512

New Holland N.V., 22 379–81. *See also* CNH Global N.V.

New Horizon Manufactured Homes, Ltd., **17** 83

New Hotel Showboat, Inc. *See* Showboat, Inc.

New Impriver NV. *See* Punch International N.V.

New Jersey Bell, **9** 321

New Jersey Educational Music Company. *See* National Educational Music Co. Ltd.

New Jersey Hot Water Heating Company, **6** 449

New Jersey Resources Corporation, 54 259–61

New Jersey Shale, **14** 250

New Jersey Tobacco Co., **15** 138

New Laoshan Brewery, **49** 418

New Line Cinema, Inc., 47 271–74; **57** 35

New London City National Bank, **13** 467

New Look Group plc, 35 308–10

New Market Development Company. *See* Cousins Properties Inc.

New Materials Ltd., **48** 344

New Mather Metals, **III** 582

New Mitsui Bussan, **III** 296

New Orleans Canal and Banking Company, **11** 105

New Orleans Saints LP, 58 255–57

The New Piper Aircraft, Inc., 44 307–10

New Plan Realty Trust, 11 345–47

New Process Company, **25** 76–77

New South Wales Health System, **16** 94

New Street Capital Inc., 8 388–90 **(upd.).** *See also* Drexel Burnham Lambert Incorporated.

New Sulzer Diesel, **III** 633

New Times, Inc., 45 288–90

New Toyo Group, **19** 227

New Trading Company. *See* SBC Warburg.

New UPI Inc., **25** 507

New Valley Corporation, 17 345–47

New Vanden Borre, **24** 266–70

New Ventures Realty Corporation, **58** 272

New World Coffee-Manhattan Bagel, Inc., **32** 15

New World Communications Group, **22** 442; **28** 248

New World Development Company Limited, IV 717–19; **8** 500; **38** 318–22 **(upd.)**

New World Entertainment, **17** 149

New World Hotel (Holdings) Ltd., **13** 66

New World Pasta Company, 53 241–44

New World Restaurant Group, Inc., 44 311–14

New York Air, **I** 103, 118, 129

New York and Richmond Gas Company, **6** 456

New York and Suburban Savings and Loan Association, **10** 91

New York Capital Bank, **41** 312

New York Central Railroad Company, **9** 228; **10** 43–44, 71–73; **17** 496

New York City Health and Hospitals Corporation, 60 214–17

New York City Off-Track Betting Corporation, 51 267–70

New York City Transit Authority, **8** 75

New York Daily News, 32 357–60

New York Electric Corporation. *See* New York State Electric and Gas.

New York Envelope Co., **32** 346

New York Evening Enquirer, **10** 287

New York Eye and Ear Infirmary. *See* Continuum Health Partners, Inc.

New York Fabrics and Crafts, **16** 197

New York Gas Light Company. *See* Consolidated Edison Company of New York.

New York Life Insurance Company, III 315–17, 332; **10** 382; **45** 291–95 **(upd.);** **63** 14

New York Magazine Co., **12** 359

New York Marine and Gotham Insurance, **41** 284

New York Presbyterian Hospital. *See* NewYork-Presbyterian Hospital.

New York Quotation Company, **9** 370

New York Restaurant Group, Inc., 32 361–63

New York Sports Clubs. *See* Town Sports International, Inc.

New York State Electric and Gas Corporation, 6 534–36

New York Stock Exchange, Inc., 9 369–72; **10** 416–17; **34** 254; **39** 296–300 **(upd.);** **54** 242

New York Telephone Co., **9** 321

The New York Times Company, IV 647–49; **15** 54; **19** 283–85 **(upd.);** **23** 158; **32** 508; **57** 243; **61** 239–43 **(upd.)**

New York Trust Co., **I** 378

New York Zoological Society. *See* Wildlife Conservation Society.

New York's Bankers Trust Co., **12** 107

New Zealand Aluminum Smelters, **IV** 59

New Zealand Countrywide Banking Corporation, **10** 336

Newa Insurance Co. Ltd., **64** 280

Newark Electronics Co., **9** 420

Newbridge & Gilbert, **56** 285

Newco Waste Systems. *See* Browning-Ferris Industries, Inc.

Newcor, Inc., 40 332–35; **65** 143, 145

Newcrest Mining Ltd., **IV** 47; **22** 107

Newell Co., 9 373–76; **12** 216; **13** 40–41; **22** 35; **25** 22; **61** 173

Newell Rubbermaid Inc., 49 253; **52 261–71 (upd.);** **53** 37, 40; **62** 231

Newfield Exploration Company, 65 260–62

Newfoundland Brewery, **26** 304

Newfoundland Energy, Ltd., **17** 121

Newfoundland Light & Power Co. *See* Fortis, Inc.

Newfoundland Processing Ltd. *See* Newfoundland Energy, Ltd.

Newhall Land and Farming Company, 14 348–50

Newman's Own, Inc., 37 272–75

Newmark & Lewis Inc., **23** 373

Newmont Mining Corporation, IV 33, 171, 576; **7** 287–89, 385–88; **12** 244; **16**

25; **23** 40; **38** 231–32; **40** 411–12; **50** 30

Newnes, **17** 397

Newpark Resources, Inc., 63 305–07

Newport News Shipbuilding and Dry Dock Co., 13 372–75; **27** 36

Newport News Shipbuilding Inc., 38 323–27 **(upd.);** **41** 42; **45** 306

News & Observer Publishing Company, **23** 343

News America Publishing Inc., 12 358–60; **27** 42; **37** 408

News Communications & Media Plc, **35** 242

News Corporation Limited, IV 650–53; **7 389–93 (upd.);** **8** 551; **9** 429; **12** 358–60; **17** 398; **18** 211, 213, 254; **22** 194, 441; **23** 121; **24** 224; **25** 490; **26** 32; **27** 305, 473; **32** 239; **35** 157–58; **37** 408; **43** 174, 433; **46** 308–13 **(upd.);** **52** 4; **60** 66

News Extracts Ltd., **55** 289

News International Corp., **20** 79

News of the World Organization (NOTW), **46** 309

Newsco NV, **48** 347

Newsfoto Publishing Company, **12** 472; **36** 469

Newspaper Co-op Couponing, **8** 551

Newspaper Enterprise Association, **7** 157–58

Newsquest plc, 32 354–56

Newth-Morris Box Co. *See* Rock-Tenn Company.

Newtherm Oil Burners, Ltd., **13** 286

Newton Yarn Mills, **19** 305

Newtown Gas Co., **6** 455

NewYork-Presbyterian Hospital, 59 309–12

Nexans SA, 54 262–64

Nexar Technologies, Inc., **22** 409

NEXCOM. *See* Navy Exchange Service Command.

Nexity S.A., 66 243–45

NeXstar Pharmaceuticals Inc., **54** 130

NeXT Incorporated, **34** 348

Next Media Ltd., 61 244–47

Next plc, 6 25; **29** 355–57

Nextel Communications, Inc., 10 431–33; **21** 239; **26** 389; **27** 341–45 **(upd.)**

Nextera Enterprises, Inc., **54** 191, 193

NEXTLINK Communications, Inc., **38** 192

Neyveli Lignite Corporation Ltd., 65 263–65

NFC plc, 6 412–14; **14** 547. *See also* Exel plc.

NFL Properties, Inc., **22** 223

NFO Worldwide, Inc., 24 352–55

NFT Distribution Limited, **61** 258, 260–61

NGC. *See* National Grid Company.

NGC Corporation, 18 365–67. *See also* Dynegy Inc.

NGI International Precious Metals, Ltd., **24** 335

NGK Insulators Ltd., 67 264–66

NHK. *See* Japan Broadcasting Corporation.

NHK Spring Co., Ltd., III 580–82

NI Industries, **20** 362

Ni-Med, **50** 122

Niagara Corporation, 28 314–16

Niagara First Savings and Loan Association, **10** 91

Niagara Mohawk Holdings Inc., 45 296–99 (upd.)

Niagara Mohawk Power Corporation, V 665–67; **6** 535; **25** 130; **51** 265
Niagara of Wisconsin, **26** 362–63
Nice Day, Inc., **II** 539
Nice Systems, **11** 520
NiceCom Ltd., **11** 520
Nichido Fire and Marine Insurance Co. *See* Millea Holdings Inc.
Nichii Co., Ltd., V 154–55; **15** 470; **36** 418
Nichimen Corporation, IV 150–52, 154; **10** 439; **24** 356–59 (upd.)
Nichimo Sekiyu Co. Ltd., **IV** 555; **16** 490
Nicholas Turkey Breeding Farms, **13** 103
Nichols & Company, **8** 561
Nichols Aluminum-Golden, Inc., **62** 289
Nichols-Homeshield, **22** 14
Nichols plc, 44 315–18
Nichols Research Corporation, 18 368–70
Nicholson File Co., **II** 16
Nicholson Graham & Jones, **28** 141
Nickelodeon, **25** 381
Nickerson Machinery Company Inc., **53** 230
Nicklaus Companies, 45 300–03
Nicolet Instrument Company, **11** 513
NICOR Inc., 6 529–31
Nidec Corporation, 59 313–16
Nielsen, **10** 358
Nielsen Marketing Research. *See* A.C. Nielsen Company.
Niemann Chemie, **8** 464
Niesmann & Bischoff, **22** 207
Nieuw Rotterdam, **27** 54
NIF Ventures Co. Ltd., **55** 118
Nigeria and West Africa Marine, **56** 383
Nigerian National Petroleum Corporation, IV 472–74
Nigerian Shipping Operations, **27** 473
Nihon Keizai Shimbun, Inc., IV 654–56
Nihon Kohden Corporation, **13** 328
Nihon Lumber Land Co., **III** 758
Nihon Noyaku Co., **64** 35
Nihon Sugar, **I** 511
Nihon Synopsis, **11** 491
Nihon Timken K.K., **8** 530
Nihon Waters K.K., **43** 456
Nihron Yupro Corp. *See* Toto Ltd.
NII. *See* National Intergroup, Inc.
NIKE, Inc., V 372–74, 376; **8** 303–04, **391–94 (upd.)**; **9** 134–35, 437; **10** 525; **11** 50, 349; **13** 513; **14** 8; **15** 397; **16** 79, 81; **17** 244–45, 260–61; **18** 264, 266–67, 392; **22** 173; **25** 352; **27** 20; **29** 187–88; **31** 413–14; **36** 343–48 (upd.)
Nikkei. *See also* Nihon Keizai Shimbun, Inc.
Nikkei Shimbun Toei, **9** 29
Nikkelverk, **49** 136
Nikken Global Inc., 32 364–67
Nikko International Hotels, **I** 106
Nikko Kido Company, **6** 431
The Nikko Securities Company Limited, II 433–35; **9** 377–79 (upd.)
Nikko Trading Co., **I** 106
Nikolaiev, **19** 49, 51
Nikon Corporation, III 583–85; **9** 251; **12** 340; **18** 93, 186, 340, 342; **43** 282; **48 292–95 (upd.)**
Nilpeter, **26** 540, 542
Niman Ranch, Inc., 67 267–69
Nimbus CD International, Inc., 20 386–90

9 Telecom, **24** 79
Nine West Group Inc., **11** 348–49; **14** 441; **23** 330; **39** 247, **301–03 (upd.)**
98 Cents Clearance Centers, **62** 104
99¢ Only Stores, 25 353–55
Ningbo General Bearing Co., Ltd., **45** 170
Nintendo Co., Ltd., III 586–88; **7** 394–96 **(upd.)**; **10** 124–25, 284–86, 483–84; **13** 403; **15** 539; **16** 168, 331; **18** 520; **23** 26; **28** 317–21 **(upd.)**; **31** 237; **38** 415; **50** 83; **67 270–76 (upd.)**
Nintendo of America, **24** 4
NIOC. *See* National Iranian Oil Company.
Nippon Breweries Ltd. *See* Sapporo Breweries Ltd.
Nippon Cable Company, **15** 235
Nippon Credit Bank, II 338–39; **38** 439
Nippon Del Monte Corporation, **47** 206
Nippon Densan Corporation. *See* Nidec Corporation.
Nippon Educational Television (NET). *See* Asahi National Broadcasting Company, Ltd.
Nippon Electric Company, Limited. *See* NEC Corporation.
Nippon Express Company, Ltd., V 477–80; **64 286–90 (upd.)**
Nippon-Fisher, **13** 225
Nippon Foundation Engineering Co. Ltd., **51** 179
Nippon Gakki Co., Ltd. *See* Yamaha Corporation.
Nippon Global Tanker Co. Ltd., **53** 116
Nippon Gyomo Sengu Co. Ltd., **IV** 555
Nippon Hatsujo Kabushikikaisha. *See* NHK Spring Co., Ltd.
Nippon Helicopter & Aeroplane Transport Co., Ltd. *See* All Nippon Airways Company Limited.
Nippon Hoso Kyokai. *See* Japan Broadcasting Corporation.
Nippon Idou Tsushin, **7** 119–20
Nippon International Container Services, **8** 278
Nippon Interrent, **10** 419–20
Nippon K.K. *See* Nikon Corporation.
Nippon Kogaku K.K. *See* Nikon Corporation.
Nippon Kogyo Co. Ltd. *See* Nippon Mining Co. Ltd.
Nippon Kokan K.K. *See* NKK Corporation.
Nippon Life Insurance Company, III 273, 288, 318–20; **60 218–21 (upd.)**
Nippon Light Metal Company, Ltd., IV 153–55
Nippon Meat Packers, Inc., II 550–51; **61** 139
Nippon Mining Co., Ltd., IV 475–77; **14** 207
Nippon Mitsubishi Oil Corporation, **49** 216
Nippon Motorola Manufacturing Co., **II** 62
Nippon Oil Company, Limited, IV 478–79; **19** 74
Nippon Oil Corporation, 63 308–13 **(upd.)**
Nippon Paint Co., Ltd, **11** 252
Nippon Paper Industries Co., Ltd., **57** 101
Nippon Phonogram, **23** 390
Nippon Polaroid Kabushiki Kaisha, **7** 437; **18** 570
Nippon Sanso Corp., **16** 486, 488
Nippon Seiko K.K., III 589–90; **47** 278
Nippon Sekiyu Co. *See* Nippon Oil Company, Limited.

Nippon Sheet Glass Company, Limited, III 714–16
Nippon Shinpan Co., Ltd., II 436–37, 442; **8** 118; **61 248–50 (upd.)**
Nippon Steel Chemical Co., **10** 439
Nippon Steel Corporation, IV 116, 130, **156–58**, 184, 212, 228, 298; **6** 274; **14** 369; **17 348–51 (upd.)**, 556; **19** 219; **24** 370; **67** 284
Nippon Suisan Kaisha, Limited, II 552–53
Nippon Telegraph and Telephone Corporation, II 51, 62; III V 305–07; **7** 118–20; **10** 119; **13** 482; **16** 224; **21** 330; **25** 301; **27** 327, 365; **50** 129; **51 271–75 (upd.)**
Nippon Television, **7** 249; **9** 29
Nippon Tire Co., Ltd. *See* Bridgestone Corporation.
Nippon Unipac Holding, **57** 101
Nippon Yusen Kabushiki Kaisha, V 481–83; **6** 398
Nippon Yusoki Company, Ltd., **13** 501
Nippondenso Co., Ltd., III 591–94. *See also* DENSO Corporation.
NIPSCO Industries, Inc., **6 532–33**
NiSource, Inc., **38** 81
Nissan Motor Acceptance Corporation, **22** 207
Nissan Motor Co., Ltd., I 183–84, III 750; **7** 111, 120, 219; **9** 243, 340–42; **10** 353; **11** 50–51, 350–52 **(upd.)**; **16** 167; **17** 556; **23** 338–40, 289; **24** 324; **27** 203; **34** 133, **303–07 (upd.)**; **59** 393–94
Nissan Trading Company, Ltd., **13** 533
Nissay Dowa General Insurance Company Ltd., **60** 220
Nisshin Flour Milling Company, Ltd., II 554. *See also* Nisshin Seifun Group Inc.
Nisshin Seifun Group Inc., 66 246–48 **(upd.)**
Nisshin Steel Co., Ltd., IV 159–60; **7** 588
Nissho Iwai K.K., I 509–11; **6** 386; **8** 75; **15** 373; **25** 449; **27** 107
Nissui. *See* Nippon Suisan Kaisha.
Nitches, Inc., 53 245–47
Nitroglycerin AB, **13** 22
Nitroglycerin Ltd., **9** 380
Nittetsu Curtainwall Corp., **III** 758
Nittetsu Sash Sales Corp., **III** 758
Nittsu. *See* Nippon Express Co., Ltd.
Niugini Mining Ltd., **23** 42
Nixdorf Computer AG, III 154–55; **12** 162; **14** 169; **26** 497
Nixdorf-Krein Industries Inc. *See* Laclede Steel Company.
Nizhny Novgorod Dairy, **48** 438
NKK Corporation, IV 161–63, 212–13; **28 322–26 (upd.)**; **53** 170, 172
NL Industries, Inc., 10 434–36; **19** 466–68
NLG. *See* National Leisure Group.
NLI Insurance Agency Inc., **60** 220
NLM City-Hopper, **I** 109
NM Acquisition Corp., **27** 346
NMC Laboratories Inc., **12** 4
NMT. *See* Nordic Mobile Telephone.
NNG. *See* Northern Natural Gas Company.
No-Leak-O Piston Ring Company, **10** 492
No-Sag Spring Co., **16** 321
Noah's New York Bagels, **13** 494. *See also* Einstein/Noah Bagel Corporation.
Nob Hill Foods, **58** 291
Nobel Drilling Corporation, **26** 243

Nobel Industries AB, **9** 380–82; **16** 69.
  See also Akzo Nobel N.V.
Nobel Learning Communities, Inc., **37** 276–79
Noble Affiliates, Inc., **11** 353–55; **18** 366
Noble Broadcast Group, Inc., **23** 293
Noble Roman's Inc., **14** 351–53
Nobles Industries, **13** 501
Noblesville Telephone Company, **14** 258
Nobleza Piccardo SAICF, **64** 291–93
Noblitt-Sparks Industries, Inc., **8** 37–38
Nobody Beats the Wiz. *See* Cablevision Electronic Instruments, Inc.
Nocibé SA, **54** 265–68
Nocona Belt Company, **31** 435–36
Nocona Boot Co. *See* Justin Industries, Inc.
Noel Group, Inc., **24** 286–88
NOK Corporation, **41** 170–72
Nokia Corporation, **II** 69–71; **IV** 296; **6** 242; **15** 125; **17** 33, 352–54 (upd.); **18** 74, 76; **19** 226; **20** 439; **38** 328–31 (upd.); **47** 318–19; **50** 510; **52** 317; **52** 333
Nokian Tyres PLC, **59** 91
NOL Group. *See* Neptune Orient Lines Limited.
Noland Company, **35** 311–14
Nolo.com, Inc., **49** 288–91
Nolte Mastenfabriek B.V., **19** 472
Noma Industries, **11** 526
Nomai Inc., **18** 510
Nomura Bank of Japan, **34** 221
Nomura Holdings, Inc., **49** 451
Nomura Securities Company, Limited, **II** 438–41; **9** 383–86 (upd.); **39** 109
Nomura Toys Ltd., **16** 267; **43** 232
Non-Fiction Book Club, **13** 105
Non-Stop Fashions, Inc., **8** 323
Noodle Kidoodle, **16** 388–91
Noodles & Company, Inc., **55** 277–79
Nooter Corporation, **61** 251–53
NOP Research Group, **28** 501, 504
Nopco Chemical Co., **7** 308
Nopri. *See* GIB Group.
Nor-Cal Engineering Co. GmbH, **18** 162
Nora Industrier A/S, **18** 395
NORAND, **9** 411
Noranda Inc., **IV** 164–66; **7** 397–99 (upd.); **9** 282; **26** 363; **49** 136; **64** 294–98 (upd.)
Norandex, **16** 204
Norbro Corporation. *See* Stuart Entertainment Inc.
Norcal Pottery Products, Inc., **58** 60
Norcal Waste Systems, Inc., **60** 222–24
Norcen Energy Resources, Ltd., **8** 347
Norco Plastics, **8** 553
Norcon, Inc., **7** 558–59
Norcore Plastics, Inc., **33** 361
Nordbanken, **9** 382
Norddeutsche Affinerie AG, **62** 249–53
Norddeutscher-Lloyd, **6** 397–98
Nordea AB, **40** 336–39
Nordic Baltic Holding. *See* Nordea AB.
Nordica S.r.l., **10** 151; **15** 396–97; **53** 24
NordicTrack, **10** 215–17; **22** 382–84; **38** 238. *See also* Icon Health & Fitness, Inc.
Nordson Corporation, **11** 356–58; **48** 296–99 (upd.)
Nordstrom, Inc., **V** 156–58; **11** 349; **13** 494; **14** 376; **17** 313; **18** 371–74 (upd.); **21** 302; **22** 173; **67** 277–81 (upd.)
Nordwestdeutsche Kraftwerke AG. *See* PreussenElektra AG.

Norelco, **17** 110
Norelco Consumer Products Co., **12** 439; **26** 334–36
Norelec, **27** 138
Norex Leasing, Inc., **16** 397
Norfolk Carolina Telephone Company, **10** 202
Norfolk Southern Corporation, **V** 484–86; **6** 436, 487; **12** 278; **22** 167; **29** 358–61 (upd.)
Norfolk Steel, **13** 97
Norge Co., **18** 173–74; **43** 163–64
Noric Corporation, **39** 332
Norinchukin Bank, **II** 340–41
Norlin, **16** 238–39
Norm Thompson Outfitters, Inc., **47** 275–77
Norma AS. *See* Autoliv, Inc.
Norman BV, **9** 93; **33** 78
Normandy Mining Ltd., **23** 42
Normark Corporation. *See* Rapala-Normark Group, Ltd.
Norment Security Group, Inc., **51** 81
Normond/CMS, **7** 117
Norrell Corporation, **25** 356–59
Norris Cylinder Company, **11** 535
Norris Grain Co., **14** 537
Norris Oil Company, **47** 52
Norshield Corp., **51** 81
Norsk Hydro ASA, **10** 437–40; **35** 315–19 (upd.); **36** 322; **61** 345–46
Norsk Rengjorings Selskap a.s., **49** 221
Norske Skogindustrier ASA, **63** 314–16
Norstan, Inc., **16** 392–94
Norstar Bancorp, **9** 229
Nortek, Inc., **14** 482; **22** 4; **26** 101; **34** 308–12; **37** 331
Nortel Inversora S.A., **63** 375–77
Nortel Networks Corporation, **36** 349–54 (upd.); **50** 130
Nortex International, **7** 96; **19** 338
North African Petroleum Ltd., **IV** 455
North American Aviation, **7** 520; **9** 16; **11** 278, 427
North American Carbon, **19** 499
North American Cellular Network, **9** 322
North American Coal Corporation, **7** 369–71
North American Company, **6** 443, 552–53, 601–02
North American Dräger, **13** 328
North American Energy Conservation, Inc., **35** 480
North American InTeleCom, Inc., **IV** 411
North American Light & Power Company, **6** 504–05; **12** 541
North American Medical Management Company, Inc., **36** 366
North American Mogul Products Co. *See* Mogul Corp.
North American Philips Corporation, **19** 393; **21** 520
North American Plastics, Inc., **61** 112
North American Printing Ink Company, **13** 228
North American Rockwell Corp., **10** 173
North American Systems, **14** 230
North American Training Corporation. *See* Rollerblade, Inc.
North American Van Lines, **14** 37. *See also* Allied Worldwide, Inc.
North American Watch Company. *See* Movado Group, Inc.
North Atlantic Energy Corporation, **21** 411

North Atlantic Laboratories, Inc., **62** 391
North Atlantic Packing, **13** 243
North Atlantic Trading Company Inc., **65** 266–68
North British Rubber Company, **20** 258
North Broken Hill Peko, **IV** 61
North Carolina Motor Speedway, Inc., **19** 294
North Carolina National Bank Corporation. *See* NCNB Corporation.
North Carolina Natural Gas Corporation, **6** 578
North Carolina Shipbuilding Co., **13** 373
North Central Financial Corp., **9** 475
North Central Utilities, Inc., **18** 405
North East Insurance Company, **44** 356
North Eastern Bricks, **14** 249
The North Face, Inc., **8** 169; **18** 375–77; **25** 206; **41** 103; **54** 400
North Fork Bancorporation, Inc., **44** 33; **46** 314–17
North New York Savings Bank, **10** 91
North of Scotland Hydro-Electric Board, **19** 389
North Pacific Group, Inc., **61** 254–57
North Pacific Paper Corp., **IV** 298
North Sea Ferries, **26** 241, 243
North Sea Oil and Gas, **10** 337
North Shore Gas Company, **6** 543–44
North Shore Land Co., **17** 357
North Star Container, Inc., **59** 290
North Star Egg Case Company, **12** 376
North Star Marketing Cooperative, **7** 338
North Star Mill, **12** 376
North Star Steel Company, **13** 138; **18** 378–81; **19** 380; **40** 87
North Star Transport Inc., **49** 402
North Star Tubes, **54** 391, 393
North Star Universal, Inc., **25** 331, 333
North State Supply Company, **57** 9
North Supply, **27** 364
The North West Company, Inc., **12** 361–63; **25** 219–20
North-West Telecommunications. *See* Pacific Telecom, Inc.
North West Water Group plc, **11** 359–62. *See also* United Utilities PLC.
Northbridge Financial Corp., **57** 137
Northbrook Corporation, **24** 32
Northbrook Holdings, Inc., **22** 495
Northcliffe Newspapers, **19** 118
Northeast Federal Corp., **13** 468
Northeast Petroleum Industries, Inc., **11** 194; **14** 461
Northeast Savings Bank, **12** 31; **13** 467–68
Northeast Utilities, **V** 668–69; **13** 182–84; **21** 408, 411; **48** 303–06 (upd.); **55** 313, 316
Northeastern New York Medical Service, Inc., **III** 246
Northern Animal Hospital Inc., **58** 355
Northern Arizona Light & Power Co., **6** 545
Northern California Savings, **10** 340
Northern Dairies, **10** 441
Northern Drug Company, **14** 147
Northern Electric Company. *See* Northern Telecom Limited.
Northern Energy Resources Company. *See* NERCO, Inc.
Northern Engineering Industries Plc. *See* Rolls-Royce Group PLC.
Northern Fibre Products Co., **I** 202

Northern Foods plc, 10 441–43; **61** 258–62 (upd.)
Northern Illinois Gas Co., **6** 529–31
Northern Indiana Power Company, **6** 556
Northern Indiana Public Service Company, **6** 532–33
Northern Infrastructure Maintenance Company, **39** 238
Northern Leisure, **40** 296–98
Northern Light Electric Company, **18** 402–03
Northern National Bank, **14** 90
Northern Natural Gas Co. *See* Enron Corporation.
Northern Pacific Corp., **15** 274
Northern Pacific Railroad, **14** 168; **26** 451
Northern Paper, **I** 614
Northern Pipeline Construction Co., **19** 410, 412
Northern Rock plc, 33 318–21
Northern Star Co., **25** 332
Northern States Power Company, V 670–72; **18** 404; **20** 391–95 (upd.)
Northern Stores, Inc., **12** 362
Northern Sugar Company, **11** 13
Northern Telecom Limited, III 164; **V** 271; **V** 308–10; **6** 242, 307, 310; **9** 479; **10** 19, 432; **11** 69; **12** 162; **14** 259; **16** 392, 468; **17** 353; **18** 111; **20** 439; **22** 51; **25** 34; **27** 342; **47** 318–20. *See also* Nortel Networks Corporation.
Northern Trust Company, 9 387–89
Northfield Metal Products, **11** 256
Northgate Computer Corp., **16** 196
Northland. *See* Scott Fetzer Company.
Northland Cranberries, Inc., 38 332–34
Northland Publishing, **19** 231
NorthPrint International, **22** 356
Northrop Corporation, I 49, 55, 59, 76–77, 80, 84, 197, 525; **9** 416, 418; **10** 162; **11** 164, 166, 266, 269, 363–65 (upd.);
Northrop Grumman Corporation, 41 43; **45** 304–12 (upd.); **49** 444
NorthStar Computers, **10** 313
Northwest Airlines Inc., I 112–14, 125, 127; **6** 103–05 (upd.), 123; **9** 273; **11** 266, 315; **12** 191, 487; **21** 141, 143; **22** 252; **26** 337–40 (upd.), 441; **27** 20; **28** 226, 265–66; **30** 447; **31** 419–20; **33** 50–51, 302; **52** 90, 93. *See also* Mesaba Holdings, Inc.
Northwest Engineering Co. *See* Terex Corporation.
Northwest Express. *See* Bear Creek Corporation.
Northwest Industries, **8** 367; **25** 165–66. *See also* Chicago and North Western Holdings Corporation.
Northwest Instruments, **8** 519
Northwest Linen Co., **16** 228
Northwest Natural Gas Company, 45 313–15
Northwest Outdoor, **27** 280
Northwest Paper Company, **8** 430
Northwest Steel Rolling Mills Inc., **13** 97
Northwest Telecommunications Inc., **6** 598
NorthWestern Corporation, 37 280–83
Northwestern Engraving, **12** 25
Northwestern Financial Corporation, **11** 29
Northwestern Flavors LLC, **58** 379
Northwestern Manufacturing Company, **8** 133

Northwestern Mutual Life Insurance Company, III 321–24, 352; **45** 316–21 (upd.); **46** 198; **52** 243–44; **67** 328–29
Northwestern National Bank, **16** 71
Northwestern National Life Insurance Co., **14** 233
Northwestern Public Service Company, **6** 524
Northwestern States Portland Cement Co., **III** 702
Northwestern Telephone Systems. *See* Pacific Telecom, Inc.
Norton Company, 8 395–97; **22** 68; **26** 70
Norton Healthcare Ltd., **11** 208
Norton McNaughton, Inc., 25 245; **27** 346–49
Norton Opax PLC, **IV** 259; **34** 140
Norton Professional Books. *See* W.W. Norton & Company, Inc.
Norton Simon Industries, **22** 513
Norwales Development Ltd., **11** 239
Norwalk Truck Lines, **14** 567
NORWEB plc, **13** 458; **24** 270
Norwegian Caribbean Line, **27** 90
Norweld Holding A.A., **13** 316
Norwest Bank, **19** 412
Norwest Corp., **16** 135
Norwest Mortgage Inc., **11** 29; **54** 124
Norwich & Peterborough Building Society, 55 280–82
Norwich-Eaton Pharmaceuticals, **III** 53; **8** 434; **26** 383
Norwich Pharmaceuticals, **9** 358
Norwich Union Fire Insurance Society, Ltd., **III** 273, 404
Norwich Winterthur Group, **III** 404
Norwood Company, **13** 168
Norwood Promotional Products, Inc., 26 341–43
Nostell Brick & Tile, **14** 249
Notre Capital Ventures II, L.P., **24** 117
Nouvelle Compagnie Havraise Pénninsulaire, **27** 514
Nouvelle Elastelle, **52** 100–01
Nouvelles Galeries Réunies, **10** 205; **19** 308; **27** 95
Nova Corporation, **18** 365–67; **24** 395; **49** 120–21
Nova Corporation of Alberta, V 673–75; **12** 364–66
Nova Information Systems, **24** 393
Nova Mechanical Contractors, **48** 238
Nova Pharmaceuticals, **14** 46
Nova Scotia Steel Company, **19** 186
NovaCare, Inc., 11 366–68; **14** 233; **33** 185; **41** 194
Novacor Chemicals Ltd., 12 364–66
Novaction Argentina SA, **48** 224
Novagas Clearinghouse Ltd., **18** 367; **49** 120
Novalta Resources Inc., **11** 441
Novamax Technologies Inc., **34** 209
Novanet Semiconductor, **36** 124
Novapak Corporation. *See* PVC Container Corporation.
Novar plc, 49 292–96 (upd.)
Novara plc, **60** 123
Novartis AG, 18 51; **34** 284; **39** 304–10 (upd.); **50** 58, 90; **55** 285
Novatec Plastics Corporation. *See* PVC Container Corporation.
Novation, **53** 346–47

Novell, Inc., 6 260, 269–71; **9** 170–71; **10** 232, 363, 473–74, 558, 565; **11** 59, 519–20; **12** 335; **13** 482; **15** 131, 133, 373, 492; **16** 392, 394; **20** 237; **21** 133–34; **23** 359–62 (upd.); **25** 50–51, 117, 499; **33** 113, 115; **34** 442–43; **36** 80; **38** 418–19; **65** 35
Novellus Systems, Inc., 18 382–85
Noven Pharmaceuticals, Inc., 55 283–85
Novgorodnefteprodukt, **48** 378
Novo Industri A/S, I 658–60, 697
Novo Nordisk A/S, 61 263–66 (upd.)
Novobord, **49** 353
Novotel. *See* Accor SA.
NOVUM. *See* Industrie Natuzzi S.p.A.
NOVUS Financial Corporation, **33** 314
NOW. *See* National Organization for Women, Inc.
Nowsco Well Services Ltd., **25** 73
Noxell Corporation, **III** 53; **8** 434; **26** 384
NPBI International B.V., **56** 141
NPC International, Inc., 40 340–42
NPD Group, **13** 4
NPD Trading (USA), Inc., **13** 367
NPI-Omnipoint Wireless LLC, **63** 132
NPR. *See* National Public Radio, Inc.
NPS Waste Technologies, **13** 366
NRC Handelsblad BV, **53** 273
NRF B.V., **56** 247
NRG Energy, Inc., **11** 401; **50** 363
NRT Incorporated, 58 76–77; **61** 267–69
NS. *See* Norfolk Southern Corporation.
NS Group, **31** 287
NS Petites Inc., **8** 323
NSG Information System Co., **III** 715
NSK. *See* Nippon Seiko K.K.
NSK Ltd., **42** 384
NSK-Warner, **14** 64
NSMO. *See* Nederlandsche Stoomvart Maatschappij Oceaan.
NSN Network Services, **23** 292, 294
NSP. *See* Northern States Power Company.
NSU Werke, **10** 261
NTC Electronics Inc., **64** 198
NTC Publishing Group, **22** 519, 522
NTCL. *See* Northern Telecom Limited.
NTL Inc., 65 269–72
NTN Corporation, III 595–96; **28** 241; **47** 278–81 (upd.)
NTRON, **11** 486
NTT. *See* Nippon Telegraph and Telephone Corp.
NTTPC. *See* Nippon Telegraph and Telephone Public Corporation.
NU. *See* Northeast Utilities.
Nu-Era Gear, **14** 64
Nu-kote Holding, Inc., 18
Nu Skin Enterprises, Inc., 27 350–53; **31** 327 386–89
Nuance Group, **63** 361, 363
Nuclear Electric, **6** 453; **11** 399–401; **12** 349; **13** 484; **50** 280–81, 361–63; **66** 282
Nuclear Power International, **19** 166
Nucor Corporation, 7 400–02; **13** 143, 423; **14** 156; **18** 378–80; **19** 380; **21** 392–95 (upd.); **26** 407; **52** 326
Nucorp Energy, **II** 620; **59** 280–81
NUG Optimus Lebensmittel-Einzelhandelgesellschaft mbH, **V** 74
NUMAR Corporation, **25** 192
NUMMI. *See* New United Motor Manufacturing, Inc.
NUR Touristic GmbH. *See* Karstadt AG.

Nurotoco Inc. *See* Roto-Rooter Service Company.
The Nut Company NV, **66** 153
Nutmeg Industries, Inc., **17** 513
Nutraceutical International Corporation, 37 284–86
NutraSweet Company, 8 398–400; 26 108; **29** 331
Nutreco Holding N.V., 56 256–59
Nutrena, **II** 617; **13** 137
Nutri-Foods International, **18** 467–68
Nutri/System Inc., **29** 258
NutriSystem, **10** 383; **12** 531
Nutrition for Life International Inc., 22 385–88
Nutron Industries, **58** 75
Nuveen. *See* John Nuveen Company.
NV Dagblad De Telegraaf. *See* N.V. Holdingmaatschappij De Telegraaf.
NVIDIA Corporation, 54 269–73
NVR L.P., 8 401–03
NWA, Inc. *See* Northwest Airlines Corporation.
NWK. *See* Nordwestdeutsche Kraftwerke AG.
NWS BANK plc, **10** 336–37
NWT Air, **56** 39
NYC OTB Racing Network, **51** 269
Nyland Mattor, **25** 464
NYLCare Health Plans, **45** 293–94
NYLife Care Health Plans, Inc., **17** 166
Nylon de Mexico, S.A., **19** 10, 12
NYMAGIC, Inc., 41 284–86
Nymofil, Ltd., **16** 297
NYNEX Corporation, V 311–13; 6 340; **11** 19, 87; **13** 176; **25** 61–62, 102; **26** 520. *See also* Verizon Communications.
NYRG. *See* New York Restaurant Group, Inc.
NYSE. *See* New York Stock Exchange.
NYSEG. *See* New York State Electric and Gas Corporation.
NZI Corp., **III** 257

O&K Rolltreppen, **27** 269
O&Y. *See* Olympia & York Developments Ltd.
O.B. McClintock Co., **7** 144–45
O.G. Wilson, **16** 560
O. Kraft & Sons, **12** 363
O.N.E. Color Communications L.L.C., **29** 306
O-Pee-Chee, **34** 447–48
O.S. Designs Inc., **15** 396
O.Y.L. Industries Berhad, **26** 3, 5
Oak Creek Homes Inc., **41** 18
Oak Harbor Freight Lines, Inc., 53 248–51
Oak Hill Investment Partners, **11** 490
Oak Hill Sportswear Corp., **17** 137–38
Oak Industries Inc., 21 396–98
Oak Technology, Inc., 22 389–93
OakBrook Investments, LLC, **48** 18
Oakhurst Dairy, 60 225–28
Oakley, Inc., 18 390–93; 49 297–302 (upd.)
OakStone Financial Corporation, **11** 448
Oaktree Capital Management, LLC, **30** 185; **59** 265, 268
OakTree Health Plan Inc., **16** 404
Oakville, **7** 518
Oakwood Homes Corporation, 13 155; 15 326–28

OAO AVTOVAZ. *See* AVTOVAZ Joint Stock Company.
OAO Gazprom, 42 261–65
OAO LUKOIL, 40 343–46
OAO NK YUKOS, 47 282–85; 49 304
OAO Severstal. *See* Severstal Joint Stock Company.
OAO Siberian Oil Company (Sibneft), 49 303–06
OAO Tatneft, 45 322–26
Oasis Group P.L.C., **10** 506
OASYS, Inc., **18** 112
Obayashi Corp., **44** 154
ÖBB. *See* Österreichische Bundesbahnen GmbH.
Oberheim Corporation, **16** 239
Oberland, **16** 122
Obi, **23** 231
Obie Media Corporation, 56 260–62
Object Design, Inc., **15** 372
O'Boy Inc. *See* Happy Kids Inc.
O'Brien Kreitzbey, Inc., **25** 130
Observer AB, 55 286–89
Obunsha, **9** 29
OCBC. *See* Overseas-Chinese Banking Corporation.
Occidental Bank, **16** 497; **50** 497
Occidental Chemical Corporation, **19** 414; **45** 254
Occidental Life Insurance Company, **26** 486–87; **41** 401
Occidental Overseas Ltd., **11** 97; **50** 179
Occidental Petroleum Corporation, IV 480–82; 7 376; **8** 526; **12** 100; **25** 360–63 (upd.); **29** 113; **31** 456; **37** 309, 311; **45** 252, 254
Occidental Petroleum Great Britain Inc., **21** 206
Océ N.V., 24 360–63
Ocean Combustion Services, **9** 109
Ocean Drilling and Exploration Company. *See* ODECO.
Ocean Group plc, 6 415–17. *See also* Exel plc.
Ocean Pacific Apparel Corporation, **51** 321
Ocean Reef Management, **19** 242, 244
Ocean Scientific, Inc., **15** 380
Ocean Specialty Tankers Corporation, **22** 275
Ocean Spray Cranberries, Inc., 7 403–05; 10 525; **19** 278; **25** 364–67 (upd.); **38** 334
Ocean Steam Ship Company. *See* Malaysian Airlines System BHD.
Ocean Transport & Trading Ltd., **6** 417
Oceaneering International, Inc., 63 317–19
Oceania Football Confederation, **27** 150
Oceanic Steam Navigation Company, **19** 197; **23** 160
Oceans of Fun, **22** 130
Ocelet Industries Ltd., **25** 232
O'Charley's Inc., 19 286–88; 60 229–32 (upd.)
OCL. *See* Overseas Containers Ltd.
Oclassen Pharmaceuticals Inc., **56** 375
Octagon Group Ltd., **51** 173
Octane Software, **49** 124
Octek, **13** 235
Octel Messaging, 14 217, 354–56; **16** 394; **41** 287–90 (upd.)
Octopus Publishing, **IV** 667; **17** 398
Ocular Sciences, Inc., 65 273–75
Oculinum, Inc., **10** 48

Odakyu Electric Railway Company Limited, V 487–89
Odd Job Trading Corp., **29** 311–12
Odda Smelteverk A/S, **25** 82
Odeco Drilling, Inc., **7** 362–64; **11** 522; **12** 318; **32** 338, 340
Odegard Outdoor Advertising, L.L.C., **27** 280
Odetics Inc., 14 357–59
Odhams Press Ltd., **IV** 259, 666–67; **7** 244, 342; **17** 397–98
ODL, Inc., 55 290–92
ODM, **26** 490
ODME. *See* Toolex International N.V.
Odwalla, Inc., 31 349–51
Odyssey Holdings, Inc., **18** 376
Odyssey Partners Group, **II** 679; **V** 135; **12** 55; **13** 94; **17** 137; **28** 218
Odyssey Press, **13** 560
Odyssey Publications Inc., **48** 99
Odyssey Re Group, **57** 136–37
OEA. *See* Autoliv, Inc.
OEC Medical Systems, Inc., 27 354–56
Oelwerken Julius Schindler GmbH, **7** 141
OEN Connectors, **19** 166
Ofek Securities and Investments Ltd., **60** 50
Off Wall Street Consulting Group, **42** 313
Office Depot, Inc., 8 404–05; 10 235, 497; **12** 335; **13** 268; **15** 331; **18** 24, 388; **22** 154, 412–13; **23** 363–65 (upd.); **27** 95; **34** 198; **43** 293; **65** 276–80 (upd.)
Office Electronics, Inc., **65** 371
Office Mart Holdings Corporation, **10** 498
Office Systems Inc., **15** 407
The Office Works, Inc., **13** 277; **25** 500
OfficeMax Inc., 8 404; **15** 329–31; **18** 286, 388; **20** 103; **22** 154; **23** 364–65; **43** 291–95 (upd.)
Official Airline Guides, Inc., **IV** 643; **7** 312, 343; **17** 399
Officine Alfieri Maserati S.p.A., 11 104; **13** 28, 376–78
Offset Gerhard Kaiser GmbH, **IV** 325
The Offshore Company, **6** 577; **37** 243
Offshore Food Services Inc., **I** 514
Offshore Logistics, Inc., 37 287–89
Offshore Transportation Corporation, **11** 523
O'Gara Company, **57** 219
Ogden Corporation, I 512–14, 701; 6 151–53, 600; **7** 39; **25** 16; **27** 21, 196; **41** 40–41; **43** 217; **59** 321. *See also* Covanta Energy Corporation.
Ogden Food Products, **7** 430
Ogden Gas Co., **6** 568
Ogden Ground Services, **39** 240, 242
Ogilvy & Mather, **22** 200
Ogilvy Group Inc., I 25–27, 31, 37, 244; **9** 180. *See also* WPP Group.
Oglebay Norton Company, 17 355–58
Oglethorpe Power Corporation, 6 537–38
Oh la la!, **14** 107
Ohbayashi Corporation, I 586–87
The Ohio Art Company, 14 360–62; 59 317–20 (upd.)
Ohio Ball Bearing. *See* Bearings Inc.
Ohio Barge Lines, Inc., **11** 194
Ohio Bell Telephone Company, 14 363–65; 18 30
Ohio Boxboard Company, **12** 376
Ohio Brass Co., **II** 2

Ohio Casualty Corp., 11 369–70
Ohio Coatings Company, 58 363
Ohio Crankshaft Co. See Park-Ohio Industries Inc.
Ohio Edison Company, V 676–78
Ohio Mattress Co., 12 438–39
Ohio Pizza Enterprises, Inc., 7 152
Ohio River Company, 6 487
Ohio-Sealy Mattress Mfg. Co., 12 438–39
Ohio Valley Electric Corporation, 6 517
Ohio Ware Basket Company, 12 319
Ohlmeyer Communications, I 275; 26 305
OHM Corp., 17 553
Ohmeda. See BOC Group plc.
Ohmite Manufacturing Co., 13 397
Ohta Keibin Railway Company, 6 430
Oil and Natural Gas Commission, IV 483–84
Oil and Solvent Process Company, 9 109
Oil-Dri Corporation of America, 20 396–99
Oil Drilling, Incorporated, 7 344
Oil Dynamics Inc., 43 178
Oil Equipment Manufacturing Company, 16 8
Oil Shale Corp., 7 537
Oilfield Industrial Lines Inc., I 477
Oilinvest. See Natinal Oil Corporation.
Oji Paper Co., Ltd., IV 320–22; 57 272–75 (upd.)
Ojibway Press, 57 13
OJSC Wimm-Bill-Dann Foods, 48 436–39
OK Turbines, Inc., 22 311
O'Keefe Marketing, 23 102
Oki Electric Industry Company, Limited, II 72–74; 15 125; 21 390
Okidata, 9 57; 18 435
Oklahoma Airmotive, 8 349
Oklahoma Entertainment, Inc., 9 74
Oklahoma Gas and Electric Company, 6 539–40; 7 409–11
Oklahoma Publishing Company, 11 152–53; 30 84
Okura & Co., Ltd., IV 167–68
Olan Mills, Inc., 62 254–56
Oland & Sons Limited, 25 281
Olathe Manufacturing, 26 494
OLC. See Orient Leasing Co., Ltd.
Old America Stores, Inc., 17 359–61
Old Colony Envelope Co., 32 345–46
Old Country Buffet Restaurant Co. (OCB). See Buffets, Inc.
Old Dominion Freight Line, Inc., 57 276–79
Old Dominion Power Company, 6 513, 515
Old El Paso, 14 212; 24 140–41
Old Harbor Candles, 18 68
Old Kent Financial Corp., 11 371–72
Old Mutual PLC, IV 535; 61 270–72
Old National Bancorp, 14 529; 15 332–34
Old Navy Clothing Company, 18 193; 55 157
Old 97 Company, 60 287
Old Quaker Paint Company, 13 471
Old Republic International Corporation, 11 373–75; 58 258–61 (upd.)
Old Spaghetti Factory International Inc., 24 364–66
Old Stone Trust Company, 13 468
Oldach Window Corp., 19 446
Oldcastle, Inc., 60 77; 64 98

Oldover Corp., 23 225
Ole's Innovative Sports. See Rollerblade, Inc.
Olean Tile Co., 22 170
Oleochim, IV 498–99
OLEX. See Deutsche BP Aktiengesellschaft.
Olex Cables Ltd., 10 445
Olin Corporation, I 379–81; IV 482; 8 23; 11 420; 13 379–81 (upd.); 16 68, 297; 32 319; 63 8
Olinkraft, Inc., 11 420; 16 376
Olive Garden Italian Restaurants, 10 322, 324; 16 156–58; 19 258; 35 83
Oliver Rubber Company, 19 454, 456
Olivetti S.p.A., 34 316–20 (upd.); 38 300; 63 379
Olivine Industries, Inc., II 508; 11 172; 36 255
Olmstead Products Co., 23 82
OLN. See Outdoor Life Network.
Olsten Corporation, 6 41–43; 9 327; 29 362–65 (upd.); 49 265. See also Adecco S.A.
Olympia & York Developments Ltd., IV 720–21; 6 478; 8 327; 9 390–92 (upd.); 30 108
Olympia Arenas, Inc., 7 278–79; 24 294
Olympia Brewing, 11 50
Olympia Entertainment, 37 207
Olympiaki, III 401
Olympic Courier Systems, Inc., 24 126
Olympic Fastening Systems, III 722
Olympic Insurance Co., 26 486
Olympic Packaging, 13 443
Olympus Communications L.P., 17 7
Olympus Optical Company, Ltd., 15 483
Olympus Partners, 65 258
Olympus Sport. See Sears plc.
Olympus Symbol, Inc., 15 483
OM Group, Inc., 17 362–64
OM Gruppen, 59 154
Omaha Public Power District, 29 353
Omaha Steaks International Inc., 62 257–59
Omega Gas Company, 8 349
Omega Protein Corporation, 25 546
OmegaTech Inc. See Martek Biosciences Corporation.
O'Melveny & Myers, 37 290–93
OMI Corporation, IV 34; 9 111–12; 22 275; 59 321–23
Omnes, 17 419
Omni ApS, 56 338
Omni Construction Company, Inc., 8 112–13
Omni Hotels Corp., 12 367–69
Omni-Pac, 12 377
Omni Services, Inc., 51 76
Omnibus Corporation, 9 283
Omnicad Corporation, 48 75
Omnicare, Inc., 13 150; 49 307–10
Omnicom Group Inc., I 28–32, 33, 36; 14 160; 22 394–99 (upd.); 23 478; 43 410; 64 73, 350. See also TBWA Worldwide.
Omnipoint Communications Inc., 18 77
OmniSource Corporation, 14 366–67
OmniTech Consulting Group, 51 99
Omnitel Pronto Italia SpA, 38 300
OMNOVA Solutions Inc., 59 324–26
Omron Corporation, 28 331–35 (upd.); 53 46

Omron Tateisi Electronics Company, II 75–77
ÖMV Aktiengesellschaft, IV 485–87
On Assignment, Inc., 20 400–02
On Command Video Corp., 23 135
On Cue, 9 360
On-Line Systems. See Sierra On-Line Inc.
Onan Corporation, 8 72
Onbancorp Inc., 11 110
Once Upon A Child, Inc., 18 207–8
Ondulato Imolese, IV 296; 19 226
1-800-FLOWERS, Inc., 26 344–46; 28 137
1-800-Mattress. See Dial-A-Mattress Operating Corporation.
180s, L.L.C., 64 299–301
One For All, 39 405
One Price Clothing Stores, Inc., 20 403–05
O'Neal, Jones & Feldman Inc., 11 142
OneBeacon Insurance Group LLC, 48 431
Oneida Bank & Trust Company, 9 229
Oneida County Creameries Co., 7 202
Oneida Gas Company, 9 554
Oneida Ltd., 7 406–08; 31 352–55 (upd.)
ONEOK Inc., 7 409–12
Onex Corporation, 16 395–97; 22 513; 24 498; 25 282; 50 275; 65 281–85 (upd.)
OneZero Media, Inc., 31 240
Onitsuka Co., Ltd., 57 52
Online Financial Communication Systems, 11 112
Only One Dollar, Inc. See Dollar Tree Stores, Inc.
Onoda Cement Co., Ltd., III 717–19. See also Taiheiyo Cement Corporation.
Onomichi, 25 469
OnResponse.com, Inc., 49 433
Onsale Inc., 31 177
Onstead Foods, 21 501
OnTarget Inc., 38 432
Ontario Hydro Services Company, 6 541–42; 9 461; 32 368–71 (upd.)
Ontario Power Generation, 49 65, 67
Ontario Teachers' Pension Plan, 61 273–75
OnTrack Data International, 57 219
OnTrak Systems Inc., 31 301
Onyx Acceptance Corporation, 59 327–29
Onyx Software Corporation, 53 252–55
O'okiep Copper Company, Ltd., 7 385–86
Opel AG. See Adam Opel AG.
Open Board of Brokers, 9 369
Open Cellular Systems, Inc., 41 225–26
Open Market, Inc., 22 522
OpenTV, Inc., 31 330–31
Operadora de Bolsa Serfin. See Grupo Financiero Serfin, S.A.
Operon Technologies Inc., 39 335
Opinion Research Corporation, 35 47; 46 318–22
Opp and Micolas Mills, 15 247–48
Oppenheimer. See Ernest Oppenheimer and Sons.
Oppenheimer & Co., Inc., 17 137; 21 235; 22 405; 25 450; 61 50
Opryland USA, 11 152–53; 25 403; 36 229
Opsware Inc., 49 311–14
Optel Corp., 17 331
OPTi Computer, 9 116
Opti-Ray, Inc., 12 215

Optical Corporation. *See* Excel Technology, Inc.
Optical Radiation Corporation, **27** 57
Optilink Corporation, **12** 137
Optima Pharmacy Services, **17** 177
Option Care Inc., 48 307–10
Optische Werke G. Rodenstock, 44 319–23
OptiSystems Solutions Ltd., **55** 67
Opto-Electronics Corp., **15** 483
Optus Communications, **25** 102
Optus Vision, **17** 150
Opus Group, 34 321–23
Oracle Corporation, 6 272–74; **10** 361, 363, 505; **11** 78; **13** 483; **14** 16; **15** 492; **18** 541, 543; **19** 310; **21** 86; **22** 154, 293; **24 367–71 (upd.)**; **25** 34, 96–97, 499; **67 282–87 (upd.)**
Orange and Rockland Utilities, Inc., **45** 116, 120
Orange Glo International, 53 256–59
Orange Julius of America, **10** 371, 373; **39** 232, 235
Orange Line Bus Company, **6** 604
Orange PLC, **24** 89; **38** 300
Orange Shipbuilding Company, Inc., **58** 70
Orb Books. *See* Tom Doherty Associates Inc.
Orb Estates, **54** 366, 368
ORBIS Corporation, **59** 289
Orbis Entertainment Co., **20** 6
Orbis Graphic Arts. *See* Anaheim Imaging.
Orbital Engine Corporation Ltd., **17** 24
Orbital Sciences Corporation, 22 400–03
Orbitz, Inc., 61 276–78
Orchard Supply Hardware Stores Corporation, 17 365–67; 25 535
Orchid Biosciences Inc., **57** 309, 311
Orcofi, **III** 48
OrderTrust LLP, **26** 440
Ore-Ida Foods Incorporated, 12 531; **13 382–83**
Orebehoved Fanerfabrik, **25** 464
Oregon Ale and Beer Company, **18** 72; **50** 112
Oregon Chai, Inc., 49 315–17
Oregon Craft & Floral Supply, **17** 322
Oregon Cutting Systems, **26** 119
Oregon Dental Service Health Plan, Inc., 51 276–78
Oregon Metallurgical Corporation, 20 406–08
Oregon Pacific and Eastern Railway, **13** 100
Oregon Steel Mills, Inc., 14 368–70; 19 380
O'Reilly Automotive, Inc., 26 347–49
Orenda Aerospace, **48** 274
Organic Valley (Coulee Region Organic Produce Pool), 53 260–62
Organización Soriana, S.A. de C.V., 35 320–22
Organizacion Techint, **66** 293–95
Organon, **63** 141
ORI. *See* Old Republic International Corporation.
Orico Life Insurance Co., **48** 328
Oriel Foods, **II** 609
Orient, **21** 122
Orient Express Hotels Inc., **29** 429–30
Orient Leasing. *See* Orix Corporation.
Orient Overseas, **18** 254
Oriental Brewery Co., Ltd., **21** 320
Oriental Precision Company, **13** 213

Oriental Trading Corp., **22** 213
Oriental Yeast Co. *See* Nisshin Seifun Group Inc.
Origin Energy Limited, **43** 75. *See also* Boral Limited.
Origin Systems Inc., **10** 285
Origin Technology, **14** 183
Original Arizona Jean Company. *See* J.C. Penney Company, Inc.
Original Cookie Co., **13** 166. *See also* Mrs. Fields' Original Cookies, Inc.
Original Musical Instrument Company (O.M.I.), **16** 239
Origins Natural Resources Inc., **30** 190
Orion Capital Corporation, **55** 331
Orion Healthcare Ltd., **11** 168
Orion Personal Insurances Ltd., **11** 168
Orion Pictures Corporation, 6 167–70; **7** 336; **14** 330, 332; **25** 326, 328–29; **31** 100; **61** 212
Orit Corp., **8** 219–20
ORIX Corporation, II 442–43, 259, 348; **44 324–26 (upd.)**
Orkem, **IV** 560; **21** 205
Orkin Pest Control, **11** 431–32, 434
Orkla A/S, 18 394–98; 25 205–07; **36** 266
Orleans Homebuilders, Inc., 62 260–62
Orlimar Golf Equipment Co., **45** 76
Orm Bergold Chemie, **8** 464
Ormco Corporation, **14** 481
ÖROP, **IV** 485–86
Orowheat Baking Company, **10** 250
La Oroya, **22** 286
ORSCO, Inc., **26** 363
Ortho Diagnostic Systems, Inc., **10** 213; **22** 75
Ortho Pharmaceutical Corporation, **10** 79–80; **30** 59–60
Orthodontic Centers of America, Inc., 35 323–26
Orthopedic Services, Inc., **11** 366
Ortloff Engineers, Ltd., **52** 103–05
Orval Kent Food Company, Inc., **7** 430
Orville Redenbacher/Swiss Miss Foods Co., **17** 241
The Orvis Company, Inc., 28 336–39
Oryx Energy Company, 7 413–15
OSA Technologies. *See* Avocent Corporation.
Osaka Gas Company, Ltd., V 679–81; **60 233–36 (upd.)**
Osaka Shinyo Kumiai, **15** 495
Osaka Shosen Kaisha. *See* Mitsui O.S.K. Lines, Ltd.
Osborn Group Inc., **48** 256
Oscar Mayer Foods Corp., 12 123, 370–72
Osco Drug, **II** 604–05
OSF Japan Ltd., **24** 365
Oshawa Group Limited, II 649–50
OshKosh B'Gosh, Inc., 9 393–95; **42 266–70 (upd.)**
Oshkosh Electric Power, **9** 553
Oshkosh Gas Light Company, **9** 553
Oshkosh Truck Corporation, 7 416–18; **14** 458
Oshman's Sporting Goods, Inc., 16 560; **17** 368–70; **27** 7
OSi Specialties, Inc., **16** 543; **36** 148–49
Osiris Holding Company, **16** 344
OSK. *See* Osaka Shosen Kaisha.
Osmonics, Inc., 18 399–401
Oster. *See* Sunbeam-Oster.

Österreichische Brau-Beteiligungs AG. *See* BBAG Österreichische Brau-Beteiligungs AG.
Österreichische Bundesbahnen GmbH, 6 418–20
Österreichische Länderbank, **23** 37
Österreichische Luftverkehrs AG. *See* Austrian Airlines AG.
Österreichische Mineralölverwaltung AG, **IV** 485
Österreichische Post- und Telegraphenverwaltung, V 314–17
Ostrada Yachts, **55** 54, 56
Ostravar A.S., **38** 77
O'Sullivan Industries Holdings, Inc., 34 313–15
Osuuskunta Metsäliito, **IV** 316
Otagiri Mercantile Co., **11** 95
OTC, **10** 492
Other Options, **29** 400
Otis Company, **6** 579
Otis Elevator Company, Inc., 13 384–86; **27** 267, 268; **29** 422; **39 311–15 (upd.)**
Otis Spunkmeyer, Inc., 28 340–42
Otosan, **I** 479–80; **54** 196–97
OTP, Incorporated, **48** 446
OTR Express, Inc., 25 368–70
Otsego Falls Paper Company, **8** 358
Ott and Brewer Company, **12** 312
Ottakar's plc, 64 302–04
Ottawa Fruit Supply Ltd., **II** 662
Ottaway Newspapers, Inc., 15 335–37
Otter Tail Power Company, 18 402–05; **37** 282
Otter-Westelaken, **16** 420; **43** 308
Otto Bremer Foundation. *See* Bremer Financial Corp.
Otto-Epoka mbH, **15** 340
Otto Sumisho Inc., **V** 161
Otto Versand GmbH & Co., V 159–61; **10** 489–90; **15 338–40 (upd.)**; **27** 427, 429; **31** 188; **34 324–28 (upd.)**; **36** 177, 180
Ottumwa Daily Courier, **11** 251
Ourso Investment Corporation, **16** 344
Outback Steakhouse, Inc., 12 373–75; 34 329–32 (upd.)
Outboard Marine Corporation, III 597–600; **8** 71; **16** 383; **20 409–12 (upd.)**; **26** 494; **42** 45; **43** 287; **45** 174
Outdoor Channel, Inc. *See* Global Outdoors, Inc.
The Outdoor Group Limited, **39** 58, 60
Outdoor Research, Incorporated, 67 288–90
Outdoor Systems, Inc., 25 371–73; 27 278–80; **48** 217
Outdoor World. *See* Bass Pro Shops, Inc.
The Outdoorsman, Inc., **10** 216
Outlet Retail Stores, Inc., **27** 286
Outlook Group Corporation, 37 294–96
Outlook Window Partnership, **19** 446
Outokumpu Metals Group. *See* OM Group, Inc.
Outokumpu Oyj, 38 335–37
Outrigger Enterprises, Inc., 67 291–93
Ovation, **19** 285
Overhill Corporation, 10 382; **51 279–81**
Overland Energy Company, **14** 567
Overland Western Ltd., **27** 473
Overnite Corporation, 58 262–65 (upd.)
Overnite Transportation Co., 14 371–73; **28** 492

Overseas-Chinese Banking Corporation, **56** 363

Overseas Containers Ltd., **6** 398, 415–16

Overseas Insurance Corporation, **58** 272

Overseas Shipholding Group, Inc., 11 376–77

Overseas Telecommunications, Inc., **27** 304

Overseas Union Bank, **56** 362–63

Ovox Fitness Clubs, **46** 432

Owen Healthcare, **50** 122

Owen Owen, **37** 8

Owen Steel Co. Inc., **15** 117

Owens & Minor, Inc., 10 143; **16 398–401**

Owens Corning Corporation, III 720–23; 8 177; **13** 169; **20 413–17 (upd.); 25** 535; **30** 283; **35** 98–99; **44** 127

Owens Country Sausage, Inc., **63** 69–70

Owens-Illinois Inc., I 609–11, 615; **III** 720–21; **IV** 343; **16** 123; **22** 254; **24** 92; **26 350–53 (upd.); 42** 438; **43** 188; **49** 253

Owensboro Municipal Utilities, **11** 37

Owosso Corporation, 29 366–68

Oxdon Investments, **II** 664

Oxfam America, **13** 13

Oxford-AnsCo Development Co., **12** 18

Oxford Bus Company, **28** 155–56

Oxford Financial Group, **22** 456

Oxford Health Plans, Inc., 16 402–04

Oxford Industries, Inc., 8 406–08; 24 158

Oxford Learning Centres, **34** 105

Oxford Paper Co., **10** 289

Oxford Realty Financial Group, Inc., **49** 26

Oxford University Press, **23** 211

Oxirane Chemical Corporation, **64** 35

OXO International, **16** 234

Oxycal Laboratories Inc., **46** 466

OxyChem, **11** 160

Oxygen Media Inc., **28** 175; **51** 220

Ozark Automotive Distributors, **26** 347–48

Ozark Utility Company, **6** 593; **50** 38

OZM. *See* OneZero Media, Inc.

P&C Foods Inc., 8 409–11; 13 95, 394

P&C Groep N.V., **46** 344

P & F Industries, Inc., 45 327–29

P&F Technologies Ltd., **26** 363

P&G. *See* Procter & Gamble Company.

P&L Coal Holdings Corporation, **45** 333

P & M Manufacturing Company, **8** 386

P & O. *See* Peninsular & Oriental Steam Navigation Company.

P&O Nedlloyd, **26** 241, 243

P.A. Bergner & Company, **9** 142; **15** 87–88

P.A. Geier Company. *See* Royal Appliance Manufacturing Company.

P.A.J.W. Corporation, **9** 111–12

P.A. Rentrop-Hubbert & Wagner Fahrzeugausstattungen GmbH, **III** 582

P.C. Richard & Son Corp., 23 372–74

P.D. Associated Collieries Ltd., **31** 369

P.D. Kadi International, **I** 580

P.E.C. Israel Economic Corporation, **24** 429

P.F. Chang's China Bistro, Inc., 37 297–99

P.G. Realty, **III** 340

P.H. Glatfelter Company, 8 412–14; 30 349–52 (upd.)

P.Ink Press, **24** 430

P.R. Mallory, **9** 179

P.S.L. Food Market, Inc., **22** 549

P.T. Asurasi Tokio Marine Indonesia, **64** 280

P.T. Bridgeport Perkasa Machine Tools, **17** 54

P.T. Darya-Varia Laboratoria, **18** 180

P.T. Gaya Motor, **23** 290

P.T. Indomobil Suzuki International, **59** 393, 397

P.T. Samick Indonesia, **56** 300

P.T. Unitex, **53** 344

P.V. Doyle Hotels Ltd., **64** 217

P.W. Huntington & Company, **11** 180

P.W.J. Surridge & Sons, Ltd., **43** 132

Paaco Automotive Group, **64** 20

Pabst Brewing Company, **I** 255; **10** 99; **18** 502; **50** 114

Pac-Am Food Concepts, **10** 178; **38** 102

Pac-Fab, Inc., **18** 161

PAC Insurance Services, **12** 175; **27** 258

PACCAR Inc., I 185–86; 10 280; **26 354–56 (upd.); 40** 135

The Pace Consultants, Inc. *See* Jacobs Engineering Group Inc.

PACE Entertainment Corp., **36** 423–24

Pace Express Pty. Ltd., **13** 20

Pace Foods Ltd., **26** 58

Pace Management Service Corp., **21** 91

PACE Membership Warehouse, Inc. *See* Kmart Corporation.

Pace Pharmaceuticals, **16** 439

Pacemaker Plastics, Inc., **7** 296

Pacer International, Inc., 54 274–76

Pacer Technology, 40 347–49

Pacer Tool and Mold, **17** 310

Pacific Advantage, **43** 253

Pacific Air Freight, Incorporated. *See* Airborne Freight Corp.

Pacific Air Transport, **9** 416

Pacific Alaska Fuel Services, **6** 383

Pacific and European Telegraph Company, **25** 99

Pacific Bell. *See* SBC Communications.

Pacific Car & Foundry Company. *See* PACCAR Inc.

Pacific Coast Feather Company, 67 209, **294–96**

Pacific Communication Sciences, **11** 57

Pacific Destination Services, **62** 276

Pacific Dry Dock and Repair Co., **6** 382

Pacific Dunlop Limited, 10 444–46. *See* *also* Ansell Ltd.

Pacific Electric Light Company, **6** 565; **50** 365

Pacific Enterprises, V 682–84; 12 477. *See also* Sempra Energy.

Pacific Finance Corp., **9** 536; **13** 529; **26** 486

Pacific Forest Products Ltd., **59** 162

Pacific Fur Company, **25** 220

Pacific Gamble Robinson, **9** 39

Pacific Gas and Electric Company, V 685–87; 11 270; **12** 100, 106; **19** 411; **25** 415. *See also* PG&E Corporation.

Pacific Glass Corp., **48** 42

Pacific Guardian Life Insurance Co., **III** 289

Pacific Home Furnishings, **14** 436

Pacific Indemnity Corp., **III** 220; **14** 108, 110; **16** 204

Pacific Integrated Healthcare, **53** 7

Pacific Lighting Corp. *See* Sempra Energy.

Pacific Linens, **13** 81–82

Pacific Link Communication, **18** 180

Pacific Lumber Company, **III** 254; **8** 348–50

Pacific Magazines and Printing, **7** 392

Pacific Mail Steamship Company. *See* APL Limited.

Pacific Media K.K., **18** 101

Pacific Monolothics Inc., **11** 520

Pacific National Insurance Co. *See* TIG Holdings, Inc.

Pacific Natural Gas Corp., **9** 102

Pacific Northwest Laboratories, **10** 139

Pacific Northwest Pipeline Corporation, **9** 102–104, 540; **12** 144

Pacific Northwest Power Company, **6** 597

Pacific Petroleums Ltd., **9** 102

Pacific Plastics, Inc., **48** 334

Pacific Power & Light Company. *See* PacifiCorp.

Pacific Pride Bakeries, **19** 192

Pacific Recycling Co. Inc., **IV** 296; **19** 226; **23** 225

Pacific Resources Inc., **IV** 47; **22** 107

Pacific Sentinel Gold Corp., **27** 456

Pacific/Southern Wine & Spirits, **48** 392

Pacific Stock Exchange, **48** 226

Pacific Sunwear of California, Inc., 28 343–45; 47 425

Pacific Telecom, Inc., 6 325–28; 25 101; **54** 62

Pacific Telesis Group, V 318–20; 6 324; **9** 321; **11** 10–11; **14** 345, 347; **15** 125; **25** 499; **26** 520; **29** 387; **47** 318. *See also* SBC Communications.

Pacific Teletronics, Inc., **7** 15

Pacific Towboat. *See* Puget Sound Tug and Barge Company.

Pacific Trail Inc., **17** 462; **29** 293, 295–96

Pacific Western Extruded Plastics Company, **17** 441. *See also* PW Eagle Inc.

Pacific Wine Co., **18** 71; **50** 112

PacifiCare Health Systems, Inc., 11 378–80

PacifiCorp, Inc., V 688–90; 7 376–78; **26 357–60 (upd.); 27** 327, 483, 485; **32** 372; **49** 363, 366

Package Products Company, Inc., **12** 150

Packaged Ice, Inc., **21** 338; **26** 449

Packaging Corporation of America, 12 376–78, 397; **16** 191; **51 282–85 (upd.)**

Packard Bell Electronics, Inc., 10 564; **11** 413; **13 387–89**, 483; **21** 391; **23** 471; **57** 263

Packard Motor Co., **8** 74; **9** 17

Packerland Packing Company, **7** 199, 201

Pacolet Manufacturing Company, **17** 327

Pact, **50** 175

PacTel. *See* Pacific Telesis Group.

Paddock Publications, Inc., 53 263–65

PAFS. *See* Pacific Alaska Fuel Services.

Page, Bacon & Co., **12** 533

Page Boy Inc., **9** 320

Page Plus NV. *See* Punch International N.V.

PageAhead Software, **15** 492

Pageland Coca-Cola Bottling Works, **10** 222

PageMart Wireless, Inc., **18** 164, 166

Paging Network Inc., 11 381–83; 39 24–25; **41** 266–67

Pagoda Trading Company, Inc. *See* Brown Group, Inc.

Paid Prescriptions, **9** 346

Paige Publications, **18** 66
PaineWebber Group Inc., II 444–46,
    449; **13** 449; **22** 352, **404–07 (upd.),**
    542; **25** 433
Painter Carpet Mills, **13** 169
PairGain Technologies, **36** 299
Paisley Products, **32** 255
La Paix, **III** 273
Pak-a-Sak, **II** 661
Pak Mail Centers, **18** 316
Pak Sak Industries, **17** 310; **24** 160
Pakhoed Holding, N.V., **9** 532; **26** 420; **41**
    339–40
Pakistan International Airlines
    Corporation, 46 323–26
Pakkasakku Oy, **IV** 471
Paknet, **11** 548
Pakway Container Corporation, **8** 268
PAL. *See* Philippine Airlines, Inc.
Palace Station Hotel & Casino. *See* Station
    Casinos Inc.
Paladar, **56** 116
Palais Royal, Inc., **24** 456
Palazzo Feroni Finanziaria SpA, **62** 313
Palco Industries, **19** 440
Pale Ski & Sports GmbH, **22** 461
Palestine Coca-Cola Bottling Co., **13** 163
The Palestine Post Limited, **62** 188
PALIC. *See* Pan-American Life Insurance
    Company.
Pall Corporation, 9 396–98
Pallas Textiles, **57** 207, 209
Palm Beach Holdings, **9** 157
Palm Harbor Homes, Inc., 39 316–18
Palm, Inc., 34 441, 445; **36 355–57; 38**
    433; **49** 184; **54** 312
Palm Shipping Inc., **25** 468–70
Palmafina, **IV** 498–99
Palmax, **47** 153
Palmer Communications, **25** 418
Palmer G. Lewis Co., **8** 135
Palmolive Co. *See* Colgate-Palmolive
    Company.
Palo Alto Brewing, **22** 421
Palo Alto Products International, Inc., **29** 6
Palo Alto Research Center, **10** 510
Palomar Medical Technologies, Inc., 22
    408–10; 31 124
PAM Group, **27** 462
Pamida Holdings Corporation, 15
    341–43; 58 331
Pampa OTT, **27** 473
The Pampered Chef, Ltd., 18 406–08
Pamplemousse, **14** 225
Pamplin Corp. *See* R.B. Pamplin Corp.
Pan-Alberta Gas Ltd., **16** 11
Pan-American Life Insurance Company,
    48 311–13
Pan American World Airways, Inc., I
    103–04, 112–13, **115–16,** 121, 124,
    126, 129, 132, 248, 530; **9** 231, 417; **10**
    561; **11** 266; **12** 191, **379–81 (upd.),**
    419; **13** 19; **14** 73; **29** 189; **36** 52–53
Pan Asia Paper Company Ltd., **63** 314–16
Pan European Publishing Co., **IV** 611
Pan Geo Atlas Corporation, **18** 513
Pan Pacific Fisheries, **24** 114
PanAgora Asset Management Inc., **60** 220
Panalpina World Transport (Holding)
    Ltd., 47 286–88; 49 81–82
Panamerican Beverages, Inc., 47 289–91;
    54 74
PanAmSat Corporation, 18 211, 213; **46**
    327–29; 54 157

Panasonic, **9** 180; **10** 125; **12** 470; **43** 427
Panavia Aircraft GmbH, **24** 84, 86–87
Panavision Inc., 24 372–74; 28 249; **38**
    295
PanCanadian Petroleum Ltd., **27** 217; **45**
    80
Pancho's Mexican Buffet, Inc., 46
    330–32
Panda Management Company, Inc., 35
    327–29
Pandair, **13** 20
Pandel, Inc., **8** 271
Pandick Press Inc., **23** 63
PanEnergy Corporation, **27** 128, 131
Panera Bread Company, 44 186, **327–29**
Panerai, **27** 489
Panhandle Eastern Corporation, IV 425;
    V 691–92; 10 82–84; **11** 28; **14** 135; **17**
    21. *See also* CMS Energy Corp.
Panhandle Oil Corp., **IV** 498
Panhandle Power & Light Company, **6** 580
Panificadora Bimbo, **19** 191
Pannill Knitting Company, **13** 531
Panocean Storage & Transport, **6** 415, 417
Panola Pipeline Co., **7** 228
Panosh Place, **12** 168
Pansophic Systems Inc., **64** 361
Pantera Energy Corporation, **11** 27
Pantheon Books, **13** 429; **31** 376
Panther, **III** 750
Pantone Inc., 53 266–69
The Pantry, Inc., 36 358–60
Pantry Pride Inc., **I** 668; **II** 670, 674; **23**
    407–08
Pants Corral, **II** 634
Papa Aldo's Pizza. *See* Papa Murphy's
    International, Inc.
Papa John's International, Inc., 15
    344–46; 16 447; **24** 295; **63** 133, 138
Papa Murphy's International, Inc., 54
    277–79
Pape and Co., Ltd., **10** 441
Papelera del Besos, **53** 24
Papelera General, S.A. de C.V., **39** 188
Papeleria Calparsoro S.A., **IV** 325
Papeles Venezolanos C.A., **17** 281
Paper Direct, **37** 107–08
The Paper Factory of Wisconsin, Inc., **12**
    209
Paper Magic Group, **35** 130–31
Paper Software, Inc., **15** 322
Paper Stock Dealers, Inc., **8** 476
PaperMate, **23** 54
Paperwork Data-Comm Services Inc., **11**
    64
Papeteries de Golbey SA, **63** 315
Les Papeteries de la Chapelle-Darblay, **IV**
    337
Papeteries de Lancey, 23 366–68
Papeteries de Malaucene S.A.S., **52**
    300–01
Les Papeteries du Limousin, **19** 227
Papetti's Hygrade Egg Products, Inc., 25
    332–33; **39 319–21**
Papierfabrik Fahrbrucke GmbH, **64** 275
Papierwaren Fleischer, **IV** 325
Papierwerke Waldhof-Aschaffenburg AG.
    See PWA Group
Papyrus Design Group, **15** 455
Par Pharmaceutical Companies, Inc., 65
    286–88
Para-Med Health Services. *See* Extendicare
    Health Services, Inc.
Parachute Press, **29** 426

ParaData Financial Systems, Inc., **57** 416
Parade Gasoline Co., **7** 228
Paradigm Entertainment, **35** 227
Paradise Creations, **29** 373
Paradise Island Resort and Casino. *See* Sun
    International Hotels Limited.
Paradise Music & Entertainment, Inc.,
    42 271–74
Paradyne, **22** 19
Paragon Communications, **44** 372
Paragon Corporate Holdings, Inc., **28** 6, 8
Paragon Vineyard Company, **36** 114
Paragren Technologies Inc., **38** 432
Parallax Software Inc., **38** 70
Parametric Integrated Circuits Inc., **63** 33
Parametric Technology Corp., 16
    405–07
Parametrics Corp., **25** 134
Paramount Communications Inc., **16** 338;
    19 403–04; **28** 296
Paramount Fire Insurance Co., **26** 486
Paramount Oil Company, **18** 467
Paramount Paper Products, **8** 383
Paramount Pictures Corporation, II
    154–56; IV 671–72, 675; **7** 528; **9** 119,
    428–29; **10** 175; **12** 73, 323; **19** 404; **21**
    23–25; **23** 503; **24** 327; **25** 88, 311,
    327–29, 418; **31** 99; **35** 279. *See also*
    Viacom Inc.
Parashop SA, **48** 279
Parasitix Corporation. *See* Mycogen
    Corporation.
Parasole Restaurant Holdings, Inc., **38** 117
Paravant Inc., **58** 101
Paravision International, **III** 48; **8** 343
PARCO Co., Ltd. *See* Seibu Department
    Stores, Ltd.
Parents and Children Together, Inc., **64**
    311
ParentWatch, **34** 105
Parfums Chanel, **12** 57
Parfums Rochas S.A. *See* Wella AG.
Pargas, **I** 378
Paribas. *See* Banque de Paris et des Pays-
    Bas, BNP Paribas Group; Compagnie
    Financiere de Paribas.
Paridoc and Giant, **12** 153
Paris Bourse, **34** 13
Paris Corporation, 22 411–13
Paris Group, **17** 137
Paris Playground Equipment, **13** 319
Parisian, Inc., 14 374–76; 19 324–25; **41**
    343–44
Park Acquisitions, Inc., **38** 308
Park-Brannock Shoe Company, **48** 69
Park Consolidated Motels, Inc., **14** 105
Park Corp., 22 414–16
Park Drop Forge Co. *See* Park-Ohio
    Industries Inc.
Park Hall Leisure, **II** 140; **24** 194
Park Inn International, **11** 178
Park-Ohio Industries Inc., 17 371–73
Park Ridge Corporation, **9** 284
Park Tower Hotel Co. Ltd., **55** 375
Parkdale State Bank, **25** 114
Parke-Bernet, **11** 453
Parke, Davis & Co. *See* Warner-Lambert
    Co.
Parker Brothers, **16** 337; **21** 375; **25** 489
Parker Drilling Company, 28 346–48
Parker Drilling Company of Canada, **9** 363
Parker-Hannifin Corporation, III
    601–03; 21 108; **24 375–78 (upd.)**
Parker Lancasters & Orleans, Inc., **62** 262

Parker Pattern Works Co., **46** 293
Parker's Pharmacy, Inc., **15** 524
Parks-Belk Co., **19** 324
Parks Box & Printing Co., **13** 442
Parkway Distributors, **17** 331
Parlex Corporation, 61 279–81
Parmalat Finanziaria SpA, 50 343–46
Parson and Hyman Co., Inc., **8** 112
Parsons Brinckerhoff, Inc., 34 333–36
The Parsons Corporation, 8 415–17; 56 263–67 (upd.)
Parsons International Trading Business, **27** 195
Parsons Place Apparel Company, **8** 289
Partech, **28** 346, 348
Partek Corporation, **11** 312; **52** 250
Parthénon, **27** 10
Participating Annuity Life Insurance Co., **21** 14
Partlow Corporation, **7** 116
Partouche SA. *See* Groupe Partouche SA.
Parts Plus, **26** 348
Party City Corporation, 54 280–82
PartyLite Gifts, Inc., **18** 67, 69
Pascagoula Lumber Company, **28** 306
Pascale & Associates, **12** 476
Pasha Pillows, **12** 393
Pasminco, **IV** 61
Pasqua Inc., **28** 64
Pasquier Nutrition, **58** 46
Pass & Seymour, **21** 348–49
Passive Power Products, Inc., **32** 41
Pasta Central, **49** 60
Patagonia, **16** 352; **18** 376; **21** 193; **25** 206. *See also* Lost Arrow Inc.
Patak Spices Ltd., **18** 247
Patch Rubber Co., **19** 277–78
Patchoque-Plymouth Co., **IV** 371
PATCO. *See* Philippine Airlines, Inc.
Patent Arms Manufacturing Company, **12** 70
Paterno Wines International, **48** 392
Paternoster Stores plc. *See* Kingfisher plc; Woolworth Corporation.
Paterson Candy Ltd., **22** 89
Pâtes Papiers et Textilose. *See* Matussière et Forest SA.
Pathe Communications Co., **IV** 676; **7** 529; **25** 329
Pathé SA, 29 369–71. *See also* Chargeurs International.
Pathfinder Pubs, **57** 411
Pathmark Stores, Inc., II 672–74; **9** 173; **15** 260; **18** 6; **19** 479, 481; **23** 369–71; **33** 436
PathoGenesis Corporation, **36** 119
Patient Care, Inc., **13** 150
Patil Systems, **11** 56
Patina Group. *See* Restaurant Associates Corporation.
Patina Oil & Gas Corporation, 24 379–81
Patino N.V., **17** 380
Pâtisserie Pasquier, **58** 46
Patrick Industries, Inc., 30 342–45
Patrick Raulet, S.A., **36** 164
Patricof & Company, **24** 45
Patriot American Hospitality, Inc., **21** 184
PATS Inc., **36** 159
Patterson Dental Co., 19 289–91
Patterson Industries, Inc., **14** 42
Patterson Pump Company, **57** 159–60
Patterson-UTI Energy, Inc., 55 293–95
Patton Electric Company, Inc., **19** 360

Patton Paint Company. *See* PPG Industries, Inc.
Paul A. Brands, **11** 19
Paul Andra KG, **33** 393
Paul Boechat & Cie, **21** 515
Paul C. Dodge Company, **6** 579
Paul Davril, Inc., **25** 258
Paul H. Rose Corporation, **13** 445
Paul Harris Stores, Inc., 15 245; **18** 409–12
Paul, Hastings, Janofsky & Walker LLP, 27 357–59
Paul Koss Supply Co., **16** 387
Paul Marshall Products Inc., **16** 36
Paul Mueller Company, 65 289–91
Paul Ramsay Group, **41** 323
The Paul Revere Corporation, 12 382–83; 52 379
Paul Revere Insurance, **34** 433
Paul-Son Gaming Corporation, 66 249–51
Paul Wahl & Co., **IV** 277
Paul, Weiss, Rifkind, Wharton & Garrison, 47 292–94
Paulaner Brauerei GmbH & Co. KG, 35 330–33
Pauls Plc, **III** 699
Pavallier, **18** 35
Pavex Construction Company. *See* Granite Rock Company.
Pawnee Industries, Inc., **19** 415
Paxall, Inc., **8** 545
Paxson Communications Corporation, 33 322–26
Pay 'N Pak Stores, Inc., 9 399–401; 16 186–88
Pay 'n Save Corp., **12** 477; **15** 274; **17** 366
Pay Less, **II** 601, 604
Paychex, Inc., 15 347–49; 46 333 36 (upd.)
PayConnect Solutions, **47** 39
Payless Cashways, Inc., 11 384–86; 13 274; **44 330–33 (upd.)**
Payless DIY. *See* The Boots Company PLC.
PayLess Drug Stores, **12** 477–78; **18** 286; **22** 39
Payless ShoeSource, Inc., 13 361; **18** 413–15; **26** 441
PayPal Inc., 58 266–69
PBF Corp. *See* Paris Corporation.
PBL. *See* Publishing and Broadcasting Ltd.
PBS. *See* Public Broadcasting Stations.
PC Connection, Inc., 37 300–04
PC Globe, Inc., **13** 114
PC Home Publishing, **61** 246
PC Realty, Canada Ltd., **III** 340
PCA. *See* Packaging Corporation of America.
PCA-Budafok Paperboard Ltd., **12** 377
PCA International, Inc., 62 263–65
PCAS. *See* Dynaction S.A.
pcBoat.com, **37** 398
PCI Acquisition, **11** 385
PCI NewCo Inc., **36** 159
PCI Services, Inc. *See* Cardinal Health, Inc.
PCL Construction Group Inc., 50 347–49
PCL Industries Ltd., **IV** 296; **19** 226
PCM Uitgevers NV, 53 270–73
PCO. *See* Corning Inc.
PCS. *See* Potash Corp. of Saskatchewan Inc.

PCS Health Systems Inc., **12** 333; **47** 115, 235–36
PCX. *See* Pacific Stock Exchange.
PDA Engineering, **25** 305
PDA Inc., **19** 290
PDI, Inc., 49 25; 52 272–75
PDO. *See* Petroleum Development Oman.
PDQ Machine, **58** 75
PDQ Transportation Inc., **18** 226
PDS Gaming Corporation, 44 334–37
PDV America, Inc., **31** 113
PDVSA. *See* Petróleos de Venezuela S.A.
Peabody Coal Company, IV 47, 576; **7** 387–88; **10 447–49**
Peabody Energy Corporation, 45 330–33 (upd.)
Peabody Holding Company, Inc., IV 19, 169–72; **6** 487; **7** 209
Peace Arch Entertainment Group Inc., 51 286–88
Peaches Entertainment Corporation, **24** 502
Peachtree Doors, **10** 95
Peachtree Federal Savings and Loan Association of Atlanta, **10** 92
Peachtree Software Inc., **18** 364
Peak Audio Inc., **48** 92
Peak Oilfield Service Company, **9** 364
The Peak Technologies Group, Inc., 14 377–80
Peapod, Inc., 22 522; **30 346–48**
Pearce-Uible Co., **14** 460
Pearl Health Services, **I** 249
Pearle Vision, Inc., 12 188; **13 390–92; 14** 214; **23** 329; **24** 140; **34** 179
Pearson plc, IV 611, 652, **657–59; 14** 414; **25** 283, 285; **32** 355; **38** 402; **46 337–41 (upd.)**
Peasant Restaurants Inc., **30** 330
Pease Industries, **39** 322, 324
Peat Marwick. *See* KPMG Peat Marwick.
Peavey Electronics Corporation, 16 408–10
Peavey Paper Mills, Inc., **26** 362
PEC Plastics, **9** 92
Pechenganickel MMC, **48** 300
Pechiney S.A., IV 173–75; **12** 253–54; **26** 403; **45 334–37 (upd.)**
PECO Energy Company, 11 387–90. *See also* Exelon Corporation.
Pediatric Services of America, Inc., 31 356–58
Pediatrix Medical Group, Inc., 61 282–85
Pedigree Petfoods, **22** 298
Peebles Inc., 16 411–13; 43 296–99 (upd.)
Peek & Cloppenburg KG, 46 342–45
Peekskill Chemical Works. *See* Binney & Smith Inc.
Peel-Conner Telephone Works, **II** 24
Peerless, **8** 74; **11** 534
Peerless Gear & Machine Company, **8** 515
Peerless Spinning Corporation, **13** 532
Peerless Systems, Inc., **17** 263
Peet's Coffee & Tea, Inc., 13 493; **18** 37; **38 338–40**
PEI. *See* Process Engineering Inc.
Pei Cobb Freed & Partners Architects LLP, 57 280–82
Peko-Wallsend Ltd., **13** 97
Pelican Homestead and Savings, **11** 107
Pelikan Holding AG, **18** 388
Pella Corporation, 10 95; **12 384–86; 22** 346; **39 322–25 (upd.)**

Pelmorex, Inc., **52** 402
Pelto Oil Corporation, **14** 455; **44** 362
PEM International Ltd., **28** 350
Pemco Aviation Group Inc., 54 283–86
Pemex. *See* Petróleos Mexicanos.
Pen Computing Group, **49** 10
Penaflor S.A., 66 252–54
Penauille Polyservices SA, 49 318–21
Penda Corp., **19** 415
Pendaflex. *See* Esselte.
Pendle Travel Services Ltd. *See* Airtours Plc.
Pendleton Grain Growers Inc., 64 305–08
Pendleton Woolen Mills, Inc., 42 275–78
Penford Corporation, 55 296–99
Pengrowth Gas Corp., **25** 232
The Penguin Group, **46** 337
Penguin Publishing Co. Ltd., **IV** 659
Penhaligon's, **24** 237
Peninsula Stores, Ltd. *See* Lucky Stores, Inc.
The Peninsular and Oriental Steam Navigation Company, V 490–93; 22 444; **26** 241, 243; **37** 137; **38 341–46 (upd.)**
Peninsular and Oriental Steam Navigation Company (Bovis Division), I 588–89
Peninsular Power, **6** 602
Peninsular Railroad Company, **17** 440
Penn Advertising, **27** 280
Penn Central Corp., **II** 255; **10** 71, 73, 547; **17** 443
Penn Champ Co., **9** 72
Penn Corp., **13** 561
Penn Cress Ice Cream, **13** 393
Penn Engineering & Manufacturing Corp., 28 349–51
Penn National Gaming, Inc., 33 327–29
Penn Traffic Company, 8 409–10; 13 95, 393–95
Penn-Western Gas and Electric, **6** 524
Pennaco Hosiery, Inc., **12** 93; **62 89–91**
PennEnergy, **55** 302
Penney's. *See* J.C. Penney Company, Inc.
Pennington Seed, Inc. of Delaware, **58** 60
Pennon Group Plc, 45 338–41
Pennsy Supply, Inc., **64** 98
Pennsylvania Blue Shield, III 325–27. *See also* Highmark Inc.
Pennsylvania Electric Company, **6** 535; **27** 182
Pennsylvania Farm Bureau Cooperative Association, **7** 17–18
Pennsylvania Gas and Water Company, **38** 51
Pennsylvania General Insurance Company, **48** 431
Pennsylvania House, Inc., **10** 324; **12** 301
Pennsylvania International Raceway. *See* Penske Corporation.
Pennsylvania Life Insurance Company, **27** 47
Pennsylvania Power & Light Company, V 693–94; 11 388
Pennsylvania Pump and Compressor Co., **II** 16
Pennsylvania Railroad, **6** 436; **10** 71–73; **26** 295
Pennsylvania Steel Foundry and Machine Co., **39** 32
Pennsylvania Water & Power Company, **25** 44

Pennwalt Corporation, I 382–84; 12 18; **21** 205
PennWell Corporation, 55 300–03
Penny Curtiss Baking Co., Inc., **13** 395
Pennzoil Company, IV 488–90, 551, 553; **10** 190; **14** 491, 493; **20 418–22 (upd.);** **23** 40–41; **25** 443, 445; **39** 330; **41** 391, 394; **47** 436
Pennzoil-Quaker State Company, 49 343; **50 350–55 (upd.)**
Penrod Drilling Corporation, **7** 228, 558
Pension Benefit Guaranty Corp., **III** 255; **12** 489
Penske Corporation, V 494–95; 19 223, **292–94 (upd.); 20** 263
Penske Motorsports, **32** 440
Penske Truck Rental, **24** 445
Pentair, Inc., 7 419–21; 11 315; **26 361–64 (upd.); 56** 18
Pental Insurance Company, Ltd., **11** 523
Pentane Partners, **7** 518
Pentastar Transportation Group, Inc. *See* Dollar Thrifty Automotive Group, Inc.
Pentech International, Inc., 14 217; **29 372–74; 52** 193
Pentes Play, Inc., **27** 370, 372
Pentland Group plc, 20 423–25; 35 204, 206–07
Penton Media, Inc., 9 414; **27 360–62; 33** 335–36
People Express Airlines Inc., I 98, 103, **117–18**, 123–24, 129–30; **21** 142; **22** 220
People That Love (PTL) Television, **13** 279
People's Drug Store, **II** 604–05; **22** 37–38
People's Ice and Refrigeration Company, **9** 274
People's Insurance Co., **III** 368
People's Radio Network, **25** 508
People's Trust Company, **49** 412
Peoples, **24** 315–16
Peoples Bancorp, **14** 529
Peoples Bank, **13** 467; **17** 302
Peoples Bank & Trust Co., **31** 207
Peoples Bank of Youngstown, **9** 474
Peoples Energy Corporation, 6 543–44
Peoples Gas Light & Coke Co., **6** 529, 543–44
Peoples Gas Light Co., **6** 455; **25** 44
Peoples Heritage Financial Group, Inc. *See* Banknorth Group, Inc.
Peoples Jewelers of Canada, **16** 561; **40** 472
Peoples National Bank, **41** 178–79
Peoples Natural Gas Company of South Carolina, **6** 576
Peoples Restaurants, Inc., **17** 320–21
Peoples Savings of Monroe, **9** 482
Peoples Security Insurance Co., **III** 219
Peoples Trust of Canada, **49** 411
PeopleServe, Inc., **29** 401
PeopleSoft Inc., 11 78; **14 381–83; 33 330–33 (upd.); 38** 432; **59** 77
The Pep Boys—Manny, Moe & Jack, 11 391–93; 16 160; **26** 348; **36 361–64 (upd.)**
PEPCO. *See* Portland Electric Power Company; Potomac Electric Power Company.
Pepe Clothing Co., **18** 85
Pepper Hamilton LLP, 43 300–03
Pepperell Manufacturing Company, **16** 533–34

Pepperidge Farm. *See* Campbell Soup Company.
The Pepsi Bottling Group, Inc., 40 350–53; 65 328, 330
PepsiAmericas, Inc., 67 297–300 (upd.)
PepsiCo, Inc., I 276–79; II 608; **III** 106, 116, 588; **7** 265, 267, 396, 404, 434–35, 466, 505–06; **8** 399; **9** 177, 343; **10** 130, 199, 324, **450–54 (upd.); 11** 421, 450; **12** 337; **13** 162, 284, 494; **15** 72, 75, 380; **16** 96; **18** 65; **19** 114, 221; **21** 143, 313, 315–16, 362, 401, 405, 485–86; **22** 95, 353; **23** 418, 420; **25** 91, 177–78, 366, 411; **28** 271, 473, 476; **31** 243; **32** 59, 205; **36** 234, 237; **38 347–54 (upd.); 40** 340–42, 350–52; **54** 72–73
Pepsodent Company, **9** 318
Perception Technology, **10** 500
Perdigao SA, 52 276–79; 59 361
Perdue Farms Inc., 7 422–24, 432; **23 375–78 (upd.); 32** 203; **64** 386
Perfect Fit Industries, **17** 182–84
Perfect-Ventil GmbH, **9** 413
Performance Contracting, Inc., **III** 722; **20** 415
Performance Food Group Company, 31 359–62
Performance Technologies, Inc., **10** 395
Perfumania, Inc., **22** 157
Pergamon Holdings, **15** 83; **50** 125
Pergamon Press, **IV** 611, 641–43, 687; **7** 311–12
Perini Corporation, 8 418–21; 38 481
The Perkin-Elmer Corporation, 7 425–27; 9 514; **13** 326
Perkins Bacon & Co., **10** 267
Perkins Cake & Steak, **9** 425
Perkins Coie LLP, 56 268–70
Perkins Engines Ltd., **10** 274; **11** 472; **19** 294; **27** 203
Perkins Family Restaurants, L.P., 22 417–19
Perl Pillow, **19** 304
Perland Environmental Technologies Inc., **8** 420
Permal Group, **27** 276, 513
Permaneer Corp. *See* Spartech Corporation.
Permanent General Companies, Inc., **11** 194
Permanent Pigments Inc., **25** 71
permanent tsb, **59** 245
Permodalan, **III** 699
Pernod Ricard S.A., I 280–81; 21 399–401 (upd.)
Pernvo Inc., **I** 387
Perot Systems Corporation, 13 482; 29 375–78
Perrier, **19** 50
Perrier Corporation of America, **16** 341
Perrier Vittel S.A., **52** 188
Perrigo Company, 12 218, **387–89; 59 330–34 (upd.)**
Perry Brothers, Inc., **24** 149
Perry Capital Corp., **28** 138
Perry Drug Stores Inc., **12** 21; **26** 476
Perry Ellis International, Inc., 16 37; **41 291–94**
Perry Manufacturing Co., **16** 37
Perry Sports, **13** 545; **13** 545
Perry Tritech, **25** 103–05
Perry's Shoes Inc., **16** 36
Perscombinatie, **IV** 611
Pershing & Co., **22** 189
Personal Care Corp., **17** 235

Personal Performance Consultants, **9** 348
Personal Products Company, **8** 511
Personnel Pool of America, **29** 224, 26–27
Perstorp AB, I 385–87; 51 289–92 (upd.)
Pertamina, IV 491–93; 56 271–74 (upd.)
Pertec Computer Corp., **17** 49; **18** 434
Pertech Computers Ltd., **18** 75
Perusahaan Otomobil Nasional Bhd., 62 266–68
Pet Food & Supply, **14** 385
Pet Foods Plus Inc., **39** 355
Pet Incorporated, 7 428–31; 10 554; **12** 124; **13** 409; **14** 214; **24** 140; **27** 196; **43** 217; **46** 290
Pet Warehouse Inc., **62** 108
Petaluma Ltd., **54** 227, 229
Petco Animal Supplies, Inc., 29 379–81
Pete's Brewing Company, 18 72, 502; **22** 420–22
Peter Cundill & Associates Ltd., **15** 504
Peter Gast Shipping GmbH, **7** 40; **41** 42
Peter J. Schmitt Co., **13** 394; **24** 444–45
Peter Kiewit Sons' Inc., I 599–600; III 198; **8 422–24; 15** 18; **25** 512, 514
Peter Norton Computing Group, **10** 508–09
Peter Paul/Cadbury, **II** 512; **15** 221; **51** 158
Peters-Revington Corporation, **26** 100. *See also* Chromcraft Revington, Inc.
Petersen Cos., **52** 192
Petersen Publishing Company, 21 402–04
Peterson American Corporation, 55 304–06
Peterson Furniture Company, **51** 9
Peterson, Howell & Heather. *See* PHH Arval.
Peterson Soybean Seed Co., **9** 411
Petit Bateau, **35** 263
La Petite Academy, **13** 299
Petite Sophisticate. *See* The United States Shoe Corporation.
Petoseed Co. Inc., **29** 435
Petrie Stores Corporation, 8 425–27
Petrini's, **II** 653
Petro-Canada Limited, IV 494–96; 13 557; **50** 172
Petro/Chem Environmental Services, Inc., **IV** 411
Petrobrás. *See* Petróleo Brasileiro S.A.
Petrocel, S.A., **19** 12
Petrochemicals Company, **17** 90–91
Petrochemicals Industry Co., **IV** 451; **55** 243
Petrochim, **IV** 498
PetroChina Company Ltd., **46** 86
Petrocorp. *See* Petroleum Company of New Zealand.
PetroCorp, **63** 409
Petroecuador. *See* Petróleos del Ecuador.
PetroFina S.A., IV 455, 495, **497–500,** 576; **7** 179; **26 365–69 (upd.)**
Petrogal. *See* Petróleos de Portugal.
Petrol Ofisi Anonim Sirketi, **IV** 564
Petrolane Properties, **17** 558
Petróleo Brasileiro S.A., IV 501–03
Petróleos de Portugal S.A., IV 504–06
Petróleos de Venezuela S.A., II 661; **IV** 391–93, **507–09**[ro; **24** 522; **31** 113
Petróleos del Ecuador, IV 510–11
Petróleos Mexicanos, IV 512–14, 528; **19** 10, **295–98 (upd.); 41** 147
Petroleum Authority of Thailand, **IV** 519; **56** 287

Petroleum Development Corp. of the Republic of Korea, **IV** 455
Petroleum Development Oman LLC, IV 515–16
Petroleum Helicopters, Inc., 35 334–36; **37** 288; **39** 8
Petroleum Projects Co., **IV** 414
Petrolgroup, Inc., **6** 441
Petroliam Nasional Bhd (Petronas), 56 275–79 (upd.)
Petrolite Corporation, 15 350–52; 57 65
Petromex. *See* Petróleos de Mexico S.A.
Petromin Lubricating Oil Co., **17** 415; **50** 416
Petron Corporation, 58 270–72
Petronas, IV 517–20; 21 501. *See also* Petroliam Nasional Bhd.
Petronor, **IV** 514, 528
Petrossian Inc., 54 287–89
PETsMART, Inc., 14 384–86; 27 95; **29** 379–80; **41 295–98 (upd.); 45** 42
Petstuff, Inc., **14** 386; **41** 297
Pettibone Corporation, **19** 365
Petzazz, **14** 386
Peugeot S.A., I 187–88; 11 104; **26** 11; **50** 197. *See also* PSA Peugeot Citroen S.A.
The Pew Charitable Trusts, 35 337–40
Pez Candy, Inc., 38 355–57
Pfaff-Pegasus of U.S.A. Inc., **15** 385
Pfaltz & Bauer, Inc., **38** 3
The Pfaltzgraff Co. *See* Susquehanna Pfaltzgraff Company.
Pfauter-Maag Cutting Tools, **24** 186
PFCI. *See* Pulte Financial Companies, Inc.
PFD Supply, Inc., **47** 304
PFI Acquisition Corp., **17** 184
Pfizer, Hoechst Celanese Corp., **8** 399
Pfizer Inc., I 367, **661–63,** 668; **9** 356, **402–05 (upd.); 10** 53–54; **11** 207, 310–11, 459; **12** 4; **17** 131; **19** 105; **38 358–67 (upd.); 44** 175; **63** 207, 233, 235
Pflueger Corporation, **22** 483
PG&E Corporation, 26 370–73 (upd.); **27** 131. *See also* Portland General Electric.
PGA. *See* The Professional Golfers' Association.
PGG/HSC Feed Company LLC, **64** 307
PHAMIS Inc., **64** 190
Phantom Fireworks. *See* B.J. Alan Co., Inc.
Phaostron Instruments and Electronic Co., **18** 497–98
Phar-Mor Inc., 12 209, **390–92,** 477; **18** 507; **21** 459; **22** 157; **50** 457
Pharma Plus Drugmarts, **II** 649–50
PharmaCare Management Services, Inc., **45** 136
Pharmaceutical Resources, Inc. *See* Par Pharmaceutical Companies, Inc.
Pharmacia & Upjohn Inc., 25 22, **374–78 (upd.); 34** 177, 179
Pharmacia A.B., I 664–65
Pharmacia Hospital Products, **56** 81
Pharmaco Dynamics Research, Inc., **10** 106–07
Pharmacom Systems Ltd., **II** 652; **51** 303
Pharmacy Corporation of America, **16** 57
Pharmanex, Inc., **27** 352
Pharmaplan Gruppe, **56** 141
Pharmaprix Ltd., **II** 663; **49** 368
Pharmedix, **11** 207
Pharos, **9** 381

Phat Fashions LLC, 49 322–24
Phelan & Collender, **III** 442
Phelan Faust Paint, **8** 553
Phelps Dodge Corporation, IV 33, **176–79,** 216; **7** 261–63, 288; **19** 375; **28 352–57 (upd.); 40** 411
Phenix Mills Ltd., **II** 662
PHF Life Insurance Co., **IV** 623
PHH Arval, V 496–97; 53 274–76 (upd.)
PHH Monomers, L.L.C., **61** 113
PHI. *See* Pizza Hut, Inc.
Phibro Corporation, **IV** 80; **21** 67
Philadelphia and Reading Corp., **25** 165
Philadelphia Carpet Company, **9** 465
Philadelphia Coke Company, **6** 487
Philadelphia Company, **6** 484, 493
Philadelphia Eagles, 37 305–08
Philadelphia Electric Company, V 695–97; 6 450. *See also* Exelon Corporation.
Philadelphia Sports Clubs. *See* Town Sports International, Inc.
Philadelphia Suburban Corporation, 39 326–29
Philco Corp., **13** 402; **50** 299
Phildar, **37** 22
Phildrew Ventures, **44** 147
PhileoAviation Sdn Bhd, **65** 350
Philip Environmental Inc., 16 414–16
Philip Morris Companies Inc., II 530–34; **V 405–07,** 409, 417; **7** 272, 274, 276, 548; **8** 53; **9** 180; **12** 337, 372; **13** 138, 517; **15** 64, 72–73, 137; **18** 72, **416–19 (upd.); 19** 112, 369; **20** 23; **22** 73, 338; **23** 427; **26** 249, 251; **29** 46–47; **32** 472, 476; **44 338–43 (upd.); 50** 144; **52** 16. *See also* Kraft Foods Inc.
Philip Smith Theatrical Enterprises. *See* GC Companies, Inc.
Philipp Brothers Chemicals, Inc., **25** 82
Philipp Holzmann AG, 14 169; **16** 284, 286; **17 374–77**
Philippine Aerospace Development Corporation, **27** 475
Philippine Airlines, Inc., 6 106–08, 122–23; **23 379–82 (upd.); 27** 464
Philippine National Oil Company, **58** 270
Philips, **V** 339; **10** 269; **22** 194
Philips Electronics N.V., 8 153; **9** 75; **10** 16; **12** 475, 549; **13** 396, **400–03 (upd.);** **14** 446; **23** 389; **26** 334; **27** 190–92; **32** 373; **34** 258; **37** 121; **47 383–86.** *See also* Koninklijke Philips Electronics N.V.
Philips Electronics North America Corp., 13 396–99; 26 334
N.V. Philips Gloeilampenfabriken, II 78–80; IV 680; **12** 454. *See also* Philips Electronics N.V.
Philips Medical Systems, **29** 299
Phillip Securities, **16** 14; **43** 8
Phillippe of California, **8** 16; **36** 24
Phillips & Jacobs, Inc., **14** 486
Phillips Colleges Inc., **22** 442; **39** 102
Phillips, de Pury & Luxembourg, 49 325–27
Phillips Foods, Inc., 63 320–22
Phillips Manufacturing Company, **8** 464
Phillips Petroleum Company, IV 414, 445, 453, 498, **521–23,** 567, 570–71, 575; **10** 84, 440; **11** 522; **13** 356, 485; **17** 422; **19** 176; **24** 521; **31** 457; **38** 407; **40 354–59 (upd.); 47** 70. *See also* ConocoPhillips.

Phillips-Van Heusen Corporation, 24 382–85; **55** 87
Phitech, Inc., **56** 112
PHLCorp., **11** 261
PHM Corp., **8** 461
Phoenicia Glass, **25** 266–67
Phoenix Assurance Co., **III** 370–74; **55** 332
Phoenix Financial Services, **11** 115
Phoenix Insurance Co., **III** 389
Phoenix Mecano AG, 61 286–88
Phoenix Microsystems Inc., **13** 8
Phoenix Mutual Life Insurance, **16** 207
Phoenix Technologies Ltd., **13** 482
Phone America of Carolina, **8** 311
Phonogram, **23** 389
Photo Corporation of America. *See* PCA International, Inc.
Photo Research Inc. *See* Excel Technology, Inc.
PhotoChannel Networks, Inc., **45** 283
Photocircuits Corp., **18** 291–93
PhotoDisc Inc., **31** 216, 218
PHP Healthcare Corporation, 22 423–25
Phuket Air Catering Company Ltd. *See* Thai Airways International.
PhyCor, Inc., 36 365–69
Physical Measurements Information, **31** 357
Physician Corporation of America, **24** 231
Physician Sales & Service, Inc., 14 387–89
Physician's Weight Loss Center, **10** 383
Physicians Formula Cosmetics, **8** 512
Physicians Placement, **13** 49
Physio-Control International Corp., 18 420–23; **30** 316
Physiotherapy Associates Inc., **29** 453
Piaget, **27** 487, 489
Piaggio & C. S.p.A., 17 24; **20 426–29**; **36** 472; **39** 36–37
Piam Pty. Ltd., **48** 364
PIC International Group PLC, 24 386–88 **(upd.)**
Pic 'N' Save, **17** 298–99
Picard Surgeles, **27** 93
Picault, **19** 50
Piccadilly Cafeterias, Inc., 19 299–302
Pick-N-Pay, **II** 642; **9** 452
Pick Pay, **48** 63
Pickands Mather, **13** 158
Picker International Corporation, **8** 352; **30** 314
Pickfords Ltd., **6** 412–14
Pickfords Removals, **49** 22
PickOmatic Systems, **8** 135
Pickwick International, **9** 360; **38** 315
Piclands Mather, **7** 308
Pico Ski Area Management Company, **28** 21
Picture Classified Network, **IV** 597
PictureTel Corp., 10 455–57; 27 363–66 **(upd.)**
Piece Goods Shops, **16** 198
Piedmont Coca-Cola Bottling Partnership, **10** 223
Piedmont Natural Gas Company, Inc., **27 367–69**
Piedmont Pulp and Paper Co. *See* Westvaco Corporation.
Pier 1 Imports, Inc., 12 179, 200, **393–95; 34 337–41 (upd.); 53** 245
Pierburg GmbH, **9** 445–46

Pierce Leahy Corporation, 24 389–92. *See also* Iron Mountain Inc.
Pierce National Life, **22** 314
Piercing Pagoda, Inc., 29 382–84; 40 472
Pierre & Vacances SA, 48 314–16
Pierre Foods, **13** 270–72; **29** 203
Pietrafesa Corporation, **29** 208
Piezo Electric Product, Inc., **16** 239
Piggly Wiggly Southern, Inc., II 624; **13** 251–52, **404–06; 18** 6, 8; **21** 455; **22** 127; **26** 47; **27** 245; **31** 406, 408; **32** 260
Pilgrim House Group, **50** 134
Pilgrim's Pride Corporation, 7 432–33; **23 383–85 (upd.); 39** 229
Pilkington plc, **II** 475; **724–27; 22** 434; **34 342–47 (upd.)**
Pillar Corp., **52** 185
Pilliod Furniture, Inc., **12** 300
Pillowtex Corporation, 19 303–05; 31 200; **41 299–302 (upd.)**
Pillsbury Company, II 555–57; 7 106, 128, 277, 469, 547; **8** 53–54; **10** 147, 176; **11** 23; **12** 510; **13 407–09 (upd.),** 516; **14** 212, 214; **15** 64; **16** 71; **17** 70–71, 434; **22** 59, 426; **24** 140–41; **25** 179, 241; **27** 196, 287; **29** 433; **32** 32, 67; **38** 100; **56** 46; **62 269–73 (upd.)**
Pillsbury Madison & Sutro LLP, 29 385–88
Pilot Air Freight Corp., 67 301–03
Pilot Corporation, 49 328–30
Pilot Freight Carriers, **27** 474
Pilsa, **55** 189
PIMCO Advisors, **57** 20
Pin 'n' Save, **50** 98
Pinault-Printemps-Redoute S.A., 15 386; **19 306–09 (upd.); 22** 362; **27** 513; **41** 185–86; **42** 171
Pincus & Co., **7** 305
Pine Tree Casting. *See* Sturm, Ruger & Company, Inc.
Pinecliff Publishing Company, **10** 357
Pinelands, Inc., **9** 119; **26** 33
Pinelands Water Company, **45** 275, 277
Ping An Insurance Company Ltd., **65** 104
Pinguely-Haulotte SA, 51 293–95
Pinkerton's Inc., 9 406–09; 13 124–25; **14** 541; **16** 48; **41** 77, 79. *See also* Securitas AB.
Pinnacle Art and Frame, **31** 436
Pinnacle Books, **25** 483
Pinnacle Distribution, **52** 429
Pinnacle Fitness, **25** 42
Pinnacle West Capital Corporation, 6 545–47; **26** 359; **54 290–94 (upd.)**
Pinole Point Steel, **63** 272
Pinto Island Metals Company, **15** 116
Pioneer Asphalt Co., **36** 146–47
Pioneer Bank, **41** 312
Pioneer Concrete Services Ltd. *See* Pioneer International Limited
Pioneer Corporations, **62** 374
Pioneer Cotton Mill, **12** 503
Pioneer Electronic Corporation, III 604–06; **28 358–61 (upd.)**
Pioneer Engineering and Manufacturing Co., **55** 32
Pioneer Federal Savings Bank, **10** 340; **11** 115
Pioneer Financial Corp., **11** 447
Pioneer Food Stores Co-op, **24** 528
Pioneer Hi-Bred International, Inc., 9 410–12; **17** 131; **21** 387; **41 303–06** **(upd.)**

Pioneer International Limited, III 728–30; **28** 83
Pioneer Natural Gas Company, **10** 82
Pioneer Natural Resources Company, 59 335–39
Pioneer Outdoor, **27** 280
Pioneer Plastics Corporation, **31** 399–400
Pioneer-Standard Electronics Inc., 13 47; **19 310–14**
Pipasa, **41** 329
Pipe Line Service Company. *See* Plexco.
Piper Aircraft Corp., **8** 49–50
Piper Impact, Inc., **62** 289
Piper Jaffray Companies Inc., 22 426–30, 465. *See also* U.S. Bancorp.
Pirelli S.p.A., V 249–51; 10 319; **15** **353–56 (upd.); 16** 318; **21** 73; **28** 262
Piscataquis Canal and Railroad Company, **16** 348
Pisces Inc., **13** 321
Pispalan Werhoomo Oy, **I** 387
Pitman Company, 58 273–75
Pitney Bowes, Inc., III 156–58, 159; **19** **315–18 (upd.); 47 295–99 (upd.)**
Pittman Company, **28** 350
Pittsburgh & Lake Angeline Iron Company, **13** 156
Pittsburgh Aluminum Alloys Inc., **12** 353
Pittsburgh Brewing Co., **10** 169–70; **18** 70, 72; **50** 111, 114
Pittsburgh Chemical Co. *See* United States Steel Corp.
Pittsburgh Consolidation Coal Co., **8** 346
Pittsburgh National Corporation. *See* PNC Financial Corporation.
Pittsburgh Paint & Glass. *See* PPG Industries, Inc.
Pittsburgh Plate Glass Co. *See* PPG Industries, Inc.
Pittsburgh Railway Company, **9** 413
Pittsburgh Steel Company, **7** 587
Pittsburgh Steelers Sports, Inc., 66 255–57
The Pittston Company, IV 180–82, 566; **10** 44; **19 319–22 (upd.).** *See also* The Brink's Company.
Pittway Corporation, 9 413–15; 27 361–62; **28** 133–34; **33 334–37 (upd.)**
Pivot Rules, Inc. *See* Bluefly, Inc.
Pivotpoint, Inc., **55** 258
Pixar Animation Studios, 34 348–51; 63 437
Pixel Semiconductor, **11** 57
Pizitz, Inc., **19** 324
Pizza Dispatch. *See* Dominos's Pizza, Inc.
Pizza Hut Inc., I 221, 278, 294; **II** 614; **7** 152–53, 267, **434–35,** 506; **10** 450; **11** 50; **12** 123; **13** 336, 516; **14** 107; **15** 344–46; **16** 446; **17** 71, 537; **21** 24–25, 315, **405–07 (upd.); 22** 353; **24** 295; **25** 179–80, 227; **28** 238; **33** 388; **40** 340; **58** 385; **63** 133, 136
Pizza Inn, Inc., 46 346–49; 16 447; **25** 179
PizzaCo, Inc., **7** 152
Pizzeria Uno, **25** 178
PJ's Coffee, **64** 327
PJS Publications, **22** 442
PKbanken, **II** 353
Place Two. *See* Nordstrom, Inc.
Placer Development Ltd., **IV** 19
Placer Dome Inc., 20 430–33; 36 314; **61** 289–93 **(upd.)**
Placid Oil Co., **7** 228

Plaid Holdings Corp., **9** 157
Plain Jane Dress Company, **8** 169
Plains Cotton Cooperative Association, **57** 283–86
Plains Dairy, **53** 21
Plainwell Paper Co., Inc., **8** 103
Planar Systems, Inc., 61 294–97
Planet Hollywood International, Inc., 18 424–26; **25** 387–88; **32** 241, 243–44; **41** 307–10 (upd.)
Planet Smoothie Franchises LLC, **64** 327–28
Planet Waves, **48** 232
Planters Company, **24** 287
Planters Lifesavers, **14** 274–75
Plas-Techs, Inc., **15** 35
Plastic Coating Corporation, **8** 483
Plastic Containers, Inc., **15** 129; **25** 512
Plastic Engineered Products Company. *See* Ballard Medical Products.
Plastic Parts, Inc., **19** 277
Plastic-Plate, Inc., **61** 158, 160
Plastics, Inc., **13** 41
Plasto Bambola. *See* BRIO AB.
Plate Glass Group, **24** 450
Plateau Holdings, Inc., **12** 260; **13** 502
Platinum Entertainment, Inc., 35 341–44
PLATINUM Technology, Inc., 14 390–92
Plato Learning, Inc., 44 344–47
Platte River Insurance Company, **60** 16
Play by Play Toys & Novelties, Inc., 26 374–76
Play It Again Sam (PIAS), **44** 164
Play It Again Sports, **18** 207–08
Playboy Enterprises, Inc., 18 427–30; **48** 148
PlayCore, Inc., 27 370–72
Players International, Inc., 16 263, 275; **19** 402; **22** 431–33; **33** 41; **43** 226–27
Playland, **16** 389
Playmates Toys, 23 386–88
Playmaxx, Inc., **55** 132
Playmobil. *See* geobra Brandstätter GmbH & Co. KG.
Playskool, Inc., 12 169; **13** 317; **25** 379–81
Playtex Products, Inc., 8 511; **15** 357–60; **24** 480; **54** 325
Playworld, **16** 389–90
Plaza Coloso S.A. de C.V., **10** 189
PLC. *See* Prescription Learning Corporation.
Pleasant Company, 25 314; **27** 373–75; **61** 202–03
Pleasant Holidays LLC, 62 274–76
Pleasurama PLC, **12** 228; **32** 243
Plessey Company, PLC, II 81–82; **33** 287–88
Plex Co., Ltd., **55** 48
Plexco, **7** 30–31
Plexus Corporation, 35 345–47
Plezall Wipers, Inc., **15** 502
Plitt Theatres, Inc. *See* Cineplex Odeon Corporation.
Plough Inc. *See* Schering-Plough.
Plum Associates, **12** 270
Plum Creek Timber Company, Inc., 43 304–06
Pluma, Inc., 27 376–78
Plumb Tool, **II** 16
Plus Development Corporation, **10** 458–59
Plus Mark, Inc., **7** 24
Plus System Inc., **9** 537
Plus-Ultra, **II** 196

Plus Vita, **36** 162
Pluto Technologies International Inc., **38** 72
Ply Gem Industries Inc., 12 396–98; **23** 225
Plymouth County Electric Co., **14** 124
Plymouth Mills Inc., **23** 66
PMC Contract Research AB, **21** 425
PMI Corporation. *See* Physical Measurements Information
The PMI Group, Inc., 49 331–33
PMI Mortgage Insurance Company, **10** 50
PMS Consolidated, **8** 347
PMT Services, Inc., 24 393–95
PN Gaya Motor, **56** 284
PNC Bank Corp., 13 410–12 (upd.); **14** 103; **18** 63; **53** 135
PNC Financial Corporation, II 342–43; **9** 476; **17** 114
The PNC Financial Services Group Inc., 46 350–53 (upd.)
Pneumo Abex Corp., **I** 456–58; **III** 512; **10** 553–54; **38** 293–94
Pneumo Dynamics Corporation, **8** 409
PNL. *See* Pacific Northwest Laboratories.
PNM Resources Inc., 51 296–300 (upd.)
PNP. *See* Pacific Northwest Power Company.
POAS. *See* Türkiye Petrolleri Anonim Ortakliği
POB Polyolefine Burghausen GmbH, **IV** 487
Pocahontas Foods USA, **31** 359, 361
Pochet SA, 55 307–09
Pocket Books, Inc., **10** 480; **13** 559–60
Poclain Company, **10** 380
Poe & Associates, Inc., **41** 63–64
Pogo Producing Company, 39 330–32
Pohang Iron and Steel Company Ltd., IV 183–85; **17** 351. *See also* POSCO.
Pohjan Sellu Oy, **IV** 316
Point Chehalis Packers, **13** 244
Polak & Schwarz Essencefabricken, **9** 290
Poland Spring Natural Spring Water Co., **31** 229
Polar Air Cargo Inc., 60 237–39
Polar Manufacturing Company, **16** 32
Polar S.A., **59** 418
Polar Star Milling Company, **7** 241
Polaris Industries Inc., 12 399–402; **35** 348–53 (upd.); **40** 47, 50
Polaroid Corporation, III 607–09; **7** 436–39 (upd.); **12** 180; **28** 362–66 (upd.); **41** 104, 106; **54** 110
Polbeth Packaging Limited, **12** 377
Polenghi, **25** 84
Policy Management Systems Corporation, 11 394–95
Policy Studies, Inc., 62 277–80
Poliet S.A., 33 175–77, 338–40; **40** 108
Polioles, S.A. de C.V., **19** 10, 12
Politos, S.A. de C.V., **23** 171
Polk Audio, Inc., 34 352–54
Pollenex Corp., **19** 360
Polo Food Corporation, **10** 250
Polo/Ralph Lauren Corporation, 9 157; **12** 403–05; **16** 61; **25** 48; **62** 281–85 (upd.)
Polser, **19** 49, 51
Polskie Linie Lotnicze S.A. *See* LOT Polish Airlines.
Poly-Glas Systems, Inc., **21** 65
Poly-Hi Corporation, **8** 359
Polyblend Corporation, **7** 4

Polydesign België, **16** 421
Polydesign Nederland, **16** 421
Polydor B.V., **23** 389
Polydor KK, **23** 390
Polydress Plastic GmbH, **7** 141
Polygon Networks Inc., **41** 73
PolyGram N.V., 13 402; **22** 194; **23** 389–92; **25** 411; **26** 152, 314, 394; **31** 269
Polyken Technologies, **11** 220
Polymer Technologies Corporation, **26** 287
Polyphase Corporation. *See* Overhill Corporation.
Polysius AG, **IV** 89
Pomeroy Computer Resources, Inc., 33 341–44
Pomeroy's, **16** 61; **50** 107
Pommery et Greno, **II** 475
Pompes Guinard S.A., **62** 217
Ponderosa Steakhouse, 7 336; **12** 373; **14** 331; **15** 361–64
Ponderosa System Inc., **12** 199
Pont-à-Mousson S.A., **16** 119, 121–22; **21** 253
Pont Royal SA, **48** 316
Pontiac, **10** 353
Ponto Frio Bonzao, **22** 321
Pontos GmbH, **56** 152
Poof-Slinky, Inc., 61 298–300
Poore Brothers, Inc., 44 348–50
Poorman-Douglas Corporation, **13** 468
Pop.com, **43** 144
Pope & Talbot, Inc., 12 406–08; **61** 301–05 (upd.)
Pope Cable and Wire B.V., **19** 45
Popeye's/Church's, **23** 115, 117
Popeyes Famous Fried Chicken and Biscuits, Inc., **7** 26–28; **32** 13
Pophitt Cereals, Inc., **22** 337
Poppe Tyson Inc., **23** 479; **25** 91
Poppin' Fresh Pies, Inc., **12** 510
Popsicle, **II** 573; **14** 205
Popular Aviation Company, **12** 560
Popular Club Plan, **12** 280; **34** 232
Popular, Inc., 41 311–13
Popular Merchandise, Inc., **12** 280
Pori, **IV** 350
Poron Diffusion, **9** 394
Poron, S.A., **42** 268–69
Porsche AG, 13 28, 219, 413–15; **31** 363–66 (upd.); **36** 198
Port Arthur Finance Corp., **37** 309
The Port Authority of New York and New Jersey, 47 359; **48** 317–20
Port Blakely Mill Company, **17** 438
Port Dickson Power Sdn. Bhd., **36** 435–36
Port of London Authority, **48** 317
Port Stockton Food Distributors, Inc., **16** 451, 453
Portage Industries Corp., **19** 415
El Portal Group, Inc., **58** 371
Portal Software, Inc., 47 300–03
Portals Water Treatment, **11** 510
Porter-Cable Corporation, **26** 361–63
Porter Chadburn plc, **28** 252
Porter Shoe Manufacturing Company, **13** 360
Portex, **25** 431
Portia Management Services Ltd., **30** 318
Portland General Corporation, 6 548–51
Portland General Electric, **45** 313; **50** 103
Portland Heavy Industries, **10** 369
Portland Plastics, **25** 430–31

Portland Shipyard LLC. *See* Cascade General Inc.
Portland Trail Blazers, 50 356–60
Portland-Zementwerke Heidelberg A.G., **23** 326
Portnet, **6** 435
Portsmouth & Sunderland, **35** 242, 244
Portucel. *See* Grupo Portucel Soporcel.
Portugalia, **46** 398
Portways, **9** 92
Posadas. *See* Grupo Posadas, S.A. de C.V.
POSCO, 57 287–91 (upd.)
Positive Response Television, Inc., **27** 337–38
Post Office Group, V 498–501
Post Properties, Inc., 26 377–79
La Poste, V 470–72
Posti- Ja Telelaitos, 6 329–31
PostScript, **17** 177
Potain SAS, **59** 274, 278
Potash Corporation of Saskatchewan Inc., 18 51, **431–33; 27** 318; **50** 90
Potlatch Corporation, 8 428–30; 19 445; **34 355–59 (upd.)**
Potomac Edison Company, **38** 39–40
Potomac Electric Power Company, 6 552–54; 25 46
Potter & Brumfield Inc., 11 396–98
Pottery Barn, **13** 42; **17** 548–50
Pottsville Behavioral Counseling Group, **64** 311
Poulan/Weed Eater. *See* White Consolidated Industries Inc.
PowCon, Inc., **17** 534
Powell Duffryn plc, 31 367–70
Powell Energy Products, **8** 321
Powell Group, **33** 32
Powell's Books, Inc., 37 181; **40 360–63**
Power Applications & Manufacturing Company, Inc., **6** 441
Power Corporation of Canada, 36 370–74 (upd.)
Power Parts Co., **7** 358
Power Products, **8** 515
Power Team, **10** 492
PowerBar Inc., 44 351–53
Powercor. *See* PacifiCorp.
PowerFone Holdings, **10** 433
Powergen PLC, 11 399–401; 12 349; **13** 458, 484; **50** 172, 280–81, **361–64 (upd.)**
Powerhouse Technologies, Inc., 13 485; **27 379–81**
PowerSoft Corp., **11** 77; **15** 374
Powerteam Electrical Services Ltd., **64** 404
Powertel Inc., **48** 130
Powerware Corporation. *See* Eaton Corporation.
Pozzi-Renati Millwork Products, Inc., **8** 135
PP&L. *See* Pennsylvania Power & Light Company.
PP&L Global, Inc., **44** 291
PPB Group Berhad, 57 292–95
PPG Industries, Inc., III 722, **731–33; 8** 222, 224; **16** 120–21; **20** 415; **21** 221, 223; **22** 147, **434–37 (upd.); 37** 73; **39** 292
PPI. *See* Precision Pattern Inc.
PPI Two Corporation, **64** 334
PPL Corporation, 41 314–17 (upd.)
PR Holdings, **23** 382
PR Newswire, 35 354–56
Practical and Educational Books, **13** 105

Practical Business Solutions, Inc., **18** 112
Prada Holding B.V., 45 342–45; **50** 215
Pragma Bio-Tech, Inc., **11** 424
Prairie Farms Dairy, Inc., 47 304–07
Prairielands Energy Marketing, Inc., **7** 322, 325
Prakla Seismos, **17** 419
Prandium Inc., **51** 70
Pratt & Whitney, 7 456; **9** 14, 16–18, 244–46, **416–18; 10** 162; **11** 299, 427; **12** 71; **13** 386; **14** 564; **24** 312; **39** 313
Pratt Hotel Corporation, **21** 275; **22** 438
Pratt Properties Inc., **8** 349
Pratta Electronic Materials, Inc., **26** 425
Praxair, Inc., 11 402–04; 16 462; **43** 265; **48 321–24 (upd.)**
Praxis Biologics, **8** 26; **27** 115
Praxis Corporation, **30** 499
Pre-Fab Cushioning, **9** 93
Pre Finish Metals Incorporated, **63** 270–71
Pre-Paid Legal Services, Inc., 20 434–37
PreAnalytiX, **39** 335
Precept Foods, LLC, **54** 168
Precise Fabrication Corporation, **33** 257
Precise Imports Corp., **21** 516
Precision Castparts Corp., 15 365–67
Precision Games, **16** 471
Precision Husky Corporation, **26** 494
Precision IBC, Inc., **64** 20–21
Precision Interconnect Corporation, **14** 27
Precision LensCrafters, **13** 391
Precision Moulds, Ltd., **25** 312
Precision Optical Industry Company, Ltd. *See* Canon Inc.
Precision Pattern Inc., **36** 159
Precision Power, Inc., **21** 514
Precision Response Corporation, **47** 420
Precision Software Corp., **14** 319
Precision Spring of Canada, Ltd., **55** 305
Precision Stainless Inc., **65** 289
Precision Standard Inc. *See* Pemco Aviation Group Inc.
Precision Studios, **12** 529
Precision Tool, Die & Machine Company Inc., **51** 116–17
Precision Tube Formers, Inc., **17** 234
Precisionaire. *See* Flanders Corporation.
Precoat Metals, **54** 331
Precor, **III** 610–11
Predica, **II** 266
Predicasts Inc., **12** 562; **17** 254
Prefco Corporation, **57** 56–57
Preferred Medical Products. *See* Ballard Medical Products.
Preferred Products, Inc., **II** 669; **18** 504; **50** 454
PREINCO Holdings, Inc., **11** 532
PREL&P. *See* Portland Railway Electric Light & Power Company.
Premark International, Inc., III 610–12; 14 548; **28** 479–80. *See also* Illinois Tool Works Inc.
Premcor Inc., 37 309–11
Premier Cement Ltd., **64** 98
Premier Health Alliance Inc., **10** 143
Premier Industrial Corporation, 9 419–21; 19 311
Premier Insurance Co., **26** 487
Premier Medical Services, **31** 357
Premier Milk Pte Ltd., **54** 117
Premier One Products, Inc., **37** 285
Premier Parks, Inc., 27 382–84
Premier Radio Networks, Inc., **23** 292, 294
Premier Rehabilitation Centers, **29** 400

Premier Sport Group Inc., **23** 66
Premiere Labels Inc., **53** 236
Premisteres S.A., **II** 663
Premium Standard Farms, Inc., 30 353–55
PremiumWear, Inc., 30 356–59
Prentice Hall Computer Publishing, **10** 24
Prentice Hall Inc., **I** 453; **IV** 672; **19** 405; **23** 503
Prescott Ball & Turben, **12** 60
Prescott Investors, **14** 303; **50** 311
Prescription Learning Corporation, **7** 256; **25** 253
Présence, **III** 211
Preserver Group, Inc., 44 354–56
President Baking Co., **36** 313
President Casinos, Inc., 22 438–40
President Riverboat Casino-Mississippi Inc., **21** 300
Presidents Island Steel & Wire Company. *See* Laclede Steel Company.
Presley Cos., **59** 422
Press Associates, **19** 334
Pressed Steel Car Co., **6** 395; **25** 169
Presses de la Cité. *See* Groupe de la Cité.
Pressman Toy Corporation, 56 280–82
Presstar Printing, **25** 183
Presstek, Inc., 33 345–48
Pressware International, **12** 377
Prestage Farms, **46** 83
Prestel Verlag, **66** 123
Prestige et Collections, **III** 48
Prestige Fragrance & Cosmetics, Inc., **22** 158
The Prestige Group plc, **19** 171
Prestige International, **33** 284
Prestige Leather Creations, **31** 435–36
Prestige Properties, **23** 388
Presto Products, Inc., **II** 609–10; **IV** 187; **19** 348; **50** 401
Preston Corporation, 6 421–23; 14 566, 568
Prestone Products Corp., **22** 32; **26** 349
Prestwick Mortgage Group, **25** 187
Pret A Manger, **63** 280, 284–85
Pretty Good Privacy, Inc., **25** 349
Pretty Neat Corp., **12** 216
Pretty Paper Inc., **14** 499
Pretzel Time. *See* Mrs. Fields' Original Cookies, Inc.
Pretzelmaker. *See* Mrs. Fields' Original Cookies, Inc.
Pretzels Incorporated, **24** 241
Preussag AG, IV 109, 201, 231; **17 378–82; 21** 370; **28** 454; **42 279–83 (upd.); 44** 432
PreussenElektra Aktiengesellschaft, V 698–700; 39 57
Preval, **19** 49–50
Previews, Inc., **21** 96
PreVision Marketing, Inc., **37** 409
Priam Corporation, **10** 458
Priba, **26** 158, 160
Pribina, **25** 85
Price Chopper Supermarkets. *See* The Golub Corporation.
Price Club. *See* The Price Company.
Price Communications Corporation, 42 284–86
Price Company Ltd. *See* Abitibi-Consoludated, Inc.
The Price Company, II 664; **V 162–64; 14** 393–94; **34** 198
Price Enterprises, Inc., **14** 395

Price, McCormick & Co., **26** 451
Price Rite, **25** 67
Price Waterhouse LLP, 9 422–24; 14 245; **26** 439. *See also* PricewaterhouseCoopers
PriceCostco, Inc., 14 393–95
Pricel. *See* Chargeurs.
Priceline.com Incorporated, 57 296–99
Priceline.com Inc., **58** 118–19
Pricesearch Ltd Co, **48** 224
PricewaterhouseCoopers, 29 389–94 (upd.); 57 166; **63** 200
PRIDE Enterprises. *See* Prison Rehabilitative Industries and Diversified Enterprises, Inc.
Pride Petroleum Services. *See* DeKalb Genetics Corporation.
Priggen Steel Building Co., **8** 545
Prima S.A., **67** 201
Primadonna Resorts Inc., **17** 318
Primagas GmbH, **55** 347
Primark Corp., 10 89–90; **13 416–18**
Primary Coatings, Inc., **51** 190
Prime Care International, Inc., **36** 367
Prime Computer, Inc. *See* Computervision Corporation.
Prime Hospitality Corporation, 52 280–83
Prime Motor Inns Inc., **IV** 718; **11** 177; **17** 238
The Prime-Mover Co., **13** 267
Prime Service, Inc., **28** 40
Prime Telecommunications Corporation, **8** 311
PrimeAmerica, **III** 340
Primedex Health Systems, Inc., 25 382–85
Primedia Inc., 7 286; **12** 306; **21** 403–04; **22 441–43; 23** 156, 158, 344, 417; **24** 274; **56** 192
Primergy Corp., **39** 261
Primerica Corporation, I 612–14; III 283 **8** 118; **9** 218–19, 360–61; **11** 29; **15** 464; **27** 47; **36** 202. *See also* American Can Co.
Primerica Financial Services, Inc., **30** 124; **59** 121, 125
PriMerit Bank, **19** 412
PrimeSource, **26** 542
Primestar, **38** 176
PRIMESTAR Partners L.P., **28** 241
PrimeWood, Inc., **61** 398
Primex Fibre Ltd., **IV** 328
Primo Foods Ltd., **7** 430
Prince Co., **II** 473
Prince Gardner Company, **17** 465; **23** 21
Prince Golf International, Ltd., **23** 450
Prince Holding Corporation, **26** 231; **59** 252
Prince of Wales Hotels, PLC, **14** 106; **25** 308
Prince Sports Group, Inc., 15 368–70
Prince Street Technologies, Ltd., **8** 271
Prince William Bank, **II** 337; **10** 425
Princess Cruise Lines, 22 444–46
Princess Hotel Group, **21** 353
Princess Hotels International Inc., **45** 82
Princess Metropole, **21** 354
Princeton Gas Service Company, **6** 529
Princeton Laboratories Products Company, **8** 84; **38** 124
The Princeton Review, Inc., 12 142; **42** 210, **287–90**

Princeton Telecommunications Corporation, **26** 38
Princeville Airlines, **24** 22
Principal Health Care, **59** 139
Principal Mutual Life Insurance Company, III 328–30
Pringle Barge Line Co., **17** 357
Print Technologies, Inc., **22** 357
Printex Corporation, **9** 363
PrintNation Inc., **58** 275
Printrak, A Motorola Company, 44 357–59
Printronix, Inc., 14 377–78; **18 434–36**
Priority Records, **22** 194
Pripps Ringnes, **18** 394, 396–97
Prison Rehabilitative Industries and Diversified Enterprises, Inc. (PRIDE), 53 277–79
Prisunic SA. *See* Pinault-Printemps-Redoute SA.
Pritchard Corporation. *See* Black & Veatch, Inc.
Private Colleges and Universities, Inc., **55** 15
Prize Energy, **59** 336
Pro-Fac Cooperative, Inc., **7** 104–06; **21** 154–55, 157
Pro-Lawn, **19** 250
Pro-Line Corporation, **36** 26
Pro-optik AG, **31** 203
Probe Exploration Inc., **25** 232
Process Engineering Inc., **21** 108
Process Systems International, **21** 108
Processing Technologies International. *See* Food Ingredients Technologies.
Procor Limited, **16** 357
Procordia Foods, **18** 396
The Procter & Gamble Company, II 684, 616; **III 50–53; 7** 277, 300, 419; **8** 63, 106–07, 253, 282, 344, 399, **431–35** **(upd.)**, 477, 511–12; **9** 291, 317–19, 552; **10** 54, 288; **11** 41, 421; **12** 126–27, 439; **13** 39, 215; **14** 121–22, 262, 275; **15** 357; **16** 302–04, 440; **18** 68, 147–49, 217, 229; **22** 146–47; **26 380–85 (upd.);** **32** 208; **35** 111, 113; **37** 270; **38** 365; **42** 51; **43** 257–58; **52** 349; **67** 116; **304–11 (upd.)**
Proctor & Schwartz, **17** 213
Proctor-Silex. *See* Hamilton Beach/Proctor-Silex Inc.
Prodega Ltd. *See* Bon Appetit Holding AG.
Prodigy Communications Corporation, 10 237–38; **12** 562; **13** 92; **27** 517; **34 360–62; 56** 312
Prodigy Consulting Inc., **51** 198
Product Components, Inc., **19** 415
Production Association Kirishinefteorgsintez, **48** 378
Production Management Companies Inc., **65** 334
Productivity Point International Inc., **54** 192–93
Produits Jaeger, **27** 258
Profarmaco Nobel S.r.l., **16** 69
Professional Bull Riders Inc., 55 310–12
Professional Computer Resources, Inc., **10** 513
Professional Detailing, Inc. *See* PDI, Inc.
Professional Education Systems, Inc., **17** 272; **53** 319
The Professional Golfers' Association of America, 41 318–21

Professional Health Care Management Inc., **14** 209
Professional Health-Care Resources, **50** 123
Professional Underwriters Liability Insurance Company, **55** 128
Proffitt's, Inc., 19 323–25, 510, 512; **63** 147. *See also* Saks Holdings, Inc.
Profile Extrusion Company, **22** 337
Profimatics, Inc., **11** 66
PROFITCo., **II** 231
Progenx, Inc., **47** 221
Progress Development Organisation, **10** 169
Progress Software Corporation, 15 371–74
Progressive Bagel Concepts, Inc. *See* Einstein/Noah Bagel Corporation.
Progressive Corporation, 11 405–07; 29 395–98 (upd.)
Progressive Distributions Systems, **44** 334
Progressive Distributors, **12** 220
Progressive Grocery Stores, **7** 202
Progressive Networks, Inc., **37** 193. *See also* RealNetworks, Inc.
Progresso, **I** 514; **14** 212
Project Carriers. *See* Hansa Linie.
Projexions Video Supply, Inc., **24** 96
Projiis, **II** 356
ProLab Nutrition, Inc., **49** 275, 277
Proland, **12** 139
Proler International Corp., **13** 98; **19** 380–81
ProLogis, 57 300–02
Promarkt Holding GmbH, **24** 266, 270
Promigas, **IV** 418
Promodès SA, **24** 475; **26** 158, 161; **37** 21; **64** 66, 69
Promotional Graphics, **15** 474
Promus Companies, Inc., 9 425–27; 15 46; **16** 263; **22** 537; **38** 76–77; **43** 225–26; **62** 179
Prontophot Holding Limited, **6** 490
Propaganda Films, Inc., **23** 389, 391
Property Automation Software Corporation, **49** 290
Prophecy Ltd., **55** 24
ProSiebenSat.1 Media AG, 46 403; **54 295–98**
Proskauer Rose LLP, 47 308–10
ProSource Distribution Services, Inc., **16** 397; **17** 475. *See also* Onex Corporation.
The Prospect Group, Inc., **11** 188
Prospect Provisions, Inc. *See* King Kullen Grocery Co., Inc.
Protan & Fagertun, **25** 464
Protection One, Inc., 32 372–75
Protective Closures, **7** 296–97
Protective Insurance Company, **51** 37, 39
Protek, **III** 633
Protogene Laboratories Inc., **17** 288
Proton. *See* Perusahaan Otomobil Nasional Bhd.
Proveedora de Seguridad del Golfo, S.A. de C.V., **45** 425–26
Provell Inc., 58 276–79 (upd.)
Proventus Handels AB, **35** 362
The Providence Journal Company, 28 367–69; **30** 15
La Providence, **III** 210–11
Providence National Bank, **9** 228
The Providence Service Corporation, 64 309–12

Providence Steam and Gas Pipe Co. *See* Grinnell Corp.

Provident Institution for Savings, **13** 467

Provident Life and Accident Insurance Company of America, III 331–33, 404; **57** 234. *See also* UnumProvident Corporation.

Provident National Corporation. *See* PNC Financial Corporation.

Provident Travelers Mortgage Securities Corp., **III** 389

Providian Financial Corporation, 52 62, **284–90 (upd.)**

Provigo Inc., II 651–53; 12 413; **51 301–04 (upd.)**

Provimi, **36** 185

Les Provinces Réunies, **III** 235

Provincetown-Boston Airlines, **I** 118

Provincial Bank of Ireland Ltd., **16** 13

Provincial Engineering Ltd, **8** 544

Provincial Gas Company, **6** 526

Provincial Newspapers Ltd., **28** 502

PROWA, **22** 89

Proximity Technology, **23** 210

Prudential Assurance Company, **24** 314

Prudential Bache Securities, **9** 441

Prudential-Bache Trade Corporation, **II** 51; **21** 331

Prudential Corporation plc, III 334–36; IV 711; **8** 276–77. *See also* Prudential plc.

Prudential Insurance Company of America, III 249, 259, 265–67, 273, 291–93, 313, 329, **337–41; 10** 199; **11** 243; **12** 28, 500; **13** 561; **14** 95, 561; **16** 135, 497; **17** 325; **22** 266; **23** 226; **25** 399; **30 360–64 (upd.); 36** 77–78; **42** 193, 196; **45** 294; **50** 153, 497; **52** 238–39; **63** 14

Prudential Oil & Gas, Inc., **6** 495–96

Prudential plc, 48 325–29 (upd.)

Prudential Steel Ltd., **59** 280, 282

Prymetall GmbH & Co. KG, **62** 253

PS Business Parks, Inc., **52** 291

PSA. *See* Pacific Southwest Airlines.

PSA Peugeot Citroen S.A., 7 35; **28 370–74 (upd.); 54** 126

PSB Company, **36** 517

PSCCo. *See* Public Service Company of Colorado.

PSE, Inc., **12** 100

PSF. *See* Premium Standard Farms, Inc.

PSI. *See* Process Systems International.

PSI Resources, 6 555–57

Psion PLC, 45 346–49

Psychological Corp., **IV** 623; **12** 223

PT Abacus Distribution System Indonesia, **58** 140

PT Aerowisata, **58** 140

PT Astra International Tbk, 56 283–86

PT Bank Buana Indonesia Tbk, 60 240–42

PT Capura Angkasa, **58** 140

PT Components, **14** 43

Ptarmigan Airways Ltd., **56** 39

PTI Communications, Inc. *See* Pacific Telecom, Inc.

PTN Publishing, Inc., **56** 73

PTT Nederland N.V., **27** 472; **30** 393–94

PTT Public Company Ltd., 56 287–90

PTT Telecom BV, **V** 299–301

PTV. *See* Österreichische Post- und Telegraphenverwaltung.

Pubco Corporation, 17 383–85

Publi-Graphics, **16** 168

Public Broadcasting Stations, **29** 426; **51** 309

Public/Hacienda Resorts, Inc. *See* Santa Fe Gaming Corporation.

Public Savings Insurance Co., **III** 219

Public Service Co., **14** 124

Public Service Company of Colorado, 6 558–60

Public Service Company of Indiana. *See* PSI Energy.

Public Service Company of New Hampshire, 21 408–12; 55 313–18 (upd.)

Public Service Company of New Mexico, 6 561–64; **27** 486. *See also* PNM Resources Inc.

Public Service Corporation of New Jersey, **44** 360

Public Service Enterprise Group Inc., V 701–03; 44 360–63 (upd.)

Public Service Market. *See* The Golub Corporation.

Public Storage, Inc., 21 476; **52 291–93,** 310–11

Publicaciones Citem, S.A. de C.V., **39** 188

Publicis S.A., 13 204; **19 329–32; 21** 265–66; **23** 478, 480; **25** 91; **33** 180; **39** 166, 168; **42** 328, 331

PubliGroupe, **49** 424

Publishers Clearing House, 23 393–95; 27 20; **64 313–16 (upd.)**

Publishers Group, Inc., 35 357–59

Publishers Paper Co., **IV** 677–78

Publishing and Broadcasting Limited, 19 400–01; **54 299–302**

Publix Super Markets Inc., II 627; **7 440–42; 9** 186; **20** 84, 306; **23** 261; **31 371–74 (upd.); 59** 425

Puck Holdings, **35** 474, 476

Puck Lazaroff Inc. *See* The Wolfgang Puck Food Company, Inc.

Pueblo Xtra International, Inc., 47 311–13; 54 73–74

Puerto Rican Aqueduct and Sewer Authority, **6** 441

Puerto Rico Electric Power Authority, 47 314–16

Puget Mill Company, **12** 406–07

Puget Sound Alaska Van Lines. *See* Alaska Hydro-Train.

Puget Sound Energy Inc., 50 365–68 (upd.)

Puget Sound National Bank, **8** 469–70

Puget Sound Power And Light Company, 6 565–67; 50 103

Puget Sound Tug and Barge Company, **6** 382

Puig Beauty and Fashion Group S.L., 60 243–46

Pulaski Furniture Corporation, 33 349–52

Pulitzer Inc., 58 280–83 (upd.)

Pulitzer Publishing Company, 15 375–77

Pullman Savings and Loan Association, **17** 529

Pullman Standard, **7** 540

Pulsar Internacional S.A., 21 413–15

Pulse Engineering, Inc., **29** 461

Pulte Corporation, **8 436–38; 22** 205, 207

Pulte Homes, Inc., 42 291–94 (upd.)

Puma AG Rudolf Dassler Sport, 35 360–63; 36 344, 346

Pumpkin Masters, Inc., 48 330–32

Punch International N.V., 66 258–60

Punchcraft, Inc., **III** 569; **20** 360

Purdue Fredrick Company, **13** 367

Pure-Gar, Inc., **49** 276

Pure Milk Products Cooperative, **11** 24

Purex Corporation, **I** 450

Purina Mills, Inc., 32 376–79

Puris Inc., **14** 316

Puritan-Bennett Corporation, 13 419–21

Puritan Fashions Corp., **22** 122

Purity Supreme, Inc., **II** 674; **24** 462

Purodenso Co., **III** 593

Purolator Courier, Inc., **6** 390; **16** 397; **18** 177; **25** 148

Purolator Products Company, 21 416–18; 28 263; **61** 66

Puros de Villa Gonzales, **23** 465

Purup-Eskofot, **44** 44

Push Records, Inc., **42** 271

Putnam Investments Inc., **25** 387; **30** 355. *See also* Marsh & McLennan Companies, Inc.

Putnam Management Co., **III** 283

Putnam Reinsurance Co., **III** 198

Putt-Putt Golf Courses of America, Inc., 23 396–98

PVC Container Corporation, 67 312–14

PW Eagle, Inc., 48 333–36

PWA Group, IV 323–25; 28 446. *See also* Svenska Cellulosa.

PWS Holding Corporation, **13** 406; **26** 47

PWT Projects Ltd., **22** 89

PWT Worldwide, **11** 510

PYA/Monarch, **II** 675; **26** 504

Pyramid Breweries Inc., 33 353–55

Pyramid Communications, Inc., **IV** 623

Pyramid Companies, 54 303–05

Pyramid Electric Company, **10** 319

Pyramid Electronics Supply, Inc., **17** 275

Pyramid Technology Corporation, **10** 504; **27** 448

Pyxis. *See* Cardinal Health, Inc.

Q&B Foods Inc., **57** 202–03

Q Lube, Inc., **18** 145; **24** 339

Q.E.P. Co., Inc., 65 292–94

Qantas Airways Limited, 6 109–13; 14 70, 73; **24 396–401 (upd.); 27** 466; **31** 104; **38** 24

Qatar General Petroleum Corporation, IV 524–26

Qiagen N.V., 39 333–35

Qingdao Haier Refrigerator Co., Ltd., **65** 167, 169

Qintex Australia Ltd., **II** 150; **25** 329

QMS Ltd., **43** 284

QO Chemicals, Inc., **14** 217

QSC Audio Products, Inc., 56 291–93

QSP, Inc., **IV** 664

Qtera Corporation, **36** 352

Quad/Graphics, Inc., 19 333–36

Quad Pharmaceuticals, Inc. *See* Par Pharmaceuticals Inc.

Quail Oil Tools, **28** 347–48

Quaker Alloy, Inc., **39** 31–32

Quaker Fabric Corp., 19 337–39

Quaker Oats Company, II 558–60, 575, 684; **12** 167, 169, **409–12 (upd.); 13** 186; **22** 131, 337–38; **25** 90, 314; **27** 197; **30** 219; **31** 282; **34 363–67 (upd.); 38** 349; **43** 121, 218; **63** 250–52

Quaker State Corporation, 7 443–45; 21 419–22 (upd.); 25 90; 26 349. See also Pennzoil-Quaker State Company.
QUALCOMM Incorporated, 20 438–41; 26 532; 38 271; 39 64; 41 289; 43 312–13; 46 410, 422; 47 317–21 (upd.)
Qualcore, S. de R.L. de C.V., 51 116
Qualipac, 55 309
QualiTROL Corporation, 7 116–17
Quality Aviation Services, Inc., 53 132
Quality Bakers of America, 12 170
Quality Chekd Dairies, Inc., 48 337–39
Quality Courts Motels, Inc., 14 105. See also Choice Hotels International, Inc.
Quality Dining, Inc., 18 437–40; 63 80
Quality Food Centers, Inc., 17 386–88; 22 271, 273
Quality Inns International, 13 363; 14 105. See also Choice Hotels International, Inc.
Quality Markets, Inc., 13 393
Quality Oil Co., II 624–25
Quality Paperback Book Club (QPB), 13 105–07
Quality Products, Inc., 18 162
Qualix S.A., 67 347–48
Quanex Corporation, 13 422–24; 62 286–89 (upd.)
Quanta Computer Inc., 47 322–24
Quanta Systems Corp., 51 81
Quanterra Alpha L.P., 63 347
Quantex Microsystems Inc., 24 31
Quantronix Corporation. See Excel Technology Inc.
Quantum Chemical Corporation, 8 439–41; 11 441; 30 231, 441
Quantum Computer Services, Inc. See America Online, Inc.
Quantum Corporation, 10 56, 403, 458–59, 463; 25 530; 36 299–300; 62 290–93 (upd.)
Quantum Health Resources, 29 364
Quantum Marketing International, Inc., 27 336
Quantum Offshore Contractors, 25 104
Quantum Overseas N.V., 7 360
Quantum Restaurant Group, Inc., 30 330
Quarex Industries, Inc. See Western Beef, Inc.
Quark, Inc., 36 375–79
Quarrie Corporation, 12 554
Quebec Credit Union League, 48 290
Quebéc Hydro-Electric Commission. See Hydro-Quebéc.
Quebecor Inc., 12 412–14; 19 333; 26 44; 29 471; 47 325–28 (upd.)
Queen City Broadcasting, 42 162
Queens Isetan Co., Ltd. See Isetan Company Limited.
Queensborough Holdings PLC, 38 103
Queensland Alumina, IV 59
Queensland and Northern Territories Air Service. See Qantas Airways Limited.
Queensland Mines Ltd., III 729
Quelle Group, V 165–67. See also Karstadt Quelle AG.
Quesarias Ibéricas, 23 219
Quest Aerospace Education, Inc., 18 521
Quest Diagnostics Inc., 26 390–92
Quest Education Corporation, 42 212
Quest Pharmacies Inc., 25 504–05
Questa Oil and Gas Co., 63 408
Questar Corporation, 6 568–70; 10 432; 26 386–89 (upd.)

Questor Management Co. LLC, 55 31
Questor Partners, 26 185
The Quick & Reilly Group, Inc., 18 552; 20 442–44; 26 65
Quick Pak Inc., 53 236
Quicken.com. See Intuit Inc.
Quickie Designs, 11 202, 487–88
The Quigley Corporation, 62 294–97
Quik Stop Markets, Inc., 12 112
Quiksilver, Inc., 18 441–43; 27 329
QuikTrip Corporation, 36 380–83
Quill Corporation, 28 375–77; 55 354
Quillery, 27 138
Quilmes Industrial (QUINSA) S.A., 57 74, 76–77; 67 315–17
Quilter Sound Company. See QSC Audio Products, Inc.
Química y Farmacia, S.A. de C.V., 59 332
Quimicos Industriales Penoles. See Industrias Penoles, S.A. de C.V.
Quincy Family Steak House, II 679; 10 331; 19 287; 27 17, 19
Quintana Roo, Inc., 17 243, 245; 25 42
Quintel Communications, Inc., 61 375
Quintex Australia Limited, 25 329
Quintiles Transnational Corporation, 21 423–25
Quintron, Inc., 11 475
Quintus Computer Systems, 6 248
Quixote Corporation, 15 378–80
Quixtar Inc., 30 62
Quixx Corporation, 6 580
The Quizno's Corporation, 32 444; 42 295–98
Quoddy Products Inc., 17 389, 390
Quotron Systems, Inc., IV 670; 9 49, 125; 30 127; 47 37
QVC Inc., 9 428–29; 10 175; 12 315; 18 132; 20 75; 24 120, 123; 58 284–87 (upd.); 67 206
Qwest Communications International, Inc., 25 499; 26 36; 32 218; 36 43–44; 37 126, 312–17; 49 312; 63 393
QwikSilver II, Inc., 37 119

R&B Falcon Corp. See Transocean Sedco Forex Inc.
R&B, Inc., 51 305–07
R & B Manufacturing Co., III 569; 20 361
R&D Systems, Inc., 52 347
R&O Software-Technik GmbH, 27 492
R&S Home and Auto, 56 352
R&S Technology Inc., 48 410
R. and W. Hawaii Wholesale, Inc., 22 15
R-Anell Custom Homes Inc., 41 19
R-B. See Arby's, Inc.
R-Byte, 12 162
R-C Holding Inc. See Air & Water Technologies Corporation.
R.B. Pamplin Corp., 45 350–52
R.C. Bigelow, Inc., 16 90; 49 334–36
R.C. Willey Home Furnishings, 18 60
R. Cubed Composites, Inc., I 387
R.E. Funsten Co., 7 429
R.G. Barry Corp., 17 389–91; 44 364–67 (upd.)
R.G. Dun-Bradstreet Corp. See The Dun & Bradstreet Corp.
R. Griggs Group Limited, 23 399–402; 31 413–14
R.H. Donnelley Corporation, 61 81–83
R.H. Macy & Co., Inc., V 168–70; 8 442–45 (upd.); 10 282; 11 349; 13 42; 15 281; 16 206–07, 328, 388, 561; 23

60; 27 60, 481; 30 379–83 (upd.); 31 190, 192–93; 45 15; 60 72
R.H. Stengel & Company, 13 479
R.J. Reynolds, I 261, 363; II 544; 7 130, 132, 267, 365, 367; 9 533; 13 490; 14 78; 15 72–73; 16 242; 21 315; 27 125; 29 195; 32 344. See also RJR Nabisco.
R.J. Reynolds Tobacco Holdings, Inc., 30 384–87 (upd.)
R.J. Tower Corporation. See Tower Automotive, Inc.
R.K. Brown, 14 112
R.L. Crain Limited, 15 473
R.L. Manning Company, 9 363–64
R.L. Polk & Co., 10 460–62
R-O Realty, Inc., 43 314
R.P.M., Inc., 25 228
R.P. Scherer Corporation, I 678–80; 33 145
R.R. Bowker Co., 17 398; 23 440
R.R. Donnelley & Sons Company, IV 660–62, 673; 9 430–32 (upd.); 11 293; 12 414, 557, 559; 18 331; 19 333; 38 368–71 (upd.)
R.S.R. Corporation, 31 48
R.S. Stokvis Company, 13 499
R. Scott Associates, 11 57
R-T Investors LC, 42 323–24
R. Twining & Co., 61 395
R.W. Beck, 29 353
R.W. Harmon & Sons, Inc., 6 410
RABA PLC, 10 274
Rabbit Software Corp., 10 474
Rabobank Group, 26 419; 33 356–58
RAC. See Ravenswood Aluminum Company.
Racal-Datacom Inc., 11 408–10
Racal Electronics PLC, II 83–84; 11 408, 547; 42 373, 376; 50 134
Race Z, Inc. See Action Peformance Companies, Inc.
Rachel's Dairy Ltd., 37 197–98
Racine Hidraulica, 21 430
Racine Threshing Machine Works, 10 377
Racing Champions. See Action Performance Companies, Inc.
Racing Champions Corporation, 37 318–20
Racing Collectables Club of America, Inc. See Action Performance Companies, Inc.
Racket Store. See Duckwall-ALCO Stores, Inc.
Rada Corp., IV 250
Radian Group Inc., 42 299–301. See also Onex Corporation.
Radian Lamp Corp., 13 398
Radio & Television Equipment Company (Radio-Tel), 16 200–01; 43 168–69
Radio Austria A.G., V 314–16
Radio Cap Company. See Norwood Promotional Products, Inc.
Radio City Productions, 30 102
Radio Corporation of America. See RCA Corporation.
Radio Flyer Inc., 34 368–70
Radio-Keith-Orpheum, 9 247; 12 73; 31 99
Radio One, Inc., 67 318–21
Radio Receptor Company, Inc., 10 319
Radio Shack, II 106–08; 12 470; 13 174
Radio Vertrieb Fürth. See Grundig AG.
Radiocel, 39 194
Radiometer A/S, 17 287
Radiometrics, Inc., 18 369
RadioShack Canada Inc., 30 391

RadioShack Corporation, 36 384–88 (upd.)
Radiotelevision Española, **7** 511
Radisson Hotels Worldwide, **22** 126–27
Radius Inc., 16 417–19
Radix Group, Inc., **13** 20
Radman Inc., **56** 247
RadNet Managed Imaging Services, Inc., **25** 382–84
Radnor Venture Partners, LP, **10** 474
Raet, **39** 177
Raffinerie Tirlemontoise S.A., **27** 436
Raffineriegesellschaft Vohburg/Ingolstadt mbH, **7** 141
RAG AG, 35 364–67; **60** 247–51 (upd.)
Rag Shops, Inc., 30 365–67
Ragan Outdoor, **27** 280
Ragazzi's, **10** 331
Ragdoll Productions Ltd., 51 308–11
Ragnar Benson Inc., **8** 43–43
Rail Link, Inc., **27** 181
Rail Van Global Logistics, **54** 276
Railroad Enterprises, Inc., **27** 347
RailTex, Inc., 20 445–47
Railtrack Group PLC, 39 238; **50** 369–72
Railway Express Agency, **6** 388–89; **25** 146–48
Railway Maintenance Equipment Co., **14** 43
Rainbow Home Shopping Ltd. *See* Otto-Versand (GmbH & Co.).
Rainbow Media, **47** 421
Rainbow Programming Holdings, **7** 63–64
Rainbow Valley Orchards, **54** 257
RainbowBridge Communications, Inc., **25** 162
Raincoast Book Distribution, **34** 5
Rainer Pulp & Paper Company, **17** 439
Rainfair, Inc., **18** 298, 300
Rainforest Café, Inc., 25 386–88; **32** 241, 244
Rainier Brewing Company, 23 403–05
Rainier Pulp and Paper Company. *See* Rayonier Inc.
Rainy River Forest Products, Inc., **26** 445
Rajastan Breweries, Ltd., **18** 502
Raky-Danubia, **IV** 485
Ralcorp Holdings, Inc., **13** 293, 425, 427; **15** 189, 235; **21** 53, 56; **22** 337; **36** 238; **43** 438; **50** 294; **55** 96; **63** 251. *See also* Ralston Purina Company.
Raleigh UK Ltd., 65 295–97
Raley's Inc., 14 396–98; **58** 288–91 (upd.)
Ralli International, **IV** 259
Rally's Hamburgers, Inc., 25 389–91; **46** 97
Rally's Inc., **14** 452; **15** 345; **16** 96–97; **23** 225
Rallye SA, 12 154; **54** 306–09; **59** 107
Ralph & Kacoo's. *See* Piccadilly Cafeterias, Inc.
Ralph Lauren. *See* Polo/Ralph Lauren Corportion.
The Ralph M. Parsons Company. *See* The Parsons Corporation.
Ralph Wilson Plastics, **III** 610–11
Ralph's Industries, **31** 191
Ralphs Grocery Company, 35 368–70
Ralston Purina Company, I 608, **II** 560, **561–63**, 617; **7** 209, 396, 547, 556; **8** 180; **9** 180; **12** 276, 411, 510; **13** 137, 270, 293, **425–27** (upd.); **14** 194–95,

558; **18** 312; **21** 56; **23** 191; **50** 294. *See also* Ralcorp Holdings, Inc.
Ramada International Hotels & Resorts, **IV** 718; **9** 426; **11** 177; **13** 66; **21** 366; **25** 309; **28** 258; **38** 320; **52** 281
Rambol, **25** 84
Rampage Clothing Co., **35** 94
Ramparts, Inc., **57** 159
Ramsay Youth Services, Inc., 41 322–24
Ranbar Packing, Inc. *See* Western Beef, Inc.
Ranchers Packing Corp. *See* Western Beef, Inc.
Rand Capital Corp., **35** 52–53
Rand McNally & Company, 28 378–81; **53** 122
Randall's Food Markets, Inc., 40 364–67
Randgold & Exploration, **63** 182–83
Random House, Inc., 13 113, 115, 178, **428–30**; **14** 260; **31** 375–80 (upd.); **42** 287; **54** 17, 22
Randon Meldkamer, **43** 307
Randstad Holding n.v., 16 420–22; **43** 307–10 (upd.)
Range Resources Corporation, 45 353–55
The Rank Group plc, 64 317–21 (upd.)
Rank Organisation PLC, II 157–59; **IV** 698; **12** 229; **14** 399–402 (upd.); **26** 543, 546; **32** 241, 243–44; **34** 140; **40** 296, 298
Ranks Hovis McDougall Limited, II 564–65; **28** 382–85 (upd.)
Ransburg Corporation, **22** 282
Ransom and Randolph Company, **10** 271
Ransom Industries LP, **55** 266
RAO Unified Energy System of Russia, 45 356–60
Rapala-Normark Group, Ltd., 30 368–71
Rapides Bank & Trust Company, **11** 107
Rapidforms, Inc., **35** 130–31
Rare Hospitality International Inc., 19 340–42
RAS. *See* Riunione Adriatica di Sicurtà SpA.
Rascal House, **24** 243
Ratin A/S, **49** 376
Rational GmbH, **22** 354
Ratti Vallensasca, **25** 312
Raufast et Fils, **35** 205
Rauma-Repola Oy, **IV** 316, 340, 349–50. *See also* Metso Corporation
Raumtechnik Messebau & Event Marketing GmbH, **60** 143
Rauscher Pierce Refsnes, Inc., **15** 233
Raven Industries, Inc., 33 359–61
Raven Press, **14** 555
Ravenna Metal Products Corp., **12** 344
Ravensburger AG, 64 322–26
Ravenseft Properties Ltd. *See* Land Securities PLC.
Ravenswood Aluminum Company, **52** 72–73
RAVIcad, **18** 20; **43** 17
Raving Brands, Inc., 64 327–29
Rawlings Sporting Goods Co., Inc., 7 177; **23** 449; **24** 402–04
Rawls Brothers Co., **13** 369
Ray Industries, **22** 116
Ray Simon, **24** 94
Ray Strauss Unlimited, **22** 123
Raychem Corporation, III 492; **8** 446–47; **63** 404
Raymar Book Corporation, **11** 194

Raymond International Inc., **28** 201
Raymond, Trice & Company, **14** 40
Raynet Corporation, **8** 447
Rayonese Textile, Inc., **29** 140
Rayonier Inc., 24 405–07
Rayovac Corporation, 13 431–34; **17** 105; **23** 497; **24** 480; **39** 336–40 (upd.)
Raytech Corporation, 61 306–09
Raytheon Aircraft Holdings Inc., 46 354–57
Raytheon Company, II 85–87; **8** 51, 157; **11** 411–14 (upd.); **12** 46; **14** 223; **17** 419, 553, 564; **21** 200; **23** 181; **24** 88; **25** 223; **36** 190–91; **38** 372–77 (upd.); **42** 373, 376; **48** 252
Razel S.A., **55** 62
Razorback Acquisitions, **19** 455
Razorfish, Inc., 37 321–24
RB&W Corp., **17** 372
RBC Dominion Securities, **25** 12
RCA Corporation, II 88–90; **III** 569; **6** 334; **7** 520; **8** 157; **9** 283; **10** 173; **11** 318, 411; **12** 204, 208, 454, 544, 548; **13** 106, 398, 429, 506, 573; **14** 357, 436; **16** 549; **17** 29; **20** 361; **21** 151; **22** 541; **23** 181; **26** 358, 511; **28** 349; **31** 376; **34** 186, 516; **38** 373; **57** 309–10
RCA Global Communications, Inc., **27** 304
RCG International, Inc., **III** 344
RCM Technologies, Inc., 34 371–74
RCN Corp., **25** 107
RDMS Direct Marketing BV, **53** 362
RDO Equipment Company, 33 362–65
RE/MAX International, Inc., 59 344–46
REA. *See* Railway Express Agency.
Rea & Derick, **II** 605
Rea Construction Company, **17** 377
React-Rite, Inc., **8** 271
Read-Rite Corp., 10 403–04, 463–64; **18** 250
The Reader's Digest Association, Inc., IV 663–64; **17** 392–95 (upd.)
Reader's Garden Inc., **22** 441
Reading Railroad, **9** 407
Ready Mixed Concrete, **28** 82
Real Color Displays, **53** 117
Real Decisions, **21** 236
Real Estate Maintenance, **25** 15
Real Fresh, **25** 85
Real Goods Trading Company, **41** 177
Real-Share, Inc., **18** 542
Real Times, Inc., 66 261–65
Real Turismo, S.A. de C.V., 50 373–75
RealCom Communications Corporation, **15** 196
Realeum, Inc., **58** 11
Reality Group Limited, **47** 165, 169
The Really Useful Group, 23 390; **26** 393–95; **34** 422
RealNetworks, Inc., 53 280–82
Realty Development Co. *See* King Kullen Grocery Co., Inc.
Realty Investment Group, **25** 127
Realty Parking Properties II L.P., **18** 104
Reavis & McGrath, **47** 139
Rebekah W. Harkness Foundation, **52** 199
Recaro North America Inc., **26** 231
Reckitt & Colman plc, II 566–67; **15** 46, 360; **18** 556; **22** 148; **27** 69
Reckitt Benckiser plc, 42 302–06 (upd.)
Reckson Associates Realty Corp., 47 329–31
Record Bar / Licorice Pizza, **9** 361

Record Merchandisers. *See* Entertainment UK.
Record World Inc., **9** 361
Recordati S.p.A., **52** 135
Recording for the Blind & Dyslexic, 51 312–14
Recoton Corp., 15 381–83
Recoupe Recycling Technologies, **8** 104
Recovery Centers of America, **III** 88
Recovery Engineering, Inc., 25 392–94
Recreational Equipment, Inc., 18 444–47; 22 173
Recticel S.A., **17** 182–84
Recubrimientos Interceramic, S.A. de C.V., **53** 175
Recycled Paper Greetings, Inc., 21 426–28
RED, **44** 164
Red & White, **II** 682
The Red Adair Company, **37** 171
Red Ant Entertainment, **17** 14
Red Apple Group, Inc., 23 406–08; 24 528–29; **31** 231
Red Ball, Inc., **18** 300
Red Brick Systems Inc., **30** 246
Red Bull GmbH, 31 244; **60 252–54**
Red Carpet Food Systems, **39** 409
Red Chisinau, **51** 389
Red-E-Food Systems, Inc. *See* Del Taco, Inc.
Red Food Stores, Inc., **19** 327–28
Red Hat, Inc., 45 361–64
Red House Books Ltd., **29** 426
Red Kap. *See* VF Corporation.
Red L Foods, **13** 244
Red Line HealthCare Corporation, **47** 236
Red Lion Entertainment, **29** 503
Red Lobster Inns of America, **16** 156–58
Red Lobster Restaurants, **19** 258
Red Oak Consulting, **42** 244
Red Owl Stores, Inc., **II** 670; **18** 506; **50** 456
Red Pepper Software Co., **59** 77
Red River Commodities, Inc. *See* Deli Universal NV.
Red Robin Gourmet Burgers, Inc., 56 294–96
Red Roof Inns, Inc., 13 363; **18 448–49; 21** 362
Red Rooster, **V** 35
Red Spot Paint & Varnish Company, 55 319–22
Red Star Express, **14** 505
Red Storm, **41** 409
Red Televisiva Megavision S.A., **67** 136–38
The Red Wing Co., Inc., **28** 382; **55** 96, 98
Red Wing Pottery Sales, Inc., 52 294–96
Red Wing Shoe Company, Inc., 9 433–35; 30 372–75 (upd.)
Redbook Florists Service, **28** 138
Redbook Publishing Co., **14** 460
Reddy Ice, **II** 661
Redgate Communications, **26** 19
Redhook Ale Brewery, Inc., 31 381–84
Reditab S.p.A., **12** 109
Redken Laboratories, **8** 131; **24** 251
Redland Plasterboard, **28** 83
Redland plc, III 734–36; 14 249, 739; **15** 154; **37** 205
Redlaw Industries Inc., **15** 247
Redman Industries, Inc., **17** 81, 83
La Redoute, S.A. *See* Pinault-Printemps-Redoute SA.

Redrow Group plc, 31 385–87
Redwood Design Automation, **11** 47; **16** 520
Redwood Fire & Casualty Insurance Co., **III** 214
Redwood Systems, **48** 112
Reebok International Ltd., V 375–77; 8 171, 303–04, 393; **9** 134–35, **436–38 (upd.); 11** 50–51, 349; **13** 513; **14** 8; **17** 244–45, 260; **18** 266; **19** 112; **22** 173; **25** 258, 352, 450; **26 396–400 (upd.); 36** 346
Reed & Barton Corporation, 67 322–24
Reed & Ellis, **17** 439
Reed & Gamage, **13** 243
Reed Elsevier plc, 19 268; **23** 271, 273; **31 388–94 (upd.); 32** 354; **33** 263, 265–66, 458; **34** 438; **43** 92–93
Reed-Hycalog, **57** 162, 164
Reed International PLC, IV 270, 642, **665–67**, 711; **7** 244–45, 343; **10** 407; **12** 359; **17 396–99 (upd.); 23** 350; **49** 408
Reeder Light, Ice & Fuel Company, **6** 592; **50** 38
Reeds Jewelers, Inc., 22 447–49
Reese Finer Foods, Inc., **7** 429
Reese Products, **III** 569; **11** 535; **20** 361
Reeves Banking and Trust Company, **11** 181
Reeves Brothers, **17** 182
Reeves Pulley Company, **9** 440
Refco, Inc., **10** 251; **22** 189
Reference Software International, **10** 558
Refinaria de Petróleo Ipiranga S.A., **67** 216
Reflectone Inc. *See* CAE USA Inc.
Reflex Winkelmann & Pannhoff GmbH, **18** 163
Refractarios Mexicanos, S.A. de C.V., **22** 285
Refrigeração Paraná S.A., **22** 27
Refrigerantes do Oeste, SA, **47** 291
Regal-Beloit Corporation, 18 450–53
Regal Entertainment Group, 59 340–43
Regal Inns, **13** 364
Regal Manufacturing Co., **15** 385
Regency Health Services Inc., **25** 457
Regency International, **10** 196
Regenerative Environmental Equipment Company, Inc., **6** 441
Regeneron Pharmaceuticals Inc., **10** 80
Regent Carolina Corporation, **37** 226
Regent Communications Inc., **23** 294
Regent International Hotels Limited, **9** 238; **29** 200
Régie Autonome des Pétroles, **IV** 544–46; **21** 202–04
Régie des Télégraphes et Téléphones. *See* Belgacom.
Régie Nationale des Usines Renault, I 145, 148, 178–79, 183, **189–91**, 207, 210; **7** 566–67; **11** 104; **12** 91; **15** 514; **19** 50; **22** 331; **50** 197. *See also* Renault SA.
Regional Bell Operating Companies, **15** 125; **18** 111–12, 373
Regis Corporation, 18 454–56; 22 157; **26** 475, 477
Register & Tribune Co. *See* Cowles Media Company.
Regnecentralen AS, **III** 164
Rego Supermarkets and American Seaway Foods, Inc., **9** 451; **13** 237
Rehab Hospital Services Corp., **III** 88; **10** 252

RehabClinics Inc., **11** 367
Rehrig Manufacturing, **51** 35
REI. *See* Recreational Equipment, Inc.
Reich, Landman and Berry, **18** 263
Reichart Furniture Corp., **14** 236
Reichhold Chemicals, Inc., 8 554; **10** 465–67
Reidman Corporation, **41** 65
Reidsville Fashions, Inc., **13** 532
Reimersholms, **31** 458–60
Reims Aviation, **8** 92; **27** 100
Rein Elektronik, **10** 459
Reinsurance Agency, **III** 204–05
Reisland GmbH, **15** 340
Reiue Nationale des Usines Renault, **7** 220
Rekkof Restart NV, **28** 327
Relational Courseware, Inc., **21** 235–36
Relational Database Systems Inc., **10** 361–62
Relational Technology Inc., **10** 361
Relationship Marketing Group, Inc., **37** 409
Release Technologies, **8** 484
Reliable Life Insurance Company, **58** 259
Reliable Stores Inc., **14** 236
Reliance Electric Company, 9 439–42
Reliance Group Holdings, Inc., III 342–44
Reliance National Indemnity Company, **18** 159
Reliance Steel & Aluminum Co., 19 343–45
Reliant Energy Inc., 44 368–73 (upd.)
ReLife Inc., **14** 233; **33** 185
Reliv International, Inc., 58 292–95
Relocation Central. *See* CORT Business Services Corporation.
Rembrandt Group Ltd., **IV** 93, 97; **50** 144
Remedy Corporation, 58 296–99
RemedyTemp, Inc., 20 448–50
Remgro, **IV** 97
Remington Arms Company, Inc., 12 415–17; 40 368–71 (upd.)
Remington Products Company, L.L.C., 42 307–10
Remington Rand, **III** 126, 148, 151, 165–66, 642; **10** 255; **12** 416; **19** 430
Remmele Engineering, Inc., **17** 534
Rémy Cointreau S.A., 20 451–53
Remy Martin, **48** 348–49
REN Corp. USA, Inc., **13** 161
REN Corporation, **49** 156
Renaissance Communications Corp., **22** 522; **63** 393
Renaissance Connects, **16** 394
Renaissance Cosmetics Inc. *See* New Dana Perfumes Co.
Renaissance Energy Ltd., **47** 181
Renaissance Hotel Group N.V., **38** 321
Renaissance Learning Systems, Inc., 39 341–43
Renal Systems, Inc. *See* Minntech Corporation.
Renault Argentina S.A., 67 325–27
Renault S.A., 26 11, **401–04 (upd.); 34** 303, 306; **61** 181–82; **63** 302, 304
Rendeck International, **11** 66
Rendic International, **13** 228
René Garraud. *See* Wella AG.
Renfro Corp., **25** 167
Rengo Co., Ltd., IV 326
Renishaw plc, 46 358–60
RENK AG, 37 325–28
Reno Air Inc., 23 409–11; 24 400; **28** 25
Reno de Medici S.p.A., 41 325–27

Réno-Dépôt Inc., **26** 306
Reno Technologies, **12** 124
Rent-A-Center, Inc., 22 194; **24** 485; **33**
    366, 368; **45 365–67**
Rent-Way, Inc., 33 366–68
Rental Service Corporation, 28 386–88
Renters Choice Inc. *See* Rent-A-Center,
    Inc.
Rentokil Initial Plc, 34 43; **47 332–35; 49**
    375–77; **64** 197
Rentrak Corporation, 35 371–74
Rentz, **23** 219
Renwick Technologies, Inc., **48** 286
Reo Products. *See* Lifetime Hoan
    Corporation.
Repairmaster Canada, Inc., **53** 359
Repco Ltd., **15** 246
Replacement Enterprises Inc., **16** 380
Repligen Inc., **13** 241
Repola Ltd., **19** 465; **30** 325
Repola Oy, **IV** 316, 347, 350
Repsol S.A., IV 527–29; 16 423–26
    (upd.); 49 211
Repsol-YPF S.A., 40 372–76 (upd.)
Repubblica, **IV** 587
Republic Airlines, **25** 421; **28** 265
Republic Aviation Corporation, **9** 205–07;
    48 167
Republic Broadcasting Corp., **23** 292
Republic Corp., **I** 447
Republic Engineered Steels, Inc., 7
    446–47 26 405–08 (upd.)
Republic Freight Systems, **14** 567
Republic Industries, Inc., 24 12; **26**
    409–11, 501
Republic Insurance, **III** 404
Republic National Bank, **19** 466
Republic New York Corporation, 11
    415–19
Republic Pictures, **9** 75
Republic Powdered Metals, Inc., **8** 454
Republic Steel Corp., **I** 491; **7** 446; **12**
    353; **13** 169, 157; **14** 155; **24** 304. *See*
    also Republic Engineered Steels, Inc.
Republic Supply Co., **63** 288
Res-Care, Inc., 29 399–402
Research Analysis Corporation, **7** 15
Research Cottrell, Inc., **6** 441
Research Genetics, Inc., **52** 183–84
Research in Motion Ltd., 54 310–14
Research Publications, **8** 526
Réseau Ferré de France, 57 328, 332; **66**
    266–68
Resecenter, **55** 90
Resem SpA, **I** 387
Reserve Mining Co., **17** 356
Reservoir Productions, **17** 150
Residence Inns, **9** 426
Residential Funding Corporation, **10** 92–93
Resin Exchange, **19** 414
ResNet Communications Inc., **28** 241
Resolution Systems, Inc., **13** 201
Resolution Trust Corp., **10** 117, 134; **11**
    371; **12** 368
Resona Holdings Inc., **53** 322
Resorts International, Inc., 12 418–20;
    19 402; **26** 462; **56** 135
Resorts World Bhd. *See* Genting Bhd.
Resource America, Inc., 42 311–14
Resource Associates of Alaska, Inc., **7** 376
The Resource Club, **32** 80
Resource Electronics, **8** 385
Resource Group International, **25** 207
ReSource NE, Inc., **17** 553

reSOURCE PARTNER, INC., **22** 95
Respond Industries, Inc., **51** 76
Response Oncology, Inc., 27 385–87
Restaurant Associates Corporation, 66
    269–72
The Restaurant Company, **22** 417
Restaurant Enterprises Group Inc., **14** 195
Restaurant Property Master, **19** 468
Restaurants Les Pres Limitée, **II** 652
Restaurants Universal Espana S.A., **26** 374
Restaurants Unlimited, Inc., 13 435–37;
    23 127–29
Restoration Hardware, Inc., 30 376–78
Resurgens Communications Group, **7** 336;
    8 311; **27** 306
Retail Association Pskovnefteprodukt, **48**
    378
Retail Concepts Inc., **55** 174
Retail Credit Company. *See* Equifax.
Retail Systems Consulting, Inc., **24** 395
Retail Ventures Inc., **14** 427; **24** 26
Retequattro, **19** 19
Retirement and Health Services
    Corporation, **57** 128
Retirement Care Associates Inc., **25** 457
Retirement Systems of Alabama, **52** 387
Retorte Ulrich Scharrer GmbH, **62** 253
Reuben H. Donnelley Corp. *See* The Dunn
    & Bradstreet Corp.
Reuters Group PLC, 63 323–27 (upd.)
Reuters Holdings PLC, IV 259, 652, 654,
    656, **668–70; 10** 277, 407; **21** 68–70; **22**
    450–53 (upd.); 34 11, 227
Revco D.S., Inc., V 171–73; 9 67, 187; **12**
    4; **16** 560; **19** 357; **32** 169–70; **45** 136
Revell-Monogram Inc., 16 427–29; 25
    71; **27** 14
Revere Copper and Brass Co. *See* The Paul
    Revere Corporation.
Revere Foil Containers, Inc., **12** 377
Revere Furniture and Equipment Company,
    14 105; **25** 307
Revere Ware Corporation, 22 454–56
Revlon Inc., I 668, 677, 693, 696; **II** 679;
    III 54–57, 727; **8** 131, 341; **9** 202–03,
    291; **11** 8, 333–34; **12** 314; **16** 439; **17**
    110, **400–04 (upd.); 18** 229; **22** 157; **25**
    55; **26** 384; **28** 246–47; **30** 188–89; **64**
    330–35 (upd.)
Rewe-Beteiligungs-Holding National
    GmbH, **53** 179; **54** 295–96
Rewe Group, **37** 241
Rewe-Liebbrand, **28** 152
Rex Pulp Products Company, **9** 304
Rex Re Insurance Ltd., **51** 143
REX Stores Corp., 10 468–69; 19 362
Rexall Drug & Chemical Co., **13** 525; **14**
    547
Rexall Drug Co., **50** 487
Rexall Sundown, Inc., **37** 340, 342
Rexam PLC, 32 380–85 (upd.); 45 337;
    50 122
Rexel, Inc., 15 384–87
Rexene Products Co., **IV** 457
Rexham Inc., **IV** 259; **8** 483–84
Rexnord Corporation, 14 43; **21 429–32;**
    37 30; **55** 324
Reycan, **49** 104
Reydel Industries, **23** 95–96
Reyes Holdings, Inc., **24** 388
The Reynolds and Reynolds Company,
    17 142, 144; **50 376–79**
Reynolds Electric Co., **22** 353

Reynolds Metals Company, IV 186–88;
    12 278; **19 346–48 (upd.); 21** 218; **22**
    455; **25** 22; **56** 9, 11
RF Communications, **II** 38
RF Micro Devices, Inc., 43 311–13
RF Monolithics Inc., **13** 193
RFF. *See* Réseau Ferré de France.
RFI Group, Inc., **54** 275
RGI. *See* Rockefeller Group Inc.
RHC Holding Corp., **10** 13; **13** 364; **27** 11
RHD Holdings, **23** 413
Rheem Manufacturing, **25** 368; **52** 398–99
Rheem South Africa Ltd., **59** 226
Rheinische Metallwaaren- und
    Maschinenfabrik AG, **9** 443–44
Rheinische Zuckerwarenfabrik GmbH, **27**
    460
Rheinmetall Berlin AG, 9 443–46
Rheinstahl Union Brueckenbau, **8** 242
Rhenus-Weichelt AG, **6** 424, 426
RHI AG, 53 283–86
RHI Entertainment Inc., **16** 257
Rhino Entertainment Company, 18
    457–60; 21 326
RHM. *See* Ranks Hovis McDougall.
Rhodes & Co., **8** 345
Rhodes Inc., 23 412–14
Rhodia SA, 38 378–80
Rhône Moulage Industrie, **39** 152, 154
Rhône-Poulenc S.A., I 388–90, 670, 672,
    692; **8** 153, 452; **9** 358; **10 470–72**
    (upd.); 16 438; **21** 466; **23** 194, 197; **34**
    284; **38** 379
Rhymney Iron Company, **31** 369
Rica Foods, Inc., 41 328–30
Ricardo Gallo. *See* Vidrala S.A.
Riccar, **17** 124; **41** 114
Riccardo's Restaurant, **18** 538
Riceland Foods, Inc., **27** 390
Rich Products Corporation, 7 448–49;
    38 381–84 (upd.)
Rich's Inc., **9** 209; **10** 515; **31** 191
Richard A. Shaw, Inc., **7** 128
Richard D. Irwin Inc. *See* Dow Jones &
    Company, Inc.
Richard P. Simmons, **8** 19
Richards & O'Neil LLP, **43** 70
The Richards Group, Inc., 58 300–02
Richardson Company, **36** 147
Richardson Electronics, Ltd., 17 405–07
Richardson Industries, Inc., 62 298–301
Richardson-Vicks Company. *See* The
    Procter & Gamble Company
Richardson's, **21** 246
Richfood Holdings, Inc., 7 450–51; 50
    458
Richland Co-op Creamery Company, **7** 592
Richland Gas Company, **8** 349
Richmon Hill & Queens County Gas Light
    Companies, **6** 455
Richmond American Homes of Florida,
    Inc., **11** 258
Richmond Carousel Corporation, **9** 120
Richmond Cedar Works Manufacturing
    Co., **12** 109; **19** 360
Richmond Corp., **15** 129
Richmond Paperboard Corp., **19** 78
Richmond Pulp and Paper Company, **17**
    281
Richton International Corporation, 39
    344–46
Richtree Inc., 63 328–30
Richway, **10** 515
Richwood Building Products, Inc., **12** 397

Richwood Sewell Coal Co., **17** 357
Rickards, Roloson & Company, **22** 427
Rickel Home Centers, **II** 673
Ricky Shaw's Oriental Express, **25** 181
Ricoh Company, Ltd., **III 159–61**; **8** 278; **18** 386, 527; **19** 317; **21** 122; **24** 429; **36 389–93 (upd.)**
Ricola Ltd., **62 302–04**
Ricolino, **19** 192
Riddell Inc., **33** 467
Riddell Sports Inc., **22 457–59**; **23** 449
Ridder Publications. *See* Knight-Ridder, Inc.
Ride, Inc., **22 460–63**
Ridge Tool Co., **II** 19
Ridgewell's Inc., **15** 87
Ridgewood Properties Inc., **12** 394
Ridgway Co., **23** 98
Ridgway Color, **13** 227–28
Ridley Corporation Ltd., **62 305–07**
Riedel-de Haën AG, **22** 32; **36** 431
Rieke Corp., **III** 569; **11** 535; **20** 361
The Riese Organization, **38 385–88**
Rieter Holding AG, **42 315–17**
Rig Tenders Company, **6** 383
Riggin & Robbins, **13** 244
Riggs National Corporation, **13 438–40**
Right Associates, **27** 21; **44** 156
Right Management Consultants, Inc., **42 318–21**
Right Source, Inc., **24** 96
RightPoint, Inc., **49** 124
RightSide Up, Inc., **27** 21
Rijnhaave Information Systems, **25** 21
Rike's, **10** 282
Riken Corp., **10** 493
Riken Kagaku Co. Ltd., **48** 250
Riklis Family Corp., **9 447–50**; **12** 87; **13** 453; **38** 169; **43** 355
Rinascente Group, **12** 153, **54** 220
Ring King Visibles, Inc., **13** 269
Ring Ltd., **43** 99
Ringier America, **19** 333
Ringköpkedjan, **II** 640
Ringling Bros., Barnum & Bailey Circus, **25** 312–13
Ringnes Bryggeri, **18** 396
Rini-Rego Supermarkets Inc., **13** 238
Rini Supermarkets, **9** 451; **13** 237
Rinker Group Ltd., **65 298–301**
Rio Grande Industries, Inc., **12** 18–19
Rio Grande Servaas, S.A. de C.V., **23** 145
Rio Sportswear Inc., **42** 269
Rio Sul Airlines. *See* Varig, SA.
Rio Tinto plc, **II** 628; **IV** 58–61, 189–91, 380; **19 349–53 (upd.)**; **21** 352; **27** 253; **42** 395; **50 380–85 (upd.)**
Riocell S.A., **57** 47
Riordan Freeman & Spogli, **13** 406
Riordan Holdings Ltd., **10** 554; **67** 298
Riser Foods, Inc., **9 451–54**; **13** 237–38
Risk Management Partners Ltd., **35** 36
Risk Planners, **II** 669
Ritchie Bros. Auctioneers Inc., **41 331–34**
Rite Aid Corporation, **V 174–76**; **9** 187, 346; **12** 221, 333; **16** 389; **18** 199, 286; **19 354–57 (upd.)**; **23** 407; **29** 213; **31** 232; **32** 166, 169–70; **63 331–37 (upd.)**
Rite-Way Department Store, **II** 649
Riteway Distributor, **26** 183
Rittenhouse Financial Services, **22** 495
Ritter Co. *See* Sybron Corp.

Ritter Sport. *See* Alfred Ritter GmbH & Co. KG.
Ritz Camera Centers, **18** 186; **34 375–77**
Ritz-Carlton Hotel Company L.L.C., **9 455–57**; **21** 366; **29 403–06 (upd.)**
Ritz Firma, **13** 512
Riunione Adriatica di Sicurtà SpA, **III 345–48**
Riva Group Plc, **53** 46
The Rival Company, **17** 215; **19 358–60**
Rivarossi, **16** 337
Rivaud Group, **29** 370
River Boat Casino, **9** 425–26
River City Broadcasting, **25** 418
River North Studios. *See* Platinum Entertainment, Inc.
River Oaks Furniture, Inc., **43 314–16**
River Ranch Fresh Foods—Salinas, Inc., **41** 11
River Thames Insurance Co., Ltd., **26** 487
Riverdeep Group plc, **41** 137
Riverside Chemical Company, **13** 502
Riverside Furniture, **19** 455
Riverside Insurance Co. of America, **26** 487
Riverside Iron Works, Ltd., **8** 544
Riverside National Bank of Buffalo, **11** 108
Riverside Press, **10** 355–56
Riverside Publishing Company, **36** 272
Riverwood International Corporation, **7** 294; **11 420–23**; **48 340–44 (upd.)**
Riviana Foods, **27 388–91**
Riyadh Armed Forces Hospital, **16** 94
Rizzoli Publishing, **23** 88
RJMJ, Inc., **16** 37
RJR Nabisco Holdings Corp., **I** 261; **II** 370, 426, 477–78, 542–44; **V 408–10, 415**; **7** 130, 132, 277, 596; **9** 469; **12** 82, 559; **13** 342; **14** 214, 274; **17** 4/1; **22** 73, 95, 441; **23** 163; **24** 273; **30** 384; **32** 234; **33** 228; **36** 151, 153; **46** 259; **49** 77–78; **56** 190–92; **63** 84. *See also* R.J Reynolds Tobacco Holdings Inc., Nabisco Brands, Inc.; R.J. Reynolds Industries, Inc.
RK Rose + Krieger GmbH & Co. KG, **61** 286–87
RKO. *See* Radio-Keith-Orpheum.
RKO-General, Inc., **8** 207
RLA Polymers, **9** 92
RMC Group p.l.c., **III 737–40**; **34 378–83 (upd.)**
RMH Teleservices, Inc., **42 322–24**
RMP International, Limited, **8** 417
Roadhouse Grill, Inc., **22 464–66**; **57** 84
Roadline, **6** 413–14
Roadmaster Industries, Inc., **16 430–33**; **22** 116
Roadmaster Transport Company, **18** 27; **41** 18
RoadOne. *See* Miller Industries, Inc.
Roadstone-Wood Group, **64** 98
Roadway Express, Inc., **25 395–98 (upd.)**
Roadway Services, Inc., **V 502–03**; **12** 278, 309; **14** 567; **15** 111
Roanoke Capital Ltd., **27** 113–14
Roanoke Electric Steel Corporation, **45 368–70**
Roanoke Fashions Group, **13** 532
Robb Engineering Works, **8** 544
Robbins & Myers Inc., **13** 273; **15 388–90**
Robeco Group, **26** 419–20

Roberds Inc., **19 361–63**
Robert Allen Companies, **III** 571; **20** 362
Robert Benson, Lonsdale & Co. Ltd. *See* Dresdner Kleinwort Wasserstein.
Robert Bosch GmbH, **I 392–93**, 411; **13** 398; **16 434–37 (upd.)**; **22** 31; **43 317–21 (upd.)**; **67** 80–82
Robert E. McKee Corporation, **6** 150
Robert Fleming Holdings Ltd., **I** 471; **11** 495
Robert Gair Co., **15** 128
Robert Garrett & Sons, Inc., **9** 363
Robert Half International Inc., **18 461–63**
Robert Hall Clothes, Inc., **13** 535
Robert Hansen Trucking Inc., **49** 402
Robert Johnson, **8** 281–82
Robert McLane Company. *See* McLane Company, Inc.
Robert McNish & Company Limited, **14** 141
Robert Mondavi Corporation, **15 391–94**; **39** 45; **50 386–90 (upd.)**; **54** 343
Robert Skeels & Company, **33** 467
Robert Stigwood Organization Ltd., **23** 390
Robert W. Baird & Co. Incorporated, **III** 324; **7** 495; **67 328–30**
Robert Watson & Co. Ltd., **I** 568
Robert Wood Johnson Foundation, **35 375–78**
Robertet SA, **39 347–49**
Roberts Express, **V** 503
Roberts Pharmaceutical Corporation, **16 438–40**
Robertson Animal Hospital, Inc., **58** 355
Robertson Building Products, **8** 546
Robertson-Ceco Corporation, **8** 546; **19 364–66**
Robertson, Stephens & Co., **22** 465
Robin Hood Flour Mills, Ltd., **7** 241–43; **25** 241
Robin International Inc., **24** 14
Robinair, **10** 492, 494
Robinson & Clark Hardware. *See* Clarcor Inc.
Robinson Helicopter Company, **51 315–17**
Robinson Industries, **24** 425
Robinson Smith & Robert Haas, Inc., **13** 428
Robinson's Japan Co. Ltd. *See* Ito-Yokado Co., Ltd.
Robinsons Soft Drinks Limited, **38** 77
Robot Manufacturing Co., **16** 8
Robotic Simulations Limited, **56** 134
Robotic Vision Systems, Inc., **16** 68
ROC. *See* Royal Olympic Cruise Lines Inc.
Roccade, **39** 177
Roch, S.A., **23** 83
Roche Biomedical Laboratories, Inc., **8** 209–10; **11 424–26**. *See also* Laboratory Corporation of America Holdings.
Roche Bioscience, **14 403–06 (upd.)**
Roche Holding AG, **30** 164; **32** 211, 213–14; **37** 113; **50** 421
Rocher Soleil, **48** 315
Rochester Gas And Electric Corporation, **6 571–73**
Rochester Group, Inc., **60** 267
Rochester Instrument Systems, Inc., **16** 357
Rochester Telephone Corporation, **6 332–34**; **12** 136; **16** 221

Röchling Industrie Verwaltung GmbH, **9** 443

Rock Bottom Restaurants, Inc., 25 399–401

Rock Island Plow Company, **10** 378

Rock of Ages Corporation, 37 329–32

Rock Systems Inc., **18** 337

Rock-Tenn Company, 13 441–43; 59 347–51 (upd.)

Rockcor Inc., **I** 381; **13** 380

Rockcote Paint Company, **8** 552–53

The Rockefeller Foundation, 34 384–87; 52 15

Rockefeller Group International Inc., 58 303–06

Rocket Chemical Company. *See* WD-40 Company.

Rockford Corporation, 43 322–25

Rockford Products Corporation, 55 323–25

Rockhaven Asset Management, LLC, **48** 18

Rocking Horse Child Care Centers of America Inc. *See* Nobel Learning Communities, Inc.

Rockland Corp., **8** 271

Rockland React-Rite, Inc., **8** 270

Rockower of Canada Ltd., **II** 649

Rockport Company. *See* Reebok International Ltd.

Rockresorts, Inc., **22** 166

RockShox, Inc., 26 412–14; 65 325–27

Rockwell Automation, 43 326–31 (upd.)

Rockwell International Corporation, I 78–80; 6 263; **7** 420; **8** 165; **9** 10; **10** 279–80; **11** 268, 278, 427–30 (upd.), 473; **12** 135, 248, 506; **13** 228; **18** 369; **22** 51, 53, 63–64; **32** 81, 84–85; **33** 27; **35** 91; **36** 121–22; **39** 30; **44** 357

Rocky Mexico, Inc., **62** 353

Rocky Mountain Bankcard, **24** 393

Rocky Mountain Financial Corporation, **13** 348

Rocky River Power Co. *See* Connecticut Light and Power Co.

Rocky Shoes & Boots, Inc., 26 415–18

Rod's Food Products, **36** 163

Rodale, Inc., 47 336–39 (upd.)

Rodale Press, Inc., 22 443; **23 415–17; 54** 22

Rodamco N.V., IV 698; **26 419–21**

Rodel, Inc., **26** 425

Röder & Co., **34** 38, 40

Rodeway Inns of America, **11** 242; **25** 309

Rodgers Instrument Corporation, **38** 391

Rodney Square Management Corp., **25** 542

Rodven Records, **23** 391

Roederstein GmbH, **21** 520

Roegelein Co., **13** 271

Roger Cleveland Golf Company, **15** 462; **43** 375–76

Roger Williams Foods, **II** 682

Rogers & Co., **63** 17–18

Rogers & Oling, Inc., **17** 533

Rogers & Phillips, Inc., **56** 383

Rogers CanGuard, Inc., **32** 374

Rogers Communications Inc., 30 388–92 (upd.); 50 275. *See also* Maclean Hunter Publishing Limited.

Rogers Corporation, 61 310–13

Rohde & Schwarz GmbH & Co. KG, 39 350–53

Rohe Scientific Corp., **13** 398

Röhm and Haas Company, I 391–93; 14 182–83; **26 422–26 (upd.)**

ROHN Industries, Inc., 22 467–69

Rohölgewinnungs AG, **IV** 485

Rohr Gruppe, **20** 100

Rohr Incorporated, 9 458–60; 11 165

The Rokke Group, **16** 546; **32** 100; **59** 431

Rokko Warehouse & Transport Co. Ltd., **56** 181

Rolamentos FAG Ltda., **62** 132

Roland Berger & Partner GmbH, 37 333–36

Roland Corporation, 38 389–91

Roland Murten A.G., 7 452–53

Roland NV, **41** 340

Rolex. *See* Montres Rolex S.A.

Roll International Corporation, 37 337–39

Rollerblade, Inc., 15 395–98; 22 202–03; 34 388–92 (upd.)

Rolling Stones Records, **23** 33

Rollins Burdick Hunter Company, **III** 204; **45** 27

Rollins, Inc., 11 431–34

Rollo's, **16** 95

Rolls-Royce Allison, 29 407–09 (upd.)

Rolls-Royce Motors Ltd., I 194–96; 9 16–18, 417–18; **11** 403; **21** 435

Rolls-Royce plc, I 81–83; 7 454–57 (upd.); 9 244; **11** 268; **12** 190; **13** 414; **21 433–37 (upd.); 24** 85; **27** 495–96; **46** 358–59; **47** 7, 9

Rolls-Royce Group PLC, 67 331–36 (upd.)

Rolm Corp., **III** 149; **18** 344; **22** 51; **34** 512

Rolodex Electronics, **23** 209, 212

Rolscreen. *See* Pella Corporation.

Romacorp, Inc., 58 307–11

Rome Network, Inc., **24** 95

Romeike Ltd., **55** 289

Romper Room Enterprises, Inc., **16** 267

Ron Tonkin Chevrolet Company, 55 326–28

Ronco, Inc., 15 399–401; 21 327

Rondel's, Inc., **8** 135

Ronel, **13** 274

Roni-Linda Productions, Inc., **27** 347

Ronnebyredds Trävaru, **25** 463

Ronrico, **58** 195

Ronson PLC, 49 337–39

Ronzoni Foods Corp., **15** 221

Roombar S.A., **28** 241

Rooms To Go Inc., 28 389–92

Rooney Brothers Co., 25 402–04

Roosevelt Hospital. *See* Continuum Health Partners, Inc.

Roots Canada Ltd., 27 194; **42 325–27**

Roper Industries, Inc., 15 402–04; 25 89; **50 391–95 (upd.)**

Ropert Group, **18** 67

Ropes & Gray, 40 377–80

RoProperty Services BV. *See* Rodamco N.V.

Rorer Group, I 666–68; 12 4; **16** 438; **24** 257

Rosaen Co., **23** 82

Rosarita Food Company, **25** 278

Rose & Co., **26** 65

Rose Acre Farms, Inc., 60 255–57

Rose Art Industries, 58 312–14

Rose Exterminator Company, **25** 15

Rose Forgrove Ltd., **51** 249, 251

Rose Foundation, **9** 348

Rose's Stores, Inc., 13 261, **444–46; 23** 215

Rosebud Dolls Ltd., **25** 312

Roseburg Forest Products Company, 58 315–17

Rosehaugh, **24** 269

RoseJohnson Incorporated, **14** 303; **50** 311

Rosemount Estates. *See* Southcorp Limited.

Rosemount Inc., 13 226; **15 405–08; 46** 171; **61** 98

Rosen Enterprises, Ltd., **10** 482

Rosenbluth International Inc., 14 407–09

Rosenfeld Hat Company. *See* Columbia Hat Company.

Rosengrens Produktions AB, **53** 158

Rosenmund-Guèdu, **31** 158

Rosenthal A.G., **34** 493, 496

Rosewood Financial, Inc., **24** 383

Roshco, Inc., **27** 288

Roslyn Bancorp, **46** 316

Ross Carrier Company, **8** 115

Ross Clouston, **13** 244

Ross Stores, Inc., 17 408–10; 43 332–35 (upd.)

Rossendale Combining Company, **9** 92

Rossignol Ski Company, Inc. *See* Skis Rossignol S.A.

Rostelecom, **59** 208–11

Rostocker Brauerei VEB, **9** 87

Rostvertol plc, 62 308–10

Roswell Public Service Company, **6** 579

Rotadisk, **16** 7

Rotary International, 31 395–97

Rotec Zug AG, **57** 402

Rotelcom Data Inc., **6** 334; **16** 222

Rotem Amfert Negev Ltd., **55** 229

Roth Co., **16** 493

Roth Freres SA, **26** 231; **59** 252

Rothmans International BV, **33** 82

Rothmans International p.l.c., IV 93; **V 411–13; 27** 488

Rothmans UK Holdings Limited, 19 367–70 (upd.)

Rothschild Financial Corporation, **13** 347

Roto-Rooter, Inc., 13 149–50; **15 409–11; 16** 387; **61 314–19 (upd.)**

Rotor Tool Co., **II** 16

Rotork plc, 46 361–64

Rotterdam Beleggings (Investment) Consortium. *See* Robeco.

Rotterdam Lloyd, **6** 403–04; **26** 241–42

The Rottlund Company, Inc., 28 393–95

Rouge Steel Company, 8 448–50

Roughdales Brickworks, **14** 249

Rougier. *See* Groupe Rougier, SA.

Roularta Media Group NV, 48 345–47

Round Hill Foods, **21** 535

Round Table, **16** 447

Roundy's Inc., 14 410–12; 58 318–21 (upd.)

Rouse & Associates, **57** 221–23

The Rouse Company, 15 412–15; 63 338–41 (upd.)

Roussel Uclaf, I 669–70; 8 451–53 (upd.); 18 236; **19** 51; **25** 285; **38** 379

Routh Robbins Companies, **21** 96

Roux Séguéla Cayzac & Goudard. *See* Euro RSCG Worldwide S.A.

Rover Group Ltd., 7 458–60; 11 31, 33; **14** 36; **21 441–44 (upd.); 24** 87–88; **38** 83, 85–86

Rowan Companies, Inc., 43 336–39

Rowe & Pitman, **14** 419

Rowe Price-Fleming International, Inc., **11** 495
Rowell Welding Works, **26** 433
Rowenta. *See* Groupe SEB.
Rowland Communications Worldwide, **42** 328, 331
Rowntree and Co., **27** 104
Rowntree Mackintosh PLC, II 548, **568–70; 7** 383; **28** 311
Roxell, N.V., **43** 129
Roxoil Drilling, **7** 344
Roy and Charles Moore Crane Company, **18** 319
Roy F. Weston, Inc., 33 369–72
Royal & Sun Alliance Insurance Group plc, 55 329–39 (upd.)
Royal Ahold N.V., **60** 17, 305. *See also* Koninklijke Ahold N.V.
Royal Appliance Manufacturing Company, 15 416–18; **17** 233
The Royal Bank of Canada, II 344–46; **21** 445–48 (upd.)
Royal Bank of Ireland Ltd., **16** 13
The Royal Bank of Scotland Group plc, 10 336–37; **12** 421–23; **38** 13, 392–99 (upd.); **42** 76
Royal Bankgroup of Acadiana, Inc., **37** 201
Royal Canin S.A., 39 354–57
Royal Caribbean Cruises Ltd., 22 444–46; 470–73; **27** 29
Royal Copenhagen A/S, **9** 99
Royal Crown Company, Inc., 8 536–37; **14** 32–33; **23** 418–20; **52** 97. *See also* Cott Corporation.
Royal Data, Inc. *See* King Kullen Grocery Co., Inc.
Royal Doulton plc, IV 659; **14** 413–15; **34** 497; **38** 400–04 (upd.)
Royal Dutch Petroleum Company, IV 530–32, 657; **24** 496. *See also* Shell Transport and Trading Company p.l.c.
Royal Dutch/Shell Group, IV 530–32; **7** 481–82; **17** 417; **19** 73, 75; **21** 203; **22** 237; **24** 520; **41** 356–57, 359; **49** 340–44 (upd.); **57** 152, 237; **59** 372
Royal Electric Company, **6** 501
Royal Exchange Assurance Corp., **III** 369–71, 373
Royal Farms, **24** 528
Royal Food Products, **24** 528–29; **36** 163
Royal Gist-brocades NV, **56** 95
Royal Grolsch NV, 54 315–18
Royal Industries, Inc., **19** 371
Royal Insurance Holdings plc, III 349–51
Royal International Optical Inc. *See* U.S. Vision, Inc.
Royal Interocean Lines, **6** 404; **26** 243
Royal Jackson, **14** 236
Royal KPN N.V., 30 393–95, 461, 463
Royal Mail Group, **6** 416; **19** 198
Royal Nedlloyd. *See* Koninglijke Nedlloyd N.V.
Royal Nepal Airline Corporation, 41 335–38
Royal Netherlands Steamship Company. *See* KNSM.
Royal Numico N.V., 33 145, 147; **37** 340–42
Royal Olympic Cruise Lines Inc., 52 297–99
Royal Orchid Holidays. *See* Thai Airways International.
Royal Ordnance plc, **13** 356; **24** 87–88

Royal Packaging Industries Van Leer N.V., 9 305; **30** 396–98; **64** 188
Royal Pakhoed N.V., **9** 532
Royal PTT Post, 30 463
Royal Securities Company, **6** 585
Royal Sporting House Pte. Ltd., **21** 483
Royal Vendex KBB N.V. *See* Koninklijke Vendex KBB N.V. (Royal Vendex KBB N.V.).
Royal Vopak NV, 41 339–41
Royal Wessanen. *See* Koninklijke Wessanen.
Royale Belge, **III** 177, 200, 394
Royale Inns of America, **25** 307
Royce Electronics, **III** 569; **18** 68; **20** 361
Royce Laboratories Inc., **56** 375
Royster-Clark, Inc., **13** 504
RPI. *See* Research Polymers International.
RPISA. *See* Refinaria de Petrólco Ipiranga S.A.
RPM Inc., 8 454–57; **36** 394–98 (upd.); **51** 369
RSA Security Inc., 46 365–68; **47** 430
RSC. *See* Rental Service Corporation.
RSI Corp., **8** 141–42; **30** 160
RSO Records, **23** 390
RSV, **26** 496
RTI Group, **58** 366
RTL Group SA, 41 29; **44 374–78**
RTL-Véeronlque, **IV** 611
RTM Restaurant Group, 58 322–24
RTS Packaging, LLC, **59** 347, 350
RTW Air Service(s) Pte. Ltd., **51** 123
RTZ Corporation PLC, IV 189–92; 7 261, 263; **27** 256. *See also* Rio Tinto plc.
Rubber Latex Limited, **9** 92
Rubbermaid Incorporated, III 613–15; **12** 168–69; **13** 317–18; **19** 407; **20** 262, **454–57 (upd.); 21** 293; **28** 479; **31** 160–61; **34** 369. *See also* Newell Rubbermaid Inc.
Rubicon Group plc, **32** 50
Rubio's Restaurants, Inc., 35 379–81
Rubo Lederwaren, **14** 225
Ruby Tuesday, Inc., 18 464–66
Rubyco, Inc., **15** 386
La Ruche Meridionale, **12** 153
Ruddick Corporation, **23** 260
Rudolf Wolff & Co. Ltd., **64** 297
Ruel Smith Transportation Services, Inc., **39** 66
Ruff Hewn, **25** 48
Rug Corporation of America, **12** 393
The Rugby Group plc, 31 398–400; 34 380
Ruger Corporation, **19** 431
Ruhrgas AG, V 704–06; 7 141; **18** 50; **38** 405–09 (upd.); **42** 263; **50** 90, 172
Ruhrkohle AG, IV 193–95. *See also* RAG AG.
Ruiz Food Products, Inc., 53 287–89
Runnymede Construction Co., **8** 544
Runo-Everth Treibstoff und Ol AG, **7** 141
Rural Cellular Corporation, 43 340–42
Rural/Metro Corporation, 28 396–98; 39 22
Rush Communications, 33 373–75. *See also* Phat Fashions LLC.
Rush Enterprises, Inc., 64 336–38
Russ Berrie and Company, Inc., 12 424–26
Russell Corporation, 8 458–59; **12** 458; **30 399–401 (upd.)**

Russell Electric, **11** 412
Russell Kelly Office Services, Inc. *See* Kelly Services Inc.
Russell Reynolds Associates Inc., 38 410–12
Russell Stover Candies Inc., 12 427–29
Rust Craft Greeting Cards Incorporated, **12** 561
Rust International Inc., 6 599–600; **11** 435–36
Rust-Oleum Corporation, **36** 396
Rütgers AG, **60** 250
Rütgerswerke AG, **8** 81
Ruth's Chris Steak House, 28 399–401; **37** 297
Rutherford Hill Winery, **48** 392
RWE Group, V 707–10; 33 194, 196; **50** 396–400 (upd.); **59** 135–37
RxAmerica, **22** 40; **25** 297
Ryan Aeronautical, **I** 525; **10** 522; **11** 428
Ryan Aircraft Company, **9** 458
Ryan Beck & Co., Inc., 66 273–75
Ryan Homes, Inc., **8** 401–02
Ryan Insurance Company, **III** 204; **45** 26
Ryan Milk Company of Kentucky, **7** 128
Ryan's Family Steak Houses, Inc., 15 419–21; **19** 287; **22** 464
Ryanair Holdings plc, 35 382–85
Ryder System, Inc., V 504–06; 13 192; **19** 293; **24** 408–11 (upd.); **25** 93, 144; **28** 3; **41** 37
Ryecroft Foods Limited, **61** 387–88
Ryerson Tull, Inc., 19 216; **40** 269, **381–84 (upd.)**
Rykoff-Sexton, Inc., **21** 497; **26** 503, 505
The Ryland Group, Inc., 8 460–61; **19** 126; **37** 343–45 (upd.)
Ryobi Ltd., **I** 202
Ryohin Keikaku Co., Ltd., **36** 420
Rypper Corp., **16** 43
Rysher Entertainment, **22** 162; **25** 329
The Ryvita Company Limited, **II** 466; **13** 52; **41** 31

S&A Restaurant Corp., **7** 336; **10** 176; **14** 331; **15** 363; **38** 100–01
S&C Electric Company, 15 422–24
S&H. *See* Sperry and Hutchinson Co.
S&H Diving Corporation, **6** 578
S&K Famous Brands, Inc., 23 421–23
S&P. *See* Standard & Poor's Corporation.
S&V Screen Inks, **13** 227–28
S&W Fine Foods, **12** 105
S + T Gesellschaft fur Reprotechnik mbH, **29** 306
S.A. CARFUEL, **12** 152
S.A. Cockerill Sambre. *See* Cockerill Sambre Group.
S.A. de C.V., **29** 461
S.A. des Ateliers d'Aviation Louis Breguet. *See* Groupe Dassault Aviation SA.
s.a. GB-Inno-BM. *See* GIB Group.
S.A. Greetings Corporation, **22** 35
S.A. Innovation—Bon Marché N.V., **26** 160
S.A. Schonbrunn & Co., **14** 18
S.B. Irving Trust Bank Corp., **II** 218
S.B. Penick & Co., **8** 548
S.C. Johnson & Son, Inc., III 58–59; 8 130; **10** 173; **12** 126–28; **17** 215; **21** 386; **28** 215, **409–12 (upd.)**
S-C-S Box Company, **8** 173
S.D. Cohn & Company, **10** 455; **27** 364
S.E. Rykoff & Co., **26** 503

S.G. Warburg and Co., **II** 629; **14** 419; **16** 377. *See also* SBC Warburg.
S. Grumbacher & Son. *See* The Bon-Ton Stores, Inc.
S.H. Kress & Co., **17** 203–04
S.I.P., Co., **8** 416
S-K-I Limited, **15** 457–59
S.K. Wellman Ltd., **14** 81; **59** 222
S. Kuhn & Sons, **13** 221
S.P. Richards Co., **45** 177–79
S Pearson & Son Ltd. *See* Pearson plc
S.R. Dresser Manufacturing Co. *See* Dresser Industries, Inc.
S.S. Kresge Company. *See* Kmart Corporation.
S.S. Pierce Company, **60** 267
S.S.V. Inc., **36** 420
S.T. Cooper & Sons, **12** 283
S.T. Dupont Company, **23** 55
S.W.M. Chard, **27** 259
SA Alliance Air, **28** 404
SA Express, **28** 404
Sa SFC NV, **18** 162–63
SAA. *See* South African Airways.
SAA (Pty) Ltd., **28** 402–04
SAAB. *See* Svenska Aeroplan Aktiebolaget.
Saab Automobile AB, **32** 386–89 (upd.); **36** 242–43; **63** 211; **64** 150
Saab-Scania A.B., **I** 197–98, 210; **10** 86; **11** 437–39 (upd.); **16** 322; **34** 117
Saarberg-Konzern, **IV** 196–99. *See also* RAG AG.
Saarstahl AG, **IV** 228
Saatchi & Saatchi plc, **I** 33–35; **6** 229; **14** 49–50; **16** 72; **21** 236; **22** 296; **33** 65, 67; **328–31** (upd.); **64** 351
SAB. *See* South African Breweries Ltd.
SAB WABCO International AB, **53** 85
Saban Entertainment, **24** 171
Sabanci Group, **54** 197–98
Sabanci Holdings. *See* Haci Omer Sabanci Holdings A.S.
Sabaté Diosos SA, **48** 348–50
Sabela Media, Inc., **49** 423
Sabena S.A./N.V., **18** 80; **33** 49, 51, 376–79; **34** 398
Saber Energy, Inc., **7** 553–54
Saber Software Corp., **25** 348
Sabi International Ltd., **22** 464
Sabian Ltd., **38** 68
SABIC. *See* Saudi Basic Industries Corporation.
SABIM Sable, **12** 152
Sabine Transportation Company. *See* Kirby Corporation.
SABMiller plc, **59** 352–58 (upd.)
SABO Maschinenfabrik AG, **21** 175
Sabratek Corporation, **29** 410–12
SABRE Group Holdings, Inc., **25** 144; **26** 427–30; **28** 22; **52** 23
Sabre Interactive, **46** 434
Sacer, **31** 127–28
Sach Bicycle Components. *See* SRAM Corporation.
Sachs-Dolmer G.m.b.H., **22** 334
Sacilor. *See* Usinor S.A.
Sacks Industries, **8** 561
OY Saco AB, **23** 268
SACOR, **IV** 250, 504–06
Sacramento Savings & Loan Association, **10** 43, 45
Saddlebag Lake Resorts, Inc., **63** 23

SADE Ingenieria y Construcciones S.A., **38** 435, 437
Sadia S.A., **59** 359–62
SAE Magnetics Ltd., **18** 250
SAFECO Corporation, **III** 352–54; **10** 44
Safeguard Scientifics, Inc., **10** 232–34, 473–75; **27** 338
Safelite Glass Corp., **19** 371–73
Safer, Inc., **21** 385–86
Safeskin Corporation, **18** 467–70
Safety Components International, Inc., **63** 342–44
Safety 1st, Inc., **24** 412–15; **46** 192; **59** 164
Safety-Kleen Corp., **8** 462–65
Safety Rehab, **11** 486
Safety Savings and Loan, **10** 339
Safeway Inc., **II** 601, 604–05, 609–10, 628, 632, 637, **654–56**; **7** 61, 569; **9** 39; **10** 442; **11** 239, 241; **12** 113, 209, 559; **13** 90, 336; **16** 64, 160, 249, 452; **22** 37; **24** 273, **416–19** (upd.); **25** 296; **27** 292; **28** 510; **30** 24, 27; **33** 305; **40** 366; **56** 87
Safeway PLC, **50** 401–06 (upd.)
Saffa SpA, **41** 325–26
Safilo SpA, **40** 155–56; **54** 319–21
SAFR. *See* Société Anonyme des Fermiers Reúnis.
Saga Communications, Inc., **II** 608; **27** 226, **392–94**
Saga Petroleum ASA, **35** 318
Sagami Optical Co., Ltd., **48** 295
Sagamore Insurance Company, **51** 37–39
The Sage Group, **43** 343–46
Sagebrush Sales, Inc., **12** 397
Sagebrush Steakhouse, **29** 201
SAGEM S.A., **37** 346–48
Saginaw Dock & Terminal Co., **17** 357
Sagitta Arzneimittel, **18** 51; **50** 90
Sahara Casino Partners L.P., **19** 379
Sahara Resorts. *See* Santa Fe Gaming Corporation.
SAI. *See* Stamos Associates Inc.
Sai Baba, **12** 228
Saia Motor Freight Line, Inc., **6** 421–23; **45** 448
Saibu Gas, **IV** 518–19
SAIC. *See* Science Applications International Corporation.
SAIC Velcorex, **12** 153; **27** 188
Saiccor, **IV** 92; **49** 353
Sainrapt et Brice, **9** 9
Sainsbury's. *See* J Sainsbury PLC.
St. Alban Boissons S.A., **22** 515
St. Andrews Insurance, **III** 397
Saint-Gobain. *See* Compagnie de Saint Gobain S.A.
Saint-Gobain Weber. *See* Weber et Broutin France.
St. Ives Laboratories Inc., **36** 26
St Ives plc, **34** 393–95
St. James Associates, **32** 362–63
The St. Joe Company, **31** 422–25
St. Joe Corporation, **59** 185
St. Joe Gold, **23** 40
St. Joe Minerals Corp., **8** 192
St. Joe Paper Company, **8** 485–88
St. John Knits, Inc., **14** 466–68
St. John's Wood Railway Company, **6** 406
St. Jude Medical, Inc., **11** 458–61; **43** 347–52 (upd.)
St. Laurent Paperboard Inc., **30** 119

St. Lawrence Cement Inc., **III** 702; **8** 258–59
St. Louis and Illinois Belt Railway, **6** 504
Saint Louis Bread Company, **18** 35, 37; **44** 327
St. Louis Concessions Inc., **21** 39
St. Louis Music, Inc., **48** 351–54
St. Louis Post-Dispatch LLC, **58** 283
St. Louis Troy and Eastern Railroad Company, **6** 504
St. Luke's-Roosevelt Hospital Center. *See* Continuum Health Partners, Inc.
St. Martin's Press, **25** 484–85; **35** 452
St. Mary Land & Exploration Company, **60** 189; **63** 345–47
St. Michel-Grellier S.A., **44** 40
St. Paul Bank for Cooperatives, **8** 489–90
St. Paul Book and Stationery, Inc., **47** 90
The St. Paul Companies, **III** 355–57; **15** 257; **21** 305; **22** 154, **492–95** (upd.)
St. Paul Fire and Marine Insurance Co. *See* The St. Paul Companies, Inc.
St. Paul Venture Capital Inc., **34** 405–06
St. Regis Paper Co., **10** 265; **12** 377
SAirGroup, **29** 376; **33** 268, 271; **37** 241; **46** 398; **47** 287
SAirLogistics, **49** 80–81
Saison Group, **V** 184–85, 187–89; **36** 417–18, 420; **42** 340–41
Sakae Printing Co., Ltd., **64** 261
Sako Ltd., **39** 151
Saks Fifth Avenue, **15** 291; **18** 372; **21** 302; **22** 72; **25** 205; **27** 329; **50** 117–19; **57** 179–80
Saks Holdings, Inc., **24** 420–23
Saks Inc., **41** 342–45 (upd.)
Sakura Bank, **39** 286. *See also* Sumitomo Mitsui Banking Corporation.
Salant Corporation, **12** 430–32; **27** 445; **51** 318–21 (upd.)
Sale Knitting Company, **12** 501. *See also* Tultex Corporation.
Salem Broadcasting, **25** 508
Salem Carpet Mills, Inc., **9** 467
Salem Sportswear, **25** 167
Salick Health Care, Inc., **21** 544, 546; **50** 58; **53** 290–92
Salim Group, **18** 180–81
Salinas Equipment Distributors, Inc., **33** 364
Sallie Mae. *See* SLM Holding Corp.; Student Loan Marketing Association.
Sally Beauty Company, Inc., **8** 15–17; **36** 23–26; **60** 258–60
Salmon Carriers, **6** 383
Salmon River Power & Light Company, **12** 265
Salomon Brothers Inc., **28** 164
Salomon Inc., **II** 426, 432, 434, 441, **447–49**; **III** 221, 215, 721; **IV** 137; **7** 114; **9** 378–79, 386; **11** 35, 371; **13** 331, **447–50** (upd.) Inc.; **18** 60, 62; **19** 293; **21** 67; **22** 102; **23** 472–74; **25** 12, 125; **42** 34
Salomon Smith Barney, **30** 124
Salomon Worldwide, **20** 458–60; **33** 7. *See also* adidas-Salomon AG.
Salt River Project, **19** 374–76
Salton, Inc., **30** 402–04
Salvagnini Company, **22** 6
The Salvation Army USA, **15** 510–11; **32** 390–93

Salvatore Ferragamo Italia S.p.A., 62 311–13
Salzgitter AG, IV 200–01; 17 381
SAM. *See* Sociedad Aeronáutica de Medellín, S.A.
Sam & Libby Inc., **30** 311
Sam Ash Music Corporation, 30 405–07
Sam Goody, **9** 360–61; **63** 65
Sam's Club, 8 555–57; **12** 221, 335; **13** 548; **14** 393; **15** 470; **16** 64; **25** 235; **40** 385–87; **41** 254–56
Samancor Ltd., **IV** 92–93
Samaritan Senior Services Inc., **25** 503
Samas-Groep N.V., **47** 91
Sambo's, **12** 510
Samcor Glass. *See* Corning Inc.
Samedan Oil Corporation, **11** 353
Sames, S.A., **21** 65–66
Samick Musical Instruments Co., Ltd., 56 297–300
Samim, **IV** 422
Sammy Corp., **54** 16
Samna Corp., **6** 256; **25** 300
Sampoerna PT, **62** 96–97
Sampson's, **12** 220–21
Samson Technologies Corp., **30** 406
Samsonite Corporation, 13 311, 451–53; **16** 20–21; **38** 169; **43** 353–57 (upd.)
Samsung-Calex, **17** 483
Samsung Display Co., Ltd., **59** 81
Samsung Electronics Co., Ltd., 14 416–18; **18** 139, 260; **41** 346–49 (upd.)
Samsung Group, I 515–17; **13** 387; **29** 207–08; **62** 68–69
Samuel Austin & Son Company, **8** 41
Samuel Cabot Inc., 53 293–95
Samuel Meisel & Company, Inc., **11** 80–81; **29** 509, 511
Samuel, Son & Co. Ltd., **24** 144
Samuels Jewelers Incorporated, 30 408–10
San Antonio Public Service Company, **6** 473
San Diego Gas & Electric Company, V 711–14; **6** 590; **11** 272; **25** 416. *See also* Sempra Energy.
San Francisco Baseball Associates, L.P., 55 340–43
San Francisco Maillots, **62** 228
San Francisco Mines of Mexico Ltd., **22** 285
San Gabriel Light & Power Company, **16** 496; **50** 496
San Giorgio Macaroni Inc., **53** 242
San Miguel Corporation, I 221; **15** 428–30; **23** 379; **57** 303–08 (upd.); **63** 227
San Paolo IMI S.p.A., **63** 52–53
Sanborn Hermanos, S.A., 20 461–63; **21** 259
Sanborn Manufacturing Company, **30** 138
Sandals Resorts International, 65 302–05
Sandcastle 5 Productions, **25** 269–70
Sanders Associates, Inc., **9** 324; **13** 127–28
Sanderson Computers, **10** 500
Sanderson Farms, Inc., 15 425–27
Sandia National Laboratories, 49 345–48
Sandiacre Packaging Machinery Ltd., **51** 249–50
Sandoz Ltd., I 671–73; **7** 315, 452; **8** 108–09, 215; **10** 48, 199; **11** 173; **12** 388; **15** 139; **18** 51; **22** 475; **27** 299; **50** 90. *See also* Novartis AG.
Sandoz Nutrition Corp., **24** 286

SandPoint Corp., **12** 562; **17** 254
Sandusky Plastics, Inc., **17** 157
Sandusky Portland Cement Company, **24** 331
Sandvik AB, IV 202–04; **32** 394–98 (upd.)
Sandwell, Inc., **6** 491
Sandwich Chef, Inc. *See* Wall Street Deli, Inc.
Sandy's Pool Supply, Inc. *See* Leslie's Poolmart, Inc.
Sanford C. Bernstein Inc., **63** 27
Sanford-Brown College, Inc., **41** 419–20
Sanichem Manufacturing Company, **16** 386
Sanitary Farm Dairies, Inc., **7** 372
Sanitation Systems, Inc. *See* HMI Industries.
Sanitec Corporation, 51 322–24
Sanko Peterson Corporation, **55** 306
Sankyo Company, Ltd., I 674–75; **56** 301–04 (upd.)
Sanlam, **IV** 535; **49** 353
SANlight Inc., **62** 293
Sano Corporation, **63** 142
Sano Railway Company, **6** 430
Sanofi Group, I 676–77; **21** 205; **23** 236, 238, 242; **35** 262–63, 265
The Sanofi-Synthélabo Group, 49 349–51 (upd.)
SanomaWSOY Corporation, 51 325–28
Sanpaolo IMI S.p.A., 50 407–11
Sanrio Company, Ltd., 38 413–15
Santa Ana Savings and Loan, **10** 339
Santa Ana Wholesale Company, **16** 451
Santa Barbara Restaurant Group, Inc., 37 349–52
The Santa Cruz Operation, Inc., 38 416–21
Santa Fe Gaming Corporation, 19 377–79
Santa Fe Gold Corporation, **38** 232
Santa Fe Industries, **12** 19; **28** 498
Santa Fe International Corporation, 38 422–24
Santa Fe Pacific Corporation, V 507–09; **24** 98. *See also* Burlington Northern Santa Fe Corporation.
Santa Fe Railway, **12** 278; **18** 4
Santa Fe Snyder Corp., **61** 75
Santa Fe Southern Pacific Corp., **III** 512; **6** 150, 599; **22** 491
Santa Margherita S.p.A. *See* Industrie Zignago Santa Margherita S.p.A.
Santa Rosa Savings and Loan, **10** 339
Santal, **26** 160
Santiago Land Development Corporation, **58** 20
Santone Industries Inc., **16** 327
Sanus Corp. Health Systems, **III** 317
Sanwa Bank, Ltd., II 347–48; **7** 119; **15** 43, 431–33 (upd.)
Sanyo Chemical Manufacturing Co., **III** 758
Sanyo Electric Co., Ltd., II 91–92; **III** 569; **14** 535; **20** 361; **36** 399–403 (upd.)
Sanyo-Kokusaku Pulp Co., Ltd., IV 327–28
Sanyo Semiconductor, **17** 33
Sanyo White Cement Co. Ltd., **60** 301
SAP AG, 11 78; **16** 441–44; **25** 34; **26** 496, 498; **43** 358–63 (upd.)
SAP America Inc., **38** 431–32
SAPAC. *See* Société Parisienne d'Achats en Commun.

Sapeksa, **55** 189
Sapirstein Greeting Card Company. *See* American Greetings Corporation.
Sappi Limited, 49 352–55
Sapporo Breweries Limited, I 282–83; **13** 454–56 (upd.); **20** 28–29; **21** 319–20; **36** 404–07 (upd.); **52** 32
SAPRA-Landauer Ltd., **51** 210
Saputo Inc., 59 363–65
Sara Lee Corporation, II 571–73, 675; **7** 113 **8** 262; **10** 219–20; **11** 15, 486; **12** 494, 502, 531; **15** 359, 434–37 (upd.), 507; **19** 192; **25** 91, 125, 166, 523; **26** 325, 503; **29** 132; **38** 381; **45** 111–12, 114; **49** 10; **52** 99, 101; **54** 322–27 (upd.); **63** 218
Saracen's Head Brewery, **21** 245
Saratoga Partners, **24** 436
Sarawak Trading, **14** 448
Sargent & Lundy, **6** 556
SARL, **12** 152
Sarma, **26** 159–61
Sarmag, **26** 161
Sarnoff Corporation, 57 309–12, 333, 335
Saros Corp., **15** 474; **62** 141
Sarotti GmbH, **53** 315
Sarpe, **IV** 591
Sarrió S.A., **41** 325–26
Sartek Industries Inc., **44** 441
The SAS Group, 34 396–99 (upd.)
SAS Institute Inc., 10 476–78; **38** 432; **64** 361
Saskatchewan Oil and Gas Corporation, **13** 556–57
Sasol Limited, IV 533–35; **47** 340–44 (upd.)
SAT. *See* Stockholms Allmänna Telefonaktiebolag.
Satcom Group of Companies, **32** 40
Satellite Business Systems, **21** 14; **23** 135; **27** 304
Satellite Software International, **10** 556
Satellite Television PLC, **23** 135
Satellite Transmission and Reception Specialist Company, **11** 184
Saturn Corporation, 7 461–64; **21** 449–53 (upd.); **22** 154; **36** 242; **64** 150
Saturn Industries, Inc., **23** 489
SATV. *See* Satellite Television PLC.
Satyam, **59** 129
Saucona Iron Co., **7** 48
Saucony Inc., 35 386–89
Sauder Woodworking Co., 12 433–34; **35** 390–93 (upd.)
Saudi Arabian Airlines, 6 114–16; **27** 132, 395–98 (upd.)
Saudi Arabian Oil Company, IV 536–39; **17** 411–15 (upd.); **50** 412–17 (upd.). *See also* Arabian American Oil Co.
Saudi Arabian Parsons Limited, **8** 416
Saudi Basic Industries Corporation (SABIC), 58 325–28
Saudi Refining Inc., **IV** 539; **17** 414
Saudia. *See* Saudi Arabian Airlines.
Sauer-Danfoss Inc., 61 320–22
Saunders Karp & Co., **26** 190
Saunders, Karp, and Megrue, LP, **28** 258
Sauza, **31** 92
Sav-on Drug, **II** 605; **12** 477
Sav-X, **9** 186
Sava Group, **20** 263
Savacentre Ltd., **II** 658; **13** 284
Savage, **19** 430

Savannah Electric & Power Company, **38** 448

Savannah Foods & Industries, Inc., 7 **465–67**; **32** 274, 277; **35** 178

Savannah Gas Company, **6** 448; **23** 29

Save & Prosper Group, **10** 277

Save-A-Lot, **II** 682; **11** 228

Save Mart, **14** 397; **27** 292

Save.com, **37** 409

Savia S.A. de C.V., **29** 435

Savio, **IV** 422

Oy Savo-Karjalan Tukkuliike, **8** 293

Savoy Group, **24** 195

Savoy Industries, **12** 495

Savoy Pictures Entertainment Inc., **25** 214

Sawdust Pencil Company, **29** 372

Sawgrass Asset Management, LLC, **48** 18

Sawhill Tubular Products, **41** 3

Sawtek Inc., 43 364–66 (upd.); **63** 398

Sawyer Electrical Manufacturing Company, **11** 4

Sawyer Industries, Inc., **13** 532

Sawyer Research Products, Inc., **14** 81

Saxby, S.A., **13** 385

Saxon Oil, **11** 97

Saxon Petroleum, Inc., **19** 162

Saxonville USA, **61** 254, 256

SB Acquisitions, Inc., **46** 74

SBAR, Inc., 30 4

Sbarro, Inc., 16 445–47; **19** 435; **27** 146; **64 339–42 (upd.)**

SBC Communications Inc., 25 498–99; **29** 62; **32 399–403 (upd.)**; **34** 362; **43** 447; **47** 10; **63** 371, 373, 384

SBC Warburg, 14 419–21; **15** 197

SBC Warburg Dillon Read, **52** 355

Sberbank, 62 314–17

SBI. *See* State Bank of India.

SBK Entertainment World, Inc., **22** 194; **24** 485; **26** 187

SBS Broadcasting, **61** 58

SBS Technologies, Inc., 25 405–07

SCA. *See* Svenska Cellulosa AB.

SCA Services, Inc., **9** 109

SCAC. *See* Société Commercial d'Affrètements et de Combustibles.

Scaldia Paper BV, **15** 229

Scan Screen, **IV** 600

SCANA Corporation, 6 574–76; **19** 499; **56 305–08 (upd.)**

Scanair, **34** 397–98

Scancem, **38** 437

Scandic Hotels AB, **49** 193

Scandinavian Airlines System, I 119–20, 121; **25** 159; **26** 113; **27** 26; **31** 305; **33** 50; **38** 105. *See also* The SAS Group.

Scandinavian Broadcasting System SA, **53** 325

ScanDust, **III** 625

Scania-Vabis. *See* Saab-Scania AB.

ScanSource, Inc., 29 413–15

Scantron Corporation, **17** 266–68

Scarborough Public Utilities Commission, 9 461–62

Scaturro Supermarkets, **24** 528

SCB Computer Technology, Inc., 29 **416–18**

SCEcorp, V 715–17; **6** 590. *See also* Edison International.

Scenic Airlines, Inc., **25** 420, 423

Scenographic Designs, **21** 277

SCG Corporation, **56** 323

Schäfer, **31** 158

Schaper Mfg. Co., **12** 168

Schauman Wood Oy, **IV** 277, 302

Schawk, Inc., 24 424–26

Scheels All Sports Inc., 63 348–50

Scheid Vineyards Inc., 66 276–78

Schein Pharmaceutical Inc., **13** 77; **56** 375

Schell Brewing. *See* August Schell Brewing Company Inc.

Schenker Deutschland AG, **59** 391

Schenker-Rhenus Ag, 6 424–26

Schenley Industries Inc., **9** 449; **24** 140

Scherer. *See* R.P. Scherer.

Schering A.G., I 681–82, 684, 701; **10** 214; **14** 60; **16** 543; **36** 92, 148; **50** **418–22 (upd.)**

Schering-Plough Corporation, I 683–85; **11** 142, 207; **14** 58, 60, **422–25 (upd.)**; **36** 91–92; **45** 382; **49 356–62 (upd.)**; **63** 232–33

Schiavi Homes, Inc., **14** 138

Schibsted ASA, 31 401–05

Schick Products, **41** 366

Schick Shaving, **38** 363, 365

Schick-Wilkinson Sword. *See* Wilkinson Sword Ltd.

Schieffelin & Somerset Co., 61 323–25

Schindler Holding AG, 27 267; **29** **419–22**

Schlitz Brewing Co., **I** 255, 268, 270, 291, 600; **10** 100; **12** 338; **18** 500; **23** 403

Schlotzsky's, Inc., 36 408–10

Schlumberger Limited, III 616–18; **13** 323; **17 416–19 (upd.)**; **25** 191; **43** 91, 338; **45** 418; **49** 305; **59** 217, **366–71** **(upd.)**

Schmalbach-Lubeca-Werke A.G., **15** 128

Schmermund Verpackungstechnik GmbH, **60** 193

Schmid, **19** 166

Schmitt Music Company, 40 388–90

Schneider National, Inc., 36 411–13; **47** 318–19; **63** 237

Schneider S.A., II 93–94; **18 471–74** **(upd.)**; **19** 165–66; **37** 39

Schneiderman's Furniture Inc., 28 **405–08**

Schnitzer Steel Industries, Inc., 19 **380–82**

Schnoll Foods, **24** 528

Schnuck Markets, Inc., **60** 256; **63** 129

Schober Direktmarketing, **18** 170

Schocken Books, **13** 429

Schoeller & Co. Bank AG, **59** 239

Schoeller & Hoesch Group, **30** 349, 352

Schoenfeld Industries, **16** 511

Scholastic Corporation, 10 479–81; **29** 143, **423–27 (upd.)**

Scholl Inc., **49** 359, 380

Schöller, **27** 436, 439

School-Tech, Inc., 62 318–20

Schott Brothers, Inc., 67 337–39

Schott Corporation, 53 296–98

Schottenstein Stores Corp., 14 426–28; **19** 108; **24** 26; **38** 475. *See also* American Eagle Outfitters, Inc.

Schreiber Foods, **26** 432

Schreiber Frères. *See* Groupe Les Echos.

Schrock Cabinet Company, **13** 564

Schroders plc, 42 332–35

Schroders Ventures, **18** 345

Schroff Inc., **26** 361, 363

Schubach, **30** 408

Schubert & Salzer GmbH, **42** 316

Schuck's Auto Supply. *See* CSK Auto Corporation.

Schuff Steel Company, 26 431–34

Schuitema, **II** 642; **16** 312–13

Schuler Chocolates, **15** 65

Schuler Homes, Inc., **58** 84

Schuller International, Inc., **11** 421

Schultz Sav-O Stores, Inc., 21 454–56; **31 406–08**

Schultz, Snyder & Steele Lumber Company, **61** 254, 256

Schuykill Energy Resources, **12** 41

Schwabe-Verlag, **7** 42

Schwabel Corporation, **19** 453

Schwan's Sales Enterprises, Inc., 7 **468–70**; **26 435–38 (upd.)**

Schwartz Iron & Metal Co., **13** 142

Schwarze Pumpe, **38** 408

Schweitzer-Mauduit International, Inc., **16** 304; **43** 258; **52 300–02**

Schweizerische Kreditanstalt, **6** 489

Schweizerische Nordostbahn, **6** 424

Schweizerische Post-, Telefon- und **Telegrafen-Betriebe, V 321–24**

Schweizerische Ruckversicherungs-Gesellschaft. *See* Swiss Reinsurance Company.

Schweppes Ltd. *See* Cadbury Schweppes PLC.

Schwinn Cycle and Fitness L.P., 16 494; **19 383–85**; **26** 412; **47** 95

The Schwinn GT Co., **26** 185

Schwitzer, **II** 420

SCI. *See* Service Corporation International; Société Centrale d'Investissement.

SCI 169 Rue de Rennes, **53** 32

SCI Systems, Inc., 9 463–64; **12** 451

Scicon International, **14** 317; **49** 165

SciCor Inc., **30** 152

Science Applications International **Corporation, 15 438–40**; **59** 399–400

Scientific-Atlanta, Inc., 6 335–37; **45** **371–75 (upd.)**; **54** 406

Scientific Communications, Inc., **10** 97

Scientific Data Systems, **10** 365

Scientific Games Corporation, 20 48; **64** **343–46 (upd.)**

Scientific Materials Company, **24** 162

Scientific Research Products, Inc. of Delaware, **60** 287

Scioto Bank, **9** 475

Scitex Corporation Ltd., 15 148, 229; **24** **427–32**; **26** 212; **43** 150; **48** 123

Scitor, **52** 108

SCM Corp., **8** 223–24; **17** 213

SCO. *See* Santa Cruz Operation, Inc.

SCOA Industries, Inc., **13** 260

Scopus Technology Inc., **38** 431

SCOR S.A., III 394; **20 464–66**

The Score Board, Inc., 19 386–88

Score Entertainment. *See* Donruss Playoff L.P.

Score! Learning, Inc., **42** 211

Scot Lad Foods, **14** 411

Scotch House Ltd., **19** 181

Scotia Securities, **II** 223

Scotiabank. *See* The Bank of Nova Scotia.

Scotsman Industries, Inc., II 420; **16** 397; **20 467–69**

Scott-Ballantyne Company. *See* Ballantyne of Omaha, Inc.

Scott Communications, Inc., **10** 97

Scott Fetzer Company, III 214; **12** **435–37**, 554–55; **17** 233; **18** 60, 62–63; **42** 33

Scott Graphics, **8** 483

Scott Health Care, **28** 445

Scott Holdings, **19** 384

Scott Paper Company, **IV** 325, 327, **329–31**; **8** 483; **16** 302, 304; **17** 182; **18** 181; **29** 333; **31** 409–12 **(upd.)**; **43** 258

Scott Transport, **27** 473

Scotti Brothers, **20** 3

Scottish & Newcastle plc, **15 441–44**; **35** **394–97 (upd.)**; **50** 201, 277; **59** 255, 296, 299

Scottish and Southern Energy plc, **66** **279–84 (upd.)**

Scottish Amicable plc, **48** 328

Scottish Brick, **14** 250

Scottish Electric, **6** 453

Scottish Hydro-Electric PLC, **13 457–59**. *See also* Scottish and Southern Energy plc.

Scottish Inns of America, Inc., **13** 362

Scottish Media Group plc, **32 404–06**; **41** 350–52

Scottish Mutual plc, **39** 5–6

Scottish Nuclear, Ltd., **19** 389

Scottish Power plc, **49 363–66 (upd.)**

Scottish Radio Holding plc, **41 350–52**

Scottish Sealand Oil Services Ltd., **25** 171

Scottish Universal Investments, **45** 189

ScottishPower plc, **19 389–91**; **27** 483, 486

Scottish Telecom plc, **19** 389

The Scotts Company, **22 474–76**

Scotty's, Inc., **12** 234; **22 477–80**; **26** 160–61

Scovill Fasteners Inc., **22** 364; **24 433–36**

SCP Pool Corporation, **39 358–60**

Scranton Corrugated Box Company, Inc., **8** 102

Scranton Plastics Laminating Corporation, **8** 359

Screg Group, **I** 563; **24** 79; **31** 128

Scriha & Deyhle, **10** 196

Scripps-Howard, Inc. *See* The E.W. Scripps Company.

Scrivner Inc., **17** 180

SCS Interactive, **44** 261

Scudder Kemper Investments. *See* Zurich Financial Services.

SD-Scicon plc, **24** 87

SD Warren, **49** 352–53

SDA Systems Inc., **48** 75

SDB Espan, **51** 16

SDGE. *See* San Diego Gas & Electric Company.

SDK Health Care Information Systems, **16** 94

SDL PLC, **67 340–42**

SDV. *See* Groupe Bolloré.

Sea Containers Ltd., **29 428–31**

Sea-Land Service Inc., **9** 510–11; **22** 164, 166

Sea Life Centre Aquariums, **10** 439

Sea Star Line, **41** 399

Sea World Property Trust, **58** 359

Seabee Corp., **18** 276

Seaboard Air Line Railroad. *See* CSX Corporation.

Seaboard Corporation, **36 414–16**

Seaboard Finance Company, **13** 63

Seaboard Surety Company, **III** 357; **22** 494

Seabourn Cruise Lines, **6** 368; **27** 90, 92

Seabrook Farms Co., **24** 527–28

Seabulk Offshore International. *See* Hvide Marine Incorporated.

SeaCat Corporation, **59** 282

Seacat-Zapata Off-Shore Company, **18** 513

Seafield Capital Corporation, **27** 385, 387. *See also* LabOne, Inc.

Seafield Estate and Consolidated Plantations Berhad, **14** 448

Seafirst. *See* Seattle First National Bank, Inc.

SeaFirst Corp., **II** 228; **17** 462

Seagate Technology, Inc., **8 466–68**; **9** 57; **10** 257, 403–04, 459; **11** 56, 234; **13** 483; **18** 250; **25** 530; **34 400–04 (upd.)**; **45** 429

The Seagram Company Ltd., **I** 284–86[ro]; **7** 155; **18** 72; **21** 26, 401; **22** 194; **23** 125; **25** 266, 268, 366, **408–12 (upd.)**; **26** 125, 127, 152; **28** 475; **29** 196; **31** 269; **33** 375, 424, 432; **46** 438; **47** 418–20; **50** 114

Seagull Energy Corporation, **11 440–42**

Seahawk Services Ltd., **37** 289

Seal Products, Inc., **12** 264

Seal Sands Chemicals, **16** 69

Sealaska Corporation, **60 261–64**

Sealed Air Corporation, **14 429–31**; **57** **313–17 (upd.)**

Sealed Power Corporation, **I 199–200**; **10** 492–94. *See also* SPX Corporation.

SeaLite Sciences, Inc., **52** 171

Sealright Co., Inc., **17 420–23**; **64** 186–87

SealRite Windows, **19** 446

Sealtest, **14** 205

Sealy Inc., **12 438–40**; **28** 416; **34** 407

Seaman Furniture Company, Inc., **28** 389; **32 407–09**

Sean John, Inc., **58** 15

Seaquist Manufacturing Corporation, **9** 413–14; **33** 335–36

Searle & Co. *See* G.D. Searle & Co.

Sears Canada Inc., **25** 221

Sears Logistics Services, **18** 225–26

Sears plc, **V 177–79**

Sears, Roebuck and Co., **II** 411, 414; **III** 259, 265, 340, 536, 598, 653–55; **V** **180–83**; **7** 166, 479; **8** 224, 287–89; **9** 44, 65–66 156, 210, 213, 219, 235–36, 430–31, 538; **10** 10, 50–52, 199, 236–37, 288, 304–05, 490–91; **11** 62, 349, 393, 498; **12** 54, 96–98, 309, 311, 315, 430–31, 439, 522, 548, 557; **13** 165, 260, 268, 277, 411, 545, 550, 562–63; **14** 62; **15** 402, 470; **16** 73, 75, 160, 327–28, 560; **17** 366, 460, 487; **18** 65, 168, 283, 445, **475–79 (upd.)**; **19** 143, 221, 309, 490; **20** 259, 263; **21** 73, 94, 96–97; **23** 23, 52, 210; **25** 221, 357, 535; **27** 30, 32, 163, 347–48, 416, 428–30; **33** 311–12; **36** 418; **50** 391; **51** 319, 321; **56 309–14 (upd.)**; **57** 11

Sears Roebuck de México, S.A. de C.V., **20 470–72**; **21** 259; **34** 302

Seashore Transportation Co., **13** 398

SEAT. *See* Sociedad Española de Automoviles de Turismo.

Seat Pagine Gialle S.p.A., **47 345–47**

Seatrain International, **27** 474

Seattle Brewing and Malting Company. *See* Rainier Brewing Company.

Seattle City Light, **50 423–26**

Seattle Coffee Company, **32** 12, 15

Seattle Electric Company, **6** 565; **50** 365–66

Seattle FilmWorks, Inc., **20 473–75**

Seattle First National Bank Inc., **8** **469–71**

Seattle Times Company, **15 445–47**

Seaview Oil Co., **IV** 393

Seaway Express, **9** 510

Seaway Food Town, Inc., **9** 452; **15** **448–50**

SeaWest, **19** 390

SEB Group. *See* Skandinaviska Enskilda Banken AB.

SEB S.A. *See* Groupe SEB.

Sebastian International, **48** 422

Sebastiani Vineyards, Inc., **28 413–15**; **39** 421

Seco Products Corporation, **22** 354

Secon GmbH, **13** 160

Second Harvest, **29 432–34**

Second National Bank of Bucyrus, **9** 474

Second National Bank of Ravenna, **9** 474

Secoroc, **III** 427

Le Secours, **III** 211

SecPac. *See* Security Pacific Corporation.

Secure Horizons, **11** 378–79

Secure Networks, Inc., **25** 349

Securicor Plc, **11** 547; **45 376–79**

Securitas AB, **41** 77, 80; **42** 165–66, **336–39**

Securities Industry Automation Corporation, **9** 370

Securities Management & Research, Inc., **27** 46

Security Bancorp, **25** 186–87

Security Capital Corporation, **17** **424–27**; **21** 476; **48** 330–31; **49** 28–29

Security Capital Group, **56** 58–59

Security Data Group, **32** 373

Security Dynamics Technologies, Inc., **46** 367

Security Express, **10** 269

Security Life and Annuity Company, **11** 213

Security Management Company, **8** 535–36

Security National Corp., **10** 246

Security Pacific Corporation, **II 349–50**, 422; **III** 366; **8** 45, 48; **11** 447; **17** 137

Security Trust Company, **9** 229, 388

Security Union Title Insurance Co., **10** 43–44

SED International Holdings, Inc., **43** **367–69**

Sedat Eldem, **13** 475

SEDCO, **17** 418

Seddon Group Ltd., **67 343–45**

Sedgwick Group PLC, **I** 427; **10** 38

Sedgwick Sales, Inc., **29** 384

SEDTCO Pty., **13** 61

See's Candies, Inc., **30 411–13**

Seeburg Corporation, **15** 538

Seed Restaurant Group Inc., **13** 321; **27** 145

Seed Solutions, Inc., **11** 491

Seeman Brothers. *See* White Rose, Inc.

SEEQ Technology, Inc., **9** 114; **13** 47; **17** 32, 34; **64** 246

Sega Enterprises, Ltd., **28** 320

Sega of America, Inc., **7** 396; **10** 124–25, 284–86, **482–85**; **18** 520; **50** 157

Sega of Japan, **24** 4

Sego Milk Products Company, **7** 428

Seguros Comercial America, **21** 413

Seguros Monterrey Aetna, **19** 189; **45** 294

Seguros Serfin S.A., **25** 290

Segway LLC, **48 355–57**

Seibels, Bruce & Co., **11** 394–95

Seibert-Oxidermo, Inc., **55** 321
Seibu Allstate Life Insurance Company, Ltd., **27** 31
Seibu Department Stores, Ltd., V 184–86; 42 340–43 (upd.)
Seibu Group, **36** 417–18; **47** 408–09
Seibu Railway Co. Ltd., V 510–11
Seibu Saison, **6** 207
Seifu Co. Ltd., **48** 250
Seigle's Home and Building Centers, Inc., 41 353–55
Seika Co., Ltd., **55** 48
Seiko Corporation, III 619–21; 11 46; **12** 317; **13** 122; **16** 168, 549; **17 428–31 (upd.); 21** 122–23; **22** 413; **41** 72
Seiko Instruments USA Inc., **23** 210
Seikosha Co., **64** 261
Seimi Chemical Co. Ltd., **48** 41
Seino Transportation Company, Ltd., 6 427–29
Seismograph Service Limited, **11** 413; **17** 419
Seita, 23 424–27
Seitel, Inc., 47 348–50
The Seiyu, Ltd., V 187–89; 36 417–21 (upd.); 63 427, 431
Seizo-sha, **12** 483
Sekisui Chemical Co., Ltd., III 741–43
Selat Marine Services, **22** 276
Selby Shoe Company, **48** 69
Select Comfort Corporation, 34 405–08
Select Energy, Inc., **48** 305
Select-Line Industries, **9** 543
Select Medical Corporation, 65 306–08
Select Theatres Corp. *See* Shubert Organization Inc.
Selection Trust, **IV** 380, 565
Selectour SA, 53 299–301
Selectronics Inc., **23** 210
Selectrons Ltd., **41** 367
Selena Coffee Inc., **39** 409
Selenia, **I** 467; **38** 374
Self Auto, **23** 232
The Self-Locking Carton Company, **14** 163
Self-Service Drive Thru, Inc., **25** 389
Self Service Restaurants, **II** 613
Selfix, Inc. *See* Home Products International, Inc.
Selfridges Plc, 34 409–11
Selig Chemical Industries, **54** 252, 254
Seligman & Latz, **18** 455
Selkirk Communications Ltd., **26** 273
Sells-Floto, **32** 186
The Selmer Company, Inc., 19 392–94, 426, 428; 55 113
Seltel International Inc., **35** 246
Sema plc, **59** 370
Semarca, **11** 523
Sematech, **18** 384, 481
SembCorp Logistics Ltd., **53** 199, 203
Sembler Company, **11** 346
SEMCO Energy, Inc., 44 379–82
Semi-Tech Global, **30** 419–20
Seminis, Inc., 21 413; **29 435–37**
Seminole Electric Cooperative, **6** 583
Seminole Fertilizer, **7** 537–38
Seminole National Bank, **41** 312
Semitic, Inc., **33** 248
Semitool, Inc., 18 480–82
Sempra Energy, 25 413–16 (upd.)
Semrau and Sons, **II** 601
Semtech Corporation, 32 410–13
Sencel Aero Engineering Corporation, **16** 483

Seneca Foods Corporation, 17 432–34; 60 265–68 (upd.)
Senega, **63** 365
Sengstacke Enterprises. *See* Real Times LLC.
Senior Corp., **11** 261
Sennheiser Electronic GmbH & Co. KG, 66 285–89
Sensi, Inc., **22** 173
Sensient Technologies Corporation, 52 303–08 (upd.)
Sensormatic Electronics Corp., 11 443–45; 39 77–79
Sensory Science Corporation, 37 353–56
Sentinel Foam & Envelope Corporation, **14** 430
Sentinel Savings and Loan, **10** 339
Sentry, **II** 624
Sentry Insurance Company, **10** 210
La Senza Corporation, 66 205–07
Sepal, Ltd., **39** 152, 154
AB Separator. *See* Alfa-Laval AB
SEPECAT, **24** 86
Sephora SA, **51** 234–35; **54** 265–67
Sepracor Inc., 45 380–83
Sept, **IV** 325
Sequa Corporation, 13 460–63; 54 328–32 (upd.)
Sequel Corporation, **41** 193
Sequent Computer Systems Inc., **10** 363
Sequoia Athletic Company, **25** 450
Sequoia Pharmacy Group, **13** 150
Sera-Tec Biologicals, Inc. *See* Rite Aid Corporation.
Seragen Inc., **47** 223
Serco Group plc, 47 351–53
Sereg Valves, S.A., **17** 147
Serewatt AG, **6** 491
Serologicals Corporation, 63 351–53
Serono S.A., 47 354–57
Serta, Inc., 28 416–18
Serval Marketing, **18** 393
Servam Corp., **7** 471–73
Service and Systems Solutions Ltd., **64** 404
Service America Corp., 7 471–73; 27 480–81
Service Co., Ltd., **48** 182
Service Control Corp. *See* Angelica Corporation.
Service Corporation International, 6 293–95; 16 343–44; **37** 66–68; **51 329–33 (upd.)**
Service Corporation of America, **17** 552
Service Games Company, **10** 482
Service Master L.P., **34** 153
Service Merchandise Company, Inc., V 190–92; 6 287; **9** 400; **19 395–99 (upd.)**
Service Products Buildings, Inc. *See* Turner Construction Company.
Service Q. General Service Co., **I** 109
ServiceMaster Inc., 6 44–46; 13 199; **23 428–31 (upd.)**
Services Maritimes des Messageries Impériales. *See* Compagnie des Messageries Maritimes.
ServiceWare, Inc., **25** 118
Servicios de Corte y Confeccion, S.A. de C.V., **64** 142
Servicios Financieros Quadrum S.A., **14** 156
Servisair Plc, **49** 320
Servisco, **II** 608

ServiStar Coast to Coast Corporation. *See* TruServ Corporation.
ServoChem A.B., **I** 387
Servomation Corporation, **7** 472–73
Servomation Wilbur. *See* Service America Corp.
Servoplan, S.A., **8** 272
SES Staffing Solutions, **27** 21
Sesame Street Book Club, **13** 560
Sesamee Mexicana, **48** 142
Sessler Inc., **19** 381
Setagaya Industry Co., Ltd., **48** 295
SETCAR, **14** 458
Seton Scholl. *See* SSL International plc.
Seven Arts Limited, **25** 328
7-Eleven, Inc., 32 414–18 (upd.); 36 358
Seven-Eleven Japan Co., **41** 115. *See also* Ito-Yokado Co., Ltd.
Seven Generation, Inc., **41** 177
Seven Hills Paperboard, LLC, **59** 350
Seven Network Limited, **25** 329
Seven-Up Co., **18** 418
SevenOne Media, **54** 297
Sevenson Environmental Services, Inc., 42 344–46
Seventh Street Corporation, **60** 130
Severn Trent PLC, 12 441–43; 38 425–29 (upd.)
Severonickel Combine, **48** 300
Seversky Aircraft Corporation, **9** 205
Severstal Joint Stock Company, 65 309–12
Sewell Plastics, Inc., **10** 222
Sextant In-Flight Systems, LLC, **30** 74
Seymour Electric Light Co., **13** 182
Seymour International Press Distributor Ltd., **IV** 619
Seymour Press, **IV** 619
Seymour Trust Co., **13** 467
SF Bio, **52** 51
SF Recycling & Disposal, Inc., **60** 224
SFI Group plc, 51 334–36
SFIC Holdings (Cayman) Inc., **38** 422
SFIM Industries, **37** 348
SFNGR. *See* Nouvelles Galeries Réunies.
SFS Bancorp Inc., **41** 212
SFX Broadcasting Inc., **24** 107
SFX Entertainment, Inc., 36 422–25; 37 383–84
SG Racing, Inc., **64** 346
SGC. *See* Supermarkets General Corporation.
SGE. *See* Vinci.
SGI, 29 438–41 (upd.)
SGL Carbon Group, **40** 83; **46** 14
SGLG, Inc., **13** 367
SGS-Thomson Microelectronics, **54** 269–70
Shakespeare Company, 16 296; **22 481–84**
Shakey's Pizza, **16** 447
Shaklee Corporation, 12 444–46; 17 186; **38** 93; **39 361–64 (upd.)**
Shalco Systems, **13** 7
Shampaine Industries, Inc., **37** 399
Shamrock Advisors, Inc., **8** 305
Shamrock Broadcasting Inc., **24** 107
Shamrock Capital L.P., **7** 81–82
Shamrock Holdings, **9** 75; **11** 556; **25** 268
Shamrock Oil & Gas Co., **7** 308
Shan-Chih Business Association, **23** 469
Shana Corporation, **62** 142
Shandwick International, **47** 97
Shanggong Co. Ltd., **65** 134

Shanghai Asia Pacific Co., **59** 59
Shanghai Crown Maling Packaging Co. Ltd., **13** 190
Shanghai Dajiang, **62** 63
Shanghai General Bearing Co., Ltd., **45** 170
Shanghai International Finance Company Limited, **15** 433
Shanghai Kyocera Electronics Co., Ltd., **21** 331
Shanghai Petrochemical Co., Ltd., 18 483–85; **21** 83; **45** 50
Shanghai Shesuo UNF Medical Diagnostic Reagents Co., **61** 229
Shanghai Tobacco, **49** 150, 153
Shangri-La Asia Ltd., **22** 305
Shanks Group plc, 45 384–87
Shannon Aerospace Ltd., 36 426–28
Shannon Group, Inc., **18** 318, 320; **59** 274, 277
Shansby Group, **27** 197; **43** 218; **64** 265
Shanshin Engineering Company Ltd., **60** 236
Share Drug plc, **24** 269
Shared Financial Systems, Inc., **10** 501
Shared Medical Systems Corporation, 14 432–34
Shared Technologies Inc., **12** 71
Shared Use Network Systems, Inc., **8** 311
ShareWave Inc., **48** 92
Shari Lewis Enterprises, Inc., **28** 160
Sharmoon, **63** 151
Sharon Steel Corp., **7** 360–61; **8** 536; **13** 158, 249; **47** 234
Sharon Tank Car Corporation, **6** 394; **25** 169
Sharp Corporation, II 95–96; **III** 14, 428, 455, 480; **6** 217, 231; **11** 45; **12** 447–49 (upd.); **13** 481; **16** 83; **21** 123; **22** 197; **40 391–95 (upd.)**
Sharp Water, Inc., **56** 62
The Sharper Image Corporation, 10 486–88; **23** 210; **26** 439; **27** 429; **62** 321–24 **(upd.)**
Sharples Separator Company, **64** 17
Shasta Beverages. *See* National Beverage Corp.
Shato Holdings, Ltd., **60** 357
Shaw Communications Inc., **26** 274; **35** 69
The Shaw Group, Inc., 50 427–30; **64** 372
Shaw Industries, Inc., 9 465–67; **19** 274, 276; **25** 320; **40 396–99 (upd.)**
Shaw's Supermarkets, Inc., II 658–59; **23** 169; **56 315–18**
Shawell Precast Products, **14** 248
Shawinigan Water and Power Company, **6** 501–02
Shea Homes. *See* J.F. Shea Co., Inc.
Sheaffer Group, **23** 54, 57
Shearman & Sterling, 32 419–22; **35** 467
Shearson Hammill & Company, **22** 405–06
Shearson Lehman Brothers Holdings Inc., I 202; **II** 398–99, 450, 478; **8** 118; **9 468–70 (upd.)**; **10** 62–63; **11** 418; **12** 459; **15** 124, 463–64
Shearson Lehman Hutton Group, **49** 181
Shearson Lehman Hutton Holdings Inc., II 339, 445, **450–52**; **9** 125; **10** 59, 63; **17** 38–39
Shedd's Food Products Company, **9** 318
Sheffield Exploration Company, **28** 470
Sheffield Forgemasters Group Ltd., **39** 32
Sheffield Silver Company, **67** 322–23

Shekou Container Terminal, **16** 481; **38** 345
Shelby Insurance Company, **10** 44–45
Shelby Steel Processing Co., **51** 238
Shelby Williams Industries, Inc., 14 435–37
Shelco, **22** 146
Sheldahl Inc., 23 432–35
Shelf Life Inc. *See* King Kullen Grocery Co., Inc.
Shell. *See* Royal Dutch/Shell Group; Shell Oil Company; Shell Transport and Trading Company p.l.c.
Shell Canada Limited, **32** 45
Shell Chemical Corporation, **IV** 531–32, 540; **8** 415; **24** 151
Shell Forestry, **21** 546; **50** 58
Shell France, **12** 153
Shell Oil Company, IV 540–41; **6** 382, 457; **8** 261–62; **11** 522; **14** 25, **438–40 (upd.)**; **17** 417; **19** 175–76; **21** 546; **22** 274; **24** 520; **25** 96, 232, 469; **26** 496; **41** 356–60 **(upd.)**, 395; **45** 54
Shell Transport and Trading Company p.l.c., IV 425, 429, 440, 454, 466, 470, 472, 474, 484–86, 491, 505, 508, **530–32**, 564; **31** 127–28; **50** 58, 355. *See also* Royal Dutch Petroleum Company; Royal Dutch/Shell.
Shell Western E & P, **7** 323
Sheller-Globe Corporation, I 201–02; **17** 182
Shells Seafood Restaurants, Inc., 43 370–72
Shelly Brothers, Inc., **15** 65
Shenzhen Namtek Co., Ltd., **61** 232–33
Shepherd Hardware Products Ltd., **16** 357
Shepherd Neame Limited, 30 414–16
Shepherd Plating and Finishing Company, **13** 233
Shepler Equipment Co., **9** 512
Sheraton Corp. of America, **III** 98–99; **11** 198; **13** 362–63; **21** 91
Sherborne Group Inc./NH Holding Inc., **17** 20
Sherbrooke Paper Products Ltd., **17** 281
Sheridan Bakery, **II** 633
Sherr-Gold, **23** 40
Sherritt Gordon Mines, **7** 386–87; **12** 260
The Sherwin-Williams Company, III 744–46; **8** 222, 224; **11** 384; **12** 7; **13** 469–71 **(upd.)**; **19** 180; **24** 323; **30** 474
Sherwood Brands, Inc., 53 302–04
Sherwood Equity Group Ltd. *See* National Discount Brokers Group, Inc.
Sherwood Medical Group, **I** 624; **10** 70; **50** 538
Sherwood Securities, **66** 308
Shiara Holdings, Inc., **53** 88
Shidler Group. *See* First Industrial Realty Trust, Inc.
Shieh Chi Industrial Co., **19** 508
Shields & Co., **9** 118
Shihen Technical Corporation, **60** 272
Shihlin Electric & Engineering Group, **49** 460
Shikoku Electric Power Company, Inc., V 718–20; **60 269–72 (upd.)**
Shiley, Inc., **38** 361
Shillito's, **31** 192
Shimano Inc., 64 347–49
Shimizu Construction Company Ltd., **44** 153

Shimotsuke Electric Railway Company, **6** 431
Shin-Nihon Glass Co., **I** 221
Shinko Rayon Ltd. *See* Mitsubishi Rayon Co., Ltd.
Shinko Securities Co. Ltd., **58** 235
Shintech, **11** 159–60
Shinwa Pharmaceutical Co. Ltd., **48** 250
Shionogi & Co., Ltd., III 60–61; **11** 90, 290; **17 435–37 (upd.)**
Ship 'n Shore, **9** 156–57
Shipley Co. Inc., **26** 425
Shipowners and Merchants Tugboat Company, **6** 382
Shipper Group, **16** 344
Shipstad & Johnson's Ice Follies, **25** 313
Shiseido Company, Limited, III 62–64; **8** 341, 343; **22 485–88 (upd.)**
Shizuoka Itaku Co., Ltd., **64** 261
SHL Systemhouse Inc., **27** 305
Shobiz, Inc., **60** 143
Shochiku Company Ltd., **28** 461
Shockley Electronics, **20** 174
Shoe Carnival Inc., 14 441–43
Shoe Supply, Inc., **22** 213
Shoe-Town Inc., **23** 310
Shoe Works Inc., **18** 415
Shonac Corp., **14** 427
Shonco, Inc., **18** 438
Shoney's, Inc., 7 474–76; **14** 453; **19** 286; **23 436–39 (upd.)**; **29** 290–91; **59** 104–06
Shop 'n Save Warehouse Foods Inc., **63** 129
Shop At Home Network LLC. *See* The E.W. Scripps Company.
SHOP Channel, **64** 185
Shop Rite Foods Inc., **II** 672–74; **7** 105; **19** 479. *See also* Big V Supermarkets, Inc.
ShopKo Stores Inc., II 669–70; **18** 505–07; **21 457–59**; **50 455–57**; **58 329–32 (upd.)**
Shoppers Drug Mart Corporation, 49 367–70
Shoppers Food Warehouse Corporation, 16 159, 161; **66 290–92**
Shoppers World Stores, Inc. *See* LOT$OFF Corporation.
ShopRite. *See* Foodarama Supermarkets, Inc.
Shopwell/Food Emporium, **II** 638; **16** 247, 249
ShopWise.com Inc., **53** 13
Shore Manufacturing, **13** 165
Shorewood Packaging Corporation, 28 419–21; **47** 189
Short Brothers, **24** 85
Shoseido Co., **17** 110
Shotton Paper Co. Ltd., **IV** 350
Showa Aluminum Corporation, **8** 374
Showa Denko, **IV** 61
Showa Marutsutsu Co. Ltd., **8** 477
Showa Products Company, **8** 476
Showa Shell Sekiyu K.K., IV 542–43; **59 372–75 (upd.)**
ShowBiz Pizza Time, Inc., 12 123; **13** 472–74; **15** 73; **16** 447. *See also* CEC Entertainment, Inc.
Showboat, Inc., 19 400–02; **43** 227
Showcase of Fine Fabrics, **16** 197
Showco, Inc., **35** 436
Showscan Entertainment Inc., **34** 230
Showscan Film Corporation, **28** 206

Showtime, **7** 222–23; **9** 74; **23** 274–75, 391, 503; **25** 329–30
Shred-It Canada Corporation, 56 319–21
Shreve and Company, **12** 312
Shreveport Refrigeration, **16** 74
Shu Uemura, **III** 43
Shubert Organization Inc., 24 437–39
Shubrooks International Ltd., **11** 65
Shuffle Master Inc., 51 337–40
Shuford Mills, Inc., **14** 430
Shugart Associates, **8** 466; **22** 189
Shulman Transport Enterprises Inc., **27** 473
Shure Inc., 60 273–76
Shurfine International, **60** 302
Shurgard Storage Centers, Inc., 21 476; **52** 293, **309–11**
Shuttleworth Brothers Company. *See* Mohawk Industries, Inc.
Shuwa Corp., **22** 101; **36** 292
SHV Holdings N.V., 14 156; **55 344–47**
SI Holdings Inc., **10** 481; **29** 425
The Siam Cement Public Company Limited, 56 322–25
Siam Makro, **62** 63
SIAS, **19** 192
SIATA S.p.A., **26** 363
SIB Financial Services, **39** 382
Sibco Universal, S.A., **14** 429
Sibel, **48** 350
Siberian Moloko, **48** 438
Sibneft. *See* OAO Siberian Oil Company.
Siboney Shoe Corp., **22** 213
SiCAP AG, **58** 338
SICC. *See* Univision Communications Inc.
Sichuan Changhong Electric Co. Ltd., **63** 36
Sichuan Station Wagon Factory, **38** 462
Sick's Brewery, **26** 304
Siclet, **25** 84
Sicma Aero Seat, **36** 529
Sideco Americana S.A., 67 346–48
Sidel. *See* Groupe Sidel S.A.
Siderar S.A.I.C., 66 293–95
Siderca S.A.I.C., **41** 405–06
Sidley Austin Brown & Wood, 40 400–03
Siebe plc, **13** 235. *See also* BTR Siebe plc.
Siebel Group, **13** 544–45
Siebel Marketing Group, **27** 195
Siebel Systems, Inc., 38 430–34
Siebert Financial Corp., 32 423–25
Siegel & Gale, 64 350–52
Siemens AG, II 97–100; **III** 154–55, 466, 482, 516; **7** 232; **9** 11, 32, 44; **10** 16, 363; **11** 59, 196, 235, 397–98, 460; **12** 546; **13** 402; **14** 169, **444–47 (upd.)**; **16** 392; **18** 32; **19** 166, 313; **20** 290; **22** 19, 373–74; **23** 389, 452, 494–95; **24** 88; **33** 225, 288; **57 318–23 (upd.)**
Siemens Solar Industries L.P., **44** 182
The Sierra Club, 28 422–24
Sierra Designs, Inc., **10** 215–16
Sierra Health Services, Inc., 15 451–53
Sierra Leone External Telegraph Limited, **25** 100
Sierra On-Line, Inc., 13 92, 114; **14** 263; **15 454–56**; **16** 146; **29** 75; **41 361–64 (upd.)**
Sierra Pacific Industries, 22 489–91
Sierra Precision, **52** 187
Sierrita Resources, Inc., **6** 590
Siete Oil and Gas Co., **63** 346
SIFCO Industries, Inc., 41

Sifo Group AB. *See* Observer AB.
Sight & Sound Entertainment, **35** 21
Sigma-Aldrich Corporation, I 690–91; 36 429–32 (upd.)
Sigma Alimentos, S.A. de C.V., **19** 11–12
Sigma Network Systems, **11** 464
Signal Companies, Inc. *See* AlliedSignal Inc.
Signal Corporation, **54** 395–96
Signal Galaxies, **13** 127
Signal Oil & Gas Inc., **7** 537; **11** 278; **19** 175
Signal Pharmaceutical Inc. *See* Celgene Corporation.
Signalite, Inc., **10** 319
SignalSoft, **63** 202
Signature Bank, **54** 36
Signature Brands USA Inc., **28** 135; **30** 139
Signature Corporation, **22** 412–13
Signature Flight Support Services Corporation, **47** 450
Signature Health Care Corp., **25** 504
Signet Banking Corporation, 11 446–48
Signet Communications Corp., **16** 195
Signet Group PLC, 61 326–28
Signetics Co., **11** 56; **18** 383; **44** 127
Signode Industries, **III** 519; **22** 282
Sika Finanz AG, **28** 195
Sikes Corporation, **III** 612
Sikorsky Aircraft Corporation, 9 416; **24 440–43**; **41** 368; **46** 65
SIL&P. *See* Southern Illinois Light & Power Company.
SILA. *See* Swedish Intercontinental Airlines.
Silband Sports Corp., **33** 102
Silenka B.V., **III** 733; **22** 436
Silex. *See* Hamilton Beach/Proctor-Silex Inc.
Silgan Holdings Inc., **26** 59
Silhouette Brands, Inc., 55 348–50
Silicon Beach Software, **10** 35
Silicon Compiler Systems, **11** 285
Silicon Energy Corporation, **64** 205
Silicon Engineering, **18** 20; **43** 17
Silicon Graphics Inc., 9 471–73; **10** 119, 257; **12** 323; **15** 149, 320; **16** 137, 140; **20** 8; **25** 96; **28** 320; **38** 69; **43** 151; **50** 322. *See also* SGI.
Silicon Light Machines Corporation, **48** 128
Silicon Magnetic Systems, **48** 128
Silicon Microstructures, Inc., **14** 183
Silit, **60** 364
Silk-Epil S.A., **51** 58
Silkies, **55** 196
Silknet Software Inc., **51** 181
Silo Electronics, **16** 73, 75
Silo Holdings, **9** 65; **23** 52
Silo Inc., **V** 50; **10** 306, 468; **19** 123; **49** 112
Silver Burdett Co., **IV** 672, 675; **7** 528; **19** 405
Silver City Airways. *See* British World Airlines Ltd.
Silver City Casino. *See* Circus Circus Enterprises, Inc.
Silver Dollar Mining Company, **20** 149
Silver Dolphin, **34** 3, 5
Silver Furniture Co., Inc., **15** 102, 104
Silver King Communications, **25** 213
Silver Screen Partners, **II** 174
Silverado Banking, **9** 199

Silverado Partners Acquisition Corp., **22** 80
Silverline, Inc., **16** 33
Silvermans Menswear, Inc., **24** 26
SilverPlatter Information Inc., 23 440–43
Silvershoe Partners, **17** 245
Silverstar Ltd. S.p.A., **10** 113; **50** 42
Silverstein Properties, Inc., 47 358–60; 48 320
Simco S.A., 37 357–59
Sime Darby Berhad, 14 448–50; 36 433–36 (upd.)
Simeira Comercio e Industria Ltda., **22** 320
SIMEL S.A., **14** 27
Simer Pump Company, **19** 360
SIMEST, **24** 311
Simi Winery, Inc., **34** 89
Simicon Co., **26** 153
Simkins Industries, Inc., **8** 174–75
Simmons Company, 34 407; **47 361–64**
Simon & Schuster Inc., IV 671–72; **13** 559; **19 403–05 (upd.)**; **23** 503; **28** 158
Simon de Wit, **II** 641
Simon DeBartolo Group Inc., **26** 146; **27** 401; **57** 234
Simon Engineering, **11** 510
Simon Marketing, Inc., **19** 112, 114
Simon Property Group, Inc., 27 399–402; 49 414
Simon Transportation Services Inc., 27 403–06
Simons Inc., **26** 412
Simple Shoes, Inc., **22** 173
Simplex Industries, Inc., **16** 296
Simplex Technologies Inc., 21 460–63
Simplex Wire and Cable Co. *See* Tyco International Ltd.
Simplicity Manufacturing, Inc., 64 353–56
Simplicity Pattern Company, **I** 447; **8** 349; **23** 98; **29** 134
Simpson Investment Company, 17 438–41
Simpson Marketing, **12** 553
Simpson Thacher & Bartlett, 27 327; **39 365–68**
Simpson Timber Company. *See* PW Eagle Inc.
Simpsons. *See* Hudson's Bay Company.
SIMS Deltec, Inc. *See* Deltec, Inc.
Sims Telephone Company, **14** 258
Simsmetal USA Corporation, **19** 380
SimuFlite, **II** 10
Simula, Inc., 41 368–70
Simulaids, Inc., **62** 18
Sinai Kosher Foods, **14** 537
Sinclair Broadcast Group, Inc., 25 417–19; 47 120
Sinclair Paint Company, **12** 219
Sinfor Holding, **48** 402
Sing Tao Holdings Ltd., **29** 470–71
Singapore Airlines Ltd., 6 117–18; **12** 192; **20** 313; **24** 399; **26** 115; **27** 26, **407–09 (upd.)**, 464, 466; **38** 26
Singapore Alpine Electronics Asia Pte. Ltd., **13** 31
Singapore Candle Company, **12** 393
Singapore Petroleum Co., **IV** 452
Singapore Shinei Sangyo Pte Ltd., **48** 369
Singapore Technologies Engineering Ltd., **61** 43
Singapore Telecom, **18** 348
Singer & Friedlander Group plc, 41 371–73

Singer Company, **9** 232; **11** 150; **13** 521–22; **19** 211; **22** 4; **26** 3; **29** 190. *See also* Bicoastal Corp.

The Singer Company N.V., **30 417–20 (upd.)**

Singer Hardware & Supply Co., **9** 542

Singer Sewing Machine Co., **12** 46

Singer Supermarkets, **25** 235

The Singing Machine Company, Inc., **60 277–80**

Singular Software, **9** 80

Sinister Games, **41** 409

Sinkers Inc., **21** 68

Sino Life Insurance Co., **64** 280

Sinochem. *See* China National Chemicals Import and Export Corp.

Sinopec. *See* China National Petroleum Corporation.

Sintel, S.A., **19** 256

Sioux City Gas and Electric Company, **6** 523–24

Sioux City Newspapers, **64** 237

SIP. *See* Società Italiana per L'Esercizio delle Telecommunicazioni p.A.

Siporex, S.A., **31** 253

Sir Speedy, Inc., **16 448–50**; **33** 231

SIRCOMA, **10** 375

SIREM, **23** 95

The Sirena Apparel Group Inc., **25** 245

Sirloin Stockade, **10** 331

Sirrine. *See* CRSS Inc.

Sirte Oil Company. *See* Natinal Oil Corporation.

Sisters Chicken & Biscuits, **8** 564

Sisters of Bon Secours USA. *See* Bon Secours Health System, Inc.

SIT-Siemens. *See* Italtel.

SITA Telecommunications Holdings. *See* Equant N.V.

Sitca Corporation, **16** 297

Sithe Energies, Inc., **24** 327

Sitintel, **49** 383

Sitmar Cruises, **22** 445

Six Continents PLC, **54** 315; **59** 298

Six Flags, Inc., **17 442–44**; **54 333–40 (upd.)**

Six Industries, Inc., **26** 433

61 Going to the Game!, **14** 293

Sixt AG, **39 369–72**

Sizeler Property Investors Inc., **49** 27

Sizzler International Inc., **15** 361–62. *See also* Worldwide Restaurant Concepts, Inc.

SJB Equities, Inc., **30** 53

The SK Equity Fund, L.P., **23** 177

Skånska Ättiksfabriken A.B. *See* Perstorp AB.

Skadden, Arps, Slate, Meagher & Flom, **10** 126–27; **18 486–88**; **27** 325, 327

Skaggs-Albertson's Properties, **II** 604

Skaggs Companies, **22** 37

Skaggs Drug Centers, Inc., **II** 602–04; **7** 20; **27** 291; **30** 25–27; **65** 22

Skagit Nuclear Power Plant, **6** 566

Skalli Group, **67 349–51**

Skandia America Reinsurance Corp., **57** 135–36

Skandia Insurance Company, Ltd., **25** 85; **50 431–34**

Skandinaviska Enskilda Banken AB, **II 351–53**, 365–66; **56 326–29 (upd.)**

Skanska AB, **IV** 204; **25** 463; **32** 396; **38 435–38**

Skanza Mammoet Transport Sdn Bhd, **26** 280

Skechers U.S.A. Inc., **31 413–15**; **62** 47

Sketchley plc, **19** 124

SKF. *See* Aktiebolaget SKF.

SKF Industries Inc. *See* AB Volvo.

Ski-Doo. *See* Bombardier Inc.

Skidmore, Owings & Merrill, **13 475–76**

Skil-Craft Playthings, Inc., **13** 560

Skillern, **16** 560

Skillware, **9** 326

Skis Rossignol S.A., **15 460–62**; **43 373–76 (upd.)**

Skoda Auto a.s., **39 373–75**

SKODA Group, **37** 399–400

SKS Group, **20** 363

SKW Nature's Products, Inc., **25** 332

Sky Chefs, Inc., **16** 397; **65** 282–84

Sky Climber Inc., **11** 436

Sky Merchant, Inc., **V** 78

Skyband, Inc., **12** 359

SkyBox International Inc., **15** 72–73

Skylight, **25** 508

Skyline Chili, Inc., **62 325–28**

Skyline Corporation, **30 421–23**

Skyline Homes, **17** 82

Skyline Transportation, **57** 277

SkyMall, Inc., **26 439–41**; **28** 241

Skypak, **27** 474

Skyservice Airlines Inc., **42** 327

SkyTel Corp., **18** 349; **23** 212

Skywalker Sound, **12** 322; **50** 320

Skyway Airlines, **11** 299; **32** 335; **35** 293–94

SkyWest, Inc., **25 420–24**

Skyy Spirits, LLC, **57** 105–06

SL Green Realty Corporation, **44 383–85**

SL Holdings. *See* Finlay Enterprises, Inc.

Slade Gorton & Company, **13** 243

Slater Co. Foods, **II** 607

Slater Electric, **21** 349

Slater Systems, Inc., **13** 48

Slater, Walker, **63** 76

Slautterback Corporation, **48** 299

Slavneft, **49** 306

SLCN Ltd., **64** 205

Sleeman Breweries of Canada, **50** 115

Sleepy's Inc., **32 426–28**

SLI, Inc., **48 358–61**

Slick Airways, **6** 388; **25** 146

Slim Jim, Inc. *See* GoodMark Foods, Inc.

Slim-Fast Foods Company, **12** 531; **18 489–91**; **27** 196; **66 296–98 (upd.)**

Slingerland Drum Company, **16** 239

Slinky, Inc. *See* Poof-Slinky, Inc.

Slip-X Safety Treads, **9** 72

SLJFB Vedrenne, **22** 344

SLM Holding Corp., **25 425–28 (upd.)**

SLM International Inc. *See* The Hockey Company.

Sloan's Supermarkets Inc. *See* Gristede's Sloan's, Inc.

Sloman Neptun Schiffahrts, **26** 279

Slope Indicator Company, **26** 42

Sloss Industries Corporation, **22** 544

Slots-A-Fun. *See* Circus Circus Enterprises, Inc.

Slough Estates PLC, **IV 722–25**; **50 435–40 (upd.)**

Slovak Air Services S.R.O., **66** 51

Slovenská Konzultacná Firma S.R.O. V Likvidácii, **66** 51

AB Small Business Investment Co., Inc., **13** 111–12

Small Tube Products, Inc., **23** 517

Small World Productions, **65** 136

SMALLCO, **III** 340

Smalley Transportation Company, **6** 421–23

SMAN. *See* Societe Mecanique Automobile du Nord.

Smart & Final, Inc., **12** 153–54; **16 451–53**

Smart Choice Automotive Group, **64** 20–21

Smart Communications, **18** 180, 182

Smart Products, **44** 261

Smart Shirts Ltd., **8** 288–89

Smart Talk Network, Inc., **16** 319

SmartCash, **18** 543

SmartForce PLC, **43 377–80**

SmarTTarget Marketing, **36** 342

SMBC. *See* Sumitomo Mitsui Banking Corporation.

Smead Manufacturing Co., **17 445–48**

Smed International, **39** 207

SMH. *See* The Swatch Group SA.

SMI Industries, **25** 15

Smiles Holdings Ltd., **38** 501

Smirnoff, **14** 212; **18** 41

Smit International, **26** 241

Smith and Bell Insurance, **41** 178, 180

Smith & Butterfield Co., Inc., **28** 74

Smith & Hawken, **10** 215, 217

Smith & Nephew plc, **17 449–52**; **41 374–78 (upd.)**

Smith & Wesson Corporation, **30 424–27**

Smith & Weston, **19** 430

Smith & Wollensky Operating Corp., **32** 362

Smith Barney Inc., **I** 614; **6** 410; **10** 63; **13** 328; **15 463–65**; **19** 385; **20** 360; **22** 406; **59** 121, 125–26

Smith Cattleguard. *See* Smith-Midland Corporation.

Smith Corona Corp., **13 477–80**; **14** 76; **23** 210

Smith International, Inc., **15 466–68**; **59** 368, **376–80 (upd.)**

Smith McDonell Stone and Co., **14** 97

Smith Meter Co., **11** 4

Smith-Midland Corporation, **56 330–32**

Smith New Court PLC, **13** 342; **40** 313

Smith Packaging Ltd., **14** 429

Smith Parts Co., **11** 3

Smith Sport Optics Inc., **54** 319–20

Smith Transfer Corp., **II** 607–08; **13** 49

Smith Wall Associates, **32** 145

Smith's Food & Drug Centers, Inc., **8 472–74**; **17** 558, 561; **24** 36; **26** 432; **57 324–27 (upd.)**

Smithfield Foods, Inc., **7 477–78**, 524–25; **22** 509, 511; **43** 25, **381–84 (upd.)**; **46** 83

SmithKline Beckman Corporation, **I 692–94**; **14** 46, 53; **26** 391; **30** 29–31. *See also* GlaxoSmithKline plc.

SmithKline Beecham plc, **III 65–67**; **8** 210; **9** 347; **10** 47, 471; **11** 9, 90, 337; **13** 77; **14** 58; **16** 438; **17** 287; **24** 88; **25** 82; **32** 212–13, **429–34 (upd.)**; **36** 91; **38** 362. *See also* GlaxoSmithKline plc.

Smiths Group plc, **56** 83

Smiths Industries PLC, **25 429–31**

Smithsonian Institution, **27 410–13**

Smithway Motor Xpress Corporation, **39** 376–79

Smitty's Super Valu Inc., **12** 391; **17** 560–61

Smittybilt, Incorporated, **40** 299–300

Smoby International SA, **56** 333–35

Smoothie Island, **49** 60

Smorgon Steel Group Ltd., **62** 329–32

SMP Clothing, Inc., **22** 462

Smucker. *See* The J.M. Smucker Company.

Smurfit Companies. *See* Jefferson Smurfit Group plc.

Smurfit-Stone Container Corporation, **26** 442–46 (upd.)

SN Repal. *See* Société Nationale de Recherche de Pétrole en Algérie.

Snack Ventures Europe, **10** 324; **36** 234, 237

Snake River Sugar Company, **19** 468

Snam Montaggi, **IV** 420

Snam Progetti, **IV** 420, 422

Snap-On, Incorporated, **27** 414–16 (upd.); **32** 397

Snap-on Tools Corporation, **7** 479–80; **25** 34

Snapper Inc., **64** 355

Snapple Beverage Corporation, **11** 449–51; **12** 411; **24** 480; **27** 153; **31** 243; **34** 366; **39** 383, 386

Snapps Drive-Thru, **25** 389

Snappy Car Rental, Inc., **6** 393; **25** 142–43. *See also* Republic Industries, Inc.

SnapTrack Inc., **63** 203

SNCF. *See* Société Nationale des Chemins de Fer Français.

SNE Enterprises, Inc., **12** 397

SNEA. *See* Société Nationale Elf Aquitaine.

Snecma Group, **17** 482; **46** 369–72

Snell & Wilmer L.L.P., **28** 425–28

Snell Acoustics, **22** 99

Snelling Personnel Services, **52** 150

SNET. *See* Southern New England Telecommunications Corporation.

SNMC Management Corporation, **11** 121; **48** 177

Snoqualmie Falls Plant, **6** 565

Snow Brand Milk Products Company, Ltd., **II** 574–75; **48** 362–65 (upd.)

Snow White Dairies Inc. *See* Dairy Mart Convenience Stores, Inc.

Snowy Mountains Hydroelectric Authority, **13** 118

Snyder Communications, **35** 462, 465

Snyder Group Company, **56** 294

Snyder Oil Company, **24** 379–81; **45** 354

Snyder's of Hanover, **35** 213

SnyderGeneral Corp., **8** 321. *See also* AAF-McQuay Incorporated.

Soap Opera Magazine, **10** 287

Sobu Railway Company, **6** 431

Socal. *See* Standard Oil Company (California).

Socamel-Rescaset, **40** 214, 216

Socar, Incorporated, **45** 370

Socata. *See* EADS SOCATA.

Sochiku, **9** 30

Sociade Intercontinental de Compressores Hermeticos SICOM, S.A., **8** 515

La Sociale di A. Mondadori & C. *See* Arnoldo Mondadori Editore S.P.A.

Sociedad Aeronáutica de Medellín, S.A., **36** 53

Sociedad Anónima Viña Santa Rita, **67** 136–37

Sociedad Financiera Mexicana, **19** 189

Sociedad Macri S.A., **67** 346

Sociedade Anónima Concessionária de Refinacao em Portugal. *See* SACOR.

Sociedade de Vinhos da Herdade de Espirra-Produçao e Comercializaçao de Vinhos, S.A., **60** 156

Società Anonima Lombarda Fabbrica Automobili, **13** 27

Societa Esercizio Fabbriche Automobili e Corse Ferrari, **13** 219

Società Finanziaria Telefonica per Azioni, **V** 325–27

Societa Industria Meccanica Stampaggio S.p.A., **24** 500

Societa Italiana Gestione Sistemi Multi Accesso. *See* Alitalia—Linee Aeree Italiana, S.P.A.

Società Italiana per L'Esercizio delle Telecommunicazioni p.A., **V** 325–27

Società Meridionale Finanziaria, **49** 31

Società Sportiva Lazio SpA, **44** 386–88

Société Africaine de Déroulage des Ets Rougier, **21** 439

Société Air France, **27** 417–20 (upd.). *See also* Groupe Air France.

Société Alsacienne de Magasins SA, **19** 308

Societe Anonima Italiana Ing. Nicola Romeo & Company, **13** 27

Societe Anonomie Alfa Romeo, **13** 28

Societe Anonyme Automobiles Citroen, **7** 35–36. *See also* PSA Peugeot Citroen S.A.

Société Anonyme Belge des Magasins Prisunic-Uniprix, **26** 159

Société Anonyme des Assurances Générales. *See* Assurances Générales de France.

Société Anonyme des Fermiers Reúnis, **23** 219

Société Anonyme Française du Ferodo. *See* Valeo.

La Societe Anonyme Francaise Holophane, **19** 211

Societe Anonyme Francaise Timken, **8** 530

Société Anonyme Telecommunications, **III** 164

Société, Auxiliaire d'Entrepreses SA, **13** 206

Société BIC, S.A., bf]VIII 60–61; **23** 55–57

Société Centrale d'Investissement, **29** 48

Société Civil des Mousquetaires. *See* ITM Entreprises SA.

Société Civile Valoptec, **21** 222

Société Commercial d'Affrètements et de Combustibles, **67** 198

Societe Commerciale Citroen, **7** 36

Société Congolaise des Grands Magasins Au Bon Marché, **26** 159

Société d'Emboutissage de Bourgogne. *See* Groupe SEB.

Société d'Exploitation AOM Air Liberté SA (AirLib), **53** 305–07

Société d'Investissement de Travaux Publics, **31** 128

Société de Collecte des Prodicteurs de Preval, **19** 50

Société de Développements et d'Innovations des Marchés Agricoles et Alimentaires. *See* SODIMA.

Société de Diffusion de Marques. *See* SODIMA.

Société de Diffusion Internationale Agro-Alimentaire. *See* SODIAAL.

Société de Fiducie du Québec, **48** 289

Société des Caves de Roquefort, **24** 444

Société des Caves et des Producteurs Reunis de Roquefort, **19** 49

Société des Ciments Français, **33** 339

Société des Etablissements Gaumont. *See* Gaumont SA.

Société des Fibres de Carbone S.A., **51** 379

Société des Grandes Entreprises de Distribution, Inno-France, **V** 58

Société des Immeubles de France, **37** 357, 359

Société des Magasins du Casino, **59** 109

Société des Moteurs Gnôme, **46** 369

Société du Figaro S.A., **60** 281–84

Société du Louvre, **27** 421–23

Société Economique de Rennes, **19** 98

Société European de Semi-Remorques, **7** 513

Société Européenne de Production de L'avion E.C.A.T. *See* SEPECAT.

Société Française de Casinos, **48** 198

Société General de Banque, **17** 324

Société Générale, **II** 354–56; **9** 148; **13** 203, 206; **19** 51; **33** 118–19; **42** 347–51 (upd.); **47** 411–12

Société Générale de Banque,. *See* Generale Bank.

Société Générale de Belgique S.A. *See* Generale Bank.

Société Générale des Entreprises. *See* Vinci.

Société Générale du Telephones, **21** 231

Societe-Hydro-Air S.a.r.L., **9** 27

Société Industrielle Belge des Pétroles, **IV** 498–99

Société Internationale Pirelli S.A., **V** 250

Société Laitière Vendômoise, **23** 219

Société Luxembourgeoise de Navigation Aérienne S.A., **64** 357–59

Societe Mecanique Automobile de l'Est/du Nord, **7** 37

Societe Nationale de Programmes de Télévision Française 1. *See* Télévision Française 1.

Société Nationale des Chemins de Fer Français, **V** 512–15; **57** 328–32 (upd.); **67** 187–88

Société Nationale des Pétroles d'Aquitaine, **21** 203–05

Société Nationale Elf Aquitaine, **IV** 535, 544–47, 559–60; **7** 481–85 (upd.); **8** 452; **11** 97; **12** 153

Société Norbert Dentressangle S.A., **67** 352–54

Société Nouvelle d'Achat de Bijouterie, **16** 207

Société Nouvelle des Etablissements Gaumont. *See* Gaumont SA.

Société Parisienne d'Achats en Commun, **19** 307

Société Parisienne Raveau-Cartier, **31** 128

Société pour l'Étude et la Realisation d'Engins Balistiques. *See* SEREB.

Société pour le Financement de l'Industrie Laitière, **19** 51

Société Samos, **23** 219

Société Savoyarde des Fromagers du Reblochon, **25** 84

Société Succursaliste S.A. d'Approvisonnements Guyenne et Gascogne. *See* Guyenne et Gascogne.

Société Suisse de Microelectronique & d'Horlogerie. *See* The Swatch Group SA.

Société Tefal. *See* Groupe SEB.

Société Tunisienne de l'Air-Tunisair, 49 371–73

Societe Vendeenne des Embalages, 9 305

Society Corporation, 9 474–77

Socma. *See* Sociedad Macri S.A.

SOCO Chemical Inc., 8 69

Socony. *See* Standard Oil Co. (New York).

Socony-Vacuum Oil Company. *See* Mobil Corporation.

Socpresse, 60 281

Sodak Gaming, Inc., 9 427; 41 216

Sodexho Alliance SA, 23 154; 29 442–44; 47 201

Sodiaal S.A., 19 50; 36 437–39 (upd.)

SODIMA, II 576–77. *See also* Sodiaal S.A.

Sodiso, 23 247

Soeker Exploration & Production Pty, Ltd., 59 336–37

Soekor, IV 93

Sofamor Danek Group, Inc. *See* Medtronic, Inc.

Soffo, 22 365

Soficom, 27 136

SOFIL. *See* Société pour le Financement de l'Industrie Laitière.

Sofimex. *See* Sociedad Financiera Mexicana.

Sofitam, S.A., 21 493, 495

Sofitels. *See* Accor SA.

Sofora Telecomunicaciones S.A., 63 377

Soft Lenses Inc., 25 55

Soft Sheen Products, Inc., 31 416–18; 46 278

Soft*Switch, 25 301

Softbank Corp., 12 562; 13 481–83; 16 168; 27 516, 518; 36 523; 38 439–44 (upd.)

Softimage Inc., 38 71–72

SoftKat. *See* Baker & Taylor, Inc.

SoftKey Software Products Inc., 24 276

Softsel Computer Products, 12 334–35

SoftSolutions Technology Corporation, 10 558

Software AG, 11 18

Software Development Pty., Ltd., 15 107

Software Dimensions, Inc. *See* ASK Group, Inc.

Software, Etc., 13 545

The Software Group Inc., 23 489, 491

Software Plus, Inc., 10 514

Software Publishing Corp., 14 262

Softwood Holdings Ltd., III 688

Sogara S.A., 23 246–48

Sogedis, 23 219

Sogo Co., 42 342

Sohio Chemical Company, 13 502

Soil Teq, Inc., 17 10

Soilserv, Inc. *See* Mycogen Corporation.

Solair Inc., 14 43; 37 30–31

La Solana Corp., IV 726

Solar Electric Corp., 13 398

Solaray, Inc., 37 284–85

Select Technology Group, 47 12

Solectron Corporation, 12 161–62, 450–52; 38 186, 189; 46 38; 48 366–70 (upd.)

Solera Capital, 59 50

Solid Beheer B.V., 10 514

Solid Cement Corporation, 59 115

Solite Corp., 23 224–25

Söll, 40 96, 98

Sollac, 24 144; 25 96

Solley's Delicatessen and Bakery, 24 243

Solo Serve Corporation, 23 177; 28 429–31

SOLOCO Inc., 63 305

Soloman Brothers, 17 561

Solomon Smith Barney Inc., 22 404

Solomon Valley Milling Company, 6 592; 50 37

Solon Automated Services, II 607

Solsound Industries, 16 393

Soltam, 25 266

Solutia Inc., 29 330; 52 312–15

Solvay & Cie S.A., I 394–96; 21 464–67 (upd.)

Solvay Animal Health Inc., 12 5

Solvay S.A., 61 329–34 (upd.)

Solvent Resource Recovery, Inc., 9 109

Solvents Recovery Service of New Jersey, Inc., 8 464

SOMABRI, 12 152

SOMACA, 12 152

Somali Bank, 31 220

Someal, 27 513, 515

Somerfield plc, 47 365–69 (upd.)

Somerville Electric Light Company, 12 45

Somerville Packaging Group, 28 420

Sommer-Allibert S.A., 19 406–09; 22 49; 25 462, 464

Sommers Drug Stores, 9 186

Sonat Exploration Company, 63 366

Sonat, Inc., 6 577–78; 22 68

Sonatrach, 65 313–17 (upd.)

Sonecor Systems, 6 340

Sonera Corporation, 50 441–44. *See also* TeliaSonera AB.

Sonergy, Inc., 49 280

Sonesta International Hotels Corporation, 44 389–91

Sonet Media AB, 23 390

SONI Ltd., 64 404

Sonic Corp., 37 14 451–53; 16 387; 360–63 (upd.)

Sonic Duo, 48 419

Sonic Innovations Inc., 56 336–38

Sonic Restaurants, 31 279

Sonnen Basserman, II 475

SonnenBraune, 22 460

Sonoco Products Company, 8 475–77; 12 150–51; 16 340

The Sonoma Group, 25 246

Sonor GmbH, 53 216

SonoSite, Inc., 56 339–41

Sony Corporation, II 101–03, 440; III 141, 143, 340, 658; 7 118; 9 385; 10 86, 119, 403; 11 46, 490–91, 557; 12 75, 161, 448, 453–56 (upd.); 13 399, 403, 482, 573; 14 534; 16 94; 17 533; 18 18; 19 67; 20 439; 21 129; 22 194; 24 4; 25 22; 26 188, 433, 489, 511; 28 241; 30 18; 31 239; 40 404–10 (upd.); 43 15; 47 318–20, 410; 63 36; 64 256–57

Sony Ericsson Mobile Communications AB, 61 137

Soo Line Corporation, 24 533. *See also* Canadian Pacific Ltd.

Soo Line Mills, II 631

Sooner Trailer Manufacturing Co., 29 367

Soparind, 25 83–85

Sope Creek, 30 457

Sophus Berendsen A/S, 49 374–77

SOPORCEL, 34 38–39

Soporcel-Sociedade Portuguesa de Papel, S.A., 60 156

Sorbents Products Co. Inc., 31 20

Sorbus, 6 242

Soreal, 8 344

Sorenson Research Company, 36 496

Sorg Paper Company. *See* Mosinee Paper Corporation.

Soriana. *See* Organización Soriana, S.A. de C.V.

Sorin S.p.A., 61 70, 72

Soros Fund Management LLC, 27 198; 28 432–34; 43 218

Sorrento, Inc., 19 51; 24 444–46; 26 505

SOS Staffing Services, 25 432–35

Sosa, Bromley, Aguilar & Associates. *See* D'Arcy Masius Benton & Bowles, Inc.

Soterra, Inc., 15 188

Sotheby's Holdings, Inc., 11 452–54; 15 98–100; 29 445–48 (upd.); 32 164; 39 81–84; 49 325

Soufflet SA. *See* Groupe Soufflet SA.

Sound Advice, Inc., 41 379–82

Sound of Music Inc. *See* Best Buy Co., Inc.

Sound Trek, 16 74

Sound Video Unlimited, 16 46; 43 60

Sound Warehouse, 9 75

Souplantation Incorporated. *See* Garden Fresh Restaurant Corporation.

The Source Enterprises, Inc., 65 318–21

Source One Mortgage Services Corp., 12 79

Source Perrier, 7 383; 24 444

Souriau, 19 166

South African Airways Ltd., 6 433, 435; 27 132

The South African Breweries Limited, I 287–89; 24 447–51 (upd.); 26 462. *See also* SABMiller plc.

South African Railways, 6 434–35

South African Transport Services, 6 433, 435

South Asia Tyres, 20 263

South Australian Brewing Company, 54 228, 230

South Bend Toy Manufacturing Company, 25 380

South Carolina Electric & Gas Company. *See* SCANA Corporation.

South Carolina National Corporation, 16 523, 526

South Carolina Power Company, 38 446–47

South Central Bell Telephone Co. *See* BellSouth Corporation.

South Central Railroad Co., 14 325

South Coast Gas Compression Company, Inc., 11 523

South Coast Terminals, Inc., 16 475

South Dakota Public Service Company, 6 524

South Florida Neonatology Associates, 61 284

South Fulton Light & Power Company, 6 514

South Jersey Industries, Inc., 42 352–55

South of Scotland Electricity Board, 19 389–90

South Overseas Fashion Ltd., 53 344

South Sea Textile, III 705

South Wales Electric Company, **34** 219
South West Water Plc. *See* Pennon Group Plc.
South Western Electricity plc, **38** 448; **41** 316
South-Western Publishing Co., **8** 526–28
Southam Inc., **7** 486–89; **15** 265; **24** 223; **36** 374
Southco, **II** 602–03; **7** 20–21; **30** 26
Southcorp Holdings Ltd., **17** 373; **22** 350
Southcorp Limited, **54** 341–44
Southdown, Inc., **14** 454–56; **59** 114–15
Southeast Bank of Florida, **11** 112
Southeast Public Service Company, **8** 536
Southeastern Freight Lines, Inc., **53** 249
Southeastern Personnel. *See* Norrell Corporation.
Southeastern Power and Light Company, **6** 447; **23** 28
Southern and Phillips Gas Ltd., **13** 485
Southern Australia Airlines, **24** 396
Southern Bank, **10** 426
Southern Bearings Co., **13** 78
Southern Bell, **10** 202
Southern Blvd. Supermarkets, Inc., **22** 549
Southern Box Corp., **13** 441
Southern California Edison Co., **11** 272; **12** 106; **35** 479. *See also* Edison International.
Southern California Financial Corporation, **27** 46
Southern California Fruit Growers Exchange. *See* Sunkist Growers, Inc.
Southern California Gas Co., **25** 413–14, 416
Southern Casualty Insurance Co., **III** 214
The Southern Company, **V** 721–23[ro; **24** 525; **38** 445–49 (upd.)
Southern Cooker Limited Partnership, **51** 85
Southern Cotton Co., **24** 488
Southern Cross Paints, **38** 98
Southern Discount Company of Atlanta, **9** 229
Southern Electric PLC, **13** 484–86. *See also* Scottish and Southern Energy plc.
Southern Electric Supply Co., **15** 386
Southern Electronics Corp. *See* SED International Holdings, Inc.
Southern Equipment & Supply Co., **19** 344
Southern Financial Bancorp, Inc., **56** 342–44
Southern Forest Products, Inc., **6** 577
Southern Gage, **III** 519; **22** 282
Southern Graphic Arts, **13** 405
Southern Guaranty Cos., **III** 404
Southern Idaho Water Power Company, **12** 265
Southern Illinois Light & Power Company, **6** 504
Southern Indiana Gas and Electric Company, **13** 487–89
Southern Lumber Company, **8** 430
Southern Manufacturing Company, **8** 458
Southern Minnesota Beet Sugar Cooperative, **32** 29
Southern National Bankshares of Atlanta, **II** 337; **10** 425
Southern Natural Gas Co., **6** 447–48, 577
Southern Nevada Power Company, **11** 343
Southern Nevada Telephone Company, **11** 343

Southern New England Telecommunications Corporation, **6** 338–40
Southern Oregon Broadcasting Co., **7** 15
Southern Pacific Communications Corporation, **9** 478–79
Southern Pacific Rail Corp., **12** 18–20. *See also* Union Pacific Corporation.
Southern Pacific Transportation Company, **V** 516–18; **12** 278; **26** 235; **37** 312
Southern Peru Copper Corp.,
Southern Peru Copper Corporation, **IV** 3; **40** 220, 222, 411–13
Southern Phenix Textiles Inc., **15** 247–48
Southern Power Company. *See* Duke Energy Corporation.
Southern Recycling Inc., **51** 170
Southern Science Applications, Inc., **22** 88
Southern States Cooperative Incorporated, **36** 440–42
Southern Sun Hotel Corporation. *See* South African Breweries Ltd.; Sun International Hotels Limited.
Southern Telephone Company, **14** 257
Southern Union Company, **12** 542; **27** 424–26
Southern Video Partnership, **9** 74
Southern Water plc, **19** 389–91; **49** 363, 365–66
Southgate Medical Laboratory System, **26** 391
Southington Savings Bank, **55** 52
The Southland Corporation, **II** 620, 660–61; **7** 114, 374, 490–92 (upd.); **9** 178; **13** 333, 525; **23** 406–07; **25** 125; **26** 447; **31** 231; **50** 487. *See also* 7-Eleven, Inc.
Southland Mobilcom Inc., **15** 196
Southland Paper, **13** 118
Southland Royal Company, **27** 86
Southland Royalty Co., **10** 190
Southmark Corp., **11** 483; **33** 398
Southport, Inc., **44** 203
Southtrust Corporation, **11** 455–57
Southwest Airlines Co., **I** 106; **6** 119–21; **21** 143; **22** 22; **24** 452–55 (upd.); **25** 404; **26** 308, 439–40; **33** 301–02; **35** 383; **44** 197, 248; **52** 167
Southwest Airmotive Co., **II** 16
Southwest Convenience Stores, LLC, **26** 368
Southwest Converting, **19** 414
Southwest Enterprise Associates, **13** 191
Southwest Forest Industries, **IV** 334
Southwest Gas Corporation, **19** 410–12
Southwest Hide Co., **16** 546
Southwest Property Trust Inc., **52** 370
Southwest Sports Group, **51** 371, 374
Southwest Water Company, **47** 370–73
Southwestern Bell Corporation, **V** 328–30; **6** 324; **10** 431, 500; **14** 489; **17** 110; **18** 22. *See also* SBC Communications Inc.
Southwestern Bell Publications, **26** 520
Southwestern Electric Power Co., **21** 468–70
Southwestern Gas Pipeline, **7** 344
Southwestern Illinois Coal Company, **7** 33
Southwestern Public Service Company, **6** 579–81
Southwestern Textile Company, **12** 393
Southwire Company, Inc., **8** 478–80; **12** 353; **23** 444–47 (upd.)

Souvall Brothers, **8** 473
Souza Cruz S.A., **65** 322–24
Sovereign Corp., **III** 221; **14** 109; **37** 84
Sovintel, **59** 209, 211
Sovran Financial, **10** 425–26
Sovran Self Storage, Inc., **66** 299–301
SovTransavto, **6** 410
Soyco Foods, Inc., **58** 137
Soyland Power Cooperative, **6** 506
SP Pharmaceuticals, LLC, **50** 123
SP Reifenwerke, **V** 253
SP Tyres, **V** 253
Space Control GmbH, **28** 243–44
Space Craft Inc., **9** 463
Space Data Corporation, **22** 401
Space Systems Corporation. *See* Orbital Sciences Corporation.
Space Systems/Loral, **9** 325
Spacehab, Inc., **37** 364–66
Spacesaver Corporation, **57** 208–09
Spaghetti Warehouse, Inc., **25** 436–38
Spagnesi, **18** 258
Spago. *See* The Wolfgang Puck Food Company, Inc.
Spalding & Evenflo, **24** 530
Spalding, Inc., **17** 243; **23** 449; **54** 73
Spanco Yarns, **62** 375
Spangler Candy Company, **44** 392–95
Spanish Broadcasting System, Inc., **41** 383–86
Spanish International Communications Corp. *See* Univision Communications Inc.
SPAO, **39** 184
Spar Aerospace Limited, **32** 435–37
SPAR Handels AG, **35** 398–401; **36** 296; **63** 431
Sparbanken Bank, **18** 543
SPARC International, **7** 499
Spare Change, **10** 282
Sparks Computerized Car Care Centers, **25** 445
Sparks-Withington Company. *See* Sparton Corporation.
Sparrow Records, **22** 194
Sparta, Inc., **18** 369
Sparta Surgical Corporation, **33** 456
Spartan Communications, **38** 308–09
Spartan Industries, Inc., **45** 15
Spartan Insurance Co., **26** 486
Spartan Motors Inc., **14** 457–59
Spartan Stores Inc., **II** 679–80; **8** 481–82; **10** 302; **14** 412; **66** 302–05 (upd.)
Spartech Corporation, **9** 92; **19** 413–15; **33** 78–79
Sparton Corporation, **18** 492–95
SPCM, Inc., **14** 477
Spear, Leeds & Kellogg, **51** 148; **66** 306–09
Spec's Music, Inc., **19** 416–18
Special Agent Investigators, Inc., **14** 541
Special Foods, **14** 557
Special Project Films, Inc., **58** 124
Special Zone Limited, **26** 491
Specialized Bicycle Components Inc., **19** 384; **50** 445–48
Specialty Brands Inc., **25** 518
Specialty Coatings Inc., **8** 483–84
Specialty Equipment Companies, Inc., **25** 439–42
Specialty Foods Corporation, **29** 29, 31
Specialty Products & Insulation Co., **59** 381–83

Specialty Products Co., **8** 386
Specialty Retailers, Inc., **24** 456
Spectra-Physics AB, **9** 380–81
Spectra Star, Inc., **18** 521
Spectradyne, **28** 241
Spectral Dynamics Corporation. *See* Scientific- Atlanta, Inc.
Spectron MicroSystems, **18** 143
Spectrum Club, **25** 448–50
Spectrum Communications Holdings International Limited, **24** 95
Spectrum Concepts, **10** 394–95
Spectrum Control, Inc., 67 355–57
Spectrum Data Systems, Inc., **24** 96
Spectrum Dyed Yarns of New York, **8** 559
Spectrum Health Care Services, **13** 48
Spectrum Medical Technologies, Inc., **22** 409
Spectrum Numismatics International, Inc., **60** 146
Spectrum Technology Group, Inc., **7** 378; **18** 112
Spectrumedia, **21** 361
Speech Design GmbH, **62** 38–39
Speed-O-Lac Chemical, **8** 553
SpeeDee Oil Change and Tune-Up, 25 443–47
Speedway Motorsports, Inc., 32 438–41
Speedway SuperAmerica LLC, **49** 330
Speedy Auto Glass, **30** 501
Speedy Europe, **54** 207
Speedy Muffler King, **10** 415; **24** 337, 339
Speizman Industries, Inc., 44 396–98
Spelling Entertainment, 14 460–62; 35 402–04 (upd.)
Spenard Builders Supply. *See* Lanoga Corporation.
Spencer & Spencer Systems, Inc., **18** 112
Spencer Gifts, Inc., **15** 464
Spencer Stuart and Associates, Inc., 14 463–65
Sperry & Hutchinson Co., **12** 299; **23** 243–44
Sperry Aerospace Group, **6** 283
Sperry Corporation, **III** 165–66, 329, 642; **8** 92; **12** 39; **13** 511; **16** 137; **18** 386, 542; **22** 379. *See also* Unisys Corporation.
Sperry New Holland. *See* New Holland N.V.
Sperry Top-Sider, Inc., **37** 377, 379
Spezialpapierfabrik Blankenstein GmbH, **64** 275
Sphere Drake Holdings Ltd., **57** 136
Sphere Inc., **8** 526; **13** 92
Sphere SA, **27** 9
Spherion Corporation, 45 272, 274; 52 316–18
Spider Software, Inc., **46** 38
Spie. *See* Amec Spie S.A.
Spie Batignolles SA, **13** 206; **24** 79
Spiegel, Inc., 8 56–58; 10 168, 489–91; 11 498; 9 190, 219; 13 179; 27 427–31 (upd.); 34 232; 36 177, 180
SPIEGEL-Verlag Rudolf Augstein GmbH & Co. KG, 44 399–402
Spin Master, Ltd., 61 335–38
SpinCircuit Inc., **38** 188
Spinelli Coffee Co., **51** 385
Spinnaker Industries, Inc., **43** 276
Spinnaker Software Corp., **24** 276
Spirax-Sarco Engineering plc, 59 384–86
SPIRE Corporation, **14** 477
Spire, Inc., **25** 183

Spirella Company of Great Britain Ltd. *See* Coats plc.
Spirit Airlines, Inc., 31 419–21
Spirit Cruises, **29** 442–43
Spliethoff, **26** 280
SPN Resources, LLC, **65** 334
Spoerle Electronic, **10** 113; **50** 42
Spokane Falls Electric Light and Power Company. *See* Edison Electric Illuminating Company.
Spokane Falls Water Power Company, **6** 595
Spokane Natural Gas Company, **6** 597
Spokane Street Railway Company, **6** 595
Spokane Traction Company, **6** 596
Spom Japan, **IV** 600
Spon Press, **44** 416
Spoornet, **6** 435
Sporis, **27** 151
Sporloisirs S.A., **9** 157
Sport Chalet, Inc., 16 454–56
Sport Developpement SCA, **33** 10
Sport Supply Group, Inc., 22 458–59; 23 448–50; 30 185
Sporting Dog Specialties, Inc., **14** 386
Sportland, **26** 160
Sportmagazine NV, **48** 347
Sportmart, Inc., 15 469–71. *See also* Gart Sports Company.
Sports & Co. *See* Hibbett Sporting Goods, Inc.
Sports & Recreation, Inc., 15 470; 17 453–55
The Sports Authority, Inc., 15 470; 16 457–59; 17 453; 18 286; 24 173; 43 385–88 (upd.)
The Sports Club Company, 25 448–51
Sports Experts Inc., **II** 652
Sports Holdings Corp., **34** 217
Sports Inc., **14** 8; **33** 10
Sports Plus, **44** 192
Sports-Tech Inc., **21** 300
Sports Traders, Inc., **18** 208
Sportservice Corporation, **7** 133–35
The Sportsman's Guide, Inc., 36 443–46
Sportstown, Inc., **15** 470
Sportsystems Corporation, **7** 133, 135
Spotless Group Limited, **62** 391
Sprague Devices, Inc., **11** 84
Sprague Technologies, **21** 520
Spraysafe, **29** 98
Sprecher & Schub, **9** 10
Spreckels Sugar Company, Inc., **32** 274, 277
Spring Co., **21** 96, 246
Spring Forge Mill, **8** 412
Spring Group plc, **54** 191–93
Spring Grove Services, **45** 139–40
Spring Valley Brewery. *See* Kirin Brewery Company, Limited.
Springer Verlag GmbH & Co., **IV** 611, 641
Springfield Bank, **9** 474
Springfield Gas Light Company, **38** 81
Springhouse Corp. *See* Reed Elsevier.
Springmaid International, Inc., **19** 421
Springs Industries, Inc., V 378–79; 19 419–22 (upd.); 29 132; 31 199
Sprint Canada Inc., **44** 49
Sprint Communications Company, L.P., 9 478–80; 10 19, 57, 97, 201–03; 11 183, 185, 500–01; 18 32, 164–65, 569–70; 22 19, 162; 24 120, 122; 25 102; 26 17; 27 365; 36 167. *See also*

Sprint Corporation; US Sprint Communications.
Sprint Corporation, 46 373–76 (upd.)
Sprint PCS, **33** 34, 36–37; **38** 433
Sprocket Systems, **50** 320
Sprout Group, **37** 121
Sprout-Matador A.S., **51** 25
SPS Technologies, Inc., 30 428–30
SPSS Inc., 64 360–63
SPT Telecom. *See* Cesky Telecom, a.s.
Spun Yarns, Inc., **12** 503
Spur Oil Co., **7** 362
SPX Corporation, 10 492–95; 47 374–79 (upd.)
SPZ, Inc., **26** 257
SQ Software, Inc., **10** 505
SQL Solutions, Inc., **10** 505
Square D Company, **18** 473
Square Industries, **18** 103, 105
Squibb Beech-Nut. *See* Beech-Nut Nutrition Corp.
Squibb Corporation, I 695–97; 8 166; 16 438–39. *See also* Bristol-Myers Squibb Company.
Squire Fashions Inc. *See* Norton McNaughton of Squire, Inc.
SR. *See* Southern Railway.
SRAM Corporation, 65 325–27
SRC Holdings Corporation, 67 358–60
SRI International, Inc., 10 139; 57 309, 311, 333–36
SRI Strategic Resources Inc., **6** 310
SS&C Technologies Inc., **66** 225
SS Cars, Ltd. *See* Jaguar Cars, Ltd.
SS Lazio. *See* Societá Sportiva Lazio SpA.
SSA. *See* Stevedoring Services of America Inc.
Ssangyong Cement Industrial Co., Ltd., III 747–50; 61 339–43 (upd.)
Ssangyong Motor Company, **34** 132
SSC Benelux & Company, **52** 310–11
SSDS, Inc., **18** 537; **43** 433
SSI Medical Services, Inc., **10** 350
SSL International plc, 49 378–81
SSMC Inc., **II** 10
SSP Company, Inc., **17** 434
St. *See under* Saint
Staal Bankiers, **13** 544
STAAR Surgical Company, 57 337–39
Stackpole Fibers, **37** 427
Stadia Colorado Corporation, **18** 140
Stadt Corporation, **26** 109
Staefa Control System Limited, **6** 490
Staff Builders Inc. *See* ATC Healthcare, Inc.
Staff International, **40** 157
StaffAmerica, Inc., **16** 50
Stafford-Lowdon, **31** 435
Stage Stores, Inc., 24 456–59
Stagecoach Holdings plc, 30 431–33; 55 103
Stags' Leap Winery, **22** 80
Stahl-Urban Company, **8** 287–88
Stahlwerke Südwestfalen AG, **IV** 89
Stainless Fabrication Inc., **65** 289
Stakis plc, **49** 193
Stamford Drug Group, **9** 68
Stamford FHI Acquisition Corp., **27** 117
Stamos Associates Inc., **29** 377
Stamps.com Inc., **34** 474
Stanadyne Automotive Corporation, 37 367–70
Stanadyne, Inc., **7** 336; **12** 344

StanCorp Financial Group, Inc., 56 345–48

Standard & Poor's Corp., **IV** 482, 636–37; **12** 310; **25** 542

Standard Aircraft Equipment, **II** 16

Standard Alaska, **7** 559

Standard Bank, **17** 324

Standard Box Co., **17** 357

Standard Brands, **7** 365, 367; **18** 538

Standard Car Truck, **18** 5

Standard Chartered plc, II 357–59, 386; **10** 170; **47** 227; **48 371–74 (upd.)**

Standard Commercial Corporation, 12 110; **13 490–92**; **27** 126; **62 333–37 (upd.)**

The Standard Companies, Inc., **58** 374

Standard Electric Time Company, **13** 233

Standard Electrica, **II** 13

Standard Federal Bank, 9 481–83

Standard Fruit and Steamship Co. of New Orleans, **31** 168

Standard Gauge Manufacturing Company, **13** 233

Standard Gypsum Corp., **19** 77

Standard Insert Co., **28** 350

Standard Kollsman Industries Inc., **13** 461

Standard Life & Accident Insurance Company, **27** 47–48

Standard Life Assurance Company, III 358–61

Standard Life Insurance Company, **11** 481

The Standard Life Insurance Company of New York, **56** 345

Standard Microsystems Corporation, 11 462–64

Standard Motor Products, Inc., 40 414–17

Standard of America Life Insurance Co., **III** 324

Standard of Georgia Insurance Agency, Inc., **10** 92

Standard Oil Co., **6** 455; **7** 169–72, 263, 414; **8** 415; **10** 110, 289; **14** 21; **25** 230; **27** 129. See also Exxon Corporation; Mobil Corporation.

Standard Oil Co. (California). See ChevronTexaco Corporation

Standard Oil Co. (Indiana). See Amoco Corporation.

Standard Oil Co. (New York), **IV** 485, 504, 537, 549, 558; **7** 171. See also Mobil Corporation.

Standard Oil Co. of New Jersey, **IV** 415–16, 419, 431–33, 438, 460, 463–64, 488, 522, 531, 537–38, 544, 558, 565, 571; **7** 170–72, 253, 351; **13** 124; **17** 412–13; **24** 521

Standard Oil Co. of Ohio, **IV** 452, 463, 522, 571; **7** 171, 263; **12** 309; **24** 521

Standard Pacific Corporation, 52 319–22

Standard Plastics, **25** 312

Standard Printing Company, **19** 333

Standard Process & Engraving, Inc., **26** 105

Standard Products Company, **19** 454

Standard Rate & Data Service, **7** 286

Standard Register Co., 15 472–74

Standard Screw Co., **12** 344

Standard Shares, **9** 413–14

Standard Steel Propeller, **9** 416; **10** 162

Standard Telephone and Radio, **II** 13

Standard Telephones and Cables, Ltd., **6** 242

Standard Tin Plate Co., **15** 127

Standard-Vacuum Oil Co. See Mobil Corporation.

Standex International Corporation, 16 470–71; **17 456–59**; **44 403–06 (upd.)**

Standish Industries Inc., **61** 295

Stanhome Inc., 9 330; **11** 94–96; **15 475–78**

Stanhome Worldwide Direct Selling, **35** 262, 264

Stanley Furniture Company, Inc., 34 412–14

Stanley Home Products, Incorporated. See Stanhome Inc.

Stanley Leisure plc, 66 310–12

Stanley Mining Services, Ltd., **19** 247

Stanley Smith Security. See Initial Security.

The Stanley Works, III 626–29; **7** 480; **9** 543; **13** 41; **20 476–80 (upd.)**

StanMont, Inc., **24** 425

Stant Corporation, **15** 503, 505

StanWest Equities, Inc., **56** 348

Staples, Inc., 8 404–05; **10 496–98**; **18** 24, 388; **20** 99; **22** 154; **23** 363, 365; **24** 270; **55 351–56 (upd.)**

Star, **10** 287–88

Star Air Service. See Alaska Air Group, Inc.

Star Alliance, **26** 113; **33** 51; **38** 36

Star Banc Corporation, 11 465–67; **13** 222; **31** 206. See also Firstar Corporation.

Star Building Systems, Inc., **19** 366

Star Cruises Ltd. See Genting Bhd.

Star Engraving, **12** 471

Star Enterprises, Inc., **6** 457

Star Finishing Co., **9** 465

Star Laboratories Inc., **24** 251

Star Markets Company, Inc., **23** 169; **56** 317

Star Medical Europe B.V., **56** 338

Star Medical Technologies, Inc., **22** 409; **31** 124

Star Paper Tube, Inc., **19** 76–78

Star Sportswear Manufacturing Corp., **29** 294

Star Systems, Inc., **52** 88

Starber International, **12** 181

Starbucks Corporation, 13 493–94; **18** 37; **22** 370; **25** 178, 501; **28** 63; **34 415–19 (upd.)**; **36** 156–57; **37** 181; **38** 340; **40** 152–53; **44** 313; **50** 97; **63** 87

Starcraft Corporation, 13 113; **30 434–36**; **66 313–16 (upd.)**

Stardent Computer Inc., **III** 553; **26** 256

Starfish Software, **23** 212

Stark Record and Tape Service. See Camelot Music, Inc.

Starkey Laboratories, Inc., 52 323–25

StarKist Foods. See H.J. Heinz Company.

Starlen Labs, Ltd., **31** 346

Starlight Networks, Inc., **27** 366

Starline Optical Corp., **22** 123

Starpointe Savings Bank, **9** 173

Starrett Corporation, 21 471–74

Star's Discount Department Stores, **16** 36

Startech Semiconductor Inc., **14** 183

Startel Corp., **15** 125

Starter Corp., 12 457–458

Starwood Capital, **29** 508

Starwood Hotels & Resorts Worldwide, Inc., 33 217; **54 345–48**

The Stash Tea Company, 50 449–52

State Bank of Albany, **9** 228

State Bank of India, 63 354–57

State Farm Insurance Companies, **27** 30; **29** 397; **39** 155

State Farm Mutual Automobile Insurance Company, III 362–64; **10** 50; **22** 266; **23** 286; **25** 155; **41** 313; **51 341–45 (upd.)**

State Finance and Thrift Company, **14** 529

State Financial Services Corporation, 51 346–48

State Leed, **13** 367

State Mutual Life Assurance Company, **63** 29

State-o-Maine, **18** 357–59

State Savings Bank and Trust Co., **11** 180; **42** 429

State Street Boston Corporation, 8 491–93

State Street Corporation, 57 340–44 (upd.)

Staten Island Advance Corp. See Advance Publications Inc.

Staten Island Bancorp, Inc., 39 380–82

Stater Bros. Holdings Inc., 17 558; **64** 364–67

Statex Petroleum, Inc., **19** 70

Static, Inc., **14** 430

Static Snowboards, Inc., **51** 393

Station Casinos Inc., 25 452–54

Stationers Distributing Company, **14** 523

Stationers, Inc., **28** 74

Statoil ASA, 54 97; **61** 238, **344–48 (upd.)**

StatScript Management Services, **26** 73

The Staubach Company, 62 338–41

Stauffer Chemical Company, **8** 105–07; **21** 545

Stauffer Communications, Inc., **36** 339–41

Stax Records, **23** 32

STC PLC, III 141, **162–64**; **25** 497; **36** 351

Stead & Miller, **13** 169

Steak & Ale, **7** 336; **12** 373

The Steak n Shake Company, 14 130–31; **41 387–90**

Steam Boiler Works, **18** 318

Steamboat Ski and Resort Corporation, **28** 21

Stearns & Foster, **12** 439

Stearns Catalytic World Corp., **II** 87; **11** 413

Stearns Coal & Lumber, **6** 514

Stearns, Inc., 43 389–91

Stearns Manufacturing Co., **16** 297

Steego Auto Paints, **24** 160

Steel Authority of India Ltd., IV 205–07; **66 317–21 (upd.)**

Steel Co. of Canada Ltd. See Stelco Inc.

Steel Dynamics, Inc., 18 380; **26** 530; **52 326–28**

Steel Technologies Inc., 63 358–60

Steelcase Inc., 7 493–95; **8** 251–52, 255, 405; **25** 500; **27 432–35 (upd.)**; **39** 205–07

Steely, **IV** 109

Steen Production Services, Inc., **51** 248

Steenfabriek De Ruiterwaard, **14** 249

Steenkolen Handelsvereniging NV, **39** 176; **50** 335

Stefanel SpA, 63 361–63

Stefany, **12** 152

Stegbar Pty Ltd., **31** 398–400

Steger Furniture Manufacturing Co., **18** 493

Steiff. *See* Margarete Steiff GmbH.
Steil, Inc., **8** 271
Steilman Group. *See* Klaus Steilmann GmbH & Co. KG.
Stein Mart Inc., 19 423–25
Stein Printing Company, **25** 183
Stein Robaire Helm, **22** 173
Steinbach Inc., **14** 427
Steinbach Stores, Inc., **19** 108
Steinberg Incorporated, II 652–53, **662–65**
Steinberger, **16** 239
Steiner Corporation (Alsco), 53 308–11
Steinheil Optronik GmbH, **24** 87
Steinmüller Verwaltungsgesellschaft. *See* Vereinigte Elektrizitaswerke Westfalen AG
Steinway & Sons, **16** 201; **43** 170
Steinway Musical Properties, Inc., 19 392, 394, **426–29**; **55** 111, 114
Stelco Inc., IV 208–10; **24** 144; **51 349–52 (upd.)**
Stella Bella Corporation, **19** 436
Stella D'Oro Company, **7** 367
Stellar Systems, Inc., **14** 542
Stelmar Shipping Ltd., 52 329–31
Stelux Manufacturing Company, **13** 121; **41** 71
Stelwire Ltd., **51** 352
Stena AB, **25** 105; **29** 429–30
Stena Line AB, **38** 345
Stena-Sealink, **37** 137
Stens Corporation, **48** 34
Stentor Canadian Network Management, **6** 310
Stenval Sud, **19** 50
Stepan Company, 30 437–39
The Stephan Company, 60 285–88
Stephen F. Whitman & Son, Inc., **7** 429
Stephens Inc., **67** 129–30
Stephenson Clarke and Company, **31** 368–69
Sterchi Bros. Co., **14** 236
Steria SA, 49 382–85
Stericycle Inc., 33 380–82
STERIS Corporation, 29 449–52
Sterling Capital Partners, **57** 56–57
Sterling Chemicals, Inc., 16 460–63; **27** 117
Sterling Drug Inc., I 698–700
Sterling Electronics Corp., 18 496–98; **19** 311
Sterling Engineered Products, **III** 640, 642; **16** 9
Sterling Forest Corp., **III** 264
Sterling House Corp., **42** 4
Sterling Inc., **61** 326–27
Sterling Industries, **13** 166
Sterling Manhattan, **7** 63
Sterling Organics Ltd., **12** 351; **50** 282
Sterling Software, Inc., 11 468–70; **31** 296
Sterling Stores Co. Inc., **24** 148
Sterling Winthrop, **7** 164; **36** 174; **49** 351
Stern & Stern Textiles, **11** 261
Stern Bros. Investment Bank, **19** 359
Stern Bros., LLC, **37** 224
Stern Publishing, **38** 478
Stern's, **9** 209
Sternco Industries, **12** 230–31
STET. *See* Società Finanziaria Telefonica per Azioni.
Stet Hellas, **63** 378–79
Steuben Glass. *See* Corning Inc.

Stevcoknit Fabrics Company, **8** 141–43
Steve's Ice Cream, **16** 54–55
Stevedoring Services of America Inc., 28 435–37; **50** 209–10
Steven Madden, Ltd., 37 371–73
Stevens Linen Associates, Inc., **8** 272
Stevens Sound Proofing Co., **7** 291
Stevens, Thompson & Runyan, Inc. *See* CRSS Inc.
Stevens Water Monitoring Systems, **52** 226
Stew Leonard's, 56 349–51
Stewart and Richey Construction Co., **51** 170
Stewart & Stevenson Services Inc., 11 471–73
Stewart Enterprises, Inc., 16 344; **20 481–83**; **37** 67
Stewart Systems, Inc., **22** 352–53
Stewart, Tabori & Chang, **58** 155
Stewart's Beverages, 39 383–86
Steyr Walzlager, **III** 625
Stichting Continuiteit AMEV, **III** 202
Stickley. *See* L. and J.G. Stickley, Inc.
Stieber Rollkupplung GmbH, **14** 63
Stihl. *See* Andreas Stihl AG & Co. KG.
Stilecraft, **24** 16
Stillwater Mining Company, 47 380–82
Stilwell Financial Inc. *See* Janus Capital Group Inc.
Stimson & Valentine, **8** 552
Stimsonite Corporation, **49** 38
Stinnes AG, 6 424, 426; **8** 68–69, **494–97**; **23** 68–70, **451–54 (upd.)**; **33** 195; **59 387–92 (upd.)**
Stirling Group plc, 62 342–44
STM Systems Corp., **11** 485
STMicroelectronics NV, 52 332–35
Stock Clearing Corporation, **9** 370
Stock Yards Packing Co., Inc., 37 374–76
Stockholder Systems Inc., **11** 485
Stockpack Ltd., **44** 318
Stoelting Brothers Company, **10** 371
Stokely Van Camp, **II** 560, 575; **12** 411; **22** 338
Stokvis/De Nederlandsche Kroon Rijwiefabrieken, **13** 499
Stoll-Moss Theatres Ltd., 34 420–22
Stollwerck AG, **53** 312–15
Stolt-Nielsen S.A., 42 356–59; **54** 349–50
Stolt Sea Farm Holdings PLC, 54 349–51
Stone & Webster, Inc., 13 495–98; **64 368–72 (upd.)**
Stone-Consolidated Corporation, **25** 9, 12
Stone Container Corporation, IV 332–34; **8** 203–04; **15** 129; **17** 106; **25** 12. *See also* Smurfit-Stone Container Corporation.
Stone Manufacturing Company, 14 469–71; **43 392–96 (upd.)**
Stonega Coke & Coal Co. *See* Westmoreland Coal Company.
Stoner Associates. *See* Severn Trent PLC.
Stonington Partners, **19** 318
StonyBrook Services Inc., **24** 49
Stonyfield Farm, Inc., 55 357–60
Stoody Co., **19** 440
Stoof, **26** 278–79
Stoomvaart Maatschappij Nederland, **6** 403–04; **26** 241
The Stop & Shop Companies, Inc., II 666–67; **9** 451, 453; **12** 48–49; **16** 160, 314; **23** 169; **24 460–62 (upd.)**

Stop N Go, **7** 373; **25** 126
Stoppenbauch Inc., **23** 202
Stora Enso Oyj, 36 128, **447–55 (upd.)**
Stora Kopparbergs Bergslags AB, IV 335–37, 340; **12** 464; **28** 445–46. *See also* Stora Enso Oyj.
Storage Dimensions Inc., **10** 404
Storage Technology Corporation, 6 275–77; **12** 148, 161; **16** 194; **28** 198
Storage USA, Inc., 21 475–77
Storebor Brux Company, **52** 406
Storehouse PLC, II 658; **13** 284; **16 464–66**; **17** 42–43, 335; **24** 75
Storer Communications, **7** 91–92, 200–1; **24** 122
Storm Technology, **28** 245
Storz Instruments Co., **25** 56; **27** 115
Stouffer Corp., 8 498–501; **28** 238
Stowe Machine Co., Inc., **30** 283
STP, **19** 223; **26** 349
STRAAM Engineers. *See* CRSS Inc.
Straits Steamship Co. *See* Malaysian Airlines System.
Stran, **8** 546
StrataCom, Inc., 11 59; **16 467–69**; **34** 113
Stratasys, Inc., 67 361–63
Strategic Implications International, Inc., **45** 44
Strategix Solutions, **43** 309
StrategyOne, **62** 115
Stratford Corporation, **15** 103; **26** 100
Stratos Boat Co., Ltd., **III** 600
Stratton Oakmont Inc., **37** 372–73; **46** 282
Stratton Ski Corporation, **15** 235
Stratus Computer, Inc., 10 499–501
Straus-Frank Company, **29** 86, 88
Strauss Discount Auto, 56 352–54
Strawberries, **30** 465
Strayer Education, Inc., 53 316–19
Stream International Inc., **48** 369
Stream Machine Co., **48** 92
Streamline Holdings, **39** 237–38
StreamScapes Media, **51** 286, 288
Street & Smith Publications, Inc., **13** 178
The Stride Rite Corporation, 8 502–04; **9** 437; **33** 244; **37 377–80 (upd.)**
Strintzis Lines Shipping S.A., **64** 45
Strix Ltd., 51 353–55
Strobbe Graphics NV. *See* Punch International N.V.
Stroehmann Bakeries, **II** 631
The Stroh Brewery Company, I 255, **290–92**; **13** 10–11, 455; **18** 72, **499–502 (upd.)**; **22** 422; **23** 403, 405; **36** 14–15
Strombecker Corporation, 60 289–91
Stromeyer GmbH, **7** 141
Strong Electric Corporation, **19** 211
Strong International, **27** 57
Stroock & Stroock & Lavan LLP, 40 418–21
Strouds, Inc., 33 383–86
Structural Dynamics Research Corporation, **10** 257
Structural Fibers, Inc. *See* Essef Corporation.
Structural Iberica S.A., **18** 163
Struebel Group, **18** 170
Strydel, Inc., **14** 361; **59** 320
Stryker Corporation, 10 351; **11 474–76**; **29 453–55 (upd.)**
Stuart & Sons Ltd., **34** 493, 496
Stuart C. Irby Company, 58 333–35
Stuart Entertainment Inc., 16 470–72

Stuart Hall Co., **17** 445
Stuart Medical, Inc., **10** 143; **16** 400
Stuckey's, Inc., **7** 429
Studebaker-Packard, **9** 118; **10** 261
Student Loan Marketing Association, II 453–55. See also SLM Holding Corp.
StudioCanal, **48** 164–65
Studley Products Inc., **12** 396
Stuffit Co., **IV** 597
Stuller Settings, Inc., 35 405–07
Sturbridge Yankee Workshop, Inc., **10** 216
Sturgeon Bay Shipbuilding and DryDock Company, **18** 320
Sturm, Ruger & Company, Inc., 19 430–32
Stussy, Inc., 55 361–63
Style Magazine BV, **48** 347
Styleclick.com, Inc., **47** 420
Stylus Writing Instruments, **27** 416
SU214, **28** 27, 30
Suave Shoe Corporation. See French Fragrances, Inc.
Sub-Zero Freezer Co., Inc., 31 426–28
Suber Suisse S.A., **48** 350
Subic Bay Energy Co., Ltd, **56** 290
The SubLine Company, Inc., **53** 340
SubLogic, **15** 455
SUBperior Distribution Systems, Inc., **53** 340
Suburban Coastal Corporation, **10** 92
Suburban Light and Power Company, **12** 45
Suburban Propane Partners, L.P., I 378; **30 440–42[ro**
Suburban Savings and Loan Association, **10** 92
Subway, 15 56–57; **32 442–44.** See also Doctor's Associates Inc.
Successories, Inc., 30 443–45[ro
Sucden. See Compagnie Financière Sucres et Denrées.
Sucesora de Jose Puig y Cia C.A., **60** 246
Suchard Co. See Jacobs Suchard.
Sudamericana Holding S.A., **63** 180
Sudbury Inc., 16 473–75; 17 373
Sudbury River Consulting Group, **31** 131
Süddeutsche Donau- Dampfschiffahrts-Gesellschaft, **6** 425
Südzucker AG, 27 436–39
Suez Lyonnaise des Eaux, 36 456–59 (upd.); 38 321; **40** 447, 449; **42** 386, 388; **45** 277; **47** 219
Suez Oil Processing Co., **IV** 413–14; **51** 113
Suffolk County Federal Savings and Loan Association, **16** 346
Sugar Entertainment, **51** 288
Sugar Land State Bank, **25** 114
Sugar Mount Capital, LLC, **33** 355
Sugarland Industries. See Imperial Holly Corporation.
SugarLoaf Creations, Inc. See American Coin Merchandising, Inc.
Sugarloaf Mountain Corporation, **28** 21
The Suit Company, **51** 253
Suito Sangyo Co., Ltd. See Seino Transportation Company, Ltd.
SUITS. See Scottish Universal Investments.
Suiza Foods Corporation, 25 512, 514; **26 447–50; 37** 197; **38** 381
Sukhoi Design Bureau Aviation Scientific-Industrial Complex, 24 463–65

Sullivan & Cromwell, 26 451–53; 27 327; **47** 437
Sullivan-Schein Dental Products Inc., **31** 256
Sullivan, Stauffer, Colwell & Bayles, **14** 314
Sulpetro Limited, **25** 232
Sulzer Brothers Limited, III 630–33, 638
Sumergrade Corporation, **19** 304; **41** 300
Suminoe Textile Co., **8** 235
Sumisei Secpac Investment Advisors, **III** 366
Sumisho Electronics Co. Ltd., **18** 170
Sumitomo Bank, Limited, II 360–62; IV 726; **9** 341–42; **18** 170; **23** 340; **26 454–57 (upd.)**
Sumitomo Chemical Company Ltd., I 397–98; II 361
Sumitomo Corporation, I 518–20; III 43, 365; **V** 161; **7** 357; **11 477–80 (upd.),** 490; **15** 340; **17** 556; **18** 170; **28** 288; **36** 420; **45** 115
Sumitomo Electric Industries, II 104–05
Sumitomo Heavy Industries, Ltd., III 634–35; 10 381; **42 360–62 (upd.)**
Sumitomo Life Insurance Company, III 365–66; 60 292–94 (upd.)
Sumitomo Metal Industries, Ltd., I 390; **II** 361; **IV 211–13,** 216; **10** 463–64; **11** 246; **24** 302
Sumitomo Metal Mining Co., Ltd., IV 214–16; 9 340; **23** 338
Sumitomo Mitsui Banking Corporation, 51 356–62 (upd.)
Sumitomo Realty & Development Co., Ltd., IV 726–27
Sumitomo Rubber Industries, Ltd., V 252–53; 20 263
Sumitomo Trading, **45** 8
The Sumitomo Trust & Banking Company, Ltd., II 363–64; IV 726; **53 320–22 (upd.)**
Summa Corporation, **9** 266; **17** 317; **50** 306
Summa International, **56** 284
Summer Paper Tube, **19** 78
SummerGate Inc., **48** 148
Summers Group Inc., **15** 386
The Summit Bancorporation, 14 472–74
Summit Constructors. See CRSS Inc.
Summit Family Restaurants Inc., 19 89, 92, **433–36**
Summit Gear Company, **16** 392–93
Summit Management Co., Inc., **17** 498
Summit Screen Inks, **13** 228
Summit Systems Inc., **45** 280
Summit Technology Inc., **30** 485
Sumolis, **54** 315, 317
Sun Aire, **25** 421–22
Sun Alliance Group PLC, III 296, **369–74,** 400; **37** 86. See also Royal & Sun Alliance Insurance Group plc.
Sun Apparel Inc., **39** 247
Sun Capital Partners Inc., **63** 79
Sun Chemical Corp. See Sequa Corp.
Sun Communities Inc., 46 377–79
Sun Company, Inc., IV 548–50; 7 114, 414; **11** 484; **12** 459; **17** 537; **25** 126. See also Sunoco, Inc.
Sun Country Airlines, I 114; **30 446–49**
Sun-Diamond Growers of California, 7 496–97. See also Diamond of California.
Sun Distributors L.P., 12 459–461
Sun Electric, **15** 288

Sun Electronics, **9** 116
Sun Equities Corporation, **15** 449
Sun-Fast Color, **13** 227
Sun Federal, **7** 498
Sun Federal Savings and Loan Association of Tallahassee, **10** 92
Sun Financial Group, Inc., **25** 171
Sun Fire Coal Company, **7** 281
Sun Foods, **12** 220–21
Sun Gro Horticulture Inc., **49** 196, 198
Sun Healthcare Group Inc., 25 455–58; 61 205
Sun International Hotels Limited, 12 420; **26 462–65; 37** 254–55
Sun Kyowa, **III** 43
Sun Life Group of America, **11** 482
Sun Live Co., **56** 201
Sun-Maid Growers of California, **7** 496–97
Sun Mark, Inc., **21** 483
Sun Media, **27** 280; **29** 471–72; **47** 327
Sun Men's Shop Co., Ltd. See Nagasakiya Co., Ltd.
Sun Microsystems, Inc., II 62; **7 498–501; 9** 36, 471; **10** 118, 242, 257, 504; **11** 45–46, 490–91, 507; **12** 162; **14** 15–16, 268; **15** 321; **16** 140, 195, 418–19; **18** 537; **20** 175, 237; **21** 86; **22** 154; **23** 471; **25** 348, 499; **26** 19; **27** 448; **30 450–54 (upd.); 36** 80–81; **38** 416, 418; **43** 238–40; **44** 97; **45** 200; **49** 124; **53** 57; **63** 296
Sun Oil Co., **IV** 371, 424, 548–50; **7** 413–14; **11** 35; **18** 233; **19** 162; **36** 86–87. See also Sunoco, Inc.
Sun Optical Co., Ltd. . See Nagasakiya Co., Ltd.
Sun Pac Foods, **45** 161
Sun Pharmaceutical Industries Ltd., 24 480; **57 345–47**
Sun Shades 501 Ltd., **21** 483
Sun Ship, **IV** 549
Sun Sportswear, Inc., 17 460–63; 23 65–66
Sun State Marine Services, Inc. See Hvide Marine Incorporated.
Sun Techno Services Co., Ltd. See Nagasakiya Co., Ltd.
Sun Technology Enterprises, **7** 500
Sun Television & Appliances Inc., 10 502–03; 19 362
Sun Valley Equipment Corp., **33** 363
SunAir, **11** 300
SunAmerica Inc., 11 481–83
Sunbeam-Oster Co., Inc., 9 484–86; 14 230; **16** 488; **17** 215; **19** 305; **22** 3; **28** 135, 246; **30** 136; **42** 309
Sunbelt Beverage Corporation, **32** 520
Sunbelt Coca-Cola, **10** 223
Sunbelt Nursery Group, Inc., **12** 179, 200, 394
Sunbelt Rentals Inc., **34** 42
Sunbird, **III** 600. See also Nagasakiya Co., Ltd.
Sunburst Hospitality Corporation, 26 458–61
Sunburst Technology Corporation, **36** 273
Sunburst Yarns, Inc., **13** 532
Sunclipse Inc., **IV** 250
Sunco N.V., **22** 515
Suncoast Motion Picture Company, **9** 360; **63** 65
SunCor Development Company, **6** 546–47
Suncor Energy Inc., 33 167; **54 352–54**
Sundance Publishing, **IV** 609; **12** 559

Sundor Group, **54** 213
Sundstrand Corporation, **7** 502–04; **21** 478–81 (upd.); **61** 320–21
Sundt Corp., **24** 466–69
Sundwig Eisenhütte Maschinenfabrik GmbH & Co., **51** 25
SunGard Data Systems Inc., **11** 484–85
Sunglass Hut International, Inc., **18** 393; **21** 482–84; **52** 227, 230
Sunkiss Thermoreactors, **21** 65
Sunkist Growers, Inc., **7** 496; **25** 366; **26** 466–69; **47** 63
Sunkus & Associates, **49** 427
Sunkus Co. Ltd. *See* Nagasakiya Co., Ltd.
Sunlight Services Group Limited, **45** 139
Sunlit Industries, **44** 132
Sunnybrook Farms, **25** 124
Sunnyside Feedmill, **60** 316
Sunoco, Inc., **28** 438–42 (upd.)
SunQuest HealthCare Corp. *See* Unison HealthCare Corporation.
Sunquest Information Systems Inc., **45** 279, 281
Sunray DX Oil Co., **7** 414
The Sunrider Corporation, **26** 316, 470–74; **27** 353
SunRise Imaging, **44** 358
Sunrise Inc., **55** 48
Sunrise Medical Inc., **11** 202, **486–88**
Sunrise Test Systems, **11** 491
Sunsations Sunglass Company, **21** 483
Sunshine Biscuit Co., **35** 181; **36** 313
Sunshine Bullion Co., **25** 542
Sunshine Jr. Stores, Inc., **17** 170
Sunshine Mining Company, **20** 149
SunSoft Inc., **7** 500; **43** 238
Sunstate, **24** 396
Sunsweet Growers, **7** 496
Suntory Ltd., **13** 454; **21** 320; **36** 404; **65** 328–31
SunTrust Banks Inc., **23** 455–58; **33** 293
Sunward Technologies, Inc., **10** 464
Supasnaps, **V** 50
Supelco, Inc., **36** 431
Super Bazars, **26** 159
Super D Drugs, **9** 52
Super Dart. *See* Dart Group Corporation.
Super 8 Motels, Inc., **11** 178
Super Food Services, Inc., **15** 479–81; **18** 8
Super Oil Seals & Gaskets Ltd., **16** 8
Super 1 Stores. *See* Brookshire Grocery Company.
Super-Power Company, **6** 505
Super Quick, Inc., **7** 372
Super Rite Foods, Inc., **V** 176; **19** 356; **63** 334
Super Sagless Spring Corp., **15** 103
Super Sol Ltd., **41** 56–57
Super Store Industries, **14** 397
Super Valu Stores, Inc., **II** 632, **668–71**; **7** 450; **8** 380; **14** 411; **17** 180; **23** 357–58. *See also* SUPERVALU INC.
Superb Manufacturing, **60** 56
Superbrix, **14** 248
La Supercalor S.P.A. *See* De'Longhi S.p.A.
Supercuts Inc., **26** 475–78
Superdrug plc, **24** 266, 269–70. *See also* Rite Aid Corporation.
Superfast Ferries SA, **64** 45
Superior Bearings Company. *See* Federal-Mogul Corporation.
Superior Energy Services, Inc., **65** 332–34

Superior Foam and Polymers, Inc., **44** 261
Superior Healthcare Group, Inc., **11** 221
Superior Industries International, Inc., **8** 505–07
Superior Oil Co., **49** 137
Superior Recycled Fiber Industries, **26** 363
Superior Transfer, **12** 309
Superior Uniform Group, Inc., **30** 455–57
SuperMac Technology Inc., **16** 419
Supermarchés GB, **26** 159
Supermarchés Montréal, **II** 662–63
Supermarkets General Holdings Corporation, **II** 672–74; **16** 160; **23** 369–70. *See also* Pathmark Stores, Inc.
Supermart Books, **10** 136
Supersaver Wholesale Clubs, **8** 555
Supersnaps, **19** 124
SuperStation WTBS. *See* Turner Broadcasting System, Inc.
Supertest Petroleum Corporation, **9** 490
SUPERVALU INC., **18** 503–08 (upd.); **21** 457–57; **22** 327; **50** 453–59 (upd.); **58** 319–20, 329
Supervalue Corp., **13** 393
SupeRx, **II** 644
Supplyon AG, **48** 450
Suprema Specialties, Inc., **27** 440–42
Supreme International Corporation, **27** 443–46; **30** 358; **41** 291
Supreme Life Insurance Company of America, **28** 212
Supron Energy Corp., **15** 129
Surety Life Insurance Company, **10** 51
SureWay Air Traffic Corporation, **24** 126
Surgical Health Corporation, **14** 233
Surgical Plastics, **25** 430–31
OAO Surgutneftegaz, **48** 375–78
Suroflex GmbH, **23** 300
Surpass Software Systems, Inc., **9** 81
Surplus Software, **31** 176
Surrey Free Inns plc. *See* SFI Group plc.
Surridge Dawson Ltd. *See* Dawson Holdings PLC.
Survey Research Group, **10** 360
SurVivaLink, **18** 423
Susan Bristol, **16** 61
Susan Kay Cosmetics. *See* The Cosmetic Center, Inc.
SuSE Linux AG, **45** 363
Susie's Casuals, **14** 294
Susquehanna Pfaltzgraff Company, **8** 508–10
Sussex Group, **15** 449
Sussex Trust Company, **25** 541
Sutherland Lumber Co., **19** 233
Sutter Corp., **15** 113
Sutter Health, **12** 175–76
Sutter Home Winery Inc., **16** 476–78
Sutton & Towne, Inc., **21** 96
Sutton Laboratories, **22** 228
Suunto Oy, **41** 14, 16
Suzannah Farms, **7** 524
Suzuki Motor Corporation, **7** 110; **8** 72; **9** 487–89; **23** 290, 459–62 (upd.); **36** 240, 243; **39** 38; **59** 393–98 (upd.); **61** 10
Suzy Shier Limited, **18** 562. *See also* La Senza Corporation.
Svea Choklad A.G., **II** 640
AB Svensk Färgämnesindustri, **50** 55
Svensk Filmindustrie, **52** 49, 51
Svensk Golvindustri, **25** 463

Svensk Pantbelåning, **61** 53
Svenska Aeroplan Aktiebolaget. *See* Saab-Scania AB.
Svenska Cellulosa Aktiebolaget SCA, **IV** 325, 336, **338–40**, 667; **17** 398; **28** 443–46 (upd.); **52** 163
Svenska Handelsbanken AB, **II** 365–67; **50** 460–63 (upd.)
Svenska Kullagerfabriken A.B., **7** 565; **26** 9. *See also* AB Volvo.
Svenska Stålpressnings AB, **26** 11
Sverdrup Corporation, **14** 475–78
SVF. *See* Société des Vins de France.
SVIDO, **17** 250
SWA. *See* Southwest Airlines.
SWALEC. *See* Scottish and Southern Energy plc.
Swallow Airplane Company, **8** 49; **27** 98
Swallow Sidecar and Coach Building Company, **13** 285
Swan, **10** 170
Swank Inc., **17** 464–66
Swarovski International Holding AG, **40** 422–25
The Swatch Group SA, **7** 532–33; **25** 481; **26** 479–81
Swearingen Aircraft Company, **9** 207; **48** 169
Swedish Ericsson Group, **17** 353
Swedish Match AB, **39** 387–90 (upd.)
Swedish Match S.A., **9** 381; **12** 462–64; **23** 55; **25** 464
Swedish Ordnance-FFV/Bofors AB, **9** 381–82
Swedish Telecom, **V** 331–33
SwedishAmerican Health System, **51** 363–66
Sweedor, **12** 464
Sweeney Specialty Restaurants, **14** 131
Sweeney's, **16** 559
Sweet & Maxwell, **8** 527
Sweet Candy Company, **60** 295–97
Sweet Life Foods Inc., **18** 507; **50** 457
Sweet Traditions LLC, **21** 323
Sweetheart Cup Company, Inc., **36** 460–64
Swenson Granite Company, Inc., **37** 331
Swett & Crawford Group, **III** 357; **22** 494
Swift & Company, **13** 351; **17** 124; **41** 114; **55** 364–67; **60** 187
Swift Adhesives, **10** 467
Swift Denim Group, **66** 134
Swift Energy Company, **63** 364–66
Swift Independent Packing Co., **13** 350, 352; **42** 92
Swift Textiles, Inc., **12** 118; **15** 247
Swift Transportation Co., Inc., **26** 533; **33** 468; **42** 363–66; **64** 218
Swinerton Inc., **43** 397–400
Swing-N-Slide, Inc. *See* PlayCore, Inc.
Swingline, Inc., **7** 3–5
Swire Pacific Ltd., **I** 521–22; **16** 479–81 (upd.); **18** 114; **57** 348–53 (upd.); **59** 261
Swisher International Group Inc., **14** 17–19; **23** 463–65; **27** 139
Swiss Air Transport Company Ltd., **I** 121–22; **24** 312; **27** 409; **33** 49, 51, 271
Swiss Banca de Gottardo, **26** 456
Swiss Bank Corporation, **II** 368–70, 378–79; **14** 419–20; **52** 354. *See also* UBS AG.
Swiss Barry Callebaut AG, **53** 315
Swiss Broadcasting Corporation, **53** 325

Swiss Federal Railways (Schweizerische Bundesbahnen), V 519–22
Swiss International Air Lines Ltd., 48 379–81
Swiss Life, **52** 357–58
Swiss Reinsurance Company (Schweizerische Rückversicherungs-Gesellschaft), III 375–78; **15** 13; **21** 146; **45** 110; **46** 380–84 (upd.)
Swiss Saurer AG, **39** 39, 41
Swiss Telecom PTT. *See* Swisscom AG.
Swiss Time Australia Pty Ltd, **25** 461
Swiss Volksbank, **21** 146–47
Swissair Associated Co., **34** 397–98; **36** 426
Swissair Group, **47** 286–87; **49** 80–81
SwissCargo, **49** 81
Swisscom AG, **58** 336–39
Switchboard Inc., **25** 52
SXI Limited, **17** 458
Sybase, Inc., **10** 361, 504–06; **11** 77–78; **15** 492; **25** 96; **27** 447–50 (upd.)
SyberVision, **10** 216
Sybra, Inc., **19** 466–68
Sybron International Corp., **14** 479–81; **19** 289–90
Sycamore Networks, Inc., **45** 388–91
SYCOM, Inc., **18** 363
Sydney Electricity, **12** 443
Sydney FM Facilities Pty. Limited, **58** 359
SYDOOG, Inc., **64** 160
Sydsvenska Kemi AB, **51** 289
Sykes Enterprises, Inc., **45** 392–95
Syllogic B.V., **29** 376
Sylvan, Inc., **22** 496–99
Sylvan Lake Telephone Company, **6** 334
Sylvan Learning Systems, Inc., **13** 299; **34** 439; **35** 408–11; **55** 213
Sylvania Companies, **7** 161; **8** 157; **11** 197; **13** 402; **23** 181; **50** 299
Symantec Corporation, **10** 507–09; **25** 348–49
Symbian Ltd., **45** 346, 348
Symbios Logic Inc., **19** 312; **31** 5
Symbiosis Corp., **10** 70; **50** 538
Symbol Technologies, Inc., **10** 363, 523–24; **15** 482–84
Symphony International, **14** 224
Syms Corporation, **29** 456–58
Symtron Systems Inc., **37** 399–400
Symtronix Corporation, **18** 515
Syn-Optics, Inc., **29** 454
Synbiotics Corporation, **23** 284
Syncordia Corp., **15** 69
Syncro Ltd., **51** 89
Syncrocom, Inc., **10** 513
Syncrude Canada Limited, **25** 232
Synercom Technology Inc., **14** 319
Synercon Corporation, **25** 538
Synergen Inc., **13** 241
Synergy Dataworks, Inc., **11** 285
Synergy Software, Inc., **31** 131
Synetic, Inc., **16** 59
Synfloor SA, **25** 464
Synopsys, Inc., **11** 489–92; **18** 20; **43** 17
SynOptics Communications, Inc., **10** 194, 510–12; **11** 475; **16** 392; **22** 52
Synovus Financial Corp., **12** 465–67; **18** 516–17; **52** 336–40 (upd.)
Synrad, Inc. *See* Excel Technology, Inc.
Syntex Corporation, I 701–03; III 53; **8** 216–17, 434, 548; **10** 53; **12** 322; **26** 384; **50** 321
Syntex Pharmaceuticals Ltd., **21** 425

Synthecolor S.A., **8** 347
Synthetic Blood Corp., **15** 380
Synthetic Pillows, Inc., **19** 304
Synthomer. *See* Yule Catto & Company plc.
Syntron, Inc., **18** 513–15
SyQuest Technology, Inc., **18** 509–12
Syracuse China, **8** 510
Syratech Corp., **14** 482–84; **27** 288
Syroco, **14** 483–84
SYSCO Corporation, II 675–76; **9** 453; **16** 387; **18** 67; **24** 470–72 (upd.), 528; **26** 504; **47** 457; **58** 241
SYSCO Security Systems, Inc., **51** 81
Syscon Corporation, **38** 227
Sysorex Information Systems, **11** 62
SysScan, V 339
Systech Environmental Corporation, **28** 228–29
System Designers plc. *See* SD-Scicon plc.
System Fuels, Inc., **11** 194
System Parking West, **25** 16
System Software Associates, Inc., **10** 513–14
Systematic Business Services, Inc., **48** 256–57
Systematics Inc., **6** 301; **11** 131
Systemax, Inc., **52** 341–44
Systembolaget, **31** 459–60
Systems & Computer Technology Corp., **19** 437–39
Systems and Services Company. *See* SYSCO Corporation.
Systems Center, Inc., **11** 469
Systems Construction Ltd., II 649
Systems Development Corp., **25** 117
Systems Engineering and Manufacturing Company, **11** 225
Systems Engineering Labs (SEL), **11** 45; **13** 201
Systems Exploration Inc., **10** 547
Systems Marketing Inc., **12** 78
Systron Donner Corp. *See* BEI Technologies, Inc.
Systronics, **13** 235
Sytner Group plc, **45** 396–98
Syufy Enterprises. *See* Century Theatres, Inc.
Szabo, II 608

T. and J. Brocklebank Ltd., **23** 160
T&N PLC, **26** 141
T-Fal. *See* Groupe SEB.
T/Maker, **9** 81
T-Netix, Inc., **46** 385–88
T-Online International AG, **61** 349–51
T-Shirt Brokerage Services, Inc., **26** 257
T-Tech Industries, **26** 363
T.G.I. Friday's, **10** 331; **19** 258; **20** 159; **21** 250; **22** 127; **44** 349
T.J. Falgout, **11** 523
T.J. Maxx. *See* The TJX Companies, Inc.
T.L. Smith & Company, **21** 502
T. Marzetti Company, **57** 354–56; **60** 199–200; **61** 172, 174
T. Rowe Price Associates, Inc., **10** 89; **11** 493–96; **34** 423–27 (upd.)
T.S. Farley, Limited, **10** 319
T. Wear Company S.r.l., **25** 121
TA Associates Inc., **10** 382; **32** 146; **54** 361
TA Logistics, **49** 402
TA Media AG, **15** 31
TA Triumph-Adler AG, **48** 382–85

TAB Products Co., **17** 467–69
Tabacalera, S.A., V 414–16; **15** 139; **17** 470–73 (upd.)
TABCORP Holdings Limited, **44** 407–10
Table Supply Meat Co. *See* Omaha Steaks International Inc.
TACA. *See* Grupo TACA.
Taco Bell Corp., **7** 267, 505–07; **9** 178; **13** 336, 494; **14** 453; **15** 486; **16** 96–97; **17** 537; **21** 315, 485–88 (upd.); **25** 178; **58** 385
Taco Cabana, Inc., **23** 466–68
Taco John's International Inc., **15** 485–87; **63** 367–70 (upd.)
Taco Kid, **7** 506
Taft Broadcasting Co. *See* Great American Broadcasting Inc.
TAG Heuer International SA, **7** 554; **25** 459–61
Tag Mex, Inc., **62** 353
TAG Pharmaceuticals, Inc., **22** 501; **54** 363
Taguchi Automobile. *See* Seino Transportation Company, Ltd.
Tahoe Joe's, Inc., **32** 102 32 249
TAI, Ltd., **34** 397
Taiba Corporation, **8** 250
Taiheiyo Bank, **15** 495
Taiheiyo Cement Corporation, **60** 298–301 (upd.)
Taiko Trading Co. Ltd., **51** 179
Taikoo Motors Limited, **57** 352
Taio Paper Mfg. Co., Ltd. *See* Daio Paper Co., Ltd.
Taisho Marine and Fire Insurance Co., Ltd., III 209, 295–96
Taisho Pharmaceutical, II 361
Taittinger S.A., **27** 421; **43** 401–05
Taiwan Aerospace Corp., **11** 279; **24** 88
Taiwan Auto Glass, III 715
Taiwan Power Company, **22** 89
Taiwan Semiconductor Manufacturing Company Ltd., **18** 20; **22** 197; **43** 17; **47** 383–87
Taiyo Fishery Company, Limited, II 578–79
Taiyo Kobe Bank, Ltd., II 371–72
Taiyo Kogyo Corporation, **35** 98, 100
Taiyo Nippon Kisen Co. Ltd., **56** 181
Takanashi Milk Products Ltd., **37** 197
Takara Holdings Inc., **25** 488; **62** 345–47
Takarazuka Hankyu Company Ltd., **62** 170
Takashimaya Company, Limited, V 193–96; **41** 114; **47** 388–92 (upd.)
Take-Two Interactive Software, Inc., **46** 389–91
Takeda Chemical Industries, Ltd., I 704–06; **46** 392–95 (upd.)
Takeda Riken, **11** 504
Takihyo, **15** 145
Takkyubin, V 537
Tako Carton Plant Ltd., **56** 255
Talanx AG, **53** 162
The Talbots, Inc., **11** 497–99; **12** 280; **31** 429–32 (upd.)
Talcott National Corporation, **11** 260–61
Talegen Holdings Inc., **26** 546
Talent Net Inc., **44** 164
Taliq Corp., III 715
Talisman Energy Inc., **9** 490–93; **47** 393–98 (upd.)
TALK Corporation, **34** 48
Talk Miramax Books, **64** 285
Talk Radio Network, Inc., **23** 294
Talkline, **63** 371–72

Talley Industries, Inc., 10 386; **16** 482–85

Tally Corp., **18** 434

Talmadge Farms, Inc., **20** 105

Taltex Ltd., **51** 379

Tama. *See* Hoshino Gakki Co. Ltd.

Tamarind International Inc., **62** 342, 344

Tamarkin Co., **12** 390

Tambrands Inc., 8 511–13; 12 439; **15** 359–60, 501; **16** 303; **26** 384; **37** 394

Tamco, **12** 390; **19** 380

Tamedia AG, 53 323–26

Tamfelt Oyj Abp, 62 348–50

Tamglass Automotive OY, **22** 436

Tampa Electric Company, **6** 582–83

Tampax Inc. *See* Tambrands Inc.

Tampimex Oil, **11** 194

TAMSA. *See* Tubos de Acero de Mexico, S.A.

Tandem Computers, Inc., 6 278–80; 10 499; **11** 18; **14** 318; **26** 93; **29** 477–79; **50** 227

Tandon, **25** 531

Tandy Corporation, II 106–08; 9 43, 115, 165; **10** 56–57, 166–67, 236; **12** 468–70 (upd.); **13** 174; **14** 117; **16** 84; **17** 353–54; **24** 502; **25** 531; **26** 18; **34** 198; **49** 183; **63** 122. *See also* RadioShack Corporation.

Tandycrafts, Inc., 31 433–37

Tangent Industries, **15** 83; **50** 124

Tanger Factory Outlet Centers, Inc., 49 386–89

Tangiers International. *See* Algo Group Inc.

Tangram Rehabilitation Network, Inc., **29** 401

Tanimura & Antle, **54** 257

Tanks Oil and Gas, **11** 97; **50** 178

Tanne-Arden, Inc., **27** 291

Tanner-Brice Company, **13** 404

Tantalum Mining Corporation, **29** 81

TAP—Air Portugal Transportes Aéreos Portugueses S.A., 46 396–99 (upd.)

Tapemark Company Inc., 64 373–75

Tapiola Insurance, **IV** 316

Tapis-St. Maclou, **37** 22

Tappan. *See* White Consolidated Industries Inc.

Tara Foods, **II** 645

Target Corporation, 10 284, **515–17; 12** 508; **13** 261, 274, 446; **14** 398; **15** 275; **16** 390; **17** 460–61; **18** 108, 283, 286; **20** 155; **22** 328; **27** 315, **451–54 (upd.); 39** 269, 271; **55** 159; **61** 352–56 (upd.); **63** 254, 262

Target Marketing and Promotions, Inc., **55** 15

Target Marketing Systems Inc., **64** 237

Target Rock Corporation, **35** 134–36

Tarkett Sommer AG, 12 464; **25** 462–64

Tarmac America, **64** 379–80

Tarmac plc, III 751–54; 14 250; **28** 447–51 (upd.); **36** 21

Taro Pharmaceutical Industries Ltd., 65 335–37

TAROM S.A., 64 376–78

Tarragon Oil and Gas Ltd., **24** 522

Tarragon Realty Investors, Inc., 45 399–402

Tarrant Apparel Group, 62 351–53

Tarsa, **63** 151

TASC. *See* Analytical Sciences Corp.

Taser International, Inc., 62 354–57

Tasman Pulp and Paper Co. Ltd. *See* Fletcher Challenge Ltd.

Tastee Freeze, **39** 234

Tasty Baking Company, 14 485–87; 35 412–16 (upd.)

Tasukara Company Ltd., **62** 170

TAT European Airlines, **14** 70, 73; **24** 400

Tata Airlines. *See* Air-India Limited.

Tata Enterprises, **III** 43

Tata Industries, **20** 313; **21** 74

Tata Iron & Steel Co. Ltd., IV 217–19; 44 411–15 (upd.)

Tate & Lyle PLC, II 580–83; 7 466–67; **13** 102; **42** 367–72 (upd.)

Tatham Corporation, **21** 169, 171

Tatham/RSCG, **13** 204

Tati SA, 25 465–67

Tatneft. *See* OAO Tatneft.

Tattered Cover Book Store, 43 406–09

Tatung Co., **13** 387; **23** 469–71

Taurus Exploration, **21** 208

Taurus Programming Services, **10** 196

TaurusHolding GmbH & Co. KG, 46 400–03

Tax Management, Inc., **23** 92

Taylor & Francis Group plc, 44 416–19

Taylor Aircraft Corporation, **44** 307

Taylor Corporation, 36 465–67; 37 108

Taylor Guitars, 48 386–89

Taylor Made Golf Co., 23 270, **472–74; 33** 7

Taylor Material Handling, **13** 499

Taylor Medical, **14** 388

Taylor Nelson Sofres plc, 34 428–30; 37 144

Taylor Petroleum, Inc., **17** 170

Taylor Publishing Company, 12 471–73; 25 254; **36** 468–71 (upd.)

Taylor Woodrow plc, I 590–91; 13 206; **38** 450–53 (upd.)

Tayto Ltd., **22** 515

Tazo Tea Company, **50** 450

TB Wood's Corporation, 56 355–58

TBC Corp., **20** 63

TBS. *See* Turner Broadcasting System, Inc.

TBWA Advertising, Inc., 6 47–49; 22 394

TBWA Worldwide, **42** 175; **43** 412

TBWA\Chiat\Day, 43 410–14 (upd.)

TC Advertising. *See* Treasure Chest Advertising, Inc.

TC Debica, **20** 264

TCA. *See* Air Canada.

TCBC. *See* Todays Computers Business Centers.

TCBY Enterprises Inc., 17 474–76

TCF. *See* Tokyo City Finance.

TCF Financial Corporation, 47 399–402

TCH Corporation, **12** 477

TCI. *See* Tele-Communications, Inc.

TCI Communications, **29** 39

TCI Inc., **33** 92–93

TCI International Inc., **43** 48

TCM Investments, Inc., **49** 159

TCPL. *See* TransCanada PipeLines Ltd.

TCS Management Group, Inc., **22** 53

TCW Capital, **19** 414–15

TD Bank. *See* The Toronto-Dominion Bank.

TDC A/S, 63 371–74

TDK Corporation, II 109–11; IV 680; **17** 477–79 (upd.); **49** 390–94 (upd.)

TDL Group Ltd., 46 404–06

TDL Infomedia Ltd., **47** 347

TDS. *See* Telephone and Data Systems, Inc.

Teachers Insurance and Annuity Association, III 379–82; 22 268; **35** 75; **47** 331; **49** 413

Teachers Insurance and Annuity Association-College Retirement Equities Fund, 45 403–07 (upd.)

Teachers Service Organization, Inc., **8** 9–10

Team America, **9** 435

Team Penske. *See* Penske Corporation.

Team Rental Group. *See* Budget Group, Inc.

Teams, Inc., **37** 247

Teamsters Central States Pension Fund, **19** 378

Teamsters Union, **13** 19

TearDrop Golf Company, 32 445–48

Tech Data Corporation, 10 518–19

Tech/Ops Landauer, Inc. *See* Landauer, Inc.

Tech Pacific International, **18** 180; **39** 201, 203

Tech-Sym Corporation, 18 513–15; 44 420–23 (upd.)

Tech Textiles, USA, **15** 247–48

Techalloy Co., **IV** 228

Techgistics, **49** 403

Techint Group, **63** 385

Technair Packaging Laboratories, **18** 216

TECHNE Corporation, 52 345–48

Technical Ceramics Laboratories, Inc., **13** 141

Technical Coatings Co., **13** 85; **38** 96–97

Technical Materials, Inc., **14** 81

Technical Olympic USA, **46** 180

Technicare, **11** 200

Technicolor Inc., **28** 246

Technicon Instruments Corporation, **III** 56; **11** 333–34; **22** 75

Technifax, **8** 483

Techniques d'Avant-Garde. *See* TAG Heuer International SA.

Technisch Bureau Visser, **16** 421

Technitrol, Inc., 29 459–62

Technology Management Group, Inc., **18** 112

Technology Resources International Ltd., **18** 76

Technology Venture Investors, **11** 490; **14** 263

Technophone Ltd., **17** 354

Technosource Services, Inc., **60** 185

TechTeam Europe, Ltd., **41** 281

Teck Corporation, 9 282; **27** 455–58

Tecnacril Ltda, **51** 6

Tecnamotor S.p.A., **8** 72, 515

Tecneco, **IV** 422

Tecnipapel-Sociedade de Transformaçao e Distribuiçao de Papel, Lda, **60** 156

Tecnipublicaciones, **14** 555

Tecnost S.p.A., **34** 319

TECO Energy, Inc., 6 582–84

Tecom Industries, Inc., **18** 513–14

Tecomar S.A., **50** 209

Tecsa, **55** 182

Tecstar Inc. *See* Starcraft Corporation.

Tectrix Fitness Equipment, Inc., **49** 108

Tecumseh Products Company, 8 72, **514–16**

Ted Bates, Inc., **10** 69; **16** 71–72; **50** 537

Teddy's Shoe Store. *See* Morse Shoe Inc.

Tee Vee Toons, Inc., 57 357–60

Teekay Shipping Corporation, **25** 468–71
Teepak International, **55** 123
Tees and Hartlepool, **31** 367, 369
Tefal. *See* Groupe SEB.
TEFSA, **17** 182
TEIC. *See* B.V. Tabak Export & Import Compagnie.
Teijin Limited, **I** 511; **V** 380–82; **61** 357–61 (upd.)
Teikoku Jinken. *See* Teijin Limited.
Teikoku Oil Co., Ltd., **63** 312
Tejas Gas Co., **41** 359
Tejas Snacks LP, **44** 349
Tejon Ranch Company, **35** 417–20
Teklogix International, **45** 346, 348
Tekmunc A/S, **17** 288
Teknekron Infoswitch Corporation, **22** 51
Teknika Electronics Corporation, **43** 459
Tekno Books, **58** 167
Tekrad, Inc. *See* Tektronix, Inc.
Tektronix, Inc., **8** 517–21; **10** 24; **11** 284–86; **36** 331; **38** 71; **39** 350, 353; **41** 235; **61** 294–95; **63** 396–97
Tel-A-Data Limited, **11** 111
TelAutograph Corporation, **29** 33–34
Telcon. *See* Telegraph Construction and Maintenance Company.
Telcordia Technologies, Inc., **59** 399–401
Tele-Communications, Inc., **II** 160–62, 167; **10** 484, 506; **11** 479; **13** 280; **15** 264–65; **17** 148; **18** 64–66, 211, 213, 535; **19** 282; **21** 307, 309; **23** 121, 502; **24** 6, 120; **25** 213–14; **26** 33; **28** 241; **38** 120; **42** 114–15; **43** 433; **50** 317
Tele Consulte, **14** 555
Tele Danmark. *See* TDC A/S.
Télé Luxembourg, **44** 376
Tele-Response and Support Services, Inc., **53** 209
Telebook, **25** 19
Telec Centre S.A., **19** 472
TeleCheck Services, **18** 542
TeleCheck Services, Inc., **11** 113
TeleChef, **33** 387, 389
Teleco Oilfield Services Inc., **6** 578; **22** 68
TeleColumbus, **11** 184
Telecom Argentina S.A., **63** 375–77
Telecom Australia, **6** 341–42
Telecom Canada. *See* Stentor Canadian Network Management.
Telecom Corporation of New Zealand Limited, **54** 355–58
Telecom Eireann, **7** 508–10. *See also* eircom plc.
Telecom Finland, **57** 363
Telecom FL AG, **58** 338
Telecom Italia Mobile S.p.A., **63** 378–80
Telecom Italia S.p.A., **15** 355; **24** 79; **34** 316, 319; **43** 415–19; **47** 345–46; **57** 67, 69
Telecom New Zealand, **18** 33
Telecom-900, **59** 303
Telecom One, Inc., **29** 252
Telecom Personal S.A., **63** 376
Telecom*USA, **27** 304
Telecom XXI, **59** 303
TelecomAsia, **62** 63
Telecommunications of Jamaica Ltd., **25** 101
Telecomunicaçoes do Paraná. *See* Brasil Telecom Participaçoes S.A.
Telecredit, Inc., **6** 25
Telectronic Pacing Systems, **10** 445

Teledyne Inc., **I** 486, 523–25; **10** 262–63, 365, **520–22 (upd.)**; **11** 265; **13** 387; **17** 109; **18** 369; **29** 400; **35** 136
Teledyne Technologies Inc., **62** 358–62 (upd.)
Teleflora LLC, **19** 12; **21** 259; **28** 138; **37** 337
Telefonaktiebolaget LM Ericsson, **V** 334–36; **46** 407–11 (upd.)
Telefónica de Argentina S.A., **61** 362–64; **63** 214, 375–77
Telefónica de España, S.A., **V** 337–40; **43** 422
Telefónica S.A., **46** 172, 412–17 (upd.); **61** 362
Telefonos de Mexico S.A. de C.V., **14** 488–90; **63** 381–84 (upd.)
Téléfrance, **25** 174
telegate AG, **18** 155; **47** 345, 347
Teleglobe Inc., **14** 512
Telegraph Construction and Maintenance Company, **25** 98–100
Telegraphic Service Company, **16** 166
Telekomunikacja Polska SA, **18** 33; **50** 464–68
Telelistas Editors Ltda., **26** 520
TeleMarketing Corporation of Louisiana, **8** 311
Telemarketing Investments, Ltd., **8** 311
Telematics International Inc., **18** 154, 156
Télémécanique, **19** 166
Telemundo Communications Group Inc., **III** 344; **24** 516; **63** 161, 166
Telenet Communications, **18** 32
Telenet Information Services, **47** 37
Telenor, **31** 221; **57** 364
Teleos Communications Inc., **26** 277
Telepar. *See* Brasil Telecom Participaçoes S.A.
Telephone and Data Systems, Inc., **9** 494–96, 527–529; **31** 449
Telephone Company of Ireland, **7** 508
Telephone Exchange Company of Indianapolis, **14** 257
Telephone Management Corporation, **8** 310
Telephone Utilities, Inc. *See* Pacific Telecom, Inc.
Telephone Utilities of Washington. *See* Pacific Telecom, Inc.
TelePizza S.A., **33** 387–89
Teleport Communications Group, **14** 253; **24** 122
Teleprompter Corp., **7** 222; **10** 210; **18** 355
Telerate Systems Inc., **IV** 603, 670; **10** 276–78; **21** 68; **47** 102–03
Telerent Europe. *See* Granada Group PLC.
TeleRep. *See* Cox Enterprises, Inc.
TeleRoss LLC, **59** 209–211
Telesat Cable TV, Inc., **23** 293
Telesis Oil and Gas, **6** 478
Telesistema, **18** 212
Telesistema Mexico. *See* Grupo Televisa.
TeleSite, U.S.A., Inc., **44** 442
TeleSphere, **8** 310; **60** 62
Telesystems SLW Inc., **10** 524
Teletrade Inc., **60** 146
Telettra S.p.A., **V** 326; **9** 10; **11** 205
Tele2 AB, **26** 331–33
Teletype Corp., **14** 569
Televimex, S.A., **18** 212
Television de Mexico, S.A., **18** 212
Television Española, S.A., **7** 511–12; **18** 211
Télévision Française 1, **23** 475–77

Television Sales and Marketing Services Ltd., **7** 79–80
Teleway Japan, **7** 118–19; **13** 482
Telex Corporation, **II** 87; **13** 127
TeleZüri AG, **53** 324
Telfin, **V** 339
Telia AB, **54** 406. *See also* TeliaSonera AB.
Telia Mobitel, **11** 19; **26** 332
TeliaSonera AB, **57** 361–65 (upd.)
Telihoras Corporation, **10** 319
Telinq Inc., **10** 19
Telios Pharmaceuticals, Inc., **11** 460; **17** 288
Tellabs, Inc., **11** 500–01; **40** 426–29 (upd.); **45** 390; **54** 69; **63** 4
TELMARK, Inc., **57** 284
Telmex. *See* Teléfonos de México S.A. de C.V.
Telpar, Inc., **14** 377
Telport, **14** 260
Telstra Corporation Limited, **50** 469–72
Teltrend, Inc., **57** 409
Telxon Corporation, **10** 523–25
Tembec Inc., **IV** 296; **19** 226; **66** 322–24
Temerlin McClain, **23** 479; **25** 91
TEMIC TELEFUNKEN, **34** 128, 133, 135
Temp Force, **16** 421–22; **43** 308
Temple, Barker & Sloan/Strategic Planning Associates, **III** 283
Temple Frosted Foods, **25** 278
Temple Inks Company, **13** 227
Temple-Inland Inc., **IV** 341–43; **8** 267–69; **31** 438–42 (upd.)
Templeton, **II** 609
TEMPO Enterprises, **II** 162
Tempo-Team, **16** 420; **43** 307
Tempur-Pedic Inc., **54** 359–61
Tempus Expeditions, **13** 358
Tempus Group plc, **48** 442
TemTech Ltd., **13** 326
Ten Speed Press, **27** 223
Tenacqco Bridge Partnership, **17** 170
Tenaris SA, **63** 385–88
Tenby Industries Limited, **21** 350
Tencor Instruments, Inc. *See* KLA-Tencor Corporation.
Tender Loving Care Health Care Services Inc., **64** 39
Tenet Healthcare Corporation, **55** 368–71 (upd.)
TenFold Corporation, **35** 421–23
Tengelmann Group, **II** 636–38; **16** 249–50; **27** 459–62; **35** 401; **55** 164
Tengelmann Warenhandelsgesellschaft OHG, **47** 197
Tennant Company, **13** 499–501; **33** 390–93 (upd.)
Tenneco Inc., **I** 182, 526–28; **IV** 152, 283, 371, 499; **6** 531; **10** 379–80, 430, **526–28 (upd.)**; **11** 440; **12** 91, 376; **13** 372–73; **16** 191, 461; **19** 78, 483; **21** 170; **22** 275, 380; **24** 358; **38** 325, 380; **40** 134; **45** 354; **51** 282–84; **65** 260–61
Tennessee Book Company, **11** 193
Tennessee Eastman Corporation. *See* Eastman Chemical Company.
Tennessee Gas Pipeline Co., **14** 126
Tennessee Gas Transmission Co., **13** 496; **14** 125
Tennessee Insurance Company, **11** 193–94
Tennessee Paper Mills Inc. *See* Rock-Tenn Company.

Tennessee Restaurant Company, **9** 426; **30** 208–9

Tennessee River Pulp & Paper Co., **12** 376–77; **51** 282–83

Tennessee Trifting, **13** 169

Tennessee Valley Authority, **22** 10; **38** 447; **50 473–77**

Tennessee Woolen Mills, Inc., **19** 304

Teoma Technologies, Inc., **65** 51–52

TEP. *See* Tucson Electric Power Company.

Tequila Sauza, **31** 91

Tequilera de Los Altos, **31** 92

TeraBeam Networks Inc., **41** 261, 263–64

Teradata Corporation. *See* NCR Corporation.

Teradyne, Inc., **11 502–04**

Terex Corporation, **7 513–15**; **8** 116; **40 430–34 (upd.)**

Teril Stationers Inc., **16** 36

The Terlato Wine Group, **48 390–92**

Terminix International, **11** 433; **25** 16

Terra Industries, Inc., **13** 277, **502–04**

Terra Lycos, Inc., **43 420–25**; **46** 416

Terracor, **11** 260–61

Terragrafics, **14** 245

Terrain King, **32** 26

Terre Haute Electric, **6** 555

Terre Lune, **25** 91

Territory Ahead, Inc., **29** 279

Terumo Corporation, **48 393–95**

Tesa, S.A., **23** 82

TESC. *See* The European Software Company.

Tesco PLC, **II 677–78**; **10** 442; **11** 239, 241; **24 473–76 (upd.)**; **54** 38, 40; **58** 102

Tesoro Bolivia Petroleum Company, **25** 546

Tesoro Petroleum Corporation, **7 516–19**; **45 408–13 (upd.)**

Tesseract Inc., **11** 78; **33** 331

Tessman Seed, Inc., **16** 270–71

The Testor Corporation, **8** 455; **51 367–70**

Tetra Pak International SA, **53 327–29**

Tetra Plastics Inc. *See* NIKE, Inc.

Tetra Tech, Inc., **29 463–65**

Tettemer & Associates. *See* The Keith Companies.

Teva Pharmaceutical Industries Ltd., **22 500–03**; **47** 55; **54 362–65 (upd.)**

Tex-Mex Partners L.C., **41** 270

Texaco Canada Inc., **25** 232

Texaco Inc., **II** 31, 313, 448; **IV 551–53**; **7** 172, 280, 483; **9** 232; **10** 190; **12** 20; **13** 448; **14 491–94 (upd.)**; **17** 412; **18** 488; **41** 359, **391–96 (upd.)** **19** 73, 75, 176; **24** 521; **27** 481; **28** 47; **47** 436; **50** 353; **63** 310. *See also* ChevronTexaco Corporation.

Texas Air Corporation, **I 123–24**, 127, 130; **12** 489; **35** 427

Texas Almanac, **10** 3

Texas Bus Lines, **24** 118

Texas Coffee Traders, **60** 210

Texas Eastern Corp., **6** 487; **11** 97, 354; **14** 126; **50** 179

Texas Eastern Transmission Company, **11** 28

Texas Gas Resources Corporation, **22** 166

Texas Homecare, **21** 335

Texas Industries, Inc., **8 522–24**; **13** 142–43

Texas Instruments Incorporated, **II 112–15**; **IV** 681; **7** 531; **8** 157; **9** 43, 116, 310; **10** 22, 87, 307; **11** 61, 308, 490, 494, **505–08 (upd.)**; **12** 135, 238; **14** 42–43; **16** 4, 333; **17** 192; **18** 18, 436; **21** 123; **23** 181, 210; **25** 96, 531; **38** 375; **43** 15; **46 418–23 (upd.)**

Texas International Airlines, **21** 142

Texas Metal Fabricating Company, **7** 540

Texas-New Mexico Utilities Company, **6** 580

Texas Pacific Group Inc., **22** 80; **23** 163, 166; **30** 171; **34** 231; **36 472–74**; **56** 44, 48; **64** 144–45

Texas Public Utilities, **II** 660

Texas Rangers Baseball, **51 371–74**

Texas Super Duper Markets, Inc., **7** 372

Texas Timberjack, Inc., **51** 279–81

Texas Trust Savings Bank, **8** 88

Texas United Insurance Co., **III** 214

Texas Utilities Company, **V 724–25**; **12** 99; **25 472–74 (upd.)**; **35** 479

Texasgulf Inc., **13** 557; **18** 433

Texboard, **IV** 296; **19** 226

Texstar Petroleum Company, **7** 516

Texstyrene Corp., **IV** 331

Textile Diffusion, **25** 466

Textile Paper Tube Company, Ltd., **8** 475

Textile Rubber and Chemical Company, **15** 490

Textron Inc., **I 529–30**; **II** 420; **8** 93, 157, 315, 545; **9** 497, 499; **11** 261; **12** 251, 382–83, 400–01; **13** 63–64; **17** 53; **21** 175; **22** 32; **27** 100; **34 431–34 (upd.)**; **35** 350–51; **46** 65

Textron Lycoming Turbine Engine, **9 497–99**

Texwood Industries, Inc., **20** 363

TFC. *See* Times Fiber Communications, Inc.

TFH Publications, Inc., **58** 60

TFM. *See* Grupo Transportación Ferroviaria Mexicana, S.A. de C.V.

TFN Group Communications, Inc., **8** 311

TF1 **24** 79. *See also* Télévision Française 1

TFP, Inc., **44** 358–59

TFS. *See* Total Filtration Services, Inc.

TG Credit Service Co. Ltd., **55** 375

TGEL&PCo. *See* Tucson Gas, Electric Light & Power Company.

TH:s Group, **10** 113; **50** 43

Thai Airways International Public Company Limited, **6 122–24**; **27 463–66 (upd.)**

Thai Lube Blending Co., **56** 290

Thai Nylon Co. Ltd., **53** 344

Thai Union International Inc., **24** 116

Thalassa International, **10** 14; **27** 11

Thales S.A., **42 373–76**; **47** 9; **49** 165, 167

Thames Trains, **28** 157

Thames Water plc, **11 509–11**; **22** 89

Thameslink, **28** 157

THAW. *See* Recreational Equipment, Inc.

Theatrical Syndicate, **24** 437

Thelem SA, **54** 267

Therm-o-Disc, **II** 19

Therm-X Company, **8** 178

Thermacore International Inc., **56** 247

Thermador Corporation, **67** 82

Thermadyne Holding Corporation, **19 440–43**

Thermal Dynamics, **19** 441

Thermal Energies, Inc., **21** 514

Thermal Power Company, **11** 270

Thermal Snowboards, Inc., **22** 462

Thermal Transfer Ltd., **13** 485

ThermaStor Technologies, Ltd., **44** 366

Thermo BioAnalysis Corp., **25 475–78**

Thermo Electron Corporation, **7 520–22**; **11** 512–13; **13** 421; **24** 477; **25** 475–76; **52** 389

Thermo Fibertek, Inc., **24 477–79**

Thermo Instrument Systems Inc., **11 512–14**; **25** 475–77

Thermo King Corporation, **13 505–07**

Thermoform Plastics, **56** 378–79

Thermoforming USA, **16** 339

Thermogas Co., **35** 175

Thermolase Corporation, **22** 410

Thermos Company, **16 486–88**

TheStreet.com, **34** 125

THHK Womenswear Limited, **53** 333

ThiemeMeulenhoff BV, **53** 273

Thies Companies, **13** 270

Thiess Dampier Mitsui, **IV** 47

Things Remembered, **13** 165–66

Think Entertainment, **II** 161

Think Technologies, **10** 508

Thiokol Corporation, **8** 472; **9** 358–59, **500–02 (upd.)**; **12** 68; **22 504–07 (upd.)**

Third Coast Capital, Inc., **51** 109

Third National Bank. *See* Fifth Third Bancorp.

Third National Bank of Dayton, **9** 475

Third Wave Publishing Corp. *See* Acer Inc.

ThirdAge.com, **49** 290

Thirteen/WNET. *See* Educational Broadcasting Corporation.

Thistle Group, **9** 365

Thistle Hotels PLC, **54 366–69**

Thom McAn, **11** 349. *See also* Melville Corporation.

Thomas & Betts Corporation, **11 515–17**; **14** 27; **54 370–74 (upd.)**

Thomas & Howard Co., **II** 682; **18** 8

Thomas and Judith Pyle, **13** 433

Thomas Bros. Maps, **28** 380

Thomas Cook Group Ltd., **17** 325; **57** 195

Thomas Cook Travel Inc., **9 503–05**; **33 394–96 (upd.)**; **42** 282

Thomas De La Rue and Company, Ltd., **44** 357–58

Thomas H. Lee Co., **11** 156, 450; **14** 230–31; **15** 309; **19** 371, 373; **24 480–83**; **25** 67; **28** 134; **30** 219; **32** 362; **52** 95; **56** 225

Thomas Industries Inc., **29 466–69**

Thomas J. Lipton Company, **II** 609, 657; **11** 450; **14 495–97**; **16** 90; **32** 474

Thomas Jefferson Life Insurance Co., **III** 397

Thomas Kinkade Galleries. *See* Media Arts Group, Inc.

Thomas Linnell & Co. Ltd., **II** 628

Thomas Nationwide Transport. *See* TNT.

Thomas Nationwide Transport Limited. *See* TNT Post Group N.V.

Thomas Nelson Inc., **8** 526; **14 498–99**; **24** 548; **38 454–57 (upd.)**

Thomas Publishing Company, **26 482–85**

Thomas Y. Crowell, **IV** 605

Thomaston Mills, Inc., **27 467–70**

Thomasville Furniture Industries, Inc., **12 474–76**; **28** 406; **31** 248; **39** 170, 174

Thompson and Formby, **16** 44

Thompson Aircraft Tire Corp., **14** 42

Thompson-Hayward Chemical Co., **13** 397

Thompson Medical Company. *See* Slim-Fast Nutritional Foods International Inc.
Thompson Nutritional Products, **37** 286
Thompson PBE Inc., **24** 160–61
Thomsen Greenhouses and Garden Center, Incorporated, 65 338–40
Thomson BankWatch Inc., **19** 34
Thomson-Brandt, **II** 13, 116–17; **9** 9
The Thomson Corporation, 8 525–28; 10 407; **12** 361, 562; **17** 255; **22** 441; **34** 435–40 (upd.); **44** 155
Thomson International, **37** 143
Thomson-Jenson Energy Limited, **13** 558
THOMSON multimedia S.A., 18 126; **36** 384; **42 377–80 (upd.)**
Thomson-Ramo-Woolridge. *See* TRW Inc.
Thomson S.A., II 31, 116–17; 7 9; **13** 402; **50** 300; **59** 81. *See also* THOMSON multimedia S.A.
Thomson Travel Group, **27** 27
Thonet Industries Inc., **14** 435–36
Thor Industries, Inc., 39 391–94
Thorn Apple Valley, Inc., 7 523–25; 12 125; **22 508–11 (upd.)**; **23** 203
Thorn EMI plc, I 52, 411, **531–32**; **19** 390; **24** 87; **26** 151; **40** 105; **59** 228. *See also* EMI plc; Thorn plc.
Thorn plc, 24 484–87
Thorncraft Inc., **25** 379
Thorndike, Doran, Paine and Lewis, Inc., **14** 530
Thornhill Inc, **64** 217
Thornton Baker. *See* Grant Thornton International.
Thornton Stores, **14** 235
Thorntons plc, 46 424–26
Thoroughgood, **II** 658
Thorpe Park, **55** 378
Thorsen Realtors, **21** 96
Thos. & Wm. Molson & Company. *See* The Molson Companies Limited.
Thousand Trails, Inc., 13 494; **33 397–99**
Thousands Springs Power Company, **12** 265
THQ, Inc., 39 395–97; **52** 191
Threads for Life, **49** 244
Threadz, **25** 300
Three-Diamond Company. *See* Mitsubishi Shokai.
The 3DO Company, 10 286; **43 426–30**
3 Guys, **II** 678, **V** 35
3 Maj, **25** 469
Three Ring Asia Pacific Beer Co., Ltd., **49** 418
Three Rivers Pulp and Paper Company, **17** 281
Three Score, **23** 100
3 Suisses International, **12** 281
3Com Corporation, 10 237; **11 518–21**; **20** 8, 33; **26** 276; **34 441–45 (upd.)**; **36** 122, 300, 357; **49** 184. *See also* Palm, Inc.
3D Planet SpA, **41** 409
3dfx Interactive Inc., **54** 269–71
3Dlabs, **57** 78, 80
3M Company, 61 365–70 (upd.)
360 Youth Inc., **55** 15
360networks inc., **46** 268
Threshold Entertainment, **25** 270
Thrift Drug, **V** 92
Thrift Mart, **16** 65
ThriftiCheck Service Corporation, **7** 145
Thriftimart Inc., **12** 153; **16** 452
Thriftway Food Drug, **21** 530

Thriftway Foods, **II** 624
Thrifty Corporation, **25** 413, 415–16; **55** 58
Thrifty PayLess, Inc., 12 477–79; **18** 286; **19** 357
Thrifty Rent-A-Car. *See* Dollar Thrifty Automotive Group, Inc.
Throwing Corporation of America, **12** 501
Thrustmaster S.A., **41** 190
Thummel Schutze & Partner, **28** 141
Thunder Bay Press, **34** 3–5
Thüringer Schokoladewerk GmbH, **53** 315
Thurmond Chemicals, Inc., **27** 291
Thurston Motor Lines Inc., **12** 310
Thyssen AG, IV 195, 221–23, 228; **8** 75–76; **14** 169
Thyssen Krupp AG, 28 104, **452–60 (upd.)**; **42** 417
Thyssen-Krupp Stahl AG, **26** 83
Thyssengas, **38** 406–07
TI. *See* Texas Instruments.
TI Corporation, **10** 44
TI Group plc, 17 480–83
TIAA-CREF. *See* Teachers Insurance and Annuity Association-College Retirement Equities Fund.
Tianjin Automobile Industry Group, **21** 164
Tianjin Bohai Brewing Company, **21** 230; **50** 202
Tianjin Paper Net, **62** 350
Tibbett & Britten Group plc, 32 449–52
Tiber Construction Company, **16** 286
Tichenor Media System Inc., **35** 220
Ticketmaster Corp., 13 508–10; **25** 214; **36** 423–24
Ticketmaster Group, Inc., 37 381–84 (upd.); **47** 419, 421
Ticketron, **13** 508–09; **24** 438; **37** 381–82
TicketsWest.com, **59** 410, 412
Tichnor & Fields, **10** 356
Ticor Title Insurance Co., **10** 45
Tidel Systems, **II** 661; **32** 416
Tidewater Inc., 11 522–24; **37 385–88 (upd.)**; **59** 402
Tidewater Utilities, Inc., **45** 275, 277
Tidi Wholesale, **13** 150
TIE. *See* Transport International Express.
Tien Wah Press (Pte.) Ltd., **IV** 600
Tierco Group, Inc., **27** 382
Tierney & Partners, **23** 480
Tiffany & Co., 12 312; **14 500–03**; **15** 95; **19** 27; **26** 145; **27** 329; **41** 256; **57** 179–80; **60** 202
TIG Holdings, Inc., 26 486–88; **57** 136–37
Tiger Accessories, **18** 88
Tiger International, Inc., **17** 505; **18** 178; **42** 141
Tiger Management Associates, **13** 158, 256
Tiger Oats, **I** 424
TigerDirect, Inc., **52** 342–44
Tigon Corporation, **41** 288
Tilcon Capaldi, Inc., **64** 98
Tilden Interrent, **10** 419
Tile & Coal Company, **14** 248
Tilia Inc., 62 363–65
Tilley Endurables, Inc., 67 364–66
Tillinghast, Nelson & Warren Inc., **32** 459
Tillotson Corp., 14 64; **15 488–90**
TIM. *See* Telecom Italia Mobile S.p.A.
Tim Horton's Restaurants, **23** 507; **47** 443. *See also* TDL Group Ltd.
Timber Lodge Steakhouse, Inc., **37** 351–52
Timber Realization Co., **IV** 305

The Timberland Company, 11 349; **13 511–14**; **17** 245; **19** 112; **22** 173; **25** 206; **54 375–79 (upd.)**
Timberline Software Corporation, 15 491–93
TIMCO. *See* Triad International Maintenance Corp.
Time Distribution Services, **13** 179
Time Electronics, **19** 311
Time Industries, **26** 445
Time-Life Books, Inc. **44** 447, 449. *See also* Time Warner Inc.
Time Life Music, **44** 242
Time Saver Stores, Inc., **12** 112; **17** 170
Time-Sharing Information, **10** 357
Time Warner Inc., II 168, 175–177, 252, 452; **IV** 341–42, 636, **673–76**; **7** 63, 222–24, 396, **526–30 (upd.)**; **8** 267–68, 527; **9** 119, 469, 472; **10** 168, 286, 484, 488, 491; **12** 531; **13** 105–06, 399; **14** 260; **15** 51, 54; **16** 146, 223; **17** 148, 442–44; **18** 66, 535; **19** 6, 336; **22** 52, 194, 522; **23** 31, 33, 257, 274, 276, 393; **24** 321–22; **25** 141, 498–99; **26** 33, 151, 441; **27** 121, 429–30; **43** 55; **54** 334, 336–37. *See also* AOL Time Warner Inc.
Timeplex, **9** 32
Times Fiber Communications, Inc., **40** 35–36
The Times Mirror Company, IV 677–78; **14** 97; **17 484–86 (upd.)**; **21** 404; **22** 162, 443; **26** 446; **35** 419; **63** 393–94
Times Newspapers, **8** 527
Times Publishing Group, **54** 116, 118
Timeshare Resale Brokers Inc. *See* ILX Resorts Incorporated.
TIMET. *See* Titanium Metals Corporation.
Timex Corporation, 25 479–82 (upd.)
Timex Enterprises Inc., 7 531–33; **10** 152; **12** 317; **25** 22
The Timken Company, 7 447; **8 529–31**; **15** 225; **42 381–85 (upd.)**; **55** 221–22
Timothy Whites, **24** 74
Tioga Gas Plant Inc., **55** 20
Tioxide Group plc, **44** 117, 119
Tip Top Drugstores plc, **24** 269
Tip Top Tailors, **29** 162
TIPC Network. *See* Gateway 2000.
Tiphook PLC, **13** 530
Tipton Centers Inc., **V** 50; **19** 123; **49** 112
Tiscali SpA, 48 396–99
TISCO. *See* Tata Iron & Steel Company Ltd.
Tishman Speyer Properties, L.P., 47 403–06
Tissue Technologies, Inc., **22** 409
Titan Acquisition Corporation, **51** 34, 36
Titan Cement Company S.A., 64 379–81
The Titan Corporation, 36 475–78; **45** 68, 70
Titan Manufacturing Company, **19** 359
Titan Sports, Inc., **52** 192
Titanium Metals Corporation, 10 434; **21 489–92**
Titanium Technology Corporation, **13** 140
Titleist. *See* Acushnet Company.
TITISA, **9** 109
Titmuss Sainer Dechert. *See* Dechert.
Tivoli Audio, **48** 85
Tivoli Systems, Inc., **14** 392
TJ International, Inc., 19 444–47

The TJX Companies, Inc., V 197–98; 13 548; **14** 426; **19 448–50 (upd.); 29** 106; **57 366–69 (upd.)**
TKR Cable Co., **15** 264
TKT. *See* Transkaryotic Therapies Inc.
TL Enterprises, Inc., **56** 5
TLC Associates, **11** 261
TLC Beatrice International Holdings, Inc., 22 512–15
TLC Gift Company, **26** 375
TLO, **25** 82
TMB Industries, **24** 144
TMC Industries Ltd., **22** 352
TML Information Services Inc., **9** 95
TMP Worldwide Inc., 30 458–60
TMS, Inc., **7** 358
TMS Marketing, **26** 440
TMS Systems, Inc., **10** 18
TMT. *See* Trailer Marine Transport.
TMW Capital Inc., **48** 286
TN Technologies Inc., **23** 479
TNT Crust, Inc., **23** 203
TNT Freightways Corporation, 14 504–06
TNT Grading Inc., **50** 348
TNT Limited, V 523–25
TNT Post Group N.V., 27 471–76 (upd.); 30 393, **461–63 (upd.).** *See also* TPG N.V.
Toa Airlines, **I** 106; **6** 427
Toa Medical Electronics Ltd., **22** 75
Toa Tanker Co. Ltd., **IV** 555
Toastmaster, **17** 215; **22** 353
Tobacco Group PLC, **30** 231
Tobacco Products Corporation, **18** 416
Tobias, **16** 239
Tobu Railway Co Ltd, 6 430–32
TOC Retail Inc., **17** 170
Tocom, Inc., **10** 320
Today's Man, Inc., 20 484–87; 21 311
Todays Computers Business Centers. *See* Intelligent Electronics, Inc.
The Todd-AO Corporation, 33 400–04. *See also* Liberty Livewire Corporation.
Todd Shipyards Corporation, 7 138; **14 507–09**
Todhunter International, Inc., 27 477–79
Todito.com, S.A. de C.V., **39** 194, 196
Toei Co. Ltd., **9** 29–30; **28** 462
Tofaş, **I** 479–80; **54** 196–97
Tofte Industrier, **63** 315
Toftejorg Group, **64** 18
Tofutti Brands, Inc., 64 382–84
Togo's Eatery, **29** 19
Toho Co., Ltd., 24 327; **28 461–63; 61** 360
Tohoku Alps, **II** 5
Tohokushinsha Film Corporation, **18** 429
Tohuku Electric Power Company, Inc., V 726–28
Tojo Railway Company, **6** 430
Tokai Aircraft Co., Ltd. *See* Aisin Seiki Co., Ltd.
The Tokai Bank, Limited, II 373–74; 15 494–96 (upd.)
Tokai Kogyo Co. Ltd., **I** 615; **48** 42
Tokheim Corporation, 21 493–95
Tokio Marine and Fire Insurance Co., Ltd., III 383–86. *See also* Millea Holdings Inc.
Tokiwa shokai Ltd., **64** 261
Tokos Medical Corporation, **17** 306, 308–09

Tokushima Automobile Service Company Inc., **60** 272
Tokyo Broadcasting System, **7** 249; **9** 29; **16** 167
Tokyo City Finance, **36** 419–20
Tokyo Dento Company, **6** 430
Tokyo Disneyland, **6** 176
Tokyo Electric Power Company, V 729–33
Tokyo Electronic Corp., **11** 232
Tokyo Gas and Electric Industrial Company, **9** 293
Tokyo Gas Co., Ltd., V 734–36; 55 372–75 (upd.)
Tokyo Ishikawajima Shipbuilding and Engineering Company, **9** 293
Tokyo Maritime Agency Ltd., **56** 181
Tokyo Motors. *See* Isuzu Motors, Ltd.
Tokyo Stock Exchange, **34** 254
Tokyo Telecommunications Engineering Corp. *See* Tokyo Tsushin Kogyo K.K.
Tokyu Corporation, V 526–28; 47 407–10 (upd.)
Tokyu Department Store Co., Ltd., V 199–202; 32 453–57 (upd.)
Tokyu Land Corporation, IV 728–29
Toledo Edison Company. *See* Centerior Energy Corporation.
Toledo Milk Processing, Inc., **15** 449
Toledo Scale Corp., **9** 441; **30** 327
Toll Brothers Inc., 15 497–99
Tollgrade Communications, Inc., 44 424–27
Tom Brown, Inc., 37 389–91
Tom Doherty Associates Inc., 25 483–86
Tom Snyder Productions, **29** 470, 472
Tom Thumb, **40** 365–66
Tom Thumb-Page, **16** 64
Tom's Foods Inc., 66 325–27
Tom's of Maine, Inc., 45 414–16
Toman Corporation, **19** 390
The Tomatin Distillery Co., Ltd., **62** 347
Tombstone Pizza Corporation, 13 515–17
Tomcan Investments Inc., **53** 333
Tomen Corporation, IV 224–25; 19 256; **24 488–91 (upd.)**
Tomkins-Johnson Company, **16** 8
Tomkins plc, 11 525–27; 28 382, 384; **30** 424, 426; **44 428–31 (upd.); 56** 78–79
Tomlee Tool Company, **7** 535; **26** 493
Tommy Armour Golf Co., **32** 446–47
Tommy Bahama. *See* Viewpoint International, Inc.
Tommy Hilfiger Corporation, 16 61; **20 488–90; 25** 258; **53 330–33 (upd.)**
Tomy Company Ltd., 65 341–44
Tone Brothers, Inc., 21 496–98; 63 83, 85
Tone Coca-Cola Bottling Company, Ltd., **14** 288; **47** 206
Tonen Corporation, IV 554–56; 16 489–92 (upd.)
TonenGeneral Sekiyu K.K., 54 380–86 (upd.)
Tong Yang Cement Corporation, 62 366–68
Tonka Corporation, 12 169; **14** 266; **16** 267; **25** 380, **487–89; 43** 229, 232
Tonkin, Inc., **19** 114
Tony Lama Company Inc., **19** 233
Tony Roma's, A Place for Ribs Inc., **40** 340–41. *See also* Romacorp, Inc.
Tony Stone Images, **31** 216–17

Too, Inc., 61 371–73
Toohey, **10** 170
Toolex International N.V., 26 489–91
Tootsie Roll Industries Inc., 12 480–82; 15 323
Top End Wheelchair Sports, **11** 202
Top Green International, **17** 475
Top Tool Company, Inc., **25** 75
Topack Verpackungstechnik, **60** 193
The Topaz Group, Inc., 62 369–71
Topco Associates LLC, 17 78; **60 302–04**
Topkapi, **17** 101–03
Toppan Printing Co., Ltd., IV 679–81; 58 340–44 (upd.)
Topps Company, Inc., 13 518–20; 19 386; **34 446–49 (upd.)**
Topps Markets, **16** 314
Tops Appliance City, Inc., 17 487–89
Tops Markets LLC, 60 305–07
TopTip, **48** 116
Topy Industries, Limited, **8** 506–07
Tor Books. *See* Tom Doherty Associates Inc.
Toray Industries, Inc., V 383–86; 17 287; **51 375–79 (upd.)**
Torchmark Corporation, 9 506–08; 11 17; **22 540–43; 33 405–08 (upd.)**
Torfeaco Industries Limited, **19** 304
The Toro Company, 7 534–36; 26 492–95 (upd.)
Toromont Industries, Ltd., 21 499–501
Toronto and Scarborough Electric Railway, **9** 461
The Toronto-Dominion Bank, II 375–77, 456; **16** 13–14; **18 551–53; 21** 447; **43** 7; **49 395–99 (upd.)**
Toronto Electric Light Company, **9** 461
Toronto Maple Leafs. *See* Maple Leaf Sports & Entertainment Ltd.
Toronto Raptors. *See* Maple Leaf Sports & Entertainment Ltd.
Toronto Sun Publishing Company. *See* Sun Media.
Torrent Systems, Inc., **59** 56
The Torrington Company, 13 521–24
Torrington National Bank & Trust Co., **13** 467
Torstar Corporation, 7 488–89; 29 470–73; 52 155. *See also* Harlequin Enterprises Limited.
Toscany Co., **13** 42
Tosco Corporation, 7 537–39; 12 240; **20** 138; **24** 522; **36** 359; **40** 358; **63** 113
Toshiba Corporation, I 533–35; II 62, 68, 73, 99, 102, 118, 122, 326, 440; **III** 298, 461, 533, 604; **6** 287; **7** 529; **9** 7, 181; **10** 518–19; **11** 46, 328; **12** 454, **483–86 (upd.),** 546; **13** 324, 399, 482; **14** 117, 446; **16** 5, 167; **17** 533; **18** 18, 260; **21** 390; **22** 193, 373; **23** 471; **40 435–40 (upd.); 43** 15; **47** 153–54; **57** 321
Toshin Kaihatsu Ltd. *See* Takashimaya Co., Limited.
Toshin Paper Co., Ltd., **IV** 285
Tostem. *See* Toyo Sash Co., Ltd.
Total Audio Visual Services, **24** 95
Total Beverage Corporation, **16** 159, 161
Total Compagnie Française des Pétroles S.A., IV 498, 504, 515, 525, 544–47, **557–61; 7** 481–84; **13** 557; **21** 203. *See also* TOTAL S.A.
Total Entertainment Restaurant Corporation, 46 427–29

Total Exploration S.A., **11** 537

Total Filtration Services, Inc., **61** 66

Total Fina Elf S.A., **47** 342, 365, 368; **50 478–86 (upd.)**; **56** 63, 65

Total Global Sourcing, Inc., **10** 498

Total Home Entertainment (THE), **39** 240, 242

Total Petroleum Corporation, **21** 500

TOTAL S.A., **24 492–97 (upd.)**, 522; **25** 104; **26** 369; **61** 238

Total System Services, Inc., **12** 465–66; **18** 168, 170, **516–18**; **52** 336

Totem Resources Corporation, **9 509–11**

Totino's Finer Foods, **26** 436

TOTO LTD., **III** 755–56; **28 464–66 (upd.)**

Touch America Inc., **37** 127; **44** 288

Touch-It Corp., **22** 413

Touche Remnant Holdings Ltd., **II** 356

Touche Ross. *See* Deloitte Touche Tohmatsu International.

Touchstone Films. *See* The Walt Disney Company.

Le Touquet's, SA, **48** 197

Tourang Limited, **7** 253

Touristik Union International GmbH. and Company K.G., **II** 163–65; **46** 460. *See also* Preussag AG.

Tourtime America, **56** 223

Toval Japon, **IV** 680

Towa Optical Manufacturing Company, **41** 261–63

Tower Air, Inc., **28 467–69**

Tower Automotive, Inc., **24 498–500**

Tower Records, **9** 361; **10** 335; **11** 558; **30** 224. *See also* MTS Inc.

Towers, **II** 649

Towers Perrin, **32 458–60**

Towle Manufacturing Co., **14** 482–83; **18** 69

Town & Country Corporation, **7** 372; **16** 546; **19 451–53**; **25** 254

Town Sports International, Inc., **46 430–33**

Townsend Hook, **IV** 296, 650, 652; **19** 226

Townsends, Inc., **64 385–87**

Toxicol Laboratories, Ltd., **21** 424

Toy Biz, Inc., **10** 402; **18 519–21**; **54** 58

Toy Liquidators, **13** 541–43; **50** 99

Toy Park, **16** 390

Toyad Corp., **7** 296

Toymax International, Inc., **29 474–76**; **52** 193

Toyo Ink Manufacturing, **26** 213

Toyo Kogyo, **II** 361

Toyo Microsystems Corporation, **11** 464

Toyo Pulp Co., **IV** 322

Toyo Rayon. *See* Toray Industries, Inc.

Toyo Sash Co., Ltd., **III 757–58**

Toyo Seikan Kaisha Ltd., **I 615–16**

Toyo Tire & Rubber Co., **V** 255–56; **9** 248

Toyo Toki Co., Ltd. *See* Toto.

Toyo Trust and Banking Co., **17** 349

Toyoda Automatic Loom Works, Ltd., **III 636–39**

Toyota Industrial Equipment, **27** 294, 296

Toyota Motor Corporation, **I 203–05**; **6** 514; **7** 111, 118, 212, 219–21; **8** 315; **9** 294, 340–42; **10** 407; **11** 351, 377, 487, **528–31 (upd.)**; **14** 321; **15** 495; **21** 162, 273; **23** 289–90, 338–40; **25** 198; **34** 303, 305–06; **38 458–62 (upd.)**; **56** 284, 286; **59** 393–94

Toyota Tsusho America, Inc., **13** 371

Toys 'R' Us, Inc., **V** 203–06; **10** 235, 284, 484; **12** 178; **13** 166; **14** 61; **15** 469; **16** 389–90, 457; **18 522–25 (upd.)**; **24** 412; **25** 314; **31** 477–78; **37** 129; **43** 385; **57 370–75 (upd.)**

TP Transportation, **39** 377

TPA. *See* Aloha Airlines Incorporated.

TPCR Corporation. *See* The Price Company.

TPG N.V., **64 388–91 (upd.)**

Trac Inc., **44** 355

Trace International Holdings, Inc., **17** 182–83; **26** 502

Tracinda Corporation, **25** 329–30

Tracker Marine. *See* Bass Pro Shops, Inc.

Tracker Services, Inc., **9** 110

Traco International N.V., **8** 250; **32** 249

Tracor Inc., **10** 547; **17 490–92**; **26** 267

Tractebel S.A., **20 491–93**. *See also* Suez Lyonnaise des Eaux.

Tractor Supply Company, **57 376–78**

Tradax, **II** 617; **13** 137

Trade Development Bank, **11** 415–17

Trade Source International, **44** 132

Trade Waste Incineration, Inc., **9** 109

Trade-Winds Environmental Restoration, Inc., **62** 389

Trader Classified Media N.V., **57 379–82**

Trader Joe's Company, **13 525–27**; **41** 422; **50 487–90 (upd.)**

Trader Media Group, **53** 152

Trader Publications, Inc., **IV** 597

Trader Publishing Company, **12** 302

Traders Group Ltd., **11** 258

Trading Post Group Pty Ltd., **57** 381

The Trading Service, **10** 278

Traex Corporation, **8** 359

Trafalgar House Investments Ltd., **IV** 259, 711; **20** 313; **23** 161; **24** 88; **36** 322

Trafalgar House PLC, **47** 178

Traffix, Inc., **61 374–76**

Trafford Park Printers, **53** 152

Trafiroad NV, **39** 239

Trailer Bridge, Inc., **41 397–99**

Trailer Marine Transport, **6** 383

Trailways Lines, Inc., **I** 450; **9** 425; **32** 230

Trak Auto Corporation, **16** 159–62

TRAK Communications Inc., **44** 420

TRAK Microwave Corporation, **18** 497, 513

Trammell Crow Company, **IV** 343; **8** 326–28, **532–34**; **49** 147–48; **54** 222–24; **57** 27, **383–87 (upd.)**; **58** 11–13

Trane Company, **10** 525; **21** 107; **22** 6; **26** 4. *See also* American Standard Companies, Inc.

Trans-Canada Air Lines. *See* Air Canada.

Trans Colorado, **11** 299

Trans-Continental Leaf Tobacco Company, (TCLTC), **13** 491

Trans Continental Records, **52** 430

Trans Freight Lines, **27** 473–74

Trans International Airlines, **41** 402

Trans Louisiana Gas Company, **43** 56–57

Trans-Lux Corporation, **51 380–83**

Trans-Mex, Inc. S.A. de C.V., **42** 365

Trans-Natal Coal Corp., **IV** 93

Trans Ocean Products, **8** 510

Trans-Pacific Airlines, **22** 251. *See also* Aloha Airlines Incorporated.

Trans-Resources Inc., **13** 299

Trans Thai-Malaysia, **56** 290

Trans Union Corp., **IV** 137; **6** 25; **28** 119

Trans Western Publishing, **25** 496

Trans World Airlines, Inc., **I 125–27**, 132; **II** 679; **6** 130; **9** 17, 232; **10** 301–03; **11** 277, 427; **12** 381, **487–90 (upd.)**; **14** 73; **15** 419; **22** 22, 219; **26** 439; **29** 190; **35 424–29 (upd.)**; **52** 21, 90, 168

Trans-World Corp., **19** 456; **47** 231

Trans World Entertainment Corporation, **24 501–03**

Trans World International, **18** 262–63

Trans World Life Insurance Company, **27** 46–47

Trans World Music, **9** 361

Trans World Seafood, Inc., **13** 244

Transaction Systems Architects, Inc., **29 477–79**

Transaction Technology, **12** 334

TransAlta Utilities Corporation, **6 585–87**

Transamerica—An AEGON Company, **41 400–03 (upd.)**

Transamerica Corporation, **I 536–38**; **III** 344; **7** 236–37; **8** 46; **11** 273, 533; **13 528–30 (upd.)**; **21** 285; **25** 328; **27** 230; **46** 48. *See also* TIG Holdings, Inc.

Transamerica Pawn Holdings. *See* EZCORP Inc.

Transamerica Retirement Services, **63** 176

TransAmerican Waste Industries Inc., **41** 414

Transat. *See* Compagnie Générale Transatlantique (Transat).

Transatlantic Holdings, Inc., **III** 198; **11 532–33**; **15** 18

Transatlantische Dampfschiffahrts Gesellschaft, **6** 397

Transatlantische Gruppe, **III** 404

Transax, **63** 102

TransBrasil S/A Linhas Aéreas, **31 443–45**; **46** 398

TransCanada PipeLines Limited, **I** 264; **V 737–38**; **17** 22–23

Transco Energy Company, **V 739–40**; **18** 366. *See also* The Williams Companies.

Transcontinental and Western Air Lines, **9** 416; **12** 487

Transcontinental Gas Pipe Line Corporation. *See* Transco Energy Company.

Transcontinental Pipeline Company, **6** 456–57

Transcontinental Services Group N.V., **16** 207

TransCor America, Inc., **23** 154

Transelco, Inc., **8** 178

Transfer Drivers, Inc., **46** 301

Transflash, **6** 404; **26** 243

Transfracht, **6** 426

Transiciel SA, **48 400–02**

Transit Homes of America, Inc., **46** 301

Transit Mix Concrete and Materials Company, **7** 541

Transitions Optical Inc., **21** 221, 223

Transitron, **16** 332

Transkaryotic Therapies Inc., **54** 111

Transking Inc. *See* King Kullen Grocery Co., Inc.

Transkrit Corp., **IV** 640; **26** 273

Translittoral, **67** 353

Transmanche-Link, **13** 206–08; **37** 135

Transmedia Network Inc., **20 494–97**

Transmedica International, Inc., **41** 225

Transmisiones y Equipos Mecanicos, S.A. de C.V., **23** 171

Transmitter Equipment Manufacturing Co., **13** 385

TransMontaigne Inc., 28 470–72

Transmontane Rod and Gun Club, **43** 435–36

Transnet Ltd., 6 433–35

Transocean Sedco Forex Inc., 45 417–19; **59** 368

Transpac, **IV** 325

Transport Corporation of America, Inc., 49 400–03

Transport International Pool, **58** 239

Transportacion Ferroviaria Mexicana, **50** 209

Transportacion Maritima Mexicana S.A. de C.V., **12** 279; **26** 236; **47** 162; **50** 208

Transportation Technologies Industries Inc., **51** 155

Transportation.com, **45** 451

Transportes Aéreas Centro-Americanos. *See* Grupo TACA.

Transportes Aereos Portugueses, S.A., 6 125–27. *See also* TAP—Air Portugal Transportes Aéreos Portugueses S.A.

Transportes Aeromar, **39** 188

Transrack S.A., **26** 363

Transue & Williams Steel Forging Corp., **13** 302

Transway International Corp., **10** 369

Transworld Communications, **35** 165

Transworld Corp., **14** 209

Transworld Drilling Company Limited. *See* Kerr-McGee Corporation.

The Tranzonic Companies, 8 512; 15 500–02; 37 392–95

Trapper's, **19** 286

Trasgo, S.A. de C.V., **14** 516; **50** 493

Travel Air Manufacturing Company, **8** 49; **27** 97

Travel Inc., **26** 309

Travel Information Group, **17** 398

Travel Ports of America, Inc., 17 493–95

Travelers/Aetna Property Casualty Corp., **63** 14

Travelers Bank & Trust Company, **13** 467

Travelers Book Club, **13** 105

Travelers Corporation, III 387–90; 15 463 124. *See also* Citigroup Inc.

Travelers/Aetna Property Casualty Corp., **21** 15

Travelocity.com, Inc., 46 434–37; 58 118–20

Travers Morgan Ltd., **42** 183

Travis Boats & Motors, Inc., 37 396–98

Travis Perkins plc, 34 450–52

Travocéan, **25** 104

Traylor Engineering & Manufacturing Company, **6** 395; **25** 169

TRC. *See* Tennessee Restaurant Company.

TRC Companies, Inc., 32 461–64

TRE Corp., **23** 225

Treadco, Inc., 16 39; **19** 38, 454–56

Treasure Chest Advertising Company, Inc., 21 60; 32 465–67

Treasure House Stores, Inc., **17** 322

Treatment Centers of America, **11** 379

Trebuhs Realty Co., **24** 438

Tredegar Corporation, 10 291; **52 349–51; 59** 24

Tree of Life, Inc., 29 480–82

Tree Sweet Products Corp., **12** 105; **26** 325

Tree Tavern, Inc., **27** 197

Trefoil Capital Investors, L.P., **8** 305

Trego Systems Inc., **64** 190

Trek Bicycle Corporation, 16 493–95; 19 384–85

Trelleborg A.B., **IV** 166

Tremec. *See* Transmisiones y Equipos Mecanicos, S.A. de C.V.

Tremont Corporation, **21** 490

Trencherwood Plc, **45** 443

Trend International Ltd., **13** 502

Trend-Lines, Inc., 22 516–18

Trends Magazine NV, **48** 347

Trendwest Resorts, Inc., 12 439; **33 409–11**. *See also* Jeld-Wen, Inc.

TrentonWorks Limited. *See* The Greenbrier Companies.

Tresco, **8** 514

Trevor Sorbie of America, Inc., **60** 287

Tri-City Federal Savings and Loan Association, **10** 92

Tri-City Utilities Company, **6** 514

Tri-County National Bank, **9** 474

Tri-Marine International Inc., **24** 116

Tri-Miller Packing Company, **7** 524

Tri-Sonics, Inc., **16** 202; **43** 170

Tri-State Baking, **53** 21

Tri-State Improvement Company, **6** 465–66

Tri-State Publishing & Communications, Inc., **22** 442

Tri State Recycling Corporation, **15** 117

Tri-Union Seafoods LLC, **24** 116

Tri Valley Growers, 32 468–71

Tri-Village Developments BV, **58** 359

Triad, **14** 224

Triad Artists Inc., **23** 514

Triad International Maintenance Corp., **13** 417

Triad Nitrogen, Inc., **27** 316, 318

Triad Systems Corp., **38** 96

The Triangle Group, **16** 357

Triangle Industries Inc., **I** 614; **14** 43

Triangle Pharmaceuticals, Inc., **54** 131

Triangle Publications, Inc., **12** 359–60

Triangle Sheet Metal Works, Inc., **45** 327

Triarc Companies, Inc., 8 535–37; 13 322; **14** 32–33; **34 453–57 (upd.)**; **39** 383, 385; **57** 227; **58** 324

Tribe Computer Works. *See* Zoom Technologies, Inc.

Tribune Company, IV 682–84; 10 56; **11** 331; **22 519–23 (upd.)**; **26** 17; **32** 358–59; **38** 306; **42** 133; **63 389–95 (upd.)**

Tricap Restructuring Fund, **59** 162

Trick & Murray, **22** 153

Trico Products Corporation, 15 503–05

Tricon Global Restaurants, Inc., **21** 313, 317, 405, 407, 485; **40** 342; **57** 228. *See also* Yum! Brands Inc.

Tridel Enterprises Inc., 9 512–13

Trident Data Systems, **54** 396

Trident II, Inc., **64** 253

Trident NGL Holdings Inc., **18** 365, 367

Trident Seafoods Corporation, 56 359–61

Trifari, Krussman & Fishel, Inc., **9** 157

Trigen Energy Corporation, 6 512; **42 386–89**

Trigon Industries, **13** 195; **14** 431

Trilan Developments Ltd., **9** 512

Trilogy Fabrics, Inc., **16** 125

Trilogy Retail Enterprises L.P., **58** 186

Trilon Financial Corporation, II 456–57

Trimac Ltd., **25** 64

TriMas Corp., III 571; **11 534–36; 20** 359, 362; **39** 266

Trimble Navigation Limited, 40 441–43

Trimel Corp., **47** 54

Trinc Company, **59** 320

TriNet Corporate Realty Trust, Inc., **65** 146

Trinidad and Tobago External Telecommunications Company, **25** 100

Trinidad-Tesoro Petroleum Company Limited, **7** 516, 518

Trinity Beverage Corporation, **11** 451

Trinity Broadcasting, **13** 279

Trinity Capital Opportunity Corp., **17** 13

Trinity Distributors, **15** 139

Trinity Industries, Incorporated, 7 540–41

Trinity Mirror plc, 49 404–10 (upd.)

TRINOVA Corporation, III 640–42, 731; **13** 8; **16** 7, 9

Triple Five Group Ltd., 49 411–15

Triple P N.V., 26 496–99

Trippe Manufacturing Co., **10** 474; **24** 29

TriQuest-Nypro Plastics, **60** 264

TriQuint Semiconductor, Inc., 63 396–99

Trisko Jewelry Sculptures, Ltd., 57 388–90

TriStar Pictures, **II** 136–37; **12** 75, 455; **23** 275; **28** 462. *See also* Columbia TriStar Motion Pictures Companies.

Triton Bioscience, **III** 53; **26** 384

Triton Cellular Partners, L.P., **43** 341

Triton Energy Corporation, 11 537–39; **55** 20

Triton Group Ltd., **I** 447; **31** 287; **34** 339

Triton Systems Corp., **22** 186

Triumph-Adler, **11** 265. *See also* TA Triumph-Adler AG.

Triumph American, Inc., **12** 199

Triumph Films, **25** 174

Triumph, Finlay, and Philips Petroleum, **11** 28

Triumph Group, Inc., 21 153; **31 446–48**

Triumph LOR, Inc., **63** 305–06

Triumph Motorcycles Ltd., 53 334–37

Trivest, Inc., **21** 531–32

Trizec Corporation Ltd., 9 84–85; **10 529–32**

TrizecHahn, **37** 311; **63** 341

TRM Copy Centers Corporation, 18 526–28

Troll, **13** 561

Trolley Barn Brewery Inc., **25** 401

Tropical Marine Centre, **40** 128–29

Tropical Shipping, Inc., **6** 529, 531

Tropical Sportswear Int'l Corporation, **42** 120

Tropicana Products, Inc., 25 366; **28** 271, 473–77; **38** 349; **45** 160–62

Trotter, Inc., **49** 108

Trotter-Yoder & Associates, **22** 88

Trottner-McJunkin SA de CV, **63** 287–88

Trouw Nutrition USA, **56** 258

Troxel Cycling, **16** 53

Troy & Nichols, Inc., **13** 147

Troy Design Group, **55** 32

Troy Metal Products. *See* KitchenAid.

Troyfel Ltd., **III** 699

TRT Communications, Inc., **6** 327; **11** 185

Tru-Run Inc., **16** 207

Tru-Stitch, **16** 545

Tru-Trac Therapy Products, **11** 486

Truck Components Inc., **23** 306

Trudeau Marketing Group, Inc., **22** 386

True Form Foundations Corporation, **59** 267

True North Communications Inc., 23 478–80; **25** 91. *See also* Foote, Cone & Belding Worldwide.

True Temper Hardware Co., **30** 241–42

True Value Hardware Stores. *See* TruServ Corporation.

Trugg-Hansa Holding AB, **III** 264

TruGreen, **23** 428, 430

Truitt Bros., **10** 382

Trump Organization, 16 262; **23 481–84**; **43** 225; **64 392–97 (upd.)**

Trunkline Gas Company, **6** 544; **14** 135

Trunkline LNG Co., **IV** 425

Trus Joist Corporation. *See* TJ International, Inc.

TruServ Corporation, 24 504–07

Trussdeck Corporation. *See* TJ International, Inc.

Trust Company of the West, **19** 414; **42** 347

Trustcorp, Inc., **9** 475–76

Trusted Information Systems, Inc., **25** 349

Trusthouse Forte PLC, III 104–06; **16** 446

TRW Inc., I 539–41; **6** 25; **8** 416; **9** 18, 359; **10** 293; **11** 68, **540–42 (upd.)**; **12** 238; **14 510–13 (upd.)**; **16** 484; **17** 372; **18** 275; **19** 184; **23** 134; **24** 480; **26** 141; **28** 119; **32** 437; **33** 47; **34** 76; **43** 311, 313; **45** 152

TRW Vehicle Safety Systems Inc., **41** 369

Tryart Pty. Limited, **7** 253

TSA. *See* Transaction Systems Architects, Inc.

TSB Group plc, 12 491–93; **16** 14

TSC. *See* Tractor Supply Company.

TSI Inc., **38** 206

TSI Soccer Corporation, **29** 142–43

Tsingtao Brewery Group, 49 416–20

TSMC. *See* Taiwan Semiconductor Manufacturing Company Ltd.

TSO. *See* Teacher's Service Organization, Inc.

TSO Financial Corp., **II** 420; **8** 10

Tsogo Sun Gaming & Entertainment, **17** 318

TSP. *See* Tom Snyder Productions.

TSR Inc., **24** 538

Tsuang Hine Co., **III** 582

Tsubakimoto-Morse, **14** 64

Tsurusaki Pulp Co., Ltd., **IV** 285

Tsutsunaka Plastic Industry Co., **8** 359

TSYS. *See* Total System Services, Inc.

TT Acquisitions, Inc., **56** 361

TTK. *See* Tokyo Tsushin Kogyo K.K.

TTX Company, 6 436–37; **66 328–30 (upd.)**

Tubby's, Inc., 53 338–40

Tube Fab Ltd., **17** 234

Tube Forming, Inc., **23** 517

Tube Reducing Corp., **16** 321

Tube Service Co., **19** 344

Tubed Chemicals Corporation, **27** 299

Tuborg, **9** 99

Tubos de Acero de Mexico, S.A. (TAMSA), 41 404–06

Tuboscope, **42** 420

Tucker, Lynch & Coldwell. *See* CB Commercial Real Estate Services Group, Inc.

TUCO, Inc., **8** 78

Tucson Electric Power Company, 6 588–91; **42** 388

Tucson Gas & Electric, **19** 411–12

Tuesday Morning Corporation, 18 529–31

Tuff Stuff Publications, **23** 101

TUI. *See* Touristik Union International GmbH. and Company K.G.

TUI Group GmbH, 42 283; **44 432–35**

Tuileries et Briqueteries d'Hennuyeres et de Wanlin, **14** 249

TUJA, **27** 21

Tully's Coffee Corporation, 51 384–86

Tultex Corporation, 13 531–33

Tumbleweed, Inc., 33 412–14

Tunhems Industri A.B., **I** 387

Tunisair. *See* Société Tunisienne de l'Air-Tunisair.

Tupolev Aviation and Scientific Technical Complex, 24 58–60

Tupperware Corporation, 15 475, 477; **17** 186; **18** 67; **28 478–81**

Turbine Engine Asset Management LLC, **28** 5

TurboLinux Inc., **45** 363

Turcot Paperboard Mills Ltd., **17** 281

Turk Telecom, **63** 378, 380

Turkish Petroleum Co. *See* Türkiye Petrolleri Anonim Ortakliği.

Turkiye Is Bankasi A.S., 61 377–80

Türkiye Petrolleri Anonim Ortakliği, IV 562–64

Turner Broadcasting System, Inc., II 166–68; **IV** 676; **6 171–73 (upd.)**; **7** 64, 99, 306, 529; **23** 33, 257; **25** 313, 329, 498; **30** 100; **47** 272; **57** 40; **66 331–34 (upd.)**

Turner Construction Company, 66 335–38

The Turner Corporation, 8 538–40; **23 485–88 (upd.)**; **25** 402; **33** 197

Turner Entertainment Co., **18** 459

Turner Glass Company, **13** 40

Turner Network Television, **21** 24

Turnstone Systems, **44** 426

TURPAS. *See* Türkiye Petrolleri Anonim Ortakliği

Turtle Wax, Inc., 15 506–09; **16** 43; **26** 349

Tuscarora Inc., 17 155; **29 483–85**

The Tussauds Group, 55 376–78

Tutt Bryant Industries PLY Ltd., **26** 231

Tuttle, Oglebay and Company. *See* Oglebay Norton Company.

TV & Stereo Town, **10** 468

TV Asahi, **7** 249

TV Azteca, S.A. de C.V., 39 194–95, **398–401**

TV Food Network, **22** 522

TV Guide, Inc., 43 431–34 (upd.)

TVA. *See* Tennessee Valley Authority.

TVE. *See* Television Española, S.A.

TVE Holdings, **22** 307

TVH Acquisition Corp., **III** 264

TVI, Inc., 15 510–12

TVN Entertainment Corporation, **32** 239

TVS Entertainment PLC, **13** 281

TVSN Ltd., **64** 185

TVT Records. *See* Tee Vee Toons, Inc.

TVW Enterprises, **7** 78

TW Services, Inc., II 679–80; **10** 301–03

TWA. *See* Trans World Airlines; Transcontinental & Western Airways.

TWC. *See* The Weather Channel, Inc.

Tweco Co., **19** 441

Tweeds, **12** 280

Tweeter Home Entertainment Group, Inc., 30 464–66; **41** 379, 381

Twentieth Century Fox Film Corporation, II 169–71; **12** 322, 359; **15** 23, 25, 234; **25** 327, **490–94 (upd.)**; **43** 173

"21" International Holdings, **17** 182

21 Invest International Holdings Ltd., **14** 322

21st Century Food Products. *See* Hain Food Group, Inc.

21st Century Mortgage, **18** 28

Twenty-third Publications, **49** 48

24/7 Real Media, Inc., 49 421–24

TWI. *See* Trans World International.

Twin City Wholesale Drug Company, **14** 147

Twin Disc, Inc., 21 502–04

Twin Hill Acquisition Company, Inc., **48** 286

Twinings Tea, **41** 31

Twinlab Corporation, 34 458–61

Twinpak, **IV** 250

Two Guys, **12** 49

2ndhead Oy, **51** 328

21st Century Mortgage, **41** 18, 20

TWW Plc, **26** 62

TXEN, Inc., **18** 370

TxPort Inc., **13** 8

Ty Inc., 33 415–17

Tyco International Ltd., III 643–46; **13** 245–47; **21** 462; **28 482–87 (upd.)**; **30** 157; **44** 6; **50** 135; **54** 236, 239, 373; **63 400–06 (upd.)**

Tyco Submarine Systems Ltd., **32** 217

Tyco Toys, Inc., 12 494–97; **13** 312, 319; **18** 520–21; **25** 314

Tyler Corporation, 23 489–91

Tymnet, **18** 542

Tyndale House Publishers, Inc., 57 391–94

Tyndall's Formal Wear, **60** 5

Tyrolean Airways, **9** 233; **33** 50

Tyskie Brewery, **24** 450

Tyson Foods, Inc., II 584–85; **7** 422–23, 432; **14 514–16 (upd.)**; **21** 535; **23** 376, 384; **26** 168; **39** 229; **50 491–95 (upd.)**; **64** 386

U.B. TUFF., **67** 339

U.C.L.A.F. *See* Roussel-Uclaf.

U-Haul International Inc. *See* Amerco.

U.K. Corrugated, **IV** 296; **19** 226

U.S. *See also* US.

U.S. Aggregates, Inc., 42 390–92

U.S. Appliances, **26** 336

U.S. Bancorp, 12 165; **14 527–29**; **36 489–95 (upd.)**

U.S. Bank of Washington, **14** 527

U.S. Banknote Company, **30** 43

U.S. Bearings Company. *See* Federal-Mogul Corporation.

U.S. Billing, Inc. *See* Billing Concepts Corp.

U.S. Biomedicals Corporation, **27** 69

U.S. Bioscience, Inc., **35** 286, 288

U.S. Borax, Inc., 42 393–96

U.S. Brass., **24** 151

U.S. Can Corporation, 30 474–76

U.S. Cellular Corporation, 31 449–52 (upd.)

U.S. Computer of North America Inc., **43** 368

U.S. Delivery Systems, Inc., 22 153, **531–33; 47** 90. *See also* Velocity Express Corporation.

U.S. Electrical Motors, **II** 19

U.S. Elevator Corporation, **19** 109–11

U.S. Envelope, **19** 498

U.S. Foodservice, 26 503–06; **37** 374, 376

U.S. Generating Company, **26** 373

U.S. Geological Survey, **9** 367

U.S. Graphite. *See* Wickes Inc.

U.S. Guarantee Co., **III** 220; **14** 108

U.S. Healthcare, Inc., 6 194–96; **21** 16

U.S. Home Corporation, 8 541–43

U.S. Industries, Inc., **7** 208; **18** 467; **23** 296; **24** 150; **27** 288

U.S. Intec, **22** 229

U.S. International Reinsurance, **III** 264

U.S. Investigations Services Inc., **35** 44

U.S. Lawns, **31** 182, 184

U.S. Lines, **III** 459; **11** 194

U.S. Lock Corporation, **9** 543; **28** 50–52

U.S. Long Distance Corp. *See* Billing Concepts Corp.

U.S. News and World Report Inc., 30 477–80

U.S. Office Products Company, 25 500–02; **41** 69, 247; **47** 91

U.S. Overall Company, **14** 549

U.S. Physical Therapy, Inc., 65 345–48

U.S. Plywood Corp. *See* United States Plywood Corp.

U.S. RingBinder Corp., **10** 313–14

U.S. Robotics Corporation, 9 514–15; **20** 8, 69; **22** 17; **24** 212; **34** 444; **36** 122, 357; **48** 369; **49** 184; **66** 339–41 **(upd.)**

U.S. Rubber Company, **10** 388

U.S. Satellite Broadcasting Company, Inc., 20 505–07

U.S. Shoe Corporation, **43** 98; **44** 365

U.S. Smelting Refining and Mining, **7** 360

U.S. Software Inc., **29** 479

U.S. Steel Corp. *See* United States Steel Corp.

U.S. Telephone Communications, **9** 478

U.S. Timberlands Company, L.P., 42 397–400

U.S. Time Corporation, **13** 120

U.S. Trust Corp., 17 496–98

U.S. Vanadium Co., **9** 517

U.S. Venture Partners, **15** 204–05

U.S. Vision, Inc., 66 342–45

U S West, Inc., V 341–43; **11** 12, 59, 547; **25** 101, 495–99 **(upd.); 32** 218; **36** 43; **37** 124–27

U.S. Windpower, **11** 222–23

U.S. Xpress Enterprises, Inc., **18** 159

U-Tote'M, **II** 620; **7** 372

UA. *See* Metro- Goldwyn-Mayer Inc., MGM/UA Communications Company; United Artists Corp.

UAA. *See* EgyptAir.

UAL Corporation, 34 462–65 **(upd.); 52** 22, 25

UAP. *See* Union des Assurances de Paris.

UAP Inc., **45** 179

UARCO Inc., **15** 473–74

UAT. *See* UTA.

Ube Industries, Ltd., III 759–61; **38** 463–67 **(upd.)**

Ubi Soft Entertainment S.A., 41 188–89, **407–09**

Ubique Ltd, **25** 301

UBL Educational Loan Center, **42** 211

UBS AG, 52 352–59 **(upd.); 59** 141, 144–45

UCAR International, Inc., **40** 83

UCI, **25** 173

Udo Fischer Co., **8** 477

UDRT. *See* United Dominion Realty Trust, Inc.

UDV. *See* United Distillers and Vintners.

Ueda Kotsu Company, **47** 408

UETA Inc., **29** 510–11

Ufa Sports, **44** 190

UFJ Bank, **61** 250

Ugg Holdings, Inc., **22** 173

UGI. *See* United Gas Improvement.

UGI Corporation, 12 498–500

Ugine S.A., 20 498–500

Ugly Duckling Corporation, 22 524–27

Uhlmans Inc., **24** 458

UI International, **6** 444

UIB. *See* United Independent Broadcasters, Inc.

UICI, 33 418–21

Uinta Co., **6** 568

Uintah National Corp., **11** 260

UIS Co., **13** 554–55; **15** 324

Uitgeversmaatschappij Elsevier. *See* Reed Elsevier.

Uitzendbureau Amstelveen. *See* Randstad Holding n.v.

UJB Financial Corp., **14** 473

UKF. *See* Unie van Kunstmestfabrieken.

Ukrop's Super Market's, Inc., 39 402–04

UL. *See* Underwriters Laboratories, Inc.

Ullrich Copper, Inc. *See* Foster Wheeler Corp.

Ullstein Langen Müller, **IV** 591

ULN. *See* Union Laitière Normande.

Ulstein Holding ASA, **27** 494

Ultimate Electronics, Inc., 18 532–34; **21** 33; **24** 52, 269

Ultra Mart, **16** 250

Ultra Pac, Inc., 24 512–14

UltraCam. *See* Ultrak Inc.

UltraCare Products, **18** 148

Ultrak Inc., 24 508–11

Ultralar, **13** 544

Ultralife Batteries, Inc., 58 345–48

Ultramar Diamond Shamrock Corporation, IV 565–68; **31** 453–57 **(upd.)**

Ultrametl Mfg. Co., **17** 234

Umacs of Canada Inc., **9** 513

Umberto's of New Hyde Park Pizzeria, **16** 447

Umbro Holdings Ltd., **43** 392. *See also* Stone Manufacturing Company.

UMC. *See* United Microelectronics Corp.

UMG. *See* Universal Music Group.

UMI Company, **29** 58

NV Umicore SA, 47 411–13

Umpqua River Navigation Company, **13** 100

Unadulterated Food Products, Inc., **11** 449

UNAT, **III** 197–98

Unbrako Socket Screw Company Ltd., **30** 429

Uncas-Merchants National Bank, **13** 467

Uncle Ben's Inc., 22 528–30

Under Armour Performance Apparel, 61 381–83

Underground Group, **6** 407

Underwood, **24** 269

Underwriter for the Professions Insurance Company, **55** 128

Underwriters Laboratories, Inc., 30 467–70

Underwriters Reinsurance Co., **10** 45

Unefon, S.A., **39** 194, 196

UNELCO. *See* Union Electrica de Canarias S.A.

Unelec, Inc., **13** 398

UNG. *See* United National Group, Ltd.

Ungaro SA, **62** 313

Uni-Cast. *See* Sturm, Ruger & Company, Inc.

Uni Europe, **III** 211

Uni-Marts, Inc., 17 499–502

Uni-President Group, **49** 460

Unibail SA, 40 444–46

Unibank, **40** 336; **50** 149–50

Unic. *See* GIB Group.

Unicapital, Inc., **15** 281

Unicare Health Facilities, **6** 182; **25** 525

Unicco Security Services, **27** 22

Unice, **56** 335

UNICEF. *See* United Nations International Children's Emergency Fund (UNICEF).

Unicel. *See* Rural Cellular Corporation.

Unicer, **9** 100

Unichem, **25** 73

Unichema International, **13** 228

Unicom Corporation, 29 486–90 **(upd.).** *See also* Exelon Corporation.

Unicon Producing Co., **10** 191

Unicoolait, **19** 51

UNICOR. *See* Federal Prison Industries, Inc.

Unicord Company, **24** 115; **64** 60

UniCorp, **8** 228

UniCredito Italiano, **50** 410

Uniden, **14** 117

Unidrive, **47** 280

UniDynamics Corporation, **8** 135

Uniface Holding B.V., **10** 245; **30** 142

Unifi, Inc., 12 501–03; **62** 372–76 **(upd.)**

Unified Energy System of Russia. *See* RAO Unified Energy System of Russia.

Unified Western Grocers, **31** 25

UniFirst Corporation, 16 228; **21** 115, **505–07**

Uniflex Corporation, **53** 236

Uniforce Services Inc., **40** 119

Unigate PLC, II 586–87; **28** 488–91 **(upd.); 29** 150. *See also* Uniq Plc.

Unigesco Inc., **II** 653

Uniglory, **13** 211

Unigro. *See* Laurus N.V.

Unigroup, **15** 50

UniHealth America, **11** 378–79

Unijoh Sdn, Bhd, **47** 255

Unik S.A., **23** 170–171

Unilab Corp., **26** 391

Unilever PLC/Unilever N.V., II 588–91; **III** 52, 495; **7** 542–45 **(upd.),** 577; **8** 105–07, 166, 168, 341, 344; **9** 449; **11** 205, 421; **13** 243–44; **14** 204–05; **18** 395, 397; **19** 193; **21** 219; **22** 123; **23** 242; **26** 306; **28** 183, 185; **30** 396–97; **32** 472–78 **(upd.); 36** 237; **49** 269; **57** 301

Unilife Assurance Group, **III** 273

UniLife Insurance Co., **22** 149

Unilog SA, 42 401–03

Uniloy Milacron Inc., **53** 230

UniMac Companies, **11** 413

Unimetal, **30** 252

Uninsa, **I** 460

Union Aéromaritime de Transport. *See* UTA.

Union Bag–Camp Paper Corp. *See* Union Camp Corporation.

Union Bank. *See* State Street Boston Corporation.

Union Bank of California, **16 496–98.** *See also* UnionBanCal Corporation.

Union Bank of New York, **9** 229

Union Bank of Scotland, **10** 337

Union Bank of Switzerland, **II 378–79;** **21** 146. *See also* UBS AG.

Union Bay Sportswear, **17** 460

Union Biscuits. *See* Leroux S.A.S.

Union Camp Corporation, **IV 344–46; 8** 102; **39** 291; **47** 189; **63** 269

Union Carbide Corporation, **I** 390, 399–401, 582, 666; **7** 376; **8** 180, 182, 376; **9** 16, **516–20 (upd.); 10** 472; **11** 402–03; **12** 46; **13** 118; **14** 281–82; **16** 461; **17** 159; **43** 265–66; **48** 321; **55** 380

Union Cervecera, **9** 100

Union Colliery Company. *See* Union Electric Company.

Union Commerce Corporation, **11** 181

Union Commerciale, **19** 98

Union Corporation. *See* Gencor Ltd.

Union des Assurances de Paris, **II** 234; **III 201, 391–94**

Union des Coopératives Bressor, **25** 85

Union des Cooperatives Laitières. *See* Unicoolait.

Union des Mines, **52** 362

Union des Transports Aériens. *See* UTA.

Union Electric Company, **V 741–43; 6** 505–06; **26** 451. *See also* Ameren Corporation.

Unión Electrica Fenosa. *See* Unión Fenosa S.A.

Union Equity Co-Operative Exchange, **7** 175

Unión Fenosa, S.A., 51 387–90; 56 216

Union Financiera, **19** 189

Union Financière de France Banque SA, 52 360–62

Union Fork & Hoe Company. *See* Acorn Products, Inc.

Union Gas & Electric Co., **6** 529

l'Union Générale des Pétroles, **IV** 560

Union Hardware, **22** 115

Union Laitière Normande, **19** 50. *See also* Compagnie Laitière Européenne.

Union Levantina de Seguros, **III** 179

Union Light, Heat & Power Company, **6** 466

Union Minière. *See* NV Umicore SA.

Union Mutual Life Insurance Company. *See* UNUM Corp.

Union National Bank of Wilmington, **25** 540

Union of European Football Association, **27** 150

Union of Food Co-ops, **II** 622

Union Oil Co., **9** 266

Union Oil Co. of California. *See* Unocal Corporation.

Union Pacific Corporation, **V 529–32; 12** 18–20, 278; **14 371–72; 28 492–500 (upd.); 36** 43–44; **58** 262

Union Pacific Resources Group, **52** 30

Union Pacific Tea Co., **7** 202

Union Paper & Co. AS, **63** 315

Union Planters Corporation, 54 387–90

Union Power Company, **12** 541

Union Pub Company, **57** 411, 413

Union Savings and Loan Association of Phoenix, **19** 412

Union Savings Bank, **9** 173

Union Savings Bank and Trust Company, **13** 221

Union Steamship Co. of New Zealand Ltd., **27** 473

Union Sugar, **II** 573

Union Suisse des Coopératives de Consommation. *See* Coop Schweiz.

Union Tank Car Co., **IV** 137

Union Telecard Alliance, LLC, **34** 223

Union Telephone Company, **14** 258

Union Texas Petroleum Holdings, Inc., 7 379; **9 521–23**

Union-Transport, **6** 404; **26** 243

Union Trust Co., **9** 228; **13** 222

The Union Underwear Company, **8** 200–01; **25** 164–66

Union Verwaltungsgesellschaft mbH, **66** 123

Unionamerica, Inc., **III** 243; **16** 497; **50** 497

UnionBanCal Corporation, 50 496–99 (upd.)

UnionBay Sportswear Co., **27** 112

Unione Manifatture, S.p.A., **19** 338

Uniphase Corporation. *See* JDS Uniphase Corporation.

Uniplex Business Software, **41** 281

Uniq Plc, **52** 418, 420

Unique Casual Restaurants, Inc., 27 480–82

Unique Pub Company, **59** 182

Uniroy of Hempstead, Inc. *See* Aris Industries, Inc.

Uniroyal Chemical Corporation, **36** 145

Uniroyal Corp., **8** 503; **11** 159; **20** 262

Uniroyal Goodrich, **42** 88

Uniroyal Holdings Ltd., **21** 73

Unishops, Inc. *See* Aris Industries, Inc.

Unison HealthCare Corporation, 25 503–05

Unisource Worldwide, Inc., **47** 149

Unistar Radio Networks, **23** 510

Unisys Corporation, **III 165–67; 6 281–83 (upd.); 8** 92; **9** 32, 59; **12** 149, 162; **17** 11, 262; **18** 345, 386, 434, 542; **21** 86; **36 479–84 (upd.)**

Unit Corporation, **6** 394, 396; **25** 170; **63 407–09**

Unit Group plc, **8** 477

Unitech plc, **27** 81

United Acquisitions, **7** 114; **25** 125

United Advertising Periodicals, **12** 231

United AgriSeeds, Inc., **21** 387

United Air Express. *See* United Parcel Service of America Inc.

United Air Fleet, **23** 408

United Aircraft and Transportation Co., **9** 416, 418; **10** 260; **12** 289; **21** 140

United Airlines, **I** 118, 124, **128–30; II** 680; **6 128–30 (upd.),** 131, 388–89; **9** 271–72, 283, 416, 549; **10** 199, 301, 561; **11** 299; **12** 192, 381; **14** 73; **22** 199, 220; **24** 21, 22; **25** 146, 148, 421–23; **26** 113, 440; **27** 20; **29** 507; **38** 105; **52** 386; **55** 10–11. *See also* UAL Corporation.

United Alaska Drilling, Inc., **7** 558

United Alloy Steel Company, **26** 405

United-American Car, **13** 305

United American Insurance Company of Dallas, **9** 508; **33** 407

United American Lines, **6** 398

United Arab Airlines. *See* EgyptAir.

United Artists Corp., **IV** 676; **9** 74; **12** 13; **13** 529; **14** 87; **21** 362; **23** 389; **26** 487; **36** 47; **41** 402. *See also* MGM/UA Communications Company; Metro-Goldwyn-Mayer Inc.

United Artists Theatre Circuit, Inc., **37** 63–64; **59** 341

United Australian Automobile Industries, **62** 182

United Auto Group, Inc., 26 500–02; 45 261

United Biscuits (Holdings) plc, **II 592–94; 26** 59; **36** 313; **42 404–09 (upd.); 64** 270

United Brands Company, **II 595–97; 7** 84–85; **12** 215; **21** 110, 112; **25** 4; **60** 132

United Breweries International, Ltd., **60** 207

United Breweries Ltd. **I** 221, 223, 288; **24** 449. *See also* Carlsberg A/S.

United Broadcasting Corporation Public Company Ltd., **31** 330

United Building Centers. *See* Lanoga Corporation.

United Business Media plc, 52 363–68 (upd.)

United Cable Television Corporation, **9** 74; **18** 65; **43** 431

United Capital Corporation, **56** 136

United Central Oil Corporation, **7** 101

United Cigar Manufacturers Company,. *See* Culbro Corporation.

United Cities Gas Company, **43** 56, 58

United Communications Systems, Inc. **V** 346

United Computer Services, Inc., **11** 111

United Consolidated Industries, **24** 204

United Corp., **10** 44

United Defense Industries, Inc., 30 471–73; 66 346–49 (upd.)

United Distiller & Vintners, **43** 215. *See also* Diageo plc.

United Distillers and Vintners, **57** 105

United Distillers Glenmore, Inc., **34** 89

United Dominion Industries Limited, **IV** 288; **8 544–46; 16 499–502 (upd.); 47** 378; **57** 87

United Dominion Realty Trust, Inc., 52 369–71

United Electric Light and Water Co., **13** 182

United Engineers & Constructors, **11** 413

United Express, **11** 299

United Factors Corp., **13** 534–35

United Federal Savings and Loan of Waycross, **10** 92

United Financial Corporation, **12** 353

United Financial Group, Inc., **8** 349

United 5 and 10 Cent Stores, **13** 444

United Foods, Inc., 21 508–11

United Fruit Co., **7** 84–85; **21** 110–11; **44** 152

United Funds, Inc., **22** 540–41

United Gas and Electric Company of New Albany, **6** 555

United Gas and Improvement Co., **13** 182

United Gas Improvement Co., **6** 446, 523; **11** 388

United Graphics, **12** 25

United Grocers, **II** 625

United Health, Inc. *See* Extendicare Health Services, Inc.

United HealthCare Corporation, **9** 524–26; **24** 229, 231. *See also* Humana Inc.

The United Illuminating Company, **21** 512–14

United Image Entertainment, **18** 64, 66

United Industrial Corporation, **37** 399–402

United Industrial Syndicate, **8** 545

United Information Systems, Inc., **V** 346

United International Holdings Inc., **28** 198

United Investors Life Insurance Company, **22** 540; **33** 407

United Iron & Metal Co., **14** 156

United Jewish Communities, **33** 422–25

United Kingdom Atomic Energy Authority, **6** 451–52

United Kingdom Hotel Investments Ltd., **64** 217

United Knitting, Inc., **21** 192, 194

United Life & Accident Insurance Co., **III** 220–21; **14** 109

United Life Insurance Company, **12** 541

United Light and Power, **6** 511

United Machinery Co., **15** 127

United Match Factories, **12** 462

United Media, **22** 442

United Merchandising Corp., **12** 477

United Merchants & Manufacturers, Inc., **13** 534–37; **31** 160

United Meridian Corporation, **8** 350

United Microelectronics Corporation, **22** 197; **47** 384, 386; **67** 38

United Mortgage Servicing, **16** 133

United National Group, Ltd., **63** 410–13

United Nations International Children's Emergency Fund (UNICEF), **58** 349–52

United Natural Foods, Inc., **32** 479–82

United Natural Gas Company, **6** 526

United Netherlands Navigation Company. *See* Vereenigde Nederlandsche Scheepvaartmaatschappij.

United News & Media plc, **28** 501–05 **(upd.)**; **35** 354. *See also* United Business Media plc.

United Newspapers plc, **IV** 685–87. *See also* United Business Media plc.

United of Omaha, **III** 365

United Office Products, **11** 64

United Optical, **10** 151

United Overseas Bank Ltd., **56** 362–64

United Pacific Financial Services, **III** 344

United Pacific Life Insurance Co., **III** 343–44

United Pan-Europe Communications NV, **47** 414–17

United Paper Mills Ltd., **IV** 316, 347–50. *See also* UPM-Kymmene Corporation.

United Paramount Network, **25** 418–19; **26** 32; **31** 109

United Parcel Service, Inc., **63** 414–19

United Parcel Service of America Inc., **V** 533–35; **6** 385–86, 390; **11** 11; **12** 309, 334; **13** 19, 416; **14** 517; **17** 503–06 **(upd.)**; **18** 82, 177, 315–17; **24** 22, 133; **25** 148, 150, 356; **27** 471, 475; **34** 473; **39** 33; **41** 245; **42** 140; **49** 460

United Power and Light Corporation, **6** 473; **12** 541

United Presidential Life Insurance Company, **12** 524, 526

United Press International, Inc., **16** 166; **25** 506–09

United Railways & Electric Company, **25** 44

United Refining Co., **23** 406, 408

United Rentals, Inc., **28** 386, 388; **34** 466–69; **48** 272

United Resources, Inc., **21** 514

United Retail Group Inc., **33** 426–28

United Retail Merchants Stores Inc., **9** 39

United Satellite Television, **10** 320

United Savings of Texas, **8** 349

United Scientific Holdings, **47** 8

United Service Organizations, **60** 308–11

United Servomation, **7** 471–72

United Shipping & Technology, Inc., **49** 440

United Shirt Shops, Inc. *See* Aris Industries, Inc.

United Skates of America, **8** 303

United Software Consultants Inc., **11** 65

United States Aluminum Co., **17** 213

United States Aviation Underwriters, Inc., **24** 176

United States Can Co., **15** 127, 129

United States Cellular Corporation, **9** 494–96, 527–29. *See also* U.S. Cellular Corporation.

United States Electric and Gas Company, **6** 447

United States Electric Light and Power Company, **25** 44

The United States Electric Lighting Company, **11** 387

United States Fidelity and Guaranty Co. *See* USF&G Corporation.

United States Filter Corporation, **20** 501–04; **38** 168, 170; **52** 189

United States Football League, **29** 347

United States Gypsum Co. *See* USG Corporation.

United States Health Care Systems, Inc. *See* U.S. Healthcare, Inc.

United States Mail Steamship Co., **23** 160

United States Medical Finance Corp., **18** 516, 518

United States National Bancshares, **25** 114

United States National Bank of Galveston. *See* Cullen/Frost Bankers, Inc.

United States National Bank of Oregon, **14** 527

The United States National Bank of Portland, **14** 527–28

United States Pipe and Foundry Company, **62** 377–80

United States Playing Card Company, **62** 381–84

United States Plywood Corp., **13** 100

United States Postal Service, **10** 60; **14** 517–20; **34** 470–75 **(upd.)**; **42** 140

United States Satellite Broadcasting Company Inc., **24** 226; **38** 176

United States Security Trust Co., **13** 466

United States Shoe Corporation, **V** 207–08; **17** 296, 390; **23** 328; **39** 301; **52** 229

United States Steel Corporation, **I** 491; **IV** 572–74; **6** 514; **7** 70–73, 401–02, 549–51; **10** 32; **11** 194; **12** 353–54; **17** 356; **18** 378; **26** 405, 451; **50** 500–04 **(upd.)**; **54** 247–48

United States Surgical Corporation, **10** 533–35; **13** 365; **21** 119–20; **28** 486; **34** 476–80 **(upd.)**

United States Tobacco Company, **9** 533

United Stationers Inc., **14** 521–23; **25** 13; **36** 508

United Steel Mills Ltd., **25** 266

United Supers, **II** 624

United Technologies Automotive Inc., **15** 513–15

United Technologies Corporation, **I** 84–86; **9** 18, 418; **10** 536–38 **(upd.)**; **11** 308; **12** 289; **13** 191, 384–86; **22** 6; **34** 371–72, 432, 481–85 **(upd.)**; **39** 311, 313

United Telecommunications, Inc., **V** 344–47; **8** 310; **9** 478–80; **10** 202; **12** 541

United Telephone Company, **7** 508; **14** 257

United Telephone Company of the Carolinas, **10** 202

United Telephone of Indiana, **14** 259

United Telephone System, Inc., **V** 346

United Television, Inc., **9** 119; **26** 32

United Thermal Corp., **42** 388

United Transportation Co., **6** 382

United Truck Lines, **14** 505

United Utilities, Inc., **10** 202

United Utilities PLC, **52** 372–75 **(upd.)**

United Van Lines, **14** 37; **15** 50

United Video Satellite Group, **18** 535–37. *See also* TV Guide, Inc.

United Water Resources, Inc., **40** 447–50; **45** 277

United Way of America, **36** 485–88

United Westburne Inc., **19** 313

United Wholesale Grocery Company. *See* Spartan Stores Inc.

United-A.G. Cooperative Inc., **65** 252

Unitel Communications Inc., **6** 311; **44** 49; **46** 401; **47** 136

Unitika Ltd., **V** 387–89; **53** 341–44 **(upd.)**

Unitil Corporation, **37** 403–06

Unitog Co., **16** 228; **19** 457–60; **21** 115; **51** 76

Unitransa, **27** 474

Unitrin Inc., **16** 503–05

Unitron Medical Communications, **29** 412

Unity Cellular Systems, Inc. *See* Rural Cellular Corporation.

Unity Financial Corp., **19** 411

Univar Corporation, **8** 99; **9** 530–32; **12** 333; **41** 340; **55** 297

Univas, **13** 203 **23** 171

Univasa, **39** 229

Univel Inc., **38** 418

Universal Belo Productions, **10** 5

Universal Cheerleaders Association. *See* Varsity Spirit Corp.

Universal Cigar Corp., **14** 19

Universal Compression, Inc., **59** 402–04

Universal Consumer Products Group, **30** 123

Universal Controls, Inc., **10** 319

Universal Cooler Corp., **8** 515

Universal Corporation, **V** 417–18; **48** 403–06 **(upd.)**

Universal Electronics Inc., **39** 405–08

Universal Foods Corporation, **7** 546–48; **21** 498. *See also* Sensient Technologies Corporation.

Universal Footcare Products Inc., **31** 255

Universal Forest Products, Inc., 10 539–40; **59** 405–09 (upd.)
Universal Frozen Foods, **23** 321
Universal Genève, **13** 121
Universal Guaranty Life Insurance Company, **11** 482
Universal Health Services, Inc., 6 191–93
Universal Industries, Inc., **10** 380; **13** 533
Universal International, Inc., 25 353, 355, **510–11**
Universal Juice Co., **21** 55
Universal Leaf Tobacco Company. *See* Universal Corporation.
Universal Manufacturing, **25** 167
Universal Marking Systems, **25** 331
Universal Match, **12** 464
Universal Matchbox Group, **12** 495
Universal Music Group, **22** 194; **26** 152; **37** 193
Universal Pictures, **10** 196; **25** 271. *See also* Universal Studios, Inc.
Universal Press Syndicate, **10** 4; **40** 38
Universal Records, **27** 123
Universal Reinsurance Corporation, **58** 20
Universal Resources Corporation, **6** 569; **26** 388
Universal Shoes, Inc., **22** 213
Universal Studios Florida, **14** 399
Universal Studios, Inc., 12 73; **21** 23–26; **25** 411; **33** 429–33; **47** 419–21
Universal Tea Co., Inc., **50** 449
Universal Telephone, **9** 106
Universal Textured Yarns, **12** 501
Universe Tankships, **59** 198
UNIVERSELLE Engineering U.N.I. GmbH, **60** 194
University HealthSystem Consortium, **53** 346
University of Phoenix, **24** 40
Univisa, **24** 516
Univision Communications Inc., 18 213; **24 515–18; 41** 150–52; **54** 72–73, 158
Unix System Laboratories Inc., **25** 20–21; **38** 418
UNM. *See* United News & Media plc.
Uno-e Bank, **48** 51
Uno Restaurant Corporation, 16 447; **18** 465, **538–40**
Uno-Ven, **IV** 571; **24** 522
Unocal Corporation, IV 569–71; **24 519–23 (upd.)**
UNR Industries, Inc. *See* ROHN Industries, Inc.
Unterberg Harris, **25** 433
UNUM Corp., 13 538–40
UnumProvident Corporation, 52 376–83 **(upd.)**
Uny Co., Ltd., II 619; **V** 209–10, 154; **13** 545; **36** 419; **49 425–28 (upd.)**
UOB. *See* United Overseas Bank Ltd.
UPC. *See* United Pan-Europe Communications NV.
UPI. *See* United Press International.
Upjohn Company, I 707–09; **III** 53; **8 547–49 (upd.); 10** 79; **12** 186; **13** 503; **14** 423; **16** 440. *See also* Pharmacia & Upjohn Inc.
UPM-Kymmene Corporation, 19 461–65; **25** 12; **30** 325; **50 505–11 (upd.)**
UPN. *See* United Paramount Network.
Upper Deck Company, LLC, **34** 448; **37** 295
Upper Peninsula Power Co., **53** 369

UPS. *See* United Parcel Service, Inc.
UPS Aviation Technologies, Inc., **60** 137
UPSHOT, **27** 195
Urban Outfitters, Inc., 14 524–26
Urbaser SA, **55** 182
Urenco, **6** 452
URS Corporation, 45 420–23
Urwick Orr, **II** 609
US. *See also* U.S.
US Airways Express, **32** 334; **38** 130
US Airways Group, Inc., 28 506–09 (upd.); 33 303; **52** 24–25, **384–88 (upd.)**
US Industrial Chemicals, Inc., **8** 440
US Industries Inc., **30** 231
US Monolithics, **54** 407
US 1 Industries, **27** 404
US Order, Inc., **10** 560, 562
US Repeating Arms Co., **58** 147
US Sprint Communications Company, **V** 346–47; **8** 310; **9** 32; **10** 543; **11** 302; **12** 136, 541; **14** 252–53; **16** 318, 392; **25** 101; **29** 44; **43** 447. *See also* Sprint Communications Company, L.P.
US Telecom, **9** 478–79
US West Communications Services, Inc., **19** 255; **21** 285; **29** 39, 45, 478; **37** 312, 315–16. *See also* Regional Bell Operating Companies.
USA Cafes, **14** 331
USA Floral Products Inc., **27** 126
USA Interactive, Inc., 47 418–22 (upd.); 58 117, 120
USA Networks Inc., **25** 330, 411; **33** 432; **37** 381, 383–84; **43** 422
USA Security Systems, Inc., **27** 21
USA Truck, Inc., 42 410–13
USAA, 10 541–43; 62 385–88 (upd.)
USAir Group, Inc., I 131–32; **III** 215; **6** 131–32 (upd.); **11** 300; **14** 70, 73; **18** 62; **21** 143; **24** 400; **26** 429; **42** 34. *See also* US Airways Group, Inc.
USANA, Inc., 27 353; **29 491–93**
USCC. *See* United States Cellular Corporation.
USCP-WESCO Inc., **II** 682
Usego AG., **48** 63
USF&G Corporation, III 395–98; **11** 494–95; **19** 190. *See also* The St. Paul Companies.
USFL. *See* United States Football League.
USFreightways Corporation, **27** 475; **49** 402
USG Corporation, III 762–64; **26 507–10 (upd.)**
USH. *See* United Scientific Holdings.
Usinger's Famous Sausage. *See* Fred Usinger Inc.
Usinor SA, 42 414–17 (upd.)
Usinor Sacilor, IV 226–28; **22** 44; **24** 144; **26** 81, 84; **54** 393
USLD Communications Corp. *See* Billing Concepts Corp.
USM, **10** 44
USO. *See* United Service Organizations.
Usource LLC, **37** 406
USPS. *See* United States Postal Service.
USSC. *See* United States Surgical Corporation.
USSI. *See* U.S. Software Inc.
UST Inc., 9 533–35; 42 79; **50 512–17 (upd.)**
UST Wilderness Management Corporation, **33** 399

Usutu Pulp Company, **49** 353
USV Pharmaceutical Corporation, **11** 333
USWeb/CKS. *See* marchFIRST, Inc.
USX Corporation, IV 572–74; **7** 193–94, **549–52 (upd.)**. *See also* United States Steel Corporation.
UT Starcom, **44** 426
Utag, **11** 510
Utah Construction & Mining Co., **14** 296
Utah Federal Savings Bank, **17** 530
Utah Gas and Coke Company, **6** 568
Utah Medical Products, Inc., 36 496–99
Utah Mines Ltd., **IV** 47; **22** 107
Utah Power and Light Company, 9 536; **12** 266; **27 483–86**. *See also* PacifiCorp.
UTI Energy, Inc. *See* Patterson-UTI Energy, Inc.
Utilicom, **6** 572
Utilicorp United Inc., 6 592–94. *See also* Aquilla.
UtiliTech Solutions, **37** 88
Utility Constructors Incorporated, **6** 527
Utility Engineering Corporation, **6** 580
Utility Fuels, **7** 377
Utility Line Construction Service, Inc., **59** 65
Utility Service Affiliates, Inc., **45** 277
Utility Services, Inc., **42** 249, 253
Utility Supply Co. *See* United Stationers Inc.
UUNET, 38 468–72
UV Industries, Inc., **7** 360; **9** 440
Uwajimaya, Inc., 60 312–14

V.L. Churchill Group, **10** 493
VA Linux Systems, **45** 363
VA TECH ELIN EBG GmbH, 49 429–31
VA Technologie AG, **57** 402
Vacheron Constantin, **27** 487, 489
Vaco, **38** 200, 202
Vaculator Division. *See* Lancer Corporation.
Vacuum Metallurgical Company, **11** 234
Vacuum Oil Co. *See* Mobil Corporation.
Vadoise Vie, **III** 273
VAE AG, **57** 402
VAE Nortrak Cheyenne Inc., **53** 352
Vail Associates, Inc., 11 543–46; 31 65, 67
Vail Resorts, Inc., 43 435–39 (upd.)
Vaillant GmbH, 44 436–39
Val Corp., **24** 149
Val-Pak Direct Marketing Systems, Inc., **22** 162
Val Royal LaSalle, **II** 652
Valassis Communications, Inc., 8 550–51; 37 407–10 (upd.)
Valcom, **13** 176
ValCom Inc. *See* InaCom Corporation.
Valdi Foods Inc., **II** 663–64
Vale do Rio Doce Navegacao SA— Docenave, **43** 112
Vale Harmon Enterprises, Ltd., **25** 204
Vale Power Company, **12** 265
Valenciana de Cementos, **59** 112
Valentine & Company, **8** 552–53
Valentino, **67** 246, 248
Valeo, 23 492–94; 66 350–53 (upd.)
Valero Energy Corporation, 7 553–55
Valhi, Inc., 10 435–36; **19 466–68**
Valid Logic Systems Inc., **11** 46, 284; **48** 77
Vality Technology Inc., **59** 56

Vallen Corporation, 45 424–26
Valley Bank of Helena, **35** 197, 199
Valley Bank of Maryland, **46** 25
Valley Bank of Nevada, **19** 378
Valley Crest Tree Company, **31** 182–83
Valley Deli Inc., **24** 243
Valley Fashions Corp., **16** 535
Valley Federal of California, **11** 163
Valley Fig Growers, **7** 496–97
Valley Media Inc., 35 430–33
Valley National Bank, **II** 420
Valley-Todeco, Inc., **13** 305–06
Valleyfair, **22** 130
Vallourec SA, 54 391–94
Valmet Corporation, III 647–49; **IV** 350, 471. *See also* Metso Corporation.
Valmont Industries, Inc., 13 276; **19** 50, 469–72
Valores Industriales S.A., 19 10, 12, 189, 473–75; **29** 219
The Valspar Corporation, 8 552–54; **32** 483–86 **(upd.)**
Valtek International, Inc., **17** 147
Value America, **29** 312
Value City Department Stores,
Value City Department Stores, Inc., 29 311; **38** 473–75
Value Foods Ltd., **11** 239
Value Giant Stores, **12** 478
Value House, **II** 673
Value Investors, **III** 330
Value Line, Inc., 16 506–08
Value Merchants Inc., 13 541–43
Value Rent-A-Car, **9** 350; **23** 354
ValueClick, Inc., 49 432–34
Valueland, **8** 482
ValueVision International, Inc., 22 534–36; **27** 337
ValuJet, Inc. *See* AirTran Holdings, Inc.
Valvtron, **11** 226
VAMED Gruppe, **56** 141
Van Ameringen-Haebler, Inc., **9** 290
Van Camp Seafood Company, Inc., 7 556–57. *See also* Chicken of the Sea International.
Van Cleef & Arpels Inc., **26** 145
Van de Kamp's, Inc., **7** 430
Van der Moolen Holding NV, **37** 224
Van Dorn Company, **13** 190
Van Gend and Loos, **6** 404; **26** 241, 243
Van Houtte Inc., 39 409–11
Van Kirk Chocolate, **7** 429
Van Kok-Ede, **II** 642
Van Leer Containers Inc., **30** 397
Van Leer Holding, Inc., **9** 303, 305
Van Leer N.V. *See* Royal Packaging Industries Van Leer N.V.; Greif Inc.
Van Mar, Inc., **18** 88
Van Nostrand Reinhold, **8** 526
Van Ommeren, **41** 339–40
Van Sickle, **IV** 485
Van Waters & Rogers, **8** 99; **41** 340
Van Wezel, **26** 278–79
Van Wijcks Waalsteenfabrieken, **14** 249
Van's Aircraft, Inc., 65 349–51
Vanadium Alloys Steel Company (VASCO), **13** 295–96
Vanant Packaging Corporation, **8** 359
Vance International Airways, **8** 349
Vance Publishing Corporation, 64 398–401
Vanderbilt Mortgage and Finance, **13** 154
Vanessa and Biffi, **11** 226

The Vanguard Group, Inc., 34 486–89 **(upd.)**
The Vanguard Group of Investment Companies, 9 239; **14** 530–32
Vanguard International Semiconductor Corp., **47** 385
Vanity Fair. *See* VF Corporation.
Vans, Inc., 16 509–11; **17** 259–61; **47** 423–26 **(upd.)**
Vanstar, **13** 176
Vantage Analysis Systems, Inc., **11** 490
Vantive Corporation, **33** 333; **38** 431–32
Varco International, Inc., 42 418–20
Varco-Pruden, Inc., **8** 544–46
Vare Corporation, **8** 366
Vari-Lite International, Inc., 35 434–36
Varian Associates Inc., 12 504–06
Varian, Inc., 48 407–11 **(upd.)**
Varibus Corporation, **6** 495
Variflex, Inc., 51 391–93
Variform, Inc., **12** 397
VARIG S.A. (Viação Aérea Rio-Grandense), 6 133–35; **26** 113; **29** 494–97 **(upd.)**; **31** 443–45; **33** 19
Varity Corporation, III 650–52; **7** 258, 260; **19** 294; **27** 203, 251
Varlen Corporation, 16 512–14
Varney Speed Lines. *See* Continental Airlines, Inc.
Varo, **7** 235, 237
Varsity Spirit Corp., 15 516–18; **22** 459
Varta AG, 9 180–81; **23** 495–99
Vascoloy-Ramet, **13** 295
VASP (Viaçao Aérea de Sao Paulo), **31** 444–45
Vasset, S.A., **17** 362–63
Vast Solutions, **39** 24
Vastar Resources, Inc., 24 524–26; **38** 445, 448
Vattenfall AB, 57 395–98
Vaughan Harmon Systems Ltd., **25** 204
Vaughan Printers Inc., **23** 100
Vaungarde, Inc., **22** 175
Vauxhall, **19** 391
VBB Viag-Bayernwerk-Beteiligungs-Gesellschaft mbH, **IV** 232; **50** 170
VCA Antech, Inc., 58 353–55
VCH Publishing Group. *See* John Wiley & Sons, Inc.
VDM Nickel-Technologie AG, **IV** 89
VEAG, **57** 395, 397
Veba A.G., I 542–43; **IV** 199, 455, 508; **8** 69, 494–495; **15** 519–21 **(upd.)**; **23** 69, 451, 453–54; **24** 79; **25** 102; **26** 423; **32** 147; **59** 389–91; **62** 14. *See also* E.On AG.
Vebego International BV, 49 435–37
VECO International, Inc., 7 558–59
Vector Automotive Corporation, **13** 61
Vector Casa de Bolsa, **21** 413
Vector Gas Ltd., **13** 458
Vector Group Ltd., 35 437–40 **(upd.)**
Vector Video, Inc., **9** 74
Vectra Bank Colorado, **53** 378
Veda International, **54** 395–96
Vedelectric, **13** 544
Vedior NV, 35 441–43; **44** 5; **62** 208
Veeco Instruments Inc., 32 487–90
Veeder-Root Company, **7** 116–17
VeggieTales. *See* Big Idea Productions, Inc.
Veit Companies, 43 440–42
Vel-Tex Chemical, **16** 270
Velcarta S.p.A., **17** 281

Velcro Industries N.V., 19 476–78
Velda Farms, Inc., **26** 448
VeloBind, Inc., **10** 314
Velocity Express Corporation, 49 438–41
Velva-Sheen Manufacturing Co., **23** 66
Vemar, **7** 558
Venator Group Inc., 35 444–49 **(upd.)**
Vencemos, **20** 124
Vencor, Inc., IV 402; **14** 243; **16** 515–17; **25** 456
Vendex International N.V., 10 136–37; **13** 544–46; **26** 160; **46** 187, 189. *See also* Koninklijke Vendex KBB N.V. (Royal Vendex KBB N.V.).
Vendôme Luxury Group plc, 27 487–89; **29** 90, 92
Vendors Supply of America, Inc., **7** 241–42; **25** 241
Venetian Casino Resort, LLC, 47 427–29
Venevision, **54** 72–73, 75
Venevision, **24** 516, 517
Ventshade Company, **40** 299–300
Ventura, **29** 356–57
Venture Out RV, **26** 193
Venture Stores Inc., 12 507–09
Ventures Limited, **49** 137
Venturi, Inc., **9** 72
Veolia Environnement SA, **66** 68
Vepco. *See* Virginia Electric and Power Company.
Vera Imported Parts, **11** 84
Verafumos Ltd., **12** 109
Veragon Corporation. *See* Drypers Corporation.
Veratex Group, **13** 149–50
Veravision, **24** 510
Verbatim Corporation, 14 533–35
Verbundnetz Gas AG, **38** 408
Verd-A-Fay, **13** 398
Vereenigde Nederlandsche Scheepvaartmaatschappij, **6** 404; **26** 242
Vereinigte Elektrizitäts und Bergwerke A.G. *See* VEBA A.G.
Vereinigte Elektrizitätswerke Westfalen AG, IV 195; **V** 744–47
Vereinigte Glanzstoff-Fabriken, **13** 21
Vereinigte Industrie-Unternehmungen Aktiengesellschaft. *See* VIAG
Vereinigte Papierwerke Schickedanz AG, **26** 384
Vereinigte Stahlwerke AG, **14** 327
Verenigde Bedrijven Bredero, **26** 280
Verenigde Nederlandse Uitgeverijen. *See* VNU N.V.
Verenigde Spaarbank Groep. *See* VSB Groep.
Veri-Best Baking Co., **56** 29
Veridian Corporation, 54 395–97
Verienigte Schweizerbahnen, **6** 424
Verifact Inc. (IVI), **46** 251
VeriFone, Inc., 15 321; **18** 541–44; **27** 219–21; **28** 191; **50** 227
Verilyte Gold, Inc., **19** 452
VeriSign, Inc., 47 430–34
Veritas Capital Fund L.P., **44** 420, 423; **59** 192
Veritas Capital Management, L.L.C., **54** 178
Veritas Capital Partners, **26** 408
Veritas Software Corporation, 45 427–31
Veritec Technologies, Inc., **48** 299
Veritus Inc., **27** 208–09

Verizon Communications, **43** 443–49
    (upd.)
Verizon Wireless, Inc., **42** 284; **63** 131
Verlagsgruppe Georg von Holtzbrinck
    GmbH, **15** 158, 160; **25** 485; **35** 450–53
Verlagsgruppe Märkische Verlags- und
    Druckgesellschaft mbH, **66** 123
Vermeer Manufacturing Company, **17**
    507–10
Vermont General Insurance Company, **51**
    248
Vermont Pure Holdings, Ltd., **51** 394–96
The Vermont Teddy Bear Co., Inc., **36**
    500–02
Verneuil Holding Co, **21** 387
Vernitron Corporation, **18** 293
Vernon and Nelson Telephone Company.
    See British Columbia Telephone
    Company.
Vernon Savings & Loan, **9** 199
Vernors, Inc., **25** 4
Verreries Brosse S.A.S., **67** 210, 212
Verreries Pochet et du Courval, **55** 309
Versace. *See* Gianni Versace SpA.
Versatec Inc., **13** 128
Versatile Farm and Equipment Co., **22** 380
Versax, S.A. de C.V., **19** 12
Verson Allsteel Press Co., **21** 20, 22
Vert Baudet, **19** 309
Vertex Data Science Limited, **52** 372,
    374–75
Vertical Technology Industries, **14** 571
Verticom, **25** 531
Verve Records, **23** 389
Vesa Energy, **57** 397
Vessel Management Services, Inc., **28** 80
Vestar Capital Partners, **42** 309
Vestek Systems, Inc., **13** 417
Vestro, **19** 309
Vesuvius USA Corporation, **8** 179
Veszpremtej, **25** 85
Veterinary Cos. of America, **III** 25
VEW AG, **39** 412–15
Vexlar, **18** 313
VF Corporation, **V** 390–92; **12** 205; **13**
    512; **17** 223, 225, **511–14 (upd.)**; **25** 22;
    31 261; **54** 398–404 **(upd.)**; **59** 267–68
VHA Inc., **53** 345–47
VHA Long Term Care, **23** 431
VH1 Inc., **23** 503
VI-Jon Laboratories, Inc., **12** 388
Via Cariane. *See* Keolis SA.
Via-Générale de Transport et d'Industrie
    SA, **28** 155
Via Verde, **64** 57
ViaAfrika. *See* Naspers Ltd.
Viacao Aerea Rio Grandense of South
    America. *See* VARIG, SA.
Viacom Enterprises, **7** 336
Viacom Inc., **23** 274–76, **500–03 (upd.)**;
    24 106, 327; **26** 32; **28** 295; **30** 101; **31**
    59, 109; **35** 402; **48** 214; **51** 218–19; **67**
    367–71 (upd.)
Viacom International Inc., **7** 222–24,
    530, **560–62**; **9** 429; **10** 175; **19** 403
Viag AG, **IV** 229–32, 323; **25** 332; **32**
    153; **43** 188–89; **59** 252. *See also* E.On
    AG.
Viajes El Corte Inglés, S.A., **26** 129
VIASA. *See* Iberia.
ViaSat, Inc., **54** 405–08
Viasoft Inc., **27** 490–93; **59** 27
VIASYS Healthcare, Inc., **52** 389–91
Viasystems Group, Inc., **67** 372–74

Viatech Continental Can Company, Inc.,
    25 512–15 **(upd.)**
Vickers Inc., **III** 640, 642; **13** 8; **23** 83
Vickers plc, **21** 435; **27** 494–97; **47** 9
VICOM, **48** 415
Vicon Industries, Inc., **44** 440–42
VICORP Restaurants, Inc., **12** 510–12;
    48 412–15 **(upd.)**
Victoire Delage, **62** 229
Victor Company, **10** 483
Victor Company of Japan, Ltd., **II**
    118–19; **12** 454; **26** 511–13 **(upd.)**
Victor Equipment Co., **19** 440
Victor Value, **II** 678
Victoria & Co., **39** 247
Victoria Coach Station, **6** 406
Victoria Creations Inc., **13** 536
Victoria Group, **44** 443–46 **(upd.)**
VICTORIA Holding AG, **III** 399–401.
    See also Victoria Group.
Victoria Ward, Limited, **57** 157
Victoria's Secret, **11** 498; **12** 557, 559; **16**
    219; **18** 215; **24** 237; **25** 120–22, 521;
    59 190, 192–93. *See also* The Limited,
    Inc.
Victorinox AG, **21** 515–17
Victory Refrigeration Company, **22** 355
Victory Savings and Loan, **10** 339
Victory Supermarket. *See* Big V
    Supermarkets, Inc.
Vidal Sassoon, **17** 110
Video Concepts, **9** 186
Video Independent Theatres, Inc., **14** 86
Video Library, Inc., **9** 74
Video News International, **19** 285
Video Superstores Master Limited
    Partnership, **9** 74
Video Trend, **60** 84
VideoFusion, Inc., **16** 419
Videotex Network Japan, **IV** 680
Videotron, **25** 102
VideV, **24** 509
Vidrala S.A., **67** 375–77
La Vie Claire, **13** 103
Vie de France Yamazaki Inc., **58** 380–82
Vielle Montaign, **22** 285
Vienna Sausage Manufacturing Co., **14**
    536–37
Viessmann Werke GmbH & Co., **37**
    411–14
Vietnam International Assurance Co., **64**
    280
Vietnam LPG Co., Ltd., **56** 290
View-Master/Ideal Group, **12** 496
Viewer's Edge, **27** 429
Viewlogic, **11** 490
Viewpoint International, Inc., **66** 354–56
ViewStar Corp., **20** 103
Viewtel, **14** 36
ViewTrade Holding Corp., **46** 282
Vigilant Insurance Co., **III** 220; **14** 108; **37**
    83
Vigoro, **22** 340
Viking, **IV** 659
Viking Building Products, **22** 15
Viking Computer Services, Inc., **14** 147
Viking Consolidated Shipping Corp, **25**
    470
Viking Direct Limited, **10** 545
Viking Foods, Inc., **8** 482; **14** 411
Viking Industries, **39** 322, 324
Viking Office Products, Inc., **10** 544–46
Viking Penguin, **IV** 611
Viking Press, **12** 25

Viking Pump Company, **21** 499–500
Viking Range Corporation, **66** 357–59
Viking Star Shipping, Inc. *See* Teekay
    Shipping Corporation.
Viktor Achter, **9** 92
Village Inn. *See* VICORP Restaurants, Inc.
Village Roadshow Ltd., **58** 356–59
Village Super Market, Inc., **7** 563–64
Village Voice Media, Inc., **38** 476–79
Villager, Inc., **11** 216; **39** 244
Villazon & Co., **27** 139
Villeroy & Boch AG, **37** 415–18
VILPAC, S.A., **26** 356
AO VimpelCom, **48** 416–19; **59** 300
Vimto. *See* Nichols plc.
Vin & Spirit AB, **31** 458–61; **58** 197
Viña Concha y Toro S.A., **45** 432–34
Vinci, **27** 54; **43** 450–52; **49** 44
Vincor International Inc., **50** 518–21
Viner Bros., **16** 546
Vinewood Companies, **53** 232
Vingaarden A/S, **9** 100
Vining Industries, **12** 128
Viniprix SA, **10** 205; **19** 309; **27** 95
Vinita Rock Company, **50** 49
Vinland Web-Print, **8** 360
Vinson & Elkins L.L.P., **28** 48; **30**
    481–83; **47** 139–40, 447
Vintage Petroleum, Inc., **42** 421–23
Vintage Yarns, **62** 374
Vintners International, **34** 89
Vinton Studios, **63** 420–22
Vipond, Inc., **64** 31
Vipont Pharmaceutical, **III** 25; **14** 122
VIPS, **11** 113
Viratec Thin Films, Inc., **22** 347
Virco Manufacturing Corporation, **17**
    515–17
Virgin Atlantic Airlines. *See* Virgin Group
    PLC.
Virgin Express, **35** 384
Virgin Group PLC, **12** 513–15; **14** 73; **18**
    80; **22** 194; **24** 486; **29** 302; **32** 491–96
    (upd.); **50** 125
The Virgin Islands Telephone Co., **19** 256
Virgin Music Group Worldwide, **52** 429
Virgin Retail Group Ltd., **9** 75, 361; **37**
    262
Virginia Eastern Shore Sustainable
    Development Corporation, **28** 307
Virginia Electric and Power Company. *See*
    Dominion Resources, Inc.
Virginia Fibre Corporation. *See* Greif Inc.
Virginia Laminating, **10** 313
Virginia Mason Medical Center, **41** 183
Virginia National Bankshares, **10** 426
Virginia Railway and Power Company
    (VR&P). *See* Dominion Resources, Inc.
Viridian Group plc, **64** 402–04
Viridor Waste Limited, **45** 338
Viromedics, **25** 382
Visa. *See* Valores Industriales S.A.
Visa International, **II** 200; **9** 333–35,
    536–38; **18** 543; **20** 59; **26** 514–17
    (upd.); **41** 200–01; **61** 249
Vishay Intertechnology, Inc., **11** 516; **21**
    518–21
Visible Impact Target Company, **62** 82
Visio Corporation, **63** 296
Vision Centers, **12** 188
Vision Hardware Group. *See* Acorn
    Products, Inc.
Vision Technologies Kinetics Inc., **61** 43

Vision Technology Group Ltd., **19** 124; **49** 113

Visionware Ltd., **38** 419

Visionworks, **9** 186

Viskase Companies, Inc., 17 157, 159; **55 379–81**

Vista Bakery, Inc., 14 306; **56 365–68**

Vista Chemical Company, I 402–03

Vista Concepts, Inc., **11** 19

Vista Resources, Inc., **17** 195

Vista 2000, Inc., **36** 444

Vistana, Inc., 22 537–39; 26 464

Visual Action Holdings plc, **24** 96, 374

Visual Information Technologies, **11** 57

VISX, Incorporated, 30 484–86

Vita-Achter, **9** 92

Vita Liquid Polymers, **9** 92

Vita Plus Corporation, 60 315–17

Vitafoam Incorporated, **9** 93; **33** 78

Vital Health Corporation, **13** 150

Vital Processing Services LLC, **18** 516, 518

Vitalink Communications Corp., **11** 520; **34** 444

Vitalink Pharmacy Services, Inc., 15 522–24; 25 309–10

Vitalscheme, **38** 426

Vitamin Shoppe Industries, Inc., 60 318–20

Vitamin World, **31** 346–48

Vitesse Semiconductor Corporation, 32 497–500

Vitex Foods, **10** 382

Vitoria-Minas Railroad, **43** 111

Vitramon, Inc., **54** 371–72

Vitro Corp., 8 178; **10 547–48; 17** 492

Vitro Corporativo S.A. de C.V., 34 490–92

Vitro S.A., **19** 189

VIVA, **23** 390

Vivarte SA, 54 409–12 (upd.)

Vivendi Universal S.A., 29 369, 371; **32** 52, 54; **33** 178, 181; **34** 83, 85; **38** 168, 170; **40** 408; **41** 361; **43** 450, 452; **44** 190; **46 438–41 (upd.); 47** 420–21; **48** 164–65; bf]LXIII 166

Vivendia, **40** 449

Vivesvata Iron and Steel Ltd., **IV** 207

Vivra, Inc., 15 119; **18 545–47**

VKI Technologies Inc., **39** 409

Vladivostok Dairy, **48** 438

Vlasic Foods International Inc., 25 516–19

VLSI Technology, Inc., 11 246; **16 518–20; 31** 300

VMG Products. See Drypers Corporation.

VMX Inc., **14** 355; **41** 289

VND, **III** 593

VNG. See Verbundnetz Gas AG.

VNS. See Vereenigde Nederlandsche Scheepvaartmaatschappij.

VNU N.V., 27 361, **498–501; 38** 8

Vobis Microcomputer, **20** 103; **23** 311

VocalTec, Inc., **18** 143

Vodac, **11** 548

Vodacom World Online Ltd., **48** 399

Vodafone Group Plc, 11 547–48; 34 85; **36 503–06 (upd.); 38** 296, 300

Vodapage, **11** 548

Vodata, **11** 548

Vodavi Technology Corporation, **13** 213

Voest-Alpine Stahl AG, IV 233–35; 31 47–48

voestalpine AG, 57 399–403 (upd.)

Vogel Peterson Furniture Company, **7** 4–5

Vogoro Corp., **13** 503

Voice Data Systems, **15** 125

Voice Powered Technology International, Inc., **23** 212

Voice Response, Inc., **11** 253

VoiceStream Wireless Corporation, **48** 130

Voith Sulzer Papiermaschinen GmbH. See J.M. Voith AG.

Volition, Inc., **39** 395

Volkswagen Aktiengesellschaft, I 206–08; 7 8; **10** 14; **11** 104, **549–51 (upd.); 13** 413; **14** 169; **19** 484; **26** 12; **27** 11, 496; **31** 363–65; **32 501–05 (upd.); 34** 55, 130; **39** 373–74

Volt Information Sciences Inc., 26 518–21

Volume Distributors. See Payless ShoeSource, Inc.

Volume Service Company. See Restaurants Unlimited, Inc.

Volume Shoe Corporation. See Payless ShoeSource,Inc.

Volunteer Leather Company, **17** 202, 205

Volunteer State Life Insurance Co., **III** 221; **37** 84

Volunteers of America, Inc., 66 360–62

AB Volvo, **I 209–11; II** 5, 366; **7 565–68 (upd.), 9** 283, 84, 350, 381; **10** 274; **12** 68, 342; **13** 30, 356; **14** 321; **15** 226; **18** 394; **23** 354; **26 9–12 (upd.)**, 401, 403; **33** 191, 364; **39** 126; **61** 179, 182; **64** 133; **67 378–83 (upd.)**

Volvo-Penta, 21 503

Von Maur Inc., 64 405–08

von Roll, **6** 599

Von Ruden Manufacturing Co., **17** 532

Von's Grocery Co., **8** 474; **17** 559

The Vons Companies, Incorporated, II 655; **7 569–71; 12** 209; **24** 418; **28 510–13 (upd.); 35** 328

VOP Acquisition Corporation, **10** 544

Vornado Realty Trust, 20 508–10; 39 211; **45** 14–16; **47** 360

Voroba Hearing Systems, **25** 56

Vortex Management, Inc., **41** 207

Vorwerk & Co., 27 502–04

Vosper Thornycroft Holding plc, 41 410–12

Vossloh AG, 53 348–52

Votainer International, **13** 20

Vought Aircraft Industries, Inc., 11 364; **45** 309; **49 442–45**

Vox, **58** 195

Voyager Communications Inc., **24** 5

Voyager Ltd., **12** 514

Voyageur Travel Insurance Ltd., **21** 447

VR&P. See Virginia Railway and Power Company.

Vratislavice A.S., **38** 77

VRG International. See Roberts Pharmaceutical Corporation.

Vriesco Plastics B.V., **53** 221

Vroom & Dreesmann, **13** 544–46

VS Services, **13** 49

VSA. See Vendors Supply of America, Inc.

VSB Groep, **III** 199, 201

VSD Communications, Inc., **22** 443

VSEL, **24** 88

VSK Group. See The Allied Defense Group, Inc.

VSM. See Village Super Market, Inc.

VST. See Vision Technology Group Ltd.

Vtel Corporation, **10** 456; **27** 365

VTR Incorporated, **16** 46; **43** 60

Vu-Tech Communications, Inc., **48** 54

Vulcan Materials Company, 7 572–75; 12 39; **25** 266; **41** 147, 149; **52 392–96 (upd.)**

Vulcan Ventures Inc., **32** 145; **43** 144

Vulcraft, **7** 400–02

VW&R. See Van Waters & Rogers.

VWR Textiles & Supplies, Inc., **11** 256

VWR United Company, **9** 531

Vycor Corporation, **25** 349

Vyvx, **31** 469

W&A Manufacturing Co., LLC, **26** 530

W&F Fish Products, **13** 103

W & J Sloane Home Furnishings Group, **35** 129

W de Argentina–Inversiones S.L., **63** 377

W.A. Krueger Co., **19** 333–35

W.A. Whitney Company, 53 353–56

W. Atlee Burpee & Co., 11 198; **27 505–08**

W.B Doner & Co., 10 420; **12** 208; **28** 138; **56 369–72**

W.B. Saunders Co., **IV** 623–24

W.C. Bradley Company, **18** 516

W.C.G. Sports Industries Ltd. See Canstar Sports Inc.

W.C. Smith & Company Limited, **14** 339

W. Duke Sons & Company, 27 128

W.E. Andrews Co., Inc., **25** 182

W.E. Dillon Company, Ltd., **21** 499

W.F. Kaiser, **60** 364

W.F. Linton Company, **9** 373

W.G. Yates & Sons Construction Company. See The Yates Companies, Inc.

W.H. Brady Co., 17 518–21

W.H. Gunlocke Chair Co. See Gunlocke Company.

W.H. Smith & Son (Alacra) Ltd., **15** 473

W H Smith Group PLC, V 211–13

W.L. Gore & Associates, Inc., 14 538–40; 26 417; **60 321–24 (upd.)**

W.M. Bassett Furniture Co. See Bassett Furniture Industries, Inc.

W.O. Daley & Company, **10** 387

W.P. Carey & Co. LLC, 49 446–48

W.R. Bean & Son, **19** 335

W.R. Berkley Corp., 15 525–27

W.R. Breen Company, **11** 486

W.R. Case & Sons Cutlery Company, **18** 567

W.R. Grace & Company, I 547–50; 11 216; **12** 337; **13** 149, 502, 544; **14** 29; **16** 45–47; **17** 308, 365–66; **21** 213, 507, 526; **22** 188, 501; **25** 535; **35** 38, 40; **43** 59–60; **49** 307; **50** 78, **522–29 (upd.); 54** 363

W. Rosenlew, **IV** 350

W.S. Barstow & Company, **6** 575

W.T. Grant Co., **16** 487

W.T. Rawleigh, **17** 105

W.W. Grainger, Inc., V 214–15; 13 297; **26 537–39 (upd.)**

W.W. Kimball Company, **12** 296; **18** 44

W.W. Norton & Company, Inc., 28 518–20

Waban Inc., V 198; **13 547–49; 19** 449. See also HomeBase, Inc.

Wabash National Corp., 13 550–52

Wabash Valley Power Association, **6** 556

Wabtec Corporation, 40 451–54

Wachbrit Insurance Agency, **21** 96

Wachovia Bank of Georgia, N.A., 16 521–23

Wachovia Bank of South Carolina, N.A., 16 524–26

Wachovia Corporation, 10 425; 12 16, **516–20**; 16 521, 524, 526; 23 455; 46 442–49 (upd.)

Wachtell, Lipton, Rosen & Katz, 47 435–38

The Wackenhut Corporation, 13 124–25; **14 541–43**; 28 255; 41 80; 63 423–26 (upd.)

Wacker-Chemie GmbH, 35 454–58

Wacker Oil Inc., 11 441

Waco Aircraft Company, 27 98

Wacoal Corp., 25 520–24

Waddell & Reed, Inc., 22 540–43; 33 405, 407

Wade Smith, 28 27, 30

Wadsworth Inc., 8 526

WaferTech, 18 20; 43 17; 47 385

Waffle House Inc., 14 544–45; 60 325–27 (upd.)

Wagenseller & Durst, 25 249

Waggener Edstrom, 42 424–26

The Wagner & Brown Investment Group, 9 248

Wagner Castings Company, 16 474–75

Wagner Litho Machinery Co., 13 369–70

Wagner Spray Tech, 18 555

Wagonlit Travel, 22 128; 55 90

Wagons-Lits, 27 11; 29 443; 37 250–52

Waha Oil Company. See Natinal Oil Corporation.

AB Wahlbecks, 25 464

Waitaki International Biosciences Co., 17 288

Waitrose Ltd. See John Lewis Partnership plc.

Wakefern Food Corporation, II 672; 7 563–64; 18 6; 25 66, 234–35; 28 143; 33 434–37

Wako Shoji Co. Ltd. See Wacoal Corp.

Wal-Mart de Mexico, S.A. de C.V., 35 322, **459–61** (upd.)

Wal-Mart Stores, Inc., II 108; V 216–17; 6 287; 7 61, 331; 8 33, 295, **555–57** (upd.); 9 187, 361; 10 236, 284, 515–16, 524; 11 292; 12 48, 53–55, 63–64, 97, 208–09, 221, 277, 333, 477, 507–08; 13 42, 215–17, 260–61, 274, 332–33, 444, 446; 14 235; 15 139, 275; 16 61–62, 65, 390; 17 297, 321, 460–61; 18 108, 137, 186, 283, 286; 19 511; 20 263; 21 457–58; 22 224, 257, 328; 23 214; 24 148, 149, 334; 25 221–22, 254, 314; 26 **522–26** (upd.), 549; 27 286, 313, 315, 416, 451; 29 230, 314, 318; 32 169, 338, 341; 33 307; 34 198; 37 64; 41 61, 115; 45 408, 412; 59 330, 425–26; 62 134–35, 144–45, 265; **63 427–32** (upd.); 64 36, 38

Walbridge Aldinger Co., 38 480–82

Walbro Corporation, 13 553–55

Walchenseewerk AG, 23 44

Waldbaum, Inc., II 638; 15 260; 16 247, 249; **19 479–81**; 24 528

Walden Book Company Inc., 10 136–37; 16 160; 17 522–24; 25 30

Waldorf Corporation, 59 350

Wales & Company, 14 257

Walgreen Co., V 218–20; 9 346; 18 199; **20 511–13** (upd.); 21 186; 24 263; 32

166, 170; **45** 133, 137; **65 352–56** (upd.)

Walk Haydel & Associates, Inc., 25 130

Walk Softly, Inc., 25 118

Walker & Lee, 10 340

Walker Dickson Group Limited, 26 363

Walker Digital, 57 296–98

Walker Interactive Systems, 11 78; 25 86

Walker Manufacturing Company, 19 482–84

Walkins Manufacturing Corp., III 571; 20 362

Walkup's Merchant Express Inc., 27 473

Wall Drug Store, Inc., 40 455–57

Wall Street Deli, Inc., 33 438–41

Wallace & Tiernan Group, 11 361; 52 374

The Wallace Berrie Company. See Applause Inc.

Wallace Computer Services, Inc., 36 507–10

Wallace International Silversmiths, 14 482–83

Wallbergs Fabriks A.B., 8 14

Wallin & Nordstrom. See Nordstrom, Inc.

Wallis. See Sears plc.

Wallis Arnold Enterprises, Inc., 21 483

Wallis Tractor Company, 21 502

Walnut Capital Partners, 62 46–47

Walrus, Inc., 18 446

Walsin-Lihwa, 13 141

The Walt Disney Company, II 156, **172–74**; 6 **174–77** (upd.); 7 305; 8 160; 10 420; 12 168, 208, 229, 323, 495–96; 13 551; 14 260; 15 197; 16 143, 336; 17 243, 317, 442–43; 21 23–26, 360–61; 23 257–58, 303, 335, 476, 514; 25 172, 268, 312–13; 27 92, 287; 30 **487–91** (upd.); 34 348; 43 142, 447; 50 322, 389; 51 218, 220; 52 3, 5, 84; 53 41; 54 333, 335–37; 56 119; 61 201; 63 **433–38** (upd.); 64 282

Walter Bau, 27 136, 138

Walter E. Heller, 17 324

Walter Herzog GmbH, 16 514

Walter Industries, Inc., III 765–67; 22 544–47 (upd.); 62 377

Walter Wilson, 49 18

Walter Wright Mammoet, 26 280

Walton Manufacturing, 11 486

Walton Monroe Mills, Inc., 8 558–60

Wang Global, 39 176–78

Wang Laboratories, Inc., III 168–70; 6 **284–87** (upd.); 8 139; 9 171; 10 34; 11 68, 274; 12 183; 18 138; 19 40; 20 237

WAP, 26 420

Waples-Platter Co., II 625

Warbasse-Cogeneration Technologies Partnership, 35 479

Warburg Pincus, 9 524; 14 42; 24 373; 61 403

Warburg USB, 38 291

Warburtons Bakery Cafe, Inc., 18 37

Ward's Communications, 22 441

Wards. See Circuit City Stores, Inc.

Waremart. See WinCo Foods.

WARF. See Wisconsin Alumni Research Foundation.

Waring and LaRosa, 12 167

The Warnaco Group Inc., 9 156; 12 521–23; 22 123; 25 122, 523; 46 **450–54** (upd.); 51 30. See also Authentic Fitness Corp.

Warner & Swasey Co., 8 545

Warner Communications Inc., II **175–77**, 452; IV 673, 675–76; 7 526, 528–30 8 527; 9 44–45, 119, 469; 10 196; 11 557; 12 495–96; 17 65, 149, 442–43; 21 23–25, 360; 22 519, 522; 23 23–24, 390, 501; 24 373; 25 327–28, 418–19, 498; 26 102, 151; 61 202. See also AOL Time Warner Inc.

Warner Cosmetics, III 48; 8 129

Warner Electric, 58 67

Warner-Lambert Co., I 710–12; 7 596; 8 62–63; **10 549–52** (upd.); 12 480, 482; 13 366; 16 439; 20 23; 25 55, 366; 34 284; 38 366; 56 303

Warner Roadshow Film Distributors Greece SA, 58 359

Warners' Stellian Inc., 67 384–87

Warrantech Corporation, 53 357–59

Warren Apparel Group Ltd., 39 257

Warren Bancorp Inc., 55 52

Warren Bank, 13 464

Warren Frozen Foods, Inc., 61 174

Warren, Gorham & Lamont, 8 526

Warren Oilfield Services, 9 363

Warren Petroleum, 18 365, 367; 49 121

Warrick Industries, 31 338

Warrington Products Ltd. See Canstar Sports Inc.

Warrior River Coal Company, 7 281

Warwick Chemicals, 13 461

Warwick International Ltd., 13 462

Warwick Valley Telephone Company, 55 382–84

Wasatch Gas Co., 6 568

Wascana Energy Inc., 13 556–58

Washburn Graphics Inc., 23 100

The Washington Companies, 33 442–45

Washington Duke Sons & Co., 12 108

Washington Federal, Inc., 17 525–27

Washington Football, Inc., 35 462–65

Washington Gas Light Company, 19 485–88

Washington Inventory Service, 30 239

Washington Mills Company, 13 532

Washington Mutual, Inc., 17 528–31

Washington National Corporation, 11 482; 12 524–26

Washington Natural Gas Company, 9 539–41

The Washington Post Company, III 214; IV 688–90; 11 331; 18 60, 61, 63; 20 515–18 (upd.); 23 157–58; 42 31, 33–34, 209–10

Washington Public Power Supply System, 50 102

Washington Railway and Electric Company, 6 552–53

Washington Scientific Industries, Inc., 17 532–34

Washington Specialty Metals Corp., 14 323, 325

Washington Sports Clubs. See Town Sports International, Inc.

Washington Steel Corp., 14 323, 325

Washington Water Power Company, 6 566, **595–98**; 50 103–04, 366

Washtenaw Gas Company. See MCN Corporation.

Wassall Plc, 18 548–50

Wasserstein Perella Partners, II 629; 17 366

Waste Connections, Inc., 46 455–57

Waste Control Specialists LLC, 19 466, 468

Waste Holdings, Inc., 41 413–15
Waste Management, Inc., V 752–54; 6
  600; 9 73, 108–09; 11 435–36; 18 10;
  50 61; 60 343
Water Engineering, 11 360
Water Pik Technologies, Inc., 34
  498–501
Water Products Group, 6 487–88
Water Street Corporate Recovery Fund, 10
  423
The Waterbury Companies, 16 482
Waterford Foods Plc, 59 206
Waterford Wedgwood Holdings PLC, IV
  296; 12 527–29
Waterford Wedgwood plc, 34 493–97
  (upd.); 38 403
Waterhouse Investor Services, Inc., 18
  551–53; 49 397
Waterlow and Sons, 10 269
Waterman Marine Corporation, 27 242
The Waterman Pen Company. See BIC
  Corporation.
WaterPro Supplies Corporation, 6 486, 488
Waters Corporation, 43 453–57
Waterstone's, 42 444. See also HMV
  Group plc.
Waterstreet Inc., 17 293
Watkins-Johnson Company, 15 528–30
Watkins-Strathmore Co., 13 560
Watney Mann and Truman Brewers, 9 99
Watsco Inc., 52 397–400
Watson & Philip. See Alldays plc.
Watson Group, 55 52
Watson-Haas Lumber Company, 33 257
Watson-Marlow Bredel, 59 384
Watson Pharmaceuticals Inc., 16
  527–29; 56 373–76 **(upd.).**
Watson-Triangle, 16 388, 390
Watson Wyatt Worldwide, 42 427–30
Watt & Shand, 16 61; 50 107
Watt AG, 6 491
Watt Electronic Products, Limited, 10 319
The Watt Stopper, 21 348, 350
Wattie Industries, 52 141
Wattie's Ltd., 7 576–78; 11 173
Watts Industries, Inc., 19 489–91
Watts/Silverstein, Inc., 24 96
Waukesha Engine Servicenter, 6 441
Waukesha Foundry Company, 11 187
Wausau Sulphate Fibre Co. See Mosinee
  Paper Corporation.
Wausau-Mosinee Paper Corporation, 60
  328–31 **(upd.)**
Wavelength Corporate Communications
  Pty Limited, 24 95
Waverly, Inc., 10 135; 16 530–32; 19 358
Waverly Pharmaceutical Limited, 11 208
Wawa Inc., 17 535–37
Waxman Industries, Inc., 9 542–44; 20
  362; 28 50–51
Wayco Foods, 14 411
Waycross-Douglas Coca-Cola Bottling, 10
  222
Wayfinder Group Inc., 51 265
Waymaker Oy, 55 289
Wayne Home Equipment. See Scott Fetzer
  Company.
Wayne Oakland Bank, 8 188
WB. See Warner Communications Inc.
WBI Holdings, Inc., 42 249, 253
WCI Holdings Corporation, V 223; 13 170;
  41 94
WCK, Inc., 14 236

WCM Beteilingungs- und Grundbesitz AG,
  58 202, 205
WCPS Direct, Inc., 53 359
WCRS Group plc. See Aegis Group plc.
WCT Live Communication Limited, 24 95
WD-40 Company, 18 554–57
We Energies. See Wisconsin Energy
  Corporation.
Wear-Ever, 17 213
WearGuard, 13 48
The Weather Channel Companies, 52
  401–04; 55 244. See also Landmark
  Communications, Inc.
The Weather Department, Ltd., 10 89
Weather Guard, IV 305
Weatherford International, Inc., 39
  416–18; 57 164; 59 403
Weathers-Lowin, Leeam, 11 408
Webb & Knapp, 10 43
Webb Corbett and Beswick, 38 402
Webber Gage Co., 13 302
Webber Oil Company, 61 384–86
WeBco International LLC, 26 530
Webco Securities, Inc., 37 225
Weber, 16 488
Weber Aircraft Inc., 41 369
Weber et Broutin France, 66 363–65
Weber Metal, 30 283–84
Weber-Stephen Products Co., 40 458–60
Weblock, I 109
WebLogic Inc., 36 81
WebMD Corporation, 65 357–60
Webtron Corp., 10 313
Webvan Group Inc., 38 223
Wedgwood. See Waterford Wedgewood
  Holdings PLC.
Weeres Industries Corporation, 52
  405–07
Weetabix Limited, 61 387–89
Wegener NV, 53 360–62
Wegert Verwaltungs-GmbH and Co.
  Beteiligungs-KG, 24 270
Wegmans Food Markets, Inc., 9 545–46;
  24 445; 41 416–18 **(upd.)**
Weichenwerk Brandenburg GmbH, 53 352
Weider Health and Fitness, Inc., 38 238
Weider Nutrition International, Inc., 29
  498–501; 33 146–47; 34 459; 61 222,
  224
Weider Sporting Goods, 16 80
Weifang Power Machine Fittings Ltd., 17
  106
Weight Watchers Gourmet Food Co., 43
  218
Weight Watchers International Inc., 10
  383; 12 530–32; 13 383; 27 197; 33
  446–49 **(upd.)**
Weil Ceramics & Glass, 52 148
Weil, Gotshal & Manges LLP, 55
  385–87
Weiner's Stores, Inc., 33 450–53
Weingart Robert Weil, 65 328, 330
Weirton Steel Corporation, IV 236–38; 7
  447, 598; 8 346, 450; 10 31–32; 12 352,
  354; 26 407, 527–30 **(upd.)**
Weis Markets, Inc., 15 531–33
The Weitz Company, Inc., 42 431–34
Welbilt Corp., 19 492–94; 27 159
Welborn Transport Co., 39 64, 65
Welch's, 25 366
Welco Feed Manufacturing Company, 60
  316
Welcome Wagon International Inc., 16 146
Weldless Steel Company, 8 530

Wella AG, III 68–70; 48 420–23 **(upd.)**
Welland Pipe Ltd., 51 352
Wellborn Paint Manufacturing Company,
  56 98
Wellby Super Drug Stores, 12 220
WellChoice, Inc., 67 388–91 **(upd.)**
Wellcome Foundation Ltd., I 713–15; 8
  210, 452; 9 265; 10 551; 32 212. See
  also GlaxoSmithKline plc.
Wellcome Trust, 41 119
Weller Electric Corp., II 16
Wellington Management Company, 14
  530–31; 23 226
Wellington Sears Co., 15 247–48
Wellman, Inc., 8 561–62; 21 193; 52
  408–11 **(upd.);** 64 86
Wellmark, Inc., 10 89
Wellness Co., Ltd., IV 716
WellPath Community Health Plans, Inc.,
  59 140
WellPoint Health Networks Inc., 25
  525–29
Wellrose Limited, 53 333
Wells Aircraft, 12 112
Wells Fargo & Company, II 380–84,
  319, 395; 10 59–60; 12 165, 533–37
  (upd.); 17 325; 18 60, 543; 19 411; 22
  542; 25 434; 27 292; 32 373; 38 44,
  483–92 **(upd.);** 41 200–01; 46 217; 54
  124. See also American Express
  Company.
Wells Fargo HSBC Trade Bank, 26 203
Wells-Gardner Electronics Corporation,
  43 458–61
Wells Rich Greene BDDP, 6 50–52
Wells' Dairy, Inc., 36 511–13
Wellspring Associates L.L.C., 16 338
Wellspring Resources LLC, 42 429
Welsbach Mantle, 6 446
Welsh Associated Collieries Ltd., 31 369
Welsh, Carson, Anderson & Stowe, 65
  128–30
Welsh Water. See Hyder plc.
Wendel Investissement, 57 381
Wendy's International, Inc., II 614–15,
  647; 7 433; 8 563–65; 9 178; 12 553;
  13 494; 14 453; 16 95, 97; 17 71, 124;
  19 215; 23 384, 504–07 **(upd.);** 26 284;
  33 240; 36 517, 519; 41 114; 46
  404–05; 47 439–44 **(upd.)**
Wenger S.A., 21 515
Wenmac Corp., 51 368
Wenner Media, Inc., 32 506–09
Werco, Inc., 54 7
Werkhof GmbH, 13 491; 62 336
Werknet, 16 420; 43 308
Werner Baldessarini Design GmbH, 48 209
Werner Enterprises, Inc., 26 531–33
Werner International, III 344; 14 225
Wertheim Schroder & Company, 17 443
Weru Aktiengesellschaft, 18 558–61; 49
  295
Wesco Financial Corp., III 213, 215; 18
  62; 42 32–34
Wesco Food Co., II 644
Wescot Decisison Systems, 6 25
Wesley Jessen VisionCare Inc., 65 274
Wesper Co., 26 4
Wesray and Management, 17 213
Wesray Capital Corporation, 13 41; 17
  443; 47 363
Wesray Corporation, 22 55
Wesray Holdings Corp., 13 255
Wesray Transportation, Inc., 14 38

Wessanen. *See* Koninklijke Wessanen nv.
Wessanen USA, **29** 480
Wesson/Peter Pan Foods Co., **17** 241
West Australia Land Holdings, Limited, **10** 169
West Bend Co., 14 546–48; 16 384; **43** 289
West Coast Entertainment Corporation, 29 502–04
West Coast Grocery Co., **II** 670; **18** 506; **50** 456
West Coast Machinery, **13** 385
West Coast Power Company, **12** 265
West Coast Restaurant Enterprises, **25** 390
West Coast Savings and Loan, **10** 339
West Company, **53** 298
West Corporation, 42 435–37
West End Family Pharmacy, Inc., **15** 523
West Fraser Timber Co. Ltd., 17 538–40
West Georgia Coca-Cola Bottlers, Inc., **13** 163
West Group, 34 438, **502–06 (upd.)**
West Harrison Gas & Electric Company, **6** 466
West Jersey Electric Company, **6** 449
West Los Angeles Veterinary Medical Group, Inc., **58** 355
West Lynn Creamery, Inc., **26** 450
West Marine, Inc., 17 541–43; 37 398
West Missouri Power Company. *See* UtiliCorp United Inc.; Aquilla, Inc.
West Newton Savings Bank, **13** 468
West Newton Telephone Company, **14** 258
West One Bancorp, 11 552–55; 36 491
West Penn Electric. *See* Allegheny Power System, Inc.
West Penn Power Company, **38** 38–40
West Pharmaceutical Services, Inc., 42 438–41
West Point-Pepperell, Inc., 8 566–69; 9 466; **15** 247; **25** 20; **28** 218. *See also* WestPoint Stevens Inc.; JPS Textile Group, Inc.
West Publishing Co., 7 579–81; 10 407; **33** 264–65. *See also* The West Group.
West Side Printing Co., **13** 559
West TeleServices Corporation. *See* West Corporation.
West Texas Utilities Company, **6** 580
West Union Corporation, **22** 517
West Virginia Bearings, Inc., **13** 78
West Virginia Pulp and Paper Co. *See* Westvaco Corporation.
Westaff Inc., 33 454–57
WestAir Holding Inc., **11** 300; **25** 423; **32** 336
Westamerica Bancorporation, 17 544–47
Westar Energy, Inc., 57 404–07 (upd.)
Westbrae Natural, Inc., **27** 197–98; **43** 218
Westburne Group of Companies, **9** 364
Westchester County Savings & Loan, **9** 173
Westchester Specialty Group, Inc., **26** 546
Westclox Seth Thomas, **16** 483
WestCoast Hospitality Corporation, 59 410–13
Westcon Group, Inc., 67 392–94
Westcor Realty, **57** 235
Westcott Communications Inc., **22** 442
Westdeutsche Landesbank Girozentrale, II 385–87; 33 395; **46 458–61 (upd.);** **47** 83
Westec Corporation. *See* Tech-Sym Corporation.

Westell Technologies, Inc., 57 408–10
Westerbeke Corporation, 60 332–34
Western Aerospace Ltd., **14** 564
Western Air Express, **9** 17
Western Air Lines, **I** 98, 100, 106; **21** 142; **25** 421–23
Western Areas Ltd., **61** 292
Western Atlas Inc., III 473; **12 538–40;** **17** 419; **57** 64
Western Australian Specialty Alloys Proprietary Ltd., **14** 564
Western Auto, **19** 223; **57** 11
Western Auto Supply Co., **8** 56; **11** 392
Western Automatic Machine Screw Co., **12** 344
Western Bank, **17** 530
Western Beef, Inc., 22 548–50
Western Bingo, **16** 471
Western Company of North America, 15 534–36; 25 73, 75
Western Crude, **11** 27
Western Data Products, Inc., **19** 110
Western Digital Corp., 10 403, 463; **11** 56, 463; **25 530–32**
Western Edison, **6** 601
Western Electric Co., **II** 57, 66, 88, 101, 112; **7** 288; **11** 500–01; **12** 136; **13** 57; **49** 346
Western Electric Manufacturing Company, **54** 139
Western Empire Construction. *See* CRSS Inc.
Western Equities, Inc. *See* Tech-Sym Corporation.
Western Family Foods, **47** 457; **53** 21
Western Federal Savings & Loan, **9** 199
Western Fire Equipment Co., **9** 420
Western Forest Products Ltd., **59** 161
Western Gas Resources, Inc., 45 435–37
Western Geophysical, **12** 538–39
Western Glucose Co., **14** 17
Western Graphics Corporation, **58** 314
Western Hotels Inc. *See* Westin Hotels and Resorts Worldwide.
Western Illinois Power Cooperative, **6** 506
Western Inland Lock Navigation Company, **9** 228
Western International Communications, **35** 68
Western International Media, **22** 294
Western International University, **24** 40
Western Kentucky Gas Company, **43** 56–57
Western Kraft Corp., **8** 476
Western Life Insurance Co., **III** 356; **22** 494
Western Light & Telephone Company. *See* Western Power & Gas Company.
Western Light and Power. *See* Public Service Company of Colorado.
Western Massachusetts Co., **13** 183
Western Medical Services, **33** 456
Western Merchandise, Inc., **8** 556
Western Merchandisers, Inc., **29** 229–30
Western Mining Corp., **IV** 61, 95
Western Mortgage Corporation, **16** 497; **50** 497
Western National Life Company, **10** 246; **14** 473
Western Natural Gas Company, **7** 362
Western Newell Manufacturing Company. *See* Newell Co.
Western Pacific, **22** 220
Western Pacific Industries, **10** 357

Western Pioneer, Inc., **18** 279
Western Platinum, **21** 353
Western Platinum Ltd. *See* Lomin plc.
Western Playing Card Co., **13** 559
Western Power & Gas Company. *See* Centel Corporation.
Western Printing and Lithographing Company, **19** 404
Western Public Service Corporation, **6** 568
Western Publishing Group, Inc., 13 114, **559–61; 15** 455; **25** 254, 313; **28** 159; **29** 76
Western Reflections LLC, **55** 291
Western Reserve Bank of Lake County, **9** 474
Western Reserve Telephone Company. *See* Alltel Corporation.
Western Reserves, **12** 442
Western Resources, Inc., 12 541–43; 27 425; **32** 372–75
Western Rosin Company, **8** 99
The WesterN SizzliN Corporation, 10 331; **19** 288; **60 335–37**
Western Slope Gas, **6** 559
Western States Fire Protection Company, **64** 30–32
Western Steel Group, **26** 407
Western Steer Family Restaurant, **10** 331; **18** 8
Western Telegraph Company, **25** 99
Western Telephone Company, **14** 257
Western Union Corporation, **6** 386; **9** 536; **10** 263; **12** 9; **14** 363; **15** 72; **17** 345–46; **21** 25; **24** 515
Western Union Financial Services, Inc., 54 413–16
Western Vending, **13** 48; **41** 22
Western Wireless Corporation, 36 514–16
Westfälische Metall-Industrie Aktien-Gesellschaft. *See* Hella KGaA Hueck & Co.
Westfälische Transport AG, **6** 426
Westfield Holdings Group, **57** 156
Westin Hotel Co., 9 283, **547–49; 21** 91; **54** 345–47
Westin Hotels and Resorts Worldwide, 29 505–08 (upd.)
Westinghouse Air Brake Company. *See* Wabtec Corporation.
Westinghouse Cubic Ltd., **19** 111
Westinghouse Electric Corporation, I 4, 7, 19, 22, 28, 33, 82, 84–85, 524; **II** **120–22; 6** 452, 483, 556; **9** 12, 17, 128, 162, 245, 417, 439–40, 553; **10** 280, 536; **11** 318; **12** 194, **544–47 (upd.); 13** 230, 398, 402, 506–07; **14** 300–01; **16** 8; **17** 488; **18** 320, 335–37, 355; **19** 164–66, 210; **21** 43; **26** 102; **27** 269; **28** 69; **33** 253; **36** 327; **41** 366; **45** 306; **48** 217; **50** 299; **57** 319, 321–22. *See also* CBS Radio Group.
WestJet Airlines Ltd., 38 493–95
WestLB. *See* Westdeutsche Landesbank Girozentrale.
Westmark Mortgage Corp., **13** 417
Westmark Realty Advisors, **21** 97
Westmark Systems, Inc., **26** 268
Westminster Press Ltd. *See* Pearson plc.
Westmoreland Coal Company, 7 582–85
Weston Bakeries, **II** 631
Weston Engineering, **53** 232
Weston Foods Inc. *See* George Weston Limited.

Weston Pharmaceuticals, **V** 49; **19** 122–23; **49** 111–12
Weston Presidio, **49** 189; **65** 257, 259
Weston Resources, **II** 631–32
Westpac Banking Corporation, II 388–90; **17** 285; **48** 424–27 (upd.)
WestPoint Stevens Inc., 16 533–36; **21** 194; **28** 219. See also JPS Textile Group, Inc.
Westport Resources Corporation, 63 439–41
Westport Woman, **24** 145
Westvaco Corporation, IV 351–54; **19 495–99 (upd.)**
The Westwood Group, **20** 54
Westwood One, Inc., 17 150; **23 508–11**
Westwood Pharmaceuticals, **III** 19
Westworld Resources Inc., **23** 41
Westwynn Theatres, **14** 87
The Wet Seal, Inc., 18 562–64; **49** 285
Wet'n Wild Inc., **64** 94
Wetterau Incorporated, II 645, 681–82; **7** 450; **18** 507; **32** 222; **50** 457
Wexpro Company, **6** 568–69
Weyco Group, Incorporated, 32 510–13
Weyerhaeuser Company, IV 298, 304, 308, **355–56**, 358; **8** 428, 434; **9 550–52** (upd.); **19** 445–46, 499; **22** 489; **26** 384; **28 514–17 (upd.)**; **31** 468; **32** 91; **42** 397; **49** 196–97
Weyman-Burton Co., **9** 533
WFP. See Western Forest Products Ltd.
WFSC. See World Fuel Services Corporation.
WGBH Educational Foundation, 66 366–68
WGM Safety Corp., **40** 96–97
WH Smith PLC, 42 442–47 (upd.)
Wham-O, Inc., 61 390–93
Wharf Holdings Limited, **12** 367–68; **18** 114
Whatman plc, 46 462–65
Wheat, First Securities, **19** 304–05
Wheaton Industries, 8 570–73
Wheaton Science Products, 60 338–42 (upd.)
Wheatsheaf Investment, **27** 94
Wheel Horse, **7** 535
Wheel Restaurants Inc., **14** 131
Wheel to Wheel Inc., **66** 315
Wheelabrator Technologies, Inc., V 754; **6 599–600**; **11** 435; **60 343–45 (upd.)**
Wheeled Coach Industries, Inc., **33** 105–06
Wheeling-Pittsburgh Corporation, 7 586–88; **58 360–64 (upd.)**
Whemco, **22** 415
Where Magazines International, **57** 242
Wherehouse Entertainment Incorporated, 9 361; **11 556–58**; **29** 350; **35** 431–32
WHI Inc., **14** 545; **60** 326
Whippoorwill Associates Inc., **28** 55
Whirl-A-Way Motors, **11** 4
Whirlpool Corporation, III 653–55; **8** 298–99; **11** 318; **12** 252, 309, **548–50** (upd.); **13** 402–03, 563; **15** 403; **18** 225–26; **22** 218, 349; **23** 53; **25** 261; **50** 300, 392; **59 414–19 (upd.)**
Whirlwind, Inc., **7** 535
Whistler Corporation, **13** 195
Whitaker-Glessner Company, **7** 586
Whitaker Health Services, **III** 389
Whitbread PLC, I 293–94; **18** 73; **20 519–22 (upd.)**; **29** 19; **35** 395; **42** 247;

50 114; **52 412–17 (upd.)**; **59** 182–83, 255
Whitby Pharmaceuticals, Inc., **10** 289
White & Case LLP, 35 466–69
White Automotive, **10** 9, 11
White Brothers, **39** 83, 84
White Castle System, Inc., 12 551–53; **33** 239; **36 517–20 (upd.)**
White Consolidated Industries Inc., III 573; **8** 298; **12** 252; **13 562–64**; **22** 216–17
White Discount Department Stores, **16** 36
The White House, Inc., 60 346–48
White Miller Construction Company, **14** 162
White Mountain Freezers, **19** 360
White Mountains Insurance Group, Ltd., 48 428–31
White-New Idea, **13** 18
White Oil Corporation, **7** 101
White Rock Corp., **27** 198; **43** 218
White-Rodgers, **II** 19
White Rose, Inc., 12 106; **24 527–29**
White Star Line, **23** 161
White Swan Foodservice, **II** 625
White Tractor, **13** 17
White Wave, 43 462–64
White-Westinghouse. See White Consolidated Industries Inc.
Whitehall Company Jewellers, **24** 319
Whitehall Labs, **8** 63
Whitewater Group, **10** 508
Whitewear Manufacturing Company. See Angelica Corporation.
Whitman Corporation, 7 430; **10** 414–15, **553–55 (upd.)**; **11** 188; **22** 353–54; **27** 196; **43** 217. See also PepsiAmericas, Inc.
Whitman Education Group, Inc., 41 419–21
Whitman Publishing Co., **13** 559–60
Whitman's Chocolates, **7** 431; **12** 429
Whitmire Distribution. See Cardinal Health, Inc.
Whitney Group, **40** 236–38
Whitney Holding Corporation, 21 522–24
Whitney National Bank, **12** 16
Whitney Partners, L.L.C., **40** 237
Whittaker Corporation, I 544–46; **III** 389, 444; **34** 275; **48 432–35 (upd.)**
Whittard of Chelsea Plc, 61 394–97
Whittle Communications L.P., IV 675; **7** 528; **13** 403; **22** 442
Whittman-Hart Inc. See marchFIRST, Inc.
Whitworth Brothers Company, **27** 360
Whole Foods Market, Inc., 19 501–02; **20 523–27**; **41** 422–23; **47** 200; **50 530–34 (upd.)**
Wholesale Cellular USA. See Brightpoint, Inc.
The Wholesale Club, Inc., **8** 556
Wholesale Depot, **13** 547
Wholesale Food Supply, Inc., **13** 333
Wholesome Foods, L.L.C., **32** 274, 277
Wholly Harvest, **19** 502
WHSC Direct, Inc., **53** 359
WHX Corporation, **58** 360
Whyte & Mackay Distillers Ltd., **V** 399; **19** 171; **49** 152
Wicanders Group, **48** 119
Wicat Systems, **7** 255–56; **25** 254
Wicell Research Institute, **65** 367
Wichita Industries, **11** 27

Wickes Inc., I 453, 483; **V 221–23**; **10** 423; **13** 169–70; **15** 281; **17** 365–66; **19** 503–04; **20** 415; **25 533–36 (upd.)**; **41** 93
Wicor, Inc., **54** 419
Wielkopolski Bank Kredytowy, **16** 14
Wiener Städtische, **58** 169
Wienerwald Holding, **17** 249
Wiesner, Inc., **22** 442
Wifstavarfs, **IV** 325
Wilbert, Inc., 56 377–80
Wilbur Chocolate Company, 66 369–71
Wild by Nature. See King Cullen Grocery Co., Inc.
Wild Harvest, **56** 317
Wild Leitz G.m.b.H., **23** 83
Wild Oats Markets, Inc., 19 500–02; **29** 213; **41 422–25 (upd.)**
WildBlue Communications Inc., **54** 406
Wildlife Conservation Society, 31 462–64
Wildlife Land Trust, **54** 172
Wildwater Kingdom, **22** 130
Wiles Group Ltd. See Hanson PLC.
Wiley Manufacturing Co., **8** 545
Oy Wilh. Schauman AB. See UPM-Kymmene
Wilhelm Weber GmbH, **22** 95
Wilhelm Wilhelmsen Ltd., **7** 40; **41** 42
Wilkins Department Store, **19** 510
Wilkinson, Gaddis & Co., **24** 527
Wilkinson Sword Ltd., 12 464; **38** 365; **60 349–52**
Willamette Falls Electric Company. See Portland General Corporation.
Willamette Industries, Inc., IV 357–59; **13** 99, 101; **16** 340; **28** 517; **31 465–68 (upd.)**
Willbros Group, Inc., 56 381–83
Willcox & Gibbs Sewing Machine Co., **15** 384
Willetts Manufacturing Company, **12** 312
Willey Brothers, Inc. See BrandPartners Group, Inc.
William B. Tanner Co., **7** 327
William Barnet and Son, Inc., **III** 246
William Benton Foundation, **7** 165, 167
The William Brooks Shoe Company. See Rocky Shoes & Boots, Inc.
William Byrd Press Inc., **23** 100
William Carter Company, **17** 224
William Cory & Son Ltd., **6** 417
William E. Pollack Government Securities, **II** 390
William E. Wright Company, **9** 375
William Esty Company, **16** 72
William George Company, **32** 519
William Grant & Sons Ltd., 22 343; **60 353–55**
William Hewlett, **41** 117
William Hill Organization Limited, 49 449–52
William Hodges & Company, **33** 150
William Hollins & Company Ltd., **44** 105
William J. Hough Co., **8** 99–100
William L. Bonnell Company, Inc., 66 372–74
William Lyon Homes, 59 420–22
William Morris Agency, Inc., 23 512–14; **43** 235–36
William Morrow & Company, **19** 201
William Odhams Ltd., **7** 244
William P. Young Contruction, **43** 400
William Penn Cos., **III** 243, 273

William Penn Life Insurance Company of New York, **24** 285
William Press, **I** 568
William S. Kimball & Co., **12** 108
William Southam and Sons, **7** 487
William Underwood Co., **7** 430
William Zinsser & Co.,
William Zinsser & Company, Inc., 8 456; **58 365–67**
Williams & Connolly LLP, 47 445–48
Williams & Glyn's Bank Ltd., **12** 422
Williams & Wilkins. *See* Waverly, Inc.
Williams Communications Group, Inc., 6 340; **25** 499; **34 507–10**
The Williams Companies, Inc., IV 575–76; 27 307; **31 469–72 (upd.)**
Williams Deacon's Bank, **12** 422
Williams Electronics, **12** 419
Williams Electronics Games, Inc., **15** 539
Williams Gold Refining Co., **14** 81
The Williams Manufacturing Company, **19** 142–43
Williams/Nintendo Inc., **15** 537
Williams Oil-O-Matic Heating Corporation, **12** 158; **21** 42
Williams plc, **44** 255
Williams Printing Company. *See* Graphic Industries Inc.
Williams Scotsman, Inc., 65 361–64
Williams-Sonoma, Inc., 13 42; **15** 50; **17 548–50; 27** 225, 429; **44 447–50 (upd.)**
Williamsburg Gas Light Co., **6** 455
Williamsburg Restoration, Incorporated, **53** 106
Williamson-Dickie Manufacturing Company, 14 549–50; 45 438–41 (upd.)
Williamsport Barber and Beauty Corp., **60** 287
Willie G's, **15** 279
Willis Corroon Group plc, 25 537–39
Willis Stein & Partners, **21** 404; **58** 318, 321
Williston Basin Interstate Pipeline Company, **7** 322, 324. *See also* WBI Holdings, Inc.
Willor Manufacturing Corp., **9** 323
Wilmington Coca-Cola Bottling Works, Inc., **10** 223
Wilmington Trust Corporation, 25 540–43
Wilsdorf & Davis, **13** 353–54
Wilshire Real Estate Investment Trust Inc., **30** 223
Wilshire Restaurant Group Inc., **13** 66; **28** 258
Wilson Bowden Plc, 45 442–44
Wilson Brothers, **8** 536
Wilson Foods Corp., **12** 124; **22** 510
Wilson Jones Company, **7** 4–5
Wilson Learning Group, **17** 272; **65** 188–89
Wilson-Maeulen Company, **13** 234
Wilson Sonsini Goodrich & Rosati, 34 511–13
Wilson Sporting Goods Company, 13 317; **16** 52; **23** 449; **24** 403, **530–32; 25** 167; **41** 14–16
Wilson's Supermarkets, **12** 220–21
Wilsons The Leather Experts Inc., 21 525–27; 58 368–71 (upd.)
WilTel Network Services, **27** 301, 307

Wimbledon Tennis Championships. *See* The All England Lawn Tennis & Croquet Club.
Wimpey International Ltd., **13** 206
Win-Chance Foods, **II** 508; **36** 255
Win Schuler Foods, **25** 517
Wincanton plc, 52 418–20
Winchell's Donut Houses Operating Company, L.P., II 680; **60 356–59**
WinCo Foods Inc., 60 360–63
Wind River Systems, Inc., 37 419–22
Windmere Corporation, 16 537–39. *See also* Applica Incorporated.
Windmere-Durable Holdings, Inc., **30** 404
WindowVisions, Inc., **29** 288
Windsong Exports, **52** 429
Windsor Forestry Tools, Inc., **48** 59
Windsor Manufacturing Company, **13** 6
Windsor Trust Co., **13** 467
Windstar Sail Cruises. *See* Carnival Corporation.
Windsurfing International, **23** 55
Windswept Environmental Group, Inc., 62 389–92
Windward Capital Partners, **28** 152, 154
The Wine Group, Inc., 39 419–21
Wine World, Inc., **22** 78, 80
Winegard Company, 56 384–87
Winfire, Inc., **37** 194
Wingate Partners, **14** 521, 523
Winget Ltd. *See* Seddon Group Ltd.
Wings & Wheels, **13** 19
Wings Luggage, Inc., **10** 181
WingspanBank.com, **38** 270
Winkelman Stores, Inc., **8** 425–26
Winlet Fashions, **22** 223
Winn-Dixie Stores, Inc., II 626–27, 670, 683–84; **7** 61; **11** 228; **15** 178; **16** 314; **18** 8; **21 528–30 (upd.); 34** 269; **59 423–27 (upd.)**
Winnebago Industries Inc., 7 589–91; 22 207; **27 509–12 (upd.)**
Winners Apparel Ltd. *See* The TJX Companies, Inc.
Winning International, **21** 403
WinsLoew Furniture, Inc., 21 531–33
Winston & Strawn, 35 470–73
Winston Furniture Company, Inc., **21** 531–33
Winston Group, **10** 333
Winter Hill Frozen Foods and Services, **55** 82
WinterBrook Corp., **26** 326
Winterflood Securities Limited, **39** 89, 91
Wintershall AG, **IV** 485; **38** 408
Winterthur Insurance, **21** 144, 146–47; **59** 144–46
Winterthur Schweizerische Versicherungs-Gesellschaft, III 402–04
Winthrop Lawrence Corporation, **25** 541
Winton Engines, **10** 273
Winyah Concrete & Block, **50** 49
Wipro Limited, 43 465–68
Wire and Cable Specialties Corporation, **17** 276
Wire and Plastic Products PLC. *See* WPP Group PLC.
Wireless Hong Kong. *See* Hong Kong Telecommunications Ltd.
Wireless LLC, **18** 77
Wireless Management Company, **11** 12
Wiron Prefabricados Modulares, S.A., **65** 363
Wirtz Productions Ltd., **15** 238

Wisconsin Alumni Research Foundation, 65 365–68
Wisconsin Bell, Inc., 14 551–53; 18 30
Wisconsin Central Transportation Corporation, 12 278; **24 533–36**
Wisconsin Dairies, 7 592–93
Wisconsin Energy Corporation, 6 601–03, 605; **54 417–21 (upd.)**
Wisconsin Gas Company, **17** 22–23
Wisconsin Power and Light, **22** 13; **39** 260
Wisconsin Public Service Corporation, 6 604–06; **9 553–54.** *See also* WPS Resources Corporation.
Wisconsin Steel, **10** 430; **17** 158–59
Wisconsin Tissue Mills Inc., **8** 103
Wisconsin Toy Company. *See* Value Merchants Inc.
Wisconsin Wire and Steel, **17** 310; **24** 160
Wise Foods, Inc., **22** 95
Wise Solutions, Inc. *See* Altiris, Inc.
Wiser's De Luxe Whiskey, **14** 141
Wispark Corporation, **6** 601, 603
Wisser Service Holdings AG, **18** 105
Wisvest Corporation, **6** 601, 603
WiSys Technology Foundation, **65** 367
Witco Corporation, I 404–06; **16 540–43 (upd.)**
Wite-Out Products, Inc., **23** 56–57
Witech Corporation, **6** 601, 603
Withington Company. *See* Sparton Corporation.
Wittgensteiner Kliniken Gruppe, **56** 141
Wittington Investments Ltd., **13** 51
The Wiz. *See* Cablevision Electronic Instruments, Inc.
Wizards of the Coast Inc., 24 537–40; 43 229, 233
WizardWorks Group, Inc., **31** 238–39
WL Ross & Co., **67** 125
WLIW-TV. *See* Educational Broadcasting Corporation.
WLR Foods, Inc., 14 516; **21 534–36; 50** 494
Wm. B. Reily & Company Inc., 58 372–74
WM Investment Company, **34** 512
Wm. Morrison Supermarkets PLC, 38 496–98
Wm. Underwood Company, **40** 53
Wm. Wrigley Jr. Company, 7 594–97; 58 375–79 (upd.)
WMC, Limited, 43 469–72
WMF. *See* Württembergische Metallwarenfabrik AG (WMF).
WMS Industries, Inc., 15 537–39; 41 215–16; **53 363–66 (upd.)**
WMX Technologies Inc., 11 435–36; **17** 551–54; **26** 409
Wolf Furniture Enterprises, **14** 236
Wolfe & Associates, **25** 434
Wolfe Industries, Inc., **22** 255
Wolff Printing Co., **13** 559
The Wolfgang Puck Food Company, Inc., 26 534–36
Wolohan Lumber Co., 19 503–05; 25 535
Wolseley plc, 64 409–12
Wolters Kluwer NV, IV 611; **14 554–56; 31** 389, 394; **33 458–61 (upd.)**
The Wolverhampton & Dudley Breweries, PLC, 57 411–14
Wolverine Equities Company, **62** 341
Wolverine Insurance Co., **26** 487
Wolverine Tube Inc., 23 515–17

Wolverine World Wide, Inc., **16** 544–47; **17** 390; **32** 99; **44** 365; **59** 428–33 (upd.)
Womack Development Company, **11** 257
Womacks Saloon and Gaming Parlor, **53** 91
Womble Carlyle Sandridge & Rice, PLLC, **52** 421–24
Women's Specialty Retailing Group. *See* Casual Corner Group, Inc.
Women's World, **15** 96
Wometco Coca-Cola Bottling Co., **10** 222
Wometco Coffee Time, **I** 514
Wometco Enterprises, **I** 514
Wonderware Corp., **22** 374
Wong International Holdings, **16** 195
Wood Hall Trust plc, **I** 592–93; **50** 200
Wood-Metal Industries, Inc. *See* Wood-Mode, Inc.
Wood-Mode, Inc., **23** 518–20
Wood River Oil and Refining Company, **11** 193
Wood Shovel and Tool Company, **9** 71
Wood, Struthers & Winthrop, Inc., **22** 189
Wood Wyant Inc., **30** 496–98
Woodbridge Winery, **50** 388
Woodbury Co., **19** 380
Woodcock, Hess & Co., **9** 370
Woodcraft Industries Inc., **61** 398–400
Woodhaven Gas Light Co., **6** 455
Woodhill Chemical Sales Company, **8** 333
Woodland Publishing, Inc., **37** 286
Woodlands, **7** 345–46
Woodmen of the World Life Insurance Society, **66** 227–28
Woods Equipment Company, **32** 28
Woodside Petroleum, **63** 440
Woodside Travel Trust, **26** 310
Woodville Appliances, Inc., **9** 121
Woodward-Clyde Group Inc., **45** 421
Woodward Governor Company, **13** 565–68; **49** 453–57 (upd.)
Woodworkers Warehouse, **22** 517
Woolco Department Stores. *See* Woolworth Corporation.
Woolrich Inc., **62** 393–96
The Woolwich plc, **30** 492–95; **64** 50
Woolworth Corporation, **6** 344; **V** 224–27; **8** 509; **14** 293–95; **17** 42, 335; **20** 528–32 (upd.); **25** 22. *See also* Kingfisher plc; Venator Group Inc.
Woolworth Holdings. *See* Kingfisher plc.
Woolworth's Ltd., **II** 656. *See also* Kingfisher plc.
Wooster Preserving Company, **11** 211
Worcester Gas Light Co., **14** 124
Worcester Wire Works, **13** 369
Word, Inc., **14** 499; **38** 456
WordPerfect Corporation, **6** 256; **10** 519, 556–59; **12** 335; **25** 300; **41** 281. *See also* Corel Corporation.
WordStar International, **15** 149; **43** 151. *See also* The Learning Company Inc.
Work Wear Corp., **II** 607; **16** 229
Workflow Management, Inc., **65** 369–72
Working Assets Funding Service, **43** 473–76
Working Title Films, **23** 389
Workscape Inc., **42** 430
World Acceptance Corporation, **57** 415–18
World Airways, **10** 560–62; **28** 404
World Bank Group, **33** 462–65

World Book Group. *See* Scott Fetzer Company.
World Book, Inc., **12** 554–56
World Championship Wrestling (WCW), **32** 516
World Color Press Inc., **12** 557–59; **19** 333; **21** 61
World Commerce Corporation, **25** 461
World Communications, Inc., **11** 184
World Duty Free Americas, Inc., **29** 509–12 (upd.)
World Duty Free plc, **33** 59
World Film Studio, **24** 437
World Flight Crew Services, **10** 560
World Foot Locker, **14** 293
World Fuel Services Corporation, **47** 449–51
World Gift Company, **9** 330
World International Holdings Limited, **12** 368
World Machinery Company, **45** 170–71
World Minerals Inc., **60** 16
World Online, **48** 398–39
World Poker Tour, LLC, **51** 205, 207
World Publications, LLC, **8** 423; **65** 373–75
World Savings and Loan, **19** 412; **47** 159–60
World Service Life Insurance Company, **27** 47
World Trade Corporation. *See* International Business Machines Corporation.
World Trans, Inc., **33** 105
World Wrestling Federation Entertainment, Inc., **32** 514–17
World Yacht Enterprises, **22** 438
The World's Biggest Bookstore, **58** 185
World's Finest Chocolate Inc., **39** 422–24
WorldCom, Inc., **14** 330, 332; **18** 33, 164, 166; **29** 227; **38** 269–70, 468; **46** 376; **61** 212. *See also* MCI WorldCom, Inc.
WorldCorp, Inc., **10** 560–62
WorldGames, **10** 560
WorldMark, The Club, **33** 409
Worlds of Fun, **22** 130
Worlds of Wonder, Inc., **25** 381; **26** 548
Worldview Systems Corporation, **26** 428; **46** 434
WorldWay Corporation, **16** 41
Worldwide Fiber Inc., **46** 267
Worldwide Insurance Co., **48** 9
Worldwide Logistics, **17** 505
Worldwide Restaurant Concepts, Inc., **47** 452–55
Worldwide Semiconductor Manufacturing Co., **47** 386
Worldwide Underwriters Insurance Co., **III** 218–19
Wormald International Ltd., **13** 245, 247; **63** 403
Worms et Cie, **27** 275–76, **513–15**
Worth Corp., **27** 274
Worthen Banking Corporation, **15** 60
Worthington Foods, Inc., **14** 557–59; **33** 170
Worthington Industries, Inc., **7** 598–600; **8** 450; **21** 537–40 (upd.)
Woven Belting Co., **8** 13
WPL Holdings, **6** 604–06
WPM. *See* Wall Paper Manufacturers.
WPP Group plc, **6** 53–54; **22** 201, 296; **23** 480; **48** 440–42 (upd.); **66** 157, 160, 378. *See also* Ogilvy Group Inc.

WPS Resources Corporation, **53** 367–70 (upd.)
Wrafton Laboratories Ltd., **59** 332
Wrather Corporation, **18** 354
Wrenn Furniture Company, **10** 184
WRG. *See* Wells Rich Greene BDDP.
Wright & Company Realtors, **21** 257
Wright Aeronautical, **9** 16
Wright Company, **9** 416
Wright Group, **22** 519, 522
Wright Manufacturing Company, **8** 407
Wright Medical Group, Inc., **61** 401–05
Wright Plastic Products, **17** 310; **24** 160
Wrightson Limited, **19** 155
WS Atkins Plc, **45** 445–47
WSGC Holdings, Inc., **24** 530
WSI. *See* Weather Services International.
WSI Corporation, **10** 88–89
WSM Inc., **11** 152
WSMC. *See* Worldwide Semiconductor Manufacturing Co.
WSMP, Inc., **29** 202
WTD Industries, Inc., **20** 533–36
Wurlitzer Co., **17** 468; **18** 45
Württembergische Metallwarenfabrik AG (WMF), **60** 364–69
WVPP. *See* Westvaco Corporation.
WVT Communications. *See* Warwick Valley Telephone Company.
WWG Industries, Inc., **22** 352–53
WWT, Inc., **58** 371
WWTV, **18** 493
Wyandotte Chemicals Corporation, **18** 49
Wyant Corporation, **30** 496–98
Wycombe Bus Company, **28** 155–56
Wyeth, **50** 535–39 (upd.)
Wyeth-Ayerst Laboratories, **25** 477; **27** 69
Wyle Electronics, **14** 560–62; **19** 311
Wyly Corporation, **11** 468
Wyman-Gordon Company, **14** 563–65; **30** 282–83; **41** 367
Wynkoop Brewing Company, **43** 407
Wynn's International, Inc., **22** 458; **33** 466–70
Wyse Technology, Inc., **10** 362; **15** 540–42

X-Acto, **12** 263
X-Chem Oil Field Chemicals, **8** 385
X-Rite, Inc., **48** 443–46
XA Systems Corporation, **10** 244
Xaos Tools, Inc., **10** 119
Xaver Fendt GmbH & Co. KG. *See* AGCO Corporation.
Xcelite, **II** 16
Xcor International, **15** 538; **53** 364–65
Xeikon NV, **26** 540–42; **66** 260
Xenell Corporation, **48** 358
Xenia National Bank, **9** 474
Xenotech, **27** 58
Xeron, Inc., **56** 62
Xerox Corporation, **II** 159, 412, 448; **III** 120–21, 157, 159, **171–73**; **6** 288–90 (upd.), 390; **7** 45, 161; **8** 164; **10** 22, 139, 430, 510–11; **11** 68, 494, 518; **13** 127, 448; **14** 399; **17** 328–29; **18** 93, 111–12; **22** 411–12; **25** 54–55, 148, 152; **26** 213, 540, 542, **543–47 (upd.)**; **28** 115; **36** 171; **40** 394; **41** 197; **46** 151
Xetra, **59** 151
Xetra, **59** 151
Xiamen Airlines, **33** 99
Xilinx, Inc., **16** 317, 548–50; **18** 17, 19; **19** 405; **43** 15–16

Xing Technology Corp., **53** 282
XMR, Inc., **42** 361
XP, **27** 474
Xpect First Aid Corp., **51** 76
Xpert Recruitment, Ltd., **26** 240
Xpress Automotive Group, Inc., **24** 339
XR Ventures LLC, **48** 446
XRAL Storage and Terminaling Co., **IV** 411
Xros, Inc., **36** 353
XTO Energy Inc., 52 425–27
XTRA Corp., **18** 67
Xtra Limited New Zealand, **54** 355–57
XTX Corp., **13** 127
Xuzhuo Liebherr Concrete Machinery Co. Ltd., **64** 241
Xynetics, **9** 251
Xytek Corp., **13** 127

Yacimientos Petrolíferos Fiscales Sociedad Anónima. *See* Repsol-YPF SA.
Yageo Corporation, 16 551–53
Yahoo! Inc., 25 18; **27 516–19; 38** 439; **45** 201
Yakovlev, **24** 60
Yale and Valor, PLC, **50** 134–35
Yamagata Enterprises, **26** 310
Yamaha Corporation, III 366, 599, **656–59; 11** 50; **12** 401; **16** 410, **554–58 (upd.); 17** 25; **18** 250; **19** 428; **22** 196; **33** 28; **40 461–66 (upd.); 49** 178
Yamaha Motor Co., Ltd., **59** 393, 397
Yamaha Musical Instruments, **16** 202; **43** 170
Yamaichi Capital Management, **42** 349
Yamaichi Securities Company, Limited, II 458–59; 9 377
Yamamotoyama Co., Ltd., **50** 449
Yamano Music, **16** 202; **43** 171
Yamanouchi Consumer Inc., **39** 361
Yamanouchi Pharmaceutical Co., Ltd., **12** 444–45; **38** 93
Yamato Transport Co. Ltd., V 536–38; 49 458–61 (upd.)
Yamazaki Baking Co., Ltd., IV 152; **24** 358; **58 380–82**
Yanbian Industrial Technology Training Institute, **12** 294
Yangzhou Motor Coach Manufacturing Co., **34** 132
The Yankee Candle Company, Inc., 37 423–26; 38 192
Yankee Energy Gas System, Inc., **13** 184
Yankee Gas Services Company, **48** 305
YankeeNets LLC, 35 474–77
Yankton Gas Company, **6** 524
Yarmouth Group, Inc., **17** 285
Yasuda Fire and Marine Insurance Company, Limited, III 405–07, 408; **45** 110
Yasuda Mutual Life Insurance Company, II 446; **III 408–09; 22** 406–07; **39 425–28 (upd.)**
The Yasuda Trust and Banking Company, Limited, II 391–92; 17 555–57 (upd.)
Yates-Barco Ltd., **16** 8
Yates Circuit Foil, **IV** 26
The Yates Companies, Inc., 62 397–99
Yearbooks, Inc., **12** 472
Yeargin Construction Co., **II** 87; **11** 413
Yellow Cab Co., **10** 370; **24** 118
Yellow Corporation, 14 566–68; 45 448–51 (upd.)

Yellow Freight System, Inc. of Deleware, V 539–41; 12 278
YES! Entertainment Corporation, 10 306; **26 548–50**
Yesco Audio Environments, **18** 353, 355
Yeti Cycles Inc., **19** 385
YGK Inc., **6** 465, 467
Yhtyneet Paperitehtaat Oy. *See* United Paper Mills Ltd.
YKK, **19** 477
YMCA of the USA, 31 473–76
Ymos A.G., **IV** 53; **26** 83
YOCREAM International, Inc., 47 456–58
Yogen Fruz World-Wide, Inc. *See* CoolBrands International Inc.
Yokado Co. Ltd. *See* Ito-Yokado Co. Ltd.
Yoko Sangyo Co., **64** 35
Yokogawa Electric Works, Limited, **13** 234
Yokohama Bottle Plant, **21** 319
The Yokohama Rubber Co., Ltd., V 254–56; 19 506–09 (upd.)
Yokohama Tokyu Deppartment Store Co., Ltd., **32** 457
Yondenko Corporation, **60** 272
Yongpyong Resort Co., **61** 342
Yoosung Enterprise Co., Ltd., **23** 269
Yoplait S.A. *See* Sodiaal S.A.
The York Bank and Trust Company, **16** 14; **43** 8
The York Group, Inc., 50 540–43
York International Corp., 13 569–71; 22 6
York Research Corporation, 35 478–80
York Manufacturing Co $$York Manufacturing Co., **13** 385
York Safe & Lock Company, **7** 144–45; **22** 184
York Steak House, **16** 157
York Wastewater Consultants, Inc., **6** 441
Yorkshire Energies, **45** 21
Yorkshire Group, **61** 133
Yorkshire Television Ltd., **IV** 659
Yorkshire-Tyne Tees Television, **24** 194
Yorkshire Water Services Ltd. *See* Kelda Group plc.
Yoshikazu Taguchi, **6** 428
Young & Co.'s Brewery, P.L.C., 38 499–502
Young & Rubicam, Inc., I 36–38; 9 314; **13** 204; **16** 166–68; **22 551–54 (upd.); 41** 89–90, 198; **66 375–78 (upd.)**
Young & Selden, **7** 145
Young Broadcasting Inc., 40 467–69; 42 163
Young Chang Akki Company, **51** 201
Young Innovations, Inc., 44 451–53
Young Readers of America, **13** 105
Young's Market Company, LLC, 32 518–20
Youngblood Truck Lines, **16** 40
Youngjin Pharmaceutical, **62** 221
Youngs Drug Products Corporation, **8** 85; **38** 124
Youngstown Sheet & Tube, **I** 490–91; **13** 157
Younkers, Inc., 19 324–25, **510–12; 41** 343–44
Your Communications Limited, **52** 372, 374
Youth Centre Inc., **16** 36
Youth Services International, Inc., 21 541–43; 30 146
Youthtrack, Inc., **29** 399–400

Yoxall Instrument Company, **13** 234
Yoyoteiki Cargo Co., Ltd., **6** 428
YPF Sociedad Anónima, IV 577–78. *See also* Repsol-YPF S.A.
Yside Investment Group, **16** 196
YTT. *See* Yorkshire-Tyne Tees Television.
The Yucaipa Cos., 17 558–62; 22 39; **32** 222; **35** 369
Yugraneft, **49** 306
Yukon Pacific Corporation, **22** 164, 166
YUKOS, **49** 305–06. *See also* OAO NK YUKOS.
Yule Catto & Company plc, 54 422–25
Yum! Brands Inc., 57 228; **58 383–85**
Yutaka Co., Ltd., **55** 48
Yves Rocher. *See* Laboratoires de Biologie Végétale Yves Rocher.
Yves Soulié, **II** 266
YWCA of the U.S.A., 45 452–54

Z Media, Inc., **49** 433
Z-Spanish Media Corp., **35** 220; **41** 151
Z.C. Mines, **IV** 61
Zagara's Inc., **35** 190–91
Zahnfabrik Weinand Sohne & Co. G.m.b.H., **10** 271
Zale Corporation, 16 206, **559–61; 17** 369; **19** 452; **23** 60; **40 470–74 (upd.)**
Zambezi Saw Mills (1968) Ltd., **IV** 241
Zambia Breweries, **25** 281
Zambia Industrial and Mining Corporation Ltd., IV 239–41
Zamboni. *See* Frank J. Zamboni & Co., Inc.
Zanders Feinpapiere AG, **IV** 288; **15** 229
Zanussi, **III** 480; **22** 27; **53** 127
Zany Brainy, Inc., 31 477–79; 36 502
Zap, Inc., **25** 546
Zapata Corporation, 17 157, 160; **25 544–46; 63** 343–44
Zapata Gulf Marine Corporation, **11** 524
Zaring Premier Homes, **41** 133
Zastron Electronic (Shenzhen) Co. Ltd., **61** 233
Zatarain's, Inc., 64 413–15
Zausner, **25** 83
Zayre Corp., **9** 20–21; **13** 547–48; **29** 106; **30** 55–56; **33** 198. *See also* The TJX Companies, Inc.
ZCE Platinum, **63** 40
ZCMI. *See* Zion's Cooperative Mercantile Institution.
ZDF, **41** 28–29
ZDNet, **36** 523
Zealand Mines S.A., **23** 41
Zebco, **22** 115
Zebra Technologies Corporation, 14 378, **569–71; 53 371–74 (upd.)**
Zecco, Inc., **6** 441
Zee Medical, Inc., **47** 235
ZeFer, **63** 151
Zell Bros., **16** 559
Zell/Chilmark Fund LP, **12** 439; **19** 384
Zellers. *See* Hudson's Bay Company.
Zellstoff-und Papierfabrik Rosenthal Gmbh & Co KG., **64** 275
Zellweger Telecommunications AG, **9** 32
Zeneca Group PLC, 21 544–46. *See also* AstraZeneca PLC.
Zengine, Inc., **41** 258–59
Zenit Bank, **45** 322
Zenith Data Systems, Inc., 10 563–65
Zenith Electronics Corporation, II 123–25; 10 563; **11** 62, 318; **12** 183; **13**

109, 398, **572–75 (upd.)**; **18** 421; **34** **514–19 (upd.)**

Zenith Media, **42** 330–31

Zentralsparkasse und Kommerzialbank Wien, **23** 37

Zentronics, **19** 313

Zep Manufacturing Company, **54** 252, 254

Zeppelin Luftschifftechnik GmbH, **48** 450

Zerex, **50** 48

Zergo Holdings, **42** 24–25

Zero Corporation, 17 563–65

Zero First Co Ltd., **62** 245

Zero Plus Dialing, Inc. *See* Billing Concepts Corp.

Zetor s.p., **21** 175

Zeus Components, Inc., **10** 113; **50** 43

Zexel Valeo Compressor USA Inc. *See* Valeo.

ZF Friedrichshafen AG, 48 447–51

Zhenjiang Zhengmao Hitachi Zosen Machinery Co. Ltd., **53** 173

Zhong Yue Highsonic Electron Company, **62** 150

Zhongbei Building Material Products Company, **26** 510

Zhongde Brewery, **49** 417

Ziebart International Corporation, 30 499–501; **66 379–82 (upd.)**

The Ziegler Companies, Inc., 24 541–45; **63 442–48 (upd.)**

Ziff Communications Company, 7 239–40; **12** 359, **560–63**; **13** 483; **16** 371; **17** 152, 253; **25** 238, 240; **41** 12

Ziff Davis Media Inc., 36 521–26 (upd.); **47** 77, 79. *See also* CNET Networks, Inc.

Ziff-Davis Publishing Co., **38** 441

Zignago Vetro S.p.A., **67** 210–12

Zila, Inc., 46 466–69

Zilber Ltd., **13** 541

Zildjian. *See* Avedis Zildjian Co.

Zilkha & Company, **12** 72

Zilog, Inc., 15 543–45; **16** 548–49; **22** 390

Zimmer AG, **IV** 142

Zimmer Holdings, Inc., 45 455–57

Zimmer Inc., **10** 156–57; **11** 475

Zinc Products Company, **30** 39

Zindart Ltd., 60 370–72

Zinsser. *See* William Zinsser & Company, Inc.

Zion Foods, **23** 408

Zion's Cooperative Mercantile Institution, 33 471–74

Zions Bancorporation, 12 564–66; **24** 395; **53 375–78 (upd.)**

Zippo Manufacturing Company, 18 565–68

Zipps Drive-Thru, Inc., **25** 389

Zippy Mart, **7** 102

Zodiac S.A., 36 527–30

Zody's Department Stores, **9** 120–22

Zolfo Cooper LLC, **57** 219

Zoll Foods, **55** 366

Zoll Medical, **18** 423

Zoloto Mining Ltd., **38** 231

Zoltek Companies, Inc., 37 427–30

Zomba Records Ltd., 52 428–31

The Zondervan Corporation, **51** 131

Zondervan Publishing House, 14 499; **24 546–49**

Zones, Inc., 67 395–97

Zoom Technologies, Inc., 53 379–82 (upd.)

Zoom Telephonics, Inc., 18 569–71

Zortech Inc., **10** 508

Zotos International, Inc., **III** 63; **17** 110; **22** 487; **41** 228

ZPT Radom, **23** 427

ZS Sun Limited Partnership, **10** 502

Zuari Cement, **40** 107, 109

Zuellig Group N.A., Inc., **46** 226

Zuivelcooperatie De Seven Provincien UA, **59** 194

Zuka Juice, **47** 201

Zumtobel AG, 50 544–48

Zurich Financial Services, 40 59, 61; **42 448–53 (upd.)**

Zurich Insurance Group, **15** 257; **25** 154, 156

Zürich Versicherungs-Gesellschaft, III 410–12. *See also* Zurich Financial Services

Zurn Industries, Inc., **24** 150

Zvezda Design Bureau, **61** 197

Zwarovski, **16** 561

Zweckform Büro-Produkte G.m.b.H., **49** 38

Zycad Corp., **11** 489–91

Zycon Corporation, **24** 201

Zygo Corporation, 42 454–57

ZymoGenetics Inc., **61** 266

Zytec Corporation, 19 513–15. *See also* Artesyn Technologies Inc.

INDEX TO INDUSTRIES

Index to Industries

ACCOUNTING

American Institute of Certified Public Accountants (AICPA), 44
Andersen Worldwide, 29 (upd.)
Automatic Data Processing, Inc., 47 (upd.)
Deloitte Touche Tohmatsu International, 9; 29 (upd.)
Ernst & Young, 9; 29 (upd.)
Grant Thornton International, 57
KPMG International, 33 (upd.)
L.S. Starrett Co., 13
McLane Company, Inc., 13
NCO Group, Inc., 42
Paychex, Inc., 46 (upd.)
PricewaterhouseCoopers, 9; 29 (upd.)
Robert Wood Johnson Foundation, 35
Univision Communications Inc., 24

ADVERTISING & OTHER BUSINESS SERVICES

ABM Industries Incorporated, 25 (upd.)
Ackerley Communications, Inc., 9
ACNielsen Corporation, 13; 38 (upd.)
Acsys, Inc., 44
Adecco S.A., 36 (upd.)
Adia S.A., 6
Administaff, Inc., 52
Advo, Inc., 6; 53 (upd.)
Aegis Group plc, 6
Affiliated Computer Services, Inc., 61
AHL Services, Inc., 27
Alloy, Inc., 55
Amdocs Ltd., 47
American Building Maintenance Industries, Inc., 6
The American Society of Composers, Authors and Publishers (ASCAP), 29
Amey Plc, 47
Analysts International Corporation, 36
The Arbitron Company, 38
Ariba, Inc., 57
Armor Holdings, Inc., 27
Ashtead Group plc, 34
The Associated Press, 13
Bain & Company, 55
Barrett Business Services, Inc., 16
Barton Protective Services Inc., 53
Bates Worldwide, Inc., 14; 33 (upd.)
Bearings, Inc., 13
Berlitz International, Inc., 13
Big Flower Press Holdings, Inc., 21
Boron, LePore & Associates, Inc., 45
The Boston Consulting Group, 58
Bozell Worldwide Inc., 25
BrandPartners Group, Inc., 58
Bright Horizons Family Solutions, Inc., 31
Broadcast Music Inc., 23
Buck Consultants, Inc., 55
Bureau Veritas SA, 55
Burns International Services Corporation, 13; 41 (upd.)
Cambridge Technology Partners, Inc., 36
Campbell-Mithun-Esty, Inc., 16

Cannon Design, 63
Career Education Corporation, 45
Carmichael Lynch Inc., 28
CDI Corporation, 54 (upd.)
Central Parking Corporation, 18
Century Business Services, Inc., 52
Chancellor Beacon Academies, Inc., 53
ChartHouse International Learning Corporation, 49
Chiat/Day Inc. Advertising, 11
Chicago Board of Trade, 41
Chisholm-Mingo Group, Inc., 41
Christie's International plc, 15; 39 (upd.)
Cintas Corporation, 21
COMFORCE Corporation, 40
Command Security Corporation, 57
Computer Learning Centers, Inc., 26
Corporate Express, Inc., 47 (upd.)
CORT Business Services Corporation, 26
Cox Enterprises, Inc., 22 (upd.)
Creative Artists Agency LLC, 38
Cyrk Inc., 19
Dale Carnegie Training, Inc., 28
D'Arcy Masius Benton & Bowles, Inc., 6; 32 (upd.)
Dawson Holdings PLC, 43
DDB Needham Worldwide, 14
Deluxe Corporation, 22 (upd.)
Dentsu Inc., I; 16 (upd.); 40 (upd.)
Deutsch, Inc., 42
Deutsche Post AG, 29
DoubleClick Inc., 46
Drake Beam Morin, Inc., 44
The Dun & Bradstreet Corporation, 61 (upd.)
Earl Scheib, Inc., 32
eBay Inc., 67 (upd.)
EBSCO Industries, Inc., 17
Ecology and Environment, Inc., 39
Edelman, 62
Edison Schools Inc., 37
Education Management Corporation, 35
Electro Rent Corporation, 58
Employee Solutions, Inc., 18
Ennis Business Forms, Inc., 21
Equifax Inc., 6; 28 (upd.)
Equity Marketing, Inc., 26
ERLY Industries Inc., 17
Euro RSCG Worldwide S.A., 13
Expedia, Inc., 58
Fallon McElligott Inc., 22
FileNet Corporation, 62
Fiserv, Inc., 33 (upd.)
FlightSafety International, Inc., 29 (upd.)
Florists' Transworld Delivery, Inc., 28
Foote, Cone & Belding Worldwide, I; 66 (upd.)
Forrester Research, Inc., 54
Frankel & Co., 39
Franklin Covey Company, 37 (upd.)
Frost & Sullivan, Inc., 53
Gage Marketing Group, 26
The Gallup Organization, 37
George P. Johnson Company, 60

George S. May International Company, 55
Gevity HR, Inc., 63
GfK Aktiengesellschaft, 49
Glotel plc, 53
Grey Global Group Inc., 6; 66 (upd.)
Group 4 Falck A/S, 42
Groupe Jean-Claude Darmon, 44
GSD&M Advertising, 44
GSI Commerce, Inc., 67
Gwathmey Siegel & Associates Architects LLC, 26
Ha-Lo Industries, Inc., 27
Hakuhodo, Inc., 6; 42 (upd.)
Hall, Kinion & Associates, Inc., 52
Handleman Company, 15
Harte-Hanks, Inc., 63 (upd.)
Havas SA, 33 (upd.)
Hays Plc, 27
Headway Corporate Resources, Inc., 40
Heidrick & Struggles International, Inc., 28
Hildebrandt International, 29
IKON Office Solutions, Inc., 50
IMS Health, Inc., 57
Interep National Radio Sales Inc., 35
International Brotherhood of Teamsters, 37
International Management Group, 18
International Total Services, Inc., 37
The Interpublic Group of Companies, Inc., I; 22 (upd.)
Ipsos SA, 48
Iron Mountain, Inc., 33
ITT Educational Services, Inc., 33
J.D. Power and Associates, 32
Jackson Hewitt, Inc., 48
Japan Leasing Corporation, 8
Jostens, Inc., 25 (upd.)
JOULÉ Inc., 58
JWT Group Inc., I
Katz Communications, Inc., 6
Katz Media Group, Inc., 35
Keane, Inc., 56
Kelly Services Inc., 6; 26 (upd.)
Ketchum Communications Inc., 6
Kinko's Inc., 16; 43 (upd.)
Kirshenbaum Bond + Partners, Inc., 57
Kohn Pedersen Fox Associates P.C., 57
Korn/Ferry International, 34
Kroll Inc., 57
Labor Ready, Inc., 29
Lamar Advertising Company, 27
Le Cordon Bleu S.A., 67
Learning Tree International Inc., 24
Leo Burnett Company Inc., I; 20 (upd.)
Lintas: Worldwide, 14
Mail Boxes Etc., 18; 41 (upd.)
Manhattan Associates, Inc., 67
Manpower, Inc., 30 (upd.)
marchFIRST, Inc., 34
Maritz Inc., 38
MAXIMUS, Inc., 43
MDC Partners Inc., 63
Mediaset SpA, 50
Milliman USA, 66
Moody's Corporation, 65

ADVERTISING & OTHER BUSINESS SERVICES (continued)

MPS Group, Inc., 49
Mullen Advertising Inc., 51
National Equipment Services, Inc., 57
National Media Corporation, 27
Neopost S.A., 53
New England Business Services, Inc., 18
New Valley Corporation, 17
NFO Worldwide, Inc., 24
Nobel Learning Communities, Inc., 37
Norrell Corporation, 25
Norwood Promotional Products, Inc., 26
Obie Media Corporation, 56
Observer AB, 55
The Ogilvy Group, Inc., I
Olsten Corporation, 6; 29 (upd.)
Omnicom Group, I; 22 (upd.)
On Assignment, Inc., 20
1-800-FLOWERS, Inc., 26
Opinion Research Corporation, 46
Oracle Corporation, 67 (upd.)
Orbitz, Inc., 61
Outdoor Systems, Inc., 25
Paris Corporation, 22
Paychex, Inc., 15
PDI, Inc., 52
Pei Cobb Freed & Partners Architects LLP, 57
Penauille Polyservices SA, 49
Phillips, de Pury & Luxembourg, 49
Pierce Leahy Corporation, 24
Pinkerton's Inc., 9
PMT Services, Inc., 24
Priceline.com Incorporated, 57
Publicis S.A., 19
Publishers Clearing House, 23; 64 (upd.)
Randstad Holding n.v., 16; 43 (upd.)
RemedyTemp, Inc., 20
Rental Service Corporation, 28
Rentokil Initial Plc, 47
The Richards Group, Inc., 58
Right Management Consultants, Inc., 42
Ritchie Bros. Auctioneers Inc., 41
Robert Half International Inc., 18
Roland Berger & Partner GmbH, 37
Ronco, Inc., 15
Russell Reynolds Associates Inc., 38
Saatchi & Saatchi, I; 42 (upd.)
Securitas AB, 42
ServiceMaster Limited Partnership, 6
Shared Medical Systems Corporation, 14
Sir Speedy, Inc., 16
Skidmore, Owings & Merrill, 13
SmartForce PLC, 43
SOS Staffing Services, 25
Sotheby's Holdings, Inc., 11; 29 (upd.)
Spencer Stuart and Associates, Inc., 14
Spherion Corporation, 52
Steiner Corporation (Alsco), 53
Strayer Education, Inc., 53
Superior Uniform Group, Inc., 30
Sykes Enterprises, Inc., 45
Sylvan Learning Systems, Inc., 35
TA Triumph-Adler AG, 48
Taylor Nelson Sofres plc, 34
TBWA\Chiat\Day, 6; 43 (upd.)
Thomas Cook Travel Inc., 33 (upd.)
Ticketmaster Group, Inc., 13; 37 (upd.)
TMP Worldwide Inc., 30
TNT Post Group N.V., 30
Towers Perrin, 32
Trader Classified Media N.V., 57
Traffix, Inc., 61
Transmedia Network Inc., 20
Treasure Chest Advertising Company, Inc., 32

TRM Copy Centers Corporation, 18
True North Communications Inc., 23
24/7 Real Media, Inc., 49
Tyler Corporation, 23
U.S. Office Products Company, 25
UniFirst Corporation, 21
United Business Media plc, 52 (upd.)
United News & Media plc, 28 (upd.)
Unitog Co., 19
Valassis Communications, Inc., 37 (upd.)
ValueClick, Inc., 49
Vebego International BV, 49
Vedior NV, 35
W.B Doner & Co., 56
The Wackenhut Corporation, 14; 63 (upd.)
Waggener Edstrom, 42
Warrantech Corporation, 53
Wells Rich Greene BDDP, 6
Westaff Inc., 33
Whitman Education Group, Inc., 41
William Morris Agency, Inc., 23
Williams Scotsman, Inc., 65
Workflow Management, Inc., 65
WPP Group plc, 6; 48 (upd.)
Young & Rubicam, Inc., I; 22 (upd.); 66 (upd.)

AEROSPACE

A.S. Yakovlev Design Bureau, 15
Aerojet-General Corp., 63
Aeronca Inc., 46
The Aerospatiale Group, 7; 21 (upd.)
Alliant Techsystems Inc., 30 (upd.)
Antonov Design Bureau, 53
Aviacionny Nauchno-Tehnicheskii Komplex im. A.N. Tupoleva, 24
Avions Marcel Dassault-Breguet Aviation, I
B/E Aerospace, Inc., 30
Banner Aerospace, Inc., 14
Beech Aircraft Corporation, 8
Bell Helicopter Textron Inc., 46
The Boeing Company, I; 10 (upd.); 32 (upd.)
Bombardier Inc., 42 (upd.)
British Aerospace plc, I; 24 (upd.)
CAE USA Inc., 48
Canadair, Inc., 16
Cessna Aircraft Company, 8
Cirrus Design Corporation, 44
Cobham plc, 30
Daimler-Benz Aerospace AG, 16
DeCrane Aircraft Holdings Inc., 36
Ducommun Incorporated, 30
EADS SOCATA, 54
EGL, Inc., 59
Empresa Brasileira de Aeronáutica S.A. (Embraer), 36
European Aeronautic Defence and Space Company EADS N.V., 52 (upd.)
Fairchild Aircraft, Inc., 9
Fairchild Dornier GmbH, 48 (upd.)
First Aviation Services Inc., 49
G.I.E. Airbus Industrie, I; 12 (upd.)
General Dynamics Corporation, I; 10 (upd.); 40 (upd.)
GKN plc, 38 (upd.)
Goodrich Corporation, 46 (upd.)
Groupe Dassault Aviation SA, 26 (upd.)
Grumman Corporation, I; 11 (upd.)
Grupo Aeropuerto del Sureste, S.A. de C.V., 48
Gulfstream Aerospace Corporation, 7; 28 (upd.)
HEICO Corporation, 30
International Lease Finance Corporation, 48

N.V. Koninklijke Nederlandse Vliegtuigenfabriek Fokker, I; 28 (upd.)
Lancair International, Inc., 67
Learjet Inc., 8; 27 (upd.)
Lockheed Martin Corporation, I; 11 (upd.); 15 (upd.)
Loral Space & Communications Ltd., 54 (upd.)
Magellan Aerospace Corporation, 48
Martin Marietta Corporation, I
Martin-Baker Aircraft Company Limited, 61
McDonnell Douglas Corporation, I; 11 (upd.)
Meggitt PLC, 34
Messerschmitt-Bölkow-Blohm GmbH., I
Moog Inc., 13
Mooney Aerospace Group Ltd., 52
The New Piper Aircraft, Inc., 44
Northrop Grumman Corporation, I; 11 (upd.); 45 (upd.)
Orbital Sciences Corporation, 22
Pemco Aviation Group Inc., 54
Pratt & Whitney, 9
Raytheon Aircraft Holdings Inc., 46
Robinson Helicopter Company, 51
Rockwell International Corporation, I; 11 (upd.)
Rolls-Royce Allison, 29 (upd.)
Rolls-Royce plc, I; 7 (upd.); 21 (upd.)
Rostvertol plc, 62
Sequa Corp., 13
Shannon Aerospace Ltd., 36
Sikorsky Aircraft Corporation, 24
Smiths Industries PLC, 25
Snecma Group, 46
Société Air France, 27 (upd.)
Spacehab, Inc., 37
Spar Aerospace Limited, 32
Sukhoi Design Bureau Aviation Scientific-Industrial Complex, 24
Sundstrand Corporation, 7; 21 (upd.)
Teledyne Technologies Inc., 62 (upd.)
Textron Lycoming Turbine Engine, 9
Thales S.A., 42
Thiokol Corporation, 9; 22 (upd.)
United Technologies Corporation, I; 10 (upd.)
Van's Aircraft, Inc., 65
Vought Aircraft Industries, Inc., 49
Whittaker Corporation, 48 (upd.)
Woodward Governor Company, 49 (upd.)
Zodiac S.A., 36

AIRLINES

Aer Lingus Group plc, 34
Aeroflot—Russian International Airlines, 6; 29 (upd.)
Aerolíneas Argentinas S.A., 33
Air Canada, 6; 23 (upd.); 59 (upd.)
Air China, 46
Air Jamaica Limited, 54
Air Mauritius Ltd., 63
Air New Zealand Limited, 14; 38 (upd.)
Air Sahara Limited, 65
Air Wisconsin Airlines Corporation, 55
Air-India Limited, 6; 27 (upd.)
AirTran Holdings, Inc., 22
Alaska Air Group, Inc., 6; 29 (upd.)
Alitalia-Linee Aeree Italiana, S.p.A., 6; 29 (upd.)
All Nippon Airways Company Limited, 6; 38 (upd.)
Aloha Airlines, Incorporated, 24
America West Holdings Corporation, 6; 34 (upd.)
American Airlines, I; 6 (upd.)
AMR Corporation, 28 (upd.); 52 (upd.)

Amtran, Inc., 34
Arrow Air Holdings Corporation, 55
Asiana Airlines, Inc., 46
Atlantic Coast Airlines Holdings, Inc., 55
Atlantic Southeast Airlines, Inc., 47
Atlas Air, Inc., 39
Austrian Airlines AG (Österreichische
    Luftverkehrs AG), 33
Aviacionny Nauchno-Tehnicheskii
    Komplex im. A.N. Tupoleva, 24
Avianca Aerovías Nacionales de Colombia
    SA, 36
Bahamas Air Holdings Ltd., 66
Banner Aerospace, Inc., 37 (upd.)
Braathens ASA, 47
Bradley Air Services Ltd., 56
British Airways PLC, I; 14 (upd.); 43
    (upd.)
British Midland plc, 38
British World Airlines Ltd., 18
Cargolux Airlines International S.A., 49
Cathay Pacific Airways Limited, 6; 34
    (upd.)
Ceské aerolinie, a.s., 66
Chautauqua Airlines, Inc., 38
China Airlines, 34
China Eastern Airlines Co. Ltd., 31
China Southern Airlines Company Ltd., 33
Comair Holdings Inc., 13; 34 (upd.)
Continental Airlines, Inc., I; 21 (upd.); 52
    (upd.)
Corporación Internacional de Aviación,
    S.A. de C.V. (Cintra), 20
Delta Air Lines, Inc., I; 6 (upd.); 39 (upd.)
Deutsche Lufthansa Aktiengesellschaft, I;
    26 (upd.)
Eastern Airlines, I
easyJet Airline Company Limited, 39
EgyptAir, 6; 27 (upd.)
El Al Israel Airlines Ltd., 23
The Emirates Group, 39
EVA Airways Corporation, 51
Finnair Oyj, 6; 25 (upd.); 61 (upd.)
Flying Boat, Inc. (Chalk's Ocean Airways),
    56
Frontier Airlines, Inc., 22
Garuda Indonesia, 6
Groupe Air France, 6
Grupo TACA, 38
Gulf Air Company, 56
HAL Inc., 9
Hawaiian Airlines, Inc., 22 (upd.)
Hong Kong Dragon Airlines Ltd., 66
Iberia Líneas Aéreas de España S.A., 6; 36
    (upd.)
Icelandair, 52
Indian Airlines Ltd., 46
Japan Air Lines Company Ltd., I; 32 (upd.)
Jersey European Airways (UK) Ltd., 61
Jet Airways (India) Private Limited, 65
JetBlue Airways Corporation, 44
Kenmore Air Harbor Inc., 65
Kitty Hawk, Inc., 22
Kiwi International Airlines Inc., 20
Koninklijke Luchtvaart Maatschappij, N.V.
    (KLM Royal Dutch Airlines), I; 28 (upd.)
Korean Air Lines Co., Ltd., 6; 27 (upd.)
Lan Chile S.A., 31
Lauda Air Luftfahrt AG, 48
LOT Polish Airlines (Polskie Linie
    Lotnicze S.A.), 33
LTU Group Holding GmbH, 37
Malév Plc, 24
Malaysian Airlines System Berhad, 6; 29
    (upd.)
Mesa Air Group, Inc., 11; 32 (upd.)
Mesaba Holdings, Inc., 28

Midway Airlines Corporation, 33
Midwest Express Holdings, Inc., 35
Northwest Airlines Corporation, I; 6 (upd.);
    26 (upd.)
Offshore Logistics, Inc., 37
Pakistan International Airlines Corporation,
    46
Pan American World Airways, Inc., I; 12
    (upd.)
Panalpina World Transport (Holding) Ltd.,
    47
People Express Airlines, Inc., I
Petroleum Helicopters, Inc., 35
Philippine Airlines, Inc., 6; 23 (upd.)
Preussag AG, 42 (upd.)
Qantas Airways Limited, 6; 24 (upd.)
Reno Air Inc., 23
Royal Nepal Airline Corporation, 41
Ryanair Holdings plc, 35
SAA (Pty) Ltd., 28
Sabena S.A./N.V., 33
The SAS Group, 34 (upd.)
Saudi Arabian Airlines, 6; 27 (upd.)
Scandinavian Airlines System, I
Singapore Airlines Ltd., 6; 27 (upd.)
SkyWest, Inc., 25
Société d'Exploitation AOM Air Liberté
    SA (AirLib), 53
Société Luxembourgeoise de Navigation
    Aerienne S.A., 64
Société Tunisienne de l'Air-Tunisair, 49
Southwest Airlines Co., 6; 24 (upd.)
Spirit Airlines, Inc., 31
Sun Country Airlines, 30
Swiss Air Transport Company, Ltd., I
Swiss International Air Lines Ltd., 48
TAP—Air Portugal Transportes Aéreos
    Portugueses S.A., 46
TAROM S.A., 64
Texas Air Corporation, I
Thai Airways International Public
    Company Limited, 6; 27 (upd.)
Tower Air, Inc., 28
Trans World Airlines, Inc., I; 12 (upd.); 35
    (upd.)
TransBrasil S/A Linhas Aéreas, 31
Transportes Aereos Portugueses, S.A., 6
TV Guide, Inc., 43 (upd.)
UAL Corporation, 34 (upd.)
United Airlines, I; 6 (upd.)
US Airways Group, Inc., I; 6 (upd.); 28
    (upd.); 52 (upd.)
VARIG S.A. (Viação Aérea Rio-
    Grandense), 6; 29 (upd.)
WestJet Airlines Ltd., 38

AUTOMOTIVE

AB Volvo, I; 7 (upd.); 26 (upd.); 67 (upd.)
Adam Opel AG, 7; 21 (upd.); 61 (upd.)
Advance Auto Parts, Inc., 57
Aisin Seiki Co., Ltd., 48 (upd.)
Alfa Romeo, 13; 36 (upd.)
Alvis Plc, 47
America's Car-Mart, Inc., 64
American Motors Corporation, I
Applied Power Inc., 32 (upd.)
Arnold Clark Automobiles Ltd., 60
ArvinMeritor, Inc., 8; 54 (upd.)
Asbury Automotive Group Inc., 60
ASC, Inc., 55
Autocam Corporation, 51
Autoliv, Inc., 65
Automobiles Citroen, 7
Automobili Lamborghini Holding S.p.A.,
    13; 34 (upd.)
AutoNation, Inc., 50
AVTOVAZ Joint Stock Company, 65

Bajaj Auto Limited, 39
Bayerische Motoren Werke AG, I; 11
    (upd.); 38 (upd.)
Bendix Corporation, I
Blue Bird Corporation, 35
Bombardier Inc., 42 (upd.)
Borg-Warner Automotive, Inc., 14; 32
    (upd.)
The Budd Company, 8
CarMax, Inc., 55
CARQUEST Corporation, 29
Caterpillar Inc., 63 (upd.)
Chrysler Corporation, I; 11 (upd.)
CNH Global N.V., 38 (upd.)
Consorcio G Grupo Dina, S.A. de C.V., 36
CSK Auto Corporation, 38
Cummins Engine Company, Inc., I; 12
    (upd.); 40 (upd.)
Custom Chrome, Inc., 16
Daihatsu Motor Company, Ltd., 7; 21
    (upd.)
Daimler-Benz A.G., I; 15 (upd.)
DaimlerChrysler AG, 34 (upd.); 64 (upd.)
Dana Corporation, I; 10 (upd.)
Deere & Company, 42 (upd.)
Delphi Automotive Systems Corporation,
    45
Don Massey Cadillac, Inc., 37
Donaldson Company, Inc., 49 (upd.)
Douglas & Lomason Company, 16
Ducati Motor Holding S.p.A., 30
Eaton Corporation, I; 10 (upd.)
Echlin Inc., I; 11 (upd.)
Edelbrock Corporation, 37
Federal-Mogul Corporation, I; 10 (upd.);
    26 (upd.)
Ferrari S.p.A., 13; 36 (upd.)
Fiat SpA, I; 11 (upd.); 50 (upd.)
FinishMaster, Inc., 24
Ford Motor Company, I; 11 (upd.); 36
    (upd.); 64 (upd.)
Ford Motor Company, S.A. de C.V., 20
Fruehauf Corporation, I
General Motors Corporation, I; 10 (upd.);
    36 (upd.); 64 (upd.)
Gentex Corporation, 26
Genuine Parts Company, 9; 45 (upd.)
GKN plc, 38 (upd.)
Group 1 Automotive, Inc., 52
Harley-Davidson Inc., 7; 25 (upd.)
Hastings Manufacturing Company, 56
Hayes Lemmerz International, Inc., 27
The Hertz Corporation, 33 (upd.)
Hino Motors, Ltd., 7; 21 (upd.)
Holden Ltd., 62
Holley Performance Products Inc., 52
Hometown Auto Retailers, Inc., 44
Honda Motor Company Limited (Honda
    Giken Kogyo Kabushiki Kaisha), I; 10
    (upd.); 29 (upd.)
Hyundai Group, 56 (upd.)
Insurance Auto Auctions, Inc., 23
Isuzu Motors, Ltd., 9; 23 (upd.); 57 (upd.)
Kawasaki Heavy Industries, Ltd., 63 (upd.)
Kelsey-Hayes Group of Companies, 7; 27
    (upd.)
Key Safety Systems, Inc., 63
Kia Motors Corporation, 12; 29 (upd.)
Kwik-Fit Holdings plc, 54
Lear Seating Corporation, 16
Les Schwab Tire Centers, 50
Lithia Motors, Inc., 41
Lotus Cars Ltd., 14
Lund International Holdings, Inc., 40
Mack Trucks, Inc., I; 22 (upd.); 61 (upd.)
The Major Automotive Companies, Inc., 45
Masland Corporation, 17

AUTOMOTIVE (continued)

Mazda Motor Corporation, 9; 23 (upd.); 63 (upd.)

Mel Farr Automotive Group, 20

Metso Corporation, 30 (upd.)

Midas Inc., 10; 56 (upd.)

Mitsubishi Motors Corporation, 9; 23 (upd.); 57 (upd.)

Monaco Coach Corporation, 31

Monro Muffler Brake, Inc., 24

Montupet S.A., 63

National R.V. Holdings, Inc., 32

Navistar International Corporation, I; 10 (upd.)

Nissan Motor Co., Ltd., I; 11 (upd.); 34 (upd.)

O'Reilly Automotive, Inc., 26

Officine Alfieri Maserati S.p.A., 13

Oshkosh Truck Corporation, 7

Paccar Inc., I

PACCAR Inc., 26 (upd.)

Pennzoil-Quaker State Company, IV; 20 (upd.); 50 (upd.)

Penske Corporation, 19 (upd.)

The Pep Boys—Manny, Moe & Jack, 11; 36 (upd.)

Perusahaan Otomobil Nasional Bhd., 62

Peugeot S.A., I

Piaggio & C. S.p.A., 20

Porsche AG, 13; 31 (upd.)

PSA Peugeot Citroen S.A., 28 (upd.)

R&B, Inc., 51

Regie Nationale des Usines Renault, I

Renault Argentina S.A., 67

Renault S.A., 26 (upd.)

Republic Industries, Inc., 26

The Reynolds and Reynolds Company, 50

Robert Bosch GmbH., I; 16 (upd.); 43 (upd.)

RockShox, Inc., 26

Rockwell Automation, 43 (upd.)

Rolls-Royce plc, I; 21 (upd.)

Ron Tonkin Chevrolet Company, 55

Rover Group Ltd., 7; 21 (upd.)

Saab Automobile AB, 32 (upd.)

Saab-Scania A.B., I; 11 (upd.)

Safelite Glass Corp., 19

Safety Components International, Inc., 63

Saturn Corporation, 7; 21 (upd.)

Sealed Power Corporation, I

Sheller-Globe Corporation, I

Sixt AG, 39

Skoda Auto a.s., 39

Spartan Motors Inc., 14

SpeeDee Oil Change and Tune-Up, 25

SPX Corporation, 10; 47 (upd.)

Standard Motor Products, Inc., 40

Superior Industries International, Inc., 8

Suzuki Motor Corporation, 9; 23 (upd.); 59 (upd.)

Sytner Group plc, 45

Tower Automotive, Inc., 24

Toyota Motor Corporation, I; 11 (upd.); 38 (upd.)

Triumph Motorcycles Ltd., 53

TRW Inc., 14 (upd.)

Ugly Duckling Corporation, 22

United Auto Group, Inc., 26

United Technologies Automotive Inc., 15

Valeo, 23; 66 (upd.)

Volkswagen Aktiengesellschaft, I; 11 (upd.); 32 (upd.)

Walker Manufacturing Company, 19

Winnebago Industries Inc., 7; 27 (upd.)

Woodward Governor Company, 49 (upd.)

ZF Friedrichshafen AG, 48

Ziebart International Corporation, 30; 66 (upd.)

BEVERAGES

A & W Brands, Inc., 25

Adolph Coors Company, I; 13 (upd.); 36 (upd.)

AG Barr plc, 64

Allied Domecq PLC, 29

Allied-Lyons PLC, I

Anchor Brewing Company, 47

Anheuser-Busch Companies, Inc., I; 10 (upd.); 34 (upd.)

Asahi Breweries, Ltd., I; 20 (upd.); 52 (upd.)

Asia Pacific Breweries Limited, 59

August Schell Brewing Company Inc., 59

Bacardi Limited, 18

Baltika Brewery Joint Stock Company, 65

Banfi Products Corp., 36

Baron Philippe de Rothschild S.A., 39

Bass PLC, I; 15 (upd.); 38 (upd.)

BBAG Osterreichische Brau-Beteiligungs-AG, 38

Beringer Blass Wine Estates Ltd., 22; 66 (upd.)

The Boston Beer Company, Inc., 18; 50 (upd.)

Brauerei Beck & Co., 9; 33 (upd.)

Brown-Forman Corporation, I; 10 (upd.); 38 (upd.)

Budweiser Budvar, National Corporation, 59

Cadbury Schweppes PLC, 49 (upd.)

Canandaigua Brands, Inc., 34 (upd.)

Canandaigua Wine Company, Inc., 13

Cantine Giorgio Lungarotti S.R.L., 67

Carlsberg A/S, 9; 29 (upd.)

Carlton and United Breweries Ltd., I

Casa Cuervo, S.A. de C.V., 31

Cerveceria Polar, I

The Chalone Wine Group, Ltd., 36

Clearly Canadian Beverage Corporation, 48

Coca Cola Bottling Co. Consolidated, 10

The Coca-Cola Company, I; 10 (upd.); 32 (upd.); 67 (upd.)

Companhia de Bebidas das Américas, 57

Corby Distilleries Limited, 14

Cott Corporation, 52

D.G. Yuengling & Son, Inc., 38

Davide Campari-Milano S.p.A., 57

Dean Foods Company, 21 (upd.)

Delicato Vineyards, Inc., 50

Deschutes Brewery, Inc., 57

Distillers Company PLC, I

Dr Pepper/Seven Up, Inc., 9; 32 (upd.)

E. & J. Gallo Winery, I; 7 (upd.); 28 (upd.)

Eckes AG, 56

Empresas Polar SA, 55 (upd.)

Faygo Beverages Inc., 55

Ferolito, Vultaggio & Sons, 27

Florida's Natural Growers, 45

Foster's Group Limited, 7; 21 (upd.); 50 (upd.)

Fuller Smith & Turner P.L.C., 38

G. Heileman Brewing Company Inc., I

The Gambrinus Company, 40

Geerlings & Wade, Inc., 45

General Cinema Corporation, I

Golden State Vintners, Inc., 33

Grand Metropolitan PLC, I

Green Mountain Coffee, Inc., 31

The Greenalls Group PLC, 21

Greene King plc, 31

Grupo Modelo, S.A. de C.V., 29

Guinness/UDV, I; 43 (upd.)

The Hain Celestial Group, Inc., 43 (upd.)

Hansen Natural Corporation, 31

Heineken N.V, I; 13 (upd.); 34 (upd.)

Heublein, Inc., I

Hiram Walker Resources, Ltd., I

illycaffè SpA, 50

Imagine Foods, Inc., 50

Interbrew S.A., 17; 50 (upd.)

Jacob Leinenkugel Brewing Company, 28

JD Wetherspoon plc, 30

Jim Beam Brands Worldwide, Inc., 58 (upd.)

Karlsberg Brauerei GmbH & Co KG, 41

Kendall-Jackson Winery, Ltd., 28

Kikkoman Corporation, 14

Kirin Brewery Company, Limited, I; 21 (upd.); 63 (upd.)

König Brauerei GmbH & Co. KG, 35 (upd.)

Labatt Brewing Company Limited, I; 25 (upd.)

Latrobe Brewing Company, 54

Laurent-Perrier SA, 42

Lion Nathan Limited, 54

The Macallan Distillers Ltd., 63

Madeira Wine Company, S.A., 49

Maison Louis Jadot, 24

Marchesi Antinori SRL, 42

Marie Brizard & Roger International S.A., 22

Martini & Rossi SpA, 63

MBC Holding Company, 40

Mendocino Brewing Company, Inc., 60

Miller Brewing Company, I; 12 (upd.)

The Minute Maid Company, 28

Mitchells & Butlers PLC, 59

Moët-Hennessy, I

The Molson Companies Limited, I, 26 (upd.)

Montana Coffee Traders, Inc., 60

Mott's Inc., 57

National Beverage Corp., 26

National Grape Cooperative Association, Inc., 20

National Wine & Spirits, Inc., 49

Nichols plc, 44

Ocean Spray Cranberries, Inc., 25 (upd.)

Odwalla, Inc., 31

Oregon Chai, Inc., 49

Panamerican Beverages, Inc., 47

Parmalat Finanziaria SpA, 50

Paulaner Brauerei GmbH & Co. KG, 35

Peet's Coffee & Tea, Inc., 38

Penaflor S.A., 66

The Pepsi Bottling Group, Inc., 40

PepsiAmericas, Inc., 67 (upd.)

PepsiCo, Inc., I; 10 (upd.); 38 (upd.)

Pernod Ricard S.A., I; 21 (upd.)

Pete's Brewing Company, 22

Philip Morris Companies Inc., 18 (upd.)

Pyramid Breweries Inc., 33

Quilmes Industrial (QUINSA) S.A., 67

R.C. Bigelow, Inc., 49

Rainier Brewing Company, 23

Red Bull GmbH, 60

Redhook Ale Brewery, Inc., 31

Rémy Cointreau S.A., 20

Robert Mondavi Corporation, 15; 50 (upd.)

Royal Crown Company, Inc., 23

Royal Grolsch NV, 54

SABMiller plc, 59 (upd.)

San Miguel Corporation, 57 (upd.)

Sapporo Breweries Limited, I; 13 (upd.); 36 (upd.)

Scheid Vineyards Inc., 66

Schieffelin & Somerset Co., 61

Scottish & Newcastle plc, 15; 35 (upd.)

The Seagram Company Ltd., I; 25 (upd.)

Sebastiani Vineyards, Inc., 28
Shepherd Neame Limited, 30
Skalli Group, 67
Snapple Beverage Corporation, 11
The South African Breweries Limited, I;
    24 (upd.)
Southcorp Limited, 54
Starbucks Corporation, 13; 34 (upd.)
The Stash Tea Company, 50
Stewart's Beverages, 39
The Stroh Brewery Company, I; 18 (upd.)
Suntory Ltd., 65
Sutter Home Winery Inc., 16
Taittinger S.A., 43
Takara Holdings Inc., 62
The Terlato Wine Group, 48
Todhunter International, Inc., 27
Triarc Companies, Inc., 34 (upd.)
Tsingtao Brewery Group, 49
Tully's Coffee Corporation, 51
Van Houtte Inc., 39
Vermont Pure Holdings, Ltd., 51
Vin & Spirit AB, 31
Viña Concha y Toro S.A., 45
Vincor International Inc., 50
Whitbread and Company PLC, I
William Grant & Sons Ltd., 60
The Wine Group, Inc., 39
The Wolverhampton & Dudley Breweries,
    PLC, 57
Young & Co.'s Brewery, P.L.C., 38

BIOTECHNOLOGY

Amersham PLC, 50
Amgen, Inc., 10; 30 (upd.)
Biogen Inc., 14; 36 (upd.)
Cambrex Corporation, 44 (upd.)
Centocor Inc., 14
Charles River Laboratories International,
    Inc., 42
Chiron Corporation, 10; 36 (upd.)
Covance Inc., 30
CryoLife, Inc., 46
Delta and Pine Land Company, 33
Dionex Corporation, 46
Enzo Biochem, Inc., 41
Genentech, Inc., 32 (upd.)
Genzyme Corporation, 38 (upd.)
Gilead Sciences, Inc., 54
Howard Hughes Medical Institute, 39
Huntingdon Life Sciences Group plc, 42
IDEXX Laboratories, Inc., 23
ImClone Systems Inc., 58
Immunex Corporation, 14; 50 (upd.)
IMPATH Inc., 45
Incyte Genomics, Inc., 52
Inverness Medical Innovations, Inc., 63
Invitrogen Corporation, 52
The Judge Group, Inc., 51
Life Technologies, Inc., 17
Martek Biosciences Corporation, 65
Medtronic, Inc., 30 (upd.)
Millipore Corporation, 25
Minntech Corporation, 22
Mycogen Corporation, 21
New Brunswick Scientific Co., Inc., 45
Qiagen N.V., 39
Quintiles Transnational Corporation, 21
Seminis, Inc., 29
Serologicals Corporation, 63
Sigma-Aldrich Corporation, 36 (upd.)
Starkey Laboratories, Inc., 52
STERIS Corporation, 29
TECHNE Corporation, 52
Waters Corporation, 43
Whatman plc, 46

Wisconsin Alumni Research Foundation,
    65
Wyeth, 50 (upd.)

CHEMICALS

A. Schulman, Inc., 8
Aceto Corp., 38
Air Products and Chemicals, Inc., I; 10
    (upd.)
Airgas, Inc., 54
Akzo Nobel N.V., 13
Albemarle Corporation, 59
AlliedSignal Inc., 22 (upd.)
American Cyanamid, I; 8 (upd.)
American Vanguard Corporation, 47
ARCO Chemical Company, 10
Asahi Denka Kogyo KK, 64
Atanor S.A., 62
Atochem S.A., I
Avecia Group PLC, 63
Baker Hughes Incorporated, 22 (upd.); 57
    (upd.)
Balchem Corporation, 42
BASF Aktiengesellschaft, I; 18 (upd.); 50
    (upd.)
Bayer A.G., I; 13 (upd.); 41 (upd.)
Betz Laboratories, Inc., I; 10 (upd.)
The BFGoodrich Company, 19 (upd.)
BOC Group plc, I; 25 (upd.)
Brenntag AG, 8; 23 (upd.)
Burmah Castrol PLC, 30 (upd.)
Cabot Corporation, 8; 29 (upd.)
Cambrex Corporation, 16
Catalytica Energy Systems, Inc., 44
Celanese Corporation, I
Celanese Mexicana, S.A. de C.V., 54
Chemcentral Corporation, 8
Chemi-Trol Chemical Co., 16
Church & Dwight Co., Inc., 29
Ciba-Geigy Ltd., I; 8 (upd.)
The Clorox Company, 22 (upd.)
Croda International Plc, 45
Crompton Corporation, 9; 36 (upd.)
Cytec Industries Inc., 27
Degussa-Hüls AG, 32 (upd.)
DeKalb Genetics Corporation, 17
The Dexter Corporation, I; 12 (upd.)
Dionex Corporation, 46
The Dow Chemical Company, I; 8 (upd.);
    50 (upd.)
DSM N.V., I; 56 (upd.)
Dynaction S.A., 67
E.I. du Pont de Nemours & Company, I; 8
    (upd.); 26 (upd.)
Eastman Chemical Company, 14; 38 (upd.)
Ecolab Inc., I; 13 (upd.); 34 (upd.)
Elementis plc, 40 (upd.)
English China Clays Ltd., 15 (upd.); 40
    (upd.)
ERLY Industries Inc., 17
Ethyl Corporation, I; 10 (upd.)
Ferro Corporation, 8; 56 (upd.)
Firmenich International S.A., 60
First Mississippi Corporation, 8
Formosa Plastics Corporation, 14; 58
    (upd.)
Fort James Corporation, 22 (upd.)
G.A.F., I
The General Chemical Group Inc., 37
Georgia Gulf Corporation, 9; 61 (upd.)
Givaudan SA, 43
Great Lakes Chemical Corporation, I; 14
    (upd.)
Guerbet Group, 46
H.B. Fuller Company, 32 (upd.)
Hauser, Inc., 46
Hawkins Chemical, Inc., 16

Henkel KGaA, 34 (upd.)
Hercules Inc., I; 22 (upd.); 66 (upd.)
Hoechst A.G., I; 18 (upd.)
Hoechst Celanese Corporation, 13
Huls A.G., I
Huntsman Chemical Corporation, 8
IMC Fertilizer Group, Inc., 8
Imperial Chemical Industries PLC, I; 50
    (upd.)
International Flavors & Fragrances Inc., 9;
    38 (upd.)
Israel Chemicals Ltd., 55
Koppers Industries, Inc., I; 26 (upd.)
L'Air Liquide SA, I; 47 (upd.)
Lawter International Inc., 14
LeaRonal, Inc., 23
Loctite Corporation, 30 (upd.)
Lubrizol Corporation, I; 30 (upd.)
Lyondell Chemical Company, 45 (upd.)
M.A. Hanna Company, 8
MacDermid Incorporated, 32
Mallinckrodt Group Inc., 19
MBC Holding Company, 40
Melamine Chemicals, Inc., 27
Methanex Corporation, 40
Minerals Technologies Inc., 52 (upd.)
Mississippi Chemical Corporation, 39
Mitsubishi Chemical Corporation, I; 56
    (upd.)
Mitsui Petrochemical Industries, Ltd., 9
Monsanto Company, I; 9 (upd.); 29 (upd.)
Montedison SpA, I
Morton International Inc., 9 (upd.)
Morton Thiokol, Inc., I
Nagase & Company, Ltd., 8
Nalco Chemical Corporation, I; 12 (upd.)
National Distillers and Chemical
    Corporation, I
National Sanitary Supply Co., 16
National Starch and Chemical Company,
    49
NCH Corporation, 8
Nisshin Seifun Group Inc., 66 (upd.)
NL Industries, Inc., 10
Nobel Industries AB, 9
Norsk Hydro ASA, 35 (upd.)
Novacor Chemicals Ltd., 12
NutraSweet Company, 8
Olin Corporation, I; 13 (upd.)
OM Group, Inc., 17
OMNOVA Solutions Inc., 59
Penford Corporation, 55
Pennwalt Corporation, I
Perstorp AB, I; 51 (upd.)
Petrolite Corporation, 15
Pioneer Hi-Bred International, Inc., 41
    (upd.)
Praxair, Inc., 11
Quantum Chemical Corporation, 8
Reichhold Chemicals, Inc., 10
Rhodia SA, 38
Rhône-Poulenc S.A., I; 10 (upd.)
Robertet SA, 39
Rohm and Haas Company, I; 26 (upd.)
Roussel Uclaf, I; 8 (upd.)
RPM, Inc., 36 (upd.)
RWE AG, 50 (upd.)
The Scotts Company, 22
SCP Pool Corporation, 39
Sequa Corp., 13
Shanghai Petrochemical Co., Ltd., 18
Sigma-Aldrich Corporation, 36 (upd.)
Solutia Inc., 52
Solvay S.A., I; 21 (upd.); 61 (upd.)
Stepan Company, 30
Sterling Chemicals, Inc., 16
Sumitomo Chemical Company Ltd., I

CHEMICALS (continued)

Takeda Chemical Industries, Ltd., 46 (upd.)
Terra Industries, Inc., 13
Teva Pharmaceutical Industries Ltd., 22
Total Fina Elf S.A., 24 (upd.); 50 (upd.)
Ube Industries, Ltd., 38 (upd.)
Union Carbide Corporation, I; 9 (upd.)
Univar Corporation, 9
The Valspar Corporation, 32 (upd.)
Vista Chemical Company, I
Witco Corporation, I; 16 (upd.)
Yule Catto & Company plc, 54
Zeneca Group PLC, 21

CONGLOMERATES

A.P. Møller - Maersk A/S, 57
Accor SA, 10; 27 (upd.)
AEG A.G., I
Alcatel Alsthom Compagnie Générale
d'Electricité, 9
Alco Standard Corporation, I
Alexander & Baldwin, Inc., 40 (upd.)
Alfa, S.A. de C.V., 19
Alleghany Corporation, 60 (upd.)
Allied Domecq PLC, 29
Allied-Signal Inc., I
AMFAC Inc., I
The Anschutz Corporation, 36 (upd.)
Antofagasta plc, 65
APi Group, Inc., 64
Aramark Corporation, 13
ARAMARK Corporation, 41
Archer-Daniels-Midland Company, I; 11
(upd.)
Arkansas Best Corporation, 16
Associated British Ports Holdings Plc, 45
BAA plc, 33 (upd.)
Barlow Rand Ltd., I
Barratt Developments plc, 56 (upd.)
Bat Industries PLC, I
Berjaya Group Bhd., 67
Berkshire Hathaway Inc., 42 (upd.)
Bond Corporation Holdings Limited, 10
Brascan Corporation, 67
BTR PLC, I
Bunzl plc, 31 (upd.)
Burlington Northern Santa Fe Corporation,
27 (upd.)
Business Post Group plc, 46
C. Itoh & Company Ltd., I
C.I. Traders Limited, 61
Cargill, Incorporated, 13 (upd.); 40 (upd.)
CBI Industries, Inc., 7
Charoen Pokphand Group, 62
Chemed Corporation, 13
Chesebrough-Pond's USA, Inc., 8
China Merchants International Holdings
Co., Ltd., 52
Cisneros Group of Companies, 54
CITIC Pacific Ltd., 18
CJ Corporation, 62
Colt Industries Inc., I
Compagnie Financiere Richemont AG, 50
The Connell Company, 29
Cox Enterprises, Inc., 67 (upd.)
Cristalerias de Chile S.A., 67
CSR Limited, 28 (upd.)
Daewoo Group, 18 (upd.); 57 (upd.)
De Dietrich & Cie., 31
Deere & Company, 21 (upd.)
Delaware North Companies Incorporated, 7
Desc, S.A. de C.V., 23
The Dial Corp., 8
Dr. August Oetker KG, 51
EBSCO Industries, Inc., 40 (upd.)
El Corte Inglés Group, 26 (upd.)
Elders IXL Ltd., I

Engelhard Corporation, 21 (upd.)
Farley Northwest Industries, Inc., I
Fimalac S.A., 37
First Pacific Company Limited, 18
Fisher Companies, Inc., 15
Fletcher Challenge Ltd., 19 (upd.)
Florida East Coast Industries, Inc., 59
FMC Corporation, I; 11 (upd.)
Fortune Brands, Inc., 29 (upd.)
Fraser & Neave Ltd., 54
Fuqua Industries, Inc., I
General Electric Company, 34 (upd.); 63
(upd.)
Genting Bhd., 65
GIB Group, 26 (upd.)
Gillett Holdings, Inc., 7
Granaria Holdings B.V., 66
Grand Metropolitan PLC, 14 (upd.)
Great American Management and
Investment, Inc., 8
Greyhound Corporation, I
Groupe Bolloré, 67
Groupe Louis Dreyfus S.A., 60
Grupo Carso, S.A. de C.V., 21
Grupo Clarín S.A., 67
Grupo Industrial Bimbo, 19
Grupo Industrial Saltillo, S.A. de C.V., 54
Gulf & Western Inc., I
Haci Omer Sabanci Holdings A.S., 55
Hagemeyer N.V., 39
Hankyu Corporation, 23 (upd.)
Hanson PLC, III; 7 (upd.)
Hanwha Group, 62
Hawk Corporation, 59
Hitachi Zosen Corporation, 53 (upd.)
Hitachi, Ltd., I; 12 (upd.); 40 (upd.)
Ho-Chunk Inc., 61
Hutchison Whampoa Limited, 18; 49
(upd.)
Hyundai Group, 56 (upd.)
IC Industries, Inc., I
Ilitch Holdings Inc., 37
Inchcape PLC, 16 (upd.); 50 (upd.)
Industria de Diseño Textil S.A. (Inditex),
64
Industrie Zignago Santa Margherita S.p.A.,
67
Ingram Industries, Inc., 11; 49 (upd.)
Instituto Nacional de Industria, I
International Controls Corporation, 10
International Telephone & Telegraph
Corporation, I; 11 (upd.)
Investor AB, 63
Istituto per la Ricostruzione Industriale, I
ITOCHU Corporation, 32 (upd.)
J.R. Simplot Company, 60 (upd.)
Jardine Matheson Holdings Limited, I; 20
(upd.)
Jason Incorporated, 23
Jefferson Smurfit Group plc, 19 (upd.)
The Jim Pattison Group, 37
Jordan Industries, Inc., 36
Justin Industries, Inc., 19
Kanematsu Corporation, 24 (upd.)
Kao Corporation, 20 (upd.)
Katy Industries, Inc., I
Kesko Ltd. (Kesko Oy), 8; 27 (upd.)
Kidde plc, I; 44 (upd.)
King Ranch, Inc., 60 (upd.)
Knowledge Universe, Inc., 54
Koç Holding A.S., I; 54 (upd.)
Koninklijke Nedlloyd N.V., 26 (upd.)
Koor Industries Ltd., 25 (upd.)
Körber AG, 60
K2 Inc., 16
The L.L. Knickerbocker Co., Inc., 25
Lancaster Colony Corporation, 8; 61 (upd.)

Larry H. Miller Group, 29
Lear Siegler, Inc., I
Lefrak Organization Inc., 26
Leucadia National Corporation, 11
Linde AG, 67 (upd.)
Litton Industries, Inc., I; 11 (upd.)
Loews Corporation, I; 12 (upd.); 36 (upd.)
Loral Corporation, 8
LTV Corporation, I
LVMH Moët Hennessy Louis Vuitton SA,
33 (upd.)
Marubeni Corporation, I; 24 (upd.)
MAXXAM Inc., 8
McKesson Corporation, I
McPherson's Ltd., 66
Melitta Unternehmensgruppe Bentz KG, 53
Menasha Corporation, 8
Metallgesellschaft AG, 16 (upd.)
Metromedia Company, 7; 61 (upd.)
Minnesota Mining & Manufacturing
Company (3M), I; 8 (upd.); 26 (upd.)
Mitsubishi Corporation, I; 12 (upd.)
Mitsubishi Heavy Industries, Ltd., 40
(upd.)
Mitsui & Co., Ltd., I; 28 (upd.)
The Molson Companies Limited, I; 26
(upd.)
Montedison S.p.A., 24 (upd.)
NACCO Industries, Inc., 7
Nagase & Co., Ltd., 61 (upd.)
National Service Industries, Inc., 11; 54
(upd.)
New World Development Company
Limited, 38 (upd.)
Nichimen Corporation, 24 (upd.)
Nissho Iwai K.K., I
Norsk Hydro A.S., 10
Novar plc, 49 (upd.)
Ogden Corporation, I
Onex Corporation, 16; 65 (upd.)
Orkla A/S, 18
Park-Ohio Industries Inc., 17
Pentair, Inc., 7
Philip Morris Companies Inc., 44 (upd.)
Poliet S.A., 33
Powell Duffryn plc, 31
Power Corporation of Canada, 36 (upd.)
PPB Group Berhad, 57
Preussag AG, 17
The Procter & Gamble Company, 67 (upd.)
PT Astra International Tbk, 56
Pubco Corporation, 17
Pulsar Internacional S.A., 21
R.B. Pamplin Corp., 45
The Rank Organisation Plc, 14 (upd.)
Red Apple Group, Inc., 23
Roll International Corporation, 37
Rubbermaid Incorporated, 20 (upd.)
Samsung Group, I
San Miguel Corporation, 15
Sara Lee Corporation, 15 (upd.); 54 (upd.)
Schindler Holding AG, 29
Sea Containers Ltd., 29
Seaboard Corporation, 36
Sealaska Corporation, 60
Sequa Corporation, 54 (upd.)
ServiceMaster Inc., 23 (upd.)
SHV Holdings N.V., 55
Sideco Americana S.A., 67
Sime Darby Berhad, 14; 36 (upd.)
Société du Louvre, 27
Standex International Corporation, 17; 44
(upd.)
Stinnes AG, 23 (upd.)
Sudbury Inc., 16
Sumitomo Corporation, I; 11 (upd.)

Swire Pacific Limited, I; 16 (upd.); 57 (upd.)
Talley Industries, Inc., 16
Tandycrafts, Inc., 31
TaurusHolding GmbH & Co. KG, 46
Teijin Limited, 61 (upd.)
Teledyne, Inc., I; 10 (upd.)
Tenneco Inc., I; 10 (upd.)
Textron Inc., I; 34 (upd.)
Thomas H. Lee Co., 24
Thorn Emi PLC, I
Thorn plc, 24
TI Group plc, 17
Time Warner Inc., IV; 7 (upd.)
Tokyu Corporation, 47 (upd.)
Tomen Corporation, 24 (upd.)
Tomkins plc, 11; 44 (upd.)
Toshiba Corporation, I; 12 (upd.); 40 (upd.)
Tractebel S.A., 20
Transamerica–An AEGON Company, I; 13 (upd.); 41 (upd.)
The Tranzonic Cos., 15
Triarc Companies, Inc., 8
Triple Five Group Ltd., 49
TRW Inc., I; 11 (upd.)
Tyco International Ltd., 63 (upd.)
Unilever, II; 7 (upd.); 32 (upd.)
Unión Fenosa, S.A., 51
United Technologies Corporation, 34 (upd.)
Universal Studios, Inc., 33
Valhi, Inc., 19
Valores Industriales S.A., 19
Veba A.G., I; 15 (upd.)
Vendôme Luxury Group plc, 27
Viacom Inc., 23 (upd.); 67 (upd.)
Virgin Group, 12; 32 (upd.)
W.R. Grace & Company, I; 50
The Washington Companies, 33
Watsco Inc., 52
Wheaton Industries, 8
Whitbread PLC, 20 (upd.)
Whitman Corporation, 10 (upd.)
Whittaker Corporation, I
WorldCorp, Inc., 10
Worms et Cie, 27
Yamaha Corporation, 40 (upd.)

CONSTRUCTION

A. Johnson & Company H.B., I
ABC Supply Co., Inc., 22
Abertis Infraestructuras, S.A., 65
Abrams Industries Inc., 23
Aegek S.A., 64
Amec Spie S.A., 57
AMREP Corporation, 21
Anthony & Sylvan Pools Corporation, 56
Asplundh Tree Expert Co., 59 (upd.)
ASV, Inc., 34; 66 (upd.)
The Austin Company, 8
Autoroutes du Sud de la France SA, 55
Balfour Beatty plc, 36 (upd.)
Baratt Developments PLC, I
Barton Malow Company, 51
Bauerly Companies, 61
Beazer Homes USA, Inc., 17
Bechtel Group, Inc., I; 24 (upd.)
Bellway Plc, 45
BFC Construction Corporation, 25
Bilfinger & Berger AG, I; 55 (upd.)
Bird Corporation, 19
Black & Veatch LLP, 22
Boral Limited, 43 (upd.)
Bouygues S.A., I; 24 (upd.)
BRISA Auto-estradas de Portugal S.A., 64
Brown & Root, Inc., 13
Bufete Industrial, S.A. de C.V., 34

Building Materials Holding Corporation, 52
Bulley & Andrews, LLC, 55
CalMat Co., 19
Cavco Industries, Inc., 65
Centex Corporation, 8; 29 (upd.)
Chugach Alaska Corporation, 60
Cianbro Corporation, 14
The Clark Construction Group, Inc., 8
Colas S.A., 31
D.R. Horton, Inc., 58
Day & Zimmermann, Inc., 31 (upd.)
Dick Corporation, 64
Dillingham Construction Corporation, I; 44 (upd.)
Dominion Homes, Inc., 19
The Drees Company, Inc., 41
Dycom Industries, Inc., 57
Edw. C. Levy Co., 42
Eiffage, 27
Ellerbe Becket, 41
EMCOR Group Inc., 60
Empresas ICA Sociedad Controladora, S.A. de C.V., 41
Encompass Services Corporation, 33
Engle Homes, Inc., 46
Environmental Industries, Inc., 31
Eurotunnel PLC, 13
Fairclough Construction Group PLC, I
Fleetwood Enterprises, Inc., 22 (upd.)
Fluor Corporation, I; 8 (upd.); 34 (upd.)
Forest City Enterprises, Inc., 52 (upd.)
Fred Weber, Inc., 61
George Wimpey plc, 12; 51 (upd.)
Gilbane, Inc., 34
Granite Construction Incorporated, 61
Granite Rock Company, 26
Grupo Dragados SA, 55
Grupo Ferrovial, S.A., 40
H.J. Russell & Company, 66
Habitat for Humanity International, 36
Heery International, Inc., 58
Heijmans N.V., 66
Hillsdown Holdings plc, 24 (upd.)
Hochtief AG, 33
Horton Homes, Inc., 25
Hospitality Worldwide Services, Inc., 26
Hovnanian Enterprises, Inc., 29
J.A. Jones, Inc., 16
J.F. Shea Co., Inc., 55
J.H. Findorff and Son, Inc., 60
Jarvis plc, 39
JLG Industries, Inc., 52
John Brown PLC, I
John Laing plc, I; 51 (upd.)
John W. Danforth Company, 48
Kajima Corporation, I; 51 (upd.)
Kaufman and Broad Home Corporation, 8
KB Home, 45 (upd.)
Kellogg Brown & Root, Inc., 62 (upd.)
Kitchell Corporation, 14
The Koll Company, 8
Komatsu Ltd., 16 (upd.)
Kraus-Anderson, Incorporated, 36
Kumagai Gumi Company, Ltd., I
L'Entreprise Jean Lefebvre, 23
Ledcor Industries Limited, 46
Lennar Corporation, 11
Lincoln Property Company, 8
Lindal Cedar Homes, Inc., 29
Linde A.G., I
MasTec, Inc., 55
Matrix Service Company, 65
McCarthy Building Companies, Inc., 48
Mellon-Stuart Company, I
Michael Baker Corp., 14
Morrison Knudsen Corporation, 7; 28 (upd.)

New Holland N.V., 22
Newpark Resources, Inc., 63
NVR L.P., 8
Ohbayashi Corporation, I
Opus Group, 34
Orleans Homebuilders, Inc., 62
The Parsons Corporation, 56 (upd.)
PCL Construction Group Inc., 50
The Peninsular & Oriental Steam Navigation Company (Bovis Division), I
Perini Corporation, 8
Peter Kiewit Sons' Inc., 8
Philipp Holzmann AG, 17
Post Properties, Inc., 26
Pulte Homes, Inc., 8; 42 (upd.)
Pyramid Companies, 54
Redrow Group plc, 31
Rinker Group Ltd., 65
RMC Group p.l.c., 34 (upd.)
Rooney Brothers Co., 25
The Rottlund Company, Inc., 28
The Ryland Group, Inc., 8; 37 (upd.)
Sandvik AB, 32 (upd.)
Schuff Steel Company, 26
Seddon Group Ltd., 67
Shorewood Packaging Corporation, 28
Simon Property Group, Inc., 27
Skanska AB, 38
Standard Pacific Corporation, 52
Stone & Webster, Inc., 64 (upd.)
Sundt Corp., 24
Swinerton Inc., 43
Taylor Woodrow plc, I; 38 (upd.)
Thyssen Krupp AG, 28 (upd.)
Toll Brothers Inc., 15
Trammell Crow Company, 8
Tridel Enterprises Inc., 9
Turner Construction Company, 66
The Turner Corporation, 8; 23 (upd.)
U.S. Aggregates, Inc., 42
U.S. Home Corporation, 8
VA TECH ELIN EBG GmbH, 49
Veit Companies, 43
Walbridge Aldinger Co., 38
Walter Industries, Inc., 22 (upd.)
The Weitz Company, Inc., 42
Willbros Group, Inc., 56
William Lyon Homes, 59
Wilson Bowden Plc, 45
Wood Hall Trust PLC, I
The Yates Companies, Inc., 62

CONTAINERS

Ball Corporation, I; 10 (upd.)
BWAY Corporation, 24
Clarcor Inc., 17
Continental Can Co., Inc., 15
Continental Group Company, I
Crown Cork & Seal Company, Inc., I; 13 (upd.); 32 (upd.)
Gaylord Container Corporation, 8
Golden Belt Manufacturing Co., 16
Greif Inc., 15; 66 (upd.)
Grupo Industrial Durango, S.A. de C.V., 37
Hanjin Shipping Co., Ltd., 50
Inland Container Corporation, 8
Kerr Group Inc., 24
Keyes Fibre Company, 9
Libbey Inc., 49
Liqui-Box Corporation, 16
The Longaberger Company, 12
Longview Fibre Company, 8
The Mead Corporation, 19 (upd.)
Metal Box PLC, I
Molins plc, 51
National Can Corporation, I

CONTAINERS (continued)

Owens-Illinois, Inc., I; 26 (upd.)
Packaging Corporation of America, 51
  (upd.)
Primerica Corporation, I
PVC Container Corporation, 67
Reynolds Metals Company, 19 (upd.)
Royal Packaging Industries Van Leer N.V.,
  30
Sealright Co., Inc., 17
Shurgard Storage Centers, Inc., 52
Smurfit-Stone Container Corporation, 26
  (upd.)
Sonoco Products Company, 8
Thermos Company, 16
Toyo Seikan Kaisha, Ltd., I
U.S. Can Corporation, 30
Ultra Pac, Inc., 24
Viatech Continental Can Company, Inc., 25
  (upd.)
Vidrala S.A., 67
Vitro Corporativo S.A. de C.V., 34

DRUGS/PHARMACEUTICALS

A.L. Pharma Inc., 12
Abbott Laboratories, I; 11 (upd.); 40 (upd.)
Akorn, Inc., 32
Alpharma Inc., 35 (upd.)
ALZA Corporation, 10; 36 (upd.)
American Home Products, I; 10 (upd.)
AmerisourceBergen Corporation, 64 (upd.)
Amersham PLC, 50
Amgen, Inc., 10
Amylin Pharmaceuticals, Inc., 67
Andrx Corporation, 55
Astra AB, I; 20 (upd.)
AstraZeneca PLC, 50 (upd.)
Barr Laboratories, Inc., 26
Bayer A.G., I; 13 (upd.)
Berlex Laboratories, Inc., 66
Biovail Corporation, 47
Block Drug Company, Inc., 8
Bristol-Myers Squibb Company, III; 9
  (upd.); 37 (upd.)
C.H. Boehringer Sohn, 39
Caremark Rx, Inc., 10; 54 (upd.)
Carter-Wallace, Inc., 8; 38 (upd.)
Celgene Corporation, 67
Cephalon, Inc., 45
Chiron Corporation, 10
Chugai Pharmaceutical Co., Ltd., 50
Ciba-Geigy Ltd., I; 8 (upd.)
D&K Wholesale Drug, Inc., 14
Discovery Partners International, Inc., 58
Dr. Reddy's Laboratories Ltd., 59
Elan Corporation PLC, 63
Eli Lilly and Company, I; 11 (upd.); 47
  (upd.)
Eon Labs, Inc., 67
Express Scripts Inc., 44 (upd.)
F. Hoffmann-La Roche Ltd., I; 50 (upd.)
Fisons plc, 9; 23 (upd.)
Forest Laboratories, Inc., 52 (upd.)
FoxMeyer Health Corporation, 16
Fujisawa Pharmaceutical Company Ltd., I
G.D. Searle & Co., I; 12 (upd.); 34 (upd.)
GEHE AG, 27
Genentech, Inc., I; 8 (upd.)
Genetics Institute, Inc., 8
Genzyme Corporation, 13
Glaxo Holdings PLC, I; 9 (upd.)
GlaxoSmithKline plc, 46 (upd.)
Groupe Fournier SA, 44
H. Lundbeck A/S, 44
Hauser, Inc., 46
Heska Corporation, 39
Huntingdon Life Sciences Group plc, 42

ICN Pharmaceuticals, Inc., 52
IVAX Corporation, 55 (upd.)
Johnson & Johnson, III; 8 (upd.)
Jones Medical Industries, Inc., 24
The Judge Group, Inc., 51
King Pharmaceuticals, Inc., 54
Kos Pharmaceuticals, Inc., 63
Kyowa Hakko Kogyo Co., Ltd., 48 (upd.)
Leiner Health Products Inc., 34
Ligand Pharmaceuticals Incorporated, 47
Marion Merrell Dow, Inc., I; 9 (upd.)
McKesson Corporation, 12; 47 (upd.)
Medicis Pharmaceutical Corporation, 59
MedImmune, Inc., 35
Merck & Co., Inc., I; 11 (upd.)
Miles Laboratories, I
Millennium Pharmaceuticals, Inc., 47
Monsanto Company, 29 (upd.)
Moore Medical Corp., 17
Murdock Madaus Schwabe, 26
Mylan Laboratories Inc., I; 20 (upd.); 59
  (upd.)
National Patent Development Corporation,
  13
Natrol, Inc., 49
Natural Alternatives International, Inc., 49
Novartis AG, 39 (upd.)
Noven Pharmaceuticals, Inc., 55
Novo Nordisk A/S, I; 61 (upd.)
Omnicare, Inc., 49
Par Pharmaceutical Companies, Inc., 65
Perrigo Company, 59 (upd.)
Pfizer Inc., I; 9 (upd.); 38 (upd.)
Pharmacia & Upjohn Inc., I; 25 (upd.)
The Quigley Corporation, 62
Quintiles Transnational Corporation, 21
R.P. Scherer, I
Roberts Pharmaceutical Corporation, 16
Roche Bioscience, 14 (upd.)
Rorer Group, I
Roussel Uclaf, I; 8 (upd.)
Sandoz Ltd., I
Sankyo Company, Ltd., I; 56 (upd.)
The Sanofi-Synthélabo Group, I; 49 (upd.)
Schering AG, I; 50 (upd.)
Schering-Plough Corporation, I; 14 (upd.);
  49 (upd.)
Sepracor Inc., 45
Serono S.A., 47
Shionogi & Co., Ltd., 17 (upd.)
Sigma-Aldrich Corporation, I; 36 (upd.)
SmithKline Beecham plc, I; 32 (upd.)
Solvay S.A., 61 (upd.)
Squibb Corporation, I
Sterling Drug, Inc., I
Sun Pharmaceutical Industries Ltd., 57
The Sunrider Corporation, 26
Syntex Corporation, I
Takeda Chemical Industries, Ltd., I
Taro Pharmaceutical Industries Ltd., 65
Teva Pharmaceutical Industries Ltd., 22; 54
  (upd.)
The Upjohn Company, I; 8 (upd.)
Vitalink Pharmacy Services, Inc., 15
Warner-Lambert Co., I; 10 (upd.)
Watson Pharmaceuticals Inc., 16; 56 (upd.)
The Wellcome Foundation Ltd., I
Zila, Inc., 46

ELECTRICAL & ELECTRONICS

ABB ASEA Brown Boveri Ltd., II; 22
  (upd.)
ABB Ltd., 65 (upd.)
Acer Inc., 16
Acuson Corporation, 10; 36 (upd.)
ADC Telecommunications, Inc., 30 (upd.)
Adtran Inc., 22

Advanced Micro Devices, Inc., 30 (upd.)
Advanced Technology Laboratories, Inc., 9
Agere Systems Inc., 61
Agilent Technologies Inc., 38
Aiwa Co., Ltd., 30
AKG Acoustics GmbH, 62
Akzo Nobel N.V., 41 (upd.)
Alliant Techsystems Inc., 30 (upd.)
AlliedSignal Inc., 22 (upd.)
Alpine Electronics, Inc., 13
Alps Electric Co., Ltd., II
Altera Corporation, 18; 43 (upd.)
Altron Incorporated, 20
Amdahl Corporation, 40 (upd.)
American Power Conversion Corporation,
  24; 67 (upd.)
American Technical Ceramics Corp., 67
AMP Incorporated, II; 14 (upd.)
Amphenol Corporation, 40
Amstrad plc, 48 (upd.)
Analog Devices, Inc., 10
Analogic Corporation, 23
Anam Group, 23
Anaren Microwave, Inc., 33
Andrew Corporation, 10; 32 (upd.)
Apex Digital, Inc., 63
Apple Computer, Inc., 36 (upd.)
Applied Power Inc., 32 (upd.)
Arrow Electronics, Inc., 10; 50 (upd.)
Ascend Communications, Inc., 24
Astronics Corporation, 35
Atari Corporation, 9; 23 (upd.); 66 (upd.)
Atmel Corporation, 17
AU Optronics Corporation, 67
Audiovox Corporation, 34
Ault Incorporated, 34
Autodesk, Inc., 10
Avnet Inc., 9
AVX Corporation, 67
Bang & Olufsen Holding A/S, 37
Barco NV, 44
Benchmark Electronics, Inc., 40
Bicoastal Corporation, II
Blonder Tongue Laboratories, Inc., 48
BMC Industries, Inc., 59 (upd.)
Bogen Communications International, Inc.,
  62
Bose Corporation, 13; 36 (upd.)
Boston Acoustics, Inc., 22
Bowthorpe plc, 33
Braun GmbH, 51
Broadcom Corporation, 34
Bull S.A., 43 (upd.)
Burr-Brown Corporation, 19
C-COR.net Corp., 38
Cabletron Systems, Inc., 10
Cadence Design Systems, Inc., 48 (upd.)
Cambridge SoundWorks, Inc., 48
Canon Inc., 18 (upd.)
Carbone Lorraine S.A., 33
Carl-Zeiss-Stiftung, 34 (upd.)
CASIO Computer Co., Ltd., 16 (upd.); 40
  (upd.)
CDW Computer Centers, Inc., 52 (upd.)
Checkpoint Systems, Inc., 39
Chubb, PLC, 50
Cirrus Logic, Inc., 48 (upd.)
Cisco Systems, Inc., 34 (upd.)
Citizen Watch Co., Ltd., 21 (upd.)
Clarion Company Ltd., 64
Cobham plc, 30
Cobra Electronics Corporation, 14
Coherent, Inc., 31
Cohu, Inc., 32
Compagnie Générale d'Électricité, II
Conexant Systems, Inc., 36
Cooper Industries, Inc., II

Cray Research, Inc., 16 (upd.)
Cree Inc., 53
CTS Corporation, 39
Cubic Corporation, 19
Cypress Semiconductor Corporation, 20; 48 (upd.)
Dai Nippon Printing Co., Ltd., 57 (upd.)
Daktronics, Inc., 32
Dallas Semiconductor Corporation, 13; 31 (upd.)
De La Rue plc, 34 (upd.)
Dell Computer Corporation, 31 (upd.)
DH Technology, Inc., 18
Digi International Inc., 9
Discreet Logic Inc., 20
Dixons Group plc, 19 (upd.)
Dolby Laboratories Inc., 20
DRS Technologies, Inc., 58
Dynatech Corporation, 13
E-Systems, Inc., 9
Electronics for Imaging, Inc., 15; 43 (upd.)
Emerson, II; 46 (upd.)
Emerson Radio Corp., 30
ENCAD, Incorporated, 25
Equant N.V., 52
Equus Computer Systems, Inc., 49
ESS Technology, Inc., 22
Everex Systems, Inc., 16
Exabyte Corporation, 40 (upd.)
Exar Corp., 14
Exide Electronics Group, Inc., 20
Flextronics International Ltd., 38
Fluke Corporation, 15
Foxboro Company, 13
Frequency Electronics, Inc., 61
Fuji Electric Co., Ltd., II; 48 (upd.)
Fujitsu Limited, 16 (upd.); 42 (upd.)
Funai Electric Company Ltd., 62
Gateway, Inc., 63 (upd.)
General Atomics, 57
General Dynamics Corporation, 40 (upd.)
General Electric Company, II; 12 (upd.)
General Electric Company, PLC, II
General Instrument Corporation, 10
General Signal Corporation, 9
GenRad, Inc., 24
GM Hughes Electronics Corporation, II
Goldstar Co., Ltd., 12
Gould Electronics, Inc., 14
Grundig AG, 27
Guillemot Corporation, 41
Hadco Corporation, 24
Hamilton Beach/Proctor-Silex Inc., 17
Harman International Industries Inc., 15
Harris Corporation, II; 20 (upd.)
Hayes Corporation, 24
Herley Industries, Inc., 33
Hewlett-Packard Company, 28 (upd.); 50 (upd.)
Holophane Corporation, 19
Hon Hai Precision Industry Co., Ltd., 59
Honeywell Inc., II; 12 (upd.); 50 (upd.)
Hubbell Incorporated, 9; 31 (upd.)
Hughes Supply, Inc., 14
Hutchinson Technology Incorporated, 18; 63 (upd.)
Hypercom Corporation, 27
IDEO Inc., 65
IEC Electronics Corp., 42
Imax Corporation, 28
In Focus Systems, Inc., 22
Indigo NV, 26
Ingram Micro Inc., 52
Integrated Defense Technologies, Inc., 54
Intel Corporation, II; 10 (upd.)

International Business Machines Corporation, III; 6 (upd.); 30 (upd.); 63 (upd.)
International Rectifier Corporation, 31
Itel Corporation, 9
Jabil Circuit, Inc., 36
Jaco Electronics, Inc., 30
JDS Uniphase Corporation, 34
Johnson Controls, Inc., 59 (upd.)
Juno Lighting, Inc., 30
Katy Industries, Inc., 51 (upd.)
Keithley Instruments Inc., 16
Kemet Corp., 14
Kent Electronics Corporation, 17
Kenwood Corporation, 31
Kimball International, Inc., 48 (upd.)
Kingston Technology Corporation, 20
KitchenAid, 8
KLA-Tencor Corporation, 45 (upd.)
KnowledgeWare Inc., 9
Kollmorgen Corporation, 18
Konica Corporation, 30 (upd.)
Koninklijke Philips Electronics N.V., 50 (upd.)
Koor Industries Ltd., II
Koss Corporation, 38
Kudelski Group SA, 44
Kulicke and Soffa Industries, Inc., 33
Kyocera Corporation, II
LaBarge Inc., 41
The Lamson & Sessions Co., 61 (upd.)
Lattice Semiconductor Corp., 16
LeCroy Corporation, 41
Legrand SA, 21
Linear Technology, Inc., 16
Littelfuse, Inc., 26
Loral Corporation, 9
Lowrance Electronics, Inc., 18
LSI Logic Corporation, 13; 64
Lucent Technologies Inc., 34
Lucky-Goldstar, II
Lunar Corporation, 29
Mackie Designs Inc., 33
MagneTek, Inc., 15; 41 (upd.)
Marconi plc, 33 (upd.)
Marquette Electronics, Inc., 13
Matsushita Electric Industrial Co., Ltd., II
Maxim Integrated Products, Inc., 16
Merix Corporation, 36
Methode Electronics, Inc., 13
Mitel Corporation, 18
MITRE Corporation, 26
Mitsubishi Electric Corporation, II; 44 (upd.)
Molex Incorporated, 54 (upd.)
Motorola, Inc., II; 11 (upd.); 34 (upd.)
Nam Tai Electronics, Inc., 61
National Instruments Corporation, 22
National Presto Industries, Inc., 16; 43 (upd.)
National Semiconductor Corporation, II; 26 (upd.)
NEC Corporation, II; 21 (upd.); 57 (upd.)
Nexans SA, 54
Nintendo Co., Ltd., 28 (upd.)
Nokia Corporation, II; 17 (upd.); 38 (upd.)
Nortel Networks Corporation, 36 (upd.)
Northrop Grumman Corporation, 45 (upd.)
Oak Technology, Inc., 22
Oki Electric Industry Company, Limited, II
Omron Corporation, II; 28 (upd.)
Otter Tail Power Company, 18
Palm, Inc., 36
Palomar Medical Technologies, Inc., 22
Parlex Corporation, 61
The Peak Technologies Group, Inc., 14
Peavey Electronics Corporation, 16

Philips Electronics N.V., II; 13 (upd.)
Philips Electronics North America Corp., 13
Pioneer Electronic Corporation, 28 (upd.)
Pioneer-Standard Electronics Inc., 19
Pitney Bowes Inc., 47 (upd.)
Pittway Corporation, 9
Planar Systems, Inc., 61
The Plessey Company, PLC, II
Plexus Corporation, 35
Polk Audio, Inc., 34
Potter & Brumfield Inc., 11
Premier Industrial Corporation, 9
Protection One, Inc., 32
Quanta Computer Inc., 47
Racal Electronics PLC, II
RadioShack Corporation, 36 (upd.)
Radius Inc., 16
Raychem Corporation, 8
Rayovac Corporation, 13
Raytheon Company, II; 11 (upd.); 38 (upd.)
RCA Corporation, II
Read-Rite Corp., 10
Reliance Electric Company, 9
Research in Motion Ltd., 54
Rexel, Inc., 15
Richardson Electronics, Ltd., 17
Ricoh Company, Ltd., 36 (upd.)
The Rival Company, 19
Rockford Corporation, 43
Rogers Corporation, 61
S&C Electric Company, 15
SAGEM S.A., 37
St. Louis Music, Inc., 48
Sam Ash Music Corporation, 30
Samsung Electronics Co., Ltd., 14; 41 (upd.)
SANYO Electric Co., Ltd., II; 36 (upd.)
Sarnoff Corporation, 57
ScanSource, Inc., 29
Schneider S.A., II; 18 (upd.)
SCI Systems, Inc., 9
Scientific-Atlanta, Inc., 45 (upd.)
Scitex Corporation Ltd., 24
Seagate Technology, Inc., 34 (upd.)
Semtech Corporation, 32
Sennheiser Electronic GmbH & Co. KG, 66
Sensormatic Electronics Corp., 11
Sensory Science Corporation, 37
SGI, 29 (upd.)
Sharp Corporation, II; 12 (upd.); 40 (upd.)
Sheldahl Inc., 23
Shure Inc., 60
Siemens AG, II; 14 (upd.); 57 (upd.)
Silicon Graphics Incorporated, 9
Smiths Industries PLC, 25
Solectron Corporation, 12; 48 (upd.)
Sony Corporation, II; 12 (upd.); 40 (upd.)
Spectrum Control, Inc., 67
SPX Corporation, 47 (upd.)
Sterling Electronics Corp., 18
STMicroelectronics NV, 52
Strix Ltd., 51
Stuart C. Irby Company, 58
Sumitomo Electric Industries, Ltd., II
Sun Microsystems, Inc., 30 (upd.)
Sunbeam-Oster Co., Inc., 9
SyQuest Technology, Inc., 18
Tandy Corporation, II; 12 (upd.)
Tatung Co., 23
TDK Corporation, II; 17 (upd.); 49 (upd.)
Tech-Sym Corporation, 18
Technitrol, Inc., 29
Tektronix, Inc., 8
Teledyne Technologies Inc., 62 (upd.)

ELECTRICAL & ELECTRONICS
(continued)

Telxon Corporation, 10
Teradyne, Inc., 11
Texas Instruments Inc., II; 11 (upd.); 46 (upd.)
Thales S.A., 42
Thomas & Betts Corporation, 54 (upd.)
THOMSON multimedia S.A., II; 42 (upd.)
The Titan Corporation, 36
Tops Appliance City, Inc., 17
Toromont Industries, Ltd., 21
Trans-Lux Corporation, 51
Trimble Navigation Limited, 40
TriQuint Semiconductor, Inc., 63
Tweeter Home Entertainment Group, Inc., 30
Ultrak Inc., 24
Universal Electronics Inc., 39
Varian Associates Inc., 12
Veeco Instruments Inc., 32
VIASYS Healthcare, Inc., 52
Viasystems Group, Inc., 67
Vicon Industries, Inc., 44
Victor Company of Japan, Limited, II; 26 (upd.)
Vishay Intertechnology, Inc., 21
Vitesse Semiconductor Corporation, 32
Vitro Corp., 10
VLSI Technology, Inc., 16
Wells-Gardner Electronics Corporation, 43
Westinghouse Electric Corporation, II; 12 (upd.)
Wyle Electronics, 14
Yageo Corporation, 16
York Research Corporation, 35
Zenith Data Systems, Inc., 10
Zenith Electronics Corporation, II; 13 (upd.); 34 (upd.)
Zoom Telephonics, Inc., 18
Zumtobel AG, 50
Zytec Corporation, 19

ENGINEERING & MANAGEMENT SERVICES

AAON, Inc., 22
Aavid Thermal Technologies, Inc., 29
Alliant Techsystems Inc., 30 (upd.)
Altran Technologies, 51
Amey Plc, 47
Analytic Sciences Corporation, 10
Arcadis NV, 26
Arthur D. Little, Inc., 35
The Austin Company, 8
Balfour Beatty plc, 36 (upd.)
Brown & Root, Inc., 13
Bufete Industrial, S.A. de C.V., 34
C.H. Heist Corporation, 24
CDI Corporation, 6
CH2M Hill Ltd., 22
The Charles Stark Draper Laboratory, Inc., 35
Coflexip S.A., 25
Corrections Corporation of America, 23
CRSS Inc., 6
Dames & Moore, Inc., 25
DAW Technologies, Inc., 25
Day & Zimmermann Inc., 9; 31 (upd.)
Donaldson Co. Inc., 16
Dycom Industries, Inc., 57
EG&G Incorporated, 8; 29 (upd.)
Eiffage, 27
Essef Corporation, 18
FKI Plc, 57
Fluor Corporation, 34 (upd.)
Forest City Enterprises, Inc., 52 (upd.)
Foster Wheeler Corporation, 6; 23 (upd.)

Framatome SA, 19
Georg Fischer AG Schaffhausen, 61
Gilbane, Inc., 34
Grupo Dragados SA, 55
Halliburton Company, 25 (upd.)
Harding Lawson Associates Group, Inc., 16
Harza Engineering Company, 14
HDR Inc., 48
HOK Group, Inc., 59
ICF Kaiser International, Inc., 28
Jacobs Engineering Group Inc., 6; 26 (upd.)
The Judge Group, Inc., 51
JWP Inc., 9
The Keith Companies Inc., 54
Klöckner-Werke AG, 58 (upd.)
Kvaerner ASA, 36
Layne Christensen Company, 19
The MacNeal-Schwendler Corporation, 25
Malcolm Pirnie, Inc., 42
McDermott International, Inc., 37 (upd.)
McKinsey & Company, Inc., 9
Michael Baker Corporation, 51 (upd.)
Nooter Corporation, 61
Oceaneering International, Inc., 63
Ogden Corporation, 6
Opus Group, 34
Parsons Brinckerhoff, Inc., 34
The Parsons Corporation, 8; 56 (upd.)
RCM Technologies, Inc., 34
Renishaw plc, 46
Rosemount Inc., 15
Roy F. Weston, Inc., 33
Royal Vopak NV, 41
Rust International Inc., 11
Sandia National Laboratories, 49
Sandvik AB, 32 (upd.)
Sarnoff Corporation, 57
Science Applications International Corporation, 15
Serco Group plc, 47
Siegel & Gale, 64
Siemens AG, 57 (upd.)
SRI International, Inc., 57
Stone & Webster, Inc., 13; 64 (upd.)
Susquehanna Pfaltzgraff Company, 8
Sverdrup Corporation, 14
Tech-Sym Corporation, 44 (upd.)
Tetra Tech, Inc., 29
Thyssen Krupp AG, 28 (upd.)
Towers Perrin, 32
Tracor Inc., 17
TRC Companies, Inc., 32
Underwriters Laboratories, Inc., 30
United Dominion Industries Limited, 8; 16 (upd.)
URS Corporation, 45
VA TECH ELIN EBG GmbH, 49
VECO International, Inc., 7
Vinci, 43
Willbros Group, Inc., 56
WS Atkins Plc, 45

ENTERTAINMENT & LEISURE

A&E Television Networks, 32
Aardman Animations Ltd., 61
ABC Family Worldwide, Inc., 52
Academy of Television Arts & Sciences, Inc., 55
Acclaim Entertainment Inc., 24
Activision, Inc., 32
AEI Music Network Inc., 35
Affinity Group Holding Inc., 56
Airtours Plc, 27
Alaska Railroad Corporation, 60
All American Communications Inc., 20

The All England Lawn Tennis & Croquet Club, 54
Alliance Entertainment Corp., 17
Alternative Tentacles Records, 66
Alvin Ailey Dance Foundation, Inc., 52
Amblin Entertainment, 21
AMC Entertainment Inc., 12; 35 (upd.)
American Golf Corporation, 45
American Gramaphone LLC, 52
American Skiing Company, 28
Ameristar Casinos, Inc., 33
AMF Bowling, Inc., 40
Anaheim Angels Baseball Club, Inc., 53
Anchor Gaming, 24
AOL Time Warner Inc., 57 (upd.)
Applause Inc., 24
Aprilia SpA, 17
Argosy Gaming Company, 21
Aristocrat Leisure Limited, 54
The Art Institute of Chicago, 29
Artisan Entertainment Inc., 32 (upd.)
Asahi National Broadcasting Company, Ltd., 9
Aspen Skiing Company, 15
Aston Villa plc, 41
The Athletics Investment Group, 62
Atlanta National League Baseball Club, Inc., 43
The Atlantic Group, 23
Autotote Corporation, 20
Aztar Corporation, 13
Bad Boy Worldwide Entertainment Group, 58
Baker & Taylor Corporation, 16; 43 (upd.)
Bally Total Fitness Holding Corp., 25
Baltimore Orioles L.P., 66
The Baseball Club of Seattle, LP, 50
The Basketball Club of Seattle, LLC, 50
Bertelsmann A.G., 15 (upd.); 43 (upd.)
Bertucci's Inc., 16
Big Idea Productions, Inc., 49
Blockbuster Inc., 9; 31 (upd.)
Boca Resorts, Inc., 37
Bonneville International Corporation, 29
Booth Creek Ski Holdings, Inc., 31
Boston Celtics Limited Partnership, 14
Boston Professional Hockey Association Inc., 39
The Boy Scouts of America, 34
British Broadcasting Corporation Ltd., 7; 21 (upd.)
British Sky Broadcasting Group plc, 20; 60 (upd.)
Cablevision Systems Corporation, 7
California Sports, 56
Callaway Golf Company, 45 (upd.)
Canterbury Park Holding Corporation, 42
Capital Cities/ABC Inc., II
Carlson Companies, Inc., 22 (upd.)
Carlson Wagonlit Travel, 55
Carmike Cinemas, Inc., 14; 37 (upd.)
Carnival Corporation, 6; 27 (upd.)
The Carsey-Werner Company, L.L.C., 37
CBS Inc., II; 6 (upd.)
Cedar Fair, L.P., 22
Central European Media Enterprises Ltd., 61
Central Independent Television, 7; 23 (upd.)
Century Casinos, Inc., 53
Century Theatres, Inc., 31
Championship Auto Racing Teams, Inc., 37
Chicago Bears Football Club, Inc., 33
Chicago National League Ball Club, Inc., 66
Chris-Craft Industries, Inc., 31 (upd.)

Chrysalis Group plc, 40
Churchill Downs Incorporated, 29
Cinar Corporation, 40
Cineplex Odeon Corporation, 6; 23 (upd.)
Cinram International, Inc., 43
Cirque du Soleil Inc., 29
Classic Vacation Group, Inc., 46
Cleveland Indians Baseball Company, Inc.,
    37
ClubCorp, Inc., 33
Colonial Williamsburg Foundation, 53
Columbia Pictures Entertainment, Inc., II
Columbia TriStar Motion Pictures
    Companies, 12 (upd.)
Comcast Corporation, 7
Compagnie des Alpes, 48
Continental Cablevision, Inc., 7
Corporation for Public Broadcasting, 14
Cox Enterprises, Inc., 22 (upd.)
Crown Media Holdings, Inc., 45
Cruise America Inc., 21
Cunard Line Ltd., 23
Dallas Cowboys Football Club, Ltd., 33
Dave & Buster's, Inc., 33
Death Row Records, 27
Denver Nuggets, 51
The Detroit Lions, Inc., 55
The Detroit Pistons Basketball Company,
    41
Detroit Tigers Baseball Club, Inc., 46
dick clark productions, inc., 16
DIRECTV, Inc., 38
Dover Downs Entertainment, Inc., 43
DreamWorks SKG, 43
E! Entertainment Television Inc., 17
edel music AG, 44
Educational Broadcasting Corporation, 48
Edwards Theatres Circuit, Inc., 31
Elektra Entertainment Group, 64
Elsinore Corporation, 48
Elvis Presley Enterprises, Inc., 61
Endemol Entertainment Holding NV, 46
Equity Marketing, Inc., 26
ESPN, Inc., 56
Esporta plc, 35
Euro Disney S.C.A., 20; 58 (upd.)
Europe Through the Back Door Inc., 65
Fair Grounds Corporation, 44
Family Golf Centers, Inc., 29
FAO Schwarz, 46
Fédération Internationale de Football
    Association, 27
Feld Entertainment, Inc., 32 (upd.)
Film Roman, Inc., 58
First Choice Holidays PLC, 40
First Team Sports, Inc., 22
Fisher-Price Inc., 32 (upd.)
Florida Gaming Corporation, 47
4Kids Entertainment Inc., 59
Fox Entertainment Group, Inc., 43
Fox Family Worldwide, Inc., 24
Gaumont SA, 25
Gaylord Entertainment Company, 11; 36
    (upd.)
GC Companies, Inc., 25
Geffen Records Inc., 26
Gibson Guitar Corp., 16
Girl Scouts of the USA, 35
Global Outdoors, Inc., 49
GoodTimes Entertainment Ltd., 48
Granada Group PLC, II; 24 (upd.)
Grand Casinos, Inc., 20
The Green Bay Packers, Inc., 32
Grévin & Compagnie SA, 56
Groupe Partouche SA, 48
Grupo Televisa, S.A., 54 (upd.)
Hallmark Cards, Inc., 40 (upd.)

Hanna-Barbera Cartoons Inc., 23
Hard Rock Cafe International, Inc., 32
    (upd.)
Harlem Globetrotters International, Inc., 61
Harpo Inc., 28; 66 (upd.)
Harrah's Entertainment, Inc., 16; 43 (upd.)
Harveys Casino Resorts, 27
Hasbro, Inc., 43 (upd.)
Hastings Entertainment, Inc., 29
The Hearst Corporation, 46 (upd.)
The Heat Group, 53
Hilton Group plc, III; 19 (upd.); 49 (upd.)
HIT Entertainment PLC, 40
HOB Entertainment, Inc., 37
Hollywood Casino Corporation, 21
Hollywood Entertainment Corporation, 25
Hollywood Media Corporation, 58
Hollywood Park, Inc., 20
Home Box Office Inc., 7; 23 (upd.)
Horseshoe Gaming Holding Corporation,
    62
Imax Corporation, 28
Indianapolis Motor Speedway Corporation,
    46
Infinity Broadcasting Corporation, 48
    (upd.)
Infogrames Entertainment S.A., 35
Integrity Inc., 44
International Creative Management, Inc.,
    43
International Family Entertainment Inc., 13
International Game Technology, 41 (upd.)
International Olympic Committee, 44
International Speedway Corporation, 19
Interscope Music Group, 31
The Intrawest Corporation, 15
Irvin Feld & Kenneth Feld Productions,
    Inc., 15
Isle of Capri Casinos, Inc., 41
iVillage Inc., 46
Iwerks Entertainment, Inc., 34
Jackpot Enterprises Inc., 21
Japan Broadcasting Corporation, 7
Jazz Basketball Investors, Inc., 55
Jazzercise, Inc., 45
Jillian's Entertainment Holdings, Inc., 40
The Jim Henson Company, 23
The Joffrey Ballet of Chicago, 52
Jurys Doyle Hotel Group plc, 64
Juventus F.C. S.p.A, 53
K'Nex Industries, Inc., 52
Kampgrounds of America, Inc. (KOA), 33
King World Productions, Inc., 9; 30 (upd.)
Knott's Berry Farm, 18
Kuoni Travel Holding Ltd., 40
The Kushner-Locke Company, 25
Ladbroke Group PLC, II; 21 (upd.)
Lakes Entertainment, Inc., 51
Las Vegas Sands, Inc., 50
Lego A/S, 13; 40 (upd.)
Liberty Livewire Corporation, 42
Liberty Media Corporation, 50
Liberty Travel, Inc., 56
Life Time Fitness, Inc., 66
Lifetime Entertainment Services, 51
Lionel L.L.C., 16
Lions Gate Entertainment Corporation, 35
LIVE Entertainment Inc., 20
LodgeNet Entertainment Corporation, 28
Lucasfilm Ltd., 12; 50 (upd.)
Luminar Plc, 40
Manchester United Football Club plc, 30
Mandalay Resort Group, 32 (upd.)
Maple Leaf Sports & Entertainment Ltd.,
    61
The Marcus Corporation, 21

Mashantucket Pequot Gaming Enterprise
    Inc., 35
MCA Inc., II
McMenamins Pubs and Breweries, 65
Media General, Inc., 7
Mediaset SpA, 50
Mega Bloks, Inc., 61
Metro-Goldwyn-Mayer Inc., 25 (upd.)
Metromedia Companies, 14
Métropole Télévision, 33
Metropolitan Baseball Club Inc., 39
The Metropolitan Museum of Art, 55
Metropolitan Opera Association, Inc., 40
MGM Grand Inc., 17
MGM/UA Communications Company, II
Midway Games, Inc., 25
Mikohn Gaming Corporation, 39
Milwaukee Brewers Baseball Club, 37
Miramax Film Corporation, 64
Mizuno Corporation, 25
Mohegan Tribal Gaming Authority, 37
Monarch Casino & Resort, Inc., 65
Motown Records Company L.P., 26
Movie Gallery, Inc., 31
Multimedia Games, Inc., 41
Muzak, Inc., 18
National Amusements Inc., 28
National Association for Stock Car Auto
    Racing, 32
National Broadcasting Company, Inc., II; 6
    (upd.)
National Football League, 29
National Hockey League, 35
National Public Radio, Inc., 19; 47 (upd.)
National Rifle Association of America, 37
National Thoroughbred Racing Association,
    58
Navarre Corporation, 24
Navigant International, Inc., 47
New Line Cinema, Inc., 47
New Orleans Saints LP, 58
New York City Off-Track Betting
    Corporation, 51
News Corporation Limited, 46 (upd.)
Nicklaus Companies, 45
Nintendo Company, Ltd., 28 (upd.); 67
    (upd.)
O'Charley's Inc., 19
Orion Pictures Corporation, 6
Outrigger Enterprises, Inc., 67
Paradise Music & Entertainment, Inc., 42
Paramount Pictures Corporation, II
Pathé SA, 29
Paul-Son Gaming Corporation, 66
PDS Gaming Corporation, 44
Peace Arch Entertainment Group Inc., 51
Penn National Gaming, Inc., 33
Philadelphia Eagles, 37
Pierre & Vacances SA, 48
Pittsburgh Steelers Sports, Inc., 66
Pixar Animation Studios, 34
Platinum Entertainment, Inc., 35
Play by Play Toys & Novelties, Inc., 26
Players International, Inc., 22
Pleasant Holidays LLC, 62
PolyGram N.V., 23
Poof-Slinky, Inc., 61
Portland Trail Blazers, 50
Powerhouse Technologies, Inc., 27
Premier Parks, Inc., 27
President Casinos, Inc., 22
Preussag AG, 42 (upd.)
Princess Cruise Lines, 22
Professional Bull Riders Inc., 55
The Professional Golfers' Association of
    America, 41
Promus Companies, Inc., 9

ENTERTAINMENT & LEISURE
(continued)

ProSiebenSat.1 Media AG, 54
Publishing and Broadcasting Limited, 54
Putt-Putt Golf Courses of America, Inc., 23
Radio One, Inc., 67
Ragdoll Productions Ltd., 51
Rainforest Cafe, Inc., 25
The Rank Group plc, II; 64 (upd.)
Rawlings Sporting Goods Co., Inc., 24
The Really Useful Group, 26
Regal Entertainment Group, 59
Rentrak Corporation, 35
Rhino Entertainment Company, 18
Ride, Inc., 22
Rollerblade, Inc., 34 (upd.)
Roularta Media Group NV, 48
Royal Caribbean Cruises Ltd., 22
Royal Olympic Cruise Lines Inc., 52
RTL Group SA, 44
Rush Communications, 33
S-K-I Limited, 15
Salomon Worldwide, 20
San Francisco Baseball Associates, L.P., 55
Santa Fe Gaming Corporation, 19
Schwinn Cycle and Fitness L.P., 19
Scientific Games Corporation, 64 (upd.)
Scottish Radio Holding plc, 41
Seattle FilmWorks, Inc., 20
Sega of America, Inc., 10
Selectour SA, 53
SFX Entertainment, Inc., 36
Showboat, Inc., 19
Shubert Organization Inc., 24
Shuffle Master Inc., 51
The Singing Machine Company, Inc., 60
Six Flags, Inc., 17; 54 (upd.)
Smithsonian Institution, 27
Società Sportiva Lazio SpA, 44
Sony Corporation, 40 (upd.)
Speedway Motorsports, Inc., 32
Spelling Entertainment Group, Inc., 14
Spin Master, Ltd., 61
The Sports Club Company, 25
Stanley Leisure plc, 66
Station Casinos Inc., 25
Stoll-Moss Theatres Ltd., 34
Stuart Entertainment Inc., 16
TABCORP Holdings Limited, 44
Take-Two Interactive Software, Inc., 46
Tee Vee Toons, Inc., 57
Tele-Communications, Inc., II
Television Española, S.A., 7
Texas Rangers Baseball, 51
Thomas Cook Travel Inc., 9
The Thomson Corporation, 8
Thousand Trails, Inc., 33
THQ, Inc., 39
Ticketmaster Corp., 13
The Todd-AO Corporation, 33
Toho Co., Ltd., 28
Tomy Company Ltd., 65
The Topps Company, Inc., 34 (upd.)
Touristik Union International GmbH. and
   Company K.G., II
Town Sports International, Inc., 46
Toy Biz, Inc., 18
Trans World Entertainment Corporation, 24
Travelocity.com, Inc., 46
Tribune Company, 63 (upd.)
TUI Group GmbH, 44
Turner Broadcasting System, Inc., II; 6
   (upd.); 66 (upd.)
The Tussauds Group, 55
Twentieth Century Fox Film Corporation,
   II; 25 (upd.)
Ubi Soft Entertainment S.A., 41

United Pan-Europe Communications NV,
   47
United States Playing Card Company, 62
Universal Studios, Inc., 33
Univision Communications Inc., 24
USA Interactive, Inc., 47 (upd.)
Vail Resorts, Inc., 11; 43 (upd.)
Venetian Casino Resort, LLC, 47
Viacom Inc., 7; 23 (upd.)
Village Roadshow Ltd., 58
Vinton Studios, 63
Vivendi Universal S.A., 46 (upd.)
The Walt Disney Company, II; 6 (upd.); 30
   (upd.); 63 (upd.)
Warner Communications Inc., II
Washington Football, Inc., 35
West Coast Entertainment Corporation, 29
WGBH Educational Foundation, 66
Wham-O, Inc., 61
Wherehouse Entertainment Incorporated,
   11
Whitbread PLC, 52 (upd.)
Wildlife Conservation Society, 31
William Hill Organization Limited, 49
Wilson Sporting Goods Company, 24
Wizards of the Coast Inc., 24
WMS Industries, Inc., 53 (upd.)
World Wrestling Federation Entertainment,
   Inc., 32
YankeeNets LLC, 35
YES! Entertainment Corporation, 26
YMCA of the USA, 31
Young Broadcasting Inc., 40
Zomba Records Ltd., 52

FINANCIAL SERVICES: BANKS

Abbey National plc, 10; 39 (upd.)
Abigail Adams National Bancorp, Inc., 23
ABN AMRO Holding, N.V., 50
Algemene Bank Nederland N.V., II
Allianz AG, 57 (upd.)
Allied Irish Banks, plc, 16; 43 (upd.)
Almanij NV, 44
Amalgamated Bank, 60
AMCORE Financial Inc., 44
American Residential Mortgage
   Corporation, 8
AmSouth Bancorporation,12; 48 (upd.)
Amsterdam-Rotterdam Bank N.V., II
Anchor Bancorp, Inc., 10
Apple Bank for Savings, 59
Astoria Financial Corporation, 44
Australia and New Zealand Banking Group
   Limited, II; 52 (upd.)
Banca Commerciale Italiana SpA, II
Banca Fideuram SpA, 63
Banca Intesa SpA, 65
Banca Monte dei Paschi di Siena SpA, 65
Banco Bilbao Vizcaya Argentaria S.A., II;
   48 (upd.)
Banco Bradesco S.A., 13
Banco Central, II
Banco Comercial Português, SA, 50
Banco do Brasil S.A., II
Banco Espírito Santo e Comercial de
   Lisboa S.A., 15
Banco Itaú S.A., 19
Banco Santander Central Hispano S.A., 36
   (upd.)
Bank Austria AG, 23
Bank Brussels Lambert, II
Bank Hapoalim B.M., II; 54 (upd.)
Bank Leumi le-Israel B.M., 60
Bank of America Corporation, 46 (upd.)
Bank of Boston Corporation, II
Bank of China, 63
Bank of East Asia Ltd., 63

Bank of Ireland, 50
Bank of Mississippi, Inc., 14
Bank of Montreal, II; 46 (upd.)
Bank of New England Corporation, II
The Bank of New York Company, Inc., II;
   46 (upd.)
The Bank of Nova Scotia, II; 59 (upd.)
Bank of the Philippine Islands, 58
Bank of Tokyo-Mitsubishi Ltd., II; 15
   (upd.)
Bank One Corporation, 10; 36 (upd.)
BankAmerica Corporation, II; 8 (upd.)
Bankers Trust New York Corporation, II
Banknorth Group, Inc., 55
Banque Nationale de Paris S.A., II
Barclays plc, II; 20; 64 (upd.)
BarclaysAmerican Mortgage Corporation,
   11
Barings PLC, 14
Barnett Banks, Inc., 9
BayBanks, Inc., 12
Bayerische Hypotheken- und Wechsel-
   Bank AG, II
Bayerische Vereinsbank A.G., II
Beneficial Corporation, 8
BNP Paribas Group, 36 (upd.)
Boatmen's Bancshares Inc., 15
Bremer Financial Corp., 45
Brown Brothers Harriman & Co., 45
Canadian Imperial Bank of Commerce, II;
   61 (upd.)
Capitalia S.p.A., 65
Carolina First Corporation, 31
Casco Northern Bank, 14
The Chase Manhattan Corporation, II; 13
   (upd.)
Cheltenham & Gloucester PLC, 61
Chemical Banking Corporation, II; 14
   (upd.)
Citicorp, II; 9 (upd.)
Citigroup Inc., 30 (upd.); 59 (upd.)
Citizens Financial Group, Inc., 42
Close Brothers Group plc, 39
Commercial Credit Company, 8
Commercial Federal Corporation, 12; 62
   (upd.)
Commerzbank A.G., II; 47 (upd.)
Compagnie Financiere de Paribas, II
Continental Bank Corporation, II
CoreStates Financial Corp, 17
Countrywide Credit Industries, Inc., 16
Crédit Agricole, II
Crédit Lyonnais, 9; 33 (upd.)
Crédit National S.A., 9
Credit Suisse Group, II; 21 (upd.); 59
   (upd.)
Credito Italiano, II
Cullen/Frost Bankers, Inc., 25
CUNA Mutual Group, 62
The Dai-Ichi Kangyo Bank Ltd., II
The Daiwa Bank, Ltd., II; 39 (upd.)
Danske Bank Aktieselskab, 50
Dauphin Deposit Corporation, 14
Deposit Guaranty Corporation, 17
Deutsche Bank AG, II; 14 (upd.); 40 (upd.)
Dexia Group, 42
Dime Savings Bank of New York, F.S.B.,
   9
Donaldson, Lufkin & Jenrette, Inc., 22
Dresdner Bank A.G., II; 57 (upd.)
Emigrant Savings Bank, 59
European Investment Bank, 66
Fifth Third Bancorp, 13; 31 (upd.)
First Bank System Inc., 12
First Chicago Corporation, II
First Commerce Bancshares, Inc., 15
First Commerce Corporation, 11

First Empire State Corporation, 11
First Fidelity Bank, N.A., New Jersey, 9
First Hawaiian, Inc., 11
First Interstate Bancorp, II
First Nationwide Bank, 14
First of America Bank Corporation, 8
First Security Corporation, 11
First Tennessee National Corporation, 11; 48 (upd.)
First Union Corporation, 10
First Virginia Banks, Inc., 11
Firstar Corporation, 11; 33 (upd.)
Fleet Financial Group, Inc., 9
FleetBoston Financial Corporation, 36 (upd.)
Fourth Financial Corporation, 11
The Fuji Bank, Ltd., II
Generale Bank, II
German American Bancorp, 41
Glacier Bancorp, Inc., 35
Golden West Financial Corporation, 47
The Governor and Company of the Bank of Scotland, 10
Grameen Bank, 31
Granite State Bankshares, Inc., 37
Great Lakes Bancorp, 8
Great Western Financial Corporation, 10
GreenPoint Financial Corp., 28
Grupo Financiero Banamex S.A., 54
Grupo Financiero Banorte, S.A. de C.V., 51
Grupo Financiero BBVA Bancomer S.A., 54
Grupo Financiero Galicia S.A., 63
Grupo Financiero Serfin, S.A., 19
H.F. Ahmanson & Company, II; 10 (upd.)
Habersham Bancorp, 25
Hancock Holding Company, 15
Hang Seng Bank Ltd., 60
Hanmi Financial Corporation, 66
Hibernia Corporation, 37
The Hongkong and Shanghai Banking Corporation Limited, II
HSBC Holdings plc, 12; 26 (upd.)
Hudson River Bancorp, Inc., 41
Huntington Bancshares Inc., 11
HVB Group, 59 (upd.)
IBERIABANK Corporation, 37
The Industrial Bank of Japan, Ltd., II
Irish Life & Permanent Plc, 59
J Sainsbury plc, 38 (upd.)
J.P. Morgan & Co. Incorporated, II; 30 (upd.)
J.P. Morgan Chase & Co., 38 (upd.)
Japan Leasing Corporation, 8
Julius Baer Holding AG, 52
Kansallis-Osake-Pankki, II
KeyCorp, 8
Kookmin Bank, 58
Kredietbank N.V., II
Kreditanstalt für Wiederaufbau, 29
Lloyds Bank PLC, II
Lloyds TSB Group plc, 47 (upd.)
Long Island Bancorp, Inc., 16
Long-Term Credit Bank of Japan, Ltd., II
Manufacturers Hanover Corporation, II
Marshall & Ilsley Corporation, 56
MBNA Corporation, 12
Mediolanum S.p.A., 65
Mellon Bank Corporation, II
Mellon Financial Corporation, 44 (upd.)
Mercantile Bankshares Corp., 11
Meridian Bancorp, Inc., 11
Metropolitan Financial Corporation, 13
Michigan National Corporation, 11
Midland Bank PLC, II; 17 (upd.)
The Mitsubishi Bank, Ltd., II

The Mitsubishi Trust & Banking Corporation, II
The Mitsui Bank, Ltd., II
The Mitsui Trust & Banking Company, Ltd., II
Mizuho Financial Group Inc., 58 (upd.)
Mouvement des Caisses Desjardins, 48
N M Rothschild & Sons Limited, 39
National Bank of Greece, 41
National City Corp., 15
National Westminster Bank PLC, II
NationsBank Corporation, 10
NBD Bancorp, Inc., 11
NCNB Corporation, II
Nippon Credit Bank, II
Nordea AB, 40
Norinchukin Bank, II
North Fork Bancorporation, Inc., 46
Northern Rock plc, 33
Northern Trust Company, 9
NVR L.P., 8
Old Kent Financial Corp., 11
Old National Bancorp, 15
PNC Bank Corp., II; 13 (upd.)
The PNC Financial Services Group Inc., 46 (upd.)
Popular, Inc., 41
PT Bank Buana Indonesia Tbk, 60
Pulte Corporation, 8
Rabobank Group, 33
Republic New York Corporation, 11
Riggs National Corporation, 13
The Royal Bank of Canada, II; 21 (upd.)
The Royal Bank of Scotland Group plc, 12; 38 (upd.)
The Ryland Group, Inc., 8
St. Paul Bank for Cooperatives, 8
Sanpaolo IMI S.p.A., 50
The Sanwa Bank, Ltd., II; 15 (upd.)
SBC Warburg, 14
Sberbank, 62
Seattle First National Bank Inc., 8
Security Capital Corporation, 17
Security Pacific Corporation, II
Shawmut National Corporation, 13
Signet Banking Corporation, 11
Singer & Friedlander Group plc, 41
Skandinaviska Enskilda Banken AB, II; 56 (upd.)
Société Générale, II; 42 (upd.)
Society Corporation, 9
Southern Financial Bancorp, Inc., 56
Southtrust Corporation, 11
Standard Chartered plc, II; 48 (upd.)
Standard Federal Bank, 9
Star Banc Corporation, 11
State Bank of India, 63
State Financial Services Corporation, 51
State Street Corporation, 8; 57 (upd.)
Staten Island Bancorp, Inc., 39
The Sumitomo Bank, Limited, II; 26 (upd.)
Sumitomo Mitsui Banking Corporation, 51 (upd.)
The Sumitomo Trust & Banking Company, Ltd., II; 53 (upd.)
The Summit Bancorporation, 14
SunTrust Banks Inc., 23
Svenska Handelsbanken AB, II; 50 (upd.)
Swiss Bank Corporation, II
Synovus Financial Corp., 12; 52 (upd.)
The Taiyo Kobe Bank, Ltd., II
TCF Financial Corporation, 47
The Tokai Bank, Limited, II; 15 (upd.)
The Toronto-Dominion Bank, II; 49 (upd.)
TSB Group plc, 12
Turkiye Is Bankasi A.S., 61
U.S. Bancorp, 14; 36 (upd.)

U.S. Trust Corp., 17
UBS AG, 52 (upd.)
Union Bank of California, 16
Union Bank of Switzerland, II
Union Financière de France Banque SA, 52
Union Planters Corporation, 54
UnionBanCal Corporation, 50 (upd.)
United Overseas Bank Ltd., 56
USAA, 62 (upd.)
Wachovia Bank of Georgia, N.A., 16
Wachovia Bank of South Carolina, N.A., 16
Washington Mutual, Inc., 17
Wells Fargo & Company, II; 12 (upd.); 38 (upd.)
West One Bancorp, 11
Westamerica Bancorporation, 17
Westdeutsche Landesbank Girozentrale, II; 46 (upd.)
Westpac Banking Corporation, II; 48 (upd.)
Whitney Holding Corporation, 21
Wilmington Trust Corporation, 25
The Woolwich plc, 30
World Bank Group, 33
The Yasuda Trust and Banking Company, Ltd., II; 17 (upd.)
Zions Bancorporation, 12; 53 (upd.)

FINANCIAL SERVICES: NON-BANKS

A.B. Watley Group Inc., 45
A.G. Edwards, Inc., 8; 32 (upd.)
ACE Cash Express, Inc., 33
Advanta Corporation, 8; 38 (upd.)
Ag Services of America, Inc., 59
Alliance Capital Management Holding L.P., 63
Allmerica Financial Corporation, 63
Ambac Financial Group, Inc., 65
America's Car-Mart, Inc., 64
American Express Company, II; 10 (upd.); 38 (upd.)
American General Finance Corp., 11
American Home Mortgage Holdings, Inc., 46
Ameritrade Holding Corporation, 34
AMVESCAP PLC, 65
Arthur Andersen & Company, Société Coopérative, 10
Avco Financial Services Inc., 13
Aviva PLC, 50 (upd.)
Bear Stearns Companies, Inc., II; 10 (upd.); 52 (upd.)
Benchmark Capital, 49
Bill & Melinda Gates Foundation, 41
Bozzuto's, Inc., 13
Bradford & Bingley PLC, 65
Capital One Financial Corporation, 52
Carnegie Corporation of New York, 35
Cash America International, Inc., 20; 61 (upd.)
Cattles plc, 58
Cendant Corporation, 44 (upd.)
Certegy, Inc., 63
Cetelem S.A., 21
The Charles Schwab Corporation, 8; 26 (upd.)
Citfed Bancorp, Inc., 16
Coinstar, Inc., 44
Comerica Incorporated, 40
Commercial Financial Services, Inc., 26
Concord EFS, Inc., 52
Coopers & Lybrand, 9
Cramer, Berkowitz & Co., 34
Credit Acceptance Corporation, 18
Cresud S.A.C.I.F. y A., 63
CS First Boston Inc., II

FINANCIAL SERVICES: NON-BANKS
(*continued*)

Dain Rauscher Corporation, 35 (upd.)
Daiwa Securities Group Inc., II; 55 (upd.)
Datek Online Holdings Corp., 32
The David and Lucile Packard Foundation, 41
Dean Witter, Discover & Co., 12
Deutsche Börse AG, 59
Dow Jones Telerate, Inc., 10
Dresdner Kleinwort Wasserstein, 60 (upd.)
Drexel Burnham Lambert Incorporated, II
DVI, Inc., 51
E*Trade Financial Corporation, 20; 60 (upd.)
Eaton Vance Corporation, 18
Edward D. Jones & Company L.P., 66 (upd.)
Edward Jones, 30
Euronext Paris S.A., 37
Experian Information Solutions Inc., 45
Fair, Isaac and Company, 18
Fannie Mae, 45 (upd.)
Federal National Mortgage Association, II
Fidelity Investments Inc., II; 14 (upd.)
First Albany Companies Inc., 37
First Data Corporation, 30 (upd.)
First USA, Inc., 11
FMR Corp., 8; 32 (upd.)
Forstmann Little & Co., 38
Fortis, Inc., 15
Frank Russell Company, 46
Franklin Resources, Inc., 9
Freddie Mac, 54
Friedman, Billings, Ramsey Group, Inc., 53
Gabelli Asset Management Inc., 30
The Goldman Sachs Group Inc., II; 20 (upd.); 51 (upd.)
Grede Foundries, Inc., 38
Green Tree Financial Corporation, 11
Gruntal & Co., L.L.C., 20
Grupo Financiero Galicia S.A., 63
H & R Block, Incorporated, 9; 29 (upd.)
H.D. Vest, Inc., 46
Hoenig Group Inc., 41
Household International, Inc., II; 21 (upd.)
Ingenico—Compagnie Industrielle et Financière d'Ingénierie, 46
Instinet Corporation, 34
Inter-Regional Financial Group, Inc., 15
Investcorp SA, 57
The Island ECN, Inc., 48
Istituto per la Ricostruzione Industriale S.p.A., 11
J. & W. Seligman & Co. Inc., 61
Janus Capital Group Inc., 57
JB Oxford Holdings, Inc., 32
Jefferies Group, Inc., 25
John Hancock Financial Services, Inc., 42 (upd.)
The John Nuveen Company, 21
Jones Lang LaSalle Incorporated, 49
Kansas City Southern Industries, Inc., 26 (upd.)
Kleiner, Perkins, Caufield & Byers, 53
Kleinwort Benson Group PLC, II
Kohlberg Kravis Roberts & Co., 24; 56 (upd.)
KPMG Worldwide, 10
La Poste, 47 (upd.)
LaBranche & Co. Inc., 37
Lazard LLC, 38
Legg Mason, Inc., 33
London Stock Exchange Limited, 34
M.H. Meyerson & Co., Inc., 46
MacAndrews & Forbes Holdings Inc., 28
MasterCard International, Inc., 9

MBNA Corporation, 33 (upd.)
Merrill Lynch & Co., Inc., II; 13 (upd.); 40 (upd.)
Metris Companies Inc., 56
Morgan Grenfell Group PLC, II
Morgan Stanley Dean Witter & Company, II; 16 (upd.); 33 (upd.)
Mountain States Mortgage Centers, Inc., 29
NASD, 54 (upd.)
National Association of Securities Dealers, Inc., 10
National Auto Credit, Inc., 16
National Discount Brokers Group, Inc., 28
National Financial Partners Corp., 65
Navy Federal Credit Union, 33
Neuberger Berman Inc., 57
New Street Capital Inc., 8
New York Stock Exchange, Inc., 9; 39 (upd.)
The Nikko Securities Company Limited, II; 9 (upd.)
Nippon Shinpan Co., Ltd., II; 61 (upd.)
Nomura Securities Company, Limited, II; 9 (upd.)
Norwich & Peterborough Building Society, 55
Old Mutual PLC, 61
Ontario Teachers' Pension Plan, 61
Onyx Acceptance Corporation, 59
ORIX Corporation, II; 44 (upd.)
PaineWebber Group Inc., II; 22 (upd.)
PayPal Inc., 58
The Pew Charitable Trusts, 35
Piper Jaffray Companies Inc., 22
Pitney Bowes Inc., 47 (upd.)
Providian Financial Corporation, 52 (upd.)
The Prudential Insurance Company of America, 30 (upd.)
The Quick & Reilly Group, Inc., 20
Resource America, Inc., 42
Robert W. Baird & Co. Incorporated, 67
Ryan Beck & Co., Inc., 66
Safeguard Scientifics, Inc., 10
Salomon Inc., II; 13 (upd.)
SBC Warburg, 14
Schroders plc, 42
Shearson Lehman Brothers Holdings Inc., II; 9 (upd.)
Siebert Financial Corp., 32
SLM Holding Corp., 25 (upd.)
Smith Barney Inc., 15
Soros Fund Management LLC, 28
Spear, Leeds & Kellogg, 66
State Street Boston Corporation, 8
Student Loan Marketing Association, II
T. Rowe Price Associates, Inc., 11; 34 (upd.)
Teachers Insurance and Annuity Association-College Retirement Equities Fund, 45 (upd.)
Texas Pacific Group Inc., 36
Total System Services, Inc., 18
Trilon Financial Corporation, II
United Jewish Communities, 33
The Vanguard Group, Inc., 14; 34 (upd.)
VeriFone, Inc., 18
Visa International, 9; 26 (upd.)
Wachovia Corporation, 12; 46 (upd.)
Waddell & Reed, Inc., 22
Washington Federal, Inc., 17
Waterhouse Investor Services, Inc., 18
Watson Wyatt Worldwide, 42
Western Union Financial Services, Inc., 54
Working Assets Funding Service, 43
World Acceptance Corporation, 57
Yamaichi Securities Company, Limited, II
The Ziegler Companies, Inc., 24; 63 (upd.)

Zurich Financial Services, 42 (upd.)

FOOD PRODUCTS

A. Moksel AG, 59
Agway, Inc., 7
Ajinomoto Co., Inc., II; 28 (upd.)
Alabama Farmers Cooperative, Inc., 63
The Albert Fisher Group plc, 41
Alberto-Culver Company, 8
Aldi Group, 13
Alfred Ritter GmbH & Co. KG, 58
Alpine Lace Brands, Inc., 18
American Crystal Sugar Company, 11; 32 (upd.)
American Foods Group, 43
American Italian Pasta Company, 27
American Maize-Products Co., 14
American Pop Corn Company, 59
American Rice, Inc., 33
Amfac/JMB Hawaii L.L.C., 24 (upd.)
Annie's Homegrown, Inc., 59
Archer-Daniels-Midland Company, 32 (upd.)
Archway Cookies, Inc., 29
Arcor S.A.I.C., 66
Arla Foods amba, 48
Arnott's Ltd., 66
Associated British Foods plc, II; 13 (upd.); 41 (upd.)
Associated Milk Producers, Inc., 11; 48 (upd.)
Atlantic Premium Brands, Ltd., 57
August Storck KG, 66
Aurora Foods Inc., 32
Awrey Bakeries, Inc., 56
B&G Foods, Inc., 40
The B. Manischewitz Company, LLC, 31
Bahlsen GmbH & Co. KG, 44
Balance Bar Company, 32
Baltek Corporation, 34
Barilla G. e R. Fratelli S.p.A., 17; 50 (upd.)
Bear Creek Corporation, 38
Beatrice Company, II
Beech-Nut Nutrition Corporation, 21; 51 (upd.)
Ben & Jerry's Homemade, Inc., 10; 35 (upd.)
Berkeley Farms, Inc., 46
Besnier SA, 19
Bestfoods, 22 (upd.)
Blue Bell Creameries L.P., 30
Blue Diamond Growers, 28
Bob's Red Mill Natural Foods, Inc., 63
Bonduelle SA, 51
Bongrain SA, 25
Booker PLC, 13; 31 (upd.)
Borden, Inc., II; 22 (upd.)
Boyd Coffee Company, 53
Brach and Brock Confections, Inc., 15
Brake Bros plc, 45
Bridgford Foods Corporation, 27
Brioche Pasquier S.A., 58
Brothers Gourmet Coffees, Inc., 20
Broughton Foods Co., 17
Brown & Haley, 23
Bruce Foods Corporation, 39
Bruegger's Corporation, 63
BSN Groupe S.A., II
Bumble Bee Seafoods L.L.C., 64
Bunge Ltd., 62
Burns, Philp & Company Ltd., 63
Bush Boake Allen Inc., 30
Bush Brothers & Company, 45
C.H. Robinson Worldwide, Inc., 40 (upd.)
Cadbury Schweppes PLC, II; 49 (upd.)
Cagle's, Inc., 20

Calavo Growers, Inc., 47
Calcot Ltd., 33
Campbell Soup Company, II; 7 (upd.); 26 (upd.)
Campofrío Alimentación S.A, 59
Canada Packers Inc., II
Cargill Inc., 13 (upd.)
Carnation Company, II
The Carriage House Companies, Inc., 55
Carroll's Foods, Inc., 46
Carvel Corporation, 35
Castle & Cooke, Inc., II; 20 (upd.)
Cattleman's, Inc., 20
Celestial Seasonings, Inc., 16
Central Soya Company, Inc., 7
Chelsea Milling Company, 29
Chicken of the Sea International, 24 (upd.)
Chiquita Brands International, Inc., 7; 21 (upd.)
Chock Full o'Nuts Corp., 17
Chocoladefabriken Lindt & Sprüngli AG, 27
CHS Inc., 60
Chupa Chups S.A., 38
Clif Bar Inc., 50
The Clorox Company, 22 (upd.)
Coca-Cola Enterprises, Inc., 13
Community Coffee Co. L.L.C., 53
ConAgra Foods, Inc., II; 12 (upd.); 42 (upd.)
The Connell Company, 29
ContiGroup Companies, Inc., 43 (upd.)
Continental Grain Company, 10; 13 (upd.)
CoolBrands International Inc., 35
CPC International Inc., II
Cranswick plc, 40
CSM N.V., 65
Cumberland Packing Corporation, 26
Curtice-Burns Foods, Inc., 7; 21 (upd.)
Czarnikow-Rionda Company, Inc., 32
Dairy Crest Group plc, 32
Dalgery, PLC, II
Danisco A/S, 44
Dannon Co., Inc., 14
Darigold, Inc., 9
Dawn Food Products, Inc., 17
Dean Foods Company, 7; 21 (upd.)
DeKalb Genetics Corporation, 17
Del Monte Foods Company, 7; 23 (upd.)
Di Giorgio Corp., 12
Diageo plc, 24 (upd.)
Diamond of California, 64 (upd.)
Dippin' Dots, Inc., 56
Dole Food Company, Inc., 9; 31 (upd.)
Domino Sugar Corporation, 26
Doskocil Companies, Inc., 12
Dreyer's Grand Ice Cream, Inc., 17
The Earthgrains Company, 36
Emge Packing Co., Inc., 11
Empresas Polar SA, 55 (upd.)
Eridania Béghin-Say S.A., 36
ERLY Industries Inc., 17
Eskimo Pie Corporation, 21
Farley's & Sathers Candy Company, Inc., 62
Farmland Foods, Inc., 7
Farmland Industries, Inc., 48
Ferrero SpA, 54
Fieldale Farms Corporation, 23
Fleer Corporation, 15
Fleury Michon S.A., 39
Florida Crystals Inc., 35
Flowers Industries, Inc., 12; 35 (upd.)
Fonterra Co-Operative Group Ltd., 58
FoodBrands America, Inc., 23
Foster Poultry Farms, 32
Fred Usinger Inc., 54

Fresh America Corporation, 20
Fresh Foods, Inc., 29
Friesland Coberco Dairy Foods Holding N.V., 59
Frito-Lay Company, 32
Fromageries Bel, 23
Fyffes Plc, 38
Galaxy Nutritional Foods, Inc., 58
Gardenburger, Inc., 33
Geest Plc, 38
General Mills, Inc., II; 10 (upd.); 36 (upd.)
George A. Hormel and Company, II
George Weston Limited, 36 (upd.)
Gerber Products Company, 7; 21 (upd.)
Ghirardelli Chocolate Company, 30
Givaudan SA, 43
Glanbia plc, 59
Global Berry Farms LLC, 62
Godiva Chocolatier, Inc., 64
Gold Kist Inc., 17; 26 (upd.)
Gold'n Plump Poultry, 54
Golden Enterprises, Inc., 26
Gonnella Baking Company, 40
Good Humor-Breyers Ice Cream Company, 14
Goodman Fielder Ltd., 52
GoodMark Foods, Inc., 26
Gorton's, 13
Goya Foods Inc., 22
Great Harvest Bread Company, 44
Grist Mill Company, 15
Groupe Danone, 32 (upd.)
Groupe Soufflet SA, 55
Gruma, S.A. de C.V., 31
Grupo Herdez, S.A. de C.V., 35
Grupo Leche Pascual S.A., 59
Guittard Chocolate Company, 55
H.J. Heinz Company, II; 11 (upd.); 36 (upd.)
The Hain Celestial Group, Inc., 27; 43 (upd.)
Hanover Foods Corporation, 35
HARIBO GmbH & Co. KG, 44
The Hartz Mountain Corporation, 12
Hazlewood Foods plc, 32
Herman Goelitz, Inc., 28
Hershey Foods Corporation, II; 15 (upd.); 51 (upd.)
Hill's Pet Nutrition, Inc., 27
Hillsdown Holdings plc, II; 24 (upd.)
Horizon Organic Holding Corporation, 37
Hormel Foods Corporation, 18 (upd.); 54 (upd.)
Hudson Foods Inc., 13
Hulman & Company, 44
Hunt-Wesson, Inc., 17
Iams Company, 26
IAWS Group plc, 49
IBP, Inc., II; 21 (upd.)
Iceland Group plc, 33
Imagine Foods, Inc., 50
Imperial Holly Corporation, 12
Imperial Sugar Company, 32 (upd.)
Industrias Bachoco, S.A. de C.V., 39
Intercorp Excelle Foods Inc., 64
International Multifoods Corporation, 7; 25 (upd.)
Interstate Bakeries Corporation, 12; 38 (upd.)
Itoham Foods Inc., II; 61 (upd.)
J & J Snack Foods Corporation, 24
The J.M. Smucker Company, 11
J.R. Simplot Company, 16
Jacobs Suchard A.G., II
Jim Beam Brands Co., 14
John B. Sanfilippo & Son, Inc., 14
Johnsonville Sausage L.L.C., 63

Julius Meinl International AG, 53
Just Born, Inc., 32
Kal Kan Foods, Inc., 22
Kamps AG, 44
Keebler Foods Company, 36
Kellogg Company, II; 13 (upd.); 50 (upd.)
Kerry Group plc, 27
Kettle Foods Inc., 48
Kewpie Kabushiki Kaisha, 57
Kikkoman Corporation, 14; 47 (upd.)
The King Arthur Flour Company, 31
King Ranch, Inc., 14
Klement's Sausage Company, 61
Koninklijke Wessanen nv, II; 54 (upd.)
Kraft Foods Inc., 45 (upd.)
Kraft General Foods Inc., II; 7 (upd.)
Kraft Jacobs Suchard AG, 26 (upd.)
Krispy Kreme Doughnuts, Inc., 21; 61 (upd.)
L.D.C. SA, 61
La Choy Food Products Inc., 25
Lam Son Sugar Joint Stock Corporation (Lasuco), 60
Lamb Weston, Inc., 23
Lance, Inc., 14; 41 (upd.)
Land O'Lakes, Inc., II; 21 (upd.)
Ledesma Sociedad Anónima Agrícola Industrial, 62
Leprino Foods Company, 28
Leroux S.A.S., 65
Lifeway Foods, Inc., 65
Lincoln Snacks Company, 24
Litehouse Inc., 60
Lucille Farms, Inc., 45
Luigino's, Inc., 64
M.A. Gedney Co., 51
Madrange SA, 58
Malt-O-Meal Company, 22; 63 (upd.)
Maple Leaf Foods Inc., 41
Mars, Incorporated, 7; 40 (upd.)
Maui Land & Pineapple Company, Inc., 29
Mauna Loa Macadamia Nut Corporation, 64
McCormick & Company, Incorporated, 7; 27 (upd.)
McIlhenny Company, 20
McKee Foods Corporation, 7; 27 (upd.)
Meiji Milk Products Company, Limited, II
Meiji Seika Kaisha, Ltd., II
Michael Foods, Inc., 25
Mid-America Dairymen, Inc., 7
Midwest Grain Products, Inc., 49
Mike-Sell's Inc., 15
Milnot Company, 46
Molinos Río de la Plata S.A., 61
Monfort, Inc., 13
Morinaga & Co. Ltd., 61
Mrs. Baird's Bakeries, 29
Mt. Olive Pickle Company, Inc., 44
MTR Foods Ltd., 55
Murphy Family Farms Inc., 22
Nabisco Foods Group, II; 7 (upd.)
Nantucket Allserve, Inc., 22
Nathan's Famous, Inc., 29
National Presto Industries, Inc., 43 (upd.)
National Sea Products Ltd., 14
Natural Selection Foods, 54
Nestlé S.A., II; 7 (upd.); 28 (upd.)
New England Confectionery Co., 15
New World Pasta Company, 53
Newhall Land and Farming Company, 14
Newman's Own, Inc., 37
Niman Ranch, Inc., 67
Nippon Meat Packers, Inc., II
Nippon Suisan Kaisha, Limited, II
Nisshin Seifun Group Inc., II; 66 (upd.)
Northern Foods plc, 10; 61 (upd.)

FOOD PRODUCTS (continued)

Northland Cranberries, Inc., 38
Nutraceutical International Corporation, 37
NutraSweet Company, 8
Nutreco Holding N.V., 56
Oakhurst Dairy, 60
Ocean Spray Cranberries, Inc., 7; 25 (upd.)
OJSC Wimm-Bill-Dann Foods, 48
Omaha Steaks International Inc., 62
Ore-Ida Foods Incorporated, 13
Organic Valley (Coulee Region Organic
    Produce Pool), 53
Oscar Mayer Foods Corp., 12
Otis Spunkmeyer, Inc., 28
Overhill Corporation, 51
Papetti's Hygrade Egg Products, Inc., 39
Parmalat Finanziaria SpA, 50
Pendleton Grain Growers Inc., 64
Penford Corporation, 55
PepsiCo, Inc., I; 10 (upd.); 38 (upd.)
Perdigao SA, 52
Perdue Farms Inc., 7; 23 (upd.)
Pet Incorporated, 7
Petrossian Inc., 54
Pez Candy, Inc., 38
Philip Morris Companies Inc., 18 (upd.)
Phillips Foods, Inc., 63
PIC International Group PLC, 24 (upd.)
Pilgrim's Pride Corporation, 7; 23 (upd.)
The Pillsbury Company, II; 13 (upd.); 62
    (upd.)
Pioneer Hi-Bred International, Inc., 9
Pizza Inn, Inc., 46
Poore Brothers, Inc., 44
PowerBar Inc., 44
Prairie Farms Dairy, Inc., 47
Premium Standard Farms, Inc., 30
The Procter & Gamble Company, III; 8
    (upd.); 26 (upd.)
Purina Mills, Inc., 32
Quaker Oats Company, II; 12 (upd.); 34
    (upd.)
Quality Chekd Dairies, Inc., 48
Ralston Purina Company, II; 13 (upd.)
Ranks Hovis McDougall Limited, II; 28
    (upd.)
Reckitt Benckiser plc, II; 42 (upd.)
Rica Foods, Inc., 41
Rich Products Corporation, 7; 38 (upd.)
Richtree Inc., 63
Ricola Ltd., 62
Ridley Corporation Ltd., 62
Riviana Foods Inc., 27
Roland Murten A.G., 7
Rose Acre Farms, Inc., 60
Rowntree Mackintosh, II
Royal Numico N.V., 37
Ruiz Food Products, Inc., 53
Russell Stover Candies Inc., 12
Sadia S.A., 59
Sanderson Farms, Inc., 15
Saputo Inc., 59
Sara Lee Corporation, II; 15 (upd.); 54
    (upd.)
Savannah Foods & Industries, Inc., 7
Schlotzsky's, Inc., 36
Schwan's Sales Enterprises, Inc., 7
See's Candies, Inc., 30
Seminis, Inc., 29
Seneca Foods Corporation, 60 (upd.)
Sensient Technologies Corporation, 52
    (upd.)
Silhouette Brands, Inc., 55
Skalli Group, 67
Slim-Fast Foods Company, 66 (upd.)
Smithfield Foods, Inc., 7; 43 (upd.)

Snow Brand Milk Products Company, Ltd.,
    II; 48 (upd.)
Sodiaal S.A., 36 (upd.)
SODIMA, II
Sorrento, Inc., 24
Spangler Candy Company, 44
Stock Yards Packing Co., Inc., 37
Stollwerck AG, 53
Stolt Sea Farm Holdings PLC, 54
Stolt-Nielsen S.A., 42
Stonyfield Farm, Inc., 55
Stouffer Corp., 8
Südzucker AG, 27
Suiza Foods Corporation, 26
Sun-Diamond Growers of California, 7
Sunkist Growers, Inc., 26
Supervalu Inc., 18 (upd.); 50 (upd.)
Suprema Specialties, Inc., 27
Sweet Candy Company, 60
Swift & Company, 55
Sylvan, Inc., 22
T. Marzetti Company, 57
Taiyo Fishery Company, Limited, II
Tasty Baking Company, 14; 35 (upd.)
Tate & Lyle PLC, II; 42 (upd.)
TCBY Enterprises Inc., 17
TDL Group Ltd., 46
Thomas J. Lipton Company, 14
Thorn Apple Valley, Inc., 7; 22 (upd.)
Thorntons plc, 46
TLC Beatrice International Holdings, Inc.,
    22
Tofutti Brands, Inc., 64
Tom's Foods Inc., 66
Tombstone Pizza Corporation, 13
Tone Brothers, Inc., 21
Tootsie Roll Industries Inc., 12
Townsends, Inc., 64
Tri Valley Growers, 32
Trident Seafoods Corporation, 56
Tropicana Products, Inc., 28
Tyson Foods, Inc., II; 14 (upd.); 50 (upd.)
U.S. Foodservice, 26
Uncle Ben's Inc., 22
Unigate PLC, II; 28 (upd.)
United Biscuits (Holdings) plc, II; 42
    (upd.)
United Brands Company, II
United Foods, Inc., 21
Universal Foods Corporation, 7
Van Camp Seafood Company, Inc., 7
Vienna Sausage Manufacturing Co., 14
Vista Bakery, Inc., 56
Vlasic Foods International Inc., 25
Wattie's Ltd., 7
Weetabix Limited, 61
Wells' Dairy, Inc., 36
White Wave, 43
Wilbur Chocolate Company, 66
Wimm-Bill-Dann Foods, 48
Wisconsin Dairies, 7
WLR Foods, Inc., 21
Wm. B. Reily & Company Inc., 58
Wm. Wrigley Jr. Company, 7; 58 (upd.)
World's Finest Chocolate Inc., 39
Worthington Foods, Inc., 14
Yamazaki Baking Co., Ltd., 58
YOCREAM International, Inc., 47
Zatarain's, Inc., 64

FOOD SERVICES & RETAILERS

Advantica Restaurant Group, Inc., 27
    (upd.)
AFC Enterprises, Inc., 32 (upd.)
Affiliated Foods Inc., 53
Albertson's, Inc., II; 7 (upd.); 30 (upd.); 65
    (upd.)

Aldi Group, 13
Alex Lee Inc., 18; 44 (upd.)
Allen Foods, Inc., 60
America's Favorite Chicken Company,
    Inc., 7
American Stores Company, II
Applebee's International, Inc., 14; 35
    (upd.)
ARA Services, II
Arby's Inc., 14
Arden Group, Inc., 29
Argyll Group PLC, II
Ark Restaurants Corp., 20
Asahi Breweries, Ltd., 20 (upd.)
ASDA Group Ltd., II; 28 (upd.); 64 (upd.)
Associated Grocers, Incorporated, 9; 31
    (upd.)
Association des Centres Distributeurs E.
    Leclerc, 37
Au Bon Pain Co., Inc., 18
Auchan, 37
Auntie Anne's, Inc., 35
Autogrill SpA, 49
Avado Brands, Inc., 31
Back Bay Restaurant Group, Inc., 20
Back Yard Burgers, Inc., 45
Bashas' Inc., 33
Bear Creek Corporation, 38
Benihana, Inc., 18
Bertucci's Corporation, 64 (upd.)
Big Bear Stores Co., 13
Big V Supermarkets, Inc., 25
Big Y Foods, Inc., 53
Blimpie International, Inc., 15; 49 (upd.)
Bob Evans Farms, Inc., 9; 63 (upd.)
Bob's Red Mill Natural Foods, Inc., 63
Bon Appetit Holding AG, 48
Boston Market Corporation, 12; 48 (upd.)
Briazz, Inc., 53
Brinker International, Inc., 10; 38 (upd.)
Brookshire Grocery Company, 16
Bruegger's Corporation, 63
Bruno's, Inc., 7; 26 (upd.)
Buca, Inc., 38
Budgens Ltd., 59
Buffalo Wild Wings, Inc., 56
Buffets, Inc., 10; 32 (upd.)
Burger King Corporation, II; 17 (upd.); 56
    (upd.)
C & S Wholesale Grocers, Inc., 55
C.H. Robinson, Inc., 11
Caffè Nero Group PLC, 63
California Pizza Kitchen Inc., 15
Captain D's, LLC, 59
Cargill, Inc., II
Caribou Coffee Company, Inc., 28
Carlson Companies, Inc., 22 (upd.)
Carr-Gottstein Foods Co., 17
Casey's General Stores, Inc., 19
Casino Guichard-Perrachon S.A., 59 (upd.)
CBRL Group, Inc., 35 (upd.)
CEC Entertainment, Inc., 31 (upd.)
Chart House Enterprises, Inc., 17
Checkers Drive-Up Restaurants Inc., 16
The Cheesecake Factory Inc., 17
Chi-Chi's Inc., 13; 51 (upd.)
Chicago Pizza & Brewery, Inc., 44
Chick-fil-A Inc., 23
Chipotle Mexican Grill, Inc., 67
Church's Chicken, 66
Cinnabon Inc., 23
The Circle K Corporation, II
CKE Restaurants, Inc., 19; 46 (upd.)
Coborn's, Inc., 30
Compass Group PLC, 34
Comptoirs Modernes S.A., 19
Consolidated Products Inc., 14

Controladora Comercial Mexicana, S.A. de C.V., 36
Cooker Restaurant Corporation, 20; 51 (upd.)
The Copps Corporation, 32
Cosi, Inc., 53
Cost-U-Less, Inc., 51
Coto Centro Integral de Comercializacion S.A., 66
Cracker Barrel Old Country Store, Inc., 10
Cremonini S.p.A., 57
Culver Franchising System, Inc., 58
D'Agostino Supermarkets Inc., 19
Dairy Mart Convenience Stores, Inc., 7; 25 (upd.)
Darden Restaurants, Inc., 16; 44 (upd.)
Dean & DeLuca, Inc., 36
Del Taco, Inc., 58
Delhaize "Le Lion" S.A., 44
DeMoulas / Market Basket Inc., 23
DenAmerica Corporation, 29
Deschutes Brewery, Inc., 57
Diedrich Coffee, Inc., 40
Dierbergs Markets Inc., 63
Doctor's Associates Inc., 67 (upd.)
Dominick's Finer Foods, Inc., 56
Domino's, Inc., 7; 21 (upd.); 63 (upd.)
Donatos Pizzeria Corporation, 58
Eateries, Inc., 33
Edeka Zentrale A.G., II; 47 (upd.)
Einstein/Noah Bagel Corporation, 29
El Chico Restaurants, Inc., 19
Elior SA, 49
Elmer's Restaurants, Inc., 42
Embers America Restaurants, 30
Etablissements Economiques du Casino Guichard, Perrachon et Cie, S.C.A., 12
Famous Dave's of America, Inc., 40
Fatburger Corporation, 64
Fazoli's Systems, Inc., 27
Flagstar Companies, Inc., 10
Flanigan's Enterprises, Inc., 60
Fleming Companies, Inc., II
The Food Emporium, 64
Food Lion LLC, II; 15 (upd.); 66 (upd.)
Foodarama Supermarkets, Inc., 28
Foodmaker, Inc., 14
The Fred W. Albrecht Grocery Co., 13
Fresh Choice, Inc., 20
Fresh Enterprises, Inc., 66
Fresh Foods, Inc., 29
Friendly Ice Cream Corp., 30
Frisch's Restaurants, Inc., 35
Fuller Smith & Turner P.L.C., 38
Furr's Restaurant Group, Inc., 53
Furr's Supermarkets, Inc., 28
Garden Fresh Restaurant Corporation, 31
The Gateway Corporation Ltd., II
Genuardi's Family Markets, Inc., 35
George Weston Limited, II; 36 (upd.)
Ghirardelli Chocolate Company, 30
Giant Food Inc., II; 22 (upd.)
Godfather's Pizza Incorporated, 25
Golden Corral Corporation, 10; 66 (upd.)
Golden State Foods Corporation, 32
The Golub Corporation, 26
Gordon Food Service Inc., 8; 39 (upd.)
The Grand Union Company, 7; 28 (upd.)
The Great Atlantic & Pacific Tea Company, Inc., II; 16 (upd.); 55 (upd.)
Greggs PLC, 65
Gristede's Sloan's, Inc., 31
Ground Round, Inc., 21
Groupe Promodès S.A., 19
Guyenne et Gascogne, 23
H.E. Butt Grocery Co., 13; 32 (upd.)
Haggen Inc., 38

Hannaford Bros. Co., 12
Hard Rock Cafe International, Inc., 12
Harris Teeter Inc., 23
Harry's Farmers Market Inc., 23
Hickory Farms, Inc., 17
Holberg Industries, Inc., 36
Holland Burgerville USA, 44
Hooters of America, Inc., 18
Hops Restaurant Bar and Brewery, 46
Houchens Industries Inc., 51
Hughes Markets, Inc., 22
Hungry Howie's Pizza and Subs, Inc., 25
Hy-Vee, Inc., 36
ICA AB, II
Iceland Group plc, 33
IHOP Corporation, 17; 58 (upd.)
Il Fornaio (America) Corporation, 27
In-N-Out Burger, 19
Ingles Markets, Inc., 20
Inserra Supermarkets, 25
Inter Link Foods PLC, 61
International Dairy Queen, Inc., 10; 39 (upd.)
ITM Entreprises SA, 36
Ito-Yokado Co., Ltd., 42 (upd.)
J Sainsbury plc, II; 13 (upd.); 38 (upd.)
J Alexander's Corporation, 65
Jamba Juice Company, 47
JD Wetherspoon plc, 30
Jerry's Famous Deli Inc., 24
Jitney-Jungle Stores of America, Inc., 27
John Lewis Partnership plc, 42 (upd.)
Johnny Rockets Group, Inc., 31
KFC Corporation, 7; 21 (upd.)
King Kullen Grocery Co., Inc., 15
Koninklijke Ahold N.V. (Royal Ahold), II; 16 (upd.)
Koo Koo Roo, Inc., 25
The Kroger Co., II; 15 (upd.); 65 (upd.)
The Krystal Company, 33
Kwik Save Group plc, 11
La Madeleine French Bakery & Café, 33
Landry's Restaurants, Inc., 15; 65 (upd.)
The Laurel Pub Company Limited, 59
Laurus N.V., 65
LDB Corporation, 53
Leeann Chin, Inc., 30
Levy Restaurants L.P., 26
Little Caesar Enterprises, Inc., 7; 24 (upd.)
Loblaw Companies Limited, 43
Logan's Roadhouse, Inc., 29
Lone Star Steakhouse & Saloon, Inc., 51
Long John Silver's, 13; 57 (upd.)
Luby's, Inc., 17; 42 (upd.)
Lucky Stores, Inc., 27
Lund Food Holdings, Inc., 22
Madden's on Gull Lake, 52
Maid-Rite Corporation, 62
Marie Callender's Restaurant & Bakery, Inc., 28
Marsh Supermarkets, Inc., 17
Max & Erma's Restaurants Inc., 19
McAlister's Corporation, 66
McDonald's Corporation, II; 7 (upd.); 26 (upd.); 63 (upd.)
Megafoods Stores Inc., 13
Meijer Incorporated, 7
Metcash Trading Ltd., 58
Metromedia Companies, 14
Mexican Restaurants, Inc., 41
The Middleby Corporation, 22
Minyard Food Stores, Inc., 33
MITROPA AG, 37
Monterey Pasta Company, 58
Morrison Restaurants Inc., 11
Morton's Restaurant Group, Inc., 30
Mrs. Fields' Original Cookies, Inc., 27

Musgrave Group Plc, 57
Nash Finch Company, 8; 23 (upd.); 65 (upd.)
Nathan's Famous, Inc., 29
National Convenience Stores Incorporated, 7
New World Restaurant Group, Inc., 44
New York Restaurant Group, Inc., 32
Noble Roman's Inc., 14
Noodles & Company, Inc., 55
NPC International, Inc., 40
O'Charley's Inc., 19; 60 (upd.)
Old Spaghetti Factory International Inc., 24
The Oshawa Group Limited, II
Outback Steakhouse, Inc., 12; 34 (upd.)
P&C Foods Inc., 8
P.F. Chang's China Bistro, Inc., 37
Pancho's Mexican Buffet, Inc., 46
Panda Management Company, Inc., 35
Panera Bread Company, 44
Papa John's International, Inc., 15
Papa Murphy's International, Inc., 54
Pathmark Stores, Inc., 23
Peapod, Inc., 30
Penn Traffic Company, 13
Performance Food Group Company, 31
Perkins Family Restaurants, L.P., 22
Petrossian Inc., 54
Phillips Foods, Inc., 63
Piccadilly Cafeterias, Inc., 19
Piggly Wiggly Southern, Inc., 13
Pizza Hut Inc., 7; 21 (upd.)
Planet Hollywood International, Inc., 18; 41 (upd.)
Players International, Inc., 22
Ponderosa Steakhouse, 15
Provigo Inc., II; 51 (upd.)
Publix Super Markets Inc., 7; 31 (upd.)
Pueblo Xtra International, Inc., 47
Quality Dining, Inc., 18
Quality Food Centers, Inc., 17
The Quizno's Corporation, 42
Rally's Hamburgers, Inc., 25
Ralphs Grocery Company, 35
Randall's Food Markets, Inc., 40
Rare Hospitality International Inc., 19
Raving Brands, Inc., 64
Red Robin Gourmet Burgers, Inc., 56
Restaurant Associates Corporation, 66
Restaurants Unlimited, Inc., 13
Richfood Holdings, Inc., 7
Richtree Inc., 63
The Riese Organization, 38
Riser Foods, Inc., 9
Roadhouse Grill, Inc., 22
Rock Bottom Restaurants, Inc., 25
Romacorp, Inc., 58
Roundy's Inc., 58 (upd.)
RTM Restaurant Group, 58
Rubio's Restaurants, Inc., 35
Ruby Tuesday, Inc., 18
Ruth's Chris Steak House, 28
Ryan's Family Steak Houses, Inc., 15
Safeway PLC, II; 24 (upd.); 50 (upd.)
Santa Barbara Restaurant Group, Inc., 37
Sbarro, Inc., 16; 64 (upd.)
Schlotzsky's, Inc., 36
Schultz Sav-O Stores, Inc., 21
Schwan's Sales Enterprises, Inc., 26 (upd.)
Seaway Food Town, Inc., 15
Second Harvest, 29
See's Candies, Inc., 30
Seneca Foods Corporation, 17
Service America Corp., 7
SFI Group plc, 51
Shaw's Supermarkets, Inc., 56
Shells Seafood Restaurants, Inc., 43

FOOD SERVICES & RETAILERS
(*continued*)

Shoney's, Inc., 7; 23 (upd.)
ShowBiz Pizza Time, Inc., 13
Skyline Chili, Inc., 62
Smart & Final, Inc., 16
Smith's Food & Drug Centers, Inc., 8; 57
   (upd.)
Sodexho Alliance SA, 29
Somerfield plc, 47 (upd.)
Sonic Corporation, 14; 37 (upd.)
The Southland Corporation, II; 7 (upd.)
Spaghetti Warehouse, Inc., 25
SPAR Handels AG, 35
Spartan Stores Inc., 8
Stater Bros. Holdings Inc., 64
The Steak n Shake Company, 41
Steinberg Incorporated, II
Stew Leonard's, 56
The Stop & Shop Companies, Inc., II
Subway, 32
Super Food Services, Inc., 15
Supermarkets General Holdings
   Corporation, II
Supervalu Inc., II; 18 (upd.); 50 (upd.)
SYSCO Corporation, II; 24 (upd.)
Taco Bell Corp., 7; 21 (upd.)
Taco Cabana, Inc., 23
Taco John's International, Inc., 15; 63
   (upd.)
TelePizza S.A., 33
Tesco PLC, II
Tops Markets LLC, 60
Total Entertainment Restaurant
   Corporation, 46
Trader Joe's Company, 13; 50 (upd.)
Travel Ports of America, Inc., 17
Tree of Life, Inc., 29
Triarc Companies, Inc., 34 (upd.)
Tubby's, Inc., 53
Tully's Coffee Corporation, 51
Tumbleweed, Inc., 33
TW Services, Inc., II
Ukrop's Super Market's, Inc., 39
Unique Casual Restaurants, Inc., 27
United Natural Foods, Inc., 32
Uno Restaurant Corporation, 18
Uwajimaya, Inc., 60
Vail Resorts, Inc., 43 (upd.)
VICORP Restaurants, Inc., 12; 48 (upd.)
Village Super Market, Inc., 7
The Vons Companies, Incorporated, 7; 28
   (upd.)
Waffle House Inc., 14; 60 (upd.)
Wakefern Food Corporation, 33
Waldbaum, Inc., 19
Wall Street Deli, Inc., 33
Wawa Inc., 17
Wegmans Food Markets, Inc., 9; 41 (upd.)
Weis Markets, Inc., 15
Wendy's International, Inc., 8; 23 (upd.);
   47 (upd.)
The WesterN SizzliN Corporation, 60
Wetterau Incorporated, II
White Castle System, Inc., 12; 36 (upd.)
White Rose, Inc., 24
Whittard of Chelsea Plc, 61
Whole Foods Market, Inc., 50 (upd.)
Wild Oats Markets, Inc., 19; 41 (upd.)
Winchell's Donut Houses Operating
   Company, L.P., 60
WinCo Foods Inc., 60
Winn-Dixie Stores, Inc., II; 21 (upd.); 59
   (upd.)
Wm. Morrison Supermarkets PLC, 38
The Wolfgang Puck Food Company, Inc.,
   26

Worldwide Restaurant Concepts, Inc., 47
Young & Co.'s Brewery, P.L.C., 38
Yucaipa Cos., 17
Yum! Brands Inc., 58

**HEALTH & PERSONAL CARE
PRODUCTS**

Akorn, Inc., 32
ALARIS Medical Systems, Inc., 65
Alberto-Culver Company, 8
Alco Health Services Corporation, III
Allergan, Inc., 10; 30 (upd.)
American Safety Razor Company, 20
American Stores Company, 22 (upd.)
Amway Corporation, III; 13 (upd.)
Atkins Nutritionals, Inc., 58
Aveda Corporation, 24
Avon Products, Inc., III; 19 (upd.); 46
   (upd.)
Bally Total Fitness Holding Corp., 25
Bausch & Lomb Inc., 7; 25 (upd.)
Baxter International Inc., I; 10 (upd.)
BeautiControl Cosmetics, Inc., 21
Becton, Dickinson & Company, I; 11
   (upd.)
Beiersdorf AG, 29
Big B, Inc., 17
Bindley Western Industries, Inc., 9
Block Drug Company, Inc., 8; 27 (upd.)
The Body Shop International plc, 53 (upd.)
The Boots Company PLC, 24 (upd.)
Bristol-Myers Squibb Company, III; 9
   (upd.)
C.R. Bard Inc., 9
Candela Corporation, 48
Cardinal Health, Inc., 18; 50 (upd.)
Carson, Inc., 31
Carter-Wallace, Inc., 8
Caswell-Massey Co. Ltd., 51
CCA Industries, Inc., 53
Chattem, Inc., 17
Chesebrough-Pond's USA, Inc., 8
Chronimed Inc., 26
Cintas Corporation, 51 (upd.)
The Clorox Company, III
CNS, Inc., 20
Colgate-Palmolive Company, III; 14 (upd.);
   35 (upd.)
Conair Corp., 17
Cordis Corp., 19
Cosmair, Inc., 8
Coty, Inc., 36
Cybex International, Inc., 49
Datascope Corporation, 39
Del Laboratories, Inc., 28
Deltec, Inc., 56
Dentsply International Inc., 10
DEP Corporation, 20
DePuy, Inc., 30
The Dial Corp., 23 (upd.)
Direct Focus, Inc., 47
Drackett Professional Products, 12
Elizabeth Arden, Inc., 8; 40 (upd.)
Empi, Inc., 26
Enrich International, Inc., 33
The Estée Lauder Companies Inc., 9; 30
   (upd.)
Ethicon, Inc., 23
Forest Laboratories, Inc., 11
Forever Living Products International Inc.,
   17
French Fragrances, Inc., 22
Gambro AB, 49
General Nutrition Companies, Inc., 11; 29
   (upd.)
Genzyme Corporation, 13
The Gillette Company, III; 20 (upd.)

Groupe Yves Saint Laurent, 23
Guerlain, 23
Guest Supply, Inc., 18
Guidant Corporation, 58
Hanger Orthopedic Group, Inc., 41
Helen of Troy Corporation, 18
Helene Curtis Industries, Inc., 8; 28 (upd.)
Henkel KGaA, III
Henry Schein, Inc., 31
Herbalife International, Inc., 17; 41 (upd.)
Inter Parfums Inc., 35
Invacare Corporation, 11
IVAX Corporation, 11
IVC Industries, Inc., 45
The Jean Coutu Group (PJC) Inc., 46
John Paul Mitchell Systems, 24
Johnson & Johnson, III; 8 (upd.); 36 (upd.)
Kanebo, Ltd., 53
Kao Corporation, III
Kendall International, Inc., 11
Kimberly-Clark Corporation, III; 16 (upd.);
   43 (upd.)
Kyowa Hakko Kogyo Co., Ltd., III
L'Oréal SA, III; 8 (upd.); 46 (upd.)
Laboratoires de Biologie Végétale Yves
   Rocher, 35
The Lamaur Corporation, 41
Lever Brothers Company, 9
Lion Corporation, III; 51 (upd.)
Luxottica SpA, 17
Mannatech Inc., 33
Mary Kay Corporation, 9; 30 (upd.)
Maxxim Medical Inc., 12
Medco Containment Services Inc., 9
Medline Industries, Inc., 61
Medtronic, Inc., 8; 67 (upd.)
Melaleuca Inc., 31
The Mentholatum Company Inc., 32
Mentor Corporation, 26
Merck & Co., Inc., 34 (upd.)
Merit Medical Systems, Inc., 29
Nature's Sunshine Products, Inc., 15
NBTY, Inc., 31
NeighborCare, Inc., 67 (upd.)
Neutrogena Corporation, 17
New Dana Perfumes Company, 37
Nikken Global Inc., 32
Nutrition for Life International Inc., 22
Ocular Sciences, Inc., 65
OEC Medical Systems, Inc., 27
Patterson Dental Co., 19
Perrigo Company, 12
Physician Sales & Service, Inc., 14
Playtex Products, Inc., 15
The Procter & Gamble Company, III; 8
   (upd.); 26 (upd.); 67 (upd.)
Reliv International, Inc., 58
Revlon Inc., III; 17 (upd.)
Roche Biomedical Laboratories, Inc., 11
S.C. Johnson & Son, Inc., III
Safety 1st, Inc., 24
Schering-Plough Corporation, 14 (upd.)
Shaklee Corporation, 39 (upd.)
Shionogi & Co., Ltd., III
Shiseido Company, Limited, III; 22 (upd.)
Slim-Fast Nutritional Foods International,
   Inc., 18
Smith & Nephew plc, 17
SmithKline Beecham PLC, III
Soft Sheen Products, Inc., 31
STAAR Surgical Company, 57
Sunrise Medical Inc., 11
Tambrands Inc., 8
Terumo Corporation, 48
Tom's of Maine, Inc., 45
The Tranzonic Companies, 37
Turtle Wax, Inc., 15

United States Surgical Corporation, 10; 34
    (upd.)
USANA, Inc., 29
Utah Medical Products, Inc., 36
VHA Inc., 53
VIASYS Healthcare, Inc., 52
VISX, Incorporated, 30
Vitamin Shoppe Industries, Inc., 60
Water Pik Technologies, Inc., 34
Weider Nutrition International, Inc., 29
Wella AG, III; 48 (upd.)
West Pharmaceutical Services, Inc., 42
Wright Medical Group, Inc., 61
Wyeth, 50 (upd.)
Zila, Inc., 46
Zimmer Holdings, Inc., 45

HEALTH CARE SERVICES

Acadian Ambulance & Air Med Services,
    Inc., 39
Adventist Health, 53
Advocat Inc., 46
Alterra Healthcare Corporation, 42
Amedysis, Inc., 53
The American Cancer Society, 24
American Healthways, Inc., 65
American Lung Association, 48
American Medical Association, 39
American Medical International, Inc., III
American Medical Response, Inc., 39
American Red Cross, 40
AmeriSource Health Corporation, 37 (upd.)
AmSurg Corporation, 48
Applied Bioscience International, Inc., 10
Assisted Living Concepts, Inc., 43
ATC Healthcare Inc., 64
Beverly Enterprises, Inc., III; 16 (upd.)
Bon Secours Health System, Inc., 24
C.R. Bard, Inc., 65 (upd.)
Caremark Rx, Inc., 10; 54 (upd.)
Children's Comprehensive Services, Inc.,
    42
Children's Hospitals and Clinics, Inc., 54
Chronimed Inc., 26
COBE Laboratories, Inc., 13
Columbia/HCA Healthcare Corporation, 15
Community Psychiatric Centers, 15
CompDent Corporation, 22
CompHealth Inc., 25
Comprehensive Care Corporation, 15
Continental Medical Systems, Inc., 10
Continuum Health Partners, Inc., 60
Coventry Health Care, Inc., 59
Easter Seals, Inc., 58
Erickson Retirement Communities, 57
Express Scripts Incorporated, 17
Extendicare Health Services, Inc., 6
FHP International Corporation, 6
Fresenius AG, 56
Genesis Health Ventures, Inc., 18
GranCare, Inc., 14
Group Health Cooperative, 41
Hazelden Foundation, 28
HCA - The Healthcare Company, 35 (upd.)
Health Care & Retirement Corporation, 22
Health Management Associates, Inc., 56
Health Risk Management, Inc., 24
Health Systems International, Inc., 11
HealthSouth Corporation, 14; 33 (upd.)
Highmark Inc., 27
The Hillhaven Corporation, 14
Hooper Holmes, Inc., 22
Hospital Central Services, Inc., 56
Hospital Corporation of America, III
Howard Hughes Medical Institute, 39
Humana Inc., III; 24 (upd.)
Intermountain Health Care, Inc., 27

Jenny Craig, Inc., 10; 29 (upd.)
Kinetic Concepts, Inc. (KCI), 20
LabOne, Inc., 48
Laboratory Corporation of America
    Holdings, 42 (upd.)
Lifeline Systems, Inc., 53
Lincare Holdings Inc., 43
Manor Care, Inc., 6; 25 (upd.)
March of Dimes, 31
Matria Healthcare, Inc., 17
Maxicare Health Plans, Inc., III; 25 (upd.)
Mayo Foundation, 9; 34 (upd.)
Medical Management International, Inc., 65
Memorial Sloan-Kettering Cancer Center,
    57
Merit Medical Systems, Inc., 29
National Health Laboratories Incorporated,
    11
National Medical Enterprises, Inc., III
New York City Health and Hospitals
    Corporation, 60
NewYork-Presbyterian Hospital, 59
NovaCare, Inc., 11
Option Care Inc., 48
Orthodontic Centers of America, Inc., 35
Oxford Health Plans, Inc., 16
PacifiCare Health Systems, Inc., 11
Palomar Medical Technologies, Inc., 22
Pediatric Services of America, Inc., 31
Pediatrix Medical Group, Inc., 61
PHP Healthcare Corporation, 22
PhyCor, Inc., 36
Primedex Health Systems, Inc., 25
The Providence Service Corporation, 64
Quest Diagnostics Inc., 26
Ramsay Youth Services, Inc., 41
Res-Care, Inc., 29
Response Oncology, Inc., 27
Rural/Metro Corporation, 28
Sabratek Corporation, 29
St. Jude Medical, Inc., 11; 43 (upd.)
Salick Health Care, Inc., 53
Select Medical Corporation, 65
Sierra Health Services, Inc., 15
Smith & Nephew plc, 41
The Sports Club Company, 25
SSL International plc, 49
Stericycle Inc., 33
Sun Healthcare Group Inc., 25
SwedishAmerican Health System, 51
Tenet Healthcare Corporation, 55 (upd.)
Twinlab Corporation, 34
U.S. Healthcare, Inc., 6
U.S. Physical Therapy, Inc., 65
Unison HealthCare Corporation, 25
United HealthCare Corporation, 9
United Nations International Children's
    Emergency Fund (UNICEF), 58
United Way of America, 36
Universal Health Services, Inc., 6
VCA Antech, Inc., 58
Vencor, Inc., 16
VISX, Incorporated, 30
Vivra, Inc., 18
Volunteers of America, Inc., 66
WellPoint Health Networks Inc., 25
YWCA of the U.S.A., 45

HOTELS

Amerihost Properties, Inc., 30
Aztar Corporation, 13
Bass PLC, 38 (upd.)
Boca Resorts, Inc., 37
Boyd Gaming Corporation, 43
Bristol Hotel Company, 23
The Broadmoor Hotel, 30
Caesars World, Inc., 6

Candlewood Hotel Company, Inc., 41
Carlson Companies, Inc., 22 (upd.)
Castle & Cooke, Inc., 20 (upd.)
Cedar Fair, L.P., 22
Cendant Corporation, 44 (upd.)
Choice Hotels International Inc., 14
Circus Circus Enterprises, Inc., 6
Club Méditerranée S.A., 6; 21 (upd.)
Doubletree Corporation, 21
Extended Stay America, Inc., 41
Fibreboard Corporation, 16
Four Seasons Hotels Inc., 9; 29 (upd.)
Fuller Smith & Turner P.L.C., 38
Gables Residential Trust, 49
Gaylord Entertainment Company, 11; 36
    (upd.)
Granada Group PLC, 24 (upd.)
Grand Casinos, Inc., 20
Grand Hotel Krasnapolsky N.V., 23
Grupo Posadas, S.A. de C.V., 57
Helmsley Enterprises, Inc., 9
Hilton Hotels Corporation, III; 19 (upd.);
    49 (upd.); 62 (upd.)
Holiday Inns, Inc., III
Hospitality Franchise Systems, Inc., 11
Howard Johnson International, Inc., 17
Hyatt Corporation, III; 16 (upd.)
ILX Resorts Incorporated, 65
Interstate Hotels & Resorts Inc., 58
ITT Sheraton Corporation, III
JD Wetherspoon plc, 30
John Q. Hammons Hotels, Inc., 24
The La Quinta Companies, 11; 42 (upd.)
Ladbroke Group PLC, 21 (upd.)
Landry's Restaurants, Inc., 65 (upd.)
Las Vegas Sands, Inc., 50
Madden's on Gull Lake, 52
Mandalay Resort Group, 32 (upd.)
Manor Care, Inc., 25 (upd.)
The Marcus Corporation, 21
Marriott International, Inc., III; 21 (upd.)
McMenamins Pubs and Breweries, 65
Mirage Resorts, Incorporated, 6; 28 (upd.)
Monarch Casino & Resort, Inc., 65
Motel 6, 13; 56 (upd.)
MWH Preservation Limited Partnership, 65
Omni Hotels Corp., 12
Park Corp., 22
Players International, Inc., 22
Preussag AG, 42 (upd.)
Prime Hospitality Corporation, 52
Promus Companies, Inc., 9
Real Turismo, S.A. de C.V., 50
Red Roof Inns, Inc., 18
Resorts International, Inc., 12
Ritz-Carlton Hotel Company L.L.C., 9; 29
    (upd.)
Sandals Resorts International, 65
Santa Fe Gaming Corporation, 19
The SAS Group, 34 (upd.)
SFI Group plc, 51
Showboat, Inc., 19
Sonesta International Hotels Corporation,
    44
Starwood Hotels & Resorts Worldwide,
    Inc., 54
Sun International Hotels Limited, 26
Sunburst Hospitality Corporation, 26
Thistle Hotels PLC, 54
Trusthouse Forte PLC, III
Vail Resorts, Inc., 43 (upd.)
WestCoast Hospitality Corporation, 59
Westin Hotels and Resorts Worldwide, 9;
    29 (upd.)
Whitbread PLC, 52 (upd.)
Young & Co.'s Brewery, P.L.C., 38

INFORMATION TECHNOLOGY

A.B. Watley Group Inc., 45
Acxiom Corporation, 35
Adaptec, Inc., 31
Adobe Systems Incorporated, 10; 33 (upd.)
Advanced Micro Devices, Inc., 6
Agence France-Presse, 34
Agilent Technologies Inc., 38
Aldus Corporation, 10
Allen Systems Group, Inc., 59
AltaVista Company, 43
Altiris, Inc., 65
Amdahl Corporation, III; 14 (upd.); 40 (upd.)
Amdocs Ltd., 47
America Online, Inc., 10; 26 (upd.)
American Business Information, Inc., 18
American Management Systems, Inc., 11
American Software Inc., 25
Amstrad PLC, III
Analytic Sciences Corporation, 10
Analytical Surveys, Inc., 33
Anker BV, 53
Ansoft Corporation, 63
Anteon Corporation, 57
AOL Time Warner Inc., 57 (upd.)
Apollo Group, Inc., 24
Apple Computer, Inc., III; 6 (upd.)
The Arbitron Company, 38
Ariba, Inc., 57
Asanté Technologies, Inc., 20
Ascential Software Corporation, 59
AsiaInfo Holdings, Inc., 43
ASK Group, Inc., 9
Ask Jeeves, Inc., 65
ASML Holding N.V., 50
AST Research Inc., 9
At Home Corporation, 43
AT&T Bell Laboratories, Inc., 13
AT&T Corporation, 29 (upd.)
AT&T Istel Ltd., 14
Attachmate Corporation, 56
Autologic Information International, Inc., 20
Automatic Data Processing, Inc., III; 9 (upd.)
Autotote Corporation, 20
Avid Technology Inc., 38
Avocent Corporation, 65
Aydin Corp., 19
Baan Company, 25
Baltimore Technologies Plc, 42
Banyan Systems Inc., 25
Battelle Memorial Institute, Inc., 10
BBN Corp., 19
BEA Systems, Inc., 36
Bell and Howell Company, 9; 29 (upd.)
Bell Industries, Inc., 47
Billing Concepts Corp., 26
Bloomberg L.P., 21
Blue Martini Software, Inc., 59
BMC Software, Inc., 55
Boole & Babbage, Inc., 25
Booz Allen & Hamilton Inc., 10
Borland International, Inc., 9
Bowne & Co., Inc., 23
Brite Voice Systems, Inc., 20
Broderbund Software, 13; 29 (upd.)
BTG, Inc., 45
Bull S.A., 43 (upd.)
Business Objects S.A., 25
C-Cube Microsystems, Inc., 37
CACI International Inc., 21
Cadence Design Systems, Inc., 11
Caere Corporation, 20
Cahners Business Information, 43
CalComp Inc., 13

Cambridge Technology Partners, Inc., 36
Candle Corporation, 64
Canon Inc., III
Cap Gemini Ernst & Young, 37
Caribiner International, Inc., 24
Catalina Marketing Corporation, 18
CDW Computer Centers, Inc., 16
Cerner Corporation, 16
Cheyenne Software, Inc., 12
CHIPS and Technologies, Inc., 9
Ciber, Inc., 18
Cincom Systems Inc., 15
Cirrus Logic, Incorporated, 11
Cisco Systems, Inc., 11
Citizen Watch Co., Ltd., 21 (upd.)
Citrix Systems, Inc., 44
CNET Networks, Inc., 47
Cogent Communications Group, Inc., 55
Cognizant Technology Solutions Corporation, 59
Cognos Inc., 44
Commodore International Ltd., 7
Compagnie des Machines Bull S.A., III
Compaq Computer Corporation, III; 6 (upd.); 26 (upd.)
Complete Business Solutions, Inc., 31
CompuAdd Computer Corporation, 11
CompuCom Systems, Inc., 10
CompUSA, Inc., 35 (upd.)
CompuServe Interactive Services, Inc., 10; 27 (upd.)
Computer Associates International, Inc., 6; 49 (upd.)
Computer Data Systems, Inc., 14
Computer Sciences Corporation, 6
Computervision Corporation, 10
Compuware Corporation, 10; 30 (upd.); 66 (upd.)
Comshare Inc., 23
Conner Peripherals, Inc., 6
Control Data Corporation, III
Control Data Systems, Inc., 10
Corbis Corporation, 31
Corel Corporation, 15; 33 (upd.)
Corporate Software Inc., 9
Cray Research, Inc., III
CTG, Inc., 11
Cybermedia, Inc., 25
Dassault Systèmes S.A., 25
Data Broadcasting Corporation, 31
Data General Corporation, 8
Datapoint Corporation, 11
Dell Computer Corp., 9
Deutsche Börse AG, 59
Dialogic Corporation, 18
DiamondCluster International, Inc., 51
Digex, Inc., 46
Digital Equipment Corporation, III; 6 (upd.)
Digital River, Inc., 50
Documentum, Inc., 46
The Dun & Bradstreet Corporation, IV; 19 (upd.)
Dun & Bradstreet Software Services Inc., 11
DynCorp, 45
E.piphany, Inc., 49
EarthLink, Inc., 36
ECS S.A, 12
Edmark Corporation, 14; 41 (upd.)
Egghead Inc., 9
El Camino Resources International, Inc., 11
Electronic Arts Inc., 10
Electronic Data Systems Corporation, III; 28 (upd.)
Electronics for Imaging, Inc., 43 (upd.)
EMC Corporation, 12; 46 (upd.)

Encore Computer Corporation, 13
Environmental Systems Research Institute Inc. (ESRI), 62
Epic Systems Corporation, 62
EPIQ Systems, Inc., 56
Evans & Sutherland Computer Corporation, 19
Exabyte Corporation, 12
Experian Information Solutions Inc., 45
First Financial Management Corporation, 11
Fiserv Inc., 11
FlightSafety International, Inc., 9
FORE Systems, Inc., 25
Franklin Electronic Publishers, Inc., 23
FTP Software, Inc., 20
Fujitsu Limited, III; 42 (upd.)
Fujitsu-ICL Systems Inc., 11
Future Now, Inc., 12
Gartner Group, Inc., 21
Gateway, Inc., 10; 27 (upd.)
GEAC Computer Corporation Ltd., 43
Gericom AG, 47
Getronics NV, 39
GFI Informatique SA, 49
Google, Inc., 50
GSI Commerce, Inc., 67
GT Interactive Software, 31
Guthy-Renker Corporation, 32
Handspring Inc., 49
Hewlett-Packard Company, III; 6 (upd.)
Hyperion Software Corporation, 22
ICL plc, 6
Identix Inc., 44
IDX Systems Corporation, 64
IKON Office Solutions, Inc., 50
Imation Corporation, 20
Infineon Technologies AG, 50
Information Access Company, 17
Information Builders, Inc., 22
Information Resources, Inc., 10
Informix Corporation, 10; 30 (upd.)
Infosys Technologies Ltd., 38
Ing. C. Olivetti & C., S.p.a., III
Inktomi Corporation, 45
Inso Corporation, 26
Intel Corporation, 36 (upd.)
IntelliCorp, Inc., 45
Intelligent Electronics, Inc., 6
Intergraph Corporation, 6; 24 (upd.)
International Business Machines Corporation, III; 6 (upd.); 30 (upd.); 63 (upd.)
Intrado Inc., 63
Intuit Inc., 14; 33 (upd.)
Iomega Corporation, 21
IONA Technologies plc, 43
J.D. Edwards & Company, 14
Jack Henry and Associates, Inc., 17
Janus Capital Group Inc., 57
The Judge Group, Inc., 51
Juniper Networks, Inc., 43
Juno Online Services, Inc., 38
Kana Software, Inc., 51
Keane, Inc., 56
KLA Instruments Corporation, 11
Knight Ridder, Inc., 67 (upd.)
KnowledgeWare Inc., 31 (upd.)
Komag, Inc., 11
Kronos, Inc., 18
Kurzweil Technologies, Inc., 51
Lam Research Corporation, 11
Landauer, Inc., 51
Lason, Inc., 31
Lawson Software, 38
The Learning Company Inc., 24
Learning Tree International Inc., 24

Legent Corporation, 10
LEXIS-NEXIS Group, 33
Logica plc, 14; 37 (upd.)
Logicon Inc., 20
Logitech International SA, 28
LoJack Corporation, 48
Lotus Development Corporation, 6; 25
  (upd.)
The MacNeal-Schwendler Corporation, 25
Macromedia, Inc., 50
Madge Networks N.V., 26
MAI Systems Corporation, 11
MAPICS, Inc., 55
Maxtor Corporation, 10
Mead Data Central, Inc., 10
Mecklermedia Corporation, 24
Medical Information Technology Inc., 64
Mentor Graphics Corporation, 11
Mercury Interactive Corporation, 59
Merisel, Inc., 12
Metatec International, Inc., 47
Metro Information Services, Inc., 36
Micro Warehouse, Inc., 16
Micron Technology, Inc., 11; 29 (upd.)
Micros Systems, Inc., 18
Microsoft Corporation, 6; 27 (upd.); 63
  (upd.)
Misys plc, 45; 46
MITRE Corporation, 26
The Motley Fool, Inc., 40
National Semiconductor Corporation, 6
National TechTeam, Inc., 41
Navarre Corporation, 24
NCR Corporation, III; 6 (upd.); 30 (upd.)
Netscape Communications Corporation, 15;
  35 (upd.)
Network Appliance, Inc., 58
Network Associates, Inc., 25
Nextel Communications, Inc., 10
NFO Worldwide, Inc., 24
Nichols Research Corporation, 18
Nimbus CD International, Inc., 20
Nixdorf Computer AG, III
Novell, Inc., 6; 23 (upd.)
NVIDIA Corporation, 54
Océ N.V., 24
Odetics Inc., 14
Onyx Software Corporation, 53
Opsware Inc., 49
Oracle Corporation, 6; 24 (upd.); 67 (upd.)
Orbitz, Inc., 61
Packard Bell Electronics, Inc., 13
Parametric Technology Corp., 16
PC Connection, Inc., 37
PeopleSoft Inc., 14; 33 (upd.)
Perot Systems Corporation, 29
Pitney Bowes Inc., III
PLATINUM Technology, Inc., 14
Policy Management Systems Corporation,
  11
Policy Studies, Inc., 62
Portal Software, Inc., 47
Primark Corp., 13
The Princeton Review, Inc., 42
Printrak, A Motorola Company, 44
Printronix, Inc., 18
Prodigy Communications Corporation, 34
Progress Software Corporation, 15
Psion PLC, 45
Quantum Corporation, 10; 62 (upd.)
Quark, Inc., 36
Racal-Datacom Inc., 11
Razorfish, Inc., 37
RCM Technologies, Inc., 34
RealNetworks, Inc., 53
Red Hat, Inc., 45
Remedy Corporation, 58

Renaissance Learning Systems, Inc., 39
Reuters Group PLC, 22 (upd.); 63 (upd.)
The Reynolds and Reynolds Company, 50
Ricoh Company, Ltd., III
RSA Security Inc., 46
SABRE Group Holdings, Inc., 26
The Sage Group, 43
The Santa Cruz Operation, Inc., 38
SAP AG, 16; 43 (upd.)
SAS Institute Inc., 10
SBS Technologies, Inc., 25
SCB Computer Technology, Inc., 29
Schawk, Inc., 24
SDL PLC, 67
Seagate Technology, Inc., 8
Siebel Systems, Inc., 38
Sierra On-Line, Inc., 15; 41 (upd.)
SilverPlatter Information Inc., 23
SmartForce PLC, 43
Softbank Corp., 13; 38 (upd.)
SPSS Inc., 64
Standard Microsystems Corporation, 11
STC PLC, III
Steria SA, 49
Sterling Software, Inc., 11
Storage Technology Corporation, 6
Stratus Computer, Inc., 10
Sun Microsystems, Inc., 7; 30 (upd.)
SunGard Data Systems Inc., 11
Sybase, Inc., 10; 27 (upd.)
Sykes Enterprises, Inc., 45
Symantec Corporation, 10
Symbol Technologies, Inc., 15
Synopsis, Inc., 11
System Software Associates, Inc., 10
Systems & Computer Technology Corp.,
  19
T-Online International AG, 61
Tandem Computers, Inc., 6
TenFold Corporation, 35
Terra Lycos, Inc., 43
The Thomson Corporation, 34 (upd.)
3Com Corporation, 11; 34 (upd.)
The 3DO Company, 43
Timberline Software Corporation, 15
Traffix, Inc., 61
Transaction Systems Architects, Inc., 29
Transiciel SA, 48
Triple P N.V., 26
Ubi Soft Entertainment S.A., 41
Unilog SA, 42
Unisys Corporation, III; 6 (upd.); 36 (upd.)
United Business Media plc, 52 (upd.)
UUNET, 38
Verbatim Corporation, 14
Veridian Corporation, 54
VeriFone, Inc., 18
VeriSign, Inc., 47
Veritas Software Corporation, 45
Viasoft Inc., 27
Volt Information Sciences Inc., 26
Wang Laboratories, Inc., III; 6 (upd.)
WebMD Corporation, 65
West Group, 34 (upd.)
Westcon Group, Inc., 67
Western Digital Corp., 25
Wind River Systems, Inc., 37
Wipro Limited, 43
Wolters Kluwer NV, 33 (upd.)
WordPerfect Corporation, 10
Wyse Technology, Inc., 15
Xerox Corporation, III; 6 (upd.); 26 (upd.)
Xilinx, Inc., 16
Yahoo! Inc., 27
Zapata Corporation, 25
Ziff Davis Media Inc., 36 (upd.)
Zilog, Inc., 15

INSURANCE

AEGON N.V., III; 50 (upd.)
Aetna Inc., III; 21 (upd.); 63 (upd.)
AFLAC Incorporated, 10 (upd.); 38 (upd.)
Alexander & Alexander Services Inc., 10
Alfa Corporation, 60
Alleanza Assicurazioni S.p.A., 65
Alleghany Corporation, 10
Allianz AG, III; 15 (upd.); 57 (upd.)
Allmerica Financial Corporation, 63
The Allstate Corporation, 10; 27 (upd.)
AMB Generali Holding AG, 51
American Family Corporation, III
American Financial Group Inc., III; 48
  (upd.)
American General Corporation, III; 10
  (upd.); 46 (upd.)
American International Group, Inc., III; 15
  (upd.); 47 (upd.)
American National Insurance Company, 8;
  27 (upd.)
American Premier Underwriters, Inc., 10
American Re Corporation, 10; 35 (upd.)
N.V. AMEV, III
Aon Corporation, III; 45 (upd.)
Assicurazioni Generali SpA, III; 15 (upd.)
Assurances Générales de France, 63
Atlantic American Corporation, 44
Aviva PLC, 50 (upd.)
Axa, III
AXA Colonia Konzern AG, 27; 49 (upd.)
B.A.T. Industries PLC, 22 (upd.)
Baldwin & Lyons, Inc., 51
Bâloise-Holding, 40
Benfield Greig Group plc, 53
Berkshire Hathaway Inc., III; 18 (upd.)
Blue Cross and Blue Shield Association,
  10
Brown & Brown, Inc., 41
Business Men's Assurance Company of
  America, 14
Capital Holding Corporation, III
Catholic Order of Foresters, 24
China Life Insurance Company Limited, 65
ChoicePoint Inc., 65
The Chubb Corporation, III; 14 (upd.); 37
  (upd.)
CIGNA Corporation, III; 22 (upd.); 45
  (upd.)
Cincinnati Financial Corporation, 16; 44
  (upd.)
CNA Financial Corporation, III; 38 (upd.)
Commercial Union PLC, III
Connecticut Mutual Life Insurance
  Company, III
Conseco Inc., 10; 33 (upd.)
The Continental Corporation, III
The Doctors' Company, 55
Empire Blue Cross and Blue Shield, III
Enbridge Inc., 43
Engle Homes, Inc., 46
The Equitable Life Assurance Society of
  the United States Fireman's Fund
  Insurance Company, III
ERGO Versicherungsgruppe AG, 44
Erie Indemnity Company, 35
Fairfax Financial Holdings Limited, 57
Farm Family Holdings, Inc., 39
Farmers Insurance Group of Companies, 25
Fidelity National Financial Inc., 54
The First American Corporation, 52
First Executive Corporation, III
Foundation Health Corporation, 12
Gainsco, Inc., 22
GEICO Corporation, 10; 40 (upd.)
General Accident PLC, III
General Re Corporation, III; 24 (upd.)

INSURANCE (*continued*)

Gerling-Konzern Versicherungs-
  Beteiligungs-Aktiengesellschaft, 51
Great-West Lifeco Inc., III
Gryphon Holdings, Inc., 21
Guardian Financial Services, 64 (upd.)
Guardian Royal Exchange Plc, 11
Harleysville Group Inc., 37
HDI (Haftpflichtverband der Deutschen
  Industrie Versicherung auf
  Gegenseitigkeit V.a.G.), 53
The Home Insurance Company, III
Horace Mann Educators Corporation, 22
Household International, Inc., 21 (upd.)
HUK-Coburg, 58
Irish Life & Permanent Plc, 59
Jackson National Life Insurance Company,
  8
Jefferson-Pilot Corporation, 11; 29 (upd.)
John Hancock Financial Services, Inc., III;
  42 (upd.)
Johnson & Higgins, 14
Kaiser Foundation Health Plan, Inc., 53
Kemper Corporation, III; 15 (upd.)
Legal & General Group plc, III; 24 (upd.)
The Liberty Corporation, 22
Liberty Mutual Holding Company, 59
Lincoln National Corporation, III; 25
  (upd.)
Lloyd's of London, III; 22 (upd.)
The Loewen Group Inc., 40 (upd.)
Lutheran Brotherhood, 31
Marsh & McLennan Companies, Inc., III;
  45 (upd.)
Massachusetts Mutual Life Insurance
  Company, III; 53 (upd.)
The Meiji Mutual Life Insurance Company,
  III
Mercury General Corporation, 25
Metropolitan Life Insurance Company, III;
  52 (upd.)
MGIC Investment Corp., 52
The Midland Company, 65
Millea Holdings Inc., 64 (upd.)
Mitsui Marine and Fire Insurance
  Company, Limited, III
Mitsui Mutual Life Insurance Company,
  III; 39 (upd.)
Modern Woodmen of America, 66
Munich Re (Münchener Rückversicherungs-
  Gesellschaft Aktiengesellschaft in
  München), III; 46 (upd.)
The Mutual Benefit Life Insurance
  Company, III
The Mutual Life Insurance Company of
  New York, III
Nationale-Nederlanden N.V., III
New England Mutual Life Insurance
  Company, III
New York Life Insurance Company, III; 45
  (upd.)
Nippon Life Insurance Company, III; 60
  (upd.)
Northwestern Mutual Life Insurance
  Company, III; 45 (upd.)
NYMAGIC, Inc., 41
Ohio Casualty Corp., 11
Old Republic International Corporation, 11;
  58 (upd.)
Oregon Dental Service Health Plan, Inc.,
  51
Pan-American Life Insurance Company, 48
The Paul Revere Corporation, 12
Pennsylvania Blue Shield, III
The PMI Group, Inc., 49
Preserver Group, Inc., 44

Principal Mutual Life Insurance Company,
  III
The Progressive Corporation, 11; 29 (upd.)
Provident Life and Accident Insurance
  Company of America, III
Prudential Corporation PLC, III
The Prudential Insurance Company of
  America, III; 30 (upd.)
Prudential plc, 48 (upd.)
Radian Group Inc., 42
Reliance Group Holdings, Inc., III
Riunione Adriatica di Sicurtà SpA, III
Royal & Sun Alliance Insurance Group
  plc, 55 (upd.)
Royal Insurance Holdings PLC, III
SAFECO Corporaton, III
The St. Paul Companies, Inc., III; 22 (upd.)
SCOR S.A., 20
Skandia Insurance Company, Ltd., 50
StanCorp Financial Group, Inc., 56
The Standard Life Assurance Company, III
State Farm Mutual Automobile Insurance
  Company, III; 51 (upd.)
State Financial Services Corporation, 51
Sumitomo Life Insurance Company, III; 60
  (upd.)
The Sumitomo Marine and Fire Insurance
  Company, Limited, III
Sun Alliance Group PLC, III
SunAmerica Inc., 11
Svenska Handelsbanken AB, 50 (upd.)
Swiss Reinsurance Company
  (Schweizerische Rückversicherungs-
  Gesellschaft), III; 46 (upd.)
Teachers Insurance and Annuity
  Association-College Retirement Equities
  Fund, III; 45 (upd.)
Texas Industries, Inc., 8
TIG Holdings, Inc., 26
The Tokio Marine and Fire Insurance Co.,
  Ltd., III
Torchmark Corporation, 9; 33 (upd.)
Transatlantic Holdings, Inc., 11
The Travelers Corporation, III
UICI, 33
Union des Assurances de Pans, III
United National Group, Ltd., 63
Unitrin Inc., 16
UNUM Corp., 13
UnumProvident Corporation, 52 (upd.)
USAA, 10
USF&G Corporation, III
Victoria Group, 44 (upd.)
VICTORIA Holding AG, III
W.R. Berkley Corp., 15
Washington National Corporation, 12
WellChoice, Inc., 67 (upd.)
White Mountains Insurance Group, Ltd., 48
Willis Corroon Group plc, 25
''Winterthur'' Schweizerische
  Versicherungs-Gesellschaft, III
The Yasuda Fire and Marine Insurance
  Company, Limited, III
The Yasuda Mutual Life Insurance
  Company, III; 39 (upd.)
''Zürich'' Versicherungs-Gesellschaft, III

LEGAL SERVICES

Akin, Gump, Strauss, Hauer & Feld,
  L.L.P., 33
American Bar Association, 35
American Lawyer Media Holdings, Inc., 32
Amnesty International, 50
Arnold & Porter, 35
Baker & Hostetler LLP, 40
Baker & McKenzie, 10; 42 (upd.)
Baker and Botts, L.L.P., 28

Bingham Dana LLP, 43
Brobeck, Phleger & Harrison, LLP, 31
Cadwalader, Wickersham & Taft, 32
Chadbourne & Parke, 36
Cleary, Gottlieb, Steen & Hamilton, 35
Clifford Chance LLP, 38
Coudert Brothers, 30
Covington & Burling, 40
Cravath, Swaine & Moore, 43
Davis Polk & Wardwell, 36
Debevoise & Plimpton, 39
Dechert, 43
Dewey Ballantine LLP, 48
Dorsey & Whitney LLP, 47
Fenwick & West LLP, 34
Fish & Neave, 54
Foley & Lardner, 28
Fried, Frank, Harris, Shriver & Jacobson,
  35
Fulbright & Jaworski L.L.P., 47
Gibson, Dunn & Crutcher LLP, 36
Greenberg Traurig, LLP, 65
Heller, Ehrman, White & McAuliffe, 41
Hildebrandt International, 29
Hogan & Hartson L.L.P., 44
Holland & Knight LLP, 60
Holme Roberts & Owen LLP, 28
Hughes Hubbard & Reed LLP, 44
Hunton & Williams, 35
Jenkens & Gilchrist, P.C., 65
Jones, Day, Reavis & Pogue, 33
Kelley Drye & Warren LLP, 40
King & Spalding, 23
Kirkland & Ellis LLP, 65
Latham & Watkins, 33
LeBoeuf, Lamb, Greene & MacRae,
  L.L.P., 29
The Legal Aid Society, 48
Mayer, Brown, Rowe & Maw, 47
Milbank, Tweed, Hadley & McCloy, 27
Morgan, Lewis & Bockius LLP, 29
O'Melveny & Myers, 37
Paul, Hastings, Janofsky & Walker LLP,
  27
Paul, Weiss, Rifkind, Wharton & Garrison,
  47
Pepper Hamilton LLP, 43
Perkins Coie LLP, 56
Pillsbury Madison & Sutro LLP, 29
Pre-Paid Legal Services, Inc., 20
Proskauer Rose LLP, 47
Ropes & Gray, 40
Shearman & Sterling, 32
Sidley Austin Brown & Wood, 40
Simpson Thacher & Bartlett, 39
Skadden, Arps, Slate, Meagher & Flom, 18
Snell & Wilmer L.L.P., 28
Stroock & Stroock & Lavan LLP, 40
Sullivan & Cromwell, 26
Vinson & Elkins L.L.P., 30
Wachtell, Lipton, Rosen & Katz, 47
Weil, Gotshal & Manges LLP, 55
White & Case LLP, 35
Williams & Connolly LLP, 47
Wilson Sonsini Goodrich & Rosati, 34
Winston & Strawn, 35
Womble Carlyle Sandridge & Rice, PLLC,
  52

MANUFACTURING

A-dec, Inc., 53
A. Schulman, Inc., 49 (upd.)
A.B.Dick Company, 28
A.O. Smith Corporation, 11; 40 (upd.)
A.T. Cross Company, 17; 49 (upd.)
A.W. Faber-Castell Unternehmensverwaltung
  GmbH & Co., 51

AAF-McQuay Incorporated, 26
AAON, Inc., 22
AAR Corp., 28
ABB Ltd., 65 (upd.)
ABC Rail Products Corporation, 18
Abiomed, Inc., 47
ACCO World Corporation, 7; 51 (upd.)
Acme-Cleveland Corp., 13
Acorn Products, Inc., 55
Acushnet Company, 64
Acuson Corporation, 36 (upd.)
Adams Golf, Inc., 37
Adolf Würth GmbH & Co. KG, 49
Advanced Circuits Inc., 67
AEP Industries, Inc., 36
Ag-Chem Equipment Company, Inc., 17
AGCO Corporation, 13; 67 (upd.)
Agfa Gevaert Group N.V., 59
Ahlstrom Corporation, 53
Airgas, Inc., 54
Aisin Seiki Co., Ltd., III
AK Steel Holding Corporation, 41 (upd.)
AKG Acoustics GmbH, 62
Aktiebolaget Electrolux, 22 (upd.)
Aktiebolaget SKF, III; 38 (upd.)
Alamo Group Inc., 32
ALARIS Medical Systems, Inc., 65
Alberto-Culver Company, 36 (upd.)
Aldila Inc., 46
Alfa Laval AB, III; 64 (upd.)
Allen Organ Company, 33
Allen-Edmonds Shoe Corporation, 61
Alliant Techsystems Inc., 8; 30 (upd.)
The Allied Defense Group, Inc., 65
Allied Healthcare Products, Inc., 24
Allied Products Corporation, 21
Allied Signal Engines, 9
AlliedSignal Inc., 22 (upd.)
Allison Gas Turbine Division, 9
Alltrista Corporation, 30
Alps Electric Co., Ltd., 44 (upd.)
Alvis Plc, 47
Amer Group plc, 41
American Axle & Manufacturing Holdings,
    Inc., 67
American Biltrite Inc., 43 (upd.)
American Business Products, Inc., 20
American Cast Iron Pipe Company, 50
American Greetings Corporation, 59 (upd.)
American Homestar Corporation, 18; 41
    (upd.)
American Locker Group Incorporated, 34
American Power Conversion Corporation,
    67 (upd.)
American Standard Companies Inc., 30
    (upd.)
American Technical Ceramics Corp., 67
American Tourister, Inc., 16
American Woodmark Corporation, 31
Ameriwood Industries International Corp.,
    17
Amerock Corporation, 53
Ameron International Corporation, 67
AMETEK, Inc., 9
AMF Bowling, Inc., 40
Ampacet Corporation, 67
Ampex Corporation, 17
Amway Corporation, 30 (upd.)
Analogic Corporation, 23
Anchor Hocking Glassware, 13
Andersen Corporation, 10
The Andersons, Inc., 31
Andreas Stihl AG & Co. KG, 16; 59 (upd.)
Andritz AG, 51
Ansell Ltd., 60 (upd.)
Anthem Electronics, Inc., 13
Apasco S.A. de C.V., 51

Apex Digital, Inc., 63
Applica Incorporated, 43 (upd.)
Applied Films Corporation, 48
Applied Materials, Inc., 10; 46 (upd.)
Applied Micro Circuits Corporation, 38
Applied Power Inc., 9; 32 (upd.)
ARBED S.A., 22 (upd.)
Arctco, Inc., 16
Arctic Cat Inc., 40 (upd.)
Ariens Company, 48
The Aristotle Corporation, 62
Armor All Products Corp., 16
Armstrong World Industries, Inc., III; 22
    (upd.)
Artesyn Technologies Inc., 46 (upd.)
ArvinMeritor, Inc., 54 (upd.)
Asahi Glass Company, Ltd., 48 (upd.)
Ashley Furniture Industries, Inc., 35
ASICS Corporation, 57
ASML Holding N.V., 50
Astronics Corporation, 35
ASV, Inc., 34; 66 (upd.)
Atlas Copco AB, III; 28 (upd.)
Atwood Mobil Products, 53
AU Optronics Corporation, 67
Aurora Casket Company, Inc., 56
Avedis Zildjian Co., 38
Avery Dennison Corporation, 17 (upd.); 49
    (upd.)
Avocent Corporation, 65
Avondale Industries, 7; 41 (upd.)
AVX Corporation, 67
B.J. Alan Co., Inc., 67
Badger Meter, Inc., 22
Baker Hughes Incorporated, III
Baldor Electric Company, 21
Baldwin Piano & Organ Company, 18
Baldwin Technology Company, Inc., 25
Balfour Beatty plc, 36 (upd.)
Ballantyne of Omaha, Inc., 27
Ballard Medical Products, 21
Bally Manufacturing Corporation, III
Baltek Corporation, 34
Baltimore Aircoil Company, Inc., 66
Bandai Co., Ltd., 55
Barmag AG, 39
Barnes Group Inc., 13
Barry Callebaut AG, 29
Bassett Furniture Industries, Inc., 18
Bath Iron Works, 12; 36 (upd.)
Beckman Coulter, Inc., 22
Beckman Instruments, Inc., 14
Becton, Dickinson & Company, 36 (upd.)
BEI Technologies, Inc., 65
Beiersdorf AG, 29
Bel Fuse, Inc., 53
Belden Inc., 19
Bell Sports Corporation, 16; 44 (upd.)
Beloit Corporation, 14
Bénéteau SA, 55
Benjamin Moore & Co., 13; 38 (upd.)
BenQ Corporation, 67
Berger Bros Company, 62
Bernina Holding AG, 47
Berry Plastics Corporation, 21
BIC Corporation, 8; 23 (upd.)
BICC PLC, III
Billabong International Ltd., 44
The Bing Group, 60
Binks Sames Corporation, 21
Binney & Smith Inc., 25
Biomet, Inc., 10
BISSELL Inc., 9; 30 (upd.)
The Black & Decker Corporation, III; 20
    (upd.); 67 (upd.)
Black Diamond Equipment, Ltd., 62
Blodgett Holdings, Inc., 61 (upd.)

Blount International, Inc., 12; 48 (upd.)
Blue Nile Inc., 61
Blyth Industries, Inc., 18
BMC Industries, Inc., 17; 59 (upd.)
Bodum Design Group AG, 47
Boral Limited, 43 (upd.)
Borden, Inc., 22 (upd.)
Borg-Warner Automotive, Inc., 14
Borg-Warner Corporation, III
Boston Scientific Corporation, 37
Bou-Matic, 62
The Boyds Collection, Ltd., 29
Brannock Device Company, 48
Brass Eagle Inc., 34
Bridgeport Machines, Inc., 17
Briggs & Stratton Corporation, 8; 27 (upd.)
BRIO AB, 24
British Vita plc, 33 (upd.)
Brother Industries, Ltd., 14
Brown & Sharpe Manufacturing Co., 23
Brown-Forman Corporation, 38 (upd.)
Broyhill Furniture Industries, Inc., 10
Brunswick Corporation, III; 22 (upd.)
BSH Bosch und Siemens Hausgeräte
    GmbH, 67
BTR Siebe plc, 27
Buck Knives Inc., 48
Buckeye Technologies, Inc., 42
Bucyrus International, Inc., 17
Bugle Boy Industries, Inc., 18
Building Materials Holding Corporation, 52
Bulgari S.p.A., 20
Bulova Corporation, 13; 41 (upd.)
Bundy Corporation, 17
Burelle S.A., 23
Burton Snowboards Inc., 22
Bush Boake Allen Inc., 30
Bush Industries, Inc., 20
Butler Manufacturing Company, 12; 62
    (upd.)
C&J Clark International Ltd., 52
C.F. Martin & Co., Inc., 42
C.R. Bard, Inc., 65 (upd.)
California Cedar Products Company, 58
California Steel Industries, Inc., 67
Callaway Golf Company, 15; 45 (upd.)
Campbell Scientific, Inc., 51
Cannondale Corporation, 21
Caradon plc, 20 (upd.)
The Carbide/Graphite Group, Inc., 40
Carbo PLC, 67 (upd.)
Carbone Lorraine S.A., 33
Cardo AB, 53
Carl-Zeiss-Stiftung, III; 34 (upd.)
Carma Laboratories, Inc., 60
Carrier Corporation, 7
Cascade Corporation, 65
Cascade General, Inc., 65
CASIO Computer Co., Ltd., III; 40 (upd.)
Catalina Lighting, Inc., 43 (upd.)
Caterpillar Inc., III; 15 (upd.); 63 (upd.)
Cavco Industries, Inc., 65
CEMEX S.A. de C.V., 59 (upd.)
Central Garden & Pet Company, 58 (upd.)
Central Sprinkler Corporation, 29
Centuri Corporation, 54
Century Aluminum Company, 52
Ceradyne, Inc., 65
Cessna Aircraft Company, 27 (upd.)
Champion Enterprises, Inc., 17
Chanel SA, 12; 49 (upd.)
The Charles Machine Works, Inc., 64
Chart Industries, Inc., 21
Chittenden & Eastman Company, 58
Chris-Craft Industries, Inc., 31 (upd.)
Christian Dalloz SA, 40
Christofle SA, 40

MANUFACTURING (*continued*)

Chromcraft Revington, Inc., 15
Ciments Français, 40
Cincinnati Milacron Inc., 12
Cinram International, Inc., 43
Circon Corporation, 21
Cirrus Design Corporation, 44
Citizen Watch Co., Ltd., III
CLARCOR Inc., 17; 61 (upd.)
Clark Equipment Company, 8
Clayton Homes Incorporated, 13; 54 (upd.)
The Clorox Company, 22 (upd.)
CNH Global N.V., 38 (upd.)
Coach, Inc., 45 (upd.)
COBE Cardiovascular, Inc., 61
Cobra Golf Inc., 16
Cockerill Sambre Group, 26 (upd.)
Cohu, Inc., 32
Colas S.A., 31
The Coleman Company, Inc., 30 (upd.)
Colfax Corporation, 58
Collins & Aikman Corporation, 41 (upd.)
Collins Industries, Inc., 33
Colorado MEDtech, Inc., 48
Colt's Manufacturing Company, Inc., 12
Columbia Sportswear Company, 19
Columbus McKinnon Corporation, 37
Compagnie de Saint-Gobain, 64 (upd.)
CompuDyne Corporation, 51
Concord Camera Corporation, 41
Congoleum Corp., 18
Conn-Selmer, Inc., 55
Conrad Industries, Inc., 58
Conso International Corporation, 29
Consorcio G Grupo Dina, S.A. de C.V., 36
Constar International Inc., 64
Converse Inc., 9
Cooper Cameron Corporation, 58 (upd.)
The Cooper Companies, Inc., 39
Cooper Industries, Inc., 44 (upd.)
Cordis Corporation, 46 (upd.)
Corning Inc., 44 (upd.)
Corrpro Companies, Inc., 20
Corticeira Amorim, Sociedade Gestora de
    Participaço es Sociais, S.A., 48
Crane Co., 8; 30 (upd.)
Creative Technology Ltd., 57
Creo Inc., 48
CRH plc, 64
Crosman Corporation, 62
Crown Equipment Corporation, 15
CTB International Corporation, 43 (upd.)
Cuisinart Corporation, 24
Culligan Water Technologies, Inc., 12; 38
    (upd.)
Cummins Engine Company, Inc., 40 (upd.)
CUNO Incorporated, 57
Curtiss-Wright Corporation, 10; 35 (upd.)
Cutter & Buck Inc., 27
Cybex International, Inc., 49
Daewoo Group, III
Daikin Industries, Ltd., III
Daisy Outdoor Products Inc., 58
Danaher Corporation, 7
Daniel Industries, Inc., 16
Danisco A/S, 44
Day Runner, Inc., 41 (upd.)
DC Shoes, Inc., 60
De'Longhi S.p.A., 66
Dearborn Mid-West Conveyor Company,
    56
Decora Industries, Inc., 31
DeCrane Aircraft Holdings Inc., 36
Deere & Company, III; 42 (upd.)
Defiance, Inc., 22
Dell Inc., 63 (upd.)
DEMCO, Inc., 60

Denby Group plc, 44
Denison International plc, 46
DENSO Corporation, 46 (upd.)
Department 56, Inc., 14
DePuy Inc., 37 (upd.)
Detroit Diesel Corporation, 10
Deutsche Babcock A.G., III
Deutz AG, 39
Devro plc, 55
Dial-A-Mattress Operating Corporation, 46
Diebold, Incorporated, 7; 22 (upd.)
Diesel SpA, 40
Dixon Industries, Inc., 26
Dixon Ticonderoga Company, 12
Djarum PT, 62
DMI Furniture, Inc., 46
Donaldson Company, Inc., 49 (upd.)
Donnelly Corporation, 12; 35 (upd.)
Dorel Industries Inc., 59
Douglas & Lomason Company, 16
Dover Corporation, III; 28 (upd.)
Dresser Industries, Inc., III
Drew Industries Inc., 28
Drexel Heritage Furnishings Inc., 12
Drypers Corporation, 18
Ducommun Incorporated, 30
Duncan Toys Company, 55
Dunn-Edwards Corporation, 56
Duracell International Inc., 9
Durametallic, 21
Duriron Company Inc., 17
Dürkopp Adler AG, 65
Dürr AG, 44
EADS SOCATA, 54
Eagle-Picher Industries, Inc., 8; 23 (upd.)
The Eastern Company, 48
Eastman Kodak Company, III; 7 (upd.); 36
    (upd.)
Easton Sports, Inc., 66
Eaton Corporation, 67 (upd.)
ECC International Corp., 42
Ecolab Inc., 34 (upd.)
Eddie Bauer Inc., 9
EDO Corporation, 46
EG&G Incorporated, 29 (upd.)
Ekco Group, Inc., 16
Elamex, S.A. de C.V., 51
Elano Corporation, 14
Electrolux AB, III; 53 (upd.)
Eljer Industries, Inc., 24
Elscint Ltd., 20
Encompass Services Corporation, 33
Energizer Holdings, Inc., 32
Enesco Corporation, 11
Engineered Support Systems, Inc., 59
English China Clays Ltd., 40 (upd.)
Ernie Ball, Inc., 56
Escalade, Incorporated, 19
Esselte, 64
Esselte Leitz GmbH & Co. KG, 48
Essilor International, 21
Esterline Technologies Corp., 15
Ethan Allen Interiors, Inc., 12; 39 (upd.)
The Eureka Company, 12
Everlast Worldwide Inc., 47
Excel Technology, Inc., 65
EXX Inc., 65
Fabbrica D' Armi Pietro Beretta S.p.A., 39
Facom S.A., 32
FAG—Kugelfischer Georg Schäfer AG, 62
Faiveley S.A., 39
Falcon Products, Inc., 33
Fanuc Ltd., III; 17 (upd.)
Farah Incorporated, 24
Farmer Bros. Co., 52
Fastenal Company, 42 (upd.)
Faultless Starch/Bon Ami Company, 55

Featherlite Inc., 28
Fedders Corporation, 18; 43 (upd.)
Federal Prison Industries, Inc., 34
Federal Signal Corp., 10
Fellowes Manufacturing Company, 28
Fender Musical Instruments Company, 16;
    43 (upd.)
Ferro Corporation, 56 (upd.)
Figgie International Inc., 7
Firearms Training Systems, Inc., 27
First Alert, Inc., 28
First Brands Corporation, 8
First International Computer, Inc., 56
The First Years Inc., 46
Fisher Controls International, LLC, 13; 61
    (upd.)
Fisher Scientific International Inc., 24
Fisher-Price Inc., 12; 32 (upd.)
Fiskars Corporation, 33
Fisons plc, 9
Flanders Corporation, 65
Fleetwood Enterprises, Inc., III; 22 (upd.)
Flexsteel Industries Inc., 15; 41 (upd.)
Flextronics International Ltd., 38
Flint Ink Corporation, 41 (upd.)
Florsheim Shoe Company, 9
Flour City International, Inc., 44
Flow International Corporation, 56
Flowserve Corporation, 33
Fort James Corporation, 22 (upd.)
FosterGrant, Inc., 60
Fountain Powerboats Industries, Inc., 28
Foxboro Company, 13
Framatome SA, 19
Frank J. Zamboni & Co., Inc., 34
Franklin Electric Company, Inc., 43
Freudenberg & Co., 41
Friedrich Grohe AG & Co. KG, 53
Frigidaire Home Products, 22
Frymaster Corporation, 27
FSI International, Inc., 17
Fuji Photo Film Co., Ltd., III; 18 (upd.)
Fujisawa Pharmaceutical Company, Ltd.,
    58 (upd.)
Fuqua Enterprises, Inc., 17
Furniture Brands International, Inc., 39
    (upd.)
Furon Company, 28
The Furukawa Electric Co., Ltd., III
G. Leblanc Corporation, 55
G.S. Blodgett Corporation, 15
Gardner Denver, Inc., 49
The Gates Corporation, 9
GE Aircraft Engines, 9
GEA AG, 27
Geberit AG, 49
Gehl Company, 19
Gemini Sound Products Corporation, 58
Gemplus International S.A., 64
GenCorp Inc., 8; 9 (upd.)
General Atomics, 57
General Bearing Corporation, 45
General Cable Corporation, 40
General Dynamics Corporation, 40 (upd.)
General Housewares Corporation, 16
Genmar Holdings, Inc., 45
geobra Brandstätter GmbH & Co. KG, 48
Georg Fischer AG Schaffhausen, 61
The George F. Cram Company, Inc., 55
Georgia Gulf Corporation, 61 (upd.)
Gerber Scientific, Inc., 12
Gerresheimer Glas AG, 43
Giddings & Lewis, Inc., 10
The Gillette Company, 20 (upd.)
GKN plc, III; 38 (upd.)
Gleason Corporation, 24
The Glidden Company, 8

Global Power Equipment Group Inc., 52
Glock Ges.m.b.H., 42
Goodman Holding Company, 42
Goodrich Corporation, 46 (upd.)
Goody Products, Inc., 12
The Gorman-Rupp Company, 18; 57 (upd.)
Goss Holdings, Inc., 43
Goulds Pumps Inc., 24
Graco Inc., 19; 67 (upd.)
Graham Corporation, 62
Grant Prideco, Inc., 57
Greene, Tweed & Company, 55
Greif Inc., 66 (upd.)
Griffon Corporation, 34
Grinnell Corp., 13
Groupe André, 17
Groupe Guillin SA, 40
Groupe Herstal S.A., 58
Groupe Legis Industries, 23
Groupe SEB, 35
Grow Group Inc., 12
Grupo Cydsa, S.A. de C.V., 39
Grupo IMSA, S.A. de C.V., 44
Grupo Industrial Saltillo, S.A. de C.V., 54
Grupo Lladró S.A., 52
Guangzhou Pearl River Piano Group Ltd.,
   49
Gulf Island Fabrication, Inc., 44
Gunite Corporation, 51
The Gunlocke Company, 23
Guy Degrenne SA, 44
H.B. Fuller Company, 8; 32 (upd.)
Hach Co., 18
Hackman Oyj Adp, 44
Haemonetics Corporation, 20
Haier Group Corporation, 65
Halliburton Company, III
Hallmark Cards, Inc., 40 (upd.)
Hansgrohe AG, 56
Hanson PLC, 30 (upd.)
Hardinge Inc., 25
Harland and Wolff Holdings plc, 19
Harmon Industries, Inc., 25
Harnischfeger Industries, Inc., 8; 38 (upd.)
Harsco Corporation, 8
Hartmarx Corporation, 32 (upd.)
The Hartz Mountain Corporation, 46 (upd.)
Hasbro, Inc., III; 16 (upd.)
Haskel International, Inc., 59
Hastings Manufacturing Company, 56
Hawker Siddeley Group Public Limited
   Company, III
Haworth Inc., 8; 39 (upd.)
Head N.V., 55
Headwaters Incorporated, 56
Health O Meter Products Inc., 14
Heekin Can Inc., 13
HEICO Corporation, 30
Heidelberger Druckmaschinen AG, 40
Hella KGaA Hueck & Co., 66
Henkel Manco Inc., 22
The Henley Group, Inc., III
Heraeus Holding GmbH, 54 (upd.)
Herman Miller, Inc., 8
Hermès International S.A., 34 (upd.)
Hillenbrand Industries, Inc., 10
Hillerich & Bradsby Company, Inc., 51
Hillsdown Holdings plc, 24 (upd.)
Hilti AG, 53
Hitachi Zosen Corporation, III
Hitchiner Manufacturing Co., Inc., 23
HMI Industries, Inc., 17
Hollander Home Fashions Corp., 67
Holnam Inc., 8
Holson Burnes Group, Inc., 14
Home Products International, Inc., 55
HON INDUSTRIES Inc., 13

The Hoover Company, 12; 40 (upd.)
Hoshino Gakki Co. Ltd., 55
Huffy Corporation, 7; 30 (upd.)
Huhtamäki Oyj, 64
Hunt Manufacturing Company, 12
Hunter Fan Company, 13
Hydril Company, 46
Hyster Company, 17
Hyundai Group, III; 7 (upd.)
Icon Health & Fitness, Inc., 38
IDEO Inc., 65
Igloo Products Corp., 21
Illinois Tool Works Inc., III; 22 (upd.)
Imatra Steel Oy Ab, 55
IMI plc, 9
Imo Industries Inc., 7; 27 (upd.)
In-Sink-Erator, 66
Inchcape PLC, III; 16 (upd.); 50 (upd.)
Industrie Natuzzi S.p.A., 18
Infineon Technologies AG, 50
Ingalls Shipbuilding, Inc., 12
Ingersoll-Rand Company Ltd., III; 15
   (upd.); 55 (upd.)
Insilco Corporation, 16
Interco Incorporated, III
Interface, Inc., 8
The Interlake Corporation, 8
Internacional de Ceramica, S.A. de C.V.,
   53
International Controls Corporation, 10
International Flavors & Fragrances Inc., 38
   (upd.)
International Game Technology, 10
Invacare Corporation, 47 (upd.)
Invensys PLC, 50 (upd.)
Invivo Corporation, 52
Ionics, Incorporated, 52
Irwin Toy Limited, 14
Ishikawajima-Harima Heavy Industries Co.,
   Ltd., III
Itron, Inc., 64
J. D'Addario & Company, Inc., 48
J.I. Case Company, 10
J.M. Voith AG, 33
Jabil Circuit, Inc., 36
Jacuzzi Inc., 23
JAKKS Pacific, Inc., 52
James Hardie Industries N.V., 56
Japan Tobacco Inc., 46 (upd.)
Jayco Inc., 13
Jeld-Wen, Inc., 45
Jenoptik AG, 33
Jervis B. Webb Company, 24
JLG Industries, Inc., 52
Johns Manville Corporation, 64 (upd.)
Johnson Controls, Inc., III; 26 (upd.); 59
   (upd.)
Johnson Matthey PLC, 49 (upd.)
Johnson Worldwide Associates, Inc., 28
Johnstown America Industries, Inc., 23
Jones Apparel Group, Inc., 11
Jostens, Inc., 7; 25 (upd.)
K'Nex Industries, Inc., 52
Kaman Corporation, 12; 42 (upd.)
Karsten Manufacturing Corporation, 51
Kasper A.S.L., Ltd., 40
Katy Industries, Inc., 51 (upd.)
Kawasaki Heavy Industries, Ltd., III; 63
   (upd.)
Kaydon Corporation, 18
KB Toys, 35 (upd.)
Kelly-Moore Paint Company, Inc., 56
Kenmore Air Harbor Inc., 65
Keramik Holding AG Laufen, 51
Kerr Group Inc., 24
Kewaunee Scientific Corporation, 25
Key Safety Systems, Inc., 63

Key Tronic Corporation, 14
Keystone International, Inc., 11
KHD Konzern, III
KI, 57
Kimball International, Inc., 12; 48 (upd.)
Kit Manufacturing Co., 18
Knape & Vogt Manufacturing Company,
   17
Knoll Group Inc., 14
Koala Corporation, 44
Kobe Steel, Ltd., IV; 19 (upd.)
Koch Enterprises, Inc., 29
Koenig & Bauer AG, 64
Kohler Company, 7; 32 (upd.)
Komatsu Ltd., III; 16 (upd.); 52 (upd.)
Kone Corporation, 27
Konica Corporation, III
KSB AG, 62
Kubota Corporation, III; 26 (upd.)
Kuhlman Corporation, 20
Kyocera Corporation, 21 (upd.)
L-3 Communications Holdings, Inc., 48
L. and J.G. Stickley, Inc., 50
L.B. Foster Company, 33
L.S. Starrett Company, 64 (upd.)
La-Z-Boy Incorporated, 14; 50 (upd.)
Lacks Enterprises Inc., 61
LADD Furniture, Inc., 12
Ladish Co., Inc., 30
Lafarge Cement UK, 28; 54 (upd.)
Lafuma S.A., 39
Lakeland Industries, Inc., 45
Lam Research Corporation, 31 (upd.)
The Lamson & Sessions Co., 13; 61 (upd.)
Lancer Corporation, 21
The Lane Co., Inc., 12
Laserscope, 67
LaSiDo Inc., 58
LeapFrog Enterprises, Inc., 54
Leatherman Tool Group, Inc., 51
Leggett & Platt, Inc., 11; 48 (upd.)
Leica Camera AG, 35
Leica Microsystems Holdings GmbH, 35
Lennox International Inc., 8; 28 (upd.)
Lenox, Inc., 12
Leupold & Stevens, Inc., 52
Lexmark International, Inc., 18
Liebherr-International AG, 64
Linamar Corporation, 18
Lincoln Electric Co., 13
Lindal Cedar Homes, Inc., 29
Lindsay Manufacturing Co., 20
Little Tikes Company, 13; 62 (upd.)
Loctite Corporation, 8
Logitech International SA, 28
The Longaberger Company, 12; 44 (upd.)
Louis Vuitton, 10
Lucas Industries PLC, III
Luxottica SpA, 52 (upd.)
Lydall, Inc., 64
Lynch Corporation, 43
M&F Worldwide Corp., 38
M.A. Bruder & Sons, Inc., 56
MacAndrews & Forbes Holdings Inc., 28
Mace Security International, Inc., 57
Mackay Envelope Corporation, 45
Madison-Kipp Corporation, 58
Mag Instrument, Inc., 67
Maidenform, Inc., 59 (upd.)
Mail-Well, Inc., 28
Makita Corporation, 22; 59 (upd.)
MAN Aktiengesellschaft, III
Manitou BF S.A., 27
The Manitowoc Company, Inc., 18; 59
   (upd.)
Mannesmann AG, III; 14 (upd.)
Marcolin S.p.A., 61

MANUFACTURING (*continued*)

Margarete Steiff GmbH, 23
Marisa Christina, Inc., 15
Mark IV Industries, Inc., 7; 28 (upd.)
The Marmon Group, 16 (upd.)
Marshall Amplification plc, 62
Martin Industries, Inc., 44
Martin-Baker Aircraft Company Limited, 61
Marvin Lumber & Cedar Company, 22
Mary Kay, Inc., 30 (upd.)
Masco Corporation, III; 20 (upd.); 39 (upd.)
Masonite International Corporation, 63
Master Lock Company, 45
Material Sciences Corporation, 63
Matsushita Electric Industrial Co., Ltd., 64 (upd.)
Mattel, Inc., 7; 25 (upd.); 61 (upd.)
Matth. Hohner AG, 53
Matthews International Corporation, 29
Maverick Tube Corporation, 59
Maxco Inc., 17
Maxwell Shoe Company, Inc., 30
Maytag Corporation, III; 22 (upd.)
McClain Industries, Inc., 51
McDermott International, Inc., III
McKechnie plc, 34
McWane Corporation, 55
Meade Instruments Corporation, 41
Meadowcraft, Inc., 29
Medtronic, Inc., 67 (upd.)
Meggitt PLC, 34
Meiji Seika Kaisha Ltd., 64 (upd.)
Menasha Corporation, 59 (upd.)
Merck & Co., Inc., 34 (upd.)
Merillat Industries Inc., 13
Mestek Inc., 10
Metso Corporation, 30 (upd.)
Mettler-Toledo International Inc., 30
Michael Anthony Jewelers, Inc., 24
Microdot Inc., 8
The Middleton Doll Company, 53
Midwest Grain Products, Inc., 49
Miele & Cie. KG, 56
Mikasa, Inc., 28
Mikohn Gaming Corporation, 39
Milacron, Inc., 53 (upd.)
Miller Industries, Inc., 26
Milton Bradley Company, 21
Mine Safety Appliances Company, 31
Minolta Co., Ltd., III; 18 (upd.); 43 (upd.)
Minuteman International Inc., 46
Mitsubishi Heavy Industries, Ltd., III; 7 (upd.)
Mity Enterprises, Inc., 38
Mobile Mini, Inc., 58
Modine Manufacturing Company, 8; 56 (upd.)
Moen Incorporated, 12
Mohawk Industries, Inc., 19; 63 (upd.)
Molex Incorporated, 11
Monnaie de Paris, 62
Montres Rolex S.A., 13; 34 (upd.)
Montupet S.A., 63
Motorcar Parts & Accessories, Inc., 47
Moulinex S.A., 22
Movado Group, Inc., 28
Mr. Coffee, Inc., 15
Mr. Gasket Inc., 15
Mueller Industries, Inc., 7; 52 (upd.)
Multi-Color Corporation, 53
Nashua Corporation, 8
National Envelope Corporation, 32
National Gypsum Company, 10
National Oilwell, Inc., 54
National Picture & Frame Company, 24

National Standard Co., 13
National Starch and Chemical Company, 49
Natrol, Inc., 49
Natural Alternatives International, Inc., 49
NCR Corporation, 30 (upd.)
Neopost S.A., 53
New Balance Athletic Shoe, Inc., 25
New Holland N.V., 22
Newcor, Inc., 40
Newell Rubbermaid Inc., 9; 52 (upd.)
Newport News Shipbuilding Inc., 13; 38 (upd.)
Nexans SA, 54
NGK Insulators Ltd., 67
NHK Spring Co., Ltd., III
Nidec Corporation, 59
NIKE, Inc., 36 (upd.)
Nikon Corporation, III; 48 (upd.)
Nintendo Company, Ltd., III; 7 (upd.); 67 (upd.)
Nippon Seiko K.K., III
Nippondenso Co., Ltd., III
NKK Corporation, 28 (upd.)
NordicTrack, 22
Nordson Corporation, 11; 48 (upd.)
Nortek, Inc., 34
Norton Company, 8
Norton McNaughton, Inc., 27
Novellus Systems, Inc., 18
NTN Corporation, III; 47 (upd.)
Nu-kote Holding, Inc., 18
O'Sullivan Industries Holdings, Inc., 34
Oak Industries Inc., 21
Oakley, Inc., 49 (upd.)
Oakwood Homes Corporation, 15
ODL, Inc., 55
The Ohio Art Company, 14; 59 (upd.)
Oil-Dri Corporation of America, 20
180s, L.L.C., 64
Oneida Ltd., 7; 31 (upd.)
Optische Werke G. Rodenstock, 44
Orange Glo International, 53
Osmonics, Inc., 18
Otis Elevator Company, Inc., 13; 39 (upd.)
Outboard Marine Corporation, III; 20 (upd.)
Outdoor Research, Incorporated, 67
Owens Corning Corporation, 20 (upd.)
Owosso Corporation, 29
P & F Industries, Inc., 45
Pacer Technology, 40
Pacific Coast Feather Company, 67
Pacific Dunlop Limited, 10
Pall Corporation, 9
Palm Harbor Homes, Inc., 39
Panavision Inc., 24
Park Corp., 22
Parker-Hannifin Corporation, III; 24 (upd.)
Parlex Corporation, 61
Patrick Industries, Inc., 30
Paul Mueller Company, 65
Pechiney SA, IV; 45 (upd.)
Pella Corporation, 12; 39 (upd.)
Penn Engineering & Manufacturing Corp., 28
Pentair, Inc., 26 (upd.)
Pentech International, Inc., 29
The Perkin-Elmer Corporation, 7
Peterson American Corporation, 55
Phillips-Van Heusen Corporation, 24
Phoenix Mecano AG, 61
Physio-Control International Corp., 18
Pilkington plc, 34 (upd.)
Pinguely-Haulotte SA, 51
Pioneer Electronic Corporation, III
Pitney Bowes, Inc., 19

Pittway Corporation, 33 (upd.)
Planar Systems, Inc., 61
PlayCore, Inc., 27
Playmates Toys, 23
Playskool, Inc., 25
Pleasant Company, 27
Ply Gem Industries Inc., 12
Pochet SA, 55
Polaris Industries Inc., 12; 35 (upd.)
Polaroid Corporation, III; 7 (upd.); 28 (upd.)
PPG Industries, Inc., 22 (upd.)
Prada Holding B.V., 45
Praxair, Inc., 48 (upd.)
Precision Castparts Corp., 15
Premark International, Inc., III
Pressman Toy Corporation, 56
Presstek, Inc., 33
Prince Sports Group, Inc., 15
Printronix, Inc., 18
Puig Beauty and Fashion Group S.L., 60
Pulaski Furniture Corporation, 33
Pumpkin Masters, Inc., 48
Punch International N.V., 66
Puritan-Bennett Corporation, 13
Purolator Products Company, 21
PVC Container Corporation, 67
PW Eagle, Inc., 48
Q.E.P. Co., Inc., 65
QSC Audio Products, Inc., 56
Quixote Corporation, 15
R. Griggs Group Limited, 23
Racing Champions Corporation, 37
Radio Flyer Inc., 34
Raleigh UK Ltd., 65
Rapala-Normark Group, Ltd., 30
Raven Industries, Inc., 33
Raychem Corporation, 8
Rayovac Corporation, 39 (upd.)
Raytech Corporation, 61
Recovery Engineering, Inc., 25
Red Spot Paint & Varnish Company, 55
Red Wing Pottery Sales, Inc., 52
Red Wing Shoe Company, Inc., 9
Reed & Barton Corporation, 67
Regal-Beloit Corporation, 18
Reichhold Chemicals, Inc., 10
Remington Arms Company, Inc., 12; 40 (upd.)
Remington Products Company, L.L.C., 42
RENK AG, 37
Revell-Monogram Inc., 16
Revere Ware Corporation, 22
Revlon Inc., 64 (upd.)
Rexam PLC, 32 (upd.)
Rexnord Corporation, 21
RF Micro Devices, Inc., 43
Rheinmetall Berlin AG, 9
RHI AG, 53
Richardson Industries, Inc., 62
Riddell Sports Inc., 22
Rieter Holding AG, 42
River Oaks Furniture, Inc., 43
RMC Group p.l.c., 34 (upd.)
Roadmaster Industries, Inc., 16
Robbins & Myers Inc., 15
Robertson-Ceco Corporation, 19
Rock-Tenn Company, 59 (upd.)
Rockford Products Corporation, 55
RockShox, Inc., 26
Rockwell Automation, 43 (upd.)
Rogers Corporation, 61
Rohde & Schwarz GmbH & Co. KG, 39
ROHN Industries, Inc., 22
Rohr Incorporated, 9
Roland Corporation, 38
Rollerblade, Inc., 15; 34 (upd.)

Rolls-Royce Group PLC, 67 (upd.)
Ronson PLC, 49
Roper Industries, Inc., 15; 50 (upd.)
Rose Art Industries, 58
Roseburg Forest Products Company, 58
Rotork plc, 46
Royal Appliance Manufacturing Company, 15
Royal Canin S.A., 39
Royal Doulton plc, 14; 38 (upd.)
RPM, Inc., 8; 36 (upd.)
Rubbermaid Incorporated, III
Russ Berrie and Company, Inc., 12
S.C. Johnson & Son, Inc., 28 (upd.)
Sabaté Diosos SA, 48
Safeskin Corporation, 18
Safety Components International, Inc., 63
Safilo SpA, 54
Salant Corporation, 12; 51 (upd.)
Salton, Inc., 30
Samick Musical Instruments Co., Ltd., 56
Samsonite Corporation, 13; 43 (upd.)
Samuel Cabot Inc., 53
Sandvik AB, 32 (upd.)
Sanitec Corporation, 51
Sanrio Company, Ltd., 38
Sauder Woodworking Company, 12; 35 (upd.)
Sauer-Danfoss Inc., 61
Sawtek Inc., 43 (upd.)
Schindler Holding AG, 29
Schlumberger Limited, III
School-Tech, Inc., 62
Schott Corporation, 53
Scotsman Industries, Inc., 20
Scott Fetzer Company, 12
The Scotts Company, 22
Scovill Fasteners Inc., 24
Sealed Air Corporation, 14; 57 (upd.)
Sealy Inc., 12
Segway LLC, 48
Seiko Corporation, III; 17 (upd.)
Select Comfort Corporation, 34
The Selmer Company, Inc., 19
Semitool, Inc., 18
Sequa Corp., 13
Serta, Inc., 28
Severstal Joint Stock Company, 65
Shakespeare Company, 22
The Shaw Group, Inc., 50
Shelby Williams Industries, Inc., 14
Sherwood Brands, Inc., 53
Shimano Inc., 64
Shorewood Packaging Corporation, 28
Shuffle Master Inc., 51
Shurgard Storage Centers, Inc., 52
SIFCO Industries, Inc., 41
Simmons Company, 47
Simplicity Manufacturing, Inc., 64
Simula, Inc., 41
The Singer Company N.V., 30 (upd.)
The Singing Machine Company, Inc., 60
Skis Rossignol S.A., 15; 43 (upd.)
Skyline Corporation, 30
SLI, Inc., 48
Smead Manufacturing Co., 17
Smith & Wesson Corporation, 30
Smith Corona Corp., 13
Smith International, Inc., 15
Smith-Midland Corporation, 56
Smiths Industries PLC, 25
Smoby International SA, 56
Snap-On, Incorporated, 7; 27 (upd.)
Sonic Innovations Inc., 56
SonoSite, Inc., 56
Sparton Corporation, 18
Specialized Bicycle Components Inc., 50

Specialty Equipment Companies, Inc., 25
Specialty Products & Insulation Co., 59
Spectrum Control, Inc., 67
Speizman Industries, Inc., 44
Spin Master, Ltd., 61
Spirax-Sarco Engineering plc, 59
SPS Technologies, Inc., 30
SPX Corporation, 47 (upd.)
SRAM Corporation, 65
SRC Holdings Corporation, 67
Stanadyne Automotive Corporation, 37
Standex International Corporation, 17
Stanley Furniture Company, Inc., 34
The Stanley Works, III; 20 (upd.)
Starcraft Corporation, 66 (upd.)
Stearns, Inc., 43
Steel Authority of India Ltd., 66 (upd.)
Steel Dynamics, Inc., 52
Steel Technologies Inc., 63
Steelcase, Inc., 7; 27 (upd.)
Steinway Musical Properties, Inc., 19
Stelco Inc., 51 (upd.)
The Stephan Company, 60
Stewart & Stevenson Services Inc., 11
STMicroelectronics NV, 52
Stratasys, Inc., 67
Strombecker Corporation, 60
Stryker Corporation, 11; 29 (upd.)
Sturm, Ruger & Company, Inc., 19
Sub-Zero Freezer Co., Inc., 31
Sudbury Inc., 16
Sulzer Brothers Limited (Gebruder Sulzer Aktiengesellschaft), III
Sumitomo Heavy Industries, Ltd., III; 42 (upd.)
Susquehanna Pfaltzgraff Company, 8
Swank Inc., 17
Swarovski International Holding AG, 40
The Swatch Group SA, 26
Swedish Match AB, 12; 39 (upd.)
Sweetheart Cup Company, Inc., 36
Sybron International Corp., 14
Syratech Corp., 14
Systemax, Inc., 52
TAB Products Co., 17
TAG Heuer International SA, 25
Taiheiyo Cement Corporation, 60 (upd.)
Taiwan Semiconductor Manufacturing Company Ltd., 47
Tarkett Sommer AG, 25
Taser International, Inc., 62
Taylor Guitars, 48
Taylor Made Golf Co., 23
TB Wood's Corporation, 56
TDK Corporation, 49 (upd.)
TearDrop Golf Company, 32
Tecumseh Products Company, 8
Tektronix, Inc., 8
Tempur-Pedic Inc., 54
Tenaris SA, 63
Tennant Company, 13; 33 (upd.)
Terex Corporation, 7; 40 (upd.)
The Testor Corporation, 51
Tetra Pak International SA, 53
Thales S.A., 42
Thermadyne Holding Corporation, 19
Thermo BioAnalysis Corp., 25
Thermo Electron Corporation, 7
Thermo Fibertek, Inc., 24
Thermo Instrument Systems Inc., 11
Thermo King Corporation, 13
Thiokol Corporation, 22 (upd.)
Thomas & Betts Corp., 11
Thomas Industries Inc., 29
Thomasville Furniture Industries, Inc., 12
Thor Industries, Inc., 39
3M Company, 61 (upd.)

Thyssen Krupp AG, 28 (upd.)
Tilia Inc., 62
Timex Corporation, 7; 25 (upd.)
The Timken Company, 8; 42 (upd.)
Titan Cement Company S.A., 64
TJ International, Inc., 19
Todd Shipyards Corporation, 14
Tokheim Corporation, 21
Tomy Company Ltd., 65
Tong Yang Cement Corporation, 62
Tonka Corporation, 25
Toolex International N.V., 26
The Topaz Group, Inc., 62
Topps Company, Inc., 13
Toray Industries, Inc., 51 (upd.)
The Toro Company, 7; 26 (upd.)
The Torrington Company, 13
TOTO LTD., 28 (upd.)
Town & Country Corporation, 19
Toymax International, Inc., 29
Toyoda Automatic Loom Works, Ltd., III
Tredegar Corporation, 52
Trek Bicycle Corporation, 16
Trico Products Corporation, 15
TriMas Corp., 11
Trinity Industries, Incorporated, 7
TRINOVA Corporation, III
TriQuint Semiconductor, Inc., 63
Trisko Jewelry Sculptures, Ltd., 57
Triumph Group, Inc., 31
Tubos de Acero de Mexico, S.A. (TAMSA), 41
Tultex Corporation, 13
Tupperware Corporation, 28
Twin Disc, Inc., 21
Ty Inc., 33
Tyco International Ltd., III; 28 (upd.)
Tyco Toys, Inc., 12
U.S. Robotics Corporation, 9; 66 (upd.)
Ube Industries, Ltd., 38 (upd.)
Ultralife Batteries, Inc., 58
United Defense Industries, Inc., 30; 66 (upd.)
United Dominion Industries Limited, 8; 16 (upd.)
United Industrial Corporation, 37
United States Filter Corporation, 20
United States Pipe and Foundry Company, 62
Unitika Ltd., 53 (upd.)
Unitog Co., 19
Utah Medical Products, Inc., 36
VA TECH ELIN EBG GmbH, 49
Vaillant GmbH, 44
Vallourec SA, 54
Valmet Corporation (Valmet Oy), III
Valmont Industries, Inc., 19
The Valspar Corporation, 8
Vari-Lite International, Inc., 35
Varian, Inc., 48 (upd.)
Variflex, Inc., 51
Varity Corporation, III
Varlen Corporation, 16
Varta AG, 23
Velcro Industries N.V., 19
Vermeer Manufacturing Company, 17
Viasystems Group, Inc., 67
Vickers plc, 27
Victorinox AG, 21
Vidrala S.A., 67
Viessmann Werke GmbH & Co., 37
Viking Range Corporation, 66
Villeroy & Boch AG, 37
Virco Manufacturing Corporation, 17
Viskase Companies, Inc., 55
Vita Plus Corporation, 60
Vitro Corporativo S.A. de C.V., 34

MANUFACTURING (*continued*)

voestalpine AG, 57 (upd.)
Vorwerk & Co., 27
Vosper Thornycroft Holding plc, 41
Vossloh AG, 53
W.A. Whitney Company, 53
W.H. Brady Co., 17
W.L. Gore & Associates, Inc., 14; 60
   (upd.)
W.W. Grainger, Inc., 26 (upd.)
Wabash National Corp., 13
Wabtec Corporation, 40
Walbro Corporation, 13
Washington Scientific Industries, Inc., 17
Wassall Plc, 18
Waterford Wedgwood plc, 12; 34 (upd.)
Waters Corporation, 43
Watts Industries, Inc., 19
WD-40 Company, 18
Weber-Stephen Products Co., 40
Weeres Industries Corporation, 52
Welbilt Corp., 19
Wellman, Inc., 8; 52 (upd.)
Weru Aktiengesellschaft, 18
West Bend Co., 14
Westell Technologies, Inc., 57
Westerbeke Corporation, 60
Western Digital Corp., 25
Wheaton Science Products, 60 (upd.)
Wheeling-Pittsburgh Corporation, 58 (upd.)
Whirlpool Corporation, III; 12 (upd.); 59
   (upd.)
White Consolidated Industries Inc., 13
Wilbert, Inc., 56
Wilkinson Sword Ltd., 60
William L. Bonnell Company, Inc., 66
William Zinsser & Company, Inc., 58
Williamson-Dickie Manufacturing
   Company, 45 (upd.)
Wilson Sporting Goods Company, 24
Windmere Corporation, 16
Winegard Company, 56
WinsLoew Furniture, Inc., 21
WMS Industries, Inc., 15; 53 (upd.)
Wolverine Tube Inc., 23
Wood-Mode, Inc., 23
Woodcraft Industries Inc., 61
Woodward Governor Company, 13; 49
   (upd.)
Wright Medical Group, Inc., 61
Württembergische Metallwarenfabrik AG
   (WMF), 60
Wyant Corporation, 30
Wyman-Gordon Company, 14
Wynn's International, Inc., 33
X-Rite, Inc., 48
Yamaha Corporation, III; 16 (upd.)
The York Group, Inc., 50
York International Corp., 13
Young Innovations, Inc., 44
Zebra Technologies Corporation, 53 (upd.)
Zero Corporation, 17
Zindart Ltd., 60
Zippo Manufacturing Company, 18
Zodiac S.A., 36
Zygo Corporation, 42

MATERIALS

AK Steel Holding Corporation, 19
American Biltrite Inc., 16
American Colloid Co., 13
American Standard Inc., III
Ameriwood Industries International Corp.,
   17
Apasco S.A. de C.V., 51
Apogee Enterprises, Inc., 8
Asahi Glass Company, Limited, III

Bairnco Corporation, 28
Bayou Steel Corporation, 31
Blessings Corp., 19
Blue Circle Industries PLC, III
Bodycote International PLC, 63
Boral Limited, III
British Vita PLC, 9
Brush Engineered Materials Inc., 67
California Steel Industries, Inc., 67
Callanan Industries, Inc., 60
Cameron & Barkley Company, 28
Carborundum Company, 15
Carl-Zeiss-Stiftung, 34 (upd.)
Carlisle Companies Incorporated, 8
Cemex SA de CV, 20
Century Aluminum Company, 52
CertainTeed Corporation, 35
Chargeurs International, 21 (upd.)
Chemfab Corporation, 35
Cold Spring Granite Company Inc., 67
   (upd.)
Compagnie de Saint-Gobain S.A., III; 16
   (upd.)
Cookson Group plc, III; 44 (upd.)
Corning Incorporated, III
CSR Limited, III
Dal-Tile International Inc., 22
The David J. Joseph Company, 14
The Dexter Corporation, 12 (upd.)
Dyckerhoff AG, 35
ECC Group plc, III
Edw. C. Levy Co., 42
84 Lumber Company, 9; 39 (upd.)
ElkCorp, 52
English China Clays Ltd., 15 (upd.); 40
   (upd.)
Envirodyne Industries, Inc., 17
Feldmuhle Nobel A.G., III
Fibreboard Corporation, 16
Florida Rock Industries, Inc., 46
Foamex International Inc., 17
Formica Corporation, 13
GAF Corporation, 22 (upd.)
The Geon Company, 11
Giant Cement Holding, Inc., 23
Gibraltar Steel Corporation, 37
Granite Rock Company, 26
Groupe Sidel S.A., 21
Harbison-Walker Refractories Company, 24
Harrisons & Crosfield plc, III
Heidelberger Zement AG, 31
Hexcel Corporation, 28
"Holderbank" Financière Glaris Ltd., III
Holnam Inc., 39 (upd.)
Holt and Bugbee Company, 66
Howmet Corp., 12
Ibstock Brick Ltd., 14; 37 (upd.)
Imerys S.A., 40 (upd.)
Internacional de Ceramica, S.A. de C.V.,
   53
International Shipbreaking Ltd. L.L.C., 67
Joseph T. Ryerson & Son, Inc., 15
Lafarge Coppée S.A., III
Lafarge Corporation, 28
Lehigh Portland Cement Company, 23
Manville Corporation, III; 7 (upd.)
Material Sciences Corporation, 63
Matsushita Electric Works, Ltd., III; 7
   (upd.)
McJunkin Corporation, 63
Medusa Corporation, 24
Mitsubishi Materials Corporation, III
Nippon Sheet Glass Company, Limited, III
North Pacific Group, Inc., 61
OmniSource Corporation, 14
Onoda Cement Co., Ltd., III
Owens-Corning Fiberglass Corporation, III

Pilkington plc, III; 34 (upd.)
Pioneer International Limited, III
PPG Industries, Inc., III
Redland plc, III
Rinker Group Ltd., 65
RMC Group p.l.c., III
Rock of Ages Corporation, 37
The Rugby Group plc, 31
Schuff Steel Company, 26
Sekisui Chemical Co., Ltd., III
Severstal Joint Stock Company, 65
Shaw Industries, 9
The Sherwin-Williams Company, III; 13
   (upd.)
The Siam Cement Public Company
   Limited, 56
Simplex Technologies Inc., 21
Solutia Inc., 52
Sommer-Allibert S.A., 19
Southdown, Inc., 14
Spartech Corporation, 19
Ssangyong Cement Industrial Co., Ltd., III;
   61 (upd.)
Steel Technologies Inc., 63
Sun Distributors L.P., 12
Tarmac PLC, III
Tarmac plc, 28 (upd.)
TOTO LTD., III; 28 (upd.)
Toyo Sash Co., Ltd., III
Tuscarora Inc., 29
U.S. Aggregates, Inc., 42
Ube Industries, Ltd., III
United States Steel Corporation, 50 (upd.)
USG Corporation, III; 26 (upd.)
voestalpine AG, 57 (upd.)
Vulcan Materials Company, 7; 52 (upd.)
Wacker-Chemie GmbH, 35
Walter Industries, Inc., III
Waxman Industries, Inc., 9
Weber et Broutin France, 66
Wolseley plc, 64
Zoltek Companies, Inc., 37

MINING & METALS

A.M. Castle & Co., 25
Aggregate Industries plc, 36
Aktiebolaget SKF, 38 (upd.)
Alcan Aluminium Limited, IV; 31 (upd.)
Alcoa Inc., 56 (upd.)
Alleghany Corporation, 10
Allegheny Ludlum Corporation, 8
Alrosa Company Ltd., 62
Altos Hornos de México, S.A. de C.V., 42
Aluminum Company of America, IV; 20
   (upd.)
AMAX Inc., IV
AMCOL International Corporation, 59
   (upd.)
Amsted Industries Incorporated, 7
Anglo American Corporation of South
   Africa Limited, IV; 16 (upd.)
Anglo American PLC, 50 (upd.)
Aquarius Platinum Ltd., 63
ARBED S.A., IV; 22 (upd.)
Arch Mineral Corporation, 7
Armco Inc., IV
ASARCO Incorporated, IV
Ashanti Goldfields Company Limited, 43
Atchison Casting Corporation, 39
Barrick Gold Corporation, 34
Battle Mountain Gold Company, 23
Benguet Corporation, 58
Bethlehem Steel Corporation, IV; 7 (upd.);
   27 (upd.)
BHP Billiton, 67 (upd.)
Birmingham Steel Corporation, 13; 40
   (upd.)

Boart Longyear Company, 26
Bodycote International PLC, 63
Boral Limited, 43 (upd.)
British Coal Corporation, IV
British Steel plc, IV; 19 (upd.)
Broken Hill Proprietary Company Ltd., IV, 22 (upd.)
Brush Engineered Materials Inc., 67
Brush Wellman Inc., 14
Buderus AG, 37
Carpenter Technology Corporation, 13
Chaparral Steel Co., 13
Christensen Boyles Corporation, 26
Cleveland-Cliffs Inc., 13; 62 (upd.)
Coal India Ltd., IV; 44 (upd.)
Cockerill Sambre Group, IV; 26 (upd.)
Coeur d'Alene Mines Corporation, 20
Cold Spring Granite Company, 16
Cold Spring Granite Company Inc., 67 (upd.)
Cominco Ltd., 37
Commercial Metals Company, 15; 42 (upd.)
Companhia Vale do Rio Doce, IV; 43 (upd.)
CONSOL Energy Inc., 59
Corporacion Nacional del Cobre de Chile, 40
Corus Group plc, 49 (upd.)
CRA Limited, IV
Cyprus Amax Minerals Company, 21
Cyprus Minerals Company, 7
Daido Steel Co., Ltd., IV
De Beers Consolidated Mines Limited/De Beers Centenary AG, IV; 7 (upd.); 28 (upd.)
Degussa Group, IV
Dofasco Inc., IV; 24 (upd.)
Echo Bay Mines Ltd., IV; 38 (upd.)
Engelhard Corporation, IV
Falconbridge Limited, 49
Fansteel Inc., 19
Fluor Corporation, 34 (upd.)
Freeport-McMoRan Copper & Gold, Inc., IV; 7 (upd.); 57 (upd.)
Fried. Krupp GmbH, IV
Gencor Ltd., IV, 22 (upd.)
Geneva Steel, 7
Gerdau S.A., 59
Glamis Gold, Ltd., 54
Gold Fields Ltd., IV; 62 (upd.)
Grupo Mexico, S.A. de C.V., 40
Handy & Harman, 23
Hanson Building Materials America Inc., 60
Hanson PLC, 30 (upd.)
Harmony Gold Mining Company Limited, 63
Hecla Mining Company, 20
Hemlo Gold Mines Inc., 9
Heraeus Holding GmbH, IV
Highveld Steel and Vanadium Corporation Limited, 59
Hitachi Metals, Ltd., IV
Hoesch AG, IV
Homestake Mining Company, 12; 38 (upd.)
Horsehead Industries, Inc., 51
The Hudson Bay Mining and Smelting Company, Limited, 12
Hylsamex, S.A. de C.V., 39
IMCO Recycling, Incorporated, 32
Imerys S.A., 40 (upd.)
Imetal S.A., IV
Inco Limited, IV; 45 (upd.)
Industrias Penoles, S.A. de C.V., 22
Inland Steel Industries, Inc., IV; 19 (upd.)
Intermet Corporation, 32

Iscor Limited, 57
Ispat Inland Inc., 30; 40 (upd.)
Johnson Matthey PLC, IV; 16 (upd.)
JSC MMC Norilsk Nickel, 48
Kaiser Aluminum & Chemical Corporation, IV
Kawasaki Heavy Industries, Ltd., 63 (upd.)
Kawasaki Steel Corporation, IV
Kennecott Corporation, 7; 27 (upd.)
Kentucky Electric Steel, Inc., 31
Kerr-McGee Corporation, 22 (upd.)
Kinross Gold Corporation, 36
Klockner-Werke AG, IV
Kobe Steel, Ltd., IV; 19 (upd.)
Koninklijke Nederlandsche Hoogovens en Staalfabrieken NV, IV
Laclede Steel Company, 15
Layne Christensen Company, 19
Lonmin plc, 66 (upd.)
Lonrho Plc, 21
The LTV Corporation, 24 (upd.)
Lukens Inc., 14
Magma Copper Company, 7
The Marmon Group, IV; 16 (upd.)
Massey Energy Company, 57
MAXXAM Inc., 8
Meridian Gold, Incorporated, 47
Metaleurop S.A., 21
Metallgesellschaft AG, IV
Minerals and Metals Trading Corporation of India Ltd., IV
Minerals Technologies Inc., 11; 52 (upd.)
Mitsui Mining & Smelting Co., Ltd., IV
Mitsui Mining Company, Limited, IV
Mueller Industries, Inc., 52 (upd.)
National Steel Corporation, 12
NERCO, Inc., 7
Newmont Mining Corporation, 7
Neyveli Lignite Corporation Ltd., 65
Niagara Corporation, 28
Nichimen Corporation, IV
Nippon Light Metal Company, Ltd., IV
Nippon Steel Corporation, IV; 17 (upd.)
Nisshin Steel Co., Ltd., IV
NKK Corporation, IV; 28 (upd.)
Noranda Inc., IV; 7 (upd.); 64 (upd.)
Norddeutsche Affinerie AG, 62
North Star Steel Company, 18
Nucor Corporation, 7; 21 (upd.)
Oglebay Norton Company, 17
Okura & Co., Ltd., IV
Oregon Metallurgical Corporation, 20
Oregon Steel Mills, Inc., 14
Outokumpu Oyj, 38
Park Corp., 22
Peabody Coal Company, 10
Peabody Energy Corporation, 45 (upd.)
Peabody Holding Company, Inc., IV
Pechiney SA, IV; 45 (upd.)
Peter Kiewit Sons' Inc., 8
Phelps Dodge Corporation, IV; 28 (upd.)
The Pittston Company, IV; 19 (upd.)
Placer Dome Inc., 20; 61 (upd.)
Pohang Iron and Steel Company Ltd., IV
POSCO, 57 (upd.)
Potash Corporation of Saskatchewan Inc., 18
Quanex Corporation, 13; 62 (upd.)
RAG AG, 35; 60 (upd.)
Reliance Steel & Aluminum Co., 19
Republic Engineered Steels, Inc., 7; 26 (upd.)
Reynolds Metals Company, IV
Rio Tinto PLC, 19 (upd.); 50 (upd.)
RMC Group p.l.c., 34 (upd.)
Roanoke Electric Steel Corporation, 45
Rouge Steel Company, 8

The RTZ Corporation PLC, IV
Ruhrkohle AG, IV
Ryerson Tull, Inc., 40 (upd.)
Saarberg-Konzern, IV
Salzgitter AG, IV
Sandvik AB, IV
Saudi Basic Industries Corporation (SABIC), 58
Schnitzer Steel Industries, Inc., 19
Severstal Joint Stock Company, 65
Siderar S.A.I.C., 66
Smorgon Steel Group Ltd., 62
Southern Peru Copper Corporation, 40
Southwire Company, Inc., 8; 23 (upd.)
Steel Authority of India Ltd., IV
Stelco Inc., IV
Stillwater Mining Company, 47
Sumitomo Metal Industries, Ltd., IV
Sumitomo Metal Mining Co., Ltd., IV
Tata Iron & Steel Co. Ltd., IV; 44 (upd.)
Teck Corporation, 27
Tenaris SA, 63
Texas Industries, Inc., 8
Thyssen AG, IV
The Timken Company, 8; 42 (upd.)
Titanium Metals Corporation, 21
Tomen Corporation, IV
Total Fina Elf S.A., 50 (upd.)
U.S. Borax, Inc., 42
Ugine S.A., 20
NV Umicore SA, 47
Usinor SA, IV; 42 (upd.)
Usinor Sacilor, IV
VIAG Aktiengesellschaft, IV
Voest-Alpine Stahl AG, IV
Vulcan Materials Company, 52 (upd.)
Walter Industries, Inc., 22 (upd.)
Weirton Steel Corporation, IV; 26 (upd.)
Westmoreland Coal Company, 7
Wheeling-Pittsburgh Corp., 7
WMC, Limited, 43
Worthington Industries, Inc., 7; 21 (upd.)
Zambia Industrial and Mining Corporation Ltd., IV

PAPER & FORESTRY

Abitibi-Consolidated, Inc., IV; 25 (upd.)
Albany International Corporation, 51 (upd.)
Amcor Limited, IV; 19 (upd.)
American Greetings Corporation, 59 (upd.)
American Pad & Paper Company, 20
Aracruz Celulose S.A., 57
Arjo Wiggins Appleton p.l.c., 34
Asplundh Tree Expert Co.,20; 59 (upd.)
Avery Dennison Corporation, IV
Badger Paper Mills, Inc., 15
Beckett Papers, 23
Bemis Company, Inc., 8
Bohemia, Inc., 13
Boise Cascade Corporation, IV; 8 (upd.); 32 (upd.)
Bowater PLC, IV
Bunzl plc, IV
Canfor Corporation, 42
Caraustar Industries, Inc., 19; 44 (upd.)
Carter Lumber Company, 45
Champion International Corporation, IV; 20 (upd.)
Chesapeake Corporation, 8; 30 (upd.)
Consolidated Papers, Inc., 8; 36 (upd.)
Crane & Co., Inc., 26
Crown Vantage Inc., 29
CSS Industries, Inc., 35
Daio Paper Corporation, IV
Daishowa Paper Manufacturing Co., Ltd., IV; 57 (upd.)
Deltic Timber Corporation, 46

PAPER & FORESTRY (*continued*)

Dillard Paper Company, 11
Doman Industries Limited, 59
Domtar Inc., IV
DS Smith Plc, 61
Enso-Gutzeit Oy, IV
Esselte Pendaflex Corporation, 11
Federal Paper Board Company, Inc., 8
FiberMark, Inc., 37
Fletcher Challenge Ltd., IV
Fort Howard Corporation, 8
Fort James Corporation, 22 (upd.)
Georgia-Pacific Corporation, IV; 9 (upd.);
    47 (upd.)
Groupe Rougier SA, 21
Grupo Portucel Soporcel, 60
Guilbert S.A., 42
Holmen AB, 52 (upd.)
Honshu Paper Co., Ltd., IV
International Paper Company, IV; 15
    (upd.); 47 (upd.)
James River Corporation of Virginia, IV
Japan Pulp and Paper Company Limited,
    IV
Jefferson Smurfit Group plc, IV; 49 (upd.)
Jujo Paper Co., Ltd., IV
Kimberly-Clark Corporation, 16 (upd.); 43
    (upd.)
Kimberly-Clark de México, S.A. de C.V.,
    54
Kruger Inc., 17
Kymmene Corporation, IV
Longview Fibre Company, 8; 37 (upd.)
Louisiana-Pacific Corporation, IV; 31
    (upd.)
M-real Oyj, 56 (upd.)
MacMillan Bloedel Limited, IV
Matussière et Forest SA, 58
The Mead Corporation, IV; 19 (upd.)
Mercer International Inc., 64
Metsa-Serla Oy, IV
Mo och Domsjö AB, IV
Monadnock Paper Mills, Inc., 21
Mosinee Paper Corporation, 15
Nashua Corporation, 8
National Envelope Corporation, 32
NCH Corporation, 8
Norske Skogindustrier ASA, 63
Oji Paper Co., Ltd., IV
P.H. Glatfelter Company, 8; 30 (upd.)
Packaging Corporation of America, 12
Papeteries de Lancey, 23
Plum Creek Timber Company, Inc., 43
Pope & Talbot, Inc., 12; 61 (upd.)
Potlatch Corporation, 8; 34 (upd.)
PWA Group, IV
Rayonier Inc., 24
Rengo Co., Ltd., IV
Reno de Medici S.p.A., 41
Rexam PLC, 32 (upd.)
Riverwood International Corporation, 11;
    48 (upd.)
Rock-Tenn Company, 13; 59 (upd.)
Rogers Corporation, 61
St. Joe Paper Company, 8
Sanyo-Kokusaku Pulp Co., Ltd., IV
Sappi Limited, 49
Schweitzer-Mauduit International, Inc., 52
Scott Paper Company, IV; 31 (upd.)
Sealed Air Corporation, 14
Sierra Pacific Industries, 22
Simpson Investment Company, 17
Specialty Coatings Inc., 8
Stone Container Corporation, IV
Stora Enso Oyj, 36 (upd.)
Stora Kopparbergs Bergslags AB, IV

Svenska Cellulosa Aktiebolaget SCA, IV;
    28 (upd.)
Tapemark Company Inc., 64
Tembec Inc., 66
Temple-Inland Inc., IV; 31 (upd.)
Thomsen Greenhouses and Garden Center,
    Incorporated, 65
TJ International, Inc., 19
U.S. Timberlands Company, L.P., 42
Union Camp Corporation, IV
United Paper Mills Ltd. (Yhtyneet
    Paperitehtaat Oy), IV
Universal Forest Products, Inc., 10; 59
    (upd.)
UPM-Kymmene Corporation, 19; 50 (upd.)
Wausau-Mosinee Paper Corporation, 60
    (upd.)
West Fraser Timber Co. Ltd., 17
Westvaco Corporation, IV; 19 (upd.)
Weyerhaeuser Company, IV; 9 (upd.); 28
    (upd.)
Wickes Inc., 25 (upd.)
Willamette Industries, Inc., IV; 31 (upd.)
WTD Industries, Inc., 20

PERSONAL SERVICES

AARP, 27
ADT Security Services, Inc., 12; 44 (upd.)
Africare, 59
American Civil Liberties Union (ACLU),
    60
American Retirement Corporation, 42
Arthur Murray International, Inc., 32
Association of Junior Leagues International
    Inc., 60
Berlitz International, Inc., 39 (upd.)
The Brink's Company, 58 (upd.)
Carriage Services, Inc., 37
CDI Corporation, 54 (upd.)
ChildrenFirst, Inc., 59
Childtime Learning Centers, Inc., 34
Chubb, PLC, 50
Corinthian Colleges, Inc., 39
Correctional Services Corporation, 30
CUC International Inc., 16
Curves International, Inc., 54
Davis Service Group PLC, 45
DeVry Incorporated, 29
Educational Testing Service, 12; 62 (upd.)
The Ford Foundation, 34
Franklin Quest Co., 11
Goodwill Industries International, Inc., 16;
    66 (upd.)
GP Strategies Corporation, 64 (upd.)
Greg Manning Auctions, Inc., 60
Gunnebo AB, 53
The Humane Society of the United States,
    54
Huntington Learning Centers, Inc., 55
Imperial Parking Corporation, 58
Initial Security, 64
Jazzercise, Inc., 45
The John D. and Catherine T. MacArthur
    Foundation, 34
Kaplan, Inc., 42
KinderCare Learning Centers, Inc., 13
Knowledge Learning Corporation, 51
The Loewen Group Inc., 16; 40 (upd.)
Mace Security International, Inc., 57
Management and Training Corporation, 28
Manpower, Inc., 9
Michael Page International plc, 45
Mothers Against Drunk Driving (MADD),
    51
National Heritage Academies, Inc., 60
National Organization for Women, Inc., 55

Prison Rehabilitative Industries and
    Diversified Enterprises, Inc. (PRIDE), 53
Recording for the Blind & Dyslexic, 51
Regis Corporation, 18
The Rockefeller Foundation, 34
Rollins, Inc., 11
Rosenbluth International Inc., 14
Rotary International, 31
The Salvation Army USA, 32
Service Corporation International, 6; 51
    (upd.)
SOS Staffing Services, 25
Stewart Enterprises, Inc., 20
Supercuts Inc., 26
United Service Organizations, 60
Weight Watchers International Inc., 12; 33
    (upd.)
The York Group, Inc., 50
Youth Services International, Inc., 21
YWCA of the U.S.A., 45

PETROLEUM

Abu Dhabi National Oil Company, IV; 45
    (upd.)
Agway, Inc., 21 (upd.)
Alberta Energy Company Ltd., 16; 43
    (upd.)
Amerada Hess Corporation, IV; 21 (upd.);
    55 (upd.)
Amoco Corporation, IV; 14 (upd.)
Anadarko Petroleum Corporation, 10; 52
    (upd.)
ANR Pipeline Co., 17
Anschutz Corp., 12
Apache Corporation, 10; 32 (upd.)
Aral AG, 62
Arctic Slope Regional Corporation, 38
Ashland Inc., 19; 50 (upd.)
Ashland Oil, Inc., IV
Atlantic Richfield Company, IV; 31 (upd.)
Baker Hughes Incorporated, 22 (upd.); 57
    (upd.)
Belco Oil & Gas Corp., 40
Benton Oil and Gas Company, 47
Berry Petroleum Company, 47
BHP Billiton, 67 (upd.)
BJ Services Company, 25
Blue Rhino Corporation, 56
BP p.l.c., 45 (upd.)
The British Petroleum Company plc, IV; 7
    (upd.); 21 (upd.)
British-Borneo Oil & Gas PLC, 34
Broken Hill Proprietary Company Ltd., 22
    (upd.)
Burlington Resources Inc., 10
Burmah Castrol PLC, IV; 30 (upd.)
Callon Petroleum Company, 47
Caltex Petroleum Corporation, 19
ChevronTexaco Corporation, IV; 19 (upd.);
    47 (upd.)
Chiles Offshore Corporation, 9
China National Petroleum Corporation, 46
Chinese Petroleum Corporation, IV; 31
    (upd.)
CITGO Petroleum Corporation, IV; 31
    (upd.)
The Coastal Corporation, IV; 31 (upd.)
Compañia Española de Petróleos S.A.
    (Cepsa), IV; 56 (upd.)
Comstock Resources, Inc., 47
Conoco Inc., IV; 16 (upd.)
ConocoPhillips, 63 (upd.)
CONSOL Energy Inc., 59
Cooper Cameron Corporation, 20 (upd.)
Cosmo Oil Co., Ltd., IV; 53 (upd.)
Crown Central Petroleum Corporation, 7
DeepTech International Inc., 21

Den Norse Stats Oljeselskap AS, IV
Denbury Resources, Inc., 67
Deutsche BP Aktiengesellschaft, 7
Devon Energy Corporation, 61
Diamond Shamrock, Inc., IV
Dynegy Inc., 49 (upd.)
E.On AG, 50 (upd.)
Edge Petroleum Corporation, 67
Egyptian General Petroleum Corporation,
  IV; 51 (upd.)
El Paso Corporation, 66 (upd.)
Elf Aquitaine SA, 21 (upd.)
Empresa Colombiana de Petróleos, IV
Enbridge Inc., 43
Energen Corporation, 21
Enron Corporation, 19
ENSCO International Incorporated, 57
Ente Nazionale Idrocarburi, IV
Enterprise Oil PLC, 11; 50 (upd.)
Entreprise Nationale Sonatrach, IV
Equitable Resources, Inc., 54 (upd.)
Exxon Corporation, IV; 7 (upd.); 32 (upd.)
Exxon Mobil Corporation, 67 (upd.)
Ferrellgas Partners, L.P., 35
FINA, Inc., 7
Flying J Inc., 19
Forest Oil Corporation, 19
OAO Gazprom, 42
General Sekiyu K.K., IV
Giant Industries, Inc., 19; 61 (upd.)
Global Industries, Ltd., 37
Global Marine Inc., 9
GlobalSantaFe Corporation, 48 (upd.)
Grey Wolf, Inc., 43
Halliburton Company, 25 (upd.); 55 (upd.)
Hanover Compressor Company, 59
Hellenic Petroleum SA, 64
Helmerich & Payne, Inc., 18
Holly Corporation, 12
Hunt Consolidated, Inc., 7; 27 (upd.)
Hurricane Hydrocarbons Ltd., 54
Husky Energy Inc., 47
Idemitsu Kosan Co., Ltd., 49 (upd.)
Idemitsu Kosan K.K., IV
Imperial Oil Limited, IV; 25 (upd.)
Indian Oil Corporation Ltd., IV; 48 (upd.)
Ipiranga S.A., 67
Kanematsu Corporation, IV
Kerr-McGee Corporation, IV; 22 (upd.)
Kinder Morgan, Inc., 45
King Ranch, Inc., 14
Koch Industries, Inc., IV; 20 (upd.)
Koppers Industries, Inc., 26 (upd.)
Kuwait Petroleum Corporation, IV; 55
  (upd.)
Libyan National Oil Corporation, IV
The Louisiana Land and Exploration
  Company, 7
OAO LUKOIL, 40
Lyondell Petrochemical Company, IV
MAPCO Inc., IV
Maxus Energy Corporation, 7
McDermott International, Inc., 37 (upd.)
Meteor Industries Inc., 33
Mitchell Energy and Development
  Corporation, 7
Mitsubishi Oil Co., Ltd., IV
Mobil Corporation, IV; 7 (upd.); 21 (upd.)
Murphy Oil Corporation, 7; 32 (upd.)
Nabors Industries, Inc., 9
National Iranian Oil Company, IV; 61
  (upd.)
National Oil Corporation, 66 (upd.)
Neste Oy, IV
Newfield Exploration Company, 65
NGC Corporation, 18

Nigerian National Petroleum Corporation,
  IV
Nippon Oil Corporation, IV; 63 (upd.)
OAO NK YUKOS, 47
Noble Affiliates, Inc., 11
Occidental Petroleum Corporation, IV; 25
  (upd.)
Oil and Natural Gas Commission, IV
ÖMV Aktiengesellschaft, IV
Oryx Energy Company, 7
Parker Drilling Company, 28
Patina Oil & Gas Corporation, 24
Patterson-UTI Energy, Inc., 55
Pennzoil-Quaker State Company, IV; 20
  (upd.); 50 (upd.)
Pertamina, IV; 56 (upd.)
Petro-Canada Limited, IV
PetroFina S.A., IV; 26 (upd.)
Petróleo Brasileiro S.A., IV
Petróleos de Portugal S.A., IV
Petróleos de Venezuela S.A., IV
Petróleos del Ecuador, IV
Petróleos Mexicanos, IV; 19 (upd.)
Petroleum Development Oman LLC, IV
Petroliam Nasional Bhd (Petronas), IV; 56
  (upd.)
Petron Corporation, 58
Phillips Petroleum Company, IV; 40 (upd.)
Pioneer Natural Resources Company, 59
Pogo Producing Company, 39
Premcor Inc., 37
PTT Public Company Ltd., 56
Qatar General Petroleum Corporation, IV
Quaker State Corporation, 7; 21 (upd.)
Range Resources Corporation, 45
Repsol-YPF S.A., IV; 16 (upd.); 40 (upd.)
Resource America, Inc., 42
Rowan Companies, Inc., 43
Royal Dutch/Shell Group, IV; 49 (upd.)
RWE AG, 50 (upd.)
St. Mary Land & Exploration Company, 63
Santa Fe International Corporation, 38
Sasol Limited, IV; 47 (upd.)
Saudi Arabian Oil Company, IV; 17 (upd.);
  50 (upd.)
Schlumberger Limited, 17 (upd.); 59 (upd.)
Seagull Energy Corporation, 11
Seitel, Inc., 47
Shanghai Petrochemical Co., Ltd., 18
Shell Oil Company, IV; 14 (upd.); 41
  (upd.)
Showa Shell Sekiyu K.K., IV; 59 (upd.)
OAO Siberian Oil Company (Sibneft), 49
Smith International, Inc., 59 (upd.)
Société Nationale Elf Aquitaine, IV; 7
  (upd.)
Sonatrach, 65 (upd.)
Statoil ASA, 61 (upd.)
Suburban Propane Partners, L.P., 30
Sun Company, Inc., IV
Suncor Energy Inc., 54
Sunoco, Inc., 28 (upd.)
Superior Energy Services, Inc., 65
OAO Surgutneftegaz, 48
Swift Energy Company, 63
Talisman Energy Inc., 9; 47 (upd.)
OAO Tatneft, 45
Tesoro Petroleum Corporation, 7; 45 (upd.)
Texaco Inc., IV; 14 (upd.); 41 (upd.)
Tidewater Inc., 37 (upd.)
Tom Brown, Inc., 37
Tonen Corporation, IV; 16 (upd.)
TonenGeneral Sekiyu K.K., 54 (upd.)
Tosco Corporation, 7
TOTAL S.A., IV; 24 (upd.)
TransMontaigne Inc., 28
Transocean Sedco Forex Inc., 45

Travel Ports of America, Inc., 17
Triton Energy Corporation, 11
Türkiye Petrolleri Anonim Ortaklığı, IV
Ultramar Diamond Shamrock Corporation,
  IV; 31 (upd.)
Union Texas Petroleum Holdings, Inc., 9
Unit Corporation, 63
Universal Compression, Inc., 59
Unocal Corporation, IV; 24 (upd.)
USX Corporation, IV; 7 (upd.)
Valero Energy Corporation, 7
Varco International, Inc., 42
Vastar Resources, Inc., 24
Vintage Petroleum, Inc., 42
Wascana Energy Inc., 13
Weatherford International, Inc., 39
Webber Oil Company, 61
Western Atlas Inc., 12
Western Company of North America, 15
Western Gas Resources, Inc., 45
Westport Resources Corporation, 63
The Williams Companies, Inc., IV; 31
  (upd.)
World Fuel Services Corporation, 47
XTO Energy Inc., 52
YPF Sociedad Anonima, IV

PUBLISHING & PRINTING

A.B.Dick Company, 28
A.H. Belo Corporation, 10; 30 (upd.)
Advance Publications Inc., IV; 19 (upd.)
Advanced Marketing Services, Inc., 34
Advanstar Communications, Inc., 57
Affiliated Publications, Inc., 7
Agence France-Presse, 34
American Banknote Corporation, 30
American Greetings Corporation, 7, 22
  (upd.)
American Media, Inc., 27
American Printing House for the Blind, 26
Andrews McMeel Universal, 40
The Antioch Company, 40
AOL Time Warner Inc., 57 (upd.)
Arandell Corporation, 37
Archie Comics Publications, Inc., 63
Arnoldo Mondadori Editore S.p.A., IV; 19
  (upd.); 54 (upd.)
The Associated Press, 31 (upd.)
The Atlantic Group, 23
Axel Springer Verlag AG, IV; 20 (upd.)
Banta Corporation, 12; 32 (upd.)
Bauer Publishing Group, 7
Bayard SA, 49
Berlitz International, Inc., 13
Bernard C. Harris Publishing Company,
  Inc., 39
Bertelsmann A.G., IV; 15 (upd.); 43 (upd.)
Big Flower Press Holdings, Inc., 21
Blue Mountain Arts, Inc., 29
Bobit Publishing Company, 55
Bonnier AB, 52
Book-of-the-Month Club, Inc., 13
Bowne & Co., Inc., 23
Broderbund Software, 13; 29 (upd.)
Brown Printing Company, 26
Burda Holding GmbH. & Co., 23
The Bureau of National Affairs, Inc., 23
Butterick Co., Inc., 23
Cadmus Communications Corporation, 23
Cahners Business Information, 43
CCH Inc., 14
Central Newspapers, Inc., 10
Champion Industries, Inc., 28
Cherry Lane Music Publishing Company,
  Inc., 62
ChoicePoint Inc., 65

PUBLISHING & PRINTING (*continued*)

The Christian Science Publishing Society, 55

The Chronicle Publishing Company, Inc., 23

Chrysalis Group plc, 40

CMP Media Inc., 26

Commerce Clearing House, Inc., 7

Concepts Direct, Inc., 39

Condé Nast Publications, Inc., 13; 59 (upd.)

Consumers Union, 26

The Copley Press, Inc., 23

Courier Corporation, 41

Cowles Media Company, 23

Cox Enterprises, Inc., IV; 22 (upd.)

Crain Communications, Inc., 12; 35 (upd.)

Current, Inc., 37

Cygnus Business Media, Inc., 56

Dai Nippon Printing Co., Ltd., IV; 57 (upd.)

Daily Mail and General Trust plc, 19

Dawson Holdings PLC, 43

Day Runner, Inc., 14

DC Comics Inc., 25

De La Rue plc, 10; 34 (upd.)

DeLorme Publishing Company, Inc., 53

Deluxe Corporation, 7; 22 (upd.)

Dennis Publishing Ltd., 62

Dex Media, Inc., 65

Donruss Playoff L.P., 66

Dorling Kindersley Holdings plc, 20

Dover Publications Inc., 34

Dow Jones & Company, Inc., IV; 19 (upd.); 47 (upd.)

The Dun & Bradstreet Corporation, IV; 19 (upd.)

Duplex Products Inc., 17

The E.W. Scripps Company, IV; 7 (upd.); 28 (upd.); 66 (upd.)

The Economist Group Ltd., 67

Edmark Corporation, 14

Electronics for Imaging, Inc., 43 (upd.)

Elsevier N.V., IV

EMAP plc, 35

EMI Group plc, 22 (upd.)

Encyclopaedia Britannica, Inc., 7; 39 (upd.)

Engraph, Inc., 12

Enquirer/Star Group, Inc., 10

Entravision Communications Corporation, 41

Essence Communications, Inc., 24

Farm Journal Corporation, 42

Farrar, Straus and Giroux Inc., 15

Flint Ink Corporation, 13

Follett Corporation, 12; 39 (upd.)

Forbes Inc., 30

Frankfurter Allgemeine Zeitung GmbH, 66

Franklin Electronic Publishers, Inc., 23

Freedom Communications, Inc., 36

Gannett Company, Inc., IV; 7 (upd.); 30 (upd.); 66 (upd.)

Geiger Bros., 60

Gibson Greetings, Inc., 12

Golden Books Family Entertainment, Inc., 28

Goss Holdings, Inc., 43

Graphic Industries Inc., 25

Gray Communications Systems, Inc., 24

Grolier Incorporated, 16; 43 (upd.)

Groupe de la Cite, IV

Groupe Les Echos, 25

Grupo Clarín S.A., 67

Grupo Televisa, S.A., 54 (upd.)

Guardian Media Group plc, 53

The H.W. Wilson Company, 66

Hachette, IV

Hachette Filipacchi Medias S.A., 21

Hallmark Cards, Inc., IV; 16 (upd.); 40 (upd.)

Harcourt Brace and Co., 12

Harcourt Brace Jovanovich, Inc., IV

Harcourt General, Inc., 20 (upd.)

Harlequin Enterprises Limited, 52

HarperCollins Publishers, 15

Harris Interactive Inc., 41

Harry N. Abrams, Inc., 58

Harte-Hanks Communications, Inc., 17

Havas SA, 10; 33 (upd.)

Hazelden Foundation, 28

The Hearst Corporation, IV; 19 (upd.); 46 (upd.)

Her Majesty's Stationery Office, 7

N.V. Holdingmaatschappij De Telegraaf, 23

Hollinger International Inc., 24; 62 (upd.)

Houghton Mifflin Company, 10; 36 (upd.)

IDG Books Worldwide, Inc., 27

Independent News & Media PLC, 61

Informa Group plc, 58

Information Holdings Inc., 47

International Data Group, Inc., 7; 25 (upd.)

IPC Magazines Limited, 7

John Fairfax Holdings Limited, 7

John H. Harland Company, 17

John Wiley & Sons, Inc., 17; 65 (upd.)

Johnson Publishing Company, Inc., 28

Johnston Press plc, 35

Jostens, Inc., 25 (upd.)

Journal Register Company, 29

Kaplan, Inc., 42

Kinko's, Inc., 43 (upd.)

Knight Ridder, Inc., 67 (upd.)

Knight-Ridder, Inc., IV; 15 (upd.)

Kodansha Ltd., IV; 38 (upd.)

Krause Publications, Inc., 35

Landmark Communications, Inc., 12; 55 (upd.)

Larry Flynt Publishing Inc., 31

Le Monde S.A., 33

Lebhar-Friedman, Inc., 55

Lee Enterprises Inc., 11; 64 (upd.)

LEXIS-NEXIS Group, 33

Lonely Planet Publications Pty Ltd., 55

M. Shanken Communications, Inc., 50

Maclean Hunter Publishing Limited, IV; 26 (upd.)

Macmillan, Inc., 7

Martha Stewart Living Omnimedia, L.L.C., 24

Marvel Entertainment Group, Inc., 10

Matra-Hachette S.A., 15 (upd.)

Maxwell Communication Corporation plc, IV; 7 (upd.)

McClatchy Newspapers, Inc., 23

The McGraw-Hill Companies, Inc., IV; 18 (upd.); 51 (upd.)

Mecklermedia Corporation, 24

Media General, Inc., 38 (upd.)

Menasha Corporation, 59 (upd.)

Meredith Corporation, 11; 29 (upd.)

Merrill Corporation, 18; 47 (upd.)

Miller Publishing Group, LLC, 57

The Miner Group International, 22

Mirror Group Newspapers plc, 7; 23 (upd.)

Moore Corporation Limited, IV

Morris Communications Corporation, 36

Multimedia, Inc., 11

Naspers Ltd., 66

National Audubon Society, 26

National Geographic Society, 9; 30 (upd.)

National Journal Group Inc., 67

New Times, Inc., 45

New York Daily News, 32

The New York Times Company, IV; 19 (upd.); 61 (upd.)

News America Publishing Inc., 12

News Corporation Limited, IV; 7 (upd.)

Newsquest plc, 32

Next Media Ltd., 61

Nihon Keizai Shimbun, Inc., IV

Nolo.com, Inc., 49

Oji Paper Co., Ltd., 57 (upd.)

Ottaway Newspapers, Inc., 15

Outlook Group Corporation, 37

Pantone Inc., 53

PCM Uitgevers NV, 53

Pearson plc, IV; 46 (upd.)

PennWell Corporation, 55

Penton Media, Inc., 27

Petersen Publishing Company, 21

Plato Learning, Inc., 44

Playboy Enterprises, Inc., 18

Pleasant Company, 27

PR Newswire, 35

Primedia Inc., 22

The Providence Journal Company, 28

Publishers Group, Inc., 35

Publishing and Broadcasting Limited, 54

Pulitzer Inc., 15; 58 (upd.)

Quad/Graphics, Inc., 19

Quebecor Inc., 12; 47 (upd.)

R.L. Polk & Co., 10

R.R. Donnelley & Sons Company, IV; 9 (upd.); 38 (upd.)

Rand McNally & Company, 28

Random House Inc., 13; 31 (upd.)

Ravensburger AG, 64

The Reader's Digest Association, Inc., IV; 17 (upd.)

Real Times, Inc., 66

Recycled Paper Greetings, Inc., 21

Reed Elsevier plc, IV; 17 (upd.); 31 (upd.)

Reuters Group PLC, IV; 22 (upd.); 63 (upd.)

Rodale, Inc., 23; 47 (upd.)

Rogers Communications Inc., 30 (upd.)

St Ives plc, 34

SanomaWSOY Corporation, 51

Schawk, Inc., 24

Schibsted ASA, 31

Scholastic Corporation, 10; 29 (upd.)

Scott Fetzer Company, 12

Scottish Media Group plc, 32

Seat Pagine Gialle S.p.A., 47

Seattle Times Company, 15

The Sierra Club, 28

Simon & Schuster Inc., IV; 19 (upd.)

Sir Speedy, Inc., 16

SkyMall, Inc., 26

Société du Figaro S.A., 60

Softbank Corp., 13

The Source Enterprises, Inc., 65

Southam Inc., 7

SPIEGEL-Verlag Rudolf Augstein GmbH & Co. KG, 44

Standard Register Co., 15

Tamedia AG, 53

Taylor & Francis Group plc, 44

Taylor Corporation, 36

Taylor Publishing Company, 12; 36 (upd.)

Thomas Nelson, Inc., 14; 38 (upd.)

Thomas Publishing Company, 26

The Thomson Corporation, 8; 34 (upd.)

The Times Mirror Company, IV; 17 (upd.)

Tom Doherty Associates Inc., 25

Toppan Printing Co., Ltd., IV; 58 (upd.)

The Topps Company, Inc., 34 (upd.)

Torstar Corporation, 29

Trader Classified Media N.V., 57

Tribune Company, IV; 22 (upd.); 63 (upd.)

Trinity Mirror plc, 49 (upd.)
Tyndale House Publishers, Inc., 57
U.S. News and World Report Inc., 30
United Business Media plc, 52 (upd.)
United News & Media plc, IV; 28 (upd.)
United Press International, Inc., 25
Valassis Communications, Inc., 8
Value Line, Inc., 16
Vance Publishing Corporation, 64
Verlagsgruppe Georg von Holtzbrinck
    GmbH, 35
Village Voice Media, Inc., 38
VNU N.V., 27
Volt Information Sciences Inc., 26
W.W. Norton & Company, Inc., 28
Wallace Computer Services, Inc., 36
The Washington Post Company, IV; 20
    (upd.)
Waverly, Inc., 16
Wegener NV, 53
Wenner Media, Inc., 32
West Group, 7; 34 (upd.)
Western Publishing Group, Inc., 13
WH Smith PLC, V; 42 (upd.)
Wolters Kluwer NV, 14; 33 (upd.)
World Book, Inc., 12
World Color Press Inc., 12
World Publications, LLC, 65
Xeikon NV, 26
Zebra Technologies Corporation, 14
Ziff Davis Media Inc., 12; 36 (upd.)
Zondervan Publishing House, 24

REAL ESTATE

Alexander's, Inc., 45
Alico, Inc., 63
AMB Property Corporation, 57
Amfac/JMB Hawaii L.L.C., 24 (upd.)
Apartment Investment and Management
    Company, 49
Archstone-Smith Trust, 49
Associated Estates Realty Corporation, 25
AvalonBay Communities, Inc., 58
Berkshire Realty Holdings, L.P., 49
Boston Properties, Inc., 22
Bramalea Ltd., 9
British Land Plc, 54
Canary Wharf Group Plc, 30
CapStar Hotel Company, 21
CarrAmerica Realty Corporation, 56
Castle & Cooke, Inc., 20 (upd.)
Catellus Development Corporation, 24
CB Commercial Real Estate Services
    Group, Inc., 21
Chateau Communities, Inc., 37
Chelsfield PLC, 67
Cheung Kong (Holdings) Limited, IV; 20
    (upd.)
Clayton Homes Incorporated, 54 (upd.)
Colonial Properties Trust, 65
The Corcoran Group, Inc., 58
Cousins Properties Incorporated, 65
Del Webb Corporation, 14
Duke Realty Corporation, 57
EastGroup Properties, Inc., 67
The Edward J. DeBartolo Corporation, 8
Enterprise Inns plc, 59
Equity Office Properties Trust, 54
Equity Residential, 49
Erickson Retirement Communities, 57
Fairfield Communities, Inc., 36
First Industrial Realty Trust, Inc., 65
Forest City Enterprises, Inc., 16; 52 (upd.)
Gecina SA, 42
General Growth Properties, Inc., 57
Griffin Land & Nurseries, Inc., 43
Grubb & Ellis Company, 21

The Haminerson Property Investment and
    Development Corporation plc, IV
Hammerson plc, 40
Harbert Corporation, 14
Helmsley Enterprises, Inc., 39 (upd.)
Home Properties of New York, Inc., 42
Hongkong Land Holdings Limited, IV; 47
    (upd.)
Hyatt Corporation, 16 (upd.)
ILX Resorts Incorporated, 65
IRSA Inversiones y Representaciones S.A.,
    63
J.F. Shea Co., Inc., 55
JMB Realty Corporation, IV
Jones Lang LaSalle Incorporated, 49
JPI, 49
Kaufman and Broad Home Corporation, 8
Kennedy-Wilson, Inc., 60
Kerry Properties Limited, 22
Kimco Realty Corporation, 11
The Koll Company, 8
Land Securities PLC, IV; 49 (upd.)
Lefrak Organization Inc., 26
Lend Lease Corporation Limited, IV; 17
    (upd.); 52 (upd.)
Liberty Property Trust, 57
Lincoln Property Company, 8; 54 (upd.)
The Loewen Group Inc., 40 (upd.)
The Macerich Company, 57
Mack-Cali Realty Corporation, 42
Manufactured Home Communities, Inc., 22
Maui Land & Pineapple Company, Inc., 29
Maxco Inc., 17
Meditrust, 11
Melvin Simon and Associates, Inc., 8
MEPC plc, IV
Meritage Corporation, 26
The Middleton Doll Company, 53
Mitsubishi Estate Company, Limited, IV;
    61 (upd.)
Mitsui Real Estate Development Co., Ltd.,
    IV
The Nature Conservancy, 28
New Plan Realty Trust, 11
New World Development Company Ltd.,
    IV
Newhall Land and Farming Company, 14
Nexity S.A., 66
NRT Incorporated, 61
Olympia & York Developments Ltd., IV; 9
    (upd.)
Park Corp., 22
Perini Corporation, 8
Post Properties, Inc., 26
ProLogis, 57
Public Storage, Inc., 52
Railtrack Group PLC, 50
RE/MAX International, Inc., 59
Reckson Associates Realty Corp., 47
Rockefeller Group International Inc., 58
Rodamco N.V., 26
The Rouse Company, 15; 63 (upd.)
Shubert Organization Inc., 24
The Sierra Club, 28
Silverstein Properties, Inc., 47
Simco S.A., 37
SL Green Realty Corporation, 44
Slough Estates PLC, IV; 50 (upd.)
Sovran Self Storage, Inc., 66
Starrett Corporation, 21
Storage USA, Inc., 21
Sumitomo Realty & Development Co.,
    Ltd., IV
Sun Communities Inc., 46
Tanger Factory Outlet Centers, Inc., 49
Tarragon Realty Investors, Inc., 45

Taylor Woodrow plc, 38 (upd.)
Tejon Ranch Company, 35
Tishman Speyer Properties, L.P., 47
Tokyu Land Corporation, IV
Trammell Crow Company, 8; 57 (upd.)
Trendwest Resorts, Inc., 33
Tridel Enterprises Inc., 9
Trizec Corporation Ltd., 10
The Trump Organization, 23; 64 (upd.)
Unibail SA, 40
United Dominion Realty Trust, Inc., 52
Vistana, Inc., 22
Vornado Realty Trust, 20
W.P. Carey & Co. LLC, 49
William Lyon Homes, 59

RETAIL & WHOLESALE

A.C. Moore Arts & Crafts, Inc., 30
A.T. Cross Company, 49 (upd.)
Aaron Rents, Inc., 14; 35 (upd.)
Abatix Corp., 57
ABC Appliance, Inc., 10
ABC Carpet & Home Co. Inc., 26
Abercrombie & Fitch Co., 15
Academy Sports & Outdoors, 27
Ace Hardware Corporation, 12; 35 (upd.)
Action Performance Companies, Inc., 27
After Hours Formalwear Inc., 60
Alabama Farmers Cooperative, Inc., 63
Alain Afflelou SA, 53
Alba-Waldensian, Inc., 30
Alberto-Culver Company, 36 (upd.)
Albertson's, Inc., 65 (upd.)
Alldays plc, 49
Allders plc, 37
Allou Health & Beauty Care, Inc., 28
Alrosa Company Ltd., 62
Amazon.com, Inc., 25; 56 (upd.)
AMERCO, 67 (upd.)
American Coin Merchandising, Inc., 28
American Eagle Outfitters, Inc., 24; 55
    (upd.)
American Furniture Company, Inc., 21
American Stores Company, 22 (upd.)
AmeriSource Health Corporation, 37 (upd.)
Ames Department Stores, Inc., 9; 30 (upd.)
Amscan Holdings, Inc., 61
Amway Corporation, 13; 30 (upd.)
The Anderson-DuBose Company, 60
The Andersons, Inc., 31
AnnTaylor Stores Corporation, 13; 37
    (upd.); 67 (upd.)
Appliance Recycling Centers of America,
    Inc., 42
Arbor Drugs Inc., 12
Arcadia Group plc, 28 (upd.)
Army and Air Force Exchange Service, 39
Art Van Furniture, Inc., 28
ASDA Group plc, 28 (upd.)
Ashworth, Inc., 26
Au Printemps S.A., V
Audio King Corporation, 24
Authentic Fitness Corporation, 20; 51
    (upd.)
Auto Value Associates, Inc., 25
Autobytel Inc., 47
AutoNation, Inc., 50
AutoZone, Inc., 9; 31 (upd.)
AVA AG (Allgemeine Handelsgesellschaft
    der Verbraucher AG), 33
Aveda Corporation, 24
Aviation Sales Company, 41
AWB Ltd., 56
B. Dalton Bookseller Inc., 25
Babbage's, Inc., 10
Baby Superstore, Inc., 15
Baccarat, 24

RETAIL & WHOLESALE (*continued*)

Bachman's Inc., 22
Bailey Nurseries, Inc., 57
Banana Republic Inc., 25
Barnes & Noble, Inc., 10; 30 (upd.)
Barnett Inc., 28
Barney's, Inc., 28
Bass Pro Shops, Inc., 42
Bear Creek Corporation, 38
Bearings, Inc., 13
bebe stores, inc., 31
Bed Bath & Beyond Inc., 13; 41 (upd.)
Belk Stores Services, Inc., V; 19 (upd.)
Ben Bridge Jeweler, Inc., 60
Benetton Group S.p.A., 67 (upd.)
Bergdorf Goodman Inc., 52
Bergen Brunswig Corporation, V; 13 (upd.)
Bernard Chaus, Inc., 27
Best Buy Co., Inc., 9; 23 (upd.); 63 (upd.)
Bhs plc, 17
Big Dog Holdings, Inc., 45
Big 5 Sporting Goods Corporation, 55
Big Lots, Inc., 50
Big O Tires, Inc., 20
Birkenstock Footprint Sandals, Inc., 42 (upd.)
Black Box Corporation, 20
Blacks Leisure Group plc, 39
Blair Corporation, 25; 31 (upd.)
Bloomingdale's Inc., 12
Blue Nile Inc., 61
Blue Square Israel Ltd., 41
Bluefly, Inc., 60
Blyth Industries, Inc., 18
The Body Shop International PLC, 11
The Bombay Company, Inc., 10
The Bon Marché, Inc., 23
The Bon-Ton Stores, Inc., 16; 50 (upd.)
Books-A-Million, Inc., 14; 41 (upd.)
The Boots Company PLC, V; 24 (upd.)
Borders Group, Inc., 15; 43 (upd.)
Boscov's Department Store, Inc., 31
Bozzuto's, Inc., 13
Bradlees Discount Department Store Company, 12
Brambles Industries Limited, 42
Brioni Roman Style S.p.A., 67
Broder Bros. Co., 38
Brooks Brothers Inc., 22
Brookstone, Inc., 18
The Buckle, Inc., 18
Buhrmann NV, 41
Build-A-Bear Workshop Inc., 62
Building Materials Holding Corporation, 52
Burdines, Inc., 60
Burlington Coat Factory Warehouse Corporation, 10; 60 (upd.)
Burt's Bees, Inc., 58
The Burton Group plc, V
Buttrey Food & Drug Stores Co., 18
buy.com, Inc., 46
C&A, V; 40 (upd.)
C&J Clark International Ltd., 52
Cabela's Inc., 26
Cablevision Electronic Instruments, Inc., 32
Cache Incorporated, 30
Caldor Inc., 12
Calloway's Nursery, Inc., 51
Camelot Music, Inc., 26
Campeau Corporation, V
Campo Electronics, Appliances & Computers, Inc., 16
Car Toys, Inc., 67
Carrefour SA, 10; 27 (upd.); 64 (upd.)
Carson Pirie Scott & Company, 15
Carter Hawley Hale Stores, Inc., V
Carter Lumber Company, 45

Cartier Monde, 29
Casual Corner Group, Inc., 43
Casual Male Retail Group, Inc., 52
Catherines Stores Corporation, 15
Cato Corporation, 14
CDW Computer Centers, Inc., 16
Celebrity, Inc., 22
Central Garden & Pet Company, 23
Chadwick's of Boston, Ltd., 29
Charlotte Russe Holding, Inc., 35
Charming Shoppes, Inc., 38
Chas. Levy Company LLC, 60
ChevronTexaco Corporation, 47 (upd.)
Chiasso Inc., 53
The Children's Place Retail Stores, Inc., 37
Christian Dior S.A., 49 (upd.)
Christopher & Banks Corporation, 42
Cifra, S.A. de C.V., 12
The Circle K Company, 20 (upd.)
Circuit City Stores, Inc., 9; 29 (upd.); 65 (upd.)
Clinton Cards plc, 39
The Clothestime, Inc., 20
CML Group, Inc., 10
Co-operative Group (CWS) Ltd., 51
Coach, Inc., 45 (upd.)
Coborn's, Inc., 30
Coinmach Laundry Corporation, 20
Coldwater Creek Inc., 21
Cole National Corporation, 13
Coles Myer Ltd., V; 20 (upd.)
Collectors Universe, Inc., 48
Comdisco, Inc., 9
Compagnie Financière Sucres et Denrées S.A., 60
CompUSA, Inc., 10
Computerland Corp., 13
Concepts Direct, Inc., 39
Conn's, Inc., 67
The Container Store, 36
Controladora Comercial Mexicana, S.A. de C.V., 36
Coop Schweiz Genossenschaftsverband, 48
Corby Distilleries Limited, 14
Corporate Express, Inc., 22; 47 (upd.)
Cortefiel S.A., 64
The Cosmetic Center, Inc., 22
Cost Plus, Inc., 27
Costco Wholesale Corporation, V; 43 (upd.)
Cotter & Company, V
County Seat Stores Inc., 9
Courts Plc, 45
CPI Corp., 38
Crate and Barrel, 9
Croscill, Inc., 42
Crowley, Milner & Company, 19
Crown Books Corporation, 21
Cumberland Farms, Inc., 17
CVS Corporation, 45 (upd.)
Daffy's Inc., 26
The Daiei, Inc., V; 17 (upd.); 41 (upd.)
The Daimaru, Inc., V; 42 (upd.)
Dairy Mart Convenience Stores, Inc., 25 (upd.)
Daisytek International Corporation, 18
Damark International, Inc., 18
Dart Group Corporation, 16
Darty S.A., 27
David Jones Ltd., 60
David's Bridal, Inc., 33
Dayton Hudson Corporation, V; 18 (upd.)
Deb Shops, Inc., 16
Debenhams Plc, 28
Deli Universal NV, 66
dELiA*s Inc., 29
Department 56, Inc., 34 (upd.)

Designer Holdings Ltd., 20
Deveaux S.A., 41
DFS Group Ltd., 66
Dick's Sporting Goods, Inc., 59
Diesel SpA, 40
Digital River, Inc., 50
Dillard Department Stores, Inc., V; 16 (upd.)
Dillon Companies Inc., 12
Discount Auto Parts, Inc., 18
Discount Drug Mart, Inc., 14
Dixons Group plc, V; 19 (upd.); 49 (upd.)
Do it Best Corporation, 30
Dollar Tree Stores, Inc., 23; 62 (upd.)
Donna Karan International Inc., 56 (upd.)
The Dress Barn, Inc., 24; 55 (upd.)
Drs. Foster & Smith, Inc., 62
Drug Emporium, Inc., 12
Du Pareil au Même, 43
Duane Reade Holding Corp., 21
Duckwall-ALCO Stores, Inc., 24
Dunnes Stores Ltd., 58
Duty Free International, Inc., 11
Dylex Limited, 29
E-Z Serve Corporation, 17
Eagle Hardware & Garden, Inc., 16
eBay Inc., 32
Eckerd Corporation, 9; 32 (upd.)
Eddie Bauer, Inc., 36 (upd.)
Edgars Consolidated Stores Ltd., 66
Egghead.com, Inc., 31 (upd.)
Eileen Fisher Inc., 61
El Corte Inglés Group, V
The Elder-Beerman Stores Corp., 10; 63 (upd.)
Electrocomponents PLC, 50
Ellett Brothers, Inc., 17
EMI Group plc, 22 (upd.)
Ermenegildo Zegna SpA, 63
Ethan Allen Interiors, Inc., 39 (upd.)
EToys, Inc., 37
Euromarket Designs Inc., 31 (upd.)
Evans, Inc., 30
EZCORP Inc., 43
Family Christian Stores, Inc., 51
Family Dollar Stores, Inc., 13; 62 (upd.)
Fastenal Company, 14; 42 (upd.)
Faultless Starch/Bon Ami Company, 55
Fay's Inc., 17
Federated Department Stores, Inc., 9; 31 (upd.)
Fielmann AG, 31
Fila Holding S.p.A., 20; 52 (upd.)
Findel plc, 60
Fingerhut Companies, Inc., 9; 36 (upd.)
The Finish Line, Inc., 29
Finlay Enterprises, Inc., 16
First Cash Financial Services, Inc., 57
Fleming Companies, Inc., 17 (upd.)
Florsheim Shoe Group Inc., 9; 31 (upd.)
FNAC, 21
Follett Corporation, 12
Footstar, Incorporated, 24
Fortunoff Fine Jewelry and Silverware Inc., 26
Frank's Nursery & Crafts, Inc., 12
Fred Meyer Stores, Inc., V; 20 (upd.); 64 (upd.)
Fred's, Inc., 23; 62 (upd.)
Frederick Atkins Inc., 16
Frederick's of Hollywood, Inc., 59 (upd.)
Fretter, Inc., 10
Friedman's Inc., 29
Fruth Pharmacy, Inc., 66
Funco, Inc., 7
Future Shop Ltd., 62
G.I. Joe's, Inc., 30

Gadzooks, Inc., 18
Gaiam, Inc., 41
Galeries Lafayette S.A., V; 23 (upd.)
Galyan's Trading Company, Inc., 47
Gander Mountain, Inc., 20
Gantos, Inc., 17
The Gap, Inc., V; 18 (upd.); 55 (upd.)
Garden Ridge Corporation, 27
Gart Sports Company, 24
GEHE AG, 27
General Binding Corporation, 10
General Host Corporation, 12
Genesco Inc., 17
Genovese Drug Stores, Inc., 18
Genuine Parts Company, 45 (upd.)
Gerald Stevens, Inc., 37
Giant Food Inc., 22 (upd.)
GIB Group, V; 26 (upd.)
Glacier Water Services, Inc., 47
The Good Guys, Inc., 10; 30 (upd.)
Goodwill Industries International, Inc., 16
Goody's Family Clothing, Inc., 20; 64
    (upd.)
Gottschalks, Inc., 18
GrandVision S.A., 43
Graybar Electric Company, Inc., 54
The Great Universal Stores plc, V; 19
    (upd.)
Griffin Land & Nurseries, Inc., 43
Grossman's Inc., 13
Groupe Alain Manoukian, 55
Groupe Castorama-Dubois Investissements,
    23
Groupe DMC (Dollfus Mieg & Cie), 27
Groupe Go Sport S.A., 39
Groupe Lapeyre S.A., 33
Groupe Zannier S.A., 35
Grow Biz International, Inc., 18
Grupo Casa Saba, S.A. de C.V., 39
Grupo Elektra, S.A. de C.V., 39
Grupo Eroski, 64
Grupo Gigante, S.A. de C.V., 34
Gruppo Coin S.p.A., 41
GT Bicycles, 26
GTSI Corp., 57
Gucci Group N.V., 15; 50 (upd.)
Guilbert S.A., 42
Guitar Center, Inc., 29
GUS plc, 47 (upd.)
Hahn Automotive Warehouse, Inc., 24
Hale-Halsell Company, 60
Half Price Books, Records, Magazines Inc.,
    37
Hallmark Cards, Inc., 40 (upd.)
Hammacher Schlemmer & Company, 21
Hancock Fabrics, Inc., 18
Hankyu Department Stores, Inc., V; 62
    (upd.)
Hanna Andersson Corp., 49
Hanover Compressor Company, 59
Hanover Direct, Inc., 36
Harold's Stores, Inc., 22
Harrods Holdings, 47
Harry Winston Inc., 45
Harvey Norman Holdings Ltd., 56
Hasbro, Inc., 43 (upd.)
Haverty Furniture Companies, Inc., 31
Hechinger Company, 12
Heilig-Meyers Company, 14; 40 (upd.)
Helzberg Diamonds, 40
Hennes & Mauritz AB, 29
Henry Modell & Company Inc., 32
Hensley & Company, 64
Hertie Waren- und Kaufhaus GmbH, V
Hibbett Sporting Goods, Inc., 26
Highsmith Inc., 60
Hills Stores Company, 13

Hines Horticulture, Inc., 49
HMV Group plc, 59
The Hockey Company, 34
Holiday RV Superstores, Incorporated, 26
Holt's Cigar Holdings, Inc., 42
The Home Depot, Inc., V; 18 (upd.)
Home Hardware Stores Ltd., 62
Home Interiors & Gifts, Inc., 55
Home Shopping Network, Inc., V; 25
    (upd.)
HomeBase, Inc., 33 (upd.)
Hot Topic, Inc., 33
House of Fabrics, Inc., 21
House of Fraser PLC, 45
HSN, 64 (upd.)
Hudson's Bay Company, V; 25 (upd.)
IKEA International A/S, V; 26 (upd.)
InaCom Corporation, 13
Indigo Books & Music Inc., 58
Insight Enterprises, Inc., 18
International Airline Support Group, Inc.,
    55
Intimate Brands, Inc., 24
Isetan Company Limited, V; 36 (upd.)
Ito-Yokado Co., Ltd., V; 42 (upd.)
J&R Electronics Inc., 26
J. Baker, Inc., 31
The J. Jill Group, Inc., 35
J.C. Penney Company, Inc., V; 18 (upd.);
    43 (upd.)
Jack Schwartz Shoes, Inc., 18
Jacobson Stores Inc., 21
Jalate Inc., 25
James Beattie plc, 43
Jay Jacobs, Inc., 15
Jennifer Convertibles, Inc., 31
Jetro Cash & Carry Enterprises Inc., 38
JG Industries, Inc., 15
JJB Sports plc, 32
John Lewis Partnership plc, V; 42 (upd.)
JUSCO Co., Ltd., V
Just For Feet, Inc., 19
K & B Inc., 12
K & G Men's Center, Inc., 21
K-tel International, Inc., 21
Karstadt Aktiengesellschaft, V; 19 (upd.)
Kash n' Karry Food Stores, Inc., 20
Kasper A.S.L., Ltd., 40
Kaufhof Warenhaus AG, V; 23 (upd.)
Kaufring AG, 35
Kay-Bee Toy Stores, 15
Kiabi Europe, 66
Kiehl's Since 1851, Inc., 52
Kingfisher plc, V; 24 (upd.)
Kinney Shoe Corp., 14
Kmart Corporation, V; 18 (upd.); 47 (upd.)
Knoll Group Inc., 14
Kohl's Corporation, 9; 30 (upd.)
Koninklijke Vendex KBB N.V. (Royal
    Vendex KBB N.V.), 62 (upd.)
Kotobukiya Co., Ltd., V; 56 (upd.)
Krause's Furniture, Inc., 27
Krispy Kreme Doughnuts, Inc., 61 (upd.)
L. and J.G. Stickley, Inc., 50
L. Luria & Son, Inc., 19
L.A. T Sportswear, Inc., 26
L.L. Bean, Inc., 38 (upd.)
La Senza Corporation, 66
La-Z-Boy Incorporated, 14; 50 (upd.)
Lamonts Apparel, Inc., 15
Lands' End, Inc., 9; 29 (upd.)
Lane Bryant, Inc., 64
Lanoga Corporation, 62
Laura Ashley Holdings plc, 37 (upd.)
Lazare Kaplan International Inc., 21
Le Chateau Inc., 63
Lechmere Inc., 10

Lechters, Inc., 11; 39 (upd.)
LensCrafters Inc., 23
Leroy Merlin SA, 54
Les Boutiques San Francisco, Inc., 62
Lesco Inc., 19
Leslie's Poolmart, Inc., 18
Leupold & Stevens, Inc., 52
Levenger Company, 63
Levitz Furniture Inc., 15
Lewis Galoob Toys Inc., 16
Li & Fung Limited, 59
Lifetime Hoan Corporation, 27
Lillian Vernon Corporation, 12; 35
The Limited, Inc., V; 20 (upd.)
Linens 'n Things, Inc., 24
Little Switzerland, Inc., 60
Littlewoods plc, V; 42 (upd.)
Liz Claiborne, Inc., 25 (upd.)
Lochmann's Inc., 24
Lojas Arapuã S.A., 22; 61 (upd.)
London Drugs Ltd., 46
Longs Drug Stores Corporation, V; 25
    (upd.)
Lost Arrow Inc., 22
LOT$OFF Corporation, 24
Lowe's Companies, Inc., V; 21 (upd.)
Luxottica SpA, 52 (upd.)
Mac Frugal's Bargains - Closeouts Inc., 17
Mac-Gray Corporation, 44
MarineMax, Inc., 30
Marionnaud Parfumeries SA, 51
Marks and Spencer p.l.c., V; 24 (upd.)
Marks Brothers Jewelers, Inc., 24
Marshall Field's, 63
Marshalls Incorporated, 13
Marui Company Ltd., V; 62 (upd.)
Maruzen Co., Limited, 18
Mary Kay, Inc., 30 (upd.)
Matalan PLC, 49
Matsuzakaya Company Ltd., V; 64 (upd.)
Maus Frères SA, 48
The Maxim Group, 25
The May Department Stores Company, V;
    19 (upd.); 46 (upd.)
Mayor's Jewelers, Inc., 41
Mazel Stores, Inc., 29
McCoy Corporation, 58
McJunkin Corporation, 63
McKesson Corporation, 47 (upd.)
McLane Company, Inc., 13
MCSi, Inc., 41
Media Arts Group, Inc., 42
Meier & Frank Co., 23
Meijer Incorporated, 27 (upd.)
Melville Corporation, V
The Men's Wearhouse, Inc., 17; 48 (upd.)
Menard, Inc., 34
Mercantile Stores Company, Inc., V; 19
    (upd.)
Merry-Go-Round Enterprises, Inc., 8
Mervyn's California, 10; 39 (upd.)
Metro AG, 50
Michael C. Fina Co., Inc., 52
Michaels Stores, Inc., 17
Micro Warehouse, Inc., 16
MicroAge, Inc., 16
Mitsukoshi Ltd., V; 56 (upd.)
MNS, Ltd., 65
Monsoon plc, 39
Montgomery Ward & Co., Incorporated, V;
    20 (upd.)
Moore-Handley, Inc., 39
Morse Shoe Inc., 13
Moss Bros Group plc, 51
Mothers Work, Inc., 18
Moto Photo, Inc., 45
Mr. Bricolage S.A., 37

RETAIL & WHOLESALE (*continued*)

MTS Inc., 37
Musicland Stores Corporation, 9; 38 (upd.)
Nagasakiya Co., Ltd., V
Nash Finch Company, 65 (upd.)
National Educational Music Co. Ltd., 47
National Home Centers, Inc., 44
National Intergroup, Inc., V
National Record Mart, Inc., 29
National Wine & Spirits, Inc., 49
Natural Wonders Inc., 14
Navy Exchange Service Command, 31
Nebraska Book Company, Inc., 65
Neff Corp., 32
NeighborCare, Inc., 67 (upd.)
The Neiman Marcus Group, Inc., 12; 49 (upd.)
Netflix, Inc., 58
New Look Group plc, 35
Next plc, 29
Nichii Co., Ltd., V
NIKE, Inc., 36 (upd.)
Nine West Group Inc., 11
99¢ Only Stores, 25
Nocibé SA, 54
Noland Company, 35
Noodle Kidoodle, 16
Nordstrom, Inc., V; 18 (upd.); 67 (upd.)
Norelco Consumer Products Co., 26
Norm Thompson Outfitters, Inc., 47
North Pacific Group, Inc., 61
The North West Company, Inc., 12
Norton McNaughton, Inc., 27
Nu Skin Enterprises, Inc., 27
Oakley, Inc., 49 (upd.)
Office Depot, Inc., 8; 23 (upd.); 65 (upd.)
OfficeMax, Inc., 15; 43 (upd.)
Olan Mills, Inc., 62
Old America Stores, Inc., 17
One Price Clothing Stores, Inc., 20
Orchard Supply Hardware Stores Corporation, 17
Organización Soriana, S.A. de C.V., 35
The Orvis Company, Inc., 28
OshKosh B'Gosh, Inc., 42 (upd.)
Oshman's Sporting Goods, Inc., 17
Ottakar's plc, 64
Otto Versand (GmbH & Co.), V; 15 (upd.); 34 (upd.)
Owens & Minor, Inc., 16
P.C. Richard & Son Corp., 23
Pamida Holdings Corporation, 15
The Pampered Chef, Ltd., 18
The Pantry, Inc., 36
Parisian, Inc., 14
Party City Corporation, 54
Paul Harris Stores, Inc., 18
Pay 'N Pak Stores, Inc., 9
Payless Cashways, Inc., 11; 44 (upd.)
Payless ShoeSource, Inc., 18
PCA International, Inc., 62
Pearle Vision, Inc., 13
Peebles Inc., 16; 43 (upd.)
Peet's Coffee & Tea, Inc., 38
Petco Animal Supplies, Inc., 29
Petrie Stores Corporation, 8
PETsMART, Inc., 14; 41 (upd.)
Phar-Mor Inc., 12
Pier 1 Imports, Inc., 12; 34 (upd.)
Piercing Pagoda, Inc., 29
Pilot Corporation, 49
Pinault-Printemps Redoute S.A., 19 (upd.)
Pitman Company, 58
Pomeroy Computer Resources, Inc., 33
Powell's Books, Inc., 40
The Price Company, V
PriceCostco, Inc., 14

Proffitt's, Inc., 19
Provell Inc., 58 (upd.)
Provigo Inc., 51 (upd.)
Publishers Clearing House, 64 (upd.)
Puig Beauty and Fashion Group S.L., 60
Purina Mills, Inc., 32
Quelle Group, V
QuikTrip Corporation, 36
Quill Corporation, 28
QVC Inc., 58 (upd.)
R.H. Macy & Co., Inc., V; 8 (upd.); 30 (upd.)
RadioShack Corporation, 36 (upd.)
Rag Shops, Inc., 30
Raley's Inc., 14; 58 (upd.)
Rallye SA, 54
Rapala-Normark Group, Ltd., 30
RDO Equipment Company, 33
Reckitt Benckiser plc, 42 (upd.)
Recoton Corp., 15
Recreational Equipment, Inc., 18
Reeds Jewelers, Inc., 22
Rent-A-Center, Inc., 45
Rent-Way, Inc., 33
Restoration Hardware, Inc., 30
Revco D.S., Inc., V
REX Stores Corp., 10
Rhodes Inc., 23
Richton International Corporation, 39
Riklis Family Corp., 9
Rite Aid Corporation, V; 19 (upd.); 63 (upd.)
Ritz Camera Centers, 34
Roberds Inc., 19
Rocky Shoes & Boots, Inc., 26
Rogers Communications Inc., 30 (upd.)
Rooms To Go Inc., 28
Roots Canada Ltd., 42
Rose's Stores, Inc., 13
Ross Stores, Inc., 17; 43 (upd.)
Roundy's Inc., 14
Rush Enterprises, Inc., 64
S&K Famous Brands, Inc., 23
Saks Inc., 24; 41 (upd.)
Sally Beauty Company, Inc., 60
Sam Ash Music Corporation, 30
Sam's Club, 40
Samuels Jewelers Incorporated, 30
Sanborn Hermanos, S.A., 20
SanomaWSOY Corporation, 51
Scheels All Sports Inc., 63
Schmitt Music Company, 40
Schneiderman's Furniture Inc., 28
Schottenstein Stores Corp., 14
Schultz Sav-O Stores, Inc., 31
The Score Board, Inc., 19
Scotty's, Inc., 22
SCP Pool Corporation, 39
Seaman Furniture Company, Inc., 32
Sears plc, V
Sears Roebuck de México, S.A. de C.V., 20
Sears, Roebuck and Co., V; 18 (upd.); 56 (upd.)
SED International Holdings, Inc., 43
Seibu Department Stores, Ltd., V; 42 (upd.)
Seigle's Home and Building Centers, Inc., 41
The Seiyu, Ltd., V; 36 (upd.)
Selfridges Plc, 34
Service Merchandise Company, Inc., V; 19 (upd.)
7-Eleven, Inc., 32 (upd.)
Shaklee Corporation, 12
The Sharper Image Corporation, 10; 62 (upd.)

Shoe Carnival Inc., 14
ShopKo Stores Inc., 21; 58 (upd.)
Shoppers Drug Mart Corporation, 49
Shoppers Food Warehouse Corporation, 66
Signet Group PLC, 61
SkyMall, Inc., 26
Sleepy's Inc., 32
Solo Serve Corporation, 28
Sophus Berendsen A/S, 49
Sound Advice, Inc., 41
Southern States Cooperative Incorporated, 36
Spartan Stores Inc., 66 (upd.)
Spec's Music, Inc., 19
Spiegel, Inc., 10; 27 (upd.)
Sport Chalet, Inc., 16
Sport Supply Group, Inc., 23
Sportmart, Inc., 15
Sports & Recreation, Inc., 17
The Sports Authority, Inc., 16; 43 (upd.)
The Sportsman's Guide, Inc., 36
Stage Stores, Inc., 24
Stanhome Inc., 15
Staples, Inc., 10; 55 (upd.)
Starbucks Corporation, 34 (upd.)
Starcraft Corporation, 30
Stefanel SpA, 63
Stein Mart Inc., 19
Stinnes AG, 8
The Stop & Shop Companies, Inc., 24 (upd.)
Storehouse PLC, 16
Strauss Discount Auto, 56
Stride Rite Corporation, 8
Strouds, Inc., 33
Stuller Settings, Inc., 35
Successories, Inc., 30
Sun Television & Appliances Inc., 10
Sunglass Hut International, Inc., 21
Supreme International Corporation, 27
Swarovski International Holding AG, 40
Syms Corporation, 29
Systemax, Inc., 52
Takashimaya Company, Limited, V; 47 (upd.)
The Talbots, Inc., 11; 31 (upd.)
Target Corporation, 61 (upd.)
Target Stores, 10; 27 (upd.)
Tati SA, 25
Tattered Cover Book Store, 43
Tech Data Corporation, 10
Tengelmann Group, 27
Tesco PLC, 24 (upd.)
Thomsen Greenhouses and Garden Center, Incorporated, 65
Thrifty PayLess, Inc., 12
Tiffany & Co., 14
The Timberland Company, 54 (upd.)
The TJX Companies, Inc., V; 19 (upd.); 57 (upd.)
Today's Man, Inc., 20
Tokyu Department Store Co., Ltd., V; 32 (upd.)
Too, Inc., 61
Topco Associates LLC, 60
Tops Appliance City, Inc., 17
Total Fina Elf S.A., 50 (upd.)
Toys "R" Us, Inc., V; 18 (upd.); 57 (upd.)
Tractor Supply Company, 57
Travis Boats & Motors, Inc., 37
Travis Perkins plc, 34
Trend-Lines, Inc., 22
TruServ Corporation, 24
Tuesday Morning Corporation, 18
Tupperware Corporation, 28
TVI, Inc., 15

Tweeter Home Entertainment Group, Inc., 30
U.S. Vision, Inc., 66
Ultimate Electronics, Inc., 18
Ultramar Diamond Shamrock Corporation, 31 (upd.)
Uni-Marts, Inc., 17
United Rentals, Inc., 34
The United States Shoe Corporation, V
United Stationers Inc., 14
Universal International, Inc., 25
Uny Co., Ltd., V; 49 (upd.)
Urban Outfitters, Inc., 14
Uwajimaya, Inc., 60
Vallen Corporation, 45
Valley Media Inc., 35
Value City Department Stores, Inc., 38
Value Merchants Inc., 13
ValueVision International, Inc., 22
Vans, Inc., 47 (upd.)
Venator Group Inc., 35 (upd.)
Vendex International N.V., 13
Venture Stores Inc., 12
The Vermont Teddy Bear Co., Inc., 36
VF Corporation, 54 (upd.)
Viewpoint International, Inc., 66
Viking Office Products, Inc., 10
Vivarte SA, 54 (upd.)
Von Maur Inc., 64
Vorwerk & Co., 27
W. Atlee Burpee & Co., 27
W.W. Grainger, Inc., V
Waban Inc., 13
Wacoal Corp., 25
Wal-Mart de Mexico, S.A. de C.V., 35 (upd.)
Wal-Mart Stores, Inc., V; 8 (upd.); 26 (upd.); 63 (upd.)
Walden Book Company Inc., 17
Walgreen Co., V; 20 (upd.); 65 (upd.)
Wall Drug Store, Inc., 40
Warners' Stellian Inc., 67
Weiner's Stores, Inc., 33
West Marine, Inc., 17
Western Beef, Inc., 22
The Wet Seal, Inc., 18
Weyco Group, Incorporated, 32
WH Smith PLC, V; 42 (upd.)
The White House, Inc., 60
Whole Foods Market, Inc., 20
Wickes Inc., V; 25 (upd.)
Williams Scotsman, Inc., 65
Williams-Sonoma, Inc., 17; 44 (upd.)
Wilsons The Leather Experts Inc., 21; 58 (upd.)
Wolohan Lumber Co., 19
Wolverine World Wide, Inc., 59 (upd.)
Woolworth Corporation, V; 20 (upd.)
World Duty Free Americas, Inc., 29 (upd.)
The Yankee Candle Company, Inc., 37
Young's Market Company, LLC, 32
Younkers, Inc., 19
Zale Corporation, 16; 40 (upd.)
Zany Brainy, Inc., 31
Ziebart International Corporation, 30
Zion's Cooperative Mercantile Institution, 33
Zones, Inc., 67

RUBBER & TIRE

Aeroquip Corporation, 16
Bandag, Inc., 19
The BFGoodrich Company, V
Bridgestone Corporation, V; 21 (upd.); 59 (upd.)
Carlisle Companies Incorporated, 8
Compagnie Générale des Établissements Michelin, V; 42 (upd.)
Continental AG, V; 56 (upd.)
Continental General Tire Corp., 23
Cooper Tire & Rubber Company, 8; 23 (upd.)
Elementis plc, 40 (upd.)
General Tire, Inc., 8
The Goodyear Tire & Rubber Company, V; 20 (upd.)
The Kelly-Springfield Tire Company, 8
Les Schwab Tire Centers, 50
Myers Industries, Inc., 19
Pirelli S.p.A., V; 15 (upd.)
Safeskin Corporation, 18
Sumitomo Rubber Industries, Ltd., V
Tillotson Corp., 15
Treadco, Inc., 19
Ube Industries, Ltd., 38 (upd.)
The Yokohama Rubber Co., Ltd., V; 19 (upd.)

TELECOMMUNICATIONS

A.H. Belo Corporation, 30 (upd.)
Abertis Infraestructuras, S.A., 65
Acme-Cleveland Corp., 13
ADC Telecommunications, Inc., 10
Adelphia Communications Corporation, 17; 52 (upd.)
Adtran Inc., 22
Advanced Fibre Communications, Inc., 63
AEI Music Network Inc., 35
AirTouch Communications, 11
Alcatel S.A., 36 (upd.)
Alliance Atlantis Communications Inc., 39
ALLTEL Corporation, 6; 46 (upd.)
American Telephone and Telegraph Company, V
American Tower Corporation, 33
Ameritech Corporation, V; 18 (upd.)
Amstrad plc, 48 (upd.)
AO VimpelCom, 48
AOL Time Warner Inc., 57 (upd.)
Arch Wireless, Inc., 39
ARD, 41
Ascom AG, 9
Aspect Telecommunications Corporation, 22
AT&T Bell Laboratories, Inc., 13
AT&T Corporation, 29 (upd.)
AT&T Wireless Services, Inc., 54 (upd.)
BCE Inc., V; 44 (upd.)
Beasley Broadcast Group, Inc., 51
Belgacom, 6
Bell Atlantic Corporation, V; 25 (upd.)
Bell Canada, 6
BellSouth Corporation, V; 29 (upd.)
BET Holdings, Inc., 18
BHC Communications, Inc., 26
Blackfoot Telecommunications Group, 60
Bonneville International Corporation, 29
Bouygues S.A., 24 (upd.)
Brasil Telecom Participaçoes S.A., 57
Brightpoint, Inc., 18
Brite Voice Systems, Inc., 20
British Columbia Telephone Company, 6
British Telecommunications plc, V; 15 (upd.)
BT Group plc, 49 (upd.)
C-COR.net Corp., 38
Cable & Wireless HKT, 30 (upd.)
Cable and Wireless plc, V; 25 (upd.)
Cablevision Systems Corporation, 30 (upd.)
The Canadian Broadcasting Corporation (CBC), 37
Canal Plus, 10; 34 (upd.)
CanWest Global Communications Corporation, 35
Capital Radio plc, 35
Carlton Communications PLC, 15; 50 (upd.)
Carolina Telephone and Telegraph Company, 10
Carrier Access Corporation, 44
CBS Corporation, 28 (upd.)
CBS Television Network, 66 (upd.)
Centel Corporation, 6
Centennial Communications Corporation, 39
Central European Media Enterprises Ltd., 61
Century Communications Corp., 10
Century Telephone Enterprises, Inc., 9; 54 (upd.)
Cesky Telecom, a.s., 64
Chancellor Media Corporation, 24
Charter Communications, Inc., 33
China Telecom, 50
Chris-Craft Industries, Inc., 9
The Christian Broadcasting Network, Inc., 52
Chrysalis Group plc, 40
Chugach Alaska Corporation, 60
CIENA Corporation, 54
Cincinnati Bell, Inc., 6
Citadel Communications Corporation, 35
Clear Channel Communications, Inc., 23
Cogent Communications Group, Inc., 55
COLT Telecom Group plc, 41
Comcast Corporation, 24 (upd.)
Comdial Corporation, 21
Commonwealth Telephone Enterprises, Inc., 25
Comsat Corporation, 23
Comverse Technology, Inc., 15; 43 (upd.)
Corning Inc., 44 (upd.)
Craftmade International, Inc., 44
Cumulus Media Inc., 37
DDI Corporation, 7
Deutsche Telekom AG, V; 48 (upd.)
Dialogic Corporation, 18
Directorate General of Telecommunications, 7
DIRECTV, Inc., 38
Discovery Communications, Inc., 42
Dobson Communications Corporation, 63
DSC Communications Corporation, 12
EchoStar Communications Corporation, 35
ECI Telecom Ltd., 18
eircom plc, 31 (upd.)
Electric Lightwave, Inc., 37
Electromagnetic Sciences Inc., 21
Emmis Communications Corporation, 47
Energis plc, 47
Entercom Communications Corporation, 58
Entravision Communications Corporation, 41
Equant N.V., 52
ESPN, Inc., 56
Eternal Word Television Network, Inc., 57
EXCEL Communications Inc., 18
Executone Information Systems, Inc., 13
Expand SA, 48
4Kids Entertainment Inc., 59
Fox Family Worldwide, Inc., 24
France Télécom Group, V; 21 (upd.)
Frontier Corp., 16
Gannett Co., Inc., 30 (upd.)
Garmin Ltd., 60
General DataComm Industries, Inc., 14
Geotek Communications Inc., 21
Getty Images, Inc., 31
Global Crossing Ltd., 32

TELECOMMUNICATIONS (*continued*)
Golden Telecom, Inc., 59
Granite Broadcasting Corporation, 42
Gray Communications Systems, Inc., 24
Groupe Vidéotron Ltée., 20
Grupo Televisa, S.A., 18; 54 (upd.)
GTE Corporation, V; 15 (upd.)
Guthy-Renker Corporation, 32
GWR Group plc, 39
Harmonic Inc., 43
Havas, SA, 10
Hispanic Broadcasting Corporation, 35
Hong Kong Telecommunications Ltd., 6
Hubbard Broadcasting Inc., 24
Hughes Electronics Corporation, 25
IDB Communications Group, Inc., 11
IDT Corporation, 34
Illinois Bell Telephone Company, 14
Indiana Bell Telephone Company, Incorporated, 14
Infineon Technologies AG, 50
Infinity Broadcasting Corporation, 11
InterDigital Communications Corporation, 61
IXC Communications, Inc., 29
Jacor Communications, Inc., 23
Jones Intercable, Inc., 21
Koninklijke PTT Nederland NV, V
Landmark Communications, Inc., 55 (upd.)
LCI International, Inc., 16
LDDS-Metro Communications, Inc., 8
Level 3 Communications, Inc., 67
LIN Broadcasting Corp., 9
Lincoln Telephone & Telegraph Company, 14
LodgeNet Entertainment Corporation, 28
Loral Space & Communications Ltd., 54 (upd.)
Manitoba Telecom Services, Inc., 61
Mannesmann AG, 38
MasTec, Inc., 19; 55 (upd.)
McCaw Cellular Communications, Inc., 6
MCI WorldCom, Inc., V; 27 (upd.)
McLeodUSA Incorporated, 32
Mercury Communications, Ltd., 7
Metrocall, Inc., 41
Metromedia Companies, 14
Métropole Télévision, 33
MFS Communications Company, Inc., 11
Michigan Bell Telephone Co., 14
MIH Limited, 31
MITRE Corporation, 26
Mobile Telecommunications Technologies Corp., 18
Mobile TeleSystems OJSC, 59
Modern Times Group AB, 36
The Montana Power Company, 44 (upd.)
Multimedia, Inc., 11
National Broadcasting Company, Inc., 28 (upd.)
National Grid USA, 51 (upd.)
NCR Corporation, 30 (upd.)
NetCom Systems AB, 26
Nevada Bell Telephone Company, 14
New Valley Corporation, 17
Nexans SA, 54
Nextel Communications, Inc., 27 (upd.)
Nippon Telegraph and Telephone Corporation, V; 51 (upd.)
Norstan, Inc., 16
Nortel Networks Corporation, 36 (upd.)
Northern Telecom Limited, V
NTL Inc., 65
NYNEX Corporation, V
Octel Messaging, 14; 41 (upd.)
Ohio Bell Telephone Company, 14
Olivetti S.p.A., 34 (upd.)

Österreichische Post- und Telegraphenverwaltung, V
Pacific Telecom, Inc., 6
Pacific Telesis Group, V
Paging Network Inc., 11
PanAmSat Corporation, 46
Paxson Communications Corporation, 33
PictureTel Corp., 10; 27 (upd.)
Posti- ja Telelaitos, 6
Price Communications Corporation, 42
ProSiebenSat.1 Media AG, 54
Publishing and Broadcasting Limited, 54
QUALCOMM Incorporated, 20; 47 (upd.)
QVC Network Inc., 9
Qwest Communications International, Inc., 37
Research in Motion Ltd., 54
RMH Teleservices, Inc., 42
Rochester Telephone Corporation, 6
Rogers Communications Inc., 30 (upd.)
Royal KPN N.V., 30
Rural Cellular Corporation, 43
Saga Communications, Inc., 27
Sawtek Inc., 43 (upd.)
SBC Communications Inc., 32 (upd.)
Schweizerische Post-, Telefon- und Telegrafen-Betriebe, V
Scientific-Atlanta, Inc., 6; 45 (upd.)
Seat Pagine Gialle S.p.A., 47
Securicor Plc, 45
Sinclair Broadcast Group, Inc., 25
Società Finanziaria Telefonica per Azioni, V
Sonera Corporation, 50
Southern New England Telecommunications Corporation, 6
Southwestern Bell Corporation, V
Spanish Broadcasting System, Inc., 41
Spelling Entertainment, 35 (upd.)
Sprint Corporation, 9; 46 (upd.)
StrataCom, Inc., 16
Swedish Telecom, V
Swisscom AG, 58
Sycamore Networks, Inc., 45
SynOptics Communications, Inc., 10
T-Netix, Inc., 46
TDC A/S, 63
Telcordia Technologies, Inc., 59
Telecom Argentina S.A., 63
Telecom Australia, 6
Telecom Corporation of New Zealand Limited, 54
Telecom Eireann, 7
Telecom Italia Mobile S.p.A., 63
Telecom Italia S.p.A., 43
Telefonaktiebolaget LM Ericsson, V; 46 (upd.)
Telefónica de Argentina S.A., 61
Telefónica S.A., V; 46 (upd.)
Telefonos de Mexico S.A. de C.V., 14; 63 (upd.)
Telekomunikacja Polska SA, 50
Telephone and Data Systems, Inc., 9
Télévision Française 1, 23
TeliaSonera AB, 57 (upd.)
Tellabs, Inc., 11; 40 (upd.)
Telstra Corporation Limited, 50
Tiscali SpA, 48
The Titan Corporation, 36
Tollgrade Communications, Inc., 44
TV Azteca, S.A. de C.V., 39
U.S. Satellite Broadcasting Company, Inc., 20
U S West, Inc., V; 25 (upd.)
U.S. Cellular Corporation, 9; 31 (upd.)
United Pan-Europe Communications NV, 47

United Telecommunications, Inc., V
United Video Satellite Group, 18
USA Interactive, Inc., 47 (upd.)
Verizon Communications, 43 (upd.)
ViaSat, Inc., 54
Vivendi Universal S.A., 46 (upd.)
Vodafone Group PLC, 11; 36 (upd.)
The Walt Disney Company, 63 (upd.)
Watkins-Johnson Company, 15
The Weather Channel Companies, 52
West Corporation, 42
Western Union Financial Services, Inc., 54
Western Wireless Corporation, 36
Westwood One, Inc., 23
Williams Communications Group, Inc., 34
The Williams Companies, Inc., 31 (upd.)
Wipro Limited, 43
Wisconsin Bell, Inc., 14
Working Assets Funding Service, 43
Young Broadcasting Inc., 40
Zoom Technologies, Inc., 53 (upd.)

TEXTILES & APPAREL

Abercrombie & Fitch Co., 35 (upd.)
adidas-Salomon AG, 14; 33 (upd.)
Alba-Waldensian, Inc., 30
Albany International Corp., 8
Algo Group Inc., 24
American Safety Razor Company, 20
Amoskeag Company, 8
Angelica Corporation, 15; 43 (upd.)
AR Accessories Group, Inc., 23
Aris Industries, Inc., 16
ASICS Corporation, 57
Authentic Fitness Corporation, 20; 51 (upd.)
Banana Republic Inc., 25
Bata Ltd., 62
Benetton Group S.p.A., 10; 67 (upd.)
Bill Blass Ltd., 32
Birkenstock Footprint Sandals, Inc., 12
Blair Corporation, 25
Brazos Sportswear, Inc., 23
Brioni Roman Style S.p.A., 67
Brooks Brothers Inc., 22
Brooks Sports Inc., 32
Brown Group, Inc., V; 20 (upd.)
Bugle Boy Industries, Inc., 18
Burberry Ltd., 17; 41 (upd.)
Burke Mills, Inc., 66
Burlington Industries, Inc., V; 17 (upd.)
Calcot Ltd., 33
Calvin Klein, Inc., 22; 55 (upd.)
Candie's, Inc., 31
Canstar Sports Inc., 16
Capel Incorporated, 45
Capezio/Ballet Makers Inc., 62
Carhartt, Inc., 30
Cato Corporation, 14
Chargeurs International, 21 (upd.)
Charming Shoppes, Inc., 8
Cherokee Inc., 18
Chic by H.I.S, Inc., 20
Chico's FAS, Inc., 45
Chorus Line Corporation, 30
Christian Dior S.A., 19; 49 (upd.)
Christopher & Banks Corporation, 42
Cintas Corporation, 51 (upd.)
Claire's Stores, Inc., 17
Coach Leatherware, 10
Coats plc, V; 44 (upd.)
Collins & Aikman Corporation, 13
Columbia Sportswear Company, 19; 41 (upd.)
Concord Fabrics, Inc., 16
Cone Mills LLC, 8; 67 (upd.)
Converse Inc., 31 (upd.)

Cotton Incorporated, 46
Courtaulds plc, V; 17 (upd.)
Croscill, Inc., 42
Crown Crafts, Inc., 16
Crystal Brands, Inc., 9
Culp, Inc., 29
Cygne Designs, Inc., 25
Dan River Inc., 35
Danskin, Inc., 12; 62 (upd.)
Deckers Outdoor Corporation, 22
Delta and Pine Land Company, 59
Delta Woodside Industries, Inc., 8; 30
   (upd.)
Designer Holdings Ltd., 20
The Dixie Group, Inc., 20
Dogi International Fabrics S.A., 52
Dolce & Gabbana SpA, 62
Dominion Textile Inc., 12
Donna Karan International Inc., 15; 56
   (upd.)
Donnkenny, Inc., 17
Duck Head Apparel Company, Inc., 42
Dunavant Enterprises, Inc., 54
Dyersburg Corporation, 21
Ecco Sko A/S, 62
Eileen Fisher Inc., 61
Ellen Tracy, Inc., 55
Eram SA, 51
Ermenegildo Zegna SpA, 63
Esprit de Corp., 8; 29 (upd.)
Etam Developpement SA, 44
Etienne Aigner AG, 52
Evans, Inc., 30
Fab Industries, Inc., 27
Fabri-Centers of America Inc., 16
Fieldcrest Cannon, Inc., 9; 31 (upd.)
Fila Holding S.p.A., 20
Florsheim Shoe Group Inc., 31 (upd.)
Fossil, Inc., 17
Frederick's of Hollywood Inc., 16
French Connection Group plc, 41
Fruit of the Loom, Inc., 8; 25 (upd.)
Fubu, 29
G&K Services, Inc., 16
G-III Apparel Group, Ltd., 22
Galey & Lord, Inc., 20; 66 (upd.)
Garan, Inc., 16; 64 (upd.)
Gerry Weber International AG, 63
Gianni Versace SpA, 22
Giorgio Armani S.p.A., 45
The Gitano Group, Inc. 8
Greenwood Mills, Inc., 14
Groupe DMC (Dollfus Mieg & Cie), 27
Groupe Yves Saint Laurent, 23
Gucci Group N.V., 15; 50 (upd.)
Guess, Inc., 15
Guilford Mills Inc., 8; 40 (upd.)
Gymboree Corporation, 15
Haggar Corporation, 19
Hampton Industries, Inc., 20
Happy Kids Inc., 30
Hartmarx Corporation, 8
The Hartstone Group plc, 14
HCI Direct, Inc., 55
Healthtex, Inc., 17
Helly Hansen ASA, 25
Hermès S.A., 14
The Hockey Company, 34
Hugo Boss AG, 48
Hyde Athletic Industries, Inc., 17
I.C. Isaacs & Company, 31
Industria de Diseño Textil S.A., 64
Interface, Inc., 8; 29 (upd.)
Irwin Toy Limited, 14
Items International Airwalk Inc., 17
J. Crew Group, Inc., 12; 34 (upd.)

JLM Couture, Inc., 64
Jockey International, Inc., 12; 34 (upd.)
Johnston Industries, Inc., 15
Jones Apparel Group, Inc., 39 (upd.)
Jordache Enterprises, Inc., 23
Jos. A. Bank Clothiers, Inc., 31
JPS Textile Group, Inc., 28
K-Swiss, Inc., 33
Karl Kani Infinity, Inc., 49
Kellwood Company, 8
Kenneth Cole Productions, Inc., 25
Kinney Shoe Corp., 14
Klaus Steilmann GmbH & Co. KG, 53
Koret of California, Inc., 62
L.A. Gear, Inc., 8; 32 (upd.)
L.L. Bean, Inc., 10; 38 (upd.)
LaCrosse Footwear, Inc., 18; 61 (upd.)
Laura Ashley Holdings plc, 13
Lee Apparel Company, Inc., 8
The Leslie Fay Company, Inc., 8; 39 (upd.)
Levi Strauss & Co., V; 16 (upd.)
Liz Claiborne, Inc., 8
London Fog Industries, Inc., 29
Lost Arrow Inc., 22
Maidenform, Inc., 20; 59 (upd.)
Malden Mills Industries, Inc., 16
Marzotto S.p.A., 20; 67 (upd.)
Milliken & Co., V; 17 (upd.)
Mitsubishi Rayon Co., Ltd., V
Mossimo, Inc., 27
Mothercare UK Ltd., 17
Movie Star Inc., 17
Naf Naf SA, 44
Nautica Enterprises, Inc., 18; 44 (upd.)
New Balance Athletic Shoe, Inc., 25
Nike, Inc., V; 8 (upd.)
Nine West Group, Inc., 39 (upd.)
Nitches, Inc., 53
The North Face, Inc., 18
Oakley, Inc., 18
OshKosh B'Gosh, Inc., 9; 42 (upd.)
Oxford Industries, Inc., 8
Pacific Sunwear of California, Inc., 28
Peek & Cloppenburg KG, 46
Pendleton Woolen Mills, Inc., 42
Pentland Group plc, 20
Perry Ellis International, Inc., 41
Phat Fashions LLC, 49
Pillowtex Corporation, 19; 41 (upd.)
Plains Cotton Cooperative Association, 57
Pluma, Inc., 27
Polo/Ralph Lauren Corporation, 12; 62
   (upd.)
Prada Holding B.V., 45
PremiumWear, Inc., 30
Puma AG Rudolf Dassler Sport, 35
Quaker Fabric Corp., 19
Quiksilver, Inc., 18
R.G. Barry Corporation, 17; 44 (upd.)
Recreational Equipment, Inc., 18
Red Wing Shoe Company, Inc., 30 (upd.)
Reebok International Ltd., V; 9 (upd.); 26
   (upd.)
Rieter Holding AG, 42
Rollerblade, Inc., 15
Russell Corporation, 8; 30 (upd.)
St. John Knits, Inc., 14
Salant Corporation, 51 (upd.)
Salvatore Ferragamo Italia S.p.A., 62
Saucony Inc., 35
Schott Brothers, Inc., 67
Shaw Industries, Inc., 40 (upd.)
Shelby Williams Industries, Inc., 14
Skechers U.S.A. Inc., 31
Sophus Berendsen A/S, 49
Springs Industries, Inc., V; 19 (upd.)
Starter Corp., 12

Stefanel SpA, 63
Steiner Corporation (Alsco), 53
Steven Madden, Ltd., 37
Stirling Group plc, 62
Stone Manufacturing Company, 14; 43
   (upd.)
The Stride Rite Corporation, 8; 37 (upd.)
Stussy, Inc., 55
Sun Sportswear, Inc., 17
Superior Uniform Group, Inc., 30
Tamfelt Oyj Abp, 62
Tarrant Apparel Group, 62
Teijin Limited, V
Thomaston Mills, Inc., 27
Tilley Endurables, Inc., 67
The Timberland Company, 13; 54 (upd.)
Tommy Hilfiger Corporation, 20; 53 (upd.)
Too, Inc., 61
Toray Industries, Inc., V
Tultex Corporation, 13
Under Armour Performance Apparel, 61
Unifi, Inc., 12; 62 (upd.)
United Merchants & Manufacturers, Inc.,
   13
United Retail Group Inc., 33
Unitika Ltd., V
Vans, Inc., 16; 47 (upd.)
Varsity Spirit Corp., 15
VF Corporation, V; 17 (upd.); 54 (upd.)
Walton Monroe Mills, Inc., 8
The Warnaco Group Inc., 12; 46 (upd.)
Wellman, Inc., 8; 52 (upd.)
West Point-Pepperell, Inc., 8
WestPoint Stevens Inc., 16
Weyco Group, Incorporated, 32
Williamson-Dickie Manufacturing
   Company, 14
Wolverine World Wide, Inc., 16; 59 (upd.)
Woolrich Inc., 62

TOBACCO

American Brands, Inc., V
B.A.T. Industries PLC, 22 (upd.)
British American Tobacco PLC, 50 (upd.)
Brooke Group Ltd., 15
Brown & Williamson Tobacco
   Corporation, 14; 33 (upd.)
Culbro Corporation, 15
Dibrell Brothers, Incorporated, 12
DIMON Inc., 27
800-JR Cigar, Inc., 27
Gallaher Group Plc, V; 19 (upd.); 49 (upd.)
General Cigar Holdings, Inc., 66 (upd.)
Holt's Cigar Holdings, Inc., 42
Imasco Limited, V
Imperial Tobacco Group PLC, 50
Japan Tobacco Incorporated, V
KT&G Corporation, 62
Nobleza Piccardo SAICF, 64
North Atlantic Trading Company Inc., 65
Philip Morris Companies Inc., V; 18 (upd.)
R.J. Reynolds Tobacco Holdings, Inc., 30
   (upd.)
RJR Nabisco Holdings Corp., V
Rothmans UK Holdings Limited, V; 19
   (upd.)
Seita, 23
Souza Cruz S.A., 65
Standard Commercial Corporation, 13; 62
   (upd.)
Swisher International Group Inc., 23
Tabacalera, S.A., V; 17 (upd.)
Universal Corporation, V; 48 (upd.)
UST Inc., 9; 50 (upd.)
Vector Group Ltd., 35 (upd.)

TRANSPORT SERVICES

Abertis Infraestructuras, S.A., 65
Aéroports de Paris, 33
Air Express International Corporation, 13
Airborne Freight Corporation, 6; 34 (upd.)
Alamo Rent A Car, Inc., 6; 24 (upd.)
Alaska Railroad Corporation, 60
Alexander & Baldwin, Inc., 10
Allied Worldwide, Inc., 49
AMCOL International Corporation, 59
    (upd.)
Amerco, 6
AMERCO, 67 (upd.)
American Classic Voyages Company, 27
American President Companies Ltd., 6
Anschutz Corp., 12
APL Limited, 61 (upd.)
Aqua Alliance Inc., 32 (upd.)
Atlas Van Lines, Inc., 14
Attica Enterprises S.A., 64
Avis Rent A Car, Inc., 6; 22 (upd.)
BAA plc, 10
Bekins Company, 15
Berliner Verkehrsbetriebe (BVG), 58
Bollinger Shipyards, Inc., 61
Boyd Bros. Transportation Inc., 39
Brambles Industries Limited, 42
The Brink's Company, 58 (upd.)
British Railways Board, V
Broken Hill Proprietary Company Ltd., 22
    (upd.)
Budget Group, Inc., 25
Budget Rent a Car Corporation, 9
Burlington Northern Santa Fe Corporation,
    V; 27 (upd.)
C.H. Robinson Worldwide, Inc., 40 (upd.)
Canadian National Railway System, 6
Canadian Pacific Railway Limited, V; 45
    (upd.)
Cannon Express, Inc., 53
Carey International, Inc., 26
Carlson Companies, Inc., 6
Carolina Freight Corporation, 6
Celadon Group Inc., 30
Central Japan Railway Company, 43
Chargeurs, 6
CHC Helicopter Corporation, 67
Chicago and North Western Holdings
    Corporation, 6
Christian Salvesen Plc, 45
Coach USA, Inc., 24; 55 (upd.)
Coles Express Inc., 15
Compagnie Générale Maritime et
    Financière, 6
Consolidated Delivery & Logistics, Inc., 24
Consolidated Freightways Corporation, V;
    21 (upd.); 48 (upd.)
Consolidated Rail Corporation, V
CR England, Inc., 63
Crowley Maritime Corporation, 6; 28
    (upd.)
CSX Corporation, V; 22 (upd.)
Danzas Group, V; 40 (upd.)
Deutsche Bahn AG, V; 46 (upd.)
DHL Worldwide Express, 6; 24 (upd.)
Dollar Thrifty Automotive Group, Inc., 25
East Japan Railway Company, V; 66 (upd.)
EGL, Inc., 59
Emery Air Freight Corporation, 6
Emery Worldwide Airlines, Inc., 25 (upd.)
Enterprise Rent-A-Car Company, 6
Eurotunnel Group, 37 (upd.)
EVA Airways Corporation, 51
Evergreen International Aviation, Inc., 53
Evergreen Marine Corporation (Taiwan)
    Ltd., 13; 50 (upd.)
Executive Jet, Inc., 36

Exel plc, 51 (upd.)
Expeditors International of Washington
    Inc., 17
Federal Express Corporation, V
FedEx Corporation, 18 (upd.); 42 (upd.)
Fritz Companies, Inc., 12
Frontline Ltd., 45
Frozen Food Express Industries, Inc., 20
Garuda Indonesia, 58 (upd.)
GATX Corporation, 6; 25 (upd.)
GE Capital Aviation Services, 36
Gefco SA, 54
General Maritime Corporation, 59
Genesee & Wyoming Inc., 27
Geodis S.A., 67
The Go-Ahead Group Plc, 28
The Greenbrier Companies, 19
Greyhound Lines, Inc., 32 (upd.)
Groupe Bourbon S.A., 60
Grupo TMM, S.A. de C.V., 50
Grupo Transportación Ferroviaria
    Mexicana, S.A. de C.V., 47
GulfMark Offshore, Inc., 49
Hanjin Shipping Co., Ltd., 50
Hankyu Corporation, V; 23 (upd.)
Hapag-Lloyd AG, 6
Harland and Wolff Holdings plc, 19
Harper Group Inc., 17
Heartland Express, Inc., 18
The Hertz Corporation, 9
Holberg Industries, Inc., 36
Hospitality Worldwide Services, Inc., 26
Hub Group, Inc., 38
Hvide Marine Incorporated, 22
Illinois Central Corporation, 11
International Shipholding Corporation, Inc.,
    27
J.B. Hunt Transport Services Inc., 12
John Menzies plc, 39
Kansas City Southern Industries, Inc., 6; 26
    (upd.)
Kawasaki Kisen Kaisha, Ltd., V; 56 (upd.)
Keio Teito Electric Railway Company, V
Kinki Nippon Railway Company Ltd., V
Kirby Corporation, 18; 66 (upd.)
Knight Transportation, Inc., 64
Koninklijke Nedlloyd Groep N.V., 6
Kuehne & Nagel International AG, V; 53
    (upd.)
La Poste, V; 47 (upd.)
Landstar System, Inc., 63
Leaseway Transportation Corp., 12
London Regional Transport, 6
Maine Central Railroad Company, 16
Mammoet Transport B.V., 26
Martz Group, 56
Mayflower Group Inc., 6
Mercury Air Group, Inc., 20
The Mersey Docks and Harbour Company,
    30
Metropolitan Transportation Authority, 35
Miller Industries, Inc., 26
Mitsui O.S.K. Lines, Ltd., V
Moran Towing Corporation, Inc., 15
The Morgan Group, Inc., 46
Morris Travel Services L.L.C., 26
Motor Cargo Industries, Inc., 35
National Car Rental System, Inc., 10
National Express Group PLC, 50
National Railroad Passenger Corporation
    (Amtrak), 22; 66 (upd.)
Neptune Orient Lines Limited, 47
NFC plc, 6
Nippon Express Company, Ltd., V; 64
    (upd.)
Nippon Yusen Kabushiki Kaisha, V

Norfolk Southern Corporation, V; 29 (upd.)
Oak Harbor Freight Lines, Inc., 53
Ocean Group plc, 6
Odakyu Electric Railway Company
    Limited, V
Oglebay Norton Company, 17
Old Dominion Freight Line, Inc., 57
OMI Corporation, 59
Österreichische Bundesbahnen GmbH, 6
OTR Express, Inc., 25
Overnite Corporation, 14; 58 (upd.)
Overseas Shipholding Group, Inc., 11
Pacer International, Inc., 54
The Peninsular and Oriental Steam
    Navigation Company, V; 38 (upd.)
Penske Corporation, V
PHH Arval, V; 53 (upd.)
Pilot Air Freight Corp., 67
Polar Air Cargo Inc., 60
The Port Authority of New York and New
    Jersey, 48
Post Office Group, V
Preston Corporation, 6
RailTex, Inc., 20
Railtrack Group PLC, 50
Réseau Ferré de France, 66
Roadway Express, Inc., V; 25 (upd.)
Royal Olympic Cruise Lines Inc., 52
Royal Vopak NV, 41
Ryder System, Inc., V; 24 (upd.)
Santa Fe Pacific Corporation, V
Schenker-Rhenus AG, 6
Schneider National, Inc., 36
Securicor Plc, 45
Seibu Railway Co. Ltd., V
Seino Transportation Company, Ltd., 6
Simon Transportation Services Inc., 27
Smithway Motor Xpress Corporation, 39
Société Nationale des Chemins de Fer
    Français, V; 57 (upd.)
Société Norbert Dentressangle S.A., 67
Southern Pacific Transportation Company,
    V
Stagecoach Holdings plc, 30
Stelmar Shipping Ltd., 52
Stevedoring Services of America Inc., 28
Stinnes AG, 8; 59 (upd.)
Stolt-Nielsen S.A., 42
Sunoco, Inc., 28 (upd.)
Swift Transportation Co., Inc., 42
The Swiss Federal Railways
    (Schweizerische Bundesbahnen), V
Teekay Shipping Corporation, 25
Tibbett & Britten Group plc, 32
Tidewater Inc., 11; 37 (upd.)
TNT Freightways Corporation, 14
TNT Post Group N.V., V; 27 (upd.); 30
    (upd.)
Tobu Railway Co Ltd, 6
Tokyu Corporation, V
Totem Resources Corporation, 9
TPG N.V., 64 (upd.)
Trailer Bridge, Inc., 41
Transnet Ltd., 6
Transport Corporation of America, Inc., 49
TTX Company, 6; 66 (upd.)
U.S. Delivery Systems, Inc., 22
Union Pacific Corporation, V; 28 (upd.)
United Parcel Service of America Inc., V;
    17 (upd.)
United Parcel Service, Inc., 63
United States Postal Service, 14; 34 (upd.)
USA Truck, Inc., 42
Velocity Express Corporation, 49
Werner Enterprises, Inc., 26
Wincanton plc, 52

Wisconsin Central Transportation
  Corporation, 24
Yamato Transport Co. Ltd., V; 49 (upd.)
Yellow Corporation, 14; 45 (upd.)
Yellow Freight System, Inc. of Delaware,
  V

UTILITIES

AES Corporation, 10; 13 (upd.); 53 (upd.)
Aggreko Plc, 45
Air & Water Technologies Corporation, 6
Alberta Energy Company Ltd., 16; 43
  (upd.)
Allegheny Energy, Inc., V; 38 (upd.)
Ameren Corporation, 60 (upd.)
American Electric Power Company, Inc.,
  V; 45 (upd.)
American States Water Company, 46
American Water Works Company, Inc., 6;
  38 (upd.)
Aquila, Inc., 50 (upd.)
Arkla, Inc., V
Associated Natural Gas Corporation, 11
Atlanta Gas Light Company, 6; 23 (upd.)
Atlantic Energy, Inc., 6
Atmos Energy Corporation, 43
Baltimore Gas and Electric Company, V;
  25 (upd.)
Bay State Gas Company, 38
Bayernwerk AG, V; 23 (upd.)
Bewag AG, 39
Big Rivers Electric Corporation, 11
Black Hills Corporation, 20
Bonneville Power Administration, 50
Boston Edison Company, 12
Bouygues S.A., 24 (upd.)
British Energy Plc, 49
British Gas plc, V
British Nuclear Fuels plc, 6
Brooklyn Union Gas, 6
Calpine Corporation, 36
Canadian Utilities Limited, 13; 56 (upd.)
Cap Rock Energy Corporation, 46
Carolina Power & Light Company, V; 23
  (upd.)
Cascade Natural Gas Corporation, 9
Centerior Energy Corporation, V
Central and South West Corporation, V
Central Hudson Gas and Electricity
  Corporation, 6
Central Maine Power, 6
Central Vermont Public Service
  Corporation, 54
Centrica plc, 29 (upd.)
Chesapeake Utilities Corporation, 56
Chubu Electric Power Company, Inc., V;
  46 (upd.)
Chugoku Electric Power Company Inc., V;
  53 (upd.)
Cincinnati Gas & Electric Company, 6
CIPSCO Inc., 6
Citizens Utilities Company, 7
City Public Service, 6
Cleco Corporation, 37
CMS Energy Corporation, V, 14
The Coastal Corporation, 31 (upd.)
Cogentrix Energy, Inc., 10
The Coleman Company, Inc., 9
The Columbia Gas System, Inc., V; 16
  (upd.)
Commonwealth Edison Company, V
Commonwealth Energy System, 14
Companhia Energética de Minas Gerais
  S.A. CEMIG, 65
Connecticut Light and Power Co., 13
Consolidated Edison, Inc., V; 45 (upd.)

Consolidated Natural Gas Company, V; 19
  (upd.)
Consumers Power Co., 14
Consumers Water Company, 14
Consumers' Gas Company Ltd., 6
Covanta Energy Corporation, 64 (upd.)
Dalkia Holding, 66
Destec Energy, Inc., 12
The Detroit Edison Company, V
Dominion Resources, Inc., V; 54 (upd.)
DPL Inc., 6
DQE, Inc., 6
DTE Energy Company, 20 (upd.)
Duke Energy Corporation, V; 27 (upd.)
E.On AG, 50 (upd.)
Eastern Enterprises, 6
Edison International, 56 (upd.)
El Paso Electric Company, 21
El Paso Natural Gas Company, 12
Electrabel N.V., 67
Electricidade de Portugal, S.A., 47
Electricité de France, V; 41 (upd.)
Electricity Generating Authority of
  Thailand (EGAT), 56
Elektrowatt AG, 6
Enbridge Inc., 43
ENDESA S.A., V; 46 (upd.)
Enron Corporation, V; 46 (upd.)
Enserch Corporation, V
Ente Nazionale per L'Energia Elettrica, V
Entergy Corporation, V; 45 (upd.)
Equitable Resources, Inc., 6; 54 (upd.)
Exelon Corporation, 48 (upd.)
Florida Progress Corporation, V; 23 (upd.)
Fortis, Inc., 15; 47 (upd.)
Fortum Corporation, 30 (upd.)
FPL Group, Inc., V; 49 (upd.)
Gaz de France, V; 40 (upd.)
General Public Utilities Corporation, V
Générale des Eaux Group, V
GPU, Inc., 27 (upd.)
Great Plains Energy Incorporated, 65
  (upd.)
Gulf States Utilities Company, 6
Hawaiian Electric Industries, Inc., 9
Hokkaido Electric Power Company Inc.
  (HEPCO), V; 58 (upd.)
Hokuriku Electric Power Company, V
Hongkong Electric Holdings Ltd., 6; 23
  (upd.)
Houston Industries Incorporated, V
Hyder plc, 34
Hydro-Québec, 6; 32 (upd.)
Iberdrola, S.A., 49
Idaho Power Company, 12
Illinois Bell Telephone Company, 14
Illinois Power Company, 6
Indiana Energy, Inc., 27
International Power PLC, 50 (upd.)
IPALCO Enterprises, Inc., 6
The Kansai Electric Power Company, Inc.,
  V; 62 (upd.)
Kansas City Power & Light Company, 6
Kelda Group plc, 45
Kenetech Corporation, 11
Kentucky Utilities Company, 6
KeySpan Energy Co., 27
Korea Electric Power Corporation (Kepco),
  56
KU Energy Corporation, 11
Kyushu Electric Power Company Inc., V
LG&E Energy Corporation, 6; 51 (upd.)
Long Island Lighting Company, V
Lyonnaise des Eaux-Dumez, V
Madison Gas and Electric Company, 39
Magma Power Company, 11
Maine & Maritimes Corporation, 56

Manila Electric Company (Meralco), 56
MCN Corporation, 6
MDU Resources Group, Inc., 7; 42 (upd.)
Middlesex Water Company, 45
Midwest Resources Inc., 6
Minnesota Power, Inc., 11; 34 (upd.)
The Montana Power Company, 11; 44
  (upd.)
National Fuel Gas Company, 6
National Grid USA, 51 (upd.)
National Power PLC, 12
Nebraska Public Power District, 29
N.V. Nederlandse Gasunie, V
Nevada Power Company, 11
New England Electric System, V
New Jersey Resources Corporation, 54
New York State Electric and Gas, 6
Neyveli Lignite Corporation Ltd., 65
Niagara Mohawk Holdings Inc., V; 45
  (upd.)
NICOR Inc., 6
NIPSCO Industries, Inc., 6
North West Water Group plc, 11
Northeast Utilities, V; 48 (upd.)
Northern States Power Company, V; 20
  (upd.)
Northwest Natural Gas Company, 45
NorthWestern Corporation, 37
Nova Corporation of Alberta, V
Oglethorpe Power Corporation, 6
Ohio Edison Company, V
Oklahoma Gas and Electric Company, 6
ONEOK Inc., 7
Ontario Hydro Services Company, 6; 32
  (upd.)
Osaka Gas Company, Ltd., V; 60 (upd.)
Otter Tail Power Company, 18
Pacific Enterprises, V
Pacific Gas and Electric Company, V
PacifiCorp, V; 26 (upd.)
Panhandle Eastern Corporation, V
PECO Energy Company, 11
Pennon Group Plc, 45
Pennsylvania Power & Light Company, V
Peoples Energy Corporation, 6
PG&E Corporation, 26 (upd.)
Philadelphia Electric Company, V
Philadelphia Suburban Corporation, 39
Piedmont Natural Gas Company, Inc., 27
Pinnacle West Capital Corporation, 6; 54
  (upd.)
PNM Resources Inc., 51 (upd.)
Portland General Corporation, 6
Potomac Electric Power Company, 6
Powergen PLC, 11; 50 (upd.)
PPL Corporation, 41 (upd.)
PreussenElektra Aktiengesellschaft, V
PSI Resources, 6
Public Service Company of Colorado, 6
Public Service Company of New
  Hampshire, 21; 55 (upd.)
Public Service Company of New Mexico, 6
Public Service Enterprise Group Inc., V;
  44 (upd.)
Puerto Rico Electric Power Authority, 47
Puget Sound Energy Inc., 6; 50 (upd.)
Questar Corporation, 6; 26 (upd.)
RAO Unified Energy System of Russia, 45
Reliant Energy Inc., 44 (upd.)
Rochester Gas and Electric Corporation, 6
Ruhrgas AG, V; 38 (upd.)
RWE AG, V; 50 (upd.)
Salt River Project, 19
San Diego Gas & Electric Company, V
SCANA Corporation, 6; 56 (upd.)
Scarborough Public Utilities Commission,
  9

UTILITIES (*continued*)

SCEcorp, V
Scottish and Southern Energy plc, 66
  (upd.)
Scottish Hydro-Electric PLC, 13
Scottish Power plc, 19; 49 (upd.)
Seattle City Light, 50
SEMCO Energy, Inc., 44
Sempra Energy, 25 (upd.)
Severn Trent PLC, 12; 38 (upd.)
Shikoku Electric Power Company, Inc., V;
  60 (upd.)
Sonat, Inc., 6
South Jersey Industries, Inc., 42
The Southern Company, V; 38 (upd.)
Southern Electric PLC, 13
Southern Indiana Gas and Electric
  Company, 13
Southern Union Company, 27
Southwest Gas Corporation, 19
Southwest Water Company, 47
Southwestern Electric Power Co., 21
Southwestern Public Service Company, 6
Suez Lyonnaise des Eaux, 36 (upd.)
TECO Energy, Inc., 6
Tennessee Valley Authority, 50
Texas Utilities Company, V; 25 (upd.)
Thames Water plc, 11
Tohoku Electric Power Company, Inc., V
The Tokyo Electric Power Company,
  Incorporated, V
Tokyo Gas Co., Ltd., V; 55 (upd.)
TransAlta Utilities Corporation, 6
TransCanada PipeLines Limited, V
Transco Energy Company, V
Trigen Energy Corporation, 42
Tucson Electric Power Company, 6
UGI Corporation, 12
Unicom Corporation, 29 (upd.)
Union Electric Company, V
The United Illuminating Company, 21
United Utilities PLC, 52 (upd.)
United Water Resources, Inc., 40
Unitil Corporation, 37
Utah Power and Light Company, 27
UtiliCorp United Inc., 6
Vattenfall AB, 57
Vereinigte Elektrizitätswerke Westfalen
  AG, V
VEW AG, 39
Viridian Group plc, 64
Warwick Valley Telephone Company, 55
Washington Gas Light Company, 19
Washington Natural Gas Company, 9
Washington Water Power Company, 6
Westar Energy, Inc., 57 (upd.)
Western Resources, Inc., 12
Wheelabrator Technologies, Inc., 6
Wisconsin Energy Corporation, 6; 54
  (upd.)
Wisconsin Public Service Corporation, 9
WPL Holdings, Inc., 6
WPS Resources Corporation, 53 (upd.)

WASTE SERVICES

Allied Waste Industries, Inc., 50
Allwaste, Inc., 18
Appliance Recycling Centers of America,
  Inc., 42
Azcon Corporation, 23
Berliner Stadtreinigungsbetriebe, 58
Brambles Industries Limited, 42
Browning-Ferris Industries, Inc., V; 20
  (upd.)
Chemical Waste Management, Inc., 9
Copart Inc., 23
E.On AG, 50 (upd.)

Ecology and Environment, Inc., 39
Industrial Services of America, Inc., 46
Ionics, Incorporated, 52
ISS A/S, 49
Kelda Group plc, 45
MPW Industrial Services Group, Inc., 53
Newpark Resources, Inc., 63
Norcal Waste Systems, Inc., 60
Pennon Group Plc, 45
Philip Environmental Inc., 16
Roto-Rooter, Inc., 15; 61 (upd.)
Safety-Kleen Corp., 8
Sevenson Environmental Services, Inc., 42
Severn Trent PLC, 38 (upd.)
Shanks Group plc, 45
Shred-It Canada Corporation, 56
Stericycle Inc., 33
TRC Companies, Inc., 32
Veit Companies, 43
Waste Connections, Inc., 46
Waste Holdings, Inc., 41
Waste Management, Inc., V
Wheelabrator Technologies, Inc., 60 (upd.)
Windswept Environmental Group, Inc., 62
WMX Technologies Inc., 17

GEOGRAPHIC INDEX

Geographic Index

Algeria

Sonatrach, IV; 65 (upd.)

Argentina

Aerolíneas Argentinas S.A., 33
Arcor S.A.I.C., 66
Atanor S.A., 62
Coto Centro Integral de Comercializacion
  S.A., 66
Cresud S.A.C.I.F. y A., 63
Grupo Clarín S.A., 67
Grupo Financiero Galicia S.A., 63
IRSA Inversiones y Representaciones S.A.,
  63
Ledesma Sociedad Anónima Agrícola
  Industrial, 62
Molinos Río de la Plata S.A., 61
Nobleza Piccardo SAICF, 64
Penaflor S.A., 66
Quilmes Industrial (QUINSA) S.A., 67
Renault Argentina S.A., 67
Sideco Americana S.A., 67
Siderar S.A.I.C., 66
Telecom Argentina S.A., 63
Telefónica de Argentina S.A., 61
YPF Sociedad Anonima, IV

Australia

Amcor Limited, IV; 19 (upd.)
Ansell Ltd., 60 (upd.)
Aquarius Platinum Ltd., 63
Aristocrat Leisure Limited, 54
Arnott's Ltd., 66
Australia and New Zealand Banking Group
  Limited, II; 52 (upd.)
AWB Ltd., 56
BHP Billiton, 67 (upd.)
Billabong International Ltd., 44
Bond Corporation Holdings Limited, 10
Boral Limited, III; 43 (upd.)
Brambles Industries Limited, 42
Broken Hill Proprietary Company Ltd., IV;
  22 (upd.)
Burns, Philp & Company Ltd., 63
Carlton and United Breweries Ltd., I
Coles Myer Ltd., V; 20 (upd.)
CRA Limited, IV
CSR Limited, III; 28 (upd.)
David Jones Ltd., 60
Elders IXL Ltd., I
Foster's Group Limited, 7; 21 (upd.); 50
  (upd.)
Goodman Fielder Ltd., 52
Harvey Norman Holdings Ltd., 56
Holden Ltd., 62
James Hardie Industries N.V., 56
John Fairfax Holdings Limited, 7
Lend Lease Corporation Limited, IV; 17
  (upd.); 52 (upd.)
Lion Nathan Limited, 54
Lonely Planet Publications Pty Ltd., 55
McPherson's Ltd., 66
Metcash Trading Ltd., 58

News Corporation Limited, IV; 7 (upd.);
  46 (upd.)
Pacific Dunlop Limited, 10
Pioneer International Limited, III
Publishing and Broadcasting Limited, 54
Qantas Airways Limited, 6; 24 (upd.)
Ridley Corporation Ltd., 62
Rinker Group Ltd., 65
Smorgon Steel Group Ltd., 62
Southcorp Limited, 54
TABCORP Holdings Limited, 44
Telecom Australia, 6
Telstra Corporation Limited, 50
Village Roadshow Ltd., 58
Westpac Banking Corporation, II; 48 (upd.)
WMC, Limited, 43

Austria

AKG Acoustics GmbH, 62
Andritz AG, 51
Austrian Airlines AG (Österreichische
  Luftverkehrs AG), 33
Bank Austria AG, 23
BBAG Österreichische Brau-Beteiligungs-
  AG, 38
Gericom AG, 47
Glock Ges.m.b.H., 42
Julius Meinl International AG, 53
Lauda Air Luftfahrt AG, 48
ÖMV Aktiengesellschaft, IV
Österreichische Bundesbahnen GmbH, 6
Österreichische Post- und
  Telegraphenverwaltung, V
Red Bull GmbH, 60
RHI AG, 53
VA TECH ELIN EBG GmbH, 49
voestalpine AG, IV; 57 (upd.)
Zumtobel AG, 50

Bahamas

Bahamas Air Holdings Ltd., 66
Sun International Hotels Limited, 26
Teekay Shipping Corporation, 25

Bahrain

Gulf Air Company, 56
Investcorp SA, 57

Bangladesh

Grameen Bank, 31

Belgium

Agfa Gevaert Group N.V., 59
Almanij NV, 44
Bank Brussels Lambert, II
Barco NV, 44
Belgacom, 6
C&A, 40 (upd.)
Cockerill Sambre Group, IV; 26 (upd.)
Delhaize "Le Lion" S.A., 44
Electrabel N.V., 67
Generale Bank, II

GIB Group, V; 26 (upd.)
Groupe Herstal S.A., 58
Interbrew S.A., 17; 50 (upd.)
Kredietbank N.V., II
PetroFina S.A., IV; 26 (upd.)
Punch International N.V., 66
Roularta Media Group NV, 48
Sabena S.A./N.V., 33
Solvay S.A., I; 21 (upd.); 61 (upd.)
Tractebel S.A., 20
NV Umicore SA, 47
Xeikon NV, 26

Bermuda

Bacardi Limited, 18
Central European Media Enterprises Ltd.,
  61
Frontline Ltd., 45
Jardine Matheson Holdings Limited, I; 20
  (upd.)
Sea Containers Ltd., 29
Tyco International Ltd., III; 28 (upd.); 63
  (upd.)
White Mountains Insurance Group, Ltd., 48

Brazil

Aracruz Celulose S.A., 57
Banco Bradesco S.A., 13
Banco Itaú S.A., 19
Brasil Telecom Participaçoes S.A., 57
Companhia de Bebidas das Américas, 57
Companhia Energética de Minas Gerais
  S.A. CEMIG, 65
Companhia Vale do Rio Doce, IV; 43
  (upd.)
Empresa Brasileira de Aeronáutica S.A.
  (Embraer), 36
Gerdau S.A., 59
Ipiranga S.A., 67
Lojas Arapua S.A., 22; 61 (upd.)
Perdigao SA, 52
Petróleo Brasileiro S.A., IV
Sadia S.A., 59
Souza Cruz S.A., 65
TransBrasil S/A Linhas Aéreas, 31
VARIG S.A. (Viaçâo Aérea Rio-
  Grandense), 6; 29 (upd.)

Canada

Abitibi-Consolidated, Inc., V; 25 (upd.)
Abitibi-Price Inc., IV
Air Canada, 6; 23 (upd.); 59 (upd.)
Alberta Energy Company Ltd., 16; 43
  (upd.)
Alcan Aluminium Limited, IV; 31 (upd.)
Algo Group Inc., 24
Alliance Atlantis Communications Inc., 39
Bank of Montreal, II; 46 (upd.)
Bank of Nova Scotia, The, II; 59 (upd.)
Barrick Gold Corporation, 34
Bata Ltd., 62
BCE Inc., V; 44 (upd.)
Bell Canada, 6

Canada (*continued*)

BFC Construction Corporation, 25
Biovail Corporation, 47
Bombardier Inc., 42 (upd.)
Bradley Air Services Ltd., 56
Bramalea Ltd., 9
Brascan Corporation, 67
British Columbia Telephone Company, 6
Campeau Corporation, V
Canada Packers Inc., II
Canadair, Inc., 16
Canadian Broadcasting Corporation (CBC),
The, 37
Canadian Imperial Bank of Commerce, II;
61 (upd.)
Canadian National Railway System, 6
Canadian Pacific Railway Limited, V; 45
(upd.)
Canadian Utilities Limited, 13; 56 (upd.)
Canfor Corporation, 42
Canstar Sports Inc., 16
CanWest Global Communications
Corporation, 35
CHC Helicopter Corporation, 67
Cinar Corporation, 40
Cineplex Odeon Corporation, 6; 23 (upd.)
Cinram International, Inc., 43
Cirque du Soleil Inc., 29
Clearly Canadian Beverage Corporation, 48
Cognos Inc., 44
Cominco Ltd., 37
Consumers' Gas Company Ltd., 6
CoolBrands International Inc., 35
Corby Distilleries Limited, 14
Corel Corporation, 15; 33 (upd.)
Cott Corporation, 52
Creo Inc., 48
Discreet Logic Inc., 20
Dofasco Inc., IV; 24 (upd.)
Doman Industries Limited, 59
Dominion Textile Inc., 12
Domtar Inc., IV
Dorel Industries Inc., 59
Dylex Limited, 29
Echo Bay Mines Ltd., IV; 38 (upd.)
Enbridge Inc., 43
Extendicare Health Services, Inc., 6
Fairfax Financial Holdings Limited, 57
Falconbridge Limited, 49
Fortis, Inc., 15; 47 (upd.)
Four Seasons Hotels Inc., 9; 29 (upd.)
Future Shop Ltd., 62
GEAC Computer Corporation Ltd., 43
George Weston Limited, II; 36 (upd.)
Great-West Lifeco Inc., III
Groupe Vidéotron Ltée., 20
Harlequin Enterprises Limited, 52
Hemlo Gold Mines Inc., 9
Hiram Walker Resources, Ltd., I
Hockey Company, The, 34
Hollinger International Inc., 62 (upd.)
Home Hardware Stores Ltd., 62
Hudson Bay Mining and Smelting
Company, Limited, The, 12
Hudson's Bay Company, V; 25 (upd.)
Hurricane Hydrocarbons Ltd., 54
Husky Energy Inc., 47
Hydro-Québec, 6; 32 (upd.)
Imasco Limited, V
Imax Corporation, 28
Imperial Oil Limited, IV; 25 (upd.)
Imperial Parking Corporation, 58
Inco Limited, IV; 45 (upd.)
Indigo Books & Music Inc., 58
Intercorp Excelle Foods Inc., 64
Intrawest Corporation, The, 15
Irwin Toy Limited, 14

Jean Coutu Group (PJC) Inc., The, 46
Jim Pattison Group, The, 37
Kinross Gold Corporation, 36
Kruger Inc., 17
La Senza Corporation, 66
Labatt Brewing Company Limited, I; 25
(upd.)
LaSiDo Inc., 58
Le Chateau Inc., 63
Ledcor Industries Limited, 46
Les Boutiques San Francisco, Inc., 62
Linamar Corporation, 18
Lions Gate Entertainment Corporation, 35
Loblaw Companies Limited, 43
Loewen Group, Inc., The, 16; 40 (upd.)
London Drugs Ltd., 46
Maclean Hunter Publishing Limited, IV; 26
(upd.)
MacMillan Bloedel Limited, IV
Magellan Aerospace Corporation, 48
Manitoba Telecom Services, Inc., 61
Maple Leaf Foods Inc., 41
Maple Leaf Sports & Entertainment Ltd.,
61
Masonite International Corporation, 63
MDC Partners Inc., 63
Mega Bloks, Inc., 61
Methanex Corporation, 40
Mitel Corporation, 18
Molson Companies Limited, The, I; 26
(upd.)
Moore Corporation Limited, IV
Mouvement des Caisses Desjardins, 48
National Sea Products Ltd., 14
Noranda Inc., IV; 7 (upd.); 64 (upd.)
Nortel Networks Corporation, 36 (upd.)
North West Company, Inc., The, 12
Northern Telecom Limited, V
Nova Corporation of Alberta, V
Novacor Chemicals Ltd., 12
Olympia & York Developments Ltd., IV; 9
(upd.)
Onex Corporation, 16; 65 (upd.)
Ontario Hydro Services Company, 6; 32
(upd.)
Ontario Teachers' Pension Plan, 61
Oshawa Group Limited, The, II
PCL Construction Group Inc., 50
Peace Arch Entertainment Group Inc., 51
Petro-Canada Limited, IV
Philip Environmental Inc., 16
Placer Dome Inc., 20; 61 (upd.)
Potash Corporation of Saskatchewan Inc.,
18
Power Corporation of Canada, 36 (upd.)
Provigo Inc., II; 51 (upd.)
Quebecor Inc., 12; 47 (upd.)
Research in Motion Ltd., 54
Richtree Inc., 63
Ritchie Bros. Auctioneers Inc., 41
Rogers Communications Inc., 30 (upd.)
Roots Canada Ltd., 42
Royal Bank of Canada, The, II; 21 (upd.)
Saputo Inc., 59
Scarborough Public Utilities Commission,
9
Seagram Company Ltd., The, I; 25 (upd.)
Shoppers Drug Mart Corporation, 49
Shred-It Canada Corporation, 56
Southam Inc., 7
Spar Aerospace Limited, 32
Spin Master, Ltd., 61
Steinberg Incorporated, II
Stelco Inc., IV; 51 (upd.)
Suncor Energy Inc., 54
Talisman Energy Inc., 9; 47 (upd.)
TDL Group Ltd., 46

Teck Corporation, 27
Tembec Inc., 66
Thomson Corporation, The, 8; 34 (upd.)
Tilley Endurables, Inc., 67
Toromont Industries, Ltd., 21
Toronto-Dominion Bank, The, II; 49 (upd.)
Torstar Corporation, 29
TransAlta Utilities Corporation, 6
TransCanada PipeLines Limited, V
Tridel Enterprises Inc., 9
Trilon Financial Corporation, II
Triple Five Group Ltd., 49
Trizec Corporation Ltd., 10
Van Houtte Inc., 39
Varity Corporation, III
Vincor International Inc., 50
Wascana Energy Inc., 13
West Fraser Timber Co. Ltd., 17
WestJet Airlines Ltd., 38

Cayman Islands

Garmin Ltd., 60
United National Group, Ltd., 63

Chile

Corporacion Nacional del Cobre de Chile,
40
Cristalerias de Chile S.A., 67
Lan Chile S.A., 31
Viña Concha y Toro S.A., 45

China

Air China, 46
Asia Info Holdings, Inc., 43
Bank of China, 63
China Eastern Airlines Co. Ltd., 31
China Life Insurance Company Limited, 65
China National Petroleum Corporation, 46
China Southern Airlines Company Ltd., 33
China Telecom, 50
Chinese Petroleum Corporation, IV; 31
(upd.)
Guangzhou Pearl River Piano Group Ltd.,
49
Haier Group Corporation, 65
Li & Fung Limited, 59
Shanghai Petrochemical Co., Ltd., 18
Tsingtao Brewery Group, 49
Zindart Ltd., 60

Colombia

Avianca Aerovías Nacionales de Colombia
SA, 36
Empresa Colombiana de Petróleos, IV

Czech Republic

Budweiser Budvar, National Corporation,
59
Ceské aerolinie, a.s., 66
Cesky Telecom, a.s., 64
Skoda Auto a.s., 39

Denmark

A.P. Møller - Maersk A/S, 57
Arla Foods amba, 48
Bang & Olufsen Holding A/S, 37
Carlsberg A/S, 9; 29 (upd.)
Danisco A/S, 44
Danske Bank Aktieselskab, 50
Ecco Sko A/S, 62
Group 4 Falck A/S, 42
H. Lundbeck A/S, 44
IKEA International A/S, V; 26 (upd.)
ISS A/S, 49
Lego A/S, 13; 40 (upd.)

Novo Nordisk A/S, I; 61 (upd.)
Sophus Berendsen A/S, 49
TDC A/S, 63

Ecuador

Petróleos del Ecuador, IV

Egypt

EgyptAir, 6; 27 (upd.)
Egyptian General Petroleum Corporation,
IV; 51 (upd.)

El Salvador

Grupo TACA, 38

Finland

Ahlstrom Corporation, 53
Amer Group plc, 41
Enso-Gutzeit Oy, IV
Finnair Oyj, 6; 25 (upd.); 61 (upd.)
Fiskars Corporation, 33
Fortum Corporation, 30 (upd.)
Hackman Oyj Adp, 44
Huhtamäki Oyj, 64
Imatra Steel Oy Ab, 55
Kansallis-Osake-Pankki, II
Kesko Ltd. (Kesko Oy), 8; 27 (upd.)
Kone Corporation, 27
Kymmene Corporation, IV
M-real Oyj, 56 (upd.)
Metsa-Serla Oy, IV
Metso Corporation, 30 (upd.)
Neste Oy, IV
Nokia Corporation, II; 17 (upd.); 38 (upd.)
Outokumpu Oyj, 38
Posti- ja Telelaitos, 6
Sanitec Corporation, 51
SanomaWSOY Corporation, 51
Sonera Corporation, 50
Stora Enso Oyj, 36 (upd.)
Tamfelt Oyj Abp, 62
United Paper Mills Ltd. (Yhtyneet
    Paperitehtaat Oy), IV
UPM-Kymmene Corporation, 19; 50 (upd.)
Valmet Corporation (Valmet Oy), III

France

Accor SA, 10; 27 (upd.)
Aéroports de Paris, 33
Aerospatiale Group, The, 7; 21 (upd.)
Agence France-Presse, 34
Alain Afflelou SA, 53
Alcatel Alsthom Compagnie Générale
    d'Electricité, 9
Alcatel S.A., 36 (upd.)
Altran Technologies, 51
Amec Spie S.A., 57
Association des Centres Distributeurs E.
    Leclerc, 37
Assurances Générales de France, 63
Atochem S.A., I
Au Printemps S.A., V
Auchan, 37
Automobiles Citroen, 7
Autoroutes du Sud de la France SA, 55
Avions Marcel Dassault-Breguet Aviation,
    I
Axa, III
Baccarat, 24
Banque Nationale de Paris S.A., II
Baron Philippe de Rothschild S.A., 39
Bayard SA, 49
Bénéteau SA, 55
Besnier SA, 19
BNP Paribas Group, 36 (upd.)

Bonduelle SA, 51
Bongrain SA, 25
Bouygues S.A., I; 24 (upd.)
Brioche Pasquier S.A., 58
BSN Groupe S.A., II
Bull S.A., 43 (upd.)
Bureau Veritas SA, 55
Burelle S.A., 23
Business Objects S.A., 25
Canal Plus, 10; 34 (upd.)
Cap Gemini Ernst & Young, 37
Carbone Lorraine S.A., 33
Carrefour SA, 10; 27 (upd.); 64 (upd.)
Casino Guichard-Perrachon S.A., 59 (upd.)
Cetelem S.A., 21
Chanel SA, 12; 49 (upd.)
Chargeurs International, 6; 21 (upd.)
Christian Dalloz SA, 40
Christian Dior S.A., 19; 49 (upd.)
Christofle SA, 40
Ciments Français, 40
Club Mediterranée S.A., 6; 21 (upd.)
Coflexip S.A., 25
Colas S.A., 31
Compagnie de Saint-Gobain, III; 16 (upd.);
    64 (upd.)
Compagnie des Alpes, 48
Compagnie des Machines Bull S.A., III
Compagnie Financiere de Paribas, II
Compagnie Financière Sucrés et Denrées
    S.A., 60
Compagnie Générale d'Électricité, II
Compagnie Générale des Établissements
    Michelin, V; 42 (upd.)
Compagnie Générale Maritime et
    Financière, 6
Comptoirs Modernes S.A., 19
Crédit Agricole, II
Crédit Lyonnais, 9; 33 (upd.)
Crédit National S.A., 9
Dalkia Holding, 66
Darty S.A., 27
Dassault Systèmes S.A., 25
De Dietrich & Cie., 31
Deveaux S.A., 41
Dexia Group, 42
Du Pareil au Même, 43
Dynaction S.A., 67
EADS SOCATA, 54
ECS S.A., 12
Eiffage, 27
Electricité de France, V; 41 (upd.)
Elf Aquitaine SA, 21 (upd.)
Elior SA, 49
Eram SA, 51
Eridania Béghin-Say S.A., 36
Essilor International, 21
Etablissements Economiques du Casino
    Guichard, Perrachon et Cie, S.C.A., 12
Etam Developpement SA, 44
Euro Disney S.C.A., 20; 58 (upd.)
Euro RSCG Worldwide S.A., 13
Euronext Paris S.A., 37
Expand SA, 48
Facom S.A., 32
Faiveley S.A., 39
Fimalac S.A., 37
Fleury Michon S.A., 39
FNAC, 21
Framatome SA, 19
France Télécom Group, V; 21 (upd.)
Fromageries Bel, 23
G.I.E. Airbus Industrie, I; 12 (upd.)
Galeries Lafayette S.A., V; 23 (upd.)
Gaumont SA, 25
Gaz de France, V; 40 (upd.)
Gecina SA, 42

Gefco SA, 54
Générale des Eaux Group, V
Geodis S.A., 67
GFI Informatique SA, 49
GrandVision S.A., 43
Grévin & Compagnie SA, 56
Groupe Air France, 6
Groupe Alain Manoukian, 55
Groupe André, 17
Groupe Bolloré, 67
Groupe Bourbon S.A., 60
Groupe Castorama-Dubois Investissements,
    23
Groupe Danone, 32 (upd.)
Groupe Dassault Aviation SA, 26 (upd.)
Groupe de la Cite, IV
Groupe DMC (Dollfus Mieg & Cie), 27
Groupe Fournier SA, 44
Groupe Go Sport S.A., 39
Groupe Guillin SA, 40
Groupe Jean-Claude Darmon, 44
Groupe Lapeyre S.A., 33
Groupe Legris Industries, 23
Groupe Les Echos, 25
Groupe Louis Dreyfus S.A., 60
Groupe Partouche SA, 48
Groupe Promodès S.A., 19
Groupe Rougier SA, 21
Groupe SEB, 35
Groupe Sidel S.A., 21
Groupe Soufflet SA, 55
Groupe Yves Saint Laurent, 23
Groupe Zannier S.A., 35
Guerbet Group, 46
Guerlain, 23
Guilbert S.A., 42
Guillemot Corporation, 41
Guy Degrenne SA, 44
Guyenne et Gascogne, 23
Hachette, IV
Hachette Filipacchi Medias S.A., 21
Havas, SA, 10; 33 (upd.)
Hermès International S.A., 14; 34 (upd.)
Imerys S.A., 40 (upd.)
Imetal S.A., IV
Infogrames Entertainment S.A., 35
Ingenico—Compagnie Industrielle et
    Financière d'Ingénierie, 46
ITM Entreprises SA, 36
Keolis SA, 51
Kiabi Europe, 66
L'Air Liquide SA, I; 47 (upd.)
L'Entreprise Jean Lefebvre, 23
L'Oréal SA, III; 8 (upd.); 46 (upd.)
L.D.C. SA, 61
La Poste, V; 47 (upd.)
Laboratoires de Biologie Végétale Yves
    Rocher, 35
Lafarge Coppée S.A., III
Lafuma S.A., 39
Laurent-Perrier SA, 42
Lazard LLC, 38
Le Cordon Bleu S.A., 67
Le Monde S.A., 33
Legrand SA, 21
Leroux S.A.S., 65
Leroy Merlin SA, 54
LVMH Möet Hennessy Louis Vuitton SA,
    I; 10; 33 (upd.)
Lyonnaise des Eaux-Dumez, V
Madrange SA, 58
Maison Louis Jadot, 24
Manitou BF S.A., 27
Marie Brizard & Roger International S.A.,
    22
Marionnaud Parfumeries SA, 51
Matra-Hachette S.A., 15 (upd.)

France (*continued*)

Matussière et Forest SA, 58
Metaleurop S.A., 21
Métropole Télévision, 33
Monnaie de Paris, 62
Montupet S.A., 63
Moulinex S.A., 22
Mr. Bricolage S.A., 37
Naf Naf SA, 44
Neopost S.A., 53
Nexans SA, 54
Nexity S.A., 66
Nocibé SA, 54
Papeteries de Lancey, 23
Pathé SA, 29
Pechiney SA, IV; 45 (upd.)
Penauille Polyservices SA, 49
Pernod Ricard S.A., I; 21 (upd.)
Peugeot S.A., I
Pierre & Vacances SA, 48
Pinault-Printemps Redoute S.A., 19 (upd.)
Pinguely-Haulotte SA, 51
Pochet SA, 55
Poliet S.A., 33
PSA Peugeot Citroen S.A., 28 (upd.)
Publicis S.A., 19
Rallye SA, 54
Regie Nationale des Usines Renault, I
Rémy Cointreau S.A., 20
Renault S.A., 26 (upd.)
Réseau Ferré de France, 66
Rhodia SA, 38
Rhône-Poulenc S.A., I; 10 (upd.)
Robertet SA, 39
Roussel Uclaf, I; 8 (upd.)
Royal Canin S.A., 39
Sabaté Diosos SA, 48
SAGEM S.A., 37
Salomon Worldwide, 20
Sanofi-Synthélabo Group, The, I; 49 (upd.)
Schneider S.A., II; 18 (upd.)
SCOR S.A., 20
Seita, 23
Selectour SA, 53
Simco S.A., 37
Skalli Group, 67
Skis Rossignol S.A., 15; 43 (upd.)
Smoby International SA, 56
Snecma Group, 46
Société Air France, 27 (upd.)
Société d'Exploitation AOM Air Liberté
    SA (AirLib), 53
Société du Figaro S.A., 60
Société du Louvre, 27
Société Générale, II; 42 (upd.)
Société Nationale des Chemins de Fer
    Français, V; 57 (upd.)
Société Nationale Elf Aquitaine, IV; 7
    (upd.)
Société Norbert Dentressangle S.A., 67
Sodexho Alliance SA, 29
Sodiaal S.A., 36 (upd.)
SODIMA, II
Sommer-Allibert S.A., 19
Steria SA, 49
Suez Lyonnaise des Eaux, 36 (upd.)
Taittinger S.A., 43
Tati SA, 25
Télévision Française 1, 23
Thales S.A., 42
THOMSON multimedia S.A., II; 42 (upd.)
Total Fina Elf S.A., IV; 24 (upd.); 50
    (upd.)
Transiciel SA, 48
Ubi Soft Entertainment S.A., 41
Ugine S.A., 20
Unibail SA, 40

Unilog SA, 42
Union des Assurances de Pans, III
Union Financière de France Banque SA, 52
Usinor SA, IV; 42 (upd.)
Valeo, 23; 66 (upd.)
Vallourec SA, 54
Vinci, 43
Vivarte SA, 54 (upd.)
Vivendi Universal S.A., 46 (upd.)
Weber et Broutin France, 66
Worms et Cie, 27
Zodiac S.A., 36

Germany

A. Moksel AG, 59
A.W. Faber-Castell Unternehmensverwaltung
    GmbH & Co., 51
Adam Opel AG, 7; 21 (upd.); 61 (upd.)
adidas-Salomon AG, 14; 33 (upd.)
Adolf Würth GmbH & Co. KG, 49
AEG A.G., I
Aldi Group, 13
Alfred Ritter GmbH & Co. KG, 58
Allianz AG, III; 15 (upd.); 57 (upd.)
AMB Generali Holding AG, 51
Andreas Stihl AG & Co. KG, 16; 59 (upd.)
Aral AG, 62
ARD, 41
August Storck KG, 66
AVA AG (Allgemeine Handelsgesellschaft
    der Verbraucher AG), 33
AXA Colonia Konzern AG, 27; 49 (upd.)
Axel Springer Verlag AG, IV; 20 (upd.)
Bahlsen GmbH & Co. KG, 44
Barmag AG, 39
BASF Aktiengesellschaft, I; 18 (upd.); 50
    (upd.)
Bauer Publishing Group, 7
Bayer A.G., I; 13 (upd.); 41 (upd.)
Bayerische Hypotheken- und Wechsel-
    Bank AG, II
Bayerische Motoren Werke AG, I; 11
    (upd.); 38 (upd.)
Bayerische Vereinsbank A.G., II
Bayernwerk AG, V; 23 (upd.)
Beiersdorf AG, 29
Berliner Stadtreinigungsbetriebe, 58
Berliner Verkehrsbetriebe (BVG), 58
Bertelsmann A.G., IV; 15 (upd.); 43 (upd.)
Bewag AG, 39
Bilfinger & Berger AG, I; 55 (upd.)
Brauerei Beck & Co., 9; 33 (upd.)
Braun GmbH, 51
Brenntag AG, 8; 23 (upd.)
BSH Bosch und Siemens Hausgeräte
    GmbH, 67
Buderus AG, 37
Burda Holding GmbH. & Co., 23
C&A Brenninkmeyer KG, V
C.H. Boehringer Sohn, 39
Carl-Zeiss-Stiftung, III; 34 (upd.)
Commerzbank A.G., II; 47 (upd.)
Continental AG, V; 56 (upd.)
Daimler-Benz Aerospace AG, 16
DaimlerChrysler AG, I; 15 (upd.); 34
    (upd.); 64 (upd.)
Degussa Group, IV
Degussa-Huls AG, 32 (upd.)
Deutsche Babcock A.G., III
Deutsche Bahn AG, 46 (upd.)
Deutsche Bank AG, II; 14 (upd.); 40 (upd.)
Deutsche BP Aktiengesellschaft, 7
Deutsche Bundesbahn, V
Deutsche Bundespost TELEKOM, V
Deutsche Börse AG, 59
Deutsche Lufthansa Aktiengesellschaft, I;
    26 (upd.)

Deutsche Post AG, 29
Deutsche Telekom AG, 48 (upd.)
Deutz AG, 39
Dr. August Oetker KG, 51
Dresdner Bank A.G., II; 57 (upd.)
Dürkopp Adler AG, 65
Dürr AG, 44
Dyckerhoff AG, 35
E.On AG, 50 (upd.)
Eckes AG, 56
Edeka Zentrale A.G., II; 47 (upd.)
edel music AG, 44
ERGO Versicherungsgruppe AG, 44
Esselte Leitz GmbH & Co. KG, 48
Etienne Aigner AG, 52
FAG—Kugelfischer Georg Schäfer AG, 62
Fairchild Dornier GmbH, 48 (upd.)
Feldmuhle Nobel A.G., III
Fielmann AG, 31
Frankfurter Allgemeine Zeitung GmbH, 66
Fresenius AG, 56
Freudenberg & Co., 41
Fried. Krupp GmbH, IV
Friedrich Grohe AG & Co. KG, 53
GEA AG, 27
GEHE AG, 27
geobra Brandstätter GmbH & Co. KG, 48
Gerling-Konzern Versicherungs-
    Beteiligungs-Aktiengesellschaft, 51
Gerresheimer Glas AG, 43
Gerry Weber International AG, 63
GfK Aktiengesellschaft, 49
Grundig AG, 27
Hansgrohe AG, 56
Hapag-Lloyd AG, 6
HARIBO GmbH & Co. KG, 44
HDI (Haftpflichtverband der Deutschen
    Industrie Versicherung auf
    Gegenseitigkeit V.a.G.), 53
Heidelberger Druckmaschinen AG, 40
Heidelberger Zement AG, 31
Hella KGaA Hueck & Co., 66
Henkel KGaA, III; 34 (upd.)
Heraeus Holding GmbH, IV; 54 (upd.)
Hertie Waren- und Kaufhaus GmbH, V
Hochtief AG, 33
Hoechst A.G., I; 18 (upd.)
Hoesch AG, IV
Hugo Boss AG, 48
HUK-Coburg, 58
Huls A.G., I
HVB Group, 59 (upd.)
Infineon Technologies AG, 50
J.M. Voith AG, 33
Jenoptik AG, 33
Kamps AG, 44
Karlsberg Brauerei GmbH & Co KG, 41
Karstadt Aktiengesellschaft, V; 19 (upd.)
Karstadt Quelle AG, 57 (upd.)
Kaufhof Warenhaus AG, V; 23 (upd.)
Kaufring AG, 35
KHD Konzern, III
Klaus Steilmann GmbH & Co. KG, 53
Klöckner-Werke AG, IV; 58 (upd.)
Koenig & Bauer AG, 64
König Brauerei GmbH & Co. KG, 35
    (upd.)
Körber AG, 60
Kreditanstalt für Wiederaufbau, 29
KSB AG, 62
Leica Camera AG, 35
Leica Microsystems Holdings GmbH, 35
Linde AG, I; 67 (upd.)
LTU Group Holding GmbH, 37
MAN Aktiengesellschaft, III
Mannesmann AG, III; 14 (upd.); 38 (upd.)
Margarete Steiff GmbH, 23

Matth. Hohner AG, 53
Melitta Unternehmensgruppe Bentz KG, 53
Messerschmitt-Bölkow-Blohm GmbH., I
Metallgesellschaft AG, IV; 16 (upd.)
Metro AG, 50
Miele & Cie. KG, 56
MITROPA AG, 37
Munich Re (Münchener Rückversicherungs-
    Gesellschaft Aktiengesellschaft in
    München), III; 46 (upd.)
Nixdorf Computer AG, III
Norddeutsche Affinerie AG, 62
Optische Werke G. Rodenstock, 44
Otto Versand GmbH & Co., V; 15 (upd.);
    34 (upd.)
Paulaner Brauerei GmbH & Co. KG, 35
Peek & Cloppenburg KG, 46
Philipp Holzmann AG, 17
Porsche AG, 13; 31 (upd.)
Preussag AG, 17; 42 (upd.)
PreussenElektra Aktiengesellschaft, V
ProSiebenSat.1 Media AG, 54
Puma AG Rudolf Dassler Sport, 35
PWA Group, IV
Qiagen N.V., 39
Quelle Group, V
RAG AG, 35; 60 (upd.)
Ravensburger AG, 64
RENK AG, 37
Rheinmetall Berlin AG, 9
Robert Bosch GmbH, I; 16 (upd.); 43
    (upd.)
Rohde & Schwarz GmbH & Co. KG, 39
Roland Berger & Partner GmbH, 37
Ruhrgas AG, V; 38 (upd.)
Ruhrkohle AG, IV
RWE AG, V; 50 (upd.)
Saarberg-Konzern, IV
Salzgitter AG, IV
SAP AG, 16; 43 (upd.)
Schenker-Rhenus AG, 6
Schering AG, I; 50 (upd.)
Sennheiser Electronic GmbH & Co. KG,
    66
Siemens AG, II; 14 (upd.); 57 (upd.)
Sixt AG, 39
SPAR Handels AG, 35
SPIEGEL-Verlag Rudolf Augstein GmbH
    & Co. KG, 44
Stinnes AG, 8; 23 (upd.); 59 (upd.)
Stollwerck AG, 53
Südzucker AG, 27
T-Online International AG, 61
TA Triumph-Adler AG, 48
Tarkett Sommer AG, 25
TaurusHolding GmbH & Co. KG, 46
Tengelmann Group, 27
Thyssen Krupp AG, IV; 28 (upd.)
Touristik Union International GmbH. and
    Company K.G., II
TUI Group GmbH, 44
Vaillant GmbH, 44
Varta AG, 23
Veba A.G., I; 15 (upd.)
Vereinigte Elektrizitätswerke Westfalen
    AG, V
Verlagsgruppe Georg von Holtzbrinck
    GmbH, 35
VEW AG, 39
VIAG Aktiengesellschaft, IV
Victoria Group, III; 44 (upd.)
Viessmann Werke GmbH & Co., 37
Villeroy & Boch AG, 37
Volkswagen Aktiengesellschaft, I; 11
    (upd.); 32 (upd.)
Vorwerk & Co., 27
Vossloh AG, 53

Wacker-Chemie GmbH, 35
Wella AG, III; 48 (upd.)
Weru Aktiengesellschaft, 18
Westdeutsche Landesbank Girozentrale, II;
    46 (upd.)
Württembergische Metallwarenfabrik AG
    (WMF), 60
ZF Friedrichshafen AG, 48

Ghana

Ashanti Goldfields Company Limited, 43

Greece

Aegek S.A., 64
Attica Enterprises S.A., 64
Hellenic Petroleum SA, 64
National Bank of Greece, 41
Royal Olympic Cruise Lines Inc., 52
Stelmar Shipping Ltd., 52
Titan Cement Company S.A., 64

Hong Kong

Bank of East Asia Ltd., 63
Cable & Wireless HKT, 30 (upd.)
Cathay Pacific Airways Limited, 6; 34
    (upd.)
Cheung Kong (Holdings) Limited, IV; 20
    (upd.)
China Merchants International Holdings
    Co., Ltd., 52
CITIC Pacific Ltd., 18
First Pacific Company Limited, 18
Hang Seng Bank Ltd., 60
Hong Kong Dragon Airlines Ltd., 66
Hong Kong Telecommunications Ltd., 6
Hongkong and Shanghai Banking
    Corporation Limited, The, II
Hongkong Electric Holdings Ltd., 6; 23
    (upd.)
Hongkong Land Holdings Limited, IV; 47
    (upd.)
Hutchison Whampoa Limited, 18; 49
    (upd.)
Kerry Properties Limited, 22
Nam Tai Electronics, Inc., 61
New World Development Company
    Limited, IV; 38 (upd.)
Next Media Ltd., 61
Playmates Toys, 23
Singer Company N.V., The, 30 (upd.)
Swire Pacific Limited, I; 16 (upd.); 57
    (upd.)
Tommy Hilfiger Corporation, 20; 53 (upd.)

Hungary

Malév Plc, 24

Iceland

Icelandair, 52

India

Air Sahara Limited, 65
Air-India Limited, 6; 27 (upd.)
Bajaj Auto Limited, 39
Coal India Limited, IV; 44 (upd.)
Dr. Reddy's Laboratories Ltd., 59
Indian Airlines Ltd., 46
Indian Oil Corporation Ltd., IV; 48 (upd.)
Infosys Technologies Ltd., 38
Jet Airways (India) Private Limited, 65
Minerals and Metals Trading Corporation
    of India Ltd., IV
MTR Foods Ltd., 55
Neyveli Lignite Corporation Ltd., 65
Oil and Natural Gas Commission, IV

State Bank of India, 63
Steel Authority of India Ltd., IV; 66 (upd.)
Sun Pharmaceutical Industries Ltd., 57
Tata Iron & Steel Co. Ltd., IV; 44 (upd.)
Wipro Limited, 43

Indonesia

Djarum PT, 62
Garuda Indonesia, 6; 58 (upd.)
PERTAMINA, IV
Pertamina, 56 (upd.)
PT Astra International Tbk, 56
PT Bank Buana Indonesia Tbk, 60

Iran

National Iranian Oil Company, IV; 61
    (upd.)

Ireland

Aer Lingus Group plc, 34
Allied Irish Banks, plc, 16; 43 (upd.)
Baltimore Technologies Plc, 42
Bank of Ireland, 50
CRH plc, 64
Dunnes Stores Ltd., 58
eircom plc, 31 (upd.)
Elan Corporation PLC, 63
Fyffes Plc, 38
Glanbia plc, 59
Harland and Wolff Holdings plc, 19
IAWS Group plc, 49
Independent News & Media PLC, 61
IONA Technologies plc, 43
Irish Life & Permanent Plc, 59
Jefferson Smurfit Group plc, IV; 19 (upd.);
    49 (upd.)
Jurys Doyle Hotel Group plc, 64
Kerry Group plc, 27
Musgrave Group Plc, 57
Ryanair Holdings plc, 35
Shannon Aerospace Ltd., 36
Telecom Eireann, 7
Waterford Wedgwood plc, 34 (upd.)

Israel

Amdocs Ltd., 47
Bank Hapoalim B.M., II; 54 (upd.)
Bank Leumi le-Israel B.M., 60
Blue Square Israel Ltd., 41
ECI Telecom Ltd., 18
El Al Israel Airlines Ltd., 23
Elscint Ltd., 20
Israel Chemicals Ltd., 55
Koor Industries Ltd., II; 25 (upd.)
Scitex Corporation Ltd., 24
Taro Pharmaceutical Industries Ltd., 65
Teva Pharmaceutical Industries Ltd., 22; 54
    (upd.)

Italy

Alfa Romeo, 13; 36 (upd.)
Alitalia-Linee Aeree Italiana, S.p.A., 6; 29
    (upd.)
Alleanza Assicurazioni S.p.A., 65
Aprilia SpA, 17
Arnoldo Mondadori Editore S.p.A., IV; 19
    (upd.); 54 (upd.)
Assicurazioni Generali SpA, III; 15 (upd.)
Autogrill SpA, 49
Automobili Lamborghini Holding S.p.A.,
    13; 34 (upd.)
Banca Commerciale Italiana SpA, II
Banca Fideuram SpA, 63
Banca Intesa SpA, 65
Banca Monte dei Paschi di Siena SpA, 65

Italy (*continued*)

Barilla G. e R. Fratelli S.p.A., 17; 50 (upd.)
Benetton Group S.p.A., 10; 67 (upd.)
Brioni Roman Style S.p.A., 67
Bulgari S.p.A., 20
Cantine Giorgio Lungarotti S.R.L., 67
Capitalia S.p.A., 65
Credito Italiano, II
Cremonini S.p.A., 57
Davide Campari-Milano S.p.A., 57
De'Longhi S.p.A., 66
Diesel SpA, 40
Dolce & Gabbana SpA, 62
Ducati Motor Holding S.p.A., 30
Ente Nazionale Idrocarburi, IV
Ente Nazionale per L'Energia Elettrica, V
Ermenegildo Zegna SpA, 63
Fabbrica D' Armi Pietro Beretta S.p.A., 39
Ferrari S.p.A., 13; 36 (upd.)
Ferrero SpA, 54
Fiat SpA, I; 11 (upd.); 50 (upd.)
Fila Holding S.p.A., 20; 52 (upd.)
Gianni Versace SpA, 22
Giorgio Armani S.p.A., 45
Gruppo Coin S.p.A., 41
Guccio Gucci, S.p.A., 15
illycaffè SpA, 50
Industrie Natuzzi S.p.A., 18
Industrie Zignago Santa Margherita S.p.A., 67
Ing. C. Olivetti & C., S.p.a., III
Istituto per la Ricostruzione Industriale S.p.A., I; 11
Juventus F.C. S.p.A., 53
Luxottica SpA, 17; 52 (upd.)
Marchesi Antinori SRL, 42
Marcolin S.p.A., 61
Martini & Rossi SpA, 63
Marzotto S.p.A., 20; 67 (upd.)
Mediaset SpA, 50
Mediolanum S.p.A., 65
Montedison SpA, I; 24 (upd.)
Officine Alfieri Maserati S.p.A., 13
Olivetti S.p.A., 34 (upd.)
Parmalat Finanziaria SpA, 50
Piaggio & C. S.p.A., 20
Pirelli S.p.A., V; 15 (upd.)
Reno de Medici S.p.A., 41
Riunione Adriatica di Sicurtè SpA, III
Safilo SpA, 54
Salvatore Ferragamo Italia S.p.A., 62
Sanpaolo IMI S.p.A., 50
Seat Pagine Gialle S.p.A., 47
Società Finanziaria Telefonica per Azioni, V
Società Sportiva Lazio SpA, 44
Stefanel SpA, 63
Telecom Italia Mobile S.p.A., 63
Telecom Italia S.p.A., 43
Tiscali SpA, 48

Jamaica

Air Jamaica Limited, 54

Japan

Aisin Seiki Co., Ltd., III; 48 (upd.)
Aiwa Co., Ltd., 30
Ajinomoto Co., Inc., II; 28 (upd.)
All Nippon Airways Co., Ltd., 6; 38 (upd.)
Alpine Electronics, Inc., 13
Alps Electric Co., Ltd., II; 44 (upd.)
Asahi Breweries, Ltd., I; 20 (upd.); 52 (upd.)
Asahi Denka Kogyo KK, 64
Asahi Glass Company, Ltd., III; 48 (upd.)

Asahi National Broadcasting Company, Ltd., 9
ASICS Corporation, 57
Bandai Co., Ltd., 55
Bank of Tokyo-Mitsubishi Ltd., II; 15 (upd.)
Bridgestone Corporation, V; 21 (upd.); 59 (upd.)
Brother Industries, Ltd., 14
C. Itoh & Company Ltd., I
Canon Inc., III; 18 (upd.)
CASIO Computer Co., Ltd., III; 16 (upd.); 40 (upd.)
Central Japan Railway Company, 43
Chubu Electric Power Company, Inc., V; 46 (upd.)
Chugai Pharmaceutical Co., Ltd., 50
Chugoku Electric Power Company Inc., V; 53 (upd.)
Citizen Watch Co., Ltd., III; 21 (upd.)
Clarion Company Ltd., 64
Cosmo Oil Co., Ltd., IV; 53 (upd.)
Dai Nippon Printing Co., Ltd., IV; 57 (upd.)
Dai-Ichi Kangyo Bank Ltd., The, II
Daido Steel Co., Ltd., IV
Daiei, Inc., The, V; 17 (upd.); 41 (upd.)
Daihatsu Motor Company, Ltd., 7; 21 (upd.)
Daikin Industries, Ltd., III
Daimaru, Inc., The, V; 42 (upd.)
Daio Paper Corporation, IV
Daishowa Paper Manufacturing Co., Ltd., IV; 57 (upd.)
Daiwa Bank, Ltd., The, II; 39 (upd.)
Daiwa Securities Group Inc., II; 55 (upd.)
DDI Corporation, 7
DENSO Corporation, 46 (upd.)
Dentsu Inc., I; 16 (upd.); 40 (upd.)
East Japan Railway Company, V; 66 (upd.)
Fanuc Ltd., III; 17 (upd.)
Fuji Bank, Ltd., The, II
Fuji Electric Co., Ltd., II; 48 (upd.)
Fuji Photo Film Co., Ltd., III; 18 (upd.)
Fujisawa Pharmaceutical Company, Ltd., I; 58 (upd.)
Fujitsu Limited, III; 16 (upd.); 42 (upd.)
Funai Electric Company Ltd., 62
Furukawa Electric Co., Ltd., The, III
General Sekiyu K.K., IV
Hakuhodo, Inc., 6; 42 (upd.)
Hankyu Department Stores, Inc., V; 23 (upd.); 62 (upd.)
Hino Motors, Ltd., 7; 21 (upd.)
Hitachi, Ltd., I; 12 (upd.); 40 (upd.)
Hitachi Metals, Ltd., IV
Hitachi Zosen Corporation, III; 53 (upd.)
Hokkaido Electric Power Company Inc. (HEPCO), V; 58 (upd.)
Hokuriku Electric Power Company, V
Honda Motor Company Limited, I; 10 (upd.); 29 (upd.)
Honshu Paper Co., Ltd., IV
Hoshino Gakki Co. Ltd., 55
Idemitsu Kosan Co., Ltd., IV; 49 (upd.)
Industrial Bank of Japan, Ltd., The, II
Isetan Company Limited, V; 36 (upd.)
Ishikawajima-Harima Heavy Industries Co., Ltd., III
Isuzu Motors, Ltd., 9; 23 (upd.); 57 (upd.)
Ito-Yokado Co., Ltd., V; 42 (upd.)
ITOCHU Corporation, 32 (upd.)
Itoham Foods Inc., II; 61 (upd.)
Japan Airlines Company, Ltd., I; 32 (upd.)
Japan Broadcasting Corporation, 7
Japan Leasing Corporation, 8

Japan Pulp and Paper Company Limited, IV
Japan Tobacco Inc., V; 46 (upd.)
Jujo Paper Co., Ltd., IV
JUSCO Co., Ltd., V
Kajima Corporation, I; 51 (upd.)
Kanebo, Ltd., 53
Kanematsu Corporation, IV; 24 (upd.)
Kansai Electric Power Company, Inc., The, V; 62 (upd.)
Kao Corporation, III; 20 (upd.)
Kawasaki Heavy Industries, Ltd., III; 63 (upd.)
Kawasaki Kisen Kaisha, Ltd., V; 56 (upd.)
Kawasaki Steel Corporation, IV
Keio Teito Electric Railway Company, V
Kenwood Corporation, 31
Kewpie Kabushiki Kaisha, 57
Kikkoman Corporation, 14; 47 (upd.)
Kinki Nippon Railway Company Ltd., V
Kirin Brewery Company, Limited, I; 21 (upd.); 63 (upd.)
Kobe Steel, Ltd., IV; 19 (upd.)
Kodansha Ltd., IV; 38 (upd.)
Komatsu Ltd., III; 16 (upd.); 52 (upd.)
Konica Corporation, III; 30 (upd.)
Kotobukiya Co., Ltd., V; 56 (upd.)
Kubota Corporation, III; 26 (upd.)
Kumagai Gumi Company, Ltd., I
Kyocera Corporation, II; 21 (upd.)
Kyowa Hakko Kogyo Co., Ltd., III; 48 (upd.)
Kyushu Electric Power Company Inc., V
Lion Corporation, III; 51 (upd.)
Long-Term Credit Bank of Japan, Ltd., II
Makita Corporation, 22; 59 (upd.)
Marubeni Corporation, I; 24 (upd.)
Marui Company Ltd., V; 62 (upd.)
Maruzen Co., Limited, 18
Matsushita Electric Industrial Co., Ltd., II; 64 (upd.)
Matsushita Electric Works, Ltd., III; 7 (upd.)
Matsuzakaya Company Ltd., V; 64 (upd.)
Mazda Motor Corporation, 9; 23 (upd.); 63 (upd.)
Meiji Milk Products Company, Limited, II
Meiji Mutual Life Insurance Company, The, III
Meiji Seika Kaisha Ltd., II; 64 (upd.)
Millea Holdings Inc., 64 (upd.)
Minolta Co., Ltd., III; 18 (upd.); 43 (upd.)
Mitsubishi Bank, Ltd., The, II
Mitsubishi Chemical Corporation, I; 56 (upd.)
Mitsubishi Corporation, I; 12 (upd.)
Mitsubishi Electric Corporation, II; 44 (upd.)
Mitsubishi Estate Company, Limited, IV; 61 (upd.)
Mitsubishi Heavy Industries, Ltd., III; 7 (upd.); 40 (upd.)
Mitsubishi Materials Corporation, III
Mitsubishi Motors Corporation, 9; 23 (upd.); 57 (upd.)
Mitsubishi Oil Co., Ltd., IV
Mitsubishi Rayon Co., Ltd., V
Mitsubishi Trust & Banking Corporation, The, II
Mitsui & Co., Ltd., 28 (upd.)
Mitsui Bank, Ltd., The, II
Mitsui Bussan K.K., I
Mitsui Marine and Fire Insurance Company, Limited, III
Mitsui Mining & Smelting Co., Ltd., IV
Mitsui Mining Company, Limited, IV

Mitsui Mutual Life Insurance Company, III; 39 (upd.)
Mitsui O.S.K. Lines, Ltd., V
Mitsui Petrochemical Industries, Ltd., 9
Mitsui Real Estate Development Co., Ltd., IV
Mitsui Trust & Banking Company, Ltd., The, II
Mitsukoshi Ltd., V; 56 (upd.)
Mizuho Financial Group Inc., 58 (upd.)
Mizuno Corporation, 25
Morinaga & Co. Ltd., 61
Nagasakiya Co., Ltd., V
Nagase & Co., Ltd., 8; 61 (upd.)
NEC Corporation, II; 21 (upd.); 57 (upd.)
NGK Insulators Ltd., 67
NHK Spring Co., Ltd., III
Nichii Co., Ltd., V
Nichimen Corporation, IV; 24 (upd.)
Nidec Corporation, 59
Nihon Keizai Shimbun, Inc., IV
Nikko Securities Company Limited, The, II; 9 (upd.)
Nikon Corporation, III; 48 (upd.)
Nintendo Co., Ltd., III; 7 (upd.); 28 (upd.); 67 (upd.)
Nippon Credit Bank, II
Nippon Express Company, Ltd., V; 64 (upd.)
Nippon Life Insurance Company, III, 60 (upd.)
Nippon Light Metal Company, Ltd., IV
Nippon Meat Packers, Inc., II
Nippon Oil Corporation, IV; 63 (upd.)
Nippon Seiko K.K., III
Nippon Sheet Glass Company, Limited, III
Nippon Shinpan Co., Ltd., II; 61 (upd.)
Nippon Steel Corporation, IV; 17 (upd.)
Nippon Suisan Kaisha, Limited, II
Nippon Telegraph and Telephone Corporation, V; 51 (upd.)
Nippon Yusen Kabushiki Kaisha, V
Nippondenso Co., Ltd., III
Nissan Motor Company Ltd., I; 11 (upd.); 34 (upd.)
Nisshin Seifun Group Inc., II; 66 (upd.)
Nisshin Steel Co., Ltd., IV
Nissho Iwai K.K., I
NKK Corporation, IV; 28 (upd.)
Nomura Securities Company, Limited, II; 9 (upd.)
Norinchukin Bank, II
NTN Corporation, III; 47 (upd.)
Odakyu Electric Railway Company Limited, V
Ohbayashi Corporation, I
Oji Paper Co., Ltd., IV; 57 (upd.)
Oki Electric Industry Company, Limited, II
Okura & Co., Ltd., IV
Omron Corporation, II; 28 (upd.)
Onoda Cement Co., Ltd., III
ORIX Corporation, II; 44 (upd.)
Osaka Gas Company, Ltd., V; 60 (upd.)
Pioneer Electronic Corporation, III; 28 (upd.)
Rengo Co., Ltd., IV
Ricoh Company, Ltd., III; 36 (upd.)
Roland Corporation, 38
Sankyo Company, Ltd., I; 56 (upd.)
Sanrio Company, Ltd., 38
Sanwa Bank, Ltd., The, II; 15 (upd.)
SANYO Electric Company, Ltd., II; 36 (upd.)
Sanyo-Kokusaku Pulp Co., Ltd., IV
Sapporo Breweries, Ltd., I; 13 (upd.); 36 (upd.)

Seibu Department Stores, Ltd., V; 42 (upd.)
Seibu Railway Co. Ltd., V
Seiko Corporation, III; 17 (upd.)
Seino Transportation Company, Ltd., 6
Seiyu, Ltd., The, V; 36 (upd.)
Sekisui Chemical Co., Ltd., III
Sharp Corporation, II; 12 (upd.); 40 (upd.)
Shikoku Electric Power Company, Inc., V; 60 (upd.)
Shimano Inc., 64
Shionogi & Co., Ltd., III; 17 (upd.)
Shiseido Company, Limited, III; 22 (upd.)
Showa Shell Sekiyu K.K., IV; 59 (upd.)
Snow Brand Milk Products Company, Ltd., II; 48 (upd.)
Softbank Corp., 13; 38 (upd.)
Sony Corporation, II; 12 (upd.); 40 (upd.)
Sumitomo Bank, Limited, The, II; 26 (upd.)
Sumitomo Chemical Company Ltd., I
Sumitomo Corporation, I; 11 (upd.)
Sumitomo Electric Industries, Ltd., II
Sumitomo Heavy Industries, Ltd., III; 42 (upd.)
Sumitomo Life Insurance Company, III; 60 (upd.)
Sumitomo Marine and Fire Insurance Company, Limited, The, III
Sumitomo Metal Industries, Ltd., IV
Sumitomo Metal Mining Co., Ltd., IV
Sumitomo Mitsui Banking Corporation, 51 (upd.)
Sumitomo Realty & Development Co., Ltd., IV
Sumitomo Rubber Industries, Ltd., V
Sumitomo Trust & Banking Company, Ltd., The, II; 53 (upd.)
Suntory Ltd., 65
Suzuki Motor Corporation, 9; 23 (upd.); 59 (upd.)
Taiheiyo Cement Corporation, 60 (upd.)
Taiyo Fishery Company, Limited, II
Taiyo Kobe Bank, Ltd., The, II
Takara Holdings Inc., 62
Takashimaya Company, Limited, V; 47 (upd.)
Takeda Chemical Industries, Ltd., I; 46 (upd.)
TDK Corporation, II; 17 (upd.); 49 (upd.)
Teijin Limited, V; 61 (upd.)
Terumo Corporation, 48
Tobu Railway Co Ltd, 6
Toho Co., Ltd., 28
Tohoku Electric Power Company, Inc., V
Tokai Bank, Limited, The, II; 15 (upd.)
Tokio Marine and Fire Insurance Co., Ltd., The, III
Tokyo Electric Power Company, Incorporated, The, V
Tokyo Gas Co., Ltd., V; 55 (upd.)
Tokyu Corporation, V; 47 (upd.)
Tokyu Department Store Co., Ltd., V; 32 (upd.)
Tokyu Land Corporation, IV
Tomen Corporation, IV; 24 (upd.)
Tomy Company Ltd., 65
TonenGeneral Sekiyu K.K., IV; 16 (upd.); 54 (upd.)
Toppan Printing Co., Ltd., IV; 58 (upd.)
Toray Industries, Inc., V; 51 (upd.)
Toshiba Corporation, I; 12 (upd.); 40 (upd.)
TOTO LTD., III; 28 (upd.)
Toyo Sash Co., Ltd., III
Toyo Seikan Kaisha, Ltd., I
Toyoda Automatic Loom Works, Ltd., III

Toyota Motor Corporation, I; 11 (upd.); 38 (upd.)
Ube Industries, Ltd., III; 38 (upd.)
Unitika Ltd., V; 53 (upd.)
Uny Co., Ltd., V; 49 (upd.)
Victor Company of Japan, Limited, II; 26 (upd.)
Wacoal Corp., 25
Yamaha Corporation, III; 16 (upd.); 40 (upd.)
Yamaichi Securities Company, Limited, II
Yamato Transport Co. Ltd., V; 49 (upd.)
Yamazaki Baking Co., Ltd., 58
Yasuda Fire and Marine Insurance Company, Limited, The, III
Yasuda Mutual Life Insurance Company, The, III; 39 (upd.)
Yasuda Trust and Banking Company, Ltd., The, II; 17 (upd.)
Yokohama Rubber Co., Ltd., The, V; 19 (upd.)

Kuwait

Kuwait Petroleum Corporation, IV; 55 (upd.)

Libya

National Oil Corporation, IV; 66 (upd.)

Liechtenstein

Hilti AG, 53

Luxembourg

ARBED S.A., IV; 22 (upd.)
Cargolux Airlines International S.A., 49
Gemplus International S.A., 64
RTL Group SA, 44
Société Luxembourgeoise de Navigation Aérienne S.A., 64
Tenaris SA, 63

Malaysia

Berjaya Group Bhd., 67
Genting Bhd., 65
Malaysian Airlines System Berhad, 6; 29 (upd.)
Perusahaan Otomobil Nasional Bhd., 62
Petroliam Nasional Bhd (Petronas), IV; 56 (upd.)
PPB Group Berhad, 57
Sime Darby Berhad, 14; 36 (upd.)

Mauritius

Air Mauritius Ltd., 63

Mexico

Alfa, S.A. de C.V., 19
Altos Hornos de México, S.A. de C.V., 42
Apasco S.A. de C.V., 51
Bufete Industrial, S.A. de C.V., 34
Casa Cuervo, S.A. de C.V., 31
Celanese Mexicana, S.A. de C.V., 54
CEMEX S.A. de C.V., 20; 59 (upd.)
Cifra, S.A. de C.V., 12
Consorcio G Grupo Dina, S.A. de C.V., 36
Controladora Comercial Mexicana, S.A. de C.V., 36
Corporación Internacional de Aviación, S.A. de C.V. (Cintra), 20
Desc, S.A. de C.V., 23
Editorial Televisa, S.A. de C.V., 57
Empresas ICA Sociedad Controladora, S.A. de C.V., 41
Ford Motor Company, S.A. de C.V., 20

Mexico (*continued*)

Gruma, S.A. de C.V., 31
Grupo Aeropuerto del Sureste, S.A. de C.V., 48
Grupo Carso, S.A. de C.V., 21
Grupo Casa Saba, S.A. de C.V., 39
Grupo Cydsa, S.A. de C.V., 39
Grupo Elektra, S.A. de C.V., 39
Grupo Financiero Banamex S.A., 54
Grupo Financiero Banorte, S.A. de C.V., 51
Grupo Financiero BBVA Bancomer S.A., 54
Grupo Financiero Serfin, S.A., 19
Grupo Gigante, S.A. de C.V., 34
Grupo Herdez, S.A. de C.V., 35
Grupo IMSA, S.A. de C.V., 44
Grupo Industrial Bimbo, 19
Grupo Industrial Durango, S.A. de C.V., 37
Grupo Industrial Saltillo, S.A. de C.V., 54
Grupo Mexico, S.A. de C.V., 40
Grupo Modelo, S.A. de C.V., 29
Grupo Posadas, S.A. de C.V., 57
Grupo Televisa, S.A., 18; 54 (upd.)
Grupo TMM, S.A. de C.V., 50
Grupo Transportación Ferroviaria Mexicana, S.A. de C.V., 47
Hylsamex, S.A. de C.V., 39
Industrias Bachoco, S.A. de C.V., 39
Industrias Penoles, S.A. de C.V., 22
Internacional de Ceramica, S.A. de C.V., 53
Kimberly-Clark de México, S.A. de C.V., 54
Organización Soriana, S.A. de C.V., 35
Petróleos Mexicanos, IV; 19 (upd.)
Pulsar Internacional S.A., 21
Real Turismo, S.A. de C.V., 50
Sanborn Hermanos, S.A., 20
Sears Roebuck de México, S.A. de C.V., 20
Telefonos de Mexico S.A. de C.V., 14; 63 (upd.)
Tubos de Acero de Mexico, S.A. (TAMSA), 41
TV Azteca, S.A. de C.V., 39
Valores Industriales S.A., 19
Vitro Corporativo S.A. de C.V., 34
Wal-Mart de Mexico, S.A. de C.V., 35 (upd.)

Nepal

Royal Nepal Airline Corporation, 41

Netherlands

ABN AMRO Holding, N.V., 50
AEGON N.V., III; 50 (upd.)
Akzo Nobel N.V., 13; 41 (upd.)
Algemene Bank Nederland N.V., II
Amsterdam-Rotterdam Bank N.V., II
Arcadis NV, 26
ASML Holding N.V., 50
Baan Company, 25
Buhrmann NV, 41
CNH Global N.V., 38 (upd.)
CSM N.V., 65
Deli Universal NV, 66
DSM N.V., I; 56 (upd.)
Elsevier N.V., IV
Endemol Entertainment Holding NV, 46
Equant N.V., 52
European Aeronautic Defence and Space Company EADS N.V., 52 (upd.)
Friesland Coberco Dairy Foods Holding N.V., 59

Getronics NV, 39
Granaria Holdings B.V., 66
Grand Hotel Krasnapolsky N.V., 23
Gucci Group N.V., 50
Hagemeyer N.V., 39
Head N.V., 55
Heijmans N.V., 66
Heineken N.V., I; 13 (upd.); 34 (upd.)
Indigo NV, 26
Ispat International N.V., 30
Koninklijke Ahold N.V. (Royal Ahold), II; 16 (upd.)
Koninklijke Luchtvaart Maatschappij, N.V. (KLM Royal Dutch Airlines), I; 28 (upd.)
Koninklijke Nederlandsche Hoogovens en Staalfabrieken NV, IV
Koninklijke Nedlloyd N.V., 6; 26 (upd.)
Koninklijke Philips Electronics N.V., 50 (upd.)
Koninklijke PTT Nederland NV, V
Koninklijke Vendex KBB N.V. (Royal Vendex KBB N.V.), 62 (upd.)
Koninklijke Wessanen nv, II; 54 (upd.)
KPMG International, 10; 33 (upd.)
Laurus N.V., 65
Mammoet Transport B.V., 26
MIH Limited, 31
N.V. AMEV, III
N.V. Holdingmaatschappij De Telegraaf, 23
N.V. Koninklijke Nederlandse Vliegtuigenfabriek Fokker, I; 28 (upd.)
N.V. Nederlandse Gasunie, V
Nationale-Nederlanden N.V., III
New Holland N.V., 22
Nutreco Holding N.V., 56
Océ N.V., 24
PCM Uitgevers NV, 53
Philips Electronics N.V., II; 13 (upd.)
PolyGram N.V., 23
Prada Holding B.V., 45
Qiagen N.V., 39
Rabobank Group, 33
Randstad Holding n.v., 16; 43 (upd.)
Rodamco N.V., 26
Royal Dutch/Shell Group, IV; 49 (upd.)
Royal Grolsch NV, 54
Royal KPN N.V., 30
Royal Numico N.V., 37
Royal Packaging Industries Van Leer N.V., 30
Royal Vopak NV, 41
SHV Holdings N.V., 55
TNT Post Group N.V., V, 27 (upd.); 30 (upd.)
Toolex International N.V., 26
TPG N.V., 64 (upd.)
Trader Classified Media N.V., 57
Triple P N.V., 26
Unilever N.V., II; 7 (upd.); 32 (upd.)
United Pan-Europe Communications NV, 47
Vebego International BV, 49
Vedior NV, 35
Velcro Industries N.V., 19
Vendex International N.V., 13
VNU N.V., 27
Wegener NV, 53
Wolters Kluwer NV, 14; 33 (upd.)

New Zealand

Air New Zealand Limited, 14; 38 (upd.)
Fletcher Challenge Ltd., IV; 19 (upd.)
Fonterra Co-Operative Group Ltd., 58
Telecom Corporation of New Zealand Limited, 54
Wattie's Ltd., 7

Nigeria

Nigerian National Petroleum Corporation, IV

Norway

Braathens ASA, 47
Den Norse Stats Oljeselskap AS, IV
Helly Hansen ASA, 25
Kvaerner ASA, 36
Norsk Hydro ASA, 10; 35 (upd.)
Norske Skogindustrier ASA, 63
Orkla A/S, 18
Schibsted ASA, 31
Statoil ASA, 61 (upd.)
Stolt Sea Farm Holdings PLC, 54

Oman

Petroleum Development Oman LLC, IV

Pakistan

Pakistan International Airlines Corporation, 46

Panama

Panamerican Beverages, Inc., 47
Willbros Group, Inc., 56

Peru

Southern Peru Copper Corporation, 40

Philippines

Bank of the Philippine Islands, 58
Benguet Corporation, 58
Manila Electric Company (Meralco), 56
Petron Corporation, 58
Philippine Airlines, Inc., 6; 23 (upd.)
San Miguel Corporation, 15; 57 (upd.)

Poland

LOT Polish Airlines (Polskie Linie Lotnicze S.A.), 33
Telekomunikacja Polska SA, 50

Portugal

Banco Comercial Português, SA, 50
Banco Espírito Santo e Comercial de Lisboa S.A., 15
BRISA Auto-estradas de Portugal S.A., 64
Corticeira Amorim, Sociedade Gestora de Participaço es Sociais, S.A., 48
Electricidade de Portugal, S.A., 47
Grupo Portucel Soporcel, 60
Madeira Wine Company, S.A., 49
Petróleos de Portugal S.A., IV
TAP—Air Portugal Transportes Aéreos Portugueses S.A., 46
Transportes Aereos Portugueses, S.A., 6

Puerto Rico

Puerto Rico Electric Power Authority, 47

Qatar

Qatar General Petroleum Corporation, IV

Romania

TAROM S.A., 64

Russia

A.S. Yakovlev Design Bureau, 15
Aeroflot—Russian International Airlines, 6; 29 (upd.)
Alrosa Company Ltd., 62

AO VimpelCom, 48
Aviacionny Nauchno-Tehnicheskii
   Komplex im. A.N. Tupoleva, 24
AVTOVAZ Joint Stock Company, 65
Baltika Brewery Joint Stock Company, 65
Golden Telecom, Inc., 59
JSC MMC Norilsk Nickel, 48
Mobile TeleSystems OJSC, 59
OAO Gazprom, 42
OAO LUKOIL, 40
OAO NK YUKOS, 47
OAO Siberian Oil Company (Sibneft), 49
OAO Surgutneftegaz, 48
OAO Tatneft, 45
OJSC Wimm-Bill-Dann Foods, 48
RAO Unified Energy System of Russia, 45
Rostvertol plc, 62
Sberbank, 62
Severstal Joint Stock Company, 65
Sukhoi Design Bureau Aviation Scientific-
   Industrial Complex, 24

Saudi Arabia

Saudi Arabian Airlines, 6; 27 (upd.)
Saudi Arabian Oil Company, IV; 17 (upd.);
   50 (upd.)
Saudi Basic Industries Corporation
   (SABIC), 58

Scotland

Arnold Clark Automobiles Ltd., 60
Distillers Company PLC, I
General Accident PLC, III
Governor and Company of the Bank of
   Scotland, The, 10
Royal Bank of Scotland Group plc, The,
   12
Scottish & Newcastle plc, 15
Scottish Hydro-Electric PLC, 13
Scottish Media Group plc, 32
ScottishPower plc, 19
Stagecoach Holdings plc, 30
Standard Life Assurance Company, The,
   III

Singapore

Asia Pacific Breweries Limited, 59
Creative Technology Ltd., 57
Flextronics International Ltd., 38
Fraser & Neave Ltd., 54
Neptune Orient Lines Limited, 47
Singapore Airlines Ltd., 6; 27 (upd.)
United Overseas Bank Ltd., 56

South Africa

Anglo American Corporation of South
   Africa Limited, IV; 16 (upd.)
Barlow Rand Ltd., I
De Beers Consolidated Mines Limited/De
   Beers Centenary AG, IV; 7 (upd.); 28
   (upd.)
Edgars Consolidated Stores Ltd., 66
Gencor Ltd., IV; 22 (upd.)
Gold Fields Ltd., IV; 62 (upd.)
Harmony Gold Mining Company Limited,
   63
Highveld Steel and Vanadium Corporation
   Limited, 59
Iscor Limited, 57
Naspers Ltd., 66
SAA (Pty) Ltd., 28
Sappi Limited, 49
Sasol Limited, IV; 47 (upd.)
South African Breweries Limited, The, I;
   24 (upd.)
Transnet Ltd., 6

South Korea

Anam Group, 23
Asiana Airlines, Inc., 46
CJ Corporation, 62
Daewoo Group, III; 18 (upd.); 57 (upd.)
Electronics Co., Ltd., 14
Goldstar Co., Ltd., 12
Hanjin Shipping Co., Ltd., 50
Hanwha Group, 62
Hyundai Group, III; 7 (upd.); 56 (upd.)
Kia Motors Corporation, 12; 29 (upd.)
Kookmin Bank, 58
Korea Electric Power Corporation (Kepco),
   56
Korean Air Lines Co., Ltd., 6; 27 (upd.)
KT&G Corporation, 62
Lucky-Goldstar, II
Pohang Iron and Steel Company Ltd., IV
POSCO, 57 (upd.)
Samick Musical Instruments Co., Ltd., 56
Samsung Electronics Co., Ltd., I; 41 (upd.)
Ssangyong Cement Industrial Co., Ltd., III;
   61 (upd.)
Tong Yang Cement Corporation, 62

Spain

Abertis Infraestructuras, S.A., 65
Banco Bilbao Vizcaya Argentaria S.A., II;
   48 (upd.)
Banco Central, II
Banco do Brasil S.A., II
Banco Santander Central Hispano S.A., 36
   (upd.)
Campofrío Alimentación S.A., 59
Chupa Chups S.A., 38
Compañia Española de Petróleos S.A.
   (Cepsa), IV; 56 (upd.)
Cortefiel S.A., 64
Dogi International Fabrics S.A., 52
El Corte Inglés Group, V; 26 (upd.)
ENDESA S.A., V; 46 (upd.)
Grupo Dragados SA, 55
Grupo Eroski, 64
Grupo Ferrovial, S.A., 40
Grupo Leche Pascual S.A., 59
Grupo Lladró S.A., 52
Iberdrola, S.A., 49
Iberia Líneas Aéreas de España S.A., 6; 36
   (upd.)
Industria de Diseño Textil S.A., 64
Instituto Nacional de Industria, I
Puig Beauty and Fashion Group S.L., 60
Repsol-YPF S.A., IV; 16 (upd.); 40 (upd.)
Tabacalera, S.A., V; 17 (upd.)
Telefónica S.A., V; 46 (upd.)
TelePizza S.A., 33
Television Española, S.A., 7
Terra Lycos, Inc., 43
Unión Fenosa, S.A., 51
Vidrala S.A., 67

Sweden

A. Johnson & Company H.B., I
AB Volvo, I; 7 (upd.); 26 (upd.); 67 (upd.)
Aktiebolaget Electrolux, 22 (upd.)
Aktiebolaget SKF, III; 38 (upd.)
Alfa Laval AB, III; 64 (upd.)
Astra AB, I; 20 (upd.)
Atlas Copco AB, III; 28 (upd.)
Autoliv, Inc., 65
Bonnier AB, 52
BRIO AB, 24
Cardo AB, 53
Electrolux AB, III; 53 (upd.)
Gambro AB, 49
Gunnebo AB, 53

Hennes & Mauritz AB, 29
Holmen AB, 52 (upd.)
ICA AB, II
Investor AB, 63
Mo och Domsjö AB, IV
Modern Times Group AB, 36
NetCom Systems AB, 26
Nobel Industries AB, 9
Nordea AB, 40
Observer AB, 55
Perstorp AB, I; 51 (upd.)
Saab Automobile AB, I; 11 (upd.); 32
   (upd.)
Sandvik AB, IV; 32 (upd.)
SAS Group, The, 34 (upd.)
Scandinavian Airlines System, I
Securitas AB, 42
Skandia Insurance Company, Ltd., 50
Skandinaviska Enskilda Banken AB, II; 56
   (upd.)
Skanska AB, 38
Stora Kopparbergs Bergslags AB, IV
Svenska Cellulosa Aktiebolaget SCA, IV;
   28 (upd.)
Svenska Handelsbanken AB, II; 50 (upd.)
Swedish Match AB, 39 (upd.)
Swedish Telecom, V
Telefonaktiebolaget LM Ericsson, V; 46
   (upd.)
TeliaSonera AB, 57 (upd.)
Vattenfall AB, 57
Vin & Spirit AB, 31

Switzerland

ABB ASEA Brown Boveri Ltd., II; 22
   (upd.)
ABB Ltd., 65 (upd.)
Adecco S.A., 36 (upd.)
Adia S.A., 6
Arthur Andersen & Company, Société
   Coopérative, 10
Ascom AG, 9
Bâloise-Holding, 40
Barry Callebaut AG, 29
Bernina Holding AG, 47
Bodum Design Group AG, 47
Bon Appetit Holding AG, 48
Chocoladefabriken Lindt & Sprüngli AG,
   27
Ciba-Geigy Ltd., I; 8 (upd.)
Compagnie Financiere Richemont AG, 50
Coop Schweiz Genossenschaftsverband, 48
Credit Suisse Group, II; 21 (upd.); 59
   (upd.)
Danzas Group, V; 40 (upd.)
De Beers Consolidated Mines Limited/De
   Beers Centenary AG, IV; 7 (upd.); 28
   (upd.)
Elektrowatt AG, 6
F. Hoffmann-La Roche Ltd., I; 50 (upd.)
Fédération Internationale de Football
   Association, 27
Firmenich International S.A., 60
Geberit AG, 49
Georg Fischer AG Schaffhausen, 61
Givaudan SA, 43
Holderbank Financière Glaris Ltd., III
International Olympic Committee, 44
Jacobs Suchard A.G., II
Julius Baer Holding AG, 52
Keramik Holding AG Laufen, 51
Kraft Jacobs Suchard AG, 26 (upd.)
Kudelski Group SA, 44
Kuehne & Nagel International AG, V; 53
   (upd.)
Kuoni Travel Holding Ltd., 40
Liebherr-International AG, 64

Switzerland (*continued*)

Logitech International SA, 28
Maus Frères SA, 48
Mettler-Toledo International Inc., 30
Montres Rolex S.A., 13; 34 (upd.)
Nestlé S.A., II; 7 (upd.); 28 (upd.)
Novartis AG, 39 (upd.)
Panalpina World Transport (Holding) Ltd., 47
Phoenix Mecano AG, 61
Ricola Ltd., 62
Rieter Holding AG, 42
Roland Murten A.G., 7
Sandoz Ltd., I
Schindler Holding AG, 29
Schweizerische Post-, Telefon- und Telegrafen-Betriebe, V
Serono S.A., 47
STMicroelectronics NV, 52
Sulzer Brothers Limited (Gebruder Sulzer Aktiengesellschaft), III
Swarovski International Holding AG, 40
Swatch Group SA, The, 26
Swedish Match S.A., 12
Swiss Air Transport Company, Ltd., I
Swiss Bank Corporation, II
Swiss Federal Railways (Schweizerische Bundesbahnen), The, V
Swiss International Air Lines Ltd., 48
Swiss Reinsurance Company (Schweizerische Rückversicherungs-Gesellschaft), III; 46 (upd.)
Swisscom AG, 58
TAG Heuer International SA, 25
Tamedia AG, 53
Tetra Pak International SA, 53
UBS AG, 52 (upd.)
Union Bank of Switzerland, II
Victorinox AG, 21
Winterthur Schweizerische Versicherungs-Gesellschaft, III
Zurich Financial Services, 42 (upd.)
Zürich Versicherungs-Gesellschaft, III

Taiwan

Acer Inc., 16
AU Optronics Corporation, 67
BenQ Corporation, 67
China Airlines, 34
Directorate General of Telecommunications, 7
EVA Airways Corporation, 51
Evergreen Marine Corporation (Taiwan) Ltd., 13; 50 (upd.)
First International Computer, Inc., 56
Formosa Plastics Corporation, 14; 58 (upd.)
Hon Hai Precision Industry Co., Ltd., 59
Quanta Computer Inc., 47
Taiwan Semiconductor Manufacturing Company Ltd., 47
Tatung Co., 23
Yageo Corporation, 16

Thailand

Charoen Pokphand Group, 62
Electricity Generating Authority of Thailand (EGAT), 56
PTT Public Company Ltd., 56
Siam Cement Public Company Limited, The, 56
Thai Airways International Public Company Limited, 6; 27 (upd.)
Topaz Group, Inc., The, 62

Tunisia

Société Tunisienne de l'Air-Tunisair, 49

Turkey

Haci Omer Sabanci Holdings A.S., 55
Koç Holding A.S., I; 54 (upd.)
Turkiye Is Bankasi A.S., 61
Türkiye Petrolleri Anonim Ortakliği, IV

Ukraine

Antonov Design Bureau, 53

United Arab Emirates

Abu Dhabi National Oil Company, IV; 45 (upd.)
Emirates Group, The, 39

United Kingdom

Aardman Animations Ltd., 61
Abbey National plc, 10; 39 (upd.)
Aegis Group plc, 6
AG Barr plc, 64
Aggregate Industries plc, 36
Aggreko Plc, 45
Airtours Plc, 27
Albert Fisher Group plc, The, 41
All England Lawn Tennis & Croquet Club, The, 54
Alldays plc, 49
Allders plc, 37
Allied Domecq PLC, 29
Allied-Lyons PLC, I
Alvis Plc, 47
Amersham PLC, 50
Amey Plc, 47
Amnesty International, 50
Amstrad plc, III; 48 (upd.)
AMVESCAP PLC, 65
Anglo American PLC, 50 (upd.)
Anker BV, 53
Antofagasta plc, 65
Arcadia Group plc, 28 (upd.)
Argyll Group PLC, II
Arjo Wiggins Appleton p.l.c., 34
ASDA Group Ltd., II; 28 (upd.); 64 (upd.)
Ashtead Group plc, 34
Associated British Foods plc, II; 13 (upd.); 41 (upd.)
Associated British Ports Holdings Plc, 45
Aston Villa plc, 41
AstraZeneca PLC, 50 (upd.)
AT&T Istel Ltd., 14
Avecia Group PLC, 63
Aviva PLC, 50 (upd.)
BAA plc, 10; 33 (upd.)
Balfour Beatty plc, 36 (upd.)
Barclays plc, II; 20 (upd.); 64 (upd.)
Barings PLC, 14
Barratt Developments plc, I; 56 (upd.)
Bass PLC, I; 15 (upd.); 38 (upd.)
Bat Industries PLC, I; 20 (upd.)
Bellway Plc, 45
Benfield Greig Group plc, 53
Bhs plc, 17
BICC PLC, III
Blacks Leisure Group plc, 39
Blue Circle Industries PLC, III
BOC Group plc, I; 25 (upd.)
Body Shop International plc, The, 11; 53 (upd.)
Bodycote International PLC, 63
Booker plc, 13; 31 (upd.)
Boots Company PLC, The, V; 24 (upd.)
Bowater PLC, IV
Bowthorpe plc, 33

BP p.l.c., 45 (upd.)
Bradford & Bingley PLC, 65
Brake Bros plc, 45
British Aerospace plc, I; 24 (upd.)
British Airways PLC, I; 14 (upd.); 43 (upd.)
British American Tobacco PLC, 50 (upd.)
British Broadcasting Corporation Ltd., 7; 21 (upd.)
British Coal Corporation, IV
British Energy Plc, 49
British Gas plc, V
British Land Plc, 54
British Midland plc, 38
British Nuclear Fuels plc, 6
British Petroleum Company plc, The, IV; 7 (upd.); 21 (upd.)
British Railways Board, V
British Sky Broadcasting Group plc, 20; 60 (upd.)
British Steel plc, IV; 19 (upd.)
British Telecommunications plc, V; 15 (upd.)
British Vita plc, 9; 33 (upd.)
British World Airlines Ltd., 18
British-Borneo Oil & Gas PLC, 34
BT Group plc, 49 (upd.)
BTR PLC, I
BTR Siebe plc, 27
Budgens Ltd., 59
Bunzl plc, IV; 31 (upd.)
Burberry Ltd., 17; 41 (upd.)
Burmah Castrol PLC, IV; 30 (upd.)
Burton Group plc, The, V
Business Post Group plc, 46
C&J Clark International Ltd., 52
C.I. Traders Limited, 61
Cable and Wireless plc, V; 25 (upd.)
Cadbury Schweppes PLC, II; 49 (upd.)
Caffè Nero Group PLC, 63
Canary Wharf Group Plc, 30
Capital Radio plc, 35
Caradon plc, 20 (upd.)
Carbo PLC, 67 (upd.)
Carlton Communications PLC, 15; 50 (upd.)
Cartier Monde, 29
Cattles plc, 58
Central Independent Television, 7; 23 (upd.)
Centrica plc, 29 (upd.)
Chelsfield PLC, 67
Cheltenham & Gloucester PLC, 61
Christian Salvesen Plc, 45
Christie's International plc, 15; 39 (upd.)
Chrysalis Group plc, 40
Chubb, PLC, 50
Clifford Chance LLP, 38
Clinton Cards plc, 39
Close Brothers Group plc, 39
Co-operative Group (CWS) Ltd., 51
Coats plc, V; 44 (upd.)
Cobham plc, 30
COLT Telecom Group plc, 41
Commercial Union PLC, III
Compass Group PLC, 34
Cookson Group plc, III; 44 (upd.)
Corus Group plc, 49 (upd.)
Courtaulds plc, V; 17 (upd.)
Courts plc, 45
Cranswick plc, 40
Croda International Plc, 45
Daily Mail and General Trust plc, 19
Dairy Crest Group plc, 32
Dalgety, PLC, II
Davis Service Group PLC, 45
Dawson Holdings PLC, 43

De La Rue plc, 10; 34 (upd.)
Debenhams Plc, 28
Denby Group plc, 44
Denison International plc, 46
Dennis Publishing Ltd., 62
Devro plc, 55
Diageo plc, 24 (upd.)
Dixons Group plc, V; 19 (upd.); 49 (upd.)
Dorling Kindersley Holdings plc, 20
Dresdner Kleinwort Wasserstein, 60 (upd.)
DS Smith Plc, 61
easyJet Airline Company Limited, 39
ECC Group plc, III
The Economist Group Ltd., 67
Electrocomponents PLC, 50
Elementis plc, 40 (upd.)
EMAP plc, 35
EMI Group plc, 22 (upd.)
Energis plc, 47
English China Clays Ltd., 15 (upd.); 40
   (upd.)
Enterprise Inns plc, 59
Enterprise Oil PLC, 11; 50 (upd.)
Esporta plc, 35
Eurotunnel Group, 13; 37 (upd.)
Exel plc, 51 (upd.)
Fairclough Construction Group PLC, I
Findel plc, 60
First Choice Holidays PLC, 40
Fisons plc, 9; 23 (upd.)
FKI Plc, 57
French Connection Group plc, 41
Fuller Smith & Turner P.L.C., 38
Gallaher Group Plc, 49 (upd.)
Gallaher Limited, V; 19 (upd.)
Gateway Corporation Ltd., The, II
Geest Plc, 38
General Electric Company PLC, II
George Wimpey PLC, 12; 51 (upd.)
GKN plc, III; 38 (upd.)
GlaxoSmithKline plc, I; 9 (upd.); 46 (upd.)
Glotel plc, 53
Go-Ahead Group Plc, The, 28
Granada Group PLC, II; 24 (upd.)
Grand Metropolitan PLC, I; 14 (upd.)
Great Universal Stores plc, The, V; 19
   (upd.)
Greenalls Group PLC, The, 21
Greene King plc, 31
Greggs PLC, 65
Guardian Financial Services, 64 (upd.)
Guardian Media Group plc, 53
Guardian Royal Exchange Plc, 11
Guinness/UDV, I; 43 (upd.)
GUS plc, 47 (upd.)
GWR Group plc, 39
Hammerson plc, 40
Hammerson Property Investment and
   Development Corporation plc, The, IV
Hanson PLC, III; 7 (upd.); 30 (upd.)
Harrisons & Crosfield plc, III
Harrods Holdings, 47
Hartstone Group plc, The, 14
Hawker Siddeley Group Public Limited
   Company, III
Hays Plc, 27
Hazlewood Foods plc, 32
Her Majesty's Stationery Office, 7
Hillsdown Holdings plc, II; 24 (upd.)
Hilton Group plc, 49 (upd.)
HIT Entertainment PLC, 40
HMV Group plc, 59
House of Fraser PLC, 45
HSBC Holdings plc, 12; 26 (upd.)
Huntingdon Life Sciences Group plc, 42
Ibstock Brick Ltd., 14; 37 (upd.)
ICL plc, 6

IMI plc, 9
Imperial Chemical Industries PLC, I; 50
   (upd.)
Imperial Tobacco Group PLC, 50
Inchcape PLC, III; 16 (upd.); 50 (upd.)
Informa Group plc, 58
Inter Link Foods PLC, 61
International Power PLC, 50 (upd.)
Invensys PLC, 50 (upd.)
IPC Magazines Limited, 7
J Sainsbury plc, II; 13 (upd.); 38 (upd.)
James Beattie plc, 43
Jarvis plc, 39
JD Wetherspoon plc, 30
Jersey European Airways (UK) Ltd., 61
JJB Sports plc, 32
John Brown PLC, I
John Laing plc, I; 51 (upd.)
John Lewis Partnership plc, V; 42 (upd.)
John Menzies plc, 39
Johnson Matthey PLC, IV; 16 (upd.); 49
   (upd.)
Johnston Press plc, 35
Kelda Group plc, 45
Kennecott Corporation, 7; 27 (upd.)
Kidde plc, 44 (upd.)
Kingfisher plc, V; 24 (upd.)
Kleinwort Benson Group PLC, II
Kvaerner ASA, 36
Kwik-Fit Holdings plc, 54
Ladbroke Group PLC, II; 21 (upd.)
Lafarge Cement UK, 54 (upd.)
Land Securities PLC, IV; 49 (upd.)
Laura Ashley Holdings plc, 13; 37 (upd.)
Laurel Pub Company Limited, The, 59
Legal & General Group plc, III; 24 (upd.)
Littlewoods plc, V; 42 (upd.)
Lloyd's of London, III; 22 (upd.)
Lloyds TSB Group plc, II; 47 (upd.)
Logica plc, 14; 37 (upd.)
London Regional Transport, 6
London Stock Exchange Limited, 34
Lonmin plc, 66 (upd.)
Lonrho Plc, 21
Lotus Cars Ltd., 14
Lucas Industries PLC, III
Luminar Plc, 40
Macallan Distillers Ltd., The, 63
Madge Networks N.V., 26
Manchester United Football Club plc, 30
Marconi plc, 33 (upd.)
Marks and Spencer p.l.c., V; 24 (upd.)
Marshall Amplification plc, 62
Martin-Baker Aircraft Company Limited,
   61
Matalan PLC, 49
Maxwell Communication Corporation plc,
   IV; 7 (upd.)
McKechnie plc, 34
Meggitt PLC, 34
MEPC plc, IV
Mercury Communications, Ltd., 7
Mersey Docks and Harbour Company, The,
   30
Metal Box PLC, I
Michael Page International plc, 45
Midland Bank PLC, II; 17 (upd.)
Mirror Group Newspapers plc, 7; 23 (upd.)
Misys plc, 45; 46
Mitchells & Butlers PLC, 59
Molins plc, 51
Monsoon plc, 39
Morgan Grenfell Group PLC, II
Moss Bros Group plc, 51
Mothercare UK Ltd., 17
N M Rothschild & Sons Limited, 39
National Express Group PLC, 50

National Power PLC, 12
National Westminster Bank PLC, II
New Look Group plc, 35
Newsquest plc, 32
Next plc, 29
NFC plc, 6
Nichols plc, 44
North West Water Group plc, 11
Northern Foods plc, 10; 61 (upd.)
Northern Rock plc, 33
Norwich & Peterborough Building Society,
   55
Novar plc, 49 (upd.)
NTL Inc., 65
Ocean Group plc, 6
Old Mutual PLC, 61
Ottakar's plc, 64
Pearson plc, IV; 46 (upd.)
Peninsular & Oriental Steam Navigation
   Company (Bovis Division), The, I
Peninsular and Oriental Steam Navigation
   Company, The, V; 38 (upd.)
Pennon Group Plc, 45
Pentland Group plc, 20
PIC International Group PLC, 24 (upd.)
Pilkington plc, III; 34 (upd.)
Plessey Company, PLC, The, II
Post Office Group, V
Powell Duffryn plc, 31
Powergen PLC, 11; 50 (upd.)
Prudential plc, 48 (upd.)
Psion PLC, 45
R. Griggs Group Limited, 23
Racal Electronics PLC, II
Ragdoll Productions Ltd., 51
Railtrack Group PLC, 50
Raleigh UK Ltd., 65
Rank Group plc, The, II; 14 (upd.); 64
   (upd.)
Ranks Hovis McDougall Limited, II; 28
   (upd.)
Really Useful Group, The, 26
Reckitt Benckiser plc, II; 42 (upd.)
Redland plc, III
Redrow Group plc, 31
Reed Elsevier plc, IV; 17 (upd.); 31 (upd.)
Renishaw plc, 46
Rentokil Initial Plc, 47
Reuters Group PLC, IV; 22 (upd.); 63
   (upd.)
Rexam PLC, 32 (upd.)
Rio Tinto PLC, 19 (upd.); 50 (upd.)
RMC Group p.l.c., III; 34 (upd.)
Rolls-Royce Group PLC, 67 (upd.)
Rolls-Royce plc, I; 7 (upd.); 21 (upd.)
Ronson PLC, 49
Rothmans UK Holdings Limited, V; 19
   (upd.)
Rotork plc, 46
Rover Group Ltd., 7; 21 (upd.)
Rowntree Mackintosh, II
Royal & Sun Alliance Insurance Group
   plc, 55
Royal Bank of Scotland Group plc, The,
   38 (upd.)
Royal Doulton plc, 14; 38 (upd.)
Royal Dutch Petroleum Company/ The
   Shell Transport and Trading Company
   p.l.c., IV
Royal Insurance Holdings PLC, III
RTZ Corporation PLC, The, IV
Rugby Group plc, The, 31
Saatchi & Saatchi PLC, I
SABMiller plc, 59 (upd.)
Safeway PLC, 50 (upd.)
Sage Group, The, 43
SBC Warburg, 14

United Kingdom (*continued*)

Schroders plc, 42
Scottish & Newcastle plc, 35 (upd.)
Scottish and Southern Energy plc, 66
  (upd.)
Scottish Power plc, 49 (upd.)
Scottish Radio Holding plc, 41
SDL PLC, 67
Sea Containers Ltd., 29
Sears plc, V
Securicor Plc, 45
Seddon Group Ltd., 67
Selfridges Plc, 34
Serco Group plc, 47
Severn Trent PLC, 12; 38 (upd.)
SFI Group plc, 51
Shanks Group plc, 45
Shepherd Neame Limited, 30
Signet Group PLC, 61
Singer & Friedlander Group plc, 41
Slough Estates PLC, IV; 50 (upd.)
Smith & Nephew plc, 17;41 (upd.)
SmithKline Beecham plc, III; 32 (upd.)
Smiths Industries PLC, 25
Somerfield plc, 47 (upd.)
Southern Electric PLC, 13
Spirax-Sarco Engineering plc, 59
SSL International plc, 49
St Ives plc, 34
Standard Chartered plc, II; 48 (upd.)
Stanley Leisure plc, 66
STC PLC, III
Stirling Group plc, 62
Stoll-Moss Theatres Ltd., 34
Stolt-Nielsen S.A., 42
Storehouse PLC, 16
Strix Ltd., 51
Sun Alliance Group PLC, III
Sytner Group plc, 45
Tarmac plc, III; 28 (upd.)
Tate & Lyle PLC, II; 42 (upd.)
Taylor & Francis Group plc, 44
Taylor Nelson Sofres plc, 34
Taylor Woodrow plc, I; 38 (upd.)
Tesco PLC, II; 24 (upd.)
Thames Water plc, 11
Thistle Hotels PLC, 54
Thorn Emi PLC, I
Thorn plc, 24
Thorntons plc, 46
TI Group plc, 17
Tibbett & Britten Group plc, 32
Tomkins plc, 11; 44 (upd.)
Travis Perkins plc, 34
Trinity Mirror plc, 49 (upd.)
Triumph Motorcycles Ltd., 53
Trusthouse Forte PLC, III
TSB Group plc, 12
Tussauds Group, The, 55
Ultramar PLC, IV
Unigate PLC, II; 28 (upd.)
Unilever PLC, II; 7 (upd.); 32 (upd.)
United Biscuits (Holdings) plc, II; 42
  (upd.)
United Business Media plc, 52 (upd.)
United News & Media plc, IV; 28 (upd.)
United Utilities PLC, 52 (upd.)
Vendôme Luxury Group plc, 27
Vickers plc, 27
Virgin Group, 12; 32 (upd.)
Viridian Group plc, 64
Vodafone Group PLC, 11; 36 (upd.)
Vosper Thornycroft Holding plc, 41
Wassall Plc, 18
Waterford Wedgwood Holdings PLC, 12
Watson Wyatt Worldwide, 42
Weetabix Limited, 61

Wellcome Foundation Ltd., The, I
WH Smith PLC, V, 42 (upd.)
Whatman plc, 46
Whitbread PLC, I; 20 (upd.); 52 (upd.)
Whittard of Chelsea Plc, 61
Wilkinson Sword Ltd., 60
William Grant & Sons Ltd., 60
William Hill Organization Limited, 49
Willis Corroon Group plc, 25
Wilson Bowden Plc, 45
Wincanton plc, 52
Wm. Morrison Supermarkets PLC, 38
Wolseley plc, 64
Wolverhampton & Dudley Breweries, PLC,
  The, 57
Wood Hall Trust PLC, I
Woolwich plc, The, 30
WPP Group plc, 6; 48 (upd.)
WS Atkins Plc, 45
Young & Co.'s Brewery, P.L.C., 38
Yule Catto & Company plc, 54
Zeneca Group PLC, 21
Zomba Records Ltd., 52

United States

A & E Television Networks, 32
A & W Brands, Inc., 25
A-dec, Inc., 53
A. Schulman, Inc., 8; 49 (upd.)
A.B. Watley Group Inc., 45
A.B.Dick Company, 28
A.C. Moore Arts & Crafts, Inc., 30
A.G. Edwards, Inc., 8; 32
A.H. Belo Corporation, 10; 30 (upd.)
A.L. Pharma Inc., 12
A.M. Castle & Co., 25
A.O. Smith Corporation, 11; 40 (upd.)
A.T. Cross Company, 17; 49 (upd.)
AAF-McQuay Incorporated, 26
AAON, Inc., 22
AAR Corp., 28
Aaron Rents, Inc., 14; 35 (upd.)
AARP, 27
Aavid Thermal Technologies, Inc., 29
Abatix Corp., 57
Abbott Laboratories, I; 11 (upd.); 40 (upd.)
ABC Appliance, Inc., 10
ABC Carpet & Home Co. Inc., 26
ABC Family Worldwide, Inc., 52
ABC Rail Products Corporation, 18
ABC Supply Co., Inc., 22
Abercrombie & Fitch Co., 15; 35 (upd.)
Abigail Adams National Bancorp, Inc., 23
Abiomed, Inc., 47
ABM Industries Incorporated, 25 (upd.)
Abrams Industries Inc., 23
Academy of Television Arts & Sciences,
  Inc., 55
Academy Sports & Outdoors, 27
Acadian Ambulance & Air Med Services,
  Inc., 39
Acclaim Entertainment Inc., 24
ACCO World Corporation, 7; 51 (upd.)
ACE Cash Express, Inc., 33
Ace Hardware Corporation, 12; 35 (upd.)
Aceto Corp., 38
Ackerley Communications, Inc., 9
Acme-Cleveland Corp., 13
ACNielsen Corporation, 13; 38 (upd.)
Acorn Products, Inc., 55
Acsys, Inc., 44
Action Performance Companies, Inc., 27
Activision, Inc., 32
Acushnet Company, 64
Acuson Corporation, 10; 36 (upd.)
Acxiom Corporation, 35
Adams Golf, Inc., 37

Adaptec, Inc., 31
ADC Telecommunications, Inc., 10; 30
  (upd.)
Adelphia Communications Corporation, 17;
  52 (upd.)
Administaff, Inc., 52
Adobe Systems Inc., 10; 33 (upd.)
Adolph Coors Company, I; 13 (upd.); 36
  (upd.)
ADT Security Services, Inc., 12; 44 (upd.)
Adtran Inc., 22
Advance Auto Parts, Inc., 57
Advance Publications Inc., IV; 19 (upd.)
Advanced Circuits Inc., 67
Advanced Fibre Communications, Inc., 63
Advanced Marketing Services, Inc., 34
Advanced Micro Devices, Inc., 6; 30 (upd.)
Advanced Technology Laboratories, Inc., 9
Advanstar Communications, Inc., 57
Advanta Corporation, 8; 38 (upd.)
Advantica Restaurant Group, Inc., 27
  (upd.)
Adventist Health, 53
Advo, Inc., 6; 53 (upd.)
Advocat Inc., 46
AEI Music Network Inc., 35
AEP Industries, Inc., 36
Aerojet-General Corp., 63
Aeronca Inc., 46
Aeroquip Corporation, 16
AES Corporation, The, 10; 13 (upd.); 53
  (upd.)
Aetna Inc., III; 21 (upd.); 63 (upd.)
AFC Enterprises, Inc., 32
Affiliated Computer Services, Inc., 61
Affiliated Foods Inc., 53
Affiliated Publications, Inc., 7
Affinity Group Holding Inc., 56
AFLAC Incorporated, 10 (upd.); 38 (upd.)
Africare, 59
After Hours Formalwear Inc., 60
Ag Services of America, Inc., 59
Ag-Chem Equipment Company, Inc., 17
AGCO Corporation, 13; 67 (upd.)
Agere Systems Inc., 61
Agilent Technologies Inc., 38
Agway, Inc., 7; 21 (upd.)
AHL Services, Inc., 27
Air & Water Technologies Corporation, 6
Air Express International Corporation, 13
Air Methods Corporation, 53
Air Products and Chemicals, Inc., I; 10
  (upd.)
Air Wisconsin Airlines Corporation, 55
Airborne Freight Corporation, 6; 34 (upd.)
Airgas, Inc., 54
AirTouch Communications, 11
AirTran Holdings, Inc., 22
AK Steel Holding Corporation, 19; 41
  (upd.)
Akin, Gump, Strauss, Hauer & Feld,
  L.L.P., 33
Akorn, Inc., 32
Alabama Farmers Cooperative, Inc., 63
Alamo Group Inc., 32
Alamo Rent A Car, Inc., 6; 24 (upd.)
ALARIS Medical Systems, Inc., 65
Alaska Air Group, Inc., 6; 29 (upd.)
Alaska Railroad Corporation, 60
Alba-Waldensian, Inc., 30
Albany International Corporation, 8; 51
  (upd.)
Albemarle Corporation, 59
Alberto-Culver Company, 8; 36 (upd.)
Albertson's, Inc., II; 7 (upd.); 30 (upd.); 65
  (upd.)
Alco Health Services Corporation, III

Alco Standard Corporation, I
Alcoa Inc., 56 (upd.)
Aldila Inc., 46
Aldus Corporation, 10
Alex Lee Inc., 18; 44 (upd.)
Alexander & Alexander Services Inc., 10
Alexander & Baldwin, Inc., 10; 40 (upd.)
Alexander's, Inc., 45
Alfa Corporation, 60
Alico, Inc., 63
All American Communications Inc., 20
Alleghany Corporation, 10; 60 (upd.)
Allegheny Energy, Inc., 38 (upd.)
Allegheny Ludlum Corporation, 8
Allegheny Power System, Inc., V
Allen Foods, Inc., 60
Allen Organ Company, 33
Allen Systems Group, Inc., 59
Allen-Edmonds Shoe Corporation, 61
Allergan, Inc., 10; 30 (upd.)
Alliance Capital Management Holding
  L.P., 63
Alliance Entertainment Corp., 17
Alliant Techsystems Inc., 8; 30 (upd.)
Allied Defense Group, Inc., The, 65
Allied Healthcare Products, Inc., 24
Allied Products Corporation, 21
Allied Signal Engines, 9
Allied Waste Industries, Inc., 50
Allied Worldwide, Inc., 49
AlliedSignal Inc., I; 22 (upd.)
Allison Gas Turbine Division, 9
Allmerica Financial Corporation, 63
Allou Health & Beauty Care, Inc., 28
Alloy, Inc., 55
Allstate Corporation, The, 10; 27 (upd.)
ALLTEL Corporation, 6; 46 (upd.)
Alltrista Corporation, 30
Allwaste, Inc., 18
Aloha Airlines, Incorporated, 24
Alpharma Inc., 35 (upd.)
Alpine Lace Brands, Inc., 18
AltaVista Company, 43
Altera Corporation, 18; 43 (upd.)
Alternative Tentacles Records, 66
Alterra Healthcare Corporation, 42
Altiris, Inc., 65
Altron Incorporated, 20
Aluminum Company of America, IV; 20
  (upd.)
Alvin Ailey Dance Foundation, Inc., 52
ALZA Corporation, 10; 36 (upd.)
Amalgamated Bank, 60
AMAX Inc., IV
Amazon.com, Inc., 25; 56 (upd.)
AMB Property Corporation, 57
Ambac Financial Group, Inc., 65
Amblin Entertainment, 21
AMC Entertainment Inc., 12; 35 (upd.)
AMCOL International Corporation, 59
  (upd.)
AMCORE Financial Inc., 44
Amdahl Corporation, III; 14 (upd.); 40
  (upd.)
Amdocs Ltd., 47
Amedysis, Inc., 53
Amerada Hess Corporation, IV; 21 (upd.);
  55 (upd.)
Amerco, 6
AMERCO, 67 (upd.)
Ameren Corporation, 60 (upd.)
America Online, Inc., 10; 26 (upd.)
America West Holdings Corporation, 6; 34
  (upd.)
America's Car-Mart, Inc., 64
America's Favorite Chicken Company,
  Inc., 7

American Airlines, I; 6 (upd.)
American Axle & Manufacturing Holdings,
  Inc., 67
American Banknote Corporation, 30
American Bar Association, 35
American Biltrite Inc., 16; 43 (upd.)
American Brands, Inc., V
American Building Maintenance Industries,
  Inc., 6
American Business Information, Inc., 18
American Business Products, Inc., 20
American Cancer Society, The, 24
American Cast Iron Pipe Company, 50
American Civil Liberties Union (ACLU),
  60
American Classic Voyages Company, 27
American Coin Merchandising, Inc., 28
American Colloid Co., 13
American Crystal Sugar Company, 9; 32
  (upd.)
American Cyanamid, I; 8 (upd.)
American Eagle Outfitters, Inc., 24; 55
  (upd.)
American Electric Power Company, Inc.,
  V; 45 (upd.)
American Express Company, II; 10 (upd.);
  38 (upd.)
American Family Corporation, III
American Financial Group Inc., III; 48
  (upd.)
American Foods Group, 43
American Furniture Company, Inc., 21
American General Corporation, III; 10
  (upd.); 46 (upd.)
American General Finance Corp., 11
American Golf Corporation, 45
American Gramaphone LLC, 52
American Greetings Corporation, 7; 22
  (upd.); 59 (upd.)
American Healthways, Inc., 65
American Home Mortgage Holdings, Inc.,
  46
American Home Products, I; 10 (upd.)
American Homestar Corporation, 18; 41
  (upd.)
American Institute of Certified Public
  Accountants (AICPA), 44
American International Group, Inc., III; 15
  (upd.); 47 (upd.)
American Italian Pasta Company, 27
American Lawyer Media Holdings, Inc., 32
American Locker Group Incorporated, 34
American Lung Association, 48
American Maize-Products Co., 14
American Management Systems, Inc., 11
American Media, Inc., 27
American Medical Association, 39
American Medical International, Inc., III
American Medical Response, Inc., 39
American Motors Corporation, I
American National Insurance Company, 8;
  27 (upd.)
American Pad & Paper Company, 20
American Pop Corn Company, 59
American Power Conversion Corporation,
  24; 67 (upd.)
American Premier Underwriters, Inc., 10
American President Companies Ltd., 6
American Printing House for the Blind, 26
American Re Corporation, 10; 35 (upd.)
American Red Cross, 40
American Residential Mortgage
  Corporation, 8
American Retirement Corporation, 42
American Rice, Inc., 33
American Safety Razor Company, 20
American Skiing Company, 28

American Society of Composers, Authors
  and Publishers (ASCAP), The, 29
American Software Inc., 25
American Standard Companies Inc., III; 30
  (upd.)
American States Water Company, 46
American Stores Company, II; 22 (upd.)
American Technical Ceramics Corp., 67
American Telephone and Telegraph
  Company, V
American Tourister, Inc., 16
American Tower Corporation, 33
American Vanguard Corporation, 47
American Water Works Company, Inc., 6;
  38 (upd.)
American Woodmark Corporation, 31
Amerihost Properties, Inc., 30
AmeriSource Health Corporation, 37 (upd.)
AmerisourceBergen Corporation, 64 (upd.)
Ameristar Casinos, Inc., 33
Ameritech Corporation, V; 18 (upd.)
Ameritrade Holding Corporation, 34
Ameriwood Industries International Corp.,
  17
Amerock Corporation, 53
Ameron International Corporation, 67
Ames Department Stores, Inc., 9; 30 (upd.)
AMETEK, Inc., 9
AMF Bowling, Inc., 40
Amfac/JMD Hawaii L.L.C., I; 24 (upd.)
Amgen, Inc., 10; 30 (upd.)
Amoco Corporation, IV; 14 (upd.)
Amoskeag Company, 8
AMP Incorporated, II; 14 (upd.)
Ampacet Corporation, 67
Ampex Corporation, 17
Amphenol Corporation, 40
AMR Corporation, 28 (upd.); 52 (upd.)
AMREP Corporation, 21
Amscan Holdings, Inc., 61
AmSouth Bancorporation, 12; 48 (upd.)
Amsted Industries Incorporated, 7
AmSurg Corporation, 48
Amtran, Inc., 34
Amway Corporation, III; 13 (upd.); 30
  (upd.)
Amylin Pharmaceuticals, Inc., 67
Anadarko Petroleum Corporation, 10; 52
  (upd.)
Anaheim Angels Baseball Club, Inc., 53
Analog Devices, Inc., 10
Analogic Corporation, 23
Analysts International Corporation, 36
Analytic Sciences Corporation, 10
Analytical Surveys, Inc., 33
Anaren Microwave, Inc., 33
Anchor Bancorp, Inc., 10
Anchor Brewing Company, 47
Anchor Gaming, 24
Anchor Hocking Glassware, 13
Andersen Worldwide, 10; 29 (upd.)
Anderson-DuBose Company, The, 60
Andersons, Inc., The, 31
Andrew Corporation, 10; 32 (upd.)
Andrews McMeel Universal, 40
Andrx Corporation, 55
Angelica Corporation, 15; 43 (upd.)
Anheuser-Busch Companies, Inc., I; 10
  (upd.); 34 (upd.)
Annie's Homegrown, Inc., 59
AnnTaylor Stores Corporation, 13; 37
  (upd.); 67 (upd.)
ANR Pipeline Co., 17
Anschutz Corporation, The, 12; 36 (upd.)
Ansoft Corporation, 63
Anteon Corporation, 57
Anthem Electronics, Inc., 13

United States (*continued*)

Anthony & Sylvan Pools Corporation, 56
Antioch Company, The, 40
AOL Time Warner Inc., 57 (upd.)
Aon Corporation, III; 45 (upd.)
Apache Corporation, 10; 32 (upd.)
Apartment Investment and Management Company, 49
Apex Digital, Inc., 63
APi Group, Inc., 64
APL Limited, 61 (upd.)
Apogee Enterprises, Inc., 8
Apollo Group, Inc., 24
Applause Inc., 24
Apple Bank for Savings, 59
Apple Computer, Inc., III; 6 (upd.); 36 (upd.)
Applebee's International Inc., 14; 35 (upd.)
Appliance Recycling Centers of America, Inc., 42
Applica Incorporated, 43 (upd.)
Applied Bioscience International, Inc., 10
Applied Films Corporation, 48
Applied Materials, Inc., 10; 46 (upd.)
Applied Micro Circuits Corporation, 38
Applied Power, Inc., 9; 32 (upd.)
Aqua Alliance Inc., 32 (upd.)
Aquila, Inc., 50 (upd.)
AR Accessories Group, Inc., 23
ARA Services, II
ARAMARK Corporation, 13; 41 (upd.)
Arandell Corporation, 37
Arbitron Company, The, 38
Arbor Drugs Inc., 12
Arby's Inc., 14
Arch Mineral Corporation, 7
Arch Wireless, Inc., 39
Archer-Daniels-Midland Company, I; 11 (upd.); 32 (upd.)
Archie Comics Publications, Inc., 63
Archstone-Smith Trust, 49
Archway Cookies, Inc., 29
ARCO Chemical Company, 10
Arctco, Inc., 16
Arctic Cat Inc., 40 (upd.)
Arctic Slope Regional Corporation, 38
Arden Group, Inc., 29
Argosy Gaming Company, 21
Ariba, Inc., 57
Ariens Company, 48
Aris Industries, Inc., 16
Aristotle Corporation, The, 62
Ark Restaurants Corp., 20
Arkansas Best Corporation, 16
Arkla, Inc., V
Armco Inc., IV
Armor All Products Corp., 16
Armor Holdings, Inc., 27
Armstrong World Industries, Inc., III; 22 (upd.)
Army and Air Force Exchange Service, 39
Arnold & Porter, 35
Arrow Air Holdings Corporation, 55
Arrow Electronics, Inc., 10; 50 (upd.)
Art Institute of Chicago, The, 29
Art Van Furniture, Inc., 28
Artesyn Technologies Inc., 46 (upd.)
Arthur D. Little, Inc., 35
Arthur Murray International, Inc., 32
Artisan Entertainment Inc., 32 (upd.)
ArvinMeritor, Inc., 8; 54 (upd.)
Asanté Technologies, Inc., 20
ASARCO Incorporated, IV
Asbury Automotive Group Inc., 60
ASC, Inc., 55
Ascend Communications, Inc., 24
Ascential Software Corporation, 59

Ashland Inc., 19; 50 (upd.)
Ashland Oil, Inc., IV
Ashley Furniture Industries, Inc., 35
Ashworth, Inc., 26
ASK Group, Inc., 9
Ask Jeeves, Inc., 65
Aspect Telecommunications Corporation, 22
Aspen Skiing Company, 15
Asplundh Tree Expert Co., 20; 59 (upd.)
Assisted Living Concepts, Inc., 43
Associated Estates Realty Corporation, 25
Associated Grocers, Incorporated, 9; 31 (upd.)
Associated Milk Producers, Inc., 11; 48 (upd.)
Associated Natural Gas Corporation, 11
Associated Press, The, 13; 31 (upd.)
Association of Junior Leagues International Inc., 60
AST Research Inc., 9
Astoria Financial Corporation, 44
Astronics Corporation, 35
ASV, Inc., 34; 66 (upd.)
At Home Corporation, 43
AT&T Bell Laboratories, Inc., 13
AT&T Corporation, 29 (upd.)
AT&T Wireless Services, Inc., 54 (upd.)
Atari Corporation, 9; 23 (upd.); 66 (upd.)
ATC Healthcare Inc., 64
Atchison Casting Corporation, 39
Athletics Investment Group, The, 62
Atkins Nutritionals, Inc., 58
Atlanta Gas Light Company, 6; 23 (upd.)
Atlanta National League Baseball Club, Inc., 43
Atlantic American Corporation, 44
Atlantic Coast Airlines Holdings, Inc., 55
Atlantic Energy, Inc., 6
Atlantic Group, The, 23
Atlantic Premium Brands, Ltd., 57
Atlantic Richfield Company, IV; 31 (upd.)
Atlantic Southeast Airlines, Inc., 47
Atlas Air, Inc., 39
Atlas Van Lines, Inc., 14
Atmel Corporation, 17
Atmos Energy Corporation, 43
Attachmate Corporation, 56
Atwood Mobil Products, 53
Au Bon Pain Co., Inc., 18
Audio King Corporation, 24
Audiovox Corporation, 34
August Schell Brewing Company Inc., 59
Ault Incorporated, 34
Auntie Anne's, Inc., 35
Aurora Casket Company, Inc., 56
Aurora Foods Inc., 32
Austin Company, The, 8
Authentic Fitness Corporation, 20; 51 (upd.)
Auto Value Associates, Inc., 25
Autobytel Inc., 47
Autocam Corporation, 51
Autodesk, Inc., 10
Autologic Information International, Inc., 20
Automatic Data Processing, Inc., III; 9 (upd.); 47 (upd.)
AutoNation, Inc., 50
Autotote Corporation, 20
AutoZone, Inc., 9; 31 (upd.)
Avado Brands, Inc., 31
AvalonBay Communities, Inc., 58
Avco Financial Services Inc., 13
Aveda Corporation, 24
Avedis Zildjian Co., 38

Avery Dennison Corporation, IV; 17 (upd.); 49 (upd.)
Aviation Sales Company, 41
Avid Technology Inc., 38
Avis Rent A Car, Inc., 6; 22 (upd.)
Avnet Inc., 9
Avocent Corporation, 65
Avon Products, Inc., III; 19 (upd.); 46 (upd.)
Avondale Industries, 7; 41 (upd.)
AVX Corporation, 67
Awrey Bakeries, Inc., 56
Aydin Corp., 19
Azcon Corporation, 23
Aztar Corporation, 13
B&G Foods, Inc., 40
B. Dalton Bookseller Inc., 25
B. Manischewitz Company, LLC, The, 31
B.J. Alan Co., Inc., 67
B/E Aerospace, Inc., 30
Babbage's, Inc., 10
Baby Superstore, Inc., 15
Bachman's Inc., 22
Back Bay Restaurant Group, Inc., 20
Back Yard Burgers, Inc., 45
Bad Boy Worldwide Entertainment Group, 58
Badger Meter, Inc., 22
Badger Paper Mills, Inc., 15
Bailey Nurseries, Inc., 57
Bain & Company, 55
Bairnco Corporation, 28
Baker & Hostetler LLP, 40
Baker & McKenzie, 10; 42 (upd.)
Baker & Taylor Corporation, 16; 43 (upd.)
Baker and Botts, L.L.P., 28
Baker Hughes Incorporated, III; 22 (upd.); 57 (upd.)
Balance Bar Company, 32
Balchem Corporation, 42
Baldor Electric Company, 21
Baldwin & Lyons, Inc., 51
Baldwin Piano & Organ Company, 18
Baldwin Technology Company, Inc., 25
Ball Corporation, I; 10 (upd.)
Ballantyne of Omaha, Inc., 27
Ballard Medical Products, 21
Bally Manufacturing Corporation, III
Bally Total Fitness Holding Corp., 25
Baltek Corporation, 34
Baltimore Aircoil Company, Inc., 66
Baltimore Gas and Electric Company, V; 25 (upd.)
Baltimore Orioles L.P., 66
Banana Republic Inc., 25
Bandag, Inc., 19
Banfi Products Corp., 36
Bank of America Corporation, 46 (upd.)
Bank of Boston Corporation, II
Bank of Mississippi, Inc., 14
Bank of New England Corporation, II
Bank of New York Company, Inc., The, II; 46 (upd.)
Bank One Corporation, 10; 36 (upd.)
BankAmerica Corporation, II; 8 (upd.)
Bankers Trust New York Corporation, II
Banknorth Group, Inc., 55
Banner Aerospace, Inc., 14; 37 (upd.)
Banta Corporation, 12; 32 (upd.)
Banyan Systems Inc., 25
BarclaysAmerican Mortgage Corporation, 11
Barnes & Noble, Inc., 10; 30 (upd.)
Barnes Group Inc., 13
Barnett Banks, Inc., 9
Barnett Inc., 28
Barney's, Inc., 28

Barr Laboratories, Inc., 26
Barrett Business Services, Inc., 16
Barton Malow Company, 51
Barton Protective Services Inc., 53
Baseball Club of Seattle, LP, The, 50
Bashas' Inc., 33
Basketball Club of Seattle, LLC, The, 50
Bass Pro Shops, Inc., 42
Bassett Furniture Industries, Inc., 18
Bates Worldwide, Inc., 14; 33 (upd.)
Bath Iron Works, 12; 36 (upd.)
Battelle Memorial Institute, Inc., 10
Battle Mountain Gold Company, 23
Bauerly Companies, 61
Bausch & Lomb Inc., 7; 25 (upd.)
Baxter International Inc., I; 10 (upd.)
Bay State Gas Company, 38
BayBanks, Inc., 12
Bayou Steel Corporation, 31
BBN Corp., 19
BEA Systems, Inc., 36
Bear Creek Corporation, 38
Bear Stearns Companies, Inc., II; 10
   (upd.); 52 (upd.)
Bearings, Inc., 13
Beasley Broadcast Group, Inc., 51
Beatrice Company, II
BeautiControl Cosmetics, Inc., 21
Beazer Homes USA, Inc., 17
bebe stores, inc., 31
Bechtel Group, Inc., I; 24 (upd.)
Beckett Papers, 23
Beckman Coulter, Inc., 22
Beckman Instruments, Inc., 14
Becton, Dickinson & Company, I; 11
   (upd.); 36 (upd.)
Bed Bath & Beyond Inc., 13; 41 (upd.)
Beech Aircraft Corporation, 8
Beech-Nut Nutrition Corporation, 21; 51
   (upd.)
BEI Technologies, Inc., 65
Bekins Company, 15
Bel Fuse, Inc., 53
Belco Oil & Gas Corp., 40
Belden Inc., 19
Belk Stores Services, Inc., V; 19 (upd.)
Bell and Howell Company, 9; 29 (upd.)
Bell Atlantic Corporation, V; 25 (upd.)
Bell Helicopter Textron Inc., 46
Bell Industries, Inc., 47
Bell Sports Corporation, 16; 44 (upd.)
BellSouth Corporation, V; 29 (upd.)
Beloit Corporation, 14
Bemis Company, Inc., 8
Ben & Jerry's Homemade, Inc., 10; 35
   (upd.)
Ben Bridge Jeweler, Inc., 60
Benchmark Capital, 49
Benchmark Electronics, Inc., 40
Bendix Corporation, I
Beneficial Corporation, 8
Benihana, Inc., 18
Benjamin Moore & Co., 13; 38 (upd.)
Benton Oil and Gas Company, 47
Bergdorf Goodman Inc., 52
Bergen Brunswig Corporation, V; 13 (upd.)
Berger Bros Company, 62
Beringer Blass Wine Estates Ltd., 66 (upd.)
Beringer Wine Estates Holdings, Inc., 22
Berkeley Farms, 46
Berkshire Hathaway Inc., III; 18 (upd.); 42
   (upd.)
Berkshire Realty Holdings, L.P., 49
Berlex Laboratories, Inc., 66
Berlitz International, Inc., 13; 39 (upd.)
Bernard C. Harris Publishing Company,
   Inc., 39

Bernard Chaus, Inc., 27
Berry Petroleum Company, 47
Berry Plastics Corporation, 21
Bertucci's Corporation, 16; 64 (upd.)
Best Buy Co., Inc., 9; 23 (upd.); 63 (upd.)
Bestfoods, 22 (upd.)
BET Holdings, Inc., 18
Bethlehem Steel Corporation, IV; 7 (upd.);
   27 (upd.)
Betz Laboratories, Inc., I; 10 (upd.)
Beverly Enterprises, Inc., III; 16 (upd.)
BFGoodrich Company, The, V; 19 (upd.)
BHC Communications, Inc., 26
BIC Corporation, 8; 23 (upd.)
Bicoastal Corporation, II
Big B, Inc., 17
Big Bear Stores Co., 13
Big Dog Holdings, Inc., 45
Big 5 Sporting Goods Corporation, 55
Big Flower Press Holdings, Inc., 21
Big Idea Productions, Inc., 49
Big Lots, Inc., 50
Big O Tires, Inc., 20
Big Rivers Electric Corporation, 11
Big V Supermarkets, Inc., 25
Big Y Foods, Inc., 53
Bill & Melinda Gates Foundation, 41
Bill Blass Ltd., 32
Billing Concepts Corp., 26
Bindley Western Industries, Inc., 9
Bing Group, The, 60
Bingham Dana LLP, 43
Binks Sames Corporation, 21
Binney & Smith Inc., 25
Biogen Inc., 14; 36 (upd.)
Biomet, Inc., 10
Bird Corporation, 19
Birkenstock Footprint Sandals, Inc., 12; 42
   (upd.)
Birmingham Steel Corporation, 13; 40
   (upd.)
BISSELL Inc., 9; 30 (upd.)
BJ Services Company, 25
Black & Decker Corporation, The, III; 20
   (upd.); 67 (upd.)
Black & Veatch LLP, 22
Black Box Corporation, 20
Black Diamond Equipment, Ltd., 62
Black Hills Corporation, 20
Blackfoot Telecommunications Group, 60
Blair Corporation, 25; 31
Blessings Corp., 19
Blimpie International, Inc., 15; 49 (upd.)
Block Drug Company, Inc., 8; 27 (upd.)
Blockbuster Inc., 9; 31 (upd.)
Blodgett Holdings, Inc., 61 (upd.)
Blonder Tongue Laboratories, Inc., 48
Bloomberg L.P., 21
Bloomingdale's Inc., 12
Blount International, Inc., 12; 48 (upd.)
Blue Bell Creameries L.P., 30
Blue Bird Corporation, 35
Blue Cross and Blue Shield Association,
   10
Blue Diamond Growers, 28
Blue Martini Software, Inc., 59
Blue Mountain Arts, Inc., 29
Blue Nile Inc., 61
Blue Rhino Corporation, 56
Bluefly, Inc., 60
Blyth Industries, Inc., 18
BMC Industries, Inc., 17; 59 (upd.)
BMC Software, Inc., 55
Boart Longyear Company, 26
Boatmen's Bancshares Inc., 15
Bob Evans Farms, Inc., 9; 63 (upd.)
Bob's Red Mill Natural Foods, Inc., 63

Bobit Publishing Company, 55
Boca Resorts, Inc., 37
Boeing Company, The, I; 10 (upd.); 32
   (upd.)
Bogen Communications International, Inc.,
   62
Bohemia, Inc., 13
Boise Cascade Corporation, IV; 8 (upd.);
   32 (upd.)
Bollinger Shipyards, Inc., 61
Bombay Company, Inc., The, 10
Bon Marché, Inc., The, 23
Bon Secours Health System, Inc., 24
Bon-Ton Stores, Inc., The, 16; 50 (upd.)
Bonneville International Corporation, 29
Bonneville Power Administration, 50
Book-of-the-Month Club, Inc., 13
Books-A-Million, Inc., 14; 41 (upd.)
Boole & Babbage, Inc., 25
Booth Creek Ski Holdings, Inc., 31
Booz Allen & Hamilton Inc., 10
Borden, Inc., II; 22 (upd.)
Borders Group, Inc., 15; 43 (upd.)
Borg-Warner Automotive, Inc., 14; 32
   (upd.)
Borg-Warner Corporation, III
Borland International, Inc., 9
Boron, LePore & Associates, Inc., 45
Boscov's Department Store, Inc., 31
Bose Corporation, 13; 36 (upd.)
Boston Acoustics, Inc., 22
Boston Beer Company, Inc., The, 18; 50
   (upd.)
Boston Celtics Limited Partnership, 14
Boston Consulting Group, The, 58
Boston Edison Company, 12
Boston Market Corporation, 12; 48 (upd.)
Boston Professional Hockey Association
   Inc., 39
Boston Properties, Inc., 22
Boston Scientific Corporation, 37
Bou-Matic, 62
Bowne & Co., Inc., 23
Boy Scouts of America, The, 34
Boyd Bros. Transportation Inc., 39
Boyd Coffee Company, 53
Boyd Gaming Corporation, 43
Boyds Collection, Ltd., The, 29
Bozell Worldwide Inc., 25
Bozzuto's, Inc., 13
Brach and Brock Confections, Inc., 15
Bradlees Discount Department Store
   Company, 12
BrandPartners Group, Inc., 58
Brannock Device Company, 48
Brass Eagle Inc., 34
Brazos Sportswear, Inc., 23
Bremer Financial Corp., 45
Briazz, Inc., 53
Bridgeport Machines, Inc., 17
Bridgford Foods Corporation, 27
Briggs & Stratton Corporation, 8; 27 (upd.)
Bright Horizons Family Solutions, Inc., 31
Brightpoint, Inc., 18
Brink's Company, The, 58 (upd.)
Brinker International, Inc., 10; 38 (upd.)
Bristol Hotel Company, 23
Bristol-Myers Squibb Company, III; 9
   (upd.); 37 (upd.)
Brite Voice Systems, Inc., 20
Broadcast Music Inc., 23
Broadcom Corporation, 34
Broadmoor Hotel, The, 30
Brobeck, Phleger & Harrison, LLP, 31
Broder Bros. Co., 38
Broderbund Software, Inc., 13; 29 (upd.)
Brooke Group Ltd., 15

United States (*continued*)

Brooklyn Union Gas, 6
Brooks Brothers Inc., 22
Brooks Sports Inc., 32
Brookshire Grocery Company, 16
Brookstone, Inc., 18
Brothers Gourmet Coffees, Inc., 20
Broughton Foods Co., 17
Brown & Brown, Inc., 41
Brown & Haley, 23
Brown & Root, Inc., 13
Brown & Sharpe Manufacturing Co., 23
Brown & Williamson Tobacco
   Corporation, 14; 33 (upd.)
Brown Brothers Harriman & Co., 45
Brown Group, Inc., V; 20 (upd.)
Brown Printing Company, 26
Brown-Forman Corporation, I; 10 (upd.);
   38 (upd.)
Browning-Ferris Industries, Inc., V; 20
   (upd.)
Broyhill Furniture Industries, Inc., 10
Bruce Foods Corporation, 39
Bruegger's Corporation, 63
Bruno's, Inc., 7; 26 (upd.)
Brunswick Corporation, III; 22 (upd.)
Brush Engineered Materials Inc., 67
Brush Wellman Inc., 14
BTG, Inc., 45
Buca, Inc., 38
Buck Consultants, Inc., 55
Buck Knives Inc., 48
Buckeye Technologies, Inc., 42
Buckle, Inc., The, 18
Bucyrus International, Inc., 17
Budd Company, The, 8
Budget Group, Inc., 25
Budget Rent a Car Corporation, 9
Buffalo Wild Wings, Inc., 56
Buffets, Inc., 10; 32 (upd.)
Bugle Boy Industries, Inc., 18
Build-A-Bear Workshop Inc., 62
Building Materials Holding Corporation, 52
Bulley & Andrews, LLC, 55
Bulova Corporation, 13; 41 (upd.)
Bumble Bee Seafoods L.L.C., 64
Bundy Corporation, 17
Bunge Ltd., 62
Burdines, Inc., 60
Bureau of National Affairs, Inc.,The 23
Burger King Corporation, II; 17 (upd.); 56
   (upd.)
Burke Mills, Inc., 66
Burlington Coat Factory Warehouse
   Corporation, 10; 60 (upd.)
Burlington Industries, Inc., V; 17 (upd.)
Burlington Northern Santa Fe Corporation,
   V; 27 (upd.)
Burlington Resources Inc., 10
Burns International Services Corporation,
   13; 41 (upd.)
Burr-Brown Corporation, 19
Burt's Bees, Inc., 58
Burton Snowboards Inc., 22
Bush Boake Allen Inc., 30
Bush Brothers & Company, 45
Bush Industries, Inc., 20
Business Men's Assurance Company of
   America, 14
Butler Manufacturing Company, 12; 62
   (upd.)
Butterick Co., Inc., 23
Buttrey Food & Drug Stores Co., 18
buy.com, Inc., 46
BWAY Corporation, 24
C & S Wholesale Grocers, Inc., 55
C-COR.net Corp., 38

C-Cube Microsystems, Inc., 37
C.F. Martin & Co., Inc., 42
C.H. Heist Corporation, 24
C.H. Robinson Worldwide, Inc., 11; 40
   (upd.)
C.R. Bard, Inc., 9; 65 (upd.)
Cabela's Inc., 26
Cabletron Systems, Inc., 10
Cablevision Electronic Instruments, Inc., 32
Cablevision Systems Corporation, 7; 30
   (upd.)
Cabot Corporation, 8; 29 (upd.)
Cache Incorporated, 30
CACI International Inc., 21
Cadence Design Systems, Inc., 11; 48
   (upd.)
Cadmus Communications Corporation, 23
Cadwalader, Wickersham & Taft, 32
CAE USA Inc., 48
Caere Corporation, 20
Caesars World, Inc., 6
Cagle's, Inc., 20
Cahners Business Information, 43
Calavo Growers, Inc., 47
CalComp Inc., 13
Calcot Ltd., 33
Caldor Inc., 12
California Cedar Products Company, 58
California Pizza Kitchen Inc., 15
California Sports, Inc., 56
California Steel Industries, Inc., 67
Callanan Industries, Inc., 60
Callaway Golf Company, 15; 45 (upd.)
Callon Petroleum Company, 47
Calloway's Nursery, Inc., 51
CalMat Co., 19
Calpine Corporation, 36
Caltex Petroleum Corporation, 19
Calvin Klein, Inc., 22; 55 (upd.)
Cambrex Corporation, 16; 44 (upd.)
Cambridge SoundWorks, Inc., 48
Cambridge Technology Partners, Inc., 36
Camelot Music, Inc., 26
Cameron & Barkley Company, 28
Campbell Scientific, Inc., 51
Campbell Soup Company, II; 7 (upd.); 26
   (upd.)
Campbell-Mithun-Esty, Inc., 16
Campo Electronics, Appliances &
   Computers, Inc., 16
Canandaigua Brands, Inc., 13; 34 (upd.)
Candela Corporation, 48
Candie's, Inc., 31
Candle Corporation, 64
Candlewood Hotel Company, Inc., 41
Cannon Design, 63
Cannon Express, Inc., 53
Cannondale Corporation, 21
Canterbury Park Holding Corporation, 42
Cap Rock Energy Corporation, 46
Capel Incorporated, 45
Capezio/Ballet Makers Inc., 62
Capital Cities/ABC Inc., II
Capital Holding Corporation, III
Capital One Financial Corporation, 52
CapStar Hotel Company, 21
Captain D's, LLC, 59
Car Toys, Inc., 67
Caraustar Industries, Inc., 19; 44 (upd.)
Carbide/Graphite Group, Inc., The, 40
Carborundum Company, 15
Cardinal Health, Inc., 18; 50 (upd.)
Career Education Corporation, 45
Caremark Rx, Inc., 10; 54 (upd.)
Carey International, Inc., 26
Cargill, Incorporated, II; 13 (upd.); 40
   (upd.)

Carhartt, Inc., 30
Caribiner International, Inc., 24
Caribou Coffee Company, Inc., 28
Carlisle Companies Incorporated, 8
Carlson Companies, Inc., 6; 22 (upd.)
Carlson Wagonlit Travel, 55
Carma Laboratories, Inc., 60
CarMax, Inc., 55
Carmichael Lynch Inc., 28
Carmike Cinemas, Inc., 14; 37 (upd.)
Carnation Company, II
Carnegie Corporation of New York, 35
Carnival Corporation, 6; 27 (upd.)
Carolina First Corporation, 31
Carolina Freight Corporation, 6
Carolina Power & Light Company, V; 23
   (upd.)
Carolina Telephone and Telegraph
   Company, 10
Carpenter Technology Corporation, 13
CARQUEST Corporation, 29
Carr-Gottstein Foods Co., 17
CarrAmerica Realty Corporation, 56
Carriage House Companies, Inc., The, 55
Carriage Services, Inc., 37
Carrier Access Corporation, 44
Carrier Corporation, 7
Carroll's Foods, Inc., 46
Carsey-Werner Company, L.L.C., The, 37
Carson Pirie Scott & Company, 15
Carson, Inc., 31
Carter Hawley Hale Stores, Inc., V
Carter Lumber Company, 45
Carter-Wallace, Inc., 8; 38 (upd.)
Carvel Corporation, 35
Cascade Corporation, 65
Cascade General, Inc., 65
Cascade Natural Gas Corporation, 9
Casco Northern Bank, 14
Casey's General Stores, Inc., 19
Cash America International, Inc., 20; 61
   (upd.)
Castle & Cooke, Inc., II; 20 (upd.)
Casual Corner Group, Inc., 43
Casual Male Retail Group, Inc., 52
Caswell-Massey Co. Ltd., 51
Catalina Lighting, Inc., 43 (upd.)
Catalina Marketing Corporation, 18
Catalytica Energy Systems, Inc., 44
Catellus Development Corporation, 24
Caterpillar Inc., III; 15 (upd.); 63 (upd.)
Catherines Stores Corporation, 15
Catholic Order of Foresters, 24
Cato Corporation, 14
Cattleman's, Inc., 20
Cavco Industries, Inc., 65
CB Commercial Real Estate Services
   Group, Inc., 21
CBI Industries, Inc., 7
CBRL Group, Inc., 35 (upd.)
CBS Corporation, II; 6 (upd.); 28 (upd.)
CBS Television Network, 66 (upd.)
CCA Industries, Inc., 53
CCH Inc., 14
CDI Corporation, 6; 54 (upd.)
CDW Computer Centers, Inc., 16; 52
   (upd.)
CEC Entertainment, Inc., 31 (upd.)
Cedar Fair, L.P., 22
Celadon Group Inc., 30
Celanese Corporation, I
Celebrity, Inc., 22
Celestial Seasonings, Inc., 16
Celgene Corporation, 67
Cendant Corporation, 44 (upd.)
Centel Corporation, 6

Centennial Communications Corporation, 39
Centerior Energy Corporation, V
Centex Corporation, 8; 29 (upd.)
Centocor Inc., 14
Central and South West Corporation, V
Central Garden & Pet Company, 23; 58 (upd.)
Central Hudson Gas and Electricity Corporation, 6
Central Maine Power, 6
Central Newspapers, Inc., 10
Central Parking Corporation, 18
Central Soya Company, Inc., 7
Central Sprinkler Corporation, 29
Central Vermont Public Service Corporation, 54
Centuri Corporation, 54
Century Aluminum Company, 52
Century Business Services, Inc., 52
Century Casinos, Inc., 53
Century Communications Corp., 10
Century Telephone Enterprises, Inc., 9; 54 (upd.)
Century Theatres, Inc., 31
Cephalon, Inc., 45
Ceradyne, Inc., 65
Cerner Corporation, 16
CertainTeed Corporation, 35
Certegy, Inc., 63
Cessna Aircraft Company, 8; 27 (upd.)
Chadbourne & Parke, 36
Chadwick's of Boston, Ltd., 29
Chalone Wine Group, Ltd., The, 36
Champion Enterprises, Inc., 17
Champion Industries, Inc., 28
Champion International Corporation, IV; 20 (upd.)
Championship Auto Racing Teams, Inc., 37
Chancellor Beacon Academies, Inc., 53
Chancellor Media Corporation, 24
Chaparral Steel Co., 13
Charles Machine Works, Inc., The, 64
Charles River Laboratories International, Inc., 42
Charles Schwab Corporation, The, 8; 26 (upd.)
Charles Stark Draper Laboratory, Inc., The, 35
Charlotte Russe Holding, Inc., 35
Charming Shoppes, Inc., 8; 38
Chart House Enterprises, Inc., 17
Chart Industries, Inc., 21
Charter Communications, Inc., 33
ChartHouse International Learning Corporation, 49
Chas. Levy Company LLC, 60
Chase Manhattan Corporation, The, II; 13 (upd.)
Chateau Communities, Inc., 37
Chattem, Inc., 17
Chautauqua Airlines, Inc., 38
Checkers Drive-Up Restaurants Inc., 16
Checkpoint Systems, Inc., 39
Cheesecake Factory Inc., The, 17
Chelsea Milling Company, 29
Chemcentral Corporation, 8
Chemed Corporation, 13
Chemfab Corporation, 35
Chemi-Trol Chemical Co., 16
Chemical Banking Corporation, II; 14 (upd.)
Chemical Waste Management, Inc., 9
Cherokee Inc., 18
Cherry Lane Music Publishing Company, Inc., 62

Chesapeake Corporation, 8; 30 (upd.)
Chesapeake Utilities Corporation, 56
Chesebrough-Pond's USA, Inc., 8
ChevronTexaco Corporation, IV; 19 (upd.); 47 (upd.)
Cheyenne Software, Inc., 12
Chi-Chi's Inc., 13; 51 (upd.)
Chiasso Inc., 53
Chiat/Day Inc. Advertising, 11
Chic by H.I.S, Inc., 20
Chicago and North Western Holdings Corporation, 6
Chicago Bears Football Club, Inc., 33
Chicago Board of Trade, 41
Chicago National League Ball Club, Inc., 66
Chick-fil-A Inc., 23
Chicken of the Sea International, 24 (upd.)
Chico's FAS, Inc., 45
Children's Comprehensive Services, Inc., 42
Children's Hospitals and Clinics, Inc., 54
Children's Place Retail Stores, Inc., The, 37
ChildrenFirst, Inc., 59
Childtime Learning Centers, Inc., 34
Chiles Offshore Corporation, 9
Chipotle Mexican Grill, Inc., 67
CHIPS and Technologies, Inc., 9
Chiquita Brands International, Inc., 7; 21 (upd.)
Chiron Corporation, 10; 36 (upd.)
Chisholm-Mingo Group, Inc., 41
Chittenden & Eastman Company, 58
Chock Full o' Nuts Corp., 17
Choice Hotels International Inc., 14
ChoicePoint Inc., 65
Chorus Line Corporation, 30
Chris-Craft Industries, Inc., 9; 31 (upd.)
Christensen Boyles Corporation, 26
Christian Broadcasting Network, Inc., The, 52
Christian Science Publishing Society, The, 55
Christopher & Banks Corporation, 42
Chromcraft Revington, Inc., 15
Chronicle Publishing Company, Inc., The, 23
Chronimed Inc., 26
Chrysler Corporation, I; 11 (upd.)
CHS Inc., 60
CH2M Hill Ltd., 22
Chubb Corporation, The, III; 14 (upd.); 37 (upd.)
Chugach Alaska Corporation, 60
Church & Dwight Co., Inc., 29
Church's Chicken, 66
Churchill Downs Incorporated, 29
Cianbro Corporation, 14
Ciber, Inc., 18
CIENA Corporation, 54
CIGNA Corporation, III; 22 (upd.); 45 (upd.)
Cincinnati Bell, Inc., 6
Cincinnati Financial Corporation, 16; 44 (upd.)
Cincinnati Gas & Electric Company, 6
Cincinnati Milacron Inc., 12
Cincom Systems Inc., 15
Cinnabon Inc., 23
Cintas Corporation, 21; 51 (upd.)
CIPSCO Inc., 6
Circle K Company, The, II; 20 (upd.)
Circon Corporation, 21
Circuit City Stores, Inc., 9; 29 (upd.); 65 (upd.)
Circus Circus Enterprises, Inc., 6

Cirrus Design Corporation, 44
Cirrus Logic, Inc., 11; 48 (upd.)
Cisco Systems, Inc., 11; 34 (upd.)
Citadel Communications Corporation, 35
Citfed Bancorp, Inc., 16
CITGO Petroleum Corporation, IV; 31 (upd.)
Citicorp, II; 9 (upd.)
Citigroup Inc., 30 (upd.); 59 (upd.)
Citizens Financial Group, Inc., 42
Citizens Utilities Company, 7
Citrix Systems, Inc., 44
City Public Service, 6
CKE Restaurants, Inc., 19; 46 (upd.)
Claire's Stores, Inc., 17
CLARCOR Inc., 17; 61 (upd.)
Clark Construction Group, Inc., The, 8
Clark Equipment Company, 8
Classic Vacation Group, Inc., 46
Clayton Homes Incorporated, 13; 54 (upd.)
Clear Channel Communications, Inc., 23
Cleary, Gottlieb, Steen & Hamilton, 35
Cleco Corporation, 37
Cleveland Indians Baseball Company, Inc., 37
Cleveland-Cliffs Inc., 13; 62 (upd.)
Clif Bar Inc., 50
Clorox Company, The, III; 22 (upd.)
Clothestime, Inc., The, 20
ClubCorp, Inc., 33
CML Group, Inc., 10
CMP Media Inc., 26
CMS Energy Corporation, V, 14
CNA Financial Corporation, III; 38 (upd.)
CNET Networks, Inc., 47
CNS, Inc., 20
Coach USA, Inc., 24; 55 (upd.)
Coach, Inc., 10; 45 (upd.)
Coastal Corporation, The, IV, 31 (upd.)
COBE Cardiovascular, Inc., 61
COBE Laboratories, Inc., 13
Coborn's, Inc., 30
Cobra Electronics Corporation, 14
Cobra Golf Inc., 16
Coca Cola Bottling Co. Consolidated, 10
Coca-Cola Company, The, I; 10 (upd.); 32 (upd.); 67 (upd.)
Coca-Cola Enterprises, Inc., 13
Coeur d'Alene Mines Corporation, 20
Cogent Communications Group, Inc., 55
Cogentrix Energy, Inc., 10
Cognizant Technology Solutions Corporation, 59
Coherent, Inc., 31
Cohu, Inc., 32
Coinmach Laundry Corporation, 20
Coinstar, Inc., 44
Cold Spring Granite Company, 16
Cold Spring Granite Company Inc., 67 (upd.)
Coldwater Creek Inc., 21
Cole National Corporation, 13
Coleman Company, Inc., The, 9; 30 (upd.)
Coles Express Inc., 15
Colfax Corporation, 58
Colgate-Palmolive Company, III; 14 (upd.); 35 (upd.)
Collectors Universe, Inc., 48
Collins & Aikman Corporation, 13; 41 (upd.)
Collins Industries, Inc., 33
Colonial Properties Trust, 65
Colonial Williamsburg Foundation, 53
Colorado MEDtech, Inc., 48
Colt Industries Inc., I
Colt's Manufacturing Company, Inc., 12

United States (*continued*)

Columbia Gas System, Inc., The, V; 16 (upd.)
Columbia Sportswear Company, 19; 41 (upd.)
Columbia TriStar Motion Pictures Companies, II; 12 (upd.)
Columbia/HCA Healthcare Corporation, 15
Columbus McKinnon Corporation, 37
Comair Holdings Inc., 13; 34 (upd.)
Comcast Corporation, 7; 24 (upd.)
Comdial Corporation, 21
Comdisco, Inc., 9
Comerica Incorporated, 40
COMFORCE Corporation, 40
Command Security Corporation, 57
Commerce Clearing House, Inc., 7
Commercial Credit Company, 8
Commercial Federal Corporation, 12; 62 (upd.)
Commercial Financial Services, Inc., 26
Commercial Metals Company, 15; 42 (upd.)
Commodore International Ltd., 7
Commonwealth Edison Company, V
Commonwealth Energy System, 14
Commonwealth Telephone Enterprises, Inc., 25
Community Coffee Co. L.L.C., 53
Community Psychiatric Centers, 15
Compaq Computer Corporation, III; 6 (upd.); 26 (upd.)
CompDent Corporation, 22
CompHealth Inc., 25
Complete Business Solutions, Inc., 31
Comprehensive Care Corporation, 15
CompuAdd Computer Corporation, 11
CompuCom Systems, Inc., 10
CompuDyne Corporation, 51
CompUSA, Inc., 10; 35 (upd.)
CompuServe Interactive Services, Inc., 10; 27 (upd.)
Computer Associates International, Inc., 6; 49 (upd.)
Computer Data Systems, Inc., 14
Computer Learning Centers, Inc., 26
Computer Sciences Corporation, 6
Computerland Corp., 13
Computervision Corporation, 10
Compuware Corporation, 10; 30 (upd.); 66 (upd.)
Comsat Corporation, 23
Comshare Inc., 23
Comstock Resources, Inc., 47
Comverse Technology, Inc., 15; 43 (upd.)
ConAgra Foods, Inc., II; 12 (upd.); 42 (upd.)
Conair Corp., 17
Concepts Direct, Inc., 39
Concord Camera Corporation, 41
Concord EFS, Inc., 52
Concord Fabrics, Inc., 16
Condé Nast Publications, Inc., 13; 59 (upd.)
Cone Mills Corporation, 8
Cone Mills LLC, 67 (upd.)
Conexant Systems, Inc., 36
Congoleum Corp., 18
Conn's, Inc., 67
Conn-Selmer, Inc., 55
Connecticut Light and Power Co., 13
Connecticut Mutual Life Insurance Company, III
Connell Company, The, 29
Conner Peripherals, Inc., 6
ConocoPhillips, IV; 16 (upd.); 63 (upd.)
Conrad Industries, Inc., 58

Conseco, Inc., 10; 33 (upd.)
Conso International Corporation, 29
CONSOL Energy Inc., 59
Consolidated Delivery & Logistics, Inc., 24
Consolidated Edison, Inc., V; 45 (upd.)
Consolidated Freightways Corporation, V; 21 (upd.); 48 (upd.)
Consolidated Natural Gas Company, V; 19 (upd.)
Consolidated Papers, Inc., 8; 36 (upd.)
Consolidated Products Inc., 14
Consolidated Rail Corporation, V
Constar International Inc., 64
Consumers Power Co., 14
Consumers Union, 26
Consumers Water Company, 14
Container Store, The, 36
ContiGroup Companies, Inc., 43 (upd.)
Continental Airlines, Inc., I; 21 (upd.); 52 (upd.)
Continental Bank Corporation, II
Continental Cablevision, Inc., 7
Continental Can Co., Inc., 15
Continental Corporation, The, III
Continental General Tire Corp., 23
Continental Grain Company, 10; 13 (upd.)
Continental Group Company, I
Continental Medical Systems, Inc., 10
Continuum Health Partners, Inc., 60
Control Data Corporation, III
Control Data Systems, Inc., 10
Converse Inc., 9; 31 (upd.)
Cooker Restaurant Corporation, 20; 51 (upd.)
Cooper Cameron Corporation, 20 (upd.); 58 (upd.)
Cooper Companies, Inc., The, 39
Cooper Industries, Inc., II; 44 (upd.)
Cooper Tire & Rubber Company, 8; 23 (upd.)
Coopers & Lybrand, 9
Copart Inc., 23
Copley Press, Inc., The, 23
Copps Corporation, The, 32
Corbis Corporation, 31
Corcoran Group, Inc., The, 58
Cordis Corporation, 19; 46 (upd.)
CoreStates Financial Corp, 17
Corinthian Colleges, Inc., 39
Corning Inc., III; 44 (upd.)
Corporate Express, Inc., 22; 47 (upd.)
Corporate Software Inc., 9
Corporation for Public Broadcasting, 14
Correctional Services Corporation, 30
Corrections Corporation of America, 23
Corrpro Companies, Inc., 20
CORT Business Services Corporation, 26
Cosi, Inc., 53
Cosmair, Inc., 8
Cosmetic Center, Inc., The, 22
Cost Plus, Inc., 27
Cost-U-Less, Inc., 51
Costco Wholesale Corporation, V; 43 (upd.)
Cotter & Company, V
Cotton Incorporated, 46
Coty, Inc., 36
Coudert Brothers, 30
Countrywide Credit Industries, Inc., 16
County Seat Stores Inc., 9
Courier Corporation, 41
Cousins Properties Incorporated, 65
Covance Inc., 30
Covanta Energy Corporation, 64 (upd.)
Coventry Health Care, Inc., 59
Covington & Burling, 40
Cowles Media Company, 23

Cox Enterprises, Inc., IV; 22 (upd.); 67 (upd.)
CPC International Inc., II
CPI Corp., 38
CR England, Inc., 63
Cracker Barrel Old Country Store, Inc., 10
Craftmade International, Inc., 44
Crain Communications, Inc., 12; 35 (upd.)
Cramer, Berkowitz & Co., 34
Crane & Co., Inc., 26
Crane Co., 8; 30 (upd.)
Crate and Barrel, 9
Cravath, Swaine & Moore, 43
Cray Research, Inc., III; 16 (upd.)
Creative Artists Agency LLC, 38
Credit Acceptance Corporation, 18
Cree Inc., 53
Crompton Corporation, 9; 36 (upd.)
Croscill, Inc., 42
Crosman Corporation, 62
Crowley Maritime Corporation, 6; 28 (upd.)
Crowley, Milner & Company, 19
Crown Books Corporation, 21
Crown Central Petroleum Corporation, 7
Crown Crafts, Inc., 16
Crown Equipment Corporation, 15
Crown Media Holdings, Inc., 45
Crown Vantage Inc., 29
Crown, Cork & Seal Company, Inc., I; 13; 32 (upd.)
CRSS Inc., 6
Cruise America Inc., 21
CryoLife, Inc., 46
Crystal Brands, Inc., 9
CS First Boston Inc., II
CSK Auto Corporation, 38
CSS Industries, Inc., 35
CSX Corporation, V; 22 (upd.)
CTB International Corporation, 43 (upd.)
CTG, Inc., 11
CTS Corporation, 39
Cubic Corporation, 19
CUC International Inc., 16
Cuisinart Corporation, 24
Culbro Corporation, 15
Cullen/Frost Bankers, Inc., 25
Culligan Water Technologies, Inc., 12; 38 (upd.)
Culp, Inc., 29
Culver Franchising System, Inc., 58
Cumberland Farms, Inc., 17
Cumberland Packing Corporation, 26
Cummins Engine Company, Inc., I; 12 (upd.); 40 (upd.)
Cumulus Media Inc., 37
CUNA Mutual Group, 62
Cunard Line Ltd., 23
CUNO Incorporated, 57
Current, Inc., 37
Curtice-Burns Foods, Inc., 7; 21 (upd.)
Curtiss-Wright Corporation, 10; 35 (upd.)
Curves International, Inc., 54
Custom Chrome, Inc., 16
Cutter & Buck Inc., 27
CVS Corporation, 45 (upd.)
Cybermedia, Inc., 25
Cybex International, Inc., 49
Cygne Designs, Inc., 25
Cygnus Business Media, Inc., 56
Cypress Semiconductor Corporation, 20; 48 (upd.)
Cyprus Amax Minerals Company, 21
Cyprus Minerals Company, 7
Cyrk Inc., 19
Cytec Industries Inc., 27
Czarnikow-Rionda Company, Inc., 32

D&K Wholesale Drug, Inc., 14
D'Agostino Supermarkets Inc., 19
D'Arcy Masius Benton & Bowles, Inc., VI; 32 (upd.)
D.G. Yuengling & Son, Inc., 38
D.R. Horton, Inc., 58
Daffy's Inc., 26
Dain Rauscher Corporation, 35 (upd.)
Dairy Mart Convenience Stores, Inc., 7; 25 (upd.)
Daisy Outdoor Products Inc., 58
Daisytek International Corporation, 18
Daktronics, Inc., 32
Dal-Tile International Inc., 22
Dale Carnegie Training, 28
Dallas Cowboys Football Club, Ltd., 33
Dallas Semiconductor Corporation, 13; 31 (upd.)
Damark International, Inc., 18
Dames & Moore, Inc., 25
Dan River Inc., 35
Dana Corporation, I; 10 (upd.)
Danaher Corporation, 7
Daniel Industries, Inc., 16
Dannon Co., Inc., 14
Danskin, Inc., 12; 62 (upd.)
Darden Restaurants, Inc., 16; 44 (upd.)
Darigold, Inc., 9
Dart Group Corporation, 16
Data Broadcasting Corporation, 31
Data General Corporation, 8
Datapoint Corporation, 11
Datascope Corporation, 39
Datek Online Holdings Corp., 32
Dauphin Deposit Corporation, 14
Dave & Buster's, Inc., 33
Davey Tree Expert Company, The, 11
David and Lucile Packard Foundation, The, 41
David J. Joseph Company, The, 14
David's Bridal, Inc., 33
Davis Polk & Wardwell, 36
DAW Technologies, Inc., 25
Dawn Food Products, Inc., 17
Day & Zimmermann, Inc., 9; 31 (upd.)
Day Runner, Inc., 14; 41 (upd.)
Dayton Hudson Corporation, V; 18 (upd.)
DC Comics Inc., 25
DC Shoes, Inc., 60
DDB Needham Worldwide, 14
Dean & DeLuca, Inc., 36
Dean Foods Company, 7; 21 (upd.)
Dean Witter, Discover & Co., 12
Dearborn Mid-West Conveyor Company, 56
Death Row Records, 27
Deb Shops, Inc., 16
Debevoise & Plimpton, 39
Dechert, 43
Deckers Outdoor Corporation, 22
Decora Industries, Inc., 31
DeCrane Aircraft Holdings Inc., 36
DeepTech International Inc., 21
Deere & Company, III; 21 (upd.); 42 (upd.)
Defiance, Inc., 22
DeKalb Genetics Corporation, 17
Del Laboratories, Inc., 28
Del Monte Foods Company, 7; 23 (upd.)
Del Taco, Inc., 58
Del Webb Corporation, 14
Delaware North Companies Incorporated, 7
dELiA*s Inc., 29
Delicato Vineyards, Inc., 50
Dell, Inc., 9; 31 (upd.); 63 (upd.)
Deloitte Touche Tohmatsu International, 9; 29 (upd.)

DeLorme Publishing Company, Inc., 53
Delphi Automotive Systems Corporation, 45
Delta Air Lines, Inc., I; 6 (upd.); 39 (upd.)
Delta and Pine Land Company, 33; 59
Delta Woodside Industries, Inc., 8; 30 (upd.)
Deltec, Inc., 56
Deltic Timber Corporation, 46
Deluxe Corporation, 7; 22 (upd.)
DEMCO, Inc., 60
DeMoulas / Market Basket Inc., 23
DenAmerica Corporation, 29
Denbury Resources, Inc., 67
Denison International plc, 46
Dentsply International Inc., 10
Denver Nuggets, 51
DEP Corporation, 20
Department 56, Inc., 14; 34 (upd.)
Deposit Guaranty Corporation, 17
DePuy Inc., 30; 37 (upd.)
Deschutes Brewery, Inc., 57
Designer Holdings Ltd., 20
Destec Energy, Inc., 12
Detroit Diesel Corporation, 10
Detroit Edison Company, The, V
Detroit Lions, Inc., The, 55
Detroit Pistons Basketball Company, The, 41
Detroit Tigers Baseball Club, Inc., 46
Deutsch, Inc., 42
Devon Energy Corporation, 61
DeVry Incorporated, 29
Dewey Ballantine LLP, 48
Dex Media, Inc., 65
Dexter Corporation, The, I; 12 (upd.)
DFS Group Ltd., 66
DH Technology, Inc., 18
DHL Worldwide Express, 6; 24 (upd.)
Di Giorgio Corp., 12
Dial Corp., The, 8; 23 (upd.)
Dial-A-Mattress Operating Corporation, 46
Dialogic Corporation, 18
Diamond of California, 64 (upd.)
Diamond Shamrock, Inc., IV
DiamondCluster International, Inc., 51
Dibrell Brothers, Incorporated, 12
dick clark productions, inc., 16
Dick Corporation, 64
Dick's Sporting Goods, Inc., 59
Diebold, Incorporated, 7; 22 (upd.)
Diedrich Coffee, Inc., 40
Dierbergs Markets Inc., 63
Digex, Inc., 46
Digi International Inc., 9
Digital Equipment Corporation, III; 6 (upd.)
Digital River, Inc., 50
Dillard Department Stores, Inc., V; 16 (upd.)
Dillard Paper Company, 11
Dillingham Construction Corporation, I; 44 (upd.)
Dillon Companies Inc., 12
Dime Savings Bank of New York, F.S.B., 9
DIMON Inc., 27
Dionex Corporation, 46
Dippin' Dots, Inc., 56
Direct Focus, Inc., 47
DIRECTV, Inc., 38
Discount Auto Parts, Inc., 18
Discount Drug Mart, Inc., 14
Discovery Communications, Inc., 42
Discovery Partners International, Inc., 58
Dixie Group, Inc., The, 20
Dixon Industries, Inc., 26

Dixon Ticonderoga Company, 12
DMI Furniture, Inc., 46
Do it Best Corporation, 30
Dobson Communications Corporation, 63
Doctor's Associates Inc., 67 (upd.)
Doctors' Company, The, 55
Documentum, Inc., 46
Dolby Laboratories Inc., 20
Dole Food Company, Inc., 9; 31 (upd.)
Dollar Thrifty Automotive Group, Inc., 25
Dollar Tree Stores, Inc., 23; 62 (upd.)
Dominick's Finer Foods, Inc., 56
Dominion Homes, Inc., 19
Dominion Resources, Inc., V; 54 (upd.)
Domino Sugar Corporation, 26
Domino's Pizza, Inc., 7; 21 (upd.)
Domino's, Inc., 63 (upd.)
Don Massey Cadillac, Inc., 37
Donaldson Company, Inc., 16; 49 (upd.)
Donaldson, Lufkin & Jenrette, Inc., 22
Donatos Pizzeria Corporation, 58
Donna Karan International Inc., 15; 56 (upd.)
Donnelly Corporation, 12; 35 (upd.)
Donnkenny, Inc., 17
Donruss Playoff L.P., 66
Dorsey & Whitney LLP, 47
Doskocil Companies, Inc., 12
DoubleClick Inc., 46
Doubletree Corporation, 21
Douglas & Lomason Company, 16
Dover Corporation, III; 28 (upd.)
Dover Downs Entertainment, Inc., 43
Dover Publications Inc., 34
Dow Chemical Company, The, I; 8 (upd.); 50 (upd.)
Dow Jones & Company, Inc., IV; 19 (upd.); 47 (upd.)
Dow Jones Telerate, Inc., 10
DPL Inc., 6
DQE, Inc., 6
Dr Pepper/Seven Up, Inc., 9; 32 (upd.)
Drackett Professional Products, 12
Drake Beam Morin, Inc., 44
DreamWorks SKG, 43
Drees Company, Inc., The, 41
Dress Barn, Inc., The, 24; 55 (upd.)
Dresser Industries, Inc., III
Drew Industries Inc., 28
Drexel Burnham Lambert Incorporated, II
Drexel Heritage Furnishings Inc., 12
Dreyer's Grand Ice Cream, Inc., 17
DRS Technologies, Inc., 58
Drs. Foster & Smith, Inc., 62
Drug Emporium, Inc., 12
Drypers Corporation, 18
DSC Communications Corporation, 12
DTE Energy Company, 20 (upd.)
Duane Reade Holding Corp., 21
Duck Head Apparel Company, Inc., 42
Duckwall-ALCO Stores, Inc., 24
Ducommun Incorporated, 30
Duke Energy Corporation, V; 27 (upd.)
Duke Realty Corporation, 57
Dun & Bradstreet Corporation, The, IV; 19 (upd.); 61 (upd.)
Dun & Bradstreet Software Services Inc., 11
Dunavant Enterprises, Inc., 54
Duncan Toys Company, 55
Dunn-Edwards Corporation, 56
Duplex Products Inc., 17
Duracell International Inc., 9
Durametallic, 21
Duriron Company Inc., 17
Duty Free International, Inc., 11
DVI, Inc., 51

United States *(continued)*

Dycom Industries, Inc., 57
Dyersburg Corporation, 21
Dynatech Corporation, 13
DynCorp, 45
Dynegy Inc., 49 (upd.)
E! Entertainment Television Inc., 17
E*Trade Financial Corporation, 20; 60 (upd.)
E. & J. Gallo Winery, I; 7 (upd.); 28 (upd.)
E.I. du Pont de Nemours & Company, I; 8 (upd.); 26 (upd.)
E.piphany, Inc., 49
E.W. Scripps Company, The, IV; 7 (upd.); 28 (upd.); 66 (upd.)
Eagle Hardware & Garden, Inc., 16
Eagle-Picher Industries, Inc., 8; 23 (upd.)
Earl Scheib, Inc., 32
Earthgrains Company, The, 36
EarthLink, Inc., 36
Easter Seals, Inc., 58
Eastern Airlines, I
Eastern Company, The, 48
Eastern Enterprises, 6
EastGroup Properties, Inc., 67
Eastman Chemical Company, 14; 38 (upd.)
Eastman Kodak Company, III; 7 (upd.); 36 (upd.)
Easton Sports, Inc., 66
Eateries, Inc., 33
Eaton Corporation, I; 10 (upd.); 67 (upd.)
Eaton Vance Corporation, 18
eBay Inc., 32; 67 (upd.)
EBSCO Industries, Inc., 17; 40 (upd.)
ECC International Corp., 42
Echlin Inc., I; 11 (upd.)
EchoStar Communications Corporation, 35
Eckerd Corporation, 9; 32 (upd.)
Ecolab, Inc., I; 13 (upd.); 34 (upd.)
Ecology and Environment, Inc., 39
Eddie Bauer, Inc., 9; 36 (upd.)
Edelbrock Corporation, 37
Edelman, 62
Edge Petroleum Corporation, 67
Edison Brothers Stores, Inc., 9
Edison International, 56 (upd.)
Edison Schools Inc., 37
Edmark Corporation, 14; 41 (upd.)
EDO Corporation, 46
Education Management Corporation, 35
Educational Broadcasting Corporation, 48
Educational Testing Service, 12; 62 (upd.)
Edw. C. Levy Co., 42
Edward D. Jones & Company L.P., 30; 66 (upd.)
Edward J. DeBartolo Corporation, The, 8
Edwards Theatres Circuit, Inc., 31
EG&G Incorporated, 8; 29 (upd.)
Egghead.com, Inc., 9; 31 (upd.)
EGL, Inc., 59
84 Lumber Company, 9; 39 (upd.)
800-JR Cigar, Inc., 27
Eileen Fisher Inc., 61
Einstein/Noah Bagel Corporation, 29
Ekco Group, Inc., 16
El Camino Resources International, Inc., 11
El Chico Restaurants, Inc., 19
El Paso Corporation, 66 (upd.)
El Paso Electric Company, 21
El Paso Natural Gas Company, 12
Elamex, S.A. de C.V., 51
Elano Corporation, 14
Elder-Beerman Stores Corp., The, 10; 63 (upd.)
Electric Lightwave, Inc., 37
Electro Rent Corporation, 58
Electromagnetic Sciences Inc., 21

Electronic Arts Inc., 10
Electronic Data Systems Corporation, III; 28 (upd.)
Electronics for Imaging, Inc., 15; 43 (upd.)
Elektra Entertainment Group, 64
Eli Lilly and Company, I; 11 (upd.); 47 (upd.)
Elizabeth Arden, Inc., 8; 40 (upd.)
Eljer Industries, Inc., 24
ElkCorp, 52
Ellen Tracy, Inc., 55
Ellerbe Becket, 41
Ellett Brothers, Inc., 17
Elmer's Restaurants, Inc., 42
Elsinore Corporation, 48
Elvis Presley Enterprises, Inc., 61
Embers America Restaurants, 30
EMC Corporation, 12; 46 (upd.)
EMCOR Group Inc., 60
Emerson, II; 46 (upd.)
Emerson Radio Corp., 30
Emery Worldwide Airlines, Inc., 6; 25 (upd.)
Emge Packing Co., Inc., 11
Emigrant Savings Bank, 59
Emmis Communications Corporation, 47
Empi, Inc., 26
Empire Blue Cross and Blue Shield, III
Employee Solutions, Inc., 18
ENCAD, Incorporated, 25
Encompass Services Corporation, 33
Encore Computer Corporation, 13
Encyclopaedia Britannica, Inc., 7; 39 (upd.)
Energen Corporation, 21
Energizer Holdings, Inc., 32
Enesco Corporation, 11
Engelhard Corporation, IV; 21 (upd.)
Engineered Support Systems, Inc., 59
Engle Homes, Inc., 46
Engraph, Inc., 12
Ennis Business Forms, Inc., 21
Enquirer/Star Group, Inc., 10
Enrich International, Inc., 33
Enron Corporation, V, 19; 46 (upd.)
ENSCO International Incorporated, 57
Enserch Corporation, V
Entercom Communications Corporation, 58
Entergy Corporation, V; 45 (upd.)
Enterprise Rent-A-Car Company, 6
Entravision Communications Corporation, 41
Envirodyne Industries, Inc., 17
Environmental Industries, Inc., 31
Environmental Systems Research Institute Inc. (ESRI), 62
Enzo Biochem, Inc., 41
Eon Labs, Inc., 67
Epic Systems Corporation, 62
EPIQ Systems, Inc., 56
Equifax Inc., 6; 28 (upd.)
Equitable Life Assurance Society of the United States, III
Equitable Resources, Inc., 6; 54 (upd.)
Equity Marketing, Inc., 26
Equity Office Properties Trust, 54
Equity Residential, 49
Equus Computer Systems, Inc., 49
Erickson Retirement Communities, 57
Erie Indemnity Company, 35
ERLY Industries Inc., 17
Ernie Ball, Inc., 56
Ernst & Young, 9; 29 (upd.)
Escalade, Incorporated, 19
Eskimo Pie Corporation, 21
ESPN, Inc., 56
Esprit de Corp., 8; 29 (upd.)
ESS Technology, Inc., 22

Essef Corporation, 18
Esselte, 64
Esselte Pendaflex Corporation, 11
Essence Communications, Inc., 24
Estée Lauder Companies Inc., The, 9; 30 (upd.)
Esterline Technologies Corp., 15
Eternal Word Television Network, Inc., 57
Ethan Allen Interiors, Inc., 12; 39 (upd.)
Ethicon, Inc., 23
Ethyl Corporation, I; 10 (upd.)
EToys, Inc., 37
Eureka Company, The, 12
Euromarket Designs Inc., 31 (upd.)
Europe Through the Back Door Inc., 65
Evans & Sutherland Computer Corporation, 19
Evans, Inc., 30
Everex Systems, Inc., 16
Evergreen International Aviation, Inc., 53
Everlast Worldwide Inc., 47
Exabyte Corporation, 12; 40 (upd.)
Exar Corp., 14
EXCEL Communications Inc., 18
Excel Technology, Inc., 65
Executive Jet, Inc., 36
Executone Information Systems, Inc., 13
Exelon Corporation, 48 (upd.)
Exide Electronics Group, Inc., 20
Expedia, Inc., 58
Expeditors International of Washington Inc., 17
Experian Information Solutions Inc., 45
Express Scripts Inc., 17; 44 (upd.)
Extended Stay America, Inc., 41
EXX Inc., 65
Exxon Corporation, IV; 7 (upd.); 32 (upd.)
Exxon Mobil Corporation, 67 (upd.)
EZCORP Inc., 43
E-Systems, Inc., 9
E-Z Serve Corporation, 17
Fab Industries, Inc., 27
Fabri-Centers of America Inc., 16
Fair Grounds Corporation, 44
Fair, Isaac and Company, 18
Fairchild Aircraft, Inc., 9
Fairfield Communities, Inc., 36
Falcon Products, Inc., 33
Fallon McElligott Inc., 22
Family Christian Stores, Inc., 51
Family Dollar Stores, Inc., 13; 62 (upd.)
Family Golf Centers, Inc., 29
Famous Dave's of America, Inc., 40
Fannie Mae, 45 (upd.)
Fansteel Inc., 19
FAO Schwarz, 46
Farah Incorporated, 24
Farley Northwest Industries, Inc., I
Farley's & Sathers Candy Company, Inc., 62
Farm Family Holdings, Inc., 39
Farm Journal Corporation, 42
Farmer Bros. Co., 52
Farmers Insurance Group of Companies, 25
Farmland Foods, Inc., 7
Farmland Industries, Inc., 48
Farrar, Straus and Giroux Inc., 15
Fastenal Company, 14; 42 (upd.)
Fatburger Corporation, 64
Faultless Starch/Bon Ami Company, 55
Fay's Inc., 17
Faygo Beverages Inc., 55
Fazoli's Systems, Inc., 27
Featherlite Inc., 28
Fedders Corporation, 18; 43 (upd.)
Federal Express Corporation, V
Federal National Mortgage Association, II

Federal Paper Board Company, Inc., 8
Federal Prison Industries, Inc., 34
Federal Signal Corp., 10
Federal-Mogul Corporation, I; 10 (upd.);
   26 (upd.)
Federated Department Stores Inc., 9; 31
   (upd.)
FedEx Corporation, 18 (upd.); 42 (upd.)
Feld Entertainment, Inc., 32 (upd.)
Fellowes Manufacturing Company, 28
Fender Musical Instruments Company, 16;
   43 (upd.)
Fenwick & West LLP, 34
Ferolito, Vultaggio & Sons, 27
Ferrellgas Partners, L.P., 35
Ferro Corporation, 8; 56 (upd.)
FHP International Corporation, 6
FiberMark, Inc., 37
Fibreboard Corporation, 16
Fidelity Investments Inc., II; 14 (upd.)
Fidelity National Financial Inc., 54
Fieldale Farms Corporation, 23
Fieldcrest Cannon, Inc., 9; 31 (upd.)
Fifth Third Bancorp, 13; 31 (upd.)
Figgie International Inc., 7
FileNet Corporation, 62
Film Roman, Inc., 58
FINA, Inc., 7
Fingerhut Companies, Inc., 9; 36 (upd.)
Finish Line, Inc., The, 29
FinishMaster, Inc., 24
Finlay Enterprises, Inc., 16
Firearms Training Systems, Inc., 27
Fireman's Fund Insurance Company, III
First Albany Companies Inc., 37
First Alert, Inc., 28
First American Corporation, The 52
First Aviation Services Inc., 49
First Bank System Inc., 12
First Brands Corporation, 8
First Cash Financial Services, Inc., 57
First Chicago Corporation, II
First Commerce Bancshares, Inc., 15
First Commerce Corporation, 11
First Data Corporation, 30 (upd.)
First Empire State Corporation, 11
First Executive Corporation, III
First Fidelity Bank, N.A., New Jersey, 9
First Financial Management Corporation,
   11
First Hawaiian, Inc., 11
First Industrial Realty Trust, Inc., 65
First Interstate Bancorp, II
First Mississippi Corporation, 8
First Nationwide Bank, 14
First of America Bank Corporation, 8
First Security Corporation, 11
First Team Sports, Inc., 22
First Tennessee National Corporation, 11;
   48 (upd.)
First Union Corporation, 10
First USA, Inc., 11
First Virginia Banks, Inc., 11
First Years Inc., The, 46
Firstar Corporation, 11; 33 (upd.)
Fiserv Inc., 11; 33 (upd.)
Fish & Neave, 54
Fisher Companies, Inc., 15
Fisher Controls International, LLC, 13; 61
   (upd.)
Fisher Scientific International Inc., 24
Fisher-Price Inc., 12; 32 (upd.)
Flagstar Companies, Inc., 10
Flanders Corporation, 65
Flanigan's Enterprises, Inc., 60
Fleer Corporation, 15

FleetBoston Financial Corporation, 9; 36
   (upd.)
Fleetwood Enterprises, Inc., III; 22 (upd.)
Fleming Companies, Inc., II; 17 (upd.)
Flexsteel Industries Inc., 15; 41 (upd.)
FlightSafety International, Inc., 9; 29 (upd.)
Flint Ink Corporation, 13; 41 (upd.)
Florida Crystals Inc., 35
Florida East Coast Industries, Inc., 59
Florida Gaming Corporation, 47
Florida Progress Corporation, V; 23 (upd.)
Florida Rock Industries, Inc., 46
Florida's Natural Growers, 45
Florists' Transworld Delivery, Inc., 28
Florsheim Shoe Group Inc., 9; 31 (upd.)
Flour City International, Inc., 44
Flow International Corporation, 56
Flowers Industries, Inc., 12; 35 (upd.)
Flowserve Corporation, 33
Fluke Corporation, 15
Fluor Corporation, I; 8 (upd.); 34 (upd.)
Flying Boat, Inc. (Chalk's Ocean Airways),
   56
Flying J Inc., 19
FMC Corporation, I; 11 (upd.)
FMR Corp., 8; 32 (upd.)
Foamex International Inc., 17
Foley & Lardner, 28
Follett Corporation, 12; 39 (upd.)
Food Emporium, The, 64
Food Lion LLC, II; 15 (upd.); 66 (upd.)
Foodarama Supermarkets, Inc., 28
FoodBrands America, Inc., 23
Foodmaker, Inc., 14
Foote, Cone & Belding Worldwide, I; 66
   (upd.)
Footstar, Incorporated, 24
Forbes Inc., 30
Ford Foundation, The, 34
Ford Motor Company, I; 11 (upd.); 36
   (upd.); 64 (upd.)
FORE Systems, Inc., 25
Forest City Enterprises, Inc., 16; 52 (upd.)
Forest Laboratories, Inc., 11; 52 (upd.)
Forest Oil Corporation, 19
Forever Living Products International Inc.,
   17
Formica Corporation, 13
Forrester Research, Inc., 54
Forstmann Little & Co., 38
Fort Howard Corporation, 8
Fort James Corporation, 22 (upd.)
Fortune Brands, Inc., 29 (upd.)
Fortunoff Fine Jewelry and Silverware Inc.,
   26
Fossil, Inc., 17
Foster Poultry Farms, 32
Foster Wheeler Corporation, 6; 23 (upd.)
FosterGrant, Inc., 60
Foundation Health Corporation, 12
Fountain Powerboats Industries, Inc., 28
4Kids Entertainment Inc., 59
Fourth Financial Corporation, 11
Fox Entertainment Group, Inc., 43
Fox Family Worldwide, Inc., 24
Foxboro Company, 13
FoxMeyer Health Corporation, 16
FPL Group, Inc., V; 49 (upd.)
Frank J. Zamboni & Co., Inc., 34
Frank Russell Company, 46
Frank's Nursery & Crafts, Inc., 12
Frankel & Co., 39
Franklin Covey Company, 11; 37 (upd.)
Franklin Electric Company, Inc., 43
Franklin Electronic Publishers, Inc., 23
Franklin Resources, Inc., 9

Fred Meyer Stores, Inc., V; 20 (upd.); 64
   (upd.)
Fred Usinger Inc., 54
Fred W. Albrecht Grocery Co., The, 13
Fred Weber, Inc., 61
Fred's, Inc., 23; 62 (upd.)
Freddie Mac, 54
Frederick Atkins Inc., 16
Frederick's of Hollywood, Inc., 16; 59
   (upd.)
Freedom Communications, Inc., 36
Freeport-McMoRan Copper & Gold, Inc.,
   IV; 7 (upd.); 57 (upd.)
French Fragrances, Inc., 22
Frequency Electronics, Inc., 61
Fresh America Corporation, 20
Fresh Choice, Inc., 20
Fresh Enterprises, Inc., 66
Fresh Foods, Inc., 29
Fretter, Inc., 10
Fried, Frank, Harris, Shriver & Jacobson,
   35
Friedman's Inc., 29
Friedman, Billings, Ramsey Group, Inc., 53
Friendly Ice Cream Corp., 30
Frigidaire Home Products, 22
Frisch's Restaurants, Inc., 35
Frito-Lay Company, 32
Fritz Companies, Inc., 12
Frontier Airlines, Inc., 22
Frontier Corp., 16
Frost & Sullivan, Inc., 53
Frozen Food Express Industries, Inc., 20
Fruehauf Corporation, I
Fruit of the Loom, Inc., 8; 25 (upd.)
Fruth Pharmacy, Inc., 66
Frymaster Corporation, 27
FSI International, Inc., 17
FTP Software, Inc., 20
Fubu, 29
Fujitsu-ICL Systems Inc., 11
Fulbright & Jaworski L.L.P., 47
Funco, Inc., 20
Fuqua Enterprises, Inc., 17
Fuqua Industries, Inc., I
Furniture Brands International, Inc., 39
   (upd.)
Furon Company, 28
Furr's Restaurant Group, Inc., 53
Furr's Supermarkets, Inc., 28
Future Now, Inc., 12
G&K Services, Inc., 16
G-III Apparel Group, Ltd., 22
G. Heileman Brewing Company Inc., I
G. Leblanc Corporation, 55
G.A.F., I
G.D. Searle & Company, I; 12 (upd.); 34
   (upd.)
G.I. Joe's, Inc., 30
G.S. Blodgett Corporation, 15
Gabelli Asset Management Inc., 30
Gables Residential Trust, 49
Gadzooks, Inc., 18
GAF Corporation, 22 (upd.)
Gage Marketing Group, 26
Gaiam, Inc., 41
Gainsco, Inc., 22
Galaxy Nutritional Foods, Inc., 58
Galey & Lord, Inc., 20; 66 (upd.)
Gallup Organization, The, 37
Galyan's Trading Company, Inc., 47
Gambrinus Company, The, 40
Gander Mountain, Inc., 20
Gannett Company, Inc., IV; 7 (upd.); 30
   (upd.); 66 (upd.)
Gantos, Inc., 17
Gap, Inc., The, V; 18 (upd.); 55 (upd.)

United States (*continued*)

Garan, Inc., 16; 64 (upd.)
Garden Fresh Restaurant Corporation, 31
Garden Ridge Corporation, 27
Gardenburger, Inc., 33
Gardner Denver, Inc., 49
Gart Sports Company, 24
Gartner Group, Inc., 21
Gates Corporation, The, 9
Gateway, Inc., 10; 27 (upd.); 63 (upd.)
GATX Corporation, 6; 25 (upd.)
Gaylord Container Corporation, 8
Gaylord Entertainment Company, 11; 36
  (upd.)
GC Companies, Inc., 25
GE Aircraft Engines, 9
GE Capital Aviation Services, 36
Geerlings & Wade, Inc., 45
Geffen Records Inc., 26
Gehl Company, 19
GEICO Corporation, 10; 40 (upd.)
Geiger Bros., 60
Gemini Sound Products Corporation, 58
GenCorp Inc., 8; 9
Genentech, Inc., I; 8 (upd.); 32 (upd.)
General Atomics, 57
General Bearing Corporation, 45
General Binding Corporation, 10
General Cable Corporation, 40
General Chemical Group Inc., The, 37
General Cigar Holdings, Inc., 66 (upd.)
General Cinema Corporation, I
General DataComm Industries, Inc., 14
General Dynamics Corporation, I; 10
  (upd.); 40 (upd.)
General Electric Company, II; 12 (upd.);
  34 (upd.); 63 (upd.)
General Growth Properties, Inc., 57
General Host Corporation, 12
General Housewares Corporation, 16
General Instrument Corporation, 10
General Maritime Corporation, 59
General Mills, Inc., II; 10 (upd.); 36 (upd.)
General Motors Corporation, I; 10 (upd.);
  36 (upd.); 64 (upd.)
General Nutrition Companies, Inc., 11; 29
  (upd.)
General Public Utilities Corporation, V
General Re Corporation, III; 24 (upd.)
General Signal Corporation, 9
General Tire, Inc., 8
Genesco Inc., 17
Genesee & Wyoming Inc., 27
Genesis Health Ventures, Inc., 18
Genetics Institute, Inc., 8
Geneva Steel, 7
Genmar Holdings, Inc., 45
Genovese Drug Stores, Inc., 18
GenRad, Inc., 24
Gentex Corporation, 26
Genuardi's Family Markets, Inc., 35
Genuine Parts Company, 9; 45 (upd.)
Genzyme Corporation, 13; 38 (upd.)
Geon Company, The, 11
George A. Hormel and Company, II
George F. Cram Company, Inc., The, 55
George P. Johnson Company, 60
George S. May International Company, 55
Georgia Gulf Corporation, 9; 61 (upd.)
Georgia-Pacific Corporation, IV; 9 (upd.);
  47 (upd.)
Geotek Communications Inc., 21
Gerald Stevens, Inc., 37
Gerber Products Company, 7; 21 (upd.)
Gerber Scientific, Inc., 12
German American Bancorp, 41
Getty Images, Inc., 31

Gevity HR, Inc., 63
Ghirardelli Chocolate Company, 30
Giant Cement Holding, Inc., 23
Giant Food Inc., II; 22 (upd.)
Giant Industries, Inc., 19; 61 (upd.)
Gibraltar Steel Corporation, 37
Gibson Greetings, Inc., 12
Gibson Guitar Corp., 16
Gibson, Dunn & Crutcher LLP, 36
Giddings & Lewis, Inc., 10
Gilbane, Inc., 34
Gilead Sciences, Inc., 54
Gillett Holdings, Inc., 7
Gillette Company, The, III; 20 (upd.)
Girl Scouts of the USA, 35
Gitano Group, Inc., The, 8
Glacier Bancorp, Inc., 35
Glacier Water Services, Inc., 47
Glamis Gold, Ltd., 54
Gleason Corporation, 24
Glidden Company, The, 8
Global Berry Farms LLC, 62
Global Crossing Ltd., 32
Global Industries, Ltd., 37
Global Marine Inc., 9
Global Outdoors, Inc., 49
Global Power Equipment Group Inc., 52
GlobalSantaFe Corporation, 48 (upd.)
GM Hughes Electronics Corporation, II
Godfather's Pizza Incorporated, 25
Godiva Chocolatier, Inc., 64
Gold Kist Inc., 17; 26 (upd.)
Gold'n Plump Poultry, 54
Golden Belt Manufacturing Co., 16
Golden Books Family Entertainment, Inc.,
  28
Golden Corral Corporation, 10; 66 (upd.)
Golden Enterprises, Inc., 26
Golden State Foods Corporation, 32
Golden State Vintners, Inc., 33
Golden West Financial Corporation, 47
Goldman Sachs Group Inc., The, II; 20
  (upd.); 51 (upd.)
Golub Corporation, The, 26
Gonnella Baking Company, 40
Good Guys, Inc., The, 10; 30 (upd.)
Good Humor-Breyers Ice Cream Company,
  14
Goodman Holding Company, 42
GoodMark Foods, Inc., 26
Goodrich Corporation, 46 (upd.)
GoodTimes Entertainment Ltd., 48
Goodwill Industries International, Inc., 16;
  66 (upd.)
Goody Products, Inc., 12
Goody's Family Clothing, Inc., 20; 64
  (upd.)
Goodyear Tire & Rubber Company, The,
  V; 20 (upd.)
Google, Inc., 50
Gordon Food Service Inc., 8; 39 (upd.)
Gorman-Rupp Company, The, 18; 57
  (upd.)
Gorton's, 13
Goss Holdings, Inc., 43
Gottschalks, Inc., 18
Gould Electronics, Inc., 14
Goulds Pumps Inc., 24
Goya Foods Inc., 22
GP Strategies Corporation, 64 (upd.)
GPU, Inc., 27 (upd.)
Graco Inc., 19; 67 (upd.)
Graham Corporation, 62
GranCare, Inc., 14
Grand Casinos, Inc., 20
Grand Union Company, The, 7; 28 (upd.)
Granite Broadcasting Corporation, 42

Granite Construction Incorporated, 61
Granite Rock Company, 26
Granite State Bankshares, Inc., 37
Grant Prideco, Inc., 57
Grant Thornton International, 57
Graphic Industries Inc., 25
Gray Communications Systems, Inc., 24
Graybar Electric Company, Inc., 54
Great American Management and
  Investment, Inc., 8
Great Atlantic & Pacific Tea Company,
  Inc., The, II; 16 (upd.); 55 (upd.)
Great Harvest Bread Company, 44
Great Lakes Bancorp, 8
Great Lakes Chemical Corporation, I; 14
  (upd.)
Great Plains Energy Incorporated, 65
  (upd.)
Great Western Financial Corporation, 10
Grede Foundries, Inc., 38
Green Bay Packers, Inc., The, 32
Green Mountain Coffee, Inc., 31
Green Tree Financial Corporation, 11
Greenberg Traurig, LLP, 65
Greenbrier Companies, The, 19
Greene, Tweed & Company, 55
GreenPoint Financial Corp., 28
Greenwood Mills, Inc., 14
Greif Inc., 15; 66 (upd.)
Grey Advertising, Inc., 6
Grey Global Group Inc., 66 (upd.)
Grey Wolf, Inc., 43
Greyhound Lines, Inc., I; 32 (upd.)
Griffin Land & Nurseries, Inc., 43
Griffon Corporation, 34
Grinnell Corp., 13
Grist Mill Company, 15
Gristede's Sloan's, Inc., 31
Grolier Incorporated, 16; 43 (upd.)
Grossman's Inc., 13
Ground Round, Inc., 21
Group 1 Automotive, Inc., 52
Group Health Cooperative, 41
Grow Biz International, Inc., 18
Grow Group Inc., 12
Grubb & Ellis Company, 21
Grumman Corporation, I; 11 (upd.)
Gruntal & Co., L.L.C., 20
Gryphon Holdings, Inc., 21
GSD&M Advertising, 44
GSI Commerce, Inc., 67
GT Bicycles, 26
GT Interactive Software, 31
GTE Corporation, V; 15 (upd.)
GTSI Corp., 57
Guangzhou Pearl River Piano Group Ltd.,
  49
Guccio Gucci, S.p.A., 15
Guess, Inc., 15
Guest Supply, Inc., 18
Guidant Corporation, 58
Guilford Mills Inc., 8; 40 (upd.)
Guitar Center, Inc., 29
Guittard Chocolate Company, 55
Gulf & Western Inc., I
Gulf Island Fabrication, Inc., 44
Gulf States Utilities Company, 6
GulfMark Offshore, Inc., 49
Gulfstream Aerospace Corporation, 7; 28
  (upd.)
Gunite Corporation, 51
Gunlocke Company, The, 23
Guthy-Renker Corporation, 32
Gwathmey Siegel & Associates Architects
  LLC, 26
Gymboree Corporation, 15

H & R Block, Incorporated, 9; 29 (upd.)
H.B. Fuller Company, 8; 32 (upd.)
H.D. Vest, Inc., 46
H.E. Butt Grocery Company, 13; 32 (upd.)
H.F. Ahmanson & Company, II; 10 (upd.)
H.J. Heinz Company, II; 11 (upd.); 36 (upd.)
H.J. Russell & Company, 66
H.W. Wilson Company, The, 66
Ha-Lo Industries, Inc., 27
Habersham Bancorp, 25
Habitat for Humanity International, 36
Hach Co., 18
Hadco Corporation, 24
Haemonetics Corporation, 20
Haggar Corporation, 19
Haggen Inc., 38
Hahn Automotive Warehouse, Inc., 24
Hain Celestial Group, Inc., The, 27; 43 (upd.)
HAL Inc., 9
Hale-Halsell Company, 60
Half Price Books, Records, Magazines Inc., 37
Hall, Kinion & Associates, Inc., 52
Halliburton Company, III; 25 (upd.); 55 (upd.)
Hallmark Cards, Inc., IV; 16 (upd.); 40 (upd.)
Hamilton Beach/Proctor-Silex Inc., 17
Hammacher Schlemmer & Company, 21
Hampton Industries, Inc., 20
Hancock Fabrics, Inc., 18
Hancock Holding Company, 15
Handleman Company, 15
Handspring Inc., 49
Handy & Harman, 23
Hanger Orthopedic Group, Inc., 41
Hanmi Financial Corporation, 66
Hanna Andersson Corp., 49
Hanna-Barbera Cartoons Inc., 23
Hannaford Bros. Co., 12
Hanover Compressor Company, 59
Hanover Direct, Inc., 36
Hanover Foods Corporation, 35
Hansen Natural Corporation, 31
Hanson Building Materials America Inc., 60
Happy Kids Inc., 30
Harbert Corporation, 14
Harbison-Walker Refractories Company, 24
Harcourt Brace and Co., 12
Harcourt Brace Jovanovich, Inc., IV
Harcourt General, Inc., 20 (upd.)
Hard Rock Cafe International, Inc., 12; 32 (upd.)
Harding Lawson Associates Group, Inc., 16
Hardinge Inc., 25
Harlem Globetrotters International, Inc., 61
Harley-Davidson Inc., 7; 25 (upd.)
Harleysville Group Inc., 37
Harman International Industries Inc., 15
Harmon Industries, Inc., 25
Harmonic Inc., 43
Harnischfeger Industries, Inc., 8; 38 (upd.)
Harold's Stores, Inc., 22
Harper Group Inc., 17
HarperCollins Publishers, 15
Harpo, 28; 66 (upd.)
Harrah's Entertainment, Inc., 16; 43 (upd.)
Harris Corporation, II; 20 (upd.)
Harris Interactive Inc., 41
Harris Teeter Inc., 23
Harry N. Abrams, Inc., 58
Harry Winston Inc., 45
Harry's Farmers Market Inc., 23
Harsco Corporation, 8

Harte-Hanks, Inc., 17; 63 (upd.)
Hartmarx Corporation, 8; 32 (upd.)
Hartz Mountain Corporation, The, 12; 46 (upd.)
Harveys Casino Resorts, 27
Harza Engineering Company, 14
Hasbro, Inc., III; 16 (upd.); 43 (upd.)
Haskel International, Inc., 59
Hastings Entertainment, Inc., 29
Hastings Manufacturing Company, 56
Hauser, Inc., 46
Haverty Furniture Companies, Inc., 31
Hawaiian Airlines, Inc., 22 (upd.)
Hawaiian Electric Industries, Inc., 9
Hawk Corporation, 59
Hawkins Chemical, Inc., 16
Haworth Inc., 8; 39 (upd.)
Hayes Corporation, 24
Hayes Lemmerz International, Inc., 27
Hazelden Foundation, 28
HCA - The Healthcare Company, 35 (upd.)
HCI Direct, Inc., 55
HDR Inc., 48
Headwaters Incorporated, 56
Headway Corporate Resources, Inc., 40
Health Care & Retirement Corporation, 22
Health Management Associates, Inc., 56
Health O Meter Products Inc., 14
Health Risk Management, Inc., 24
Health Systems International, Inc., 11
HealthSouth Corporation, 14; 33 (upd.)
Healthtex, Inc., 17
Hearst Corporation, The, IV; 19 (upd.); 46 (upd.)
Heartland Express, Inc., 18
Heat Group, The, 53
Hechinger Company, 12
Hecla Mining Company, 20
Heekin Can Inc., 13
Heery International, Inc., 58
HEICO Corporation, 30
Heidrick & Struggles International, Inc., 28
Heilig-Meyers Company, 14; 40 (upd.)
Helen of Troy Corporation, 18
Helene Curtis Industries, Inc., 8; 28 (upd.)
Heller, Ehrman, White & McAuliffe, 41
Helmerich & Payne, Inc., 18
Helmsley Enterprises, Inc., 9; 39 (upd.)
Helzberg Diamonds, 40
Henkel Manco Inc., 22
Henley Group, Inc., The, III
Henry Modell & Company Inc., 32
Henry Schein, Inc., 31
Hensley & Company, 64
Herbalife International, Inc., 17; 41 (upd.)
Hercules Inc., I; 22 (upd.); 66 (upd.)
Herley Industries, Inc., 33
Herman Goelitz, Inc., 28
Herman Miller, Inc., 8
Hershey Foods Corporation, II; 15 (upd.); 51 (upd.)
Hertz Corporation, The, 9; 33 (upd.)
Heska Corporation, 39
Heublein, Inc., I
Hewlett-Packard Company, III; 6 (upd.); 28 (upd.); 50 (upd.)
Hexcel Corporation, 28
Hibbett Sporting Goods, Inc., 26
Hibernia Corporation, 37
Hickory Farms, Inc., 17
Highmark Inc., 27
Highsmith Inc., 60
Hildebrandt International, 29
Hill's Pet Nutrition, Inc., 27
Hillenbrand Industries, Inc., 10
Hillerich & Bradsby Company, Inc., 51
Hillhaven Corporation, The, 14

Hills Stores Company, 13
Hilton Hotels Corporation, III; 19 (upd.); 62 (upd.)
Hines Horticulture, Inc., 49
Hispanic Broadcasting Corporation, 35
Hitchiner Manufacturing Co., Inc., 23
HMI Industries, Inc., 17
Ho-Chunk Inc., 61
HOB Entertainment, Inc., 37
Hoechst Celanese Corporation, 13
Hoenig Group Inc., 41
Hogan & Hartson L.L.P., 44
HOK Group, Inc., 59
Holberg Industries, Inc., 36
Holiday Inns, Inc., III
Holiday RV Superstores, Incorporated, 26
Holland & Knight LLP, 60
Holland Burgerville USA, 44
Hollander Home Fashions Corp., 67
Holley Performance Products Inc., 52
Hollinger International Inc., 24
Holly Corporation, 12
Hollywood Casino Corporation, 21
Hollywood Entertainment Corporation, 25
Hollywood Media Corporation, 58
Hollywood Park, Inc., 20
Holme Roberts & Owen LLP, 28
Holnam Inc., 8; 39 (upd.)
Holophane Corporation, 19
Holson Burnes Group, Inc., 14
Holt and Bugbee Company, 66
Holt's Cigar Holdings, Inc., 42
Home Box Office Inc., 7; 23 (upd.)
Home Depot, Inc., The, V; 18 (upd.)
Home Insurance Company, The, III
Home Interiors & Gifts, Inc., 55
Home Products International, Inc., 55
Home Properties of New York, Inc., 42
Home Shopping Network, Inc., V; 25 (upd.)
HomeBase, Inc., 33 (upd.)
Homestake Mining Company, 12; 38 (upd.)
Hometown Auto Retailers, Inc., 44
HON INDUSTRIES Inc., 13
Honda Motor Company Limited, I; 10 (upd.); 29 (upd.)
Honeywell Inc., II; 12 (upd.); 50 (upd.)
Hooper Holmes, Inc., 22
Hooters of America, Inc., 18
Hoover Company, The, 12; 40 (upd.)
Hops Restaurant Bar and Brewery, 46
Horace Mann Educators Corporation, 22
Horizon Organic Holding Corporation, 37
Hormel Foods Corporation, 18 (upd.); 54 (upd.)
Horsehead Industries, Inc., 51
Horseshoe Gaming Holding Corporation, 62
Horton Homes, Inc., 25
Hospital Central Services, Inc., 56
Hospital Corporation of America, III
Hospitality Franchise Systems, Inc., 11
Hospitality Worldwide Services, Inc., 26
Hot Topic, Inc., 33
Houchens Industries Inc., 51
Houghton Mifflin Company, 10; 36 (upd.)
House of Fabrics, Inc., 21
Household International, Inc., II; 21 (upd.)
Houston Industries Incorporated, V
Hovnanian Enterprises, Inc., 29
Howard Hughes Medical Institute, 39
Howard Johnson International, Inc., 17
Howmet Corp., 12
HSN, 64 (upd.)
Hub Group, Inc., 38
Hubbard Broadcasting Inc., 24
Hubbell Incorporated, 9; 31 (upd.)

United States (*continued*)

Hudson Foods Inc., 13
Hudson River Bancorp, Inc., 41
Huffy Corporation, 7; 30 (upd.)
Hughes Electronics Corporation, 25
Hughes Hubbard & Reed LLP, 44
Hughes Markets, Inc., 22
Hughes Supply, Inc., 14
Hulman & Company, 44
Humana Inc., III; 24 (upd.)
Humane Society of the United States, The, 54
Hungry Howie's Pizza and Subs, Inc., 25
Hunt Consolidated, Inc., 27 (upd.)
Hunt Manufacturing Company, 12
Hunt Oil Company, 7
Hunt-Wesson, Inc., 17
Hunter Fan Company, 13
Huntington Bancshares Inc., 11
Huntington Learning Centers, Inc., 55
Hunton & Williams, 35
Huntsman Chemical Corporation, 8
Hutchinson Technology Incorporated, 18; 63 (upd.)
Hvide Marine Incorporated, 22
Hy-Vee, Inc., 36
Hyatt Corporation, III; 16 (upd.)
Hyde Athletic Industries, Inc., 17
Hydril Company, 46
Hypercom Corporation, 27
Hyperion Software Corporation, 22
Hyster Company, 17
I.C. Isaacs & Company, 31
Iams Company, 26
IBERIABANK Corporation, 37
IBP, Inc., II; 21 (upd.)
IC Industries, Inc., I
ICF Kaiser International, Inc., 28
ICN Pharmaceuticals, Inc., 52
Icon Health & Fitness, Inc., 38
Idaho Power Company, 12
IDB Communications Group, Inc., 11
Identix Inc., 44
IDEO Inc., 65
IDEXX Laboratories, Inc., 23
IDG Books Worldwide, Inc., 27
IDT Corporation, 34
IDX Systems Corporation, 64
IEC Electronics Corp., 42
Igloo Products Corp., 21
IHOP Corporation, 17; 58 (upd.)
IKON Office Solutions, Inc., 50
Il Fornaio (America) Corporation, 27
Ilitch Holdings Inc., 37
Illinois Bell Telephone Company, 14
Illinois Central Corporation, 11
Illinois Power Company, 6
Illinois Tool Works Inc., III; 22 (upd.)
ILX Resorts Incorporated, 65
Imagine Foods, Inc., 50
Imation Corporation, 20
IMC Fertilizer Group, Inc., 8
ImClone Systems Inc., 58
IMCO Recycling, Incorporated, 32
Immunex Corporation, 14; 50 (upd.)
Imo Industries Inc., 7; 27 (upd.)
IMPATH Inc., 45
Imperial Holly Corporation, 12
Imperial Sugar Company, 32 (upd.)
IMS Health, Inc., 57
In Focus Systems, Inc., 22
In-N-Out Burger, 19
In-Sink-Erator, 66
InaCom Corporation, 13
Incyte Genomics, Inc., 52
Indiana Bell Telephone Company, Incorporated, 14

Indiana Energy, Inc., 27
Indianapolis Motor Speedway Corporation, 46
Industrial Services of America, Inc., 46
Infinity Broadcasting Corporation, 11; 48 (upd.)
Information Access Company, 17
Information Builders, Inc., 22
Information Holdings Inc., 47
Information Resources, Inc., 10
Informix Corporation, 10; 30 (upd.)
Ingalls Shipbuilding, Inc., 12
Ingersoll-Rand Company Ltd., III; 15 (upd.); 55 (upd.)
Ingles Markets, Inc., 20
Ingram Industries, Inc., 11; 49 (upd.)
Ingram Micro Inc., 52
Initial Security, 64
Inktomi Corporation, 45
Inland Container Corporation, 8
Inland Steel Industries, Inc., IV; 19 (upd.)
Inserra Supermarkets, 25
Insight Enterprises, Inc., 18
Insilco Corporation, 16
Inso Corporation, 26
Instinet Corporation, 34
Insurance Auto Auctions, Inc., 23
Integrated Defense Technologies, Inc., 54
Integrity Inc., 44
Intel Corporation, II; 10 (upd.); 36 (upd.)
IntelliCorp, Inc., 45
Intelligent Electronics, Inc., 6
Inter Parfums Inc., 35
Inter-Regional Financial Group, Inc., 15
Interco Incorporated, III
InterDigital Communications Corporation, 61
Interep National Radio Sales Inc., 35
Interface, Inc., 8; 29 (upd.)
Intergraph Corporation, 6; 24 (upd.)
Interlake Corporation, The, 8
Intermet Corporation, 32
Intermountain Health Care, Inc., 27
International Airline Support Group, Inc., 55
International Brotherhood of Teamsters, 37
International Business Machines Corporation, III; 6 (upd.); 30 (upd.); 63 (upd.)
International Controls Corporation, 10
International Creative Management, Inc., 43
International Dairy Queen, Inc., 10; 39 (upd.)
International Data Group, Inc., 7; 25 (upd.)
International Family Entertainment Inc., 13
International Flavors & Fragrances Inc., 9; 38 (upd.)
International Game Technology, 10; 41 (upd.)
International Lease Finance Corporation, 48
International Management Group, 18
International Multifoods Corporation, 7; 25 (upd.)
International Paper Company, IV; 15 (upd.); 47 (upd.)
International Rectifier Corporation, 31
International Shipbreaking Ltd. L.L.C., 67
International Shipholding Corporation, Inc., 27
International Speedway Corporation, 19
International Telephone & Telegraph Corporation, I; 11 (upd.)
International Total Services, Inc., 37
Interpublic Group of Companies, Inc., The, I; 22 (upd.)
Interscope Music Group, 31

Interstate Bakeries Corporation, 12; 38 (upd.)
Interstate Hotels & Resorts Inc., 58
Intimate Brands, Inc., 24
Intrado Inc., 63
Intuit Inc., 14; 33 (upd.)
Invacare Corporation, 11; 47 (upd.)
Inverness Medical Innovations, Inc., 63
Invitrogen Corporation, 52
Invivo Corporation, 52
Iomega Corporation, 21
Ionics, Incorporated, 52
IPALCO Enterprises, Inc., 6
Iron Mountain, Inc., 33
Irvin Feld & Kenneth Feld Productions, Inc., 15
Island ECN, Inc., The, 48
Isle of Capri Casinos, Inc., 41
Ispat Inland Inc., 40 (upd.)
Itel Corporation, 9
Items International Airwalk Inc., 17
Itron, Inc., 64
ITT Educational Services, Inc., 33
ITT Sheraton Corporation, III
IVAX Corporation, 11; 55 (upd.)
IVC Industries, Inc., 45
iVillage Inc., 46
Iwerks Entertainment, Inc., 34
IXC Communications, Inc., 29
J & J Snack Foods Corporation, 24
J&R Electronics Inc., 26
J. & W. Seligman & Co. Inc., 61
J. Alexander's Corporation, 65
J. Baker, Inc., 31
J. Crew Group Inc., 12; 34 (upd.)
J. D'Addario & Company, Inc., 48
J. Jill Group, Inc., The, 35
J.A. Jones, Inc., 16
J.B. Hunt Transport Services Inc., 12
J.C. Penney Company, Inc., V; 18 (upd.); 43 (upd.)
J.D. Edwards & Company, 14
J.D. Power and Associates, 32
J.F. Shea Co., Inc., 55
J.H. Findorff and Son, Inc., 60
J.I. Case Company, 10
J.M. Smucker Company, The, 11
J.P. Morgan & Co. Incorporated, II; 30 (upd.)
J.P. Morgan Chase & Co., 38 (upd.)
J.R. Simplot Company, 16; 60 (upd.)
Jabil Circuit, Inc., 36
Jack Henry and Associates, Inc., 17
Jack Schwartz Shoes, Inc., 18
Jackpot Enterprises Inc., 21
Jackson Hewitt, Inc., 48
Jackson National Life Insurance Company, 8
Jaco Electronics, Inc., 30
Jacob Leinenkugel Brewing Company, 28
Jacobs Engineering Group Inc., 6; 26 (upd.)
Jacobson Stores Inc., 21
Jacor Communications, Inc., 23
Jacuzzi Inc., 23
JAKKS Pacific, Inc., 52
Jalate Inc., 25
Jamba Juice Company, 47
James River Corporation of Virginia, IV
Janus Capital Group Inc., 57
Jason Incorporated, 23
Jay Jacobs, Inc., 15
Jayco Inc., 13
Jazz Basketball Investors, Inc., 55
Jazzercise, Inc., 45
JB Oxford Holdings, Inc., 32
JDS Uniphase Corporation, 34

Jefferies Group, Inc., 25
Jefferson-Pilot Corporation, 11; 29 (upd.)
Jeld-Wen, Inc., 45
Jenkens & Gilchrist, P.C., 65
Jennifer Convertibles, Inc., 31
Jenny Craig, Inc., 10; 29 (upd.)
Jerry's Famous Deli Inc., 24
Jervis B. Webb Company, 24
JetBlue Airways Corporation, 44
Jetro Cash & Carry Enterprises Inc., 38
JG Industries, Inc., 15
Jillian's Entertainment Holdings, Inc., 40
Jim Beam Brands Worldwide, Inc., 14; 58
    (upd.)
Jim Henson Company, The, 23
Jitney-Jungle Stores of America, Inc., 27
JLG Industries, Inc., 52
JLM Couture, Inc., 64
JMB Realty Corporation, IV
Jockey International, Inc., 12; 34 (upd.)
Joffrey Ballet of Chicago, The 52
John B. Sanfilippo & Son, Inc., 14
John D. and Catherine T. MacArthur
    Foundation, The, 34
John H. Harland Company, 17
John Hancock Financial Services, Inc., III;
    42 (upd.)
John Nuveen Company, The, 21
John Paul Mitchell Systems, 24
John Q. Hammons Hotels, Inc., 24
John W. Danforth Company, 48
John Wiley & Sons, Inc., 17; 65 (upd.)
Johnny Rockets Group, Inc., 31
Johns Manville Corporation, 64 (upd.)
Johnson & Higgins, 14
Johnson & Johnson, III; 8 (upd.); 36 (upd.)
Johnson Controls, Inc., III; 26 (upd.); 59
    (upd.)
Johnson Publishing Company, Inc., 28
Johnson Worldwide Associates, Inc., 28
Johnsonville Sausage L.L.C., 63
Johnston Industries, Inc., 15
Johnstown America Industries, Inc., 23
Jones Apparel Group, Inc., 11; 39 (upd.)
Jones, Day, Reavis & Pogue, 33
Jones Intercable, Inc., 21
Jones Lang LaSalle Incorporated, 49
Jones Medical Industries, Inc., 24
Jordache Enterprises, Inc., 23
Jordan Industries, Inc., 36
Jos. A. Bank Clothiers, Inc., 31
Joseph T. Ryerson & Son, Inc., 15
Jostens, Inc., 7; 25 (upd.)
JOULÉ Inc., 58
Journal Register Company, 29
JPI, 49
JPS Textile Group, Inc., 28
Judge Group, Inc., The, 51
Juniper Networks, Inc., 43
Juno Lighting, Inc., 30
Juno Online Services, Inc., 38
Just Born, Inc., 32
Just For Feet, Inc., 19
Justin Industries, Inc., 19
JWP Inc., 9
JWT Group Inc., I
K & B Inc., 12
K & G Men's Center, Inc., 21
K'Nex Industries, Inc., 52
K-Swiss, Inc., 33
K-tel International, Inc., 21
Kaiser Aluminum & Chemical Corporation,
    IV
Kaiser Foundation Health Plan, Inc., 53
Kal Kan Foods, Inc., 22
Kaman Corporation, 12; 42 (upd.)
Kampgrounds of America, Inc. 33

Kana Software, Inc., 51
Kansas City Power & Light Company, 6
Kansas City Southern Industries, Inc., 6; 26
    (upd.)
Kaplan, Inc., 42
Karl Kani Infinity, Inc., 49
Karsten Manufacturing Corporation, 51
Kash n' Karry Food Stores, Inc., 20
Kasper A.S.L., Ltd., 40
Katy Industries, Inc., I; 51 (upd.)
Katz Communications, Inc., 6
Katz Media Group, Inc., 35
Kaufman and Broad Home Corporation, 8
Kaydon Corporation, 18
KB Home, 45 (upd.)
KB Toys, 15; 35 (upd.)
Keane, Inc., 56
Keebler Foods Company, 36
Keith Companies Inc., The, 54
Keithley Instruments Inc., 16
Kelley Drye & Warren LLP, 40
Kellogg Brown & Root, Inc., 62 (upd.)
Kellogg Company, II; 13 (upd.); 50 (upd.)
Kellwood Company, 8
Kelly Services Inc., 6; 26 (upd.)
Kelly-Moore Paint Company, Inc., 56
Kelly-Springfield Tire Company, The, 8
Kelsey-Hayes Group of Companies, 7; 27
    (upd.)
Kemet Corp., 14
Kemper Corporation, III; 15 (upd.)
Kendall International, Inc., 11
Kendall-Jackson Winery, Ltd., 28
Kenetech Corporation, 11
Kenmore Air Harbor Inc., 65
Kennedy-Wilson, Inc., 60
Kenneth Cole Productions, Inc., 25
Kent Electronics Corporation, 17
Kentucky Electric Steel, Inc., 31
Kentucky Utilities Company, 6
Kerr Group Inc., 24
Kerr-McGee Corporation, IV; 22 (upd.)
Ketchum Communications Inc., 6
Kettle Foods Inc., 48
Kewaunee Scientific Corporation, 25
Key Safety Systems, Inc., 63
Key Tronic Corporation, 14
KeyCorp, 8
Keyes Fibre Company, 9
KeySpan Energy Co., 27
Keystone International, Inc., 11
KFC Corporation, 7; 21 (upd.)
KI, 57
Kidde, Inc., I
Kiehl's Since 1851, Inc., 52
Kikkoman Corporation, 47 (upd.)
Kimball International, Inc., 12; 48 (upd.)
Kimberly-Clark Corporation, III; 16 (upd.);
    43 (upd.)
Kimco Realty Corporation, 11
Kinder Morgan, Inc., 45
KinderCare Learning Centers, Inc., 13
Kinetic Concepts, Inc. (KCI), 20
King & Spalding, 23
King Arthur Flour Company, The, 31
King Kullen Grocery Co., Inc., 15
King Pharmaceuticals, Inc., 54
King Ranch, Inc., 14; 60 (upd.)
King World Productions, Inc., 9; 30 (upd.)
Kingston Technology Corporation, 20
Kinko's, Inc., 16; 43 (upd.)
Kinney Shoe Corp., 14
Kirby Corporation, 18; 66 (upd.)
Kirkland & Ellis LLP, 65
Kirshenbaum Bond + Partners, Inc., 57
Kit Manufacturing Co., 18
Kitchell Corporation, 14

KitchenAid, 8
Kitty Hawk, Inc., 22
Kiwi International Airlines Inc., 20
KLA-Tencor Corporation, 11; 45 (upd.)
Kleiner, Perkins, Caufield & Byers, 53
Klement's Sausage Company, 61
Kmart Corporation, V; 18 (upd.); 47 (upd.)
Knape & Vogt Manufacturing Company,
    17
Knight Ridder, Inc., 67 (upd.)
Knight Transportation, Inc., 64
Knight-Ridder, Inc., IV; 15 (upd.)
Knoll Group Inc., 14
Knott's Berry Farm, 18
Knowledge Learning Corporation, 51
Knowledge Universe, Inc., 54
KnowledgeWare Inc., 9; 31 (upd.)
Koala Corporation, 44
Koch Enterprises, Inc., 29
Koch Industries, Inc., IV; 20 (upd.)
Kohl's Corporation, 9; 30 (upd.)
Kohlberg Kravis Roberts & Co., 24; 56
    (upd.)
Kohler Company, 7; 32 (upd.)
Kohn Pedersen Fox Associates P.C., 57
Koll Company, The, 8
Kollmorgen Corporation, 18
Komag, Inc., 11
Koo Koo Roo, Inc., 25
Koppers Industries, Inc., I; 26 (upd.)
Koret of California, Inc., 62
Korn/Ferry International, 34
Kos Pharmaceuticals, Inc., 63
Koss Corporation, 38
Kraft Foods Inc., II; 7 (upd.); 45 (upd.)
Kraus-Anderson, Incorporated, 36
Krause Publications, Inc., 35
Krause's Furniture, Inc., 27
Krispy Kreme Doughnuts, Inc., 21; 61
    (upd.)
Kroger Company, The, II; 15 (upd.); 65
    (upd.)
Kroll Inc., 57
Kronos, Inc., 18
Krystal Company, The, 33
K2 Inc., 16
KU Energy Corporation, 11
Kuhlman Corporation, 20
Kulicke and Soffa Industries, Inc., 33
Kurzweil Technologies, Inc., 51
Kushner-Locke Company, The, 25
L-3 Communications Holdings, Inc., 48
L. and J.G. Stickley, Inc., 50
L. Luria & Son, Inc., 19
L.A. Gear, Inc., 8; 32 (upd.)
L.A. T Sportswear, Inc., 26
L.B. Foster Company, 33
L.L. Bean, Inc., 10; 38 (upd.)
L.L. Knickerbocker Co., Inc., The, 25
L.S. Starrett Company, 13; 64 (upd.)
La Choy Food Products Inc., 25
La Madeleine French Bakery & Café, 33
La Quinta Companies, The, 11; 42 (upd.)
La-Z-Boy Incorporated, 14; 50 (upd.)
LaBarge Inc., 41
LabOne, Inc., 48
Labor Ready, Inc., 29
Laboratory Corporation of America
    Holdings, 42 (upd.)
LaBranche & Co. Inc., 37
Lacks Enterprises Inc., 61
Laclede Steel Company, 15
LaCrosse Footwear, Inc., 18; 61 (upd.)
LADD Furniture, Inc., 12
Ladish Co., Inc., 30
Lafarge Corporation, 28
Lakeland Industries, Inc., 45

United States (*continued*)

Lakes Entertainment, Inc., 51
Lam Research Corporation, 11; 31 (upd.)
Lamar Advertising Company, 27
Lamaur Corporation, The, 41
Lamb Weston, Inc., 23
Lamonts Apparel, Inc., 15
Lamson & Sessions Co., The, 13; 61 (upd.)
Lancair International, Inc., 67
Lancaster Colony Corporation, 8; 61 (upd.)
Lance, Inc., 14; 41 (upd.)
Lancer Corporation, 21
Land O'Lakes, Inc., II; 21 (upd.)
Landauer, Inc., 51
Landmark Communications, Inc., 12; 55 (upd.)
Landry's Restaurants, Inc., 65 (upd.)
Landry's Seafood Restaurants, Inc., 15
Lands' End, Inc., 9; 29 (upd.)
Landstar System, Inc., 63
Lane Bryant, Inc., 64
Lane Co., Inc., The, 12
Lanoga Corporation, 62
Larry Flynt Publishing Inc., 31
Larry H. Miller Group, 29
Las Vegas Sands, Inc., 50
Laserscope, 67
Lason, Inc., 31
Latham & Watkins, 33
Latrobe Brewing Company, 54
Lattice Semiconductor Corp., 16
Lawson Software, 38
Lawter International Inc., 14
Layne Christensen Company, 19
Lazare Kaplan International Inc., 21
LCI International, Inc., 16
LDB Corporation, 53
LDDS-Metro Communications, Inc., 8
LeapFrog Enterprises, Inc., 54
Lear Seating Corporation, 16
Lear Siegler, Inc., I
Learjet Inc., 8; 27 (upd.)
Learning Company Inc., The, 24
Learning Tree International Inc., 24
LeaRonal, Inc., 23
Leaseway Transportation Corp., 12
Leatherman Tool Group, Inc., 51
Lebhar-Friedman, Inc., 55
LeBoeuf, Lamb, Greene & MacRae, L.L.P., 29
Lechmere Inc., 10
Lechters, Inc., 11; 39 (upd.)
LeCroy Corporation, 41
Lee Apparel Company, Inc., 8
Lee Enterprises Inc., 11; 64 (upd.)
Leeann Chin, Inc., 30
Lefrak Organization Inc., 26
Legal Aid Society, The, 48
Legent Corporation, 10
Legg Mason, Inc., 33
Leggett & Platt, Inc., 11; 48 (upd.)
Lehigh Portland Cement Company, 23
Leiner Health Products Inc., 34
Lennar Corporation, 11
Lennox International Inc., 8; 28 (upd.)
Lenox, Inc., 12
LensCrafters Inc., 23
Leo Burnett Company Inc., I; 20 (upd.)
Leprino Foods Company, 28
Les Schwab Tire Centers, 50
Lesco Inc., 19
Leslie Fay Companies, Inc., The, 8; 39 (upd.)
Leslie's Poolmart, Inc., 18
Leucadia National Corporation, 11
Leupold & Stevens, Inc., 52
Level 3 Communications, Inc., 67

Levenger Company, 63
Lever Brothers Company, 9
Levi Strauss & Co., V; 16 (upd.)
Levitz Furniture Inc., 15
Levy Restaurants L.P., 26
Lewis Galoob Toys Inc., 16
LEXIS-NEXIS Group, 33
Lexmark International, Inc., 18
LG&E Energy Corporation, 6; 51 (upd.)
Libbey Inc., 49
Liberty Corporation, The, 22
Liberty Livewire Corporation, 42
Liberty Media Corporation, 50
Liberty Mutual Holding Company, 59
Liberty Property Trust, 57
Liberty Travel, Inc., 56
Life Technologies, Inc., 17
Life Time Fitness, Inc., 66
Lifeline Systems, Inc., 53
Lifetime Entertainment Services, 51
Lifetime Hoan Corporation, 27
Lifeway Foods, Inc., 65
Ligand Pharmaceuticals Incorporated, 47
Lillian Vernon Corporation, 12; 35 (upd.)
Limited, Inc., The, V; 20 (upd.)
LIN Broadcasting Corp., 9
Lincare Holdings Inc., 43
Lincoln Electric Co., 13
Lincoln National Corporation, III; 25 (upd.)
Lincoln Property Company, 8; 54 (upd.)
Lincoln Snacks Company, 24
Lincoln Telephone & Telegraph Company, 14
Lindal Cedar Homes, Inc., 29
Lindsay Manufacturing Co., 20
Linear Technology, Inc., 16
Linens 'n Things, Inc., 24
Lintas: Worldwide, 14
Lionel L.L.C., 16
Liqui-Box Corporation, 16
Litehouse Inc., 60
Lithia Motors, Inc., 41
Littelfuse, Inc., 26
Little Caesar Enterprises, Inc., 7; 24 (upd.)
Little Tikes Company, 13; 62 (upd.)
Litton Industries, Inc., I; 11 (upd.)
LIVE Entertainment Inc., 20
Liz Claiborne, Inc., 8; 25 (upd.)
Lockheed Martin Corporation, I; 11 (upd.); 15 (upd.)
Loctite Corporation, 8; 30 (upd.)
LodgeNet Entertainment Corporation, 28
Loehmann's Inc., 24
Loews Corporation, I; 12 (upd.); 36 (upd.)
Logan's Roadhouse, Inc., 29
Logicon Inc., 20
LoJack Corporation, 48
London Fog Industries, Inc., 29
Lone Star Steakhouse & Saloon, Inc., 51
Long Island Bancorp, Inc., 16
Long Island Lighting Company, V
Long John Silver's, 13; 57 (upd.)
Longaberger Company, The, 12; 44 (upd.)
Longs Drug Stores Corporation, V; 25 (upd.)
Longview Fibre Company, 8; 37 (upd.)
Loral Space & Communications Ltd., 8; 9; 54 (upd.)
Lost Arrow Inc., 22
LOT$OFF Corporation, 24
Lotus Development Corporation, 6; 25 (upd.)
Louisiana Land and Exploration Company, The, 7
Louisiana-Pacific Corporation, IV; 31 (upd.)

Lowe's Companies, Inc., V; 21 (upd.)
Lowrance Electronics, Inc., 18
LSI Logic Corporation, 13; 64
LTV Corporation, The, I; 24 (upd.)
Lubrizol Corporation, I; 30 (upd.)
Luby's, Inc., 17; 42 (upd.)
Lucasfilm Ltd., 12; 50 (upd.)
Lucent Technologies Inc., 34
Lucille Farms, Inc., 45
Lucky Stores, Inc., 27
Luigino's, Inc., 64
Lukens Inc., 14
Lunar Corporation, 29
Lund Food Holdings, Inc., 22
Lund International Holdings, Inc., 40
Lutheran Brotherhood, 31
Lydall, Inc., 64
Lynch Corporation, 43
Lyondell Chemical Company, IV; 45 (upd.)
M&F Worldwide Corp., 38
M. Shanken Communications, Inc., 50
M.A. Bruder & Sons, Inc., 56
M.A. Gedney Co., 51
M.A. Hanna Company, 8
M.H. Meyerson & Co., Inc., 46
Mac Frugal's Bargains - Closeouts Inc., 17
Mac-Gray Corporation, 44
MacAndrews & Forbes Holdings Inc., 28
MacDermid Incorporated, 32
Mace Security International, Inc., 57
Macerich Company, The, 57
Mack Trucks, Inc., I; 22 (upd.); 61 (upd.)
Mack-Cali Realty Corporation, 42
Mackay Envelope Corporation, 45
Mackie Designs Inc., 33
Macmillan, Inc., 7
MacNeal-Schwendler Corporation, The, 25
Macromedia, Inc., 50
Madden's on Gull Lake, 52
Madison Gas and Electric Company, 39
Madison-Kipp Corporation, 58
Mag Instrument, Inc., 67
Magma Copper Company, 7
Magma Power Company, 11
MagneTek, Inc., 15; 41 (upd.)
MAI Systems Corporation, 11
Maid-Rite Corporation, 62
Maidenform, Inc., 20; 59 (upd.)
Mail Boxes Etc., 18; 41 (upd.)
Mail-Well, Inc., 28
Maine & Maritimes Corporation, 56
Maine Central Railroad Company, 16
Major Automotive Companies, Inc., The, 45
Malcolm Pirnie, Inc., 42
Malden Mills Industries, Inc., 16
Mallinckrodt Group Inc., 19
Malt-O-Meal Company, 22; 63 (upd.)
Management and Training Corporation, 28
Mandalay Resort Group, 32 (upd.)
Manhattan Associates, Inc., 67
Manitowoc Company, Inc., The, 18; 59 (upd.)
Mannatech Inc., 33
Manor Care, Inc., 6; 25 (upd.)
Manpower, Inc., 9; 30 (upd.)
Manufactured Home Communities, Inc., 22
Manufacturers Hanover Corporation, II
Manville Corporation, III; 7 (upd.)
MAPCO Inc., IV
MAPICS, Inc., 55
March of Dimes, 31
marchFIRST, Inc., 34
Marcus Corporation, The, 21
Marie Callender's Restaurant & Bakery, Inc., 28

MarineMax, Inc., 30
Marion Laboratories, Inc., I
Marisa Christina, Inc., 15
Maritz Inc., 38
Mark IV Industries, Inc., 7; 28 (upd.)
Marks Brothers Jewelers, Inc., 24
Marmon Group, The, IV; 16 (upd.)
Marquette Electronics, Inc., 13
Marriott International, Inc., III; 21 (upd.)
Mars, Incorporated, 7; 40 (upd.)
Marsh & McLennan Companies, Inc., III; 45 (upd.)
Marsh Supermarkets, Inc., 17
Marshall & Ilsley Corporation, 56
Marshall Field's, 63
Marshalls Incorporated, 13
Martek Biosciences Corporation, 65
Martha Stewart Living Omnimedia, L.L.C., 24
Martin Industries, Inc., 44
Martin Marietta Corporation, I
Martz Group, 56
Marvel Entertainment Group, Inc., 10
Marvin Lumber & Cedar Company, 22
Mary Kay Corporation, 9; 30 (upd.)
Masco Corporation, III; 20 (upd.); 39 (upd.)
Mashantucket Pequot Gaming Enterprise Inc., 35
Masland Corporation, 17
Massachusetts Mutual Life Insurance Company, III; 53 (upd.)
Massey Energy Company, 57
MasTec, Inc., 19; 55 (upd.)
Master Lock Company, 45
MasterCard International, Inc., 9
Material Sciences Corporation, 63
Matria Healthcare, Inc., 17
Matrix Service Company, 65
Mattel, Inc., 7; 25 (upd.); 61 (upd.)
Matthews International Corporation, 29
Maui Land & Pineapple Company, Inc., 29
Mauna Loa Macadamia Nut Corporation, 64
Maverick Tube Corporation, 59
Max & Erma's Restaurants Inc., 19
Maxco Inc., 17
Maxicare Health Plans, Inc., III; 25 (upd.)
Maxim Group, The, 25
Maxim Integrated Products, Inc., 16
MAXIMUS, Inc., 43
Maxtor Corporation, 10
Maxus Energy Corporation, 7
Maxwell Shoe Company, Inc., 30
MAXXAM Inc., 8
Maxxim Medical Inc., 12
May Department Stores Company, The, V; 19 (upd.); 46 (upd.)
Mayer, Brown, Rowe & Maw, 47
Mayflower Group Inc., 6
Mayo Foundation, 9; 34 (upd.)
Mayor's Jewelers, Inc., 41
Maytag Corporation, III; 22 (upd.)
Mazel Stores, Inc., 29
MBC Holding Company, 40
MBNA Corporation, 12; 33 (upd.)
MCA Inc., II
McAlister's Corporation, 66
McCarthy Building Companies, Inc., 48
McCaw Cellular Communications, Inc., 6
McClain Industries, Inc., 51
McClatchy Newspapers, Inc., 23
McCormick & Company, Incorporated, 7; 27 (upd.)
McCoy Corporation, 58
McDermott International, Inc., III; 37 (upd.)
McDonald's Corporation, II; 7 (upd.); 26 (upd.); 63 (upd.)
McDonnell Douglas Corporation, I; 11 (upd.)
McGraw-Hill Companies, Inc., The, IV; 18 (upd.); 51 (upd.)
MCI WorldCom, Inc., V; 27 (upd.)
McIlhenny Company, 20
McJunkin Corporation, 63
McKee Foods Corporation, 7; 27 (upd.)
McKesson Corporation, I; 12; 47 (upd.)
McKinsey & Company, Inc., 9
McLane Company, Inc., 13
McLeodUSA Incorporated, 32
McMenamins Pubs and Breweries, 65
MCN Corporation, 6
MCSi, Inc., 41
McWane Corporation, 55
MDU Resources Group, Inc., 7; 42 (upd.)
Mead Corporation, The, IV; 19 (upd.)
Mead Data Central, Inc., 10
Meade Instruments Corporation, 41
Meadowcraft, Inc., 29
Mecklermedia Corporation, 24
Medco Containment Services Inc., 9
Media Arts Group, Inc., 42
Media General, Inc., 7; 38 (upd.)
Medical Information Technology Inc., 64
Medical Management International, Inc., 65
Medicis Pharmaceutical Corporation, 59
MedImmune, Inc., 35
Meditrust, 11
Medline Industries, Inc., 61
Medtronic, Inc., 8; 30 (upd.); 67 (upd.)
Medusa Corporation, 24
Megafoods Stores Inc., 13
Meier & Frank Co., 23
Meijer Incorporated, 7; 27 (upd.)
Mel Farr Automotive Group, 20
Melaleuca Inc., 31
Melamine Chemicals, Inc., 27
Mellon Bank Corporation, II
Mellon Financial Corporation, 44 (upd.)
Mellon-Stuart Company, I
Melville Corporation, V
Melvin Simon and Associates, Inc., 8
Memorial Sloan-Kettering Cancer Center, 57
Men's Wearhouse, Inc., The, 17; 48 (upd.)
Menard, Inc., 34
Menasha Corporation, 8; 59 (upd.)
Mendocino Brewing Company, Inc., 60
Mentholatum Company Inc., The, 32
Mentor Corporation, 26
Mentor Graphics Corporation, 11
Mercantile Bankshares Corp., 11
Mercantile Stores Company, Inc., V; 19 (upd.)
Mercer International Inc., 64
Merck & Co., Inc., I; 11 (upd.); 34 (upd.)
Mercury Air Group, Inc., 20
Mercury General Corporation, 25
Mercury Interactive Corporation, 59
Meredith Corporation, 11; 29 (upd.)
Meridian Bancorp, Inc., 11
Meridian Gold, Incorporated, 47
Merillat Industries Inc., 13
Merisel, Inc., 12
Merit Medical Systems, Inc., 29
Meritage Corporation, 26
Merix Corporation, 36
Merrell Dow, Inc., I; 9 (upd.)
Merrill Corporation, 18; 47 (upd.)
Merrill Lynch & Co., Inc., II; 13 (upd.); 40 (upd.)
Merry-Go-Round Enterprises, Inc., 8
Mervyn's California, 10; 39 (upd.)
Mesa Air Group, Inc., 11; 32 (upd.)
Mesaba Holdings, Inc., 28
Mestek Inc., 10
Metatec International, Inc., 47
Meteor Industries Inc., 33
Methode Electronics, Inc., 13
Metris Companies Inc., 56
Metro Information Services, Inc., 36
Metro-Goldwyn-Mayer Inc., 25 (upd.)
Metrocall, Inc., 41
Metromedia Company, 7; 14; 61 (upd.)
Metropolitan Baseball Club Inc., 39
Metropolitan Financial Corporation, 13
Metropolitan Life Insurance Company, III; 52 (upd.)
Metropolitan Museum of Art, The, 55
Metropolitan Opera Association, Inc., 40
Metropolitan Transportation Authority, 35
Mexican Restaurants, Inc., 41
MFS Communications Company, Inc., 11
MGIC Investment Corp., 52
MGM Grand Inc., 17
MGM/UA Communications Company, II
Michael Anthony Jewelers, Inc., 24
Michael Baker Corporation, 14; 51 (upd.)
Michael C. Fina Co., Inc., 52
Michael Foods, Inc., 25
Michaels Stores, Inc., 17
Michigan Bell Telephone Co., 14
Michigan National Corporation, 11
Micro Warehouse, Inc., 16
MicroAge, Inc., 16
Microdot Inc., 8
Micron Technology, Inc., 11; 29 (upd.)
Micros Systems, Inc., 18
Microsoft Corporation, 6; 27 (upd.); 63 (upd.)
Mid-America Dairymen, Inc., 7
Midas Inc., 10; 56 (upd.)
Middleby Corporation, The, 22
Middlesex Water Company, 45
Middleton Doll Company, The, 53
Midland Company, The, 65
Midway Airlines Corporation, 33
Midway Games, Inc., 25
Midwest Express Holdings, Inc., 35
Midwest Grain Products, Inc., 49
Midwest Resources Inc., 6
Mikasa, Inc., 28
Mike-Sell's Inc., 15
Mikohn Gaming Corporation, 39
Milacron, Inc., 53 (upd.)
Milbank, Tweed, Hadley & McCloy, 27
Miles Laboratories, I
Millennium Pharmaceuticals, Inc., 47
Miller Brewing Company, I; 12 (upd.)
Miller Industries, Inc., 26
Miller Publishing Group, LLC, 57
Milliken & Co., V; 17 (upd.)
Milliman USA, 66
Millipore Corporation, 25
Milnot Company, 46
Milton Bradley Company, 21
Milwaukee Brewers Baseball Club, 37
Mine Safety Appliances Company, 31
Miner Group International, The, 22
Minerals Technologies Inc., 11; 52 (upd.)
Minnesota Mining & Manufacturing Company (3M), I; 8 (upd.); 26 (upd.)
Minnesota Power, Inc., 11; 34 (upd.)
Minntech Corporation, 22
Minute Maid Company, The, 28
Minuteman International Inc., 46
Minyard Food Stores, Inc., 33
Mirage Resorts, Incorporated, 6; 28 (upd.)
Miramax Film Corporation, 64
Mississippi Chemical Corporation, 39

United States (*continued*)

Mitchell Energy and Development Corporation, 7
MITRE Corporation, 26
Mity Enterprises, Inc., 38
MNS, Ltd., 65
Mobil Corporation, IV; 7 (upd.); 21 (upd.)
Mobile Mini, Inc., 58
Mobile Telecommunications Technologies Corp., 18
Modern Woodmen of America, 66
Modine Manufacturing Company, 8; 56 (upd.)
Moen Incorporated, 12
Mohawk Industries, Inc., 19; 63 (upd.)
Mohegan Tribal Gaming Authority, 37
Molex Incorporated, 11; 54 (upd.)
Monaco Coach Corporation, 31
Monadnock Paper Mills, Inc., 21
Monarch Casino & Resort, Inc., 65
Monfort, Inc., 13
Monro Muffler Brake, Inc., 24
Monsanto Company, I; 9 (upd.); 29 (upd.)
Montana Coffee Traders, Inc., 60
Montana Power Company, The, 11; 44 (upd.)
Monterey Pasta Company, 58
Montgomery Ward & Co., Incorporated, V; 20 (upd.)
Moody's Corporation, 65
Moog Inc., 13
Mooney Aerospace Group Ltd., 52
Moore Medical Corp., 17
Moore-Handley, Inc., 39
Moran Towing Corporation, Inc., 15
Morgan Group, Inc., The, 46
Morgan Stanley Dean Witter & Company, II; 16 (upd.); 33 (upd.)
Morgan, Lewis & Bockius LLP, 29
Morris Communications Corporation, 36
Morris Travel Services L.L.C., 26
Morrison Knudsen Corporation, 7; 28 (upd.)
Morrison Restaurants Inc., 11
Morse Shoe Inc., 13
Morton International Inc., 9 (upd.)
Morton Thiokol, Inc., I
Morton's Restaurant Group, Inc., 30
Mosinee Paper Corporation, 15
Mossimo, Inc., 27
Motel 6, 13; 56 (upd.)
Mothers Against Drunk Driving (MADD), 51
Mothers Work, Inc., 18
Motley Fool, Inc., The, 40
Moto Photo, Inc., 45
Motor Cargo Industries, Inc., 35
Motorcar Parts & Accessories, Inc., 47
Motorola, Inc., II; 11 (upd.); 34 (upd.)
Motown Records Company L.P., 26
Mott's Inc., 57
Mountain States Mortgage Centers, Inc., 29
Movado Group, Inc., 28
Movie Gallery, Inc., 31
Movie Star Inc., 17
MPS Group, Inc., 49
MPW Industrial Services Group, Inc., 53
Mr. Coffee, Inc., 15
Mr. Gasket Inc., 15
Mrs. Baird's Bakeries, 29
Mrs. Fields' Original Cookies, Inc., 27
Mt. Olive Pickle Company, Inc., 44
MTS Inc., 37
Mueller Industries, Inc., 7; 52 (upd.)
Mullen Advertising Inc., 51
Multi-Color Corporation, 53
Multimedia Games, Inc., 41

Multimedia, Inc., 11
Murdock Madaus Schwabe, 26
Murphy Family Farms Inc., 22
Murphy Oil Corporation, 7; 32 (upd.)
Musicland Stores Corporation, 9; 38 (upd.)
Mutual Benefit Life Insurance Company, The, III
Mutual Life Insurance Company of New York, The, III
Muzak, Inc., 18
MWH Preservation Limited Partnership, 65
Mycogen Corporation, 21
Myers Industries, Inc., 19
Mylan Laboratories Inc., I; 20 (upd.); 59 (upd.)
Nabisco Foods Group, II; 7 (upd.)
Nabors Industries, Inc., 9
NACCO Industries, Inc., 7
Nalco Chemical Corporation, I; 12 (upd.)
Nantucket Allserve, Inc., 22
NASD, 54 (upd.)
Nash Finch Company, 8; 23 (upd.); 65 (upd.)
Nashua Corporation, 8
Nathan's Famous, Inc., 29
National Amusements Inc., 28
National Association for Stock Car Auto Racing, 32
National Association of Securities Dealers, Inc., 10
National Audubon Society, 26
National Auto Credit, Inc., 16
National Beverage Corp., 26
National Broadcasting Company, Inc., II; 6 (upd.); 28 (upd.)
National Can Corporation, I
National Car Rental System, Inc., 10
National City Corp., 15
National Convenience Stores Incorporated, 7
National Discount Brokers Group, Inc., 28
National Distillers and Chemical Corporation, I
National Educational Music Co. Ltd., 47
National Envelope Corporation, 32
National Equipment Services, Inc., 57
National Financial Partners Corp., 65
National Football League, 29
National Fuel Gas Company, 6
National Geographic Society, 9; 30 (upd.)
National Grape Cooperative Association, Inc., 20
National Grid USA, 51 (upd.)
National Gypsum Company, 10
National Health Laboratories Incorporated, 11
National Heritage Academies, Inc., 60
National Hockey League, 35
National Home Centers, Inc., 44
National Instruments Corporation, 22
National Intergroup, Inc., V
National Journal Group Inc., 67
National Media Corporation, 27
National Medical Enterprises, Inc., III
National Oilwell, Inc., 54
National Organization for Women, Inc., 55
National Patent Development Corporation, 13
National Picture & Frame Company, 24
National Presto Industries, Inc., 16; 43 (upd.)
National Public Radio, Inc., 19; 47 (upd.)
National R.V. Holdings, Inc., 32
National Railroad Passenger Corporation (Amtrak), 22; 66 (upd.)
National Record Mart, Inc., 29
National Rifle Association of America, 37

National Sanitary Supply Co., 16
National Semiconductor Corporation, II; VI, 26 (upd.)
National Service Industries, Inc., 11; 54 (upd.)
National Standard Co., 13
National Starch and Chemical Company, 49
National Steel Corporation, 12
National TechTeam, Inc., 41
National Thoroughbred Racing Association, 58
National Wine & Spirits, Inc., 49
NationsBank Corporation, 10
Natrol, Inc., 49
Natural Alternatives International, Inc., 49
Natural Selection Foods, 54
Natural Wonders Inc., 14
Nature Conservancy, The, 28
Nature's Sunshine Products, Inc., 15
Nautica Enterprises, Inc., 18; 44 (upd.)
Navarre Corporation, 24
Navigant International, Inc., 47
Navistar International Corporation, I; 10 (upd.)
Navy Exchange Service Command, 31
Navy Federal Credit Union, 33
NBD Bancorp, Inc., 11
NBTY, Inc., 31
NCH Corporation, 8
NCNB Corporation, II
NCO Group, Inc., 42
NCR Corporation, III; 6 (upd.); 30 (upd.)
Nebraska Book Company, Inc., 65
Nebraska Public Power District, 29
Neff Corp., 32
NeighborCare, Inc., 67 (upd.)
Neiman Marcus Group, Inc., The, 12; 49 (upd.)
NERCO, Inc., 7
Netflix, Inc., 58
Netscape Communications Corporation, 15; 35 (upd.)
Network Appliance, Inc., 58
Network Associates, Inc., 25
Neuberger Berman Inc., 57
Neutrogena Corporation, 17
Nevada Bell Telephone Company, 14
Nevada Power Company, 11
New Balance Athletic Shoe, Inc., 25
New Brunswick Scientific Co., Inc., 45
New Dana Perfumes Company, 37
New England Business Services, Inc., 18
New England Confectionery Co., 15
New England Electric System, V
New England Mutual Life Insurance Company, III
New Jersey Resources Corporation, 54
New Line Cinema, Inc., 47
New Orleans Saints LP, 58
New Piper Aircraft, Inc., The, 44
New Plan Realty Trust, 11
New Street Capital Inc., 8
New Times, Inc., 45
New Valley Corporation, 17
New World Pasta Company, 53
New World Restaurant Group, Inc., 44
New York City Health and Hospitals Corporation, 60
New York City Off-Track Betting Corporation, 51
New York Daily News, 32
New York Life Insurance Company, III; 45 (upd.)
New York Restaurant Group, Inc., 32
New York State Electric and Gas, 6

New York Stock Exchange, Inc., 9; 39 (upd.)
New York Times Company, The, IV; 19 (upd.); 61 (upd.)
Newcor, Inc., 40
Newell Rubbermaid Inc., 9; 52 (upd.)
Newfield Exploration Company, 65
Newhall Land and Farming Company, 14
Newman's Own, Inc., 37
Newmont Mining Corporation, 7
Newpark Resources, Inc., 63
Newport News Shipbuilding Inc., 13; 38 (upd.)
News America Publishing Inc., 12
NewYork-Presbyterian Hospital, 59
Nextel Communications, Inc., 10; 27 (upd.)
NFO Worldwide, Inc., 24
NGC Corporation, 18
Niagara Corporation, 28
Niagara Mohawk Holdings Inc., V; 45 (upd.)
Nichols Research Corporation, 18
Nicklaus Companies, 45
NICOR Inc., 6
NIKE, Inc., V; 8 (upd.); 36 (upd.)
Nikken Global Inc., 32
Niman Ranch, Inc., 67
Nimbus CD International, Inc., 20
Nine West Group, Inc., 11; 39 (upd.)
99¢ Only Stores, 25
NIPSCO Industries, Inc., 6
Nitches, Inc., 53
NL Industries, Inc., 10
Nobel Learning Communities, Inc., 37
Noble Affiliates, Inc., 11
Noble Roman's Inc., 14
Noland Company, 35
Nolo.com, Inc., 49
Noodle Kidoodle, 16
Noodles & Company, Inc., 55
Nooter Corporation, 61
Norcal Waste Systems, Inc., 60
NordicTrack, 22
Nordson Corporation, 11; 48 (upd.)
Nordstrom, Inc., V; 18 (upd.); 67 (upd.)
Norelco Consumer Products Co., 26
Norfolk Southern Corporation, V; 29 (upd.)
Norm Thompson Outfitters, Inc., 47
Norrell Corporation, 25
Norstan, Inc., 16
Nortek, Inc., 34
North Atlantic Trading Company Inc., 65
North Face, Inc., The, 18
North Fork Bancorporation, Inc., 46
North Pacific Group, Inc., 61
North Star Steel Company, 18
Northeast Utilities, V; 48 (upd.)
Northern States Power Company, V; 20 (upd.)
Northern Trust Company, 9
Northland Cranberries, Inc., 38
Northrop Grumman Corporation, I; 11 (upd.); 45 (upd.)
Northwest Airlines Corporation, I; 6 (upd.); 26 (upd.)
Northwest Natural Gas Company, 45
NorthWestern Corporation, 37
Northwestern Mutual Life Insurance Company, III; 45 (upd.)
Norton Company, 8
Norton McNaughton, Inc., 27
Norwood Promotional Products, Inc., 26
NovaCare, Inc., 11
Novell, Inc., 6; 23 (upd.)
Novellus Systems, Inc., 18
Noven Pharmaceuticals, Inc., 55
NPC International, Inc., 40

NRT Incorporated, 61
Nu Skin Enterprises, Inc., 27
Nu-kote Holding, Inc., 18
Nucor Corporation, 7; 21 (upd.)
Nutraceutical International Corporation, 37
NutraSweet Company, 8
Nutrition for Life International Inc., 22
NVIDIA Corporation, 54
NVR L.P., 8
NYMAGIC, Inc., 41
NYNEX Corporation, V
Oak Harbor Freight Lines, Inc., 53
Oak Industries Inc., 21
Oak Technology, Inc., 22
Oakhurst Dairy, 60
Oakley, Inc., 18; 49 (upd.)
Oakwood Homes Corporation, 15
Obie Media Corporation, 56
Occidental Petroleum Corporation, IV; 25 (upd.)
Ocean Spray Cranberries, Inc., 7; 25 (upd.)
Oceaneering International, Inc., 63
O'Charley's Inc., 19; 60 (upd.)
Octel Messaging, 14; 41 (upd.)
Ocular Sciences, Inc., 65
Odetics Inc., 14
ODL, Inc., 55
Odwalla, Inc., 31
OEC Medical Systems, Inc., 27
Office Depot, Inc., 8; 23 (upd.); 65 (upd.)
OfficeMax, Inc., 15; 43 (upd.)
Offshore Logistics, Inc., 37
Ogden Corporation, I; 6
Ogilvy Group, Inc., The, I
Oglebay Norton Company, 17
Oglethorpe Power Corporation, 6
Ohio Art Company, The, 14; 59 (upd.)
Ohio Bell Telephone Company, 14
Ohio Casualty Corp., 11
Ohio Edison Company, V
Oil-Dri Corporation of America, 20
Oklahoma Gas and Electric Company, 6
Olan Mills, Inc., 62
Old America Stores, Inc., 17
Old Dominion Freight Line, Inc., 57
Old Kent Financial Corp., 11
Old National Bancorp, 15
Old Republic International Corporation, 11; 58 (upd.)
Old Spaghetti Factory International Inc., 24
Olin Corporation, I; 13 (upd.)
Olsten Corporation, 6; 29 (upd.)
OM Group, Inc., 17
Omaha Steaks International Inc., 62
O'Melveny & Myers, 37
OMI Corporation, 59
Omni Hotels Corp., 12
Omnicare, Inc., 49
Omnicom Group, I; 22 (upd.)
OmniSource Corporation, 14
OMNOVA Solutions Inc., 59
On Assignment, Inc., 20
180s, L.L.C., 64
One Price Clothing Stores, Inc., 20
1-800-FLOWERS, Inc., 26
Oneida Ltd., 7; 31 (upd.)
ONEOK Inc., 7
Onyx Acceptance Corporation, 59
Onyx Software Corporation, 53
Opinion Research Corporation, 46
Opsware Inc., 49
Option Care Inc., 48
Opus Group, 34
Oracle Corporation, 6; 24 (upd.); 67 (upd.)
Orange Glo International, 53
Orbital Sciences Corporation, 22
Orbitz, Inc., 61

Orchard Supply Hardware Stores Corporation, 17
Ore-Ida Foods Incorporated, 13
Oregon Chai, Inc., 49
Oregon Dental Service Health Plan, Inc., 51
Oregon Metallurgical Corporation, 20
Oregon Steel Mills, Inc., 14
O'Reilly Automotive, Inc., 26
Organic Valley (Coulee Region Organic Produce Pool), 53
Orion Pictures Corporation, 6
Orleans Homebuilders, Inc., 62
Orthodontic Centers of America, Inc., 35
Orvis Company, Inc., The, 28
Oryx Energy Company, 7
Oscar Mayer Foods Corp., 12
OshKosh B'Gosh, Inc., 9; 42 (upd.)
Oshkosh Truck Corporation, 7
Oshman's Sporting Goods, Inc., 17
Osmonics, Inc., 18
O'Sullivan Industries Holdings, Inc., 34
Otis Elevator Company, Inc., 13; 39 (upd.)
Otis Spunkmeyer, Inc., 28
OTR Express, Inc., 25
Ottaway Newspapers, Inc., 15
Otter Tail Power Company, 18
Outback Steakhouse, Inc., 12; 34 (upd.)
Outboard Marine Corporation, III; 20 (upd.)
Outdoor Research, Incorporated, 67
Outdoor Systems, Inc., 25
Outlook Group Corporation, 37
Outrigger Enterprises, Inc., 67
Overhill Corporation, 51
Overnite Corporation, 14; 58 (upd.)
Overseas Shipholding Group, Inc., 11
Owens & Minor, Inc., 16
Owens Corning Corporation, III; 20 (upd.)
Owens-Illinois, Inc., I; 26 (upd.)
Owosso Corporation, 29
Oxford Health Plans, Inc., 16
Oxford Industries, Inc., 8
P&C Foods Inc., 8
P & F Industries, Inc., 45
P.C. Richard & Son Corp., 23
P.F. Chang's China Bistro, Inc., 37
P.H. Glatfelter Company, 8; 30 (upd.)
Paccar Inc., I; 26 (upd.)
Pacer International, Inc., 54
Pacer Technology, 40
Pacific Coast Feather Company, 67
Pacific Enterprises, V
Pacific Gas and Electric Company, V
Pacific Sunwear of California, Inc., 28
Pacific Telecom, Inc., 6
Pacific Telesis Group, V
PacifiCare Health Systems, Inc., 11
PacifiCorp, V; 26 (upd.)
Packaging Corporation of America, 12; 51 (upd.)
Packard Bell Electronics, Inc., 13
Paddock Publications, Inc., 53
Paging Network Inc., 11
PaineWebber Group Inc., II; 22 (upd.)
Pall Corporation, 9
Palm Harbor Homes, Inc., 39
Palm, Inc., 36
Palomar Medical Technologies, Inc., 22
Pamida Holdings Corporation, 15
Pampered Chef, Ltd., The, 18
Pan American World Airways, Inc., I; 12 (upd.)
Pan-American Life Insurance Company, 48
Panamerican Beverages, Inc., 47
PanAmSat Corporation, 46
Panavision Inc., 24

United States (*continued*)

Pancho's Mexican Buffet, Inc., 46
Panda Management Company, Inc., 35
Panera Bread Company, 44
Panhandle Eastern Corporation, V
Pantry, Inc., The, 36
Papa John's International, Inc., 15
Papa Murphy's International, Inc., 54
Papetti's Hygrade Egg Products, Inc., 39
Par Pharmaceutical Companies, Inc., 65
Paradise Music & Entertainment, Inc., 42
Parametric Technology Corp., 16
Paramount Pictures Corporation, II
Paris Corporation, 22
Parisian, Inc., 14
Park Corp., 22
Park-Ohio Industries Inc., 17
Parker Drilling Company, 28
Parker-Hannifin Corporation, III; 24 (upd.)
Parlex Corporation, 61
Parsons Brinckerhoff, Inc., 34
Parsons Corporation, The, 8; 56 (upd.)
Party City Corporation, 54
Pathmark Stores, Inc., 23
Patina Oil & Gas Corporation, 24
Patrick Industries, Inc., 30
Patterson Dental Co., 19
Patterson-UTI Energy, Inc., 55
Paul Harris Stores, Inc., 18
Paul, Hastings, Janofsky & Walker LLP, 27
Paul Mueller Company, 65
Paul Revere Corporation, The, 12
Paul, Weiss, Rifkind, Wharton & Garrison, 47
Paul-Son Gaming Corporation, 66
Paxson Communications Corporation, 33
Pay 'N Pak Stores, Inc., 9
Paychex, Inc., 15; 46 (upd.)
Payless Cashways, Inc., 11; 44 (upd.)
Payless ShoeSource, Inc., 18
PayPal Inc., 58
PC Connection, Inc., 37
PCA International, Inc., 62
PDI, Inc., 52
PDS Gaming Corporation, 44
Peabody Coal Company, 10
Peabody Energy Corporation, 45 (upd.)
Peabody Holding Company, Inc., IV
Peak Technologies Group, Inc., The, 14
Peapod, Inc., 30
Pearle Vision, Inc., 13
Peavey Electronics Corporation, 16
PECO Energy Company, 11
Pediatric Services of America, Inc., 31
Pediatrix Medical Group, Inc., 61
Peebles Inc., 16; 43 (upd.)
Peet's Coffee & Tea, Inc., 38
Pei Cobb Freed & Partners Architects LLP, 57
Pella Corporation, 12; 39 (upd.)
Pemco Aviation Group Inc., 54
Pendleton Grain Growers Inc., 64
Pendleton Woolen Mills, Inc., 42
Penford Corporation, 55
Penn Engineering & Manufacturing Corp., 28
Penn National Gaming, Inc., 33
Penn Traffic Company, 13
Pennsylvania Blue Shield, III
Pennsylvania Power & Light Company, V
Pennwalt Corporation, I
PennWell Corporation, 55
Pennzoil-Quaker State Company, IV; 20 (upd.); 50 (upd.)
Penske Corporation, V; 19 (upd.)

Pentair, Inc., 7; 26 (upd.)
Pentech International, Inc., 29
Penton Media, Inc., 27
People Express Airlines, Inc., I
Peoples Energy Corporation, 6
PeopleSoft Inc., 14; 33 (upd.)
Pep Boys—Manny, Moe & Jack, The, 11; 36 (upd.)
Pepper Hamilton LLP, 43
Pepsi Bottling Group, Inc., The, 40
PepsiAmericas, Inc., 67 (upd.)
PepsiCo, Inc., I; 10 (upd.); 38 (upd.)
Perdue Farms Inc., 7; 23 (upd.)
Performance Food Group Company, 31
Perini Corporation, 8
Perkin-Elmer Corporation, The, 7
Perkins Coie LLP, 56
Perkins Family Restaurants, L.P., 22
Perot Systems Corporation, 29
Perrigo Company, 12; 59 (upd.)
Perry Ellis International, Inc., 41
Pet Incorporated, 7
Petco Animal Supplies, Inc., 29
Pete's Brewing Company, 22
Peter Kiewit Sons' Inc., 8
Petersen Publishing Company, 21
Peterson American Corporation, 55
Petrie Stores Corporation, 8
Petroleum Helicopters, Inc., 35
Petrolite Corporation, 15
Petrossian Inc., 54
PETsMART, Inc., 14; 41 (upd.)
Pew Charitable Trusts, The, 35
Pez Candy, Inc., 38
Pfizer Inc., I; 9 (upd.); 38 (upd.)
PG&E Corporation, 26 (upd.)
Phar-Mor Inc., 12
Pharmacia & Upjohn Inc., I; 25 (upd.)
Phat Fashions LLC, 49
Phelps Dodge Corporation, IV; 28 (upd.)
PHH Arval, V; 53 (upd.)
Philadelphia Eagles, 37
Philadelphia Electric Company, V
Philadelphia Suburban Corporation, 39
Philip Morris Companies Inc., V; 18 (upd.); 44 (upd.)
Philips Electronics North America Corp., 13
Phillips, de Pury & Luxembourg, 49
Phillips Foods, Inc., 63
Phillips Petroleum Company, IV; 40 (upd.)
Phillips-Van Heusen Corporation, 24
PHP Healthcare Corporation, 22
PhyCor, Inc., 36
Physician Sales & Service, Inc., 14
Physio-Control International Corp., 18
Piccadilly Cafeterias, Inc., 19
PictureTel Corp., 10; 27 (upd.)
Piedmont Natural Gas Company, Inc., 27
Pier 1 Imports, Inc., 12; 34 (upd.)
Pierce Leahy Corporation, 24
Piercing Pagoda, Inc., 29
Piggly Wiggly Southern, Inc., 13
Pilgrim's Pride Corporation, 7; 23 (upd.)
Pillowtex Corporation, 19; 41 (upd.)
Pillsbury Company, The, II; 13 (upd.); 62 (upd.)
Pillsbury Madison & Sutro LLP, 29
Pilot Air Freight Corp., 67
Pilot Corporation, 49
Pinkerton's Inc., 9
Pinnacle West Capital Corporation, 6; 54 (upd.)
Pioneer Hi-Bred International, Inc., 9; 41 (upd.)
Pioneer Natural Resources Company, 59
Pioneer-Standard Electronics Inc., 19

Piper Jaffray Companies Inc., 22
Pitman Company, 58
Pitney Bowes Inc., III; 19; 47 (upd.)
Pittsburgh Steelers Sports, Inc., 66
Pittston Company, The, IV; 19 (upd.)
Pittway Corporation, 9; 33 (upd.)
Pixar Animation Studios, 34
Pizza Hut Inc., 7; 21 (upd.)
Pizza Inn, Inc., 46
Plains Cotton Cooperative Association, 57
Planar Systems, Inc., 61
Planet Hollywood International, Inc., 18; 41 (upd.)
Platinum Entertainment, Inc., 35
PLATINUM Technology, Inc., 14
Plato Learning, Inc., 44
Play by Play Toys & Novelties, Inc., 26
Playboy Enterprises, Inc., 18
PlayCore, Inc., 27
Players International, Inc., 22
Playskool, Inc., 25
Playtex Products, Inc., 15
Pleasant Company, 27
Pleasant Holidays LLC, 62
Plexus Corporation, 35
Plum Creek Timber Company, Inc., 43
Pluma, Inc., 27
Ply Gem Industries Inc., 12
PMI Group, Inc., The, 49
PMT Services, Inc., 24
PNC Financial Services Group Inc., The, II; 13 (upd.); 46 (upd.)
PNM Resources Inc., 51 (upd.)
Pogo Producing Company, 39
Polar Air Cargo Inc., 60
Polaris Industries Inc., 12; 35 (upd.)
Polaroid Corporation, III; 7 (upd.); 28 (upd.)
Policy Management Systems Corporation, 11
Policy Studies, Inc., 62
Polk Audio, Inc., 34
Polo/Ralph Lauren Corporation, 12; 62 (upd.)
PolyGram N.V., 23
Pomeroy Computer Resources, Inc., 33
Ponderosa Steakhouse, 15
Poof-Slinky, Inc., 61
Poore Brothers, Inc., 44
Pope & Talbot, Inc., 12; 61 (upd.)
Popular, Inc., 41
Port Authority of New York and New Jersey, The, 48
Portal Software, Inc., 47
Portland General Corporation, 6
Portland Trail Blazers, 50
Post Properties, Inc., 26
Potlatch Corporation, 8; 34 (upd.)
Potomac Electric Power Company, 6
Potter & Brumfield Inc., 11
Powell's Books, Inc., 40
PowerBar Inc., 44
Powerhouse Technologies, Inc., 27
PPG Industries, Inc., III; 22 (upd.)
PPL Corporation, 41 (upd.)
PR Newswire, 35
Prairie Farms Dairy, Inc., 47
Pratt & Whitney, 9
Praxair, Inc., 11; 48 (upd.)
Pre-Paid Legal Services, Inc., 20
Precision Castparts Corp., 15
Premark International, Inc., III
Premcor Inc., 37
Premier Industrial Corporation, 9
Premier Parks, Inc., 27
Premium Standard Farms, Inc., 30
PremiumWear, Inc., 30

Preserver Group, Inc., 44
President Casinos, Inc., 22
Pressman Toy Corporation, 56
Presstek, Inc., 33
Preston Corporation, 6
Price Communications Corporation, 42
Price Company, The, V
PriceCostco, Inc., 14
Priceline.com Incorporated, 57
PricewaterhouseCoopers, 9; 29 (upd.)
Primark Corp., 13
Prime Hospitality Corporation, 52
Primedex Health Systems, Inc., 25
Primedia Inc., 22
Primerica Corporation, I
Prince Sports Group, Inc., 15
Princess Cruise Lines, 22
Princeton Review, Inc., The, 42
Principal Mutual Life Insurance Company,
   III
Printrak, A Motorola Company, 44
Printronix, Inc., 18
Prison Rehabilitative Industries and
   Diversified Enterprises, Inc. (PRIDE), 53
Procter & Gamble Company, The, III; 8
   (upd.); 26 (upd.); 67 (upd.)
Prodigy Communications Corporation, 34
Professional Bull Riders Inc., 55
Professional Golfers' Association of
   America, The, 41
Proffitt's, Inc., 19
Progress Software Corporation, 15
Progressive Corporation, The, 11; 29 (upd.)
ProLogis, 57
Promus Companies, Inc., 9
Proskauer Rose LLP, 47
Protection One, Inc., 32
Provell Inc., 58 (upd.)
Providence Journal Company, The, 28
Providence Service Corporation, The, 64
Provident Life and Accident Insurance
   Company of America, III
Providian Financial Corporation, 52 (upd.)
Prudential Insurance Company of America,
   The, III; 30 (upd.)
PSI Resources, 6
Pubco Corporation, 17
Public Service Company of Colorado, 6
Public Service Company of New
   Hampshire, 21; 55 (upd.)
Public Service Company of New Mexico, 6
Public Service Enterprise Group Inc., V;
   44 (upd.)
Public Storage, Inc., 52
Publishers Clearing House, 23; 64 (upd.)
Publishers Group, Inc., 35
Publix Supermarkets Inc., 7; 31 (upd.)
Pueblo Xtra International, Inc., 47
Puget Sound Energy Inc., 6; 50 (upd.)
Pulaski Furniture Corporation, 33
Pulitzer Inc., 15; 58 (upd.)
Pulte Corporation, 8
Pulte Homes, Inc., 42 (upd.)
Pumpkin Masters, Inc., 48
Purina Mills, Inc., 32
Puritan-Bennett Corporation, 13
Purolator Products Company, 21
Putt-Putt Golf Courses of America, Inc., 23
PVC Container Corporation, 67
PW Eagle, Inc., 48
Pyramid Breweries Inc., 33
Pyramid Companies, 54
Q.E.P. Co., Inc., 65
QSC Audio Products, Inc., 56
Quad/Graphics, Inc., 19
Quaker Fabric Corp., 19

Quaker Oats Company, The, II; 12 (upd.);
   34 (upd.)
Quaker State Corporation, 7; 21 (upd.)
QUALCOMM Incorporated, 20; 47 (upd.)
Quality Chekd Dairies, Inc., 48
Quality Dining, Inc., 18
Quality Food Centers, Inc., 17
Quanex Corporation, 13; 62 (upd.)
Quantum Chemical Corporation, 8
Quantum Corporation, 10; 62 (upd.)
Quark, Inc., 36
Quest Diagnostics Inc., 26
Questar Corporation, 6; 26 (upd.)
Quick & Reilly Group, Inc., The, 20
Quigley Corporation, The, 62
Quiksilver, Inc., 18
QuikTrip Corporation, 36
Quill Corporation, 28
Quintiles Transnational Corporation, 21
Quixote Corporation, 15
Quizno's Corporation, The, 42
QVC Inc., 9; 58 (upd.)
Qwest Communications International, Inc.,
   37
R&B, Inc., 51
R.B. Pamplin Corp., 45
R.C. Bigelow, Inc., 49
R.G. Barry Corporation, 17; 44 (upd.)
R.H. Macy & Co., Inc., V; 8 (upd.); 30
   (upd.)
R.J. Reynolds Tobacco Holdings, Inc., 30
   (upd.)
R.L. Polk & Co., 10
R.P. Scherer, I
R.R. Donnelley & Sons Company, IV; 9
   (upd.); 38 (upd.)
Racal-Datacom Inc., 11
Racing Champions Corporation, 37
Radian Group Inc., 42
Radio Flyer Inc., 34
Radio One, Inc., 67
RadioShack Corporation, 36 (upd.)
Radius Inc., 16
Rag Shops, Inc., 30
RailTex, Inc., 20
Rainforest Cafe, Inc., 25
Rainier Brewing Company, 23
Raley's Inc., 14; 58 (upd.)
Rally's Hamburgers, Inc., 25
Ralphs Grocery Company, 35
Ralston Purina Company, II; 13 (upd.)
Ramsay Youth Services, Inc., 41
Rand McNally & Company, 28
Randall's Food Markets, Inc., 40
Random House, Inc., 13; 31 (upd.)
Range Resources Corporation, 45
Rapala-Normark Group, Ltd., 30
Rare Hospitality International Inc., 19
Raven Industries, Inc., 33
Raving Brands, Inc., 64
Rawlings Sporting Goods Co., Inc., 24
Raychem Corporation, 8
Rayonier Inc., 24
Rayovac Corporation, 13; 39 (upd.)
Raytech Corporation, 61
Raytheon Aircraft Holdings Inc., 46
Raytheon Company, II; 11 (upd.); 38
   (upd.)
Razorfish, Inc., 37
RCA Corporation, II
RCM Technologies, Inc., 34
RDO Equipment Company, 33
RE/MAX International, Inc., 59
Read-Rite Corp., 10
Reader's Digest Association, Inc., The, IV;
   17 (upd.)
Real Times, Inc., 66

RealNetworks, Inc., 53
Reckson Associates Realty Corp., 47
Recording for the Blind & Dyslexic, 51
Recoton Corp., 15
Recovery Engineering, Inc., 25
Recreational Equipment, Inc., 18
Recycled Paper Greetings, Inc., 21
Red Apple Group, Inc., 23
Red Hat, Inc., 45
Red Robin Gourmet Burgers, Inc., 56
Red Roof Inns, Inc., 18
Red Spot Paint & Varnish Company, 55
Red Wing Pottery Sales, Inc., 52
Red Wing Shoe Company, Inc., 9; 30
   (upd.)
Redhook Ale Brewery, Inc., 31
Reebok International Ltd., V; 9 (upd.); 26
   (upd.)
Reed & Barton Corporation, 67
Reeds Jewelers, Inc., 22
Regal Entertainment Group, 59
Regal-Beloit Corporation, 18
Regis Corporation, 18
Reichhold Chemicals, Inc., 10
Reliance Electric Company, 9
Reliance Group Holdings, Inc., III
Reliance Steel & Aluminum Co., 19
Reliant Energy Inc., 44 (upd.)
Reliv International, Inc., 58
Remedy Corporation, 58
RemedyTemp, Inc., 20
Remington Arms Company, Inc., 12; 40
   (upd.)
Remington Products Company, L.L.C., 42
Renaissance Learning Systems, Inc., 39
Reno Air Inc., 23
Rent-A-Center, Inc., 45
Rent-Way, Inc., 33
Rental Service Corporation, 28
Rentrak Corporation, 35
Republic Engineered Steels, Inc., 7; 26
   (upd.)
Republic Industries, Inc., 26
Republic New York Corporation, 11
Res-Care, Inc., 29
Resorts International, Inc., 12
Resource America, Inc., 42
Response Oncology, Inc., 27
Restaurant Associates Corporation, 66
Restaurants Unlimited, Inc., 13
Restoration Hardware, Inc., 30
Revco D.S., Inc., V
Revell-Monogram Inc., 16
Revere Ware Corporation, 22
Revlon Inc., III; 17 (upd.); 64 (upd.)
REX Stores Corp., 10
Rexel, Inc., 15
Rexnord Corporation, 21
Reynolds and Reynolds Company, The, 50
Reynolds Metals Company, IV; 19 (upd.)
RF Micro Devices, Inc., 43
Rhino Entertainment Company, 18
Rhodes Inc., 23
Rica Foods, Inc., 41
Rich Products Corporation, 7; 38 (upd.)
Richards Group, Inc., The, 58
Richardson Electronics, Ltd., 17
Richardson Industries, Inc., 62
Richfood Holdings, Inc., 7
Richton International Corporation, 39
Riddell Sports Inc., 22
Ride, Inc., 22
Riese Organization, The, 38
Riggs National Corporation, 13
Right Management Consultants, Inc., 42
Riklis Family Corp., 9
Riser Foods, Inc., 9

United States (*continued*)

Rite Aid Corporation, V; 19 (upd.); 63 (upd.)
Ritz Camera Centers, 34
Ritz-Carlton Hotel Company L.L.C., 9; 29 (upd.)
Rival Company, The, 19
River Oaks Furniture, Inc., 43
Riverwood International Corporation, 11; 48 (upd.)
Riviana Foods Inc., 27
RJR Nabisco Holdings Corp., V
RMH Teleservices, Inc., 42
Roadhouse Grill, Inc., 22
Roadmaster Industries, Inc., 16
Roadway Express, Inc., V; 25 (upd.)
Roanoke Electric Steel Corporation, 45
Robbins & Myers Inc., 15
Roberds Inc., 19
Robert Half International Inc., 18
Robert Mondavi Corporation, 15; 50 (upd.)
Robert W. Baird & Co. Incorporated, 67
Robert Wood Johnson Foundation, 35
Roberts Pharmaceutical Corporation, 16
Robertson-Ceco Corporation, 19
Robinson Helicopter Company, 51
Roche Bioscience, 11; 14 (upd.)
Rochester Gas and Electric Corporation, 6
Rochester Telephone Corporation, 6
Rock Bottom Restaurants, Inc., 25
Rock of Ages Corporation, 37
Rock-Tenn Company, 13; 59 (upd.)
Rockefeller Foundation, The, 34
Rockefeller Group International Inc., 58
Rockford Corporation, 43
Rockford Products Corporation, 55
RockShox, Inc., 26
Rockwell Automation, 43 (upd.)
Rockwell International Corporation, I; 11 (upd.)
Rocky Shoes & Boots, Inc., 26
Rodale Press, Inc., 23
Rodale, Inc., 47 (upd.)
Rogers Corporation, 61
Rohm and Haas Company, I; 26 (upd.)
ROHN Industries, Inc., 22
Rohr Incorporated, 9
Roll International Corporation, 37
Rollerblade, Inc., 15; 34 (upd.)
Rollins, Inc., 11
Rolls-Royce Allison, 29 (upd.)
Romacorp, Inc., 58
Ron Tonkin Chevrolet Company, 55
Ronco, Inc., 15
Rooms To Go Inc., 28
Rooney Brothers Co., 25
Roper Industries, Inc., 15; 50 (upd.)
Ropes & Gray, 40
Rorer Group, I
Rose Acre Farms, Inc., 60
Rose Art Industries, 58
Rose's Stores, Inc., 13
Roseburg Forest Products Company, 58
Rosemount Inc., 15
Rosenbluth International Inc., 14
Ross Stores, Inc., 17; 43 (upd.)
Rotary International, 31
Roto-Rooter, Inc., 15; 61 (upd.)
Rottlund Company, Inc., The, 28
Rouge Steel Company, 8
Roundy's Inc., 14; 58 (upd.)
Rouse Company, The, 15; 63 (upd.)
Rowan Companies, Inc., 43
Roy F. Weston, Inc., 33
Royal Appliance Manufacturing Company, 15
Royal Caribbean Cruises Ltd., 22

Royal Crown Company, Inc., 23
RPM, Inc., 8; 36 (upd.)
RSA Security Inc., 46
RTM Restaurant Group, 58
Rubbermaid Incorporated, III; 20 (upd.)
Rubio's Restaurants, Inc., 35
Ruby Tuesday, Inc., 18
Ruiz Food Products, Inc., 53
Rural Cellular Corporation, 43
Rural/Metro Corporation, 28
Rush Communications, 33
Rush Enterprises, Inc., 64
Russ Berrie and Company, Inc., 12
Russell Corporation, 8; 30 (upd.)
Russell Reynolds Associates Inc., 38
Russell Stover Candies Inc., 12
Rust International Inc., 11
Ruth's Chris Steak House, 28
Ryan Beck & Co., Inc., 66
Ryan's Family Steak Houses, Inc., 15
Ryder System, Inc., V; 24 (upd.)
Ryerson Tull, Inc., 40 (upd.)
Ryland Group, Inc., The, 8; 37 (upd.)
S&C Electric Company, 15
S&K Famous Brands, Inc., 23
S-K-I Limited, 15
S.C. Johnson & Son, Inc., III; 28 (upd.)
Saatchi & Saatchi, 42 (upd.)
Sabratek Corporation, 29
SABRE Group Holdings, Inc., 26
SAFECO Corporaton, III
Safeguard Scientifics, Inc., 10
Safelite Glass Corp., 19
Safeskin Corporation, 18
Safety Components International, Inc., 63
Safety 1st, Inc., 24
Safety-Kleen Corp., 8
Safeway Inc., II; 24 (upd.)
Saga Communications, Inc., 27
St. Joe Company, The, 31
St. Joe Paper Company, 8
St. John Knits, Inc., 14
St. Jude Medical, Inc., 11; 43 (upd.)
St. Louis Music, Inc., 48
St. Mary Land & Exploration Company, 63
St. Paul Bank for Cooperatives, 8
St. Paul Companies, Inc., The, III; 22 (upd.)
Saks Inc., 24; 41 (upd.)
Salant Corporation, 12; 51 (upd.)
Salick Health Care, Inc., 53
Sally Beauty Company, Inc., 60
Salomon Inc., II; 13 (upd.)
Salt River Project, 19
Salton, Inc., 30
Salvation Army USA, The, 32
Sam Ash Music Corporation, 30
Sam's Club, 40
Samsonite Corporation, 13; 43 (upd.)
Samuel Cabot Inc., 53
Samuels Jewelers Incorporated, 30
San Diego Gas & Electric Company, V
Sandals Resorts International, 65
Sanderson Farms, Inc., 15
Sandia National Laboratories, 49
Santa Barbara Restaurant Group, Inc., 37
Santa Cruz Operation, Inc., The, 38
Santa Fe Gaming Corporation, 19
Santa Fe International Corporation, 38
Santa Fe Pacific Corporation, V
Sara Lee Corporation, II; 15 (upd.); 54 (upd.)
Sarnoff Corporation, 57
SAS Institute Inc., 10
Saturn Corporation, 7; 21 (upd.)
Saucony Inc., 35

Sauder Woodworking Company, 12; 35 (upd.)
Sauer-Danfoss Inc., 61
Savannah Foods & Industries, Inc., 7
Sawtek Inc., 43 (upd.)
Sbarro, Inc., 16; 64 (upd.)
SBC Communications Inc., 32 (upd.)
SBS Technologies, Inc., 25
SCANA Corporation, 6; 56 (upd.)
ScanSource, Inc., 29
SCB Computer Technology, Inc., 29
SCEcorp, V
Schawk, Inc., 24
Scheels All Sports Inc., 63
Scheid Vineyards Inc., 66
Schering-Plough Corporation, I; 14 (upd.); 49 (upd.)
Schieffelin & Somerset Co., 61
Schlotzsky's, Inc., 36
Schlumberger Limited, III; 17 (upd.); 59 (upd.)
Schmitt Music Company, 40
Schneider National, Inc., 36
Schneiderman's Furniture Inc., 28
Schnitzer Steel Industries, Inc., 19
Scholastic Corporation, 10; 29 (upd.)
School-Tech, Inc., 62
Schott Brothers, Inc., 67
Schott Corporation, 53
Schottenstein Stores Corp., 14
Schuff Steel Company, 26
Schultz Sav-O Stores, Inc., 21; 31 (upd.)
Schwan's Sales Enterprises, Inc., 7; 26 (upd.)
Schweitzer-Mauduit International, Inc., 52
Schwinn Cycle and Fitness L.P., 19
SCI Systems, Inc., 9
Science Applications International Corporation, 15
Scientific Games Corporation, 64 (upd.)
Scientific-Atlanta, Inc., 6; 45 (upd.)
Score Board, Inc., The, 19
Scotsman Industries, Inc., 20
Scott Fetzer Company, 12
Scott Paper Company, IV; 31 (upd.)
Scotts Company, The, 22
Scotty's, Inc., 22
Scovill Fasteners Inc., 24
SCP Pool Corporation, 39
Seaboard Corporation, 36
Seagate Technology, Inc., 8; 34 (upd.)
Seagull Energy Corporation, 11
Sealaska Corporation, 60
Sealed Air Corporation, 14; 57 (upd.)
Sealed Power Corporation, I
Sealright Co., Inc., 17
Sealy Inc., 12
Seaman Furniture Company, Inc., 32
Sears, Roebuck and Co., V; 18 (upd.); 56 (upd.)
Seattle City Light, 50
Seattle FilmWorks, Inc., 20
Seattle First National Bank Inc., 8
Seattle Times Company, 15
Seaway Food Town, Inc., 15
Sebastiani Vineyards, Inc., 28
Second Harvest, 29
Security Capital Corporation, 17
Security Pacific Corporation, II
SED International Holdings, Inc., 43
See's Candies, Inc., 30
Sega of America, Inc., 10
Segway LLC, 48
Seigle's Home and Building Centers, Inc., 41
Seitel, Inc., 47
Select Comfort Corporation, 34

Select Medical Corporation, 65
Selmer Company, Inc., The, 19
SEMCO Energy, Inc., 44
Seminis, Inc., 29
Semitool, Inc., 18
Sempra Energy, 25 (upd.)
Semtech Corporation, 32
Seneca Foods Corporation, 17; 60 (upd.)
Sensient Technologies Corporation, 52 (upd.)
Sensormatic Electronics Corp., 11
Sensory Science Corporation, 37
Sepracor Inc., 45
Sequa Corporation, 13; 54 (upd.)
Serologicals Corporation, 63
Serta, Inc., 28
Service America Corp., 7
Service Corporation International, 6; 51 (upd.)
Service Merchandise Company, Inc., V; 19 (upd.)
ServiceMaster Inc., 6; 23 (upd.)
7-11, Inc., 32 (upd.)
Sevenson Environmental Services, Inc., 42
SFX Entertainment, Inc., 36
SGI, 29 (upd.)
Shakespeare Company, 22
Shaklee Corporation, 12; 39 (upd.)
Shared Medical Systems Corporation, 14
Sharper Image Corporation, The, 10; 62 (upd.)
Shaw Group, Inc., The, 50
Shaw Industries, Inc., 9; 40 (upd.)
Shaw's Supermarkets, Inc., 56
Shawmut National Corporation, 13
Shearman & Sterling, 32
Shearson Lehman Brothers Holdings Inc., II; 9 (upd.)
Shelby Williams Industries, Inc., 14
Sheldahl Inc., 23
Shell Oil Company, IV; 14 (upd.); 41 (upd.)
Sheller-Globe Corporation, I
Shells Seafood Restaurants, Inc., 43
Sherwin-Williams Company, The, III; 13 (upd.)
Sherwood Brands, Inc., 53
Shoe Carnival Inc., 14
Shoney's, Inc., 7; 23 (upd.)
ShopKo Stores Inc., 21; 58 (upd.)
Shoppers Food Warehouse Corporation, 66
Shorewood Packaging Corporation, 28
ShowBiz Pizza Time, Inc., 13
Showboat, Inc., 19
Shubert Organization Inc., 24
Shuffle Master Inc., 51
Shure Inc., 60
Shurgard Storage Centers, Inc., 52
Sidley Austin Brown & Wood, 40
Siebel Systems, Inc., 38
Siebert Financial Corp., 32
Siegel & Gale, 64
Sierra Club, The, 28
Sierra Health Services, Inc., 15
Sierra On-Line, Inc., 15; 41 (upd.)
Sierra Pacific Industries, 22
SIFCO Industries, Inc., 41
Sigma-Aldrich Corporation, I; 36 (upd.)
Signet Banking Corporation, 11
Sikorsky Aircraft Corporation, 24
Silhouette Brands, Inc., 55
Silicon Graphics Incorporated, 9
SilverPlatter Information Inc., 23
Silverstein Properties, Inc., 47
Simmons Company, 47
Simon & Schuster Inc., IV; 19 (upd.)
Simon Property Group, Inc., 27

Simon Transportation Services Inc., 27
Simplex Technologies Inc., 21
Simplicity Manufacturing, Inc., 64
Simpson Investment Company, 17
Simpson Thacher & Bartlett, 39
Simula, Inc., 41
Sinclair Broadcast Group, Inc., 25
Singing Machine Company, Inc., The, 60
Sir Speedy, Inc., 16
Six Flags, Inc., 17; 54 (upd.)
Skadden, Arps, Slate, Meagher & Flom, 18
Skechers USA Inc., 31
Skidmore, Owings & Merrill, 13
Skyline Chili, Inc., 62
Skyline Corporation, 30
SkyMall, Inc., 26
SkyWest, Inc., 25
SL Green Realty Corporation, 44
Sleepy's Inc., 32
SLI, Inc., 48
Slim-Fast Foods Company, 18; 66 (upd.)
SLM Holding Corp., 25 (upd.)
Smart & Final, Inc., 16
SmartForce PLC, 43
Smead Manufacturing Co., 17
Smith & Wesson Corporation, 30
Smith Barney Inc., 15
Smith Corona Corp., 13
Smith International, Inc., 15; 59 (upd.)
Smith's Food & Drug Centers, Inc., 8; 57 (upd.)
Smith-Midland Corporation, 56
Smithfield Foods, Inc., 7; 43 (upd.)
SmithKline Beckman Corporation, I
Smithsonian Institution, 27
Smithway Motor Xpress Corporation, 39
Smurfit-Stone Container Corporation, 26 (upd.)
Snap-On, Incorporated, 7; 27 (upd.)
Snapple Beverage Corporation, 11
Snell & Wilmer L.L.P., 28
Society Corporation, 9
Soft Sheen Products, Inc., 31
Solectron Corporation, 12; 48 (upd.)
Solo Serve Corporation, 28
Solutia Inc., 52
Sonat, Inc., 6
Sonesta International Hotels Corporation, 44
Sonic Corp., 14; 37 (upd.)
Sonic Innovations Inc., 56
Sonoco Products Company, 8
SonoSite, Inc., 56
Soros Fund Management LLC, 28
Sorrento, Inc., 24
SOS Staffing Services, 25
Sotheby's Holdings, Inc., 11; 29 (upd.)
Sound Advice, Inc., 41
Source Enterprises, Inc., The, 65
South Jersey Industries, Inc., 42
Southdown, Inc., 14
Southern Company, The, V; 38 (upd.)
Southern Financial Bancorp, Inc., 56
Southern Indiana Gas and Electric Company, 13
Southern New England Telecommunications Corporation, 6
Southern Pacific Transportation Company, V
Southern States Cooperative Incorporated, 36
Southern Union Company, 27
Southland Corporation, The, II; 7 (upd.)
Southtrust Corporation, 11
Southwest Airlines Co., 6; 24 (upd.)
Southwest Gas Corporation, 19
Southwest Water Company, 47

Southwestern Bell Corporation, V
Southwestern Electric Power Co., 21
Southwestern Public Service Company, 6
Southwire Company, Inc., 8; 23 (upd.)
Sovran Self Storage, Inc., 66
Spacehab, Inc., 37
Spaghetti Warehouse, Inc., 25
Spangler Candy Company, 44
Spanish Broadcasting System, Inc., 41
Spartan Motors Inc., 14
Spartan Stores Inc., 8; 66 (upd.)
Spartech Corporation, 19
Sparton Corporation, 18
Spear, Leeds & Kellogg, 66
Spec's Music, Inc., 19
Specialized Bicycle Components Inc., 50
Specialty Coatings Inc., 8
Specialty Equipment Companies, Inc., 25
Specialty Products & Insulation Co., 59
Spectrum Control, Inc., 67
SpeeDee Oil Change and Tune-Up, 25
Speedway Motorsports, Inc., 32
Speizman Industries, Inc., 44
Spelling Entertainment, 14; 35 (upd.)
Spencer Stuart and Associates, Inc., 14
Spherion Corporation, 52
Spiegel, Inc., 10; 27 (upd.)
Spirit Airlines, Inc., 31
Sport Chalet, Inc., 16
Sport Supply Group, Inc., 23
Sportmart, Inc., 15
Sports & Recreation, Inc., 17
Sports Authority, Inc., The, 16; 43 (upd.)
Sports Club Company, The, 25
Sportsman's Guide, Inc., The, 36
Springs Industries, Inc., V; 19 (upd.)
Sprint Corporation, 9; 46 (upd.)
SPS Technologies, Inc., 30
SPSS Inc., 64
SPX Corporation, 10; 47 (upd.)
Squibb Corporation, I
SRAM Corporation, 65
SRC Holdings Corporation, 67
SRI International, Inc., 57
STAAR Surgical Company, 57
Stage Stores, Inc., 24
Stanadyne Automotive Corporation, 37
StanCorp Financial Group, Inc., 56
Standard Commercial Corporation, 13; 62 (upd.)
Standard Federal Bank, 9
Standard Microsystems Corporation, 11
Standard Motor Products, Inc., 40
Standard Pacific Corporation, 52
Standard Register Co., 15
Standex International Corporation, 17; 44 (upd.)
Stanhome Inc., 15
Stanley Furniture Company, Inc., 34
Stanley Works, The, III; 20 (upd.)
Staples, Inc., 10; 55 (upd.)
Star Banc Corporation, 11
Starbucks Corporation, 13; 34 (upd.)
Starcraft Corporation, 30; 66 (upd.)
Starkey Laboratories, Inc., 52
Starrett Corporation, 21
Starter Corp., 12
Starwood Hotels & Resorts Worldwide, Inc., 54
Stash Tea Company, The, 50
State Farm Mutual Automobile Insurance Company, III; 51 (upd.)
State Financial Services Corporation, 51
State Street Corporation, 8; 57 (upd.)
Staten Island Bancorp, Inc., 39
Stater Bros. Holdings Inc., 64
Station Casinos Inc., 25

United States (*continued*)

Staubach Company, The, 62
Steak n Shake Company, The, 41
Stearns, Inc., 43
Steel Dynamics, Inc., 52
Steel Technologies Inc., 63
Steelcase, Inc., 7; 27 (upd.)
Stein Mart Inc., 19
Steiner Corporation (Alsco), 53
Steinway Musical Properties, Inc., 19
Stepan Company, 30
Stephan Company, The, 60
Stericycle Inc., 33
STERIS Corporation, 29
Sterling Chemicals, Inc., 16
Sterling Drug, Inc., I
Sterling Electronics Corp., 18
Sterling Software, Inc., 11
Stevedoring Services of America Inc., 28
Steven Madden, Ltd., 37
Stew Leonard's, 56
Stewart & Stevenson Services Inc., 11
Stewart Enterprises, Inc., 20
Stewart's Beverages, 39
Stillwater Mining Company, 47
Stock Yards Packing Co., Inc., 37
Stone & Webster, Inc., 13; 64 (upd.)
Stone Container Corporation, IV
Stone Manufacturing Company, 14; 43
   (upd.)
Stonyfield Farm, Inc., 55
Stop & Shop Companies, Inc., The, II; 24
   (upd.)
Storage Technology Corporation, 6
Storage USA, Inc., 21
Stouffer Corp., 8
StrataCom, Inc., 16
Stratasys, Inc., 67
Stratus Computer, Inc., 10
Strauss Discount Auto, 56
Strayer Education, Inc., 53
Stride Rite Corporation, The, 8; 37 (upd.)
Stroh Brewery Company, The, I; 18 (upd.)
Strombecker Corporation, 60
Stroock & Stroock & Lavan LLP, 40
Strouds, Inc., 33
Stryker Corporation, 11; 29 (upd.)
Stuart C. Irby Company, 58
Stuart Entertainment Inc., 16
Student Loan Marketing Association, II
Stuller Settings, Inc., 35
Sturm, Ruger & Company, Inc., 19
Stussy, Inc., 55
Sub-Zero Freezer Co., Inc., 31
Suburban Propane Partners, L.P., 30
Subway, 32
Successories, Inc., 30
Sudbury Inc., 16
Suiza Foods Corporation, 26
Sullivan & Cromwell, 26
Summit Bancorporation, The, 14
Summit Family Restaurants, Inc. 19
Sun Communities Inc., 46
Sun Company, Inc., IV
Sun Country Airlines, 30
Sun Distributors L.P., 12
Sun Healthcare Group Inc., 25
Sun Microsystems, Inc., 7; 30 (upd.)
Sun Sportswear, Inc., 17
Sun Television & Appliances Inc., 10
Sun-Diamond Growers of California, 7
SunAmerica Inc., 11
Sunbeam-Oster Co., Inc., 9
Sunburst Hospitality Corporation, 26
Sundstrand Corporation, 7; 21 (upd.)
Sundt Corp., 24
SunGard Data Systems Inc., 11

Sunglass Hut International, Inc., 21
Sunkist Growers, Inc., 26
Sunoco, Inc., 28 (upd.)
Sunrider Corporation, The, 26
Sunrise Medical Inc., 11
SunTrust Banks Inc., 23
Super Food Services, Inc., 15
Supercuts, Inc., 26
Superior Energy Services, Inc., 65
Superior Industries International, Inc., 8
Superior Uniform Group, Inc., 30
Supermarkets General Holdings
   Corporation, II
SUPERVALU Inc., II; 18 (upd.); 50 (upd.)
Suprema Specialties, Inc., 27
Supreme International Corporation, 27
Susquehanna Pfaltzgraff Company, 8
Sutter Home Winery Inc., 16
Sverdrup Corporation, 14
Swank Inc., 17
SwedishAmerican Health System, 51
Sweet Candy Company, 60
Sweetheart Cup Company, Inc., 36
Swift & Company, 55
Swift Energy Company, 63
Swift Transportation Co., Inc., 42
Swinerton Inc., 43
Swisher International Group Inc., 23
Sybase, Inc., 10; 27 (upd.)
Sybron International Corp., 14
Sycamore Networks, Inc., 45
Sykes Enterprises, Inc., 45
Sylvan Learning Systems, Inc., 35
Sylvan, Inc., 22
Symantec Corporation, 10
Symbol Technologies, Inc., 15
Syms Corporation, 29
Synopsis, Inc., 11
SynOptics Communications, Inc., 10
Synovus Financial Corp., 12; 52 (upd.)
Syntex Corporation, I
SyQuest Technology, Inc., 18
Syratech Corp., 14
SYSCO Corporation, II; 24 (upd.)
System Software Associates, Inc., 10
Systemax, Inc., 52
Systems & Computer Technology Corp.,
   19
T-Netix, Inc., 46
T. Marzetti Company, 57
T. Rowe Price Associates, Inc., 11; 34
   (upd.)
TAB Products Co., 17
Taco Bell Corp., 7; 21 (upd.)
Taco Cabana, Inc., 23
Taco John's International, Inc., 15; 63
   (upd.)
Take-Two Interactive Software, Inc., 46
Talbots, Inc., The, 11; 31 (upd.)
Talley Industries, Inc., 16
Tambrands Inc., 8
Tandem Computers, Inc., 6
Tandy Corporation, II; 12 (upd.)
Tandycrafts, Inc., 31
Tanger Factory Outlet Centers, Inc., 49
Tapemark Company Inc., 64
Target Corporation, 10; 27 (upd.); 61
   (upd.)
Tarragon Realty Investors, Inc., 45
Tarrant Apparel Group, 62
Taser International, Inc., 62
Tasty Baking Company, 14; 35 (upd.)
Tattered Cover Book Store, 43
Taylor Corporation, 36
Taylor Guitars, 48
Taylor Made Golf Co., 23
Taylor Publishing Company, 12; 36 (upd.)

TB Wood's Corporation, 56
TBWA\Chiat\Day, 6; 43 (upd.)
TCBY Enterprises Inc., 17
TCF Financial Corporation, 47
Teachers Insurance and Annuity
   Association-College Retirement Equities
   Fund, III; 45 (upd.)
TearDrop Golf Company, 32
Tech Data Corporation, 10
Tech-Sym Corporation, 18; 44 (upd.)
TECHNE Corporation, 52
Technitrol, Inc., 29
TECO Energy, Inc., 6
Tecumseh Products Company, 8
Tee Vee Toons, Inc., 57
Tejon Ranch Company, 35
Tektronix, Inc., 8
Telcordia Technologies, Inc., 59
Tele-Communications, Inc., II
Teledyne Technologies Inc., I; 10 (upd.);
   62 (upd.)
Telephone and Data Systems, Inc., 9
Tellabs, Inc., 11; 40 (upd.)
Telxon Corporation, 10
Temple-Inland Inc., IV; 31 (upd.)
Tempur-Pedic Inc., 54
Tenet Healthcare Corporation, 55 (upd.)
TenFold Corporation, 35
Tennant Company, 13; 33 (upd.)
Tenneco Inc., I; 10 (upd.)
Tennessee Valley Authority, 50
Teradyne, Inc., 11
Terex Corporation, 7; 40 (upd.)
Terlato Wine Group, The, 48
Terra Industries, Inc., 13
Tesoro Petroleum Corporation, 7; 45 (upd.)
Testor Corporation, The, 51
Tetra Tech, Inc., 29
Texaco Inc., IV; 14 (upd.); 41 (upd.)
Texas Air Corporation, I
Texas Industries, Inc., 8
Texas Instruments Inc., II; 11 (upd.); 46
   (upd.)
Texas Pacific Group Inc., 36
Texas Rangers Baseball, 51
Texas Utilities Company, V; 25 (upd.)
Textron Inc., I; 34 (upd.)
Textron Lycoming Turbine Engine, 9
Thermadyne Holding Corporation, 19
Thermo BioAnalysis Corp., 25
Thermo Electron Corporation, 7
Thermo Fibertek, Inc., 24
Thermo Instrument Systems Inc., 11
Thermo King Corporation, 13
Thermos Company, 16
Thiokol Corporation, 9; 22 (upd.)
Thomas & Betts Corporation, 11; 54 (upd.)
Thomas Cook Travel Inc., 9; 33 (upd.)
Thomas H. Lee Co., 24
Thomas Industries Inc., 29
Thomas J. Lipton Company, 14
Thomas Nelson, Inc., 14; 38 (upd.)
Thomas Publishing Company, 26
Thomaston Mills, Inc., 27
Thomasville Furniture Industries, Inc., 12
Thomsen Greenhouses and Garden Center,
   Incorporated, 65
Thor Industries, Inc., 39
Thorn Apple Valley, Inc., 7; 22 (upd.)
Thousand Trails, Inc., 33
THQ, Inc., 39
3Com Corporation, 11; 34 (upd.)
3DO Company, The, 43
3M Company, 61 (upd.)
Thrifty PayLess, Inc., 12
Ticketmaster Group, Inc., 13; 37 (upd.)
Tidewater Inc., 11; 37 (upd.)

Tiffany & Co., 14
TIG Holdings, Inc., 26
Tilia Inc., 62
Tillotson Corp., 15
Timberland Company, The, 13; 54 (upd.)
Timberline Software Corporation, 15
Time Warner Inc., IV; 7 (upd.)
Times Mirror Company, The, IV; 17 (upd.)
Timex Corporation, 7; 25 (upd.)
Timken Company, The, 8; 42 (upd.)
Tishman Speyer Properties, L.P., 47
Titan Corporation, The, 36
Titanium Metals Corporation, 21
TJ International, Inc., 19
TJX Companies, Inc., The, V; 19 (upd.); 57 (upd.)
TLC Beatrice International Holdings, Inc., 22
TMP Worldwide Inc., 30
TNT Freightways Corporation, 14
Today's Man, Inc., 20
Todd Shipyards Corporation, 14
Todd-AO Corporation, The, 33
Todhunter International, Inc., 27
Tofutti Brands, Inc., 64
Tokheim Corporation, 21
Toll Brothers Inc., 15
Tollgrade Communications, Inc., 44
Tom Brown, Inc., 37
Tom Doherty Associates Inc., 25
Tom's Foods Inc., 66
Tom's of Maine, Inc., 45
Tombstone Pizza Corporation, 13
Tone Brothers, Inc., 21
Tonka Corporation, 25
Too, Inc., 61
Tootsie Roll Industries Inc., 12
Topco Associates LLC, 60
Topps Company, Inc., The, 13; 34 (upd.)
Tops Appliance City, Inc., 17
Tops Markets LLC, 60
Torchmark Corporation, 9; 33 (upd.)
Toro Company, The, 7; 26 (upd.)
Torrington Company, The, 13
Tosco Corporation, 7
Total Entertainment Restaurant Corporation, 46
Total System Services, Inc., 18
Totem Resources Corporation, 9
Tower Air, Inc., 28
Tower Automotive, Inc., 24
Towers Perrin, 32
Town & Country Corporation, 19
Town Sports International, Inc., 46
Townsends, Inc., 64
Toy Biz, Inc., 18
Toymax International, Inc., 29
Toys ''R'' Us, Inc., V; 18 (upd.); 57 (upd.)
Tracor Inc., 17
Tractor Supply Company, 57
Trader Joe's Company, 13; 50 (upd.)
Traffix, Inc., 61
Trailer Bridge, Inc., 41
Trammell Crow Company, 8; 57 (upd.)
Trans World Airlines, Inc., I; 12 (upd.); 35 (upd.)
Trans World Entertainment Corporation, 24
Trans-Lux Corporation, 51
Transaction Systems Architects, Inc., 29
Transamerica–An AEGON Company, I; 13 (upd.); 41 (upd.)
Transatlantic Holdings, Inc., 11
Transco Energy Company, V
Transmedia Network Inc., 20
TransMontaigne Inc., 28
Transocean Sedco Forex Inc., 45
Transport Corporation of America, Inc., 49

Tranzonic Companies, The, 37
Travel Ports of America, Inc., 17
Travelers Corporation, The, III
Travelocity.com, Inc., 46
Travis Boats & Motors, Inc., 37
TRC Companies, Inc., 32
Treadco, Inc., 19
Treasure Chest Advertising Company, Inc., 32
Tredegar Corporation, 52
Tree of Life, Inc., 29
Trek Bicycle Corporation, 16
Trend-Lines, Inc., 22
Trendwest Resorts, Inc., 33
Tri Valley Growers, 32
Triarc Companies, Inc., 8; 34 (upd.)
Tribune Company, IV; 22 (upd.); 63 (upd.)
Trico Products Corporation, 15
Trident Seafoods Corporation, 56
Trigen Energy Corporation, 42
TriMas Corp., 11
Trimble Navigation Limited, 40
Trinity Industries, Incorporated, 7
TRINOVA Corporation, III
Triple Five Group Ltd., 49
TriQuint Semiconductor, Inc., 63
Trisko Jewelry Sculptures, Ltd., 57
Triton Energy Corporation, 11
Triumph Group, Inc., 31
TRM Copy Centers Corporation, 18
Tropicana Products, Inc., 28
True North Communications Inc., 23
Trump Organization, The, 23; 64 (upd.)
TruServ Corporation, 24
TRW Inc., I; 11 (upd.); 14 (upd.)
TTX Company, 6; 66 (upd.)
Tubby's, Inc., 53
Tucson Electric Power Company, 6
Tuesday Morning Corporation, 18
Tully's Coffee Corporation, 51
Tultex Corporation, 13
Tumbleweed, Inc., 33
Tupperware Corporation, 28
Turner Broadcasting System, Inc., II; 6 (upd.); 66 (upd.)
Turner Construction Company, 66
Turner Corporation, The, 8; 23 (upd.)
Turtle Wax, Inc., 15
Tuscarora Inc., 29
TV Guide, Inc., 43 (upd.)
TVI, Inc., 15
TW Services, Inc., II
Tweeter Home Entertainment Group, Inc., 30
Twentieth Century Fox Film Corporation, II; 25 (upd.)
24/7 Real Media, Inc., 49
Twin Disc, Inc., 21
Twinlab Corporation, 34
Ty Inc., 33
Tyco Toys, Inc., 12
Tyler Corporation, 23
Tyndale House Publishers, Inc., 57
Tyson Foods, Inc., II; 14 (upd.); 50 (upd.)
U S West, Inc., V; 25 (upd.)
U.S. Aggregates, Inc., 42
U.S. Bancorp, 14; 36 (upd.)
U.S. Borax, Inc., 42
U.S. Can Corporation, 30
U.S. Cellular Corporation, 31 (upd.)
U.S. Delivery Systems, Inc., 22
U.S. Foodservice, 26
U.S. Healthcare, Inc., 6
U.S. Home Corporation, 8
U.S. News and World Report Inc., 30
U.S. Office Products Company, 25
U.S. Physical Therapy, Inc., 65

U.S. Robotics Corporation, 9; 66 (upd.)
U.S. Satellite Broadcasting Company, Inc., 20
U.S. Timberlands Company, L.P., 42
U.S. Trust Corp., 17
U.S. Vision, Inc., 66
UAL Corporation, 34 (upd.)
UGI Corporation, 12
Ugly Duckling Corporation, 22
UICI, 33
Ukrop's Super Market's, Inc., 39
Ultimate Electronics, Inc., 18
Ultra Pac, Inc., 24
Ultrak Inc., 24
Ultralife Batteries, Inc., 58
Ultramar Diamond Shamrock Corporation, 31 (upd.)
Uncle Ben's Inc., 22
Under Armour Performance Apparel, 61
Underwriters Laboratories, Inc., 30
Uni-Marts, Inc., 17
Unicom Corporation, 29 (upd.)
Unifi, Inc., 12; 62 (upd.)
UniFirst Corporation, 21
Union Bank of California, 16
Union Camp Corporation, IV
Union Carbide Corporation, I; 9 (upd.)
Union Electric Company, V
Union Pacific Corporation, V; 28 (upd.)
Union Planters Corporation, 54
Union Texas Petroleum Holdings, Inc., 9
UnionBanCal Corporation, 50 (upd.)
Unique Casual Restaurants, Inc., 27
Unison HealthCare Corporation, 25
Unisys Corporation, III; 6 (upd.); 36 (upd.)
Unit Corporation, 63
United Airlines, I; 6 (upd.)
United Auto Group, Inc., 26
United Brands Company, II
United Defense Industries, Inc., 30; 66 (upd.)
United Dominion Industries Limited, 8; 16 (upd.)
United Dominion Realty Trust, Inc., 52
United Foods, Inc., 21
United HealthCare Corporation, 9
United Illuminating Company, The, 21
United Industrial Corporation, 37
United Jewish Communities, 33
United Merchants & Manufacturers, Inc., 13
United National Group, Ltd., 63
United Nations International Children's Emergency Fund (UNICEF), 58
United Natural Foods, Inc., 32
United Parcel Service of America Inc., V; 17 (upd.)
United Parcel Service, Inc., 63
United Press International, Inc., 25
United Rentals, Inc., 34
United Retail Group Inc., 33
United Service Organizations, 60
United States Cellular Corporation, 9
United States Filter Corporation, 20
United States Pipe and Foundry Company, 62
United States Playing Card Company, 62
United States Postal Service, 14; 34 (upd.)
United States Shoe Corporation, The, V
United States Steel Corporation, 50 (upd.)
United States Surgical Corporation, 10; 34 (upd.)
United Stationers Inc., 14
United Technologies Automotive Inc., 15
United Technologies Corporation, I; 10 (upd.); 34 (upd.)
United Telecommunications, Inc., V

United States (*continued*)

United Video Satellite Group, 18
United Water Resources, Inc., 40
United Way of America, 36
Unitil Corporation, 37
Unitog Co., 19
Unitrin Inc., 16
Univar Corporation, 9
Universal Compression, Inc., 59
Universal Corporation, V; 48 (upd.)
Universal Electronics Inc., 39
Universal Foods Corporation, 7
Universal Forest Products, Inc., 10; 59 (upd.)
Universal Health Services, Inc., 6
Universal International, Inc., 25
Universal Studios, Inc., 33
Univision Communications Inc., 24
Uno Restaurant Corporation, 18
Unocal Corporation, IV; 24 (upd.)
UnumProvident Corporation, 13; 52 (upd.)
Upjohn Company, The, I; 8 (upd.)
Urban Outfitters, Inc., 14
URS Corporation, 45
US Airways Group, Inc., I; 6 (upd.); 28 (upd.); 52 (upd.)
USA Interactive, Inc., 47 (upd.)
USA Truck, Inc., 42
USAA, 10; 62 (upd.)
USANA, Inc., 29
USF&G Corporation, III
USG Corporation, III; 26 (upd.)
UST Inc., 9; 50 (upd.)
USX Corporation, IV; 7 (upd.)
Utah Medical Products, Inc., 36
Utah Power and Light Company, 27
UtiliCorp United Inc., 6
UUNET, 38
Uwajimaya, Inc., 60
Vail Resorts, Inc., 11; 43 (upd.)
Valassis Communications, Inc., 8; 37 (upd.)
Valero Energy Corporation, 7
Valhi, Inc., 19
Vallen Corporation, 45
Valley Media Inc., 35
Valmont Industries, Inc., 19
Valspar Corporation, The, 8; 32 (upd.)
Value City Department Stores, Inc., 38
Value Line, Inc., 16
Value Merchants Inc., 13
ValueClick, Inc., 49
ValueVision International, Inc., 22
Van Camp Seafood Company, Inc., 7
Van's Aircraft, Inc., 65
Vance Publishing Corporation, 64
Vanguard Group, Inc., The, 14; 34 (upd.)
Vans, Inc., 16; 47 (upd.)
Varco International, Inc., 42
Vari-Lite International, Inc., 35
Varian, Inc., 12; 48 (upd.)
Variflex, Inc., 51
Varlen Corporation, 16
Varsity Spirit Corp., 15
Vastar Resources, Inc., 24
VCA Antech, Inc., 58
VECO International, Inc., 7
Vector Group Ltd., 35 (upd.)
Veeco Instruments Inc., 32
Veit Companies, 43
Velocity Express Corporation, 49
Venator Group Inc., 35 (upd.)
Vencor, Inc., 16
Venetian Casino Resort, LLC, 47
Venture Stores Inc., 12
Verbatim Corporation, 14
Veridian Corporation, 54

VeriFone, Inc., 18
VeriSign, Inc., 47
Veritas Software Corporation, 45
Verizon Communications, 43 (upd.)
Vermeer Manufacturing Company, 17
Vermont Pure Holdings, Ltd., 51
Vermont Teddy Bear Co., Inc., The, 36
VF Corporation, V; 17 (upd.); 54 (upd.)
VHA Inc., 53
Viacom Inc., 7; 23 (upd.); 67 (upd.)
ViaSat, Inc., 54
Viasoft Inc., 27
VIASYS Healthcare, Inc., 52
Viasystems Group, Inc., 67
Viatech Continental Can Company, Inc., 25 (upd.)
Vicon Industries, Inc., 44
VICORP Restaurants, Inc., 12; 48 (upd.)
Vienna Sausage Manufacturing Co., 14
Viewpoint International, Inc., 66
Viking Office Products, Inc., 10
Viking Range Corporation, 66
Village Super Market, Inc., 7
Village Voice Media, Inc., 38
Vinson & Elkins L.L.P., 30
Vintage Petroleum, Inc., 42
Vinton Studios, 63
Virco Manufacturing Corporation, 17
Visa International, 9; 26 (upd.)
Vishay Intertechnology, Inc., 21
Viskase Companies, Inc., 55
Vista Bakery, Inc., 56
Vista Chemical Company, I
Vistana, Inc., 22
VISX, Incorporated, 30
Vita Plus Corporation, 60
Vitalink Pharmacy Services, Inc., 15
Vitamin Shoppe Industries, Inc., 60
Vitesse Semiconductor Corporation, 32
Vitro Corp., 10
Vivra, Inc., 18
Vlasic Foods International Inc., 25
VLSI Technology, Inc., 16
Volt Information Sciences Inc., 26
Volunteers of America, Inc., 66
Von Maur Inc., 64
Vons Companies, Incorporated, The, 7; 28 (upd.)
Vornado Realty Trust, 20
Vought Aircraft Industries, Inc., 49
Vulcan Materials Company, 7; 52 (upd.)
W. Atlee Burpee & Co., 27
W.A. Whitney Company, 53
W.B Doner & Co., 56
W.H. Brady Co., 17
W.L. Gore & Associates, Inc., 14; 60 (upd.)
W.P. Carey & Co. LLC, 49
W.R. Berkley Corp., 15
W.R. Grace & Company, I; 50 (upd.)
W.W. Grainger, Inc., V; 26 (upd.)
W.W. Norton & Company, Inc., 28
Waban Inc., 13
Wabash National Corp., 13
Wabtec Corporation, 40
Wachovia Bank of Georgia, N.A., 16
Wachovia Bank of South Carolina, N.A., 16
Wachovia Corporation, 12; 46 (upd.)
Wachtell, Lipton, Rosen & Katz, 47
Wackenhut Corporation, The, 14; 63 (upd.)
Waddell & Reed, Inc., 22
Waffle House Inc., 14; 60 (upd.)
Waggener Edstrom, 42
Wakefern Food Corporation, 33
Wal-Mart Stores, Inc., V; 8 (upd.); 26 (upd.); 63 (upd.)

Walbridge Aldinger Co., 38
Walbro Corporation, 13
Waldbaum, Inc., 19
Walden Book Company Inc., 17
Walgreen Co., V; 20 (upd.); 65 (upd.)
Walker Manufacturing Company, 19
Wall Drug Store, Inc., 40
Wall Street Deli, Inc., 33
Wallace Computer Services, Inc., 36
Walt Disney Company, The, II; 6 (upd.); 30 (upd.); 63 (upd.)
Walter Industries, Inc., II; 22 (upd.)
Walton Monroe Mills, Inc., 8
Wang Laboratories, Inc., III; 6 (upd.)
Warnaco Group Inc., The, 12; 46 (upd.)
Warner Communications Inc., II
Warner-Lambert Co., I; 10 (upd.)
Warners' Stellian Inc., 67
Warrantech Corporation, 53
Warwick Valley Telephone Company, 55
Washington Companies, The, 33
Washington Federal, Inc., 17
Washington Football, Inc., 35
Washington Gas Light Company, 19
Washington Mutual, Inc., 17
Washington National Corporation, 12
Washington Natural Gas Company, 9
Washington Post Company, The, IV; 20 (upd.)
Washington Scientific Industries, Inc., 17
Washington Water Power Company, 6
Waste Connections, Inc., 46
Waste Holdings, Inc., 41
Waste Management, Inc., V
Water Pik Technologies, Inc., 34
Waterhouse Investor Services, Inc., 18
Waters Corporation, 43
Watkins-Johnson Company, 15
Watsco Inc., 52
Watson Pharmaceuticals Inc., 16; 56 (upd.)
Watson Wyatt Worldwide, 42
Watts Industries, Inc., 19
Wausau-Mosinee Paper Corporation, 60 (upd.)
Waverly, Inc., 16
Wawa Inc., 17
Waxman Industries, Inc., 9
WD-40 Company, 18
Weather Channel Companies, The 52
Weatherford International, Inc., 39
Webber Oil Company, 61
Weber-Stephen Products Co., 40
WebMD Corporation, 65
Weeres Industries Corporation, 52
Wegmans Food Markets, Inc., 9; 41 (upd.)
Weider Nutrition International, Inc., 29
Weight Watchers International Inc., 12; 33 (upd.)
Weil, Gotshal & Manges LLP, 55
Weiner's Stores, Inc., 33
Weirton Steel Corporation, IV; 26 (upd.)
Weis Markets, Inc., 15
Weitz Company, Inc., The, 42
Welbilt Corp., 19
WellChoice, Inc., 67 (upd.)
Wellman, Inc., 8; 52 (upd.)
WellPoint Health Networks Inc., 25
Wells Fargo & Company, II; 12 (upd.); 38 (upd.)
Wells Rich Greene BDDP, 6
Wells' Dairy, Inc., 36
Wells-Gardner Electronics Corporation, 43
Wendy's International, Inc., 8; 23 (upd.); 47 (upd.)
Wenner Media, Inc., 32
Werner Enterprises, Inc., 26
West Bend Co., 14

West Coast Entertainment Corporation, 29
West Corporation, 42
West Group, 34 (upd.)
West Marine, Inc., 17
West One Bancorp, 11
West Pharmaceutical Services, Inc., 42
West Point-Pepperell, Inc., 8
West Publishing Co., 7
Westaff Inc., 33
Westamerica Bancorporation, 17
Westar Energy, Inc., 57 (upd.)
WestCoast Hospitality Corporation, 59
Westcon Group, Inc., 67
Westell Technologies, Inc., 57
Westerbeke Corporation, 60
Western Atlas Inc., 12
Western Beef, Inc., 22
Western Company of North America, 15
Western Digital Corp., 25
Western Gas Resources, Inc., 45
Western Publishing Group, Inc., 13
Western Resources, Inc., 12
WesterN SizzliN Corporation, The, 60
Western Union Financial Services, Inc., 54
Western Wireless Corporation, 36
Westin Hotels and Resorts Worldwide, 9;
   29 (upd.)
Westinghouse Electric Corporation, II; 12
   (upd.)
Westmoreland Coal Company, 7
WestPoint Stevens Inc., 16
Westport Resources Corporation, 63
Westvaco Corporation, IV; 19 (upd.)
Westwood One, Inc., 23
Wet Seal, Inc., The, 18
Wetterau Incorporated, II
Weyco Group, Incorporated, 32
Weyerhaeuser Company, IV; 9 (upd.); 28
   (upd.)
WGBH Educational Foundation, 66
Wham-O, Inc., 61
Wheaton Industries, 8
Wheaton Science Products, 60 (upd.)
Wheelabrator Technologies, Inc., 6; 60
   (upd.)
Wheeling-Pittsburgh Corporation, 7; 58
   (upd.)
Wherehouse Entertainment Incorporated,
   11
Whirlpool Corporation, III; 12 (upd.); 59
   (upd.)
White & Case LLP, 35
White Castle System, Inc., 12; 36 (upd.)
White Consolidated Industries Inc., 13
White House, Inc., The, 60
White Rose, Inc., 24
Whitman Corporation, 10 (upd.)
Whitman Education Group, Inc., 41
Whitney Holding Corporation, 21
Whittaker Corporation, I; 48 (upd.)
Whole Foods Market, 20; 50 (upd.)
Wickes Inc., V; 25 (upd.)
Wilbert, Inc., 56
Wilbur Chocolate Company, 66
Wild Oats Markets, Inc., 19; 41 (upd.)
Wildlife Conservation Society, 31
Willamette Industries, Inc., IV; 31 (upd.)
William L. Bonnell Company, Inc., 66
William Lyon Homes, 59
William Morris Agency, Inc., 23
William Zinsser & Company, Inc., 58
Williams & Connolly LLP, 47
Williams Communications Group, Inc., 34
Williams Companies, Inc., The, IV; 31
   (upd.)
Williams Scotsman, Inc., 65
Williams-Sonoma, Inc., 17; 44 (upd.)

Williamson-Dickie Manufacturing
   Company, 14; 45 (upd.)
Wilmington Trust Corporation, 25
Wilson Sonsini Goodrich & Rosati, 34
Wilson Sporting Goods Company, 24
Wilsons The Leather Experts Inc., 21; 58
   (upd.)
Winchell's Donut Houses Operating
   Company, L.P., 60
WinCo Foods Inc., 60
Wind River Systems, Inc., 37
Windmere Corporation, 16
Windswept Environmental Group, Inc., 62
Wine Group, Inc., The, 39
Winegard Company, 56
Winn-Dixie Stores, Inc., II; 21 (upd.); 59
   (upd.)
Winnebago Industries Inc., 7; 27 (upd.)
WinsLoew Furniture, Inc., 21
Winston & Strawn, 35
Wisconsin Alumni Research Foundation,
   65
Wisconsin Bell, Inc., 14
Wisconsin Central Transportation
   Corporation, 24
Wisconsin Dairies, 7
Wisconsin Energy Corporation, 6; 54
   (upd.)
Wisconsin Public Service Corporation, 9
Witco Corporation, I; 16 (upd.)
Wizards of the Coast Inc., 24
WLR Foods, Inc., 21
Wm. B. Reily & Company Inc., 58
Wm. Wrigley Jr. Company, 7; 58 (upd.)
WMS Industries, Inc., 15; 53 (upd.)
WMX Technologies Inc., 17
Wolfgang Puck Food Company, Inc., The,
   26
Wolohan Lumber Co., 19
Wolverine Tube Inc., 23
Wolverine World Wide, Inc., 16; 59 (upd.)
Womble Carlyle Sandridge & Rice, PLLC,
   52
Wood-Mode, Inc., 23
Woodcraft Industries Inc., 61
Woodward Governor Company, 13; 49
   (upd.)
Woolrich Inc., 62
Woolworth Corporation, V; 20 (upd.)
WordPerfect Corporation, 10
Workflow Management, Inc., 65
Working Assets Funding Service, 43
World Acceptance Corporation, 57
World Bank Group, 33
World Book, Inc., 12
World Color Press Inc., 12
World Duty Free Americas, Inc., 29 (upd.)
World Fuel Services Corporation, 47
World Publications, LLC, 65
World Wrestling Federation Entertainment,
   Inc., 32
World's Finest Chocolate Inc., 39
WorldCorp, Inc., 10
Worldwide Restaurant Concepts, Inc., 47
Worthington Foods, Inc., 14
Worthington Industries, Inc., 7; 21 (upd.)
WPL Holdings, Inc., 6
WPS Resources Corporation, 53 (upd.)
Wright Medical Group, Inc., 61
WTD Industries, Inc., 20
Wyant Corporation, 30
Wyeth, 50 (upd.)
Wyle Electronics, 14
Wyman-Gordon Company, 14
Wynn's International, Inc., 33
Wyse Technology, Inc., 15
X-Rite, Inc., 48

Xerox Corporation, III; 6 (upd.); 26 (upd.)
Xilinx, Inc., 16
XTO Energy Inc., 52
Yahoo! Inc., 27
Yankee Candle Company, Inc., The, 37
YankeeNets LLC, 35
Yates Companies, Inc., The, 62
Yellow Corporation, 14; 45 (upd.)
Yellow Freight System, Inc. of Delaware,
   V
YES! Entertainment Corporation, 26
YMCA of the USA, 31
YOCREAM International, Inc., 47
York Group, Inc., The, 50
York International Corp., 13
York Research Corporation, 35
Young & Rubicam, Inc., I; 22 (upd.); 66
   (upd.)
Young Broadcasting Inc., 40
Young Innovations, Inc., 44
Young's Market Company, LLC, 32
Younkers, Inc., 19
Youth Services International, Inc., 21
Yucaipa Cos., 17
Yum! Brands Inc., 58
YWCA of the United States, 45
Zale Corporation, 16; 40 (upd.)
Zany Brainy, Inc., 31
Zapata Corporation, 25
Zatarain's, Inc., 64
Zebra Technologies Corporation, 14; 53
   (upd.)
Zenith Data Systems, Inc., 10
Zenith Electronics Corporation, II; 13
   (upd.); 34 (upd.)
Zero Corporation, 17
Ziebart International Corporation, 30; 66
   (upd.)
Ziegler Companies, Inc., The, 24; 63 (upd.)
Ziff Davis Media Inc., 12; 36 (upd.)
Zila, Inc., 46
Zilog, Inc., 15
Zimmer Holdings, Inc., 45
Zion's Cooperative Mercantile Institution,
   33
Zions Bancorporation, 12; 53 (upd.)
Zippo Manufacturing Company, 18
Zoltek Companies, Inc., 37
Zondervan Publishing House, 24
Zones, Inc., 67
Zoom Technologies, Inc., 18; 53 (upd.)
Zygo Corporation, 42
Zytec Corporation, 19

Venezuela

Cerveceria Polar, I
Cisneros Group of Companies, 54
Empresas Polar SA, 55 (upd.)
Petróleos de Venezuela S.A., IV

Vietnam

Lam Son Sugar Joint Stock Corporation
   (Lasuco), 60

Virgin Islands

Little Switzerland, Inc., 60

Wales

Hyder plc, 34
Iceland Group plc, 33
Kwik Save Group plc, 11

Zambia

Zambia Industrial and Mining Corporation
   Ltd., IV

NOTES ON CONTRIBUTORS —————————————————————

Notes on Contributors

COHEN, M. L. Novelist and researcher living in Paris.

COVELL, Jeffrey L. Seattle-based writer.

CULLIGAN, Susan B. Minnesota-based writer.

DINGER, Ed. Writer and editor based in Bronx, New York.

HALASZ, Robert. Former editor in chief of *World Progress* and *Funk & Wagnalls New Encyclopedia Yearbook*; author, *The U.S. Marines* (Millbrook Press, 1993).

HEER-FORSBERG, Mary. Minneapolis-based researcher and writer.

INGRAM, Frederick C. Utah-based business writer who has contributed to *GSA Business, Appalachian Trailway News,* the *Encyclopedia of Business,* the *Encyclopedia of Global Industries,* the *Encyclopedia of Consumer Brands,* and other regional and trade publications.

PEIPPO, Kathleen. Minneapolis-based writer.

RHODES, Nelson. Editor, writer, and consultant in the Chicago area.

ROTHBURD, Carrie. Writer and editor specializing in corporate profiles, academic texts, and academic journal articles.

SALAMIE, David E. Part-owner of InfoWorks Development Group, a reference publication development and editorial services company.